INSIGNIA

BELGIUM
BENIN
BOLIVIA
BOSNIA
BOSNIAN SERBIA
BOTSWANA
BRAZIL
BRUNEI
BULGARIA
CHINA
COLOMBIA
CONGO
MINISTERIO DE SEGURIDAD PUBLICA SECION AEREA
COSTA RICA
CROATIA
CUBA
CYPRUS
CZECH
DENMARK
FINLAND
GABON
GERMANY
GHANA
GREECE
GUATEMALA
GUINEA
GUINEA-BISSAU
GUYANA
IVORY COAST
JAMAICA
JAPAN
JORDAN
KENYA
KOREA (NORTH)
KOREA (SOUTH)
KUWAIT
LAOS
MAURITANIA
MEXICO
MONGOLIA
MOROCCO
MOZAMBIQUE
NEPAL
NETHERLANDS
NEW ZEALAND
NICARAGUA
PHILIPPINES
POLAND
PORTUGAL
QATAR
ROMANIA
RUSSIA (C.I.S.)
RWANDA
SAUDI ARABIA
SENEGAMBIA
SWEDEN
SWITZERLAND
SYRIA
TAIWAN
TANZANIA
THAILAND
TOGO
TRINIDAD & TOBAGO
TUNISIA
YEMEN
YUGOSLAV REPUBLIC
ZAIRE
ZAMBIA
ZIMBABWE

BRASSEY'S WORLD AIRCRAFT & SYSTEMS DIRECTORY

BRASSEY'S

WORLD AIRCRAFT & SYSTEMS DIRECTORY

1996/97

This inaugural edition of the ***Brassey's World Aircraft & Systems Directory*** is the result of over two years work by a highly-dedicated team headed by Michael Taylor. Work began in 1993 and continued through to the winter of 1995 when details of last-minute developments and sales were incorporated into this present volume. Michael's international team of specialist contributors provided expertise and assistance in their respective fields. The august Editorial Board brought their many years of experience in the Services and aerospace industry to the project, and offered essential support and advice throughout the development of this directory. John Lee co-ordinated the many facets of the project and was assisted by Nicki Marshall.

The invaluable contributions of the following individuals must also be acknowledged: AVM Hurrell, Isobel Taylor, Jim Sutton, Malcolm English, Clive Rigden, Ruth Binney, Ken Webb, Peter Champion, Paul Effeny, Gary Grant, Nicky Cartwright, Judit Budinszky, Gill Paul, David Woodvine, Pushpindar Singh, Peter Selinger, Arnold W.L. Nayler, Mario B. de M. Vinagre, Peter Middleton, Alan Brothers. Finally, thanks are due to the employees of the many companies covered in this first edition for the time and effort they expended in fulfilling the requests for information that ultimately make such a publication possible.

Chief Editor
Michael Taylor

Managing Editor
John Lee

Assistant Editor
Nicki Marshall

CHIEF EDITOR: MICHAEL TAYLOR

Michael Taylor had his first aviation book published when he was 19 years old. At the same time he was also contributing important sections to *Jane's All the World's Aircraft*, *Jane's Fighting Ships* and other books.

In 1976 he became Editor of the magazine *Aircraft Illustrated*, while still compiling sections for various Jane's yearbooks and writing on average four books a year. In 1981 he was appointed Editor of *Jane's Aviation Review* and conceived and masterminded *Jane's Encyclopedia of Aviation*. In the late 1980s Michael Taylor became Assistant Editor to *Jane's All the World's Aircraft*, by which time his output of aviation books had passed 100. In 1993 he left this position to become Chief Editor of the *Brassey's World Aircraft and Systems Directory*.

SPECIALIST CONTRIBUTORS

Piotr Butowski: Russian and Polish Military Aircraft

Piotr Butowski is a resident of Gdansk, Poland. He is the author of several books on Russian aviation history and several hundred articles for a variety of notable periodicals in Polish, English, French, Japanese and Russian. He is in close contact with many chief designers and military officers in Russia and the Ukraine.

David Mondey: Helicopters

David Mondey remembers seeing the 1929 Schneider Trophy Contest for seaplanes at Calshot as an eleven year old. After serving in the Royal Airforce Volunteer Reserve, he began aviation writing in the late 1950s and has compiled or edited almost 50 books including many editions of the *Guinness Book of Aircraft Facts and Feats* produced jointly with Michael Taylor.

Neville Beckett: British Aerospace (Military)

Neville Beckett was an engineer with British Aerospace for 37 years mostly working at Brough in Humberside but latterly at Warton in Lancashire where his activities related to future projects. Since retirement, he continues to write for a number of aviation publications.

Geoffrey P. Jones: Recreational Aircraft

Currently the Managing Director of a civil engineering company in Guernsey, Geoffrey P. Jones is a private pilot and well-known aviation photographer. He is also European Editor for *Kit Planes* magazine.

Joachim Ewald: Sailplanes and Motorgliders

A renowned sailplane and motorglider test pilot, Joachim Ewald is an experienced writer and is a regular contributor to the German magazine *Fliegermagazin*.

Doug Richardson: Missiles and Radars

Following a distinguished career as an electronics engineer, Doug Richardson became a journalist and writer in 1976. His work on avionics, communications, navigation systems, satellites and a wide range of military technologies including electronic and space warfare has appeared in an array of international magazines. Formerly Defence Editor of *Flight International* and Editor of the *Military Technology* journal he currently edits *Telecommunications Development Asia Pacific*.

Mike Jerram: Runway Bearing Strengths

Mike Jerram is an aviation journalist, author and photographer. He is Deputy Editor of the UK's leading General Aviation magazine *Pilot*, European Correspondent for *Flying* in the USA, and serves as a consultant to the General Aviation & Traders Association.

EDITORIAL BOARD

Air Vice-Marshal AFC Hunter CBE AFC MA LLB DL

Director of Public Relations (Royal Air Force); Commandant Royal Air Force Staff College; Commander and Administrator of Sovereign Base Areas, British Forces, Cyprus.

Barry Wheeler

Editor - *Air International*; Editor of M.O.D. in-house Joint Services Recognition classified publications; Current Editor of *Air Pictorial*.

Derek Wood

Conceived and published *Jane's Defence Weekly*; *Sunday Telegraph* Aviation Correspondent; Historian for Royal Observer Corps; Editor - Royal Air Force Historical Society; Contributor to *Interavia Aerospace World*.

Jeremy Gambrill

Sales and Marketing Director - Jane's Information Group 1981-88; Publisher of *Air International*; currently runs Nunnleigh Enterprises a marketing services company for defence and aerospace publishers; heads the marketing team at Brassey's and edits *Billing Systems Review* for Corby Communications.

First published 1996 by Brassey's (UK) Ltd;
33 John Street, London WC1N 2AT
United Kingdom

ISBN 1 85753 198 1

British Library Cataloguing in Publication Data
is available on request

First published 1996 in North America by Brassey's, Inc.
1313 Dolley Madison Blvd., Suite 401, McLean, VA 22101,
United States of America

ISBN 1 57488 063 2

Library of Congress Cataloging-in-Publication Data

World aircraft and systems directory,1996–97 / Michael J. H. Taylor:

p. cm.
Includes index .
ISBN 1-57488-063-2
1. Aircraft industry—Directories. I. Taylor, Michael John Haddrick.
TL512.W65 195
629.133'34'0294 — dc20 95–37193
CIP

Design and typesetting by Book Creation Services, London

Index by Indexing Specialists, Hove

Airforce Insignia illustrations provided by Key Publishing

Reprographics by KPL, Tunbridge Wells

Printed and bound in the United Kingdom

The second edition of the *Brassey's World Aircraft & Systems Directory* is scheduled for publication in January 1998.
Contributors should write to:

The Editor
Brassey's World Aircraft & Systems Directory
Brassey's (UK) Ltd;
33 John Street
London WC1N 2AT
United Kingdom

CONTENTS

BRASSEY'S WORLD AIRCRAFT & SYSTEMS DIRECTORY

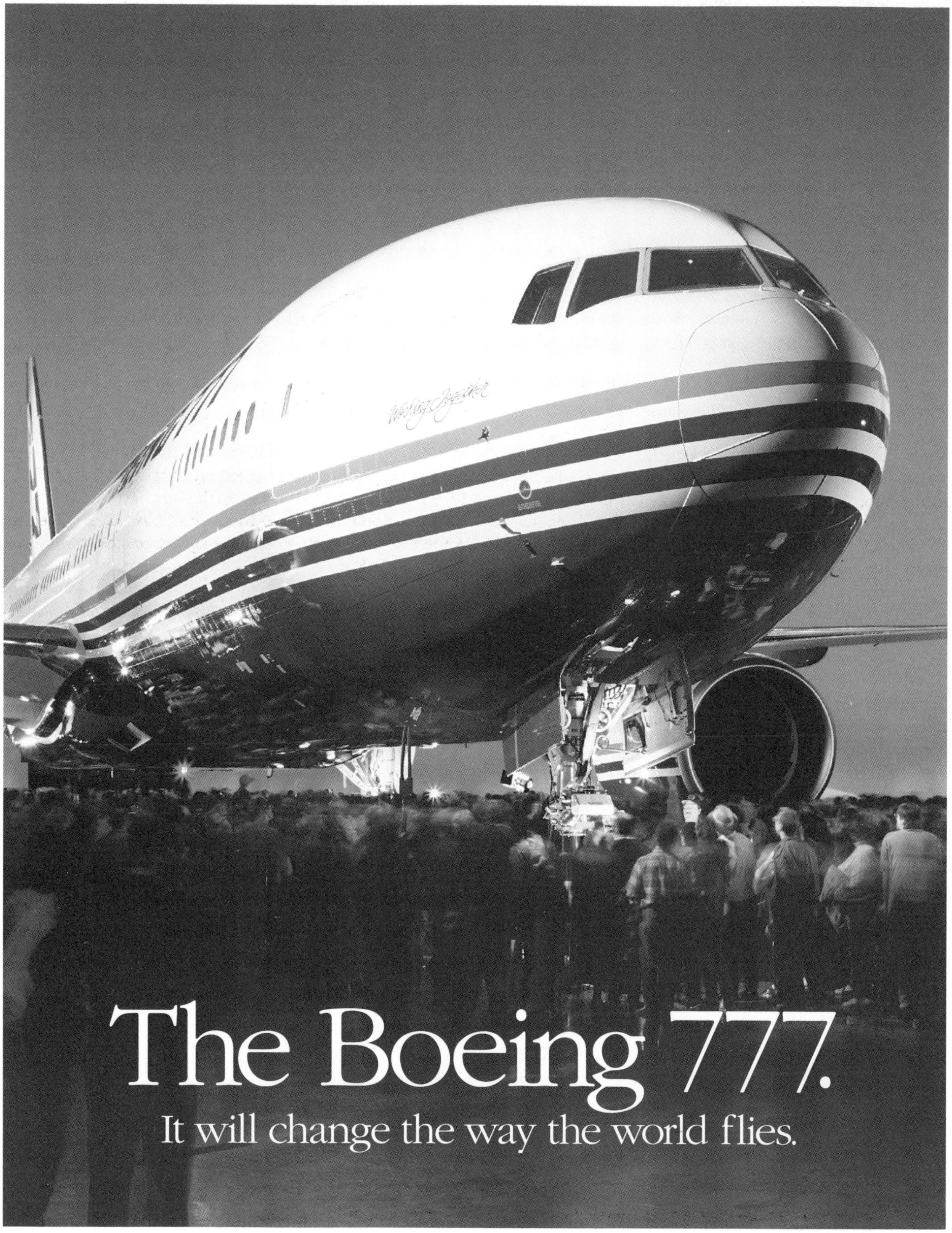
The Boeing 777.
It will change the way the world flies.

FOREWORD

There has rarely, if ever, been a time of greater opportunity for the world's aerospace industries, or one of greater challenge. Many of the world's major aircraft have been flying since the 1970s, and some vital to everyday operations and security are much older than that. The venerable C/KC-135s, for example, of which well over 500 are in active USAF and reserve use, have an average age of about 33 years, yet are always much in evidence round-the-clock when called upon. Similarly, despite many past attempts, nobody has built a successor to the indispensable Harrier family of jump jets conceived in the 1950s. On the commercial front, Boeing's 747, the standard international airliner for heavy loads and long ranges, first flew over a quarter of a century ago. The supersonic Concorde needs a replacement around the turn of the century, and there will not be one.

It can take up to 12 years to develop a major aircraft from project definition stage to production. There is no question the aircraft manufacturers know how to build the types required for the 21st century. They can already offer the right blends of high performance, precision navigation and stores delivery, enormously powerful engines of unprecedented fuel economy, and new weight-saving and high-strength materials. Paper projects abound for 650- to 1,000-passenger airliners, and almost every other conceivable type of aircraft where a market niche exists. They are commonplace and convincing.

In a real world, decisions to manufacture or not are made by businessmen and accountants, and not simply by engineers or even patriots. Those controlling the purse strings, be they in government or in industry, take a hard-nosed view of costs and/or profitability which, almost invariably, will be long-term matters. It might sometimes seem that the importance of aviation in making social progress or even ensuring military survival is a matter of secondary significance.

The businessmen and accountants plainly did not trust the aviation industry in 1966 when Pan American, then synonymous with much that was best in US airline flying, ordered 25 of Boeing's proposed Model 747s. Other operators felt compelled to order 'Jumbos' or risk losing business. One of their top men commented: "We are buying aircraft that have not yet been fully designed, with millions of dollars we don't have. We have to operate them into airports that are too small, in an air traffic control system that is too slow. And we must fill them with more passengers than we have ever carried."

Since then the 747 has grown steadily in size and capacity to meet the seemingly insatiable demand for extra capacity. Approximately 1,200 have been sold and orders continue to be placed, airline fares have been slashed, and safety records have been set that seemed unattainable in the 1960s. Only speculators have learned nothing from this.

Supersonic Concorde can claim very similar accolades, having carried passengers between Europe and North America, at twice the speed of sound, as day-to-day routine in perfect safety, and has done so for nearly two decades. Flights by British Airways are in constant operating profit, because most people who can afford to fly the Atlantic in pampered luxury choose to do so.

And that brings us back to economics. It is estimated to have cost over a billion pounds (1970s value) to develop and produce Concorde – a figure which today would be many times that. It was not possible to recoup this investment when fourteen of the aircraft were delivered to Air France and British Airways, and nobody bought any more, claiming that Concorde was too small, too noisy, too costly to operate, or too something else. Of course, with hindsight the environmental impact has proved to be manageable and operating profits were there for the taking. Arguably Concorde is indeed too small. That is why manufacturers in France, the USA, Japan, Germany and Russia have all conceived second-generation SSTs with seating of typically 250. Only France and Britain have wide experience of designing, building and operating SSTs, but NASA is attempting to help bridge the gap by leasing a re-engined Russian Tupolev Tu-144D airliner with only 87 flying hours clocked-up since construction in 1982 to assist the US High-Speed Civil Transport programme in association with Boeing, McDonnell Douglas, Rockwell, General Electric and Pratt & Whitney. But at the end of the day, the willingness and ability to produce such an aircraft mean nothing without funding, and no significant proportion has yet been forthcoming.

The design and final assembly of large subsonic airliners in the West is very largely the preserve of three giant companies – Boeing, McDonnell Douglas and Airbus. But, increasingly, production of subassemblies for their products are being entrusted in part to manufacturers in the Pacific Rim where labour costs are low and quality is high.

International co-operation is not new and will continue to create goodwill and interdependence between nations of the world and can promote faster economic development. But where should it end? Co-operation brings many benefits. It is advantageous politically, fostering relations through trade. It also makes sound economic sense, allowing companies to produce high quality products at lower costs, if sometimes at a price to the domestic labour market. Collaboration can also spread development costs and

Brazil's Embraer EMB-145 regional airliner, successfully developed with international risk-sharing partners, shown here making its first flight on 11 August 1995

Roll-out of the first Lockheed Martin C-130J-30 Hercules for the RAF on 18 October 1995. This option was chosen in preference to the planned European alternative

risk, either of which may be unacceptable for a single company or nation. It shares expertise and eliminates or reduces competition. If there is a downside, it is that junior partners may be enriched by technology transfer, to become the manufacturing competitors of the future.

Europe, for all its apparent obstacles to political union, has already been extremely successful in setting the pace of aviation collaboration. Tornado has defied its early critics and has been an outstandingly successful programme. And Airbus has not only produced highly effective aircraft but has done so profitably. This amazing example of large scale co-operation sees major subassemblies flown from manufacturers across Europe to final assembly lines in France and Germany. This "industrial shuttle" has worked so well that veteran Guppy outsized transports used for years to ferry subassemblies between nations are being replaced by a small fleet of 4 new and specially prepared SATIC Airbus A300-600ST Belugas.

The latest in the successful Hornet series is the F/A-18E, rolled out on 18 September 1995

It is not only large and highly expensive aircraft that have benefited from international collaboration. For example, Dassault's new Falcon 900EX, first flown in 1995, has 20% of total investment from Alenia (Italy), AlliedSignal (USA), Hellenic Aircraft Industries (Greece), Honeywell (USA), Latécoère (France) and Sabca (Belgium).

But not everything in Europe is perfect by any means. Eurocopter was hardly thrilled at the British Government's decision in July 1995 to buy US Apache as the Army's attack helicopter, following an earlier and similar decision by the Netherlands. Though the UK is not a shareholder in Eurocopter, British Aerospace had been associated with the Eurocopter Tiger bid. Clearly the term "Euro" does not guarantee anything even within the close community, as also discovered by Euroflag when Britain chose the Lockheed Martin C-130J over the FLA (now an Airbus project) as the RAF's replacement transport. But loss for Eurocopter was gain for Westland, which will build the Apaches. For BAe, this came in a period that saw its former Hawker business aircraft jetting off to the USA under Raytheon ownership and the remainder of its regional aircraft business merging with Aerospatiale/Alenia's ATR company to create the Aero International Regional consortium.

On the military scene, the Eurofighter programme continues to be dogged by political and funding problems. In-service dates have slipped and its future depends on a complex web of international and domestic factors. Not all or even many of these are military, and the programme illustrates graphically at one and the same time the advantages and disadvantages of collaborative projects. The massive costs of going it alone have to be set against the inherent risks of such a project which, arguably, are quite beyond the control of any individual partner. What are the real effects on the national security of the participants? At their simplest, delays can require the fielding of interim aircraft, as is the case with Spain's use of the Hornet and Italy's leasing of Tornado F3.

It is even possible to conceive of long-term replacement or logistic problems, if international circumstances were to change and partners were to become unreliable. Such may be one of the considerations behind Sweden's decision to go ahead alone with Gripen. Certainly, Sweden's stance of non-alignment has served well the aviation industry of a country of less than nine million souls. It has been necessary to overcome major financial and technical problems to produce the Gripen, designed in Sweden, built in Sweden, powered by a Swedish engine and equipped with Swedish avionics and in doing so it has met the needs of its own government, and produced what is probably the world's best light multi-role fighter. Even without the prospect of foreign sales, Sweden would still have built Gripen because it needs it. The icing on the cake is that British Aerospace is so impressed with Gripen that it is now a partner for the international marketing effort.

In the mid-1990s, what the aviation industry is capable of producing may fall at the first budgetary hurdle; the technically possible may prove to be financially insupportable, and the gulf between what is possible and what can be afforded may be wider today than ever before. That sobering fact alone demands close attention to the world aviation industry by men and women of vision and imagination. Only people such as they can bring to decision making bodies the qualities necessary to placate financial and business factors which could otherwise stifle progress. Such vision may demand too much of the culture and attitudes of an internationalized industry where, even more than in a national enterprise, the cult of the bottom line and 'national' interests are inevitable.

Michael Taylor
November 1995

DIRECTORY USER'S GUIDE

The *Brassey's World Aircraft & Systems Directory 1996/97* details aircraft in production or under development worldwide – military, commercial, general aviation, helicopters, autogyros, updates and modifications, sporting, homebuilts, microlights, gliders and airships. All categories are important to the industry and enthusiast alike. In addition the directory contains all relevant older combat aircraft, whether undergoing upgrade or not. The specification of an aircraft is insufficient knowledge if the performance details of the radar it carries and missiles it launches (if military) are not available at source for half the knowledge is half the capability revealed. Essential also are details of the engines too. To address all these the book contains sections on commercial, military and light aircraft engines, missiles, and commercial and military radars, plus runway bearing strengths.

The book has been divided into 12 sections, to enable the reader to see and compare at a glance aircraft of similar purpose built throughout the world. Within each section, countries are listed alphabetically and within each country, aircraft manufacturers are listed alphabetically.

Important company information (such as a contact address, telephone/facsimile number and information officer) is provided for each manufacturer, but where a manufacturer's products fall into more than one section (for example, McDonnell Douglas in Combat, Airliners and Helicopters) the company details are given in the first section containing any of that company's aircraft, with cross references thereafter. A comprehensive index is also provided.

The book has been designed for easy reference and usability. Each new company entry starts with a heading arranged across the entire page. This prevents the products of different companies merging. The significant development dates of an aircraft are listed, rather than written in paragraph form, with a distinctive ▲ icon by each date to make it easily distinguished. Therefore, by looking for the ▲ symbol throughout the book, the development dates of all aircraft can be found at a glance. Other distinctive icons have been adopted for the various business ● **Activities** of a company, its ■ **Facilities**, and the design ★**Aims** of individual aircraft.

Within the individual aircraft entries, information is presented in a way intended to help resolve readers' queries with ease. For example, there are separate sub-headings for **"fixed"** and **"expendable weapons"** of a combat aircraft, as well as for its **"radar"**, **"flight instruments/avionics"** and **"self-protection systems"**. Similarly, there are separate sub-headings for the **"engine"**, its **"power rating"**, **"fuel system"** and **"refuelling probe"**. Specification data (such as dimensions, weights and performance) is provided in a shaded box for speedy reference.

GLOSSARY OF ABBREVIATIONS

The following abbreviations are used throughout the directory:

2-D Two dimensional
3-D Three dimensional
AAM Air-to-air missile
AC Alternating current
ACLS Automatic carrier landing system
ACN Aircraft classification number
ACO Airborne commanding officer
ACT Active control technology
ADC Air data computer
ADF Automatic direction finder
ADI Attitude director indicator
ADV Air defence variant
AEW Airborne early warning
AEW&C Airborne early warning & control
AFCS Automatic flight control system
AFDS Autopilot and flight director system
Afterburning Augmented thrust
AGM Air-to-ground missile
AHRS Attitude heading reference system
AIDS Airborne integrated data system
Airstairs Passenger boarding stairs built as an integral part of the aircraft
ALCM Air launched cruise missile
ALCS Active lift control system
ALFS Airborne low frequency sonar
Alt Altitude
AM Amplitude modulation
Amp Ampére
ANG Air National Guard (US)
Anhedral Inclined downward from root to tip
AoA Angle of attack
AOC Air officer commanding
APU Auxiliary power unit
ARCS Acquisition radar and control system
ARIA Advanced range instrumentation aircraft
ARM Anti-radiation missile
ARS Attack radar set
Articulated rotor With blades able to flap, drag and feather
ARV Air recreational vehicle
ASARS Advanced synthetic aperture radar system
ASI Airspeed indicator
ASM Air-to-surface missile
ASO Acoustic systems officer
ASRAAM Advanced short range air-to-air missile
ASST Anti-ship surveillance & targeting. Also, advanced supersonic transport
ASTOVL Advanced short take-off and vertical landing
ASUW Anti surface warfare. See ASV
ASV Anti surface warfare (anti ship)
ASW Anti submarine warfare
ATC Air traffic control. Also, approved type certificate
ATDS Airborne tactical data system
ATF Advanced tactical fighter
ATGW Anti-tank guided weapon
ATHS Airborne target handover system
ATO Assisted take-off. RATO (rocket) and JATO (jet, often meaning rocket)
Autogyro US gyroplane
AUW All up weight
Avionics Aviation electronics
AVLF Airborne very low frequency
AWACS Airborne warning & control system
AWAC Automatic weapons control system
AWR Airborne weather radar

BCAR British Civil Airworthiness Requirements
BERP British experimental rotor programme
BHP Brake horsepower
BIT Built in test
BITE Built in test equipment
BLC Boundary layer control
Bleed air Hot compressed air taken from turbine engines
Blimp Non-rigid buoyant aircraft (airship)
Blind flying Flying using instruments, without outside visual references
BVR Beyond visual range

C^2 Command and control
C^3 Command, control and communications
C^3I Command, control, communications and intelligence
CAA Civil Aviation Authority (UK)
CAD Computer aided design
CAM Computer aided manufacture
Canard Foreplane
CAP Combat air patrol
CAS Calculated airspeed
Casevac Casualty evacuation
Cat Category
CB Chemical biological
CBU Cluster bomb unit
CBW Chemical, biological warfare
CCD Charge coupled device
CCV Control configured vehicle
CDU Cockpit display unit
CEO Chief executive officer
CEP Concurrent evaluation phase
CFT Conformal fuel tank
CG Centre of gravity
Chord Width between the leading and trailing edges of an aerofoil
CIS Commonwealth of independent states
CKD Component knock down (parts for assembly)
Clean Flying with flaps, slats and undercarriage retracted (if u/c retractable). No external stores
CNI Communications navigation identification
CO Commanding officer
COD Carrier on-board delivery
C of A Certificate of airworthiness
COIN Counter insurgency
Combi Combined passengers and freight
Comint Communications intelligence
com or **comm** Communications
CCP Cost per passenger
cm Centimetre
Combat SAR Combat search and rescue
CPS Central processing system
CPU Central processing unit
CSRL Common strategic rotary launcher
CRT Cathode ray tube
CW Continuous wave. Also chemical warfare
CWR Colour weather radar

DADC Digital air data computer
DADS Digital air data system
dB Decibel
DC Direct current
Derated Output power of an engine deliberately restricted to under its full possible rating
DF Direction finder
DID Data insertion device
Difar Directional acoustic frequency analysis and recording
Dihedral Inclined upwards from root to tip
DIN(S) Digital inertial navigation (system)
DLC Direct lift control
DME Distance measuring equipment
DMU Distance measuring unit. Also data management unit
DoD Department of Defense (US)
DRU Direct reporting unit

EAA Experimental Aircraft Association
EAS Equivalent airspeed
ECCM Electronic counter countermeasures
ECM Electronic countermeasures
ECR Electronic combat and reconnaissance
EEZ Exclusive economic zone
EFIS Electronic flight instrumentation system
EGT Exhaust gas temperature.
ehp. Equivalent horsepower
EHSI Electronic horizontal situation indicator
EICAS Engine indication/instrument and crew alerting system
EICMS Engine in-flight monitoring system
ekW Equivalent Kilowatt
ELF Extremely low frequency
Elint Electronic intelligence
ELT Emergency locator transponder
EM Electromagnetic
EMS Emergency medical service
EO Electro-optical
EOC Early operational capability
EPNdB Equivalent perceived noise decibel
ER Extended range
ERU Ejector release unit
eshp Equivalent shaft horsepower
ESM Electronic (support or surveillance) measures
Esmo ESM operator
ETOPS Extended range twin operations
EW Electronic warfare

FAA Federal Aviation Administration (US) or Fleet Air Arm (UK)
FAC Forward air control
FADEC Full authority digital engine control
FAR Federal aviation regulations
FBL Fly by light
FBW Fly by wire
FCS Flight control system
FDAS Flight director acquisition system
FDC Flight director coupler
FDI Flight director indicator
FDS Flight director system
ff First flight
FFAR Folding fin (or forward firing or free flight) aircraft rocket
FGA Fighter and ground attack
FGR Fighter, ground (attack) and reconnaissance
FLIR Forward looking infra-red
FM Frequency modulation
FMC(S) Flight management computer (system)
FMD Flight management display
FMS Foreign military sales (US) or flight management system
FSD Full scale development
ft Foot (12 ins)
FY Fiscal year

g Gramme
G limit Acceleration due to gravity
GAC Gust alleviation control
glove Non-moving root section of a variable-geometry wing
GNS Global navigation system
GP General purpose
GPS Global positioning system
GPU Ground power unit
GPWS Ground proximity warning system
GRP Flas reinforced plastics
GW Guided weapon

HARS Heading and attitude reference system
HDD Head down display
HE High explosive
HF High frequency
HMD or **HMS** Helmet mounted display (or sight)
HOCAC Hands on cyclic and collective
HOTAS Hands on throttle and stick
HOTCC Hands on throttle/collective/cyclic
hp Horsepower
HSD Horizontal situation display
HSI Horizontal situation indicator
HUD Head up display
HUDWAC HUD weapon aiming computer
HUMS Health and usage monitoring system
HVAR High velocity aircraft rocket
Hz Hertz

IAS Indicated airspeed
ICAO International Civil Aviation Organization
IDS Interdiction strike
IF Intermediate frequency
IFF Identification friend or foe
IFR Instrument flight rules
IGE In ground effect
IIR Imaging infra-red
IIRS Instrument inertial reference set
ILS Instrument landing system
IMS Information (or integrated) management system
INS Inertial navigation system
ins Inches
IOC Initial operational capability
IR Infra-red
IRCCD Infra-red charged coupled device
IRCM Infra-red countermeasures
IRLS Infra-red linescan
IRS Inertial reference system
IRST Infra-red search track
ISA International standard atmosphere
ISAR Inverse synthetic aperture radar
IRU Inertial reference unit

JAR Joint Airworthiness Requirements
JATO Jet assisted take off (see ATO)

K Kelvin
kg Kilogramme
km Kilometre
km/h Kilometre per hour
kN Kilonewtons
kts Knots
kVA Kilovolt ampere
kW Kilowatt

LAMPS Light airbirne multi-purpose system
LANTIRN Low altitude navigation and targeting infra-red (at) night
lbf Pounds force (engine thrust rating)
LCD Liquid crystal display
LCN Load classification number
LED Light emitting diode
LERX Leading-edge route extension
Litres Litres x 0.264177 = US gallons. Litres x 0.219975 = Imperial gallons
LGB Laser guided bomb
Litter Stretcher
LLL(TV) Low light level (TV)
Loran Long range navigation
Low observables Stealth
LRU Line replaceable unit

m Metre
Mach Mach number
MAD Magnetic anomaly detector
MCP Maximum continuous power
MCU Management control unit
Medevac Medical evacuation
MEP Mission equipment package
MF Medium frequency
MFD Multi-function display
MGT Motor gas temperature
MGTOW Maximum gross take-off weight
MIL-STD Military standard
MLS Microwave landing system
MLW Maximum landing weight
mm Millimetre
Mмо (Mmo) Maximum operating Mach number
MMS Mast mounted sight
mod Modified
MoU Memorandum of understanding
MPD Multi-purpose display
mph Miles per hour
MR Medium range or maritime reconnaissance
MSIP Multi stages improvement programme
MTOW Maximum take-off weight
MW Medium wave

N/A Not applicable
NACA National Advisory Committee for Aeronautics
NAS Naval air station
NASA National Aeronautics and Space Administration
NATO North Atlantic Treaty Organization
nav Navigation
navaid Navigation aid
nav/com(m) Navigation and communications
NBC Nuclear, biological, chemical
NEDS Narcotics eradication delivery system
Ni-cd Nickel cadmium
NOE Nap of the earth
NOS Night observation surveillance
Notar No tail rotor (McDonnell Douglas)
NVG Night vision goggles
NVS Night vision system

OBOGS On-board oxygen generating system
OCU Operational conversion unit
OEI One engine inoperative
OGE Out of ground effect
Omega Long-range radio navigation aid
OMI Omnibearing magnetic indicator
OTH(T) Over the horizon (targeting)
OTPI On top position indicator
OTU Operational training unit

PCN Pavement classification number
PFCS Primary flight control (or computer) system
PFD Primary flight display
PGM Precision guided munition
PRDS Processed radar display system
psi Pounds per square inch. psi x 0.06895 = bars
PWR Passive warning receiver

R&D Research & development
RAF Royal Air Force
RAM Radar absorbing material. Also random access memory
RAWS Radar altitude warning system. Also radar attack and warning system
RCS Radar cross section
RF Radio frequency
RFP Request for proposals
RHWR Radar homing and warning receiver
RHWS Radar homing and warning system
RMI Remote or radio magnetic indicator
Root Innermost part of a aerofoil where it attaches to the supporting airframe
rpm Revolutions per minute
RPV Remotely piloted vehicle (drone/UAV)
RWR Radar warning receiver. Also rear warning radar

SALT Strategic arms limitation talks
SAM Surface-to-air missile
SAR Search and rescue. Also synthetic aperture radar and semi-active radar
SARH Semi-active radar homing
SAS Stability augmentation system
Satcom. Satellite communications.
SCAS Stability and control augmentation system
SEAD Suppression of enemy air defenses
Senso Sensor operator
SFC Specific fuel consumption
shp Shaft horsepower
SIF Selective identification (interrogation) facility
Sigint Signals intelligence
SLAR Side looking airborne radar
SLEP Service life extension programme
SOF Special operations forces
SPILS Stall protection and incidence limiting system
SR Short range or strategic reconnaissance
SRAM Short range attack missile
SSB Single sideband
SST Supersonic transport
STA Supplementary Type Approval
STC Supplemental Type Certificate
STO Short take off
STOL Short take off and landing
STOVL Short take off and vertical landing
Swing wing Variable geometry wing

Tacamo Take charge and move out (US Navy)
Tacan Tactical air navigation
Tacco Tactical commander or co-ordinator
TANS Tactical air navigation system
TAS True airspeed
TBO Time between overhauls
TCAS Traffic alert and collision avoidance system
TDS Tactical data system
TET Turbine entry temperature
TGT Turbine gas temperature
TGW Terminally guided weapon
TIALD Thermal imaging airborne laser designator
TIAS Target identification and acquisition system
TIT Turbine entry temperature
TLS Tactical landing system
TOGW Take off gross weight
tonne 1,000 kilogrammes
TSD Tactical situation display
TV Television
TWR Threat warning radar

UAV Unmanned aerial vehicle
UHF Ultra high frequency
USAF United States Air Force
USMC United States Marine Corps
USN United States Navy
USCG United States Coast Guard

V Volts
VA Volt amperes
Variable geometry "Swing" wing
Vd Maximum permitted diving speed
VDU Visual or video display unit
Vertrep Vertical replenishment
VFR Visual flight rules
VHF Very high frequency
VIP Very important person. Also value improvement programme
VLF Very low frequency
Vмо (Vmo) Maximum permitted operating speed
Vɴᴇ (Vne) Never-exceed speed
VOD Vertical on-board delivery
VOR VHF omnidirectional (radio) range
VPU Video processing unit
VSD Vertical situation display
VSI Vertical speed indicator
V/STOL Vertical or short take-off and landing
VTO(L) Vertical take-off (and landing)

WA&SD World Aircraft & Systems Directory
WDNS Weapon delivery and navigation system
WSI Windshear indicator
WSO Weapon system operator

Micky Blackwell, President, Lockheed Martin Aeronautics Sector

Combat Aircraft (and Modern Turbine Trainers)

Lockheed Aircraft Argentina SA (LAASA) (Argentina)

Corporate address: c/o Area de Material Córdoba (AMC), Avenida Fuerza Aérea Argentina km 5.2, 5103 Córdoba.
Telephone: +54 51 650 594
Facsimile: +54 51 654 486
Founded: 1 July 1995, to manage the Fábrica Militar de Aviones SA (FMA) that had first formed in 1927 under Argentine Air Force control via its Area de Material Córdoba (AMC). Unlike other divisions of Lockheed Martin, LAASA has not adopted "Martin" in its name.
Employees: 1,250.
CEO: Harry Q. Radcliffe (Managing Director).
Information: Ronald Lindeke at LMAS, California (see Lockheed Martin under USA).

● Activities

● On 15 December 1994 the Government of Argentina and former Lockheed Aircraft Service Company (now Lockheed Martin Aircraft Services) of the USA signed contracts to privatize the Government's Fábrica Militar de Aviones SA (FMA) aircraft factory and maintenance depot at Córdoba, to modify A-4M Skyhawk attack aircraft under a $200 million (approximately) contract, and provide aircraft maintenance services for the Argentine Air Force for 5 years under a similarly priced contract. Consequently, Lockheed established LAASA (Lockheed Aircraft Argentina SA) for operating purposes, beginning management on 1 July 1995.
● Lockheed Martin's A-4M Skyhawk contract covers the refurbishment and modernization of 36 ex-US Navy aircraft for Argentina (stored in Arizona in 1994) over a 3 year period. The work includes depot level inspections and rewiring, engine refurbishment, avionics upgrade, pilot and mechanic training, spares provisioning and technical documentation. The initial 18 A-4Ms will be upgraded at Chino, California, USA, and 18 at the Area de Material Córdoba (AMC) using Lockheed kits.
● Under depot privatization, LAASA has a 25-year concession. Córdoba is expected to become an international C-130 maintenance centre, attracting also other fabrication, maintenance and modification work, including commercial.
Comments: In November 1995, the Editor was informed by Lockheed Martin that the company considered the Pucará to be an ideal low-intensity conflict attack aircraft.

Fábrica Militar de Aviones SA (FMA) IA.58A Pucará

First flight: 20 August 1969 (with original Garrett TPE331 engines).
Role: Attack, counter-insurgency, close air support, photographic reconnaissance and special operations.
Chief designer: Comandante Héctor Ruiz.

★ Aims

★ Uncomplicated, low-cost and compact counter-insurgency aircraft to meet a requirement of the Argentine Air Force, capable of flying from grass and other unprepared strips.
★ Short take-off distance, reduced to about 265 ft (80m) when using underfuselage JATO boosters.
★ 2 crew shared workload, although often flown in combat as a single seater to allow for an increased fuel/weapon load.
★ Low level operations, requiring an armoured floor and resistant windscreen to protect the crew against 0.30-calibre bullets, plus self-sealing fuel tanks.
★ Substantial built-in gun armament, plus a wide range of expendable weapons.

▲ Development

▲1966. Programme started, initially producing a twin-boom design.
▲ 26 December 1967. Flight of an unpowered aerodynamic prototype in revised conventional-fuselage form. Then known as the A-X2 Delfin.
▲ 1968. Metal cut for the first prototype.
▲ 6 September 1970. First flight of a prototype with production-standard Astazou engines.
▲ 8 November 1974. First flight of a production Pucará.
▲ 1976. Initial deliveries to the Air Force.
▲ 15 May 1979. First flight of the IA.58B prototype, featuring 30-mm instead of 20-mm cannon with fewer rounds of ammunition, slightly heavier expendable load, some avionics upgrade, and resultant airframe changes. Did not progress to production.
▲ April 1982. Pucarás of Grupo 3 were flown to the Falkland/Malvinas Islands as part of the Argentine military presence, thereafter operating from Goose Green, Pebble Island and Port Stanley.
▲ Resulting from Falkland/Malvinas operations, 48 more Pucarás were ordered (many more than were lost), making 108 production total.
▲ 30 December 1985. First flight of the single-seat and heavier-armed IA.58C. Not adopted.

Sri Lanka Air Force IA.58A Pucará carrying 8 bombs (Denis Hughes)

Also cancelled was the IA.66 with more powerful Garrett engines.
▲ 1993. As the latest Pucará operator, Sri Lanka received the first of 4 ex-Argentine aircraft. These operate with No 1 Wing from Anuradhapura.
Sales/users: Production ended 1986. Argentine Air Force had approximately 40 in 1995, Colombia 3, Sri Lanka 4, and Uruguay 6. Sri Lanka has options for a further 6.
Crew: 2 crew, with rear cockpit raised by 250-mm to offer good forward visibility.
Cockpits: Conventional, with dual controls, under a single-piece upward-hinged canopy. Armour protection (see Aims).
Crew escape: Martin-Baker AP06A zero-zero ejection seats.
Fixed guns: 2 x 20-mm Hispano DCA804 cannon and 4 x 7.62-mm FN-Browning M2-30 guns in the nose.
Ammunition: 270 rounds per cannon and 900 rounds per gun.
Number of weapon pylons: 3, with up to a 2,205 lb (1,000 kg) load under the fuselage and up to half that weight under each wing, with a total load not exceeding 3,307 lb (1,500 kg).
Expendable weapons and equipment: Bombs of up to 500 kg weight each (including SITEA BK-BR series of 50 to 500 kg general purpose and BRP/BRPS/FAS parachute retarded bombs of 50 to 500 kg), napalm, air-to-surface missiles including Pescador, torpedoes for an anti-shipping role, rocket launchers each with 19 x 2.75-ins rockets, other larger rockets, various gun and cannon pods, and/or drop tanks within the total load limit. Any combination of release modes.
Additional stores: Includes reconnaissance pods.
Flight/weapon system avionics/instrumentation: Navigation avionics include, amongst others, an instrument landing system (ILS) with VOR/Loc (navigational guidance using VHF omnidirectional radio range — VOR) and glideslope. Automatic direction finder (ADF). SFOM 83A3 reflector sight originally fitted. ECM can be carried.
Wing characteristics: Straight low-mounted, with dihedral on the tapering outer sections.
Wing control surfaces: Ailerons and slotted flaps.
Tail control surfaces: T-tail with rudder and elevators.
Construction materials: Metal.
Engines: 2 Turbomeca Astazou XVIG turboprops.
Engine rating: Each 965 shp (720 kW).
Fuel system: 1,280 litres standard internal capacity, rising to a maximum of 3,016 litres with a combination of 318 and/or 1,100 litre drop tanks carried under the

Sri Lanka Pucará with rocket pods (Denis Hughes)

DETAILS FOR IA.58A PUCARÁ.

Principal dimensions:
Wing span: 47 ft 7 ins (14.5 m)
Maximum length: 46 ft 9 ins (14.25 m)
Maximum height: 17 ft 7 ins (5.36 m)

Wings:
Aerofoil section: NACA 64_2A215 and 64_1A212 (root/tip)
Area: 326.15 sq ft (30.3 m^2)
Aspect ratio: 6.94
Incidence: 2°
Dihedral: 7° on outer tapering sections

Tail unit:
Tailplane span: 15 ft 5 ins (4.7 m)
Tailplane area: 49.514 sq ft (4.6 m^2)
Fin area: 41.44 sq ft (3.85 m^2)
Fin angle: approx 35° sweepback

Undercarriage:
Type: Retractable, with twin mainwheels and nosewheel
Tyre size: 7.5 x 10
Wheel base: 12 ft 9 ins (3.89 m)
Turning circle: 21 ft 4 ins (6.5 m)

Weights:
Empty, operating: 8,863 lb (4,020 kg)
Maximum take-off: 15,000 lb (6,800 kg)

Performance:
Maximum speed: 270 kts (311 mph) 500 km/h
Stall speed: 77 kts (89 mph) 143 km/h with flaps, at light weight
Take-off distance: 984 ft (300 m) without JATO, 265 ft (80 m) with JATO
Landing distance: 660 ft (201 m) at light weight
Maximum climb rate: 3,550 ft (1,075 m) per minute
G limits: +6, -3
Ceiling: over 32,000 ft (9,750 m)
Range with 1,730 litres fuel: 310-525 naut miles (356-605 miles) 574-972 km, depending on mission altitude
Radius of action with full payload: typically 190 naut miles (218 miles) 350 km on 98% internal fuel (with reserve), to and from target at high altitude, with low-level attack

fuselage and wings. Accumulator tanks for 30 seconds of inverted flying.
Electrical system: 28.5 volt DC supply with 2 engine-driven starter-generators. 24 volt/36 amp-hours ni-cd battery. 2 static inverters for AC supply.
Hydraulic system: 2,540 psi.
Braking system: Hydraulic disc on main units.
Oxygen system: Bendix.
Aircraft variants:
IA.58A Pucará as detailed, the only production and in-service model.

FMA IA.63 Pampa

First flight: 6 October 1984.
Role: Basic, advanced and weapon training, and light attack.

★ Aims
★ To provide the Argentine Air Force with a modern jet trainer and light attack aircraft to replace the Morane-Saulnier MS.760 Paris and possibly other aircraft.
★ Capable of operating from grass and other unprepared strips.

▲ Development
▲ 1979. Programme begun. 7 designs submitted in single- and twin-jet configurations, with selection in the following year.
▲ 1981. Full-scale development initiated after wind-tunnel testing of scale models and further design work. Participation by Dornier of Germany (with Alpha Jet experience, and having also designed under German Government funding a transonic supercritical wing), provided technical back-up in addition to manufacturing the wings and other surfaces for the prototypes. The chosen aerofoil was of advanced Dornier type.
▲ March 1981. Metal cut for the first of what became 5 prototypes (3 flying and 2 ground test).
▲ 6 October 1984. First flight of a prototype, although the sixth flight on 10 October marked the recognized first flight date.
▲ 7 August 1985. First flight of the second prototype. A Government order for production aircraft was placed 2 months later.
▲ April 1988. 3 of an initial 18 production Pampas ordered were received by the IV Brigada Aérea (the M-S Paris operating Brigada at Mendoza). 1 squadron fully equipped by May 1992, then unarmed and without HUDs or weapon delivery systems (see Avionics).
▲ May 1990. LTV (later renamed Vought and now part of Northrop Grumman) and FMA became partners to offer the Pampa 2000-International for the USAF's JPATS programme.
▲ 31 August 1992. Second prototype in provisional Pampa 2000-International form was lost in an accident in Britain, while preparing for the Farnborough Air Show.
▲ 26 May 1993. First flight of a Pampa 2000-International prototype proper, prepared from an Argentine production Pampa.
▲ 22 November 1994. Vought informed of the USAF's decision to withdraw Pampa 2000-International from the continuing JPATS competition.
▲ 1995. Continuing programme to upgrade Pampa, based around the Elbit lightweight weapon delivery and navigation system (see Avionics), to provide an advanced interface system that familiarizes trainee pilots with a WDNS.
Sales/users: 18 ordered for the Argentine Air Force by early 1995, with up to 46 more expected to be funded later. Early consideration by Brazil to buy Pampas did not materialize, but more recently other nations have expressed interest. The Argentine Navy has also sought funding for 12 naval training variants, modified for landing on the deck of *25 de Mayo* but also for shore use. Former contender for the US JPATS programme but not selected.
Crew: 2, trainee normally in the front cockpit and instructor in the tandem rear cockpit that is raised to provide improved forward visibility.
Cockpit: Dual controls. Rear cockpit has a multi-function display.
Crew escape: UPC S-III-S3IA63 zero-zero ejection seats.
Fixed guns: None internally, but retrofitted with an underfuselage 30-mm cannon pod.
Number of weapon pylons: 5, comprising 1 under the fuselage (882 lb, 400 kg maximum weapon load), and 4 under the wings (2 x 882 lb, 400 kg and 2 x 550 lb, 250 kg). Maximum weapon load is believed to be restricted to 2,558 lb (1,160 kg) when Pampa carries 968 litres of fuel.
Expendable weapons and equipment: Container for practice bombs or rockets, 250 lb and/or 500 lb bombs (including SITEA BK-BR series of general purpose and BRP/BRPS/FAS parachute retarded bombs), rockets, gun pod with two 7.62-mm machine-guns, or other weapons. See Fixed guns.
Flight/weapon system avionics/instrumentation: As part of an upgrade programme, a head-up display has been fitted to in-service and new Pampas, together with the Elbit lightweight weapon delivery and navigation system which could include an up-front control panel, central mission computer, ring laser gyro/inertial navigation system, video camera and VTR, and rear cockpit multi-function display.
Wing characteristics: High-mounted transonic, straight tapered, with slight anhedral.
Wing control surfaces: Ailerons and single-slotted Fowler flaps.
Tail control surfaces: Slab tailplane. Rudder.
Airbrakes: 2, on the fuselage near the tail.
Fuselage: Conventional, with a slim, almost boom-like aft end carrying the tail, allowing for the efflux from the underfuselage engine nozzle.
Construction materials: All metal.
Engine: AlliedSignal TFE731-2N turbofan.
Engine rating: 3,500 lbf (15.57 kN).
Fuel system: 1,375 litres maximum. Inverted flying permitted (10 seconds).
Electrical system: 28 volt DC supply with engine-driven starter-generator. 2 x 27 amp-hours ni-cd batteries. 2 static inverters for AC supply.
Hydraulic system: 3,000 psi (dual).
Braking system: Messier-Bugatti discs on main units, with anti-skid.

Aircraft variants:
IA.63 Pampa is the standard Argentine Air Force version, as detailed. The naval variant had not been designated at the time of writing, thought to have been originally planned with a higher-thrust TFE731 engine but now similarly rated.
Pampa 2000-International was the combined Vought/FMA version for the USAF's JPATS competition, the offered training system including aircraft, trainers, instructional material and logistics support. AlliedSignal TFE731-2B and AlliedSignal equipment and air-conditioning system. 3 prototypes, 1 modified from the second Pampa prototype and 2 from production aircraft.

FMA 63 Pampa with the IV Brigada Aérea

DETAILS FOR IA.63 PAMPA.

Principal dimensions:
Wing span: 31 ft 9 ins (9.69 m)
Maximum length: 35 ft 9 ins (10.9 m)
Maximum height: 14 ft 1.25 ins (4.3 m)

Wings:
Aerofoil section: Dornier A-7/-8
Area: 168.272 sq ft (15.63 m^2)
Aspect ratio: 6.01
Anhedral: 3°

Tail unit:
Tailplane span: 15 ft (4.58 m)
Tailplane area: 46.866 sq ft (4.35 m^2)

Undercarriage:
Type: Retractable, with steerable nosewheel
Main wheel tyre size: Goodrich 6.5 x 10
Wheel base: 14 ft 6 ins (4.42 m)
Wheel track: 8 ft 9 ins (2.66 m)

Weights:
Empty, operating: 6,217 lb (2,820 kg)
Normal take-off: 9,200 lb (4,173 kg)
Maximum take-off: 11,025 lb (5,000 kg)

Performance:
Maximum speed: 400 kts (460 mph) 741 km/h at sea level
Cruise speed: 300 kts (345 mph) 556 km/h TAS
Stall speed: 79 kts (91 mph) 147 km/h CAS
Approach speed (1.3Vs), at 7,275 lb (3,300 kg) weight: 103 kts (118 mph) 191 km/h
Take-off distance, at 7,715 lb (3,500 kg) weight: 1,315 ft (400 m) nominal
Landing distance: 460 m (1,510 ft)
Maximum climb rate: 5,200 ft (1,584 m) per minute
Roll rate: 150° per second
G limits: +7, -3 without external stores
Ceiling: 42,300 ft (12,900 m)
Range with full fuel: 1,000 naut miles (1,150 miles) 1,850 km
Radius of action with full fuel and 2,205 lb (1,000 kg) of bombs: 194 naut miles (223 miles) 359 km

Promavia S.A. (Belgium)

Corporate address: Chaussée de Fleurus 181, B-6200 Gosselies-Aéroport.
Telephone: +32 71 35 08 29
Facsimile: +32 71 35 79 54
Telex: 51872 squal b
Founded: 1984.
Information: André Delhamende (Chairman and CEO).

● Activities
● Jet Squalus in Belgium and including the civil pilot training programme/Jet Air Academy (see General Aviation), and the ATTA/MiG 815 as a collaborative programme, with prototypes being built in Russia (see Multi-national at the end of the section).

Promavia Jet Squalus

First flight: 30 April 1987.
Role: Screening, primary, basic, part-advanced and weapon trainer. Potential for reconnaissance, maritime surveillance, search and rescue, counter-insurgency and target towing.

★ Aims
★ For both military and civil training (see also General Aviation), with no earlier piston aircraft training requirements for student pilots.
★ Direct operating cost said to be about $150 per hour.
★ Simple, efficient and safe airframe and systems, with safe engine-out landing.
★ All-weather flying.
★ Fully aerobatic.
★ Performance sufficient for an all-through trainer: screening, primary, basic and part advanced.

▲ Development
▲ Design and construction of 2 proof-of-concept prototypes in collaboration with Dr Stelio Frati of Italy, the first in military form and the second now featuring an airline pilot training cockpit. Another prototype will have cockpit pressurization.
▲ In the process (in 1994-95) of changing over from the original Garrett (AlliedSignal) TFE109 engine to a higher-thrust Williams-Rolls FJ44 engine.
Sales/users: Purchase price approximately $2 million.
Crew: 2, side-by-side.
Cockpit: Dual controls.
Crew escape: Martin-Baker Mk 11 ejection seats
Number of weapon pylons: 4 underwing if required, each 331 lb (150 kg).

Promavia Jet Squalus military and civil jet trainer

Expendable weapons and equipment: Light weapons for training and possible counter-insurgency.
Additional stores: Special mission equipment is pod-mounted and could include day and night optical/infra-red reconnaissance equipment, photographic/low light level TV cameras, side-looking airborne radar (in an underfuselage pod for surveillance), and more.
Radar: Provision for weather radar.
Flight/weapon system avionics/instrumentation: Customer's option. Typically dual VHF com, VHF nav 1 with EHSI and MB lights, VHF nav 2 with VOR/ILS indicator, ADF with RMI transponder, DME, radio altimeter and VLF/Omega RNAV. Optional UHF com, Tacan and IFF.
Wing characteristics: Straight tapered.
Wing control surfaces: Ailerons (with tabs) and flaps.
Tail control surfaces: Elevators (with starboard tab) and rudder. VOR/LOC/GS antenna carried on the tailfin.
Airbrakes: Dual, under the fuselage.
Flight control system: Electrical for ailerons, electrical/mechanical for elevators, and hydraulic for flaps, airbrakes and undercarriage.
Construction materials: Basically an all-aluminium alloy riveted structure. Composites for nose section, engine air-inlets, wingtips, elevator tips and tail fairing.
Engine: Williams-Rolls FJ44 (originally 1,330 lbf, 5.92 kN Garrett/AlliedSignal TFE109-1).
Engine rating: 1,900 lbf (8.45 kN).
Air intakes: Fuselage sides.
Flight refuelling probe: None.
Fuel system: 720 litres. Single point gravity refuelling.
Electrical system: DC supply with 28 volt/300 amp starter-generator. 23 volt/43 amp-hours battery. AC supply with 2 static inverters, 26 volt/400Hz and 115 volt/400Hz.
Hydraulic system: Electro-hydraulic power pack, detached from the engine.
Braking system: Hydraulic disc, toe operated.

DETAILS FOR JET SQUALUS WITH TFE109 ENGINE.
PERFORMANCE FIGURES IN ITALICS ARE CALCULATED WITH THE CURRENT FJ44 ENGINE.

Principal dimensions:
Wing span: 29 ft 8 ins (9.04 m)
Maximum length: 30 ft 8.5 ins (9.36 m)
Maximum height: 11 ft 10 ins (3.6 m)

Wings:
Aerofoil section: Supercritical
Area: 146.17 sq ft (13.58 m^2)
Aspect ratio: 6.018
Incidence: 1° and 1° 45′ (root/tip)
Dihedral: 6°

Undercarriage:
Type: Retractable trailing-arm type, with steerable nosewheel
Main wheel tyre size: 6.00 x 6
Nose wheel tyre size: 5.00 x 5
Wheel base: 11 ft 9 ins (3.58 m)
Wheel track: 11 ft 9.25 ins (3.59 m)

Weights:
Empty, operating: 3,086 lb (1,400 kg)
Maximum take-off and landing: 5,291 lb (2,400 kg)
Maximum take-off aerobatic: 4,409 lb (2,000 kg)

Performance:
Maximum dive speed: 380 kts (437 mph) 703 mph, *the same*
Never-exceed speed (VNE): 345 kts (397 mph) 639 km/h, *the same*
Normal operating speed: 280 kts (322 mph) 519 km/h, *320 kts (368 mph) 593 km/h*
Design manoeuvring speed: 210 kts (242 mph) 389 km/h, *the same*
Stall speed: 67 kts (77 mph) 124 km/h with full flaps, *the same*
Take-off distance: 1,200 ft (366 m) at sea level, ISA, *the same*
Landing distance: 1,100 ft (335 m) at sea level, ISA, *the same*
Maximum climb rate: 2,500 ft (762 m) per minute, *3,600 ft (1,100 m) per minute*
G limits: +7, -3.5
Ceiling: 34,000 ft (10,350 m) at sea level, *40,000 ft (12,200 m)*
Ferry range: 1,000 naut miles (1,150 miles) 1,850 km at 20,000 ft (6,100 m) altitude, *750 naut miles (863 miles) 1,389 km*

Oxygen system: Gaseous.
Ice protection system: TKS fluid for leading edges. Optional electrically heated windscreen.

Aircraft variants:
Jet Squalus is the standard side-by-side military and civil pilot trainer.
ATTA/MiG is a tandem two-seat derivative for advanced training (see Multi-national entries at the end of this section).

Promavia ARA-3600

First flight: Not flown at the time of writing.
Role: Tactical aircraft for light attack and reconnaissance.

★ Aims:
★ Based on the ATTA design, but with a pilot only.
★ Carriage of 2,205 lb (1,000 kg) of weapons and/or other stores.

▲ Development
▲ 1989. Programme started but progress held up by delays in the ATTA-4000 project.

SABCA (Belgium)

Full name: Société Anonyme Belge de Constructions Aéronautiques.
Corporate address: Chaussée de Haecht 1470, B-1130, Bruxelles. Charleroi plant: Rue des Fusillés 11, B-6041 Gosselies.
Telephone: +32 2 729 55 11 or 59 01 (Bruxelles). +32 71 25 42 11 or 43 39 (Gosselies).
Facsimile: +32 2 216 15 70 (Bruxelles). +32 71 34 42 14 or 35 48 27 (Gosselies).
Telex: 21237 SABCA B.
Founded: December 1920. Major shareholders are Dassault Aviation and Fokker NV.
Employees: 1,550.
Information: Claude Baudrenghien (Marketing Manager, aircraft repair and modernization).

SABCA Mirage 5 MIRSIP upgrade for Chile, becoming the Elkan

■ Facilities
■ Brussels plant (Bruxelles) is the corporate HQ, engineering, design, development and test facility, and manufactures aerospace structures, servo systems and electronics.
■ Charleroi plant, inaugurated in 1954, is for assembly and integration, retrofit, mid-life updates, and maintenance and overhaul of aeroplanes and helicopters.
■ SABCA Limburg NV plant (Dellestraat 32, B-3560 Lummen) was founded in 1989 as a fully-owned subsidiary. It designs, develops and manufactures composite aerofoil skins by automated tape-laying, monolithic and honeycomb structures.

● Activities
● Production of servo actuators, and is the world's second largest source of integrated servo actuators for the F-16 programme.
● Limburg activities include producing the Rafale vertical fin, Boeing AWACS antenna fairings, A330/A340 tailcone access doors, Falcon 900 bell fairing engine cowls, Fokker 50 wing trailing edges, and Ariane 5 space booster nosecone and fairings.
● Electronics and electro-optics, including SIB 92 controls for the Mirage V MIRSIP (see below).
● Research and Development.
● Aircraft modernization and repair.

This includes:
A 109. Design and development of the military cockpit front panel for the Belgian Army.
F-5. Update, including new avionics (HUD, HOTAS, INS and more) and industrial co-operation with the customer.
F-16. SABCA delivered 222 F-16s to Lockheed Martin and co-operates with Lockheed Martin in the Mid-Life Update programme.
Mirage 5. MIRSIP (MIRage System Improvement Programme) is the latest SABCA upgrade, having previously modernized 10 former Belgian Air Force Mirage 5s under a safety improvement programme. Almost the entire fleet of Belgian Mirage 5s has been withdrawn from service, many having been offered for sale. Chile has purchased 25, including 4 Mirage 5BRs and a Mirage 5BD. The remaining 15 single-seaters and 5 two-seat operational trainers are all undergoing upgrade under the current SABCA MIRSIP, becoming Mirage 5M Elkans to serve with Grupo 8 of Ala 1. The first Elkan was rolled-out on 11 October 1994, and Elkans have been airlifted to Chile by Antonov transports during 1995. The SABCA MIRSIP for Chilean Mirage 5s includes canards; nose strakes; HOTAS; new avionics encompassing weapon delivery, navigation, UHF/VHF communications, cockpit displays and IFF; active/passive ECM; a laser designator; zero-zero ejection seats; and system improvements. SABCA claims that the standardization of equipment and firing performances with the F-16 makes the Mirage 5 MIRSIP a suitable F-16 lead-in aircraft.

EMBRAER (Brazil)

Full name: Empresa Brasileira de Aeronáutica S.A.
Corporate address: Av. Brig. Faria Lima 2.170 (Caixa Postal 343), 12227-901 São José dos Campos SP.
Telephone: +55 123 21 8842 or 25 1000/1529
Facsimile: +55 123 21 5339/8466
Telex: 1233589 EBAE BR
Founded: 19 August 1969.
Employees: 5,700.
Information: Rogério Stolle de Andrade (Marketing and Sales Division).

● Activities
● Privatization of Embraer was completed on 7 December 1994. Previously the company was a mixed capital corporation established with funds from the Brazilian Government and the private sector. The Government was the major shareholder and retained 96.5% of its voting stock. At privatization, 55.5% of the voting stock was sold for R$154.1 million. A consortium led by bank Bozano Simonsen, representing local pension funds plus leasing and investment banks (acting on behalf of foreign investors), acquired 45.44% of the stock put up for auction and assumed a controlling interest. The remaining 9.96% was acquired by investment banks and private investors. The total stock sold represented 67% to national investors and 33% to foreign investors. In addition to the stock purchase, the new owners injected R$30 million to capitalize the company. Some weeks later, a further 10% of the voting shares was sold, leaving the Government 18.4% of the voting stock and the employees 10%.
● Under a June 1987 contract with McDonnell Douglas, Embraer has been manufacturing carbon/epoxy outboard flaps for the MD-11 airliner, with 200 shipsets ordered and 100 on option, deliveries having begun in October 1988.
● Under a 1989 contract with Boeing, Embraer has been supplying machined flap supports for the 747 and 767 airliners.
● Under a 16 December 1991 contract with Boeing, Embraer is producing wing tips and dorsal fins for the 777 airliner, deliveries lasting from 1993 to 1999.
● Multi-national programme is the AMX (see Multi-national in this section). Development of the CBA-123 Vector has ended.
● The EMB-120EW and EMB-120SR surveillance versions of the Brasilia can be found in the Reconnaissance section.

DIVISIONS

Embraer Divisão Equipamentos
HQ address: São José dos Campos SP.

● Activities
● Equipment division.

Indústria Aeronáutica Neiva S.A.
HQ Address: See General Aviation section.

● Activities
● Subsidiary of Embraer, producing the EMB-202 Ipanema agricultural aircraft and a line of light aircraft built under licence from Piper (which see). Also now marketing PZL Warszawa-Okecie aircraft.

EAC-Embraer Aircraft Corporation
HQ Address: 276 South West 34th Street, Fort Lauderdale, FL 33315, USA.

● Activities
● Subsidiary for sales and after-sale support of Embraer products in North America.

EAI-Embraer Aviation International
HQ Address: Aeroport du Bourget, Zone d'Aviation d'Affaires, 93 350 Le Bourget, France.

● Activities
● Subsidiary for sales and after-sale support of Embraer products in Europe and Asia.

Embraer EMB-111A Patrulha

First flight: 15 August 1977.
Role: Maritime surveillance, patrol, surface vessel attack, and search and rescue.

Embraer EMB-111A (P-95) Patrulha of the Brazilian Air Force

★ Aims

⋆ To meet a requirement of the Brazilian Coastal Command.
⋆ Based on the commercial Bandeirante airframe but with a nose radome, wingtip fuel tanks to increase flight duration (internal fuel capacity also increased) and other modifications.

▲ Development

▲ 11 April 1978. The Brazilian Air Force received its first Patrulha. After all 19 P-95s had been delivered to operating countries (by 1981), no further Patrulha deliveries took place for 7 years.
▲ October 1989. Delivery of the first P-95B version to the Brazilian Air Force, with the remaining 9 following in 1990.
Sales/users: 29 delivered in both versions; in 1995, the Brazilian Air Force operated 21, Chilean Navy 6 and Gabonese Air Force 1.
Flight crew: 2.
Mission crew: 3 crew to operate the radar-radio and ECM work stations, plus 1 or 2 observers. Can carry troops or paratroops.
Fixed guns: None.
Number of weapon pylons: 4.
Expendable weapons and equipment: 2 x 5-ins HVAR rockets or a launcher containing 7 x 2.75-ins rockets on each pylon. Other mission equipment can include flares, buoys, smoke grenades and an SST-121 transponder for day or night illuminating or marking (see also Self-protection). Other expendable equipment can include rescue gear and survival packs.
Additional stores: A wing-mounted searchlight can be carried for night spotting and SAR, when only 3 pylons can be used.
Radar: AIL APS-128 (P-95) or Thorn EMI Super Searcher (P-95B) search radar carried in the extended nose radome.
Flight/weapon system avionics/instrumentation: IFR. See radar. Passive ECM fitted to EMB-111ANs.
Self-protection systems: Chaff dispenser.
Wing control surfaces: See Bandeirante.
Tail control surfaces: See Bandeirante.
Engines: See Bandeirante.
Fuel system: 2,550 litres internally and in wingtip tanks, of which 2,454 are usable.
Systems: See Bandeirante.

Aircraft variants:
P-95 was the Brazilian military designation for the first series EMB-111A aircraft, known to the Chilean Navy as EMB-111AN. Based on the short-fuselage Bandeirante. Some upgraded to P-95B standard.
P-95B covers the final 10 for Brazil with improved radar and other avionics changes.

DETAILS FOR EMB-111A. SEE ALSO BANDEIRANTE.

Principal dimensions:
Wing span: 52 ft 4 ins (15.95 m)
Maximum length: 48 ft 11 ins (14.91 m)
Maximum height: 16 ft 2 ins (4.92 m)

Weights:
Empty, operating: 8,290-8,598 lb (3,760-3,900 kg)
Maximum take-off: 15,430 lb (7,000 kg)

Performance:
Maximum cruising speed: 194 kts (223 mph) 359 km/h
Stall speed: 73 kts (84 mph) 135 km/h CAS
Take-off distance: 2,133 ft (650 m)
Landing distance: 1,477 ft (450 m) minimum
Maximum climb rate: 1,188 ft (362 m) per minute
Range with full fuel: 1,590 naut miles (1,829 miles) 2,945 km

Embraer EMB-312 Tucano

First flight: 16 August 1980.
Role: Basic and advanced training, and capable of armament and target towing, day and night instrument flying, aerobatic visual flights, and ferry flights.

★ Aims

⋆ First military trainer designed from the outset to use turboprop engines.
⋆ Operation within the temperature ranges of +50° C and -45° C. Altitude operational range 30,000 ft (9,145 m) to -1,000 ft (-305 m) below sea level.
⋆ Structure designed originally for a safe life of 6,000 hours, based on 82% basic/advanced training, 15% weapon and tactics training, and 3% logistics. EMB-312F has 10,000 hour and Shorts Tucano 12,000 hour structural life (see Aircraft variants).

Camouflaged Embraer EMB-312 Tucano in Brazilian service as the T-27, with machine-gun and rocket pods

▲ Development

▲ 1978. Design was initiated, at first intended as a replacement for Brazilian Cessna T-37s.
▲ 6 December 1978. Brazilian Ministry of Aeronautics awarded a contract for 4 prototypes, 2 flying and 2 test.
▲ 16 September 1980. First flight of a prototype. Second prototype flew on 10 December that year.
▲ 16 August 1982. Pre-series Tucano flew.
▲ September 1983. Deliveries began to the Brazilian Air Force under the designation T-27, with 6 officially handed to the EDA-Esquadrão de Demonstração Aerea (air display squadron). The first export customer was Honduras, which ordered 10.
▲ October 1983. First major export breakthrough, with Egypt ordering 120 for itself and Iraq, the first 10 delivered from Brazil, leading to the Arab Organization for Industrialization assembling the remainder (later increased to 124 assembled by AOI).
▲ 21 March 1985. The Tucano was chosen against stiff competition to equip the RAF as the British-built Shorts Tucano (not S312), replacing the Jet Provost (see Aircraft variants). 130 were delivered up to 25 January 1993.
▲ 14 February 1986. First flight of a Tucano with the RAF's required Garrett engine.
▲ 30 December 1986. First flight of a Shorts Tucano.
▲ 7 April 1993. First flight (2 hours duration) of a French Air Force EMB-312F.
Sales/users: 655 ordered by November 1995 (650 delivered), serving with Argentina, Brazil, Colombia, Egypt, France, Honduras, Iran, Iraq, Kenya, Kuwait, Paraguay, Peru, the UK and Venezuela. (See Aircraft variants.). No orders placed by Mexico by February 1995, despite reports.

TYPE	QUANTITY	MANUFAC-TURER	MODEL	TOTAL EXTERNAL STORES (Kg)
EXTERNAL TANK	2	EMBRAER	320 L	586
MACHINE-GUN	2	FNH AEROTEC	HMP .50'' C2 .30''	232 82
	2	FNH	TMP .30''	228
MACHINE - GUN WITH ROCKET LAUNCHER	2	FNH	HMP/MRL 70 50''/70 mm	368
ROCKET LAUNCHER	4	AVIBRÁS	LM 37/7 7 x 37 mm	128
	4	FNH AVIBRÁS	LAU 32 7 x 70 mm LM 70/7 7 x 70 mm	402 344
	4	MATRA	F2/6 6 x 68 mm	232
PRACTICE BOMB	4	MATRA FNH	SAMP 6 MK 76	45 45
BOMB	4	MATRA FNH	SAMP 120 MK 81	480 472
	2	MATRA FNH	SAMP 250 MK 82	500 482

External weapon/drop-tanks configurations using pylons with standard release unit 2610 (49 lb, 23 kg) (courtesy Embraer)

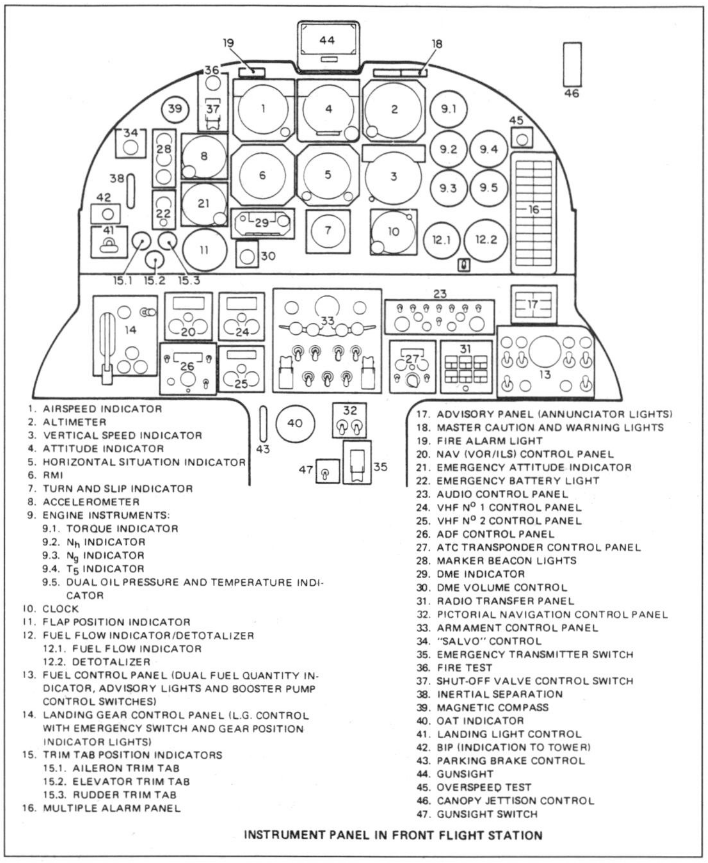

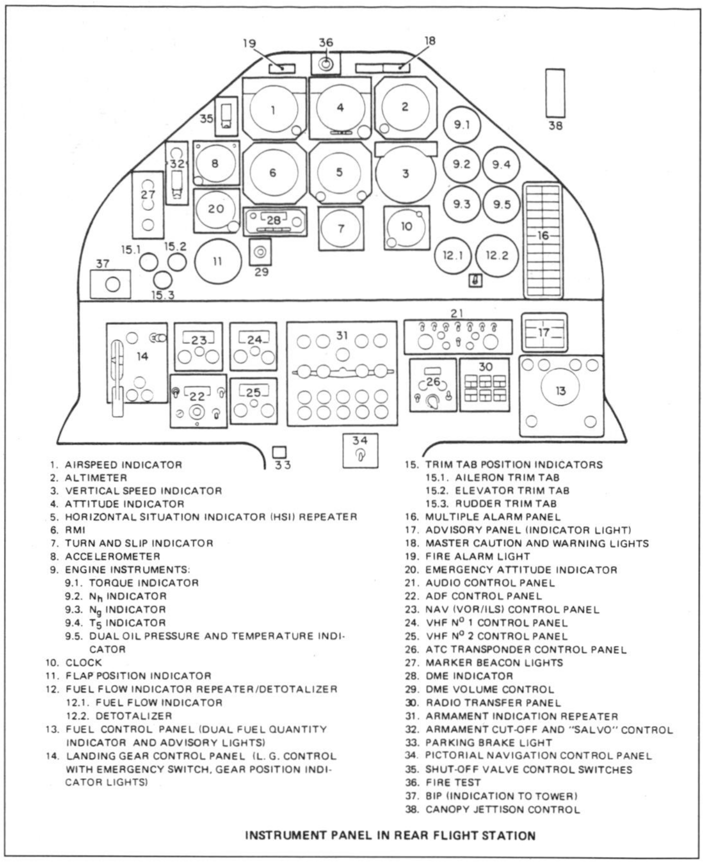

Embraer Tucano front and rear cockpit instrument panel layouts (courtesy Embraer)

Crew: 2 in tandem, with rear seat raised to allow a visibility of 4° 30′ below horizontal when the aircraft is level.
Crew escape: Martin-Baker MKBR8LC ejection seats, allowing safe ejection at any speed in flight at altitude but at speeds above 70 kts (81 mph) 130 km/h at ground level. Each seat has a pilot parachute and jungle survival kit.
Fixed guns: None.
Number of weapon pylons: 4, each limited to 551 lb (250 kg) in weapon configuration, or 408 lb (185 kg) in aerobatic configuration. 2 stores only for ferry flights, each inboard point carrying 694 lb (315 kg).
Expendable weapons and equipment: See diagram.
Radar: None.
Flight/weapon system avionics/instrumentation: Communications (including Collins/Engetronica VHF20B VHF transceiver), navigation and identification. Navigation system consists of a Collins PN-101 gyromagnetic compass, Collins/Engetronica TDR-90 transponder, Collins/Engetronica automatic digital ADF-60A, Collins/Engetronica VIR-30A VOR/ILS/marker beacon receiver and DME-40 subsystems, and Ametek C-5D magnetic compass, among others.
Wing control surfaces: Ailerons (deflection 15° down, 17° up), with tabs. Single-slotted flaps with 35° maximum deflection (25% relative chord).
Tail control surfaces: Elevators (deflection 20° down, 18° up) with port tab, and rudder (25° deflection), with tab.
Airbrakes: Ventral type on French and UK Tucanos.

DETAILS FOR EMB-312.

Principal dimensions:
Wing span: 36 ft 6.5 ins (11.14 m)
Maximum length: 32 ft 4 ins (9.86 m)
Maximum height: 11 ft 2 ins (3.4 m)

Cockpit:
Length: 9 ft 6 ins (2.9 m)
Width: 2 ft 9.5 ins (0.85 m)
Height: 5 ft 1 ins (1.55 m) stepped
Canopy: 8 ft 4.5 ins (2.55 m) free length, 2 ft 7 ins (0.85 m) maximum free width. Side hinged
Baggage: 6 cu ft (1.17 m^3), with 66 lb (30 kg) capacity, with fixture net

Wings:
Aerofoil section: NACA 63_2A-415 root at centre line, 63A-212 tip
Area: 208.8 sq ft (19.4 m^2)
Aspect ratio: 6.397
Sweepback: 0° 43′ 26″ at 25% chord
Chord at root: 7 ft 6.5 ins (2.3 m)
Chord at tip: 3 ft 6 ins (1.07 m) structural
Chord at centre line: 7 ft 11.5 ins (2.43 m)
Incidence: 1° 25′ at centre line
Geometric twist: 2° 13′
Dihedral: 5° 30′ at 30% chord

Tail unit:
Tailplane span: 15 ft 3.5 ins (4.66 m)
Tailplane area: 49.19 sq ft (4.57 m^2) without fillets
Fin area: 15.72 sq ft (1.46 m^2)

Undercarriage:
Type: Retractable, with nosewheel
Main wheel tyre size: 6.50-10, 8 ply, Type III Nylon, rib, tube
Nose wheel tyre size: 5.00-5, 8 ply, Type III Nylon, rib, tube
Wheel base: 10 ft 4.5 ins (3.16 m)
Wheel track: 12 ft 4 ins (3.76 m)

Weights:
Empty, equipped: 4,123 lb (1,870 kg) ± 2%
Maximum zero-fuel weight: 4,519 lb (2,050 kg)
Maximum take-off: 7,000 lb (3,175 kg) or 5,622 lb (2,550 kg) in aerobatic configuration
Maximum landing weight: 6,173 lb (2,800 kg), or 5,622 lb (2,550 kg) in aerobatic configuration

Performance:
Never-exceed speed (VNE): 280 kts (322 mph) 518 km/h, or 291 kts (335 mph) 539 km/h design
Maximum speed: 242 kts (278 mph) 448 km/h at 8,000 ft and 5,622 lb AUW, 227 kts (261 mph) 420 km/h at 7,000 ft and 7,000 lb AUW, ISA
Maximum cruise speed: 222 kts (255 mph) 411 km/h at 10,000 ft, or 240 kts (276 mph) 444 km/h design
Stall speed: 72 kts (83 mph) 134 km/h *clean*, 75 kts (87 mph) 139 km/h *design clean* at 5,622 lb AUW, 67 kts (77 mph) 124 km/h *with flaps*, 69 kts (80 mph) 128 km/h *design with flaps* at 5,622 lb AUW
Manoeuvring speed: 98 kts (113 mph) 181 km/h *design with flaps* at 5,622 lb AUW
Take-off distance: 1,227 ft (374 m) at 5,622 lb AUW, 1,811 ft (552 m) at 7,000 lb AUW, ISA. 1,962 ft (598 m) at 7,000 lb AUW at ISA + 15° C
Landing distance: 1,276 ft (389 m) at 5,622 lb AUW, brakes only (no thrust reverse) at sea level, ISA, or 1,493 ft (455 m) at 6,173 lb AUW, brakes only, at sea level, ISA + 15° C
Take-off distance over a 50 ft (15 m) obstacle: 2,103 ft (641 m) at 5,622 lb AUW, sea level, ISA, or 3,717 ft (1,133 m) at 7,000 lb AUW, sea level, ISA + 15° C
Landing distance over a 50 ft (15 m) obstacle: 1,716 ft (523 m) at 5,622 lb AUW, with brakes and reverse thrust, sea level, ISA, or 2,323 ft (708 m) at 6,173 lb AUW, brakes only, sea level, ISA + 15° C
Maximum climb rate: 2,230 ft (680 m) per minute at sea level at 5,622 lb AUW, or 1,460 ft (445 m) per minute at sea level at 7,000 lb AUW, ISA
G limits: +4.4, -2.2 weapon configuration, or +6, -3 aerobatic configuration
Ceiling: 30,000 ft (9,145 m)
Range with full internal fuel: 1,111 naut miles (1,278 miles) 2,057 km at long-range cruise speed, 30 minutes reserve, at 25,000 ft altitude, 5,622 lb AUW, ISA, or 1,764 naut miles (2,030 miles) 3,267 km at long-range cruise speed, 30 minutes reserve, at 17,000 ft altitude, 7,000 lb AUW, ISA + 15° C

Flight control system: Mainly mechanical, with electromechanical flaps and tabs.
Construction materials: Basically 2024 aluminium alloy, with steel alloys and glassfibre where advantageous to strength, structure, shape, weight and heat protection.
Engine: Pratt & Whitney Canada PT6A-25C turboprop, with a Hartzell HC-B3TN-3C/T10178-8R 3-blade propeller. Allows 30 seconds of inverted flight, 15 seconds vertical nose up, 20 seconds vertical flight nose down, 10 seconds zero G.
Engine rating: 750 shp (559.3 kW), with 700 shp (522 kW) maximum climb and cruise rating.
Fuel system: 694 litres in 2 wing tanks. Provision 2 x 330 litre drop tanks, carried on inboard pylons.
Electrical system: 28 volt DC, with a 25.2 volt/26 amp-hours BTCA-9-20 alkaline (ni-cd) battery, an emergency battery, and a 200 amp starter-generator. AC system furnished by a main 250 volt-amp inverter, generating 115 and 26 volt/400Hz. A 125 volt-amp standby inverter supplies some AC essential loads in an electrical emergency.
Hydraulic system: 2,100 psi.
Braking system: Single disc on each main unit.
Oxygen system: Low pressure (450 psi) diluter-demand system for both crew members. 6 or 7 x 200 litre cylinders.

Aircraft variants:
EMB-312 is Embraer's designation for the standard PT6A-25C-powered version, as detailed.
EMB-312F is the French Air Force model, receiving 80 with extended fatigue life airframes (see Aims), a ventral airbrake, French avionics and other changes. First delivery batch comprised 2 pre-series aircraft for evaluation at French Ministry of Defence organizations. All 80 to be delivered by February 1998. Replaces Fouga Magisters.
Shorts Tucano (not S312, as often quoted) is the RAF version, with differences including a 1,100 shp (820.3 kW) Garrett (now AlliedSignal) TPE331-12B turboprop to improve performance, airframe strengthening for 12,000 hours, ventral airbrake, 37 ft (11.28 m) wing span, redesigned cockpits with much UK equipment, and more. Also sold to Kuwait. Maximum speed 274 kts (315 mph) 507 km/h.

Embraer EMB-312 H/ALX Super Tucano

First flight: 15 May 1993 for genuine Super Tucano prototype (see Development).
Role: Training (similar to Tucano) and day/night operational missions including anti-guerrilla (see Development – 1993).

★ Aims:
★ Advanced version of the Tucano, with a strengthened airframe.
★ 1,600 shp (1,193 kW) Pratt & Whitney Canada PT6A-68R turboprop engine in the proof-of-concept prototype, with a 5-blade propeller (see Engine).
★ Fuselage lengthened by 4 ft 6 ins (1.37 m), made up of 1 ft 2 ins (0.37 m) ahead of and 3 ft 4 ins (1 m) aft of the cockpit.
★ Electrically-actuated, upward hinged canopy.
★ New cockpit layout.
★ Global Positioning System (GPS), Traffic Collision Avoidance System (TCAS).
★ Pressurized cockpit.
★ On-board oxygen generating system.
★ Air-cycle air-conditioning system.
★ Crew anti-G system.
★ Zero-zero ejection seats.
★ Redesigned engine cowling to improve

EMB-312H Super Tucano first prototype

maintainability.
★ Standard ventral airbrake.
★ Single and two-seat versions of the ALX, for armed operational missions in addition to training (see Aircraft variants).

▲ Development
▲ January 1991. Development began, with public disclosure of the programme in June at the Paris Air Show.
▲ 9 September 1991. First flight of the Super Tucano proof-of-concept aircraft, modified from the RAF Shorts Tucano prototype. Pilot was Gilberto Pedrosa Schittini.
▲ May 1992. Embraer and Northrop of the USA signed a preliminary agreement to jointly tender a version of Super Tucano for the USAF's JPATS programme.
▲ 1993. 2 prototype Super Tucanos proper appeared, the first making its maiden flight on 15 May and the second on 14 October. Public deput 20 May at the Embraer works. The second prototype was fitted out to take part in the USAF's JPATS programme, in co-operation with team-member Northrop, the Embraer/ Northrop association having been formalized in July 1993.
▲ 1993. Studies begun of the ALX derivative model for advanced training (including weapon familiarization and conversion to advanced navigation/attack systems), plus operational light attack missions by day or night. Development contract was signed on 18 August 1995. First prototype expected to fly in early 1996.
▲ 26 August 1994. Provisional certification by the Brazilian CTA. The 2 prototypes had flown over 500 flight hours in 396 missions, 20 of which were certification oriented and flown by CTA representatives.
Sales/users: Brazilian Air Force plans to purchase 100 ALXs, for delivery from about 1996-97, to perform some duties currently undertaken by Xavantes. Single-seaters to be designated A-29s and two-seaters AT-29s in Brazilian service.
Crew: 2 normally. ALX will be available in both single and 2-seat versions.
Number of weapon pylons: See Aims and Aircraft variants.
Flight/weapon system avionics/instrumentation: See Aims and Aircraft variants.
Engine: 1,600 shp (1,193 kW) Pratt & Whitney Canada PT6A-68R turboprop engine in the proof-of-concept prototype. EMB-312HJ had a 1,300 shp (969.4 kW) PT6A-68A engine and ALX has a PT6A-68/1.
Fuel system: 694 litres.

Aircraft variants:
ALX is the designation of a special-application version of Super Tucano for the Brazilian Air Force and export, intended for operational missions in addition to training. Structural and system modifications, including 5 hardpoints for weapons/drop tanks, and the cockpit will have crew ballistic protection. Advanced navigation/attack systems including a head-up display, multi-function displays, central mission computer, inertial reference system, GPS and an air-data computer. Provision for FLIR, a radar warning receiver and chaff dispenser. Able to operate with weapons from unpaved runways. 1,600 shp (1,193 kW). PT6A-68/1 engine.
EMB-312H is the designation of the standard dedicated trainer version, capable of carrying weapons.
EMB-312HJ was the JPATS version with a 1,300 hp (969.4 kW) PT6A-68A engine.

DETAILS FOR EMB-312H, INDICATING STANDARD TUCANO DIFFERENCES.

Principal dimensions:
Maximum length: 37 ft 5.5 ins (11.42 m)
Maximum height: 12 ft 9.5 ins (3.9 m)

Undercarriage:
Wheel base: 11 ft (3.36 m)

Weights:
Empty, operating: 5,335 lb (2,420 kg)
Maximum take-off: 7,032 lb (3,190 kg)

Performance:
Maximum speed: 301 kts (346 mph) 557 km/h at 20,000 ft
Maximum cruise speed: 286 kts (329 mph) 530 km/h at 20,000 ft
Long-range cruise speed: 228 kts (262 mph) 422 mph at 20,000 ft
Stall speed: 85 kts (98 mph) 157 km/h *clean*, 78 kts (90 mph) 145 km/h *with flaps and undercarriage down*, EAS
Take-off distance: 1,148 ft (350 m)
Landing distance: 1,805 ft (550 m)
Take-off over a 50 ft (15 m) obstacle: 1,805 ft (550 m)
Landing over a 50 ft (15 m) obstacle: 2,822 ft (860 m)
Maximum climb rate: 2,935 ft (895 m) per minute
G limits: +7, -3.5 aerobatic
Ceiling: 35,000 ft (10,650 m)
Range with full fuel: 847 naut miles (975 miles) 1,568 km at 30,000 ft, with 30 minutes reserve
Ferry range: 1,495 naut miles (1,721 miles) 2,768 km at 25,000 ft, with underwing tanks and 30 minutes reserve
Duration: 6 hours on internal fuel, at long-range cruise speed, 30 minutes reserve

Bristol Aerospace Ltd (Canada)

Corporate address: PO Box 874, 660 Berry Street, Winnipeg, Manitoba R3C 2S4.
Telephone: +1 204 788 2831
Facsimile: +1 204 775 7494
Founded: Origins in McDonald Brothers Aircraft of 1930 founding. Purchased by Rolls-Royce in 1966 and operating under Rolls-Royce Industries Canada Ltd.
Information: Robert C. Walker (public relations).

DIVISIONS

Aircraft

● Activities

● Modernization of the F-5.
● Repair and overhaul for Canadian Forces' Bell helicopters, including refurbishment of airframe structures, repair and overhaul of structural and dynamic components, avionics upgrade integration and development of night vision goggles cockpit compatibility.
● Development of the Wire Strike Protection System (WSPS®) for helicopters, offering protection against inadvertent flight into horizontal power and communications wires and cables.

Aerocomponents

● Activities

● Major aero-engine and aero-structure design and manufacturing programmes, working with a wide range of materials. Offers advanced techniques for forming, welding, brazing, heat treat, coating and chemical processing. Comprehensive machining facilities. Manufacture of components using both composite and metal to metal bonding.

Rockets & Space

● Activities

● Owns and operates Canada's only solid fuel propellant plant, providing motors for many of this division's products. These include Black Brant sounding rockets, space payloads, small satellites, CRV7 rocket weapon system, and remotely controlled targets. Included among 4 air, 1 sea and 2 land targets is the Pop-Up Helicopter land target, aimed at helping air-defence gunners learn and maintain skills needed to meet the challenge of nap-of-the-earth mission combat helicopters that pop-up for target search and missile firing.

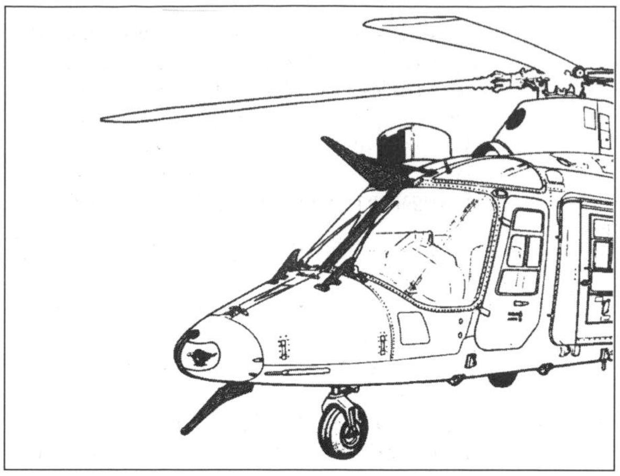

Bristol Aerospace Wire Strike Protection System (WSPS®), comprising a roof-mounted cutter-deflector, lower cutter-deflector, and windshield deflector (courtesy Bristol Aerospace)

Bristol Aerospace F-5 Modernization

First flight: 14 June 1991.
Role: Modernization of F-5s for enhanced combat capability or for a lead-in trainer role, as detailed below.

★ Aims

★ Refurbishment with redesigned parts for up to 4,000 additional hours of airframe life. Major modification and improvements include new wing, dorsal longeron, vertical and horizontal stabilizers, undercarriage, aft fuselage formers and complete rewiring. All major structural and aged components are repaired or replaced using new processes, procedures and materials. Major elements are designed and manufactured in accordance with MIL-Standard procedures.
★ Installation of an advanced avionics suite, putting navigation accuracy and weapon delivery in the same class as modern fighters, with 88% fewer passes required to disable a hard point target and 64% fewer passes to disable a soft area target.
★ Alternative avionics upgrade and structural improvements in a re-lifed F-5 to produce a cost-effective supersonic lead-in trainer (as for modernized Canadian CF-116s).

Bristol Aerospace working on structural improvements to F-5s

▲ Development

▲ 14 June 1991. First Canadian Forces' modernized CF-116 prototype flew, against a 1990 order for upgrade as lead-in trainers of its Canadair/Northrop CF-5s. Redeliveries took place between 1993 and 1995, initially to No 419 Squadron.
▲ May 1994. Bristol Aerospace and Northrop Grumman announced a teaming agreement to jointly pursue the F-5E/F modernization market. Bristol is the principal subcontractor to Northrop Grumman.
Sales/users: Canadian Forces CF-116 modernization encompassed 34 CF-5s plus 2 used in a flight test programme. Supply of 15 sets of improved design wings for Norwegian F-5A/Bs, delivered 1995-96, follow the earlier installation of new dorsal longerons. Spanish F-5s are undergoing the structural life extension, with Bristol as prime subcontractor to CASA and responsible for new manufacture and repair of the wings and other major assemblies, plus providing engineering work, life cycle support and spare parts. Other programmes undertaken or underway for Singapore, Thailand, the USAF and US Navy.

Bristol Aerospace upgraded cockpit for a Canadian lead-in trainer, showing the HUD

Flight/weapon system avionics/instrumentation: Upgraded, with 1553B MUX bus interface avionics suite. Cockpit features a head-up display, high situation awareness, head-up nav/attack and HOTAS. Laser inertial navigation system and weapon aiming computer (4-6 MIL weapon delivery accuracy). Configuration flexibility for 1 or 2 multi-function displays, radar, laser ranger, radar warning receiver, chaff/flare dispenser, and additional weapons.
Wing characteristics: Replacement of the lower skin, 15% spars (inboard and outboard), 44% spars (inboard), 66% spars (complete), wing attachment root ribs, and main undercarriage uplock ribs.
Tail surfaces: New tailfin with redesigned skin that extends fatigue life at the critical radius. New tailplane.
Fuselage: Original aluminium dorsal longeron is replaced with a steel reinforced version, extending the time between inspections. Aft fuselage section is reinforced with redesigned formers. New skins (FS 436-531).
Undercarriage: New.
Fuel system: New fuel cells and tip-tank repair and overhaul (or exchange).
Electrical system: Rewired.

Empresa Nacional de Aeronáutica (ENAER) (Chile)

Corporate address: Avda J.M.Carrera, 11087 Paradero 36½, Santiago.
Telephone: +56 2 5282823, 5282735 and 5282599.
Facsimile: +56 2 5282699
Telex: 645157 ENAER PCT
Founded: 1984.
Employees: 1,700.
Information: Alejandro Vargas (commercial), and Felipe Fernandez mesa (aircraft maintenance division).

● Activities

- ENAER's first and principal programme was the piston-engined T-35 Pillán basic trainer, developed jointly by ENAER and Piper of the USA but completely manufactured and assembled by ENAER (except for knock-down kits supplied to CASA in Spain – see General Aviation section). This followed the assembly of Piper Dakotas by the Ala de Mantenimiento of the Chilean Air Force, the nation's first experience of aircraft manufacture, a programme begun in 1979 and which led to the creation of ENAER as a national aeronautical company.
- Part manufacture and assembly of A-36 Halcón attack aircraft was completed in 1995, having previously assembled related T-36 jet trainers. This was ENAER's second industrial programme.
- Current principal programmes are the development of the T35 DT Pillán Turbo trainer and development/production of the Ñamcu light plane (see General Aviation section), the latter as the first aircraft to be entirely designed and built by ENAER.
- Modernization, upgrading and structural life extension programmes are offered for civil and military aircraft, encompassing the Hawker Hunter (including self-defence EW equipment), the conversion of the Beech 99 to a maritime surveillance aircraft and also for electronic intelligence (with an ENAER ITATA radar detection sytem), modernization of the Mirage 50 to Pantera 50C form and upgrade of the Northrop F-5. The latter includes upgrade to F-5 Plus standard of all of the Chilean Air Force's F-5E/Fs (14 or 15), in co-operation with IAI, having Elta EL/M-2032B Doppler radar, enhanced weapon delivery and navigation systems, inertial navigation system, air data computer, El-Op head-up and 2 head-down displays, HOTAS, radar warning receiver, chaff/flare dispenser, jammer, and deletion of 1 cannon. 2 modernized by IAI and redelivered in 1993, with all further conversions in Chile.
- Other activities encompass aircraft maintenance and repair (A-37, C-130, CASA 212, UH-1H and others), engine maintenance (repair, overhaul and inspection of over 20 different types), accessories maintenance, component production (including tail parts for the CN-235 and EMB-145 commercial transports), and commercialization services covering technical training, field support, provision of spare parts and more.
- In September 1994 ENAER signed a contract with the Chilean Air Force for the manufacture of mechanical components for FASat-Alfa, the first Chilean satellite (a collaborative programme with Surrey Satellite Technology of the UK), launched in July 1995 carrying experiments for ozone layer monitoring, data transfer, GPS navigation and student educational experiments.

ENAER T-35 DT Pillán Turbo (courtesy ENAER)

ENAER T-35 DT Pillán Turbo

First flight: February 1986 (T-35 Pillán with an Allison engine as the first prototype, then known as the T-35TX Aucán). March 1991 (second prototype, as the Pillán Turbo proper).
Role: Military and civil primary and basic trainer, including screening, familiarization, aerobatics, formation flying, navigation, instrument and night flying, plus utility and rescue operations, reconnaissance and patrol.

★ Aims

- ★ Turboprop version of the T-35 Pillán (originally known as the T-35TX Aucán before considerable modification), designed and developed to maximize flight similarities whilst providing an advanced aircraft. Basing the new aircraft on an existing and proven aircraft (the Pillán) avoided the outlay in engineering and design costs involved in producing a completely new aircraft. Structural components and systems remain unchanged.
- ★ High manoeuvrability, fully aerobatic, and fully equipped for instrument flying.
- ★ Cockpit design and flight characterlstlcs similar to turbojet/turbofan trainers.
- ★ All systems and avionics are standard aeronautical components, readily available and in general use worldwide.

▲ Development

- ▲ See First flight (above).
- ▲ Developed under a joint programme between ENAER, Allison and Soloy.
- ▲ 1990. Soloy Corporation of the USA contracted to develop a turboprop conversion kit for the Pillán.

Sales/users: Available for purchase.
Crew: 2, at a total weight of 380 lb (172 kg).
Cockpit: Tandem, with flight and engine controls designed to familiarize the student-pilot with single-pilot operation. Instructor's rear seat is stepped up by 8.66 ins (220 mm) for visual control over the student. Duplicated instruments, avionics and flight controls.
Fixed guns: None.
Number of weapon pylons: None indicated at prototype stage.
Flight/weapon system avionics/instrumentation: Standard configuration includes audio selector panels, VHF/VOR, transponder, ADF, HSI, RMI, DME, marker beacon, slave meters and gyro unit. Audio stall warning is activated at 5-8 kts above the aerodynamic stall speed.
Wing characteristics: Straight, low mounted, with compound leading edges. Single spar, attached to the fuselage spar box.
Wing control surfaces: Ailerons (with port tab) and single-slotted flaps.
Tail control surfaces: Variable incidence tailplane, single-section elevator and rudder, with tabs.
Flight control system: Mechanical for ailerons, elevator and rudder, the remainder electrical.
Fuselage: Semi-monocoque, built in 2 parts (front fuselage and tail cone).
Construction materials: All metal, except for glassfibre wing/tailplane tips and engine cowl.
Engine: Allison 250-B17D turboprop, with a 3-blade Hartzell HC-B3TF-7A/T9212K-2 propeller.
Engine rating: 420 shp (320.2 kW).
Fuel system: 291.5 litres in 2 wing and 1 central tanks, of which 278 litres are usable. Weight of usable fuel 494 lb (224 kg); 30 lb (13.6 kg) unusable fuel.
Electrical system: DC supply using a 28 volt 80 amp starter-generator and 24 volt 20 amp-hour acid lead battery. Socket on starboard fuselage side for electrical power from an external source.

Details for Pillán Turbo.

Principal dimensions:
Wing span: 29 ft (8.84 m)
Length: 27 ft 7 ins (8.41 m)
Maximum height: 8 ft 8 ins (2.64 m)

Wings:
Aerofoil section: NACA 65_2415
Area: 147.36 sq ft (13.69 m^2)
Aspect ratio: 5.708
Incidence: 2° root, -30′ at wingtip
Dihedral: 7°

Tail unit:
Tailplane span: 10 ft (3.05 m)
Tailplane area: 16.9 sq ft (1.57 m^2)
Fin area: 7.427 sq ft (0.69 m^2)

Undercarriage:
Type: Retractable, with steerable nosewheel
Main wheel tyre size: 6.00-6.
Nose wheel tyre size: 5.00-5
Wheel base: 6 ft 7 ins (2 m)
Wheel track: 9 ft 10 ins (3.01 m)
Turning radius: 20 ft 4 ins (6.2 m)

Weights:
Empty: 2,079 lb (943 kg)
Maximum take-off and landing: 2,950 lb (1,338 kg)
Maximum aerobatic: 2,900 lb (1,315 kg)

Performance:
Maximum permissible speed: 241 kts (277 mph) 446 km/h
Cruise speed: 169 kts (194 mph) 313 km/h at 55% power
Maximum speed: 230 kts (254 mph) 426 km/h
Landing speed: 90 kts (104 mph) 166 km/h
Stall speed: 62 kts (72 mph) 115 km/h *with flaps and undercarriage lowered*, 66 kts (76 mph) 123 km/h *clean*
Maximum undercarriage extension speed: 138 kts (159 mph) 256 km/h
Take-off distance: 640 ft (195 m)
Landing distance: 420 ft (128 m) ground roll.
Take-off over a 50 ft (15 m) obstacle: 1,171 ft (357 m)
Landing over a 50 ft (15 m) obstacle: 1,820 ft (555 m)
Maximum climb rate: 2,200 ft (671 m) per minute at sea level
Time to 9,845 ft (3,000 m): 5.5 minutes
Inverted flight time: 15 seconds
G limits: +6, -3
Ceiling: 25,000 ft (7,622 m) *service*, 26,500 ft (8,079 m) *absolute*
Range at 75% power: 350 naut miles (403 miles) 648 km, at 8,000 ft and 45 minutes reserve
Range at 55% power: 410 naut miles (472 miles) 759 km at 13,000 ft and 45 minutes reserve
Range at 65% power: 579 naut miles (666 miles) 1,072 km, at 18,000 ft and no reserve
Duration: 3 hours 30 minutes at 12,000 ft

Hydraulic system: 1,800 psi (only for undercarriage actuation).
Braking system: Hydraulic disc on main units.
Oxygen system: Fitted.

ENAER T-36/A-36 Halcón

Role: Advanced jet trainer (T-36) and light tactical attack (A-36).

C16. ENAER A-36 Halcón (Denis Hughes)

★ Aims

⋆ Licence built Spanish CASA C-101BB and C-101CC respectively, that became ENAER's second industrial programme.
⋆ Chosen for co-production because of the aircraft's characteristics and because it allowed ENAER to take part in a technological exchange programme.
⋆ ENAER manufactured the front fuselage, tail unit, flight control surfaces, electric and hydraulic systems, and assembled the entire structure under the final phase of the Halcón programme, having begun by assembling CASA-produced kits for the first few aircraft and thereafter progressively introduced locally-produced components.

▲ Development

▲ 1980. Chilean Air Force signed a development and co-production contract with CASA for the C-101.
▲ 1983. First of 4 T-36s produced by CASA entered Air Force service with the Escuela de Aviación Capitan Avalos. In November, the first A-36 flew.
▲ 1989. Final phase of production/assembly, with ENAER contributing its highest number of components (see Aims).
▲ 1995. Production/assembly of the A-36 completed, having previously delivered all T-36s.
Sales/users: 14 T-36s and 23 A-36s produced, 10 and 19 respectively under the co-production arrangements. Used by the Escuela de Aviación Capitan Avalos as trainers, and by 2 squadrons (1° Esquadrão of Brigada Aérea I and 12° Esquadrão of Brigada Aérea IV) in A-36 tactical form.
Further details: See CASA entry under Spain.

ENAER Pantera 50

First flight: 1986 (in aerodynamic prototype form).
Role: Interceptor-fighter.

★ Aims:

⋆ Upgrade of the Chilean Air Force's Mirage 50 interceptors and operational trainers (16 aircraft) to third generation aircraft, to enhance capabilities, improve manoeuvrability and give a long operational life. *Programme has progressed very slowly, and conversion of the entire fleet could be in doubt following the purchase by the Air Force of SABCA-upgraded Mirage 5 Elkans (see SABCA).

▲ Development

▲ 1985. Programme initiated, with technical support from Israel Aircraft Industries.
▲ 1986. First Pantera prototype conversion flown for aerodynamic testing, incorporating just the Israeli-developed fixed canards on the air intake sides.
▲ 1988. First flight of a full Pantera conversion, featuring some Israeli Kfir avionics including Elta EL/M-2001B ranging radar in a lengthened nose, new weapon delivery and navigation system, computerized head-up display and Israeli Python 3 missiles, and also with locally-developed Caiquen III radar warning receiver and Eclipse chaff/flare dispensers.
Sales/users: Only about one-third of the Mirage 50 fleet had been converted to Panteras by early 1995, and continued upgrade may be in doubt following receipt of upgraded Mirage 5s from SABCA in Belgium.

ENAER Pantera 50 upgrade (courtesy ENAER)

Aviation Industries of China (China)

Corporate address: PO Box 33, 67 Jiao Nan Street, Beijing 100712.
Telephone: +86 1 401 3322
Facsimile: +86 1 401 3648
Founded: June 1993.
CEO: Zhu Yuli.

● Activities

● Established to oversee the growth of China's aviation industry, and encourage foreign investment and collaboration. High-level deligations have been received from Europe (including BAe, CASA, DASA, GEC-Marconi, Rolls-Royce and many others), North America (including Boeing, McDonnell Douglas, GE and P&W), Israel, Japan, South Korea and elsewhere. Risk-sharing joint ventures are being established with Chengdu, Changhe, Xi'an and other manufacturers.
● AVIC's principal operating organization is CATIC (which see).
● Announcement has been made of the development of a 100-120 seat regional transport between AVIC, Fokker, Daimler-Benz and Samsung.
Important recent developments in China to assist the process include:
● Approval issued by the State Council, CAAC and Ministry of Foreign Trade and Economic Co-operation on 6 May 1994, allowing foreign investment in the development of civil airports and air transport companies. (Boeing, with representatives from China Aviation Supplies Corp, opened a parts centre at Beijing's capital airport on 1 December 1994.)
● The civil aircraft import licensing system was abolished from 1 January 1994, to open the aviation market in China.
● On 1 April 1994 air traffic control over the Beijing-Guangzhou-Shenzhen route was transferred from Air Force to civilian operation.
● On 13 April 1994 Chuncheng civil airport at Tongshi in Hainan became the first privately run civil airport in China.

China National Aero-Technology Import and Export Corporation (CATIC) (China)

Corporate address: 5 Liangguochang, Dongcheng Qu, Beijing 100010 (PO Box 647).
Telephone: +86 1 401 7722
Facsimile: +86 1 401 5381, 4015682
Telex: 210403 CATIC CN/22318 AEROT CN
Cable: CAID BEIJING
Founded: 1979, becoming the CATIC Group under AVIC on 26 August 1993.
Employees: 10,000.
CEO: Liu Guomin (President).

● Activities

● Established to integrate Chinese industry and technology with trade. Deals with the export of aero and non-aero products (including Chinese manufactured aircraft), and imports modern aero and civilian technologies. Also develops co-production and joint-venture programmes.
● Has 11 subsidiaries in China (3 in Beijing and others in Shenzhen, Guangzhou, Shanghai, Zhuhai, Fuzhou, Xiamen, Hangzhou and Harbin), and has overseas representatives in 21 countries and regions.
● Has over 120 joint ventures and sole ventures operating worldwide. The agreement covering development of the K-8 jet trainer (see Multi-national section) was signed by CATIC and the Defence Production Division of the Pakistan Government, although recent changes have led to the reported abandonment of plans for K-8 production in Pakistan in favour of a greater component manufacturing role.
● Current international sub-contracting of aircraft, engine and airborne system components is undertaken on behalf of companies from Canada, France, Germany, Italy, the UK and USA, including for the Airbus A300, A310 and A320, various Boeing airliners and the MD-80/90 series.
● The Technical Support Division provides technical services, after-sales service, spares supply, overhaul/repair, flight crew/ground crew training and more.

Chengdu Aircraft Industry (China)

Corporate address: PO Box 800, Chengdu, Sichuan 610092.
Telephone: +86 28 769461
Facsimile: +86 28 769816
Founded: 1958.
Information: Wang Yinggong.

● Activities

● In addition to building and developing versions of the Jianjiji-7 fighter and modest production of the Jianjiji Jiaolianji-5 (JJ-5) trainer, Chengdu has been entrusted with development of the new "FC-1" fighter. It also produces McDonnell Douglas MD-80 and 90 series airliner nose structures for Chinese and US production.

Chengdu J-7 and Super-7

First flight: 17 January 1966.
Role: Tactical fighter and air defence interceptor.

★ Aims

★ Jianjiji-7 (J-7) was developed from the Mikoyan MiG-21F-13, after the Soviet Government agreed to Chinese manufacture.
★ Super-7 is aimed at producing a more modern fighter using foreign technologies, based on the exported Airguard but with major structural and avionics differences and using a Klimov engine.

▲ Development

▲ 1960-61. Discussions between the USSR and both Czechoslovakia and China on local co-production of the new MiG-21 fighter in its early form started almost immediately after Soviet production began. Interest centred on the second production version, the MiG-21F-13, the first model to have missile armament.
▲ Chinese programme began with the receipt from the USSR of both completed test aircraft and components for Chinese assembly and familiarization. However, technical transfer had not been completed before co-operation ended, forcing a delay in the programme while the extra engineering and development work was undertaken.
▲ 17 January 1966. First J-7 flown, having been assembled from Chinese parts at Shenyang, where most fighter production was then centred and where the first few production J-7s were built. Production at Chengdu started in the following year.
▲ 30 December 1978. Maiden flight of the much improved J-7 II, leading to substantial production for the Chinese air force and modest export.
▲ 26 April 1984. Maiden flight the J-7 III, the final development of the basic MiG-21 concept with the traditional nose intake.
▲ 1989. Co-operation with Grumman of the USA on development of the radically-altered Super-7 was terminated at government level, with Chengdu thereafter joining Pakistan Aeronautical Complex in its development and with Israel probably supplying the avionics. Engines from Russia.
▲ 1996. Maiden flight of the multi-role Super-7 prototype anticipated.

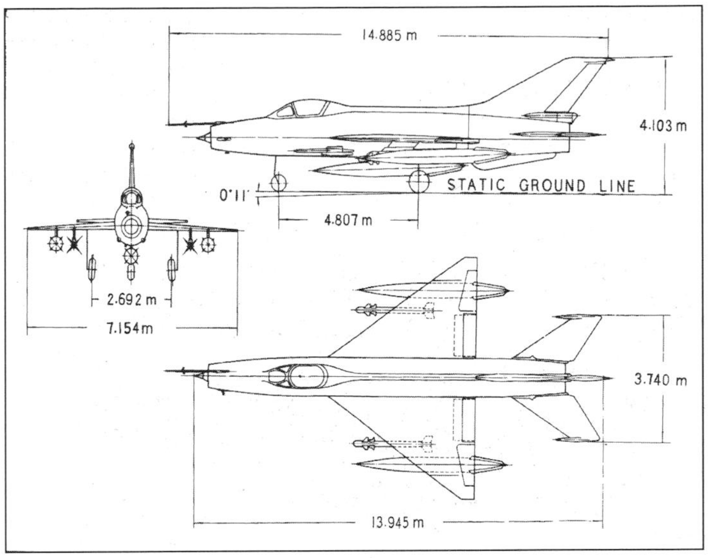

Chengdu A-7M Airguard drawing (courtesy CATIC)

Sales/users: Chinese production is thought to total about 1,000 aircraft, of which more than half that number remain in Air Force service as interceptors. All nations to have received exported F-7s appear to continue to operate them. These include Albania (operating about 15 F-7As at Durres-Shijak), Bangladesh (16 F-7Ms, operated by No 5 Squadron at Dhaka and No 35 at Chittagong), Egypt (about 90), Iran (18 F-7Ms), Iraq (over 60), Myanmar (30 F-7Ms – probably not all delivered by early 1995), Pakistan (95 F-7P/MP, received from July 1988 and first serving with No 20 Squadron at Rafiqui – now also with No 18 Squadron at the same base, No 2 at Masroor and No 25 OCU at Mianwali), Sri Lanka (4 F-7BSs operated by No 5 Squadron at Katunayake as part of a mixed squadron with FT-5s), Tanzania (11 F-7As), and Zimbabwe (20 F-7Ms).
Details: Principally for the F-7M, but not exclusively (as indicated).
Crew: Pilot.
Crew escape: Chengdu zero-altitude ejection seat, for use at speeds not less than 70 kts (81 mph)130 km/h. Martin Baker seat in other versions (see Aircraft variants).
Fixed guns: 2 x 30-mm Type 30-1 cannon. 1 x 23-mm cannon in J-7 III.
Ammunition: 120 rounds total.
Number of weapon pylons: 4, plus underfuselage station for an auxiliary fuel tank.
Expendable weapons and equipment: 1 Chinese PL-2 to PL-7 or French (Matra Magic) air-to-air missile, or a pod for 57-mm or 90-mm rockets (air-to-air or air-to-ground), or a 50-500 kg bomb under each inboard wing pylon (full range of Norinco bombs, including fuel-air, concrete penetration cluster, anti-armour cluster, general purpose). 1 x 50-150 kg bomb, or rockets or an auxiliary fuel tank under each outboard pylon. F-7P can carry 4 US Sidewinder AAMs (see Aircraft variants).
Radar: Skyranger. F-7P/MP now with replacement FIAR Grifo.
Flight/weapon system avionics/instrumentation: GEC-Marconi suite, encompassing Type 956 head-up display and weapon-aiming computer, and air data computer. Other avionics include locally produced Model 602 IFF.
Wing characteristics: Mid mounted delta. J-7E has radically-redesigned "cranked" deltas, with less leading-edge sweep at about half-span and forward-sweep on the trailing edge from the ailerons outward.
Wing control surfaces: Ailerons and trailing-edge flaps.
Tail control surfaces: Highly swept slab tailplane and rudder.
Airbrakes: 3 mounted on the fuselage.
Flight control system: Hydraulically actuated.
Construction materials: All metal.
Engine: Liyang WP-13F turbojet in F-7M and F-7 III, with power to weight ratio of 6. Single 9,689 lbf/13,443 lbf (43.1 kN/59.8 kN) WP7B in F-7A, and similarly rated WP7B M batch in F-7B and WP7B (BM) in F-7L and some F-7Ms. Single 9,037 lbf/14,815 lbf (40.2 kN/65.9 kN) in some F-7 IIIs, with 5.9 power to weight ratio. See Aircraft variants for Liming WP7C and F-engined J-7 II and J-7E and Klimov-engined Super-7.

Sri Lanka Air Force F-7BS operated by No 5 Squadron at Katunayake (Denis Hughes)

Chengdu Super-7 (courtesy CATIC)

Engine rating: 9,690 lbf (43.1 kN) dry, 14,815 lbf (65.9 kN) with afterburning (WP-13F).
Air intakes: At nose, with a central radar-carrying shock-cone.
Fuel system: 2,385 litres in the wings and fuselage. 1 x 800 litre or 500 litre auxiliary fuel tank under the fuselage, and/or 1 x 500 litre tank under each outboard wing pylon. Internal fuel for Super-7 is 5,130 lb (2,327 kg).
Braking system: LS-16 disc brakes on main undercarriage units and LS-15 on nosewheel. Drag-chute carried in a pod under the rudder.

Aircraft variants:

J-7 I (Jianjiji-7 I) was the first major Chinese version, though numbers remained limited. Short range, 2 wing pylons, and the ejection seat/forward-hinged canopy caused difficulties. Exported in small numbers as the F-7A.
J-7 II (Jianjiji-7 II) was produced with the improved M batch engine of similar rating, the option of a 720 litre auxiliary fuel tank carried under the fuselage, jettisonable rear-hinged canopy, new ejection seat capable of use at lower speed (135 kts, 155 mph, 250 km/h), and other refinements. Exported as the F-7B with optional French AAMs. Another export version was the F-7BS, specially produced for Sri Lanka with 4 underwing pylons. Information received by WA&SD from China indicated also the use of the WP7C, rated at 9,590 lbf (42.66 kN) dry and 13,625 lbf (60.6 kN) with afterburning. This is probably fitted to the last production aircraft or by retrofit.
F-7L is an export version about which nothing much is known. It uses a WP7B (BM) engine. It is almost certainly an Airguard variant.
F-7M Airguard became the first truly modernized version, intended to attract export interest. Increased range, advanced weapons control system, greater weapons fit options and improved engine and pilot ejection seat. Skyranger ranging radar and other western avionics, including a HUD, requiring a better electrical system. 4 underwing weapon/tank pylons, and the availability of PL-7 missiles. Stronger undercarriage.
F-7P Airguard is an upgrade of the F-7M for Pakistan, sometimes referred to as Skybolt. Martin Baker 10L ejection seat. 4 US Sidewinder AAMs. Grifo radar being retrofitted. A sub-variant is the F-7MP, featuring an important avionics upgrade and a revised cockpit layout. In addition to Grifo, it has Collins ARN-147 VOR/ILS, ARN-149 automatic direction finder and Pro Line II digital distance measuring equipment.
J-7 III (Jianjiji-7 III) became the first all-weather variant of the J-7 for Chinese service, featuring JL-7 radar, improved fire control system, KJ-11 autopilot, radar warning receiver, GT4 ECM, new Model 605A IFF, WP13F engine with a power-to-weight ratio of 6 and more internal fuel, blown flaps (possibly 25° deflection for take-off and 45° for landing), HTY-4 ejection seat, ability to carry 4 missiles or other loads, 23-mm Type 23-3 twin-barrel cannon carried under the fuselage and other updates. A further upgraded model has also joined the Chinese air force and navy, the designation of which is uncertain. Normal take-off weight 17,968 lb (8,150 kg) with 2 missiles.
J-7E (Jianjiji-7E) of 1990 appearance has an entirely new wing shape, in the form of a cranked delta of 27 ft 4 ins (8.32 m) span and 267.81 sq ft (24.88 m^2) area (see Wing characteristics). HUD, air data computer, PL-7 missile option (4 underwing pylons), and 9,920 lbf (44.13 kN) dry and 14,330 lbf (63.75 kN) with afterburning Liming WP7F turbojet.

Chengdu FC-1 next-generation Chinese fighter

Super-7 is the most radical modernization of the F-7, said in brochure material to be an advanced all-weather light fighter which meets the mission requirements around the year 2000. It offers air-to-air and air-to-ground multi-role capabilities at low cost, and has potential for further development. Incorporating foreign technologies, its development was begun with assistance from Grumman, but is now associated with PAC (see Development). "Solid" nose housing fire control radar, and resulting side air intakes. New larger-area wings with leading-edge slats, wingtip missile launchers and root extensions. J-7 III cannon pack. Greater fuel capacity, Martin Baker ejection seat, advanced off-the-shelf avionics (some reports suggest Israeli origin but with the possibility of the British GEC Blue Hawk), and reportedly an 11,100 lbf (49.42 kN) dry and 18,300 lbf (81.4 kN) with afterburning Klimov RD-33 turbojet engine. New undercarriage and ground arrester hook. Was to fly in 1996 but programme could have ended.

DETAILS FOR F-7M, *WITH SUPER-7 IN ITALICS.*

Principal dimensions:
Wing span: 23 ft 5.5 ins (7.154 m), *29 ft 5.5 ins (8.98 m)*
Maximum length: 45 ft 9 ins (13.945 m) tail to shock cone, or 48 ft 10 ins (14.885 m) including nose probe, *50 ft 2 ins (15.3 m)*
Maximum height: 13 ft 5.5 ins (4.103 m), *13 ft 6.5 ins (4.13 m)*

Wings:
Area: 247.57 sq ft (23 m^2), *265 sq ft (24.6 m^2)*
Aspect ratio: 2.225
Sweepback: 49° 6' at 25% chord
Incidence: 0°
Anhedral: 2°

Tail unit:
Tailplane span: 12 ft 3 ins (3.74 m)
Tailplane area: 42.41 sq ft (3.94 m^2)
Fin area: 37.46 sq ft (3.48 m^2)

Undercarriage:
Type: Retractable, with steerable nosewheel
Main wheel tyre size: 600 x 200 mm
Nose wheel tyre size: 500 x 180 mm
Wheel base: 15 ft 9 ins (4.807 m), *18 ft 4 ins (5.59 m)*
Wheel track: 8 ft 10 ins (2.692 m), *9 ft 2 ins (2.79 m)*
Turning radius: 23 ft 1 ins (7.04 m)

Weights:
Empty: 11,629 lb (5,275 kg)
Normal take-off: 16,603 lb (7,531 kg) with 2 x PL-7s
Take-off weight for Super-7: *20,062-24,900 lb (9,100- 11,295kg)*

Performance (F-7M with 2 x PL-7s):
Maximum Mach number: Mach 2.05, *1.8+*
Maximum speed: 1,174 kts (1,351 mph) 2,175 km/h
Take-off distance: 2,300-3,120 ft (700-950 m), *1,820 ft (555 m)*
Landing distance: 1,970-2,955 ft (600-900 m) with drag-chute, *2,825 ft (860 m)*
Maximum climb rate: 35,435 ft (10,800 m) per minute
Level flight acceleration time from Mach 0.9-1.2: 35 seconds at 16,400 ft (5,000 m)
Maximum sustained rate of turn: 14.7° per second at Mach 0.7, 9.5° per second at Mach 0.8 and 5,000 m
G limits: +8, *+8.5*
Ceiling: 59,710 ft (18,200 m) service, or 61,350 ft (18,700 m) absolute (static), *55,000 ft (16,760 m)*
Range with 2 x PL-7s and 3 x 500 litre drop tanks: 939 naut miles (1,081 miles) 1,740 km
Range with 2 x PL-7s and 2 x 500 litre plus 1 x 800 litre drop tanks: 1,204 naut miles (1,385 miles) 2,230 km

Chengdu FC-1

First flight: Early 1997.
Role: Advanced multi-role fighter, capable of air superiority, interdiction and air support.

★ Aims

★ To become operational early next century as a replacement for the J-7, and possibly also to replace J-6s and Q-5s. Almost certainly replaces Super-7 development.

▲ Development

▲ 1991. Development began.
▲ Being developed in co-operation with MAPO-MiG of Russia, with part funding believed to come from Pakistan (to be an early export user).
Crew: Pilot, but with a two-seater also anticipated.
Number of weapon pylons: 7, including wingtip.
Fixed guns: 23-mm twin-barrel cannon.
Expendable weapons and equipment: To include wingtip PL-7s or PL-10s. Weapon load 7,716 lb (3,500 kg).
Radar: Pulse Doppler multi-mode.
Flight/weapon system avionics/instrumentation: Modern cockpit layout.
Wing characteristics: Cropped delta type, with swept leading edges and straight trailing edges. Wing root extensions.
Tail control surfaces: All moving tailplane and rudder.
Engine: Klimov RD-93 turbofan.
Engine rating: 17,985 lbf (80 kN). To be built by Liyang.
Air intakes: On the fuselage sides with splitter plates.

DETAILS FOR FC-1.

Principal dimensions:
Wing span: 29 ft 6 ins (9 m)
Length: 45 ft 9 ins (13.952 m)
Height: 16 ft 5 ins (5.014 m)

Undercarriage:
Type: Retractable, with nosewheel
Wheel base: 16 ft 10 ins (5.137 m)
Wheel track: 7 ft 6 ins (2.3 m)

Weights:
Maximum take-off: 26,675 lb (12,100 kg)

Performance:
Maximum speed: Mach 1.6-1.8
Take-off distance: 1,640 ft (500 m)
Landing distance: 2,300 ft (700 m)
Ceiling: 52,500 ft (16,000 m)
G limits: +8
Radius of action: 648 naut miles (745 miles) 1,200 km for air-to-air, 378 naut miles (435 miles) 700 km for attack

Chengdu JJ-5

First flight: 8 May 1966.
Role: Advanced lead-in/fighter conversion trainer.

★ Aims

★ Based on the Shenyang Jianjiji-5A (or J-5A – a Chinese-built MiG-17PF variant) single-seat interceptor and attack aircraft, but modified to incorporate a MiG-15UTI-type tandem cockpit arrangement for 2 crew.

▲ Development

▲ Most production JJ-5s were built over 2 decades from 1967.

Sales/users: China has a mix of over 600 J-5 single-seaters and JJ-5 two-seaters remaining available to the air force and navy as interceptors, attack aircraft and trainers. Exported FT-5 trainers are thought to remain only with Pakistan (about 20), Sri Lanka (2, also with a combat role and flown by No 5 Squadron as part of a mixed squadron – see the J-7 entry), Sudan (a mix of 10 or more F-5 and FT-5 single/two-seaters for attack and training) and Zimbabwe (2). Almost certainly now unavailable, except as ex-service aircraft, and those exported to Pakistan and Sudan may well be replaced by K-8s.
Crew: 2.
Cockpit: Tandem cockpits, with a slightly elevated rear instructor's seat. Dual controls. Split canopy, with a side-hinged front section and rearward-sliding aft section.
Fixed guns: 23-mm Type 23-1 cannon in a detachable pack under the fuselage.
Number of weapon pylons: 2 under the wings, usually for 400 litre drop tanks.
Radar: Ranging type, for use with the gunsight.
Airframe characteristics: Similar to the Russian Mikoyan MiG-17.
Construction materials: All metal.
Engine: Liming WP5D non-augmented turbojet.
Engine rating: 5,950 lbf (26.48 kN).
Air intakes: At the fuselage nose.
Flight refuelling probe: None.

One of 2 Sri Lanka Air Force Chengdu FT-5s, the export Jianjiji Jiaolianji-5 trainer (Denis Hughes)

Details for JJ-5.

Principal dimensions:
Wing span: 31 ft 7 ins (9.63 m)
Maximum length: 37 ft 9 ins (11.5 m)
Maximum height: 12 ft 5 ins (3.8 m)

Undercarriage:
Type: Retractable, with nosewheel

Weights:
Empty, operating: 8,994 lb (4,080 kg)
Maximum take-off: 13,702 lb (6,215 kg)

Performance:
Mission speed: 418 kts (481 mph) 775 km/h
Take-off distance: 2,500 ft (760 m)
Landing distance: 2,725 ft (830 m)
Maximum climb rate: 5,300 ft (1,620 m) per minute
Duration: 2.6 hours with maximum fuel

Guizhou Aviation Industry Corporation (China)

Corporate address: PO Box 38, Anshun, Guizhou 561000.
Telephone: +86 851 551027
Texex: 66018 AIMGA CN

● Activities

● Produces two-seat operational training variants of the Chengdu J-7 fighter, in addition to work on the main J-7 programme, and is engaged in development of a new combat version of the two-seater with a lengthened fuselage.
● Other activities include weaponry and turbine engines.

Guizhou FT-7 in service with Sri Lanka Air Force, armed with 57-2 rocket pods (Denis Hughes)

Guizhou JJ-7

First flight: 5 July 1985 (JJ-7).
Role: Supersonic lead-in/fighter conversion trainer, with combat capability. New and lengthened two-seat combat variant is under development.

★ Aims

★ JJ-7/FT-7 is capable of duplicating all the flying and combat techniques of the J-7/F-7, and a major part of F-8 training.

▲ Development

▲ 1982. Development work on the JJ-7 started, based on the J-7 II.
▲ 1986. Production initiated, with the first series-built FT-7 making its maiden flight at the end of 1987.
▲ 9 November 1990. Maiden flight of a production FT-7P for Pakistan.
▲ 1994. Development of a lengthened two-seat operational combat version announced.
Sales/users: No indication of Chinese use of the JJ-7. Export of the FT-7 to Myanmar, Pakistan (15 FT-7Ps), Sri Lanka (1) and Zimbabwe (2).
Details: For the FT-7.
Crew: 2.
Cockpit: Twin tandem cockpits, equipped with duplicated instrumentation and controls, the rear having a retractable periscope for improving the forward view. Red lighting. Starboard-hinged canopies. Cockpit pressure differential 4.35 psi.
Crew escape: Ejection seats.
Fixed guns: Optional weaponry, including a 23-mm twin-barrel 23-3 cannon pack carried under the fuselage.
Number of weapon pylons: Normally 2 under the wings plus an underfuselage station for a drop tank, but 4 underwing pylons on the FT-7P.
Expendable weapons and equipment: Typical choice of 2 x PL-2B air-to-air missiles, 2 x 18 round 57-2 rocket packs or 2 x 100-250 kg bombs.
Radar: See J-7 entry.
Flight/weapon system avionics/instrumentation: Includes a "trouble simulator" system. Pakistan's FT-7Ps incorporate avionics in keeping with its F-7 models.
Fuselage: Similar to the J-7 but with larger ventral fins of angular shape. Very slightly shorter overall length including nose probe.
Engine: Liyang WP7B (BM) turbojet.
Engine rating: 9,689 lbf (43.1 kN) dry, 13,443 lbf (59.8 kN) with afterburning.

Air intakes: At fuselage nose.
Flight refuelling probe: None.
Fuel system: 560 litres in wing tanks and 1,880 litres in the fuselage. Removable metal "saddle-back" tank to the rear of the cockpits. Optional 500 litre drop tanks under the wings and/or a 720 litre underfuselage tank. FT-7P has greater tankage.
Electrical system: 28.5 volt DC supply. Engine-driven starter-generator, with static inverters.
Hydraulic system: 3,000 psi.
Braking system: See J-7 entry.

Aircraft variants:
JJ-7 is the Chinese designation but with no known production for the domestic forces.
FT-7 is the standard export version, with only 2 underwing pylons.
FT-7P is a structurally upgraded version for Pakistan, with avionics compatible with its Airguard fighters and 4 underwing pylons. Empty weight reduced by some 418 lb (190 kg), and with a maximum take-off weight of 18,960 lb (8,600 kg), allowing for increased armament and/or fuel.
Operational combat variant of the JJ-7 is under development, with a longer fuselage. Its purpose is unknown.

DETAILS FOR FT-7.

Principal dimensions:
Wing span: 23 ft 5.5 ins (7.154 m)
Maximum length: 45 ft 9 ins (13.945 m) tail to shock cone, 48 ft 9.5 ins (14.874 m) including nose probe
Maximum height: 13 ft 5.5 ins (4.103 m)

Wings:
Area: 247.57 sq ft (23 m^2)
Aspect ratio: 2.225
Sweepback: 49° 6' at 25% chord
Incidence: 0°
Anhedral: 2°

Tail unit:
Tailplane span: 12 ft 3 ins (3.74 m)
Tailplane area: 42.41 sq ft (3.94 m^2)
Fin area: 37.46 sq ft (3.48 m^2)

Undercarriage:
Type: Retractable, with steerable nosewheel
Main wheel tyre size: 600 x 200 mm
Nose wheel tyre size: 500 x 180 mm
Wheel base: 15 ft 9 ins (4.807 m)
Wheel track: 8 ft 10 ins (2.6924 m)
Turning radius: 23 ft 1 ins (7.04 m)

Weights:
Empty, operating: 12,167 lb (5,519 kg)
Maximum take-off: 18,860 lb (8,555 kg)

Performance:
Maximum speed: Mach 2.05 (CATIC brochure quotes speed at above 1.25 km altitude or 4,100 ft, 1,250 m, but it is probable that it should be above 12.5 km or 41,000 ft, 12,500 m)
Take-off speed: 170-181 kts (196-208 mph) 315-335 km/h
Landing speed: 165-175 kts (190-202 mph) 306-324 km/h
Stall speed: 135 kts (155 mph) 250 km/h
Take-off distance: 2,955-3,610 ft (900-1,100 m)
Landing distance: 2,790-3,610 ft (850-1,100 m) with drag-chute and braking
Maximum climb rate: 30,512 ft (9,300 m) per minute
G limits: +7
Ceiling: 56,760 ft (17,300 m) service, 58,070 ft (17,700 m) theoretical absolute
Range with full internal fuel: 545 naut miles (627 miles) 1,010 km, at 36,000 ft (11,000 m)
Range with full internal fuel plus a 720 litre drop tank: 788 naut miles (906 miles) 1,459 km, at 36,000 ft (11,000 m)
Range with maximum weapon load: 709 naut miles (816 miles) 1,313 km

Harbin Aircraft Manufacturing Corporation (China)

Corporate address: PO Box 201, 15 Youxie Street, Pingfang, Harbin 150066.
Telephone: +86 451 8602122
Facsimile: +86 451 8602061
Telex: 87082 HAF CN
Founded: 1952.
Employees: 16,100.
Information: Xu Zhanbin (Director of aircraft sales).

● Activities
● Main transport aircraft production centres on the Y-12 (including the latest Y-12 (IV) that obtained its type certificate from the CAAC on 3 July 1994). The Y-11B had not entered production in early 1995.
● The SH-5 flying-boat remains important to the Chinese navy but went out of production after a small number of aircraft had been produced.
● Helicopter production now includes Z-9Bs, while the new EC-120 has also flown. The much publicized Polar Star designed by Harbin and the Nanjing University of Aeronautics and Astronautics did not succeed. China is also developing a dedicated attack helicopter, about which very little is known and may not be a Harbin project.
● Harbin first flew a new propulsive-wing ultralight on 8 October 1994, known as the HFY-5, initial production examples of which were delivered at the end of 1994.

Harbin H-5 bomber (Denis Hughes)

Harbin H-5 (NATO name *Beagle*)

Role: Strategic and tactical bomber, reconnaissance and naval anti-shipping.

★ Aims
★ Derived from the Soviet Ilyushin Il-28 bomber that had first flown as a prototype in the USSR on 8 August 1948.

▲ Development
▲ Manufactured in various H-5 models from 1966 to the early 1980s.
Sales/users: It is believed that over 300 H-5s remain in service with the Chinese air force and at least 140 with the navy, equipping a total of 12 regiments. Exported H-5s are retained by Egypt (a tiny number for maritime reconnaissance), North Korea (perhaps as many as 80) and a dozen or so HZ-5s operate in Romania.
Crew: 3, comprising pilot under the bubble canopy, navigator-bombardier in a nose compartment with extensive glazing, and radio operator tail gunner towards the rear of the fuselage.
Cockpit: See Crew. Dual controls in the training version. Cockpit/cabin pressure differential 5.8 psi.
Crew escape: Ejection seats for the pilot and navigator, and parachute escape through the underfuselage compartment entrance hatch for the radio operator.
Fixed guns: 4 x 23-mm Norinco Type 23 cannon, 2 in a tail turret and 2 in the fuselage.
Ammunition: 225 rounds and 100 rounds per cannon in each position respectively.
Expendable weapons and equipment: Up to 6,620 lb (3,000 kg) of free-fall nuclear or general purpose (including new low drag type) bombs, 250 kg incendiary bombs, possibly fuel/air bombs, 1 large or 2 small torpedoes, mines, depth charges or other loads carried in the weapon bay.
Additional stores: Reconnaissance cameras.
Radar: Ground-mapping type. (See Self-protection.)
Flight/weapon system avionics/instrumentation: Conventional, including radio compass and altimeter.
Self-protection systems: Tail warning radar.
Wing characteristics: Straight, high mounted, of 2-spar torsion-box construction.
Wing control surfaces: Ailerons (with tabs) and 2-section slotted flaps.
Tail control surfaces: Swept tail unit, with a fixed incidence dihedral tailplane, elevators and rudder (both with tabs).
Flight control system: Mechanical, with hydraulically actuated flaps.
Construction materials: Metal, principally duralumin.
Engines: 2 Liming or Xi'an WP5 series turbojets. JATO available to boost take-off.
Engine rating: Each 5,950 lbf (26.5 kN).
Flight refuelling probe: None.
Fuel system: 7,900 litres maximum.
Electrical system: 28 volt DC, with a starter-generator and 2 x 30 amp-hour batteries.
Hydraulic system: 1,600 psi.
De-icing system: Hot air for wing and tail leading edges.

Aircraft variants:
H-5 is the production bomber and torpedo bomber version, though no longer built.
HJ-5 is a dual-control training model, named *Mascot* by NATO.
HZ-5 is the photographic reconnaissance version, with up to 5 cameras.

DETAILS FOR H-5.

Principal dimensions:
Wing span: 70 ft 4 ins (21.45 m)
Maximum length: 57 ft 11 ins (17.65 m)
Maximum height: 22 ft (6.7 m)

Wings:
Aerofoil section: Based on the Russian SR-5S.
Area: 654.4 sq ft (60.8 m^2)
Aspect ratio: 7.57
Incidence: 0° 38′
Anhedral: 3°

Undercarriage:
Type: Retractable, with twin nosewheels
Main wheel tyre size: 1,150 x 355 mm
Nose wheel tyre size: 600 x 180 mm
Wheel track: 24 ft 3 ins (7.4 m)

Weights:
Empty, operating: 28,440 lb (12,900 kg)
Maximum take-off: 46,740 lb (21,200 kg)

Performance:
Maximum speed: 486 kts (559 mph) 900 km/h at 14,750 ft (4,500 m)
Take-off distance: 3,775 ft (1,150 m)
Landing distance: 3,840 ft (1,170 m)
Maximum climb rate: 2,950 ft (900 m) per minute at sea level
Ceiling: 40,355 ft (12,300 m)
Range with full payload: 1,296 naut miles (1,491 miles) 2,400 km at long-range cruise speed

Harbin SH-5

Harbin SH-5 in Fire-fighting water-bomber and Navy forms (Xinhua News Agency)

First flight: 3 April 1976.
Role: Principally for anti-submarine work, mine warfare, anti-shipping and maritime patrol, but also capable of search and rescue and cargo-carrying.

★ Aims
★ To supplement at least 12 remaining radial-engined Beriev Be-6 (NATO *Madge*) flying-boats of 1950s vintage.
★ Larger, heavier and much faster than the Be-6, with 4 turboprop engines and modern detection systems. An upgrade of its systems is believed to be wanted.

▲ Development
▲ December 1968. Design began.
▲ October 1971. First prototype appeared for static testing.
▲ December 1973. Second, flying prototype appeared.
▲ May 1975. Water trials began, lasting some 10 months.
▲ 30 July 1984. First flight of the first production SH-5.
▲ 3 September 1986. First and only production batch of 4 in full military form were received by the PLA Navy.

Sales/users: 1 static test prototype, 1 flying prototype and 5 production SH-5s (confirmed). 4 of the latter are operated at the Tuandao base. Production has ended. 1 of the non-military flying-boats has been tested as a fire-fighter for water bombing (see Aircraft variants for details).
Crew: 2 pilots, navigator (in glazed nose cabin), radio operator and flight engineer, plus typically 3 operators of mission equipment.
Fixed guns: 2 cannon in a remote turret between the wings and tail, probably of 23-mm.
Number of weapon pylons: 4.
Expendable weapons and equipment: Weapon bay can house up to 13,230 lb (6,000 kg) of bombs, mines, depth charges, sonobuoys, signal bombs, possibly torpedoes, or droppable survival equipment. Underwing stores can include 2 x C-101 or other anti-ship missiles and up to 6 light torpedoes, or other combinations of torpedoes and bombs.
Radar: Doppler search type in nose.
Flight/weapon system avionics/instrumentation: Magnetic anomaly detector (MAD) in the tail extension ("sting"). Conventional instrumentation and avionics that include inertial navigation and air data computer. Equipment for programmed dropping of sonobuoys.
No upgrade is planned using foreign avionics.
Wing characteristics: Straight, high mounted, with tapering and anhedral outer panels. Fixed single-step floats near the tips.
Wing control surfaces: Ailerons (with tabs), 2-section trailing-edge flaps and spoilers.
Tail control surfaces: Twin unit, comprising a dihedral tailplane and rounded endplate fins with rudders (with tabs). Elevators (with tabs). Endplate location in line with the propellers offers better efficiency at low speed.
Flight control system: Hydraulic.
Fuselage: Hull is of conventional configuration, with a single-step planing bottom. Unpressurized. Spray suppression strakes each side of the hull, immediately aft of the nose glazing, to prevent spray reaching the engines at slow taxi speed. Spray suppressing "cut-outs" in the chine approximately level with the propellers, intended to prevent spray at high water speed. Water rudder aft of the hull, under the long MAD "sting". Internal arrangement includes 3 cargo compartments in the forward hull for up to a total 22,050 lb (10,000 kg) load, with mission stations and equipment aft, all interconnected and capable of being sealed in an emergency. Cargo compartments are probably convertible for litters when required. Weapon bay to the rear.
Construction materials: Metal.
Engines: 4 Dongan WJ5A turboprops, with 12 ft 10 ins (3.9 m) Boading 4-blade propellers. 2 engines can be shut down to extend mission duration.
Engine rating: Each 3,150 ehp (2,349 ekW) to 30° C.
Flight refuelling probe: None.
Fuel system: About 21,000 litres (confirmed by Harbin). No carriage of drop tanks.

Aircraft variants:
SH-5 for the PLA Navy 4 aircraft as detailed.
Fire-fighting variant has been tested, able to carry 17,635 lb (8,000 kg) of water, scooped during a taxi run and taking 15 seconds to fill using this method.

DETAILS FOR SH-5.

Principal dimensions:
Wing span: 118 ft 1 ins (36 m)
Maximum length: 127 ft 7 ins (38.9 m)
Maximum height: 32 ft 2 ins (9.802 m)

Wings:
Area: 1,550 sq ft (144 m^2)
Aspect ratio: 9
Anhedral: On outer panels

Undercarriage:
Type: Retractable beaching undercarriage, with twin nosewheels and single main wheel units. Not amphibious for shore landing

Weights:
Empty, operating: 58,400 lb (26,500 kg) in anti-submarine configuration, or lighter in other non-combat roles
Maximum take-off: 99,200 lb (45,000 kg)

Performance:
Maximum speed: 300 kts (346 mph) 556 km/h
Cruise speed: 243 kts (280 mph) 450 km/h
Minimum patrol speed: 125 kts (143 mph) 230 km/h
Take-off distance: 1,585 ft (482 m)
Landing distance: 2,145 ft (653 m)
Ceiling: 33,625 ft (10,250 m)
Range with full fuel: 2,564 naut miles (2,950 miles) 4,750 km
Duration: up to 15 hours

Nanchang Aircraft Manufacturing Company (China)

Corporate address: PO Box 5001-506, Nanchang, Jiangxi 330024.
Telephone: +86 791 8451833 – 3737, 4515, 4390, 3892
Facsimile: +86 791 8451491
Telex: 95068 NAMC CN
Founded: 1951.
Employees: About 20,000.
Information: Feng Jinghua.

● Activities

● Includes the development/production of the N-5A agricultural aircraft and CJ-6A primary trainer (see General Aviation section).
● In partnership with Pakistan Aeronautical Complex on the K-8 jet trainer programme.

Nanchang A-5C carrying PL-7 missiles, rocket launchers, 760 litre drop tanks and 4 bombs

Nanchang Q-5/A-5M (NATO name *Fantan*)

First flight: 5 June 1965.
Role: Supersonic attack and strike aircraft, anti-shipping, and with the capability of limited air defence.

★ Aims

★ To develop a dedicated attack aircraft using enhanced Shenyang J-6 technology and based on that airframe.
★ Transonic speed at low level.
★ Minimum transonic drag by adopting an area ruled fuselage configuration.
★ Cockpit armour to protect the pilot from ground fire during low-level close support missions.
★ To offer the potential of carrying a nuclear weapon at high speed.

▲ Development

▲ 1958. Very limited design work on the Q-5 began at Shenyang, but the project was transferred to Nanchang for further development by the Ministry of Aviation.
▲ 1961. Project cancelled but revived 2 years later.
▲ 1965. First flight of a prototype, but the intended early production was deferred after trials indicated that modifications to several of the aircraft's systems should be undertaken.
▲ 1969. Prototypes reappeared, with modifications to the armament, hydraulic and other systems. Production authorized.
▲ 1970. Early production Q-5s appeared as conventionally-armed attack/strike aircraft, each with a fuselage weapon bay. Availability of a small free-fall nuclear bomb soon led to several being modified for trials and service.
▲ 1980. The improved Q-5 I appeared, with greatly increased internal fuel tankage to cure the Q-5's lack of range, but requiring deletion of the bomb bay and addition of 2 more underwing pylons to make good the loss of internal weapon attachment points.
▲ January 1983. First exports, with upgraded A-5Cs being delivered over the next 12 months to the Pakistan Air Force.
▲ 1984. Appearance of the Q-5 IA, also adopting 6 underwing pylons and some other A-5C-type upgrades. Certified early the following year.
▲ 30 August 1988. First flight of an A-5M prototype, produced by modification of a Q-5 II by Aeritalia (now Alenia) of Italy under a CATIC agreement of 1986. Based on the need for a modern navigation/attack system.
▲ 17 September 1988. First Q-5K Kong Yun prototype made its maiden flight, having undergone an extensive navigation/attack avionics upgrade by Thomson-CSF of France (under a CATIC agreement) that included a laser rangefinder, head-up-display, INS and much more, together with the required improved electrical supply system. This programme was, however, abandoned in 1990.
▲ 17 October 1988. First A-5M prototype was lost in an accident.
▲ 8 March 1989. First flight of the second A-5M prototype. Development was completed in 1991 but further upgrades were anticipated.
▲ 1993. Myanmar became the first A-5M recipient.
Sales/users: Bangladesh (A-5Cs with 2 squadrons at Dhaka and Chittagong), China (well over 500 in air force service, and over 100 with the navy for anti-shipping, the latter confirmed by Nanchang to have no special designation), Myanmar (A-5Ms), North Korea (40 Q-5 IAs), and Pakistan (perhaps 45 A-5Cs remaining with 3 squadrons at Masroor and Peshawar).

Nanchang A-5C in Pakistan Air Force service (Denis Hughes)

Crew: Pilot.
Cockpit: Armoured and pressurized.
Crew escape: The standard Chinese ejection seat is a zero-altitude Type I, with safe operation between 135 and 459 kts (155 and 528 mph) 250 and 850 km/h . A-5C and M use a Martin Baker zero-zero ejection seat.
Fixed guns: 2 x 23-mm Norinco 23-2K cannon in the wing roots.
Ammunition: 100 rounds per cannon.
Number of weapon pylons: 8 on Q-5 (2 in weapon bay, 2 underfuselage and 4 under the wings). 8 on Q-5 I/IA/II, with no weapon bay but 4 externally under the fuselage plus 4 under the wings. 10 on A-5C/A-5 III, all external, including 6 under the wings. 12 on A-5M, including 8 under the wings.
Expendable weapons and equipment: 4,409 lb (2,000 kg) total weight. Early Q-5s could carry up to 2 x 500 kg general-purpose bombs in the bay, plus lighter bombs under the fuselage and wings. However, as the normal operational load was 1,000 kg, it can be supposed that the planned configuration was to remain "clean", with no external stores beyond perhaps drop tanks unless on a close support mission. Fuselage pylons can each carry up to a 250 kg general purpose bomb, incendiary bomb, or other types including foreign special-purpose weapons such as Durandal penetration bombs for disabling airfields. Inner wing stations for light weapons, including pods for 57-mm, 68-mm, 90-mm or 130-mm rockets, practice or light fragmentation bombs. Centre wing pylons each have the greatest carrying capacity, suited to a C-801 or similar anti-ship missile, various types of bombs including 350 kg Norinco anti-tank/anti-runway cluster types or foreign, fuel/air bomb of up to 500 kg, 760 litre (or 1,140 litre on the A-5M) auxiliary fuel tank or other load. Outboard pylons are each normally used to carry an air-to-air missile for self-defence or for limited air-defence duty, including the PL-2/2B or PL-7 range (plus PL-5B for A-5M) of Chinese AAMs, or alternatively Sidewinder or Magic on exported aircraft. A number of Chinese aircraft may carry up to a 20 kiloton nuclear weapon. At least the A-5M could be equipped to carry anti-radiation missiles and laser-guided weapons.
Radar: No radar in Q-5 models, except possibly in the Navy's aircraft compatible with an anti-ship role. Pointer 2500 I-band ranging radar in the modified nose of the A-5M.
Flight/weapon system avionics/instrumentation: Conventional instrumentation in all Q-5/A-5C models, including a WL-7 radio compass, AR-3201/CT-3 VHF and HF/SSB transceiver, marker beacon receiver and IFF. Chinese aircraft have a gun camera at the nose. ABS1A or SH-1J optical bombing sight. Very much improved A-5M has a modern navigation/attack system interfaced with retained Chinese avionics, based on the principal subsystems of: Chinese VHF communications and IFF; Litton LN-39A inertial navigation system; 2 Singer digital computers and dual-redundant 1553B databus,

with computer based weapon aiming and delivery, incorporating the Pointer 2500 ranging radar and a new stores management system; Alenia head-up-display and other cockpit changes; data processing, with an air data computer; ECM (existing or Italian type) and radar warning receiver. Changes required an improved electrical system. Further A-5M improvements could include (now, or as a later development) night vision systems and a laser rangefinder.
Self-protection systems: Type 930 radar warning receiver. ECM pod can be carried on the centre wing pylon (of Italian manufacture on the A-5M). Chaff/flare dispenser available to at least the A-5M.
Wing characteristics: Sharply swept, mid mounted, with a mid-span fence, configured from J-6 wings.
Wing control surfaces: Ailerons (port tab) and Gouge area-increasing trailing-edge flaps.
Tail control surfaces: Anhedral slab tailplane with anti-flutter devices, and rudder (with tab).
Airbrakes: Under fuselage, hydraulically actuated.
Flight control system: Hydraulic for ailerons, flaps and boosted tailplane, mechanical for rudder, and electric tabs.
Fuselage: Lengthened and considerably altered area-ruled J-6 type for minimum transonic drag, leaving almost no ancestral likeness. "Solid" metal pointed nose on all versions except the A-5M.
Construction materials: Metal, but with the possible use of composites for future A-5M developments to reduce the radar signature.
Engines: 2 Liming WP6 turbojets. Alternative WP6As for export A-5s and possibly available for retrofit to Q-5s. Hydraulically operated afterburner nozzle.
Engine rating: Each 5,400 lbf (24.03 kN) dry and 7,165 lbf (31.87 kN) with afterburning. WP6As have an afterburning rating of 8,930 lbf (39.72 kN).
Air intakes: Each side of the forward fuselage, level with the cockpit, with splitter plates.
Flight refuelling probe: A system to allow the Q-5/A-5 to receive fuel from H-6 tankers was designed by Flight Refuelling Ltd in the 1980s but never adopted.
Fuel system: 3,648 litres internally. 2 x 760 litre or 2 x 400 litre auxiliary fuel tanks (middle or outer pylons respectively), or up to 2 x 1,140 litre tanks for the A-5M.
Electrical system: 28 volt DC supply with 2 engine-driven starter-generators. 2 static inverters for the AC supply.
Hydraulic system: Primary and secondary systems, at 3,000 psi. Emergency back-up pressure of 1,565 psi for undercarriage extension.
Braking system: Disc on main units. Drag-chute housed in a tail fairing, typically positioned (except in the oldest aircraft) under the rudder.

Aircraft variants:
Q-5 was the original version with a fuselage bomb bay.
Q-5 I was the first model to have the bay removed and fuel tankage increased, becoming the standard configuration.
Q-5 IA introduced several important refinements, including 2 extra underwing pylons, improved optical sights, and better self protection among other changes.
Q-5 II appears to be almost identical to the Q-5 IA except for having a RWR.
A-5C (or A-5 III) is the major export model, with many refinements dictated by the requirements of the Pakistan Air Force. Marginally greater length and span. These include improved avionics, the ability to carry Western-manufactured weapons, and a Martin Baker zero-zero ejection seat.
A-5M is the latest model, developed in association with Aeritalia (now Alenia) of Italy. Many avionics improvements, as noted previously, and 12 pylons. Extended time between overhaul for the engines and greater drop tank capacity.

Details for A-5 models.

Principal dimensions:
Wing span: 31 ft 10 ins (9.7 m)
Maximum length: 53 ft 4 ins (16.255 m) for A-5C/A-5 III with probe, 50 ft 7 ins (15.415 m) without, or 50 ft 5 ins (15.366 m) for A-5M
Maximum height: 14 ft 10 ins (4.516 m) for A-5C/A-5 III, 14 ft 10.5 ins (4.53 m) for A-5M

Wings:
Area: 300.9 sq ft (27.95 m^2)
Aspect ratio: 3.366
Sweepback: 52° 30' at 25% chord
Chord at root: 13 ft 7.5 ins (4.15 m)
Chord at tip: 5 ft 1 ins (1.55 m)
Incidence: 0°
Anhedral: 4°

Undercarriage:
Type: Retractable, with nosewheel (not steerable) that rotates through nearly 90° during retraction
Main wheel tyre size: 830 x 205 mm
Nose wheel tyre size: 595 x 230 mm
Wheel base: 13 ft 2 ins (4.01 m)
Wheel track: 14 ft 5 ins (4.4 m)

Weights:
Empty: 14,317 lb (6,494 kg) for A-5C/A-5 III, or 14,625 (6,634 kg) for A-5M
Maximum take-off: 26,455 lb (12,000 kg)

Performance:
Maximum level flight Mach number: Mach 1.12 for A-5C/A-5 III, Mach 1.2 for A-5M, at 36,000 ft (11,000 m)
Maximum speed: 653 kts (752 mph) 1,210 km/h for A-5C/A-5 III, or 661 kts (761 mph) 1,225 km/h for A-5M, at sea level
Take-off distance: 4,101 ft (1,250 m) for A-5C/A-5 III, or 3,937 ft (1,200 m) for A-5M, at maximum weight
Landing distance: 2,638-3,478 ft (804-1,060 m) ground roll
Maximum climb rate: 20,275 ft (6,180 m) per minute for A-5C/A-5 III, or 22,640 ft (6,900 m) per minute for A-5M, clean, at 16,405 ft (5,000 m)
G limits: +7.5
Ceiling: 52,000 ft (15,850 m) for A-5C/A-5 III, 52,490 ft (16,000 m) for A-5M
Range with full fuel: 1,080 naut miles (1,242 miles) 2,000 km, with 1,520 litres of auxiliary fuel, at 11,000 m and best range cruise speed
Radius of action: 216-324 naut miles (248-373 miles) 400-600 km for A-5C/A-5 III, or 173-279 naut miles (200-321 miles) 320-518 km for A-5M, depending on mission profile, with a 2,000 kg payload

Shenyang Aircraft Corporation (China)

Corporate address: PO Box 328, Shenyang, Liaoning 110034.
Telephone: +86 24 6896680
Facsimile: +86 24 6896689
Employees: Approximately 30,000.

● Activities
● Has been responsible for producing the great majority of Chinese fighters and fighter-bombers since the mid-1950s, including huge numbers of J-5s (MiG-17F/PFs) and J-6s (MiG-19s), of which several thousand remain available to the PLA Air Force and to the Navy for various duties including interception, attack, reconnaissance and training. In addition, Shenyang built JJ-2 two-seat trainers remain active (MiG-15UTIs), as are JJ-6s for a similar role. Current fighter work is based on the J-8 II and intended F-8 II export model.
● Sub-contract work includes components for several European and North American aircraft programmes, including the Airbus A320, Boeing 757, DHC Dash 8 and Jetstream ATP airliners.

Shenyang F-6 operated by Pakistan, an exported J-6 for interceptor and attack duties (Denis Hughes)

Shenyang J-8 II (NATO name *Finback*)

First flight: 5 July 1969.
Role: Multi-role fighter, for interception, air superiority, battlefield interdiction, and close air support.

★ Aims
★ Enlarged, twin-engined development of the J-7, initially with a similar nose air intake and shock-cone.
★ J-8 II reconfigured to make space for a more capable fire-control radar, and provide greater airflow via 2 side air intakes to feed engines with higher augmented ratings.

▲ Development

▲ 1964. Work on the J-8 programme began.
▲ 1969. Flight trials with the prototypes began and continued over several years, while further development work and construction was halted for political reasons.
▲ 1979. Construction of 3 pre-series aircraft began, 1 being destroyed before flight.
▲ 24 April 1981. First flight of a pre-series J-8 I
▲ 12 June 1984. First flight of the first of four J-8 II prototypes, with 2 others being built for ground testing.
▲ 1985. Production began of early model J-8s, followed by J-8 Is.
▲ 5 August 1987. Contract signed between CATIC and Grumman of the USA , covering the development of an upgrade package for the J-8 II funded under a USAF foreign military sales programme named *Peace Pearl*, involving 50 sets. Included in the upgrade were to be a modified Westinghouse APG-66 radar, fire control computer, a Litton LN-39 inertial navigation system and head-up display. Two J-8 IIs were delivered to the USA for development purposes.
▲ 1989. *Peace Pearl* programme was put on hold by the US Government following events in China, leading to Chinese termination of the project in the following year. The prototypes were sent back to China 4 years later. Production of the J-8 II continued despite the lack of upgrade, but in very small numbers.
▲ 1994. First appearance of the F-8 II export version of the J-8 II, with many upgrades.

Sales/users: Early J-8 day fighters have largely been withdrawn or were upgraded to J-8 I standard for all-weather operations, joined by small numbers of J-8 IIs. Reported numbers in service in early 1995 vary greatly between 125 and well over 200. Low volume production is said to continue, including in F-8 II export and possibly naval variants. Iran is rumoured to be an export customer.
Crew: Pilot, under an upward-hinged canopy.
Cockpit: Modern head-up and head-down displays in the export F-8 II (see Avionics and Aircraft variants).
Crew escape: Ejection seat.
Fixed guns: Underfuselage 23-mm twin-barrel 23-3 cannon.
Ammunition: 200 rounds.
Number of weapon pylons: 7, with the single underfuselage pylon typically carrying a drop tank to extend range.
Expendable weapons and equipment: 9,920 lb (4,500 kg) maximum load, including PL-2B and PL-7 air-to-air missiles, HF-16A or B launchers each for 12 x 57-mm air-to-air rockets fired in salvos of 4, 8 or 12, or HF-7 launchers for 90-mm air-to-surface rockets to attack armoured or installation targets, or bombs and/or drop tanks.
Radar: China Leihua SR-4 I/J-band air-to-air fire control radar with single-target tracking and engagement in the J-8 I, and an unidentified monopulse radar (possibly China Leihua Type 317a) in the J-8 II to offer single target tracking/engagement, ground mapping, terrain avoidance and ranging. Doppler radar in F-8 II.
Flight/weapon system avionics/instrumentation: Includes tactical air navigation system, instrument landing system, marker beacon receiver, and IFF. Gun camera. Autopilot for maintaining altitude, heading and level flight. F-8 II has a new digital avionics package, with a navigation/attack system using a dual redundant MIL-STD-1553B databus and Doppler radar. Head-up display and 2 head-down displays. Optical gyro sight.
Self-protection systems: Radar warning receiver and ECM. Chaff/flare dispensers.
Wing characteristics: Delta, mid mounted, with upper-surface fences towards the wingtips.
Wing control surfaces: Ailerons and single-slotted trailing-edge flaps. F-8 II has leading-edge flaps.

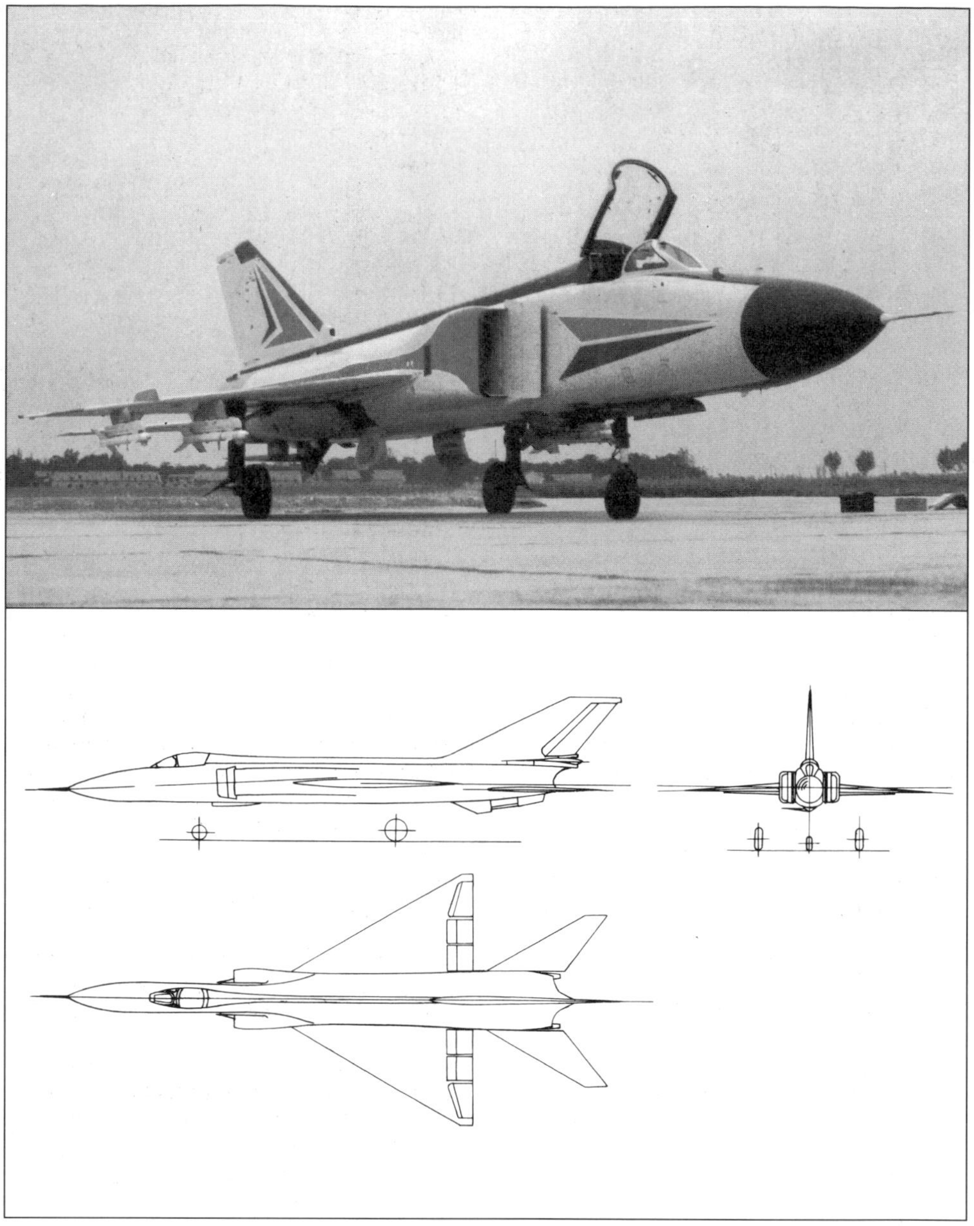

Shenyang J-8 II multi-role fighter drawing and photograph (courtesy Shenyang)

Tail control surfaces: Slab tailplane and rudder. A large stabilizing fin under the rear fuselage is deployed from its folded position only once the aircraft is airborne.
Airbrakes: 4, under the fuselage.
Flight control system: Hydraulic.
Fuselage: Area-ruled for minimum transonic/supersonic drag, with an upper-surface spine running from the cockpit to the fin-root airscoop. 2 further airscoops on the aft fuselage, 1 each side of the fin.
Construction materials: All metal, principally aluminium alloy, with the ailerons and portions of the tail unit of weight-saving honeycomb construction.
Engines: 2 Liyang WP13A II turbojets in the J-8 II, with a power-to-weight ratio of 5.6. Information from China gave the same engines for the F-8 II, though some reports suggest a WP13B version with augmented thrust raised to 15,430 lbf (68.649 kN).
Engine rating: Each 9,600 lbf (42.7 kN) dry, 14,815 lbf (65.9 kN) with afterburning.
Air intakes: Fuselage sides on the J-8 II/F-8 II, with splitter plates (in the nose with a shock-cone on the J-8 I).
Flight refuelling probe: Fitted to F-8 II only.
Fuel system: Estimated to be at least 4,350 litres internally, plus optionally, auxiliary fuel carried under the fuselage and on the outer underwing pylons.
Electrical system: 28.5 volt DC supply with 2 engine-driven starter generators. 2 alternators for 3-phase AC supply.
Hydraulic system: 2 systems, each 3,000 psi.
Braking system: Disc brakes. Drag-chute housed in an under-rudder fairing.

Aircraft variants:

J-8 and J-8 I *(Finback-A)* were early production versions with nose air intakes, the former for day/fair weather operations and equipped with a ranging radar, 2 x 30-mm cannon and 4 x PL-2B missiles or 2 missiles and 2 drop tanks. Probably no F-8s in service, as most were converted to F-8 II standard with a new air-to-air radar in the air intake shock cone (see Radar), one 23-mm cannon and other changes for all-weather use. 2 engines of J-7 type.
J-8 II *(Finback-B)* is the much modified development with multi-role capability, partly due to its change of radar (see Radar) in a new "solid" nose. Side air intakes, new engines and greater weapon carrying capability on 7 pylons.
F-8 II *(Finback-B)* is the CATIC-advertized export version. New digital avionics package, with a navigation/attack system using a dual redundant MIL-STD-1553B databus and Doppler radar. Head-up display and 2 head-down displays. Possibly higher augmented-thrust engines (see Engines) and in-flight refuelling probe. Leading-edge flaps. Could be related to a similarly-upgraded naval variant that is believed to be under development.

DETAILS FOR J-8 II/F-8 II.

Principal dimensions:
Wing span: 30 ft 8 ins (9.344 m)
Maximum length: 70 ft 10 ins (21.59 m)
Maximum height: 17 ft 9 ins (5.41 m)

Wings:
Area: 454.24 sq ft (42.2 m²)
Aspect ratio: 2.07
Sweepback: 60°
Anhedral: From roots

Undercarriage:
Type: Retractable, with steerable nosewheel
Wheel base: 24 ft 1 ins (7.337 m)
Wheel track: 12 ft 3 ins (3.741 m)

Weights:
Empty: 21,650 lb (9,820 kg)
Normal take-off weight: 31,525 lb (14,300 kg)
Maximum take-off: 39,240 lb (17,800 kg)

Performance:
Maximum operating Mach number: Mach 2.2
Maximum indicated speed: 702 kts (808 mph) 1,300 km/h
Take-off speed: 175 kts (202 mph) 325 mph
Landing speed: 157 kts (180 mph) 290 km/h
Take-off distance: 2,203 ft (670 m)
Landing distance: 3,280 ft (1,000 m) with drag-chute
Maximum climb rate: 39,375 ft (12,000 m) per minute
Ceiling: 65,615 ft (20,000 m)
Range with full fuel: 1,188 naut miles (1,367 miles) 2,200 km
Radius of action: 432 naut miles (497 miles) 800 km

Xi'an Aircraft Company (China)

Full name: Xi'an Aircraft Industrial Group of China.
Corporate address: PO Box 140-84, Xi'an 710000.
Telephone: +86 29 7216929
Facsimile: +86 29 6203707
Telex: 70101 XAC CN
Founded: 1958.
Employees: over 19,000.
Information: Wang Zhigang.

● Activities

- In addition to development of the JH-7, current manufacturing activities centre on the Y7 series of military and civil transports. Xi'an will also become the principal Chinese company involved in the development of a 100-120 seat regional jet (see Fokker/Daimler-Benz/AVIC/Samsung in the Airliners section).
- Manufactures the Eaglet 100 2-seat light aircraft, of which the first 3 production aircraft were ordered by the Shantou flying club in early 1995.
- Sub-contracting work includes parts for the Airbus A300, ATR 42, Boeing 737 and 747, and Canadair amphibians. The Boeing 737 work is particularly significant, having begun many years ago and covering tail fins and tailplanes, but under a new agreement worth US$600 million that was officially launched on 8 August 1994, Xi'an will assemble the B737's aft section.

Xi'an H-6 (NATO name *Badger*)

First flight: 24 December 1968.
Role: Intermediate-range strategic and tactical bomber, reconnaissance, and anti-shipping.

★ Aims

★ Developed from the Russian Tupolev Tu-16.

▲ Development

▲ 27 April 1952. First flight date for the Soviet Type 88 prototype of the Tu-16, piloted by Nikolai Rybko.
▲ 1953. Soviet production began at Kazan aircraft factory No 22.
▲ 1957. China received a licence from the USSR to manufacture the Tu-16 bomber. 1 dismantled Tu-16 and another in component form were handed over for familiarization in 1959.
▲ 27 September 1959. The reassembled Tu-16 made its maiden flight in China.
▲ 1961. Xi'an took over the entire programme, leaving Harbin clear to continue its work on the separate H-5 (Il-28) bomber and Z-5 (Mi-4) helicopter.

Sales/users: Production believed to have ended. Estimates vary as to the number of H-6s in Chinese military service, but it is likely to stand at more than 100 in bomber and anti-shipping versions and possibly as high as 125. Iraq operates some 8 aircraft, undoubtedly a mix of Russian Tu-16s and B-6Ds.
Crew: 7.
Crew escape: All crew are equipped with ejection seats, both pilots ejected upward and the remaining crew downwards.
Fixed guns: 7 x 23-mm cannon, mounted as 1 in the nose (deleted from H-6D/B-6D), and twin installations in the tail, remotely controlled dorsal and ventral positions.
Number of weapon pylons: 2 on H-6D/B-6D.
Expendable weapons and equipment: Typical 6,614 lb (3,000 kg) load, but rising to 19,842 lb (9,000 kg) maximum for H-6D/B-6D which can alternatively carry 2 x C-601 anti-shipping missiles mid-wing. Norinco-produced bombs can include 250 kg, 500 kg, 1,500 kg, and 3,000 kg Type 2 general purpose; 250 kg, 500 kg and 1,000 kg low-drag; 250 kg incendiary; and nuclear.
Additional stores: Marine markers and flares, deployed via an aft fuselage chute.
Radar: Doppler navigation type of unspecified origin. Missile guidance radar on some H-6D/B-6Ds.
Flight/weapon system avionics/instrumentation: Conventional, including autopilot, attitude/heading reference system, inertial navigation system and more.
Wing characteristics: Swept, mid mounted, of 2-spar construction.
Wing control surfaces: Ailerons (15° deflection) and 2-section TsAGI (Fowler type) trailing-edge flaps (35°).
Tail control surfaces: Swept, 2-spar structure, with elevators (-26°, +16° deflection) and rudder (25°).
Flight control system: Mechanical/hydraulically boosted.
Construction materials: Metal.
Engines: 2 Xi'an WP8 turbojets.
Engine rating: Each 20,945 lbf (93.167 kN).
Air intakes: Forward of the wing roots.
Flight refuelling probe: None.
Fuel system: 43,800 litres maximum in 27 wing and fuselage tanks, but normally 39,600 litres (weighing 68,453 lb, 31,050 kg).

Tupolev Tu-16K-11-16s, perhaps still operational with Egypt, indicating the general appearance of the Chinese-built H-6 (US Air Force)

DETAILS FOR H-6 AND B-6D (EXPORT MODEL).

Principal dimensions:
Wing span: 108 ft 3 ins (32.989 m) or 112 ft 2 ins (34.189 m)
Maximum length: 114 ft 2 ins (34.8 m)
Maximum height: 33 ft 11.5 ins (10.355 m)

Wings:
Aerofoil section: Based on Soviet PR-1-10S-9 root, SR-11-12 tip
Area: 1,772.3 sq ft (164.65 m²) or 1,803.49 sq ft (167.55 m²)
Aspect ratio: 6.5-6.61
Sweepback: 35° at 25% chord. Leading-edge sweepback 41° from root to 7th rib, 37° outboard
Incidence: 1°
Anhedral: 3°

Tail unit:
Tailplane span: 38 ft 7 ins (11.75 m)
Fin area: 250.85 sq ft (23.305 m²)
Fin angle: 42°

Undercarriage:
Type: Retractable, with twin nosewheels. 4-wheel main bogies retract into wing trailing-edge fairings
Main wheel tyre size: 1,100 x 330 mm
Nose wheel tyre size: 900 x 275
Wheel base: 35 ft 10 ins (10.913 m)
Wheel track: 32 ft (9.775 m)

Weights:
Empty: 80,690 lb (36,600 kg) for early aircraft, rising to 83,180 lb (37,730 kg) for the late H-6s, and 84,945 lb (38,530 kg) for the H-6D/B-6D
Maximum take-off: 158,730 to possibly 171,960 lb (72,000 to possibly 78,000 kg) for the H-6, 167,100 lb (75,800 kg) for the H-6D/B-6D

Performance:
Maximum allowable Mach number: Mach 0.9
Maximum speed: 567 kts (652 mph) 1,050 km/h
Cruise speed: 424 kts (488 mph) 785 km/h for the armed H-6D/B-6D
Landing speed: 120 kts (139 mph) 223 km/h
Take-off distance: 6,900 ft (2,100 m)
Landing distance: 5,055 ft (1,540 m)
Maximum climb rate: 3,740 ft (1,140 m) per minute for H-6D/B-6D
Ceiling: 49,215 ft (15,000 m)
Range with full fuel: 2,322 naut miles (2,671 miles) 4,300 km for H 6D/B-6D. Possibly 3,110 naut miles (3,579 miles) 5,760 km for the H-6 with a 6,614 lb (3,000 kg) payload at 158,730 lb (72,000 kg) take-off weight
Duration: 5.7 hours

Braking system: Main wheel brakes. Drag-chute (PTK-16 type on Russian Tu-16s).

Aircraft variants:
H-6A bomber was the principal Chinese production model, first flown in 1968.
H-6D or B-6D was produced into the 1990s, introducing a greater wing span, heavier take-off weight, and with the option of C-601 missiles and associated systems for an anti-shipping role.

Xi'an JH-7

First flight: Probably late 1988.
Role: Supersonic strike, interdiction, ground attack, and maritime strike.

▲ Development

▲ August 1988. First prototype was completed at Xi'an.
▲ September 1988. News of the development of this important aircraft was released at the Farnborough Air Show, UK, in the form of a model and very basic details.
▲ 1992. Intended initial service entry, but it is believed none had reached air regiments by early 1995.

Sales/users: 2 prototypes have almost certainly flown, and may have been followed by a small pre-series batch for trials, but this is unconfirmed. Reports in 1995 suggested that the PLA Navy might no longer want JH-7s.
Crew: 2, in tandem, with a slightly raised rear cockpit.
Crew escape: HTY-4 zero-zero ejection seats.
Fixed guns: 1 x 23-mm cannon.
Number of weapon pylons: 4 underwing and 2 AAM launch rails at the wingtips, as shown on the model. The possibility of weapon/stores stations under the fuselage cannot be overlooked.
Expendable weapons and equipment: Bombs of various types, air-to-surface missiles (including C-801 anti-ship) and/or auxiliary fuel tanks (outer pylons) underwing, plus 2 air-to-air missiles (probably PL-5s on the model) at the wingtips for self-defence and limited air defence.
Radar: Navigation/attack and terrain following/clearance.
Flight/weapon system avionics/instrumentation: Prototypes are fitted with Chinese avionics. Foreign suite must be a possibility for production aircraft.

Wing characteristics: Shoulder mounted anhedral wings, of almost swept-delta planform. Compound leading edge, incorporating a dogtooth extension at about two-thirds span, above which is an overwing fence.
Wing control surfaces: Ailerons and flaps of unknown characteristics.
Tail control surfaces: Slab tailplane and rudder.
Canard: None.
Fuselage: Area-rule design.
Construction materials: Principally metal.
Engines: 2 Xi'an WS9 turbofans in the prototypes. Reports suggest more powerful Liming engines are intended for production aircraft or higher rated foreign engines.
Engine rating: Each 12,550 lbf (55.83 kN) dry, 20,515 lbf (91.26 kN) with afterburning.
Air intakes: Fuselage sides, with splitter plates.
Flight refuelling probe: None shown on the model.
Fuel system: Internal plus optional auxiliary tanks under the outboard wing pylons.

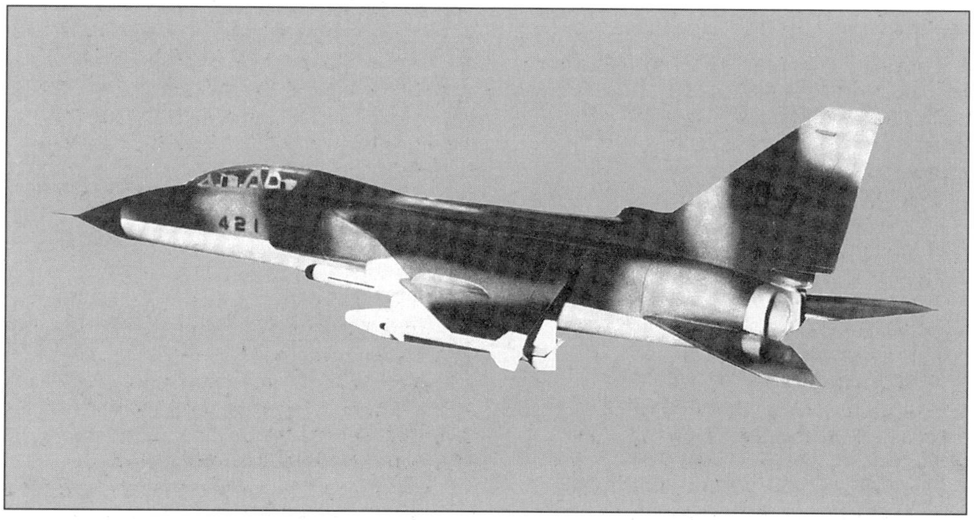

Xi'an JH-7 Model (courtesy Air International)

DETAILS FOR JH-7.

Principal dimensions:
Wing span: 42 ft (12.8 m)
Maximum length: 69 ft (21 m)
Maximum height: 20 ft 5 ins (6.22 m)

Wings:
Area: 563 sq ft (52.3 m^2)
Aspect ratio: 3.13
Anhedral: From roots

Undercarriage:
Type: Retractable, with steerable nosewheel/s

Weights:
Maximum take-off: Believed to be substantially over 59,500 lb (27,000 kg)

Performance:
Maximum speed: Mach 1.7
Ceiling: 52,500 ft (16,000 m)

Aero Holding Prague (Czech Republic)

Corporate address: Beranovych 130, 199 04 Praha 9 – Letnany.
Telephone: +42 2 882747, 884065
Facsimile: +42 2 882747, 881340
Telex: 121893 vzlu c
Founded: 1 December 1990.
Employees: 43. Over 10,000 employees in the 8 subsidiaries.
Information: Zdenek Burian (marketing, communications and public relations).

● Activities

● Parent company of the holding group that forms the main part of the Czech aero industry. It has major stakes in Aero Vodochody, Let Kunovice, Letov Prague, Motorlet Prague, Technometra Prague – Radotín, Teset Semily, Cenkovské Strojirny Cenkov, and Aeronautical Research and Test Institute (VZLÚ) Prague.
● Aero Holding is partly privatized, with 35.2% owned by individual shareholders.
● Principal business is the organization, co-ordination and financing of activities connected with research development, production, sales and operation of aircraft and other aeronautical products including international co-operation programmes.

SUBSIDIARIES

Aero Vodochody
HQ address: See entry.

Let Kunovice
HQ address: See entry.

Letov Prague
HQ address: Beranovych 65, 199 02 Praha 9 – Letnany.
Telephone: +42 2 66311933, 66311902
Facsimile: +42 2 8587175

● Activities

● Some 1,146 employees, producing the TL-X flight simulator, NKTL-29/39 ejection seat simulator, and LK-2 Sluka and LK-3 Nova ultralights.

Motorlet Prague
HQ address: Jinonická 329, 158 01 Praha 5 – Jinonice.
Telephone: +42 2 52961111
Facsimile: +42 2 526060

● Activities

● Engine production. Some 1,395 employees.

Technometra Prague – Radotín
HQ address: Vrázská 239, 153 05 Praha 5 – Radotín.

● Activities

● Undercarriage production and maintenance, plus other products.

Teset Semily
HQ address: ul. 3. kvetna, 513 28 Semily

● Activities

● Undercarriage production and maintenance, plus other products.

Cenkovske Strojírny
HQ address: 262 24 Cenkov.

● Activities

● Aircraft seat production and maintenance.

VZLÚ
HQ address: Beranovych 130, 199 05 Praha 9 – Letnany.
Telephone: +42 2 6847580, 6847836, 6848256
Facsimile: +42 2 6835905, 8590653

● Activities

● Development and testing of aircraft aerodynamics and strength, propulsion units, electrical equipment and hydraulic systems; flight tests; charter air transport; joint development projects with Hamilton Standard of the USA, and other work.

Aero Vodochody Ltd (Czech Republic)

Corporate address: 250 70 Odolena Voda.
Telephone: +42 2 66410041 (marketing), 66410122 (sales) 66410971, 66411140
Facsimile: +42 2 823 172
Telex: 121 169
Founded: 28 April 1953, originally as Rudy Letov Vodochody (marking the day the first Vodochody-assembled MiG-15/S-102 took off). Vodochody and Aero Vysocany organizations merged on 1 July 1954, becoming Aero Vodochody.
Employees: 2,750.
Information: Milos Valis (marketing).

● Activities

● Produces a range of jet trainers/light attack aircraft, and has the Ae-270 civil utility aircraft under development.

Aero L-39 C in Czech Republic service

Aero L-39 Albatros

First flight: 4 November 1968.
Role: Training and light attack.

★ Aims:

★ Rugged and simple design, to take over from the L-29 Delfin.
★ Suited to operations in hard climates and conditions, from hot and dusty to frosty winters or tropical.
★ Thoroughly designed airframe and systems for easy maintenance, good reliability, simple pre-flight checks and full autonomy. Mean time between failure in flight is higher than 300 flight hours.
★ Low foreign object damage to the engine by the high position of the air intakes, protected by the low-mounted wings.
★ Proven airframe service life of 6,000 flight hours.

▲ Development

▲ 1974. L-39 C entered military service.
▲ 25 August 1975. Maiden flight of the L-39 ZO.
▲ 29 September 1976. Maiden flight of the L-39 ZA.
Sales/users: 2,838 sold by early 1995, including 4 L-39 MS that became the L-59 in developed form, to Afghanistan (12 C), Algeria (32 ZA), Bulgaria (36 ZA), Cambodia (6, upgraded by Elbit), Czech Republic/Slovakia (85 C, V, ZA and MS), Cuba (30 C), Ethiopia (20 C), Germany (52 ZO), Iraq (81 ZO), Libya (181 ZO), Nigeria (24 ZA), Romania (32 ZA), USSR/Russia (2,094, some now used by other CIS states), Syria (99 ZA and ZO), Thailand (36 ZA) and Vietnam (24 ZA and ZO).
Crew: 2, in tandem, the rear instructor's seat raised.
Cockpit: Pressurized, with automatic pressure and temperature regulation. Pneumatic canopy seals are supplied by a 2 litre compressed air bottle in the nose compartment. Anti-g suits with automatic regulation protects the crew from the effect of high load factors during manoeuvres.
Crew escape: VS1-BRI ejection seats (with survival kits), suitable at all heights from zero and from 81 kts (93 mph) 150 km/h to the maximum permissible speed.
Fixed guns: L-39 ZA/MP has a 23-mm GSh-23 gun in a detachable fuselage pod.
Ammunition: 150 rounds.
Number of weapon pylons: 2 underwing on L-39 C, 4 on ZO, ZA and ZA/MP.
Expendable weapons and equipment: 626 lb (284 kg) on L-39 C, and up to 2,844 lb (1,290 kg) on ZO, ZA and ZA/MP. Compatibility with NATO standard weapons. See weapon chart for combinations.
Flight/weapon system avionics/ instrumentation: LPR 80 (LUN 3520) communication, RV-5M radio altimeter and KXP 756 transponder. General avionics configurations at customer's request; customized options can include Aero/Flight Visions Combat Training System, Weapon Delivery and Navigation System, and Advanced Weapons Delivery System options, the latter with a mission computer, HUD, 2 multi-function displays in each cockpit and video display in the rear cockpit, and able to be combined with radar, FLIR, laser rangefinder, warning systems, GPS and more. L-39 ZA/MP is equipped with an integrated digital nav/attack system, incorporating a head-up display. The front pilot's view and HUD symbology are registered by video camera and are displayed in the instructor's rear cockpit. Gyro gunsight or HUD with mission computer for weapon delivery.
Wing characteristics: Straight, low mounted, with tip-tanks.
Wing control surfaces: Ailerons (with tabs) and double-slotted flaps.
Tail control surfaces: Elevators and rudder (with tabs).
Airbrakes: 2 under centre fuselage.
Flight control system: Mechanical for ailerons, elevator and rudder; electrohydraulically for flaps and airbrakes. In case of failure, the functions can be performed by the emergency hydraulic system.
Construction materials: Aluminium alloy.
Engine: Ivchenko PROGRESS AI-25TL turbofan, with hydromechanical control and emergency backup circuit. Starting using a Saphir 5 APU; when airborne, the engine can be restarted by both the APU or by autorotation.
Engine rating: 3,792 lbf (16.87 kN).
Fuel system: 1,955 litres usable in 5 fuselage, 2 fixed wingtip and 2 optional drop tanks. Fuselage fuel 1,817 lb (824 kg), 2 x 100 litre wingtip tanks for 344 lb (156 kg), 2 x 150 litre underwing tanks for 516 lb (234 kg) or 2 x 350 litre underwing tanks for 1,221 lb (554 kg).
Electrical system: Main supply is 28 volt DC, with an engine-driven generator (emergency back-up V 910 ram air turbine producing 3kVA). 12 volt 28 amp-hour SAM 28 lead-acid battery for APU starting and standby. AC supply is 3-phase of 3 x 115/200 volt-400Hz.
Hydraulic system: 2,000 psi. Emergency circuit is supplied by an hydraulic accumulator.
Braking system: Hydraulic double disc brakes on main units, with an anti-skid system. Nosewheel has a shimmy damper.
De-icing system: Windshield and air intakes by hot air.
Oxygen system: Oxygen masks in both cockpits.

Aircraft variants:
L-39 C is the basic training version.
L-39 V is a single-seater for target towing.
L-39 ZO is an improved basic trainer with reinforced wings with 4 pylons.
L-39 ZA is the ground attack and reconnaissance version with an underfuselage gun pod and 4 pylons on the reinforced wings.
L-39 ZA/MP is a multi-purpose version with Western avionics and head-up display. 36 ZAs for Thailand delivered during 1993-94 are known as L-39 ZA/ARTs and have Elbit avionics (see Elbit). Suited to basic pilot training, combat manoeuvre/attack/weapon training, and light attack.

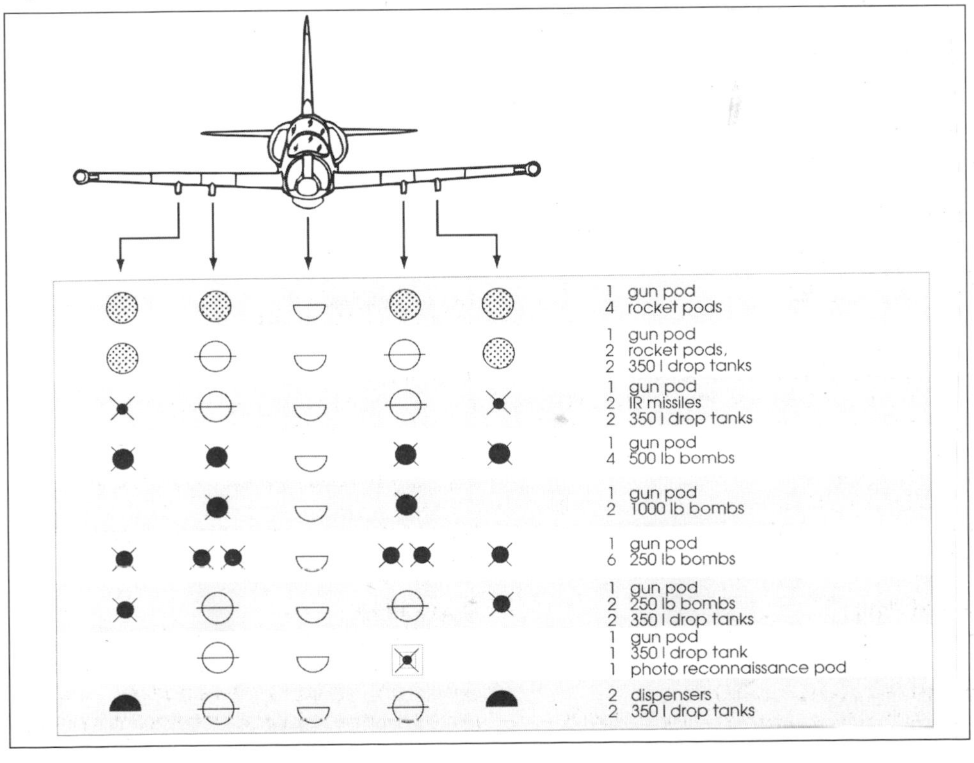

Aero L-39 ZA armament options (courtesy Aero)

DETAILS FOR L-39.

Principal dimensions:
Wing span: 31 ft (9.46 m)
Maximum length: 39 ft 10 ins (12.13 m)
Maximum height: 15 ft 8 ins (4.77 m)

Wings:
Aerofoil section: NACA 64A012 mod 5
Area: 202.36 sq ft (18.8 m^2)
Aspect ratio: 4.76
Sweepback: 1° 45′ on leading-edge
Incidence: 2°
Dihedral: 2° 20′

Tail unit:
Tailplane span: 14 ft 5 ins (4.4 m)
Tailplane area: 42.3 sq ft (3.93 m^2)

Undercarriage:
Type: Retractable, with castering/centring nosewheel
Designed to withstand hard conditions and operations from paved/unpaved and grass airfields
Main wheel tyre size: 610 x 185 mm for C, 610 x 215 mm for ZA
Nose wheel tyre size: 430 x 150 mm for C, 450 x 165 mm for ZA
Wheel base: 14 ft 5 ins (4.39 m)
Wheel track: 8 ft (2.44 m)

Weights:
Empty, equipped: 7,584-7,892 lb (3,440-3,580 kg)
Maximum ramp weight: 12,500 lb (5,670 kg) for ZA
Maximum take-off: 10,362 lb (4,700 kg) for C, 12,346 lb (5,600 kg) for ZA

Performance (at 9,480 lb, 4,300 kg take-off weight):
Maximum dive speed: 491 kts (565 mph) 910 km/h
Maximum speed: 407 kts (469 mph) 755 km/h
Stall speed: 91kts (104 mph) 169 km/h for C, 103 kts (118 mph) 190 km/h for ZA, both with flaps
Take-off distance over a 50 ft (15 m) obstacle: 2,625 ft (800 m)
Landing distance over a 50 ft (15 m) obstacle: 3,051 ft (930 m)
Maximum climb rate: 4,330 ft (1,320 m) per minute
Climb to 16,400 ft (5,000 m): 6 minutes
G limits: +8, -4
Ceiling: 36,000 ft (11,000 m)
Range with full fuel: 971 naut miles (1,118 miles) 1,800 km
Duration: 4 hours

Aero L-59 E delivered to Egypt (Aero/Jan Kouba)

Aero L-59

First flight: 30 September 1986 (in X-22/L-39 MS prototype form).
Role: Training, light attack/COIN, shore defence and limited air defence.

★ Aims

★ Development of the L-39, with additional thrust, modernized cockpit instrumentation, and broader combat capabilities.
★ Incorporates diagnostic system for evaluation of technical condition. Maintenance requirements 4.2 hours per flight hour.
★ 15 minute turn-around between sorties.

▲ Development

▲ 3 prototypes, the second and third as X-24/25 flying on 26 June and 6 October 1987.
▲ 1 October 1989. Maiden flight of a production L-59, with deliveries of 6 to the Czech air force during 1991-92.
▲ 29 January 1993. First of 48 L-59 Es for Egypt were delivered.

Sales/users: Czech Republic (6 L-59s), Egypt (48 L-59 Es) and Tunisia (12 L-59s).
Details: Generally as for the L-39, except in the following ways:
Crew escape: VS-2 zero-zero ejection seats.
Number of weapon pylons: 4.
Expendable weapons and equipment: 3,307 lb (1,500 kg) of stores, in similar combinations as shown on the L-39 chart, but with no reconnaissance pod indicated and with the option of 4 x 350 litre drop tanks. In weapon training form, typical armament could include 2 x SUU 20s with 12 practice bombs.
Flight/weapon system avionics/instrumentation: VHF and UHF radio communications equipment, and radio-navigation systems. Optional integrated nav/attack system. Up-front control panel, ring laser gyro/INS, video camera and VTR. HUD is basic flight instrumentation, with all data for symbology computed via a central digital computer. System can work in air-to-ground, air-to-air and navigation modes. Attitude and horizontal situations are displayed on 4 x 4 ins (10 x 10 cm) EFIS displays. Options include Stand-Alone Autonomous Air Combat Manoeuvring Instrumentation (A^2CMI), HUD-projected on visor, and full display and sight helmet (DASH).
Self-protection systems: Optional radar warning receiver.
Wing control surfaces: Aileron deflection ±16°.
Tail control surfaces: Elevator deflection +30°, -20°. Rudder deflection ±30°.
Flight control system: Similar to L-39, but irreversible power-operated by actuators.

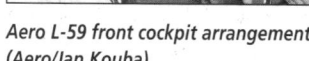

Aero L-59 front cockpit arrangement (Aero/Jan Kouba)

Fuselage: Strengthened.
Construction materials: Aluminium alloy, with the ailerons and elevators adopting a honeycomb form of construction.
Engine: Ivchenko PROGRESS DV-2 turbofan. Saphir 5M APU. A new variant with an AlliedSignal engine will fly in 1996 as the L-59 F.
Engine rating: 4,850 lbf (21.58 kN).
Fuel system: Up to 2,937 litres, as 1,225 litres internal and 700 litres external (possible 1,400 litres external). 30 seconds of inverted flight.
Electrical system: Main supply is 27 volt DC, with a 9 kW engine-driven generator. Stand-by source is APU driven. Emergency source is a 25 amp-hour ni-cd battery. AC supply via inverters is 115 volt single-phase and 3 x 36 volt three-phase.
Braking system: 3 disc brakes with anti-skid system, allowing differential braking for steering.

DETAILS FOR L-59.

Principal dimensions:
Wing span: 31 ft 4 ins (9.54 m)
Maximum length: 40 ft (12.2 m)
Maximum height: 15 ft 8 ins (4.77 m)

Tail unit:
Tailplane area: 57 sq ft (5.3 m^2)

Weights:
Empty: 8,885 lb (4,030 kg)
Maximum take-off: 12,258 lb (5,660 kg) clean, 13,196 lb (5,986 kg) with gun and 2 rocket pods, 14,579 lb (6,613 kg) with gun, rockets and 2 drop tanks, 15,432 lb (7,000 kg) maximum
Maximum take-off weight from grass: 13,228 lb (6,000 kg)
Maximum landing weight: 13,228 lb (6,000 kg) concrete, 12,566 lb (5,700 kg) unpaved

Performance:
Maximum limiting Mach number: Mach 0.82
Maximum speed: 472 kts (544 mph) 875 km/h
Stall speed: 117-129 kts (135-148 mph) 216-238 km/h *clean*, 99-110 kts (113-126 mph) 182-203 km/h with *flaps*
Take-off distance: 2,100-3,543 ft (640-1,080 m) concrete, 2,822 ft (860 m) unpaved at clean weight
Landing distance: 2,363-2,510 ft (720-765 m) at 12,257 lb (5,560 kg) weight
Maximum climb rate: 4,920 ft (1,500 m) per minute at sea level, at 5,560 kg weight
Climb to 5,000 m: 3 minutes 30 seconds at 5,560 kg weight
G limits: +8, -4 up to 5,560 kg; +6, -3 to 7,000 kg; in turn at sea level, ISA, 2.25-3.42
Ceiling: 40,000 ft (12,200 m)
Range with full fuel: 653-796 naut miles (752-916 miles) 1,210-1,475 km, depending on weight, at 5,000 m, ISA, 5% reserve
Duration: 3 hours 50 minutes at 12,202 lb (5,535 kg) take-off weight

Aero L-139 Albatros 2000

First flight: 10 May 1993.
Role: Basic/advanced training and light attack.

▲ Development

▲ Straightforward development of the L-39, customized to use a US engine and avionics.
Details: Generally similar to the L-39, except in the following ways:
Crew escape: VS-2 A ejection seats.
Number of weapon pylons: 4, outer pylons 551 lb (250 kg) capacity, inner 1,102 lb (500 kg) capacity.
Expendable weapons and equipment: Weight as for L-59, with similar options.
Flight/weapon system avionics/ instrumentation: VCS 40 A VFF, KTR 909 UHF, MST

Aero L-139 Albatros 2000 front cockpit

67A transponder, RMS 555 central panel radio and identification equipment. Radio-navigation equipment encompasses DFS 43A radio-compass, VNS 41 VOR/ILS, DMS 44 DME, KNS 660 FMS+GPS, EFS 40 EFIS, KAH 560 AHRS, and KAT 480 ADC. Available weapon delivery and navigation system and HUD as detailed for L-59, from Western supplier.

Engine: AlliedSignal TFE731-4-1T turbofan.

Engine rating: 4,080 lbf (18.15 kN).

Fuel system: 1,100 litres in the fuselage, 200 litres in the wingtip tanks, plus optionally 4 x 600 litre or 350 litre drop tanks. Allowable 20 seconds of inverted flight.

Electrical system: 28 volt/12kW DC system using a Lucas 23080-023 starter-generator with 51539-020A control unit, or 28 volt/6kW Lusas 23081-040A auxiliary generator as a back-up. Emergency 24 volt/43 amp-hour ni-cd battery. 115 volt/400Hz AC supply, using Maraton PC-250 and Mesit LUN 2463.01 converters.

Hydraulic system: 2,175 psi normal pressure, 2,390 psi maximum.

Braking system: Hydraulic discs on mainwheels. No nosewheel brake.

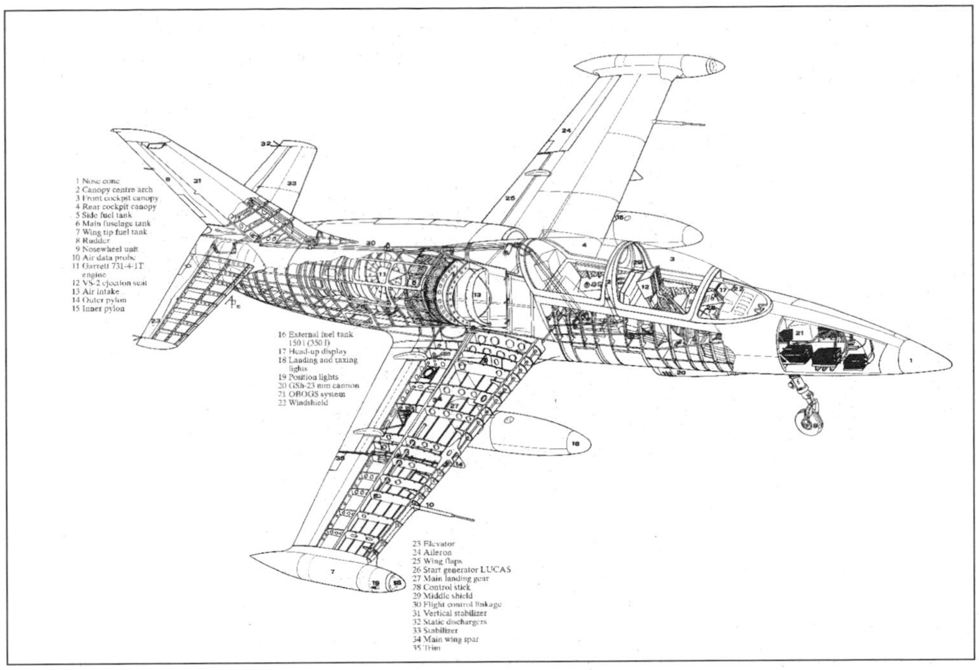

Aero L-139 Albatros 2000 cutaway (courtesy Aero Vodochody)

Details for L-139 Albatros 2000.

Weights:
Empty: 7,624 lb (3,458 kg)
Ramp weight: 10,005-13,228 lb (4,538-6,000 kg)
Take-off: 10,026 lb (4,548 kg) clean
Maximum landing weight: 10,582 lb (4,800 kg)

Performance:
Maximum limiting Mach number: Mach 0.8
Maximum speed: 410 kts (472 mph) 760 km/h at 20,000 ft (6,100 m)
Stall speed: 90 kts (104 mph) 167 km/h
Landing speed: 99 kts (114 mph) 183 km/h
Take-off distance: 1,640 ft (500 m)
Landing distance: 2,000 ft (610 m)
Maximum climb rate: 4,200 ft (1,278 m) per minute
G limits: +8, -4
Ceiling: 38,700 ft (11,800 m)
Range with full internal fuel: 869 naut miles (1,000 miles) 1,610 km
Duration: 3 hours 32 minutes

Aero L-159

First flight: Expected April 1996.

Role: Single-seat light multi-role combat, and two-seat training variant, suited to close air support, air defence, tactical reconnaissance, counter insurgency, border patrol, anti-ship, and lead-in fighter and weapons training.

★ Aims

★ Based on the L-59 configuration but with accommodation for a pilot only in the combat version.
★ Tactical mobility, including ability to use semi-prepared airstrips.
★ Latest generation turbofan engine.
★ NATO compatible.
★ Equipped with advanced avionics and sensors, including radar.

Aero L-139 Albatros 2000 in camouflage (Aero/Jan Kouba)

▲ Development

▲ April 1996. First flight expected.
▲ 1998. Initial operational capability.

Sales/users: Czech air force is to receive 72.

Crew: Pilot.

Cockpit: See avionics for displays. Ballistic protection.

Number of weapon pylons: 7, 6 under the wings and 1 under the fuselage centreline.

Expendable weapons and equipment: 5,159 lb (2,340 kg), including air-to-air and air-to-surface missiles. Provision for future weapons and special pods.

Radar: Multi-mode pulse Doppler type.

Flight/weapon system avionics/instrumentation: Integration via an MIL-STD-1553 databus, allowing future growth. Ring laser gyro INS with integral GPS, head-up display with raster capability, and colour multi-function

Aero L-159 single-seat multi-role combat aircraft with AAMs and a centreline sensor pod

head-down displays. A team led by Rockwell Aerospace has signed a US$ 18.6 million contract to design and fit a new avionics suite into the prototype, to include multi-function displays, air data computer, IFF fire-control radar, stores management system and RWR.

Self-protection systems: Radar warning receiver and countermeasures dispensers. See Cockpit and Fuel system for OBIGGS elements.

Fuselage: Forward section redesigned for 1 cockpit and a nose radome.

Engine: AlliedSignal/ITEC F124-GA-100 turbofan. APU fitted.

Engine rating: 6,300 lbf (28.02 kN).

Fuel system: 3,307 lb (1,500 kg) of internal fuel. 5,705 lb (2,588 kg) of auxiliary fuel in 4 tanks. Tank inerting system for protection.

Oxygen: On-board oxygen generating system.

Details for L-159.

Principal dimensions:
Wing span: 31 ft 4 ins (9.54 m)
Maximum length: 41 ft 1 ins (12.53 m)
Maximum height: 15 ft 8 ins (4.77 m)

Weights:
Empty: 9,171 lb (4,160 kg)
Maximum ramp weight: 17,637 lb (8,000 kg)

Performance:
Maximum speed: 502 kts (578 mph) 930 km/h at sea level
Take-off distance: 1,608 ft (490 m)
Maximum climb rate: 9,250 ft (2,820 m) per minute
G limits: +8, -4 structural
Ceiling: 43,300 ft (13,200 m)
Range with full internal fuel: 848 naut miles (975 miles) 1,570 km

Arab Organization for Industrialization (AOI) (Egypt)

Corporate address: 2 D Abbassiya Square, PO Box 770, Cairo – A.R.E.
Telephone: +20 2 932822, 823377
Facsimile: +20 2 826010
Telex: 92090, 92014 AOI UN
Founded: November 1975.
Employees: Some 20,000.
Information: Mahmoud El-Refai (Director of Operations & Marketing).

DIVISIONS

<u>Aircraft Factory</u>
HQ address: PO Box 11722, Helwan, Cairo.
Telephone: +20 2 780114, 782407
Facsimile: +20 2 782408

● Activities
● Assembled both the Alpha Jet and Tucano trainers.
● Currently produces the Helwan 2 and Helwan 3 multi-purpose light aircraft, and manufactures Mirage 2000 components plus auxiliary fuel tanks for F-16s, various Mirages and old Mikoyan types.

<u>Helwan Factory</u>

● Activities
● Has assembled, ground/flight tested, overhauls and repairs SA-342L Gazelle helicopters (airframe and some dynamic parts).

<u>Kader Factory</u>
HQ address: PO Box 287, Heliopolis.

● Activities
● Contributed to the AOI Tucano programme, and produced the Gomhouria primary trainer.

<u>Engine Factory</u>
HQ address: PO Box 12, Helwan.
Telephone: +20 2 781088, 781404.
Facsimile: +20 2 781236

● Activities
● Assembles the Larzac 04 and PT6A-25E. Overhauls and repairs the Larzac, PT6A-25E, Atar 09C and CT-64.

<u>Arab British Engine Co (ABECO)</u>
HQ address: See Engine section.

● Activities
● Overhauls and repairs helicopter engines, as a joint venture organization.

Dassault Aviation (France)

Corporate address: 9 rond-point des Champs-Elysées/Marcel Dassault, 75008 Paris.
Telephone: +33 1 43 59 14 70
Facsimile: +33 1 42 56 20 01
Founded: 14 December 1971 as Avions Marcel Dassault-Breguet Aviation, changing to the present name in 1990. The merger brought together the post-war Dassault company and the Société des Avions Louis Breguet, one of France's oldest established aircraft companies, dating from 1911. 35% of the company's shares are held by the state-owned Société de Gestion de Participations Aeronautiques (SOGEPA) organization, which performs as a holding company to co-ordinate R&D between France's 2 largest aerospace concerns, Dassault and Aerospatiale.
Information: Christine Mougin (Director of Communications).
Press communications address: 27 rue du Professeur Victor Pauchet – 92420 Vaucresson.
Telephone: +33 1 47 95 86 91
Fax: +33 1 47 95 87 40

■ Facilities
■ Argenteuil, Argonay, Biarritz-Parme, Bordeaux-Mérignac, Martignas and Poitiers.

● Activities
● Designs, develops and manufactures military and civil aircraft (see Falcon series of business jets and derivatives in the General Aviation section).
● Researches artificial intelligence techniques for the aeronautical and space industries, designs and manufactures flight control systems, undertakes weapon system design and integration, develops new materials and related technologies for aircraft structures, and more.

SUBSIDIARIES

<u>Dassault Systèmes</u>
HQ address: 24-28 av. du Général de Guelle, 92150 Suresnes
Telephone: +33 1 40 99 40 99
Facsimile: +33 1 42 04 45 81

● Activities
● Computer aided design and manufacturing (CAD/CAM).
● Related companies are **Dassault Systemes Services** (East 15 Midland Avenue, Paramus, NJ 07652, USA) and **Dassault Systemes of America** (2500 West Empire Avenue, Burbank, CA 91504, USA).

<u>Sogitec</u>
HQ address: 4 rue Marcel-Monge – Immeuble Nobel, 92158 Suresnes Cedex.
Telephone: +33 1 41 18 57 00
Facsimile: +33 1 41 18 57 18, 18 59 19.

■ Facilities
■ Suresnes, Rennes and Bordeaux.

● Activities
● Specializes in simulation and integrated logistics. 2 main divisions, Electronic and Communication.

Dassault Atlantic, Atlantique 2 and 3

First flight: 7 May 1981 for Atlantique 2, 21 October 1961 for Atlantic.
Role: Long-range maritime patrol, anti-submarine warfare, minelaying and bombing, maritime and signal intelligence, strike aircraft guidance, and search and rescue.

★ Aims
★ Original Atlantic was designed by Breguet in France,

DETAILS FOR ATLANTIQUE 2.

Principal dimensions:
Wing span: 122 ft 10 ins (37.45 m)
Maximum length: 123 ft 9 ins (37.71 m)
Maximum height: 35 ft 9 ins (10.9 m)

Wings:
Aerofoil section: NASA 64 type
Area: 1,295.33 sq ft (120.34 m^2)
Aspect ratio: 11
Sweepback: 9° at leading edge
Incidence: 3°
Dihedral: 6°

Tail unit:
Tailplane span: 40 ft 5 ins (12.31 m)
Tailplane area: 260.5 sq ft (24.2 m^2)

Undercarriage:
Type: Retractable, with twin nosewheels
Wheel base: 30 ft 10 ins (9.4 m)
Wheel track: 29 ft 6 ins (9 m)

Weights:
Empty, equipped: 56,659 lb (25,700 kg), with 3,500 kg of mission avionics
Normal take-off: 97,444 lb (44,200 kg)
Maximum take-off: 101,853 lb (46,200 kg)

Performance:
Maximum speed: 350 kts (403 mph) 648 km/h
Cruise speed: 300 kts (345 mph) 556 km/h
Economical patrol speed: 170 kts (196 mph) 315 km/h
Stall speed: 90 kts (104 mph) 167 km/h with flaps
Balanced runway length: 7,875 ft (2,400 m), at maximum take-off weight, ISA
Take-off distance over a 35 ft (11 m) obstacle: 6,040 ft (1,840 m)
Landing distance over a 35 ft (11 m) obstacle: 4,920 ft (1,500 m)
Maximum climb rate: 2,000 ft (610 m) per minute, at 88,185 lb (40,000 kg) weight
Ceiling: 30,000 ft (9,150 m)
Range with full fuel: 4,200 naut miles (4,836 miles) 7,778 km
On station duration at normal take-off weight: 8 hours at low altitude, 600 naut miles from base, with 4 torpedoes, 2 Exocets and 100 sonobuoys
On station duration with full fuel: 8 hours , with 2 torpedoes and 1 Exocet, at 1,000 naut miles from base. 4 hours at 1,500 naut miles from base, same weapons
Maximum duration: 18 hours

Dassault Atlantique 2 in French Navy service, with Iguane lowered

but followed a policy aim of NATO to realize the design of a standardized maritime patrol aircraft to replace the Lockheed Neptune. In the event, the Atlantic was only bought by France, Germany, Italy and the Netherlands, totalling 87 aircraft.

⋆ Atlantique 2 is derived from Atlantic. Its main characteristics are, like Atlantic, a sturdy airframe, high aspect ratio wing, single large weapon bay with high load carrying capability, and Tyne Mk 21 turboprops. Mission systems avionics are new and of the latest technology.

⋆ Atlantique 2 airframe is produced by a European consortium, comprising Aerospatiale, Dassault, Dornier, MBB, Alenia, and Sabca-Sonaca. A new Atlantique 3 version is being studied.

▲ Development

▲ 19 July 1965. First production Atlantic flew.
▲ 19 July 1974. Final Atlantic delivered, going to the Italian Navy.
▲ September 1978. Development of Atlantique 2 began, born out of the former Atlantic II programme, in which an Atlantic prototype had been assigned for modification to this standard in 1974.
▲ 7 May 1981. First flight of the Atlantique 2.
▲ 19 October 1988. First production Atlantique 2 flew.
▲ October 1989. First Atlantique 2 delivery.
▲ 1 February 1991. First Atlantique 2 operational unit, as 23 Flottille of the French Navy.

Sales/users: France (some 16 Atlantics remaining in early 1995 of 40 received, but being withdrawn as the last of 28 Atlantique 2s are received), Germany (19 Atlantics remaining operational of 20 received, including 5 modified for signal intelligence), Italy (18 Atlantics), and Pakistan (4 ex-French Atlantics, plus 2 for spares).
Details: Principally for Atlantique 2.
Crew: 10-12, according to mission. 2 pilots, flight engineer, mission tactical co-ordinator, nav/comms operator, ESM-MAD operator, radar operator, 2 acoustic operators, and 1-3 observers. Up to 24 persons can be carried on deployment flights.
Fixed guns: None.
Number of weapon pylons: 4 under the wings, for a total external stores weight of 7,716 lb (3,500 kg).
Expendable weapons and equipment: Single weapon bay for a 5,511 lb (2,500 kg) load, including up to 8 torpedoes (Mk 46 or V9) , 8 depth charges, 8 bombs (typically 125 kg), 6 250 kg mines, 2 Exocet anti-ship missiles, 8 air-sea rescue containers, or a combination that could be, typically, 3 torpedoes or mines or depth charges and an Exocet. Underwing loads can include 2 or 4 Magic, ARMAT or other weapons.
Additional stores: Rear fuselage encompasses 4 day/night marker compartments (capacity 69), 4 automatic sonobuoy launchers (capacity 72 A or F size chutes), 4 reloadable sonobuoy launchers of A/F/G size and 1 free-fall chute, sonobuoy storage (60), retro launcher and storage (32), and flare launcher and storage (60).
Radar: Thomson-CSF Iguane, in a retractable radome.
Flight/weapon system avionics/instrumentation: Weapon system based on a distributed computer system, and comprising a tactical system with a central processing unit and tactical display, and decentralized sub-systems (detection, navigation, weapons, communications, etc), each with its own control and processing computer. Data exchanges between the sub-systems and to/from the tactical system are made through a digital databus. 2 INS (SEGEM Uliss 53). Mission system avionics sub-systems include 2 acoustic processing units for detecting, locating, identifying and tracking submarines through a network of sonobuoys; a compressed pulse radar able to detect small targets in heavy sea states; a radar emission detection system (ESM – ARAR 13A); a magnetic anomaly detector (MAD), used to classify and locate submarines; and an infra-red sensor under the nose (FLIR – Tango) for long-range, day/night detection of surface vessels. The navigation system comprises redundant inertial platform, coupled to GPS Navstar satellite equipment and air data unit automatic navigation plotter. The communications system comprises redundant equipment, such as HF, VHF and UHF (with HAVE QUICK II) with secure devices (voice and TTY). It also includes data link capability (NATO Link II). Omera 35 cameras in the nose and vertically in an aft compartment.
Self-protection systems: See above. Capable of carrying air-to-air missiles under the wings.
Wing characteristics: Straight, low mounted. Wingtip pods.
Wing control surfaces: Ailerons, 3-section slotted flaps and 3 spoilers per wing.
Tail control surfaces: Elevators and rudder.
Airbrakes: Use of spoilers.
Flight control system: Hydraulic.
Construction materials: Extensive use of bonded light alloy honeycomb panels.

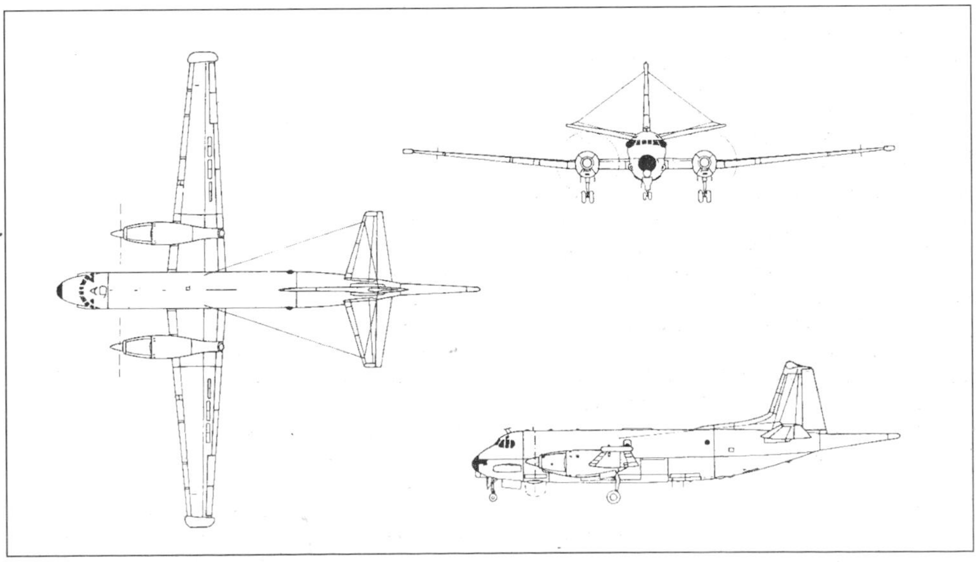

Dassault Atlantique 2 (courtesy Dassault)

Engines: 2 Rolls-Royce Tyne Mk 21 turboprops.
Engine rating: Each 6,100 ehp (4,549 ekW).
Flight refuelling probe: None. See Aircraft variants.
Fuel system: 23,120 litres (40,785 lb, 18,500 kg maximum).
Electrical system: 28 volt DC supply, with 4 x 6kW transformer/rectifiers and a 40 amp-hour battery. Dual AC supplies, 115/200 volt variable frequency 3-phase, with 2 alternators; 115/200 volt, 400Hz 3-phase , with 4 engine-driven generators. APU-driven emergency AC generator.
Hydraulic system: 2,700 psi (dual).
Braking system: Discs, with anti skid.
De-icing system: Electric for air intakes and propellers, pneumatic for wing/tail leading edges.

Aircraft variants:

Atlantic is the original version, entering service in 1966 and the fleet having logged over 800,000 flight hours. French and Italian aircraft have undergone, or are undergoing, avionics upgrade, while 5 German aircraft have been modified for sigint.
Atlantique 2 is the newly built upgraded version, for French Navy service, as detailed.
Atlantique 3 is a proposed new updated version of Atlantique 2, to take advantage of new off-the-shelf technologies. These could include Allison AE2100 turboprop engines that could increase duration by up to 1.5 hours and allow an ASW radius of up to 1,000 naut miles (1,151 miles) 1,852 km with 11,023 lb (5,000 kg) of external weapons and remain on-station for 7 hours, in-flight refuelling capability, new or improved sensors (radar with imagery, acoustics with enhanced sonobuoy processing, SATCOM/communications systems, etc), and improved self-protection (ESM with DASS, new AAMs, etc). EFIS. Anti-ship capability. Proposed as a Nimrod replacement for the RAF.

Dassault Mirage III, 5 and 50

First flight: 17 November 1956 (Mirage III), 19 May 1967 (Mirage 5), and 15 April 1979 (Mirage 50).
Role: Interceptor-fighter and reconnaissance (Mirage III), ground attack and interceptor (Mirage V) and multi-mission fighter (Mirage 50).
Sales/users: Out of production but many are undergoing significant upgrade; about 615 of the 1,420 or so III/5/50s built remain available for service or are complete but assigned for cannibalization. Argentina (III and 5, retrofitted with refuelling probes), Brazil (III–Es and two-seaters modernized using Dassault kits), Colombia (5, being upgraded by IAI, including canards), Egypt (5, upgraded), Gabon (5), Lebanon (III, remaining handful in storage), Libya (5), Pakistan (III and 5, largest "on-paper" force, but including ex-Australian III-Os used in part for spares – upgrade of some IIIs was specified to include HOTAS, inertial navigation system, GPS, FLIR, enhanced ECM and possibly improved radar), Peru (5, upgraded by Dassault and including digital avionics, laser rangefinder, improved RWR and flight refuelling probe), Switzerland (III, being upgraded with canards, zero-zero ejection seat, drag-chute and better self-protection systems), United Arab Emirates (5, upgraded in Pakistan), and Venezuela (50, including upgraded III/5s to 50 standard by Dassault, with Cyrano IV-M3 radar and Atar 09K-50 engine).
Further upgrades producing newly-named aircraft (see separate company entries), as follows:
ENAER of Chile Pantera.
Atlas of South Africa Cheetahs.
SABCA of Belgium. Includes Chilean Elkans.
See also:
Israel Aircraft Industries.
Pakistan Aeronautical Complex.
Swiss Federal Aircraft Factory.
Details: Principally for the Mirage III-E.
Crew: Pilot.
Crew escape: Martin Baker RM4 zero-height ejection seat, offering safe ejection at over 90 kts (103 mph) 167 km/h.
Fixed guns: 2 x 30-mm DEFA 552A cannon.
Ammunition: Each 125 rounds.
Number of weapon pylons: 5, including 1 under the fuselage.
Expendable weapons and equipment: 8,818 lb (4,000 kg) load, including air-to-air or air-to-surface missiles, bombs, multi-store carrier for rockets and fuel or rockets and bombs, CC 630 gun pod (2 x 30-mm) and more.
Radar: Thomson-CSF Cyrano II.
Wing characteristics: Low mounted delta.
Wing control surfaces: 2 elevons and a trailing-edge flap.
Tail control surfaces: Rudder only.
Canard: Often retrofitted.
Airbrakes: On upper and lower surfaces of the wings, near the leading edge.
Flight control system: Hydraulic.
Fuselage: Area rule design.
Construction materials: Metal.
Engines: SNECMA Atar 09C turbojet. Can use a jettisonable SEPR 844 RATO system.
Engine rating: 9,702 lbf (43.16 kN) dry, 13,672 lbf (60.82 kN) with afterburning.
Air intakes: Ahead of wing roots.
Flight refuelling probe: Sometimes retrofitted during upgrade.
Fuel system: 2,940 litres. Provision for 2 drop tanks, of 250 (in multi-store carrier), 625, 1,100, 1,300 or 1,700 litres capacity each.
Electrical system: DC supply using a 26.5 volt generator and 24 volt 40 amp-hour batteries.
200 volt/400Hz AC supply using a transformer and alternator.
Hydraulic system: 3,000 psi (dual).
Braking system: Includes drag-chute.

DETAILS FOR MIRAGE III-E.

Principal dimensions:
Wing span: 27 ft (8.22 m)
Maximum length: 49 ft 4 ins (15.03 m)
Maximum height: 14 ft 9 ins (4.5 m)

Wings:
Area: 376.74 sq ft (35 m^2)
Aspect ratio: 1.931
Incidence: 0°
Anhedral: 1°

Undercarriage:
Type: Retractable, with nosewheel
Main wheel tyre size: 750 x 230 mm
Wheel base: 16 ft (4.87 m)
Wheel track: 10 ft 4 ins (3.15 m)

Weights:
Empty: 15,543 lb (7,050 kg)
Maximum take-off: 30,203 lb (13,700 kg)

Performance:
Maximum speed: Mach 2.2
Maximum speed at sea level: 750 kts (864 mph) 1,390 km/h
Take-off distance: 5,250 ft (1,600 m) at maximum weight
Landing distance: 2,300 ft (700 m) with drag-chute
Time to 36,100 ft (11,000 m): 3 minutes
Ceiling: 55,775 ft (17,000 m) with RATO
Radius of action: 648 naut miles (746 miles) 1,200 km

Dassault Mirage 5PA.3 of 8 TAS, Pakistan Air Force, carrying an Exocet anti-ship missile, 2 AIM-9P Sidewinders and 2 x 1,300 litre drop tanks (Denis Hughes)

Dassault Mirage IV-P

First flight: 17 June 1959.
Role: Supersonic bomber and strategic reconnaissance.

★ Aims:

★ Scaled-up Mirage III, originally for strategic nuclear role, later tactical nuclear/conventional and strategic reconnaissance.

▲ Development

▲ 62 production Mirage IV-As were delivered to the French Force de Frappe between 1964-68.
▲ 1 October 1964. Initial operational capability of the Mirage IV-A, carrying the AN-11 nuclear bomb.
▲ 1983. Modification programme began of 18 IV-As to IV-Ps to carry the ASMP nuclear missile, with 1 more to make good an attrition loss. 12 further modified to have the capability of carrying the CT-52 strategic reconnaissance pod.
▲ 1 May 1986. Initial operational capability with the Mirage IV-P.
▲ December 1987. Last of 18 IV-Ps received by the Air Force.

Dassault Mirage IV-P armed with an ASMP missile (SIRPA "AIR")

▲ 1996. Expected retirement as a bomber, but with reconnaissance (and emergency bomber) role likely to continue until about 1998.

Users: 18 remaining in French service, with 14 operational with 2 squadrons (1/91 Gascogne and 2/92 Bretagne). 4 with OCU.

Crew: 2.

Cockpit: Fighter type cockpit and canopy for the pilot, with the navigator to his rear under a semi-glazed cover.

Crew escape: Martin Baker ejection seats.

Number of weapon pylons: 5, 4 under the wings for self-protection systems and drop tanks, and 1 underfuselage for an ASMP missile or reconnaissance pod.

Expendable weapons and equipment: ASMP thermonuclear stand-off missile of 300 kiloton. Presumably still capable of carrying 16 x 450 kg conventional bombs.

Additional stores: See earlier paragraphs.

Radar: Thomson-CSF Arcana.

Self-protection systems: Thomson-CSF Serval radar warning receivers. Thomson-CSF TMV 015 Barem jammer and Philips BOZ-100 chaff/flare dispenser on the outer pylons.

Construction materials: Metal.

Engines: 2 SNECMA Atar 9K-14 turbojets.

Engine rating: Each 14,837 lbf (66 kN). Provision for 12 rocket RATO system.

Flight refuelling probe: At nose (see photograph).

Fuel system: 1,650 litre or 2,500 litre drop-tanks on the inner pylons.

Details for Mirage IV-P.

Principal dimensions:
Wing span: 38 ft 11 ins (11.85 m)
Maximum length: 76 ft 5 ins (23.3 m)
Maximum height: 17 ft 9 ins (5.4 m)

Weights:
Empty, operating: 31,960 lb (14,500 kg)
Maximum take-off: 72,752 lb (33,000 kg)

Performance:
Maximum speed: Mach 2.2
Maximum speed at low altitude: 648 kts (746 mph) 1,200 km/h IAS
Ceiling: 54,125 ft (16,500 m)
Radius of action: 810 naut miles (932 miles) 1,500 km

Dassault Mirage 2000

First flight: 10 March 1978.

Role: Air superiority/defence, long-range strike, multi-role (with priorities according to version – see Aircraft variants), reconnaissance and electronic warfare.

★ Aims

★ Advanced aerodynamics, and extensive use of composites.
★ Low wing loading, high thrust-to-weight ratio.
★ Full fly-by-wire control system.
★ Extensive use of integrated maintenance to minimize the required ground operations, and thereby the number of technicians and amount of ground equipment (during the 1992 Gulf conflict, a 98% readiness rate was achieved).

▲ Development

▲ 18 December 1975. Mirage 2000 development approved as the French Air Force's next-generation combat aircraft.
▲ 10 March 1978. First flight of the first of 4 single-seat and 1 two-seat prototypes.
▲ 11 October 1980. First flight of a Mirage 2000 B prototype.
▲ November 1982. First Mirage 2000 C delivery to the French Air Force, following the first flight on the 20th.
▲ 3 February 1983. First flight of the Mirage 2000 N.
▲ 1984. Initial operational capability with the French Air Force's 1/2 Cigognes squadron at Dijon.
▲ 1984. Delivery and IOC of the Mirage 2000 E.
▲ 1985. IOC with the first exported Mirage 2000s.
▲ January 1987. Initial delivery of the Mirage 2000 N to the French Air Force.
▲ 24 October 1990. First flight of the Mirage 2000-5.
▲ February 1991. First flight of a Mirage 2000 D.
▲ July 1993. First delivery of a Mirage 2000 D.
▲ 1996. First Mirage 2000-5 deliveries.

Sales/users: Some 547 full production aircraft ordered by 1995 (plus 13 original development aircraft), including well over 100 Mirage 2000-5s), of which more than 400 had been delivered. Abu Dhabi (E and ED, known as EAD, RAD and DAD for interception, reconnaissance and training), Egypt (B/ED and E), French Air Force (318 B, C, D, and 2000-5), Greece (E and B/ED), India (E and ED, known as H and TH Vajra), Peru (E and ED, known as P and DP), Qatar (2000-5), Taiwan (2000-5). Pakistan is negotiating for 44 Mirage 2000-5s.

Crew: Pilot or 2 crew (see Aircraft variants).

Cockpit: Mirage 2000-5 differs from previous versions by having a "glass cockpit" arrangement and interface intended to lighten the pilot's tasks in a hostile environment, with 5 displays: HUD, head-down display, 2 lateral displays, and a head-level display. HOTAS. Mirage 2000 N cockpit installations were designed for two-person missions, the rear cockpit mainly for navigation, ECM management and weapon preparation; 2 head-down displays. 2000 C has head-up and head-down displays. 2000 D has 2 head down displays.

Crew escape: Martin-Baker F10Q zero-zero type.

Fixed guns: 2 x DEFA 554 30-mm cannon in single-seaters.

Ammunition: Each 125 rounds.

Number of weapon pylons: 9, 4 under the wings and 5 under the fuselage.

Expendable weapons and equipment: Maximum load 13,890 lb (6,300 kg). Mirage 2000-5 can carry

The latest Dassault Mirage 2000-5 in single-seat form (Dassault Aviation/Aviaplans)

Dassault Mirage 2000 D two-seater (Dassault Aviation/Aviaplans)

4 Mica and 2 Magic 2 AAMs plus up to 3 drop tanks; other Mirage 2000s can carry Magic 2 and Super 530D missiles. Standard available air-to-surface weapons include up to 18 x 250 kg bombs, 6 x 400 kg modular stand-off/area bombs, 18 x BAP 100 or Durandel anti-runway bombs, up to 6 Beluga or 18 x BAT 120 cluster bombs; laser-guided weapons (1 or 2 x 1,000 kg Matra LGB, or 1 or 2 Aerospatiale AS 30L); or 1 or 2 Armat anti-radiation or Exocet anti-ship missiles; 1 x 30-mm CC 630 twin-gun pod; and/or 2 or 4 rocket pods. ASMP available on French Air Force Ns and Ds, and Apache submunition missile for D from 1996.
Additional stores: Available pods, according to the aircraft version, include 1 or 2 self-defence or 1 offensive ECM, laser designator or FLIR. Alternative optical/IR, SLAR and electronic intelligence reconnaissance pods. Mirage 2000-5 has an integrated FLIR pod and LDP laser designator pod (IR and EO), and EW system.
Radar: Thomson-CSF RDM radar in a small number of Mirage 2000-Cs, thereafter Thomson-CSF/Dassault Electronique RDI. RDM in 2000 Es. Dassault Electronique Antilope V in 2000 N and Antilope 50 in 2000 D. Thomson-CSF RDY in 2000-5.
Flight/weapon system avionics/instrumentation: Dassault Electronique 2084 digital central computer (2084XR in 2000 D), and digital databus. SFENA 605 autopilot (2000 C), 606 (2000 N), 607 (2000 D) and 608 (2000-5). Other systems include Deltac Tacan and Socrat 8900 VOR/ILS. See Aircraft variants.
Self-protection systems: Mirage 2000-5 has a comprehensive internal and fully integrated self-protection system (radar warning receiver, advanced jammer, chaff/flare dispensers, etc), with no need for external pods, to be operated in conjunction with a new proficient and programmable mission planning and debriefing system. Mirage 2000 C/N use Serval RWR, Caméléon jamming system, and Spirale chaff/flare. Internal integrated ECM system in E, and some with Spirale. Matra DDM missile launch warning receiver on some French Air Force 2000D/Ns from Spring 1995.
Wing characteristics: Low mounted, variable camber delta type with high-lift devices.
Wing control surfaces: 2-section elevons (16° up, 25° down). Automatic slats along the entire leading edge, inboard section drooping up to 17° 30', outboard 30°.
Tail control surfaces: Rudder only.
Airbrakes: On upper and lower wing surfaces.
Flight control system: Fly-by-wire.
Fuselage: Area-ruled type.
Construction materials: Metal, including lightweight honeycomb cores for the elevons, rudder and avionics bay cover. Extensive use of carbon and boron fibre, particularly for the rudder, fin and elevon skins, providing a 20% weight reduction for those parts.
Engine: SNECMA M53-5 or M53-P2.
Engine rating: 12,235 lbf (54.43 kN) dry, 19,840 lbf (88.26 kN) with afterburning for M53-5. 14,400 lbf (64.05 kN) dry, 21,400 lbf (95.19 kN) with afterburning for M53-P2. New version with an augmented rating of 22,050 lbf (98.07 kN) will be made available.
Air intakes: Side mounted, with moving centrebodies. Externally fixed strakes to create vortices at high AoA.
Flight refuelling probe: Many on-line French Air Force single and two-seat Mirage 2000s are capable of in-flight refuelling. Most multi-role Mirage 2000s are capable of flight refuelling, or use as "buddy" system tankers.
Fuel system: 3,978 litres internally in 2000 C/E wing and fuselage tanks, 3,904 litres in other versions. 1,300 litre drop tank under the fuselage and 2 x 1,700 or 2,000 litre tanks under the wings.
Electrical system: Twin 20kVA or 25kVA/400Hz alternators, twin DC transformers, static inverter and 40 amp-hour ni-cd battery.
Hydraulic system: 4,000 psi (dual).
Braking system: Disc brakes on main units, with anti-skid system. Provision for a drag-chute or arrester hook.
Oxygen system: Eros type.

300	1 800	400	400	1 800	400	400	1 800	300	EXTERNAL LOADS (kg)
		●	●		●	●			MICA ACTIVE AIR-TO-AIR MISSILE
●	●						●	●	MAGIC IR MISSILE
	●						●		UNDERWING EXTRA FUEL TANK
				●					FUSELAGE EXTRA FUEL TANK
	●●●●	●	●	●●●●	●	●	●●●●		500 lb / 250 kg BOMB
	●			●			●		2,000 lb / 1,000 kg LASER GUIDED BOMB
		●	●	●●●●	●	●			DURANDAL BOMB
				18					BAP 100 PENETRATION BOMB
	●	●	●	●	●	●	●		BELUGA GRENADE DISPENSER
				●					F 2 PRACTICE BOMB LAUNCHER
●	●						●	●	F 4 (18) 68 mm ROCKET LAUNCHER
			●						E.O. OR I.R. WEAPON GUIDANCE POD
	●						●		AS 30 L LASER GUIDED MISSILE
				●					APACHE System
	●						●		ANTI-RADIATION MISSILE
	●						●		AIR-TO-SEA ACTIVE MISSILE
					●				FLIR POD
				●					TWIN GUN POD
				●					RECCE POD
				●					OFFENSIVE OR INTELLIGENCE ECM POD
				●					BUDDY REFUELLING POD

Dassault Mirage 2000-5 stores inventory (courtesy Dassault). Stores configuration capabilities according to aircraft specifications

Aircraft variants:

<u>Mirage 2000 B</u> is a 2-seat operational trainer, based on the C. The B and C versions are together known as DAs. French Air Force ordered some 27 aircraft.
<u>Mirage 2000 C</u> is a single-seat air-defence version, the initial 37 produced with the Thomson-CSF RDM radar and SNECMA M53-5 engine, and thereafter with Thomson-CSF/Dassault Electronique RDI radar and M53-P2 engine. Early RDM aircraft are having RDI installed during 1994-97, taken from a similar number of RDI-equipped aircraft that are undergoing upgrade to Mirage 2000-5 standard. 2 x 30-mm DEFA cannon, Magic 2 and Super 540D AAMs. Internal countermeasures system. The B and C versions are together known as DAs. French Air Force ordered some 126 aircraft, of which 37 are being modified to 2000–5
<u>Mirage 2000 D</u> ("diversified") is based on the N but is dedicated to all-weather day and night air-to-surface attack. High speed and very low altitude automatic terrain-following capability. Fully redesigned cockpit offers an advanced interface between the crew and the weapons system. Capable of launching conventional weapons or the most sophisticated modern weapons, including laser-guided and submunitions, and retains the N's nuclear capability. Some 90 ordered by the French Air Force. A version without nuclear capability is proposed for export.
<u>Mirage 2000 E</u> is a single-seat multi-role export version of the C, with M53-P2 engine, multimode RDM radar, and Magic 2 and Super 530D AAMs. Can be used for air-to-air, air-to-ground, air-to-surface and reconnaissance missions. Numerous standard and sophisticated weapon options, including laser guided.
<u>Mirage 2000 ED</u> (or B/ED) is a two-seat operational training version of the E, similar in concept to the 2000 B.
<u>Mirage 2000 N</u> is a two-seat all-weather, very low altitude penetration version with nuclear capability. Equipped with Dassault Electronique Antilope V terrain-following radar, Sagem twin-inertial navigation system, TRT radar-altimeter, autopilot, Thomson-CSF displays, Dassault Electronique ECM, Omera vertical camera and an M53-P2 engine, and carries an ASMP medium-range nuclear missile and 2 x Magic 2 AAMs for self defence.

BASIC DETAILS FOR ALL MIRAGE 2000s, OR AS SPECIFIED.

Principal dimensions:
Wing span: 29 ft 11 ins (9.13 m)
Maximum length: 48 ft 1 ins (14.65 m) for Mirage 2000-5 and D, 47 ft 1.5 ins (14.36 m) for C and E, and 47 ft 9 ins (14.55 m) for two-seaters
Maximum height: 17 ft 1 ins (5.2 m) for single-seaters, 16 ft 11 ins (5.15 m) for two-seaters

Wings:
Area: 441.32 sq ft (41 m^2)
Aspect ratio: 2.033
Sweepback: 58° on the leading edge
Anhedral: From roots

Undercarriage:
Type: Retractable, with twin steerable nosewheels
Main wheel tyre size: 750 x 230 mm
Nose wheel tyre size: 360 x 135 mm
Wheel base: 16 ft 5 ins (5 m)
Wheel track: 11 ft 2 ins (3.4 m)

Weights:
Empty: 16,535 lb (7,500 kg) for single-seaters, 16,755 lb (7,600 kg) for two-seaters
Typical combat: 21,000 lb (9,525 kg)
Maximum take-off: 23,942 lb (10,860 kg) for single-seaters, 24,163 lb (10,960 kg) for two-seaters

Performance:
Maximum, and maximum sustained speed: over Mach 2.2
Maximum speed at sea level: Mach 1.2
Minimum stable speed: 100 kts (115 mph) 186 km/h
Approach speed: 140 kts (161 mph) 260 km/h
Maximum climb rate: 58,000-60,000 ft (17,680-18,300 m) per minute
Climb to 49,000 ft (14,935 m)/Mach 2: 4 minutes
Roll rate: 270° per second
G limits: +9, -4.5
Operational Ceiling: 59,000-60,000 ft (18,000-18,300 m)
Operational loiter time: 150 minutes for Mirage 2000-5 at Mach 0.8/25,000 ft (7,620 m) with 3 drop tanks and 6 AAMs
Operational range for 5 minutes combat (Mirage 2000-5): 780 naut miles (898 miles) 1,445 km at Mach 0.8/30,000 ft (9,145 m), 6 AAMs, drop tanks released
Range (Mirage 2000 E): Over 850 naut miles (979 miles) 1,574 km with drop tanks on an air-to-ground mission, ISA
Maximum range: over 1,900 naut miles (2,188 miles) 3,520 km, with drop tanks

French Air Force ordered some 75 aircraft.
Mirage 2000-5 is the latest advanced multi-role combat version, featuring enhanced capabilities. Derived from the 2000 DA (B and C versions), primarily for air superiority/defence but with extensive multi-role capabilities consistent with those developed for the E. Thomson-CSF RDY Doppler radar with automatic selection of waveform, allowing all-altitude and all-weather lookdown/shootdown multi-target detection and tracking (up to 24 targets and track-while-scan 8), capable of interfacing with an IFF. "Glass cockpit" with 5 displays and an improved fully integrated countermeasures system. New Matra Mica active interception-combat missiles in an air-to-air role (4 Micas, 2 Magic 2s and up to 3 drop tanks for an additional 5,300 litres of fuel). Two-seat version also available. Deliveries from 1996.

Dassault F1 CTs of the French Air Force (SIRPA "AIR")

Dassault Mirage F1

First flight: 23 December 1966.
Role: Interceptor, fighter and attack.

★ Aims

★ Designed to supersede the Mirage III.
★ Dassault-funded scaled-down, single-seat and single-engined version of the two-seat Mirage F2 prototype, the officially contracted replacement fighter ordered for development by the French Government.
★ New wing design incorporating high-lift devices, to reduce take-off landing distances.

▲ Development

▲ 7 January 1967. Mach 2+ achieved by the F1 prototype on its fourth test flight.
▲ 20 March 1969. Maiden flight of the first of 3 pre-production F1s, fitted with a 14,771 lbf (65.71 kN) Atar 09K-31 turbojet. Engine replaced with an Atar 09K50 the same year.
▲ 18 September 1969. Maiden flight of the second pre-production F1, featuring a revision to the dogtooth wing leading edge.
▲ 15 February 1973. Maiden flight of a full production F1 C.
▲ 14 March 1973. French Air Force received its first F1 C.
▲ 26 May 1976. Maiden flight of a two-seat F1 B operational trainer.
▲ February 1992. First upgraded F1 CT redelivered to the French Air Force's 1/13 Normandie-Niemen.
Sales/users: Out of production, after 731 aircraft. Users are Ecuador (B and E), France (B, C, C-200, CR-200 and CT – see Aircraft variants), Greece (C), Iraq (B and E), Jordan (B, C and E), Kuwait (B and C – to be sold), Libya (A, B, and E), Morocco (B, C and E – being refurbished by Dassault), Qatar (see comments that follow), South Africa (A and C – see later comments) and Spain (B, C, D and E – being upgraded – includes recently purchased ex-French and ex-Qatar aircraft). Qatar has sold 11 Mirage F1 Es and 2 F1 Bs to Spain, the first arriving on 23 August 1994 for 111 Escuadrón; the final 5 from this purchase will be delivered in 1997, after Qatar has received its Mirage 2000s. Spain has also acquired 4 ex-French F1 Cs and an F1 B. South Africa retains its As in service for ground attack; its 13 Cs were withdrawn as interceptors but 2 were flying again in 1994 fitted with Russian Klimov SMR 95 (RD-33) engines, which may later power the remainder. The Philippines has been offered surplus French F1s, against the same requirements that has encouraged IAI to offer Kfir 2000s.
Details: Principally for the F1 CT.
Crew: Pilot.
Crew escape: Martin Baker F10M ejection seat in the F1 CT and more recent examples of the other versions. F1 C-200 has the Martin Baker F1RM4 of earlier-built examples.
Fixed guns: 1 x 30-mm DEFA 553 cannon. 2 cannon in other versions.
Ammunition: 135 rounds.
Number of weapon pylons: 7, comprising 1 under the fuselage (maximum load 4,630 lb, 2,100 kg), 4 under the wings (2,865 lb, 1,300 kg inboard and 1,212 lb, 550 kg outboard), and 2 air-to-air missile wingtip launchers.
Expendable weapons and equipment: 13,890 lb (6,300 kg) maximum stores load. Hundreds of possible combinations for weapons and other stores, including 14 x 250 kg bombs, CEM 1 multi-store carriers for 18 rockets plus BAP 100 or Durandel anti-runway/conventional/training bombs or anti-vehicle grenade launcher, CC 420/630 gun pods with twin 30-mm DEFA 553 or 554 guns, air-to-surface missiles, and more.
Additional stores: Reconnaissance pods, electronic warfare pods, FLIR, and drop tanks. Include the COR 2 optical reconnaissance pod for cameras and an IR scanner, for day or night use, and a Raphael SLAR pod (side-looking airborne radar).
Radar: Cyrano IV fire control radar updated to IVMR form.
Flight/weapon system avionics/instrumentation: Sagem Uliss 47 INS, Dassault Electronique 182 digital nav/attack computer, improved HUD, Tacan, IFF, Thomson-CSF laser rangefinder and more.
Self-protection systems: Radar warning receiver, and optional jammer pods and chaff/flare dispensers; Matra Corail decoy system, with 252 electromagnetic cartridges or 112 infra-red or optronic cartridges.
Wing characteristics: Swept, shoulder mounted, with dogtooth leading edge. Anhedral from roots.
Wing control surfaces: Ailerons, 2-section differentially-controlled double-slotted flaps, spoilers, and drooping leading edges.
Tail control surfaces: Slab tailplane and rudder.
Airbrakes: 1 under each air intake.
Flight control system: Hydraulically actuated, with manual or electric command.
Construction materials: Mostly metal, with minor use of some carbonfibre skins.
Engine: SNECMA Atar 09K50 turbojet.
Engine rating: 11,060 lbf (49.2 kN) dry, 15,846 lbf (70.49 kN) with afterburning.
Air intakes: Fuselage side, with centrebody.
Flight refuelling probe: Removable.
Fuel system: 4,300 litres. Optional 2,200 litre underfuselage drop tank and 1,200 litre underwing drop tanks.
Electrical system: DC supply using transformer/rectifiers and a ni-cd battery.
Hydraulic system: 3,000 psi (dual).
Braking system: With anti-skid system.

Aircraft variants:
F1 A was conceived as a day fighter and ground attack aircraft, of reduced specification. Included licensed production by Atlas in South Africa.
F1 B is a two-seat operational trainer, based on the F1 C.
F1 C was produced as an all-weather interceptor, with attack capability. Cyrano IV radar, but with Cyrano IVM in some exports. 2 cannon. French Air Force Cs with flight refuelling probes (increasing length from 50 ft to 50 ft 2.5 ins, 15.23 to 15.3 m, because of a fuselage insert) became F1 C-200s. Refuelling probes were also fitted to some exported F1s. Standard air-to-air missiles are 2 x Super 530s and 2 Magics/Sidewinders.
F1 CR-200 is the French Air Force's reconnaissance equivalent of the F1-C-200 but with Cyrano IVMR radar. Carries Matra Corail decoy system (see Avionics).
F1 CT is the new designation of about 55 French Air Force F1 C-200 interceptors modified to basically F1 E standard for ground attack. Most work was carried out by Atelier Industriel de l'Air, following a Dassault-produced pattern conversion of 1991.
F1 D is the two-seat training variant of the F1 E.

DETAILS FOR F1 CT.

Principal dimensions:
Wing span: 27 ft 7 ins (8.4 m) without wingtip missiles
Maximum length: 50 ft 2.5 ins (15.3 m)
Maximum height: 14 ft 9 ins (4.5 m)

Wings:
Area: 269.1 sq ft (25 m^2)

Undercarriage:
Type: Retractable, with twin nosewheels

Weights:
Empty: above 16,300 lb (7,400 kg)
Maximum take-off: 35,700 lb (16,200 kg)

Performance:
Maximum speed: Mach 2.2
Maximum speed at low level: 799 kts (920 mph) 1,480 km/h
Take-off distance: 1,969 ft (600 m)
Landing distance: 2,198 ft (670 m)
Maximum climb rate: 42,000 ft (12,780 m) per minute at sea level
Ceiling: 65,615 ft (20,000 m)
Radius of action with full internal fuel: 229 naut miles (264 miles) 425 km, with 7,716 lb (3,500 kg) bombload, flying at high altitude to and from the target

F1 E was produced as a multi-role export fighter, equally suited to interceptor, attack and reconnaissance duties. Features the radar, INS, nav/attack computer and HUD as detailed for the F1 CT.

Dassault Rafale

First flight: 4 July 1986.
Role: Air superiority, air defence, air-to-ground, air-to-surface (anti-ship), reconnaissance, and strike/nuclear strike.

★ Aims:

★ To equip the French Air Force and Navy with a similar combat aircraft capable of performing a wide range of missions with all present and near future armaments, in all weathers and by day or night. To supersede Jaguars with the Air Force and Crusaders and Super Etendards with the Navy.
★ 25-30 year life cycle.
★ Rapid reconfiguration for changes of role.
★ Survivability through EW systems, terrain masking by very low altitude flying, stealth through the airframe shaping, choice of materials, and design of aerials and external load carriage.
★ Inter-operability with NATO air forces.
★ Achieve total integration of all conventional aircraft systems: fuel, hydraulics, electrics, air conditioning and communication.

▲ Development

▲ December 1983. Decision made to construct a technology demonstrator (ACX/Rafale A), with manufacture beginning in April 1984 and the first flight on 4 July 1986.
▲ December 1986. Start of the M88-2 engine development programme.
▲ 21 April 1988. Order for Rafale C01, an Air Force prototype. First flown on 19 May 1991.
▲ 6 December 1988. Order for the first Rafale M (01), a Navy prototype. The Rafale M02 was ordered on 4 July 1990. M 01 first flown on 11 December 1991, M 02 on 8 November 1993.
▲ 19 July 1989. Order for Rafale B 01, an Air Force two-seat prototype. First flown 30 April 1993.
▲ 27 February 1990. First flight of Rafale with an M88-2 engine in place of 1 previous F404.
▲ 15 June 1992. First operational evaluation by the CEV, DGA, Air Force and Navy, at Istres, lasting until 26 June.
▲ 8 July 1992. Start of Rafale M's USC1 verification programme, lasting until 23 August . Rafale M 01 at Lakehurst (New Jersey, USA) and then Patuxent River (Maryland, USA), undertaking 39 catapults, 69 rolling strand engagements, 14 simulated deck landings on a runway, and 6 deck landings.
▲ 30 October 1992. 1,000th Rafale flight (Rafale A 708, C 01 195, and M 01 97).
▲ 23 December 1992. Industrialization of the Rafale programme was notified to Dassault, leading to future production.
▲ 31 December 1992. Order for the first production M88 engines.
▲ 15 January 1993. Start of the USC2 programme to extend Rafale M's "clean" flight envelope, lasting until 18 February. Included 42 catapults, 19 simulated deck landings on a runway, 24 rolling strand engagements, and 45 deck landings.
▲ 5 March 1993. First Rafale gun firing by C 01 at Cazaux, followed by Magic 2 firing on 26 March.
▲ 26 March 1993. First 2 production aircraft ordered, as B 1 and M 1.
▲ 19 April 1993. Start of the PA1 programme covering aircraft carrier compatibility using Rafale M 01 on *Foch*, lasting until 7 May. Included 31 deck landings and 31 catapults.
▲ 8 November 1993. Start of the USC3 programme with Rafale M 01 at Lakehurst, lasting until 15 December, to open the flight envelope with external loads (5 configurations). Included 59 catapults, 49 rolling strand engagements and 40 deck landings.
▲ 27 January 1994. Start of the PA2 programme with Rafale M 01 and 02, to open the flight envelope, test carrier compatibility with attachments, and VAMOM (inspections of fitness for operation and maintenance). Lasted until 7 February, and then repeated 11 April-3 May. Included 62 deck landings and catapults.

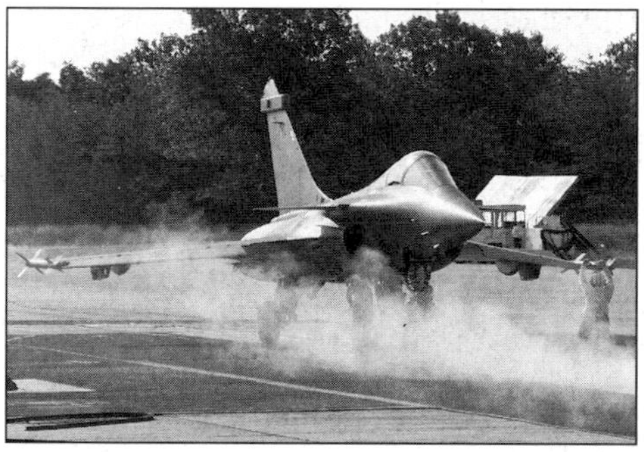

Dassault Rafale M 01 during carrier compatibility trials in the USA

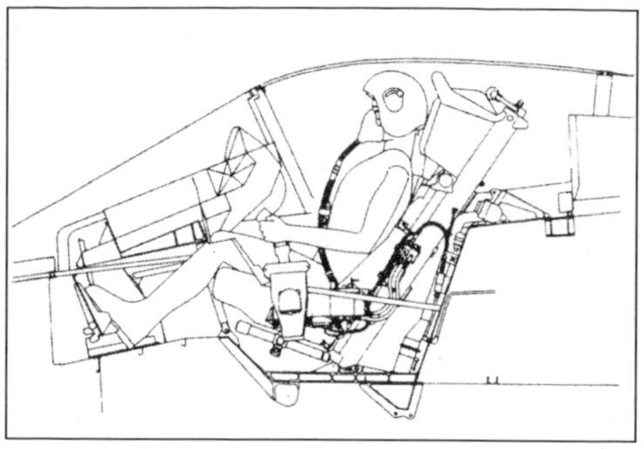

Dassault Rafale seating layout, with the pilot tilted 29° to resist g loads (courtesy Dassault)

▲ 17 February 1994. Orders placed for production Rafale M 2, M 3 and B 2.
▲ 5 September 1994. Rafale's 2,000th flight, at Farnborough Air Show.
▲ 1997. IOC of the naval Rafale M.
Sales/users: French Air Force (94 single-seat and 140 two-seat) and Navy (86). Air Force expected to order 16 per year from 1998, though recent recommendations have suggested the need for 20. Offered for export, with possible initial contracts agreed in 1995 for 1999 delivery.
Crew: Pilot, or 2 crew (pilot and weapon system operator, or pilot and trainee) in Rafale B.
Cockpit: Seat tilted 29° to assist the pilot in resisting g loads (by limiting the vertical distance between the heart and the brain). Wide-field holographic collimated head-up display. Images from the sensors and the weapons system status are shown on 2 lateral colour touch-screens. Principal screen is a mid-head colour display, collimated to avoid too-frequent adjustment, showing elements of the tactical situation. Helmet-mounted display (see Avionics). Controls situated on the single engine-control lever or on the side stick controller, in accordance with HOTAS. Canopy is gold coated to reduce signature.
Crew escape: SEMMB/Martin Baker Mk 16 ejection seat.
Fixed guns: 1 x 30-mm DEFA 791B cannon, with a rate of fire of 2,500 rounds per minute.
Number of weapon pylons: 14 on Rafale B and C, 13 on M, 5 of which are heavy (over 1,000 kg) and wet for drop tanks (underfuselage centre line, and inner/centre underwing pylons).
Expendable weapons and equipment: Up to 17,637 lb (8,000 kg). Typically 8 Mica air-to-air missiles, or 2 x AS 30L laser-guided missiles and 2 x 1,000 kg laser-guided bombs plus 4 Micas, or 2 Apache submunition missiles and 2 Micas, or 16 x 225 kg bombs and 2 Micas, or 2 anti-ship missiles and 4 Micas, or ASMP, among other options (ASMP will not be available initially on the first Rafales for each force), all in combination with drop tanks and/or mission pods.
Additional stores: Photographic or electromagnetic reconnaissance pod, FLIR pod, targeting/navigation pods, etc.
Radar: GIE Radar RDE2, the first European radar to have an antenna with electronic scanning in 2 planes and a very high computing power.
Flight/weapon system avionics/instrumentation: 2 mission computers managing the high-output digital lines. Sextant Avionics voice-activated controls (not on the first production aircraft – see Weapons). 2 Sagem Uliss 52X (Sigma FL90 ring-laser gyro) INS, and GPS coupled to the lasergyro platforms. GIE IFF. "Glass cockpit" (see Cockpit). Images of the external scene from an infra-red camera can be superimposed on the HUD. Forward-looking optronic sensor (OSF – not to be fitted initially to the first production aircraft) allows passive visible and infra-red detection at long range, multi-target angular tracking, and ranging on air, sea and ground targets (complements the capabilities of the radar in

Dassault Rafale C 01 (foreground) and B 01 two-seater, both with their flight refuelling probes removed

clear weather or in conditions of very severe electromagnetic jamming, and on penetration missions in clear weather it increases the stealth of the navigation and weapons system by allowing the use of the RBE2 to limited checks). Compatible with the Sextant Avionics OPSIS helmet-mounted sight.
Self-protection systems: Spectra (protection and fire control avoidance) is an internal system that is integrated with the navigation and weapons system, to enhance survivability against air-to-air and surface-to-air threats. It monitors the whole range of electromagnetic threats and reports missile launches (by the use of missile departure detectors – DDMs) or laser illuminations (by laser warning detectors – DAL). Following detection and identification, electromagnetic jamming, chaffing or evasive manoeuvres can be effected. This system is unlikely to be fitted to the first production aircraft (see Weapons).
Wing characteristics: Mid-mounted clipped delta, with extended leading-edges near the roots.
Wing control surfaces: Each wing has 2 elevons and 2-section leading-edge slats.
Tail control surfaces: Rudder.
Canard: Active, of swept delta planform, located to optimize aerodynamic efficiency and stability control without impeding the pilot's view. Automatic 20° incidence setting when the undercarriage is lowered.
Airbrakes: 2, on the fuselage each side of the fin.
Flight control system: Fly-by-wire. 3 digital channels and 1 analog channel, connected to the complete navigation and weapons system. Linked to the control of the engines, the system allows actuation of all control surfaces throughout the flight envelope, from zero speed to Mach 1.8 and -3 to +9g. System allows attitude control in all 3 axes, automatic limitation control, flight control at high angles of attack, co-ordinated turns, speed vector control, and approach with thrust/drag ratio monitoring. It can also be applied to other functions, including low altitude, high speed gust-load alleviation. Control surface deflection results from comparison between the pilot input and the actual motion of the aircraft as detected by the various sensors (accelerometers, rate gyros, probes, etc). Flight controls check between missions is automatic.
Construction materials: Much use of carbonfibre, even for large components such as the rear fuselage, wing panels, elevons, fin, rudder (with aluminium honeycomb core), etc. Kevlar for wing root/fuselage fairings and wingtips. Superplastic formed/diffusion bonded canards. Metals include titanium for the slats.
Engines: 2 SNECMA M88-2 turbofans in the prototypes. Production Rafales will use M88-3s of 19,560 lbf (87 kN) augmented thrust.
Engine rating: Each 11,250 lbf (50.04 kN) dry, 16,850 lbf (74.95 kN) with afterburning. During Rafale's first flight, Mach 1 was attained in "super-cruise" (without engine afterburning).
Air intakes: Semi ventral, with no moving parts or bleeds, for optimum performance trade-off at all speeds. Specially designed for stealth qualities.
Flight refuelling probe: Probe on starboard side of nose.
Fuel system: Over 5,325 litres internally. Refuelling between missions takes 4 to 7 minutes, depending on the configuration. Optional auxiliary fuel comprises a 1,700 litre underfuselage drop tank, 2 x 2,000 litre and/or 2 x 1,300 litre underwing tanks, all combinations to a maximum of 6,600 litres (see Number of pylons). Removable (non-retractable) flight refuelling probe.
Electrical system: Auxilec system, with 2 x 30/40kVA alternators.
Hydraulic system: Aviac dual system. 4,000 psi.
Braking system: High power carbon brakes on all wheels. Drag-chute available.
Oxygen system: Autonomous oxygen generation (OBOGS). Air Liquide generating equipment and Eros system equipment.

Aircraft variants:
Rafale B is the two-seat dual-control operational trainer and operational combat aircraft.
Rafale C is the French Air Force single-seater.
Rafale M is the French Navy's single-seater for aircraft carrier operations. Only some 1,322 lb (600 kg) heavier than the Rafale C, with the fuselage structure reinforced for carrier operations and the undercarriage modified, plus an arrester hook. Other changes include an electrically-folding ladder, a unit to align gyro platforms with those of the ship, and deck landing aids.

DETAILS FOR RAFALE.

Principal dimensions:
Wing span: 35 ft 9 ins (10.9 m)
Maximum length: 50 ft 2.5 ins (15.3 m)
Maximum height: 17 ft 6 ins (5.34 m) for Rafale D

Wings:
Area: 495.14 sq ft (46 m^2)
Aspect ratio: 2.5
Anhedral: From roots

Undercarriage:
Type: Retractable, with twin steerable nosewheels. Naval Rafale M have been designed to withstand hard landings on deck of 6 m per second vertical drop. Rafale M nosewheel leg has energy restitution to optimize take-off at the end of the deck, to create a "jump"
Main wheel tyre size: 810 x 275 mm
Nose wheel tyre size: 550 x 200 mm

Weights:
Empty, operating: 19,974 lb (9,060 kg) for Rafale D, 21,320 lb (9,670 kg) for M
Maximum ramp weight: 42,990 lb (19,500 kg). Growth potential to 47,400 lb (21,500 kg)

Performance:
Maximum speed: Mach 1.8-Mach 2
Maximum low-altitude speed: 750 kts (864 mph) 1,390 km/h
Approach speed: 115 kts (132 mph) 213 km/h
Take-off/landing distance: under 1,312 ft (400 m) with AAMs
G limits: +9, -3.6
Maximum angle of attack: 32°
Radius of action: 1,000 naut miles (1,150 miles) 1,850 km with maximum internal/external fuel and 8 Mica missiles

Dassault Super Etendard

First flight: 28 October 1974.
Role: Carrier-borne strike-fighter for fleet protection against surface-ship attack, attack of sea and land targets, air cover, and photographic reconnaissance.

★ Aims
★ To replace the Etendard IV (in use from 1962 – see Aircraft variants), as an upgraded development. 2 Super Etendard prototypes were produced by conversion of existing Etendard IV-Ms, 1 for engine and weapon development (including Exocet compatibility) and the second for navigation, ship-borne and other trials.

▲ Development
▲ 25 March 1975. Second Super Etendard prototype made its maiden flight.
▲ 24 November 1977. First flight of a newly-manufactured production Super Etendard.
▲ 28 June 1978. Receipt of the first Super Etendards by the French Navy.
▲ 1979. 14 ordered for the Argentine Navy, for eventual aircraft carrier operations from *25 de Mayo* and shore basing.
▲ November 1981. First Argentine Super Etendards delivered.
▲ April 1982. The 5 Argentine Super Etendards delivered were moved with the 2nd Naval Fighter Attack Escuadrilla to Rio Grande on Tierra del Fuego, for the defence of the Malvinas/Falkland Islands. 1 was used for spares.
▲ 4 May 1982. An Argentine Super Etendard attacked HMS *Sheffield* with an Exocet, causing a fire which eventually destroyed the ship. Other actions followed.
▲ 1983. Production of the Super Etendard ended after 85 aircraft. The proposed land-based version has not progressed to production.
▲ 5 October 1990. First flight of an upgraded French Navy Super Etendard, with new radar, computer, INS and more.
Sales/users: Argentina (12 in service) and France (71 built, of which 70 were delivered; 54 are earmarked for upgrade to extend service to 2007-2010, of which about 5 had been redelivered by early 1995; 7 are carrier-borne at any time).
Crew: Pilot.
Cockpit: Armoured for protection during low-level missions. Upgraded cockpit on upgraded French aircraft (see Avionics).
Crew escape: Martin Baker CM4-A ejection seat.
Fixed guns: 2 DEFA 30-mm cannon rack-mounted under the fuselage.

Dassault Super Etendards with wings folded (left rear) and wings spread (right), plus 2 Etendard IV-Ps (foreground) (courtesy Dassault)

Ammunition: Each 125 rounds.
Number of weapon pylons: 5 originally, 6 on upgraded aircraft (including 4 under the wings).
Expendable weapons and equipment: Up to 4,630 lb (2,100 kg). Exocet, AS 30L or ASMP nuclear stand-off missile (latter 2 French Navy only), bombs (typically 4 x 250 kg or 400 kg), 4 pods for 18 x 68-mm rockets, 2 Matra Magic air-to-air missiles, and/or drop tanks. Typically 1 Exocet and a drop tank under the wings.
Additional stores: Reconnaissance pod under the fuselage.
Radar: Thomson-CSF Agave or retrofitted Dassault Electronique Anémone I/J-band multi-function.
Flight/weapon system avionics/instrumentation: Includes UAT 90 air data computer (Type 66 on pre-upgraded aircraft), wide-angle head-up display, head-down EW display, radar altimeter and Sagem inertial navigation system offering high-precision navigation and bombing. IFF. HOTAS on French upgraded Super Etendards.
Self-protection systems: Thomson-CSF Sherloc RWR. Optional jamming pod or chaff/flare pod.
Wing characteristics: Swept, mid mounted, with anhedral. Foldable outer panels for stowage on board ship.
Wing control surfaces: Ailerons with irreversible power operated actuators, double-slotted trailing-edge flaps, spoilers, and drooping leading-edges with dogtooth.
Tail control surfaces: Slab tailplane (with trim) and rudder.
Airbrakes: 2, under the fuselage.
Flight control system: Hydraulic.
Fuselage: Area rule design.
Construction materials: Metal.
Engine: SNECMA Atar 08K50 turbojet.
Engine rating: 11,023 lbf (49 kN).
Air intakes: Each side of the fuselage, level with the canopy.
Flight refuelling probe: Retractable, on the nose.
Fuel system: 3,200 litres in wing and fuselage tanks. 1 or 2 underwing 625 litre or 1,100 litre drop tanks (see Weapons), and a 600 litre tank under the fuselage or a detachable "buddy" flight refuelling system).
Braking system: Disc brakes. Drag-chute in the tail for shore operations. Arrester hook.

Aircraft variants:
Etendard IV-P and MP remain available to the French Navy (21 in total, 10 of which have been modernized for service to the end of the century, with 7 active) for unarmed reconnaissance and tanker roles. Developed from the armed Etendard IV-M, first flown in 1958.
Super Etendard is the principal service model, as detailed.

DETAILS FOR SUPER ETENDARD.

Principal dimensions:
Wing span: 31 ft 6 ins (9.6 m)
Maximum length: 46 ft 11 ins (14.31 m)
Maximum height: 12 ft 8 ins (3.86 m)

Wings:
Area: 305.69 sq ft (28.4 m^2)
Aspect ratio: 3.245
Sweepback: 45° at 25% chord
Anhedral: 3° 30′

Undercarriage:
Type: Retractable, with nosewheel
Main wheel tyre size: 760 x 195 mm
Nose wheel tyre size: 490 x 155 mm
Wheel base: 15 ft 9 ins (4.8 m)
Wheel track: 11 ft 6 ins (3.5 m)

Weights:
Empty: 14,330 lb (6,500 kg)
Maximum take-off: 26,455 lb (12,000 kg)

Performance:
Maximum speed: Transonic (about Mach 1)
Maximum speed at low level: 648 kts (746 mph) 1,200 km/h
Ship approach speed: 135 kts (155 mph) 250 km/h, at 17,195 lb (7,800 kg) weight
Ceiling: 44,950 ft (13,700 m)
Radius of action: 475 naut miles (547 miles) 880 km with drop tanks and an Exocet

Socata (France)

Full name: Société de Construction d'Avions de Tourisme et d'Affaires.
Corporate address: Le Terminal, Bâtiment 413, Zône d'Aviation d'Affaires, F-93350 Aéroport du Bourget.
Telephone: +33 1 49 34 69 70
Facsimile: +33 1 49 34 69 71
Telex: 520 828 F
Founded: 1966.
Employees: Approximately 1,000 technicians at Tarbes.
Information: Caroline Vallette (Promotion and Communication).
International sales: 12 rue Pasteur, BP 76, F-92152 Suresnes Cedex.

■ Facilities
■ Production unit: Aéroport de Rarbes-Ossun-Lourdes, BP 930, 65009 Tarbes Cedex (*telephone* +33 62 41 76 00, *Facsimile* +33 62 41 76 54). Customer operations and product support also at Tarbes.

● Activities
● Socata is Aerospatiale's general aviation subsidiary, producing a range of light aircraft (see General Aviation section). The Epsilon trainer is also detailed in that section.
● Pre-project activities include CAD designing, computing, static endurance testing, in-flight testing and more, networked to Aerospatiale's computing centre and computerized design and engineering departments.
● Sub-contract work includes parts for Eurocopter Dauphin, Ecureuil and Super Puma helicopters plus for Airbus and ATR airliners, Dassault Falcon and Lockheed Martin Hercules, and the CFM 56 engine.

Socata Omega

First flight: 30 April 1989 (with original TP 319 Arrius engine).
Role: Primary and basic military trainer, also for full aerobatics, formation flying, and patrol and surveillance.

★ Aims
★ Turboprop development of the Epsilon.
★ Expanded manoeuvre envelope.
Crew: 2, in tandem, the rear seat raised.
Cockpit: Dual controls. HOTAS concept.
Crew escape: Optional Martin Baker Mk 15PC ejection seats, and detonating microcord canopy jettisoning.
Number of weapon pylons: 4 optionally.
Expendable weapons and equipment: Optional light weapons for training and armed patrol.
Flight/weapon system avionics/ instrumentation: IFR. VOR/ILS/MKR VIR 32, ADF 60 A, TDR 90 transponder, Collins ETC 500F, EDU 500F cathode tube display, TNC 500 Tacan, IFF, and UHF Magnavox ARC 164 and VHF ARC 186 radio communications.
Wing characteristics: Straight, low mounted, with dihedral from roots and upturned wingtips.
Wing control surfaces: Ailerons (with tabs) and single-slotted flaps.
Tail control surfaces: Elevators (with tabs) and rudder.
Flight control system: Mechanical, but with electrically actuated tabs and flaps.
Construction materials: Metal, except for polyester-skinned elevators and rudder.
Engine: Turbomeca Arrius 1D or 2D turboprop, with a 6 ft 8 ins (2.03 m) Hartzell 3-blade constant-speed propeller.
Engine rating: 488 shp (364 kW) or flat rated at 360 shp (268 kW), or 600 shp (447 kW) with same flat rating, respectively. Engine has FADEC.
Fuel system: 276 litres in 2 structural tanks in the wing leading edges, of which 210 litres are usable. Collector cells in each tank for 9 minutes of inverted flight.
Electrical system: 24 volt/17 amp-hour ni-cd battery, 4.8kW/28 volt starter-generator, emergency alternator, electrical power centre, and with distribution through bus bars.

Socata Omega two-seat turboprop trainer with an Arrius 1D engine fitted

DETAILS FOR OMEGA.

Principal dimensions:
Wing span: 26 ft (7.92 m)
Maximum length: 26 ft 4 ins (8.026 m)
Maximum height: 8 ft 8 ins (2.64 m)

Wings:
Area: 96.88 sq ft (9 m^2)
Aspect ratio: 6.97

Undercarriage:
Type: Retractable, with nosewheel, electrohydraulically actuated
Wheel base: 5 ft 11 ins (1.8 m)
Wheel track: 7 ft 6.5 ins (2.3 m)

Weights:
Empty, operating: 2,381 lb (1,080 kg), with ejection seats fitted
Maximum take-off and landing: 3,307 lb (1,500 kg) aerobatic, 3,637 lb (1,650 kg) with full weapon options

Performance:
Maximum operating speed: 280 kts (322 mph) 518 km/h
Maximum cruise speed: 262 kts (302 mph) 485 km/h at 20,000 ft (6,100 m), ISA
Maximum flap or undercarriage extended speed: 130 kts (150 mph) 240 km/h
Stall speed: 68 kts (79 mph) 126 km/h with flaps
Take-off distance over a 50 ft (15 m) obstacle: 1,657 ft (505 m)
Landing distance over a 50 ft (15 m) obstacle: 1,394 ft (425 m)
Maximum climb rate: 2,200 ft (670 m) per minute
Time to 20,000 ft (6,100 m): 11 minutes
G limits: +7, -3.5
Ceiling: 30,000 ft (9,145 m)
Range with full fuel: 706 naut miles (813 miles) 1,308 km, cruise at 20,000 ft (6,100 m), with reserve

Daimler-Benz Aerospace AG (Germany)

Corporate address: Postfach 801109, D-81663 Munich.
Telephone: +49 89 6 07-0
Facsimile: +49 89 6 07 26481
Founded: Renamed Daimler-Benz Aerospace on 1 January 1995, from the former Deutsche Aerospace AG corporate unit of the Daimler-Benz Group that had been founded in 1989. Oldest operating unit of the Aircraft section of Daimler-Benz is Dornier Luftfahrt GmbH of the Regional Aircraft Division, which dates from 1922.
Employees: Over 60,000.
Information: Detmar Grosse-Leege (Senior Vice President, Corporate Communications – *telephone* +49 89 6 07-3 42 50); Christian Poppe (Vice President, Corporate Press Department – *telephone* +49 89 6 07-3 42 35); Heinz Skrzipietz (Vice President, Corporate Public Relations – *telephone* +49 89 6 07-3 42 83); and Eckehart Rotter (Vice President, Aircraft Public Affairs – *telephone* +49 89 6 07-3 44 15).

● Activities

● In addition to the divisions detailed below, on 9 November 1994 DASA signed an agreement with Hellenic Aerospace Industry of Greece covering future co-operation over civil and military programmes, defence technology and satellite communication, while another agreement with the DLR German aerospace research establishment covers co-operation in R&D. About 75% of Daimler-Benz Aerospace's turnover is in international industrial structures (EurasSpace, Eurocopter, Fokker).
● Debis (Daimler-Benz Inter Services), the service division, took the lead in establishing a new leasing company for Fokker aircraft (see Fokker).

AIRCRAFT DIVISIONS

Daimler-Benz Aerospace Airbus GmbH
HQ address: Postfach 950109, Kreetslag 10, D-21111 Hamburg.
Telephone: +49 40 74 37-30 16 (press office)
Facsimile: +49 40 74 37-25 22 (press office)

● Activities

● Undertakes the German interest in the multi-national Airbus airliner programmes, and is responsible for an important share in Fokker 100 manufacturing. Other interests include the FLA, Super Transporter, and working with Tupolev of Russia on the Cryoplane powered by liquid hydrogen.

Regional Aircraft (administered by Dornier Luftfahrt GmbH)
HQ address: Postfach 3, D-82230 Wessling.
Telephone: +49 81 53 30 0 (+49 89 6 07-3 44 15 for press office)
Facsimile: +49 8153 30 2055 (+49 89 6 07-2 56 65 for press office)
Telex: 526 450 doas d

● Activities

● Dornier 228 and 328 transports, including border patrol and other specialized variants (see Airliners section).
● Supports NATO aircraft, particularly the E-3 fleet, shares manufacture of the Dassault Atlantique 2 and supports German Navy Atlantics, and is undertaking a life extension programme on the German Army's UH-1D Iroquois helicopters.

Military Aircraft
HQ address: PO Box 801160, D-81663 Munich 80.
Telephone: +49 89 6 07-2 57 11 (press office)
Facsimile: +49 89 6 07-2 24 55 (press office)

● Activities

● Undertakes work on the Eurofighter 2000 and Panavia Tornado, modernizes German Air Force F-4F Phantoms under the ICE programme, contributes to both the Rockwell Ranger 2000 and NASA X-31A, manufactures Airbus airliner components, and produces reconnaissance, training/simulation and other systems.

Fokker Holding
HQ address: See Fokker.
Telephone: +31 20 6 05 78 60
Facsimile: +31 20 6 05 75 99

● Activities

● Daimler-Benz Aerospace has a 78% share-holding in Fokker Holding, which in turn has 51% of Fokker's share capital.

Helicopters – Eurocopter D
HQ address: Postfach 9801140, Munich 80.
Telephone: +49 89 60 00-64 88
Facsimile: +49 89 60 00-44 37

● Activities

● As the Eurocopter Deutschland component of Eurocopter SA, it was tasked to undertake development and production of helicopters of German origin.

SPACE DIVISIONS

Space Transportation and Propulsion Systems

Orbital Infrastructure

Satellites and Application Systems

DEFENSE AND CIVIL SYSTEMS DIVISIONS

Dynamic Systems

Radar and Radio Systems

Command and Information Systems

Energy and Systems Technology

PROPULSION SYSTEMS DIVISIONS

Aircraft Applications

Land/Marine Applications

Daimler-Benz F-4 ICE upgrade

First flight: 2 May 1990.

▲ Development

▲ Prior to the ICE programme, DASA performed structural life extension programmes from 1980 on German Air Force RF-4Es and F-4Fs.
▲ To improve the self-defence capability of the F-4Fs, the German Federal Ministry of Defence awarded DASA a contract in 1985 for the upgrade of the AN/ALQ 101 and ALQ 119 systems. The work was completed with demonstration of the performance improvements against modern threat radars. Series production for the Air Force started in 1994.
▲ Since the configuration of the F-4F in an air-to-air role was considered inadequate to counter the anticipated threats until Eurofighter 2000 appeared in service, a

F-4F ICE with missiles including 4 AMRAAMs

tactical requirement to improve the capabilities was established. The main aims were to improve the fire control system for all-weather operations, allow beyond-visual-range enemy detection, defeat the enemy beyond its firing range, track-while-scan, track multiple targets, have look-down/shoot-down, permit more accurate navigation and air-to-ground attack, to integrate the AIM-120 AMRAAM missile, and improve the navigation subsystem with new IN and ADC sensors for more accurate data for radar signal processing and for better overall reliability.

F-4F ICE conversions 13 and 15

▲ 1986. DASA was awarded a contract by the MoD to upgrade the avionics system on more than 150 F-4Fs. In performing this upgrade, known as the Improved Combat Efficiency (ICE) programme, the company successfully completed the conceptual, definition, development and test phases, and by March 1995 more than 130 modernized aircraft had been redelivered to the German Air Force (having started April 1992), including those fitted-out at the second source Air Force Depot Maintenance Facility. Successful live firings of AMRAAM were conducted between October 1991 and September 1992 at Point Mugu in the USA, and Initial Operational Capability has been declared.

▲ The ICE programme introduced and integrated:
- AIM-120 AMRAAM missiles and launchers.
- Multi-function AN/APG-65GY pulse-Doppler radar.
- New Litef digital fire control computer.
- H-423 ring laser IN set.
- New standard GEC-Marconi CPU-143/A air data computer.
- Modified display system.
- MIL-STD-1553B multiplex data bus.

RFB Rhein-Flugzeugbau GmbH (Germany)

Corporate address: Krefelder Strasse 840, D-11066 Mönchengladbach.
Telephone: +49 21 61 682-0 (682-175 – sales department).
Facsimile: +49 21 61 68 22 44 or 682-273
Founded: 1957.
Employees: 133.
Information: Hartmut Stiegler (President and owner).

● Activities

- Aircraft maintenance and repair, airline support, and maintenance and overhaul of various items of search and rescue equipment.
- RFB has not had an aircraft in production for 3 years (to 1995), but recently produced the tail and canopy for the Rockwell Ranger 2000.
- Has proposed production of the Swedish MFI-10 light plane as the MFI-10C Vipan (see General Aviation section).
- Is offering a new version of the Fantrainer known as the Fantrainer 800, but no prototype had been built up to mid-1995. Is also offering the Williams turbofan-powered Tiro-Trainer, with 75% commonality with the FT-600.
- Manufactures airframe structures and components under contract, specializing in composites materials but also built in metal.
- Operates target-towing and other specialized aircraft under contract from the German Government.
- Has extensive maintenance, overhaul, repair and service facilities for military, commercial and general aviation aircraft, plus engines, avionics and components.

RFB Fantrainer 800 (+ 400 and 600)

First flight: Fantrainer 800 not flown by early 1995.
Role: Primary and basic trainer.

★ Aims

★ Differs from the FT-600 (see Aircraft variants) in having an uprated Allison C-30 engine, to provide constant performance over a wide temperature range up to an altitude of 15,000 ft (4,570 m), resulting in a higher cruise speed and improved climb rate.

Sales/users: No prototype built by early 1995. Available. 47 earlier Fantrainer 400s and 600s are in use with the Royal Thai Air Force, while Lufthansa became a commercial user for instructor training.
Crew: 2.
Cockpit: Tandem cockpits, the rear instructor's seat raised by 3 ins (8 cm) to improve the forward view.
Crew escape: No ejection seats, but use of the UPC zero-zero rocket extraction system.
Fixed guns: None.
Flight/weapon system avionics/instrumentation: IFR equipped.
Wing characteristics: Mid mounted, with straight leading edges and forward-swept trailing edges.
Wing control surfaces: Ailerons (with port tab) and split flaps.
Tail control surfaces: T-tail, with elevators (with tabs) and rudder.
Airbrakes: 2, hydraulically actuated, on the fan duct.
Flight control system: Mechanical.
Fuselage: Pod-type, load-bearing forward section and unusual cruciform rear section, attached at 3 positions. Non-structural fan duct at the point of join, with the shape of the rear fuselage not impeding thrust.
Construction materials: Forward fuselage load-bearing keel and skins, plus wings, of composites (mostly glassfibre). Metal rear fuselage and tail.
Engine: Allison 250-C30 turboshaft mounted in the rear of the forward fuselage section, with a Hoffmann 5-blade ducted fan.
Engine rating: 650 shp (484.7 kW).
Air intakes: Just aft of the rear cockpit canopy.
Flight refuelling probe: None.
Fuel system: 480 litres in 4 wing tanks. Provision for drop tanks, offering an additional 440 litres. Fuel weights are 388 lb (176 kg) of internal fuel for aerobatics, 847 lb (384 kg) utility; maximum auxiliary fuel weight (utility only) 882 lb (400 kg).
Electrical system: Starter-generator and battery.
Braking system: Fitted.

Aircraft variants:

Fantrainer 800 is the latest version of Fantrainer, for which no actual prototype has yet been built. Based on the Fantrainer 600 but with the forward fuselage adopting composites for its load-bearing structure in addition to the skins. Fantrainer 400 and 600 were ordered into component production in 1982, with those for Thailand mostly being assembled from kits by an offshoot of the Royal Thai Air Force. Only a small number were assembled by RFB. First flight of a prototype built by RFB under German Defence Ministry contract took place on 27 October 1977. The first RFB production Fantrainer (a 600) flew on 12 August 1984. All have metal load-bearing fuselage structures, and the 400s were originally assembled with Thai-produced

RFB Fantrainer in Royal Thai Air Force service (Denis Hughes)

DETAILS FOR FANTRAINER 800.

Principal dimensions:
Wing span: 31 ft 11.5 m (9.74 m)
Maximum length: 31 ft 1 ins (9.48 m)
Maximum height: 10 ft 4.5 ins (3.16 m)

Wings:
Aerofoil section: Eppler 502
Area: 150.69 sq ft (14 m^2)
Aspect ratio: 6.776
Incidence: 0°
Dihedral: 3°

Tail unit:
Tailplane span: 11 ft 10 ins (3.59 m)
Tailplane area: 33.6 sq ft (3.12 m^2)

Undercarriage:
Type: Retractable, with castering nosewheel
Wheel base: 12 ft 9 ins (3.89 m)
Wheel track: 6 ft 4 ins (1.94 m)

Weights:
Empty: 2,600 lb (1,180 kg)
Maximum take-off: 5,092 lb (2,310 kg) utility, or 3,527 lb (1,600 kg) for aerobatic
Maximum landing weight: 4,409 lb (2,000 kg)

Performance (at aerobatic take-off weight):
Maximum speed: 259 kts (298 mph) 480 km/h at 15,000 ft (4,570 m)
Cruise speed: 243 kts (280 mph) 450 km/h at 15,000 ft
Stall speed: 61 kts (70 mph) 113 km/h
Take-off and landing distance: 821 ft (250 m)
Maximum climb rate: 2,950 ft (900 m) per minute at sea level
G limits: +6, -3 aerobatic, +4.4, -1.76 utility
Ceiling: 25,000 ft (7,620 m)
Range with full fuel: 560 naut miles (646 miles) 1,040 km, no drop tank, 10,000 ft (3,050 m), with 45 minutes reserve
Duration: 4 hours 6 minutes, conditions as above

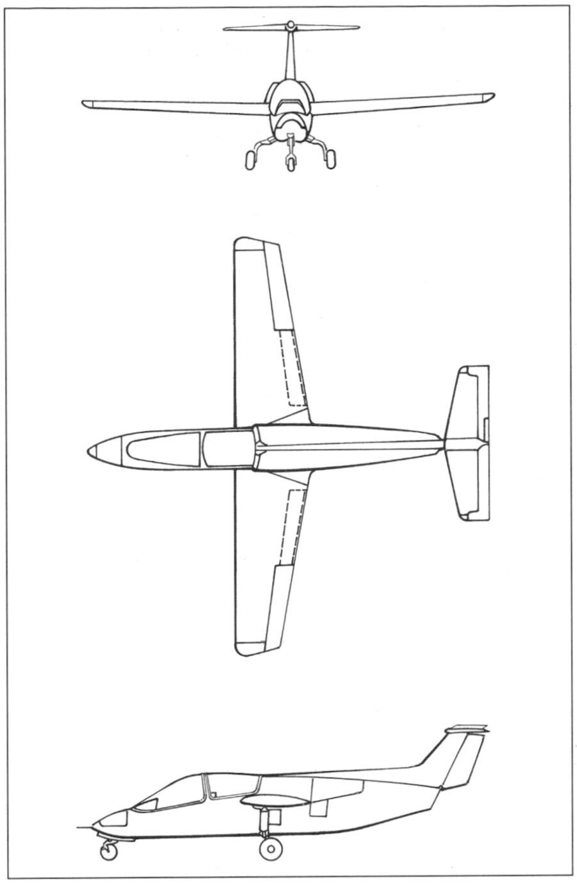

RFB Tiro-Trainer drawing (Bill Hobson)

metal wings. Out of production. Fantrainer 400 engine is a 420 shp (313 kW) Allison 250-C20B, providing a maximum speed of 200 kts (230 mph) 370 km/h at 10,000 ft (3,050 m) at 3,527 lb (1,600 kg) take-off weight. Fantrainer 600 uses a 250-C30, offering 225 kts (259 mph) 417 km/h at 18,000 ft (5,500 m) at 3,527 lb (1,600 kg) weight.

RFB Tiro-Trainer

First flight: Not flown by mid 1995.
Role: Student pilot screening, primary and basic training.

★ Aims

★ 75% commonality of parts with the Fantrainer, from which it is derived. Identical empty, maximum take-off and useful weights as FT-600.
★ Provide jet "habits" from the initial training period, to minimize the problems associated with transition to advanced equipment, and thereby requiring only the Tiro-Trainer and a 2-seat operational jet to cover all aspects of training.
★ Low-cost flight hours for maintaining pilot proficiency.

▲ Development

▲ Began 1994.
Details: Configuration and accommodation are basically similar to the Fantrainer, except that a turbofan engine has replaced the turboshaft, requiring changes to the fuselage aft of the cockpit and to the base area of the vertical tail.
Engine: Williams-Rolls FJ44 turbofan.
Engine rating: Flat rated to 1,525 lbf (6.78 kN)

Details for Tiro-Trainer.

Principal dimensions:
Wing span: 31 ft 11.5 m (9.74 m)
Maximum length: 31 ft 6 ins (9.6 m)
Maximum height: 11 ft 8 ins (3.55 m)

Undercarriage:
Type: Retractable, with nosewheel
Wheel base: 12 ft 9 ins (3.89 m)
Wheel track: 6 ft 4 ins (1.94 m)

Weights:
Empty: 2,557 lb (1,160 kg)
Maximum take-off: 5,070 lb (2,300 kg), utility
Useful load: 2,513 lb (1,140 kg)

Performance (at 3,968 lb, 1,800 kg weight):
Maximum speed: 338 kts (389 mph) 626 km/h at 25,000 ft (7,620 m)
Cruise speed: 318 kts (366 mph) 589 km/h at 10,000 ft (3,050 m)
Stall speed: 61 kts (70 mph) 113 km/h
Maximum climb rate: 3,175 ft (968 m) per minute
Range with full fuel: 910 naut miles (1,048 miles) 1,685 km at 20,000 ft (6,100 m), 50% power
Duration: 3 hours 30 minutes at above conditions

Hellenic Aerospace Industry Ltd (Greece)

Corporate address: Athens Tower, Messogion 2-4, GR-115 270 Athens.
Telephone: +30 1 7799679, 7799654, 7799622 and 7799506
Facsimile: +30 1 7797670
Telex: 219528 HAI GR
Founded: 1975.
Employees: Approximately 3,000.
Information: Athanasios Nezis (Chairman and Managing Director).

■ Facilities

■ Tanagra, PO Box 23, GR-320 09 Schimatari (*telephone* +30 1 8836711, 0262-52000, *facsimile* +30 1 8838714, 0262-52170). Divided into 4 major facilities: Aircraft with 33 production shops and capable of supporting virtually all Western fighter, commercial, cargo and helicopter types; Engine with 18 shops providing inspection, repair, overhaul, modification, testing and trouble shooting services to over 23 types of engines and their components/accessories; Electronics (plus Electronics Manufacturing, producing parts including Hawk radar modules, Stinger missile launch tubes and grip stocks, and AIM-9P Sidewinder missile cable assemblies and upgrade kits) and Airframe Manufacturing.

● Activities

● Maintenance, overhaul and modification of fighter and commercial aircraft and helicopters, engines, aircraft and engine accessories and components, avionics, airborne and ground navigation/communication systems and equipment.
● Fabrication and assembly of aircraft structural parts and major assemblies, and engine parts.
● Manufacturing of complete electronics and telecommunications products and systems, and parts for weapon systems.
● Training in a wide range of aviation disciplines at HAI Training Services.
● Non-aviation products include an artillery laser range finder, night vision equipment, communications equipment, Hermes digital message device, and more.
● On 9 November 1994, DASA of Germany (Daimler-Benz) signed an agreement with HAI covering future co-operation over civil and military programmes, defence technology and satellite communication.

Hellenic Aerospace Industry's Aircraft maintenance facility keeps A-7E and H Corsair II attack aircraft flying with 7 operational squadrons

Aeronautical Development Agency (India)

Corporate address: PO Box 1718, Vimanapura Post Office, Bangalore 560017.
Telephone: +91 80 556 0642
Telex: 0845 8114 ADA IN
Information: T. Prakash.

ADA Light Combat Aircraft

First flight: June 1996.
Role: Lightweight multi-mission tactical fighter, for close air support and capable of air defence.

★ Aims

★ To replace the MiG-21s and MiG-23s in Indian service. Ajeet replacement, as originally intended for LCA, has already taken place (completed 1991 by the MiG-23).
★ Advanced design, using weight-saving composites materials and with an Indian-developed engine.
★ Unstable design for high manoeuvrability, requiring computer control.
★ Small radar signature.
★ 3,000 hour service life. Less than 10 ground maintenance hours per flight hour.
★ Capable of operating from paved, unpaved and grass airstrips, and in hot and high conditions.
★ 95% mission reliability during 1 hour sorties.

▲ Development

▲ 1983. Project started following receipt of Indian Government go-ahead. Feasibility studies were assisted by Dornier, MBB and MTU.
▲ 5 January 1985. The Scientific Adviser to the Indian Defence Ministry announced research development of the LCA at the 71st Indian Science Congress.

ADA Light Combat Aircraft mock-up (Denis Hughes)

▲ 1990. Initial design completed, leading to the start of prototype construction by Hindustan Aeronautics Ltd in the following year.
▲ 1993. Mock-up displayed to the public at the Avia India show.
▲ 1 April 1993. The expected roll-out date for LCA was given as June 1996 at the Parliamentary Consultative Committee for Defence, 6 months ahead of schedule.
▲ 1994. First test run of the Kaveri engine.
▲ 1995. LCA flight control software tested in the USA, initially by using an NT-33 and later an F-16.
▲ 1995. Programme partners were still being sought.
▲ March 1998. Production go-ahead expected.
▲ 2005. Probable service entry.

Sales/users: 2 prototypes under construction. About 200 production aircraft are required by the Indian Air Force.
Crew: Pilot.
Cockpit: See Avionics.
Crew escape: Zero-zero ejection seat.
Fixed guns: 23-mm GSh-23 twin-barrel cannon.
Ammunition: 220 rounds.
Number of weapon pylons: 7 (1 under the fuselage and 6 under the wings).
Expendable weapons and equipment: Over 8,820 lb (4,000 kg), including laser-guided weapons, anti-ship missile, medium and short-range AAMs, and rocket pods. Rearmament and refuelling takes under 15 minutes.
Radar: Indigenous multi-mode type.
Flight/weapon system avionics/instrumentation: Includes an EFIS cockpit with holographic head-up display and CRTs, mission computer with 3 1553B-standard databuses, INS, Tacan, IFF and FLIR. Night vision equipment will be available. Israel has been approached to offer both hardware and technical assistance.
Self-protection systems: Radar warning receiver, jammer and chaff/flare dispenser.
Wing characteristics: Mid-to-shoulder mounted compound delta type, with varying degrees of anhedral from the roots, root slots, and considerable twist. Designed for vortex lift, to shed vortex evenly over both wings to increase lift and decrease the stalling speed.
Wing control surfaces: Entire trailing-edge is taken up with 2-section elevons. 3-section leading-edge slats.
Tail control surfaces: Rudder.
Flight control system: Lockheed Martin integrated digital, quadruplex redundant fly-by-wire.
Construction materials: Carbonfibre wings and tail unit, constituting 30% of the airframe (possibly to be increased). Kevlar radome. Aluminium-lithium and titanium alloys.
Engine: Prototypes each use a General Electric F404-F2J3 turbofan. Production aircraft will have the Gas Turbine Research Establishment Kaveri turbofan (previously designated GTX-35VS), rated at about 11,530 lbf (51.3 kN) dry and 18,078 lbf (80.4 kN) with afterburning.
Engine rating: 18,100 lbf (80.51 kN) for GE type.
Air intakes: On the fuselage sides, almost level with the wing leading edge. Fixed geometry, with splitter plates.
Flight refuelling probe: Non-retractable type (probably removable), on the starboard side of the nose.
Fuel system: Internal fuel plus up to 5 x 800 litre drop tanks.
Braking system: Kevlar drag-chute.

Aircraft variants:
LCA for the Indian Air Force and to be offered for export, as detailed (figures are provisional).
Future naval variant, with a strengthened undercarriage, arrester hook, anti-corrosion materials, and a developed Kaveri engine.

DETAILS FOR LIGHT COMBAT AIRCRAFT.

Principal dimensions:
Wing span: 26 ft 11 ins (8.2 m)
Maximum length: 43 ft 4 ins (13.2 m)
Maximum height: 14 ft 5 ins (4.4 m)

Wings:
Area: about 403.65 sq ft (37.5 m^2)
Aspect ratio: 1.79

Undercarriage:
Type: Retractable, with twin nosewheels

Weights:
Empty: 12,125 lb (5,500 kg)
Take-off: 18,739 lb (8,500 kg) without stores

Performance:
Maximum speed: Mach 1.6
Take-off distance: 2,000 ft (610 m) from a hot and high airfield with full fuel and 5,300 lb (2,400 kg) payload
Sustained turn rate: 13-17° per second; instantaneous 30°
G limits: +8, -3
Ceiling: 50,000 ft (15,250 m)

Hindustan Aeronautics Limited (HAL) (India)

Corporate address: 15/1 Cubbon Road, Bangalore 560 001.
Telephone: +91 812 2256901 (80 2205197, 2261158 and 2268629 marketing department)
Facsimile: +91 80 2258758 and 5777533
Founded: 1 October 1964, from the merger of Aeronautics India Ltd and other established manufacturing concerns.
Employees: over 37,000.
Information: Cmdr M. Nirmal (Deputy General Manager, Public Relations).

■ Facilities
■ Aircraft activities are divided into 4 Complex groupings: Accessories, Bangalore, Design and MiG, all based in Bangalore but with individual divisions in Bangalore and elsewhere.
■ Design Complex is charged with the design of aeroplanes, helicopters, avionics and engines, with present activities based around the Advanced Light Helicopter, a tandem two-seat attack helicopter development, and the HTT-35.

● Activities
● In addition to the programmes listed, HAL is co-operating internationally in the development of new regional airliners, and has begun the process of establishing refurbishing and overhaul facilities for commercial jetliners.
● On 25 January 1993 a Memorandum of Understanding was signed between HAL and British Aerospace to establish BAe HAL Software Ltd, to manufacture and export computer software.

DIVISIONS

Aircraft (part of the Bangalore Complex)
HQ address: Bag 1788, Bangalore 560 017.

● Activities
● Jaguar programme.
● Work on the LCA tactical fighter programme (see Aeronautical Development Agency).
● Development of an AWACS aircraft, in co-operation with the Hyderabad Division.
● Component manufacturing under contract from various European and US aerospace companies.

Helicopter (part of the Bangalore Complex)
HQ address: Bag 1790, Bangalore 560 017.

● Activities
● Cheetah and Chetak helicopter programmes.

Other Bangalore Complex divisions are:
Aerospace, Engine, Overhaul, and Foundry & Forge.

Hyderabad, Kanpur, Korwa and Lucknow (parts of the Accessories Complex)
HQ address: Bag 225, Kanpur 208 008 (for Kanpur Division).

● Activities
● Radars, nav/attack systems, INS, and other avionics from Hyderabad and Korwa; Dornier 228, HPT-32 Deepak and other programmes from Kanpur; principally undercarriages from Lucknow.

Koraput (part of the MiG Complex)

● Activities
● Engines for MiG aircraft.

Nasik (part of the MiG Complex)
HQ address: Nasik 422 207, Maharashtra.

● Activities
● MiG-21 and MiG-27 programmes. Production of the latter is believed to have ended in late 1994.

Aircraft Design, Helicopter Design, Engine Design and Avionics Design (parts of the Design Complex)

HAL HTT-35

First flight: About 1996.
Role: Student pilot screening, primary and basic training, and some advanced elements.

★ Aims
★ To be used in conjunction with the proposed Advanced Jet Trainer purchase, leading to the eventual

replacement of both the HPT-32 and Kiran trainers.
⋆ 7,000 flying hour structural life.
Crew: 2, in tandem, the instructor's rear cockpit raised to improve forward vision.
Cockpit: Dual controls.
Crew escape: Lightweight ejection seats.
Fixed guns: None.
Number of weapon pylons: 2, under the wings.
Expendable weapons and equipment: 1,103 lb (500 kg) load, including bombs, rocket and gun pods for weapons training and potentially light attack.
Flight/weapon system avionics/instrumentation: Includes an automatic direction finder.
Wing characteristics: Straight, low mounted, with dihedral.
Wing control surfaces: Ailerons and flaps.

Details for HTT-35.

Principal dimensions:
Wing span: 34 ft 1 ins (10.4 m)
Maximum length: 31 ft 3 ins (9.527 m)
Maximum height: 12 ft 8 ins (3.86 m)

Wings:
Area: 193.75 sq ft (18 m^2)
Aspect ratio: 6
Incidence: 2°
Dihedral: 5° 40'

Undercarriage:
Type: Retractable, with nosewheel
Wheel base: 9 ft 3 ins (2.825 m)
Wheel track: 10 ft 6 ins (3.2 m)

Weights:
Empty: 3,840 (1,742 kg)
Maximum take-off: 6,228 lb (2,825 kg) with 500 kg of weapons

Performance:
Maximum speed: over 270 kts (311 mph) 500 km/h at 10,000 ft (3,050 m)
Stall speed: 76 kts (87 mph) 140 km/h clean
Take-off distance over a 50 ft (15 m) obstacle: 855 ft (260 m)
Landing distance over a 50 ft (15 m) obstacle: 1,900 ft (578 m)
Maximum climb rate: 4,000 ft (1,220 m) per minute
G limits: +6, -3
Ceiling: over 29,500 ft (9,000 m)
Range with full fuel: 685 naut miles (789 miles) 1,270 km
Duration: 4 hours

Tail control surfaces: Elevators and rudder, with tabs.
Flight control system: Mechanical, except for hydraulically-actuated flaps.
Construction materials: Metal.
Engine: AlliedSignal TPE331-12D or Pratt & Whitney Canada PT6A-62 turboprop.
Engine rating: 1,100 shp (820.3 kW) or 950 shp (708.4 kW) respectively, with a 4-blade propeller.
Fuel system: 992 lb (450 kg) weight of usable fuel. Capable of 30 seconds of inverted flight.
Electrical system: 28 volt DC supply using an engine driven starter-generator. Back-up 40 amp-hour ni-cd battery. AC supply using 2 static inverters.
Braking system: Discs on main units.

HAL Jaguar International Shamsher

Following delivery to the Indian Air Force of 40 fly-away SEPECAT Jaguar Internationals built in Europe, HAL began assembly of a further 45 Shamshers (progressively with some indigenous components, including Hyderabad Division avionics), the first making its maiden flight at Bangalore on 31 March 1982 in the hands of the company's Chief Test Pilot. Subsequent manufacturing by HAL has covered a further 46. In-service Jaguars include a number of maritime strike examples (12 to 17) with Thomson-CSF Agave radar, DARIN nav/attack system and armed with Sea Eagle anti-ship missiles. Further details on the Jaguar can be found under SEPECAT in the Multi-national section.

HAL MiG-21 and MiG-27M

MiG-21 assembly in India began with the MiG-21FL, in November 1966, following the import of Soviet-built aircraft that went to No 28 Squadron, IAF. MiGs built entirely from Indian components were delivered from October 1970, with nearly 200 being completed by March 1974. Production subsequently centred on the MiG-21M (delivered from February 1973), followed by the MiG-21bis. A programme to upgrade MiG-21bis fighters to MiG-21-93 standard is progressing in co-operation with Mikoyan (needed due to delays in the LCA programme – see Russia), while it has been suggested that HAL should put the MiG-21 back into production for export to countries that require an inexpensive fighter, perhaps incorporating some LCA technology.
MiG-27M assembly at HAL's MiG Complex began in 1984, leading to manufacture with indigenously-built components from 1988. Just 1 MiG-27M was completed in 1994, and production has ended. Details of the MiG-27 can be found under Mikoyan in the Russian section. An upgrade programme for India's operational MiG-27Ms is likely.

HAL Jaguar International Shamsher (Denis Hughes)

Elbit Ltd (Israel)

Corporate address: PO Box 539, Haifa 31053.
Telephone: +972 4 315315
Facsimile: +972 4 550002, 551623
Also: PO Box 650, Karmiel 20101 (*telephone* +972 4 901111, *facsimile* +972 4 986522)
Founded: 1971.
Information: Ilana Gelfer (Marketing promotion manager).

● Activities

- Modernization programmes for the A-4, F-4, F-5, F-15, F-16, Kfir, L-39, Mirage and MiG-21.
- Integrating weapon delivery and navigation, stores management and display systems, mission computers and more.
- Provides ground support, test and training equipment and depot maintenance procedures.
- Offers the HALO advanced helicopter avionics suite for safe night-time nap-of-the-earth flying.
- Produces a wide range of products, including mission computers, stores management systems, modular multi-role computer, multi-function displays, integrated communication/radio navigation and identification system, digital image processing and communication system, and OPHER autonomous terminal guidance for general purpose bombs.

F-4 Phantom upgrades include Elbit avionics interface computer and missile control system, as selected for the USAF and ANG. Upgrade of the F-4 2000 weapon delivery system includes radar display processor, HUD electronic unit integration, multi-function displays, digital data link (alphanumeric video), avionics interface computer, and operational flight programmes software.
F-5 upgrades are intended to provide a multi-role fire control radar, structural modifications for new aerodynamic capabilities and life extension, electronic warfare suite, HOTAS, head-out flight, reduced pilot workload, improved weapon delivery and navigation system, up-front controls and displays, multi-function colour displays, and incorporation of comm and R-nav.
F-16 avionics work includes providing advanced stores management systems (SMS) under sub-contract to Lockheed Martin, multi-function displays as a co-producer and Elbit developed fire control computers. Elbit has also participated in several Israeli Air Force programmes, integrating display and sight helmet systems (DASH), digital communications systems, and supporting the IAF's improved Operational Capability Upgrade (OCU) of F-16A/Bs.
L-39 avionics and cockpit instrumentation upgrade is intended to provide an advanced interface system that familiarizes student pilots with a full weapon delivery and navigation system and HUD. It comprises a HUD, up-front control panel, central mission computer, ring

laser gyro/inertial navigation system, video camera and VTR, and multi-function display in the rear cockpit. Additional features that can be integrated include stand-alone autonomous air combat manoeuvring instrumentation (A^{2}CMI), HUD projected on the pilot's visor, full display and sight helmet, and radar warning receiver. 6 L-39s bought by Cambodia for delivery in 1995 are being upgraded to some extent.

MiG-21 step-by-step upgrades offer integration of an advanced multi-role radar for air-to-air/range radar for close air support and HUD, navigation sensors (such as INS, ring laser gyro, GPS), computerized air data centre, stores management system for computerized armament management, communications system and radio/navigation suite, modular multi-role computer, modernized cockpit with HOTAS, advanced display and control systems (including multi-function colour displays, up-front control panel, HUD and helmet mounted display), structural improvements for extended life, enhanced reliability including advanced test equipment and simplified maintenance of aircraft systems, modern integrated briefing/debriefing capability, and experience in operational flight programme software.

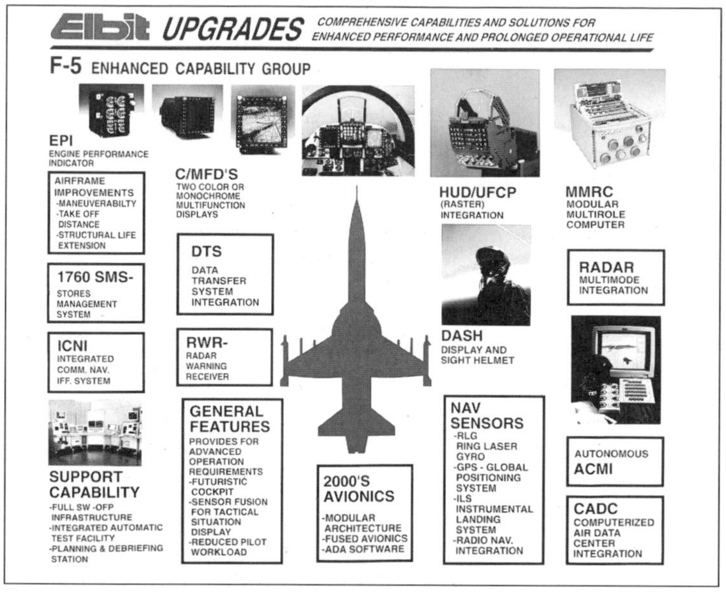

Elbit F-5 enhanced capability upgrade

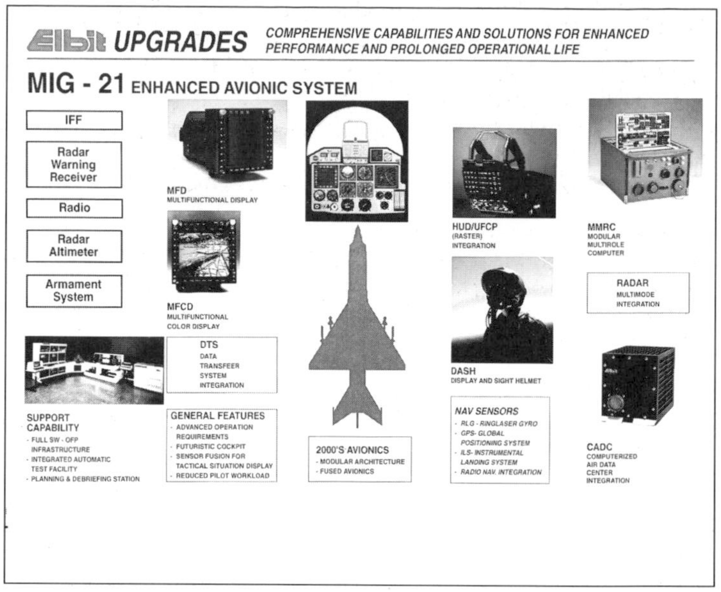

Elbit MiG-21 enhanced avionics system upgrade

Israel Aircraft Industries Ltd (IAI) (Israel)

IAI's Lahav Division's upgraded MiG-21bis on its first flight on 24 May 1995, featuring Western avionics

Corporate address: Ben-Gurion International Airport, 70100.
Telephone: +972 3 935 8509, 8514 and 936 8541
Facsimile: +972 3 935 8512 and 3882
Telex: 381033 ISRAV IL
Founded: 1 April 1967, from the former Bedek Aviation of 1953 founding.
Employees: Over 16,000.
Information: Doron Suslik (Director of Corporate Communication).

● Activities

● In addition to the various programmes detailed below, IAI has received a US Army contract to overhaul Black Hawk main rotor blades, and on 1 March 1995 signed a Memorandum of Understanding with McDonnell Douglas to jointly enter the USAF's T-38 Avionics Upgrade Programme competition.

DIVISIONS

Aircraft

HQ address: As above.
Telephone: +972 3 934 4136 or 971 1471

■ Facilities

■ Lahav undertakes military aircraft programmes, including the Kfir and MiG-21. It is now also offering an upgrade package for the Sukhoi Su-22, developed during 1994. At least 1 country was near to ordering the upgrade in early 1995. The upgrade enables the Su-22 to launch modern laser-guided precision weapons, and other gains include an advanced EW system.

■ Malat for UAVs, including the new Heron long-duration UAV that was unveilled during a 30 minute flight on 18 October 1994.

■ Malkam specializes in airframe components built to contract/sub-contract.

■ Matan handles civil programmes, currently centred on the Astra and Astra Galaxy.

■ Tashan undertakes engineering programmes related to aircraft and systems, from analysis through to integration and testing.

Bedek Aviation

HQ address: As above.
Telephone: +972 3 935 8964
Facsimile: +972 3 971 2298

● Activities

● Extensive aircraft, engine and systems servicing, overhaul and modification.

● Offers a large number of upgrade and modification programmes, often in co-operation with Elta Electronic Industries (a subsidiary of IAI's Electronics Division), including those for the A-4, Boeing 707 and 720, Boeing 747 (conversion of an ex-Pan Am 747-100 into a freighter for GATX-Airlog among the latest), DC-10, F-4, F-5 (to F-5 Plus – see ENAER of Chile), F-15, F-16, Hercules, MiG-21 (including MiG-21-2000 in co-operation with Aerostar of Romania), MiG-23, Mirage III and 5, and S-2 Tracker.

● Supplied the complete avionics package to produce the Antonov An-72P, modified a Romanian Soim trainer to become the prototype IAR 109 Swift, and is upgrading South African Air Force Cheetah Es to have the Elta EL/M-2035 radar and ex-F1 09K50 engines.

● Co-operation with Elta has produced the Phalcon airborne early warning conversion of the Boeing 707, first flown on 12 May 1993. A Chilean Air Force B707 has been converted to Phalcon configuration. It is rumoured that 2 South African B707 tanker/transports

Israeli Air Force Phantom 2000, modified to extend service life into the next century by having a strengthened airframe, wiring and hydraulic improvements. Avionics integrator is Elbit, basing the upgrade on its ACE-3 package, with a 1750 avionics interface computer as the core of the suite, a multi-mode radar, El-Op HUD, multi-function cockpit displays and HOTAS, a digital weapon delivery and navigation system, and enhanced self-protection suite

IAI modified S-2E/UP Tracker carrier-borne anti-submarine aircraft belonging to the Argentine Navy (temporarily in Israeli markings), with 1,645 shp (1,227 kW) AlliedSignal TPE331-15 turboprops, searchlight on the starboard wing and upgrades to the systems. All 5 others are being upgraded in Argentina using supplied kits

have been installed with some elements of the system. Other air forces showing interest are the Italian and Israeli. IAI is reportedly looking into the possibility of adapting the Airbus A321 as a Phalcon system carrier.

<u>Electronics</u>
HQ address: PO Box 105, Yahud IZ, 56000.
Telephone: +972 3 531 5555 and 4021
Facsimile: +972 3 536 5205 and 3975

■ Facilities

■ Elta Electronic Industries, MBT Systems and Space Technology, Tamam Precision Instruments Industries, and MLM System Engineering and Integration.

<u>Technologies</u>
HQ address: PO Box 190, Lod IZ, Lod 71101.
Telephone: +972 8 23 9111
Facsimile: +972 8 22 2792

■ Facilities

■ Golan Industries, MATA Helicopters, Ramta Structures and Systems, and Servo Hydraulics Lod.

● Activities

● Includes upgrade of Israeli Sikorsky CH-53D Stallion helicopters to Yasur 2000 standard.

IAI Kfir C2, C7, C10 and Kfir 2000

First flight: 1973 in C1 prototype form, 1974 in C2 form, 1983 in C7 form, and C10 not known to have flown by early 1995.
Role: Multi-role tactical fighter for interception and attack.

★ Aims

★ Developed from the basic Mirage 5 airframe and with many changes, including the adoption of canards and a dogtooth wing leading edge from the C2 version, and those needed to install a General Electric J79 engine in place of a SNECMA Atar.
★ New cockpit layout, with adoption of Israeli-supplied avionics. HOTAS.
Sales/users: Colombia (13 C7/TC-7), Ecuador (10 C2/TC2), and Israel (about 100 operational C7/TC7s plus stored C2s and C7s). The purchase of 18 C10s (upgraded to Kfir 2000 form) by the Philippines had not occurred at the time of writing, while Taiwan reportedly required 40 similar aircraft but these too had not materialized at the time of writing.
Details: Principally for the C7.
Crew: Pilot.
Cockpit: See Avionics.
Crew escape: Martin Baker IL10P zero-zero ejection seat.
Fixed guns: 2 x 30-mm Israeli-built DEFA 552 cannon in the bottom of the air intake ducts.
Ammunition: 140 rounds per cannon.
Number of weapon pylons: 9, including 5 under the fuselage.
Expendable weapons and equipment: 13,415 lb (6,085 kg) load. Many armament and store options, including 2 x Python 3, Shafrir 2 or Sidewinder air-to-air missiles, bombs of up to 3,000 lb (1,360 kg) weight (including general purpose, ATAP-1000 and TAL-1/2 cluster, Griffin and Guillotine laser-guided, Elbit OPHER-fitted guided, and Pyramid TV-guided), rocket launchers, Maverick or Shrike or other air-to-surface missiles, and more often in combination with drop tanks.
Radar: Elta EL/M-2021 pulse Doppler fire control type. Elta EL/M-2032 multi-mode pulse Doppler in the C10/Kfir 2000.
Flight/weapon system avionics/instrumentation: WDNS 341 weapon delivery and navigation system. Elbit 82 stores management system incorporating a stores management computer (SMC) and armament control and display panel (ACDP), and handling smart weapon delivery, for programmed accuracy and precise delivery.
Self-protection systems: EW suite.
Wing characteristics: Low-mounted delta, with dogtooth leading edge.
Wing control surfaces: 2-section elevons and inboard flap.
Tail control surfaces: Rudder only.
Canard: Non-movable but detachable, of swept delta planform, on the air intake ducts.
Airbrakes: On each upper and lower wing surface.
Flight control system: Hydraulically actuated.
Construction materials: Metal.
Engine: General Electric J79-J1E turbojet.
Engine rating: 11,890 lbf (52.89 kN) dry, 18,750 lbf (83.41 kN) with afterburning.
Air intakes: Side mounted, with adjustable centre-cones.
Flight refuelling probe: Available for the C7 and C10.
Fuel system: 3,243 litres. Various drop tanks of 500-1,700 litres capacity can be carried on 1 underfuselage and 2 underwing pylons, to a maximum total of 4,700 litres.
Electrical system: 28 volt DC supply with 2 transformer-rectifiers and ni-cd battery. Alternators and static inverter for AC supply.
Hydraulic system: 2 systems.
Braking system: Disc brakes and an anti-skid system. Drag-chute in an under-rudder pod.

IAI Kfir C-7

Aircraft variants:

<u>C2</u> is the oldest available version which, along with its TC2 two-seat counterpart for operational training, only serves operationally with Ecuador. Others in store in Israel. Became the principal production model after a relatively small number of C1s had been built, introducing canards, dogtooth wings and other improvements. 7 pylons.
<u>C7</u> was produced by modification of the C2, with a higher-rated engine, 9 pylons, and significant avionics and cockpit upgrades. TC7 became the equivalent operational trainer.
<u>C10/Kfir 2000</u> are the latest upgraded models offered by IAI's Aircraft Division, the former available since 1993 and Kfir 2000 as the latest variant. Incorporate Elta EL/M-2032 multi-mode, track-while-scan radar (see Radar), new multi-role computer for fire control, stores management and display functions, ring laser gyro/inertial navigation system RLG/INS), and a modernized cockpit with an up-front control panel, head-up display, and monochromatic and colour multi-function displays; MILstd 1553B digital databus. The Philippines is being offered also the Python 3 missile with the Kfir 2000.

DETAILS FOR C7.

Principal dimensions:
Wing span: 27 ft (8.22 m)
Maximum length: 51 ft 4 ins (15.65 m)
Maximum height: 14 ft 11 ins (4.55 m)

Wings:
Area: 374.58 sq ft (34.8 m^2)
Aspect ratio: 1.942
Sweepback: 60° 35′ on the leading edge
Incidence: 1°
Anhedral: 1°

Undercarriage:
Type: Retractable, with steerable nosewheel
Wheel base: 16 ft (4.87 m)
Wheel track: 10 ft 6 ins (3.2 m)

Weights:
Maximum take-off: 36,375 lb (16,500 kg)

Performance:
Maximum speed: above Mach 2.3 at over 36,000 ft (11,000 m)
Maximum speed at sea level: 750 kts (864 mph) 1,389 km/h
Take-off distance: 4,760 ft (1,450 m)
Landing distance: 4,200 ft (1,280 m) in interceptor configuration
Maximum climb rate: 46,000 ft (14,000 m) per minute
Turn rate: 18.9° per second instantaneous, 9.6° per second sustainable, in an interceptor configuration with 50% internal fuel
G limits: +7.5
Operational ceiling: 58,000 ft (17,700 m)
Radius of action: 419 naut miles (482 miles) 776 km in interceptor configuration with 3,425 litres of auxiliary fuel, or 640 naut miles (736 miles) 1,186 km with maximum internal and external fuel, a 2,600 lb (1,180 kg) bomb load, 2 x AAMs and flying to/from the target at high altitude

Aeronautica Macchi Holding Group (Italy)

Corporate address: Via Paolo Foresio 1, 21040 Venegono Superiore (Varese).
Telephone: +39 331 865910
Facsimile: +39 331 827595
Founded: 1912 origin in the Società Anonima Nieuport-Macchi.

● Activities

● Holding company to Aermacchi (see below), Logic SpA (an avionics company; Via Brescia 29, 20063 Cernusco S/N, MI; *telephone* +39 2 921 02551; *facsimile* +39 2 921 02528), and SICAMB SpA (a joint-venture with Martin Baker producing ejection seats, crashworthy helicopter seats, and aerostructures including participation in MB-339, AMX, Atlantique, ATR 42, DC-8, Airbus, MD-11, Falcon 200 and G-222 programmes; Via Eschido 1, 04100 Latina; *telephone* +39 773 6541; *facsimile* +39 773 654 200).

Aermacchi SpA (Italy)

Corporate address: As for Aeronautica Macchi.
Telephone: +39 331 813 111
Facsimile: +39 331 813 450, 827 595
Employees: 2,000, including 400 specialized technical personnel devoted to aerospace design activities (as of 1995).
Information: Marketing Department; *facsimile* +39 331 813 152.

● Activities

● Leading company of the Group. Apart from the aircraft detailed below, Aermacchi is involved in the AMX, Eurofighter 2000, PTS-2000, Tornado (technology and manufacturing contribution; is the designer and sole source manufacturer of the underwing pylons) and Yak/Aem-130 programmes.
● Under a contract with Daimler-Benz Aerospace, is responsible for the design and production of the front fuselage of the Dornier 328 airliner and for assembly of the pressurized fuselage.
● With Daimler-Benz and Dassault, is studying a future generation new training system, designated TS-21.
● Aermacchi, Lockheed Martin, Rolls-Royce and Textron Aerostructures developed a variant of the MB-339 for the USAF's JPATS competition, as the T-Bird II (not selected), and Aermacchi is also co-operating with Hawker de Havilland Ltd and Honeywell Australia Ltd in proposing the MB-339FD for the Royal Australian Air Force.
● Has produced test benches to service Tornado and Eurofighter hydraulic systems, designed/qualified firewall bulkheads for rocket booster engines of Ariane 4, and conducts other non-aerospace activities.

Aermacchi MB-339 series

First flight: 12 August 1976 in MB-339X prototype form.
Role: Primary, basic and advanced trainer, lead-in fighter trainer, light attack, aerobatic display and radio calibration.

★ Aims

★ Modern replacement for the MB-326 series.
★ 12,000 flying hours, 24,000 landings, structural life for the MB-339A.

▲ Development

▲ 20 May 1977. First flight of the second MB-339X prototype.
▲ 20 July 1978. First flight of a production MB-339A, entering service with the Italian Air Force in August that year.
▲ 17 December 1985. First flight of a more powerful MB-339C.
▲ October 1989. A teaming agreement was signed between Aermacchi and Lockheed (LASC) to prepare a missionized version of the MB-339A for entry in the USAF's JPATS competition. Rolls-Royce officially joined the team in 1990, followed by Textron Aerostructures in mid-1993.
▲ May 1992. An MB-339A demonstrator was delivered to Lockheed's Marietta facility for the JPATS competition. Not selected in 1995.
▲ September 1994. Aermacchi, Hawker de Havilland and Honeywell Australia signed a Memorandum of Understanding to co-operate in proposing the MB-339FD as a replacement for the MB-326H in the RAAF's Project Air 5367 lead-in fighter trainer programme.

Aermacchi MB-339FD with refuelling probe attached

Aermacchi MB-339As in Italian Air Force service

Sales/users: 207 ordered by March 1995, including 2 MB-339X and 1 MB-339C prototypes. Argentina (Navy, 10), Dubai (7), Ghana (4), Italy (124, including 19 delivered to the Frecce Tricolori display team, and 15 MB-339CDs), Malaysia (13), New Zealand (18 MB-339C advanced trainers), Nigeria (12) and Peru (16).

Aermacchi MB-339C advanced and fighter lead-in trainer with the Royal New Zealand Air Force

Details: Principally for the MB-339A.
Crew: 2, with rear instructor's seat raised by 12.8 ins (32.5 cm).
Cockpit: See Avionics.
Crew escape: Martin Baker IT10F (16L on T-Bird) zero-zero ejection seats.
Fixed guns: None.
Number of weapon pylons: 6 under the wings, outboard pylons for up to a 750 lb (340 kg) load each and 4 inner pylons for up to 1,000 lb (454 kg) load each. Centre pylon on each wing is wet for a drop tank.
Expendable weapons and equipment: Many combinations up to 4,500 lb (2,040 kg) for the MB-339A and 4,000 lb (1,815 kg) on MB-339C. Cannon and machine-gun options include 2 Aermacchi pods each with a 12.7-mm Browning M-3 gun and 350 rounds of ammunition or 30-mm DEFA 553 cannon and 120 rounds (each weighing 251 lb, 114 kg and 551 lb, 250 kg respectively), or 6 General Electric SUU-11 Minigun pods

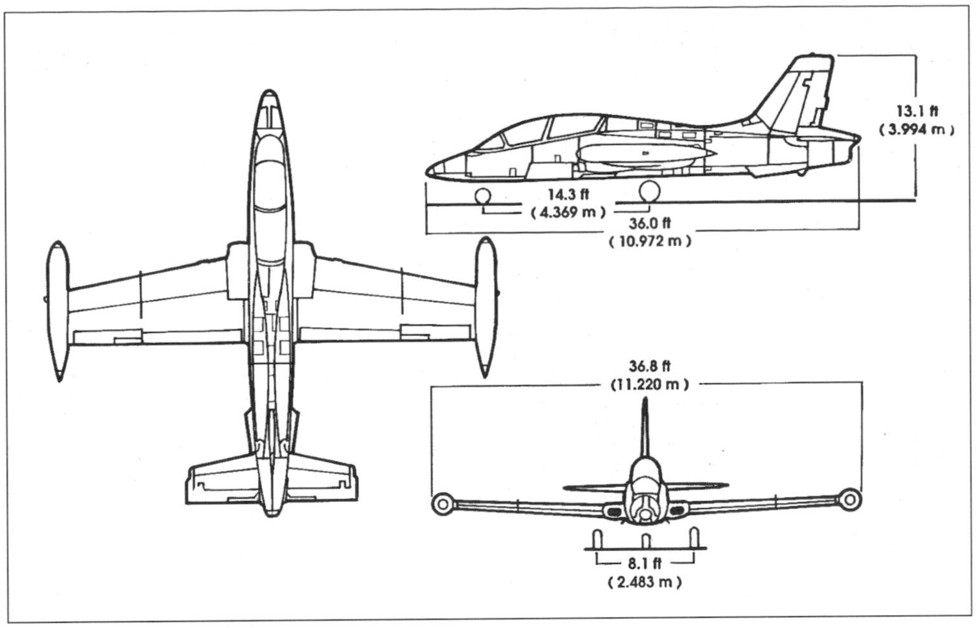

Aermacchi MB-339A drawing

each with a 7.62-mm gun and 1,500 rounds (each weighing about 325 lb, 147 kg). Many rocket pod options include 6 Aerea AL-12-80 (each 12 x 81-mm rockets), 6 Aerea AL-18-50 (each 18 x 50-mm rockets), 6 Aerea AL-25-50 (each 25 x 50-mm rockets), 6 Bristol Aerospace LAU launchers (each 7 x 2.75-ins, or 4 x 5-ins, or 6 x 70-mm rockets), 6 Matra launchers (each 18 x 68-mm) or 6 Matra F2 launchers (6 x 68-mm), or 4 TBA launchers (each 4 x 100-mm). Missile choices include 2 Magic or Sidewinder air-to-air missiles, Marte Mk-2A anti-ship or AGM-65 Maverick air-to-surface (MB-339C/CD). Other weapon options include 4 x 1,000 lb or 6 x 750 lb general purpose bombs, 6 TBA multi-bomb carriers (each with 6 x BAP 100 airfield attack penetration or BAT-120 anti-tank fragmentation bombs), or 6 dispensers for combinations of bombs and rockets or bombs and flares. Alenia 8.105.924 reflector or Saab RGS 2 gyroscopic sight in the forward cockpit (optional rear).

Additional stores: Optional pod with 4 x 70-mm Vinten cameras. See also Avionics and Self-protection.

Radar: MB-339AM carries Doppler radar.

Flight/weapon system avionics/instrumentation: IFR, including Tacan or DME, VOR/ILS, ADF and marker beacon receiver. GEC-Marconi 620C navigation computer in the MB-339A, or 620K in the C which also has inertial reference unit, digital nav/attack system with navigation computer and weapon-aimimg computer, HUD, HOTAS, CRT display, stores management system, RWR, ECM, and laser rangefinder. MB-339FD and CD have HOTAS, 3 liquid-crystal multi-function displays in each cockpit, ring laser gyro platform with embedded GPS, powerful mission processor which acts as the main bus controller, and HUD in each cockpit; digital data transfer in accordance with MIL-STD-1553B using dual redundant data bus.

Self-protection systems: ELT-156 RWR, ELT-555 ECM pod and ALE-40 chaff/flare dispenser in MB-339C/CD.

Wing characteristics: Straight, low mounted, with fixed tiptanks (2 sizes). 1 upper-surface fence on each wing.

Wing control surfaces: Ailerons (with balance tabs) and single-slotted flaps.

Tail control surfaces: Elevators and rudder, all with balance/trim tabs. Outward-canted shallow ventral fins under the rear fuselage.

Airbrake: Under the mid-fuselage.

Flight control system: Mechanical, with hydraulically-actuated aileron servos and flaps. Electro-hydraulic airbrake. Electrically actuated tabs.

Construction materials: Metal, with stressed wing and tail skins strengthened by lateral stringers.

Engine: Rolls-Royce Viper 632-43, built by Rinaldo Piaggio SpA. Similar engine for MB-339A (PAN). MB-339C, CD and FD have 4,360 lbf (19.39 kN) Viper 680-43, and T-Bird had 4,000 lbf (17.79 kN) Viper 680-582 with improved maintainability.

Engine rating: 3,970 lbf (17.66 kN) for Mk 632-43.

Air intakes: In the leading edges of the wing roots.

Flight refuelling probe: MB-339FD and CD have a detachable probe; in-flight refuelling probe has become optional on other models.

Fuel system: 1,413-1,781 litres, including tiptanks. 2 drop tanks, each 325 litres capacity.

Electrical system: 28 volt DC supply with 2 engine-driven starter-generators. 2 ni-cd batteries for engine start-up. 2 single-phase static inverters for AC supply.

Hydraulic system: 2,500 psi.

Braking system: Hydraulic disc, with anti-skid system.

Aircraft variants:

MB-339A is the standard advanced trainer version, capable of light ground attack. Also included are Radiomisure radio calibration aircraft operated by the Italian Air Force.

MB-339AM is the anti-shipping version, qualified to carry Marte Mk-2A missiles and with upgraded avionics including radar. Test aircraft was an Italian Air Force MB-339A modified to C standard, with trials in collaboration with the force's Experimental Test Centre.

MB-339A (PAN) is the Italian Air Force's aerobatic display team version.

MB-339C is the advanced and fighter lead-in trainer version, also for light attack, with avionics upgrade (see Avionics). Uprated Viper 680-43 engine.

MB-339CD is a version of the FD for the Italian Air Force, for service use from late 1996.

Marte Mk-2A anti-ship missile launched from an MB-339 test aircraft for the MB-339AM programme

MB-339FD (Full Digital) is the latest and most advanced version, based on the C and intended to meet the Royal Australian Air Force's Project Air 5367 Lead-In Fighter requirement, for which it has been short-listed. To replace MB-326Hs by the end of the century, for pilot transitioning from the PC-9 to the Hornet or F-111. Collaborating companies are Hawker de Havilland and Honeywell Australia.

T-Bird II was the version for the USAF/USN JPATS competition, missionized from the MB-339A. Collaborating in the Lockheed-Martin led team were Aermacchi, Rolls-Royce and Textron Aerostructures. Viper 680-582 engine. Not selected.

DETAILS PRINCIPALLY FOR THE MB-339A.

Principal dimensions:
Wing span: 35 ft 5 ins (10.8 m) for MB-339A, 32 ft 10 ins (10 m) for A (PAN), 36 ft 10 ins (11.22 m) for C/CD/ FD
Maximum length: 36 ft (10.972 m) for MB-339A and A (PAN), 36 ft 10.5 ins (11.24 m) for C/CD/FD
Maximum height: 13 ft 1 ins (3.994 m)

Wings:
Aerofoil section: Modified NACA 64A-114 and 64A-212 (tip)
Area: 207.743 sq ft (19.3 m^2)
Aspect ratio: 6.04
Sweepback: 11° 18′ leading-edge
Dihedral: From roots

Undercarriage:
Type: Retractable, with steerable nosewheel
Main wheel tyre size: 545 x 175 mm
Nose wheel tyre size: 380 x 150 mm
Wheel base: 14 ft 4 ins (4.369 m)
Wheel track: 8 ft 2 ins (2.483 m)

Weights:
Empty, operating: 6,890 lb (3,125 kg) for MB-339A, 7,560 lb (3,430 kg) for MB-339C
Maximum take-off: 13,007 lb (5,900 kg) for MB-339A/A (PAN), 14,000 lb (6,350 kg) for C/CD/FD

Performance:
Maximum operating Mach number (MMO): Mach 0.85
Maximum speed: 484 kts (557 mph) 897 km/h for MB-339A/A (PAN), 486 kts (559 mph) 900 km/h for C, and 497 kts (572 mph) 920 km/h for CD and FD
Stall speed: 81 kts (93 mph) 149 km/h for MB-339A, 85 kts (98 mph) 157 km/h for C
Take-off distance: 3,002 ft (915 m) at gross weight for MB-339A, 1,610 ft (490 m) for C at 10,983 lb (4,982 kg) weight with no external weapons/pods/equipment, at sea level
Landing distance: 1,365 ft (415 m) for MB-339A at gross weight, 1,510 ft (460 m) for C at above conditions, at sea level
Maximum climb rate: 6,600 ft (2,010 m) for MB-339A, 7,100 ft (2,160 m) for C, at sea level
G limits: +8, -4
Ceiling: 48,000 ft (14,630 m) for MB-339A, 46,720 ft (14,240 m) for C
Range with full internal fuel: 950 naut miles (1,094 miles) 1,759 km for MB-339A

Aermacchi TS-21

Role: Study into a 21st Century training system for NATO air forces.

★ Aims:

★ Integrated training system that can reduce the total cost of producing a "mission ready" pilot.

SIAI Marchetti (Italy)

Corporate address: Via Indipendenza 2, 21018 Sesto Calende (VA).
Telephone: +39 331 929111
Facsimile: +39 331 922525
Telex: 331848 SIAICO
Founded: 1915. Now part of Agusta (see Helicopter section) but responsible for the management of aircraft production.

● Activities

- Manufacturing at Sesto Calende, and flight testing prior to delivery at the Vergiate factory.
- Component production has included wing root trailing edge, flaps and wingtips for the Panavia Tornado, tail section of the G222, flaps and central fuselage sections for the F-104S, and tailcone and inspection door for the Airbus A310.
- Maintenance, overhaul and training activities at Malpensa Airport.

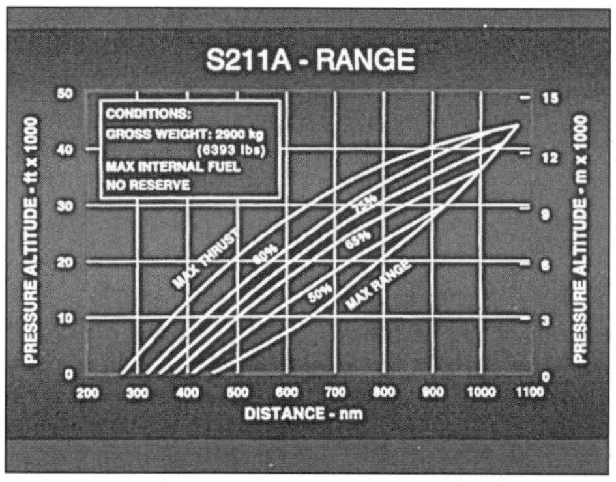

SIAI Marchetti S211A range graph (courtesy SIAI Marchetti)

SIAI Marchetti S211A

First flight: 10 April 1981 in S211 prototype form; 1992 for S211A.
Role: Trainer (fully aerobatic) and light ground attack.

★ Aims

★ 14,400 flying hours structural life.

▲ Development

▲ 1984. Delivery of S211s to Singapore in component form began in November. Assembly by a subsidiary of Singapore Aircraft Industries (now Singapore Technologies Aerospace) allowed delivery to the Republic of Singapore Air Force from 1985.
▲ 1992. First flight of the S211A, and delivery of the first of 2 aircraft to Grumman of the USA for the JPATS competition.

Sales/users: Philippines (24 S211/S211A) and Singapore (30 S211, of which 29 were operated in early 1995). All those for Singapore and the majority for the Philippines were assembled locally. Haiti received 4 but these were given up.

SIAI Marchetti S211A in JPATS colours

Crew: 2, with instructor's rear seat raised by 11 ins (28 cm). 15° downward view over the nose from the front cockpit. 5° downward view over the front cockpit seat from the rear cockpit, and 20° forwards beneath the canopy frame.
Cockpit: Integration of freon cycle for cooling with engine bleed air for heating and cockpit pressurization (max differential 3.5 psi).The second JPATS S211A was given an EFIS cockpit layout (see Aircraft variants).
Crew escape: Martin Baker Mk 10 zero-zero ejection seats.
Fixed guns: Uses a detachable 12.7-mm gun pod under the fuselage.
Number of weapon pylons: 4 under the wings, plus an underfuselage centreline position for the gun pod or ferry pod.
Expendable weapons and equipment: Up to 1,455 lb (660 kg). See diagram for weapon options.
Radar: Capable of having Doppler radar.
Flight/weapon system avionics/instrumentation: Different equipment, according to requirements. Typically VHF/UHF com; AHRS (HSI, ADI), ADF, VOR-ILS/Tacan navigation; ATC/IFF. Capable of having a wide-angle head-up display and ISIS D-211 optical weapon aiming system.
Self-protection systems: Optional radar warning system and ECM.
Wing characteristics: Shoulder-mounted, swept back, with anhedral. Upper surface fences on the leading edge, above the outer pylon positions.
Wing control surfaces: Ailerons and Fowler type flaps.
Tail control surfaces: Variable incidence tailplane, horn-balanced elevators (with tabs) and horn-balanced rudder.
Airbrakes: Under the fuselage.
Flight control system: Push-pull rod primary controls, boosted ailerons, electrically operated flaps and three-axis trims, and hydraulically operated airbrake.
Construction materials: Wide use of structural bonding and composite materials (Kevlar, Nomex and carbonfibre). Metal wings, with one-piece skins.
Engine: Pratt & Whitney Canada JT15D-5C turbofan.
Engine rating: 3,190 lbf (14.19 kN) at take-off.
Air intakes: Ahead of, and below, the wings. Splitter plates.
Flight refuelling probe: Not fitted.
Fuel system: Integral wing tank and fuselage sump, with total capacity of 900 litres. Ejection pumps used for fuel transfer from wing to fuselage tank and for engine feed. Electric fuel pump for engine starting and emergency conditions. Refuelling by gravity via a single point in the wing. Provision for 2 x 270 litre drop tanks. Optional pressure refuelling system.
Electrical system: 28 volt DC negative ground system powered by an engine-driven starter-generator. Ni-cd battery for engine starting and operation in emergency conditions. 2 static inverters for the AC supply for the instruments and avionics.
Hydraulic system: 3,000 psi. For undercarriage, airbrake, freon compressor and aileron booster.
Braking system: Hydraulically actuated.

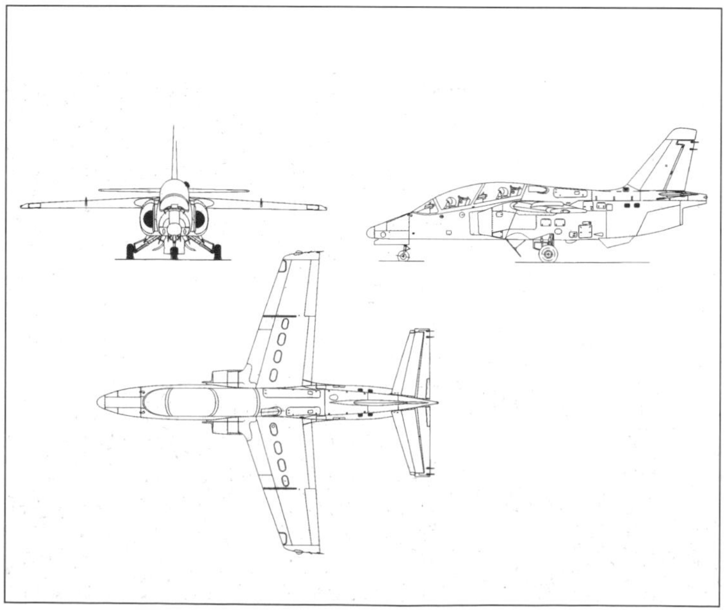

SIAI Marchetti S211A drawing (courtesy SIAI Marchetti)

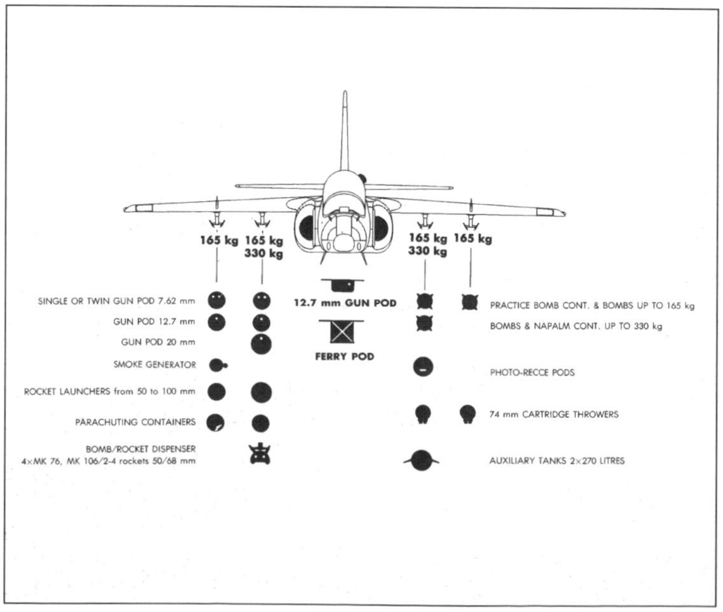

SIAI Marchetti S211A weapon options (courtesy SIAI Marchetti)

Aircraft variants:
S211 was the initial version, generally similar to the described S211A but with a 2,500 lbf (11.12 kN) JT15D-4C engine providing lower performance, 800 litres of fuel, and different supercritical wing section.
S211A is the current version, as described. Also the basis of the JPATS entry led by Northrop Grumman; 2 S211As were delivered to the USA, the second with an EFIS cockpit. Not selected.

Details for S211A.

Principal dimensions:
Wing span: 27 ft 9.5 ins (8.47 m)
Maximum length: 31 ft 2 ins (9.5 m)
Maximum height: 12 ft 5.5 ins (3.8 m)

Wings:
Aerofoil section: Modified GAW-1
Area: 136.27 sq ft (12.66 m^2)
Aspect ratio: 5.67
Sweepback: 15° 30′ at 25% chord
Chord at root: 7 ft 1 ins (2.151 m)
Chord at tip: 3 ft 3 ins (1 m)
Anhedral: 2°

Tail unit:
Tailplane span: 13 ft (3.96 m)

Undercarriage:
Type: Retractable, with steerable nosewheel. Optional powered nosewheel steering
Wheel base: 13 ft 2 ins (4.02 m)
Wheel track: 7 ft 6 ins (2.29 m)

Weights:
Empty: 4,453 lb (2,020 kg)
Maximum take-off: 6,393 lb (2,900 kg) trainer, 7,716 lb (3,500 kg) armed

Performance (trainer at take-off weight, clean, ISA):
Maximum dive speed: Mach 0.8
Maximum speed: 410 kts (472 mph) 760 km/h at 25,000 ft (7,620 m)
Stall speed: 82 kts (95 mph) 152 km/h
Take-off distance: 1,450 ft (440 m)
Landing distance: 1,362 ft (415 m)
Maximum climb rate: 4,920 ft (1,500 m) per minute
G limits: +7, -3; 4.2, sustained at sea level; 3, sustained at 15,000 ft (4,570 m)
Ceiling: 42,000 ft (12,800 m)
Duration: 3 hours 25 minutes, with 10% reserve

SIAI Marchetti SF260E/F and SF260TP

First flight: 15 July 1964 in SF250 prototype form.
Role: Fully aerobatic primary military/civil trainer (SF260E/F), armed trainer capable of light attack (SF260E/F Warrior), and turboprop trainer/attack aircraft (SF260TP). Typical training syllabus covers proficiency, solo, aerobatic, instrument, night, formation and navigation.

★ Aims
★ Latest available versions of the SF260 series (see Aircraft variants)
★ SF260E/F certified to FAA Part 23.
★ ST260TP based on a safe-life philosophy of 8,000 flying hours/20 years, and corresponding to relevant FAA regulations integrated with MIL-A-8866 specifications. Internal and external finish in accordance with MIL-F-7179D.
Sales/users: Over 870 sold, among the latest being 18 SF260TPs going to the 100th Training Wing of the Philippine Air Force from late 1994. Current military operators include Belgium (SF260D and M), Bolivia (C), Brunei (Warrior), Burundi (Warrior and TP), Burkina Faso (Warrior), Chad (Warrior), Ecuador (ME), Ethiopia (TP), Haiti (TP), Ireland (Warrior), Italy (AM), Libya (Warrior), Myanmar (includes Warrior), Nicaragua (Warrior), Philippines (M Warrior and TP), Singapore (M and Warrior), Somalia (Warrior), Sri Lanka (M and TP), Thailand (M), Togo (C and Warrior), Tunisia (C and Warrior), Turkey (D), UAE (TP), Uganda (Warrior), Zaïre (M), Zambia (M) and Zimbabwe (C and Warrior).
Details: Principally for the current SF260E/F and SF260TP.
Crew: 3, with side-by-side seating for the pilot and co-pilot/student, and passenger at rear. Heated and ventilated. Optional freon air conditioning.
Cockpit: Ergonomic damper-mounted instrument panel provides space for a complete set of instruments and avionics for dual pilot operation.
Fixed guns: None.
Number of weapon pylons: 2 standard NATO MA4A under the wings on SF260E/F Warrior. 4 similar NATO pylons on SF260TP.
Expendable weapons and equipment: 661 lb (300 kg) for SF260E/F Warrior and SF260TP Warrior, with release and firing via a trigger on the control stick; selection control on the armament panel. See armament diagram for weapon options.
Flight/weapon system avionics/instrumentation: To customers' requirements. See Cockpit.
Wing characteristics: Straight, low mounted, with dihedral and fixed tip-tanks.

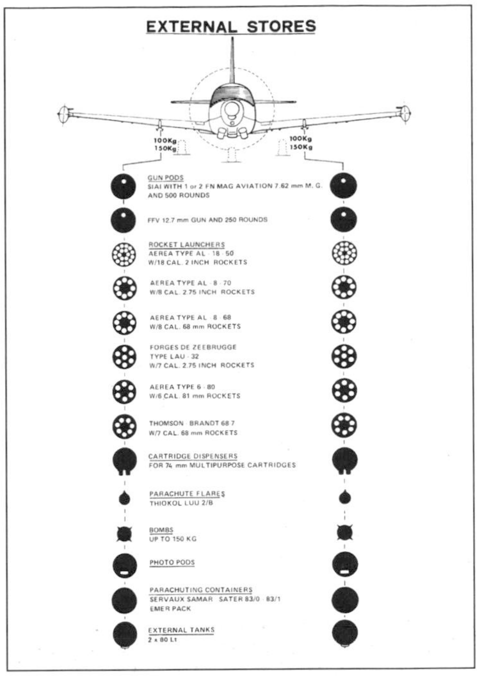

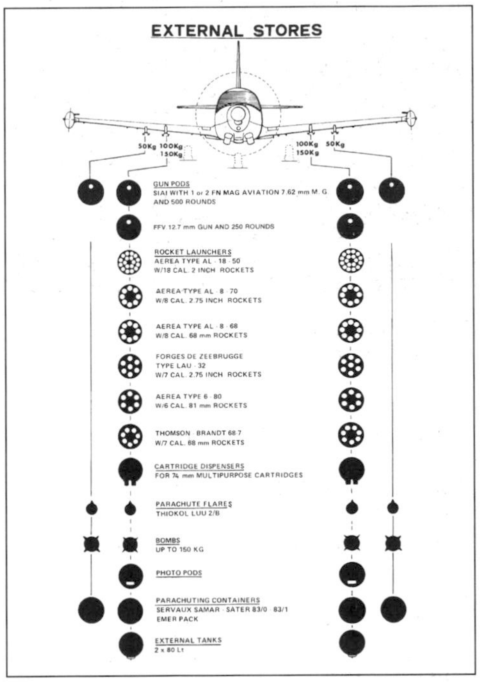

SIAI Marchetti SF260E/F Warrior (top) and SF260TP Warrior weapon options (courtesy SIAI Marchetti)

SIAI Marchetti SF260Ds in Turkish Air Force use

SIAI Marchetti SF260TP in full camouflage

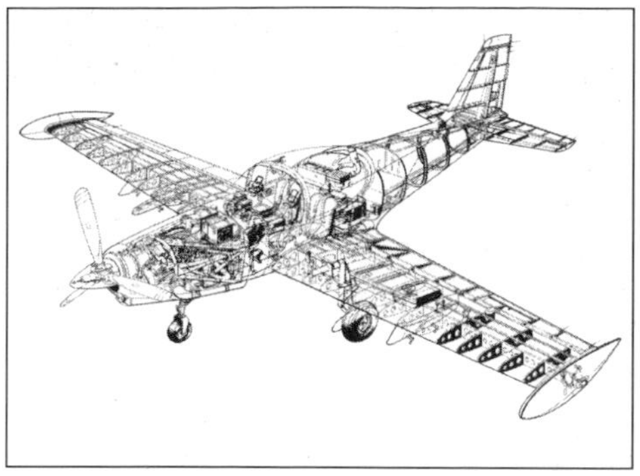

SIAI Marchetti SF260TP cutaway (courtesy SIAI Marchetti)

Wing control surfaces: Frise type ailerons (with tabs) and slotted flaps.
Tail control surfaces: Horn balanced elevators (starboard tab on SF260E/F, port on SF260TP), and horn balanced rudder (with tab on TP).
Flight control system: Dual cable primary controls, with 3-axis trim. Electric flaps.
Construction materials: Metal, stressed skin.
Engine: 260 hp (194 kW) Textron Lycoming AIO-540-D4A5 in SF260E, O-540-E4A5 for SF260F, with a fuel injected version available as an option, using a Hartzell HC-C2YK-1BF/8477-8R 2-blade constant-speed propeller. SF260TP uses a 350 shp (261 kW) Allison 250-B17D fully aerobatic turboprop, with a 76 ins (1.93 m) Hartzell HC-B3TF-7A/T10173-25R 3-blade propeller.
Engine rating: See above.
Fuel system: 243 litres in 4 aluminium alloy tanks: 2 wing tanks of 99 litres the pair and 2 fixed tip-tanks of 144 litres the pair, with fuel selector, filter and booster pumps.
Electrical system: 24 volt DC, with an alternator-rectifier and 24 amp-hour ni-cd battery.
Braking system: Mainwheel discs.
De-icing system: Electrical for the engine air intake of the SF260TP available.

Aircraft variants:
SF260A, B, C and D are unarmed versions principally for civil customers, but are also found in military service. A, B and C are out of production, and the final Ds going to the air forces of Turkey and Belgium from 1992-94.
SF260E and F are current production versions of the piston trainer, as described, for civil and military use. Different engine models.
SF260M, first flown in 1970, was produced as a military version of the A. Out of production.
Warrior is the name of military versions intended to be armed.
SF260TP is the turboprop version, also available in Warrior form. As described.

DETAILS FOR SF-260E/F, *WITH SF260TP IN ITALICS*

Principal dimensions:
Wing span: 27 ft 5 ins (8.35 m)
Maximum length: 23 ft 3.5 ins (7.1 m), *24 ft 3.5 ins (7.4 m)*
Maximum height: 7 ft 11 ins (2.41 m)

Wings:
Aerofoil section: Modified NACA 64_1212, 64_1210 at root/tip
Area: 108.72 sq ft (10.1 m^2)
Aspect ratio: 6.9 with tip-tanks

Undercarriage:
Type: Retractable, with steerable nosewheel. Electrical retraction
Wheel base: 5 ft 5 ins (1.66 m)
Wheel track: 7 ft 5.5 ins (2.274 m)

Weights:
Empty: 1,717 lb (779 kg)
Maximum take-off: 2,645 lb (1,200 kg) for SF260E/F *and SF260TP as trainer, 2,866 lb (1,300 kg) armed*

Performance (SF260E/F at 2,425 lb, 1,100 kg weight; SF260TP at 2,645 lb, 1,200 kg weight):
Maximum speed: 187 kts (216 mph) 347 km/h, *230 kts (265 mph) 426 km/h at 10,000 ft (3,000 m)*
Cruise speed: *216 kts (249 mph) 400 km/h at 10,000 ft (3,050 m)*
Stall speed: 60 kts (69 mph) 111 km/h with full flaps, *68 kts (79 mph) 126 km/h with full flaps*
Take-off distance: 1,575 ft (480 m), *978 ft (298 m)*
Landing distance: 1,460 ft (445 m), *1,008 ft (307 m)*
Maximum climb rate: 1,800 ft (546 m) per minute, *2,165 ft (660 m) per minute*
G limits: +6. -3
Ceiling: 19,000 ft (5,800 m), *24,600 ft (7,500 m)*
Range with full fuel: 805 naut miles (926 miles) 1,490 km, *512 naut miles (590 miles) 950 km*
Ferry range: 596 naut miles (686 miles) 1,104 km
SF260E/F typical training mission: 50 naut miles (57.6 miles) 93 km distance at 170 kts (196 mph) 315 km/h and 3,000 ft (914 m) altitude (2,513 lb, 1,140 kg take-off weight), with 2 hours 42 minutes over the operating area before return, with total elapsed time of 3 hours 19 minutes, allowing a 44 lb (20 kg) fuel reserve
SF260E/F typical aerobatic training mission: 25 naut miles (29 miles) 46 km distance at 150 kts (173 mph) 278 km/h at 3,000 ft (914 m) altitude (2,293 lb, 1,040 kg take-off weight), with 40 minutes over the operating area before return, with total elapsed time of 1 hour, allowing a 33 lb (15 kg) fuel reserve
SF260TP typical armed mission: Cruise at 180 kts (207 mph) 333 km/h and 200 ft (61 m) altitude to target at 80 naut miles (92 miles) 148 km distance, 20 minutes over target before return at 145 kts (167 mph) 268 km/h and 10,000 ft (3,050 m), with a total elapsed time of 1 hour 25 minutes, allowing a 44 lb (20 kg) fuel reserve

Alenia (Italy)

Corporate address: Via E. Petrolini 2, 00197 Roma.
Telephone: +39 6 807781
Facsimile: +39 6 8072215, 8075184
Telex: 611395 Alenia I
Founded: 20 December 1990, following the merger of Aeritalia and Selenia. Undergoing further changes in 1995. Part of the Finmeccanica SpA group.
Employees: Approximately 25,000.
Information: Riccardo Rovere.

● Activities
- Main non-US subcontractor to McDonnell Douglas on the MD-11 programme, amounting to 12.11% of the airframe value. Includes 300 series of winglets, fins and rudders, and fuselage panels. Also, the first cargo hatch (the largest ever fitted on a commercial aircraft), manufactured at the Capodichino factories, for the combi version was delivered in October 1990. Alenia is also contracted to produce fuselage sections for the MD-95.
- G222 production and support, with the latest order for 6 coming from Thailand (see Freighter section).
- F-104ASA and TF-104G modernization (see below).
- Boeing 707 tanker conversions (see Freighter section).
- Boeing 727 re-engining programme through Dee Howard Co, a subsidiary company (see Airlines section).
- Participation in the Dassault 2000 programme, including Alenia personnel working at Dassault during the definition phase, and development at Alenia's Turin factories and at Piaggio's Finale Ligure factories.
- Multi-national programmes include Airbus A321, AMX, ATR series, Eurofighter 2000, FLA and Tornado.

Alenia F-104ASA M

▲ Development
▲ In 1982 it was decided to modernize the Aeritalia-built F-104S interceptors and attack aircraft to new ASA (Aggiornamento Sistema d'Arma) standard, by upgrading the weapon system. The modernization affected mainly the radar (new FIAR R21G/M1 Setter), which now allows the F-104ASA to operate against aircraft flying at extremely low altitudes. The upgraded aircraft were redelivered to the Italian Air Force between December 1986 and February 1993.
▲ To extend the F-104ASA's operational life until Eurofighter 2000 is available, the ASA M (maintainability) modernization programme has been drafted to keep 100 F-104ASA Ms operational into the next century. The number, which could rise to 108, includes TF-104G two-seat operational trainers.
▲ The ASA M programme calls for the installation of equipment similar to that in Tornado and AMX. This is aimed at ensuring better maintenance due to the availability of spares, lower costs, and maximum commonality in substitute components. The modernization entails rewiring of the power system and the substitution of navigation avionics.
▲ Alenia is producing a retrofit kit for the ASA M, with certification expected in late 1995 and initial operational capability of F-104ASA Ms two years later. Immediate plans cover 30 F-104ASA Ms and 18 TF-104G upgrades.

Alenia F-104ASA interceptor ready for ASA M modernization

Fuji Heavy Industries Ltd (Japan)

Fuji T-5 JMSDF trainer at Shimofusa air base (K. Hinata)

Corporate address: Subaru Building, 7-2, Nishishinjuku 1-chome, Shinjuku-ku, Tokyo 160.
Telephone: +81 3 3347 2111, 2525 (2513 for Aerospace Division)
Facsimile: +81 3 3347 2338, 2588
Telex: 232 2268 FUJI J
Founded: 15 July 1953.
Employees: Approximately 15,300, of which over 3,000 in the aerospace division.
Information: Publicity office +81 3 3347 2023.

DIVISIONS

Utsunomiya Manufacturing Division

HQ address: 1-11, Yonan 1-chome, Utsunomiya, Tochigi 320.
Telephone: +81 286 58 1114

● Activities

● Subordinate to the Aerospace/Transportation Equipment (Rolling Stock) Division. Major participant in FS-X development, and manufactures components for Boeing 747 (aileron), 757 (outboard flap), 767 (wing/body fairing and main undercarriage door) and 777 (wing/body fairing and main undercarriage door), McDonnell Douglas MD-11 (outboard aileron) and Fokker 50 airliners. These include over 40,000 hybrid honeycomb panels of carbonfibre/Kevlar for Boeing 767/777 wing/body fairings.

● Prime contractor for Japanese-built AH-1S and UH-1 helicopters, and developed the T-5 trainer for the Maritime Self Defence Force.

● Undertakes subcontract work within the Japanese industry on the Kawasaki-led P-3C and Mitsubishi-led F-15J programmes, plus the T-4 trainer (fin, tailplane, tailcone, fairings, wingtips, wing/flap trailing edge), and the Patriot air defence system.

● J/AQM-1 and Flying Forward Observation System UAV systems.

● Develops high-performance composite materials and structures for space vehicles and plays an important development role in projects of Japan's National Aerospace Development Agency and National Aerospace Laboratory.

Non-aerospace divisions are:

Automobile Division

Transportation Equipment (Bus) Division

Industrial Products Division

Fuji T-5

First flight: 27 April 1988, following trials with a re-engined KM-2 from 1984.
Role: Primary/basic trainer and utility aircraft, capable of aerobatics.

★ Aims

★ Lighter and higher-performing development of the KM-2, with a turboprop engine, sliding blister-type canopy, and upgraded cockpit with more room.

▲ Development

▲ 30 August 1988. First production T-5 was delivered to the JMSDF.
Sales/users: 32 for the JMSDF. Further 5 aircraft have been requested from FY1995 funding.
Crew: 2 for training and aerobatics, and 4 persons in a utility role.
Cockpit: Dual controls. Upgraded from the KM-2.
Fixed guns: None.
Number of weapon pylons: None.
Flight/weapon system avionics/instrumentation: IFR.
Wing characteristics: Straight, low mounted, with dihedral.
Wing control surfaces: Ailerons (with tabs) and single-slotted flaps.
Tail control surfaces: Horn-balanced elevators and rudder, all with tabs.
Flight control system: Mechanical.
Construction materials: Metal.
Engine: Allison 250-B17D turboprop.
Engine rating: 420 shp (313.3 kW), flat rated to 350 shp (261 kW).
Fuel system: 363 litres in the wings.
Electrical system: 30 volt DC supply via a starter-generator. Ni-cd battery for engine starting and operation in emergency conditions. 2 static inverters for AC supply.
Braking system: Hydraulic disc type.

DETAILS FOR T-5.

Principal dimensions:
Wing span: 32 ft 11 ins (10.04 m)
Maximum length: 27 ft 8 ins (8.44 m)
Maximum height: 9 ft 9 ins (3 m)

Wings:
Aerofoil section: NACA 23016.5/23012 (root/tip)
Area: 177.6 sq ft (16.5 m^2)
Aspect ratio: 6.109
Sweepback: 0°
Incidence: 4°/1° (root/tip)
Dihedral: 6°

Undercarriage:
Type: Retractable, with steerable nosewheel
Main wheel tyre size: 6.50 x 8
Nose wheel tyre size: 5.00 x 5
Wheel base: 7 ft 5 ins (2.27 m)
Wheel track: 9 ft 7 ins (2.92 m)

Weights:
Empty: 2,385 lb (1,082 kg)
Maximum take-off: 3,980 lb (1,805 kg)

Performance:
Maximum speed: 192 kts (221 mph) 356 km/h
Stall speed: 56 kts (65 mph) 104 km/h with flaps
Take-off distance: 991 ft (302 m) at 3,494 lb (1,585 kg) aerobatic weight
Landing distance: 571 ft (174 m) at aerobatic weight
Maximum climb rate: 1,700 ft (518 m) per minute, at aerobatic weight
Ceiling: 25,000 ft (7,620 m)
Range with full payload: 509 naut miles (586 miles) 944 km

Kawasaki Heavy Industries Ltd (Japan)

Corporate address: Tokyo Head Office: World Trade Centre Building, 4-1, Hamamatsu-cho 2-chome, Minato-ku, Tokyo 105. Kobe Head Office: Kobe Crystal Tower, 1-3, Higashikawasaki-cho 1-chome, Chuo-ku, Kobe 650-91.
Telephone: +81 3435 2111 (Tokyo), +81 78 371 9530 (Kobe)
Facsimile: +81 3 3436 3037 (Tokyo), +81 78 371 9568 (Kobe)
Telex: 242 4371 (Tokyo), 5622 355 (Kobe)
Founded: 1918 an aircraft department of Kawasaki Dockyard was founded at the Hyogo Works; 1937 the aircraft department separated from then-Kawasaki Rolling Stock Manufacturing Co at Hyogo to form Kawasaki Aircraft Co Ltd; 1969 Kawasaki Aircraft, Rolling Stock Manufacturing and Dockyard merged to form Kawasaki Heavy Industries.
Employees: 17,400, of which nearly 5,000 are in aerospace activities.
Information: Toshiyuki Nagai (Helicopter Sales, Aircraft Sales Division).

AEROSPACE DIVISION

■ Factories at

■ Gifu (1, Kawasaki-cho, Kakamigahara, Gifu 504) for manufacturing, repair and overhaul of equipment for commercial aircraft, anti-submarine aircraft, fighters, trainers and helicopters, plus missiles and space equipment.

■ Nogoya 1 (11, Kusunoki 3-chome, Yatomi-cho, Ama-gun, Aichi 498) and Nagoya 2 (7-4, Kanaoka, Tobishima-mura, Ama-gun, Aichi 490-14), for manufacturing and assembly of airframes.

■ Akashi and Seishin for manufacturing and overhaul of jet engines, helicopter transmissions, and more.

● Activities

● Aerospace accounts for about 24.2% of Kawasaki's total group sales.

● Manufactures the T-4 trainer, and is prime contractor for Japanese P-3C anti-submarine aircraft and Boeing Chinook helicopters (following earlier production of 160 KV107IIAs). Undertakes parts production and partial assembly for F-15J fighters, and supplies components for the Boeing 767 and 777 plus part of the fuselage for the Airbus A321. Manufactures the BK 117 helicopter (with Eurocopter) plus versions of the McDonnell Douglas MD 500 helicopter under licence. Also prime contractor for the tandem-seat OH-X Kongata Kansoku, the armed small observation helicopter programme.

Kawasaki-produced Lockheed P-3C anti-submarine and patrol aircraft. Operated since the early 1980s, deliveries of the final specialized variants to the JMSDF are still underway, with the last 2 aircraft (an EP-3 electronic intelligence and a UP-3D EW trainer) requested from FY1995 funding. The total of 109 JMSDF P-3 types includes 4 EP-3s, 1 UP-3C testbed and 2 UP-3Ds. 10 crew, T56-IHI-14 turboprop engines, 410 kts maximum speed and 4,200 naut mile range (K. Hinata)

Kawasaki T-4 with underwing load at Hyakuri air base in October 1994 (K. Hinata)

● Engine development and manufacture includes participation in the multi-national V2500 turbofan programme. It is also engaged in research for Supersonic Transport/Hypersonic Transport engines.
● Space activities include overseeing construction of the H-II launch vehicle complex, and development and manufacture of payload fairings. Other space programmes include the HOPE-X orbiting spaceplane, Japanese Experiment Module (JEM) as part of the Space Station programme, and rendezvous and docking systems.

Kawasaki T-4 and AT-X

First flight: 29 July 1985.
Role: Intermediate trainer.

★ Aims

★ To replace the T-33 operating with the JASDF, and subsequently the T-1 primary jet trainer.
★ Good flying characteristics over a broad speed range, to ease student pilots from primary trainers and on to advanced trainers.

▲ Development

▲ 4 September 1981. Japan Defence Agency officially designated Kawasaki prime contractor for development of the T-4, covering FY1981-1988.
▲ October 1981. Development was initiated, basic design taking 12 months.
▲ Early 1988. Testing of 4 flying prototypes completed.
▲ 28 June 1988. Maiden flight of a series-built T-4, with deliveries starting that September.

Sales/users: Some 200 required by the JASDF, of which 154 have been funded, including 9 ordered in 1994 and 10 in FY1995.
Details: T-4.
Crew: 2, with rear instructor's seat raised by 10.5 ins (27 cm). Baggage hold provided.
Crew escape: UPC SHIS-3J ejection seats.
Fixed guns: None.
Number of pylons: 5, with underfuselage pylon for EW dispenser, target towing gear or other pod, and 2 under each wing for auxiliary fuel tanks or equipment pods.
Expendable weapons and equipment: Not armed.
Radar: None.
Flight/weapon system avionics/instrumentation: Includes air data computer, Tacan, VOR/ILS and AHRS. Shimadzu-built J/AVQ-1 head-up display.
Wing characteristics: Shoulder mounted, sweptback, with anhedral. Dog-tooth leading edges. Root extensions merge leading edges with air intakes.
Wing control surfaces: Ailerons and double-slotted flaps.
Tail control surfaces: Slab tailplane and rudder.
Airbrakes: 2, on the rear fuselage.
Flight control system: Hydraulic.
Construction materials: Metal, except for composites ailerons, airbrakes, fin, sections of the flaps/tailplane, and rudder.
Engines: 2 x Ishikawajima-Harima F3-IHI-30 turbofans.
Engine rating: Each 3,682 lbf (16.38 kN) at take-off.
Air intakes: Fuselage sides, ahead of the wings.
Fuel system: Over 2,240 litres. Optional 454 litre drop tanks.
Electrical system: 2 engine-driven starter generators.
Hydraulic system: 3,000 psi (dual).
Braking system: Mainwheel brakes and anti-skid system.

Aircraft variants:
T-4 is the standard intermediate jet trainer, as described.
AT-X is a projected advanced training and upgraded derivative of the T-4, to replace the supersonic T-2 trainer by the year 2002. Another contender is a variant of the FS-X.

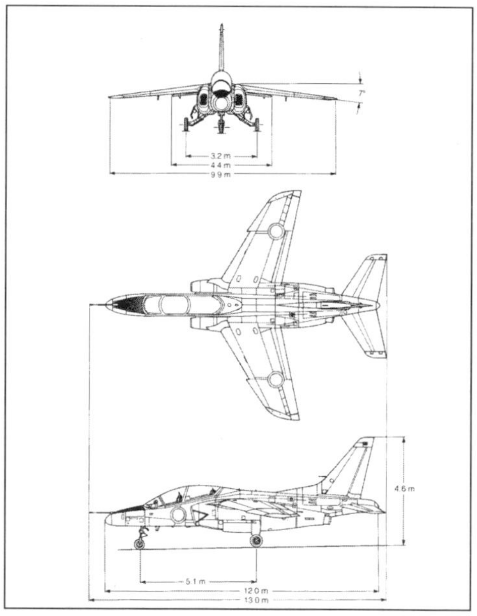

Kawasaki T-4 intermediate trainer drawing (courtesy Kawasaki)

DETAILS FOR T-4.

Principal dimensions:
Wing span: 32 ft 6 ins (9.9 m)
Maximum length: 42 ft 8 ins (13 m) including probe
Maximum height: 15 ft 1 ins (4.6 m)

Wings:
Aerofoil section: Supercritical
Area: 226.04 sq ft (21 m^2)
Aspect ratio: 4.67
Sweepback: 27.5° at 25% chord
Incidence: 0°
Anhedral: 7°

Tail unit:
Tailplane span: 14 ft 5 ins (4.4 m)

Undercarriage:
Type: Retractable, with nosewheel
Wheel base: 16 ft 9 ins (5.1 m)
Wheel track: 10 ft 6 ins (3.2 m)
Turning radius: 31 ft (9.45 m)

Weights:
Empty: 8,355 lb (3,790 kg)
Maximum take-off: 12,544 lb (5,690 kg) clean, 16,535 lb (7,500 kg) design

Performance:
Maximum speed: Mach 0.9, at 10,692 lb (4,850 kg) all-up weight with 50% fuel load
Maximum speed at sea level: 560 kts (645 mph) 1,038 km/h, weight and fuel as above
Cruise speed: Mach 0.75, at 12,544 lb (5,690 kg) all-up weight
Stall speed: 90 kts (104 mph) 167 km/h at 10,692 lb (4,850 kg) weight
Take-off distance: 2,001 ft (610 m) at 12,544 lb (5,690 kg) weight, 35° C
Landing distance: 2,100 ft (640 m) at 10,692 lb (4,850 kg) weight
Maximum climb rate: 10,000 ft (3,050 m) per minute, at 12,544 lb (5,690 kg) weight
Ceiling: 50,000 ft (15,240 m) at 12,544 lb (5,690 kg) weight
Range with full fuel: 700 naut miles (806 miles) 1,297 km, at 12,544 lb (5,690 kg) weight and cruise speed
Range with 2 x 454 litre drop tanks: 900 naut miles (1,036 miles) 1,667 km

Mitsubishi Heavy Industries Ltd (Japan)

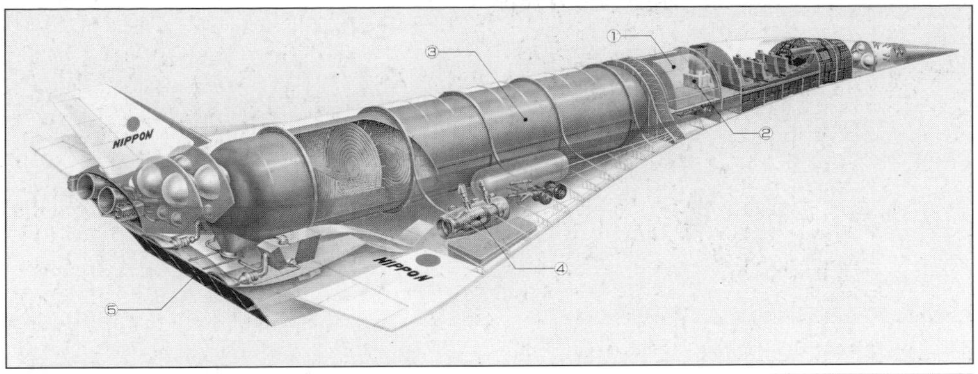

Conceptual drawing of the manned space shuttle under study for development in the 21st century by the National Aerospace Laboratory, Science and Technology Agency, in co-operation with Mitsubishi. Take off and landing would be similar to a conventional aeroplane. Liquified air cycle engine (LACE) for low speeds and in vacuum, and scramjet for high speed in air. 1 Cargo bay; 2 air lock; 3 fuel tank for slush hydrogen; 4 jet engine for return; 5 air intake (courtesy Mitsubishi)

Corporate address: 5-1, Marunouchi 2-chome, Chiyoda-ku, Tokyo 100.
Telephone: +81 3 3212 3111
Facsimile: +81 3 3212 9865
Telex: J22282, J22443
Founded: Aerospace division had its foundations in 1921 and by 1945 had produced over 18,000 aircraft; reorganized in December 1952.
Employees: Over 44,800 total employees.
Information: Wataru Tsunefuka (Aerospace & Special Vehicle Administration Department).

AEROSPACE & SPECIAL VEHICLE DIVISION

● Activities

- Undertaking development of the FS-X (Fighter Support Experimental), leading the nation's team that includes Fuji, Japan Aviation Electronics Industry Ltd (1-21-6 Dogenzaka, Shibuya-ku, Tokyo 150) and Kawasaki among others.
- Prime contractor for Japanese licence-built H-60J helicopters and F-15J fighters (again involving Fuji, Kawasaki and ShinMaywa), and also modernizing the JASDF's F-4EJ fleet.
- Active in development and production of the Canadian Global Express.
- Subcontract activities include parts for the Boeing 737-700/800 (wing flaps), 747 (inboard wing flap), 767 (rear fuselage sections) and 777 (passenger doors and panels), and McDonnell Douglas MD-11 (tailcone) and MD-80 (wing trailing edge).
- Aero engines (including the V2500) and space vehicle construction, serving as systems' integrator to Japan's National Space Development Agency; the first H-II vehicle was launched from Tanegashima on 4 February 1994.

Mitsubishi F-1

Photograph shows F-1 single-seat close support fighters, developed from the Mitsubishi T-2 supersonic trainer. The first of 77 built was flown on 16 June 1977, and deliveries to the JASDF took place between 26 September 1977 and March 1987. It has a fully automatic navigation system, and uses Mitsubishi J/AWG-12 radar. 1 x 20-mm JM61 cannon and 6,000 lb (2,720 kg) of weapons on 5 pylons. Wing span 25 ft 10 ins (7.88 m), length 58 ft 7 ins (17.85 m), and height 14 ft 8.5 ins (4.48 m). 2 x 7,305 lbf (32.5 kN) TF40-IHI-801A turbofan engines (see Adour in the Engines section). Empty weight 14,017 lb (6,358 kg) and maximum weight 30,200 lb (13,700 kg). Maximum speed Mach 1.5. To be replaced by FS-X

Mitsubishi F-4EJKai

Photograph shows an F-4EJKai, one of the 87 F-4Es being modernized (of 104 required) with Westinghouse APG-66J radar, Litton INS, Kaiser head-up-display, radar warning receiver and more, for improved fighter (AIM-7E/F Sparrows and AIM-9P/L Sidewinders), attack and anti-ship (ASM-1 missiles) roles. Another 17 F-4Es are being modernized independently into RF-4EJ tactical reconnaissance aircraft, with Texas APQ-172 radar and electronic sensor pod. Airframe life is extended to 5,000 flight hours

Mitsubishi F-15J and F-15DJ

Photograph shows F-15J Eagles, 2 of the 205 single-seat F-15Js and 2-seat F-15DJs ordered or requested for the JASDF to fiscal year 1995, of 223 required. First 2 (funded under FMS) were delivered complete from McDonnell Douglas in March 1981, followed by 8 aircraft in kit form for Japanese assembly and delivered for service to the Nyutabaru air base on 11 December 1982. 12 DJs were also delivered in assembled form. 180 F-15J/DJs had been delivered to the JASDF by 1994. They are equivalent to the US F-15C/D, but without conformal auxiliary fuel tanks and powered by Ishikawajima-Harima built F100-IHI-100 engines. Kawasaki plays a major production role, with inputs also from Fuji and ShinMaywa. Future plans include incorporation of some FS-X technologies into F-15Js, including "stealth materials" and avionics. A prototype F-15J upgrade could be ready by 1996. In a further programme, the JDA is funding an electronic countermeasures pod to be carried on an F-15J "wet" pylon, to enable an ECM escort role. Housing active phased-array radar, the pod would allow mixed FS-X/F-15J squadrons to counter heavy electronic jamming during anti-ship missions

Mitsubishi FS-X

First flight: Expected late 1995.
Role: Fighter Support Experimental – close support and anti-shipping.

★ Aims

★ To replace the F-1 with an aircraft based on the F-16 but incorporating advanced technologies from both Japan and the USA.
★ Mach 2 performance, approximately a 9 tonne payload, CCV flight mode, and ability to launch air-to-surface, medium range and short range missiles, including anti-ship.
★ Use of advanced materials and structural technology to the airframe, and incorporating cocured composite technology. Increased wing area compared to the F-16C.
★ Modification of the F-16's nose configuration, lengthened fuselage, adoption of a strengthened windshield, and use of a drag-chute.
★ Installation of advanced avionics systems, including active phased array radar.
★ Use of improved performance engines.
★ First major military aircraft development programme conducted jointly by the USA and Japan.

▲ Development

▲ October 1987. Development initiated as a modified variant of the F-16.
▲ November 1988. Memorandum of Understanding signed between the Japanese and US Governments on production work share. Separately, Mitsubishi was made prime contractor by the JDA.
▲ January 1989. Licence agreement signed between Mitsubishi and General Dynamics, allowing some design to start in the following year.
▲ February 1990. Agreement signed between Japan and the USA over technology transfer and work sharing, with the USA receiving a 40% share. General Dynamics (later Lockheed Martin) received the first of 5 development subcontracts, with work including airframe parts, various avionic systems including the stores management system, and ground test equipment.
▲ March 1990. Mitsubishi and Lockheed joint development activity began.
▲ June 1994. The rear fuselage of the first flyable FS-X prototype was handed over to Mitsubishi by Lockheed. In July Lockheed installed an F110-GE-129 engine during "fit checks". Lockheed was also to provide 16 wing leading-edge flaps (9 left hand and 7 right hand) and left-hand wingbox components, with the first flap delivered on 28 July 1994 and all shipped by mid-1995. These include some for ground testing, prototype flying and spares.
▲ 12 January 1995. Roll out of the first prototype at Mitsubishi's Komaki Minami plant. 2 static test and 3 further flying prototypes delivered from April.
▲ February 1995. Ground structural testing of FS-X began at JDA's Tachikawa centre.
▲ 12 September 1995. High speed taxi trials began.

Mitsubishi FS-X at roll-out in 1995

▲ February 1996. Expected delivery of the first prototype to the JASDF for a 1,000 hour flight testing and evaluation programme lasting until 1998.
▲ 1999. Possible delivery of initial production aircraft to the JASDF, though 2000 is more likely.
Sales/users: 2 static prototypes for a 6,000 hour test programme, and 4 flying prototypes. 130 production aircraft required, but a pending 1 year procurement delay and other governmental considerations might lead to a reduction to 65-70 aircraft for 3 operational squadrons. 12-14 are expected to be ordered in FY 1996.
Crew: Pilot, or 2 in the TFS-X.
Cockpit: HUD and displays, see Avionics. Strengthened windshield.
Crew escape: Ejection seat.
Fixed guns: 1 x 20-mm M61A1 multi-barrel cannon.

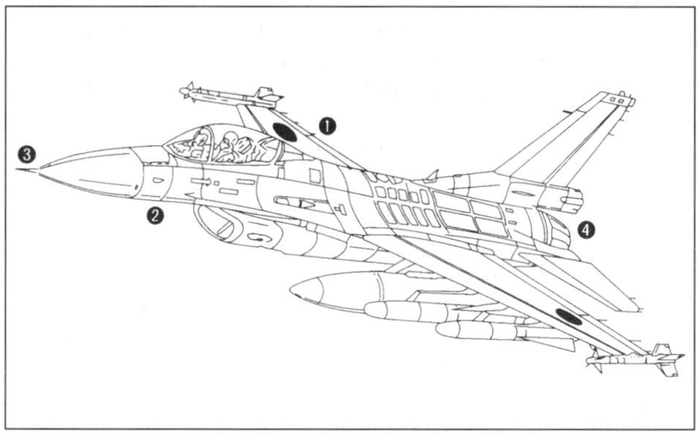

Mitsubishi FS-X drawing, showing particularly the pylon arrangements with drop tanks, missiles and wingtip AAMs (courtesy Mitsubishi)

Number of weapon pylons: 9, as 3 under each wing, 2 wingtip launch rails for air-to-air missiles, and 1 under the fuselage.
Expendable weapons and equipment: 19,840 lb (9,000 kg) payload. Wide range of possible weapons including air-to-surface, medium range and short range missiles, anti-ship missiles (ASM-2), and Sparrow or other air-to-air missiles for self defence.
Radar: Mitsubishi Electric active phased array.
Flight/weapon system avionics/ instrumentation: Japan Aviation Electronics/AlliedSignal digital flight control computers. Radar with integrated EW system, laser gyro INS, Shimadzu holographic HUD, and 3 Yokogawa liquid-crystal multi-function displays. Lockheed Martin has design responsibility for the stores management system and some other avionics and avionics support equipment items, including certain software test stations and factory test equipment.

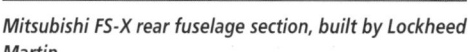

Mitsubishi FS-X rear fuselage section, built by Lockheed Martin

Self-protection systems: See Avionics, and also the previous entry for escorting F-15Js with ECM pods.
Wing characteristics: Built by Lockheed Martin (cocured wing box and lower skin), Fuji (upper skin and wing fairings).
Wing control surfaces: Flaperons (Fuji built) and 2-section leading-edge flaps (Lockheed Martin built).
Tail control surfaces: Fuji built tail unit. Slab tailplane and rudder.
Flight control system: Fly-by-wire.
Fuselage: Produced by Mitsubishi (forward section), Kawasaki (centre) and Lockheed Martin (rear). Radome manufactured by Fuji.
Construction materials: Includes advanced cocured composites, whereby the wing box and lower skin are cured and bonded in one process. Radar absorbent material for the air intake and surface leading edges. Flaps have aluminium skins and spars bonded to an aluminium honeycomb core.
Engine: General Electric F110-GE-129 turbofan.
Engine rating: 17,000 lbf (75.62 kN) dry, 29,000 lbf (128.93 kN) with afterburning.
Air intake: Under the fuselage, F-16 style, with some use of radar absorbent materials (built by Fuji).
Flight refuelling probe: Not specified at present.
Fuel system: 4,675 litres. Drop tanks can more than double fuel capacity.

Aircraft variants:
FS-X is the single-seat combat version, as described.
TFS-X is the two-seat operational training version. Advanced trainer derivative is possible, based on the TFS-X, as a contender in the T-2 replacement programme.

DETAILS FOR FS-X.

Principal dimensions:
Wing span: 36 ft 6 ins (11.13 m)
Maximum length: 50 ft 1 ins (15.27 m)
Maximum height: 16 ft 4 ins (4.97 m)

Wings:
Area: 357 sq ft (33.17 m^2)
Aspect ratio: 3.73
Sweepback: 33° 12′
Incidence: 2° 30′

Undercarriage:
Type: Retractable, with steerable nosewheel

Weights:
Empty: 21,000 lb (9,525 kg)
Maximum take-off: 48,700 lb (22,100 kg)
Payload: 19,840 lb (9,000 kg)

Performance:
Maximum speed: Quoted by Mitsubishi as approximately Mach 2

Daewoo Heavy Industries Ltd (South Korea)

Corporate address: 6 Manseok-Dong, Dong-gu, Incheon.
Telephone: +82 32 760 1114
Facsimile: +82 32 762 1546
Telex: DHILTD K28473
Cable: DHILTD INCHEON
Founded: Aerospace Division within the group founded in 1984.
Information: Kyory Do Park (Manager, Sales Department, Aerospace Division).

AEROSPACE DIVISION

HQ address: Daewoo Center Building, 20th FL.541.5-GA, Namdaemu-ro, Jung-gu, CPO Box 7955, Seoul.
Telephone: +82 2 726 3114
Telex: DHILTD K23301

● Activities

● In addition to the various helicopter programmes (described in the Helicopter section), DHI is developing the KTX-1 Yeo-Myung trainer for the indigenous air force, constructs centre fuselages for Samsung F-16 assembly, is playing an important role in the Samsung KTX-II programme, and produces components for the Boeing 747 and Dornier 328. It has reportedly also proposed fitting new wings and a tandem cockpit to existing F-5As as an alternative lead-in fighter trainer to the KTX-2, should the latter programme be cancelled.
● DHI is participating with Samsung and Korean Air in a projected 120-passenger regional airliner programme, to be developed jointly with AVIC of China and others.
● Is expected to co-build the MiG 822 trainer.
● Under South Korea's foreign military purchases, DHI has produced components for the BAe Hawk Mk 67, Bell Canada helicopters, Lockheed Martin P-3C Update III and Westland Super Lynx Mk 99.

Daewoo KTX-1 Yeo-Myung

First flight: 12 December 1991.
Role: Primary trainer, capable of aerobatics. Can be armed.

▲ Development

▲ 1988. Programme to develop a Korean trainer began. Daewoo's first complete aircraft project as prime contractor and South Korea's first indigenous aircraft. Also participating in the programme are Korean Air, Samsung and GSP.
▲ 12 December 1991. First flight of the first of 6 prototypes. Flight testing will last until 1997.
▲ 1998. Start of KT-1 production. These aircraft will feature a Fairey Hydraulics undercarriage among other changes to the prototypes.
Sales/users: Up to 100 production KT-1 Yeo-Myungs are expected to be produced for the Air Force.
Crew: 2, in tandem, with the instructor having a raised cockpit to improve forward vision.
Number of weapon pylons: Probably 4 under the wings, 2 "wet".
Expendable weapons and equipment: Machine-guns and rockets.
Flight/weapon system avionics/instrumentation: IFR, including VOR/ILS, Tacan and marker beacon receiver.
Wing characteristics: Straight, low mounted, with dihedral.
Wing control surfaces: Ailerons with tabs and split flaps.

Daewoo KTX-1 Yeo-Myung trainer with test equipment attached

Tail control surfaces: Elevators and rudder (with tab).
Airbrake: Under the fuselage. Actuator by Fairey Hydraulics.
Flight control system: Hydraulic, except for electrically actuated tabs.
Engine: Prototype 01 has a 560 shp (417.6 kW) Pratt & Whitney Canada PT6A-25A turboprop. 02 has a 1,000 shp (745.7 kW) PT6A-60A. O3 has a 950 shp (708 kW) PT6A-62. Also to be tested is the AlliedSignal TPE331 turboshaft.
Fuel system: 640 litres, mainly carried in the wings. Provision for 2 x 189 litre drop tanks.
Hydraulic system: 3,000 psi. Fairey Hydraulics accumulator, power package, sampling and shut-off valves, selector manifold, and actuators for the airbrake and flaps.
Braking system: Hydraulic type on main units.

Details for KTX-1.

Principal dimensions:
Wing span: 33 ft 3.5 ins (10.12 m)
Maximum length: 33 ft 9.5 ins (10.3 m)
Maximum height: 12 ft 3 ins (3.74 m)

Wings:
Aerofoil section: Modified NACA 63-128
Area: 166.95 sq ft (15.51 m2)
Aspect ratio: 6.603

Tail unit:
Tailplane span: 13 ft 2 ins (4 m)

Undercarriage:
Type: Retractable, with steerable nosewheel. Production aircraft will have new undercarriage designed by Fairey Hydraulics
Main wheel tyre size: 18 x 5.5
Wheel base: 9 ft 9 ins (2.96 m)
Wheel track: 9 ft (2.75 m)

Weights:
Empty: 3,152 lb (1,430 kg)
Maximum take-off: 5,470 lb (2,480 kg), or 4,250 lb (1,930 kg) for aerobatic

Performance:
Maximum speed: 310 kts (357 mph) 574 km/h
Take-off distance over a 50 ft (15 m) obstacle: 1,300 ft (400 m)
Landing distance over a 50 ft (15 m) obstacle: 1,600 ft (478 m)
Maximum climb rate: 3,500 ft (1,065 m) per minute
Ceiling: 38,000 ft (11,600 m)
Range with full fuel: 900 naut miles (1,036 miles) 1,666 km

Samsung Aerospace Industries Ltd (South Korea)

Corporate address: Samsung Life Building, 250, 2-ka, Taepyung-ro, Chung-ku, Seoul 100716.
Telephone: +82 2 751 8583, 8584
Facsimile: +82 2 751 8590, 8633, 8723
Founded: Samsung was founded in 1938, with aerospace activities from the 1980s.

● Activities

● Consortium leader/integrator in the development of the KTX-2, prime contractor for Lockheed Martin F-16Cs and Ds being constructed under licence for the Republic of Korea Air Force, and prime contractor for the proposed upgrade of the Air Force's F-5Es and F-5Fs in co-operation with Northrop Grumman, Bristol Aerospace of Canada and CASA of Spain (avionics and probable 4,000 hour airframe life extension).
● Heads the South Korean team collaborating with AVIC of China in the development of a new 120-seat regional aircraft, with signature of a collaborative agreement on 31 October 1994.
● Manufactures components for the Bell Canada 212 and 412, Boeing 757 and 767, and de Havilland DHC-8 Dash 8.

Samsung KTX-2

First flight: Year 2000.
Role: Lead-in fighter trainer and light combat.

★ Aims

★ To replace the T-33A and T-37C, of which over 70 remain.
★ Mach 1.4 maximum speed and 1,000 naut mile range.

Samsung KTX-2 impression (Bill Hobson)

▲ Development

▲ 1992. Initial design work started by South Korea's Defence Development Agency and Samsung, with major participation by Lockheed under an F-16C/D offset deal.
▲ July 1994. Selection of the present mid-mounted wing and single fin design, over the high-wing and twin fin alternative layout.
▲ 1995. Preliminary design completed. A foreign partner is being sought, with British Aerospace, Daimler-Benz and Dassault in contact.
▲ 2000. Likely first flight date.
▲ 2003. Initial operational capability.

Sales/users: Proposed for the Republic of Korea Air Force.
Crew: 2, in tandem, under a large bubble canopy.
Crew escape: Ejection seats.
Number of weapon pylons: 4 under the wings plus wingtip missile rails.
Wing characteristics: Mid mounted and sweptback, with wingtip launch rails.
Tail control surfaces: Tailplane, and single fin and rudder.
Flight control system: Fly-by-wire.
Engine: 16,000 lbf (71.2 kN) class turbofan.
Air intakes: Fuselage sides, just ahead and below of the wing roots.

Details for KTX-2.

Principal dimensions:
Wing span: 25 ft 7 ins (7.8 m)
Maximum length: 45 ft (13.7 m)

Performance:
Maximum speed: Mach 1.4
Range with full fuel: 1,000 naut miles (1,150 miles) 1,850 km

Fokker (Netherlands)

Full name: N.V. Koninklijke Nederlandse Vliegtuigenfabriek Fokker.
Corporate address: PO Box 12222, NL-1100 AE Amsterdam-Zuidoost, but to move in 1996.
Telephone: +31 20 6056666
Facsimile: +31 20 5647015
Telex: 11526 fmhs nl
Founded: 21 July 1919.
Employees: 7,300.
Information: Leo J.N. Steijn (Corporate Communications Officer – *telephone* +31 20 6057887, *facsimile* +31 20 6057599).

● Activities

● Oldest aircraft manufacturer in the world still producing aircraft under is own name. It is a publicly-held stock corporation.
● Fokker Holding, owned 78% by Daimler-Benz Aerospace and 22% by the Dutch State, has a 51% majority interest in the Fokker company. Through German participation, Fokker is part of the Daimler-Benz group.
● A separate leasing company was proposed in 1994, to acquire aircraft then leased out by Fokker, to reduce capital employed by some NLG 1 billion at the end of that year. It was expected that over the coming years the new company will finance some NLG 5 billion worth of leasing contracts for Fokker aircraft. Debis (Daimler-Benz Inter Services), the service division of Daimler-Benz, took the lead in setting up the leasing company, with Fokker itself becoming a minority shareholder.
● New Fokker Training Centre has become operational at Hoofddorp, providing training for maintenance personnel, flight crews, flight attendants and flight operations personnel of present and future F27, F28, 50, 70, 100 and derivative operators. Jointly owned by Fokker and the Friendship Simulation Company (FSC), undertaking all training (including flight) and operating the simulator facility respectively. FSC is itself a joint venture company of Fokker and the Schreiner Aviation Group. The first Fokker 70/100 full-flight simulator was installed in early 1995.
● Restructuring of the company will see the head office moved, Ypenburg plant closed, and an aerostructures division take over component manufacturing.
● In addition to the Maritime Enforcer Mk 2 detailed here, information on the Maritime Mk 2 maritime surveillance aircraft, Kingbird Mk 2 early warning and control aircraft, Sentinel Mk 2 surveillance/ reconnaissance aircraft, and Black Crow Mk 2 signal intelligence aircraft can be found in the Reconnaissance section. Fokker airliners and military transports are detailed in the Airliners section.

DIVISIONS

Fokker Aircraft B.V.
HQ address: As above.
Telephone: +31 20 605 7115
Facsimile: +31 20 605 7015

■ Facilities

■ 4 plants in early 1995 (see below for planned changes to this), at Schiphol (engineering and final assembly), Drechtsteden (parts production and component assembly) but to become part of an aerostructures division (see Activities), Ypenburg (composite structures and bonding) but scheduled to close and its work taken over at another plant, and ELMO at Woensdrecht (wire assemblies and electronics).

● Activities

● The largest operating company of Fokker, responsible for all commercial and military aircraft programmes. Its activities include design, development, production, marketing, sales and product support.
● Pioneer of hot metal bonding to produce durable, lightweight structures.
● Over 30 years, 786 Fokker F27 Friendship and 241 F28 Fellowship transports were sold to 170 customers in some 70 countries, becoming the world's top-selling civil turboprop and world's first short-haul jet respectively. Now superseded by the Fokker 50 and 60, and Fokker 70, 100 and 130 (see Airliners section).
● Also participates in multi-national programmes. Produces wing moving parts and undercarriage doors for the Airbus A300-600 and A310; is a partner in the Gulfstream V, responsible for the tail unit; builds components for the F-16 (having assembled 300 for the air forces of the Netherlands, Norway and Denmark); and collaborates in the NH90 helicopter programme.

Fokker Aircraft Services B.V.
Fokker Special Products B.V.
Fokker Space & Systems B.V.
Avio Diepen B.V.

Fokker Maritime Enforcer Mk 2

Fokker Maritime Enforcer Mk 2 operating with N°121 Squadron, Singapore Air Force, which achieved IOC in September 1995

First flight: 30 November 1992.
Role: Anti-submarine, anti-surface vessel and maritime patrol.

★ Aims

★ Based on the Fokker 50, serving as a versatile and cost-effective platform carrying dedicated mission equipment.
★ Search at sea level or cruise at altitudes up to 25,000 ft (7,620 m).
★ Loiter at 1,500 ft (460 m) or lower at speeds between 140 and 200 kts (161 and 230 mph) 259 and 370 km/h.
★ Mission endurance of up to 8 hours, 200 naut miles (230 miles) 370 km from base.

▲ Development

▲ 9 March 1991. Launch of the Fokker Maritime Enforcer Mk 2 programme.
Sales/users: In production. Orders include 5 for Singapore, operated by N°121 Squadron.

Crew: 2 pilots, plus the Tactical Co-ordinator (TACCO) responsible for tactical navigation and mission co-ordination, 2 non-acoustic sensor operators with displays and control consoles (1 monitors the search radar and IRDS, the other the ESM systems), an acoustic systems operator monitoring the processed signals from the sonobuoys dropped by the aircraft, and 2 observers who look for visual contacts through large windows in the forward fuselage (also load sonobuoys into the rotary launcher in the rear of the cabin).
Cockpit: Electronic Flight Instruments System (EFIS) cockpit displays, comprising a primary flight display and a navigation display for each pilot. Weather information can be superimposed on both navigation displays. Primary flight and navigation information can be switched from one display to the other.
Fixed guns: None.
Number of weapon pylons: 6 or 8, with 2 or 3 under each wing (including optional outer pylon) and 2 fuselage stub-wing stations (each fuselage station up to a 2,000 lb, 907 kg load).
Expendable weapons and equipment: Includes 2 Harpoon anti-ship missiles, or up to 8 homing torpedoes or depth charges. Mixed loads are possible. See Avionics for sonobuoys.
Radar: Texas Instruments AN/APS-134 search radar with 4 modes: detection of periscopes or other small targets at ranges out to 32 naut miles (37 miles) 59 km, long-range search and navigation, maritime surveillance out to 150 naut miles (173 miles) 278 km, and a track-while-scan mode. In sea state 3, the radar will detect a snorkel at 33 naut miles (38 miles) 61 km from 2,000 ft (610 m) and a patrol boat at 54 naut miles (62 miles) 100 km from 20,000 ft (6,100 m).
Flight/weapon system avionics/instrumentation: See Radar and Cockpit. Embodies the latest advances in solid state electronics, processors and displays. All mission systems are integrated via a dual redundant MIL-STD-1553B databus system. Dornier Central Tactical System is the core of the integrated mission sensor systems, and processes and correlates all input data for presentation on the colour multi-function displays fitted in the operator consoles and cockpit. On a large full-colour display, it presents the realtime tactical situation, including aircraft position, target tracks, prediction of target positions, location of sonobuoys, bearing/range circles from sonobuoys, ESM bearings, radar contact range and bearing and visual sighting (event) marks. IFF. Infra-red Detection System with zoom facility, mounted under the nose, presents passive day/night thermal images of boats and other objects on the sea surface. It complements the search radar at shorter ranges for tasks such as identification of vessels or locating survivors. Video infra-red images can be displayed in both the cockpit and cabin. Electronic Support Measures (ESM) system can detect and identify transmitting radars across the 0.5-18 GHz frequency range. Principal sensors for detecting and tracking submerged submarines are the various types of sonobuoys. The Computing Devices AN/UYS-503 Acoustical Signal Processor provides contact indentification, range and bearing information on a submarine. Magnetic anomaly detector (MAD). Automatic Flight Control System (AFCS) provides flight director and autopilot functions. The dual-channel fail-passive autopilot is certified to Cat II operation. Integrated Alerting System provides graded warning signals of abnormal operational or systems conditions by means of visual and aural warnings. Wide range of communications systems, comprising dual HF, triple V/UHF and single VHF backup, permits exchange of tactical information with co-operating sea, air and ground forces, as well as providing communication with civil/ATC authorities. Tactical Data Links and Radio Teletype (RTT) in HF and UHF bands, both secure and clear communications. Primary means of navigation is the dual inertial/GPS system.
Airframe: See Fokker 50 in the Airliners section.
Engines: 2 Pratt & Whitney Canada PW125B or PW127B turboprops (see Fokker 50 entry in the Airliners section), driving 6-blade Dowty Aerospace carbonfibre propellers.
Fuel system: 7,450 litres internally. 2 optional drop tanks, each 938 litres.

DETAILS FOR ENFORCER MK 2.

Principal dimensions: See Fokker 50 in the Airliners section

Weights:
Empty, operating: 32,620 lb (14,795 kg)
Maximum take-off: 47,500 lb (21,545 kg)
Performance: See Aims, and Fokker 50 entry in the Airliners section

Philippine Aerospace Development Corporation (Philippines)

Corporate address: Box 7395, Domestic Airport Post Office, Lock Box 1300, Domestic Road, Pasay City, Metro Manila.
Telephone: +63 2 832 37 57 or 832 27 41
Facsimile: +63 2 832 25 68
Founded: 1973.
Information: Prudencio M. Reyes Jr (President).

● Activities

● Has most recently assembled 24 SIAI-Marchetti S211 jet trainers, 18 SF260TP turboprop trainers and a number of Lancair lightplanes for the air force and police.
● Following PADC's assembly of Pilatus Britten-Norman Islanders for the armed forces and others, operates a service centre and also maintains the engines.
● Following PADC's assembly of BO 105 helicopters for the armed forces and others, Philippine Helicopter Services Inc subsidiary undertakes repair, maintenance and servicing, and acts as a spares depot. Also maintains MD 500 rotor blades.
● Undertakes repair and maintenance of Allison turboshaft and also reciprocating engines (see above).

Instytut Lotnictwa (Poland)

Corporate address: Aleja Krakowska nr 110/114, 02-256 Warszawa.
Telephone: +48 22 460 011, 460 801 (Director 460 993)
Facsimile: See Information.
Telex: 813 537
Founded: 1926.
Information: +48 22 464 432 (Marketing, *telephone* and *facsimile*).

● Activities

● In addition to wide-ranging research and development, and testing, in the fields of aircraft, engines, instrumentation and materials, several engines (see Engines section) and aircraft have been built (see General Aviation).

Instytut Lotnictwa 'Kobra 2000'

First flight: Expected 1999-2000.
Role: Close air support.
Chief designer: Włodzimierz Gnarowski.

★ Aims

★ Proposed as a replacement for Iryda in air-to-ground operations, and originally designed as a competitor to the PZL-230 Skorpion.

▲ Development

▲ Early design stage of the project.
Crew: Pilot.
Number of weapon pylons: 8, with 6 under the wings plus 2 wingtip launch rails.
Expendable weapons and equipment: Probably 8,818 lb (4,000 kg) of air-to-surface missiles, unguided rockets or bombs suspended under the wings, plus 2 air-to-air missiles at the wingtips.
Wing characteristics: Shoulder mounted, with moderate sweptback and wingroot extensions.
Tail control surfaces: Slab tailplane (possibly taileron), carried on twin rear fuselage/ventral fins. Swept fin and rudder.
Fuselage: Highly curved, with a large dorsal common air intake for the engines ahead of the tailfin.
Engines: 2 turbofans mounted in the rear fuselage, developed from the 3,970 lbf (17.65 kN) IL D-18A.

Aircraft variants:
Kobra 2000 was first named MT-2000 (myśliwiec taktyczny, tactical fighter).

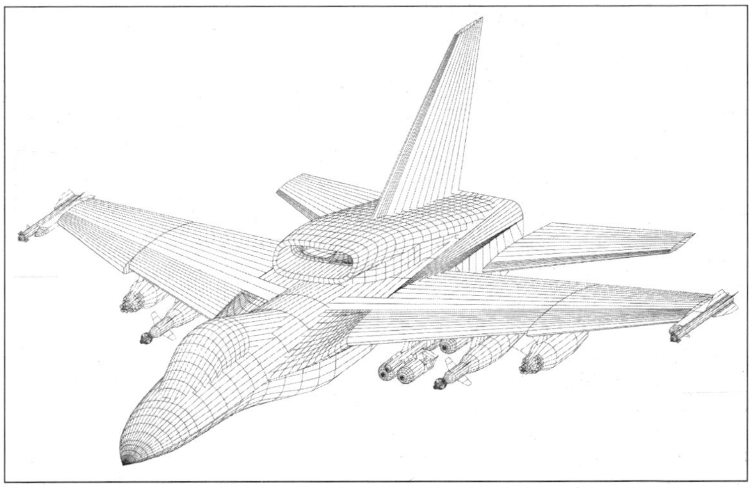

Instytut Lotnictwa Kobra 2000 computer drawing, indicating substantial armament options (courtesy Instytut Lotnictwa/via Piotr Butowski)

PZL-Mielec S.A. (Poland)

Full name: Joint Stock Company PZL-Mielec S.A., formerly known as Wytwórnia Sprzetu Komunikacyjnego PZL-Mielec (Transport Equipment Works).
Corporate address: ul. Wojska Polskiego 3, 39-300 Mielec.
Telephone: +48 196 7000, 7819
Facsimile: +48 14 214785 or 196 7226
Telex: 632293
Founded: 1938.
Information: Grazyna Utracka (Sales and Marketing Manager).

● Activities

● In addition to Iryda variants, PZL-Mielec has manufactured many thousands of An-2 Antek general-purpose transports, and continues to produce the M-28/Skytruck, M-18A Dromader agricultural aircraft and M-26 Iskierka piston trainer, plus the M-20 Mewa developed from the Piper Seneca II and now the Tampico Club TB 9 lightplane under Socata contract (see General Aviation section). Other work includes parts for the Ilyushin Il-86 and Il-96.

PZL-Mielec I-22 Iryda first production aircraft for the Polish Air Force

PZL-Mielec I-22 Iryda and Iryda M-93, M-95 and M-97

First flight: 3 March 1985 (I-22 prototype; pilot Ludwik Natkaniec).
Role: Advanced trainer and light attack, with projected dedicated combat and reconnaissance versions.

★ Aims

★ Modern replacement for the TS-11 Iskra.
★ Capable of day/night and adverse weather flying, and able to use unprepared airfields.
★ Built according to UK AP-970 regulations. Flight handling characteristics conform to the requirements of US military standards MIL-F-8785 b/ASG.
★ Structural life of 2,500 flight hours or 10,000 take-off/landings.
★ Roomy cockpits. Oxygen, fire-fighting, de-icing, air-conditioning and other airborne systems are installed.

▲ Development

▲ 15 December 1975. Governmental decision to design a new jet trainer, provisionally named Iskra-22. Design team of Instytut Lotnictwa led initially by R. Oriowski, then from 1979 by Alfred Baron, and since December 1987 by Wíodzimierz Gnarowski.
▲ 1979. Following the negative opinion of a state commission, work started on a new project. Air Force requirements were stated as: maximum speed 900 km/h, maximum Mach number 0.85, climb rate 40 metres per second, take-off distance 750 m, landing distance 900 m, and operational radius of 220 km.
▲ 1982. Technical design accepted by the Polish Air Force.
▲ 3 March 1985. First flight by prototype 02. 2 x SO-3W-22 (later renamed PZL-5) turbojets.
▲ 30 January 1987. 02 prototype crashed, killing the pilot.
▲ 1990. Work started on the I-22M-93 modernized version with Larzac 04C20 engines and Israeli avionics. Later other engines and avionics analyzed.
▲ March 1992. Joint factory and state acceptance tests of I-22 completed.
▲ 14 April 1992. I-22 Iryda officially commissioned by Polish Air Force.
▲ 5 May 1992. First flight of the first production aircraft, side number 103, c/n *AN001-03*.
▲ 24 October 1992. First 2 production aircraft, 103 and 105, ceremonially assigned to Polish Air Force.
▲ 22 December 1992. First flight of the Iryda M-93,

PZL-Mielec I-22 Iryda under construction (Piotr Butowski)

powered by K-15 turbojets (installed in *SP-PWD* prototype).

▲ 25 April 1994. First flight of the Iryda M-93V prototype, powered by Rolls-Royce Viper 545 engines (installed in *SP-PWE* prototype, piloted by Ludwik Natkaniec). Also featured new Martin Baker Mk 10L ejection seats (will be standard for the M-93).

▲ 26 May 1994. First flight of the M-93S prototype with Sagem avionics (installed in *SP-PWD*)

▲ 6 July 1994. First flight of the first production M-93K with K-15 engines (c/n *AN002-04*, registration *SP-PWF*), now used for tests by PZL Mielec.

▲ September 1994. Iryda was presented abroad for the first time (*SP-PWE* M-93V prototype) at the Farnborough Air Show in the UK.

Sales/users: 7 prototypes built as: c/n *1ANP01-01* for static tests; c/n *1ANP01-02*, side number 02, the first flying prototype; c/n *1ANP01-03*, registration *SP-PWB*, no longer flyable; c/n *1ANP01-04*, *SP-PWC*; 5th prototype initially with c/n *1ANP01-05*, later renumbered *AN001-01*, and after receiving K-15 engines renumbered again *ANAP1-01*, but with the continuous side registration *SP-PWD*, and now with K-15 engines and Sagem avionics; c/n *1ANP01-06*, later *AN001-02*, now with Viper engines and renumbered *ANBP1-01*, side registration *SP-PWE*; c/n *AN001-04*, used for fatigue tests. 6 full production aircraft built by the end of 1994 (Nos 103, 105, 201-204) and 9 aircraft per year planned against a Polish Air Force requirement of 42 aircraft for pilot schools and about 20 for training within Air Force units. All production aircraft up to 203 are in I-22 Iryda form with PZL-5 turbojets. Number 204 (c/n *AN002-04*) is the first production Iryda M-93K with PZL K-15 engines.

Details: Principally for the Iryda I-22.

Crew: 2, in tandem, the instructor's rear seat considerably stepped up by 16 ins (40 cm). See Aircraft variants for single-seat models.

Cockpit: See Aims. Cockpit pressurized.

Crew escape: VS1-BRI/P zero height ejection seats, capable of use down to 150 km/h. Martin Baker Mk 10L ejection seats are standard for the M-93.

Fixed guns: 1 x 23-mm GSz-23L 2-barrel gun in an under-fuselage pack.

Ammunition: 50-200 rounds.

Number of weapon pylons: 4 under the wings, each capable of carrying a 1,100 lb (500 kg) load; 2 are "wet".

Expendable weapons and equipment: Up to 2,646 lb (1,200 kg), typically including single bombs of 50 kg to 500 kg weight each or up to 4 x 50 kg to 100 kg bombs on each pylon using multi-store carriers, launchers for 16 or 32 x 57-mm rockets, or 2 R-60 air-to-air missiles, or a combination of weapons. Other options include gun pods or a munition dispenser.

Additional stores: Camera pods.

Radar: None.

Flight/weapon system avionics/instrumentation: IFR-rated front cockpit. Includes SOD-57M ILS, ARK-15M ADF and ORS-2M marker beacon receiver. IFF. S-13-100 gun camera and ASP PFD-122 gyro gunsight.

Self-protection systems: SPO-10 RWR.

Wing characteristics: High mounted, with swept leading-edge and straight trailing edge. Anhedral.

PZL-Mielec M-93V with Viper engines (Piotr Butowski)

Wing control surfaces: Hydraulically boosted ailerons (capable of differential operation, and with ground-adjustable tabs), and single-slotted flaps.

Tail control surfaces: Variable incidence tailplane, elevators and rudder (with ground adjustable tab).

Airbrakes: 2, aft of the wings.

Flight control system: Mechanical, except for hydraulic flaps, tailplane incidence and airbrakes.

Construction materials: Metal stressed skin, but including minor use of metal honeycomb in the elevators and non-structural composites.

Engines: 2 PZL-5 turbojets (previously known as SO-3W22s).

Engine rating: Each 2,425 lbf (10.79 kN).

Air intakes: Fuselage sides, well below and ahead of the wings.

Flight refuelling probe: None.

Fuel system: 2,430 litres in wing and fuselage tanks; maximum internal fuel weight 4,351 lb (1,974 kg). 30 seconds inverted flight allowable. 2 x 380 litre drop tanks can be carried.

Electrical system: 115 volt/400 Hz single-phase and 36 volt/400Hz 3-phase AC supply using 2 starter generators and principal and stand-by static converters. Emergency DC supply using 2 x 24 volt/25 amp-hour batteries.

Hydraulic system: 3,046 psi.

Braking system: Hydraulic disc type on main units. Parking brakes. SH21U-1 drag-chute in the tailcone.

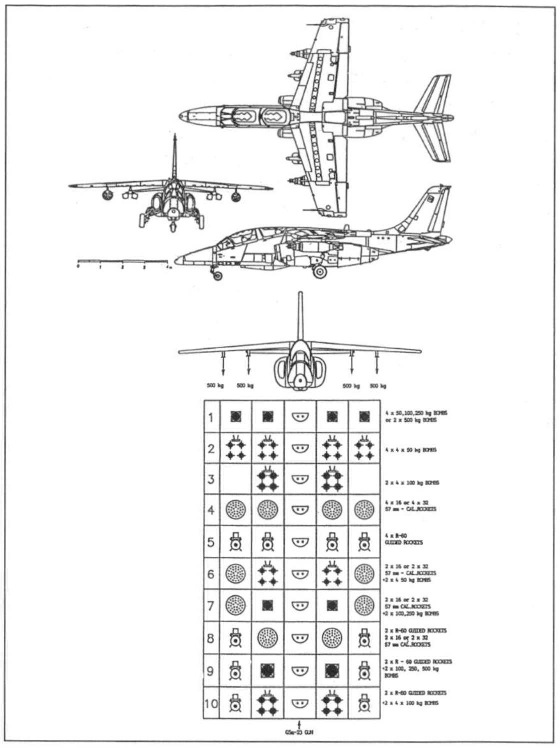

PZL-Mielec M-93 drawing and weapon choice diagram (courtesy PZL-Mielec)

De-icing system: Electrically heated front transparencies, and bleed air for the canopy and air intakes.

Details for the I-22 Iryda.

Principal dimensions:
Wing span: 31.6 ft (9.6 m)
Maximum length: 43 ft 4.5 ins (13.22 m)
Maximum height: 14 ft 1 ins (4.3 m)

Wings:
Aerofoil section: NACA 64A010, NACA 64A210 (root/tip)
Area, gross: 214.4 sq ft (19.92 m^2)
Aspect ratio: 4.627
Sweepback: 18° on leading edge
Chord at root: 9 ft 6 ins (2.9 m)
Chord at tip: 4 ft (1.25 m)
Incidence: 0°
Anhedral: 4° 30′
Twist: 1° 44′

Tail unit:
Tailplane span: 16 ft 1 ins (4.9 m)
Tailplane and elevators area: 52 sq ft (4.83 m^2)
Fin and rudder area: 39.6 sq ft (3.68 m^2)
Fin angle: 29° 48′ at 25% chord

Undercarriage:
Type: Retractable, with steerable nosewheel
Main wheel tyre size: 670 x 210 mm
Nose wheel tyre size: 430 x 170 mm
Wheel base: 16 ft 2 ins (4.92 m)
Wheel track: 8 ft 11 ins (2.71 m)

Weights:
Empty, operating: 10,141 lb (4,600 kg)
Normal take-off: 14,660 lb (6,650 kg)
Maximum take-off: 15,212 lb (6,900 kg)

Performance (clean):
Maximum operating Mach number (MMO): Mach 0.8
Maximum diving speed: 513 kts (590 mph) 950 km/h
Maximum speed at sea level: 424 kts (488 mph) 785 km/h
Maximum speed at 16,400 ft (5,000 m): 451 kts (519 mph) 835 km/h
Stalling speed: 110 kts (127 mph) 203 km/h
Time to 16,400 ft (5,000 m): 4 minutes 24 seconds
Take-off distance: 2,395 ft (730 m)
Landing distance: 2,100 ft (640 m)
Take-off distance over a 50 ft (15 m) obstacle: 3,937 ft (1,200 m)
Landing distance over a 50 ft (15 m) obstacle: 4,397 ft (1,340 m)
Maximum climb rate: 4,920 ft (1,500 m) per minute, at sea level
G limits: +7.3, -4
Service ceiling: 39,370 ft (12,000 m)
Range: 621 naut miles (715 miles) 1,150 km, at 16,400 ft (5,000 m) altitude
Duration: 2 hours 33 minutes, at 16,400 ft (5,000 m) altitude

Performance with standard weapon load of 8 x 50 kg bombs plus 2 x UB-16 rocket launchers (1,808 lb, 820 kg):
Maximum operating Mach number (MMO): Mach 0.7
Maximum diving speed: 446 kts (513 mph) 826 km/h
Maximum speed at sea level: 369 kts (425 mph) 684 km/h
Maximum speed at 13,125 ft (4,000 m): 375 kts (431 mph) 694 km/h
Time to 16,400 ft (5,000 m): 6 minutes 48 seconds
Take-off distance: 4,101 ft (1,250 m)
Landing distance: 2,494 ft (760 m)
Take-off distance over a 50 ft (15 m) obstacle: 7,218 ft (2,200 m)
Landing distance over a 50 ft (15 m) obstacle: 5,151 ft (1,570 m)
Maximum climb rate: 3,307 ft (1,008 m) per minute at sea level
G limits: +6, -3
Ceiling: 31,170 ft (9,500 m)
Range: 327 naut miles (376 miles) 605 km, at 16,400 ft (5,000 m) altitude
Radius of action: 108 naut miles (124 miles) 200 km
Duration: 1 hour 32 minutes at 16,400 ft (5,000 m) altitude

Aircraft variants:
I-22 Iryda (code named W-300) is the standard training version, with 2 x PZL-5 (SO-3W-22) turbojets.
Iryda M-93 (originally named I-22M-93) is a modified combat trainer with new engines, intended to train pilots in operational flights and also to perform tactical operational missions. The following engines have been tested: IL K-15 (3,307 lbf, 14.72 kN), IL D-18A (3,970 lbf, 17.65 kN), SNECMA Larzac 04-C20 (3,174 lbf, 14.1 kN), Rolls-Royce Viper 535 (3,360 lbf, 14.95 kN) and Pratt & Whitney Canada JT15D-5C (3,190 lbf, 14.19 kN). Due to financial restrictions, work on D-18A ceased; more powerful versions of the K-15, named K-16 (3,527 lbf, 15.69 kN) and K-18 (3,968 lbf, 17.65 kN), are under development.
Iryda M-93K is an M-93 sub-variant with K-15 Kaszub engines, for Polish Air Force.
Iryda M-93M is a projected marine attack/reconnaissance version, similar to the M-93 but with specialized equipment or armament.
Iryda M-93S is similar to the M-93 but with a French Sagem MAESTRO nav/attack system that includes Uliss 92 inertial navigation system, multi-channel GPS, wide-view HUD and EFIS colour displays. WDNS allows actual weapon delivery as well as simulated firing through state-of-the-art technology. HOTAS control.
Iryda M-93V is the export sub-variant of the M-93, with Rolls-Royce Viper 535 engines. Empty weight 9,920 lb (4,500 kg). Take-off weight 19,180 lb (8,700 kg). Maximum speed 515 kts (593 mph) 955 km/h. Take-off run 2,445 ft (745 m). Service ceiling 45,000 ft (13,700 m). Ferry range 648 naut miles (745 miles) 1,200 km.
Iryda M-95 (originally named I-22M-95) is a projected two-seat tactical reconnaissance/ground attack version. Similar to the M-93 but with new swept wings with supercritical aerofoil sections, modified tail unit, updated avionics, and special reconnaissance equipment. Fixed 30-mm cannon, provision for AAMs, ASMs and bombs. Design data figures includes a maximum speed of 502-540 kts (578-621 mph) 930-1,000 km/h (depending on the engines), combat radius with 4,409 lb (2,000 kg) of armament of 135-189 naut miles (155-217 miles) 250-350 km, maximum take-off weight of 19,180-20,944 lb (8,700-9,500 kg), and weapon load of 4,850-6,614 lb (2,200-3,000 kg). Programme frozen due to a lack of financial support.
Iryda M-97S (szturmowy, attack) is a projected single-seat light ground attack aircraft, similar to the M-95 but with a reconfigured fuselage nose with single cockpit. Design data figures are similar to the M-95 except for a maximum take-off weight of 19,180-21,605 lb (8,700-9,800 kg) and weapon load of 5,512-7,716 lb (2,500-3,500 kg).
Iryda M-97MS (myśliwsko-szturmowy, fighter-attack) is a projected fighter-attack version, differing from the M-97S in armament system only.

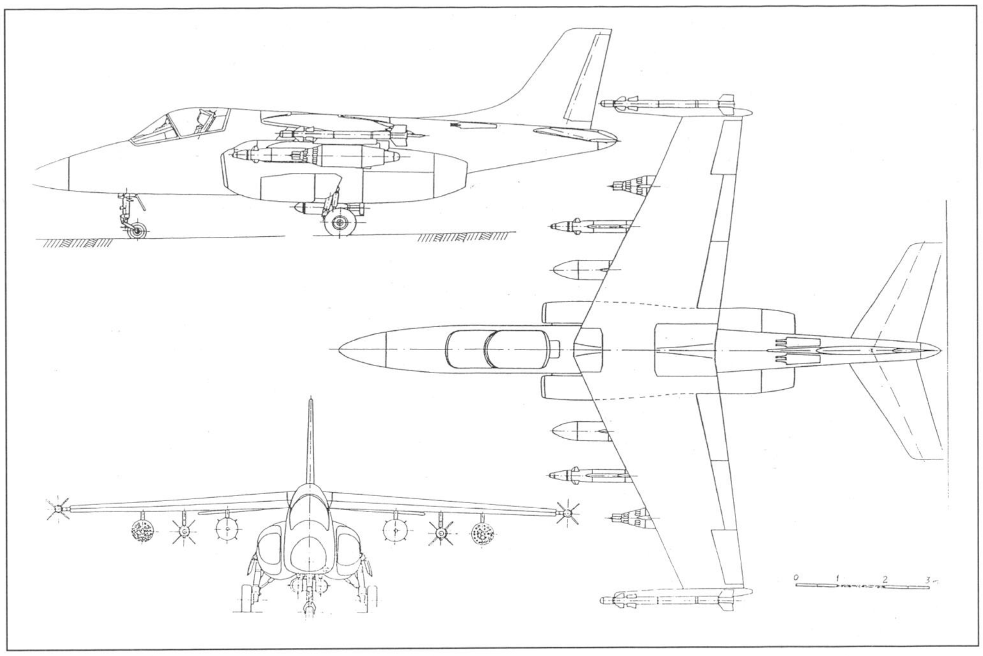

PZL-Mielec M-99 Orkan drawing (courtesy PZL-Mielec)

M-99 Orkan is a ground attack aircraft, detailed in a separate entry.

PZL-Mielec M-99 Orkan

First flight: Not yet flown.
Role: Close air support; derived from I-22 Iryda (or, more exactly, from the Iryda M-97 project).

▲ Development
▲ Project stage.
Crew: Pilot only.
Fixed guns: 30-mm cannon.
Ammunition: 250 rounds.
Number of weapon pylons: 10, comprising 3 under each wing, wingtip AAM launch rails, and 2 under the fuselage.
Expendable weapons and equipment: Up to 9,039 lb (4,100 kg). Standard light weapons of Polish, Russian and Western origin, including infra-red air-to-air missiles (for example, Magic 2), laser-guided air-to-surface missiles (for example, Kh-25ML, AS-10 *Karen*), ZK-300 Kisajno submunitions dispensers, bombs, rockets, etc.
Airframe: As for the M-97 Iryda, although the fuselage has been modified around the engine nacelles because of the more powerful turbofans. Strengthened undercarriage.
Engines: 2 x 4,851 lbf (21.58 kN) Povazské Strojárne DV-2 turbofans, or 5,990 lbf (26.65 kN) Rolls-Royce Turbomeca Adour Mk 871 turbofans.

DETAILS FOR M-99 ORKAN WITH ADOUR ENGINES (*DETAILS WITH DV-2S IN ITALICS IF DIFFERENT*).

Principal dimensions:
Wing span: 35 ft 6.5 ins (10.83 m)
Maximum length: 43 ft 4.5 ins (13.22 m)
Maximum height: 15 ft 2 ins (4.62 m)

Wings:
Area: 247.57 sq ft (23 m^2)
Aspect ratio: 5.1

Weights:
Maximum take-off: 26,301 lb (11,930 kg), 25,794 lb *(11,700 kg)*

Performance:
Maximum speed: 551 kts (634 mph) 1,020 km/h, *505 kts (581 mph) 935 km/h*
Take-off distance: 1,378 ft (420 m), *1,739 ft (530 m)*
Maximum climb rate: 15,550 ft (4,740 m) per minute, *7,875 ft (2,400 m) per minute*, at sea level
Ceiling: 47,245 ft (14,400 m)
Radius of action: 162-243 naut miles (186-280 miles) 300-450 km, at low altitude and with 6,614 lb (3,000 kg) of weapons

PZL-Warszawa Okecie (Poland)

Full name: Panstwowe Zaklady Lotnicze Warszawa Okecie SA.
Corporate address: Aleja Krakowska nr 110/114, 00-971 Warszawa.
Telephone: +48 22 460 031
Facsimile: +48 22 462 701
Founded: 1 January 1928.

● Activities
● Produces a range of light and agricultural aircraft in addition to the trainers detailed here (see also the General Aviation section). The PZL-230 Skorpion ground attack aircraft project will now encompass AlliedSignal engines and avionics.

PZL-Warszawa Okecie PZL-130 Orlik

First flight: 12 October 1984 (original piston-engined Orlik, with pilot Witold Lukomski). 16 July 1986 for the Orlik Turbo (pilot Jerzy Wojnar), now known simply as Orlik.
Role: Fully aerobatic basic, advanced and combat trainer, plus counter-insurgency (TC-3).

★ Aims
★ Original piston-engined Orlik was designed for both civil and military training and limited operational roles, with the cockpit instrumentation configured to permit easy transition to jet aircraft. Difficulty obtaining the required AOOT M-14PM radial engine led to its demise after prototype flying.
★ Orlik Turbo, already well under development when Orlik was cancelled, offered jet-like handling combined with turboprop efficiency.
★ Designed to comply with US FAR 23, Amdt 28.

▲ Development
▲ 1979. Design work on the PZL-130 Orlik (Eaglet) piston-engined trainer began. The chief designer was Andrzej Frydrychewicz, assisted by Tomasz Wolf.
▲ July 1982. Full-scale mock-up commissioned.
▲ 12 October 1984. First flight of prototype c/n 002, side-marked *SP-PCA*, powered by an M-14PM radial piston engine.

▲ 1985. *SP-PCC* (c/n *004*) was presented at the Paris Air Show.
▲ November 1985. Design of the PZL-130T Orlik Turbo offered.
▲ November 1985. *SP-PCC* shipped to Canada to be fitted with a turboprop engine.
▲ 16 July 1986. First flight of *SP-PCC* (later redesignated *SP-RCC*), with a Pratt & Whitney PT6A-25A turboprop.
▲ 20 January 1987. *SP-RCC* was lost in Colombia, killing the pilots.
▲ 19 February and 19 March 1988. Two follow-up piston-engined aircraft built, Nos 005 and 006. Both later converted into PZL-130TMs, re-engined with M-601E turboprops.
▲ 12 January 1989. First flight of the PZL-130TM prototype (007) powered by a Motorlet Walter M-601E turboprop. Pilot Jan Gawęcki.
▲ January 1990. Polish Air Force acceptance tests of the PZL-130TM began.
▲ 4-9 November 1990. Flight testing of PZL-130T (*SP-WCA*, 008) in Israel. Here, Israeli military pilots made about 100 flights totalling 23 flight hours.
▲ 18 September 1991. First flight of PZL-130TB prototype (*009, SP-PRF*).
▲ October 1992. 2 PZL-130TMs (*005* and *006*) were delivered to the Polish Air Force for qualification tests.
▲ 2 June 1993. First flight of the PZL-130TC prototype (011, *SP-PCE*), pilots Tadeusz Dunowski and Jerzy Wojnar.
▲ June 1993. PZL-130TB (second production aircraft, 0*13, SP-PCF*) displayed at the Paris Air Show.
▲ November 1993. Polish Air Force qualification tests of PZL-130TB completed.
▲ 4 March 1994. First PZL-130TBs delivered to the Polish Air Force.
▲ 7 July 1994. First PZL-130TC-1s delivered to the Polish Air Force.

Sales/users: In November 1991, PZL-130T (*008*) was lent to the Polish Military Pilot Academy at Deblin by PZL-Warszawa Okecie. Next 3 PZL-130TMs (005, 006, 007) were delivered to Deblin in October 1992 for evaluation tests. Normal deliveries began 4 March 1994, when a batch of 9 PZL-130TBs (*012* to *021*, excluding *014*) were delivered to the Polish Air Force (021 lost 30 April 1994). The following 7 PZL-130TC-1s (*022* to *028*) were delivered on 7 July 1994. 15 aircraft are in service with the 60th Training Air Regiment in Radom, and the remaining aircraft in Deblin.

Details: Principally for the current production PZL-130TC-1 Orlik.

Crew: 2, in tandem, the rear instructor's seat raised by 2.5 ins (6.5 cm).

Crew escape: Martin Baker CH15A ejection seats on production TC-1s and converted TBs that formerly had LFK-F1 ejection seats.

Fixed guns: None.

Number of weapon pylons: 6 under the wings (see Aircraft variants), 2 of which are "wet" for drop tanks.

Expendable weapons and equipment: 1,764 lb (800 kg).

Flight/weapon system avionics/instrumentation: AlliedSignal Bendix/King avionics, including KTR908 VHF communications. See Aircraft variants for navigation avionics. EFIS cockpit layout tested on the TC-2 in 1995 (see Aircraft variants). S-17 gunsight. Gun camera.

Wing characteristics: Straight, low mounted, with dihedral. Removable leading edges for easy repair or replacement.

Wing control surfaces: Frise type ailerons and 3-position double-slotted flaps, with new servo tabs.

Tail control surfaces: Elevators and rudder, with new servo tabs. A special trim system has been flight tested to counter propeller torque, comprising a Lear Astronics computer controlling a ventral tail fin.

Flight control system: Mechanical, except for electrically actuated flaps and tabs.

Construction materials: Metal, but with broad glassfibre wingtips.

Engine: Motorlet Walter M-601T turboprop, with a 5-blade propeller.

Engine rating: 751 shp (560 kW).

Fuel system: 560 litres. 2 x 340 litre drop tanks can be carried.

Electrical system: 27.5 volt DC supply powered by a starter generator and 2 x 24 volt/15 amp-hour ni-cd batteries. Inverter for 115 volt/26 volt AC supply.

Braking system: Multi-disc type. Parking brakes.

Aircraft variants:

PZL-130 Orlik was the designation of the M-14PM piston-engined prototypes, with a single aircraft (006) tested with Polish K-8AA derivative engine.

PZL-Warszawa Okecie PZL-130TC-1 Orliks

PZL-130T Orlik Turbo was given a 550 shp (410 kW) Pratt & Whitney Canada PT6A-25A turboprop. Other changes included increased dorsal fin leading-edge forward sweep, changes to the systems (the pneumatic system replaced by hydraulic, the electric system redesigned, and an oxygen system added). New equipment was fitted, and the wing structure was strengthened in order to allow underwing stores. 2 prototypes only (004, *SP-RCC* converted from PZL-130, and 008, *SP-WCA*).

PZL-130TM was similar to the PZL-130T, but fitted with a Motorlet Walter M-601E engine of similar power and a 5-blade propeller. Prototype was 007, and later 005 and 006 were converted into this standard.

PZL-130TB (originally named Orlik Turbo Bis, currently simply Orlik) became the standard version for the Polish Air Force, with an M-601T engine and 5-blade propeller. Much heavier than the PZL-130T/TM, with the take-off weight increased from 3,527 to 5,952 lb (1,600 to 2,700 kg). The wing span was extended by 3 ft 3 ins (1 m), and new double-slotted flaps of greater span installed. The position of the ailerons changed, and the aerodynamic twist increased, but the torque box remained unchanged. Weapon load and number of pylons increased from the previous 1,411 lb (640 kg) and 4 pylons (see Weapons). Also, to improve visibility, the rear seat was raised and a single-piece canopy adopted (without the fixed windscreen). Lightweight LFK-F1 ejection seats. Main undercarriage was given increased tyre pressure and new multi-disc brakes. The nosewheel was changed to be of similar size to the main wheels, with steering instead of self-centring.

PZL-130TBH is the proposed version for Hungary. Brochure used the name Turbo Orlik.

PZL-130TC is the most advanced version, intended for export. 950 shp (708.4 kW) Pratt & Whitney PT6A-62 with a 4-blade Hartzell propeller. 2 aircraft built so far (010 and 011), one for static tests. AlliedSignal Bendix/King avionics, including KNR634 navigation glideslope, KTU709 Tacan, KDF806 ADF, KDM706 DME, KXP756 transponder, and Omega navigation system. Flight Vision HUD in the front cockpit. Martin Baker CH15A ejection seats. Maximum take-off weight 5,952 lb (2,700 kg) with 560 litres of fuel and up to 1,764 lb (800 kg) of external stores. Maximum speed 335 kts (385 mph) 620 km/h, take-off distance 722 ft (220 m), landing distance 1,280 ft (390 m), climb rate 3,878 ft (1,182 m) per minute, ceiling 32,800 ft (10,000 m), and range 594 naut miles (684 miles) 1,100 km.

PZL-130TC-1 is similar to the PZL-130TB but with Martin Baker CH15A ejection seats and other minor alterations including AlliedSignal GPS and transponder, and servo tabs on the control surfaces. This is the current production version, and all the PZL-130TBs will be converted to this standard.

PZL-130TC-2 has an EFIS cockpit layout, and it is probable that this upgrade will eventually be adopted by the Polish Air Force. Flight testing took place during the Spring of 1995.

PZL-130TC-3 is a proposed counter-insurgency version of TC-1, due to fly in 1995. Flight Vision HUD, and 1,543 lb (700 kg) of weapons including Zeus 7.62-mm gun pods, rockets, Strela type AAMs, bombs of up to 200 kg weight each, or submunition dispensers.

PZL-130TD is similar to the PZL-130TC but with a less powerful 750 shp (559.3 kW) PT6A-25C turboprop and 3-blade Hartzell propeller. Project only.

PZL-130TE is a proposed economic version, with a 560 shp (417.6 kW) PT6A-25 engine. Due to the available power, this version has no ejection seats and its equipment has been considerably reduced.

DETAILS FOR PZL-130TC-1 ORLIK.

Principal dimensions:
Wing span: 29 ft 7 ins (9 m)
Maximum length: 29 ft 7 ins (9 m)
Maximum height: 11 ft 7 ins (3.53 m)

Wings:
Aerofoil section: Modified NACA 64_2215
Area: 139.9 sq ft (13 m^2)
Aspect ratio: 6.231
Twist: +3° root, -3° tip,
Dihedral: 5°

Undercarriage:
Type: Retractable, with all wheels of similar size and steerable nosewheel
Main wheel tyre size: 500 x 200 mm
Nose wheel tyre size: 500 x 200 mm
Wheel base: 9 ft 6 ins (2.9 m)
Wheel track: 10 ft 2 ins (3.1 m)

Weights:
Empty, operating: 3,196 lb (1,450 kg)
Maximum take-off: 5,952 lb (2,700 kg), or 4,410 lb (2,000 kg) for aerobatics

Performance:
Maximum speed: 302 kts (348 mph) 560 km/h at 19,700 ft (6,000 m) altitude, 274 kts (315 mph) 508 km/h at sea level
Take-off distance: 564 ft (172 m)
Landing distance: 605 ft (184 m)
Maximum climb rate: 4,050 ft (1,235 m) per minute
G limits: +6, -3 aerobatic or +4.4, -1.76 utility
Ceiling: 33,000 ft (10,000 m)
Range with full internal and external fuel: 1,242 naut miles (1,429 miles) 2,300 km

S.C. Avioane S.A. (Romania)

Avioane IAR-99 Soim showing the weapon options for attack. The underfuselage cannon pod is just visible

Corporate address: 1100 Craiova, Str Aeroportului nr 1.
Telephone: +40 51 12 41 70
Facsimile: +40 51 12 43 82
Founded: 1 February 1972 (named IAv Craiova until 1991).
Information: Nicolae Deneanu (General Manager).

● Activities

● In addition to the aircraft detailed here, Avioane is technically still constructing IAR-93s (see Multi-national part of this section), although its programme partners in former-Yugoslavia have been unable to keep production going. This has resulted in many Romanian-built fuselages and wings being stored against future need. The work force has accordingly been dramatically reduced, and much of the remaining manufacturing output has been geared to non-aviation items, including prefabricated buildings.

Avioane IAR-99 Soim and IAR-109 Swift

First flight: 21 December 1985 (Soim) and 1992 (Swift).
Role: Advanced trainer and close support.

★ Aims

★ Soim presumably to replace the L-29 Delfin, though both types (and L-39s) were in service in early 1995.
★ Swift is a more capable aircraft than Soim, with a modern glass cockpit layout and greatly improved avionics, aimed principally at export markets. Soims could be upgraded to this standard.
Sales/users: 2 flying and 1 static test Soim prototypes. Up to 50 Soims may be in service with the Romanian Air Force, although this number may include aircraft still undelivered from a second order. Negotiations for 40 with an unnamed country were reported in late 1994. 2 Swift test aircraft, configured from existing Soims.
Details: Principally for the Soim.
Crew: 2, in tandem, with the rear instructor's seat raised by 14 ins (35 cm). Only a pilot is carried during attack missions.
Cockpit: Pressurized. Split canopy in attack models.
Crew escape: Zero-zero ejection seats. Swift uses Martin Baker Mk 10L zero-zero seats.
Fixed guns: 23-mm GSh-23 cannon in a detachable underfuselage pod.
Ammunition: 200 rounds.
Number of weapon pylons: 4, including 2 "wet" for drop tanks.
Expendable weapons and equipment: Up to 2,205 lb (1,000 kg) total load, including 2 pods each with 2 x 7.62-mm guns, bombs of 50 kg to 250 kg weight on single or multi-store carriers, 42-mm or 57-mm rocket launchers, or other options. The gun pods or the drop tanks are suited only to the inner pylons, not a combination of these on all 4 pylons. See Aircraft variants for Swift's weapon options.
Radar: None.
Flight/weapon system avionics/instrumentation: Conventional, including ADF, radio altimeter and marker beacon receiver. IFF. AA-1F gyroscopic sight. Gun camera. See Aircraft variants for Swift's avionics.
Wing characteristics: Straight, low mounted, with slight dihedral from the roots.
Wing control surfaces: Ailerons (port tab) and single-slotted flaps.
Tail control surfaces: Elevators and rudder, with tabs.
Airbrakes: 2, under the aft fuselage.
Flight control system: Hydraulic ailerons, flaps and airbrakes, mechanical elevators and rudder, electric tabs.
Construction materials: Metal, with honeycomb sandwich construction used for various components including all the control surfaces except for the flaps.
Engine: Rolls-Royce Viper 632-41M turbojet, built indigenously by Intreprinderea Turbomecanica Bucuresti.
Engine rating: 3,970 lbf (17.66 kN).
Air intakes: Fuselage sides, above the wings, with small splitter plates.
Flight refuelling probe: None.
Fuel system: 1,370 litres in wing and fuselage tanks. 2 x 225 litre auxiliary fuel tanks can be carried. Swift can carry 300 litre drop tanks.
Electrical system: 28 volt DC supply using a starter generator. Ni-cd battery for engine starting and operation under emergency conditions. AC supply of 115 volt/400Hz and 26 volt/400Hz using 2 static inverters.
Hydraulic system: 2,987 psi.
Braking system: Hydraulic disc type. Anti-skid system.
De-icing system: Bleed air for windshield.

Aircraft variants:

IAR-99 Soim is the current production version, as described.
IAR-109 Swift is an upgrade of Soim, based on the same airframe and engine but with new avionics installed by Israel Aircraft Industries' Bedek Aviation Division. 2 versions, both heavier than Soim, as the IAR-109T trainer and the IAR-109TF combat trainer and attack aircraft. Avionics integrated via a MIL-STD-1553B databus system. Astronautics air-data computer, ring laser gyro inertial navigation system, head-up display, EFIS, TV monitor, HOTAS, up-front control panel and more. IFF transponder. Laser rangefinder. Weapon options to include guided bombs or ASMs, and IR air-to-air missiles (presumably 2 on the inner pylons, as stated to be an option for Soim).

DETAILS FOR IAR-99 SOIM.

Principal dimensions:
Wing span: 32 ft 4 ins (9.85 m)
Maximum length: 36 ft 1.5 ins (11.009 m)
Maximum height: 12 ft 10 ins (3.898 m)

Wings:
Aerofoil section: Modified NACA 64_1A214, 64_1A212 (root/tip)
Area: 201.39 sq ft (18.71 m^2)
Aspect ratio: 5.186
Sweepback: 6° 35' at 25% chord
Incidence: 1°
Dihedral: 3°

Undercarriage:
Type: Retractable, with castering nosewheel. Swift has a steerable nosewheel
Main wheel tyre size: 552 x 164 mm
Nose wheel tyre size: 445 x 150 mm
Wheel base: 14 ft 4 ins (4.378 m)
Wheel track: 8 ft 10 ins (2.686 m)

Weights:
Empty, operating: 7,054 lb (3,200 kg)
Maximum take-off: 12,257 lb (5,560 kg) for attack, 9,700 lb (4,400 kg) training. 10,580 lb (4,800 kg) for IAR-109T Swift

Performance:
Maximum operating Mach number (MMO): Mach 0.76
Maximum speed: 467 kts (538 mph) 865 km/h clean
Take-off distance: 1,475-3,150 ft (450-960 m), depending upon weight
Landing distance: 1,800-1,970 ft (550-600 m), depending upon weight
Maximum climb rate: 6,900 ft (2,100 m) per minute
G limits: +7, -3.6
Ceiling: 42,300 ft (12,900 m)
Range with full fuel: 594 naut miles (683.5 miles) 1,100 km, clean
Radius of action: 208 naut miles (239 miles) 385 km, at high altitude with maximum weapon load and 2,249 lb (1,020 kg) of internal fuel

Aeroprogress Inc (Russia)

Corporate address: 65A Volokolamskoye Highway, Moscow 123424.
Telephone: +7 095 145 8860
Facsimile: +7 095 145 9477
Founded: 1990.
Information: Evgeny P. Grunin (President and General Designer).

● Activities

- Undertakes the design and construction of a wide range of different types of aircraft, from military to commuter and wing-in-ground-effect, many of which are still in the development stage. See General Aviation section for the greatest coverage of these types.
- All aircraft have been or will be certified by the Aviation Design Bureau ROKS-AERO, which is incorporated in the Aeroprogress Corporation.
- Associated with Aeroprogress are Washington Aeroprogress Inc in the USA (initially offering kits of the T-411 Wolverine – which see), and the Khrunichev State Space Research Centre (which see), which manufactures aircraft and is the source of the Russian model T-411 Volverin.
- Member of the Business Aviation Association, an important grouping of production facilities in Russia to co-operate over civil production. The BAA includes among many facilities those of Myasishchev, Yakovlev and MAPO-MiG, the latter where most Aeroprogress manufacture takes place. Orders total hundreds of aircraft.
- In addition to those aircraft detailed here, it should be noted that T-130 is being revised to have weapon options under the requirements of the Frontier Forces (with Chinese manufacture also under negotiation).

DIVISIONS

<u>Amphibious and Special Aircraft</u>
<u>Business and Touring Aircraft</u>
<u>Replica Aircraft</u>
<u>Trainer and Aerobatics</u>
<u>Utility Aircraft</u>

Aeroprogress T-501

First flight: Originally planned for 1993, but changes to Russian Air Force requirements and competition from other manufacturers has led to the schedule being revised.

DETAILS FOR T-501.

Principal dimensions:
Wing span: 36 ft 1 ins (11 m)
Maximum length: 31 ft 8 ins (9.66 m)
Maximum height: approx 13 ft 1 ins (4 m)

Wings:
Area: 177.6 sq ft (16.5 m^2)
Aspect ratio: 7.3

Undercarriage:
Type: Retractable, with nosewheel
Wheel base: approx 9 ft 5 ins (2.88 m)
Wheel track: approx 9 ft 5 ins (2.88 m)

Weights:
Maximum take-off: 5,886 lb (2,670 kg)

Performance:
Maximum speed: approx 308 kts (354 mph) 570 km/h
Take-off distance: 525 ft (160 m)
Landing distance: 623 ft (190 m)
Maximum climb rate: 4,100 ft (1,260 m) per minute
Range with full fuel: 972 naut miles (1,118 miles) 1,800 km at height, with drop tanks

Role: Basic trainer, with armament capability.

▲ Development

- ▲ Being co-ordinated with the Russian Air Force.
- ▲ 1992. Metal cut for the first of 3 prototypes (1 for static testing) at MAPO-MiG.
- ▲ Manufacture will take place at Khrunichev (which see).

Crew: 2, in tandem, the rear instructor's seat raised.
Crew escape: Lightweight ejection seats.
Fixed guns: None.
Number of weapon pylons: 6 under the wings, 2 "wet" for drop tanks.
Expendable weapons and equipment: 1,102 lb (500 kg) of light weapons, including multi-barrel gun pods or rockets.
Wing characteristics: Straight, low mounted, without dihedral/anhedral.
Wing control surfaces: Horn-balanced ailerons and possibly flaps, with tabs.
Tail control surfaces: Horn-balanced elevators and rudder, with tabs.
Engine: OMSK/Glushenkov TVD-10B turboprop, with 3-blade propeller.
Engine rating: 1,011 shp (754 kW).
Fuel system: 1,102 lb (500 kg) of internal fuel. Can carry 2 drop tanks.

Aeroprogress Roks-Aero T-504 Borets

Role: Two-seat, twin-boom (Bronco-like) combat trainer project.
Engines: 2 x 960 shp (716 kW) OMSK TVD-10B turboprops.
Specifications: MTOW 16,095 lb (7,300 kg); fuel 3,307 lb (1,500 kg); payload 5,510 lb (2,500 kg); maximum speed 297 kts (342 mph) 550 km/h; range 1,080 naut miles (1,242 miles) 2,000 km; g limits +5, -2; and ceiling 19,685 ft (6,000 m).

Aeroprogress T-710 Anaconda

First flight: Project only.
Role: All-weather, day/night STOL strike aircraft for local conflicts and peacekeeping, possibly also for forward air control and observation. Can also undertake transport duties.

★ Aims

- ★ Spin-proof due to extensive leading-edge slats.
- ★ Short take-off and landing due to efficient high-lift devices.

Aeroprogress T-710 Anaconda

Aeroprogress T-501 basic trainer

Aeroprogress T-720 projected lightweight two-seat combat aircraft, with 8 underwing pylons and an under-fuselage gun pod. Take-off weight 9,920 lb (4,500 kg), maximum speed 405 kts (466 mph) 750 km/h, range 756 naut miles (870 miles) 1,400 km, and powered by a 1,300 shp (970 kW) RKBM TVD-1500 turboprop engine with a 6-blade pusher propeller

Aeroprogress T-730, presumably a projected side-by-side two-seat very light attack aircraft and trainer, featuring a stealth-like blended fuselage with chines, swept-forward wings, active canards, slab tailplane (possibly tailerons), twin fins and a 450 shp (335.6 kW) Soyuz TVD-450 turboprop engine with a 6-blade pusher propeller. Take-off weight 2,645 lb (1,200 kg), maximum speed 281 kts (323 mph) 520 km/h, and range 540 naut miles (621 miles) 1,000 km

⋆ Survivability due to titanium and composites cockpit armour, overwing engine exhaust pipe nozzles for low IR signature, polyurethane foam filled fuel tanks, and triple redundant flight control system.

Crew: 2, in tandem, under separate canopies.
Passengers/freight: 9 airborne troops can be accommodated in a cabin behind the cockpit. Alternatively, freight can be carried on a special ventral lifting platform.
Cockpit: Armour protected, using titanium and composites.
Fixed guns: Carried in an unspecified position.

DETAILS FOR ANACONDA.

Undercarriage:
Type: Retractable, with nosewheel

Weights:
Maximum take-off: 16,535 lb (7,500 kg)

Performance:
Cruise speed: 389 kts (447 mph) 720 km/h
Overland speed: 313 kts (360 mph) 580 km/h
Landing distance: 1,640 ft (500 m) at airstrip with ground pressure of 5 kg/cm^2
G limits: +5, -2.5
Ceiling: 19,700 ft (6,000 m)
Radius of action: 243 naut miles (280 miles) 450 km, with 2,205 lb (1,000 kg) load

Expendable weapons and equipment: 2,205 lb (1,000 kg) normal, 5,511 lb (2,500 kg) maximum weapon load. Weapons include bombs and missiles.
Flight/weapon system avionics/instrumentation: Include a weapon control system.
Wing characteristics: Straight, high mounted, without anhedral/dihedral. High-lift devices.
Wing control surfaces: Ailerons, flaps and leading-edge slats.
Tail control surfaces: Twin tail booms and twin fins, with single joining tailplane. Elevator and rudders.
Canard: None.
Airbrakes: Airbrakes in wing upper surface.
Flight control system: Triple redundant.
Fuselage: Pod type, as for US Bronco. Twin probes at the nose.
Engines: 2 Klimov TV7-117M turboprops, with 11 ft 10 ins (3.6 m) 5 or 6-blade propellers.
Engine rating: Each 2,500 shp (1,864 kW).
Fuel system: 3,309 lb (1,500 kg) in polyurethane foam filled tanks.

Aeroprogress T-752 Shtyk

First flight: Project only.
Role: All-weather, day/night, wing-in-ground-effect strike aircraft, for use in local conflicts, and anti-helicopter/light aircraft.

★ Aims

⋆ Tandem wing and V tail configuration for high CG and minimum induced drag.
⋆ Effective balancing without rudders, with high-lift devices deflected during take-off, landing and in normal flight.
⋆ Survivability due to titanium and composites cockpit armour, overwing engine exhaust pipe nozzles for low IR signature, polyurethane foam filled fuel tanks, and triple redundant flight control system.

Crew: 2.
Passengers/freight: 5 airborne troops or 2 litters and an attendant in the cargo compartment aft of the cockpit.
Expendable weapons and equipment: 2,205 lb (1,000 kg) normal, 4,409 lb (2,000 kg) maximum weapon load. Weapons include bombs and AAM/ASM missiles carried on 6 underwing pylons and 6 under-canard pylons.

DETAILS FOR SHTYK.

Weights:
Maximum take-off: 16,094 lb (7,300 kg)

Performance:
Maximum speed: 400 kts (460 mph) 740 km/h
Minimum speed: 38 kts (44 mph) 70 km/h
Landing distance: 656 ft (200 m), at airstrip with ground pressure of 5 kg/cm^2
G limits: +6, -3.5
Ceiling: 19,700 ft (6,000 m)
Radius of action: 216 naut miles (248 miles) 400 km, with a 2,205 lb (1,000 kg) load

Flight/weapon system avionics/instrumentation: Weapon control system, with aiming sensors in the nosecone and sidebody fairings.
Wing characteristics: Wing-in-ground-effect, triple configuration.
Control surfaces: Variable-incidence, main, rear-mounted wing, with forward sweep to increase the critical angles of attack without a tip stall and to increase aileron efficiency. High-lift devices (see Aims) and slotted wing effect. High-lift devices deflected during take-off, landing and in normal flight. Lateral control using vertical surfaces found at the aircraft's CG.
Engines: 2 Klimov TV7-117M2 turboprops, with 11 ft 10 ins (3.6 m) 3-blade propellers.
Engine rating: 2,800 shp (1,864 kW).
Fuel system: 3,307 lb (1,500 kg).

Aeroprogress T-752 Shtyk, a projected and highly futuristic two-seat wing-in-ground-effect strike aircraft

Beriev Joint-Stock Company (Russia)

Full name: Joint Stock Company "TANTK named after G.M. Beriev".
Corporate address: 1 Aviatorov Square, 347928 Taganrog.
Telephone: +7 86344 49839 or 49901
Facsimile: +7 86344 41454
Founded: 1932.
Information: Gennady S. Panatov (General Director).

■ Facilities

■ Include the design bureau departments, laboratory complex, flight test complex, experimental production plant, and test base at Gelenjic on the Black Sea.
■ Beriev also became a component of the Beta Air Limited Joint Venture (originally Association), along with the Taganrog aircraft production plant, Irkutsk aircraft production plant (IAPO) and Geneva ILTA Trade Finance SA, a Russian-Swiss venture. Through Beta Air, other western companies are becoming involved in Be-200 development.

Beriev Be-12 and Be-14 (NATO name *Mail*)

First flight: 18 October 1960 (pilot Piotr Bobro).
Role: Shore-based, short-range anti-submarine warfare (ASW) and search and rescue amphibian. Also converted for fire-fighting, civil transport and patrol, and ecological monitoring.

★ Aims

⋆ Replacement for the Be-6 and Be-10.

▲ Development

▲ 1958. Work began.
▲ 18 October 1960. First flight.
▲ July 1961. First public presentation, during a fly-past at Tushino airfield in Moscow.
▲ 24 November 1961. First prototype crashed, with the loss of 3 crew.
▲ 1962. Second prototype built.
▲ 1963-1972. Series manufacturing.
▲ 1992. Civil conversion programme started, particularly aimed at the fire-fighting version.
▲ 13 July 1993. The effectiveness of the Be-12P fire-

Beriev Be-12 Mail in the Caspian Sea (Piotr Butowski)

fighter was demonstrated, when it dropped 252 tonnes of water in 2 runs during a fire at the village of Listvianka.

▲ 1 June 1994. The Russian Government voted the declaration "On Fighting the Forest Fire". According to this declaration, in 1994 naval aviation was to hand over a further 8 Be-12s to be converted to fire-fighting versions.

▲ 6-11 October 1994. Be-12NKh delivered some 30 tonnes of cargo to earthquake victims in Yuzhno-Kurilsk.

Sales/users: Manufactured between 1963-72 in Taganrog. A total of 132 was built, of which about 90 were still in service with Russian and Ukrainian naval aviation prior to the civil conversion programme (see Development and Aircraft variants). Some 12 are operated by Vietnam and possibly also Syria. 10 Be-12NKh and Be-12P conversions by May 1995.

Crew: 4 (2 pilots side-by-side, navigator in the glazed fuselage nose, under the radar antenna, and a radio officer in the cabin). Crew of 6 in the Be-12PS (rescue system operator and stretcher-bearer added).

Fixed guns: None.

Expendable weapons and equipment: Weapons/stores bay in the bottom of the fuselage, aft of the step, for AT-1 torpedoes, APR-2 missile-torpedoes, depth charges, mines, sonobuoys, signal bombs and more. Further weapons/stores can be suspended on 4 pylons under the outer wing panels. Maximum load is 6,614 lb (3,000 kg) but normally 3,307 lb (1,500 kg). The Be-12P fire-fighter can take in 6,000 litres of water during the take-off run

Additional stores: KAS-90 motorboat in the rescue variant. See Aircraft variants.

Radar: Leninets PSRS-2 Initsiativa-2B search/attack radar in the fuselage nose.

Flight/weapon system avionics/instrumentation: Baku search/attack system integrating radar, magnetic anomaly detector (MAD) and radio sonobuoys systems. Orsha (APM-60) MAD antenna extends rearward from tail. Equipment for programmed dropping of radio sonobuoys, and onboard SPARU-55 receiver.

Self-protection systems: None.

Wing characteristics: High-mounted, cranked wings to keep the propellers clear of the water.

Wing control surfaces: 2-section trailing-edge flaps and aileron (with tabs) on each wing.

Tail control surfaces: H-type tail unit with sharply dihedral tailplane. 2 oval endplates located in line with the propellers for better efficiency at low speed on water. Elevators and rudders, with tabs.

Flight control system: Mechanical for ailerons, elevators and rudders, with hydraulic boost. Hydraulic flaps and electric tabs.

Fuselage: Single step boat hull, with 2 anti-spray strakes each side of the forward section.

Construction materials: All metal.

Engines: 2 Ivchenko PROGRESS AI-20D (series 4) turboprops located over the highest point of the wings, with 4-blade variable-pitch propellers. AI-8 auxiliary power unit (APU).

Engine rating: Each 5,180 ehp (3,863 ekW).

Flight refuelling probe: None.

Fuel system: 19,842 lb (9,000 kg) of internal fuel. Provision for 2 additional tanks inside the cabin, 1,800 litres each.

Electrical system: 28 volt DC, with 2 engine-driven generators.

Aircraft variants:

Prototype was powered by 2 VK-2 turboprops located in nacelles under the wings. No nose radar.

Be-12 *Mail* is the standard ASW version, powered by AI-20s transferred to the upper surface of the wings. Nicknamed Chaika (Seagull).

Be-12EKO (ekologichesky) is a projected ecological monitoring version.

Be-12I (issledovatelsky, research) is a projected civil version.

Be-12N has the Nartsiss (narcissus) search/attack system.

Be-12NKh (narodno-khoziaystvennyi, economical) is a civil transport/multipurpose conversion, already used for relief work (see Development). Viktor Ponomaryov (Deputy General Designer) is responsible for conversions; 10 Be-12NKh/Be-12P conversions by May 1995.

Be-12P (pozharnyi, fire-fighting) is the fire-fighting conversion. Prototype (c/n 9601404, side number 40) first flew in about 1991. Work is financed by the administration of Irkutsk district and by the Federal Forestry Service of Russia. 3 aircraft had been converted by early 1995. First, with factory number 2602505, was presented to the public in August and September 1993 in Zhukovsky near Moscow. A further 8 Be-12s are believed to have been assigned to fire-fighting versions (see Development). The aircraft takes in 6,000 litres of water during the take-off run. When extinguishing an actual fire in the Irkutsk district, with 9,921 lb (4,500 kg) of fuel and a distance flown from the water to the fire equal to 8 naut miles (9.3 miles) 15 km, a Be-12P dropped 120 tonnes of water onto the burning forest (see Development – 13 July 1993). Leasing arrangements are likely for this and possibly other versions.

Be-14 (design designation or military) Be-12PS (poiskovo-spasatelnyi, search-and-rescue), used for SAR and built in small quantity. No weapons bay; instead, a floor is installed inside the fuselage. Special search, rescue and medical equipment. Large door on port side of the fuselage. No MAD tail sting. Crew of 6 (rescue system operator and stretcher-bearer added).

M-12 was produced for record breaking, setting 42 international records for turboprop-powered amphibians, including 39,975 ft (12,185 m) altitude, 305.2 kts (351.3 mph) 565.3 km/h speed, 1,429.61 naut miles (1,645.163 miles) 2,647.634 km distance, and 22,267 lb (10,100 kg) payload.

Beriev Be-12P fire-fighting conversion (Piotr Butowski)

DETAILS FOR BE-12 MAIL.

Principal dimensions:
Wing span: 97 ft 11 ins (29.842 m)
Maximum length: 98 ft 9 ins (30.11 m)
Maximum height, on the ground: 29 ft 10 ins (9.1 m)

Wings:
Area, gross: 1,066 sq ft (99 m²)

Undercarriage:
Type: Retractable, with retracting tailwheel. Non-retractable wingtip floats
Wheel base: 47 ft 4 ins (14.436 m)
Wheel track: 16 ft 5 ins (5.00 m)

Weights:
Empty, operating: 54,013 lb (24,500 kg)
Maximum take-off from concrete runway: 79,366 lb (36,000 kg)
Maximum take-off from water: 77,162 lb (35,000 kg)
Maximum landing: 67,241 lb (30,500 kg)

Performance:
Never-exceed speed (V_{NE}): 313 kts (360 mph) 580 km/h
Maximum operating speed: 255 kts (294 mph) 473 km/h
Required sea run length: 5,906 ft (1,800 m)
Required minimum depth of water: 10 ft (3 m)
Take-off to 50 ft (15 m) from concrete runway: 6,562 ft (2,000 m)
Take-off to 50 ft (15 m) from water: 7,546 ft (2,300 m)
Landing from 50 ft (15 m) at 67,241 lb (30,500 kg) weight, on shore: 5,906 ft (1,800 m)
Landing from 50 ft (15 m) at 67,241 lb (30,500 kg), on water: 6,890 ft (2,100 m)
Allowable wave height: 2.62 ft (0.8 m)
Time of climb to service ceiling: 20 minutes
Ceiling: 36,090 ft (11,000 m), reduced to 26,245 ft (8,000 m) during service
Minimum level flight altitude over sea: 66 ft (20 m)
Range with full payload: 810 naut miles (932 miles) 1,500 km
Range with 3,307 lb (1,500 kg) payload, at 13,125 ft (4,000 m) altitude: 1,469 naut miles (1,690 miles) 2,720 km, with 5% fuel reserve
Range with 3,307 lb (1,500 kg) payload, at 22,965-26,250 ft (7,000-8,000 m) altitude: 1,782 naut miles (2,051 miles) 3,300 km, with 5% fuel reserve
Maximum range, without auxiliary tanks: 1,944 naut miles (2,237 miles) 3,600 km

Beriev A-40/Be-40 Albatross, Be-42 and Be-44 (NATO name *Mermaid*)

First flight: 8 December 1986 (pilot Yevgeni Lakhmastov).
Role: Intermediate-range anti-submarine warfare/mine laying, search and rescue and patrol/reconnaissance amphibian.
Chief designer: Alexei Konstantinov.

Beriev A-40 (Be-40 prototype) with extended flaps and slats. Note the hull shape, including wedges (Piotr Butowski)

★ Aims

★ Designed as the replacement for both the Be-12 *Mail* amphibian and Il-38 *May*.
★ Ability to alight on water, yet possess a range of 5,000 km needed to satisfy the Il-38-replacement requirement.
★ Ability to take-off from rough sea with wave heights exceeding 2 m.

▲ Development

▲ 1983. Work started.
▲ 1985. Metal cut for the first prototype.
▲ 1988. Design of a search and rescue variant began.
▲ Early 1992. The Russian Navy ordered about 20 aircraft, widely publicized to be for search and rescue.
▲ 22 June 1993. An A-40 prototype was displayed at the Woodford Air Base in the UK, marking the Be-40's promotion as a possible replacement for RAF Nimrods, with British equipment and armament.

Sales/users: 2 of 3 existing A-40 prototypes are used as flying test-beds, while the third is for static testing. By early 1995 none of these carried any special equipment or weapons. In 1992, the Russian Navy ordered a certain number (reportedly 20), the first being completed in late 1994/early 1995. Beriev has obtained the permission of the Russian Government to sell the Be-40 abroad, and the aircraft has visited several international expositions (see Development). The most likely foreign purchaser could be India, where the Il-38 and Tu-142M ASW aircraft have been in service for many years.

Details: Principally for the Be-40.
Crew: 8 (2 pilots, radio operator, navigator, engineer and 3 observers).
Cockpit: Conventional instrumentation.
Fixed weapons: None.
Expendable weapons and equipment: Up to 14,330 lb (6,500 kg) carried in the fuselage bay, including ASW torpedoes and missiles, depth bombs, mines, etc. The list of Be-40 weapons includes 3 Orlan ASW torpedoes or 4 to 6 ASW missiles of Korshun, Yastreb and Oriol types, but no further details are available.
Radar: Undernose radome covers search/attack, surveillance, navigation and wave measuring radar.
Flight/weapon system avionics/ instrumentation: Inertial flight/navigation system. IFF.
Self-protection systems: Probably active electronic jammers standard.
Wing characteristics: Slightly swept, shoulder mounted. No dihedral/anhedral. Wingtip floats and jammer pods. Optimized for 2 speeds: maximum cruising speed (760 km/h) and patrol speed (Mach 0.3-0.35).
Wing control surfaces: Each wing has an aileron, 2-section double-slotted flaps, spoilers and full leading-edge slats.
Tail control surfaces: T-tail with variable incidence swept tailplane with elevators, and swept fin with rudder.
Fuselage: Semi-monocoque, of high length-over-beam ratio. The fuselage height was made as low as possible (maximum height 13 ft 5 ins, 4.1 m), making the planing bottom relatively flat; the so called "boat pitch" is 1% at the stern and 6.5% at the bow. A flat bottom, however, means much greater dynamic load on the hull when taking-off and alighting. Therefore special profiles were designed to reduce these loads by half, the so-called "variable-rise bottom". The hull is of single step type, double-chine forward of the step (like a flattened "W") and a simple "V" aft of the step. 2 wedges are attached at the rear of the step, near the bomb bay, to assist take off. Anti-spray strakes are carried near the nose and forward of the step, the forward strakes acting at low speed and the rear at high speed to protect the engines from water inhalation. Main cabin area is divided into 2 pressurized and unpressurized compartments.
Construction materials: Mostly metal, but with honeycomb core/composites used where structurally acceptable.
Engines: 2 Aviadvigatel D-30KPV turbofans carried above the fuselage, aft of the wings. 2 Rybinsk/Novikov RD-38K turbojet boosters (each 6,581 lbf, 29.27 kN) are installed below the main engines. D-30KPVs are reportedly to be replaced with higher rated engines. TA-12 APU.

Beriev A-40 second prototype, originally numbered 20 but now 378 (Piotr Butowski)

Engine rating: Each 26,455 lbf (117.68 kN) at take off and 6,062 lbf (26.97 kN) cruise forD-30KPV.
Engine nozzles: Toed out.
Flight refuelling probe: Mounted on the nose, forward of the cockpit.
Fuel system: 35,100 litres.
Electrical system: 27 volt DC system, and 115 volt/400Hz single-phase and 115-220 volt/400Hz three-phase AC systems, using 2 engine-driven 60kVA AC generators, 3 static inverters and 3 batteries.
Hydraulic system: 3,000 psi.
Braking system: Discs on the main units, with anti-skid.
De-icing system: For cockpit windows, tail, wing slats and air intakes.
Oxygen system: Gaseous.

DETAILS FOR A-40/BE-40.

Principal dimensions:
Wing span: 136 ft 7 ins (41.62 m)
Maximum length: 143 ft 10 ins (43.84 m)
Maximum height: 36 ft 4 ins (11.07 m)

Wings:
Aerofoil section: Supercritical
Area: 2,152.78 sq ft (200 m^2)
Aspect ratio: 8.6
Sweepback: 23° 13′
Incidence: 3° 23′ at root
Twist: 4° 30′
Dihedral/Anhedral: 0°

Tail unit:
Tailplane span: 38 ft 11 ins (11.87 m)
Tailplane area: 302.31 sq ft (28.086 m^2)
Fin area: 225.93 sq ft (20.99 m^2)

Undercarriage:
Type: Retractable, with twin steerable nosewheels. Main units have tandem pairs of wheels. Fixed wingtip floats
Main wheel tyre size: 1,030 x 350 mm
Nose wheel tyre size: 840 x 290 mm
Wheel base: 48 ft 8 ins (14.835 m)
Wheel track: 16 ft 3 ins (4.96 m)
Turning radius: 63 ft 2 ins (19.25 m)

Weights:
Maximum take-off: 189,597 lb (86,000 kg)
Maximum landing: 187,393 lb (85,000 kg) on water, 160,937 lb (73,000 kg) on shore

Performance:
Maximum operating Mach number (M_{MO}): Mach 0.79
Maximum cruise speed: 410 kts (472 mph) 760 km/h
Patrol speed: Mach 0.3-0.35
Stall speed: 146 kts (168 mph) 270 km/h *clean*, 98 kts (113 mph) 182 km/h *with flaps*
Take-off distance: 3,281-3,937 ft (1,000-1,200 m)
Landing distance: 2,300-2,953 ft (700-900 m)
Ceiling: 31,825 ft (9,700 m)
Range with full fuel: 2,970 naut miles (3,418 miles) 5,500 km
Range with full payload: 2,214 naut miles (2,547 miles) 4,100 km, also quoted in brochures as 2,538 naut miles (2,920 miles) 4,700 km

Beriev A-40 engine arrangement, with the D-30KPV above the RD-38K booster (the nozzle protected here by a spherical titanium cover)

Polish MiG-21bis Fishbed-L with a single R-13M Atoll and 2 R-60MK Aphids under the wing, plus bombs, unguided rockets and cannon ammunition on the ground (Piotr Butowski)

14-17 km, and search area 28° in azimuth and 17° 40' in elevation. MiG-21-93 has the small Kopyo radar, made according to design and technology of the MiG-29M's N-010 Zhuk unit. Weight 364 lb (165 kg). Mean time between failures (MTBF) 120 hours. Kopyo can also engage targets at altitudes from 100 ft (30 m), whereas RP-22 detects targets at above 3,280 ft (1,000 m). Kopyo can track-while-scan up to 8 targets simultaneously and engage 2, whereas RP-22 could trace only 1. It can alsobe used to detect ground targets and for ground mapping (with freeze picture, zooming, etc.). At the September 1994 Farnborough Air Show, the Phazotron company gave details of the improved radar for MiG-21-93, called Super Kopyo. Due to a new processor, the maximum range has increased to 40.5 naut miles (46.6 miles) 75 km in the forward hemisphere and 24.3 naut miles (28 miles) 45 km in the rearward hemisphere. It is probable that Super Kopyo is another name for the Phathom radar designed jointly by Phazotron and Thomson-CSF of France (See Sukhoi Su-17/Su-20/Su-22 entry). MiG-21-2000 has Elta EL/M-2032 radar.

Flight/weapon systems avionics/instrumentation: MiG-21bis has the ASP-PFD-21 gun sight, AP-155SN autopilot (KAP-2K for old versions, up to MiG-21PFM *Fishbed F*), R-832M com radio, RV-UM radio altimeter, ARK-10 radiocompass, SOD-57M transponder, MRP-56P beacon receiver, and Lazur-M data link. SRZO-2 IFF standard, although Hungarian MiGs are receiving USAF Electronic Systems Center IFF under the Peace Pannon system (similar Western IFF may eventually also be fitted to Czech, Polish and Slovakian aircraft). MiG-21-93 has a Shchel-3UM helmet mounted sight, and infra-red search/track system combined with a laser rangefinder for close air combat and engagement of ground/sea targets. MiG-21-93 can co-ordinate interceptions with MiG-31 lead aircraft. See MiG-21-2000 under IAI.

Self-protection systems: MiG-21bis and older versions have SPO-10 Sirena radar warning receiver. SM-1 suspended pod containing SPS-141M response electronic jammer and 2 x 32-cartridge ASO-2I chaff/flare dispensers. MiG-21-93 has BVP-1F chaff/flare dispensers installed on the upper surface of the wingroots, with 120 x 26-mm cartridges.

Wings: Mid-mounted delta, with anhedral.

Wing control surfaces: Ailerons, and blown flaps (deflection 25° for take-off and 45° for landing).

Tail control surfaces: Sweptback slab tailplane (deflection +7° 30', -16° 30') and rudder (±25°).

Airbrakes: 2 airbrakes on lower front fuselage, each 4.76 sq ft (0.442 m^2) and deflected 35°; third airbrake under the rear fuselage, 5.06 sq ft (0.47 m^2), deflected 40°.

Flight control system: Mechanical, hydraulically actuated (BU-210 boosters for tailplane, BU-45 boosters for ailerons).

Fuselage: Semi-monocoque elliptic sections.

Construction materials: Aluminium alloys (mainly D16), steel (mainly 30KhGSNA) and magnesium alloys.

Engine: MiG-21bis has a Soyuz/Gavrilov R-25-300 turbojet. See Aircraft variants for other versions.

Engine rating: 9,039 lbf (40.21 kN) dry, 15,100 lbf (67.18 kN) with afterburning. As the result of short duration increase of rpm up to 106% and with second afterburner, the ground level thrust at near sonic speed has been increased to 21,825 lbf (97.09 kN) for several seconds.

Air intake: In the nose, with adjustable cone.

Fuel system: 11 internal tanks (7 fuselage, 4 wings). MiG-21bis capacity is 2,885 litres, plus 3 drop tanks (1 x 800 litres under the fuselage and 2 x 490 litres under the wings). MiG-21SM/M/MF capacity is 2,600 litres plus 1 x 800 litre drop tank. MiG-21PF/PFM capacity is 2,680 litres, plus 1 x 490 litre drop tank.

Flight refuelling probe: None.

Electrical system: DC supply using 1 x 28.5 volt generator and 2 x 24 volt batteries. 115 volt/400 Hz AC supply with a generator.

Hydraulic system: Dual, AMG-10 oil, pressure 3,045 psi.

Braking system: Brake on each wheel. PT-21UK drag-chute of 204.5 sq ft (19 m^2).

Aircraft variants (main, in order of appearance, not alphabetical, but with U series trainers last):

MiG-21F (E-6, izdelye 72) *Fishbed-C* was the initial production model, manufactured 1959-60. No radar, no guided weapons, and 1 or 2 x 30-mm cannon. Powered by a 12, 677 lbf (56.39 kN) Tumansky R-11F-300.

MiG-21F-13 (E-6T, izdelye 74) *Fishbed-C* was similar to MiG-21F but armed with 2 x K-13 (AA-2 *Atoll*) AAMs. Manufactured 1960-62 in the Soviet Union and later in Czechoslovakia and China.

MiG-21PF (E-7, izdelye 76) *Fishbed-D* was given RP-21 (TsD-30) radar, more internal fuel, and 13,614 lbf (60.56 kN) R-11F2-300 engine. Manufactured 1962-64.

MiG-21PFV is similar to MiG-21PF, for Vietnam.

MiG-21PFS (E-7SPS) is similar to MiG-21PF but with blown wing flaps instead of former Fowler type.

MiG-21PFM (izdelye 77) *Fishbed-E* is similar to MiG-21PFS but with increased tailfin area.

MiG-21FL was the export designation of MiG-21PFM (77) for India.

MiG-21PFM (izdelye 94) *Fishbed-F* is similar to MiG-21PFM (77) but with RP-21M radar, new ASP-PF-21 gunsight and Sirena-3M radar warning receiver. Provision for jet-assisted take-off (JATO) rockets. KM-1 ejection seat since 15th production series. Manufactured 1964-65 for Soviet Air Force, 1966-68 for export.

MiG-21R (E-7R, izdelye 94R) *Fishbed-H* is a reconnaissance variant. Larger dorsal spine. Provision for 2 underwing drop tanks. Reconnaissance pod suspended under the fuselage. Manufactured 1965-71.

MiG-21S (E-7S, izdelye 95) has improved RP-22M radar, AP-155 autopilot (also borrowed from the MiG-25), and more fuel. Manufactured 1965-68.

MiG-21SM (izdelye 15, initially 95M) *Fishbed-J* is similar to MiG-21S but has a more powerful 14,308 lbf (63.65 kN) R-13-300 turbojet, built-in GSh-23L cannon, and 4 underwing pylons instead of 2. Manufactured 1968-74.

Details for MiG-21bis Fishbed-L.

Principal dimensions:
Wing span: 23 ft 6 ins (7.154 m)
Maximum length: 51 ft 8 ins (15.75 m)
Maximum length without probe: 47 ft 5 ins (14.457 m)
Maximum height: 13 ft 6 ins (4.103 m)

Wings:
Aerofoil section: TsAGI C-96
Area: 247.6 sq ft (23.0 m^2)
Wing aspect ratio: 2.225
Sweepback: 57° leading edge
Mean aerodynamic chord: 13 ft 2 ins (4.002 m)
Incidence: 0°
Anhedral: 2°

Tail unit:
Tailplane aerofoil section: A6A
Tailplane area (moving sections): 40.3 sq ft (3.74 m^2)
Tailplane sweepback: 55°
Fin aerofoil section: S-11
Fin area: 57.05 sq ft (5.3 m^2)
Fin sweepback: 61° 27'
Rudder area: 10.4 sq ft (0.965 m^2)

Undercarriage:
Type: Retractable, with steerable nosewheel (47°)
Main wheel tyre size: 800 x 200 mm
Nose wheel tyre size: 500 x 180 mm
Wheel base: 15 ft 5 ins (4.71 m)
Wheel track: 9 ft 2 ins (2.787 m)

Weights:
Empty, operating: 12,882 lb (5,843 kg)
Normal take-off: 19,235 lb (8,725 kg)
Maximum take-off: 22,928 lb (10,400 kg)
Landing: 16,094 lb (7,300 kg)

Performance:
Maximum speed: Mach 2.05 or 1,174 kts (1,351 mph) 2,175 km/h
Maximum speed at sea level: Mach 1.05 or 702 kts (808 mph) 1,300 km/h
Landing speed: 146 kts (168 mph) 270 km/h
Take-off distance: 2,953 ft (900 m)
Take-off distance with JATO rockets: 1,640 ft (500 m)
Landing distance: 2,133 ft (650 m) with drag-chute
Maximum climb rate: 44,300 ft (13,500 m) per minute at sea level
G limits: +8
Ceiling: 57,415 ft (17,500 m)
Range: 661 (761 miles) 1,225 km clean
Range with 2 AAMs: 605 naut miles (696 miles) 1,120 km
Range with 2 AAMs and a 800 litre drop tank: 794 naut miles (913 miles) 1,470 km
Ferry range: 1,026 naut miles (1,181 miles) 1,900 km

MiG-21M (E-7M, izdelye 96 or izdelye 88) *Fishbed-J* was the export version of MiG-21SM, with downgraded RP-21MA radar, and R-11F2S-300 engine. Manufactured 1968-71 in the USSR and from 1973 in India.

MiG-21MF (izdelye 96F) *Fishbed-J* was the export variant of MiG-21SM. RP-22 or RP-21MA radar, and R-13-300 or R-11F2SK-300 engine.

MiG-21SMT (izdelye 50) *Fishbed-K* is similar to MiG-21SM but with an extremely large dorsal spine containing more fuel. Manufactured 1971-72, subsequently with the spine tank reduced.

MiG-21ST is a conversion of MiG-21SMT with smaller dorsal spine tank.

MiG-21MT (izdelye 96T) was the export version of MiG-21SMT. Small quantity produced in 1971 but never delivered.

MiG-21-93 upgraded cockpit (Piotr Butowski)

MiG-21US Mongol-B two-seater being refuelled (Piotr Butowski)

MiG-21bis (E-7bis, izdelye 75) *Fishbed-L* is similar to MiG-21SM but with the R-25-300 engine and lengthened dorsal spine fuel tank. New R-13M, R-55 and R-60 short-range AAMs. Manufactured 1972-74 for Soviet Air Force, later for export. About 200 manufactured in India during 1980-87. Izdelye 75A version for WarPact countries, 75B for others. See description above.
MiG-21bis (izdelye 75P) *Fishbed-N* is similar to izdelye 75 but with additional RSBN-6S short range radio navigation and instrument landing system.
MiG-21U (izdelye 66) *Mongol-A* is a two-seat trainer based on the MiG-21F-13. Manufactured 1962-66 for the USSR, and 1964-68 for export.
MiG-21US (izdelye 68) *Mongol-B* is the training version with blown flaps, R-11F2S-300 engine and KM-1 ejection seats. Manufactured 1966-71.
MiG-21UM (izdelye 69) *Mongol-B* is the modified training version with AP-155 autopilot and ASP-PFD gunsight (trainers have no radar).
MiG-21-93 (initially named MiG-21I for India) is the proposed Mikoyan mid-life upgrade of MiG-21, principally MiG-21bis. For the Indian upgrade requirement, the Mikoyan tender was forwarded to India in September 1991. The initial contract between HAL and MiG was finally signed in April 1993.
MiG-21-93 prototype was presented for the first time in May 1994 during ILA'94, Berlin. First flight 25 May 1995. On 3 May 1994 the Indian deputy minister of defence informed the parliament about the acceptance of the Mikoyan tender for updating 100, and perhaps several dozen more. It has the airframe and engine of MiG-21bis, and is equipped with new coherent pulse-Doppler Kopyo radar (previously called Komar). Armed with R-77 and R-27 AAMs, as well as Kh-31P and Kh-25MP anti-radiation ASMs, and Kh-31A and Kh-35 anti-ship missiles. Normal take-off weight is 19,456 lb (8,825 kg). Maximum speed 1,174 kts (1,351 mph) 2,175 km/h at high altitude and 702 kts (808 mph) 1,300 km/h at sea level. Practical ceiling is 56,760 ft (17,300 m), practical range on internal fuel as an interceptor with 2 missiles is 540 naut miles (621 miles) 1,000 km at high altitude and 302 naut miles (348 miles) 560 km at low altitude. Ferry range is 1,134 naut miles (1,305 miles) 2,100 km. However, In 1995 Israel was allowed to submit further proposals for the avionics to upgrade Indian MiG-21s, which is in keeping with the agreement with Mikoyan, which allows India to select different avionics if desired.
MiG-21-2000 is the IAI (Israel Aircraft Industries) upgrade with Elta EL/M-2032 radar, new cockpit instrumentation with HUD and 2 CRT displays, and new weapons including Israeli Rafael Python 3 AAMs and laser-guided bombs. MiG-21-2000 demonstrator was presented for the first time during the 1993 Paris Air Show (upgraded MiG-21MF delivered from Romania). Up to 110 Romanian aircraft are expected to be upgraded, of which 85 will be assigned to a ground attack role. First flown in 1995.

Mikoyan MiG-23 (NATO name *Flogger*)

First flight: 10 June 1967 (variable geometry prototype), piloted by Alexander Fedotov.
Role: Variable-geometry wing fighter; with MiG-23B/BN ground attack versions.
Chief Designer: Grigori Sedov.

★ Aims

★ To replace the MiG-21 in tactical and air defence units.
★ Mikoyan's first and only production swing-wing fighter.

MiG-23MF Flogger-B of the Polish 28th Fighter Air Regiment at Slupsk in combat readiness. Armed with 2 R-23R Apex and 4 R-60MK Aphid AAMs (Piotr Butowski)

▲ Development

▲ April 1965. Programme 23 started, intended to produce an aircraft with R-23 AAMs, Kh-23 ASMs, Sapfir-23 radar, ASP-23 gunsight, TP-23 IRST device, and AVM-23 analog computer.
▲ 3 April 1967. First flight of the 23-01 prototype *Faithless*. Delta wings. Single Tumansky R-27-300 turbojet (17,200 lbf, 76.5 kN) and 2 Kolesov RD36-35 lift engines (each 5,180 lbf, 23 kN).
▲ 10 June 1967. First flight of the 23-11 swing-wing prototype *Flogger-A*. Prototype now in the Monino museum. Single R-27F-300 turbojet. Take-off weight 29,320 lb (13,300 kg). Mach 2.13.
▲ 9 July 1967. 23-01 and 23-11 displayed during the Aviation Day in Moscow.
▲ March 1969. First flight of a MiG-23UB two-seat trainer prototype.
▲ 28 May 1969. First flight of production MiG-23S aircraft.
▲ 20 August 1970. First flight of the MiG-23B attack version, piloted by Piotr Ostapenko.
▲ June 1972. First flight of the large-scale production version, the MiG-23M.
▲ 1974. Seen abroad for the first time (Egyptian MiG-23BNs over Cairo).
▲ 1976. Production switched to the MiG-23ML lightened version.
▲ August 1978. MiG-23ML presented abroad for the first time (Finland).
▲ 1994. Finally withdrawn from Russian service.
▲ 27 September 1994. India and Russia (Mikoyan) signed a co-operation agreement, covering among several programmes an avionics upgrade of Indian MiG-23s (and MiG-27s).
Sales/users: Manufactured between 1969 and 1985, with 4,278 single-seaters and 769 trainers. Single-seat versions were manufactured at the Znamya Truda factory in Moscow (now MAPO), and MiG-23UB trainers at Irkutsk. In 1990 Soviet aviation in Europe operated 1,180 MiG-23s, including 749 by Air Defence Troops, 422 by the Air Force (mainly for training purposes) and 9 by the Navy. In the Asian sector of the country 400 MiG-23s were then flown. Between then and 1994 all MiG-23s were withdrawn from Russian operational service, although a certain number have been preserved for strategic reserve until the year 2000. The first foreign users of

DETAILS FOR MIG-23MLD FLOGGER-K, UNLESS STATED.

Principal dimensions:
Wing span: 25 ft 6 ins (7.779 m) *fully swept*, 45 ft 10 ins (13.965 m) *fully spread*
Maximum length: 54 ft 10 ins (16.7 m)
Maximum height: 15 ft 10 ins (4.82 m)

Wings:
Area, wings fully swept: 367.7 sq ft (34.16 m^2)
Area, wings fully spread: 402 sq ft (37.35 m^2)
Sweepback at leading edge, fixed glove: 70°
Sweepback at quarter chord, movable panels: Manually variable to 16°, 45° and 72° (in the first service period additional 33° introduced, but later deleted)
Sweepback at leading edge, movable panels: 18° 40', 47° 40' and 74° 40'
Incidence: 0°
Anhedral: 4°
Trailing-edge flaps area: 63.5 sq ft (5.9 m^2)
Leading-edge slats area: 14.2 sq ft (1.32 m^2)
Spoilers area: 6.45 sq ft (0.6 m^2)

Tail unit:
Tailplane span: 18 ft 1 ins (5.51 m)
Tailplane area: 74.6 sq ft (6.93 m^2)
Tailplane sweepback: 55° 40'
Fin area: MiG-23M/MF/MS/BN/UB 77.6 sq ft (7.21 m^2)
Fin sweepback: 65°
Fin forward extension sweepback: MiG-23M/MF/MS/BN/UB 72° 20'
Rudder area: 10.0 sq ft (0.93 m^2)
Ventral fin area: 15.7 sq ft (1.46 m^2)

Undercarriage:
Type: Retractable, with twin steerable nosewheels
Main wheel tyre size: 840 x 290 mm
Nose wheel tyre size: 520 x 125 mm
Wheel base: 18 ft 11 ins (5.772 m)
Wheel track: 8 ft 9 ins (2.658 m)

Weights:
Empty, operating (MiG-23MF): 23,910 lb (10,845 kg)
Maximum take-off: 39,242 lb (17,800 kg)
Maximum take-off (MiG-23MF): 40,234 lb (18,250 kg)
Normal take-off: 32,717 lb (14,840 kg)
Normal take-off (MiG-23MF): 34,723 lb (15,750 kg)

Performance:
Maximum speed: Mach 2.35 or 1,350 kts (1,553 mph) 2,500 km/h at height, Mach 1.1 or 729 kts (839 mph) 1,350 km/h at sea level
Maximum climb rate: 45,275 ft (13,800 m) per minute at sea level
Take-off distance: 1,640 ft (500 m)
Landing distance: 2,461 ft (750 m)
G limit: +8.5
Ceiling: 60,000 ft (18,300 m)
Range: 1,026 naut miles (1,181 miles) 1,900 km, clean
Range with standard armament: 810 naut miles (932 miles) 1,500 km, no drop tanks
Range with 3 drop tanks, no armament: 1,523 naut miles (1,752 miles) 2,820 km
Range with 3 drop tanks and standard armament: 1,377 naut miles (1,584 miles) 2,550 km

MiG-23s (MiG-23BN, MiG-23MS and MiG-23UB) were Egypt and Libya, from 1974. Warsaw Pact countries purchased MiG-23s in the late 1970s; MiG-23MF, MiG-23ML, MiG-23BN and MiG-23UB were used by the air forces of Czechoslovakia and East Germany, while Bulgaria also took the MiG-23MLD. It has been reported that Czech MiG-23s are being withdrawn from service, though recent Magic 2 missile tests have been conducted (see Weapons). The fighter was less popular in Poland (42 MiG-23MF/UBs purchased, of which 37 remain in service), Romania and Hungary. Other MiG-23 operators in early 1995 are Afghanistan, Algeria, Angola, Cuba, Ethiopia, India (MiG-23BN Vijay, later as MiG-23MF Rakshak and MiG-23UB), Iraq, Libya, North Korea, Sudan, Syria, Vietnam and Yemen. Non-typical owners (for non-operational use) of small numbers are the USA, China and Israel; 1 MiG-23 was flown to Israel on 11 October 1989 while China bought at least 2 aircraft from Egypt (paying with spare parts for old type MiGs) and the USA bought more aircraft from Egypt in 1978 and later obtained several others from Germany.

MiG-23UB Flogger-C combat trainer with separate canopies (Piotr Butowski)

Crew: Pilot or 2 in the MiG-23UB operational trainer.
Crew escape: Mikoyan KM-1M ejection seat, operable from zero height to 65,600 ft (20,000 m), and between 70-648 kts (81-746 mph) 130-1,200 km/h.
Fixed guns: Gryazev/Shipunov GSh-23L twin-barrel 23-mm cannon mounted under the fuselage.
Ammunition: 200 rounds.
Number of weapon pylons: 4, 2 under the wing gloves (2,205 lb, 1,000 kg each) and 2 under the fuselage (1,102 lb, 500 kg each).

Hungarian MiG-23MF with wings swept, showing the dogtooth leading edges and rear lower airbrakes extended (Piotr Butowski)

Expendable weapons and equipment: Up to 4,409 lb (2,000 kg) total despite pylon capacity, or 6,614 lb (3,000 kg) for the MiG-23B/BN. Standard armament for air-to-air missions comprises 2 medium range R-23 (AA-7 *Apex*) missiles in infra-red R-23T or semi-active radar R-23R versions, plus 4 close-air combat R-60Ms (AA-8 *Aphid*). Later fighter versions, from MiG-23MLA, can use modified R-24 (AA-7 *Apex*) AAMs. MiG-23MLD was adapted to R-73 (AA-11 *Archer*) in the place of the R-60M. Czech MiG-23s have been tested with Magic 2 AAMs in place of *Aphids* (see Users). Air-to-ground weapons include bombs (up to 500 kg each, with 2 in tandem under wing gloves), unguided rockets and 2 Kh-66/Kh-23 (AS-7 *Kerry*) radio-command homing air-to-surface missiles (fighter version needs suspended Delta radio-command pod for *Kerry* launch; MiG-23B/BN/UB/S have Delta as standard).
Radar and weapon system avionics: See Aircraft variants.
Flight avionics/ instrumentation (fighter versions): Polyot flight/navigation system. ARK-15M radio compass, RV-4 radio altimeter, MRP-56P beacon marker receiver, RSBN-6S short range navigation and ILS. SO-69 transponder. Parol IFF (SRZO-2 on early versions). Lazur data link for ground controlled intercept. R-862 com radio (R-832M on early aircraft).
Self-protection systems: SPO-10 Sirena (later SPO-15 Beryoza) radar warning receiver. Some MiG-23MLDs were equipped with BVP-50-60 chaff/flare dispensers on the rear fuselage and Gardenia active jamming pod. SPS-141FSh Siren electronic jammer standard for the MiG-23B/BN, built into the nose of the fuselage.
Wing characteristics: Variable-geometry, high-wing monoplane, with small fixed wing gloves. Movable panels powered by SPK-1 hydraulic gearbox. 2 dogtooth leading edges for each wing, 1 on the movable panel and seen when swept, and another on the wingroot.
Wing control surfaces: 4-section slats (20°) on the leading edge of each movable panel. 3-section, full-span (movable panel), single-slotted trailing edge flaps (25° for take-off and 50° for landing). 2-section spoilers (45°) on the upper surface of each movable panel, forward of the inner flap.
Tail control surfaces: Slab tailplane (taileron), deflected evenly (+8° 30', -24° 30') or differentially (6° 30'). Rudder (25° deflection). Large folding underfuselage ventral fin, deployed after the undercarriage has been retracted.
Airbrakes: 2 pairs on the rear fuselage, upper of 4.52 sq ft (0.42 m^2) and deflected 45°, and lower of 8.61 sq ft (0.80 m^2) and deflected 35°.
Flight control system: Mechanical, hydraulically actuated. 3-channel autopilot.
Construction materials: All-metal, using aluminium alloys, steel centre fuselage torsion box and titanium in rear fuselage.
Engine: MiG-23M/MF/BN: 27,558 lbf (122.59 kN) with afterburning Soyuz/Khachaturov R-29-300 (izdelye 55) turbojet. MiG-23ML/MLA/MLD/P/PD: 28,660 lbf (127.49 kN) with afterburning R-35-300 (izdelye 77). MiG-23MS/S/UB: 22,046 lbf (63.75 kN) R27F2M-300 (izdelye 47M). Variable geometry nozzles.
Air intakes: Variable geometry side intakes, with 3° forward slant.
Flight refuelling probe: Not fitted normally, but some Iraqi MiG-23BNs have a French Mirage F1 probe installed.
Fuel system: MiG-23ML/MLA/MLD/P/PD: 4,260 litres of internal fuel, including 3,550 litres in 3 fuselage tanks and 710 litres in 6 wing tanks. Provision for 3 x 800 litre auxiliary tanks, 1 under the fuselage and 2 under the wings when fully spread. MiG-23M/MF/MS/BN: as above plus 4th rear fuselage tank of 470 litres capacity.
Electrical system: 28 volt DC supply. 208 volt/400Hz, 115 volt/400Hz and 36 volt/400Hz AC supply.
Hydraulic system: 2, main and for control system actuators.
Braking system: Each wheel. Twin drag-chute in the finroot.

Aircraft variants (in NATO name sequence):
MiG-23S (23-11S, or izdelye 2) *Flogger A* was the first production version, equipped with Sapfir-21 radar and armament system of the MiG-21. R-27F2M-300 engine. Mach 2.27 and ceiling 59,000 ft (18,000 m).
MiG-23M (23-11M, or izdelye 2M) *Flogger-B* was the basic production version with Sapfir-23D radar (NATO *High Lark*), ASP-23D gunsight, TP-23-1 infra-red search and track device (IRST) and R-23 (AA-7 *Apex*) AAMs. Extended chord of movable wing panel and R-29-300 engine. Take-off weight 34,723 lb (15,750 kg) clean, maximum 45,569 lb (20,670 kg). Mach 2.35.
MiG-23MF *Flogger-B* was produced as an export version of MiG-23M for WarPact countries.
MiG-23UB (23-51) *Flogger-C* is the tandem two-seat operational trainer. No radar. R27F2M-300 engine.
MiG-23MS *Flogger-E* was the export version for Third World countries, having a MiG-23M airframe combined with MiG-23S radar/armament and engine.
MiG-23B (32-24) *Flogger-F* was produced as a ground-attack version. Lyulka AL-21F3 turbojet. Sokol-23S attack system instead of radar, and KN-23 navigation system. Just 24 aircraft produced in 1971.
MiG-23BN (32-23) *Flogger-F* was the modified ground-attack version, manufactured mainly for export. Wings as for the MiG-23M. R-29B-300 engine. Sokol-23N attack system with Fon-1400 laser rangefinder in the nose.
MiG-23ML (23-12, izdelye 3) *Flogger-G* was produced as a lightened version with shorter tailfin than MiG-23M. Sapfir-23ML (N-003– NATO *High Lark 2*) radar of 46 naut miles (53 mile) 85 km range, improved TP-23M IRST and ASP-17ML gunsight.
MiG-23MLA (23-12A) *Flogger-G* is similar to MiG-23ML but with improved RP-23MLA Ametist (N-008) radar, TP-26 IRST and R-24 (AA-7 *Apex*) AAMs.
MiG-23P (23-14, izdelye 6) *Flogger-G* was an MiG-23ML derivative specially adapted for Air Defence Troops. RP-23P (N-006) radar and digital computer.
MiG-23PD is the MiG-23P converted to MiG-23MLD standard.
MiG-23BN (32-23) *Flogger-H* is similar to *Flogger-F* but with Beryoza RWR in the place of Sirena.
MiG-23MLD (23-18) *Flogger-K* is an upgrade of MiG-23ML and MiG-23MLA, with vortex generators at the wingroots and at the nose probe. Radar modified for close-air combat, added Shchel-3U helmet-mounted sight, and R-73 (AA-11 *Archer*) missiles.
MiG-23MLDG is similar to the MiG-23MLD, but with Gardenia ECM jammer built into the airframe. Prototype only.
MiG-23I is the proposed upgrade of export MiG-23s, with MiG-29's Topaz radar and R-27 (AA-10 *Alamo*) and R-77 (AA-12 *Adder*) missiles.

Mikoyan MiG-25 (NATO name *Foxbat*)

First flight: 6 March 1964 (pilot Alexander Fedotov).
Role: Supersonic reconnaissance, interception, strike and air-defence suppression.
Chief designer: Nikolai Matyuk; deputy Lev Shengelaya.

★ Aims

★ Originally conceived to counter the US B-70 Valkyrie bomber then under development (later cancelled).
★ Maximum speed of 3,000 km/h, service ceiling of 20,000 m and range of 4,000 km (range not achieved).
★ MiG-25RB able to cruise at Mach 2.35 with bombs suspended.
★ MiG-25RB equipped with accurate Peleng nav/attack system, with automatic release of bombs at preset co-ordinates, operating by day or night and in any weather. Bombs dropped from over 65,600 ft (20,000 m) altitude at supersonic speed.

Details for the MiG-25RB (applies also to derived versions such as MiG-25RBV, RBK, RBS, etc).

Principal dimensions:
Wing span: 43 ft 11 ins (13.38 m)
Wing span for MiG-25P/PDS: 46 ft 2 ins (14.062 m)
Wing span for MiG-25PD: 46 ft (14.015 m)
Maximum length: 70 ft 8.5 ins (21.55 m)
Maximum length for MiG-25PD: 70 ft 8 ins (21.53 m)
Maximum height: 19 ft 8 ins (6.0 m)
Maximum height for MiG-25PD: 20 ft 7 ins (6.28 m)

Wings:
Aerofoil section: P-44M, P-101M (root/tip)
Area: 660.9 sq ft (61.40 m^2)
Area for MiG-25P/PD/PDS: 664.46 sq ft (61.73 m^2)
Aspect ratio: 2.92
Sweepback at leading edge: 41° 02′
Sweepback at leading edge for MiG-25P/PD/PDS: 42° 30′ inner section, 41° 02′ outer section
Incidence: 2°
Anhedral: 5°

Tail unit:
Tailplane span: 28 ft 8 ins (8.74 m)
Tailplane area: 105.6 sq ft (9.81 m^2)
Tailplane sweepback: 50° 22′
Fin sweepback at leading edge: 54°
Fins cant angle: outward 8°

Undercarriage:
Type: Retractable, with twin nosewheels
Main wheel tyre size: 1,300 x 360 mm
Nose wheel tyre size: 700 x 200 mm
Wheel base: 16 ft 10.5 ins (5.144 m)
Wheel base for MiG-25PD: 16 ft 10 ins (5.139 m)
Wheel track: 12 ft 7.5 ins (3.85 m)
Stationary angle of pitch: 2° 28′

Weights:
Take-off: 77,294 lb (35,060 kg) clean
Take-off for MiG-25PD: 76,964 lb (34,920 kg) clean
Take-off with 4 R-40 AAMs, for MiG-25PD: 80,800 lb (36,650 kg)
Take-off with drop tank: 87,810 lb (39,830 kg)
Take-off, maximum: 90,830 lb (41,200 kg)
Take-off, maximum, for MiG-25PD: 90,389 lb (41,000 kg)

Performance:
Maximum limiting Mach number at 42,600 ft (13,000 m): Mach 2.83
Maximum speed at 42,600 ft (13,000 m): 1,620 kts (1,864 mph) 3,000 km/h
Supersonic cruise Mach number, at high altitude: Mach 2.35
Supersonic cruise speed, at high altitude: 1,350 kts (1,553 mph) 2,500 km/h
Maximum Mach number with 4 FAB-500 bombs, at 42,600 ft (13,000 m): Mach 2.35
Maximum Mach number with 4 x FAB-500 bombs and drop tank, at 42,600 ft (13,000 m): Mach 1.5
Maximum speed at sea level: 648 kts (746 mph) 1,200 km/h
Maximum climb rate for MiG-25PD: 25,600 ft (7,800 m) per minute, at sea level
Time to Mach 2.35 at 65,600 ft (20,000 m) altitude: 6 minutes 36 seconds, clean
Time to Mach 2.35 at 65,600 ft (20,000 m) altitude, with 4 x FAB-500 bombs: 8 minutes 12 seconds
Time to Mach 2.35 at 65,600 ft (20,000 m) altitude, with 4 x R-40 AAMs, for MiG-25PD: 9 minutes 30 seconds
G limit: 3.8, with 4 x FAB-500 bombs
Ceiling: 75,460 ft (23,000 m)
Ceiling with 4 x FAB-500 bombs: 67,900 ft (20,700 m)
Range with 4 x FAB-500s, Mach 2.35: 891 naut miles (1,025 miles) 1,650 km
Range with 4 x FAB-500s and drop tank, Mach 2.35: 1,150 naut miles (1,324 miles) 2,130 km
Range with 4 x FAB-500s, subsonic speed: 1,007 naut miles (1,159 miles) 1,865 km
Range with 4 x FAB-500s and drop tank, subsonic speed: 1,296 naut miles (1,491 miles) 2,400 km

▲ Development

▲ 1961. Work started.
▲ February 1962. Official governmental order.
▲ 6 March 1964. First flight of the E-155R-1 reconnaissance prototype.
▲ 9 September 1964. First flight of the E-155P-1 interceptor prototype, piloted by Piotr Ostapenko.
▲ 9 July 1967. First public showing, with a fly-pass of 4 aircraft over Domodedovo airport, Moscow.
▲ 13 June 1972. MiG-25P interceptor officially commissioned into service with Soviet Air Defence Troops.
▲ December 1972. MiG-25RB, MiG-25RBK and MiG-25RBS reconnaissance versions commissioned into the Soviet Air Force.
▲ 20 March 1971-6 June 1972. 4 MiG-25Rs were operated in Egypt (with Soviet crews).
▲ 19 October 1973-June 1974. 4 MiG-25RBVs were operated in Egypt (with Soviet crews).
▲ 6 September 1976. A MiG-25P was covertly flown to Japan by a Soviet pilot, allowing the first detailed examination outside of the USSR.
▲ 4 November 1976. Programme for the MiG-25P update, as the MiG-25PD, was accepted in USSR.
▲ 19 November 1977. First flight of a MiG-25PD, piloted by Valeri Menitsky.
▲ 1980-1982. MiG-25P upgraded to MiG-25PD standard (named MiG-25PDS).
▲ 1985. Series production completed.
▲ 1994. MiG-25PD/PDS interceptors finally withdrawn from the service with Russian Air Defence Troops.

Sales/users: 1,186 MiG-25s were built. Full-scale production in Gorki (now Nizhni Novgorod) lasted until 1982, and later a small quantity of MiG-25BM anti-radar aircraft were manufactured up to 1985. In 1990, of over 800 operational Soviet MiG-25s, 544 were in the European part of the USSR, split as 382 interceptors of Air Defence Troops and 162 reconnaissance/strike versions. The remainder was based in the Asian areas of the USSR. In 1993 Belarus had 75 aircraft and Ukraine 107. MiG-25PDs and PDS were recently withdrawn from service with Russian Air Defence and replaced by MiG-31s and Su-27s. The reconnaissance version of MiG-25 will remain in service for some time, since there is no replacement. In the late 1970s several other countries purchased MiG-25s. MiG-25P interceptors were delivered in 1979 to Algeria and Syria and, a little later, to Iraq and Libya (the latter obtained also MiG-25PDs). Reconnaissance MiG-25RBs are used by Algeria, India, Iraq, Libya and Syria. India also obtained 2 training aircraft of MiG-25RU type. Although MiG-25 was offered to the Warsaw Pact countries, only Bulgaria bought 3 MiG-25RBs and 1 MiG-25RU, and these were later returned.
Crew: Pilot, except for MiG-25PU/RU two-seat trainers.
Cockpit: Conventional.
Crew escape: Mikoyan KM-1M ejection seat, operable from zero height and over 70 kts (81 mph) 130 km/h. Early aircraft had the KM-1.
Fixed guns: None.
Number of weapon pylons: 4 under the wings. Underfuselage stations on MiG-25RB.
Expendable weapons and equipment: MiG-25P is armed with 4 R-40 (AA-6 *Acrid*) medium range AAMs,

MiG-25RBF Foxbat-D reconnaissance-bomber (Piotr Butowski)

usually 2 infra-red R-40Ts and 2 semi-active radar R-40Rs. MiG-25PD and PDS carry 4 improved R-40Ds (R-40TD and R-40RD versions) or 2 R-40Ds and 4 short range R-60Ms (AA-8 *Aphid*). MiG-25RB and its sub-variants are armed with up to 10 FAB-500T demolition bombs (4 under the wings and 6 under the fuselage), or with single nuclear bomb. MiG-25BM is armed with 4 Kh-58 (AS-11 *Kilter*) anti-radar missiles.

Radar and weapon system avionics: See Aircraft variants.

Flight system avionics/instrumentation: MiG-25P/PD/PDS are equipped with the Polyot-1I flight/navigation system enabling, among other modes, flight along a preset path with 3 waypoints, return to 1 of 4 programmed airfields, and landing approach down to 164 ft (50 m) altitude. Interceptor versions have used the Vozdukh-1M ground controlled intercept (GCI) system. Standard equipment includes the SO-69 transponder, SRO-2N and SRZO-15 IFF, RV-3 or RV-4 altimeter, ARK-10 or ARK-19 radio compass, MRP-56P beacon receiver, and RSBN-6S short range radio navigation and approach system. R-832M (or R-802) and R-864 (or R-847) com radio. Radar and GCI systems are deleted from reconnaissance/strike versions, but the Peleng-D/DR/DM nav/attack system with TsVM-10-155 Orbita digital computer is added, plus DISS-7 (DISS-3S on early aircraft) Doppler navigation radar.

Self-protection systems: Active ECM jammers (MiG-25RB/BM family only) built into the nose: SPS-141 Siren on early production aircraft, later SPS-151 Lyutik. SPO-10 Sirena or SPO-15 Beryoza radar warning receiver. Some late production MiG-25PDs are equipped with chaff/flare dispensers built into the wing fences (as for the MiG-29).

Wing characteristics: Modestly sweptback, high mounted. Longer, bended leading edges on interceptor versions. Aerodynamic fence on the upper surface of each wing; anti-flutter system on the wingtips.

Wing control surfaces: Blown trailing-edge flaps (25° for take-off, 45° for landing) and ailerons (25°).

Tail control surfaces: Slab tailplane (taileron), deflected evenly or differentially, +13°, -32° for take-off and +5°, -12.5° in flight. Twin fins (rudders 25° deflection) and 2 ventral fins.

Airbrakes: Door-type airbrake on top of the rear fuselage, deflecting 45°.

Flight control system: Mechanical, hydraulically actuated. SAU-155 automatic control system.

Fuselage: Rectangular cross section, the welded structure forming a tank occupying some three-quarters of the volume and which is subdivided into compartments and reinforced by internal longitudinals. The spacing of the longitudinals is very dense, at 0.9 ins (25 mm).

Construction materials: Nickel steel of VNS-2, VNS-4 and VNS-5 type (80%), D19 thermo-resistant aluminium alloy (11%) and titanium (8%).

Engines: 2 Soyuz/Tumansky R-15BD-300 turbojets, side-by-side in the fuselage rear, R-15B-300 in early aircraft.

Engine rating: Each 24,692 lbf (109.84 kN) with afterburning.

Air intakes: Wedge-type, with electronically-controlled lower intake lip.

Flight refuelling probe: Test aircraft only. See MiG-25PDZ below.

Fuel system: Fuel located in 6 fuselage compartments (including tanks around the air intakes), 4 wing tanks and in the tailfins. Total of 31,900 lb (14,470 kg) of internal fuel for the MiG-25PD interceptor; 33,609 lb (15,245 kg) for the reconnaissance MiG-25RB. Provision for extra-large underfuselage auxiliary tank, of 9,855 lb (4,470 kg) capacity. Thermal resistant fuel of T-6 or T-7P type

Electrical system: 2 engine-driven 27 volt DC generators. 1 or 2 AC generators. 2 emergency batteries and transformers.

Hydraulic system: Main and secondary for flight control units, with main supplying also other systems and secondary for emergency brake back-up.

MiG-25BM Foxbat-F air-defence suppression aircraft (Dmitri Grinyuk/via Piotr Butowski)

Braking system: On all units, with main and emergency. Twin drag-chutes, 646 and 538 sq ft (60 and 50 m²), housed in the tailcone between and above the engine nozzles.

Aircraft variants:

MiG-25P (E-155P, izdelye 84) *Foxbat-A* interceptor with Smerch-A radar and 4 R-40 (AA-6 *Acrid*) AAMs. Manufactured until 1978; converted 1982-84 into MiG-25PDS. Smerch-A has a search range of 54 naut miles (62 miles) 100 km for bomber-size targets, and automatic tracking over 27 naut miles (31 miles) 50 km. Search angles 60° each side in azimuth, +6°, -6° in elevation.

MiG-25R (E-155R, izdelye 02) *Foxbat-B* was the initial reconnaissance version. 3 cameras and SRS-4 Romb electronic intelligence (elint) device. Manufactured until 1970.

MiG-25RB (izdelye 02B) *Foxbat-B* is the 1970 reconnaissance-bomber version. As MiG-25R but armed with up to 11,023 lb (5,000 kg) of bombs.

MiG-25RBN (izdelye 02B) *Foxbat-B* is the night reconnaissance version. As MiG-25RB but specialized cameras.

MiG-25RBV (izdelye 02B) *Foxbat-B* is similar to the MiG-25RB but with SRS-9 Virazh instead of Romb.

MiG-25RBK (izdelye 02K or izdelye 51) *Foxbat-D* is similar to MiG-25RB but without cameras. Kub elint. Manufactured 1972-80.

MiG-25RBS (izdelye 02S or izdelye 52) *Foxbat-D* has no cameras but has Sabla side-looking airborne radar (SLAR). Manufactured 1972-77.

MiG-25RBT (izdelye 02T) *Foxbat-D* has Tangazh elint.

MiG-25RBSh *Foxbat-D* is a 1981 version, converted from MiG-25RBS with Shompol SLAR instead of Sabla.

MiG-25RBF (izdelye 02F) *Foxbat-D* is a 1981 version, converted from MiG-25RBK with Shar elint instead of Kub.

MiG-25BM (izdelye 02M or izdelye 66) *Foxbat-F* is an air defence suppression version, armed with 4 Kh-58 (AS-11 *Kilter*) anti-radar missiles. Prototype appeared in 1977, and manufactured 1982-85. Also some MiG-25RBs were converted into MiG-25BMs.

MiG-25PD (izdelye 84D) *Foxbat-E* is an updated air defence version with Sapfir-25 radar instead of Smerch-A, R-40D AAMs, and a TP-26Sh1 infra-red search and track (IRST) device with a 24.3 naut mile (28 mile) 45 km maximum range. Manufactured 1978-82. Sapfir-25 (S-500, N-005) is a look-down/shoot-down pulse Doppler radar with a search range for bomber-size targets at high altitude of 56.7-62 naut miles (65.2-71.5 miles) 105-115 km, and tracking range of 40.5-43.2 naut miles (46.6-50 miles) 75-80 km. Search angles 30-60° each side in azimuth (depending of operation mode), +14°, -14° in elevation; the centre line of radar search sector can be moved 56° in azimuth and +52°, -42° in elevation.

MiG-25PDS (izdelye 84DS) *Foxbat-E* is similar to MiG-25PD but converted from the MiG-25P.

MiG-25I is a proposed conversion of the MiG-25P/PD with the MiG-29's Topaz radar and R-27 (AA-10 *Alamo*) and R-77 (AA-12 *Adder*) missiles. Not ordered.

MiG-25RU (izdelye 39) *Foxbat-C* is the two-seat trainer.

MiG-25PU (izdelye 22) *Foxbat-C* is similar to MiG-25RU but for combat training also, having 4 underwing pylons.

Izdelye 99 was an experimental aircraft with 3 MiG-31-type D-30F-6 turbofans. 2 built.

MiG-25SOTN (samolot optiko-televizyonnogo nabludenya) is a converted MiG-25PU (side number 22, c/n *22040578*) used to record the final landing phase of the Buran space shuttle.

MiG-25PDZ (Z stands for zapravka) is a converted MiG-25PD with flight refuelling probe. Additional 250-mm compartment set into the fuselage nose.

MiG-25PDSL is an MiG-25PD with added ECM systems. Prototype only.

Mikoyan MiG-27 (*Flogger-D/J*)

First flight: 20 August 1970, piloted by Piotr Ostapenko (MiG-23B prototype).
Role: Supersonic ground attack aircraft based on the MiG-23.
Chief designer: Grigori Sedov.

★ Aims

⋆ Alterations over the MiG-23 in accordance with its role, including strengthened undercarriage, external steel plate cockpit armour, deletion of the multi-mode radar, reshaping of the shortened nose to improve downward vision, changes to wing sweep and flap control, long wingroot extensions, non-variable air intakes, 2-position afterburner nozzles, new avionics, and larger low-pressure tyres.

▲ Development

▲ 1969. Work started.
▲ 1971. Series of 24 MiG-23Bs manufactured.
▲ 1973. MiG-23BM entered the service with the Soviet Air Force, renamed MiG-27.
▲ 1983. Production in the Soviet Union completed and transferred to India.
▲ 11 January 1986. First Indian MiG-27L assembled from Soviet MiG-27M parts (produced by Irkutsk) left the Nasik factory.
▲ 1988. First all-Indian MiG-27L (export M, also known as ML) was completed.
▲ 1994. Withdrawn from service in the CIS.
▲ Late 1994. Production of the MiG-27 was completed in India, with just 1 new aircraft reportedly accepted for military service that year.

Sales/users: Manufactured at the Irkutsk and Ulan-Ude factories, with a total of about 910 built between 1973 and 1983, including 560 MiG-27s, 200 of the most sophisticated MiG-27Ks and 150 MiG-27Ms. During 1982-85, standard MiG-27 *Flogger-D*s were converted into MiG-27D *Flogger-J*s at the Ulan-Ude factory. Production of MiG-27, after completion in the USSR, was transferred to India. These were manufactured at Nasik until 1994, while R-29B-300 engines are built at Koraput. The production programme provided for 165 aircraft of this type, the 100th leaving the production line in May 1992. Production had been expected to continue until 1997. India has plans to modernize these aircraft, equipping them with Indian or Western avionics such as IFF-405A, VUC-201A com radio, ARC-610A beacon receiver, RAM-700A radio altimeter, flight recorder, etc. Indian MiG-27s are the only examples now in service, the type having been withdrawn in the CIS.
Crew: Pilot.
Crew escape: Mikoyan KM-1M ejection seat.
Fixed guns: 6-barrel 30-mm GSh-6-30 cannon under the fuselage.
Ammunition: 265 rounds.
Number of weapon pylons: 7.
Expendable weapons and equipment: 6,614 lb (3,000 kg), though up to 8,818 lb (4,000 kg) had been standard on CIS models. Guided air-to-surface weapons can include Kh-23 (AS-7 *Kerry*), Kh-25ML (AS-10 *Karen*) Kh-29L/T (AS-14 *Kedge*), Kh-25MP/Kh-27 (AS-12 *Kegler*), and KAB-500Kr TV-guided bombs. (MiG-27K had the ability to carry laser guided KAB-500L bombs and new generation Kh-31P *Krypton* anti-radiation and Kh-59M *Kazoo* TV missiles.) Can carry 4 R60 *Aphid* air-to-air missiles for self defence. Standard unguided weapons include bombs, submunitions dispensers, incendiary tanks, and gun packs (including SPPU-22-01 with computer controlled movable barrels).
Radar: No multi-mode radar (see below for navigation).
Other sensors or mission equipment: Reconnaissance pod.
Flight/weapon system avionics/instrumentation: PrNK-23M nav/attack system. Inertial navigation system, SAU-23B1 control system/autopilot, A-321 (Korall-I) short-range radio navigation, and DISS-7 Doppler navigation radar. A-031 altimeter. R-862 and R-864 com radios. Klon laser rangefinder/target designator.
Self-protection systems: SPO-15 Beryoza RWR. SPS-141M Siren-FSh active jammer built into the fuselage nose and another jammer suspended in pods. Possibly BVP-50-60 chaff/flare dispensers on the top of the rear fuselage.
Engine: Soyuz/Khachaturov R-29B-300.
Engine rating: 17,637 lbf (78.46 kN) dry, 25,353 lbf (112.778 kN) with afterburning.
Nozzles/air intakes: Simple 2-position engine nozzle. Fixed geometry air intakes.

Mikoyan MiG-27L, the licence-build version of the M, also known as ML (Piotr Butowski)

Details for MiG-27 are similar to MiG-23 except as follows.

Principal dimensions:
Wing span: 25 ft 6 ins (7.779 m) *fully swept*, 45 ft 10 ins (13.965 m) *fully spread*
Maximum length: 56 ft (17.076 m)
Maximum height: 16 ft 5 ins (5 m)

Undercarriage:
Main wheel tyre size: 840 x 360 mm
Nose wheel tyre size: 570 x 140 mm
Wheel base: 19 ft 8 ins (5.991 m)
Wheel track: 8 ft 11 ins (2.728 m)

Weights:
Empty, operating: 26,676 lb (12,100 kg)
Maximum take-off: 39,903 lb (18,100 kg), unprepared runway
Maximum take-off with 8 x FAB-500 bombs: 45,569 lb (20,670 kg)
Landing (normal): 31,306 lb (14,200 kg)

Performance:
Maximum operating Mach number (Mmo): Mach 1.7
Maximum speed: 1,015 kts (1,168 mph) 1,880 km/h
Maximum Mach number at sea level: Mach 1.1
Maximum speed at sea level: 729 kts (839 mph) 1,350 km/h
Stalling speed: 170 kts (196 mph) 315 km/h
Landing speed: 146 kts (168 mph) 270 km/h
Take-off distance: 2,625 ft (800 m)
Landing distance: 3,117 ft (950 m) with drag-chute, 4,265 ft (1,300 m) brakes only
G limits: +7.5
Radius of action, with 2 Kh-29 ASMs: 121 naut miles (140 miles) 225 km, at low altitude
Radius of action, with 2 Kh-29 ASMs and 3 drop tanks: 292 naut miles (336 miles) 540 km
Maximum range: 945 naut miles (1,087 miles) 1,750 km
Maximum range with 3 drop tanks: 1,350 naut miles (1,553 miles) 2,500 km

Aircraft variants (in service):

MiG-27M (32-29) *Flogger-J* was developed as a simplified version of the MiG-27K, with provision for laser guided missiles but no laser guided bombs. MiG-27K's Kayra (K for Kayra) laser/optical sight/target designator was replaced by a Klon laser rangefinder/target designator. PrNK-23M nav/attack system.
MiG-27L (32-29L, sometimes called MiG-27ML) is the licence-build version of MiG-27M, manufactured by the Nasik Division of HAL in India, and named Bahadur.

Mikoyan MiG-29 (NATO name *Fulcrum*)

First flight: 6 October 1977, piloted by Alexander Fedotov.
Role: Lightweight close-air combat fighter, and attack.
Chief designer: Rostislav Belyakov until 1982, Mikhail Valdenberg from 1982-93, Valeri Novikov since May 1993.

★ Aims

⋆ Extremely high manoeuvrability, with high angles of attack.
⋆ Thrust to weight ratio of 1.1.
⋆ Wide fuselage/wing centre section providing 40% of the lifting force.
⋆ Complex weapon control system comprising radar, infra-red search-track and helmet mounted target designator.
⋆ Operation from rough unprepared runways, due to separate take-off air intakes that allow main intake blanking.
⋆ Structural life of 2,500 flight hours (20 years).

▲ Development

▲ 1969. Soviet Air Force competition opened for an PFI (perspektivnyi frontovoi istrebitel – advanced tactical fighter) of similar class to the US F-15. First MiG-29 design was a heavy air-superiority fighter.
▲ 1971. PFI programme was subdivided into 2 independent sections: TPFI (T for tyazholyi– heavy) and LPFI (L for logkiy – lightweight), similar to the US F-15 and F-16. MiG-29 was accordingly designed as a lightweight fighter.
▲ 1974. Preliminary design accepted.
▲ 6 October 1977. First flight of 9-01 prototype, the first of 14 prototypes.
▲ March 1979. First information published in the West, provisionally named Ram-L.
▲ 29 April 1981. First flight of the MiG-29UB combat trainer, piloted by Alexander Fedotov.
▲ 1982. Beginning of series production at Moscow's Znamya Truda aircraft plant (now MAPO).
▲ August 1983. First aircraft delivered to the Soviet Air Force.
▲ 1984. State Acceptance Trials completed.
▲ 13 February 1985. First flight of the izdelye 9-14 experimental version of the MiG-29 with air-to-surface attack systems in a suspended pod. Pilot Toktar Aubakirov. Prototype only.
▲ 25 April 1986. First flight of MiG-29M (MiG-33). See separate entry.

DETAILS FOR MIG-29 FULCRUM-A.

Principal dimensions:
Wing span: 37 ft 3 ins (11.36 m)
Maximum length: 56 ft 10 ins (17.32 m)
Length without probe: 53 ft 5 ins (16.28 m)
Maximum height: 15 ft 6 ins (4.73 m)

Wings:
Area: 410.1 sq ft (38.1 m^2)
Aspect ratio: 3.39
Sweepback at leading edge: 42°
Sweepback of LERX, at leading edge: 73° 30′
Incidence: 0°
Anhedral: 3°

Tail unit:
Tailplane span: 25 ft 6 ins (7.78 m)
Fins cant angle: 6° outward
Distance between fins, at roots: 11 ft 1 ins (3.38 m)

Undercarriage:
Type: Retractable, with twin steerable nosewheels
Main wheel tyre size: 840 x 290 mm
Nose wheel tyre size: 570 x 140 mm
Wheel base: 12 ft (3.645 m)
Wheel track: 10 ft 2 ins (3.09 m)

Weights:
Empty, operating: 24,030 lb (10,900 kg)
Take-off, clean: 31,526 lb (14,300 kg)
Take-off with 2 R-27 and 4 R-60M AAMs: 34,392 lb (15,600 kg)
Maximum take-off: 40,741 lb (18,480 kg)
Maximum take-off for MiG-29S: 43,431 lb (19,700 kg)
Maximum landing: 31,306 lb (14,200 kg)
Normal landing: 27,117 lb (12,300 kg)

Performance:
Maximum operating Mach number (MMO): Mach 2.3
Maximum operating speed: 1,296 kts (1,491 mph) 2,400 km/h
Maximum Mach number at sea level: Mach 1.2
Maximum speed at sea level: 810 kts (932 mph) 1,500 km/h
Maximum climb rate: 65,750 ft (20,040 m) per minute, at sea level
Stalling speed: 130 kts (149 mph) 240 km/h
Landing speed, normal landing weight: 135 kts (155 mph) 250 km/h
Landing speed, maximum landing weight: 146 kts (168 mph) 270 km/h
Take-off distance, maximum afterburning: 820 ft (250 m)
Take-off distance, without afterburning: 1,805 ft (550 m)
Landing distance, normal landing weight, with drag-chute: 2,165 ft (660 m)
Landing distance, normal landing weight: 2,953-3,117 ft (900-950 m)
Acceleration time from 600 to 1,000 km/h at 3,280 ft (1,000 m) height: 13.5 seconds
Acceleration time from 1,100 to 1,300 km/h at 3,280 ft (1,000 m) height: 8.7 sec
Maximum angle of attack, Mach < 0.85: 26°
Maximum angle of attack, Mach > 0.85: 15°
Maximum angle of attack, with 4,409 lb (2,000 kg) of bombs: 19°
G limits at Mach < 0.85, at 31,306 lb (14,200 kg) weight: +9, -3
G limits at Mach > 0.85, weight 31,306 lb (14,200 kg): +7/-1.5
Ceiling, clean: 59,050 ft (18,000 m)
Ceiling, with 2 AAMs: 57,400 ft (17,500 m)
Range at high altitude, Mach 0.8: 772 naut miles (889 miles) 1,430 km
Range at 660 ft (200 m), Mach 0.5: 383 naut miles (441 miles) 710 km
Maximum range with drop tank: 1,134 naut miles (1,305 miles) 2,100 km
Maximum range with drop tanks, MiG-29S: 1,566 naut miles (1,802 miles) 2,900 km

▲ 1 July 1986. MiG-29 first seen abroad, in Finland.
▲ 1992. Production switched to MiG-29S.

Sales/users: Single-seat fighter versions manufactured in Moscow and MiG-29UB combat trainers in Nizhni Novgorod (former Gorki). Total of 1,216 MiG-29 single-seaters and 197 MiG-29UBs built by January 1995. Since about 1990 production has continued for export only. In 1990 some 768 Soviet MiG-29s were based in Europe (704 Air Force, 64 Navy; never used by Air Defence Troops), plus an estimated 250 in the Asian sector of the USSR. By 1994, 71 of these were in Belarus, 33 Moldova, 236 Ukraine, about 30 in Turkmenistan, about 30 in Uzbekistan, Kazakhstan, and the remaining quantity in Russia. Exports had been made to Bulgaria, Cuba, Czech Republic (reserve, reportedly for sale), Germany (now integrated into the Luftwaffe), Hungary, India (80-85 aircraft when including 10 more ordered in January 1995; first delivered 1986, and to be built in that country), Iran, Iraq, North Korea, Poland, Romania, Slovakia, Syria, and former Yugoslavia. Total of about 270 exported to 14 countries. New export deliveries began after several years of inactivity. At the beginning of 1994, Slovakia obtained the first 6 MiG-29s of a new batch (1 MiG-29UB training aircraft and 5 single-seaters), as payment for Russian debts, and within this scheme Slovakia will purchase a total of 20. The purchase of 20 MiG-29s (most with inflight refuelling capability) by Malaysia was signed on 7 June 1994 in Kuala Lumpur (first deliveries in April 1995), the contract including 16 MiG-29S single seaters, 2 MiG-29UB two-seaters and a further 2 MiG-29UBs for training the ground staff. The Malaysians also stipulated in the contract an RD-33 engine lifetime of up to 2,000 hours, adaptation of the airframe to wet climate conditions, and installation of a satellite navigation system. Moldova sold some MiG-29s to Yemen in 1994.

Mikoyan MiG-29 (9-13) Fulcrum-C in Ukrainian markings, with drag-chute deployed (Piotr Butowski)

Crew: Pilot, or 2 in the MiG-29UB.
Cockpit: Conventional instrumentation, with HUD.
Crew escape: Zvezda zero-zero K-36DM/2-06 ejection seat.
Fixed guns: Gryazev/Shipunov GSh-30-1 (9A-4071K) single-barrel 30-mm cannon, built into the port wing LERX. Rate of fire 1,800 rounds per minute, and effective range of 3,900-5,900 ft (1,200-1,800 m) against air targets and 656-2,625 ft (200-800 m) against ground targets.
Ammunition: 150 rounds.
Number of weapon pylons: 6 under the wings; BD3-UMK2B pylons; APU-470, APU-73-1D and APU 68-85E launching devices.
Expendable weapons and equipment: Standard air-combat armament comprises 2 medium-range radar or infra-red R-27R (AA-10 *Alamo*) AAMs on the inner pylons, plus 4 R-73 (AA-11 *Archer*) or R-60M (AA-8 *Aphid*) short-range infra-red missiles on the outer pylons. Air-to-ground weapons include up to 4,409 lb (2,000 kg) of 250 kg and 500 kg free-fall bombs, ZB-500 incendiary tank, KMGU-2 submunitions dispenser, and 57-mm to 240-mm unguided rockets (S-8 and S-24B); load increased to 6,614 lb (3,000 kg) on *Fulcrum-C*. No smart weapons. Because of its improved radar, MiG-29S can be armed with new-generation active radar medium-range R-77 (RVV-AE, AA-12 *Adder*) and extended-range R-27ER (AA-10C *Alamo-C*) AAMs. Maximum bomb load is increased to 8,816 lb (4,000 kg), due to tandem bomb racks on the 4 innermost pylons. TV guided bombs, ASMs and active radar Kh-31A for MiG-29SM.
Radar: RLPK-29 (radiolokatsyonnyi pritselnyi kompleks) radar attack system includes coherent pulse Doppler S-29 (N-019, NATO *Slot Back*) look-down/shoot-down radar and Ts100.02-06 digital computer. Search range (fighter-type target) is 38 naut miles (43.5 miles) 70 km in front hemisphere and 19 naut miles (21.75 miles) 35 km in rear hemisphere, with an increase of about 50% for larger bomber-size targets. Radar can track up to 10 targets simultaneously and engage the one chosen by the computer as the most important. Search angles 67° each side in azimuth, +60°, -38° in elevation. MiG-29S is equipped with the more jam-resistant N-019M Topaz radar, able to track 10 and engage 2.
Flight/weapon system avionics/instrumentation: RLPK-29 radar system is supported by the OEPrNK-29 (optiko-elektronnyi pritselno-navigatsyonnyi kompleks) opto-electronic nav/attack system, which comprises the OEPS-29 sighting system, SN-29 navigation system, Ts100.02-02 digital computer, SUO-29M2 weapons control system and SYeI-31E2 data presentation system with ILS-31 head-up-display. OEPS-29 (optiko-elektronnaya pritselnaya sistema) comprises the KOLS-29 infra-red/laser search and track device (tracking range 10 naut miles, 11.2 miles, 18 km, rear hemisphere only, distance accuracy 10 ft, 3 m) and Shchel-3UM helmet-mounted target designator. SN-29 (sistema navigatsi) includes the ARK-19 radio compass, A-037/06 altimeter, A-611 marker beacon receiver, and A-323 short-range navigation and instrument landing system. E502-20/04 Turkus data link for target indication from land-based radars. R-862 com radio, SO-69M transponder. Parol IFF (SRO-2 transponder, SRZ-15 interrogator).
Self-protection systems: SPO-15 (L006-LM/101) Beryoza radar warning receiver. 20SP passive countermeasures system with 2 BVP-30-26M (blok vybrosa pomekh) chaff/flare dispensers built into the wing upper surface fence; each dispenser contains 30 x 26-mm PPI-26 flares or PPR-26 chaff cartridges. MiG-29 (9-13) and MiG-29S (9-13S) also have the Gardenia-1 active electronic jammer built into the airframe.
Wing characteristics: Swept-back, mid mounted. Wide fuselage/wing centre section provides 40% of the lifting force. Leading-edge root extensions (LERX). Outer wing panels of conventional 3-spar construction.
Wing control surfaces: 3-section, full-span (except wingtips) manoeuvring flaps (20°). Slotted trailing-edge flaps (25°), and ailerons (+25°, -15°, neutral +5°) with tabs. Vortex generators on forward fuselage prevents aileron reversal at near maximum angles of attack.
Tail control surfaces: Tail surfaces are mounted on booms alongside the engine nacelles. Slab (taileron) tailplane, deflected +5° 45′, -17° 45′ evenly or differentially. Twin fins and rudders, outward canted by 6°. Rudders have 25° deflection.

Airbrakes: Above and below the rear fuselage, between the engine nozzles; upper flap deflects 56° and has an area of 7.9 sq ft (0.73 m^2), lower deflects 60° and has an area of 8.6 sq ft (0.795 m^2).
Flight control system: Mechanical, hydraulically actuated. SAU-451-04 (sistema avtomaticheskogo upravlenya) automatic control system includes SOS-3M (sistema ogranichitelnykh signalov) angle of attack/ g-load dumper.
Construction materials: Mainly aluminium-lithium alloys, steel, with some composites (used in parts of the ailerons, trailing-edge flaps and tail) and titanium.
Engines: 2 widely spaced Klimov/Sarkisov RD-33 turbofans.
Engine rating: Each 11,100 lbf (49.42 kN) dry, and 18,300 lbf (81.4 kN) with afterburning.
Air intakes: Wedge main air intakes, which are blanked off by doors with many small apertures when the nosewheel is lowered, at which point air for the engines is supplied via the apertures plus louvres on the upper surface of each LERX. ARV-29D air-intake control.
Flight refuelling probe: Fitted to some aircraft.
Fuel system: 4,300 litres of internal fuel in 3 tanks inside the fuselage/wing centre section (650, 870 and 2,120 litres) and 2 outer wing tanks (each 330 litres). Provision for a single underfuselage drop tank between the engines, of 1,520 litres capacity on *Fulcrum-C*. 2 more 1,150 litre underwing tanks can be carried by MiG-29S only.
Hydraulic system: 3,002 psi.
Braking system: Mainwheels brakes. 183 sq ft (17 m^2) drag-chute housed in a tailcone, aft of the airbrakes.

Aircraft variants:

MiG-29 (izdelye 9-12 or izdelye 5) *Fulcrum-A* was the first production model, early series aircraft having detachable ventral tail fins and no chaff/flare overwing dispensers. Extended-chord rudders later retrofitted on all aircraft. Export variants were designated 9-12A (with N-019EA radar) for WarPact countries, or 9-12B for other countries.
MiG-29 (izdelye 9-13 or izdelye 7) *Fulcrum-C* is similar to 9-12 but with Gardenia active ECM system installed in the more heavily curved top of fuselage decking.
MiG-29UB (izdelye 9-51 or izdelye 30) *Fulcrum-B* is the two-seat trainer. Radar removed, and no chaff/flare dispensers.
MiG-29KVP (korotkiy vzlot i posadka, STOL), aircraft 9-18 is a technology demonstrator for the ship-borne MiG-29K, converted from an early production MiG-29 (9-12). Arrester hook added under the tail. Tested on land at Saki, Ukraine, with the first ski-jump take-off on 21 August 1982, piloted by Aviard Fastovets. Prototype only.
MiG-29S (izdelye 9-13S) is externally similar to MiG-29. Modified N-019M Topaz radar. Improved weapons include R-27RE extended-range and R-77 medium-range missiles; maximum weapons load 8,818 lb (4,000 kg). Improved flight control system, allowing a 30° angle of attack (instead of 26°). Provision for 2 x 1,150 litre drop tanks under the wings, supplementing the previous underfuselage tank, offering a ferry range of 1,566 naut miles (1,802 miles) 2,900 km.
MiG-29SD is similar to MiG-29S but converted from the MiG-29. Avionics changes include IFF and active jamming. Conversions apply to both 9-12 and 9-13 models. Rudders have greater travel.
MiG-29SE (izdelye 9-13SE) is the export version of MiG-29S. Added Tacan AN/APN-118 navigation system, TNL-1000 GPS receiver, ILS-71, R-800L1 radio with emergency frequency of 243 MHz, and SO-69M transponder. Downgraded N-019ME radar.
MiG-33 (MiG-29M) and MiG-29K– see separate entry.
MiG-29SM is similar to MiG-29S but has extended air-to-surface capabilities. TV display for use with KAB-500KR guided bomb and Kh-29T or Kh-31A missiles. Displayed June 1995. 44,090 lb (20,000 kg) take-off weight.

DETAILS FOR MiG-29M FULCRUM-E.

Principal dimensions:
Wing span: 37 ft 3 ins (11.36 m)
Maximum length: 57 ft (17.37 m)
Maximum height: 15 ft 6 ins (4.73 m)

Wings:
Sweepback: 42° leading edge
Anhedral: 3°

Undercarriage:
Type: Strengthened MiG-29 type
Wheel base: 11 ft 11 ins (3.64 m)
Wheel track: 10 ft 2 ins (3.10 m)

Weights:
Normal take-off: 37,038 lb (16,800 kg)
Maximum take-off: 48,502 lb (22,000 kg)

Performance:
Maximum operating Mach number (MMO): Over Mach 2.2
Maximum speed: 1,323 kts (1,522 mph) 2,450 km/h
Maximum speed at sea level: 810 kts (932 mph) 1,500 km/h
Maximum climb rate: 64,960 ft (19,800 m) per minute, at sea level
Turn rate at 9,850 ft (3,000 m): 23° per second
Maximum angle of attack, Mach < 0.85: 30°
G limit at Mach < 0.85: +9
Ceiling: 55,775 ft (17,000 m)
Radius of action, air combat mission, with 2 medium-range and 2 short-range AAMs, 3 drop tanks, and 5 x 360° turns during combat: 675 naut miles (777 miles) 1,250 km
Radius of action, air intercept mission with 4 medium-range AAMs, 3 drop tanks, Mach 0.85: 778 naut miles (895 miles) 1,440 km
Radius of action, ground attack mission with 2 ASMs, 2 short-range AAMs, and 3 drop tanks: 642 naut miles (739 miles) 1,190 km
Radius of action, ground attack mission with 4,409 lb (2,000 kg) of bombs, 2 short-range AAMs, and 3 drop tanks: 632 naut miles (727 miles) 1,170 km
Maximum range: 1,188 naut miles (1,367 miles) 2,200 km, on internal fuel
Range at low altitude: 486 naut miles (559 miles) 900 km on internal fuel
Ferry range with 3 drop tanks: 1,728 naut miles (1,988 miles) 3,200 km

Mikoyan MiG-33, MiG-29M and MiG-29K (NATO name *Fulcrum-E*)

First flight: 25 April 1986, piloted by Valeri Menitsky.
Role: Lightweight tactical fighter and ground attack aircraft; MiG-29K is a ship-borne version.
Chief designer: Mikhail Valdenberg (1982-93) and Valeri Novikov since May 1993.

★ Aims

★ According to data from the design bureau, the close air combat effectiveness of MiG-29M is 1.8 times better than that of MiG-29 and 3.5 times more effective in ground attack.
★ Necessary ground service for the MiG-29M is 11.5 man hours per 1 flight hour.
★ Mean time for flight preparation of the MiG-29M is 30 minutes.
★ 15-25 minutes turnaround between missions.

▲ Development

▲ 1982. Start of work on a highly modified and advanced MiG-29 derivative with air-to-surface capabilities added. Also start of development of a ship-borne version as the MiG-29K.
▲ 25 April 1986. First flight of the MiG-29M prototype (side number 151, first aircraft of 9-15 type).
▲ 23 July 1988. First flight of the MiG-29K, piloted by Toktar Aubakirov (side number 311, first aircraft of 9-31 type).
▲ September 1992. First seen abroad, at the Farnborough Air Show (MiG-29M side number 156).
Sales/users: 6 aircraft built for trials. Small-scale production expected for the Russian Air Force and export.
Crew: Pilot.
Cockpit: 15° visibility over the nose (1.5° more than MiG-29), due to the higher seat position. 2 cathode-ray tube (CRT) multi-function displays and improved HUD, with conventional instrumentation as stand-by. Cockpit differs from aircraft to aircraft; for example, CRT displays in 156 (sixth aircraft) are located about 8 ins (20 cm) lower than in 155. First MiG with HOTAS.
Crew escape: Zvezda K-36DM zero-zero ejection seats.
Fixed guns: GSh-30-1 single-barrel 30-mm cannon.
Ammunition: 100 rounds.
Number of weapon pylons: 9, 4 under each wing and 1 under the fuselage.
Expendable weapons and equipment: Up to 12,125 lb (5,500 kg). Air-to-air weapons are those detailed in the previous MiG-29 entry or 2 improved range R-27ER/R-27ETs (AA-10 *Alamo-C/D*), or up to 8 active-radar medium range R-77s (AA-12 *Adder*); maximum quantity of R-27R/R-27T1s (AA-10 *Alamo-A/B*)

Fifth MiG-29M prototype Fulcrum-E, armed with Kh-31 ASMs and R-77. Note the sharp "chine" of the wing LERX (Piotr Butowski)

Kh-29T (AS-14 Kedge) heavy TV-guided ASM on a MiG-29M, with an R-77 AAM at left (Piotr Butowski)

missiles is 4 rather than 2 for MiG-29. Air-to-surface weapons options include up to 6 Kh-25ML/MP (AS-10 *Karen*/AS-12 *Kegler*) laser guided/ anti-radar missiles, up to 6 Kh-29L/T (AS-14 *Kedge*) laser/TV guided missiles, up to 4 Kh-31A/P (AS-17 *Krypton*) anti-ship/anti-radar missiles, or up to 6 KAB-500Kr TV-guided bombs, as well as free-fall bombs, submunitions dispensers, rockets, incendiary tanks, etc.
Radar: Phazotron S-29M (N-010) Zhuk lookdown/ shootdown pulse Doppler radar. Search range for fighter-size targets 48.6 naut miles (56 miles) 90 km in the forward hemisphere, 21.6 naut miles (25 miles) 40 km in rear hemisphere. Can track-while-scan 10 targets and engage 4 simultaneously. Mapping with the resolution of 49-66 ft (15-20 m), image freezing and terrain following in the air-to-ground mode.
Flight/weapon system avionics/instrumentation: Improved opto-electronic search and track device has a range of 16.2 naut miles (18.6 miles) 30 km in the rear and 5.4 naut miles (6.2 miles) 10 km in the forward hemispheres. Moreover, it may be used for laser designation of surface targets to be attacked by Kh-25ML and Kh-29L laser-guided missiles. The new TV channel is used for increasing the range of visual observation (for identification of targets without switching-on the radar IFF unit) as well as for designation of targets for TV guided Kh-29T air-to-surface missiles and KAB-500Kr bombs.
Self-protection systems: The improved radar warning receiver is also used for programming the seekers of Kh-25MP and Kh-31P anti-radiation missiles immediately before launch. Gardenia-1 active jammer built into the airframe. Chaff/flare system built into the dorsal spine, with 120 x 26-mm flares/cartridges rather than 60 in MiG-29.
Wing characteristics: Chine type LERX from the wing leading-edge creates strong vortex.
Wing control surfaces: Similar to MiG-29 but with elongated ailerons.
Tail control surfaces: Slab tailplane of greater chord, with dogtooth leading edges.
Airbrakes: Single door-type airbrake on fuselage dorsal spine (see photograph).
Flight control system: Analog fly-by-wire. Quadruple redundant pitch control; dual roll and yaw control with stand-by mechanical system (up to half of normal deflection of control surfaces).
Fuselage: Enlarged dorsal spine, the fuselage structure ending beyond the engine nozzles (see photograph).
Construction materials: Lightweight aluminium/lithium alloy centre-section.

MiG-29M cockpit (Piotr Butowski)

Rear view of the MiG-29K, showing the redesigned rear fuselage, raised single airbrake, and stowed arrester hook (Piotr Butowski)

Kh-25ML (AS-10 Karen) laser-guided ASM (rear) and R-77 (AS-12 Adder) AAM under a MiG-29K with wingtips folded (Piotr Butowski)

Engines: 2 Klimov/Sarkisov RD-33K turbofans (engine life 1,400 hours, including general overhaul after first 700 hours).
Engine rating: Each 19,400 lbf (86.3 kN) with afterburning; 22,050 lbf (98.07 kN) version is under test.
Air intakes: Larger than for MiG-29, in accordance with the increased engine rating. Original MiG-29 blanking doors deleted, as are the overwing louvres and associated ducting (see Fuel system below), replaced by blanking grids and electronically-controlled lower intake lip (to further increase orifice area when required) that together provide sufficient air flow during take off. Curiously, to camouflage MiG-29M against identification, false louvres were painted on the upper surface of the LERX to make the aircraft appear similar to MiG-29.
Fuel system: 5,700 litres (1,400 litres more than MiG-29) of internal fuel, due to the freeing of space in the LERX. Provision for 3 drop tanks, 1 x 1,520 litre under the fuselage and 2 x 1,150 litre under the wings.
Flight refuelling probe: MiG-29K only.
Braking system: Twin drag-chutes, 280 sq ft (26 m^2) area.

Aircraft variants:

MiG-29M (izdelye 9-15 or izdelye 9) *Fulcrum-E* , as described.
MiG-29EM (izdelye 9-15E) is the projected export version of MiG-29M, equipped with the downgraded radar/weapons of the MiG-29S.
MiG-29MR is the projected reconnaissance version.
MiG-29UM (izdelye 9-16) is the projected two-seat combat trainer.
MiG-33 is the export version of MiG-29M, with fully rated radar/weapon system.
MiG-29K (izdelye 9-31) *Fulcrum-D* was produced as a carrier-borne version, similar to the MiG-29M. Work began in 1984, and the maiden flight was achieved on 23 July 1988. The first landing on the carrier *Tbilisi* (now *Admiral Kuznetsov*) was made on 1 November 1989. 2 prototypes only, with the programme terminated in the Summer of 1993 in favour of Su-27K (Su-33). Construction commonality between MiG-29K and MiG-29M is 80-85%. RD-33K engines have an additional special mode of operation, offering 20,723 lbf (92.19 kN) of thrust. In-flight refuelling and an emergency fuel tank emptying system are installed. Wing span increased to 39 ft 4.5 ins (12.0 m); extended chord trailing edge flaps; leading-edge flaps extended to the wing tips, but the ailerons are unchanged. The wings fold for stowage on board ship (the folded span is 25 ft 7 ins, 7.80 m). The nose radome also folds, reducing length from 56 ft 8 ins (17.27 m) to 49 ft 6.5 ins (15.10 m). Rear fuselage is reinforced, and an arrester hook installed. The S-29K radar is similar to S-29M Zhuk, and the navigation system is improved. Nominal take-off weight is 39,022 lb (17,700 kg); maximum 49,163 lb (22,300 kg). Maximum speed is 1,242 kts (1,429 mph) 2,300 km/h; maximum speed at sea level is 756 kts (890 mph) 1,400 km/h. Ceiling 57,000 ft (17,400 m); climb rate at 1,000 m altitude is 51,180 ft (15,600 m) per minute. G limit at Mach < 0.85 is +8.5; G limit at Mach > 0.85 is +6. Ferry range is 1,620 naut miles (1,864 miles) 3,000 km.
MiG-29KU (korabelnyi uchebnyi) is the projected ship-borne training version of MiG-29K, with a redesigned nose section containing a separate stepped cockpit with individual canopy for the instructor, forward and below of the standard cockpit, as for the MiG-25PU/RU. Programme cancelled.
Projected further developments of MiG-29M include a version with added canard surfaces.

Mikoyan MiG-31 (NATO name *Foxhound*)

First flight: 16 September 1975, piloted by Alexander Fedotov.
Role: Long-range interceptor for autonomous operation with or without GCI (ground-controlled interception) system support, mainly for Russia's northern regions for protection against cruise missile attack.

★ Aims

★ Mach 2.35 cruise speed with 4 R-33 long-range AAMs.
★ 720 km supersonic combat radius.
★ 3 hours 36 minutes subsonic flight endurance.
★ All-altitude weapons system.
★ Electronically-scanned phased array fire control radar, enabling true multi-target engagement.
★ Group operations of up to 4 aircraft, with common information area (data exchange system).
★ Heaviest, most heavily armed, and fastest fighter aircraft in the world.
★ Loss coefficient: 11.7 aircraft for 100,000 flight hours.

▲ Development

▲ 1972. Work began on a MiG-25 replacement with added all-altitude multi-target capability and extended flight endurance. Chief designer, Gleb Lozino-Lozinski, was replaced in the mid-1970s by Konstantin Vasilchenko; now Anatoli Belosvet.

▲ 16 September 1975. First flight of MiG-25MP (E-155MP) prototype.

▲ 1976. First knowledge in the West of a MiG-25 development came from a defecting Soviet MiG-25 pilot.

▲ December 1976. First pre-production MiG-31 built by Gorki (now Nizhny Novgorod) aircraft plant.

▲ December 1981. State acceptance trials were completed and the MiG-31-33 intercept system (which includes MiG-31 aircraft, R-33 missiles and control systems) was accepted into service with Soviet Air Defence Troops.

▲ 1983. Initial operational capability achieved by the first MiG-31 unit, the 786th Air Defence Fighter Regiment in Pravdinsk.

▲ Autumn 1985. MiG-31 was photographed for the first time by a Norwegian F-16 over the Barents Sea.

▲ 21 December 1985. First flight of the MiG-31M, piloted by Boris Orlov.

▲ 1986. First flight of the MiG-31D satellite interceptor.

▲ 1990. MiG-31B replaced MiG-31 on the production line.

▲ June 1991. MiG-31 was exhibited for the first time in the West (Paris Air Show).

▲ Spring 1994. First successful launches of R-37 missiles from the MiG-31M, at a distance of over 162 naut miles (186 miles) 300 km.

Sales/users: About 400 built by early 1995, and series production continues in small quantities at Nizhny Novgorod. In service with Russian Air Defence Troops only, located in the Moscow region and Northern Russia. A contract for the delivery of 24 to China was reported in 1992.

Crew: 2, in tandem cockpits, pilot (front) and weapons systems officer (rear).

Cockpit: Separate rearward-hinged canopies. Controls in both cockpits. Conventional instrumentation.

Crew escape: Zvezda K-36 zero-zero ejection seats (Mikoyan KM-1M in early aircraft).

Fixed guns: 6-barrel 23-mm GSh-6-23 (9YeYu) cannon at the starboard side of MiG-31's fuselage. No cannon in the MiG-31M.

Ammunition: 260 rounds.

Number of weapon pylons: 8, or 10 for MiG-31M (6 instead of 4 under the fuselage, and 4 under the wings)

Expendable weapons and equipment: 4 semi-active radar R-33 (AA-9 *Amos*) AAMs of 65 naut mile (74.6 mile) 120 km range, carried in tandem pairs under the fuselage (the front pair semi-recessed), plus 2 medium-range R-40TD (AA-6 *Acrid*) or 4 self-defence R-60M (AA-8 *Aphid*) AAMs on the wing pylons. MiG-31B/BS have R-33S instead of R-33 missiles. MiG-31M is armed with 6 active-radar R-37 AAMs of 189 naut mile (217 mile) 350 km of range and 4 medium-range R-77s (AA-12 *Adders*).

Mikoyan MiG-31 Foxhound-A 2-seat interceptor (Piotr Butowski)

Radar: Zaslon (or N-007, or S-800, NATO name *Flash Dance*) fire control radar, the first ever operational electronically-scanned phased array type (chief designer Alfred Fedotchenko). Can track 10 targets and engage 4 well-spread targets simultaneously. Search range for bomber-sized targets is 108 naut miles (124 miles) 200 km, and tracking range 65 naut miles (74.6 miles) 120 km, in the forward hemisphere, or 49 naut miles (56 miles) 90 km search and 38 naut miles (43.5 miles) 70 km tracking in the rear hemisphere. Search range of fighter-size targets in the forward hemisphere is 49 naut miles. Search angles are 70° each side in azimuth, and +70°, -60° in elevation. Zaslon weighs more than 2,205 lb (1,000 kg), of which 661 lb (300 kg) is the antenna of 43 in (110 cm) diameter. MiG-31M is equipped with Zaslon-M radar, capable of tracking 10 targets and engaging 6 simultaneously, and has extended range; about 55 in (140 cm) diameter antenna.

Flight/weapon system avionics/instrumentation: Argon-K digital weapon computer. Tropik (Loran-type) and Marshrut (Omega-type) long-range navigation systems. 8TP retractable infra-red search and track device under fuselage nose, with search angles of 60° each side in azimuth, and +6°, -13° in elevation.

Self-protection systems: SPO-15 Beryoza radar warning receiver, and active electronic countermeasures.

Wing characteristics: Modestly swept-back, high mounted, with short leading-edge root extensions. Single fence on the upper surface of each wing.

Wing control surfaces: Ailerons (+20°, -20°) and slotted trailing-edge flaps (30°). 4-section leading-edge slats (13°).

Tail control surfaces: Slab (taileron) tailplane, operating both symmetrically (+9°, -30°) and differentially (+1° 50', -1° 50') to simulate elevator and aileron functions when flying at supersonic speed. Twin outward-canted fins with rudders (25° deflection), and 2 ventral stabilizing fins.

Details for MiG-31B/MiG-31BS Foxhound-A.

Principal dimensions:
Wing span: 44 ft 2 ins (13.464 m)
Maximum length: 74 ft 5 ins (22.688 m)
Length without probe: 67 ft 8 ins (20.62 m)
Maximum height: 20 ft 2 ins (6.150 m)

Wings:
Area: 663 sq ft (61.6 m^2)
Aspect ratio: 2.943
Sweepback at leading edge: 41°
Sweepback at trailing edge: 9° 30'
Twist: 0° root
Anhedral: 4°
Aileron span: 5 ft 7 ins (1.7 m)
Trailing-edge flap span: 8 ft 10 ins (2.682 m)

Tail unit:
Tailplane span: 28 ft 8 ins (8.740 m)
Tailplane sweepback: 50° 22'
Tailplane dihedral: 1° 25'
Fins area: 168 sq ft (15.6 m^2)
Fin sweepback: 54°
Fins cant angle: 8° outward
Rudders area: 22.8 sq ft (2.12 m^2)
Ventral fins area: 32.3 sq ft (3.0 m^2)
Ventral fins cant angle: 12° outward

Undercarriage:
Type: Retractable, with twin nosewheels. Each main unit has 2 offset tandem wheels
Main wheel tyre size: 950 x 300 mm
Nose wheel tyre size: 660 x 200 mm
Wheel base: 23 ft 4 ins (7.113 m)
Wheel track: 11 ft 11 ins (3.638 m)

Weights:
Empty, operating: 48,105 lb (21,820 kg)
Maximum take-off: 101,853 lb (46,200 kg)

Performance:
Maximum Mach number: Mach 2.83
Maximum speed at high altitude: 1,620 kts (1,864 mph) 3,000 km/h
Maximum speed at sea level: 810 kts (932 mph) 1,500 km/h
Supersonic cruise Mach number at high altitude: Mach 2.35
Supersonic cruise speed at high altitude: 1,350 kts (1,553 mph) 2,500 km/h
Subsonic cruise Mach number: Mach 0.85
Landing speed: 151 kts (174 mph) 280 km/h
Take-off distance: 3,937 ft (1,200 m)
Landing distance: 2,625 ft (800 m)
Climb time to 32,810 ft (10,000 m): 7.9 minutes
G limit: +5
Combat radius at Mach 2.35, with 4 R-33s and no drop tanks: 389 naut miles (447 miles) 720 km
Combat radius at Mach 0.85, with 4 R-33s, 2 drop tanks, and one in-flight refuelling: 1,188 naut miles (1,367 miles) 2,200 km
Combat radius at Mach 0.85, with 4 R-33s and 2 drop tanks: 756 naut miles (870 miles) 1,400 km
Combat radius at Mach 0.85, with R-33s and no drop tanks: 648 naut miles (746 miles) 1,200 km
Ferry range, unrefuelled: 1,782 naut miles (2,050 miles) 3,300 km
Duration with drop tanks: 3 hours 36 min

MiG-31B front cockpit (Piotr Butowski)

MiG-31B rear cockpit (Piotr Butowski)

MiG-31M Foxhound-B with a more convex dorsal spine and long curved wingroot extensions. The "fat" nose contains Zaslon-M radar. Note the wingtip pods, lowered airbrake, and electronically controlled lower air intake lip (Piotr Butowski)

Airbrakes: 2, forward-hinged, under the air-intake ducts (44°). Airbrakes area 29.9 sq ft (2.78 m^2)
Flight control system: Conventional, hydraulically actuated.
Construction materials: 50% steel, 33% aluminium and 16% titanium by weight.
Engines: 2 Aviadvigatel/Solovyov D-30F-6 (izdelye 48) turbofans. MiG-31M uses 2 advanced D-30F-6Ms (izdelye 64) of 38,580 lbf (171.62 kN) with afterburning.
Engine rating: Each 20,944 lbf (93.17 kN) dry, and 34,172 lbf (152 kN) with afterburning.
Air intakes: Wedge-type, with electronically-controlled lower intake lip to increase the orifice area when required.
Flight refuelling probe: MiG-31B/BS are equipped with a semi-retractable probe on the port side of the nose. MiG-31M has a starboard-side retractable probe.
Fuel system: 36,045 lb (16,350 kg) of fuel inside the fuselage and fins. 2 x 2,500 litre drop tanks can be carried under the wings. MiG-31M has a 39,683 lb (18,000 kg) internal fuel capacity.
Braking system: Mainwheels brakes. Twin drag-chute in a fairing between the engine nozzles.

Aircraft variants:

E-155MP (MiG-25MP, izdelye 83) prototype had no wingroot extensions.
MiG-31 (izdelye 01) *Foxhound-A*, as described (see MiG-31B).
MiG-31B (izdelye 01B or izdelye 12) *Foxhound-A* has radar and missile changes. New navigation system. Flight-refuelling probe added.
MiG-31BS (izdelye 01BS) *Foxhound-A* is similar to the MiG-31B, but upgraded from the MiG-31. A-723 navigation system. Software-enhanced Zaslon radar.
MiG-31E is an export version.
MiG-31F is a proposed mid-life upgrade for interceptors, with MTOW increased to 110,230 lb (50,000 kg). Armament includes 6 Kh-31s, 3 Kh-59s, 2 Kh-59Ms, 3 Ch-27T/Ls or other ASMs (including projected anti-ballistic missile weapons), or AA-12 *Adder* or AA-11 *Archer* AAMs.
MiG-31FE is the export version of MiG-31F.
MiG-31M (izdelye 05) *Foxhound-B* has a modified weapons system with Zaslon-M radar, and up to 6 R-37 plus 4 R-77 AAMs. No fixed cannon. Wingroot extensions with lengthened curved leading edges, wider dorsal spine, cylindrical wingtip pods on some aircraft, reduced glazing for the rear cockpit, and increased-area rudders. More powerful engines, more fuel, and refuelling probe transferred to starboard side. Take-off weight increased to about 114,640 lb (52,000 kg). 7 built by early 1995, with production continuing.
MiG-31D (izdelye 07) was developed as an anti-satellite version, armed with 2 Vympel missiles on wing pylons. 2 prototypes cancelled.

Mikoyan 1-42

First flight: Expected in 1995, but not flown by July.
Role: Advanced tactical fighter with attack capability.

★ Aims

★ Supersonic cruise speed.
★ High manoeuvrability at supersonic speed.
★ Control retained at angles of attack up to 60-70° (so called super-manoeuvrability).
★ Safe flying at hypercritical angles of attack (about 100-120°), with stability but not controllability (so-called hyper-manoeuvrability).
★ Final configuration to have vectoring engine nozzles.
★ Built with so-called "second generation stealth technology" (special radar absorbing materials and coatings, with minimal airframe changes that impair aircraft performance).
★ Air-to-air missiles carried in the fuselage weapons bay, in order to reduce the aircraft's radar signature.
★ New radars, including a tail unit for rearward coverage.
★ New weapon systems with next-generation missiles of each range-class.

▲ Development

▲ 1983. Work began on the new MFI (mnogo-funktsyonalnyi istrebitel, multifunction fighter) according to programme I-90 (istrebitel, fighter for the nineties).
▲ 1986. Mikoyan design bureau began the detailed design.
▲ 1991. First flight originally planned, but completion of the prototypes has been delayed through financial restrictions, especially for engine development.
▲ 1994. Revised first flight date, (but again delayed).
▲ December 1994. Performed high-speed taxi trials.
▲ 1998-2000. Possible initial Russian deployment, according to reported comments of Col Gen Piotr Deinekin.

Sales/users: 2 prototypes built by Mikoyan experimental works in Moscow.
Crew: Pilot.
Fixed guns: Probably a single 30-mm cannon.
Expendable weapons and equipment: Standard air-to-air armament includes 162 naut mile (186 mile) 300 km range R-37 missiles, medium/intermediate range R-77/R-77M missiles, and R-73 close air combat missiles, housed in the fuselage. The Vympel design bureau is working on a successor to the R-73 short-range missile for use on 1-42 and other aircraft. The first tests of this new high-manoeuvrability missile are expected in near future.
Radar: N-014 electronically-scanned phased array type in the nose. Rearward-looking self-defence radar in the tail.
Wing characteristics: Shoulder mounted, with moderate sweepback. Little or no anhedral or dihedral. Clipped wingtips.

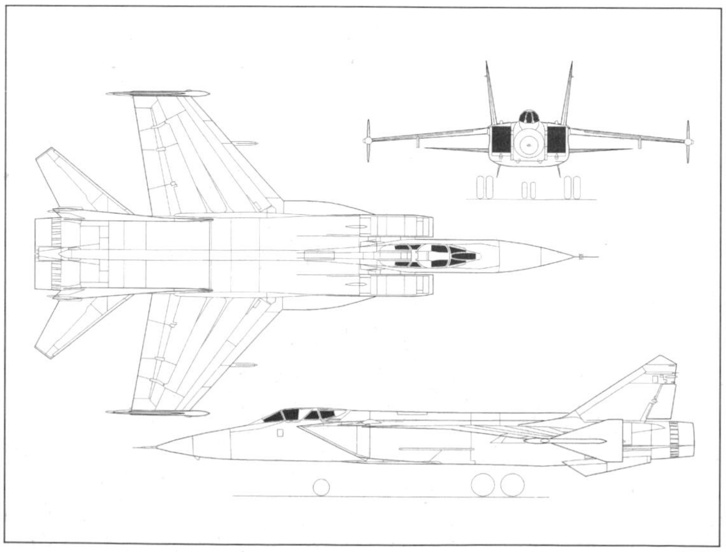

MiG-31D (07) anti-satellite interceptor (Piotr Butowski)

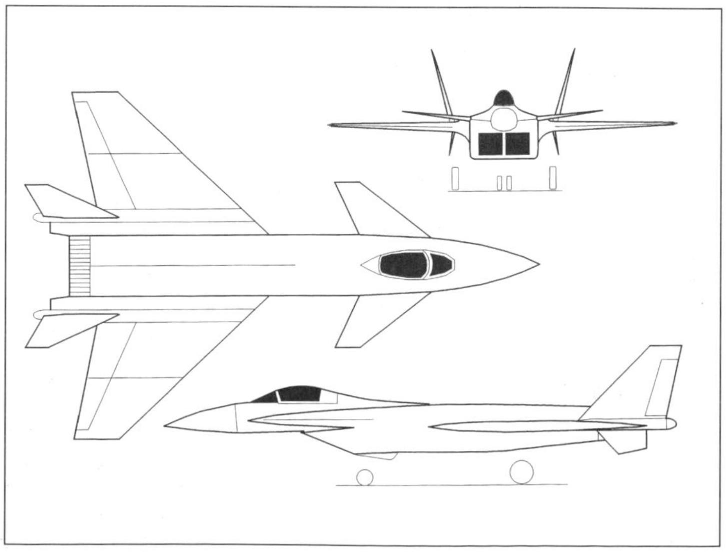

Mikoyan 1-42 fifth-generation fighter (provisional drawing as of early 1995 via Piotr Butowski)

Wing control surfaces: Multi-segment leading-edge flaps. Trailing-edge ailerons and flaps, with possible spoilers.
Tail control surfaces: Twin outward-canted dorsal fins and inset rudders, possibly carried on short fuselage booms of MiG-29 type. Twin outward-canted ventral fins.
Canard: Swept, near the nose.
Fuselage: Rectangular cross section, though blended on the upper decking. Additional flaps, functioning as elevators, are installed on the rear fuselage, thus increasing the allowable centre of gravity range.
Airbrakes: Large airbrake on the upper fuselage.
Engines: 2 Saturn AL-41F turbofans.
Engine rating: Each about 40,785 lbf (181.4 kN).
Air intakes: Box-type under the forward fuselage, with large side-by-side inlets.
Nozzles: Vectoring nozzles will be fitted to the final configuration.

Aircraft variants:
1-44 prototype, without some advanced systems. MTOW over 77,160 lb (35,000 kg).
1-42 (MFI) final production configuration.

Mikoyan 701 and 701P

Role: Projected long-range and high-altitude interceptor (successor to the MiG-31 but not a derivative), and 16-passenger supersonic business jet (701P).

▲ Development
▲ Late 1980s. Initial design began.
▲ September 1993. Picture of the 701P projected passenger aircraft was published in Moscow.
▲ 1994. Reportedly cancelled through lack of financial support.
Crew: probably 2.
Wing characteristics: Cranked delta type.
Tail unit: No tailplane.
Engines: 2 turbofans carried above the wings.
Air intake: Dorsal type.

Aircraft variants:
701 or MDP (mnogofunktsyonalnyi dalnyi pierekhvatchik) intended as a multi-role long-range and high-altitude interceptor.
701P was a proposed supersonic business/executive version for 16 passengers. Range of 3,780 naut miles (4,350 miles) 7,000 km. Cruise speed 1,242-1,350 kts (1,429-1,553 mph) 2,300-2,500 km/h at 55,800 ft (17,000 m) altitude. Subsonic range of 5,940 naut miles (6,835 miles) 11,000 km.

DETAILS FOR MIKOYAN 701, PROVISIONAL.

Principal dimensions:
Wing span: 62 ft 4 ins (19 m)
Maximum length: 98 ft 5 ins (30 m)
Maximum height: 26 ft 3 ins (8 m)

Performance:
Cruise speed: 1,350 kts (1,553 mph) 2,500 km/h
Supersonic range: 3,780 naut miles (4,350 miles) 7,000 km
Subsonic range: 5,940 naut miles (6,835 miles) 11,000 km

Mikoyan MiG-AT (821 and 822)

First flight: 1995, following 18 May roll-out.
Role: Advanced trainer and light attack.

★ Aims
★ To replace the L-29 Delfin and L-39 Albatros in Russian Air Force service.
★ To be capable of various aspects of training, including flying, air combat and weapons.
★ Requirements of the Russian Air Force are (in summarized form):
a) 2 non-afterburning engines, with 0.6-0.7 power-to-weight ratio. Take-off weight 11,023-12,125 lb (5,000-5,500 kg).
b) 459 kts (528 mph) 850 km/h maximum speed. Landing speed not exceeding 92 kts (106 mph) 170 km/h, and take-off and landing runs not exceeding 1,640 ft (500 m). Provision for operation from unpaved runways.
c) Normal range of 648 naut miles (746 miles) 1,200 km at Mach 0.5 and 19,700 ft (6,000 m) altitude. Ferry range of 1,350 naut miles (1,553 miles) 2,500 km.
d) G limits of +8, -3.
e) High manoeuvrability, similar to that of new generation fighters.
f) Pre-programmable control system imitating aircraft with different longitudinal stability coefficient.
g) 10,000 flying hours structural life over 25 years, with possible extension to 15,000 hours.

▲ Development
▲ January 1991. Competition for a new generation jet trainer (UTS, uchebno-trenirovochnyi samolyot) was initiated by the Russian Air Force. UTK (uchebno-trenirovochnyi komplex) training system has been ordered which includes flight simulators.
▲ January 1992. First stage of the competition summarized. Mikoyan 821, Myasishchev M-200, Sukhoi S-54 and Yakovlev Yak-130 took part in the design competition. The designs were judged in 8 technical and economic categories. The Sukhoi S-54 was reportedly judged winner in 4 of the 8 categories (technical perfection, flight safety, combat capability and technical training). But, at the same time, the S-54 was disqualified for having only a single engine. Both Mikoyan and Yakovlev were approved to continue the development of prototypes.
▲ 14 September 1992. Agreement signed between Mikoyan and SNECMA concerning use of Larzac 04-R20 engines in the MiG-AT. The Larzac powers the 821.1 first prototype and export aircraft. Also, Mikoyan, SNECMA and Sextant Avionique signed an agreement to jointly develop and market the trainer.
▲ 1995. Despite expected final selection in 1994, the final choice between the MiG-AT (821) and Yak-130 will not be made until after testing of the flying prototypes.
▲ January 1995. Ground testing took place of the MiG-AT prototype in France with production Larzac 04-R20 engines. Aircraft shipped to Russia for the first flight and subsequently returned for exhibition at the 1995 Paris Air Show.
Sales/users: Estimated requirement under UTS is for 800-1,000 aircraft before the year 2000 (because of a planned quick withdrawal of the L-29 and L-39).
The potential export market is for 1,200 aircraft over 20 years. Export interest includes that from South Africa and South Korea.
Crew: 2, in tandem, the rear instructor's seat raised.
Crew escape: Zvezda K-93 ejection seats.
Fixed guns: None.
Number of weapon pylons: 6 under the wings.
Expendable weapons and equipment: Up to 4,409 lb (2,000 kg), including the usual light weapons.
Flight and weapon system avionics/instrumentation: 821.1 prototype and export MiG-ATFs will receive Sextant Avionique avionics, including colour multi-function liquid crystal displays (LCD), HUD, inertial navigation system and mission computer. ILS, Tacan and IFF. Laser rangefinder. Integration using MIL-STD-1553B databus. MiG-ATRs
Self-protection system: Radar warning receivers.
Wing characteristics: Straight, low-mounted, with slight wingroot extensions.
Wing control surfaces: Ailerons and flaps.
Tail control surfaces: Elevators and rudder. Ventral fin.
Airbrakes: 2, forming the tailcone.
Flight control system: Fly-by-wire (originally to be mechanical).
Construction materials: Metal for the wings (honeycomb core), tail and 60% of the fuselage of the prototypes. Remaining fuselage content, plus wing control surfaces, of carbonfibre and glassfibre composites. See Aircraft variants for composite wing notes.
Engines: 2 SNECMA Larzac 04-R20 turbofans for prototype and export aircraft. Russian AI-25TL, R-35K and R-35M turbofans were analyzed for 821 aircraft

DETAILS FOR 821.

Principal dimensions:
Wing span: 33 ft 4 ins (10.16 m)
Maximum length: 39 ft 5 ins (12.01 m)
Maximum height: 15 ft 2 ins (4.623 m)

Wings:
Aspect ratio: 5.84
Area: 190.2 sq ft (17.67 m²)

Undercarriage:
Type: Retractable, with nosewheel
Main wheel tyre size: 660 x 200 mm
Nose wheel tyre size: 500 x 150
Wheel base: 14 ft 8 ins (4.477 m)
Wheel track: 12 ft 6 ins (3.8 m)

Weights:
Normal take-off: 10,163 lb (4,610 kg)
Maximum take-off: 15,432 lb (7,000 kg)

Performance:
Max operating Mach number (MMO): Mach 0.85
Maximum speed at sea level: 459 kts (528 mph) 850 km/h
Stalling speed: 97 kts (112 mph) 180 km/h
Landing speed: 94 kts (109 mph) 175 km/h
Take-off distance: 1,018 ft (310 m)
Landing distance: 1,870 ft (570 m), ground roll
G limits: +8, -3
Ceiling: 50,850 ft (15,500 m)
Practical range at Mach 0.5, 19,700 ft (6,000 m) altitude: 648 naut miles (746 miles) 1,200 km

Mikoyan MiG-AT

for the Russian Air Force, but probably the same Larzac engines will eventually be selected if agreement can be reached covering production in Russia.
Engine rating: Each 3,175 lbf (14.21 kN).
Air intakes: Each side of the fuselage, above the wing roots. See Aircraft variants.
Fuel system: 1,874 lb (850 kg) capacity.

Aircraft variants:
821 is the basic variant proposed for the Russian Air Force. Prototype differs from the previously exhibited models by having shorter wings with slight wingroot extensions (formerly 35 ft 4 ins, 10.76 m span and entirely straight) and a lower tailplane instead of the former T-tail. Also, the air intakes are now shorter and straight (previously diagonal type), and the movable section of the cockpit canopy has been strengthened.
MiG-ATF is the commercial name for the trainer with French avionics.
MiG-ATR is the commercial name with Russian avionics.
822 is a developed version for South Korea. The internal wing structure has been slightly altered and construction is of composites. 822 will be manufactured by Daewoo.
MiG-ATC proposed two-seat combat training version.
MiG-AC (or ATB) proposed single-seat combat version.

Myasishchev Design Bureau (Russia)

Corporate address: 140160 Zhukovsky, Moscow Region.
Telephone: +7 095 2726041 or 5567776
Facsimile: +7 095 5565583
Founded: 1951.
Information: Alexander Brook (Chief Designer). Stanislav G. Smirnov (Chief expert of conversion).

Myasishchev M-200 Master

Role: Civil and military jet trainer.

★ Aims
★ The same requirements as for the Yakovlev Yak-130 (which see).
★ Adaptive wing. Reprogrammable flight control system.
★ 15,000 flying hour service life.

▲ Development
▲ UTS competition (see Mikoyan MiG-AT entry).
Details: Brief details follow, as R&D has reportedly ended.
Wing control surfaces: Automatic operation of the leading-edge slats, trailing-edge flaps, ailerons and spoilers. This allows (in combination with the reprogrammable control system) the trainer to simulate various flight conditions (including extreme), with sufficient margin of stability.
Engines: 2 Ivchenko PROGRESS/Klimov/ Sarkisov R-35M turbofans.
Engine rating: Each 3,748 lbf (16.67 kN).

Aircraft variants:
M-200 Master aircraft and NUTK-200 ground system together make the UTK-200 training system.

Myasishchev M-200 Master advanced trainer in model form (Piotr Butowski)

DETAILS FOR M-200.

Principal dimensions:
Wing span: 30 ft 10 ins (9.40 m)
Maximum length: 34 ft (10.37 m)
Maximum height: 13 ft 9 ins (4.20 m)

Undercarriage:
Type: Retractable, with nosewheel
Wheel base: 14 ft 1 ins (4.30 m)
Wheel track: 8 ft 10 ins (2.70 m)

Weights:
Empty, operating: 8,389 lb (3,805 kg)
Normal take-off: 10,362 lb (4,700 kg)

Performance:
Maximum speed: 459 kts (528 mph) 850 km/h at sea level
Cruise speed: 378 kts (435 mph) 700 km/h
Take-off speed: 97 kts (112 mph) 180 km/h
Landing speed: 84 kts (96 mph) 155 km/h
Take-off distance: 656 ft (200 m)
Landing distance: 1,575 ft (480 m)
G limits: +8, -3
Allowable angle-of-attack: 28-30°
Operating ceiling: 42,980 ft (13,100 m)
Normal range: 756 naut miles (870 miles) 1,400 km
Ferry range: 1,188 naut miles (1,367 miles) 2,200 km

Sukhoi Shturmoviks consortium (Russia)

● Activities
● In March 1992, 47 companies, including the Sukhoi design bureau, Tiblisi and Ulan-Ude aircraft factories, Ufa engine factory and many others formed the Sukhoi Shturmoviks consortium. The main objective is the manufacturing and sale of Su-25 and Su-25T aircraft, plus later designs.

Sukhoi Design Bureau (Russia)

Corporate address: 23A Polikarpov Str, Moscow 125284.
Telephone: +7 095 945 65 25
Facsimile: +7 095 200 42 43
Telex: 414716 SUHOI SU
Founded: 1939.
Information: Mikhail Petrovich Seemonov (General Designer).

● Activities
● In addition to the combat aircraft and trainers detailed here, Sukhoi piston-engined trainers and aerobatic aircraft, plus various transports, can be found in the Freighter and General Aviation sections.

Note: Sukhoi Su-7B/BM/BMK/U *Fitter* attack aircraft remain in very small numbers with a few air forces, including Algeria, Iraq and North Korea. Not subject to upgrade, these are approaching the end of their service life.

Sukhoi Su-17, Su-20 and Su-22 (NATO name *Fitter*)

First flight: 2 August 1966, piloted by Vladimir Ilyushin.
Role: Ground attack and reconnaissance, with limited use for interception (Peru). Su-22M5 upgrade can be multi-role, including full air-to-air combat (see Aircraft variants).
Chief designer: Nikolai Zyrin until the 1980s, now Alexander Slezev.

★ Aims
★ Variable geometry (swing-wing) development of the Su-7, improving payload, take-off/landing distances, range and other performances.

▲ Development
▲ May 1965. Work started on a variable-geometry wing derivative of the Su-7 *Fitter-A*.
▲ 2 August 1966. First flight of the S-22I technology demonstrator, seen to have only the outer wing panels moving.
▲ 1968. Prototype of the production version appeared, as the S-32.
▲ 1972. More powerful AL-21F-3 turbojet introduced (Su-17M).
▲ 1974. Fon (Background) laser rangefinder and KN-23 navigation system introduced (Su-17M2).
▲ 1976. Klon (Maple tree) laser rangefinder/target designator and K-36DM ejection seat introduced (Su-17M3).
▲ 1978. Computerized PrNK-54 navigation/attack system introduced (Su-17M4).
▲ 1990. Series manufacturing completed.
Sales/users: All versions were produced at the Komsomolsk-on-Amur plant. Production ended (see Development). In 1995 the Su-17 was being withdrawn from service with CIS air forces except in reconnaissance form. At that time Ukraine had 41 aircraft in service and Russia not more than 100. Others are in Kazakhstan, Turkmenistan and Uzbekistan. In 1974-76 Poland purchased 27 Su-20s, which are now being withdrawn, the last going in 1995. Other users of Su-20s are Algeria,

Sukhoi Su-22M4 Fitter-K armed with 50 kg bombs under the fuselage and 4 of the 6 underwing pylons (Waclaw Holys/via Piotr Butowski)

DETAILS FOR SU-17M4 FITTER-K.

Principal dimensions:
Wing span: 44 ft 11 ins (13.68 m) *fully spread*, 32 ft 11 ins (10.025 m) *fully swept*
Maximum length: 62 ft 5 ins (19.02 m)
Length without probe: 56 ft 11 ins (17.341 m)
Maximum height: 16 ft 10 ins (5.129 m)

Wings:
Aspect ratio: 4.862 *spread*, 2.884 *swept*
Area: 414.3 sq ft (38.49 m^2) *fully spread*, 375 sq ft (34.85 m^2) *fully swept*
Sweepback of fixed panel: 63°
Sweepback of variable panels: 30° to 63°, leading edges
Twist: +1° root
Anhedral: 3°

Tail unit:
Tailplane span: 15 ft 3 ins (4.646 m)

Undercarriage:
Type: Retractable, with steerable nosewheel
Main wheel tyre size: 800 x 360 mm
Nose wheel tyre size: 640 x 200 mm
Wheel base: 17 ft 3 ins (5.247 m)
Wheel track: 12 ft 7 ins (3.83 m)

Weights:
Empty, operating: 23,457 lb (10,640 kg)
Nominal take-off: 36,156 lb (16,400 kg) with 2,204 lb (1,000 kg) of weapons
Maximum take-off: 42,990 lb (19,500 kg)

Performance:
Maximum operating Mach number (MMO): Mach 1.77
Maximum operating speed at high altitude: 999 kts (1,150 mph) 1,850 km/h
Maximum speed at sea level, clean: 729 kts (839 mph) 1,350 km/h
Maximum speed at sea level, with armament: 675 kts (777 mph) 1,250 km/h
Landing speed: 154 kts (177 mph) 285 km/h
Take-off distance: 1,969 ft (600 m)
Landing distance: 3,117 ft (950 m)
G limit: +7
Ceiling: 49,871 ft (15,200 m)
Practical range with 2,204 lb (1,000 kg) of weapons, at low altitude: 756 naut miles (870 miles) 1,400 km
Practical range with 2,204 lb (1,000 kg) of weapons, at high altitude: 1,242 naut miles (1,429 miles) 2,300 km
Maximum range: 1,377 naut miles (1,584 miles) 2,550 km

Egypt and Iraq. In 1985 2 Egyptian aircraft were bought by West Germany for testing in the experimental unit Erprobungsstelle 61 (1 for flying and 1 for spares). The total number of Su-22s in service throughout the world, except CIS, is over 300. In early 1995 Poland had 83 Su-22M4 single-seaters and 19 Su-22UM3K trainers; in 1994 the Polish Air Force awarded IDS-PZL Aerospace Industries a contract for an Su-22 simulator. Other Su-22 operators are Afghanistan, Angola, Czech Republic, Hungary, Libya, North Korea, Peru, Slovakia, Syria, Vietnam and Yemen.

Details: Principally for Su-17M4 *Fitter-K*, unless stated.
Crew: Pilot, or 2 in trainer versions.
Cockpit: Conventional. Su-22M5 upgrade offers a glass cockpit option and HOTAS (see Aircraft variants).
Crew escape: Zvezda K-36DM zero-zero ejection seat.
Fixed guns: 2 Nudelman/Rikhter single-barrel 30-mm NR-30 cannon, 1 in each wingroot. Only starboard cannon in two-seaters.
Ammunition: 80 rounds each.
Number of weapon pylons: 10, as 4 under the fuselage in tandem pairs, 4 under the fixed sections of the wings plus 2 small underwing pylons exclusively for R-60 (AA-8 *Aphid*) self-defence AAMs (*Atolls* on some exported aircraft).
Expendable weapons and equipment: Up to 9,370 lb (4,250 kg). Smart weapons include laser-guided Kh-25ML (AS-10 *Karen*) and Kh-29L (AS-14 *Kedge*) ASMs, anti-radar Kh-25MP (AS-12 *Kegler*) requiring a Vyuga guidance pod, and radio-command Kh-25MR (AS-10 *Karen*) requiring a Delta guidance pod. Aircraft from 30th production series can carry TV-guided Kh-29T (AS-14 *Kedge*) missiles. Standard Russian unguided weapons include bombs of up to 500 kg, KMGU submunition dispensers, 57-mm to 370-mm rockets, and UPK-23-250 and SPPU-22-01 gun pods (up to 4, with the option of 2 firing backwards). Russian aircraft formerly able to deliver nuclear weapons. Air-to-air missiles (see Weapon pylons). It is of interest to note that Konstrukta-Defence of Slovakia has developed the Phobos anti-runway system (comprising 6 or 9 rocket-powered bombs), suited to the Su-22 and other aircraft.
Additional stores: Any Su-17M4 and Su-17M3 can carry the large KKR-1 (konteyner kompleksnoi razvedki) reconnaissance pod suspended beneath the fuselage. The pod contains 3 cameras (A-39, UA-47 and PA-1), KDF-38 flare dispenser, and SRS-9 Virazh elint or SRS-13 in later versions. FLIR pods, etc, see Su-22M5 upgrade under Aircraft variants.
Radar: DISS-7 Doppler navigation radar only. Su-22M5 upgrade offers a pulse Doppler Phathom radar (see Aircraft variants).
Flight/weapon system avionics/instrumentation: PrNK-54 nav/attack system with TsVM20-22 computer. Klon-54 laser rangefinder/target designator in the nosecone. A-720 long-range radio navigation, A-312 (Radikal-NP) short-range radio navigation, ARK-22 radiocompass, MRP-66 marker beacon receiver, A-035 altimeter, and SO-69 transponder. SRO-2 IFF. R-862 and R-855UM (stand-by) com radios. See Aircraft variants for avionics differences between versions. Su-22s operated by Peru later had some western avionics installed, as both the RWR and navigation systems were considered inadequate. Proposed Su-22M5 upgrade with improved Russian and French avionics is detailed under Aircraft variants.
Self-protection systems: SPO-15 (L-006) Beryoza radar warning receiver. 2 KDS-23 chaff/flare dispensers (6 x 50-mm cartridges each) built into the dorsal spine and 8 ASO-2V dispensers (each with 32 x 26-mm) cartridges, mounted on rear fuselage.
Wing characteristics: Variable geometry outer panels (variable sweep from 30° to 63°) and large fixed inner panels. Outer panels are powered by GMP-22 hydraulic motors. 2 large aerodynamic fences on the upper surface of each fixed wing panel, allowing 3 weapon pylons beneath.
Wing control surfaces: 2-section double-slotted trailing-edge flaps on each fixed panel, deflecting 25° (inner section) or 26° (outer section). Slats on the leading edge of the movable outer panels, and ailerons on the trailing edge (+22°, -22° when the wings are fully spread, +21°, -15° when swept).
Tail control surfaces: Slab tailplane (+26.5°, -10°), and rudder (25° deflection). Ventral fin.
Airbrakes: 4, symmetrically mounted on the rear fuselage, deflecting 50°, each of 3.55 sq ft (0.33 m^2).
Fuselage: Area ruled, circular section.
Flight control system: Mechanical, hydraulically actuated.
Construction materials: All metal, using aluminium alloys and steel.
Engine: Saturn/Lyulka AL-21F-3 or AL-21F-3A turbojet. Some export Su-22s use the 25,353 lbf (112.78 kN) with afterburning Soyuz/Khachaturov R-29BS-300. Optionally 2 RATO units.
Engine rating: 17,196 lbf (76.49 kN) dry and 24,692 lbf (109.84 kN) with full afterburning.
Air intake: Nose type with conical shock cone; shock cone was principally non-adjustable, but remaining versions have adjustable cones.
Flight refuelling probe: None.
Fuel system: 8,311 lb (3,770 kg) of fuel in 4 fuselage tanks and the 2 outer wing panel tanks. Normal provision for a single PTB-1150 (1,150 litre) or PTB-800 (820 litre) drop tank beneath the outer wing pylons. Also see Aircraft variants.
Hydraulic system: 3,002 psi (dual systems).
Braking system: Main wheel brakes, not on nosewheel. Drag-chute (area 269 sq ft, 25 m^2) housed in a pod at the tailfin root.

Aircraft variants (in order of appearance):
Su-7IG (S-22I) *Fitter-B* first prototype, used as a variable-wing technology demonstrator.
Su-17 (S-32) *Fitter-B* had a 21,164 lbf (94.15 kN) with full afterburning AL-7F1-250 turbojet. Manufactured 1970-72. 6,614 lb (3,000 kg) weapon load. 6,173 lb (2,800 kg) of internal fuel.
Su-17M (S-32M) *Fitter-C* appeared in 1972 as the first large-scale production version. 24,692 lbf (109.84 kN) with afterburning AL-21F-3 engine. 8,818 lb (4,000 kg) of weapons. 8,003 lb (3,630 kg) of internal fuel.
Su-20 (S-32MK) *Fitter-C* became the export version of Su-17M, with slightly downgraded equipment and weapons.
Su-17M2 (S-32M2) *Fitter-D* appeared in 1974 and was manufactured 1975-79. 8 ins (200 mm) lengthened nose. Fon-1400 laser rangefinder and DISS 7 Doppler navigation radar added, and new ASP-17 gun sight.
Su-22 (Su-17M2D, S-32M2K) *Fitter-F* is the export

KKR-2 reconnaissance pod on an Su-22. Note the UB-22 rocket pack and UZR-60 practice AAM under the wing (Piotr Butowski)

version of the Su-17M2, powered by an R-29B-300 engine instead of the standard AL-21F-3.
Su-17UM (S-52U, S-52UM) *Fitter-E/G* appeared from 1976 as two-seat combat trainers, with weapon systems retained but only 1 cannon. Much larger dorsal spine, and new K-36 ejection seats instead of the former KS-4. Early version with short tailfin was named S-52U *Fitter-E*, followed by S-52UM *Fitter-G* with a lengthened fin.
Su-17M3 (S-52) *Fitter-H* is externally similar to the Su-17UM but is a single seater. New weapon system including Klon laser rangefinder/target designator, and new KN-23 navigation system.
Su-22M (S-52K) *Fitter-J* is the export derivative of the Su-17M3, powered by the R-29B-300 engine.
Su-22UM (S-52UMK) *Fitter-E* is the export name of the Su-17UM.
Su-17UM3 (S-52UM3) *Fitter-G* appeared in 1978 as a 2-seat trainer similar to the Su-17UM, but with the weapon system of the Su-17M3.
Su-22UM3 (S-52UM3K) *Fitter-G* is the export version of the Su-17UM3, powered by the R-29BS-300 turbojet.
Su-17M4 (S-54) *Fitter-K* was manufactured during 1980-90. Most advanced production version. As described.
Su-22UM3K (S-52UM3K) *Fitter-G* is similar to Su-22UM3 but with the AL-21F3 engine. Appeared in 1983.
Su-22M4 (S-54K) *Fitter-K* is the export version of the Su-17M4.
Su-22M5 (S-55) is the proposed conversion of existing aircraft. Project prepared jointly by Sukhoi, Thomson-CSF and Sextant Avionique. In the initial basic stage of the upgrade programme, the existing nav/attack system will be replaced by the advanced PrNK-55, but with no change to aircraft functions. Russian head-up display will be replaced by a new smart HUD for day and night operations, and a lightweight OTA (OTA-200 monochrome or OTA-1300 colour) camera for HUD picture recording can be installed. Klon-54 laser rangefinder/target designator will be superseded by a Thomson-CSF TMV 630 unit of 10.8 naut miles (12.4 miles) 20 km maximum range. The new Sextant Avionique mission computer weighs no more than 17.6 lb (8 kg); before operation it is programmed by a CINNA 3PN multi-aircraft mission planning system as used by the French Air Force, allowing the flight path and weapons use to be defined and optimized. Sherloc radar warning receiver (RWR) will replace the Beryoza, offering precise identification and location of enemy radars. Changes in the navigation systems includes NSS100-P Navstar/Glonass GPS receiver, AHV6 radio altimeter, Totem inertial navigation system, and ADU 300 air data unit. Optionally, conventional cockpit instrumentation can be replaced by 2 MFD55 multi-function colour 5 ins x 5 ins (13 x 13 cm) liquid crystal active matrix displays derived from the French Rafale. Radio, VOR, navigation and IFF systems can be also improved. The next stage proposal significantly expands the combat potential, offering beyond visual range (BVR) air-to-air plus all-weather round-the-clock air-to-surface capability. The core of this upgrade is the lightweight (about 264 lb, 120 kg) Phathom radar located in the air intake shock cone, in the place of Klon-54 laser rangefinder. Phathom is a product of the Russian Phazotron and French Thomson-CSF organizations. Russia supplies the elements of MiG-21-93's Kopyo radar, including antenna, receiver, transmitter and primary power distributor. Thomson provides data and signal processors; the analog processor will be jointly developed by Phazotron and Thomson. Pulse Doppler Phathom is a multi-function radar, which in air-to-air mode enables the Su-22M5 to track-while-scan 8 targets and engage 4. In the air-to-surface mode it can perform ground mapping, terrain avoidance and missile guidance with multi-target capacity. It is probable that Phathom has similar parameters to Super Kopyo presented in leaflet form during the 1994 Farnborough Air Show. If so, maximum air-to-air search range will be 40.5 naut miles (46.6 miles) 75 km in the forward hemisphere and 24.3 naut miles (28 miles) 45 km in the rearward hemisphere. When used against air targets, upgraded *Fitter* can be equipped with a helmet-mounted display (HMD), which was qualified on Mirage 2000. HMD is connected to the system through the 1553B dual redundant databus interface. The display's field of view is 20°, when sight line is 0° 15'. The flight/navigation data, weapon system status and warnings are also presented on the HMD. During air-to-ground operations the aircraft can carry a Rubis FLIR pod connected to the system through the common databus, a laser target designation pod, and Barem jamming pod. Barem performs the detection, analyses and identification of enemy radar signals of H to J bands and responds with active electronic jamming.
Further proposals include changes to the electrical system, in-flight refuelling capability, and HOTAS. Weapons may possibly include R-77 (AA-12 *Adder*) and R-27 (AA-10 *Alamo*) AAMs, Kh-31P (AS-17 *Krypton*) anti-radar and Kh-31A and Kh-35 anti-ship missiles. With the laser target designation pod, laser-guided missiles and bombs may be carried (including possibly Western types).

Sukhoi Su-24 (NATO name *Fencer*)

First flight: 2 July 1967 for the T6-1 delta-winged prototype, piloted by Vladimir Ilyushin. 17 January 1970 for the T6-2I variable-geometry prototype.
Role: Nuclear strike, tactical bomber, reconnaissance and electronic warfare.
Chief designer: Yevgeni Felsner until 1989, then Leonid Logvinov.

★ Aims

★ To penetrate enemy defences for 5 minutes at 1,400 km/h and 200 m altitude.
★ Supersonic replacement for the near-obsolete Ilyushin Il-28 and Yakovlev Yak-28, originally intended to be developed from the Su-7.

▲ Development

▲ 1961. Initial requirements for an Su-7 development equipped with nav/attack radar.
▲ Autumn 1963. Full-scale mock-up of the S-6 project.
▲ August 1965. Governmental order for the T-6 (T-58M) tactical nuclear strike aircraft.
▲ Autumn 1966. Full-scale mock-up of the T-6 accepted.
▲ 2 July 1967. 5 am first flight of the T6-1 prototype with fixed delta wings and 4 lift engines built into the fuselage.
▲ August 1968. Official governmental order for a variable-geometry derivative.
▲ 17 January 1970. Maiden flight of the T6-2I variable-geometry wing prototype, piloted by Vladimir Ilyushin.
▲ December 1971. First production aircraft left the factory in Novosibirsk.
▲ July 1974. State Acceptance Trials completed.
▲ 1974. Su-24 attained initial operational capability with the first unit.
▲ February 1975. Su-24 officially commissioned into Soviet Air Force service.
▲ February 1975. Requirements for Su-24M modification issued, including new smart weapons, more precise nav/attack system, powerful self-protection system, and increased range.
▲ 24 June 1977. Maiden flight of the first Su-24M prototype.
▲ Summer 1979. First production Su-24M left the factory.
▲ November 1979. Trials with Su-24M completed.
▲ December 1979. First flight of the Su-24MP electronic warfare version.
▲ March 1980 to May 1981. Supplementary tests of the weapon system.
▲ May 1980. First flight of the first prototype Su-24MR reconnaissance aircraft, piloted Anatoli Ivanov.
▲ June 1983. Su-24M officially commissioned.
▲ 1987. First Su-24MK export aircraft manufactured.
▲ August 1988. First public showing of the Su-24, at Zhukovsky outside Moscow.
Sales/users: Su-24 was manufactured at Novosibirsk during 1972-74, before production changed to the SU-27IB. In 1990 the Soviet Air Force in Europe had 760 Su-24s, with 99 more in Naval Aviation. A further 120-150 Su-24s were based in the Asian sector of the USSR, bringing the total number then in service to about 1,000, including more than 130 Su-24MR *Fencer-E* reconnaissance and 8 Su-24MP *Fencer-F* electronic warfare versions. Since then there has been no significant changes in the total number, although their basing has altered considerably. Many Su-24s were taken over by Belarus and Ukraine, the latter keeping all the aircraft stationed on its territory (except for 6 Su-24Ms, which flew back to Russia). Russia itself has been withdrawing aircraft from all its foreign bases (except several taken over by Azerbaijan at the Dallyar Air Base in June 1992 – which reportedly are not airworthy). In October 1992 Belarus had 40 aircraft and the Ukraine 257, with all other flyable former Soviet Su-24s in Russia. This general situation is probably unaltered. The Su-24MK export version acquired by Algeria (10), Iraq (24 aircraft, all of which are now thought to be in Iran), Libya (6 aircraft delivered against 15 ordered), and Syria (reportedly 42).

Sukhoi Su-24M Fencer-D with twin drag-chute deployed (Piotr Butowski)

Under the fuselage of the Sukhoi Su-24M Fencer-D, with wide Kayra window, gun fairing (left) and bomb pylons (Piotr Butowski)

Crew: Pilot and navigator/weapons system officer, side-by-side (pilot to port). SPU-9 intercom.
Cockpit: 2 separate rearward-hinged canopies. Dual controls.
Crew escape: Zvezda K-36DM zero-zero ejection seats (K-36D on the first series of *Fencer*-As).
Fixed guns: 6-barrel 23-mm GSh-6-23 or GSh-6-23M (AO-19) gun in a fairing under the starboard side of the under fuselage. Similar fairing on the port side contains an AKS-5 photo-gun.
Ammunition: 500 rounds.
Number of weapon pylons: 8, as 4 under the fuselage, 2 under the wing gloves, and 2 pivoting pylons under the outer wing panels (see also Su-24MR).

Sukhoi Su-24M Fencer-D refuelling a similar aircraft using the Sakhalin pod

Expendable weapons and equipment: Up to 17,637 lb (8,000 kg) for *Fencer-D*; 15,432 lb (7,000 kg) for *Fencer-A/B/C*. Principal weapons in a nuclear role are the TN-1000 and TN-1200. Conventional options for *Fencer-D* include a wide range of smart weapons such as anti-radiation Kh-58U (AS-11 *Kilter*), Kh-25MP (AS-12 *Kegler*) and Kh-31P (AS-17 *Krypton*) ASMs; laser-guided Kh-25ML (AS-10 *Karen*) and Kh-29L (AS-14 *Kedge*) missiles plus KAB-500L and KAB-1500L bombs; and TV-guided Kh-29T (AS-14 *Kedge*), Kh-59 (AS-13 *Kingbolt*) and Kh-59M (AS-18 *Kazoo*) missiles plus KAB-500Kr and KAB-1500TK bombs. *Fencer-A/B/C* are armed with older weapons such as Kh-28 (AS-9 *Kyle*) anti-radiation missiles, but no laser or TV weapons. Unguided weapons for *Fencer* include bombs up to 1,500 kg, RBK-250 and RBK-500 cluster bombs, KMGU-2 submunitions dispensers, incendiary tanks, 80-mm to 420-mm rockets, and UPK-23 or SPPU-6 (with flexible GSh-6-23) gun packs. 2 R-60 (AA-8 *Aphid*) AAMs can be carried for self protection, or older R-55s on *Fencer-A/B/C*. Su-24MR *Fencer-E* and Su-24MP *Fencer-F* carry no air-to-surface weapons.
Additional stores: See Aircraft variants, particularly Su-24MR and MP.
Radar: See Flight/weapon system avionics.

Flight/weapon system avionics/instrumentation (principally Su-24M *Fencer-D*): PNS-24M Tigr-NS nav/attack system includes Orion-A air-to-surface radar (81 naut mile, 93 mile, 150 km range), Relyef terrain-avoidance radar, DISS-7 Doppler navigation radar, and Kayra-24 laser-TV sight/target designator. TsVM-10-058K Orbita (tsentralnaya vychislitelnaya mashina) digital weapons system computer. Less sophisticated PNS-24 Puma nav/attack system on *Fencer-A/B/C*. R-862 and R-864G radios, SO-69 transponder, ARK-15M radio compass, RV-21 Impuls altimeter, Klistron short range radio navigation system, and RSDN-10 long-range navigation system. Vstrecha all-weather radio navigation system (range 162 naut miles, 186 miles, 300 km) for automatic search and lead to tanker. Further systems suspended in the pods include Fantasmagoria (L-080 or L-081) passive radar associated with anti-radiation missiles and APK-9 data-link pod associated with Kh-59M (AS-18 *Kazoo*) ASM.
Self-protection systems: *Fencer-A/B/C* have no integrated self-protection systems, but use separate devices such as SPO-10 Sirena RWR (*Fencer-C* has SPO-15 Beryoza) and suspended ECM pods. *Fencer-D* has BKO-2 (L-167) Karpaty computer-controllable self-protection system comprising SPO-15S (L-006) Beryoza radar warning receiver (RWR), Mak (L-082) infra-red launch and approach warning device (small blister on the upper fuselage aft of the cockpit), SPS-161/SPS-162 Geran (L-101/L-102) active response jammer, and APP-50A chaff/flare dispensers (four cassettes with 3 x 50-mm cartridges each, built into the fuselage near the tailfin root).
Wing characteristics: Shoulder mounted, with small fixed gloves and variable-geometry main panels. Movable outer panels are controlled (4 wing angles – see data table) by SPK-2-3 (sistema povorota kryla) hydraulic actuators. Large aerodynamic fence in line with the weapon pylon on early series Su-24M/MR/MP.
Wing control surfaces: 3-section (4-section on early aircraft) leading-edge slats (27°) over the full span of the outer panels. Double-slotted 2-section (3-section on early aircraft) trailing-edge flaps (34°) on each outer wing panel. 2-section differential spoilers (43°) forward of the flaps for roll control at low speed and lift dumping on landing. No ailerons.
Tail control surfaces: All-moving horizontal stabilizer deflected +11°/-25° evenly or differentially; conventional tail with rudder (24° each). 2 ventral fins.
Airbrakes: Front covers of main undercarriage bays, hinged 62°; 18.1 sq ft (1.68 m²) total area.
Flight control system: Mechanical, hydraulically actuated. SAU-6M1 automatic control system (SAU-6 in early aircraft) with terrain avoidance capability using Relyef radar.
Fuselage: Semi-monocoque, of rectangular section. Fuselages of Su-24M/MR/MP *Fencer-D/E/F* are lengthened over earlier versions, by the addition of a 29.5 ins (750 mm) fuselage plug added in front of the cockpit, containing new avionics and the flight refuelling set.
Construction materials: All metal, mainly aluminium alloys.
Engines: 2 Saturn AL-21F-3 or AL-21F-3A (izdelye 89) turbojets.
Engine rating: Each 17,196 lbf (76.49 kN) dry, 24,692 lbf (109.8 kN) with afterburning.
Air intakes: Fixed geometry (standard from the 22nd production series, and later older aircraft similarly modified, with controls removed), with splitter plates.
Flight refuelling probe: Provision for in-flight refuelling on Su-24M/MR/MP *Fencer-D/E/F* only, with the probe mounted centrally in front of the cockpit. Su-24M *Fencer-D* can also act as a buddy tanker to another aircraft through the UPAZ-1A (unifitsyrovannyi podvesnoi agregat zapravki) Sakhalin refuelling pack suspended beneath the fuselage (see photograph).
Fuel system: 11,860 litres (21,715 lb, 9,850 kg) of fuel in 3 fuselage tanks (10,860 litres in early Su-24

DETAILS FOR Su-24M FENCER-D.

Principal dimensions:
Wing span: 34 ft (10.366 m) *fully swept*, 57 ft 10.5 ins (17.64 m) *fully spread*
Maximum length: 80 ft 6 ins (24.532 m)
Maximum height: 20 ft 4 ins (6.193 m)

Wings:
Aerofoil section: SR14S-5.376 for gloves; SR14S-9.226/SR16M-10 movable sections
Area: 549.2 sq ft (51.024 m²) *swept*, 593.8 sq ft (55.168 m²) *spread*
Aspect ratio: 2.106 *swept*, 5.64 *spread*
Sweepback of fixed centre-section: 69°, at leading edge
Sweepback of movable panel: 16°, 35°, 45° and 69° at leading edge
Incidence: 0°
Anhedral: 4.5°
Leading-edge slats area: 32.68 sq ft (3.036 m²)
Spoilers area: 32.97 sq ft (3.063 m²)
Trailing-edge flaps area: 109.9 sq ft (10.21 m²)

Tail unit:
Tailplane span: 27.56 ft (8.40 m)
Tailplane area: 147.6 ft (13.707 m²)
Tailplane sweepback: 55°, at quarter chord
Fin sweepback: 55°, at quarter chord
Ventral fins area, total: 23.7 sq ft (2.2 m²)

Undercarriage:
Type: Retractable, with steerable nosewheel. Twin wheels on each unit. Mudguard on front wheels. Low-pressure tyres of main undercarriage
Main wheel tyre size: 950 x 300 mm
Nose wheel tyre size: 660 x 200 mm
Wheel base: 27.92 ft (8.510 m)
Wheel track: 10.88 ft (3.317 m)

Weights:
Empty, operating: 49,207 lb (22,320 kg)
Nominal take-off, with 6,612 lb (3,000 kg) of weapons: 79,300 lb (35,970 kg)
Maximum take-off: 87,523 lb (39,700 kg)

Performance:
Maximum operating Mach number (MMO): Mach 1.35
Maximum speed: 783 kts (901 mph) 1,450 km/h
Maximum speed at sea level, clean: 737 kts (848 mph) 1,365 km/h
Maximum speed at sea level with armament: 715 kts (823 mph) 1,325 km/h
Take-off distance: 2,789-2,953 ft (850-900 m)
Landing distance with drag-chute: 2,625-2,789 ft (800-850 m)
Landing distance without drag-chute: 4,265 ft (1,300 m)
G limit: +6.5
Ceiling: 54,135 ft (16,500 m)
Maximum range at high altitude with 2 x 3,000 litre drop tanks: 1,350 naut miles (1,553 miles) 2,500 km
Maximum range with single in-flight refuelling: 2,306 naut miles (2,653 miles) 4,270 km
Radius of action, at 650 ft (200 m) altitude, no drop tanks: 221 naut miles (255 miles) 410 km
Radius of action, at 650 ft (200 m), with drop tanks: 302 naut miles (348 miles) 560 km

Kh-58 (AS-11 Kilter), the standard anti-radiation weapon of the Su-24M (Piotr Butowski)

Fencer-A. Up to 3 auxiliary tanks, as 2 PTB-3000 (3,000 litres each) on wing pylons and a single PTB-2000 (2,000 litres) under the fuselage, when maximum fuel is 19,860 litres. See also Aircraft variants.

Electrical system: 2 DC and AC generators, plus 2 stand-by batteries.

Hydraulic system: 3 separate systems. AMG-10 liquid, pressure 2,986 psi.

Braking system: PTK-6M twin drag-chutes in the tailfin root, 495 sq ft (46 m^2) total area.

Aircraft variants:

T6-1 was the first prototype with fixed delta wings, powered by 2 R-27 (later AL-27) main engines and 4 R36-35 lift engines inside the fuselage. Now in the Monino museum.

Su-24 was named *Fencer-A*, *B* and *C* in the West: *Fencer-A* covers the first 15 production series. Rectangular rear fuselage box enclosing the engine nozzles. First 4 series powered by 2 AL-21F (izdelye 85) engines of 19,620 lbf (87.28 kN) each; later standard AL-21F3s and widened air intakes. An additional 1,000 litres of internal fuel was provided from the 8th production series. RSDN-10 long-range navigation system retrofitted.

Fencer-B covers aircraft from the 16th to 21st production series. Drag-chute container increased in size and raised, and the rear fuselage rounded. RSDN-10 long-range navigation system retrofitted.

Fencer C covers aircraft of the 22nd to 27th series. Improved equipment with SPO-15 Beryoza RWR instead of SPO-10 Sirena, RSDN-10 long-range navigation system (later retrofitted to older aircraft), and new IFF. Manufactured up to 1983, parallel with the first Su-24Ms. Fixed air intakes (intake controls removed also from existing aircraft).

Su-24M *Fencer-D* has a modified nav/attack system, new weapons, provision for flight refuelling, and lengthened forward fuselage (by 29.5 ins, 750 mm). See general description.

Su-24MK *Fencer-D* is the export version of Su-24M, K standing for kommercheskiy or commercial. As for Su-24M but with minor differences in radio and IFF equipment.

Su-24MR *Fencer-E* is the reconnaissance version, designed for all-weather, day and night, multi-system reconnaissance operations. Radar, infra-red, TV, laser, radio, radiation and photo-reconnaissance equipment integrated into the united BKR-1 system. Relyef terrain-avoidance radar remains, whereas the Orion nav/attack radar was replaced with Shtyk side-looking radar. A-100 camera under the port air intake. Kayra-24 removed to make room for the AP-402P panoramic camera. Aist-M TV-camera and Zima infra-red scanner installed under the fuselage. Further equipment carried in suspended pods includes Shpil-2M laser or Tangazh electronic intelligence (elint) under the centre fuselage, and the Efir-1M radiation reconnaissance system under the starboard outer wing panel. 2 R-60 self-defence AAMs under the port wing. Inner wing pylons can carry 2 PTB-3000 fuel tanks. Reconnaissance information is transmitted to the ground stations by the ShRK-1 Posrednik-1 transmitter. The photographs are developed on board the aircraft and dropped to the ground in a Kadr container. No air-to-surface attack capabilities since Orion radar and Kayra laser/TV system were removed. NK-24 navigation system.

Su-24MP *Fencer-F* covers only 8 aircraft built up to the end of 1990, and in service with the 118th Electronic Warfare Air Regiment in Chertkov in the Ukraine. Landysh electronic warfare system, comprising the Los, Fasol and Mimoza subsystems built into the fuselage and suspended in pods. Su-24MP can be distinguished externally by a narrow longitudinal fairing under the nose, sword type aerials of the Fasol unit at the sides of the air intakes, and radio transparent fairing at the back of the fuselage just behind the cockpit. No attack capability, but can carry 2 R-60 AAMs for self protection.

Sukhoi Su-25 (and Su-28) (NATO name *Frogfoot*)

First flight: 22 February 1975, piloted by Vladimir Ilyushin.

Role: Subsonic close-air support, and target towing.

Chief designer: Yuri Ivashechkin, replaced in 1983 by Vladimir Babak.

★ Aims

★ 4,000 kg of offensive weapons, including laser-guided missiles.

★ High manoeuvrability.

★ Full armour protection for the pilot.

★ Extensive protection of systems, including fuel tanks filled with anti-explosive reticulated polyurethane foam and constructed to prevent large leaks, control system partially doubled with large-diameter steel pushrods, engines spaced widely apart in stainless steel compartments to prevent simultaneous damage from ground fire (capable of using any available fuel), and basic items of equipment armour protected.

★ Maintenance system/equipment housed in 4 containers fitted to the pylons for 5-day autonomous operation away from base.

▲ Development

▲ March 1968. Start of work on the T-8 (or SPB) design for a subsonic attack aircraft (without an order for the Air Force). 2 x 3,858 lbf (17.16 kN) AI-25T turbojets, and 18,078 lb (8,200 kg) take-off weight.

▲ March 1969. Official competition for a close air support aircraft announced by the Soviet Air Force.

▲ Autumn 1969. Sukhoi T-8 project selected for further development.

▲ 22 February 1975. First flight of the T8-1 prototype. 2 x 5,512 lbf (24.52 kN) RD-9 turbojets, 26,896 lb (12,200 kg) take-off weight, and 540 kts (621 mph) 1,000 km/h target speed.

▲ December 1975. T8-2 second prototype began flight tests.

▲ March 1976. 9,039 lbf (40.21 kN) R-95Sh engines installed in the T8-2, renamed T8-2D.

▲ 1977. Su-25 identified in the West. Provisionally named Ram-J.

▲ 26 April 1978. Aircraft submitted for state acceptance trials.

▲ 18 June 1979. T8-3 built, the first Su-25 from the Tbilisi aircraft factory.

▲ 16 April-5 June 1980. T8-1D and T8-3 tested in Afghanistan, based at the Shindand Air Base.

▲ 30 December 1980. State acceptance trials completed.

▲ 4 February 1981. First operational unit became the 200th Independent Attack Air Flight, with 12 aircraft formed at the Sital-chai airfield in Azerbaijan.

▲ 18 June 1981. Su-25s of the 200th Independent Attack Air Flight flew to Shindand in Afghanistan for initial combat operations.

▲ 1984. First series of modified aircraft with hydraulic actuators. Maximum speed increased from 459 kts (528 mph) 850 km/h to 540 kts (621 mph) 1,000 km/h.

▲ 17 August 1984. First flight of the Su-25T tank-buster version (see separate entry)

▲ 6 August 1985. First flight of the Su-25UB combat trainer.

▲ 1987. Su-25UB production started.

▲ 1987. Su-25BM replaced the Su-25 on the production line at Tbilisi.

▲ August 1987. First flight of the Su-28/Su-25UT.

▲ June 1989. Su-25 and Su-25UT (Su-28) displayed abroad for the first time (Paris Air Show).

▲ 1 November 1989. Su-25UTG landed for the first time on board the aircraft carrier *Tbilisi* (now *Admiral Kuznetsov*).

▲ 1992. Production ended.

Sales/users: Single-seat combat versions were manufactured at the Tbilisi aircraft plant between 1979 and 1992, while two-seaters came from the Ulan-Ude factory between 1987 and 1992. More than 700 Su-25s were built. According to official data of 1990, 385 Su-25s were then in active service in the European sector of the USSR, with some 100 more outside Europe. With the break-up of the USSR, Ukraine took over 80 and Belarus 99, those remaining belonging to Russia, though several are used in Georgia. About 210 aircraft were exported to Afghanistan, Angola (12 Su-25K and 2 Su-25UBK in 1988-89), Bulgaria, Czech Republic, Hungary, Iraq, North Korea and Slovakia. Czechoslovakia received its first Su-25K on 2 April 1984, later also receiving Su-25UBK trainers. Afghanistan received 60 aircraft between 1986-90. Bulgaria bought a regiment in 1985, comprising 36 combat Su-25Ks and 4 Su-25UBKs. Iraq had about 45 Su-25s, which were used during the Iraq-Iran war. On 25 January 1991, 7 Iraqi Su-25Ks flew to Iran; 2 others were lost on 6 February 1991.

Slovakian Sukhoi Su-25K Frogfoot-A. Note the ladder spread from the port fuselage side (Piotr Butowski)

Crew: Pilot; or instructor (rear) and pupil (front) in the trainer versions. Projected 3-seat tandem trainer was Su-25U3.

Cockpit: Self-contained compartment of welded titanium plates (10 to 24-mm

Details for Su-25.

Principal dimensions:
Wing span: 47 ft 1 ins (14.36 m)
Maximum length: 50 ft 11.5 ins (15.53 m), 50 ft 5 ins (15.36 m) for Su-25UB
Fuselage length: 47 ft 10.5 ins (14.59 m)
Maximum height: 15 ft 9 ins (4.80 m), 17 ft 1 ins (5.2 m) for Su-25UB

Wings:
Area: 324 sq ft (30.10 m^2)
Aspect ratio: 6.85
Taper ratio: 3.38
Sweepback at leading edge: 19° 54′
Sweepback at trailing edge: 0°
Chord at root: 11 ft 4 ins (3.457 m)
Chord at tip: 3 ft 4.5 ins (1.023 m)
Anhedral: 2° 30′
Twist: 0° root
Leading-edge slats area, total: 34 sq ft (3.16 m^2)
Ailerons area, total: 16.28 sq ft (1.512 m^2)
Trailing-edge flaps area, total: 47.82 sq ft (4.443 m^2)

Tail unit:
Tailplane span: 15 ft 3 ins (4.652 m)
Tailplane area: 69.7 sq ft (6.473 m^2)
Tailplane dihedral: 5°
Tailplane sweepback: 23° 17′
Elevators area: 20.26 sq ft (1.882 m^2)
Fin height: 8 ft 6 ins (2.58 m)
Fin area: 50.05 sq ft (4.65 m^2)
Rudder area: 8.11 sq ft + 2.22 sq ft upper section (0.7534 m^2+ 0.206 m^2)
Fin sweepback: 35° 47′

Undercarriage:
Type: Retractable, with steerable nosewheel (with mudguard)
Main wheel tyre size: 840 x 360 mm
Nose wheel tyre size: 660 x 200 mm
Wheel base: 11 ft 9 ins (3.574 m)
Wheel track: 8 ft 2 ins (2.506 m)

Weights:
Normal, take-off: 32,023 lb (14,530 kg), or 31,416 lb (14,250 kg) for early aircraft
Maximum take-off: 38,647 lb (17,530 kg) or 38,250 lb (17,350 kg) for early aircraft
Landing, normal: 23,810 lb (10,800 kg)

Performance:
Maximum allowable Mach number: Mach 0.82, or 0.71 for early aircraft
Maximum operating speed, with 4 x 250 kg bombs plus 2 x R-60 AAMs: 513 kts (590 mph) 950 km/h, or 459 kts (528 mph) 850 km/h for early aircraft
Take-off speed: 130-135 kts (149-155 mph) 240-250 km/h
Landing speed: 121-124 kts (140-143 mph) 225-230 km/h
Take-off distance, normal weight: 1,969 ft (600 m)
Take-off distance, maximum weight: 2,953 ft (900 m)
Landing distance: 1,969 ft (600 m)
G limits with normal weapons load and 80% internal fuel: +6.5
Ceiling: 22,950 ft (7,000 m)
Range with maximum internal fuel, at low altitude: 275 naut miles (317 miles) 510 km, or 270 naut miles (311 miles) 500 km for early aircraft
Maximum range, with drop tanks: 999 naut miles (1,450 miles) 1,850 km, or 1,053 naut miles (1,212 miles) 1,950 km for early aircraft

thick). Starboard-opening canopy, and ladder on the port side of the fuselage.
Crew escape: Zvezda K-36L (light) zero-zero ejection seat.
Fixed guns: Double-barrel 30-mm GSh-2-30 (AO-17A) cannon built into the port front fuselage, under the pilot's cockpit.
Ammunition: 250 rounds.
Number of weapon pylons: 8 under the wings, each able to carry a 1,102 lb (500 kg) load, plus 2 small outboard pylons for R-60 (AA-8 *Aphid*) AAMs only.
Expendable weapons and equipment: Normal weapon load is 2,954 lb (1,340 kg), comprising 4 x 250 kg bombs plus 2 x R-60 AAMs. Maximum load is 9,568 lb (4,340 kg). The most advanced weapons are laser-guided Kh-25ML (AS-10 *Karen*) and Kh-29L (AS-14 *Kedge*) ASMs. Unguided weapons include 57 to 370-mm rockets, standard Russian free-fall bombs up to 500 kg weight each, KMGU submunitions dispensers, incendiary tanks, and UPK-23-250 and SPPU-22-01 gun containers. R-60 (AA-8 *Aphid*) AAMs for self-protection only.
Additional stores: Include 4 rocket-propelled PM-6 diving targets, or 4 M-6 parachute targets, or the TL-70 towing system carried under the wings, the latter carried under the port wing and towing a Kometa target.
Radar: Doppler navigation radar (see below).
Flight/weapon system avionics/instrumentation: ASP-17BC-8 gunsight, Klon-PS laser rangefinder/target designator (small window in the nose), and AKS-5 photographic camera. Navigation system derived from the KN-23 system of the MiG-27/Su-17M3; RSBN-6S short-range navigation and instrument landing system, A-031 (early aircraft had RV-5M) altimeter, DISS-7 Doppler navigation radar, and ARK-15M radio compass. SRO-2 Khrom IFF transponder. R-862 radio.

Sukhoi Su-25UB Frogfoot-B trainer (Piotr Butowski)

Self-protection systems: SPO-15L Beryoza (early aircraft: SPO-10 Sirena) radar warning receiver. 8 (early aircraft 4) ASO-2V chaff/flare dispensers (32 x 26-mm rounds each) mounted on the rear upper fuselage at the tailfin sides and above the rear engine ducts. Provision for a container with SPS-141MVG Gvozdika response electronic jammer.
Wing characteristics: Straight, shoulder mounted, with dogtooth leading edge. Tip pods (see Airbrakes).
Wing control surfaces: Each wing has 5-section leading-edge slats across the full span (12° for landing, 6° for manoeuvring), 2-section double-slotted trailing-edge flaps (40° inner and 35° outer sections for landing, 10° all sections for manoeuvring), and ailerons (+20°, -20°).
Tail control surfaces: Variable incidence tailplane (1° 40′, -3° 17′ or -7° 56′), with elevators (+23°, -14°) and tabs (15°). 2-section rudder (25° deflection) with tab, upper section operated as an automatic yaw dumper.
Airbrakes: Crocodile-type, forming split wingtip pods (110°), with area of 13 sq ft (1.2 m^2).
Flight control system: Manually operated elevators and rudder, and ailerons with BU-45 hydraulic actuators (early series aircraft, up to 1984, fully manually operated).
Construction materials: Aluminium alloys and steel.
Fuselage: Semi-monocoque, with flat sides.
Engines: 2 Soyuz/Gavrilov R-95Sh turbojets (the non-afterburning version of the MiG-21's R-13-300 engine) in long nacelles at the fuselage sides, each 9,039 lbf (40.21 kN). Upgraded R-195s in the Su-25BM and last series Su-25, offering 9,921 lbf (44.13 kN) and significantly reduced exhaust gas temperature; cool air from a tailpipe is mixed with the hot engine efflux to further reduce the possibility of infra-red detection.
Engine rating: See Engines.
Air intakes: Fuselage sides, under the wings.
Flight refuelling probe: None.
Fuel system: 6,614 lb (3,000 kg), or 6,008 lb (2,725 kg) for the Su-25UB, in 2 centre-fuselage and 1 wing centre-section tanks. Provision for 4 x 820 litre PTB-800 drop tanks beneath the wings.
Electrical system: 2 engine-driven AC generators, 2 x 28 volt DC generators and 2 batteries.
Hydraulic systems: 2 independent engine-driven systems.
Braking system: Main wheel brakes plus a twin drag-chute.

Aircraft variants:
T8-1 and T8-2 prototypes used RD-9 turbojets.
Su-25 *Frogfoot-A* became the standard single-seater, powered by R-95Sh turbojets. Longer wings than the prototypes (wing aspect ratio raised from 5 to 6.85), and weapon system modernized.
Su-25K (kommercheski) export version of Su-25.
Su-25UB (uchebno-boevoi) *Frogfoot-B* is the tandem two-seat combat trainer, with weapon systems retained. Larger tailfin.
Su-25UBK is the export version of Su-25UB.
Su-25BM (buksir mishenei) *Frogfoot-A* is the modernized single-seat attack version, but also specialized for target towing. R-95Sh engines replaced by R-195s with lower IR-signature and higher thrust. Also used for target towing (see Additional stores). 50 built.
Su-25BMK is the export version of Su-25BM.
Su-25UT (uchebno-trenirovochnyi, Su-28) is a two-seat jet aerobatic aircraft based on the Su-25UB, with weapon system and some equipment removed. Only 1 built.
Su-25UTG (G for gak) is a shipborne trainer. Weapon system removed, and instrument landing system and arrester hook added. Series of 10 built at the Ulan-Ude plant during 1989-90. 5 at the Saki (Ukraine) training centre, 4 on board *Admiral Kuznetsov*, and 1 lost in an accident.
Su-25U3 was a projected three-seat tandem trainer of 1991. Work stopped.
Su-25T is a specialized tank-buster version (see separate entry).

Sukhoi Su-25T (NATO name *Frogfoot*)

First flight: 17 August 1984, piloted by Alexander Isakov.
Role: Export subsonic, armoured close-air support and anti-tank aircraft, used also as lead aircraft for groups of Su-25Ks.
Chief designer: Vladimir Babak.

Sukhoi Su-25TM with Kopyo-25 radar pod (Piotr Butowski)

★ Aims

- ★ Expanded navigation/attack system compared with Su-25.
- ★ New smart weapons, including laser-beam riding Vikhr anti-tank missiles
- ★ Increased range.

▲ Development

▲ 1980. Work started on a dedicated anti-tank aircraft.
▲ 17 August 1984. First flight of prototype T8M-1.
▲ 26 July 1990. First flight of a production Su-25T, at Tbilisi, Georgia.
▲ November 1991. First public presentation (Dubai, UAE) with the export name Su-25TK. Provisionally designated Su-34 by Sukhoi, later officially Su-25T.
▲ December 1992. State Acceptance Tests completed.

Sales/users: In 1990-91 the factory in Tiblisi, Georgia, manufactured the first series of 8 Su-25Ts. The Russian Air Force is not intending to purchase Su-25Ts, as it has sufficient numbers of subsonic close-air support aircraft in respect of limits agreed during disarmament talks in Paris. In December 1993 the Sukhoi Shturmoviks consortium opened talks with Bulgaria, which are expected to result in the lease of 2 or 4 Su-25Ts, and similar talks were in progress with Slovakia in 1995. With these air forces, Su-25Ts would probably be used as homing and lead aircraft for groups of Su-25Ks. It is said that the present Su-25T production rate at Ulan-Ude in Russia (transferred from Tbilisi) is very low. A tender for production in Poland, submitted in Summer 1994, did not arouse great interest.

Crew: Pilot.
Crew escape: K-36 ejection seat.
Cockpit: Fully armoured.
Fixed guns: 1 x 30-mm twin-barrel GSh-2-30 cannon installed under the starboard side of the fuselage, requiring the nosewheel leg to be moved left.
Number of weapon pylons: 10, including 2 wingtip stations for air-to-air missiles only.
Expendable weapons and equipment: Up to 8,818 lb (4,000 kg) of weapons on the 8 main pylons, plus 794 lb (360 kg) at the wingtips (see above). The basic anti-tank armament is 16 Vikhr missiles carried in 2 x APU-8 clusters under the wings. The aircraft can also carry all types of Russian tactical air-to-ground missiles, such as versions of Kh-25, Kh-29, Kh-31, Kh-35, Kh-58 with laser, TV and passive or active radar homing. Also available are guided bombs, such as the KAB-500L laser-guided or KAB-500Kr TV-guided bomb.
Radar: None usually, see Su-25TM below.
Flight/weapon system avionics/instrumentation: Inertial stabilized platform with Voskhod navigation system, with 2 computers. The system has the I-251 Shkval optical-TV subsystem used for target detection, automatic tracking and homing the laser-guided missiles. The Shkval unit includes 3 interconnected channels: TV channel for observation and tracking, Prichal laser rangefinder/target designator, and laser-beam homing system for the Vikhr missile. A large, common window for the TV camera and laser unit is installed in the aircraft's nose. The viewing angles for the Shkval optical-TV system can be adjusted for wide range (observation) 27° x 36°, or for narrow range (tracking) 0.7° x 1.0°. The optical axis of Shkval can be moved vertically from +15° through to -80°, and horizontally by 35° each side. Shkval can track a movable target (such as a tank) with an accuracy of 2 ft (0.6 m) at a distance of 4.3 naut miles (5 miles) 8 km. A container with Merkuriy TV equipment (13.7° x 18.2° or 5.5° x 7.3° respective angles of view) can be suspended under the fuselage for night missions. Merkuriy allows the pilot to see a large target (such as a bridge) from a distance of 5.4-6.5 naut miles (6.2-7.5 miles) 10-12 km or a tank from the distance of 1.6 naut miles (1.9 miles) 3 km. For protection against possible damage during taking-off or landing, the nose of the container is enclosed with a strong steel cover that is opened during operation of the system. The optical system of Merkuriy is not stabilized. TV information is displayed on a monochrome display on the right-hand side of the control panel, except for information from the wide angle channel, which is displayed on the HUD. The Su-25TM additionally has suspended pods with Kindzhal radar and Khod infra-red systems (instead of the Merkuriy container).
Self-protection systems: Irtysh electronic counter-measures system, which includes Beryoza radar warning receiver, L-166S1, UV-26 and Gardenia active electronic jammer. UV-26 chaff/flare dispenser system contains 192 x 26-mm PPI-26 infra-red or PPR-26 chaff cartridges and is installed in a large fairing at the tailfin root. Next to the UV-26 is an L-166S1 active infra-red jamming unit, generating signals inside the rear cone with apex angle of 50°. The 5 kW unit weighs 62 lb (28 kg).
Airframe: As for Su-25UB, but with additional equipment and fuel in the place of the rear cockpit.
Engines: 2 Soyuz R-195 turbojets. Cold air bleed to reduce the infra-red signature.
Engine rating: Each 9,921 lbf (44.13 kN).
Flight refuelling probe: None.
Fuel system: 4,890 litres (8,466 lb, 3,840 kg) of internal fuel, equivalent to 1,000 litres more than Su-25. Provision for 4 x 820 litre PTB-800 or 2 x 1,150 litre PTB-1150 drop tanks under the wings.

DETAILS FOR Su-25T.

Principal dimensions as Su-25 except:
Maximum length: 50 ft 1.5 ins (15.28 m)
Maximum height: 17 ft 1 ins (5.20 m)
Fin area: 56.84 sq ft (5.28 m^2)

Weights:
Nominal take-off: 36,376 lb (16,500 kg), with 5,203 lb (2,360 kg) of weapons
Maximum take-off: 42,990 lb (19,500 kg)
Maximum landing: 29,100 lb (13,200 kg)

Performance:
Maximum allowable Mach number: Mach 0.82
Maximum speed: 513 kts (590 mph) 950 km/h
Maximum cruise speed at 656 ft (200 m): 378 kts (435 mph) 700 km/h
Maximum climb rate: 11,400 ft (3,480 m) per minute, at sea level
Take-off distance: 1,969-2,297 ft (600-700 m)
Landing distance: 1,969-2,297 ft (600-700 m)
G limits: +6.5
Ceiling: 32,810 ft (10,000 m)
Radius of action with 5,203 lb (2,360 kg) of armament at low altitude: 216 naut miles (249 miles) 400 km
Radius of action with 5,203 lb (2,360 kg) of armament at high altitude: 378 naut miles (435 miles) 700 km
Range: 1,350 naut miles (1,553 miles) 2,500 km with maximum fuel

Khod pod under the fuselage of an Su-25TM (Piotr Butowski)

Aircraft variants:

Su-25T (T-8M) is the initial version.
Su-25TM (T-8TM) is the developed production version. Kinzhal and Khod pods added. It features a Kopyo-25 radar pod as seen at Zhukovsky in August 1995. This bestows all-weather and day/night capability. Missiles can include R-27R, R-27ER and R-77 AAMs. Tests to be completed in 1997.
Su-25TK is the export designation, K meaning kommercheskiy or commercial.
Su-25TP Projected ship-borne attack version, featuring an arrester hook and strengthened undercarriage. Armed with Kh-31A (AS-17 *Krypton*) and Kh-35 missiles. Programme has been terminated.

Sukhoi Su-27 (NATO name *Flanker*)

First flight: 20 May 1977, piloted by Vladimir Ilyushin.
Role: Long-range air-superiority fighter.
Chief designers: Naum Chernyakov (up to 1975), Mikhail Simonov (January 1976-December 1979), Artyom Kolchin (December 1979-October 1981), and Alexei Knyshev (since October 1981).

★ Aims

- ★ To counter the US F-15 and other advanced aircraft.
- ★ To destroy enemy strike aircraft at altitudes from 30 m to 17-18 km
- ★ Attain 1,350-1450 km/h at sea level and 2,300-2,500 km range at height.
- ★ Thrust to weight ratio of 1.2:1.
- ★ To operate from third class airfields with runway lengths of 1,200 m.

▲ Development

▲ 1969. PFI (perspektivnyi frontovoi istrebitel) advanced tactical fighter programme started to produce a fighter in the class of the US F-15 Eagle.
▲ 1971. Sukhoi T-10 project selected.

Sukhoi Su-27 Flanker-B operated by Ukraine (Piotr Butowski)

Sukhoi Su-27 Flanker-B landing with airbrake raised (Piotr Butowski)

▲ 20 May 1977. First flight of the T10-1 prototype.
▲ 7 July 1978. T10-2 second prototype crashed, with the loss of the pilot.
▲ March 1979. First information published in the West, with the fighter provisionally named Ram-K.
▲ 23 August 1879. First flight of the AL-31F turbofan-powered prototype, T10-3.
▲ 1980-82. Series of 5 Su-27s (T-10) were built at the Komsomolsk-on-Amur factory.
▲ 20 April 1981. First flight of the totally redesigned T10S-1 (T10-7) production prototype, piloted by Vladimir Ilyushin.
▲ 3 September 1981. T10S-1 was lost, but the pilot survived.
▲ 23 December 1981. T10S-2 second prototype crashed, with the loss of the pilot.
▲ 1982. Production of the Su-27 (T-10S) began.
▲ December 1984. Initial operational capability of the first Su-27 unit.
▲ 7 March 1985. First flight of the Su-27UB combat trainer, piloted by Nikolai Sadovnikov.
▲ Spring 1990. First Su-27 military unit sent abroad, 159th Fighter Air Regiment of the Soviet Air Force based at Kluczewo, Poland.
▲ 7 January 1987. A Norwegian F-16 made the first contact with an Su-27, over the Barents Sea.
▲ 13 September 1987. Collision of a Soviet Su-27 and Norwegian P-3B Orion.
▲ May 1989. Su-27 was displayed abroad for the first time as "Pugachev's cobra", at the Paris Air Show.
▲ 19 March 1993. First known combat loss, when a Russian Su-27 was struck by a surface-to-air missile near Sukhumi.

Sales/users: Production of Su-27 *Flanker-B* started in 1982 at the Komsomolsk-on-Amur plant. Su-27UB *Flanker-C* combat trainer entered production in 1986 at the Irkutsk production plant. In October 1990 the Soviet Union had 413 Su-27s in Europe, of which two-thirds belonged to Air Defence Troops and the remainder to the Air Force, including 2 regiments stationed abroad in Poland (159th Regiment in Kluczewo, 37 aircraft, and 582nd Regiment in Chojna, 34 aircraft). In October 1993 Ukraine had 67 aircraft and Belarus 25, the rest remaining with Russia's armed forces and by then totalling about 500-550 aircraft when including those in the Asian sector of the country. During 1993-94, because of financial restrictions, the Russian Air Force received no further Su-27s, the Komsomolsk factory undertaking only those still being built for China plus a small series of shipborne Su-27Ks. The 24 Chinese Su-27SKs and 2 Su-27UBKs were the first exports, and China ordered a second batch in early 1995 covering 22 SKs and 2 UBKs (delivered 1995-96), plus possible licence manufacture. All initially served with the 3rd Division at Wuhu AFB. Syria has a requirement for 14. Vietnam has purchased about 6.

Details for Su-27 Flanker-B.

Principal dimensions:
Wing span: 48 ft 3 ins (14.7 m)
Length without probe: 72 ft (21.935 m)
Maximum height: 19 ft 6 ins (5.932 m)

Wings:
Area: 667.8 sq ft (62.037 m²)
Aspect ratio: 3.48
Sweepback at leading edge: 42°
Sweepback at trailing edge: 15°
Incidence: 0°
Dihedral/anhedral: 0°
Leading edge slats area, gross: 49.51 sq ft (4.6 m²)
Trailing-edge flaperons area, gross: 52.74 sq ft (4.9 m²)

Tail unit:
Tailplane span: 32 ft 5 ins (9.88 m)
Tailplane area: 131.75 sq ft (12.24 m²)
Fins area, gross: 165.76 sq ft (15.4 m²)
Fins cant angle: 0°
Rudders area, gross: 37.57 sq ft (3.49 m²)
Ventral fins area, gross: 26.91 sq ft (2.5 m²)

Undercarriage:
Type: Retractable, with steerable nosewheel with mudguard
Main wheel tyre size: 1,030 x 350 mm
Nose wheel tyre size: 680 x 260 mm
Wheel base: 19 ft 4 ins (5.88 m)
Wheel track: 14 ft 3 ins (4.34 m)

Weights:
Empty, operating: 36,112 lb (16,380 kg)
Normal take-off: 51,015 lb (23,140 kg)
Maximum take-off: 62,391 lb (28,300 kg)
Maximum allowable take-off for last production series: 72,752 lb (33,000 kg)

Performance:
Maximum operating speed: 1,350 kts (1,553 mph) 2,500 km/h
Maximum speed at sea level: 756 kts (870 mph) 1,400 km/h
Landing speed: 121 kts (140 mph) 225 km/h
Take-off distance: 2,133-2,297 ft (650-700 m)
Landing distance: 2,034-2,297 ft (620-700 m)
Roll rate: about 270° per second
G limit: +9
Ceiling: 60,700 ft (18,500 m)
Maximum range, clean: 2,008 naut miles (2,312 miles) 3,720 km
Maximum range with 10 AAMs: 1,512 naut miles (1,740 miles) 2,800 km
Radius of action at high altitude: 589 naut miles (677 miles) 1,090 km
Radius of action at low altitude: 227 naut miles (261 miles) 420 km

Details for Su-27UB Flanker C.

Principal dimensions:
Maximum height: 20 ft 10 ins (6.357 m)

Weights:
Empty, operating: 38,580 lb (17,500 kg)
Normal take-off: 53,220 lb (24,140 kg)
Maximum take-off: 67,130 lb (30,450 kg)
Maximum allowable take-off for last production series: 73,854 lb (33,500 kg)

Performance:
Max operating speed: 1,161 kts (1,336 mph) 2,150 km/h
Maximum speed at sea level: 756 kts (870 mph) 1,400 km/h
Landing speed: 124 kts (143 mph) 230 km/h
G limit: +9
Ceiling: 57,400 ft (17,500 m)
Maximum range, clean: 1,620 naut miles (1,864 miles) 3,000 km
Take-off distance: 2,461-2,625 ft (750-800 m)
Landing distance: 2,133-2,297 ft (650-700 m)

Long tail 'sting' between the engine nozzles of Su-27 contains the drag-chute, a fuel tank, Beryoza RWR antennae and APP-50 chaff/flare unit (Piotr Butowski)

Crew: Pilot, or 2 in the Su-27UB trainer. Crew has the NAZ-8 portable life pack containing Komar-2M radio, PSN-1 dinghy, medicine, food, signal flares, etc.
Cockpit: Conventional, with analog indicators and switches.
Crew escape: K-36DM series 2 zero-zero ejection seat.
Fixed guns: Single-barrel 30-mm GSh-301 cannon in the starboard LERX.
Ammunition: 150 rounds.
Number of weapon pylons: 10 (or 12 in the last production series), comprising 2 under the fuselage in tandem between the engine nacelles, 2 under the air ducts, 4 (or 6) under the wings, and 2 at the wingtips.
Expendable weapons and equipment: Maximum allowable load is 17,636 lb (8,000 kg), but the maximum load in normal operations is 8,818 lb (4,000 kg). Typical armament for air-combat missions comprises 10 (or 12) AAMs, including up to 4 extended-range R-27ER/ETs (AA-10 *Alamo-C/D*) and up to 6 medium-range R-27R/Ts (AA-10 *Alamo-A/B*). Outer underwing pylons and wingtip pylons normally carry R-73 close-air combat AAMs. Only unguided air-to-ground weapons can be used, including bombs and rockets. See upgrade under Aircraft variants.
Radar: RLPK-27 (radiolokatsyonnyi pritselnyi kompleks) radar attack system includes NIIP S-27 Myech (N-001) coherent pulse Doppler look-down/shoot-down radar (designed by Viktor Grishin) and a TsVM-80 digital computer. Search range 130 naut miles (149 miles) 240 km and tracking range 92 naut miles (105.6 miles) 170 km, both in the forward hemisphere. Radar can track up to 10 targets simultaneously and engage 2. See upgrade under Aircraft variants.
Flight/weapon system avionics/instrumentation: RLPK-27 radar system is supported by OEPS-27 (optiko-elektronnaya pritselnaya sistema) which comprises an OLS-27 (optiko-lokatsyonnaya stantsya, or 36Sh) infra-red search/track device coupled with a laser rangefinder (tracking range 27 naut miles, 31 miles, 50 km in the rearward hemisphere and 8.1 naut miles, 9.3 miles, 15 km in the forward hemisphere), Shchel-3U helmet-mounted target designator and Ts-100 computer. Head-up-display showing integrated information from the various sensors. R-800 and R-864 com radios, Parol IFF, TKS-2 secure data link for group operations, and Spektr data link for target indication from land-based radars. Navigation equipment includes 2 altimeters, ARK-22 radio compass, marker beacon receiver, A-317 short range radio navigation, and SO-69 transponder.

Sukhoi Su-27UB Flanker-C operated by the Russkiye Vityazi aerobatic team (Piotr Butowski)

Self-protection systems: SPO-15 Beryoza (L-006) radar warning receiver with sensors on the sides of the air intakes and on the tailboom. Pallad electronic countermeasures (ECM) system (only rearward hemisphere is jammed when board radar is active). Provision for suspended ECM jamming pods, including 2 Sorbtsya-S (L-005) on the wingtips. APP-50 (L-O29) chaff/flare system built into the tailboom. 8 dispensers, each with 3 x 50-mm cartridges in early aircraft; from the 18th production series, 32 dispensers in expanded tailboom sides.
Wing characteristics: Swept, mid mounted, with 3-spar structure. Low wing loading. Sharp-edged wingroot extensions.
Wing control surfaces: Flaperon (+35°, -20°) occupies about 60% of each wing trailing edge from root. Full-span leading-edge slats (30°).
Tail control surfaces: Mounted on booms alongside the engine nacelles. Twin uncanted fins and rudders (25° deflection). Slab (taileron) tailplane, deflecting symmetrically (+15°, -20°) or differentially (+10°, -10°). Twin ventral fins.
Airbrakes: Single door-type airbrake on the fuselage dorsal spine, hydraulically actuated 54°. Area 28 sq ft (2.6 m^2).
Flight control system: Designed to be inherently unstable. SDU-10-27 (sistema distantsyonnovo upravlenya) quadruple redundant analog fly-by-wire, with no mechanical backup. RPD-1 electro-hydraulical power units. Flaperons and slats are controlled manually for take-off and landing, computer-assisted control (fly-by-wire) in flight. Tailplane computer controlled, except when operated differentially. Rudder has manual control. Automatic control system includes OPR (ogranichitel predelnykh rezhimov) angle of attack/g-load limiter, which can be overruled manually.
Fuselage: Airframe designed from similar national research that aided the MiG-29. Wide fuselage/wing centre section provides considerable lifting force. Fuselage is of semi-monocoque construction, technologically divided into 3 sections. Nose section contains the radar, cockpit, front undercarriage unit and equipment boxes; sloping centre section houses 2 fuel tanks, airbrake, equipment boxes and main undercarriage compartment; the rear section houses widely spaced engine nacelles and a central rearward-protruding boom containing a fuel tank, equipment, chaff/flare dispensers and drag-chute.
Construction materials: All metal, mainly aluminium alloy, but with titanium in the engine nacelles.
Engines: 2 Saturn/Lyulka AL-31F (izdelye 99V) turbofans.
Engine rating: Each 16,755 lbf (74.53 kN) dry, 27,558 lbf (122.59 kN) with afterburning.
Air intakes: 3 ramp adjustable type. Intakes semi-blanked during take-off and landing by a grid, when additional air is provided by sets of louvres around the intake.
Flight refuelling probe: None.
Fuel system: Up to 12,000 litres (20,723 lb, 9,400 kg) of fuel in 5 tanks: 2 in the wing centre section, 2 in the outer wings and 1 in the tailboom. Nominal fuel is 13,227 lb (6,000 kg), while the remaining 7,496 lb (3,400 kg) is called the "internal auxiliary tank". No external drop tanks are carried. Tanks are filled with anti-explosive reticulated polyurethane foam.
Electrical system: 27 volt DC supply. 2 AC generators, 115 volt/400 Hz. 2 x 20NKBN-25 stand-by batteries.
Hydraulic system: Dual systems, pressure 3,983 psi, used for the tailplane, rudders, flaperons, slats, airbrake, undercarriage, undercarriage doors, mainwheel brakes, air intakes and air-intake grids (see Flight control system).
Braking system: Mainwheel brakes. Twin drag-chutes, 538.2 sq ft (50 m^2) gross area, housed in the tailboom.

Aircraft variants:

T-10 *Flanker-A* appeared in 1977. 4 prototypes, plus first 5 pre-production aircraft built at Komsomolsk-on-Amur. Ogival wing and AL-21F3 turbojets (except T10-3 and T10-4 with AL-31Fs). First prototype now in the Monino museum. Possibly up to 15 prototype/development aircraft.
Su-27S (T-10S) *Flanker-B* became the basic production tactical dual-role model, as described. The basic air defence version of the same aircraft is Su-27P *Flanker-B.*
Su-27UB *Flanker-C* is a two-seat combat trainer. Prototype appeared in 1985. In production since 1986 at Irkutsk. Second cockpit added by reducing fuel capacity. Full combat capability, with radar/weapons system retained.
Su-27UB vectoring-thrust test-bed, see Su-35.
Su-27SK (K for kommerchesky) is the export version of Su-27s.
Su-27UBK is the export version of Su-27UB.
P-42 is the 3rd prototype (T10S-3) prepared for record flights, with radar, weapons system, antennas, paint, etc removed. During 1986-87 it set a series of 27 records for climb and altitude.
T10-20R became another special conversion (though record-breaking flights were not performed), destined for long-range supersonic flight. Reduced weight, and fuel added in the nose (in place of the radar) and tail (in the "sting" between the engines), offering 26,455 lb (12,000 kg) of fuel at 58,643 lb (26,600 kg) take-off weight. Now in the museum at Khodinka airfield in Moscow.
Su-27PD became the personal aircraft of Anatoli Kvochur, well-known test pilot. Standard Su-27, but with the weapon system removed and flight-refuelling probe added (D for dozapravka).
Projected life-time upgrade for the Su-27 by installing new Zhuk-27 radar, R-77 (AA-12) AAMs and air-to-surface weapons.
Su-30 (Su-27PU) is a two-seat interceptor/multi-role fighter derivative. See separate entry.
Su-32FN is a two-seat maritime strike derivative. See separate entry.
Su-33 (Su-27K) is a shipborne fighter derivative. See separate entry.
Su-34 (Su-27IB) is a two-seat tactical bomber derivative. See separate entry.
Su-35 (Su-27M) is an advanced air-superiority fighter with ground attack capability derivative. See separate entry.

Sukhoi Su-30 (NATO name *Flanker*)

First flight: 30 December 1989.
Role: Two-seat long-range multi-role interceptor (Su-30), two-seat fighter with ground attack capability (Su-30MK), and combat trainer.

Sukhoi Su-30MK with a KAB-500T bomb and APK-9 data link pod (rear) between engines, Kh-29T Kedge missile under the starboard air intake, multiple bomb rack under the port intake, Kh-31 Krypton and R-27 Alamo under the inner port-side wing pylons, Kh-59M Kazoo and R-77 Adder under the inner starboard-side wing pylons, and 4 x R-73s on the outer and wingtip pylons (Piotr Butowski)

Chief designers: Alexei Knyshev (supervisor), Igor Yemelyanov (Su-30) and Viktor Galushko (air-to-surface weapon system for Su-30MK).

★ Aims

⋆ Ability to carry high-accuracy air-to-ground/surface missiles.
⋆ In-flight refuelling.

▲ Development

▲ 1987. First tests with a flight refuelling system on the Su-27 (Su-27UB side number 02). The aircraft was also used as a buddy tanker with a UPAZ-1A Sakhalin refuelling pack.
▲ 23 June 1987. Aircraft flew from Moscow to Komsomolsk on Amur and back, remaining airborne for 15 hours 31 minutes, after being flight refuelled 4 times. Total distance 7,238 naut miles (8,329 miles) 13,404 km.
▲ 30 December 1989. First flight of the T-10PU (Su-27PU) prototype (side number 05).
▲ Early 1992. 2 production aircraft were built at the Irkutsk factory.
▲ May-June 1993. Su-27UB (ex side number 389, now 321) was presented as an Su-30MK at the Paris Air Show, with the suspended weapons and equipment pods of the proposed Su-30MK, but no flight refuelling probe or ground-attack weapons control system.

DETAILS FOR SU-30MK.
AS SU-27UB EXCEPT:

Weights:
Normal take-off: 55,115 lb (25,000 kg)
Maximum take-off: 74,957 lb (34,000 kg)

Performance:
Maximum operating Mach number (MMO): Mach 2.0
Maximum speed: 1,147 kts (1,320 mph) 2,125 km/h
Maximum speed at low altitude: 729 kts (839 mph) 1,350 km/h
Take-off distance: 1,805 ft (550 m)
Landing dustance: 2,198 ft (670 m)
G limit: +8
Ceiling: 57,400 ft (17,500 m)
Maximum range without flight refuelling: 1,620 naut miles (1,864 miles) 3,000 km
Range with 1 flight refuelling: 2,808 naut miles (3,231 miles) 5,200 km
Range with 2 flight refuellings: 3,774 naut miles (4,343 miles) 6,990 km

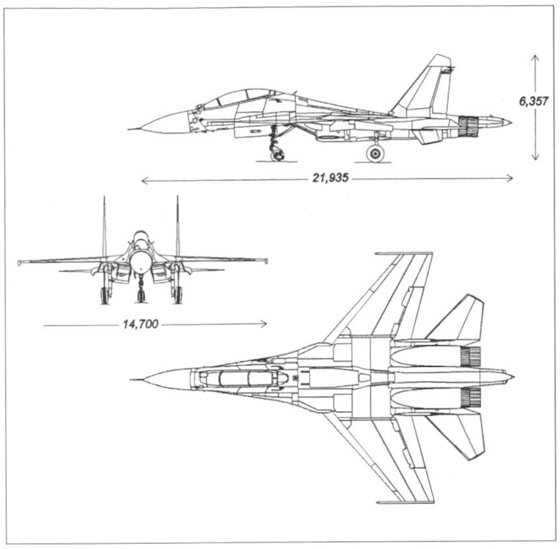

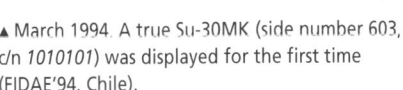

Sukhoi Su-30 drawing (courtesy Sukhoi)

Sukhoi Su-30MK (Piotr Butowski)

▲ March 1994. A true Su-30MK (side number 603, c/n *1010101*) was displayed for the first time (FIDAE'94, Chile).
▲ Indian Air Force pilots tested the Su-30MK at Irkutsk, as a possible first step towards licensed production by HAL in India.
Sales/users: Only a few aircraft have been manufactured at Irkutsk, with 1 used by the Russian aerobatic team. Negotiations with India for about 20-35 Su-30MKs, with possible licence production of 60 more in India, reportedly ended in early 1995.
Crew: 2, in tandem cockpit.
Cockpit: Full avionics/instrumentation in both cockpits.
Crew ejection: As for Su-27/Su-27UB.
Fixed guns: As for Su-27/Su-27UB.
Number of weapon pylons: 12.
Expendable weapons and equipment: Su-30 has the same weapons as the Su-27/Su-27UB. Su-30MK can carry up to a 17,637 lb (8,000 kg) load. Besides the standard air-to-air armament of the Su-27, it carries guided air-to-surface missiles and weapon guidance pods. Kh-31P (AS-17 *Krypton*) anti-radar missiles are controlled by the SPO-32 Pastel radar warning receiver (RWR) pod, which detects the targets and programmes the missile before launch. The SPO-32 pod is suspended on the front pylon between the air intake ducts. TV-guided Kh-29T (AS-14 *Kedge*) missiles and KAB-500Kr bombs use guidance cameras, the picture from the missile being projected on the TV screen situated on the upper right side of the instrument panel in the cockpit. The longer-range (62 naut mile, 71.5 mile, 115 km) Kh-59M (AS-18 *Kazoo*) TV-guided missile requires an APK-9 data link pod, suspended on the rear underfuselage pylon. Kh-29L (AS-14 *Kedge*) laser-guided missile uses the laser channel of the OLS-27 for target designation.
Radar: As for Su-27/Su-27UB.
Flight/weapon system avionics/instrumentation: Extended navigation equipment and tactical data exchange set, enabling a group commander on board an Su-30 to assign targets to other fighters.
Self-protection systems: As for Su-27 plus SPS-161 ECM jammer in a common pod with SPO-32 Pastel RWR.
Wing characteristics: As for Su-27/Su-27UB.
Tail control surfaces: As for Su-27UB.
Flight control system: As for Su-27/Su-27UB.
Fuselage: As for Su-27UB.
Construction materials: As for Su-27/Su-27UB.
Engines: As for Su-27/Su-27UB.
Flight refuelling probe: See below.
Fuel system: As for Su-27UB, but provision for in-flight refuelling with a standard probe on the port side of the nose. On the Su-30 (and other versions of the Su-27 equipped with a refuelling probe), the IRST is moved to the right side of the windscreen (instead of centre).

Aircraft variants:
Su-30 (Su-27PU, T-10PU) is a two-seat long range interceptor.
Su-30M is a multi-role export version, but with unguided weapons.
Su-30MK (T-10PMK) is a multi-role export version with guided weapons. Mid-life upgrade of Russian AF Su-27/Su-27UBs is to Su-30MK standard.

Sukhoi Su-32FN (NATO name *Flanker*)

First flight: 28 December 1994. Fifth aircraft (T10B-5) shown at Paris in June 1995.
Role: Specialized long-range maritime strike, as a variant of Su-34, with the same engines and seating.
Fixed guns: GSh-301 30-mm cannon.
Number of weapon pylons: 12.
Expendable weapons and equipment: Wide range of sophisticated weapons, including a single Kh-41 Moskit under the fuselage, or 6 Kh-25Ms, 2 Kh-35s, 2 Kh–59Ms or other types.
Radar: High-resolution, multi-function nav/attack radar, with terrain following/avoidance.
Flight/weapon system avionics/instrumentation: Include 7-CRT liquid crystal EFIS. Internal ECM.

Kh-59T Kazoo arming a Sukhoi Su-30MK (Piotr Butowski)

DETAILS FOR Su-32N.

Principal dimensions:
Wing span: 48 ft 3 ins (14.7 m)
Length: 82 ft 8 ins (25.2 m)
Maximum height: 20 ft 3 ins (6.2 m)

Weights:
Maximum take-off: 99,208 lb (45,000 kg)

Sukhoi Su-33 (service designation Su-27K) (NATO name *Flanker-D*)

First flight: 17 August 1987, piloted by Viktor Pugachov.
Role: Carrier-borne air-superiority/air defence and anti-ship aircraft.
Chief designer: Konstantin Marbashev.

★ Aims
★ Modified ship-borne derivative of the Su-27. Bureau designation Su-33, Russian Navy designation Su-27K.

▲ Development
▲ 28 August 1982. First take-off of Su-27 (T10-3, third prototype) from a dummy flight deck marked out on the runway at Saki, Ukraine, the Naval aviation test centre. Piloted by Nikolai Sadovnikov.
▲ 1984. Official government order for the Su-27K and MiG-29K ship-borne fighters.
▲ 1 September 1984. First landing of Su-27 (T10-25 test aircraft) with use of an arrester hook, piloted by Viktor Pugachov.

Heavy Moskit (officially ASM-MSS) anti-ship missile under an Su-33 (Su-27K). Note the aircraft's canard and leading-edge slat (Piotr Butowski)

Sukhoi Su-33/Su-27K with wings and tail folded, and refuelling probe visible on the port side of the cockpit (Piotr Butowski)

▲ 25 September 1984. First take-off from the new ski-jump built at Saki, an exact copy the flight deck of the aircraft carrier *Tbilisi,* by T10-25.
▲ May 1985. First flight of T10-24 test aircraft, the first Su-27 with canard surfaces, piloted by Viktor Pugachov.
▲ 1987. First fully-automatic landings of the Su-27 on the Saki runway using the Rezystor radio system, and the first night landing using the Luna-3 optical-laser system.
▲ 17 August 1987. First flight of T10K-1, the first proper prototype (designated also T10-37, side number 37); this was lost in 1988, the pilot surviving.
▲ Spring 1988. First information published on the Su-27K, named *Flanker-B variant 2*, later *Flanker-D*.
▲ 1 November 1989. First landing on the deck of *Tbilisi*, piloted by Viktor Pugachov. The aircraft was T10K-2 (T10-39, side number 39)
▲ 18 August 1991. First public presentation, a fly-pass at the Zhukovsky test centre.
▲ 26 September 1991. First flights by military pilots (not test pilots) on the deck of an aircraft carrier; the first was Col Timur Apakidze.
▲ October 1994. State acceptance trials were completed successfully (started Autumn 1992). The aircraft was officially commissioned and accepted into service with the Russian Navy as the Su-27K (names T-10K and Su-33 are from the Design Bureau).
▲ Summer 1994. Saki airfield leased to Russia from Ukraine for aircraft carrier pilot training.

Sales/users: 6 test aircraft plus an initial first batch of 18 built during 1992-93 at Komsomolsk-on-Amur plant (see Su-27 for plant information). Subsequent production terminated due to financial cutbacks, but production could be re-established to provide for a full unit and also a reserve unit (52 aircraft of all types make up the air element on board the *Admiral of the Fleet Kuznetsov* aircraft carrier).
Crew: Pilot.
Cockpit: As for Su-27, plus some new navigation instrumentation.
Crew escape: Zvezda K-36DM ejection seat.
Fixed guns: As for Su-27 (single GSh-30-1 cannon).
Number of weapon pylons: 12.
Expendable weapons and equipment: Maximum weapon load of 14,330 lb (6,500 kg). In addition to standard Su-27 weapons, the Su-27K can carry R-27EM air-to-air missiles specialized for use over the sea against air targets flying at low altitude, as well as 4 x Kh-31A anti-ship missiles of 38 naut mile (43.5 mile) 70 km range and 1 heavy Moskit (ASM-MSS) missile weighing 9,921 lb (4,500 kg) and with a range of 135 naut miles (155 miles) 250 km.
Radar: As for Su-27.
Flight/weapon system avionics/ instrumentation: Su-27K carries a special device, allowing fully automatic, command controlled or manual controlled landing. On board ship are 2 landing systems that combine with the aircraft's system: Rezistor automatic radio approach and landing system, and Luna-3 optical-laser system warning the pilot by means of lights of various colours against deviations from the best landing approaching path.
Self-protection systems: As for Su-27.
Wing characteristics: In spite of external similarity to Su-27, the internal wing structure of Su-27K is quite different. Outer wing panels fold for stowage on board ship.
Wing control surfaces: A conventional trailing-edge flap and aileron occupy the full trailing edge, instead of the Su-27's approximately 60% span flaperon.
Tail control surfaces: As for Su-27, but folding outer tailplane panels are standard. The folded tailplane seems to have caused problems, indicated by the alterations to T10K-6 (side number 79); when presented to CIS leaders at Machulishche in February 1992, T10K-6 had a folded horizontal tail, but 2 months later the same aircraft was displayed at the Kubinka Air Base with a one-piece unit.
Canard: All-moving, swept, deflected symmetrically only (about +7°, -70°).
Airbrakes: As for Su-27.
Flight control system: Adapted from the Su-27.
Fuselage: Upward folding nose radome. Folding tailboom, which is much shorter than that of Su-27.
Construction materials: Greater use of anti-corrosion materials.
Engines: As for Su-27. 2 x AL-35Fs, each 30,865 lbf (137.3 kN), are expected to be the definitive engines.
Flight refuelling probe: Mounted on the port side of the nose. The lights on both sides in the front fuselage are for illuminating the tanker's drogue during night refuelling. UPAZ-A Sakhalin 'buddy' refuelling pod can be carried under the fuselage of Su-27K. Flight refuelling is a very important feature of the Su-27K, since it cannot take off with full fuel from the carrier if heavily armed.
Braking system: Arrester hook under the tailboom. No drag-chute.

Aircraft variants:
Su-27K (Su-33, K stands for korabelnyi, ship-borne), as described.

Sukhoi Su-34 first prototype, designated T10B-1, with single mainwheels (Dmitri Grinyuk/via Piotr Butowski)

DETAILS FOR SU-33 (SU-27K).

Principal dimensions:
Wing span: 48 ft 3 ins (14.70 m)
Span with wings and tailplane folded: 24 ft 3 ins (7.40 m)
Length without probe: 69 ft 6 ins (21.185 m)
Maximum height: 19 ft 2 ins (5.85 m)

Wings:
Sweepback at leading edge: 42°
Dihedral/Anhedral: 0°

Tail unit:
Tailplane span: 32 ft 2 ins (9.80 m)

Undercarriage:
Type: Strengthened retractable type, with twin nosewheels
Main wheel tyre size: 1,030 x 350 mm
Wheel base: 19 ft 3 ins (5.872 m)
Wheel track: 14 ft 5 ins (4.40 m)

Weights:
Maximum take-off: 66,000 lb (29,940 kg)
Maximum in flight, after refuelling: 72,752 lb (33,000 kg)

Performance:
Maximum speed: 1,242 kts (1,429 mph) 2,300 km/h
Maximum speed at sea level: 756 kts (870 mph) 1,400 km/h
Approach speed: 130 kts (149 mph) 240 km/h
G limit: +9
Ceiling: 55,775 ft (17,000 m)
Maximum range without flight refuelling: 1,620 naut miles (1,864 miles) 3,000 km

Sukhoi Su-34 (Su-27IB)

First flight: 13 April 1990, piloted by Anatoli Ivanov.
Role: Supersonic tactical, theatre bomber, to replace MiG-27 *Flogger*, Su-17 *Fitter* and Su-24 *Fencer*.
Chief designer: Rollan Martirosov.

Sukhoi Su-34 first production aircraft, designated T10B-1, with tandem mainwheels and a large tailboom containing rear radar (Alexei Mikheyev/via Piotr Butowski)

DETAILS FOR Su-34 (PRELIMINARY).

Principal dimensions:
Wing span: 48 ft 3 ins (14.7 m)
Length without probe: 76 ft 5 ins (23.3 m)
Length overall: 81 ft 4 ins (24.8 m)
Maximum height: 20 ft (6.1 m)
Canards span: 21 ft (6.4 m)

Undercarriage:
Type: Retractable, with twin nosewheels. Single mainwheels on the T10-42 prototype but tandem mainwheels on production aircraft

Weights:
Maximum take-off: 97,000 lb (44,000 kg)

Performance:
Maximum speed: 972 kts (1,118 mph) 1,800 km/h
Maximum speed at sea level: 702 kts (808 mph) 1,300 km/h
Range with maximum fuel: 2,160 naut miles (2,485 miles) 4,000 km

★ Aims
⋆ Developed from the general Su-27 fighter type but with significant airframe redesign offering side-by-side seating.
⋆ Titanium armour plating around the cockpit.
⋆ Additional rearward-facing air-to-air radar in a long tailboom.

▲ Development
▲ 13 April 1990. First flight of the T10B-1 prototype.
▲ 1991. First photograph published by the TASS press agency.
▲ 14 February 1992. T10B-1 displayed at Machulishche, Belarus, to CIS leaders. Officially named Su-27IB.
▲ 18 December 1993. First flight of first production aircraft (T10B-1), piloted by Igor Votintsev and Yevgeni Revunov.
▲ 3 March 1994. T10B-1 flew from Novosibirsk to Zhukovsky for testing.
▲ 28 December 1994. Second production aircraft flew, manufactured at Novosibirsk.
Sales/users: Series manufacturing began at the Novosibirsk aircraft plant, replacing Su-24 *Fencer*. Up to 13 Su-34s are expected to be built by 1998. India has expressed interest in the aircraft.
Crew: Pilot (port side) and the weapons operator (starboard seat) side by side.
Cockpit: Very high cockpit arranged to allow the crew to stand and undertake relaxing exercises during long-duration flights. Aft of the cockpit is a toilet and galley compartment. Cockpit conditions at 32,800 ft (10,000 m) are the same as at 7,875 ft (2,400 m), allowing the crew to work without oxygen masks. Crew enter the cockpit via the front wheel bay; the canopy is not opened. The entire cockpit is located inside a 17 mm thick titanium alloy "box", protecting the crew from anti-aircraft fire.
Crew escape: Zvezda K-36DM zero-zero ejection seats.
Fixed guns: GSh-301 cannon built into starboard wingroot.
Number of weapon pylons: 12.
Expendable weapons and equipment: Up to 17,637 lb (8,000 kg). The aircraft presented at Machulishche carried Kh-31P (AS-17 *Krypton*) anti-radar, Kh-29L (AS-14 *Kedge*) laser-guided and Kh-29T TV guided air-to-surface missiles, KAB-500L laser-guided bombs, plus R-73 (AA-11 *Archer*) and R-77 (*Adder*) air-to-air missiles. According to General Designer Seemonov, the maximum range of the missiles carried by Su-34 is 250 km, so additional weapons must be carried. From currently known Russian ASMs, this range is attainable by AFM-L (Alfa) and Kh-65.
Radar: Leninets phased-array radar in the nose, with automatic terrain following and terrain avoidance capability. Rear-facing air-to-air radar installed in the tailboom tip.
Flight/weapon system avionics/ instrumentation: Inertial navigation system integrated with GLONASS satellite navigation. According to Mikhail Seemonov, the aircraft navigational system "with principally new computer" is capable of navigation "with accuracy of up to 1 m".
Self-protection system: Pastel radar warning receiver, Mak infra-red missile launch and approach warning device, laser warning device. Sorptsya-S ECM containers can be mounted at the wing tips. Chaff/flare dispensers tested on T10B-1.
Wing characteristics: As for Su-27.
Tail control surfaces: As for Su-27UB for T10-42 prototype, and as for Su-27 for production aircraft.
Canard: Similar to that of Su-33 and Su-35.
Construction materials: 3,263 lb (1,480 kg) of the overall weight is taken by the protection system (armoured cockpit, etc.)
Engines: Intended engines are 2 Saturn AL-35Fs (each 30,865 lbf, 137.3 kN); at present AL-31Fs (each 27,558 lbf, 122.59 kN) are fitted.
Air intakes: Non adjustable.
Flight refuelling probe: Standard, on the port side of the nose.
Braking system: Drag-chute is housed on top of the fuselage, between the engine nacelles.

Aircraft variants:
Su-34 (Su-27IB, istriebitiel-bombardirovshchik, fighter-bomber). The first prototype was the 42nd test aircraft of Su-27 family, with side number 42 and called T10-42. The first production aircraft was T10-43 and numbered 43. See below.
T10B-1 (T10-42) was produced as a conversion of an Su-27UB, with the front fuselage replaced (up to frame No 18). T10B-2 (T10-43) is a newly-built production aircraft.
Su-27KU. Projected ship-borne version. Programme was terminated by early 1995.
Reconnaissance and Electronic warfare versions are being developed as replacements for the Su-24MR/MP *Fencer-E/F.*
Su-32FN is a specialized maritime strike variant. See separate entry.

Sukhoi Su-35 (Su-27M) and Su-37 (NATO name *Flanker*)

First flight: 28 June 1988.
Role: Advanced air-superiority fighter, with ground-attack capability.
Chief designer: Nikolai Nikitin.

★ Aims
⋆ Instability some 3 to 5 times greater than for the Su-27, to increase manoeuvrability. Maximum angle of attack 30° in steady subsonic conditions. Angles of attack may reach 120° in "non-steady" combat conditions, with no stalling or spin.
⋆ Improved avionics including track-while-scan radar for up to 15-24 targets (see Radar) and rear radar.
⋆ Vectored thrust for developed models.

▲ Development
▲ 28 June 1988. Maiden flight of the T10M-1 first prototype.
▲ 1989. Vectored thrust trials began with a modified Su-27UB as T10-16 (Su-27LL-PS) (see Nozzles).
▲ 14 February 1992. Su-27M (side number 706) was presented to CIS leaders at Machulishche.
▲ September 1992. First public presentation, with T10M-3 (side number 703, c/n *79371010102*), Sukhoi designated Su-35, at the Farnborough Air Show.
▲ 1995. Su-35/Su-27M expected to enter Russian Air Force service.
Sales/users: 2 prototypes built at the Sukhoi test production facility in Moscow, and a further 9 pre-production aircraft at the Komsomolsk-on-Amur plant. India has expressed interest in the aircraft, while the Russian State Committee for Defence Branches of Industry has suggested the United Arab Emirates is likely to purchase Su-35s. Su-37 has been suggested as a variant of the Su-35 for the UAE, possibly to meet the known long-range strike requirement.
Crew: Pilot.
Cockpit: Glass cockpit with 4 multi-function displays (front panel and side panels, the exact positioning varying from aircraft to aircraft). Monochrome displays in current aircraft, colour displays for production aircraft. Starboard side-stick controller planned for operational aircraft, but current test aircraft have the conventional central stick.

Sukhoi Su-35 (Su-27M) as T-10M-11. Note the thrust vectoring nozzles (Alexei Mikheyev)

Details for Su-35.

Principal dimensions:
Wing span: 48 ft 3 ins (14.7 m)
Maximum length: 72 ft 6 ins (22.1 m)
Maximum height: 20 ft 9 ins (6.32 m)

Wings:
Sweepback at leading edge: 42°

Undercarriage:
Type: Retractable, with single nosewheel on 706 and 707 prototypes, and twin wheels on the following aircraft

Weights:
Empty, operating: 40,565 lb (18,400 kg)
Normal take-off, air-combat mission: 56,659 lb (25,700 kg)

Performance:
Maximum speed: 1,350 kts (1,553 mph) 2,500 km/h
Maximum speed at sea level: 756 kts (870 mph) 1,400 km/h
Required runway length: 3,937 ft (1,200 m)
G limit: +10
Ceiling: 59,000 ft (18,000 m)
Range with maximum fuel: 2,160 naut miles (2,485 miles) 4,000 km
Range with single flight refuelling: 3,510 naut miles (4,039 miles) 6,500 km

Sukhoi Su-27UB used as a vectoring thrust test-bed, with the port engine equipped with a special end piece for duplicating any type and configuration of nozzle (Piotr Butowski)

Crew escape: K-36DM zero-zero ejection seat, inclined 30° for better g-force tolerance and adapted for long-duration flights. PPK-15 anti-G suit for pilot.
Fixed guns: As for Su-27 (GSh-30-1 30-mm cannon).
Number of weapon pylons: 14.
Expendable weapons and equipment: Up to 17,634 lb (8,000 kg) of weapons. All types of modern Russian air-to-air missiles, including 189 naut mile (217 mile) 350 km range R-37s, medium/extended range R-77/R-77Ms (AA-12 *Adder*) and short-range R-73 (AA-11 *Archer*). All types of Russian tactical air-to-surface missiles, including anti-radar/active radar Kh-31 (AS-17 *Krypton*) and Kh-59M (AS-18 *Kazoo*) TV-guided missiles, plus bombs, rockets, etc.
Radar: NIIP N-011 multi-mode look-down/shoot-down radar with aperture antenna, designed by Tamerlan Bekerbayev. Coverage ±85°. Maximum search range for an air target is 216 naut miles (249 miles) 400 km. Track-while-scan mode allows tracking of 15 air targets and engaging 6 simultaneously (including motionless targets such as helicopters). In an air-to-ground mode, it can acquire surface targets at ranges up to 108 naut miles (124 miles) 200 km, and undertake ground mapping, terrain following and terrain avoidance. Su-35 also carries rear-looking N-012 radar with a 1.6-2.2 naut mile (1.9-2.5 mile) 3-4 km range, carried in the thicker tailboom. Phazotron company offers the competitive Zhuk-Ph radar with phased-array electronically-scanned antenna (coverage ±60° currently, but to be substantially increased mechanically), with an anticipated detection range of 89-132 naut miles (103-152 miles) 165-245 km, and a reported capability to detect 24 targets and engage 6 to 8.
Flight/weapon system avionics/instrumentation: Improved opto-electronic search/track device includes TV channel, IR channel and laser rangefinder/target designator.

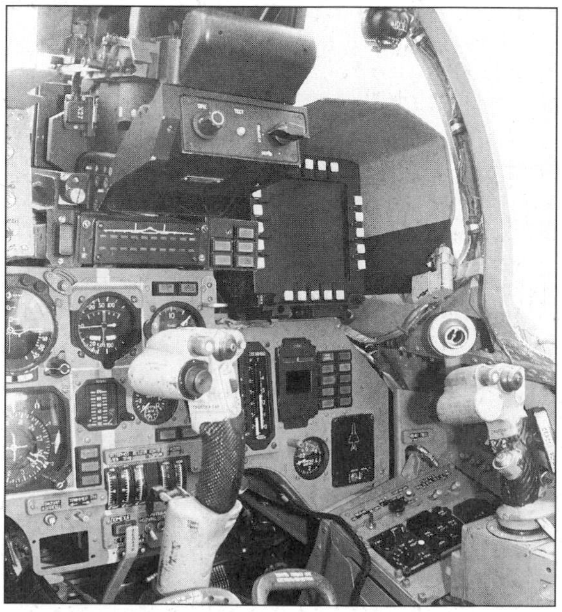

Cockpit of the Su-27 test-bed (designated LMK-2405), equipped with a side-stick controller of the type destined for Su-35 (in addition to the normal central stick) (Piotr Butowski)

Self-protection systems: Improved, including wingtip jammer pods, Mak infra-red sensor on the fuselage and Pastel RWR.
Wing characteristics: As for Su-27.
Tail control surfaces: As for Su-27 on the T10M-1 (706) prototype, but higher and thicker fins with internal fuel tankage on other aircraft.
Canard: All-moving, swept (-50°, +10°).
Airbrakes: As for Su-27.
Fuselage: Longer and thicker nose, with no Pitot tube.
Construction materials: Increased use of composites and aluminium-lithium alloy.
Flight control system: Quadruple redundant digital fly-by-wire for the longitudinal control channel (tailplane when deflected symmetrically), triple redundant digital fly-by-wire in other channels.
Engines: 2 Saturn AL-31FM (AL-35F) turbofans on the production version, but the Su-27's standard AL-31F engines are installed in the pre-production aircraft.
Engine rating: Each 30,865 lbf (137.3 kN).
Nozzles: Circular 3-dimensional vectored-thrust nozzles (15° deflection) are to be fitted to production aircraft. In 1989 Sukhoi began trials with a vectored-thrust test-bed based on the Su-27UB, the port engine of which was equipped with a special end piece for duplicating any type and configuration of nozzle (the other engine remained unchanged). First Su-35/Su-27M (T10M-11, side number 711) with thrust vectoring was expected to make its first flight in late 1994, but this flight had not yet taken place by mid-1995.
Flight refuelling probe: Standard, on the port side of the front fuselage.
Fuel system: Fuel capacity is about 3,307 lb (1,500 kg) greater than for Su-27.

Aircraft variants:
Su-35 is named Su-27M by the Russian Air Force, and Su-35 and T-10M by Sukhoi.
Su-37 is the designation of a proposed strike variant for export. It has slight changes in avionics compared to the Su-35, but not extended range.

Sukhoi S-32

First flight: Late 1990s/early 2000s?
Role: Advanced tactical fighter.

★ Aims
★ Project to replace the Mikoyan 1-42.

▲ Development
▲ 1991. Work started on the new generation fighter. The continuation of the full development programme for the Mikoyan 1-42 was reportedly seen to exceed the present funding capability of Russia, leading to this reportedly cheaper and less sophisticated fighter.
▲ 2006. Expected operational capability.
Wing characteristics: Canard type, with negative wing sweep.

Sukhoi S-54

Role: Advanced trainer and light combat aircraft.
Chief designer: Igor Yemelyanov.

★ Aims
★ See Mikoyan MiG-AT for Russian Air Force requirements.

Details for S-54.

Principal dimensions:
Wing span: 31 ft 6 ins (9.595 m)
Maximum length: 43 ft 5 ins (13.24 m)
Maximum height: 14 ft 6 ins (4.41 m)

Wings:
Chord at root: 15 ft 3 ins (4.64 m)
Chord at tip: 3 ft 11 ins (1.18 m)

Tail unit:
Tailplane span: 18 ft (5.49 m)
Tailplane area: 48 sq ft (4.46 m^2)
Fins area, gross: 69.53 sq ft (6.46 m^2)
Rudders area, gross: 16.6 sq ft (1.54 m^2)

Undercarriage:
Type: Retractable, with nosewheel
Wheel base: 11 ft 4 ins (3.45 m)
Wheel track: 8 ft 3 ins (2.52 m)

Weights:
Empty, operating: 10,560 lb (4,790 kg)
Maximum take-off: 20,745 lb (9,410 kg)
Maximum landing: 15,719 lb (7,130 kg)

Performance:
Maximum operating Mach number (MMO): Mach 1.55
Maximum speed: 891 kts (1,025 mph) 1,650 km/h
Maximum speed at sea level: 648 kts (746 mph) 1,200 km/h
Stalling speed: 97 kts (112 mph) 180 km/h
Landing speed: 92 kts (106 mph) 170 km/h
Take-off distance: 1,181 ft (360 m)
Landing distance: 1,640 ft (500 m)
G limits: +9, -3
Ceiling: 59,000 ft (18,000 m)
Range with maximum internal fuel, at high altitude: 1,080 naut miles (1,242 miles) 2,000 km
Range with maximum internal fuel, at sea level: 443 naut miles (509 miles) 820 km

Sukhoi S-54 combat trainer in latest 1995 configuration (Piotr Butowski)

Crew: 2, in tandem cockpits, the rear seat raised.
Crew escape: Zvezda K-36 zero-zero ejection seats.
Fixed guns: None.
Number of weapon pylons: 6, comprising 2 under each wing and 2 wingtip AAM launch rails.
Expendable weapons and equipment: Missiles, unguided rockets and other light armament. A model presented by Sukhoi carried medium-range R-77 (AA-12 *Adder*) and close-range R-73 (AA-11 *Archer*) AAMs, plus TV-guided bombs.

⋆ Contrary to stated Air Force requirements, Sukhoi consciously selected a single-engined layout for reasons of lower cost.
⋆ Now with an Su-27 type engine.
⋆ Supersonic speed to make real-time combat training possible.
⋆ Programmable stability, with switch-operated attitude and spin recovery.
⋆ Seen as a scaled-down Su-27 type.

Radar: NIIP S-27 Myech (N-001).
Flight/weapon system avionics/instrumentation: Instrumentation similar to that of the Su-35, with "glass" cockpit.
Wing characteristics: Swept, mid mounted, with small wingroot extensions. Canards.
Wing control surfaces: Leading-edge flaps, and trailing-edge flaperons.
Tail control surfaces: 2 outward-canted fins and inset rudders are mounted at the wing trailing edges, while the aft-mounted tailplane is slab type.
Airbrake: Fitted.
Flight control system: Fly-by-wire.
Engine: Saturn/Lyulka AL-31F turbofan.
Engine rating: 16,755 lbf (74.53 kN) dry rating.
Flight refuelling probe: None.
Fuel system: 3,660 lb (1,660 kg) of internal fuel.

Sukhoi T-60S

First flight: After the year 2000.
Role: Medium-range strike aircraft.

⋆ Aims

⋆ Replacement for the Tupolev Tu-16 *Badger* and Tu-22 *Blinder*, plus eventually the Tu-22M *Backfire*.

▲ Development

▲ 1983. Initial design started.
Sales/users: Komsomolsk-on-Amur factory was constructing the first prototype (see Su-27 entry for plant information).
Wing characteristics: Almost certainly rear-mounted delta type, with LERX and chines.
Canard: Sweptback.
Engines: 2 augmented engines.
Air intakes: Dorsal type.

Tupolev Joint-Stock Company (Russia)

Corporate address: 7 Academician Tupolev Embankment (Naberejnaia Akademika Tupoleva), Moscow 111250.
Telephone: +7 095 261 24 36, 261 69 80, 283 23 35, or 267 25 08
Facsimile: +7 095 261 71 41 or 08 68
Telex: 412439 YAUZA SU
Founded: Lineage can be traced to Andrei Nikolayevich Tupolev's leadership of the AGOS department of the Moscow TsAGI from 1922. Tupolev name was adopted in the 1940s.
Information: Valentin Shoubin (Chief of Information); E. Kutcherenko (Deputy Chief of Information – *telephone* +7 095 263 77 26).
General Note: An agreement was reached between Russia and the Ukraine in early 1995 concerning strategic bombers based in the Ukraine. It appears that 25 Tu-96MS *Bear-H*s and 19 Tu-160 *Blackjacks* will be repurchased by Russia at about one-fifth their cost, possibly to be paid in full or part with spares and maintenance agreements for other Ukrainian weapon systems.

Tupolev Tu-16 (NATO name *Badger*)

First flight: 27 April 1952, piloted by Nikolai Rybko.
Role: Intermediate-range bomber (virtually out of service, except in Chinese Xi'an H-6 form – which see for general dimensions, etc), reconnaissance, electronic warfare and tanker.
Chief designer: Dmitri Markov.

▲ Development

▲ 27 April 1952. First flight of prototype 88 or izdelye N free-fall bomber (*Type 39* in the old NATO coding system).
▲ 1952. State acceptance trials of the first prototype completed. Speed 510 kts (587 mph) 945 km/h rather than the required 540 kts (621 mph) 1,000 km/h, and range less than the required 2,700 naut miles (3,107 miles) 5,000 km with 11,023 lb (5,000 kg) of bombs.
▲ Spring 1953. First flight of the second prototype. Weight reduced by 12,125 lb (5,500 kg), and speed 546 kts (629 mph) 1,012 km/h during factory trials and 536 kts (616 mph) 992 km/h during state acceptance trials.
▲ 1953. Production started at Kazan aircraft factory No 22.
▲ 1954. Production started at Kuibyshev (becoming Samara) aircraft factory No 1.
▲ 1 May 1954. 9 aircraft flew over Red Square.
▲ August 1954. First flight of the Tu-16KS missile carrier.
▲ July 1961. Tu-16KS *Badger-B* and Tu-16K-10 *Badger-C* were presented to the public for the first time at the Tushino Aviation Day.
Sales/users: Production took place between 1953 and 1963 at 2 aircraft plants, Kazan No 22 and Kuibyshev (becoming Samara) No 1. About 1,500 were manufactured as Tu-16s, Tu-16As, Tu-16Rs, Tu-16Ts, Tu-16KSs and Tu-16K-10s, with all the remaining versions produced by mid-life conversions. According to official Soviet data, in October 1990 the total number of Tu-16s in the European sector of the USSR was 173, including 81 flown by the Air Force and 92 by Naval Aviation. In addition, approximately 60 aircraft were stationed in the Asian sector. All combat Tu-16s are now withdrawn from active service with CIS Air Forces, though it is possible that some remain with naval forces (in October 1993 the Ukrainian Navy operated 19 Tu-16s as trainers with the 540th Missile Carriers Regiment in Kulbakino; there is no data for the Russian Navy).

Tupolev Tu-16RM Badger-D maritime reconnaissance aircraft

In addition, Egypt may still operate 8 or more Tu-16K-11-16s for anti-ship missions, while Iraq is believed to have a similar number with *Kingfish* among weapon options. The Iraqi force includes Chinese-built B-6Ds, the exported H-6, the latter of which still forms an important element of the Chinese forces. See Xi'an for H-6 details and a photograph of Egyptian Tu-16K-11-16s.

Details: See Xi'an H-6 for general airframe details, which in most respects can be applied to the original Tu-16.

Fixed guns: PV-23Tu-16 self-defence cannon system comprising 7 x 23-mm AM-23 cannon, installed as 1 single cannon in the nose (removed from some aircraft) and 3 flexible twin-cannon turrets (the rear gunner position was replaced by an ECM unit on some aircraft). Argon (NATO *Bee Hind*) radar sight in the tailfin root, above the tail-gun position.

Expendable weapons and equipment: See Aircraft variants.

Radar: RBP-4 Rubidiy (NATO *Mushroom*) nav/attack radar for early series, later improved Rubin-A (NATO *Short Horn*) in a small undernose radome. Tu-16K-10 *Badger-C* and Tu-16RM *Badger-D* were given YeN (NATO *Puff Ball*) radar occupying the whole fuselage nose (deleting the glazed navigator's station).

Flight/weapon system avionics/instrumentation: Navigation system comprises a gyro-compass, astro-compass, 2 radio-compasses (ARK-15), radio altimeters (RV-5 and RV-18), Doppler navigation DISS Trassa, SP-50M instrument approach and landing system, and Chayka long-rang radio navigation or later Glonass/ Navstar receiver. AP-6E autopilot. Communication equipment includes R-807 and R-808 HF radios, RSIU-3M UHF radio, and SPU-10 intercom.

Self-protection systems: Sirena-3 radar warning receiver. SPS-5 Fasol (bean) active jammer later became standard (2 sword-type antennae under the front fuselage), some aircraft having more powerful Rezeda (reseda) or Fyalka (violet) jammers in the place of the tail cannon turret.

Engines: 2 Soyuz/Mikulin RD-3M-500 turbojets inside the wingroots.

Engine rating: Each 20,945 lbf (93.17 kN) take off, 16,865 lbf (75.02 kN) normal.

Aircraft variants:

Those possibly still in service include:

Tu-16N *Badger-A* probe-and-drogue tanker, most recently for flight refuelling Tu-22M *Backfire* bombers and training purposes. Small series originally built in 1963 to service Tu-22 *Blinders*.

Tu-16RM (razvedchik morskoi, sea reconnaissance) *Badger-D* with *Puff Ball* and elint antennae under the fuselage. First seen in 1962.

Tu-16R (razvedchik, project 92) *Badger-E* reconnaissance aircraft with 6 photographic cameras inside the weapon bay, later 3 or 4 cameras and 2 electronic intelligence (elint) sensors. First flown in 1955.

Tu-16RM-2 *Badger-F* sea reconnaissance version, converted from *Badger-A*. Elint antennae under the fuselage and in 2 teardrop-shaped fairings under the wing pylons.

Tu-16K-11-16 *Badger-G* is armed with 2 underwing missiles, either KSR-2 anti-radar or KSR-11 anti-ship, both known as AS-5 *Kelt* in the West. Glazed nose, and Rubin-1A undernose radar. Officially commissioned in 1962, but not recognized in the West until September 1968.

Tu-16K-26 *Badger-G mod* is similar to Tu-16K-11-16 but with KSR-6 (AS-6 *Kingfish*) missiles.

Tu-16KSR-2-5 *Badger-G* mod is similar to Tu-16K-26, but converted from the Tu-16K-11-16.

Tu-16K-26P *Badger-G mod* is similar to Tu-16K-26, but armed with KSR-5P passive anti-radar missiles.

Tu-16P Buket *Badger-J* is an electronic jamming aircraft, converted from the Tu-16P Yolka (Christmas Tree) jammer (using chaff) during the 1970s. This variant has a long and streamlined fairing covering the aerials of the SPS-44 Buket (bouquet) noise jamming unit located directly under the bomb bay. The Buket unit, very advanced at that time, is capable of operating in A to I frequencies against detected radars. It emits continuous or pulse jamming signals.

Tu-16Ye and Tu-16Ye Azalya *Badger-K* is an electronic intelligence aircraft converted from *Badger-A,* and has many small antennae under the fuselage.

Tu-16 *Badger-L* is a naval electronic version, identified by a tail "sting" housing specialized equipment and a "thimble" nose radome. Other fairings, plus optional underwing equipment pods.

Tupolev Tu-22M (NATO name *Backfire*)

First flight: 30 August 1969, piloted by V. Borisov.

Role: Intermediate range bomber/missile carrier, with an electronic warfare version under tests in 1995.

Chief designer: Dmitri Markov until January 1992; thereafter Boris Levanovich.

★ Aims

★ To replace Tu-16 *Badger* and Tu-22 *Blinder* medium bombers in performing nuclear/conventional strike against targets in Western Europe and China, as well in anti-ship missions when the main targets are aircraft carriers.

★ 2,000 km/h dash speed.

★ Mach 0.9 low-level penetration of enemy air defences with wings fully swept.

★ 900 km/h high-altitude flight with wings at 30°.

★ Compatibility with previously used Kh-22 missile system of the Tu-22 *Blinder*.

★ Maximum armament of 3 Kh-22 (AS-4 *Kitchen*) missiles.

Tupolev Tu-22M2 Backfire-B. Note the opened canopy (Anatoli Andreyev/via Piotr Butowski)

▲ Development

▲ 1965. Tupolev began work on the variable-geometry medium bomber project 145, or izdelye (product) 45, or aircraft A. Target data for project 145 in 1965 were as follows: length 134 ft 6 in (41.0 m), wing span 77 ft 7 ins to 120 ft 5 ins (23.66 m to 36.7 m), take-off weight 231,485 lb (105,000 kg), and armament of a single Kh-22 missile. The design speed was 2,000 km/h, ceiling 17,000 m, supersonic range 4,000 km, and subsonic range 6,000 km.

▲ 1967. Final design was approved by the State Commission. Required speed 2,000 km/h and maximum range 7,000 km.

▲ 30 August 1969. First flight of Tu-22M0 prototype.

▲ July 1971. First flight of a Tu-22M pre-production aircraft. Series manufacturing carried out at Kazan.

▲ 1973. First flight of the Tu-22M2 large-scale production version.

▲ 1975. First delivery to 185th Heavy Bomber Regiment of Guards stationed in Poltava, Ukraine.

▲ 1975. Work began on a modernization version designated Tu-22M3 (or aircraft AM, or izdelye 45.03).

▲ 20 June 1977. Maiden flight of the AM prototype.

▲ 18 June 1979. According to SALT-2 treaty, Soviets were obliged to delete the in-flight refuelling capability and not to increase the production rate of the Tu-22M.

▲ 1983. Tu-22M3 officially accepted for the service with the Soviet Air Force.

▲ December 1987-January 1988. Two squadrons of Tu-22M2s of 185th Regiment stationed in Poltava, operating from Mary air base in Turkmenistan, took action against forces blocking Khost, Afghanistan. Other combat missions were performed from October 1988 to January 1989 by 16 Tu-22M3s, including attacks on approaches to the roads being used by departing Soviet troops. Heavy and very heavy bombs (500-3,000 kg) were dropped from high altitude.

▲ 1990. Series manufacturing was thought to have ended, but it is now believed that some production continues.

Sales/users: Manufactured between 1971-90 at the Kazan plant named after Sergei Gorbunov. Total of 512 produced, only for the Soviet Air Force and Navy and never exported. According to official data, in 1990 there were 257 Tu-22M2/Tu-22M3s in active service in the European sector of the USSR, plus some 60 more aircraft stationed in the Far East. At that time the total number of *Backfire* regiments in the European sector was 12, including: 52nd Training Heavy Bomber Regiment in Shaykovka (Russia) with 19 aircraft, 185th Heavy Bomber Regiment in Poltava (Ukraine) with 22 aircraft, 200th Heavy Bomber Regiment in Bobruisk (Belorussia) with 20 aircraft, 260th Heavy Bomber Regiment in Stryi (Ukraine) with 20 aircraft, 132nd Heavy Bomber Regiment in Tartu (Estonia) with 20 aircraft, 402nd Heavy Bomber Regiment in Balbasovo (Belorussia) with 21 aircraft, and 840th Heavy Bomber Regiment in Soltsi (Russia) with 20 aircraft. Naval aviation then had: 540th Missile Carrier Regiment in Kulbakino (Ukraine) with 29 aircraft, 5th Missile Carrier Regiment in Vesioloye (Ukraine) with 20 aircraft, 943rd Missile Carrier Regiment in Oktyabrskoye (Ukraine) with 23 aircraft, 924th Missile Carrier Regiment in Oleni (Russia) with 23 aircraft, and 574th Missile Carrier Regiment in Lakhta (Russia) with 20 aircraft. After the break-up of the USSR, the aircraft were divided between Russia and Ukraine. The aircraft from Estonia and Belorussia were assigned to the Russian Air Force (2 Belorussian regiments are still stationed there for the time being). In October 1993 Ukraine had 54 aircraft (14 with the 184th Heavy Bomber Regiment in Priluki, 16 with the 185th Heavy Bomber Regiment in Poltava and 24 with the 540th Naval Missile Regiment in Kulbakino),

Tupolev Tu-22M3 Backfire-C modified to carry a 6-round launcher for Kh-15 (AS-16 Kickback) short-range attack missiles in the weapon bay (Dmitri Grinyuk/via Piotr Butowski)

Details for Tu-22M3 Backfire-C.

Principal dimensions:
Wing span: 76 ft 5 ins (23.3 m) *swept (65°)*, 112 ft 6 ins (34.28 m) *fully spread (20°)*
Maximum length: 139 ft 4 ins (42.46 m)
Fuselage length: 126 ft 4 ins (38.5 m)
Maximum height: 36 ft 3 ins (11.05 m)

Wings:
Area: 1,892-1,976 sq ft (175.78-183.58 m^2)
Aspect ratio: 3.088 *swept*, 6.401 *spread*
Sweepback of fixed glove: 56° at leading edge
Sweepback of movable panels: 20°, 30°, 50°, 60° and 65° at leading edge
Anhedral/dihedral: 0°
Twist: -4° at tip

Tail unit:
Tailplane span: 36 ft 11 ins (11.26 m)
Tailplane area: 664.13 sq ft (664 m^2)
Fin area: 355 sq ft (32.98 m^2)
Fin angle: 57° 15' leading-edge sweepback

Undercarriage:
Type: Retractable, with nosewheel. Main legs are attached to the fixed wing gloves, retracted into the wings while the wheels are partly retracted into the fuselage; each main bogie comprises 3 pairs of wheels in tandem. Nose leg has double wheels, rearward-retracted into the fuselage. *Backfire-A* pre-production aircraft had big wing trailing-edge fairings to enclose the retracting gear; the main gear comprised 6-wheel units with the central pair of wheels moved aside by 29.5 ins (75 cm) during extension.
Main wheel tyre size: 1,030 x 350 mm
Nose wheel tyre size: 1,000 x 280 mm
Wheel base: 44 ft 4 ins (13.51 m)
Wheel track: 23 ft 11 ins (7.3 m)

Weights:
Maximum take-off: 273,373 lb (124,000 kg)
Maximum take-off with JATO rockets: 278,665 lb (126,400 kg)
Normal landing: 171,960 lb (78,000 kg)
Maximum landing: 194,007 lb (88,000 kg); can land at full weight in an emergency.

Performance:
Maximum operating Mach number (MMO): Mach 1.88
Maximum speed at high altitude: 1,080 kts (1,243 mph) 2,000 km/h, or 1,242 kts (429 mph) 2,300 km/h*
Cruising speed: 486 kts (559 mph) 900 km/h
Take-off speed: 200 kts (230 mph) 370 km/h
Time to climb to 26,245 ft (8,000 m) without afterburning: 20 minutes
Time to climb to 42,650 ft (13,000 m) without afterburning: 25-30 minutes
Turning radius at supersonic speed: 8.1-10.8 naut miles (9.3-12.4 miles) 15-20 km
Turning radius at subsonic speed: 2.7-3.24 naut miles (3.1-3.73 miles) 5-6 km
Take-off distance: 6,562-6,890 ft (2,000-2,100 m), or 6,300 ft (1,920 m)*
Landing distance: 4,100-4,757 ft (1,250-1,450 m)*
G limits: +1.6 *fully spread*, +2.0 *fully swept*
Ceiling at supersonic speed: 43,635 ft (13,300 m), or 45,930 ft (14,000 m)*
Ceiling at subsonic speed: 33,465 ft (10,200 m)
Radius of action at high altitude, some supersonic flight, with 1 x Kh-22, unrefuelled: 1,188 naut miles (1,367 miles) 2,200 km

* Performances marked with * come from a table shown with a Tu-22M3 outside Kubinka air base in April 1992.

and all or most remained in 1995. The future of 2 units belonging to Black Sea Fleet (5th and 943rd Missile Carrier Regiments) stationed in Crimea is not clear.

Crew: 4, with 2 pilots side by side, the navigator and weapon system operator to their rear.

Cockpit: Conventional instrumentation and control wheels. Air conditioning, using engine compressor-stage bleed air; also for maintaining correct temperature for specialist avionics in other parts of the aircraft.

Crew escape: Tupolev KT-1 ejection seats (kreslo Tupoleva, Tupolev's seats), connected into the ASS automatic rescue system. A minimum speed of 70 kts (81 mph) 130 km/h is necessary for safe ejection at below 200 ft (60 m) altitude; at greater altitude there is no speed limit. LAS-5M life saving dinghies.

Fixed weapons: Defensive armament of Tu-22M3 includes 23-mm GSh-23 double-barrel cannon (1 barrel above the other), with a firing rate equal to 4,000 rpm, installed in a UK-9A-802 tail turret that is remotely controlled by means of a PRS-4 radar sight (NATO *Fan Tail*) and TP-1 TV sight. Tu-22M2 has 2 x GSh-23 cannon in the tail turret and older *Box Tail* radar (the pre-production Tu-22M was given a large container with jamming equipment instead of cannons).

Expendable weapons and equipment: 52,910 lb (24,000 kg) normal maximum load, including conventional or nuclear free-fall bombs or mines, or 3 x Kh-22 (AS-4 *Kitchen*) missiles, 1 semi recessed under the fuselage and 2 under the fixed wing glove. The normal weapon load is 26,455 lb (12,000 kg) of bombs or a single Kh-22. Raduga Kh-22 is used in 3 versions: nuclear Kh-22N with inertial guidance, Kh-22M conventional anti-ship missile with active radar seeker, and Kh-22MP anti-radiation missile. In the Tu-22M3's low-level penetration (air defence suppression) role, the fuselage Kh-22 is replaced by an MKU rotary launcher (MKU stands for mnogozaryadnaya katapultnaya ustanovka, multiple launching device) carrying 6 x Kh-15P (AS-16 *Kickback*) short-range attack missiles inside the weapon bay. It is also possible to replace all 3 Kh-22s with 10 Kh-15P missiles (6 inside the fuselage and 4 under the wings). Bombs can be carried suspended on KD-3-22R or KD-4-105A pylons inside the bomb bay as well as on 4 external MBD3-U9-68 multiple racks (2 under the engine air intake trunks and 2 under the wings, each rack carrying 6 x 500 kg bombs). Maximum bomb loads are, for instance, 69 x 250 kg, or 42 x 500 kg, or 8 x 1,500 kg (including guided bombs – according to some sources the aircraft carries UPAB-1500s), or 2 x 3,000 kg. The practical armament load does not exceed 12,000 kg, however, as a greater load compromises the fuel carried.

Radar: Leninets/St Petersburg PN-A navigation/attack radar (NATO *Down Beat*) installed under dielectric nose cone. No automatic terrain avoidance capability. See also Fixed weapons for tail radar.

Flight/weapon system avionics/ instrumentation: OBP-15 optical bomb sight in the fairing under the crew cockpit. AFA-15 photographic camera installed under the fuselage nose. The Tu-22M3 aircraft together with Kh-22 missiles and respective homing systems form the K-22M missile complex (K for kompleks, complex). Communication equipment (some secure type) includes 2 x UHF R-832M radios, 1 x HF R-846 radio and SPU-10 intercom. Autonomous and highly accurate navigation system with automatic high/low altitude pre-programming, and automatic approach, includes a long-range navigation system, short-range navigation system, ARK-15 radio compass, SP-50 instrument landing system, and 2 x RV-18 radio altimeters. RI-65 voice information device.

Tupolev Tu-22M3 Backfire-C with wings spread, operated by the Russian Air Force (Piotr Butowski)

Self-protection systems: Ural system consists of active and passive jamming, including SPS-171 and SPS-172 response jammers, AG-56 noise jamming generator with automatic tuning, and chaff/flare dispensers installed under the tailplane roots. L-082 Mak infra-red missile launch and approach sensor on top of the fuselage just behind the rear crew, and Sirena-3 radar warning receiver.

Wing characteristics: Variable geometry (see table). Large fixed glove centre-section. Hydraulic wing-sweep motors; wings panels motion synchronized.

Wing control surfaces: Fowler-type trailing-edge flaps (62° deflection) on the fixed glove sections. Each movable panel has 3 sections of double-slotted flaps (deflected by 23° for take-off and 40° for landing), and 3-section full-span leading-edge slats. No ailerons; control is performed by 3 sections of spoilers/lift dumpers on the outer panels and by differential deflection of the elevators.

Tail control surfaces: Slab type (tailerons), deflected +9°, -20° symmetrically or differentially. Large tailfin with rudder.

Flight control system: Hydraulic/electric.

Fuselage: Conventional semi-monocoque type. Circular cross section forward and more rectangular at the centre and rear.

Engines: Tu-22M3 is powered by 2 Samara NK-25 afterburning turbofans (designed by the SGNPP Trud team of Nikolai Kuznetsov in Samara, former Kuibyshev). Time from low to full thrust is 9 seconds; 18 seconds to full thrust with afterburning. TA-6 auxiliary power unit, installed in front of the tailfin root, supplies power for engine starting and for onboard systems. Tu-22M and Tu-22M2 used NK-22 turbofans of 44,090 lbf (196.14 kN – see Aircraft variants).
Engine rating: 31,526 lbf (140.2 kN) without afterburning and 55,115 lbf (245.18 kN) with afterburning.
Air intakes: Wedge-type on Tu-22M3. Tu-22M/M2 were given slightly inclined intakes, with large vertical splitter plates.
Flight refuelling probe: Above-nose fairing replaced the in-flight refuelling probe after the 1980 treaty, but can be re-equipped.
Fuel system: 118,057 lb (53,550 kg) of fuel in tanks located in the fuselage and wings (including outer panels), plus in the fence in front of the tailfin. Standard fuel: T-1, TS-1 or RT.
Electrical system: 27 volt DC supply with 4 x GSR-20BK engine-driven generators (2 per engine) and 2 ni-cd batteries. AC supply with 2 x GT 60 NZHCH 12P generators for 3-phase 200/115 volt 400Hz, and 2 x TS 350SO4A transformers for 36 volt/400Hz 3-phase.
Hydraulic system: 3 separate systems, each 3,046 psi, for flight controls, wing sweep, undercarriage and brakes.
Braking system: Hydraulic wheel brakes. Drag-chute carried in an under rear fuselage bay.
De-icing system: Electro-thermal de-icing of cockpit and sight windows, plus air intakes. Hot air deicing of inlet guide vanes.

Aircraft variants:
Tu-22M0 *Backfire-A* (or Tu-22KM, or izdelye 45.00, or 145, or A) prototype of 1969. NK-144-22 turbofans. Range 2,235 naut miles (2,570 miles) 4,140 km. Maximum speed 826 kts (951 mph) 1,530 km/h. Span 103 ft 8 ins (31.6 m).
Tu-22M *Backfire A* (or 45.01) pre-series aircraft of 1971 appearance. Modified NK-22 engines and lengthened movable wing panels (maximum span 112 ft 6 ins, 34.28 m). Maximum range 2,700 naut miles (3,107 miles) 5,000 km, and maximum speed 896 kts (1,031 mph) 1,660 km/h.
Tu-22M2 *Backfire-B* (or 45.02) of 1973 appearance was the first large-scale production version. Equipped with new flight/navigational systems. 2 x GSh-23 cannon in the tail replacing the electronic jamming unit. Maximum range 2,753 naut miles (3,170 miles) 5,100 km, and maximum speed 972 kts (1,118 mph) 1,800 km/h.
Tu-22M2Ye, 1974. Experimental aircraft powered by NK-25 turbofans.
Tu-22M3 *Backfire-C* (or 45.03, or AM) of 1977 appearance, is the improved version with more powerful NK-25 engines, and redesigned forward fuselage with larger wedge-type air intakes and upturned nosecone
Tu-22MP electronic warfare version equipped with Miass jamming system, developed from the Tu-22M3. Identified by US intelligence in February 1986 at Kazan. The second and third prototypes of Tu-22MP, built in 1992, were under test in 1994-95.
Tu-22MR is a reconnaissance version that entered service in the late 1980s. About 12 built.

Tupolev Tu-95 (NATO name *Bear*)

First flight: 12 November 1952, piloted by Alexei Perelet. Current Tu-95MS first flew in August 1979.
Role: Long-range bomber, strategic, maritime and photographic reconnaissance, and electronic intelligence.
Chief designer: Nikolai Bazenkov (1951-1976), later Dmitri Antonov.

★ Aims
★ Required speed of 900-950 km/h, and range of 14,000-15,000 km with a single nuclear bomb.

▲ Development
▲ 11 July 1951. Andrei Tupolev assigned to build the Tu-95 intercontinental bomber.
▲ 12 November 1952. Maiden flight of the Tu-95/1 first prototype, powered by TV-2F turboprops.
▲ May 1953. Tu-95/1 was lost in an accident.
▲ 16 February 1955. First flight of the Tu-95/2 production prototype, with four NK-12 turboprops.
▲ Summer 1955. First public presentation, during the Tushino Aviation Day fly-pass.
▲ Autumn 1955. First production aircraft left factory No 18 in Kuibyshev (Samara).
▲ August 1957. Tu-95M officially entered Soviet Air Force service.
▲ 1965. Series production completed (restarted later).
▲ Summer 1968. First flight of the Tu-142 anti-submarine warfare derivative. See separate entry.
▲ October 1975. First flight of the Tu-95K-22.
▲ 1978. First test launches of the Kh-55 (AS-15 *Kent*) cruise missile from a Tu-95M-55 test bed.
▲ August 1979. First flight of the Tu-95MS.
▲ 1984. Initial operational capability of the first unit equipped with Tu-95MS heavy bombers, as the 182nd Heavy Bomber Regiment in Uzin-Shepelovka, Ukraine.
▲ February 1992. Final end to Tu-95MS production announced by President Yeltsin.

Sales/users: Production at Kuibyshev (becoming Samara) aviation plant. During the first production period (1955-1965) about 140 aircraft were built. Approximately 70 of these are still in service (15 Tu-95RTs with Russian Naval Aviation and 55 Tu-95K-22s). After a gap of about 15 years, series production of the Tu-95 was re-established in Kuibyshev (Samara). During 1983-92 some 80 Tu-95MS *Bear-H* bombers were produced and are currently in service with the air forces of Ukraine (25 aircraft) and Russia. However, under an agreement of early 1995, Ukraine is to return all the *Bear-Hs* to Russia (see the start of the Tupolev entry for further details). In addition, Kazakhstan inherited 40 Tu-95MSs and these were operated by the 79th Heavy Bomber Division in Semipalatynsk, but most have been handed back to Russia, with the last 4 Tu-95MSs flying to Russia on 19 February 1994; only several Tu-95s of old types, practically without combat value, remain in Kazakhstan. Russia had (in April 1995) 89 Tu-95s with strategic forces, as 24 Tu-95K-22s at Ryazan air base, and 28 Tu-95MS6s and 37 Tu-95MS16s at Mozdok and Ukrainka.
Details: General description applies to the Tu-95MS *Bear-H*.
Crew: 2 pilots, navigation/defence systems operator, navigation/offensive weapons operator (with access to the astrodome), observer, flight engineer, and tail gunner.
Cockpit: 2 separate pressurized compartments (cockpit and the isolated tail gunner's); 3 compartments in early aircraft produced between 1955-65. All crew (except tail gunner) enter the cockpit via the front undercarriage bay. Conventional instrumentation.
Crew escape: No ejection seats.
Fixed guns: 1 or 2 self-defence twin-barrelled 23-mm GSh-23 cannon in the tail turret, controlled by a radar sight *(Box Tail)*. Tu-95RT and MR have full defensive armament of tail, dorsal and ventral turrets, with twin cannon in each. Tu-95K-22 has only the ventral turret.
Expendable weapons and equipment: 6 x Kh-55 (AS-15 *Kent*) cruise missiles on the MKU-6 rotary launcher inside the fuselage. Tu-95MS16 has an additional 10 x Kh-55s under the wings in four clusters (2 on each inner pylon and 3 on each pylon between the engines).
Radar: Obzor navigation/attack radar *(Clam Pipe)* at the nose, with weather radar above. See Fixed guns.
Flight/weapon system avionics/instrumentation: Satellite communication system. The aircraft is capable of taking-off with just 1,312 ft (400 m) visibility, and a 100 ft (30 m) cloud base, and land under 3,280 ft (1,000 m) and 328 ft (100 m) respective conditions. IFF antenna is mounted near the root of the in-flight refuelling probe.
Self-protection systems: Active electronic countermeasures system. ECM sensors at the nose (twin), jammers at the nose and rear fuselage, and in pods under the tail turret. Radar warning receivers at the nose and tail, and Mak infra-red missile launch and approach sensor under the nose. 50-mm chaff/flare dispensers in the undercarriage fairings.
Wing characteristics: Swept, mid mounted, with marginal anhedral. 3 boundary layer fences on each wing. 4-spar 35° (at 25% chord) inner wing panels; 3-spar 33.5° outer wing panels.
Wing control surfaces: 2-section double-slotted trailing-edge flaps (Fowler-type flaps in aircraft produced between 1955-65) and 3-section ailerons (with tabs) on each wing. Spoilers on upper wing surface.

DETAILS FOR Tu-95MS BEAR-H.

Principal dimensions:
Wing span: 164 ft 2 ins (50.04 m)
Maximum length: 161 ft 2 ins (49.13 m)
Maximum height: 43 ft 8 ins (13.301 m)
Fuselage diameter: 9 ft 6 ins (2.9 m) maximum

Wings:
Area: 3,1210.5 sq ft (289.9 m²)
Aspect ratio: 8.64
Sweepback: 35° (inner panel), 33° 30′ (outer panel), at 25% chord

Undercarriage:
Type: Retractable, with steerable twin nosewheels. 4-wheel bogies on each main unit, retracted into the large fairings on the wing trailing edges, in line with the inner engines.
Main wheel tyre size: 1450 x 450 mm
Nose wheel tyre size: 1140 x 350 mm
Wheel base: 48 ft 8 ins (14.827 m)
Wheel track: 41 ft 2 ins (12.55 m)

Weights:
Maximum take-off: 407,885 lb (185,000 kg)
Maximum in flight: 412,264 lb (187,000 kg), after in-flight refuelling.
Maximum landing: 297,624 lb (135,000 kg)

Performance:
Maximum speed: 448 kts (516 mph) 830 km/h
Take-off speed at 185,000 kg: 162 kts (186 mph) 300 km/h
Landing speed at 135,000 kg: 148 kts (171 mph) 275 km/h
Take-off distance at 185,000 kg: 8,334 ft (2,540 m)
G limit: +2
Ceiling: 34,450 ft (10,500 m)
Range without in-flight refuelling: 5,670 naut miles (6,524 miles) 10,500 km
Range with single in-flight refuelling: 7,613 naut miles (8,761 miles) 14,100 km
Flight duration without in-flight refuelling: 14 hours

Tupolev Tu-95MS Bear-H during in-flight refuelling (Anatoli Andreyev/via Piotr Butowski)

Tupolev Tu-95MS Bear-H taking off. Note the various fairings and antennae around the nose and all along the upper fuselage

Tail control surfaces: Variable incidence tailplane, adjustable in flight according to the fuel used (1° down, 3° up). Elevators and rudder, all with tabs.
Flight control system: Mechanical, hydraulically actuated.
Fuselage: Semi-monocoque, circular section. About a 36 ft (11 m) long bomb bay in the centre.
Construction materials: Metal.
Engines: 4 Samara/Kuznetsov NK-12MP turboprops. Each 8-blade AV-60 K propeller unit comprises 2 x 4-blade co-axial contra-rotating reversible-pitch propellers.
Engine rating: Each 14,805 ehp (11,040 ekW) maximum power, 9,870 ehp (7,360 ekW) cruise.
Flight refuelling probe: Ahead of the cockpit, on the nose.
Fuel system: About 165,345 lb (75,000 kg) of internal fuel. No auxiliary tanks.
Hydraulic system: For actuators and undercarriage.
Braking system: Mainwheel brakes.
De-icing system: Thermal for wing and tailplane leading edges.

Aircraft variants:
Tu-95 (izdelye V) *Bear-A* appeared in 1955. Out of service.
Tu-95M *Bear-A* appeared in 1957. Production version with NK-12M engines. Out of service.
Tu-95K (izdelye VK) *Bear-B* appeared in 1956. Missile carrier, armed with Mikoyan Kh-20 (AS-3 *Kangaroo*) heavy stand-off missile. Out of service.
Tu-95KD *Bear-B* appeared in 1963. Similar to Tu-95K but with flight refuelling probe added. Out of service.
Tu-95KM *Bear-C* appeared in 1963. Similar to Tu-95K, but with photographic and electronic reconnaissance equipment added. Out of service.
Tu-95RTs (razvedchik-tseleukazatel) *Bear-D* appeared in 1962. Maritime reconnaissance/sea target acquisition version. Uspekh-1 *Big Bulge* reconnaissance radar under the fuselage in line with the wing roots, *Short Horn* navigation radar, A-322Z Doppler radar, and *Box Tail* tail radar. Automatic data link with missile forces for target acquisition. About 15 still in service with the Russian Navy.
Tu-95MR *Bear-E* became a photographic reconnaissance version. Few only. In service.
Tu-142 *Bear-F.* See separate entry.
Tu-95K-22 (izdelye VK-22) *Bear-G* appeared in 1975. Conversion of the Tu-95K/KD/KM armed with 2 Kh-22 (AS-4 *Kitchen*) ASMs. Also for electronic intelligence. ECM in the extended tailcone and nose thimble. *Down Beat* nose radar. Few dozen still in service.
Tu-95M5 was a Tu-95M conversion armed with KSR-5 (AS-6 *Kingfish*) missiles. Prototype only.
Tu-95M-55 appeared in 1976 as a Tu-95M conversion armed with Kh-55 (AS-15 *Kent*) cruise missiles. Prototype only.
Tu-95MS (izdelye VP) *Bear-H* appeared in 1979. In service, and one of the main operational versions. As described.
Tu-96MS16 *Bear-H* is armed with 16 cruise missiles rather than 6. In service.
Tu-95U is a training conversion of M series aircraft.

Tupolev Tu-142 (NATO name *Bear-F/J*)

First flight: Summer 1968.
Role: Long-range anti-submarine warfare and communications relay, derived from the Tu-95.

★ Aims
★ All-ocean operation at a distance of 4,000 km from base.

▲ Development
▲ 1963. Work began on a long-range ASW aircraft based on the Tu-95 strategic bomber.
▲ Summer 1968. First flight of the prototype.

Tupolev Tu-142MZ Bear F mod 4. Note the large underfuselage radome (Piotr Butowski)

DETAILS FOR Tu-142MZ BEAR-F MOD 4, UNLESS STATED.

Principal dimensions:
Wing span: 164 ft 2 ins (50.04 m)
Maximum length: 174 ft 1 ins (53.07 m)
Maximum height: 41 ft 4 ins (12.59 m)

Wings:
Area: 3,121 sq ft (289.9 m^2)

Undercarriage:
Type: Similar to Tu-95, but with larger main wheels
Main wheel tyre size: 1,500 x 500 mm
Nose wheel tyre size: 1,140 x 350 mm

Weights:
Maximum take-off: 407,885 lb (185,000 kg)
Payload of Tu-142MZ-K: 37,479 lb (17,000 kg)

Performance:
Maximum speed: 462 kts (531 mph) 855 km/h
Cruise speed, Tu-142MZ-K: 400 kts (460 mph) 740 km/h
Take-off distance, Tu-142MZ-K: 8,335 ft (2,540 m)
Range without flight refuelling, Tu-142MZ-K: 4,941 naut miles (5,685 miles) 9,150 km, with 15,432 lb (7,000 kg) fuel reserve
Duration, without flight refuelling, Tu-142MZ-K: 12 hours 36 minutes
Duration with single flight refuelling: 17 hours

▲ December 1972. Tu-142 *Bear-F* was officially accepted for service with Soviet Naval Aviation.
▲ 1973. First identified in the West.
▲ 4 November 1975. First flight of the modified Tu-142M *Bear-F mod 2*, piloted by I. Vedernikov.
▲ 1980. Tu-142M entered service.
▲ 1986. Tu-142MR *Bear-J* communications relay aircraft was first identified in the West.
Sales/users: Produced during the 1970s, with relaunch of second-series production in the mid-1980s (Tu-142MZ *Bear F mod 4*) which continued up to 1992-1993. About 55 Tu-142 ASW aircraft are in current service with Russian Naval Aviation, divided between the Pacific and Northern Fleets, plus a few Tu-142MRs. Eight Tu-142MK-Es are operated by India.
Crew: 10.
Fixed guns: 2 twin-barrel 23-mm GSh-23 cannon in the tail turret, controlled by a radar sight.
Expendable weapons and equipment: Located inside 2 fuselage weapon bays (1 in place of the removed ventral cannon turret), with options including torpedoes, missiles, depth charges (nuclear or conventional), mines, and sonobuoys.
Radar: Korshun J-band 360° search/attack radar in an underfuselage radome. Small weather radar in the nose.
Flight/weapon system avionics/instrumentation: Automatic data link for target acquisition. Satellite communication system.
Self-protection systems: Active electronic jammers, and 50-mm chaff/flare dispensers inside the main undercarriage fairings. Mak infra-red missile launch and approach warning sensor is located under the nose just aft of the weather radar.
Airframe and engines: As for Tu-95MS *Bear-H* (which see).

Aircraft variants:
Tu-142 *Bear-F* is a long-range ASW aircraft, with the Berkut search/attack system of the Ilyushin Il-38 *May.* Early

Tupolev Tu-142MR Bear-J communications relay aircraft. Note the underfuselage VLF antenna system

Tupolev Tu-142MZ tail-gunner's position. Note the 2 twin-barrel cannon, fire control radar antenna above the glazing and with the short-range navigation antenna directly below, and 2 ECM pods under the tail (Piotr Butowski)

Large number of 50-mm chaff/flare dispensers carried in 3 rows in the top and bottom of the main undercarriage fairings (at the rear), each with 3 tubes (Piotr Butowski)

Tupolev Tu-142MZ Bear-F mod 4. Note the refuelling probe, ECM antenna on the fuselage nose, weather radar just below the glazed navigator's compartment, and the bulged antenna radome of the Korshun search/attack radar deep under the fuselage (Piotr Butowski)

aircraft were able to operate from unprepared runways due to larger nosewheel tyres and 6-wheel rather than 4-wheel main undercarriage bogies (the undercarriage fairings on the wing trailing edges were much larger). Later, the standard undercarriage was fitted *(Bear F mod 1)*.

Tu-142M (design bureau name Tu-142MK, for Korshun) *Bear-F mod 2* and *mod 3* were given new Korshun anti-submarine search/attack system capable of detecting low-noise new-generation submarines. Ladoga magnetic anomaly detector, inertial navigation system, and new communication systems. Completely redesigned and more comfortable flight deck. Flight refuelling probe inclined 4° downward. During production the MAD antenna was relocated from the tailplane tip *(Bear F mod 2)* to the tailfin tip *(Bear F mod 3)*.

Tu-142MK-E is the export derivative of Tu-142MK, for India.

Tu-142MZ *Bear-F mod 4* was the last production version, appearing in the mid-1980s. New Zarechye (therefore Z in the name) radio sonobuoys system, and new self-defence systems. Chin mounted weather radar reintroduced (having been deleted on *Mod 1, 2* and *3* versions). ECM thimble radome on the nose. As described.

Tu-142MZ-K (K from kommerchesky) is a proposed civil transport derivative of Tu-142MZ.

Tu-142MR *Bear-J* is a communications relay aircraft. The main task is to ensure a communications link between the Russian authorities and the commanders of strategic nuclear missile submarines. The most important features include a ventral pod for the very low frequency trailing wire antenna installed in the forward bomb bay, satellite communications dome on the upper forward fuselage, and a forward-pointing pod on the tailfin.

Tupolev Tu-160 (NATO name *Blackjack*)

First flight: 17 December 1981, piloted by Boris Veremei
Role: Supersonic heavy missile carrier (not yet adapted for free-fall bombing). Projected escort interceptor and Burlak spacecraft launch platform.
Chief designer: Valentin Bliznyuk

Tupolev Tu-160 Blackjack with wings at 20° (Piotr Butowski)

★ Aims

★ Original aim was for a supersonic strategic bomber able to cruise at 3,200-3,500 km/h, and with a 16,000-18,000 km maximum range. Sukhoi T-4MS became the winning design before the requirements were scaled down (see below and Development).
★ 2 flight profiles to overcome enemy air defences: Mach 1.8 at high altitude armed with long-range stand-off missiles, or high subsonic speed at low altitude to defeat defences with short-range missiles or soften defences in preparation for the main attacking force.
★ Cruise at Mach 0.77 at high altitude.
★ Long-range platform for cruise missiles.
Note. Maintaining a good safety record in service, with pilots finding the aircraft easy to fly.

▲ Development

▲ 1967. Competition opened for a supersonic strategic bomber (see first entry under Aims). Sukhoi T-4MS (winner) and Myasishchev M-20 projects participated.
▲ 1970. Revised (scaled down) requirements called for a dash speed of 2,000 km, and maximum range of 14,000-16,000 km. In this stage of the competition, the Myasishchev M-18 was judged winner against Tupolev's Tu-144 airliner variant. Reportedly, because of inadequate production capabilities of the Myasishchev team, the design was handed over to Tupolev.
▲ 1975. Technical design work began.
▲ 1977. Full-scale mock-up accepted.
▲ 25 November 1981. Tu-160 was reportedly photographed at the Zhukovsky test centre by an airline passenger. This was the first Tu-160 photograph published in the West. Provisionally named Ram-P.
▲ 17 December 1981. First flight of the 70-01 prototype.
▲ 6 October 1984. First flight of the second prototype 70-03 (70-02 was used for static tests).
▲ February 1985. First supersonic flight.
▲ May 1987. First Tu-160 entered service with the 184th Heavy Bomber Regiment of Guards at Priluki, Ukraine. First 10-aircraft Flight established before the end of 1987.
▲ June 1987. First launches of Kh-55 (AS-15 *Kent*) cruise missiles from the Tu-160 performed by military pilots.
▲ 2 August 1988. Frank C. Carlucci, US Defense Secretary, became the first person from the West to be given a close view of a Tu-160 (aircraft side number 12, Kubinka air base near Moscow).
▲ 20 August 1989. Tu-160 was shown to the public for the first time during a fly-pass over Tushino airfield in Moscow.
▲ 1989-90. Series of 44 speed, payload and altitude records were claimed, including a speed of 935 kts (1,075.8 mph) 1,731.4 km/h over a 1,000 km closed circuit with a 66,139 lb (30,000 kg) payload (class C-1-r, take-off weight up to 240,000 kg).
▲ May 1991. An F-16A of 331 Sqn, Royal Norwegian Air Force, intercepted a Tu-160 off the coast near Tromsø.
▲ May 1992. 184th Regiment in Priluki was taken over by Ukraine. Russia formed its own Tu-160 unit at Engels with 6 aircraft (1,096th Heavy Bomber Regiment). See Sales/users.
▲ August 1992. First public static presentation, at the MosAeroshow'92 exhibition in Zhukovsky.
▲ 22 October 1992. First launch of Kh-55 missiles by Russian pilots (Lieutenant Colonel A. Zhikharev, commanding officer of the 1,096th Regiment).
▲ June 1994. Manufacturing of Tu-160 in Kazan was halted

Details for Tu-160 Blackjack bomber.

Principal dimensions:
Wing span: 116 ft 9.5 ins (35.6 m) *at 65° sweep*, 166 ft 4 ins (50.7 m) at *35° sweep*, and 182 ft 9 ins (55.7 m) *at 20° sweep*
Maximum length: 177 ft 6 ins (54.1 m)
Maximum height: 44 ft (13.1 m)
Length of engine nacelle: 43 ft 7 ins (13.28 m)

Wings:
Area: 2,497.2 sq ft (232 m^2)
Aspect ratio: 13.373 at 20° sweep.
Sweepback: fixed at 20°, 35° or 65°

Tail unit:
Tailplane span: 43 ft 6 ins (13.25 m)

Undercarriage:
Type: Retractable, with twin nosewheels. 6-wheel main bogies (3 tandem pairs) retracting into the wing centre section between the weapon bay and engine nacelles
Main wheel tyre size: 1,260 x 425 mm
Nose wheel tyre size: 1,080 x 400 mm
Wheel base: 58 ft 8 ins (17.88 m)
Wheel track: 17 ft 9 ins (5.4 m)
Allowed angle of attack when landing: 12° 30'

Weights:
Empty: 242,508 lb (110,000 kg)
Maximum take-off: 606,270 lb (275,000 kg)
Maximum landing: 341,716 lb (155,000 kg)

Performance:
Maximum operating Mach number (Mmo): Mach 2.35 is the latest quoted maximum speed. Other sources have suggested Mach 1.8 and Mach 2.05
Normal maximum speed: 1,080 kts (1,243 mph) 2,000 km/h
Cruise Mach number: Mach 0.77
Minimum speed at 308,650 lb (140,000 kg): 140 kts (162 mph) 260 km/h
Take-off distance: 2,953-7,218 ft (900-2,200 m) at 150-275 tonnes weight respectively
Landing distance: 3,937-5,250 ft (1,200-1,600 m) at 140-155 tonnes weight respectively
Maximum climb rate: 13,800 ft (4,200 m) per minute
Practical ceiling: 49,200 ft (15,000 m)
G limit: 2
Practical range without in-flight refuelling, Mach 0.77, and 6 x Kh-55SM missiles dropped mid range: 6,641 naut miles (7,643 miles) 12,300 km, with 5% fuel reserve
Maximum theoretical range: 7,532 naut miles (8,668 miles) 13,950 km
Maximum duration without in-flight refuelling: 15 hours
Combat radius at Mach 1.5: 1,080 naut miles (1,243 miles) 2,000 km

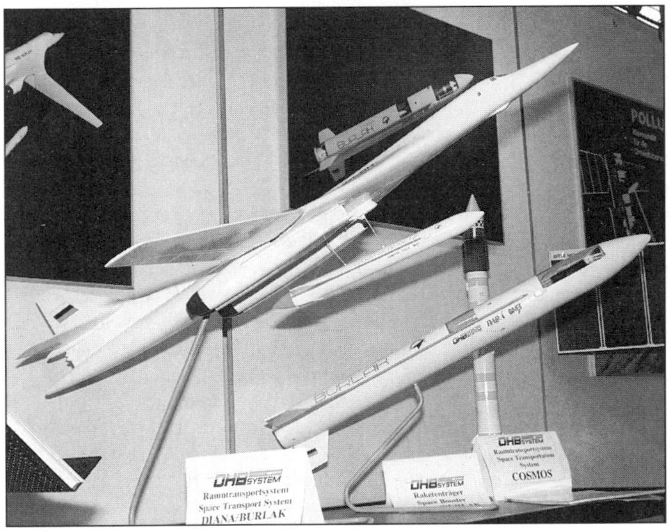

Model of the Tu-160SK with the Burlak space vehicle suspended under the fuselage (Piotr Butowski)

temporarily due to financial restrictions.
▲ Early 1995. Agreement between Russia and the Ukraine covered the return of all 19 available Ukrainian Tu-160s to the Russian Air Force (see Notes at the start of the Tupolev entry).

Sales/users: Series manufacturing at the Kazan aircraft plant named after S. Gorbunov. More than 30 built before June 1994. 19 in service with the 184th Heavy Bomber Regiment of the Ukrainian Air Force in Priluki (rarely flying, and being returned to Russia), and at least 5 with the 1,096th Regiment of Heavy Bombers of Russian Air Force in Engels. Several Tu-160s (perhaps 12) are reportedly at the Kazan factory airfield awaiting payment, and a small number are at the Zhukovsky test centre.

Crew: 4, all in the nose cockpit. The front port-side seat is occupied by the commander-pilot, with the co-pilot at his side. The rear seats are occupied by the navigator/offensive weapons operator and the navigator/EW and communications operator.

Cockpit: Access via the nosewheel undercarriage bay. Small galley and toilet. Fighter-type sticks rather than the usual wheels or yokes. Conventional analog instrumentation, with no CRT displays.

Crew escape: Zvezda K-36DM zero-zero ejection seats, ejecting upwards.

Fixed guns: None.

Expendable weapons and equipment: Weapons are carried exclusively inside the fuselage in 2 tandem weapon bays, each 37 ft (11.28 m) long and 6 ft 4 ins (1.92 m) wide. Basic armament comprises 12 Raduga Kh-55SM (AS-15B *Kent*) cruise missiles installed on 2 x MKU-6 revolving launchers (MKU stands for mnogozaryadnaya katapultnaya ustanovka, multi-round catapulting device), 1 x 6-round launcher in each of the bays. Each missile is dropped mechanically from the lowest point of the revolving drum and then fired. Afterwards the drum is revolved 60° ready for the next launch. The weight of 12 x Kh-55s is 44,974 lb (20,400 kg). Alternative armament is the Raduga Kh-15P (AS-16 *Kickback*) short-range attack missile. Kh-15Ps are used to suppress enemy air defence systems, by destroying the radars and thereby open the way for other attacking aircraft. 24 x Kh-15P missiles can be carried on 4 short revolving drums (in tandem pairs), the total load weighing 63,493 lb (28,800 kg). Theoretically, the Tu-160 is capable of carrying free-fall nuclear or conventional bombs but, as yet, has not been adapted for these types of weapons.

Radar: Obzor-K navigation/attack radar in the nose. Terrain following capability.

Flight/weapon system avionics/instrumentation: OPB-15 optical bomb sight in the fairing under the nose. Astro-inertial long-range navigation system, plotting the current position on the map. About 100 computers are used for the control of various onboard systems (including 12 computers for the fire control system). Interestingly, a single central computer concept was considered and abandoned during the course of aircraft design, believing a multi-computer system more reliable.

Self-protection systems: Electronic countermeasures system and chaff/flare dispensers in the fuselage tailcone.

Wing characteristics: Variable geometry, with slight anhedral. Outer, movable panels are set for 3 manually-selected positions: 20° for take-off and landing, 35° for Mach 0.77 cruise speed, and 65° for supersonic flight. With the wings fully swept, the inner section of each 3-section trailing-edge flap is raised to become a large aerodynamic fence between the wing and the fixed glove to improve directional stability.

Wing control surfaces: Each movable wing panel has 4-section leading-edge slats, a 3-section double-slotted trailing-edge flap, and aileron. 5-section spoilers ahead of the flaps.

Tail control surfaces: Mid-mounted slab (taileron) tailplane, deflecting symmetrically or differentially. All-moving upper section of the tailfin, above the tailplane, forms the rudder.

Flight control system: Quadruple fly-by-wire, plus stand-by mechanical. Since the aircraft is statically unstable, the use of the mechanical control system is considerably limited.

Fuselage: The long and narrow fuselage/wing centre section (LERX type), blended for maximum radar deflection, is subdivided into 4 compartments: nose (radar unit, crew cockpit and nosewheel undercarriage unit), front (fuel tanks and front weapon bay), centre (main undercarriage units, engine nacelles and rear weapon bay) and rear (fuel tanks and equipment).

Construction materials: Mainly, if not entirely, metal.

Engines: 4 Samara NK-32 turbofans in widely separated pairs (to make room in the fuselage for the weapon bay) under the wing centre section, with the nacelles protruding far beyond wing trailing edge.

Engine rating: Each 30,865 lbf (137.3 kN) dry, 55,115 lbf (245.18 kN) with afterburning.

Nozzles/air intakes: Automatically adjustable nozzles. Adjustable air intake with vertical wedge for each pair of engines.

Flight refuelling probe: Retractable probe mounted in the upper part of nose.

Fuel system: 309,970 lb (140,600 kg) of fuel in 13 tanks installed in the fuselage/wing centre section and the movable wing panels. The fuel transfer system is used to balance the aircraft when accelerating into supersonic speed.

Braking system: 3 drag-chutes of 1,130 sq ft (105 m^2) gross area.

Aircraft variants:
Tu-160 (izdelye 70) strategic bomber, as described.
Tu-160P was a projected escort interceptor, armed with medium and long range AAMs. Programme has been cancelled.
Tu-160SK is a projected commercial version for use as a launching platform for the Burlak space vehicle (similar to the US Pegasus), as presented as a full-scale mock-up in Paris in 1995. Burlak was designed by the Raduga missile design bureau as an inexpensive low-Earth-orbital vehicle to carry a 1,819-2,425 lb (825-1,100 kg) load, depending to the orbital altitude. Projected Burlak-M with the additional hypersonic ram-jet engine will carry 50% more payload. Weighing 70,550 lb (32,000 kg), Burlak is suspended under the fuselage of the Tu-160, between the engine nacelles. Range of the Tu-160SK with Burlak will be 2,997 naut miles (3,450 miles) 5,550 km, and the spacecraft will be launched at 44,300 ft (13,500 m) altitude and 972 kts (1,118 mph) 1,800 km/h speed.

Yakovlev Aircraft Corporation (Russia)

Corporate address: 68 Leningradsky Prospekt, 125315 Moscow.
Telephone: +7 095 157 1734
Facsimile: +7 095 157 4726
Founded: 1992, from the former A.S. Yakovlev design bureau.
Information: Yuri V. Zasypkin.

• Activities

- Yakovlev forms part of the Skorost association, bringing together the design bureau, the Saratov and Smolensk airframe manufacturing factories, and the Ivchenko PROGRESS engine company in the Ukraine.
- It is a partner in Hyundai-Yak Aerospace Co Ltd, a South Korean based company aimed at developing, marketing and selling a wide range of small and medium sized aircraft. Initial products are the Yak-54, Yak-58 and Yak-112.
- Markets the Israel Aircraft Industries Astra Galaxy in the CIS as a risk-sharing partner.

Yakovlev Yak-36M/38 (NATO name *Forger*)

This ship-borne VSTOL combat aircraft, that first flew on 15 January 1971 (231 built), has been withdrawn from service with the Russian Navy.

Yakovlev 41/141 (NATO name *Freestyle*)

First flight: 9 March 1987 (pilot Andrei Sinitsyn).
Role: ship-borne VTOL supersonic fighter, with air-to-sea capability. Shore-based short take-off version proposed.
Chief designers: Sergei Yakovlev, Alexander Levinskikh, Victor Pavlov and, since 1987, Konstantin Popovich.

▲ Development

▲ 1975. Work started on the Yak-41 as a ship-borne VTOL supersonic interceptor.
▲ 9 March 1987. First flight, by prototype number *75*, using conventional take-off techniques.
▲ Spring 1988. Development announced in the West by US Rear Admiral William O. Studeman. Temporarily named *Ram-T* by NATO.
▲ 12 April 1989. First flight of second prototype number *77* (conventional take-off).
▲ Summer 1989. Mach 1 exceeded for the first time.
▲ 29 December 1989. First hovering flight.
▲ 13 June 1990. First full profile flight.
▲ April 1991. Andrei Sinitsyn set 12 world records in class H for VTOL aircraft. 11 records were set for the first time and the twelfth was taken from the British Harrier (time of climb to 12,000 m, equal to 116.2 seconds, the former record was 122.6 seconds). The records were for maximum altitude (42,980 ft, 13,100 m), rate of climb without load and also with a 1,000 kg and 2,000 kg load, plus maximum load (2,500 kg) lifted to 2,000 m altitude.
▲ June 1991. Model and video film showing the testing of the Yak-141 appeared at the Paris Air Show.
▲ 26 September 1991. First landing onboard the aircraft carrier *Admiral Gorshkov*.
▲ 5 October 1991. Prototype *77* damaged when hard landed on the carrier (later restored for static show purposes and delivered to the Khodynka museum).
▲ November 1991. Russian Government financial support for the programme stopped.
▲ September 1992. Yak-141 presented at Farnborough in the UK.

Details for the naval Yak-141 (Yak-41M) Freestyle.

Principal dimensions:
Wing span: 33 ft 2 ins (10.105 m)
Wing span with wings folded: 19 ft 4 ins (5.9 m)
Maximum length: 60 ft 3 ins (18.36 m)
Maximum height: 16 ft 4 ins (4.985 m)

Wings:
Area: 341.2 sq ft (31.7 m^2)
Aspect ratio: 3.22
Anhedral: From roots

Undercarriage:
Type: Retractable, with nosewheel
Wheel base: 22 ft 9 ins (6.945 m)
Wheel track: 9 ft 10 ins (3.00 m)
Main wheel tyre size: 880 x 230 mm
Nose wheel tyre size: 500 x 150 mm

Weights:
Empty, operating: 25,684 lb (11,650 kg)
Maximum vertical take-off (VTO): 34,823 lb (15,800 kg)
Maximum rolling take-off (RTO): 42,990 lb (19,500 kg)

Performance:
Maximum operating Mach number (Mmo): Mach 1.7
Maximum operating speed: 972 kts (1,118 mph) 1,800 km/h
Maximum speed at sea level: 675 kts (777 mph) 1,250 km/h
Take-off distance: 98-328 ft (30-100 m) for STOL operations; otherwise vertical
Landing distance: 787 ft (240 m) with brakes for STOL operations; otherwise vertical
G limit: +7
Ceiling: 49,215 ft (15,000 m)
Range, VTO, clean, at sea level: 351 naut miles (404 miles) 650 km
Range, VTO, clean, at high altitude: 756 naut miles (870 miles) 1,400 km
Range, RTO, 2,205 lb (1,000 kg) of weapons, at sea level: 545 naut miles (628 miles) 1,010 km
Range, RTO, 2,205 lb (1,000 kg) of weapons, at high altitude: 1,134 naut miles (1,305 miles) 2,100 km
Typical combat radius, RTO, 4,409 lb (2,000 kg) of weapons: 373 naut miles (429 miles) 690 km

▲ 1993. Work on the Yak-141 terminated.
▲ 1-2 September 1994. Following a meeting between Yakovlev officials and those of the Russian defence ministry and security council, it has been suggested that the Yak-141 programme has been revived.
▲ 1995. Development continued also on a higher-performance, reconfigured land-based STOL variant (see Aircraft variants).

Sales/users: 4 prototypes built, including 2 for flight testing. In 1991, the Soviet Navy ordered a small series as Yak-141s for military purposes. Full production equipment was prepared in Smolensk. The first series-built aircraft was expected in 1993, providing initial operational capability in 1995. However, in November 1991, as a result of reduced military expenditure, production was halted. When new production will begin is, as yet, unclear.
Crew: Pilot.
Crew escape: SK-EM automatic ejection system, with K-36LV ejection seat.
Fixed guns: GSh-301 30-mm cannon under the port engine intake.
Ammunition: 120 rounds.
Number of weapon pylons: 4 underwing.
Expendable weapons and equipment: Can include R-77 (AA-12 *Adder*) and R-27 (AA-10 *Alamo*) medium range and R-73 (AA-11 *Archer*) short range AAMs. Anti-ship attacks can be mounted using Kh-31A (AS-17 *Krypton*) and Kh-35 missiles, while Kh-31P and Kh-58 (AS-11 *Kilter*) are for attacking radar sites. Unguided weapons include rockets, bombs or cannon pods. Total payload 5,732 lb (2,600 kg) for a rolling take-off, or 2,205 lb (1,000 kg) for VTO. See Aircraft variants for the land-based version.
Radar: Phazotron M-002, similar to the Zhuk in the MiG-29M.
Flight/weapon system avionics/instrumentation: Automatic flight control system during ship-board operations. Computer-integrated information displayed on the EFIS and HUD, with inputs also from the IFF, helmet-mounted display and laser/TV designator. GPS.
Wing characteristics: Shoulder mounted, with swept leading edges and straight trailing edges for the inboard panels and swept for the outer. Folding outer panels for ship-board stowage.
Wing control surfaces: Ailerons, trailing-edge flaps and leading-edge slats.
Tail control surfaces: Twin-boom type tail unit, with all-moving tailplane (2 separate halves) and twin outward-canted fins with rudders. Inner edges of the booms are heat protected from the main engine efflux.

Yakovlev Yak-141 (ex 75) first prototype with lift-jet nozzle doors opened and the upper air intake door raised (Piotr Butowski)

Flight control system: Triple redundant digital fly-by-wire. Puffer jets at wingtips and nose, for stability.
Construction materials: Mostly aluminium and lithium, but with considerable use of carbonfibre (26% of structural weight) for wing and tail components.
Engines: 3. Single Soyuz/Kobchyenko R-79V-300 lift/cruise turbofan with afterburner located horizontally inside the rear fuselage and 2 Rybinsk/Novikov RD-41 lift engines mounted 15° off vertical behind the cockpit. Engine thrust/aircraft weight

ratio in VTO operation is 1.31:1. The R-79 is a mixed-flow afterburning turbofan with a by-pass ratio of 0.9-1.2 in forward flight. It has a single vectoring nozzle, exhausting between the 2 halves of the tail unit for horizontal flight, or vectored slightly forward-of-vertical (95°) for vertical flying and 65° for short take offs. The engine has a triple redundant analog electronic control system, duplicated by a hydro-mechanical unit. The R-79 is rated at 34,172 lbf (152.1 kN) with afterburning and 24,250 lbf (107.88 kN) dry. The afterburner can be used during all modes of flight. An uprated version with FADEC is being developed as the R-79M, offering about 39,680 lbf (176.5 kN) with afterburning. Each RD-41 lift engine (with triple redundant digital control) has a maximum thrust of 9,039 lbf (40.2 kN) and vectoring range of +17° and -9°. The nozzle itself is variable by 10%.
Air intakes: Wedge-type on the fuselage sides for the main engine. Door aft of the cockpit is raised when lift-jets are operated, to provide air.
Flight refuelling probe: None.
Fuel system: 9,700 lb (4,400 kg) of internal fuel. 3,858 lb (1,750 kg) of auxiliary fuel, carried as a 2,000 litre conformal tank.
Braking system: Main wheel brakes. Brake-chute carried in a pod above the rear fuselage.

Yakovlev Yak-141 (ex 77) prototype restored after being damaged in a hard landing (Piotr Butowski)

Aircraft variants:

Yak-41 was the projected interceptor version.
Yak-41M added air-to-surface anti-ship missile capability. 2 flying prototypes built, originally numbered 75 and 77 but now both *141*.
Yak-141 is the official and export designation of Yak-41M.
Land-based version of Yak-41 will have increased weapon load and longer range, and will take-off under normal conditions after a 394 ft (120 m) ground run. Vertical take-off will still be possible with reduced load or fuel reserve. The new airframe configuration resembles a latest-generation fighter, and thereby the effective radar signature will be considerably reduced. It will have greater internal fuel capacity and larger-area wings. There will be no changes in the propulsion system. Improved undercarriage and brakes, with the landing run not exceeding 394 ft (120 m). Landing speed will not be higher than 43 kts (50 mph) 80 km/h. According to information from Yakovlev, the aircraft will be capable of carrying 9,259 lb (4,200 kg) of weapons for STOL operations. Typical radius of action with 4,409 lb (2,000 kg) of bombs increases to 486 naut miles (559 miles) 900 km.

Yakovlev Yak-43

First flight: Not yet flown.
Role: Projected next-generation STOVL fighter.
Crew: Pilot only.
Engine: 1 Samara/Kuznetsov NK-32 turbofan. This engine combines the functions of lift and cruise and has been tested on a full scale stand.
Airframe: Stealth configuration, using radar absorbing materials.
Radar: 2 radars (one in front and another in the tail).
Expendable weapons and equipment: Normal weapon load is carried inside a bay to retain stealth features.

Yakovlev Yak-130

First flight: Expected late 1995 for Yak-130D demonstrator.
Role: Two-seat jet trainer, and light combat and reconnaissance aircraft (see Aircraft variants).

Yakovlev Yak-130 (Piotr Butowski)

★ Aims

★ To replace the L-29 Delfin and L-39 Albatros in Russian Air Force service.
★ To be capable of various aspects of training, including flying, air combat and weapons.
★ Requirements of the Russian Air Force are (in summarized form):
a) 2 non-afterburning engines, with 0.6-0.7 power-to-weight ratio. Take-off weight 11,023-12,125 lb (5,000-5,500 kg).
b) 459 kts (528 mph) 850 km/h maximum speed. Landing speed not exceeding 92 kts (106 mph) 170 km/h, and take-off and landing runs not exceeding 1,640 ft (500 m). Provision for operation from unpaved runways.
c) Normal range of 648 naut miles (746 miles) 1,200 km at Mach 0.5 and 19,700 ft (6,000 m) altitude. Ferry range of 1,350 naut miles (1,553 miles) 2,500 km
d) G limits of +8, -3.
e) High manoeuvrability, similar to that of new generation fighters.
f) Pre-programmable control system imitating aircraft with different longitudinal stability coefficient.
g) 10,000 flying hours structural life over 25 years, with possible extension to 15,000 hours.

▲ Development

▲ January 1991. Competition for a new generation jet trainer (UTS, uchebno-trenirovochnyi samolyot) was initiated by the Russian Air Force. UTK (uchebno-trenirovochnyi komplex) training system has been ordered which includes (besides the UTS aircraft) flight simulators.
▲ January 1992. First stage of the competition summarized. Mikoyan 821, Myasishchev M-200, Sukhoi S-54 and Yakovlev Yak-130 took part in the design competition. The designs were judged in 8 technical and economic categories. The Sukhoi S-54 was reportedly judged winner in 4 of the 8 categories (technical perfection, flight safety, combat capability and technical-training). But, at the same time, the S-54 was disqualified for having only a single engine. From the remaining designs, the Yak-130 reportedly came out best, but its advantage over the Mikoyan 821 was not decisive and it was decided to postpone the competition result. Both Mikoyan and Yakovlev were approved to continue the development of prototypes.
▲ May 1994. Next stage summarized. 200 Yak-130s were initially ordered but the final choice between the Yak-130 and MiG-AT (821) will now not be made until after testing of the flying prototypes.
▲ 30 November 1994. The first Yak-130D prototype under construction was displayed, prior to having its engines and avionics installed. Aermacchi of Italy is co-operating in development.
▲ 29 May 1995. Yak-130D was presented to the press in Moscow.
Sales/users: Estimated requirement under UTS is for 800-1,000 aircraft before the year 2000 (because of a planned quick withdrawal of the L-29 and L-39). The potential export market is for 1,200 aircraft over 20 years.
Crew: Student-pilot (front) and instructor (rear) in tandem cockpits. 17° look-down visibility from front seat and 9° from rear raised seat.
Crew escape: Zvezda K-36 zero-zero ejection seats.
Fixed guns: Laser imitation of cannon for training.
Number of weapon pylons: 7.
Expendable weapons and equipment: Can include guided missiles, unguided rockets, bombs and gun pods. 6,614 lb (3,000 kg) load.
Radar: Planned for possible single-seat combat derivative.
Flight/weapon system avionics/instrumentation: Automatic flight and training procedure control system with 2 digital computers. HUD in the front cockpit. 2 cathode-ray tube displays in each cockpit, with conventional instrumentation as stand-by. Navigation system including GPS, short range radio navigation and instrument landing, radio-compass, radio altimeter, etc. The aircraft has a combat simulator system which includes close air combat with use of infra-red and other guided missiles and cannon, attack against ground targets with various types of guided missiles, as well as passive and active jamming. Helmet mounted sight. Com radio, intercom, IFF, flight data recorder, and video recording of student-pilot behaviour.
Wing characteristics: Mid-mounted, with swept leading edges and wingroot extensions. Winglets.
Wing control surfaces: Automatic slats on leading edges. Ailerons and Fowler type trailing-edge flaps.
Tail control surfaces: All-moving slab tailplane, with dogtooth extended chord leading edges. Tall fin and rudder.
Airbrakes: Door-type on the upper fuselage .
Flight control system: Fly-by-wire (originally to be mechanical). Longitudinal stability can be programmed within 0-10% range.
Engines: 2 Klimov/Sarkisov RD-35M turbofans (developed version of DV-2S). Previously, as originally planned, the prototype was to be powered by 2 AI-25TLMs (3,792 lbf, 16.87 kN) and production aircraft by 2 R-35s (4,300 lbf, 19.12 kN).
Engine rating: Each 4,850 lbf (21.58 kN).
Air intakes: Main air intakes are located under the leading-edge root extensions (LERX). Take-off intakes for unpaved runway operations are on the upper surface of LERX (solution similar to that of the MiG-29 but much simpler).
Flight refuelling probe: None.
Fuel system: 3,638 lb (1,650 kg) of fuel in 3 internal tanks (1 in the fuselage behind the cockpit and 1 inside each wing). Provision for auxiliary conformal tank containing 1,213 lb (550 kg) of fuel.

Aircraft variants:

Yak-130D is the first prototype (Demonstrator). Length 39 ft (11.9 m), longer LERXs, and no dogtooth at tailplane.
Basic Yak-130 is intended for pilot training, but other specialized versions and derivatives are also offered, including those for:

Details for Super Skyhawk.

Principal dimensions:
Wing span: 27 ft 6 ins (8.382 m)
Maximum length: 41 ft 8.5 ins (12.7 m)
Maximum height: 15 ft (4.57 m)

Wings:
Area: 260 sq ft (24.15 m^2)
Aspect ratio: 2.91
Sweepback: 33° at 25% chord
Dihedral: From roots

Undercarriage:
Type: Retractable, with steerable nosewheel
Wheel base: 12 ft (3.66 m)
Wheel track: 7 ft 9.5 ins (2.37 m)
Turning circle: 12 ft 4 ins (3.76 m)

Weights:
Empty, operating: 10,250 lb (4,650 kg)
Maximum take-off: 22,500 lb (10,200 kg)

Performance:
Maximum speed: 609 kts (700 mph) 1,128 km/h
Stall speed: 134 kts (154 mph) 247 km/h
Maximum climb rate: 10,900 ft (3,325 m) per minute
Ceiling: 40,000 ft (12,190 m)
Range with full payload: 625 naut miles (720 miles) 1,160 km

Singapore Technologies Aerospace Super Skyhawks flown by the Black Knights

the Black Knights official Air Force display team.
Crew: Pilot.
Cockpit: Armour protected. Modernized with head-up and head-down displays, and more (see Avionics).
Crew escape: Escapac Zero-zero ejection seat.
Fixed guns: 2 x 30-mm Aden cannon housed in the wing roots.
Number of weapon pylons: 5, 4 under the wings and 1 under the fuselage.
Expendable weapons and equipment: Many weapon options including Maverick missiles, free-fall bombs, rockets, and laser-guided bombs (requiring a laser designator or the designator of an accompanying aircraft).
Flight/weapon system avionics/instrumentation: Litton LN-93 laser inertial navigation, air data computer, stores management system, GEC-Marconi 4150 head-up display, and head-down display.
Wing characteristics: Low mounted, cropped delta, with slight dihedral.
Wing control surfaces: Ailerons (port tab), flaps, leading-edge slats, and split spoilers ahead of the flaps.
Tail control surfaces: Variable incidence tailplane, elevators and rudder.
Airbrakes: Rear of fuselage sides.
Construction materials: All metal.
Engine: General Electric F404-GE-100D non-augmented turbofan.
Engine rating: 11,000 lbf (48.93 kN).
Nozzle/air intakes: A long tailpipe helps attract heat-seeking missiles away from the main airframe area. Fuselage side air intakes were modified when the F404 was installed.
Flight refuelling probe: Non-retractable at the nose.
Fuel system: About 3,000 litres. Drop tanks can be carried.

AIRASA (South Africa)

Full name: Aerospace Industry Representative Association of South Africa.
Corporate address: PO Box 7810, Bonaero Park 1622.
Telephone: +27 11 395 1848
Facsimile: +27 11 973 4116
Founded: 7 February 1992
Information: Petro Geyer (Secretary).

● Activities
- Approximately 400 companies in South Africa are involved to varying degrees in the aviation and aerospace industries. AIRASA was founded to unify the interests of companies and organizations engaged in research, design, development, production, assembly, test, maintenance and logistic support, project management, education and training, trading and dealing.
- The specific aims are: the unification, protection and growth of the South African aerospace industry and its entities; the establishment of an information base for use in promoting AIRASA and its members; the co-ordination of strategic planning to stimulate the development of the aerospace industry; the promotion of international contacts to increase market potential and encourage foreign investment and trade; the collective provision of inputs/viewpoints to the authorities for legislation and the creation of a favourable business environment; and provision of special services to members of the association according to common requirements.

Denel (Pty) Ltd (South Africa)

Corporate address: Denel Building, Jochemus Street, Erasmuskloof, PO Box 8322, Hennopsmeer, 0046.
Telephone: +27 12 428 0604
Facsimile: +27 12 428 0947
Employees: 14,000.
Information: P. P. Holtzhausen (Group Executive Manager: Public Relations and Environmental Affairs – *telephone* +27 12 428 0911, *facsimile* +27 12 428 0662).

● Activities
- Independent, diversified industrial group and one of South Africa's leading manufacturers and suppliers of high technology industrial and military products, systems and services.
- Presently converting its technology base for the manufacture of non-military products.
- Comprises 21 operating and industrial divisions structured as individual business units in 6 categories: aerospace, systems (mechanical and electronic), informatics and properties, manufacturing, business development and international marketing.

AEROSPACE GROUP DIVISIONS

Atlas Aviation (which see).

OTB
HQ address: Overberg Test Range, Bredasdorp.
Telephone: +27 2847 5 9010
Facsimile: +27 2847 5 9256

● Activities
- Supports the aerospace industry by conducting flight tests and satellite launches.

Simera (see the Freighter section).

Atlas Aviation (South Africa)

Corporate address: Astro Park, Atlas Road, Bonaero Park, PO Box 11, Kempton Park, 1620.
Telephone: +27 11 927 9111
Facsimile: +27 11 395 1103
Telex: 742403
Founded: 1964 registered as a private company.
Employees: Over 5,000.
Information: Mike Weeks (Senior Public Relations Officer – *telephone* +27 11 927 2236, *facsimile* +27 11 395 1725).

● Activities
- Development, production and logistical support of fixed and rotary-wing aircraft, plus production of gas turbine engines and related subsystems.
- State-of-the-art maintenance services.
- Products and capabilities include the ACE (All Composite Evaluator) trainer; Rooivalk attack helicopter; Puma gunship; modification and upgrading of aircraft and their subsystems; manufacture of fixed-wing and rotary-wing aircraft, engines, composite material structures and components, and aerospace quality sand castings; precision and vacuum investment castings; service and overhaul of airframes, engines, components and accessories including avionics, hydraulics, pneumatics, navigation and fuel systems; full-scale repair; flight testing under hot and high conditions; logistical support; and provision of manpower and training.

Atlas Aviation ACE (All Composite Trainer)

First flight: 29 April 1991.
Role: Trainer.

★ Aims

- ★ 15,000 flying hour service life.
- ★ Low maintenance costs, and good fatigue and corrosion resistance due to the carbonfibre/epoxy airframe.
- ★ Good power to weight ratio.
- ★ Good gliding performance to enhance flight safety, due to the good lift/drag ratio.
- ★ Aerobatic.

▲ Development

▲ 1986. Design was initiated by Aerotek (a government research agency), as a composites technology demonstrator under Project Ovid.

▲ 1991. First flight. Offered to the South African Air Force as a military trainer to replace Harvards, but Pilatus PC-7 Mk IIs selected.

▲ 14 January 1995. Loss of the demonstrator, after a wheels-up forced landing at Jan Smuts Airport in Johannesburg caused extensive damage. Earlier loss of pitch control reportedly forced the emergency landing. Second demonstrator to fly in the latter part of 1996, with new engine, upgraded avionics and a lengthened fuselage.

Atlas Aviation ACE trainer

Sales/users: Available for purchase.
Crew: 2, with raised rear seat.
Cockpit: Non-jettisonable canopy, with straight-through ejection in an emergency.

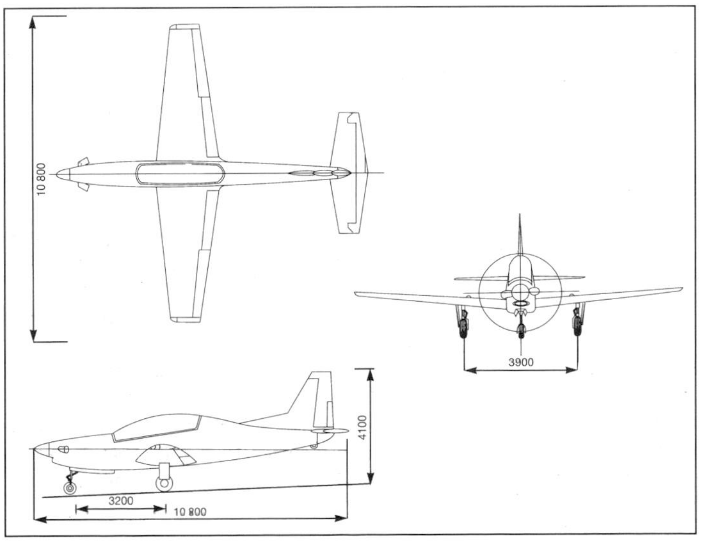

Atlas Aviation ACE drawing

Crew escape: Ejection seats.
Wing characteristics: Straight, low mounted, with dihedral from the roots.
Wing control surfaces: Ailerons and flaps.
Tail control surfaces: Single-piece horn-balanced elevator, and rudder with tab.
Construction materials: Carbonfibre composites with honeycomb inserts. Wing, fuselage, tailplane and control surfaces are all manufactured as single-piece items.
Engine: Pratt & Whitney Canada PT6A-34 turboprop with a 7 ft 9 ins (2.36 m) propeller in the first prototype. Second demonstrator has a PT6A-68 engine. PT6A-25C for subsequent aircraft.
Engine rating: 750 shp (559.3 kW) take-off, 700 shp (522 kW) cruise.

Details for Ace.

Principal dimensions:
Wing span: 35 ft 5 ins (10.8 m)
Maximum length: 35 ft 5 ins (10.8 m)
Maximum height: 13 ft 5 ins (4.1 m)

Wings:
Area: 193.75 sq ft (18 m^2)
Aspect ratio: 6.5
Dihedral: From roots

Tail unit:
Tailplane span: 14 ft 1 ins (4.3 m)
Tailplane area (including elevators): 46.5 sq ft (4.32 m^2)
Vertical tail chord: 5 ft 8 ins (1.72 m)
Fin and rudder area: 21.53 sq ft (2 m^2)

Undercarriage:
Type: Retractable, with nosewheel
Wheel base: 10 ft 6 ins (3.2 m)
Wheel track: 12 ft 10 ins (3.9 m)

Weights:
Empty: 3,406 lb (1,545 kg)
Maximum take-off: 4,850 lb (2,200 kg)

Performance:
Maximum operating speed: 300 kts (345 mph) 555 km/h
Maximum speed at sea level: 255 kts (294 mph) 472 km/h
Maximum speed at 5,000 ft (1,525 m): 270 kts (311 mph) 500 km/h
Take-off distance over a 50 ft (15 m) obstacle: 1,380 ft (420 m) clean, 1,200 ft (365 m) with take-off flaps
Landing distance over a 50 ft (15 m) obstacle: 1,410 ft (430 m) clean, 1,230 ft (375 m) with landing flaps
Maximum climb rate: 2,750 ft (838 m) per minute
Time to 25,000 ft (7,620 m): under 15 minutes
Roll rate: 150° per second, maximum, at 180 kts (207 mph) 333 km/h
Sustained turn rate: 20.7° per second, at 5,000 ft (1,525 m)
G limits: +7, -3.5
Ceiling: 33,000 ft (10,000 m)
Range with full fuel: 1,100 naut miles (1,266 miles) 2,037 km, at 25,000 ft (7,620 m)
Duration: 5 hours 30 minutes at 25,000 ft

Atlas Aviation Cheetah

First flight: 1986.
Role: Multi-role fighter, fighter-bomber, and reconnaissance.

Possible general configuration of the definitive Cheetah, with compound wing leading edges and wingtip missiles (courtesy Atlas Aviation)

★ Aims

- ★ Highly modified Mirage III, to maintain combat efficiency at a time when replacement aircraft were unavailable, through very extensive airframe, engine and avionics upgrades.
- ★ Continued development based on newly designed high-efficiency wings and a further avionics upgrade (including radar).

▲ Development

▲ 1984. Launch of the Cheetah programme, as an upgrade of the Mirage IIIEZ, DZ, D2Z, RZ and R2Z. Becomes almost a totally new design. Subsequent conversions also included 9 or more Cheetah D/Es from ex-Israeli Kfirs.

▲ July 1986. First Cheetah is rolled out, as a conversion of a Mirage III-D2Z two-seat operational trainer.

▲ 1987. Initial operational capability.

▲ 1994. Funding costs and figures for the continuing Cheetah programme were announced in the South African parliament, confirming the intention to re-wing aircraft and install new Elta radar.

Sales/users: 38 for the SAAF under a 6,500 million Rand programme, including the latest multi-role Cheetah Cs; 24 were thought to be operational in early 1995 with No 2 Squadron. 20 Cheetah Ds, Es, Rs and R2s were put up for sale in 1994.
Crew: Pilot, or 2 in operational training versions.
Radar: Elta EL/M-2001, and EL-M-2035 on Cheetah Cs.
Wing characteristics: Modified Mirage III low-mounted delta type, with a fence and dog-tooth leading edge. The Advanced Combat Wing, first seen on a modified R2, has drooped leading-edges and an extended outer section giving greater tip chord. It offers the capability of stable flight at speeds as low as 80 kts (92 mph) 148 km/h at 33° angle of attack, a higher sustained turn rate, and extra fuel capacity. A further modification has been proposed, whereby the outer panel of each wing has less sweep and a squared-off tip to mount an AAM launch rail.
Canard: Swept, clipped delta type, fixed to the air intake sides.

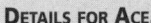

Engine: SNECMA Atar 09K50 turbojet, taken from decommissioned Mirage F1s. The Russian Klimov RD-33 of approximately similar dry thrust but with much higher augmented rating, has been flight tested in a Cheetah as a possible new power source; decision expected in 1995.
Engine rating: 11,060 lbf (49.2 kN) dry, 15,846 lbf (70.49 kN) with afterburning.
Flight refuelling probe: Fixed to the starboard side of the cockpit.

Aircraft variants:
Cheetah C is the latest multi-role combat version, representing modified Es with Elta EL/M-2035 radar and the new low-drag wings. Avionics installed by IAI's Bedek Aviation.
Cheetah D is the two-seat operational trainer, converted from the Mirage III-D2Z and Kfir.
Cheetah E is a single-seat interceptor and fighter-bomber, converted from Mirages and Kfirs.
Cheetah R/R2 are the reconnaissance fighter versions.

Atlas Aviation Cheetah D (courtesy Atlas Aviation)

Construcciones Aeronáuticas, S.A. (CASA) (Spain)

Corporate address: Avda. Aragón, 404– 28022 Madrid.
Telephone: +34 1 585 70 00, 585 77 89
Facsimile: +34 1 585 74 57
Telex: 41696/41726 CASA E
Founded: 1923.
Employees: over 8,000.
Information: Leopoldo Avila Casuso (Sales Technology, Marketing).

DIVISIONS

Aircraft Division

● Activities

- Complete design of aircraft and integrated structures (its own and those related to multi-national manufacturing programmes), with a high degree of industrial automation in the production processes. At the forefront of the design and manufacture of large composite material structural elements.
- Product Support Service puts the aircraft into service and integrates it into the operator's organization. Offers an integral package of courses for all levels of flight and ground crews.
- Multi-national programmes include Airbus, Eurofighter and FLA.
- Research, design and manufacture of structural parts and components for other aircraft, including contracts with Boeing (B757 flaps), Eurocopter, McDonnell Douglas (MD-11 tailplane and Spanish Hornets), Northrop Grumman, Saab (Saab 2000 wings) and Sikorsky (including Spanish Navy HS.23/S-70B-1 components).
- In addition to the aircraft detailed here and under the Multi-national part of this section, see also Airliners.
- A proposed attack aircraft is the AX, which could replace upgraded F-5s early next century. No firm commitment to the project has yet been taken, and partners are being sought. It is known that Samsung of South Korea has approached CASA as a potential partner for its similar-class KTX-II (which see) programme, but no news of the outcome was available at the time of writing.

Maintenance Division

● Activities

- Modernization of aircraft and weapon systems. Over 7,900 aircraft have passed through this division's facilities to be serviced, checked or modernized, including AV-8 Harrier, BO 105, Super Puma, F-4, F-5, F-15, F/A-18, and Mirage III/F1s.
- Current work includes a life extension programme for Spanish F-5s, and modernization of Mirage F1s.

Space Division

● Activities

- Develops high stability mechanical subsystems, service modules, direct broadcasting reflector antennae, power distribution networks, robotics and animation software.
- In co-operation with the European Space Agency, participates on scientific programmes, telecommunications ventures, transport systems, platform and earth tracking instrument programmes, and a large number of technologically related projects.
- Produces the first-stage skirts (forward and intertank) for Ariane 4, plus the equipment bay structure, payload adaptors, safety and switching boxes, and a set of POGO valves. For Ariane 5, develops the upper stage EPS-support and equipment-bay structures, and more.
- Also participates in the Helios, Spot 4, Eutelsat II, Hispasat, Huygens, Soho, Envisat, Metop and Polar Platform programmes.

CASA C-101 Aviojet

First flight: 27 June 1977.
Role: Basic, advanced and lead-in trainer, ground attack and tactical support, and special missions including target towing; can undertake reconnaissance, armed patrol, point defence, and forward air control.

★ Aims

- ★ Optimum cost/efficiency ratio.
- ★ Modular airframe design.
- ★ 10,000 flight hour structural life.
- ★ Minimum maintenance using a Progressive Maintenance Programme, allowing a rate of under 4 man-hours per flight hour, including third level.

▲ Development

▲ 16 September 1976. Spanish Ministry of Air and CASA signed an agreement for development and 6 prototypes (4 flying, 2 static). Northrop of the USA and MBB of Germany assisted design.
▲ 27 June 1977. First flight of the first flying prototype.
▲ 30 September 1977. First flight of the second flying prototype.
▲ 1978. Third and fourth flying prototypes made their maiden flights on 26 January and 17 April.
▲ 17 March 1980. First production C-101 EBs entered service with the Spanish General Air Academy to equip Squadron 793.
▲ 16 November 1983. Maiden flight of the C-101 CC attack version.

Sales/users: 92 C-101 EBs have been delivered to the Spanish Air Force as E.25 Mirlos, serving with the General Air Academy (see Development), plus the Practice Group where refresher courses are undertaken together with a series of special missions including target towing, and also equips the Aguila aerobatic display team. ENAER in Chile has built examples as Halcóns for the Chilean Air Force (which see), and CASA exported 4 C-101BBs to Honduras (operating from Comayagua) and 16 to Jordan in C-101 CC form.
Crew: 2, the instructor's rear seat raised by 13 ins (32 cm).
Cockpit: HOTAS, etc (see Avionics). Accommodates crew members between the 3rd and 99th percentiles. Front cockpit vision below the horizon is 15°, 9° from the rear seat. Duplicated instruments and controls in the cockpits, with rear cockpit command priority for flight safety. 2 independent canopy sections, hinged sideways. Internal transparent screen protects the instructor in the event of front pilot ejection. Automatic pressurization at 8,000 ft (2,440 m), maintained to 19,685 ft (6,000 m), above which 4.07 psi pressure differential is maintained; bleed air system.
Crew escape: Martin Baker Mk 10 zero-zero ejection seats.
Fixed guns: See below.
Ammunition: 130 cannon rounds, or 220 rounds per machine-gun.
Number of weapon pylons: 6 under the wings (500kg, 375 kg and 250 kg capacity each wing set) plus a central fuselage station for a 30-mm DEFA 553 cannon or 2 x 12.7-mm Browning machine-gun pod.
Expendable weapons and equipment: 4,000 lb (1,814 kg) at maximum take-off weight. Options include rocket launchers, bombs, 2 Maverick air-to-surface missiles or 2 air-to-air missiles (Magic or Sidewinder).
Flight/weapon system avionics/instrumentation: C-101 CC version includes communication and identification system, as well as a navigation system built around a flight director and gyroscope platform. DD version is equipped with an integrated nav/attack system built around a HUD, and interconnected through a 1553B digital databus. Standard C-101 communications equipment comprises

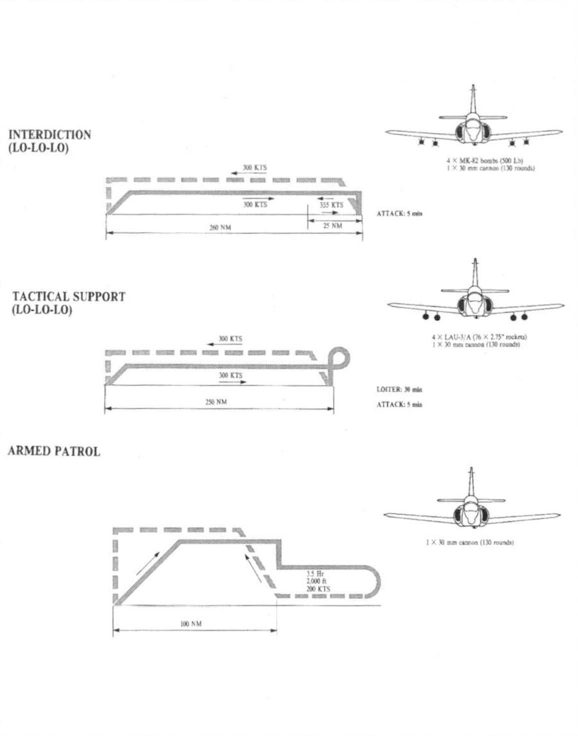

CASA C-101 Aviojet mission profiles (courtesy CASA)

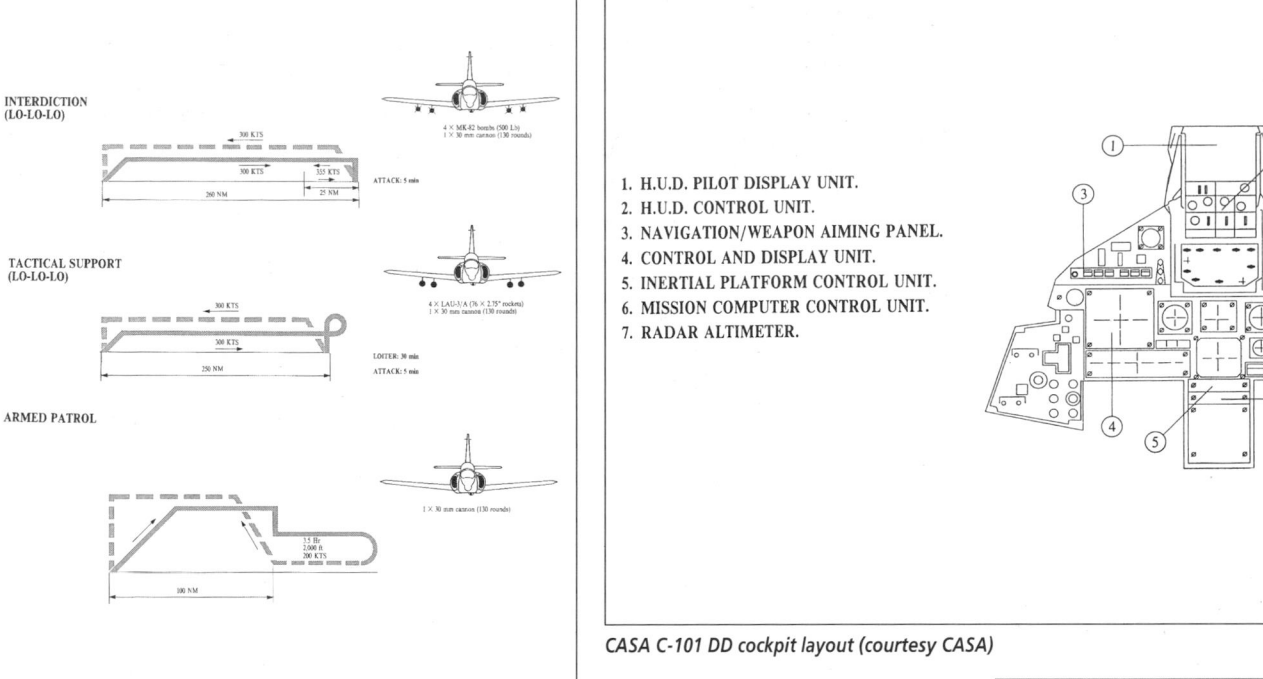

1. H.U.D. PILOT DISPLAY UNIT.
2. H.U.D. CONTROL UNIT.
3. NAVIGATION/WEAPON AIMING PANEL.
4. CONTROL AND DISPLAY UNIT.
5. INERTIAL PLATFORM CONTROL UNIT.
6. MISSION COMPUTER CONTROL UNIT.
7. RADAR ALTIMETER.

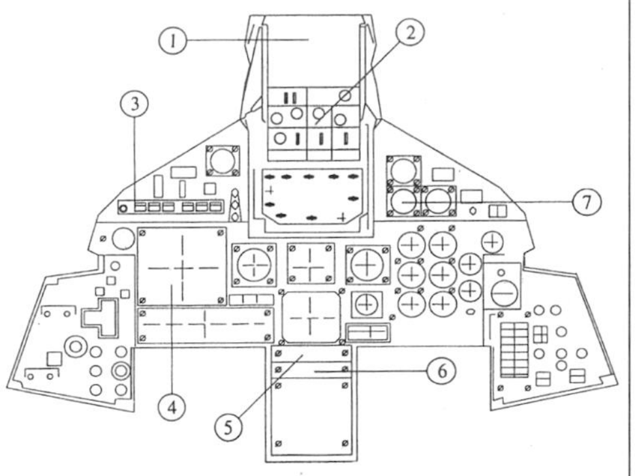

CASA C-101 DD cockpit layout (courtesy CASA)

Andrea intercom, Collins VHF, Magnavox/Collins UHF, Teledyne IFF/SIF and Dorne Margolin ELT. Nav/attack comprises Collins Tacan, VOR/ILS/MK, DME and ADF, plus CASA armament control. C-101 CC has an Avimo gunsight, Lear Siegler gyro platform and Sperry flight director. C-101 DD has a GEC-Marconi FD4513 HUD, Litton inertial platform, Alenia mission computer, Microtecnica air data computer, Alenia radar altimeter, MIL-STD-1553B digital databus, and HOTAS.
Self-protection systems: Optional Gen. Instrument radar warning receiver, and Vinten chaff/flare system.
Wing characteristics: Single-piece, 3-spar, straight, and low mounted, attached to the fuselage by 6 bolts. Use of advanced aerofoil technology offers lower aerodynamic drag with greater thickness and structural strength.
Wing control surfaces: Ailerons (with tabs) and flaps.
Tail control surfaces: Variable incidence tailplane. Elevator and rudder, both with tabs. 2 ventral fins at the rear fuselage increase directional stability (particularly for weapon launching).
Airbrakes: Under the central fuselage, hydraulically operated.
Flight control system: Mechanical, except for hydraulically actuated ailerons and flaps. Electric trim tabs and electrically actuated tailplane incidence.
Construction materials: Conventional, but using modern manufacturing techniques and materials such as numerically controlled integral machining, honeycomb and composites.
Engine: AlliedSignal TFE731-5J in the C-101CC and DD (see Aircraft variants for other engines)
Engine rating: 4,300-4,750 lbf (19.13-21.13 kN) at take off.
Air intakes: Above the wings, ahead of the leading edges, at sufficient height to eliminate all FOD problems.
Flight refuelling probe: None.
Fuel system: Flexible bag fuselage tank and 3 integral wing tanks. Normal capacity (no outer wing tankage) of 1,730 litres; 2,972 lb (1,348 kg). Total internal capacity 2,414 litres; 4,148 lb (1,881 kg). Single pressure refuelling point, providing 1,670 litres in 3 minutes; also independent gravity point for each tank. Allowable 30 seconds inverted flight. No drop tanks.
Electrical system: 28 volt, 9kW DC starter-generator, driven by the engine high-pressure spool acting through the accessory gearbox. 2 x 24 volt, 23 amp-hour ni-cd batteries for emergency use, and can be used to start the engine. 2 x 700 VA static inverters with 115 volt and 26 volt single-phase current outputs for the AC supply for the lighting and navigation equipment.
Hydraulic system: 3,000 psi. In the event of a failure, back-up systems operate the undercarriage, aileron boosters and wheel brakes. Nitrogen reservoir supplies the pressure needed to lower the under-carriage, the aileron booster subsystem has an accumulator to provide power for roll control in an emergency, and an accumulator provides emergency power for the brakes.
Braking system: Hydraulic brakes, and anti-skid devices.
Oxygen system: Gaseous, in 2 high-pressure bottles, for up to 8 hours for both crew members. An emergency bottle by each seat.

CASA C-101 Aviojet in full camouflage, with a gun pod and underwing stores

DETAILS FOR C-101 CC AND DD.

Principal dimensions:
Wing span: 34 ft 9.5 ins (10.6 m)
Maximum length: 41 ft (12.5 m)
Maximum height: 13 ft 11.5 ins (4.25 m)

Wings:
Aerofoil section: NORCASA-15
Area: 215.28 sq ft (20 m^2)
Aspect ratio: 5.618
Incidence: 1°
Dihedral: 5°

Tail unit:
Tailplane span: 14 ft 2 ins (4.32 m)
Tailplane area: 37.028 sq ft (3.44 m^2)

Undercarriage:
Type: Retractable, with nosewheel
Wheel track: 10 ft 5 ins (3.18 m)

Weights:
Empty, operating: 7,650 lb (3,470 kg)
Typical training weight: 9,590 lb (4,350 kg) with 50% normal fuel
Maximum take-off and landing: 13,889 lb (6,300 kg)

Performance:
Maximum dive speed: Mach 0.8
Maximum speed: 450 kts (518 mph) 833 km/h
Take-off speed: 110 kts (127 mph) 204 km/h
Undercarriage retraction speed: 200 kts (230 mph) 370 km/h
Stall speed: 85 kts (98 mph) 158 km/h, with flaps
Landing speed: about 90 knots (104 mph) 167 km/h
Take-off distance: 1,838 ft (560 m)
Landing distance: 1,575 ft (480 m)
Maximum climb rate: 6,400 ft (1,950 m) per minute
Time to 25,000 ft (7,620 m): 6 minutes 30 seconds
Roll rate: 180° per second
G limits: +7.5, -3.9
Maximum sustained load factor: 4.6
Ceiling: 44,000 ft (13,400 m)
Training mission time: 2 hours 15 minutes, with full normal fuel
Range with full fuel: 2,000 naut miles (2,300 miles) 3,700 km
Duration: 7 hours

Aircraft variants:
C-101EB trainer, used by Spain as the E.25 Mirlo. 3,500 lbf (15.57 kN) AlliedSignal TFE731-2J turbofan engine.
C-101 BB armed trainer, powered by a 3,700 lbf (16.46 kN) TFE731-3J engine. Used by Chile as the Halcón, and Honduras.
C-101 CC is a higher performing attack and training version, operated by Chile as the Halcón and Jordan. TFE731-5J engine.
C-101 DD is the latest version, equipped with an integrated nav/attack system built around a HUD (see Avionics). TFE731-5J engine. The Continuously Computed Impact Point (CCIP) mode for air-to-ground attack and the Continuous Tracking (CT) and Continuous Computed Impact Line (CCIL) modes for air-to-air combat, enable training in most modern combat techniques.

CASA C-212 M Patrullero

Role: Anti-submarine, maritime patrol, counter-insurgency, search and rescue, and electronic warfare variants of the Aviocar STOL transport.

★ Aims
★ See C-212 Aviocar entry in the Freighters section for more general Aims and Development.
★ High-wing configuration, together with FOD resistant engines and tough, wide-track undercarriage with low-pressure tyres, offer easy operation from unpaved airstrips (up to 150 passes over CBR = 3.5).
★ Good low-altitude flight capability, good cabin visibility, and over 9 hours endurance (with drop tanks) for special missions.
★ Possible use of FLIR, search radar and related systems, plus weapons capability.
★ Effective for electronic warfare, including electronic support measures, electronic countermeasures, electronic intelligence, and airborne early warning. Other missions can include photogrammetric, navigation training, and geophysical survey.
Sales/users: Derived from the 100, 200 and the latest 300 series Aviocar. Operators in early 1995 were Angola (MP), Argentina (coast guard, C-212 MP), Jordan (survey), Mexico (navy, MP), Portugal (MP and DE), Spain (customs MP, air force MP/DE), Sudan (MP), Sweden (navy, MP but used also for ASW), Uruguay (MP), and Venezuela (navy, MP).

CASA C-212 MP operated by the Prefectura Naval Argentina, based on the latest Aviocar Series 300 with winglets. Note the underwing auxiliary tanks. Weapon outriggers have been removed

Crew: 2 pilots, plus a radar operator and 2 observers (with use of bulged windows) in the main maritime patrol version; pilots plus a radar/ESM operator, tactical controller with MAD, and acoustic controller, plus 1 more for anti-submarine warfare; or pilot plus up to 4 persons in the main cabin of the photogrammetric version.
Fixed guns: None.
Number of weapon pylons: 2, on fuselage outriggers.
Expendable weapons and equipment: 1,102 lb (500 kg) load on the outrigger pylons for 2 Sea Skua anti-ship missiles, 2 Mk 46 Sting Ray smart torpedoes, 2 bombs of up to 250 kg each, LAU-3A or LAU-32 rocket launchers, 20-mm cannon pods, or 2 x 12.7 or 2 x twin 7.62-mm machine-gun pods. Equipment for the maritime patrol and anti-submarine versions also includes sonobuoys and smoke markers.
Radar: See below and Aircraft variants.
Flight/weapon system avionics/instrumentation: Communications equipment includes interphone, 2 VHF, HF and ATC/transponder. Navigation includes 2 VOR/ILS, 2 ADF, DME and weather radar. Flight control includes AFCS and radio altimeter. Optional avionics include VHF/UHF-AF/FM comm, IFF/SIF, VLF/Omega, Tacan and an emergency locator transmitter. See also Aircraft variants.

DETAILS AS FOR C-212 AVIOCAR IN THE AIRLINERS SECTION. The following differences come from specific CASA C-212 M literature.

Weights:
Maximum take-off: 17,637 lb (8,000 kg)
Normal take-off weight: 16,975 lb (7,700 kg)
Maximum landing weight: 16,424 lb (7,450 kg)
Maximum payload: 5,952 lb (2,700 kg)
Maximum weapon load: 1,102 lb (500 kg)

Performance:
Maximum cruise speed: 190 kts (219 mph) 352 km/h
Take-off distance over a 50 ft (15 m) obstacle: 1,884 ft (574 m)
Landing distance over a 50 ft (15 m) obstacle: 1,703 ft (519 m)
Maximum climb rate: 1,600 ft (488 m) per minute
Ceiling: 26,000 ft (7,925 m), or 11,400 ft (3,475 m) on 1 engine
Range with full internal/external fuel: 1,370 naut miles (1,577 miles) 2,537 km
Range with full payload: 430 naut miles (495 miles) 796 km
Search duration: over 9 hours, with drop tanks

Fuel system: 2,000 litres (usable) in the wings, plus 1,000 litres in 2 underwing drop tanks.

Aircraft variants:
Maritime patrol version (MP) has a 360° APS-128 search radar in the nose radome (can be housed under the fuselage, but not typically), with options including FLIR. Also used for search and rescue. Sonobuoys, smoke markers and a searchlight. Bulged observers' windows. Radar operator is positioned immediately behind the flight deck.
Electronic warfare versions for ESM, electronic counter-measures (including jammers), electronic intelligence, and airborne early warning.
Photogrammetric version.
Anti-submarine version is designed to have a 360° search radar under the fuselage, magnetic anomaly detector (MAD), sonobuoys, ESM, on-top position indicator, and IFF/SIF. This version was not among the cabin layout drawings received from CASA. Not believed to be in use.

FFA (Sweden)

Full name: Flygtekniska Försöksanstalten (Aeronautical Research Institute of Sweden).
Corporate address: PO Box 11021, S-161 11 Bromma.
Telephone: +46 8 634 10 00
Facsimile: +46 8 25 34 81
Telex: 107 25 FFA S
Founded: 1940.
Information: Major General Lars B. Persson (Director General).

● Activities
● Central government agency for aeronautical research in Sweden. Its principal role is to provide scientific support and technical assistance to Swedish Government authorities, to domestic and foreign industries and to other organizations.
● Aeronautical research and testing, as a part of the development of Swedish military and civil aircraft, is the core business. The number of international aerospace customers is also increasing.
● Main areas of research are aerodynamics, structures, acoustics and flight systems.

Industrigruppen JAS (Sweden)

Founded: 1981, by a number of Swedish companies to create an industrial group to develop and produce the Gripen, namely Saab AB (until 1995 known as Saab-Scania, and with 65% programme delivery value), Volvo Aero Corporation (15% delivery value), Ericsson Radar Electronics AB (16% delivery value) and FFV Aerotech AB (4% delivery value). See this section for Saab details, Engine section for Volvo, and Radar section for Ericsson.
International marketing/sales: Saab AB, Saab Military Aircraft and British Aerospace signed a joint venture agreement in June 1995 covering international marketing and sales, export adaptation and production of Gripen.

IG JAS 39 Gripen

First flight: 9 December 1988.
Role: Lightweight multi-role fighter, maritime or ground attack, and reconnaissance aircraft.

★ Aims
★ World's first production combat aircraft of a completely new generation.
★ First multi-role fighter combining interceptor, attack and reconnaissance roles in a single aircraft.
★ One aircraft to perform fighter, attack and reconnaissance missions, with the same pilot. By push-button control, the pilot chooses the system function in the computer programs, giving the Gripen the characteristics needed for that particular mission.
★ Canard and delta wing configuration with a large number of control surfaces and a digital control system to provide unique handling characteristics. High manoeuvrability.

IG JAS 39-2 Gripen painted for advanced tests during 1995 and carrying AMRAAM and Sidewinders

⋆ Small radar cross-section, making detection difficult.
⋆ Totally integrated avionics structure, with a common software language for all important functions.
⋆ Dispersed operation from short and narrow runways, including Sweden's V90 roads under emergency conditions with 2,625 ft (800 m) long and 30 ft (9 m) wide strip segments.
⋆ 8,000 flight hour economic life cycle (calculated from fatigue tests begun in December 1993).
⋆ Under 10 minute combat turnaround by a single technician and 5 conscripts, including refuelling, rearming, essential servicing and inspection. Built-in AUP, for independent alert and engine start-up.
⋆ Built-in test and monitoring system, with any failure localized and displayed on a HDD. Line replaceable units for fast repair. Monitoring system, together with in-depth maintenance analysis (MSG-3), optimizes the balance between preventive and on-condition maintenance.

▲ Development

▲ Mid-1980. Definition phase was initiated.
▲ 3 June 1981. Proposals to the customer, FMV (Försvarets Materielverk – Swedish Defence Materiel Administration).
▲ 30 June 1982. FMV and Industry Group JAS signed a contract to develop Gripen, covering 5 test aircraft and an initial batch of 30 fixed-price production aircraft. Long term intention is to replace AJ, SH, SF, JA and then AJS Viggens plus older J 35J Draken interceptors.
▲ 26 April 1987. Prototype 39-1 roll out, with the first flight at the end of the following year (see First flight).
▲ 2 February 1989. First prototype Gripen was lost in a landing accident.
▲ 4 May 1990-23 October 1991. 4 other prototypes made their maiden flights.
▲ 26 June 1992. Contracts signed for batch 2 production covering 110 aircraft, including development and production of 14 JAS 39B two-seaters and support systems.

IG JAS 39 Gripen armed with wingtip Sidewinders, outboard Mavericks and inboard RBS-15Fs. Note the cannon under the port side of the nose (Hans-Olof Arpfors/Saab)

▲ 10 September 1992. Maiden flight of the first production Gripen (JAS 39.101). Replaced JAS 39-1 for trials.
▲ 8 June 1993. First delivery of a Gripen to the FMV (JAS 39.102, first flown 4 March).
▲ 8 August 1993. JAS 39.102 (second production aircraft) crashed during a flying display in Stockholm. The test pilot ejected safely. Following a Swedish Board of Accident Investigation report (dated 18 August) and implementation of the recommendations, a Government Commission report of 11 January 1994 stated that the programme should be continued. Modified flight control software improves low speed and low altitude handling; new non-linear filter has been added and phase-lag deleted.
▲ 29 December 1993. Flight tests resumed with JAS 39-2.
▲ 1994. During this year, about 85% of the agreed verification work included in Gripen development was completed. 443 test flights took place, representing 70% of the planned total. Firing tests of Rb75 Maverick air-to-surface missile from Gripen were completed at the end of the year. A major part of the cold weather tests had been completed by August, and taxiing in water and slush had also been performed. Weapon tests were undertaken in Northern Sweden.

IG JAS 39A in F7 Wing markings. Note the air intake pylon

▲ 1 September 1994. AMRAAM missiles ordered by the FMV for Gripen, following a governmental decision that July.
▲ February 1995. 2 more production Gripens were delivered, making 5 for F7 Wing.
▲ March 1995. Test Gripens 1 to 4 had completed 2,316 flights, accumulating 3,737 flying hours.
▲ 22 March 1995. New P.11 flight control software was flown for the first time, to be incorporated into production aircraft later that year.
▲ 1995-96. Start of pilot conversion at F7's Satenäs Air Force Base, with the first Viggen pilots converting from October 1995 and thereby providing Gripen IOC.
▲ 29 September 1995. Roll-out of the JAS 39B. First flight expected 1996.
▲ 1997. Full F7 operational capability with Gripen.
▲ 1998. First delivery of a production JAS 39B.
▲ 2002. Delivery of the 140th Gripen anticipated.

Sales/users: 5 test aircraft, plus 140 production aircraft under batches 1 and 2 to be used by 8 operational squadrons (total includes 14 JAS 39Bs – see Development). Third production batch of 120 Gripens will be to JAS 39C standard, with an eventual intention to provide for 280-300 aircraft and 16 operational squadrons. JAS 39.108 flew on 11 April 1995. First deliveries to F7 Wing (home base at Satenäs) in 1994, though initially operated from Linköping and used to train ground personnel. Further early production aircraft based at FMV's Malmen and used by F7's TU39 tactical development squadron. Test aircraft No 2 (39-2) has been used for opening up the speed and altitude flight envelope, weapon and separation tests (with dispenser pod, drop tanks, and Maverick, Sidewinder and RBS15 missiles), and flutter tests with all load alternatives. It was later converted for spin tests. Test aircraft No 3 (39-3) is a complete system aircraft with radar and full presentation equipment, and has been used for testing radar, weapons and navigation systems. No 4 (39-4) was primarily for testing performance and engine operation (including in-flight engine restart tests in 1993). No 5 (39-5) has similar functions to No 3. Aircraft 39.101 is the first production Gripen fitted with data acquisition equipment and used for testing production functions. By September 1995, 12 production Gripens had been delivered and 15 from batch 2 were in structural or final assembly. The first JAS 39-B two-seater was rolled out that month. Production is building to 20 aircraft a year. On 13 September 1995 the Hungarian Government and Saab signed an MoU which included the purchase of Gripens.

Crew: Pilot, or 2 crew for JAS 39B.

Cockpit: 0.7 ins (17 mm) longer and redesigned HOTAS centrally-mounted hand-stick controller has replaced the original stick to improve pilot comfort. Identical cockpits in the JAS 39B, except the HUD is omitted from the rear cockpit but, instead, the front pilot's HUD and exterior view can be presented on the rear cockpit's Flight Data Display.

Crew escape: Martin Baker S10LS zero-zero ejection seats.

Fixed guns: 27-mm Mauser Bk27 cannon, which can operate in an automatic radar-guided aiming mode.

Number of pylons: 9, comprising 4 under the wings, 2 at the wingtips, 2 under the air intakes (principally for avionics pods), and 1 under the fuselage

Expendable weapons and equipment: Wingtip Rb 74 (AIM-9L) Sidewinder air-to-air missiles (plus cannon) is the basic armament of all models. Additional armament can include AMRAAM air-to-air (Mica is an option), RBS-15F anti-ship, Rb75 Maverick air-to-surface or other missiles, DWS39 cluster weapons dispensers, conventional or retarded bombs, rockets and more.

Additional stores: Camera and sensor pods (reconnaissance and electronic warfare).

Radar: Ericsson PS-05/A pulse-Doppler.

Flight/weapon system avionics/instrumentation: Ericsson DS80E system

DETAILS FOR JAS 39A, *WITH JAS 39B IN ITALICS.*

Principal dimensions:
Wing span: 27 ft 7 ins (8.4 m)
Maximum length: 46 ft 3 ins (14.1 m), *48 ft 7 ins (14.8 m)*
Maximum height: 14 ft 9 ins (4.5 m)

Undercarriage:
Type: Retractable, with steerable twin nosewheels
Wheel base: 17 ft 1 ins (5.2 m), *19 ft 4 ins (5.9 m)*
Wheel track: 7 ft 10.5 ins (2.4 m)

Weights:
Empty, operating: 14,600 lb (6,620 kg)
Take-off: about 17,639 lb (8,000 kg) clean
Maximum take-off: about 27,558 lb (12,500 kg)

Performance:
Maximum speed: Supersonic at high, medium and low altitudes
Take-off distance: See Aims
G limits: +9

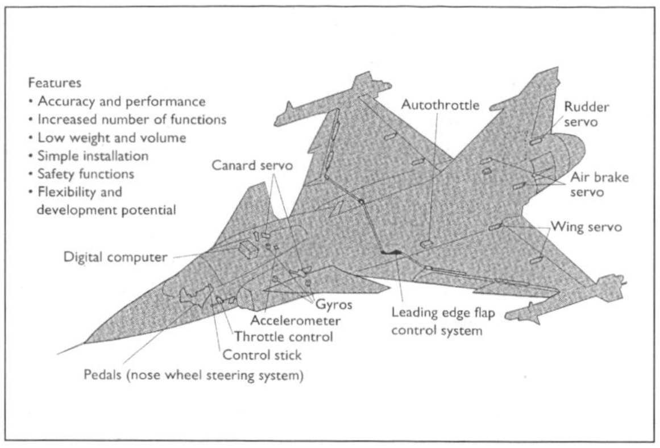

IG JAS 39A Gripen features (courtesy Saab)

comprising radar (see above), EP-17 electronic display system, SDS 80 computing system, and TV camera and video cassette recorder for intelligence gathering and training. 3 1553 databuses. 3 colour head-down displays (in-flight reconfigurable) with soft keys in the front frames for selectable and interchangeable presentations. Wide-angle HUD for both flight and weapon-aiming symbology and, if wanted, raster video images from electro-optical sensors such as FLIR. A helmet sighting system is under development, and a fully integrated helmet-mounted display including weapon aiming symbology is under consideration for the future. See also Cockpit. For attack and reconnaissance, data link permits transfer of tactical information in real or near-real time; radar-derived surface target data can be transferred from one Gripen to another group of "radar silent" attacking aircraft. Honeywell laser inertial navigation system and radar altimeter. (Gripen mock-up has been fitted with a Saab OTIS infra-red search/track system mock-up on the nose.)

Self-protection systems: Ericsson EW suite.

Wing characteristics: Rear-mounted delta, with clipped tips for missile rails. Dogtooth leading edge.

Wing control surfaces: Automatic, 2-section leading-edge flaps. 2 elevons on each wing trailing edge. Any 2 control surfaces (wing, canard or tail) can be lost without affecting the ability to return to base.

Tail control surfaces: Rudder.

Canard: Close coupled, all moving, swept type. Can be heavily tilted for braking during the landing roll.

Airbrakes: Rear fuselage sides. See Canards.

Flight control system: Initially Lear Astronics triplex redundant fly-by-wire; Lockheed Martin is under contract to produce an upgraded control computer.

Construction materials: Carbonfibre used for about 30% of the airframe, including the wings, canards, fin and more. Static load testing of the complete airframe at 230% of load limit has been undertaken.

Engine: Volvo RM12 (F404 type).

Engine rating: 12,141 lbf (54 kN) dry, 18,105 lbf (80.54 kN) with afterburning.

Nozzle: Variable.

Flight refuelling probe: None.

Fuel system: 5,000 lb (2,268 kg) capacity in the wings and fuselage, plus optional drop tanks.

Electrical system: 40 kVA, 400Hz system with generator and transformer. 10 kVA generator for back-up AC supply.

Hydraulic system: 2 independent systems.

Braking system: Disc type on all wheels, and anti-skid devices.

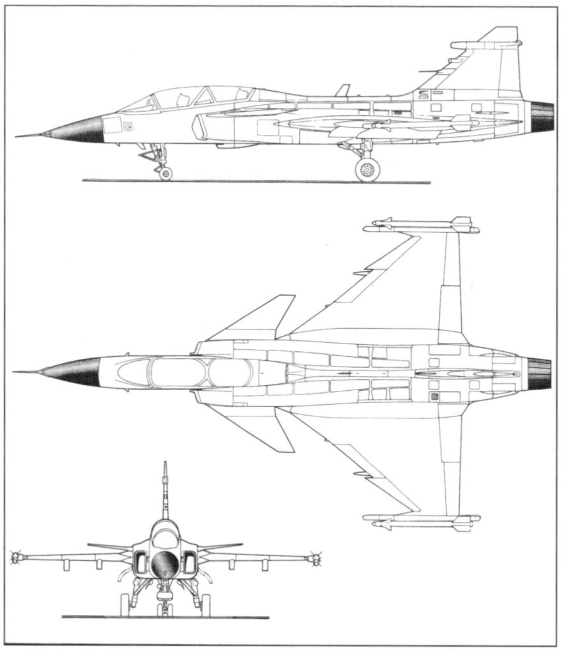

IG JAS 39B Gripen two-seater drawing (Gunnar Jansson/courtesy Saab)

Aircraft variants:

JAS 39A is the initial production single seater, as described.

JAS 39B is the two-seater for tactical training and operational missions requiring a 2-person crew. Identical cockpits, except the HUD is omitted from the rear cockpit (see Cockpit). No internal cannon. Eventual extra tasks for two-seaters could include a flying air-defence tactical control centre role.

JAS 39C is the third-phase upgraded single-seater, with a more powerful engine and higher weights. Engine options under examination include the Volvo RM12 Plus, Eurojet EJ200, General Electric F414 and SNECMA M88-3 (to be decided in 1996). Also upgraded avionics and other systems.

JAS 39X is the export version.

Saab Aircraft AB (Saab Military Aircraft) (Sweden)

Corporate address: S-581 88 Linköping.
Telephone: +46 13 18 00 00, 18 70 00
Facsimile: +46 13 18 18 02, 18 21 42, 18 71 70
Telex: 50040 saabblg s, 50153 SAABAC S
Founded: 16 May 1995 as Saab Aircraft AB, following a split of the former Saab-Scania Group into 2 companies. Saab has its foundations in Svenska Aeroplan AB of 1937, itself formed out of Svenska Aero AB of 1921.
Employees: 7,800.
Information: Kai Hammerich (Chief of Central Information – *telephone* +46 13 18 71 61).

BRIEF DETAILS FOR J35 J DRAKEN. SEE PHOTOGRAPH FOR MORE INFORMATION.

Principal dimensions:
Wing span: 30 ft 11 ins (9.42 m)
Maximum length: 50 ft 4 ins (15.34 m)
Maximum height: 12 ft 9 ins (3.89 m)

Engine:
Volvo RM6C (Rolls-Royce Avon) turbojet, of 17,085 lbf (76 kN) with afterburning

Armament:
1 x 30-mm cannon plus 6 Sidewinder/Falcon air-to-air missiles

Weights:
Maximum take-off: about 27,557 lb (12,500 kg)

Performance:
Maximum speed: over Mach 2
Maximum landing speed: 162 kts (186 mph) 300 km/h
Ceiling: 42,650-49,200 ft (13,000-15,000 m)
Range with full fuel: 742-1,485 naut miles (855-1,710 miles) 1,375-2,750 km

Saab J35 J Draken interceptors, over 60 remaining with the Swedish Air Force, plus SK35 C trainers. To be replaced eventually by Gripens. Last Danish Drakens were withdrawn by Esk 729 squadron on 31 December 1994. Drakens are being replaced in Finland by Hornets, but the type remains active with Austria in 35OE form (see accompanying data table)

■ Facilities

■ Linköping, Malmö, Ödeshög, Göteborg, Jönköping, Huskvarna and Kista.

DIVISIONS

Note. Saab Aircraft AB comprises 5 product companies plus Service Partner, of which Military Aircraft, Dynamics and Training Systems jointly form Business Area Saab Defence. Since 1991, Saab-Scania (and now Saab AB) has been wholly owned by Investor.

Saab Military Aircraft
Address: As for Corporate.
Telephone: +46 13 18 00 00
Facsimile: +46 13 18 18 02
Information: Jan Ahlgren (Public Relations Director – *telephone* +46 13 18 39 07, *facsimile* +46 13 18 54 27).

● Activities

● Gripen development and production (see IG JAS), continuous up-dating of Viggen, and re-engining Sk60 trainers.

Saab Dynamics
Address: As for Corporate.
Telephone: +46 13 28 60 00
Facsimile: +46 13 28 60 06

Saab Sk60 trainers, of which 115 in Swedish service are being re-engined with Williams-Rolls FJ44 turbofans. Modification work and engine replacement is by Saab Military Aircraft and the workshops of the Air Force Flight Training School, F5, at Ljungbyhed. First flown on 6 October 1995, 9 will be delivered in 1996 and the remainder by 1998

● Activities

● Autonomous guided weapons, defence electronics and optronics.

Saab Training Systems
Address: S-561 85 Huskvarna.
Telephone: +46 36 19 46 00
Facsimile: +46 36 14 32 85

● Activities

● Include the BT 46 laser simulator.

Saab Aircraft
Address: As for Corporate.
Telephone: +46 13 18 20 00
Facsimile: +46 13 18 27 22

● Activities

● Commercial aircraft.

Saab Combitech
Address: Box 1017, S-551 11 Jönköping.
Telephone: +46 36 19 40 00
Facsimile: +46 36 19 45 10

● Activities

● Products and systems in the space, industry, and automotive and traffic sectors.

Saab Service Partner

Saab 37 Viggen

First flight: 8 February 1967.
Role: All-weather air defence, attack, reconnaissance and training.

★ Aims

★ Unusual (at the time of design) wing/canard configuration, intended to provide a good combination of high maximum speed, low sensitivity to turbulent air, and low landing speed with retained design simplicity.

★ Wing/canard configuration also chosen to delay "super stall" at high angles of incidence, due to the vortexes on the canard and main wings mutually stabilizing each other.

★ Good take-off and landing performance, allowing straight stretches of road to be used for dispersion under emergency conditions, instead of building large numbers of unaffordable and well-defended air bases. Short landing performance results from a high-lift and low landing speed wing planform, engine thrust reversing that remains efficient even on icy surfaces, automatic speed control in approach, HUD to give high touch-down precision, and an undercarriage dimensioned for carrier-type landings to eliminate the need for a flare-out before touch-down. Landing can be made in about 1,640 ft (500 m), and take-off in a shorter distance.

★ Modular electronic equipment for very rapid replacement.

★ Under 10 minute turnaround time by 5 conscripts under a chief mechanic.

▲ Development:

▲ 8 February 1967. First prototype made its maiden flight.

▲ 2 July 1970. Last of the original 7 prototypes first flew, representing the SK37 trainer.

▲ 23 February 1971. First production Viggen flew, an AJ37 attack aircraft. Deliveries to the Swedish Air Force began that June.

▲ 21 May 1973. First SF37 flew, with production deliveries from 1977.

▲ 19 June 1975. First production SH37 was delivered.

▲ 4 November 1977. Maiden flight of a production JA37. Deliveries started in 1979, with F13 Wing at Norrköping operating the type from 1980.

▲ 29 June 1990. Delivery of the final newly-built Viggen, a JA37 interceptor.

▲ 1995. Continuous series of upgrades over the years, currently up to number 32, has given Viggen double its original combat efficiency.

Sales/users: 329 Viggens were delivered to the Swedish Air Force between 1971 and 1990, the final version as the JA37 interceptor. 14 Viggen squadrons were available in 1995, of which 8 have the JA37 interceptor. However, the first Viggen pilots were converting to Gripens from October 1995. Although JA37s will be the last Viggens to be replaced by Gripens, 75 of the older AJ, SH and SF37 Viggens have also been converted to AJS37 form and redelivered between 1993-95, leaving Sweden with a substantial JA37 and AJS37 force for continued service. (see Aircraft variants).
Details: Principally for JA37, unless stated.
Crew: Pilot, but 2 crew in tandem stepped cockpits on the SK37 trainer.
Cockpit: Throttle used for engine control, select weapons, lock the radar, choose sighting functions, range the sight and insert of span of target (in radar-off mode), extend airbrakes, disengage auto-throttle and control the recorder. See Avionics.
Crew escape: Saab rocket-assisted zero-zero ejection seat.
Fixed guns: 30-mm Oerlikon Automatic cannon in an underfuselage pack (see drawing). Muzzle velocity 1,200 m per second. Fire rate 22 rounds per second.
Ammunition: 150 rounds.
Number of weapon pylons: 7, 4 under the wings and 3 under the fuselage.
Expendable weapons and equipment: 6 Sky Flash

DETAILS FOR JA37.

Principal dimensions:
Wing span: 34 ft 9.5 ins (10.6 m)
Maximum length: 53 ft 10 ins (16.4 m)
Maximum height: 19 ft 4.5 ins (5.9 m)

Wings:
Area: 495.14 sq ft (46 m^2)
Aspect ratio: 2.443
Canard span: 17 ft 10.5 ins (5.45 m)
Canard area: 66.736 sq ft (6.2 m^2)
Dihedral: 0°
Anhedral: 0°

Undercarriage:
Type: Retractable, with twin steerable nosewheels. Tandem mainwheels
Main wheel tyre size: 660 x 165 mm
Nose wheel tyre size: 460 x 140 mm
Wheel base: 18 ft 8 ins (5.69 m)
Wheel track: 15 ft 7.5 ins (4.76 m)

Weights:
Maximum take-off: 44,092 lb (20,000 kg)

Performance:
Maximum speed: over Mach 2
Maximum speed at low altitude: Mach 1.2
Landing speed: 119 kts (137 mph) 220 km/h
Time to 32,810 ft (10,000 m): under 100 seconds
Take-off distance: See Aims
Landing distance: See Aims
Ceiling: 59,055 ft (18,000 m)
Range with full fuel: over 1,080 naut miles (1,243 miles) 2,000 km
Radius of action: 270 naut miles (311 miles) 500 km for a low altitude mission

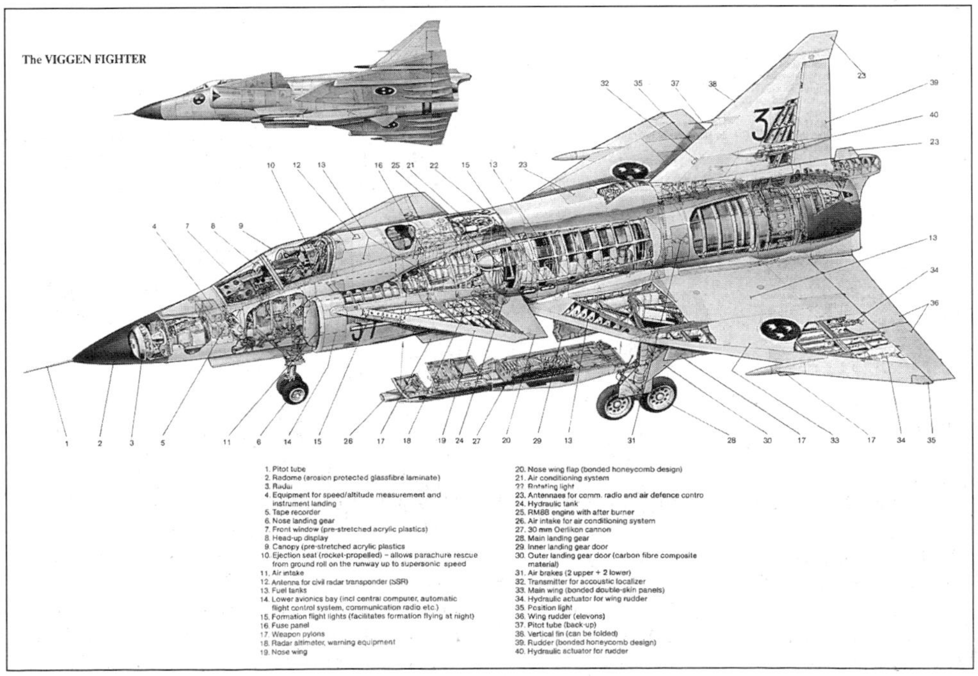

Saab JA37 Viggen drawing (courtesy Saab)

and Sidewinder air-to-air missiles, or 4 launchers or 6 x 135-mm rockets each to attack ground or sea targets. See Aircraft variants for expanded choices.
Additional stores: Reconnaissance pods, etc (see Aircraft variants).
Radar: Ericsson PS-46/A pulse-Doppler, with medium pulse repetition frequency.
Flight/weapon system avionics/instrumentation: Ericsson EP-12 electronic display system, with 3 CRTs. Also conventional instrumentation. See Aircraft variants. Saab/Honeywell digital automatic flight control system.
Self-protection systems: SATT radar warning system.
Wing characteristics: Rear mounted cranked-arrow delta, with dogtooth leading edge.
Wing control surfaces: 2-section elevons. (See also canard.)
Tail control surfaces: Rudder (fin can be folded).
Canard: Fixed on the air intake side, with trailing-edge flaps.
Airbrakes: 4, 2 upper and 2 lower on the rear fuselage.
Flight control system: Hydraulic.

Saab SK37 Viggen tandem cockpit trainer

Construction materials: Mainly aluminium alloys, with steel for highly stressed parts or areas with high temperatures, titanium for the tailcone and elsewhere, nickel alloys for components taking extremely high temperatures such as the engine outlet, glassfibre reinforced plastics for the radome and other electrical covers, and carbonfibre reinforced plastics for some components. Bonded honeycomb canard flaps and rudder.
Engine: Volvo RM8A in AJS37 and SF/SH37, or RM8B in JA37. Over a 2 year period from 1992, the cost of RM8 maintenance was cut in half.
Engine rating: 14,750 lbf (65.61 kN) dry, 26,000 lbf (115.7 kN) with afterburning for RM8A; 16,200 lbf (72.06 kN) dry, 28,110 lbf (125.04 kN) with afterburning for RM8B.
Flight refuelling probe: None.
Fuel system: Tanks in the wings and fuselage.
Electrical system: 28 volt DC supply with a rectifier and 24 volt ni-cd batteries, and 210/115 volt 400Hz 3-phase AC supply, via a generator.
Hydraulic system: Twin systems, each 3,002 psi.
Braking system: Brakes, with anti-skid devices.

Aircraft variants

AJS37 is a common conversion of 75 AJ, SH and SF early production versions of Viggen, adapting the aircraft to modern technology with a new computer, new reconnaissance equipment and a new mission data entry method. The conversion allows the AJS to undertake air defence, attack or reconnaissance roles with equal capability upon requirement (instead of each previous model having a main task). The new computer allows the AJS37 to be armed with the RBS15F anti-ship missile and DWS39 cluster weapons dispenser, or other missile options. In addition, AJS37 is able to carry an increased interception weapons load. Also, the PLA mission planning system is being introduced in the Swedish Air Force. This system allows the pilot to plan his entire mission while on the ground and enter the data to the AJS's computer via a portable computer memory. It is a first step towards Gripen capability, since interception and reconnaissance missions can be performed by the same aircraft.
JA37 is the fighter version for all-weather air defence, especially at low altitude. Principal missions are ground-vectored intercept, combat air patrol, fighter sweep and attack against ground or naval targets. Taller tailfin, built-in automatic cannon, more powerful engine, different radar and avionics, and reinforced to fly faster at low altitude and for more violent manoeuvring. Additional hydraulic actuator under each wing. Upgrade has involved mainly the computer programs, developed to improve the tactical use of the aircraft. The existing computer has been given increased capacity, mainly to enhance the radar system. The faster memories now installed have also improved the performance of the computer, autopilot and display equipment. The latest version has been fitted with an automatic sighting function, which allows the radar system to send direct signals to the flight control system for better and faster target sighting. Development work on a further upgrade began in 1994, involving change to a more modern computer and a new communications system.
SF37 is a photo-reconnaissance version with camera sight, low and high-altitude cameras, night cameras, infra-red camera, illumination EQ, ECM pod and self-defence missiles.
SH37 is a sea surveillance version. Long-distance camera, night reconnaissance pod, modified radar, ECM pod and self-defence missiles.
SK37 is a tandem cockpit trainer. External fuel tank.

F + W (Switzerland)

Full name: Eidgenössisches Flugzeugwerk, Fabrique Federale d'Avions, Fabbrica Federale di Aeroplani.
Corporate address: CH-6032, Emmen.
Telephone: +41 41 59 41 11
Facsimile: +41 41 55 25 88
Founded: 1934 for aircraft production as EFW. Adopted the brief F + W organization title in 1972 from the 3 separate full names.
Employees: over 600.

● Activities

- Government research and development organization, also undertaking manufacture, component production, maintenance and upgrading.
- Is assembling all but 2 of the 26 F/A-18Cs and 8 F/A-18Ds chosen to replace Swiss F-5Es, plus is developing and constructing low-drag pylons. BAe Hawk Mk 66 assembly has finished.
- Produces components under contract, including A320 airliner wingtips, auxiliary fuel tanks for the Dassault Rafale, and wing slats for McDonnell Douglas MD-80 series of airliners.
- Upgrade of Swiss Mirage IIIS/RSs includes F + W developed small and fixed canards mounted on the air intake sides, new self-protection systems, limited avionics upgrade (including audio and visual warning indicators to highlight potentially dangerous flight situations), Martin Baker Mk 6 zero-zero ejection seats, drag-chute, and provision for underwing/under fuselage auxiliary fuel tanks.
- Manufactures various missiles, including the anti-armour Dragon.

Pilatus Aircraft Ltd (Switzerland)

Full name: Pilatus Flugzeugwerke AG (member of the Oerlikon-Bührle Group).
Corporate address: CH-6370 Stans.
Telephone: +41 63 61 11
Facsimile: +41 61 33 51
Telex: 866 202-PIL CH
Cable: PILATUSAIR STANS
Founded: 1939.
Information: W. J. Cato (Manager, Marketing Services).

● Activities

- In addition to the trainers detailed here, the PC-6 Turbo Porter and PC-12 can be found in the General Aviation section.
- A production line for turboprop trainers could be opened at the Pilatus Britten-Norman subsidiary.

DIVISIONS

Pilatus Britten-Norman Ltd
HQ address: See UK section.

Pilatus PC-7 Turbo Trainer

First flight: 18 August 1978 (production model).
Role: Basic through to advanced flying training, including aerobatic, tactical and instrument.

★ Aims

★ Noise levels at 2,200 rpm: 73 dB(A) aerobatic weight, 79.5 dB(A) utility weight.
★ Approved manoeuvres in aerobatic category are steep turn, looping positive, roll off the top (Immelmann), lazy eight, cuban eight, climbing half-roll, aileron roll, barrel roll, hesitation roll, slow roll, wing over, inverted flight (30 seconds maximum), and spins. Manoeuvres in utility category are steep turn, looping positive, roll off the top (Immelmann), lazy eight and roll.

▲ Development

▲ 5 December 1978. FOCA type certification, Aerobatic category.
▲ 6 April 1979. FOCA type certification, utility category.
Sales/users: Several hundred built. Operators include the forces of Angola, Austria, Bolivia, Botswana, Chile (navy), Guatemala, Iran, Iraq, Malaysia, Mexico, Myanmar, Netherlands, Suriname, Switzerland and UAE.
Crew: Student pilot and instructor in tandem. Solo flights from the front cockpit.
Cockpit: 55 lb (25 kg) of baggage.
Crew escape: Optional Martin Baker CH 15A ejection seats.
Fixed guns: None.
Number of weapon pylons: 6; 551 lb (250 kg) inboard, 353 lb (160 kg) centre and 243 lb (110 kg) outboard capacities per wing.

DETAILS FOR PC-7.

Principal dimensions:
Wing span: 34 ft 1.5 ins (10.4 m)
Maximum length: 32 ft 1 ins (9.775 m)
Maximum height: 10 ft 6.5 ins (3.21 m)

Wings:
Aerofoil section: NACA 64_2A-415, 64_1A-612 (root/tip)
Area: 178.68 sq ft (16.6 m^2)
Aspect ratio: 6.516
Dihedral: 7°

Undercarriage:
Type: Retractable, with castering nosewheel. Electric operation, with manual back-up
Wheel base: 7 ft 7 ins (2.31 m)
Wheel track: 8 ft 4 ins (2.54 m)

Weights:
Empty*: typically 2,976 lb (1,350 kg), but depends on avionics fit
Maximum take-off: 4,189 lb (1,900 kg) *aerobatic*, 5,952 lb (2,700 kg) *utility*, with underwing stores
Maximum landing weight (FAR 23): 4,189 lb (1,900 kg) *aerobatic*, 5,652 lb (2,700 kg) *utility* with underwing stores, 10 ft (3 m) per second sink rate
Maximum landing weight (MIL SPEC): 3,977 lb (1,804 kg) *aerobatic*, 13 ft (4 m) per second sink rate
Centre of gravity range:
Aerobatic: 18 to 28% MGC
Utility: 22 to 28% MGC

Performance (EAS at maximum operating weights):
Design diving speed: 300 kts (345 mph) 556 km/h
Maximum operating Mach number (MMO): Mach 0.55
Maximum permitted operating speed, and maximum design cruise speed: 270 kts (311 mph) 500 km/h
Design manoeuvring speed: 175 kts (202 mph) 324 km/h *aerobatic*, 181 kts (208 mph) 335 km/h *utility*
Maximum speed with flaps and/or undercarriage extended: 135 kts (155 mph) 250 km/h
Maximum cruise speed: 209-225 kts (241-259 mph) 387-417 km/h, *aerobatic*
Maximum range cruise speed: 150-171 kts (173-197 mph) 278-317 km/h
Stall speed, clean: 71 kts (82 mph) 132 km/h *aerobatic*, 83 kts (96 mph) 154 km/h *utility*
Stall speed, flaps and undercarriage down: 63.5 kts (73 mph) 118 km/h *aerobatic*, 74 kts (86 mph) 137 km/h *utility*
Take-off distance: 787 ft (240 m) *aerobatic* with flaps, 2,559 ft (780 m) *utility* with 6 pylon stores and no flaps, both at sea level
Landing distance: 968 ft (295 m) *aerobatic*, 1,657 ft (505 m) *utility* with 6 pylon stores, with brakes, at sea level
Take-off over a 50 ft (15 m) obstacle: 1,312-1,936 ft (400-590 m) *aerobatic*, 3,871-5,906 ft (1,180-1,800 m) *utility* with 6 pylon stores, both at sea level to 8,000 ft (2,440 m)
Landing over a 50 ft (15 m) obstacle: 1,673-2,051 ft (510-625 m) *aerobatic*, 2,625-3,248 ft (800-990 m) *utility* with 6 pylon stores, both at sea level to 8,000 ft (2,440 m)
Maximum climb rate: 2,150 ft (655 m) per minute *aerobatic*, 1,290 ft (393 m) per minute *utility* with 6 pylon stores, at sea level
G limits: +6, -3 *aerobatic*; +4.5, -2.25 *utility*; +2 with flaps
Ceiling: 25,000 ft (7,620 m) *operating*, 33,000 ft (10,000 m) *service*
Still air range with full fuel: 407-730 naut miles (468-840 miles) 754-1,353 km, sea level to 20,000 ft (6,100 m) altitude, with reserve
Still air duration: 1 hour 54 minutes at sea level and maximum cruise speed, to 4 hours 22 minutes at 20,000 ft (6,100 m) and maximum range cruise speed

*Empty weight is defined as the complete aircraft, without usable fuel, and no crew, baggage or underwing stores, but including engine oil and unusable fuel

Pilatus PC-7s with drop tanks under the wings, ready for long-distance delivery

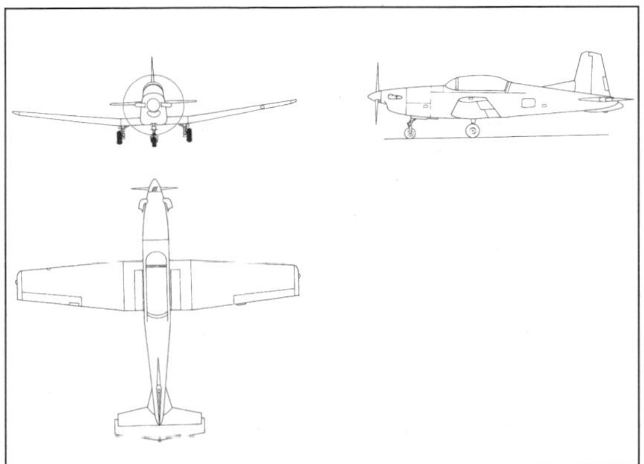

Pilatus PC-7 drawing (courtesy Pilatus)

Expendable weapons and equipment: 2,293 lb (1,040 kg) total permissible pylon load.
Flight/weapon system avionics/instrumentation: Optional ranges of communications and navigation avionics. Standard instrumentation in each cockpit includes an airspeed indicator, attitude indicator, turn and bank indicator, altimeter, vertical speed indicator, angle of attack indexer, magnetic compass, trim position indicators and much more.
Self-protection systems: Swiss Air Force aircraft use the Ericsson Erijammer pod for ECM training.
Wing characteristics: Straight, low mounted, with dihedral outboard of the centre section.
Wing control surfaces: Ailerons with tabs, and split flaps.
Tail control surfaces: Elevators and rudder, with tabs.
Flight control system: Manual, but with electrically actuated (mechanically operated) flaps and electric tabs.
Construction materials: Aluminium alloy. Single-piece wing formed by a main spar, auxiliary spar, ribs and stringer-reinforced skin.
Engine: Pratt & Whitney Canada PT6A-25A turboprop, with a 7 ft 9 ins (2.362 m) Hartzell HC-B3TN-2 constant-speed propeller.
Engine rating: 560 shp (417.6 kW).
Air intakes: Engine intake air inertial separation system for ice protection.
Fuel system: 474 litres of usable fuel in 2 tanks. 30 seconds maximum inverted flight due to a 12 litre aerobatic tank. Can carry 2 x 152 or 240 litre drop tanks.
Electrical system: 28 volt DC supply via dual-role starter-generator, and a secondary 24 volt supply using a 24 volt 40 amp-hour ni-cd battery. 2 (main and stand-by) AC output static inverters, each providing 2 outputs of 115 volt/400Hz and 26 volt/400Hz.
Hydraulic system: For brakes only (see below).
Braking system: Hydraulic on mainwheels.
De-icing system: See air intakes. Electrically heated pitot tube, static ports, fuel sense lines and angle-of-attack transmitter. Optional propeller de-icing. Flight into known or forecast icing conditions is not approved.
Oxygen system: Gaseous.

Pilatus PC-7 Mk II

First flight: 28 September 1992.
Role: Civil and military trainer (see PC-7).

★ Aims

★ Based on the PC-7 but developed to include an advanced airframe with stepped cockpits, better aerodynamics (and including an improved tail unit), improved handling qualities and higher manoeuvrability, a robust undercarriage for grass operation and featuring nosewheel steering, advanced cockpit layout, more powerful engine with a 4-blade propeller, addition of an airbrake and standard ejection seats, and improved access for easier maintenance.

DETAILS FOR PC-7 MK II.

Principal dimensions:
Wing span: 33 ft 2.5 ins (10.12 m)
Maximum length: 33 ft 3 ins (10.13 m)
Maximum height: 10 ft 8.5 ins (3.26 m)

Wings:
Area: 175.34 sq ft (16.29 m^2)
Aspect ratio: 6.287

Tail unit:
Tailplane span: 12 ft 2 ins (3.7 m)

Undercarriage:
Type: Retractable, with steerable nosewheel
Wheel base: 7 ft 7 ins (2.312 m)
Wheel track: 8 ft 4 ins (2.54 m)

Weights:
Empty: typically 3,682 lb (1,670 kg), but depending on avionics fit
Maximum take-off: 4,960 lb (2,250 kg) *aerobatic*, 5,952 lb (2,700 kg) *utility*

Performance (aerobatic weight, ISA, at sea level unless stated):
Maximum operating speed: 300 kts (345 mph) 555 km/h
Maximum cruise speed at 10,000 ft (3,050 m): 250 kts (288 mph) 463 km/h
Stall speed: 79 kts (91 mph) 147 km/h *clean*, 70 kts (81 mph) 130 km/h *with flaps and undercarriage down*
Take-off distance over a 50 ft (15 m) obstacle: 1,740 ft (530 m)
Landing distance over a 50 ft (15 m) obstacle: 1,592 ft (485 m)
Maximum climb rate: 2,705 ft (824.5 m) per minute
G limits: +7, -3.5 *aerobatic*; +4.5, -2.25 *utility*
Range with full fuel: over 770 naut miles (886 miles) 1,426 km at 25,000 ft (7,620 m) and cruise power

Pilatus PC-7 Mk II demonstrator with South African Air Force marking

▲ Development

▲ 1992. Conceived initially to meet a South African Air Force requirement for a Harvard replacement.
▲ 1993. Ordered by South Africa against competition from the indigenous Atlas ACE.
▲ 1994. Production began.

Sales/users: 60 ordered by South Africa (to replace over 100 surviving Harvards).
Crew: 2, in tandem, the rear seat raised.
Crew escape: Martin Baker CH11A ejection seats fitted as standard.
Fixed guns: None.
Number of weapon pylons: 2 "wet" pylons on SAAF aircraft, for drop tanks only.
Flight/weapon system avionics/instrumentation: Improved avionics and layout, including optional HUD.
Airbrake: Under the fuselage, directly aft of the wing.
Engine: Pratt & Whitney Canada PT6A-25C turboprop, with an 8 ft (2.43 m) 4-blade propeller.
Engine rating: 700 shp (522 kW) cruise.
Fuel system: 470 litres in 2 wing tanks, plus a 12 litre aerobatic tank allowing 30 seconds of inverted flight. Optional 155 or 246 litre drop tanks.
Hydraulic system: 3,002 psi for undercarriage operation and steering, and airbrake.

Pilatus PC-9 and PC-9 Mk II

First flight: 7 May 1984.
Role: Basic to advanced flying training, and target towing.

★ Aims

★ Approved manoeuvres in aerobatic category are stall turn, steep turn, loop positive, roll off the top (Immelmann), lazy eight, cuban eight, vertical roll, rolling turn, climbing half-roll, aileron roll, barrel roll, hesitation roll, slow roll, wing over, inverted flight (60 seconds maximum), erect spin and Derry turn. Manoeuvres with underwing stores are steep turn, loop positive, roll off the top (Immelmann), chandelle, aileron roll, barrel roll, cuban eight and lazy eight.

▲ Development

▲ 19 September 1985. FOCA type certificate gained in the aerobatic category.
▲ 2 April 1987. FOCA type certificate gained for operation with underwing stores installed.

Sales/users: In addition to non-military sales, PC-9s are operated by the forces of Angola, Australia (assembled locally), Myanmar, Saudi Arabia (original 30, plus 20 more ordered in late 1994), Switzerland, Thailand, USA (army, non-operational chase aircraft), and others. German plus Swiss Air Force aircraft undertake target-towing roles. The expected South Korean purchase of PC-9s has been withdrawn (with a review by the South Korean Government in 1997). The PC-9 Mk II was also entered by Raytheon-Pilatus in the US military JPATS competition as the Beech Mk II, being announced winner on 22 June 1995. Up to 711 will be built for the USAF and US Navy a Raytheon's Wichita works, for delivery to the forces between 1999 and 2017.

Expendable weapons and equipment: 2,293 lb (1,040 kg) total permissible load.
Flight/weapon system avionics/instrumentation: Except for the audio system, the communication system is optional. Standard navigation system comprises a pitot-static system with Mach/airspeed indicators, altimeters, vertical speed indicators, angle of attack system, attitude indicators and stand-by magnetic compass. Other navigation equipment is optional. Each cockpit is equipped with an engine and secondary display panel (ESDP) with liquid crystal displays. PC-9 Mk II has a steerable FLIR system, which displays images in either cockpit.
Wing characteristics: Straight, low mounted, with dihedral outboard of the centre section.
Wing control surfaces: Ailerons with tabs, and split flaps.

DETAILS FOR PC-9.

Principal dimensions:
Wing span: 33 ft 2.5 ins (10.124 m)
Maximum length: 33 ft 4.5 ins (10.175)
Maximum height: 10 ft 8 ins (3.26 m)

Wings:
Aerofoil section: PIL15M825, PIL12M850 (root/tip)
Area: 175.34 sq ft (16.29 m^2)
Aspect ratio: 6.292
Incidence: 1°
Dihedral: 7°

Tail unit:
Tailplane span: 11 ft 2 ins (3.4 m)
Tailplane area: 19.375 sq ft (1.8 m^2)

Undercarriage:
Type: Retractable, with steerable nosewheel
Wheel base: 7 ft 7 ins (2.312 m)
Wheel track: 8 ft 4 ins (2.54 m)

Weights:
Empty*: typically 3,715 lb (1,685 kg), depending on avionics fit
Maximum take-off: 4,960 lb (2,250 kg) aerobatic, 7,055 lb (3,200 kg) with underwing stores
Maximum landing weight: 4,960 lb (2,250 kg) aerobatic, 6,834 lb (3,100 kg) with underwing stores
Centre of gravity range:
Aerobatic: 22 to 30% MAC
Utility: 24 to 28% MAC

Performance (EAS at maximum operating weights):
Design diving speed: 360 kts (414 mph) 666 km/h
Design diving Mach number: Mach 0.73
Maximum operating Mach number (MMO): Mach 0.68
Maximum operating speed: 320 kts (368 mph) 593 km/h
Design cruise speed: 320 kts (368 mph) 593 km/h
Maximum speed with flaps and/or undercarriage extended: 150 kts (173 mph) 278 km/h
Maximum cruise speed: 298 kts (343 mph) 552 km/h at 25,000 ft (7,620 m)
Long-range cruise speed: 208 kts (240 mph) 385 km/h at 25,000 ft (7,620 m)
Manoeuvring speed: 210 kts (242 mph) 389 km/h, 200 kts (230 mph) 370 km/h with underwing stores
Stall speed, clean: 79 kts (91 mph) 146 km/h, 93 kts (107 mph) 173 km/h with underwing stores
Stall speed, flaps and undercarriage down: 70 kts (81 mph) 130 mph, 86 kts (100 mph) 160 km/h with underwing stores
Take-off distance: 755 ft (230 m) at sea level, aerobatic
Landing distance: 1,378 ft (420 m) at sea level, aerobatic
Take-off over a 50 ft (15 m) obstacle: 1,230 ft (375 m) at sea level, aerobatic
Landing over a 50 ft (15 m) obstacle: 1,772 ft (540 m) at sea level, aerobatic
Maximum climb rate: 4,100 ft (1,250 m) per minute at sea level, 3,100 ft (945 m) per minute at 10,000 ft (3,050 m)
G limits: +7, -3.5 aerobatic; +4.5, -2.25 with underwing stores; +2, -0 with flaps and undercarriage extended
Ceiling: 25,000 ft (7,620 m) operating, 38,000 ft (11,600 m) service
Still-air range with full internal fuel, at sea level: 358-401 naut miles (412-461 miles) 663-743 km, with reserve
Still-air range with full internal fuel, at 25,000 ft (7,620 m): 732-847 naut miles (843-975 miles) 1,356-1,569 km, with reserve
Duration: 1 hour 19 minutes to 4 hours 6 minutes, on internal fuel and with reserve, depending on speed and altitude

*see PC-7 for basic weight criteria

Pilatus PC-9 operated by the Royal Australian Air Force. 2 were delivered by Pilatus in 1987, followed by kits and parts for 17 units, with the remaining 48 built locally by HDH and ASTA

Details: Principally for the PC-9.
Crew: 2, in tandem stepped cockpits. Pilot in the front cockpit when flying solo.
Crew escape: Martin Baker CH 11A ejection seats, operational from zero height to 40,000 ft (12,200 m), and 60 to 400 kts EAS.
Fixed guns: None.
Number of weapon pylons: 6; 551 lb (250 kg) inboard, 551 lb (250 kg) centre "wet", and 243 lb (110 kg) outboard capacities per wing.
Tail control surfaces: Elevators and rudder, with tabs.
Flight control system: Manual, but with hydraulically operated flaps and airbrake, and electric tabs.
Airbrake: Single, plate type under the fuselage.
Construction materials: Aluminium alloy. Single-piece wing formed by a main spar, auxiliary spar, ribs and stringer-reinforced skin.
Engine: Pratt & Whitney Canada PT6A-62 turboprop, with an 8 ft (2.44 m) constant-speed propeller.
Engine rating: 950 shp (708.4 kW).
Air intakes: Engine intake air inertial separation system for ice protection.
Fuel system: 535 litres of usable fuel in 2 tanks, plus a 12 litre aerobatic tank allowing a maximum 60 seconds of inverted flight. 2 optional 154 litre or 248 litre drop tanks.
Electrical system: 28 volt DC supply via dual-role

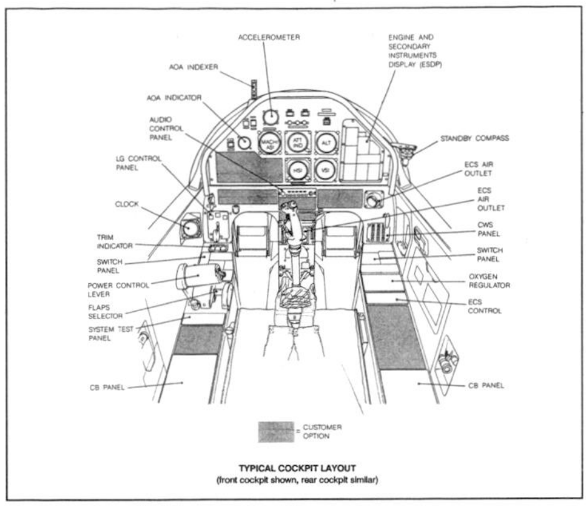

Pilatus PC-9 typical cockpit layout (courtesy Pilatus)

starter-generator, and a secondary 24 volt supply using a 24 volt 40 amp-hour ni-cd battery. 2 (main and standby) AC output static inverters, each providing 2 outputs of 115 volt/400Hz and 26 volt/400Hz.
Hydraulic system: 3,002 psi.
Braking system: Hydraulic mainwheel brakes.
De-icing system: See air intakes. Electrically heated pitot tube, static ports, and angle-of-attack transmitter. Optional propeller de-icing. Flight into known or forecast icing conditions is not approved.
Oxygen system: Gaseous. Emergency oxygen is fitted to each ejection seat.

Aircraft variants:
PC-9 is the standard version, as detailed.
PC-9B is the designation of commercially-operated target-towing aircraft supporting the German forces.
PC-9 Mk II is the version that won the USAF/US Navy JPATS competition in 1995, known as the Beech Mk II. First flown in December 1992. Improved performance due to the 1,250 shp (932.1 kW) PT6A-68 turboprop. Pressurized cockpits, improved birdstrike capability, Martin Baker Mk 16 ejection seats, AlliedSignal state-of-the-art optimized avionics and increased crew comfort, plus maintenance features to reduce still further the operating costs. Can carry several types of ordnance utilizing various kinds of optical sight. Complete day/night training with the addition on FLIR.

Han Hsiang Aerospace Industry Co Ltd (Taiwan)

Corporate address: No 111, Lane 68, Fuw-Shing North Road, Taichung, Taiwan 40722 (*postal address* PO Box 90008-10, Taichung).
Telephone: +886 4 2523051, 2562379, 2562210, 2562325, 2562327
Facsimile: +886 4 2562282, 2562261, 2562268
Telex: 51142AIDC
Founded: March 1969 as AIDC (Aero Industry Development Center). Renamed in 1995.
Employees: About 6,000.
Information: Johnny Hung (Deputy Director, New Business Development).

■ Facilities
■ Chin Chuan Kang for aircraft assembly, development test facilities and flight test centre.
■ Taichung for HQ, aeronautical research laboratory, component factories and avionics factory.
■ Kaoshiung for the aero engine factory.

● Activities
● On 17 May 1995 it was announced that AIDC had been granted government approval to widen its activities into civil and component manufacture. Renamed HHAI, it continues to be state owed at present, but will become privatized by 1999.
● Present products include manufacture of AlliedSignal TFE731 and TFE1042 engines, the AT-3 trainer and the Ching-Kuo Indigenous Defence Fighter, while past programmes have included the Bell UH-1H, Northrop F-5E/F and T53 engine.

DIVISIONS (in 1995)

Aircraft Factory

● Activities
● Over 2,200 employees at 2 complexes with 18 manufacturing plants. Parts fabrication, testing, assembly, maintenance, production planning, support and services facilities.

Aeronautical System Development

● Activities
● Research, development and production of numerous aviation programmes, including AT-3 and IDF.

Aero Engine Factory

● Activities
● Established September 1973 and now with over 600 employees for modern engine manufacturing.

Aeronautical Research Laboratory

● Activities
● Founded in 1939 and became part of the former AIDC in 1969. Water and wind tunnels (subsonic and supersonic), fatigue/load/static testing laboratory, electrical power testing laboratory, flight control centre, dual-dome flight simulator, engine test facility, flight test range, material laboratory, computer centre and more.

Avionics Factory

● Activities
● Founded April 1980. Meets MIL-STD specifications and ISO-9000 production requirements for the IDF avionics systems. 7 current co-production programmes for the IDF including the digital flight control computer, mission computer, radar, integrated air data computer, bus interface unit, Tacan radio and the fuel measuring and indicating control system.

Administration and Operations Support

HHAI AT-3 Tzu-Chung

First flight: 16 September 1980.
Role: Trainer, light attack and target towing.

▲ Development
▲ 1975. Development began of the AT-CH-3.
▲ 1977. Construction of 2 prototypes began.
▲ 1980-81. 2 prototypes appeared, the second making its maiden flight on 30 October 1981.
▲ 6 February 1984. Maiden flight of a production AT-3, with deliveries beginning the following month.
▲ 1989. Production ended after 62 examples.
Sales/users: 62 built between 1977 and 1989, 60 for Air Force service. No exports.

HHAI AT-3 in full camouflage for attack, with a trainer parked just in view. Note the one-piece canopy (Denis Hughes)

Crew: 2, in tandem, the rear seat stepped up by 11.8 ins (30 cm)
Cockpit: Pressurization differential 5 psi. One-piece canopy (see photograph).
Crew escape: Zero-zero ejection seats.
Fixed guns: See below.
Number of weapon pylons: Underfuselage bay for a machine-gun pack or other equipment. 9 pylons for the usual range of light weapons; 6 under the wings (inner "wet" each 1,400 lb, 635kg capacity; centre the same capacity; outer 600 lb, 272 kg capacity), wingtip launchers for AAMs, and 1 under the fuselage (2,000 lb, 907 kg capacity). Total load must not exceed 6,000 lb (2,722 kg).
Additional stores: Include pylon-mounted target systems or drop tanks.
Flight/weapon system avionics/instrumentation: IFR equipped. VOR/ILS and marker beacon indicator. Company produced avionics include IFF (with Teledyne), Tacan (with Collins), undercarriage warning, variable gain control, stability augmentation, radio communication, caution panel, hydraulic pressure/cabin pressure/fuel indicators, and inter-communications. Gunsight and camera.
Wing characteristics: Straight, low-mounted, with slight dihedral from the roots. Thought to be undergoing modification.
Wing control surfaces: Ailerons and single-slotted flaps.
Tail control surfaces: Slab tailplane and rudder (with yaw damper).
Airbrakes: 2 under the centre fuselage.
Flight control system: Hydraulic, but with electric flap actuation.
Construction materials: Mostly metal, including honeycomb sandwich for the ailerons, but with composites airbrakes and some fuselage parts.
Engines: 2 AlliedSignal TFE731-2L turbofans.
Engine rating: Each 3,500 lbf (15.57 kN) take-off, 755 lbf (3.36 kN) cruise at 40,000 ft (12,200 m) and Mach 0.8.
Air intakes: Fuselage sides, ahead and above the wing, with splitter plates.
Flight refuelling probe: None.
Fuel system: 1,630 litres in 2 fuselage bag tanks. 2 optional 568 litre drop tanks under the wings.
Electrical system: 28 volt DC supply via engine-driven starter-generators. 40 amp-hour ni-cd battery for engine start-up. AC supply via 2 static inverters.
Hydraulic system: Dual, each 3,002 psi, with the ailerons, tailplane and rudder served by both.
Braking system: Disc type.
Oxygen system: Liquid.

DETAILS FOR THE AT-3.

Principal dimensions:
Wing span: 34 ft 4 ins (10.46 m)
Maximum length: 42 ft 4 ins (12.9 m)
Maximum height: 14 ft 4 ins (4.36 m)

Wings:
Aerofoil section: Supercritical.
Area: 236 sq ft (21.93 m^2)
Aspect ratio: 4.989
Incidence: 1.5°

Tail unit:
Tailplane span: 15 ft 10 ins (4.83 m)

Undercarriage:
Type: Retractable, with steerable nosewheel that is also extendable to raise the nose by 3.5° during the ground run to reduce the take-off distance
Main wheel tyre size: 24 x 8 ins
Nose wheel tyre size: 18 x 6.5 ins
Wheel base: 18 ft (5.49 m)
Wheel track: 13 ft (3.96 m)

Weights:
Empty, operating: 8,500 lb (3,855 kg)
Flying training take-off: 11,500 lb (5,215 kg) clean
Maximum take-off: 17,500 lb (7,940 kg) for attack

Performance:
Maximum speed: Mach 0.85 at 36,100 ft (11,000 m)
Maximum cruise speed: 476 kts (548 mph) 882 km/h
Stall speed: 100 kts (116 mph) 185 km/h without flaps and undercarriage retracted
Take-off distance: 1,500 ft (460 m)
Landing distance: 2,200 ft (670 m)
Maximum climb rate: 10,105 ft (3,080 m) per minute
Ceiling: 48,000 ft (14,630 m)
Range with full fuel: 1,230 naut miles (1,416 miles) 2,275 km
Duration: 3.2 hours

Aircraft variants:

AT-3 is the basic version, as described, some 20 camouflaged for attack.
AT-3A is a dedicated single-seater for attack and anti-ship roles (latter presumably with Hsiung Feng II), the prototype and so far only confirmed example being prepared from the second AT-3 prototype. Avionics changes included a new nav/attack system. Named Lui-Meng.
AT-3B is an upgrade of a number of AT-3s, retrofitted with AT-3A nav/attack.

HHAI Ching-Kuo indigenous defence fighter

First flight: 28 May 1989.
Role: Air defence fighter, anti-ship and ground attack.

★ Aims

★ Replacement for Taiwan's F-5E/F Tiger IIs and Starfighters, following US government blocks on Northrop F-20 Tigershark licence production and the sale of other advanced fighters.
★ To carry indigenous Sky Sword and Hsiung Feng II missiles.
★ 8,000 flying hour structural life.

HHAI Ching-Kuo indigenous defence fighter (courtesy HHAI)

▲ Development

▲ 1982. IDF programme begun. Allowed assistance came from Garrett (now AlliedSignal) with the engines, General Dynamics with the airframe, Westinghouse with the radar, and others. Newly founded Avionics Factory undertook substantial IDF work.
▲ 28 May 1989. Maiden flight of the first of 4 flying prototypes, as the *10001* single-seater.
▲ 10 July 1990. Maiden flight of the first two-seat and final prototype (*10004*).
▲ 12 July 1991. Second prototype was lost.
▲ 19 November 1993. Last of 10 pre-series Ching-Kuos was received by the Air Force.
▲ January 1994. Production deliveries began. All to be delivered by late 1977.
▲ January 1995. IOC with No 8 Squadron at Chin Chuan Kang, replacing Starfighters.
Sales/users: Original figure of 250 production IDFs was cut to 130 in 1993 following the availability of F-16s and Mirage 2000-5s and reportedly also because of concerns over engine rating. In early 1995, 102 single-seaters and 28 two-seaters remained the number planned, though funding cutbacks could reduce this further. 22 IDFs equip No 8 Squadron, declared operational in January 1995. Offered for export.
Crew: Pilot, or 2 crew in tandem.
Cockpit: 2 AlliedSignal head-down displays plus a head-up display. Side-stick controller.
Crew escape: Martin Baker Mk 12 zero-zero ejection seats.
Fixed guns: 20-mm M61A cannon in the fuselage.
Number of weapon pylons: 6, 2 under the wings, 2 wingtip and 2 under the fuselage.
Expendable weapons and equipment: For air defence, 4 Sky Sword I air-to-air missiles under the wings and on the wingtip launchers, plus 2 Sky Sword IIs under the fuselage. Alternative weapons can include 2 Maverick air-to-ground, 3 Hsiung Feng II anti-ship or other missiles, rocket launchers and bombs.
Radar: Golden Dragon 53 pulse-Doppler, based on the US APG-67(V).
Flight/weapon system avionics/instrumentation: HHAI's Avionics Factory has 7 current co-production programmes for the IDF, including the digital flight control computer, mission computer, radar, integrated air data computer, bus interface unit, Tacan radio and the fuel measuring and indicating control system. Honeywell H423 INS. Gun camera. See also Cockpit.
Wing characteristics: Straight, mid-mounted, with no dihedral/anhedral, blended into the fuselage. LERX. Wingtip launch rails.
Wing control surfaces: Flaperons and leading-edge flaps.
Tail control surfaces: Slab tailplane (tailerons) and inset rudder.
Flight control system: Digital fly-by-wire (Lear Astronics).
Construction materials: Mostly metal, but with some composites including the tailplane.
Engines: 2 AlliedSignal (ITEC) TFE1042-70 turbofans.
Engine rating: Each 6,025 lbf (26.8 kN) dry, 9,460 lbf (42.08 kN) with afterburning.
Air intakes: Oval, with splitter plates, on the fuselage sides.
Flight refuelling probe: None.
Fuel system: Over 2,500 litres. Provision for drop tanks under the wings.

DETAILS FOR CHING KUO.

Principal dimensions:
Wing span: 28 ft (8.53 m) without wingtip AAMs
Maximum length: 47 ft 6 ins (14.48 m) with probe
Maximum height: approximately 13 ft 2 ins (4 m)

Undercarriage:
Type: Retractable, with steerable nosewheel
Wheel base: estimated 16 ft 5 ins (5 m)
Wheel track: estimated 6 ft 7 ins (2 m)

Weights:
Maximum take-off: estimated 20,000 lb (9,070 kg)

Performance:
Maximum speed: estimated Mach 1.65
G limits: +6.5
Ceiling: estimated over 50,000 ft (15,250 m)

TUSAS Aerospace Industries (Turkey)

Full name: TUSAS Havacilik ve Uzay Sanayi AS.
Corporate address: PO Box 18, 06692 Kavaklidere, Ankara.
Telephone: +90 312 811 1800
Facsimile:+90 312 811 1425
Founded: 1984. Joint-venture company, with Lockheed Martin as one shareholder.
Employees: over 2,000.

● Activities

● F-16 production for the Turkish and Egyptian air forces, plus major airframe sections for US production lines. Under the original US Peace Onyx I programme, the Turkish Air Force (THK) has been receiving 136 F-16Cs and 24 F-16Ds since 1987, all but 8 assembled by TAI at Mürted, where 2 Ana Jet Ü F-16 squadrons and the OCU are based. An additional 80 ordered in 1992 and 1994 includes 46 for Egypt, the first delivered on 29 March 1994.
● CN-235M transport production under licence from CASA, with Spain having delivered only 2 of the 52 destined for the THK. These include replacements for C-47s, plus 16 assigned to an electronic warfare role.
● UH-60L Black Hawk production, with TAI assembling 50 of the 95 ordered, mostly for Army service.
● Other work includes aircraft modernization, commuter aircraft development (a 19-passenger aircraft, suited also to freighting, is underway), and work on the European FLA.
● The THK is modernizing its F-4s fleet to have new radar and other improved avionics, for which TAI is involved alongside foreign companies. Plans to upgrade F-5s may be affected by further F-16 purchases.

British Aerospace plc (UK)

Corporate address: Warwick House, Farnborough Aerospace Centre, Farnborough, Hampshire GY14 6YU.
Telephone: +44 1252 373232
Facsimile: +44 1252 383000
Founded: 29 April 1977 by the amalgamation of BAC, Hawker Siddeley Aviation, Hawker Siddeley Dynamics and Scottish Aviation.
Employees: Approximately 50,000.
Information: Locksley C. Ryan (Director of Communications).

DIVISIONS

British Aerospace Defence Ltd
HQ address: Lancaster House, Farnborough Aerospace Centre, Farnborough, Hants GU14 6YU.
Telephone: +44 1252 373232
Facsimile: +44 1252 384812
With:

Military Aircraft Division
HQ address: Warton Aerodrome, Preston, Lancashire PR4 1AX.
Telephone: +44 1772 633333
Facsimile: +44 1772 643724
Information: Maria Gill (Head of Public Affairs and Communications – *telephone* +44 1772 852714, *facsimile* +44 1772 854289).
Also:
Address: Brough, North Humberside HU15 1EQ.
Telephone: +44 1482 667121
Facsimile: +44 1482 666625

Address: Dunsfold Aerodrome, Godalming, Surrey GU8 4BS.
Telephone: +44 1483 272121
Facsimile: +44 1483 200341

Address: Hertford House, Farnborough Aerospace Centre, Farnborough, Hampshire GU14 6YU.
Telephone: +44 1252 373232
Facsimile: +44 1252 383000

Address: Samlesbury Aerodrome, Balderstone, Lancashire BB2 7LF.
Telephone: +44 1254 812371
Facsimile: +44 1254 768000

● Activities
● In addition to the aircraft detailed here, see also Eurofighter 2000, McDonnell Douglas/BAe Harrier II, Harrier II Plus and STOVL Strike Fighter, SEPECAT Jaguar and Tornado in the multi-nation part of this section.

Systems & Services Division
HQ address: Mill Lane, Warton Aerodrome, Preston, Lancashire PR4 1AX.
Telephone: +44 1772 633333
Facsimile: +44 1772 855286

● Activities
● Prime contractor for the Saudi Arabian Al Yamamah contract, was teamed with Eurocopter in proposing the Tiger for the British Army, and has naval interests including Project Horizon , the Common New Generation Frigate for which BAe is a partner in the UK prime contractorship role.

Dynamics Division
HQ address: Six Hills Way, Stevenage, Herts SG1 2DA.
Telephone: +44 1438 312422
Facsimile: +44 1438 753377

Also
Address: Lostock Lane, Lostock, Bolton, Lancashire BL6 4BR.
Telephone: +44 1204 696551
Facsimile: +44 1204 693908

Address: PO Box 5, Filton, Bristol BS12 7QW.
Telephone: +44 1272 693866
Facsimile: +44 1272 692055

● Activities
● Develops and supplies air, ground and ship launched guided weapon systems, including Jernas, Merlin and Seawolf, plus the collaborative Trigat, Active Sky Flash and ASRAAM. A co-operation agreement with GEC-Marconi covers development of the Pegasus conventionally armed stand off missile.

Royal Ordnance Division
HQ address: Euxton Lane, Chorley, Lancashire PR7 6AD.
Telephone: +44 1257 265511
Facsimile: +44 1257 242609

British Aerospace (Systems & Equipment) Ltd
HQ address: Clittaford Road, Southway, Plymouth, Devon PL6 6DE.
Telephone: +44 1752 695695
Facsimile: +44 1752 695500

And:
National Remote Sensing Centre Ltd
Address: Delta House, Southwood Crescent, Southwood, Farnborough, Hampshire GU14 0NL.
Telephone: +44 1252 541464

● Activities
● Navigation, radomes, recorders, motion sensing, weapon sub-systems, tracking and databus equipment, communications and magnetic components. Recent contracts include those from Lockheed Martin for integration of TERPROM digital terrain system into the F-16.

BAe Flying College
HQ address: Prestwick Airport, Ayrshire KA9 2RW.
Telephone: +44 1292 671022
Facsimile: +44 1292 671010

BAeSEMA Ltd
HQ address: Biwater House, Portsmouth Road, Esher, Surrey KT10 9SJ.
Telephone: +44 1372 466660
Facsimile: +44 1372 466566
(jointly owned by BAe and Sema Group plc.)

● Activities
● Integrated logistics support, electronic warfare, reliability engineering, Liftspan CM system, operational analysis, defence facilities engineering and more.

British Aerospace Inc
HQ address: 22070 Broderick Drive, Sterling, Virginia 20166, USA.
Telephone: +1 703 406 2000
Facsimile: +1 703 243 3097

Also:
Government programmes office
1101 Wilson Boulevard, Suite 1200, Rosslyn, Virginia 22209, USA.

BAe Australia
HQ address: 14 Parkway, Technology Park, The Levels, South Australia 5095.
Telephone: +61 8 343 8221
Facsimile: +61 8 349 6629

British Aerospace Airbus Ltd
HQ address: PO Box 77, Bristol BS99 7AR.
Telephone: +44 1272 693831

Also:
Broughton, nr Chester, Clwyd CH4 0DR.
Telephone: +44 1244 522713
Facsimile: +44 1244 523031
Information: Sue Cutts (Manager, Public Affairs).

● Activities
● See Airliners section. Also the FLA military transport programme through Airbus (see Freighters).

British Aerospace Regional Aircraft Ltd*
**Note:* Avro International and Jetstream Aircraft are merging with ATR to form a new regional transport company, as Aero International Regional. Further details of this company can be found under the Aero International Regional heading in the Multi-national part of the Airliners section (which see).

With:
Avro International Aerospace Division
HQ address: Marketing Operations Centre, Chester Road, Woodford, Manchester SK7 1QR.
Telephone: +44 161 439 5050

● Activities
● See Airliners section. See also Fokker of the Netherlands.

Jetstream Aircraft Ltd
HQ address: Preswick International Airport, Ayrshire KA9 2RW.
Telephone: +44 1292 79888

● Activities
● See Airliners and Reconnaissance sections.

British Aerospace Hawk T Mk 1/1A, 50, 60 and 100 series

First flight: 21 August 1974; May 1976 for Mk 50 demonstrator, 1 April 1982 for Mk 60, and 1 October 1987 for Mk 100.
Role: Basic and advanced trainer, with operational air defence and attack roles (see Aircraft variants).

★ Aims
★ Modern, high-subsonic, advanced flying trainer, and also weapons and navigation trainer with potential for further development.
★ Uncompromized configuration, with tandem seating in an "ideal" cockpit.
★ Fuel-efficient turbofan engine.
★ 6,000 flying hour safe fatigue life.

▲ Development
▲ Original design and development was by Hawker Siddeley Aviation (see Founded).
▲ October 1971. HS 1182 selected to fulfil requirement ASR 397, as a replacement for Folland Gnat and Hawker Hunter advanced trainers.
▲ October 1973. HS 1182 given the name Hawk.
▲ 4 November 1976. First deliveries to No 4 Flying Training School at RAF Valley.
▲ 1980. First export deliveries, as Mk 51s for Finland.
▲ 18 November 1981. Winner of a US Navy's VTXTS competition for a new carrier-capable trainer. Became

British Aerospace Hawk Mk 63C for Abu Dhabi

the T-45A Goshawk. Full scale development began in 1984. (See McDonnell Douglas/BAe T-45 Goshawk in the multi-national section).

▲ 13 July 1982. First Mk 60 delivery, as Mk 61 for Zimbabwe.

▲ 19 May 1986. First flight of the Hawk Mk 200 single-seater (which see).

▲ 4 December 1991. First aircraft carrier landing by a Hawk variant, a US Goshawk (which see).

▲ April 1993. First Mk 100 delivery, as Mk 102 for Abu Dhabi.

Sales/users: T Mk 1: UK (176, with 88 redelivered as T Mk 1As). Series 50: Finland (50 Mk 51s and 7 Mk 51As), Indonesia (20 Mk 53s) and Kenya (12 Mk 52s). Series 60: Abu Dhabi (12 Mk 63As, 4 Mk 63Bs plus 4 new Mk 63Cs), Dubai (9 Mk 61s), Kuwait (12 Mk 64s), Saudi Arabia (30 Mk 65s plus 20 65As), Switzerland (20 Mk 66s), South Korea (20 Mk 67s) and Zimbabwe (8 Mk 60s and 5 Mk 60As). Series 100: Abu Dhabi (18 Mk 102s), Indonesia (8 Mk 109s), Malaysia (10 Mk 108s), and Oman (4 Mk 103s). By early 1995 all had been delivered, except for final Mk 109s to Indonesia in 1996. 1 Mk 100 used by BAe for development flying.

Crew: 2 in tandem, with the rear instructor's seat stepped up. Usually flown as a single-seater in combat.

Cockpit: Single-piece windshield with frame, hinging forward for maintenance only. Single-piece canopy with mid arch, sideways (starboard) opening. Rear cockpit has a protective front screen integral with the canopy arch.

Crew escape: Martin Baker Mk 10B zero-zero ejection seats in early aircraft, Mk 10LH later. Canopy fracturing system (miniature detonating cord - MDC).

Fixed guns: None, although a self-contained single 30-mm Aden cannon pod can be carried on the centreline attachment. *Mk 51* uses a 12.7-mm gun.

Ammunition: Up to 150 rounds.

Number of weapon pylons: *T Mk 1/1A* have 3 (2 under the wings and 1 under the fuselage), but with the ability to have 2 more under the wings. *Series 50/60* have all 5 in use, each underwing pylon with a 1,135 lb (515 kg) capacity. *Series 50/60* introduced "wet" pylons and an increased overall load. *Series 100* adds wingtip AAM launch rails, making 7 weapon points. Utilization of twin-store carriers enables *Hawk 100* and *Mk 63A/C* to carry a maximum of 11 stores.

Expendable weapons and equipment: *Mk 1/1A:* typically 1,500 lb (680 kg) of practice bombs or rocket pods on the wing pylons and a gun pod under the fuselage, with optional AIM-9L Sidewinders for *Mk 1A*. *Series 50/60/100* are able to carry an extensive range of NATO and US stores, including gun pod, rocket launchers (68-mm, 81-mm or 100-mm rockets), bombs (250 lb, 500 lb or 1,000 lb), cluster bombs, runway cratering bombs, practice bomb/rocket carriers, air-to-surface missiles (including Maverick) and Sidewinder or Magic AAMs. *Series 100* has standard wingtip launch rails for additional Sidewinders or Magics, although 12 Abu Dhabi *Mk 63s* have also been given new wings of Series 100 type plus the higher-rated engine (becoming *Mk 63As*), as have newly-built *Mk 63Cs*. Maximum warload for *Series 60/100s* is 6,600 lb (3,000 kg). Twin-store carriers can be adopted (see above).

Additional stores: Reconnaissance pod, ECM pod or target-towing system.

Radar: None. See Hawk 200.

Flight/weapon system avionics/instrumentation: Conventional dial-type flight instrumentation on all but *Series 100* aircraft. *T Mk 1/1A* and *Series 50* have UHF, VHF, VOR/ILS/DME and IFF. No HUD. Gunsight. *Series 60* incorporates attitude and heading reference system (AHRS), ISIS gunsight and a comprehensive stores management system. *Series 100* offers an advanced state-of-the-art fit, including wide-angle HUD, new generation weapon aiming computer, and head-down multi-purpose display. HOTAS. Optional FLIR/laser ranging in the nose. Laser inertial navigation. High accuracy air data. MIL-STD-1553B dual redundant digital databus. Development continues to provide laser INS for Hawk.

Self-protection systems: Radar warning receiver. IR flares and chaff on *Series 100*. Possible ECM.

Wing characteristics: Slightly swept, low mounted, with dihedral. 2 spar, single-piece continuous wing structure. Skin with integral stiffeners. Undercarriage accommodated ahead of the front spar, avoiding a cut-out in the main wing box. Fences, stall strips and vortex generators. *Series 100* wing has leading-edge droop to enhance lift and manoeuvrability, and full flap vanes.

Wing control surfaces: Ailerons outboard of trailing-edge flaps (single-slotted plus fixed vane, effectively double slotted); *Series 60* and *100* have 4-position flaps, including combat settings, instead of the earlier 3-position.

Tail control surfaces: Slab tailplane and rudder (with tab). 2 canted ventral underfuselage strakes. Aerodynamic "SMURF" surfaces immediately ahead of and lower than the tailplane on *Series 100* aircraft, intended to inhibit tailplane stall and thereby increase trimming ability in flapped configurations.

Airbrakes: Single petal under the rear fuselage. Cannot be used for landing.

Flight control system: Hydraulic for ailerons, tailplane plus flap actuation. Manual only for rudder, but a powered rudder was introduced on *Series 60/100*, with yaw damper. Electric trimming about all axes.

Fuselage: Manufacture breakdown: cockpit to aft of the rear pressure bulkhead and nose section, centre fuselage, separate intake nacelles, and rear fuselage aft of the wing trailing edge. Equipment (depending on variant) in the nose, under and aft of the rear cockpit, and in the fuselage dorsal spine. Centre fuselage accommodates a large bag fuel tank and intake ducts, the wing being a continuous carry-through structure.

Construction materials: Principally aluminium alloys.

Engine: Rolls-Royce Turbomeca Adour turbofan (see below).

Engine rating: *Mk 1/1A* have Adour 151 of 5,240 lbf (23.31 kN). *Series 50* has Adour 851 of similar rating. *Series 60* has Adour 861 of 5,710 lbf (25.4 kN). *Series 100* has Adour 871 of 5,990 lbf (26.65 kN), as have Mk 63As.

Nozzles: Fixed, plain.

Air intakes: Bifurcated pitots, with vertical bodyside diverters.

Flight refuelling probe: Flight tested on Hawk 100 only.

Fuel system: 1,659 litres in integral wing and centre section tanks, plus fuselage bag tank. *Series 50/60/100* have "wet" inner wing pylons; *Series 50* can carry 450 litre combat drop tanks, and *Series 60/100* can carry 591 litre drop tanks.

Electrical system: Single 9kW DC generator. AC power via 2 x 500 VA inverters. Emergency power from 2 x 18 amp-hour batteries. Increased power on *Series 60* via a single 12kW DC generator, 2 IKVA inverters. 2 batteries supply 20 minutes power for essential services in the event of primary supply failure. *Series 100* has AC power from 2 x 3KVA inverters.

Hydraulic system: 2 independent systems, at 3,000 psi, provide power to aileron and tailplane PCUs. No 1 system also supplies general services (airbrake, undercarriage, flaps and wheel brakes). No 2 system supplies PCUs in the event of No 1 failure. Ram air turbine supplies power in the event of both systems or engine failure.

Braking system: Main wheel brakes, with anti-skid. Drag-chute on most versions but not on RAF *Mk 1/1As*.

Oxygen system: Gaseous, capacity 1,400 litres, for up to 4 hours duration.

BAe Hawk typical mission radius, or duration/ferry range

Version	Weapons	Fuel	Mission	naut miles (miles) km
Series 50	2 x 1,000 lb bombs	internal	Lo-Lo-Lo-Lo	187 (215) 346
	4 x 1,000 lb bombs	internal	Lo-Lo-Lo-Lo	162 (186) 300
	6 x 1,000 lb bombs	internal	Lo-Lo-Lo-Lo	140 (161) 259
	2 x 1,000 lb bombs	+2 drop tanks	Lo-Lo-Lo-Lo	278 (320) 515
	4 x 1,000 lb bombs	+2 drop tanks	Lo-Lo-Lo-Lo	250 (288) 463
	2 x 1,000 lb bombs	internal	Hi-Lo-Lo-Hi	406 (467) 752
	4 x 1,000 lb bombs	internal	Hi-Lo-Lo-Hi	337 (388) 624
	6 x 1,000 lb bombs	internal	Hi-Lo-Lo-Hi	280 (322) 519
	2 x 1,000 lb bombs	+2 drop tanks	Hi-Lo-Lo-Hi	608 (699) 1,126
	4 x 1,000 lb bombs	+2 drop tanks	Hi-Lo-Lo-Hi	500 (575) 926
	Gun + 2 Sidewinders	internal	1 crew, combat air patrol	70 minutes, at 100 naut miles
	Gun + 2 Sidewinders	internal	1 crew, combat air patrol	40minutes, at 200 naut miles
	Gun + 2 Sidewinders	+2 drop tanks	1 crew, combat air patrol	130 minutes, at 100 naut miles
	Gun + 2 Sidewinders	+2 drop tanks	1 crew, combat air patrol	98 minutes, at 200 naut miles
			ferry range	about 1,400 (1,610) 2,593
Series 60	Gun + 4 Sidewinders	+2 drop tanks	air defence, Hi-Hi	2.7 hours at 100 naut miles
			interdiction, Hi-Lo-Lo-Hi.	415 (478) 768
	2 x rocket pods	+2 drop tanks	maritime attack	455 (524) 842
			ferry range	1,575 (1,813) 2,917
Series 100	Gun + 4 Sidewinders	+2 drop tanks	air defence, Hi-Hi	2 hours at 100 naut miles
			close air support	125 (144) 231.5
			interdiction, Hi-Lo-Lo-Hi.	345 (397) 639
		+2 drop tanks	ferry range	1,360 (1,566) 2,519

DETAILS FOR HAWK (NOT HAWK 200).

Principal dimensions:
Wing span: 30 ft 10 ins (9.39 m), 32 ft 7.5 ins (9.94 m) over AAMs
Maximum length: 38 ft 10.5 ins (11.85 m), or 40 ft 9 ins (12.42 m) *Series 60/100*
Maximum height: 13 ft 1 ins (3.99 m)

Wings:
Area: 179.64 sq ft (16.69 m^2)
Aspect ratio: 5.28
Sweepback: 21.5° at 25% chord
Chord at root: 8 ft 8 ins (2.64 m)
Chord at tip: 3 ft (0.91 m)
Dihedral: 2°

Tail unit:
Tailplane span: 14 ft 5 ins (4.39 m)
Tailplane area: 46.6 sq ft (4.33 m^2)
Fin area: 27 sq ft (2.51 m^2), or 28.1 sq ft (2.61 m^2) *Series 100*

Undercarriage:
Type: Retractable, with castering or steerable nosewheel
Main wheel tyre size: 22 x 6.50-10
Nose wheel tyre size: 18 x 5.5-16
Wheel base: 14 ft 9 ins (4.5 m)
Wheel track: 11 ft 5 ins (3.48 m)

Weights:
Empty: 7,700 lb (3,493 kg) approximately *for Series 50*, 8,845 lb (4,012 kg) *Series 60*, 9,700 lb (4,400 kg) *Series 100*
Design trainer take-off: 11,100 lb (5,035 kg) *Series 50*
Maximum take-off: 17,085 lb (7,750 kg) *Series 50*, 20,062 lb (9,100 kg) *Series 60/100*

Performance:
Maximum level Mach number: Mach 0.82 *for Series 100*
Maximum speed (*Series 50*): 540 kts (622 mph) 1,000 km/h clean, or 485 kts (558 mph) 898 km/h with 1 crew, 2 Sidewinders and 60% fuel
Stall speed: 96 kts (110 mph) 177 km/h
Take-off distance: 1,500 ft (457 m) *Series 50* at design trainer weight, ISA+ 15°, or 4,200 ft (1,280 m) at 17,000 lb (7,711 kg) weight
Landing distance: 1,800 ft (549 m) *Series 50*, at 10,000 lb (4,536 kg) weight, or 1,500 ft (457 m) with drag-chute
Time to 30,000 ft (9,145 m): 8 minutes 30 seconds for *Series 50* with 1 crew, gun, 2 Sidewinders and internal fuel, or 6 minutes 54 seconds for *Series 60*, or 7 minutes 30 seconds for *Series 100*
G limits: +8, -4 for *Series 50*, +6 -3 for *Series 100* with 6 x 1,000 lb bombs and 60% fuel
G limit, sustained: 4.6, *Series 50* at sea level, mean combat weight
Ceiling: 46,000 ft (14,000 m) for *Series 60*

British Aerospace Hawk Mk 103 for Oman

British Aerospace Hawk 100 cutaway (courtesy British Aerospace)

Aircraft variants:
Hawk T Mk 1 is the RAF's advanced flying and weapon training version.
Hawk T Mk 1A covers 88 T Mk 1s modified and redelivered to carry AIM-9L Sidewinders on the inner wing pylons and the option of using outer pylons, for an operational point air defence role under emergency conditions or co-operating with radar-equipped Tornados in a Mixed Fighter Force. All returned to service by 1986.
Hawk Mk 50 is the export trainer, with similarly rated engines to the T Mk 1. Higher weights and with limited attack capability.
Hawk Mk 60 is an export variant with greater engine power and higher performance, significant airframe changes (see Wing characteristics and other headings) and increased weapon options.
Hawk Mk 100 has another increase in engine power, greater operational fighter and attack capabilities through improved weapon system management and avionics, and with further airframe changes including a new wing with leading-edge droop to improve manoeuvrability plus manual combat flaps. HOTAS. Provision for nose-mounted FLIR/laser ranging.

British Aerospace Hawk 200

First flight: 19 May 1986 (demonstrator).
Role: Multi-role for air defence, close air support, battlefield interdiction, maritime support, maritime strike, reconnaissance and more.

★ Aims
★ Exploitation of the proven two-seat Hawk design, producing a single-seat, lightweight, subsonic combat variant with significantly increased air-to-air and air-to-ground capability by the provision of radar. Increased fuel load for longer range.

▲ Development
▲ June 1984. BAe private venture decision to enhance the export potential of the Hawk.
▲ 2 July 1986. First demonstrator was lost barely 8 weeks after the first flight, due to G-induced loss of consciousness.
▲ July 1990. First order placed by Oman.
▲ 13 February 1992. Third Hawk 200 flew (the 2nd in April 1987), featuring a complete avionics fit, including radar.
▲ 11 September 1993. First flight of a full production Hawk 200, as a Mk 203 for Oman.
▲ 1995. Development flying with the company demonstrator continued.
Sales/users: Ordered by Indonesia (16 Mk 209s), Malaysia (18 as Hawk Mk 208s), and Oman (12 as Hawk Mk 203s). 2 Mk 200s used by BAe for development flying.
Crew: Pilot.
Cockpit: Smaller canopy with MDC, retaining good field of view. Sideways opening.
Crew escape: Martin Baker Mk 10LH.
Fixed guns: None, but 30-mm gun pod under the fuselage.
Ammunition: Up to 150 rounds.
Number of weapon pylons: 7, as for Hawk 100. Utilization of twin-store carriers enables a maximum of 11 stores to be carried. Maximum 2,000 lb (907 kg) load on each underwing pylon.
Expendable weapons and equipment: Extensive range of NATO and US stores as detailed under the earlier Hawk entry. Normal maximum 6,600 lb (3,000 kg).
Additional stores: Reconnaissance pod, target towing system, etc. Optional ECM pod.
Radar: Westinghouse APG-66H multi-mode radar, offering 8 air-to-surface and 10 air-to-air modes with fixing, target detection and target ranging sub modes. Derivative of the APG-66 in the F-16.

DETAILS FOR HAWK 200.

Principal dimensions:
Wing span: 30 ft 10 ins (9.39 m), 32 ft 7.5 ins (9.94 m) over AAMs
Maximum length: 37 ft 3 ins (11.35 m)
Maximum height: 13 ft 7 ins (4.14 m)

Wings:
Area: 179.64 sq ft (16.69 m^2)
Aspect ratio: 5.28
Sweepback: 21.5° at 25% chord
Chord at root: 8 ft 8 ins (2.64 m)
Chord at tip: 3 ft (0.91 m)
Dihedral: 2°

Tail unit:
Tailplane span: 14 ft 5 ins (4.39 m)
Tailplane area: 46.6 sq ft (4.33 m^2)

Weights:
Empty: 9,810 lb (4,450 kg)
Maximum take-off: 20,060 lb (9,100 kg)

Performance:
Maximum speed: 540 kts (621 mph) 1,000 km/h at sea level
Take-off distance: 2,070 ft (631 m)
Landing distance: 1,960 ft (597 m)
Time to 30,000 ft (9,145 m): under 7.5 minutes
G limits: +8, -4
G limit with 1,102 lb (500 kg) load on individual underwing pylons: +8
Sustained G limit: over +5, at 300 kts at sea level
Ceiling: 44,500 ft (13,500 m)

BAe Hawk 200 typical mission radius, or duration/ferry range

Weapons	Fuel	Mission	naut miles (miles) km
4 x 1,000 lb bombs, gun and 2 Sidewinders	internal	close air support	100 (115) 185
2,000 lb (907 kg) of bombs and 2 Sidewinders	+2 drop tanks	battlefield interdiction	290 (334) 537
2 rocket launchers and 2 Sidewinders	+2 drop tanks	maritime support	315 (363) 583
Reconnaissance pod and 2 Sidewinders	+2 drop tanks	fighter reconnaissance	490 (564 miles) 907
4 Sidewinders and gun	+2 drop tanks	air defence	2 hours loiter at radius of 100 (115) 185
	+2 drop tanks	ferry range	1,300 (1,497) 2,407

British Aerospace Hawk Mk 208 of Malaysia

Flight/weapon system avionics/instrumentation: Based on the Hawk 100 fit, except for the addition of display of radar data.
Self-protection systems: Radar warning receiver, and chaff/flare dispenser.
Wing characteristics: Based on the Hawk 100.
Engine: Rolls-Royce Turbomeca Adour 871 turbofan.
Engine rating: 5,990 lbf (26.65 kN).
Flight refuelling probe: Optional and proven, with fixed probe.
Fuel system: 3,000 lb (1,361 kg) of usable fuel. Provision for drop tanks.
Oxygen system: 1,400 litres capacity, for up to 7 hours duration.

British Aerospace Harrier I

Of the original versions of Harrier still used, the Royal Navy has two-seat T Mk 4A (ex-RAF)/T Mk 4N trainers, a number recently converted to T Mk 8s for F/A Mk 2 compatibility, Indian Navy two-seat T Mk 60 trainers, and the Royal Thai Navy has taken over 8 ex-Spanish AV-8S and TAV-8S Matadors for use from a new light aircraft carrier.

British Aerospace Sea Harrier FRS and F/A Mk 2

First flight: 20 August 1978 (FRS Mk 1).
Role: STOVL ship-based fleet air defence, surface ship attack and reconnaissance.

★ Aims

★ Derived from Harrier GR Mk 3, incorporating radar for surface search and air-to-air intercept, avionics and weapons appropriate to role.

▲ Development

▲ 15 May 1975. Programme announced as the P1184 Sea Harrier, with the eventual intention to replace the FAA's large-carrier combat aircraft (F-4 Phantoms and Buccaneers), and to be flown from new light and small carrier-cruisers.
▲ 18 June 1979. FRS Mk 1 entered Royal Navy service, with initial trials from HMS *Hermes* starting November.
▲ 22 September 1980. The Royal Navy's last large aircraft carrier, HMS *Ark Royal,* sailed to the scrapyard.
▲ 30 October 1980. First "ski jump" trial from HMS *Hermes,* the end of deck ramp allowing short-run take-offs at increased weights.
▲ 26 February 1981. A new variable-angle ski-jump (7-15°) became operational at RNAS Yeovilton, to help in the development of the optimum deck angle for the new *Invincible* class carriers. HMS *Ark Royal* built with a 12° ski jump, *Invincible* refitted with a 13° ramp and *Illustrious* returned to service in 1994 with a 13° ramp.
▲ 1 May 1982. Sea Harrier recorded its first air victory, against a Mirage IIIEA during the South Atlantic conflict.
▲ 6 August 1982. Export FRS Mk 51 for the Indian Navy first flew. Delivered 22 December.
▲ 19 September 1988. Under a Ministry of Defence mid-life upgrade contract with BAe, the first flight took place of the FRS Mk 2 aerodynamic development aircraft.
▲ 7 December 1988. MoD contract with BAe to upgrade 29 Royal Navy FRS Mk 1s to Mk 2 standard. Upgraded aircraft were redesignated F/A Mk 2s.
▲ 1990. MoD ordered 18 newly built Mk 2s. Entered service from 1995, when delivery of five T Mk 8N trainers were also due.
▲ 7 November 1990. First carrier landing by a Mk 2, on *Ark Royal.*
▲ 29 March 1993. First AMRAAM air-to-air missile fired from a Mk 2.
▲ 2 April 1993. First F/A Mk 2 was handed over to the Royal Navy at Dunsfold.
▲ 1994. MoD ordered a further 5 F/A Mk 2s.
▲ 1994. Russia agreed to sell India the Kiev-class carrier-cruiser *Admiral Gorshkov*, which is likely to deploy some of India's Sea Harriers.
▲ 1995. Newly built F/A Mk 2s and T Mk 8N trainers entered service.
▲ April 1995. Royal Navy accepted into service the VEGA F/A Mk 2 training system for maintenance technicians.
Sales/users: 57 FRS Mk 1s were delivered to the Royal Navy between 1979-88, of which 29 are being upgraded to F/A Mk 2s and a further 18 Mk 2s newly built (21 FRS Mk 1s and 15 F/A Mk 2s were in service by March 1995). Indian Navy received 23 FRS Mk 51s between 1982-92 (19 in service in March 1995) plus 4 Harrier T Mk 60 trainers. India's plan to purchase F/A Mk 2s to replace FRS Mk 51s has been abandoned, deciding instead on a navalized LCA. A limited upgrade of FRS Mk 51s will keep them operational until the year 2010.

Details for Sea Harrier.

Principal dimensions:
Wing span: 25 ft 3 ins (7.7 m)
Maximum length: 47 ft 7 ins (14.5 m) Mk 1, 46 ft 5 ins (14.15 m) Mk 2
Length, nose folded: 42 ft 3 ins (12.88 m) Mk 1, 42 ft 10 ins (13.06 m) Mk 2
Maximum height: 11 ft 10 ins (3.61 m)

Wings:
Aerofoil section: Hawker design (10% t/c root, 5% tip)
Area: 201 sq ft (18.67 m^2)
Aspect ratio: 3.17
Sweepback: 34° at 25% chord
Chord at root: 11 ft 8 ins (3.56 m)
Chord at tip: 4 ft 2 ins (1.27 m)
Incidence: 1°
Anhedral: 12°

Tail unit:
Tailplane span: 13 ft 11 ins (4.24 m)
Tailplane area: 47.5 sq ft (4.41 m^2)
Fin area: 25.8 sq ft (2.4 m^2)

Undercarriage:
Type: Retractable bicycle type, with twin main wheels retracting aft and single nosewheel retracting forward. Single outrigger wheel near each wingtip, retracting aft into a fairing
Main wheel tyre size: 27 x 7.74-13
Nose wheel tyre size: 26 x 8.75-11
Outrigger tyre size: 13.5 x 6.4
Wheel base: 11 ft 4 ins (3.45 m)
Wheel track: 22 ft 2 ins (6.76 m)

Weights:
Empty, operating: 13,885 lb (6,298 kg) Mk 1, 14,585 lb (6,616 kg) Mk 2
Maximum take-off: 26,200 lb (11,884 kg)

Ski-jump:
Incremental weight for 12° ski-jump take-off: 2,500 lb (1,134 kg)
Take-off with the VTO payload of 5,000 lb (2,268 kg): 50-60% reduction in run

Performance:
Maximum speed at altitude: <Mach 1
Maximum speed at sea level: 635 kts (731 mph) 1,176 km/h
STO take-off distance: 1,000 ft (305 m) at maximum weight
Radius of action (attack): 300 naut miles (345 miles) 555 km, Hi-Lo-Hi mission
Radius of action (intercept): 400 naut miles (460 miles) 741 km, Hi-Hi mission
Duration (combat air patrol): 1.7 hours at 100 naut miles (115 miles) 185 km

British Aerospace F/A Mk 2s, the first European combat aircraft fitted with Advanced Medium Range air-to-air missiles (AMRAAMs)

British Aerospace FRS Mk 51 Sea Harrier of the Indian Navy (Denis Hughes)

Crew: Pilot only.
Cockpit: Seat raised by 11 ins (28 cm) compared to the land-based Harrier, to improve view.
Crew escape: Martin Baker Mk 10H zero-zero ejection seat.
Fixed guns: None, but provision for 2 x 30-mm Aden gun pods in a ventral position, replacing strakes.
Number of weapon pylons: 7, 4 under the wings (inner pylons "wet" and each capable of a 2,000 lb, 907 kg load; outer 650 lb, 295 kg load on the FRS Mk 1 or 1,000 lb, 454 kg on F/A Mk 2) and 3 under the fuselage (standard centreline plus 2 positions after removing the strakes).
Expendable weapons and equipment: Maximum weapon/stores load 8,500 lb (3,856 kg) for STO, or 5,000 lb (2,268 kg) for VTO. Range of free fall, retarded and cluster bombs (WE177 nuclear weapon for the FRS Mk 1, with S denoting strike). Also rockets, flares, etc. FRS Mk 1 air-to-air armament comprises 4 Sidewinders on the outer wing pylons (Magics on Indian Mk 51s). F/A Mk 2 air-to-air armament comprises 4 AMRAAMs (2 under the wings and 2 instead of the underfuselage strakes) or 2 underfuselage AMRAAMs plus 4 Sidewinders. Other options include 2 Sea Eagle anti-ship, ASRAAM or anti-radar ALARM missiles.
Additional stores: Reconnaissance pod.
Radar: FRS Mk 1 has GEC-Marconi Blue Fox multi-mode, and F/A Mk 2 has Blue Vixen multi-mode pulse-Doppler.
Flight/weapon system avionics/instrumentation: FRS Mk 1 has HUD/weapon aiming computer, stores management system, NAVHARS pulse Doppler, radar altimeter, MADGE (microwave airborne digital guidance equipment), Tacan, autopilot, UHF/VHF and IFF.
F/A Mk 2 has, in addition, MIL-STD-1553B databus and revised cockpit layout with new head-down displays and HOTAS. GPS to be added.
Self-protection systems: Radar warning receiver. Chaff/flare dispenser on Mk 2.
Wing characteristics: Marginally swept, shoulder-mounted, with heavy anhedral. 2 fences per wing (3 on Mk 2) and a series of small vortex generators (Mk 1 has 12, Mk 2 has 11 per wing). Mk 2 has a variable wing leading edge, plus the dogtooth moved closer to the root. Wing extension panels can be fitted for long-range ferry flights.
Wing control surfaces: The flight control system is a combination of aerodynamic surfaces and reaction controls. Plain ailerons and flaps. Autostabilizer jet reaction control system ("puffer jets"), with valves at the nose, tailpipe and near the wingtips. Bleed air from the engine HP compressor. Stability Augmentation and Attitude Hold System (SAAHS) comprises the Automatic Flight Control System (AFCS) and Stability Augmentation System (SAS), offering stability about all axes over the complete flight envelope.
Tail control surfaces: Variable-incidence slab tailplane and rudder (with tab).
Airbrakes: Single petal type under the fuselage.
Flight control system: Hydraulic powered control units.
Fuselage: Folding nose radome for access and below-deck storage ("spotting").
Construction materials: All metal, with enhanced corrosion protection over the land-based Harrier, including elimination of all magnesium components. Single-piece, 3-spar wing. Mainly aluminium alloy (including honeycomb sandwich for parts of the control surfaces) but using titanium in areas of extreme heat.
Engine: Rolls-Royce Pegasus 11 Mk 104 or 106 vectored turbofan.
Engine rating: 21,500 lbf (95.64 kN).
Nozzles: 4 rotatable thrust-vectoring, made of steel, with 98.5° movement from aft to forward of vertical, enabling flight in any direction, including backwards.
Air intakes: Bifurcated, pitots, with internal throat bleed slot; series of 8 section relief doors around each intake (varying sizes) offers increased airflow during vertical or slow flying.
Flight refuelling probe: None.
Fuel system: 2,864 litres in 5 fuselage and 2 wing tanks. Provision for 2 x 454.6, 863.7 or 1,500 litre drop tanks.
Electrical system: Main AC supply using 2 x 15kVA generators. DC supply via transformer/rectifiers. 2 x 28 volt 25 amp-hour batteries.
Hydraulic system: 2 independent systems, each 3,000 psi.
Braking system: Mult-disc brakes, with anti-skid.
Oxygen system: Liquid for Mk 1/Mk 2, gaseous for Mk 51.

Aircraft variants:
FRS Mk 1 was the original Royal Navy version, with all delivered by 1988. Assigned for upgrade, as detailed previously.
FRS Mk 51 is the Indian Navy version, armed with Magic AAMs. Operated from *Viraat* (ex-*Hermes*) and *Vikrant.*
F/A Mk 2 was formerly known as FRS Mk 2. Latest Royal Navy version, upgraded from FRS Mk 1s and newly built.
Two-seat trainers delivered to the 2 navies were T Mk 4N corresponding to FRS Mk 1, T Mk 8N corresponding to Mk 2, and T Mk 60 for India. Radar/weapon training for the Royal Navy is undertaken on the Hunter T Mk 8M.

British Aerospace Nimrod MR Mk 2P and R Mk 1P

First flight: 23 May 1967 (first of 2 prototypes utilizing existing de Havilland Comet 4C airframe).
Role: Maritime patrol, anti-submarine warfare, anti-ship attack, maritime reconnaissance, and search and rescue control post (MR), and signal/electronic intelligence (R Mk 1P).

★ Aims
★ Exploitation of the payload, range/duration and volumetric capacity of the existing Comet jet airliner, to derive a fast, efficient and economic (Spey engines instead of Avons) maritime patrol aircraft but with a low wing loading and good low-speed manoeuvrability.
★ Large, unpressurized, external lower fuselage pannier "grafted" onto the newly built and shorter Comet 4C-type fuselage of production aircraft, housing a capacious weapons bay and nose radome. Other airframe changes.

▲ Development
▲ 4 June 1964. Air Staff Requirement 381 issued, for development of a replacement for the Shackleton Mk 3 (phased out by December 1971). Project became the Hawker Siddeley 801.
▲ 31 July 1967. First flight of the second prototype, retaining Avon engines and used for avionic system testing.
▲ 28 June 1968. First flight of a true MR Mk 1.

DETAILS FOR NIMROD MR MK 2P.

Principal dimensions:
Wing span: 114 ft 10 ins (35 m)
Maximum length: 129 ft (39.32 m) MR, 120 ft (36.58 m) R Mk 1P, including refuelling probes
Maximum height: 30 ft (9.14 m)

Wings:
Area: 2,121 sq ft (197.05 m^2)
Aspect ratio: 6.2
Sweepback: 20° at 25% chord
Chord at root: 29 ft 6 ins (8.99 m)
Chord at tip: 6 ft 9 ins (2.06 m)

Tail unit:
Tailplane span: 47 ft 7 ins (14.5 m)
Tailplane area: 435 sq ft (40.41 m^2)
Fin area: 179 sq ft (16.63 m^2), including dorsal fin

Undercarriage:
Type: Retractable, with twin steerable nosewheels. 4-wheel main bogies
Main wheel tyre size: 36 x 10
Nose wheel tyre size: 30 x 9-15
Wheel base: 46 ft 9 ins (14.25 m)
Wheel track: 28 ft 3 ins (8.61 m)

Weights:
Empty, operating: 86,000 lb (39,009 kg)
Normal take-off: 177,500 lb (80,513 kg)
Maximum take-off: 192,000 lb (87,090 kg)

Performance:
Maximum speed at altitude: 500 kts (576 mph) 926 km/h
Maximum cruise speed: 475 kts (547 mph) 880 km/h
Typical patrol speed: 200 kts (230 mph) 370 km/h
Take-off distance: 4,800 ft (1,465 m)
Ceiling: 42,000 ft (12,800 m)
Ferry range: up to 4,998 naut miles (5,755 miles) 9,262 km
Duration: 12 hours

▲ 2 October 1969. First newly-built MR Mk 1 was delivered to RAF Strike Command (OCU St Mawgan).
▲ 1971. R Mk 1 special sigint variant delivered, later given flight refuelling to become R Mk 1P.
▲ 23 August 1979. Redelivery of the first upgraded MR Mk 1 to Mk 2 standard, featuring new tactical, ESM, navigation and communications avionics.
▲ 1982. MR Mk 2P (MR Mk 2 modified for in-flight refuelling). 13 initially converted for operation during the Falklands conflict. Anti-ship and AAM self-defence missile capability added later that year.
▲ 1983-86. Improved ESM self-defence suite and infra-red detection system added, plus further improvements to the communications, and battle management aids.
▲ 1995. Bids submitted for the replacement or refurbishment of 25 Nimrod MR Mk 2Ps, with interested companies including Lockheed Martin.
Sales/users: RAF only. 46 MR Mk 1s built but no longer in service. 35 Mk 1s re-equipped to Mk 2 standard, becoming the current Mk 2P after further changes (see before). 25 available in 1995 with 3 squadrons at Kinloss, Scotland, plus the OCU. 2 of 3 R Mk 1Ps built (with flight refuelling) remain in operation, one having been lost in a sea ditching on 16 May 1995. Abortive AEW Mk 3 programme of 1977-86 involved 11 Mk 1 airframes.
Crew: Flight crew of 4 (pilot, co-pilot, flight engineer and navigator), plus 8 "warfare" crew (see Cabin).
Cockpit: Flight deck for the pilot, co-pilot and flight engineer.
Cabin: Main cabin, aft of the flight deck, is divided into 3 areas: forward Tactical Compartment, mid Rest Quarters and rear Store Loading Area. Tactical

British Aerospace Nimrod MR Mk 2P

compartment accommodates the navigator plus the warfare crew comprising the tactical navigator, radar operator, communications operator, 2 sonobuoy systems operators, and the ESM/MAD operator. 2 observers/ expendables handlers in the rest area.
Fixed guns: None.
Number of weapon pylons: 6 rows of store carriers in the roof of the 48 ft 6 ins (14.78 m) weapons bay. Pylon under each wing on the MR Mk 2P and R Mk 1P.
Expendable weapons and equipment: 13,500 lb (6,123 kg). Torpedoes (Stringray), depth charges, mines and cluster bombs. Probably nuclear depth bomb. Anti-ship Harpoon can be carried in the bay.
2 Sidewinder AAMs can be carried for self-defence under each wing pylon. Other expendables include sonobuoys and markers stored and launched from the 30 ft (9.14 m) stores loading area.
Radar: Thorn EMI Searchwater surface search radar in the nose, replacing the original Mk 1's ASV Mk 21.
Flight/weapon system avionics/instrumentation: Magnetic anomaly detection (MAD system sensor in the glassfibre tail boom "sting"). Loral Yellowgate in the wingtip pods. ESM also in the glassfibre fin-tip pod. Instrumentation includes acoustic processors and displays for passive and active sonobouys. Much enhanced capability introduced on the MR Mk 2 covered navigational, radar and acoustic systems; new acoustic monitoring system, and 50-fold increase in sensor computing power. Additional conditioning system introduced into the rear fuselage to accommodate increased heat load. Associated air intake on the rear fuselage port side. Onboard self-contained ASW simulation training system. Inertial navigation. Twin HF transceivers. Twin UHF/VHF radios. Automatic flight control system. Electro-optical IR sensor dome in an underwing fairing immediately outboard of the starboard wing pylon. Day/night cameras. Searchlight ahead of the starboard wing tank.
Self-protection systems: Chaff dispensing BOZ pods may be carried on the wing pylons. GEC-Marconi Ariel towed active-radar decoy.
Wing characteristics: Slightly swept, low mounted, with marginal dihedral. 2-spar structure, continuous through fuselage. Wingtip pods.
Wing control surfaces: Ailerons outboard of 2-section plain trailing-edge flaps. Spoiler airbrakes, mid span, on upper and lower surfaces immediately ahead of the outer flap sections. 11 vortex generators per outer wing panel.
Tail control surfaces: Full-span elevator (with tabs) and rudder. Large dorsal fin extension, needed to offset the directionally destabilizing effect of the pannier. Finlets on the upper and lower surfaces of the tailplane and a shallow ventral fin, to improve handling when refuelling operations are underway (this introduced in 1982).
Airbrakes: See Wings.
Flight control system: Powered hydro-mechanical units on all surfaces. Automatic flight control via a 3-axis autopilot integrated with the navigation and tactical system. Specifically tailored for safe low-altitude flying.
Fuselage: Pressurized main cabin and unpressurized pannier/weapons bay.
Construction materials: Principally aluminium alloy, but with other materials including glassfibre for the radome and various pods. Redux adhesive bonding extensively used in place of riveting.
Engines: 4 Rolls-Royce RB168 Spey 250 turbofans.
Engine rating: Each 11,995 lbf (53.36 kN).
Air intakes: Wing root leading-edge intakes, enlarged from those of the Comet for higher mass flow of Spey engines.
Flight refuelling probe: Above the flight deck.
Fuel system: 48,778 litres in the wings, lower fuselage and permanent wing leading-edge (external) tanks. Provision for up to 6 auxiliary tanks in the weapons bay.
Electrical system: 60 kVA alternator on each engine, any of which can meet normal power demands.
Hydraulic system: Lockheed system, working at 2,500 psi for the powered units of the flying controls, weapons bay doors, steering, undercarriage and various doors, etc. Either inboard engine can supply full hydraulic power for the entire aircraft.
Braking system: Main wheel braking, with anti-skid. Thrust reversers on outer engines only.

Aircraft variants:

MR Mk 2P is the maritime patrol version, its features including an additional conditioning air intake on the rear fuselage (port side), adjacent to the fin extension.
R Mk 1P is the sigint/elint variant, distinguishable by the forward pointing radomes in front of the wing pods and a similar radome pointing rearward at the rear of the fuselage. MAD boom deleted. Additional small antennae and special EW pods on underwing pylons. Wingtip ESM as for MR Mk 2P. Only 2 aircraft remaining as of 17 May 1995.

The Boeing Company (USA)

Corporate address: PO Box 3707, Seattle, WA 98124-2207 (mailing).
Telephone: +1 206 655 2121
Facsimile: +1 206 655 1171
Telex: 329430
Cable: BOEINGAIR

General Offices
Address: 7755 East Marginal Way South, Seattle, Washington 98108.
Telephone: +1 206 655 2121
Founded: 15 July 1916, with 26 April 1917 for adoption of the name Boeing Airplane Company, formed out of Pacific Aero Products Company.
Employees: Approximately 115,000.
Information: Paul Binder (Director, Public Relations – *telephone* +1 206 655 6123, *facsimile* +1 206 655 3987).

DIVISIONS

Boeing Defense & Space Group
HQ address: PO Box 3999, MS 80-RF, Seattle, WA 98124-2499 (mailing).

General Offices
Address: 20403 68th Avenue S, Kent, WA 98032.
Telephone: +1 206 773 0530 (Public Relations)
Facsimile: +1 206 773 4261
Information: Pete Dakan (Public Relations)
Employees: under 30,000.

With
Boeing Aerospace Operations
HQ address: PO Box 320220, Cocoa Beach, FL 32932-0220.
Telephone: +1 407 783 0220
Facsimile: +1 407 783 6090

● Activities
● Provides flight equipment processing contract support to Johnson Space Center.

AGROSystems Inc
HQ address: 324 North Mary Avenue, Sunnyvale, CA 94088-3452.
Telephone: +1 408 737 200

● Activities
● Design and manufacture of electronic warfare and signal intelligence systems.

Electronic Systems Division
HQ address: PO Box 3999, MS 3F-61, Seattle, WA 98124-2499.
Telephone: +1 206 657 3046, 773 2121
Facsimile: +1 206 657 3033
Information: Susan Bradley (Public Relations).

● Activities
● Include working with Product Support on the E-3 and 767 AWACS programmes. Also Maritime Patrol Avionics and design/manufacture of electronics for all Divisions.

Helicopters Division
HQ address: PO Box 16858, MS P30-01, Philadelphia, PA 19142-0858.
Telephone: +1 610 591 2864, 2121
Facsimile: +1 610 591 4820
Information: Madelyn Bush (Public Relations – *telephone* +1 610 591 2864).

■ **Facilities**
■ Ridley Township, PA, for manufacturing and administration.
■ Wilmington, Delaware County, for the Flight Test Centre.

● **Activities**
● Include CH-47 and CH-46, V-22 Osprey and RAH-66 Comanche.

Military Airplanes Division
HQ address: PO Box 3999, MS 4C-98, Seattle, WA 98124-2499 (mailing).

General Offices
Address: 9725 E Marginal Way S, Seattle, WA 98108.
Telephone: +1 206 655 1198, 2121
Facsimile: +1 206 662 0660
Information: Randy Harrison (Public Relations – *telephone* +1 206 655 1198).

● **Activities**
● Teamed with Lockheed Martin to produce the F-22 next-generation air superiority fighter. Has produced B-2 large structural components.
● Develops military derivatives of Boeing commercial aircraft, including military equipped transports, electronic mission platforms and aerial refuelling tankers.
● JAST/ASTOVL fighter concepts. Has also studied a carrier-capable surveillance and AEW aircraft with a joined wing, as a possible future Hawkeye replacement under the USN's EX programme.
● Proposal to the USAF to explore the concept of an aircraft-carried, high-energy Airborne Laser that could engage and destroy ballistic missiles while still in their boost phase.

Missiles and Space Division
Address: PO Box 240002, MS JW-49, Huntsville, AL 35824-6402.
Telephone: +1 205 461 2803
Facsimile: +1 205 461 2252, 2121
Information: James Keller (Public Relations – *telephone* +1 205 461 2803).

● **Activities**
● Prime contractor for the redesigned Space Station.
● Support of the Inertial Upper Stage booster.
● Production of the Avenger air-defence system.

Product Support Division
HQ address: PO Box 7730, MS K-12-12, Wichita, KS 67277-7730.
Information: Dick Ziegler (Manager, Public Relations – *telephone* +1 316 526 3153, 2121, *facsimile* +1 316 526 1845).

● **Activities**
● Modification and post-product support work, including E-6 TACAMO (see Electronic section) and KC-135 (see Freighter section).
● Logistics support for the USAF's special air mission fleet.
● Modification of French Air Force C-135FR tankers with wing-mounted hose and drogue refuelling pods (11 kits).
● Support the Electronics Systems Division 767 AWACS (as ordered by Japan) with engineering design for the environmental control, oxygen, hydraulics and fuel systems, and wiring integration and aircraft interiors, plus structural modifications.
● Modernization of B-52 bombers for conventionally armed missions (CMUP – see below).
● B-1B bomber support, mainly by sustaining engineering services, and the conventional mission upgrade programme (CMUP).

Boeing Commercial Airplane Group
HQ address: PO Box 3707, Seattle, Washington 98124-2207 (mailing).

General offices
Address: N 8th & Park Avenue. N Renton, WA 98055.
Telephone: +1 206 237 2121
Facsimile: +1 206 237 3544
Employees: Approximately 70,000.
Information: Bill Curry (Public Relations).

● **Activities**
● Manufactures and develops the Boeing 737 (300 to 800 series), 747-400 series, 757, 767-200 and -300 series, 767-200 and -300, and 777-200.

With
Customer Services Division
HQ address: 2925 S, 112th, Seattle, WA 98168.
Telephone: +1 206 655 2121
Facsimile: +1 206 544 9550

● **Activities**
● Provides training, field support and spare parts.

Engineering Division
HQ address: N 8th & Park Avenue, Renton, WA 98055.
Telephone: +1 206 234 3535

Everett Division
HQ address: 3003 West Casino Road, Everett, WA 98203.
Telephone: +1 206 294 4088
Facsimile: +1 206 342 1756

● **Activities**
● Responsible for 747 and 767 design and production.

Fabrication Division
HQ address: 1002 15th Street W, Auburn, WA 98002.
Telephone: +1 206 931 5834
Facsimile: +1 206 931 9500

● **Activities**
● Component production.

Materiel Division
HQ address: 20818 44th Avenue W, Lynnwood, WA.
Telephone: +1 206 655 2121

● **Activities**
● Materials and subcontracted components used for Boeing aircraft.

Propulsion Systems Division
HQ address: 7600 212th Avenue SW, Kent, WA 98032.
Telephone: +1 206 393 8000

● **Activities**
● Preparation of all jet engines for installation in Boeing aircraft.

Renton Division
HQ address: N 8th & Park Avenue N, Renton, WA 98055.
Telephone: +1 206 237 2121
Facsimile: +1 206 237 1379

● **Activities**
● Design and production of 737 and 757.

777 Division
HQ address: PO Box 3707, Seattle, WA 98124 (mailing).
Telephone: +1 206 294 4088

● **Activities**
● Design and development of the 777.

Wichita Division
HQ address: PO Box 7730, M/S K12-12, Wichita, KS 67277-7730 (mailing).
Telephone: +1 316 526 3153

● **Activities**
● Production of components for Boeing aircraft.

Boeing Georgia Inc
HQ address: 7979 NE Industrial Blvd, Macon, GA 31297.
Telephone: +1 912 781 3000
Facsimile: +1 912 781 3052

● **Activities**
● Manufacture of sub-assemblies.

Boeing Information and Support Services
Address: PO Box 24346, MS 7A-16, Bellevue, WA 98124-0346.
Telephone: +1 206 763 5166
Facsimile: +1 206 865 2958
Information: Karen Burt (Public Relations – *telephone* +1 206 865 4653).

● **Activities**
● Provides computing and telecommunications support to all operating elements of Boeing.
● Develops and manages large-scale information systems for selected agencies of the federal government.

Boeing B-52H Stratofortress

First flight: 15 April 1952 (YB-52).
Role: Conventional and nuclear strategic bomber.

★ **Aims**
Features of the B-52H over previous B-52 models are:
★ Increased range made possible by more powerful TF-33 turbofan engines.
★ 20-mm Gatling cannon (replacing 4 x 50-calibre machine-guns) in the tail turret.
★ More refined electronic defensive and offensive systems.
★ Extreme low-altitude capabilities.

▲ **Development**
▲ 18 March 1954. First B-52A production aircraft rolled out, first flying on 5 August.
▲ 18 June 1965. First combat use in Vietnam, armed with conventional weapons.
▲ 1991. First US aircraft launched during the Gulf War.
▲ August 1994. 2 B-52s from Barksdale AFB flew the first round-the-world bombing flight, dropping 27,000 lb (12,247 kg) of bombs in the Kuwait desert as part of the 47-hour practice mission.
▲ September 1994. Redelivery of the first conventional mission upgrade programme (CMUP) conversion.

DETAILS FOR B-52H.

Principal dimensions:
Wing span: 185 ft (56.39 m)
Maximum length: 160 ft 11 ins (49.04 m)
Maximum height: 40 ft 8 ins (12.4 m)

Wings:
Area: 4,000 sq ft (371.61 m^2)
Aspect ratio: 8.56
Sweepback: 35°

Undercarriage:
Type: Retractable, with 8 main wheels in double tandem bogies, plus 2 small protection wheels at the wingtips. Main wheels are housed 2-each in 4 fuselage wheel wells
Wheel base: 50 ft 3 ins (15.32 m)
Wheel track: 8 ft 3 ins (2.51 m)

Weights:
Maximum take-off: over 488,000 lb (221,353 kg)

Performance:
Maximum speed at high altitude: 517 kts (595 mph) 958 km/h
Maximum low-level speed: 365 kts (420 mph) 675 km/h
Cruise speed: 443 kts (510 mph) 820 km/h
Take-off distance: 9,500 ft (2,895 m)
Ceiling: 55,000 ft (16,750 m)
Operational range, with 1 flight refuelling: 7,500 naut miles (8,636 miles) 13,890 km
Maximum range: over 8,684 naut miles (10,000 miles) 16,090 km

Boeing B-52H Stratofortress of the 5th Bomb Wing at Minot AFB (Peter R. March)

*Note: Past and present upgrade programmes have added new offensive avionics, environmental control, fuel quantity, autopilot, radar, enhanced ECM, upgraded all-weather and stand-off capabilities (resulting in a decreased risk to the aircraft from enemy defences), plus improved reliability and support/maintenance. 1995-96 plans are to enhance the B-52H's conventional roles for low-threat bombing and stand-off attack.

Sales/users: 85 remained in the active inventory of Air Combat Command in early 1995, including 47 previously marked for retirement storage at AMARC Davis-Monthan. Of these, 57 are primary aircraft authorized (PAA) for operational missions and serve with the 2nd Bomb Wing at Barksdale AFB and 5th Bomb Wing at Minot AFB; 410th Bomb Wing at K.I.Sawyer AFB closed on 30 September 1995. In addition, the US Air Force Reserve operates 9.

Crew: 5, as 2 pilots, navigator, radar operator and EW operator.
Fixed guns: 20-mm Gatling cannon in the tail turret.
Expendable weapons and equipment: Over 50,000 lb (22,680 kg) conventional load. Current CMUP programme by the Product Support Division to transfer the conventional weapon capability of B-52Gs to B-52Hs. The modification provides the capability to accommodate AGM-142A HAVE NAP and Harpoon missiles and the universal bomb bay adapter, and well as integrated conventional stores management and global positioning systems. Common strategic rotary launcher (CSRL) fitted, designed to carry nuclear missiles as well as gravity nuclear bombs. Typical conventional armament of 51 x 500 lb bombs, 24 on external wing pylons and 27 in the bomb bay. Alternatively, 20 AGM-86B/AGM-129A ALCM nuclear missiles (12 under wing and 8 in the bay) or a combination of 12 missiles and 8 gravity nuclear bombs. Intended for deployment are GBU-30 (formerly JDAM), AGM-154A JSOW and from 1998 the WCMD (Wind Corrected Munition Dispenser).
Radar: See below.
Flight/weapon system avionics/instrumentation: Many modernization programmes have retained combat efficiency. To the current integrated conventional stores management, secure radios, MIL-STD-1760 interfaces and global positioning systems upgrade programmes for up to 47 aircraft, previous programes added the AN/ASQ-151 electro-optical viewing system (EVS) to assist low-altitude flying (comprising a Hughes AAQ-6 FLIR and Westinghouse AVQ-22 low light level TV system in twin steerable nose turrets), ALQ-122 Smart Noise Operation Equipment, ALQ-155(V) ECM, AFSATCOM satellite communications, and a digital navigation/weapon delivery suite, including Tercom, Doppler radar, INS, AHRS and more.
Self-protection systems: Dalmo Victor ALR-46 radar warning receiver, Westinghouse ALQ-153 tail warning radar and ALQ-172 ECM jamming system.
Wing characteristics: Swept, high mounted, with anhedral. Kinked trailing edges.
Wing control surfaces: 2 sets of flaps per wing, with ailerons between. Spoiler/airbrakes on the upper surface.
Tail control surfaces: Variable-incidence tailplane. Elevators (with tabs) and rudder.
Airbrakes: Symmetric use of spoilers.
Construction materials: Metal.
Engines: 8 Pratt & Whitney TF33-P-3 turbofans.
Engine rating: Each 17,000 lbf (75.62 kN).
Flight refuelling probe: Fitted.
Fuel system: 174,129 litres. Provision for 2 x 2,650 litre auxiliary fuel tanks.

Cessna Aircraft Company (USA)

Corporate address: One Cessna Boulevard, Wichita, KS 67215 (mailing address: PO Box 7706, Wichita, KS 67277-7706).
Telephone: +1 316 941 6056, from outside the USA; 1 800 4 within the USA.
Facsimile: +1 316 941 6640
Founded: 18 December 1927.
Information: David Franson (Director of Public Relations – *telephone* +1 316 941 6488).

● Activities

● Light, business and corporate aircraft (see General Aviation section).

Cessna 526 CitationJet

First flight: 20 December 1993.
Role: Primary jet trainer, intended initially for the JPATS competition. Since not selected, programme will probably be terminated.

★ Aims

★ Designed and built in the USA, specifically as a contender for the USAF/USN JPATS trainer competition. Cessna was teamed with Williams-Rolls, AlliedSignal and Universal Propulsion Company.
★ Built with low-risk technology.
★ "Missionization" of the Cessna 525 CitationJet business aircraft.
★ Common components with the 525 CitationJet transport (75%), including wings, engines, undercarriage, hydraulic system, electrical system, flight controls, and fuel system.
★ New components for the JPATS CitationJet include the fuselage, tail unit, cockpit, canopy, escape system, avionics and on-board oxygen generating system.
★ Structure built to USAF ASIP criteria for fail-safe design, and damage tolerance, plus overall durability and economic life.
★ Optimized for 2-level maintenance, and extended inspection and overhaul intervals.

Cessna 526 CitationJet prototypes

▲ Development

▲ 2 March 1994. First flight of the second prototype.
▲ 22 June 1994. Certified under FAR Pt 23 Aerobatic category.

Sales/users: Intended for the USAF and US Navy (projected 711 JPATS aircraft) but not selected.
Crew: 2, in tandem stepped cockpits.
Cockpit: Clam-shell canopy, jettisoned for ejection. Pressurized 5 psi.
Crew escape: Universal Propulsion Company zero-zero ejection seats.
Fixed guns: None.
Number of weapon pylons: None disclosed.
Expendable weapons and equipment: None disclosed.
Flight/weapon system avionics/instrumentation: "Glass" cockpit with AlliedSignal Bendix/King avionics and 5 ins EFIS displays.
Wing characteristics: Straight, low mounted, with dihedral. 3-spar design. 22 small vortex generators per wing at mid chord.
Wing control surfaces: Horn-balanced ailerons (with tabs) and flaps. Spoilers.
Tail control surfaces: Horn-balanced elevator and horn-balanced rudder, with tabs.
Flight control system: Mechanical.
Fuselage: Windscreen tilts forward for access behind instrument panel, nose section tilts up for complete access to the pneumatic, brake and IBOGS systems, side panels fold down to access to avionics LRUs, and stand-up access hatch in the tailcone.
Construction materials: Principally aluminium alloy, with minimal use of composites (non-structural components only).
Engines: 2 Williams-Rolls F129 turbofans.
Engine rating: Each derated to 1,500 lbf (6.672 kN). Engine replacement in under 60 minutes by 2 experienced technicians.
Fuel system: Multi-cell single-tank arrangement, with no fuel management system.
Electrical system: 28 volt DC supply, with 2 x 300 kVA starter-generators and a 28 volt sealed lead acid battery. No AC supply.
Hydraulic system: 1,500 psi.
Oxygen system: On-board oxygen generating system.

Details for 526 CitationJet.

Principal dimensions:
Wing span: 37 ft (11.28 m)
Maximum length: 40 ft 8 ins (14.4 m)
Maximum height: 12 ft 6 ins (3.81 m)

Wings:
Aerofoil section: Cessna/NASA laminar flow

Undercarriage:
Type: Retractable, with nosewheel

Weights:
Empty: 4,920 lb (2,232 kg)
Maximum take-off: 7,400 lb (3,357 kg)

Performance:
Maximum speed: Mach 0.7 or 270 kts (311 mph) 500 km/h CAS
Stall speed: 76 kts (88 mph) 141 km/h CAS, with full flaps, 50% fuel
Approach speed: 99 kts (114 mph) 183 km/h CAS, with full flaps, 50% fuel
Time to 18,000 ft (5,486 m): 5.8 minutes
G limits: +7
Ceiling: over 35,000 ft (10,668 m)
Range with full fuel: 1,050 naut miles (1,209 miles) 1,944 km, with IFR reserve

Lockheed Martin (USA)

Corporate address: 6801 Rockledge Drive, Bethesda, MD 20817.
Telephone: +1 301 897 6561 (Corporate Communications)
Facsimile: +1 301 897 6252
Founded: 15 March 1995, as a merger of the Lockheed Corporation (founded 1926) and Martin Marietta (founded 1965 but with roots going back to 1911).
Employees: 170,000.
Information: Susan Pearce (Vice President, Corporate Communications) and Keith Mordoff (Director, International Public Relations – *telephone* +1 301 897 6387).

SECTORS AND DIVISIONS

Aeronautics Sector
Information: Phil Giaramita (Vice President, Communications)
Telephone: +1 301 897 6121
Comprising:

Lockheed Martin Skunk Works
HQ address: 1011 Lockheed Way, Palmdale, CA 93599-3740.
Information: James Ragsdale
Telephone: +1 805 572 4153
Facsimile: +1 805 572 4163

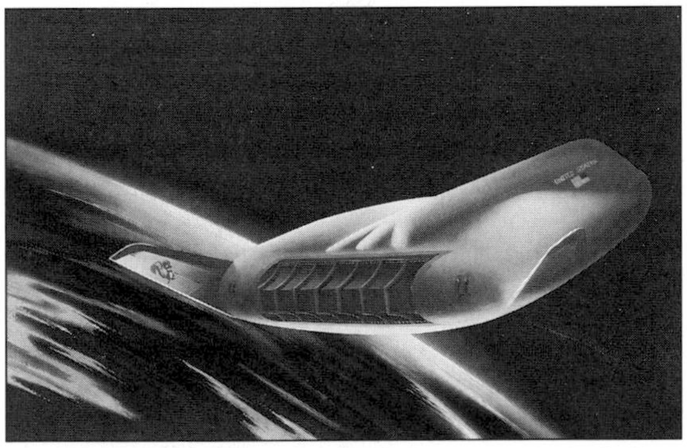

Lockheed Martin Skunk Works concept for a reusable aeroballistic rocket lifting-body vehicle. Normally pilotless, it could carry up to a 40,000 lb (18,140 kg) load into low Earth orbit

Lockheed Martin Aircraft Services
HQ address: PO Box 33, Ontario, CA 91761-0033.
Information: Ron Lindeke
Telephone: +1 909 989 7984
Facsimile: +1 909 395 2334

Lockheed Martin Logistics Management
HQ address: 1600 East Pioneer Pkwy., Arlington, TX 76010-6594.
Information: Kathryn Hayden
Telephone: +1 817 548 2442
Facsimile: +1 817 860 7930

Lockheed Martin Aeronautical Systems
HQ address: 86 South Cobb Drive, Marietta, GA 30063-0264.
Information: Brian Johnstone (Executive Director, Public Affairs).
Telephone: +1 404 494 4124
Facsimile: +1 404 494 7656
Information (Airlift programmes): Julius Alexander (*telephone* +1 404 494 9818)
Information (P-3, S-3, MPA/AEW programmes): Doug Oliver (*telephone* +1 404 494 6208)
Information (F-22, Advanced Tactical programmes, and L-1011): Jeff Rhodes (*telephone* +1 404 494 2702)

Lockheed Martin Tactical Aircraft Systems
HQ address: Lockheed Blvd., Fort Worth, TX 76108.
Information: Joseph W. Stout
Telephone: +1 817 763 4086
Facsimile: +1 817 763 4797
Also:

LMTAS Abilene Facility
Address: PO Box 1401, Abilene, TX 79604.
Telephone: +1 915 691 2022
Facsimile: +1 915 691 2127
Information: Steve Abel.

Lockheed Martin Aero & Naval Systems
HQ address: 103 Chesapeake Park Plaza, Baltimore, MD 21220.
Telephone: +1 410 682 1120
Facsimile: +1 410 682 3276
Information: Don Carson.

● Activities

- Include C-130 production and modernization, F-16, F-22, F-117A, Mitsubishi FS-X co-development and component manufacture, P-3, and U-2 upgrade; engine thrust reversers; Samson "open skies" surveillance pod; contract field services; aircraft modification and maintenance (including upgrade of 36 Argentine A-4M Skyhawks under an agreement of 15 December 1994 – see Argentina); and UAVs. Oportunities include JAST (Joint Attack Strike Technology), and NDAA (Non-Developmental Airlift Aircraft) with the possibility of C-5 restart, C-5 modernization or additional C-130s. See also Reconnaissance and Freighter sections.

Electronics Sector
Information: James Tierney (Vice President, Communications).
Telephone: +1 301 897 6480
Comprising:

Lockheed Martin Armament Systems

Lockheed Martin Communications Systems

Lockheed Martin Control Systems

Lockheed Martin Defense Systems

Lockheed Martin Electronics & Missiles
HQ address: 5600 West Sand Lake Road, Orlando, FL 32819-8907.
Telephone: +1 407 356 2207
Facsimile: +1 407 356 0919
Information: Al Kamhi.

Lockheed Martin Government Electronics Systems

Lockheed Martin Ocean, Radar & Sensor Systems

Sanders
HQ address: NHQ Spit Brook Road, Nashua, NH 03061-0868.
Telephone: +1 603 885 2817
Facsimile: +1 603 885 2813
Information: Marv Braman.

Information & Technology Service Sector
Telephone: +1 301 897 6482
Information: Laurie Tolleson (Vice President).
Comprising:

Lockheed Martin Management & Data Systems

Lockheed Martin Information Sciences Group
With:

FORMTEK Inc

Enterprise Info Systems Company

Informations Systems Company

Lockheed Martin Services Group
HQ address: 2339 Route 70 West, Cherry Hill, NJ 08358
Telephone: +1 609 486 5126
Facsimile: +1 609 486 5270
Information: Neal Linkon.
With:

KAPL

Lockheed Martin Services Company

Lockheed Martin Engineering & Sciences

Lockheed Martin IMS

Lockheed Martin Commercial Products Group
With:

CalComp

Lockheed Martin Commercial Electronics

Access Graphics Inc

MountainGate Inc

Lockheed Martin Manned Space Systems

Lockheed Martin Space Operations Company

Space & Strategic Missiles Sector

Telephone: +1 301 897 6493
Information: Virnell Bruce (Vice President).
Comprising:

Lockheed Martin Missiles & Space
HQ address: PO Box 3504, Sunnyvale, CA 94088-3504.
Telephone: +1 408 742 5113
Facsimile: +1 408 743 2239
Information: Janet Wrather.
Also:

Address: PO Box 17100, Austin, TX 78760-7100.
Telephone: +1 512 386 1401
Facsimile: +1 512 386 1800
Information: Ken Wood.

Lockheed Martin Astronautics

Lockheed Martin Astro Space

Lockheed Martin Technical Operations

Note:* See also **Lockheed Aircraft Argentina SA (LAASA)** under Argentina.

Energy and Environmental sector

Lockheed Martin Energy Systems

Lockheed Martin Specialty Components

Lockheed Martin Environmental Systems & Technologies

Lockheed Martin Idaho Technologies

Lockheed Martin Utility Services

M4 Environmental L.P.

Sandia Corporation

Lockheed AC-130H and Rockwell AC-130U Spectre

Role: Heavy gunship for special operations by day or night, including close air support, interdiction, armed reconnaissance, escort and area defence.
Sales/users: 16th Special Operations Wing, Special Operations Command, USAF, out of Hurlburt Field, Florida (Rockwell AC-130U) and 919th Special Operations Wing, US Air Force Reserve, out of Duke Field, Florida (LMAS AC-130H, replacing AC-130As in 1995). Total force of 21 Spectres.
Crew: 13, including 3 on the flight deck and 7 in the battle management centre. Aft observer occupies a tail-ramp station.
Expendable weapons and equipment: AC-130H has a trainable 105-mm howitzer and 40-mm cannon, plus 2 M61 Vulcan multi-barrel 20-mm cannon, all projecting from the port side of the fuselage, for concentrated heavy fire on ground targets. AC-130U has the 20-mm cannon replaced by a single GAU-12/U 6-barrel 25-mm cannon. Aircraft circles around the target, concentrating fire at the centre. Integration of the primary sensors and weapons through mission computers allows the AC-130U to strike 2 separate targets simultaneously.
Flight/weapon system avionics/instrumentation: Digital fire control radar (APQ-150 on AC-130H and APQ-180 on AC-130U) and digital computer for accurate weapons use. Integrated electro-optical sensors that include FLIR and low light level TV. Side-mounted head-up display for visual gun training.
Self-protection systems: Sprectra ceramic armour, chaff/flare dispensers, ITT Enhanced AN/ALQ-172 electronic countermeasures system, infra-red receiver, radar warning receiver, and more. The AN/ALQ-172 was first fitted to the new AC-130U, but a contract of 18 October 1994 with Chrysler Technologies Airborne Systems (plus options) will see similar systems fitted to AC-130Hs from 1995-1999.

LMAS AC-130H Spectre, a gunship conversion of the Hercules transport. Note the howitzer and 40-mm cannon seen protruding from the rear fuselage, the radome housing tracking radar, and other sensors

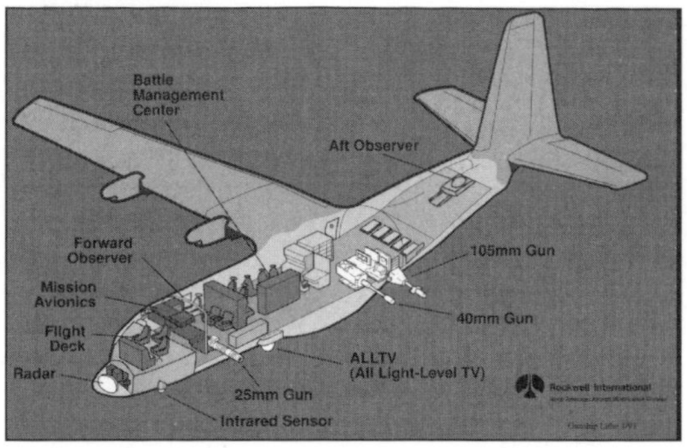

Rockwell Aerospace's North American Aircraft Modification Division AC-130U Spectre

Flight refuelling probe: Fitted to both versions.

Aircraft variants:
AC-130H was produced by Lockheed, with avionics upgrading in 1993 of the computer, sensors, navigation and communications equipment.
AC-130U is the latest version, produced by Rockwell Aerospace's North American Aircraft Modification Division as conversions of 13 Lockheed C-130H transports. Replacing the AC-130H with the active USAF. First flown in late 1990, but further modification delayed deliveries until 1994-95. Improved radar and weapon changes.

Lockheed Martin (LMTAS) F-16 Fighting Falcon

First flight: 20 January 1974.
Role: Fighter, air defence, close air support, battlefield interdiction and reconnaissance.

★ Aims

⋆ Originally intended as a lightweight and low-cost day fighter. Role subsequently expanded to include all-weather operations and ground attack.
⋆ Relaxed stability for reduced tail drag and improved manoeuvrability, requiring fly-by-wire control.
⋆ 8,000 hour structural life.
⋆ Mishap rate per 100,000 flight hours: 4.5 (USAF), 5.4 (worldwide).

▲ Development

▲ 28 February 1972. Proposals for the Lightweight Fighter programme received by the USAF from 5 manufacturers.
▲ 13 April 1972. General Dynamics and Northrop contracted to develop competing prototypes (2 each as YF-16s and YF-17s).
▲ 2 February 1974. Recognized and scheduled first flight at Edwards AFB.
▲ 11 March 1974. First Mach 2 test flight.
▲ 13 January 1975. YF-16 chosen for EMD, under the renamed Air Combat Fighter programme. Role expanded to include ground attack, and with provision for radar and navigation avionics suited to all-weather operations.
▲ 8 December 1976. Maiden flight of the first of 8 EMD aircraft (including 2 two-seaters).
▲ 8 August 1977. Maiden flight of the first EMD F-16B two-seater.
▲ 7 August 1978. Maiden flight of the first full production F-16A.
▲ 6 January 1979. First delivery to the USAF, going to the 388th TFW at Hill AFB.
▲ 26 January 1979. Belgian Air Force became the first foreign recipient. Final assembly of European F-16s was undertaken in Belgium and the Netherlands.
▲ 1983. F-16s joined the US Air National Guard, followed by the US Air Force Reserve the next year.
▲ 1993. F-16s were assigned to the new battlefield air support composite Wing at Pope AFB, NC. Also the first AFRES unit deployment on peacekeeping duties.
▲ Late 1993. F-16s around the world passed 5 million flight hours.
▲ December 1993. Lockheed Fort Worth awarded Honeywell Defense Avionics Systems a contract for design of a liquid-crystal flat panel colour display for the F-16.
▲ 11 February 1994. First launch demonstration of high off-boresight missile capability, at Tyndall AFB. Launching an AIM-9 derivative, the pilot used his helmet-mounted display to slew a missile seeker to his line of sight and achieve seeker lock-on at high angles off the nose of the F-16B.
▲ March 1994. Multi-Axis Thrust Vectoring (MATV) F-16 completed its 95-flight test programme.
▲ March 1994. Integration of Harpoon onto USAF F-16s.
▲ 19 May 1994. AFTI/F-16 launched a HARM missile using off-board sensor data, in the Talon Sword Bravo demonstration. Target data, transmitted to a US Navy Prowler via a satellite, was correlated by the aircrew to identify and locate an appropriate threat emitter, sending the target data through an Improved Data Modem to the AFTI/F-16.
▲ August 1994. F-16 selected by the USAF to perform SEAD (Suppression of Enemy Air Defences) missions, following demonstrations that May.
▲ April 1995. First Mid-Life Update F-16 was flown.
▲ 26 April 1995. First flight of an F-16C of the ANG equipped with a special recon-optical pod.
▲ 27 April 1995. 3,500th production F-16 delivered, an F-16C Block 50D.
▲ 2,025. Expected final retirement of F-16s from the USAF.
Sales/users: Deliveries of 3,500 production F-16s of all versions by 27 April 1995. Ordered by Bahrain (12 F-16C/Ds with GE-100 engines), Belgium (160 F-16A/Bs with PW-200/220s), Denmark (70 F-16A/Bs, some assigned to reconnaissance, plus 3 ex-USAF F-16As, with PW-200/220s), Egypt (175 F-16A/B/C/Ds with GE-100/129 and PW-200/220s, including 46 produced by TAI), Greece (80 F-16C/Ds with GE-100/129s), Indonesia (12 F-16A/Bs with PW-220s), Israel (210 A/B/C/Ds with GE-100 and PW-200s, plus 50 ex-USAF F-16s from August 1994), South Korea (40 plus 120 further F-16C/Ds with PW-220/229s being delivered – first export customer with Block 52 aircraft), Netherlands (213 F-16A/Bs with PW-200/220s), Norway (74 F-16A/Bs with PW-200/220s), Pakistan (71 F-16A/Bs initially

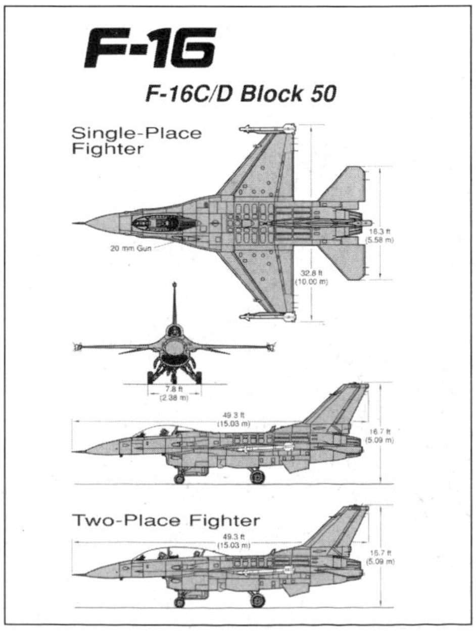

Lockheed Martin F-16C/D Block 50 drawing (courtesy Lockheed Martin)

ordered but embargoed; 36 may be delivered in 1996 with PW-200/220s), Portugal (20 F-16A/Bs with PW-220Es, delivered from 18 February 1994), Singapore (26, as 8 F-16A/Bs with PW-220s and 18 F-16C/Ds ordered July 1994 with PW-229 engines), Taiwan (150 F-16A/Bs), Thailand (36 F-16A/Bs), Turkey (236 with GE-100/129s), USA (2,196 A/B/C/Ds to the USAF with all engine options, of which 777 were in the active inventory but only 663 primary aircraft authorized (PAA) for combat with the active USAF in early 1995, plus 121 with the AFRES and 742 with the ANG, including the Thunderbirds display team – 272 A/Bs were modified into F-16ADF air defence fighters for the ANG, and others have replaced or are replacing A-10As and F-111E/Fs for close air support/interdiction; 26 F-16N/TFs for US Navy with GE-100s), and Venezuela (24 F-16A/Bs with PW-200s). F-16A/Bs withdrawn from USAF service have been offered for sale. See Aircraft variants for F-16U proposal to UAE. Czech Air Force has expressed an interest in purchasing 24 stored Belgian F-16As.

Details: Principally F-16C Block 50, unless stated.
Crew: Pilot, reclining at 30° to help withstand high g forces. 2 crew in tandem in two-seaters.
Cockpit: Side stick controller. Monchrome CRT displays being replaced by colour liquid crystal displays on some aircraft.
Crew escape: McDonnell Douglas ACES II zero-zero ejection seat (see above).
Fixed guns: 20-mm General Electric M61A1 multi-barrel gun in the port wing root. Those USAF F-16s modified for close air support and battlefield interdiction (replacing A-10A Thunderbolts) carry a GPU-5/A 30-mm cannon under the fuselage.
Ammunition: 511 rounds.
Number of weapon pylons: 9, as 6 under the wings (capacities 4,500 lb, 2,040 kg inner; 3,500 lb, 1,588 kg middle; 700 lb, 317 kg outer), 1 under the fuselage (2,200 lb, 998 kg capacity), and 2 wingtip AAM launch rails.
Expendable weapons and equipment: 12,000 lb (5,443 kg) load. Typical air-to-air armament is 6 AIM-9L, M or P Sidewinders, though other deployments include Sparrow and AMRAAM, and Python 3s on Israeli aircraft. The adoption of French MICA air-to-air missiles has been studied against possible foreign requirement. Captive testing of the BAe ASRAAM was completed on an F-16 at Eglin AFB in early 1995. Air-to-ground armament includes free-fall and smart bombs, and missiles including Shrike and HARM anti-radiation, Harpoon and Penguin anti-ship, and Maverick. Future weapons will include GBU-30, JSOW and WCMD (wind corrected munition dispenser). South Korea may deploy Popeye on its F-16C/Ds.
Additional stores: Can include LANTIRN, FLIR, laser designator, reconnaissance and other systems.
Radar: F-16C/D have Westinghouse AN/APG-68 coherent, multi-mode, digital fire control radar, from

Details for F-16C Block 50.

Principal dimensions:
Wing span: 32 ft 9.5 ins (10 m) over missiles
Maximum length: 49 ft 3.5 ins (15.02 m)
Maximum height: 16 ft 8.5 ins (5.09 m)

Wings:
Aerofoil section: NACA 64A-204
Area: 300 sq ft (27.87 m^2)
Aspect ratio: 3.2 without missiles
Sweepback: 40° leading edge

Tail unit:
Tailplane span: 18 ft 3.5 ins (5.58 m)
Tailplane area: 63.7 sq ft (5.918 m^2)
Fin area: 43.1 sq ft (4.004 m^2) dorsal and ventral

Undercarriage:
Type: Retractable, with steerable nosewheel
Main wheel tyre size: 27.75 x 8.75-14.5
Nose wheel tyre size: 18 x 5.7-8
Wheel base: 13 ft 2 ins (4 m)
Wheel track: 7 ft 9.5 ins (2.38 m)

Weights:
Empty: 18,600 lb (8,437 kg) with GE-129 or PW-229 engine
Maximum take-off: 42,300 (19,187 kg)

Performance:
Maximum speed: Mach 2+
G limits: +9 design
Ceiling: over 50,000 ft (15,240 m)
Ferry range: over 1,737 naut miles (2,000 miles) 3,218 km

F-16B No 2 technology demonstrator fires a Raytheon prototype AAM in the first US launch demonstration of high off-boresight missile capability

Block 50 production aircraft incorporating the Westinghouse Advanced Programmable Signal Processor.
Flight/weapon system avionics/instrumentation: Avionics integrated via 2 x 1553B databuses. Improved data modem for faster data transmission and demonstrated near real time linking and receiving data. Litton inertial navigation system (LN-39 or ring-laser gyro LN-93) or Honeywell H-523, Collins AN/ARN-108 instrument landing system, and Collins AN/ARN-118 tactical air navigation system. Terprom digital terrain profile matching system on European and some USAF upgrades and incorporated in new production Block 20 F-16A/Bs. Honeywell air data computer. New modular mission computer under Mid-Life Upgrade for European F-16A/Bs and retrofit to 229 USAF F-16C/Ds. 128K data transfer cartridge. Magnavox Have Quick transceiver. Teledyne AN/APX-101 IFF (APX-109 V3 IFF for US FMS sales). GEC-Marconi wide-angle holographic head-up display. Honeywell Defense Avionics Systems monochrome CRT displays; European aircraft are also receiving other new equipment under the MLU (as detailed under Aircraft variants), including Honeywell 4 ins x 4 ins liquid-crystal flat panel colour displays and enhanced upgraded programmable display generator to replace the CRTs from 1996; similar colour fit is being offered to other F-16A/B/C/D operators. Horizontal situation display for increased situation awareness and tactical flexibility on all missions. Lockheed Martin Enhanced Envelope Gunsight now used by some USAF F-16C/Ds, and may be retrofitted to others. USAF IOC in 1994 for the AN/ASQ-213 HARM Targeting System (initally used by 20th FW F-16C/Ds of Block 50). LANTIRN for night and precision-guided weapon cabability. Many variations of equipment on international aircraft.

Lockheed Martin F-16 with AN/ASQ-213 HARM Targeting System and AGM-88 HARM missiles

Self-protection systems: Dalmo Victor AN/ALR-69 RWR or Loral AN/ALR-56M, Westinghouse AN/ALQ-131 jammer pod (AN/ALQ-184 available), AN/ALQ-126B deceptive ECM, and chaff/flare.
Wing characteristics: Mid mounted, blended with the fuselage, with swept leading edges and no anhedral/dihedral. Vortex control surfaces from the wingroots to a point on the fuselage sides level with the cockpit, to enhance lift and increase stability at high alpha. F-16U has a delta wing (see Aircraft variants).
Wing control surfaces: Flaperons and automatic leading-edge manoeuvring flaps.
Tail control surfaces: Slab tailplane (tailerons) and rudder. VHF/FM antenna, with extended operating distance, incorporated into the leading edge of the fin.
Canard: None.
Airbrakes: Each side between the engine and the tailplane.
Flight control system: Digital fly-by-wire.
Construction materials: Principally aluminium alloy, with honeycomb core for the leading-edge flaps, leading-edges of the tailplane, and twin ventral fins. Graphite/epoxy fin and tailplane skins. Air intake construction and gold-coated canopy on many F-16C/Ds reduce radar signature.
Engine: General Electric F110-GE-100 or later GE-129, or Pratt & Whitney F100-PW-200, 220 or 229 turbofan.
Engine rating: 28,000 lbf (124.55 kN), 29,000 lbf (128.93 kN), 23,770 lbf (105.74 kN), the same, and 29,100 lbf (129.445 kN) with afterburning respectively. GE-129 and PW-229 fitted to F-16C/Ds from Block 50/52. See Engine section for F100 upgrades.
Air intakes: Large intake under the fuselage, with splitter plate.
Fuel system: 3,986 litres in wing and fuselage tanks, reduced to 3,297 on two-seaters. 3 drop tanks, as 1,135.6 litre tank under the fuselage, and a 1,400 litre or 2,271 litre tank under each wing.
Electrical system: 60kVA and 10 kVA principal and back-up generators. 17 amp-hour battery, plus 4 stand-by batteries for the fly-by-wire system.
Hydraulic system: 2 systems, each 3,000 psi.
Braking system: Brakes, with anti-skid. Drag-chute available in a pod beneath the fin, as used by 6 export customers. Arrester hook.

Aircraft variants:

AFTI/F-16 is an Advanced Fighter Technology Integration aircraft, a one-off operated by the USAF for test programmes (see Development).

F-16ES with overwing conformal fuel tanks

YF-22 (PAV-2) showing the 2D engine nozzles, wing control surfaces and undercarriage position (F-22 Photo Team)

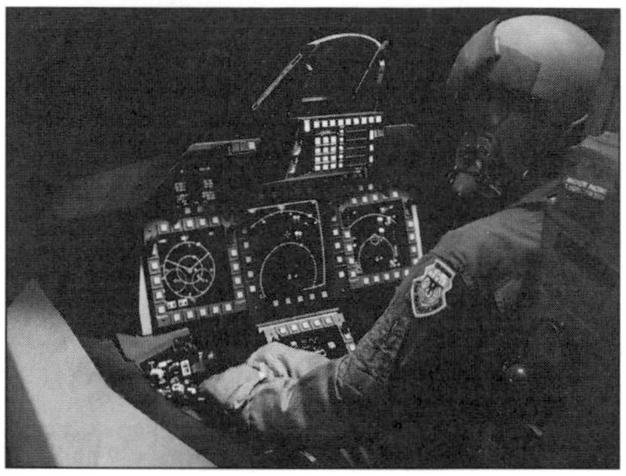

F-22 cockpit concept demonstrator, with a wide-angle HUD, CNI/ICAWS display to the left, flight instrument display to the right, 200 mm central primary multi-function display, defensive display (left of PMFD), attack display (right), and systems display below

F-16A was the initial production version, though still available (as delivered to Portugal from February 1994). AN/APG-66 radar. Many upgraded (see below). Originally analog fly-by-wire control system.
F-16B is the two-seat version of F-16A.
F-16ADF was the designation given to 272 USAF F-16A/Bs when modified for air defence with the ANG, armed with Sidewinders, Sparrow and AMRAAM. IOC 1989. Improved AN/APG-66 radar and ECCM, IFF, and other upgrades, and with the ability to receive GPS.
F-16C has developed through a series of 3 staged improvement programmes to enhance combat efficiency (particularly attack by day or night, and beyond-visual range), in current Block 50/52D form with more powerful engine, improved AN/APG-68 radar and other avionics, enhanced situation awareness displays, autonomous HARM missile capability and more. Proposed future Block improvements will offer the ability to carry GBU-30 among other features.
F-16D is the two-seat equivalent of F-16C. Same principal dimensions.
F16C/D CAS applies to USAF F-16C/Ds to be modified for close air support.
F-16ES is the Enhanced Strategic version under test in 1995, offering a radius of action of 890 naut miles (1,025 miles) 1,650 km with 2 x 2,000 lb bombs and 4 AAMs. Features 2 conformal fuel tanks fitted to the above-wing/fuselage blend, adding 3,200 lb (1,451 kg) of fuel, plus 2 drop tanks. Nose-mounted FLIR. Offered (but not adopted) to Israel.
F-16N and TF-16N are the US Navy designations for 22 F-16Cs and 4 F-16Ds used as supersonic adversary readiness and training aircraft. AN/APG-66 radar, F110-GE-100 engine and no fitted gun.
F-16U is a unique two-seat delta-wing and 20 hardpoint variant of F-16, proposed for the United Arab Emirates as a long-range strike aircraft but not taken up. Also being proposed for the USAF as a JAST substitute as the Falcon 2000.
NF-16D is variable stability in-flight simulator test aircraft (USAF/Calspan), a converted F-16D. Present proposals are to have a thrust vectoring engine fitted and programmable cockpit displays. Currently used for flight control development in connection with the F-22 and Indian LCA programmes.
European upgrade for F-16A/Bs of Belgium (48), Denmark (61), Norway (56) and the Netherlands (136), with AN/APG-66(V2A) radar improvements, a new modular mission computer, Honeywell liquid-crystal flat panel colour displays and enhanced upgraded programmable display generator, Terprom terrain profile matching system, ring-laser gyro INS, GPS, microwave landing system and more. Upgraded aircraft will be capable of carrying advanced AAMs and ASMs.
USAF upgrade programmes include 229 F-16C/Ds receiving the new modular mission computer, and 125 F-16A/Bs flown by the US Air Force Reserve receiving Terprom. Also, several hundred older USAF F-16C/Ds are being modified for close air support and battlefield interdiction, with Pave Penny laser spot tracker, new VHF anti-jam radio, improved data modem for faster data transmission and demonstrated near real time linking and receiving data, LANTIRN and night vision goggles for night missions, missile warning receiver, radar warning receiver and chaff/flare for added self protection.
Other upgrade programmes include Israel fitting an infra-red targeting and nav pod to its F-16C/Ds.

Lockheed Martin (LMAS) F-22

First flight: 29 September 1990.
Role: Advanced tactical fighter (ATF), with ground attack capability. See Development (April 1995) below.

★ Aims

★ To conform to specific weight and fly-away cost constraints, initially targeted at 50,000 lb take-off gross weight and $35 million in FY1985 dollars.
★ Sufficient fuel for mission radius.
★ Supersonic cruise without engine afterburning (supercruise); Mach 1.58 supercruise demonstrated.
★ Low supersonic drag.
★ Internal weapons carriage in air superiority configuration. 4 x F-15-type 610 US gallon (2,309 litre) external tanks or 2 tanks plus GBU-30 (JDAM) weapons can be carried underwing.
★ Unrestricted manoeuvrability, including use of 2-dimensional (2D) convergent/divergent exhaust nozzles (see Engines) for thrust vectoring. Latter used to reduce take-off and landing runs, assist aerodynamic pitch control, and enhance control during high angles of attack and at low flying speed. Sufficient nose-up pitch control power with thrust vectoring and horizontal tails to allow trimmed flight at extreme angles of attack.
★ Thrust/weight ratio of 1.4.
★ Spin resistance and ability to recover from a spin with control surfaces neutralised.
★ Low observables (stealth) through airframe configuration and avionics, including care in design of weapons carriage arrangement, supersonic inlet, augmentor and engine nozzles, canopy, conformal avionics apertures and maintenance areas. Particular emphasis on low radar cross section (RCS).
★ High survivability, through low observables, high manoeuvrability and state-of-the-art integrated avionics for first-look/first-shoot/first-kill, with beyond-visual-range (BVR) engagement capability.
★ Fully integrated common module avionics. Liquid cooling of avionics for reliability.
★ Ada (US DoD) real-time software for all functions, including vehicle management, flight controls, sensors processing and mission avionics integration, as part of VHSIC (very-high-speed integrated circuit) technology.
★ Fully integrated cockpit displays and controls.
★ High level of reliability and supportability, at least twice as good as current fighters.

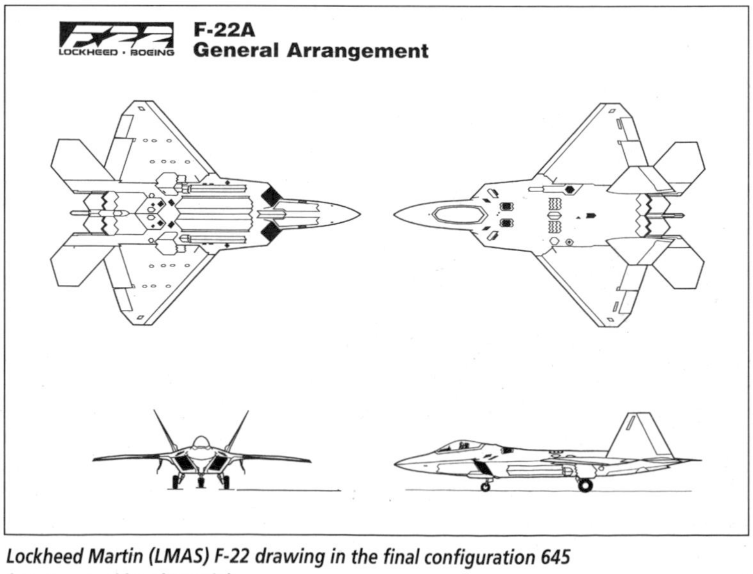

Lockheed Martin (LMAS) F-22 drawing in the final configuration 645 (courtesy Lockheed Martin)

Lockheed Martin (LMAS) YF-22 (PAV-2)

★ 15 minute turnaround time for high sortie rates.
★ All maintenance "on the plane" or at depot level, with exceptions of tyres and battery. Ground support equipment not needed as near-elimination of wing-level maintenance shops and personnel. Portable maintenance aid (lap top). Fuselage height from ground 3 ft (0.91 m).
★ Self sufficiency, with APU, OBOGS, OBIGGS and engine start.
★ Squadron of 24 F-22s require less than the capacity of 8 C-141 transports and 258 support personnel for a 30-day airlift deployment.
★ 8,000 hour structural, systems and avionics life.
★ Compatible with existing aircraft shelters.

▲ Development

▲ November 1981. USAF identified the requirement for a new air superiority fighter to replace the F-15.
▲ September 1983. Air Force awarded concept definition contracts to 7 aircraft manufacturers for the ATF.
▲ September 1985. Formal ATF request for proposals was issued.
▲ May 1986. Edward Aldridge, Secretary of the Air Force, announced that as part of the Packard Commission guidelines, the ATF demonstration/ validation programme would include prototype aircraft and engines as well as a prototype avionics demonstration.
▲ September 1986. Lockheed, Boeing and General Dynamics signed an MoU leading to a teaming agreement. Original YF-22 configuration was Lockheed 638.
▲ 31 October 1986. Lockheed/Boeing/GD team and Northrop/McDonnell Douglas team were selected to compete in the dem/val phase. Each was to build 2 prototypes (YF-22A and YF-23A respectively) plus an avionics testbed under $818 million 4 year 6 month study contracts (Lockheed team's own investment totalled $675 million).

Computer-generated rendering of F-22s engaged in combat. Picture does not have 100% fidelity with Model 645 design (courtesy Lockheed Martin)

▲ 3 November 1986. Lockheed, Boeing and GD exchanged preliminary design data.
▲ 10 July 1987. Original design was determined by the Lockheed team to be technically and competitively unacceptable.
▲ 13 July 1987. Lockheed team initiated a new YF-22 design, approved that October.
▲ April 1988. YF-22 prototype configuration was "unfrozen" to reduce supersonic drag. Redesign of the forebody and aft fuselage took place the following month.
▲ December 1988. First YF119 engine sea level bench test.
▲ 17 July 1989. Initial tests began on YF-22 avionics system in a Lockheed-owned Boeing 757.
▲ 11 October 1989. ATF evaluation phase given a 6-month extension.
▲ November 1989. System review with the USAF.
▲ January 1990. Final assembly of the first YF-22 prototype began at Palmdale, followed by the second in February.
▲ April 1990. Initial Engineering and Manufacturing Development proposals (EMDs) requested. F-22 configuration for EMD proposal frozen that August.
▲ 29 August 1990. YF-22 Prototype Air Vehicle (PAV-1) was unveiled at Lockheed Plant 10 in Palmdale. YF120-GE-100 engines fitted.
▲ 29 September 1990. Lockheed test pilot, Dave Ferguson, made the first flight in YF-22 (PAV-1), during ferry from Palmdale to Edwards AFB flight test center. Test flying by 6511st Test Squadron, USAF.
▲ 25 October 1990. First supersonic flight (PAV-1, test flight 9).
▲ 26 October 1990. First aerial refuelling of the YF-22 (PAV-1, test flight 11) from a KC-135. Aerial refuelling qualification completed on 31 October.
▲ 30 October 1990. Lockheed test pilot, Tom Morganfield, first flew the second YF-22 prototype PAV-2 from Palmdale to Edwards. YF119-PW-100 engines.
▲ 3 November 1990. PAV-1 first demonstrated supercruise (test flight 14).
▲ 15 November 1990. General Electric-powered PAV-1 first demonstrated thrust vectoring capability (test flight 15).
▲ 19 November 1990. First AFOTEC piloted flight (PAV-1, test flight 19).
▲ 20 November 1990. First in-flight weapon bay opening (PAV-2, test flight 6).
▲ 28 November 1990. General Dynamics' test pilot, Jon Beesley, fired an unarmed AAM at Mach 0.7 at 20,000 ft (6,100 m) over China Lake, California, (PAV-2, test flight 11).
▲ 10 December 1990. PAV-1 began YF-22 high angle of attack (high alpha) trials (test flight 28). Completed 17 December (test flight 38) after attaining unprecedented 60° AoA attitude while remaining in full control. (Production configuration models attained over 85° angle of attack in wind tunnel testing.)
▲ 20 December 1990. PAV-2 fired an unarmed AMRAAM missile over the Pacific Missile Test Range at Point Mugu, California (test flight 24).
▲ 28 December 1990. Mach 2+ was achieved (PAV-1, test flight 43). PAV-1 also demonstrated maximum positive g. During dem/val, PAV-1 was flown 43 times for 52.8 hours and PAV-2 31 times for 38.8 hours. YF-22 flying temporarily ended.
▲ 23 April 1991. Air Force Secretary, Dr Donald Rice, announced at a Pentagon briefing that the F-22/P&W F119 combination was winner of the ATF competition.
▲ 23 June 1991. PAV-1 was flown by C-5 to Marietta, to become a non-flying engineering mockup.
▲ 2 August 1991. USAF awarded the Lockheed team a $9.55 billion contract to begin EMD of the F-22. 11 flyable (including two 2-seaters) aircraft, 1 static test and 1 fatigue test airframe to be built (reduced January 1993 to 9). Separate $1.4 billion contract to P&W for engine development, including 33 flightworthy engines (reduced January 1993 to 27).
▲ 30 October 1991. PAV-2 began new 100 hour test programme, covering aerodynamic effects of control actuation, aerodynamic loads, vibration and acoustic fatigue, and maximum lift coefficient.
▲ 16 December 1991. External design of the F-22 frozen during air vehicle requirements/design review update. This allowed wind tunnel and radar cross section models to be built, the internal design to be completed and tooling preparations begun.
▲ 25 April 1992. Returning to Edwards AFB after a test flight, PAV-2 experienced series of pitch oscillations at about 40 ft (12 m) above the runway. With the undercarriage retracted, it hit the runway, caught fire and slid about 8,000 ft (2,440 m). No longer flight-worthy, it was taken by C-5 to Rome Air Development Center at Griffiss ARB to be used in antenna tests. External damage was repaired. On 70 flights, it had totalled 100.4 hours.
▲ 4 June 1992. Design review update completed.
▲ January 1993. Resulting from FY1993 funding shortfall, F-22 EMD programme was rephased. Key events were put back between 6 and 18 months and the number of development aircraft and engines reduced. Second rephase in mid-1994.
▲ 30 April 1993. Air vehicle Preliminary Design Review finished. Final development phase covering detailed design began.
▲ May 1993. Addition of ground attack capability.
▲ 8 December 1993. First F-22 parts fabrication began at Boeing's Kent facility.
▲ February 1995. Critical air vehicle design review begun, after 231 critical design reviews of software and subsystems. Production configuration is Lockheed 645.
▲ April 1995. Lockheed received a $9 million 2-year contract from the USAF to initiate development of F-22 variants for SEAD (suppression of enemy air defences), non-lethal suppression of enemy defences, reconnaissance, attack/interdiction, and surveillance.
▲ 1997. Anticipated date for contract to build 4 pre-production F-22s (previously January 1996).
▲ May 1997. First flight of the EMD F-22 anticipated (previously mid-1996).
▲ Mid-1997. First production F119-PW-100 engine deliveries anticipated.
▲ Late 1997. First flight of an EMD F-22 with full avionics suite anticipated.
▲ Early 1998. Start of pre-production verification with 4 aircraft.
▲ Early 1999. Start of low-rate production.
▲ March 2002. High-rate production decision (DoD "Milestone III") anticipated (previously July 2001).
▲ 2004. Anticipated entry into USAF service; in 1994, the General Accounting Office recommended initial operational capability delay to 2010.
▲ 2012. Last delivery.

Sales/users: Originally planned 750 F-22A/Bs reduced to 648, with first 4 production aircraft to be ordered in 1997, followed by 2-yearly orders of 12, reaching a total of 136 by 2002, with the first high-rate batch of 48 ordered that year. Number required was reduced in 1993 to 442 (including the 4 pre-production aircraft and 58 two-seaters), with yearly high-rate batches of 24 or 36 rather than 48. Initially 4 full production in FY1998, 12 in FY1999, followed by high rate production. In September 1994, Lockheed quoted the EMD contract value at about $11 billion. FY1995 appropriation for the F-22 programme was $2.3 billion, $111 million less than expected.

Edo hydraulic trapeze AAM launcher for the F-22

Lockheed Martin (LMAS) A/F-22X (configuration 653), a naval variable-geometry Derivative Strike/Fighter conceived out of the F-22 and former USN AFX programmes. Programme confirmed to be in "deep freeze" in November 1995

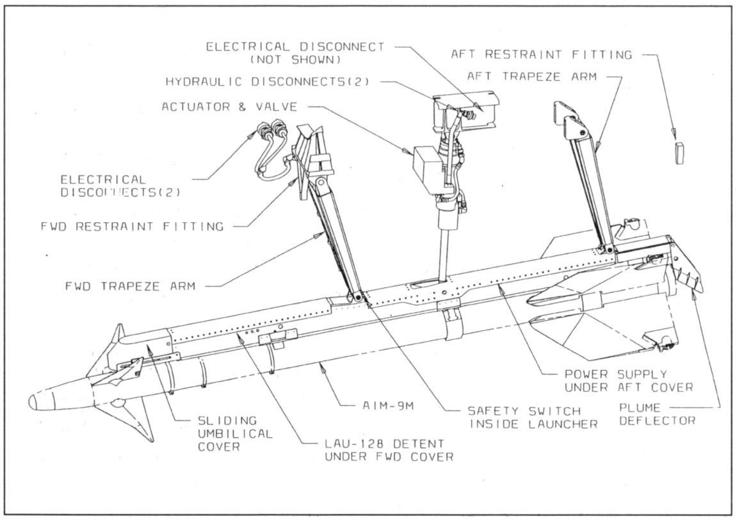

F-22 AIM-9M Trapeze launcher (courtesy Lockheed Martin)

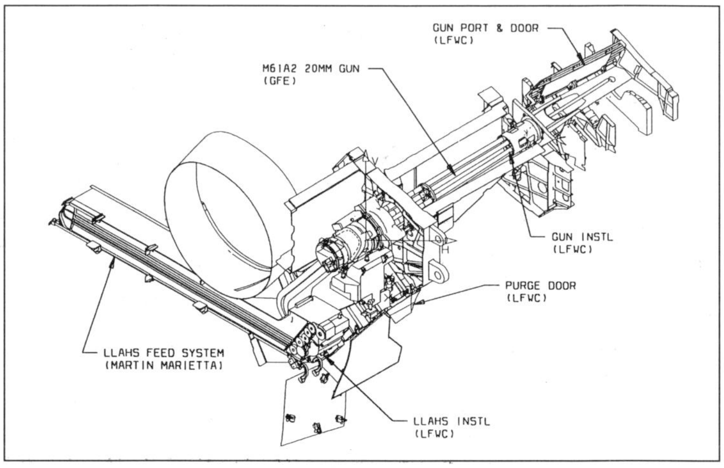

F-22 gun system installation – Isometric (courtesy Lockheed Martin)

Crew: Pilot in the F-22A, 2 in F-22B. No pilot check list. Cold start to ready to go in 4 steps (typically 17 for other aircraft).

Cockpit: 15° pilot look-down visibility over the nose through the Sierracin/Sylmar one-piece canopy with serrated leading edge. Meta Research life support system pressure suit. ILC Dover life support chemical/biological/cold water immersion gear.

Crew escape: McDonnell Douglas modified ACES II zero-zero ejection seat, with restraint webbing over the arms. Non-articulated seat in production F-22A/B; articulated system conceived for YF-22s.

Fixed gun: 20-mm M61A2 6-barrel gun concealed behind door in the starboard wing root, with firing rate of 4,000 to 6,000 rounds per minute.

Ammunition: 480 rounds.

Number of weapon pylons: 4 under the wings, plus weapon bays (see below). Each wing pylon has 5,000 lb (2,268 kg) capacity.

Expendable weapons and equipment: All air-to-air missiles are carried internally during stealth missions, in 2 side of air intake and 1 underfuselage bays, with missiles fired from Edo trapeze hydraulic launchers. For non-stealth missions, 8 additional AMRAAMs can be carried in pairs under the wings. 1 AIM-9M Sidewinder AAM in each side bay and 4 AIM-120A or 6 AIM-120C AMRAAMs in the underfuselage bay (see armament diagram). Under the May 1993 ground attack additions, provision was made for 2 AGM-137A TSSAM stand-off missiles carried under the wings (since cancelled); the underfuselage bay can house 2 x 1,000 lb GBU-30s (formerly known as JDAM or Joint Direct Attack Munitions). GBU-30s displace 2 of the AMRAAMs during attack missions. Provision was also made (mostly software) for AIM-9X. All 4 underwing stations may carry F-15 Eagle type 610 US gallon (2,309 litre) drop tanks. Ground attack provision added just 23 lb (11 kg) to weight. For ferry flights, 4 drop tanks plus 8 external (inert – fins removed) AMRAAMs may be carried in addition to bay weapons.

Radar: Westinghouse/Texas Instruments AN/APG-77 active VLO electrically-scanned active array system integrated with the radome design, and integrated with the CIP (common integrated processor).

Flight/weapon system avionics/instrumentation: Integrated avionics suite, centred on the Hughes Radar Systems Group common integrated processor (CIP – developed using very high speed integrated circuit technology) with memory of 300 Mbytes and capable of 4 billion signal processing operations each second per CIP (2 CIPs on board, with capacity for 3). CIP uses mission planable software for sensor emitter management and integration, fed via Fairchild Defense Data Transfer Unit (DTU); CIP is not fully populated, allowing further development. Sanders/General Electric radio frequency and countermeasures, and TRW Avionics & Surveillance Group communications/ navigation identification (CNI) subsystems. Integrated CNI uses multi-function antennae and shared assets to provide multiple integrated com/nav functions. In-flight data link with LPI (low probability of intercept), allowing secure monitoring of the fuel and weapon situations, whether radar is active or passive, and what targets have been selected, of other accompanying friendly aircraft. Integrated electronic combat avionics uses multi-function apertures and shared assets to perform multiple functions of radar-track warning, IR warning, missile launch detection, and threat identification. Sorted and fused information is displayed on 6 Sanders/Kaiser (OIS) colour active-matrix multi-function displays. Litton inertial reference system (IRS). GEC-Marconi wide-angle HUD. Sanders Graphics Processor Video Inferface (GPVI). Fibre network interface unit (FNIU), avionics bus interface (ABI) and fibre optic bus components by Harris Government Aerospace. Liquid cooling of avionics.

Self-protection systems: IR warning, missile launch detection, AN/ALR-94 RWR/ESM, and chaff/flare.

Wing characteristics: Modified diamond planform. Low wing loading and sufficient wing camber to meet sustained and instantaneous load factor requirements. Scrafed wingtips to house antennae.

Wing control surfaces: Ailerons (20°), flaperons (+20°, -40°), and leading-edge flaps (+3° and -35° normal, and +5°, -37° maximum).

Tail control surfaces: Virtually all-moving tailplane (+30°, -25°). Twin fins and rudders, outward canted by 28°. Rudders (30° movement). No airbrake on production aircraft (fitted to prototypes), FBW system allows aircraft deceleration at idle engine power through extension and/or movement of control surfaces, primarily asymmetric rudders (see Aircraft variants). 4-surface tail configuration provides necessary manoeuvrability and control at minimum structural weight. Using thrust vectoring to control pitch at high angle of attack, horizontal tails can be deflected differentially for high roll rates.

DETAILS FOR F-22A.

Principal dimensions:
Wing span: 44 ft 6 ins (13.564 m)
Maximum length: 62 ft 1 ins (18.923 m)
Maximum height: 16 ft 5 ins (5.004 m)

Wings:
Aerofoil section: Special, biconvex, unspecified
Area: 840 sq ft (78.039 m^2)
Aspect ratio: 2.357
Sweepback: 42° at 25% chord
Chord at root: 32 ft 3.5 ins (9.842 m)
Chord at tip: 3 ft 11 ins (1.194 m)
Twist: 0° 30', 3° 6' (root/tip)
Anhedral: 3° 15'
Ailerons area: 21.4 sq ft (1.988 m^2)
Flaperons area: 55 sq ft (5.11 m^2)
Leading-edge flaps area: 51.2 sq ft (4.757 m^2)

Tail unit:
Tailplane span: 29 ft (8.839 m)
Tailplane area: 136 sq ft (12.635 m^2)
Fin height: 19 ft 7 ins (5.969 m)
Fin area: 178 sq ft (16.537 m^2)
Fin cant angle: 28° outward

Undercarriage:
Type: Retractable, with nosewheel. Menasco Aerosystems legs
Main wheel tyre size: AlliedSignal 37 x 11.5-18
Nose wheel tyre size: AlliedSignal 23.5 x 7.5-10
Wheel base: 19 ft 9.625 ins (6.032 m)

Weights:
Empty, operating: 31,670 lb (14,365 kg)
Maximum take-off: 55,000 lb (24,950 kg)

Performance:
Maximum operating Mach number (MMO): Mach 2+ with afterburning, Mach 1.58 supercruise
Maximum operating speed: 800 kts (921 mph) 1,483 km/h at sea level
Stall speed: classified
Take-off/landing distances: less than F-15, otherwise classified
Maximum climb rate: classified
Roll rate: 100° per second at 120 kts, demonstrated
G limits: +9 target, 7.9 achieved by YF-22
Ceiling: over 50,000 ft (15,240 m)
Range with full fuel: over 1,735 naut miles (2,000 miles) 3,220 km

Canard: None.
Airbrakes: None on production aircraft but above the fuselage between the fins on the prototypes. See Tail control surfaces.
Flight control system: Quad-redundant digital fly-by-wire. Integrated electronic flight/propulsion control system, totally controlled by software. Parker-Berttea Aerospace flight control actuators. Leading-edge flap drive system by Curtiss-Wright Flight Systems.
Fuselage: Blended fuselage/wing design, with chined forebody and conformal sensors. Freestream fixed geometry supersonic air intakes. All exterior edge angles aligned with either the wing leading or trailing edges. 2 side and 1 main underfuselage weapons bays. Retractable spoiler for main bay used for aircraft deceleration with rudders. Fuselage shields some RCS return from wing trailing edges. Rosemount Aerospace air data probes.
Construction materials: The production F-22 (Model 645) comprises 23% thermoset and 1% thermoplastic composites, 15% aluminium, 5% TI 6Q2 titanium, 36% Ti 6-4 titanium, 6% steel and 14% other materials (coatings, paint, transparency, radome, tyres, brakes, sealant, adhesives, seals, actuators, gases and fluids). Composites components include bismaleimide (BMI) wing skins, mid-fuselage fuel floors and exterior skins, inlet duct skins, thermoplastic weapons bay door skins, dual resin bonded battery access panels, tailplane bonded assembly, RTM bulkheads/frames/spars, co-cured BMI/HC skin panels and doors, and BMI taco shell edge skins and spars. Wing spars and some other components are constructed using the new resin transfer moulding process. Boeing is responsible for development and construction of the wings and aft fuselage, and structures for the installation of the engines, nozzles and APU.
Engines: 2 Pratt & Whitney F119-PW-100 augmented turbofans. All engine accessories placed at the bottom of the engine for easy maintenance. Engine change in under 90 minutes using a single trailer. APU in port wing root.
Engine rating: Each 35,000 lbf (155.7 kN) range.
Nozzles: 2D convergent/divergent (±20°) with independent throat and exit area actuation and pitch-axis thrust vectoring.
Air intakes: Freestream fixed geometry supersonic intakes with swept cowl lips, boundary layer bleed and overboard bypass systems, and relatively long subsonic diffuser offering 100% line-of-sight RF blockage. Thrust vectoring adds 30-50 lb (13.6-22.7 kg) to the nozzles.
Flight refuelling probe: B.F.Goodrich Aerospace fuel interface set. XAR flight refuelling receptacle.
Fuel system: Aft of cockpit fuel tank removed from F-22B, to allow for second cockpit.
Electrical system: Originally Sundstrand main electrical power generating system; Smiths 270 volt DC distribution system.
Hydraulic system: High pressure, non-inflammable system. Dowty Decoto actuators.
Braking system: AlliedSignal.
Oxygen system: Normalair-Garrett onboard oxygen generating system.

Aircraft variants:
YF-22 designation covers the 2 original prototypes (PAV-1 and -2), both now non-flying. GE YF120 and P&W YF119 engines tested. Straight trailing edges to trapezoid wings and tailplane. More pointed nosecone. Airbrake. Serrated edges to cockpit canopy. Bolt-on spoiler on underfuselage between intakes, permanently hanging in slipstream on some test flights, to assist in collecting weapons bay acoustic and vibration data. Wing span 43 ft (13.11 m), length 64 ft 2 ins (19.56 m), same area as F-22, wing/stabilizer sweepback 48°.
F-22A will be the production single-seater. EMDs, pre-production and production aircraft will have reprofiled wings and tail surfaces, and reprofiled ailerons (constant chord). Reduced wingroot thickness and sweepback, changes to camber and twist, and increased anhedral. Modified undercarriage with shorter wheel track and wheel base, modified legs and doors. Increased fin area. Air inlets farther back, approximately level with the rear of the canopy. Serrated edges to the canopy and nosecone retained. Airbrake deleted, with deceleration through extension and/or movement of the rudders, weapon bay spoiler, open nozzle exit area and open bleed and bypass doors to increase buzz free operation range of inlet.
F-22B will be the two-seat operational training version. Same length as F-22A, with aft-of-fuselage fuel tank removed.
Future variants for lethal/non-lethal suppression of enemy defences, reconnaissance, attack/interdiction and surveillance (see Development).

Lockheed Martin (General Dynamics) F-111

First flight: 21 December 1964 (F-111A, piloted by Richard Johnson and Val Prahl).
Role: Fighter-bomber, nuclear or conventional strike, and reconnaissance.

★ Aims
★ First modern variable-geometry aircraft, and first operational variable-geometry combat aircraft, originally to replace the F-105 Thunderchief.
★ Sufficient range to ferry unrefuelled across the Pacific or Atlantic.
★ Carriage of conventional or nuclear weapons.
★ Above Mach 2 maximum speed at altitude, and supersonic low-level dash.
★ Short take-off and landing distances, and good rough field performance.
★ Unique rocket-boosted cockpit escape system.

▲ Development
▲ 1960. Specific Operational Requirement 183 issued by the USAF and USN, the latter planning a carrier-capable version to replace Phantom.
▲ 24 November 1962. DoD selected General Dynamics (over Boeing) to undertake development of the TFX tactical fighter, assisted by Grumman.
▲ 21 December 1964. Maiden flight of an F-111A, its variable geometry wings fixed at 26°.
▲ 6 January 1965. Wing sweep was tested in flight for the first time.
▲ 20 October 1967. First emergency ejection of the nose module.
▲ 17 March 1968. First operational mission by F-111As in Vietnam.
▲ 12 September 1970. First UK basing of the F-111, when F-111Es flew in to Upper Heyford.
▲ 1 June 1973. First 6 of 24 F-111Cs for the Royal Australian Air Force arrived at Amberley.
▲ September 1989. Rockwell received a contract to begin the USAF's Pacer Strike upgrade programme on 84 F-111Fs over the coming decade.
▲ August 1990. First flight of an RAAF F-111C with Rockwell Aerospace avionics upgrade. All F-111Cs, F-111A(C)s and RF-111Cs had been similarly upgraded in Australia using locally produced kits by the end of 1995.
▲ 1991. Over 100 USAF F-111s undertook nearly 5,000 sorties during the Gulf War (14,000 mission hours), mostly at night. These included sorties to stop oil flowing into the Persian Gulf. 85% mission capability rate attained.
▲ July 1992. Flight trials began under the F-111F's Pacer Strike modernization programme.
▲ 16 September 1992. UK deployment of F-111s ended, when the last F-111E returned to the USA.
▲ 1993. All USAF F-111 squadrons were brought together at Cannon AFB, NM.
▲ 28 September 1993. The first 2 of 15 ex-USAF F-111Gs (stored) destined for the RAAF, that had flown from McClellan AFB, arrived in Amberley, Australia.
▲ December 1993. Operational capability with the GBU-15 on USAF F-111s, followed by AGM-130 in July 1994.
▲ 1994. Delivery of the first Pacer Strike upgraded F-111F to the USAF.
▲ April 1994. F-111Es and Fs of the 27th FW won the grand prize and several top trophies in Air Combat Command's 1994 Proud Shield bombing and navigation competition, flying against F-15Es, B-52 and B-1Bs.
▲ 1995-96. The start of F-111E/F withdrawal from active service (see Users). This had not been expected until well into the next century. A government bill had prevented bomber retirements in FY1995.
▲ 2020. Expected retirement of RAAF F-111s.
Sales/users: 104 F-111s serve with the USAF in 1995. F-111Fs serve with the 27th Fighter Wing, 8th Air Force, of the USAF's Air Combat Command, at Cannon AFB, NM, alongside EF-111A EW aircraft. F-111Es are operated by the 27th FW for training. Total of about 74 F-111s on the active USAF list in 4 squadrons (plus EF-111A Ravens – see Electronic section); F-111E/F units are 428th Fighter Squadron for training and possible combat, 522nd, 523rd and 524th. Retirement will start in 1995-96, replaced by F-16C/Ds. RAAF has 36 F-111

Lockheed Martin (General Dynamics) F-111F (Alex H. Porteous)

types, as 4 F-111A(C)s, 13 F-111Cs, 15 F-111Gs (ex-USAF) and 4 RF-111Gs for strike and reconnaissance.
Crew: 2, side by side.
Crew escape: Zero-zero rocket-assisted cockpit ejection module, in which the crew remain until lowered to the ground by parachute.
Number of weapon pylons: 4 pivoting.
Expendable weapons and equipment: Up to 25,000 lb (11,340 kg), carried under the wings and in the fuselage bay. Options include 6 nuclear weapons (2 in the bay), missiles, smart bombs (including GBU-28), free-fall bombs, Gator mine dispenser, or 12 Durandel anti-runway weapons. Recent deployments have included AGM-130 and GBU-15 precision-guided munitions. Can carry AIM-9M Sidewinders for self-defence. Future weapons will include the stand-off AGM-154A JSOW, but not now the expected GBU-30s (former JDAM).
Radar: Terrain-following radar.
Flight/weapon system avionics/instrumentation: See Aircraft variants.
Wing characteristics: Variable-geometry outer panels, shoulder mounted. No anhedral or dihedral. Large fixed wing gloves.
Wing control surfaces: Double-slotted trailing-edge flaps, leading-edge slats and above-wing spoilers, used also for lift dumping and as airbrakes.
Tail control surfaces: Slab (taileron) tailplane and rudder.
Engines: See Aircraft variants.
Flight refuelling probe: Retractable, in the upper decking.
Air intakes: Variable.

DETAILS FOR F-111F.

Principal dimensions:
Wing span: 31 ft 11 ins (9.73 m) *swept (72° 30')*, 63 ft (19.2 m) *fully spread (16°)*
Maximum length: 73 ft 6 ins (22.4 m)
Maximum height: 17 ft 2 ins (5.23 m)

Wings:
Aerofoil section: NACA 64A
Area: 525 sq ft (48.77 m^2)
Aspect ratio: 7.56 *spread*
Sweepback: 16° to 72° 30'

Undercarriage:
Type: Retractable, with twin nosewheels

Weights:
Empty, operating: 47,840 lb (21,535 kg)
Maximum take-off: 100,000 lb (45,360 kg)

Performance:
Maximum speed at altitude: Mach 2.5
Maximum speed at low level: Mach 1.2
Ceiling: about 60,000 ft (18,290 m)
Range with full fuel: over 2,518 naut miles (2,900 miles) 4,667 kM

Aircraft variants:
F-111A(C) is the RAAF designation of 4 ex-USAF F-111As received and modernized to make good attrition losses.
F-111C is the principal RAAF version, retrofitted with Pave Tack (see below) and other avionics improvements, including Rockwell Aerospace-integrated digital avionics system with MIL STD 1553B databus. 18,500 lbf (82.29 kN) with afterburning Pratt & Whitney TF30-P-3 turbofan engines.
RF-111C covers 4 RAAF F-111Cs converted to reconnaissance aircraft (all still in service) with IR linescan, various cameras and TV.
F-111E is now used as a trainer by the USAF, having replaced the F-111G. Original analog bombing and navigation suite replaced during 1989-93 with a digital system, allowing use of GPS, improved sensors and advanced weapons. 2 x 19,600 lbf (87.19 kN) with afterburning Pratt & Whitney TF30-P-103 turbofan engines.
F-111F is the only version remaining on active strength with the USAF. 2 x 25,100 lbf (95.64 kN) with after-burning TF30-P-111s. Pave Tack in the fuselage bay for use with smart weapons. Under the Pacer Strike modernization programme to bring the aircraft further inline with the F-111E (which also helps commonality for maintenance), F-111Fs received digital communications and navigation equipment, ring-laser gyro/INS, GPS, new computer software, and more. A further upgrade introduces the ALQ-131/184 ECM podded system.
F-111G was the conversion of strategic FB-111As for conventional attack. Retired by the USAF, but 15 surplus aircraft were received by the RAAF. Rotation allows for extended service well into the next century. Upgraded by Rockwell with digital avionics and new nav/attack system.

Lockheed Martin (LMSW) F-117 Nighthawk and A/F-117X

First flight: 18 June 1981 (FSD, flown by Hal Farley).
Role: Subsonic night attack (F-117A), and carrier-capable day/night attack (A/F-117X).
Details: Principally for F-117A.

DETAILS FOR F-117A.

Principal dimensions:
Wing span: 43 ft 3.5 ins (13.2 m)
Maximum length: 65 ft 11 ins (20.09 m)
Maximum height: 12 ft 5 ins (3.78 m)

Wings:
Aerofoil section: Special, comprising 3 upper and 2 lower flat surfaces joined spanwise
Area: 913 sq ft (84.82 m^2)
Aspect ratio: 2.054
Sweepback: 67° 30'

Tail unit:
Fin cant angle: Outward, approximately 42° 30' from vertical

Undercarriage:
Type: Retractable, with steerable noswheel

Weights:
Maximum take-off: 52,500 lb (23,814 kg)

Performance:
Maximum speed: 561 kts (646 mph) 1,040 km/h
Landing speed: 150 kts (173 mph) 278 km/h
G limits: +6
Radius of action: 600 naut miles (691 miles) 1,111 km with full weapon load, unrefuelled

★ Aims
★ First operational aircraft to fully exploit low observable (LO or stealth) technology.
★ To penetrate dense threat environments at night, and attack high-value targets with pinpoint accuracy, using stealth technology and intelligent mission planning.
★ 7 observable signatures to defeat, namely radar, infra-red, visual, contrails, engine smoke, acoustic and electromagnetic emissions. Achieved by faceted airframe with many angled skin plates to reflect any incoming radar beam away from its source, radar absorbing edges and coatings (including those to the airframe and gold-coated canopy), gridded inlets, unique nozzle design and special antennae. Low RCS principally aimed at avoiding AWACS detection. Low IR signature due to non-afterburning engines and efflux cooling, above-wing air intakes with heated gridding, and shielded exhaust nozzles. Contrail dispersal through nozzle design (see Nozzles). Low noise.
★ Almost "Lifting body" airframe, using integrated vortexes created by the many angles.
★ Unstable in all axes, relying on fly-by-wire control.
★ Internal weapons carriage.
★ Use of proven systems to reduce overall system development risk, including cockpit components, flight control system and computers from the F-16A and F/A-18, navigation system of developed B-52 type, and C-130 environmental control system.
★ Deployment to forward operating locations. Modular, air-transportable vans were developed for support of the avionics, subsystems and the mission planning system. 5 maintenance vans and 2 mission-data-planning-system vans that can be airlifted by C-5, C-141 or C-130.

▲ Development
▲ 1974. DARPA requested studies from 5 aircraft manufacturers for a reduced radar signature fighter. Lockheed's Advanced Development Projects organization was not among those approached. Lockheed submitted an independent proposal in 1975.
▲ April 1976. Lockheed "Skunk Works" was selected by DARPA to develop a stealth fighter under the Have Blue programme.
▲ 1 December 1977. Maiden flight of the first of 2 XST

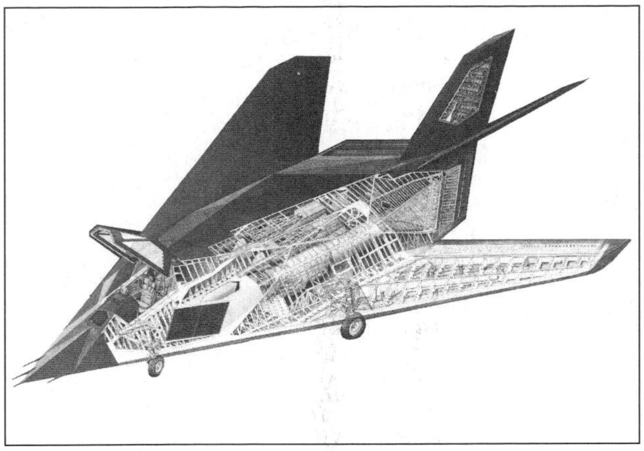

Lockheed Martin (LMSW) F-117A Nighthawk cutaway (courtesy Lockheed Martin)

Have Blue technology demonstrators, at Groom Lake, Nevada. Each 12,000 lb (5,443 kg) weight aircraft was powered by 2 General Electric CJ610 turbojets, each engine rated at 2,850 lbf (12.68 kN).
▲ 4 May 1978. First XST lost in an accident.
▲ 16 November 1978. Start of full-scale engineering development and fabication of 5 FSD flight test vehicles and 15 production F-117As, under the Senior Trent programme.
▲ July 1979. Second XST was lost.
▲ 15 October 1979. The 4450th Tactical Group was founded, eventually to receive F-117As (see below).
▲ 16 January 1981. First FSD F-117 was taken to the Tonopah test range, where it flew mid-year.
▲ 22 March 1982. First night flight by an EMD aircraft.
▲ 20 April 1982. Loss of the first F-117A prior to delivery due to a control connection problem, resulting in a replacement being built.
▲ 7 July 1982. Weapon release trials began.
▲ 23 August 1982. Deliveries began to the USAF. First operational pilot to fly an F-117A was Major Al Whitley of the 4450th on 15 October. Initial operational capability with the 4450th Test Squadron was declared in October 1983.
▲ 1987. RAF personnel first received opportunities to fly the F-117A in the USA.
▲ 10 November 1988. First public announcement of the F-117A.
▲ 20-21 December 1989. First operational use of the F-117A, when 2 dropped 2,000 lb laser-guided bombs on the Rio Hato barrack area in Panama during Operation Just Cause.
▲ 1 December 1988. First flight of an F-117A upgraded for trials under the Offensive Capability Improvement Programme. Upgrade of the F-117A fleet continues, with Phase V for completion by March 1997.
▲ 21 April 1990. First public viewing, at Nellis AFB.
▲ 12 July 1990. Final F-117 delivered, making 64 aircraft (including FSD prototypes).
▲ 19 August 1990. 21 F-117As of the 37th TFW left Tonopah for Operation Desert Shield, stopping overnight at Langley before flying non-stop to King Khalid Air Base in Saudi Arabia, refuelled from KC-10As. 21 more arrived on 4 December and 26 January, the latter from the 417th Tactical Fighter Training Squadron.
▲ 1991. 42 F-117As of the 37th TFW operated during the Gulf War, flying 1,271 missions. First missions were on 16 January, when 30 aircraft flew 37 sorties.
▲ August 1991. Modernization of the navigation suite began.
▲ 24 June 1994. USAF officially adopted the name Nighthawk.
▲ April-May 1995. 2 F-117As lost, 1 in an emergency landing accident and the other over New Mexico.

Sales/users: 60 full-production F-117As were built but only 59 accepted by the USAF and given serial numbers (as the first was lost on its maiden flight at Groom Lake prior to delivery), of which 53 remain on strength and 45 are primary aircraft authorized (PAA) for operational missions. Currently operated by the 49th Fighter Wing (12th Air Force), Air Combat Command, USAF, out of Holloman AFB, New Mexico.

Crew: Pilot.

Cockpit: Centre-stick control. Throttles on the left console, and pilot interface to the flight control and mission computers on the right console. Flat plate, gold coated, canopy glazing. Saw-tooth leading edge to the canopy frame to direct radar reflections.

Crew escape: McDonnell Douglas ACES II zero-zero ejection seat.

Fixed guns: None.

Expendable weapons and equipment: Weapon bay in the flat underside of the mid-fuselage, 15 ft 5 ins (4.7 m) long. Houses an extendable weapons rack, known as a trapeze. Targeting and weapon delivery by use of an infra-red acquisition and designation system. 5,000 lb (2,268 kg) load. Laser-guided conventional bombs of up to 2,000 lb (907 kg) weight each (typically GBU-10 and -27), tactical munitions dispensers, missiles including Maverick or HARM, and nuclear bombs. Can carry Sidewinders for self protection. New weapons include GBU-30s (JDAM) and JSOW.

Radar: None.

Flight/weapon system avionics/instrumentation: Sophisticated navigation and attack systems integrated into a digital avionics suite. MIL STD 1760 interface. Automated mission planning; before a mission, planning computers define the detailed parameters, after which the data is transferred to the electronic data transfer module (a portable cartridge) used for loading the aircraft's computers. Following take off, the mission programme (integrated with the autothrottle and autopilot) permits hands-off flying. Recently revised flight management system as part of the on-going upgrades. Recently upgraded computer (IBM AP-102). Honeywell H-423/E ring laser gyro inertial navigation system. GPS. AHRS. Forward-looking, and downward-looking, upgraded infra-red systems (FLIR inset ahead of the canopy, and DLIR in a steerable underfuselage turret) each with a boresight laser designator and autotracker. Pilot Activated Automatic Recovery System to regain level attitude. 4-dimensional cockpit instrumentation, with up-front data entry panel, Kaiser HUD, central video monitor to display infra-red imagery, 2 colour multi-function displays and digital moving map. Retractable radio antennae under the fuselage, but most missions are flown in radio silence.

Wing characteristics: Extremely swept wings, low mounted, with no anhedral/dihedral. Leading edges form a straight line with the triangular fuselage nose. A/F-117X is projected with larger wings of much reduced sweep, with leading- and trailing-edge control surfaces and possibly a curved aerofoil. Straight wingtips.

Wing control surfaces: 2-section elevons.

Tail control surfaces: V tailplane, comprising upper-section slab "ruddervators" that combine the functions of rudders and elevators. Fixed lower section. New construction, using composites, and are faceted and have very sharp edges. Ruddervators also help obstruct infra-red and radar returns from the nozzle area. F/A-117X adds a slab tailplane to the ruddervators.

Canard: None.

Flight control system: GEC quadruple redundant fly-by-wire.

Fuselage: Faceted airframe of pyramidical shape, with the outer skin formed by many flat-plate surfaces set at angles to dissipate signals from hostile radars. Black-finished, mainly radar-absorbing composite skin material, with a new resin-based, stronger and more heat-resistant material used for the trailing-edge segments. Subsystems access within the undercarriage and weapon bay for servicing, plus the single avionics bay, help minimize the need to remove RAM coatings. 4 faceted and heated nose pitot tubes provide air data to the flight control computer. All doors and removable panels have saw-tooth leading and trailing edges.

Construction materials: Mainly aluminium alloy, with a complicated internal structure to support the flat panels (see drawing). Graphite-thermoplastic box structure to the twin fins, with stainless steel base. Composite bay and undercarriage doors.

Engines: 2 General Electric F404-GE-F1D2 turboshafts.

Engine rating: Each 10,800 lbf (48.04 kN). No afterburning.

Air intakes: Each side of the cockpit, with (heated) grids that block and disperse radar energy. Horizontal 6-sided doors set into the upper intake surface form

F-117A Nighthawk, showing the broad "platypus" nozzles to produce a wide, thin plume for fast dispersion in the aircraft's wake

F-117A Nighthawk with drag-chute deployed

Lockheed Martin A/F-117X proposed naval derivative of the F-117A

auxiliary intakes. Internal trunking diverts some air to the exhaust nozzles for efflux cooling.

Nozzles: Horizontal "slot" type nozzles form the fuselage trailing edges, with protruding lower lips, and 11 vertical guide vanes within each nozzle. Cold-air efflux cooling. Nozzles nicknamed "platypus" type. Nozzles produce a wide, thin plume, directed marginally upward, for fast dispersion in the aircraft's wake. Wide expanse of the airframe is to obstruct direct infra-red and radar detection of the aft engine section. New constructional materials for the trailing edges (see fuselage) may replace the original heat tiles. F/A-117X appears to have 2D thrust vectoring nozzles of F-22 type, though still shielded.

Flight refuelling probe: Rollover, aft of cockpit. Rear-facing light to illuminate the receptacle.

Fuel system: Auxiliary fuel tanks carried internally in the bay.

Braking system: Carbon brakes, with anti-skid system. Drag-chute. Runway arrester hook.

Aircraft variants:

F-117A Nighthawk is the operational USAF stealth fighter, as described.

A/F-117X is the proposed derivative for the US Navy, as an affordable attack aircraft for carrier deployment by the year 2002. A land-based variant is also proposed.

Lockheed Martin (LASC) P-3 Orion

First flight: 19 August 1958 (Electra *N1883* aerodynamic prototype with simulated MAD tail boom), 25 November 1959 (YP3V-1, becoming YP-3A from 1962).

Role: Maritime patrol, anti-submarine, anti-surface vessel, sea control and fisheries protection, mine-laying, search and rescue, over the horizon targeting, and much more including airborne early warning (see Electronics section).

★ Aims

★ To replace the land-operated P2V Neptune and P5M Marlin flying-boat, to be based on an existing aircraft to save time and development costs.

★ Long loiter time.

★ Larger than Neptune, with longer range and higher speed.

▲ Development

▲ August 1957. Design proposals requested under Specification 146 by the US Navy for a new ASW aircraft.

▲ 24 April 1958. Lockheed was announced winner with its Electra airliner variant, the main change being a shorter fuselage incorporating an internal weapons bay, plus new avionics and equipment to suit its role.

▲ 15 April 1961. First flight of the first of 7 pre-production P3V-1 Orions.

▲ 15 April 1962. Board of Inspection and Survey trials at Patuxent River began, to eventually total 2,521 hours.

▲ 23 July 1962. Production deliveries began to the US Navy, initially to VP-8 at NAS Patuxent River, followed by VP-44.

▲ January 1966. Initial deliveries of the P-3B, to VP-8 at NAS Moffett Field.

▲ 18 September 1968. Maiden flight of the P-3C, with deliveries first going to VP-56 in June 1969.

▲ July 1970. First Orions into Naval Air Reserve service, in P-3A form, becoming l VP-91 at Moffett Field.

▲ 13 November 1978. P-3A Orions were finally withdrawn from active US Navy service, replaced by P-3Bs and Cs.

▲ 18 September 1968. Maiden flight of the P-3C Orion, entering US Navy service the following year.

▲ 17 April 1990. Final production P-3C for the US Navy.

▲ 1991. During Operation Desert Shield/Desert Storm, US Navy Orions operated over the eastern Mediterranean, Red Sea, Gulf Oman and Persian Gulf, undertaking surveillance, identification and interdiction of surface shipping, plus over-the-horizon targeting and damage assessment.

▲ May 1991. Last production P-3C delivery from Palmdale; the follow-on P-7A LRAACA had been cancelled in 1990.

▲ June 1994. The first of 8 P-3Cs for South Korea was rolled-out, representing the first newly built Orions from Marietta (where production had been transferred).

▲ 1994. Under Project Sword, a US Navy P-3C was used as a command, control, communications and intelligence aircraft to rely real-time information to the cockpit instrumentation of a USAF F-16. A Navy Hornet was used in a similar demonstration in 1995.

Sales/users: Total sales are 649 by 1995, the final 8 going to South Korea. Argentina (ex-US Navy P-3s), Australia (P-3C Update II/II.5; 18 to receive avionics upgrade, the first by E-Systems in the USA and the remainder in Australia), Canada (CP-140 Aurora plus CP-140A Arcturus for long-range coastal surveillance), Chile (P/UP-3A), Greece (4 ex-US Navy P-3Bs, plus 2 P-3As for training and 2 for spares), Iran (P-3F), Japan (Kawasaki P-3C Update II.5/III, EP-3, UP-3), South Korea (8 new P-3C Update III), Netherlands (P-3C Update II.5), New Zealand (P-3K), Norway (P-3C Update III and P-3N), Pakistan (P-3C Update II.75), Portugal (P-3P), Spain (P-3A and B), Thailand (5 ex-US Navy as 3 P-3T and 2 UP-3T, plus 2 for spares – all based on the P-3A), and USA (Navy, P-3Bs and 247 P-3C Upgrade IIIs on strength with active squadrons and Navy Reserve – no P-3Bs with active first-line squadron – plus specialized variants as detailed under Aircraft variants, and including US Customs P-3 AEW). US Navy P-3C Update IIIs being further upgraded by Unisys to have AN/APS-137 Inverse Synthetic-Aperture Radar, improved infra-red detection, improved communications to allow co-ordinated operations with surface and sub-surface vessels, and standard Loral AN/ALR-66 ESM. Upgraded P-3s in storage have been suggested as a possibility to meet Air Staff Requirement 420 for an RAF Nimrod replacement. Several Middle Eastern nations are said to have expressed interest in Orions.

Crew: Typically 10, as pilot, co-pilot and flight engineer in the flight station, tactical co-ordinator (TACCO) and navigator/communicator aft, MAD operator next in a separate cabin, then a large cabin for the 2 acoustic sensor stations, and finally the ordnance station, plus the flight technician. Observer stations aft, followed by a toilet, galley and rest area with bunks and seats. Up to 13 other persons can be carried, including a relief crew for extended missions.

Fixed guns: None.

Number of weapon pylons: 10 under the wings, plus a 12 ft 10 in (3.91 m) long weapons bay in the forward fuselage.

DETAILS FOR P-3C UPDATE III.

Principal dimensions:
Wing span: 99 ft 8 ins (30.38 m)
Maximum length: 116 ft 10 ins (35.61 m)
Maximum height: 33 ft 8.5 ins (10.27 m)

Wings:
Aerofoil section: Modified NACA 0014, 0012 (root/tip)
Area: 1,300 sq ft (120.77 m^2)
Aspect ratio: 7.64
Incidence: 3° and 0.5° (root/tip)
Dihedral: 6°

Tail unit:
Tailplane span: 42 ft 10 ins (13.06 m)
Tailplane area: 241 sq ft (22.39 m^2)

Undercarriage:
Type: Retractable, with twin wheels on each unit
Wheel base: 29 ft 9 ins (9.07 m)
Wheel track: 31 ft 2 ins (9.5 m)

Weights:
Empty: 61,491 lb (27,892 kg)
Normal take-off: 139,760 lb (63,394 kg)
Maximum take-off: 142,000 lb (64,410 kg)

Performance:
Maximum speed: 405 kts (466 mph) 750 km/h at 15,000 ft (4,570 m)
Long-range cruise speed: 350 kts (403 mph) 648 km/h at 25,000 ft (7,620 m)
Patrol speed: 209 kts (241 mph) 387 km/h
Stall speed: 133 kts (153 mph) 248 km/h *clean*, 112 kts (129 mph) 208 km/h *with flaps*
Take-off distance: 4,240 ft (1,292 m)
Landing distance over a 50 ft (15 m) obstacle: 2,770 ft (844 m)
Maximum climb rate: 2,600 ft (792 m) per minute at sea level
Ceiling: 34,400 ft (10,485 m)
Maximum radius of action: 2,070 naut miles (2,384 miles) 3,836 km
Ferry range: 4,500 naut miles (5,182 miles) 8,334 km
Duration: 14 hours 30 minutes on all engines, 17 hours 12 minutes on 2 engines

Expendable weapons and equipment: Up to 20,000 lb (9,072 kg). Weapon options include 8 Harpoon anti-ship missiles under the wings, 8 x Mk 46 or 6 x Mk 50 torpedoes in the bay or 6 x Mk 60s under the wings, 3 nuclear depth bombs in the bay, up to 20 depth bombs, 11 Mk 83 bombs, up to 20 destructors, up to 11 mines underwing and in the bay, rockets, flares and sonobuoys (52 launch chutes, of which 51 computer controlled – 48 can be loaded before take-off). AGM-65D Maverick capability is being added to US Navy P-3C-IIIs. 2 AIM-9L Sidewinders can be carried for self protection.

Radar: AN/APS-115 search radar, with 360° scanning, or AN/APS-137 ISAR for upgraded US Navy P-3C-IIIs. Australian aircraft are likely to be fitted with Elta EL/M-2022A.

Flight/weapon system avionics/instrumentation: AN/AYA-8 data processing system comprises the AN/ASQ-114 central digital computer or proposed AN/ASQ-212 under the US Navy ASUW Improvement Programme, 3 or 4 logic units, 2 magnetic tape transports, and signal data converter. Navigation system includes dual LTN-72 INS, LTN-211 Omega, AN/APN-227 Doppler radar, AN/ARN-81 Loran A/C, true airspeed computer, AN/ARN-118 Tacan, VOR/ILS, AN/ARN-83 LF-ADF, AN/ARA-50 UHF-DF, AN/AJN-15 flight direction indicator and OTPI. Communications system includes 2 AN/ARC-143 UHF transceivers, AN/ARC-101 VHF

Lockheed Martin P-3C Update III Orion, armed with Harpoon

transceiver, 2 AN/ARC-161 HF transceivers, AN/ACQ-5 data link, AN/AGC-6 teletype, integrated acoustic comm system, and sucure KY-75 HF and UHF voice. US Navy P-3C-IIIs are receiving a communications upgrade. IFF/SIF. Acoustic sensors are 2 AN/AQA-7 sonar computer recorders or an IBM AN/UYS-1 Proteus acoustic processor in Update III, 2 AN/ARR-72 or -78 (Update III) sonobuoy receivers, command actuated sonobuoy system, time code generator, acoustic tape recorder, ambient sea noise meter, bathythermograph recorder and acoustic source signal generator. Non-acoustic sensors are radar (see Radar), AN/ALQ-78 (or AN/ALR-66(V)3 for upgraded US Navy P-3C-IIIs) electronic support measures in a pod on the port inboard wing pylon (interfaces with the computer which aids in the automatic classification and analysis of radiated electron signals), AN/ASQ-81 magnetic anomaly detector (MAD) or CAE Electronics MAD for Australian upgraded P-3Cs, MAD compensation group adapter, AN/ASA-64 submarine anomaly detector, and retractable infra-red detecting set (scans for surface or partially submerged targets and resolves a target image for visual presentation on the Sensor Station 3 and TACCO displays). All US Navy P-3C-IIIs are receiving long-range electro-optical sensors. KA-74 camera and KB-18A strike assessment camera. A US Navy P-3B is being tested with laser airborne depth sounding (LADS) equipment.
Self-protection systems: See above and Weapons.
Wing characteristics: Straight, low mounted, with dihedral.
Wing control surfaces: Ailerons (with tabs) and flaps.
Tail control surfaces: Elevators and rudder, with tabs.
Flight control system: Hydraulic, with boosters.
Construction materials: Metal.
Engines: 4 Allison T56-A-14 turboprops, with Hamilton Standard 56H60-77 propellers. APU.
Engine rating: Each 4,910 shp (3,661 kW).
Flight refuelling probe: Not fitted as standard. See Aircraft variants
Fuel system: 34,825 litres usable.
Electrical system: 24 volt DC supply. 120/208 volt 400 Hz AC supply.
Hydraulic system: 3,000 psi.
Braking system: Hydraulic brakes.
De-icing system: Bleed air for wings, and electric for tail unit and propeller spinners.

Aircraft variants:

CP-140 Aurora is the Canadian version of Orion. AYK-10 computer, APS-126 radar, ASQ-501 MAD, and other systems from the S-3 Viking. ALR-66(V)3 displays.
CP-140A Arcturus is a Canadian P-3C-based long-range coastal surveillance and EEZ protection variant, with no ASW equipment.
EP-3 is Kawasaki's electronic surveillance version. 3 delivered from 1991.
EP-3E Aries II is the US Navy designation of 12 P-3Cs modified for electronic surveillance (see Electronic section).
EP-3J is a US Navy EW trainer (2).
NP-3 applies to US Navy Orions modified into testbed aircraft.
P-3A was the first production model, upgraded for current operators. Fitted with 4,500 shp (3,356 kW) T56-A-10W turboshafts. P-3T/UP-3Ts are modernized P-3As.
P-3B was the first model to use T56-A-14 engines. Most US Navy aircraft in storage, the remainder with Reserve units. P-3K and P-3Ps are upgraded P-3Bs.
P-3C version was initiated with the development of the A-NEW advanced ASW avionics system at the Naval Air Development Center at Warminster. Became the first ASW aircraft in the world with a centralized computer. Directional acoustic frequency analysis and recording processing (Difar). With this computer-integrated system, crew were relieved of the heavy task of interpreting the raw intelligence data provided by the aircraft's sensors. Instead of charts, logs and other data, the computer handled the data, allowing the crew to concentrate on tactical planning.
P-3C Update I was introduced to the US Navy in January 1975, with new avionics and software designed to increase effectiveness. Added equipment included a magnetic memory drum that expanded the computer memory 7-fold, Difar improvements, Omega navigation, and AN/ASA-66 tactical displays for 2 sensor stations.
P-3C Update II was introduced in August 1977, with new infra-red detection and sonobuoy reference systems (IRDS/SRS); Harpoon anti-ship missiles; AQH-4(V)2 28-channel magnetic tape recorder/ reproducer; LTN-72 inertial navigation system; VHF/VOR, Tacan, Doppler replacement; Triple Vernier Difar; Mad-CGA; and DMTS.
P-3C Update II.5 was an interim modernization, with improved nav/com, IACS communications link with submarines, wing pylons and other changes. Version for Kawasaki production, beginning with 5 aircraft produced from Lockheed knockdown components *(5004-5008)*; Kawasaki-produced aircraft to undertake modernization to Upgrade III standard from 1996. ALR-66(V)3 displays (similar displays are also used by Australia, Canada and Norway).
P-3C Update II.75 refers to Pakistan's aircraft, based on the Update III but with some minor downgrade of equipment.
P-3C Update III is the latest version, as flown by the active US Navy, entering service in 1984. Features an IBM Proteus acoustic processor and new sonobuoy receiver (supplanting Difar), and other changes including LTN-211 Omega and KY-75 secure HF voice. Newly built and produced by retrofit as Upgrade IIIR.
P-3F is the version used by Iran, similar to P-3C base but with in-flight refuelling.
P-3K is New Zealand's version. Receiving new wings built by Daewoo of South Korea under Project Kestrel.
P-3N refers to 2 Norwegian P-3Bs operated by the Coast Guard without ASW capability.
P-3P is the designation of 6 ex-RAAF P-3Bs operated by Portugal, with ALR-66(V)3 displays.
P-3T is Thailand's version.
P-3 AEW is the airborne early warning and control variant, with AN/APS-138 surveillance radar in a 24 ft (7.32 m) rotating dome antenna. 4 operated by the US Customs Service. Last delivered in 1993. See Electronics section.
RP-3A/C are US Navy variants for oceanographic research.
RP-3D is operated by the US Navy for atmospheric research and magnetic survey work.
TP-3A is a US Navy pilot trainer, converted from P-3As.
UP-3 designation covers various mission training, ECM training, utility transport and test aircraft versions.
VP-3A is a US Navy VIP transport.
WP-3D is an atmospheric and weather research variant of P-3C, used by the US Department of Commerce.

Lockheed Martin (LMAS) S-3B, ES-3A and US-3A Viking

First flight: 21 January 1972.
Role: Carrier-borne sea control (anti-submarine, anti-ship, mine warfare, over-the-horizon targeting and strike support) aircraft (S-3B), electronic reconnaissance and signal/communications intelligence (ES-3A) aircraft, and carrier onboard delivery aircraft (US-3A). All S-3B/EA-3As have aerial refuelling receiver/ tanker capabilities.

★ Aims

⋆ Initially to replace the Grumman S-2 Tracker as the standard US Navy fixed-wing, carrier-borne anti-submarine aircraft.
⋆ Enhanced performance coupled to newly-developed turbofan engines.
⋆ ES-3A to take over the role left by the EA-3B Skywarrior.
⋆ Due to modifications encompassed into the S-3B to increase reliability, maintainability and sustainability, S-3B operations have shown a 45% reduction in weapons avionics maintenance man-hours per flight over the S-3A, and a sustained 20% increase in operational readiness.

▲ Development

▲ 1964. US Navy announced the requirements for the VSX carrier-borne ASW aircraft.
▲ April 1968. Proposals submitted to the US Navy by the industry. Lockheed's team included Univac Federal Systems Division of Sperry Rand and Vought Systems

DETAILS FOR S-3B.

Principal dimensions:
Wing span: 68 ft 8 ins (20.93 m)
Wing span, folded: 29 ft 6 ins (8.99 m)
Maximum length: 53 ft 4 ins (16.26 m)
Maximum height: 22 ft 9 ins (6.93 m)
Height, wings/tail folded: 15 ft 3 ins (4.65 m)

Wings:
Area: 598 sq ft (55.555 m^2)
Aspect ratio: 7.88
Dihedral: 0°

Tail unit:
Tailplane span: 27 ft (8.23 m)

Undercarriage:
Type: Retractable, with twin nosewheels. Arrester hook

Weights:
Maximum take-off: 47,600 lb (21,590 kg)

Performance:
Maximum speed: 450 kts (518 mph) 834 km/h at 25,000 ft (7,620 m)
Loiter speed at sea level: 160 kts (184 mph) 296 km/h
Stall speed: 85 kts (97 mph) 156 km/h
Landing distance: 1,600 ft (488 m) on land, at 36,500 lb (16,555 kg) weight
Maximum climb rate: above 4,200 ft (1,280 m) per minute
Ceiling: 35,000 ft (10,668 m)
Combat range: 1,997 naut miles (2,300 miles) 3,700 km
Loiter duration at sea level: 7 hours 30 minutes

Lockheed Martin S-3B Viking sea control aircraft

Division of LTV Aerospace.
▲ 4 August 1969. Lockheed announced to be the winner of the VSX competition, and 8 development aircraft were ordered.
▲ 8 November 1971. First R&D YS-3A Viking was rolled out at Burbank, then trucked to Palmdale.
▲ 21 January 1972. John Christiansen and Lyle Schaefer crewed the YS-3A on its first flight, lasting 90 minutes.
▲ 28 April 1972. US Navy authorization for an initial 13 production aircraft.
▲ 19 May 1972. First flight of the second R&D S-3.
▲ 17 July 1972. First flight of the third R&D S-3, the first with full avionics suite and an APU.
▲ November 1973. First landing on an aircraft carrier, USS *Forrestal*.
▲ 20 February 1974. S-3A officially introduced to the US Navy during a ceremony at NAS North Island, initially going to VS-41 Air Antisubmarine Training Squadron.
▲ 7 July 1975. S-3As first went to sea operationally with VS-21 on board USS *John F. Kennedy*.
▲ 8 July 1978. 187th and final S-3A was delivered to the US Navy.
▲ 18 August 1981. Lockheed received a $14.5 million contract from the US Naval Air Systems Command to begin engineering development of a Viking weapon system improvement programme (WSIP) upgrade to include improved acoustic processor, expanded electronic support measure coverage, increased radar processing, sonobuoy receiver system, and provision for carrying Harpoon missiles. The first of 2 development aircraft flew on 13 September 1984 at Palmdale. Flight testing and technical/ operational evaluation ended at Patuxent River in 1986. The manufacture of kits to upgrade S-3As to S-3B standard followed.
▲ 17 December 1987. VS-27 of the US Navy's Atlantic Fleet became the first squadron to receive redelivered S-3Bs.
▲ 1990. VS-31 became the first S-3B squadron, deploying on USS *Dwight D. Eisenhower*.
▲ 19 February 1991. VS-32 sank a patrol boat during the Gulf War.
▲ 15 May 1991. ES-3A prototype made its first flight at Palmdale.
▲ 17 July 1991. S-3B sets the longest distance and duration flight records from an aircraft carrier, at 5,100 naut miles (5,873 miles) 9,445 km and 15.5 hours.
▲ 21 January 1992. First flight of an ES-3A electronic reconnaissance Viking conversion from NAS Cecil Field, to provide essential organic electronic reconnaissance capability (lost after the removal of EA-3Bs) for carrier operations.
▲ 11 February 1992. First ES-3A was redelivered to the US Navy.
▲ April 1993. VQ-5 made the first ES-3A deployment, on board USS *Independence*.
▲ 31 August 1994. 121st and final S-3B was redelivered to VS-41 in a ceremony at NAS North Island.
▲ November 1994. S-3B Viking was stated by COMCRUDESGRU FIVE to be "already the undisputed multi-mission champ of the Battle Group".
▲ 1994. Under WSIP II, Lockheed Martin is preparing 3 new phases of improvements: 1) wings, engines and related systems (structural analysis to keep the S-3 flying well into the next century); 2) reliability/ maintainability and system obsolescence; 3) mission effectiveness and response to emerging requirements, probably concentrating on littoral operations and co-operative engagements.

Sales/users: 8 research and development aircraft plus 179 full production S-3As delivered by 1978. 121 S-3A Vikings had been upgraded to S-3Bs with WSIP kits by 1994, also making S-3Bs suited to in-flight refuelling other US Navy aircraft (8 S-3Bs per squadron). Installation work carried out at NAS Cecil Field (83) and NAS North Island (38), as "the most complex modification programmes ever accomplished in the field". After the prototype ES-3A was produced by Lockheed's Skunk Works, 15 additional aircraft were modified at Cecil Field (operated by VQ-5 based at NAS North Island and VQ-6 at NAS Cecil Field). Current US Navy strength technically includes also 5 stored US-3As. Requests have been made to increase VS(S-3B) and VQ(ES-3A) squadron complements.
Details: Principally for S-3B.
Crew: 4, comprising 2 pilots on the flight deck, and TACCO and SENCO stations in an cabin immediately behind. Pilot and 3 sensor station operators in ES-3A.
Crew escape: McDonnell Douglas zero-zero ejection seats, each containing a survival kit/life raft.
Fixed guns: None.
Number of weapon pylons: 2, under the wings.
Expendable weapons and equipment: 3,080 lb (1,397 kg) load. Divided weapon bay for 4 torpedoes, 4 Mk 82 bombs, 2,000 lb Mk 84 bomb, 4 mines, 4 destructors or 2-4 depth charges. Harpoon anti-ship missiles, SLAM missiles, rockets, Rockeye II cluster bomb dispensers, mines or other stores under the wings.
Radar: AN/APS-137(V)1 Inverse Synthetic Aperture Radar.
Flight/weapon system avionics/instrumentation: Original S-3A equipment included AN/ASQ-81 MAD. Modification of the S-3A to S-3B required 10 major upgrades in the weapon system capability. Included integration of the ISAR radar, ALR-76 ESM and FLIR into a sensor suite with enhanced identification capabilities; highly sensitive direction finding systems, additional ESM systems, enhanced multistatic acoustic processor (AN/UYS-1 Proteus), Hazeltine AN/ARR-78 sonobuoy receiver, Cubic AN/ARS4 sonobuoy reference system, new tape recorder, GPS receiver, satellite communications, and a variety of long-range secure voice/data systems including Joint Tactical Information Distribution System.
Self-protection systems: Goodyear AN/ALE-39 ECM integrated with the ESM suite, with chaff/flare dispensers.
Wing characteristics: Straight type, high mounted, with swept leading edges and straight trailing edges. Hydraulic wing folding.
Wing control surfaces: Ailerons, Fowler trailing-edge flaps, and leading-edge flaps. Spoilers above and beneath the wings augment roll control.
Tail control surfaces: Variable-incidence tailplane with elevators (with tabs), and rudder (with tabs). Vertical tail folds for stowage.
Construction materials: Metal.
Engines: 2 General Electric TF34-GE-400 turbofans. Increased power APU under WSIP.
Engine rating: Each 9,275 lbf (41.26 kN).
Flight refuelling probe: Above the cockpit.
Fuel system: 7,192 litres. Provision for 2 x 1,136 litre drop tanks. D-704 buddy refuelling pod system for the tanker role.
Braking system: Hydraulic brakes. Arrester hook.

Aircraft variants:
ES-3A is the new electronic reconnaissance conversion of 16 S-3As. See Reconnaissance section.
S-3 AEW was conceived as a carrier AEW aircraft to replace Hawkeye. See Reconnaissance section.
S-3B is the WSIP upgraded S-3A, for carrier-borne anti-submarine, anti-ship and tanker duties. As described. As a result of the sensors, S-3Bs were flown for nearly twice the planned utilization rates during 1994.
US-3A is the transport conversion of S-3As for carrier operations. 6 passengers or 7,480 lb (3,393 kg) of freight in the fuselage and 2 freight pods. Of 6 produced, all 5 remaining aircraft are stored at North Island.

Lockheed Martin S-3B Viking with wings folded but able to retain weapons. Note the Intruders in the background

Lockheed Martin S-3B Viking coming in to land, its arrester hook lowered

Lockheed Martin (LMSW) 86% aerodynamic and propulsion X-32B wind tunnel model , with a shaft-driven lift fan aft of the cockpit (LMSW/Lenny Lombard)

Lockheed Martin (LMSW) X-32A and X-32B

First flight: Anticipated October 1999.
Role: Multi-service strike fighter, for interdiction, escort fighter, counter-air and more.

★ Aims

★ X-32A as a possible future lightweight, single-engined replacement for the F-16 with the USAF, and the X-32B as a potential short take-off and vertical landing replacement for the F/A-18 and AV-8B with the US Navy and Marine Corps, under the Common Affordable Lightweight Fighter programme. Also considered as a possible successor for Royal Navy Sea Harriers.
★ X-32 is being developed for both the Department of Defense's JAST (Joint Advanced Strike Technology) and ARPA Common Affordable Lightweight Fighter programmes.
★ Empty weight below 24,000 lb (10,886 kg).
★ Loiter time for defensive counter air missions twice that of current fighters.
★ Acceleration to supersonic speed faster than current fighters, and sustain supersonic speed 3 times as far.
★ Single point turnaround servicing. Removal of engine in under 30 minutes.
★ If the X-32 is selected for production, LMTAS will undertake high-rate production.

▲ Development

▲ Following a study for ARPA by NASA engineers, ARPA requested ideas from the industry for a Common Affordable Lightweight Fighter, receiving 5 proposals. Contracts were awarded to 2 teams with similar fan-lift concepts, the former Lockheed Advanced Development Company and McDonnell Douglas. Separately, Boeing and Northrop Grumman are studying alternative concepts under cost-sharing research agreements.
▲ Lockheed Martin teamed with Allison, Pratt & Whitney and Rolls-Royce to win a $40 million development contract from the Advanced Research Projects Agency (ARPA). Yakovlev of Russia joined the JAST programme in 1995.
▲ August 1994. ARPA signed an agreement with the UK Ministry of Defence to co-operate in the X-32 flight demonstration programme, with the objective of developing a supersonic successor to the Sea Harrier.
▲ 1994. Mock-up of the X-32B was begun.
▲ March 1995. Sea level testing of the 45 ft (13.72 m) length and 86% scale aerodynamic and propulsion wind-tunnel model of X-32 had been completed.
▲ June-October 1995. Large-scale mock-ups from Lockheed Martin and McDonnell Douglas were tested at NASA's Ames Research Centre.
▲ 1996. Winning team to be chosen to build 2 demonstrators, 1 in USAF and 1 in Marine form. Lockheed Martin's Skunk Works will build X-32 demonstrators and conduct flight tests (and undertake eventual low rate production for an operational squadron), if selected.
▲ October 1999. Proposed first flight of both versions, the X-32A first.
▲ 2005. Operational production aircraft.
Sales/users: Proposed for the USAF, US Navy and Marine Corps, Royal Navy and others.
Crew: Pilot only.
Cockpit: Self-contained boarding ladder. Canopy of production aircraft will have a saw-tooth serrated leading edge.
Crew escape: Ejection seat.
Fixed gun: 20-mm.
Number of weapon pylons: Wing and fuselage stations (plus weapon bay).
Expendable weapons and equipment: 2 AIM-120 AMRAAM or bombs, plus 2 Sidewinders in the weapons bay. Full range of conventional, guided and anti-radiation weapons externally. Integral weapons loading to minimize support equipment.
Radar: Smaller than F-22's, but with air-to-ground modes.
Flight/weapon system avionics/instrumentation: Target designators for precision guided weapons.
Wing characteristics: Shoulder mounted, delta planform (almost diamond), blended with the fuselage. Aerodynamically thin to minimize supersonic drag. Folding wings for all versions.
Wing control surfaces: Ailerons, trailing-edge flaps and leading-edge flaps. Back up systems include use of thrust vectoring engine nozzle for pitch control in the event of flap damage.
Tail control surfaces: Twin, outward canted fins, with rudders.
Canard: All moving, continuously adjusted by the fly-by-wire control system to trim wing lift efficiency and to optimize the lift-drag ratio throughout the speed range, for optimum subsonic range, extended supersonic flight, and manoeuvrability.
Flight control system: Fly-by-wire.
Fuselage: Blended, with chines. Artist's impression of August 1994 showed doors enclosing the lift fan during conventional flight.
Construction materials: Aluminium and titanium, plus carbonfibre for the wing skins, flaps, ailerons, canards, vertical tail, inlets and many access panels.
Engine: Pratt & Whitney F119-PW-220+, a higher bypass ratio version of the F119-PW-100 turbofan. Also drives the Allison vertical lift fan in the X-32B via a shaft and gearbox, with vectoring nozzle for pitch and yaw control. Has an APU. X-32 aerodynamic and propulsion model used an F100 engine for engine ground runs in Florida (see March 1995).
Engine rating: 30,000 lb (133.45 kN), but with 25% more thrust than the basic F119 in intermediate and military power.
Air intakes: Integrated with the fuselage forebody.
Nozzle: Pratt & Whitney/Rolls-Royce 2-dimensional lift/cruise thrust vectoring primary nozzle, with variable area control (see Wing control surfaces and Engine).
Fuel system: X-32A will have an internal fuel capacity near one-third of F-16. X-32A carries about 3,000-4,000 lb (1,361-1,814 kg) of extra fuel in the space used by the X-32B's lift fan. Self-sealing tanks and lines. Using a centreline tank, has the interdiction radius of current USAF fighters.
Oxygen system: On-board oxygen and inerting gas generating systems (requiring no recharging).

Aircraft variants:
X-32A is seen as the US Air Force version, with conventional take-off.
X-32B differs by having a lift fan behind the cockpit to offer STOL capabilities. Lift fan and drive gear, needed only for Navy/Marine Corps STOVL versions, adds 2,500 lb (1,134 kg) to the basic X-32A weight.

Details for X-32.

Principal dimensions:
Maximum length: See Development – March 1995

Undercarriage:
Type: Retractable, with twin nosewheels

Weights
Empty: Below 21,600 lb (9,798 kg) for X-32A, 24,000 lb (10,886 kg) for X-32B

Performance: See Aims

McDonnell Douglas Corporation (USA)

Corporate address: PO Box 516, St Louis, MO 63166-0516.
Telephone: +1 314 232 0232
Facsimile: +1 314 234 3826
Founded: 28 April 1967, as a merger of McDonnell Aircraft Corporation (founded 1939) and Douglas Aircraft Company (founded 1920).
Employees: about 17,000.

● Activities

● In addition to the civil and military aircraft and helicopters, and other activities outlined below and in the various sections, McDonnell Douglas has signed agreements with Russia to assist in the development of future US/Russian space programmes. It also offers the KMD-11 airborne tanker/cargo aircraft (configurationally similar to the KC-10 Extender – see Freighters).

DIVISIONS

McDonnell Douglas Aerospace
HQ address: 1510 Hughes Way, Long Beach CA 90810-1870 (general HQ, and administration address for McDonnell Douglas Aerospace East, and includes the Phantom Works manufacturing and prototype centre; McDonnell Douglas Aerospace West is at 5301 Bolsa Avenue, Huntington Beach, CA 92647).
Information: Lawrence L. McCracken (Director of Communications– *telephone* +1 310 522 2552, *facsimile* +1 310 522 4785).
Comprising:

McDonnell Aircraft Company
Address: PO Box 516, St Louis, MO 63166-0516

● **Activities**

● Production of the F-15 Eagle and F/A-18 Hornet; production of the Harrier II series and T-45 Goshawk (see multi-national); development of the Common Affortable Lightweight Fighter under ARPA contract (see Multi-national); and various non-aircraft products including the ACES II ejection seat, Delta II medium launch vehicle (rocket), Modular Aircrew Simulation System (MASS), missiles (including Harpoon, SLAM and Tomahawk), advanced laser products including the electro-optical NightHawk sighting system, and other equipment including the Mast Mounted Sight. An MoU with Israel Aircraft Industries was announced on 1 March 1995, to pursue the USAF's T-38 trainer Avionics Upgrade Programme.

<u>McDonnell Douglas Helicopter Systems</u>
Address: 5000 East McDowell Road, Mesa, AZ 85215-9797.

● **Activities**

● Various helicopters, including Apache (see Helicopter section).

<u>McDonnell Douglas Transport Aircraft</u>
Information: Lawrence L. McCracken (as above).

● **Activities**

● C-17 Globemaster III military transport programme (see Freighters section).

Douglas Aircraft Company
HQ address: 3855 Lakewood Boulevard, Long Beach, CA 90846.
Telephone: +1 310 593 5511
Facsimile: +1 310 497 8720
Information: Doug Jacobsen (General Manager – *telephone* +1 310 496 7473).

● **Activities**

● Airliners and associated aircraft (see Airliners and Freighters section).

McDonnell Douglas A-4 Skyhawk

First flight: 22 June 1954.
Role: Light, carrier-capable, attack bomber.

★ **Aims**

★ Simplicity and small size, allowing aircraft carrier operations with the US Navy and US Marine Corps without the complication of wing folding.

▲ **Development**

▲ 21 June 1952. Against the official requirement for a 30,000 lb (13,600 kg) weight naval attack jet to replace the AD-1 Skyraider, Douglas proposed a design at vastly reduced weight, receiving a contract for prototypes on this date as A4Ds.
▲ 26 October 1956. Initial production deliveries of A4D-1s (later redesignated A-4Bs) to US Navy Attack Squadron VA-72.
▲ 1979. Skyhawk production ended, with the 2,960th aircraft (including 555 two-seat operational trainers).

Sales/users: Still on strength in early 1995 with Argentina (A-4M/OA-4M and A-4P from land and sea), Indonesia (A-4E and TA-4H), Israel (A-4H and N, TA-4H and J), Kuwait (A-4KU and TA-4KU), New Zealand (A-4K and TA-4K), Singapore (A-4S-1 and SU), and USA (Navy/USMC, principally for aggressor and other training). Malaysia has withdrawn its Skyhawks (put up for sale).

Upgrade programmes:
Argentine aircraft are the subject of current upgrade in association with Lockheed Martin (see Lockheed Martin and Argentina).
Israel Aircraft Industries offers a Skyhawk upgrade, which see.
New Zealand's Skyhawks have undergone modernization under Project Kahu , in association with Smith's Industries, including the receipt of Westinghouse APG-66 radar with small antenna, MIL STD 1553 databus, digital flight control system, Litton LN-93 ring laser gyro INS, VOR/ILS, HUD/WAC, CRT cockpit displays, HOTAS, radar warning receiver and chaff/flare. New weapon options include Maverick ASM and Sidewinder AAMs, and laser-guided bombs.
Singapore's Skyhawks have become Super Skyhawks under the modernization programme by Singapore Technologies Aerospace (which see for details).

McDonnell Douglas F-4 Phantom

First flight: 27 May 1958 (as the F4H-1 Phantom II).
Role: Interceptor, tactical fighter, reconnaissance fighter, and radar suppression.

▲ **Development**

▲ August 1953. McDonnell Aircraft initiated studies for a twin-jet, all weather, attack fighter, to replace the F3H Demon. Initially designated AH-1.
▲ September 1955. Ordered into development by the US Navy's Bureau of Aeronautics as the F4H-1, with emphasis as a fighter.
▲ 29 December 1960. First production Phantom was received by the US Navy's VF-11 Squadron.
▲ 17 January 1962. Following evaluation of the naval Phantom II, the selection of the aircraft for the USAF was announced.
▲ 27 May 1963. Maiden flight of a USAF's F-4C.
▲ June 1979. Production of the F-4 in the USA ended after 5,057 aircraft. Production in Japan continued until 1981.

Details: Brief details for the F-4E, unless stated. Many Phantoms have undergone significant upgrade (see Upgrades), which makes further description of the basic Phantom unnecessary.
Sales/users: Egypt (F-4E), Germany (F-4E for training, F-4F ICE – RF-4Es phased out), Greece (F-4E and RF-4E), Iran (F-4D, E and RF-4E), Israel (see IAI), Japan (see Mitsubishi), South Korea (F-4D, E and RF-4C – additional spares are being provided by the USA), Spain (RF-4C), Turkey (F-4E and RF-4E), and the USA (F-4G and RF-4C).
Crew: 2, in tandem, as pilot and weapons systems officer.
Crew escape: Ejection seats.

DETAILS FOR F-4E.

Principal dimensions:
Wing span: 38 ft 5 ins (11.71 m)
Maximum length: 62 ft 11 ins (19.18 m)
Maximum height: 16 ft 4 ins (4.98 m)

Wings:
Aerofoil section: NACA modified 0006.4-64, 0004-64, (root/tip)
Area: 530 sq ft (49.24 m²)
Aspect ratio: 2.78
Sweepback: 45° leading edges
Dihedral: 12° on outer panels only

Undercarriage:
Type: Retractable, with steerable and centring nosewheel

Weights:
Empty: 30,328 lb (13,756 kg)
Maximum take-off: 47,300-61,795 lb (21,455-28,030 kg)

Performance:
Maximum speed: Mach 2+
Stall speed: 159 kts (183 mph) 295 km/h
Take-off distance: 4,390 ft (1,340 m)
Landing distance: 3,780 ft (1,153 m)
Maximum climb rate: 6,170 ft (1,880 m) per minute at maximum weight
Ceiling: over 60,000 ft (18,290 m)
Combat radius: 618 naut miles (712 miles) 1,146 km, interdiction mission

Fixed guns: 20-mm M-61A1 6-barrel cannon.
Ammunition: 1,020 rounds.
Number of weapon pylons: 8, as 4 under the wings and 4 under the fuselage.
Expendable weapons and equipment: 16,000 lb (7,257 kg) load, including Sidewinder and Sparrow AAMs, bombs or air-to-surface missiles. See Aircraft variants and Upgrades.
Radar: AN/APQ-120 fire control radar.
Wing characteristics: Low mounted, with dihedral outer panels.
Wing control surfaces: Ailerons (no upward movement), flaps and leading-edge manoeuvring slats. Upper surface spoilers, functioning in part as ailerons for upward deflection.
Tail control surfaces: Anhedral slab tailplane (with slotted leading-edges) and rudder.
Airbrakes: 2, under the wings.
Engines: 2 General Electric J79-GE-17A turbojets.
Engine rating: Each 11,870 lbf (52.8 kN) dry, 17,900 lbf (79.62 kN) with afterburning.
Air intakes: Variable, on fuselage sides.
Flight refuelling probe: Retractable, on starboard side.
Fuel system: 7,022 litres in wings and fuselage. Optional 2,271 litre drop tank under the fuselage and 2 x 1,401 litre tanks under the wings.

IAI (Bedek) modernized Skyhawk, operated by the Israeli Air Force

Daimler-Benz upgraded F-4F ICE with APG-65 radar

Aircraft variants:

F-4D was delivered with AN/APQ-109 radar. 17,000 lbf (75.62 kN) J79-GE-15 engines.
F-4E was produced as a multi-role aircraft, suited to fighter, close air support and interdiction.
F-4F services with Germany, now upgraded under the ICE programme.
F-4G Advanced Wild Weasel is the USAF's electronic/anti-radar attack development of the F-4E, intended to locate hostile radars for attack with its own HARM missiles or those of other accompanying aircraft. AN/APR-47 electronics suite in the former gun position, capable of transmitting real-time target data. Operated by 561st FS at Nellis AFB (to be part of the US Gulf force, carrying AN/ALQ-131 and AN/ALQ-184 ECM pods) and the 124th FG, ANG, at Boise.
RF-4C is the multi-sensor reconnaissance version, with forward-looking radar, infra-red sensors and day cameras. ARN-101 digital avionics suite, ring laser gyro, and more. Operated by the US ANG's 117th RW and 152nd RG. Also, versions operated by foreign air forces.
RF-4E is another reconnaissance version, based on the F-4E.

Upgrade programmes:

Daimler-Benz in Germany under the ICE programme, which see.
IAI in Israel, for the Israeli Air Force and available to others, which see. New to include upgrade of 54 Turkish aircraft, said to include Westinghouse Norden APG-7 radar.
Mitsubishi of Japan to F-4EJKai standard, which see.
Rockwell International modernization programme, which see.

McDonnell Douglas F-15 Eagle

First flight: 27 July 1972.
Role: Air superiority fighter with ground attack capability (F-15A/B/C/D), and dual-role air superiority/long-range interdiction fighter (F-15E). SEAD (suppression of enemy air defence) role for converted F-15Cs, planned to replace F-4G Wild Weasels at the end of this decade, has been reinstated. A reconnaissance pod for the F-15D is being evaluated.

★ Aims

★ Advanced tactical fighter to replace the F-4 Phantom with the USAF.
★ F-15E designed for advanced air-to-air performance combined with improved air-to-ground capability in a single tactical aircraft.
★ F-15E needs no fighter escort, and can (if required) fly interdiction missions without electronic jamming aircraft or AWACS support.
★ F-15E has a strengthened airframe to allow take off at higher weight, and manoeuvre to 9g at combat weight throughout the flight envelope.
★ Over 65 design changes incorporated into the F-15E (from the F-15C) to improve reliability and reduce maintenance. 95.9% mission capable rate achieved during the Gulf conflict.

McDonnell Douglas F-15E Eagle with CFTs, drop tanks and AAMs

Details for F-15E, *with F-15C in italics.*

Principal dimensions:
Wing span: 42 ft 9.5 ins (13.05 m), *F-15C the same*
Maximum length: 63 ft 9.5 ins (19.45 m), *F-15C the same*
Maximum height: 18 ft 5.5 ins (5.63 m), *F-15C the same*

Wings:
Aerofoil section: NACA 64A
Area: 608 sq ft (56.49 m^2), *F-15C the same*
Aspect ratio: 3.014, F-15C *the same.*
Sweepback: 38° 42' leading edge, *F-15C the same*
Incidence: 0°, *F-15C the same*
Anhedral: 1°, *F-15C the same*

Tail unit:
Tailplane span: 28 ft 3 ins (8.61 m), *F-15C the same*
Tailplane area: 111.36 sq ft (10.346 m^2), *F-15C the same*

Undercarriage:
Type: Retractable, with nosewheel, *F-15C the same*
Main wheel tyre size: 36 x 11-18, *34.5 x 9.75-18*
Nose wheel tyre size: 22 x 7.75-9, *22 x 6.6-10*
Wheel base: 17 ft 9.5 ins (5.42 m), *F-15C the same*
Wheel track: 9 ft (2.75 m), *F-15C the same*

Weights:
Empty, operating: 32,000 lb (14,515 kg), *28,600 lb (12,975 kg)*
Maximum take-off: 81,000 lb (36,740 kg), *68,000 lb (30,844 kg)*

Performance:
Maximum speed: Mach 2.5, *F-15C the same*
Take-off distance: *900 ft (275 m) with AAMs*
Landing distance: *3,500 ft (1,070 m) without drag-chute*
G limits: +9 for F-15E throughout flight envelope, *+9, -3*
Ceiling: 60,000 ft (18,290 m)
Radius of action: 686 naut miles (790 miles) 1,271 km
Range with full fuel: 2,400 naut miles (2,764 miles) 4,445 km
Ferry range: 3,100 naut miles (3,570 miles) 5,740 km

▲ Development

▲ 1965. Programme was initiated.
▲ 23 December 1969. McDonnell Douglas was announced winner of the USAF competition, against definition phase projects by Fairchild Hiller and North American Rockwell.
▲ 27 July 1972. Maiden flight of an F-15A development aircraft, one of 18 FSD F-15As and 2 TF-15A two-seaters contracted.
▲ 14 November 1974. Hand-over of the first full production Eagle to the USAF, an F-15B (formerly TF-15A).
▲ 26 February 1979. Maiden flight of the F-15C, featuring increased internal fuel and the ability to carry low-drag Conformal Fuel Tanks (CFT) attached to the air intake nacelles (also suited to the carriage of sensors).
▲ 19 June 1979. Maiden flight of the F-15D two-seat variant of the C.
▲ February 1983. The F-15 Multi-Stage Improvement Programme was initiated by the receipt of a USAF contract.
▲ 11 December 1986. Maiden flight of a production dual-role F-15E at St Louis.
▲ 12 April 1988. First F-15E handed-over to the USAF, going initially to the 461st Tactical Fighter Training Squadron of the 405th Tactical Training Wing at Luke AFB, Arizona.
▲ 10 May 1989. First flight with 2D nozzles of the F-15SMTD (Short take-off and landing Manoeuvre Technology Demonstrator), an experimental vectored-thrust conversion of an F-15B.
▲ 1989. 336th FS of the 4th Wing at Seymour Johnson AFB, became the first operational F-15E unit.
▲ October 1994. McDD received a USAF contract of $189.8 million to upgrade the AN/APG-63 radar on over 350 F-15C/Ds.
▲ 1995. Deliveries began of export F-15Es, as F-15Is for Israel. F-15Ss for Saudi Arabia will be delivered 1996-98.
▲ 19 April 1995. Demonstration of a manned tactical reconnaissance capability, when an F-15D AFTD (advanced fighter technology demonstrator) took a series of high-resolution tactical images with electro-optical linear array reconnaissance systems in a conformal centreline pod of 23 ft (7.01 m) length. The pod is capable of carrying a complete Loral ATARS (advanced tactical airborne reconnaissance system) sensor suite.
▲ August 1997. Flight testing of the new F-15C/D radar (see above) will begin at Edwards AFB, with retrofits to start in 1999 at a rate of 72 per year.

Sales/users: Israel (received 81 new and ex-USAF F-15A/B/C/Ds, plus 21 dual-role F-15Is), Japan (14 F-15J/DJs built in the USA plus 191 assembled/built in Japan by Mitsubishi against orders to FY1995 – which see; 5 more requested under FY1996; 8 Squadrons by 1998), Saudi Arabia (received 98 new and ex-USAF F-15C/Ds and has ordered 72 dual-role F-15Ss), and the USAF (some 870 production F-15A/B/C/Ds and 209 F-15Es delivered, and further F-15Es are wanted). 645 F-15s of all versions were in the USAF's active inventory in early 1995, of which 549 were primary aircraft authorized for combat missions, plus 140 with the ANG including F-15A/Bs with the 102nd Fighter Wing at Otis AFB in Massachusetts and 123rd Fighter Squadron at Portland OR, for Air Defence.
Details: Principally F-15E.
Crew: Pilot and weapon systems officer in tandem, under a bubble canopy.
Crew escape: McDonnell Douglas ACES II zero-zero ejection seats.
Fixed guns: 1 x 20-mm M61A1 Vulcan 6-barrel cannon in the starboard wing.
Ammunition: 512 rounds.
Number of weapon pylons: Maximum of 18, comprising 1 under each wing, 1 under each air intake, 2 centreline, and 6 on each of the 2 CFTs. Each CFT (conformal fuel tank) has the ability to carry 6 air-to-ground weapons, 3 on stub pylons and 3 on a long pylon. However, the long pylon more usually carries 2 air-to-air missiles in tandem. CFTs are available to F-15C/D/Es. In addition, the wing and centreline pylons can use multiple ejectors, in the case of the wing pylons each with perhaps 4 bombs plus 2 Sidewinders or a drop tank plus 2 Sidewinders. CFT pylons cause less drag than conventional multi-ejection racks.
Expendable weapons and equipment: 24,500 lb (11,113 kg) stores load. Maximum air-to-air missile configurations are 8 AMRAAMs, or 4 Sidewinders under the wings and 4 Sparrows/AMRAAMs on the intakes. Air-to-surface missiles include Maverick (up to 3 per wing) and HARM (F-15Es and converted F-15Cs for SEAD), with future missiles to encompass JSOW. Another future weapon will be WCMD (wind corrected munitions dispenser), while a large range of current smart guided bombs include the new GBU-30 (formerly JDAM). Alternative weapons include up to 5 nuclear bombs, AGM-130 rocket-powered bombs, and conventional free-fall bombs up to the Mk 84 (2,000 lb).
Additional stores: Various mission pods, including LANTIRN (see below) carried on the 2 under front intake pylons, AXQ-14 data link to provide guidance updates for the GBU-15 guided bomb, and Texas

McDonnell Douglas F-15C Eagles

Instruments ASQ-213 high-speed anti-radar missile targeting system (HTS). Towed target. F-15D being evaluated with a reconnaissance pod (see Development – 19 April 1995).
Radar: F-15A/B/C/D have AN/APG-63 radar, except APG-70 was installed in a few late Cs and Ds; more than 350 USAF F-15C/Ds will be upgraded from 1999 with a new radar using components from the F/A-18E/F Hornet's AN/APG-73 and the transmitter and some software from the AN/APG-70 radar. F-15E's AN/APG-70 has air-to-air and air-to-ground modes, including high-resolution ground mapping and freezing to permit the crew to create an image of the target location (45° either side of the aircraft) in a short burst of radar activity. Advanced Electronics Company of Saudi Arabia is producing components for the F-15S's radar.
Flight/weapon system avionics/instrumentation: F-15E has 7 software-controlled avionics systems, comprising the IBM CP-1075C VHSIC central computer, multi-purpose display processor, avionics interface unit, radar (see above), Honeywell ring laser gyro INS, programmable armament control system, and Lear Siegler Astronics triple-redundant digital flight control system encompassing automatic terrain following that is linked to the LANTIRN navigation pod. Lockheed Martin LANTIRN (low-altitude navigation and targeting infra-red for night) itself has 2 pods: the navigational pod has FLIR for high-speed and low-altitude flight at night, its images displayed onto the pilot's Kaiser holographic wide-angle HUD, and terrain-following radar; the targeting pod has tracking FLIR and a laser designator for use with smart weapons. LANTIRN targeting pod is integrated with the main radar mapping mode, allowing the tracking FLIR to be slaved to targets selected by the aircrew on the radar display. Honeywell ASK-6 air data computer. AHRS, HSI, Tacan, ADF and ILS. Weapon System Officer has 2 Sperry colour and 2 Kaiser monochrome CRTs (to display radar, EW and IR data in addition to aircraft, weapon and threat information), plus a new Honeywell digital map display (previously Bendix). Pilot has 1 colour and 2 monochrome CRTs, plus Kaiser holographic wide-angle HUD. IFF. GPS to be installed, and a weapons-control computer link with spaceborne/airborne sensors. Elisra is supplying the EW suite for F-15Is.
Self-protection systems: Northrop Grumman AN/ALQ-135 fully automatic, software-controlled and reprogrammable, dual-mode internal electronic countermeasures system for radar jamming, covering all major threat bands, with 20 processors. RWR. Chaff/flares.
Wing characteristics: Shoulder mounted, cropped delta type, with slight anhedral.
Wing control surfaces: Plain ailerons and trailing-edge flaps.
Tail control surfaces: Slab tailplane (tailerons), currently with ±12° deflection when the aircraft is at high angle of attack but expected to rise to ± 32° after control system modifications. Pronounced dogtooth leading edges. Twin fins and inset rudders, without inward or outward cant.
Canard: None.
Airbrakes: Single large airbrake above centre fuselage.
Flight control system: New system being evaluated for the F-15E, reportedly to allow the aircraft to go well beyond the 20° angle of attack limit currently imposed to prevent the onset of spin.
Construction materials: Mostly metal (aluminium alloy and titanium, and including honeycomb core for ailerons, flaps, airbrake and wingtips), but composites airbrake skins.
Engines: 2 Pratt & Whitney F100-PW-220 or F100-PW-229 turbofans, latter allowing acceleration from idle to full afterburning in 4 seconds.
Engine rating: Each 14,590 lbf (64.9 kN) dry, 23,770 lbf (105.74 kN) with afterburning, or 17,800 lbf (79.18 kN) dry, 29,100 lbf (129.445 kN) with afterburning, respectively.
Air intakes: Variable, 2-dimensional, horizontal wedge type on the fuselage sides, with 2 ramps.
Fuel system: 6,756 litres in F-15A, 7,836 litres in F-15C, and 7,643 litres in F-15E. Fire retardant foam under the fuselage fuel tanks. Conformal Fuel Tanks (CFTs) on the F-15C house 5,542 litres of fuel, and 5,509 litres on the F-15E. Up to 3 x 2,309 litre drop tanks. CFTs (Conformal Fuel Tanks) are secured to the sides of the air intakes, offering far less drag than drop tanks and with the same g limits as the airframe, and can also house electronic systems (see Weapons).
Electrical system: 2 generators, either able to provide sufficient power for all systems.
Hydraulic system: 3 independent systems of 3,000 psi each, any able to provide safe control.
Braking system: Carbon disc brakes, with anti skid.
Oxygen system: Liquid oxygen systems in F-15A/B/C/D; molecular sieve oxygen generating system in F-15E.

Aircraft variants:
F-15A was the initial single-seat version, with AN/APG-63 radar and 14,670 lbf (65.26 kN) dry, 23,770 lbf (105.74 kN) with afterburning F100-PW-100 engines. Still in use, including with US Air Defence units.
F-15B is the two-seat training variant of F-15A, in similar use.
F-15C and F-15D became the standard production single and two seat models from 1979, with F100-PW-100, 200 and 220 engines during production. 100 and 200 series engines being upgraded to 220 standard (see Engine section).
F-15E dual-role two-seater has a modified airframe to allow higher gross weight at take off, and manoeuvre to 9g at gross combat weight throughout the flight envelope. Heaviest version, with weapon-carrying CFTs and larger rear-canopy section.
F-15J and DJ are Mitsubishi-built F-15C and D versions for the JASDF.
F-15I and S are exported F-15Es for Israel and Saudi Arabia. The first F-15S flew on 19 June 1995 and was delivered 12 September.
F-15U Plus is a projected long-range strike version for possible future use with the United Arab Emirates (in competition with other types), with new larger wings, and increased weapon and fuel loads.
F-15SMTD is a Short take-off and landing Manoeuvre Technology Demonstrator, converted from an F-15B and first flown in the 1980s. F100-PW-229 engines being fitted with new axisymmetric multi-directional thrust-vectoring pitch yaw balanced beam nozzles (PYBBN) in early 1995, under the ACTIVE (Advanced Control Technology for Integrated VEhicles) programme. Flight testing to start about September 1995.

McDonnell Douglas F/A-18 Hornet

First flight: 18 November 1978.
Role: Multi-mission, land and carried-borne fighter, attack and reconnaissance; missions include air superiority, fighter escort, suppression of enemy air defences, forward air control, close air support and day/night strike.

★ Aims
★ Replaced the A-7 Corsair II and F-4 Phantom with the USN/USMC.
★ Idle to maximum thrust in 4 seconds, and combat thrust-to-weight ratio of greater than 1 to 1.
★ Built-in test system (BITS) to check the avionics and mechanical systems. 85-89% readiness rate achieved.
★ Can operate in temperatures ranging from -51° C to +51.7° C, and survive landing descents of over 17 ft (5.2 m) per second.
★ 12,000 flying hour structural lifetime (demonstrated), equivalent to nearly 30 years USN service.

▲ Development
▲ McDonnell Douglas is prime contractor, with Northrop Grumman as principal sub-contractor producing the centre and aft fuselage, twin vertical tails and all associated subsystems.
▲ 1974. US Navy VFAX low cost, lightweight fighter programme was superseded by a plan to develop a navalized variant of the General Dynamics F-16 or Northrop F-17, then in prototype form for a USAF competition. McDD's proposal for a navalized derivative of the YF-17 was accepted, with Northrop becoming prime sub-contractor and also prime contractor on the land-based version (later abandoned). Expected separate A-18 attack and F-18 fighter variants were merged to form a single F/A-18 multi-role fighter.
▲ May 1980. The US Navy began receiving F/A-18A single-seaters and two-seat B trainers, initially operated by VFA-125 at NAS Lemoore as a development unit.
▲ 8 September 1980. Loss of a TF-18A (original designation of F/A-18B) in the UK, after flying at Farborough Air Show. Hornet flying resumed on the 20th.
▲ 28 July 1982. First of Canada's CF-18s was rolled out. Canada was the first export customer.
▲ 1983. F/A-18A/Bs entered US Marine Corps and US Navy operational service, initially with VMFA-314 (7 January) and VFA-113 (October) respectively.
▲ 3 September 1987. First production F/A-18C flew.
▲ November 1989. Deliveries began of Hornets with night strike capability.
▲ February 1992. USMC began receiving Hornets capable of integrating a reconnaissance pallet.
▲ October 1992. Delivery of Hornets with Enhanced Performance Engines.
▲ 1992. $3.88 billion contract for engineering and manufacturing development (EMD) of the F/A-18E/F advanced versions of Hornet. 7.5 year development and support programme. 7 flight test aircraft and 3 ground test.
▲ 1993. US Hornets began receiving a laser designator housed within the targeting forward-looking infra-red sensor, for laser-guided bomb carriage.
▲ 17 September 1993. 2 million F/A-18 flight hours were recorded, during a USMC flight over Bosnia-Hercegovina.
▲ May 1994. Delivery of Hornets to the US Navy with upgraded AN/APG-73 radar.
▲ May 1994. Production of the first F/A-18E/F centre/aft fuselage was started by Northrop Grumman.
▲ 23 September 1994. F/A-18E/F assembly began at McDD's St Louis facility, marking the establishment of a second Hornet production line.
▲ June 1994. Critical Design Review passed for the F/A-18E/F.
▲ 1995. See Lockheed Martin P-3C Orion entry for

McDonnell Douglas F/A-18C Hornet with centreline pod and dual-ejectors under the pylons. This view shows off the cambered LERX

McDonnell Douglas F/A-18D two-seater (foreground) and F/A-18C in USMC markings

Project Sword information relay trials involving an F/A-18A.

▲ 21 April 1995. First flight of a Finnish Hornet, an F/A-18D.

▲ 8 May 1995. Final assembly began of the F/A-18E/F.

▲ 18 September 1995. Roll-out of the first F/A-18E. First flight December.

▲ 1996. Initial low-rate F/A-18E/F production began.

▲ Late 1998. Expected start of F/A-18E/F deliveries to the US Navy.

▲ 2001. IOC of F/A-18E/F.

Sales/users: 1,263 delivered by May 1995, comprising Australia (75 between 1984-90 as AF-18As and ATF-18As), Canada (138 between 1982-88 as CF-18A/Bs, known as CF-188A/Bs), Kuwait (40 between 1992-93), Spain (72 EF-18A/Bs between 1986-90 and known as C.15s and CE.15s), and USA (938, operated by 22 Navy and 16 Marine Corps squadrons – the US Navy plans an all late-production F/A-18C/D force for carrier operations prior to E/F deliveries). On order are Hornets for Finland (64 F/A-18C/Ds, to be delivered 1995-99 and first serving with HävLLv 21 at Tampere to replace Drakens; McDD is delivering the first 7 structurally complete F/A-18Ds, with Valmet assembling all F/A-18Cs locally), Malaysia (8 F/A-18Ds between 1996-97, with a further 10-16 requested), Switzerland (34 F/A-18C/Ds between 1996-99), and further F/A-18C/Ds for the USN/USMC (24 in next FY). In addition, Spain is purchasing a number (perhaps 21) of US Navy F/A-18As to fill the gap caused by Eurofighter delays, though these were not surplus to USN requirements. For the F/A-18E/F development programme, 7 flight test aircraft and 3 ground test aircraft are being built. US Navy plans call for receipt of about 1,000 F/A-18E/Fs by 2015.

Details: Current F/A-18C/D, unless stated.

Crew: Pilot, or 2 in tandem in the F/A-18B/D/F.

Crew escape: Martin Baker SJU-5-6 zero-zero ejection seat/s.

Fixed guns: 20-mm M61A1 Vulcan cannon in the nose. Upgrade will introduce a new lightweight cannon, as to be used in E/F.

Ammunition: 570 rounds.

Number of weapon pylons: 9, as 2 wingtip for Sidewinders, 2 outboard for weapons, 2 inboard "wet" for drop tanks or weapons, 2 nacelle stations for AMRAAMs/Sparrows or sensor pods, and 1 fuselage centreline for a drop tank or air-to-ground weapon. F/A-18E/F has 2 extra wing pylons, each for up to a 1,000 lb (454 kg) load.

Expendable weapons and equipment: Current F/A-18C and D has a normal load of 13,700 lb (6,214 kg). Wingtip Sidewinders, AMRAAM or Sparrow AAMs on the nacelle pylons, and AAMs or attack weapons on the underwing and centreline pylons. Maximum air-to-air armament is 10 AMRAAMs and 2 Sidewinders. Attack weapons include IR Maverick, anti-ship Harpoon and HARM missiles, laser-guided/free fall/cluster bombs and including the latest GBU-30 (formerly JDAM for the USN), or rocket pods. Future weapons will include JSOW, and could include the Israeli Python 4. F/A-18E/F has a 17,750 lb (8,050 kg) payload.

Additional stores: FLIR pod (see Avionics) or Martin Marietta ASQ-173 laser spot tracker and strike camera.

Radar: Hughes AN/APG-65 digital multi-mode, superseded by AN/APG-73 with increased speed and memory capacity processors from May 1994 deliveries. APG-73 also used on the F/A-18E/F.

Flight/weapon system avionics/ instrumentation: Includes MIL-STD-1553B databus, and MIL-STD-1760 to provide a common electrical and digital interface between the weapons and the aircraft. Control Data AYK-14 digital computers. Digital (computer-generated) colour moving map. Navigation forward looking infra-red (NAVFLIR) sensor, with imagery on the pilot's Kaiser HUD and combined with navigation and weapon delivery symbology (the NAVFLIR pod also houses a laser designator and ranger). Loral colour video/TV mission recording system (ordered for the US Navy). Litton ASN-130A INS or more recent ASN-139 ring laser INS, GPS, Tacan, horizontal situation display, and horizontal situation indicator. 2 Kaiser multi-function displays (monochrome or colour), GEC-Marconi central CRT, and HOTAS. IFF. Spar flight incident recorder (US aircraft). Horizons Technology integrated mission support system on F/A-18s of Finland, Malaysia, Spain and Switzerland. Night vision goggles for the pilot or weapon systems officer, and compatible cockpit lighting. F/A-18C/D upgrade programmes include mission computer improvements with VHSIC technology (current XN-8), and reconnaissance capability. US Hornets use an automatic carrier landing system. Canadian F/A-18A/Bs have an instrument landing system.

DETAILS FOR F/A-18C/D, *WITH E/F IN ITALICS.*

Principal dimensions:
Wing span: 37 ft 6 ins (11.43) without wingtip missiles, 40 ft 5 ins (12.32 m) including missiles. *44 ft 8.5 ins (13.62 m) including missiles for E/F*
Span, wings folded: 27 ft 6 ins (8.38 m), *30 ft 7 ins (9.32 m) for E/F*
Maximum length: 56 ft (17.07 m), *60 ft 1 ins (18.31 m) for E/F*
Maximum height: 15 ft 3.5 ins (4.66 m), *16 ft (4.88 m) for E/F*

Wings:
Area: 400 sq ft (37.16 m^2), *500 sq ft (46.45 m^2) for E/F*
Aspect ratio: 3.516, *3.996 for E/F*
Sweepback: 20° at 25% chord
Anhedral: from root

Tail unit:
Tailplane span: 21 ft 7 ins (6.58 m)
Tailplane area: 88.1 sq ft (8.185 m^2)

Undercarriage:
Type: Retractable, with twin steerable nosewheels. Tyre pressures greatly increased for aircraft carrier operations. Can survive landing descents of over 17 ft (5.2 m) per second
Main wheel tyre size: 30 x 11.5-14.5
Nose wheel tyre size: 22 x 6.6-10
Wheel base: 17 ft 9.5 ins (5.42 m)
Wheel track: 10 ft 2.5 ins (3.11 m)

Weights:
Empty: 23,832 lb (10,810 kg), approximately *30,500 lb (13,834 kg) for E/F*
Take-off (air superiority): 36,700 lb (16,647 kg)
Maximum take-off: 56,000 lb (25,400 kg), or 51,900 lb (23,540 kg) for typical air-to-surface mission. *Approximately 66,000 lb (29,940 kg) for E/F*

Performance:
Maximum speed: over Mach 1.8
Take-off distance: less than 1,400 (426 m)
Ceiling: About 50,000 ft (15,240 m)
Radius of action (intercept): over 400 naut miles (461 miles) 741 km, internal fuel
Radius of action (attack): over 470 naut miles (541 miles) 870 km, *over 660 naut miles (760 miles) 1,222 km*

McDonnell Douglas F/A-18E Hornet during roll-out on 18 September 1995

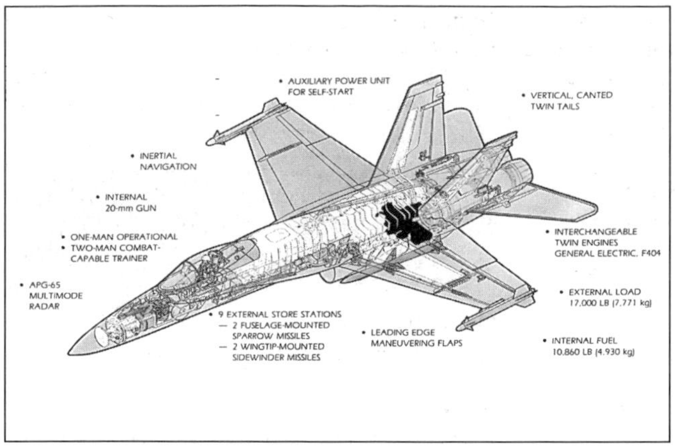

McDonnell Douglas F/A-18C Hornet cutaway, with APG-65 radar

Self-protection systems: Litton ALR-67 radar warning, Magnavox ALR-50 alerting, and Sanders ALQ-126B jamming. ALQ-162 continuous wave jammers fitted to CF-18s and some EF-18s. Westinghouse/ITT ALQ-165 for Finland. Chaff/flares. ADM-141 TALD (tactical air launched decoys). F/A-18E/F to have an Integrated Defense Electronic Countermeasures (IDECM) system, with radar, jammer, RWR, chaff/flares and towed decoy.
Wing characteristics: Straight, shoulder mounted, with long leading-edge root extensions (LERX). Slots at wing/fuselage blend. Fence added to the LERX of US F/A-18Cs improves longitudinal control during high alpha. Folding wings for carrier stowage, and standard on all aircraft.
Wing control surfaces: Ailerons, automatic trailing-edge flaperons and automatic leading-edge manoeuvre flaps.
Tail control surfaces: Slab tailplane (tailerons) and twin outward-canted fins with inset rudders. Rudders are toed-in during take-off/landing for trimming effect.
Canard: None.
Airbrakes: 1 above the extreme rear fuselage.
Flight control system: 4-channel, dual computer, digital fly-by-wire. US Hornets use an automatic carrier landing system. Emergency electric provisions. Mechanical link to tailerons for "get home" capability.
Fuselage: Northrop Grumman as principal subcontractor produces the centre and aft fuselage sections.
Construction materials: Structure has 50% by weight aluminium alloy, 13% titanium, 10% carbonfibre/epoxy composites, and the remaider of steel, glassfibre, aramid and other materials. 40% of the outer skin is carbonfibre/epoxy.
Engines: 2 General Electric F404-GE-400 turbofans, or 402s from 1992. F/A-18E/F has F414-GE-400, of 22,000 lbf (97.86 kN) with afterburning. APU. Under ideal conditions, an engine can be changed in under 21 minutes.
Engine rating: 16,000 lbf (71.17 kN) with afterburning or 17,700 lbf (78.73 kN) with afterburning respectively for GE-400 and -420.
Air intakes: Non-variable with splitters, under the wings, each side of the fuselage.
Flight refuelling probe: Retractable, in the starboard side of the nose.
Fuel system: 10,860 lb (4,926 kg) internally, equivalent to about 6,325 litres. Self-seal tanks. No fuel stored between engines. Fire retardant foam under the fuselage fuel tanks. Optional 3 x 1,249 litre drop tanks. Approximately 8,420 litres internal capacity for F/A-18E/F.
Hydraulic system: 2 independent systems, each 3,000 psi. Damage isolation of hydraulics.
Braking system: Bendix brakes. Arrester hook.

Aircraft variants:
F/A-18A was the initial production single-seater, delivered up to 1987. XN-5 mission computer.
F/A-18B was the initial 2-seat operational training version of A (originally TF-18A). Similar dimensions but with a second tandem cockpit and 6% less fuel.
F/A-18C and F/A-18D became the standard production single-seat and two-seat models from 1987, with night attack capability added from the 139th aircraft. Improved armament options include AMRAAM and IR Maverick, while many important avionics updates include huge leaps in memory for the weapon management system and mission computer (XN-6 and later XN-8). Small airframe changes. Higher rated engines from 1992. APG-73 radar (instead of APG-65) from May 1994 deliveries, with earlier aircraft being upgraded (see earlier paragraphs).
F/A-18E/F have greater range and payload, significantly increased carrier suitability and survivability (added defence electronics – see Self protection – and fuel protection). Avionics and software are over 90% common with those of F/A-18C/D. Cockpit upgrades include a larger (6.25 x 6.25 ins) tactical situation display and touch-screen upfront control panel. Fuel increased by 3,600 lb (1,633 kg) to extend mission radius by up to 60%, depending on the mission profile. 34 ins (86 cm) longer fuselage, larger wings with 100 sq ft (9.3 m^2) more area, 2 extra weapon stations, more powerful engines (see Engines), and enlarged air inlets to provide greater airflow to the engines. Horizontal tail and wing leading-edge extensions are enlarged to maintain handling qualities. Increase in the use of advanced composite materials in the airframe, and greater electrical and hydraulic capacity.
AF-18A and ATF-18A are the Australian designations of its F/A-18A/Bs, most assembled locally by ASTA. All remaining aircraft are being upgraded with C/D avionics.
CF-18A and CF-18B are the Canadian F/A-18A/Bs, known locally as CF-188A/Bs. Minor differences from US Hornets include an instrument landing system. 1,817 litre drop tanks.
EF-18A and EF-18B are the Spanish F/A-18A/Bs, known locally as C.15 and CE.15. Remaining aircraft are being upgraded to near C/D standard.
Electronic warfare (C^2W) variant of F/A-18F is proposed as a future Prowler replacement.

Northrop Grumman Corporation (USA)

Corporate address: 1840 Century Park East, Los Angeles, CA 90067-2199.
Telephone: +1 310 553 6262
Facsimile: +1 310 556 4561
Founded: 18 May 1994, following Northrop's (founded 1928) purchase of Grumman (founded 1929).
Employees: over 43,000.
Information: Mike Greywitt.

DIVISIONS

B-2 Division
HQ address: 8900 East Washington Boulevard, Pico Rivera, CA 90660-3737.
Telephone: +1 310 942 3000
Facsimile: +1 310 942 6478
Information: Edward L. Smith.

● Activities
● Development and production of the B-2 Spirit stealth bomber.
● Northrop Grumman Advanced Technology and Design Center.

Commercial Aircraft Division
HQ address: 9314 West Jefferson Boulevard, PO Box 655907, Dallas, TX 75265-5907.
Telephone: +1 214 266 2543
Facsimile: +1 214 266 4982

● Activities
● Northrop Grumman acquired the remaining interest in Vought Aircraft Company (it previously held 49%) in late 1994, thereafter making it the headquarters for the Commercial Aircraft Division that had already been established on 2 January 1993.

● Northrop Grumman produces main fuselage sections, cargo and passenger doors, floor beams and smaller structural components for the Boeing 747.
Grumman Corporation, subsidiary of Northrop Grumman, produces 747 wing centre sections, spoilers for the 757, components for the 767 and inboard flaps and spoilers for the 777, control surfaces for the McDonnell Douglas C-17, and nacelles and thrust reversers for the Fokker 70 and 100 plus Gulfstream IV. Former Vought plant manufactures major subassemblies for the Boeing 747, 757 and 767, and develops and builds wings for the Gulfstream V (first G V wing was delivered in June 1995).
● 17 F-8E(FN) Crusader variable-incidence-wing carrier interceptors, belonging to the French Navy, remain in service and have undergone upgrade, including some new components in the APQ-104 radar.

Data Systems and Services Division
HQ address: 1111 Stewart Avenue, Bethpage, New York 11714.
Telephone: +1 516 575 0574
Facsimile: +1 516 575 2164

● Activities
● Grumman Data Systems, Grumman Services and Information Service Centre.

Electronics and Systems Integration Division
HQ address: 1111 Stewart Avenue, Bethpage, New York 11714.
Telephone: +1 516 575 0574
Facsimile: +1 516 575 2164

● Activities
● Grumman Electronics.
● J-STARS, E-2C Hawkeye, EA-6B Prowler, and EF-111A (see Electronic section).
● BAT munitions, Jammers, test equipment, communications and sensors.

Military Aircraft Division
HQ address: One Northrop Avenue, Hawthorne, CA 90250.
Telephone: +1 310 332 1000
Facsimile: +1 310 332 3396
Information: Jim Taft (*telephone* +1 310 201 3335)

● Activities
● F-14 Tomcat, and F/A-18 (principal sub-contractor to McDonnell Douglas). The company's JPATS aircraft were not selected for the USAF/US Navy.
● Modification and support of the A-6, A-10 and F-5.
● Possible future development of an Affordable Lightweight Fighter, now in the study phase. Northrop Grumman and Boeing have had cost-sharing research agreements (see also Lockheed Martin and McDonnell Douglas).
● Missiles and unmanned vehicles.
● Other aerostructures.

Northrop Grumman A-6E/TRAM Intruder

First flight: 9 April 1960 (A-6A), 1970 (A-6E).
Role: Carrier-borne all-weather attack-bomber.

★ Aims

★ Long-range strike aircraft for aircraft carrier operations.
★ High subsonic performance at very low level, enabling it to fly under an enemy's radar.
★ Capable of locating and attacking even small targets in all weather conditions.

▲ Development

▲ December 1957. Grumman's G-128 was chosen by the US Navy for development against 10 other proposals.
▲ 1 February 1963. VA-42 became the first US Navy squadron to receive the original A-6A Intruder. Production of 482 A-6As ended in late 1969.
▲ 22 March 1974. First flight of an A-6E fitted with TRAM (Target Recognition Attack Multi-Sensor).
▲ 1989-92. Boeing's Product Support Division delivered 179 composite wings (see Construction materials). These wings added 8,800 flight hours to the A-6E's operational life.
▲ 3 February 1992. Last newly-built Intruder (an A-6E/TRAM) was delivered.
▲ 1997. Possible early retirement of A-6E/TRAM Intruder (previously 1999).

Sales/users: 205 A-6E and A-6E/TRAMS were built, while a large number of A-6As were brought up to this standard (or modified to other A-6 versions – see Aircraft variants). In service with the US Navy.
Crew: Pilot and navigator/bombardier, side by side.
Crew escape: Martin Baker GRU7 ejection seats.
Fixed guns: None.
Number of weapon pylons: 5 (all "wet"), each capable of carrying a 3,600 lb (1,633 kg) load simultaneously.
Expendable weapons and equipment: Up to 18,000 lb (8,164 kg) load. Typically laser-guided smart weapons, or 3 x 2,000 lb bombs plus 2 long-range drop tanks, or 28 x 500 lb bombs, or 4 Harpoon anti-ship missiles. Some were equipped for HARM anti-radar missiles under the Systems Weapon Integration Program (SWIP), and possible Maverick deployment. Optional Sidewinder AAMs for self-protection. Future weapons will include JSOW.
Additional stores: ADM-141 TALD towed decoys, fitted under the Integrated Defense Avionics Program.
Radar: Norden AN/APQ-148 or AN/APQ-156 multi-mode radar.
Flight/weapon system avionics/instrumentation: SWIP (see Weapons) provided for the modernization of some A-6Es, with avionics integration using a MIL-STD 1553B databus. IBM AN/ASQ-133 or -155 digital computer; GEC-Marconi air data computer under SWIP. AN/ARN-118 Tacan, AN/ASN-139 inertial navigation system, GPS, HUD and multi-function displays. CNI, IFF. TRAM (Target Recognition Attack Multi-Sensor) is standard, with FLIR, laser designator and laser spot detector in a small ball turret under the forward fuselage. Combined with the radar, this helps the bombardier identify, acquire and designate a target for attack in any weather.

Northrop Grumman A-6E/TRAM Intruder

Self-protection systems: Litton AN/ALR-67 radar warning receiver,
Wing characteristics: Slightly swept, mid mounted, with upper surface fences. Stall strips on the leading-edges of the wing-root extensions, inboard of a small dropped area. Wing folding for stowage. Lightning protection (nickel-coated fabric) in the composite wing design.
Wing control surfaces: Fowler type flaperons, similar-span spoilers and leading-edge slats.
Tail control surfaces: Slab tailplane and inset rudder.
Airbrakes: Split type, in the trailing-edge of the wingtips.
Flight control system: Hydraulic.
Construction materials: Metal, except for graphite/epoxy composite wings (built by Boeing) for the final production A-6Es and retrofit to older aircraft; the composite wings have aluminium control surfaces and titanium for the wing-folding fittings and other high stress areas.
Engines: 2 Pratt & Whitney J52-P-8B turbojets. See Engine section for available later-version retrofits.
Engine rating: Each 9,300 lbf (41.37 kN).
Air intakes: Fuselage sides.
Flight refuelling probe: Detachable, ahead of the cockpit.
Fuel system: 8,873 litres. Optional drop tanks on all pylons, each 1,136 or 1,514 litres capacity.
Electrical system: 2 x 30kVA generators, also for engine start-up.
Hydraulic system: 2 independent systems.
Braking system: Arrester hook.

DETAILS FOR A-6E/TRAM.

Principal dimensions:
Wing span: 53 ft (16.15 m)
Maximum length: 54 ft 9 ins (16.69 m)
Maximum height: 16 ft 2 ins (4.93 m)

Wings:
Area: 529 sq ft (49.15 m^2)
Aspect ratio: 5.31
Sweepback: 25° at 25% chord
Anhedral: Slight

Tail unit:
Tailplane span: 20 ft 4.5 ins (6.2 m)

Undercarriage:
Type: Retractable, with twin nosewheels
Wheel base: 17 ft 2 ins (5.23 m)
Wheel track: 10 ft 10.5 ins (3.31 m)

Weights:
Empty: 27,613 lb (12,525 kg)
Maximum take-off: 58,600 lb (26,580 kg) for carrier operations, or 60,400 lb (27,396 kg) from land

Performance:
Maximum speed: 559 (644 mph) 1,036 km/h
Cruise speed: 419 kts (482 mph) 776 km/h at 35,000 ft (10,670 m)
Approach speed: 110 kts (127 mph) 204 km/h
Stall speed: 137 kts (157 mph) 253 km/h *clean*, 98 kts (113 mph) 182 km/h *with flaps*
Take-off distance: 3,900 ft (1,189 m) minimum on land
Landing distance: 1,710 ft (522 m) minimum on land
Maximum climb rate: 8,600 ft (2,620 m) per minute
Ceiling: 44,600 ft (13,600 m)
Range with full payload: 877-938 naut miles (1,010-1,080 miles) 1,625-1,738 km

Aircraft variants:
A-6E/TRAM, as described, for attack.
KA-6D is a carrier-capable tanker conversion of Intruder, with a drogue housed in the under-fuselage. Operated by the US Navy.

Northrop Grumman (Fairchild Republic) A-10A/OA-10A Thunderbolt II

First flight: 10 May 1972 (YA-10A)
Role: Close air support and forward air control.

★ Aims

★ High thrust-to-weight ratio offering a very heavy and wide-ranging weapon load.
★ Long combat radius, with substantial loiter time.
★ High subsonic speed and good low-speed manoeuvrability.
★ Survivability features, including titanium cockpit armour, armoured flight control system, jammer pods and chaff/flares. Also engines well clear of the ground to prevent foreign object ingestion during operation from semi-prepared airfields, spaced to prevent simultaneous damage, and with the wings and tail offering some blockage against IR homing.

▲ Development

▲ 1974. Initial production order for 22 A-10As placed with Fairchild Republic, following selection by the USAF to meet A-X programme requirements against the competing Northrop A-9A.
▲ 21 October 1975. Maiden flight of a production A-10A. Initial recipient was the 354th TFW at Myrtle Beach AFB in South Carolina, in March 1977. IOC declared that June.
▲ 20 March 1984. USAF received its last production A-10A.
▲ 1987. OA-10 conversion for forward air control duties rejoined the USAF.
▲ 1991. A-10As flew 8,100 sorties during Operation Desert Storm, achieving nearly 96% combatability. Historically, recorded the only air-to-air gun victories of the conflict.

Sales/users: 713 built. Operated only by the USA, the active USAF retaining 131 A-10As and 101 OA-10As in 1995, of which 106 A-10As and 78 OA-10As are primary aircraft authorized (PAA) for combat missions. These serve with the 57th Wing (Headquarters); 23rd Wing, 347th Wing and 20th Fighter Wing of the 9th Air Force; 355th Wing of the 12th Air Force; 51st Fighter Wing based in South Korea and 354th Fighter Wing in Alaska of Pacific Air Forces; and the 52nd Fighter Wing in Germany of US Air Forces in Europe. In addition, 105 A-10As are with the Air National Guard, and 44 A-10As and OA-10As with Air Force Reserve. A-10As and OA-10As were continuing to be based in Italy in early 1995, in support of United Nations operations over Bosnia-Hercegovina, and 24 will be based in Kuwait. Greece, South Korea, Thailand and Turkey have been offered surplus USAF A-10As, but none have yet been accepted.
Crew: Pilot only.
Cockpit: Titanium armoured, to resist up to 23-mm shells.
Crew escape: McDonnell Douglas ACES II zero-zero ejection seat.
Fixed guns: 30-mm GAU-8/A Avenger 7-barrel cannon in the nose, installed off-centre and at a 2° depressed angle for attacking ground targets.
Ammunition: 1,174 armour-piercing rounds.
Number of weapon pylons: 11, as 8 under the wings and 3 under the fuselage (not all 3 in use simultaneously).
Expendable weapons and equipment: 16,000 lb (7,257 kg) maximum load, reduced to 12,086 lb (5,482 kg) with maximum fuel. Can include 6 Maverick ASMs, Combined Munition Dispensers, conventional and smart bombs, gun pods, and 4 AIM-9M Sidewinder AAMs for self-protection.

Fairchild Republic A-10A Thunderbolt II

Northrop Grumman B-2A Spirit

Additional stores: See Self-protection.
Radar: None.
Flight/weapon system avionics/instrumentation: Tacan, INS, ILS/FDC, AHRS, and LASTE (Low Altitude Safety and Targeting Enhancement system) for ground collision warning, better stability during weapon firing/release, and more accurate manoeuvre bombing. Optical sight and Pave Penny laser pod. IFF/SIF. HUD. Some to receive night vision goggles.
Self-protection systems: ECM jammer pod and chaff/flares.
Wing characteristics: Straight, low mounted, with down-turned wingtips and thick section for low wing loading. Dihedral on the main outer panels only.
Wing control surfaces: Ailerons that split to form upper and lower airbrakes, 2-section trailing-edge slotted flaps (3 position), and leading-edge slats.
Tail control surfaces: Elevators (with tabs) and twin rudders.
Airbrakes: See Wing control surfaces.
Flight control system: Hydraulic, with armour protection.
Construction materials: Metal.
Engines: 2 General Electric TF34-GE-100 turbofans.
Engine rating: Each 9,065 lbf (40.32 kN).
Flight refuelling probe: Optional, using UARRSI equipment.
Fuel system: 10,700 lb (4,853 kg) of internal fuel. Optionally, 3 x 2,271 litre drop tanks.

DETAILS FOR A-10A.

Principal dimensions:
Wing span: 57 ft 6 ins (17.53 m)
Maximum length: 53 ft 4 ins (16.26 m)
Maximum height: 14 ft 8 ins (4.47 m)

Wings:
Aerofoil section: NACA 6716, 6713 (root/tip)
Area: 506 sq ft (47 m²)
Aspect ratio: 6.53
Incidence: -1°
Dihedral: 7° on outer sections

Undercarriage:
Type: Retractable, with steerable offset nosewheel
Main wheel tyre size: 36 x 11
Nose wheel tyre size: 24 x 7.7
Wheel base: 17 ft 9 ins (5.41 m)
Wheel track: 17 ft 2.5 ins (5.24 m)

Weights:
Empty: 28,000 lb (12,700 kg)
Maximum take-off: 52,000 lb (23,586 kg)

Performance:
Maximum speed: 381 kts (439 mph) 707 km/h without external stores
Mission speed: 380 kts (437 mph) 704 km/h with 6 x 500 lb bombs, at 5,000 ft (1,525 m)
Take-off distance: 4,000 ft (1,220 m) at maximum weight
Landing distance: 2,000 ft (610 m) at maximum weight
Maximum climb rate: 6,000 ft (1,830 m) per minute at 32,472 lb (14,730 kg) weight
Typical mission: 130 naut miles (150 miles) 241 km to target area, 1 hour loiter, and return
Radius of action (A-10A): 412 naut miles (474 miles) 763 km
Radius of action (OA-10A): 480 naut miles (553 miles) 889 km

Aircraft variants:

A-10A is the principal version, for close air support.
OA-10A is for forward air control, without other modification but carrying only AIM-9M Sidewinder weapons and AN/ALQ-119 ECM pods for self protection, and rocket pods for target marking.

Northrop Grumman B-2A Spirit

First flight: 17 July 1989.
Role: Subsonic strategic stealth bomber.

★ Aims

★ To supplement existing bomber forces with Air Combat Command, USAF (originally intended to eventually replace the B-1B).
★ To strike maximum defended and moving targets prior to the deployment of the main non-stealth combat assets, with growing emphasis on conventional weaponry.
★ High survivability through low observable technology and defensive avionics systems.
★ Very wide wheel track, enabling the bomber to use any runway suited to a B727 airliner.
★ Requires less tanker support than other bombers.
★ Achieved maintenance hours per flight hour for the development aircraft was 63.5 in 1994, improving upon required R&M levels.

▲ Development

▲ Northrop Grumman became prime contractor on the B-2 programme, with Boeing, Vought, Hughes, CAE-Link and General Electric as principal team members, plus approximately 4,000 subcontractors.
▲ 1978. Programme was initiated, originally to be a high altitude bomber but revised in 1983 to include low level.
▲ October 1981. Development contract issued by the US Air Force Systems Program Office.
▲ January 1987. Flight testing of the integrated navigation and radar systems began, using a modified C-135 out of Edwards AFB.
▲ 22 November 1988. Roll-out of the first B-2 (AV-1) at Palmdale, under strict security.
▲ 17 July 1989. First B-2 (AV-1) made its maiden flight, of 2 hours 20 minutes, landing at Edwards AFB.
▲ 8 November 1989. First daytime flight refuelling test, using a KC-10 Extender.
▲ 13 June 1990. Block 1 testing completed (16 flights, accumulating 67 flight hours), verifying the B-2's basic flight worthiness (certified by the US General Accounting Office).
▲ 19 October 1990. First flight of the second B-2 (AV-2). Heavily instrumented and serving as the loads test aircraft, in addition to performance and weapons carriage and further envelope expansion trials. Undertook flutter (air flow induced resonance) tests, proving the B-2 to be flutter-free for its entire operational envelope.
▲ 23 October 1990. Block 2 trials began, including low observable tests (AV-1). In March 1991, Secretary of Defense certified that early Block 2 testing, including flying qualities and performance, were satisfactory, with no significant technical or operational problems. AV-1 went on to complete its development test programe in March 1992. AV-1 now in long-term "temporary" storage, awaiting future flight test assignments, having flown 81 times and accumulating more than 352 flight hours.
▲ 5 June 1991. First cross-country flight.
▲ 18 June 1991. Third B-2 (AV-3) first flew. First B-2 to be equipped with a full complement of avionics equipment (initially radar and navigation avionics, with defensive aids added in February 1993).
▲ 17 April 1992. Fourth B-2 (AV-4) first flew, used for avionics and armament testing.
▲ 4 June 1992. First night flight.
▲ 2 July 1992. First night refuelling flight.
▲ 3 September 1992. First bomb (inert) release.
▲ 5 October 1992. First flight of the 5th B-2 (AV-5), used for armament, climatic and low observable test phases.
▲ December 1992. The static test airframe was intentionally taken to the breaking point of 161% of the operational load as a test of ultimate strength. Testing confirmed that the B-2 airframe can safely take 150% of the operational load and in-flight stress that it will endure in operational service. This airframe was one of 2 ground test airframes (durability and static) that had been funded alongside the full-scale development aircraft. These were essentially airframes without internal components. Durability test airframe completed its second lifetime of fatigue testing, which simulated 20,000 flight hours or about 30 years of operational use.
▲ 2 February 1993. Sixth and last development B-2 flew as AV-6, used for technical order validation, weapons and avionics testing, including terrain following.
▲ 1-5 March 1993. The highest number of B-2 flights in a week were recorded, at 8.
▲ 13 October 1993. Longest flight to date, at 9 hours 12 minutes.

Northrop Grumman B-2A Spirit flying with an F-117A stealth fighter. Note the split outer control surfaces

▲ December 1993. A B-2 completed a 6-month programme at the Climatic Testing Laboratory at Eglin AFB, Florida.
▲ 17 December 1993. First production B-2A was delivered to the 509th Bomb Wing at Whiteman AFB. Previously that year, it had undergone a 4 month flight test programme and then electromagnetic-interference and ECM trials.
▲ 22 December 1993. First training flight by the 509th.
▲ August 1994. 40% of the B-2 flight test hours had been completed, using the 6 full-scale development aircraft at Edwards Air Force Base, logging over 1,800 hours in more than 395 flights (see June 1990 and March 1991).
▲ July 1996. First delivery of a Block 20 B-2A.
▲ 1996. Qualification to carry B-61 and B-83 nuclear weapons.
▲ 1997. Initial Operational Capability by the 393rd Bomb Squadron of the 509th Bomb Wing.
▲ August 1997. First delivery of a Block 30 B-2A (AV-20).

Sales/users: Current plans call for 20 operational B-2As (including 5 of the B-2 development aircraft brought up to operational standard), the final 4 B-2As funded under FY1994 budget. Funding for further aircraft was blocked in early 1995. The B-2 industrial base tooling is being preserved; Northrop Grumman has offered a further 20 B-2As at $12 billion. Original plans had envisaged 133 aircraft. 5 flying development B-2s (AV-2 to AV-6) have been operated by the 420th Test Squadron of Materiel Command, at the Air Force Flight Test Centre, Edwards AFB (formerly 6520th TS) as part of the Combined Test Force fleet. Block 10 aircraft (10 B-2As, plus AV-2 to AV-6 development aircraft brought up to operational standard), are being followed by Block 20s (from AV-17) and 2 final Block 30s, the latter Blocks including upgrading of earlier aircraft so that the entire fleet will be at Block 30 standard by the year 2000 (see Weapons and Avionics). 509th Bomb Wing at Whiteman AFB will have 2 squadrons, 393rd and 715th, each with 8 aircraft.

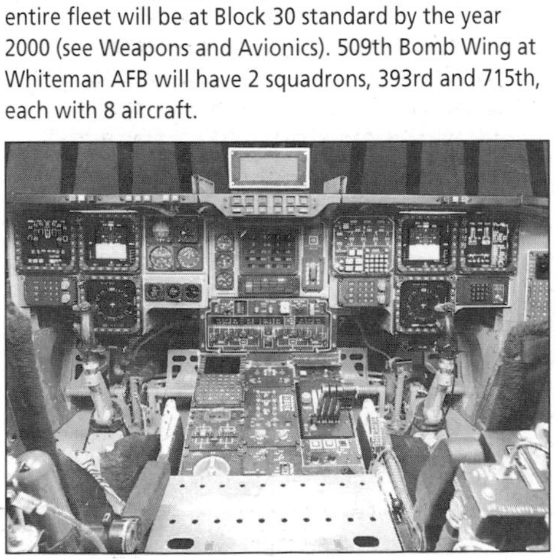

Northrop Grumman B-2A Spirit cockpit

Crew: 2, pilot on the port side of the flight deck and mission commander to starboard. Provision for a 3rd person as an extra pilot or EW officer.
Cockpit: Rounded windshield glazing, with integral mesh to disperse radar. Centre sticks with artificial feel. Self-contained ladder in the crew entrance hatch.
Crew escape: McDonnell Douglas ACES II zero-zero ejection seats.
Fixed guns: None.
Number of weapon pylons: None.
Expendable weapons and equipment: Up to a 40,000 lb (18,145 kg) load in 2 side-by-side bays in the centre fuselage area, carried on racks or rotary launchers. Vortex-generating spoilers in front of the bays are lowered when the saw-tooth edged doors are opened. Under the US Single Integrated Operational Plan (SIOP), the normal nuclear load would be about 25,000 lb (11,340 kg). B-61 and B-83 nuclear weapon representation shapes, and 2,000 lb Mk 84 conventional bomb shapes, were released from the rotary launcher during weapon separation tests. By August 1994, over 75% of weapon bay door testing for destructive acoustic vibrations (when doors are open at high speed) had been completed. Block 10 B-2As carry 16 x B-83 nuclear or Mk 84 conventional weapons on rotary launchers (or a mixed load), with room for other weapons remaining in the bay. Block 20s add the B-61 nuclear weapon (up to 20) to the options, CBU-87/89/97 cluster bomb munitions, GBU-30s (formerly JDAM) and GAMS (GPS-Aided Munitions). 128 GAM kits are to be delivered in 1996-97. Block 30 aircraft add the opportunity to carry 80 x 500 lb Mk 82 bombs, or 36 x 750 lb M117 bombs, or 80 x Mk 62 aerial mines, plus enhanced GBU-30 capability. Future weapons will include WCMD (wind corrected munition dispenser).
Radar: Hughes AN/APG-181 low-probability-of-intercept radar, with 21 modes.
Flight/weapon system avionics/instrumentation: Martin Marietta digital computers. TCN-250 Tacan, VIR-130A ILS, radar altimeter. EFIS cockpit displays (4 per side, including vertical sitation display, port MDU with engine instrumentation data, and starboard MDU for status including control surface position). IFF transponder. No HUD. Selector on the panel provides easy transition from normal flight to an operational "penetration mode", that restricts flight control surface movement and use of avionics to minimize radar and other signals. On-board test system. Angle-of-attack limiter. GPS-Aided Targeting System or GATS (using the synthetic aperture mode of the radar) allows conventional bombing (with GBU-30 or GAM) to 20 ft (6 m) accuracy.
Self-protection systems: Loral AN/APR-50 RWR. Northrop Grumman ZSR-63 defensive aids system, possibly to defeat incoming radar energy by emitting radar waves.

DETAILS FOR B-2A.

Principal dimensions:
Wing span: 172 ft (52.43 m)
Maximum length: 69 ft (21.03 m)
Maximum height: 17 ft (5.18 m)
Height to wingtip: 9 ft (2.74 m)
Height to nose: 10 ft (3.05 m)

Wings:
Area: 5,140 sq ft (477.52 m^2) estimated
Aspect ratio: 5.76 estimated
Sweepback: 33°

Undercarriage:
Type: Retractable Boeing 767 type of extremely wide track, with twin nosewheels. Tandem twin main bogies (4 wheel). Saw-tooth nosewheel door
Wheel track: 40 ft (12.19 m)

Weights:
Empty: 100,000-125,000 lb (45,359-56,700 kg)
Unarmed take-off weight: 277,000 lb (125,644 kg)
Maximum take-off: 305,000 lb (138,345 kg), to be increased to 336,500 lb (152,633 kg)

Performance:
Maximum speed: Mach 0.8
Cruise speed: Mach 0.78 at 37,000 ft (11,275 m)
Low level training speed: 420 kts (484 mph) 778 km/h
Economic cruise speed: 300-320 kts (345-368 mph) 556-593 km/h
Rotation speed: 139 kts (160 mph) 257 km/h at 277,000 lb weight
Climb-out speed: 280 kts (322 mph) 519 km/h
In flight refuelling speed: 255 kts (294 mph) 472 km/h, with a KC-135 tanker
Approach/landing speed: 130-145 kts (150-167 mph) 240-269 km/h
Take-off distance: 5,500 ft (1,676 m) at 277,000 lb weight
Maximum climb rate: 3,000 ft (915 m) per minute at sea level, at 277,000 lb weight
G limits: 2
Ceiling: 50,000 ft (15,240 m)
Range: 6,000 naut miles (6,900 miles) 11,110 km with a 32,000 lb (14,515 kg) payload, at high altitude
Range with 1 air refuelling: over 10,000 naut miles (11,515 miles) 18,520 km

Wing characteristics: Flying-wing airframe, with straight leading edges and "saw tooth" trailing edges (see drawing). Entire leading edge and wingtip returns comprise dielectric panels that mask the radar-deflecting triangulated internal wing structure. 2 large dielectric panels on the undersurface, each side of the nose, cover the radar antennae. Northrop Grumman claim that manufacturing was done to the tightest tolerances ever achieved on an aircraft system, with the B-2 accurate to within one-quarter of an inch wingtip-to-wingtip.
Wing control surfaces: All control surfaces are horizontal and form the entire trailing edges of the large outer V sections. The inboard control surfaces are 2-section elevons (functioning as ailerons and elevators), all 4 sections deployed during low-speed flight but with only the outer sections used thereafter. The two 2-section outer control surfaces perform the functions of drag rudders, spoilers and airbrakes, and are split horizontally into upper and lower sections. These are normally in use during flight, with a lower section deflecting up to 90° and an upper section as needed to perform the turn. During landing, the outer surfaces are each deployed at 45° (up and down) as airbrakes, via a panel button. Beaver tail gust load alleviation system (GLAS) with hydraulic actuator forms the centre trailing-edge point of the airframe, aft of the

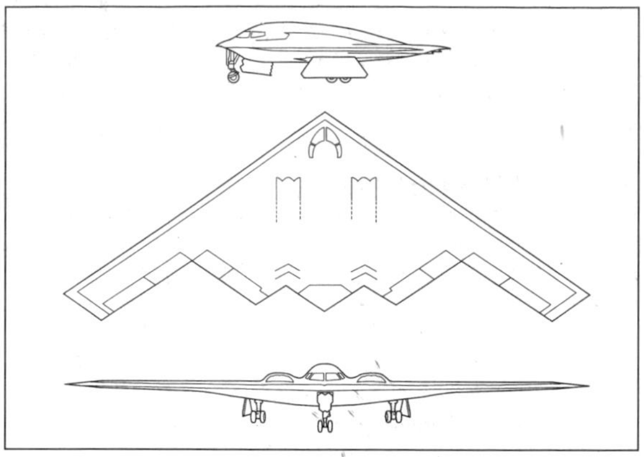

Northrop Grumman B-2A Spirit layout drawing (courtesy Northrop Grumman)

"fuselage"; it is set at about 11° down with the undercarriage deployed, and is also used for pitch trimming in normal flight.
Tail control surfaces: No vertical tail surfaces.
Airbrakes: See Wing control surfaces.
Flight control system: Lockheed Martin quadruple redundant fly-by-wire. Control stick steering.
Fuselage: Blended into the centre section of the wing.
Construction materials: Principally composite materials, including some newly developed, with wide use of graphite and epoxy. Internal honeycomb structure and honeycomb skin, with triangulated leading edges, help deflect and reduce radar returns. RAM top skin and coating, except for the dielectric leading edges. Titanium heat protection for the upper wing immediately aft of the nozzles. Nearly 900 new materials and processes were developed in the B-2 programme.
Engines: 4 General Electric F118-GE-100 non-afterburning turbofans. New tailpipe coating tested from September 1994 to remedy a low observable problem. APU.
Engine rating: Each 19,000 lbf (84.518 kN).
Air intakes: 2 paired S-duct intakes of W planform, rounded and blended into the upper wing surface. Saw-tooth boundary layer splitter plates, also to provide cool air for lower infra-red detectability. Auxiliary air inlets about one-third the way back along the intake nacelles open during take-off and low speed flight.
Nozzles: Paired in the wing upper surface, well forward of the wing trailing edges, to mask the efflux from IR detection from below. Nozzles probably produce a wider and thinner plume than usual, possibly directed marginally upward, for fast dispersion in the aircraft's wake.
Flight refuelling probe: Rotating receptacle, aft of cockpit.
Fuel system: 130,000 lb (58,967 kg) of JP-8 in 8 tanks, with automatic fuel management (manual back-up). Pressure refuelling in port wheel well. (By August 1994, flight testing had covered 100% of the air refuelling envelope with the KC-135 and over 80% of the envelope with the KC-10, showing the B-2 to be stable and easy to refuel.)
Hydraulic system: 4,000 psi.
Braking system: Brakes, with anti-skid system.

Northrop Grumman F-5 series and Modernization Programmes

First flight: 30 July 1959 (N-156 prototype for the F-5A).
Role: Lightweight tactical fighter and fighter bomber.

★ Aims

★ Inexpensive and simple supersonic aircraft, with development funded by the US Government, for export under Military Assistance Programmes.

▲ Development

▲ 31 July 1963. First flight of a production F-5A at Edwards Air Force Base.
▲ 24 February 1964. First flight of an F-5B two-seat training version.
▲ April 1964. First F-5 deliveries to Williams AFB, Arizona, for USAF personnel to train pilots and ground crew of foreign air forces.
▲ 1 February 1965. Iran became the first MAP nation to operate the F-5.
▲ 11 August 1972. First flight of the much improved F-5E Tiger II, funded by the US Government as an International Fighter Aircraft to replace the F-5A. First deliveries to the USAF to train foreign personnel in 1973.

Sales/users: Over 2,600 F-5s of all versions were built by Northrop and under co-production programmes and licensing agreements with Canada, Taiwan, South Korea, the Netherlands, Spain and Switzerland. It is estimated by Northrop Grumman that about 1,700 remain in use with Bahrain (F-5E/F), Brazil (F-5B, F-5E), Canada (CF-5A/D, being withdrawn), Chile (F-5E/F), Greece (F-5A/B, RF-5A and NF-5A/B), Honduras (F-5E/F), Indonesia (F-5E/F), Iran (F-5E/F), Jordan (F-5E/F), Kenya (F-5E/F), South Korea (F-5A/B, F-5E/F), Malaysia (F-5E/F and RF-5E TigerEye), Mexico (F-5E/F), Morocco (F-5A/B, F-5E/F), Norway (F-5G/B), Philippines (F-5A/B), Saudi Arabia (F-5B, F-5E/F and RF-5E TigerEye), Singapore (F-5E/F), Switzerland (F-5E/F), Spain (F-5A/B and RF-5A), Taiwan (F-5A/B, F-5E/F), Thailand (F-5A/B, F-5E/F), Tunisia (F-5E/F), Turkey (F-5A/B and RF-5A), Uruguay (F-5E?), USA (Navy/USMC, F-5E/F for aggressor training), Venezuela (CF-5A/D, NF-5A), Vietnam (F-5A/B, RF-5A and F-5E) and Yemen (F-5B and F-5E).
Details: Principally for F-5E Tiger II.
Crew: Pilot.
Crew escape: Ejection seat.
Fixed guns: 2 x M39A2 20-mm cannon in the nose.
Ammunition: 280 rounds each.
Number of weapon pylons: 7, as 2 wingtip AAM launch rails, 4 under the wings and 1 under the fuselage.
Expendable weapons and equipment: 7,000 lb (3,175 kg) load plus wingtip AAMs, comprising various types of bombs (including a 2,000 lb Mk 84 under fuselage), French Durandel concrete penetration weapons, Maverick or other missiles, rocket launchers, etc.
Radar: Originally Emerson AN/APQ-159.
Flight/weapon system avionics/instrumentation: Air data computer, AN/ARA-50 ADF, AN/ARN-118 Tacan, AHRS, angle-of-attack equipment and AN/ASG-31 sight. Offered options included Litton LN-33 INS, VOR/ILS with DME, and CRT with converter for radar or Maverick missile display.
Self-protection systems: Optional RWR and AN/ALE-40 countermeasures.
Wing characteristics: Straight, low mounted, with no anhedral or dihedral. Small LERX.
Wing control surfaces: Ailerons, single-slotted trailing-edge flaps, and leading-edge flaps.
Tail control surfaces: Slab tailplane and rudder.
Canard: None.
Airbrakes: 2, under the fuselage.
Flight control system: Hydraulic, with electrically operated leading-edge flaps.
Fuselage: Area ruled. Fail-safe, pressurized cockpit and avionics bay.
Construction materials: Metal.
Engines: 2 General Electric J85-GE-21B turbojets.
Engine rating: Each 3,500 lbf (15.57 kN) dry, 5,000 lbf (22.24 kN) with afterburning.
Air intakes: Fuselage sides, plus small louvred panels on the rear of the intake nacelle to provide additional air below Mach 0.4.
Flight refuelling probe: Optional, see Aircraft versions.
Fuel system: 3 fuselage bag tanks, one of 1,120 litres supplying the port engine and the other 2 totalling 1,442 litres for the starboard engine, with cross-feeding. 568 and 1,041 litres capacity drop tanks can be carried under 2 "wet" wing pylons and the fuselage.
Braking system: Disc. Drag-chute.

Aircraft variants:

F-5A Freedom Fighter was the original Mach 1.4 single-seat day fighter, powered by 2 x J85-GE-13 turbojets, each 2,720 lbf (12.1 kN) dry and 4,080 lbf (18.15 kN) with afterburning. Basic instrumentation, including Tacan and optical sight. 6,200 lb (2,812 kg) weapon load on 5 pylons, plus 2 x 20-mm cannon and wingtip Sidewinders. Built in Canada as the CF-5A with more powerful Orenda-produced J85-CAN-15 engines and refuelling probe, in the Netherlands as the NF-5A with Doppler navigation equipment and refuelling probe, and in Spain as the SF-5A. Norwegian aircraft known as F-5Gs.
F-5B was produced as the tandem two-seat version of the F-5A, shorter despite the stepped second cockpit. Also manufactured in Canada, Netherlands and Spain as the CF-5D, NF-5B and SF-5B.
RF-5A was built as the reconnaissance version, with 4 x KS-92 cameras in the extended nose and other special equipment. Spanish SRF-5As.
F-5E Tiger II was developed from the F-5A to improve general performance and manoeuvrability, and provide for all-weather flying. More engine power, increased wing area and automatic manoeuvring flaps. As detailed.
F-5F Tiger II became the two-seat training version, lengthened and heavier, with only 1 cannon, but otherwise generally similar.
RF-5E TigerEye was given an extended nose to house an exchangeable camera/IR sensor pallet for its armed reconnaissance role. Few were produced.

Upgrade programmes:

Bristol Aerospace in Canada, which see.
CASA of Spain, which see (and see also Samsung).
Elbit in Israel, which see.
Embraer may become involved in the possible upgrade of Brazil's F-5Es with AMX avionics.
ENAER in Chile, which see.
IAI in Israel, which see.
SABCA in Belgium, which see. Also recently chosen to perform upgrades on Indonesia's F-5E/Fs.
Northrop Grumman's own programmes include structural modifications and avionics upgrade of US Navy F-5Es from VFA-127 aggressor squadron (with AlliedSignal mission computer and display processor,

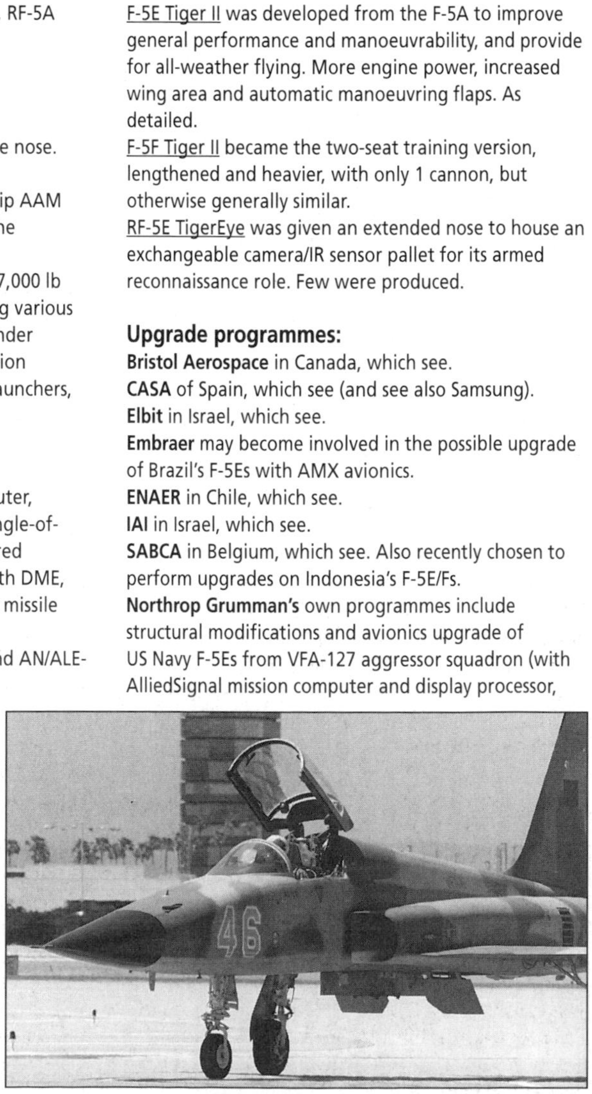

Northrop Grumman F-5E Tiger II loaned to the company by the US Navy for the avionics development and integration programme. Note the auxiliary air intake louvres on the rear of the intake nacelle

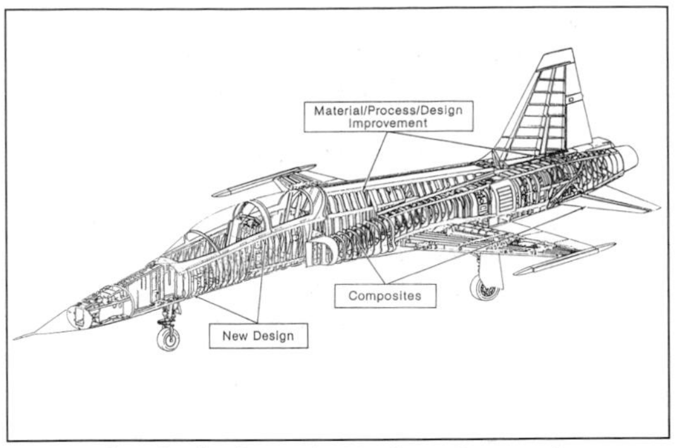

Structural modernization under Northrop Grumman's F-5 programme (courtesy Northrop Grumman)

Bristol Aerospace working on CF-5s

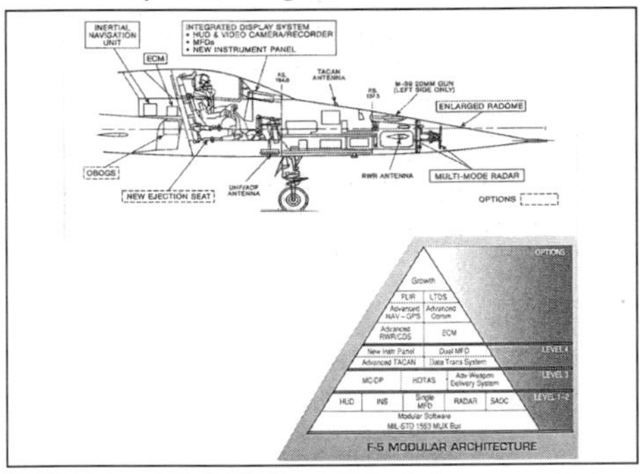

Avionics upgrade and other internal changes under the Northrop Grumman F-5 modular upgrade

air data computer, AN/APG-66 radar, Honeywell ring laser gyro and multi-function displays). See also USAF, below. The company's Tactical Fighter Modification Programme offered to F-5 operators includes 4 levels of upgrade (modular) or total modernization, covering avionics tied together with a MIL-STD-1553B databus and operational flight programme mission software from the F-20 (new radar, mission computer, multi-function cockpit displays, HUD, navigation system and weapons management system), plus on-board oxygen generating system, ejection seat and HOTAS. In addition, modern aluminium alloys and some composites will be used in the proposed structural enhancements. The Northrop Grumman team includes Bristol Aerospace, CASA and Samsung, plus subsystem suppliers. Modernization includes conversion of Tiger IIs into RF-5Es with infra-red line scanners and long-range cameras (including real-time data transmission).
Rockwell International of the USA, which see.
Samsung of South Korea, which see.
Sierra Industries of the USA for Norwegian upgrades (though 10 or more sets of new wings are coming from Bristol Aerospace).
Singapore Technologies Aerospace, which see.
The USAF has sought proposals for the upgrade of foreign F-5s, for retrofit as kits under continuing foreign military sales agreements. In July 1994, the USAF's San Antonio Air Logistics Center entered into a partnership agreement with Northrop Grumman to design, develop, conduct, analyze, demonstrate and document a total avionics system enhancement for the F-5E.

Details for F-5E Tiger II.

Principal dimensions:
Wing span: 26 ft 8 ins (8.13 m)
Wing span over missiles: 28 ft (8.53 m)
Maximum length: 48 ft 2 ins (14.68 m)
Maximum height: 13 ft 4 ins (4.06 m)

Wings:
Aerofoil section: Modified NACA 65A004.8
Area: 186 sq ft (17.28 m²)
Aspect ratio: 3.82 without missiles
Sweepback: 24° leading edge
Chord at root: 11 ft 8.5 ins (3.57 m)
Chord at tip: 2 ft 3 ins (0.68 m)
Dihedral: 0°
Anhedral: 0°

Tail unit:
Tailplane span: 14 ft 1.5 ins (4.31 m)
Tailplane area: 59 sq ft (5.48 m²)

Undercarriage:
Type: Retractable, with steerable nosewheel. Extendable nosewheel to increase wing angle of attack at take-off
Main wheel tyre size: 24 x 8-13
Nose wheel tyre size: 18 x 6.5-8
Wheel base: 17 ft (5.18 m)
Wheel track: 12 ft 5 ins (3.8 m)

Weights:
Empty: 9,583 lb (4,347 kg)
Maximum zero fuel weight: 17,534 lb (7,953 kg)
Maximum take-off: 24,675 lb (11,192 kg)

Performance:
Never-exceed speed (VNE): 710 kts (817 mph) 1,315 km/h
Maximum speed: Mach 1.63 at 36,000 ft (10,975 m)
Maximum cruise speed: Mach 0.98 at 36,000 ft
Take-off distance: 2,000 ft (610 m)
Landing distance: 2,500 ft (762 m) with drag-chute
Maximum climb rate: 34,500 ft (10,500 m) per minute
Ceiling: 51,800 ft (15,800 m)
Radius of action (attack Hi Lo Lo Hi): 480 naut miles (552 miles) 889 km, with 1,060 lb (480 kg) bomb load and 2 Sidewinders, 5 minutes over target, with reserve fuel
Range with full internal/external fuel: 1,545 naut miles (1,780 miles) 2,861 km

Northrop Grumman F-14 Tomcat

First flight: 21 December 1970.
Role: Carrier-borne, and land-based, long-range air superiority fighter with secondary long-range air-to-ground capability and reconnaissance, with planned but unfunded modification to include advanced strike.

★ Aims

⋆ Variable-geometry deck-based fighter, developed after the abandonment of the planned naval F-111B in 1968. Grumman's participation in the General Dynamics F-111 programme, plus its experience with building the experimental XF10F Jaguar, left the company in a strong position to win the US Navy's VFX competition with a variable-geometry design against competing McDonnell Douglas.
⋆ Rapid development, to meet the US Navy's need for a new aircraft, leading to selection of the F-111's Pratt & Whitney TF30 engines.
⋆ Deployment of the very long-range Phoenix air-to-air missile, as intended for F-111B, its use made possible by the new and advanced Hughes AN/AWG-9 look-down radar.

▲ Development

▲ 15 January 1969. Grumman was announced winner of the US Navy's VFX competition.
▲ 21 December 1970. First of 12 development F-14s flew at Bethpage, but was lost on its second flight on 30 December after experiencing hydraulic failure.
▲ 24 May 1971. Second development aircraft flew, followed by 7 more that year.
▲ 1972. Production deliveries of F-14As began, initially going to VF-124 for crew training.
▲ June 1972. Aircraft carrier trials were initiated.
▲ October 1972. First operational squadron deployments, to VF-1 and VF-2 at NAS Miramar.
▲ June 1973. Launch of an AIM-54 Phoenix AAM from an F-14 against a drone target with countermeasures some 109 naut miles (126 miles) 203 km from the fighter. Phoenix became operational on F-14 in 1974.
▲ 12 September 1973. Initially planned re-engined version with F401-PW-400 engines was flown in prototype form, as the F-14B. This programme did not proceed, and this F-14B variant should not be mistaken for the subsequently-produced F-14B with General Electric engines.
▲ January 1976. The first of 79 F-14As for Iran arrived at the Khatami air base in Isfahan.
▲ 14 November 1987. Maiden flight of a full production F-14B. Deliveries of F-14Bs took place between April 1988 and May 1990, initially to VF-101.
▲ 7 October 1992. Initial sea deployment of F-14As modified for bombing, nicknamed "Bombats", on

Details for F-14A.

Principal dimensions:
Wing span: 38 ft 2.5 ins (11.65 m) *swept*, 64 ft 1.5 ins (19.55 m) *spread*
Maximum length: 62 ft 8 ins (19.1 m)
Maximum height: 16 ft (4.88 m)

Wings:
Area: 565 sq ft (52.49 m²)
Aspect ratio: 7.278 *spread*, 2.584 *spread*
Sweepback: 20° *spread*, 68° *spread*

Tail unit:
Tailplane span: 32 ft 8 ins (9.96 m)

Undercarriage:
Type: Retractable, with twin nosewheels
Wheel base: 23 ft (7.01 m)
Wheel track: 16 ft 5 ins (5 m)

Weights:
Empty: 38,910 lb (17,650 kg)
Maximum take-off: 74,350 lb (33,725 kg)

Performance:
Maximum speed: Mach 2.34 clean for 2 minute dash, Mach 2.17 prolonged, Mach 1.88 with external stores, or Mach 1.2 at low altitude
Cruise speed: Mach 0.72
Approach speed: 125 kts (144 mph) 231 km/h
Take-off distance: 1,400-2,500 ft (427-762 m) on shore
Landing distance: 2,400-2,900 ft (732-885 m) on shore
Maximum climb rate: 48,200 ft (14,690 m) per minute
Sustained turn rate: 12.6° per second
G limits: +7.5, -2.4
Ceiling: 64,000 ft (19,500 m)
Typical air-to-air mission range: 460 naut miles (530 miles) 852 km
Range with full internal and external fuel: 1,600-1,737 naut miles (1,840-2,000 miles) 2,960-3,318 km

Northrop Grumman T-38A Talon trainers

board USS *John F. Kennedy*.

▲ 20 July 1992. Final newly built F-14 was handed over to the US Navy, as the last of 37 F-14Ds.

▲ 1995. Plans to modify some 200 US Navy F-14s into advanced strike aircraft, to compensate for the pending withdrawal of the A-6E/TRAM Intruder, were still in the balance. As yet unfunded by the US Navy, the US General Accounting Office considered the programme should not go ahead while waiting for the introduction of the F/A-18E and F. Upgrade of all 200 or thereabouts would take a decade. Life extension programme has been committed.

Sales/users: Iran (believed to have over 20 in active use, and a further larger quantity in store or cannibalized for spares to keep the active force flying). and US Navy (over 250 active F-14As and Bs, plus 44 F-14Ds).

Crew: Pilot and flight officer in tandem, the rear seat raised.

Cockpit: Single-piece, rear-hinging canopy

Crew escape: Martin Baker zero-zero ejection seats.

Fixed guns: 20-mm General Electric M61A-1 Vulcan cannon in the port side of the nose.

Ammunition: 675 rounds.

Number of weapon pylons: 6, 2 under the wing gloves and 4 under the fuselage, the wing pylons with optional multiple ejectors.

Expendable weapons and equipment: 14,500 lb (6,577 kg) load. 4 AIM-54C Phoenix very long range AAMs (in side by side pairs), or 4 AIM-7F/M Sparrow medium range AAMs (forward pair plus tandem centreline), or 2 Phoenix and 1 Sparrow under the fuselage. Each underwing pylon can carry a Phoenix and AIM-9M Sidewinder dogfight AAMs (larger missile under the pylon and the Sidewinder on a separate horizontal "sub-pylon" attached to the top of the main pylon), or a Sparrow and Sidewinder, or 2 Sidewinders. F-14D carries AIM-120 AMRAAM (integration by Northrop Grumman under a $12.2 million contract) in addition to Phoenix AAMs, or air-to-ground weapons including laser-guided smart weapons, cluster bombs or other stores. HARM may become available, to allow a SEAD (suppression of enemy air defences) role.

Additional stores: Tactical Air Reconnaissance Pod System with cameras and infra-red equipment, can be carried under the fuselage of all F-14Ds and a number of F-14As and Bs.

Radar: Hughes AN/AWG-9 look-down radar. F-14D has AN/APG-71 radar.

Flight/weapon system avionics/instrumentation: INS (originally AN/ASN-92(V), with ASN-139 on later models) AHRS, Tacan, ADF, radar altimeter and beacon augmentor. Autopilot, autostabilization, and automatic carrier landing system. Most F-14A/Bs now have MIL-STD-1553B databus, new AN/AYK-14 mission computer and tactical information display. Kaiser HUD. AN/ASW-27B digital data link. Undernose Northrop Television Camera Set with automatic target search/lock-on and picture display in both cockpits. GPS being fitted. IFF. F-14D is also equipped with a joint tactical information distribution system, dual chin pod (DCP) with infra-red search/track sensor and TV camera (missile launch restrictions, imposed after concern that the pod could have an effect on firing because of flow field changes, were lifted in late 1994), night vision goggles and compatible cockpit lighting.

Self-protection systems: Sanders deception jamming unit housed under the TCS. AN/ALR-67 radar warning receiver. Chaff/flare dispensers. Litton AN/ALR-67 threat warning and recognition.

Wing characteristics: Automatic variable geometry tapering outer panels (manual override) without anhedral/dihedral, with automatic manoeuvre device system to schedule high-lift devices. Large-area fixed centre-section gloves with dihedral to minimize aerodynamic drag caused by shockwave formation (so called "wave drag"). Extendable vane-strakes in the gloves only on F-14As, for supersonic trimming. Wings can be further swept to 75° for compact stowage on board ship without wing-folding mechanisms.

Wing control surfaces: Trailing-edge flaps, near full-span spoilers, and automatic leading-edge manoeuvring slats on the movable panels.

Tail control surfaces: Slab tailplane (tailerons), able to be controlled symmetrically or asymmetrically. Twin fins and rudders. Twin fixed ventral fins.

Canard: See Wing characteristics.

Airbrakes: 2, above and below the rear fuselage.

Construction materials: Principally aluminium alloy and titanium, including honeycomb core for areas of the tail unit, with composites used for the tailplane skins.

Engines: 2 x 20,900 lbf (92.97 kN) with afterburning Pratt & Whitney TF30-P-412As originally, changing to similarly rated TF30-P-414As for production aircraft built from 1984. F-14B and D new production aircraft and upgrades have 16,000 lbf (71.17 kN) dry and 27,000 lbf (120.1 kN) with afterburning General Electric F110-GE-400 turbofans.

Engine rating: See above.

Air intakes: 2D wedge, each side of the fuselage, canted at the glove dihedral angle to provide a gap between the intake trunk and the fuselage to allow turbulent air from the fuselage to pass freely. Automatically operated ramp adjusts airflow.

Flight refuelling probe: Retractable, on the starboard side of the upper nose.

Fuel system: 9,028 litres in the wings and fuselage. 2 x 1,010 litre auxiliary tanks carried under the intakes.

Braking system: Carbon brakes. Arrester hook.

Aircraft variants:

F-14A Tomcat was the original and principal production version for the US Navy and Iran, with P&W engines. Surviving US Navy aircraft have received avionics upgrading. See Avionics.

F-14B Tomcat (not to be mistaken for the F-14B prototype of 1973) turned to General Electric engines, and was originally known as F-14A(Plus). Avionics upgrading (see Avionics). New production plus modified F-14As.

F-14D "Super Tomcat" is the latest version, the small number produced by new production and conversion of earlier aircraft. Only 37 factory built and 18 F-14D(R)s produced through upgrade of earlier versions. Digital avionics replaced much of the previous analog equipment.

Northrop Grumman T-38 Talon Modernization Programmes

First flight: 10 April 1959.

Role: Advanced trainer (T-38A) and Introduction to Fighter Fundamentals trainer (AT-38B)

★ Aims

★ Developed from the Northrop N-156 lightweight tactical fighter that became the exported F-5, but with tandem cockpits.

★ First USAF supersonic trainer.

▲ Development

▲ 17 March 1961. First production T-38A was delivered, serving with the 3510th Flying Training Wing.

▲ 1972. Final T-38A deliveries.

Sales/users: 1,187 built (1,189 with prototypes), of which well over 400 were active in 1995 with FTWs of Air Education and Training Command, USAF. In addition, Taiwan is leasing 40-ex-USAF T-38As until 1997-98, about 41 German-owned aircraft are US based for training Luftwaffe pilots, and Turkey operates some 20.

Aircraft variants:

T-38A Talon is the standard advanced training version.

AT-38B Talon has practice bomb dispensers and a gunsight for lead-in fighter training.

Upgrade programmes:

Pacer Classic service life extension programme has included Northrop (Grumman) constructing over 1,300 replacement wings since the 1980s.

Avionics Upgrade Programme to keep the Talon flying until 2020 was being planned by the USAF in early 1995. Northrop Grumman has proposed a "glass" cockpit with liquid-crystal displays and a HUD, plus further structural modifications and possibly new engines. Competitively, McDonnell Douglas signed an MoU with Israel Aircraft Industries (announced March 1995) to offer collaborative modification of USAF aircraft and provide new ground-based training devices.

Northrop Grumman F-14D Tomcat

Rockwell International Corporation (USA)

Corporate address: 2201 Seal Beach Boulevard, Seal Beach, CA 90740-8250.
Telephone: +1 310 797 3311
Founded: 16 February 1973 (with roots in the North American Rockwell of 1967 formation).
Employees: More than 75,000.

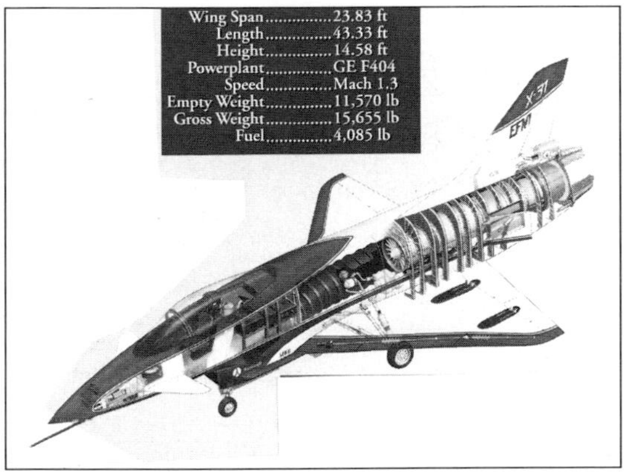
Wing Span.................23.83 ft
Length.................43.33 ft
Height.................14.58 ft
Powerplant.................GE F404
Speed.................Mach 1.3
Empty Weight.................11,570 lb
Gross Weight.................15,655 lb
Fuel.................4,085 lb

Rockwell/Daimler-Benz X-31A Enhanced Fighter Manoeuvrability experimental aircraft, the first of 2 first flown on 11 October 1990. Features fly-by-wire flight controls, thrust vectoring and other techniques to enable the aircraft to turn tighter and aim at targets more quickly than current conventional fighters. Has initiated combat manoeuvring at 70° angle of attack, demonstrated controlled flight in the post-stall regime, and became the first aircraft to complete a radical 180° minimal radius turn (courtesy Rockwell International)

Rockwell/Daimler-Benz X-31A EFM set a new record for X-Plane flights, by recording its 438th flight on 4 August 1994

DIVISIONS

Aerospace

North American Aircraft Division
HQ address: 201 North Douglas Street, El Segundo, CA 90245.
Telephone: +1 213 647 1000

■ Facilities

■ North American Aircraft Modification Division (3370 Miraloma Avenue, Anaheim, CA 92803-4921, *telephone* +1 714 762 6523). Marketing Manager Peter A. Fleury.
■ Palmdale Facility (2825 East Avenue, Palmdale, CA 93550, *telephone* +1 805 273 6000).
■ Tulsa Facility (2000 North Memorial Drive, Tulsa, OK 74115, *telephone* +1 918 835 3111, *facsimile* +1 918 834 7722).

● Activities

● Designs, builds and modifies military aircraft, and supplies metal and composite military and commercial aerostructures. A Rockwell-led team won a $4.7 million contract to update Russia's air traffic control system, under a US DoD co-operative threat reduction programme contract.
● Current programmes include support for the B-1B Lancer, X-31A Enhanced Fighter Manoeuvrability experimental programme with Daimler-Benz Aerospace of Germany, Ranger 2000 trainer, Boeing 737, 747 and 777 structural components, and more.
● Modification Division currently offers F-4 Phantom and F-5 Tiger modernization programmes (see below), has undertaken preparation of the AC-130U Spectre gunship (see Lockheed Martin), and offers a wide range of design, analysis, logistics support, flight test, installation, modification and test, and system integration and test services. It is partnered with AlliedSignal to supply the avionics for the Czech Aero L-159.
● F-4 Phantom and F-5 Tiger II modernization covers replacement of selected analog subsystems with highly reliable digital avionics; improvement in air-to-air capability by encompassing new weapons and increasing radar range; improvement in air-to-ground precision by new central mission computer, ring laser INS, more accurate air-to-ground ranging, better ground map for radar bombing, and use of smart stand-off weapons; reduces aircrew workload by HOTAS, multifunction displays, HUD, data transfer unit and mission planning systems; structural life extension programme.
● Space Systems activities include Space Shuttle orbiters and their main engines, designing the power system for the US Space Station, propulsion systems for expendable launch vehicles, and developing advanced technologies.

Automotive Division

Electronics Division

Includes the Collins Avionics & Communications Division
Address: 350 Collins Road NE, Cedar Rapids, Iowa 52498.
Telephone: +1 319 395 5775
Facsimile: +1 319 395 5111
Telex: 6871757 COLLINSSVC CDR
Information: James M.Thebeau (Manager, Marketing Communications).

● Activities

● Avionics, including flight control, display, navigation, voice and data communication, and other systems.
● Telecommunications.
● Defence electronics produced by the Electronics Division as a whole include C3 devices and systems, aircraft upgrades and modifications, tactical weapons, space defence sensors and electronics, navigation and guidance systems, naval combat systems, commercial products, etc. Produces the AGM-130 and AGM-114F Hellfire missiles, GBU-15 guided weapon, and other types.
● Industrial automation.

Graphics Division

Rockwell B-1B Lancer

First flight: 18 October 1984.
Role: Long-range penetration and stand-off strategic bomber, with current emphasis on conventional mission enhancement (though remaining nuclear capable). Also capable of long-range sea surveillance, anti-submarine patrol and aerial mine laying.

★ Aims

★ Developed from the abandoned B-1 that had been flown to prototype stage against the USAF's 1965 requirement for an Advanced Manned Strategic Bomber to supersede the B-52, but had fallen victim to funding diversion to cruise missiles.
★ Bomber development reactivated in 1981, but with only 100 revised B-1Bs to supplement B-52s as the most capable element of a composite bomber force, instead of the former 244 B-1s to replace B-52s.
★ B-1B was developed within the continuing emphasis for high subsonic speed at extremely low altitudes for penetration bombing, using an automatic terrain following system. Maximum speed at high altitude fell dramatically, due in part to a major increase in take-off weight (necessitating a strengthened undercarriage), but survivability was enhanced by improved low observable technologies applied to the airframe, the use of radar absorbent materials, and sophisticated avionics suites including electronic jamming, infra-red countermeasures and other systems to detect, evade and defeat enemy defences. Airframe changes encompassed redesigned engine nacelles with fixed inlets (instead of variable), wing-glove revisions, and the opportunity to carry a greater variety of weapons through varying bulkhead positions between the front 2 tandem weapon bays, plus the carriage of external weapons under the fuselage. To cater for increased fuel usage, front bays became "wet", allowing installation of auxiliary tanks when required.
★ Intercontinental range without refuelling.
★ Variable geometry (swing) wings, in fully spread position offering shorter take off and rapid clearance from the main operating base or airfield coming under attack. In swept configuration, the wings become suited to high altitude supersonic cruise flight or low-level/high subsonic penetration flight.
★ Radar signature 1% that of the B-52.
★ Designed to cope with overpressure from the blast of a conventional or nuclear explosion.

▲ Development

▲ 1981. Rockwell received a full-scale development contract for the B-1B's airframe plus weapon system integration. Boeing received a contract for production, acquisition and integration of the offensive avionics and supporting elements of the defensive avionics system. Eaton AIL received a contract for the defensive avionics, and General Electric a contract for the engines.
▲ 4 May 1985. Maiden flight of the second production B-1B, becoming the first into USAF service on 7 July that year when it was handed over to the 96th BW at Dyess AFB.
▲ September 1986. Initial operational capability.
▲ 16 January 1987. First SRAM (Short Range Attack Missile) launch from a B-1B.
▲ 1987. Set 36 world records for speed, payload and distance, adding 12 for time-to-climb records in 1992, and 11 speed records over a 10,000 km course in April 1994. 1992 time to climb records in Category C-1Q (over 330,000 lb weight) included attaining an altitude of 10,000 ft in 1 minute 59 seconds and 40,000 ln 9 minutes 42 seconds.
▲ 24 November 1987. First launch by a B-1B of an inert AGM-86B air-launched cruise missile.
▲ 30 April 1988. The last B-1B joined the USAF.
▲ August 1993. Rockwell, with Boeing as subcontractor, entered a teaming agreement to initiate the USAF's CMUP programme (Conventional Mission Upgrade

Rockwell B-1B Lancer with wings swept, showing the rounded wingroot leading edge and nose surfaces

Program) for the B-1B. Phase I of the CMUP, completed in 1995, included Boeing's development of software to provide for manual selection of and insertion of ballistic information into the system to accommodate various free-fall weapons, such as cluster bombs. See Weapons and Avionics, and below.

▲ 1994. Cluster bomb units (CBUs) were released during trials at Edwards Air Force Base, as part of the continuing CMUP programme.

▲ July 1994. First B-1B into reserve force service, transferring to the Kansas ANG.

▲ 1995. The CMUP (see above) continues, including $74 million for R&D under the FY1995 budget. In April 1995, Rockwell and Boeing received much larger CMUP contracts for EMD and systems integration.

Rockwell B-1B Lancer with wings spread

Sales/users: 84 remain on the active inventory of Air Combat Command in 1995, of which 82 are primary aircraft authorized (PAA) for operational use with the 7th Wing at Dyess AFB in Texas and 28th Bomb Wing at Ellsworth AFB in South Dakota (both 8th Air Force). A further 11 are with the Kansas Air National Guard. ANG B-1Bs will eventually operate from both McConnell AFB in Kansas and Robins AFB in Georgia. ACC aircraft are expected to maintain a 75% mission capable rate.

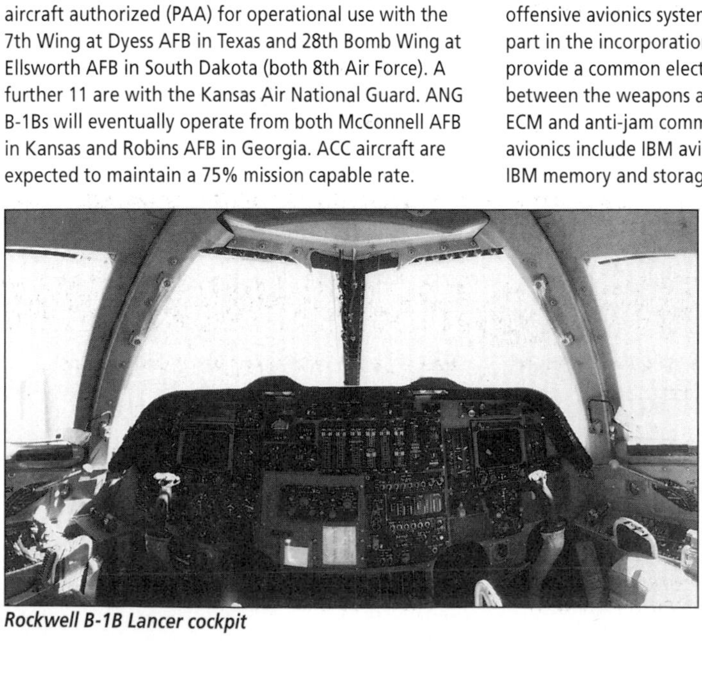

Rockwell B-1B Lancer cockpit

Crew: 4, comprising 2 pilots, offensive systems officer and defensive systems officer.

Cockpit: Radiation glareshield. Control sticks.

Crew escape: McDonnell Douglas ACES II zero-zero ejection seats.

Fixed guns: None.

Number of weapon pylons: Formerly 6, in pairs under the fuselage, for ALCMs.

Expendable weapons and equipment: 2 weapon bays in tandem under the forward fuselage (with repositionable bulkhead), and 1 bay between the paired engines. Under the CMUP, which provides in part the interfaces and systems needed to deploy GBU-30 and other new weapons, modification of the bomb rack and launcher was put in hand to handle multiple weapons and maximize payload. Normal weapon load is 42,000-64,000 lb (19,050-29,030 kg), with maximum of 75,000 lb (34,020 kg) in the bays. Absolute maximum load internal/external is 125,000 lb (56,700 kg). Conventional or nuclear weapons can be carried, with emphasis on improving conventional under the CMUP. Options include 24 x B-61 or B-83 nuclear bombs, 84 x Mk82 500 lb bombs, GBU-30s (former JDAM – Joint Direct Attack Munition) or Mk 62 mines. SRAM (Short Range Attack Missile) and AGM-86B air-launched cruise missiles (carried in the bays and on 6 underfuselage stations) are no longer part of the B-1B's inventory. Future weapons will include JSOW (Joint Standoff Weapon) and WCMD (Wind Corrected Munition Dispenser). See Development for the CMUP, Phase I.

Radar: Westinghouse AN/APQ-164 offensive radar.

Flight/weapon system avionics/instrumentation: Offensive avionics system allows the B-1B to follow the terrain at low altitude, navigate precisely to the targets, align and launch weapons, escape the target area, and return to a recovery air base. Offensive avionics system is controlled by 4 central computers operating on multiple data buses (formerly MIL-STD-1553B). These link with the 2 terrain following computers, a central integrated test system computer (CITS – which logs all flight failures and sustained damage), a defensive system computer, 2 micro-computers and 31 processors in the system line-replaceable units. Some 330,000 lines of software code containing more than 513,000 words are required to program the computers. Under the on-going CMUP (see Development), Phase IIA included recommendations for navigation, communications and offensive avionics systems (OAS) upgrades, resulting in part in the incorporation of MIL-STD-1760 capability, to provide a common electrical and digital interface between the weapons and the aircraft, plus improved ECM and anti-jam communications, and GPS. Original avionics include IBM avionics computer control, IBM memory and storage unit, Kearfott Guidance and Navigation inertial navigation unit, Sperry Flight Systems digital computer, Sperry multi-function displays (2 for the offensive system operator and 1 for the defensive system operator), Sperry video recorder, Sanders Associates electronic display units, Sundstrand Data Corporation data transfer units, Teledyne Ryan AN/APN-218 Doppler data antenna-receiver-transmitter, instrument landing system, Honeywell AN/ASN-131 radar altimeter, and IFF.

Self-protection systems: Eaton AIL AN/ALQ-161 defensive avionics suite, encompassing AN/ASQ-184 management system and chaff/flares, AN/ALQ-161A radio-frequency surveillance and electronics counter-measures system, Northrop jammers, Raytheon phased array antenna and tail warning system. A Status Test and Evaluation System within ALQ-161 co-ordinates with the CITS to allow jamming to continue after failure/damage, by re-routing electronic signals to bypass the failures.

Wing characteristics: Low mounted, variable geometry, with no dihedral/anhedral when the outer wing panels are spread, but with anhedral when swept. Small, rounded outermost sections of the fixed centre-section gloves (that house the hydraulic screwjack actuators for wing sweeping), fair the leading-edge roots of the moving panels during sweepback. Wing gloves are blended into the fuselage.

Wing control surfaces: 6-section single-slotted trailing-edge flaps (40° deflection), 4-section spoilers (70° deflection) immediately ahead of flaps, and 7-section leading-edge slats.

Tail control surfaces: Slab tailerons, operated symmetrically for pitch (10° up, 25° down) and asymmetrically for roll (±20°). 3-section inset rudder.

Canard: Very small, sweptback, anhedral "vane" surfaces on the nose ahead of the cockpit, for yaw/pitch damping.

Airbrakes: Use of spoilers.

Flight control system: Principally hydraulic, but with fly-by-wire control of the 4 outer spoiler sections and as a stand-by for the tail surfaces.

Fuselage: Area ruled and blended, coated with radar-absorption materials. Structurally produced in 5 sections.

Construction materials: Metal (principally aluminium alloy and titanium), but with composites

DETAILS FOR B-1B LANCER.

Principal dimensions:
Wing span: 78 ft 2.75 ins (23.84 m) *swept*, 136 ft 8 ins (41.66 m) *spread*
Maximum length: 145 ft 9 ins (44.426 m) actual for production aircraft, but 147 ft (44.806 m) quoted
Maximum height: 33 ft 7 ins (10.24 m) actual for production aircraft

Wings:
Area: 1,950 sq ft (181.16 m^2)
Aspect ratio: about 9.58 *spread*
Sweepback: 15° *spread*, 67° 30' *swept*

Tail unit:
Tailplane span: 44 ft 10 ins (13.67 m)

Undercarriage:
Type: Retractable, with twin steerable nosewheels. Main units comprise 4-wheel bogies
Main wheel tyre size: 46 x 16
Nose wheel tyre size: 35 x 11.5-16
Wheel base: 56 ft 5.5 ins (17.21 m) actual, main gear strut to nosewheel axle
Wheel track: 14 ft 6 ins (4.42 m)

Weights:
Empty, operating: 192,000 lb (87,090 kg)
Maximum take-off: 477,000 lb (216,363 kg)

Performance:
Maximum speed: Mach 1.2 at altitude, over 520 kts (600 mph) 966 km/h at very low level
Low level penetration altitude: about 150-200 ft (46-61 m)
Range with full fuel: about 6,500 naut miles (7,500 miles) 12,000 km, without in-flight refuelling

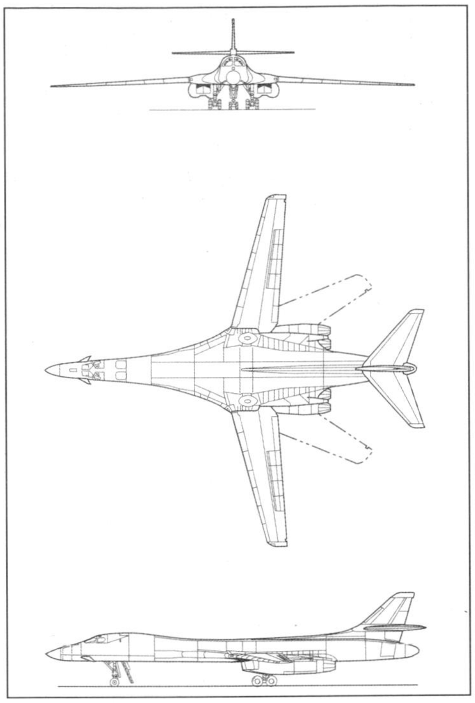

Rockwell B-1B Lancer (courtesy Rockwell Aerospace)

used for the wing-to-fuselage fairings, small areas of the wing skins and wingtips, nosecone and elsewhere.
Engines: 4 General Electric F101-GE-102 turbofans, paired in nacelles under the wing gloves.
Engine rating: Each 30,780 lbf (136 kN).
Air intakes: Non-variable.
Flight refuelling probe: Retractable, above nose radome.
Fuel system: 195,000 lb (88,450 kg) of fuel in wing and fuselage tanks. Auxiliary long-range tanks can be installed in the front weapon bays and externally under the fuselage.
Electrical system: 3-phase AC supply of 230/400 volt 400Hz, via 3 x 115kVA generators.
Hydraulic system: 4 systems, each 4,000 psi.
Braking system: Carbon brakes, with anti-skid devices.

Rockwell Ranger 2000

First flight: 15 January 1993.
Role: Primary jet trainer.

★ Aims

★ Developed for the USAF/USN JPATS competition, but was not selected for production.
★ Uses some RFB structural technology (see RFB in Germany and Fuselage below).
★ 30 year airframe service life.

DETAILS FOR RANGER 2000.

Principal dimensions:
Wing span: 34 ft 3.5 ins (10.45 m)
Maximum length: 35 ft 9.5 ins (10.91 m)
Maximum height: 12 ft 9.5 ins (3.9 m)

Wings:
Area: 167.4 sq ft (15.55 m^2)
Aspect ratio: 7.03
Dihedral: From root

Undercarriage:
Type: Retractable, with nosewheel

Weights:
Maximum take-off: 7,900 lb (3,583 kg)

Performance:
Maximum speed (IAS): 340 kts (392 mph) 630 km/h, at sea level
Maximum speed (TAS): 392 kts (451 mph) 726 km/h at 30,000 ft (9,145 m)
Stall speed: 92 kts (106 mph) 170 km/h, at gross take-off weight, sea level, IAS
Approach speed: 110 kts (127 mph) 204 mph IAS
Take-off distance over a 50 ft (15 m) obstacle: 1,400 ft (427 m) at sea level
Time to climb to 18,000 ft (5,485 m): 7 minutes
Roll rate: 180° per second
G limits: 3.1 at 15,000 ft (4,570 m), 2.3 at 25,000 ft (7,620 m)
Range with full fuel: 976 naut miles (1,124 miles) 1,807 km

Rockwell Ranger 2000 primary jet trainer

Rockwell Ranger 2000 cutaway, showing the forward fuselage keel beam (courtesy Rockwell)

▲ Development

▲ 1991. Programme initiated, originally as the FanRanger. Jointly financed by Deutsche Aerospace (now Daimler-Benz), with the German company constructing major structural airframe components and assembling the prototypes using RFB-produced tail and canopy. DASA also undertook testing and certification.
▲ 25 July 1993. Second prototype was lost in an accident. First prototype flight testing restarted that December.
▲ 20 June 1994. First flight of the third prototype, lasting 2 hour 5 minutes. Shipped to the USA for the JPATS competition on 30 June.
▲ 9 July 1994. Ranger 2000 made its US debut at Tulsa.
Sales/users: Future outside of JPATS is unclear. Any production will be by Rockwell.
Crew: 2, with the rear instructor's seat raised 12 ins (30.5 cm) to offer a minimum 3° visibility over the front seat for the smallest instructor over the largest pupil.
Cockpit: Pressurized. Transparency system designed to reduce injury from bird strike.
Crew escape: Stencel zero-zero ejection seat.
Flight/weapon system avionics/instrumentation: Collins EFIS. Large instrument panel for future growth potential.
Wing characteristics: Straight, low mounted, with forward-swept trailing edges.
Wing control surfaces: Ailerons, with tabs.
Tail control surfaces: T-tail, with elevator and rudder (tabs on both).
Airbrakes: Now beneath the fuselage, replacing former wing spoilers.
Flight control system: Manual.
Fuselage: Based on the RFB-conceived load-bearing keel beam forward section. Rear fuselage section forms a boom over the engine to support the tail.
Construction materials: Aluminium rear fuselage and fixed sections of the tail unit. Graphite composites for the remaining fuselage and flight control surfaces. Glassfibre wings.
Engine: Pratt & Whitney Canada JT15D-5C turbofan.
Engine rating: 3,190 lbf (14.19 kN).
Air intakes: Fuselage sides.
Flight refuelling probe: None.
Fuel system: 860 litres.

Multi-national

Aircraft Technology Industries (Airtech) (Indonesia/Spain)

Corporate address: Founded by IPTN of Indonesia and CASA of Spain as an equal joint venture. See Spain in this section for CASA company details, and IPTN in the Airliners section.
Founded: 1980.

● Activities

● The CN 235 is basically an airliner and freighter, and full details of these are given in the Airliners section. The following information applies only to the maritime patrol versions, of which the Irish Air Corps has received 2 in CN 235-100MPA Persuader form.

Airtech CN 235 MP and CN 235 MPA

Role: Medium-range maritime patrol, maritime surveillance for fishing control and EEZ protection, and search and rescue. Short-range submarine detection/tracking/attack, anti-surface vessel, and over-the-horizon targeting.

★ Aims

★ Based on the CN 235 M military transport.
★ User friendly integrated and modular mission system.
★ Highly interoperable software – Ada high level soft language.
★ Mission sensor NATO compatible.
★ Built-in expansion capability.

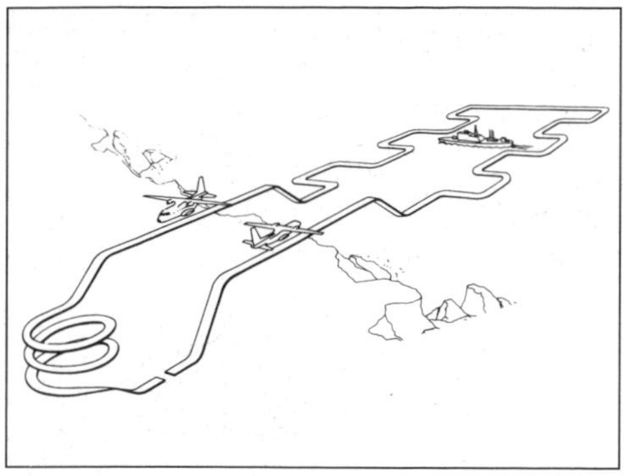

CASA CN 235 MP typical ASW mission profile, with search area 100 naut miles (115 miles) 185 km from base, patrol altitude 2,000 ft (610 m), and holding altitude 5,000 ft (1,525 m). 6 crew, 2 torpedoes and 20 sonobuoys, and 45 minutes fuel reserve. Time on task 9 hours (courtesy CASA)

★ Ready to launch weapons in the torpedo bay.
★ C³I interoperable system, with data link.
★ Maritime surveillance time on target >10 hours. ASW/ASUW range up to 500 naut miles (576 miles) 926 km, and 4 to 8 hours time on target.

Aircraft variants:
CN 236 MP has 360° scan Litton APS-504(V)5 search radar in an underfuselage radome, FLIR Systems FLIR-2000 in a "chin" ball turret (integrated with radar for better mission co-ordination), Litton/CASA TDMS mission processor, AGI Agiflite hand-held camera, and liferaft/survival kit deployment for maritime surveillance and SAR missions. Normal crew of 6. For ASW/ASUW, mission equipment includes search radar, IFF/interrogator, infra-red detecting set/FLIR, Litton ALR-85(V) ESM, acoustic receiver, on-top position indicator, and MAD. Weapons bay.
CN 235 MPA differs mainly in having the Litton radar and IFF in an enlarged nose, GEC-Marconi FLIR in an underfuselage "thimble", Argosystems ESM sensors in an above-cockpit fairing and at the tail, and extra mission crew.

CASA-produced CN 235 MP

AMX International Ltd (Brazil/Italy)

Corporate address: AMX International is a partnership of Aermacchi and Alenia of Italy and Embraer of Brazil. Addresses and Telephone/Facsimile numbers can be found under the individual companies in the earlier pages of this section.

● Activities
● The original agreement defined the workshare in the AMX programme at 23.6% Aermacchi (front fuselage and tail cone), Aeritalia (which became Alenia) at 46.7% (central fuselage, stabilizers and rudder), and 29.7% Embraer (wings, engine air intakes, pylons and drop tanks). The workshare was assigned according to the number of aircraft required by the Italian and Brazilian air forces, planned at 187 and 79 respectively.

AMX International AMX/A-1

First flight: 15 May 1984.
Role: Close air support, interdiction, close interdiction against forces behind the battlefield area, and reconnaissance, with secondary counter-air role. Developments are to include electronic combat, anti-ship and night attack.

★ Aims
★ Series production integrated and based at 3 final assembly lines, 2 in Italy and 1 in Brazil, also covering production of two-seaters.
★ Survival in a hostile environment, with minimal vulnerability, aided by low-level flight and good low-level flying characteristics, high speed, low detectability, low infra-red signature, integrated ECM, IR warning, radar warning, chaff and flares.
★ High state of readiness and safety. Pre-flight built-in test equipment. 15-minute reaction time can be maintained for 30 days with only limited servicing being provided. With systems activated on standby, AMX can be held at 5 minutes readiness for 6 hours at full performance or, with systems not activated, can be scrambled in 5 minutes with decreased performance.
★ Good take-off and landing performance. Self-starting, high-lift wing devices and brakes.
★ High speed penetration with heavy military loads.
★ High navigation and attack accuracy.
★ Post-failure operability. Ability to recover to base even if damaged. Multipath structures and systems protection. Should a double failure of both the hydraulic and electrical systems occur, the aircraft remains controllable through manual back-up of flight controls.
★ Integrated penetration aids.

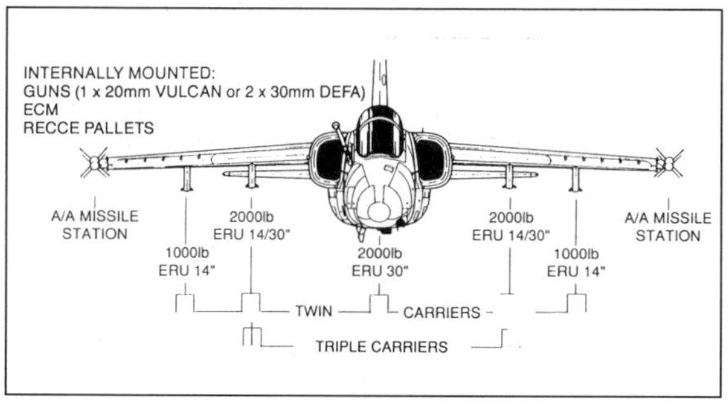

Weapon pylon arrangement and possible loads on the AMX/A-1 (courtesy Embraer)

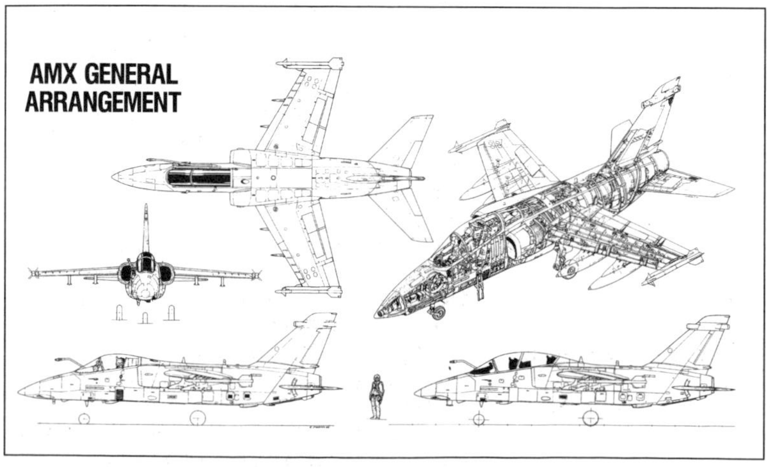

Views of the single-seat AMX/A-1 with refuelling probe, with additional AMX-T two-seater (courtesy Embraer)

▲ Development
▲ 1977. A weapon system specification was issued by the Italian Air Force for a tactical fighter-bomber to replace the F-104G Starfighter and G91, and the resulting programme involved Aermacchi and Alitalia. About the same time the Brazilian Air Force defined a requirement for a similar aircraft to replace the Xavante. The common need resulted in Embraer's involvement in the joint programme.
▲ July 1980. Aermacchi, Aeritalia and Embraer signed an agreement defining their respective participation in the development phase. An industrial agreement was then ratified by a Memorandum of Intent between the Brazilian and Italian Governments. The agreement included provisions for performing an intensive flight test programme based on 6 prototypes, 4 operating in Italy and 2 in Brazil. A seventh was built (see 1 June).
▲ 15 May 1984. First flight of an AMX, performed from Aeritalia's Turin-Caselle facility.
▲ 1 June 1984. The first prototype was lost in an accident on its fifth test flight.
▲ 19 November 1984. First flight of the second prototype, assembled by Aermacchi.
▲ 16 October 1985. First flight of a Brazilian prototype (FAB YA-1 4200) from Embraer's facility, the fifth aircraft to fly but officially the fourth prototype. Officially presented to Brazilian and Italian authorities on the 22nd.
▲ 11 May 1988. First flight of a production AMX in Italy.
▲ April 1989. The Italian Air Force began receiving its first service AMXs.
▲ 12 August 1989. First flight of a Brazilian production A-1.
▲ 17 October 1989. Brazil's 1° Esquadrão, 16° Grupo of Comando Aérotático (1°/16° GAv) received the first 2 production A-1s. This unit had been created at Santa Cruz to operate AMX.
▲ 14 March 1990. First flight of an AMX-T two-seater.
▲ 1995. First SCP-01-equipped A-1 entered Brazilian service (see Radar), having been tested on a modified BAe 125.

Sales/users: Brazil had ordered 45 single-seaters (A-1s) and 11 two-seaters at the time of writing from 94 required, with 25 single- and 3 two-seaters delivered to 1°/16° GAv. Italy had then received 73 of 120 single- and 26 two-seaters ordered, from 238 needed. Delivery of the third batch of AMX/A-1s against the number of aircraft presently ordered began in 1994. Italy is expected to convert 10 two-seaters to an EW role (see Aircraft Variants).
Crew: Pilot, with an 18° below horizon downward view over the nose. Tandem seats for the two-seater (see Aircraft variants).
Cockpit: HOTAS.
Crew escape: Martin-Baker Mk 10L zero-zero ejection

AMX International A-1, armed with bombs on single and twin carriers plus AAMs

seat, cleared up to 560 kts and 50,000 ft.
Fixed guns: 2 x 30-mm DEFA 554 cannon in A-1s, and 1 x 20-mm M61A1 Vulcan multi-barrel cannon in Italian AMX.
Ammunition: 350 rounds for M61.
Number of weapon pylons: 5, each station able to have twin carriers (2 inboard wing stations able to have triple), plus wingtip rails for 2 AIM-9L Sidewinder, Piranha or Mol AAMs. See diagram.
Expendable weapons and equipment: Up to 8,378 lb (3,800 kg) weight. Can include Mk 82/83/84 free-fall or retarded bombs, cluster bombs, rockets, stand-off weapons dispenser, precision-guided munitions (would require electro-optical guidance), air-to-ground missiles, anti-radiation missiles, or anti-ship missiles (would require radar or electro-optical guidance), plus short-range air-to-air missiles on the wingtip stations.
Additional stores: Reconnaissance packages (cameras and other sensors) are carried internally, leaving the centreline and underwing hardpoints free for weapons or fuel tanks. Palletized camera sets can be supported by an infra-red and optical reconnaissance pod installed on the centreline station. See Fuel System.
Radar: SMA/Tecnasa SCP-01 Scipio multi-mode coherent radar in the A-1. FIAR Grifo F/X plus multi-mode pulse Doppler radar in Italian AMX.
Flight/weapon system avionics/instrumentation: Databus and modular concept of the avionics system provide the capacity for future growth or new roles. Includes 2 electronic flight computers/digital bus system (MIL STD 1553 B) to provide redundancy to tolerate battle damage. Instrumentation includes TV/IR and map head-down displays and HUD. Italian AMXs are receiving Thomson-CSF CLDP laser designator pods.
Self-protection systems: Active and passive ECM, radar warning devices, missile launch and approach warning receiver, chaff and IR flares.
Wing characteristics: Shoulder-mounted, moderately sweptback, with high-lift devices.
Wing control surfaces: Ailerons, double-slotted Fowler trailing-edge flaps and leading-edge slats. Twin spoilers ahead of each pair of flaps.
Tail control surfaces: Elevators, rudder and variable-incidence tailplane.
Airbrakes: See spoilers under Wing control surfaces.
Flight control system: Fly-by-wire system for tailplane, rudder and spoilers. Hydraulically actuated ailerons and elevators. Electro-hydraulic flaps and slats. Mechanical back-up of principal surfaces (see Aims).
Construction materials: Principally aluminium alloy, with composites fin and elevators.
Engine: One Rolls-Royce Spey RB168-807 turbofan, built by FiatAvio and Celma-Cia.
Engine rating: 11,030 lbf (49.06 kN).
Flight refuelling probe: Probe to the starboard side of the cockpit when fitted.
Fuel system: 3,500 litres. Inboard wing pylons can carry 1,100- litre drop tanks, and outboard 580 litre.
Electrical system: In a total electrical loss, electro-avionic loads are fed by a battery.
Hydraulic system: 2 independent systems powered by by engine-driven pumps. In the event of damage or failure of the pumps, accumulators provide emergency supply for undercarriage extension, braking and steering, and flight control actuation in critical phases.
Braking system: Hydraulic with anti-skid, plus ground arrester hook capability.

Aircraft variants:
AMX and A-1 are the Italian and Brazilian single-seaters, used for attack and reconnaissance, with secondary counter-air.
AMX-T is the two-seat advanced trainer, suited to operational conversion and full combat use. It has the internal cannon, wingtip missiles, internal electronic warfare equipment, and chaff and flares of the single-seater, with extensive avionics. The second cockpit is placed in tandem with the normal single-seat cockpit, having had 1 fuel tank deleted and the environmental control system repositioned. It has full duplication of displays and controls, including a colour TV head-down display repeater. See next for Italian EW modifications.
Developments of AMX/A-1/AMX-T will include models for:
Electronic combat with anti-radiation missiles, emission location system, data link and soft-kill jammer pod (it is believed 10 Italian two-seaters are being modified for this role, as replacements for Piaggio PD808GEs.
Anti-ship with new radar offering sea search and possibly armed with Exocet, Kormoran, Harpoon or Sea Eagle missiles.
Night attack carrying FLIR, wide-angle HUD, laser designator and night vision goggles.

DETAILS FOR AMX/A-1.

Principal dimensions:
Wing span: 32 ft 8.5 ins (9.97 m) with wingtip missiles, 29 ft 1.5 ins (8.87 m) without
Maximum length: 43 ft 5 ins (13.23 m)
Maximum height: 14 ft 11 ins (4.55 m)

Wings:
Area: 226 sq ft (21 m^2)
Aspect ratio: 3.75
Sweepback: 27° 30′ at 25% chord

Tail unit:
Tailplane span: 17 ft 1 ins (5.2 m)
Tailplane area: 54.9 sq ft (5.1 m^2)
Fin area: 45.9 sq ft (4.27 m^2)

Undercarriage:
Type: Retractable, with steerable nosewheel
Main wheel tyre size: 670 x 210-12
Nose wheel tyre size: 18 x 5.5-8
Wheel base: 15 ft 5 ins (4.7 m)
Wheel track: 7 ft 1 ins (2.15 m)
Turning radius: 24 ft 9 ins (7.53 m)

Weights:
Empty, operating: 14,771 lb (6,700 kg)
Maximum take-off: 28,660 lb (13,000 kg)
Landing: 15,430 lb (7,000 kg) typically

Performance:
Maximum speed: Mach 0.86
Take-off distance: 3,222 ft (982 m) at sea level
Landing distance: 1,523 ft (464 m) at sea level
Maximum climb rate: 10,250 ft (3,124 m) per minute at sea level
G limits: +7.33, -3
Ceiling: 42,650 ft (13,000 m)
Radius of action: up to 500 naut miles (575 miles) 926 km

Dassault Aviation/Daimler-Benz Aerospace (France/Germany)

Corporate address: The Alpha Jet was developed and produced as an international programme between Dassault Aviation of France and Dornier of Germany. Addresses and Telephone/Facsimile numbers for Dassault and Dornier (under Daimler-Benz) can be found in the earlier pages of this section.

● Activities
● Despite Germany withdrawing the last of its Alpha Jets in 1995 (the last 35 of 175 having been used as lead-in trainers for Tornado aircrew), and sales remaining at 504, Alpha Jet brochure material was still being offered by the companies dated September 1994.

Dassault/Daimler-Benz Alpha Jet

First flight: 26 October 1973.
Role: Basic and advanced jet trainer, suited to ground support.

★ Aims
★ Extensive stores load.
★ Store versatility owing to the high wing position.
★ Twin engine safety.
★ Modern gunsight and avionics.
★ High stability.
★ Easy field maintenance.
★ Possible turnaround time between training missions of under 10 minutes.

▲ Development
▲ 4 November 1977. Maiden flight of the first production Alpha Jet.
▲ May 1982. First flight of the Alpha Jet 2, with testing at Istres lasting from May 1982 to January 1983.
▲ June 1983. Egypt became the first customer for the Alpha Jet with the Alpha Jet 2 weapon system, followed by Cameroon.
Sales/users: 504 delivered to Belgium, Cameroon, Egypt (many assembled by the Arab Organization for Industrialization – which see), France, Germany, Ivory Coast, Morocco, Nigeria, Qatar and Togo. Germany has now withdrawn the aircraft from its last Alpha Jet unit, the 49th Fighter-Bomber Wing at Fürstenfeldbruck. 50 earlier German Alpha Jets were received by Portugal, and in early 1995 Greece was negotiating the purchase of 60 German aircraft.
Details: Offered Alpha Jet 2 and Alpha Jet ATS (Air Training System).
Crew: 2, in tandem, the rear seat raised to offer improved vision.
Crew escape: Zero-zero ejection seats. Fitting of seats from different manufacturers is possible.
Fixed guns: None, but has a quickly removable underfuselage container for a 30-mm or 27-mm gun.
Ammunition: 150 rounds.
Number of weapon pylons: 5, as 4 under the wings and 1 under the fuselage (for a gun pod, etc).
Expendable weapons and equipment: 5,512 lb (2,500 kg) maximum load. See diagrams for rocket,

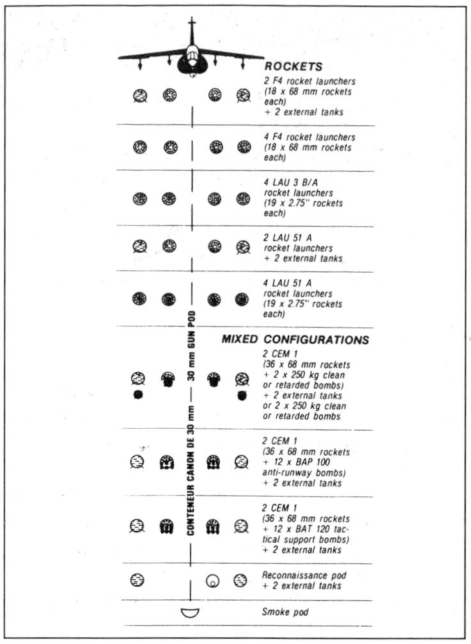

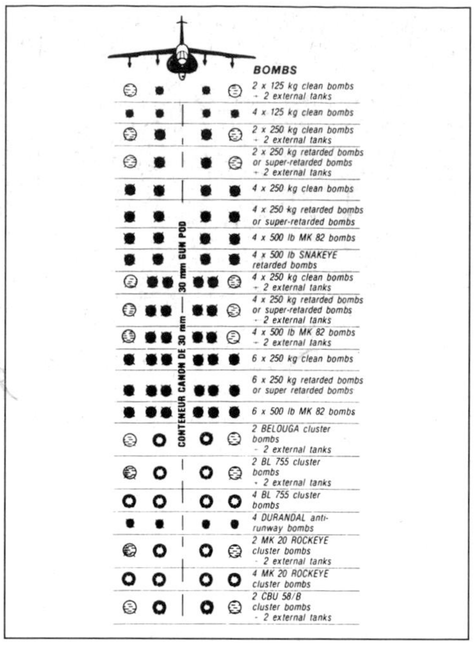

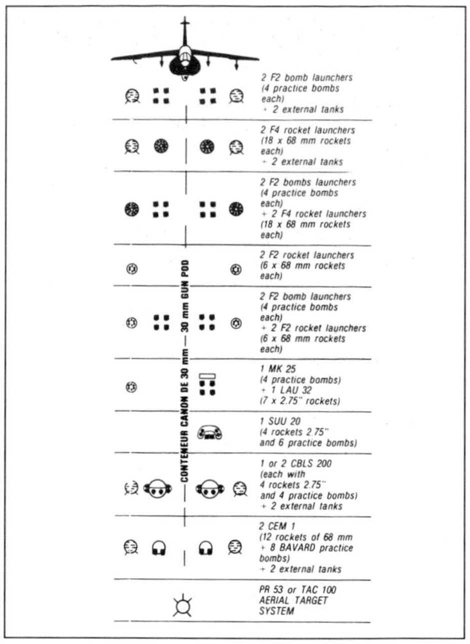

Alpha Jet stores combinations: 1. rockets and mixed; 2. bombs; 3. training (courtesy Dassault Aviation)

Alpha Jet with under-fuselage gun

bomb and training options. Also, Magic AAMs can be carried for self defence. For ground attack, 2 nav/attack system modes can be used. The first is the direct mode for gun or rocket firing in a dive, or retarded bomb release in level flight, using the Continuous Computation of Impact Point (CCIP) mode of the nav/attack system, with automatic designation through the laser or radio altimeter; alternatively, Continuous Computation of Release Point (CCRP) which allows automatic release of clean bombs during pull-up, after designation of the target through the laser (or with the radio altimeter as a back-up sensor). The second is Initial Point (IP) acquisition mode, for release of retarded or super-retarded bombs (mode CCIP/IP) or automatic release of clean bombs (mode CCRP/IP) after designation of an IP whose co-ordinates in relation to the targets are known.

Radar: None.

Flight/weapon system avionics/instrumentation: Alpha Jet 2 has a Sagem Uliss 81 nav/attack system with inertial platform and a nav/attack computer, Sextant Avionique VE 110 CRT HUD, Thomson-CSF TMV 630 laser rangefinder housed in the fuselage nose, Thomson-CSF/CNI and AHV 9 radio altimeter. System management by a digital databus. System allows fully autonomous navigation, with navigation accuracy better than 0.8 naut miles/hr without updating. Optional CCTL (continuously computed tracer line) displayed on the HUD for snap air-to-air shooting. See Weapons. See Aircraft variants for ATS avionics.

Wing characteristics: Lightly swept, shoulder mounted, with anhedral. Dogtooth leading edge and rounded tips.

Wing control surfaces: Ailerons and slotted split flaps.

Tail control surfaces: Slab tailplane and rudder.

Airbrakes: 2, on the rear upper fuselage.

Flight control system: Double-body irreversible servo controls.

Construction materials: Metal, with limited use of composites in the tail unit and airbrakes.

Engines: 2 Turbomeca-SNECMA Larzac 04-C6 or 04-C20 turbofans. C20 offers a 15% gain in take-off performance fully loaded, 10-15% gain in climb rate to 30,000 ft (9,150 m), increased manoeuvrability, better acceleration and higher speed with full load.

Engine rating: Each 2,965 lbf (13.19 kN) or 3,174 lbf (14.12 kN) respectively.

Air intakes: Each side of the fuselage, with splitter plates.

Fuel system: 2,040 litres. Can carry 2 x 310 litre or larger drop tanks in combination with weapons (see diagrams).

Electrical system: 28 volt DC supply via 2 engine-driven starter-generators. Ni-cd battery for self start. 115 volt 400Hz AC supply via static inverters.

Hydraulic system: 2 systems, each 3,002 psi.

Braking system: Disc brakes, with anti-skid. Arrester hook available.

Oxygen system: Liquid oxygen converter.

Aircraft variants:

Alpha Jet 2 was originally conceived to develop a new aircraft from the well-proven original Alpha Jet, mainly for weapon system training and tactical support, with a fully integrated inertial navigation and attack system.

Alpha Jet ATS (Advanced Training System) was previously known as Alpha Jet 3. State-of-the-art controls and displays, including CRT HUD (possibly combined with collimated head-level display) combined with rear cockpit TV monitor, lateral multifunction displays and multifunction control keyboards, to match the navigation/attack systems of the latest and future combat aircraft. This allows the possible addition of FLIR, laser designation, ECM and other equipment.

Details for Alpha Jet 2.

Principal dimensions:
Wing span: 29 ft 11 ins (9.1 m)
Maximum length: 38 ft 6.5 ins (11.75 m)
Maximum height: 13 ft 9.5 ins (4.2 m)

Wings:
Area: 188.37 sq ft (17.5 m^2)
Aspect ratio: 4.73
Sweepback: 28° at 25% chord

Tail unit:
Tailplane span: 14 ft 2.5 ins (4.33 m)

Undercarriage:
Type: Retractable, with nosewheel. Optional nosewheel steering. Low-pressure tyres
Main wheel tyre size: 615 x 255
Nose wheel tyre size: 380 x 150
Wheel base: 15 ft 6 ins (4.72 m)
Wheel track: 8 ft 11 ins (2.71 m)

Weights:
Empty, operating: 7,716 lb (3,500 kg)
Take-off: 11,023 lb (5,000 kg) training mission

Performance (C20 engines):
Maximum speed: Mach 0.85
Approach speed: about 110 kts (127 mph) 204 km/h
Stall speed: 117 kts (134 mph) 216 km/h *clean*, 90 kts (104 mph) 167 km/h *with flaps and undercarriage lowered*
Take-off distance: 1,148 ft (350 m) with C20 engine.
Landing distance: 1,510 ft (460 m)
Roll rate: nearly 250° per second, *clean*, at 350 kts (403 mph) 648 km/h, low altitude
Ceiling: 48,000 ft (14,630 m)
Duration: over 4.5 hours

EuroFighter Jagdflugzeug GmbH (Germany/Italy/Spain/UK)

Corporate address: im Airport Business Centre, Am Söldnermoos 17, 85399 Hallbergmoos, Germany.
Founded: 1986.

● Activities

● Design, development and production of Eurofighter 2000 has been undertaken as a collaborative programme between Daimler-Benz (formerly Deutsche Aerospace) of Germany (33% shareholding), Alenia of Italy (21%), CASA of Spain (13%) and British Aerospace of the UK (33%). See earlier pages for company details. The programme management structure means that the 4 companies report to NEFMA, which co-ordinates the interests of the respective governments. NEFMA also oversees the Eurojet engine programme.

Eurofighter 2000

First flight: 27 March 1994 (development aircraft 1 or DA1).
Role: Air superiority fighter, with secondary surface attack and reconnaissance.

★ Aims

★ Optimized for supersonic, beyond-visual-range (BVR) air defence.
★ High performance and agility in subsonic close air combat.
★ Relatively short field capability, also dispersability to unimproved strips.
★ Canard-delta configuration for optimum supersonic performance.
★ Naturally longitudinally unstable for high lift/drag with full authority, digital, quadruplex fly-by-wire flight control system.
★ Reduced radar cross section.
★ Advanced technology in all areas for the highest capability in a relatively small, light airframe.
★ Double engine change by 4 persons in 45 minutes. Also, 9 maintenance hours per flying hour.

▲ Development

▲ 1983. Feasibility studies were initiated by UK, Germany, Italy, Spain and France for a European Fighter Aircraft (EFA). Initial Staff Requirements were issued on 16 December.
▲ 1984. France technically withdrew to pursue Rafale as a somewhat smaller, lighter and carrier-capable fighter, made official in the following year prior to the founding of the EuroFighter company.
▲ 2 August 1985. Project definition commenced after agreement between Germany, Italy and the UK, completed in September of the following year.
▲ 1987. European Staff Requirement was formulated and issued that September with envisaged in-service date of 1997.
▲ 23 November 1988. Airframe and engine (development only) contracts were placed for work to the year 2000.

Eurofighter 2000 2-seater (Neville Beckett)

Eurofighter 2000 DA1 with 6 missiles

▲ 1992. Renamed Eurofighter 2000, but essentially unchanged, following programme review including alternative possible solutions.
▲ 27 March 1994. Maiden flight of DA1 at Manching in Germany, piloted by Peter Weger.
▲ 6 April 1994. Maiden flight of DA2 at Warton in the UK, piloted by Chris Yeo.
▲ 1994. Following 9 flights each on DA1 and DA2, both aircraft were stood down in June for fit of updated FCS and certain avionics.
▲ 15 May 1995. Flying resumed, in time for display at the June Paris Air Show.
▲ 17 March 1995. Fatigue tests on the static Eurofighter airframe at Ottobrunn exceeded 5,000 hours. Tests are to continue until early 1997, accumulating some 18,000 hours.
▲ 1995. All 7 development aircraft were due to fly before the end of the year in respective countries, to begin a 2,800 hour flight test programme. DA3 was first to have EJ200 engines installed. The German stake in the programme continued to require agreement with its partners in early 1995 (since Germany's production total fell), perhaps falling from 33% to 23-28%.
▲ 4 June 1995. DA3 first flew, the first Eurofighter 2000 with Eurojet EJ 200 engines.
▲ 1996. Production investment due.
▲ 2000. Currently planned in-service date, initially with the UK and Italy.

Sales/users: Procurement envisaged in May 1995 (to be confirmed) as UK (250, possibly rising to 290), Germany (140), Italy (130) and Spain (82). Total programme cost £14.9 billion (1995 price). Unit flyaway cost £28 million (1994 price).
Crew: Pilot, or 2 in tandem in the operational training variant.
Cockpit: Excellent all-round view, said to be better than current operational fighters. Fixed front screen with anti-bird strike canopy arch. Rear-hinged clamshell canopy. Access by integral ladder on port side. Pressurized. Centre stick. Pilot back angle limited to 18°, for good view over the nose. Enhanced pilot G protection by full coverage anti-G trousers and chest counter pressure garment.
Crew escape: Martin Baker Mk 16A zero-zero lightweight ejection seat of advanced design.
Fixed guns: Internal 27-mm Mauser cannon in the starboard wing root.
Ammunition: 150 rounds.
Number of weapon pylons: 13, as 5 under the fuselage and 4 under each wing. 3 stations are "wet", as centreline and second wing pylons from roots.
Expendable weapons and equipment: 14,300 lb (6,500 kg) load. 4 MRAAMs semi-recessed under the fuselage in low-drag configuration. Centreline bomb or 1,000 litre drop tank. 2 ASRAAMs on dedicated outboard pylons. MRAAM, SRAAM or bombs on other pylons. A mix of at least 10 air-to-air missiles can be carried. 2 x 1,500 litre tanks on "wet" wing pylons. Attack stores include 1,000 lb or 500 kg bombs, BL755, laser-guided bombs, ALARM missiles and more.
Additional stores: Laser designator pod or reconnaissance pod.
Radar: ECR 90 radar from the Euroradar consortium led by GEC-Marconi (UK), also comprising Telefunken Systemtechnik (Germany), FIAR (Italy) and INISEL (Spain). Multi-mode, pulse Doppler, with look-up and look-down capability. Long range detection and

DETAILS FOR EUROFIGHTER 2000.

Principal dimensions:
Wing span over tip-pods: 35 ft 11 ins (10.95 m)
Wing span, reference: 34 ft 5.5 ins (10.5 m)
Maximum length: 52 ft 4.5 ins (15.96 m)
Maximum height: 17 ft 4 ins (5.28 m)

Wings:
Aerofoil section: Modified standard type, approximately 4% mean thickness/chord
Area: 551.1 sq ft (51.2 m^2)
Aspect ratio: 2.205
Sweepback: 53° leading edge
Chord at root: 23 ft 7.5 ins (7.2 m)
Chord at tip: 4 ft 1.5 ins (1.26 m)
Incidence: 0°
Dihedral: 1-2°

Canard:
Span: 12 ft 6 ins (3.8 m)
Area: 25.83 sq ft (2.4 m^2) exposed

Tail unit:
Fin area: 69.97 sq ft (6.5 m^2)

Undercarriage:
Type: Retractable, with steerable nosewheel. Main gear pintle in inner wing, lateral retraction of each single wheel to horizontal in centre fuselage below air duct. Nose gear retraction aft, with wheel vertical below intake duct
Main wheel tyre size: 28 x 9.5-15
Nose wheel tyre size: 18 x 7.75-6
Wheel base: 13 ft 9.5 ins (4.2 m)
Wheel track: 13 ft 2 ins (4 m) approximately

Weights:
Empty: 22,043 lb (9,999 kg) basic mass
Take-off: 34,282 lb (15,550 kg) estimated, with full internal fuel and 6 AAMs
Maximum take-off: 46,297 lb (21,000 kg)

Performance:
Maximum speed: Mach 2, with 6 AAMs
Landing speed: 130-135 kts (150-155 mph) 241-250 km/h, estimated
Normal take-off distance: 984 ft (300 m)
Operating strip length: 2,297 ft (700 m)
Time to Mach 1.5 and over 35,000 ft (10,670 m): 2 minutes 30 seconds from brakes off
Time from 200 kts to Mach 1: 30 seconds, at low level
G limits: +9, -3
Radius of action (Lo-Lo)*: >325 naut miles (374 miles) 602 km
Radius of action (Hi-Lo-Hi)*: >1,000 naut miles (1,151 miles) 1,852 km
Radius of action (air-to-air)*: >1,000 naut miles (1,151 miles) 1,852 km
Combat air patrol time*: >3.25 hours

*unspecified load and missile profile

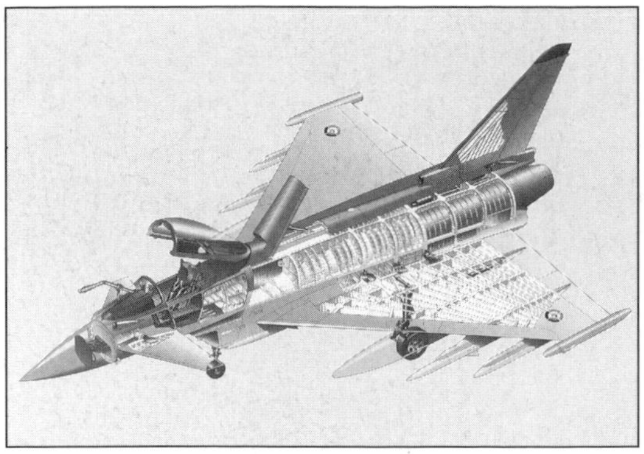

Eurofighter 2000 cutaway (courtesy British Aerospace)

tracking of airborne targets, with also air-to-surface mode. Multi-target search and track while scan. ECM resistant. Threat analysis and identification and target prioritization. Power and antenna size for active AMRAAM but provision for continuous wave illumination for semi-active missiles also. Much technology from Blue Vixen radar of Sea Harrier.

Flight/weapon system avionics/instrumentation: Displays comprise a wide-angle HUD for flight reference, weapon aiming and FLIR imagery. 3 large multi-function head-down displays (MFHDD), full colour, for tactical, navigation, radar and systems information. Helmet mounted visor display incorporates night vision aids and protection from flash and optical (laser) threats. HOTAS, with more than 20 additional functions. Automation of systems and mission management. Direct voice input for "non flight safety critical" systems. MIL-STD-1553 databus. Passive, forward-looking infra-red search and tracking sensor in a fairing on the port side of the nose, adjacent to the canopy front screen. Dual mode for airborne targets and air-surface role. Target identification facility is incorporated.

Self-protection systems: Integrated into the airframe, making add-on pods unnecessary. Defensive Aids Sub System (DASS) comprises radar warning, missile approach warning, active ECM, and laser threat warning. Chaff/flare dispensers. Auto or manual defensive control. Towed decoy intended.

Wing characteristics: Low mounted, cropped delta, with integral tip-pods for DASS. 3 main body side joints.

Wing control surfaces: Full-span, inner and outer trailing-edge flaperons, and leading-edge flap (zero slot slat), per wing.

Tail control surfaces: Fixed fin with rudder. Cooling air intake in root.

Canard: All moving (symmetrically).

Airbrakes: Single, forward hinged, dorsal petal immediately behind the canopy.

Flight control system: Full authority, digital, quadruplex fly-by-wire. "Carefree handling" control of incidence and G. Auto-recovery mode on pilot selection in case of disorientation. Air speed and flow angle data transducers under the nose.

Fuselage: Manufacture breakdown is radome and cockpit, centre fuselage with tanks and air intake ducts and with nose and main undercarriage stowage, rear fuselage housing engines.

Construction materials: Extensive use of carbon reinforced composites, comprising 70% of the total aircraft surface area (or about 40% of structure weight). Remainder of surface area is metal (15%), glassfibre reinforced plastics (12%) and other (3%). Wings have CFC skins and multiple spars with alloy ribs. Leading-edge flaps are aluminium-lithium, and outer flaperons are titanium. Canards are superplastic formed, diffusion bonded, titanium. Fin has CFC skins and multiple spars with aluminium-lithium leading edges.

Engines: 2 Eurojet EJ200 turbofans. Designed specifically for the EF2000 and optimized for air-to-air missions. Thrust/weight >9. DA1 and 2 fitted with Turbo Union RB199s.

Engine rating: Each 13,500 lbf (60 kN) dry, 20,250 lbf (90 kN) with afterburning, raising to 23,000 lbf (102.31 kN).

Air intakes: Single fixed-wedge in ventral position, incorporating bleed holes. Bleed slot at throat. "Varicowl" drooping leading edge for high incidence manoeuvring and take-off/landing. Bifurcated, with vertical external splitter. Horizontal diverter with system air intake in leading edge. No auxiliary intakes for ground running. "Arched" duct path to obscure engine face.

Nozzles: Fully variable, convergent-divergent, to maximize thrust at supersonic speed and high altitude.

Flight refuelling probe: Retractable probe on the starboard side, adjacent to the front canopy screen.

Fuel system: Integral tanks in the centre fuselage and in the wings for about 5,640 litres. External fuel in 3 x 3,500 litre drop tanks (see Weapons).

Electrical system: Engine-driven generators. APU. Hydraulic system: Fully duplicated systems. Engine-driven pumps. All primary and secondary control surfaces, and the undercarriage, actuated by power control units.

Braking system: Carbon disc brakes on the main wheels only. Drag-chute of 13 ft (4 m) diameter in the fin root fairing.

Oxygen system: On-board oxygen generating system (OBOGS).

Aircraft variants:

Single-seater, as described, with some differences between national variants in capability, avionics and weapon system.

Two-seater is the training variant, with a modest reduction in internal fuel and repositioning of avionics to retain full operational capability.

McDonnell Douglas/British Aerospace (USA/UK)

Corporate address: See under UK and USA for company details.

● Activities

● Co-operative programmes between these companies follow. Company details can be found in the UK and USA sections under individual headings.

McDonnell Douglas/British Aerospace Harrier II

First flight: 5th November 1981 (full-scale development AV-8B).

Role: Close air support and interdiction, with unique basing flexibility offered by STOVL capability (including small and/or remote forward fields and small ships).

★ Aims

★ Extensively modified and developed derivative of the Harrier I (GR Mk 3/AV-8A), incorporating much technological innovation, including lift improvement devices, larger wings with LERX, and wide use of composites.

★ Offers twice the payload/range by means of new wings, increased engine thrust, and overall performance improvements.

★ Increased operational effectiveness due to improved avionics.

▲ Development

▲ Joint BAe/McDonnell Douglas programme. McDD is prime contractor, with BAe as sub-contractor for the AV-8B/EAV-8B. BAe is prime contractor and McDD sub-contractor for RAF aircraft.

▲ October 1976. Harrier II programme was instituted, following the success of the Harrier I. Full scale development funded.

▲ 9 November 1978. Maiden flight of the first of 2 YAV-8B aerodynamic prototypes, modified from AV-8As.

▲ 1981. UK selected Harrier II for service with the RAF.

▲ 5 November 1981. First of 4 full-scale development AV-8Bs flew.

BAe/McDonnell Douglas Harrier GR Mk 7, with refuelling probe

▲ 29 August 1983. First flight of a production AV-8B, delivered in November 1983 and officially entering USMC service with VMAT-203 on 12 January 1984.

▲ 30 January 1985. USMC commissioned VMA-331 as its first non-training AV-8B squadron, at MCAS Cherry Point in North Carolina, gaining initial operational capability in August of the following year.

▲ 30 April 1985. Maiden flight of an RAF Harrier GR Mk 5 development aircraft.

▲ 21 October 1986. Maiden flight of a TAV-8B.

▲ 1 July 1987. GR Mk 5 entered RAF service, joining No 233 OCU at Wittering.

▲ 24 July 1987. First production TAV-8B was received by VMAT-23 at MCAS Cherry Point.

▲ September 1987. Maiden flight of a Spanish EAV-8B.

▲ 18 May 1990. Maiden flight of an RAF production GR Mk 7.

▲ 17 January 1991. 4 aircraft of VMA-311, USMC, undertook the first AV-8B sorties of the Gulf War. During this conflict, 86 AV-8Bs flying from Saudi Arabia and off an amphibious assault ship in the Persian Gulf, flew 3,383 sorties, accumulating 4,112 combat hours.

▲ 7 April 1994. Maiden flight of an RAF T Mk 10 trainer.

▲ 30 November 1994. Maiden flight of McDD's technology demonstrator, used initially for trials with inert wingtip Sidewinder AAMs.

▲ February 1995. McDD's technology demonstrator began evaluation of "zero scarf" rear nozzles to boost engine thrust, as already used for the forward nozzles.

▲ March 1995. Flight testing began of improved underfuselage lift improvement devices (LIDS) on the McDD demonstrator, intended to maximize VTO lift to allow higher take-off weight, by catching efflux gases

BAe/McDonnell Douglas Harrier T Mk 10 2-seat operational trainer (front) and single-seat GR Mk 7

under the fuselage that have reflected off the ground. LIDS encompassed small strakes positioned near the nosewheel doors and a crossways fence.

▲ 1998. Evaluation to take place of a lengthened centre fuselage section (see Fuselage).

Sales/users: Ordered by the Italian Navy (2 TAV-8Bs plus AV-8Bs ex-USMC), Spanish Navy (12 EAV-8Bs and 1 TEAV-8B), RAF (61 GR Mk 5/5As, since converted to GR Mk 7s, 34 newly-built GRMk 7s and 13 T Mk 10s), and USMC (252 production AV-8Bs and 24 TAV-8Bs, of which 200 and 22 were in active service in May 1995).

Crew: Pilot, or 2 in the "T" training versions.

Cockpit: Single piece front screen. Single piece bubble canopy, sliding up and aft to open on single-seaters, with MDC fragmentation for ejection. Much improved all-round view compared with Harrier I, with the pilot sitting 12 ins (30 cm) higher. Separate sideways opening canopies on two-seaters. Vertical stagger affords the instructor a good view in the two-seaters.

Crew escape: Martin Baker Mk 12H zero-zero ejection seat.

Fixed guns: None, but with provision for 2 x 25-mm Aden cannon pod on RAF aircraft and a 25-mm multi-barrel cannon on USMC variants, in ventral fuselage location.

Ammunition: 100 rounds per cannon for GRs, 300 rounds for AV-8Bs.

Number of weapon pylons: 9 on GR Mk 7 and 7 on AV-8B. Increased wing span over Harrier I allows 3 or 4 per wing, plus fuselage centreline. Intermediate and inboard wing pylons are "wet".

Expendable weapons and equipment: 13,234 lb (6,003 kg) maximum load for Pegasus 11-61-engined aircraft, 9,200 lb (4,173 kg) normal load for early AV-8Bs and 10,800 lb (4,900 kg) for GR Mk 7 and similarly engined aircraft for STO. VTO payload up to 4,000 lb (1,814 kg). Range of free fall and retarded bombs, including 1,000 lb, laser guided, cluster and practice. Alternatively, or as a mix, rocket launchers, ASMs, Sidewinder/Magic AAMs or other stores. AV-8B has, typically, a choice of 15 x Mk 82 500 lb bombs, 6 BL-755 cluster bombs, 6 x Mk 83 1,000 lb bombs, 4 Maverick ASMs, 6 Sidewinders or 12 rocket pods. McDD technology demonstrator has flown with wingtip Sidewinders.

Additional stores: Sanders AN/ALQ-164 deceptive ECM pod carried on the centreline, for protection against pulse radar threats, power modulated jamming and multiple programmable jamming techniques (ALQ-126B sub-system) and for protection against terminal CW radar threats, with threat ID techniques and priorities programmed by user (ALQ-162 sub-system). Vinten VICON 18 reconnaissance pod for RAF. GEC-Marconi TIALD (Thermal Imaging and Laser Designation) pod has been evaluated for GR Mk 7s.

Radar: None (see Harrier II Plus).

Flight/weapon system avionics/instrumentation: Integrated, computer controlled navigation/attack system. Hughes ASB-19(V)2 or 3 Angle Rate Bombing System (ARBS), with tracking by laser spot or TV. Litton ASN-130A (AV-8B) or GEC-Marconi FIN 1075/1075G (GR.Mk7) inertial navigation system (INS). ARN-118 (AV-8B) or ARI 23368 (GR Mk 7) Tacan. GEC-Marconi Moving Map Display (not on AV-8B). AiResearch digital air data computer. Unisys AYK-14(V) mission computer. MIL-STD-1553 databus. Smiths AYQ-13 stores management system (SMS) with combining HUD (for flight, threat and weapon delivery information) and display computer, and digital display indicator; SMS control via panel, MPD and HOTAS. APN-194(V) (AV-8B) or ARI 23388 (GR Mk 7) radar altimeter. VHF/UHF radio. Multi-Purpose Displays (MPD) for ARBS data, radar warning, navigation, stores management, etc. IFF. GRMk 7 and AV-8B Night Attack have GEC-Marconi FLIR, with images on the HUD or either of 2 head-down Multi-Purpose Colour Displays, including digital colour map. Night vision goggles and compatible instrumenta tion in cockpit. See also Flight controls.

Self-protection systems: GEC-Marconi Zeus electronic warfare system on RAF aircraft, including radar warning receiver, pulse Doppler missile approach warner, electronic jamming, and chaff/flare. See also Additional stores. USMC aircraft carry Litton forward/backward radar warning receiver, optical missile approach warning, FLIR receiver and ALE-39 chaff/flare.

Wing characteristics: Shoulder mounted, with swept leading edges and swept trailing edges outboard of the undercarriage outriggers. Considerable anhedral. Wing gross area increased by some 14% and span 20% relative to Harrier I, and with increased thickness/chord ratio. Outriggers moved inboard from tip (Harrier I) to nearer mid-span. Leading-edge root extensions (LERX) ahead of wing root to increase manoeuvre lift and improve handling. Continuous one-piece wing with multiple spars.

BAe/McDonnell Douglas Harrier GR Mk 7 cutaway (courtesy British Aerospace)

Wing control surfaces: Ailerons (outboard and "droopable"), and inboard slotted flaps for "positive circulation" (lift) and also with auto manoeuvre mode. Reaction controls at the wingtips, as for Harrier I, for lateral control in jet borne flight/transition.

Tail control surfaces: Slab tailplane and rudder.

Airbrakes: Single petal type under the rear fuselage.

Flight control system: Combination of conventional aerodynamic surfaces and reaction controls ("puffer jets"). Ailerons, tailplane and rudder operated by powered flying control units. Reaction control jets at each wingtip, in the nose and tail; bleed air from the engine HP compressor. Honeywell ASW-46(V)2 Stability Augmentation and Attitude Hold System (SAAHS), comprising Automatic Flight Control System (AFCS) and Stability Augmentation System (SAS), provides stability augmentation about all axes over the complete flight envelope; also provides attitude, altitude and heading hold.

Fuselage: Redesigned forward fuselage and stretched rear fuselage compared with Harrier I. Underfuselage Lift Improvement Devices (LIDS); improvements under test in 1995 (see Development). A redesigned centre fuselage will be evaluated in 1998, with 12 ins (30 cm) plug and lengthened air inlets.

Construction materials: First production combat aircraft to make extensive use of composite materials (graphite epoxy), offering considerable weight saving compared with conventional aluminium alloy airframe of Harrier I. Wing structure/LERX largely graphite epoxy, with claimed saving of 330 lb (150 kg) relative to metal. Leading edges and tips of aluminium alloy for bird strike resistance; also house hot, high pressure reaction control ducting. Tailplane, rudder and flaps, cockpit, nose section and access panels are also constructed of composites. More than 26% of structure weight comprises carbon epoxy composites, resulting in 480 lb (218 kg) weight saving.

Details for Harrier II.

Principal dimensions:
Wing span: 30 ft 4 ins (9.25 m)
Maximum length: 47 ft 1 ins (14.35 m) for *GR Mk 7*, 46 ft 4 ins (14.12 m) *for AV-8B*, 50 ft 3 ins (15.32 m) *for TAV-8B*, and 51 ft 9 ins (15.77 m) *for T Mk* 10
Maximum height: 11 ft 8 ins (3.56 m) for *GR Mk 7 and AV-8B*, and 13 ft 5 ins (4.1 m) for *T Mk 10*

Wings:
Aerofoil section: Thick supercritical (root thickness/ chord ratio 11.5%, tip 7.5%)
Area: 230 sq ft (21.37 m^2)
Aspect ratio: 3.99

Tail unit:
Tailplane span: 13 ft 11 ins (4.24 m)

Undercarriage:
Type: As for Sea Harrier, except outriggers moved inboard to reduce track
Wheel track: 17 ft (5.18 m)

Weights:
Empty: 15,060 lb (6,831 kg) *GR Mk 7* basic mass, 13,971 lb (6,337 kg) *AV-8B*
Maximum vertical take-off: 19,180 lb (8,700 kg) *GR Mk 7*, 20,595 lb (9,341 kg) *AV-8B* with Pegasus 11-61 engine
Maximum short run take-off: 29,750 lb (13,494 kg) *GR Mk* 7, 31,000 lb (14,061 kg) *AV-8B*
Maximum vertical landing mass: about 19,940 lb (9,044 kg)

Performance:
Maximum speed at altitude: Mach 0.91-0.98
Maximum speed at sea level: 585 kts (674 mph) 1,083 km/h, quoted by McDD for AV-8B as 570 kts (656 mph) 1,056 km/h
Take-off distance: 1,400-1,500 ft (427-457 m) ground run at maximum take-off weight
G limits: +8, -3
Radius of action (attack – Hi-Lo-Hi): 600 naut miles (691 miles) 1,111 km with 2 x 1,000 lb bombs, 3 x BL 755s and 2 drop tanks
Combat air patrol duration: about 3 hours, 100 naut miles (115 miles) 185 km from base, with 2 Sidewinders and 2 drop tanks
Ferry range: over 1,600 naut miles (1,842 miles) 2,963 km *quoted for GR Mk 7*, over 1,800 naut miles (2,073 miles) 3,334 km quoted by McDD *for AV-8B*

Engine: Rolls-Royce Pegasus 11 high-bypass ratio, non-afterburning, vectoring thrust turbofan. See below. Gas turbine starter and APU.
Engine rating: 21,550 lbf (95.86 kN) for Pegasus 11 Mk 105 in RAF aircraft. Similar rating for Spanish Mk 152-42. Early USMC AV-8Bs use 21,450 lbf (95.42 kN) Pegasus 11-21 (F402-RR-406A), as also for some Italian used aircraft. 23,800 lbf (105.89 kN) Pegasus 11-61 (F402-RR-408A) for USMC aircraft from No 167; ordered for Spanish Matador IIs.
Air intakes: Bifurcated, pitots, with internal throat bleet slot. New inlet featuring increased capture area, new lip profile, improved internal shaping, and only a single row of auxiliary inlet doors. These revisions produce 300 lbf (1.33 kN) additional static thrust.
Nozzles: 4 rotatable nozzles for thrust vectoring. Front pair are of zero-scarf type (cut off square) producing 200 lbf (0.89 kN) increase in static thrust. Rear zero-scarf nozzles are under test (see Development). Steel construction. See Sea Harrier for details of movement. A ceramic matrix composite blast shield for the rear nozzles was to be tested in late 1995 (titanium blast shield at present).
Flight refuelling probe: Provision for extendable probe mounted externally on the port upper intake nacelle.
Fuel system: 5 fuselage and 2 integral wing tanks. Internal capacity 4,406 litres in single-seaters, 4,149 litres in two-seaters. 4 x 1,136 litre drop tanks can be carried underwing on inner and intermediate pylons.
Electrical system: Single engine-driven AC generator.
Hydraulic system: 2 independent systems, each with an engine-driven pump and delivering 3,000 psi. Each is capable of operating power controls should the other system fail.
Braking system: Multi-disc carbon brakes, with anti-skid devices.
Oxygen system: On-board oxygen generating system.

Aircraft variants:
AV-8B is the USMC designation, with differences as noted previously. Night Attack equipped from the 167th production aircraft, which also received the uprated Pegasus 11-61 engine.
TAV-8B is the USMC's two-seat training version.
EAV-8B is the Spanish Navy version, Spanish military designated VA.2 Matador II. Operated from the aircraft carrier *Principe de Asturias*. These may be upgraded to Harrier II Plus (which see).
TEAV-8B is the single Spanish two-seat trainer.
GR Mk 7 is the RAF's version, suited to night attack. First production GR Mk 5s and then 5As have been modified to Mk 7 standard, making this the sole single-seat version in RAF service.
T Mk 10 is the RAF's two-seat training version of the GR Mk 7. Effective for day and night operational missions.

McDonnell Douglas/ British Aerospace Harrier II Plus

First flight: 22 September 1992.
Role: All-weather, day and night, attack and air-to-air STOVL combat.

★ Aims
★ Radical extension of Harrier II's combat effectiveness by the addition of proven multi-mode radar.
★ Enhanced air-to-air capability includes beyond-visual-range missile engagement.

▲ Development
▲ June 1987. Launched as a private venture by the 2 companies.
▲ 28 September 1990. Tri-national Memorandum of Understanding between USA, Italy and Spain. Funding for development and integration of radar. Funding came from all 3 countries, with $17 million of US investment from Nunn Amendment funding (for military programmes developed with NATO allies).
▲ 3 December 1990. US Navy contract awarded for the construction of a prototype and completion of a batch of AV-8Bs then on order to Plus standard.
▲ 1992. Tri-national production MoU.
▲ 1993. Entry into USMC service.
▲ December 1994. Initial deliveries to the Italian Navy, for Gruppo Aeri Imbarcati.
▲ January 1995. 3 Italian Navy Harrier II Plus aircraft left Brindisi on the carrier *Guiseppe Garibaldi* (alongside 4 Army Mangusta attack helicopters) to provide part of the air cover for UN forces leaving Somalia.
▲ 1995. No RAF requirement to date.
Sales/users: Italian Navy (16 ordered, 3 delivered by March 1995; final assembly of 13 by Alenia in Italy), Spanish Navy (9), and USMC (27 ordered of which 23 had been delivered by March 1995, plus possible remanufacture of 70+ AV-8Bs).
Details: Principal differences to Harrier II.
Number of weapon pylons: 9.
Expendable weapons and equipment: 13,234 lb (6,003 kg), including gun and ammunition. Enhanced capabilities include ability to launch AMRAAM, SRAAM, Harpoon and Maverick; Italian Navy has ordered AMRAAMs and Mavericks.
Additional stores: ECM pods.
Radar: Hughes AN/APG-65 multi-mode, pulse Doppler.
Flight/weapon system avionics/instrumentation: Similar to Harrier II but radar replaces ARBS. Enhancements will include GPS and an automatic target handoff system (ATHS).

Details for Harrier II Plus.

Principal dimensions:
Maximum length: 47 ft 9 ins (14.55 m)

Weights:
Empty, operating: 14,867 lb (6,743 kg)
Maximum useful load: 16,133 lb (7,318 kg)
Maximum take-off: 31,000 lb (14,062 kg)

Performance:
Radius of action (close air support, Lo-Lo-Lo): 200 naut miles (230 miles) 370 km, with 4 bombs, gun pod and ammunition, and 2 drop tanks
Radius of action (interdiction): 400 naut miles (461 miles) 741 km, with 4 bombs, 2 missiles and 2 drop tanks.
Radius of action (anti-ship): 540 naut miles (621 miles) 1,000 km, with 2 anti-ship missiles, 2 other missiles and 2 drop tanks
Duration (combat air patrol, Hi): over 2 hours at 100 naut miles (115 miles) 185 km, with 4 MRAAMs, 2 other missiles and 2 drop tanks; or 1.5 hours at 200 naut miles (230 miles) 370 km; or 1.5 hours at 100 naut miles with 6 MRAAMs and 2 other missiles

McDonnell Douglas/BAe Harrier II Plus operated by the USMC

Self-protection systems: ECM, infra-red suppression and 3 times more upward and downward firing chaff/flares are available than for earlier Harriers. Survivability enhancements will include missile approach warning system.
Engine: Rolls-Royce Pegasus 11-61 (F402-RR-408).

McDonnell Douglas/British Aerospace X-32A and X-32B

First flight: 1998-99?
Role: Air defence, combat air patrol, deck-launched intercept, close air support, interdiction, strike, SEAD (suppression of enemy air defences), and reconnaissance.

★ Aims
★ Common Affordable Lightweight CTOL/ASTOVL multi-role fighter with supersonic performance.
★ ASTOVL variant, as a possible replacement for Harrier/Sea Harrier and F/A-18, to be compatible with steel ship decks and concrete runways.
★ High commonality (80%?) airframe/engine with CTOL multi-role fighter for possible use with the USAF, as an F-16 replacement.
★ "Conventional" airframe and propulsion configuration for supersonic flight. Vertical lift from aft vectoring nozzles plus remote forward lift fan, under the gas-coupled propulsive lift concept.
★ Naturally unstable canard/trapezoidal wing configuration for optimum supersonic lift/drag and good subsonic manoeuvrability, including high usable alpha.
★ Reduced radar cross section by configuration geometry (external and internal), internal air-to-air missile carriage, and construction materials.

▲ Development
▲ McDonnell Douglas and British Aerospace are partnered for the airframe, and General Electric and Rolls-Royce for the engine.
▲ 1991. Phased development programme initiated with contracts from the US Advanced Research Development Agency (ARPA). Phase I of 1991-92, including Propulsion Concepts Selection. Rolls-Royce involved in Phase I, but not BAe.
▲ March 1993. Phase II, Critical Technology Evaluation and Configuration Refinement for the Common Affordable Lightweight Fighter, began with a 3-year $27.7 million contract from ARPA, to run until 1996. Full scale airframe powered lift wind tunnel testing at NASA, Ames, in 1995. Powered lift system demonstrated on a static rig.
▲ December 1993. ASTOVL programme became an integral part of the work at the McDonnell Douglas Aerospace V/STOL R&D Center, formed that month.
▲ 1996-2000. Phase III, Flight Demonstration Programme, initially in non-STOVL configuration.
▲ 1998-99. CTOL aircraft, X-32A, to fly.
▲ 2000-2001. ASTOVL aircraft, X-32B, to fly.
▲ 2010. In service date for the CTOL production fighter.
▲ 2015. In service date for the ASTOVL production fighter.
Sales/users: Potential users for the STOVL Strike Fighter (SSF) include USMC and Royal Navy. Potential users of the MRF include USAF and USN.
Crew: Pilot, or 2 for a probable tandem-seat trainer.
Cockpit: All round field of view.
Crew escape: Advanced ejection seat.
Fixed guns: Internal 20-mm cannon.
Ammunition: 400 rounds.
Expendable weapons and equipment: Limited

McDonnell Douglas/BAe ASTOVL Strike Fighter

internal carriage for air-to-air missiles, typically AMRAAM (at least 2) and AIM-9X Sidewinders. External carriage of air-to-surface weapons under the wings and fuselage (possibly also internal carriage of ASMs), bombs, rockets, etc.
Radar: Multi-mode radar.
Flight/weapon system avionics/instrumentation: Advanced "glass" displays.
Self-protection systems: Radar and infra-red receivers, ECM and chaf/flares integrated into the airframe.
Wing characteristics: Rear mounted trapezoidal wing planform, with medium sweep, of low thickness/chord ratio.
Wing control surfaces: Trailing-edge flaperons and leading-edge manoeuvre flaps.
Tail control surfaces: Twin fins and rudders, outward canted.
Canard: All moving trapezoidal, with same sweep as wings.
Flight control system: Fly-by-wire integrated flight and propulsion control system.
Fuselage: Chine on forward fuselage running into blended cross section aft. Internal weapon bay aft of engine air intakes.
Construction materials: High proportion of advanced composites and titanium alloys.
Engine: Propulsion engine derived from the General Electric YF120 variable cycle, advanced tactical fighter engine. Lift fan horizontally orientated immediately behind the cockpit, driven by gas offtake from propulsion engine.
Engine rating: 37,000 lbf (164.57 kN) class.

Details for X-32B SSF, estimated.

Principal dimensions:
Wing span: 40 ft (12.19 m)
Maximum length: 52 ft (15.85 m)

Undercarriage:
Type: Retractable, with nosewheel

Weights:
Empty: 24,000 lb (10,886 kg) basic mass
Maximum: 50,000 lb (22,680 kg) all up mass

Performance
Maximum speed at altitude: >Mach 1.7-1.8
Supercruise speed: Mach 1.5
Maximum speed at sea level: >Mach 1.2
G limits: +8
Radius of action (intercept): 300 naut miles (345 miles) 556 km, including supercruise
Radius of action (ground attack): 200-500 naut miles (230-575 miles) 370-926 km, depending on weapon load and flight profile
Radius of action (combat air patrol): up to 400 naut miles (461 miles) 741 km

Air intakes: Propulsion engine in inlets, twin bifurcated. Possible auxiliary intakes on upper surfaces for STOVL. Intake for the lift fan immediately behind the cockpit in a dorsal position, blanked off in "up and away" flight.
Nozzles: Fully variable. Possible multi-axis vectoring for "up and away" flight.
2 retractable nozzles well aft for vectoring engine flow with propulsion nozzle closed off (said to be similar to those used on Harrier II). Lift fan exit in ventral location on the fuselage, with blanking doors.
Flight refuelling probe: Retractable probe is likely.

Aircraft variants:
X-32A will be the conventional non-STOVL configuration (MRF), for the USAF. US Navy interest as an F/A-18 replacement, and for the (then) out of service A-6E.
X-32B will be the ASTOVL (Advanced Short Take Off/Vertical Landing) fighter version (SSF), for the USMC and possibly Royal Navy to replace Harrier/Sea Harrier.

McDonnell Douglas/British Aerospace T-45 Goshawk

First flight: 16 April 1988
Role: Carrier-capable undergraduate jet pilot trainer.

★ Aims
★ To replace the T-2C Buckeye and TA-4J Skyhawk, under the US Navy's VTXTS programme. Developed initially from the Hawk 60.
★ Part of the general T45TS training system, which encompasses the trainer itself, flight simulators, instructional programmes using computer-assisted techniques, a computerized training integration system, and a contractor logistics support package.
★ 14,400 hour fatigue life.

▲ Development
▲ 18 November 1981. Winner of a US Navy's VTXTS competition for a new carrier-capable trainer. Became the T-45A Goshawk. Full scale development began in 1984.
▲ October 1989. Expected Goshawk production deliveries to the US Navy, but delayed due to performance and flying shortcomings identified in operational flight testing and evaluation. Subsequent modifications included an uprated engine of Hawk 100 type, addition of wing leading-edge slats, fin and tailplane modifications, improved control harmonization, and airbrake/tailplane movement interconnected.
▲ October-November 1990. 2 US production Goshawks were delivered to the Naval Air Test Center at Patuxent River.

McDonnell Douglas/BAe T-45A Goshawk landing on USS John F. Kennedy

Details for Goshawk.

Principal dimensions:
Wing span: 30 ft 10 ins (9.39 m).
Maximum length: 39 ft 3 ins (11.96 m)
Maximum height: 14 ft (4.27 m) *for Hawk*

Wings:
Area: 190.1 sq ft (17.66 m^2)
Aspect ratio: 4.993
Sweepback: 21.5° at 25% chord
Chord at root: 8 ft 8 ins (2.64 m)
Chord at tip: 3 ft (0.91 m)
Dihedral: 2°

Tail unit:
Tailplane span: 15 ft 1 ins (4.6 m)

Undercarriage:
Type: Strengthened, high sink rate undercarriage with lengthened main oleos and twin steerable (digital) nosewheels, plus arrester hook
Main wheel tyre size: 24-7.7-10
Nose wheel tyre size: 19 x 5.25-10
Wheel base: 14 ft 0.375 ins (4.28 m)
Wheel track: 12 ft 9 ins (3.89 m)

Weights:
Empty: 9,834 lb (4,461 kg)
Normal take-off: 12,750 lb (5,783 kg)
Maximum take-off: 14,080 lb (6,386 kg)

Performance:
Stalling speed: 93 kts (107 mph) 172 km/h
Catapult launch speed: 121 kts (139 mph) 224 km/h typically
Carrier approach speed: 115 kts (132 mph) 213 km/h typically
Duration: over 3 hours
Typical carrier training mission: 100 naut miles (115 miles) 185 km radius of action, Hi-Lo-Hi, with several arrested landings, catapult launches and waveoffs

▲ 4 December 1991. First development Goshawk made a trial landing on the aircraft carrier USS *John F. Kennedy*. Declared "safe and suitable" after testing.
▲ 23 July 1992. First production aircraft were officially handed over to the US Navy at St Louis.
▲ 1994. Training system approved for service early in the year, following operational evaluation.
▲ 11 February 1994. First US Navy student flight in a Goshawk, with the first solo on 23 March.
▲ 19 March 1994. First Cockpit 21 Goshawk demonstrator flew, introducing a "glass" cockpit and digital avionics. This improved cockpit is to become the standard fit for all production Goshawks from the 73rd aircraft, with earlier Goshawks to be upgraded from 1998.
▲ 5 October 1994. The first class of US Navy pilots to use the T-45 training system (T45TS) received their "Wings of Gold".
▲ 17 January 1995. Authorization for full-rate production following a successful DoD Milestone III review of the T45TS.
▲ October 1996. First Cockpit 21 to be delivered, as Goshawk No 73.
▲ 2003. Final Goshawk delivery.
Sales/users: US Navy. Planned Goshawk inventory now be 174, of which funding cover for 84 released up to fiscal year 1995. Production rate confirmed in 1995 at 12 per year. Training Squadron Twenty-One (VT-21), part of Training Air Wing Two at Naval Air Station Kingsville, was the first squadron to employ the T45TS. NAS Kingsville had 44 T-45As by January 1995.

By April 1995, 54 Goshawks had been delivered (2 for trials and 52 others). 2 service aircraft have been lost in a collision.
Details: See British Aerospace Hawk entry for general details.
Crew: 2, in tandem, with the rear instructor's seat stepped up.
Cockpit: Retractable step/foot/hand hold for cockpit access.
Crew escape: Martin Baker Mk 14 Navy Aircrew Common Ejection Seats. Canopy fracturing system (miniature detonating cord - MDC).
Number of weapon pylons: Single pylon under each wing, stressed for 1,000 lb (454 kg) load, plus a centreline pylon.
Expendable weapons and equipment: Practice bombs or rocket pods under wings.
Additional stores: Optional baggage pod.
Radar: None.
Flight/weapon system avionics/instrumentation: Revised cockpit layout, with avionics including attitude and heading reference system (AHRS), mini HUD, UHF/VHF communication, VOR/ILS, radar altimeter, IFF and GPS. Further planned developments include MIL-STD-1553B databus, and Cockpit 21 "glass" cockpit from the 73rd production aircraft with 2 multi-function monochrome displays, HUD velocity vector and GPS.
Self-protection systems: Radar warning receiver. IR flares and chaff on Series 100. Possible ECM.
Wing characteristics: Hawk wing but with completely straight leading-edges and addition of leading-edge slats (for lower approach speeds). No wing fences, but with stall strip and vortex generators.
Wing control surfaces: See Aircraft variants.
Tail control surfaces: See Aircraft variants.
Airbrakes: 2 airbrakes (with ventilation slots) on the fuselage sides.
Engine: Rolls-Royce Turbomeca F405-RR-401 engine (Adour Mk 871) with strengthened casing for carrier-borne operations.
Engine rating: 5,845 lbf (26 kN).
Fuel system: 1,768 litres of fuel (2,900 lb, 1,315 kg). Planned modest increase in fuel capacity through use of "wet" air intakes has been dropped.
Hydraulic system: 2 independent systems, each 3,000 psi.
Braking system: Goodrich, hydraulically operated.
Oxygen system: Onboard oxygen generation system (OBOGS).

Aircraft variants:
T-45A Goshawk is the US Navy's carrier-capable version of the BAe Hawk, built by McDonnell Douglas. Increased tailplane span, and 6 ins (15 cm) fin height increase. Revised wings. Single large vertical underfin (strake) in place of Hawk's 2 smaller strakes. SMURFs. Aileron/rudder interconnect, airbrakes/tailplane (with autotrim) interconnect, improved yaw damper and aileron gearing for lower flight speeds.
T-45B Goshawk is a land-based variant of T-45A, excluded from the US Navy programme but being offered on the export market by McDonnell Douglas.

Nanchang Aircraft Manufacturing Company/Pakistan Aeronautical Complex (China/Pakistan)

Corporate address: See Nanchang in the main Chinese section.
Also
Pakistan Aeronautical Complex, Kamara, District Attock, Pakistan.
Telephone: +92 51 584212, 580261 to 580265 (5 lines) for AMF
Facsimile: +92 51 583837 for AMF
Telex: 5601 PAC KAMRA PK
Founded: 1978.
Information: Sqn Ldr S. Zahid Rahman (AD technical co-ordinator).

■ Facilities (PAC)

- Aircraft Manufacturing Factory (AMF) produces the Saab MFI 17 Supporter under licence as the Mushshak, together with the Shahbaz upgraded version (see General Aviation section). It partners Nanchang/AVIC in the development of the K-8 Karakorum jet trainer (25% of the programme), but co-manufacture/ assembly of the aircraft has not been decided yet. PAC hopes to increase its component production role to 45%. PAC already builds the horizontal stabilizer. Production of the engine cowling was expected to start by August 1995, whereas production of fin, access panels and rear fuselage section is planned for early 1996.
- Kamra Avionics and Radar Factory manufactures avionics components and complete systems, plus other varied work, and has contributed to Mirage III modernization.
- Mirage Rebuild Factory undertakes structural work, engine, avionics and systems modernization and overhaul for Mirage III and 5 fighters. Upgrade programmes include ex-Australian Mirage IIIs now belonging to Pakistan, receiving Sagem avionics, INS, GPS, upgraded ECM, FLIR, HOTAS and more. This project was still underway in late 1995. Also supports the Air Force's F-16 engines.
- F-6 Rebuild Factory is the oldest of the 4 PAC operations and manufactures components for, and overhauls, the Air Force's Chinese-built combat aircraft.

NAMC/PAC K-8 Karakorum

First flight: 21 November 1990.
Role: Basic jet trainer, also suited to more advanced training and light attack.

Nanchang/Pakistan Aeronautical Complex K-8 Karakorum (courtesy Pakistan Aeronautical Complex/CATIC)

★ Aims

- ★ Developed to MIL-F-8785C IV requirements.
- ★ Low purchase cost and minimum operational costs.

▲ Development

▲ 1987. Programme initiated, with the first metal cut at the start of 1989.
▲ 18 October 1991. Maiden flight of the second of 3 flying and 1 static test prototypes.
▲ 1992. US Government halted TFE731 engine sales to China, reportedly because of transfer of technology considerations, but allowed sales to resume from 1994.
▲ 9 April 1994. CATIC and the Pakistan Government signed an agreement at Rawalpindi covering the purchase of the first 6 K-8s for the Pakistan Air Force.
▲ 21 September 1994. Acceptance of the first 6 K-8s for the Pakistan Air Force, at Nanchang.
Sales/users: 6 ordered initially for the Pakistan Air Force from a first production batch of 15; deliveries started in September 1994. These have been used by the Air Force Academy at Risalpur for a 1,200 hours evaluation, pending further orders. It is expected that Pakistan will order the remaining 9 from the first batch, plus up to 60 others to eventually replace Shenyang FT-5s and Cessna T-37s. China is to evaluate a DV-2 powered derivative for its own forces. Export opportunities are seen as Bangladesh, Malaysia, Myanmar, Sri Lanka, Syria, Thailand and African nations.
Crew: Student and instructor in tandem, with rear seat raised by 11 ins (28 cm) to improve forward vision.
Cockpit: AlliedSignal ECS 51833 environmental control system.
Crew escape: Martin Baker Mk 10LZ zero-zero ejection seats.
Fixed guns: None, but 23-mm gun pod can be installed on the centreline, with 80 rounds of ammunition.
Number of weapon pylons: 4 under the wings, outer pylons "wet", plus centreline for gun pod or possibly other store (up to 1,543 lb, 700 kg).
Expendable weapons and equipment: 2,080 lb (943 kg) load, including bombs up to a 610 lb BL755 cluster bomb, rocket pods or 2 PL-7 AAMs.
Flight/weapon system avionics/instrumentation: AlliedSignal Bendix-King flight avionics, including Tacan, VOR/ILS, ADF. Air data computer. AHRS. Rockwell/Collins EFIS-86 display set, manufactured (and software altered) in China at the Sushi Aircraft Instrument Factory, incorporating 2 CRTS in each cockpit. Computing optical gunsight. A HOTAS system is under study.
Wing characteristics: Straight, low mounted, with slight dihedral.
Wing control surfaces: Boosted ailerons and Fowler type flaps (2 position).
Tail control surfaces: Variable incidence tailplane with horn-balanced elevators (port tab). Rudder with tab.
Airbrakes: 1, beneath the rear fuselage.
Flight control system: Mechanical, with hydraulic aileron, flap and airbrake actuation.
Construction materials: Primarily metal, including honeycomb core for the ailerons, but with composites vertical tail. PAC-built components are detailed in the introduction.
Engine: AlliedSignal TFE731-2A-2A turbofan. China to evaluate the Ivchenko PROGRESS DV-2 turbofan, of 4,850 lbf (21.58 kN).
Engine rating: 3,764 lbf (16.74 kN) take-off, 755 lbf (3.36 kN) cruise.
Air intakes: Fuselage sides, level with rear of canopy, with splitter plates.
Fuel system: 1,720 lbs (780 kg) in the wings and 2 bag tanks in the fuselage. 2 x 250 litre drop tanks optional.
Electrical system: 28.5 volt DC supply, with 24 volt back-up. AC supply comprises 400Hz frequency single-phase and 3-phase. Power-generated through engine-driven generator and static invertors.

Details for K-8.

Principal dimensions:
Wing span: 31 ft 7 ins (9.63 m)
Maximum length: 38 ft 1 ins (11.6 m)
Maximum height: 13 ft 10 ins (4.21 m)

Wings:
Aerofoil section: NACA 64A-114, NACA 64A-412 (root/tip)
Area: 183.2 sq ft (17.02 m^2)
Aspect ratio: 5.449
Sweepback: 2.219 ° at 25% chord
Incidence: 1.5 °
Dihedral: 3 °

Tail Unit:
Tailplane span: 13 ft 9 ins (4.2 m)

Undercarriage:
Type: Retractable, with steerable nosewheel.
Main wheel tyre size: 561 x 169 mm
Wheel base: 14 ft 4.5 ins (4.38 m)
Wheel track: 8 ft (2.43 m)

Weights:
Empty: 5,924 lb (2,687 kg)
Normal take-off: 8,003 lb (3,630 kg)
Maximum take-off: 9,850 lb (4,468 kg)

Performance:
Maximum speed: 432 kts (497 mph) 800 km/h
Landing speed: 89 kts (103 mph) 165 km/h
Take-off distance: 1,345 ft (410 m)
Landing distance: 1,680 ft (512 m)
Maximum climb rate: 5,900 ft (1,800 m) per minute at sea level
G limits: +7.33
Maximum roll rate: 200° per second
Ceiling: 42,650 ft (13,000 m)
Range with full fuel: 756 naut miles (870 miles) 1,400 km
Duration: 3 hours

Nanchang/Pakistan Aeronautical Complex K-8 Karakorum front and rear cockpits (courtesy CATIC)

Hydraulic system: 3,002 psi.
Braking system: Hydraulically actuated disc brakes, with anti-skid devices.
Oxygen system: Gaseous supply.

Panavia Aircraft GmbH (Germany/Italy/UK)

Corporate address: im Airport Business Centre, Am Söldnermoos 17, 85399 Hallbergmoos, Germany.
Telephone: +49 811 80 0 (main switchboard)
Founded: 26 March 1969.
Information: Dieter Gnamm (Public Relations – *telephone* +49 811 80 1238/9, *facsimile* +49 811 80 1386).

● Activities

● Partnership of Alenia of Italy (15%), Daimler-Benz of Germany (42.5%) and British Aerospace of the UK (42.5%); see these companies in the earlier pages of this section for individual details.
● Formed for the management of the Tornado design programme, initial build, full production, marketing, public relations and in-service support.

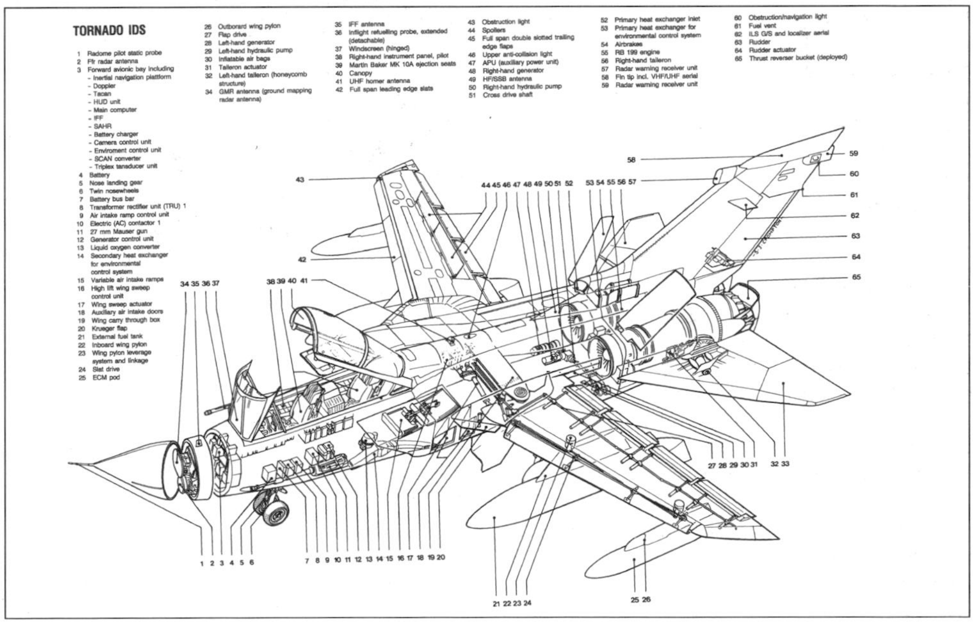

Panavia Tornado IDS cutaway (courtesy Panavia)

Panavia Tornado Interdictor Strike (IDS) and Electronic Combat and Reconnaissance (ECR)

First flight: 14 August 1974.
Role: Interdiction, strike, maritime strike and reconnaissance (IDS), and electronic combat and reconnaissance (ECR).

★ Aims

★ European tri-national collaborative programme to satisfy the needs of the UK, Germany and Italy. Netherlands withdrew.
★ Multi-role potential basic airframe, reconciling the design requirements of transonic flight at sea level, good field performance, manoeuvrability, high supersonic speed and loiter.
★ 2 crew to ease workload, and 2 engines for survivability.
★ Radar and comprehensive avionics for all weather operations, with auto-terrain following for enhanced survivability.
★ Advanced high by-pass turbofan engines optimized for aircraft, offering low cruise fuel consumption with high augmentation.
★ Design fatigue life 16,000 flying hours; scatter factor 4; minimum service life 4,000 flying hours.

Panavia Tornado GR Mk 1

▲ Development

▲ 26 March 1969. Panavia formed to handle the MRCA (Multi-Role Combat Aircraft) contract from the involved governments. Originally comprised BAC, MBB, Fiat (later Aeritalia) and Fokker-VFW, with the Netherlands withdrawing that July (now BAe, Daimler-Benz and Alenia).
▲ May 1969. Project definition phase began
▲ 1 June 1969. Turbo Union Ltd formed to design, develop and produce the MRCA engine.
▲ July 1970. Pre-development phase began.
▲ September 1971. Intention To Proceed (ITP) declared by the involved governments.
▲ 27 September 1971. First ground test run of the RB199 engine at Bristol.
▲ August 1972. Full development contract awarded.
▲ March 1973. Production investment decision made.
▲ 14 August 1974. First flight of prototype PO1 at Manching in Germany, crewed by Paul Millet (pilot) and Nils Meister.
▲ 30 October 1974. First flight of prototype PO2 at Warton in the UK.
▲ 5 December 1975. First flight of prototype PO5 at Turin in Italy.
▲ 29 July 1976. Signature of a contract covering the first production batch of 40 aircraft.
▲ 5 February 1977. First flight of a pre-series IDS (P11).
▲ 5 June 1979. First Tornado IDS handed over to the RAF

Details for Tornado IDS.

Principal dimensions:
Wing span: 45 ft 7.5 ins (13.91 m) *spread*, 28 ft 2.5 ins (8.6 m) *fully swept*
Maximum length: 54 ft 9.5 ins (16.7 m) with probe
Maximum height: 19 ft 6 ins (5.95 m)

Wings:
Area: 286.3 sq ft (26.6 m^2)
Aspect ratio: 7.274 *spread*
Sweepback: 25° *spread*, 67° *fully swept*

Tail unit:
Tailplane span: 22 ft 4 ins (6.81 m)

Undercarriage:
Type: Retractable, with twin steerable nosewheels
Main wheel tyre size: 30 x 11.5-14.5
Nose wheel tyre size: 18 x 5.5
Wheel base: 20 ft 4 ins (6.2 m)
Wheel track: 10 ft 2 ins (3.1 m)

Weights:
Empty: 30,864-31,967 lb (14,000-14,500 kg)
Maximum take-off: 61,729 lb (28,000 kg)

Performance:
Maximum operating Mach number (Mmo): Mach 2.2 *clean*, Mach 1.8 *with stores*
Maximum speed: 800 kts (921 mph) 1,482 km/h IAS
Take-off distance: 1,510 ft (460 m), or under 1,970 ft (600 m) with heavy weapon load
Landing distance: less than 1,640 ft (500 m)
G limits: +7.8, -1.5
Ceiling: above 50,000 ft (15,240 m)
Radius of action (interdiction, Lo-Lo-Lo-Lo): 600 naut miles (691 miles) 1,111 km*
Radius of action (interdiction, Hi-Lo-Lo-Hi): 800 naut miles (921 miles) 1,482 km*
Radius of action (maritime attack, Hi-Lo-Lo-Hi): over 700 naut miles (806 miles) 1,296 km
Ferry range: 2,050 naut miles (2,360 miles) 3,797 km

*with 4 x 1,000 lb bombs, 2 Sidewinders and 2 drop tanks

at Warton, followed the next day by the first to the Luftwaffe at Manching.

▲ 29 January 1981. The Tri-national Tornado Training Establishment was officially opened at RAF Cottesmore, Tornados having been received since July 1980.

▲ 25 September 1981. First production IDS for Italy flew.

▲ 6 January 1982. Tornado IDSs joined 9 Squadron, RAF, followed by the German Navy and Italy that Summer.

▲ 8 November 1982. An RAF GR Mk 1 of 9 Squadron made a non-stop return flight between England and Cyprus, refuelled by Victors and a Buccaneer. No 9 Squadron had gained IOC on 1 June.

▲ 11 July 1985. First flight of an RAF Tornado GR Mk 1A, deliveries starting on 3 April 1987.

▲ 26 September 1985. MoU signed between the UK Government and HRH Prince Sultan Bin Abdul Aziz of Saudi Arabia, covering 48 IDS and 24 ADV Tornados, worth an estimated £5 billion (including support).

▲ 26 March 1986. First flight of a Royal Saudi Air Force IDS.

▲ 24 May 1989. The first Tornado Squadron, the Germany's MFG 1, completed 50,000 Tornado flying hours.

▲ 21 May 1990. First Tornado ECR was handed over to the Luftwaffe's JaboG 38.

▲ 17 March 1992. Roll-out of the first Italian IDS conversion into an ECR test aircraft took place at Alenia's Caselle flight test centre.

▲ 29 May 1993. First flight of the RAF's GR Mk 4 Mid-Life Update test aircraft at Warton.

▲ 14 February 1994. Delivery of the first GR Mk 1B Maritime Strike Tornado to the RAF.

▲ 29 July 1994. UK contracts for the Mid-Life Update of GR Mk 1/1As to GR Mk 4/4A standard were signed with Panavia.

▲ 1997. Tornado GR Mk 4 due to enter RAF service.

▲ 1998. In-service date for the first of 40 Luftwaffe Tornados with new reconnaissance pods (see Aircraft variants).

Sales/users: 781 production IDS/ECR aircraft ordered, of which 733 had been delivered by early 1995. Orders by Germany (air force 210 IDS and 35 ECR; navy 112), Italy (99), Saudi Arabia (48, with further 48 for 1995-97 delivery), and UK (229). Some 40 German Navy maritime strike aircraft have been transferred to the Luftwaffe, and Italy has modified 16 IDSs into ECRs, as the prototype plus 15 more. The United Arab Emirates might lease up to 19 RAF GR Mk 1s, with new Hakim stand-off weapon capability.

Crew: Pilot and navigator in tandem.

Cockpit: Front screen in 3 panels, and hinges forward for maintenance access. Single-piece clamshell canopy, hinged at rear. "Two stick" trainer variant retains operational capability.

Crew escape: Martin Baker Mk 10A fully automatic ejection seats, zero-zero to 625 kts CAS/Mach 2 and 50,000 ft (15,240 m). Canopy jettison prior to ejection, but MDC assists egress in unlikely case of jettison failure.

Fixed guns: 2 x 27-mm Mauser cannon, in the sides of the lower fuselage. Selectable high and low rate of fire. No guns in the GR Mk 1A reconnaissance version or ECR.

Ammunition: 180 rounds per gun.

Number of weapon pylons: 7. Flat fuselage underside is suited to the carriage of long-range weapons, and has 3 "wet" stations (centreline and 2 outer). Dependent on the stores carried, all 3 may be used simultaneously. Each moving wing panel has inner and outer swivelling pylons; inner are "wet" and outer dedicated to ECM and chaff/flare pods. Twin or triple stores carriers can be fitted. Inner wing pylons have adapters for Sidewinders in addition to the main store.

Expendable weapons and equipment: Maximum payload of about 19,842 lb (9,000 kg) for both IDS and ECR. Extremely wide range of weapons, including all standard high-explosive bombs, cluster bombs, retarded and low-drag bombs, and laser-guided bombs; programme currently underway in 1995 to integrate Paveway III low-level LGB. WE177B tactical nuclear weapon used by RAF (until 1998). Practice bomb carriers. Alternative weapons include rocket pods, large weapon dispensers including JP233 and MW-1 for airfield attack and Matra Apache for stand-off attack, and various air-to-surface missiles including Maverick, anti-ship Kormoran and Sea Eagle, and ALARM and HARM for anti-radar. Future weapons will include the US JSOW. Sidewinders provide self defence. Typical configurations are: 8 x 1,000 lb bombs plus 2 Sidewinders, 2 ECM pods and 2 drop tanks; 2 JP-233 dispensers, 2 Sidewinders, 2 ECM pods and 2 tanks; 4 HARM missiles and 2 ECM pods; 2 Kormoran or Sea Eagle missiles and 2 tanks; MW-1, 2 AIM-9L Sidewinders, ECM pod, chaff/flare dispenser and 2 tanks; and 7 ALARM missiles, ECM pod, chaff/flare dispenser and 2 tanks.

Additional stores: Reconnaissance pod on centreline, equipped with wide-angle cameras and infra-red linescan, developed by MBB for German service; new pods being delivered for the Luftwaffe (see Aircraft variants). Buddy-buddy refuelling pod available on centreline. Thermal Imaging and Airborne Laser Designator (TIALD) pod. RSAF IDSs have Thomson-CSF designator pod.

Radar: Ground Mapping Radar (GMR) for blind navigation and targeting, and Terrain Following Radar (TFR) with auto-terrain following capability. Signals from the high resolution mapping radar and TF radar are processed in a shared LRU. Doppler radar for navigational use.

Flight/weapon system avionics/instrumentation: Principal to the avionics system is a 256 kilobyte Litef Spirit 3 digital main computer (being replaced on German and Italian IDSs by an 8 megabyte computer with Ada software), which handles the navigation, flight direction and terrain following, weapon aiming and delivery, computing, communications and defensive aids sub-systems. The sub-systems are interlinked with the GMR and TRF (see Radar), autopilot and flight director system (AFDS), digital inertial navigation system (INS), Tacan, Doppler radar, secondary altitude and heading reference system (SAHRS), air data computer, laser ranger/marked target seeker (LRMTS), ECM/ECCM, communications transmitters and receivers, IFF and ILS. Later production aircraft were also given MIL-STD-1553B (see German MLU under Aircraft variants) databus architecture, enlarged main computer memory, digital missile control unit, advanced displays, new stores management system, a solid state mission data transfer system, improved radar warning system and active ECM. On-board check-out and monitoring system (OCAMS). German ECR is equipped with FLIR, which will be introduced on the RAF's GR Mk 4 variant. Pilot's displays are HUD, head-down moving map, terrain-following E-scope and radar threat warning. Navigator's displays are centrally-located combined mapping radar and moving map display, with identical CRT display either side for navigation and mission planning. May also be used to display electro-optic sensor data (such as FLIR). "Two stick" trainer variants have port CRT display removed and flight instruments installed in the rear cockpit. See Mid-Life Updates under Aircraft variants.

Self-protection systems: Threat radar warning receivers are incorporated, forward and rearward antennae of which are mounted high on the fin leading and trailing edges. A mix of active ECM pods and chaff/flare pods is normal. RAF aircraft usually carry Sky Shadow ECM pod on the port outer wing pylon and BOZ-100 chaff/flare on the starboard wing. German aircraft carry CERBERUS ECM pod and BOZ pod. Italian aircraft are equipped with internally carried self protection jammer and may carry 2 BOZ pods. RAF has deployed an infra-red towed decoy.

Wing characteristics: Variable-geometry outer wing panels. Inboard fixed highly swept "nibs" (gloves), housing the bodyside wing pivots. 2 spars and machined skin/ribs with integral stiffeners. Swivelling pylon spigots.

Wing control surfaces: Full-span, 4-segment, double-slotted trailing-edge flaperons. Full-span, 3-segment, leading-edge slats. 2-segment lateral control spoilers/lift dumpers at mid span ahead of the flaps. Krueger flaps on the "nib" leading-edges. Fixed "nib" has feather fairings to conform to wing contour change with sweep.

Tail control surfaces: Slab tailplane (tailerons), actuated symmetrically for pitch control and differentially for roll. Characteristically large area dictated by short tail arm when wings swept and need to trim effective wing flaps. Tall and large area fin with rudder, dictated by short "fin arm" when wings swept fully aft at supersonic speeds.

Airbrakes: Petal type, in shoulder position each side of the rear fuselage.

Flight control system: All electrical, triplexed fly-by-wire system, with electrical and mechanical back-up modes. Command Stability Augmentation System (CSAS) employs Manoeuvre Demand control and optimizes aircraft flying qualities regardless of speed, height and stores load. Also Gust Alleviation. In the event of multiple failure, mechanical back-up allows a "get home" capability. Spin Prevention and Incidence Limiting System (SPILS) prevents loss of control or spin

Panavia Tornado ECR in German service, with HARM missiles

entry at high incidence. Autopilot and Flight Director System (AFDS).
Fuselage: Manufacture breakdown as: front fuselage, comprising cockpit aft of the rear pressure bulkhead to nose radome (accommodating radar, guns and nose undercarriage); centre fuselage with fuel tankage, intakes and inlet ducting, wing carry-through structure and undercarriage bays, dorsal fairing for services; rear fuselage comprising engine installation with bottom drop-out doors and fin and tailplane spigot mountings.
Construction materials: By weight, aluminium alloy (72%), titanium (17%), steel (6%) and non-metallics (5%). Titanium mainly in the wing carry-through structure incorporating wing pivots, which are Teflon coated, and the engine compartment.
Engines: 2 Turbo Union RB199 turbofans. APU.
Engine rating: 9,100 lbf (40.5 kN) dry, 16,000 lbf (71.2 kN) with afterburning in Mk 103 form for IDS, and 9,550 lbf (42.5 kN) dry and 16,700 lbf (74.3 kN) with afterburning for Mk 105 form for ECR.
Air intakes: Variable 2-dimensional, horizontal wedge type, with fixed first ramp and controlled second ramp and diffuser ramp beyond the throat bleed slot. Swept side walls. 2 auxiliary intake doors on the outer nacelle walls. Bodyside diverter.
Flight refuelling probe: Retractable (and removable) probe on the starboard side of the cockpit.
Fuel system: 5,842 litres in fuselage bag tanks and integral wing tanks, except for RAF and RSAF aircraft which have additional fuel in the fin, making 6,393 litres. Optional drop tanks in 2 underfuselage and 2 wing positions, of 1,500 or 2,250 litre capacities; RAF aircraft can carry 2,250 litre tanks (but wing sweep restricted to 63°). Maximum external fuel weight 12,897 lb (5,850 kg).
Electrical system: 115/220 volt AC 3-phase, 400 Hz constant frequency sub-system and a 28 volt DC sub-system. Power generated by 2 automatically controlled, brushless AC engine-driven generators integrated with a constant speed drive unit. Ni-cd battery for basic flight line servicing functions and APU starting. Emergency power system comprises a single shot battery, emergency hydraulic pump and emergency fuel pump, providing hydraulic power and/or fuel pressure following a double engine flame-out, double generator failure or a double transformer/rectifier unit failure.
Hydraulic system: Fully duplicated, 4,000 psi system.
Braking system: Anti-skid wheel braking, supplemented by thrust reversal and lift dumping. Target type thrust reversers are deployable from a "pre-armed" condition following main wheel contact. Emergency arrester hook. Studies into a new main undercarriage and braking system are underway, to allow increased take-off weight.
Oxygen system: 10 litre liquid oxygen converter. Each seat has an emergency supply.

Aircraft variants:
GR Mk 1 is the basic RAF combat type, with "two stick" trainer variants. As described.
GR Mk 1A is the RAF reconnaissance version, retaining external stores capability and operational characteristics. Day and night, low-level, high speed, horizon to horizon coverage by 3 internal infra-red sensors with comprehensive video recording. Displaces guns and ammunition. This type is also used by the RSAF.
GR Mk 1B is the RAF maritime attack variant, carrying 2 Sea Eagles on the outer fuselage pylons and with drop tanks on the inner wing pylons. 4 missiles are possible.
GR Mk 4/4A are the RAF's Mid-Life Update versions of the Mk 1/1A to provide covert operational capability. The programme will run from 1996-2002. FLIR sensor giving image on a wide-angle HUD. Night Vision Goggles compatible cockpit. New colour multi-function HDD for pilot. TIALD for autonomous target acquisition, designation and weapon guidance. GPS. New avionics integration system. 142 to be updated from 1/1As.
German IDS, as generally described previously. Luftwaffe force now includes ex-naval aircraft. Mid-Life Update is underway under ("Neue Avionsstruktur"), with improvements including a new 8-megabyte computer (see avionics) with Ada software, MIL-STD-1760 databus, integrated laser inertial navigation/GPS, FLIR, defensive aids computer, missile warner, improved radar warning system, and displays. To include a new reconnaissance role with a podded day/night sensor package with 2 optical cameras and infra-red line-scanner for 40 aircraft. The remaining Navy force is operated for missions against ship (with Kormoran missiles) and land targets, plus reconnaissance using pods.
Italian IDS force is being upgraded with the German IDSs.
ECR is the dedicated electronic combat and reconnaissance version. Suite of reconnaissance and EW equipment is housed in the front fuselage, displacing the guns and ammunition. Threat radar emitter located in the wing root, infra-red imaging linescan, ODIN operational data link (air-to-air and air-to-ground), FLIR and HARM missiles.
35 received by the Luftwaffe, and 16 produced for Italy as IDS conversions.

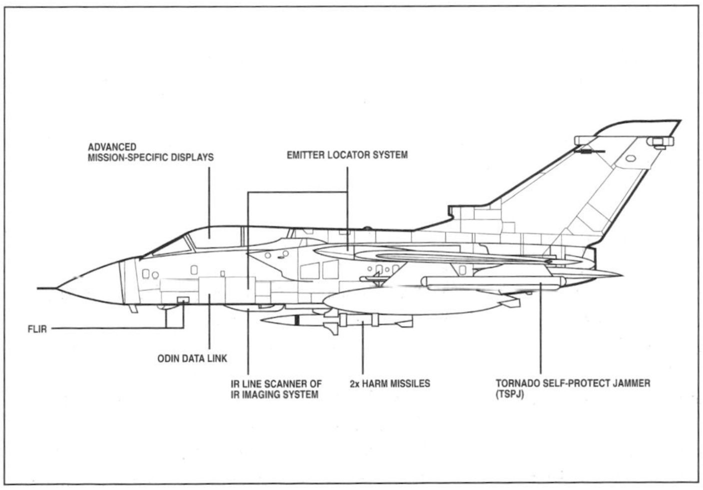

Panavia Tornado ECR system drawing (courtesy Panavia)

Panavia Tornado Air Defence Variant (ADV)

First flight: 27 October 1979 (pilot David Eagles).
Role: Long-range/duration air defence interceptor.

★ Aims
★ Significantly different variant of the Tornado airframe, exploiting the multi-role potential. High commonality with IDS, about 80% achieved.
★ Variable sweep wing for high supersonic speed and high loiter duration, ideally suited to over-ocean intercepts of attacking bombers.
★ Autonomous all-weather and day/night air defence, with beyond-visual-range engagement.
★ Patrols for over 3 hours at 300 naut miles from base with 4 Sky Flash and 4 Sidewinder AAMs.

▲ Development
▲ 4 March 1976. FSD initiated, with 3 prototypes included in the first Tornado production contract.
▲ 9 August 1979. Roll-out of the first ADV prototype at Warton (F Mk 2).
▲ 5 November 1984. Delivery of the first F Mk 2 to RAF Coningsby.
▲ 26 September 1985. MoU signed with Saudi Arabia for Tornados (see IDS), including 24 ADVs.
▲ 20 November 1985. Maiden flight of an F Mk 3 for the RAF.
▲ 9 February 1989. First ADV for the RSAF handed over.
▲ 24 March 1993. 170th and last full production ADV delivered to the RAF.
Sales/users: RAF received 21 F Mk 2s (not in service) and 152 F Mk 3s, including 52 in "2 stick" operational training configuration; 24 being leased by the Italian Air Force pending Eurofighter 2000 deliveries, with the first handed over on 7 July 1995 for use by 36° Stormo at Gioia del Colle. Royal Saudi Air Force received 24.
Details: Similar to IDS except:
Fixed guns: 1 x 27-mm Mauser cannon, on starboard side.
Ammunition: 180 rounds.
Number of weapon pylons: Flat underside of the fuselage modified to accommodate 4 medium-range

DETAILS FOR TORNADO F MK 3.
(WHERE DIFFERENT FROM IDS)

Principal dimensions:
Maximum length: 61 ft 1 ins (18.62 m)

Weights:
Empty: 31,800 lb (14,450 kg)
Maximum take-off: 61,700 lb (28,000 kg)

Performance:
Maximum operating Mach number (MMO): Mach 2.2 *clean*, Mach 1.8 *with stores*
Maximum speed: 800 kts (921 mph) 1,482 km/h IAS
Time to 30,000 ft (9,145 m): under 2 minutes from brakes off
Take-off distance: less than 3,000 ft (915 m) in full combat configuration
Landing run: less than 2,130 ft (650 m), or 1,214 ft (370 m) using brakes and thrust reversers
Roll rate: 180° per second at 750 kts (863 mph) 1,389 km/h
G limits: +7.6, -3
Ceiling: 50,000-70,000 ft (15,240-21,300 m)
Radius of action (point intercept): 900 naut miles (1,036 miles) 1,667 km subsonic*, or 200 naut miles (230 miles) 370 km supersonic*
Duration (combat air patrol): 3 hours at 300 naut miles (345 miles) 556 km from base*

*4 Sky Flash missiles, Sidewinders, gun/ammunition and 2 drop tanks

Panavia Tornado F Mk 3 with 4 Sky Flash and 2 Sidewinder AAMs

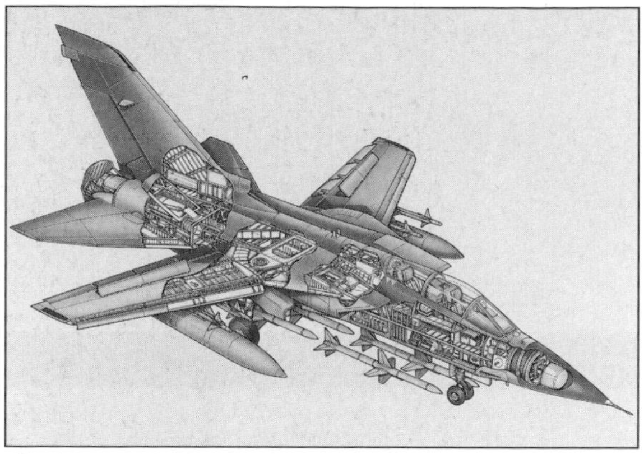

Panavia Tornado F Mk 3 cutaway (courtesy British Aerospace)

missiles in a semi-recessed, staggered, low-drag arrangement. Special long stroke Frazer Nash extensible ejector/launchers provide safe launch throughout the entire flight envelope. Inner wing pylons only, for external tanks or missiles. Twin Sidewinders may be carried on each wing pylon, using adaptors.
Expendable weapons and equipment: 4 Sky Flash and 4 AIM-9L Sidewinders. AMRAAM and ASRAAM compatibility.
Additional stores: See Self protection.
Radar: GEC-Marconi AI-24 Foxhunter multi-mode, track-while-scan, pulse Doppler, with frequency modulated interrupted continuous wave (FMICW). ECCM features. Integrated IFF. Ground mapping mode.
Flight/weapon system avionics/instrumentation: Much of the IDS hardware used, but software optimized for ADV role. Pilot has HUD, electronic HDD and threat warning displays. Weapon system operator has 2 multi-function display screens with multi-function keys, threat warning display and radar control panel. Secure data link (JTIDS).
Self-protection systems: Radar homing and warning receivers, with antennae on the fin and in the fixed "nib" (glove) leading edges. Chaff/flare dispensers on the underside of the engine bay doors.
Wing characteristics: Wing root "nib" (glove) extended forward, with leading edge sweep increased from 60° to 67°. No outer wing pylons.
Wing control surfaces: Krueger flaps deleted.
Flight control system: Automatic wing sweep and manoeuvre device system, to optimize close combat performance.
Fuselage: Plug of some 1 ft 9 ins (0.54 m) inserted aft of the rear cockpit for ADV, allowing an increase in internal fuel and the carriage of under-fuselage missiles. Longer radome, and small changes at the rear to allow for lengthened jetpipes.
Engines: 2 Turbo Union RB199 Mk 104 turbofans.
Engine rating: Each 9,100 lbf (40.5 kN) dry, 16,410 lbf (73 kN) with afterburning.
Fuel system: Internal capacity increased to 7,270 litres.

Promavia ATTA/Mikoyan 815 (Belgium/Russia)

Promavia ATTA-4000/Mikoyan 815 advanced jet trainer and tactical aircraft in model form

Corporate address: All company details can be found under Promavia and Mikoyan in this section.
First flight: 1995.
Role: Advanced training and tactical missions. Projected also as a basic jet trainer for similar uses to those outlined in the USAF's JPATS programme.

★ Aims

★ Based on the Jet Squalus but with tandem cockpits, to operate at higher altitudes and simulate combat missions.
★ Designed to be the world's lowest cost advanced trainer/tactical aircraft.
★ Direct operating costs of $300 per hour.

▲ Development

▲ 1988. Programme commencement announced by Promavia.
▲ 18 July 1992. Collaboration agreement signed between Promavia of Belgium and Mikoyan of Russia to jointly develop a jet trainer based on the Promavia Jet Squalus. Assembly of 3 prototypes by Mikoyan, 2 flying and 1 ground test.
▲ 1993. Original first flight date, reset to late 1994.
Sales/users: Purchase price aimed at $3 million. Manufacture under licence offered.
Crew: 2, student in front and instructor behind in raised cockpit.
Crew escape: Zero-zero ejection seats.
Fixed guns: None.
Number of weapon pylons: Presumably 4.
Expendable weapons and equipment: Provision for up to 4 single/double 7.62-mm machine-gun pods, or 2 single 20-mm cannon pods, or 4 rocket launchers each with seven 70-mm rockets, or 2 infra-red air-to-air missiles, or 4 Mk 82 or lighter bombs.
Flight/weapon system avionics/instrumentation: EFIS cockpit displays.
Wing characteristics: Low-mounted, straight, tapered.
Wing control surfaces: Conventional.
Tail control surfaces: Elevators (port tab) and rudder.
Engines: 2 Williams-Rolls FJ44s (previously to use either AlliedSignal TFE109-2s or more powerful TFE109-3s).
Engine rating: Each 1,900 lbf (8.45 kN).
Air intakes: Fuselage sides, at wing roots.
Flight refuelling probe: None.
Fuel system: 1,720 lb (780 kg) of fuel.

Aircraft variants:
Mikoyan 815 *izdelye 815* is the Russian designation for the ATTA.
Promavia ATTA-3000 was the original designation from Belgium of the ATTA using the AlliedSignal TFE109-2 or 3 engines.
Promavia ATTA-4000 is reportedly the current Promavia designation for the FJ44-powered trainer.

DETAILS FOR MIG-815 (PROVISIONAL).

Principal dimensions:
Wing span: 31 ft 11 in (9.73 m)
Maximum length: 34 ft 2.25 ins (10.42 m)
Maximum height: 12 ft 4 ins (3.76 m)

Wings:
Area: 170.7 sq ft (15.86 m^2)
Dihedral: Yes.

Undercarriage:
Type: retractable, with nosewheel
Wheel base: 12 ft 5 ins (3.79 m)
Wheel track: 10 ft 4 ins (3.16 m)

Weights:
Empty, operating: 3,900 lb (1,769 kg)
Maximum take-off: 6,724 lb (3,050 kg)

Performance:
Maximum speed at sea level: 378 kts (435 mph) 700 km/h
Maximum speed at 30,000 ft (9,145 m): 432 kts (497 mph) 800 km/h
Stall speed: reportedly 92 kts (106 mph) 170 km/h *presumably clean*, 78 kts (90 mph) 145 km/h *with flaps*
Landing speed: 89 kts (103 mph) 165 km/h
Take-off distance: 1,280 ft (390 m)
Landing distance: 1,362 ft (415 m)
Time to 18,000 ft (5,485 m): 3 mins 30 seconds
G load in constant turn: 4.5 at sea level, 2.6 at 22,000 ft (6,710 m), 2.4 at 25,000 ft (7,625 m)
G limits: +6, -3
Ceiling: 45,000 ft (13,720 m)
Range with full fuel: 1,188 naut miles (1,367 miles) 2,200 km

SEPECAT (France/UK)

Full name: Société Européene de Production de l'Avion Ecole de Combat et d'Appui Tactique.
Founded: 1966.

● Activities

● SEPECAT founded to manage the Anglo-French Jaguar programme. See British Aerospace (UK) and Dassault Aviation (France) for company details.

SEPECAT Jaguar

First flight: 8 September 1968.
Role: Strike fighter and maritime strike, plus advanced/operational trainer.

★ Aims

★ Efficient low-level, high-subsonic flight, and supersonic speed at altitude using augmented high by-pass turbofans optimized for the design with modest dry thrust but high boost.
★ Good field performance by means of effective wing high-lift system, drag-parachute and rugged undercarriage.
★ Navigation and weapon system tailored for accurate, low-level, first pass attack (not all-weather, except Indian maritime strike types).
★ Derived from the then-current Breguet 121 project, but increased size, weight and cost.

▲ Development

▲ May 1965. Programme initiated by the British and French defence ministries, with decision to merge the French ECAT and UK advanced trainer with attack capability requirements.
▲ 8 September 1968. First flight of prototype E-01, French two-seater for the Jaguar E, at the Istres flight test centre, piloted by Bernard Witt.
▲ 23 March 1969. First flight of the French A-03 single-seat prototype for the Jaguar A.
▲ 12 October 1969. First flight of a British prototype, a Jaguar S single-seater.
▲ 30 August 1971. First flight of prototype B-08, the British two-seater for Jaguar B.
▲ May 1972. Entered service with the French Armee de l'Air, with the CEAM at Mont de Marsan receiving the Jaguar E.

SEPECAT Jaguar GR Mk 1B with TIALD, LGB, ECM pod and Phimat pod (crown/via Neville Beckett)

▲ 11 October 1972. Maiden flight of a production Jaguar S, becoming GR Mk 1 when entering service in March 1974.
▲ June 1973. Initial operating squadron was Esc 1/7 at St Dizier.
▲ 19 August 1976. First flight of a Jaguar International, offering more thrust and greater versatility.
▲ 1977. First export deliveries of Jaguar Internationals, to Ecuador in January, followed by Oman in March (and Nigeria in 1984).
▲ 31 March 1982. First flight of an Indian-built Jaguar (Shamsher) at Bangalore, in the hands of HAL's Chief Test Pilot.
▲ 1985. British/French production completed.
▲ 1995. Number of RAF aircraft were being modified to carry the GEC-Marconi TIALD (thermal imaging airborne laser designation) pod, redesignated Mk 1Bs. See Avionics.

Sales/users: Deliveries to Ecuador (12), France (200), Nigeria (18), Oman (24) and the UK (203). In addition, India received 40 fly-away SEPECAT Jaguar Internationals built in Europe, and thereafter HAL began assembly of a further 45 under the local name Shamsher (progressively with some indigenous components, including Hyderabad Division avionics). Subsequent manufacturing by HAL has covered a further 46 (making 131 in total). See India.
Crew: Pilot, or 2 in tandem in the trainer, the rear seat raised by 16 ins (40 cm) to imprive forward view.
Cockpit: Fixed front screen with arch frame and 3 transparencies. Rear-hinged clamshell canopy.
Crew escape: Martin Baker Mk 9 zero-zero ejection seat.
Fixed guns: 2 x 30-mm Aden or DEFA cannon in the fuselage of single-seaters. Single Aden in two-seaters.
Ammunition: 150 rounds per gun.
Number of weapon pylons: 5 (or 7 – see below), as an underfuselage "wet" centreline pylon for a large store or tandem arrangement for shorter stores, and 2 pylons under each wing, the inner "wet". Unique over-wing launch rails for air-to-air missiles on some aircraft (some others carry AAMs on the outer underwing pylons).
Expendable weapons and equipment: Maximum 10,000 lb (4,536 kg) load. Full range of free-fall and retarded bombs, including 1,000 lb, 250 kg, 400 kg, and 600 lb cluster bombs, plus laser-guided, Durandel airfield cratering and practice bombs. Alternative weapons include rocket launchers, air-to-surface missiles, anti-ship missiles (Harpoon, Exocet and Kormoran, plus Sea Eagle on Indian maritime Shamshers), and provision for Sidewinder or Magic air-to-air missiles. Future weapons will include JSOW.
Additional stores: Self contained reconnaissance pack available, carried on the centreline, with up to 5 low and high altitude cameras plus infra-red linescan.
Radar: Generally none, but Indian maritime strike Shamshers have Thomson-CSF Agave radar.
Flight/weapon system avionics/instrumentation: Comprehensive integrated navigation/weapons system of British S and B variants (made available to Jaguar International) comprises digital computer control of the inertial navigation and weapon aiming sub-system. HUD. Projected head-down map display. Laser ranger and marked target seeker. Air data computer. Tacan. VOR/ILS. Radar altimeter. IFF. HF/VHF/UHF radios. With exceptions above, all other instrumentation is of conventional dial type. Indian maritime-strike Shamshers have DARIN nav/attack system. Less sophisticated systems in French variants. Number of RAF aircraft are being modified to carry GEC-Marconi TIALD (thermal imaging airborne laser designation) pod. Associated with this fit are the additions of HOTAS, wide-angle HUD, head down displays, and GPS.
Self-protection systems: Westinghouse ECM pod. Phimat chaff dispenser on out pylons. Chaff/flare dispensers on lower engine bay doors. Radar warning receiver.
Wing characteristics: Shoulder mounted, medium sweep and medium aspect ratio wings of about 5% thickness/chord ratio. Upper surface fence on each wing, in line with the leading-edge dogtooth and trailing-edge kink. Continuous spanwise structure, with machined skins and ribs.
Wing control surfaces: Full-span, double-slotted trailing-edge flaps. Part-span leading-edge slat. Lateral control spoilers immediately ahead of the outboard flaps.
Tail control surfaces: Slab tailplane (tailerons), operated asymmetrically to supplement the wing spoilers for roll control. Inset rudder.
Airbrakes: 2 petals, on the fuselage lower sides aft of the undercarriage.
Flight control system: All surfaces are powered. Artificial feel. Autostabilization about all axes.
Construction materials: Largely aluminium alloy.

DETAILS FOR JAGUAR.

Principal dimensions:
Wing span: 28 ft 6 ins (8.69 m)
Maximum length: 50 ft 11 ins (15.52 m) *single-seater*, 53 ft 10.5 ins (16.42 m) *two-seater*, both excluding probe
Maximum height: 16 ft 0.5 ins (4.89 m)

Wings:
Area: 258.33 sq ft (24 m^2)
Aspect ratio: 3.147
Sweepback: 40° leading edge
Chord at root: 11 ft 9 ins (3.58 m)
Chord at tip: 3 ft 9 ins (1.143 m)
Anhedral: 3°

Tail unit:
Tailplane span: 14 ft 10 ins (4.53 m)
Tailplane area: 84 sq ft (7.8 m^2)
Fin area: 42 sq ft (3.9 m^2)

Undercarriage:
Type: Retractable, with nosewheel. Twin main wheels with low pressure types (73 psi); nosewheel 51 psi
Main wheel tyre size: 615 x 225-10
Nose wheel tyre size: 550 x 250-6
Wheel base: 18 ft 8 ins (5.69 m)
Wheel track: 7 ft 11 ins (2.4 m)

Weights:
Empty: 15,400 lb (6,985 kg)
Normal take-off: 24,250 lb (11,000 kg)
Maximum take-off: 34,613 lb (15,700 kg)

Performance:
Maximum speed: Mach 1.6 at 36,000 ft (11,000 m), Mach 1.1 at sea level
Take-off distance: 2,887 ft (880 m) with 4 x 1,000 lb bombs
Landing distance: 1,542 ft (470 m) with 4 x 1,000 lb bombs
G limits: +8.6, -4.3
Radius of action (Lo-Lo-Lo): 290-495 naut miles (334-570 miles) 537-917 km*
Radius of action (Lo-Lo-Lo): 325 naut miles (374 miles) 602 km with 4 x 1,000 lb bombs
Radius of action (Hi-Lo-Hi): 460-760 naut miles (530-875 miles) 852-1,407 km*
Radius of action (Hi-Lo-Hi): 432 naut miles (497 miles) 800 km, with 4 x 1,000 lb bombs
Ferry range: 1,575 naut miles (1,814 miles) 2,917 km, with 3 drop tanks

*Dependent on mission profile, weapon load and tanks carried

Engines: 2 Rolls-Royce Turbomeca Adour turbofans.
Engine rating: Mk 102 of 7,305 lbf (32.5 kN) each initially for British and French Jaguars, with many British aircraft later receiving the Mk 104 of 7,900 lbf (35.14 kN). Internationals have Mk 804 of 8,040 lbf (35.76 kN) (Ecuador, India and Oman), Mk 811 of 8,400 lbf (37.37 kN) (HAL assembled Shamshers), and Mk 815 of 8,400 lbf (37.37 kN) (Nigeria and Oman). All ratings are with afterburning.
Air intakes: Rectangular fixed pitots with body side diverters. 2 auxiliary inlets on each outer wall.
Nozzles: Variable area, convergent only.
Flight refuelling probe: Provision for a retractable probe on the starboard side, adjacent to the cockpit.
Fuel system: 4,200 litres in 6 centre fuselage and wing tanks. Optional 3 x 1,200 litre drop tanks.
Electrical system: Alternator on each engine, with adequate power in the event of single failure. Emergency battery for essential services in the event of total generation failure.
Hydraulic system: 2 independent systems, with engine-driven pumps, at 3,000 psi. Battery powered electric pump in the event of a double engine failure.
Braking system: Anti-skid main wheel braking. 14 ft (4.27 m) drag-chute. Emergency arrester hook.
Oxygen system: Liquid oxygen system (LOX). Emergency oxygen on seat.

Aircraft variants:
Jaguar A is the French single-seater.
Jaguar B is the RAF two-seater, designated T.Mk 2.
Jaguar E is the French two-seater.
Jaguar S is the RAF single-seater, originally designated GR Mk 1. Became 1A as updated with inertial navigation, and latest 1B with TIALD.
Jaguar International is the exported version, with more engine power and other changes as detailed previously. Overwing AAMs.
Shamsher is the Indian Air Force name for its Jaguar Internationals with Adour 811 engines. See HAL.

S.C. Avioane S.A./Soko/UTVA (Romania/former Yugoslavia/Serbia)

Corporate address: For company details, see S.C. Avioane and UTVA in the earlier pages of this section.

Avioane IAR-93 and Soko J-22 Orao

First flight: 31 October 1974 (IAR-93 and Orao prototypes).
Role: Attack, close air support and reconnaissance, with some air defence capability.
Sales/users: Romania (air force received 36 IAR-93As in single and two-seat forms, plus a quantity of the 165 IAR-93Bs required), and Serbia (former Yugoslavia received about 124 J-22s in all versions before production by Soko ended). Current status uncertain. Reports suggest continued work by UTVA.
Crew: Pilot, or 2 crew in training and reconnaissance forms.
Cockpit: Pressurized to 3.1 psi differential.
Crew escape: Martin Baker Mk 10 zero-zero ejection seats.
Fixed guns: 2 x 23-mm GSh-23L twin-barrel guns on the lower fuselage sides.
Ammunition: 200 rounds.
Number of weapon pylons: 5, comprising 1 under-fuselage centreline (capacity 1,102 lb, 500 kg for IAR-93 and 1,764 lb, 800 kg for Orao 2), 2 underwing inner stations (1,102 lb, 500 kg each), and 2 outer (661 lb, 300 kg each for IAR-93, and 1,102 lb, 500 kg for Orao 2).
Expendable weapons and equipment: 4,630 lb (2,100 kg) load for IAR-93B and 6,173 lb (2,800 lb) for Orao 2. Typical mix of bombs encompassing cluster, fragmentation (including M-72/FAB250), PLAB series of 150, 200 and 350 litre napalm, and dispensers for anti-tank, anti-runway and anti-personnel bomblets, rockets, gun pods, and air-to-ground missiles, with Serbian aircraft including TV-guided Maverick, French Durandal concrete penetrating weapons and Grom. IAR-93Bs can undertake air defence missions, carrying 2 AAMs on each underwing pylon using multiple ejectors.

Soko J-22 Orao 2 (Austin J. Brown/Aviation Picture Library)

Additional stores: Reconnaissance pod (see Self protection).
Radar: None.
Flight/weapon system avionics/instrumentation: 3-axis stability augmentation system, ADF, marker beacon receiver, radio altimeter and radio compass. VHF and UHF comm. Oraos have Collins VOR/ILS and distance measuring equipment. Thomson-CSF HUD in Orao 2. IFF in IAR-93s.
Self-protection systems: Radar warning receiver. Centreline jammer pod on Oraos. Chaff/flares.
Wing characteristics: Shoulder mounted, sweptback, with small and straight root extensions on the IAR-93B and Orao 2. Upper surface fence aft of outer section slat on all versions, with IAR-93As and Orao 1s also having a larger fence in line with the inner wing pylon.
Wing control surfaces: Ailerons, single-slotted flaps, and 2-section leading-edge slats.
Tail control surfaces: Slab tailplane and rudder. 2 shallow ventral fins on all Oraos and single-seat IAR-93As.
Airbrakes: 2, under the forward fuselage.
Flight control system: Hydraulic, except for electrically actuated slats.
Construction materials: Principally aluminium alloy, with some use of honeycomb core for the tail control surfaces.
Engines: 2 licence-built Rolls-Royce Viper 600s (see Aircraft variants).
Flight refuelling probe: Simple, fuselage side type.
Fuel system: 3,120 litres of internal fuel. Optional 3 x 500 litre drop tanks.
Electrical system: 28 volt DC supply via 2 x 9kW engine-driven starter-generators. 24 volt ni-cd battery. 4 static inverters for 115 volt 400Hz AC supply.
Hydraulic system: 2 separate systems, each 3,002 psi.
Braking system: Hydraulic, on main units, with anti-skid. Drag-chute housed beneath the rudder.
Oxygen system: Gaseous.

Aircraft variants:
IAR-93A was the original Avioane production version built in single and two-seat forms. 3,970 lbf (17.66 kN) Viper Mk 632-41 non-augmented turbojets. Being updated to IAR-93B standard.
IAR-93B is the higher performing Avioane version, built in single and two-seat forms, with 5,030 lbf (22.37 kN) with afterburning Viper Mk 633-47 turbojets.
IJ-22 Orao *(Izvidac)* applied to early non-augmented Oraos used for training. 3,970 lbf (17.66 kN) Viper Mk 632-41s. Were being updated to Orao 2 standard.
NJ-22 Orao *(Nastavi)* was the early non-augmented version for reconnaissance. Were being updated to Orao 2 standard.
INJ-22 Orao *(Izvidac Nastavi)* applied to non-augmented aircraft for both reconnaissance and training. Were being updated to Orao 2 standard.
J-22 Orao 2 was the Soko-produced improved single-seater, installed with 5,030 lbf (22.37 kN) with afterburning Viper 633-41s. Greater fuel capacity.
NJ-22 Orao 2D was the Soko produced two-seat reconnaissance version, with the Viper 633-41s.

DETAILS FOR IAR-93/J-22.

Principal dimensions:
Wing span: 30 ft 6 ins (9.3 m)
Maximum length: 48 ft 11 ins (14.9 m) single-seaters, 50 ft 5.5 ins (15.38 m) for two-seaters
Maximum height: 14 ft 10 ins (4.52 m)

Wings:
Aerofoil section: Modified NACA 65A-008
Area: 279.9 sq ft (26 m^2)
Aspect ratio: 3.327
Sweepback: 35° at 25% chord
Chord at root: 19 ft 9.5 ins (4.2 m)
Chord at tip: 4 ft 7 ins (1.4 m)
Anhedral: 3.5°

Tail unit:
Tailplane span: 15 ft 1 ins (4.59 m)
Tailplane area: 78.684 sq ft (7.31 m^2)

Undercarriage:
Type: Retractable, with steerable nosewheel. Twin mainwheels
Main wheel tyre size: 615 x 225
Nose wheel tyre size: 450 x 190
Wheel base: 17 ft 8.5 ins (5.4 m)
Wheel track: 8 ft 2.5 ins (2.5 m)

Weights:
Empty, operating: 12,677 lb (5,750 kg) for IAR-93B, 12,125 lb (5,500 kg) for Orao
Maximum take-off: 24,030 lb (10,900 kg) for IAR-93B, 24,430 lb (11,080 kg) for Orao

Performance (IAR-93B at 18,518 lb; 8,400 kg) AUW:
Maximum speed: 586 kts (675 mph) 1,086 km/h
Stall speed: 148 kts (170 mph) 274 km/h
Take-off distance: 2,625 ft (800 m)
Landing distance: more than 3,300 ft (1,000 m)
Maximum climb rate: 12,795 ft (3,900 m) per minute
G limits: +8, -4.2
Ceiling: 44,300 ft (13,500 m)
Radius of action (Hi-Hi-Hi-Hi): 286 naut miles (330 miles) 530 km with a 2,205 lb (1,000 kg) bomb load and 1 drop tank

Special Electronic and Reconnaissance Aircraft

Note that this section details only special purpose-designed electronic warfare and reconnaissance aircraft, and not EW and reconnaissance sub-variants of operational combat aircraft (which can be found under the main aircraft headings in the Combat section). The only exceptions to this rule are ES-3A, electronic P-3s and EF-111A, all of which are particularly specialized. Highly specialized electronic variants of freighters and airliners are detailed here, but not electronic and other special helicopters, such as the Ka-31, which remain with all other helicopters in that section.

Embraer (Brazil)

Corporate address: See Combat section for full company details.
Prime contractor for the EMB-120EW/SR: Raytheon (see Development below).

Embraer EMB-120EW and SR

First delivery: 1997, to the Brazilian Air Force.
Role: *EMB-120EW*: Early warning as a remote sensor platform, to detect and track all kinds of aircraft within the surveillance area. *EMB-120SR*: Remote sensing, including exploitation of natural resources, environmental control, river pollution control, economic activities and ground occupation monitoring, and illegal activities surveillance.
Based on: EMB-120 Brasilia (see Airliners section). Structural changes for the installation of mission systems, including an over-fuselage radar scanner housing. Increased maximum take-off weight. More powerful APU.

★ Aims

★ To co-ordinate and support actions for the protection, rational exploitation of natural resources and sustained development of the Amazonian region.
★ In the EW system, data are transmitted real-time over VHF data-link. Target data from primary and secondary radar and communications scanner are combined. Final identification, situation evaluation and decisions are made in the 3 regional co-ordination centres (CRVs), to be established in the Amazonian region, and the central co-ordination centre will be stationed in Brasilia. Direction of intercept aircraft onto targets can be carried out from the aircraft or from the CRV.

▲ Development

▲ September 1994. News released. Embraer was selected by the Brazilian Government to develop these versions under the SIVAM-Sistema de Vigilância da Amazônia (Amazon Surveillance System) programme.

Embraer EMB-120EW

▲ Development is in co-ordination with Raytheon of the USA, the prime contractor. Raytheon is providing Brazil with an advanced Air Traffic Control (ATC) environmental surveillance and early warning system. A communications network, remote earth-sensing satellite information, and other ground and airborne sensor systems will form the SIVAM system.
Users: 5 EMB-120EWs and 3 EMB-120SRs initially.
Crew: 2 pilots and 1 to 3 system operators, depending on the mission. All information in the command and control system is available on all 3 work stations, which are programmable to allow an operator to use any station.
Radar: *EMB-120EW* will use a new-generation Ericsson Erieye surveillance radar. Major differences from the version used by the Swedish Air Force are optimization to lower speed targets and adaptation of the man-machine interface to the roles of the SIVAM operators. Radar control functions are to be performed in the aircraft instead of at ground centres, in case the data link to the ground centres fails or is out of range. All changes are software related. The Erieye pulse-doppler radar has coverage to about 82,000 ft (25,000 m) altitude and at ranges exceeding 162 naut miles (186 miles) 300 km. Mission avionics system creates a real-time air situation picture for local display as well as for transmission to the ground-based CRV. *EMB-120SR* will have a Synthetic Aperture Radar (SAR). This will provide all-weather day and night maps of the ground over all terrain, allowing observation, classification, localization and eventual movement over ground and water.
Other mission sensors: The *EMB-120EW* will have an on-board command and control system with 3 multi-function operator work stations, plus a communications and non-communications exploitation system (COMMS/ NON-COMMS). The *EMB-120SR* will have an ultraviolet/visible/infra-red line scanner, high-sensitivity TV/FLIR and a COMMS/NON-COMMS system. Line scanner allows a high-resolution image and simultaneously collects and records up to 6 spectral bands.
Fuel system: Adoption of an additional fuel tank.
Flight avionics/instrumentation: Adoption of new navigation and communication systems, including laser gyro, GPS, FMS and data link.
Aircraft variants: See Role.

de Havilland Inc. (Canada)

Corporate address: Unit of Bombardier Aerospace Group, Bombardier Inc (see Airliner section for all company details).

de Havilland E-9A and CT-142

Role: *E-9A:* Airborne over-the-horizon telemetry relay, to relay manned/unmanned air vehicle control data, and gather data, during missile trials at the Gulf Test Range. Also used to sea-search for intruders during tests. Can relay data from 5 pairs of vehicles flying at over Mach 5. *CT-142*: Navigation trainer.
Based on: DHC-8 Dash 8M series 100.
Users: Canada (4 CT-142s) and USA (USAF 2, operated by the 475th Weapons Evaluation Group at Tyndall AFB, Florida).
Crew: *E-9A:* 2 pilots and a systems operator.
Radar: *E-9A*: AN/APS-128D sea surveillance radar in an underfuselage radome. *CT-142:* Mapping radar in the extended nose.
Other mission sensors: *E-9A*: 5 beam, 75 ft (22.86 m) steerable phased-array telemetry antenna in a box fairing on the starboard side of the fuselage.

de Havilland E-9A with its steerable phased-array telemetry antenna exposed

Shaanxi Aircraft Company (China)

Corporate address: See Airliners section for full company details.

Shaanxi Y8AEW?

Note: It is known that China is developing an AEW aircraft, using foreign assistance with the radar and installation. Varied reports suggest the Y8 or Ilyushin Il-76 as the carrier aircraft. Either is possible, but the Y8 may be more likely, as it is built in China.
First flight: 1994-95?
Role: Airborne early warning and control.
Based on: See Note above.

▲ Development

▲ 1993. Representatives from GEC-Marconi visited China to present details of the Argus S-band AEW radar system (see UK).
Radar: Manufacturer uncertain but possibly GEC-Marconi, with likely programme participation by China Leihua Electronic Technology Research Institute. S-band, probably mounted in nose and tail positions (not over the fuselage) to avoid interference from the airframe, each with a 180° scan in azimuth.

Daimler-Benz Aerospace AG (Germany)

Corporate address: See Combat section for full company details.

Dornier 228 special missions versions

Role: Day/night maritime patrol, border patrol and surveillance, pollution control, aerial survey and mapping.
Based on: Dornier 228 (see Airliners section).
Radar: See Aircraft variants.
Other mission sensors: See Aircraft variants.
Aircraft variants:
Border patrol version has an integrated sensor suite comprising a stabilized long-range observation system (SLOS), FLIR (with a gimballed sensor head under the fuselage), remotely stabilized (Forward Motion Compensation) aerial survey camera in a floor cut-out and which can be controlled by a viewfinder/navigation sight (with 4 different lens assemblies, and interfaced to the VLF-Omega navigation system to provide navigational data on the film), night vision goggles, plus work stations for sensor control and real-time imagery exploitation, data recording, communications equipment, and C-band real-time air-to-ground data link. SLOS consists of a stabilized telescope unit (STU) with remote-mounted joystick, 2 monitors for image display which are coupled to the video tape recorder, interface to the VLF-Omega navigation system (to allow annotation of the images with the navigation data), turret for the STU, and SLOS operator console. Colour weather radar.
Maritime patrol version is offered with AlliedSignal RDR-1500B, Thorn EMI Super Searcher, Litton APS-504(V)5, or Eaton APS-128 surveillance radar. Other optional equipment includes FLIR, SLOS, night vision goggles, camera, searchlight, smoke markers and flares, etc. Also built in India by HAL for the Indian Navy and Coast Guard, originally with Thorn EMI Marec 2 radar; Super Marec radars were ordered by India for both upgrading Indian maritime patrol aircraft and equipping new anti-shipping 228s (27 radars ordered by mid-1994).
Aerial survey/mapping versions have the options (as appropriate) of cameras, stabilized telescope unit (STU), VLF magnetometer in nose radome, tail and wingtip positions (or proton at wingtips), and gamma ray detector.

Dornier 228 Maritime Patrol version operated by the Royal Thai Navy

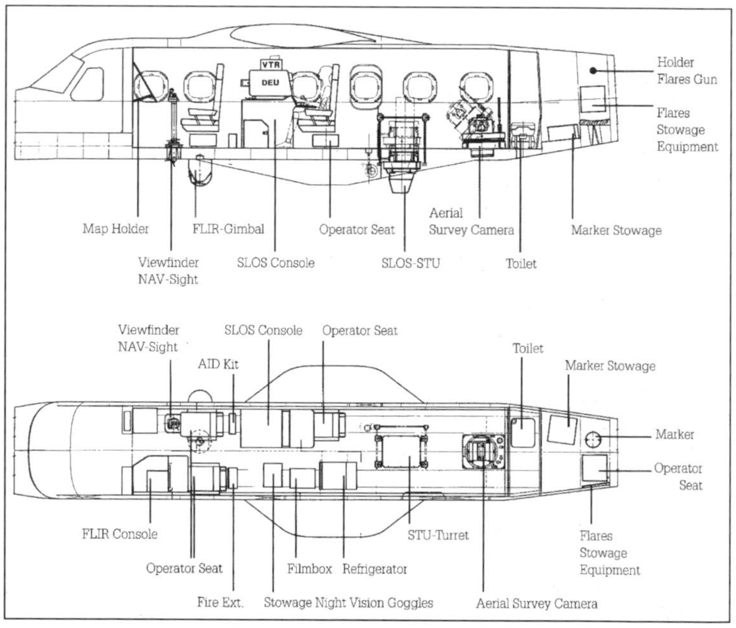

Dornier 228 Border Patrol layout (courtesy Daimler-Benz Aerospace)

Burkhart Grob Luft- und Raumfahrt GmbH & Co KG (Germany)

Corporate address: Am Flugplatz, 86874 Tussenhausen-Mattsies.
Telephone: +49 8268 998-0
Facsimile: +49 8268 998-114
Telex: 539623 grobf d
Founded: 1971.
Employees: About 2,800.

● Activities

● See also General Aviation and Glider sections.

DIVISIONS

Grob-Werke GmbH & Co KG
Mindelheim and München.

Grob Systems Inc
Bluffton, OH 45817, USA.

B. Grob do Brasil S/A
Sao Paulo, Brazil.

Grob G-520 Egrett and Strato 1

First flight: 24 June 1987 (Egrett 1).
Role: Strato 1 is a high-altitude/long-duration mission platform for a variety of applications, including research.

▲ Development

▲The name Egrett came from the 3 companies co-operating in development of the proof-of-concept aircraft, namely E-Systems (of Greenville, Texas, USA), Grob and Garrett (since AlliedSignal).
▲ 1986. Development began.
▲ 1 September 1988. Egrett 1 POC aircraft set world records for altitude, time-to-altitude and duration.
▲ 20 April 1989. First Egrett 2 flew equipped with pressurized cabin, lightning protection, retractable undercarriage and ice protection systems.
▲ 22 March 1991. LBA certification of D-500 Egrett 2, followed by FAA of the G-520 Egrett 2 on 13 September, and LBA of the G-520T on 22 December 1993.
▲ 31 March 1994. G-520 Strato 1 set 2 more world records (1,000 kg to 15,150 m).
Users: Present family comprises 4 single-seat and a two-seater, as 2 D-500 Egrett 2s, 2 G-520 Strato 1s (Grob and E-Systems operated) and the G-520T 2-seater. Egrett 1 Proof-of-concept aircraft is not operated. According to latest reports, a G-520 had been sold in late 1995 to FTN Atlas (unconfirmed).
Details: G-520 Strato 1.
Crew: Pilot, or 2 in G-520T (raised rear seat). S-1031 pressure suit for flights above 25,000 ft (7,620 m).
Cockpit: Maximum pressurization differential 6 psi.
Mission equipment: 6 payload compartments in the

Grob G-520 Strato 1 with winglets (courtesy Grob)

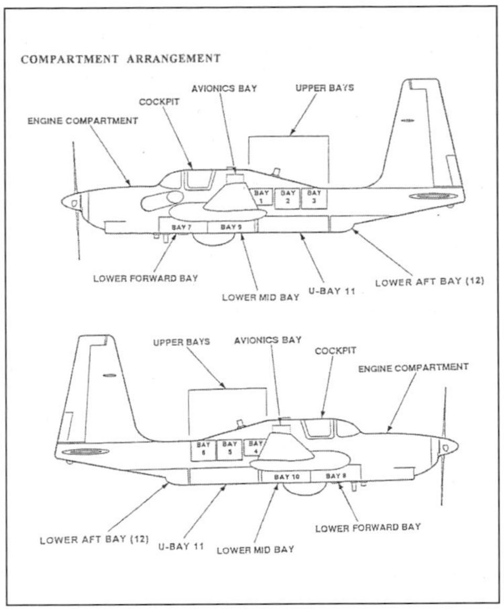

Grob G-520 Strato 1 equipment compartment arrangement (courtesy Grob)

upper fuselage, 4 in the lower forward fuselage sides, an aft fuselage bay (number 12 on the drawing) and the main removable U-shaped bay (number 11) as part of the lower centre fuselage. Capacities in mm/kg: 1 and 4 (615 x 940 x 450/68), 2 and 5 (625 x 940 x 415 or 540/102), 3 and 6 (645 x 940 x 545/102), 7 and 8 (1,450 x 250 x 500/68), 9 and 10 (1,100 x 250 x 500/68), 12 (1,000 x 750 x 530/22) and 11 (1,950 x 800 x 530/238).
Wing characteristics: Mid-mounted, high aspect ratio. Removable wingtips, allowing winglets. Inner section fairings to house undercarriage.
Wing control surfaces: Ailerons, split flaps and leading-edge slats.
Tail control surfaces: Horn-balanced elevators and rudder, all with tabs.
Flight control system: Mechanical/manual.
Construction materials: Composites.
Engine: AlliedSignal TPE331-14F-801L turboprop, with a Hartzell HC-E4P-5/E11990K 4-blade propeller.
Engine rating: Derated to 750 shp (559.3 kW) continuous.
Fuel system: 1,117 litres, of which 1,090 litres are usable. Optional 1,382 litres (1,355 litres usable).
Flight avionics/instrumentation: AlliedSignal Bendix/King KFC325 flight director and autopilot system standard. Tacan, UHF, IFF/SIF, nav/com and identification equipment optional.
Electrical system: DC supply as a 250 amp starter-generator, 24 volt lead-acid battery, 24 volt sealed lead-acid emergency battery, and DC external power connection. AC supply as 115 volt, 400 Hz 3-phase generator (10kVA, or 40 kVA optionally), 250 volt inverter and external power connection.
Oxygen system: 10 litre liquid system (LOX), with pressurized oxygen for emergency supply.
Aircraft variants: See Users.

DETAILS FOR G-520 STRATO 1, *WITH 520T IN ITALICS (WHERE DIFFERENT).*

Principal dimensions:
Wing span: 108 ft 3 ins (33 m)
Maximum length: 39 ft 4.5 ins (12 m), *44 ft 10 ins (13.67 m)*
Maximum height: 18 ft 8 ins (5.68 m), *18 ft 7 ins (5.66 m)*

Wings:
Aerofoil section: Modified Eppler E580
Area: 427.08 sq ft (39.677 m^2)
Aspect ratio: 27.445

Undercarriage:
Type: Retractable, with steerable nosewheel. Operation from unpaved runways is not authorized
Wheel base: 12 ft 2 ins (3.71 m), *14 ft (4.26 m)*
Wheel track: 15 ft 4 ins (4.68 m), *15 ft (4.57 m)*
Turning radius: 14 ft 3 ins (4.35 m)

Weights:
Empty: 6,393 lb (2,700 kg)
Maximum take-off: 10,362 lb (4,700 kg)
Maximum landing: 9,843 lb (4,465 kg)

Performance:
Maximum operating speed: Mach 0.448 or 153 kts (176 mph) 283 km/h IAS
Recommended rotation speed: 65-77 kts (75-89 mph) 120-143 km/h IAS
Recommended climb speed: 95 kts (109 mph) 176 km/h IAS from sea level to 30,000 ft (9,145 m), reducing by 1 kts per 1,000 ft (305 m) thereafter.
Stall speed: 66 kts (76 mph) 123 km/h *clean*, 60 kts (69 mph) 111 km/h *with flaps*
Take-off distance: 1,000 ft (305 m) at 9,370 lb (4,250 kg) AUW
Time to climb from 10,000 to 35,000 ft (3,050 to 10,670 m): 21 minutes at maximum weight
G limits: +3.28, -1.31 *clean*
Ceiling: 52,500 ft (16,000 m)
Range with full fuel: 1,930 naut miles (2,222 miles) 3,574 km
Duration: 13 hours, *11 hours*

Grob Strato 2C

First flight: 31 March 1995 (in proof of concept form, without mission avionics fitted).
Role: High-altitude, long-duration atmospheric/stratospheric/climatic research, earth observation and communications.

▲ Development

▲ Built under contract from the Deutsche Forschungsanstalt für Luft- und Raumfahrt (DLR). IABG is responsible for the propulsion system and sub-systems.
▲ April 1992. Design initiated, with manufacture of airframe moulds starting in mid-November.
▲ April 1993. Construction began, initially the tailplane.
▲ 1994. Construction completed and engine installation undertaken.
▲ 1995. Mission avionics fit completed, with hand-over in about October.
Users: DLR (see Development).
Crew: 2 pilots and 2 scientists.
Cockpit/cabin: Pressure cabin (including flight deck), with work stations for scientists. Toilet, galley and rest facilities.
Mission equipment: Currently available equipment includes cryogen collectors for air samples, pyranometers and pyrgeometers, scanning radiometers, mass spectrometers, and sensors for pressure, temperature and wind measurement. New equipment might include infra-red interferometers, microwave radiometers and scanners, long-distance absorption cells, active chemical ionization spectrometers, optical multi-zone analyzers, Lyman alpha equipment, light detection and ranging (LIDAR), and fast ozone probes.
Wing characteristics: High mounted, straight, with dihedral. Winglets. High aspect ratio, low wing loading.
Wing control surfaces: Ailerons with tabs, outboard spoilers, and 2-section speed brakes.
Tail control surfaces: T-tail with horn-balanced elevators and rudder, with tabs.
Flight control system: Mechanical.
Construction materials: Composites, mainly carbonfibre but also glassfibre and aramid reinforced plastics.
Engines: Compound propulsion system, suited to very high altitude. 2 Teledyne Continental TSIOL-550 turbocharged piston engines with reduction gearboxes. Each engine has an additional 2-stage turbocharger with intercooler to maintain power at a constant level up to 78,740 ft (24,000 m) altitude. 5-blade pusher propellers of 19 ft 8 ins (6 m) diameter.
Engine rating: Each 402.3 hp (300 kW).
Fuel system: 12,566 lb (5,700 kg).

DETAILS FOR STRATO 2C.

Principal dimensions:
Wing span: 185 ft 4.5 ins (56.5 m)
Fuselage length: 78 ft 9 ins (24 m)
Pressure cabin length: 18 ft 2.5 ins (5.55 m)
Fuselage diameter: 7 ft 6.5 ins (2.3 m)

Wings:
Aerofoil section: Laminar flow, high lift.
Area: 1,614.59 (150 m^2)

Aspect ratio: 21.28

Weights:
Empty: 14,660 lb (6,650 kg)
Maximum take-off: 29,432 lb (13,350 kg)
Payload: 2,205 lb (1,000 kg), or 331 lb (150 kg) to 85,300 ft (26,000 m) altitude

Performance:
Ceiling: 52,500-85,300 ft (16,000-26,000 m), *design 78,740 ft (24,000 m)*

Range with full fuel: 9,773 naut miles (11,246 miles) 18,100 km
Typical long-range mission: 2,205 lb (1,000 kg) payload and 12,346 lb (5,600 kg) of fuel (220 lb, 100 kg reserve), cruising at 186 kts (214 mph) 345 km/h at 59,000 ft (18,000 m), offering a 48 hour duration
Duration: 48 hours at 59,000 ft (18,000 m) altitude, 8 hours at 24,000 m

Grob Strato 2C (courtesy Grob)

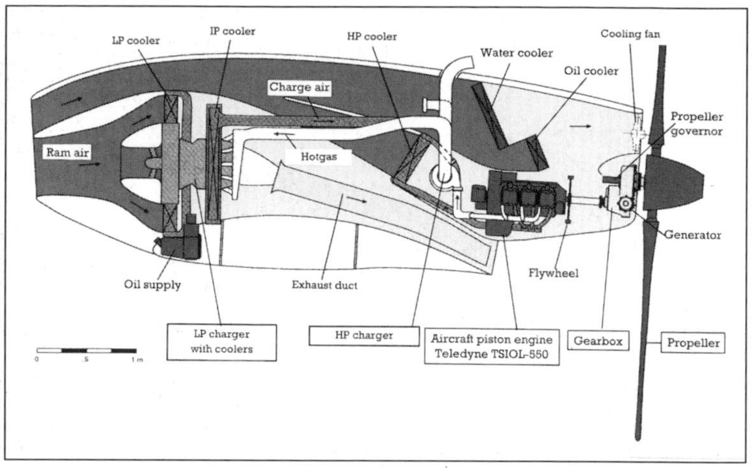

Grob Strato 2C compound propulsion system (courtesy Grob)

Hindustan Aeronautics Limited (HAL) (India)

Corporate address: See Combat section for full company details.

Hal (BAe) 748 ASWAC and CABS Phase II A320/B737

First flight: 5 November 1990 (ASWAC for aerodynamic trials).
Role: ASWAC technology demonstrator. Based on British Aerospace 748 airliner (ASWAC).

▲ Development

▲ 1985. Development was initiated by the Aerospace Surveillance Warning and Control (ASWAC) organization, under the auspices of the Defence Research and Development Organization. Modification of the borrowed 748 took place at the Aeronautical Development Establishment (ADE) in Bangalore. The above-fuselage rotating "saucer" radome was designed and manufactured jointly with MBB of Germany. However, the aircraft had no surveillance radar, nor other substantial mission equipment or sensors. Phase II of the programme was to be an ASWAC system on a Boeing 737, Airbus A320 or similar transport.
▲1989-90. ASWAC programme "went on hold", though some flying took place from 1990, but work on an ASWAC system continues at low pace at the Centre for Airborne Systems (CABS) at Bangalore.

HAL/BAe 748 ASWAC technology demonstrator landing at Bangalore Airport (Pushpindar Singh/VAYU)

Iraqi Air Force (Iraq)

Address: Baghdad.

Baghdad-1 and Adnan-1

Aircraft variants:
Baghdad-1 was the first indigenous AEW conversion of a Russian Ilyushin Il-76 transport in Iraqi Air Force service, making its public debut in 1989. Fitted with a locally-produced Thomson-CSF Tigre-G radar, with signal processor and ESM modifications to make it suitable for its new airborne application, installed (inverted) in the aircraft's tail-ramp position, with a glassfibre radome over the antennae. Scan coverage has been reported at better than 180°. Rear strakes were fitted to counteract any induced instability. Real-time data link.
Adnan-1 followed Baghdad-1 as a more sophisticated conversion of the Il-76, suited to full AWACS (able to vector friendly aircraft onto detected targets). Flight trials began on 15 December 1990. The most important feature is the above-fuselage rotating "saucer" radome, housing 2 antennae to provide full 360° coverage. 3 Adnan-1s are known to have been produced, of which 2 are in Iran. The fate of the third, damaged in 1991, is unclear.

Israel Aircraft Industries Ltd (IAI) (Israel)

Corporate address: See Combat section for company details.

IAI (Bedek Aviation Division) Phalcon

First flight: 12 May 1993
First delivery: 2 May 1995.

Role: Airborne early warning, and intelligence.
Based on: First conversion based on a Boeing 707-320C.

▲ Development

▲ Co-operation with Elta of IAI's Electronics Division has produced the Phalcon radar system, suited for installation on aircraft of varying sizes.
Users: A Chilean Air Force B707-320C has been converted to Phalcon configuration, handed over in May 1994 but returned for further work, with redelivery a year later. It is rumoured that 2 South African B707-320 tanker/transports have been installed with some elements of the system, including only the fuselage-side antennae. Other air forces showing interest are the Italian and Israeli. IAI is reportedly looking into the possibility of adapting the Airbus A321 as a Phalcon system carrier.
Crew: Flight crew, plus operators for 11 mission stations, each having 2 graphic colour displays and associated equipment. Stations comprise 5 radar, 2 communications/communications intelligence, 2 electronic intelligence/electronic support measures, and data link management.
Radar: Elta EL/M-2075 L-band radar, with up to 6 conformal airframe-mounted solid-state phased arrays (carried in 4 separate fuselage side fairings, 1 under the tail and 1 in the nose radome). Each electronically-scanned array covers a given sector in azimuth and elevation, thereby requiring all 6 arrays to provide 360° coverage. Partial fits are considered suitable to certain applications, and it is believed the Chilean B707-320C was originally delivered with 3 arrays. Maximum radar range is reportedly 215 naut miles (249 miles) 400 km, though this would depend on the profile of the targets.
Other mission sensors: Monopulse IFF, integrated with the radar arrays. Elta EL/L-8312 ESM/elint with wingtip, nose and tail antennae, Elta HF/UHF/VHF communications intelligence and other systems, with MIL-STD-1553B databus.

IAI (Bedek) Phalcon system fitted to a B707-320C, with 3 antennae only in forward fuselage sides and nose positions, providing a reported 260° scan coverage

Fokker (Netherlands)

Full name: N.V. Koninklijke Nederlandse Vliegtuigenfabriek Fokker.
Corporate address: See Combat section for company details.

● Activities

● See also Combat (for Maritime Enforcer Mk 2) and Airliners sections.

Fokker Black Crow Mk 2

Role: Signal intelligence (sigint), capable of communication intelligence (comint) and electronic intelligence (elint).
Based on: Fokker 50.
Mission equipment: Sigint system, integrated with the required subsystems, enables automatic real-time acquisition, identification, direction finding, geolocation, analysis and recording of radar transmissions in the 0.5 to 18 GHz frequency range, and computer-directed search, interception, direction finding, geolocation, analysis and recording of communications signals in the 20 to 1,000 MHz frequency range. The computer assists command and control for data fusion, geographic presentation, interactive operator tasking based on scenario recognition, automatic logging/reporting, and interpretation. Post mission processing and reporting can be performed in the aircraft.
Engines: 2 Pratt & Whitney Canada PW125B or PW127B turboprops (see Fokker 50 entry in the Airliners section), driving 6-blade Dowty Aerospace carbonfibre propellers.
Fuel system: 7,450 litres internally. 2 optional drop tanks, each 938 litres.

Fokker KingBird Mk 2

Role: Airborne early warning and airborne command and control.
Based on: Fokker 50.

★ Aims

★ Typical "time-on-station" of 8 hours, 300 naut miles (345 miles) 555 km from base (ISA + 20).
Crew: 2 pilots on the flight deck and operator consoles in the cabin for the mission commander and 3 systems operators.
Radar: Ericsson Erieye, featuring S-band frequency, low sidelobe phased array antenna (26 ft, 8 m aperture) in an overfuselage box radome, electronic scanning and adaptive sidelobe cancelling, adaptive mode selection, pulse compression, frequency agility, Doppler processing (low and medium PRF), and automatic target tracking. Detection ranges are 190 naut miles for a fighter-bomber, and 80 naut miles for a cruise missile. It also provides surveillance of low-flying aircraft, with height finding and helicopter classification, and surveillance of low radar-cross-section targets. Its primary functions are search and tracking of multiple air, sea and landborne targets.
Mission equipment: Sensor suite comprises the surveillance radar (see Radar), IFF interrogator, and electronic support missions (ESM) to detect/analyze/identify transmitting radars in the 0.5 to 18 GHz frequency range. The common display and control capability provided by the central tactical system (CTS)

Fokker KingBird Mk 2 (courtesy Fokker)

makes efficient coverage of airspace possible, with different search areas allocated to the relevant systems operators.
Engines and Fuel system: As above.

Fokker Maritime Mk 2

Role: Maritime and coastal surveillance, fishery and oilfield protection, anti-smuggling, search and rescue, and pollution control.
Based on: Fokker 50, as an unarmed variant of the Maritime Enforcer Mk 2.

★ Aims

⋆ Similar to the Maritime Enforcer Mk 2 (see in Combat section), but unarmed.
⋆ Typical 12 hour duration, ample cruise speed, and the ability to fly "low and slow" when required.

▲ Development

▲ Based on experience with the F27 Maritime (as operated by Netherlands, Nigeria, Pakistan, Peru, Philippines, Spain and Thailand).
Radar: Texas Instruments AN/APS-134 search radar, with track-while-scan.
Other mission sensors: Infra-red detection system (IRDS) for passive night identification/tracking.
Flight avionics/instrumentation: Dual mode INS and integrated GPS. HF/VHF/UHF communications to permit exchange of information with co-operating sea, air and ground forces in addition to civil/ATC authorities.
Engines and **Fuel system:** As above.

Fokker Sentinel Mk 2

Role: Border surveillance and reconnaissance.
Based on: Fokker 50.

★ Aims

⋆ Long-range operation, of over 2,000 naut miles (2,303 miles) 3,700 km per mission.
Radar: Motorola APS-135(V) side-looking airborne multi-mission radar (SLAMMR), capable of detecting moving targets beyond the line-of-sight of ground positions, or detecting cleared forests and military sites, using Doppler Moving Target Indication (MTI) processing. Detection range of moving vehicles is up to 81 naut miles (93 miles) 150 km, or shorter range for moving troops. Alternatively Texas Instruments APS-134(V)7 synthetic aperture radar.
Other mission sensors: Stand-off Electro-Optical (EO) imaging using a pod-mounted reconnaissance system. For real-time viewing at command-post level, a radio link can be made available for instant transmission of EO data.
Engines and **Fuel system:** As above.

Fokker Maritime Mk 2 (courtesy Fokker)

Fokker Sentinel Mk 2 SLAMMR and EO pods (courtesy Fokker)

Beriev Joint-Stock Company (Russia)

Corporate address: See Combat section for all company details.

Beriev A-50 and 976 (NATO name *Mainstay*)

First flight: 19 December 1978.
Role: Strategic airborne early warning and control aircraft.
Based on: Ilyushin Il-76 *Candid*.

★ Aims

⋆ To replace the Tu-126 *Moss*, based around the new Shmel radar system.
⋆ Effective operation over land and sea.

▲ Development

▲ 1965. Vega radar design bureau started work on the Shmel AEW&C system (chief designer of the system was Vladimir Ivanov, radar by V. Pogreshayev, and on-board computer by O. Rezepov).
▲ 1984. Initial operational capability.
▲ 1987. First photo-graphs published.
▲ August 1992. Presented for the first time in public (MosAeroshow in Zhukovsky).
Sales/users: Manufactured at Taganrog. About 15 in service with Russian Air Defence Troops, providing interception data to the latest Russian defence fighters. Also available to tactical forces. Production and development continues. The A-50 was used during the Gulf conflict of 1991; 2 crews under command of Major Alexei Serebrov and Major Vasili Kubasov flew by rotation over the Black Sea to monitor the situation and track cruise missiles.

Beriev A-50 Mainstay AEW&C aircraft with Sukhoi fighter escort. Note the added stub wings, fin-root intake, displaced rear gun turret, and Shmel radar antenna dome (Piotr Butowski)

Beriev 976, a civil derivative of the A-50, of which 5 have been built (Piotr Butowski)

Flight crew: 4.
Mission crew: 11 systems operators.
Radar: Rotating dome of 32 ft 10 ins (10 m) diameter and 8 ft 2 ins (2.5 m) maximum thickness carried above the fuselage, housing the Shmel radar S-band antenna. Rotation rate is 6 revolutions per minute. The radar can track up to 150 targets simultaneously; search range is 108-216 naut miles (124-248 miles) 200-400 km for fighter size targets at low altitude, and 162-324 naut miles (186-373 miles) 300-600 km for targets at high altitude.
Other mission sensors: Metre and decametre wave-length data link of 189 naut miles (217 miles) 350 km range, or unlimited range via a satellite. New type of IFF.
Self-protection systems: Oborona warning system and packs of chaff/flares on the fuselage sides.
Fixed weapons: None.
Expendable weapons and equipment: None.
Flight refuelling probe: On the nose, ahead of the cockpit. See Aircraft variants – A-50.
Aircraft variants:
A-50 *Mainstay*, as detailed. Based on the Il-76 transport but stretched using a plug ahead of the wings, no nose glazing, stub-wings added to the undercarriage nacelles and small surfaces near the fuselage tail (both undoubtedly to help prevent known buffeting during flight refuelling operations), and a fin-root air intake to cool the avionics.
A-50M is an updated version with the Shmel-2 radar system and more powerful computer.
A-50U is a projected improved version, with Shmel-M radar.
976 is a civil derivative, used as a control and data recording station during the tests flights of aircraft at the Flight Test Institute in Zhukovsky. It has, unlike the A-50, the glazed nose of the Il-76, but no in-flight refuelling capability and thereby no added aerodynamic surfaces at the undercarriage nacelle and fuselage tail. 5 built in the latter 1980s, but possibly only 1 in current use.

Details for A-50.
Typical patrol altitude: 32,810 ft (10,000 m)
*See Ilyushin Il-76 for general details in the Airliners section

Ilyushin Aviation Complex (Russia)

Corporate address: See Combat section for all company details.

Ilyushin Il-20 and Il-24 (NATO name *Coot-A*)

Role: Reconnaissance, electronic intelligence (elint), and communications relay; at present used mainly as an ordinary passenger/VIP aircraft.
Based on: Ilyushin Il-18D *Coot.*

★ Aims
★To produce a fuel-efficient and thereby long-range EW aircraft, at low cost by modifying an existing airliner airframe.

▲ Development
▲ 1978. Identified in the West.
Sales/users: Built at the Znamya Truda plant (now MAPO) in Moscow in the mid-1970s. Russian Air Force has a few, including those with the 390 Independent Reconnaissance Aviation Squadron. See Role.
Radar: Nit (thread) side-looking radar, designed at the Vega bureau, housed inside the cylindrical 32 ft 10 ins (10 m) long fairing under the forward fuselage. Wave length 2 cm. Vega Igla (needle) phased array side-looking radar with antennae on the sides of the nose in long radomes.
Other mission sensors: Electronic intelligence sensors with small bulge antennae under the rear of the fuselage.
Fixed weapons: None.
Expendable weapons and equipment: None.
Engines: 4 Ivchenko PROGRESS AI-20M turboprops.
Engine rating: Each 4,250 ehp (3,169 ekW).
Flight refuelling probe: None.
Aircraft variants:
Il-20 Coot-A is the base version, as described.
Il-20M has improved mission systems.
Il-20RT is used by the Russian Space Forces as a data collecting and relay point when ICBMs and space missiles are launched. 32 ft 10 ins (10 m) long (approximately) canoe type fairing above the centre fuselage. Nit, Igla and other sensors removed. 4 based at the Leninsk airfield near the Baykonur cosmodrome.
Il-22 Coot-B airborne command post – see Myasishchev.
Il-24N is the civil derivative of the Il-20, used for over-sea fishery observation. Nit radar retained, but Igla radar and elint sensors removed.

Details for Il-20 Coot-A.

Principal dimensions:
Wing span: 122 ft 9 ins (37.42 m)
Maximum length: 117 ft 9 ins (35.9 m)
Maximum height: 33 ft 4 ins (10.17 m)

Wings:
Area, gross: 1,507 sq ft (140 m^2)
Aspect ratio: 10.002

Weights (approx):
Empty, operating: 77,162 lb (35,000 kg)
Maximum take-off: 141,095 lb (64,000 kg)

Performance (approx):
Cruising speed: 324 kts (373 mph) 600 km/h
Take-off distance: about 4,265 ft (1,300 m)
Range with maximum fuel: 3,240 naut miles (3,728 miles) 6,000 km

Ilyushin Il-20 Coot-A (Alexei Mikheyev via Piotr Butowski)

Ilyushin Il-76 Relay Aircraft (not Il-92 – see note)

Ilyushin Il-76 relay aircraft (Piotr Butowski)

Ilyushin Il-76 relay aircraft showing the 2 blade-type aerials and trailing wire communications antenna point at the rear of the fuselage (Piotr Butowski)

Note: It is now known that this relay conversion of the Il-76 is not designated Il-92. Other quoted designations have included the Il-82.
Role: Communication relay aircraft associated with the Il-86 command post.
Based on: Ilyushin Il-76MD.

▲ Development
▲ 1992. Seen by Western observers at the Zhukovsky test centre (see Sales/users).
Sales/users: 2 aircraft built, civil registered Aeroflot Il-76MD *CCCP-76450* and *76451*. Formerly used for airborne data collecting at the flight test centre in Zhukovsky. Now used as relay aircraft for Il-86

command posts, usually based at Chkalovskaya outside Moscow, but recently seen back at the factory.
Mission equipment: The most outstanding feature of its external appearance (like the Il-86 command post) is a large canoe-shaped fairing containing a set of aerials, above the forward fuselage. 2 x AI-24 turbine engines are used to supply power for the onboard equipment, installed in long undercarriage nacelles. 2 additional long and narrow fairings are installed under the front fuselage and 2 more ahead of the tailfin. A trailing wire antenna with stabilization cone, used for low frequency radio communication, is released from beneath the rear fuselage. A sword-type aerial is fitted each side of the wire antenna. Streamlined containers, with long forward protruding rods, are installed under the wing tips. The usual nose glazing of the Il-76 has been deleted.

Ilyushin Il-86(?) Maxdome strategic airborne command post (Piotr Butowski)

Ilyushin Il-86 (NATO name *Maxdome* – see note)

Note: It is now known that this command post conversion of the Il-86 airliner has its own designation, but this was not available for publication at the time of writing.
First flight: Summer 1985.
Role: Strategic command post, subordinated to the General Staff of the Russian Armed Forces.
Based on: Ilyushin Il-86 airliner.

▲ Development
▲ Summer 1985. First flight.
▲ 5 March 1987. First flight of a fully equipped prototype.
▲ 1992. Noticed by Western observers at the Zhukovsky test centre.
Sales/users: 4 aircraft converted, all with civil markings and registered *RA-86146* to *RA-86149*. Usually based on Chkalovskaya airfield outside Moscow.
Mission equipment: The most outstanding external feature is a large canoe-shaped fairing on top of the front fuselage. The first 2 (*-146* and *-147*) have large sword-type aerials installed in various positions on the fuselage, particularly in the upper section, whilst the remaining 2 have small aerials. Longitudinal fairings are mounted in front of the tailfin and under the rear part of the fuselage. Extremely long trailing wire antenna is used for very low frequency radio (for instance, for communication with submerged submarines), released from the pod installed on the port side of the rear fuselage. See Self-protection systems.
Self-protection systems: A large, cigar shaped container is suspended near the root of each wing. The air intakes suggest electronic equipment, probably an electronic warfare system.
Flight refuelling probe: Fitted.

MAPO-MiG (Russia)

Corporate address: See Combat section for company details.

Mikoyan 301 and 321

Role: Projected hypersonic aircraft, probably for reconnaissance.

▲ Development
▲ Work began in the mid 1980s. Programme may now be terminated.
Construction materials: Mainly steel and titanium.
Engines: Conventional jet engines (not cryogenic fuel).

Performance:
Maximum operating Mach number: Mach 4
Maximum speed: 2,430 kts (2,796 mph) 4,500 km/h

Myasishchev Design Bureau (Russia)

Corporate address: See Combat section for full company details.

Myasishchev Il-22 (NATO name *Coot-B*)

Role: Airborne command post.
Based on: Ilyushin Il-18D airframe.

▲ Development
▲ Conversion of the Il-18D airliner, undertaken by Myasishchev.
Users: A dozen or so aircraft were converted and are used by the Russian armed forces. The mission equipment has been modernized many times. All Il-22/Il-22Ms are flying in civil Aeroflot markings and inscribed Il-18.
Mission equipment: Il-22 can be identified by the bullet-shaped fairing on top of the tailfin, and the shallow pod under the fuselage, about 65 ft 8 ins (20 m) long for the Il-22 and about 29 ft 7 ins (9 m) for the Il-22M. Numerous other blade-type antennae can be seen on the fuselage.
Aircraft variants:
Il-22 and Il-22M, as detailed above.

Myasishchev Il-22M (with civil Il-18 markings), featuring a shorter underfuselage antenna housing than the Il-22 (Piotr Butowski)

Myasishchev M-17 and M-55 (NATO name *Mystic*)

First flight: 26 May 1982 (M-17); piloted by Eduard Cheltsov.
Role: M-17 role is high-altitude reconnaissance aircraft, a component of a Russian reconnaissance and strike system equivalent to the US Assault Breaker or Precision Location Strike System. The system consists of the high altitude aircraft used for reconnaissance and target indication, a ground control post, launchers for surface-to-surface missiles, and strike aircraft. Due to real-time updating of reconnaissance information, the accuracy of hit is better than several metres. Ecological monitoring for M-55.

★ Aims
★ 5 hours operation at an altitude of 55,775 ft (17,000 m), with long loiter.
★ 3,307 lb (1,500 kg) of interchangeable reconnaissance and data transfer equipment.
★ Basing at second-category airfield (concrete).

▲ Development
▲ 1970. Start of work on the M-17 high-altitude balloon interceptor, intended to intercept US unmanned reconnaissance balloons.
▲ December 1978. Loss of the M-17 prototype before its first flight.
▲ 26 May 1982. First flight of the M-17 (civil

Myasishchev M-17RM (M-55) Mystic-B at Berlin Shoenefeld in June 1994 (Piotr Butowski)

registration *CCCP-17103*).

▲ 1982. M-17 detected in the West and provisionally named Ram-M.

▲ 16 September 1988. First flight of the M-17RM (M-55) reconnaissance aircraft (registration *CCCP-01552*, now *RF-01552*). Piloted by Eduard Cheltsov.

▲ 1989. M-17 (*CCCP-17103*) displayed at the Monino museum.

▲ 28 March-14 May 1990. M-17 (*CCCP-17401*) sets 25 world records in sub-class C-1i/j.

▲ November 1993. M-55 was shown for the first time abroad (in Italy). ILS-80 system installed for flights abroad. Displayed at the Farnborough Air Show in the UK the following year.

Sales/users: First prototype M-17-1 was built at the Kumertau aircraft production plant in 1978. Later, the manufacturing was transferred to Smolensk, where 2 more M-17s (plus 1 for static testing) and at least 5 M-55s were built. Production at the Smolensk factory is now continuing for the Russian air forces, with about 10 single-seaters and perhaps 2 M-55Us under construction in 1995.

Crew: Single pilot, except in the M-55U and Geofizika-2 two-seaters. VKK-6D or VK-3M pilot suit.

Cockpit: Pressurized. At maximum altitude the conditions inside the cockpit are the same as external conditions at 16,400 ft (5,000 m) altitude. Rearward hinged canopy.

Crew escape: Severin/Zvezda K-36L zero-zero ejection seat.

Mission equipment: Up to 3,306 lb (1,500 kg) of interchangeable reconnaissance sensors, including SLAR (side-looking airborne radar), infra-red scanner and photographic cameras housed inside the non-hermetic fuselage nose compartment of 318 cu ft (9 m^3) volume. Data link.

Fixed guns: See Aircraft variants.

Wing characteristics: High aspect ratio, high-wing monoplane. Built in 5 sections (centre-section plus 2 outer panels each side). Torsion box construction, with integral fuel tanks.

Wing control surfaces: No high-lift devices. Ailerons at outer trailing edge (+20°, -16°). 3-section spoilers on the upper surface of each wing (50°).

Tail control surfaces: T-type, carried on twin tailbooms, with 2-section elevator (+13° 30′, -7° 30′) and 2 rudders (±20°). Tabs on elevator and rudders.

Flight control system: Manual (without boosters); push-pull rods.

Fuselage: Nacelle built in 3 sections and housing the cockpit, sensors and engines. Dense framing without longitudinals. Twin tailbooms.

Construction materials: All-metal, mainly D16 aluminium alloy.

Engines: 2 Aviadvigatel/ Solovyov D-30V (izdelye 75) non-afterburning turbofans (D-30V10 in the prototype and D-30V12 in production aircraft). Engines mounted side-by-side in the rear fuselage. *Mystic-A* had a single RD-36-51V (see Aircraft variants).

Engine rating: Each 9,921 lbf (44.13 kN) maximum thrust at sea level and 739 lbf (3.29 kN) at 68,900 ft (21,000 m).

Fuel system: 10,000 litres of internal fuel in 5 wing tanks; 17,416 lb (7,900 kg) of special high altitude T-8V fuel or 18,298 lb (8,300 kg) of standard RT fuel.

Braking system: On main units.

Flight avionics/instrumentation: Korall short-range navigation system, R-863 and R-864 radios, Parol IFF, and digital computer.

Aircraft variants:

M-17 *Mystic-A* was the original version, built as a high-altitude reconnaissance and balloon interceptor. PrNK-17 nav/attack system with electro-optical search and track device, and armed with a flexible GSh-23 cannon with 500 rounds of ammunition in a turret. Single 15,432 lbf (68.65 kN) RD-36-51V high-altitude engine. Wing span 132 ft 3 ins (40.32 m), length overall 73 ft 1 ins (22.27 m), maximum take-off weight 40,565 lb (18,400 kg), service ceiling 70,700 ft (21,550 m), maximum speed 401 kts (462 mph) 743 km/h at 65,625 ft (20,000 m), maximum range 710 naut miles (817 miles) 1,315 km with 5% fuel reserve, and duration of 2 hours 14 minutes. Military programme terminated in 1987. Later renamed Stratosfera and used as a research aircraft for ozone-layer analysis. 2 flying prototypes built, 1 now in a museum and 1 scrapped.

M-17RM (razvedchik modifitsirovannyi, modified reconnaissance aircraft) or M-55 *Mystic-B* has a signifi-cantly redesigned airframe and twin engines. Weapon system removed. Lengthened and raised front fuselage with special equipment compartment.

M-55A Geofizika is the civil version for lower-stratosphere ecological monitoring.

M-55B Geofizika is another civil version for earth surface monitoring, using the following systems: 2-frequency synthetic aperture side-looking radar with 16.4-32.8 ft (5-10 m) resolution at 1.6 in (4 cm) wavelength or 65.6-131.2 ft (20-40 m) resolution at 49 ins (1.25 m) wavelength; A-84 photographic camera with 2.6-5.3 ft (0.8-1.6 m) resolution; Argos optical scanner with 98.4 ft (30 m) resolution; or infra-red scanner with 45.9 ft (14 m) resolution and Radius scanning radiometer with 886-6,562 ft (270-21,000 m) resolution. Geofizika can also be used for weather control, by spraying chemical agents into cloud to generate rain (used to prevent potential hailstorm clouds damaging cultivation). In this role the aircraft flies above the cloud and drops the container with chemical agent, which is opened automatically at isotherm level. Cloud height is 7-14 km and isotherm -6°C is at 4 km altitude. In development of this role, Myasishchev is in partnership with Krasnodar (The Application of Civil Aviation in National Economy) and Nalchik (Alpine Geophysic Research Institute).

M-55U was designed as a two-seat trainer, similar to the M-55 but also used as a trainer for the military versions.

MS-55 is an Antarctic surveillance version.

Geofizika-2 is a third civil research version, expected to become operational in 1997. Increased possibilities by carrying a second crew member (researcher), 4,409 lb (2,000 kg) of equipment rather than 3,307 lb (1,500 kg), and with range and flight duration increased by 25%. The forward section of the fuselage is lengthened and redesigned, using an hermetic 4.9 ft (1.50 m) plug inserted between the cockpit and equipment compartment, allowing for the installation of the second cockpit in the upper part and additional equipment in the lower. Accordingly the front undercarriage leg has been moved forward, thereby increasing the wheel base to about 24 ft (7.3 m). The lengthened fuselage and tailbooms provide 399 cu ft (11.3 m^3) of space for special equipment, including 46 cu ft (1.3 m^3) in an hermetic segment (the M-55 has only 318 cu ft, 9 m^3 of available space, all non-hermetic). Moreover the Geofizika-2 can carry measuring equipment in 2 containers, 53 cu ft (1.5 m^3) each, suspended under the wings. The wings themselves are longer, at 131 ft 4 ins (40.0 m), with upper winglets. Wing fuel capacity is increased to 22,267 lb (10,100 kg). Maximum take-off weight is 59,525 lb (27,000 kg), and maximum flight duration at altitude 62,335-65,625 ft (19,000-20,000 m) is 6 hours 30 minutes.

Myasishchev M-55B Geofizika deploying an anti-hail system (courtesy Myasishchev)

DETAILS FOR M-17RM (M-55) *MYSTIC-B.*

Principal dimensions:
Wing span: 122 ft 11 ins (37.464 m)
Maximum length without probe: 75 ft (22.8675 m)
Maximum height: 15 ft 10 ins (4.83 m)

Wings:
Aerofoil section: Supercritical P-173-9
Area, gross: 1,417 sq ft (131.6 m^2)
Aspect ratio: 10.665
Incidence: 5°
Anhedral: 2° 30′

Tail unit:
Tailplane span: 39 ft 3 ins (11.96 m)
Tailplane area: 297 sq ft (27.62 m^2)
Fin area: 156.8 sq ft (14.57 m^2)

Undercarriage:
Type: Retractable, with twin steerable nosewheels
Main tyre size: 660 x 200 mm
Nose wheel tyre size: 520 x 125 mm
Wheel base: 18 ft 10 ins (5.735 m)
Wheel track: 21 ft 8 ins (6.6 m)

Weights:
Empty, operating: 30,865 lb (14,000 kg)
Maximum take-off: 52,470 lb (23,800 kg)
Payload: 3,307 lb (1,500 kg)

Performance:
Maximum and cruise speed: 405 kts (466 mph) 750 km/h at 65,620 ft (20,000 m)
Take-off distance: 2,953 ft (900 m)
Landing distance: 2,560-5,742 ft (780-1,750 m)
Ceiling: 68,900 ft (21,000 m)
Range: 2,681 naut miles (3,085 miles) 4,965 km maximum
Duration with payload: 4 hours 12 minutes at 20,000 m, 5 hours at 55,775 ft (17,000 m)
Duration without payload: 6 hours 30 minutes at 17,000 m

Tupolev Joint-Stock Company (Russia)

Tupolev Tu-135 military transport and communications conversion of a Tu-134A (Piotr Butowski)

Corporate address: See Combat section for company details.

Tupolev Tu-135

Role: Military high command executive transport with long-range communications system.
Based on: Tupolev Tu-134A airliner (NATO name *Crusty*).
Users: Several used by the CIS armed forces (carrying civil registrations and marked Tu-134As).
Crew: As for a Tu-134A, but with the passenger cabin divided into 3 compartments, with tables, charts, rest area and communication system room.

Mission equipment: Long-range communications system added, including Baykal radio, distinguished by the long antenna "sting" protruding from the rear fuselage.

Baykal long-range communications antenna "sting" on a Tu-135 (Piotr Butowski)

Yakovlev Aircraft Corporation (Russia)

Corporate address: See Combat section for company details.

Yakovlev Yak-44

First flight: Not flown at the time of writing.
Role: Carrier-borne early warning and control aircraft, plus land-based surveillance.

★ Aims

★ Similar use to the US Navy Hawkeye.
★ Folding wings, and above-fuselage radar saucer capable of being lowered to fin height, for ship-board stowage.
★ Added land-based surveillance role (particularly border), as possible production for a single aircraft carrier would be insufficient and uneconomic.

▲ Development

▲ 1980?. Programme started.
▲ 1992. Models of Yak-44 were displayed at MosAeroshow.
▲ 27 May 1993. A full-scale mock-up numbered 77 was shown on Russian TV. It was used during development on board the deck of *Admiral Kuznetsov*.
▲ 1993. Funding for the programme was halted by the

Yakovlev Yak-44 full-scale mock-up (Piotr Butowski)

Russian Government, though Yakovlev is believed to have continued limited work against possible exports.
▲ 1-2 September 1994. Following a meeting between Yakovlev officials and those of the Russian defence ministry and security council, it was suggested that the Yak-44 programme could be revived.
Radar: Kvant radar system, with the rotating antenna in an above-fuselage saucer of 24 ft (7.3 m) diameter, installed on a single streamline support. The radar saucer can be lowered for stowage.
Mission equipment: Long-range communication equipment includes satellite communications.
Fixed weapons: None
Wing characteristics: Straight, high mounted, with outer panel folding. Winglets.
Wing control surfaces: 2-section ailerons, trailing-edge flaps, spoilers and leading-edge slats.
Tail control surfaces: H-shaped tail, with widely spaced twin fins, each with a 2-section split rudder, and dihedral tailplane with 2-section elevators.
Engines: 2 Ivchenko PROGRESS/Muravchenko D-27 propfans, with 14 ft 9 ins (4.5 m) Stupino SV-27 coaxial contra-rotating propellers, each propeller having 8 composite blades in the forward disc and 6 blades in the rear disc.
Engine rating: Each 14,000 ehp (10,440 ekW).
Flight refuelling probe: None.
Aircraft variants:
Yak-44 was designed to be the standard tactical AEW&C aircraft for the Russian navy and air force.
Yak-44E was to be the export version.

DETAILS FOR YAK-44.

Principal dimensions:
Wing span: 84 ft 4 ins (25.7 m)
Span with wings folded: 41 ft (12.5 m)
Maximum length: 67 ft 3 ins (20.5 m)
Maximum height: 23 ft (7.0 m)

Undercarriage:
Type: Retractable, with twin nosewheels. Arrester hook under the tail
Wheel base: 30 ft 9 ins (9.37 m)
Wheel track: 26 ft 4 ins (8.02 m)

Weights:
Maximum take-off: 88,185 lb (40,000 kg)

Performance:
Maximum cruising speed: 400 kts (460 mph) 740 km/h
Required runway length: 4,265 ft (1,300 m)
Ceiling: 42,653 ft (13,000 m)
Patrol duration: 6 hours 30 minutes, at 36,090 ft (11,000 m) altitude and 162 naut miles (186 miles) 300 km from base
Ferry range: 2,160 naut miles (2,485 miles) 4,000 km

Saab AB (Saab Military Aircraft) (Sweden)

Saab 340 AEW&C before delivery to the Swedish Air Force

Corporate address: See Combat section for company details.

Saab 360 AEW&C

First flight: 1 July 1994 (with radar).
First delivery: 1995.
Role: Airborne early warning and control.
Based on: Saab 340B airliner.

▲ Development
▲ 1982. Development began with Fairchild Aircraft of the USA receiving an order from the Swedish Defence Materiel Administration (FMV) to develop a trials AEW&C aircraft based around the Swedish Ericsson Erieye radar then under development. Initial plans covered the adaptation of a Fairchild Metro III with an over-fuselage box radome for the radar antenna, able to scan over a 120° sector.
▲ January 1991. Following wind-tunnel testing in 1983 and flight trials of the Metro III with an empty radome during 1986-87, trials began with a prototype radar installed.
▲ December 1992. 6 Erieye radars were ordered by the FMV, plus work on new adaptive control.
▲ 8 January 1993. Plans for an operational system involved changing the carrier aircraft to the Saab 340, the prototype of which was ordered.
▲ 23 December 1993. 5 production Saab 340 AEW&Cs were ordered for the Swedish Air Force, to be joined by the prototype.
▲ 17 January 1994. Maiden flight of a strengthened Saab 340 intended as the pre-series prototype to the AEW&C variant. Also featured enlarged ventral fins, and a new tailcone to house the APU for electrical power generation and cooling air for the avionics, but no radar or antenna.
▲ 1 July 1994. Maiden flight of the complete working system (Saab 340 AEW&C plus Erieye) at Linkoping. Being used for trials by the FMV while production deliveries are underway.
▲ 1995. Production deliveries began.
▲ 1997. Sixth and final delivery to the Swedish Air Force, comprising the FMV's prototype aircraft.
Users: Swedish Air Force (6).
Radar: Ericsson FSR-890 Erieye phased array radar, with the antenna in a 29 ft 6 ins (9 m) box radome on struts above the fuselage, with sector scanning. Said to detect fighter-bomber sized targets at about 184 naut miles (211 miles) 340 km range, and cruise missiles at 81 naut miles (93 miles) 150 km.

Performance:
On-station duration: about 6 hours, at 100 naut miles (115 miles) 185 km from base

Antonov Design Bureau (Ukraine)

Corporate address: 1 Tupolev Street, Kiev 252062.
Telephone: +7 044 442 61 24
Facsimile: +7 044 449 99 96
Telex: 131048, 132792 ozon
Founded: 1946.
Information: P. Balabuev (General Designer)

● Activities
● Principally known for transport aircraft (see Airliners section).
● Co-operates with Israel Aircraft Industries to offer an upgraded maritime patrol variant of the An-72P.

Antonov An-72P (NATO name *Coaler*)

Role: Armed surveillance and maritime patrol (day-and-night, and all-weather), especially for the 200 naut mile (230 mile) 370 km coastal zone.

Antonov An-72P armed surveillance and maritime patrol aircraft (Piotr Butowski)

▲ Development
▲ Late 1980s. Entered service with the Soviet armed forces.
▲ August 1992. Presented to the public for the first time, at Moscow.
▲ September 1992. Presented at the Farnborough Air Show.

DETAILS AS FOR THE AN-72, EXCEPT.

Weights:
Maximum take-off: 72,752 lb (33,000 kg)
Payload: 11,023 lb (5,000 kg)

Performance:
Maximum cruise speed: 389 kts (447 mph) 720 km/h
Patrol speed: 162-189 kts (186-217 mph) 300-350 km/h
Required runway length: 4,593 ft (1,400 m)
Ceiling: 33,135 ft (10,100 m), at 72,732 lb (33,000 kg) take-off weight
Patrol altitude: 1,640-3,280 ft (500-1,000 m)
Patrol duration, fuel rest for 1 hour: 5 hours to 5 hours 18 minutes

▲ February 1994. Co-operation between Antonov and Israel Aircraft Industries (IAI) announced during Asian Aerospace in Singapore. Israel is supplying complete

Antonov An-72P UPK-23 cannon pod installed forward of the starboard undercarriage nacelle (Piotr Butowski)

equipment, including EL/M-2022A maritime surveillance radar (installed in the nose), stabilized opto-electronic system for observation and tracing, programmed chaff/flare system, Elisra EW suite, etc. Upgraded cockpit with digital avionics. The aircraft will be armed with the Rafael Popeye missile; the former armament will remain.

Sales/users: Manufactured at the Kharkov aircraft plant. Dozen or so aircraft in Russian military service. Being marketed by IAI under a co-operation agreement, with new equipment (see Development).

Crew: 5, comprising 2 pilots, navigator, onboard engineer and radio operator. Navigator has a port side station and the radio operator a starboard station aft of the pilots, with bulged blister windows. Rear cabin compartment, length 22 ft 11.5 ins (7.0 m), remains a cargo hold.

Radar: Standard navigation/weather radar in the nose, to be replaced by Israeli EL/M-2022A in IAI upgraded version.

Mission equipment: OTV-124 optical-TV sensor (weighing 551 lb, 250 kg), with resolution of 33 ft (10 m) at a distance of 9,843 ft (3,000 m), is installed in the port undercarriage nacelle for observation (including night observation). It has an automatic tracing system that keeps the target in the sight. The recording equipment consists of 3 photographic cameras; 2 of type A-86P are used for daylight photography, with 1 installed in the tail (used when the cargo hold cover is opened) and the other in the port side. The third camera, a UA-47, is used for night photography and is installed near the A-86P camera in the tail. This camera is used after dropping SFP-2A flares carried inside the cargo hold (instead of bombs). Communication equipment is expanded, including instrument target indication to assist supporting coast guard ships.

Payload: Up to 11,023 lb (5,000 kg), and can include 40 troops or 22 paratroops, or 16 litter patients.

Fixed guns: UPK-23-250 cannon pod containing a twin-barrel 23 mm GSh-23 cannon, housed in the starboard side of the lower fuselage, just in front of the undercarriage nacelle.

Ammunition: 250 rounds.

Expendable weapons and equipment: Up to 1,433 lb (650 kg), suspended on 2 underwing pylons (100 kg bombs or UB-32M rocket packs) and 4 racks inside the cargo cabin above the ramp (100 kg bombs) which can be used when the ramp is slid under the cabin.

Airframe and Engines: As for the An-72.

Flight avionics/instrumentation: Inertial navigation system added.

Antonov An-30 (NATO name Clank) was developed from the An-24RT/An-26 as a dedicated civil and military survey/photogrammetry aircraft with cameras or other sensors, though still usable as a transport. First flown in 1974; out of production and not widely operated. The navigator occupies a glazed nose station. An on-board computer maintains the required flight mode during the pre-programmed mission. This An-30 is flown by the Czech Air Force (Piotr Butowski)

GEC-Marconi Avionics Ltd (UK)

Corporate address: Foxhunter Drive, Linford Wood, Milton Keynes, Buckinghamshire MK14 6LA.
Telephone: +44 1908 220044
Facsimile: +44 1908 317137

● Activities

● The GEC-Marconi Argus modular AEW system may be configured for a basic airborne surveillance platform or as a very sophisticated, multi-sensor, multi-role system. When fitted in a suitable aircraft, it offers 360° scan cover, and can provide AEW, tactical control of friendly forces, and perform a wide range of missions. It is a new generation, high performance, pulse-Doppler radar system incorporating fully-programmable signal processing, optional IFF and ESM, ergonomically efficient data processing and communications, and advanced multi-function colour displays. This may be the system being installed in the new Chinese AEW (see Shaanxi).

Pilatus Britten-Norman Ltd (UK)

Corporate address: Bembridge, Isle of Wight PO35 5PR.
Telephone: +44 1983 872511
Facsimile: +44 1983 873246
Telex: 86277/86866
Founded: Late 1950s (as Britten-Norman), becoming Pilatus Britten-Norman in 1979.
Information: Sheila Dewart (Marketing Services Co-ordinator).

● Activities

● Subsidiary of Oerlikon-Bührle Holding Ltd.

● See also Airliners section for the BN2B and BN2T Islander.

DIVISIONS

PBN USA
HQ address: 1725 Jefferson Davis Highway, Suite 400, Arlington, VA 22202.
Telephone: +1 703 413 0210
Facsimile: +1 703 413 7408

Pilatus Britten-Norman Defender

First flight: 1971 introduction of the Defender based on the piston-engined BN2B, and 1981 based on the turbine-engined BN2T.

Role: Includes border surveillance, battlefield observation, maritime patrol, urban/rural policing, customs and coast guard, EEZ and fishery protection, smuggling interdiction, and search and rescue.

Based on: BN2B and BN2T Islander STOL transports, but now principally the latter. For a general description of Islander/Defender, see the Airliners section.

★ Aims

★ Maximum surveillance capability at minimum cost, with the options of a wide range of simple to sophisticated equipment and sensors.

★ High wing permits unobstructed all-round downward view. Cabin blister windows for observation stations.

★ Operates from 1,150 ft (350 m) unprepared strips (including beaches, jungle clearings and grass).

▲ Development

▲ Developed from the Islander for specific government

Pilatus Britten-Norman BN2T Defender with the Moroccan Ministry of Fisheries, 1 of 14 used for EEZ protection (the largest BN2T Defender fleet). Equipment includes FLIR Systems' 2000G FLIR

and law enforcement agency requirements.
Users: Large number of operating countries. Operators of Defenders as surveillance/observation and photography platforms include Belgium, Cyprus, Netherlands, Oman and the UK (including Army Air Corps Defenders, which were used on active service during the Gulf conflict). Coast guard and customs versions include those with Australia (6 delivered May-August 1995), Mauritius and Pakistan, while full naval operators include India.
Radar and mission sensors: *Detection* equipment can be mounted externally on 4 underwing pylons or on/in the fuselage. Sector-scan low-cost radar can be fitted, or full 360° scanning systems with advanced processing and display units, integrated with video and thermal imaging cameras. Vertically mounted cameras can also be installed for photography through floor apertures. Other available systems include FLIR (see photograph). For monitoring and tracking, electronic sensors can be data-linked with the ground. Surveillance data collection uses video tapes and film for future intelligence assessment or as evidence in prosecutions. If required for military surveillance and tactical support, Defender can act as a targeting system for long-range weapons and land-based aircraft. Specialist trials variants have included a Skymaster radar-equipped Defender, developed with Thorn EMI, to offer standoff battlefield surveillance, and an Elint Defender for locating and identifying radio and radar transmissions, carrying a Racal Kestrel electronic warfare suite.
Mission equipment: For search and rescue, survival packs and extra dinghies can be carried and dropped through the sliding door.
Flight avionics/instrumentation: Omega, GPS, DME, VOR and ILS, and can be combined in a flight management system coupled to an autopilot to minimize pilot workload. Radar altimeter. Optional communications equipment covers UHF, VHF, MF and HF. Night vision goggles among other options.

DEFENDER DETAILS AS FOR ISLANDER (WHICH SEE), EXCEPT.

Principal dimensions:
Maximum length: Length may vary, according to the use of nose radar

Weights:
Payload with maximum fuel: 1,096 lb (497 kg) *for Defender based on the BN2B-26*, 966 lb (438 kg) *for BN2B 20*, and 1,520 lb (689 kg) *for BN2T*.
Disposable load: 2,386 lb (1,082 kg) for *Defender based on the BN2B-26*, 2,256 lb (1,023 kg) *for BN2B-20*, and 2,960 lb (1,343 kg) *for BN2T*.

Performance:
On task duration: typically 4 hours at 100 naut miles (115 miles) 185 km from base.

Defender 4000 (BN2T-4S)

First flight: 17 August 1994 (piloted by Iain Young).
Role: Surveillance, including border and maritime patrol, policing and environmental protection.
Based on: BN2T Defender.

★ Aims
★ To carry sophisticated navigation and sensor systems, including thermal imaging and radar.
★ Lengthened fuselage, larger wings and tailplane, and enhanced visibility cockpit with deep windshield.
★ Powerful turbine engines for greater sortie time and payload.
★ Advanced avionics, including EFIS and a full range of communication equipment.
★ Transit speed of 160 kts (184 mph) 296 km/h from base to the patrol area.

Crew: Airline-type seating. Space for at least 2 consoles and operators in tandem along 1 side of the cabin. Tactical seating for up to 16 personnel.
Radar: Westinghouse radar with a 360° rotating antenna in a new nose structure. Alternatively weather or simple search radar, and possible additional sensors.
Other mission sensors: Thermal imaging system, and video and film cameras (hand-held or podded).
Expendable weapons and equipment: Anti-submarine and anti-ship weapon systems on 4 underwing pylons (750 lb and 350 lb, 340 kg and 159 kg capacities each side).
Fuselage: New nose, able to fit a 27 ins (0.69 m), 360° rotating antenna.
Engines: 2 Allison B250-17F turboprops.
Engine rating: Each 400 shp (298 kW).
Fuel system: 2,002 lb (908 kg) usable.
Electrical system: 200 amp engine-driven generators.
Flight avionics/instrumentation: EFIS cockpit. Full range of UHF/ VHF/HF/VHF(FM) communications. Open radio or secure voice. Fully integrated autopilot. GPS integrated with Omega or INS.
Aircraft variants:
Border surveillance/internal security role uses visual search, thermal imaging systems, and video and fixed cameras. Can patrol 130 naut miles (150 miles) 241 km of border per flying hour, by day or night, or conduct a fixed patrol along a 43.4 naut mile (50 mile) 80 km sector for up to 6 hours, revisiting each point every 30 minutes.
Environmental role, surveying at least 1,000 sq miles (2,590 km^2) per hour.
Maritime role for fishery protection, pollution detection, search and rescue, sovereignty patrol, maritime surveillance with search radar and visual identification of each target and covering up to 3,000 sq miles (7,770 km^2) per hour in average sea traffic density, radar-only survey using a modern maritime radar and covering 6,000 sq miles (15,540 km^2) per hour, and anti-submarine/anti-ship.

Pilatus Britten-Norman Defender 4000 (BN2T-4S)

DETAILS FOR DEFENDER 4000

Principal dimensions:
Wing span: 53 ft (16.15 m)
Maximum length: 40 ft 0.5 ins (21.21 m)
Maximum height: 14 ft 3.5 ins (4.35 m)

Weights:
Maximum zero fuel: 8,300 lb (3,764 kg)
Maximum take-off and landing: 8,500 lb (3,855 kg)
Payload with maximum fuel: 1,590 lb (721 kg)
Disposable load: 3,600 lb (1,633 kg)

Performance:
Cruise speed: 176 kts (203 mph) 326 km/h
Economic cruise speed: 150 kts (173 mph) 278 km/h
Stall speed: 59 kts (68 mph) 119 km/h *clean, power off*, or 52 kts (60 mph) 96 km/h *with flaps, power off*
Take-off distance: 1,550 ft (473 m)
Landing distance: 1,450 ft (442 m)
Take-off over a 50 ft (15 m) obstacle: 1,998 ft (609 m)
Landing over a 50 ft (15 m) obstacle: 2,220 ft (677 m)
Maximum climb rate: 1,210 ft (369 m) per minute, or 223 ft (68 m) per minute with 1 engine inoperable
Ceiling: 25,000 ft (7,620 m) absolute
Range: 850 naut miles (979 miles) 1,574 km *IFR*, 993 naut miles (1,143 miles) 1,839 km *VFR*
Duration: 7 hours, or 4 hours on task 100 naut miles (115 miles) 185 km from base

Pilatus Britten-Norman MSSA (Multi-Sensor Surveillance Aircraft)

Role: STOL battlefield surveillance, border/maritime patrol, AEW, smuggling interdiction, law enforcement, environmental protection, and disaster control/relief management.
Based on: BN2T Defender.

★ Aims
★ 360° multi-mode radar, day/night TV/IR imaging system, and advanced communications.
★ Real-time reception and display of surveillance and intelligence information on a digital map.
★ Mobile or fixed ground command terminal station, or interface into existing command and control system.
★ Over 200,000 sq naut miles coverage on a single mission.
★ Positionable sector scan (20°, 60°, 120° and 240°) in addition to full 360° scanning, suited to battlefield surveillance and command and control.
★ Over 8 hour mission duration.

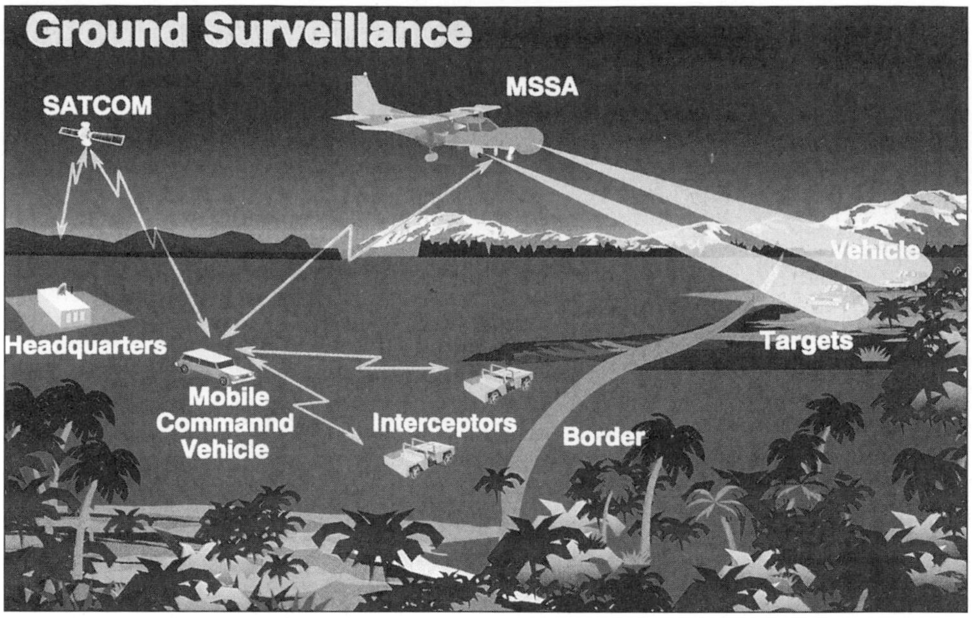

Pilatus Britten-Norman MSSA undertaking ground surveillance, with data-link to a mobile command terminal vehicle (courtesy Pilatus Britten-Norman)

▲ Development
▲ Developed in association with Westinghouse Electronic Systems Group, Law Enforcement Systems Division, Baltimore, MD, USA.
Users: First 2 sold in 1994, possibly to Turkey.
Crew: Minimum of 1 pilot and 1 systems operator.
Radar: Westinghouse APG-66SR multi-mode, with 360° scanning or sector scanning, and single or multiple track for air-to-air modes. Air-to-surface modes are real beam map and enhanced ground map (providing all weather, drift stabilized, improved resolution ground mapping capability, displayed in a video window on the Sensor Fusion Work Station – SFWS), ground moving target indicator (using Doppler processing to discriminate between moving targets and clutter and detects ground or maritime targets in excess of 6 kts at a range of 80 naut miles), sea search 1 and 2, and maritime target track.
Other mission sensors: TV and infra-red system in an underfuselage gimballed turret, to provide close-in identification and tracking of targets by day or night. Provides 360° azimuth and +30° to -75° elevation coverage. Can be slaved to the radar for identification of radar targets. Infra-red sensor is operated in the 8 to 12 micron wavelength and has 2.7x to 11.0x magnification, and is sensitive to temperature differences of 0.1° C. The TV system provides high-resolution imaging in daylight and low-light-level conditions, and is boresighted with the IR system. A contrast tracker tracks targets and a 2x and 12x magnification zoom feature is optional.
Mission equipment: SFWS (mission console), and video and audio data link for real-time transmission.
Expendable weapons and equipment: 4 NATO pylons.
Engines: 2 Allison B250-17F-1 turboprops, with 6 ft 8 ins (2.03 m) 3-blade fully-feathering propellers.
Engine rating: 400 shp (298 kW).
Fuel system: 2,000 lb (907 kg).
Electrical system: 2 engine-driven generators, providing 28 volts and 400 amps total. 24 volt/30 amp lead-acid battery.
Flight avionics/ instrumentation: EFIS 40. AlliedSignal Bendix-King KRA10A radar altimeter. LTN92 INS, with GPS. 9 ins (23 cm) cockpit mission monitor. Nav/com system comprises 2 VHF navigation receivers integrated with marker beacon receivers, 2 digital ADF systems, DME, AlliedSignal/Bendix-King KLN90 GPS, and 2 KTR908 VHF, KHF950 HF, KTR909 UHF and KFM985 VHF/FM transceivers.
Aircraft variants:
Ground surveillance role with mapping resolution, moving target indicator (MTI) out to 80 naut miles (92 miles) 148 km, infra-red and day imaging system able to identify personnel at 2 naut miles (2.3 miles) 3.7 km and vehicles at 7 naut miles (8 miles) 13 km, data-link in real-time to mobile or fixed ground command terminal, and data recording for post-mission analysis. Maritime surveillance role with real-time data-link to surface vessels, day/night imaging system, multi-mode 360° scanning radar to search out to 140 naut miles (161 miles) 259 km and track ships out to 80 naut miles (92 miles) 148 km in all sea states, and infra-red/TV system with auto-track slaved to the radar.
Airborne early warning role, able to detect targets out to 80 naut miles (92 miles) 148 km, track over 100 targets, data link interface into C³ air defence system, and control friendly aircraft for targeting and interception.

Pilatus Britten-Norman MSSA

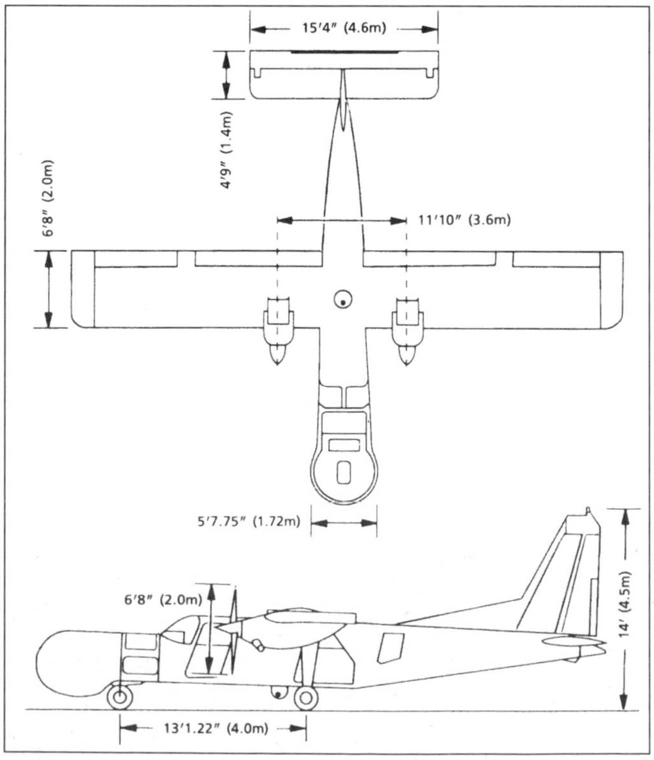

Pilatus Britten-Norman MSSA layout (courtesy Pilatus Britten-Norman)

Details for MSSA.

Principal dimensions:
Wing span: 53 ft (16.15 m)
Maximum length: 48 ft (14.63 m)
Maximum height: 14 ft (4.27 m)
Width of radome: 5 ft 7.75 ins (1.72 m)

Undercarriage:
Type: Fixed, with steerable nosewheel
Wheel base: 13 ft 1.22 ins (4 m)

Weights:
Maximum take-off: 8,500 lb (3,855 kg)

Performance:
Cruise speed: 150 kts (173 mph) 278 km/h
Patrol speed: 90-110 kts (104-127 mph) 167-204 km/h
Take-off and landing distance: <1,500 ft (457 m)
Ferry range: 1,100 naut miles (1,267 miles) 2,037 km
Duration: 8 hours

The Boeing Company (USA)

Corporate address: See Combat section for company details.

Boeing 767 AWACS about to take on fuel from a 767 tanker/transport

Boeing 767 AWACS (E-767)

First flight: November 1994 in unmodified transport form, and 1996 with structural AWACS features.
First delivery: 1998.
Role: Airborne early warning and control, for surveillance and C^3 (command, control and communications) functions for tactical and air defence forces.
Based on: Boeing 767-200ER.

★ Aims

⋆ 50% more floor space and nearly twice the volume of the B707/E-3, with a heavier payload, and greater range and operating altitude.
⋆ Uses similar proven mission avionics to the E-3, with which it will be interoperable.

▲ Development

▲ December 1991. Following the end of Boeing 707 airframe production in May, Boeing announced the 767 would become the next-generation AWACS platform.
▲ 1992. Wind tunnel testing took place, including rotodome location.
▲ November 1993. First order for two 767 AWACS (as E-767s) from the Japan Defence Agency, for JASDF service. Separate contracts covered the air vehicle and mission system equipment.
▲ November 1994. First Boeing 767 (for AWACS installation) for Japan made its first flight from Everett to Wichita, where the Product Support Division assists the Electronic Systems Division in adapting the aircraft for its role by undertaking engineering design for the environmental control, oxygen, hydraulics and fuel systems, and for wiring integration and aircraft interiors. In addition, PSD undertakes extensive airframe modification, with structural changes to Section 46 of the fuselage which carries the rotodome.
▲ 28 October 1994. 2 further E-767s ordered by the Japan Defence Agency through C Itoh Corporation, Boeing's representative in Japan.
▲ Late 1995. Second 767 arrived at Wichita, to be the first to have the mission avionics fitted.
▲ 1996. First 767 AWACS with the empty rotodome fitted will leave Wichita for Seattle for aerodynamic testing, and subsequently to have mission equipment fitted.
▲ Early 1998. Delivery of the first two 767 AWACS to Japan.

Users: Japan (4, designated E-767). Interest has been expressed from Italy, South Korea and Saudi Arabia.
Crew: 20, comprising 2 flight crew plus 18 AWACS mission specialists.
Radar: Westinghouse AN/APY-2 (see E-3 entry).
Other mission sensors and equipment: Similar to E-3, which see.
Expendable weapons and equipment: No armament.
Airframe: See Boeing 767-200ER in the Airliners section.
Engines: 2 General Electric CF6-80C2 turbofans.
Engine rating: Each 61,500 lbf (273.57 kN).
Flight refuelling probe: Fitted.
Electrical system: 4 engine-driven 150kVA 3-phase 400Hz AC generators.
Flight avionics/instrumentation: Similar to E-3, which see. Hughes Technology audio distribution systems.
Aircraft variants:
767 AWACS, as detailed.
Other future 767 military derivatives could include Joint-STARS, tankers, freighters and executive transports.

DETAILS FOR 767 AWACS.

Principal dimensions:
Wing span: 156 ft 1 ins (47.57 m)
Maximum length: 159 ft 2 ins (48.51 m)
Maximum height: 52 ft (15.85 m)
Rotodome diameter: 30 ft (9.14 m)
Rotodome thickness: 6 ft (1.83 m)

Weights:
Maximum take-off: 377,000 lb (171,000 kg)

Performance:
Maximum speed: over 434 kts (500 mph) 804 km/h
Ceiling: 34,000-43,000 ft (10,360-13,100 m)
Range: 4,500-5,000 naut miles (5,182-5,758 miles) 8,330-9,260 km
Duration: 7 hours on station, at 1,000 naut miles (1,150 miles) 1,850 km radius, or 10 hours at 300 naut miles (345 miles) 556 km radius.
Maximum duration: 22 hours with air refuelling

Boeing EC-135/137, RC-135 and OC-135

Role: See Aircraft variants.
Based on: C-135 tanker/transport (see Airliners section).
Users: USAF (17 EC-135s and 1 EC-137 are on the active inventory, of which 11 are primary aircraft authorized for operational missions; 19 RC-135s are on the active inventory, of which 15 are PAA.
Aircraft variants:
EC-135A/E ARIA are advanced range instrumentation aircraft, with huge steerable antenna in the nose. Operate as telemetry/voice relay stations in support of NASA, Department of Defense and others during missile and space programmes. 5 used by the 452nd FTS, 412th TW, Flight Test Center, Edwards AFB in California.
EC-135C/E/H/J/P/Y are strategic command and control posts, able to operate as airborne launch control centres for Air Combat Command bombers and Space Command Minuteman missiles under emergency conditions (with Peacekeeper upgrades underway), plus PACAF and USAFE forces. Continuous alert status ended in 1990, but 1 EC-135C mission is flown each day. Operated by 55th Wing from Offutt AFB, Nebraska (EC-135C) and 355th Wing out of Davis-Monthan AFB, Arizona (EC-130E/H) of ACC, plus PACAF and USAFE deployments. Flight crew of 4, the mission commander and 18 other personnel. Upgrading continues, including Milstar satellite communications, and UHF, LF/VLF radio/antennae improvements.
EC-135K is a tactical control variant for overseas deployment of fighters, operated by the 552nd Air Control Wing at Tinker AFB in Florida.
OC-135B is operated by the 55th Wing from Offutt AFB to monitor the Open Skies Treaty. To be 3 aircraft, each with synthetic aperture radar, IR linescan, and forward/vertical-looking video cameras.
RC-135S/U/V/W/X are specialized reconnaissance/intelligence aircraft, operated by the 55th Wing from Offutt AFB. Lengthened noses and various blister, radome and blade antennae. RC-135U has a larger tailcone and fin fairing. Various sensor systems that differ between versions include infra-red telescopes with associated wide-angle tracking/high resolution cameras on the RC-135S Cobra Ball, which also has 4 optical ports, and a series of horizontal fairings and a box fairing on the port front fuselage side for its role of tracking and recording ballistic missile re-entry vehicles. A new tactical role for the RC-135S includes ballistic/cruise missile detection, particularly in concert with AWACS and other specialized aircraft to track mobile launchers. JTIDS data link has been added.

Boeing RC-135V (David J. March)

Boeing E-3A operated by NATO. This aircraft was the first NATO E-3A to be upgraded for testing in 1995 with colour displays, Have Quick radios, and Link 16. Note the radomes on the fuselage sides forward of the wings, indicating AYR-1 ESM

DETAILS FOR E-3B/C.

Principal dimensions:
Wing span: 145 ft 9 ins (44.42 m)
Maximum length: 152 ft 11 ins (46.61 m)
Maximum height: 41 ft 9 ins (12.73 m)
Rotodome diameter: 30 ft (9.14 m)
Rotodome thickness: 6 ft (1.83 m)
Rotodome height above fuselage: 11 ft (3.35 m)
Radar antenna face width: 24 ft (7.32 m)
Radar antenna face height: 5 ft (1.52 m)

Weights:
Maximum: 335,000 lb (151,953 kg)
Radar system: 8,250 lb (3,742 kg)

Performance:
Maximum speed: 460 kts (530 mph) 853 km/h
Ceiling: about 30,000 ft (9,145 m)
Range with full fuel: over 5,000 naut miles (5,760 miles) 9,260 km, without in-flight refuelling
Duration: 11 hours unrefuelled

Boeing E-3 Sentry

First delivery: 22 March 1977.
Role: Airborne early warning and control, for surveillance and C^3 (command, control and communications) functions for tactical and air defence forces.
Based on: Boeing 707-320B.

★ Aims

★ Quick-reaction surveillance and C^3 needed to manage tactical and defensive fighter forces in a tactical role. Detect, identify, track and control the interception of airborne threats in a strategic role, with mobility for rapid deployment where needed.

▲ Development

▲ 26 January 1973. Full-scale development began.
▲ 1978. USAF declared initial operational capability with Core E-3As.
▲ May 1987. Long-term multi-stage improvement programme (MSIP) began with a USAF award of the ICON (Integration Contract) to Boeing, to provide USAF and NATO E-3s with an ESM passive surveillance capability, and offer other block enhancements including upgrading of the Joint Tactical Information Distribution System (JTIDS) to TADIL-J (Tactical Digital Information Link-J) or Link 16 (NATO) standard, increased computer capacity, and worldwide use of GPS. Following the first upgrade and testing of a NATO E-3 with colour displays, Have Quick radios and Link 16 (see Mission equipment) in 1994-95, Daimler-Benz Aerospace began retrofitting the remaining NATO fleet in 1996.
Users: 68 E-3 variants in use with the USAF (34 E-3B/Cs on the active inventory, of which 29 are primary aircraft authorized for operational missions, serving with the 552nd Air Control Wing based at Tinker AFB, Oklahoma; the 961st and 962nd Airborne Air Control Squadrons are deployed to Japan and Alaska), NATO (18 improved E-3As, with main operating base at Geilenkirchen, Germany), Saudi Arabia (5 AWACS plus 6 related KE-3 in-flight refuelling tankers under the Peace Sentinel programme, delivered June 1986-September 1987), France (4 E-3Fs, delivered May 1991-February 1992, operating with 36e Escadre), and the UK (7 E-3D Sentry AEW Mk 1s, delivered March 1991 to May 1992, serving with 8 Squadron at RAF Waddington).
Crew: 21, comprising 4 flight crew plus 17 AWACS specialists.
Radar: Westinghouse AN/APY-2 S-band, high-PRF, pulse-Doppler, multi-mode lookdown radar (with inherent ECCM), able to separate maritime and airborne targets from ground and sea clutter (E-3Bs have upgraded AN/APY-1s). Radar comprises 3 major subsystems, the slotted planar array antenna, radar receivers and processors located in the centre of the aircraft cabin, and the radar transmitter located in the lower cargo bay. Operating modes are *pulse-Doppler nonelevation* with high-PRF Doppler to provide lookdown surveillance to the radar horizon but does not measure target elevation, *pulse-Doppler elevation* scan which is similar to the previous mode but includes electronic vertical scan of the radar beam to provide target elevation (vertical scanning and height finding using ferrite phase-shifters), *beyond the horizon operation* for long-range surveillance of medium and high altitude aircraft (as the radar beam is above the horizon, there is no ground clutter and a low-PRF radar pulse is used to obtain range and azimuth of the target), *passive scanning* with the radar transmitter off and the receiver on to obtain ECM information (such as enemy jammer location), and *maritime mode* using a very short radar pulse to provide the high resolution required to detect moving or anchored surface ships. Liquid-cooled, slotted planar array surveillance antenna (the antenna face comprises 30 slotted waveguide sticks) and IFF/data-link fighter-control TADIL-C (tactical digital information link/command) or TADIL-J antennae are housed in the glassfibre rotodome, which turns at 6 rpm during active use but only 1 revolution every 4 minutes when unused to maintain bearing lubrication. 360° scanning, able to detect targets about 213 naut miles (245 miles) 394 km away when flying at 30,000 ft (9,145 m) operating altitude. Mission equipment can separate, manage and display these targets individually on situation displays.
Other mission sensors: AN/AYR-1 electronic support measures (ESM) fitted under MSIP to US/NATO aircraft, for passive listening and detection, enabling aircraft to detect, identify and track electronic transmissions from ground, airborne and maritime sources (enabling radar and weapon system type to be determined).
Mission equipment: Navigation, communications, data processing, identification and display equipment (colour displays under the NATO MSIP). Central to the processing network is an advanced airborne version of the IBM CC2 command and control multi-processing computer (NATO E-3 computers upraded since 1993 to CC2E model, with 380% increase in memory using bubble memory technology). Under the MSIP, Boeing produced Have Quick A-NETS, an improved communications system that provides secure, anti-jam radio contact with other AWACS, friendly aircraft and ground stations for US and NATO aircraft. Also JTIDS is being upgraded to TADIL-J (US) and Link 16 (NATO) standards to increase the amount of information that can be collected and distributed among other AWACS, friendly aircraft and ground stations.
Self-protection systems: Can carry self-defence AAMs.
Fixed guns: None.
Engines: US and NATO E-3s have 4 Pratt & Whitney TF33-PW-100 or 100A turbofans (each 21,000 lbf, 93.41 kN). Others use CFM56-2A-2 or 3 turbofans (each 24,000 lbf, 106.76 kN) offering higher operating altitudes to extend the surveillance horizon (over 35,000 ft, 10,668 m).
Flight avionics/instrumentation: Includes weather radar, dual Delco AN/ASN-119 IN, and Northrop Omega.
Aircraft variants:
E-3A is the NATO standard, representing an improved version of the original (and since upgraded) USAF Core E-3A, featuring the larger memory IBM CC-2 computer, etc.
E-3B represents 24 earliest production USAF E-3As (Cores, including 2 EC-137D prototypes) upgraded with a CC-2 computer, much improved radio communications, austere maritime capability for the radar, 14 (instead of 9) display consoles, and more.
E-3C is the other USAF version, produced by conversion of the 10 E-3As originally built to improved standard (as for NATO aircraft), featuring better command and control capability. Redelivered 1984-88.
E-3D is known to the RAF as Sentry AEW Mk 1. Wing span increased to 147 ft 7 ins (44.98 m) due to wingtip Loral Yellow Gate ESM pods.
E-3F is the French variant.

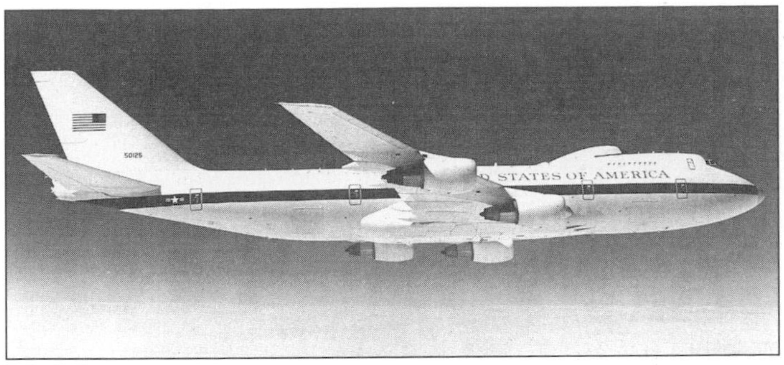

Boeing E-4B NAOC

Boeing E-4B

First flight: 13 June 1973 (in E-4A form); 1979 for E-4B.
Role: National Airborne Operations Center (NAOC) aircraft, as a survivable airborne link between the national command authorities and strategic forces during an attack.
Based on: Boeing 747-200.

★ Aims

⋆ Hardened against electromagnetic pulse and other effects of nuclear explosions (includes thermal shielding).
⋆ Over 12 hour duration without refuelling, or possible 72 hours with in-flight refuelling.

▲ Development

▲ January 1980. First E-4B entered USAF service, developed from the former E-4A (3 former E-4As were brought up to E-4B standard).
Users: USAF (4 on the active inventory, of which 3 are primary aircraft authorized for operational use with the 55th Wing of ACC out of Offutt AFB, Nebraska).
Crew: About 94.
Mission equipment: Specialized communications and data processing equipment include dual low frequency and very low frequency systems with trailing wire antennae (the short wire of just under 0.87 naut miles, 1 mile, 1.6 km length and the other of about 4.34 naut miles, 5 miles, 8 km length), Milstar satellite communications and more. When deployed, the wire antennae trail behind and below the aircraft. Can also be used to broadcast nationally by connecting with the radio and telephone networks. In August 1995, Boeing received a US$8 million contract to produce 4 tri-band radomes for E-4Bs (each having 3 different-frequency antennae).
Engines: 4 General Electric F103-GE-100 (CF6-50E2) turbofans.
Engine rating: Each 52,500 lbf (233.54 kN).
Electrical system: 1,200 kVA.

Boeing E-6A Mercury

First flight: 19 February 1987.
First delivery: August 1989.
Role: Survivable airborne communications system, supporting the US Navy's ballistic missile submarine force by providing a link between the force and national command authorities.
Based on: Boeing E-3 airframe (without rotodome), as a 707-320B derivative.

★ Aims

⋆ Faster and longer-range aircraft to replace the EC-130Q TACAMO (in keeping with support of Trident submarines).
⋆ Nuclear hardened.
⋆ Carries essential spares and can operate from short airfields in emergencies.

▲ Development

▲ 1983. Boeing was awarded a full-scale development contract.
▲ 1986. Boeing received a production contract; prototype E-6A rolled out at Renton in December 1986, produced on the same production line as E-3.
▲ 1995. Modification work and post-production support continued.
Users: US Navy (16 delivered between 1989 and 28 May 1992). Fleet can provide continuous airborne alert coverage for both Atlantic and Pacific Oceans.
Mission equipment: Dual very-low-frequency trailing-wire antennae system for one-way, emergency communications. System uses an onboard power amplifier-coupler that is connected to the antennae (the short wire of under 0.87 naut miles, 1 mile, 1.6 km length and the other of about 4.34 naut miles, 5 miles, 8 km length). When deployed, the antennae trail behind and below the aircraft. After deployment, the E-6A enters an orbit that causes the longer wire to assume a near vertical position to enhance signal transmission.
Engines: 4 CFM International F108-CF-100 (CFM56-2) turbofans.
Engine rating: Each 24,000 lbf (106.76 kN).
Modification programmes:
Tail section modifications to 3 aircraft at Seattle and 13 at Wichita, completed 1993.
New digital autopilot system to replace the analog system was flight tested by May 1994. This improves reliability and maintainability, while providing the capability for future modifications to the E-6A to improve its orbit capabilities.
Orbit improvement system (OIS) work under a $20 million contract covered the design, development, production, integration and installation of an OIS. The system suppresses "yo-yo" of the antennae caused by wind shear, improving communications effectiveness. Modification included adaptations of the 737 auto-throttle for the E-6A systems and its orbit flight profiles, as well as modification of the flight management computer (incorporating auto-throttle Built-In Test-Equipment). First E-6A installation was completed in September 1995. The upgrade improves the E-6A's ability to perform manoeuvres at high bank angles. Both the auto-throttle and FMC were developed and procured under subcontract to Smiths Industries of the UK. OIS modification of the 15 other E-6As is anticipated.
Electronic horizontal situation indicator (EHSI) and attitude direction indicator (EADI) installations are replacing the analog systems, needed for incorporation of GPS, and to provide flight deck commonality and improve maintainability respectively.

Boeing E-6A Mercury, its wingtip pods housing UHF satellite communications aerials, with HF communication aerials below, giving the aircraft a 148 ft 2 ins (45.16 m) span

Boeing EC-18B and D

Role: Advanced range instrumentation aircraft (EC-18B ARIA), and cruise missile mission control aircraft (EC-18D CMMCA).
Based on: Ex-commercial Boeing 707-320s.
Users: USAF (4 EC-18Bs and 2 EC-18Ds, operated by the 452nd FTS, 412th TW, Flight Test Center, Edwards AFB in California). All 6 are primary aircraft authorized.
Crew: 16-24 in the EC-18B.
Aircraft variants:
EC-18B is the designation of 4 ex-commercially operated Boeing 707-320s used to supplement EC-135A/Es for the ARIA role. Similar steerable antenna in the nose. Operational since 1986. Modification by McDonnell Douglas.
EC-18D covers 2 Boeing 707s modified by Chrysler Technologies Airborne Systems to carry AN/APG-63 surveillance radar for a CMMCA (plus UAV control/monitoring) role in support of both the USAF and US Navy. Other equipment includes a telemetry receiver.

Boeing common support aircraft

Role: Proposed carrier – and land-based airborne early warning and surveillance aircraft, to replace the E-2C Hawkeye in the 21st century.

DETAILS FOR COMMON SUPPORT AIRCRAFT.

Principal dimensions:
Wing span 63 ft 4 ins (19.3 m)
Maximum length: 51 ft 2 ins (15.6 m)
Maximum height: 18 ft 6 ins (5.64 m)

Undercarriage:
Type: Retractable, with twin nosewheels

Weights:
Maximum take-off: 56,300 lb (25,535 kg)

Performance:
Maximum speed: Up to an estimated Mach 0.8
On station speed: Mach 0.38

▲ Development

▲ 1988. Initial design phase was begun, originally as the EX.
▲ 1992. Public debut of the Boeing EX design.
▲ 1994. Further work probably slowed after the US Navy chose to extend Hawkeye production into the next century.
Users: Potentially the US Navy in the next century.
Crew: Pilot and 3 mission operators, in heavily glazed cockpit/cabin areas.
Crew escape: Zero-zero ejection seats.
Radar: Active phased-array radar with conformal antennae, offering 360° scanning.

Boeing common support aircraft, a follow-on concept from the former EX

Expendable weapons and equipment: 2 wing pylons for detachable equipment/sensor pods, 1,514 litre auxiliary fuel tanks or perhaps weapons.
Wing characteristics: "Joined wing" technology, with 40° sweepback forward wings (with heavy dihedral) meeting 40° forward-swept (anhedral) rear wings. Rear wings are joined to the tailfin. All 4 wings support conformal antennae for the radar, providing all-sector scanning. Wings designed to fold for ship-board operations.
Wing control surfaces: Include ailerons at the wing join.
Tail control surfaces: No separate horizontal tail surfaces. Fin with 2-section rudder.
Engines: 2 General Electric TF34-GE-400 turbofans, suspended beneath forward-swept stub wings on the mid-fuselage sides.
Engine rating: Each 9,275 lbf (41.26 kN).
Electrical system: General Electric T700-GE-401 turboshaft engine (1,723 shp, 1,285 kW) in the fuselage functions to provide electrical power for the radar.

Fairchild Aircraft Incorporated (USA)

Corporate address: PO Box 790490, San Antonio, TX 78279-0490
Telephone: +1 210 824 9421
Facsimile: +1 210 820 8656
Founded: 1959 formation of predecessor company, sold to Fairchild Hiller in 1972. 1990 sale to Fairchild Aircraft Incorporated.
Information: William S. Harris (Regional Sales Manager, North America – *telephone* +1 210 820 8613).

Fairchild Aircraft MMSA with a Lockheed Martin underfuselage pod

DIVISIONS

Fairchild Aircraft
● **Activities**
• Metro 23, C-26B Military Special Mission Aircraft, and MMSA Multi-Mission Surveillance Aircraft.

Fairchild Aircraft Services
HQ address: 9623 W. Terminal Drive, San Antonio, TX 78216
Telephone: +1 800 327 2313, 210 824 2313
Facsimile: +1 210 824 3462
● **Activities**
• Provides airlines, lessors, and Metro and Merlin operators with Factory Service performing all inspections, structural repairs and modifications.

Fairchild Financial

Merlin Express Inc
● **Activities**
• Responsible for operation, maintenance and management of the UPS Express Package Expediter fleet and provides Contractor Logistics Support for the C-26 fleet. Also a charter cargo/passenger airline.

Fairchild MMSA

Based on: Metro 23.
Aircraft variants:
MMSA is a Multi-Mission Surveillance Aircraft that can be reconfigured in under 2 hours for C^3, surveillance, reconnaissance, maritime patrol, contraband interdiction, 18 passenger or VIP, medical evacuation, cargo or utility roles. Avionics and sensors, according to the customer's requirements, can include tactical air-to-air, sea surveillance or weather avoidance radar, plus equipment for visual and infra-red surveillance and reconnaissance (carried in an underfuselage sensor pod and including camera, FLIR and linescan), sigint system for electronic reconnaissance, multi-spectral mapping, and near real-time image transmission. 8 hour endurance.

Lockheed Martin (USA)

Corporate address: See Combat section for company details.

Lockheed Martin EC-130 series

Role: See Aircraft variants.
Based on: C-130E or H Hercules.
Users: Morocco (2 civil-registered Hercules carrying side-looking airborne radar for surveillance duties) and USA (Coast Guard, USAF and ANG, as detailed).
Aircraft variants:
EC-130E ABCCC III is the designation of 8 recently upgraded (by Unisys) USAF Airborne Battlefield Command and Control Center aircraft operated by the 7th ACCS at Keesler AFB in Mississippi. Based on the C-130E, but with underfuselage antennae, podded ABCCC equipment carried in the cargo cabin, and some with replacement T56-A-15 engines.
EC-130E Comfy Levi is believed to be an electronic intelligence gathering/jamming variant of the C-130E, operated by the 193rd Special Operations Group of the US Air National Guard, from Harrisburg IAP, Pennsylvania. 2 are probably operational, re-engined with T56-A-15s, supplemented by 2 C-130Hs converted to this configuration.
EC-130E Commando Solo is operated by the 193rd SOG, ANG (see above) for psychological warfare operations by broadcasting radio or television pictures over targeted areas, but also for broadcasting during time of national emergencies. LAS is upgrading 6 to WWCTV (World Wide Color Television) configuration. Each currently has 4 tailfin-mounted antennae and underwing pods for UHF/VHF antennae. Previously known in earlier configurations as Rivet Rider and Volant Solo.
EC-130H Compass Call is a C^3 jamming aircraft, of which 14 are operated by the 41st, 42nd and 43rd squadrons of the 355th Wing, USAF, from Davis-Monthan AFB.
EC-130V first flew on 31 July 1991 as a single HC-130H conversion to AEW role for the US Coast Guard, using an above-fuselage radome and radar of E-2C Hawkeye type; 8 Hawkeyes had been received by the USCG for

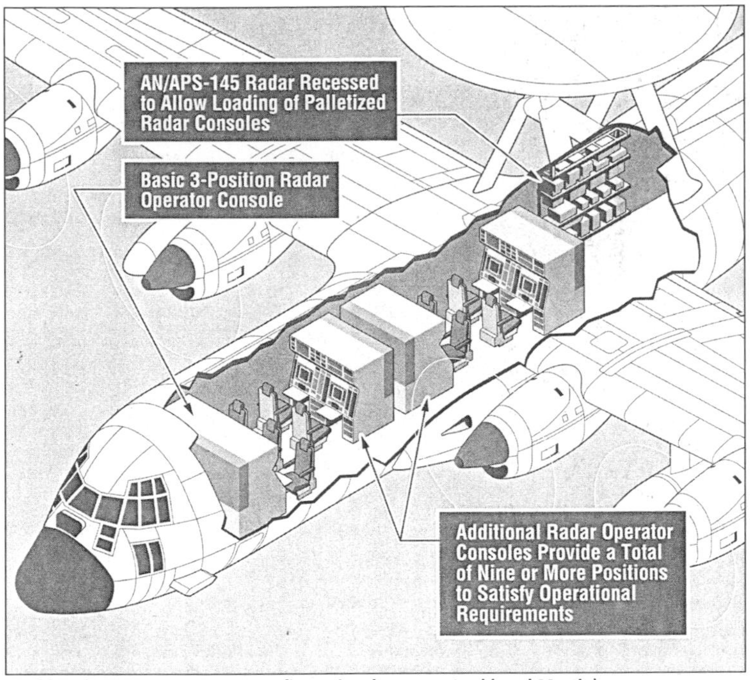

Lockheed Martin C-130 AEW configuration (courtesy Lockheed Martin)

2 Lockheed SR-71A Blackbird strategic reconnaissance aircraft (17967 and 971) have been reactivated for the USAF under a January 1995 contract with LMSW. The Air Force is sharing an SR-71B trainer with NASA, which operates its own SR-71A. The Mach 3+ "stealthy" aircraft have each been given a data link for near real-time radar image transmission. Sensors are ASARS-1 (advanced synthetic aperture radar system), or Itek camera with a gimballed head that scans to the horizon each side of the aircraft, and 2 high-resolution, preprogrammable cameras

use in its anti-smuggling operations but lacked the range offered by the EC-130V. Budget cutbacks saw the EC-130V transfer to USAF service, going to the 514th Test Squadron at Hill AFB. However, a new HC-130H conversion for the Coast Guard was begun in 1994 under new funding. Australia, Italy, South Korea and Turkey are among countries interested in new AEW&C aircraft, with the C-130 AEW&C in contention. The currently offered version is designed on a palleted system to allow easy reconfiguration. It has AN/APS-145 radar recessed to allow loading of palletized radar consoles, combined with IFF to allow automatic target detection and tracking of ships out of the radar horizon and aircraft at ranges greater than 300 naut miles. Other features are an integrated passive detection system to augment target identification, GPS integrated with dual INS, number and mix of HF, VHF and UHF radios, data links for the transmission of radar pictures to the ground and other AEW&C aircraft, and more. Unrefuelled flight time is over 11 hours.
EC-130Q was the US Navy's TACAMO version for airborne strategic communications relay between the national command authority and ballistic missile submarines up to 1992. With the arrival of the Boeing E-6A Mercury, some have been mothballed (presumably recoverable or stored for conversion), 3 converted to transports for NASA and perhaps 3 modified into TC-130Q support transports.
C-130 Samson is Lockheed Martins's own name for the C-130H carrying the Samson "Open Skies" pod. The LMAS-manufactured Samson surveillance pod, used by Belgium and 9 other countries to verify the new European Open Skies Treaty, carries 3 Recon-Optical KS-87B framing film cameras, a KS-116A panoramic film camera and 2 video cameras.

Lockheed Martin EC-130E Commando Solo. Note the tailfin antennae, ram air scoops on the rear fuselage to cool the electronics, and underwing UHF/VHF antennae pods (Daniel J. March)

Lockheed Martin ES-3A and S-3 AEW Viking

First flight: August 1991.
Role: Multirole electronic for ES-3A, including intelligence gathering/processing/evaluation/reporting, airborne command and control, over-the-horizon targeting, and battlefield management.
Based on: S-3A Viking.
Users: US Navy (16 ES-3As, operated by VQ-5 at NAS North Island and VQ-6 at NAS Cecil Field).
Aircraft variants:
ES-3A is the new electronic reconnaissance conversion of 16 S-3As, taking over the role of the former EA-3B Skywarrior on deck, incorporating S-3B surveillance systems and unique passive electronic emission capabilities to provide "a new dimension to littoral maritime battle group operations, while allowing real-time tactical information to the Carrier Battle Group and Joint Task Force Commanders". As a result of the sensors, ES-3As were flown for nearly 3 times the planned utilization rates during 1994. Modification from S-3A involved the complete cutting of the aircraft and repopulation of every available bay with new avionics, 63 antennae, and over 60 miles of new wiring. Former S-3A bomb bays were converted into avionics bays, co-pilot's station was replaced with a third sensor station, and new avionics, sensors and displays were fitted. Includes the avionics suite developed for the EP-3E Aries II. MIL-STD-1553 databus. FLIR, AN/APS-137 inverse synthetic aperture radar, AN/ALR-52 frequency measuring radar, AN/ALR-81 ESM, AN/ALD-9 direction finding system, and AN/ALR-60 communications analysis equipment.
S-3 AEW was conceived as a carrier AEW aircraft to replace Hawkeye, the principal features being the fixed triangular and aerodynamic above-fuselage radome housing 3 active electronically-scanned radar arrays and an X-band radar in the nose for missile targeting. Other avionics include infra-red search/track and electronic support measures. Turbofans would be of higher rating, and structural modifications would include general strengthening. Further development is believed to be unlikely.

Lockheed Martin ES-3A Viking

Artist's drawing of the proposed Lockeed Martin S-3 AEW

Lockheed Martin P-3 AEW, CEC, ASARS and *Slicks*, and Lockheed/Kawasaki EP-3

Based on: P-3 Orion.
Users: Japan Maritime Self Defence Force (3 Kawasaki-built EP-3s), US Customs Service (4 P-3 AEWs including 1 CEC, 1 P-3 ASARS, and 3 other special surveillance P-3s known as *Slicks*. A fifth P-3 AEW was authorized in FY1994 but unfunded; all based at the Southern Surveillance Center at NAS Corpus Christi, and US Navy (12 EP-3Es with VQ-1 and 2, and 2 EP-3Js).
Aircraft variants:
EP-3 is Kawasaki's electronic surveillance version. 3, delivered from 1991.
EP-3E Aries II is the US Navy designation of 12 P-3Cs modified for electronic surveillance under the Conversion-In-Lieu-Of-Procurement programme. Most equipment was transferred from earlier EP-3E Aries Is, with antennae in dorsal and ventral "canoe" and forward fuselage ventral dome radomes, plus the modified tailcone. Texas Instruments AN/APS-115 search radar with scan converter, and Honeywell AN/ASQ-114 computer. Other equipment includes AN/ALQ-76 noise jammer, AN/AAR-37 IR detector, AN/ALR-132 IR jammer, possibly AN/ALR-81 ESM and radar warning receiver in wingtip pods (AN/ALR-76), AN/ALQ-108 IFF, AN/ALD-9 direction finding system, AN/ALQ-110 radar signal analyzer, AN/ALR-52 frequency measuring radar, and AN/ALR-60 communications analysis equipment. MIL-STD-1553 databus. Flight crew (with a pilot as Electronic Warfare Aircraft Commander), Mission Commander and up to 15 others.
EP-3J is a US Navy EW trainer, with AN/USQ-113 and other systems.

Lockheed Martin P-3 AEW in US Customs Service use

Kawasaki-built EP-3C in JMSDF service (K. Hinata)

P-3 AEW is the airborne early warning and control conversion of Orion, with a 24 ft (7.32 m) above-fuselage dome antenna for the AN/APS-138 surveillance radar that can scan 196,000 sq miles (507,640 km^2) of airspace from sea level to 100,000 ft (30,480 m). The addition of a scan converter to the radar and has optimized the use of the 2 Lockheed Sanders miligraphic display screens by digitizing analog images to facilitate radar use over land and water; with the capability of the AYK-14 central computer, the aircraft can monitor up to 2,000 potential targets at once. The original P-3 ASW acoustic systems were removed during AEW conversion, flight control systems modernized (including EFIS), and new avionics, sensor and communication equipment added. The upgraded communications suite has 4 VHF/UHF radios, 2 FM radios, 2 HF radios, a Customs Over-The-Horizon Enforcement Network (COTHEN) radio and SATCOM. A Communication Improvement Programme to add DAMA SATCOM is underway. Deliveries to the USCS during 1988-93 (as converted P-3Bs).
P-3 ASARS is a USCS P-3 *Slick* fitted with a Loral Advanced Synthetic Aperture Radar System (ASARS) 1A, originally developed for the SR-71. This enhances its ability to locate, identify and track suspects from safe distances.
P-3 CEC refers to a US Customs Service P-3 AEW modified to test a Co-operative Engagement Capability (CEC) under a joint USN/Customs Service programme conceived to change the way the US Navy will conduct future anti-air warfare, as well as enhancing the Customs Service P-3 AEW's ability to conduct anti-smuggling activities along the US southern border. Programme funding is via the US Navy Program Executive Office, Theater Air Defense, while Customs co-operates by supplying a P-3 AEW and crew for demonstrations/validation. Trials have shown the ability of an CEC airborne platform to provide increased over-the-horizon coverage for shipboard sensors, as well as acting as a link between surface, airborne and land-based components engaged in military operations. Dem/val phase has been conducted at Virginia Capes. After dem/val, CEC-equipped aircraft will undertake "real-time" operations with ships at sea, then deploy with a battle group for tactics exploration. Modifications to the trials aircraft include addition of the CEC equipment set consisting of a data distribution system, a co-operative engagement processor with 2 new workstations, and an active aperture antenna installed under the weapon bay. Upgrades were also made to the surveillance radar, to emulate selected functions of the AN/APS-145 radar.

P-3 *Slick* is the nickname given to the 4 non-AEW USCS P-3s (including ASARS), used for surveillance.

Lockheed Martin U-2S

First delivery: October 1994 (redelivery of upgraded U-2R to S standard).
Role: Very high altitude, all-weather strategic reconnaissance, and day or night battlefield surveillance.
Based on: U-2R (former strategic U-2s and tactical reconnaissance TR-1s, all redesignated U-2Rs in 1992) and the two-seat U-2RT trainer.

★ Aims

★ Re-engined U-2R, offering a weight reduction of 1,200 lb (544 kg), fuel saving of over 15%, increase of range by 1,200 naut miles (1,380 miles) 2,200 km, increase of duration by 3 hours, and increase of altitude by 3,500 ft (1,060 m).
★ Upgrade of the sensors, though initially only the electro-optical cameras.

Details for U-2R and U-2S.

Principal dimensions:
Wing span: 103 ft (31.39 m)
Maximum length: 63 ft (19.2 m)
Maximum height: 17 ft (5.18 m)

Undercarriage:
Type: Retractable, with 1 set of twin mainwheels, and small balancing wheels under the rear fuselage and at mid-span

Weights:
Empty: 19,000 lb (8,618 kg) *for U-2R*, and 17,800 lb (8,074 kg) for *U-2S*
Maximum take-off: 40,000 lb (18,145 kg) for *U-2R*

Performance:
Maximum cruise speed: 373 mph (430 mph) 692 km/h for U-2R
Operating ceiling: 70,000 ft (21,335 m) *for U-2R*, 73,500 ft (22,400 m) for U-2S, with capability of reaching an estimated 90,000 ft (27,430 m)
G limits: +2.5
Range: 2,600 naut miles (3,000 miles) 4,830 km *for U-2R*, 3,800 naut miles (4,380 miles) 7,050 km for U-2S
Duration: about 12-15 hours

▲ Development

▲ Upgrading by Lockheed Martin's Advanced Development Company "Skunk Works" to U-2S standard takes place during depot level maintenance, so as to keep the fleet active. Work to be completed by 1998.

Users: USAF (33 U-2Rs, 3 U-2RT trainers and a rebuilt U-2R are being upgraded to 33 U-2Ss and 4 U-2STs; all single-seaters are primary aircraft authorized, operated by the 9th Reconnaissance Wing from Beale AFB, California, with detachments to Cyprus, South Korea and Saudi Arabia).

Crew: Pilot only in U-2R and S.

Crew escape: Ejection seat.

Radar: Hughes ASARS-2 (advanced synthetic aperture radar system).

Other mission sensors: New U-2S equipment includes 5 Senior Year electro-optical multi-spectral cameras. Equipment is carried in interchangeable noses, mission bay hatches and wing pods.

Fixed guns: None.

Wing characteristics: High aspect ratio straight wings, to permit power-off gliding during missions. Retractable leading-edge stall strips.

Wing control surfaces: Each wing has an aileron with tab, 2 x 2-section trailing-edge flaps, and 2 spoilers.

Tail control surfaces: Variable incidence tailplane, elevators with tabs, and rudder.

Flight control system: Manual.

Fuselage: Slender, with 2 side airbrakes towards the rear.

Construction materials: Metal.

Engine: General Electric F118-GE-101 turbofan, replacing 17,000 lbf (75.62 kN) Pratt & Whitney J75-P-13B.

Engine rating: 19,000 lbf (84.518 kN).

Lockheed Martin U-2R, still operated but the entire fleet will become U-2Ss by 1998. Note the fuel vent fairings at mid span

Flight avionics/ instrumentation: INS, Tacan, ILS, ADF and more. Future upgrades for the U-2S could include GPS, digital processing for the ASARS-2 instead of analog and new moving target indicator.

Aircraft variants:

U-2R is the J75-engined single-seater, being upgraded to U-2S. Some will remain active through 1997.

U-2RT is the J75-engined two-seat trainer, being upgraded to U-2ST.

U-2S is the upgraded model (eventually 33 aircraft), currently being redelivered, as detailed.

U-2ST is the designation of 4 upgraded two-seaters.

Northrop Grumman Corporation (USA)

Corporate address: See Combat section for company details.

Northrop Grumman E-2C Hawkeye and Hawkeye II

First flight: 21 October 1960 (original W2F-1 prototype).

Role: Carrier-borne and land-based airborne early warning/command and control (AEW/CC), primarily for wide-area air defence and strike control. Secondary missions include surface surveillance, search-and-rescue, air traffic control, and communications relay.

★ Aims

★ Highly automated system, requiring a small crew.

★ 10,000 flight hour design life for Group II aircraft, calculated at 55,000 lb (24,947 kg) gross weight.

▲ Development

▲ 29 April 1961. First flight of a W2F-1 prototype with full avionics suite.

▲ 19 January 1964. Initial delivery of an E-2A, the first operational US Navy squadron becoming VAW-11.

▲ 20 January 1971. Maiden flight of the E-2C prototype, followed by a production aircraft on 23 September 1972.

▲ May 1994. First Group II E-2C was delivered, to Taiwan (as part of that nation's *Strong Net* air defence programme).

▲ December 1994. US Navy awarded Northrop Grumman a $122.5 million contract for long-lead procurement and production start-up for 7 new Group II+ E-2C Hawkeyes (all Group II types known by Northrop Grumman as Hawkeye IIs), for delivery during 1997-98. Further US Navy procurement will take place to keep Hawkeye in production into the next century. New USN Hawkeye IIs will be the first built at the new E-2C production facility in St Augustine, Florida.

Users: 139 delivered to the US Navy by 1995 (some 70 in active service), with production restarted – instead of older aircraft modernization – to provide an additional 34 and 36 new Group II+ aircraft into the next century, beginning with 7 ordered under an initial 2 year programme from FY1995. US Navy has 11 E-2C air wings. US Coast Guard operated 4 Hawkeyes but these were returned to the US Navy, and no more are being received. 31 exported, going to Egypt (5 + 1 replacement, and is looking to buy another), Israel (4, with APS-125 radar), Japan (13), Singapore (4) and Taiwan (4, delivered 1994-96). In addition, France has ordered 2 for operation from the aircraft carrier *Foch* and later for transfer *to Charles de Gaulle,* with 2 more possibly to follow from a 1997 order. Other interested nations include South Korea, Thailand and Australia.

Crew: 5, comprising pilot, co-pilot, combat information centre officer, air control officer, and radar operator. The 3 system operators work independently in all operational roles (sensor utilization, monitoring/control of the tactical situation, and data exchange).

Crew escape: Ditching hatches above the pilots, pulled by handles into the cockpit and moved aft. CIC compartment ditching hatch on starboard side of the fuselage. For airborne escape, main port door is blown using explosive charges, after alarm has been sounded and cabin unpressurized.

Radar: Currently AN/APS-145 radar with fully automatic system optimization for continuous overland and overwater detection and tracking, the radar and IFF offering a detection volume of 6 million cubic miles. Can track over 2,000 targets and simultaneously control friendly forces to over 40 interceptions. APS-145 uses Loral-Randtron AN/APA-171 rotating antennae for the radar (TRAC-A – Total Radiation Aperture Control Antenna) and IFF. Majority of production E-2Cs (118 to the USN) were delivered with earlier and less capable APS-120, -125, -138 and recent -139 (latter for Group I E-2C variant) radars; APS-120 and -125 (latter the first digital version) are out of USN service.

Mission equipment: With the latest APS-145 radar comes enhanced high-speed processors, new high-target-capacity colour displays, JTIDS for improved secure anti-jam voice and data communications, and GPS. Also, Northrop Grumman has received a development contract for a mission computer upgrade

Northrop Grumman E-2C Hawkeye II

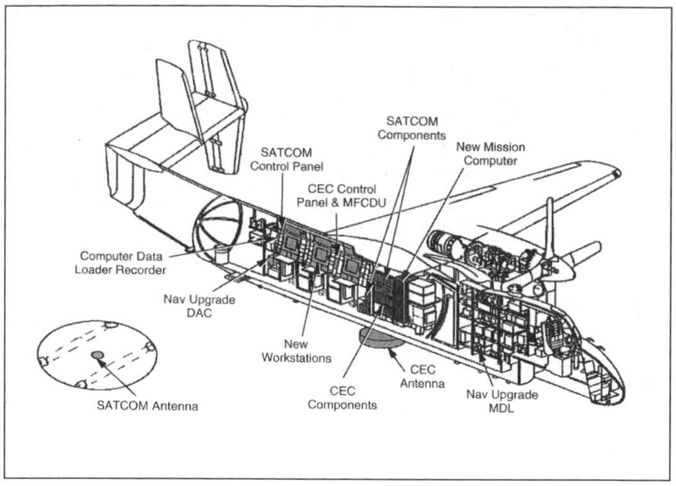

Northrop Grumman E-2C Hawkeye Group II+ upgrade with CEC cutaway (courtesy Northrop Grumman)

(MCU) for "new-build" aircraft and retrofit, to replace the Litton L-304, offering improved memory and processing capabilities in a smaller and lighter (300 lb, 136 kg instead of 750 lb, 340 kg) unit that is easier to maintain (subcontracted to Raytheon's Equipment Division). This will be based on the DEC Alpha chip processing element. Northrop Grumman is also working on a CEC suite (co-operative engagement capability) based around an underfuselage fixed active array antenna, for high speed and secure passing of radar reports between ship and air elements of the carrier battle group. Another programme which is separate to the MCU and CEC programmes, and has yet to be contracted, would see the substitution of the current operators' displays and panels for 3 new lightweight operator stations in the rear compartment, each with a flat-panel plasma screen and processor. In addition, a small workstation is proposed for the co-pilot who can often be under utilized during typical operations, allowing the co-pilot to undertake data processing.

Fixed guns: None.

Wing characteristics: Shoulder mounted, straight, with dihedral. Wings fold and turn to stow horizontally (hydraulically).

Wing control surfaces: Ailerons and Fowler flaps, the former with automatic drooping when the flaps are operated. Leading-edge de-icing boots.

Tail control surfaces: Dihedral tailplane supporting 4 sets of fins, the largest outer fins having dorsal and ventral surfaces and double-hinged rudders. 2 smaller inboard fins, only 1 having a horn-balanced double-hinged rudder. All fins cant inward.

Fuselage: Above fuselage heat exchanger for avionics cooling, being upgraded by 50% capability from 1996 production. Pylon-mounted radome.

Construction materials: All metal, except for some composites in the tail unit.

Engines: 2 Allison T56-A-427 turboprops, with 4-blade constant-speed propellers.

Engine rating: Each 5,100 eshp (3,803 ekW).

Flight refuelling probe: Retrofitted to Israeli aircraft. US Navy system has been designed but not funded.

Fuel system: Maximum 12,800 lb (5,806 kg).

Electrical system: Primary 3-phase 400 Hz AC system using 2 x 90kVA engine-driven generators and 28 volt rectifier for instruments. Emergency 10kVA generator for unfeathering the propellers. E-2C+ is receiving 225kVA generators.

Braking system: Hydraulic brakes and arrester hook.

Flight avionics/instrumentation: Manual/automatic landing system with AN/ARA-64 enhancer, using a data link with the aircraft carrier to allow the pilot to put the aircraft on the glideslope. See Mission equipment for mission computer. Navigation update for Groups II/II+ includes GEC-Marconi CP-140/A air data computer, and dual Litton AN/ASN-139 laser ring gyro INS (in place of single ASN-92) under the ECP (Engineering Change Proposal) with backing HARS. AN/ALR-73 passive detection unit. SATCOM kits already supplied for voice mini-dama hardware. Under MCU, permanent digital SATCOM links (with MATT) will follow. ADF and radar altimeter. Lockheed Martin autopilot as part of the current navigation upgrade. Communications equipment on latest aircraft comprises 2 HF and 6 UHF radios, 3 of the latter also for VHF and 1 usable for SATCOM. See Mission equipment for JTIDS (which incorporates Tacan) and CEC. Several 1553 buses and new high speed bus allows expansion of systems.

Aircraft variants:

E-2C is the standard service version, currently in Group II+ (Hawkeye II) form.

TE-2C is a training variant, of which 2 are in active USN service.

DETAILS FOR E-2C.

Principal dimensions:
Wing span: 80 ft 7 ins (24.56 m)
Maximum length: 57 ft 9 ins (17.6 m)
Maximum height: 18 ft 4 ins (5.59 m)
Radar dome diameter: 24 ft (7.32 m)

Wings:
Area: 700 sq ft (65.032 m^2)
Aspect ratio: 9.276

Undercarriage:
Type: Retractable, with steerable twin nosewheels
Wheel base: 23 ft 2 ins (7.06 m)
Wheel track: 19 ft 6 ins (5.94 m)

Weights:
Empty: 40,484 lb (18,363 kg)
Maximum take-off: 54,300 lb (24,630 kg) for Group II aircraft, with 55,000 lb (24,947 kg) as the design maximum

Performance (data received June 1995):
Maximum speed: 333 kts (383 mph) 617 km/h at 16,900 ft (5,150 m)
High cruise speed: 325 kts (374 mph) 600 km/h
Average cruise speed: 250 kts (288 mph) 463 km/h
Typical low cruise speed: 200 kts (230 mph) 370 km/h
Stall speed: 75 kts (87 mph) 139 km/h
Climb rate: 3,360 ft (1,024 m) per minute at sea level.
Take-off distance: 1,850 ft (564 m)
Landing distance over a 50 ft (15 m) obstacle: 1,360 ft (415 m) ground roll, 2,420 ft (738 m) required runway length
G limits: +3 design, +2 normal
Ceiling: 37,000 ft (11,278 m)
Ferry range: 1,540 naut miles (1,773 miles) 2,852 km
Duration: 5.3 hours at service ceiling, 200 naut miles (230 miles) 370 km from base/ship, with USN reserves

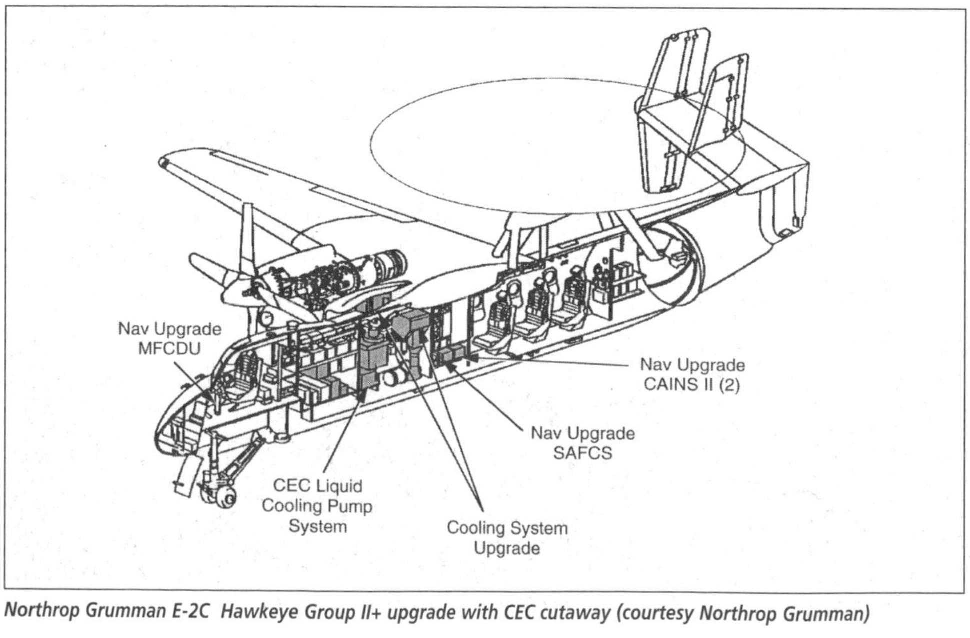

Northrop Grumman E-2C Hawkeye Group II+ upgrade with CEC cutaway (courtesy Northrop Grumman)

Northrop Grumman EA-6B Prowler

First flight: 25 May 1968.

First delivery: 1971.

Role: Naval carrier-based electronic warfare aircraft to degrade/suppress enemy defences; also deployed from land as needed. May also eventually become a principal land-based ECM aircraft with the USAF.

Based on: A-6 Intruder and the EA-6A 2-seat ECM development.

★ Aims

★ More specialized, capable and lengthened development of EA-6A, with 2 additional crew to operate the ECM systems.

Users: US Navy and US Marine Corps (170 received, with about 102 used in early 1995 by 11 active US Navy squadrons as VAQ-130 to VAQ-141, 4 USMC squadrons as VMAQ-1 to VMAQ-4, plus USN Reserve, training and other units). Overseas deployments include a Navy and Marine squadron in Japan (see photo of VMAQ-2 at Nyutabaru air base in December 1994) and Aviano in Italy to support UN operations (starting with VAQ-130, from shore and from USS *Eisenhower* in 1995).

Crew: 4, comprising the pilot, a navigation/communications and defensive ECM operator to his right, and 2 specialist ECM officers (ECMOs) in a separate heavily-glazed cabin aft of the cockpit.

Crew escape: Martin Baker ejection seats.

Mission equipment: Newest tactical communications countermeasures system is the Lockheed Sanders AN/ALQ-149, being fitted to ADVCAP (advanced capability) upgraded EA-6Bs. Housed in the fuselage, it is used to detect, identify, evaluate and jam hostile

communication signals and long-range early-warning radars. It has separate communications and radar intercept elements. The analysis subsystem examines each new signal to determine its identity, and periodically re-examines previously identified signals for updating. The subsystem also performs direction finding. After analysis, the resulting data are transferred to the aircraft's AN/AYK-14 computer for determination of threat, jamming priority and jamming response. Detailed commands are then sent to the jammer pods. The AN/ALQ-149 also provides for the controls and displays which enable the ECMO operator to interact and, if required, modify or override any automated action taken by the system. AN/ALQ-149 has been designed to be compatible with the existing (and future versions of) AN/ALQ-99 jammer. Co-operative jam/look-through cycles allow the 2 systems to function simultaneously without interference, with AN/ALQ-149 data integrated with AN/ALQ-99 to maximize co-ordination and correlation of information and minimize workload. AN/ALQ-149 has 8 weapon replaceable assemblies (WRAs), each of which plugs into a rack in the aft equipment bay. AN/ALQ-99F has 10 jamming transmitters in 5 pods. Fin-tip pod houses surveillance receivers for radar detection. Other systems are the Teledyne AN/ASN-123 navigation and AN/TSQ-142 tactical mission support, while ADVCAP adds improved Tacan, GPS and more. Future improvements in addition to current ADVCAP may include JTIDS.
Self-protection systems: Include chaff dispensers (see above).
Fixed guns: None.
Expendable weapons and equipment: 4 underwing pylons standard, with 6 on ADVCAP conversions, for pods, HARM anti-radar missiles or drop tanks. Underfuselage pylon for pod or tank.
Wing characteristics: Mid mounted, slightly swept, with root extensions and (on ADVCAP) drooped leading edges.
Wing control surfaces: Similar to Intruder. ADVCAP has modified flaps and slats.
Airbrakes: Split type, with aileron function on ADVCAP upgrade.
Engines: 2 Pratt & Whitney J52-P-408 or 409 turbojets.
Engine rating: Each 11,200 lbf (49.82 kN) or 12,000 lbf (53.38 kN) respectively.
Flight refuelling probe: At nose.
Fuel system: 15,422 lb (6,995 kg) plus optional drop tanks.

Northrop Grumman EA-6B operated by VMAQ-2 at Nyutabaru air base in December 1994 (K. Hinata)

DETAILS FOR PROWLER.

Principal dimensions:
Wing span: 53 ft (16.15 m)
Maximum length: 59 ft 10 ins (18.24 m)
Maximum height: 16 ft 3 ins (4.95 m), or 17 ft 11 ins (5.46 m) for ADVCAP

Weights:
Empty: 31,572 lb (14,320 kg)
Maximum take-off: 65,000 lb (29,480 kg)
Maximum landing: 45,500 lb (20,638 kg), or 47,500 lb (21,545 kg) for ADVCAP

Performance:
Maximum speed: 565 kts (651 mph) 1,047 km/h
Cruise speed: 417 kts (481 mph) 774 km/h
Stall speed: 124 kts (143 mph) 230 km/h *clean*
Take-off distance: 2,670 ft (814 m)
Landing distance: 2,150 ft (656 m)
Maximum climb rate: 12,900 ft (3,930 m) per minute
G limits: 5.5
Ceiling: 41,200 ft (12,560 m)
Range with full payload: 955 naut miles (1,100 miles) 1,770 km

Northrop Grumman E-8C Joint STARS

First flight: December 1988 (fully configured E-8A prototype).
First delivery: 1996.
Role: Joint Surveillance and Target Attack Radar System (J-STARS) platform, as a powerful airborne surveillance and target acquisition system to provide real-time, accurate, battle management information.
Based on: Remanufactured ex-commercial Boeing 707-300 airframes.

★ Aims

★ To detect, locate, classify, track and target hostile ground movement in all weather conditions. Operates around-the-clock, in constant communication through secure data links with Air Force command posts and Army mobile ground stations which can call upon aircraft, missiles and artillery for fire support.

▲ Development

▲ 1991. The 2 E-8A prototypes accumulated 535 flying hours over 49 sorties during the Gulf conflict, based in Saudi Arabia with the 4411th Joint STARS Squadron.
▲ 1997. Initial operational capability with E-8C.
Users: USAF (2 E-8A prototypes, 1 test aircraft and 19 production E-8Cs).
Crew: 21 for a standard mission, comprising 3 flight crew and 18 operators. 34 for a long-duration mission, comprising 6 flight crew and 28 operators (including relief crew).
Radar: Westinghouse Norden AN/APY-3 side-looking, phased array radar with antenna scanned electronically in azimuth and steered mechanically in elevation from either side of the aircraft, with wide-area surveillance, fixed target indication, synthetic aperture, moving target indicator and target classification modes. Remainder of Joint-STARS system includes 3 load-sharing, programmable signal processors (each containing 5 high-speed, fixed point distributed processors, capable of over 600 million operations per second), operator consoles, secure voice and data links, and other subsystems. Data from the 24 ft (7.32 m) long radar antenna (which is housed under the fuselage) is processed and displayed to the operators as moving or fixed target reports, target tracks, and synthetic aperture radar images. This radar data is distributed simultaneously to ground stations. In addition to ground targets, the radar can detect helicopters and has a limited maritime capability.
Mission equipment: 18 consoles, comprising 17 identical operation station consoles and a navigation/self-defence console (E-8A prototypes have

DETAILS FOR E-8C.

Principal dimensions:
Wing span: 145 ft 9 ins (44.42 m)
Maximum length: 152 ft 11 ins (46.61 m)
Maximum height: 42 ft 6 ins (12.95 m)

Wings:
Area: 3,050 sq ft (283.35 m^2)
Aspect ratio: 6.965

Weights:
Empty: 171,000 lb (77,560 kg)
Maximum take-off: 336,000 lb (152,400 kg)

Performance:
Maximum speed: Mach 0.84
Ceiling: 42,000 ft (12,800 m)
Duration: 11 hours, or 20 hours with in-flight refuelling

Northrop Grumman E-8 Joint-STARS, with a 24 ft (7.32 m) radar antenna in an underfuselage pod

10 operations consoles and 2 communications consoles). Each operator workstation can undertake flight path planning and monitoring, generation and display of cartographic and hypsographic map data, radar management, surveillance and threat analysis, radar data review, time-of-arrival calculation, jammer location, distance and azimuth calculation, pairing of weapons and targets, and other functions. Digital data links are surveillance and control link (SCDL) for transmission to mobile ground stations, JTIDS for Tacan operation and TADIL-J (tactical data information data link J) generation and processing, and satellite communications link. Voice communications encompass 12 encrypted UHF radios, 2 encrypted HF radios, 3 encrypted VHF radios with provision for single channel ground and airborne radio system (SINCGARS), and multiple intercom nets.
Engines: 4 Pratt & Whitney JT3D-3B turbojets.
Engine rating: Each 18,000 lbf (80.07 kN).
Fuel system: 155,000 lb (70,307 kg)

Northrop Grumman (General Dynamics) EF-111A Ravens

Northrop Grumman EF-111A Raven

First flight: 17 May 1977 (full prototype conversion).
First delivery: November 1981.
Role: Tactical radar jamming (defence suppression); as standoff jammer, it can loiter miles from enemy territory and maximize duration by adopting wing forward sweep, or as a fighter-bomber escort it can adopt full wingsweep for high-speed deep penetration flights, to provide close-in radar jamming.
Based on: General Dynamics (Lockheed Martin) F-111A. (See F-111 in the Combat section.)

▲ Development

▲ January 1975. Grumman won the USAF contract to convert 2 F-111A fighter-bombers into EF-111A EW prototypes.
▲ 1981. Start of deliveries, with all 42 handed over by December 1985.
▲ December 1983. Initial operational capability with the 390th Electronic Combat Squadron.
▲ March 1991. Northrop Grumman was awarded a System Improvement Program (SIP), covering 5 years, to develop and upgrade hardware and software to improve jamming, reliability, maintainability, and enhance its capacity to defeat current and future radar threats. Also airframe improvements.
▲ November 1994. EF-111As were deployed to Aviano in Italy to support regional United Nations operations. They gave way to Navy Prowlers in 1995.
▲ 1995. Planned upgrades included modernization of the jamming equipment and computers, and other improvements as noted below.
▲ Late 1990s. Despite being among the busiest aircraft in the USAF, EF-111As may be retired alongside F-111s, their role rumoured to be taken over by Prowlers.
Users: USAF (40 in the active inventory in mid-1995, with 27 primary aircraft authorized for operational missions; active force serves with the 429th Electronic Combat Squadron out of Cannon AFB, New Mexico. Others with the 79th Test & Evaluation Group at Eglin AFB).
Crew: 2, comprising the pilot and EW officer who controls both active and passive equipment through the on-board computer.
Radar: Texas Instruments AN/APQ-110 terrain-following and AN/APQ-160 attack radars, the former planned for upgrade.
Mission equipment: 3 tons of sophisticated electronic equipment, including transmitters, receivers, antennae, computers and displays, much of it redesigned from Prowler systems. Equipment includes a thin, 16 ft (4.88 m) canoe-shaped radome under the fuselage to house antennae for high-powered jamming transmitters and a tailfin pod to enclose receiving antennae and associated equipment. Eaton AN/ALQ-99E automated primary jammer with 10 transmitters.
Self-protection systems: Lockheed Sanders AN/ALQ-137(V)4 ECM, AN/ALR-62(V)4 terminal threat warning system, AN/ALR-23 radar countermeasures receiver system, and AN/ALE-47 tactical countermeasures dispenser.
Flight avionics/instrumentation: Pre-flight programmable computer, allowing known radars to be entered, enabling the EW officer to concentrate on unanticipated threat radars. Plans in 1995 called for upgrade of the terrain-following radar, computers, new inertial navigation system, and GPS.
Engines: 2 Pratt & Whitney TF30-P-103 turbofans.
Engine rating: Each 20,840 lbf (92.7 kN) with afterburning.
Fuel system: 32,493 lb (14,739 kg).

Joint-STARS operator stations, offering real-time battle management information

DETAILS FOR EF-111A.

Principal dimensions:
Wing span: 31 ft 11 ins (9.73 m) *swept (72° 30')*, 63 ft (19.2 m) *fully spread (16°)*
Maximum length: 76 ft (23.16 m)
Maximum height: 20 ft (6.1 m)

Weights:
Empty: 55,275 (25,072 kg)
Maximum take-off: 88,948 lb (40,346 kg)

Performance:
Maximum speed: 1,227 kts (1,413 mph) 2,272 km/h
Cruise speed: 436 kts (502 mph) 807 km/h
Take-off distance over a 50 ft (15m) obstacle: 5,825 ft (1,775 m)
Combat ceiling: 44,050 ft (13,425 m), service ceiling 29,500 ft (8,990 m)
Ferry range: 2,000 naut miles (2,300 miles) 3,704 km
Duration: over 4 hours without refuelling.

Northrop Grumman OV-1D and RV-1D Mohawk

First flight: 14 April 1959 (YOV-1A development aircraft).
Role: Observation, surveillance, forward air control and electronic intelligence.
Users: Argentine Army (about 20 OV-1s, as ex-US Army aircraft received from 1993) and US Army (over 50 OV-1Ds produced as newly-built aircraft and upgrades of older versions, plus some 13 RV-1Ds).
Crew: 2, side-by-side. Cockpit has armour, flak curtains and bullet-resistant glazing.
Crew escape: Martin Baker ejection seats.
Mission equipment: OV-1D features interchangeable AN/APS-94F side-looking airborne radar (SLAR) in the undernose container, or AN/AAS-24 IR surveillance/detection equipment. 2 KA-60C panoramic cameras and a KA-76 frame camera. AN/ALQ-147A(V)1 IR jamming equipment. Optional ECM pods and photo-flash equipment on underwing pylons. RV-1D includes AN/ALQ-133 for its elint role.
Fixed guns: None.
Self-protection systems: RWR.
Wing characteristics: Mid-mounted, straight.
Wing control surfaces: 2 sets of ailerons per wing, the outer with trim and servo tabs. Flaps.
Tail control surfaces: Triple tail unit, with single rudder with tab. Elevators with tabs.
Fuselage: Side airbrakes.
Engines: 2 AlliedSignal T53-L-701 turboprops.
Engine rating: Each 1,400 shp (1,044 kW).
Fuel system: 1,045 litres. Optional 2 x 568 litre drop tanks.
Flight avionics/instrumentation: Includes Tacan, VOR, radar altimeter, VHF-FM homing equipment, glideslope/marker beacon, ADF, and IFF.

Northrop Grumman OV-1D Mohawk

DETAILS FOR OV-1D.

Principal dimensions:
Wing span: 48 ft (14.63 m)
Maximum length: 41 ft (12.5 m)
Maximum height: 12 ft 8 ins (3.86 m)

Wings:
Area: 360 sq ft (33.445 m^2)
Aspect ratio: 6.4

Undercarriage:
Type: Retractable, with steerable nosewheel
Wheel base: 11 ft 8 ins (3.56 m)
Wheel track: 9 ft 2 ins (2.79 m)

Weights:
Empty, operating: 11,747 lb (5,328 kg)
Maximum take-off: 18,000 lb (8,165 kg)

Performance:
Maximum speed: 264 kts (305 mph) 490 km/h
Stall speed: 73 kts (84 mph) 135 km/h
Take-off over a 50 ft (15 m) obstacle: 1,175 ft (359 m)
Maximum climb rate: 3,620 ft (1,100 m) per minute
Ceiling: 25,000 ft (7,620 m)
Range with maximum fuel: 937 naut miles (1,080 miles) 1,738 km

Schweizer Aircraft Corporation (USA)

Corporate address: Box 147, Elmira, NY 14902.
Telephone: +1 607 739 3821
Facsimile: +1 607 796 2488
Telex: 932459
Founded: 1939.
Information: Barbara J. Tweedt (Manager, Marketing/Communications).

● Activities

● See also Helicopter, General Aviation and Gliders sections.

Schweizer SA 2-37A

First flight: 1986.
Role: Low noise, special missions aircraft for surveillance, EEZ protection, pollution control, training, towing and cargo carrying.
Based on: Developed from the SGM 2-37 motor-glider.

★ Aims

★ "Silent" from the ground when flying at 2,000 ft (610 m) with engine power low.
★ FAR Pt 23 certification.

Users: Mexico (air force, 2 delivered in late 1994) and unspecified US customer (1995 delivery). 2 US Coast Guard anti-narcotics aircraft, transferred from the USAF in 1987 and designated RG-8As, have been converted into RU-38As.
Crew: 2, side-by-side under a large canopy, as pilot and equipment operator. Seat armour available.
Mission equipment: Forward looking infra-red (FLIR), low-light-level TV, cameras or other sensors or cargo are pallet-mounted (for quick removal and replacement) to fit into the 65 cu ft (1.84 m^3) bay aft of the cockpit, accessed from below the fuselage. Maximum payload is 800 lb (363 kg). Above-fuselage blade antennae and below-fuselage turret on former USCG aircraft.
Wing characteristics: Low mounted, high aspect ratio, with dihedral main outer sections. Drooped leading-edge sections from mid span (see photograph).
Wing control surfaces: Ailerons and upper/lower airbrakes. No flaps.
Tail control surfaces: Slab tailplane with large anti-servo tab. Rudder with tab.
Construction materials: All metal.
Engine: Textron Lycoming IO-540 or TIO-540 piston engines, with exhaust silencers and 3-blade "quiet" propeller.

Schweizer SA 2-37A. Note the wing droop sections

Engine rating: 235 hp (175.2 kW) or 250 hp (186.4 kW) respectively.
Fuel system: Maximum 600 lb (272 kg). Usual capacity 197 litres.
Electrical system: 28 volt DC supply, with alternator or more powerful generator. Static inverter for AC supply available.
Braking system: Cleveland disc brakes. Parking brake.
Flight avionics/instrumentation: IFR equipped. Litton INS and AlliedSignal Bendix/King suite including VOR/ILS, ILS, ADF, marker beacon receiver, and transponder. Other equipment to customer's requirements, including night vision goggles and suitable cockpit lighting, autopilot and radar altimeter.

DETAILS FOR SA 2-37A.

Principal dimensions:
Wing span: 61 ft 6 ins (18.75 m)
Maximum length: 28 ft 1 ins (8.56 m)
Maximum height: 7 ft 9 ins (2.36 m)

Wings:
Aerofoil section: Wortmann FX-61-163 and modified FX-60-126 (root/tip)
Area: 199.41 sq ft (18.53 m^2)
Aspect ratio: 18.97

Undercarriage:
Type: Fixed, with tailwheel. Optional wheel fairings
Wheel base: 19 ft 8 ins (5.99 m)
Wheel track: 9 ft 2 ins (2.79 m)

Weights:
Empty: 2,260 lb (1,025 kg)
Maximum take-off: 4,100 lb (1,860 kg)
Payload: 800 lb (363 kg)

Performance (IO-540 engine)**:**
Cruise speed: 138 kts (159 mph) 256 km/h at 75% power
Stall speed: 72 kts (82 mph) 132 km/h *with airbrakes deployed*
Take-off distance: 1,750 ft (534 m) *from grass,* 1,270 ft (387 m) *from paved airstrip*
Maximum climb rate: 960 ft (293 m) per minute
G limits: +6.6, -3.3

Schweizer RU-38A

First flight: 31 May 1995 (unofficial technical) and June 1995 (official).
Role: Covert day/night patrol and surveillance. Also EEZ protection, pollution patrol and more will be able to jettison payloads for SAR at a later date.
Based on: SA 2-37A/RG-8A.

★ Aims

★ Modification of the USCG's RG-8As to twin-engined configuration, providing for an increased payload and improved sensor arrangement, increased over-water safety (especially at night), and better engine maintenance through geared engines to prevent valve coking at low power settings for slow-speed mission flight.

▲ Development

▲ 24 January 1994. First USCG SA 2-37A received by Schweizer for conversion into the RU-38A under USAF contract.
▲ June 1995. Flight testing began at Edwards AFB. To be operated by the USCG over the Gulf of Mexico and Caribbean for the above-mentioned roles.
Users: US Coast Guard (2 conversions of RG-8As, plus a third aircraft). It is believed that Schweizer has at least

Schweizer RU-38A, first flown on 31 May 1995

1 other national and an international customer.
Crew: 2, comprising pilot and sensor operator.
Radar: AlliedSignal Bendix/King AN/APN-215 sea search, mapping and weather radar in a radome below the nose of the port fuselage boom.
Other mission sensors: FLIR in the starboard boom, plus LLTV and dual recorder. Boom pod sensors are interchangeable.
Wing characteristics: SA 2-37A wings, with span increased by the addition of the fuselage booms.
Wing control surfaces: As for SA 2-37A.
Tail control surfaces: Twin fins and horn-balanced rudders, and single joining tailplane with elevator.
Fuselage: Pod and twin-boom type, using only the forward section of the SA 2-37A.
Engines: 2 Teledyne Continental GIO-550A piston engines in "push and pull" tandem layout, but with only 1 used during typical cruise flight. 3:2 gear reduction to 2,267 rpm.
Engine rating: Each 350 hp (261 kW).
Fuel system: 375 litres.
Flight avionics/instrumentation: Typical USCG avionics include Omega, GPS, AlliedSignal Bendix/King KY58 and KY75 communications encryption devices, Wolfsberg RT9600 Maritime band radio, Rockwell Collins ARC182 VHF/UHF, AlliedSignal HF-900 radios, and VHF/UHF direction finders. Night vision goggles optional.

DETAILS FOR RU-38A.

Principal dimensions:
Wing span: 64 ft (19.51 m)
Maximum length: 30 ft 2 ins (9.19 m)

Wings:
Area: 225.86 sq ft (20.98 m^2)
Aspect ratio: 18.135

Undercarriage:
Type: Fixed, with nosewheel

Weights:
Empty: 3,360 lb (1,524 kg)
Maximum take-off: 5,300 lb (2,404 kg)
Payload: 900 lb (408 kg)

Performance:
Never-exceed speed (Vne): 165 kts (190 mph) 305 km/h IAS
Mission speed: 90 kts (104 mph) 167 km/h
Stall speed: 75 kts (87 mph) 139 km/h IAS
Take-off distance: 960 ft (293 m) roll
Landing distance: 1,350 ft (411 m) roll
Mission altitude: Below 10,000 ft (3,050 m)
Ceiling: 24,000ft (7,315 m), service
Duration: 6 to 10 hours

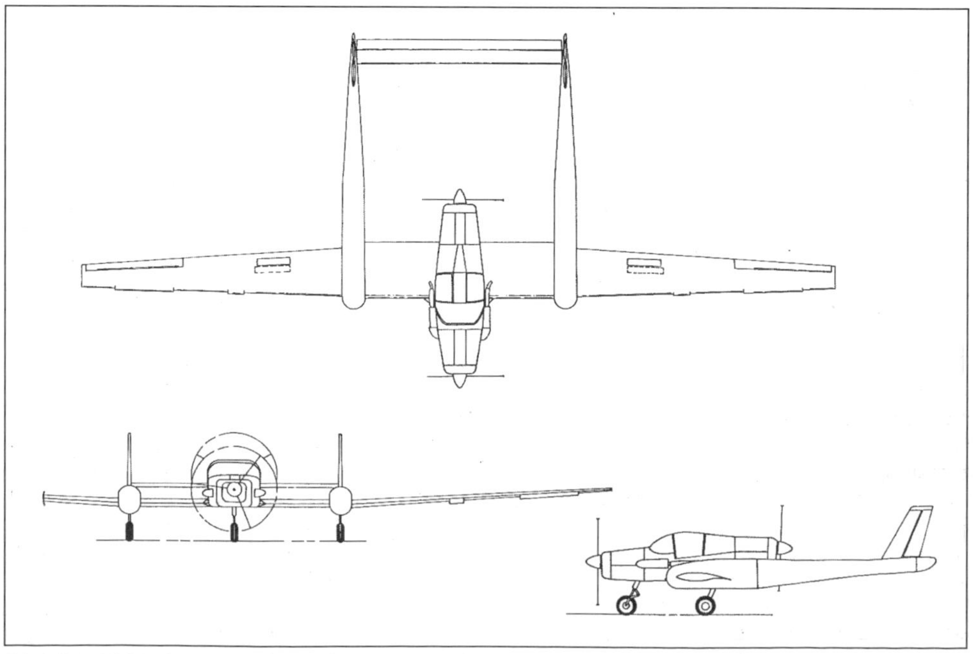

Schweizer RU-38A (courtesy Schweizer)

Airliners, Freighters and Tankers

As a guide, the term "airliner" has been determined to mean transports with seating capacities of 18/19 seats or more, though there are a number of exceptions where deemed necessary. Many component manufacturing companies are also included for reference.

AeroSpace Technologies of Australia Ltd (ASTA) (Australia)

Corporate address: Private Bag 226, Port Melbourne, Victoria 3207.
Telephone: +61 3 647 3111
Facsimile: +61 3 646 2253
Founded: 1987 to succeed GAF (Government Aircraft Factories) and Aircraft Technologies of Australia.
Information: Andrea Edwards (Communications).

● Activities

• Put on the market in 1994 for privatization through the Government Finance Minister. Rockwell Australia Ltd (part of Rockwell International) purchased the Commonwealth's shares of ASTA Components, Defence and Engineering divisions.

DIVISIONS

ASTA Aircraft Services Pty Ltd (ASTAAS)
HQ address: Avalon Airport, Private Bag 2, Lara, Victoria 3212.
Telephone: +61 52 27 9370
Facsimile: +61 52 82 3892

● Activities

• Undertakes aircraft maintenance, repair and modification for Airbus, Boeing and McDonnell Douglas types. Recent work has included 18 Boeing 747 Section 41 modifications and participation in the Pylon Validation programmes conducted by Boeing for the 747.
Commonwealth-owned shares remained available for sale in mid-1995 for the following divisions:
ASTA Avalon Airport.
Pacific Aerospace Corporation Ltd (New Zealand).

Hawker de Havilland Ltd (Australia)

Corporate address: 361 Milperra Road, Bankstown, NSW 2200.
Telephone: +61 2 772 8111
Facsimile: +61 2 7923604
Information: Ken Sayers (New Projects Manager)

● Activities

• Member of the BTR Nylex Group. Activities include production of aerostructures for various Airbus, Boeing and McDonnell Douglas civil/military aeroplanes and helicopters, aircraft upgrading (including current participation in the RAAF F-111C/G and P-3 Orion programmes), and has undertaken complete licence production of aircraft for the RAAF.
• Hawker de Havilland Victoria Ltd subsidiary closed its Engine Parts Division in late 1993, and is currently operating in 3 units, namely Airframe Manufacturing, Systems Engineering, and Repair & Overhaul.

Rockwell Australia Ltd (Australia)

Corporate address: 3 Thomas Holt Drive, PO Box 165, North Ryde, NSW 2113.
Telephone: +61 2 805 5555
Facsimile: +61 2 805 5599

● Activities

• In 1995, Rockwell Australia (part of Rockwell International) bought the Government-owned shares in 3 divisions of ASTA (which see), namely: ASTA Components (at Port Melborne), ASTA Defence (at Lara) and ASTA Engineering (at Port Melborne). These are now operated as ASTA Components and ASTA Defence business units, together with Collins Avionics and Communications and 2 other units.
• In addition to work with Hawker de Havilland on upgrade of RAAF F-111s and other military programmes, purchase of the Commonwealth's shares in ASTA has enhanced Rockwell Australia's aerostructures base. Component manufacture through ASTA shares purchase includes parts for the Airbus A320/A330/A340, Boeing 747/757/777, McDonnell Douglas MD-11/MD-80 and Hornet wing flaps, Pilatus PC-9/A, and Sikorsky helicopters.

SONACA (Belgium)

Full name: Société Nationale de Construction Aérospatiale.
Corporate address: 6041 Gosselies.
Telephone: +32 71 25 51 11
Facsimile: +32 71 34 40 35
Telex: 51241
Founded: 1978.
Information: Marcel Devresse (Marketing and Programmes Director).

● Activities

• Various fabrication, overhaul and modification programmes include fabrication of the leading-edge moving surfaces and systems for the A310/A320/A321/A330/A340, skis for the C-130, fuselage sections/wing leading edge/anti-icing system for the EMB-145, wing flaps/leading edge/trailing edge for the Atlantique, cabin panels and pilot doors for the A 109, reinforcing frames for the Saab 340/2000, and aft fuselage/fin plus final mating and repair, overhaul and modification for the F-16.

Embraer (Brazil)

Corporate address: See Combat section for all company details.

Embraer EMB-110 Bandeirante and C-95 series

First flight: 26 October 1968 (EMB-100/YC-95 *2130* prototype).
First delivery: 9 February 1973 (C-95).
Role: Short-haul passenger or cargo transport with quick-change capability. Military versions for transport and other roles. Can operate from unprepared strips and without ground support equipment.
Airframe life: 30,000 hours.
Sales: 469 delivered to civil and military customers in 37 countries, plus 29 related EMB-111s (see Combat section). Out of production by 1994. The major commercial operator has been WestAir of Fresno, CA.
Details: For the P1 and later series.
Crew: 2 flight crew.
Passengers: Typically 18-19 passengers or cargo (fewer in earlier versions and up to 21 in the final P2A version). Boarding via the main passenger door aft of the cockpit, with airstairs, allowing simultaneous cargo/baggage loading through the hydraulically-operated rear cargo door. Alternatively, some versions have 2 passenger doors and no cargo door (see Aircraft variants).
Seat pitch: *P1/41* (18 passengers): 32 ins (81 cm) right hand, 30 ins (76 cm) left hand. *P1/41* (19 passengers): 32 ins (81 cm) both. *P2/41* (18 passengers): 32 ins (81 cm) right hand, 31 ins (79 cm) left hand. See diagram.
Baggage compartment: *P1*: 113 cu ft (3.2 m^3), with 705 lb (320 kg) capacity. *P2* 70.6 cu ft (2 m^3), with 529 lb (240 kg) capacity.
Wing control surfaces: Frise ailerons (with port aileron) and double-slotted flaps.
Tail control surfaces: Elevators (starboard tab) and rudder (with tab).
Flight control system: Mechanical, with electrically-operated flaps.
Construction materials: All metal.
Engines: Two Pratt & Whitney Canada PT6A-34 turboprops, with 7 ft 9 ins (2.36 m) Hartzell propellers.

Embraer EMB-110 P1A Bandeirante used as a VIP transport

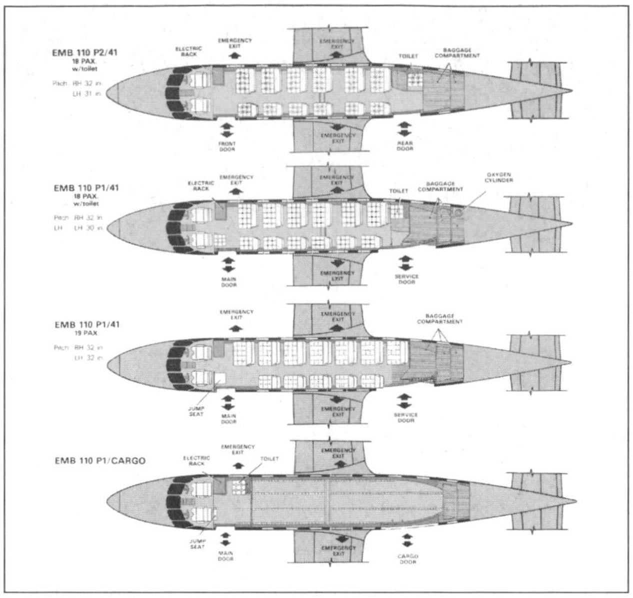

Embraer EMB-110 P1/41, P2/41 and P1 cargo cabin layouts (courtesy Embraer)

Engine rating: Each 750 shp (559.3 kW).
Fuel system: 1,720 litres (1,660 usable).
Electrical system: 2 engine-driven 28 volt DC, 200 amp generators, connected independently and in parallel with the main busbar. 24 volt, 34 amp-hours alkaline (ni-cd) battery for emergency power. Secondary system to power the AC equipment, supplied by 1 of 2 x 600 volt-amps static inverters, furnishing 115V/400Hz and 26V/400Hz AC.
Hydraulic system: 3,000 psi, generated by 2 engine-driven pumps.
Braking system: Disc on main units.
De-icing system: Inflatable de-icer boots on the wing and tail leading edges. Electrical heaters bonded to the engine air intakes. Electrical anti-icers bonded to the propeller blade leading edges. Electrically heated stall detector and windshields.
Fire system: Pneumatic, continuous type. Warning setting valves at 160°C and 450°C for average and discrete conditions respectively. Each engihe is equipped with a single discharge Halon 1301 agent bottle.
Radar: Bendix RDR-1200 or RDR-160.
Flight avionics/instrumentation: Rockwell Collins Pro Line, Microline and other systems were made available.
Aircraft variants:
EMB-110 was the initial version seating 12 passengers, sold to the Brazilian Air Force as the C-95. 680 shp (507 kW) PT6A-27 turboprop engines, as retained on early versions until the P1.
EMB-110A was produced for the Brazilian Air Force as the EC-95 for calibration.
EMB-110B was produced for the Brazilian Air Force as the R-95 for photogrammetry and in the B1 version for a private operator, the latter with a quick-change interior for carrying 14 passengers instead of camera equipment. The Uruguayan Air Force also operates a B1 for survey.
EMB-110C was built as a 15-passenger transport for commercial use from 1973. The Chilean Navy retains 3 as EMB-110CNs and the Uruguayan Air Force 3 for transport duties.
EMB-110E was built as a 7-passenger executive transport.
EMB-110K1 is a lengthened all-cargo transport, carrying a 3,422 lb (1,552 kg) load. This became the standard length for P1 and subsequent series. Brazilian military designation C-95A.
EMB-110P for 18 passengers was the last short-fuselage version, at 46 ft 8 ins (14.23 m) overall length.
EMB-110P1 was produced as an 18-passenger/cargo transport with quick-change capability. Certified under the FAA's FAR-23/135 Appendix A. Same lengthened fuselage as the K1 and PT6A-34 engines that became standard for subsequent versions. Military versions are the P1K for transport and search and rescue, Brazilian designated SC-95B.
EMB-110 P1/41 was certified under the FAA's SFAR-41 regulations for a higher maximum take-off weight. 18/19 passengers.
EMB-110 P1A incorporates a 10° dihedral tailplane and improved acoustic insulation for lower noise and vibration levels in the cabin. Was made available in FAR-23/135 and SFAR-41 versions.
EMB-110 P2 was produced as an 18-passenger version only and no cargo, with front and rear doors for passenger loading with airstairs, enabling quick turnarounds with flexibility for passenger and baggage boarding. Certified to FAR-23/135.
EMB-110 P2/41 is similar to the P2 but certified under SFAR-41.
EMB-110 P2A has the tailplane dihedral and noise/vibration reduction detailed under P1A, with similar certification. Maximum 21 passengers.
EMB-110S1 was produced for geophysical survey, with P1 engines and 54 ft 7.5 ins (16.65 m) overall length.

DETAILS FOR EMB-110 P1 AND LATER SERIES.

Principal dimensions:
Wing span: 50 ft 3 ins (15.32 m)
Maximum length: 49 ft 6.5 ins (15.1 m)
Maximum height: 16 ft 2 ins (4.92 m)

Cabin:
Length: 31 ft 2 ins (9.5 m)
Width: 5 ft 3 ins (1.6 m)
Height: 5 ft 3 ins (1.6 m)
Volume: 724 cu ft (20.5 m^3)
Main passenger door: 55.9 x 24.8 ins (1.42 x 0.63 m)
Cargo door: 55.9 x 70.9 ins (1.42 x 1.8 m)

Wings:
Aerofoil section: NACA 23016 modified/23012 modified
Area: 313.23 sq ft (29.1 m^2)
Aspect ratio: 8.1
Incidence: 3°
Dihedral: 7°

Tail unit:
Tailplane span: 24 ft 9 ins (7.54 m)
Tailplane area: 59.31 sq ft (5.51 m^2)

Undercarriage:
Type: Retractable, with steerable nosewheel
Wheel base: 16 ft 9 ins (5.1 m)
Wheel track: 16 ft 2.5 ins (4.94 m)

Weights:
See separate table

Performance:
Maximum speed: 248 kts (285 mph) 459 km/h
Maximum cruise speed: 225 kts (259 mph) 417 km/h
Long-range cruise speed: 176 kts (203 mph) 326 km/h
Stall speed: 69 kts (80 mph) 128 km/h for P2A
Take-off distance: 1,414 ft (431 m) at sea level
Take-off over a 50 ft (15 m) obstacle: 2,215 ft (675 m) at sea level
Landing distance: 1,854 ft (565 m) at sea level.
Landing distance over a 50 ft (15 m) obstacle: 2,789 ft (850 m) at sea level.
Maximum climb rate: 1,787 ft (545 m) per minute at sea level
Maximum climb rate, one engine: 428 ft (130 m) per minute at sea level
Ceiling: 21,490-22,500 ft (6,550-6,860 m)
Range: 1,025 naut miles (1,179 miles) 1,898 km with 45 minutes reserve

EMB-110 P1/P2 WEIGHT TABLE	EMB-110 P1	EMB-110 P1/41 with 18 passengers	EMB-110 P1/41 with 19 passengers	EMB-110 P2	EMB-110 P2/41 with 18 passengers	EMB-110 P2/41 with 19 passengers
Maximum ramp	12,632 lb (5,730 kg)	13,073 lb (5,930 kg)	13,073 lb (5,930 kg)	12,566 lb (5,700 kg)	13,073 lb (5,930 kg)	13,073 lb (5,930 kg)
Maximum take-off	12,500 lb (5,670 kg)	13,007 lb (5,900 kg)	13,007 lb (5,900 kg).	12,500 lb (5,670 kg)	13,007 lb (5,900 kg)	13,007 lb (5,900 kg)
Maximum landing	12,500 lb (5,670 kg)	12,566 lb (5,700 kg)	12,566 lb (5,700 kg)	12,500 lb (5,670 kg)	12,566 lb (5,700 kg)	12,566 lb (5,700 kg)
Maximum zero fuel weight	12,015 lb (5,450 kg)	12,015 lb (5,450 kg)	12,015 lb (5,450 kg)	12,015 lb (5,450 kg)	12,015 lb (5,450 kg)	12,015 lb (5,450 kg)
Empty, equipped	7,857 lb (3,564 kg)	8,007 lb (3,632 kg)	7,985 lb (3,622 kg)	7,751 lb (3,516 kg)	7,914 lb (3,590 kg)	7,892 lb (3,580 kg)
Basic operating	8,415 lb (3,817 kg)	8,565 lb (3,885 kg)	8,543 lb (3,875 kg)	8,309 lb (3,769 kg)	8,472 lb (3,843 kg)	8,450 lb (3,833 kg)
Usable fuel	2,884 lb (1,308 kg)	2,884 lb (1,308 kg)	2,884 lb (1,308 kg)	2,884 lb (1,308 kg)		

Embraer EMB-120 Brasilia

First flight: 27 July 1983.
Certification: 10 May 1985 for Brazilian CTA. 9 July 1985 for FAA Type Approval, followed in 1986 by European certification. 26 August 1986 for hot-and-high version with PW118A engines, which maintain maximum output up to a temperature of ISA+15°C at sea level.
First delivery: August 1985 to Atlantic Southeast Airlines of the USA.
Role: Regional airliner and cargo transport, with corporate and other special versions. (EMB-120EW and SR surveillance versions are detailed in the Reconnaissance Section.)
Airframe life: Designed for 40,000 flight hours or 60,000 flights with minimum structural repairs or replacements due to fatigue.
Noise levels: 82.0 EPNdB take-off, 83.5 EPNdB sideline, 92.3 EPNdB approach, with PW118 engine.

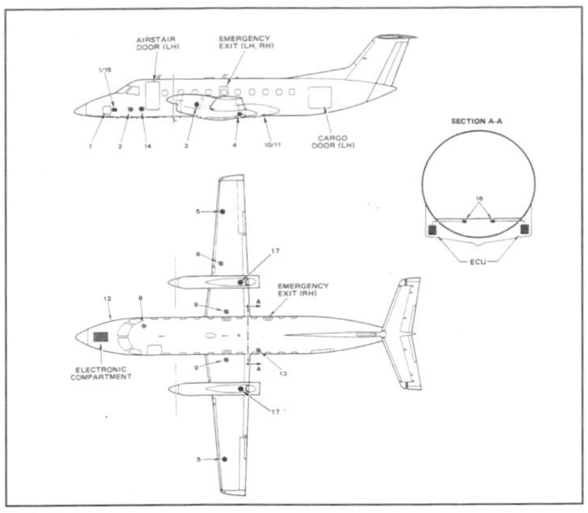

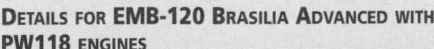

Embraer EMB-120 Brasilia ground service connections key (courtesy Embraer):

1. Electrical power DCreceptacle.
2. Oxygen supplyreceptacle.
3. Engine oil supply panels (RH, LH).
4. Hydraulic power supply connection (LH, RH).
5. Overwing gravity fuel fillers.
6. Pressure refuelling and defuelling control panel and connection.
7. Battery access.
8. Emergency gear selector valve.
9. Fuel dump valves.
10. Air conditioning connection.
11. Pressurized test connection (RH).
12. Gear doors safety valve, gear/passenger door accumulator.
13. Test connection for hydraulic reservoir pressurization and emergency brake accumulator.
14. Door control.
15. Ramp interphone jacks.
16. Air conditioning test connection.
17. Hydraulic reservoirs fillers.

Embraer EMB-120 Brasilia Advanced for United Express, one of 5 ordered in August 1994

Sales: 283 Brasilias had been delivered at the time of writing, when 32 were on order. Among the latest deliveries have been 3 EMB-120QCs for Interbrasil Star, the first received on 18 April 1995.
Details: Principally for the latest EMB-120 Brasilia Advanced, unless stated.
Crew: 2 pilots, 1 flight observer.
Passengers: 30. Passenger or cargo quick-change cabin layout are available in aircraft with a forward galley and toilet, offering 30 passengers plus 1,543 lb (700 kg) of baggage, or 7,716 lb (3,500 kg) of cargo. Conversion takes about 50 minutes by 3 persons. Removable bulkhead. Cargo restraint net system.
Seat pitch: 31 ins (79 cm) except last 2 on starboard side.
Baggage compartment: 6-section overhead compartment, each section 5.3 cu ft (0.15 m^3) and with 73 lb (33 kg) capacity. Main compartment complies with class D of FAR-25.857. *Volume* 222.5 cu ft (6.3 m^3) and 1,543 lb (700 kg) capacity. Service door 4 ft 5.5 x 4 ft 3 ins (1.36 x 1.3 m).
Cabin pressurization: 7 psi differential maintains the cabin at sea level up to 17,000 ft (5,200 m).
Wing control surfaces: Ailerons (with tabs), outboard and inboard double-slotted Fowler flaps, plus nacelle flap.
Tail control surfaces: T-tail, with rudder and elevators (with tabs).
Flight control system: Mechanical, except for hydraulically-operated rudder.
Construction materials: Mostly metal, the fuselage having chemically milled skin reinforced by extruded stiffeners. Composite wing and tailplane leading edges (detachable/interchangeable), fin leading edge and dorsal fin.
Engines: 2 Pratt & Whitney Canada PW118 or PW118A turboprops, with 10 ft 6 ins (3.2 m) Hamilton Standard 14 RF-9 propellers.
Engine rating: Each 1,800 shp (1,342 kW)
Fuel system: 3,312 litres usable, of 3,340 capacity.
Electrical system: Primary 28 volts DC supply. Power sources are 2 x 400 amp, 28 volt DC starter-generators; 2 x 150 amp, 28 volt DC auxiliary generators. The AC supply (115 and 26V) is by 2 x 250 volt-amp/400Hz single-phase static inverters, 1 as a standby.
24 volt/40 amp-hour ni-cd battery is connected to the central DC bus in parallel with the starter-generators, assisting each starter-generator during engine starting in case of no external power supply.
Hydraulic system: 3,000 psi normal pressure, with 2 independent systems.
Braking system: Hydraulically-operated disc.
De-icing system: Electrically-heated windshields and electrically de-iced propeller blades. Wings, fin and tailplane leading edges, air inlet and induction by-pass ducts are protected by inflatable de-icers.
Oxygen system: Option 1: Chemical, with 979 litres of usable oxygen for the crew and 11 oxygen generators for the passenger cabin. Option 2: Gaseous, with 11 dispensing units for the passenger cabin.
Fire system: Halon 1301.
Radar: See below.
Flight avionics/instrumentation: Digital navigation and communications systems. Collins configuration is based on the Pro Line II, with 270 naut mile colour weather radar. Options to this include a complete set of 6 EFIS. Alternative Bendix configuration centres on the CNI-3 and EFIS-10 lines, with weather radar.

Details for EMB-120 Brasilia Advanced with PW118 engines
(for PW118A engines, 9 lb, 4.08 kg should be added to equipped empty and basic operating weights, and the same amount deducted from the payload)

Principal dimensions:
Wing span: 64 ft 11 ins (19.78 m)
Maximum length: 65 ft 8 ins (20 m)
Maximum height: 20 ft 10 in (6.35 m)

Cabin:
Length: 30 ft 9 ins (9.38 m)
Width: 6 ft 11 ins (2.1 m)
Height: 5 ft 9 ins (1.76 m)
Volume: 967.62 cu ft (27.4 m^3)
Main door size: 66.9 x 30.57 ins (1.7 x 0.77 m)

Wings:
Aerofoil section: NACA 23018 modified/23012 (root/tip).
Area: 424.42 sq ft (39.43 m^2)
Aspect ratio: 9.923
Incidence: 2°
Dihedral: 6° 30′

Tail unit:
Tailplane span: 22 ft 9 ins (6.94 m)
Tailplane area: 107.64 sq ft (10 m^2)
Vertical tail area: 74.27 sq ft (6.9 m^2)

Undercarriage:
Type: Retractable, with steerable nosewheels
Main wheel tyre size: 24 x 7.25-12 12PR
Nose wheel tyre size: 18 x 5.5
Wheel base: 22 ft 1 ins (6.98 m)
Wheel track: 21 ft 7 ins (6.58 m)
Turning radius: 51 ft 8 ins (15.76 m) wingtip, no slip angle

Weights:
Empty, equipped: 15,807 lb (7,170 kg)
Basic operating: 16,711 lb (7,580 kg)
Maximum take-off: 26,433 lb (11,990 kg)
Maximum landing: 25,794 lb (11,700 kg)
Payload: 7,319 lb (3,320 kg)

Performance:
Maximum cruise speed: 298 kts (343 mph) 552 km/h ISA
Long-range speed: 264 kts (304 mph) 489 km/h ISA
Stall speed: 90 kts (104 mph) 167 km/h *with full flaps,* 17% CG
Take-off distance: 5,118 ft (1,560 m) ISA
Landing field length: 4,528 ft (1,380 m) ISA
Maximum climb rate: 2,000 ft (610 m) per minute, sea level, ISA
Maximum climb rate, one engine: 540 ft (165 m) per minute, sea level, ISA
Ceiling: 30,000 ft (9,145 m) ISA
Range with full fuel: 1,640 naut miles (1,887 miles) 3,037 km at basic operating weight, with reserve
Range with 30 passengers: 800 naut miles (920 miles) 1,481 km, at basic operating weight, with reserve

Aircraft variants:
EMB-120 was the initial production version, with 1,500 shp (1,118.6 kW) Pratt & Whitney Canada PW115 engines.
EMB-120RT quickly became the standard version, offered with either PW118 or PW118A engines. Maximum take-off weight 25,353 lb (11,500 kg). Take-off distance reduced to 4,659 ft (1,420 m). Maximum cruising speed 300 kts and 315 kts with PW118 and 118A engines respectively.
EMB-120 Cargo is the all-cargo version with a 8,818 lb (4,000 kg) payload.
EMB-120QC is the quick-change version available from 1993, with floor plus sidewall protection, fire protection system, smoke curtain separating the cockpit from the cargo compartment, a 9g removable rear bulkhead and cargo restraint net.
EMB-120ER (provisionally known as EMB-120X) became available from 1994 as an enhanced range version, with PW118 and PW118A engines and, most importantly, increased take-off weight. With PW118As, maximum cruising speed is 314 kts, ceiling 32,000 ft (9,750 m) and range slightly reduced compared with ER with PW118s under ISA conditions, but range increases at ISA+20°C with maximum fuel to 1,460 naut miles (from 1,370 naut miles for ER with PW118s at ISA+15°C).
EMB-120 Basilia Advanced became available in late 1994. Based on the ER, it has redesigned leading edges for all flying surfaces, improved passenger door sealing for better noise reduction, redesigned interior with new overhead bins of increaed capacity, improved crew seating, redesigned cockpit floor, improved flap system, increased cargo compartment capacity and more. Same maximum take-off weight and range as the EMB-120ER.
EMB-120EW and SR are surveillance versions, described in the Reconnaissance section.

Embraer EMB-145

First flight: 11 August 1995.
Certification: Flight test and certification are being conducted with the single prototype and 3 pre-series aircraft, plus a static airframe, and will take 13 months and 1,100 flight hours. Pre-series aircraft will be refurbished for delivery to early customers.
First delivery: Second half of 1996.
Role: 50-seat regional airliner.
Airframe life: Designed for 75,000 flight hours or 60,000 flights, with minimum structural repairs or replacement due to fatigue, when used in the commuter role.
Airport limits: Standard version maximum take-off weight and main LDG tyres (30 x 9.5-14) at 130 psi:

RIGID PAVEMENT	K(M N/m^3)	ACN
	150	11.0
	80	11.7
	40	12.3
	20	12.9
FLEXIBLE PAVEMENT	California Bearing Ratio	ACN
	15%	9.4
	10%	10.1
	6%	11.6
	3%	13.1

Noise levels: Predicted levels are 82 EPNdB take-off, 87 EPNdB sideline, 92 EPNdB approach. Predicted average cabin noise level during maximum cruise is 75.7 dBA.
Sales/users: Sales are expected to be over 400 aircraft in 10 years. By August 1995 Embraer held 18 firm orders, 16 options and 127 letters of intent from 18 customers in 9 countries. Launch airlines will be Australia's Flight West Airlines and TransBrasil.

Embraer EMB-145 regional twin-jet prototype

The first order from Europe came in late 1994, from Regional Airlines of Nantes (3), followed by Eastern Trade Wings of Denmark (3, for operation in India). Cost US$13 million per unit (1992 dollars).
Crew: 2 pilots and 1 flight observer.
Passengers: 50.
Seat pitch: 31 ins (79 cm).
Baggage compartment: 325 cu ft (9.2 m^3), 2,205 lb (1,000 kg). Overhead bin in 11 sections with 67.1 cu ft (1.9 m^3) of space, 635 lb (288 kg) capacity. Under-seat volume 79.8 cu ft (2.26 m^3), 992 lb (450 kg). Wardrobe and stowage compartment 48.9 cu ft (1.38 m^3). Total volume 520.8 cu ft (14.74 m^3).
Galley: 42 cu ft (1.2 m^3), catering 353 lb (160 kg) normal. Optional configurations allow 50, 56 and 81 cu ft (1.4, 1.6 and 2.3 m^3) of volume, with catering 441, 529 and 705 lb (200, 240 and 320 kg) respectively, retaining 50 passengers but reducing to 48-49 with increased half trolley capacity and/or increased wardrobe space.
Cabin pressurization: 7.8 psi differential to maintain cabin at maximum 8,000 ft to an operational ceiling of 37,000 ft.
Wing control surfaces: Aileron, 2 double-slotted flaps and 2 ground spoilers (external panel also acts as a flight speed brake) per wing.
Tail control surfaces: 2-segment rudder (tandem) where the trailing rudder is automatically deflected as a function of the forward rudder deflection, and elevators (with tabs).
Fuselage: Basically a lengthened Brasilia structure, with 3 x 7050 hand forged/machined frames providing the necessary basis for the continuous wing to fuselage attachments, and special 7050 machined frames at the tail cone providing the basis for similar attachments of the pylons and fin.
Flight control system: Mechanically actuated elevators, and the dual rudder and ailerons are power operated. For the rudder and aileron control systems, artificial feel and centring units are provided. All trims are electrically actuated. Flap panels are electrically actuated and electronically controlled. Speed brake/ground spoilers are hydraulically actuated and electronically controlled. Automatic flight control system. Stall protection system with stick shaker and stick pusher.
Construction materials: Mostly metal (generally aluminium alloy), with extensive chemical milling. Composites aft wing-stub cell upper skin (carbonfibre/Nomex honeycomb sandwich), wing

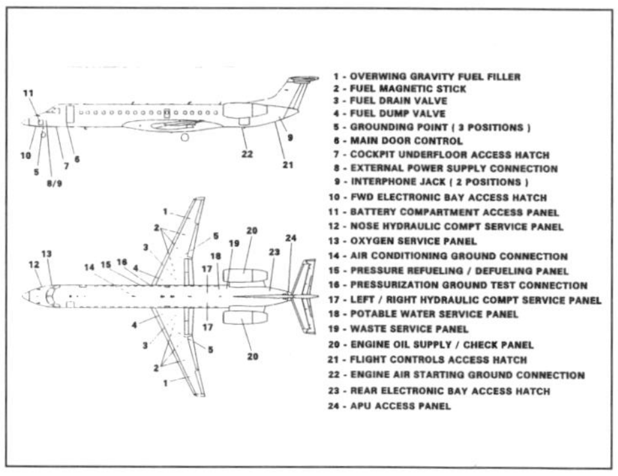

Servicing and maintenance points positioning and definitions (Courtesy Embraer)

control surfaces, fin leading edge and dorsal fin (Kevlar/glassfibre/Nomex honeycomb sandwich), fin-to-tailplane fairing (Kevlar/glassfibre) and elevator tabs. (In October 1994 Enaer of Chile began assembly of the prototype's tailplane, having earlier started assembly of the tailfin. December 1994 saw the first shipset of AE 3007 engines sent from Allison to Embraer. In January 1995 Spain's Gamesa delivered the first set of prototype wings from its newly built Vitoria EMB-145 parts plant. In March 1995 Sonaca of Belgium delivered 2 fuselage sections for the first pre-series aircraft.)
Engines: 2 Allison AE 3007A turbofans.
Engine rating: Each 7,040 lbf (31.32 kN) sea level static, ISA, with FADEC.
Fuel system: In wing tanks, each half wing tank holding 2,621 litres of usable fuel. Usable fuel 9,374 lb (4,252 kg).
Electrical system: 4 x 28 volt DC, 400 amp brushless generators. Also 400 amp/28 volt DC APU starter-generator. AC power (115 VAC) using 1 x 250 volt-amps/400Hz single-phase static inverter. 2 x 24 VDC/43 amp-hour ni-cd batteries. An independent back-up 24 VDC lead-acid sealed battery is installed to supply stabilized power for equipment that may be affected by electrical transients in the main generation system.
Hydraulic system: 3,000 psi normal pressure.
Braking system: Multi-disc type, with hydraulic and mechanical actuation, with carbon heatsink. Main brake system and an emergency/parking brake subsystem.
De-icing system: Air intake of the nacelles, and wing and tailplane leading edges use bleed air anti-icing. Electrically heated windshields, pitot-static tubes, angle-of-attack sensors, total air temperature probe, etc.

Oxygen system: Gaseous crew system. Passenger system consists of chemical generators.
Radar: Weather radar.
Flight avionics/instrumentation: Main characteristics are dual central integrated avionics computer, encompassing functions such as displays driving, autopilot/flight director, and EICAS. All glass cockpit based on five 8 x 7 ins (20 x 18 cm) CRT displays with multi-reversionary capabilities (2 primary flight displays, 2 multi-function displays and 1 EICAS display, Standard and optional equipment satisfies FAR-25, IFR operation and FAR-121.
Aircraft variants:
EMB-145 is the standard version, with an 800 naut mile range with 50 passengers.
EMB-145ER is the extended range version, offering a full-passenger range of 1,180 naut miles while retaining the same maximum operating and landing weights and payload.

Details for EMB-145.

Principal dimensions:
Wing span: 65 ft 9 ins (20.04 m)
Maximum length: 98 ft (29.87 m)
Maximum height: 22 ft 2 ins (6.75 m)

Cabin:
Length: 54 ft 1 ins (16.49 m)
Width: 6 ft 11 ins (2.1 m), and 5 ft 1 ins (1.56 m) at floor
Height: 6 ft (1.82 m)
Volume: 1,871.7 cu ft (53 m^3)
Main door size: 5 ft 7 ins x 2 ft 4 ins (1.7 x 0.71 m)
Height to sill: 5 ft 4 ins (1.63 m).

Wings:
Aerofoil section: Supercritical.
Area: 551 sq ft (51.19 m^3)
Aspect ratio: 7.85
Sweepback: about 22° 44′

Tail unit:
Tailplane span: 24 ft 9 ins (7.55 m)
Tailplane area: 120.6 sq ft (11.2 m^2)
Fin area: 77.5 sq ft (7.2 m^2)

Undercarriage:
Type: Retractable, with steerable nosewheels
Main wheel tyre size: 30 x 9.5-14
Nose wheel tyre size: 19.5 x 6.75-8
Wheel base: 47 ft 5 ins (14.45 m)
Wheel track: 13 ft 5.5 ins (4.1 m)
Turning radius: 98 ft 10 ins (29.22 m) for 180° turn

Design weights:
Empty, equipped: 24,436 lb (11,084 kg)
Ramp: 42,549 lb (19,300 kg) standard, 45,645 lb (20,700 kg) extended range
Basic operating: 25,540 lb (11,585 kg) for both versions
Maximum take-off: 42,328 lb (19,200 kg) standard, 45,415 lb (20,600 kg) extended range
Maximum landing: 41,226 lb (18,700 kg) for both versions
Payload: 12,158 lb (5,515 kg) for both versions

Design performance:
Maximum operating speed: Mach 0.78
Maximum cruise speed: Mach 0.75, or 430 kts (495 mph) 796 km/h standard, 416 kts (479 mph) 770 km/h extended range, 95% power
Stall speed: 117 kts (135 mph) 217 km/h *clean*, 97 kts (112 mph) 180 km/h *with flaps*
Take-off field length: 4,921 ft (1,500 m) standard, 5,741 ft (1,750 m) extended range at sea level, ISA
Landing field length: 4,232 ft (1,290 m)
Maximum climb rate: 2,380 ft (725 m) per minute standard, 2,150 ft (655 m) per minute extended range
Maximum climb rate, one engine: 660 ft (201 m) per minute standard, 520 ft (158 m) per minute extended range
Time to climb to 30,000 ft, MTOW: 16 minutes
Ceiling: 37,000 ft (11,280 m)
Range with full fuel: 1,430 naut miles (1,645 miles) 2,648 km at sea level, with 15 passengers, with reserve
Range with 50 passengers: 800 naut miles (920 miles) 1,480 km standard, 1,200 naut miles (1,379 miles) 2,220 km extended range

Bombardier Inc (Canada)

Corporate address: 800 René-Lévesque Blvd West, Montreal, Quebec H3B 1Y8.
Telephone: +1 514 861 9481
Facsimile: +1 514 861 7053
Employees: 36,500 in all groups, with over 24,000 in the Aerospace Group.

DIVISIONS

Aerospace Group – North America
comprising:

Bombardier Inc. Canadair
HQ address: 400 Côte-Vertu Road, Dorval, Quebec H4S 1Y9.
Telephone: +1 514 855 5000
Facsimile: +1 514 744 6586

● Activities
● See Bombardier Regional Aircraft Division and Bombardier Inc Canadair.

de Havilland Inc
HQ address: 123 Garratt Boulevard, Downsview, Ontario M3K 1Y5.
Telephone: +1 416 633 7310
Facsimile: +1 416 375 4546

● Activities
● See Bombardier Regional Aircraft Division.

Learjet Inc
HQ address: One Learjet Way, Wichita, KS 67277.
Telephone: +1 316 946 2000
Facsimile: +1 316 946 2220

● Activities
● See General Aviation section – USA.

Shorts Group
including
Short Brothers PLC
HQ address: Airport Road, Belfast, Northern Ireland BT3 9DZ.
Telephone: +44 1232 458 444
Facsimile: +44 1232 732 974

● Activities
● See UK.

Bombardier Capital Group
Bombardier Eurorail
Motorized Consumer Products Group
Transport Equipment Group - North America

Bombardier Regional Aircraft Division (Canada)

Corporate address: Garratt Boulevard, M/S N16-14, Downsview, Ontario M3K 1Y5.
Founded: August 1992.
Information: Colin S. Fisher (Manager, Public Relations – *telephone* +1 416 375 3026, *facsimile* +1 416 375 4529).

● Activities
● Marketing, sales, contracts and customer support for the Canadair Regional Jet and de Havilland Dash 8 series.

Bombardier Canadair Regional Jet, Corporate Jetliner and CRJ-X

Details: For Regional Jet (see Aircraft variants).
First flight: 10 May 1991.
Certification: 31 July 1992 (Transport Canada Type Approval based on FAA FAR 25, Amendment 62), 14 January 1993 for European JAA change 13, and 21 January 1993 for FAA.
First delivery: 19 October 1992 to Lufthansa CityLine of Germany, starting services on 1 November.
Role: Medium-range regional airliner.
Details: Regional Jet.
Airframe life: Economic repair life of 80,000 cycles.
Noise levels: 78.6 EPNdB and 89 FAR EPNdB take off, 92.1 EPNdB and 98 FAR EPNdB approach, 82.2 EPNdB and 94 FAR EPNdB sideline.
Sales: 67 delivered and 49 on order by June 1995.
Crew: 2 pilots.
Passengers: 50. Drop-down air stair for open ramp parking.
Seat pitch: 31 ins (79 cm).
Galley: Forward galley or hot double galley with reduced baggage area.
Pressurization: 8.3 psi maximum cabin differential.

Bombardier Canadair Regional Jet with Comair, the largest operator with 30 aircraft delivered/ordered

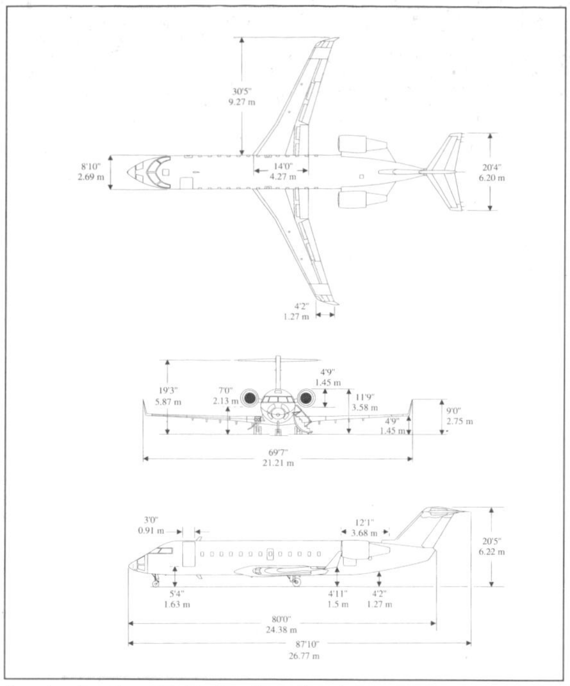

Bombardier Canadair Regional Jet drawing (courtesy Bombardier)

Bombardier Canada CRJ-X 70-seat airliner

Baggage volume: 496 cu ft (14.04 m^3) total, comprising wardrobe, overhead bin, under seat and in 314 cu ft (8.89 m^3) compartment.
Baggage hold capacity: 3,400 lb (1,542 kg).
Size of baggage door: 2 ft 9 ins height x 3 ft 7 ins width (0.84 x 1.09 m). Height to sill 5 ft 4 ins (1.63 m).
Wing control surfaces: Ailerons, and double-slotted flaps with 2 independent motors and 2 channel electric control unit. Flight spoilers and spoilerons, with 2 power control units per surface.
Tail control surfaces: Elevators and rudder with 2 channel yaw dampers.
Flight control system: Multiple redundancy. 2 or 3 power control units per surface. Mechanical, except for fly-by-wire spoilers/spoilerons. Automatic flight control system, with 2 independent flight directors and a fail-safe autopilot.
Construction materials: Metal, with considerable use of composites for the winglets, wing to fuselage fairings, tailcone, various doors and panels, main cabin floor, and more.
Engines: 2 General Electric CF34-3A1 turbofans.
Engine rating: Each 8,729 lbf (38.83 kN).
Fuel system: 9,380 lb (4,255 kg) or 5,500 litres *for Series 100*, 14,305 lb (6,489 kg) or 8,082 litres *for Series 100ER*.
Electrical system: 3-phase 115 volt/400 Hz AC supply with 2 x 30 kVA engine-driven generators, with APU and air-driven generator back-up. 28 volt DC supply using transformer/rectifiers. 17 amp-hour ni-cd battery.
Hydraulic system: 3 systems, each 3,000 psi.
Braking system: Multiple discs and anti skid.
De-icing system: Bleed air anti-icing for wing leading edges and engine air intakes, and electric system for cockpit glazing and sensors.
Fire system: Engine and APU fire protection comprises 2 loop detection and 3 extinguishing bottles.
Radar: Weather radar standard. Optional split-scan radar.
Flight avionics/instrumentation: Collins Pro Line 4 integrated digital avionics, with standard equipment of 2 primary flight displays, 2 multi-function displays, and 2 engine indication and crew alert system displays, each 7 ins x 6 ins (18 x 15 cm). Autopilot, flight management and central avionics maintenance functions are handled by an integrated avionics processing system (IAPS). Factory fitted navigation system comprises dual air data computers, dual AHRS, dual VHF nav receivers, dual ADF receivers, dual DME transceivers, 2 Mode S transponders, radio altimeter, traffic alert and collision avoidance system (TCAS), and a ground proximity warning system with windshear detection and warning. Standard communications equipment consists of dual VHF comm transceivers, digital audio system, cockpit voice recorder, emergency locater transmitter and more. Other avionics upon request, including optional single or dual flight management system, dual INS, Cat IIIa with head-up guidance system, single HF radio system, single selective calling system, third VHF comm radio, and third data concentrator unit.

Aircraft variants:

Series 100 is the standard version.

Series 100ER has increased weights to offer a higher fuel load for longer range.

Series 100LR is the latest production version, certificated in 1994. Take off weight increased to 53,000 lb (24,040 kg), allowing the longest range.

Corporate Jetliner is a business version of the Regional Jet, seating 18-50 persons. In 30 passenger form it has a weight of 31,800 lb (14,424 kg), range of 2,017 naut miles (2,322 miles) 3,735 km and can cruise at 458 kts (528 mph) 850 km/h. First delivery to the Xerox Corporation in June 1993.

Canadair Special Edition (SE), is a version of Regional Jet for trans-Atlantic corporate travel. 3,000 naut miles (3,455 miles) 5,556 km range, state-of-the-art avionics,

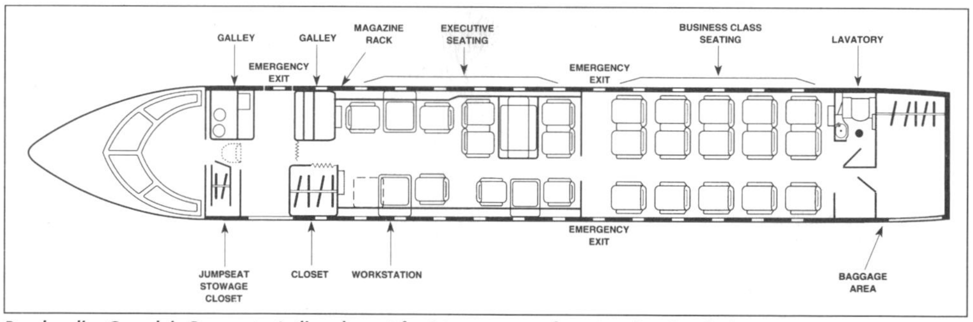

Bombardier Canadair Corporate Jetliner layout for 24 passengers (courtesy Bombardier)

DETAILS FOR REGIONAL JET.

Principal dimensions:
Wing span: 69 ft 7 ins (21.21 m)
Maximum length: 87 ft 10 ins (26.77 m)
Maximum height: 19 ft 3 ins (5.87 m)

Cabin:
Length: 48 ft 5 ins (14.76 m) excluding cockpit
Width: 8 ft 5 ins (2.57 m) maximum, 7 ft 2 ins (2.18 m) floor
Height: 6 ft 1.5 ins (1.87 m) maximum
Floor area: 346 sq ft (32.14 m^2) excluding cockpit
Volume: 2,015 cu ft (57.06 m^3)
Main passenger door: 5 ft 10 ins height x 3 ft width (1.78 m x 0.91 m).
Height to sill: 5 ft 4 ins (1.63 m)
Cargo door: airliners only

Wings:
Area: 520.4 sq ft (48.35 m^2) net
Aspect ratio: 8.85
Sweepback: 24.8° at 25% chord
Dihedral: 2.33°

Tail unit:
Tailplane span: 20 ft 4 ins (6.2 m)

Undercarriage:
Type: Retractable, with steerable nosewheels. Twin wheels of each unit
Wheel base: 37 ft 4.5 ins (11.39 m)
Wheel track: 10 ft 5 ins (3.18 m)
Turning circle: 75 ft (22.86 m) for 180° turn, with 11 ft (3.35 m) margin

Weights:
Empty, operating: 30,100 lb (13,653 kg) *Series 100*, 30,122 lb (13,663 kg) *for Series 100ER*
Maximum ramp: 47,700 lb (21,636 kg) *Series 100*, 51,250 lb (23,247 kg) *for Series 100ER*
Maximum take-off: 47,450 lb (21,523 kg) *Series 100*, 51,000 lb (23,133 kg) *for Series 100ER*
Maximum landing: 44,700 lb (20,276 kg) *Series 100*, 47,000 lb (21,319 kg) *for Series 100ER*
Payload: 12,100 lb (5,489 kg) maximum or 8,220 lb (3,729 kg) with full fuel *for Series 100*, 13,878 lb (6,295 kg) maximum or 6,823 lb (3,095 kg) with full fuel *for Series 100ER*

Performance:
High cruise speed: Mach 0.8, 459 kts (528 mph) 850 km/h
Long-range cruise speed: Mach 0.74, 424 kts (488 mph) 786 km/h
FAR take-off field length at MTOW: 5,265 ft (1,605 m) *for Series 100*, 6,090 ft (1,856 m) *for Series 100ER*, both at sea level, ISA
FAR landing field length at MLW: 4,725 ft (1,440 m) *for Series 100*, 4,900 ft (1,494 m) *for Series 100ER*
Time to climb to FL350 at MTOW: 19.2 minutes *for Series 100*, 22.3 minutes *for Series 100ER*
Ceiling: 41,000 ft (12,496 m), maximum operating
Range: 980 naut miles (1,128 miles) 1,815 km *for Series 100*, 1,620 naut miles (1,864 miles) 3,000 km *for Series 100ER*, both with 50 passengers, FAR 121 reserve, long-range cruise speed
Range (*Series 100LR*): 1,970 naut miles (2,268 miles) 3,648 km, conditions as above

and typically priced at US$21-22 million. First customer is TAG Aeronautics Ltd. CF34-3A1 turbofans. Take-off weight 53,000 lb (24,040 kg), and additional 4,000 lb (1,814 kg) of fuel in 2 new aft auxiliary tanks. Payload 8,100 lb (3,674 kg).

CRJ-X is a 70-passenger "stretched" derivative of the RJ, the design of which is well advanced. Powered by General Electric CF34-8C1 turbofans of 13,070 lbf (58.14 kN) each, it is expected to enter service in 1998. Length 106 ft 4 ins (32.41 m), wing span 75 ft 6 ins (23.01 m), MTOW 72,500 lb (32,885 kg), maximum cruise speed 467 kts (538 mph) 865 km/h and range 1,540 – 1,880 naut miles (1,773 – 2,165 miles) 2,850 – 3,480 km

Bombardier de Havilland Dash 8

First flight: 20 June 1983 (Series 100), 15 May 1987 (Series 200)
Certification: September 1984 (Series 100 – Transport Canada),14 February and 8 June 1989 (Series 300 – Transport Canada and FAA respectively).
First delivery: December 1984 service entry for Series 100 (norOntair), 27 February 1989 first delivery for Series 300 (Time Air), 1995 for Series 200.
Role: Short-range regional airliner.
Airframe life: Economic life of 160,000 landings. Dash 8-400 has crack-free life 40,000 flying hours or 80,000 flights, and economic life of 80,000 hours or 160,000 flights.
Noise levels: 81 EPNdB take off, 95 EPNdB approach, 86 EPNdB sideline.
Sales: 443 ordered by June 1995 (294 Series 100, 31 Series 200, and 11 Series 300), with 401 delivered. Production increased from 2 aircraft per month to 3 from 1995.
Crew: 2 pilots plus attendant.
Passengers: See table.
Seat pitch: 31 ins (79 cm) for Series 100/200, and 32 ins (81 cm) for Series 300.
Galley: Buffet type.
Pressurization: 5.5 psi cabin differential.
Baggage compartment volume: 300 cu ft (8.495 m^3) for Series 100/200, and 320 cu ft (9.06 m^3) for Series 300.
Size of baggage door: 4 ft 2 ins x 5 ft (1.27 x 1.52 m)
Baggage compartment: 2,000 lb (907 kg) capacity for Series 100/200, and 2,500 lb (1,134 kg) for Series 300.
Wing control surfaces: Horn-balanced ailerons (with tabs), 2-section slotted flaps, spoilers and lift dumpers. Leading-edge stall strips.
Tail control surfaces: Horn-balanced elevator (with 4 tabs) and 2-section rudder.
Flight control system: Mechanical/hydraulic.
Construction materials: Include allodyned alloys, carbonfibre, Kevlar, and Nomex honeycomb. Composites for fin/tailplane fairing, tailplane/fin leading edges, elevator tips, tailcone, dorsal fin, cabin bulkhead, luggage bins, floor panels, engine nacelles, flap shrouds and trailing edges, wingtip fairings, wing leading edges, wing/fuselage fairings, nose bay and radome.
Engines: See table.
Fuel system: 3,160 litres standard for Series 100/200/300, 5,806 litres optional for Series 100/300 and 5,700 litres optional for Series 200.
Electrical system: DC supply via dual starter-generators, dual transformer/rectifiers and dual ni-cd batteries. AC supply via dual engine-driven generators and 3 static inverters.
Braking system: With anti-skid.
Deicing system: Boots for wing, tailplane and fin leading edges. Electric propeller blade deicing.
Radar: Primus 800 weather radar.

Bombardier de Havilland Dash 8 Series 100B

Dash 8 basic configurations

	Series 100A	Series 100B	Series 200A	Series 200B	Series 300A	Series 300B	Series 300E	Series 400
Passengers (data for lower number)	37-39	37-39	37-39	37-39	50-56	50-56	50-56	70
Engines (2 turboprops)	P&WC PW120A	P&WC PW121	P&WC PW123C	P&WC PW123D	P&WC PW123	P&WC PW123B	P&WC PW123E	P&WC PW150
Rating (each)	2,000 shp (1,491 kW)	2,150 shp (1,603 kW)	2,150 shp (1,603 kW)	2,150 shp (1,603 kW) to 45° C OAT @ SL	2,380 shp (1,775 kW) to 35° C OAT @ SL	2,500 shp (1,864 kW) to 30° C OAT @ SL	2,380 shp (1,775 kW)	4,830 shp (3,602 kW)
Wing span	85 ft (25.91 m)	85 ft (25.91 m)	85 ft (25.91 m)	85 ft (25.91 m)	90 ft (27.43 m)	90 ft (27.43 m)	90 ft (27.43 m)	92 ft 3 ins (28.12 m)
Length	73 ft (22.25 m)	73 ft (22.25 m)	73 ft (22.25 m)	73 ft (22.25 m)	84 ft 3 ins (25.68 m)	84 ft 3 ins (25.68 m)	84 ft 3 ins (25.68 m)	106 ft 11 ins (32.59 m)
Height	24 ft 7 ins (7.49 m)	24 ft 7 ins (7.49 m)	24 ft 7 ins (7.49 m)	24 ft 7 ins (7.49 m)	24 ft 7 ins (7.49 m)	24 ft 7 ins (7.49 m)	24 ft 7 ins (7.49 m)	27 ft 2 ins (8.28 m)
Wing area	585 sq ft (54.35 m^2)	585 sq ft (54.35 m^2)	585 sq ft (54.35 m^2)	585 sq ft (54.35 m^2)	605 sq ft (56.21 m^2)	605 sq ft (56.21 m^2)	605 sq ft (56.21 m^2)	668 sq ft (62.06 m^2)
Wing aspect ratio	12.35	12.35	12.35	12.35	13.39	13.39	13.39	12.74
Empty weight, operating	22,600 lb (10,251 kg)	22,648 lb (10,273 kg)	22,886 lb (10,381 kg)	22,886 lb (10,381 kg)	25,720 lb (11,666 kg)	25,743 lb (11,677 kg)	25,720 lb (11,667 kg)	35,000 lb (15,875 kg)
Maximum take off weight	34,500 lb (15,649 kg)	36,300 lb (16,465 kg)	36,300 lb (16,465 kg)	36,300 lb (16,465 kg)	41,100 lb (18,643 kg)	43,000 lb (19,505 kg)	41,100 lb (18,643 kg)	59,500 lb (26,989 kg)
Maximum landing weight	33,900 lb (15,377 kg)	33,900 lb (15,377 kg)	33,900 lb (15,377 kg)	33,900 lb (15,377 kg)	40,000 lb (18,144 kg)	42,000 lb (19,051 kg)	40,000 lb (18,144 kg)	59,000 lb (26,762 kg)
Payload	8,400 lb (3,810 kg)	9,352 lb (4,242 kg)	9,114 lb (4,134 kg)	9,114 lb (4,134 kg)	11,480 lb (5,207 kg)	13,757 lb (6,240 lb)	11,480 lb (5,207 kg)	18,000 lb (8,165 kg)
Payload with maximum fuel		8,025 lb (3,640 kg)		7,740 lb (3,511 kg)		11,620 lb (5,271 kg)		
Cruise speed kts (mph) km	265 (305) 491	270 (311) 500	300 (345) 556	300 (345) 556	287 (330) 532	285 (328) 528	287 (330) 532	over 350 (403) 648 high speed
Stalling speed, with flaps kts (mph) km	72 (83) 133	72 (83) 133	72 (83) 133	72 (83) 133	77 (88) 142	77 (88) 142	77 (88) 142	
Take-off field length, SL, ISA (for 200 naut miles)	2,750 ft (838 m)	2,550 ft (777 m)	2,610 ft (796 m)	3,950 ft (1,204 m) at ISA +25° C, elevation 6,000 ft	3,035 ft (925 m)	2,920 ft (890 m)	6,650 ft (2,027 m) ISA +25° C, elevation 6,000 ft	4,000 ft (1,220 m) ISA, sea level, FAR 25
Take-off distance at MTOW	3,150 ft (960 m)	3,150 ft (960 m)	3,150 ft (960 m)	3,150 ft (960 m)	3,870 ft (1,180 m)	3,870 ft (1,180 m)	3,870 ft (1,180 m)	
Landing field length, SL, ISA	2,870 ft (875 m)	2,870 ft (875 m)	2,910 ft (887 m)	3,300 ft (1,006 m), ISA +25° C, elevation 6,000 ft	3,250 ft (991 m)	3,250 ft (991 m)	3,920 (1,195) ISA +25° C, elevation 6,000 ft	4,242 ft (1,293 m) ISA, sea level, FAR 25
Operating ceiling	25,000 ft (7,620 m)	25,000 ft (7,620 m)	25,000 ft (7,620 m)	25,000 ft (7,620 m)	25,000 ft (7,620 m)	25,000 ft (7,620 m)	25,000 ft (7,620 m)	
Range naut miles (miles) km	760 (875) 1,407	1,035 (1,192) 1,917	935 (1,076) 1,732	935 (1,076) 1,732	825 (950) 1,528	1,180 (1,359) 2,185 with optional long-range tanks	825 (950) 1,528	1,300 (1,497) 2,407 at high gross weight, reserves, MCR

Bombardier de Havilland Dash 8 Series 400

Flight avionics/instrumentation: Certified for Category II approaches. Now all Dash 8 variants certified for Category IIIa weather operations with the Flight Dynamics Head-Up Guidance System offered as an option; Horizon Air Dash 8-100 was the first to be certified by the FAA for Category IIIa operations, using a Flight Dynamics HGS 2000. Standard full complement of digital avionics, including dual channel autopilot/flight director system. Primary flight information can be displayed on EFIS. Can accommodate an expansion of navigational capability to include MLS, RNAV, and long-range systems.

Aircraft variants:

Dash 8 Series 100 has been offered in basic 100, improved range 100A and additional take-off power/payload 100B versions. Good rough field capability and hot-and-high performance.

Dash 8 Series 200 was designed for 300 kts cruise and high commonality with Series 300A, and superior payload-range capability. 200A is the basic model, with 200B offering additional take-off power for improved take-off and single-engine ceiling performance out of hot-and-high airfields.

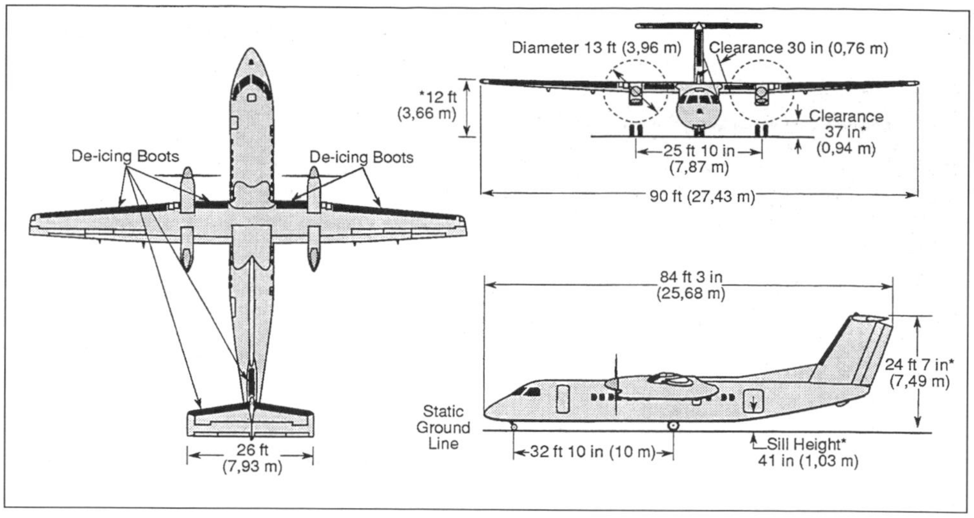

Bombardier de Havilland Dash 8 Series 300 drawing (courtesy Bombardier)

Dash 8 Series 300 is offered in 3 versions, as A and additional take-off power B and E, the latter with a further increase in hot-and-high capability. Intended for more densely travelled routes requiring higher capacity.

Dash 8 Series 400 is the latest "stretched" version, seating 70. Length increased by 18 ft 11 ins (5.77 m), wing span increased, new cargo and baggage doors, and new main undercarriage. PW150 engines with 6-blade propellers (moved 8 ins, 20.3 cm further from the fuselage). 3 configurations, basic gross weight at 59,500 lb (26,989 kg), intermediate at 61,000 lb (27,669 kg) and high at 62,500 lb (28,350 kg), with respective payloads of 18,000 lb (8,165 kg), 18,750 lb (8,505 kg) and 19,500 lb (8,845 kg). First order of 12 from Great China Airlines, launching the programme in April 1995. First flight 1997, certification 1998 and with deliveries to Great China Airlines from 1999.

Dash 8M is the military version (see also Electronic section).

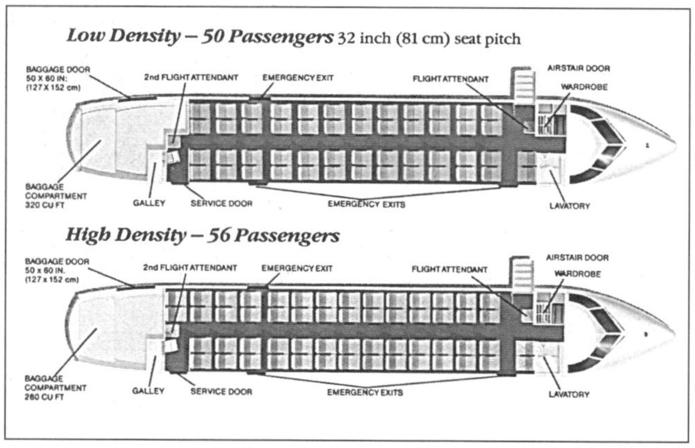

Bombardier de Havilland Dash 8 Series 300 layouts (courtesy Bombardier)

DETAILS FOR DASH 8, WITH FURTHER INFORMATION IN THE TABLE ON PAGE 203.

Cabin:

Length: 39 ft (11.89 m) *for Series 100/200*, 50 ft 3 ins (15.32 m) *for Series 300*

Width: 8 ft 2 ins (2.49 m) centreline, 6 ft 8 ins (2.03 m) floor

Height: 6 ft 4.5 ins (1.94 m)

Volume: 1,690 cu ft (47.86 m^3) *for Series 100/200*, 2,200 cu ft (62.3 m^3) *for Series 300*

Main passenger door: 2 ft 6 ins x 5 ft 9.7 ins (0.762 x 1.77 m) airstair

Tail unit:

Tailplane span: 26 ft (7.92 m)

Horizontal area: 150 sq ft (13.94 m^2)

Vertical area: 152 sq ft (14.12 m^2)

Undercarriage:

Type: Retractable, with steerable nosewheels. Twin wheels on each unit

Wheel base: 26 ft 1 ins (7.95 m) *for Series 100/200*, 32 ft 10 ins (10 m) *for Series 300.*

Wheel track: 25 ft 10 ins (7.87 m)

Bombardier Inc Canadair (Canada)

Corporate address: See Bombardier Inc for company details.

Founded: 5 August 1988, but with foundations as Canadair Ltd that formed on 3 October 1944.

Employees: Some 8,000 at facilities in Dorval, Mirabel and Saint-Laurent.

● Activities

- Constructs several fuselage and wing subassemblies for the Airbus A330/340, wing structures for the Boeing 737-500/700/800, fuselage section for the 767, and nose barrel for the F/A-18C Hornet.
- Under a 1995 $75 million contract, Canadair is to convert 4 Canadian Department of National Defence Airbus A310s into combi transports with 3 quick-change interiors, each convertible within 48 hours to full freighter configuration for 16 pallets, combi for 60 passengers and 12 pallets, or 194 passengers.
- Supports CF-18s, including current full-scale fatigue tests as part of the structural life extension programmes by the Defence Systems Division, the latter also offering other support and customizing services. Also provides training programmes, and builds UAVs.

Canadair Challenger

First flight: 8 November 1978. 18 September 1994 for latest Challenger 604 prototype (converted 601-3R).

Certification: 11 August 1980 (Canada), 7 November 1980 (USA). To FAR Pt 25.

First delivery: 30 December 1980 (Challenger 600).

Role: Wide-body business jet, regional and cargo transport.

Noise levels: 79.7 EPNdB take-off, 90.8 EPNdB approach, 85.7 EPNdB sideline.

Sales: 327 delivered by June 1995, including 134 Challenger 601-3As and 43 Challenger 601-3Rs.

Details: Challenger 601-3R.

Crew: 2 (flight).

Passengers: 5-19. Up to 7 litters in air ambulance layout, with attendants, and equipment that can include respiration apparatus, ECG and defibrillators, infusion pumps and more.

Galley: Buffet type.

Baggage volume: 115 cu ft (3.26 m^3)

Pressurization: Maximum 8.8 psi differential.

Wing control surfaces: 2-section double-slotted flaps, ailerons, inner spoiler/lift dumper and outer spoiler/airbrake.

Tail control surfaces: Variable incidence tailplane. Elevators and rudder.

Flight control system: Hydraulic, except for electrically actuated tailplane incidence.

Engines: 2 General Electric CF34-3A1 turbofans.

Bombardier Inc Canadair Challenger 604

Rockwell Collins Pro Line 4 avionics in Challenger 604

Engine rating: Each 8,729 lbf (38.83 kN), with APR rating of 9,220 lbf (41 kN).
Fuel system: 17,900 lb (8,119 kg), or 14,250 lb (6,464 kg) with maximum payload.
Electrical system: 3-phase 115/200 volt, 400 Hz AC supply via 2 x 30 kVA engine-driven generators. 28 volt DC supply via 4 transformer/rectifiers. 43 amp-hour ni-cd battery. APU and stand-by air-driven generator.
Hydraulic system: 3 systems, each 3,000 psi.
Braking system: Multiple disc brakes with anti-skid.
De-icing system: Bleed air for wing leading edges and engine air intakes. Electric de-icing for cockpit glazing and pitots.
Oxygen system: Gaseous.
Radar: Honeywell Primus 870 weather radar.
Flight avionics/instrumentation: Rockwell Collins Pro Line II suite with 5 CRT displays, dual channel digital flight guidance system, dual laser inertial reference units, dual flight management systems with worldwide database, and LASERTRAK backup navigation display unit. Challenger 604 has Pro Line 4 suite featuring 6 CRT displays with EICAS. Standard avionics for Challenger 604 include dual autopilot, dual air data systems, dual Collins FMS-6000, TWR-850 turbulence weather radar, dual Litton Flagship inertial reference systems, dual Collins radio tuning units, plus dual Collins Pro Line VHF comm, Nav, DME, ADF, Mode S transponders, dual HF-9000 high frequency comm, and improved Avtech audio control.

Aircraft variants:
Challenger 600 was the initial version, with 7,500 lbf (33.36 kN) Textron Lycoming ALF502L-2 turbofans. 11,142 litres of fuel with optional 1,186 litre tank included. Range 2,800 naut miles. 84 delivered, the last on 22 June 1983.
Challenger 601-1A was built with 8,650 lbf (38.48 kN) General Electric CF34-1As. Standard fuel capacity of 11,142 litres, for 3,440 naut mile range. Winglets added. 66 delivered between 6 May 1983 and 29 May 1987.
Challenger 601-3A has 8,650 lbf (38.48 kN) General Electric CF34-3As, offering 9,220 lbf (41 kN) with APR. Digital avionics suite including 5-tube EFIS, turbulence detecting 4-colour digital radar (other avionics as detailed for 601-3R). 134 delivered between 6 May 1987 and 29 October 1993. Version also offered with 11,979 litres of fuel for 3,585 naut mile range.
Challenger 601-3R was evolved from the 601-3A, with airliner-proven engines, intercontinental 3,585 naut mile range, and increased engine power, take-off weight and reliability. As detailed. First delivery 14 July 1993.
Challenger 604 prototype (converted 601-3R) first flew in 1994. Certification under Transport Canada received 20 September 1995, followed by FAA in October. Deliveries from late 1995. 8-19 passengers, plus 2/3 crew. Designed for a 4,000 naut mile intercontinental range. Increased fuel capacity, including saddle tanks in rear fuselage. Undertook a 10-month flight test and certification programme at Learjet's Wichita, USA, test centre. CF34-3B engines. Strengthened undercarriage, 27 ins (68.58 cm) diameter wheels and low pressure (175 psi) tyres. Improved brakes, with 3,000 psi pressure. Airline-proven components to improve reliability. New wing-to-fuselage and underbelly fairing. New avionics (see Avionics).
Challenger Cargo Variant was announced in June 1995, offered jointly with Pemco World Air Services which performs the installation.

Canadair Global Express

First flight: 1996.
First delivery: 1997.
Role: Long-range and high-speed business and VIP transport, with a very large cabin.

▲ Development
▲ October 1991. Project Global Express was introduced at the National Business Aircraft Association meeting in Texas.
▲ 20 December 1993. Programme was launched with 30 orders and 8 options.
Sales: See above. Has been promoted by potential prime contractors as a possible aircraft to meet the UK Ministry of Defence's ASTOR programme for a long-range surveillance system.
Crew: 3 + 1 (flight), with forward rest area (for 2) and toilet. Sidestick controllers.

Bombardier Canadair Global Express

DETAILS FOR 601-3R, *WITH 604 IN ITALICS WHERE DIFFERENT.*

Principal dimensions:
Wing span: 64 ft 4 ins (19.6 m)
Maximum length: 68 ft 5 ins (20.85 m),
Maximum height: 20 ft 8 ins (6.3 m)

Cabin:
Length: 28 ft 4 ins (8.64 m)
Width: 8 ft 2 ins (2.49 m) centreline, 7 ft 2 ins (2.18 m) floor
Height: 6 ft 1 ins (1.85 m)
Volume: 1,150 cu ft (32.56 m^3)
Main passenger door: 5 ft 10 ins x 3 ft (1.78 x 0.91 m)

Wings:
Area: 492 sq ft (45.71 m^2)
Aspect ratio: 8.41

Undercarriage:
Type: Retractable, with steerable/self-centring nosewheels. Twin wheels on each unit
Wheel base: 26 ft 2.5 ins (7.99 m)
Wheel track: 10 ft 5 ins (3.18 m)
Turning circle: 40 ft (12.19 m)

Weights *(604 only where shown and based on engineering projections)*:
Empty, operating: 25,760 lb (11,685 kg)
Maximum ramp weight: 45,250 lb (20,525 kg)
Maximum take-off: 45,100 lb (20,457 kg), *47,600 to optional 48,200 lb (21,592 to 21,863 kg)*
Maximum landing: 36,000 lb (16,329 kg), *38,000 lb (17,236 kg)*
Payload: 5,240 lb (2,377 kg), or 1,590 lb (721 kg) with full fuel

Performance *(604 based on engineering projections)*:
High cruise speed: Mach 0.83, 476 kts (548 mph) 882 km/h
Normal cruise speed: Mach 0.8, 459 kts (528 mph) 850 km/h
Long-range cruise speed: Mach 0.74, 425 kts (489 mph) 787 km/h
Balanced field length: 6,050 ft (1,844 m) at MTOW, sea level, ISA. 601-3R can use a 3,400 ft (1,036 m) runway according to June 1995 performance revisions, significantly adding to the possible range
Take-off distance: *6,150 ft (1,875 m), gross take-off weight, sea level, ISA*
Landing distance: 3,300 ft (1,006 m) at MLW
G limits: 2.6 design
Ceiling: 41,000ft (12,500 m)
Range with full fuel: 3,585 naut miles (4,128 miles) 6,639 km with 2 crew and 5 passengers, *4,000 naut miles (4,606 miles) 7,408 km with reserves, 7 crew and passengers, at Mach 0.8, or 3,745 naut miles (4,312 miles) 6,936 km at Mach 0.8*

Passengers: 8-19 typically, with possible 30. 8 passengers with maximum fuel load.
Galley: Fully equipped in the forward part of the cabin.
Baggage volume: 324 cu ft (9.17 m^3).
Wing characteristics: New wings and winglets, having an advanced aerofoil section with thick chord and low taper ratio to increase lift, lower drag and provide good low/high speed performances. 35° sweepback. Features 28 composite control surfaces (14 per wing).
Flight control system: Sextant Avionique primary and secondary systems, including spoilers and trim controls.
Construction materials: Subcontractors include Mitsubishi of Japan, which had expected to work on wing and centre fuselage sections from November 1994, for delivery from 1996.
Engines: 2 BMW Rolls-Royce BR710 turbofans.
Engine rating: Each 14,680 lbf (65.3 kN).
Fuel system: Parker Bertea Aerospace system.
Electrical system: Lucas Aerospace and Leach Corporation system with variable frequency generating and advanced automated power management system. AlliedSignal (team leader) RE220(GX) APU.
Hydraulic system: Abex system.
Braking system: Dowty Aerospace brake-by-wire system, with anti-skid.
Environmental control system: ABG-Semca integrated air management system, with dual environmental control, cabin pressure, and pneumatic systems. Provides bleed air anti-icing.

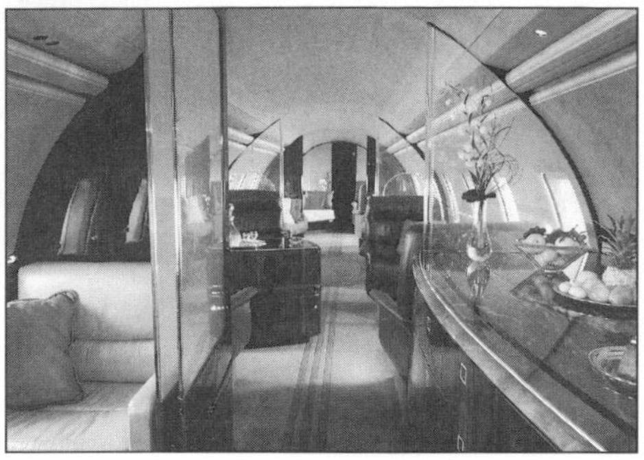

Global Express 48 ft (14.63 m) cabin

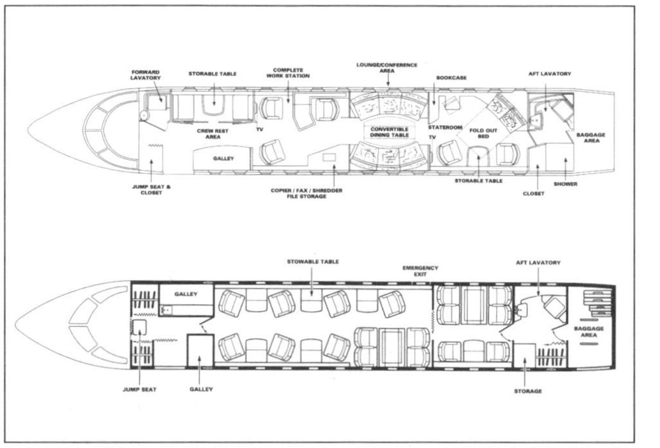

Two of many possible Global Express cabin layouts for 15-17 passengers (courtesy Bombardier)

Flight avionics/instrumentation: Honeywell Primus 2000 XP suite (suited to ETOPS), including dual fail-operational automatic flight control system, 6 CRT EFIS, an engine indication and crew alerting system (EICAS) with synoptics, a dual flight management system with "SmartPerf" software for performance calculations and dual auto-throttles. GPS, 3 inertial reference systems, 3 air data computers, 2 VHF navigation and communications systems, and traffic collision avoidance and ground proximity warning systems. Optional Sextant Avionique head-up flight display system (HFDS) for Category IIIa operations, comprising 4 LRUs, combiner, flight display computer, optical projector unit and head-up control panel.

Details for Global Express.

Principal dimensions:
Wing span: 91 ft 11 ins (28.01 m)
Maximum length: 99 ft (30.18 m)
Maximum height: 24 ft 5 ins (7.44 m)

Cabin:
Length: 48 ft (14.63 m)
Width: 8 ft 2 ins (2.49 m) centreline, 6 ft 11 ins (2.11 m) floor
Height: 6 ft 3 ins (1.91 m)
Volume: 2,077 cu ft (58.81 m^3)

Weights:
Maximum take-off: 91,000 lb (41,277 kg)
Maximum landing: 78,600 lb (35,632 kg)
Payload: 1,600 lb (726 kg) with maximum fuel

Performance:
High cruise speed: Mach 0.88
Normal cruise speed: Mach 0.85
Long-range cruise speed: Mach 0.8
Approach speed: 104-127 kts (120-146 mph) 193-235 km/h
Take-off distance: 5,540 ft (1,689 m)
Landing distance: 2,556 ft (779 m), as Part 91
Ceiling: 51,000 ft (15,545 m)
Range: 5,000-6,500 naut miles (5,758-7,485 miles) 9,260-12,038 km

Canadair CL-215 and CL-215T

First flight: 23 October 1967 (CL-215), and 8 June 1989 (CL-215T).
Certification: 27 March 1969 (CL-215), and 28 March 1991 (Transport Canada, restricted category - CL-215T), 24 December 1991 (utility category - CL-215T), 30 March 1993 (FAA, restricted category - CL-215T).
First delivery: 6 June 1969 (CL-215), and June 1991 (CL-215T, to Spain).
Role: Firefighting, transport, utility, and search and rescue amphibian.
Sales: 124 piston-engined CL-215s were delivered to customers in Canada (49), Spain (30), Greece (16), France (15), Italy (5), former Yugoslavia (5), Thailand (2) and Venezuela (2), the final delivered to Greece on 3 May 1990. By early 1995, 17 CL-215T retrofits had been ordered (Spain 15 and Province of Quebec 2), all delivered. Portugal and Sweden signed leasing agreements in 1995, covering the use of 2 CL-215s for firefighting and 1 for firefighting/maritime surveillance/SAR respectively (owned by Canadian provincial governments). Also, in 1995 Croatia became the first customer for a refurbished CL-215.
Aircraft variants:
CL-215 was the original version, powered by 2 x 2,100 hp (1,566 kW) Pratt & Whitney R-2800-83AM piston engines. Firefighting productivity in 3 hours, at 10 naut miles water-to-fire distance, is 106,930 litres.
CL-215T is the designation of CL-215s retrofitted with 2,380 shp (1,775 kW) P&WC PW123AF turboprops using kit modification and added improvements. Firefighting productivity in 3 hours, at 10 naut miles water-to-fire distance, is 133,625 litres.

Details for CL-215/CL-215T

Performance
Maximum speed: 165 kts (190 mph) 306 km/h *for CL-215*, 204 kts (235 mph) 378 km/h *for CL-215T*.
Maximum climb rate: 1,000 ft (305 m) per minute *for Cl-215*, 1,375 ft (419 m) per minute *for CL-215T*.
Water drop pattern: 400 ft (122 m)

Quebec's Fond du service aérien gouvernement Canadair CL-215T dropping 5,000 litres of foam

Canadair CL-415 and CL-415M

First flight: 6 December 1993.
Certification: 24 June 1994 (Canada), September 1994 (FAA).
First delivery: October 1994 (to France).
Role: Turboprop amphibian for firefighting, plus multi-role including EEZ protection, transport, and search and rescue. Incorporates significant modernization and upgrading compared to CL-215/T.

★ Aims:
★ Scooping water for firefighting from nearby sources and providing sustained water-bombing to contain fires. An average mission could be 5.2 naut miles (6 miles) 10 km from water to fire, with the CL-415 making 9 drops in an hour, delivering 55,170 litres of fire suppressant.
★ Land, loiter and take-off in sea conditions of 4 to 6 ft (1.22 to 1.83 m) waves and gusting winds of 35 kts, and operate from water only 6 ft (1.83 m) deep.
Sales: Governments of Quebec (8), France (12), and Italy (4). Italy first used its aircraft to fight fires in March 1995.
Crew: 2. CL-415M may have 3 flight crew, 2 observers and a specialist.
Passengers: 30 passengers (with toilet, galley, etc) with water tanks deleted, or 14 troops with quick-change fittings.
Firefighting capacity: 6,132 litres of water in 4 compartments. Foam chemical is located in left and right-hand reservoirs feeding respective tanks. Total 600 litres of usable concentrate should provide 16 foam drops at 0.6:99.4 mix ratio before replenishment. Scoop reloading of water or on the ground via adapters on the fuselage sides. Drop options are selectable by the flight crew.
Wing characteristics: High mounted, straight, with endplates and fences. Strengthened over CL-215. Leading edge extended and drooped locally just outboard of engine nacelles.
Wing control surfaces: Powered aileron (with tabs), and single-slotted flaps.
Tail control surfaces: Powered elevators and rudder (all with tabs), plus automatic rudder trim compensator. Small slat on starboard side of tailplane, inboard of finlet, to eliminate flow separation. Finlets canted 5° to port to improve directional stability. Bullet fairing at junction of tailplane/fin to eliminate airflow separation.
Construction materials: Metal.
Engines: 2 Pratt & Whitney Canada PW123AF turboprops, with Hamilton Standard 4-blade composite propellers.
Engine rating: Each 2,380 shp (1,775 kW).
Fuel system: 5,792 litres.
Electrical system: Split AC-DC bus-bar system. 2 x 400 amp, 28 volt engine-driven starter-generators. 2 x 800 volt-amp static inverters. 2 x 40 amp-hour 20-cell ni-cd batteries and battery chargers. GAPU.
Braking system: Hydraulic disc, with increased reservoir capacity over CL-215.
De-icing system: Pneumatic boot for engine air intakes, plus electric anti-ice adapter at engine inlets.
Fire system: Detection system in fire zones of engines, with 2 Halon 1301 bottles.
Flight avionics/instrumentation: Honeywell 4-tube EFIS, and 3-tube IIDS. Honeywell Primus 2 radio nav/comm management system, plus Global Wulfsberg V-UHF/FM radio, Collins HF-230 HF radio, and Honeywell AA-300 radio altimeter. Angle-of-attack indicator. Flight data recorder, radar, Omega and GPS among options.
Mission equipment: CL-415M can carry searchlight, litters, liferafts and other disaster relief/search and rescue equipment. Many other options include stores on 4 available underwing pylons.

Bombardier Canadair CL-415M with nose radar, deploying a motorized boat

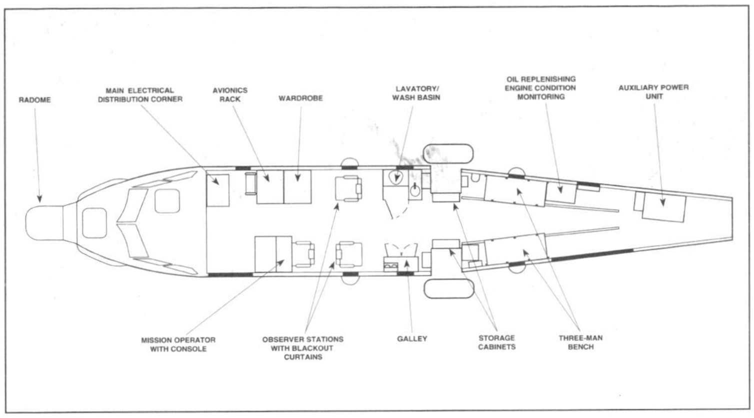

Bombardier Canadair CL-415M possible hull layout

Aircraft variants:
CL-415 is the standard firefighting version, as detailed.
CL-415M is the new multi-role variant, for military and non-military uses.

DETAILS FOR CL-415.

Principal dimensions:
Wing span: 93 ft 11 ins (28.63 m)
Maximum length: 65 ft 0.5 ins (19.82 m)
Maximum height: 29 ft 5.5 ins (8.98 m)

Wings:
Area: 1,080 sq ft (100.335 m^2)
Aspect ratio: 8.17

Undercarriage:
Type: Retractable, with steerable and self-centring twin nosewheels. Non-retactable wingtip floats
Wheel base: 23 ft 9 ins (7.24 m)
Wheel track: 17 ft 4 ins (5.28 m)

Weights:
Empty, operating: 27,783 lb (12,602 kg)
Maximum ramp: 44,000 lb (19,958 kg) land, 38,000 lb (17,237 kg) water
Pre-water scooping weight: 37,000 lb (16,783 kg)
Maximum take-off (from land): 43,850 lb (19,890 kg) *with disposable load*, 37,850 lb (17,168 kg) *with non-disposable load.*
Maximum lift, after scooping: 46,000 lb (20,865 kg)
Maximum landing: 37,000 lb (16,783 kg)
Payload: 13,500 lb (6,123 kg)

Performance:
Maximum cruise speed: 197 kts (227 mph) 365 km/h at 5,000 ft (1,525 m), ISA
Take-off distance: 2,700 ft (823 m) *disposable load*, 2,300 ft (701 m) *non-disposable load* (land), 2,670 ft (814 m) *non-disposable load* (water).
Landing distance: 2,200 ft (671 m)
Scooping distance (50 ft to 50 ft, 15 m to 15 m): 4,240 ft (1,292 m)
Scooping time: 12 seconds to refill tanks
Maximum climb rate: 1,375 ft (419 m) per minute at sea level, at 46,000 lb (20,865 kg) weight
Operating ceiling: 10,000 ft (3,050 m)
Water drop pattern: 153,309 litres in 3 hours at 10 naut miles water-to-fire distance
Ferry range: 1,310 naut miles (1,508 miles) 2,426 km
Typical time on fire: 4 hours

Kelowna Flightcraft Group (Canada)

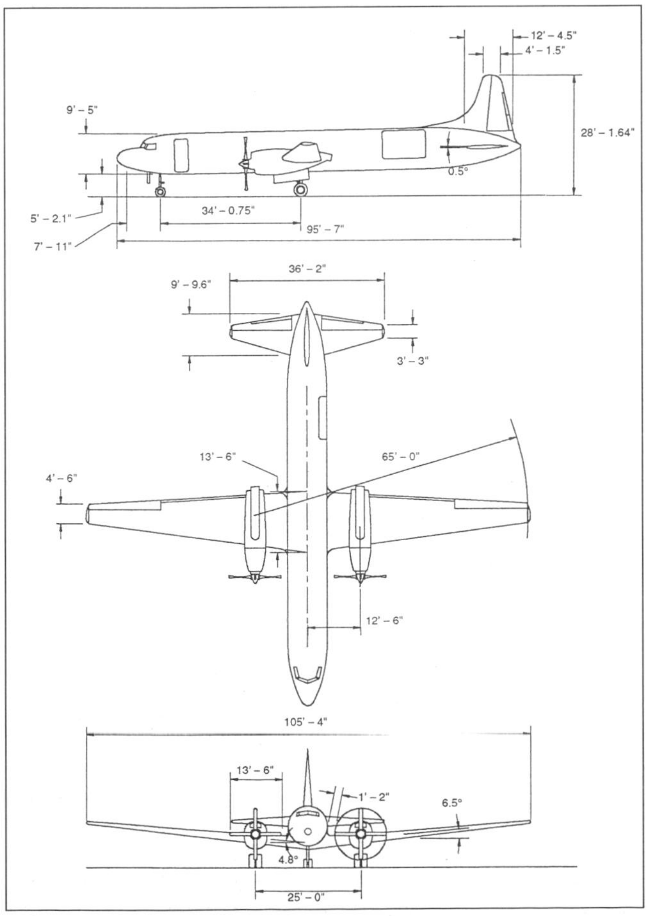

Kelowna Flightcraft CV5800 drawing (courtesy Kelowna)

Corporate address: #1 5655 Kelowna Airport, Kelowna, British Columbia VIV 1S1.
Telephone: +1 604 765 1481
Facsimile: +1 604 765 1489
Information: Bill De Meester (Director of Maintenance).

DIVISIONS

Kelowna Flightcraft Air Charter Ltd

● **Activities**
• Operates 2 Boeing 727s, 12 CV580s, 2 Cessna 402Bs, a DC-3 and Gulfstream I for charter services.

Kelowna Flightcraft Ltd

● **Activities**
• Maintains air charter fleet and performs outside customer work.

Kelowna Flight-Comm Avionics Inc

● **Activities**
• Avionics engineering, with participation in the CV5800 programme and other outside work.

Kelowna Flightcraft R&D Ltd

● **Activities**
• R&D of major aircraft modifications, including STCs and STAs. Current programmes include CV5800, long-range fuel capacity for the CV580, cargo door conversions, and more.

Kelowna Flightcraft CV5800

First flight: 11 February 1982.
Certification: Gained December 1993. CV5800 designed to meet stage 3 noise and CAT II landing standards.
First delivery: 1994.
Role: Lengthened and modernized Convair CV580 for freight or passenger uses. Similar conversions can be performed on the CV340 and CV440.
Airframe life: Modification is claimed to extend the aircraft life by a further 100,000 hours.
Conversion includes:
⋆ Complete removal of all components, including flight controls, stabilizers, systems and wiring.
⋆ Extension of the fuselage by 14 ft 3 ins (4.34 m), with intensive structural work as per Convair Engineering to accept the increased gross weight of 63,000 lb (28,576 kg).
⋆ Incorporation of a Honeywell SPZ-4500 digital AFCS, EDZ-803 4 tube EFIS, and Primus II nav/comm/ident radio package. These avionics include dual FZ-450 flight guidance computers, manually switching into a single control surface servo drive system, Primus 650 weather radar, dual VG-14A/C-14A attitude/heading package and an A-A300 radio altimeter.
⋆ Installation of Allison 501-D22G turboprop engines with Hamilton Standard 54H60 propellers.
Sales: Prototype and 1 "production" aircraft completed, both as cargo aircraft. Next conversion is

for a passenger version. Kelowna is negotiating with several sources on future production.

Aircraft variants:

CV5800 cargo version is configured to a Class E standard and is available with a cargo conveyance system. It has a cabin volume of 3,096 cu ft (87.67 m^3), operating empty weight of 33,166 lb (15,044 kg), and payload of 21,834 lb (9,904 kg).

CV5800 passenger version is for 76 passengers at 32 ins (81 cm) seat pitch.

Kelowna Flightcraft CV5800

Harbin Aircraft Manufacturing Corporation (China)

Corporate address: See Combat section for company details.

● Activities

● See also Y-11B in the General Aviation and EC-120 in the Helicopter sections.

Harbin Y-12 (II) and Y-12 (IV)

Harbin Y-12(II) (courtesy Harbin)

First flight: June 1984 (actual), 16 August (often quoted).

Certification: *Y-12 (II)*: December 1995 (Tc from CAAC), December 1986 (Pc from CAAC), and 20 June 1990 (Tc from CAA). *Y-12 (IV)*: 3 July 1994 (Tc from CAAC) and 26 March 1995 from FAA. Designed to the requirements of FAR Pt 23 and FAR Pt 135 Appendix A. Conforms to CCAR-3 and BCAR-K (CAA).

Role: Light general purpose transport with STOL characteristics, for passengers or cargo, air dropping, parachute jumping, forest seeding and agricultural, cloud seeding, geological survey, aerial photography, maritime surveillance and more. AEW and calibration versions are under development.

Harbin Y-12 (II) in AEW form, with nose radar and 2 operator stations in the main cabin (courtesy Harbin)

Sales: 85 Y-12 (II)s sold by the start of 1995, with 23 operated in China and 62 in 16 other countries including Laos, Peru, Mongolia, Fiji, Nepal, Tanzania and Zambia.

Details: For Y-12 (II).

Crew: 2 (flight).

Passengers: 17, or 15 parachutists.

Seat pitch: 29.5 ins (79 cm).

Size of baggage doors: *Front:* 1 ft 7 ins x 2 ft 4.5 ins (0.48 x 0.72 m). *Rear:* 4 ft 1 ins x 1 ft 10 ins (1.25 x 0.55 m).

Baggage compartments: *Front:* 27.2 cu ft (0.77 m^3) volume, and 220 lb (100 kg) load. *Rear:* 66.6 cu ft (1.89 m^3), and 573 lb (260 kg) load.

Wing control surfaces: Ailerons (starboard tab) and 2 section double-slotted flaps.

Tail control surfaces: Horn-balanced elevators and rudder (with tabs).

Flight control system: Mechanical, but with electrically actuated flaps.

Construction materials: Metal. Composite materials may be introduced later.

Engines: 2 Pratt & Whitney Canada PT6A-27 turboprops.

Engine rating: Each 620 shp (462.3 kW), with Hartzell 8 ft 2 ins (2.49 m) 3-blade propellers.

Fuel system: 2,712 lb (1,230 kg).

Braking system: Hydraulic.

De-icing system: Can fly into icing conditions when optional de-icing equipment for the wings and tail unit is installed.

Radar: Optional AlliedSignal Bendix/King RDR-1400C weather radar.

Flight avionics/instrumentation: VFR and IFR. Standard comm/nav equipment is VHF-251 radio, HF-230 SSB radio, ADF-650A radio compass, AUD-251H intercom, ALT-50A radio altimeter, TDR-950 transponder, DME-451 distance-measuring equipment, MKR-350 beacon marker receiver, VOR-351, PN-101 gyro magnetic compass, 101420-11934 encoding altimeter, GLS-350 glideslope receiver, and G8400A-36-24 anti-collision light. Options include APS-65 autopilot and GNS-500A-4 Omega. Y-12 (IV) to receive traffic alert and collision avoidance system (TCAS 1), and voice/digital flight data recorders.

Mission equipment: Depends on role. Forest seeding and agricultural equipment includes a 1,200 litre hopper. Radar in a bulbous nose for AEW.

Aircraft variants:

Y-12 (II) is the standard current version, as detailed.

Y-12 (IV) was developed from the Y-12 (II) and has new "shearing" wingtips to increase take-off weight to 12,500 lb (5,670 kg), 19 passenger seats, 4,374 lb (1,984 kg) payload, and the addition of a baggage door in the rear fuselage to ease loading/unloading.

DETAILS FOR Y-12 (II).

Principal dimensions:
Wing span: 56 ft 6.5 ins (17.235 m)
Maximum length: 48 ft 9 ins (14.86 m)
Maximum height: 18 ft 7.5 ins (5.675 m)

Cabin:
Length: 15 ft 10 ins (4.82 m)
Width: 4 ft 9.5 ins (1.46 m)
Height: 5 ft 7 ins (1.7 m)
Volume: 454.7 cu ft (12.9 m^3)
Main passenger/cargo door: 4 ft 6 ins x 4 ft 9 ins (1.38 x 1.45 m)

Wings:
Aerofoil section: LS(1)-0417
Area: 368.9 sq ft (34.27 m^2)
Aspect ratio: 8.668

Undercarriage:
Type: Fixed, with nosewheel. Suited to grass, sand, earth or prepared airstrips
Main wheel tyre size: 640 x 230 mm
Nose wheel tyre size: 480 x 200 mm
Wheel base: 15 ft 1 ins (4.6 m)
Wheel track: 11 ft 10 ins (3.6 m)
Turning circle: 55 ft (16.75 m)

Weights:
Maximum take-off and landing: 11,684 lb (5,300 kg)
Payload: 3,748 lb (1,700 kg)

Performance:
Maximum cruise speed: 177 kts (204 mph) 328 km/h, at 9,840 ft (3,000 m)
Economic cruise speed: 135 kts (155 mph) 250 km/h, at 9,840 ft (3,000 m)
Take-off distance: 1,395 ft (425 m), *with 15° flaps*
Landing distance: 2,034 ft (620 m) with brakes only, 1,575 ft (480 m) with brakes and reversed propellers
Maximum climb rate: 1,595 ft (486 m) per minute
Maximum climb rate, one engine: 276 ft (84 m) per minute
Cruise altitude and single-engine ceiling: 9,840 ft (3,000 m)
Ceiling: 23,000 ft (7,000 m)
Range: 723 naut miles (832 miles) 1,340 km, at economic cruise speed and 3,000 m, 45 minutes reserve
Duration: 5.2 hours, with above conditions

Shaanxi Aircraft Company (China)

Corporate address: PO Box 34, Chenggu, Shaan-Xi 723213, or PO Box 35, Chenggu, Shaan-Xi 723215.
Telephone: +86 916 216301, 214974
Facsimile: +86 916 216302, 202031
Cable: 3400, 3500
Information: Li Yousheng (Marketing Manager).

● Activities

● Production of standard and special mission aircraft, ground support equipment, and offering improvements and modifications. In addition to the Y8, Shannxi produces the Hanjiang 1,323 lb (600 kg) small commercial vehicle, SFJ6800 36-seat coach, and SFJ6120 tourist bus.

Shaanxi Y8

First flight: 25 December 1974.
Role: Medium-range transport, with special mission variants. Developed from the Antonov An-12B.
Airport limits: ACN rating of 15.
Crew: 2 pilots, engineer, navigator and radio operator.
Passengers: 121 passengers in the Y8K. 96 troops or 60 paratroops or 60 litters plus 20 seated casualties and 3 attendants in the Y8 and Y8C. Other transport versions can accommodate 14 persons in a pressurized forward compartment.
Pressurization: Fully pressurized cabin in Y8C, Y8D, Y8K and Y8X.
Size of rear ramp door: 25 ft 2 ins (7.67 m) long, 7 ft 1 ins to 10 ft 2 ins (2.16 to 3.1 m) wide, that hinges upward inside the hold to provide direct loading.
Loading facilities: Overhead conveyor with 5,070 lb (2,300 kg) capacity, and optional 4-track roller mats.
Construction materials: Metal.
Engines: 4 South Aero Engine Company WJ6 turboprops, with 4-blade reversible-pitch propellers.
Engine rating: Each 4,250 eshp (3,169 kW).
Fuel system: 50,505 lb (22,909 kg).
Braking system: Discs, with anti-skid system.
Radar: Honeywell colour weather radar in an under-nose radome.
Flight avionics/instrumentation: Y8C includes Collins flight director system, air data system, ILS, ATC and UHF radio; Honeywell magnetic heading reference system, vertical gyro; Litton Omega/VLF navigation system; AlliedSignal Bendix/King HF comm; and Sunstrand flight data recorder and CVR.

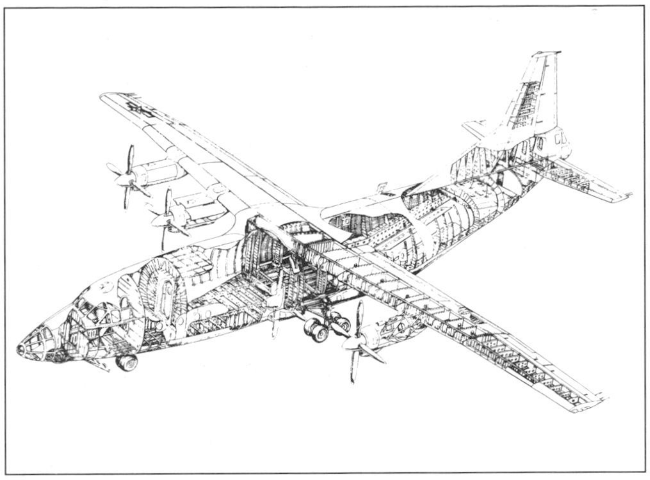

Shaanxi Y8 structure (courtesy CATIC)

Shaanxi Y8C pressurized transport

Aircraft variants:
Y8 was the original unpressurized-hold version, sometimes with tail gun turret. Prototype and production aircraft.
Y8A is a helicopter and general unpressurized-hold transport, the cabin height slightly increased by removal of the unnecessary internal cargo handling system.
Y8B was produced for civil use, with empty weight reduced by 3,792 lb (1,720 kg) by removal of military gear.
Y8C introduced pressurization for the lengthened cargo cabin of 50 ft 10 ins (15.5 m), new cargo ramp/door, new environmental control system, conveyor system for standard containers, modified undercarriage for increased airframe fatigue life, new fuel burn sequence for longer wing life, and improved comm/nav and ATC equipment. First flown on 17 December 1990.
Y8D is the export version of Y8C, reportedly operated by Myanmar, Sri Lanka and Sudan.
Y8E is a UAV launch/control aircraft.
Y8F is a livestock transport, for 500 sheep or other animals. Certification by CAAC on 26 January 1994.
Y8H carries survey equipment.
Y8K is an airliner version, with rear ramp/door deleted. 121 passengers.
Y8X is a maritime surveillance version, with Litton APS-504(V)3 surveillance radar, infra-red sensors, cameras, sonobuoys and other equipment.
Y8 AEW is a speculated version, with possible GEC-Marconi Argus radar (see Reconnaissance section – China and UK).

DETAILS FOR Y8.

Principal dimensions:
Wing span: 124 ft 8 ins (38 m)
Maximum length: 111 ft 7.5 ins (34.02 m)
Maximum height: 36 ft 7 ins (11.16 m)

Cabin:
Length: 44 ft 3.5 ins (13.5 m)
Width: 9 ft 10 ins to 11 ft 6 ins (3 to 3.5 m)
Height: 7 ft 10.5ins to 8 ft 6.5 ins (2.4 to 2.6 m)

Undercarriage:
Type: Retractable, with steerable twin nosewheels. 4-wheel main bogies with low-pressure tyres suited to unpaved airfields

Weights:
Empty, operating: 77,382 lb (35,100 kg)
Maximum take-off: 134,482 lb (61,000 kg)
Maximum landing: 127,868 lb (58,000 kg)
Payload: 44,092 lb (20,000 kg) distributed, 35,274 lb (16,000 kg) bulk item
Airdrop payload: 29,100 lb (13,200 kg), or 16,314 lb (7,400 kg) for a single item

Performance:
Maximum speed: 357 kts (411 mph) 662 km/h
Cruise speed: 297 kts (342 mph) 550 km/h
Take-off distance: 4,035 ft (1,230 m) at sea level, MTOW
FAR take-off field length: 6,234 ft (1,900 m)
Landing distance: 3,609 ft (1,100 m) at sea level, MLW
FAR landing field length: 5,414 ft (1,650 m)
Ceiling: 34,120 ft (10,400 m)
Range with full fuel: 3,032 naut miles (3,489 miles) 5,615 km

Shanghai Aviation Industrial Corporation (China)

Corporate address: PO Box 232-007, Shanghai 200232.
Telephone: +86 21 438 3311
Facsimile: +86 21 665 8103

● Activities

● Shanghai Aircraft Manufacturing Factory division produced 35 MD-82 and MD-83 airliners under licence from McDonnell Douglas of the USA, mostly for Chinese operation but including 5 MD-83s purchased by TWA. The first MD-82, built using US supplied assemblies, made its maiden flight on 2 July 1987 and entered service with China Northern Airlines on 4 August that year. Late aircraft are of mostly Chinese manufacture and assembly. On 25 April 1994, SAIC signed a sales agreement with China Northern Airlines and China Aviation Supplies Corporation, covering the last of the 35 MD-80s (going to CNA on 18 October 1994, with roll-out on 31 August). A further 20 MD-82T Trunkliners were being negotiated in 1994 but plans may have been abandoned due to MD-90 production. Trunkliner differs from the other versions in having 4-wheel main undercarriage bogies to allow operation from low bearing strength runways.

● On 25 June 1992 the MD-90-30T was chosen to be the second form of Trunkliner for Chinese assembly, with Shanghai as prime contractor (also mostly Chinese manufacture of subassemblies, with subcontracts to Chengdu, Shenyang and Xi'an), and with Chinese-assembled 25,000 lbf (111.21 kN) International Aero Engines V2525 engines. Negotiations were concluded and contracts signed on 4 November 1994 covering co-production of 20 from 1995, for delivery from 1998.

● As a third step in China's efforts to meet its fast-growing air transport requirements, a new 180-seat airliner is under consideration, to be mostly of Chinese development.

Xi'an Aircraft Company (China)

Corporate address: See Combat section for company details.

Xi'an Y7 and Y7H

First flight: 25 December 1970 for Y7, 26 December 1993 for Y7-200A.
Certification: 1980.
First delivery: 1984.

Xi'an Y7-100 transport

Role: *Y7/Y7-100/200B* are short/medium-range passenger, executive commuter, and civil/military cargo transports, developed from the Antonov An-24. Also for scientific research, pilot training, rescue, aerial mapping and more. *Y7-200A* is a convertible passenger/cargo or cargo variant. *Y7H/Y7H-500* are military/civil freighters based on the An-26 (with rear ramp/door), also suited to air-dropping, parachuting and medevac. All versions listed by Xi'an as the Y7 family.
Airframe life: 30,000 flight hours or 15,000 landings or 15 years.
Airport limits: LCN/radius of relative stiffness for *Y7-100* at MTOW (rigid runway): 64/16.5, 79/17 and 94/17.3.
Noise levels: Average below 85 dB for Y7-100.
Crew: 2 flight crew for *Y7-200A* plus observer, 3 for *Y7/-100/-200B*, or 5 crew for *Y7-100C* series. *Y7H* has 2 pilots, navigator, radio operator and air-mechanic.
Passengers: *Y7/-100/-200B* accommodate 48, 50 or 52 passengers, or 20-22 for the executive commuter variant and 38 for VIP, and *Y7-200A* has 52-56. Environmental control system automatically controls cabin temperature within 20° ±2° C. *Y7H* can carry 39 paratroops, 38 fully-armed troops, or 24 litters and an attendant.
Seat pitch: 30.7 ins (78 cm) for 52 seats and 28.3 ins (72 cm) for 56 seats in *Y7-200A*.
Galley: With food cabinets and electric kettles, aft of passenger cabin.
Pressurization: Cockpit and cabin pressurized.
Freight hold access: Y7H and Y7H-500 have a rear ramp/door, which can also be retracted under the fuselage for direct loading from trucks.
Loading facilities: For freight handling, a DJC-2 electric winch (with 4,409 lb, 2,000 kg lifting capacity, and maximum 4m/minute powered speed with a 1,168 lb, 530 kg load) and floor-mounted KSY-1 hydraulic conveyor (10,031 lb, 4,550 kg capacity) are in the Y7H cabin.
Baggage holds: 2, totalling 370.8 cu ft (10.5 m^3).
Wing control surfaces: Ailerons (21° up, 16° down, ±1°) with tabs, single-slotted inboard and double-slotted outboard flaps (all 15° for take-off and 38° landing). Winglets reduce drag by 4%, offering 5% fuel saving.
Tail control surfaces: Elevators (30° up, 15° down, ±1°) with tabs, and rudder (25°, ±1°) with tabs.
Flight control system: Mechanical for ailerons/elevators/rudder, with electric servo motor for autopilot operation. Hydraulic flap actuation.
Construction materials: Fuselage has 49 frames. Metal, but Y7-200B has carbonfibre tailplane and fin tips.
Engines: *Y7-100* and *Y7H-500* each have 2 x 2,900 ehp (2,162 ekW) Dongan WJ5A-1 turboprops with J16-G10A 4-blade auto-feathering propellers. *Y7-200B* has WJ5A-1G engines. *Y7H* has 2 x 2,790 shp (2,080 kW) WJ5A-1(M)s. All have a 1,984 lbf (8.826 kN) PY19A-300 turbojet for engine starting and performance boosting.
Fuel system: 10,560 lb (4,790 kg) for *Y7-100*. 12,125 lb (5,500 kg) for *Y7H-500*.
Electrical system: 28.5 volt DC supply via 2 engine-driven QF-18 generators (each 18kW). Emergency 24 volt power via 2 x 12HK-28 batteries. Main single-phase 115 volt, 400 Hz AC supply via JF-30A generator system, but also with 3 static inverters (1 for emergency) and 3-phase 36 volt, 400 Hz supply via an SBL-500 converter. Y7H-500 differs in having an additional DC-24B generator for auxiliary power supply (9kW) and 3 batteries.
Hydraulic system: Main system pressure 2,205 psi (±71), and emergency 2,275 psi (±213).
Braking system: Electronic anti-skid system on Y7-200B.
De-icing system: Hot air for wings and tail leading edges, turbine generator oil, engine guide vanes and inlet lips. Electric for propeller blades, spinners, windshield, air pressure sensors and pilot clock.
Fire system: HG-11 and HG-12 fire warning sensors and 4 extinguisher bottles for engines, and portable extinguishers on bulkheads of frames 7 and 34 for cabin in Y7-100.
Radar: Primus 90 colour weather radar.
Flight avionics/instrumentation: *Y7-100* principal navigation and air data equipment comprises Honeywell VG-311 dual attitude reference system and dual MHRS; Collins DF-206, ILS with 51Z-4 marker beacon receiver, AL-101 radio altimeter, DME-42, dual 51RV-4B VOR/ILS, ADI-84A, dual EHSI-74, 2 RMI-36, FGS-65 and CWS-80; Litton LTN-211 Omega/VLF; SFENA H321AKM emergency horizon, IDC air data instrument, Sundstrand 980-4100-FWXS flight data recorder, and Chinese KJ-6A autopilot and XLG-2A stall warning system with stick shaker. *Y7-200B* has EFIS-85B14, APS-85 digital flight control system, AHS-85 strapdown heading attitude system, and ADC-82A air data system, with data bus. Communication equipment for *Y7-100* comprises Collins 628T-3 HF, 618M-3 VHF, Becker 3100 audio system and Sundstrand AV-557C voice recorder. Collins 621A-6A air traffic control transponder. *Y7H-500* has KHF-950 HF. All information on a CRT.
Aircraft variants:
Y7 is the basic 3-crew version, based on the An-24.
Y7-100 is an upgraded Y7, featuring winglets, and updated cockpit and cabin systems of Western origin. Also for combi loads.
Y7-100C1, C2 and C3 are 5-crew versions with different levels of equipment.
Y7-200A is a new convertible commuter airliner/cargo or all cargo aircraft, developed with Boeing consultation. P&WC engines, lengthened fuselage (81 ft 1 ins, 24.708 m), redesigned forward fuselage to improve view from the cockpit, modified wing leading edges and flaps, vertical control sticks, and more.
Y7-200B has a fuselage lengthened by 29 ins (74 cm), new wing leading-edge profile, ground spoiler added, and 1% larger tailplane. Some use of composites (see Construction). Anti-skid system for undercarriage. Forward cargo door and emergency exit enlarged. EFIS cockpit instrumentation. WJ5A-1G engines.
Y7H is a 5-crew military cargo transport, based on the Antonov An-26. Has external suspension points for airdropping loads of up to 4,409 lb (2,000 kg). Rear ramp/door.
Y7H-500 is a civil version of Y7H. Certificated 15 June 1994.

Xi'an Y7H-500 freighter

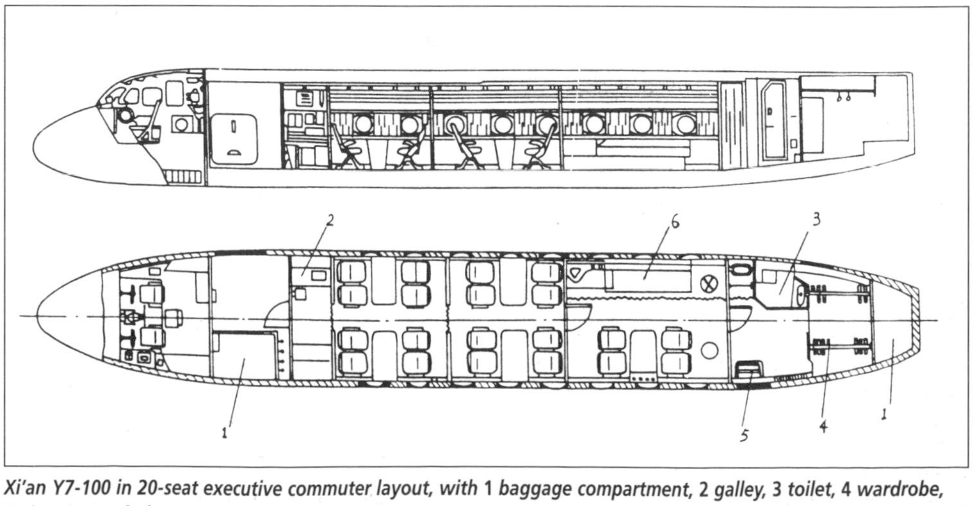

Xi'an Y7-100 in 20-seat executive commuter layout, with 1 baggage compartment, 2 galley, 3 toilet, 4 wardrobe, 5 airstair, 6 sofa (courtesy Xi'an)

Details for Y7-100, *with Y7H-500 in italics.*

Principal dimensions:
Wing span: 97 ft 4 ins (29.666 m), *95 ft 9.5 ins (29.2 m)*
Maximum length: 79 ft 5.5 ins (24.218 m), *79 ft 9 ins (24.31 m)*
Maximum height: 28 ft 1 ins (8.553 m), *29 ft 2 ins (8.89 m)*

Cabin:
Length: 32 ft 6 ins (9.91 m), *37 ft 6 ins (11.43 m)*
Width: 9 ft 1 ins (2.76 m), *9 ft 1.5 ins (2.78 m)*
Height: 6 ft 1 ins (1.86 m), *6 ft 3 ins (1.91 m)*
Volume: 1,822 cu ft (51.6 m^3)
Main passenger door: *2 ft x 4 ft 7 ins (0.6 x 1.4 m)*
Cargo door: *10 ft x 7 ft 10.5 ins (3.05 x 2.4 m), with sill height of 5 ft 8.5 ins (1.74 m)*

Wings:
Area: 810.09 sq ft (75.26 m^2), also documented as 812.78 sq ft (75.51 m^2), *807.08 sq ft (74.98 m^2)*
Aspect ratio: 11.694, *11.37*

Undercarriage:
Type: Retractable, with steerable and castering nosewheels. Twin wheels on each unit, with low-pressure tyres. Can operate from grass, soil, crushed stone or paved runways
Main wheel tyre size: 900 x 300 to 370 mm, *1,050 x 400 mm*
Nose wheel tyre size: 700 x 250 to 350 mm, *700 x 250 mm*
Wheel base: *27 ft 5 ins (8.366 m)*
Wheel track: *25 ft 11 ins (7.9 m)*
Turning circle: *36 ft 11 ins (11.25 m) radius minimum*

Weights:
Empty, operating: 33,153 lb (15,038 kg), with 3 crew, *34,773 lb (15,773 kg)*
Maximum ramp: *53,241 lb (24,150 kg)*
Maximum take-off and landing: 48,060 lb (21,800 kg), *52,910 lb (24,000 kg)*
Payload: 10,362 lb (4,700 kg), *12,125 lb (5,500 kg)*

Performance:
Maximum speed: 272 kts (312 mph) 503 km/h, *237 kts (272 mph) 438 km/h*
Cruise speed: 257 kts (296 mph) 476 km/h, at 21,000 kg and 6,000 m
Economic cruise speed: 228 kts (263 mph) 423 km/h, at 21,000 kg and 6,000 m
Stall speed: 85-110 kts (98-126 mph) 157-203 km/h, with 38° and 0° flaps respectively, at MTOW
Take-off distance: 2,100 ft (640 m), at 21,800 kg, *2,812 ft (857 m)*
Landing distance: 2,116 ft (645 m), at 21,800 kg, *2,080 ft (634 m)*
Maximum climb rate: 1,503 ft (458 m) per minute, at 21,000 kg
Ceiling: 28,700 ft (8,750 m), at 21,000 kg
Ceiling, one engine: 12,630 ft (3,850 m), at 19,000 kg
Range with full fuel: 1,297 naut miles (1,493 miles) 2,403 km
Range with full payload: 491 naut miles (565 miles) 910 km

Let Aeronautical Works Ltd (Czech Republic)

Corporate address: 686 04 Kunovice.
Telephone: +42 632 411111
Facsimile: +42 632 61352
Founded: 1950 under its own name, though an enterprise in Kunovice started in 1936 as Avia Aviation Works.

● Activities

- See also Gliders section.

Let L 410 UVP-E and L 420

First flight: 16 April 1969 (L 410 prototype), 30 December 1984 for L 410 UVP-E, and 10 November 1993 for L 420.
Certification: 1986 in UVP-E form (Russian NLGS-2). L 410 UVP-E20 improved version certified 34 July 1990 in Sweden (according to FAR 23/Amendment 34). L 420 certified to FAA FAR 23 Amendment 41 requirements in 1994.

Let L-410UVP-E

Role: STOL short-haul commuter, executive and cargo transport, with medevac, ambulance, paratroop and photogrammetric versions. Operating temperatures -50° to +42° C.
Airframe life: 20,000 flight hours or 20,000 cycles or 20 years.
Airfield limits: Minimum strength of 6 kg/cm^2 for L-420.
Noise levels: Reduced on L 420.
Sales: 1,000 L 410s of all versions delivered by 28 November 1990, with UVP-E production since 1986. Among the latest deliveries have been 3 UVP-E20G VIP transports for the Tunisian Air Force.
Details: L 410 UVP-E, except where stated.
Crew: 2.
Passengers: Up to 19. See Aircraft variants.
Seat pitch: 29.9 ins (76 cm) in 17 passenger layout.
Pressurization: None.
Baggage compartment: 24.72 cu ft (0.7 m^3) front, 47.67 cu ft (1.35 m^3) rear.
Wing control surfaces: Double-slotted flaps, ailerons, ground spoilers and ABC tabs.
Tail control surfaces: Elevators and rudder with tabs. Small ventral fin.
Flight control system: Mechanical, except for hydraulic flaps and spoilers.
Construction materials: Aluminium alloy, except for fabric-covered flaps, rudder and elevators.
Engines: 2 Motorlet Walter M 601 E turboprops, with Avia V 510 5-blade, reversible-pitch, constant-speed propellers. L 420 has 778 shp (580 kW) M 601 Fs.
Engine rating: Each 751 shp (560 kW).
Fuel system: 2,866 lb (1,300 kg) maximum. Wingtip tanks 200 litres each are optional.
Braking system: Disc brakes with anti-skid on mainwheels only.
De-icing system: Wing leading-edge rubber boots. Tailplane and fin leading edges have pneumatic de-icing. Electric propeller de-icing.
Radar: Optional AlliedSignal Bendix/King RDS 81 weather radar.
Flight avionics/instrumentation: IFR. AlliedSignal Bendix/King Gold Crown or optional EFIS Gold nav avionics, with optional KFC 325 autopilot, or Silver Crown with optional KFC 275 autopilot. Standard are ADF, VOR/ILS/MKR, NAV/RNAV/IL, transponder, DME, 2 VHF transceivers, 2 intercom, 2 public address, 2 gyro-compass, and standby head set. Other options include GPS.
Aircraft variants:
UVP-E commuter has 19 passengers plus 21.1 and 27.2 cu ft (0.6 and 0.77 m^3) baggage holds with inside

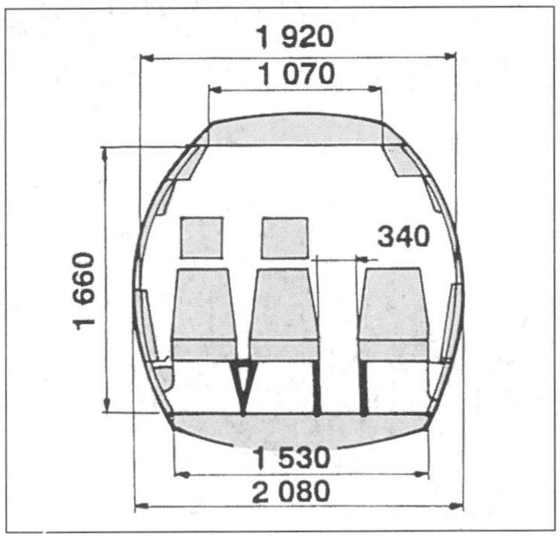

Let L 410/420 cabin cross section (courtesy Let)

access. Alternatively 17 passengers plus 21.2 and 47.7 cu ft (0.6 and 1.13 m^3) holds with outside access, tables and seats for attendant and stewardess. Toilet.
UVP-E Executive has 15 passengers (4 with armchairs) plus attendant, choice of holds as for commuter, tables, buffet and toilet.
UVP-E Cargo for a 8 ft 10 ins x 3 ft 11 ins x 1 ft (2.7 x 1.19 x 0.3 m) container, accompanying passenger seats and toilet.
UVP-E Fast Medical Aid with adjustable table and bed, 4 patient seats, foldable seats, doctor and attendant seats, toilet, and equipment. Alternatively 3 litters instead of patient seats.
UVP-E Ambulance with 6 litters, 5 seated patients and an attendant, a table and toilet.
UVP-E Paratroop with in-flight openable door, toilet and observation blisters. 15 persons.
UVP-E Photogrammetric with apertures for 2 vertical cameras, camera control unit, aiming device and side camera. 2 operator control panels, navigator workstation, blister, 551 lb (250 kg) auxiliary fuel tank, and toilet.
L 420 is a derivative of L 410 with higher-rated engines and other improvements.

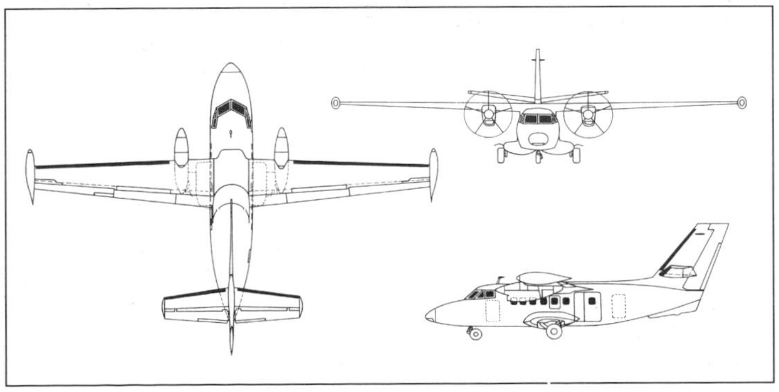

Let L 420 drawing (courtesy Let)

Details for L 410 UVP-E, *with L 420 in italics.*

Principal dimensions:
Wing span: 65 ft 6.5 ins (19.98 m) with tip tanks, 63 ft 11 ins (19.48 m) without; *L 420 the same*
Maximum length: 47 ft 4 ins (14.424 m), *the same*
Maximum height: 19 ft 1.5 ins (5.83 m), *the same*

Cabin:
Length: 18 ft 7 ins (5.655 m), *the same*
Width: 6 ft 3.5 ins (1.92 m), *the same*
Height: 5 ft 5.5 ins (1.66 m), *the same*
Volume: 632.13 cu ft (17.9 m^3), *the same*
Main passenger door/cargo: 4 ft 9.5 ins (1.46 m) height, and 2 ft 7.5 to 4 ft 1 ins (0.8 to 1.25 m) extendible width, *the same*

Wings:
Aerofoil section: NACA 63A418, 63A412 (root/tip), *the same*
Area: 378.67 sq ft (35.18 m^2), *the same*
Aspect ratio: 10.79 without tip tanks, *the same*
Dihedral: 7°, *the same*

Undercarriage:
Type: Retractable, with steerable nosewheel. Low pressure tyres for unpaved runway use, *the same.*
Main wheel tyre size: 718 x 306 mm, *720 x 310 mm*
Nose wheel tyre size: 548 x 221 mm, *550 x 225 mm*
Wheel base: 12 ft (3.666 m), *the same*
Wheel track: 11 ft 11.5 ins (3.65 m), *the same*

Weights:
Empty: 8,862 lb (4,020 kg) with tip tanks, *9,094 lb (4,125 kg)*
Maximum take-off: 14,109 lb (6,400 kg), *14,550 lb (6,600 kg)*
Maximum landing: 13,668 lb (6,200 kg), *14,110 lb (6,400 kg)*
Payload: 3,560 lb (1,615 kg), *3,770 lb (1,710 kg)*

Performance:
Continuous cruise speed: 205 kts (236 mph) 380 km/h, *210 kts (241 mph) 388 km/h*, both at 13,780 ft (4,200 m) altitude
Economic cruise speed: 197 kts (227 mph) 365 km/h, at 13,780 ft (4,200 m)
Runway length: *at least 3,297 ft (1,005 m)*
Take-off distance over a 35 ft (11 m) obstacle: *1,820 ft (555 m)*
Landing distance over a 50 ft (15m) obstacle: *1,640 ft (500 m)*
Maximum climb rate: 1,420 ft (432 m) per minute, *1,400 ft (426 m) per minute*
Maximum climb rate, one engine: 355 ft (108 m) per minute, *the same*
Ceiling: 23,785 ft (7,250 m) for 100 ft (30 m) per minute climb, 11,975 ft (3,650 m) single engine for 50 ft (15 m) per minute climb
Operating altitude: 13,780 ft (4,200 m), 19,685 ft (6,000 m) technical
Range with full fuel (UVP-E): 711 naut miles (819 miles) 1,318 km, with 2,028 lb (920 kg) payload, 45 minutes reserve, with tip tanks
Range with full fuel (L 420): *737 naut miles (849 miles) 1,366 km, with 45 minutes reserve.*
Range (L 420): *367 naut miles (422 miles) 680 km without tip tanks, 17 passengers and 45 minutes reserve*

Let L 610

First flight: 30 December 1988 (prototype with M602 engines). 18 December 1992 for L 610G (technical) and 6 January 1993 (official).
Certification: December 1994 under FAR Pt 25 and SLI.
First delivery: April 1995.
Role: Regional airliner, with quick change for cargo carrying.
Airframe life: 50,000 flight hours.
Sales: 9 L 610Ms have been delivered to the Czech Air Force (trials at Kbely). Further production of this version rests on joint venture plans with Russia's Smolensk plant, and with possible engine production in Russia or use of the Klimov-built PT6. Czech production is based on the L 610G.
Crew: 2.
Passengers: 40.
Pressurization: 5.22 psi cabin differential.
Baggage compartment: 211.9 cu ft (6 m^3) aft of the toilet.
Wing control surfaces: Ailerons (port tab), single-slotted flaps (12° take-off, 26° landing) and ground/lateral control spoilers ahead of flaps.
Tail control surfaces: Elevators (each with trim and geared tabs) and rudder (trim and spring balance tabs).
Flight control system: Mechanical, except for hydraulic flaps and spoilers.
Construction materials: Aluminium alloy, with some composites.
Engines: 2 General Electric CT7-9D turboprops, with Hamilton Standard HS-14RF-23 reversible-pitch 4-blade propellers in L 610G. Motorlet Walter M602 turboprops or possibly Klimov PT6s (see Sales) in L 610M.

Let L 610G

Engine rating: Each 1,750 shp (1,305 kW) and 1,823 shp (1,360 kW) for CT7 and M602 respectively.
Fuel system: 3,420 litres in the wings.
Electrical system: ECE 28 volt DC system, with 2 engine-driven starter-generators. 2 ni-cd batteries. Airsupply 115/200 volt AC system, with 2 x 26kVA variable frequency alternators and 1 x 8 kVA 3-phase system. 2 inverters.
Hydraulic system: Principal and back-up systems, each 3,036 psi.
Braking system: Hydraulic disc, with anti-skid system.
De-icing system: Pneumatic for wing and tail unit leading edges, operating in 1 and 3 minute cycles. Electric windshield, propellers and pitots, air intakes and horn balances.
Radar: Weather radar.
Flight avionics/instrumentation: EFIS. Rockwell Collins Pro Line II. Meets FAR Pt 121.
Aircraft variants:
L 610G became the "westernized" production version, with GE engines.
L 610M is the Walter-engined version, now possibly for Russian joint venture production.

Details for L 610G.

Principal dimensions:
Wing span: 84 ft (25.6 m)
Maximum length: 71 ft 3 ins (21.72 m)
Maximum height: 27 ft 10 ins (8.19 m)

Cabin:
Length: 25 ft 9 ins (7.84 m) for passenger area, not including galley, toilet and baggage area to the rear
Width: 8 ft 4 ins (2.54 m)
Height: 6 ft 0.25 ins (1.835 m)

Wings:
Aerofoil section: MS(1)-0318D, 0312 (root/tip)
Area: 602.78 sq ft (56 m^2)
Aspect ratio: 11.703

Undercarriage:
Type: Retractable, with steerable nosewheel. Low pressure tyres for unpaved airfields
Wheel base: 21 ft 8 ins (6.596 m)
Wheel track: 15 ft 1 ins (4.59 m)
Turning circle: 60 ft 2 ins (18.33 m)

Weights:
Empty, operating: 20,326 lb (9,220 kg)
Maximum take-off: 31,967 lb (14,500 kg)
Maximum landing: 30,864 lb (14,000 kg)
Payload: 9,260 lb (4,200 kg)

Performance:
Maximum speed: 258 kts (297 mph) 478 km/h
Economical cruise speed: 152 kts (175 mph) 281 km/h
Stall speed: 95 kts (110 mph) 176 km/h, *clean*, EAS
Landing distance over a 35 ft (11 m) obstacle: 2,172 ft (662 m)
Maximum climb rate: 1,673 ft (510 m) per minute
Ceiling: 27,560 ft (8,400 m)
Range with full fuel: 1,280-1,365 naut miles (1,473-1,572 miles) 2,370-2,530 km
Range: 664-718 naut miles (764-826 miles) 1,230-1,330 km with 40 passengers, 45 minutes plus 116 miles (185 km) reserve

Daimler-Benz Aerospace AG (Germany)

Corporate address: See Combat section for company details, particularly the Regional Aircraft Division details.

Dornier 228

First flight: 28 March 1981.
Role: STOL light commuter and cargo transport, with special mission variants.
Sales: 230 firm orders from over 70 customers in 70 countries, with 213 delivered (65% commuter version). Current production version is the 228-212. Licence production of the earlier 228-101/201 types by HAL of India has ended. Simera of South Africa has been discussing potential production arrangements for the 228, possibly encompassing joint development of a "stretched" version; Dornier opened an office in Johannesburg on 19 August 1994.
Details: 228-212.
Crew: 1 or 2 pilots.
Passengers: 19 in commuter version. Other layouts provide for up to 22 troops or 21 parachutists and a jumpmaster, or 6 litters and 9 seated persons in a medevac role.

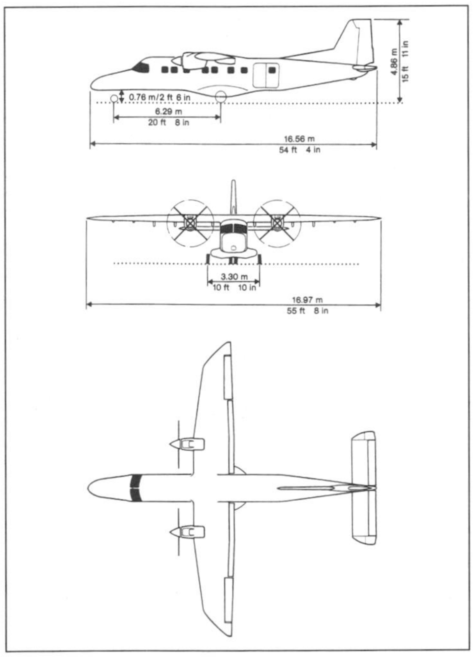

Dornier 228-212 drawing (courtesy Dornier)

Dornier 228-212 for Bavaria and to be used for measuring the ozone layer

Baggage compartments: 463 lb (210 kg) in rear cabin, plus 265 lb (120 kg) in nose.
Wing control surfaces: Drooping ailerons, and single-slotted flaps.
Tail control surfaces: Variable incidence tailplane, elevators (port tab) and rudder (with tab).
Flight control system: Mechanical.
Construction materials: Mainly aluminium alloy, but with composites contributing to the wing structure, and for the undercarriage nacelles, fuselage nose, and the tips of the wings and all fixed/moving tail surfaces.
Engines: 2 AlliedSignal TPE331-5-252D turboprops.
Engine rating: Each 840 shp (626 kW) for take off, with 776 shp (578 kW) gearbox limit.
Fuel system: 4,156 lb (1,885 kg), or 4,960 lb (2,250 kg) with optional tank.
Electrical system: 28 volt DC supply by 2 engine-driven starter-generators. 2 x 25 amp-hour ni-cd batteries. 2 static inverters for AC supply.
Hydraulic system: 3.002 psi.
Braking system: Carbon disc brakes on main units.
De-icing system: Engine intakes. Others items optional.
Radar: Optional weather radar.
Flight avionics/instrumentation: IFR equipped. Standard equipment includes VOR/ILS, marker beacon receiver, transponder, DME, RMI, HSI and ADI.
Mission equipment: See Reconnaissance section.
Aircraft variants:
Dornier 228-212 current production version, which succeeded the 228-202 from aircraft No 176. Forms the basis for all currently offered special versions (see Passengers, and below).
Cargo layout provides for up to 5,158 lb (2,340 kg) of freight in the cabin.
Border Patrol and Maritime Patrol are among several special mission military/civil variants on offer and in service. See Reconnaissance section.
Stretched 228 is a possibility, under a projected Dornier/Simera joint venture.

Details for 228-212.

Principal dimensions:
Wing span: 55 ft 8 ins (16.97 m)
Maximum length: 54 ft 4 ins (16.56 m)
Maximum height: 15 ft 11 ins (4.86 m)

Cabin:
Length: 23 ft 3 ins (7.08 m)
Width: 4 ft 5 ins (1.346 m)
Height: 5 ft 1 ins (1.55 m)
Volume: 519 cu ft (14.7 m^3)
Main passenger door: 4 ft 5 ins x 2 ft 1 ins (1.34 x 0.64 m)
Cargo door: airliners only

Wings:
Aerofoil section: A-5
Area: 344.44 sq ft (32 m^2)

Undercarriage:
Type: Retractable, with steerable nosewheel
Wheel base: 20 ft 8 ins (6.29 m)
Wheel track: 10 ft 10 ins (3.3 m)

Weights:
Empty: 8,243 lb (3,739 kg)
Maximum take-off: 14,109-14,550 lb (6,400-6,600 kg)
Maximum landing: 13,448 lb (6,100 kg)
Payload: 4,852 lb (2,201 kg)

Performance:
Maximum cruise speed: 234 kts (269 mph) 433 km/h
Long-range cruise speed: 164 kts (189 mph) 304 km/h
Maximum duration speed: 105 kts (121 mph) 195 km/h
Minimum control speed: 79 kts (91 mph) 147 km/h, *clean*
Stall speed: 81 kts (93.5 mph) 150 km/h, *with flaps*
Take-off distance: 2,600 ft (793 m)
Take-off distance (Mil STOL): 1,477 ft (450 m)
Landing distance: 1,477 ft (450 m)
Maximum climb rate: 1,870 ft (570 m) per minute
Ceiling: 28,000 ft (8,535 m)
Range with full payload: typically 600 naut miles (691 miles) 1,111 km with reserve
Range with 1,709 lb (775 kg) payload: up to 1,320 naut miles (1,520 miles) 2,444 km

Dornier 328

First flight: 6 December 1991.
Certification: 15 October 1993 (JAR 25), 10 November 1993 (FAR 25). 3/4 November 1994 LBA/FAA certification for the Improved Performance 328-110. Late 1995 for 328-120.
First delivery: 21 October 1993 to Air Engiadina. First 328-120 to Formosa Airlines.

Dornier 328 for Afrimex Aviation of Nigeria, handed over in August 1994

Role: Regional transport.
Noise levels: 81 dB take off, 87 dB sideline, and 95 dB approach. Interior below 78 dB(A) for most passengers.
Sales: 76 firm orders and 75 options from 17 customers by June 1995, with Air Scotland among the most recent. First newly-available 328-120s delivered in 1995. Interest from Simera for a co-developed military version (see 228 entry).
Crew: 2.
Passengers: 30-33. Cabin arrangements on a modular design, allowing adaptability to changing market needs. Stretched version being evaluated.
Seat pitch: 30 ins (76 cm) for 33 passengers, 30.7 ins (78 cm) for 30 passengers.
Galley: See diagram.
Pressurization: Maximum 6.75 psi cabin differential.
Baggage compartment: 8 ft 8 ins x 6 ft (2.64 x 1.83 m), with 222.48 cu ft (6.3 m^3) volume. Sill height 3 ft 10.5 ins (1.18 m).
Wing control surfaces: Ailerons (with geared tabs), flaps and available spoilers (ground/lateral control). Improved Performance 328-110 adds ground spoilers among other changes (see Aircraft variants).
Tail control surfaces: Elevators and rudder, with geared tabs.
Flight control system: Mechanical, except for hydraulic (mechanically interconnected) flaps, spoilers and electric tabs.
Construction materials: Composites (23% structural weight) for the entire rear fuselage and tail unit, including rear pressure bulkhead (aramid/carbonfibre), undercarriage and wing/fuselage fairings, and all control surfaces.
Engines: 2 Pratt & Whitney Canada PW119B or C turboprops, with 11 ft 6 ins (3.5 m) Hartzell 6-blade composite propellers.

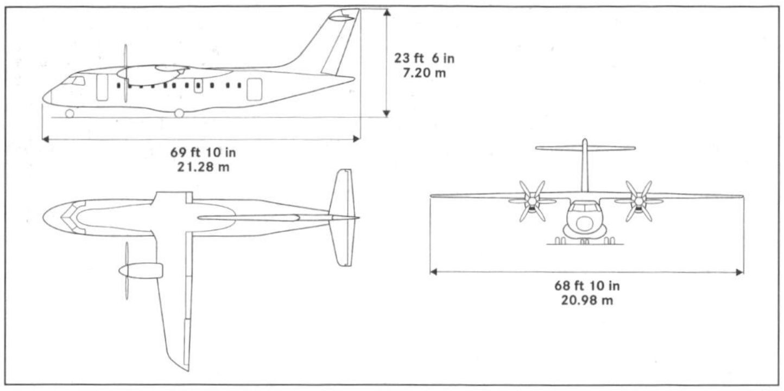

Dornier 328 drawing (courtesy Dornier)

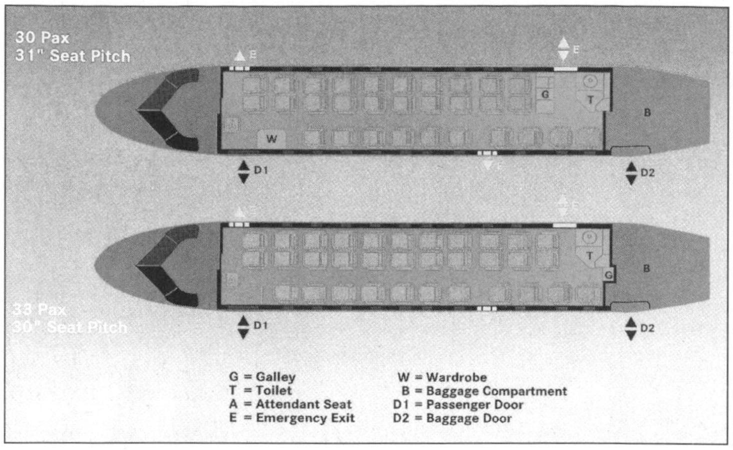

Dornier 328 cabin layouts (courtesy Dornier)

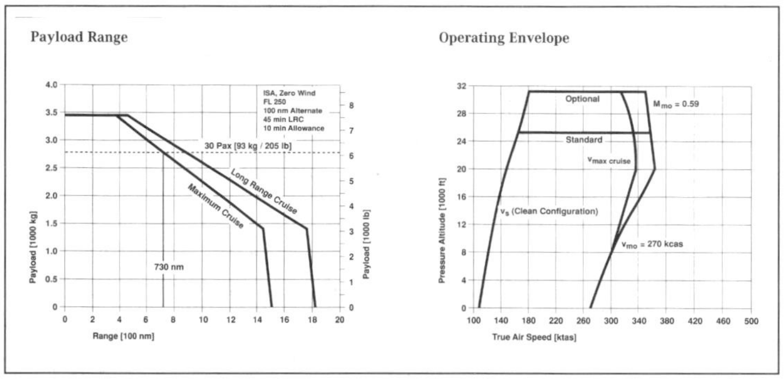

Dornier 328-100 payload/range and operating envelope graphs (courtesy Dornier)

Engine rating: Each 2,180 shp (1,626 kW).
Fuel system: Usable 4,268 litres in the wings. Under 8 minute pressure refuelling. Block fuel for a 300 naut mile (345 mile) 555 km sector (ISA, FL 200) weighing 1,437 lb (652 kg).
Electrical system: Primary DC system with 2 engine-driven starter-generators of 28 volt/400 A each. Secondary DC with 2 x 40 amp-hour ni-cd batteries. AC system has 2 x 20kVA brushless alternators. Optional AlliedSignal 36-150(DD) APU in tailcone for air conditioning bleed air, generator back-up and battery assistance during engine starting; can provide higher climb rates.
Hydraulic system: Main, and hand-pump auxiliary for emergency undercarriage extension.
Braking system: Segmented, multi-disc on mainwheels, with 2,000 landings design life.
De-icing system: Pneumatic boots for wing and tail leading edges, and air intakes. Electric mats for propeller leading edges, and electric windscreen de-icing.
Radar: Honeywell Primus 650 weather radar, or optional Primus 870.
Flight avionics/instrumentation: Honeywell Primus 2000 system, including EFIS with five 8 x 7 ins (20 x 18 cm) CRTs, EICAS, flight management system (database including VOR, VORTAC, VOR/DME, airport reference points, etc), Primus II integrated comm/nav/transponder radios, integrated avionics computer, flight director and autopilot, fibre-optic gyro AHRS, and Micro air data computer. Full range of options, including traffic alert and collision avoidance system, GPS, ground proximity warning system, microwave landing system, laser INS, head-up guidance system, and VLF/Omega nav. The Hughes/Flight Dynamics head-up guidance system (as ordered by Horizon Air) allows Cat IIIa landings.
Aircraft variants:
328-100 is the basic version, as detailed.
328-110 is the Improved Performance version, with changes including spoilers, larger dorsal and ventral fins, increased rudder travel, larger-diameter propellers and more. Flaps can be extended to 32° on approach. MTOW increased to 30,843 lb (13,990 kg), take-off distance reduced to 3,570 ft (1,088 m), landing distance 3,825 ft (1,166 m), and range 999 naut miles (1,149 miles) 1,850 km.
328-120 offers further improvements in take-off/landing performance, with 5% extra thermodynamic engine power from the PW119C engines. Certified May 1995.
328-200 was to have been the designation of the Improved Performance Kit version, with extra modifications. Programme ended in 1994.
328 hydrogen-powered testbed will fly in 1998, with a possible production version in 2005. P&WC engines.

DETAILS FOR 328-100, UNLESS STATED.

Principal dimensions:
Wing span: 68 ft 10 ins (20.98 m)
Maximum length: 69 ft 10 ins (21.28 m)
Maximum height: 23 ft 7.5 ins (7.2 m)

Cabin:
Length: 33 ft 8 ins (10.27 m)
Width: 7 ft 2 ins (2.18 m)
Height: 6 ft 2.5 ins (1.89 m)
Volume: 1,183 cu ft (33.5 m^3)
Cargo door: airliners only

Undercarriage:
Type: Retractable, with electro-hydraulically steerable nosewheels. Twin wheels on each unit
Wheel base: 24 ft 4 ins (7.41 m)
Wheel track: 10 ft 7 ins (3.22 m)
Turning circle: under 49 ft 4 ins (15 m) for 180°

Weights:
Empty, operating: 19,423 lb (8,810 kg)
Maximum take-off: 30,071 lb (13,640 kg)
Maximum landing: 29,167 lb (13,230 kg)
Payload: 7,606 lb (3,450 kg)

Performance:
Maximum operating speed: 255 kts (294 mph) 472 km/h IAS
Maximum cruise speed: 335 kts (386 mph) 620 km/h
Required field length (JAR 25/FAR 25): 3,610 ft (1,100 m) take off, ISA, sea level
Take-off distance: 3,570 ft (1,088 m) for 328-110
Landing distance: 3,825 ft (1,166 m) for 328-110
Cruise altitude: 25,000-31,160 ft (7,600-9,500 m)
Single engine ceiling: 17,000 ft (5,180 m)
Range: 730 naut miles (840.5 miles) 1,352 km, with 30 passengers 205 lb (93 kg each), maximum cruise speed, FL 250, 100 naut mile alternate and 45 minutes reserve
Range out of hot-and-high airfields: 710 naut miles (817 miles) 1,315 km, from airfields 6,000 ft (1,830 m) above sea level and at 20° C above standard
Block time for a 300 naut mile sector: 70 minutes, ISA, FL 200

PT Industri Pesawat Terbang Nusantara (IPTN) (Indonesia)

Corporate address: PO Box 1562, Jalan Pajajaran 154, Bandung 40174.
Telephone: +62 22 633900, 633911
Facsimile: +62 22 632145
Telex: 28295 IPTNBD IA
Founded: 1976.
Employees: over 15,000.
Information: Djoko Sartono (programme manager).

● Activities

- IPTN is a partner in the Airtech CN-235 programme. It also undertakes licence production of the CASA C-212. Bell 412, and Eurocopter BO-105 and Super Puma and supports the new Bell 407T and 430.
- In 1994, the Government announced its intention to sell 20% of IPTN shares to foreign investors.
- A second N-250 assembly line is to be established in the USA under a new company named American Regional Aircraft Industry (AMRAI). The location was announced on 13 June 1995 as Mobile, Alabama, with IPTN intending to retain a 40% shareholding. General Electric has offered to take a 10% stake. All primary subassemblies will be built in Indonesia, for shipping to the USA in knock-down form. A foothold in the USA had already been established with the subsidiary IPTN North America Inc, operating from Seattle.

IPTN N-250-100 and N-2130

Details: For N-250-100 (except under Aircraft variants).
First flight: 10 August 1995; roll-out of the prototype took place on 10 November 1994.
Certification: Late 1997 (to FAA Pt 25, Pt 36 and ICAO Annex 16 standards).
First delivery: Early 1998.
Role: Regional airliner.

Noise levels: Interior 78 dB.
Sales: 50-seat N-250 prototype, 3 N-250-100 flying development aircraft, and 2 static development aircraft for the 120,000 hour fatigue test programme at the National Research Centre in Serbong. All development aircraft have production-standard lengthened fuselages; first development aircraft (expected to fly May 1996) for handling and performance envelope testing, second for avionics trials, and third for final certification (1,600-2,000 hour flight test programme using the prototype and all 3 development aircraft). 188 orders/options by June 1995. Announced orders at the time of writing were from Bouraq Airlines, Merpati Nusantara and Sempati Air of Indonesia (jointly 16 firm, with many options), FFV of Sweden (MoU for 24), and Gulfstream International Airlines of the USA (4 firm plus 6 options). 1998 production covers 6 aircraft, 12 in 1999, and increasing thereafter. Projected sales of over 700.

IPTN N-250-100

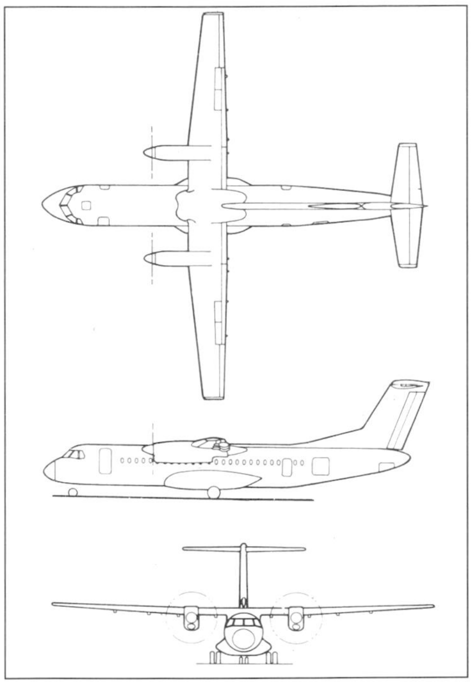

IPTN N-250-100 drawing (courtesy IPTN)

DETAILS FOR N-250-100.

Principal dimensions:
Wing span: 91 ft 10 ins (28 m)
Maximum length: 92 ft 6.25 ins (28.2 m)
Maximum height: 28 ft 10 ins (8.785 m)

Cabin:
Width: 8 ft 9.5 ins (2.68 m)
Height: 6 ft 3.5 ins (1.92 m)

Wings:
Area: 699.65 sq ft (65 m^2)
Aspect ratio: 12.062

Tail unit:
Tailplane span: 30 ft 10 ins (9.4 m)

Undercarriage:
Type: Retractable, with steerable nosewheels. Twin wheels on each unit
Wheel base: 33 ft 8 ins (10.253 m)
Wheel track: 13 ft 5.5 ins (4.1 m)

Weights:
Empty, operating: 34,612 lb (15,700 kg)
Ramp: 54,895 lb (24,900 kg)
Maximum take-off: 54,675 lb (24,800 kg)
Maximum landing: 54,233 lb (24,600 kg)

Performance:
Cruise speed: 330 kts (380 mph) 611 km/h
Long-range cruise speed: 300 kts (345 mph) 555 km
Take-off and landing distance: 4,000 ft (1,219 m)
Maximum climb rate: 1,850 ft (564 m) per minute
Maximum climb rate, one engine: 520 ft (158 m) per minute
Ceiling: 25,000 ft (7,620 m), or 20,000 ft (6,100 m) with one engine
Range with full payload: 800 naut miles (921 miles) 1,481 km

Crew: 2 (flight).
Passengers: 64-68.
Seat pitch: 31.9 ins (81 cm) for 64-seat layout, or 29.9 ins (76 cm) for 68-seat layout.
Pressurization: AlliedSignal cabin control pressure system.
Baggage volume: 7.06 cu ft (0.2 m^3) per passenger, plus a further 1.73 cu ft (0.049 m^3) per passenger in overhead bins.
Wing control surfaces: Horn-balanced ailerons with tabs, double-slotted flaps and 2-section spoilers.
Tail control surfaces: Elevators with tabs and 2-section rudder.
Flight control system: Lucas Aerospace/Liebherr-Aero-Technik fly-by-wire. Mechanical back-up for the ailerons and elevators.
Construction materials: Mostly metal, but with 10% composites used for control surfaces, wing leading edges and tips, wingroot fairings, various parts of the tail unit, tailcone and more.
Engines: 2 Allison AE 2100C turboprops, with FADEC, and driving Dowty 6-blade composite propellers.
Engine rating: Each 3,271 shp (2,365 kW) at 1,100 propeller rpm. APIC auxiliary power unit.
Fuel system: 9,259 lb (4,200 kg). Cobham system.
Radar: Optional Rockwell Collins TWR-850 doppler turbulence weather radar.
Flight avionics/instrumentation: Rockwell Collins Pro Line 4, with 5 CRTs and EICAS. Optional FMS-4050 flight management system and TCAS-94 traffic alert and collision avoidance system.

Aircraft variants:
N-250-100 is the production-standard version, longer than the first prototype (with 1 ft 8 ins and 3 ft 3 ins, 0.5 m and 1 m plugs) and originally known as N-270.
N-250-200 is a projected longer range/payload variant for delivery in the next century.
N-250 Cargo is a proposed all-cargo variant of the -100, with reinforced cabin floor and a large side-loading door.
N-2130 is a proposed 100-seat stretched derivative for service from about 2006. Wing span 95 ft (28.95 m) and length 97 ft 3 ins (29.65 m).

Alenia (Italy)

Corporate address: See Combat section for company details.

● Activities

- Alenia's Capodichino Nord factories converted 4 ex-TAP Boeing 707s into flight refuelling tankers/transports for the Italian Air Force, between 1989-93. Another has since been ordered. 3 refuelling points per aircraft, each supplying 1,600 litres of fuel per minute, with a total of 56,000 litres of transferable fuel.
- Other modification work includes converting McDonnell-Douglas DC-10/MD-11s into freighters by Alenia's Aeronavali Venezia subsidiary, and upgrading the UPS B727/DC-8 parcel-carrier fleet by its Dee Howard Co subsidiary in the USA. In addition to new digital avionics, 44 B727s are receiving new Rolls-Royce Tay 651-54 engines to comply with FAA Level III noise levels and reduce operating costs. First re-engined B727 flew in April 1992, with certification that November.

Alenia G222

First flight: 18 July 1970.
First delivery: 1976 (to Dubai).
Role: Medium-range tactical military transport, with STOL characteristics. Also used for firefighting, calibration, EW and more.
Sales: Latest order for 6 for the Royal Thai Air Force, all delivered within 18 months of the 1994 contract

Alenia converted Boeing 707 tanker-transport

date. 86 previously built, including 46 for the Italian Air Force in transport (30), G222SAA firefighting, G222RM navaid calibration and G222VS electronic countermeasures versions. 20 G222Ts with Rolls-Royce Tyne engines went to Libya, while other users include Argentina, Dubai, Nigeria, Somalia and Venezuela. In August 1990, 10 G222s were ordered by the USAF as C-27A Spartans, with 8 more on option. Chrysler Technologies Airborne Systems became prime contractor for C-27As, responsible for installation of communication and navigation equipment. Based in Panama.

Details: Standard G222 transport.
Crew: 2 or 3, plus loadmaster.
Passengers: Up to 53 fully-equipped troops, 42 paratroops, or 36 stretchers plus 4 attendants.
Pressurization: 5.95 psi cabin differential.
Freight hold volume: 2,048.25 cu ft (58 m^3)
Freight hold capacity: 19,840 lb (9,000 kg). Can include 2 trucks or 1 truck towing a trailer or howitzer gun, armoured vehicle, or many other varied loading including 5 x A-22 containers or pallets of up to 7 ft 4 ins (2.24 m) wide. Items up to 11,020 lb (5,000 kg) weight can be air dropped.
Freight hold access: Door and ramp (hydraulically operated) under the rear fuselage.
Size of freight doors: Full height and width of cabin, at 8 ft 0.5 ins x 7 ft 4.5 ins (2.45 x 2.25 m).
Wing control surfaces: Ailerons (with tabs), double-slotted flaps and 2-section spoilers.
Tail control surfaces: Variable-incidence tailplane. Elevators (with tabs) and rudder.
Flight control system: Hydraulic flaps, spoilers and rudder. Mechanical ailerons and elevators.
Construction materials: Aluminium alloy, with some honeycomb cores.
Engines: 2 General Electric T64-P4D turboprops.
Engine rating: Each 3,400 shp (2,535 kW).
Fuel system: 12,000 litres.
Electrical system: 28 volt DC supply via AC system using 2 transformer/rectifiers. 24 volt ni-cd battery and static inverter for back-up. 115/200 volt, 400 Hz 3-phase AC supply via 2 engine and 1 APU driven alternators.
Hydraulic system: 2 systems, each 3,002 psi.
Braking system: Hydraulic multi-disc type.
De-icing system: Pneumatic boots for wing, tailplane and fin leading edges. Electric for propellers, and electric plus bleed air for engine intakes.
Oxygen system: Liquid standard, with gaseous as option.
Radar: Meteo weather and mapping radar.
Flight avionics/instrumentation: Navigation suite includes autopilot, Omega, dual VOR, dual ILS, dual Tacan or DME, ADF, marker beacon receiver, HSI, flight director and more. Communications suite includes HF/SSB, UHF, VHF-AM and FM.
Mission equipment: 3 life-rafts as standard equipment.
Aircraft variants:
G222 versions, see Sales and above.
C-27A Spartan is the USAF version, delivered from April 1991.

Alenia G222, serving with the USAF as the C-27A Spartan

DETAILS FOR G222.

Principal dimensions:
Wing span: 94 ft 2 ins (28.7 m)
Maximum length: 74 ft 6 ins (22.7 m)
Maximum height: 34 ft 8 ins (10.57 m)

Cabin:
Length: 28 ft 2 ins (8.58 m)
Width: 8 ft 0.5 ins (2.45 m)
Height: 7 ft 4.5 ins (2.25 m)
Floor area: 276.42 sq ft (25.68 m^2), including ramp/door

Wings:
Area: 882.64 sq ft (82 m^2)
Aspect ratio: 10.045

Undercarriage:
Type: Can operate from semi-prepared and grass airstrips
Wheel base: 20 ft 5 ins (6.23 m)
Wheel track: 12 ft 0.5 ins (3.67 m)

Weights:
Empty, operating: 34,612 lb (15,700 kg)
Maximum take-off: 61,729 lb (28,000 kg), or 56,879 lb (25,800 kg) for C-27A
Maximum landing: 58,422 lb (26,500 kg)
Payload: 19,840 lb (9,000 kg)

Performance:
Maximum speed: 263 kts (303 mph) 487 km/h
Cruise speed: 238 kts (273 mph) 440 km/h
Stall speed: 92 kts (106 mph) 170 km/h
Take-off distance: 2,251 ft (686 m), or under 2,000 ft (610 m) for C-27A
Landing distance: 2,861 ft (872 m) at MLW, or under 2,000 ft (610 m) for C-27A
Maximum climb rate: 1,250 ft (380 m) per minute
Ceiling: 24,935 ft (7,600 m)
Range with full fuel: 2,160 naut miles (2,485 miles) 4,000 km
Range with full payload: 680 naut miles (783 miles) 1,259 km

Partenavia Costruzioni Aeronautiche SpA (Italy)

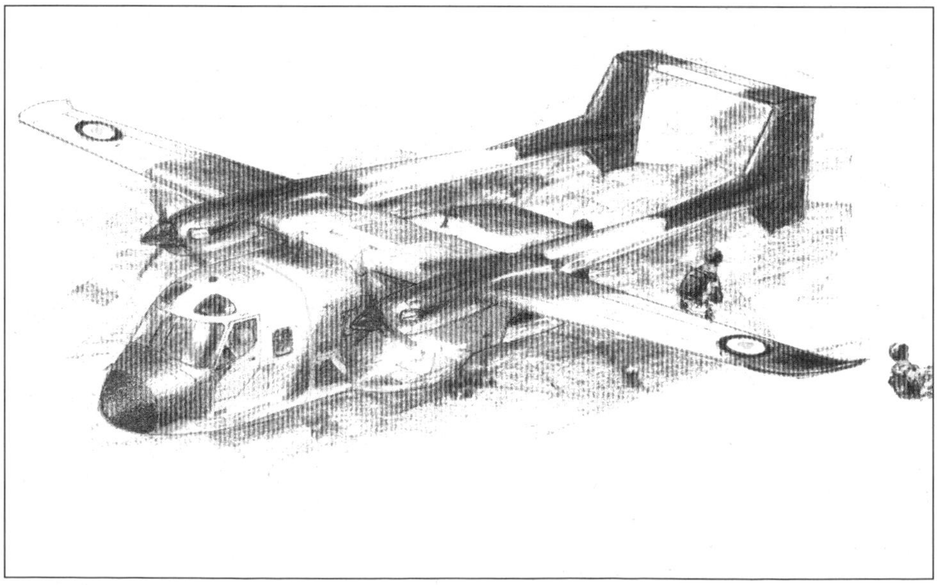

Partenavia PD 90 Tapete Air Truck

Corporate address: 24 Corso Vittorio Emanuele, 20122 Milano.
Telephone: +39 2 76001847
Facsimile: +39 2 783147
Founded: 1949.
Information: Barbara Contini (Marketing Communication Director).

■ Facilities:
■ Manufacturing plant at Naples Capodichino Airport, 102 via Ruffo di Calabria, 80143 Napoli.

● Activities
● See also General Aviation section.

Partenavia PD 90 Tapete Air Truck

First flight: Design stage.
Role: Unpressurized light transport for commuter, cargo, air ambulance, parachuting, tactical transport, maritime surveillance and firefighting roles.
Passengers: 18 in commuter configuration.
Freight hold access: Rear cargo door/ramp. Port side-loading doors.
Wing control surfaces: Ailerons and flaps.
Tail control surfaces: Joining elevator with tab, and twin rudders with tabs.
Fuselage: Pod and twin boom.
Construction materials: Metal, with stressed skin wings.
Engines: 2 Pratt & Whitney Canada PT6 turboprops.
Engine rating: Each 750 shp (559 kW).
Fuel system: 1,810 litres.

Details for PD 90 Air Truck.

Principal dimensions:
Wing span: 59 ft 1 ins (18 m)
Maximum length: 43 ft 11.5 ins (13.4 m)
Maximum height: 15 ft 5 ins (4.7 m)

Cabin:
Length: 16 ft 5 ins (5 m)
Width: 6 ft 7 ins (2 m)
Height: 5 ft 7 ins (1.7 m)

Wings
Area: 405.91 sq ft (37.71 m^2)
Aspect ratio: 8.59

Undercarriage:
Type: Retractable, with twin wheels on all units

Weights:
Empty: 7,937 lb (3,600 kg)
Maximum ramp: 13,977 lb (6,340 kg)
Maximum take-off and landing: 13,889 lb (6,300 kg)
Useful load: 6,041 lb (2,740 kg)
Payload: 3,946 lb (1,790 kg)

Performance:
Maximum speed: 240 kts (276 mph) 444 km/h at 14,000 ft (4,267 m)
Maximum cruise speed: 232 kts (267 mph) 430 km/h, at 12,000 ft (3,660 m)
Stall speed: 83 kts (96 mph) 154 km/h, *clean*, 70 kts (81 mph) 130 km/h *landing configuration*
Take-off distance: 1,050 ft (320 m)
Take-off over a 50 ft (15 m) obstacle: 1,476 ft (450 m)
Landing distance: 1,640 ft (500 m)
Landing distance over a 50 ft (15 m) obstacle: 1,968 ft (600 m)
Maximum climb rate: 1,900 ft (579 m) per minute
Maximum climb rate, one engine: 400 ft (122 m) per minute
Ceiling: 30,000 ft (9,145 m), or 14,000 ft (4,267 m) with single engine
Range with full fuel: 1,058 naut miles (1,218 miles) 1,960 km, at long-range cruise speed, 10,000 ft (3,050 m) altitude, 45 minutes reserve
Range with full payload: 418 naut miles (481 miles) 775 km, at maximum cruise speed, conditions as above

ShinMaywa Industries Ltd (Japan)

Corporate address: Nihon Building, 2-6-2 Ohtemachi, Chiyoda-Ku, Tokyo 100.
Telephone: +81 3 3245 6611
Facsimile: +81 3 3245 6616
Founded: October 1949.

● Activities

- Manufactures aircraft and subassemblies, industrial machinery and truck bodies.
- Components include contributions to aeroplanes and helicopters being assembled in Japan. McDonnell-Douglas MD-11 engine pylon, is a risk-sharing partner on the MD-95 (pylons and horizontal stabilizers), builds trailing edges for Boeing 757s and 767s, 777 wing/body fairings and components for Gulfstream business aircraft.

All 15 ShinMaywa US-1/1As have been delivered to the JMSDF, mainly for search and rescue with No 71 Squadron. A former similar PS-1 ASW amphibian, and more recently a US-1A, have been modified for firefighting, the latter (shown) carrying over 30,000 lb (13,600 kg) of water (courtesy ShinMaywa)

Fokker (Netherlands)

Full name: N.V. Koninklijke Nederlandse Vliegtuigenfabriek Fokker.
Corporate address: See Combat section for company details. See also Multi-national in this section.

Fokker 50

First flight: 28 December 1985.
Certification: 15 May 1987 (RLD), 8 February 1989 (FAA).
First delivery: 7 August 1987, to DLT/Lufthansa.
Role: Short-range airliner, and multi-purpose government/military/corporate utility transport.
Airframe life: 45,000 cycles, and economic repair life of 90,000 cycles or hours.

Fokker 50 operated by the newly founded Air Nostrum of Spain

Airport limits: LCN 18.4 at optional take-off weight, 16.9 at 41,998 lb (19,050 kg) TOW.
Noise levels: 81 EPNdB fly-over, 85.2 EPNdB sideline, 96.8 EPNdB approach, certified for standard weight.
Sales: 212 Fokker 50s sold plus 15 options by October 1995 (including 4 Fokker 60s), when about 190 had

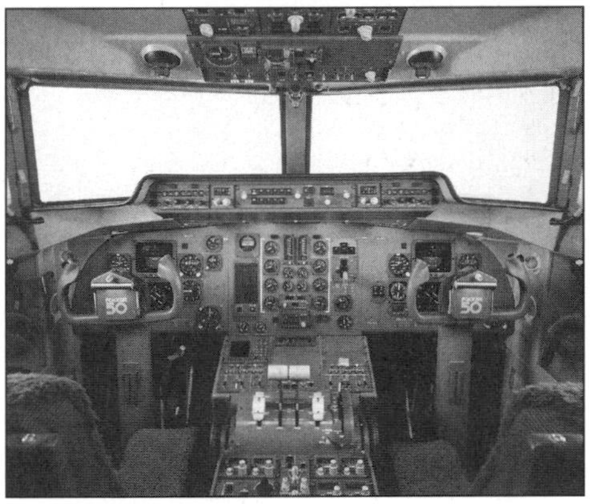

Fokker 50 EFIS cockpit

been delivered, the largest number going to Lufthansa CityLine (with 28). Among the latest operators is Skyways of Sweden, which began Fokker 50 operations in May 1995. Utility sales include the air forces of Singapore and Taiwan, Government of Tanzania, Royal Thai Police, National Iranian Oil Company and Sonangol in Angola,
Crew: 2 (flight), plus seat for observer, in low noise and "dark philosophy" cockpit.
Passengers: 46, 50 or 58 three or 4 doors, with multi-purpose door option on 3-door layouts (see below). Utility can accommodate up to 50 passengers, 40 troops, 24 stretchers plus attendants, or almost 7 tonnes of cargo.
Seat pitch: 32 ins (81 cm) in 50 seat layout, 30 ins (76 cm) in 58-seat layout.
Galley: Fully equipped for hot meals.
Pressurization: 5.5 psi maximum cabin differential.
Freight hold access: Multi-purpose rear door of 5 ft 5 ins x 4 ft 3 ins (1.65 x 1.3 m) optional for Fokker 50 and standard for the Utility version, for loading palletized cargo or containers, and also used by paratroops or for air-dropping.
Baggage compartment: 260.62 cu ft (7.38 m^3) in 50-seat layout, and 276.87 cu ft (7.84 m^3) in 58-seat layout. Total baggage volume, when including wardrobe and 6 ft 7 ins (2 m) wide/168 lb (76 kg) capacity overhead bins, is 368 cu ft (10.42 m^3) for the 50-seat layout and 372.2 cu ft (10.54 m^3) for the 58-seat layout, translating to 7.4 cu ft (0.21 m^3) and 6.4 cu ft (0.18 m^3) per passenger respectively for the 50/58 seat versions.
Wing control surfaces: Ailerons (with spring and geared tabs) and single-slotted flaps.
Tail control surfaces: Elevators (starboard tab) and rudder (trim and geared tabs).
Flight control system: Mechanical, except for hydraulic flaps with electric stand-by.
Construction materials: Principally metal, but with composites for the wing leading and trailing edges and some internal structure, tail unit and aileron leading edges, wingtips, cabin floor, various doors and fairings, engine cowlings and intakes, and more.

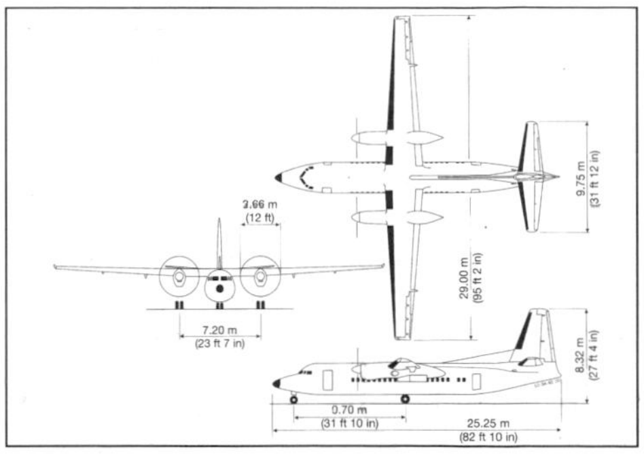

Fokker 50 drawing (courtesy Fokker)

Details for Fokker 50 with PW125Bs.

Principal dimensions:
Wing span: 95 ft 2 ins (29 m)
Maximum length: 82 ft 10 ins (25.25 m)
Maximum height: 27 ft 3.5 ins (8.32 m)

Cabin:
Length: 52 ft 4.5 ins (15.96 m)), excluding flight deck
Width: 8 ft 2.5 ins (2.5 m)
Height: 6 ft 5.2 ins (1.96 m)
Floor area: 325.07 sq ft (30.2 m^2)
Main passenger door: 5 ft 10 ins x 2 ft 6 ins (1.78 x 0.76 m)
Cargo door: See Freight hold for multi-purpose door

Wings:
Aerofoil section: modified NACA 64_4-421, 64_4-415 (root/tip)
Area: 753.47 sq ft (70 m^2)
Aspect ratio: 12.01
Incidence: 3.5°
Dihedral: 2.5°

Tail unit:
Tailplane span: 32 ft (9.75 m)
Tailplane area: 172.2 sq ft (16 m^2)

Undercarriage:
Type: Retractable, with steerable nosewheels. Twin wheels on each unit. Can operate from almost any airfield.
Main wheel tyre size: 34 x 10.75 ins
Nose wheel tyre size: 24 x 7.7 ins
Wheel base: 31 ft 10 ins (9.7 m)
Wheel track: 23 ft 7.5 ins (7.2 m)
Turning circle: 59 ft 4 ins (18.07 m) for 180° turn

Weights:
Empty, operating: 27,602 lb (12,520 kg)
Maximum ramp: 44,070 lb (19,990 kg) *standard,* 46,000 lb (20,865 kg) *optional*
Maximum take-off: 43,982 lb (19,950 kg) *standard,* 45,900 lb (20,820 kg) *optional*
Maximum landing: 42,990 lb (19,500 kg) *standard,* 43,500 lb (19,730 kg) *optional*
Payload: 13,404 lb (6,080 kg)

Performance:
Maximum permitted operating speed (VMO): 227 kts (261 mph) 420 km/h EAS
Maximum operating Mach number (MMO): Mach 0.507
Cruise speed: 282 kts (325 mph) 522 km/h TAS
Take-off field length: 2,920 ft (890 m), at sea level, ISA
Landing field length: 3,337 ft (1,017 m) at sea level, ISA, or 3,461 ft (1,055 m) at 2,000 ft (610 m), ISA + 20° C
Maximum operating altitude: 25,000 ft (7,620 m)
Range at standard take-off weight: 1,216 naut miles (1,400 miles) 2,252 km, with 50 passengers, reserves for 87 naut mile diversion at minimum fuel speed schedule, and 45 minutes continued cruise
Range at optional take-off weight: 1,665 naut miles (1,917 miles) 3,083 km, passengers and reserves as above
Out and return range: 563 naut miles (648 miles) 1,042 km *at standard MTOW,* 788 naut miles (907 miles) 1,459 km *at optional MTOW*
Multi-sector capability: 7 x 100 naut mile stages, 5 x 150 naut mile stages, or 5 x 200 naut mile stages, at optional MTOW and no refuelling at intermediate stops

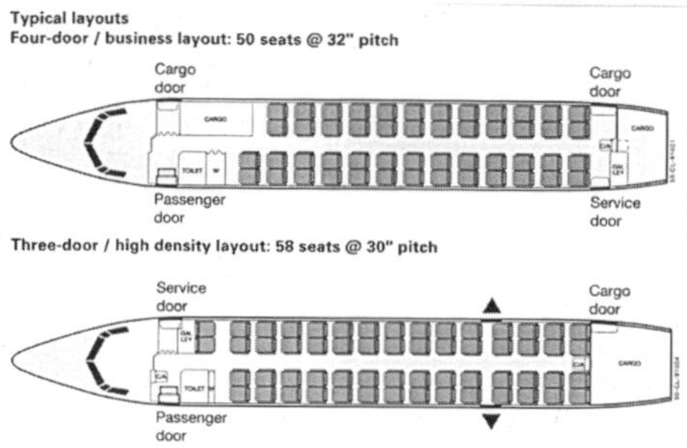

Fokker 50 typical seating layouts (courtesy Fokker)

Engines: 2 Pratt & Whitney Canada PW125B turboprops standard, or PW127Bs for High Performance, with 12 ft (3.66 m) Dowty R352/6-123-F/2 6-blade propellers. To reduce interior noise levels, propellers have electronic phase synchronization and a blade matching system.
Engine rating: Each 2,500 shp (1,864 kW) and 2,750 shp (2,051 kW) respectively.
Fuel system: 9,090 lb (4,123 kg).
Electrical system: 115/200 volt, 400 Hz 3-phase AC supply via 2 x 40kVA engine-driven generators. 28 volt DC supply via 2 x 300 amp transformer/rectifiers and 2 x 43 amp-hour ni-cd batteries. Optional APS 1000 APU (first APU-equipped Fokker 50 went to Malaysia Airlines on 25 August 1989).
Hydraulic system: 3,002 psi.
Braking system: Hydraulic, with anti-skid.
De-icing system: Bleed air for tail unit and wing leading edges. Electric for propellers and engine intakes.
Radar: Honeywell Primus P-650 weather radar.
Flight avionics/instrumentation: Honeywell EDZ-806 EFIS, with 4 colour displays on the main instrument panel for primary flight and navigation information. Automatic flight control system (AFCS) comprises 2 flight director computers and includes a dual channel autopilot system and Cat II automatic approach capability. A central multi-function display can be fitted to present the checklist, navigation data and weather radar image. Push-button engine power management, automatic systems monitoring, sound and visual alerting, and built-in test equipment. Utility can be equipped with state-of-the-art military navigation and communications equipment, such as INS, GPS, Tacan, IFF and V/UHF.
Self-protection systems: Utility can carry chaff/flares.
Aircraft variants:
Fokker 50 with standard PW125B engines (has also been referred to as the 50-100). Programme launched 24 November 1983. Launch customer Ansett of Australia.
Fokker 50 High Performance with optional PW127B engines (has been referred to as the 50-300) offers improved take-off performance under all temperature or elevation conditions.
Fokker 50 Utility has a multi-purpose rear door and sill at truckbed level, heavy-duty impact-resistant floor, and a wide range of cabin configurations. Virtually

Fokker 60 Utility in RNAF markings, with self-protection systems at the wingtips

independent of ground support equipment. Good rough-field performance. Standard PW125B engines, but optional High Performance PW127Bs. Increased take-off weight option at 47,498 lb (21,545 kg). Programme launched 8 August 1991, with first flight 11 November 1992.
Fokker Maritime Enforcer Mk 2, Maritime Mk 2, Kingbird Mk 2, Sentinel Mk 2 and Black Crow Mk 2, see Combat and Reconnaissance sections.

Fokker 60 Utility

First flight: About September 1995.
Certification: 1996.
First delivery: May 1996.
Role: Government/military/corporate personnel transport, logistics and tactical cargo transport, trooping, paratrooping or medevac.
Airframe life: 45,000 cycles, and economic repair life of 90,000 cycles or hours.

★ Aims

★ Based on the Fokker 50 Utility with PW127B engines, but with a 5 ft 4 ins (1.62 m) fuselage stretch, comprising 3 ft 4 ins (1.02 m) fore and 2 ft (0.6 m) aft of the wings.
Sales: First 4 Fokker 60 Utilities ordered for the Royal Netherlands Air Force.
Crew: 2-3.
Passengers: In military form, can accommodate 58 staff at 32 ins (81 cm) pitch, 50 fully-armed troops or 27 litters and 6 seated persons. As a freighter, can accommodate 2 jet engines or other cargoes. Fokker 60 airliner under study, with 52 seats at 35 ins (89 cm) pitch, or 10 VIPs and 28 staff.
Freight hold capacity: 17,639 lb (8,000 kg) as logistics transport, with the large freight door (see below) allowing outsized cargo including LD3 containers, fully built-up jetfreighter engines, civil engines such as the CFM56, industrial compressors or small jeeps.
Size of freight door: Large freight door in the front starboard fuselage, 10 ft x 5 ft 10 ins (3.03 x 1.78 m). The multi-purpose door, detailed under Fokker 50, is also available.
Engines: 2 Pratt & Whitney PW127B turboprops, with 12 ft (3.66 m) Dowty R352/6-123-F/2 six-blade propellers.
Engine rating: Each 2,750 shp (2,051 kW).
Fuel system: 9,090 lb (4,123 kg), with optional 13,184 lb (5,980 kg).

Details for Fokker 60 where different from Fokker 50.

Principal dimensions:
Maximum length: 88 ft 2 ins (26.87 m)
Height: 27 ft 4.5 ins (8.34 m)

Cabin:
Length: 55 ft 4 ins (16.87 m)
Floor area: 370.28 sq ft (34.4 m^2)
Volume: 2,295.5 cu ft (65 m^3)
Cargo door: 10 ft x 5 ft 10 ins (3.05 x 1.78 m). Also multi-purpose door (see Fokker 50)

Undercarriage:
Wheel base: 35 ft 2 ins (10.72 m)

Weights:
Empty, operating: 28,404 lb (12,884 kg)
Maximum take-off: 50,596 lb (22,950 kg)
Maximum landing: 47,950 lb (21,750 kg)
Payload: 17,331 lb (7,861 kg)

Performance:
Range with full payload: 1,400-1,750 naut miles (1,612-2,015 miles) 2,593-3,241 km

Fokker 70

First flight: 2 April 1993.
Certification: 14 October 1994 (RLD and FAA).
First delivery: 25 October 1994 (to Ford Motor Company).
Role: Short-medium range regional airliner, as reduced-length variant of the Fokker 100.
Airframe life: 45,000 cycles, and economic repair life of 90,000 cycles or hours.
Noise levels: 78.9 EPNdB fly-over, 89.9 EPNdB sideline, 91.9 EPNdB approach, standard weights, estimated.
Sales: 67 orders by September 1995. Launch customers were Sempati Air and Pelita Air Service, ordered in mid-1993. Lastest customers include Vietnam Airlines. Ford Motor Company became Executive Jet 70 launch customer (48-seat version).
Crew: 2 (flight).
Passengers: 70-79. Alternatively, 30-52 in the Executive Jet version.

DETAILS FOR FOKKER 70.

Principal dimensions:
Wing span: 92 ft 1.5 ins (28.08 m)
Maximum length: 101 ft 5 ins (30.91 m)
Maximum height: 27 ft 11 ins (8.51 m)

Cabin:
Length: 54 ft 4.5 ins (16.57 m)
Width: 10 ft 2 ins (3.10 m)
Height: 6 ft 7 ins (2.01 m)

Undercarriage:
Wheel base: 37 ft 10.5 ins (11.54 m)
Wheel track: 16 ft 6.5 ins (5.04 m)

Weights:
Empty, operating: 49,984 lb (22,673 kg)
Maximum taxi: 81,494 lb (36,965 kg) *standard*, 84,492 lb (38,325 kg) *intermediate optional*, or 88,493 lb (40,140 kg) *high optional*
Maximum take-off: 81,000 lb (36,740 kg) *standard*, 83,996 lb (38,100 kg) *intermediate optional*, or 87,997 lb (39,915 kg) *high optional*
Maximum landing: 75,000-78,992 lb (34,020-35,830 kg) *standard*, 78,992-81,000 lb (35,830-36,740 kg) *intermediate optional*, or 81,000 lb (36,740 kg) *high optional*
Payload: 20,507 lb (9,302 kg) *standard*, 22,007 lb (9,982 kg) *intermediate optional*, or 24,008 lb (10,890 kg) *high optional*

Performance:
Maximum permitted operating speed (MMO): 320 kts (368 mph) 593 km/h CAS
Maximum operating Mach number (MMO): Mach 0.77
Maximum speed: 462 kts (532 mph) 856 km/h TAS
Take-off field length: 3,675-5,160 ft (1,120-1,573 m) *at sea level*, 4,660-5,415 ft (1,420-1,650 m) *at 2,000 ft (610 m) elevation*
Landing field length: 3,822 ft (1,165 m) *sea level*, 3,970 ft (1,210 m) *at 2,000 ft (610 m) elevation*
Maximum operating altitude: 35,000 ft (10,670 m)
Range at 36,740 kg MTOW: 1,080 naut miles (1,243 miles) 2,000 km, with 79 passengers, minimum fuel speed schedule, reserves for overshoot to 1,500 ft, 200 naut mile diversion and 45 minutes hold
Range at 38,100 kg MTOW: 1,415 naut miles (1,629 miles) 2,620 km, passengers and reserves as above
Range at 39,915 kg MTOW: 1,840 naut miles (2,118 miles) 3,407 km
Out and return range: 825 naut miles (950 miles) 1,528 km at 83,996 lb (39,915 kg) MTOW

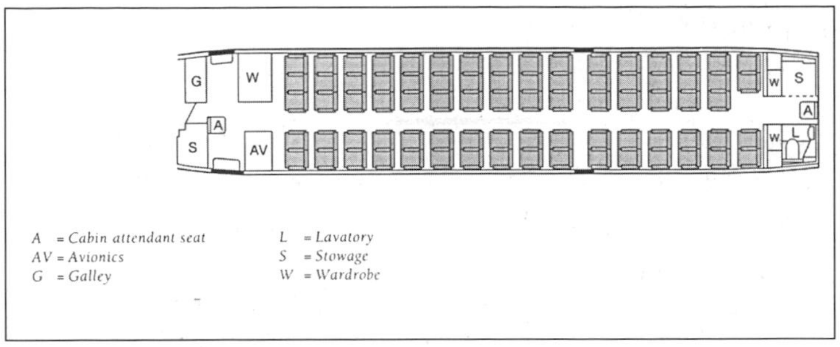

Fokker 70 cabin layout for 79 passengers (courtesy Fokker)

Seat pitch: 31/32 ins (79/81 cm) in 79-seat form.
Freight hold volume: 287.8 cu ft (8.15 m³) forward, 163.5 cu ft (4.63 m³) aft.
Baggage capacity: 310.8 cu ft (8.8 m³) in overhead bins, stowages and wardrobes.
Engines: 2 Rolls-Royce Tay Mk 620 turbofans.
Engine rating: Each 13,850 lbf (61.61 kN).
Fuel system: 9,640 litres (17,064 lb, 7,740 kg) standard or 13,365 litres (23,658 lb, 10,731 kg) optional.
Radar: Weather radar.
Flight avionics/instrumentation: ARINC 700 avionics. Automatic flight control and augmentation system, EFIS, multi-function display system and flight warning system. Cat II approach capability. Avionics can be extended to full Fokker 100 level, including Cat III autoland and flight management system.
Aircraft variants:
Fokker 70 is the basic airliner, as detailed. Variant (particularly for the North American market) is 70A, with 70 seats but greater freight capacity.
Fokker 70ER is the Extended Range version, with 4 modular fuel tanks in the forward cargo hold, providing over 3,240 naut miles (3,728 miles) 6,000 km range. First delivery 1996.
Fokker Executive Jet 70 is the corporate shuttle (30-52 passengers), business and VIP (up to 30) version. Intercontinental range in the Extended Range version. Cat III capability.

Fokker 70 operated by America West Express from 12 June 1995 (78 seats), the first in the USA

Fokker 100 and 130

Details: Fokker 100, except under Aircraft variants.
First flight: 30 November 1986.
Certification: 20 November 1987 (RLD), 30 May 1989 (FAA).
First delivery: 29 February 1988, to Swissair.
Role: Short-medium range airliner.
Airframe life: 45,000 cycles, and economic repair life of 90,000 cycles or hours.
Noise levels: 81.8 EPNdB fly-over, 91.7 EPNdB sideline and 93 EPNdB approach, certificated, at 98,000 lb (44,450 kg) MTOW and 88,000 lb (39,915 kg) MLW.
Sales: 276 ordered by June 1995.
Crew: 2 (flight).
Passengers: 107 standard, with options from 97-109.
Seat pitch: 32 ins (81 cm) standard layout.
Galleys: 2.
Pressurization: 7.54 psi cabin differential.
Freight capacity: 334.7 cu ft (9.48 m³) forward hold, or 437.9 cu ft (12.4 m³) if avionics are repositioned to the main deck. 255.7 cu ft (7.24 m³) aft hold.
Baggage capacity: 287.8 cu ft (8.15 m³) in overhead bins, stowages, wardrobes and carry-on baggage compartment.
Wing control surfaces: Ailerons (with servo tabs), double-slotted Fowler flaps, and 5-section lift dumpers. (Prototype with laminar flow wing section was used in the ELFIN European research project during 1991-92.)
Tail control surfaces: Variable incidence tailplane, elevators and inset rudder.
Flight control system: Hydraulic/manual for the principal control surfaces, with hydraulic/electric for flaps.
Construction materials: Metal, except for composites ailerons, flaps, rudder, fin extension, wing-to-fuselage fairings, floor panels and other non-structural components.
Engines: 2 Rolls-Royce Tay 620 or Tay 650 turbofans.
Engine rating: Each 13,850 lbf (61.61 kN) or 15,100 lbf (67.17 kN) respectively.
Fuel system: 13,365 litres (23,658 lb, 10,731 kg).
Electrical system: Includes engine-driven generators. AlliedSignal GTCP36-150RR APU.
Braking system: Carbon multi-disc type, with anti-skid. Clamshell speed brakes in the tailcone.
Radar: Weather radar.
Flight avionics/instrumentation: ARINC 700 avionics plus built-in test equipment. Not more than 18 instruments, including 6 colour displays, present information. EFIS and fully digital cockpit, with "dark cockpit philosophy" with no indication lights on during normal operations. Dual flight management system. Cat IIIB autoland.
Aircraft variants:
Fokker 100 is the basic version, as detailed.
A proposed Quick Change version for 88 passengers on palletized seats or containers (11 x LD3, or 5 x LD7 or LD9), and with a large cargo door, has been proposed, with structural modifications contracted out.
Fokker Executive Jet 100 is the corporate shuttle, business and VIP version. Intercontinental range in the Extended Range version with 4 modular fuel tanks in the forward cargo hold. Cat III capability.
Fokker 130 is a proposed "stretched" 116–137-passenger derivative of the Fokker 100. Project had not been launched by June 1995.

Fokker 100 EFIS cockpit

DETAILS FOR FOKKER 100.

Principal dimensions:
Wing span: 92 ft 1.5 ins (28.08 m)
Maximum length: 116 ft 7 ins (35.53 m)
Maximum height: 27 ft 10.5 ins (8.5 m)

Cabin:
Length: 69 ft 6.2 ins (21.19 m)
Width: 10 ft 2 ins (3.1 m)
Height: 6 ft 7 ins (2.01 m)
Volume: 3,799.2 cu ft (107.58 m^3)
Main passenger door: 6 ft x 2 ft 7 ins (1.82 x 0.78 m)

Wings:
Area: 1,006.42 sq ft (93.5 m^2)
Aspect ratio: 8.433
Dihedral: 2.5°

Tail unit:
Tailplane span: 32 ft 11.5 ins (10.04 m)
Tailplane area: 191.17 sq ft (17.76 m^2)

Undercarriage:
Type: Retractable, with steerable nosewheels. Twin wheels on each unit
Main wheel tyre size: 40 x 14 ins (1.01 x 0.35 m)
Nose wheel tyre size: 24 x 7.7 ins (0.61 x 0.19 m)
Wheel base: 45 ft 11.5 ins (14.01 m)
Wheel track: 16 ft 6.5 ins (5.04 m)
Turning circle: 73 ft (22.2 m) for 180° turn

Weights:
Empty, operating: 54,218 lb (24,593 kg) *with Tay 620s,* 54,514 or 54,558 lb (24,727 or 24,747 kg) *with Tay 650s*
Maximum ramp: 95,500 lb (43,320 kg) *standard,* 98,500 lb (44,680 kg) *intermediate optional,* and 101,500 lb (46,040 kg) *high optional with Tay 650s only*
Maximum take-off: 95,000 lb (43,090 kg) *standard,* 98,000 lb (44,450 kg) *intermediate optional,* or 101,000 lb (45,810 kg) *high optional with Tay 650s*
Maximum landing: 85,500 lb (38,780 kg) *standard,* 88,000 lb (39,915 kg) *intermediate and high optional*
Payload: 24,784 lb (11,242 kg) *standard with Tay 620s,* 26,780 lb (12,147 kg) *optional with Tay 620s,* 24,489 lb (11,108 kg) *standard with Tay 650s,* 26,484 lb (12,013 kg) *maximum optional with Tay 650s*

Performance:
Maximum permitted operating speed (V_{MO}): 320 kts (368 mph) 593 km/h CAS
Maximum operating Mach number (M_{MO}): Mach 0.77
Maximum speed: 462 kts (532 mph) 856 km/h TAS
Landing field length: 4,183 ft (1,275 m) *at sea level,* 6,365 ft (1,330 m) *at 2,000 ft (610 m) elevation*
Maximum operating altitude: 35,000 ft (10,670 m)
Range with Tay 620s, at 43,090 kg MTOW: 1,290 naut miles (1,485 miles) 2,389 km, with 107 passengers, minimum fuel speed schedule, reserves for overshoot to 1,500 ft, 200 naut mile diversion and 45 minutes hold
Range with Tay 620s, at 44,450 kg MTOW: 1,575 naut miles (1,813 miles) 2,917 km, conditions as above
Range with Tay 650s, at 43,090 kg MTOW: 1,260 naut miles (1,451 miles) 2,333 km
Range with Tay 650s, at 45,810 kg MTOW: 1,680 naut miles (1,934 miles) 3,111 km

Fokker 100, one of 7 operated by China Eastern Airlines

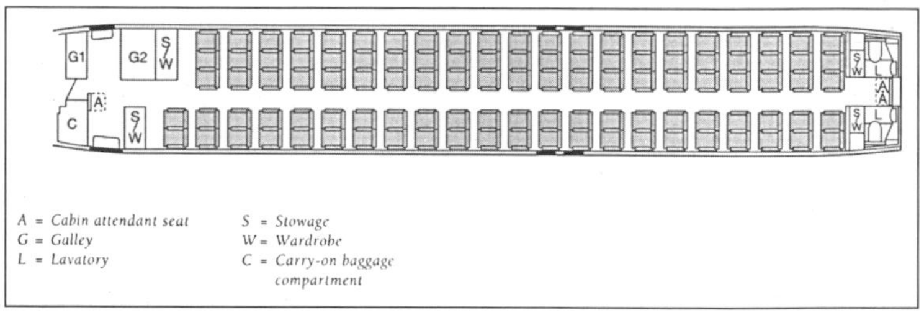

Fokker 100 cabin layout for 107 passengers (courtesy Fokker)

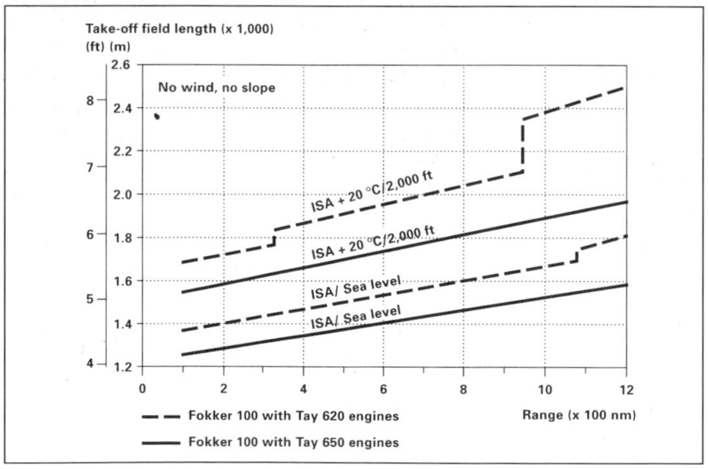

Fokker 100 take-off field length vs range chart (courtesy Fokker)

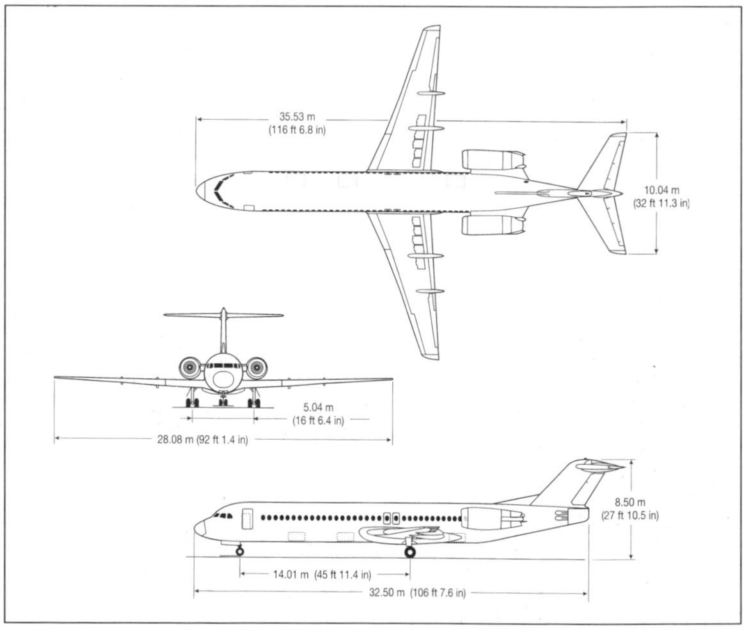

Fokker 100 drawing (courtesy Fokker)

PZL-Mielec S.A. (Poland)

Full name: Joint Stock Company PZL-Mielec S.A., formerly known as Wytwórnia Sprzetu Komunikacyjnego PZL-Mielec (Transport Equipment Company).
Corporate address: See Combat section for company details.

PZL-Mielec/Antonov M-28 and Skytruck PT (NATO name *Cash*)

First flight: 23 April 1975 (Antonov prototype), 22 July 1984 (Polish built An-28), 28 July 1993 for An-28PT Piryt (now named M-28).
Certification: 7 February 1986. Skytruck PT gained Temporary Polish Type Certificate in March 1994 and full IKCSP certification to FAR Pt 23 in mid-1995.
Role: Light passenger or cargo transport, with special military versions. An-28 now redesignated M-28.
Sales: About 160 delivered to the USSR before 1989, when production for Russia terminated, leaving several aircraft at the factory. Several purchased by the Polish armed forces, including 3 by the Navy to replace An-2s, and 2 Bryza-1Rs by the Air Force for search and rescue missions plus Bryza-1TD transports (see Aircraft variants). 6 Skytrucks sold by mid-1995 to customers in Africa and Asia, plus to the Polish Airtech company.
Details: Skytruck PT.
Crew: 2 (flight).
Passengers: 18 in Skytruck PT, 17 in other versions, or cargo (seats folded along cabin wall).
Freight hold access: Clamshell rear doors or sliding doors.
Wing control surfaces: Ailerons (port tab), 2-section double-slotted flaps (15° for take-off), manual/automatic spoilers, and leading-edge slats.
Tail control surfaces: Elevators (with tabs) and twin horn-balanced rudders (with tabs).
Flight control system: Hydraulic.

Engines: 2 Pratt & Whitney Canada PT6A-65B turboprops.
Engine rating: Each 1,100 shp (820.3 kW).
Fuel system: 3,351 lb (1,520 kg).
Electrical system: 3-phase 200/115 volt AC via engine-mounted alternators, and 3-phase 36 volt AC using TS10SO4B transformer. Under emergency conditions, PO-250A converter can supply single-phase 115 volt, 400 Hz AC power. 27 volt DC via rectifiers. 20NKBN-25 batteries for emergency power and engine start when needed.
Hydraulic system: 2,233 psi.
Braking system: Hydraulic multi-disc, with anti-skid system.
De-icing system: Thermal/pneumatic for slats, tail unit, inlet ducts, oil coolers and air intakes. Electric for propellers/spinners, windshield and pitot heads.
Radar: RDS-81 digital weather radar.
Flight avionics/instrumentation: AlliedSignal Bendix/King KFC 275 or 325 automatic flight control, radar altimeter and transponder. Navigation suite comprises dual VOR/ILS, DME, ADF, marker beacon, RMI, and dual KCS-55A plus KNS 81 digital area navigation system and GC 381 A radar graphics computer. Communications suite comprises VHF/AM (KY 196/KX 165), HF comm, audio selector panel and interphone, and dual emergency VHF.
Aircraft variants:
M-28 (formerly An-28) is the standard transport version, with 945 shp (705 kW) PZL TWD-10B engines with AW-24AN propellers.
M-28A is a Polar region transport, with increased fuel capacity.
M-28P (Pozarniczy) is a paratroop version for firefighting.
M-28TD Bryza-1 (transportowo-desantowy, cargo-assault) is a military transport/paratroop version, tested in 1992. Prototype was the converted 23rd aircraft of the seventh production series. First production M-28TD (side number 1003) was delivered October 1994 to the 13th Transport Air Regiment of Polish Air Force. Rear clamshell doors replaced by ramp sliding forward under the fuselage. 4 variants, accommodating 13 paratroops and 2 x 100 kg parachute containers, or 17 parachutists, or 6 litters and 7 seated persons, or 3,858 lb (1,750 kg) of cargo, or a special version for transporting air-to-air missiles (up to 1,102 lb, 500 kg each).
M-28RM Bryza-1R (ratowniczy morski, sea rescue) is the maritime patrol/rescue co-ordination version for the Polish Navy. 2 pilots, technician and 3 systems operators. Prototype tested in Autumn 1992, equipped with Polish made SRN-441XA 360° navigation radar in an underfuselage radome. First production aircraft was delivered on 27 October 1994 to the 7th Special Air Regiment of the Polish Navy in Siemirowice. Production version differs in having ARS-100 radar derived from the SRN-441. Radar has modified X-band antenna, rotating 7.5 or 15 times per minute. Maximum search range is 60 naut miles (69 miles) 111 km. Later version will have the ARS-400 radar, a new data transfer and command system. New wings are also being studied, with increased fuel for 5 hours duration. Chelton DF-707-1 radio system is also used for locating shipwrecked persons. Can carry ACR/RLB-14 radio marker buoys, and 2 x 100 kg SAB-100NM bombs to illuminate the rescue area (racks are on undercarriage supports, and a light PKV bombsight is located at the convex window at rear starboard of fuselage). AFA-39 photo-camera. Can also drop 3 x 6-person Mewa-6 dinghies (in addition to crew dinghies). Flight/navigation equipment includes RDS-81 weather radar, KNS-81S navigation system, KLN-90A GPS receiver, KT-71 transponder, and ARK-15 radio-compass. 2 PZL-10B turboprop engines, each rated at 900 shp (671 kW).
M-28B-2 Bryza-2 is a projected military electronic warfare version.
M-28PT Piryt prototype (SP-PDF) first flew on 28 July 1993. Westernized version. More comfortable cabin.
M Skytruck PT is the commercial name for the M-28PT Piryt (see above).

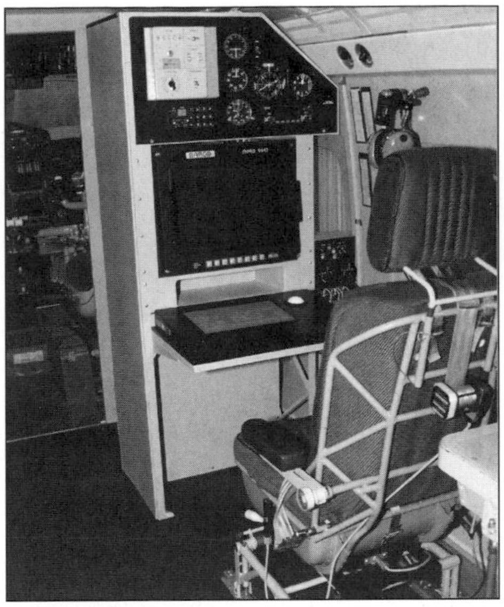

System operator's station in the M-28RM (Piotr Butowski)

First PZL-Mielec M-28RM delivered to the Polish Navy. Note the radar and illumination bombs (Piotr Butowski)

Details for Skytruck PT.

Principal dimensions:
Wing span: 72 ft 5 ins (22.07 m)
Maximum length: 43 ft (13.1 m)
Maximum height: 16 ft 1 ins (4.9 m)

Cabin:
Length: 17 ft 3 ins (5.26 m)
Width: 5 ft 8.5 ins (1.74 m)
Height: 5 ft 3 ins (1.6 m)
Cargo door: Clamshell 7 ft 10.5 ins (2.4 m) length, with 4 ft 7 ins (1.4 m) width at sill, narrowing at top to 3 ft 3.25 ins (1 m)

Wings:
Area: 427.54 sq ft (39.72 m^2)
Aspect ratio: 12.26

Undercarriage:
Type: Fixed, with castering nosewheel
Main wheel tyre size: 720 x 320 mm
Nose wheel tyre size: 595 x 185 mm
Wheel base: 14 ft 5 ins (4.4 m)
Wheel track: 11 ft 2 ins (3.4 m)
Turning circle: 45 ft 11 ins (14 m) for 180° turn

Weights:
Empty: 8,635 lb (3,917 kg)
Maximum take-off: 15,432 lb (7,000 kg)
Maximum landing: 14,661 lb (6,650 kg)
Payload: 4,409 lb (2,000 kg)
Maximum unit cargo floor loading: 882 lb (400 kg)

Performance:
Maximum cruise speed: 181 kts (208 mph) 335 km/h
Maximum airfield elevation: 8,530 ft (2,600 m)
Take-off distance: 870 ft (265 m)
Take-off over a 50 ft (15 m) obstacle: 1,100 ft (335 m)
Landing distance: 607 ft (185 m)
Landing distance over a 50 ft (15 m) obstacle: 1,920 ft (585 m)
Maximum climb rate: 2,657 ft (810 m) per minute
G limits: +3
Cruise altitude: 9,840 ft (3,000 m)
Ceiling: 20,340 ft (6,200 m)
Range: 765 naut miles (881 miles) 1,417 km, with 1,984 lb (900 kg) cargo

Romaero S.A. (Romania)

Corporate address: Bulevardul Ficusului Nr 44 Sector 1, COD 71544, Bucuresti.
Telephone: +40 1 633 50 82, 666 60 90
Facsimile: +40 1 679 44 56
Telex: 11691 IAVB-R
Founded: 1979.
Information: Constatin Dinischiotu (Sales and Marketing Executive Director).

● Activities

- Licence manufacture of the BAC One-Eleven (see below), and Pilatus Britten-Norman Islander for marketing by PBN (500 built, with 6 BN-2Bs being built in 1995 plus 9 Defender kits).
- Repair/overhaul work, nuclear power plant components, and construction of subassemblies for Boeing (agreement signed March 1994). Under a joint venture with Florida West Aircraft Services Ltd, has a new facility to work on Boeing and McDonnell Douglas aircraft, beginning with conversion of 2 Boeing 727-200s into freighters.

Romaero 1-11

First flight: 18 September 1982.
Certification: November 1982.
Role: Short-medium range airliner.
Airframe life: 85,000 hours or landings predicted.
Noise levels: 85 EPNdB fly-over, 93 EPNdB sideline, 92 EPNdB approach.
Sales: 9 Romaero 1-11s delivered by early 1995, all of Series 561RC type. Kiwi International Air Lines of the USA has ordered 11 Airstar 2500s, with production

Details for Airstar 2500, unless stated.

Principal dimensions:
Wing span: 93 ft 6 ins (28.5 m)
Maximum length: 107 ft (32.61 m)
Maximum height: 24 ft 6 ins (7.47 m)

Cabin:
Length: 70 ft 4 ins (21.44 m)
Width: 10 ft 4 ins (3.15 m)
Height: 6 ft 6 ins (1.98 m)
Volume: 4,434 cu ft (125.56 m^3)
Main passenger door: 2 ft 9 ins x 5 ft 8 ins (0.83 x 1.73 m)
Cargo doors: 3 ft 1 ins x 2 ft 7 ins (0.94 x 0.79 m) forward, 3 ft x 2 ft 2 ins (0.91 x 0.66 m) aft

Wings:
Area: 1,031 sq ft (95.78 m^2)
Aspect ratio: 8.48

Undercarriage:
Type: Retractable, with nosewheel steering. Twin wheels on each unit
Wheel base: 41 ft 5 ins (12.62 m)
Wheel track: 14 ft 3 ins (4.34 m)

Weights:
Empty, operating: 52,199 lb (23,677 kg)
Maximum ramp: 105,000 lb (47,630 kg)
Maximum take-off: 104,500 lb (47,400 kg)
Maximum landing: 90,000 lb (40,823 kg)
Payload: 21,800 lb (9,888 kg)

Performance:
Maximum and cruise speed: 470 kts (541 mph) 870 km/h, for Series 561RC
Long-range cruise speed: 410 kts (472 mph) 759 km/h, for Series 561RC
Stall speed: 100 kts (115 mph) 185 km/h, *with flaps* , for Series 561RC
Cruise altitude: 35,000 ft (10,670 m)
Range: 1,639 naut miles (1,887 miles) 3,035 km, with reserves

expected to start in 1995.
Details: Airstar 2500.
Crew: 2 (flight).
Passengers: 109 standard, with variants of 86-119. 2 entrance doors of airstep type.
Seat pitch: 30 ins (76 cm) for 109-seat layout.
Galley: Immediately aft of cockpit.
Pressurization: 7.5 psi maximum cabin differential.
Baggage/freight compartments: 451 cu ft

Romaero 1-11 Series 561RC under construction, with an Islander to the rear

(12.77 m^3) forward, 236 cu ft (6.68 m^3) aft. Capacities 5,634 lb (2,555 kg) and 4,302 lb (1,951 kg) respectively.
Wing control surfaces: Ailerons (with tabs), Fowler flaps (6° take-off, 45° approach), spoilers and lift dumpers.
Tail control surfaces: Variable incidence tailplane, elevators and rudder.

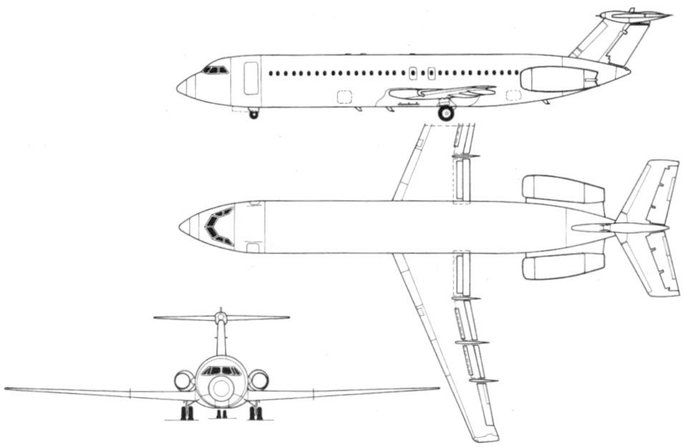

Romaero 1-11 Airstar 2500 (courtesy Romaero)

Flight control system: Hydraulic, except for mechanical ailerons.
Construction materials: Metal.
Engines: 2 Rolls-Royce Tay Mk 650-14 turbofans. Dee Howard target type thrust reversers.
Engine rating: Each 15,100 lbf (67.17 kN).
Fuel system: 14,129 litres. Optional 1,591 litre auxiliary tank to extend range.
Electrical system: AC supply via 2 x 30 kVA generators, plus an APU-mounted generator. 2 x 40 amp-hour batteries. New 450 VA standby inverter replaces older 300 VA unit.
Hydraulic system: 3,000 psi.
Braking system: Hydraulic disc, with anti-skid.
De-icing system: Bleed air for engine inlet, wing and tail unit leading edges.
Radar: Weather radar.
Flight avionics/instrumentation: Honeywell SPZ8000 EFIS, 3-axis autopilot, and dual laser inertial reference system. Primus II integrated navigation system with VHF Nav, 6-channel scanning DME and ADF modules. Nav receiver module provides VOR/LOC, glideslope, and marker beacon functions to meet Cat II requirements. VHF communications of Primus II features an integrated transceiver and fully compatible ATCRBS Mode S transponder. HF transceiver. Other standard equipment includes dual radio altimeters, digital flight data recorder, cockpit voice recorder, ground proximity/ windshear warning computer and static discharge system. Options available include microwave landing system, TCAS II, GPS, Inmarsat, VLF/Omega, additional HF, triple redundant Laseref and more.
Aircraft variants:
Series 497 is a convertible variant for passengers and cargo. Expected to be the next aircraft off the production line prior to the Airstars. Length 93 ft 6 ins (28.5 m).
Series 561RC is the basic 1-11 model, of similar length and accommodation to the later Airstar but using 12,550 lbf (55.83 kN) Spey Mk 512-14DW turbofans.
Airstar 2500 follows the Series 500/560, incorporating Tay engines (in place of Spey), ungraded flight deck and new-look interior. Has significant noise reduction with substantial margins under FAR/ICAO regulation limits, 17% less fuel burn, 20% increase in range, 32% reduction in time to climb, and lower maintenance costs.

Aeroprogress Inc (Russia)

Corporate address: See Combat section for company details.

Aeroprogress T-274 Titan

First flight: 1996.
Role: STOL civil and military freighter.
Sales: Manufacture at Omsk plant (Polyot) in co-operation with Khrunichev plant.
Crew: 2 (flight).
Pressurization: Cockpit and cabin.
Freight hold access: Under-tail ramp/door, with ramp stowed under the cabin when direct loading from vehicles is required.
Wing control surfaces: Ailerons (port tab), triple-slotted trailing-edge flaps, leading-edge slats, and 4-section spoilers. Winglets to reduce drag.
Tail control surfaces: Variable incidence T-type

Details for Titan.

Principal dimensions:
Wing span: 104 ft 8 ins (31.89 m)
Maximum length: 92 ft 1 ins (28.07 m)
Maximum height: 28 ft 5 ins (8.65 m)

Cabin:
Length: 34 ft 5 ins (10.5 m)
Width: 7 ft (2.15 m)
Height: 7 ft 3 ins (2.2 m)

Wings:
Area: 1,061.5 sq ft (98.62 m^2)
Aspect ratio: 10.31

Undercarriage:
Type: Retractable, with steerable twin nosewheels. Tandem twin mainwheels
Wheel base: 26 ft 8 ins (8.12 m)
Wheel track: 13 ft 7 ins (4.15 m)

Weights:
Maximum take-off: 79,366 lb (36,000 kg)
Payload: 28,660 lb (13,000 kg)

Performance:
Maximum speed: 340 kts (392 mph) 630 km/h
Range with full fuel: 3,565 naut miles (4,100 miles) 6,600 km
Range with full payload: 486 naut miles (559 miles) 900 km

tailplane, with elevators (2 tabs in each), and 2-section rudder (with tab).
Flight control system: Hydraulic.
Engines: 4 Klimov TV7-117 turboprops.
Engine rating: Each 2,500 shp (1,864 kW).
Radar: Navigation and/or weather radar.
Flight avionics/instrumentation: Modern avionics, probably including EFIS.

Aeroprogress T-720DP Korshun

First flight: Under development.
Role: Multi-purpose transport, using elements of the Antonov An-28 and Aeroprogress T-101, plus a US Soloy Dual Pac power plant.
Sales: Being assembled by Washington Aeroprogress at Seattle, USA or Vancouver, Canada (see General Aviation section).
Crew: 2.
Passengers: 17 passengers or 4,409 lb (2,000 kg) of cargo. Air conditioning using bleed air.
Freight hold access: Sliding cargo door in the tail section.
Wing characteristics: Modified from the An-28. Detachable outer panels.
Wing control surfaces: Ailerons (maximum 22° up, 23° down), double-slotted trailing-edge flaps (15° take-off, 40° landing), automatic leading-edge slats and interceptors.
Tail control surfaces: Fin from the T-101. Horn-balanced rudder (35°), with trim tab (15°). Horn balanced elevators (+15°, -30°), with trim tab (15°).
Flight control system: Electric/hydraulic.

DETAILS FOR KORSHUN.

Principal dimensions:
Wing span: 72 ft 5 ins (22.063 m)
Maximum height: 18 ft 2.5 ins (5.55 m)

Cabin:
Width: 6 ft 2.75 ins (1.9 m)
Height: 7 ft 0.25 ins (2.14 m)

Wings:
Area: 428.4 sq ft (39.8 m^2)
Aspect ratio: 12.23
Incidence: 4°
Dihedral: 1° 30′

Tail unit:
Tailplane span: 28 ft 6 ins (8.68 m)
Tailplane area: 134.55 sq ft (12.5 m^2)
Fin area: 67.7 sq ft (6.29 m^2)

Undercarriage:
Type: Fixed, with nosewheel. Suited to unprepared airfields. Provision for floats
Main wheel tyre size: 720 x 320 mm
Nose wheel tyre size: 595 x 185 mm
Wheel base: 12 ft 0.5 ins (3.665 m)

Weights:
Maximum take-off: 12,566 lb (5,700 kg)
Payload: 3,968 lb (1,800 kg) of cargo

Performance:
Maximum speed: 189 kts (217 mph) 350 km/h
Take-off distance: 1,903 ft (580 m) *wheels*, 2,297 ft (700 m) *floats*
Landing distance: 1,640 ft (500 m) *wheels*, 2,034 ft (620 m) *floats*
Range: 842 naut miles (969 miles) 1,560 km

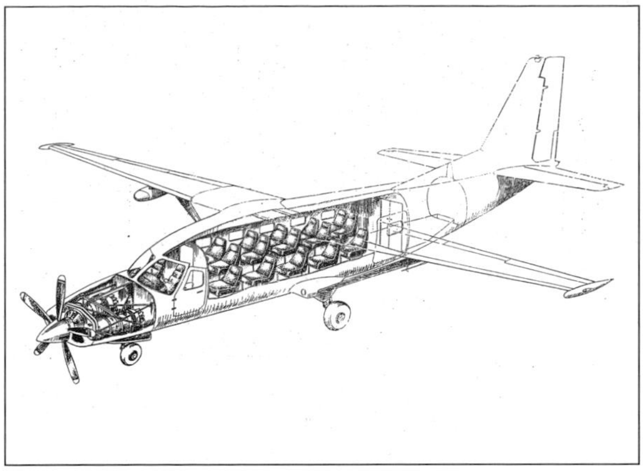

Aeroprogress T-720DP Korshun in passenger layout (courtesy Aeroprogress)

Fuselage: Mid-fuselage and tail section from the An-28 with minor modifications.
Construction materials: Fabric-covered tailplane.
Engines: 2 TVD PT6A-114 turboprops, coupled to drive a single 5-blade Hartzell propeller. Single shaft rpm 1,700. Russian engine is an AL-34.
Engine rating: Each 675 shp (503.3 kW).
Fuel system: 2,645 lb (1,200 kg).
Electrical system: 28 volt system, with generator and ni-cd battery.
Hydraulic system: 1,565-2,133 psi
De-icing system: Pneumatic and electrical.
Aircraft variants:
T-720DP Corshun is the standard version, as detailed.
Floatplane version has increased area fin and rudder, and hydraulic system modifications for the actuation of retractable wheels into the floats.

Aeroprogress T-724

First flight: Not yet flown.
Role: Light passenger and cargo transport.
Crew: 2 (flight) + 1.
Passengers: 19 passengers or cargo plus 2 accompanying persons. Toilet provided at the rear of the cabin.
Galley: Small galley aft of flight deck.
Freight hold access: Direct loading from trucks via an upward-opening cargo door with pulley system.

DETAILS FOR T-724.

Principal dimensions:
Wing span: 75 ft 1.5 ins (22.9 m)
Maximum length: 55 ft 9.5 ins (17 m)
Maximum height: 19 ft 9.5 ins (6.025 m)

Cabin:
Length: 23 ft (7 m)
Width: 6 ft 9 ins (2.05 m)
Height: 6 ft 2 ins (1.87 m)
Floor area: 129.2 sq ft (12 m^2)
Volume: 801.6 cu ft (22.7 m^3)

Undercarriage:
Type: Retractable, with nosewheel
Wheel base: 17 ft 8.5 ins (5.4 m)
Wheel track: 10 ft 6 ins (3.2 m)

Weights:
Maximum take-off: 16,534 lb (7,500 kg)
Payload: 3,770 lb (1,710 kg)

Performance:
Maximum speed: 270 kts (310 mph) 500 km/h
Take-off distance: 1,640 ft (500 m)
Landing distance: 1,970 ft (600 m)
Ceiling: 26,250 ft (8,000 m)
Range: 1,890 naut miles (2,175 miles) 3,500 km

Wing control surfaces: Ailerons, 2 section trailing-edge flaps, spoilers and leading-edge slats. Winglets.
Tail control surfaces: Elevators (with tabs) and horn-balanced rudder (with tab).
Engines: 2 turboprop engines, with 8 ft 2 ins (2.5 m) propellers. APU in the tailcone.
Engine rating: Each believed to be 1,300 shp (969 kW).
Electrical system: 115/220 volt, 400Hz AC supply.
Flight avionics/instrumentation: Includes weather radar.

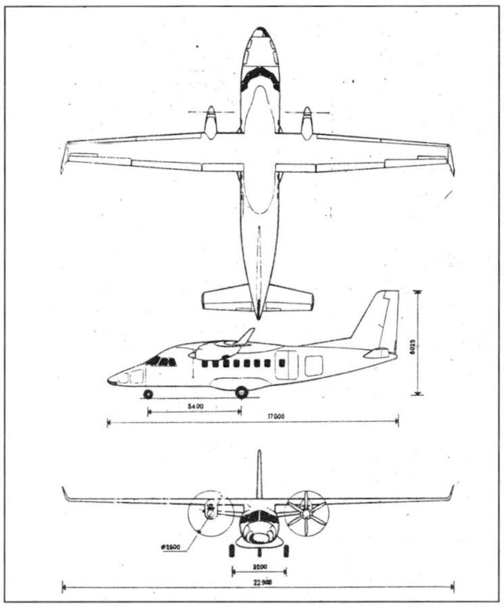

Aeroprogress T-724 19-passenger or cargo transport (courtesy Aeroprogress)

Aeroprogress T-2000 Barracuda

Role: Amphibious wing-in-ground-effect off-shore patrol vehicle, also suited to rescue and passenger transport.

▲ Development

▲ August 1994. Research and development started.
Sales: Estimated unit cost US$3.5 million.
Crew: 2.
Passengers: 40 or cargo for air routes, or up to 60 for rescue.
Wing characteristics: Rear-mounted main wings, with long-chord anhedral centre section and high aspect ratio dihedral outer panels with winglets. Forward anhedral wings and float-mounted dihedral stub wings. Produces dynamic air cushion during ground-effect flight at heights down to 2 ft 8 ins (0.8 m). Typical WIG mode flying height is 5 ft (1.5 m).
Wing control surfaces: 4-section surfaces on the trailing-edges of the main outer wing panels, plus surfaces on all 4 parts of the forward wings.
Tail control surfaces: Twin fins and high-mounted tailplane, with rudders and elevator.
Fuselage: Main fuselage pod plus large amphibious float sections.
Engines: 2 turboprops, driving 5-blade shrouded pusher propellers.
Engine rating: Each 1,850 shp (1,380 kW).
Fuel system: Can operate on kerosene, gasoline, diesel, gas or conventional aviation fuels.

Aeroprogress T-2000 Barracuda

DETAILS FOR BARRACUDA.

Undercarriage:
Type: Can operate from unprepared ground, water, snow and ice-covered surfaces, using the integral floats, integral wheels, or skis. Up to wave height 3 or 4 for water take-off/landing

Weights:
Maximum take-off: 33,070 lb (15,000 kg)
Payload: 8,818 lb (4,000 kg)

Performance:
Maximum speed: 270 kts (310 mph) 500 km/h
Operating altitude in non-WIG flight: 13,125 ft (4,000 m)
Range in WIG mode: 2,430 naut miles (2,796 miles) 4,500 km
Range in aircraft mode: 1,458 naut miles (1,677 miles) 2,700 km
Loiter duration: 24 hours in WIG mode, 10 hours in aircraft mode

Aeroprogress T-2010

Role: Projected wing-in-ground-effect cargo and troop transport.

★ Aims

★ Weight of 88,185 lb (40,000 kg).
Engines: Propfans.

Aeroprogress T-2010 WIG transport

Aeroprogress T-2402 Dinosaur and T-2414

Details: For T-2402 Dinosaur, except in Aircraft variants.
Role: Medium/long-range multi-purpose military/civil transport, also suited to paradropping/parachuting, forest patrol, visual and instrument survey, aerial photography, medevac and EEZ patrol.

▲ Development

▲ 1995. Detail design began.

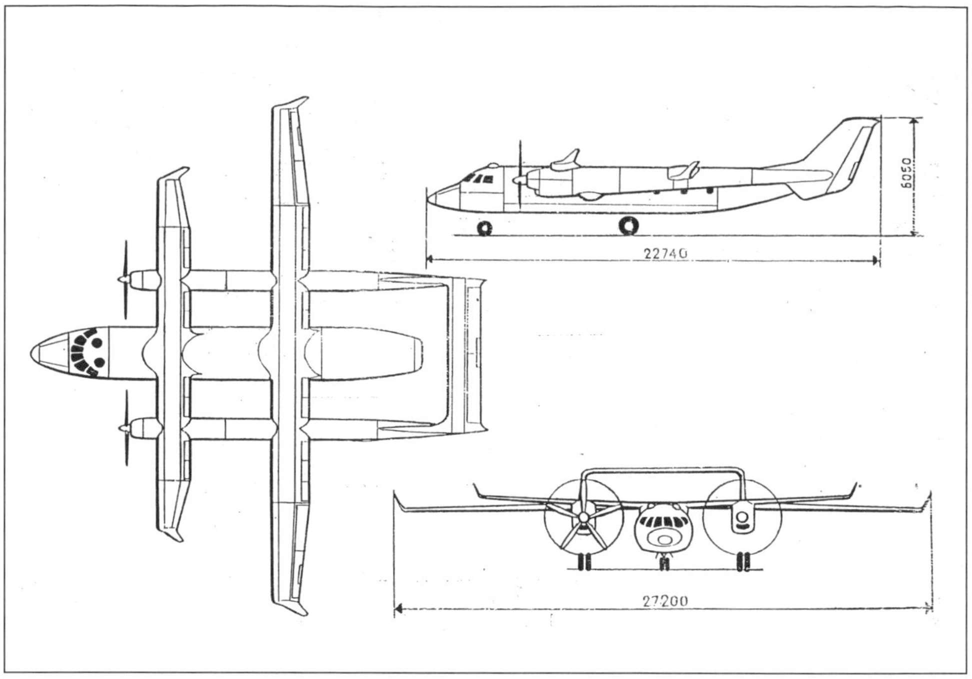

Aeroprogress T-2402 Dinosaur (courtesy Aeroprogress)

DETAILS FOR T-2402.

Principal dimensions:
Wing span: 89 ft 3 ins (27.2 m)
Maximum length: 74 ft 7 ins (22.74 m)
Maximum height: 19 ft 10 ins (6.05 m)

Weights:
Maximum take-off: 54,013 lb (24,500 kg)
Payload: 13,228 lb (6,000 kg)

Performance:
Maximum speed: 292 kts (336 mph) 540 km/h
Cruise speed: 270 kts (311 mph) 500 km/h
Take-off over a 50 ft (15 m) obstacle: 2,625 ft (800 m)
Landing distance over a 50 ft (15 m) obstacle: 1,970 ft (600 m)
Range with full fuel: 2,430 naut miles (2,796 miles) 4,500 km
Range with full payload: 864 naut miles (994 miles) 1,600 km

Sales: Estimated unit cost US$8.5 million.
Crew: 5.
Passengers: 56. In military transport form, a typical layout could be 2 armed jeeps and accompanying troops.
Freight hold access: Rear ramp/door.
Engines: 2 Klimov TV7-117 turboprops, with 11 ft 10 ins (3.6 m) SV-34 6-blade propellers (4-blade in photograph, 5-blade in received drawing).
Engine rating: Each 3,000 shp (2,237 kW).
Fuel system: 12,125 lb (5,500 kg).

Aeroprogress T-2414 in model form

Aircraft variants:
T-2402 Dinosaur, as detailed.
T-2414 is a projected STOL freighter with a hinged rear fuselage section that makes it suitable for carrying large containers. When no containers are carried, the rear section is moved forward to serve as a cockpit fairing. 2 x 6,000 shp (4,474 kW) Rolls-Royce turboprops. Take-off weight 88,185 lb (40,000 kg).

Aeroprogress T-2412 Harpoon

First flight: Under development.
Role: Multi-purpose amphibian for passengers/cargo, EEZ and forest patrol, rescue, survey, aerial photography and special applications.
Sales: Reported prospective customers in Indonesia, Malaysia and Latin America.
Crew: 2, with pilot left and co-pilot right, on seats able to tilt 35°. Control wheels. Special applications freighter/passenger convertible version will have ejection seats.
Pressurization: Flight deck and cabin.
Freight hold access: Rear ramp/door as an extension of the cabin pressure floor, with 2 floor-strengthening beams and 10 frames. Patrol version will have an extendable ramp for launching/recovering a 6-seat boat.
Wing characteristics: Cantilever, cranked high-aspect-ratio (2 spar) wings in tandem, mounted above the fuselage. Forward wing has detachable Whitcomb wingtip fences. Designed for outstanding take-off and landing performances due to efficient high-lift devices and wing profile. Detachable wing panels.
Wing control surfaces: 2 three-section trailing-edge flaps on forward wing, 5-section trailing-edge flaps and 2-section ailerons on main wings. See Engines.
Tail control surfaces: Twin fins and high-mounted tailplane.
Fuselage: Semi-monocoque, divided into nose, instrument bay, cockpit, passenger cabin and tail sections. Double deck. Unique load-carrying structure comprising a system of cross-beams. Divided into 25 pressurized compartments to make the aircraft virtually unsinkable. Rigid planing step, except for a depress step on the special-applications model. Sponsons on the hull sides for improving stability, housing undercarriage units and fuel, and contributing 7% of lift.

DETAILS FOR HARPOON.

Undercarriage:
Type: Retractable, with steerable (electromechanical, hand or foot operated, to ±50°) nosewheel

Construction materials: Metal fuselage with 42 frames, stringers, and riveted L16T skins, except for the rear ramp/door which has a hinged section of glassfibre, T-shaped longitudinal members of carbonfibre, and skin of multilayer glassfibre with foam-rubber filling. Composites sponsons with 4-mm walls to allow unpaved runway and rough water operation. Flaps, wingtips, front wing spars, and wing rear area skins of composites. Total glassfibre tail unit, with foam-rubber filling.
Engines: 2 TV7-117 turboprops, with wide rectangular exhaust nozzles divided into 12 channels by vertical partitions and masked by a slotted flap to lower the infra-red signature; wide efflux quickly mixes with cold air. Upper protruding edges of the nozzles are of titanium and faced with ceramic tiles.
Braking system: Mainwheel discs and automatic anti-skid.
Radar: Weather radar in nose.
Flight avionics/instrumentation: Includes 2 large-screen multi-purpose displays. Satellite communications.

Aeroprogress T-2418

Role: Projected STOL transport.

★ Aims

★ Weighing 48,500 lb (22,000 kg), this is a canard monoplane with a rear loading ramp and facilities for in-flight parachute cargo deliveries.
Engines: 2 Klimov TV7-117 turboprops.

Aviaspetstrans Consortium (Russia)

Corporate address: Zhukovsky 5, Moscow Region.
Telephone: +7 095 556 59 93
Facsimile: +7 095 292 65 11
Founded: 1990.

Aviaspetstrans (Myasishchev) Yamal

First flight: 1998.
Role: Multi-purpose amphibian for passenger/cargo transportation into remote areas, medevac, ice and EEZ patrol, ecological survey, firefighting, air/sea rescue and more.

▲ Development

▲ Under the auspices of Gosaviaregistr, involving 4 Russian scientific/research organizations, and with Myasishchev undertaking actual aircraft development.

Crew: 2.
Passengers: 15 passengers as a flying-boat, 18 when operated from land. Alternatively, medevac and other layouts.
Wing control surfaces: Ailerons (with tabs) and 2-section flaps.
Tail control surfaces: T-tail, with elevators (with tabs) and split rudder, the lower half with tab (rudder split each side of the propeller housing).
Fuselage: Single-step hull, with side sponsons for stability and to house the main undercarriage units.
Engines: 2 RKBM RD-600S turboshafts, driving a single tail-mounted 6-blade pusher propeller through a combining reduction gearbox.
Engine rating: Each 1,300 shp (969.4 kW).
Fuel system: 5,291 lb (2,400 kg).

DETAILS FOR YAMAL.

Principal dimensions:
Wing span: 70 ft 2.5 ins (21.4 m)
Maximum length: 55 ft 2.5 ins (16.825 m)
Maximum height: 17 ft 7 ins (5.367 m)

Cabin:
Volume: 826.36 cu ft (23.4 m^3)
Main passenger door: On the port side of the upper hull, above the sponson

Wings:
Area: 558.65 sq ft (51.9 m^2)
Aspect ratio: 8.824

Undercarriage:
Type: Retractable main wheels and fixed tailwheel

Nosewheel undercarriage being developed. Maximum ground pressure 64 psi

Weights:
Payload: 4,409 lb (2,000 kg)

Performance:
Maximum cruise speed: 235 kts (270 mph) 435 km/h, at 24,600 ft (7,500 m)
Long-range cruise speed: 202 kts (233 mph) 375 km/h
Take-off distance: 738 ft (225 m) *land,* 755 ft (230 m) *water*
Operating altitude: 24,600 ft (7,500 m)
Range with full payload: 632 naut miles (727 miles) 1,170 km, at *maximum cruise speed,* or 756 naut miles (870 miles) 1,400 km at *long-range cruise speed*

Aviaspetstrans (Myasischev) Yamal (Piotr Butowski)

Beta Air Limited Joint Venture (Russia)

Corporate address: Beta Air Scientific-Technical Complex, 347923 Taganrog.
Telephone: + 7 86344 49853
Facsimile: +7 86344 41454

● Activities

● Beta Air Limited Joint Venture combines Beriev, the Taganrog aircraft production association, Irkutsk aircraft production association (IAPO) and Geneva ILTA Trade Finance SA of Switzerland.

Beta Air (Beriev) Be-200

First flight: June 1994 announcement by the Irkutsk aircraft production association that construction of 4 Be-200s would begin in 1995. Work on the first 2 prototypes began in 1994 (flying and static test). Originally, the first flight was expected in late 1994.

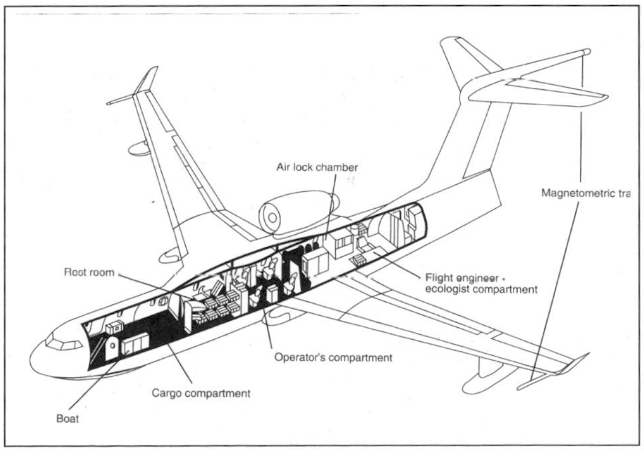

Beta Air (Beriev) Be-200 in ecological configuration (courtesy Beriev)

Certification/first delivery: 1997 planned certification, start of series production, and initial deliveries.
Role: Multi-purpose amphibian, initially for fire-fighting but to be offered for passenger and/or cargo carrying, search and rescue, environmental and maritime patrol, and ice reconnaissance.
Sales: 109 reported orders by early 1995, including 55 for the Irkutsk and Sakhlan regional administrations and 54 for the state forestry organization.
Crew: 2 flight crew for each version.
Passengers: 2 cabin attendants and 68 passengers in all-tourist layout. Ambulance configuration has 30 litters and seats for 7 casualties/attendants.

DETAILS FOR BE-200.

Principal dimensions:
Wing span: 107 ft 3 ins (32.7 m) over winglets
Maximum length: 105 ft 2 ins (32.049 m)
Maximum height: 29 ft 2 ins (8.9 m)

Cabin:
Length: 55 ft 9 ins (17 m)
Width: 8 ft 6.5 ins (2.6 m)
Height: 6 ft 3 ins (1.9 m)
Volume: 2,966.4 cu ft (84 m^3) in cargo transport configuration
Main passenger door: 5 ft 7 ins x 2 ft 11.5 ins (1.7 x 0.9 m)

Wings:
Aerofoil section: Supercritical
Area: 1,264.1 sq ft (117.44 m^2)
Aspect ratio: 9.1

Tail unit:
Tailplane span: 33 ft 2 ins (10.114 m)
Tailplane area: 193.32 sq ft (17.96 m^2)

Undercarriage:
Type: Retractable, with twin steerable nosewheels
Main wheel tyre size: 950 x 300 mm
Nose wheel tyre size: 620 x 180 mm
Wheel base: 36 ft 6.5 ins (11.143 m)
Wheel track: 14 ft 1 ins (4.3 m)
Turning radius: 57 ft 1 ins (17.4 m)

Weights:
Maximum: 92,594 lb (42,000 kg), said to be take-off weight but likely lift weight after water scooping for fire-fighting
Normal take-off: 79,366 lb (36,000 kg)
Maximum landing: 77,162 lb (35,000 kg)
Payload: 17,637 lb (8,000 kg) of cargo

Performance:
Cruise speed: 405 kts (466 mph) 750 km/h
Stall speed: 116 kts (134 mph) 215 km/h *clean*, 84 kts (97 mph) 155 km/h *with flaps*
Take-off distance: 2,953 ft (900 m) *from shore*, 3,281 ft (1,000 m) *from water*
Landing distance: 3,445 ft (1,050 m) *to shore*, 3,609 ft (1,100 m) *to water*
Maximum wave height: 3 ft 1 ins (1.2 m)
Maximum climb rate: 2,756 ft (840 m) per minute
Ceiling: 36,000 ft (11,000 m)
Range with 64 passengers: 1,674 naut miles (1,926 miles) 3,100 km
Range with 6 tonnes of cargo: 1,620 naut miles (1,864 miles) 3,000 km
Range with full fuel: 2,160 naut miles (2,485 miles) 4,000 km

Seat pitch: 29.5 ins (75 cm).
Fire-fighting tanks volume: 423.8 cu ft (12 m^3) of water in 2 tanks, and 42.38 cu ft (1.2 m^3) of liquid chemical in 3 tanks. 320 tonnes of water can be dropped without refuelling during repeated missions, assuming an airfield to reservoir distance of 108 naut miles (124 miles) 200 km and a reservoir to fire distance of 5.4 naut miles (6.2 miles) 10 km.
Freight hold capacity: 8 tonnes of cargo in freighter configuration, with a hold of 55 ft 9 ins (17 m) length x 8 ft 6 ins (2.6 m) width x 6 ft 3 ins (1.9 m) height.
Wing control surfaces: Ailerons, single-slotted flaps, spoilers and leading-edge slats. Winglets.
Tail control surfaces: Elevators and rudder.
Engines: 2 Ivchenko PROGRESS D-436T1 turbofans, carried as for the A-40/Be-40 (which see in Combat section). BMW Rolls-Royce BR710S are proposed as alternative engines.
Engine rating: Each 16,865 lbf (75 kN).
Electrical system: As for Be-40.
Hydraulic system: 3,000 psi.
De-icing system: As for Be-40.
Radar: MN-85 weather radar.
Flight avionics/instrumentation: ARIA (joint venture between AlliedSignal and National Institute of Aircraft Equipment) integrated avionics, including 6 EFIS flat-panel displays, each 6 x 8 ins (15 x 20 cm), and a flight management system. Satellite communication for ecological role.
Mission equipment: For search and rescue, the aircraft carries appropriate sensors, searchlights for night illumination and medical equipment.
Aircraft variants: See previous paragraphs and Role.

Beriev Joint-Stock Company (Russia)

Corporate address: See Combat section for company details. See also Reconnaissance and General Aviation.

Beriev Be-32

First flight: 3 March 1967 for Be-30 commuter transport (production halted after 8 aircraft).
Certification: 1995 for Be-32.
Role: Light passenger/cargo commuter transport, 7-passenger business aircraft, and with adoption to ambulance and forest/economic monitoring.

▲ Development

▲ 1993. Be-32 launched as a modestly revised version of the Be-30, having secured an initial order for 50 from Moscow Airways. A Be-30 became Be-32 demonstrator, displayed at the Paris Air Show.
Crew: 2.
Passengers: 14 and 17 passenger versions, 7 passengers in the business model, 9 litters plus 6 seats and a medical attendant in an ambulance role, and 12 paratroops/parachutists or 17 troops.
Freight hold access: 2 large port-side freight doors.
Wing control surfaces: Ailerons and double-slotted flaps.

DETAILS FOR BE-32.

Principal dimensions:
Wing span: 55 ft 9 ins (17 m)
Maximum length: 51 ft 6 ins (15.7 m)
Maximum height: 18 ft 1.5 ins (5.52 m)

Cabin:
Length: 18 ft 7 ins (5.66 m)
Width: 5 ft (1.52 m)
Height: 5 ft 11 ins (1.81 m)
Floor area: 39.18 sq ft (3.64 m^2)
Volume: 459.1 cu ft (13 m^3)
Door size: 4 ft 3 ins x 2 ft 5.5 ins (1.3 x 0.75 m)

Wings:
Aerofoil section: P-20
Aspect ratio: 9
Twist: 3°
Anhedral: On outer panels.

Undercarriage:
Type: Retractable, with twin nosewheels. Can operate from natural ground airfields, or in Northern and Arctic regions using floats and skis
Main wheel tyre size: 720 x 320 mm
Nose wheel tyre size: 500 x 150 mm
Wheel base: 15 ft 7 ins (4.75 m)
Wheel track: 17 ft 1 ins (5.2 m)

Weights:
Empty: 10,494 lb (4,760 kg)
Maximum take-off: 15,432-16,094 lb (7,000-7,300 kg)
Maximum landing: 14,991 lb (6,800 kg)
Payload: 4,409 lb (2,000 kg)

Performance:
Maximum cruise speed: 237-259 kts (273-298 mph) 440-480 km/h
Economic cruise speed: 202 kts (233 mph) 375 km/h
Take-off distance over a 35 ft (11 m) obstacle: 1,969 ft (600 m)
Landing distance over a 50 ft (15 m) obstacle: 2,034 ft (620 m)
Maximum climb rate: 1,476 ft (450 m) per minute at sea level
Range with 17 passengers: 351 naut miles (404 miles) 650 km
Range with 7 passengers: 864 naut miles (994 miles) 1,600 km

Beriev Be-32 light commuter and general transport (Piotr Butowski)

Tail control surfaces: Elevators (port tab) and rudder (with tab).
Construction materials: Mostly metal, including honeycomb panels for part of the wings and tail unit. Glassfibre for non-structural wing and tail tips plus wing-root fillets.
Engines: 2 Pratt & Whitney-Klimov PT6A-65B turboprops; originally planned with OMSK TVD-10Bs or TVD-20s.
Engine rating: 1,100 shp (820.3 kW).
Fuel system: 2,250 litres.
Electrical system: DC power by 25.5 volt/12 kW rectifiers. AC power by 115-200 volt/ 400Hz three-phase system with 2 x 16 kW alternators.
Braking system: On main units.
De-icing system: Electro-thermal for cockpit windows and propellers. Hot air for wing/tail leading edges, air intakes and oil cooler.
Radar: Weather type.
Flight avionics/instrumentation: Automatic flight control system.

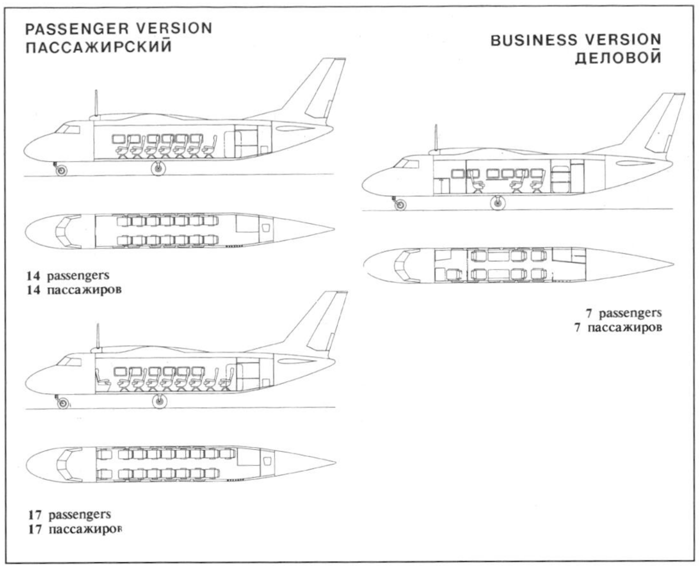

Beriev Be-32 in 14, 17 and 7 passenger layouts (courtesy Beriev)

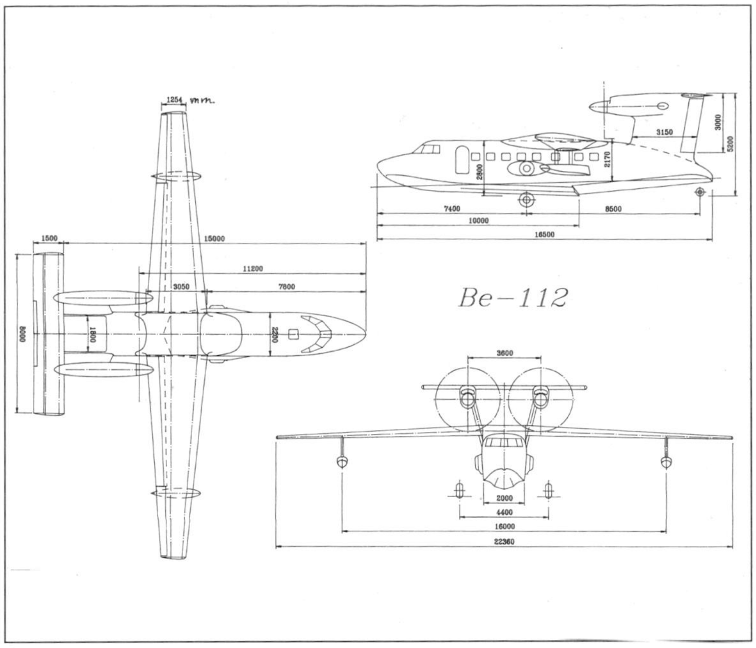

Beriev Be-112 amphibian (courtesy Beriev)

Beriev Be-112

First flight: Not yet flown.
Role: Multi-purpose amphibian for passenger/cargo carrying, ambulance and veterinary support to far-off regions, geological support, ice and fishery surveillance, EEZ patrol, and ecological monitoring.
Crew: 2.
Passengers: 21-24. Ambulance version carries 5 seated casualties/attendants and a light all-terrain vehicle. Patrol version has 4 mission stations plus an inflatable boat. Cargo version has 3 passengers plus cargo.
Wing control surfaces: Ailerons and flaps.
Tail control surfaces: Twin outward-canted fins, each 10 ft 4 ins (3.15 m) chord, carrying the engines. Twin rudders. Constant-chord tailplane attached to the rear of the engines/top of the fins, with a single wide elevator and tab.
Fuselage: Large hatch in the rear hull, between the fins, for paratroops/parachutists and airdropped cargo, and also useful to load long items, and make on-water unloading easier.
Engines: 2 OMSK TVD-20 (each 1,380 shp, 1,029 kW) or Rybinsk TVD-1500 (each 1,300 shp, 969.4 kW) mounted on top of the tailfins.
Flight avionics/instrumentation: Russian or Western digital flight/navigation equipment with electronic displays.

Beriev Be-112 amphibian model (courtesy Beriev)

DETAILS FOR BE-112.

Principal dimensions:
Wing span: 73 ft 4 ins (22.36 m)
Maximum length: 54 ft 1.5 ins (16.5 m)
Maximum height: 17 ft 1 ins (5.2 m) with undercarriage retracted

Hull/fuselage:
Width: 6 ft 7 ins (2 m) at planing bottom, 7 ft 3 ins (2.2 m) at top decking.
Height: 9 ft 2 ins (2.8 m) maximum
Cargo door: 5 ft 11 ins (1.8 m) width

Wings:
Area: 538.2 sq ft (50 m^2)
Aspect ratio: 10
Anhedral: Slight

Tail unit:
Tailplane span: 26 ft 3 ins (8 m)

Undercarriage:
Type: Retractable, with tailwheel. Twin floats under the outer wing panels, 52 ft 6 ins (16 m) apart
Wheel base: 27 ft 11 ins (8.5 m)
Wheel track: 14 ft 5 ins (4.4 m)

Weights:
Maximum take-off: 18,739 lb (8,500 kg)
Payload and fuel: 6,393 lb (2,900 kg)
Commercial payload: 4,762 lb (2,160 kg)

Performance:
Cruise speed: 194 kts (224 mph) 360 km/h
Landing speed: 76 kts (87 mph) 140 km/h
Take-off and landing distance: 1,870 ft (570 m)
Maximum wave height: 3 ft 3 ins (1 m), sea state 3
Range with 24 passengers: 351 naut miles (404 miles) 650 km, 30 minutes reserve
Range with 20 passengers: 580 naut miles (668 miles) 1,075 km, with 30 minutes reserve

Ilyushin Aviation Complex (Russia)

Corporate address: See Combat section for all company details. See also Reconnaissance and General Aviation sections.

Ilyushin Il-76 (NATO name *Candid*)

First flight: 25 March 1971 (piloted by Eduard Kuznetsov). 8 May 1973 for the first production aircraft, manufactured at the Tashkent plant.
Chief designer: Radiy Papkovsky.
Role: Medium/long-range civil and military transport, also used for firefighting, medical evacuation, astronaut training, electronic countermeasures and more. Able to operate in severe weather conditions.
Sales: In production since 1973 at the Tashkent aircraft factory named after V. Chkalov. More than 850 manufactured, of which up to 500 are in current service with military transport aviation and about 200 with civil companies in the CIS. 122 exported to Algeria, China (10), Cuba (2), India (24 named Gajaraj, operated since July 1985), Iraq (more than 30), Libya (21) and Syria (4); some returned to Russia, leaving about 90 abroad.
Details: Principally for the Il-76MD.
Crew: 6/7. Twin-deck, upper for pilots, lower for navigator.
Pressurization: 7.25 psi differential for freight hold.
Freight hold capacity: For payload, see Aircraft variants. Typical loads include standard Russian containers, each 8 ft (2.44 m) width and height by the following lengths: 40 ft (12.19 m) (UAK-20), 19 ft 11 ins (6.06 m) (UAK-10 and UUK-20), and 9 ft 10 ins (2.99 m) (UAK-5 and UUK-10). Also smaller UAK-5A and UAK-2.5 containers and PA-6.8, PA-5.6, PA-4.5, PA-3.6, PA-2.5 pallets. Alternatively up to 126 paratroops, or 167 troops, or 245 troops when the second deck is installed. It takes 30 minutes to convert the standard Il-76 into a passenger aircraft using 3 modules installed into the cabin (105 passengers), or into an evacuation aircraft for litter patients.
Freight hold access: Rear loading ramp, and a small door each side of the front cabin.
Size of freight doors: Rear opening 11 ft 2 ins x 11 ft 4 ins (3.4 x 3.45 m).
Loading facilities: 2 floor electrical winches, each 6,614 lb (3,000 kg), and 4 electrical telphers, each 5,512 lb (2,500 kg). Roller tracks on the floor. Rear loading ramp can lift up to 66,139 lb (30,000 kg). 4 toe plates to load self-propelled and towed vehicles.
Wing control surfaces: Full-span leading-edge slats (15% of wing chord, deflected 25°). Each wing has 2 sections of triple-slotted trailing-edge flaps, occupying 73.5% of the span, with maximum deflection of 43° for the inner section and 40° for the outer. Ailerons (+16°, -28°) with tabs. Forward of the flaps are

Ilyushin Il-76MF, the lengthened freighter seen at NAKS' 95 in Zhukovsky in August 1995 (Piotr Butowski).

4 sections of spoilers (20°, deflected differentially to support ailerons or evenly as airbrakes when landing) and 4 sections of airbrakes (40°).

Tail control surfaces: T-tail, with a variable incidence tailplane (+2°, -8°), elevators (+15°, -21°) with tabs, and rudder (± 27°) with tab.

Ilyushin Il-76TD converted to fire-fighting configuration (Piotr Butowski)

Flight control system: Mechanical, power operated; manual control as stand-by.

Construction materials: All-metal; aluminium alloy, steel and titanium. Metal honeycomb used for the detachable panels of the wings, tail unit, pylons and undercarriage fairings.

Engines: 4 Aviadvigatel D-30KP II turbofans, with thrust reversers. TA-6A auxiliary power unit in the starboard main undercarriage fairing. The Il-76M/Il-76T are powered by D-30KP turbofans of the same thrust but inferior high temperature characteristics (take-off thrust to ISA +15° C, while D-30KP IIs are to ISA +23° C). Proposed mid-life upgrade by installing CFM International CFM56-5C2s (31,217 lbf, 138.87 kN). Another upgrade offer uses Russian PS-90A12 turbofans, each 26,455 lbf (117.68 kN), as Il-76TD-90.

Engine thrust: Each 26,455 lbf (117.68 kN) at take-off.

Fuel system: Up to 109,480 litres (187,040 lb, 84,840 kg) of fuel in 12 tanks along the whole span of the wings.

Flight refuelling: None.

Electrical system: 115/120 volt, 400Hz AC supply has 4 x 60 kVA generators (1 on each engine). 1 x 40 kVA generator (AC 115/220 volt, 400 Hz), and 1 x DC 12 kW generator on APU, as stand-by. 4 batteries and DC/AC converters as an emergency power source.

Hydraulic system: 2 independent systems, with 2 hydraulic pumps each. Operating pressure 2,990 psi.

Braking system: Hydraulically operated, with anti-skid system.

Radar: Kupol-3-76 navigation radar in an undernose radome that is also used as a sight when paradropping. Kupol-2-76 for civil aircraft.

Flight avionics/instrumentation: SAU-76 automatic control system. R-838 and R-847 communication radios.

Fixed weapons: Many military aircraft and a few civil have a rear gun turret with 2 twin-barrel GSh-23 cannon.

Expendable weapons and equipment: Up to 4 x 500 kg flares for illumination of the landing area.

Self-protection systems: See cannon under Fixed weapons. Some military aircraft have radar warning receivers in large fairings on the sides of the nose. During the conflict in Afghanistan, chaff/flare dispensers were carried (pack of 96 x 50-mm projectiles on each side of the fuselage and/or on the undercarriage fairings).

Aircraft variants:

Il-76 *Candid-A* prototypes had a maximum take-off weight of 374,785 lb (170,000 kg) and a payload of 72,752 lb (33,000 kg).

Il-76LL (letayushchaya laboratoria or flying test bed) covers several aircraft used at the Russian Flight Test Centre in Zhukovsky as engine test beds. D-18T, D-236, D-27, etc have been installed in place of the standard starboard inner engine. Measurement equipment in the cabin.

Il-76M *Candid-B* military transport features slight strengthening of the wings, wider rear fuselage, new equipment, and a maximum take-off weight of 374,785 lb (170,000 kg) but a maximum payload of 103,617 lb (47,000 kg). Range 3,510 naut miles (4,039 miles) 6,500 km with a 44,092 lb (20,000 kg) payload. Tail gun turret on some aircraft. Production switched to this version and its Il-76T civil derivative in 1977.

Il-76MD *Candid-B* (D for dalniy or long range) was given considerably strengthened wings. Maximum allowable take-off weight increased to 418,878 lb (190,000 kg), which made possible provision for more fuel (this tankage volume was left unused in previous versions). Range 3,942 naut miles (4,536 miles) 7,300 km with a 20,000 kg payload. Improved D-30KP II engines.

Il-76MDK and IL-76K (K for kosmos) versions were prepared for cosmonaut training. In the cabin of the diving aircraft a state of weightlessness is created, lasting 22-24 seconds a dozen or so times during each flight.

Il-76MDPS (PS for poiskovo-spasatelnyi or search and rescue) is able to patrol for 3 hours at a distance of 1,620 naut miles (1,864 miles) 3,000 km from base. Group of 40 rescue paratroopers can be dropped as well as a Gagara motor boat (22,046 lb, 10,000 kg weight, with a crew of 3 – allowable wave height 10 ft, 3.0 m) plus dinghies for 1,000 people.

Il-76MF has a fuselage lengthened by 21 ft 8 ins (6.6 m) by the insertion of 2 plugs, becoming 164 ft 8 ins (50.2 m) fuselage length and 174 ft 6 ins (53.194 m) overall length. The cargo hold is 102 ft 2 ins (31.14 m) long, including the ramp. The basic Russian variant is powered by 4 Aviadvigatel PS-90A76 turbofans, each 35,300 lbf (157 kN), but a later variant is planned using CFM56-5C2s. Fuel efficiency improved by 12%. Take-off weight 462,970 lb (210,000 kg), empty weight 222,667 lb (101,000 kg), and maximum payload 114,640 lb (52,000 kg). Practical range with a 40,000 kg load is 3,132 naut miles (3,610 miles) 5,800 km with 1 hour reserve. Cruise speed 405-421 kts (466-485 mph) 750-780 km/h. Updated avionics include Kupol-3-76MF radar, SAU-76Ts automatic control system and BASK-124 flight data recorder borrowed from the Antonov An-124. The prototype first flew on 1 August 1995.

Il-76P or Il-76TP (P stands for pozharnyi or fire-fighting) was developed in 1989. 97,003 lb (44,000 kg) of fire-extinguishing mixture, in 2 tanks, can be released from 66-330 ft (20-100 m) at 150-160 kts. Time of discharge is 6-7 seconds, covering an area of 1,640 x 328 ft (500 x 100 m). Refill takes between 10 and 15 minutes. Any Il-76 can be converted to a fire-fighting version in field conditions. Equipment

DETAILS FOR Il-76MD CANDID-B, UNLESS STATED OTHERWISE.

Principal dimensions:
Wing span: 165 ft 8 ins (50.5 m)
Maximum length: 152 ft 10 ins (46.594 m)
Maximum height: 48 ft 5 ins (14.76 m)

Cabin:
Length, maximum: 80 ft 6 ins (24.54 m)
Length, without ramp: 65 ft 7 ins (20.0 m)
Width: 11 ft 4 ins (3.45 m) at floor
Height, maximum: 11 ft 2 ins (3.4 m)
Main door: 11 ft 2 ins x 11 ft 4 ins (3.4 x 3.45 m)
Side doors: 6 ft 3 ins x 2 ft 10 ins (1.9 x 0.86 m)

Wings:
Aerofoil section: TsAGI P-151
Area, gross: 3,242 sq ft (301.2 m^2)
Aspect ratio: 8.467
Sweepback: 25° at 25% chord
Twist: +3° root, 0° tip
Anhedral: 3°
Ailerons area: 142.84 sq ft (13.27 m^2)
Spoilers area: 116.9 sq ft (10.86 m^2)
Airbrakes area: 170.07 sq ft (15.8 m^2)
Trailing-edge flap area: approx 710.4 sq ft (66 m^2)

Tail unit:
Tailplane span: 57 ft 1 ins (17.4 m)
Tailplane area: 678.1 sq ft (63 m^2)
Elevators area: 184.8 sq ft (17.17 m^2)
Fin height: 23 ft 9 ins (7.245 m)
Fin sweepback: 38° 10' at 25% chord
Fin area: 538.2 sq ft (50 m^2)

Undercarriage:
Type: Retractable, with steerable nosewheel unit consisting of a 4-wheel bogie. Each main unit consists of 2 such bogies in tandem
Main wheels tyre size: 1,300 x 480 mm
Nose wheel tyre size: 1,100 x 330 mm
Wheel base: 46 ft 6 ins (14.17 m)
Wheel track: 26 ft 9 ins (8.16 m)

Weights:
Empty, operating: 196,211 lb (89,000 kg)
Maximum take-off: 418,878 lb (190,000 kg)
Maximum allowable take-off: 462,970 lb (210,000 kg) for no more than 15% of take-offs
Maximum take-off from unprepared runway: 347,228 lb (157,500 kg)
Maximum landing: 341,716 lb (155,000 kg)
Payload: 103,617 lb (47,000 kg) maximum

Performance:
Maximum allowable Mach number: 0.77
Maximum cruising speed: 405-421 kts (466-485 mph) 750-780 km/h at 39,370 ft (12,000 m)
Take-off run: 5,578 ft (1,700 m)
Landing run: 2,953-3,281 ft (900-1,000 m)
Cruise altitude (Il-76MF): 29,525-39,370 ft (9,000-12,000 m)
Range with maximum fuel: 4,212 naut miles (4,847 miles) 7,800 km
Range with 44,092 lb (20,000 kg) payload: 3,942 naut miles (4,536 miles) 7,300 km
Range with 88,184 lb (40,000 kg) payload: 2,570 naut miles (2,958 miles) 4,760 km
Range with maximum payload: 2,052 naut miles (2,361 miles) 3,800 km

Ilyushin Il-76LL test-bed, installed with a D-27 propfan engine (Piotr Butowski)

weight is about 11,023 lb (5,000 kg). Can carry 40 paratroopers/firefighters and 384 weather cartridges with silver iodide. Leading designer Nikolai Talikov. Demonstrated to the US Forest Service and British officials at Boscombe Down, UK, on 9 September 1994. Cost about US$9,000 to US$10,000 per hour.

Il-76PP (postanovshchik pomekh or jammer) is the electronic countermeasures aircraft, conceived as an escort aircraft for the A-50 AEW&C. Prototype only, appearing in about 1985.

Il-76 Scalpel was developed as a medical version, using 3 container-type modules with a surgical room, recovery room, etc, mounted inside the cabin. Medical crew of 12. Used during the conflict in Afghanistan.

Il-76T *Candid-A* became the civil derivative of the Il-76M, with assault/paratroop equipment removed and no tail turret. Maximum payload 110,231 lb (50,000 kg).

Il-76TD *Candid-A* is the civil derivative of the Il-76MD.

Il-76TF is a projected commercial MF. Available in 1996.

Il-82 Relay Aircraft – see Electronic section.

Beriev A-50 *Mainstay*/Be-976, see Reconnaissance section.

Il-78 *Midas* – see separate entry.

Bagdad-1 and Adnan-1 are AEW&C derivatives developed in Iraq. See Reconnaissance section.

Ilyushin Il-78 and Il-76M (NATO name *Midas*)

First flight: June 1983.
Chief designer: Radiy Papkovsky
Role: In-flight refuelling tanker, (replaced 3MS-2 and 3MN-2 *Bison-B*).
Based on: Il-76MD.
Sales: About 40 in service, divided equally between Ukraine (409th Air Tanker Regiment at Uzin; first unit, gaining IOC in 1987) and Russia (230th Regiment at Engels). Production completed.
Crew: 6, including refuelling operator in the place usually occupied by the tail gunner.
Freight holds: The Il-78 is similar to the Il-76 when the additional fuel tanks are removed. The Il-78M version carries no freight, as the fuel tanks are fixed.
Size of freight doors: Il-78 is similar to the Il-76. The Il-78M has no doors.
Fuel system: 2 cylindrical fuel tanks mounted inside the cabin (removable in Il-78, fixed in Il-78M), each carrying 30,865 lb (14,000 kg) of fuel for the Il-78 and 39,683 lb (18,000 kg) for the Il-76M. Both versions can also transfer fuel from the standard wing torsion box tanks.
Fuel transfer: Fuel is transferred via 3 UPAZ-1A Sakhalin refuelling pods (unifitsirovannyi podvesnoi agregat zapravki – unified suspended refuelling gear), designed by the Zvezda bureau. 2 are installed under the wings, each at the distance of 53 ft 10 ins (16.40 m) from the aircraft centre line. The third pod is suspended from the port side of the rear fuselage at a distance of 9 ft 10 ins (3 m) from the centre line. The central pod was designed for refuelling 1 heavy aircraft, whereas the underwing pods transfer fuel to 2 lighter aircraft (in combat conditions 3 tactical aircraft can be refuelled simultaneously). At least 85 ft (26 m) of the UPAZ-1A's hose has to be unwound prior to the start of refuelling, which starts automatically after the drogue has captured the probe and is stopped after transferring the preset volume of fuel. The refuelling operation can also be stopped manually by the operator, or automatically after the whole hose length is unwound or when the difference in speed of the aircraft exceeds 591 ft (180 m) per minute. Refuelling can only be carried out during direct visibility (for night operations, lights are used). Il-78 can also be used as a ground refuelling station for 4 aircraft, usually on front line airfields. The refuelling pods are then replaced by 4 hoses connected directly to the valves of the internal fuel storage tanks.
Flight avionics/instrumentation: As for Il-76, plus Vstrecha short-range radio navigation system for all weather, day and night mutual detection and approach from 162 naut miles (186 miles) 300 km distance. The system controls automatically the distance between the aircraft and generates a warning signal if the aircraft are too close (closest allowable distance is 42.8 ft, 13 m).
Aircraft variants:
Il-78 *Midas* was the initial version, with a maximum allowable take-off weight of 418,878 lb (190,000 kg). Convertible between transport/tanker.
Il-78M *Midas* is the standard, strengthened production version. Maximum allowable take-off weight is 462,970 lb (210,000 kg). Non-convertible. No cabin doors or ramp, resulting in a reduced structural weight.
Il-78MK (Kommerchesky) is the export version.
Il-78V has modified refuelling pods of MK-32B type.

Ilyushin Il-76M Midas tanker about to transfer fuel to a Tu-95 heavy bomber (Anatoli Andreyev)

UPAZ-1A Sakhalin refuelling pod on the port side of the Il-78 Midas rear fuselage (Piotr Butowski)

Ilyushin Il-86-300 (NATO name *Camber*)

First flight: 22 December 1976.
First delivery: September 1979, with Aeroflot passenger services starting on 26 December 1980 between Moscow and Tashkent.
Chief designer: G. V. Novozhilov.
Role: Medium/long-range widebody airliner.
Sales: Some 92 in current airline service of 99 delivered before production ended in 1994, plus 4 delivered as strategic command posts with civil markings and registered *RA-86146* to *RA-86149*. Largest current operators are Aeroflot Russian International Airlines (23) and Vnukovo Air Lines (20).
Crew: 2 pilots, engineer and optional navigator.
Passengers: Passenger accommodation in compartments on the upper deck, with entrance on lower deck. "Luggage by themselves" system adopted, whereby personal baggage is loaded and unloaded by the passengers using racks on the lower deck. Internal stairs connect the decks. Seating options include 28 first class and 206 economy at 6 and 8 abreast respectively, 259 in mixed layout when entering directly to the upper deck (allowing deletion of lower deck access), and 350 maximum in an all-economy layout at 9 abreast.

DETAILS FOR *MIDAS*.

Principal dimensions: As for Il-76MD

Weights:
Maximum allowable take-off (Il-78): 418,878 lb (190,000 kg)
Maximum allowable take-off (Il-78M): 462,970 lb (210,000 kg)
Maximum from unprepared runway: 347,228 lb (157,500 kg)
Maximum landing: 334,000 lb (151,500 kg)
Maximum fuel in standard wing tanks: 187,040 lb (84,840 kg)
Maximum fuel in additional cabin tanks (Il-78): 61,729 lb (28,000 kg)
Maximum fuel in additional cabin tanks (Il-78M): 79,366 lb (36,000 kg)

Performance:
Cruising speed: 405 kts (466 mph) 750 km/h
Refuelling speed: 232-319 kts (267-367 mph) 430-590 km/h IAS
Take-off distance (Il-78): 5,578 ft (1,700 m) at MTOW
Take-off distance (l-78M): 6,824 ft (2,080 m) at MTOW
Landing distance: 2,953 ft (900 m)
G limit: 2.0 at 379,195 lb (172,000 kg)
Refuelling altitude: 6,562-29,525 ft (2,000-9,000 m)
Refuelling radius, 44,092 lb (20,000 kg) of fuel delivered (Il-78): 1,998 naut miles (2,299 miles) 3,700km
Refuelling radius, 20,000 kg of fuel delivered (Il-78M): 2,727 naut miles (3,138 miles) 5,050 km
Refuelling radius, 66,139 lb (30,000 kg) of fuel delivered (Il-78): 1,080 naut miles (1,243 miles) 2,000km
Refuelling radius, 30,000 kg of fuel delivered (Il-78M): 2,268 naut miles (2,610 miles) 4,200 km
Refuelling radius, 88,185 lb (40,000 kg) of fuel delivered (Il-78): 1,134 naut miles (1,305 miles) 2,100 km
Refuelling radius, 40,000 kg of fuel delivered (Il-78M): 1,863 naut miles (2,144 miles) 3,450 km
Refuelling radius, 110,231 lb (50,000 kg) of fuel delivered (Il-78): 756 naut miles (870 miles) 1,400 km
Refuelling radius, 110,231 lb 50,000 kg of fuel delivered (Il-78M): 1,404 naut miles (1,616 miles) 2,600 km

Galley: On lower deck.
Freight hold access: Lower deck holds for containers, comprising 8 LD3s (or pallets), which can be doubled if light luggage racks are reduced in number.
Wing control surfaces: Ailerons, 2-section double-slotted trailing-edge flaps, leading-edge slats, 2-section and 4-section airbrakes/spoilers. 4 over-wing fences.
Tail control surfaces: Variable incidence tailplane, 2-section elevators and 2-section inset rudder.
Flight control system: Hydraulic, with manual back-up for ailerons, elevators and rudder.
Construction materials: Metal, except for composites used in the cabin floors.
Engines: 4 Samara NK-86 turbofans standard, but some re-engined with Aviadvigatel PS-90As of 35,274 lbf (157 kN) or CFM56s.
Engine rating: Each 29,320 lbf (130.43 kN) for NK-86.
Fuel system: 114,000 litres, weighing 194,778 lb (88,350 kg).
Electrical system: 200/115 volt, 400Hz AC supply, using a 40 kVA generator driven by each engine. Back-up 36 volt 3-phase AC. 27 volt DC supply. APU.
De-icing system: Pulse type.
Radar: Weather/navigation.
Flight avionics/instrumentation: ICAO Cat IIIA.

Details for Il-86-300.

Principal dimensions:
Wing span: 157 ft 8 ins (48.06 m)
Maximum length: 195 ft 4 ins (59.54 m)
Maximum height: 51 ft 10 ins (15.81 m)

Wings:
Area: 3,444.5 sq ft (320 m^2) accepted, but quoted by a Moscow source as 330 m^2
Aspect ratio: 7.218

Undercarriage:
Type: Retractable, with twin steerable nosewheels and 3 sets of 4-wheel main bogies to reduce runway loading
Main wheel tyre size: 1,300 x 480 mm
Nose wheel tyre size: 1,120 x 450 mm
Wheel base: 70 ft 0.25 ins (21.34 m)
Wheel track: 36 ft 7 ins (11.15 m)

Weights:
Maximum take-off: 458,560-462,970 lb (208,000-210,000 kg)
Maximum landing: 385,808 lb (175,000 kg)
Payload: 92,594 lb (42,000 kg)

Performance:
High cruise speed: 513 kts (590 mph) 950 km/h
Typical cruise speed: 486 kts (560 mph) 900 km/h
Required field length: 8,530 ft (2,600 m)
Cruise altitude: 32,150-36,000 ft (9,800-11,000 m)
Range with full fuel: 2,483 naut miles (2,858 miles) 4,600 km, also reported to be 5,800 km (but unlikely)
Typical range with full payload: over 1,350 naut miles (1,553 miles) 2,500 km

Ilyushin Il-86-300, the first Russian wide-body airliner

Ilyushin Il-96

First flight: 28 September 1988.
Certification: 29 December 1992.
First delivery: 1993 to Aeroflot, with services starting that July.
Chief designer: G. V. Novozhilov.
Role: Long-range widebody airliner.
Airframe life: 60,000 flying hours.
Noise levels: Meets ICAO Chapter 3 Annex 16.

★ Aims

★ Derived from the Il-86 but with very significant changes including supercritical wings, increase in wing aspect ratio, winglets, wide adoption of composites materials, new and more efficient high-bypass-ratio turbofans, advanced flight deck with CRT displays, and fly-by-wire control.
★ Fuel consumption per passenger/km of the Il-96-300 is approximately half that of the long-range Il-62M.
Sales: Aeroflot Russian International Airlines 7 and Domodedovo 2 by early 1995. Il-96M is likely to become the main production version, for delivery from 1995-96.
Details: Il-96-300.
Crew: 2 pilots and an engineer, with 2 optional seats.
Passengers: Passengers on upper deck, with Il-86's "Luggage by themselves" system abandoned. Typical layouts are 22 first (6 abreast), 40 business (8 abreast) and 173 economy (9 abreast) classes, or 300 economy (9 abreast).
Seat pitch: 40.2 ins (102 cm), 35.5 ins (90 cm), 34.3 ins (87 cm) and 34.3 ins (87 cm) respectively.
Galley: On lower deck.
Freight hold capacity: Up to 16 LD3 containers or pallets.
Wing control surfaces: Inner and outer ailerons, the latter to provide damping moment. Double-slotted and 2-section single-slotted trailing-edge flaps. Multi-section leading-edge slats. 3-section airbrakes and multi-section spoilers.
Tail control surfaces: Variable-incidence tailplane. Elevators and inset 2-section rudder.
Flight control system: Triplex fly-by-wire, with manual back-up.
Construction materials: Metal, but with composites for areas of the tail unit, wing flaps, cabin floors and cargo holds.
Engines: 4 Aviadvigatel PS-90A turbofans. APU.
Engine rating: Each 35,274 lbf (157 kN), with thrust reversers.
Fuel system: 148,260 litres or 253,315 lb (114,900 kg).
Hydraulic system: 3,002 psi.
Radar: Weather/navigation.
Flight avionics/instrumentation: Electronic flight deck with 3 pairs of colour CRT screens. Satellite navigation receivers, Omega, INS and flight management system. Head-up flight display system (HFDS) for Category IIIA operations.
Aircraft variants:
Il-96-300 is the initial production version, as detailed.
Il-96M/MO is a westernized version for Category IIIB operations, using 38,250 lbf (170.1 kN) Pratt & Whitney PW2337 turbofans and Rockwell Collins avionics (ARINC 700). 2-crew flight deck. First flown 6 April 1993 as the Il-96MO prototype. Lengthened to 209 ft 9.3 ins (63.939 m) to accommodate 311, 335 or 386 passsengers. MTOW 595, 250 lb (270,000 kg) and maximum payload 127,868 lb (58,000 kg). Cruise speed 459-470 kts (528-540 mph) 850-870 km/h, take-off distance 11,000 ft (3,350 m) and range with 30 tonne payload 6,480-7,020 naut miles (7,456-8,077 miles) 12,000-13,000 km. A variant with ducted engines has been proposed as the MK.
Il-96T is a freighter conversion, with a 202,825 lb (92,000 kg) payload and 11 ft 10 ins x 8 ft 6.5 ins (3.6 x 2.6 m) loading door. PW2337 engines and Rockwell Collins avionics.

Ilyushin Il-96M (Piotr Butowski)

Details for Il-96-300.

Principal dimensions:
Wing span: 197 ft 2.3 ins (60.105 m)
Maximum length: 181 ft 7 ins (55.35 m)
Maximum height: 57 ft 8 ins (17.57 m)

Cabin:
Volume: 12,360 cu ft (350 m^3)
Main passenger doors: 3, each 6 ft x 3 ft 6 ins (1.83 x 1.07 m)

Wings:
Aerofoil section: Supercritical.
Area: 4,215.14 sq ft (391.6 m^2) accepted, with 350 m^2 quoted by a Moscow source
Aspect ratio: 9.225
Sweepback: 30° at 25% chord

Tail unit:
Tailplane span: 67 ft 6 ins (20.57 m)

Undercarriage:
Type: As for Il-86-300, but with larger 1,260 x 460 mm nosewheel tyres
Wheel base: 65 ft 10 ins (20.065 m)
Wheel track: 34 ft 1 ins (10.4 m)

Weights:
Empty: 257,941 lb (117,000 kg)
Maximum take-off: 476,198 lb (216,000 kg)
Maximum landing: 385,808 lb (175,000 kg)
Payload: 88,185 lb (40,000 kg)

Performance:
High cruise speed: 486 kts (560 mph) 900 km/h
Typical cruise speed: 459 kts (528 mph) 850 km/h
Take-off field length: 8,530 ft (2,600 m)
Landing field length: 6,496 ft (1,980 m)
Cruise altitude: 32,800-39,370 ft (10,000-12,000 ft)
Maximum range: 5,940 naut miles (6,835 miles) 11,000 km
Range with full payload: 4,050 naut miles (4,660 miles) 7,500 km

Ilyushin Il-106

First flight: Expected 1998-2000.
Chief designer: G. V. Novozhilov.
Role: Heavy military transport.
Wing control surfaces: Each wing has 6 sections of leading-edge slats, 2 sections of trailing-edge flaps and an aileron. 6 sections of spoilers/airbrakes forward of the flaps.
Engines: 4 Samara/Kuznetsov NK-92 turbofans (each 39,685 lbf, 176.53 kN) or Aviadvigatel/Reshetnikov D-100s (each 41,888 lbf, 186.33 kN).

DETAILS FOR Il-106.

Principal dimensions:
Wing span: 191 ft 11 ins (58.5 m)
Wing span, without winglets: 182 ft 8 ins (55.68 m)
Maximum length: 189 ft (57.6 m)
Fuselage length: 182 ft 1 ins (55.5 m)
Maximum height: 65 ft 4 ins (19.925 m)

Cabin:
Length: 111 ft 7 ins (34 m)
Width: 19 ft 8 ins (6 m)
Height: 15 ft 1 ins (4.6 m)

Weights:
Maximum take-off: 568,792 lb (258,000 kg)

Performance:
Cruising speed: 443-459 kts (510-528 mph) 820-850 km/h
Take-off distance: 5,085 ft (1,550 m)
Landing distance: 4,593 ft (1,400 m)
Range with maximum payload: 2,700 naut miles (3,107 miles) 5,000 km

Ilyushin Il-106 projected heavy military transport in model form (Piotr Butowski)

Ilyushin Il-112

First flight: Project.
Chief designer: G. V. Novozhilov.
Role: Short-haul regional airliner, VIP transport and freighter.

▲ Development
▲ 1994. Preliminary design began.
Crew: 2.
Passengers: 11, 21 and 32 seat versions anticipated.
Pressurization: Flight deck and cabin.
Freight hold access: Freighter version would have a rear ramp/door and large side-loading door.
Wing characteristics: Straight, high mounted, with no dihedral/anhedral.
Wing control surfaces: Ailerons, long-chord flaps, and 2-section spoilers.
Tail control surfaces: T tail, with elevators and rudder.
Engines: 2 Klimov TV7-117 turboshafts.
Engine rating: Each 2,500 shp (1,864 kW).

DETAILS FOR Il-112.

Principal dimensions:
Wing span: 68 ft 11 ins (21 m)
Maximum length: 65 ft 7 ins (20 m)
Maximum height: 27 ft 11 ins (8.5 m)

Undercarriage:
Type: Retractable, with nosewheel. Main units to retract into fairings on the fuselage sides
Wheel track: 11 ft 10 ins (3.6 m)

Weights:
Empty: 16,755 lb (7,600 kg)
Maximum take-off: 28,660 lb (13,000 kg)
Payload: up to 7,716 lb (3,500 kg)

Performance:
Maximum cruise speed: 324 kts (373 mph) 600 km/h
Take-off distance: 1,345 ft (410 m)
Landing distance: 1,148 ft (350 m)
Cruise altitude: 26,245 ft (8,000 m)
Range with 32 passengers: 810 naut miles (932 miles) 1,500 km
Range with 11 passengers: 1,944 naut miles (2,237 miles) 3,600 km, at 270 kts (311 mph) 500 km/h

Ilyushin Il-114

First flight: 29 March 1990.
Certification: 1993.
First delivery: 1993.
Chief designer: G. V. Novozhilov.
Role: Short-haul pressurized transport to replace the An-24, able to operate from airfields with low support levels.
Sales: Built at the Tashkent plant. Ordered by independent Russian airlines, including Uzbekistan Airways. Sale of some 350 anticipated for domestic services in Russia. Among the latest operators is Archangelsk Airlines, which received 2 in March 1995.
Crew: 2 (flight).
Passengers: 60-64 standard, but can be reconfigured for fewer or extra passengers or freight. Airsteps.
Pressurization: 6.4psi cabin differential.
Seat pitch: 29.5 ins (75 cm).
Galley: Towards the rear of the cabin.
Wing control surfaces: Ailerons (with servo and trim tabs), double-slotted flaps, spoiler and 2 airbrakes.
Tail control surfaces: Elevators and rudder, with tabs.
Flight control system: Mechanical, but with hydraulic flaps.
Construction materials: Principally metal, but with 10% by weight composites.
Engines: 2 Klimov TV7-117-3 (C type) turboprops, with SV-34 six-blade high-technology composites propellers. APU housed in the tailcone for engine starting. Western engines to be available as an option for export aircraft (see Aircraft variants).
Engine rating: Each 2,500 shp (1,864 kW) at take off, 1,800 shp (1,342 kW) cruise.
Fuel system: 8,360 litres.
Electrical system: 115/220 volt, 400Hz AC supply via 2 x 40 kVA generators. 24 volt DC supply.
Hydraulic system: Dual systems, each 3,002 psi.
Braking system: Hydraulic disc.
De-icing system: Bleed air for engine inlets and electro/thermal for propellers and cockpit glazing.
Radar: Weather radar.

Ilyushin Il-114 at Farnborough in September 1994

DETAILS FOR Il-114.

Principal dimensions:
Wing span: 98 ft 5 ins (30 m)
Fuselage length: 85 ft (25.9 m)
Maximum length: 88 ft 2 ins (26.877 m)
Maximum height: 30 ft 7 ins (9.324 m)

Cabin:
Length: 73 ft (22.24 m)
Height: 6 ft 3.5 ins (1.92 m)
Main passenger door: 2, each 5 ft 7 ins x 2 ft 11.5 ins (1.7 x 0.9 m)

Wings:
Area: 881.56 sq ft (81.9 m^2)
Aspect ratio: 10.99

Tail unit:
Tailplane span: 36 ft 5 ins (11.1 m)

Undercarriage:
Type: Retractable, with steerable nosewheels. Twin wheels on each unit. Can operate from unpaved airfields.
Main wheel tyre size: 880 x 305 mm
Wheel base: 30 ft (9.13 m)
Wheel track: 27 ft 7 ins (8.4 m)

Weights:
Empty, operating: 33,069 lb (15,000 kg)
Maximum take-off: 46,297-50,045 lb (21,000-22,700 kg)
Payload: 14,330 lb (6,500 kg)

Performance:
Cruise speed: 270 kts (311 mph) 500 km/h
Take-off distance: 5,100 ft (1,550 m)
Landing distance: 4,100 ft (1,250 m)
Cruise altitude: 23,625 ft (7,200 m)
Range with full fuel: 2,592 naut miles (2,982 miles) 4,800 km
Range with 5.76 tonne payload: 648 naut miles (745 miles) 1,200 km
Range with full payload: 540 naut miles (621 miles) 1,000 km

Flight avionics/instrumentation: IFR. Modern digital suite. Meets ICAO Cat I and II standards. Glass cockpit, with 5 CRT displays presenting navigation, flight, engine and systems information. Western avionics to be made available as an option for exported aircraft.
Aircraft variants:
Il-114 is the standard TV7-117-3 version, as described.
Il-114M has higher rated TV7 engines and 1,102 lb (500 kg) extra payload.
Il-114PC is a version with P&WC PW127C turboprops, new avionics and improved systems. First flight 1996.
Il-114 Cargo variant is being developed with 51,800 lb (23,500 kg) MTOW and a 10 ft 10 ins x 5 ft 10 ins (3.31 x 1.78 m) cargo door.

MAPO-MiG (Russia)

Corporate address: See Combat section for company details.

Mikoyan MiG-110

First flight: 1996.
Chief designers: Nikolai Matyuk and Lev Shengelaya.
Role: Light multi-purpose civil/military transport.
Airframe life: 25,000 flying hours.

★ Aims

★ Minimum unit and operating costs. Strictly defined specific fuel consumption of 222 g per km/tonne payload.
★ High payload and range capabilities combined with short take-off and landing. Can be used from unprepared airfields.
★ Easy conversion between cargo, passenger and passenger/cargo versions.

▲ Development

▲ 1980. Counter-insurgency (COIN) aircraft similar to the US OV-10 Bronco was thrown open to competition to meet the needs of the Afghanistan conflict. The Mikoyan design, called izdelye 101, won the competition against Sukhoi and Ilyushin designs. Later, when interest in the COIN aircraft faded, the 101 was transformed into 101M and 101N designs for general purpose aircraft with a 4,409 lb (2,000 kg) payload.
▲ February 1992. Design work on izdelye 110 (MiG-110) began on the basis of 101, with the maximum payload increased to 11,023 lb (5,000 kg).
▲ 30 December 1993. The Russian Government elected to offer financial aid and preferential loans to the Nizhnyi Novgorod factory to prepare for series manufacture of the MiG-110.
Sales: Demand estimated at more than 1,000 aircraft for CIS civil aviation and more than 300 for the armed forces.
Crew: 2.

Mikoyan MiG-110 multi-purpose transport (Piotr Butowski)

Passengers: 39 or mixed passenger/cargo layout. See Freight hold capacity.
Pressurization: Flight deck and cabin.
Freight hold capacity: Up to 11,023 lb (5,000 kg), including a UAZ-452 truck/pickup plus ZAK-1 container, or 4 ZAK-1 containers, or bulk freight. See Passengers.
Freight hold access: Beaver-tail rear fuselage, with built-in ramp in the hinged lower section. Side door of 2 ft 4 ins x 1 ft 8 ins (0.7 x 0.5 m) for crew and passengers is located in port side of the forward fuselage.
Wing characteristics: High mounted, with approximately 7° anhedral for the inner sections from the fuselage to the booms, thereafter 0° or slight anhedral only for the outer panels.
Wing control surfaces: Aileron, 2-section double-slotted trailing-edge flaps, and leading-edge slats (about 75% span of outer panels).
Tail control surfaces: 2-section elevator (with tab) on the joining tailplane. Twin fins and rudders, canted slightly inward.
Engines: 2 Klimov/Sarkisov TV7-117SV turboprops.
Engine rating: Each 2,500 shp (1,864 kW).

DETAILS FOR MIG-110.

Principal dimensions:
Wing span: 72 ft 7 ins (22.12 m)
Maximum length: 60 ft 8 ins (18.5 m)
Maximum height: 17 ft 8.5 ins (5.4 m)

Cabin:
Length: 29 ft 6 ins (9 m) with ramp, 24 ft 3 ins (7.4 m) without ramp
Width: 9 ft 1 ins (2.76 m) maximum, 7 ft 3 ins (2.2 m) at floor
Height: 7 ft 3 ins (2.2 m)

Undercarriage:
Type: Retractable, with twin wheels on each unit.

Weights:
Maximum take-off: 33,731 lb (15,300 kg)
Payload: 11,023 lb (5,000 kg)

Performance:
Cruise speed: 270 kts (311 mph) 500 km/h
Required runway length, concrete: 1,970 ft (600 m) with full payload
Required runway length, unprepared: 1,542 ft (470 m) with a 7,716 lb (3,500 kg) payload
Required runway length, hot-and-high conditions: 2,395 ft (730 m) with 3,500 kg payload
Ceiling: 26,245-36,090 ft (8,000-11,000 m)
Range with full fuel: 2,187 naut miles (2,516 miles) 4,050 km, with 30 minutes reserve
Range with full payload: 837 naut miles (963 miles) 1,550 km, with 30 minutes reserve

NPO Molniya (Russia)

Full name: Molniya Scientific and Industrial Enterprise.
Corporate address: 4 Novoposelkovaja, Moscow 123459.
Telephone: +7 095 493 3335, 5093 and 497 4760
Facsimile: +7 095 492 9371
Information: Michael Gofin (Marketing Director).

● Activities

● To supplement reduced work on the Buran Space Shuttle programme, Molniya now develops civil aircraft.
● See also General Aviation section for the Molniya 1, 100 and 300.

Molniya 400

Role: Freighter, with possible passenger/cargo combi derivative.

Molniya 400 in airliner configuration (courtesy Molniya)

▲ Development

▲ 1994. Feasibility study has been completed, leading to preliminary design.
▲ 2000. Possible start of production, given adequate funding.
Freight hold access: Ramp/door under the rear fuselage on freighter version. Airliner does not have this facility.
Wing characteristics: Swept, high mounted, with drag-reducing winglets. Slightly swept, low-mounted canards with winglets.
Wing control surfaces: Appears to have ailerons, flaps and multi-section spoilers.
Tail control surfaces: Mid-mounted tailplane with 2-section elevators. Rudder.

DETAILS FOR MOLNIYA 400.

Principal dimensions:
Wing span: 140 ft 1 ins (42.7 m)
Maximum length: 136 ft 2 ins (41.5 m)
Maximum height: 51 ft 0.5 ins (15.56 m)

Cabin:
Length: 65 ft 8 ins (20 m)
Width: 13 ft 2 ins (4 m)
Height: 13 ft 6 ins to 14 ft 5 ins (4.1 to 4.4 m)

Undercarriage:
Type: Retractable, with twin nosewheels and 6-wheel main bogies

Weights:
Maximum take-off: 242,067 lb (109,800 kg)
Overload take-off weight: 266,759 lb (121,000 kg)
Payload: 66,139 lb (30,000 kg)
Overload payload: 110,230 lb (50,000 kg)

Performance:
Maximum speed: 502 kts (578 mph) 930 km/h
Cruise speed: 410-432 kts (472-497 mph) 760-800 km/h
Take-off distance: 4,035 ft (1,230 m)
Required runway length at overload weight: 8,530 ft (2,600 m)
Range with full fuel: 6,048 naut miles (6,960 miles) 11,200 km
Range with full payload: 2,700 naut miles (3,106 miles) 5,000 km
Range at overload weights 1,620 naut miles (1,864 miles) 3,000 km

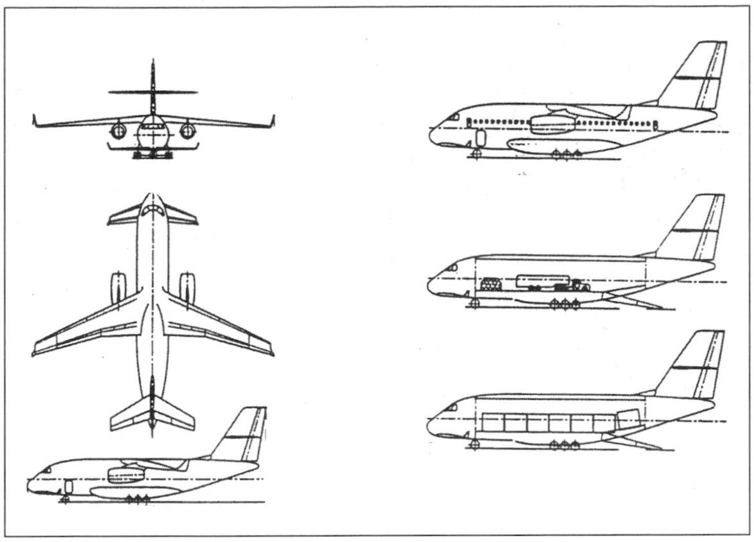

Molniya 400 views, with and without rear loading ramp (courtesy Molniya)

Engines: 2 Aviadvigatel PS-90A turbofans.
Engine rating: Each 35,274 lbf (156.9 kN).
Fuel system: 106,924 lb (48,500 kg).
Flight avionics/instrumentation: IFR and ICAO Category II landing. Modern suite.

Molniya 1000 Heracles

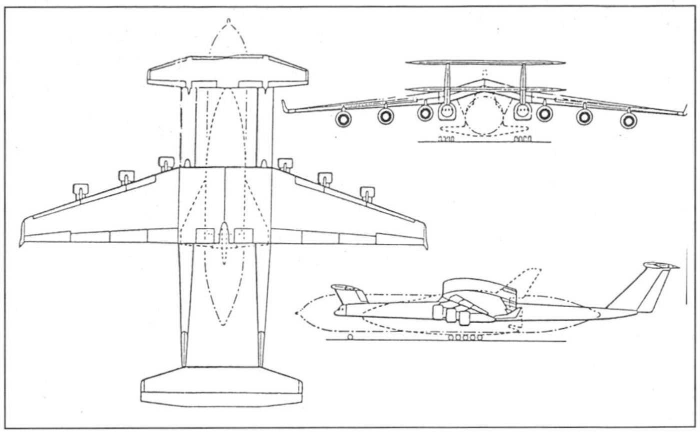

Molniya 1000 Heracles super heavy freighter (courtesy Molniya)

Role: Super-heavy freighter, as a follow-on to the Myasishchev VM-T Atlant and Antonov An-225 Mriya as a space payload carrier.

▲ Development

▲ 1994. Feasibility study underway.
▲ 2002. Possible production start-up, if funded.

Crew: Unique crew accommodation, with a cockpit in each of the 2 fuselage boom noses.
Payloads: Similar to those detailed under the Myasishchev Atlant.
Freight hold access: Open airframe, with booms/wings attaching to the space shuttle or other payload.
Wing characteristics: Large single piece canard on fin-type pylons at the nose, above the cockpits. Huge high-mounted wing, forming an inverted V at the centre section and with anhedral outer panels, with winglets.
Wing control surfaces: Multi-section leading- and trailing-edge control surfaces on both the wings and canard (see drawing).
Tail control surfaces: Huge twin fins supported on the booms, with rudders, carring a single-piece high-mounted tailplane with full-width elevator.
Engines: 6 Samara turbojets in pods under the wing. Alternatively, General Electric CF6-90VH or Pratt & Whitney PW4084 turbofans.
Fuel system: 789,250 lb (358,000 kg)

DETAILS FOR HERACLES.

Principal dimensions:
Wing span: 296 ft 7 ins (90.4 m)
Maximum length: 240 ft 10 ins (73.4 m)
Maximum height: 57 ft 5 ins (17.5 m)

Undercarriage:
Type: Retractable, with 5 rows of 4 wheels under the payload plus nosewheels

Weights:
Maximum take-off: 1,984,150 lb (900,000 kg)
Payload: 992,080 lb (450,000 kg)

Performance:
Maximum speed: 454 kts (522 mph) 840 km/h
Take-off distance: 7,775 ft (2,370 m)
Range with full fuel: 4,210-5,560 naut miles (4,846-6,400 miles) 7,800-10,300 km, with 240,000 kg payload
Range with full payload: 1,242-1,674 naut miles (1,430-1,926 miles) 2,300-3,100 km

Myasishchev Design Bureau (Russia)

Corporate address: See Combat section for all company details.

Myasishchev 3MS-2 and VM-T Atlant (NATO name *Bison*)

First flight: 20 January 1953 (M-4 *Bison-A* bomber), piloted by Fyodor Opadchiy. 29 April 1981 for the first flight of the VM-T without a load (under Commander Pilot A. Kucherenko) and 6 April 1982 for the first flight with a load (fuel tank of an Energia rocket).
Role: Ex-heavy free-fall bomber, converted into a flight refuelling tanker and now also a special transport aircraft supporting activities at the Baikonur cosmodrome.
Sales: 92 *Bisons* of all versions were manufactured between 1954 and 1963 by Factory No 23 in Moscow-Fili. At present only a few remain with the Russian Air Force. These are known as 3MS-2 *Bison-B* tankers, operated by the 1230th Tanker Air Regiment at Engels air base but now grounded and utilized as reserve aircraft. 2 *Bisons* were converted into VM-T transports for use by the Myasishchev design bureau.
Crew: 7, occupying 2 pressurized cabins, all with downward ejection seats.
Freight capacity (VM-T): 4 types of load, maximum length 147.6 ft (45 m), maximum diameter 26 ft (8 m), and maximum frontal area 506 sq ft (47 m^2), can be carried on over-fuselage mounts, as follows:
Type 0GT, the Buran space shuttle airframe, without tailfin, weighing 99,869 lb (45,300 kg).

Myasishchev 3MS-2 tanker, one of the last photographs of a military Bison in flight (Piotr Butowski)

Type 1GT, the central hydrogen fuel tank of the Energia rocket, with nose and rear fairings added, weighing 69,445 lb (31,500 kg).
Type 2GT, the oxygen tank, instrument compartment, engine compartment and head of the central stage of the Energia rocket, connected into one unit with nose fairing added weighing 66,138 lb (30,000 kg).
Type 3GT, the connected nose and rear fairings of the 1GT load, for return from Baikonur cosmodrome to the rocket factory, weighing 33,069 lb (15,000 kg).
Tail unit: Conventional swept tailplane and single fin for tanker versions. VM-T has a large-span H-type tail unit, with a heavily-dihedral tailplane and inward-canted endplate fins and rudders.
Fuselage: VM-T was given a completely new rear fuselage of strengthened type.
Engines: 3MS-2 has 4 Zubets RD-3M-500A turbojets (each 20,945 lbf, 93.17 kN). VM-T has 4 Rybinsk/Dobrynin VD-7MDs (each 23,700 lbf, 105.43 kN).
Radar: Rubin nav/attack radar in the nose.
Fixed weapons: 3MS-2 has 3 cannon turrets, each with 2 x 23-mm AM-23 cannon. VM-T has none.
Aircraft variants:
3MS-2 *Bison-B* is the tanker conversion of the 3MS bomber.
VM-T (Vladimir Myasishchev, Transportnyi, originally named 3M-T, izdelye 3-35) Atlant is the heavy-lift transport conversion of the 3M, as detailed previously. Development began Autumn 1978. The rear fuselage is completely new, the wing structure strengthened, the control system altered, and new VD-7MD engines installed. Since the load generates a strong air turbulence, the classic tail unit of the 3M was replaced by a double (H-shaped) empennage. Over 200 flights by early 1995, accumulating some 800 flying hours.
Demonstrator is a proposed flying test bed derivative of the VM-T for launching multi-use space vehicles (reusable ejection system). The aircraft would be the subsonic first-stage, the winged hypersonic booster with liquid-propellant rocket engine the second stage, and the scaled orbital vehicle (Horus, Hermes, Hotol,

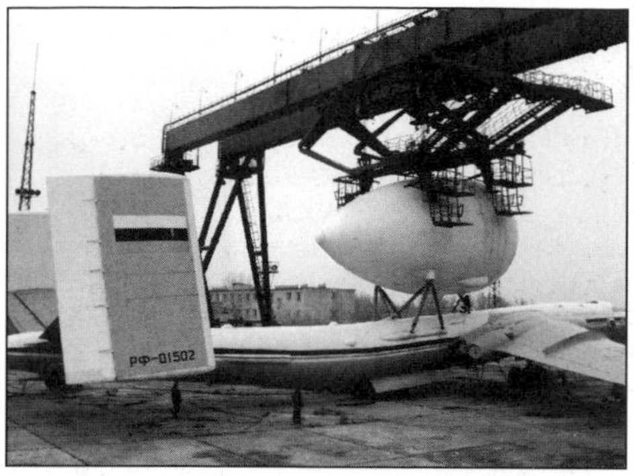

Myasishchev VM-T Atlant with a 3GT cargo, the connected nose and rear fairings of a 1GT load (Piotr Butowski)

etc) or expendable booster rocket the third stage. The Demonstrator could be responsible for launching up to 2,866 lb (1,300 kg) payloads into orbit. The rocket-space vehicle weight in all versions could be 50-60 tonnes (orbiter 18 tonnes).

DETAILS FOR 3MS-2 BISON-B.

Principal dimensions:
Wing span: 174 ft 4 ins (53.14 m)
Maximum length: 159 ft 11.5 ins (48.76 m)
Maximum height: 37 ft 9 ins (11.50 m)

Wings:
Area, gross: 3,787 sq ft (351.78 m^2)
Aspect ratio: 8.03
Sweepback: 34° 48′

Undercarriage:
Type: Retractable single-track type, with underwing supports
Wheel track (wingtip supports): 171 ft 8.5 ins (52.34 m)

Weights:
Empty, operating: 166,978 lb (75,740 kg)
Maximum take-off: 423,287 lb (192,000 kg)

Performance:
Maximum speed: 491 kts (565 mph) 910 km/h
Take-off speed: 167 kts (193 mph) 310 km/h
Landing speed: 113 kts (130 mph) 210 km/h
Ceiling: 40,190 ft (12,250 m)
G limits: 2.0

DETAILS FOR VM-T ATLANT.

Principal dimensions:
Wing span: 174 ft 4 ins (53.16 m)
Maximum length: 168 ft (51.2 m)
Maximum height: 34 ft 9 ins (10.6 m)

Wings:
Area, gross: 3,787 sq ft (351.78 m^2)
Aspect ratio: 8.033
Sweepback: 34° 48′

Weights:
Maximum take-off (0GT type load): 411,162 lb (186,500 kg)
Maximum landing weight (0GT type load): 305,340 lb (138,500 kg)

Performance:
Typical cruise speed: 243 kts (280 mph) 450 km/h
Required runway length: 11,485 ft (3,500 m)
Range with maximum load (0GT type): 810 naut miles (932 miles) 1,500 km

Myasishchev M-90 Air Ferry (MGS)

First flight: Project only; not flown.
Role: Multi-purpose very-heavy-lift transportation system for outsized equipment, cargo containers, liquid and granular loads, and passengers.
Crew: 4.

★ Aims

★ Modular construction using independent trailer-platforms which form part of the aircraft's structure, allowing the aircraft to be configured according to the cargo to be airlifted.
★ Nacelle-modules could include cylindrical modules for bulk goods requiring no special packaging. Alternative containers in 5, 10, 20 and 30 tonne units.
★ Trailer-platform for operations from unimproved runways.
★ Projected need for 30-35 in Russia.

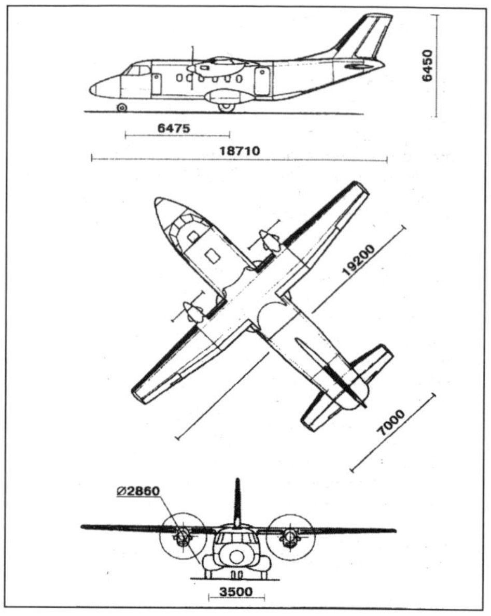

Myasishchev M-112 convertible cargo/28 passenger transport (courtesy Myasishchev)

M-90 AIR FERRY	MGS-6	MGS-8
Wing span	315 ft (96 m)	315 ft (96 m)
Length overall	210 ft (64 m)	210 ft (64 m)
Height overall	64 ft 3 ins (19.6 m)	64 ft 3 ins (19.6 m)
Tailplane span	118 ft (36 m)	118 ft (36 m)
Wheel base	210 ft (64 m)	210 ft (64 m)
Wheel track	51 ft 5 ins (15.66 m)	51 ft 5 ins (15.66 m)
Take-off weight	1,433,000 lb (650,000 kg)	1,873,925 lb (850,000 kg)
Payload	551,150 lb (250,000 kg)	up to 881,850 lb (400,000 kg)
Maximum cargo dimensions (width x height x length)	40 x 26.25 x 197 ft (12 x 8 x 60 m)	40 x 26.25 x 197 ft (12 x 8 x 60 m)
Cruise speed	356 kts (410 mph) 660 km/h	356 kts (410 mph) 660 km/h
Cruise altitude	up to 32,800 ft (10,000 m)	up to 32,800 ft (10,000 m)
Range	2,590 naut miles (2,980 miles) 4,800 km	2,430 naut miles (2,800 miles) 4,500 km
Required runway length	8,200 ft (2,500 m)	9,850 ft (3,000m)
Engines	6 x 55,100 lbf (245.2 kN) Samara NK-62 or 66,140 lbf (294.2 kN) NK-63 propfans	8 x NK-62 or 63 propfans

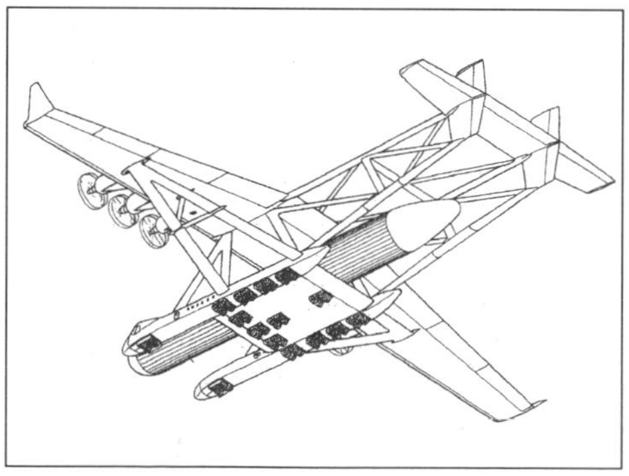

Myasishchev M-90 Air Ferry in MGS-6 configuration (courtesy Myasishchev)

Myasishchev M-112

First flight: Not flown at the time of writing.
Certification: To meet FAR/JAR Pt 25 requirements, and those of the Russian Aviaregister.
Role: Multi-purpose wide-body transport, primarily for cargo carrying but with a quickly convertible interior for passenger carrying or ambulance. Other possible roles could include training and patrol. Envisaged operations require independence from ground support equipment.
Airframe life: 30,000 flying hours.

▲ Development

▲ Developed from the initial 24-passenger MM-1 project.
▲ Development began in association with Tec Avia Inc Management Group of Germany.
▲ Quick conversion from cargo to passenger layout. Conversion takes 1 hour 30 minutes.
▲ 1994. Model displayed at Berlin ILA-94.

Crew/passengers: 1 or 2 pilots. Up to 28 passengers in the cabin at 30 ins (76 cm) pitch, Passenger door with airstair.
Freight hold: Up to 6,614 lb (3,000 kg) of cargo in the cabin. Hoist is fitted for mechanically-assisted loading/unloading. Hatch under the upswept tail with a ramp/door, allowing straight in loading of cargo, including vehicles.
Pressurization system: 5.8 psi cabin differential.
Wing control surfaces: Ailerons (port tab) and single-slotted Fowler flaps.

Details for M-112.

Principal dimensions:
Wing span: 63 ft (19.2 m)
Maximum length: 61 ft 5 ins (18.71 m)
Maximum height: 21 ft 2 ins (6.45 m)

Cabin:
Length: 24 ft 3 ins (7.4 m)
Width: 8 ft 2.5 ins (2.5 m)
Height: 6 ft 7 ins (2 m)

Undercarriage:
Type: Retractable, with twin steerable nosewheels. Low pressure tyres for operation from unpaved airfields
Wheel base: 21 ft 3 ins (6.475 m)
Wheel track: 11 ft 6 ins (3.5 m)

Weights:
Maximum take-off: 20,283 lb (9,200 kg)
Payload: 6,614 lb (3,000 kg) maximum, 5,291 lb (2,400 kg) normal

Performance:
Cruise speed: 243 kts (280 mph) 450 km/h
Take-off distance over a 50 ft (15 m) obstacle: 2,870 ft (875 m)
Landing distance over a 50 ft (15 m) obstacle: 2,034 ft (620 m)
Operating ceiling: 24,935 ft (7,600 m)
Range: 448 naut miles (516 miles) 830 km
Ferry range: 1,728 naut miles (1,988 miles) 3,200 km

Tail control surfaces: Elevators and rudder, all with tabs.
Engines: 2 Pratt & Whitney Canada PT6A turboprops. Alternatively, TVD-20M or TVD-1500 engines.
Engine rating: 1,657 shp (1,235.6 kW) for PT6As (see Engine tables for others), with 5/6-blade constant-speed low-noise propellers.
Fuel system: 2,500 litres.
Flight control system: All manual except for hydraulic flaps and electric tabs.
Electrical system: 28 volt DC supply, including 4 x 25 amp-hour batteries. 115 volt/400Hz and 26 volt/400Hz AC supplies, using 2 x 30 volt/400 amp engine-driven starter-generators. Available APU.
Braking system: Hydraulic type.
De-icing system: Electric for cockpit windows, propellers and pitot. Engine bleed air for all leading edges and air intakes.
Radar: Weather type.
Flight avionics/instrumentation: IFR. AlliedSignal Bendix/King. Optional avionics of Russian manufacture.

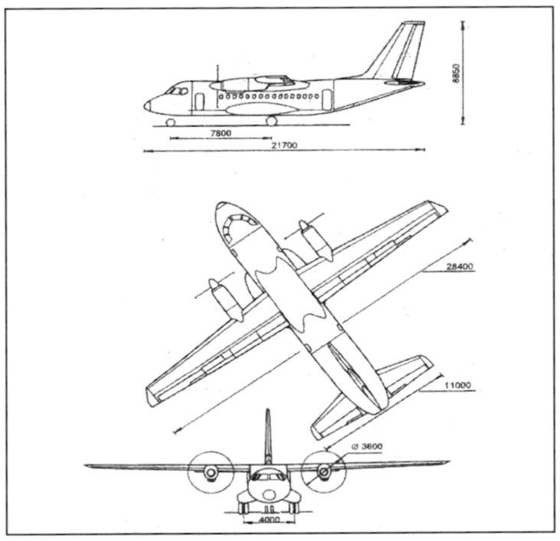

Myasishchev M-150 convertible commuter transport (courtesy Myasishchev)

Myasishchev M-150

First flight: Not flown at the time of writing.
Role: Projected convertible commuter/cargo transport, also for executive, military transport, ambulance, polar, patrol, reconnaissance, and search and rescue. Suited to hot-and-high operations, and capable of using unpaved airfields at up to 6,900 ft (2,100 m) in hot climates.
Crew: 2.
Passengers: 55 normal, or 60 maximum. Passenger doors on both sides of the fuselage.
Freight hold access: Hatch under the upswept rear fuselage for straight-in loading of cargo, when operating as a freighter.
Wing control surfaces: Believed to be ailerons (with tabs), multi-section flaps and multi-section spoilers.
Tail control surfaces: Elevators (with tabs) and rudder.
Engines: 2 Klimov TV7-117-3 turboprops or Pratt & Whitney Canada PW127 turboprops.
Engine rating: Each 2,500 shp (1,864 kW) TV7, 2,750 shp (2,051 kW) PW127.
Aircraft variants:
Passenger/cargo as detailed previously.
Rescue version can air-drop survival and other equipment.

Details for M-150.

Principal dimensions:
Wing span: 93 ft 2 ins (28.4 m)
Maximum length: 71 ft 2 ins (21.7 m)
Maximum height: 29 ft (8.85 m)

Cabin:
Length: 36 ft 1 ins (11 m)
Width: 9 ft 10 ins (3 m)
Height: 6 ft 7 ins (2 m)

Tail unit:
Tailplane span: 36 ft 1 ins (11 m)

Undercarriage:
Type: Retractable, with twin steerable nosewheels. Main units retract into large nacelles on the fuselage sides to keep the main cabin clear of obstructions
Wheel base: 25 ft 7 ins (7.8 m)
Wheel track: 13 ft 2 ins (4 m)

Weights:
Maximum take-off: 42,990 lb (19,500 kg)
Payload: 12,346 lb (5,600 kg)

Performance:
Maximum speed: 297 kts (342 mph) 550 km/h
Cruise altitude: 19,700-23,000 ft (6,000-7,000 m)
Range with full payload: 648 naut miles (746 miles) 1,200 km

Sukhoi Design Bureau (Russia)

Corporate address: See Combat section for company details. See also General Aviation section.

Sukhoi S-80

First flight: Had been expected in 1994. Now 1995?
Role: Light military/civil multi-purpose cargo and passenger transport, with STOL features. Also suitable to patrol, surveillance, survey, medevac and more.
Sales: First production aircraft is under construction at the Komsomolsk-on-Amur plant (no prototype built by Sukhoi design bureau). Full production to start in 1997. Demand in the CIS for 1,800-2,000 aircraft of this class.
Passengers: 26, or 21 paratroops, or 10 litters.
Freight hold capacity: Nearly 6,834 lb (3,100 kg) of cargo.
Freight hold access: Rear loading ramp/door, plus door on the port side of the mid fuselage.
Wing control surfaces: Ailerons, double-slotted trailing-edge flaps, and leading-edge slats between engine nacelles and wingtips. Winglets.
Tail control surfaces: Tail unit supported by twin booms. Slightly inward canted fins. Additional aerodynamic surface/support between the rear fuselage and booms. Horn-balanced rudders with tabs and narrow-chord elevator.
Engines: 2 turboprops, initially Rybinsk/Novikov TVD-1500Bs with 6-blade AV-36 propellers. 1,870 shp

Details for S-80.

Principal dimensions:
Wing span: 76 ft 0.5 ins (23.177 m)
Maximum length: 54 ft 9 ins (16.68 m)
Maximum height: 18 ft 3 ins (5.56 m)

Cabin:
Length: 20 ft 8 ins (6.3 m)
Width: 7 ft 1 ins (2.15 m)
Height: 6 ft 3 ins (1.9 m)

Wings:
Area: 473.61 sq ft (44 m^2)
Aspect ratio: 12.208
Anhedral: About 1° 30′ on outer panels

Tail unit:
Tailplane span: 16 ft (4.88 m)
Fin area: 71.47 sq ft (6.64 m^2)

Undercarriage:
Type: Retractable, with steerable nosewheels (38°). Twin wheels on each unit
Main wheel tyre size: 660 x 200 mm
Nose wheel tyre size: 500 x 180 mm
Wheel base: 21 ft 4 ins (6.5 m)
Wheel track: 18 ft 4.5 ins (5.6 m)

Weights:
Empty, operating: 14,330 lb (6,500 kg)
Maximum take-off: 24,251 lb (11,000 kg)
Maximum landing: 22,928 lb (10,400 kg)
Payload: Nearly 6,834 lb (3,100 kg) with CT7 engines, 5,512 lb (2,500 kg) otherwise

Performance:
Maximum speed: 270 kts (311 mph) 500 km/h
Cruise speed: 194-259 kts (224-298 mph) 360-480 km/h
Take-off speed: 65 kts (75 mph) 120 km/h
Take-off distance: 1,181 ft (360 m)
Take-off over a 50 ft (15 m) obstacle: 2,723 ft (830 m)
Landing distance: 591 ft (180 m)
Landing distance over a 50 ft (15 m) obstacle: 2,494 ft (760 m)
Maximum climb rate: 2,953 ft (900 m) per minute
Ceiling: 26,245 ft (8,000 m)
Range with full fuel: 2,430 naut miles (2,796 miles) 4,500 km
Range with full payload: 675 naut miles (777 miles) 1,250 km

Sukhoi S-80 multi-purpose transport (Piotr Butowski)

(1,394.5 kW) General Electric CT7-9Bs will become an alternative, with flight testing to start in 1996 (Rybinsk will offer overhaul and support for the CT7 in Russia). Power reserve permits extended capabilities in the future.
Engine rating: Each 1,300 shp (969.4 kW).
Fuel system: 2,500 litres in 2 tanks, weighing 5,225 lb (2,370 kg).
Radar: Navigation/weather radar in undernose radome.
Flight avionics/instrumentation: Rockwell Collins suite on first aircraft. Automatic systems testing.

Aircraft variants:
S-80A (arkticheskiy) is for Arctic operations.
S-80GP (gruzo-passazhirskiy, cargo-passenger) is the standard freighter version.
S-80GR (geologicheskoi razvedki) is for geological exploration.
S-80M (meditsinskiy, medical) is an air ambulance for 10 litters.
S-80P is a passenger version.
S-80PT (patrulno-transportnyi) is a patrol/transport.
S-80R (rybopoiskovyi) is for EEZ/fishery surveillance.
S-80TD (transportno-desantnyi) is the military assault-transport.

Tupolev Joint-Stock Company (Russia)

Tupolev Tu-134UBL Crusty is a modification of the airliner for use as a pilot trainer for Backfire and Blackjack bomber crews. It entered service in 1977 and was assigned to the 184th Regiment in Priluki in 1991 (as illustrated). A navigation trainer variant is the Tu-134Sh, with 12 stations, enlarged radar antenna under the nose plus wing bomb pylons. A naval pilot trainer prototype became the Tu-134UBK. Another militarized Tu-134 variant, with a tail-sting, is the Tu-135 (Piotr Butowski)

Corporate address: See Combat section for company details.

● Activities

- See also General Aviation section.
- A Tu-144D supersonic airliner (1 of 13 Tu-144s built and long out of service but among those maintained at the Zhukovsky Flight Test Centre) is now known to have been the aircraft numbered 101 that set a series of height with payload and speed records in 1983.
- Under a 15 September 1994 agreement, NASA is using a Tu-144D airliner (with 87 flying hours since construction in 1982) to assist the US High-Speed Civil Transport programme in association with Boeing, McDonnell Douglas, Rockwell, General Electric and Pratt & Whitney. It is being re-engined with NK-25s under the US$8 million 3-year programme.

Tupolev Tu-130 and Tu-132

First flight: Project announced in 1993. Could fly in 1996?
Role: Light civil/military convertible cargo/passenger transport, for autonomous operation.
Crew: 2
Passengers: As an alternative to freight, can be configured for 53 passengers.
Seat pitch: 30.7 ins (78 cm).
Freight hold volume: 1,850.5 cu ft (52.4 m^3)
Freight hold capacity: Up to 11,020 lb (5,000 kg) of cargo, including 4 containers, pallets or light vehicles.
Freight hold access: Beaver-tail rear fuselage, with rear loading ramp for straight-in loading. Ramp size 11 ft 6 ins x 9 ft 2 ins (3.5 x 2.8 m). Side loading door in forward fuselage, port side.
Wing control surfaces: Looks to be an aileron and 2-section flaps per wing. No slats.
Tail control surfaces: Conventional elevators and rudder.
Fuselage: Circular front fuselage cross-section, squaring off towards the rear.
Engines: 2 Klimov/Sarkisov TV7-117-3 turboprops.
Engine rating: Each 2,500 shp (1,864 kW).
Aircraft variants:
Tu-130 is the standard propulsion version, as detailed.
Tu-132 is similar but has its turboprops adapted for liquefied gas fuel.

Tupolev Tu-130 (Piotr Butowski)

Tupolev Tu-154M, M2 and S Freighter (NATO name *Careless*)

First flight: 4 October 1968 for Tu-154 prototype, 1982 for the Tu-152M. 1995 for Tu-154M2?
First delivery: 1971 (Tu-154 for early cargo, airmail and passenger flights, with scheduled services by Aeroflot from February 1972). Tu-154M first delivered on27 December 1984.
Role: Medium-range airliner.
Airframe life: 20,000 flying hours or 15,000 cycles.
Sales: Some 900 Tu-154s of all versions were built up to early 1995, of which around 180 were Tu-154Ms. Approximately 760 remain in service. Converted models include the noteworthy Tu-155 for trials with cryogenic fuels, having deep-cooled (lower than 120K) liquefied hydrogen (one NK-88 engine) and methane (one NK-89 engine).
Details: Tu-154M.
Crew: 2 pilots and a flight engineer.
Passengers: Various layouts including 24 first and 154 tourist class, 164 all-tourist class, and 180 all-economy class (6 abreast).
Galley: To the customer's requirements.
Pressurization: 8.41 psi.
Freight hold volume: 176.6 cu ft (5 m^3) under the cabin floor, at rear. Unpressurized.
Size of freight doors: 3 ft x 3 ft 7 ins (0.9 x 1.1 m).
Baggage holds: 759.3 cu ft (21.5 m^3) forward, 582.7 cu ft (16.5 m^3) aft. Pressurized. 2 access doors, each 3 ft 11 ins x 4 ft 5 ins (1.2 x 1.35 m).
Wing control surfaces: Ailerons (with tabs), triple-slotted trailing-edge flaps, leading-edge slats and 4-section spoilers. 4 overwing fences.
Tail control surfaces: T tail, with variable incidence tailplane, elevators with tabs, and rudder.
Flight control system: Hydraulic, but with electric slat, tailplane incidence and tab actuation.
Construction materials: Metal, with tail moving surfaces using honeycomb cores.

DETAILS FOR TU-130.

Principal dimensions:
Wing span: 87 ft 1 ins (26.54 m)
Maximum length: 74 ft 8 ins (22.75 m)
Maximum height: 27 ft 3 ins (8.3 m)

Cabin:
Length: 27 ft 11 ins (8.5 m)
Width: 9 ft 2 ins (2.8 m)
Height: 7 ft 3 ins (2.2 m)
Floor area: 256.18 sq ft (23.8 m^2)

Undercarriage:
Type: Retractable, with twin steerable nosewheels. Twin wheels on each main unit, in tandem, retracted into fairings on the fuselage sides

Weights:
Maximum take-off: 46,297 lb (21,000 kg)
Payload: 11,020 lb (5,000 kg)

Performance:
Cruise speed: 270 kts (311 mph) 500 km/h
Required runway length: 5,910 ft (1,800 m)
Ceiling: 22,965 ft (7,000 m)
Range with full payload: 1,080 naut miles (1,243 miles) 2,000 km

DETAILS FOR Tu-154M.

Principal dimensions:
Wing span: 123 ft 2.4 ins (37.55 m)
Maximum length: 157 ft 3 ins (47.925 m)
Maximum height: 37 ft 5 ins (11.4 m)

Cabin:
Width: 11 ft 9 ins (3.58 m)
Height: 6 ft 7.5 ins (2.02 m)
Volume: 5,763.4 cu ft (163.2 m^3)
Main passenger doors: 5 ft 8 ins x 2 ft 7.5 ins (1.73 x 0.8 m)

Wings:
Area: 2,168.4 sq ft (201.45 m^2)
Aspect ratio: 6.999

Tail unit:
Tailplane span: 44 ft (13.4 m)

Undercarriage:
Type: Retractable, with steerable twin nosewheels. 6-wheel main bogies
Wheel base: 62 ft 1 ins (18.92 m)
Wheel track: 37 ft 9 ins (11.5 m)

Weights:
Empty, operating: 121,915 lb (55,300 kg)
Maximum take-off: 220,462 lb (100,000 kg)
Maximum landing: 176,370 lb (80,000 kg)
Payload: 39,683 lb (18,000 kg)

Performance:
Maximum cruise speed: 513 kts (590 mph) 950 km/h
Required field length: 8,205 ft (2,500 m)
Operating ceiling: 39,040 ft (11,900 m)
Range with full fuel: 3,564 naut miles (4,100 miles) 6,600 km
Range with full payload: 2,106 naut miles (2,423 miles) 3,900 km

Tupolev Tu-154M with thrust reversers deployed

Engines: 3 Aviadvigatel D-30KU-154 II by-pass turbojets (turbofans).
Engine rating: Each 23,149 lbf (103 kN) at take-off. TA-92 APU.
Fuel system: 87,634 lb (39,750 kg). To ensure reliability, fuel from all 6 wing tanks is routed via a collector tank.
Electrical system: 3-phase AC supply via a 40 kVA alternator to each engine, producing 200/115 volt at 400Hz. 36 volt, 400Hz stand-by AC supply. 27 volt DC supply. 4 batteries.
Hydraulic system: Triple, each 3,002 psi.
Braking system: Disc, with anti-skid on main units.
De-icing system: Bleed air for engine inlets, wing and tail unit leading edges. Electric for slats.
Radar: Weather radar.
Flight avionics/instrumentation: Meets ICAO Cat II. Includes autopilot, triple inertial navigation system, ground proximity warning system, and HF/VHF communications.
Aircraft variants:
Tu-154M is the standard airliner, as described.
Tu-154M2 is a new version in 1995, with Aviadvigatel/ Perm Motors PS-90A turbofans, each 35,274 lbf (156.9 kN) for better fuel economy.
Tu-154S is a freighter conversion of any selected variant, but aimed principally at the Tu-154B. 4,061.2 cu ft (115 m^3) of useful volume in the Tu-154B conversion, comprising 2,542.7 cu ft (72 m^3) in the cabin with loading via a 9 ft 2 ins x 6 ft 2 ins (2.8 x 1.87 m) port-side cargo door, and 1,518.5 cu ft (43 m^3) under the floor. Roller tracks and ball matting to ease loading of pallets or other cargoes into the main cabin.

Tupolev Tu-156-M2

Role: Cargo variant of the Tu-154, with NK-89 engines and liquefied natural gas (LNG) fuel (or kerosene).
Engines: 3 Samara NK-89 turbofans.

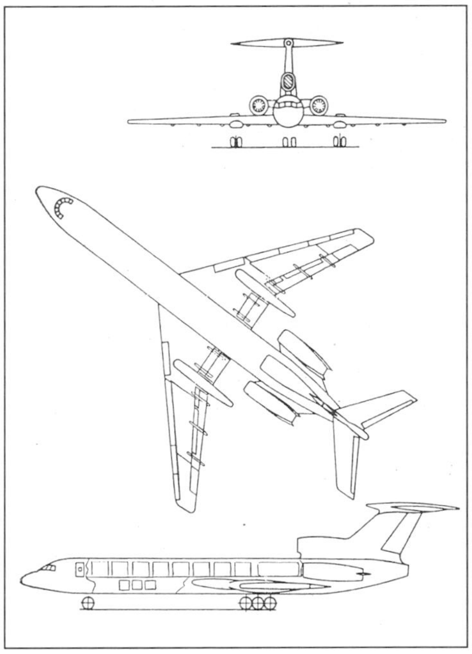

Tupolev Tu-156 LNG cargo transport (courtesy Tupolev)

Engine rating: Each 23,150 lbf (102.97 kN).
Fuel system: 28,880 lb (13,100 kg) of liquefied natural gas fuel, or 24,250 lb (11,000 kg) of kerosene. Specific fuel flow at 36,100 ft (11,000 m), Mach 0.8 with LNG 0.74; fuel flow 400 g/t-km for LNG, 438.8 g/t-km for kerosene.

DETAILS FOR Tu-156M2.

Principal dimensions: As for Tu-154M

Cabin:
Length: 60 ft (18.3 m) cargo compartment
Cargo door: 8 ft 2.5 ins x 5 ft 4 ins (2.5 x 1.62 m)

Weights:
Empty, operating: 126,545 lb (57,400 kg)
Maximum take-off: 220,462 lb (100,000 kg)
Payload: 32,187 lb (14,600 kg)

Performance:
Flight speed: 459 kts (528 mph) 850 km/h
Required runway length: 8,205 ft (2,500 m) at sea level, ISA
Range with full payload: 1,863 naut miles (2,144 miles) 3,450 km

Tupolev Tu-204 and Oriol-Avia Airlines Tu-204 Freighter

First flight: 2 January 1989 (piloted by A. Talalakine).
Certification: 29 December 1994 for Tu-204-100.
First delivery: 1994.
Role: Medium-range airliner, and freighter conversion.
Airframe life: 60,000 flying hours or 45,000 cycles.
Sales: Deliveries up to early 1995 to Vnukovo Airlines (3, with 3 more on order), Rossiya (2, plus 2 on order), Uzbekistan Airways (1, with 2 on order), Oriol-Avia (2 plus 1 freighter, with 3 more ordered), Aeroflot Russian International Airlines (4 Tu-204Cs, the first received on 7 April 1995), Kazakhstan Airlines (3), and Aviastar/ Volga Dnepr (1). Further firm orders then held plus 268 options; some 21 "white tail" airliners were reportedly awaiting delivery at the Ulyanovsk Aviation Industrial Complex Aviastar in late 1994/early 1995. The Russian Government has ordered 15 for 1995 delivery, plus 15 in 1996, for a newly created state leasing company. Production expected to rise to 35 per year, including those from the second line at KAPO in Kazan (started 1994 with the Tu-204-200). Up to 500 Tu-204s are expected to be built for CIS operators. Major maintenance facility for Russian and East European aircraft at Minsk aviation repair factory.
Details: Principally Tu-204 and Tu-204-100. See Aircraft variants.
Crew: 2 pilot operation. Engineer and observer can be carried.
Passengers: 170-214. Typically 214 in all-tourist class layout (6 abreast), or 190 in mixed layout with 12 first class (4 abreast), 35 business and 143 tourist classes (6 abreast). The Ulyanovsk Aviation Industrial Complex Aviastar has formed a joint company with Diamonite Aircraft Furnishings of the UK as Aviastar Interior Corp, to design, develop, certify and manufacture new interiors for the Tu-204, to FAR Pt 25 standards.
Seat pitch: 31.9 ins (81 cm) tourist, 37.8 ins (96 cm) business and 39 ins (99 cm) first class.
Galleys: 2 buffet galleys standard, forward and rear of the passenger cabins, but with customer options.
Freight/baggage hold volume: 388.46 cu ft (11 m^3) nose for 3 x LD3-46 containers, and 543.85 cu ft (15.4 m^3) tail for 5 x LD3-46s, both under the cabin floor.
Wing control surfaces: Aileron, 2-section double-slotted trailing-edge flap, 5-section spoiler, 4-section leading-edge slat, and 2-section airbrake per wing. Drag reducing winglets.
Tail control surfaces: Elevators and rudder.
Flight control system: Triplex digital fly-by-wire, with analog stand-by.
Construction materials: Metal, including aluminium-lithium and titanium, but with composites used for the wingroot fairings, parts of the tail unit, plus various skins and panels, representing some 18% of the structural weight.
Engines: 2 Aviadvigatel PS-90A turbofans. TA-12-60 APU housed in the tailcone.
Engine rating: Each 35,583 lbf (158.3 kN) at take-off.
Fuel system: 72,090 lb (32,700 kg) or equivalent for series 100 and 200. See Aircraft variants.
Electrical system: 200/115 volt AC supply at 400 Hz via 2 generators. 27 volt DC supply.
Hydraulic system: Triple system, each 3,002 psi.
Braking system: Carbon discs, with anti-skid system.
Fire system: 2 litre Halon portable extinguisher in the cockpit, 3 x 6 litre extinguishers on the 9g bulkhead restraint barrier in the courier compartment, 2 x 2 litre Halon and water extinguishers in the emergency equipment closet, and 6 litre Halon extinguisher in the main cargo compartment of the freighter versions.
Flight avionics/instrumentation: ICAO Cat IIIa standards. 6 CRT displays for flight, navigation, engine and systems information, triplex autopilot, Honeywell

Tupolev Tu-204 used as a Russian Presidential transport (Piotr Butowski)

Tupolev Tu-204C cabin, with cargo door open. Note the sill protectors and pallet guides hinged up at the door, the mat and main roller tracks (Piotr Butowski)

inertial reference system, VOR, DME, satellite navigation, and more. HF/VHF communications.

Aircraft variants:

Tu-204 was the initial version built, with PS-90A engines, 208,557 lb (94,600 kg) take-off weight, 46,297 lb (21,000 kg) payload and 52,910 lb (24,000 kg) of fuel.

Tu-204-100 is a principal PS-90A-engined version with a maximum take-off weight of 227,075 lb (103,000 kg), allowing an increase in fuel load for longer range. A prototype derivative with Rolls-Royce RB211-535 engines made its maiden flight on 14 August 1992 as the Tu-204-120, while this variant with Rockwell Collins avionics became Tu-204-122.

Tu-204-100C has a 51,108 lb (23,500 kg) payload and 1,944 naut miles (2,237 miles) 3,600 km range.

Tu-204-200 has PS-90A engines but with a take-off weight of 244,162 lb (110,750 kg), allowing the payload to increase to 55,556 lb (25,200 kg) and fuel load to rise to 40,730 litres. 212-214 passengers.

Tu-204-200C has a 64,595 lb (29,300 kg) payload and 2,608 naut miles (3,000 miles) 4,830 km range.

Tu-204-220 is now redesignated Tu-224 (which see). A variant with Rockwell Collins avionics was initially known as Tu-204-222. Available from 1996. Projected variant has Pratt & Whitney PW 2240 engines.

Tu-204-230 is a projected variant with 2 x NK-93 propfans.

Tu-204-300 is now redesignated Tu-234 (which see).

Tu-204C is a windowless (in cabin) freighter variant of any model (including Tu-224 and 234), built as such and not a subsequent conversion but with most of the features first worked into the Oriol-Avia Freighter conversion. Large port-side cargo door. Floor-mounted ball mat at the cargo door entrance and thereafter roller tracks.

Oriol-Avia Airlines Freighter is a conversion of the Tu-204, initially developed from Tupolev engineering data by Aviastar for Oriol-Avia use. The initial conversion has the same take-off, landing and fuel weights, and engines, as the Tu-204 it has been produced from. Cargo door 11 ft 2 ins x 7 ft 2 ins (3.405 x 2.19 m), with 73° upward-hinging movement. All passenger doors deactivated except for those forward and aft. Courier compartment, with 3 airline seats and a tip-up seat. Allowable floor loading up to 57.35 lb/sq ft (280 kg/m^2), with maximum pallet weight (7 ft 4 ins x 9 ft, 2.235 x 2.743 m) of 3,307 lb (1,500 kg) for the initial conversion, with subsequent freighters having up to 83.97 lb/sq ft (410 kg/m^2), and pallet weight up to 5,512-6,834 lb (2,500-3,100 kg), including larger pallet size. Operating empty weight of the Tu-204 Freighter is 123,106 lb (55,840 kg), allowing a 51,720 lb (23,460 kg) payload.

Details for Tu-204-100, *with Tu-204-200 in italics.*

Principal dimensions:
Wing span: 137 ft 10 ins (42 m)
Maximum length: 150 ft 11 ins (46 m)
Maximum height: 45 ft 7 ins (13.9 m)

Cabin:
Length: 99 ft (30.18 m)
Width: 11 ft 8.5 ins (3.57 m)
Height: 7 ft 6 ins (2.28 m)
Main passenger doors: 6 ft 1 ins x 2 ft 9 ins (1.85 x 0.84 m)
Cargo door: See Aircraft variants for freighter conversions

Wings:
Area: 1,915.97 sq ft (178 m^2)
Aspect ratio: 9.91
Sweepback: 28°

Tail unit:
Tailplane span: 49 ft 3 ins (15 m)

Undercarriage:
Type: Retractable, with twin steerable nosewheels. 4-wheel main bogies.
Main wheel tyre size: 1,070 x 390 mm
Nose wheel tyre size: 840 x 290 mm
Wheel base: 55 ft 9 ins (17 m)
Wheel track: 25 ft 8 ins (7.82 m)

Weights:
Empty, operating: 128,529 lb (58,300 kg), *130,073 lb (59,000 kg)*
Maximum take-off: 227,075 lb (103,000 kg), *244,162 (110,750 kg)*
Maximum landing: 194,447 lb (88,200 kg)
Payload: 46,297 lb (21,000 kg), *55,556 lb (25,200 kg)*

Performance:
Cruise speed: 437-459 kts (503-528 mph) 810-850 km/h, *448 kts (516 mph) 830 km/h*
Required runway length: 7,382 ft (2,250 m), *8,200 ft (2,500 m)*, at 30° C, 730 mmHg.
Cruise altitude: 36,420-41,340 ft (11,100-12,600 m), *the same*
Range with full payload: 2,700 naut miles (3,107 miles) 5,000 km, *3,418 naut miles (3,933 miles) 6,330 km)*

Tupolev Tu-224

Chief designer: Yuri Vorobjov.
Role: Rolls-Royce engined variant of the Tu-204, developed in co-operation with AlliedSignal.
Airframe life: 60,000 flight hours or 45,000 landings.
Sales: Marketing by Bravia (British Russian Aviation Corp), an organization comprising Tupolev, Aviastar, Avia-export and the Russian branch of Flemings (UK). Initial order for 2 cargo variants anticipated in early 1995.
Passengers: 170-214. See Tu-204.
Pressurization: AlliedSignal/Liebherr/ TEPLOOBMENNIK pressurization and air-conditioning systems, 10-15% more effective than Tu-204's, and 20-30% lighter.
Freight hold volume: 1,191.9 cu ft (33.75 m^3). Volume of bulk cargo 201.29 cu ft (5.7 m^3).
Freight hold capacity: LD3-46 containers.
Engines: 2 Rolls-Royce RB211-535E4 turbofans. GTCP 31-200/260 APU.
Fuel system: 72,091 lb (32,700 kg).
Braking system: Brakes fitted with AlliedSignal Landing Systems developed Carbenix 4000 (carbon-carbon material).
Radar: RDR-4B weather radar.
Flight avionics/instrumentation: Integrated system developed for Tupolev by AVIA, the joint venture of Russia's Avionics Research Institute (NIIAO) and AlliedSignal of the USA. EFIS with 6 liquid-crystal displays, dual ARINC 739 flight management system with GPS and compliant multi-purpose control and display units, advanced radio management system, traffic alert and collision avoidance system (TCAS II), wide range of CNI options, and Litton or Honeywell inertial reference system.

Details for Tu-224.

Principal dimensions:
Wing span: 137 ft 1.7 ins (41.8 m)
Maximum length: 151 ft 3 ins (46.1 m)
Maximum height: 45 ft 7 ins (13.9 m)

Cabin:
Length: 101 ft 8 ins (31 m)
Width: 11 ft 8.5 ins (3.57 m)
Height: 7 ft 6 ins (2.28 m)
Side door: Enlarged at mid-fuselage, that may be used as an entrance

Wings:
Area: 1,814.79 sq ft (168.6 m^2)
Aspect ratio: 10.36
Sweepback: 28°

Undercarriage:
Type: Reinforced.
Wheel base: 55 ft 9 ins (17 m)
Wheel track: 25 ft 8 ins (7.82 m)

Weights:
Empty: 121,695 lb (55,200 kg)
Maximum ramp: 244,933 lb (111,100 kg)
Maximum take-off: 244,160 lb (110,750 kg)
Maximum landing: 197,313 lb (89,500 kg)
Payload: 55,556 lb (25,200 kg)

Tupolev Tu-234

First flight: Rolled-out at the MosAeroshow on 25 August 1995.
Role: Shorter length variant of the Tu-204, originally known as Tu-204-300.
Passengers: 160-180 in 3 class layout, with 166 typically in short-range version. Reduced to 99-160 for long-range version.
Seat pitch: 39 ins (99 cm).
Engines: 2 Aviadvigatel PS-90A turbofans.
Engine rating: Each 35,583 lbf (158.3 kN) at take-off.
Aircraft variants:
Short-range version with 186,950 lb (84,800 kg) MTOW, 39,863 lb (18,000 kg) payload, maximum payload range of 1,295 naut miles (1,491 miles) 2,400 km, and design range of 1,835 naut miles (2,112 miles) 3,400 km.
Medium range version with 227,075 lb (103,000 kg) MTOW, 39,863 lb (18,000 kg) payload, and maximum payload and design ranges of 3,590 naut miles (4,132 miles) 6,650 km and 4,075 naut miles (4,691 miles) 7,550 km respectively.
Long-range version with 227,075 lb (103,000 kg) MTOW, 35,274 lb (16,000 kg), and maximum payload and design ranges of 3,888 naut miles (4,473 miles) 7,200 km and 4,995 naut miles (5,747 miles) 9,250 km respectively.

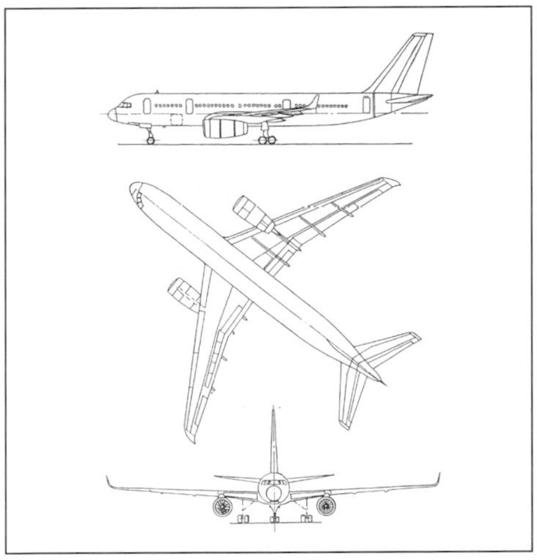

Tupolev Tu-234 drawing (courtesy Tupolev)

DETAILS FOR TU-234.

Principal dimensions:
Wing span: 134 ft 1.5 ins (40.88 m)
Maximum length: 131 ft 11 ins (40.2 m)
Maximum height: 45 ft 7 ins (13.9 m)

Weights: See Aircraft variants

Performance:
Cruise speed: 448-459 kts (516-528 mph) 830-850 km/h
Approach speed: 121 kts (140 mph) 225 km/h
Take-off distance: 6,726 ft (2,050 m), 30° C
Landing distance: 5,906 ft (1,800 m)
Operating altitude: 41,340 ft (12,600 m)
Range: See Aircraft variants

Tupolev Tu-244

Role: Supersonic airliner.
Noise levels: To meet FAR Pt 36 Chapter 3.

★ Aims
★ High fuel-to-weight ratio, quoted by Tupolev as 51-52% fuel to take-off weight, which is 1.5-2% greater than for first-generation SSTs.
★ High lift/drag ratio, quoted by Tupolev as K=9.5 at Mach 2 and K=15 at Mach 0.9.

▲ Development
▲ Project stage.
Passengers: About 300.
Wing characteristics: Cranked delta, with 7 trailing-edge control surfaces per wing and 4-section leading-edge slats.
Tail control surfaces: 2-section rudder.
Fuselage: Long, narrow and pointed, as for Tu-144 and Concorde first-generation SSTs.

DETAILS FOR TU-244.

Principal dimensions:
Wing span: 178 ft 8 ins (54.47 m)
Maximum length: 291 ft (88.7 m)
Maximum height: 51 ft 10 ins (15.8 m)

Wings:
Area: 12,916.68 sq ft (1,200 m^2)
Aspect ratio: 2.472
Sweepback: 75°, cranking to 35° for outer panels

Weights:
Zero fuel weight: 379,195 lb (172,000 kg)
Maximum take-off: 771,617 lb (350,000 kg)

Performance:
Maximum speed: above Mach 2
Operating altitude: 59,050-62,335 ft (18,000-19,000 m)
Range with full fuel: 4,968 naut miles (5,717 miles) 9,200 km

Tupolev Tu-304

Role: Long-range airliner.
Certification: 2001.
Airport limits: ACNR (A=80 mN/m^3) <68.
Passengers: 312-400.
Construction materials: Metal, except 15% composites.
Engines: 2 Rolls-Royce Trent 884 turbofans.
Engine rating: Each 86,500 lbf (384.78 kN).
Fuel system: 194,007 lb (88,000 kg).
Flight avionics/instrumentation: Suited to ICAO Cat IIIa landing.

DETAILS FOR TU-304.

Principal dimensions:
Wing span: 187 ft (57 m)
Maximum length: 203 ft 5 ins (62 m)
Maximum height: 62 ft 4 ins (19 m)

Wings:
Area: 3,659.7 sq ft (340 m^2)
Aspect ratio: 9.56
Sweepback: 33.3°

Undercarriage:
Type: Retractable, with twin steerable nosewheels. 6-wheel main bogies

Weights:
Maximum take-off: 540,130 lb (245,000 kg)
Payload: 121,255 lb (55,000 kg)

Performance:
Maximum speed: Mach 0.85
Required runway length: 10,500 ft (3,200 m) at 30° C and 1,115 ft (340 m) above sea level
Cruise altitude: 36,090 ft (11,000 m)
Range with full payload: 5,508 naut miles (6,338 miles) 10,200 km

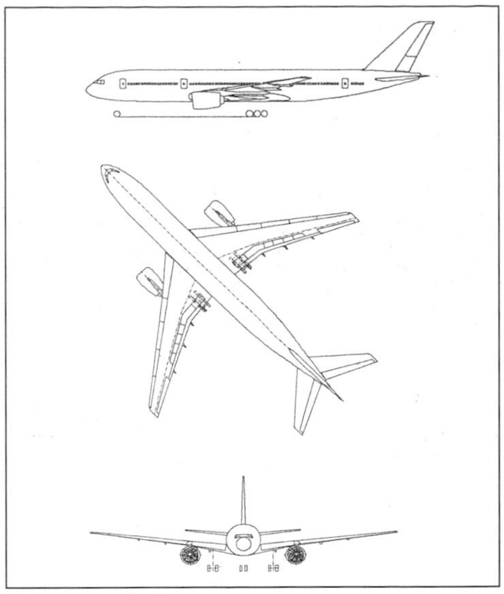

Tupolev Tu-304 long-range airliner (courtesy Tupolev)

Tupolev Tu-324

Role: Regional and business transport.
Passengers: 50 standard or 30 business in Regional layout, or 8-10 business or 1-4 VIPs.

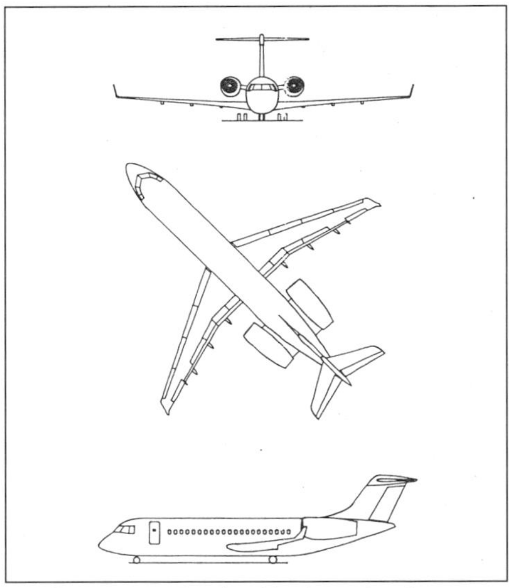

Tupolev Tu-324 regional and business aircraft (courtesy Tupolev)

DETAILS FOR TU-324, *WITH TU-324A IN ITALICS.*

Principal dimensions:
Wing span: 81 ft 1 ins (24.7 m), *the same*
Maximum length: 86 ft (26.2 m), *76 ft 1 ins (23.2 m)*
Maximum height: 24 ft (7.3 m), *the same*

Weights:
Maximum take-off: 54,300 lb (24,630 kg), *56,000 lb (25,400 kg)*
Payload: 11,023 lb (5,000 kg), *6,614 lb (3,000 kg)*

Performance:
Cruise speed: 432 kts (497 mph) 800 km/h
Required runway length: 5,910 ft (1,800 m), *6,400 ft (1,950 m)*
Range with full payload: 1,350 naut miles (1,553 miles) 2,500 km, *3,186 naut miles (3,666 miles) 5,900 km*
Range with reduced payloads: 2,457 naut miles (2,827 miles) 4,550 km with 30 passengers, *4,265 naut miles (4,910 miles) 7,900 km with 2,205 lb (1,000 kg) payload*

Wing control surfaces: Ailerons, 2-section flaps, 4-section spoilers and 4-section leading-edge slats. Winglets.
Tail control surfaces: Elevators and rudder.
Engines: 2 Soyuz R-126-300 turbofans.
Tu-324 standard regional airliner, as detailed.
Tu-324A business version, with typically 4,050 naut miles (4,660 miles) 7,500 km range but also as detailed below.

Tupolev Tu-330 and Tu-338

First flight: 1996.
Certification: 1998.
First delivery: 1998.
Chief designer: Valentin Bliznyuk, leading designer Dmitri Demenko.
Role: Medium freighter, competitor to the Ukrainian An-70.

Tupolev Tu-330 freighter (Piotr Butowski)

▲ Development

▲ Spring 1993. Project announced.
▲ 23 April 1994. Russian Prime Minister, Victor Chernomyrdin, signed a governmental resolution to finance the Tu-330 programme. According to this, the Tupolev Design Bureau and KAPO production plant in Kazan are obliged to complete the tests and obtain the certificate for the Tu-330 in 1998.
▲ 1996. Flight crew simulator to be delivered for state trials by NPO Era of Penza in 1996.

Sales: Series of 10 aircraft will be completed at the Gorbunov plant in Kazan before 1998. The total possible production run is estimated at 500-600 aircraft for military and civil use.
Freight hold access: Rear loading ramp/ door of 13 ft 2 ins x 13 ft 2 ins (4 x 4 m). Side loading door.
Wing characteristics: High-mounted super-critical, with anhedral, based on the Tu-204 wing. Large over-fuselage fairing to blend the carry-through structure. Substantial leading-edge sweepback (probably 28°), and trailing-edge sweepback on the outer panels only. Winglets.
Wing control surfaces: Ailerons, 2 or 3-section trailing-edge double-slotted flaps, multi-section airbrakes and 5-section spoilers, plus 4-section leading-edge slats.
Tail control surfaces: 2-section elevators on the dihedral tailplane, and 2-section rudder.
Construction materials: About 70% of construction elements are taken over from Tu-204 airliner, to reduce design and construction cost and time.
Engines: 2 Aviadvigatel PS-90AT turbofans. Alternative engines could be Rolls-Royce RB211-535s or Pratt & Whitney PW2000s.
Engine rating: Each 35,583 lbf (158.3 kN).
Radar: Gukol navigation/weather radar.
Aircraft variants:
Tu-330 is the standard medium transport, as detailed.
Tu-338 is a projected version with liquid gas fuelled engines.

DETAILS FOR TU-330.

Principal dimensions:
Wing span: 138 ft 9 ins (42.3 m)
Maximum length: 137 ft 9.5 ins (42 m)
Maximum height: 45 ft 11 ins (14 m)

Cabin:
Length: 64 ft (19.5 m)
Width: 13 ft 2 ins (4 m)
Height: 11 ft 8 ins to 13 ft 2 ins (3.55 to 4 m)

Wings:
Area: 2,115.1 sq ft (196.5 m^2)
Aspect ratio: 9.106

Undercarriage:
Type: Retractable, with twin steerable nosewheels. 6-wheel main bogies

Weights:
Maximum take-off: 228,178 lb (103,500 kg)
Payload: 77,162 lb (35,000 kg)

Performance:
Cruise speed: 432-459 kts (497-528 mph) 800-850 km/h
Cruise altitude: 36,090 ft (11,000 m)
Range with full fuel: 4,644 naut miles (5,344 miles) 8,600 km
Range with 66,139 lb (30,000 kg) payload: 1,620 naut miles (1,864 miles) 3,000 km
Range with 44,092 lb (20,000 kg) payload: 3,024 naut miles (3,480 miles) 5,600 km

Tupolev Tu-334

First flight: Rolled-out at MosAeroshow on 26 August 1995.
Certification: 1997.
First Delivery: Late 1997 or early1998.
Role: Medium-range airliner.

★ Aims

★ To replace the Tu-134.

▲ Development

▲ 1994. Intended first flight, but delayed. All 3 prototypes to be flying in 1995. First prototype fitted out at the Zhukovsky Flight Test Centre. Static testing at TSAGI.

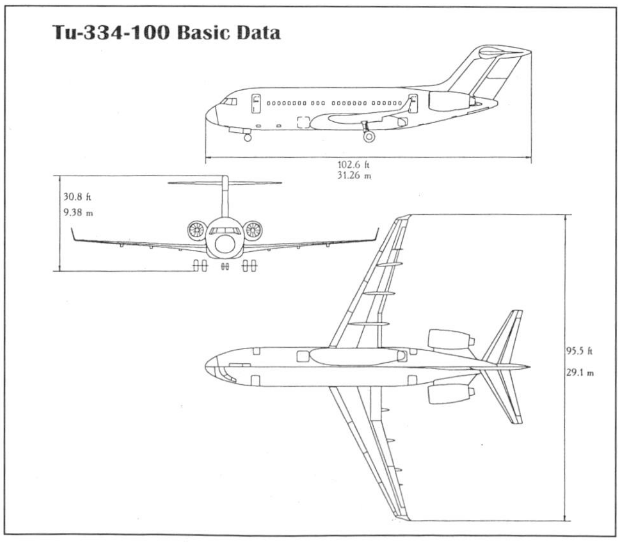

Tupolev Tu-334-100 (courtesy Tupolev)

DETAILS FOR TU-334-100, *WITH TU-334-200 IN ITALICS.*

Principal dimensions:
Wing span: 97 ft 8 ins (29.77 m), *107 ft (32.607 m)*
Maximum length: 102 ft 7 ins (31.26 m), *115 ft 4.5 ins (35.164 m)*
Maximum height: 30 ft 9 ins (9.38 m) or 28 ft 4 ins (8.625 m)?, *29 ft 9 ins (9.05 m)*

Cabin:
Length: 58 ft 6 ins (17.84 m)
Width: 11 ft 8 ins (3.57 m) at floor, *the same*
Height: 7 ft 1 ins (2.155 m), *the same*
Volume: 4,167.13 cu ft (118 m^3)

Wings:
Aerofoil section: Supercritical
Area: 895.84 sq ft (83.226 m^2), *1,076.4 sq ft (100 m^2)*
Aspect ratio: 10.649, *10.632*
Sweepback: 24°

Undercarriage:
Type: Retractable, with twin wheels on each unit. Lever type main legs. *Tu-334-200 has 4-wheel main bogies*
Wheel base: 38 ft 7 ins (11.75 m)

Weights:
Empty: 66,249 lb (30,050 kg), *75,783 lb (34,375 kg)*
Maximum take-off: 101,633 lb (46,100 kg), *120,813 lb (54,800 kg)*
Payload: 24,251 lb (11,000 kg), *29,762 lb (13,500 kg)*

Performance:
Cruise speed: 432-443 kts (497-510 mph) 800-820 km/h, *432 kts (497 mph) 800 km/h*
Balanced runway length: 7,546 ft (2,300 m) at 30° C
Cruise altitude: 34,775-36,420 ft (10,600-11,100 m), *the same*
Range with full payload: 1,080 naut miles (1,242 miles) 2,000 km, *1,188 naut miles (1,367 miles) 2,200 km*

Sales: 3 flying prototypes plus 2 static test airframes; 2 flying prototypes constructed at the Tupolev works in Moscow, 2 other aircraft in Kiev and 1 at Taganrog. Series production tooling ready.
Details: Tu-334-100 (see Aircraft variants).
Crew: 2 or 3, with additional provision for an observer or instructor.
Passengers: 102 in all-tourist class layout. Passenger doors in the forward and aft port fuselage. Alternatives include 92 mixed class, comprising 8 first class (4 abreast) and 84 tourist (6 abreast).
Seat pitch: 34 ins (87 cm) tourist, 39 ins (99 cm) first class, and 37.8 ins (96 cm) business class when provided. See Aircraft variants.
Galleys: Buffet galley aft of cockpit, with a second in the tail section.
Freight hold access: Starboard side doors for underfloor baggage/cargo compartments.
Baggage compartment/hold: 572.1 cu ft (16.2 m^3), length 13 ft 5.5 ins (4.1 m) + 9 ft 11 ins (3 m), height 3 ft 11 ins (1.2 m).
Wing characteristics: Derived from Tu-204 wing. Dihedral. Winglets.
Wing control surfaces: Aileron, 2-section flap, 4-section leading-edge slat, 2-section spoiler (with aileron functions) and 2-section airbrakes ahead of inboard flap section.
Tail control surfaces: Elevators and 2-section rudder.

Flight control system: Fly-by-wire. Emergency mechanical/hydraulic back-up for elevators and rudder.
Construction materials: Principally metal, but with 20% composites and other materials by structure weight.
Engines: 2 Ivchenko PROGRESS/Zaporozhye D-436T1 turbofans. Alternative BMW Rolls-Royce BR715-55. See Aircraft variants.
Engine rating: Each 16,535-16,865 lbf (73.55-75 kN).
Fuel system: 21,032 lb (9,540 kg).
Flight avionics/instrumentation: Meets ICAO Cat IIIa for landing. EFIS cockpit with 6 displays.
Aircraft variants:
Tu-334-100 is the standard version with D-436T1 engines, as detailed.
Tu-334-100D has the same length fuselage and seating capacity as the -100, but with D-436T2 or BMW Rolls-Royce engines (see below). Take-off weight 119,975 lb (54,420 kg). Fuel capacity increased to 30,402 lb (13,790 kg) for a 2,214 naut mile (2,547 mile) 4,100 km range. Expected service 1998.
Tu-334-200 has 18,078 lbf (80.42 kN) D-436T2 engines or BR715-55s, 30,402 lb (13,790 kg) fuel, and 4-wheel main undercarriage bogies. Standard accommodation for 126 in an all-tourist layout at 32 ins (81 cm) seat pitch, or 110 in a mixed layout with 8 first class at 39 ins (99 cm) pitch and 102 tourist.

Tupolev Tu-404

★ Aims

★ Active project, under the design leadership of Yuri Vorobjov, for a 600-850 seat giant airliner. Various configurations are under study, including huge flying-wings.

Tupolev Tu-414

Role: Regional and business transport.
Crew: 2.
Passengers: 50 (possibly 60-70) as a regional transport, 12-19 for business.
Wing control surfaces: Ailerons, multi-section flaps, leading-edge slats and spoilers. Winglets.
Tail control surfaces: Elevators and rudder.
Engines: 2 BMW Rolls-Royce BR710 turbofans. Alternative Ivchenko PROGRESS D-436T1s.
Engine rating: Each 14,680 lbf (65.3 kN).

Details for Tu-414 in regional form.

Principal dimensions:
Wing span: 92 ft (28.04 m)
Maximum length: 99 ft 1 ins (30.2 m)
Maximum height: 27 ft 9 ins (8.15 m)

Weights:
Maximum take-off: 77,380 lb (35,100 kg)
Payload: 15,430 lb (7,000 kg)

Performance:
Cruise speed: 432 kts (497 mph) 800 km/h
Required runway length: 5,900 ft (1,800 m)
Range with full Payload: 1,890 naut miles (2,174 miles) 3,500 km

Tupolev C-Prop

Role: Light passenger or cargo transport, using liquefied gas cryogenic fuel.

▲ Development

▲ Actual programme.
Passengers/cargo: 32 passengers or 3 pallets of 88 x 125 ins (2.24 x 3.175 m) or 88 x 108 ins (2.24 x 2.74 m) each.
Freight hold access: Rear ramp/door under the tail.
Wing characteristics: Low-mounted, straight main wings, with dihedral. High-mounted canards, joined to the 2 booms that are supported at the rear on wing-mounted pylons.
Wing control surfaces: Horn-balanced ailerons (with port tab) and flaps on the main wings. Canards carry trailing-edge surfaces.
Tail control surfaces: T-tail with elevators (port tab) and rudder (with tab).
Engines: 2 Pratt & Whitney Canada PT6A-67 turboprops, with pusher propellers.
Engine rating: Each 1,500 shp (1,118 kW).
Fuel system: 5,291 lb (2,400 kg) of liquified gas fuel.

Details for C-Prop.

Principal dimensions:
Wing span: 73 ft 10 ins (22.5 m)
Maximum length: 68 ft 11 ins (21 m)
Maximum height: 21 ft 8 ins (6.6 m)

Cabin:
Length: 31 ft 9 ins (9.68 m)
Width: 8 ft 6.5 ins (2.6 m)
Height: 7 ft 3 ins (2.2 m)

Weights:
Maximum take-off: 29,762 lb (13,500 kg)
Payload: 7,496 lb (3,400 kg)

Performance:
Cruise speed: 243 kts (280 mph) 450 km/h
Required runway length: 2,035 ft (620 m)
Cruise altitude: 26,250 ft (8,000 m)
Range with full payload: 810 naut miles (932 miles) 1,500 km

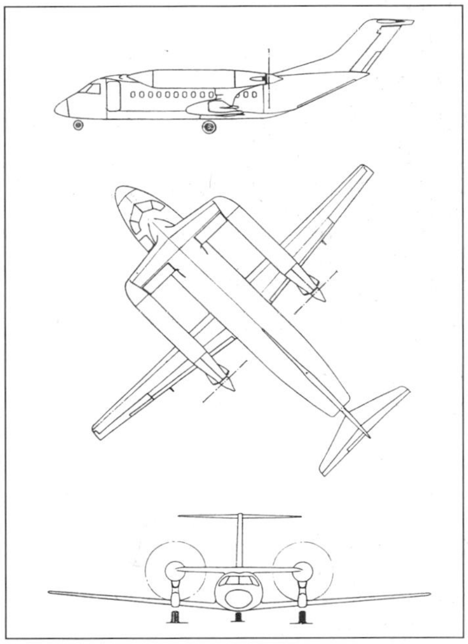

Tupolev C-Prop cryogenic fuelled transport (courtesy Tupolev)

Yakovlev Aircraft Corporation (Russia)

Corporate address: See Combat section for all company details. See also General Aviation section.

Yakovlev Yak-40 and Yak-40TL (NATO name *Codling*)

First flight: 21 October 1966.
First delivery: 1968, allowing commercial passenger flights with Aeroflot to start on 30 September.
Role: Short-haul regional and government VIP transport.
Airframe life: 30,000 flying hours.
Sales: Well over 1,000 built. Long out of production but the Yak-40TL modification is available (see Aircraft variants). An estimated 560 remain in commercial use, plus small numbers in military/government use with Bulgaria, Cambodia, Cuba, Ethiopia, Madagascar, Poland, Syria, Vietnam and Zambia.
Flight crew: 2, with third seat available.
Passengers: 16-27 normally, 32 maximum.
Seat pitch: 30 ins (75.5 cm).
Galley: Standard.
Pressurization: 4.26 psi cabin differential.
Freight holds: All-cargo version was made available.

Yakovlev Yak-40 in Slovakia (Piotr Butowski)

Wing control surfaces: 2-section ailerons (with tabs) and 3-section flaps.
Tail control surfaces: T-tail with variable-incidence tailplane. Elevators and rudder (with tab).
Flight control system: Mechanically actuated ailerons, elevators and rudder. Hydraulically actuated flaps and tailplane (electrically operated). Electrically actuated tabs.
Construction materials: All duralumin.
Engines: 3 Ivchenko PROGRESS AI-25 turbofans. Able to take-off on any 2 of the 3 engines.
Engine rating: Each 3,307 lbf (14.71 kN) at take off.
Fuel system: 3,910 litres.
Electrical system: DC system via 3 engine-driven VG-7.500-1a generators and 2 batteries. AC system via 2 x 115 volt single-phase inverters and 2 x 36 volt three-phase inverters.
Hydraulic system: 2,132 psi.
Braking system: Hydraulic.
De-icing system: Hot air for wings and tail, and electric for cockpit windows.
Radar: Grosa 40 weather radar.
Flight avionics/instrumentation: IFR.
Aircraft variants:
Yak-40 is the standard version, formerly available in VIP, airliner and cargo layouts.
Yak-40TL is the latest twin-engined configuration, modified from existing aircraft using AlliedSignal LF507-1H turbofans of 7,000 lbf (31.14 kN). Development details released in 1991.

DETAILS FOR YAK-40, UNLESS STATED.

Principal dimensions:
Wing span: 82 ft (25 m)
Maximum length: 66 ft 9.5 ins (20.36 m)
Maximum height: 21 ft 4 ins (6.5 m)

Cabin:
Length: 23 ft 2 ins (7.07 m)
Width: 7 ft 1 ins (2.15 m)
Height: 6 ft 1 ins (1.85 m)
Main door size: 5 ft 9 ins (1.74 m) x 3 ft 1 ins (0.94 m)

Wings:
Area: 753.47 sq ft (70 m^2)
Aspect ratio: 8.93
Dihedral: From root

Tail unit:
Tailplane span: 24 ft 7 ins (7.5 m)

Undercarriage:
Type: Retractable, with steerable nosewheel. Can operate from unimproved airfields
Main wheel tyre size: 1,120 x 450 mm
Nose wheel tyre size: 720 x 310 mm
Wheel base: 24 ft 6 ins (7.47 m)
Wheel track: 14 ft 10 ins (4.52 m)

Weights:
Empty, operating: 19,864-21,716 lb (9,010-9,850 kg) depending on cabin layout. 23,953 lb (10,865 kg) for TL
Maximum take-off: 35,274 lb (16,000 kg). 36,542 lb (16,575 kg) for TL
Payload: 5,997 lb (2,720 kg) for both versions

Performance:
Maximum cruise speed: 297 kts (342 mph) 550 km/h at 22,965-26,245 ft (7,000-8,000 m)
Typical take-off distance: 2,300 ft (700 m)
Required runway length: 4,594 ft (1,400 m) for TL
Landing distance: 1,181 ft (360 m)
Maximum climb rate: 1,575 ft (480 m) per minute
Range with full fuel: 972 naut miles (1,118 miles) 1,800 km. 1,053 naut miles (1,211 miles) 1,950 km for TL
Range with full payload: 783 naut miles (901 miles) 1,450 km with 32 passengers. 675 naut miles (777 miles) 1,250 km for TL

Yakovlev Yak-42 and Yak-142 (NATO name *Clobber*)

First flight: 7 March 1975 (Yak-42).
First delivery: 1980 start of Yak-42 scheduled services with Aeroflot, between Moscow and Krasnodar.
Role: Short-medium range airliner, with freighter version. Able to operate in remote regions, in temperatures of up to ±50° C.
Airframe life: 30,000 flying hours or 30,000 cycles.
Sales: Approximately 132 Yak-42s were in commercial use in early 1995, 113 of these in the CIS (largest numbers with Aeroflot and Air Ukraine), and foreign operators including China General Aviation (6), Cubana (4) and Kish Air (3). A number of Yak-42Ds were reportedly unsold at Samara in late 1994.
Crew: 2 pilots plus optional flight engineer.
Passengers: 104-120.
Seat pitch: 29.5 ins (75 cm).
Galley: 1, aft of the cockpit.
Freight holds: 2 under the cabin floor of all versions, for a total of 8 x 77.69 cu ft (2.2 m^3) containers, or baggage or other loads.

Yakovlev Yak-42 (Denis Hughes)

Freight capacity: 26,455 lb (12,000 kg) for the Yak-42T.
Size of freight door: Standard passenger Yak-42 hold door (starboard side) of 4 ft 5 ins x 3 ft 9 ins (1.35 x 1.145 m). Convertible version has a 6 ft 8 ins x 10 ft 7 ins (2.025 x 3.23 m) port-side cargo-loading door. Yak-42T has an 8 ft 2 ins x 6 ft 7 ins (2.5 x 2 m) access door to the main cabin in addition to the undercabin hold door.
Loading facilities: Floor-mounted chain drive in the undercabin holds.
Wing control surfaces: 2-section ailerons (with tabs), 2-section single-slotted trailing-edge flaps and full-width leading-edge flaps, plus 3-section spoilers.
Tail control surfaces: T-tail with a variable incidence tailplane, elevators (with tabs) and rudder (with tab).
Flight control system: Hydraulic.
Construction materials: Metal.
Engines: 3 Ivchenko PROGRESS D-36 Series I turbofans.
Engine rating: Each 14,330 lbf (63.745 kN) at take off and 3,527 lbf (15.69 kN) ideal cruise.
Fuel system: About 23,200 litres.
Electrical system: Includes TA-12 APU.
Braking system: Hydraulic disc on main units.
Radar: Weather radar. See Yak-142 under Aircraft variants.
Flight avionics/instrumentation: IFR. SAU-42 Cat II flight control system.
Aircraft variants:
Yak-42 is the standard and most produced version, available in all-passenger or passenger/cargo configurations.
Yak-42A/B have appeared since 1993 as demonstrators with AlliedSignal avionics, including EFIS in the B.
Yak-42D is a production version that carries extra fuel for an additional 108 naut miles (124 miles) 200 km range with full load. Built at Samara.
Yak-42E is an engine testbed, with an Ivchenko PROGRESS D-236 propfan replacing the starboard turbofan.
Yak-42F is a multispectral resources/environmental survey aircraft, with 2 underwing equipment pods. 17 equipment operators. Several are operated in Aeroflot markings. MTOW 124,560 lb (56,500 kg).
Yak-42T is an all-cargo version.
Yak-142 is the latest version based on the Yak-42D, featuring a full range of AlliedSignal digital avionics, RDR-4A weather radar and a 5-screen EFIS cockpit display, as developed on the Yak-42A/B demonstrators. Take-off and landing performances improved by a new wing spoiler system and a wide range of flap settings. ICAO Ch 3-16 noise levels. Improved cabin features.

DETAILS FOR YAK-42, UNLESS STATED.

Principal dimensions:
Wing span: 114 ft 5 ins (34.88 m)
Maximum length: 119 ft 4 ins (36.38 m)
Maximum height: 32 ft 3 ins (9.83 m)

Cabin:
Length: 65 ft 3 ins (19.89 m)
Width: 11 ft 10 ins (3.6 m)
Height: 6 ft 10 ins (2.08 m)
Main passenger door size: 4 ft 11 ins x 2 ft 9 ins (1.5 x 0.83 m). *5 ft 7 ins x 2 ft 10 ins (1.7 x 0.85 m) for Yak-142*

Wings:
Area: 1,614.6 sq ft (150 m^2)
Aspect ratio: 8.11
Sweepback: 23° at 25% chord

Tail unit:
Tailplane span: 35 ft 5 ins (10.8 m)

Undercarriage:
Type: Retractable, with twin steerable nosewheels and 4-wheel main units. Able to land on prepared or unimproved runways under ICAO Category II
Tyre size: 930 x 305 mm
Wheel base: 48 ft 6 ins (14.78 m)
Wheel track: 18 ft 6 ins (5.63 m)

Weights:
Empty, operating: 76,090 lb (34,515 kg)
Maximum take-off: 125,665 lb (57,000 kg)
Maximum landing: 112,435 lb (51,000 kg)
Payload: 28,660 lb (13,000 kg)

Performance:
Maximum cruise speed: 437 kts (503 mph) 810 km/h. *400 kts (460 mph) 740 km/h for Yak-142*
Economical cruise speed: 405 kts (466 mph) 750 km/h
Required runway length: 7,218 ft (2,200 m). *5,906 ft (1,800 m) for Yak-142 at sea level, ISA*
Cruise ceiling: 31,500 ft (9,600 m)
Range with full fuel: 2,214 naut miles (2,547 miles) 4,100 km
Range with full payload: 1,026 naut miles (1,180 miles) 1,900 km

Yakovlev Yak-46-1

Role: Short-medium range passenger airliner, with convertible, evacuation and other versions planned.

▲ Development
▲ 1992. Received Russian Government approval for full development.
Flight crew: 2, with optional flight engineer.
Passengers: 126 (12 first class and 114 economy), 150 and 168-passenger layouts known to date.
Wing characteristics: Similar to Yak-242 but with different control surfaces arrangement.
Tail control surfaces: Similar arrangement to Yak-242 but of differing sizes.
Flight control system: Digital fly-by-wire.
Engines: 2 Samara turbofans.
Engine rating: Each 24,251 lbf (107.88 kN).
Flight avionics/instrumentation: ICAO Category IIIa landing.

DETAILS FOR YAK-46-1.

Principal dimensions:
Wing span: 118 ft 11 ins (36.25 m)
Maximum length: 127 ft 3.5 ins (38.8 m)

Wings:
Aerofoil section: Supercritical
Area: 1,291.7 sq ft (120 m^2)
Aspect ratio: 10.95
Sweepback: 25°

Weights:
Empty, operating: 76,809 lb (34,840 kg)
Maximum take-off: 132,718 lb (60,200 kg)
Payload: 38,581 lb (17,500 kg)

Performance:
Cruise speed: 429 kts (528 mph) 850 km/h
Required runway length: 6,890 ft (2,100 m)
Cruise ceiling: 36,425 ft (11,100 m)
Range with full payload: 1,188 naut miles (1,367 miles) 2,200 km

Yakovlev Yak-46-2

Yakovlev Yak-46-2 (Piotr Butowski)

Role: Short-medium range airliner.
▲ Development
▲ 1990. Model shown at MosAeroshow.
Wing characteristics: Very similar configuration and control surfaces to the Yak-46-1.
Tail control surfaces: T-tail, with 2-section elevators and multi-section rudder.
Flight control system: Digital fly-by-wire.
Fuselage: Similar to Yak-46-1.
Engines: 2 rear-mounted Ivchenko PROGRESS D-27 propfans, with 12 ft 6 ins (3.8 m) 8-blade and 6-blade coaxial contra-rotating composites pusher propellers.
Engine rating: Each 14,000 ehp (10,440 kW).

DETAILS FOR YAK-46-2.

Principal dimensions:
Wing span: 116 ft 6 ins (35.5 m)
Maximum length: 134 ft 6 ins (41 m)

Wings:
Area: 1,291.7 sq ft (120 m^2)
Aspect ratio: 10.5

Weights:
Empty, operating: 82,232 lb (37,300 kg)
Maximum take-off: 135,143 lb (61,300 kg)
Payload: 38,581 lb (17,500 kg)

Performance:
Cruise speed: 448 kts (516 mph) 830 km/h
Required runway length: 6,890 ft (2,100 m)
Cruise altitude: 36,425 ft (11,100 m)
Range with full payload: 972 naut miles (1,118 miles) 1,800 km

Yakovlev Yak-77

First flight: 1996.
Certification: To comply with FAR/JAR Pt 25.
Role: Small regional airliner and executive/business transport.
Crew: 2
Passengers: 32 in regional layout, or 8 as a business/executive jet. Starboard airstair main passenger door.
Galley: Galley and toilet standard.
Wing control surfaces: Ailerons, trailing-edge flaps and multi-section spoilers.
Tail control surfaces: Rudder and mid-mounted swept tailplane with elevators.
Engines: 2 Allison AE 3000 series turbofans, possibly AE 3007Cs of 6,440 lbf (28.65 kN) or similar.
Flight avionics/instrumentation: Collins Pro Line 4.
Aircraft variants:
Yak-77, as detailed.
Future 50/70-seat versions, speculatively with Allison AE 3010 active growth engines, as being developed for regional jets of this size, of 9,500-11,000 lbf (42.26-48.93 kN).

DETAILS FOR YAK-77.

Principal dimensions:
Wing span: 70 ft 9 ins (21.55 m)
Maximum length: 67 ft 1 ins (20.45 m)
Maximum height: 24 ft 6 ins (7.46 m)

Wings:
Aerofoil section: TsAGI type

Tail unit:
Tailplane span: 21 ft 5 ins (6.53 m)

Undercarriage:
Type: Retractable, with twin nosewheels

Weights:
Maximum take-off: 55,556 lb (25,200 kg)
Payload: 7,716 lb (3,500 kg) maximum

Performance:
Cruise speed: Mach 0.75
Required runway length: 7,218 ft (2,200 m)
Range with full passenger payload: 3,240 naut miles (3,728 miles) 6,000 km
Range in executive/business configuration: 5,400 naut miles (6,214 miles) 10,000 km

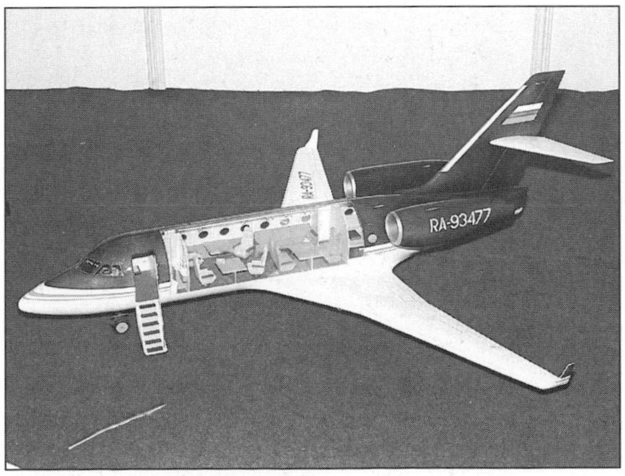

Yakovlev Yak-77 (Piotr Butowski)

Yakovlev Yak-242

First flight: Possibly 1995.
Certification: 1997.
Role: Short-haul airliner.
Crew: 2, with optional flight engineer.
Passengers: Typically 132 (including 12 First and 26 Business classes), 138 (including 12 First class), 156, 162 or 180 maximum.
Seat pitch: 29.5 ins (75 cm) in 180 passenger layout, 32 ins (81 cm) in 156 passenger layout. First class pitch 37.75 ins (96 cm) and Business 34.25 ins (87 cm).
Wing control surfaces: Ailerons, double-slotted trailing-edge flaps and leading-edge surfaces. Winglets.

Yakovlev Yak-242 (Piotr Butowski)

DETAILS FOR YAK-242.

Principal dimensions:
Wing span: 118 ft 11 ins (36.25 m)
Maximum length: 124 ft 8 ins (38 m)

Wings:
Aerofoil section: Supercritical
Area: 1,291.7 sq ft (120 m^2)
Aspect ratio: 10.95
Dihedral: From roots

Undercarriage:
Type: Retractable, with twin steerable nosewheels and 4-wheel main units

Weights:
Empty, operating: 84,657 lb (38,400 kg)
Maximum take-off: 142,418 lb (64,600 kg)
Payload: 39,683 lb (18,000 kg)

Performance:
Cruise speed: 459 kts (528 mph) 850 km/h
Required runway length: 7,218 ft (2,200 m)
Range with full fuel: 2,699 naut miles (3,106 miles) 5,000 km
Range with full payload: 864 naut miles (994 miles) 1,600 km

Tail control surfaces: 2-section elevators and rudder.
Flight control system: Digital fly-by-wire.
Fuselage: Based on the Yak-42 but lengthened.
Engines: 2 Aviadvigatel PS-90A12 turbofans.
Engine rating: Each 26,455 lbf (117.68 kN) at take off, 5,070 lbf (22.56 kN) cruise.
Fuel system: 48,502 lb (22,000 kg).
Radar: Weather radar.
Flight avionics/instrumentation: IFR. Meets ICAO Category IIIa. AlliedSignal EFIS.

Professional Aviation Services (Pty) Ltd (South Africa)

Corporate address: Terminal Building, Lanseria Airport, PO Box 3171, Randburg 2125, Johannesburg.
Telephone: +27 11 701 3320, 659 2860
(24 hrs: +27 82 410 1818)
Facsimile: +27 11 659 1336
Information: R. C. H. Garbett.

● Activities

- Charter services (with 2 AMI-converted turbine and lengthened DC-3s, Cessna Citation II, King Airs and Learjets), sales, aircraft broking and consulting.
- According to correspondence, the company is not currently involved in DC-3 modifications, but could possibly be so in the future.

Simera (South Africa)

Corporate address: PO Box 117, 1620 Kempton Park.
Telephone: +27 11 927 9111
Facsimile: +27 11 395 1017
Information: P.P. Holtzhausen (Denel Group Executive Manager: Public Relations and Environmental Affairs – *telephone* +27 12 428 0911, *facsimile* +27 12 428 0662)

● Activities

- Undertakes maintenance, refurbishment and upgrading of fixed and rotary wing aircraft, engines, sub-systems and components.
- Agreements signed in 1994 with Deutsche Airbus (now Daimler-Benz) include the conversion of Airbus A300s and A310s into freighters for the African market. First contract covers 4 A300B-4s for delivery in 1996 to BankAmerica Leasing and Capital. Future joint programmes could include participation on existing and stretched versions of the Dornier 228, a military variant of the Dornier 328, and in the FLA programme.
- Other international co-operation agreements have made Simera the sole supplier of the accessory gearbox on the Rolls-Royce RB211-535 engine, and in 1993 the company became a risk and revenue sharing partner in the Rolls-Royce Trent programme.
- In 1994, Simera jointly purchased Anglo American Airmotive, an engine maintenance company.

Simera aircraft maintenance in progress

Construcciones Aeronáuticas, S.A. (CASA) (Spain)

Corporate address: See Combat section for company details.

● Activities

- See Combat section. Development of the CASA 3000 regional airliner was halted in 1995, possibly temporarily if CASA eventually joins the Aero International Regional consortium at a future date.

CASA 3000 70-78 passenger regional airliner, its development temporarily halted in 1995

CASA 3000 cabin mockup, offering 30-32 ins (76-81 cm) seat pitch and 18 ins (45.7 cm) aisle

CASA C-212 Series 300 Aviocar

First flight: 26 March 1971 in original prototype form.
Certification: 1987 for Series 300, to FAR Pt 25/121/135.
First delivery: 1974 in original C-212A production form.
Role: STOL light passenger and cargo transport, and military freighter. Special purpose military versions are detailed in the Combat section. Other roles currently employed include medevac and civil protection, emergency hospital, aerial photography, rainmaking, geophysical survey, remote areas support, and aerial delivery.
Noise levels: FAR Pt 36.
Sales: More than 450 sold in all versions.
Crew: 2 (flight).
Passengers: 26, with optional air conditioning and noise isolation kit; cabin noise 10 dB. Airstairs. C-212M can carry 25 fully armed troops or paratroops on foldable seats, or 26 passengers in airline-style seats. Can deploy and give air support to advanced patrols of 10 troops and light vehicles, air-drop loads up to 4,409 lb (2,000 kg) at high or low altitudes (HAD, LAPES), or carry 12 litters and 4 attendants for medevac.
Seat pitch: 28.3 ins (72 cm).
Galley: Optional galley and toilet.

DETAILS FOR C-212 SERIES 300, *WITH C-212M IN ITALICS.*

Principal dimensions:
Wing span: 66 ft 6 ins (20.275 m)
Maximum length: 53 ft (16.154 m)
Maximum height: 21 ft 8 ins (6.6 m)

Cabin:
Length: 23 ft 10.5 ins (7.275 m) passenger layout, 21 ft 6 ins (6.55 m) cargo layout, *21 ft 6 ins (6.55 m).*
Width: 6 ft 11 ins (2.1 m), or 6 ft 2 ins (1.87 m) at floor, *the same*
Height: 5 ft 11 ins (1.8 m)
Volume: 840.5 cu ft (23.8 m^3)
Main passenger door: 5 ft 2 ins x 2 ft 3.5 ins (1.58 x 0.7 m)

Wings:
Area: 441.32 sq ft (41 m^2)
Aspect ratio: 10.026

Tail unit:
Tailplane span: 27 ft 7 ins (8.4 m)
Tailplane area: 96.98 sq ft (9.01 m^2)

Undercarriage:
Type: Fixed, with steerable nosewheel
Wheel base: 17 ft 11 ins (5.46 m)
Wheel track: 10 ft 2 ins (3.1 m)

Weights:
Empty: 8,333 lb (3,780 kg)
Max zero-fuel weight: 15,653 lb (7,100 kg), the same
Maximum take-off: 16,975 lb (7,700 kg), *17,857 lb (8,100 kg)*
Maximum landing: 16,424 lb (7,450 kg), *the same*
Payload: 5,115 lb (2,320 kg) passengers, 6,172 lb (2,800 kg) cargo, *5,952 lb (2,700 kg)*

Performance:
Maximum cruise speed: 191 kts (220 mph) 354 km/h, ISA, 10,000 ft (3,050 m) altitude, 97% MTOW, *190 kts (218 mph) 352 km/h, 97% MTOW*
Stall speed: 78 kts (90 mph) 145 km/h
Balanced field length: 2,936 ft (895 m), hard runway surface
Take-off distance: 2,680 ft (817 m), hard surface, TORA=ASDA criterion, FAR 25-121, *1,307 ft (398 m)* ground roll
Take-off over a 50 ft (15 m) obstacle: *1,950 ft (594 m)*
Climb gradient second segment: 3.3%.
Approach climb gradient: 3.9%, conditions as above
Landing distance: 2,840 ft (865 m), ISA, sea level, hard surface, FAR 25-121, *810 ft (247 m) ground roll*
Landing distance over a 50 ft (15 m) obstacle: *1,610 ft (490 m)*
Maximum climb rate: 1,630 ft (497 m) per minute
Maximum climb rate, one engine: 311 ft (95 m) per minute
Ceiling: 26,000 ft (7,925 m), the same
Ceiling, one engine: 11,100 ft (3,383 m), *11,400 ft (3,475 m)*
Range with 3,776 lb (1,713 kg) payload: 769 naut miles (885 miles) 1,424 km, at 10,000 ft (3,050 m), reserves
Range with 25 passengers: 190 naut miles (219 miles) 352 km, at 10,000 ft (3,050 m), reserves
Duration: *over 9 hours with underwing tanks*

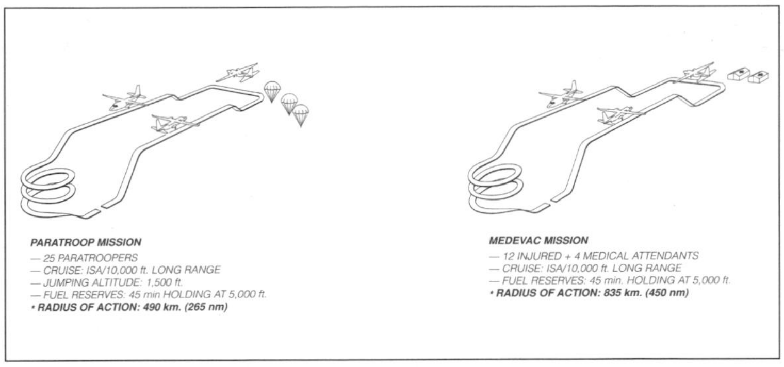

PARATROOP MISSION
— 25 PARATROOPERS
— CRUISE: ISA/10,000 ft. LONG RANGE
— JUMPING ALTITUDE: 1,500 ft.
— FUEL RESERVES: 45 min HOLDING AT 5,000 ft.
• RADIUS OF ACTION: 490 km. (265 nm)
MEDEVAC MISSION
— 12 INJURED + 4 MEDICAL ATTENDANTS
— CRUISE: ISA/10,000 ft. LONG RANGE
— FUEL RESERVES: 45 min. HOLDING AT 5,000 ft.
• RADIUS OF ACTION: 835 km. (450 nm)

CASA C-212M mission profiles (courtesy CASA)

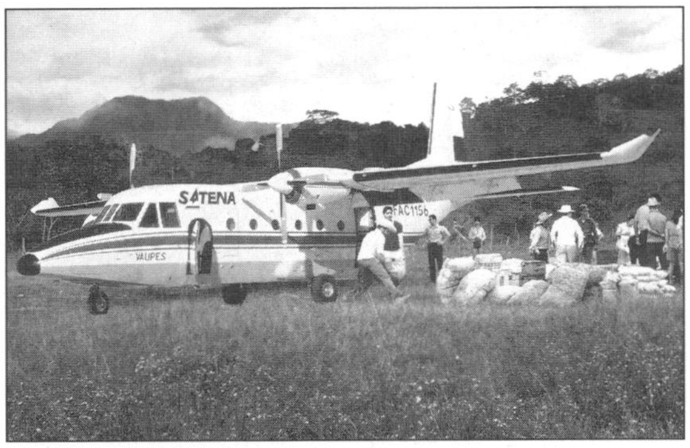

CASA C-212 Series 300 (courtesy CASA)

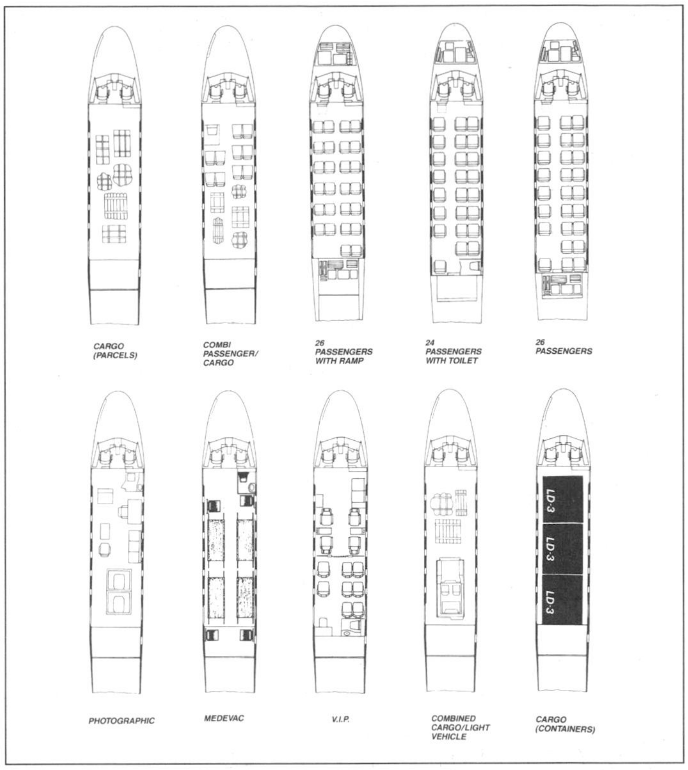

CASA C-212 Series 300 cabin configurations (courtesy CASA)

Freight hold volume: 776.92 cu ft (777 m^3).
Freight hold capacity: Optional full-freighter kit, allowing 3 LD3 containers, LD-1 or LD-727/DC-8 containers, standard 88 x 54 ins (2.24 x 1.37 m) pallets, light vehicles, military engines in their cradles, or other loads.
Freight hold access: Rear 2-section ramp/door (see below).
Size of freight doors: 95.67 x 66.14 ins (2.43 x 1.68 m) upper ventral door section, plus 54.33 x 66.14 ins (1.38 x 1.68 m) rear ramp lower door section.
Loading facilities: Roller system for cargo handling.
Baggage compartment: 123.6 cu ft (3.5 m^3).
Wing control surfaces: Ailerons (port tab) and double-slotted flaps. Winglets.
Tail control surfaces: Elevators and rudder with trim and servo tabs.
Flight control system: Mechanical (including servo tabs), but with hydraulic flaps and electric trim tabs.
Construction materials: Aluminium alloy, stressed skin.
Engines: 2 AlliedSignal TPE331-10R-513C turboprops, with 9 ft 2 ins (2.79 m) Dowty R.334/4-82-F/13 4-blade propellers.
Engine rating: Each 900 shp (671 kW).
Fuel system: 2,040 litres, of which 2,000 litres are usable (equivalent to 3,527 lb, 1,600 kg usable). C-212M can carry 2 auxiliary tanks, providing 1,000 litres.
Electrical system: DC supply by 2 engine-driven generators. AC supply via inverters. 2 x 24 volt, 40 amp-hour batteries for self-start and aircraft operability under any conditions.
Hydraulic system: 2,000 psi.
Braking system: Hydraulic discs on mainwheels. Anti-skid system available.
De-icing system: Pneumatic boot and bleed air for wing and tail unit leading edges. Electric for windshield and propellers.
Oxygen system: Standard.
Fire system: Fire extinguishing system standard.
Radar: AlliedSignal Bendix/King weather radar standard.
Flight avionics/instrumentation: Interphone, 2 VHF comm, 2 VOR-ILS, 2 ADF, DME, transponder, AFCS, radio altimeter and ELT. Optional Omega, CVR, FDR and HF. C-212M has interphone, 2 VHF, HF, ATC/transponder, 2 VOR-ILS, 2 ADF, DME, AFCS and radio altimeter plus options of VHF/UHF-AM/FM comm. IFF/SIF, VLF/Omega, Tacan and ELT.
Expendable weapons and equipment: C-212M can carry up to 1,102 lb (500 kg) of external stores on 2 outrigger pylons, including twin 7.62-mm machine-gun pod, 12.7-mm gun pod, 20-mm cannon pod, LAU-3A or 32 rocket launcher, up to 250 kg bomb, Sea Skua or similar light missile, or smart torpedo on each outrigger.
Aircraft variants:
C-212 Series 300 is the standard current version, as detailed.
C-212M is the military version for transport and many more specialized roles (see also Combat section). Can be armed.

Saab Aircraft AB (Sweden)

Corporate address: S-581 88 Linköping.
Telephone: +46 13 18 24 03, 20 00
Facsimile: +46 13 18 27 22
Telex: 50153 SAABAC

● Activities

- See also Combat section.

Saab 340B and Saab 340B Plus

First flight: 25 January 1983 in Saab-Fairchild 340 prototype form.
Certification: 15 May 1984.
First delivery: June 1984 in Saab 340A form.
Role: Regional airliner, business and cargo transport.
Airframe life: 45,000 flying hours or 90,000 landings.
Airport limits: Rigid pavement ACN < 9, unpaved (5,000 passes) CBR < 11.
Noise levels: ICAO 78.4 EPNdB flyover, 86 EPNdB sideline and 91.8 EPNdB approach. FAR Pt 36 Appendix C 78.6 EPNdB flyover, 85.9 EPNdB sideline and 91.6 EPNdB approach.
Sales: 445 firm orders for all variants (including out of production), with 82 awaiting delivery in early 1995.
Details: Principally based on the Saab 340B (see Aircraft variants).
Crew: 3, as 2 pilots plus observer.
Passengers: 30-37, with typically 33-35, all 3 abreast with aisle.
Seat pitch: 30 ins (76 cm) standard, 33 ins (84 cm) business class.
Galley: Standard (see drawings).
Pressurization: 7 psi cabin differential.
Baggage compartment: At rear of passenger cabin, with volume varying between 240.14 and 293.11 cu ft (6.8 and 8.3 m^3) depending upon a forward or rear positioned toilet. Additional baggage stowing in the forward wardrobe and overhead bins.
Wing control surfaces: Ailerons with geared tabs, and flaps.
Tail control surfaces: Elevators with geared tabs, and rudder with spring tab.
Flight control system: Primary flight controls are all manual. Hydraulic flaps, and electric tabs for trimming.
Construction materials: Metal to metal bonding is used extensively, and aluminium alloy honeycomb for doors, wing flaps, and areas of the tail unit. Kevlar (including sandwich) and carbonfibre composites for the control surfaces, fairings, engine inlets, nose and cabin fittings.
Engines: 2 General Electric CT7-9B turboprops, with Dowty 4-blade composites propellers. Optional APU.
Engine rating: Each 1,750 shp (1,305 kW).
Fuel system: 5,690 lb (2,581 kg).
Electrical system: Primary split-busbar system giving regulated DC supply via 2 x 28 volt, 400 amp starter-generators mounted on the engine accessory gearboxes, with 2 ni-cd batteries providing back-up power and engine starting. 24 volt, 5 amp-hour lead-acid battery for supply to an emergency bus. The 26 volt and 115 volt, 400 Hz supply required for certain instrumentation and avionics is derived from the 28 volt DC left-hand main bus by a solid-state inverter. A standby inverter can derive 26 volt AC from right-hand bus. 2 x 115/200 volt AC generators power a separate system for ice protection.
Hydraulic system: 3,000 psi. Designed around a single electric pump and 4 accumulators, with all feedlines located outside the pressure fuselage.
Braking system: Hydraulically operated carbon disc brakes, with anti-skid.

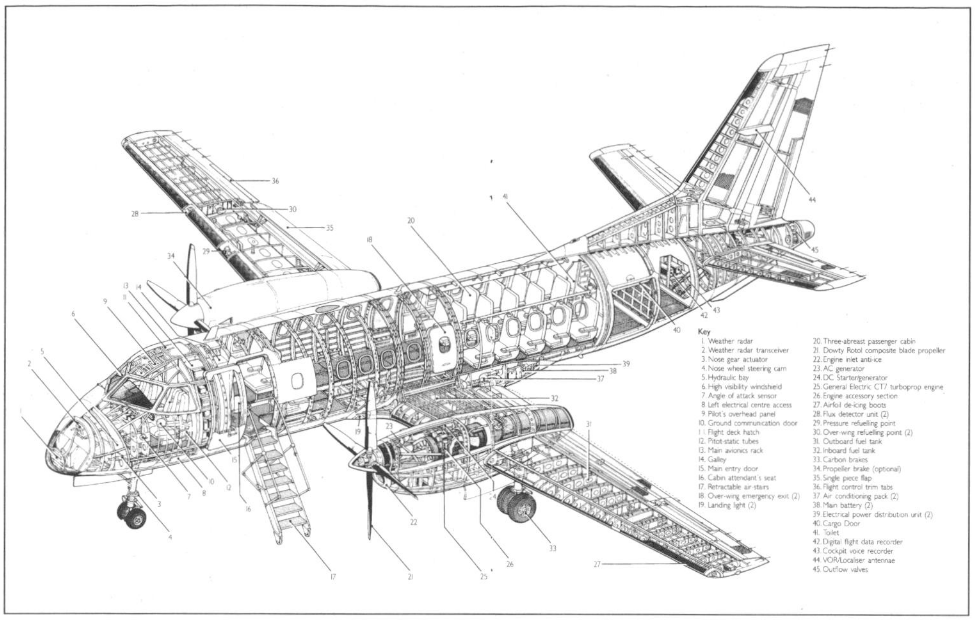

Saab 340B cutaway drawing (courtesy Saab)

Saab 340B Plus in Calm Air livery

De-icing system: Pneumatic boots actuated by engine bleed air for wing and tail unit leading edges. Electric for cockpit glazing, pitot tubes, engine intakes and propellers.
Radar: Weather radar.
Flight avionics/instrumentation: Digital avionics suite with autopilot and EFIS (pilot and co-pilot with an HSI and ADI CRT display, with an optional fifth display for secondary information). Rockwell Collins Pro Line 2 navigation and communications equipment, with AlliedSignal Gold Crown III optional. Provision for additional equipment, including second DME, ADF and transponder, HF and Area Nav. Air data computer is linked to the flight director, and information on attitude and heading is generated by the AHRS. Digital autopilot.
Aircraft variants:
340B was the standard version between 1989-94.
340B Plus is the latest version, introducing a Generation III interior of modern design and with new lighting. Other Plus improvements include 20% increase in overhead luggage bins volume, improved short field and hot-and-high performance using 2 ft (0.6 m) wingtip extensions to reduce field length by up to 400 ft (122 m) and increase take-off weight at restricted airfields by up to 1,500 lb (680 kg), new 84 psi low pressure tyre option, extended maintenance intervals, and active noise control using a system of 45 microphones and 26 speakers to produce an overall cabin noise reduction of 6 dB(A).
340QC is the quick-change version, allowing operators the option to fly passengers by day and cargo by night. Conversion takes under an hour by 2 persons. Up to 24 cargo containers can be loaded with no structural reinforcement.

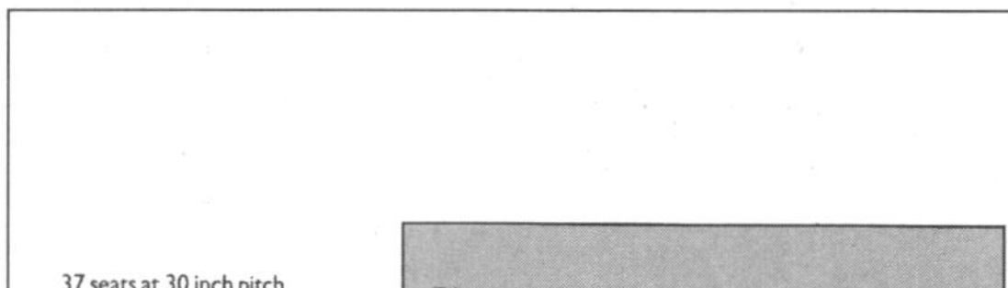

Saab 340B cabin layouts (courtesy Saab)

DETAILS FOR SAAB 340B.

Principal dimensions:
Wing span: 70 ft 4 ins (21.44 m)
Maximum length: 64 ft 9 ins (19.73 m)
Maximum height: 22 ft 6.5 ins (6.87 m)

Cabin:
Length: 34 ft 1 ins (10.39 m)
Width: 7 ft 1 ins (2.16 m)
Height: 6 ft (1.83 m) maximum, 5 ft 7 ins (1.7 m) at floor
Volume: 1,179.51 cu ft (33.4 m^3)
Main passenger door: 5 ft 3 ins x 2 ft 3 ins (1.6 x 0.69 m)
Cargo door: 4 ft 3 ins x 4 ft 5 ins (1.3 x 1.35 m)

Wings:
Aerofoil section: NASA MS(1)-0313
Area: 450 sq ft (41.81 m^2)
Aspect ratio: 10.99
Dihedral: 7°

Tail unit:
Tailplane span: 30 ft 4 ins (9.24 m)
Tailplane area: 121.42 sq ft (11.28 m^2)

Undercarriage:
Type: Retractable, with steerable nosewheels. Twin wheels on each unit
Main wheel tyre size: 24 x 7.7 ins
Nose wheel tyre size: 17.5 x 6.25 ins
Wheel base: 23 ft 5 ins (7.14 m)
Wheel track: 22 ft (6.71 m)
Turning circle: 29 ft 3 ins (8.9 m) minimum

Weights:
Empty, operating: 17,945 lb (8,140 kg)
Maximum zero-fuel: 26,500 lb (12,020 kg)
Maximum take-off: 29,211 lb (13,250 kg)
Maximum landing: 28,505 lb (12,930 kg)
Payload: 8,554 lb (3,880 kg)

Performance:
Typical cruise speed: 285 kts (328 mph) 528 km/h
Long-range cruise speed: 252 kts (290 mph) 467 km/h
Stall speed: 106 kts (122 mph) 197 km/h *clean*, 89 kts (102 mph) 164 km/h *in landing configuration*
Balanced field length for take-off (sea level): 4,233 ft (1,290 m) *JAR*, 4,335 ft (1,321 m) *FAR*
Balanced field length for take-off (5,000 ft, 1,525 m): 6,020 ft (1,835 m) *JAR with low flap setting*, 5,435 ft (1,657 m) *FAR*
Landing field length (sea level): 3,395 ft (1,035 m) *JAR*, 3,495 ft (1,065 m) *FAR*
Landing field length (5,000 ft, 1,525 m): 3,822 ft (1,165 m) *JAR*, 3,940 ft (1,201 m) *FAR*
Maximum climb rate: 2,000 ft (610 m) per minute
Ceiling: 25,000 ft (7,620 m), with 31,000 ft (9,450 m) as option
Ceiling, one engine: 12,500 ft (3,810 m) ISA, or 10.500 ft (3,200 m) at ISA + 10° C, both at 95% MTOW, 1.1% net gradient
Range with 37 passengers: 695 and 795 naut miles (800 and 915 miles) 1,287 and 1,472 km, at maximum cruise speed and FL200 and long-range cruise speed and FL250 respectively
Range with 35 passengers: 805 and 935 naut miles (927 and 1,076 miles) 1,490 and 1,731 km, conditions as above

340 Combi is another layout for the convertible interior, offering 19 passengers plus 3,307 lb (1,500 kg) of cargo.
340 AEW&C, see Reconnaissance section.

Saab 2000

First flight: 26 March 1992.
Certification: 31 March 1994 (JAA) and 29 April 1994 (FAA). PECS certification (see Tail control surfaces) December 1994.
First delivery: 30 August 1994 to Crossair.
Role: Regional airliner.
Airframe life: 60,000 flight hours or 75,000 landings.
Airport limits: Rigid pavement ACN < 15, unpaved (5,000 passes) CBR < 18.
Noise levels: 78 EPNdB flyover, 84 EPNdB lateral, 88 EPNdB approach (estimated). 76 dB(A) typical cabin level.
Sales: 39 firm orders, of which 15 delivered, by June 1995. First 3 flying aircraft built were used in the test programme (plus 2 airframes for static test), with the fourth used temporarily for function and reliability tests and for autopilot certification.
Crew: 2 (flight).
Passengers: 50-58, 3 abreast with aisle. Active noise control (see Saab 340B).
Seat pitch: 32 ins (81 cm) and 30 ins (76 cm) for 50 and 58 passengers respectively.

Saab 2000 cockpit layout (courtesy Saab)

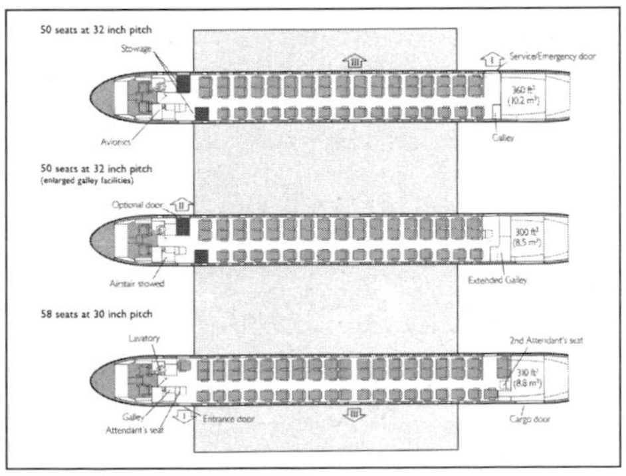

Saab 2000 cabin layouts (courtesy Saab)

DETAILS FOR SAAB 2000.

Principal dimensions:
Wing span: 81 ft 3 ins (24.76 m)
Maximum length: 88 ft 8 ins (27.03 m)
Maximum height: 25 ft 4 ins (7.73 m)

Cabin:
Length: 54 ft 9 ins (16.7 m)
Width: 7 ft 1 ins (2.16 m)
Height: 6 ft (1.83 m)
Volume: 1,861 cu ft (52.7 m^3)

Wings:
Area: 599.55 sq ft (55.7 m^2)
Aspect ratio: 11.01

Tail unit:
Tailplane span: 34 ft (10.36 m)

Undercarriage:
Type: Similar to Saab 340B
Wheel base: 36 ft (10.97 m)
Wheel track: 27 ft (8.23m)
Turning circle: 61 ft 10 ins (18.85 m) minimum

Weights:
Empty, operating: 29,762 lb (13,500 kg)
Maximum zero fuel: 42,770 lb (19,400 kg)
Maximum take-off: 48,502 lb (22,000 kg)
Maximum landing: 47,399 lb (21,500 kg)
Payload: 13,007 lb (5,900 kg)

Performance:
Typical cruise speed: 365 kts (420 mph) 676 km/h
Balanced field length for take-off (sea level): 4,662 ft (1,360 m)
Balanced field length for take-off (5,000 ft, 1,525 m): 5,512 ft (1,680 m)
Landing field length (sea level): 4,100 ft (1,250 m)
Landing field length (5,000 ft, 1,525 m): 4,560 ft (1,390 m)
Maximum climb rate: 2,379 ft (725 m) per minute
Ceiling: 31,000 ft (9,450 m)
Ceiling, one engine: 21,800 ft (6,645 m) ISA, or 19,600 ft (5,975 m) at ISA + 10° C, both at 95% MTOW, 1.1% net gradient
Range with 58 passengers: 935 and 1,045 naut miles (1,076 and 1,203 miles) 1,731 and 1,935 km, at maximum cruise speed and FL310 and long-range cruise speed and FL310 respectively
Range with 50 passengers: 1,255 and 1,425 naut miles (1,445 and 1,641 miles) 2,324 and 2,639 km, conditions as above

Saab 2000, the first delivered to Crossair

Galley: Aft of cockpit. Extended galley can be situated at the rear of the passenger cabin in 50 seat layout.
Pressurization: 7 psi cabin differential.
Freight/baggage hold Volume: 360 cu ft (10.2 m^3), or 300 cu ft (8.5 m^3) with extended galley.
Wing control surfaces: Ailerons (with trim tabs) and single-slotted flaps.
Tail control surfaces: Elevators (with geared trim and spring tabs) and rudder. Early certificated aircraft delivered with spring tab control had some limitations in loadability which have been eliminated since the retrofit of a powered elevator control system (PECS) in 1995; first test flight with PECS 19 May 1994.
Flight control system: Mechanical ailerons. Dual hydraulic fly-by-wire controlled rudder system. Now electro/ hydraulic for elevator. Hydraulic flaps. Manual geared tabs.
Construction materials: Similar to Saab 340B Plus.
Engines: 2 Allison AE 2100A turboprops, with Dowty 6-blade composite propellers. Optional APU.
Engine rating: Each 4,152 shp (3,096 kW)
Fuel system: 9,370 lb (4,250 kg) capacity.
Electrical system: 3-phase AC supply via 2 x 45kVA engine-driven generators. DC supply via 3 x 28 volt batteries.
Braking system: Carbon disc brakes and anti-skid system.
De-icing system: Similar to Saab 340B, except bleed air for engine intakes.
Radar: Rockwell Collins WXR-840 weather radar.
Flight avionics/instrumentation: Rockwell Collins Pro Line 4 suite, with 6 CRT displays and EICAS. Autopilot/flight director, flight management and centralized maintenance functions are provided by the integrated avionics processing system. Traffic alert and collision avoidance system (TCAS) is available and an aircraft communication and reporting system (ACARS) can be integrated. Category IIIa operation is optional.

Antonov Design Bureau (Ukraine)

Corporate address: See Reconnaissance section for full company details.

Antonov An-12 (NATO name *Cub*)

First flight: 16 December 1957.
First delivery: 1959 for start of operational service with Soviet Military Transport Aviation.
Role: Medium-transport/assault, electronic intelligence and electronic warfare. Also civil operated. Was the first Soviet specialized military assault transport.
Airframe life: Antonov offers a service-life extension programme.
Sales: Series manufactured at 3 production plants in the former USSR: Irkutsk Factory No 39 (1958-63), Voronezh Factory No 64 (1961-65) and Tashkent Factory No 84 (1961-72). Total of about 1,400 built, 130 of which remain in service with CIS air forces (mostly replaced by the Il-76). Exported to 14 countries. Also build in China, as Y8 (Yunshuji-8). On 6 September 1994 the final Russian An-12 based in Germany (Sperenberg) was withdrawn.
Details: Generally for the An-12BK.
Crew: 6, comprising 2 pilots, navigator, 2 on-board technicians and communication operator. Rear gunner on some aircraft.

Antonov An-12BP Cub-A of the Russian Air Force, with an unofficial tricolour on the tailfin (Piotr Butowski)

Pressurization: None for hold, but the small front compartment for 14 persons is pressurized to 7.1 psi differential. Heating system and oxygen masks for paratroops installed inside the cargo cabin.
Freight hold volume: 3,433 cu ft (97.2 m^3).

DETAILS FOR AN-12BK.

Principal dimensions:
Wing span: 124 ft 9 ins (38.028 m)
Maximum length: 108 ft 7.5 ins (33.11 m)
Maximum height: 34 ft 7 ins (10.53 m)

Cabin:
Length, without ramp: 44 ft 3 ins (13.5 m)
Width: 10 ft 2 ins (3.1 m)
Height: 8 ft 6 ins (2.6 m)
Volume: 3,433 cu ft (97.2 m^3)
Volume with ramp: 4,351 cu ft (123.2 m^3)

Wings:
Aerofoil section: TsAGI S-5-18, S-3-16, S-3-14 (root to tip)
Area, gross: 1,310 sq ft (121.73 m^2)
Aspect ratio: 11.88
Sweepback: 0° centre section; middle and outer panels 9° 41′ at leading edge and 6° 50′ at quarter chord
Incidence: 3°
Anhedral: 0° centre section and middle panels, 2° outer panels

Tail unit:
Tailplane span: 40 ft (12.196 m)

Undercarriage:
Type: Retractable, with steerable twin nosewheels. Each main unit consists of a 4-wheel bogie, retracting into the fuselage side nacelles
Main wheels tyre size: 1,050 x 300 mm
Wheel base: 35 ft 6 ins (10.82 m)
Wheel track: 16 ft 2 ins (4.92 m)

Weights:
Empty, operating: 77,382 lb (35,100 kg)
Maximum take-off: 134,482 lb (61,000 kg)
Maximum landing: 127,888 lb (58,000 kg)
Maximum payload: 44,092 lb (20,000 kg)

Performance:
Maximum speed: 418 kts (482 mph) 775 km/h
Cruising speed: 297-373 kts (342-373 mph) 550-600 km/h
Take-off distance: 4,036 ft (1,230 m)
Landing distance: 3,691 ft (1,125 m)
Service ceiling: 33,465 ft (10,200 m)
Range with full fuel: 3,132 naut miles (3,604 miles) 5,800 km
Range with full payload: 1,080 naut miles (1,243 miles) 2,000 km

Freight hold capacity: 44,092 lb (20,000 kg). Equipped for paradropping of troops (60) or military hardware (2 platforms, 35,274 lb, 16,000 kg total). 91 troops when landing conventionally.
Freight hold access: Rear doors.
Loading facilities: See Aircraft variants.
Wing control surfaces: Double-slotted trailing-edge flaps on the centre section, single-slotted flap on each middle wing panel, and 2-section aileron (with tab) on each outer panel.
Tail control surfaces: Elevators (with tabs) and rudder (with tab).
Flight control system: Mechanical; trailing-edge flaps are hydraulically actuated.
Engines: 4 Ivchenko PROGRESS AI-20M turboprops, with a 14 ft 9 ins (4.5 m) 4-blade variable-pitch AV-68 propeller. TG-16M auxiliary power unit in the port undercarriage nacelle.
Engine rating: Each 4,250 ehp (3,169 ekW) at take-off.

Antonov An-12BK Cub-A used at the Zhukovsky Flight Test Centre for ejector seat research. The seat can be launched from the tail stand in any direction (Piotr Butowski)

Fuel system: 29,600 litres in the wings and 2 tanks under the cabin floor (48,633 lb, 22,066 kg). Auxiliary fuel tanks can be installed in the cargo hold.
Flight refuelling probe: None.
Radar: RBP-3 navigation/sight radar under the nose. Some aircraft have more powerful Initsiativa-4 radar, distinguished by a much larger radome. Simple ROZ-1 observation radar instead of RBP-3/Initsiativa-4 in civil aircraft.
Flight avionics/instrumentation: NAS-1B1-28 or DISS-013-12 navigation system, KS-SG course system, AP-28D1 autopilot, ARK-11 radio compass, RV-2 or RV-5M radio altimeter, SP-50 instrument landing system, and RSBN-2S short-range radio navigation system. R-832M or R-863 plus R-837 or R-856MA communications radios. Sirena radar warning receiver.
Fixed weapons: Some aircraft have a DB-65U tail turret containing 2 flexible AM-23 23-mm cannon, KPS-53A optical sight and radio rangefinder.
Expendable weapons and equipment: Small bomb rack (2 on older aircraft) under each main undercarriage nacelle for FOTAB-100-80 flare bombs to light the landing area at night.
Aircraft variants:
An-12 *Cub-A* was the early production model, powered by 4 x 4,000 shp (2,983 kW) Kuznetsov NK-4 turboprops. Maximum take-off weight 119,050 lb (54,000 kg).
An-12A *Cub-A* (1962) was produced with heavier but more reliable Ivchenko AI-20A turboprops of the same power. Maximum take-off weight 123,459 lb (56,000 kg), later raised to 134,481 lb (61,000 kg) when the wing centre-section was strengthened. Fuel capacity 16,690 litres inside wing tanks.
Payload 44,092 lb (20,000 kg).
An-12B *Cub-A* (1963) was one of the most widespread versions, powered by AI-20M engines. Fuel capacity increased to 19,490 litres (all in wings). TG-16 APU added in port undercarriage nacelle for autonomous operation. More powerful BL-1500 winches instead of the former BL-52 inside the cargo cabin.
An-12BP *Cub-A* was similar to the An-12B, but with a dinghy as standard because of its over sea operations.
An-12BPL *Cub-A* (polarnyi lyzhnyi, polar region, ski) was produced as a variant of the An-12B but with a fixed ski undercarriage.
An-12BK *Cub-A* became a much used version. Fuel capacity increased to 29,600 litres, cargo cabin widened by 3.9 ins (100 mm) to 10 ft 2 ins (3.10 m), and rear doors widened. GL-1500DP remotely controlled winches, and telpher capacity 5,071 lb (2,300 kg). Hermetic compartment established for cargo personnel (14 people) aft of the flight deck.
An-12BK-IS is similar to the An-12BK but with self-defence ECM systems added.
An-12PS *Cub-A* (1969) became the search and rescue version, carrying a dropped Yorsh motor boat for 3 rescuers and 11 survivors.
An-12BK-VKP Zebra (1970) was produced as an airborne command post, a competitor to the Il-22 *Coot-B*. Prototype only.
An-12BL (1970) was an experimental air-defence suppression version, armed with Kh-28 (AS-9 *Kyle*) anti-radiation missiles.
An-12BSh and An-12BKSh (Sh for shturmanskiy or navigator) were developed as training aircraft for navigators of transport aviation. 10 navigator stations inside the cabin.
An-12 Tsiklon (1979) became a meteorological research aircraft.
An-12 *Cub-B* is an electronic intelligence aircraft, recognized by the West in the late 1960s. Cub-Bs were met over the Baltic Sea and Indian Ocean during Western naval exercises. Typical of elint versions are numerous antennae, in many forms. Only a dozen or so aircraft were converted for elint.
An-12PP *Cub-C* is another electronic warfare aircraft, a conversion of the An-12B or An-12BK. Several longitudinal aerials are installed under the front and middle sections of the fuselage. At the both sides of the front fuselage are 6 additional air inlets for cooling the equipment and there are 2 more inlets in the rear area. Fewer windows than in the standard transport version. A jamming unit is installed in place of the tail gunner turret.
An-12PPS (or An-12BK-PPS) *Cub-D* is a more recent EW version, converted from the An-12BK. It has similar longitudinal aerials and cooling air inlets. 4 additional cigar-shaped containers with jamming equipment, 2 suspended under the front fuselage ahead of the undercarriage nacelles and 2 at the tailfin root.
Y 8 (Yunshuji-8) covers Chinese versions and derivatives, in production.

Antonov An-22 (NATO name *Cock*)

First flight: 27 February 1965 (piloted by Yuri Kurlin).
First delivery: First production aircraft left the Tashkent factory in 1966. State Acceptance Trials in October 1967, when a 221,344 lb (100,400 kg) payload was lifted to 25,750 ft (7,848 m). First aircraft delivered to the Soviet Air Force in 1969.
Role: Heavy military transport.
Sales: Preparations for series production began in Tashkent in Uzbekistan in 1962, with the construction of a new large assembly facility as Factory No 84. More than 60 produced. First participation in the extensive Dvina exercises in March 1970. About 50 are still used by the Russian Air Force. 5 aircraft have been lost during service, in 1970 (2), 1976, 1980 and 1992. Not exported. An An-22 was the final Russian military

DETAILS FOR AN-22A.

Principal dimensions:
Wing span: 211 ft 3 ins (64.40 m)
Maximum length: 188 ft (57.31 m)
Maximum height: 41 ft 1.5 ins (12.535 m)

Wings:
Area, gross: 3,714 sq ft (345 m^2)
Aspect ratio: 12.02

Cabin:
Length, maximum: 107 ft 3 ins (32.7 m)
Length, without rear ramp: 86 ft 7 ins (26.4 m)
Width: 14 ft 5 ins (4.4 m)
Height: 14 ft 5 ins (4.4 m)
Volume: 22,601 cu ft (640 m^3)

Undercarriage:
Type: Retractable, with steerable twin nosewheels. Main units are carried inside 2 long nacelles at the sides of the fuselage. Each nacelle contains 6 pairs of braked wheels, in tandem. Due to the independent suspension of each pair, the aircraft can operate and run smoothly off runways. The undercarriage doors are opened only for the short time of lowering or raising in order to protect the inside of the bays against dust and mud. Tyre pressure can be controlled by the pilot, to make adjustments for different airfields.
Main wheel tyre size: KT-109 of 1,750 x 730 mm
Nose wheel tyre size: KT-110 of 1,450 x 580 mm

Weights:
Empty, operating: 261,748 lb (118,727 kg)
Nominal take-off: 451,947 lb (205,000 kg)
Maximum take-off: 496,040 lb (225,000 kg)
Payload: 132,240 lb (60,000 kg)

Performance:
Maximum speed: 324 kts (373 mph) 600 km/h
Cruise speed: 313 kts (360 mph) 580 km/h
Take-off speed: 138 kts (158 mph) 255 km/h
Landing speed: 130 kts (149 mph) 240 km/h
Take-off run: 4,790 ft (1,460 m)
Landing run: 3,412 ft (1,040 m)
Range with full fuel: 5,940 naut miles (6,835 miles) 11,000 km
Range with full payload: 2,700 naut miles (3,107 miles) 5,000 km

aircraft to leave former bases in Germany, on 7 September 1994.
Crew: 5, with the navigator in the nose. Cockpit deck followed by pressurized compartment for 29 passengers (freight service, stand-by crew) and the freight cabin.
Freight hold volume: 22,601 cu ft (640 m^3).
Freight hold capacity: 132,277 lb (60,000 kg), including large and heavy vehicles, missile systems, etc.
Freight hold access: Rear loading doors.
Loading facilities: Loading ramp under the tail, with the fuselage door retracting upwards to leave unrestricted space for easy loading of vehicles or other cargoes. Cargo handling gear includes equipment for parachute landing of heavy items. Travelling cranes are suspended under the cargo hold ceiling, each with a 5,512 lb (2,500 kg) capacity winch.
Wing control surfaces: Ailerons (with tabs) and double-slotted trailing-edge flaps.
Tail control surfaces: H-type unit, with elevators (with tabs) and dorsal/ventral-section rudders (with tabs).
Fuselage: Semi-monocoque, circular section.
Construction: All metal.
Engines: 4 Samara/Kuznetsov NK-12MA turboprops. Each 8-blade AV-90 propeller unit consists of 2x 4-blade co-axial contra-rotating reversible-pitch propellers.

Antonov An-22 Cock heavy transport (Piotr Butowski)

Engine rating: Each 14,805 shp (11,040 kW).
Fuel system: 211,644 lb (96,000 kg) of fuel in 40 fuel tanks inside wings and undercarriage nacelles.
Flight refuelling probe: None.
Radar: Kupol-22 navigation/sight radar under the nose. Early aircraft have Initsiativa-4-100 radar, initially located in the starboard undercarriage nacelle, later under the fuselage nose.
Fixed weapons: None.
Aircraft variants:
An-22 Antei *Cock* was the first production model.
An-22A *Cock* became the principal production version, with systems changes (mainly fuel system) and upgraded equipment.

Antonov An-24 (NATO name *Coke*)

First flight: 1960.
First delivery: Commercial services with Aeroflot began September 1963, between Moscow and Voronezh and Saratov.
Role: Short-haul passenger or cargo transport, plus fire-fighting.
Airframe life: Design life of 20,000 cycles or 22,000 flight hours. Antonov offers a life extension programme, increasing life to 40,000 cycles or 45,000 flight hours.
Sales: An estimated 1,100 were built up to 1978, of which nearly 850 remained in commercial use in early 1995 plus others with the Russian Air Force and elsewhere.
Crew: 2 to 5 (pilot, co-pilot/navigator/radio operator, or separate navigator, radio operator and engineer).
Passengers: 44-52, or 36 in combi form (see Aircraft variants for freighter versions).
Seat pitch: 28.3 ins (72 cm).
Pressurization: 4.27 psi cabin differential.
Freight hold volume: Small hold in passenger versions. Combi layout provides for a larger 494.4 cu ft (14 m^3) hold. An-24T and RT freighters have 51 ft 5 ins length x 5 ft 9.5 ins height x 7 ft 2 ins width hold (15.68 x 1.77 x 2.17 m) of 1,766 cu ft (50 m^3) volume.
Freight hold capacity: 10,168 lb (4,612 kg) in T, and 12,566 lb (5,700 kg) in RT, allowing for cargo, 30 paratroopers on folding seats, 38 troops, 24 litters and attendant, or other loads.
Freight hold access: Under rear fuselage cargo hatch in the T/RT, with upward-hinging door. Used also for paradropping. Smaller conventional door in the starboard side of the hold.
Size of freight doors: 9 ft 4 ins length x 4 ft 7 ins maximum width (2.85 x 1.4 m) tail cargo door in the T/RT. Sill height 5 ft 4 ins (1.62 m) maximum.
Loading facilities: Electric telpher in the ceiling to hoist and position cargoes, capacity 3,307 lb (1,500 kg) in T/RT, which also have a floor-mounted 9,921 lb (4,500 kg) capacity electric/manual conveyor.
Wing control surfaces: Ailerons (with tabs), single-slotted flaps in the wing centre-section and double-slotted flaps on outer panels.
Tail control surfaces: Elevators and rudder, with tabs.
Flight control system: Hydraulically-operated wing surfaces, manual tail surfaces.
Construction materials: All metal, except for composites tabs.
Engines: 2 Ivchenko PROGRESS AI-24A turboprops.
Engine rating: Each 2,550 ehp (1,902 ekW).
Fuel system: 5,550 litres.
Electrical system: DC system comprises 2 x 27 volt starter-generators. AC system comprises 2 alternators for 115 volt/400Hz, and 2 inverters for 36 volt/400Hz 3-phase.
Hydraulic system: 2,200 psi.
Braking system: Disc brakes on main units.
De-icing system: Thermal on wings and tail.
Radar: RPSN-2AN weather/navigation/avoidance radar.
Flight avionics/instrumentation: IFR. AP-28L1 autopilot. Offered with the OPB-1R sight for accurate paradropping and navigation.
Aircraft variants:
An-24P was offered as a fire-fighting conversion, undergoing trials in the early 1970s.
An-24RV is a higher weight version of the An-24V/V II, featuring an RU-19-300 auxiliary turbojet in place of the V's starter-generator, allowing take-off with a full load from airfields 9,845 ft (3,000 m) above sea level and at ISA + 30°, better take-off/climb performance generally, auxiliary power in cases of a main engine failure, and engine start-up.

DETAILS FOR AN-24V II.

Principal dimensions:
Wing span: 95 ft 9.5 ins (29.2 m)
Maximum length: 77 ft 2 ins (23.53 m)
Maximum height: 27 ft 4 ins (8.32 m)

Cabin:
Length: 31 ft 10 ins (9.69 m)
Width: 9 ft 1 ins (2.76 m)
Height: 6 ft 3 ins (1.91 m)
Main door: 4 ft 7 ins x 2 ft 5.5 ins (1.4 x 0.75 m)

Wings:
Area: 807.08 sq ft (74.98 m^2)
Aspect ratio: 11.37
Sweepback: 6° 50' at 25° outer-section chord
Incidence: 3°
Anhedral: 2°

Tail unit:
Tailplane span: 29 ft 1 ins (9.08 m)

Undercarriage:
Type: Retractable, with steerable nosewheels
Wheel base: 25 ft 10.5 ins (7.89 m)
Wheel track: 25 ft 11 ins (7.9 m)

Weights:
Empty: 29,321 lb (13,300 kg)
Maximum take-off: 46,297 lb (21,000 kg)
Payload: 12,125 lb (5,500 kg)

Performance:
Cruise: 243 kts (280 mph) 450 km/h
Take-off distance: 1,969 ft (600 m)
Maximum climb rate: 374 ft (114 m) per minute
Ceiling: 27,550 ft (8,400 m)
Range with full fuel: 1,296 naut miles (1,491 miles) 2,400 km, with reserve
Range with full payload: 297 naut miles (342 miles) 550 km, with reserve

Antonov An-24 of Ukrainian Airlines (Piotr Butowski)

An-24T and RT are freighter versions of the V and RV.
An-24V was the initial passenger version, with similarly rated AI-24 engines.
An-24V II became the standard passenger version from 1968.
Xi'an Y7 is a Chinese derivative still in production and development, which see.

Antonov An-26 (NATO name *Curl*)

First flight: 21 May 1969.
First delivery: Entered service with the Soviet Air Force in early 1970s.
Role: Light, short-haul transport based on the An-24.
Airframe life: Antonov offers a service-life extension programme.
Sales: More than 1,700 An-26s were manufactured. Adopted by the Soviet military and Aeroflot, and exported to 27 countries for military and civil use. Currently used by the CIS armed forces as auxiliary aircraft assigned individually to Air Force regiments or to staffs at various levels of command. About 200 aircraft of this type are also used commercially in Russia (some 171 with Aeroflot), and form a reserve for the armed forces. About 425 commercial An-26s were in service worldwide in early 1995. Also produced in China as the Y7H.
Crew: 3-5 (2 pilots and an onboard technician as standard; additionally a navigator and communications operator).
Passengers: See Freight hold capacity.
Pressurization: 4.27 psi cabin differential.
Freight hold volume: 2,118.9 cu ft (60 m^3)
Freight hold capacity: Up to 12,125 lb (5,500 kg) of cargo, including small military cars (up to 2,866 lb, 1,300 kg weight) or 40 troops (folding seats along the cabin sides), or 30 paratroops. In rescue configuration, 24 litter patients and 1-3 litter-bearers.
Freight hold access: Hydraulically opened rear loading ramp. When opened, the ramp can take 2 positions: lowered for roll-on from the ground or slid back horizontally under the fuselage for air-dropping or for loading directly from trucks. Door 2 ft x 4 ft 7 ins (0.6 x 1.4 m) at the starboard side of the front freight hold, used also by the crew. Emergency exits in the floor and in starboard and port sides of the hold.
Size of freight door: Rear ramp entrance width 7 ft 10.5 ins (2.40 m) at floor, 6 ft 11 ins (2.10 m) at top; height 10 ft 4 ins (3.15 m) or 5 ft 2 ins (1.564 m) in a vertical line.

Antonov An-26P fire-fighting aircraft (Piotr Butowski)

Antonov An-26RT Curl-B relay aircraft (Piotr Butowski)

Loading facilities: Single cabin-top electrical telpher, 3,306 lb (1,500 kg) capacity. 2 roller tracks on the floor (can be stowed against the cabin walls), tie-down positions and mats. Early An-26s were given a 9,921 lb (4,500 kg) electric/manual floor conveyor system.
Wing control surfaces: Single-slotted trailing-edge flaps on the centre section, tracked double-slotted flaps on the middle panels (15° for take-off, 38° for landing). 2-section ailerons (+24°, -16°) on each wing outer panel.
Tail control surfaces: Elevators (+30°, -15°). Rudder (±25°).
Flight control system: Mechanical.
Engines: 2 Ivchenko PROGRESS AI-24VT turboprops, with 12 ft 9.5 ins (3.9 m) 4-blade AV-72T propellers. In the rear of the right engine nacelle is housed a Soyuz/Tumansky RU-19A-300 turbojet (1,984 lbf, 88.3 kN) to provide additional thrust during take-off and climb, or in case of failure of one of the main engines. It is also used as an APU for starting the main engines and to drive the electric generators.
Engine rating: Each 2,820 ehp (2,103 ekW).
Fuel system: 7,100 litres in 14 wing tanks (12,125 lb, 5,500 kg).
Flight refuelling probe: None.
Electrical system: 28 volt DC. 115 volt/ 400 Hz and 36 volt/400 Hz AC supply.
Hydraulic system: 2 independent systems (basic and stand-by), pressure 2,204 psi.
Braking system: On main undercarriage units.
Radar: RPSN-3N Emblema navigation/weather radar in the nose.
Flight avionics/instrumentation: Typical set of flight/navigation instruments include ARK-11 radio compass, MRP-56P marker beacon receiver, and SP-50M instrument landing system. IFF. UHF R-802GM and HF R-836/US-SK com radios. OPB-1R bomb sight for paratroop operations.
Fixed weapons: None.
Expendable weapons and equipment: 2 racks can be mounted on each side of the fuselage, usually for SAB-100 100 kg flare bombs for illuminating of the landing area.

Antonov An-26 Curl-A rear loading ramp (Piotr Butowski)

Details for An-26 Curl-A.

Principal dimensions:
Wing span: 95 ft 9.5 ins (29.2 m)
Maximum length: 78 ft 1 in (23.8 m)
Maximum height: 28 ft 1.5 ins (8.575 m)

Cabin:
Length: 36 ft 5 ins (11.1 m)
Length, including ramp: 51 ft 5 ins (15.68 m)
Width: 9 ft 1.5 ins (2.78 m) maximum
Height: 6 ft 3 ins (1.91 m) maximum
Volume: 2,118.9 cu ft (60 m^3)

Wings:
Area, gross: 807.1 sq ft (74.98 m^2)
Aspect ratio: 11.37
Sweepback: 0° at centre section, outer panel leading edge 9° 41′, outer panel at quarter chord 6° 50′
Incidence: 3°
Anhedral: 2° outer panels

Tail unit:
Tailplane span: 32 ft 8.5 ins (9.973 m)
Tailplane area: 213.45 sq ft (19.83 m^2)
Fin area, including dorsal fin: 170.61 sq ft (15.85 m^2)

Undercarriage:
Type: Retractable, with steerable nosewheels. Twin wheels on each unit
Main wheel tyre size: 1,050 x 400 mm
Nose wheel tyre size: 700 x 250 mm
Wheel base: 25 ft 1 ins (7.651 m)
Wheel track: 25 ft 11 ins (7.90 m)
Turning circle: 36 ft 11 ins (11.25 m)

Weights:
Empty, operating: 37,289 lb (16,914 kg)
Maximum take-off: 52,910 lb (24,000 kg)
Payload: 12,125 lb (5,500 kg)

Performance:
Maximum speed: 292 kts (336 mph) 540 km/h
Cruise speed: 232-235 kts (267-270 mph) 430-435 km/h at 19,685 ft (6,000 m)
Take-off speed, at maximum take-off weight: 111 kts (127 mph) 205 km/h
Landing speed, maximum take-off weight: 105 kts (121 mph) 195 km/h
Take-off distance, concrete runway: 2,854 ft (870 m) at MTOW
Take-off distance, concrete runway: 1,739 ft (530 m) at 44,092 lb (20,000 kg) take-off weight
Take-off distance over a 50 ft (15 m) obstacle, concrete runway: 4,495 ft (1,370 m)
Landing distance: 3,806 ft (1,160 m)
Maximum climb rate: 1,417 ft (432 m) per minute at sea level, nominal engine rating, MTOW
Ceiling: 25,260 ft (7,700 m) at MTOW
Ceiling at 44,092 lb (20,000 kg): 29,530 ft (9,000 m)
Range with full fuel: 1,458 naut miles (1,678 miles) 2,700 km

Aircraft variants:
An-26 *Curl-A* was presented at the 1969 Paris Air Show as the An-24RT with enlarged loading doors. Entirely redesigned rear fuselage with flat ramp and reinforced structure. See general description.
An-26B appeared in 1978 with improved freight handling equipment, enabling 2 persons to load 3 standard freight pallets in 30 minutes.
An-26P is the fire-fighting version, with 8,818-9,700 lb (4,000-4,400 kg) of fire-extinguishing mixture.
An-26PS (pasazhirsky, svyaz) is the military executive version, with cabin seating and improved communication equipment.
An-26M Spasatel appeared in 1980 as a rescue version prepared specially for the conflict in Afghanistan. Surgical cabin.
An-26RT (relay) *Curl-B* is operated for increasing the range of communications at the tactical level of command. Externally it differs from the standard An-26 by having a great number of sword-type aerials installed on the airframe.
An-26Sh (shturmansky) appeared in 1975 as a training version for navigators destined for transport aircraft and bombers.
An-26Z-1 (zastavba) is for electronic intelligence, prepared in the Czech Republic. Large bulbous radomes on both sides of the centre fuselage.
Xi'an Y7H is a Chinese derivative, still in production and development, which see.

Antonov An-32 (NATO name *Cline*)

First flight: 9 July 1976.
First delivery: 1984, to India.
Role: Light short/medium-range freighter or airliner. Based on the An-26, with hot-and-high features added for operation from airfields at 4,500 m above sea level. Built specially against an order from India.
Sales: Manufactured continuously since 1984 at Kiev, Ukraine, aircraft plant. Most importantly for export, with only a few aircraft in Russian Air Force use and perhaps more than 60 with CIS airline operators plus others with the Department of Agriculture. 123 used by India with the local name Sutlej. Others in Afghanistan, Bangladesh, Peru (which ordered 3 more and 3 on option in 1994) and Sri Lanka.
Crew: 2 pilots and a navigator, plus optional on-board technician.
Pressurization: 4.27 psi cabin differential.
Freight hold volume: 2,331 cu ft (66 m^3)
Freight hold capacity: Up to 14,771 lb (6,700 kg), with possible loads including 50 troops, 42 paratroops, 24 litter patients plus 1-3 litter bearers, 4 x PAV-2.5 pallets, 12 MG paradropping platforms (1,102 lb, 500 kg each), or 2 x BG modular paradropping platforms (6,614 lb, 3,000 kg each).
Freight hold access: Rear loading ramp, 18 ft 6 ins (5.633 m) length, 7 ft 10.5 ins (2.4 m) bottom to 6 ft 7 ins (2 m) top width. Side doors 2 ft x 4 ft 7 ins (0.60 x 1.40 m).

Antonov An-32B Cline hot-and-high derivative of the An-26 (Piotr Butowski)

DETAILS FOR AN-32 CLINE.

Principal dimensions:
Wing span: 95 ft 9.5 ins (29.20 m)
Maximum length: 77 ft 8 ins (23.68 m)
Maximum height: 28 ft 8.5 ins (8.75 m)

Cabin:
Length, including ramp: 51 ft 6 ins (15.685 m)
Length, excluding ramp: 40 ft 11 ins (12.48 m)
Width: 9 ft 1.5 ins (2.78 m) maximum
Height: 6 ft 0.5 ins (1.84 m) maximum
Volume: 2,331 cu ft (66 m^3)

Wings:
Area, gross: 807.1 sq ft (74.98 m^2)
Aspect ratio: 11.37
Sweepback: 0° centre section, 9° 41′ outer panel leading edges
Mean aerodynamic chord: 9 ft 3 ins (2.813 m)
Anhedral: 2° outer panels
Incidence: +3°

Tail unit:
Tailplane span: 33 ft 7 ins (10.235 m)
Tailplane area: 218.5 sq ft (20.3 m^2)
Fin height: 21 ft 6 ins (6.56 m)
Fin area: 185.35 sq ft (17.22 m^2)

Undercarriage:
Type: as for An-26
Main wheel tyre size: 1,050 x 390 mm
Nose wheel tyre size: 700 x 250 mm
Wheel base: 25 ft 1 ins (7.652 m)
Wheel track: 25 ft 11 ins (7.90 m)
Turning circle: 83 ft 1 ins (25.335 m) at wingtip

Weights:
Empty, operating: 37,038 lb (16,800 kg)
Maximum take-off: 59,525 lb (27,000 kg)
Maximum landing: 55,116 lb (25,000 kg)
Payload: 14,771 lb (6,700 kg)

Performance (with AI-20D engines; *data in italics for An-32 with AI-20M engines;* all ISA):
Cruise speed: 254-286 kts (292-329 mph) 470-530 km/h, *254-270 kts (292-311 mph) 470-500 km/h*
Take-off speed: 116 kts (134 mph) 215 km/h, *116 kts (134 mph) 215 km/h*
Landing speed: 100 kts (115 mph) 185 km/h, *100 kts (115 mph) 185 km/h*
Take-off distance: 3,937 ft (1,200 m), *4,101 ft (1,250 m)*
Landing distance: 3,117 ft (950 m), *3,215 ft (980 m)*
Time to 19,685 ft (6,000 m): 11 minutes, *15 minutes.*
Ceiling: 30,840 ft (9,400 m), *27,890 ft (8,500 m)*
Range with full fuel: 1,280 naut miles (1,473 miles) 2,370 km, *1,350 naut miles (1,553 miles) 2,500 km*
Range with full payload: 659 naut miles (758 miles) 1,220 km, *702 naut miles (808 miles) 1,300 km*

UVP-26 chaff/flare dispenser can be used by the An-32 for rain-making, when MP-26 chemical cartridges are shot into clouds (Piotr Butowski)

Loading facilities: Single cabin-top electric telpher of 6,612 lb (3,000 kg) capacity. 2 stowable roller tracks on the floor, tie-down positions and mats.
Wing and tail control surfaces: As for An-26 except for triple-slotted trailing-edge flaps, and automatic slats along the entire leading-edge span.
Engines: 2 Ivchenko PROGRESS AI-20 turboprops in 2 variants: AI-20M (4,250 ehp, 3,169 ekW) for temperate climates and AI-20D (5,180 ehp, 3,863 ekW) for hot climates. 15 ft 5 ins (4.7 m) 4-blade propellers. TG-16M APU.
Fuel system: 12,004 lb (5,445 kg). Fuel with maximum payload 4,998 lb (2,267 kg).
Flight avionics/instrumentation: NK-32 navigation system, NKPB-7 sight (for paradropping), Mikron HF com, ARK-15M radio compass, DISS-013-26Sh Doppler speed and drift meter.
Fixed weapons: None.
Expendable weapons and equipment: Provision for 4 x 100 kg flare bombs.
Aircraft variants:
An-32 standard version, as detailed.
An-32B has 1,102 lb (500 kg) more payload.
An-32P (pozharnyi) Firekiller is a fire-fighting version. *UR-48004* prototype only. Carries up to 17,637 lb (8,000 kg) of water and extinguishing agents in 2 side-of-fuselage nacelles; typical speed when releasing water is 117-124 kts (135-143 mph) 217-230 km/h at 98 ft (30 m) altitude. Can also carry 27-30 firefighters to be parachuted near the fire. An-32P can also be used for weather adjustment purposes, with rain produced by means of MP-26 chemical cartridges (UVP-26 containers fixed to the fuselage sides) shot into clouds.

Antonov An-38

First flight: 22 June 1994 (Novosibirsk, Russia).
Certification: Early 1996. Certification by the Russian Interstate Registry.
First delivery: To Vostok Airlines in October 1996.
Role: Commuter airliner, utility and special mission aircraft. Capable of operating in vastly differing temperatures, from -50° C to +45° C.
Sales: Launch customer is Vostok Airlines. Series production at the Novosibirsk Aircraft Production Association (NAPA) plant in Siberia. Expected to replace many An-24s and Let L 410s. Market for 600 is anticipated. Development in association with NAPA and AlliedSignal, the latter integrating the entire power plant package, encompassing the engines, propellers, starter generators, pumps, cockpit indicators and more.
Flight crew: 2.
Passengers: 26-27. Executive layout provides for 8-10. Ambulance layout for 6 litters, 9 seated casualties and an attendant.
Galley: Warm drinks from a position immediately aft of the flight deck.
Baggage area: At the rear of the cabin, aft of the toilet.
Freight capacity: 5,512 lb (2,500 kg) of freight, either with passenger seats and baggage hold stowed against the cabin sides or in an unrestricted freighter layout for containerized cargo.
Size of freight door: Under rear fuselage door, 7 ft 3 ins x 4 ft 7 ins (2.2 x 1.4 m), slid under the cabin for straight-through loading.
Wing control surfaces: Ailerons, 2-section slotted flaps, and leading-edge slats over the entire wing outboard of the engines, plus spoilers.

Antonov An-38-100 (Piotr Butowski)

Tail control surfaces: Elevators and twin rudders, with tabs.
Engines: 2 AlliedSignal TPE331-14GR turboprops. Optional OMSK TVD-20s or Rybinsk TVD-1500Bs.
Engine rating: 1,760 shp (1,312.4 kW), with 1,650 shp (1,230 kW) gearbox limit.
Electrical system: Lucas starter-generators.
Radar: Weather radar.
Flight avionics/instrumentation: AlliedSignal flight and navigation equipment to category II minimums. AMETEK cockpit indicators.
Aircraft variants:
An-38 is presumably to be offered with OMSK TVD-20 turboprops (1,380 shp, 1,029 kW) or Rybinsk TVD-1500B turboprops (1,300 shp, 969.4 kW).
An-38-100 or An-38K is the designation of the initial production version with AlliedSignal engines, becoming the first completely new CIS aircraft to be launched with Western engines. All early flight testing of the An-38 was with these engines, accumulating 112 flying hours in almost 90 flights by early 1995.
Special missions will include fishery/forest/ice patrol, survey, photographic, ambulance and more.

DETAILS FOR AN-38.

Principal dimensions:
Wing span: 72 ft 5 ins (22.06 m)
Maximum length: 51 ft (15.54 m)
Maximum height: 14 ft 1 ins (4.3 m)

Tail unit:
Tail span: 16 ft 10 ins (5.14 m)

Undercarriage:
Type: Retractable, with nosewheel. Alternative ski gear

Weights:
Empty: 11,215 lb (5,087 kg)
Maximum take-off: 19,401 lb (8,800 kg)

Performance:
Cruise speed: 205 kts (236 mph) 380 km/h at 9,850 ft (3,000 m)
Required runway length: 2,592 ft (790 m)
Range: 1,188 naut miles (1,367 miles) 2,200 km maximum
Range with full payload: 324 naut miles (373 miles) 600 km

Antonov An-70 and An-77

First flight: 16 December 1994 (pilot Sergei Maksimov).
First delivery: 1997.
Role: Medium transport to replace remaining An-12 *Cubs*, and take over some tasks from heavier Il-76 *Candids*. Offered also as a replacement for the C-130 Hercules and C-160 Transall.
Chief designer: Vasiliy Teplov.
Airframe life: 45,000 flying hours and 20,000 cycles life over 25 years.

★ Aims

★ Ability to carry a 44,092 lb (20,000 kg) payload over 1,620 naut miles (1,864 miles) 3,000 km when operated from unprepared runways with allowed surface pressure of 0.8 MPa and with a take-off run of 1,969-2,625 ft (600-800 m).
★ Range of 2,700 naut miles (3,107 miles) 5,000 km with a 66,120 lb (30,000 kg) payload when operated from a concrete runway 5,905-7,220 ft (1,800-2,200 m) long.
★ Unusually large cargo cabin, the internal volume equal to that of the An-22, exceeding by one-third the volume of the Il-76, and 2 or 3 times greater than that of the An-12, C-130 Hercules or C-160 Transall.
★ Specific fuel consumption of 165 g per tonne kilometre, 25% less than that of the An-12 and about 50% less than for the Il-76.

▲ Development

▲ 1975. Work began. Original design was to be powered by 4 D-236 turboprop engines, fuselage diameter was to be 16 ft 5 ins (5.0 m), and the structure was to be all metal.
▲ 1985. New requirements issued, including STOL capability and new payload specifications. Work began on a new design at much higher technological level, including fly-by-wire control system, fuselage diameter increased to 18 ft 4.5 ins (5.6 m), wide use of composite materials, and adoption of D-27 propfan engines.
▲ 24 June 1993. Prime Ministers of Russia and Ukraine signed the agreement providing financial support for the An-70 (80% from Russia, 20% from Ukraine). The original agreement lapsed when Russia began work on its own Tu-330 project.
▲ 20 January 1994. Roll-out of the prototype at the Antonov works in Kiev.
▲ 14 July 1994. Establishment of a consortium of design bureaux, production plants and banks from Ukraine, Russia and Uzbekistan, for development and manufacturing of the An-70.
▲ 16 December 1994. First flight lasting 26 minutes.
▲ 10 February 1995. First prototype crashed at Kiev during its fourth test flight, with the loss of its crew of 7. Cause was a collision with a video recording aircraft which landed safely.
▲ 1997. Planned first aircraft to be delivered to an air force.

Sales: Kiev aircraft production plant was designated to be the manufacturer in 1988. Later, following the regional changes, it was decided to have simultaneous production in Kiev (Ukraine) and Samara (Russia). The wings are constructed in Tashkent (Uzbekistan). The first An-70 prototype was built by the experimental plant of Antonov in Kiev, engaged in 1995 in building 2 prototypes of the civil An-70T, while the first series production An-70 was then being manufactured in the Kiev factory. The demand for the An-70 is estimated to be for 2,000 aircraft. Discussions with Daewoo and Samsung of South Korea have taken place, covering the possibility of programme partners.
Crew: 3 (2 pilots and an on-board engineer).
Pressurization: Cockpit and freight hold are pressurized.
Freight hold capacity: 66,139 lb (30,000 kg) nominal, 77,162 lb (35,000 kg) maximum payload (see data column). Loads can include UAK-2.5, -5 and -10 containers, PA-3, 5.6 and 6.8 pallets, vehicles or many other combinations, 110 paratroops, or double-deck configuration for 300 troops.
Freight hold access: Under-tail doors and ramp for straight-in loading.
Loading facilities: Full cargo handling system.
Wing characteristics: Slightly sweptback, with thick supercritical profile. High lift devices assisted by strong airflow from the propfans which double the lifting force during take-off and landing (the lifting force coefficient then becomes 5.6).
Wing control surfaces: Ailerons, multi-slotted flaps and leading-edge slats.
Construction materials: Composites account for about 24% of the aircraft weight, used not only for fairings and other non-structural elements but also for important structures including the entire tail unit, wing flaps and ailerons of Organit composite material. Structural elements using composites are made as "integral structures" where, for instance, the tailplane skeleton forms an integral structure without mechanical connections by means of bolts or rivets.
Engines: 4 Ivchenko PROGRESS/Muravchenko D-27 propfans, with 14 ft 9 ins (4.5 m) Stupino SV-27 propellers each comprising 2 coaxial contra-rotating fans with 8 and 6 composite blades (front and rear fans respectively). Blades are attached diagonally to the hub

DETAILS FOR THE AN-70.

Principal dimensions:
Wing span: 144 ft 6.5 ins (44.06 m)
Maximum length: 132 ft 1 ins (40.25 m)
Fuselage length: 130 ft 11 ins (39.91 m)
Maximum height: 52 ft 10 ins (16.10 m)

Cabin:
Length: 61 ft (18.60 m)
Length including ramp: 71 ft 10 ins (21.90 m)
Width, at floor: 13 ft 1.5 ins (4.00 m)
Width, maximum: 15 ft 9 ins (4.80 m)
Height: 13 ft 5.5 ins (4.10 m)

Wings:
Aerofoil section: Supercritical.
Area: about 2,196 sq ft (204 m²)
Aspect ratio: 9.5

Undercarriage:
Type: Retractable, with steerable nosewheels. Multi-wheel of typical Antonov type. Nose leg has 1 twin-wheel bogie; main units comprise 3 such bogies
Wheel base: 59 ft 6.6 ins (18.15 m)
Wheel track: 17 ft 1 ins (5.20 m)

Weights:
Maximum take-off: 271,168 lb (123,000 kg)
Maximum take-off from unprepared runway: 220,462 lb (100,000 kg)
Payload, maximum: 77,162 lb (35,000 kg)
Payload, nominal: 66,139 lb (30,000 kg)
Payload, from unprepared runway: 44,092 lb (20,000 kg)

Performance:
Max operating speed: 405-432 kts (466-497 mph) 750-800 km/h
Landing speed: 86-89 kts (99-103 mph) 160-165 km/h
Take-off distance: 5,906 ft (1,800 m)
Landing distance: 6,234 ft (1,900 m)
Ceiling: 28,215-31,500 ft (8,600-9,600 m)
Range from 5,250 ft (1,600 m) concrete runway: 2,700 naut miles (3,107 miles) 5,000 km with a 66,139 lb (30,000 kg) payload, 3,321 naut miles (3,821 miles) 6,150 km with a 55,116 lb (25,000 kg) payload, 3,915 naut miles (4,505 miles) 7,250 km with a 44,080 lb (20,000 kg) payload
Range: 3,914 naut miles (4,500 miles) 7,250 km with a 20,000 kg payload, or 2,986 naut miles (3,436 miles) 5,530 km with a 30,000 kg payload, both at gross weight
Range from a 1,969-2,625 ft (600-800 m) unprepared runway: 1,620 naut miles (1,864 miles) 3,000 km with a 20,000 kg payload
Range, maximum: 4,698 naut miles (5,406 miles) 8,700 km

Antonov An-70 at Kiev (Piotr Butowski)

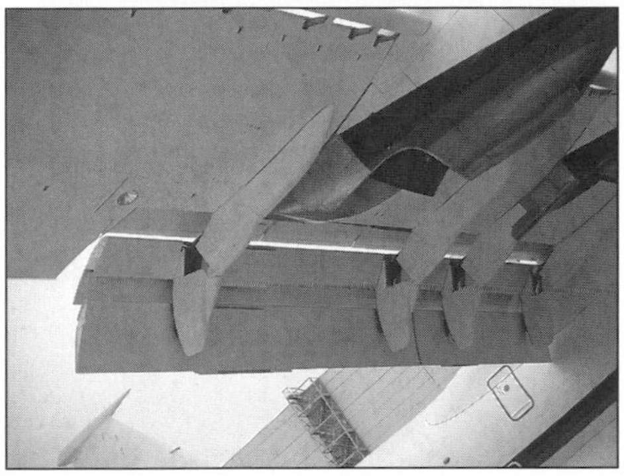

Antonov An-70 trailing-edge flaps are located behind the engines to increase lift for short-field operation (Piotr Butowski)

(the blade axis does not intersect the hub axis). Propeller efficiency 0.9.
Engine rating: each 14,000 shp (10,440 kW) take-off power.
Flight refuelling probe: None.
Flight control system: Fly-by-wire type with multiple redundancy (3 digital and 6 analog channels). A special hydraulic stand-by system is connected to the main control system in such a way as to allow changeover in an emergency without any noticeable alteration for the pilots, the commands of the crew or autopilot being relayed to the actuators via hydraulic control channels that are impervious to disturbances such as electromagnetic radiation. By virtue of this control system, a fixed, non-adjustable tailplane could be adopted.
Radar: Leninets Kupol was originally planned, but now Phazotron Gukol navigation radar derived from the MiG-29M's Zhuk radar is also proposed.
Flight avionics/instrumentation: Integrated digital system, with common databus (for the first time in the CIS); due to this system, the length of connections could be reduced by 70% and their weight by 40%, and it makes for easy adoption of foreign equipment. Colour cockpit displays. SKI-77 head-up-display for greater accuracy when taking-off and landing. The navigation system allows the aircraft to fly inside and outside the air traffic lines at any time and in any geographical region, with programmable flight path and optimization of fuel consumption. The instrument landing system meets the requirements of ICAO categories II and IIIA. The integrated in-flight automatic inspection system BASK-70 records and processes 8,000 parameters from all on-board systems (this is a version of the BASK-124 used on the An-124).
Aircraft variants:
An-70 (izdelye 77) is the basic military version.
An-70T is the commercial transport version, without military landing/troop equipment or military communication systems. 2 prototypes under construction.
An-70T-100 is a projected twin-engined low-cost civil derivative of the An-70T with no STOL abilities and lower cruising speed. 2 x D-27 propfans. Fuselage as for the An-70T, but each main undercarriage unit has 4 instead of 6 mainwheels. Winglets and tail unit changes. Crew of 2. Cruising speed 100 km/h less than for the An-70T, and payload at 5,000 km range is reduced to 44,092 lb (20,000 kg). Specific fuel consumption reduced from 165 to 125 g per tonne kilometre. Aircraft length 130 ft 1.5 ins (39.66 m), wing span 148 ft 7.5 ins (45.30 m), and height 50 ft 5 ins (15.36 m).
An-70TK is the projected convertible cargo/passenger version, using fully-equipped and removable passenger containers in the cargo cabin.
An-77 is the export designation of the An-70 (when work began the designation An-70 was classified and so izdelye 77 was adopted for the export version). Possible use of CFM56-5A1 turbofan engines.

Antonov An-72 and An-74 (NATO name *Coaler*)

First flight: 31 August 1977 (piloted by Vladimir Tersky). 22 December 1985 for the first flight of a production An-72, manufactured at the Kharkov aircraft plant. December 1989 for the first flight of a production An-74.
Role: Light freight and passenger transport, and military executive aircraft.
Chief designer: Ya. Orlov.
Sales: 7 prototypes built at the Kiev aircraft plant (including 2 for static tests). Because the Kiev factory was occupied with the export-capable An-32, production of the An-72 was transferred to Kharkov, which previously built the Tupolev Tu-104/124/134 series. Different technology caused significant delay. About 145 aircraft of all versions had been built before mid-1993 in Kharkov, mostly for military service. Factories in Arsenyev and Omsk are now producing the An-74T (the first An-74 built in Omsk made its maiden flight in 1994). The export price of the An-72/74 is about US$12.5 million.
Details: Principally for the An-72 *Coaler-C*.
Crew: 3, comprising pilot, pilot-navigator and on-board engineer. Other versions may have different numbers of crew; for instance, An-72V has 2, while An-74 has 5.
Passengers: Up to 38 (An-72S military executive version), or 52 (An-74TK). For other configurations, see Aircraft variants.
Freight hold capacity: Hermetic cargo hold is air conditioned. The various internal configurations, according to requirement and variant, allow for 22,046 lb (10,000 kg) of freight (23,149 lb, 10,500 kg in An-72G), including 4 x PAV-2.5 pallets or a similar number of UAK-2.5 containers, 57 paratroopers or 68 persons on folding seats, or 36 wounded (including 24 litter cases). Comfortable executive versions exist. See Aircraft variants for An-72AT and An-74 combi layout.
Loading facilities: A travelling crane, 5,512 lb (2,500 kg) lifting capacity, is attached to the ceiling and can work in conjunction with a removable winch of similar capacity. Floor-mounted roller tracks are optional.
Wing characteristics: High-mounted with anhedral. Position of the engines forward of the wing leading edges allows the efflux to flow over the wing and flaps to increase lift.
Wing control surfaces: Double-slotted trailing-edge flaps on the wing centre section, triple-slotted flap and 4 sections of spoilers on each middle panel (2 raised prior to landing and 2 open automatically on landing via an undercarriage sensor), and 2-section aileron (with tabs) on the outer panels. 3 sections of slats occupy the entire leading-edge span outboard of engine nacelles.
Tail control surfaces: T-tail has the tailplane located beyond the zone of exhaust gas and aerodynamic disturbances behind the wing; tailplane has a unique inverted leading-edge slat co-ordinated with the wing flaps. 2-section rudder; the rear section is subdivided into 2 parts, the lower (with tab) activated manually by the pilot and used for directional control in normal flight, the other adjusted by means of actuators. The upper part of the rear section is used for low speed flights, whereas the front section is used only for

DETAILS FOR AN-72 COALER-C.

Principal dimensions:
Wing span: 104 ft 7.5 ins (31.89 m)
Maximum length: 92 ft 1 ins (28.068 m)
Maximum height: 28 ft 8.5 ins (8.75 m)

Cabin:
Length, including ramp: 34 ft 5.5 ins (10.50 m)
Width: 7 ft 1 ins (2.15 m)
Height: 7 ft 3 ins (2.20 m)

Wings:
Area, gross: 1,060.6 sq ft (98.53 m^2)
Aspect ratio: 10.32
Sweepback: 17°
Anhedral: 10°

Undercarriage:
Type: Retractable, with steerable twin nosewheels. Low-pressure tandem mainwheels
Main wheel tyre size: 1,050 x 390 mm
Nose wheel tyre size: 720 x 310 mm
Wheel base: 26 ft 8 ins (8.12 m)
Wheel track: 13 ft 7.5 ins (4.15 m)

Weights:
Empty, operating: 42,990 lb (19,500 kg)
Maximum take-off: 76,059 lb (34,500 kg)
Maximum take-off (An-72G): 80,468 lb (36,500 kg)
Take-off from a 3,281 ft (1,000 m) runway: 60,627 lb (27,500 kg)
Payload, nominal: 11,023 lb (5,000 kg)
Payload, maximum: 22,046 lb (10,000 kg)
Payload, maximum (An-72G): An-72G: 23,149 lb (10,500 kg)

Performance:
Maximum speed: 381 kts (438 mph) 705 km/h at 32,810 ft (10,000 m)
Cruise speed: 297-374 kts (342-373 mph) 550-600 km/h at 37,810 ft (10,000 m)
Landing speed: 97 kts (112 mph) 180 km/h
Take-off distance at 72,732 lb (33,000 kg) weight: 3,051 ft (930 m)
Take-off distance at 60,627 lb (27,500 kg) weight: 2,034 ft (620 m)
Landing distance: 1,378-1,526 ft (420-465 m)
Ceiling, at 72,732 lb (33,000 kg) weight: 35,105 ft (10,700 m)
Ceiling, at 60,627 lb (27,500 kg) weight: 38,715 ft (11,800 m)
Range with full fuel: 2,592 naut miles (2,983 miles) 4,800 km, with 45 minutes reserve
Range with full fuel (An-72G): 2,484 naut miles (2,858 miles) 4,600 km
Range at 72,732 lb (33,000 kg) weight, including 22,046 lb (10,000 kg) payload: 432 naut miles (497 miles) 800 km, with 45 min reserve
Range at 80,468 lb (36,500 kg) weight, including 23,149 lb (10,500 kg) payload (An-72G): 1,053 naut miles (1,212 miles) 1,950 km, with 45 minutes reserve
Range at 72,732 lb (33,000 kg) weight, including 16,530 lb (7,500 kg) payload: 1,080 naut miles (1,243 miles) 2,000 km, with 45 minutes reserve
Range at 60,627 lb (27,500 kg) weight, including 11,023 lb (5,000 kg) payload: 432 naut miles (497 miles) 800 km, with 45 minutes reserve

Antonov An-72 Coaler-C in military executive form despite civil registration (Piotr Butowski)

compensation for thrust asymmetry in case of failure of 1 engine. Elevators (with tabs).
Construction materials: Mainly metal, but with 2,161 lb (980 kg) of composite materials.
Engines: 2 Ivchenko PROGRESS/Lotarev D-36 series 1A turbofans. Thrust reversers.
Engine rating: Each 14,330 lbf (63.745 kN).
Fuel system: 7 tanks inside the wing torsion box, total of 16,250 litres (28,550 lb, 12,950 kg).
Flight refuelling probe: None.
De-icing system: Thermal for cockpit glazing, wing and tail leading edges, and air intakes.
Radar: Navigation/weather radar in the nose.
Flight avionics/instrumentation: Malva-4 Doppler navigation. SAU-72 automatic control system provides flight along a programmed path and landing approach to an altitude of 98 ft (30 m).
Fixed weapons: None.
Aircraft variants:
An-72 *Coaler-A.* was the prototype; the first prototype had a shorter wing span (84 ft 9 ins, 25.83 m), shorter rear fuselage, 2 ventral fins and a braking chute.
An-72 *Coaler-C* is the standard military transport, as detailed.
An-72S is the military executive version with 38 passenger seats and a small cargo compartment large enough for a small vehicle or other load.
An-72AT is a freighter adapted for standard airborne containers.
An-72V is an export version with crew of 2.
An-72G is the latest transport version, with take-off weight increased to 80,469 lb (36,500 kg). 2 D-36 series 3A turbofans.
An-72PS is a proposed search and rescue version.
An-72P was an electronic countermeasures prototype, tested in mid-1980s.
An-72P patrol version (using the same designation as the EW prototype). See separate entry.
An-71 *Madcap* airborne early warning and control aircraft was based on the An-72, but with a shortened rear fuselage and forward-canted tailfin to maintain the CG. 2 prototypes only, first flown in September 1985. Kvant radar system with a 24 ft 7 ins (7.5 m) tail-mounted rotodome.
An-74 (prototype named An-72A, from Arktichesky or Arctic) is a civil version for use in polar regions, announced in February 1984. First production aircraft manufactured December 1989.
The de-icing systems as well as cabin heating and ventilation have been improved in respect of the An-72. The cabin layout has been changed, with 8 armchairs forward, a small bedroom and 3 stations for hydrologists carrying out surveillance of surface ice or navigating the ship convoys. The undercarriage can have ski/wheel units. Fuel capacity has been increased considerably. Navigation system improved. Also, special equipment for precise dropping of loads (for instance, to ice floats). During tests, the crew of S. Gorbik landed the aircraft with a 4,409 lb (2,000 kg) load of scientific equipment on a 1,969 ft (600 m) long icefield and then took off taking a group of polar scientists.
An-74P-100 is an executive transport for 16 passengers.
An-74T (transportyi) is a standard civil freight version of the An-74, with no Arctic equipment or systems. Crew of 3.
An-74TK (konvertiruyemyi) is a convertible cargo/passenger version of the An-74T with 52 folding seats.
An-74T-100 and An-74TK-100 are the An-74T and TK (respectively) with a navigator completing a crew of 4.
An-74-200, An-74T-200 and An-74TK-200 are the An-74, T and TK, with changes in equipment and new series engines. Crew of 2 in T-200 and TK-200; 5 in -200.

Antonov An-74 Coaler-B for Polar operations (Piotr Butowski)

Antonov An-124 (NATO name *Condor*)

First flight: 26 December 1982 (prototype *CCCP-680125* commanded by Vladimir Tersky).
Certification: 30 December 1992. Civil certification was awarded to the An-124-100 by the Aviaregistr of the Interstate Aviation Committee, CIS.
First delivery: February 1987, to Soviet Voyenno-Transportnaya Aviatsya (Military Transport Aviation).
Role: Very heavy, long-range military/civil freighter.
Chief Designer: Viktor Tolmachev.

▲ Development

▲ 1977. Work began on the An-124 (izdelye 400). First project had wings with sweepback of 25°, but a projected later passenger version required higher speed and the wings were redesigned to 30°. The passenger version never materialized
▲ Early 1980s. First information published in the West, quoted as An-40, later An-400.
▲ 26 July 1985. 21 records set, including a 377,473 lb (171,219 kg) payload lifted to 35,270 ft (10,750 m). Pilot V. Tersky.
▲ 6-7 May 1987. Closed distance of 10,881 naut miles (12,521 miles) 20,151 km achieved.
▲ September 1990. 451 refugees were emergency airlifted from Amman to Dacca in one An-124, with only basic amenities hastily added.
▲ 1993. The heaviest single load ever transported by air up to that time was a 124 tonne power plant generator core secured on a specially built load-spreading skid, totalling 135.2 tonnes. This was carried from Dusseldorf in Germany to New Delhi in India on an An-124-100 on behalf of the Power Generation Group of Siemens AG.
Sales: Few prototypes built at the Kiev aircraft plant. Production transferred to the newly-constructed Ulyanovsk factory (now Aviastar). First Ulyanovsk-built An-124 flew in October 1985. Wings are produced in Tashkent, Uzbekistan, with 33 sets produced by May 1995. Russian Air Force has 16 An-124s in operation, with 17 others in use with 6 civil operators (see below). Budget restraints have meant that the Russian Air Force is not purchasing further An-124s. Production, at a rate of 4/5 aircraft per year, is continuing for civil operation. 2 An-124-100s were delivered in 1994 to Rossiya (the Russian Government Air Services unit in Aeroflot) for Presidential/VIP use, with 2 more then under construction; they can be used commercially when not officially required and at least 2 are now used that way. Full commercial operators include AJAX (an Aeroflot subsidiary) which received 2 for commercial services in 1994 (a third planned), Air Foyle of the UK which leases 3, and HeavyLift of the UK and VolgaDnepr of Russia which co-operate with 6 (2 UK based); VolgaDnepr is reportedly seeking up to 4 more.
Crew: 6 or 7, comprising pilot, co-pilot, navigator, communication officer, on-board engineer and electrical engineer, with additional loadmaster in the military version. For long distance flights the aircraft takes a rest crew. Up to a dozen cargo handlers may accompany commercial loads.
Passengers: See Fuselage.
Pressurization: Normal pressure differential (7.8 psi) in the crew and passenger compartments but lowered to 3.6 psi in the cargo hold. The lower hold pressure allowed structural weight savings.
Freight hold volume: 35,315 cu ft (1,000 m^3).
Freight hold capacity: 4 platforms of P-7 or P-16 type, when equipment or cargo can be paradropped. Alternatively 12 ISO containers or other heavy/bulky cargoes including battle tanks, construction vehicles, heavy guns, missile systems, Shtil-3A ballistic missile satellite launcher, generators, etc. Paratroop operations are limited by the low hold pressurization, but when conducted the paratroopers exit in 2 files via the rear hatch with D-5 parachutes of forced opening type. (See Fuselage for passenger capacity.)
Freight hold access: Cargo is rolled or drawn into the hold via a visor-type upward-hinging fuselage nose (7 minute opening time). Unloading (or simultaneous loading) is via the standard rear door ramp.
Loading facilities: 2 travelling cranes, 22,046 lb (10,000 kg) capacity each, are installed on the cargo hold ceiling. 2 electric winches each have a 6,614 lb (3,000 kg) pulling capacity. The floor height may be adjusted in order to make cargo handling easier: the main undercarriage unit oleos may be compressed to lower the cargo hold threshold; alternatively, the nose unit can retract after extendable "rests" have been deployed, offering a sloping hold of 3° 30′. Due to 2 APUs, the cargo handling can be carried out without ground power sources.
Wing control surfaces: Each wing trailing edge has 3 sections of extended-area single-slotted flaps, with diversified deflection angle, and 2 sections of ailerons (with dampers). 12 spoilers on the upper surface of each wing. 6 sections of leading-edge flaps.
Tail control surfaces: Elevators and rudder. Fixed incidence tailplane.
Flight control system: Near-zero static stability. Quadruple-redundant fly-by-wire with mechanical backup. Control-wheels for pilots.
Fuselage: Double-deck fuselage, the upper diameter 12 ft 5.5 ins (3.8 m) and the lower 23 ft 7 ins (7.2 m). The upper contains the crew cockpit and a compartment for an alternate relief crew with a galley and toilet. A cabin for 88 persons is located on the upper deck behind the wings. The lower deck contains the cargo hold.
Construction materials: Mainly light metal alloys, but with a titanium cargo hold floor and about 12,125 lb (5,500 kg) of composites.
Engines: 4 Ivchenko PROGRESS/Lotarev D-18T turbofans. Thrust reversers of outer (cold) flow type are standard for all engines. 2 TA-12 APUs in the main undercarriage nacelles. VolgaDnepr has proposed replacing D-18Ts with Rolls-Royce RB211-524Gs.
Engine rating: Each 51,654 lbf (229.78 kN).
Fuel system: 10 integral tanks in the wings, with a total capacity of 471,215 lb (213,740 kg). Maximum

practical fuel weight for the An-124-100 is 468,151 lb (212,350 kg).
Flight refuelling probe: None.
De-icing system: Bleed air for wing leading edges and electro-impulse for tailplane leading edges and the fin.
Radar: 2 radars under a common nose radome, comprising a navigation unit and weather unit.

DETAILS FOR THE AN-124, *WITH AN-124-100 IN ITALICS FOR WEIGHTS.*

Principal dimensions:
Wing span: 240 ft 6 ins (73.3 m)
Maximum length: 226 ft 8.5 ins (69.1 m)
Maximum height: 69 ft 2 ins (21.08 m)

Cabin:
Length, at floor: 119 ft 9 ins (36.5 m)
Length, including front and rear ramps: 142 ft 7 ins (43.45 m)
Width, maximum: 21 ft 11 ins (6.68 m)
Width at floor: 21 ft (6.4 m)
Height, maximum: 14 ft 5 ins (4.4 m)

Wings:
Aerofoil section: Supercritical
Area, gross: 6,760 sq ft (628 m^2)
Aspect ratio: 8.556
Sweepback at quarter chord: 25°
Sweepback at leading edge: 33° root, 30° outer
Incidence: +3° 30′

Undercarriage:
Type: Retractable, with steerable nosewheels. Each main unit comprises 5 tandem sets of twin wheels housed inside nacelles on the fuselage sides (each set of twin wheels is independent of the others). Despite size, the An-124A has the ability to operate from unprepared strips and other surfaces. For height and slope adjustments, see Loading facilities.
Main wheel tyre size: 1,270 x 510 mm
Nose wheel tyre size: 1,120 x 450 mm
Wheel track: 29 ft (8.84 m)
Turning circle: Requires a 147 ft 8 ins (45 m) wide area

Weights:
Empty, operating: 385,800 lb (175,000 kg)
Maximum take-off: 892,871 lb (405,000 kg)
Max ramp weight (An-124-100): *877,439 lb (398,000 kg)*
Normal maximum take-off: 864,210 lb (392,000 kg), *same for An-124-100 as max certificated take-off*
Maximum landing: 727,525 lb (330,000 kg), *same for An-124-100*
Payload, maximum: 330,693 lb (150,000 kg)
Payload, normal maximum: 264,554 1b (120,000 kg), *same for An-124-100*

Performance::
Maximum Mach number: 0.77
Maximum speed: 459 kts (528 mph) 850 km/h
Cruise speed: 405 kts (466 mph), 750 km/h
Landing speed: 119-151 kts (137-174 mph) 220-280 km/h
Required runway length: 9,843 ft (3,000 m)
Ceiling: 31,170 ft (9,500 m)
Range with 330,693 lb (150,000 kg) payload: 2,430 naut miles (2,796 miles) 4,500 km
Range with 264,554 lb (120,000 kg) payload: 2,700 naut miles (3,107 miles) 5,000 km
Range with 88,185 lb (40,000 kg) payload: 6,480 naut miles (7,456 miles) 12,000 km
Maximum range: 8,688 naut miles (9,998 miles) 16,090 km
Duration, maximum: 20 hours

Flight avionics/instrumentation: SAU-3-400 automatic control system, inertial navigation, Loran and Omega navigation. Programmed flight path with more than 30 waypoints. Cockpit instrumentation is conventional. BASK-124 integrated automatic inspection system records and processes parameters picked up from more than 1,200 sensors.

Antonov An-124 Condor, the world's largest production aircraft (Piotr Butowski)

Aircraft variants:
An-124 (izdelye 400, Ruslan) *Condor* is the basic military transport version for autonomous operation.
An-124A has 6 tandem wheel sets. An-124-200 is civil variant.
An-124-100 is the civil version adapted to extended loading infrastructure of commercial airports.
An-124-100M was put under development in 1994 with Litton GPS/IRS and Collins SATCOM, ACARS and TCAS-2.
An-124-102 is under development with a 3-crew cockpit.
An-124AK is a version designed as a platform for the Shtil-3A ballistic missile that is used for carrying satellites to Earth orbit. The missile can be carried in the aircraft hold to a distance of 2,214 naut miles (2,548 miles) 4,100 km. Then, at an altitude of 36,090 ft (11,000 m) and speed of 410 kts (472 mph) 760 km/h, it is withdrawn from the cargo hold by means of a parachute. It is then stabilized in a vertical position and its engines started. The weight of Shtil-3A is 100,531 lb (45,600 kg), and length 61 ft 4 ins (18.7 m). It was originally designed for strategic submarines by the V. Makeyev bureau.
An-124FFR was put under development in 1994 as a fire-fighting version, capable of delivering 200 tonnes of water plus retardants, using the cargo hold plus 70 tonnes stored in the wing centre section. A kit would be provided to re-convert the aircraft to cargo carrying for off-season operations. An estimated 16 could be required in the next 5 years, at about $100-120 million each.

Antonov An-124-100 with nose visor raised, prior to loading a 135.2 tonne generator/skid single payload

Antonov An-140

First flight: Mid-1996.
Certification: 1996-7. Certification to ICAO Category II anticipated about 18 months after the first flight.
Role: Short-haul regional airliner.
Sales: Series aircraft are being built at the KhAPA production centre. Production committed in 1994 , after the receipt of orders from Ukrainian and Russian airline operators.
Passengers: 44-52.
Seat pitch: 32 ins (81 cm) or 29.5 ins (75 cm).
Pressurization: Standard.
Wing control surfaces: Ailerons and 2-section flaps.
Tail control surfaces: Elevators and rudder.
Engines: 2 Klimov TV3-117 turboprops.
Engine rating: Each 1,800 shp (1,342 kW), with a 6-blade advanced propeller.
Aircraft variants:
An-140 is the standard version with Klimov engines.
An-140? (designation not known at the time of writing) will have Pratt & Whitney Canada engines, presumably produced at the new joint P&WC/Klimov plant. Study project only in early 1995.

Antonov An-140 (Piotr Butowski)

DETAILS FOR AN-140.

Principal dimensions:
Wing span: 76 ft 5 ins (23.29 m)
Maximum length: 68 ft 7 ins (20.9 m)
Maximum height: 25 ft 3 ins (7.7 m)

Undercarriage:
Type: Retractable, with twin steerable nosewheels

Performance: (anticipated):
Cruise speed: 324 kts (373 mph) 600 km/h
Required runway length: 4,266 ft (1,300 m)
Range with full fuel: 1,728 naut miles (1,988 miles) 3,200 km
Range with full payload: 486 naut miles (559 miles) 900 km

Antonov An-180

First flight: Not yet flown. Design was completed in 1994.
Role: Medium-range propfan airliner. To meet ICAO Category IIIa requirements.
Airframe life: 60,000 flying hours.
Flight crew: 2 or 3.
Passengers: 150-156, 163-175, 180 and 200 passenger configurations. Also to be made available in combi form with passengers and cabin freight.

Details for the An-180.

Principal dimensions:
Wing span: 117 ft 7 ins (35.83 m)
Maximum length: 134 ft 2 ins (40.9 m)
Maximum height: 36 ft 7 ins (11.148 m)

Undercarriage:
Type: Retractable, with twin steerable nosewheels and tandem pairs of mainwheels

Weights:
Maximum take-off: 148,812 lb (67,500 kg)
Payload: 39,683 lb (18,000 kg)

Performance:
Cruise speed: 432 kts (497 mph) 800 km/h
Required runway Length: 7,218-8,530 ft (2,200-2,600 m)
Cruise ceiling: 29,855-33,125 ft (9,100-10,100 m)
Range with full fuel: 4,050-4,157 naut miles (4,660-4,784 miles) 7,500-7,700 km
Range with 163 passengers: 2,619 naut miles (3,013 miles) 4,850 km
Range with full payload: 1,781 naut miles (2,051 miles) 3,300 km

Antonov An-180 twin-propfan airliner (courtesy Antonov)

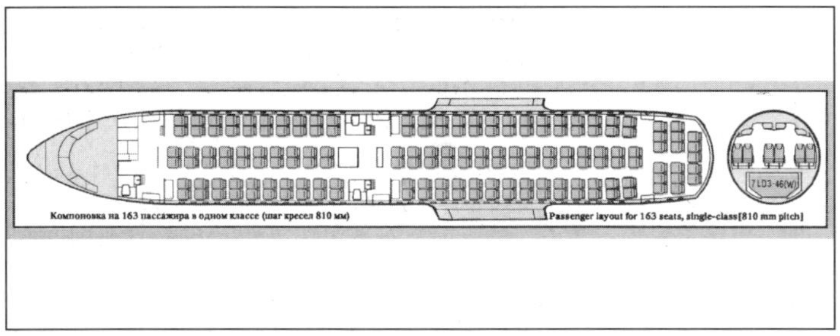

Antonov An-180 cabin layout for 163 passengers in single-class (courtesy Antonov)

Seat pitch: 32 ins (81 cm) in 163 passenger single class layout.
Freight hold capacity: 7 x LD3 containers under the cabin floor. An all-cargo version has been projected.
Wing control surfaces: Ailerons, flaps and 3-section spoilers.
Tail control surfaces: Multi-section elevators and rudder.
Engines: 2 Ivchenko PROGRESS D-27 propfans, with co-axial contra-rotating tractor propellers, mounted at the tips of the swept tailplane.
Engine rating: Each 13,819 ehp (10,305 ekW) at take-off.
Flight avionics/instrumentation: Automated navigation throughout the flight regime.

Antonov An-218

First flight: Originally expected 1996, but programme believed to have been terminated in 1995.
Role: Medium/long-range airliner. Intended to meet ICAO Category IIIa.
Sales: 1997 was the earliest possible date for production to have begun.
Flight crew: 2.

Details for the An-218-100.

Principal dimensions:
Wing span: 164 ft (50 m)
Maximum length: 196 ft 2 ins (59.79 m)
Maximum height: 51 ft 6 ins (15.7 m)

Undercarriage:
Type: Retractable, with twin steerable nosewheels. Each main unit comprises 3 pairs of wheels in tandem

Weights:
Payload: 92,594 lb (42,000 kg)

Performance:
Typical cruise speed: 470 kts (541 mph) 870 km/h
Required runway length: 9,515 ft (2,900 m)
Range with 350 passengers: 4,050 naut miles (4,660 miles) 7,500 km maximum
Range with 220 passengers (An-218-200): 5,724 naut miles (6,587 miles) 10,600 km

Passengers: 195, or 292 in a mixed class layout (comprising 210 economy class, 64 business and 18 first), 350 or 400 (economy), depending on the version (see Aircraft variants).
Seat pitch: 29.5 or 31.9 ins (75 or 81 cm) economy, 40.2 ins (102 cm) first class and 34.3 ins (87 cm) business.
Freight hold volume: Possible 6,367.2 cu ft (180.3 m^3) in 2 main under-cabin holds plus the baggage hold.
Freight hold capacity: 24 containers beneath the cabin floor.
Wing control surfaces: Ailerons, flaps, 7-section spoilers, and leading-edge slats.
Tail control surfaces: Elevators and rudder.
Engines: Ivchenko PROGRESS D-18T1 (also referred to as TM) turbofans.
Engine rating: Each 57,320 lbf (254.98 kN) max contingency, 48,149 lbf (214.18 kN) take-off.
Fuel system: Low fuel-burn, anticipated at about 18g per passenger-km.
Flight avionics/ instrumentation: Electronic cockpit displays.
Aircraft variants:
An-218-100 is the base version with D-18T1 (TM) turbofans, as detailed.
An-218-200 is a long-range 220 passenger version with more powerful 60,627 lbf (269.7 kN) D-18TR engines, with alternative General Electric CF6-80C2B6, Pratt & Whitney PW4060 or Rolls-Royce RB211-524H4s. Increased fuel capacity.
An-218-300 is the projected extended range model, carrying sufficient fuel in the standard and new freight-hold tanks for 6,048 naut miles (6,959 miles) 11,200 km. Length reduced to 158 ft 5 ins (48.29 m), with consequent reduction in passenger capacity to 195.
An-218-400 is a projected 400-seater.

Antonov An-218 (Piotr Butowski)

Antonov An-225 Mriya (NATO name *Cossack*)

First flight: 21 December 1988 (piloted by Aleksandr Galunienko).
First delivery: 1989.
Role: Extreme heavy-lift transport.
Leading Designer: Anatoli Vovnianko

★ Aims

★ External carrying of cargo with length of 196 ft 10 ins (60 m) and diameter of 26 ft 3 ins (8 m). To replace the Myasishchev Atlant.
★ Internal or external cargo of 551,000 lb (250,000 kg).
★ Maximum use of elements from the existing An-124 heavy-lift aircraft.

▲ Development

▲ Spring 1985. Work started.
▲ 30 November 1988. Roll-out of the prototype at the Antonov works in Kiev, Ukraine. Named Mriya (Ukr, meaning dream).
▲ 21 December 1988. First flight, in Kiev. Take-off run of 3,120 ft (950 m), duration 74 minutes.
▲ 22 March 1989. Undertook a 3 hours 47 minutes flight from Kiev to Leningrad and back, setting 110 world records.
▲ 13 May 1989. First flight with the Buran space shuttle on its back, in Baykonur.
▲ May 1990. First commercial flight (see Sales).

Sales: Designed specially for carrying the Buran space shuttle and Energia rocket elements from the production plant in Moscow to the Baykonur cosmodrome. This original task is no longer of the same importance, though the An-225 will continue to make flights with elements of Buran/Energia but on a reduced scale. An-225 is now also used for other tasks; for instance, in May 1990 in its first commercial flight, it airlifted a 100-tonne T-800 tractor from Chelabinsk to Yakutia, and in 1991-92 made 9 flights with humanitarian aid from Canada and USA to the Ukraine. It also offers a launching platform for space vehicles (see Aircraft variants). Only 1 An-225 has been built, but a second was being assembled in 1994-95 (its wing centre section was delivered from Tashkent to Kiev on the back of an An-22 in March 1993).
Crew: 6.
Passengers: See Fuselage.
Freight hold capacity: 551,000 lb (250,000 kg). See Fuselage.
Freight hold access: An-124-type visor nose but no rear ramp entry.
Loading facilities: as An-124.
Wing characteristics: New centre section, 70 ft 10 ins (21.6 m) span and 7 ft 10.5 ins (2.4 m) maximum thickness. Outer panels with insignificant changes.
Tail control surfaces: Fully redesigned tail unit compared to An-124, of H-type double-fin configuration to avoid airflow disturbances caused by the external cargo. 3-section elevator and 2-section rudder on each side.
Fuselage: Lengthened by 23 ft (7 m), with neatly faired external payload attachment points on the upper surface. Enlarged upper deck relief crew cabin, and passenger cabin for 60-70 persons (see An-124).
Flight control system: Quadruple-redundant fly-by-wire with mechanical backup. Doubled fly-by-wire control of wing flaps and interceptors.
Engines: 6 Ivchenko PROGRESS D-18T turbofans (see An-124).
Fuel system: Additional tankage, estimated to be considerably more than 661,390 lb (300,000 kg).
Electrical system: 27 voltDC, 115/200 volt, 400 Hz, AC.
Hydraulic system: 4 basic and 2 stand-by.
Aircraft variants:
An-225 *Cossack*, as detailed.
Various projects are envisaged using the An-225

Details for the An-225 Cossack.

Principal dimensions:
Wing span: 290 ft (88.4 m)
Maximum length: 275 ft 7 ins (84.0 m)
Maximum height: 59 ft 8 ins (18.2 m)

Cabin:
Length, at floor: 142 ft 9 ins (43.5 m)
Width, maximum: 21 ft 11 ins (6.68 m)
Width, at floor: 21 ft (6.4 m)
Height, maximum: 14 ft 5 ins (4.4 m)

Wings:
Aerofoil section: Supercritical
Area, gross: 9,742 sq ft (905 m^2)
Aspect ratio: 8.635
Sweepback at quarter chord: 25°
Sweepback at leading edge: 33° root, 30° outer

Tail Unit:
Tailplane span: 107 ft 1 ins (32.65 m)

Undercarriage:
Type: As for An-124 except: 7 pairs of wheels on each main unit. Tyre pressure 163.5 psi
Main wheel tyre size: 1,270 x 510 mm
Nose wheel tyre size: 1,120 x 450 mm
Wheel track: 29 ft (8.84 m)
Turning radius: 196.86 ft (60 m) about nosewheels

Weights:
Maximum take-off: 1,322,770 lb (600,000 kg)
Maximum payload (external or internal): 551,000 lb (250,000 kg)

Performance:
Cruising speed: 432-459 kts (497-528 mph) 800-850 km/h
Required runway length: 11,483 ft (3,500 m)
Range with full payload: 1,350 naut miles (1,553 miles) 2,500 km
Range with 440,924 lb (200,000 kg) payload: 2,430 naut miles (2,796 miles) 4,500 km
Range with 220,400 lb (100,000 kg) payload: 5,184 naut miles (5,965 miles) 9,600 km
Range with full fuel: 8,315 naut miles (9,569 miles) 15,400 km

as a launching platform. These include:
1) British Aerospace Interim Hotol space shuttle which, launched from an An-225 at 29,530 ft (9,000 m) altitude, would reach any earth orbit. Project companies from UK, Russia and Ukraine.
2) MAKS, where an An-225 would carry a Russian Molnia-1 space vehicle built by the Gleb Lozino-Lozinski team. A Russian-Ukrainian project.
3) Svityaz ballistic missile, based on the military Zenit type, proposed as a space launcher.
4) Mriya-Orlyonok as a sea rescue system, with an A-90 Orlyonok wing-in-ground effect craft carried on the back of an An-225. The weight of Orlyonok, built by the Rostislav Alekseyev team, is equal to 110 tonnes, and the entire payload would be 30 tonnes.
5. Radem testbed for space technologies.

Antonov An-225 Mriya, proposed as a launching platform for the Svityaz rocket (Piotr Butowski)

Antonov An-225 Mriya, the world's largest aircraft (Piotr Butowski)

Avro International Aerospace (UK)

Corporate address: Marketing Operations Centre, Chester Road, Woodford, Manchester SK7 1QR.
Telephone: +44 161 439 5050
Facsimile: +44 161 955 3008
Telex: 667545
USA marketing and support: PO Box 16039, Washington Dulles International Airport, Washington DC 20041.
Founded: 1993 as the British Aerospace regional jet company, following the consolidation of RJ assembly at Woodford, closure of Hatfield and separation of BAe's commercial aircraft activities into designated businesses. AMO was established at the same time to manage the BAe 146 leased fleet. The original Avro company was founded in 1910, moving to Woodford in 1924.
Employees: Some 2,000.
Information: Howard Borrington (Head of Marketing Communications) and Terry Taylor (Public Relations Manager – *telephone* +44 161 957 4634, *facsimile* +44 161 955 4131).

● Activities

● A division of British Aerospace in 1995 (see Combat section). To become part of the Aero International Regional multi-national consortium in 1996, though expected to continue assembling RJ (or renamed) jets at Woodford under AIR contract.

Avro International/Aero International Regional RJ Avroliner series

First flight: 23 March 1992 (RJ85 development aircraft – see Development).
Certification: 4 February 1983 for original BAe 146 Series 100; CAA certification of all Avroliners completed by 1 October 1993, and FAA by 10 June 1994.
First delivery: 2 April 1993 (RJ85 for Crossair).
Role: Short-range regional airliner and freighter.
Noise levels: See tables.

▲ Development

▲ Developed from, and succeeding, the British Aerospace 146 (first flown 3 September 1981), with principal changes including LF507 engines; all digital avionics including Cat IIIa, updated EFIS displays, TCAS and windshear detection, and digital flight guidance system; new wide-look "Spaceliner" interior with new overhead bins, centralized Passenger Service Units and more (for 4, 5 or 6 abreast seating); new customer support packages including JetSpares for fixed maintenance costs and more, JetStart start-up airline support package, and JetKey fleet management package.
Sales: Total of 61 ordered by June 1995, of which 34 delivered, comprising 10 RJ100s to Turkish Airlines, 8 RJ100s to SAM of Colombia, 10 RJ85s to Lufthansa of Germany, 12 RJ100s and 4 RJ85s to Crossair of Switzerland, 1 RJ85 to Pelita Air Service of Indonesia, 4 RJ70s to Air Malta and 12 RJ70s to Business Express of the USA.
Crew: 2 (flight).
Passengers: See tables.
Seat pitch: See tables.
Galleys: 2 basic cold galleys standard (1R/4R). Choice of a full transverse galley at the rear of the cabin, with the rear toilet positioned forward of the passenger door.
Pressurization: 6.75 psi, with studies to increase this to 7.46 psi.
Baggage compartments: 479 cu ft (13.6 m^3) total for RJ70, 645 cu ft (18.3 m^3) total for RJ85, and 812 cu ft (23 m^3) total for RJ100 and RJ115, comprising overhead bins, vestibule and front/rear baggage holds.
Wing control surfaces: Aileron (with trim and servo tabs), Fowler flap, roll spoiler and 3 automatic lift-spoilers per wing.
Tail control surfaces: T-tail with elevators (with trim and servo tabs) and rudder.
Flight control system: Manual/mechanical, except for hydraulic flaps and spoilers.
Construction materials: Conventional metal alloy.
Engines: See tables. Sundstrand/APIC APS1000 APU.
Fuel system: 11,729 litres standard for RJ70, RJ85 and RJ100, with 12,901 litres optional. 12,901 litres standard for RJ115.
Electrical system: 3-phase 115/200 volt AC supply at 400 Hz, via 2 x 40 kVA alternators. 28 volt DC supply, via 2 transformer/rectifiers. Emergency battery option for on-board engine start.
Hydraulic system: 3,000 psi.
Braking system: Carbon multi-discs, with anti-skid system. Split tailcone airbrakes.
De-icing system: Bleed air for wing and tailplane leading edges. Electric for cockpit glazing.
Oxygen system: Chemical.
Radar: Honeywell Primus 708 weather radar.
Flight avionics/instrumentation: Standard avionics are Honeywell digital flight guidance system, Honeywell IRS, Rockwell Collins ARINC 700 dual VHF comm/nav, Rockwell Collins dual radio altimeter, Sundstrand Mk 5 GPWS, Rockwell Collins ARINC 700 dual DME and ARINC 700 dual mode S transponder, Honeywell windshear detection and guidance, Rockwell Collins dual ADF, Global GNX-X dual FMS, and Rockwell Collins radio management panel. Dual Honeywell EFIS displays, and Smiths LED engine data displays. Options include ACARS, third VHF, TCAS and displays, single/dual HF, SELCAL, GPS, checklist facility, engine health and monitoring, quick access recorder, and ELT.
Aircraft variants:
RJ70, RJ85, RJ100 and RJ115 passenger airliners, as detailed.
QC quick-change passenger/cargo variant available for all models.
Combi combined passenger and cargo variants are available for all models.
QT "Quiet Trader" dedicated freighter variants are

Avroliner details

	RJ70	RJ85	RJ100	RJ115
Noise levels take-off, sideline, approach (EPNdB)	81.8, 87.3, 97.5	83.3, 88.1, 97.6	84.9, 87.8, 97.6	86.3, 87.6, 97.6
Passengers (typically); 5 abreast business, 6 abreast economy. 4-abreast first class	70 business or 82 economy	85 business or 100 economy	100 business, 112 economy	116 (featuring mid-cabin Type 3 emergency exits) or 128 high capacity
Seat pitch	31 ins (79 cm)	31 ins (79 cm)	31 ins (79 cm) or 32 ins (81 cm) respectively	31 ins (79 cm) or 29 ins (74 cm) respectively
Engines	4 AlliedSignal LF507-1F turbofans	4 AlliedSignal LF507-1F turbofans	4 AlliedSignal LF507-1F turbofans	4 AlliedSignal LF507-1F turbofans
Engine rating (each)	Derated to 6,130 lbf (27.27 kN), but optional full rating	7,000 lbf (31.14 kN)	7,000 lbf (31.14 kN)	7,000 lbf (31.14 kN)
Principal dimensions				
Wing span	86 ft 5 ins (26.34 m)	86 ft 5 ins (26.34 m)	86 ft 5 ins (26.34 m)	86 ft 5 ins (26.34 m)
Length	85 ft 10 ins (26.16 m)	93 ft 8 ins (28.55 m)	101 ft 8 ins (30.99 m)	101 ft 8 ins (30.99 m)
Maximum height	28 ft 3 ins (8.61 m)	28 ft 3 ins (8.61 m)	28 ft 2 ins (8.59 m)	28 ft 2 ins (8.59 m)
Cabin				
Length	50 ft 7 ins (15.42 m)	58 ft 5 ins (17.81 m)	66 ft 3 ins (20.19 m)	66 ft 3 ins (20.19 m)
Maximum width	11 ft 2.8 ins (3.42 m)	11 ft 2.8 ins (3.42 m)	11 ft 2.8 ins (3.42 m)	11 ft 2.8 ins (3.42 m)
Height	6 ft 9.3 ins (2.07 m)	6 ft 9.3 ins (2.07 m)	6 ft 9.3 ins (2.07 m)	6 ft 9.3 ins (2.07 m)
Main passenger doors	6 ft x 2 ft 9.5 ins (1.83 x 0.85 m)	6 ft x 2 ft 9.5 ins (1.83 x 0.85 m)	6 ft x 2 ft 9.5 ins (1.83 x 0.85 m)	6 ft x 2 ft 9.5 ins (1.83 x 0.85 m)
Wings				
Area	832 sq ft (77.295 m^2)	832 sq ft (77.295 m^2)	832 sq ft (77.295 m^2)	832 sq ft (77.295 m^2)
Aspect ratio	8.98	8.98	8.98	8.98
Undercarriage Can operate from unpaved runways.	Retractable, with steerable nosewheels. Twin wheels on each unit	Retractable, with steerable nosewheels. Twin wheels on each unit	Retractable, with steerable nosewheels. Twin wheels on each unit	Retractable, with steerable nosewheels. Twin wheels on each unit
Wheel base	33 ft 1.5 ins (10.1 m)	36 ft 9 ins (11.2 m)	41 ft 1 ins (12.52 m)	41 ft 1 ins (12.52 m)
Wheel track	15 ft 6 ins (4.72 m)	15 ft 6 ins (4.72 m)	15 ft 6 ins (4.72 m)	15 ft 6 ins (4.72 m)
Weights				
Empty, operating	52,300 lb (23,723 kg)	54,000 lb (24,494 kg)	55,900 lb (25,356 kg)	56,500 lb (25,628 kg)
Maximum zero-fuel	71,500 lb (32,432 kg) standard, 74,500 lb (33,793 kg) optional	79,000 lb (35,834 kg)	82,500 lb (37,421 kg)	82,500 lb (37,421 kg)
Maximum take-off	84,000 lb (38,102 kg) standard, 90,000-95,000 lb (40,823-43,091 kg) optional	93,000 lb (42,184 kg) standard, 97,000 lb (43,998 kg) optional	97,500 lb (44,225 kg) standard, 101,500 lb (46,040 kg) optional	101,500 lb (46,040 kg)
Maximum landing	83,500 lb (37,875 kg)	85,000 lb (38,555 kg)	88,500 lb (40,143 kg)	88,500 lb (40,143 kg)
Performance				
Maximum operating Mach number (MMO), JAR/FAR	Mach 0.72/0.73	Mach 0.72/0.73	Mach 0.72/0.73	Mach 0.72/0.73
Maximum permitted operating speed (VMO), IAS. kts (mph) km/h	300 (345) 555	300 (345) 555	305 (351) 565	305 (351) 565
Cruise speed. kts (mph) km/h	356-432 (410-497) 659-800	364-432 (419-497) 674-800	371-432 (427-497) 687-800	371-432 (427-497) 687-800
Take-off field length	4,190 ft (1,277 m) standard, 3,410 ft (1,039 m) optional	3,920 ft (1,195 m)	4,430 ft (1,350 m)	4,580 ft (1,396 m)
Landing field length dry/wet (350 naut mile sector), sea level	3,480/4,000 ft (1,061/1,220 m)	3,680/4,230 ft (1,122/1,290 m)	3,910/4,495 ft (1,195/1,370 m)	3,970/4,565 ft (1,210/1,391 m)
Range, sea level with reserves. naut miles (miles) km	1,175 (1,353) 2,176 *standard*, 1,550 (1,785) 2,870 *optional*, with 70 passengers; or 920 (1,059) 1,704 *standard*, 1,505 (1,733) 2,787 *optional*, with 82 passengers	1,290 (1,485) 2,389 *standard*, 1,450 (1,670) 2,685 *optional*, with 85 passengers; or 1,145 (1,318) 2,120 *standard*, 1,390 (1,600) 2,575 *optional*, with 100 passengers	1,210 (1,393) 2,241 *standard*, 1,355 (1,560) 2,509 *optional*, with 100 passengers; or 1,100 (1,266) 2,037 *standard*, 1,315 (1,514) 2,435 *optional*, with 112 passengers	1,250 (1,439) 2,315 with 116 passengers

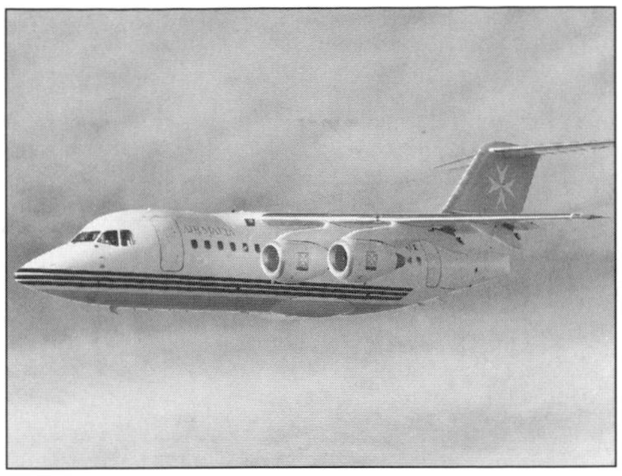

Avro International/Aero International Regional RJ70

RJ70 cockpit layout for Air Malta

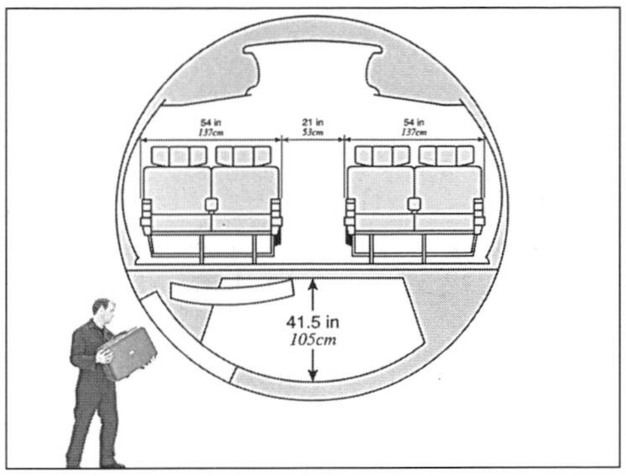

RJ Avroliner in 4-abreast first-class layout, showing rear baggage/freight hold access (courtesy Avro International)

available for all models. Typical RJ85 QT can carry a 28,195 lb (12,789 kg) payload, including LD3 containers in 1,422 cu ft (40.27 m³) volume and pallets in 2,145 cu ft (60.74 m³) volume. Cargo door for this version is 6 ft 4 ins x 10 ft 11 ins (1.93 x 3.33 m).

Jetstream Aircraft Ltd (UK)

Corporate address: Preswick International Airport, Ayrshire KA9 2RW, Scotland.
Telephone: +44 1292 479888
Facsimile: +44 1292 479703
Telex: 77432
Founded: 1 January 1993.
Employees: 2,400.
Information: Robert Gillies (Manager Product Promotion and Advertising) and Robert S. Biggart (Manager, Special Projects).

● Activities

- A division of British Aerospace in 1995 (see Combat section). To become part of the Aero International Regional multi-national consortium in 1996.
- Affiliated companies in 1995 were Jetstream Aircraft Inc of the USA for sales and marketing of Jetstream Corporate aircraft worldwide plus sales, marketing and support of Jetstream airliners in the Western hemisphere, and JSX Capital Corporation of the USA for management of fleet of BAe turboprops and remarketing of traded aircraft.
- Jetstream 31, 61 and ATP production has ended (see below), with only the Jetstream 41 going into the new Aero International Regional consortium. However, several remaining examples of these aircraft were for sale in June 1995, and the 31 can be built to order.
- The 72-78 seat **Jetstream 71** and 50-52 seat **Jetstream 51** programmes, anticipated to replace older generation turboprops and jets and originally expected to enter service in 1998, are at present on hold while the new Aero International Regional consortium decides on its future marketing strategy. Brief details for reference, issued in October 1994, can be found in the accompanying table.

Jetstream Aircraft Jetstream 31 and Super 31

First flight: 28 March 1980, as Jetstream 1 modified into the Jetstream 31 development aircraft. 18 March 1982 for production Jetstream 31. 13 April 1988 for Jetstream Super 31.
Certification: 22 June 1982 for Jetstream 31. 4 September 1988 for Jetstream Super 31 to BCAR Section D, and 30 September 1988 by the FAA to Pt 23 Commuter Category.
First delivery: 1982 in Jetstream 31 form.
Role: Short/medium-range regional airliner, corporate transport, medevac or special missions.
Details: Super 31, except where indicated.
Airframe life: 45,000 flights without major structural repair.
Noise levels: To BCAR Section N and FAR Pt 36 (Appendix F as amended by Amendments up to 36-13).
Sales: 381 Jetstream 31s and Super 31s had been delivered by June 1995. Full production has now ended but the aircraft remains available to order.
Crew: 1 or 2 pilots.
Passengers: Up to 19 in high-density airliner form, with business/corporate layouts for 8, 10, 12 or 15 passengers. Medevac layouts for 1 litter and 13 seated casualties/attendants, 2 litters and 7 seats, or 4 litters and 1 seat.
Pressurization: 5.56 psi cabin differential.
Baggage compartment: 96.7 cu ft (2.74 m³) volume for aft baggage compartment, capacity 694 lb (315 kg). Optional baggage pod of 49 cu ft (1.39 m³) volume, capacity 435 lb (197.3 kg).
Wing control surfaces: Frise aileron with geared tab, and double-slotted flap (made in 2 sections and with 10° take-off, 35°-50° landing, 20° approach, and 70° lift dump settings) per wing.
Tail control surfaces: Elevators with geared tabs and rudder with combined spring/trim tab. Underfin.
Flight control system: Manual, with aerodynamically- and mass-balanced control surfaces, except for hydraulically operated flaps.
Construction materials: Primarily aluminium alloy, but with glassfibre for the undercarriage bay fairing, slat to each flap, radome, and leading-edge fairing between fin and tailplane. Kevlar replaceable panels electrically bonded to sections of the fuselage skin to protect against gravel or ice thrown up by the propellers.
Engines: 2 AlliedSignal TPE331- 12UAR turboprops, with 8 ft 10 ins (2.69 m) McCauley or Dowty Rotol 4-blade propellers.
Engine rating: Each 1,100 shp (820.3 kW).
Fuel system: 3,248 lb (1,473 kg) usable for Jetstream Super 31 (equal to 1,846 litres), 3,024 lb (1,371 kg) for Jetstream 31.
Electrical system: Main DC supply via 2 engine-driven 30 volt, 9kW starter-generators. 2 x 24 volt, 25 amp-hour lead-acid batteries, with optional ni-cd; engine starting using battery power at temperatures down to -10° C; at lower temperatures, external electrical power is required. AC supply using 2 inverters for single-phase 115 volt and 26 volt at 400Hz, and 2 inverters each for single-phase 93 volt at 1,000 Hz.
Hydraulic system: 2,000 psi.
Braking system: Hydraulically-operated Dunlop cintered-iron, multi-piston, plate type. Maxaret anti-skid system. Parking/emergency brake.
De-icing system: Rubber boots on wing and tail unit leading edges. Electric elevator horn anti-icing mats, and electric pitot heads and stall warning vanes. Heated windshield. Bleed air for engine compressor air inlet, inlet duct and fuel control sensor probe. Propeller de-icing boots.
Oxygen system: Not provided in baseline aircraft, but with provision for drop-out system and portable cylinders.
Fire system: BTM extinguishant in bottles for engines. Portable extinguishers for the cabin.
Radar: Honeywell WXR-270/IND-270 weather radar.
Flight avionics/instrumentation: Rockwell Collins dual VHF-22A/CTL-22 comm, dual VIR-32/CTL-32 VHF nav, dual TDR-94/single CTL-92 Mode S transponder, ADF-60A/CTL-62, DME-42, and RMI-36 radio magnetic compass. Honeywell dual GH-14 gyro horizon, dual RD-450 HSI, dual C-14 compass system, and FZ-500 flight director sub-system. SFENA H.301 standby artificial horizon, Kollsman encoding altimeter, dual Kollsman VSI, dual Kollsman airspeed indicator, and Sundstrand Mk VI GPWS. Enhanced specification avionics include Honeywell SPZ 500 autopilot, second

	Jetstream 71	Jetstream 51
Passengers	72-78	50-52
Wing span	95 ft 1 ins (28.98 m)	95 ft 1 ins (28.98 m)
Length	101 ft 8 ins (31 m)	80 ft 5 ins (24.51 m)
Height	23 ft 11 ins (7.29 m)	23 ft 11 ins (7.29 m)
Empty weight, operating	36,000 lb (16,329 kg)	30,000 lb (13,608 kg)
Maximum zero fuel weight	54,200 lb (24,585 kg)	43,000 lb (19,505 kg)
Maximum take-off weight	60,000 lb (27,215 kg)	49,000 lb (22,226 kg)
Maximum payload	18,200 lb (8,255 kg)	13,000 lb (5,897 kg)
Maximum cruise speed	350 kts (403 mph) 648 km/h	360 kts (415 mph) 667 km/h
Take-off field length, ISA, sea level	4,000 ft (1,220 m)	4,000 ft (1,220 m)
IFR range	950 naut miles (1,094 miles) 1,759 km	990 naut miles (1,140 miles) 1,833 km

ADF, second DME, TCAS, cockpit voice recorder and AlliedSignal Bendix EFIS.

Aircraft variants:

Jetstream 31 has 940 shp (701 kW) TPE331-10UR-513H engines, WXR-300 radar and other differences from Super 31. Brochure figures quoted in italics in the tables are for Corporate aircraft effective May 1994.

Super 31 Airliner has 3-abreast seating for 18-19.

Super 31 Business/Corporate version for 8-15 persons in 2 or 3-abreast layouts, with toilet, galley, coat closet and baggage stowage.

Super 31 Corporate Shuttle is typically a 10-12-seater for business and charter use.

Super 31 Quick change for conversion from 12 passenger layout to 18/19 passenger airliner in just over 1 hour. Rapid role changes offered on an aircraft in Central Africa include provision for both casualty evacuation and freight operations.

Super 31 Special missions, including maritime patrol, photo reconnaissance, training, comint/sigint, flight inspection, air ambulance and more.

Jetstream Super 31s destined for J-Air in Japan, with baggage pods

DETAILS FOR JETSTREAM SUPER 31.

Principal dimensions:
Wing span: 52 ft (15.85 m)
Maximum length: 47 ft 1.5 ins (14.36 m)
Maximum height: 17 ft 8 ins (5.38 m)

Cabin:
Length: 24 ft 3 ins (7.39 m)
Width: 6 ft 1 ins (1.85 m)
Height: 5 ft 11 ins (1.8 m)
Volume: about 600 cu ft (16.99 m^3)
Main passenger door: 4 ft 8 ins x 2 ft 10 ins (1.42 x 0.86 m)

Wings:
Aerofoil section: NACA 63A418, 63A412 (root/tip)
Area: 271.3 sq ft (25.2 m^2)
Aspect ratio: 9.97

Tail unit:
Tailplane span: 21 ft 8 ins (6.6 m)

Undercarriage:
Type: Retractable, with steerable (45° each side) twin nosewheels. For ground manoeuvring, nosewheels will rotate through 360° without disconnecting the steering mechanism.
Main wheel tyre size: 28 x 9.00-12
Nose wheel tyre size: 6.00-6
Wheel base: 15 ft 1 ins (4.6 m)
Wheel track: 19 ft 6 ins (5.94 m)
Turning radius: 25 ft 1 ins (7.65 m) wheel clearance, 41 ft 2 ins (12.55 m) wingtip clearance

Weights (Jetstream Super 31, *with Jetstream 31 Corporate aircraft in italics*):
Typical empty, operating: 10,533 lb (4,778 kg) UK, 10,136 lb (4,598 kg) USA, with baggage pod, *10,800 lb (4,898 kg)*
Maximum zero fuel: 14,330 lb (6,500 kg) UK, 14,850 lb (6,736 kg) USA, *13,889 lb (6,300 kg)*
Maximum ramp: 16,314 lb (7,400 kg), *15,322 lb (6,950 kg)*
Maximum take-off: 16,204 lb (7,350 kg), *15,212 lb (6,900 kg)*
Maximum landing: 15,609 lb (7,080 kg), *14,900 lb (6,759 kg)*

Performance (Jetstream Super 31, *with Jetstream 31 Corporate aircraft in italics*):
Maximum speed: *266 kts (306 mph) 492 km/h*
Maximum cruise speed: 244-264 kts (281-304 mph) 452-489 km/h, with baggage pod, at 25,000 ft (7,620 m) down to 15,000 ft (4,572 m) respectively.
High cruise speed: *252-262 kts (290-302 mph) 467-486 km/h, at 25,000 ft (7,620 m) down to 16,000 ft (4,875 m) respectively*
Long-range cruise speed: *218-231 kts (251-266 mph) 404-428 km/h, at 16,000 ft up to 25,000 ft respectively.*
Stall speed: *84-96 kts (97-111 mph) 156-178 km/h, with 50° flaps to clean respectively, at 14,500 lb (6,577 kg) weight, idle power*
Take-off over a 50 ft (15 m) obstacle: *3,225 ft (983 m)*
Landing distance: *2,457 ft (749 m), with 50° flaps, at 14,500 lb (6,577 kg) weight*
Maximum climb rate: 2,240 ft (683 m) per minute, *2,290 ft (698 m) per minute at 13,000 lb (5,897 kg) weight*
Maximum climb rate, one engine: *662 ft (202 m) per minute, at 13,000 lb weight*
Ceiling: 25,000 ft (7,620 m), *the same*
Ceiling, one engine: *15,100 ft (4,600 m) at 13,000 lb weight*
Maximum range: up to 680 naut miles (783 miles) 1,259 km with 18/19 passengers and IFR reserves, 1,050 naut miles (1,209 miles) 1,945 km in corporate/business layout
Range at high cruise power: *1,014-1,254 naut miles (1,167-1,443 miles) 1,878-2,322 km*
Range at long-range cruise power: *1,176-1,297 naut miles (1,353-1,493 miles) 2,177-2,403 km*
Duration: *5 hours 5 minutes with 8 occupants, baggage and 3,024 lb (1,372 kg) of fuel before engine start*

Jetstream Aircraft/Aero International Regional Jetstream 41

First flight: 25 September 1991.
Certification: 23 November 1992 (JAA) and 9 April 1993 (FAA).
First delivery: 25 November 1992 to Manx Airlines.
Role: Regional transport.
Airframe life: At least 30,000 crack-free flights, and economic repair life of at least 60,000 flights.
Noise levels: 83.5 EPNdB lateral, 85.8 EPNdB flyover, and 87.8 EPNdB approach.
Sales: 144 ordered, of which 54 had been delivered by June 1995, including those to Atlantic Coast Airlines, Manx Airlines, Sun-Air of Scandinavia and Impulse Airlines.

Jetstream 41 in 30-passenger layout with Sun-Air prior to delivery

Crew: 2 (flight).
Passengers: 30 maximum, but 29 with forward galley or 29 with enhanced catering capability as standard.
Seat pitch: Standard 29-seat layout has 30 ins (76.2 cm) for 20 seats and 31 ins (78.7 cm) for 9 seats. Optional 31 ins throughout by reducing width of the galley and adjusting 2 bulkheads.
Galley: See above and diagram.
Pressurization: 5.7 psi cabin differential.
Baggage compartments: Pressurized 170 cu ft (4.81 m^3) compartment aft of cabin. 48 x 52 ins (1.22 x 1.32 m) door. 47.5 cu ft (1.35 m^3) in unpressurized ventral bay.
Wing control surfaces: Frise ailerons with trim tab, double-slotted flaps and ground spoilers.
Tail control surfaces: Elevators and rudder, with tabs.
Flight control system: Manual, except for hydraulic flaps and spoilers. Elevator and aileron control are split, with manual disconnection to enable the 2 control columns to be decoupled because of a circuit jam.
Construction materials: Principally aluminium alloy, but with titanium engine cowls, glassfibre with Nomex honeycomb core floor panels and fairings, and Kevlar main undercarriage doors (plus similar Kevlar fuselage protection panels in the propeller plane as for Jetstream 31).
Engines: 2 AlliedSignal TPE331-14GR/HR turboprops, with 9 ft 6 ins (2.9 m) McCauley C1101/1102 5-blade constant-speed propellers.
Engine rating: Each 1,650 shp (1,230 kW).
Fuel system: 3,305 litres or 5,818 lb (2,639 kg) usable.

Jetstream 41 cockpit, with GNS option

Jetstream 41 interior

Electrical system: DC supply has 2 independent channels, each powered by a 28 volt, 550/825 amp starter/generator. 2 x 24 volt, 28 amp-hour ni-cd batteries. Larger ni-cd or sealed lead-acid batteries optional. 115 volt and 26 volt, 400Hz AC supply via an inverter in each DC channel.

Hydraulic system: Single 2,000 psi system with 2 engine-driven pumps.
Braking system: Dunlop hydraulic steel rotor brake on mainwheels, with electronic anti-skid system. Parking/emergency brake.
De-icing system: Pneumatic boots for wing and tail unit leading edges, and electric for propellers, elevator horns, pitot heads, static plates and stall vanes.
Oxygen system: Optional portable and passenger emergency systems available. Space in the PSU covers for drop-out face masks.
Fire system: Fire detection system for each engine, with engine and nacelle extinguishing using Halon 1301 (BTM). Fire detection systems in the rear baggage, ventral baggage and toilet compartments, with hand-held extinguishers for the rear baggage compartment, toilet, flight deck and cabin.

Details for Jetstream 41 Airliner.

Principal dimensions:
Wing span: 60 ft 5 ins (18.42 m)
Maximum length: 63 ft 2 ins (19.25 m)
Maximum height: 18 ft 10 ins (5.74 m)

Cabin:
Length: 31 ft 4 ins (9.55 m), excluding flight deck
Width: 6 ft 1 ins (1.85 m)
Height: 5 ft 10 ins (1.78 m)
Volume: 1,040 cu ft (29.45 m^3)
Main passenger door: 4 ft 8 ins x 2 ft 5 ins (1.42 x 0.74 m)

Wings:
Aerofoil section: NACA 63A418, 63A412 (root/tip)
Area: 348.5 sq ft (32.38 m^2)
Aspect ratio: 10.5
Dihedral: 7°

Tail unit:
Tailplane span: 21 ft 11 ins (6.68 m)

Undercarriage:
Type: Retractable, with steerable nosewheels (42.5° each side). Nosewheels can caster up to 100° each side when manoeuvring with asymmetric braking or power. Twin wheels on each unit
Main wheel tyre size: 22 x 6.75-10 PR
Nose wheel tyre size: 18 x 6-6 PR
Wheel base: 24 ft (7.32 m)
Wheel track: 20 ft (6.1 m)
Turning radius: 35 ft 7.7 ins (10.86 m) wheel clearance, 56 ft 4.4 ins (17.18 m) wingtip clearance

Weights:
Empty, operating: 14,144 lb (6,416 kg)
Maximum zero fuel: 21,400 lb (9,707 kg)
Maximum ramp: 24,110 lb (10,936 kg)
Maximum take-off: 24,000 lb (10,886 kg)
Maximum landing: 23,300 lb (10,569 kg)
Payload: 7,256 lb (3,291 kg)

Performance:
Maximum operating speed (MMO/VMO): Mach 0.52, or 250 kts (288 mph) 463 km/h IAS
Maximum cruise speed: 295 kts (340 mph) 546 km/h
Take-off runway length: Minimum 3,937 ft (1,200 m) at MTOW
Maximum climb rate: 2,200 ft (671 m) per minute, sea level, 9° flap
Maximum climb rate, one engine: 400 ft (122 m) per minute, sea level, 9° flap
Ceiling: 25,000 ft (7,620 m) standard
Range: 774 naut miles (891 miles) 1,433 km
Typical operation: At least 2 x 1 hour sectors from airfields at 2,000 ft (610 m) elevation and ISA +25° C (36° C)

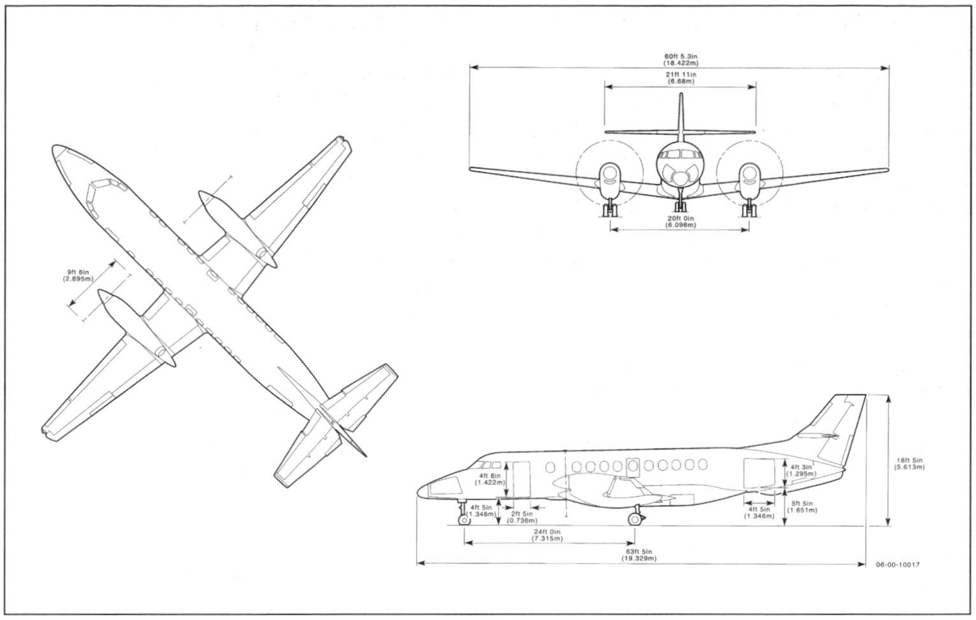

Jetstream 41 drawing (courtesy British Aerospace)

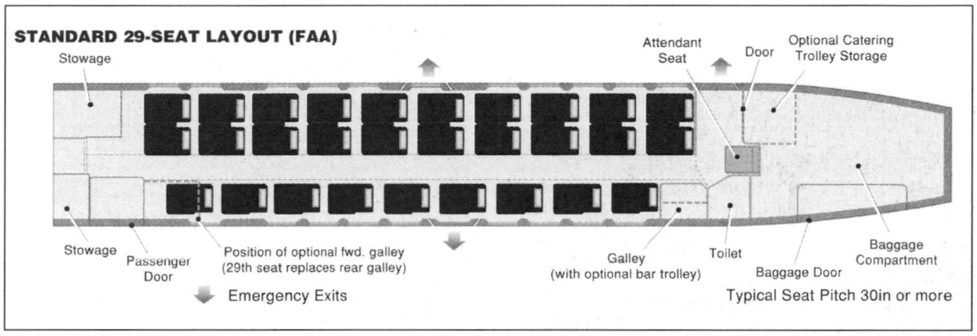

Jetstream 41 in 29-seat layout (FAA) (courtesy Jetstream Aircraft)

Radar: Honeywell Primus 650 colour weather radar.
Flight avionics/ instrumentation: Honeywell SPZ-4500 digital avionics suite with DFZ-450 digital flight director/control system, EDZ-805 4-tube EFIS, dual AHS 600 AHRS, dual DC 800 digital air data computers, RT 300 digital audio and integrated radio system, and yaw damper. Options include 3-axis autopilot, GPWS, GPS, TCAS I and a multi-function display.
Aircraft variants:
Airliner for up to 29/30 passengers, as detailed.
Corporate is typically configured for 8-14 passengers in a luxurious cabin with recline/swivel/tracking seats, at 34 ins (86 cm) seat pitch for 14-seat layout. Operating empty weight in 14-seat layout is 15,850 lb (6,736 kg), and maximum payload is 6,548 lb (2,970 kg).
Corporate Shuttle was displayed in October 1994 as a 14-seater with cabin noise reduction and weight savings.
Combi and Quick change versions are available, as are Special missions variants for roles similar to those detailed under Jetstream Super 31.

Jetstream Aircraft ATP and Jetstream 61

First flight: 6 August 1986 (ATP), 10 May 1994 (Jetstream 61).
Certification: 1988 (JAR and FAR 25 for ATP); 15 June 1995 (Jetstream 61).
First delivery: April 1988 (ATP) to British Midland Airways.
Role: Regional airliners.
Airframe life: 30,000 flying hours crack-free warranty, with economic repair life of 80,000 hours quoted for Jetstream 61.
Noise levels: Complies with requirements of BCAR Section N Issue 4, Chapter N3-3, 4 and those of

Jetstream Aircraft ATP in Merpati livery

FAR Pt 36, Appendix C, Stage 3 (to Amendment 36-16).
Sales: 55 ATPs delivered by June 1995, including 2 to Euro Direct in September 1994. Others to British Airways, Manx Airlines, United Feeder Services, Merpati, SATA, and Bangladesh Biman. Production ended, but 3 or 4 airframes remaining for sale in mid-1995. 3 options placed by Manx Airlines converted to Jetstream 41s. No Jetstream 61s ordered or delivered, but 4 or 5 airframes remained for sale in mid-1995.
Crew: 2 (flight).
Passengers: Typically 64-72 for ATP at 31 or 30 ins (79 or 76 cm) seat pitch respectively. 70 seats at 31 ins (79 cm) pitch for Jetstream 61.
Galley: Options to offer services from light snacks to full hot meals. Own servicing access door of 4 ft 1 ins x 2 ft (1.24 x 0.61 m).
Pressurization: 5.5 psi cabin differential.
Baggage compartment: Forward 128 cu ft (3.62 m^3) and rear 180 cu ft (0.509 m^3) for ATP. Forward 130 cu ft (3.68 m^3) for 1,323 lb (600 kg) load, rear 190 cu ft (5.38 m^3) for 1,874 lb (850 kg) load, with external loading, for Jetstream 61. Overhead bins with 106.6 cu ft

(3.02 m^3) volume for ATP, 125 cu ft (3.54 m^3) for Jetstream 61.
Wing control surfaces: Aerodynamically and statically balanced ailerons (geared tabs in ATP, starboard trim tab in J61), and Fowler flaps.
Tail control surfaces: Elevators with tabs, and rudder with trim/spring tabs (23° movement each way).
Flight control system: Manual, but with electric elevator trim. Mechanically interconnected flaps.
Construction materials: Metal.
Engines: 2 Pratt & Whitney Canada PW126A turboprops (ATP), and 2 PW127D turboprops (Jetstream 61), with Hamilton Standard 6-blade composite propellers. Optional APU (ATP).
Engine rating: Each 2,653 shp (1,978 kW) for ATP, 2,750 shp (2,050.7 kW) for Jetstream 61.
Fuel system: 6,364 litres maximum. 11,220 lb (5,089 kg) usable.
Electrical system: Primary 200 volt, 3-phase variable-frequency AC supply using a 49 kVA generator mounted on each propeller reduction gearbox. AC system feeds a 28 volt DC supply via 2 transformer rectifiers and a 115 volt single-phase 400 Hz sub-system via 2 static inverters. 2 x 37 amp-hour ni-cd batteries for engine starting and emergency power.
Hydraulic system: 2,450 psi. Each engine drives a variable delivery pump.
Braking system: Carbon mainwheel brakes with Maxaret anti-skid.
De-icing system: Pneumatic rubber boot system for wing and tail unit leading edges. Electric for engine intakes, propellers, pitot heads, stall warning vane, forward static plates and cockpit glazing.
Fire system: First and second shot fire extinguishing system for each engine. Halon portable extinguishers for the flight compartment, forward and rear vestibules, and water glycol for the passenger cabin.
Radar: AlliedSignal Bendix/King RDS-86 colour weather radar in ATP.
Flight avionics/instrumentation: Smiths EFIS. Digital avionics with ARINC 429 data transmission and a Cat II capable autopilot standard. VHF navigation with dual VOR/LOC/glideslope/marker receivers. DME, ATC transponder, ADF, and ground proximity warning system. Communications include dual AlliedSignal VCS-40A VHF, VC-40B transceiver, Collins 346D passenger address, and Blaupunkt tape replay system, audio. Flight data recorder, cockpit voice recorder.

Aircraft variants:
ATP was developed to replace the BAe Super 748. Euro Direct became a recent customer, receiving 2 ATPs in September 1994. Last few available in 1995 (see Sales).
Jetstream 61 was developed as a more powerful derivative of the ATP, as detailed. New extra wide seats (17.8 ins, 45 cm). Special missions versions made available. No further production, but several airframes for finishing in 1995.

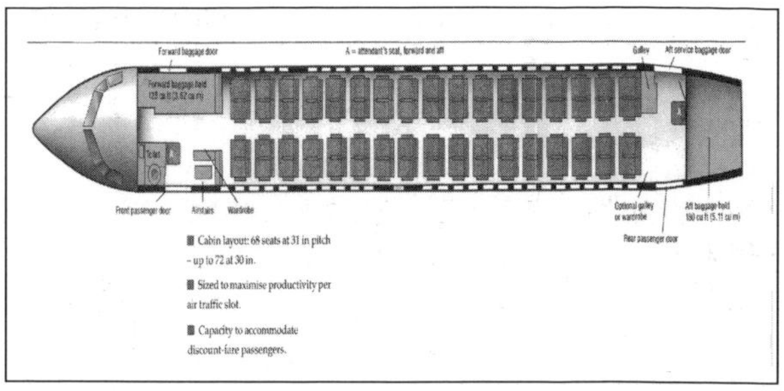

Jetstream ATP 68-passenger layout (courtesy Jetstream Aircraft)

DETAILS FOR ATP, *WITH JETSTREAM 61 IN ITALICS.*

Principal dimensions:
Wing span: 100 ft 6 ins (30.63 m), *the same*
Maximum length: 85 ft 4 ins (26.01 m), *the same*
Maximum height: 24 ft 11 ins (7.59 m), *the same*

Cabin:
Length: 63 ft (19.2 m), *the same*
Width: 8 ft 2.6 ins (2.5 m) maximum and 6 ft 9 ins (2.06 m) at floor, *the same*
Height: 6 ft 3.75 ins (1.93 m), *the same*
Volume: 2,652 cu ft (75.1 m^3) *the same*
Main passenger door: 5 ft 8 ins x 2 ft 4 ins (1.73 x 0.71 m), *the same*
Baggage door: 3 ft 7 ins x 2 ft 9 ins (1.09 x 0.84 m) forward, 5 ft 2 ins x 2 ft 4 ins (1.575 x 0.71 m) rear

Wings:
Area: 842.83 sq ft (78.3 m^2), *the same*
Aspect ratio: 11.984, *the same*
Sweepback: 2.92° at 25% chord, *the same*
Dihedral: 7°, *the same*

Tail unit:
Tailplane span: 36 ft (10.97 m), *the same*
Tailplane area: 243 sq ft (22.57 m^2), *the same*
Fin/rudder area: 148 sq ft (13.75 m^2) *the same*

Undercarriage:
Type: Retractable, with steerable (±47°) nosewheels. Twin wheels on each unit
Main wheel tyre size: 34.5 x 12-14, *the same*
Nose wheel tyre size: 22 x 6.75-10, *the same*
Wheel base: 31 ft 9.7 ins (9.7 m), *the same*
Wheel track: 27 ft 9 ins (8.46 m), *the same*
Turning radius: 31 ft 10 ins (9.7 m) about nosewheel. 79 ft 11 ins (24.36 m) powered steering (47° angle) and 64 ft 8 ins (19.71 m) free castering (67° angle), from centre of rotation to wingtip. *The same.*

Weights:
Empty, operating: 31,400 lb (14,243 kg), *31,800 lb (14,424 kg)*
Maximum zero fuel: 47,200 lb (21,409 kg), *48,000 lb (21,772 kg)*
Maximum ramp: *52,350 lb (23,745 kg)*
Maximum take-off: 52,200 lb (23,677 kg), *the same*
Maximum landing: 51,000 lb (23,133 kg), *the same*
Payload: 15,800 lb (7,166 kg), *16,430 lb (7,452 kg)*

Performance:
Maximum cruise speed: 271 kts (312 mph) 502 km at 13,000 ft (3,962 m), *270 kts (311 mph) 500 km/h*
Long-range cruise speed: 236 kts (271 mph) 437 km/h
Take-off field length: 4,410 ft (1,344 m), *4,360 ft (1,329 m)* at MTOW, ISA and sea level
Landing field length: 3,818 ft (1,164 m)
Range with full payload: 619 naut miles (713 miles) 1,146 km, with reserves for 100 naut mile diversion and 45 minutes hold
Range with 70 x 100 kg passengers: *637 naut miles (733.5 miles) 1,180 km with IFR reserves, or 2 x 275 naut mile (316.7 mile) 509 km sectors*
Range with 70 x 95 kg passengers: *777 naut miles (895 miles) 1,439 km with IFR reserves, or 2 x 335 naut mile (386 mile) 620 km sectors*

Pilatus Britten-Norman Ltd (UK)

Corporate address: See Reconnaissance section for company details.

● Activities

● The Defender, Defender 4000 and MSSA can be found in the Reconnaissance section.

Pilatus Britten-Norman BN2B and BN2T Islander series

First flight: 13 June 1965.
Certification: 10 August 1967 (UK), 19 December 1967 (USA). Manufactured in accordance with BCAR Section K and FAR Pt 23 with Pt 135 approval.
First delivery: 1967, to Loganair and Aurigny.
Role: STOL, piston-or turboprop-engined unpressurized commuter, feederline, cargo and executive transport, ambulance, crop spraying, parachuting and more.
Sales: Tótal Islander and Defender sales by March 1995 stood at 1,198, including 81 triple engined Trislanders build between 1971 and 1984. Main version is now the turboprop-engined BN2T and Defender derivatives.
Crew: Pilot.
Passengers: 9 commuter passengers or 6 in executive layout, or 3 litters and attendant, or 10 parachutists plus a jumpmaster.
Freight hold volume: 166 cu ft (4.7 m^3) with all seats removed behind pilot.
Baggage area: 49 cu ft (1.388 m^3)
Wing control surfaces: Ailerons (with starboard ground-adjustable tab) and single-slotted flaps.
Tail control surfaces: Single piece elevator and rudder, both with trim tabs.
Flight control system: Manual, except for electric flaps.
Construction materials: Aluminium alloy.
Engines: See tables.
Electrical system: DC supply via 2 x 24 volt, 50 amp engine-driven alternators. 24 volt, 17 amp-hour lead-acid battery for emergency power.
Braking system: Hydraulic.
De-icing system: Optional pneumatic boot in wing and tail unit leading edges. Optional electric propellers and windshield.
Oxygen system: Optional.
Radar: Optional weather radar.
Flight avionics/instrumentation: Standard avionics are dual VHF nav/comm with ILS, marker beacon receiver, ADF, VOR, DME, transponder and encoding altimeter. Options include ELT, autopilot, HF/MF radios, RNAV, Omega and GPS.

Aircraft variants:
Islander refers to both the piston- and turboprop-powered versions, though the name Turbine Islander is commonly used for the Allison-engined model. In civil and military/government use. As detailed.
Defender, Defender 4000 and MSSA are detailed in the Reconnaissance section.

Pilatus Britten-Norman BN2B-26 Islander in British Airways livery

Islander engine, weight and performance figures

	BN2B-26	BN2B-20	BN2T
Engines	2 Textron Lycoming O-540-E4C5 piston engines	2 Textron Lycoming IO-540-K1B5 piston engines	2 Allison 250-B17C turboprops
Engine rating (each)	260 hp (194 kW)	300 hp (224 kW)	320 shp (238.6 kW)
Weights			
Maximum zero fuel	6,300 lb (2,857 kg)	6,300 lb (2,857 kg)	6,600 lb (2,994 kg)
Maximum take-off	6,600 lb (2,994 kg) with or without tip tanks	6,600 lb (2,994 kg) with or without tip tanks	7,000 lb (3,175 kg), tip tanks standard
Maximum landing	6,600 lb (2,994 kg) with or without tip tanks	6,600 lb (2,994 kg) with or without tip tanks	6,800 lb (3,084 kg)
Payload with maximum fuel	1,706 lb (774 kg), or 1,096 lb (497 kg) with tip tanks	1,576 lb (715 kg), or 966 lb (438 kg) with tip tanks	1,520 lb (689 kg)
Disposable load	2,486 lb (1,128 kg), or 2,386 lb (1,082 kg) with tip tanks	2,356 lb (1,069 kg), or 2,256 lb (1,023 kg) with tip tanks	2,960 lb (1,343 kg)
Usable fuel	492 litres, or 814 with tip tanks	492 litres, or 814 with tip tanks	814 litres
Performance			
Maximum cruise speed at 8,000 ft (2,440 m) kts (mph) km/h	142 (164) 263	143 (165) 265	170 (196) 315
Economical cruise speed at 8,000 ft (2,440 m) kts (mph) km/h	126 (145) 233	128 (147) 237	150 (173) 278
Stall speed, power off, IAS a) clean b) with flaps kts (mph) km/h	a) 50 (58) 93 b) 40 (46) 74	a) 50 (58) 93 b) 40 (46) 74	a) 52 (60) 96 b) 45 (52) 83
Take-off distance a) ground roll b) over a 50 ft (15 m) obstacle	a) 621 ft (189 m) b) 1,218 ft (371 m)	a) 704 ft (215 m) b) 1,166 ft (355 m)	a) 837 ft (255 m) b) 1,250 ft (381 m)
Landing distance a) ground roll b) over a 50 ft (15 m) obstacle	a) 459 ft (140 m) b) 980 ft (299 m)	a) 459 ft (140 m) b) 980 ft (299 m)	a) 747 ft (228 m) b) 1,110 ft (338 m)
a) Climb rate b) Climb rate, one engine	a) 860 ft (262 m) per minute b) 145 ft (44 m) per minute	a) 1,130 ft (344 m) per minute b) 198 ft (60 m) per minute	a) 1,050 ft (320 m) per minute b) 215 ft (66 m) per minute
a) Ceiling b) Ceiling, one engine	a) 13,600 ft (4,145 m) b) 4,400 ft (1,340 m)	a) 19,700 ft (6,005 m) b) 6,150 ft (1,875 m)	a) over 25,000 ft (7,620 m) b) 10,000 ft (3,050 m)
IFR range naut miles (miles) km	539 (620) 998, or 952 (1,096) 1,763 with tip tanks	503 (579) 932, or 896 (1,032) 1,659 with tip tanks	590 (679) 1,093
VFR range naut miles (miles) km	675 (777) 1,250, or 1,130 (1,301) 2,093 with tip tanks	639 (736) 1,183, or 1,075 (1,238) 1,991 with tip tanks	728 (838) 1,348

DETAILS FOR ISLANDER.

Principal dimensions:
Wing span: 49 ft (14.94 m)
Maximum length: 35 ft 8 ins (10.87 m)
Maximum height: 14 ft 6 ins (4.42 m)

Cabin:
Length: 15 ft 2 ins (4.62 m) including baggage bay, 10 ft (3.05 m) for main passenger area only
Width: 3 ft 7 ins (1.09 m)
Height: 4 ft 2 ins (1.27 m)
Floor area: 47.2 sq ft (4.38 m^2)
Volume: 183.5 cu ft (5.2 m^3) including baggage bay, 130 cu ft (3.68 m^3) for main passenger area
Main passenger doors: 3 ft 7.5 ins x 2 ft 10 ins (1.1 x 0.86 m) starboard, and 3 ft 7.5 ins x 2 ft 1 ins (1.1 x 0.64 m) port

Wings:
Aerofoil section: NACA 23012
Area: 325 sq ft (30.19 m^2)
Aspect ratio: 7.388
Incidence: 2°

Tail unit:
Tailplane span: 15 ft 4 ins (4.67 m)
Tailplane area: 73 sq ft (6.78 m^2)

Undercarriage:
Type: Fixed, with steerable nosewheel. Twin mainwheels. Can operate from beaches, grass and other surfaces. Low pressure tyres (35 psi) for soft-field operation
Tyre size: 16 x 7-7 ins
Wheel base: 13 ft 1 ins (3.99 m)
Wheel track: 11 ft 10 ins (3.61 m)
Turning radius: 31 ft (9.45 m) minimum

Basler Turbo Conversions Inc (USA)

Corporate address: 255 West 35th Avenue, PO Box 2305, Oshkosh, WI 54903-2305.
Telephone: +1 414 236 7820
Facsimile: +1 414 235 0381
Founded: 1957.
Information: Warren Basler (Chairman)

● Activities

● Also produces the Basler Turbo-34, a lengthened Cessna Model 337 Skymaster with the twin piston engines replaced by a single rear-mounted P&WC PT6A turboprop.

Basler Turbo-67

First flight: July 1989
Certification: 27 February 1990 for Supplemental Type Certificate
First delivery: August 1990
Role: Highly modified DC-3 used for cargo and passenger carrying, troop/paratroop transport, firefighting, drug enforcement, disaster relief, geophysical survey, gunship and more.
Airframe life: Inspection includes documented 12,000 hour airframe overhaul.

★ Aims

★ Compared with the DC-3, has 35% more cabin volume, 43% increase in useful load, 24% higher speed. 76% more productivity, higher single-engine ceiling, up to 100% more fuel, lower approach speed, 34% reduction in mission fuel cost at normal cruise speeds, and all-weather capability.
★ Newly certified systems, including engines, fuel, de-icing, fire protection, stall warning, electrical, avionics, oxygen, air conditioning and Cat II autopilot.
★ Inspected, overhauled, new and upgraded parts, including undercarriage, hydraulics, wheels and brakes, and flight controls.

Sales: Operators include the US Forest Service, Turbo Power & Marine (International Red Cross), Aerocontractors, Aerial Services, Colombian Poolice, and the air forces of Bolivia, El Salvador and Guatemala.
Crew: 3.
Passengers: Optional 38 passenger interior.
Freight hold: Can accommodate 5 LD3 containers or other loads. Optional reworked cargo floor, cargo compartment liner, top cargo door, and electric cargo winch.
Size of freight doors: Oversized door option for cargo carrying, 7 ft 9.5 ins x 6 ft 7.5 ins (2.37 x 2.02 m) maximum (reduces with tapering fuselage).
Loading facilities: Cargo tracks, guide rails, pulley, and optional 8,000 lb (3,629 kg) capacity electric winch.
Airframe upgrades: Fully engineered, designed and strengthened airframe after total inspection and rework of normal wear items. Includes a structural

reinforcement conversion package. Fuselage stretched by 40 ins (1.03 m) forward of the wing and cockpit bulkhead moved forward 60 ins (1.52 m) to provide greater cabin volume and optimum centre of gravity parameters. Redesigned outer wing leading edges and wingtips. All-metal control surfaces. Centre and outer wing panels reinforced.
Engines: 2 Pratt & Whitney Canada PT6A-67R turboprops (replacing the former piston engines) with Hartzell HC-B5MA-3/M11276 5-blade propellers.
Engine rating: Each 1,424 shp (1,062 kW).
Fuel system: Engineered to FAR Pt 25, including new filler caps. Standard 2,922 litres. Optional long-range tanks of 1,514 litres or 3,028 litres.
Electrical system: Replaced with new system designed to FAR Pt 25. 4 bus system with 2 x 300 amp starter generators and 2 x 12 volt, 88 amp-hour batteries.
Braking system: B.F.Goodrich H2-445 Expander tube assembly.
Deicing system: Optional boots for wing and tail unit leading edges, and electrically headed windshield.
Radar: AlliedSignal Bendix/King RDS81 colour weather radar.
Flight avionics/instrumentation: New instrument panel and control pedestal. AlliedSignal Bendix/King standard and customized packages, including KX165 nav/comm, KR87 ADF, KNI-582 RMI, KT70 transponder, KR21 marker beacon, KRA405 radar altimeter, autopilot for Cat II minima, ground proximity warning system, Omega/GPS, flight data and cockpit voice recorders.

Basler Turbo-67

DETAILS FOR TURBO-67.

Principal dimensions:
Wing span: 95 ft 8 ins (29.16 m)
Maximum length: 67 ft 9.5 ins (20.66 m)
Maximum height: 17 ft (5.18 m) at rest, 23 ft 6 ins (7.16 m) tail up

Cabin:
Length: 42 ft 2 ins (12.85 m)
Width: 7 ft (2.13 m) at floor
Height: 6 ft 6 ins (1.98 m) varies.
Volume: 1,225 cu ft (34.69 m^3)

Weights:
Empty, operating: 15,750 lb (7,144 kg) cargo configuration, 15,000 lb (6,804 kg) empty
Maximum zero fuel: 26,200 lb (11,884 kg)
Maximum take-off and landing: 28,750 lb (13,041 kg)
Useful load: 13,750 lb (6,237 kg) maximum

Performance:
Maximum speed: 210 kts (242 mph) 388 km/h at 10,000 ft (3,050 m)
Maximum cruise speed: 205 kts (236 mph) 380 km/h, at 12,500 ft (3,810 m)
Standard cruise speed: 199 kts (229 mph) 368 km/h, 12,500 ft
Economical cruise speed: 176 kts (203 mph) 326 km/h
Take-off distance: 1,296 ft (395 m) at MTOW
Take-off over a 50 ft obstacle: 1,932-1,991 ft (590-607 m) at MTOW
Landing distance: 1,610 ft (491 m) at 28,450 lb (12,905 kg)
Landing distance over a 50 ft obstacle: 1,980 ft (604 m) at 28,650 lb (12,995 kg)
Maximum climb rate: 700-1,000 ft (213-305 m) per minute at MTOW
Ceiling, one engine: 14,000 ft (4,270 m) at 27,000 lb (12,247 kg) weight
Range: 950 naut miles (1,094 miles) 1,759 km, at standard cruise speed, with 45 minutes reserve
Range with long-range fuel: 2,140-2,260 naut miles (2,464-2,600 miles) 3,963-4,185 km

The Boeing Company (USA)

Corporate address: See Combat section for all company, group and divisions details.

● Activities

● See also Combat and Reconnaissance sections, plus Helicopter section for details of the Bell Boeing V-22 Osprey. 212 jetliners ordered in the first 8 months of 1995.

New Small Airplane (NSA)

Role: Sub-Boeing 737 size regional airliner in the 70-80 seat (5 abreast?) range, to be developed with partners.

★ Aims

★ To enter service after the year 2002. At the study stage in October 1995, including exploratory discussions with China, Japan, South Korea, Taiwan and perhaps other potential partners. May have some commonality with the third-generation 737 to keep costs low, mainly systems, but not in any form that would compromize the design of an otherwise totally new airliner.
★ A worldwide market for nearly 3,000 aircraft of this size is envisaged over 20 years. Though it is expected that Boeing would integrate the programme and offer new technologies, sales and support, actual assembly is likely to be abroad.

Boeing 707 and C-135/C-137 series

Sales and Upgrades: 1,010 Boeing 707s and related B720s in airliner and military guises were built up to 1992, since 1982 only as airframes for various military developments (the last an RAF AWACS aircraft). In early 1995, a total of about 132 B707s and four 720s remained in commercial use, often as freighters (with several companies offering freighter conversions for former passenger aircraft), while by far the greatest fleet remained with the USAF as flight refuelling

Boeing C-135FR of the French Air Force, with CFM56 engines and recently provided with wing-mounted hose and drogue pods

tankers, transports, and in various specialized variants. The latter include electronic and reconnaissance models, detailed in the Reconnaissance section. In addition, the USAF has a single OC-135B Open Skies treaty verification aircraft, which is receiving a Quiet Nacelles Stage 3 hush-kit in 1995. In May 1995 the active USAF had 264 KC-135 tankers, of which 239 were primary aircraft authorized for use, plus 8 C-135 and 7 C-137 transports. In addition, the Air National Guard then had 225 and the Air Force Reserve 62, including KC-135Rs which, as with KC-135Ts, have been re-engined with CFM56 (F108-CF-100) turbofans. Gross weight of the KC-135R/T is 322,000 lb (146,056 kg), with 120,000 lb (54,431 kg) of fuel for transfer. B707/C-135 tankers are also used by other air forces, including Turkey amongst the latest. Earlier USAF programmes re-skinned the C/KC-135s' lower wing surfaces, and future programmes are being studied, including adding wing-mounted hose and drogue refuelling pods and new digital cockpit avionics.

Boeing 727

Sales and Upgrades: 1,831 B727s were delivered up to 1984, of which more than 1,250 remain in commercial use. Various conversion programmes are offered (as detailed elsewhere), including re-engining and conversion to freighters, and a 2-man flightdeck by Aeroworks and Gull Electronic Systems.

Boeing 737

First flight: 9 April 1967 in original 737-100 form. 24 February 1984 for 737-300, 19 February 1988 for 737-400, and 20 June 1989 for 737-500.
Certification: 15 December 1967 in original 737-100 form. 14 November 1984 for 737-300, 2 September 1988 for 737-400 and 12 February 1990 for 737-500.
First delivery: 28 November 1984 to USAir for 737-300.
Role: Short/medium range airliner.
Noise levels: Meets FAR Pt 36 Stage 3/ICAO Annex 16 Chapter 3 requirements in take-off, sideline and approach with 30° flaps, but marginally exceeds the approach limit with 40° flaps. 85 dBA at take-off.
Sales: Total of 3,139 B737s had been ordered by 20 May 1995 (1,372 US and 1,767 non-US customers), comprising 30 B737-100s, 1,114 B737-200s, 1,054 B737-300s, 431 B737-400s, 357 B737-500s, 35 B737-600s, 85 B737-700s, 22 B737-800s and 11 B737-TBDs. Of these, 2,720 had been delivered (the 2,500th on 16 June 1993 to Southwest Airlines).
Crew: 2 (flight).
Passengers: 120-149 seats for 737-300 (typically 128 in 2-class and 149 inclusive tour layouts), 135-172 seats for 737-400 (typically 146 in 2-class and 168 in inclusive tour layouts), 100-132 seats for 737-500 (typically 108 in 2-class and 132 in inclusive tour layouts). 4 abreast seating with aisle for first class layout, 5 abreast with aisle for business class, and 6 abreast with aisle for economy. Movable cabin divider (can be repositioned by 1 person between flights) to adjust the ratio of premium and economy seating. Variable-geometry convertible seats are available to change the seat counts and seating proportions, the latter by increasing/decreasing spaces between the individual seats. Airstairs.

Seat pitch: 36 ins (91 cm) first class, 32 ins (81 cm) economy, and 30 ins (76 cm) inclusive tour.
Galleys: 2, forward and aft of cabin. Options available.
Toilets: 3 typically in forward and aft positions. Options available.
Pressurization: 7.5 psi cabin differential.
Freight hold volume: Lower deck volume of 1,068 cu ft (30.24 m^3) basic, or 917 or 792 cu ft (25.97 or 22.43 m^3) when auxiliary fuel tanks are installed for 737-300. 1,373 cu ft (38.88 m^3) basic, or 1,222 or 1,097 cu ft (34.6 or 31 m^3) when auxiliary fuel tanks are installed for 737-400. 822 cu ft (23.28 m^3) basic, or 671 or 546 cu ft (19 or 15.46 m^3) when auxiliary fuel tanks are installed for 737-500.
Size of freight doors: 35 x 48 ins (89 x 122 cm) forward, and 33 x 48 ins (84 x 122 cm) aft.
Loading facilities: Partial provision (wiring and relays) are available in all models to permit aftermarket installation of the Air Cargo Equipment (ACE) telescoping-shelf baggage handling equipment. Accommodated ACE in the aft compartment when auxiliary fuel tanks are not installed. Optional sliding carpet loading system for both holds.
Wing control surfaces: Ailerons with tabs, triple-slotted trailing-edge flaps, Krueger leading-edge flaps, 3-section leading-edge slats, multi-section spoilers (assisting ailerons and functioning as speed brakes) and 2 lift-dumpers/speed brakes. Next Generation 737-600/700/800 will have new double-slotted flaps with 37% fewer parts and 33% fewer bearings.
Tail control surfaces: Variable incidence tailplane. Elevators with servo tabs and and rudder.
Flight control system: Hydraulic.
Construction materials: Incorporates advanced aluminium alloys in the wings; glassfibre or glassfibre/graphite in the flap track fairings, other wing parts, wing/body fairing, nosecone, and fin tip and extension; graphite/Kevlar/glassfibre in the tailfin; Kevlar in some

Note: Pax = Passengers	**737-300**	**737-400**	**737-500**	**737-600**	**737-700**	**737-800**
Wing span	94 ft 9 ins (28.88 m)	94 ft 9 ins (28.88 m)	94 ft 9 ins (28.88 m)	112 ft 7 ins (34.32 m)	112 ft 7 ins (34.32 m)	112 ft 7 ins (34.32 m)
Maximum lenght	109 ft 7 ins (33.4 m)	119 ft 7 ins (36.45 m)	101 ft 9 ins (29.95 m)	102 ft 6 ins (31.24 m)	110 ft 4 ins (33.63 m)	129 ft 6 ins (39.47 m)
Maximum height	36 ft 6 ins (11.13 m)	36 ft 6 ins (11.13 m)	36 ft 6 ins (11.13 m)	41 ft 3 ins (12.57 m)	41 ft 2 ins (12.55 m)	41 ft 2 ins (12.55 m)
Cabin length	77 ft 2 ins (23.52 m)	89 ft 2 ins (27.18 m)				
Cabin width	11 ft 4 ins (3.45 m)	11 ft 4 ins (3.45 m)	11 ft 4 ins (3.45 m)	11 ft 7 ins (3.53 m)	11 ft 7 ins (3.53 m)	11 ft 7 ins (3.53 m)
Cabin height	7 ft (2.13 m)	7 ft (2.13 m)	7 ft (2.13 m)			
Passenger doors	6 ft x 2 ft 10 ins (1.83 x 0.86 m) and 6 ft x 2 ft 6 ins (1.83 x 0.76 m)	6 ft x 2 ft 10 ins (1.83 x 0.86 m) and 6 ft x 2 ft 6 ins (1.83 x 0.76 m)	6 ft x 2 ft 10 ins (1.83 x 0.86 m) and 6 ft x 2 ft 6 ins (1.83 x 0.76 m)			
Wing area	1,135 sq ft (105.44 m^2)	1,135 sq ft (105.44 m^2)	1,135 sq ft (105.44 m^2)	1,340 sq ft (124.5 m^2)	1,340 sq ft (124.5 m^2)	1,340 sq ft (124.5 m^2)
Wing aspect ratio	7.91	7.91	7.91	9.46	9.46	9.46
Tailplane span	41 ft 8 ins (12.7 m)	41 ft 8 ins (12.7 m)	41 ft 8 ins (12.7 m)	47 ft 2 ins (14.38 m)	47 ft 1 ins (14.35 m)	47 ft 1 ins (14.35 m)
Undercarriage type	Retractable, with steerable nosewheels. Twin wheels on each unit	Retractable, with steerable nosewheels. Twin wheels on each unit	Retractable, with steerable nosewheels. Twin wheels on each unit	Retractable, with steerable nosewheels. Twin wheels on each unit	Retractable, with steerable nosewheels. Twin wheels on each unit	Retractable, with steerable nosewheels. Twin wheels on each unit
Wheel base	40 ft 10 ins (12.45 m)			36 ft 10 ins (11.23 m)	41 ft 3 ins (12.57 m)	51 ft 2 ins (15.6 m)
Wheel track	17 ft 2 ins (5.23 m)	17 ft 2 ins (5.23 m)	17 ft 2 ins (5.23 m)	18 ft 9 ins (5.72 m)	18 ft 8 ins (5.69 m)	18 ft 9 ins (5.72 m)
Weight empty, operating	72,100 lb (32,704 kg) basic, 73,340 lb (33,266 kg) optional for long range	75,800 (34,382 kg) basic, 77,520 lb (35,162 kg) optional for long range				
Maximum taxi or brake release weight	125,000 lb (56,700 kg) basic, to 139,000-140,000 lb (63,050-63,500 kg) optional taxi	139,000 lb (63,050 kg) basic, to 150,500 lb (68,265 kg) optional taxi	116,000 lb (52,616 kg) basic, to 134,000 lb (60,780 kg) optional taxi	124,000 lb (56,245 kg) standard, 143,500 lb (65,090 kg) high gross weight	133,000 lb (60,328 kg) standard, 153,000 lb (69,400 kg) high gross weight	155,500 lb (70,533 kg) standard, 172,500 lb (78,244 kg) high gross weight
Maximum zero fuel weight	105,000 lb (47,627 kg) basic, 109,600 lb (49,713 kg) optional	113,000 lb (51,255 kg) basic, 117,000 lb (53,070 kg) optional	102,500 lb (46,493 kg) basic, 103,000 lb (46,720 kg) optional			
Maximum take-off weight	124,500 lb (56,472 kg) basic, to 138,000 lb (62,820 kg) optional	138,500 lb (62,822 kg) basic, to 150,000 lb (68,040 kg) optional	115,500 lb (52,390 kg) basic, 133,500 lb (60,555 kg) optional			
Maximum landing weight	114,000 lb (51,710 kg) basic, 116,600 lb (52,888 kg) optional	121,000 lb (54,885 kg) basic, 124,000 lb (56,245 kg) optional	110,000 lb (49,895 kg)			
Typical cruise speed	Mach 0.745 economical	Mach 0.745 economical	Mach 0.745 economical	Mach 0.79 economical cruise speed, Mach 0.82 maximum speed	Mach 0.79 economical cruise speed, Mach 0.82 maximum speed	Mach 0.79 economical cruise speed, Mach 0.82 maximum speed
Approach speed kts (mph) km/h	133 (153) 246 or 135 (155) 250 at long-range weight	137 (158) 254, or 139 (160) 257	128 (147) 237			
Take-off field length (sea level, 29° C)	6,660-7,500 ft (2,030-2,286 m) with 128 pax	7,730-8,740 ft (2,356-2,664 m) with 146 pax	6,100-8,640 ft (1,860-2,634 m) with 108 pax			
Landing field length	4,580-4,700 ft (1,396-1,433 m) with 128 pax	4,880-5,050 ft (1,488-1,540 m)	4,450 ft (1,357 m)			
Initial cruise altitude (or as specified)	35,700 ft (10,880 m), or 33,450 ft (10,195 m) at long-range weight	33,400 ft (10,180 m), or 31,700 ft (9,662 m) at long range weight	37,000 ft (11,275 m), or 34,250 ft (10,440 m) at long-range weight			
Altitude, OEI	17,400 ft (5,210 m)	16,200 ft (4,938 m), or 17,000 ft (5,180 m) at long range weight	18,400 ft (5,610 m), or 18,100 ft (5,515 m) at long range weight			
Design range naut miles (miles) km	1,625-2,520 (1,871-2,902) 3,009-4,667 with 128 pax	1,960-2,500 (2,257-2,879) 3,630-4,630 with 146 pax	1,520-2,775 (1,750-3,195) 2,815-5,139 with 108 pax	1,505-3,195 (1,733-3,679) 2,787-5,917	1,585-3,200 (1,825-3,685) 2,935-5,926	1,925-2,900 (2,216-3,339) 3,565-5,370

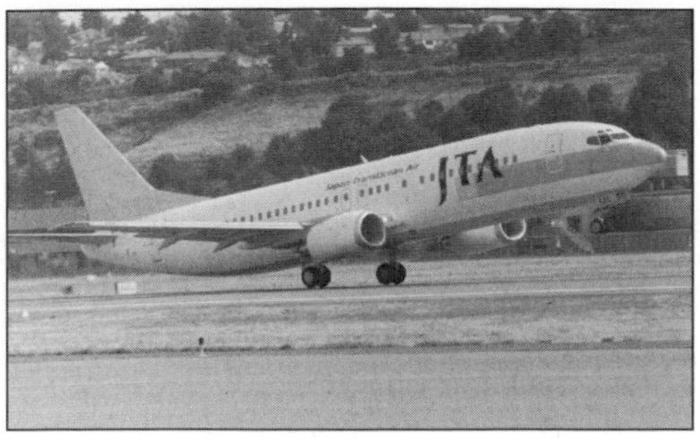

Boeing 737-400 of JTA

interior components; and graphite in the ailerons, elevators and rudder.

Engines: 2 x CFM International CFM56-3C1 turbofans operated at 20,000 lbf (88.97 kN) basic or 22,000 lbf (97.86 kN) optional for 737-300, at 22,000 lbf (97.86 kN) basic or 23,500 lbf (104.54 kN) optional for 737-400 and 737-400 high gross weight model, and 18,500 lbf (82.29 kN) basic or 20,000 lbf (88.97 kN) optional for 737-500. Customer unique engine options are CFM56-3B1 of 20,000 lbf (88.97 kN) or CFM56-3B2 of 22,000 lbf (97.86 kN) for 737-300, CFM56-3B2 of 22,000 lbf (97.86 kN) for 737-400, and CFM56-3B1 of 18,500 or 20,000 lbf (82.29 or 88.97 kN) for 737-500. APU. 120-minutes ETOPS.

Engine rating: See above.

Fuel system: 20,104 litres basic or 21,967 or 23,829 litres optional with auxiliary tanks for 737-300/400/500.

Electrical system: 2 engine-driven 50 kVA generators.

Hydraulic system: 2 independent systems, each 3,000 psi.

De-icing system: Bleed air.

Radar: Colour weather radar.

Flight avionics/instrumentation: EFIS with EADI and EHSI (with map, flight plan, nav partial compass rose, VOR/ILS full compass rose and weather modes). Wide choice of PIN-selectable display options. Flight management system (single or dual flight computers providing performance and navigation data, with GPS), full-range digital autothrottle, laser gyro inertial reference system, LED engine instrument system, aircraft condition monitoring system/ACARS, windshear alerting and guidance, time-control navigation (T-NAV), and centralized built-in test equipment (BITE) on CDU. Cat II landing standard, with Cat IIIa optional. New Generation 737s are to receive Common Display System flight decks, using Honeywell flat panel liquid crystal display technology, offering the ability to emulate electromechanical, EFIS or Primary Flight Display-Navigation Display (PFD-ND) formats for customers wanting commonality and to use the same pilot type rating.

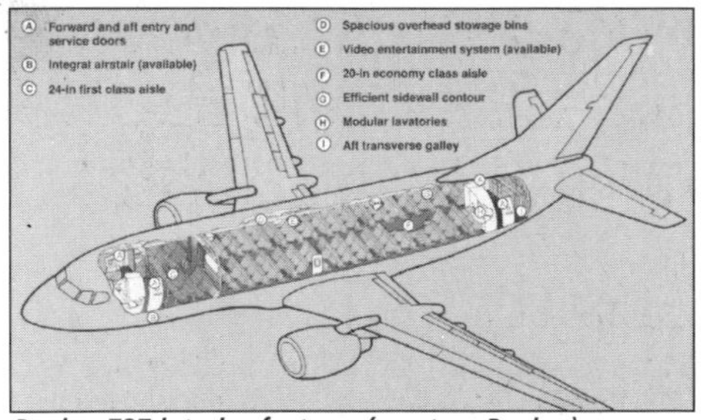

Boeing 737 interior features (courtesy Boeing)

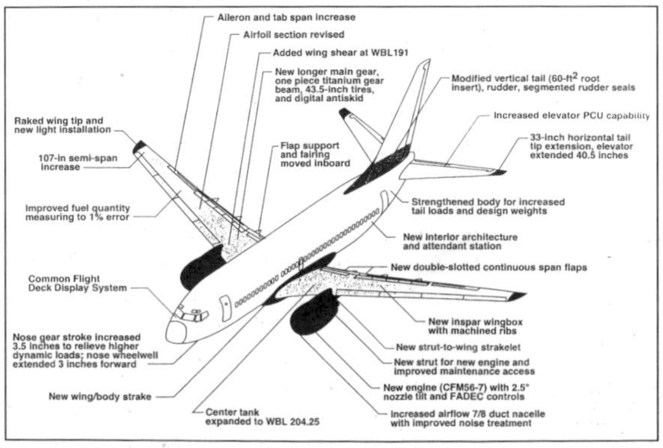

Principal changes introduced on the 737-700 (courtesy Boeing)

Aircraft variants:

737-300 is the currently available 120-149 passenger version. As detailed.

737-400 is the currently available 135-172 passenger version. As detailed.

737-500 is the currently available 100-132 passenger version. As detailed.

737-600 was known as the 737-500X before programme launch in 1995. Launch customer is SAS, which ordered 35 on 15 March 1995. 108-132 passengers. Lower hold volume 822 cu ft (23.28 m^3). Engine ratings 18,500 lbf, 20,000 lbf and 22,000 lbf (82.29, 88.97 and 97.86 kN).

737-700 will be the first of the new Next Generation 737s to enter service. The programme was launched in November 1993 and the -700 is expected to enter service in October 1997 with Southwest Airlines as first customer (intends to purchase 63). 128-149 passengers. New wings of increased chord and span, increased fuel capacity (26,136 litres), new CFM56-7 engines with noise improvements, and more. About 3,000 naut mile range. Lower hold volume 1,068 cu ft (30.24 m^3). Engine ratings 20,000 lbf, 22,000 lbf and 24,000 lbf (88.97, 97.86 and 106.76 kN).

737-800 was officially launched on 5 September 1994, with commitments for over 40 aircraft. First delivery to Hapag-Lloyd in early 1998. Longest version, with seating for 160-189 passengers. Lower hold volume 1,662 cu ft (47.06 m^3). Engine ratings 24,000 lbf and 26,400 lbf (106.76 and 117.44 kN).

Boeing 747-400, "500" and "600"

First flight: 29 April 1988 for 747-400 (original 747 prototype on 9 February 1969).

Certification: 10 January 1989 with PW4000 engines, 18 May 1989 with CF6-80C2s, and 8 June 1989 with RB211-524Gs (original 747 prototype certification 30 December 1969).

First delivery: 26 January 1989 for 747-400 to Northwest Orient Airlines, with initial services on 9 February 1989 (original 747 delivery 12 December 1969 to Pan Am).

Role: Long-range (International model) and short-range (Domestic), high capacity, airliner and freighter.

Details: 747-400 airliner, unless stated to be otherwise.

Noise levels: Meets FAA Stage 3 and ICAO Chapter 3 requirements.

▲ Development

▲ Compared with earlier versions, the 747-400 features a new interior (plus longer upper deck), advanced APU, reduced weight, aerodynamic improvements (wing extensions and winglets on International models), advanced flight deck, advanced engines with reduced fuel burn, and increased fuel capacity and range.

Sales: 1,165 ordered of all versions by 20 May 1995 (231 US and 934 non-US), comprising 248 B747-100s and 2 Freighters, 322 B747-200s and 71 Freighters, 81 B747-300s, 425 B747-400s and 16 Freighters. Of these, 1,058 had been delivered. Special variants include the USAF's 2 VC-25A (747-200) "Air Force One" executive/ presidential transports, operated by the 89th Airlift Wing from Andrews AFB.

Crew: 2 (flight), with 2 observer seats. 2-bunk crew rest area accessible from the flight deck, or optional larger rest area with 8 bunks and 2 seats or other layouts in an overhead position (no loss of passenger seats) in the rear fuselage.

Passengers: Typical 3 class arrangement is 420 passengers as 21 first class, 77 business and 322 economy. Alternative layouts include 566-568 passengers in the Domestic short-range model (24 first class at 39 ins seat pitch and 544 economy at 32 ins pitch). 4 abreast with single aisle and 6 abreast with 2 aisles normal first class sleeper seating, 7 abreast business class on main deck with 2 aisles and 4 abreast with single aisle on upper deck, and 10 abreast economy class with 2 aisles.

Boeing 747-400 International

Seat pitch: 61 ins (155 cm) first, 39 ins (99 cm) business and 32 ins (81 cm) economy. See above for first class alternative.

Galleys: 1 upper deck galley. 9 or 10 main deck galleys in centre-line and sidewall positions in 293 possible positions.

Toilets: 2 upper deck toilets in 10 possible positions. 14 main deck toilets in 11 possible positions.

Freight hold volume and capacity: In underfloor container configuration, the forward hold has a 2,768 cu ft (78.38 m^3) capacity for 16 x LD1 containers and the aft hold has a 2,422 cu ft (68.58 m^3) capacity for 14 containers, plus 835 cu ft (23.64 m^3) of bulk cargo, making 6,025 cu ft (170.6 m^3). In mixed pallet (96 x 125 ins, 244 x 318 cm) and container configuration, forward hold has a 2,075 cu ft (58.76 m^3) capacity for 5 pallets and the aft hold a 2,422 cu ft (68.58 m^3) capacity for 14 containers, plus bulk cargo, totalling 5,332 cu ft (150.98 m^3). Optionally, the aft hold can carry 16 LD1 containers for 2,768 cu ft (78.38 m^3) capacity, but then the bulk cargo volume is reduced to 490 cu ft (13.88 m^3), totalling 5,333 cu ft (151 m^3). Maximum lower hold payloads are 58,400 lb (26,490 kg) forward, 50,570 lb (22,938 kg) aft, and 14,880 lb (6,749 kg) bulk, totalling 123,850 lb (56,177 kg). Domestic model can carry 5 pallets and 14 LD-1 containers plus bulk in the lower holds, at 5,332 cu ft (150.98 m^3) volume.

Wing characteristics: Compared with earlier 747s, 747-400 International (not Domestic) has a 6 ft (1.8 m) wingtip extension and 6 ft winglet, improving take-off characteristics and offering higher cruise speed and lower drag.

Wing control surfaces: Each wing has inner and outer ailerons, with outer used only during low-speed flight. 2 flaps per wing, each sub-divided into forward/ mid/rear sections; each flap operates as a single unit up to 5° deflected angle, thereafter separating into triple-slotted. 6 spoiler sections, the inner used as a ground spoiler only. Krueger leading-edge flaps inboard, and 2 sections of leading-edge variable camber slats.

Tail control surfaces: Variable incidence tailplane. 2-section elevators. 2-section rudder of improved design, with ±30° movement (instead of 25°), new actuators (triple for upper section and dual for lower), with the former upper-section balance weights deleted.

Flight control system: Mechanical/hydraulic.

Construction materials: Includes advanced aluminium alloys for the wing upper/lower spar chords and stringers, graphite composites for the winglets and main deck passenger compartment floor panels,

Details for 747-400 airliner.

Principal dimensions:
Wing span: 211 ft 5 ins (64.44 m), becoming 213 ft (64.92 m) fully fuelled. Domestic model has no winglets and 195 ft 8 ins (59.64 m) span
Maximum length: 231 ft 10 ins (70.66 m), or 225 ft 2 ins (68.63 m) for the fuselage
Maximum height: 63 ft 8 ins (19.41 m)
Main passenger door: 6 ft 4 ins x 3 ft 6 ins (1.93 x 1.07 m)
Cargo door: 10 ft x 11 ft 2 ins (3.05 x 3.4 m)

Wings:
Area: 5,600 sq ft (520.25 m^2)
Aspect ratio: 7.98
Sweepback: 37.5 ° at 25% chord
Incidence: 2 °
Dihedral: 7 °

Tail unit:
Tailplane span: 72 ft 9 ins (22.17 m)

Undercarriage:
Type: Retractable, with twin steerable nosewheels. 4 main units comprise 4-wheel bogies, the 2 inner units steerable (±13°) when nosewheels are steered between 20-70° (20 kts speed restriction)
Main wheel tyre size: 22 ins (55.9 cm) diameter wheels, instead of former 20 ins (50.8 cm). 32-ply tyres for International model, 24-ply for Domestic
Wheel base: 84 ft (25.6 m)
Wheel track: 36 ft 1 ins (11 m)
Turning radius: 159 ft (48.46 m) wingtip

Weights (International model, unless stated to be Domestic):
Empty, operating (P&W 4056s): 402,400 lb (182,526 kg), or 403,500 lb (183,025 kg) for heaviest option, both when including overhead crew rest area
Empty, operating (CF6-80C2B1Fs): 401,800 lb (182,253 kg), or 402,900 lb (182,752 kg) for heaviest option, both when including overhead crew rest area
Empty, operating (RB211-524G/Hs): 404,000 lb (183,251 kg), or 405,100 lb (183,750 kg) for heaviest option, both when including overhead crew rest area.
Maximum zero fuel: 535,000 lb (242,670 kg)
Maximum take-off: 800,000 lb (362,880 kg) basic, with options for 833,000/850,000 lb (377,840/385,555 kg), or 870,000 lb (394,625 kg) maximum, but 875,000 lb (396,893 kg) possible with loading restrictions
Maximum take-off (Domestic): 600,000 lb (272,155 kg)
Maximum landing: 574,000 lb (260,360 kg) basic, and 630,000 lb (285,760 kg) optional
Maximum landing (Domestic): 574,000 lb (260,360 kg)

Performance (International model, unless stated to be Domestic):
Typical cruise speed: Mach 0.85
Approach speed: 146 and 153 kts (168 and 176 mph) 270 and 283 km/h at basic and all optional MTOWs respectively
Approach speed (Domestic model): 148 kts (170 mph) 274 km/h
Take-off field length (PW4056s): 9,250, 10,550 and 11,000 ft (2,819, 3,216 and 3,353 m) at basic MTOW and 850,000 lb/875,000 lb options respectively, at 30°C
Take-off field length (CF6-80C2B1Fs): 9,200, 10,550 and 11,000 ft (2,804, 3,216 and 3,353 m) at basic MTOW and 850,000 lb/875,000 lb options respectively, at 30°C
Take-off field length (RB211-524Gs): 9,300, 10,650 and 11,100 ft (2,835, 3,246 and 3,383 m) at basic MTOW and 850,000 lb/875,000 lb options respectively, at 30°C
Take-off field length (RB211-524Hs): 8,800, 10,050 and 10,500 ft (2,682, 3,063 and 3,200 m) at basic MTOW and 850,000 lb/875,000 lb options respectively, at 30°C
Take-off field length (CF6-80C2B1Fs), Domestic model: 5,850 ft (1,783 m), at 30°C, VMCG limit
Landing field length: 6,250, 6,800 and 6,800 ft (1,905, 2,073 and 2,073 m) at MTOW basic and options respectively
Landing field length (Domestic model): 6,350 ft (1,935 m)
Initial cruise altitude: 34,700, 33,400 and 32,800 ft (10,577, 10,180 and 9,997 m) at MTOW basic and options respectively
Initial cruise altitude (Domestic model): 39,100 ft (11,920 m)
Design range (PW4056s): 6,055, 6,900 and 7,270 naut miles (6,972, 7,943 and 8,371 miles) 11,214, 12,779 and 13,464 km at MTOW basic and options respectively
Design range (CF6-80C2B1Fs): 6,050, 6,880 and 7,245 naut miles (6,966, 7,922 and 8,342 miles) 11,205, 12,742 and 13,418 km at MTOW basic and options respectively
Design range (RB211-524G/Hs): 5,930, 6,765 and 7,130 naut miles (6,828, 7,790 and 8,210 miles) 10,982, 12,529 and 13,205 km at MTOW basic and options respectively
Design range (CF6-80C2B1Fs), Domestic model: 1,720 naut miles (1,980 miles) 3,185 km

Boeing 747 Freighter, with upward-hinging nose

advanced thermoplastics for the PSUs and window reveals, and hybrid composites (graphite/phenolic or Kevlar/graphite) for the engine nacelles, cabin sidewall panels, ceiling panels and stowage bins.

Engines:
Currently listed as available are 4 x
- General Electric CF6-80C2B1F (56,500 lbf, 251.33 kN); certified.
- CF6-80C2B1F1 (60,200 lbf, 267.79 kN); not certified.
- CF6-80C2B7F (62,100 lbf, 276.24 kN); not certified.
- Pratt & Whitney PW4056 (57,100 lbf, 254 kN); certified.
- PW4060 (60,200 lbf, 267.79 kN); not certified.
- PW4062 (62,900 lbf, 279.8 kN); not certified.
- Rolls-Royce RB211-524G (58,000 lbf, 258 kN); certified
- RB211-524H (60,600 lbf, 269.6 kN); certified.

Boeing 747-400 flight deck

Engine rating: See above.
Fuel system: 204,355 litres basic with P&W and R-R engines or 203,522 litres basic with GE engines, with options of 216,847 litres for P&W and R-R engines or 216,000 litres with GE engines using the tailplane fuel tank.
Electrical system: AC supply via 4 engine-driven 90 kVA generators. Pratt & Whitney Canada PW901A APU, offering 180 kVA power generation.
Hydraulic system: 4 independent systems.
Braking system: Carbon (replacing steel) brakes with anti-skid system. Domestic model has brake cooling fans.
De-icing system: Bleed air for wing leading-edge and engine inlet,
Radar: Weather radar.
Flight avionics/instrumentation: Flight management system (see illustration) with EFIS and EICAS. Dual digital air data computers, triple ring laser inertial reference system, triple ILS, dual VOR with marker receiver, dual ADF, dual DME, GPWS and TCAS. Central maintenance computer monitors over 75 aircraft systems, with satcom datalink to ground crews. GPS and FANS (future air navigation system).

Possible configuration for a New Large Airplane based on the 747, with a full-length upper deck

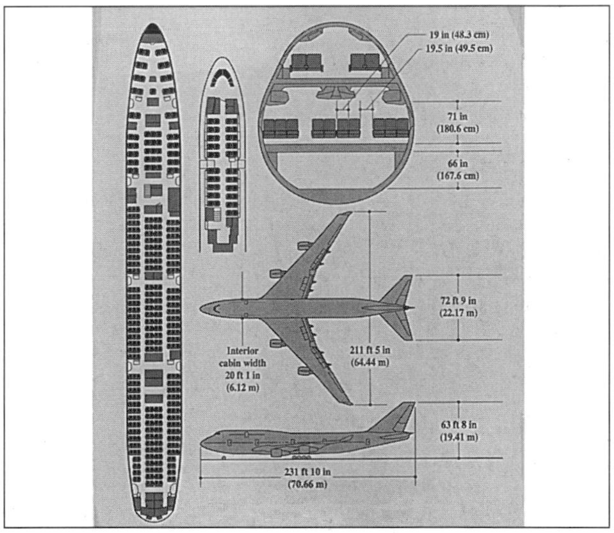

Boeing 747-400 layouts, the cabin cross-section with business-class upper deck and economy class main deck seating arrangements (courtesy Boeing)

Aircraft variants:
747-400 International with winglets, as detailed.
747-400 Domestic models without wingtip extensions and winglets (having 747-200/300 tip fairings), added upper deck windows (3 starboard, 2 port), revised avionics software and cabin pressure schedules, strengthened upper deck floor, 24-ply tyres and brake cooling fans, rear spar bulkhead fitting, re-rated engine thrust, reinforced trailing-edge flap tracks, and reinforced fuselage frames and crown stringers.
747-400 Freighter first went to Cargolux in 1993. Can fly 4,300 naut miles with 244,000 lb (110,675 kg) of revenue payload. Main deck volume is 21,550 cu ft (610.23 m^3), supplemented by 6,060 cu ft (171.6 m^3) for containers and bulk cargo in the lower holds.
747-400 Combi is the mixed passenger/cargo version, with typically 266 passengers plus cargo. Maximum passenger capacity is 413 with no main

deck cargo, though lower hold capacity is similar to the standard airliner. Maximum 60,000 lb (27,216 kg) of palleted cargo on the main deck.
747 NDAA is a proposed version of the 747 Freighter to fulfil the USAF Air Mobility Command's Non-Developmental Airlift Aircraft requirement.
Projected "stretched" version for 500-600 passengers, using a new wing based on B777 technologies. Mistakenly referred to as 747-500 by some sources, and Boeing confirmed no such designation.
Projected "stretched" version for nearly 800 passengers, with B777 type wing technology. Seen as a possible solution to the NLA (New Large Airplane) proposal. Mistakenly referred to as 747-600 by some sources, and Boeing confirmed no such designation.

Boeing 757

First flight: 19 February 1982 (Rolls-Royce engines).
Certification: 21 December 1982 (FAA), 14 January 1983 (CAA).
First delivery: December 1982, with Eastern Air Lines starting scheduled services on 1 January 1983.
Role: Medium-range airliner and freighter.
Airport limits: LCN 36 at 221,000 lb (100,244 kg) taxi weight and grade C flexible pavement.
Noise levels: 86.2 EPNdB (PW2037s) and 82.2 EPNdB (RB211-535E4s) take-off, 94 EPNdB and 93.3 EPNdB (PW and R-R) sideline, 97.7 EPNdB and 95 EPNdB (PW and R-R) approach.
Sales: 833 ordered by 20 May 1995 (587 by US and 246 by non-US customers), comprising 761 B757-200s, 2 B757-200ERs and 70 B757 Freighters. Of these, 672 had been delivered.

Boeing 757-200 medium-range airliner

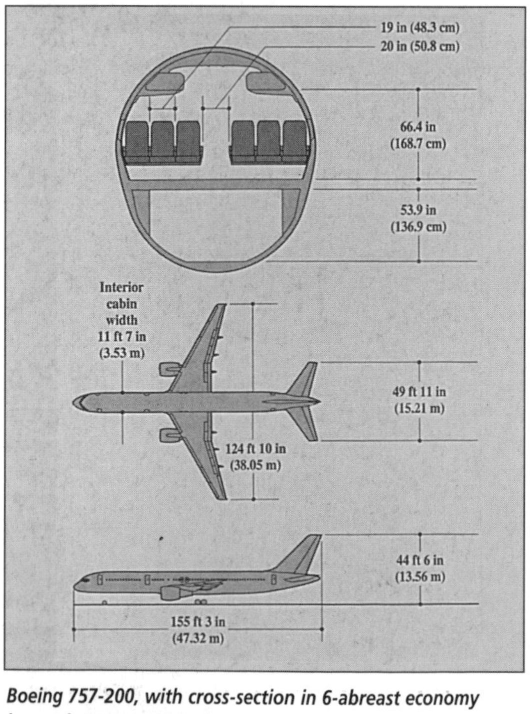

Boeing 757-200, with cross-section in 6-abreast economy layout (courtesy Boeing)

Crew: 2 pilots plus optional observer.
Passengers: 150 or 178 (16 first class and 162 economy) to a maximum of 239 in all inclusive tour layout, with typical intermediate layouts including 194 (12 first and 182 economy), 217 (all economy) and 231 (inclusive tour). 4 abreast first class, 5 abreast business and 6 abreast economy layouts, all with an aisle. Movable cabin divider (can be repositioned by 1 person between flights) to adjust the ratio of premium and economy seating.
Seat pitch: 38 ins (96.5 cm) first, 32 ins (81 cm) economy, and 28/29 ins (71/73.7 cm) inclusive tour.
Galleys: 2 to 4 galleys in 7 possible locations, with 2 standard positions (at the extreme front and extreme rear of the cabin). See drawing.
Toilets: 3 or 4 in 12 possible locations.
Freight hold volume (757-200): 1,790 cu ft (50.69 m^3) underfloor.
Freight hold volume (757-200F): See Aircraft variants.
Size of freight doors (757-200F): 134 x 86 ins (340 x 218 cm) main cargo door, and 2 lower deck doors of 105 x 97 ins (267 x 246 cm) and 99 x 93 ins (251 x 236 cm).
Loading facilities: Lower hold can have hand loading for bulk cargo, Air Cargo Equipment (ACE) telescoping-shelf system, sliding carpet as a continuous-belt-with-backstop system, or Aeroveyor belt-driven system. Aeroveyor system for container loading.
Wing control surfaces: Aileron, double-slotted trailing-edge flaps, 6-section spoilers (for aileron, speed brake and ground functions), and 5-section leading-edge slats per wing.
Tail control surfaces: Variable incidence tailplane, elevators and rudder.
Construction materials: Employs advanced aluminium alloys for wing skins, wing spars and spar chords, and composites for wing trailing-edge control surfaces, wing/body fairings, undercarriage doors, engine struts and nacelles, elevators and rudder.
Engines: Standard 2 x 40,100 lbf (178.38 kN) Rolls-Royce RB211-535E4 or 38,250 lbf (170.1 kN) Pratt & Whitney PW2037 turbofans, with optional 43,100 lbf (191.72 kN) RB211-535E4-B or 41,700 lbf (185.5 kN) PW2040s. 180 minutes ETOPS with all engines.
Engine rating: See above.
Fuel system: 42,684 litres for 757-200 and F.
Hydraulic system: 3,000 psi.
Braking system: Carbon.
De-icing system: Bleed air for wing leading edges.
Radar: Colour weather radar.
Flight avionics/instrumentation: Cat IIIb instrument landing system. EFIS-700 with 6-colour CRT displays, featuring selectable modes and ranges, moving map. weather radar image over map/VOR/ILS displays, EICAS, and built-in test features. Windshear system with visual and audio warning. Rockwell Collins FCS-700 AFDS.
Aircraft variants:
757-200 is the passenger airliner, as detailed.
757-200F Freighter can fly 3,360 naut miles (3,869 miles) 6,222 km with a maximum revenue payload of 87,500 lb (39,690 kg); normal revenue payloads of 72,210 lb (32,755 kg) based on 9 lb/cu ft cargo density or 7 lb/cu ft bulk, 79,850 or 79,400 lb (36,220 or 36,015 kg) containers (P&W and R-R engines respectively), or 84,350 or 83,900 lb (38,260 or 38,056 kg) pallets (with P&W and R-R engines respectively). Main deck container volume is 6,600 cu ft (186.89 m^3), with 15 positions for containers/pallets, while the lower holds provide 1,830 cu ft (51.82 m^3) bulk cargo volume. Same engine options. 112,350-112,800 lb (50,960-51,165 kg) empty

DETAILS FOR 757-200 WITH PW2037s, *AND 757-200 WITH RB211-535E4s IN ITALICS.*

Principal dimensions:
Wing span: 124 ft 10 ins (38.05 m), *the same*
Maximum length: 155 ft 3 ins (47.32 m), *the same*
Maximum height: 44 ft 6 ins (13.56 m), *the same*

Cabin:
Length: 118 ft 5 ins (36.09 m), *the same*
Width: 11 ft 7 ins (3.53 m), *the same*
Height: 7 ft (2.13 m), *the same*
Volume: 8,140 cu ft (230.5 m^3), *the same*
Main passenger door: 6 ft x 2 ft 9 ins (1.83 x 0.84 m) forward, and 6 ft x 2 ft 6 ins (1.83 x 0.76 m) rear, *the same*

Wings:
Area: 1,994 sq ft (185.25 m^2), *the same*
Aspect ratio: 7.815, *the same*
Sweepback: 25° at 25% chord, *the same*
Incidence: 32°, *the same*
Dihedral: 5°, *the same*

Tail unit:
Tailplane span: 49 ft 11 ins (15.21 m), *the same*
Tailplane area: 542 sq ft (50.35 m^2), *the same*

Undercarriage:
Type: Retractable, with twin steerable nosewheels. 4-wheel main bogies.
Wheel base: 60 ft (18.29 m), *the same*
Wheel track: 24 ft (7.32 m), *the same*

Weights:
Empty, operating: 127,800 lb (57,970 kg) standard or 128,900 lb (58,468 kg) optional, *128,100 lb (58,105 kg) standard or 129,200 lb (58,604 kg) optional*
Maximum zero fuel: 184,000 lb (83,460 kg) standard or 186,000 lb (84,368 kg) optional, *184,000 lb (83,460 kg) standard or 188,000 lb (85,275 kg) optional*
Maximum taxi: *221,000 lb (100,244 kg) standard or 256,000 lb (116,120 kg) optional*
Maximum take-off: 220,000 lb (99,790 kg) standard or 255,000 lb (115,666 kg) optional, *the same*
Maximum landing: 198,000 lb (89,811 kg) standard or 210,000 lb (95,255 kg) optional, *the same*

Performance:
Cruise speed: Mach 0.8-0.86, *the same*
Approach speed: 132 kts (152 mph) 244 km/h, *the same*
Take-off field length: 5,900 ft (1,800 m) or 10,000 ft (3,048 m) at optional weight, *5,430 ft (1,655 m) or 7,580 ft (2,310 m) at optional weight,* all at sea level, 29°C
Landing field length: 4,800 ft (1,463 m), *4,650 ft (1,418 m),* both with 194 passengers
Initial cruise altitude: 38,300 ft (11,675 m) standard weight or 35,400 ft (10,790 m) optional weight, *38,750 ft (11,810 m) standard weight or 35,700 ft (10,880 m) optional weight*
Altitude, OEI: 23,650 ft (7,210 m) standard weight or 23,600 ft (7,195 m) optional weight, *23,850 ft (7,270 m) standard weight or 23,800 ft (7,255 m) optional weight*
Range with full payload: 2,720 naut miles (3,132 miles) 5,037 km standard weight or 3,930 naut miles (4,525 miles) 7,278 km optional weight, *2,550 naut miles (2,936 miles) 4,722 km standard weight or 3,710 naut miles (4,272 miles) 6,870 km optional weight,* both with 194 passengers

weight (tare not included), 200,000 lb (90,718 kg) maximum zero-fuel weight, and 250,000-255,000 lb (113,400-115,665 kg) maximum take-off weight. See earlier for door sizes. Package Freighter was the original cargo model, as acquired by UPS.
757-200 Combi offers combined accommodation for passengers and cargo, typically 150 passengers and 3 containers on the main deck. Large cargo door as detailed for 757-200F.
757 FTB is a flying avionics testbed to support the F-22 fighter programme. F-22 forward fuselage is carried on the airliner's front pressure bulkhead, 28 ft (8.5 m) sensor wing is mounted above the front fuselage, APG-77 radar has been added to the nose, and the main cabin has seating for 25 engineers.

Boeing 767

First flight: 26 September 1981.
Certification: 30 July 1982 with Pratt & Whitney JT9D engines, September 1982 with General Electric engines , February 1990 with Rolls-Royce engines, January 1984 for 767-200ER, September 1986 for 767-300, December 1987 for 767-300ERs, and October 1995 for 767-300 Freighter.
First delivery: 19 August 1982 to United Airlines, starting scheduled services September 1982.
Role: Medium-long range airliner and freighter.
Noise levels: 90.4 EPNdB take-off, 96.6 EPNdB sideline, 101.7 EPNdB approach for 767-200ER with CF6-80C2B4 engines.
Sales: Total of 696 B767s ordered by 20 May 1995 (281 US and 415 non-US customers), comprising the first 767, 158 B767-200s, 69 B767-200ERs, 133 B767-300s, 327 B767-300ERs and 8 B767-TBDs. Of these, 572 had been delivered. First B767-300 Freighter went to United Parcel Service in October 1995 (from an order for 30).
Crew: 2 or 3 (flight).
Passengers: *767-200/200ER* typical 3-class 181-seat layout provides for 15 first class (60 ins, 152 cm seat pitch), 40 business (38 ins, 96.5 cm) and 126 economy (32 ins, 81 cm) passengers; or 2-class 224-seat layout for 18 first class (38 ins, 96.5 cm) and 206 economy (32 ins, 81 cm); or 1 class 247-seat layout (32 ins, 81 cm); or inclusive tour 285-seat layout (30 ins, 76 cm). First class double and single sleeper seats (5 abreast), 6 abreast business class, 7 abreast economy class, and 8 abreast inclusive-tour seating, all with 2 aisles. *767-300/300ER* typical 3-class 218-seat layout provides for 18 first, 46 business and 154 economy passengers (same pitches); or 2-class 269-seat layout for 24 first class (38 ins, 96.5 cm) and 245 economy (32 ins, 81 cm); or 1-class 290-seat (32 ins, 81 cm); or inclusive tour 325-seat layout (30 ins, 76 cm). 767-300 can accommodate up to a maximum of 350 passengers.
Seat pitch: See above.
Galleys: 767-200 has forward and aft galleys and a mid-cabin service station offered in 104 possible positions, and 767-300 has 116 possible positions.
Toilets: 5 toilets, with 767-200 having 56 possible positions, and 767-300 having 69.
Pressurization: 8.6 psi cabin differential.
Freight hold capacity: *767-200/200ER*: Typically 3 pallets (96 x 125 ins, 2.44 x 3.18 m) or 6 half-pallets (96 x 61.5 ins, 2.44 x 1.56 m) in forward hold and 10 LD-2 containers plus bulk in aft hold, with 2,800-2,875 cu ft (79.2-81.4 m^3) volume, or alternatively 22 LD-2 containers plus bulk in holds, volume 3,070 cu ft (86.9 m^3). *767-300/300ER:* Typically 4 pallets or 8 half-pallets in forward hold and 14 LD-2 containers plus bulk in aft hold, volume 3,670-3,770 cu ft (103.9-106.8 m^3), or alternatively 30 LD-2 containers plus bulk in holds, volume 4,030 cu ft (114.1 m^3). Alternative LD-3 or LD-4 containers. Freight hold payloads are 21,600 lb (9,798 kg) forward compartment, 18,000 lb (8,165 kg) aft compartment and 6,450 lb (2,926 kg) bulk compartment for the *767-200/200ER*, with alternates of 33,750 lb (15,309 kg), 27,000 lb (12,247 kg) and 6,450 lb (2,926 kg) depending on the number of passengers and galley weights. For the *767-300/300ER*, these are 28,800 lb (13,063 kg), 25,200 lb (11,431 kg) and 6,450 lb (2,926 kg) standard, or 45,000 lb (20,412 kg), 38,745 lb (17,575 kg) and 6,450 lb (2,926 kg) alternate respectively.
Size of freight doors: 70 ins (178 cm) or 134 ins (340 cm) width, when raised providing a vertical access height of 66 ins (168 cm).
Loading facilities: Ball mat at entrance and roller tracks in holds.
Wing control surfaces: Inner and outer ailerons, double-slotted inner and single-slotted outer trailing-edge flaps, multi-section spoilers (speed brakes and lift dumper functions), and leading-edge slats.
Tail control surfaces: Variable incidence tailplane, elevators and rudder.
Flight control system: Hydraulic.
Construction materials: Metal (including advanced alluminium alloy in the wings and keel beam chords), except for graphite used in parts of the floor panels, shock strut doors, ailerons, spoilers, rudder and elevators; aramid in the engine pylons and flaps; and hydrid composites in the engine nacelles, main

Note: Pax = Passengers	**767-200ER**	**767-300**	**767-300ER**
Wing span	156 ft 1 ins (47.57 m)	156 ft 1 ins (47.57 m)	156 ft 1 ins (47.57 m)
Maximum length	159 ft 2 ins (48.51 m)	180 ft 3 ins (54.94 m)	180 ft 3 ins (54.94 m)
Maximum height	52 ft (15.85 m)	52 ft (15.85 m)	52 ft (15.85 m)
Cabin length	111 ft 4 ins (33.93)	132 ft 5 ins (40.36 m)	132 ft 5 ins (40.36 m)
Cabin width	15 ft 6 ins (4.72 m)	15 ft 6 ins (4.72 m)	15 ft 6 ins (4.72 m)
Cabin height	9 ft 5 ins (2.87 m)	9 ft 5 ins (2.87 m)	9 ft 5 ins (2.87 m)
Cabin volume	15,121 cu ft (428.18 m^3)	17,088 cu ft (483.88 m^3)	17,088 cu ft (483.88 m^3)
Passenger doors	6 ft 2 ins x 3 ft 6 ins (1.88 x 1.07 m)	6 ft 2 ins x 3 ft 6 ins (1.88 x 1.07 m)	6 ft 2 ins x 3 ft 6 ins (1.88 x 1.07 m)
Wing area	3,050 sq ft (283.35 m^2)	3,050 sq ft (283.35 m^2)	3,050 sq ft (283.35 m^2)
Wing aspect ratio	7.98	7.98	7.98
Wing sweepback	31.5° at 25% chord	31.5° at 25% chord	31.5° at 25% chord
Incidence	4.25°	4.25°	4.25°
Dihedral	6°	6°	6°
Tailplane span	61 ft 1 ins (18.62 m)	61 ft 1 ins (18.62 m)	61 ft 1 ins (18.62 m)
Tailplane area	644.5 sq ft (59.876 m^2)	644.5 sq ft (59.876 m^2)	644.5 sq ft (59.876 m^2)
Undercarriage type	Retractable, with twin steerable nosewheels. 4-wheel main bogies	Retractable, with twin steerable nosewheels. 4-wheel main bogies	Retractable, with twin steerable nosewheels. 4-wheel main bogies
Main wheel tyre size	45 x 17-20	45 x 17-20	45 x 17-20
Nosewheel tyre size	37 x 14-15	37 x 14-15	37 x 14-15
Wheel base	64 ft 7 ins (19.69 m)	74 ft 8 ins (22.76 m)	74 ft 8 ins (22.76 m)
Wheel track	30 ft 6 ins (9.3 m)	30 ft 6 ins (9.3 m)	30 ft 6 ins (9.3 m)
Weight empty, operating	186,200 lb (84,460 kg) standard, 186,600 lb (84,642 kg) optional	191,700 lb (86,954 kg)	199,600 lb (90,537 kg)
Maximum ramp weight	388,000 lb (175,993 kg)	347,000 lb (157,936 kg)	401,000 lb (181,890 kg)
Maximum zero fuel weight	253,000 lb (114,760 kg) standard, 260,000 lb (117,936 kg) optional	278,000 lb (126,100 kg)	278,000 lb (126,100 kg) standard 295,000 lb (133,812 kg) optional
Maximum take-off weight	345,000 lb (156,492 kg) standard, 387,000-395,000 lb (175,543-179,172 kg) optional	345,000 lb (156,492 kg) standard, 351,000 lb (159,213 kg) optional	380,000 lb (172,368 kg) standard, 408,000-412,000 lb (185,068-186,883 kg) optional
Maximum landing weight	278,000 lb (126,100 kg) standard 285,000 (129,276 kg) optional	300,000 lb (136,080 kg)	300,000 lb (136,080 kg) standard 320,000 (145,152 kg) optional
Typical cruise speed	Mach 0.8	Mach 0.8	Mach 0.8
Approach speed kts (mph) km/h	139 (160) 257	141 (162) 261	145 (167) 268
Take-off field length (sea level, 29° C)	8,600-9,300 ft (2,621-2,835 m)	8,100 ft (2,470 m)	9,800-10,200 ft (2,987-3,109 m)
Landing field length	4,900 ft (1,494 m), 181 pax, PW4056s		5,200 ft (1,585 m), 218 pax, PW4060s
Initial cruise altitude (or as specified)	34,800-35,300 ft (10,600-10,760 m), 181 pax, PW4056s	37,200 ft (11,340 m), with CF6-80C2B2s	33,400-33,700 ft (10,180-10,270 m), 218 pax, PW4060s
Altitude, OEI	24,000 ft (7,315 m)	20,200 ft (6,157 m)	22,500 ft (6,860 m)
Range naut miles (miles) km	6,615-6,625 (7,617-7,629) 12,251-12,270 (design), with 181 pax and PW4056s	4,285 (4,934) 7,936 typically (design), with 218 pax	6,140 (7,070) 11,371 (design), with 218 pax and PW4060s

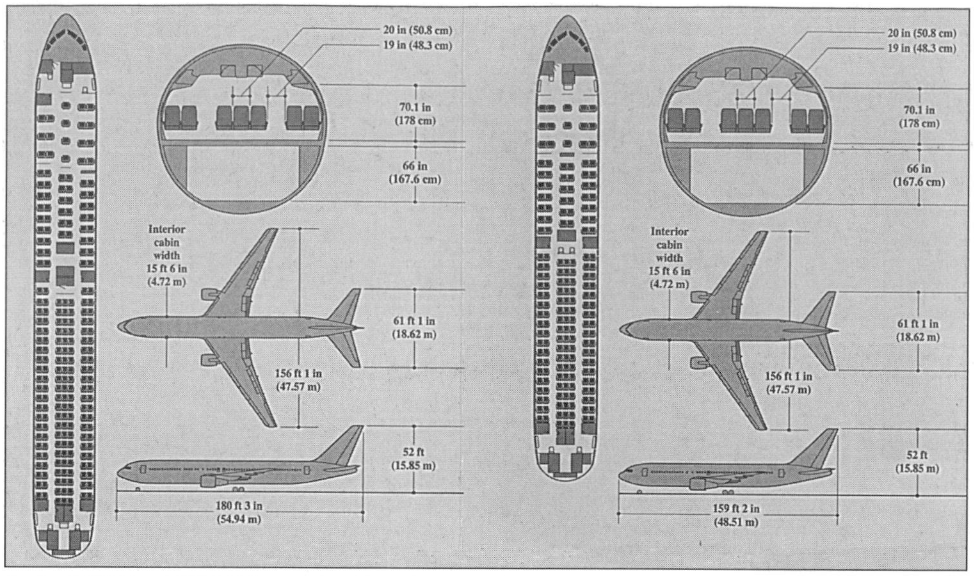

Boeing 767-300 and 767-200 layouts for 218 passengers and 181 passengers respectively, with economy class cross-sections (courtesy Boeing)

undercarriage doors, wing root/tailplane fairings, and part of the wings and fin.

Engines:

Currently listed as available to all versions except Freighter are 2 x

- General Electric CF6-80C2B2 (52,500 lbf, 233.5 kN)
- CF6-80C2B4 (57,900 lbf, 257.6 kN)
- CF6-80C2B6 (61,500 lbf, 273.6 kN)
- CF6-80C2B2F (52,500 lbf, 233.5 kN)
- CF6-80C2B4F (57,900 lbf, 257.6 kN)
- CF6-80C2B6F (61,500 lbf, 273.6 kN)
- CF6-80C2B7F (61,500 lbf, 273.6 kN +2/3% at take-off)
- Pratt & Whitney PW4050 (50,000 lbf, 222.4 kN)
- PW 4052 (52,000 lbf, 231.3 kN)
- PW4056 (56,750 lbf, 252.4 kN)
- PW4060 (60,000 lbf, 266.9 kN)
- PW4062 (62,000 lbf, 275.8 kN).

Also available to 767-300/300ER are:

- Rolls-Royce RB211-524G4 (58,000 lbf, 258 kN)
- RB211-524H (60,600 lbf, 269.6 kN)

Available to 767-300 Freighter are:

CF6-80C2B6F, CF6-80C2B7F, PW4060, PW4062, and RB211-524H.

Other engine types used include P&W JT9D-7R4 and GE CF6-80A.

ETOPS approval of 120 or 180 minutes with certain engine options.

Fuel system: 63,216 litres (767-200), 77,412 or optional 91,378 litres (-200ER), 63,216 litres (-300), and 91,378 litres (-300ER).

Electrical system: 115/200 volt, 400 Hz 3-phase AC supply, via 2 x 90 kVA engine-driven generators. APU with 90 kVA generator.

Hydraulic system: 3 systems, each 3,000 psi.

Braking system: Steel or carbon brakes, with electronic anti-skid system.

De-icing system: Wing outer leading-edges, engine inlets, cockpit glazing and data sensors.

Oxygen system: Nitrogen chlorate generators for passengers, gaseous for crew.

Radar: AlliedSignal Bendix/king RDR-4A colour weather radar or similar.

Flight avionics/instrumentation: Cat IIIb instrument landing system. All-digital electronic flight deck with EFIS colour displays, CRT engine instrument display, integrated caution/warning system and display on CRT, "Quiet dark" flight deck concept, and common pilot type rating between multiple models technologies. Full flight management system with laser gyro inertial reference system, EADI, EHSI, EICAS, ARINC 700 (digital databus), navigation radio autotuning, and certified windshear system. TCAS, ACARS, satcom, and GPS.

Aircraft variants:

767-200 is the basic medium-range version (see Passengers). Maximum take-off weight typically 300,000 lb (136,077 kg). Typical range 4,568 naut miles (5,260 miles) 8,465 km. 767 has considerable commonality with the 757.

767-200ER offers extended range through higher weight and fuel options.

767-300 is a "stretched" variant of the 767-200, with increased seating capacity as detailed under Passengers. Higher weights, as detailed in tables.

767-300R is an extended range variant of 767-300.

767-200/300ERY are projected new extended range models, undergoing wind tunnel and flutter dynamics model testing in 1994-95.

767-300 Freighter has a 8 ft 9 ins x 11 ft 8 ins (2.67 x 3.456m) cargo door. First of 30 (plus options) for United Parcel Service flew on 21 June 1995 (deliveries to UPS from 12 October 1995). 10,080 cu ft (285.43 m^3) in cargo containers on the main deck and 3,157 cu ft (89.4 m^3) in the 2 lower holds. Can carry 112,000 lb (50,800 kg) maximum revenue payload over 3,000 naut miles or 100,800 lb (45,720 kg) over 4,000 naut miles.

767 AWACS is detailed in the Reconnaissance section.

767 tanker/transport is being developed, based on the 767-200ER/300ER. 767-30ER will have up to 7 cargo hold tanks, each 3,748 litres.

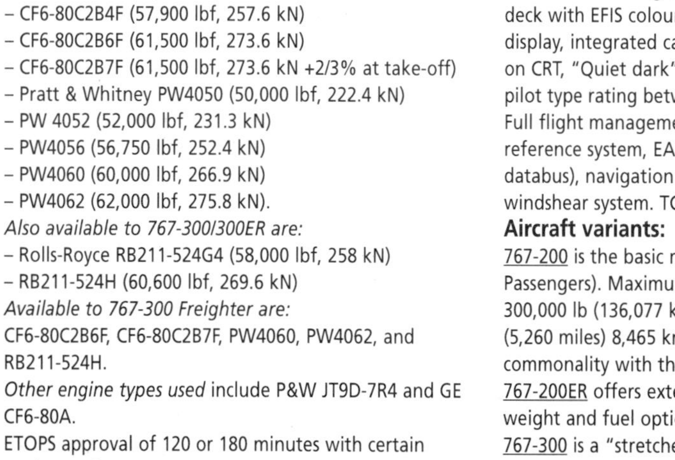

Boeing 767-300ERs, the first delivered to Aeroflot in early September 1994

Boeing 777

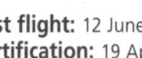

First flight: 12 June 1994 (lasting 3 hours 48 minutes).

Certification: 19 April 1995 (simultaneous FAA and JAA). Received 180 minutes ETOPS approval on 30 May.

First delivery: 17 May 1995 to United Airlines (official ceremony, following 15 May actual delivery). Revenue services began 7 June.

Role: Long-range wide-body airliner.

Sales: 167 ordered by 6 August 1995, including 23 B777-200s ordered by Saudi Arabian Airlines (Saudi) on 18 June 1995 and 31 B777-300s (for ANA, Cathay Pacific, KAL and Thai Airways). 19 B777s to be delivered in 1995.

Crew: 2 (flight).

Passengers: *777-200* accommodates 305-328 in 3-class layout (typically 24 first, 54 business and 227 economy), 375-400 in 2-class layout (typically 30 first and 345 economy), and 418-440 all-economy. *777-300* will carry 369 passengers in 3-class layout or 451 in 2-class, and the 777-100X 259 in 3-class layout.

Seat pitch: 60 ins (152 cm) first class, 38 ins (96.5 cm) business, and 32 ins (81 cm) economy.

Freight hold volume: 5,656 cu ft (160.16 m^3), or 5,300 cu ft (150.1 m^3) with 96 x 125 ins (2.44 x 3.18 m) pallets and containers.

Freight hold capacity: 32 LD-3 containers plus 600 cu ft (16.99 m^3) of bulk cargo.

Size of freight doors: 8 ft 10 ins x 5 ft 7 ins (2.69 x 1.7 m) forward, 5 ft 10 ins x 6 ft 2 ins (1.78 x 1.88 m) aft.

Loading facilities: Mechanized handing system.

Wing characteristics: Long span of increased thickness (compared with 757/767 wings) and offering higher cruise speeds, allowing full passenger loads out of many high elevation and high temperature airfields. Optional feature is a hinge and actuation mechanism to enable almost 22 ft (6.7 m) of each wingtip to fold upwards, reducing wing span to 155 ft 3 ins (47.32 m) when on the ground, to allow it to use existing gate and taxiway space.

Wing control surfaces: Aileron (30° up, 10° down), outboard Fowler-type single-slotted and inboard Fowler-type double-slotted trailing-edge flaps (6 settings), flaperon (10° up, 36° droop), 7-section spoilers (speed brakes and lift dumper functions – 60° up), Krueger leading-edge flap, and 7-section leading-edge slats (3 position) per wing.

Tail control surfaces: Variable incidence tailplane (4° up, 11° down) , elevators (30° up, 25° down), and rudder (27.3° either way) with anti-servo tab.

Flight control system: Digital fly-by-wire.

Construction materials: Use of new lightweight structural materials, including 7055 aluminium alloy for the upper wing skin and stringers. Carbonfibre and toughened carbonfibre reinforced plastics for sections of the tail unit, wing trailing-edge control surfaces, fin, elevators, engine nacelles main undercarriage doors and nosewheel doors. Hybrid composites for the floor beams, wing/body fairings and flap track fairings. Glassfibre for the nose radome, parts of the engine pylons, and areas of the wings and tail unit. Composites account for 9% of structural weight.

Engines: 2 General Electric GE90-75B (78,700 lbf, 350.08 kN), Pratt & Whitney PW4074 (74,000 lbf, 329.17 kN) or Rolls-Royce Trent 875 (77,900 lbf, 346.52 kN) turbofans for A-market. GE90-85B (84,700 lbf, 376.77 kN), PW4084 (84,000 lbf, 373.66 kN) or Trent 884s (86,500 lbf; 384.78 kN) for B-market. AlliedSignal GTCP331-500 APU. First flight of a Rolls-Royce powered B777 on 26 May 1995.

Engine rating: See above.

Fuel system: 117,348 litres A-market, 169,208 litres B-market.

Electrical system: AC supply using 2 engine-driven and 1 APU-driven 120 kVA constant-frequency generators. VSCF units generate 20 kVA per engine,

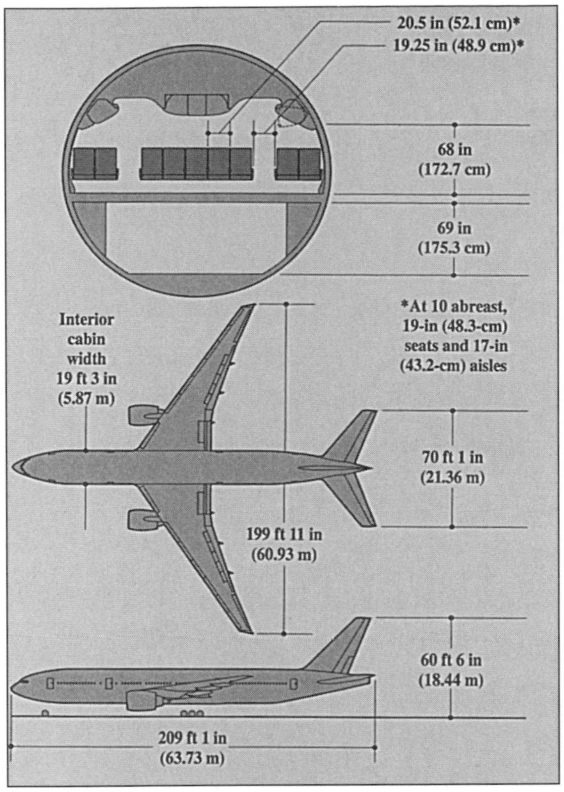

Boeing 777-200 general arrangements (courtesy Boeing)

Boeing 777-200 first delivered to United Airlines

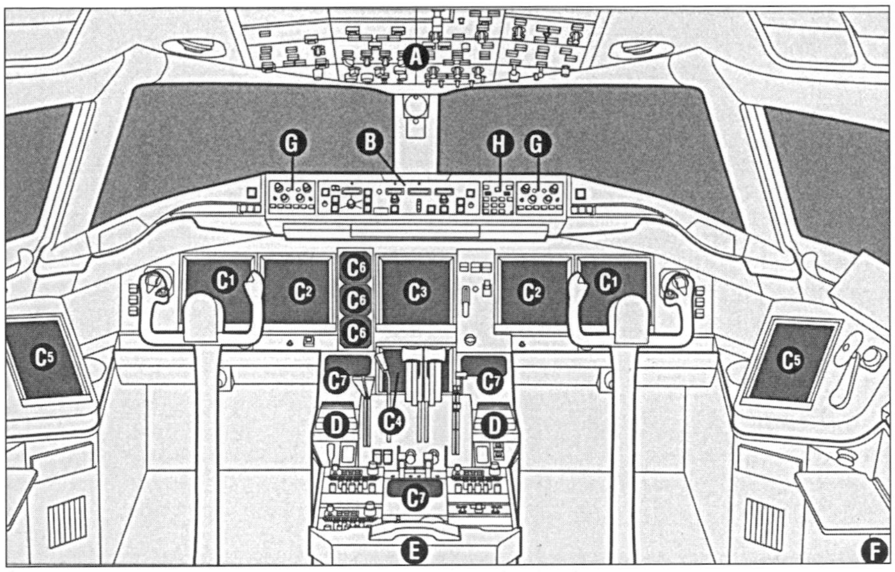

Boeing 777-200 flight deck layout (see Flight avionics for key) (courtesy Boeing)

while the shafts also produce fly-by-wire power via separate magnet systems. Emergency ram-air turbine system.
Hydraulic system: 3 independent systems, each 3,000 psi.
Braking system: AlliedSignal multi-disc carbon brakes.
De-icing system: Thermal for engine intakes and wing slats. Electric for cockpit glazing and pitot heads.
Radar: Weather radar.
Flight avionics/ instrumentation: See diagram: **A** overhead panel with larger nomenclature, cool LED lighted switches and lightplates, and flight deck lighting master brightness control; **B** full-time, triple-channel autopilot with selectable flight path angle and track modes; **C** colour flat-panel liquid-crystal displays (6) comprising C1 primary flight displays, C2 navigation/multifunction displays, C3 engine indicating and crew alerting system (EICAS), C4 multifunction display, C5 optional side LCDs, C6 standby flight instruments, and C7 flight management control display units; **D** touch-pad cursor control devices; **E** full-size printer; **F** maintenance station; **G** EFIS control panel; and **H** display select panel. ARINC 2-way digital data bus (11 such pathways to connect computers with systems). Common crew rating.

Aircraft variants:
777-100X is a projected short fuselage version for 259 passengers in 3-class layout, for ranges of up to 8,600 naut miles (9,903 miles) 15,927 km.
777-200 is the initial standard version, with a 4,000-4,820 naut mile range in A-market form (as of May 1995), rising to 6,030-7,380 naut miles in longer-range B-market form. The first B-Market 777-200 will be delivered to British Airways in December 1996. C-market will have a range above 7,000 naut miles.
777-300 is a "stretched" version, with a length of 242 ft 4 ins (73.86 m), for delivery from May 1998. Launched June 1995. In 3-class layout, it will carry 368 passengers up to 5,700 naut miles (6,563 miles) 10,556 km. Accommodation in 2-class layout is 451-479, allowing ranges of 3,740-4,000 naut miles (4,307-4,606 miles) 6,926-7,408 km. Maximum 550 passengers in all-economy layout.

DETAILS FOR 777-200.

Principal dimensions:
Wing span: 199 ft 11 ins (60.93 m), 155 ft 3 ins (47.32 m) folded
Maximum length: 209 ft 1 ins (63.73 m)
Maximum height: 60 ft 9 ins (18.52 m)

Cabin:
Length: 160 ft 8 ins (48.97 m)
Width: 19 ft 3 ins (5.87 m)
Main passenger door: 6 ft 2 ins x 3 ft 6 ins (1.88 x 1 m)

Wings:
Area: 4,605 sq ft (427.82 m^2)
Aspect ratio: 8.68
Sweepback: 31.1 ° at 25% chord

Tail unit:
Tailplane span: 70 ft 7.5 ins (21.53 m)

Undercarriage:
Type: Retractable, with twin steerable nosewheels (±70°). 6-wheel main bogies, with rear wheel steering (±8°).
Main wheel tyre size: 49 x 19-22
Nosewheel tyre size: 44 x 18-18
Wheel base: 84 ft 11 ins (25.88 m)
Wheel track: 36 ft (10.97 m)

Weights:
Empty, operating: 297,600 lb (134,990 kg) A-market, 304,790 lb (138,250 kg) B-market
Maximum zero fuel: 420,000 lb (190,510 kg) A-market, or 430,000 lb (195,050 kg) B-market
Maximum take-off: 506,000 lb (229,518 kg) standard or 515,000-535,000 lb (233,600-242,672 kg) optional in A-market, 580,000-632,500 lb (263,083-286,900 kg) in B-market
Maximum landing: 445,000 (201,850 kg) A-market, or 460,000 lb (208,652 kg) B-market

Performance:
Cruise speed: Mach 0.84
Approach speed: 138 kts (159 mph) 255 km/h
Landing field length: 5,600 ft (1,706 m)
Ceiling: about 43,000 ft (13,100 m)
Range: 3,930-4,785 naut miles (4,520-5,500 miles) 7,274-8,850 km A-market, 5,990-7,335 naut miles (6,890-8,435 miles) 11,090-13,575 km B-market

Burbank Aeronautical Corporation (USA)

Corporate address: 3000 North Clybourn Avenue, Hangar 34, Burbank, CA 91505.
Telephone: +1 818 843 8242
Facsimile: +1 818 843 4510

● Activities
• Member of the ABS consortium offering Stage 3 hushkit for the McDonnell Douglas DC-9 Series 10 to 40. (See McDonnell Douglas DC-9X).

Comtran International Inc (USA)

Corporate address: 1770 Sky Place Boulevard, International Airport, San Antonio, TX 78216.
Telephone: +1 210 821 6301
Facsimile: +1 210 822 7766
Telex: 767438 COMTRAN UD

• Activities

• Has marketed a Stage 3 hushkit plus cockpit avionics upgrading and main passenger cabin improvements or Combi conversion for the Boeing 707, in association with Rohr Industries and Shannon Engineering.

The Dee Howard Company (USA)

Corporate address: PO Box 469001, 9610 John Saunders Road, International Airport, San Antonio, TX 78246.
Telephone: +1 210 828 1341
Facsimile: +1 210 821 4008
Founded: Became a subsidiary of Alenia in 1989, when the Italian company acquired a majority shareholding.

• Activities

• Upgrading the UPS B727/DC-8 parcel-carrier fleet. In addition to new digital avionics, 44 B727s are receiving Rolls-Royce Tay 651-54 engines to comply with FAA Level III noise levels and reduce operating costs. First re-engined B727-100 flew in April 1992, with certification that November.

• Also undertakes performance improvements for Learjet 24 and 25s, avionics upgrading and re-engining for the BAC One-Eleven, and has upgraded the avionics of UPS's DC-8s.

Fairchild Aircraft Incorporated (USA)

Corporate address: See Reconnaissance section for company details, and description of MMSA.

Fairchild Metro 23, C-26 and Expediter

Certification: June 1990 to FAR Pt 23 Commuter Category, following earlier SFAR 41 and CAA for Metro III. Also ICAO Annex 8.
Role: Commuter airliner.
Details: Metro 23, unless stated.
Airframe life: 35,000 flight hours.
Airport limits: 19-passenger operations into airports under FAR Pt 23 Commuter Category requirements without off-loading.
Sales: Over 950 operating with 48 passenger and cargo airlines in many countries. European marketing and support facility in Belgium (Henneaulaan 366, 1930 Zaventem, Brussels).
Crew: 1 or 2 pilots.
Passengers: Typically 19, or 20 with 1 pilot.
Seat pitch: Typical 30 ins (76 cm).
Pressurization: 7 psi cabin differential. Sea level cabin is maintained to 16,800 ft (5,120 m).
Baggage compartments: Nose compartment of 30 cu ft (0.85 m^3) volume, for 600 lb (272 kg) of baggage/ cargo/equipment, with door of 18 x 25 ins (46 x 64 cm). Aft pressurized compartment of 143.5 cu ft (4.063 m^3) volume, for 850 lb (385.5 kg) of baggage/cargo, with a large cargo door as detailed in the table. Carry-on closet opposite the passenger door.
Wing control surfaces: Ailerons (with trim tabs) and double-slotted flaps.
Tail control surfaces: Variable incidence tailplane. Elevators and rudder (with trim tab).
Flight control system: Mechanical, except for hydraulic flaps and electrically actuated tailplane.
Construction materials: Aluminium alloy except for nosecone.
Engines: 2 AlliedSignal TPE331-12UHR turboprops, or TPE331-11Us for those not requiring hot-and-high capability. McCauley 8 ft 10 ins (2.69 m) diameter 4-blade full-feathering, reversible-pitch propellers.
Engine rating: Each TPE331-12 is rated at 1,100 shp (820.32 kW) with continuous alcohol/water injection and reserve power or 1,000 shp (745.7 kW) dry, and the TPE331-11s are each 1,000 shp (745.7 kW).
Fuel system: 2,453 litres, equivalent to 4,342 lb (1,969 kg).
Electrical system: 28 volt DC supply via 2 x 300 amp starter-generators. 2 x 24 volt and 23 amp-hour ni-cd batteries. 115 volt and 26 volt AC supply via 2 inverters.
Hydraulic system: 2,000 psi.

DETAILS FOR METRO 23.

Principal dimensions:
Wing span: 57 ft (17.37 m)
Maximum length: 59 ft 5 ins (18.1 m)
Maximum height: 16 ft 8 ins (5.08 m)

Cabin:
Length: 25 ft 5 ins (7.75 m)
Width: 5 ft 2 ins (1.57 m)
Height: 4 ft 9 ins (1.45 m)
Floor area: 140 sq ft (13.006 m^2)
Volume: 490 cu ft (13.88 m^3)
Main passenger door: 2 ft 1 ins x 4 ft 5 ins (0.64 x 1.35 m)
Cargo door: 4 ft 5 ins x 4 ft 3.25 ins (1.35 x 1.3 m)

Wings:
Area: 309 sq ft (28.707 m^2)
Aspect ratio: 10.515

Tail unit:
Tailplane span: 16 ft (4.88 m)
Tailplane area: 54.7 sq ft (5.08 m^2)

Undercarriage:
Type: Retractable, with steerable (±63°) nosewheels; optional tiller steering system for optimum ground handling. Twin wheels on each unit
Main wheel tyre size: 19.5 x 6.75-10
Nose wheel tyre size: 18 x 4.4-10
Wheel base: 19 ft 1 ins (5.82 m)
Wheel track: 15 ft (4.57 m)
Turning radius: 38 ft 6 ins (11.73 m) wingtip radius

Weights:
Empty, operating: 9,480 lb (4,300 kg) including crew
Maximum zero fuel: 14,500 lb (6,577 kg)
Maximum ramp: 16,600 lb (7,530 kg)
Maximum take-off: 16,500 lb (7,484 kg)
Take-off weight for 200 naut mile sector with 19 passengers: 14,560 lb (6,604 kg)
Maximum landing: 15,675 lb (7,110 kg)
Useful load: 7,120 lb (3,229 kg)
Payload: 5,020 lb (2,277 kg)

Performance (Metro 23 with TPE331-12UHR engines, for 200 naut mile sector with 19 passengers at 3,800 lb, 1,723 kg payload, unless stated)**:**
Cruise speed: 287-290 kts (330-334 mph) 531-537 km/h, at 14,232 lb (6,455 kg) mid-cruise weight
Stall speed: 103 kts (119 mph) 191 km/h IAS *clean*, 89 kts (102 mph) 165 km/h IAS *with flaps and undercarriage lowered*
Take-off distance: 4,400 ft (1,341 m) balanced field
Landing distance over a 50 ft (15 m) obstacle: 2,500 ft (762 m), factored (1.67) 4,175 ft (1,273 m)
Maximum climb rate: 2,700 ft (823 m) per minute at sea level (engine bleed on)
Maximum climb rate, one engine: 800 ft (244 m) per minute, sea level (engine bleed off)
Typical cruise altitude: 14,000 ft (4,267 m)
Ceiling: 25,000 ft (7,620 m)
Ceiling (C-26A): 26,700 ft (8,140 m)
Ceiling, one engine: 11,600 ft (3,535 m)
Sector totals over 200 naut miles: flight time 44.7 minutes, average flight speed 268.5 kts (309 mph) 497 km/h, and 664 lb (301.1 kg) Jet A fuel burn (including 10 minutes taxi)
Range: over 1,000 naut miles (1,151 miles) 1,852 km with IFR reserves
Range with full payload: more than 534 naut miles (615 miles) 990 km
Range (C-26A): 1,063 naut miles (1,224 miles) 1,970 km with 19 passengers
Typical profile: 4 x 150 naut mile sectors without refuelling

Fairchild Metro 23 commuter airliner

Braking system: Hydraulic disc brakes.
De-icing system: Electrically heated windscreen.
Oxygen system: 49 cu ft or optional 178 cu ft (1.39 or 5.04 m^3) capacity.
Fire system: Includes fire zone isolation and a dual engine fire extinguisher system.
Radar: Weather radar.
Flight avionics/instrumentation: Equipped with full array of instrumentation for monitoring engines, flight conditions and systems. Can accommodate EFIS, global communications, navigation and positioning systems, and flight management packages.

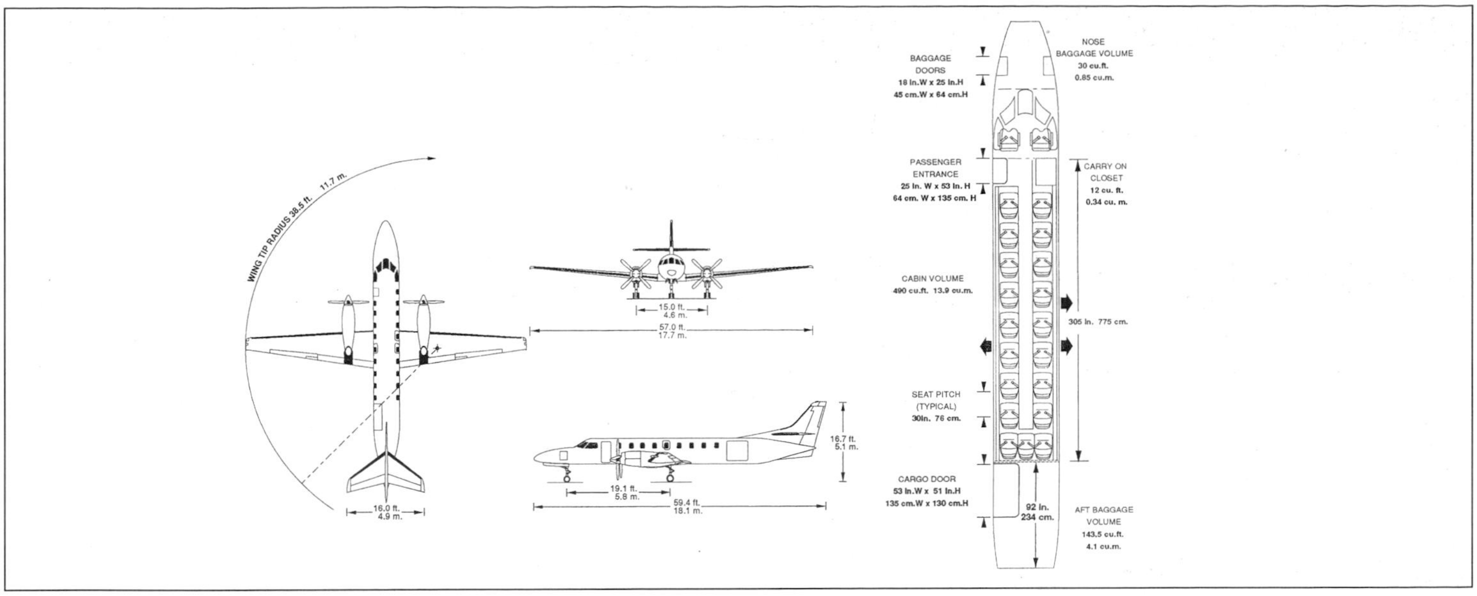

Fairchild Metro 23 (courtesy Fairchild Aircraft)

Aircraft variants:
Metro 23 commuter airliner, as detailed.
Special mission configurations for combi, air ambulance, photographic, airborne early warning, sigint or other electronic roles, and more. See also specialized MMSA.
C-26 is the US military designation for 13 original C-26As operated in the Air National Guard Operational Support Transport Aircraft role since 1989, with quick-change interiors, and 30 C-26Bs (with 23 options) ordered by the National Guard Bureau in 1991 for the ANG and Army National Guard, featuring TCAS II, GPS and microwave landing systems. 34 C-26s were operational with the ANG in May 1995. TPE331-11U-612G engines, each 1,100 shp (820.32 kW).
Expediter is an all-cargo version, with 605 cu ft (17.13 m^3) of usable volume for over 5,500 lb (2,500 kg) of package payload with package densities as low as 8.26 lb/cu ft.
Merlin 23 is the executive version, for 12-14 passengers with tables.
MMSA Multi-Mission Surveillance Aircraft, able to be reconfigured to passenger, medical evacuation and cargo configurations in 24 hours if required. See Reconnaissance section.

Lockheed Martin (USA)

With a payload of 265,000 lb (120,200 kg) and 261,000 lb (118,390 kg) respectively, the USAF's C-5A and C-5B Galaxy transports provide the main heavy lift capability to Air Mobility Command. AMC has 82 C-5s, of which 74 are primary aircraft authorized. 2 have been modified into C-5Cs for space cargoes. A further 12 operate with the Air National Guard. Lockheed has offered the new C-5D variant with CF6-80C2 engines (replacing TF39s) against the USAF's NDAA (non-developmental airlift aircraft) requirement, which will be detailed in a later edition of WA&SD if placed under development.

It was announced on 27 January 1995 that the entire USAF fleet of C-141B StarLifters had become operational without restrictions. The restrictions had been placed because of cracks originating from weep holes in the wing structures. Subsequent inspection, repair and component replacement (where necessary) has cured this. The average C-141 accumulated flying hours is over 37,000, 7,000 hours more than the original design life, and modifications are allowing 45,000 hours. Built between 1962-68 (about 227 remaining), the C-141 has a maximum payload of 94,508 lb (42,868 kg).

Corporate address: See Combat section for company details.

Lockheed-Martin C-130 and L-100 Hercules

First flight: 23 August 1954 (YC-130 prototype).
Certification: 16 February 1965 for commercial L-100 Hercules in original FAA class A category. 4 October 1968 in current commercial L-100-20 form.
Deliveries: December 1956 to November 1959 for C-130A, 1959 to March 1963 for C-130B, 1962 to March 1974 for C-130E, 1964 and continuing for C 130H, 1980 and continuing for C-130H-30, September 1996 for trials before RAF service in 1997 for C-130J.
Role: Tactical military and medium commercial freighter, with many specialized variants.
Airport limits: Typically LCN 22 at landing weight of 122,950 lb (55,770 kg) for C-130H-30, with tyre deflections of 39% assuming rigid pavement stiffness of L=30 and flexible pavement thickness of 20 ins over CBR 6 subsurface.
Noise levels: 96.7 EPNdB take-off sideline, 97.8 EPNdB take-off flyover at take-off power, 94.8 take-off flyover at cutback power, and 98.1 approach flyover, all for L-100 at MTOW and MLW.
Sales: 2,100th Hercules was delivered in June 1995, going to the Colorado Air Force Reserve. Total includes well over 100 commercial variants. Currently operated by 64 nations. Current production is based on the military C-130H, C-130H-30 and C-130J versions, with special derivatives, plus the commercial L-100 and L-100J (some military users) and derivatives.
Details: C-130H and C-130H-30, unless stated.
Crew: 4, comprising 2 pilots, flight engineer and navigator.
Passengers: 64 paratroops, 92 ground troops or 74 litters and 2 attendants in the C-130H, and 92, 128 and 74/2 respectively in the C-130H-30. See Freight hold capacity.
Pressurization: 7.5 psi cabin differential. Maintains sea level cockpit/cabin altitude to 18,000 ft (5,485 m).
Freight hold capacity: In place of troops/paratroops, palleted, containerized or bulk cargo can be carried, or wheeled, self-propelled, pushed or towed vehicles and equipment. Can airdrop loads of 42,000 lb (19,051 kg).
Freight hold access: Straight-in loading via the rear ramp/door. Floor sides of hold are strengthened as vehicle treadways, and have aluminium slide strips. Auxiliary ground loading ramps and truck loading ramps are supplied to bridge the sill height from the ground to the ramp.
Size of freight doors: Lower ramp/door 123 ins (3.12 m) wide and 124 ins (3.15 m) long, plus upper door. Lower door can be opened to any position, with a slope of 11.5° when fully lowered on level ground.

Lockheed-Martin C-130H Hercules transport delivered in 1995 to the 167th Airlift Group of the West Virginia ANG, to replace C-130Es

Mock up of the Lockheed Martin C-130J flight deck

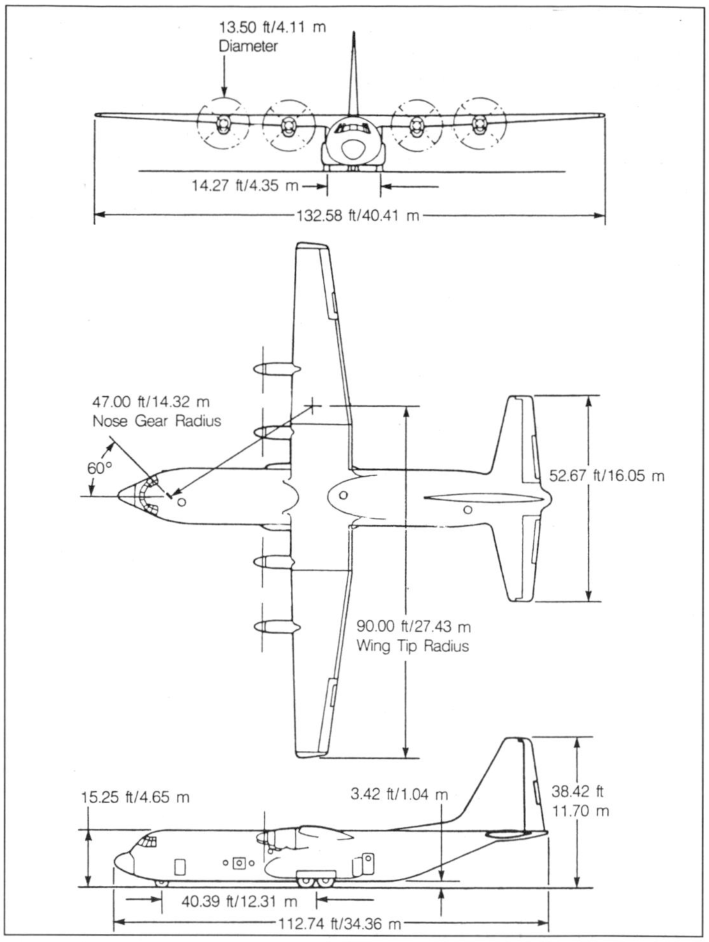

Lockheed Martin L-100-30 Super Hercules arrangement (courtesy Lockheed Martin)

When fully raised, the internal slope is 21°. Maximum ramp load in flight is 5,000 lb (2,268 kg), and during airdrop operations it is lowered level with the floor, with curbs to restrict the width of airdrop items to 9 ft 6 ins (2.9 m).

Loading facilities: A/A32H-4A mechanical dual-rail cargo handling system for pallets of 88 x 54 ins (2.24 x 1.37 m) and 88 x 108 ins (2.24 x 2.74 m) or containers. Portable electric winch of 4,000 lb (1,814 kg) capacity, wheeled pray bar of 2,000 lb (907 kg) capacity, and 2 snatch block pulleys. 10,000 lb (4,536 kg) capacity D-ring tiedown fittings on the floor, 25,000 lb (11,340 kg) capacity rings along the sides of the floor, and 5,000 lb (2,268 kg) capacity rings along the fuselage sides and on the ramp. Fitting provided for troop seats and litter racks. C-130H has 242 tiedown rings and C-130H-30 has 305.

Wing control surfaces: Aileron (with trim tab) and 2 Fowler-type flaps (inboard and outboard) per wing.

Tail control surfaces: Elevators and rudder, all with trim tabs.

Flight control system: Mechanical primary controls, with hydraulic boosters. Hydraulic flaps and electric tabs.

Construction materials: Metal.

Engines: 4 Allison T56-A-15LFE turboprops, with 13 ft 6 ins (4.11 m) diameter propellers. APU.

Engine rating: Each 4,508 shp (3,362 kW), rated in technical specification documents as 4,300 shp (3,207 kW).

Fuel system: 35,961 litres for C-130H, or 36,416 for C-130H-30, with optional underwing auxiliary tanks.

Flight refuelling/fuel transfer: See Aircraft variants.

Electrical system: AC supply via 5 x 40 kVA alternators (on engines and APU), with conversion to DC via transformer-rectifiers.

Hydraulic system: Booster, utility and auxiliary systems, at 3,000 psi.

Braking system: Hydraulic multi-disc on mainwheels, with anti-skid system.

De-icing system: Bleed air for windscreen defogging, and deicing of engine air and oil cooler inlets, forward radome, and wing and tail unit leading edges. Electric for forward and lower cockpit windscreens, propeller blades and spinners, and pitot static heads.

Oxygen system: 300 psi liquid system providing 96 hours of oxygen at 25,000 ft (7,620 m). Gaseous system optional.

Fire system: Engines, APU and bleed air powered

DETAILS FOR C-130H,
WITH C-130H-30 IN ITALICS WHERE DIFFERENT.

Principal dimensions:
Wing span: 132 ft 7 ins (40.41 m)
Maximum length: 97 ft 9 ins (29.79 m)
Maximum height: 38 ft 1 ins (11.61 m)

Cabin:
Length: 41 ft (12.5 m) actual and 40 ft 5 ins (12.32 m) usable to ramp, *56 ft (17.07 m) actual and 55 ft 5 ins (16.89 m) usable,* with additional 10 ft (3.05 m) available on the ramp
Width: 10 ft 3.2 ins (3.13 m) maximum and 9 ft 11.5 ins (3.03 m) adjacent to mainwheels
Height: 9 ft (2.74 m) maximum, with slight drop at wing point
Floor area: 425 sq ft (39.48 m^2), without ramp
Volume without ramp: 3,621 cu ft (102.53 m^3), *4,966 cu ft (140.62 m^3),* clear cube volume
Volume with ramp: 4,351 cu ft (123.2 m^3), *5,696 cu ft (161.29 m^3),* clear cube volume.
Cheek volume: 200 cu ft (5.7 m^3), *326 cu ft (9.23 m^3)*

Wings:
Aerofoil section: NACA 64A318, 64A412 (root/tip)
Area: 1,745 sq ft (162.116 m^2)
Aspect ratio: 10.08
Incidence: 3°, 0° (root/tip)
Dihedral: 2° 30′

Tail unit:
Tailplane span: 52 ft 8 ins (16.05 m)

Undercarriage:
Type: Retractable, with twin steerable nosewheels (±60°). Tandem mainwheel units.
Main wheel tyre size: 56 x 20.00-20
Nose wheel tyre size: 39 x 13
Wheel base: 29 ft 6 ins (8.99 m) from nosewheels to forward main wheels
Wheel track: 14 ft 3 ins (4.34 m)
Turning radius: 85 ft (25.91 m) wingtip, *90 ft (27.43 m) wingtip*

Weights:
Empty, operating: 76,505 lb (34,702 kg), *80,152 lb (36,356 kg)*
Maximum zero fuel: 119,142 lb (54,042 kg)
Maximum take-off: 155,000 lb (70,307 kg) for 2.5g, 175,000 lb (79,379 kg) for 2.25g
Maximum landing: 155,000 lb (70,307 kg), for 5 ft/second sink rate
Normal landing: 130,000 lb (58,967 kg), for 9 ft/second sink rate
Payload: 42,637 lb (19,340 kg), *38,990 lb (17,686 kg)*

Performance:
Maximum cruise speed: *335 kts (385 mph) 620 km/h*
Long-range cruise speed: 300 kts (345 mph) 556 km/h
Stall speed: 100 kts (115 mph) 185 km/h
Normal take-off distance: 3,585 ft (1,093 m)
Take-off over a 50 ft (15 m) obstacle: *4,700 ft (1,433 m)*
Landing distance over a 50 ft (15 m) obstacle: 2,750 ft (839 m) at 130,000 lb (58,967 kg) landing weight, *2,370 ft (723 m) at 122,950 lb (55,769 kg) landing weight*
Maximum climb rate: 1,900 ft (579 m) per minute at sea level
Time to 23,000 ft (7,010 m): 22 minutes
Cruise altitude: 24,000 ft (7,315 m), 33,000 ft (10,058 m) ceiling
Range: 1,945 naut miles (2,240 miles) 3,602 km with 40,000 lb (18,143 kg) payload, *1,740 naut miles (2,003 miles) 3,222 km with maximum payload, or 4,200 naut miles (4,836 miles) 7,778 km with an 8,430 lb (3,824 kg) payload*

systems are monitored for fire and overheat. Engines and APU are protected by a fire suppression system.
Radar: RDR-1F weather radar. 2 Rockwell Collins 621A-6A air traffic control radar transponders.
Flight avionics/instrumentation: Communications equipment includes AN/AIC-18 intercommunication, AN/AIC-13 public address, 2 Rockwell Collins 628T-2A HF transceivers and 2 618M-3A VHF command transceivers, and provision for AN/ARC-164(V)4 UHF transceiver. Navigation equipment includes Litton LTN-72 INS and LTN-211 Omega, 2 Rockwell Collins 51RV-4B VHF nav/ILS, 2 x 860E-5 DME, 2 DF-206 ADFS, and 51Z-4 marker beacon. Flight displays are dual Rockwell Collins FD-109 flight director system, 2 C-12 gyro compass systems, 860F-4/AL-101 radio altimeter, GPWS Mk II, and Kollsman altitude alerter/preselect system. Automatic flight control system with AP 105V autopilot, guidance display and sensors (2 ADI, 2 HSI).
Mission equipment: See Aircraft variants.
Self-protection systems: Some military versions carry missile warning system and chaff/flare dispensers.
Fixed guns: See AC-130 Spectre in the Combat section.
Aircraft variants:
C-130A was the original version, though later aircraft were considerably improved. 3,750 eshp (2,796 ekW) Allison T56A-9 or 11 engines. Some still with Bolivia, Honduras, Mexico, Peru and Vietnam. Gross weight 124,200 lb (56,335 kg).
C-130B entered service from 1959, featuring 4,050 eshp (3,020 ekW) T56A-7 engines, additional fuel, 135,000 lb (61,235 kg) gross weights and strengthened undercarriage. Still operated by 7 or 8 air forces.
C-130E was delivered from 1962 with T56A-7 engines, and take-off weights similar to later C-130H, extra fuel for longer range, plus other structural and avionics improvements. Still in US service plus 8 other air forces.
MC-130E Combat Talon I is a USAF special operations version, used for air-refuelling helicopters, aerial delivery and exfiltration. Much specialized equipment.
WC-130E is a USAF weather reconnaissance variant.
C-130H is a current production version, available since 1965. As detailed. Known as C-130Ks for the RAF, with Marshall of Cambridge "stretching" the fuselages to become Hercules Mk 3s.
C-130H-30 is the C-130H with a 100 ins (2.54 m) plug inserted aft of the cockpit and an 80 ins (2.03 m) plug just forward of the ramp.
AC-130H and U Spectre are gunships. See Combat section.
DC-130s are UAV control aircraft with the USAF/USN.
EC-130s are electronic warfare variants. See Reconnaissance section.
HC-130H, N and P Combat Shadow are special operations versions with the USAF, ANG, AFRES and US Coast Guard, for refuelling helicopters and rescue and recovery of equipment and personnel.
JC-130H was built for the USAF to recover parachute-borne space capsules.
KC-130F/R/T are probe-and-drogue flight refuelling tankers used by the USMC and acquired in KC-130H form by Argentina, Brazil, Israel, Morocco, Saudi Arabia, Singapore and Spain. The US Navy has KC-130T-30s.
LC-130 is a ski/wheel-equipped transport for Arctic operations with the US ANG and Antarctic with the USN.
C-130T is a transport and tanker with the US Navy Air Reserve.
C-130J is the latest version for delivery from 1996, also offered in C-130J-30 lengthened form. 25 C-130J-30s were chosen for the RAF to replace C-130Ks in December 1994, with roll-out of the first on 18 October 1995. Advanced 2-pilot flight deck with fully integrated digital avionics, MIL-STD-1553B databus architecture, colour multi-function liquid crystal displays and head-up-displays; modern navigation systems with dual INC/GPS, mission planning system, low power colour radar and digital moving map display; 4,591 shp (3,424 kW) Allison AE 2100D3 engines with Dowty 6-blade composite propellers and new digital autopilot; built-in test equipment (BITE) and integrated diagnostics with a maintenance data recorder; and improved fuel, environmental and ice protection systems. Of the first 5 constructed in 1995, 3 are for the RAF and 2 for the USAF. Take-off distance 1,950-3,125 ft (595-953 m), time to 28,000 ft (8,535 m) initial cruise altitude is 14 minutes, and range 2,835 naut miles (3,265 miles) 5,250 km.
L-100 and L-100-30 Super Hercules are commercial versions of Hercules, currently based on the C-130H and C-130H-30 military equivalents. Currently 4,508 shp (3,362 kW) Allison 501-D22A turboprops. L-100-30 ramp weight, MTOW, MLW and payload are 155,800 lb (70,670 kg), 155,000 lb (70,307 kg), 135,000 lb (61,235 kg), and 50,676 lb (22,986 kg) respectively. Special variants include an HS hospital model operated in Saudi Arabia.
L-100J is a commercial variant of the new C-130J-30.

McDonnell Douglas Corporation (USA)

Corporate address: See Combat section for company details. See also Helicopters.

● Activities

● In addition to the aircraft detailed below and in other sections, McDD and United Airlines have undertaken development of an avionics upgrade for the DC-10 to meet the Future Air Navigation System (FANS) requirement. Initially a United DC-10-10 has been fitted with a Trimble TNL-8100 nav system and GPS, with Honeywell/Racal MCS-6000 satcoms, Canadian Marconi CMA-2102 antenna and an Electronic Resource System to follow.

McDonnell Douglas C-17A Globemaster III

McDonnell Douglas C-17A Globemaster III during low-altitude parachute extraction system (LAPES) trials

First flight: 15 September 1991.
First delivery: First operational delivery on 14 June 1993 to the 437th Air Wing. First actual delivery to the 6517th Test Squadron on 15 September 1991.
Role: Heavy lift, long-range and air refuellable military transport, for intertheatre and intratheatre airlift.
Airframe life: C-17 airframe reached 45,000 hours of simulated flight on 28 November 1994 (12,819 flights/ 28,500 landings).

▲ Development

▲ Stems from the original C-X transport programme, for which McDD was chosen to be prime contractor on 28 August 1981, although the full-scale engineering and development contract was not signed until December 1985.
Sales: DoD requirement for the USAF is 120 aircraft, with 40 authorized and 32 contracted through fiscal year 1995 (21 delivered by August 1995, including 6 for flight testing at Edwards AFB). Further 8 requested by the USAF for FY1996. First operational unit was the 17th Airlift Squadron, 437th Airlift Wing at Charleston AFB, with initial operational capability achieved on 17 January 1995. Second unit was the Air Force Reserve's 315th AW. Export sales of up to 50 are possible, according to McDD.
Crew: 2 flight, plus 2 observer positions. Loadmaster in cargo crew compartment.
Passengers: 54 troops along sidewalls (27 each side), 48 troops along centreline in 8 sets of 6 seats back-to-back, or 100 troops on 10 palleted passenger packs plus 54 on sidewalls. Total capacity depending on layout 102-154. In an aeromedical evacuation role, 3 on-board litter kits (each with 4 litters) can be joined by 9 additional kits, making 48 litters in total. Contingency allows for 102 ambulatory seated patients to be caried in addition to the litters.

McDonnell Douglas C-17A Globemaster III conducting airlift defensive system demonstrations at Eglin AFB, dispensing flares

Freight hold volume: 20,900 cu ft (591.82 m^3)
Freight hold capacity: 18 x 463L pallets, including 4 on ramp. See also Passengers. Can alternatively carry Army wheeled vehicles in 2 side-by-side rows, 3 Bradley infantry fighting vehicles, an M1 main battle tank with other vehicles, or other loads such as Apache helicopters and missile systems.
Freight hold access: Rear lower ramp/door, 10° internal upsweep when closed, 9° to ground when lowered, and with ramp toes of 15° to bridge the ground with the ramp sill. Cabin floor height to the ground 5 ft 4 ins (1.62 m). Rear upper door is hinged to the cabin ceiling when open, to provide a total vertical freight loading opening of 10 ft 6 ins (3.2 m). Ramp capacity 40,000 lb (18,144 kg). Side doors for paratroop dropping.
Loading facilities: Rails, rollers and tiedown rings (25,000 lb, 11,340 kg capacity).
Aerial delivery system: 9 x 463L pallets plus 2 on ramp. Single load airdrop limit 60,000 lb (27,215 kg) platform. Sequential loads drop 110,000 lb (49,896 kg), 60 ft (18.29 m) of platform. C-17 is said to be the only aircraft that can airdrop outsize

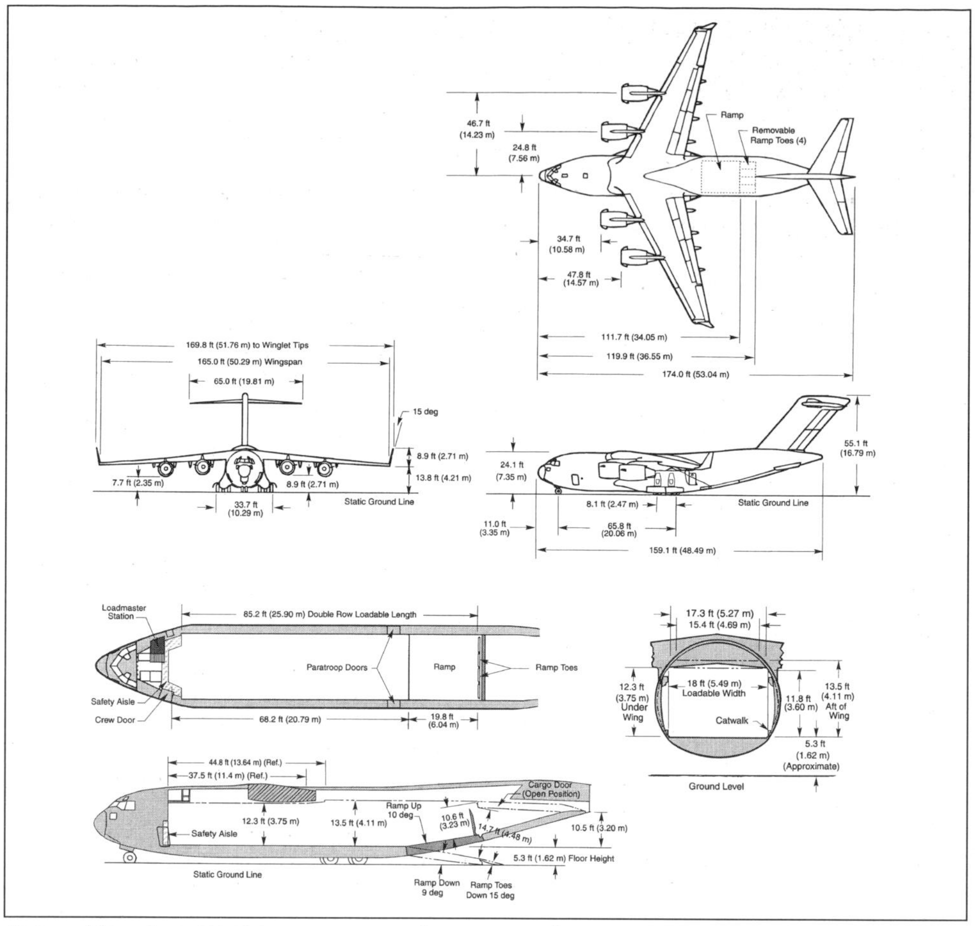

McDonnell Douglas C-17A Globemaster III general arrangements (courtesy McDonnell Douglas)

DETAILS FOR GLOBEMASTER III.

Principal dimensions:
Wing span: 165 ft (50.29), or 169 ft 10 ins (51.76 m) to winglet tips
Maximum length: 174 ft (53.04 m)
Maximum height: 55 ft 1 ins (16.79 m)

Cabin:
Length: 68 ft 2.5 ins (20.79 m) aft of flight deck to start of ramp. Ramp adds a further 19 ft 9.5 ins (6.04 m) length. Double row loadable length 85 ft 2 ins (25.96 m) including ramp
Width: 18 ft (5.49 m) loadable width (not maximum).
Height: 13 ft 6 ins (4.11 m) aft of the wing, 12 ft 3.5 ins (3.75 m) forward of wing

Wings:
Aerofoil section: Supercritical
Area: 3,800 sq ft (353.03 m^2)
Aspect ratio: 7.165
Static ground height to wingtips: 13 ft 10 ins (4.22 m)
Sweepback: 25°

Tail unit:
Tailplane span: 65 ft (19.81 m)
Tailplane area: 845 sq ft (78.5 m^2)

Undercarriage:
Type: Retractable high-sink-rate undercarriage (15 ft, 4.6 m per second), with twin nosewheels and 2 twin-strut main bogies, each strut carrying 3 wheels. Can operate from unpaved airfields
Main wheel tyre size: 50 x 21-20
Nose wheel tyre size: 40 x 15.5-16
Wheel base: 65 ft 10 ins (20.07 m)
Wheel track: 33 ft 8 ins (10.26 m)

Weights:
Design empty, operating: 269,000 lb (122,015 kg)
Maximum take-off: 585,000 lb (265,351 kg)
Payload: 169,000 lb (76,657 kg) for 2.25g

Performance:
Maximum speed: Mach 0.875
Cruise speed: Mach 0.74-0.77
Take-off field length: 8,200 ft (2,500 m), at MTOW
Landing field length: 3,000 ft (915 m), with maximum payload
Ceiling: 45,000 ft (13,715 m) service, 41,000 ft (12,500 m) operating
Range: 2,400 naut miles (2,763 miles) 4,445 km, with 157,000 lb (71,214 kg) payload
Ferry range: 4,300 naut miles (4,951 miles) 7,963 km

firepower, such as the Bradley infantry fighting vehicle.
Wing control surfaces: Externally blown flap system which allows a steep, low-speed final approach and low landing speeds for routine short field landings. With this powered lift system, the engine exhaust flow is directed through the double-slotted fixed-vane simple-hinged flaps to produce additional lifting force. Full-span leading-edge slats, aileron and 4 spoilers per wing. Winglets (9 ft 2.5 ins, 2.8 m span and 35.85 sq ft, 3.33 m^2 area) are outward canted by 15°.
Tail control surfaces: T-tail, with 2-section elevators and 2-section rudder further split into upper and lower portions.
Flight control system: Quadruple-redundant fly-by-wire, with mechanical override.
Construction materials: Aluminium alloy, steel and titanium, but with 8.1% composites (particularly for the control surfaces).
Engines: 4 Pratt & Whitney F117-PW-100 (PW2040) turbofans. Direct-flow thrust reversers capable of deployment in flight. On the ground, a fully loaded aircraft using thrust reversers can back up a 2% slope.
Engine rating: Each 41,700 lbf (185.5 kN).
Fuel system: 182,720 lb (82,880 kg).
Flight refuelling: Provision.
Electrical system: 115/200 volt, 400 Hz, 3-phase AC supply via 4 x 90 kVA engine-driven generators. Inverter for emergency AC supply and ground power. 28 volt DC supply from AC supply using 4 transformer rectifiers. 2 x 40 amp-hour ni-cd batteries for APU start-up and emergency DC power. AlliedSignal APU.
Hydraulic system: 4 independent systems, each 4,000 psi.
Braking system: Carbon type.
Fire system: Detection and suppression systems. Onboard inert gas generating system, pressurized by bleed air at 60 psi, for explosion protection.
Radar: AlliedSignal AN/APS-133(V) weather and mapping radar.
Flight avionics/instrumentation: 2 full-time all-function GEC-Marconi HUDs. 4 colour multi-function CRT displays plus conventional instruments as a backup. Delco mission computer. Honeywell air data computers. Digital navigation electronics including 4 inertial reference units, Tacan, VOR/DME, radar altimeter, ILS/marker beacon, and UHF-DF. Integrated radio communications management system, including satcom, UHF, VHF-AM/FM, HF, IFF/SIF and more. Ground proximity warning system.
Self-protection systems: See photograph and caption.

McDonnell Douglas DC-9X

Role: DC-9 Life Enhancement Programme.

★ Aims

★ With over 760 DC-9s remaining in service, of which about 660 are Series 30/40/50s, McDD is offering a life enhancement programme to extend operational life well past the year 2000 (zero time airframe structure package).
★ McDD has defined a range of structural and systems upgrades that permit operators to forward plan operation of aircraft in the 100-seat class, by either interim upgrading of DC-9s to bridge to the future acquisition of MD-95s or to undertake a more extensive upgrade suited to long-term DC-9 operations.
★ McDD offers as part of the programme features which enable the DC-9 to meet FAR Pt 36 Stage 3 and ICAO Annex 16 Chapter 3 noise regulations within the prescribed regulatory timetables. Compliance is through the addition of currently available ABS consortium hushkits (See Burbank) or, in the case of larger DC-9s such as the Series 50, re-engining with new BMW Rolls-Royce BR715, Pratt & Whitney JT8D-218B, Rolls-Royce Tay or similar engines. Maintainability and reliability improvement package.
★ DC-9X programme also offers flight deck upgrade with Euronav and operation in Cat IIIa weather conditions, plus cabin improvements (new interior affecting ceiling, bagracks and sidewalls), and increased operating weights and auxiliary fuel for longer range.
★ (Separately, Honeywell has developed a digital air data computer for the DC-9, with USAir as the intial customer.)
Sales: Among potential and actual customers, Northwest reportedly might apply structural, avionics

McDonnell Douglas DC-9X modernized DC-9

and systems upgrades, hushkits and new cabin interiors to some 90 DC-9-30s, said to increase structural life to 105,000 hours.

McDonnell Douglas KDC-10

Role: Advanced flight refuelling tanker/transport conversion of commercial DC-10-30 convertible freighters.

★ Aims/features

⋆ Maximum gross weight 565,000 lb (256,280 kg), maximum fuel capacity 246,000 lb (111,584 kg), operating weight empty 250,000 lb (113,400 kg) and maximum cargo payload 151,000 lb (68,492 kg).

⋆ Air refuelling receptacle allows the aircraft to be refuelled by other tankers.

McDonnell Douglas KDC-10

⋆ Entire main deck (less 1 pallet position) is available for various cargo and/or passenger configurations. Carries up to 30 pallets (88 x 108 ins, 2.44 x 2.74 m) in all cargo mode or up to 240 passengers and 4 pallets.

⋆ 885,786 litres (234,000 US gallons internal fuel load). Option for 3 x 15,028 litre (3,970 US gallon auxiliary) tanks in the lower lobe.

⋆ Independent hose/drogue system, with 600 gpm maximum delivery flow rate in 2 independent wing pod positions.

⋆ Advanced air refuelling boom with 1,500 gpm maximum flow rate, active fly-by-wire control, independent disconnect capability, and automatic load alleviation.

⋆ Portable remote air refuelling operator's station, providing cameras and video monitors for remote viewing, in forward cargo area of the main deck.

Sales: KLM Engineering and Maintenance is converting 2 ex-KLM DC-10s into tanker-transports for the Royal Netherlands Air Force under McDD contract, the first such civil DC-10 conversions. (For information only, the USAF retains 59 KC-10A Extender tanker-transports, based on the DC-10-30CF but newly built when delivered from 1981.)

Engines: 3 x 52,500 lbf (233.54 kN) CF6-50C2 turbofans.

McDonnell Douglas MD-11

First flight: 10 January 1990.

Certification: 8 November 1990 (FAA), April 1991 for Cat IIIb and September 1991 for JAA.

First delivery: 7 December 1990 to Finnair, starting operations on 20 December.

Role: Medium-long range passenger airliner, freighter and tanker/transport.

Sales: At least 264 commitments by 27 customers in 18 countries, with about half delivered.

Crew: 2 (flight).

Passengers: 1996 level specifications state 250 to 410, with typical 298 passenger 3-class arrangement as 16 first class (60 ins, 152 cm seat pitch), 56 business (38 ins, 96.5 cm pitch) and 226 economy (32 ins, 81 cm pitch). Typical 2-class arrangement for 323 passengers comprising 34 first (41/42 ins, 104/107 cm pitch) and 289 economy (33/34 ins, 84/86 cm pitch). All economy layout for 410 (30/31/32 ins, 76/79/81 cm pitch). 6 to 10 abreast seating with 2 aisles. Combi accommodates 181-214, and Convertible Freighter in passenger mode 350-410.

McDonnell Douglas MD-11 in passenger form

Seat pitch: See above.

Galleys and toilets: Track-mounted, interchangeable equipment.

Pressurization: 8.6 psi cabin differential.

Lower hold volume: Up to 5,566 cu ft (157.61 m^3), comprising 2,844 cu ft (80.53 m^3) in forward hold, 2,212 cu ft (62.64 m^3) in centre hold and 510 cu ft (14.44 m^3) of aft bulk. Maximum of 32 LD-3 containers plus bulk, or 10 pallets of 96 x 125 ins (2.44 x 3.18 m), or 10 pallets of 88 x 125 ins (2.24 x 3.18 m) plus 2 LD-3s and bulk. 5,164 cu ft (146.23 m^3) taken in Freighter and Convertible freighter by 6 pallets and 14 LD-3 containers. All bulk cargo volume on each model 6,850 cu ft (194 m^3).

Main deck capacity (Freighter/Convertible Freighter): 15,722 and 14,508 cu ft (445.2 and 410.82 m^3) respectively.

McDonnell Douglas MD-11 flight deck

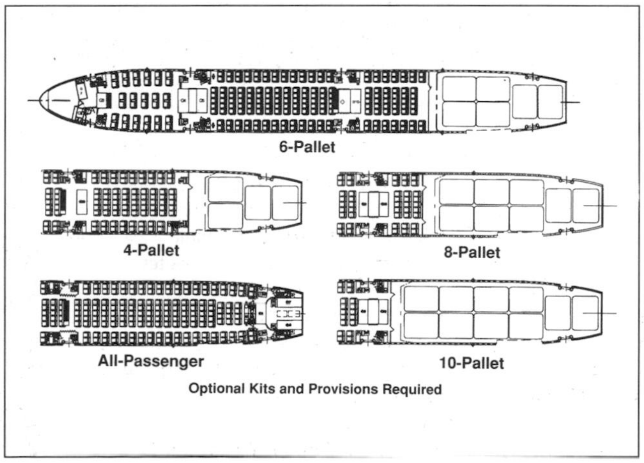

McDonnell Douglas MD-11 Combi configurations (courtesy McDonnell Douglas)

Wing control surfaces: Inner and outer ailerons (outer for low speeds only) which droop with the double-slotted flaps at take off, leading-edge slats, and 5 spoilers per wing.

Tail control surfaces: Variable-incidence tailplane, 2-section slotted elevators, and 2-section split rudder.

Flight control system: Hydraulic/electric actuation.

Construction materials: Metal, but with substantial use of composites in the control surfaces, winglets, tailplane trailing edge, wing/body fairings, engine inlets, nacelles and more.

Engines: 3 x 60,960 lbf (217.17 kN) General Electric CF6-80C2D1F, 60,000 lbf (266.9 kN) Pratt & Whitney PW4460 or 62,000 lbf (275.8 kN) PW4462 turbofan engines.

Engine rating: See above.

Fuel system: 258,721 lb (117,354 kg) without auxiliary tank, 272,014 lb (123,383 kg) with auxiliary tank. 30% fuel burn/seat improvement over DC-10.

Electrical system: AC supply via 3 x 100/120 kVA, 400 Hz engine-driven generators and 1 x 90 kVA APU-driven generator. DC supply via transformer rectifiers. 50 amp-hour battery. Emergency 25 kVA ram-air generator.

Hydraulic system: 3 independent systems.

Braking system: Carbon.

De-icing system: Bleed air for wing and tailplane leading edges. Electric for windscreen and sensors.

Oxygen system: Chemical for passengers, gaseous for flight crew and portable bottles for cabin crew.

Fire system: See Aircraft variants.

Radar: Weather radar.

Flight avionics/instrumentation: EFIS, with six 8 ins (20 cm) colour CRT flight, engine and systems displays. Dual advanced flight management systems with multifunction control/display units. Dual advanced digital flight control systems. Pilot has full override authority (not computers), and control column always indicates actual flight control position. Windshear detection. See also Aircraft variants.

Aircraft variants:

MD-11 is the standard passenger version.

MD-11 Extended Range has the additional capabilities of extra fuel for longer range, reduced drag, increased take-off weight, satcom, future air navigation system (FANS) and GPS, low noise levels, electronic flight manual, weight reduction, and improved brakes. Announced 1994. 7,255 naut mile (8,354 miles) 13,436 km range.

MD-11 Combi can carry 4, 6, 8 or 10 pallets on the main deck in addition to reduced passenger loads. Class C fire detection and extinguishing in main deck cargo space.

MD-11 Convertible Freighter can accommodate all passengers or all cargo (298 in 3 class or 193,154 lb, 87,613 kg gross weight-limited cargo). Total cargo volume of 19,672 cu ft (557.05 m^3) for pallets/containers. Conversion from passenger to cargo interior takes 2.24 days; reverse conversion takes 4 days. Complete palletized cargo capability. Main deck engine transportation capability.

MD-11 Freighter has a total cargo volume of 20,886 cu ft (591.42 m^3) for pallets/containers.

	MD-11 with 298 passengers	MD-11 Combi with 183 passengers and 6 pallets on main deck	MD-11 Freighter	MD-11 Convertible Freighter
Wing span	169 ft 10 ins (51.77 m)*	169 ft 10 ins (51.77 m)	169 ft 10 ins (51.77 m)	169 ft 10 ins (51.77 m)
Maximum length	201 ft 4 ins (61.37 m) with GE engines, 200 ft 11 ins (61.24 m) with P&W engines	201 ft 4 ins (61.37 m) with GE engines, 200 ft 11 ins (61.24 m) with P&W engines	201 ft 4 ins (61.37 m) with GE engines, 200 ft 11 ins (61.24 m) with P&W engines	201 ft 4 ins (61.37 m) with GE engines, 200 ft 11 ins (61.24 m) with P&W engines
Maximum height	57 ft 11 ins (17.65 m)	57 ft 11 ins (17.65 m)	57 ft 11 ins (17.65 m)	57 ft 11 ins (17.65 m)
Cabin length	152 ft 7 ins (46.51 m)			
Cabin width	18 ft 9 ins (5.72 m)	18 ft 4 ins (5.59 m) at floor	18 ft 4 ins (5.59 m) at floor	18 ft 4 ins (5.59 m) at floor
Cabin height	7 ft 11 ins (2.41 m)	8 ft 1.5 ins (2.47 m) stack height	8 ft 1.5 ins (2.47 m) stack height	8 ft 1.5 ins (2.47 m) stack height as Freighter
Main doors	6 ft 4 ins x 2 ft 8 ins (1.93 x 0.81 m) forward, and 6 ft 4 ins x 3 ft 6 ins (1.93 x 1.07 m) rear	13 ft 4 ins x 8 ft 6 ins (4.04 x 2.59 m) main rear cargo door	11 ft 8 ins x 8 ft 6 ins (3.56 x 2.59 m) main forward cargo door.	11 ft 8 ins x 8 ft 6 ins (3.56 x 2.59 m) main forward cargo door
Wing area, not including winglets but including ailerons	3,648 sq ft (338.91 m^2)	3,648 sq ft (338.91 m^2)	3,648 sq ft (338.91 m^2)	3,648 sq ft (338.91 m^2)
Winglet height and area	7 ft (2.13 m) and 40 sq ft (3.72 m^2)	7 ft (2.13 m) and 40 sq ft (3.72 m^2)	7 ft (2.13 m) and 40 sq ft (3.72 m^2)	7 ft (2.13 m) and 40 sq ft (3.72 m^2)
Wing aspect ratio	7.876, calculated at *span and above area criterion	7.876, calculated at *span and above area criterion	7.876, calculated at *span and above area criterion	7.876, calculated at *span and above area criterion
Wing sweepback	35°	35°	35°	35°
Tailplane span	59 ft 2 ins (18.03 m)	59 ft 2 ins (18.03 m)	59 ft 2 ins (18.03 m)	59 ft 2 ins (18.03 m)
Tailplane area	920 sq ft (85.47 m^2)	920 sq ft (85.47 m^2)	920 sq ft (85.47 m^2)	920 sq ft (85.47 m^2)
Undercarriage type	Retractable, with twin steerable (±70°) nosewheels. Main units have 4-wheel bogies, plus twin-wheel bogie under the mid fuselage	Retractable, with twin steerable (±70°) nosewheels. Main units have 4-wheel bogies, plus twin-wheel bogie under the mid fuselage	Retractable, with twin steerable (±70°) nosewheels. Main units have 4-wheel bogies, plus twin-wheel bogie under the mid fuselage	Retractable, with twin steerable (±70°) nosewheels. Main units have 4-wheel bogies, plus twin-wheel bogie under the mid fuselage
Main wheel tyre size	54 x 21-24	54 x 21-24	54 x 21-24	54 x 21-24
Nose wheel tyre size	40 x 15.5-16	40 x 15.5-16	40 x 15.5-16	40 x 15.5-16
Wheel base	80 ft 10 ins (24.64 m)	80 ft 10 ins (24.64 m)	80 ft 10 ins (24.64 m)	80 ft 10 ins (24.64 m)
Wheel track	34 ft 8 ins (10.57 m)	34 ft 8 ins (10.57 m)	34 ft 8 ins (10.57 m)	34 ft 8 ins (10.57 m)
Operating empty weight, without auxiliary tank	286,965 lb (130,165 kg)	288,885 lb (131,036 kg)	251,149 lb (113,919 kg)	289,965 lb (131,526 kg) passenger mode, 254,372 lb (115,381 kg) freight
Operating empty weight, with auxiliary tank	290,498 lb (131,768 kg) with GE engines, 290,182 lb (131,624 kg) with P&W engines			
Maximum zero fuel weight	400,000 lb (181,437 kg)	430,000 lb (195,045 kg)	451,300 lb (204,706 kg)	451,300 lb (204,706 kg)
Maximum take-off weight	602,555 lb (273,314 kg) standard, 630,500 lb (285,990 kg) optional	602,555 lb (273,314 kg) standard, 630,500 lb (285,990 kg) optional	602,555 lb (273,314 kg) standard, 630,500 lb (285,990 kg) optional	602,555 lb (273,314 kg) standard, 630,500 lb (285,990 kg) optional
Maximum landing weight	430,000 lb (195,045 kg)	458,000 lb (207,745 kg) optional	471,500 lb (213,868 kg) standard, 481,500 lb (218,405 kg) optional	471,500 lb (213,868 kg) standard, 481,500 lb (218,405 kg) optional
Payload	113,035 lb (51,272 kg)	141,115 lb (64,009 kg)	200,151 lb (90,787 kg) including tare weight	161,335 lb (73,180 kg) passenger mode, 196,928 lb (89,325 kg) cargo mode, including tare weight
Maximum speed	Mach 0.87 or 511 kts (588 mph) 946 km/h at 31,000 ft (9,450 m)	Mach 0.87 or 511 kts (588 mph) 946 km/h at 31,000 ft (9,450 m)	Mach 0.87 or 511 kts (588 mph) 946 km/h at 31,000 ft (9,450 m)	Mach 0.87 or 511 kts (588 mph) 946 km/h at 31,000 ft (9,450 m)
FAA take-off field length	10,220 ft (3,115 m) at MTOW, sea level, 30° C, with PW4462s	10,220 ft (3,115 m) at MTOW, sea level, 30° C, with PW4462s	10,220 ft (3,115 m) at MTOW, sea level, 30° C, with PW4462s	10,220 ft (3,115 m) at MTOW, sea level, 30° C, with PW4462s
FAA landing field length, MLW, sea level	6,950 ft (2,118 m)	7,330 ft (2,234 m)	7,620 ft (2,323 m)	7,620 ft (2,323 m)
Range, international reserves naut miles (miles) km	6,835 (7,871) 12,667	6,715 (7,733) 12,445	3,948 (4,546) 7,316 with weight limited payload	6,795 (7,825) 12,594 with 298 passengers, 3,948 (4,546) 7,316 with weight limited payload
Range, with auxiliary tanks naut miles (miles) km	7,245 (8,343) 13,427	5,736 (6,605) 10,630 with space limited payload		

Note: Pax = Passengers.
*1996 level specifications state 169.5 ft (51.7 m) span.

Performance Enhancement Programmes:
Phase I drag reduction with 0.7% benefit, restored initial drag deficiency by outboard wing trailing-edge splitter of 1.5 ins (3.8 cm) inboard and 0.5 in (1.3 cm) outboard.
Phase II drag reduction with 1.5% benefit, encompassing outboard slat seals and outboard ailerons drooped 4°.
CPIP Phase IIIa with 0.2% benefit introducing aileron seal plates, and 0.8% benefit with pylon fillets.
Engine and Nacelle improvements, 1.5%-2.7% benefit.
Maximum take-off weight options of 605,500 lb, 610,000 lb, 618,000 lb and 625,500 lb (274,650, 276,691, 280,320 and 283,722 kg).
Take-off field length shortened by 500-900 ft (152-274 m).
Supplemental fuel tanks made available, with 1,984 or 3,969 US gallon (7,510 or 15,024 litres) options. Quick removal capability, or 2 to 4 LD-3 containers.
KMD-11 is a flight refuelling/cargo transport variant, offered as a modern development of the KC-10 Extender.

Twin-engined MD-11 variant has been proposed, for medium ranges of 4,500-6,000 naut miles (5,180-6,900 miles) 8,335-11,100 km with 220-260 passengers. 2 engines in the 74,000 lbf (329 kN) range. A long-range version is also being studied.

McDonnell Douglas MD-12 series

Role: Full-length double-deck, high-capacity intercontinental airliner and freighter.

★ Aims

★ 2 passenger decks to offer the latest amenities, including sleeping berths, office in the sky, exercise room, in-seat videos, and seat telephones.
★ Extra wide passenger doors, aisles and stairway between decks to speed loading/unloading.

▲ Development

▲ To be developed with partners, and built at a new production facility yet to be selected.
Details: MD-12, except where stated.
Passengers: 481 in long-range (8,000 naut mile) form, with up to 579 passengers in 3-class high-capacity layout. Combi seating for 428.

McDonnell Douglas MD-12 two-deck airliner

DETAILS FOR MD-12, UNLESS STATED.

Principal dimensions:
Wing span: 229 ft (69.8 m)
Maximum length: 210 ft (64 m)
Maximum height: 76 ft (23.16 m)

Cabin:
Width: 24 ft 6 ins (7.47 m)
Height: 27 ft 11 ins (8.51 m) total internal height for all decks

Wings:
Area: 6,761 sq ft (628.12 m^2), including ailerons.
Sweepback: 35°

Undercarriage:
Wheel base: 88 ft (26.82 m)
Wheel track: 38 ft (11.58 m)

Weights:
Empty, operating: 442,000 lb (200,488 kg)
Maximum zero fuel: 640,000 lb (290,300 kg)
Maximum take-off: 1,022,000 lb (463,570 kg)
Maximum landing: 680,000 lb (308,440 kg)

Performance:
Maximum speed: Mach 0.85 or 500 kts (575 mph) 925 km/h, *same for all versions*
FAA take-off field length: 10,400 ft (3,170 m), MTOW, sea level, 30° C, *same for all versions*
FAA landing field length: 8,800 ft (2,682 m), same for HC
Design range: 8,076 naut miles (9,300 miles) 14,967 km

Freight hold volume: Lower deck hold volume 4,920 cu ft (139.32 m^3). See Aircraft variants.
Wing characteristics: All new, advanced technology, patented wing design. Winglets.
Flight control system: Fly-by-wire.
Construction materials: Extensive use of composite materials.
Engines: 4 x 60,960 lbf (217.17 kN) General Electric CF6-80C2D1F, 60,000 lbf (266.9 kN) Pratt & Whitney PW4460 or 64,000 lbf (284.89 kN) Rolls-Royce Trent 764 turbofan engines.
Engine rating: See above.
Flight avionics/instrumentation: Similar to MD-11.
Aircraft variants:
MD-12 standard airliner.
MD-12 LR will be the long-range version.
MD-12 HC will offer the high capacity seating arrangements. Same weights as MD-11, except operating empty weight 460,000 lb (208,652 kg). Design range 7,121 naut miles (8,200 miles) 13,197 km.
MD-12 HC/ER will combine high capacity with extended range.
MD-12 ST will be a stretched version.
MD-12 Twin is a projected twin-engined version.
Freighter will offer an upper deck volume of 7,030 cu ft (199.07 m^3), main deck volume of 19,030 cu ft (538.86 m3), and 4,920 cu ft (139.32 m^3) lower deck. MLW 765,000 lb (347,000 kg), maximum zero fuel weight 725,000 lb (328,855 kg) and operating empty weight 423,000 lb (191,869 kg). FAA field landing length 9,600 ft (2,926 m). Design range 4,993 naut miles (5,750 miles) 9,253 km with cargo density of 8.5 lb/cu ft.
Combi versions will offer a main deck volume of 5,530 cu ft (156.59 m^3) and 4,920 cu ft (139.32 m^3) lower deck. Maximum landing weight 695,000 lb (315,245 kg), maximum zero fuel weight 655,000 lb (297,100 kg) and operating empty weight 461,000 lb (209,106 kg). FAA field landing length 9,000 ft (2,743 m). Design range 6,340 naut miles (7,300 miles) 11,748 km with 430 passengers plus cargo and baggage at 10 lb/cu ft.

McDonnell Douglas MD-80 series

First flight: 18 October 1979.
Certification: 26 August 1980 (FAA).
First delivery: 12 September 1980 to Swissair, for services from October 1980.

McDonnell Douglas MD-80

Role: Short-medium range airliner.
Noise levels: MD-81, -82 and -83 (possibly -88) are take-off 90.4 EPNdB, sideline 94.6 EPNdB, and approach 93.3 EPNdB.
Sales: Over 1,225 ordered.
Crew: 2 (flight).
Passengers: 172 maximum, 155 typical economy for MD-81, -82, -83 and -88. 139 maximum and 130 typical economy for MD-87.
Pressurization: 7.8 psi cabin differential.
Freight hold volume: 1,253 cu ft (35.48 m^3) for MD-81, -82 and -88. 1,013 cu ft (28.68 m^3) for MD-83, and 937 cu ft (26.53 m^3) for MD-87.
Wing control surfaces: Ailerons, double-slotted flaps, full-span 3-position leading-edge slats, and 3 section spoilers (2 functioning as speed brakes and 1 for lift dumping).
Tail control surfaces: Variable incidence tailplane. Elevators and rudder, with tabs.
Flight control system: Manual ailerons and elevators. Hydraulic rudder, flaps and slats. Electric tailplane and tabs.
Construction materials: Mostly metal, but with composites used in areas of the wings, control surfaces, wing/body fairings, cabin floor and more.
Engines: 2 x 18,500 lbf (82.29 kN) Pratt & Whitney JT8D-209 turbofans for MD-81, 20,000 lbf (88.97 kN) JT8D-217A/Cs for MD-82/88, 21,000 lbf (93.41 kN) JT8D-219s for MD-83, and 20,000 lbf (88.97 kN) JT8D-217Cs for MD-87. Target type reversers, for ground operation only.
Engine rating: See above.
Fuel system: 22,107 litres for MD-81, -82 and -88. 26,498 litres for MD-83. 22,107 litres for MD-87, with optional 26,498 litres.
Electrical system: 3-phase 400 Hz supply via 2 engine-driven and 1 APU-driven 40 kVA alternators.

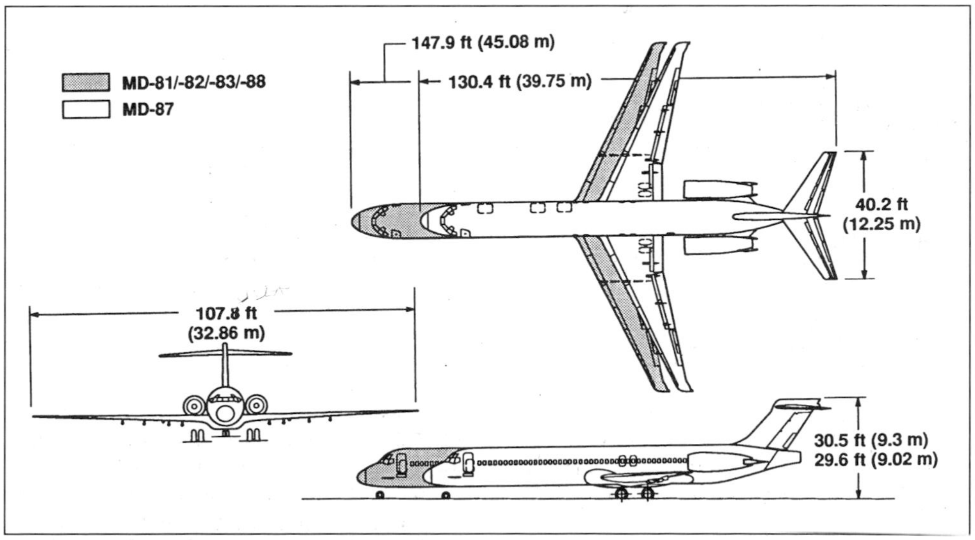

McDonnell Douglas MD-80 series drawing, showing the differences between the short-fuselage MD-87 and all other versions (courtesy McDonnell Douglas)

	MD-81 with 155 pax + baggage	MD-82 and MD-88 with 155 pax + baggage	MD-83 with 155 pax + baggage	MD-87 with 130 pax + baggage
Wing span	107 ft 10 ins (32.87 m)	107 ft 10 ins (32.87 m)	107 ft 10 ins (32.87 m)	107 ft 10 ins (32.87 m)
Maximum length	147 ft 10 ins (45.06 m)	147 ft 10 ins (45.06 m)	147 ft 10 ins (45.06 m)	130 ft 5 ins (39.75 m)
Maximum height	29 ft 7 ins (9.02 m)	29 ft 7 ins (9.02 m)	29 ft 7 ins (9.02 m)	30 ft 6 ins (9.3 m)
Cabin length	101 ft (30.78 m)	101 ft (30.78 m)	101 ft (30.78 m)	
Cabin width	10 ft 4 ins (3.15 m)	10 ft 4 ins (3.15 m)	10 ft 4 ins (3.15 m)	10 ft 4 ins (3.15 m)
Cabin height	6 ft 9 ins (2.06 m)	6 ft 9 ins (2.06 m)	6 ft 9 ins (2.06 m)	6 ft 9 ins (2.06 m)
Cabin volume	6,778 cu ft (191.93 m^3)	6,778 cu ft (191.93 m^3)	6,778 cu ft (191.93 m^3)	
Main passenger door	6 ft x 2 ft 10 ins (1.83 x 0.86 m)	6 ft x 2 ft 10 ins (1.83 x 0.86 m)	6 ft x 2 ft 10 ins (1.83 x 0.86 m)	6 ft x 2 ft 10 ins (1.83 x 0.86 m)
Wing area, including ailerons	1,209 sq ft (112.32 m^2)	1,209 sq ft (112.32 m^2)	1,209 sq ft (112.32 m^2)	1,209 sq ft (112.32 m^2)
Wing aspect ratio	9.61	9.61	9.61	9.61
Wing sweepback	24.5° at 25% chord	24.5° at 25% chord	24.5° at 25% chord	24.5° at 25% chord
Tailplane span	40 ft 2 ins (12.24 m)	40 ft 2 ins (12.24 m)	40 ft 2 ins (12.24 m)	40 ft 2 ins (12.24 m)
Undercarriage type	Retractable, with steerable nosewheels. Twin wheels on each unit	Retractable, with steerable nosewheels. Twin wheels on each unit	Retractable, with steerable nosewheels. Twin wheels on each unit	Retractable, with steerable nosewheels. Twin wheels on each unit
Main wheel tyre size	44.5 x 16.5-20	44.5 x 16.5-20	44.5 x 16.5-20	44.5 x 16.5-20
Nose wheel tyre size	26 x 6.6-14	26 x 6.6-14	26 x 6.6-14	26 x 6.6-14
Wheel base	72 ft 5 ins (22.07 m)	72 ft 5 ins (22.07 m)	72 ft 5 ins (22.07 m)	62 ft 11 ins (19.18 m)
Wheel track	16 ft 8 ins (5.08 m)	16 ft 8 ins (5.08 m)	16 ft 8 ins (5.08 m)	16 ft 8 ins (5.08 m)
Maximum zero fuel weight	118,000 lb (53,524 kg)	122,000 lb (55,339 kg)	122,000 lb (55,339 kg)	118,000 lb (53,524 kg)
Maximum ramp weight	141,000 lb (63,956 kg)	150,500 lb (68,266 kg)	161,000 lb (73,028 kg)	141,000 lb (63,956 kg)
Maximum take-off weight	140,000 lb (63,503 kg)	149,500 lb (67,812 kg)	160,000 lb (72,575 kg)	140,000 lb (63,503 kg) or 149,500 lb (67,812 kg) with auxiliary fuel tanks
Maximum landing weight	128,000 lb (58,060 kg)	130,000 lb (58,967 kg)	139,500 lb (63,276 kg)	128,000 lb (58,060 kg)
Space limited payload	38,105 lb (17,284 kg)	38,105 lb (17,284 kg)	35,705 lb (16,196 kg)	30,820 lb (13,980 kg)
Maximum speed	Mach 0.76 or 438 kts (504 mph) 811 km/h	Mach 0.76 or 438 kts (504 mph) 811 km/h	Mach 0.76 or 438 kts (504 mph) 811 km/h	Mach 0.76 or 438 kts (504 mph) 811 km/h
FAA take-off field length	7,250 ft (2,210 m) MTOW, sea level 30° C	7,450 ft (2,271 m), MTOW, sea level 30° C	8,375 ft (2,553 m), MTOW, sea level 30° C	6,100 ft (1,859 m), MTOW, sea level 30° C
FAA landing field length	4,850 ft (1,478 m) , MLW, sea level	4,920 ft (1,500 m), MLW, sea level	5,200 ft (1,585 m), MLW, sea level	4,690 ft (1,430 m), MLW, sea level
Design range, international reserves	1,563 naut miles (1,800 miles) 2,897 km	2,049 naut miles (2,360 miles) 3,798 km	2,501 naut miles (2,880 miles) 4,635 km	2,371 naut miles (2,730 miles) 4,394 km
Note: Pax = Passengers.				

Hydraulic system: 2 independent systems, each 3,000 psi.
Braking system: Disc brakes, with anti-skid system.
De-icing system: Bleed air for wing and tailplane leading edges and engine inlets. Electrical for windscreen.
Radar: Colour weather radar.
Flight avionics/instrumentation: Digital, with integrated flight systems. Cat IIIa. Late versions have EFIS, FMS, windshear detection system and more.
Aircraft variants:
MD-81 high-capacity short-range version, with JT8D-209 engines.
MD-82 and MD-88 are more powerful versions, of higher weights for longer range. MD-82 appeared in 1981 and MD-88 in 1987. See also Shanghai Aviation Industrial Corporation for MD-82/83 and MD-82T versions built in China.
MD-83 is the most powerful long-fuselage version, with the highest weights for longest range. Appeared 1984.
MD-87 is the short-fuselage version with reduced accommodation, with standard fuel capacity of the MD-82/83/88 but with optional auxiliary tanks. Appeared 1986.
Executive and business versions of the MD-83 and MD-87 became available, with luxurious cabins for small numbers of passengers (many configurations possible).

McDonnell Douglas MD-90 series

First flight: 22 February 1993, with the first production aircraft (third to fly) on 21 September 1994.
Certification: November 1994.
First delivery: February 1995, to Delta Air Lines.
Role: Medium range airliner.
Airframe life: 90,000 hours or 60,000 landings.
Noise levels: 86 EPNdB take-off, 92 EPNdB sideline, 96 EPNdB approach.

★ Aims

★ Compared with MD-80, has electronic engine controls, updated flight deck, stretched fuselage for 10 extra passengers, all-new cabin interior, vacuum toilets, upgraded digital environmental control system, carbon brakes with digital anti-skid system, improved hydraulic system, new APU, new VSCF electrical power system, V2500 engines, and powered flight controls.

McDonnell Douglas MD-90

Sales: 72 firm and 84 options at time of writing.
Crew: 2 (flight).
Passengers: 153 mixed class or 172 maximum, 5 abreast. MD-90-55 can have a high-density layout for up to 187 passengers. Airstair.
Seat pitch: 35 ins (90 cm) first class, 31 ins (80 cm) coach.
Galleys: 2 forward and 2 rear.
Toilets: 3, 1 forward and 2 aft.
Freight hold volume: 1,300 cu ft (36.81 m^3) for MD-90-30, and 822 cu ft (23.28 m^3) for MD-90-50 with optional 6,738 litre auxiliary tank installed.
Wing control surfaces: Ailerons with tabs, double-slotted fixed-vane Fowler-type flaps, full-span 3-position leading-edge slats, and spoilers (functioning as speed brakes and lift dumpers).
Tail control surfaces: T-tail, with elevators (with tabs) and rudder (with tab).
Engines: MD-90-30 has 25,000 lbf (111.21 kN) International Aero Engines V2525-D5 turbofans, and MD-90-55 has 28,000 lbf (124.55 kN) V2528-D5 turbofans. Target type thrust reversers for ground operation only. AlliedSignal 131-9(D), with 75 kVA generator (90 kVA for 5 minutes).

DETAILS FOR MD-90-30, *WITH MD-90-50 IN ITALICS WHERE DIFFERENT.*

Principal dimensions:
Wing span: 107 ft 10 ins (32.87 m)
Maximum length: 152 ft 7 ins (46.51 m)
Maximum height: 30 ft 7 ins (9.32 m)

Cabin:
Length: 105 ft 9 ins (32.23 m)
Width: 10 ft 4 ins (3.14 m)
Height: 6 ft 9 ins (2.06 m)
Main passenger door: 6 ft x 2 ft 10 ins (1.83 x 0.86 m) forward
Cargo doors: 4 ft 5 ins x 4 ft 2 ins (1.35 x 1.27 m)

Wings:
Area: 1,209 sq ft (112.32 m^2)
Aspect ratio: 9.61
Sweepback: 24.5 ° at 25% chord

Tail unit:
Tailplane span: 40 ft 2 ins (12.24 m)

Undercarriage:
Type: Retractable, with steerable nosewheels. Twin wheels on each unit
Tyre sizes: Based on MD-80.
Wheel base: 77 ft 2 ins (23.52 m)
Wheel track: 16 ft 8 ins (5.08 m)

Weights:
Empty, operating: 88,000 lb (39,916 kg), *91,900 lb (41,685 kg)*
Maximum zero fuel: 130,000 lb (58,967 kg), *135,000 lb (61,235 kg)*
Maximum ramp: 157,000 lb (71,214 kg), *173,500 lb (78,698 kg)*
Maximum take-off: 156,000 lb (70,760 kg), *172,500 lb (78,245 kg)*
Maximum landing: 142,000 lb (64,410 kg), *150,000 lb (68,039 kg)*
Space limited payload: 38,250 lb (17,350 kg), *33,500 lb (15,195 kg)*

Performance:
Maximum speed: Mach 0.84
Economic cruise speed: Mach 0.76, or 438 kts (504 mph) 811 km/h at 35,000 ft (10,670 m), ISA standard day
Landing speed: 138 kts (159 mph) 256 km/h
FAA take-off field length: 7,000 ft *(2,134 m), 7,700 ft (2,347 m)*, at MTOGW, sea level
FAA landing field length: 5,130 ft (1,564 m), *5,340 ft (1,628 m)*, at MLW, sea level
Climb rate: 2,200 ft (670 m) per minute at 17,500 ft (5,335 m)
Ceiling: 37,000 ft (11,275 m)
Range: 2,275 naut miles (2,620 miles) 4,216 km, *3,022 naut miles (3,480 miles)* 5,600 km, with international reserves

McDonnell Douglas MD-90 advanced flight deck

Fuel system: 22,107 litres for MD-90-30, and 28,845 litres for MD-90-50.
Electrical system: Variable speed/constant frequency system.
Hydraulic system: 2 systems, each 3,000 psi.
Braking system: Carbon brakes, with digital anti-skid system. Parking brake.
De-icing system: Overwing ice sensors. Electric heating of nose strakes. Warm fuel from engine oil coolers is recirculated to the wing tanks.
Radar: Weather radar.
Flight avionics/instrumentation: Advanced flight deck with EFIS (6 x 5 ins, 15 x 13 cm screens), including PFDs for radio altitude and navigation data. Full-flight management system (FMS), electronic overhead annunciator panel, INS, and LED dot-matrix displays for engine and systems monitoring. Altimeter, airspeed and vertical speed indicators. Modified windshear computer, new air data computers, and new master warning and caution system (compared with MD-80).
Aircraft variants:
MD-90-30 is the baseline version, as detailed.
MD-90-30T Trunkliner was chosen on 25 June 1992 to be the second form of Trunkliner for Chinese assembly, with Shanghai as prime contractor (also mostly Chinese manufacture of subassemblies, with subcontracts to Chengdu, Shenyang and Xi'an), and with Chinese-assembled 25,000 lbf (111.21 kN) International Aero Engines V2525 engines. Negotiations were concluded and contracts signed on 4 November 1994 covering co-production of 20 from 1995, for delivery from 1998.
MD-90-50 has, compared with the MD-90-30, a heavier gross weight for a substantial increase in range; strengthened wing, tail unit and fuselage; strengthened undercarriage, provisions for up to 6,738 litres of auxiliary fuel, and 28,000 lbf (124.55 kN) V2528-D5 turbofan engines.
MD-90-55 is similar to MD-90-50 but has additional emergency exits, permitting higher density charter configurations of up to 187 passengers.

McDonnell Douglas MD-95

First flight: 1996 in first prototype form as a modified DC-9.
First delivery: 1998.
Role: 99-passenger airliner.

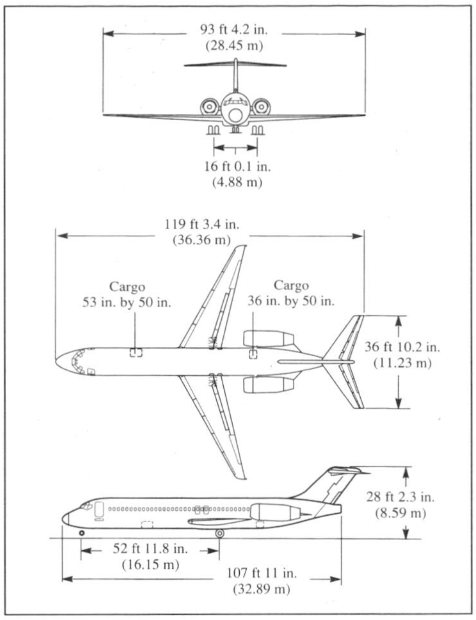

McDonnell Douglas MD-95 general arrangement (courtesy McDonnell Douglas)

Airframe life: Anticipated 100,000 hours.
Noise levels: 7 dB sideline, 7 dB take-off with cutback, and 6 dB approach below ICAO Annex 16 Chapter 3 and FAR Pt 36 Stage 3 requirements.

★ Aims
★ Replacement for Stage 2/Chapter 2 aircraft.
★ New interior design, with quiet cabin and high-level 100-passenger seating comfort.
★ Hydrocarbons 80%, carbon monoxides 70%, oxides of nitrogen 40% and smoke 42% below ICAO emission limits.

▲ Development
▲ Known major partners include Alenia of Italy (to build the fuselage), AlliedSignal (environmental control system), British Aerospace (tail unit), BMW Rolls-Royce (engines), Halla of South Korea (later wing sets), Honeywell (avionics), Korean Air (nose with forward door area), McDonnell Douglas Canada (early wing sets), ShinMaywa of Japan (engine pylons and horizontal stabilizers), SHL Servo Systems of Israel (undercarriage), Sundstrand (electrical system).
Sales: Some 200 outline sales. Possible early customers are AeroMexico, Aviaco, Finnair, Meridiana, SAS and International Lease Finance.
Crew: 2 (flight).
Passengers: 99, typically as 8 first class and 91 economy, seated 5 abreast.
Freight hold volume: 860 or 884 cu ft (24.35 or 25 m^3) for MD-95-30, and 604 or 644 cu ft (17.1 or 18.24 m^3) for ER.

McDonnell Douglas MD-95

DETAILS FOR MD-95-30, *WITH ER IN ITALICS WHERE DIFFERENT.*

Principal dimensions:
Wing span: 93 ft 4.2 ins (28.45 m)
Maximum length: 119 ft 3.4 ins (36.36 m)
Maximum height: 28 ft 2.3 ins (8.59 m)

Cabin:
Cargo doors: 53 x 50 ins (1.35 x 1.27 m) forward, 36 x 50 ins (0.91 x 1.27 m) aft

Wings:
Area: 1,000.7 sq ft (92.97 m²), including ailerons
Sweepback: 24.5° at 25% chord

Tail unit:
Tailplane span: 36 ft 10.2 ins (11.23 m)

Undercarriage:
Type: Retractable, with steerable nosewheels. Twin wheels on each unit
Wheel base: 52 ft 11.8 ins (16.15 m)
Wheel track: 16 ft 0.1 ins (4.88 m)

Weights:
Empty, operating: 66,300 lb (30,073 kg), *68,000 lb (30,844 kg)*
Maximum zero fuel: 96,000 lb (43,544 kg), *98,500 lb (44,679 kg)*
Maximum ramp: 115,000 lb (52,163 kg), *122,000 lb (55,338 kg)*
Maximum take-off: 114,000 lb (51,709 kg), *121,000 lb (54,885 kg)*
Maximum landing: 102,000 lb (46,266 kg), *110,000 lb (49,895 kg)*
Space limited payload: 23,590 lb (10,700 kg)

Performance:
Maximum speed: Mach 0.76, or 438 kts (504 mph) 811 km/h
FAA take-off field length: 6,400 ft (1,950 m), *6,600 ft (2,012 m)*, MTOW, sea level, 30° C
FAA landing field length: 5,130 ft (1,564 m), MLW, sea level
Range: See Aircraft variants

Wing control surfaces: Ailerons, double-slotted flaps, 2-position and 5-section full-span leading-edge slats, and 3-section spoilers (functioning as speed brakes).
Tail control surfaces: T-tail with elevators (2 tabs each) and rudder (with tab).
Construction materials: Lightweight airframe.
Engines: 2 BMW Rolls-Royce BR715 turbofans. Target-type thrust reversers.
Engine rating: Each 18,500 lbf (82.29 kN), with possible increase to 20,000 lbf (88.97 kN) for the ER version.
Fuel system: 13,927 litres for MD-95-30, 18,204 litres for ER.
Flight avionics/instrumentation: MD-90 avionics suite. Cat IIIa autoland. EFIS, FMS and IRS. Crew commonality with MD-80 and MD-90.
Aircraft variants:
MD-95-30 has range of 1,368 naut miles (1,575 miles) 2,535 km.
MD-95-30 ER extended range has an optional auxiliary fuel tank for up to 1,758 naut miles (2,024 miles) 3,257 km.

McDonnell Douglas MD-XX Advanced Commercial Transport

First delivery: After the year 2000.
Role: Short-medium range transcontinental airliner family.

McDonnell Douglas MD-XX Advanced Commercial Transport

★ Aims
★ Larger companion to the other new MD twin-jets under development.
★ Use of advanced technologies that benefit passengers, improve productivity of air and ground crews, enhance operational performance, and satisfy low noise and emission standards.
★ Mach 0.8 cruise, with basic range of 3,000 naut miles and extended range capability of over 4,500 naut miles.
★ Under consideration is the use of 2 geared very-high-bypass turbofan engines mounted on an advanced high aspect ratio supercritical wing (span possibly 129 ft, 39.32 m) which uses composite materials to reduce weight. Fuselage of basic model possibly about 144 ft (44 m).
★ 2-crew flight deck with advanced integrated avionics and display systems, and fly-by-light signalling for virtually all control, sensing and data distribution functions.

▲ Development
▲ 1994. Start of preliminary conceptual studies for an all-new twin-engined airliner.
Crew: 2 flight crew.
Passengers: 200-220 passengers in flexible 2-class, 2-aisle layouts, with stretched versions carrying upwards of 250 passengers.

McDonnell Douglas High Speed Civil Transport

First flight: 2003.
Certification: Projected for 2005-2006.
First delivery: 2007.
Role: Supersonic airliner.

★ Aims
★ Design goals of 300 passengers and 5,000 naut mile range.
★ Cruise speed of Mach 1.6 to Mach 2.4.

▲ Development
▲ McDD is conducting internal and NASA contract studies to determine the market requirements for an HSCT and resolve environmental, economic and technical issues.
▲ McDD is participating in an international study group exploring the HSCT concept, with Aerospatiale, Boeing, British Aerospace, Daimler-Benz, Japan Aircraft Industries, Alenia and Tupolev. (see Tupolev Tu-244.)
Sales: Possible market for 500 to 1,500.

McDonnell Douglas conceptual design for a 300-passenger HSCT

Nordam Group (USA)

Corporate address: 510 South Lansing, Tulsa, OK 74120.
Telephone: +1 918 587 4105
Facsimile: +1 918 438 9543
Telex: 158105

● Activities
● Include noise-reduction kits for JT8D-engined Boeing 737s, and manufacture/repair of General Electric CF6-50 exhaust components.

Pemco World Air Services (USA)

Corporate address: PO Box 2287, Birmingham, AL 35201-2287.
Telephone: +1 205 591 7870, or 592 0031
Facsimile: +1 205 592 6306
Founded: Took its present name in September 1994 as the commercial aircraft maintenance and modification branch of Pemco Aeroplex. A Precision Standard Inc company.
Information: Michelle Azzi (Manager, Public Relations).

● Activities
● Conversion of passenger aircraft to quick-change or freighter configurations, interior reconfigurations, galley installations, airstair installations, avionics upgrades, and hushkit installations. Aircraft maintenance and repair. Facilities in Dothan (Alabama) and Copenhagen (Denmark).

OTHER PEMCO OPERATIONS

Pemco Aeroplex

● Activities

● Undertakes military aircraft maintenance and modification at facilities in Birmingham (Alabama) and Clearwater (Florida). Announced a 7-year contract for the Programmed Depot Maintenance of the USAF's KC-135 aircraft in September 1994.

One of 7 Boeing 737-300QCs converted for Lufthansa by Pemco (courtesy Pemco)

Pemco Air Support Services

● Activities

● Product support. Large spare parts inventories in Clearwater (Florida) and Copenhagen (Denmark).

Pemco Engineers

● Activities

● Designs and manufactures aircraft cargo handling systems and components.

Pemco Nacelle Services

● Activities

● Repairs and overhauls nacelles and thrust reversers for GE, IAE, P&W, and R-R engines.

Raytheon Aircraft Company (USA)

Corporate address: PO Box 85, Wichita, KS 67201-0085.
Telephone: +1 316 676 7111
Facsimile: +1 316 676 8286
Founded: 1994, as a division of Raytheon International Inc, to merge the Beech Aircraft Corporation (acquired in 1980 but previously operated as an independent company) and Raytheon Corporate Jets (former British Aerospace Corporate Jets purchased on 6 August 1993).
Employees: 10,000.
Information: Jim Gregory (Director of Corporate Affairs – *telephone* +44 316 676 7689, *facsimile* +1 316 676 8867) and Pat Zerbe (Media Manager, *telephone* +1 316 676 7603).

■ Facilities

■ Final assembly, engineering and support activities for the Hawker corporate jets are being relocated from the UK to Wichita. BAe continues to provide fabricated parts and major subassemblies. The Little Rock, Arkansas facility of the former Raytheon Corporate Jets operates a sales force, customer service facility, aircraft painting operation, and supplies custom interiors and avionics for the Hawker line.

● Activities

● A division of Raytheon International Inc. Reported US$222 million in commercial sales during the first 3 months of 1995, including 24 business aircraft (jetprops, light jets and medium jets), with other aircraft including 8 military trainers to the USAF, 53 commercial aircraft, and 16 regional airliners (Beech 1900D Airliners).
● See General Aviation section for most aircraft types. See also Combat section for the Beech-Pilatus PC-9 Mk II trainer for the US JPATS programme.
● Produces the AQM-37C and MQM-107 missile targets.

Beech 1900D Airliner

First flight: 1 March 1990.
Certification: March 1991 to FAR Pt 23 Amendment 34.
First delivery: 1991, to Mesa Air Group.
Role: Regional airliner and executive shuttle.
Sales: 156 1900Ds delivered by 28 June 1995. First Executive shuttle was delivered to Ashanti Goldfields Company Ltd of Ghana in April 1995.
Crew: 1 or 2 pilots.
Passengers: Up to 19 passengers, 2 abreast.
Seat pitch: 30 ins (76 cm).
Galley: Optional self-service commissary and toilet.
Pressurization: 5 psi cabin differential.
Baggage compartments: 17 cu ft (0.48 m^3) forward cabin, for 250 lb (113.4 kg) of baggage. 175 cu ft (4.96 m^3) aft area, for 1,630 lb (739 kg).

DETAILS FOR 1900D AIRLINER.

Principal dimensions:
Wing span: 57 ft 10 ins (17.63 m)
Maximum length: 57 ft 10 ins (17.63 m)
Maximum height: 15 ft 6 ins (4.72 m)

Cabin:
Length: 33 ft 11 ins (10.34 m)
Width: 4 ft 6 ins (1.37 m), or 4 ft 1 ins (1.24 m) at floor
Height: 5 ft 11 ins (1.8 m)
Volume: 584 cu ft (16.54 m^3) main cabin, 103 cu ft (2.92 m^3) crew station
Main passenger door: 5 ft 4.2 ins x 2 ft 3 ins (1.63 x 0.69 m)
Cargo door: 4 ft 4 ins x 4 ft 4 ins (1.32 x 1.32 m) aft door, and 4 ft 9 ins x 4 ft 4 ins (1.45 x 1.32 m) forward door

Wings:
Aerofoil section: Modified NACA 23018, 23012 (root/tip)
Area: 310 sq ft (28.8 m^2)
Aspect ratio: 10.79
Incidence: 3° 29' root, -1° 4' tip.
Dihedral: 6°

Tail unit:
Tailplane span: 18 ft 5.75 ins (5.63 m)

Undercarriage:
Type: Retractable, with steerable nosewheel. Twin main wheel units
Wheel base: 23 ft 9.5 ins (7.25 m)
Wheel track: 17 ft 2 ins (5.23 m)
Turning radius: 41 ft 1 ins (12.53 m) wingtip

Weights:
Empty, operating: 10,550 lb (4,785 kg) typically
Maximum zero fuel: 15,000 lb (6,804 kg)
Maximum ramp: 17,060 lb (7,738 kg)
Maximum take-off: 16,950 lb (7,688 kg)
Maximum landing: 16,100 lb (7,303 kg)
Useful load: 6,510 lb (2,953 kg)
Payload: 1,887 lb (856 kg) with full fuel

Performance:
Maximum cruise speed: 281 kts (324 mph) 520 km/h *at 10,000 ft (3,050 m)*, 288 kts (332 mph) 533 km/h *at 15,000 ft (4,570 m)*, 285 kts (328 mph) 528 km/h *at 20,000 ft (6,100 m)*, 278 kts (320 mph) 515 km/h *at 25,000 ft (7,620 m)*, all at 15,000 lb (6,804 kg)
Stall speed: 82 kts (95 mph) 152 km/h, with 35° flaps, at 16,100 lb (7,303 kg)
Field length: 3,470 ft (1,058 m) with 17° flaps, sea level, ISA, at 16,000 lb (7,257 kg)
Field length: 5,717 ft (1,743 m) with 17° flaps, 5,000 ft (1,525 m), ISA + 30° C, at MTOW
Maximum climb rate: 2,625 ft (800 m) per minute at MTOW
Maximum climb rate, one engine: 675 ft (206 m) per minute at MTOW
Ceiling: 25,000 ft (7,620 m) certified, 33,000 ft (10,060 m) service, at MTOW, ISA
Ceiling, one engine: 17,500 ft (5,335 m)
Range: 481 naut miles (554 miles) 891 km at *8,000 ft (2,440 m)*, 518 naut miles (596 miles) 959 km at *12,000 ft (3,660 m)*, 571 naut miles (657 miles) 1,057 km at *16,000 ft (4,875* m), 705 naut miles (812 miles) 1,305 km at *25,000 ft (7,620* m), all at high cruise power, typical operating weight with 19 passengers, and 45 min reserve

Wing control surfaces: Ailerons (with port trim tab) and 2-section single-slotted Fowler-type flaps. Winglets.
Tail control surfaces: T-tail, with tailets, and stabilons to improve pitch stability and widen CG range (4% to 40% of MAC). Elevators and rudder, all with trim tabs.
Flight control system: Mechanical for primary controls, trimmed by mechanical servo tabs. Flaps are electro-mechanically controlled and automatically protected against asymmetric actuation. Standard electric elevator trim.
Construction materials: Aluminium alloy.
Engines: 2 Pratt & Whitney Canada PT6A-67D turboprops, with Hartzell 4-blade composite propellers.
Engine rating: Each derated to 1,279 shp (953.75 kW).
Fuel system: 2,517 litres usable.
Electrical system: 28 volt DC quadruple bus system supplied by 2 engine-driven generators and a 34 amp-hour ni-cd battery. 2 solid state 250VA SPC-10(P) inverters with failure lights supply 115 volt AC and 26 volt AC power for the avionics and instruments.

Raytheon Beech 1900D Airliner, delivered January 1995

Hydraulic system: 3,000 psi, with dual reservoir and driven by 28 volt DC electric pump.
Braking system: Goodyear multiple disc brakes on main wheels. Optional electro-hydraulic anti-skid.
De-icing system: Electric for propellers, brakes, windshield, pitot/static masts, alternate static sources and stall warning vanes. Pneumatic for wing and tail unit leading-edges. Engine intake protected from ice and FOD by inertial separators.
Oxygen system: Automatic overhead drop-down passenger system, deployed from the cockpit. Crew masks. 2 x 76.5 cu ft (2.17 m^3) bottles supply crew and passengers for 68 minutes at 25,000 ft (7,620 m).
Fire system: Continuous fire detection loop and 1-shot fire extinguisher in each nacelle. Self monitoring system discriminates between true and false warnings.
Radar: Collins WXR-350 colour weather radar standard, with WXR-840 digital radar and TWR-850 turbulence radar optional.
Flight avionics/instrumentation: Collins Pro-Line package. Flight director systems comprising dual EFIS-84 4-tube EFIS, with 4 x 4 ins (10 x 10 cm) colour CRT displays for attitude director instrument (EADI) and horizontal situation instrument (EHSI), and dual ADS-65 air data computers. Communications suite has VHF-22A transceiver with CLT-222 control and antenna. Navigation suite has VIR-32 VOR/LOC/glideslope/marker beacon receiver with CLT-32 control and antenna, ADF-462 with CLT-62 control and antenna, dual DME-42, dual RMI-36s with VOR-1/ADF on single needle and VOR-2/ADF on double needle, dual MCS-65 digital compass systems, and dual TDR-94 transponders. Sundstrand Mk VI GPWS. Provision for Goodrich TCAS 791. Other non-Collins equipment includes standby gyro horizon, cockpit voice recorder, flight data recorder, cabin briefer, and altimeters. Audio system. Optional available avionics include Collins APS-65H autopilot and AlliedSignal Bendix/King KLN-90B GPS.
Aircraft variants:
1900D Airliner is the regional transport. Quick change interior allows conversion from passenger to cargo configuration.
1900D Executive is a business version, the first going to Ashanti Goldfields Company Ltd in April 1995. This has 8 airline seats and 6 club seats, plus galley and toilet.

Quiet Nacelle (USA)

Corporate address: 8000 North-West 56th Street, Miami, FL 33166.
Telephone: +1 305 593 0731
Facsimile: +1 305 592 8265

● Activities

- Includes hushkits for the DC-8 and Boeing 707 (including a Stage 3 hushkit for the USAF OC-135B Open Skies aircraft). New hushkits will include those for the BAC One-Eleven and Fokker F28.

Multi-national

Aero International Regional (France/Italy/UK)

Corporate address: 1 Allee Pierre-Nadot, 31712 Blagnac Cedex, France.
Telephone: +33 61 93 13 01
Founded: 1996.

● Activities

- Avions de Transport Regional (ATR), owned by Alenia of Italy and Aerospatiale of France, is to merge its activities with the British regional aircraft manufacturers Avro International and Jetstream Aircraft (of British Aerospace) in early 1996 under this new consortium name. AIR is jointly and equally owned by Alenia, Aerospatiale and British Aerospace, having its HQ in Toulouse.
- The "Heads of Agreement" was signed in January 1995, the consortium name was announced in June 1995, and the joint venture organization was to be formalized late that same year.
- Production will centre on the ATR 42 and ATR 72, Avro RJ70, RJ85, RJ100 and RJ115, and Jetstream 41. Sales and marketing of all aircraft will be brought together, with actual production sub-contracted to the individual existing manufacturing plants. For this edition of WA&SD, the aircraft remain under their Summer 1995 company names (which see).

Airbus Industrie (France/Spain/Germany/UK)

Corporate address: 1 Rond Point Maurice Bellonte, 31707 Blagnac Cedex, France.
Telephone: +33 61 93 33 33
Facsimile: +33 61 93 37 92
Telex: AIRBU 530526 F
Founded: 1970.
Employees: About 32,000 work directly on Airbus aircraft within the participating companies.
Information : Barbara Kracht (Manager, Press and Information – *telephone* +33 61 93 33 87).

● Activities

- Airbus Industrie is a consortium company owned by Aerospatiale of France (37.9%), Daimler-Benz of Germany through its Daimler-Benz Aerospace Airbus GmbH division (37.9%), British Aerospace (20%) and CASA of Spain (4.2%). They not only own the shares but are industrial participants, conducting most of the design and all manufacture, co-ordinated and managed by Airbus Industrie. Associate members are Fokker of the Netherlands and Belairbus of Belgium.
- Airliner sections produced in the various countries are transported to Aerospatiale in Toulouse (headquarters) for final assembly (A300/310, A320 and A330/A340) or Dailmer-Benz in Hamburg (A319/A321). Sections have been transported by Super Guppy aircraft or by road, but the new SATIC Airbus A300-600ST Super Transporter is taking over (See final entry in this section).

DIVISIONS

Customer Services Directorate

● Activities

Undertakes support services, engineering and technical support, transition and recurrent training (formerly by Aeroformation but since May 1994 as part of CSD's activities – conducted at Toulouse in France and Miami in the USA) and flight operations support, materiel support, and business management.

Airbus Industrie China

● Activities

- Established at Beijing in 1996 as a training centre, with its own simulator and Mandarin-speaking personnel.

Airbus Military Aircraft

●Activities:

- Expected to be established in 1995-96 to take over the FLA military transport programme initiated by Euroflag. In addition to the existing Airbus partners, Alenia of Italy also has an interest in FLA.

Airbus A300B2 and B4 freighter conversions

Role: Freighter conversion of A300 ex-passenger airliners.

Details for A300B2/B4 types as indicated.

Weights:
Maximum zero fuel: 265,657 lb (120,500 kg) *for B2-200,* 273,373 lb (124,000 kg) *for B4-100,* or 295,419-299,828 lb (134,000-136,000 kg) *for B4-200*
Maximum take-off: 313,056 lb (142,000 kg) *for B2-200,* 347,228 lb (157,500 kg) *for B4-100,* or 363,762 lb (165,000 kg) *for B4-200*
Structural payload: 90,169 lb (40,900 kg) *for B2-200,* 93,917 lb (42,600 kg) *for B4-100,* or 93,035-97,444 lb (42,200-44,200 kg) *for B4-200.*

Performance:
Range with maximum payload: 1,000 naut miles (1,151 miles) 1,852 km *for B2-200,* 1,750 naut miles (2,015 miles) 3,240 km *for B4-100,* or 2,050-2,200 naut miles (2,360-2,533 miles) 3,796-4,074 km *for B4-200*
Range with 80,028 lb (36,300 kg) payload: 1,350 naut miles (1,554 miles) 2,500 km *for B2-200,* 2,200 naut miles (2,533 miles) 4,074 km *for B4-100,* 2,650 naut miles (3,051 naut miles) 4,908 km *for B4-200*

Sales: Deliveries of the A300B2/B4 early series airliners took place between 1974 and 1986. Since 1992, conversion kits have been available to permit any A300B2/B4 model to be retrofitted as freighters.
Freight hold capacity: Main deck can accommodate 9 pallets of 88 or 96 ins x 125 ins (2.23 or 2.44 x 3.18 m) plus 3 or 5 pallets of 88 x 125 ins (2.24 x 3.18 m). Lower deck can accommodate 4 pallets plus 8 LD3 containers, or 20 LD3s.

Freighter conversion of an A300B series airliner (courtesy Airbus Industrie)

Conversion kit: Comprises an upper deck cargo door of 141 x 101 ins (3.58 x 2.57 m) with 70° or 145° opening angle, floor reinforcements to increase running loads, Class E fire protection on the main deck including a smoke detection system, safety barrier net and smoke curtain, and systems adaptation/ simplification for weight reduction. Optional packs include a selection of cargo loading system packages (single row or side-by-side, engine transportation pack).
Fuel system: 43,000 litres for B2-200, and 62,000 litres for B4-100/-200.

Airbus A300-600

First flight: 8 July 1983.
Certification: 9 March 1984 with original JT9D engines.

Airbus A300-600R extended-range airliner

First delivery: 26 March 1984 to Saudi .
Role: Medium-long range widebody airliner and freighter.
Airport limits: Flexible runway ACN (Cat B) for A300-600 is 56 with standard undercarriage and 52 with optional wider main bogies. For A300-600R is 59 standard and 55 optional.
Noise levels: A300-600R with GE/P&W engines: 91.1/92.2 EPNdB at take-off, 98.6/97.7 EPNdB sideline, 99.8/101.7 EPNdB approach.
Sales: 474 A300s of all versions ordered by August 1995, of which 443 had been delivered and 428 were operating.
Details: Passenger versions; see Aircraft variants for convertible and freighter details.

Crew: 2 (flight).
Passengers: Typically 266 seats in 2-class layout (26 first at 40 ins/103 cm seat pitch and 240 economy at 32 ins/81 cm pitch), 231 in 3-class (18 sleeper first at 57 ins/ 145 cm pitch, 35 business at 40 ins/103 cm pitch and 178 economy at 32 ins/81 cm pitch), 298 all-economy (at 32 ins/81 cm pitch), and 361 high-density (current certification limit, at 29 ins/73.7 cm or 30 ins/76 cm pitch). 6 abreast first class, 7 abreast executive or business, 8 abreast economy, and 9 abreast high-density, with 2 aisles.
Seat pitch: See above.
Pressurization: 8.3 psi cabin differential.
Freight hold volume: 5,205 cu ft (147.4 m^3).
Freight hold capacity: LD3 containers are carried 2 abreast in the underfloor holds, and full-sized pallet capability is a standard feature of the forward hold. Full range of existing containers and pallets can be loaded. Forward underfloor hold loads can be 12 LD3 containers or 4 pallets (88 or 96 x 125 ins, 2.23 or 2.44 x 3.18 m), and rear hold can be 10 LD3s and 610 cu ft (17.3 m^3) of bulk or optionally 11 LD3s and 318 cu ft (9 m^3) of bulk.
Freight hold access: 106 ins x 67.5 ins (2.69 x 1.71 m) forward cargo door.
Wing characteristics: Wing derived from the previous A300B but with aerodynamic improvements by introducing a new inner wing section and also wingtip fences to reduce cruise drag (1°), while deleting the slat fence and outboard aileron.
Flight controls and system: Mechanically controlled and hydraulically operated ailerons, elevators and rudder. Fly-by-wire for tailplane incidence (with mechanical back-up), flaps and Krueger flaps, 2 position slats, spoilers/speedbrakes and lift-dumpers.
Construction materials: Includes 14,550 lb (6,600 kg) of composites for some primary and secondary structures, including fin (carbonfibre), floor struts and panels, spoilers and main undercarriage doors.
Engines: 2 x 56,000 lbf (249.1 kN) Pratt & Whitney PW4156 or 58,000 lbf (258 kN) PW4158 turbofans. Alternatively 59,000 lbf (262.45 kN) General Electric CF6-80C2A1, 60,200 lbf (267.79 kN) CF6-80C2A3, or 61,500 lbf (273.57 kN) CF6-80C2A5 turbofans. AlliedSignal APU.
Engine rating: See above.
Fuel system: 62,000 litres. A300-600R adds a 6,150 litre tank in the tailplane, with a computerized fuel transfer system for active centre-of-gravity control. Optional 73,000 litres for -600R.

Airbus A300-600F freighter

DETAILS FOR A300-600, *WITH -600R IN ITALICS WHERE DIFFERENT.*

Principal dimensions:
Wing span: 147 ft 1 ins (44.84 m)
Maximum length: 177 ft 5 ins (54.08 m)
Maximum height: 54 ft 2 ins (16.52 m)
Fuselage diameter: 18 ft 6 ins (5.64 m)

Cabin:
Length: 131 ft 11 ins (40.21 m)
Width: 17 ft 4 ins (5.28 m)
Height: 8 ft 4 ins (2.54 m)
Main passenger doors: 6 ft 4 ins x 3 ft 6 ins (1.93 x 1.07 m)

Wings:
Area: 2,798.61 sq ft (260 m^2)
Aspect ratio: 7.733
Sweepback: 28° at 25% chord

Tail unit:
Tailplane span: 53 ft 4 ins (16.26 m)
Tailplane area: 482.2 sq ft (44.8 m^2)

Undercarriage:
Type: Retractable, with twin steerable nosewheels. 4-wheel main bogies of standard 3 ft 1 ins x 4 ft 7 ins (0.927 x 1.397 m) size, but optional wider units with larger low-pressure tyres to reduce runway ACN
Main wheel tyre size: 49 x 17-20 standard, or 49 x 19-20
Nose wheel tyre size: 40 x 14-16
Wheel base: 61 ft (18.6 m)
Wheel track: 31 ft 6 ins (9.6 m)
Turning radius: 114 ft (34.75 m) wingtip

Weights:
Empty, operating: typically 198,636 lb (90,100 kg), *199,077 lb (90,300 kg)*
Maximum zero fuel: 286,600 lb (130,000 kg), *the same standard and 271,168 lb (123,000 kg) optional*
Maximum take-off: 363,762 lb (165,000 kg), *375,888 lb (170,500 kg) standard or 378,533 lb (171,700 kg) optional*
Maximum landing: 304,238 lb (138,000 kg), *308,647 lb (140,000 kg)*

Performance:
Maximum cruise speed: Mach 0.82 at 30,000 ft (9,145 m)
Economical cruise speed: Mach 0.8
Approach speed: 135 kts (155 mph) 250 km/h, *136 kts (157 mph) 252 km/h*
Take-off field length: up to 7,480 ft (2,280 m), *7,515 ft (2,290 m),* but depends on engines fitted
Landing field length: 5,040 ft (1,536 m), *5,100 ft (1,555 m)*
Initial cruise altitude: 35,000 ft (10,670 m) westbound, 33,000 ft (10,060 m) eastbound
Operating ceiling: 40,000 ft (12,200 m)
Range with 266 passengers and GE engines: 3,700 naut miles (4,260 miles) 6,852 km, *4,050 naut miles (4,663 miles) 7,500 km,* with reserves
Range with 266 passengers and P&W engines: 3,650 naut miles (4,203 miles) 6,760 km, *4,050 naut miles (4,663 miles) 7,500 km, with reserves*

Electrical system: AC supply via 2 engine-driven and 1 APU-driven 90 kVA generators, with time-limited overload ratings up to 150 kVA. fourth hydraulically-driven AC generator (5kVA) for ETOPS. 28 volt DC supply from AC system via 3 transformer rectifiers. 3 x 25 amp-hour ni-cd batteries for APU start-up and emergency power.

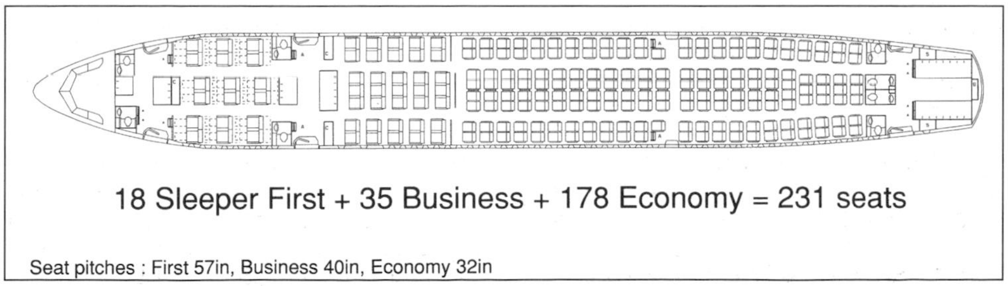

18 Sleeper First + 35 Business + 178 Economy = 231 seats
Seat pitches : First 57in, Business 40in, Economy 32in

Airbus A300-600 in typical 231 seat 3-class arrangement (courtesy of Airbus Industrie)

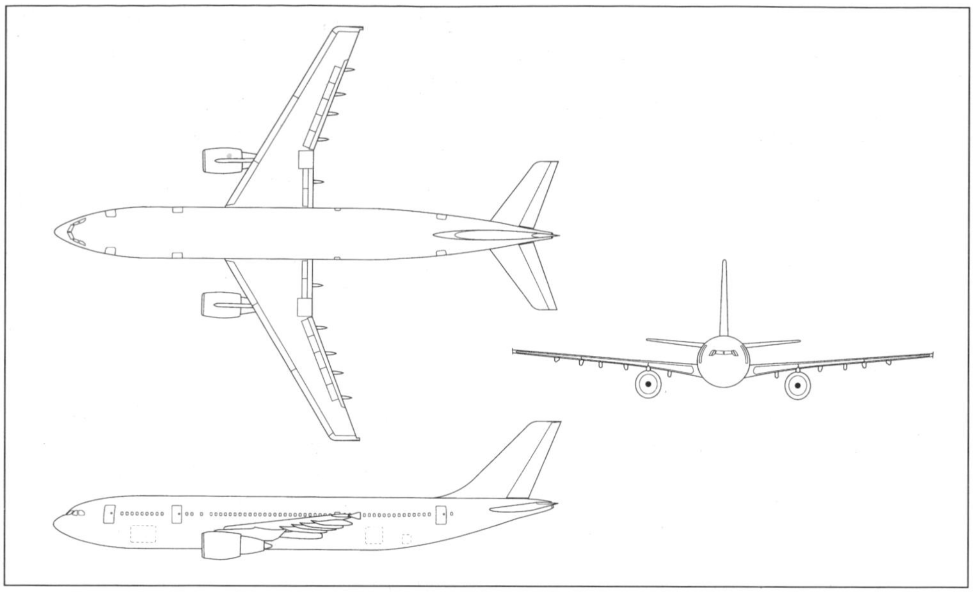

Airbus A300-600 general arrangement (courtesy Airbus Industrie)

Hydraulic system: 3 independent systems, each 3,000 psi. 1 also provides for ETOPS generator (see Electrical).
Braking system: Carbon discs, with anti-skid. Optional automatic system.
De-icing system: Bleed air for wing leading edges and engine intakes. Electric for cockpit glazing, sensors, static vents and pitots.
Fire system: See Aircraft variants.
Radar: Weather radar.
Flight avionics/instrumentation: Fully digital avionics and flight management systems. EFIS with primary flight displays (PFD) and navigation displays (ND) CRTs. Electronic centralized aircraft monitor (ECAM). Cat IIIb autoland. Windshear warning and guidance system. Common type rating with A310.
Aircraft variants:
A300-600 is the basic passenger version, also available in convertible passenger/freight versions.
A300-600R is the extended range model, available in passenger and convertible passenger/freight versions. Active centre-of-gravity control system. 180 minutes ETOPS equipped, with fourth AC generator and extra cargo hold fire suppression bottle.
A300-600C is the convertible passenger or freight version of either the standard A300-600 or -600R. Maximum structural payload is 106,042 lb (48,100 kg) in freighter mode.
A300-600F is the dedicated all-freight version of the A300-600 or -600R. Main deck compartment can be configured to carry a single row of 88/96 x 125 ins pallets or a double row of 88 x 125 ins pallets. Differences from the passenger aircraft are the addition of a large cargo door on the main deck, reinforced main deck floor, deletion of passenger doors numbers 2, 3 and 4 (left and right), deletion of cabin windows except as required for maintenance, deletion of all passenger-associated systems and equipment, addition of a semi-automatic cargo loading system, Class E main deck fire protection and Class C lower deck, and active centre-of-gravity control system on the maximum-range model. Main deck accommodates 9 pallets of 88/96 x 125 ins (2.23/2.44 x 3.18 m) and 6 of 88 x 125 ins (2.23 x 3.18 m). Lower deck accommodates 4 pallets plus 10 LD3 containers or 22 LD3s. Powered by 58,000 to 61,500 lbf (258 to 273.57 kN) CF6-80C2A5 or PW4158 engines. Maximum take-off weights are 375,888 lb (170,500 kg) for the basic maximum range version, and 363,982 lb (165,100 kg) for the optional maximum payload version. Maximum range version range 2,650 naut miles (3,051 miles) 4,908 km, and maximum payload version range 1,950 naut miles (2,245 miles) 3,611 km. Standard fuel 68,150 litres, with 44,400 litres in optional. First example to Federal Express in April 1994.

Airbus A310

First flight: 3 April 1982.
Certification: 11 March 1983.
First delivery: 29 March 1983 to Swissair and Lufthansa, starting commercial services that April.
Role: Short-medium range widebody airliner.
Airport limits: Flexible runway ACN (Cat B) for A310-200 is 43 with standard undercarriage and 41 with optional wider main bogies.
Noise levels: A310-200 with GE engines: 89.6 EPNdB at take-off, 96.4 EPNdB sideline, 98.6 EPNdB approach.
Sales: 259 ordered by August 1995, with 250 delivered and 247 operating. Military users include Canada, France and Germany, the 2 Armée de l'Air A310-300s having replaced DC-8s as VIP and cargo transports in 1994 (ex-Jordanian commercial airliners).
Details: A310 passenger versions.
Crew: 2 (flight).
Passengers: Typically 220 in 2-class layout (20 first class at 40 ins/103 cm seat pitch, and 200 economy at 32 ins/81 cm pitch), 191 in 3-class layout (12 first at 62 ins/157 cm pitch, 32 business at 40 ins/103 cm pitch, and 147 economy at 32 ins/81 cm pitch), 240 in 2-class regional layout (28 business at 36 ins/91 cm pitch, and 212 economy at 30 ins/76 cm or 31 ins/79 cm pitch), and 279 high-density layout (all economy at 29/30 ins, 73.7/76 cm pitch). Emirates A310 was (in 1992) the first airliner to offer every passenger in all classes their own video display and choice of programmes. Same airline pioneered multichannel telephone calls (via satellite) in 1993. 6 abreast first class seating, 7 abreast business, 8 abreast coach/economy, and 9 abreast high-density, all with 2 aisles.
Seat pitch: See above.

DETAILS FOR A310-200, *WITH A310-300 IN ITALICS WHERE DIFFERENT.*

Principal dimensions:
Wing span: 144 ft (43.9 m)
Maximum length: 153 ft 1 ins (46.66 m)
Maximum height: 51 ft 10 ins (15.8 m)

Cabin:
Length: 109 ft (33.24 m)
Width: 17 ft 4 ins (5.28 m)
Main passenger door: 6 ft 4 ins x 3 ft 6 ins (1.93 x 1.07 m)

Wings:
Area: 2,357.29 sq ft (219 m^2)
Aspect ratio: 8.8

Tail unit:
Tailplane span: As for A300-600

Undercarriage:
Type: As for A300-600, but with smaller main wheel tyres standard and both A300-600 tyre sizes as options to reduce runway ACN
Main wheel tyre size: 46 x 16-20
Nose wheel tyre size: As for A300-600
Wheel base: 49 ft 11 ins (15.21 m)
Wheel track: As for A300-600
Turning radius: 108 ft 3 ins (33 m) wingtip

Weights:
Empty, operating: typically 177,692 lb (80,600 kg), *178,133 lb (80,800 kg)*
Maximum zero fuel: 249,122 lb (113,000 kg) standard, 251,326 lb (114,000 kg) optional
Maximum take-off: 313,056 lb (142,000 kg), *330,693 lb standard or 337,307 lb, 346,125 lb, or 361,558 lb options (150,000 kg, 153,000 kg, 157,000 kg, or 164,000 kg)*
Maximum landing: 271,168 (123,000 kg) standard, 273,373 lb (124,000 kg) optional

Performance:
Economical cruise speed: Mach 0.8
Approach speed: 135 kts (155 mph) 250 km/h
Take-off field length: 5,900-6,100 ft (1,800-1,860 m) depending on engines, *7,300-about 9,600 ft (2,225-2,926 m), depending on engines and standard/ optional weights,* sea level and ISA + 15°
Landing distance: under 4,500 ft (1,375 m) at typical landing weight, and just over 5,000 ft (1,525 m) at optional MLW, sea level
Initial cruise altitude: 37,000 ft (11,275 m) eastbound, 35,000 ft (10,670 m) westbound
Range with 220 passengers and GE engines: 3,600 naut miles (4,145 miles) 6,667 km, *4,300-5,150 naut miles (4,951-5,930 miles), 7,963-9,538 km*
Range with 220 passengers and P&W engines: 3,650 naut miles (4,203 miles) 6,760 km, *4,350-5,200 naut miles (5,009-5,988 miles) 8,056-9,630 km*

Pressurization: 8.3 psi cabin differential.

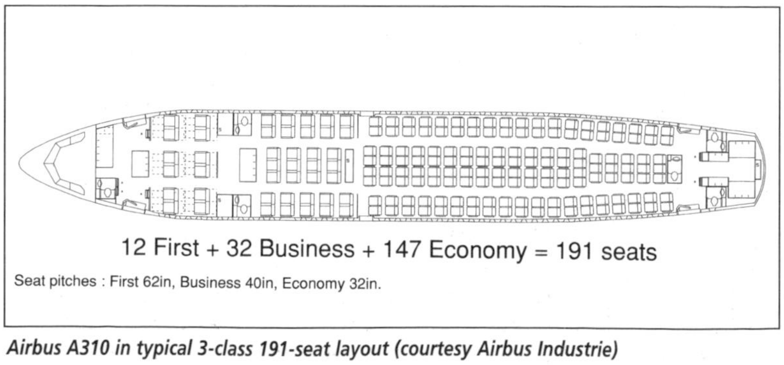

12 First + 32 Business + 147 Economy = 191 seats
Seat pitches : First 62in, Business 40in, Economy 32in.

Airbus A310 in typical 3-class 191-seat layout (courtesy Airbus Industrie)

Freight hold capacity: LD3 containers are carried 2-abreast in the underfloor holds, and full-sized pallet capability is a standard feature of the forward hold. Full range of existing containers and pallets can be loaded. Forward underfloor hold

loads can be 8 LD3 containers, or 4 LD6 containers, or 3 pallets (88 or 96 x 125 ins, 2.23 or 2.44 x 3.18 m). Rear hold loads can be 6 LD3s or 3 LD6s plus 610 cu ft (17.3 m^3) of bulk, or optionally 7 LD3s and 318 cu ft (9 m^3) of bulk.
Freight hold access: 106 ins x 67.5 ins (2.69 x 1.71 m) forward cargo door.
Wing characteristics: Outer wing design is aerodynamically clean, with no vortex generators.
Wing control surfaces: Generally similar to A300-600.
Tail control surfaces: Generally similar to A300-600.
Flight control system: Generally similar to A300-600.
Construction materials: Includes 13,670 lb (6,200 kg) of composites for some primary and secondary structures, including fin (carbonfibre), floor struts and panels, spoilers and main undercarriage doors. A310 was the first commercial airliner to be certified with a composite primary structure (fin). Wing/body, wing/pylon/nacelle, and inner wing areas incorporate an advanced 3-dimensional aerodynamic design.
Engines: 2 x 52,000 lbf (231.3 kN) Pratt & Whitney PW4152 or 56,000 lbf (249.1 kN) PW4156A turbofans. Alternatively 53,500 lbf (238 kN) General Electric CF6-80C2A2, or 59,000 lbf (262.45 kN) CF6-80C2A8 turbofans. AlliedSignal APU. 180 minutes ETOPS.
Fuel system: A310-200 has 54,920 litres usable. A300-300 adds a 6,150 litre tank in the tailplane, with a computerized fuel transfer system for active centre-of-gravity control. In addition, extra fuel volume for -300 can be provided by fitting 1 or 2 x 7,200 litre usable fuel ACTs (additional centre tanks) in the aft main cargo compartment, raising usable fuel to 68,470 or 75,470 litres. ACTs can be fitted/removed overnight, with a removable bulkhead installed behind the tanks, and feed to/from the centre wing tank.
Electrical system: AC supply via 2 engine-driven and 1 APU-driven 90 kVA generators, with time-limited overload ratings up to 180 kVA. fourth hydraulically-driven AC generator (5kVA) for ETOPS. 28 volt DC supply from AC system via 3 transformer rectifiers. 3 x 25 amp-hour ni-cd batteries for APU start-up and emergency power.
Hydraulic system: 3 independent systems, each 3,000 psi. 1 also provides for ETOPS generator (see Electrical).
Braking system: Generally similar to A300-600.
De-icing system: Generally similar to A300-600.
Flight avionics/instrumentation: Same cockpit as the A300-600.
Aircraft variants:
A310-200 is the standard version, with many features of the larger A300.
A310-300 is the extended-range version with 2 further fuel options. Active centre-of-gravity control system. 180 minutes ETOPS equipped, with fourth AC generator and extra cargo hold fire suppression bottle.
A310C is the convertible version of either model, with a large main deck door, for all-passengers or all-freight operations. Maximum structural payload is 91,490 lb (41,500 kg). 3,000 naut mile (3,454 mile) 5,556 km range with a 40 tonne load.
A310F is the dedicated freighter variant. Same range as Convertible.
Freighter Retrofit conversion kit, as detailed under A300B2/B4, is also available for the A310.

Airbus A310-300 in Diamond Sakha livery

Airbus A319

First flight: 25 August 1995.
Certification: Expected before April 1996.
First delivery: April 1996 to Swissair.
Role: Short-medium range, reduced-length and lower-capacity variant of the A320.
Airframe life: Service life before major repair of 48,000 flights of 1.25 hours average, 24,000 flights crack-free fatigue life, and 20,000 flights initial threshold for inspection.
Airport limits: Flexible runway ACN (Cat B) is 34 at standard MTOW and 37 at optional MTOW with standard undercarriage, or 19 and 18 respectively with 4-wheel main bogie undercarriage option.
Noise levels: Estimated for CFM/IAE engines as FAR 36 Stage 3 and ICAO Annex 16 Chapter 3 limits -4.5/-7.9 take-off, -3.2/-5.4 sideline, and -4.4/-4.7 approach.

Airbus Industrie A319, the smallest of the single-aisle Airbus family, during its first flight in August 1995.

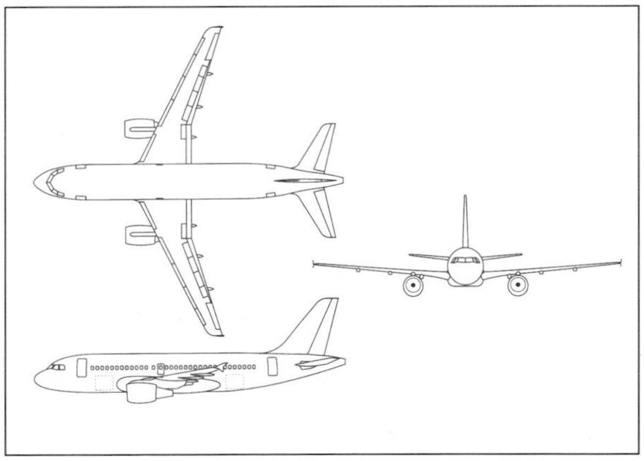
Airbus A319 general arrangement (courtesy Airbus Industrie)

▲ Development

▲ 23 March 1995. Final assembly of the first A319 (CFM56-5B engines) at Daimler-Benz Aerospace's Hamburg plant began. Final assembly of the second A319 started on 21 June.
▲ August 1995. Roll-out of the first A319.
Sales: 81 orders by August 1995. A319 gained more orders in 1994 than any other Airbus airliner.
Details: See A320 entry for other common details.
Passengers: Typically 134 seats in single-class layout (32 ins, 81 cm seat pitch), 124 seats in 2-class layout (8 first at 36 ins, 91 cm pitch and 116 economy at 32 ins, 81 cm pitch), 129 seats in alternative 2-class (55 business at 34 ins, 86 cm pitch and 74 economy at 31ins, 79 cm or 32ins, 81 cm pitch), or 148 seats in high-density layout (29 ins, 74 cm or 30 ins, 76 cm pitch). 4 abreast first class, 5 abreast international business class, and 6-abreast economy, the latter with either 19 ins (48 cm) or alternative 25 ins (64 cm) aisle. All single aisle.
Seat pitch: See above.
Freight hold capacity: 11 ft (3.35 m) long forward hold with a capacity of 301 cu ft (8.52 m^3), and 25 ft 2 ins (7.67 m) long aft hold with a capacity of 675 cu ft (19.12 m^3), giving a total of 976 cu ft (27.64 m^3) or 4 LD3-46 or LD3-46W containers plus bulk.
Loading facilities: Optional widebody-compatible mechanized semi-automatic cargo container system.
Fuselage: 3 frames removed forward of the wings (5 ft 3 ins, 1.6 m) and 4 frames aft of the wings (7ft, 2.13 m) compared with the A320. Modified rear cargo hold door, with deleted bulk hold door. Forward overwing emergency exit deleted.
Engines: 2 x 22,000 lbf (97.86 kN) CFM International CFM56-5A4 turbofans, or similarly rated International Aero Engine V2522s. Optional 23,500 lbf (104.54 kN) CFM56-5A5s, 22,000 lbf (97.86 kN) CFM56-5B5s, 23,500 lbf (104.54 kN) CFM56-5B6s or 23,500 lbf (104.54 kN) V2524-A5s. AlliedSignal 36-300 APU.
Engine rating: See above.
Fuel system: 23,860 litres.
Flight avionics/instrumentation: Almost identical to the A320/A330/A340. Similar pilot type rating for A319, A320 and A321.

DETAILS FOR A319.

Principal dimensions:
Wing span: 111 ft 10 ins (34.1 m)
Maximum length: 111 ft (33.84 m)
Maximum height: 38 ft 7 ins (11.76 m)
Fuselage width: 12 ft 11 ins (3.95 m)

Undercarriage:
Turning radius: 39 ft 8 ins (12.1 m) from centre of turn to nose gear. Nosewheels steering angle 75°, with 70° effective turn. 67 ft 7 ins (20.6 m) minimum pavement width for a 180° turn

Weights:
Empty, operating: typically 88,400 lb (40,100 kg)
Maximum zero fuel: 125,663 lb (57,000 kg)
Maximum take-off: 141,110 lb (64,000 kg) basic, 149,914 lb (68,000 kg) optional
Maximum landing: 134,448 lb (61,000 kg)

Performance:
Take-off field length: approximately 6,400-7,750 ft (1,950-2,360 m), sea level, ISA + 15° C, depending on engines
Landing field length (CFM-56-5 engines): 4,000 ft (1,220 m) at typical landing weight of 120,000 lb (54,430 kg), sea level
Landing field length (V2500 engines): about 3,900 ft (1,190 m), conditions as above.
Landing field length at MLW (CFM56-5 engines): 4,500 ft (1,372 m), at sea level
Landing field length at MLW (V2500 engines): about 4,400 ft (1,342 m), at sea level
Initial cruise altitude: 37,000 ft (11,275 m) eastbound, 35,000 ft (10,670 m) westbound
Range with 124 passengers: 1,900 naut miles (2,188 miles) 3,519 km at basic MTOW, 2,650 naut miles (3,051 miles) 4,908 km at optional MTOW

Airbus A320

First flight: 22 February 1987.
Certification: 26 February 1988.
First delivery: 28 March 1988 to Air France.
Role: Short-medium range airliner.
Airframe life: Service life before major repair of 48,000 flights of 1.25 hours average, 24,000 flights crack-free fatigue life, and 20,000 flights initial threshold for inspection.
Airport limits: Flexible runway ACN (Cat B) is 41 at standard MTOW and 42 at optional MTOW with standard undercarriage, or 22 and 23 respectively with 4-wheel main bogie undercarriage option.
Noise levels: CFM/IAE engines as FAR 36 Stage 3 and ICAO Annex 16 Chapter 3 limits -3.7/-4.9 take-off, -2.5/-4 sideline, and -4.1/-3.9 approach, at basic MTOW. For derated A321 (IAE) type engines at 75,500 kg MTOW the figures are -5.9 take-off, -4.1 sideline and -4.7 approach.
Sales: 665 ordered by August 1995, of which 506 had been delivered and 502 were in operation.
Crew: 2 (flight).
Passengers: Typically 164 seats in single-class layout (32 ins, 81 cm pitch), 150 seats in 2-class layout (12 super first class at 36 ins, 91 cm pitch, and 138 economy at 32 ins, 81 cm pitch), 137 in alternative 2-class layout (30 business at 38 or 39 ins, 97 or 99 cm pitch, and 107 economy at 32 ins, 81 cm pitch), and 180 in high-density layout (29 ins, 74 cm pitch). 4 abreast in super first class seating arrangement, with 57 ins (145 cm) double seats and 27 ins (69 cm) aisle. 5 abreast in business class and 6 abreast in economy, the latter with standard 19 ins (48 cm) aisle or alternative 25 ins (64 cm) aisle. A320 pioneered digital cabin management systems with cabin intercommunication data system (CIDS). The CIDS is responsible for the operation of cabin lighting, pre-recorded messages, emergency evacuation signalling and other tasks. It can also verify the amount of portable water on board and allow cabin staff to preselect the quantity to be uplifted. CIDS is linked to the centralized fault display system.
Seat pitch: See above.
Galleys and toilets: Modular concept for interior fittings, easing reconfiguration.
Freight hold volume: Forward hold of 16 ft 3 ins (4.95 m) length for 469 cu ft (13.28 m^3) volume, and 32 ft 2 ins (9.8 m) length aft hold for 900 cu ft (25.48 m^3), giving a total bulk volume of 1,369 cu ft (38.76 m^3).
Freight hold capacity: 3 LD3-46 or 46W containers in the forward hold and 4 aft, plus 208 cu ft (5.89 m^3) of bulk.
Loading facilities: Optional semi-automatic container system.
Wing characteristics: Introduced a totally new higher aspect ratio wing. Winglets.
Wing control surfaces: Aileron, 2-section Fowler flaps, 5-section leading-edge slats and 5 spoilers per wing. Spoilers are divided as 4 on the swept wing panels and 1 on the inner panel, functioning for auxiliary roll control, wing load alleviation in gusts (with the ailerons), lift dumpers, and speedbrakes.
Tail control surfaces: Trimmable tailplane, elevators and rudder.
Flight control system: Electronic flight control system (EFCS) with fly-by-wire control for all wing and tail surfaces, with hydraulic actuation, except for the rudder which is mechanically operated but connected to the EFCS system via the flight augmentation computer (FAC). Mechanical signalling is also retained as a stand-by mode for the trimmable tailplane. High level of redundancy, with 5 EFCS computers installed, of which 2 are ELAC (elevator and aileron computer) and 3 SEC (spoiler and elevator computer). Spoiler and elevator reversionary mode has been retained as an independent system. The EFCS system is said to offer total flight envelope protection, as the aircraft cannot be stalled or overspeeded, and offers windshear protection. It also prevents structural overstressing, offers better obstacle avoidance capability, and the load alleviation system reduces wing loads in gusts by aileron and spoiler deflection.
Construction materials: Includes improved aluminium alloys and extensive use of composites, the latter for the tail unit, wing control surfaces, wing/body fairings, engine pylons and nacelles, undercarriage doors and fairings, nosecone, and furnishings and floor panels. Weight saving of 1,764 lb (800 kg).
Engines: 2 x 25,000 lbf (111.21 kN) CFM International CFM56-5A1 or International Aero Engines V2500-A1 turbofans standard, with options of 26,500 lbf (117.88 kN) CFM56-5A3s, CFM56-5B4s, V2500-A1bumps or V2527-A5s, with FADEC.
Engine rating: See above.
Fuel system: 23,860 litres.
Electrical system: 115/200 volt, 400 Hz AC supply via 2 engine-driven and 1 APU-driven 90 kVA generators. DC supply via transformer rectifiers.

Details for A320.

Principal dimensions:
Wing span: 111 ft 10 ins (34.1 m)
Maximum length: 123 ft 3 ins (37.57 m)
Maximum height: 38 ft 7 ins (11.76 m)
Fuselage width: 12 ft 11 ins (3.95 m)

Cabin:
Length: 89 ft 10 ins (27.38 m)
Width: 12 ft 1 ins (3.7 m)
Height: 7 ft 3.5 ins (2.22 m)
Main passenger doors: 6 ft 1 ins x 2 ft 8 ins (1.85 x 0.81 m)

Tail unit:
Tailplane span: 40 ft 10 ins (12.45 m)

Undercarriage:
Type: Retractable, with twin steerable nosewheels Standard twin main wheel units but optional 4-wheel bogies to reduce runway ACN
Main wheel tyre size: 45 x 16-R20 standard, but various options available
Nose wheel tyre size: 30 x 8.8-R15, but options available
Wheel base: 41 ft 5.25 ins (12.63 m)
Wheel track: 24 ft 11 ins (7.59 m)

Weights:
Empty, operating: typically 92,153 lb (41,800 kg)
Maximum zero fuel: 134,480 lb (61,000 kg)
Maximum take-off: 162,040 lb (73,500 kg) basic, 166,450 or 169,755 lb (75,500 or 77,000 kg) optional
Maximum landing: 142,200 lb (64,500 kg)

Performance:
Cruise speed: Mach 0.78 to 0.8
Take-off field length: Minimum 6,700 ft (2,337 m) and maximum over 8,000 ft (2,440 m) with 150 passengers, sea level, ISA + 15°, depending on engines fitted
Landing field length: Meets FAR Pt 25 Amendment 42 requirements
Cruise altitude: 37,000 ft (11,275 m) eastbound, with full passenger load on sectors up to 2,500 naut miles
High cruise altitude: 35,000-39,000 ft (10,670-11,890 m), former achievable at all weights
Range (CFM engines): 2,700-2,850 naut miles (3,109-3,282 miles) 5,000-5,278 km, standard to maximum optional take-off weights
Range (IAE engines): 2,750-2,950 naut miles (3,166-3,397 miles) 5,093-5,463 km, standard to maximum optional take-off weights

Airbus A320 in United Airlines livery

Airbus A320 cockpit, with EFIS

Braking system: Carbon wheel brakes.
Flight avionics/instrumentation: ARINC 700 digital suite, incorporating SFENA autopilot. Advanced flight deck with sidestick controllers for the pilots and only 12 front-panel instruments with CRTs that are identical and interchangeable, with automatic display reconfiguration in the event of a CRT failure. Thomson-CSF/VDO EFIS has 6 CRT displays, comprising 2 primary flight displays (PFDs), 2 navigation displays (NDs), and 2 multi-purpose displays for engine/warning (ECAM upper screen) and systems data (lower screen). The multi-purpose displays access the Honeywell flight management system (FMS) and are also used to provide maintenance data in the air and on the ground, upon request. The system is coupled to a printer and can also be coupled to an optional Aircraft Communication Addressing and Reporting System (ACARS) link. Common crew type rating with A319 and A321, and cross-crew qualification with the A330 and A340. Centralized fault display system.

Airbus A321

First flight: 11 March 1993 (as first Airbus assembled in Germany).
Certification: 17 December 1993 (European certification, with IAE V2530 engines). European certification with CFM56-5Bs 17 February 1994.
First delivery: 27 January 1994, to Lufthansa.
Role: Lengthened version of the A320, with major changes relating principally to size and capacity.
Details: A321-100.
Airframe life: As for A320.
Airport limits: Flexible runway (Cat B) ACN 48 at basic weight.
Noise levels: CFM56-5B1/V2500-A5 engines as FAR 36 Stage 3 and ICAO Annex 16 Chapter 3 limits -5.3/-6.8 take-off, -1.7/-2.7 sideline, and -5.5/-5.5 approach.

★ Aims

★ Offers 24% more seats and 40% more hold volume than A320, whilst retaining maximum commonality with the A320/A319. Uprated undercarriage, modified wing trailing edges, local structural reinforcement, repositioned and larger emergency exits, and uprated engines.
Sales: 159 ordered and 29 delivered by August 1995.
Crew: 2 (flight).

Airbus A321 in Alitalia livery

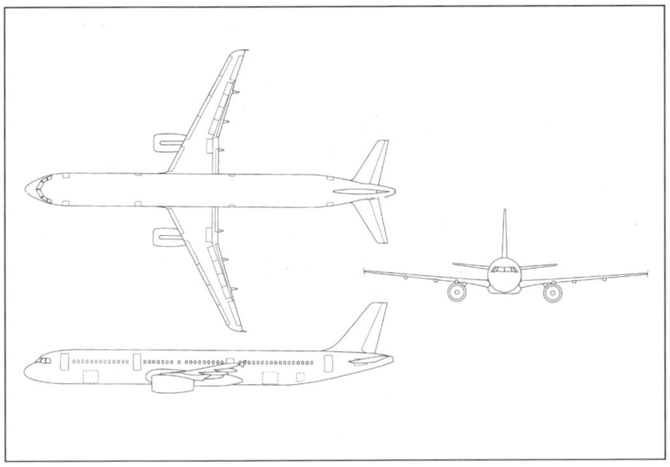

Airbus A321 general arrangement (courtesy Airbus)

Passengers: Typically 199 seats in single-class layout (32 ins, 81 cm pitch), 185 seats in 2-class layout (16 super first class at 36 ins, 91 cm pitch, and 169 economy at 31 or 32 ins, 79 or 81 cm pitch), and 107 economy at 32 ins, 81 cm pitch), and 220 in high-density layout (28 or 29 ins, 71 or 74 cm pitch). 4 abreast in super first class seating arrangement, with 57 ins (145 cm) double seats and 27 ins (69 cm) aisle. 5 abreast in business class and 6 abreast in economy, the latter with standard 19 ins (48 cm) aisle or alternative 25 ins (64 cm) aisle. CIDS as for A320.
Seat pitch: See above.
Freight hold volume: Forward hold of 27 ft 1 ins (8.27 m) length for 806 cu ft (22.82 m^3) volume, and 37 ft 5 ins (11.39 m) length aft hold for 1,022 cu ft (28.94 m^3), giving a total bulk volume of 1,828 cu ft (51.76 m^3).

Freight hold capacity: 5 LD3-46 or 46W containers in the forward hold and 5 aft, plus 208 cu ft (5.89 m^3) of bulk.
Loading facilities: Optional semi-automatic container system.
Flight control system: As for A320.
Fuselage: A320 fuselage lengthened by the addition of 8 frames forward of the wings (14 ft, 4.26 m) and 5 frames aft (8 ft 9 ins, 2.67 m).
Construction materials: As for A320.
Engines: 2 CFM International CFM56-5B1 or International Aero Engines V2530-A5 turbofans, each 30,000 lbf (133.45 kN). Optional 31,000 lbf (137.9 kN) CFM56-5B2s. AlliedSignal or APIC APU.
Engine rating: See above.
Fuel system: 23,700 litres.
Systems: Generally as for A320 but adapted as necessary.
Flight avionics/ instrumentation: As for A320.
Aircraft variants:
A321-100 is the original version, as detailed.
A321-200 is the extended range version, with 33,000 lbf (146.79 kN) International Aero Engines V2533 turbofans and an additional 2,900 litre fuel tank. Launch customer is Aero Lloyd of Germany, which placed firm orders for 4 in 212-seat single-class layout. Maximum take-off weight is 196,200 lb (89,000 kg), maximum landing weight 166,450 lb (75,500 kg), and maximum zero fuel weight 157,630 lb (71,500 kg). Range is extended by about 400-600 naut miles.
A321 is reportedly being considered by IAI as a possible airframe for the Phalcon AEW system.

DETAILS FOR A321-100.

Principal dimensions:
Wing span: 111 ft 10 ins (34.1 m)
Maximum length: 146 ft (44.51 m)
Maximum height: 38 ft 9 ins (11.81 m)
Fuselage width: 12 ft 11 ins (3.95 m)

Cabin:
Length: 112 ft 10 ins (34.39 m)
Width: 12 ft 1 ins (3.7 m)
Height: 7 ft 3.5 ins (2.22 m)
Main passenger doors: 6 ft 1 ins x 2 ft 8 ins (1.85 x 0.81 m)

Undercarriage:
Type: Uprated from A320 type, with larger tyres
Turning radius: 59 ft (18 m) radius from centre of turn to nose gear. Minimum pavement width for a 180° turn 95 ft (29 m)

Weights:
Empty, operating: typically 105,600 lb (47,900 kg)
Maximum zero fuel: 153,220 lb (69,500 kg) basic, 155,425 lb (70,500 kg) optional
Maximum take-off: 182,983 lb (83,000 kg) basic, 187,393 lb (85,000 kg) optional
Maximum landing: 162,039 lb (73,500 kg) basic, 164,244 lb (74,500 kg) optional

Performance:
Cruise speed: Mach 0.78 to 0.8
Take-off field length: typically 4,925-5,580 ft (1,500-1,700 m), sea level, ISA + 15°C, for 500-1,000 naut mile ranges
Landing field length: typically 4,925 ft (1,500 m)
Initial cruise altitude: 37,000 ft (11,275 m) eastbound, 35,000 ft (10,670 m) westbound
Range with 185 passengers (CFM engines): 2,200-2,300 naut miles (2,533-2,648 miles) 4,074-4,259 km, basic-optional MTOW
Range with 185 passengers (IAE engines): 2,250-2,350 naut miles (2,591-2,706 miles) 4,167-4,352 km, basic-optional MTOW
Maximum range: 2,650 naut miles (3,051 miles) 4,908 km

Airbus A330

First flight: 2 November 1992 (CF6 engines).
Certification: 21 October 1993 with GE engines, the first aircraft ever to gain simultaneous European and US certification. 3 June 1994 with PW4000 engines, and 22 December 1994 with Trent 700 engines.
First delivery: 30 December 1993 to Air Inter, starting commercial services in January 1994.
Role: Medium-extended range widebody airliner, with some airlines operating short-haul high-density routes.
Airport limits: A330-300 flexible pavement (Cat B) ACN is 59 at MTOW, and 64 for the higher gross weight version.

★ Aims

★ A330 technologies include advanced aerofoil sections, high-lift devices from root to tip on both leading and trailing edges to ensure optimum low-speed efficiency, centre-of-gravity management system via fuel in the tailplane and a computerized fuel transfer system, extended fly-by-wire/computer system, maximum use of new airframe materials and processes, and increased thrust versions of proven engines.
Sales: 114 ordered by August 1995, with 33 delivered.
Details: A300-300.
Crew: 2 (flight)
Passengers: Typically 335 seats in 2-class layout (30 first class at 40 ins, 103 cm seat pitch and 305 economy at 33 or 34 ins, 84 or 86 cm pitch), 295 seats in 3-class layout (18 sleeperette at 60 ins, 152 cm pitch, 81 business at 36 ins, 91 cm pitch, and 196 economy at 34 ins, 86 cm pitch), and 398 or 440 seats in high-density layouts (31 ins, 79 cm pitch). 6 abreast sleeperette/ international first class, 7 abreast business, 8 abreast economy, and 9 abreast high-density, all with 2 aisles. CIDS system (see A320).
Seat pitch: See above.
Galleys: Alternative galley locations.
Toilets: Many possible cabin positions. Special facilities for handicapped passengers and availability of on-board wheelchairs.
Freight hold capacity: Forward hold accommodates 18 LD3 containers or 6 pallets (each 88 or 96 ins, 2.24 or 2.44 m), and rear hold accommodates 14 LD3s or 5 pallets of 88 ins. Alternative rear hold layouts for 3 larger 96 ins and 2 small 88 ins pallets, or 4 large pallets and 2 LD3s. Optional additional LD3 in the separate 695 cu ft (19.7 m^3) rear bulk hold, reducing bulk volume to 486 cu ft (13.8 m^3).
Loading facilities: Large cargo doors are standard in both forward and aft holds, allowing any mix of pallets and containers in either hold. Can carry any standard unit load device, using standard ground equipment.
Wing characteristics: All-new wing with high levels of efficiency. High-lift devices over the root-to-tip of both leading and trailing edges, with leading-edge slats (typically 21°), flaps (typically 26°) and aileron droop (typically 15°). Winglets.
Wing control surfaces: 2-section outboard ailerons, 2-section single-slotted flaps, 7-section leading-edge slats, and 6 spoiler sections (latter functioning for roll control with the ailerons, and as speed brakes and lift dumpers).
Tail control surfaces: Trimmable tailplane, elevators and rudder.
Flight control system: Electronic flight control system (EFCS) with fly-by-wire control for all wing and tail surfaces, with hydraulic actuation (3 hydraulic systems), except for the rudder which is connected to the EFCS system but has a mechanical link, while stabilizer trimming is also mechanically backed-up. The pilots' sidestick controllers and the autopilot link to 3 flight control primary computers (FCPC), which serve the spoilers, ailerons, elevators, rudder and stabilizer. The sidestick controllers also link to 2 flight control secondary computers (FCSC), which serve the spoilers, rudder (trim/travel limit), and are stand-by for the ailerons and elevators. The EFCS system is said to offer total flight envelope protection, as the aircraft cannot be stalled or overspeeded, and offers windshear protection. It also prevents structural overstressing, and offers better obstacle avoidance capability.
Construction materials and processes: Include aluminium-lithium, and superplastic forming and

DETAILS FOR A330-300, *WITH HIGHER GROSS WEIGHT VERSION IN ITALICS.*

Principal dimensions:
Wing span: 197 ft 10 ins (60.3 m)
Maximum length: 208 ft 11 ins (63.6 m)
Maximum height: 54 ft 11 ins (16.7 m)
Fuselage diameter: 18 ft 6 ins (5.64 m)

Wings:
Area: 3,908.37 sq ft (363.1 m^2)
Aspect ratio: 10.014

Undercarriage:
Type: Retractable, with twin steerable nosewheels and 4-wheel main bogies
Wheel track: 34 ft 5 ins (10.5 m)

Weights:
Empty, operating: typically 261,250 lb (118,500 kg), *266,760 lb (121,000 kg)*
Maximum zero fuel: 361,560 lb (164,000 kg), *379,200 lb (172,000 kg)*
Maximum take-off: 467,380 lb (212,000 kg), *491,630 lb (223,000 kg)*
Maximum landing: 383,600 lb (174,000 kg), *405,650 lb (184,000 kg)*

Performance:
Take-off field length: about 7,350-9,000 ft (2,240-2,745 m) with CF6-80E engines, sea level, ISA + 15°
Landing field length: about 5,365 ft (1,635 m) at MLW, sea level, ISA + 15°
Initial cruise altitude: 37,000 ft (11,275 m) eastbound, 39,000 ft (11,890 m) westbound
Range with 335 passengers (GE or P&W standard engines): 4,750 naut miles (5,470 miles) 8,797 km
Range with 335 passengers and 33,290 lb (15,100 kg) of cargo (GE standard engines): 3,300 naut miles (3,800 miles) 6,110 km
Range with 335 passengers and 32,408 lb (14,700 kg) of cargo (P&W standard engines): 3,300 naut miles (3,800 miles) 6,110 km
Range with 335 passengers (R-R standard engines): 4,650-4,750 naut miles (5,355-5,470 miles) 8,611-8,797 km, depending on current or post-1996 delivered engines
Range with 335 passengers and 33,950 lb (15,400 kg) of cargo (R-R standard engines): 3,250-3,350 naut miles (3,742-3,857 miles) 6,019-6,204 km, depending on current or post-1996 delivered engines

Airbus A330-300 in Cathay Pacific livery

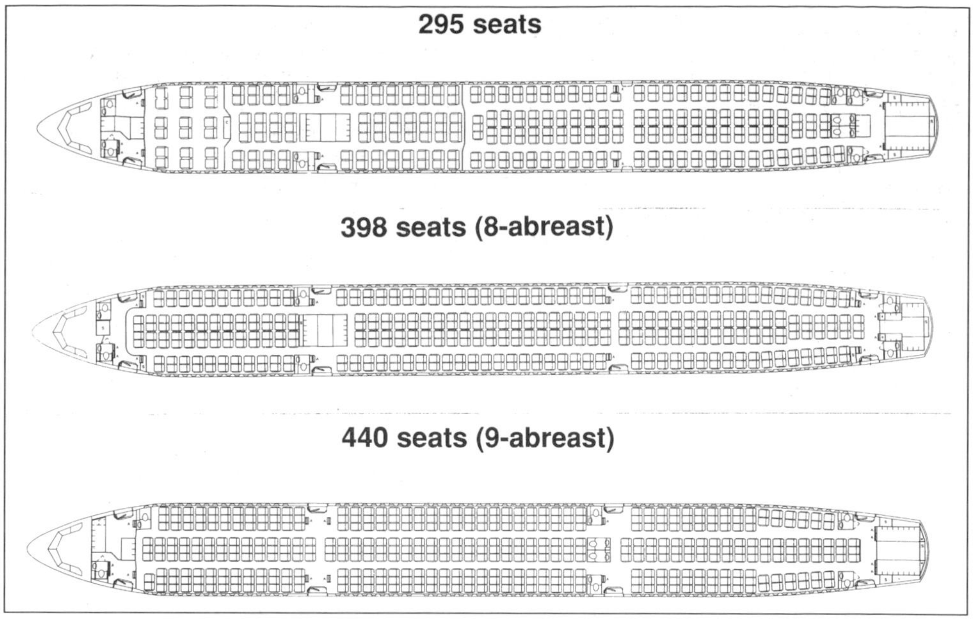

Airbus A330-300 cabin arrangements for 295 passengers in 3 class, 398 in single class, and 440 in high-density single class arrangements (courtesy Airbus)

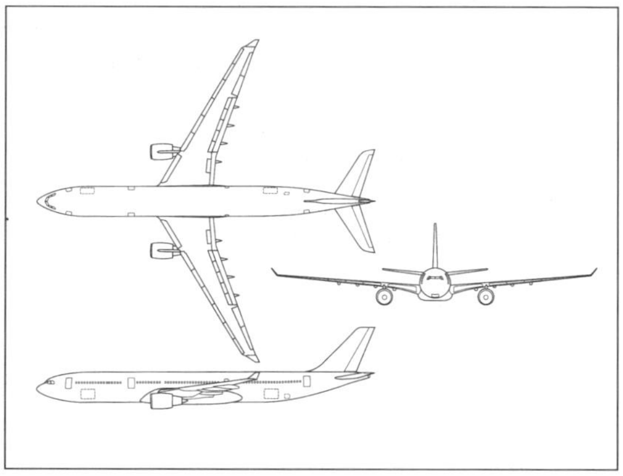

Airbus A330-300 general arrangement (courtesy Airbus)

diffusion bonding techniques for the inspection hatches, tailcone cap, slat mechanism cans and canopy parts. Composites used on the vertical and horizontal tail, moving surfaces, fairings and cabin floor panels.
Engines: 2 x 67,500 lbf (300.26 kN) General Electric CF6-80E1A2, 64,000 lbf (284.7 kN) Pratt & Whitney PW4164, or 67,500 lbf (300.26 kN) Rolls-Royce Trent 768 turbofans are standard on the A330-300. Optional engines for the A330-300 and standard for the higher gross weight version are 72,000 lbf (320.28 kN) CF6-80E1A3s, 68,000 lbf (302.48 kN) PW4168s, and 71,100 lbf (316.27 kN) Trent 772s. 180 minutes ETOPS approval with CF6-80E1 engines, 120 minutes with PW4164/4168s and 90 minutes with Trent 700s by February 1995.
Engine rating: See above.
Fuel system: 93,500 litres. Tailplane trim tank.
Radar: Weather radar.
Flight avionics/instrumentation: Flight deck derived from the A320. Cross-crew qualification with the A320, A321 and A340. Central Maintenance System (CMS) (first used on the A340 and derived from the A320's CFDS) incorporates the central maintenance computer (CMC), which is the interface between the aircraft systems, built-in test equipment (BITE) and the multi-purpose control and display unit (MCDU) located on the centre pedestal. CMC reports on the air conditioning, autopilot, electrical power, fire protection, flight controls, fuel, hydraulics and undercarriage systems among others, with data display, data print-out and real-time reporting to the ground; optional ACARS.
Aircraft variants:
A330-300 is the basic version, as detailed.
Higher gross weight version was previously designated A330-300X. It can carry 335 passengers over a range of 5,500 naut miles, or 335 passengers plus 20.3 to 21 tonnes of cargo over 3,350-3,400 naut miles. Available from 1995/6.
Shortened A330 is being studied, with slightly higher seating capacity than the A300-600 and a range of 6,000 naut miles.

Airbus A340

First flight: 25 October 1991.
Certification: 22 December 1992 (European). May 1993 for FAA.
First delivery: February 1993 to Lufthansa, entering service in March. 1,000th Airbus of all types was an A340-300 for Air France.
Role: Long-range, medium-density airliner.

★ Aims
★ 4-engined A340 and twin-engined A330 were developed simultaneously after joint launch on 5 June 1987, but with the A340 making the first flight.
★ A340-300 and A330 of the same dimensions, but with A340-200 having 8 fewer frames for reduced length. Common flight deck, fuselage, wings except for engine installations, undercarriage, tail unit, and systems except for differences caused by engine interface.
Sales: 147 ordered and 65 delivered by August 1995, with 64 operated. On 17 June 1995 Air Canada took delivery of its first A340-300 as a leased aircraft prior to its own deliveries in 1996-97, becoming the first North American operator of the type.
Crew: 2 (flight).
Passengers: Typically 250 to 350 passengers, depending on version, but with the A340-300 able to accommodate up to 440 in single-class high-density layout (see Aircraft variants). 6 abreast sleeperette/international first class, 7 abreast business, 8 abreast economy, and 9 abreast high-density, all with 2 aisles. CIDS system (see A320).
Wing/tail control surfaces: Similar to A330.
Engines: 4 CFM International CFM56-5C turbofans.
Engine rating: Each 31,200 lbf (138.79 kN) initially.
Fuel system: 138,600 litres.
Flight avionics/instrumentation: As for A330.
Aircraft variants:
A340-200 is the reduced capacity version, with 8 fewer fuselage frames for a length of 194 ft 10 ins (59.39 m). Underfloor cargo holds accommodate a total of 26 LD3 containers or 9 pallets. Optional additional LD3 in the separate 695 cu ft (19.7 m^3) rear bulk hold, reducing bulk volume to 486 cu ft (13.8 m^3). During 16-18 June 1993, A340-200 *World Ranger* is said to have broken all records for long-distance flight by a civil airliner, by flying around the world with 1 stop in New Zealand, in 48 hours 22 minutes.

DETAILS FOR A340-300, WITH *A340-200* *IN ITALICS.*

Principal dimensions: As for A330-300, *see Aircraft variants*

Undercarriage:
Type: As for A330, but with additional twin-wheel bogie under the fuselage, between the main units

Weights:
Empty, operating: 279,700 lb (126,870 kg) basic, *271,168 lb (123,000 kg)*
Maximum zero fuel: 383,600 lb (174,000 kg), *372,580 lb (169,000 kg)*
Maximum take-off: 566,587 lb (257,000 lb), the same
Maximum landing: 410,000 lb (186,000 kg), *399,000 lb (181,000 kg)*

Performance:
Cruise speed: Mach 0.82
Range: 6,600 naut miles (7,600 miles) 12,225 km, 7,350 naut miles (8,463 miles) 13,610 km
Range (in airline service): typical long-ranges are 5,730 and 5,990 naut miles (6,598 and 6,897 miles) 10,610 and 11,090 km, quoted for Gulf Air's Bahrain-New York and Air France's Paris-Buenos Aires routes respectively

A340-300 is the standard length version, corresponding in size to the A330 and with similar underfloor holds.
Higher gross weight version of the A340-300 was previously designated A340-300X. 597,452 lb (271,000 kg) maximum take-off weight. 34,000 lbf (151.24 kN) CFM56-5C4 engines certified in late 1994. Typically to carry 295 passengers over a 7,150 naut mile range. Delivery of the first to Singapore Airlines expected April 1996.
A340-8000 is one of the proposed future growth versions, intended to offer an 8,000 naut mile range with 232 passengers in 3 classes. Possible engines could include the CFMXX turbofan, rated at 40,000-50,000 lbf (177.9-222.4 kN). Could enter service in 1997. Up to 2 ACTs and an increased MTOW of 606,270 lb (275,000 kg).

Airbus A340-300

Airbus A3XX

First delivery: 2003.
Role: Very high capacity, double-deck, long-range airliner.

▲ Development

▲ 1989. Initial studies started for a 500-1,000 seat airliner, with potential fuselage cross-sections including "double bubbles".
▲ 1993. Feasibility studies initiated by Airbus Industrie and a partner for the more conventional A3XX layout.
▲ 26 May 1994. Airbus Industrie's Executive Board decided to continue the A3XX feasibility study until June 1995.
▲ 1998. Intention to proceed expected.
▲ 2003. Entry into service.

Sales: Expected airline requirement for about 1,000 very high capacity airliners by the year 2020.
Passengers: See Aircraft variants for passenger numbers. *Upper deck*: 4 abreast first class, 6 abreast business class, and 7-8 abreast economy class. *Main deck*: 6 abreast first class, 7 abreast business class, and 9-10 abreast economy class. All with 2 aisles.
Freight hold capacity: Underfloor capacity for 30 LD3 containers/10 pallets plus 530 cu ft (15 m^3) of bulk in A3XX-100. 36 LD3/12 pallets plus 530 cu ft (15 m^3) of bulk in A3XX-200.
Engines: 4 Rolls-Royce Trent 700, Pratt & Whitney PW4168 or General Electric CF6-80E1 turbofans.
Aircraft variants:
A3XX-100 to cruise at Mach 0.85 and carry 530-570 passengers over a 7,400 naut mile (8,520 mile) 13,700 km range. High-density layout for 854 passengers. Wing span 253 ft (77.1 m), length overall 228 ft 8 ins (69.7 m), height overall 74 ft 10 ins (22.8 m), and fuselage height 28 ft (8.53 m). Middle deck cabin height 8 ft (2.44 m).
A3XX-100R extended range development, to carry 530-570 passengers over an 8,400 naut mile (9,670 mile) 15,560 km range.
A3XX-200 could carry 630-670 passengers over 7,400 naut miles. High-density layout for 960 passengers. Wing span 253 ft (77.1 m), length 250 ft (76.2 m), and height 74 ft 10 ins (22.8 m).
A3XX-300 is projected to carry some 700 passengers over 7,000 naut miles (8,060 miles)12,960 km.

DETAILS FOR A3XX-100, WITH *A3XX-200* *IN ITALICS.*

Principal dimensions: See Aircraft variants

Weights:
Empty, operating: typically 531,300 lb (241,000 kg), *573,200 lb (260,000 kg)*
Maximum zero fuel: 707,700 lb (321,000 kg), *771,600 lb (350,000 kg)*
Maximum take-off: 1,049,400 lb (476,000 kg), *1,135,380 lb (515,000 kg)*
Performance: See Aircraft variants

Model of the Airbus Industrie A3XX very high capacity double-deck airliner

Airbus/Daimler-Benz Aerospace Cryoplane

First flight: The year 2000?
Role: Airbus airliner converted to fly on ecological liquefied hydrogen fuel, as a first-generation Cryoplane.

▲ Development

▲ Research project by Daimler-Benz Aerospace Airbus GmbH, in co-operation with Tupolev and Samara of Russia and several German companies and organizations.

Fuel system: Liquid hydrogen (at -253°C) has 3 times the energy of kerosene but requires 4 times the tankage volume. Fuel for Cryoplane is therefore stored in special over-cabin tanks, leaving the main cabin free for revenue payload. In the event of an accident or leak, the hydrogen evaporates upwards.

Daimler-Benz Aerospace Airbus Cryoplane

Airbus (Euroflag) Future Large Aircraft (FLA)

First delivery: 2002.
Role: Long-range logistic and tactical transport, tanker/transport and possibly maritime patrol.

▲ Development

▲ 1993. Year-long pre-feasibility study was completed into a European transport to replace the C-160 Transall and C-130 Hercules. Additional associate partners on the project became Flabel (SABCA and Sonaca) of Belgium, OGMA of Portugal and Tucas of Turkey.
▲ October 1993. Following the signing of inter-government agreements, a feasibility study was initiated, completed under auspice of Airbus in 1995.
▲ September 1994. A full-scale mock-up was displayed at Farnborough air show.
▲ 1996. Definition phase began, following establishment of an Airbus military aircraft company to take over from Euroflag srl.
▲ 1998. Full development phase to begin.
▲ 2003. Expected service entry.

Crew: 2 (flight).
Passengers: Can accommodate 126 paratroops, or a detachment of 62 troops plus 8 pallets of equipment or relief supplies. See Freight hold capacity.
Freight hold capacity: Can accommodate all major army vehicles, armoured vehicles, helicopters (2 of Super Puma size), air defence missile units and other loads. Light vehicles can be loaded side-by-side.

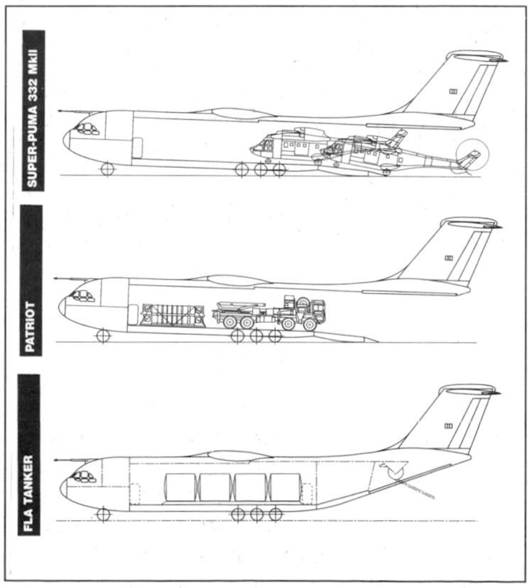

Airbus (Euroflag) FLA with Super Puma, Patriot missile and tanker payloads (courtesy Euroflag)

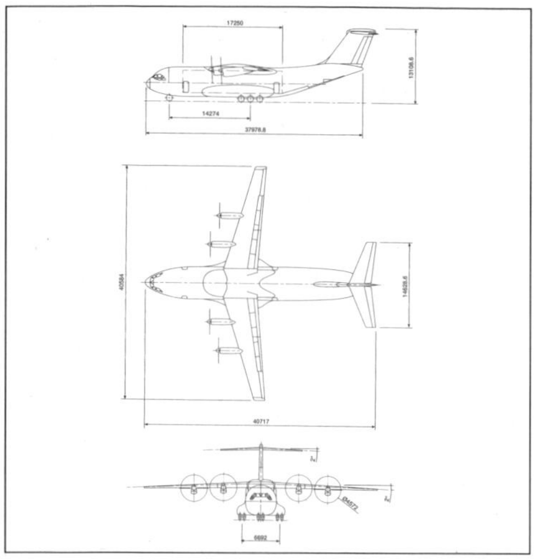

Airbus (Euroflag) FLA transport (courtesy Euroflag)

Airbus (Euroflag) FLA transport

Alternatively, 88 x 108 ins (2.24 x 2.74 m) 463L type pallets or 96 x 125 ins (2.44 x 3.18 m) 3610 type pallets. See also passengers.
Size of freight doors: Rear ramp/door, 15 ft 7 ins (4.74 m) length.
Loading facilities: Autonomous loading and cross loading capability.
Wing control surfaces: Ailerons, 2-section flaps and multi-section spoilers.
Tail control surfaces: T-tail with elevators and a 2-section rudder.
Engines: 4 advanced turboprops in the 8,000-9,000 shp (5,966-6,711 kW) range, possibly derivatives of the SNECMA M88-2 or BMW Rolls-Royce BR715 turbofan cores. However, it is believed SNECMA prefers a 2 turbofan solution, based on the CFM International CFM56, offering 42,900 lbf (191 kN).
Flight refuelling: Over-cockpit central probe.
Flight avionics/instrumentation: Advanced flight deck with integrated avionics. EFIS.
Aircraft variants:
FLA transport, as detailed. Capable of operations from unprepared runways, low and high altitude air-dropping of cargo or paratroops, casualty evacuation, flying hospital, and more.
FLA convertible tanker/ transport could offer 2-point refuelling.
FLA tanker could offer 3-point refuelling, 3 hour loiter at 450 naut miles, and transfer 81,570 lb (37,000 kg) of fuel. Fuel capacity 98,251 litres in 8 t 6 ins x 8 ft 10 ins (2.6 x 2.7 m) fuselage tanks.
FLA maritime patrol variant could offer 11 hours 30 minutes patrol time at 1,000 naut miles.

Details for FLA.

Principal dimensions:
Wing span: 133 ft 1.8 ins (40.584 m)
Maximum length: 133 ft 7 ins (40.717 m), fuselage length 124 ft 7.2 ins (37.9788 m)
Maximum height: 43 ft 1 ins (13.1086 m)
Fuselage diameter: 17 ft 10 ins (5.424 m)

Cabin:
Length: 56 ft 7 ins (17.25 m) from aft of the cockpit to the ramp/door, plus 15 ft 7 ins (4.74 m) on the ramp
Width: 13 ft 1.5 ins (4 m)
Height: 12 ft 7.5 ins (3.85 m)
Volume: 12,078 cu ft (342 m^3)

Wings:
Anhedral: 2°

Tail unit:
Tailplane span: 48 ft (14.6286 m)

Undercarriage:
Type: Retractable, with twin nosewheels and 6-wheel main units
Wheel base: 46 ft 10 ins (14.274 m)
Wheel track: 21 ft 11.5 ins (6.692 m)

Weights:
Payload: 66,186 lb (30,000 kg)

Performance:
Maximum speed: above Mach 0.7
Take-off distance: can operate from unprepared runways of over 3,500 ft (1,067 m)
Range: over 3,000 naut miles (3,455 miles) 5,556 km, with nominal payload
Ferry range: over 4,000 naut miles (4,606 miles) 7,408 km

Aircraft Technology Industries (Airtech) (Indonesia/Spain)

Corporate address: See CASA of Spain in the Combat section and IPTN of Indonesia in this section for company details.

Airtech CN 235

First flight: 11 November 1983.
Certification: 20 June 1986. Certified under FAA Pt 25 and Pt 36, and ICAO Annex 16, and designed to meet JAR requirements.

Airtech CN 235 M built by CASA in Spain

First delivery: 15 December 1986.
Role: Regional transport.
Airframe life: 50,000-60,000 cycles economical repair life.
Noise levels: FAR Pt 36: 84 EPNdB take-off, 86 EPNdB sideline, and 87 EPNdB approach.
Sales: Over 200 delivered by mid 1995 of all versions, including 2 recent CN 235 MPA Persuader maritime patrol aircraft to the Irish Air Corps.
Details: Current production CN 235, with CN 235 M under Aircraft variants.
Crew: 2 (flight).
Passengers: 44 maximum. Environmental control system. Integral stairs.
Seat pitch: 30 ins (76 cm) with 44 passengers, or 33 ins (84 cm) with 40 passengers.
Galley and toilet: See drawing.
Pressurization: 3.63 psi cabin differential.
Freight hold capacity: 4 LD3 containers, plus optional ramp container, or 2 pallets of 88 ins x 125 ins (2.24 x 3.18 m).
Size of freight doors: Rear lower ramp/door, 10 ft x 7 ft 8.5 ins (3.04 x 2.35 m). Upper section door 7 ft 9 ins x 7 ft 8.5 ins (2.36 x 2.35 m).
Wing control surfaces: Ailerons (with servo and trim tabs) and single-slotted flaps.
Tail control surfaces: Elevators (trim tab in port, servo and trim tab in starboard) and rudder (servo and trim tabs).
Flight control system: Mechanical, except for hydraulic flaps and electric trim tabs.
Construction materials: Includes wide use of composites (glassfibre, carbonfibre and Kevlar).
Engines: 2 General Electric CT7-9C turboprops, with Hamilton Standard 14RF-21 4-blade propellers. Optional propeller brake. APU.
Engine rating: Each 1,750 shp (1,305 kW) normal take-off power.
Fuel system: 5,264 litres.
Electrical system: Primary DC supply, using 2 engine-driven generators. AC power via inverters to supply circuits with constant-frequency requirements. In the event of failure in the DC generators, power can be obtained from the variable frequency AC systems through transformer rectifiers. 2 x 24 volt, 37 amp-hour ni-cd batteries for engine starting and emergency use.
Hydraulic system: 3,000 psi, with 2 parallel axial pumps, with either pump able to maintain system pressure in the event of a pump failure.
Braking system: Hydraulic disc with anti-skid system Optional nosewheel anti-spin brake.
De-icing system: Optional ice detection system.
Radar: Collins WXR-350.

DETAILS FOR CN 235, *WITH CN 235 M IN ITALICS WHERE DIFFERENT.*

Principal dimensions:
Wing span: 84 ft 8 ins (25.81 m)
Maximum length: 70 ft 2.5 ins (21.4 m)
Maximum height: 26 ft 9.8 ins (8.17 m)

Cabin:
Length: 32 ft 9 ins (9.98 m)
Width: 8 ft 10.3 ins (2.7 m), 7 ft 9.1 ins (2.36 m) at floor
Height: 6 ft 2 ins (1.88 m) at aisle
Volume: 1,578 cu ft (44.68 m^3)
Main passenger doors: 2 ft 3.6 ins x 5 ft 7 ins (0.7 x 1.7 m), and 1 ft 11.6 ins x 4 ft 2 ins (0.6 x 1.27 m)

Wings:
Aerofoil section: NACA 65_3-218
Area: 636.15 sq ft (59.1 m^2)
Aspect ratio: 11.272
Dihedral: 3°

Tail unit:
Tailplane span: 34 ft 9 ins (10.6 m)
Tailplane area: 273.4 sq ft (25.4 m^2)

Undercarriage:
Type: Retractable, with single steerable nosewheel and tandem twin mainwheel units. Optional low-pressure tyres
Main wheel tyre size: 28 x 9.0-12
Nose wheel tyre size: 24 x 7.7
Wheel base: 22 ft 8 ins (6.919 m)
Wheel track: 12 ft 9.5 ins (3.9 m)
Turning radius: 62 ft 3 ins (18.98 m) wingtip

Weights:
Empty, operating: 21,605 lb (9,800 kg) in passenger configuration
Maximum zero fuel: 31,085 lb (14,100 kg), *32,628 lb (14,800 kg)*
Maximum ramp: 34,943 lb (15,850 kg)
Maximum take-off: 34,833 lb (15,800 kg), *36,376 lb (16,500 kg)*
Maximum landing: 34,392 lb (15,600 kg), *36,376 lb (16,500 kg)*
Payload: 11,067 lb (5,020 lb) cargo version, 9,480 lb (4,300 kg) passenger version, *13,228 lb (6,000 kg)*

Performance:
Maximum cruise speed: 244 kts (281 mph) 452 km/h, at 15,000 ft (4,570 m), ISA, *240 kts (276 mph) 445 km/h, 95% MTOW*
Stall speed: 100 kts (115 mph) 185 km/h clean, 84 kts (97 mph) 156 km/h with flaps, IAS
Take-off balanced field length: 4,180 ft (1,274 m), ISA, sea level, MTOW
Take-off ground roll: *1,680 ft (512 m), MTOW, sea level, ISA*
Take-off over a 50 ft (15 m) obstacle: 2,657 ft (810 m), MTOW, sea level, ISA
Landing distance: 2,198 ft (670 m), ISA, sea level, MLW
Landing distance over a 50 ft (15 m) obstacle: *2,025 ft (617 m), MLW, sea level, ISA*
Maximum climb rate: 1,525 ft (465 m) per minute
Ceiling: 25,000 ft (7,620 m) service, *27,000 ft (8,230 m) service, 95% MTOW*
Ceiling, OEI: 14,750 ft (4,500 m)
Range with 44 passengers: 957 naut miles (1,102 miles) 1,772 km at maximum cruise speed, 1,079 naut miles (1,242 miles) 1,998 km at long-range cruise speed, with reserves
Range with 22 passengers: 1,974 naut miles (2,273 miles) 3,656 km at maximum cruise speed, 2,291 naut miles (2,638 miles) 4,243 km at long-range cruise speed
Range with maximum cargo: 843 naut miles (971 miles) 1,561 km
Range with 5,635 lb (2,556 kg) cargo: 2,474 naut miles (2,848 miles) 4,582 km
Range with 7,826 lb (3,550 kg) payload: *2,400 naut miles (2,763 miles) 4,445 km*

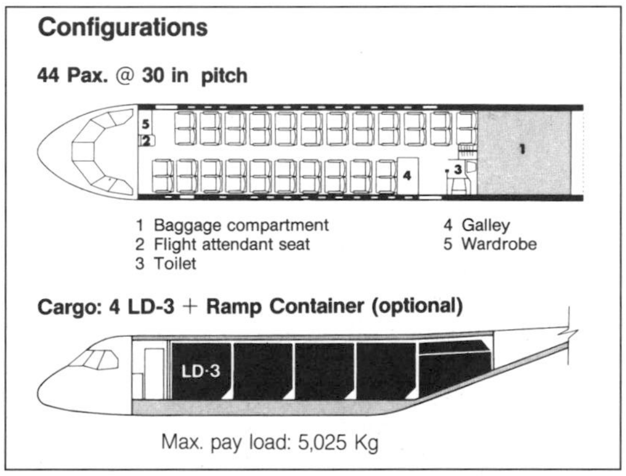

Airtech CN 235 seating and cargo arrangements (courtesy CASA)

Flight avionics/instrumentation: Avtech DADS and PACIS; Collins EFIS-85 electronic flight instruments, VHF-22B, dual TDR-90 ATC transponder, dual VIR-32 VOR/ILS/marker beacon, dual ADF-60A, dual DME-42, ALT-55B radio altimeter, APS-65 FD & AP; Motorola N-1335B SEL-CAL; Dorne & Margolin DM ELT 8.1 ELT; Fairchild A-100 A CVR and F-800 FDR; and Sundstrand Mk II GPWS. Optional Collins HF and Omega with GPS.

Aircraft variants:
CN 235 commercial version, available in passenger, cargo, and quick-change (QC) passenger/cargo variant with a reconfiguration time by 2 groundcrew of under 30 minutes using a low-weight roller system over which the passenger configuration can be installed (baggage container, modular galley and seat platforms). QC has a range of 1,075 and 2,340 naut miles (1,238 and 2, 694 miles) 1,990 and 4,333 km, with 40 and 17 passengers respectively at long-range cruise speed, or 843 and 2,474 naut miles (970 and 2,848 miles) 1,561 and 4,581 km, with a 10,648 lb (4,830 kg) and 5,216 lb (2,366 kg) payload respectively at long-range cruise speed.
CN 235 M is the military version. Airdrop capability in HAD or LAPES missions. 48 troops/paratroops with 2 jump doors. Medevac version for 21 stretchers and 4 seated attendants. 2 pallets of 88 x 108 ins (2.24 x 2.74 m) or 6 pallets of 88 x 54 ins (2.24 x 1.37 m), or vehicles, etc. Payload 13,228 lb (6,000 kg).
CN 235 MP and MPA are maritime patrol versions. See Combat section.

Avions de Transport Regional (ATR) (France/Italy)

Corporate address: 1, Allee Pierre-Nadot, 31712 Blagnac Cedex, France.
Telephone: +33 61 93 13 16
Facsimile: +33 61 93 13 18
Telex: 533 984 F/ATR
Founded: 1982.
Information: Marie-Noëlle Cabanie (Corporate Image and Video).

● Activities

● Founded by Aerospatiale of France and Alenia of Italy. ATR is merging into the new Aero International Regional consortium (which see for details), but the ATR range is detailed here until agreements have been finalized.

ATR 42

First flight: 16 August 1984.
Certification: 24 September 1985 (JAR Pt 25), 25 October 1985 (FAR Pt 25).
First delivery: October 1989.
Role: Regional airliner, or cargo transport. Can be adapted for nav aid calibration, VIP transport and other uses.
Noise levels: 82.8 EPNdB take-off, 83.7 EPNdB sideline, 96.7 EPNdB approach.
Sales: 289 ordered by September 1994.
Details: ATR 42-300/320.
Crew: 2 (flight).
Passengers: Basic version for 48 seats (30 ins, 76 cm pitch). Alternative 42 seats (33 ins, 84 cm pitch), 46 seats (30 ins, 76 cm pitch), and 50 seats (30 ins, 76 cm pitch). With the latter configuration, the forward cargo areas are reduced.
Seat pitch: See above.
Galley: At the rear of the cabin.
Toilets: At the rear of the cabin.
Pressurization: 5.95 psi cabin differential.
Freight hold volume: All seating arrangements allow for 169.5 cu ft (4.8 m^3) of cargo area aft of the cabin. 2 forward cargo areas each provide 106 cu ft (3 m^3) of space, except in 50-seat arrangement when each forward area is reduced to 63.57 cu ft (1.8 m^3).
Freight hold capacity: Simple operational system can be installed to convert the aircraft into a 9-container transport, with an 8,818 lb (4,000 kg) payload.
Wing control surfaces: Aileron (with trim tab), 2 double-slotted flaps and a spoiler per wing, the latter assisting the aileron.
Tail control surfaces: Elevators and rudder, with trim tabs.
Flight control system: Mechanical, except for hydraulic flaps and spoilers, and electric tabs.
Construction materials: Aluminium alloy, but with substantial use of composites (see diagram for the ATR 72, to which ATR 42 is similar except for the degree of carbonfibre in the wings).
Engines: 2 Pratt & Whitney Canada PW120 for the ATR 42-300, PW121 or PW121A turboprops for the ATR 42-320, with Hamilton Standard 12 SF 4-blade propellers.
Engine rating: Each 2,000 shp (1,491 kW), 2,100 shp (1,566 kW) or 2,200 shp (1,640 kW) respectively.
Fuel system: 9,920 lb (4,500 kg).
Electrical system: Principal 28 volt DC supply, via 2 engine-driven starter-generators. 2 ni-cd batteries, of 15 amp-hour and 43 amp-hour. 115/26 volt single-phase AC supply via 2 static inverters. 115/200 volt 3-phase AC supply via 20 kVA engine-driven alternators.
Hydraulic system: 2 independent systems, each 3,000 psi.
Braking system: Hydraulic discs, with anti-skid system.
De-icing system: Pneumatic boots for outer wing and tailplane leading edges, and engine intakes.

DETAILS FOR ATR 42-300, *WITH THE -320 IN ITALICS WHERE DIFFERENT.*

Principal dimensions:
Wing span: 80 ft 7 ins (24.57 m)
Maximum length: 74 ft 4.5 ins (22.67 m)
Maximum height: 24 ft 11 ins (7.59 m)

Cabin:
Length: 48 ft 1 ins (14.66 m)
Width: 8 ft 5.2 ins (2.57 m), 7 ft 5 ins (2.263 m) at floor
Height: 6 ft 3.2 ins (1.91 m)
Volume: 2,048.3 cu ft (58 m^3)
Main passenger door: 5 ft 9 ins x 2 ft 5.5 ins (1.75 x 0.75 m)

Wings:
Area: 586.63 sq ft (54.5 m^2)
Aspect ratio: 11.077
Incidence: 2° at root
Dihedral: 2.5° on outer wing panels

Undercarriage:
Type: Retractable, with steerable nosewheels. Twin wheels on each unit
Main wheel tyre size: 32 x 8.8-10
Wheel base: 28 ft 10 ins (8.78 m)
Wheel track: 13 ft 5.5 ins (4.1 m)
Turning radius: 56 ft 1 ins (17.08 m) minimum

Weights:
Empty, operating: 22,675 lb (10,285 kg), *22,685 lb (10,290 kg)*
Maximum zero fuel: 33,510 lb (15,200 kg)
Maximum take-off: 36,817 lb (16,700 kg)
Maximum landing: 36,155 lb (16,400 kg)
Payload: 10,835 lb (4,915 kg), *10,825 lb (4,910 kg)*

Performance:
Cruise speed: 265 kts (304 mph) 490 km/h, *269 kts (309 mph) 497 km/h*
Stall speed: 104 kts (120 mph) 193 km/h clean, 81 kts (93 mph) 150 km/h with 30° flaps
Balanced take-off field length: 3,576 ft (1,090 m), *3,412 ft (1,040 m)*, sea level, ISA
Balanced take-off field length: 4,265 ft (1,300 m), *4,052 ft (1,235 m)*, 3,000 ft (915 m) altitude, ISA + 10°
Landing field length: 3,380 ft (1,030 m)
Maximum operational cruise ceiling: 25,000 ft (7,600 m)
Range with 48 passengers: 920 naut miles (1,059 miles) 1,704 km

ATR 42 in British Airways Express livery

Fin and wing inner sections can have similar system. Larger boots fitted to US operating aircraft by June 1995, under FAA instruction, certified on 20 March 1995. Electric for cockpit glazing, pitots, propeller blades, and aileron/fin/elevator horn balances.

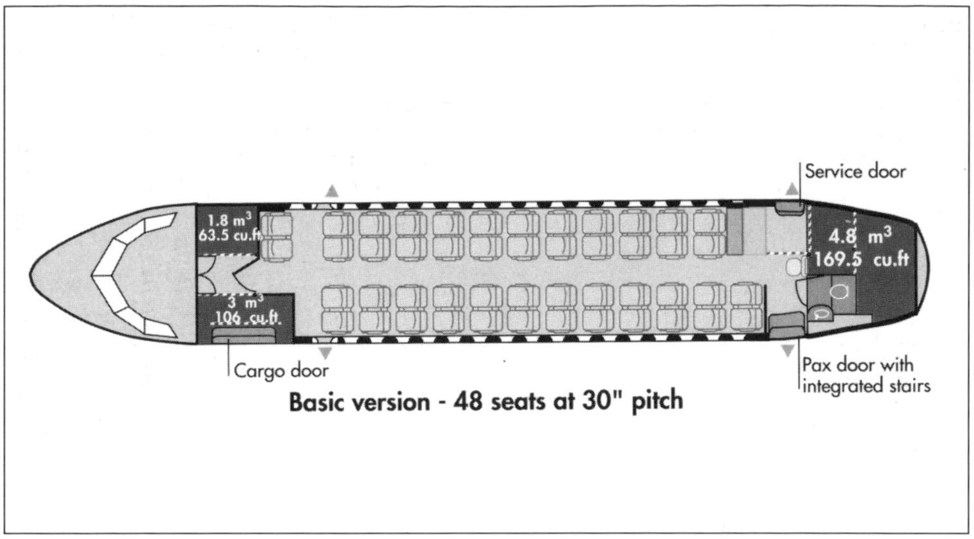

ATR 42 in 48-seat configuration (courtesy ATR)

Radar: Weather radar.
Flight avionics/instrumentation: Fully digital avionics suite, organized around the bi-directional ASCB bus. AlliedSignal Bendix/King Gold Crown III, but Collins Pro Line II is optional. 2 AZ 800 air data computers, 2 AH 600 AHRS systems, DFZ 600 automatic flight control system for Cat I approaches or as an option for Cat II approaches, and EDZ 820 EFIS with 4 CRTs and 2 symbol generator units (each SGU drives 2 CRTs). AlliedSignal Bendix/King KLN 90A GPS available, coupled to the EFIS and autopilot.
Aircraft variants:
ATR 42-300 uses PW120 engines. See Freight hold capacity for quick-change capabilities.
ATR-42-320 uses PW121 engines. Slight differences to operating empty weight and payload.
ATR-42-500, see next entry.

ATR 42-500

First flight: 16 September 1994.
Certification: 1995.
First delivery: June 1995 to Aeromar.
Role: Regional/commuter transport.

★ Aims
★ New version of ATR 42, offering increased performance and levels of comfort, with reduced operating costs. Benefits from improvements already incorporated into the ATR 72-210, but also integrates new developments.
Can operate with full payload from hot-or-high runways.
Crew: 2 (flight).
Passengers: New cabin, with all elements redesigned, reshaped and redecorated. Overall carry-on baggage capacity in 48-passenger configuration is 79.46 cu ft (2.25 m^3). New sound-proofing materials. Optional active noise control system.
Engines: 2 Pratt & Whitney Canada PW127E turboprops, with Hamilton Standard 568 F 6-blade propellers featuring a new electronic regulation system for improved blade synchronization.
Engine rating: Each 2,400 shp (1,790 shp).
Fuel system: 9,921 lb (4,500 kg)

DETAILS FOR ATR-42-500.

Weights:
Empty, operating: 24,800 lb (11,250 kg)
Maximum zero fuel: 36,817 lb (16,700 kg)
Maximum take-off: 41,005 lb (18,600 kg)
Maximum landing: 40,344 lb (18,300 kg)
Payload: 12,015 lb (5,450 kg)

Performance:
Cruise speed: 305 kts (351 mph) 565 km/h, at 17,000 ft (5,180 m)
Take-off field length: 3,710 ft (1,130 m) at sea level, ISA, MTOW; or 3,150 ft (960 m) at sea level, take-off weight for 300 naut miles with 48 passengers; or 4,626 ft (1,410 m) at 3,000 ft (915 m) altitude, ISA + 20° C
Landing field length: 3,510 ft (1,070 m) at sea level, MLW; or 3,183 ft (970 m) at sea level, ISA, at landing weight for a 300 naut mile stage length
Time to 17,000 ft (5,180 m): 9.2 minutes
Range with full payload: 1,010 naut miles (1,163 miles) 1,870 km

ATR 42-500 new cabin design (courtesy ATR)

ATR 52C

First flight: Not yet flown.
Role: Multi-purpose transport, suited to civil and military operations. Uses include cargo and vehicle carrying, troop or passenger transport, paratroop and load airdropping, and medevac.

★ Aims
★ Special configuration for its multi-purpose role, particularly a rear-loading ramp.
Passengers: 41 paratrops plus 2 jumpmasters, 54 passengers at 30 ins (76 cm) seat pitch, or 27 stretchers plus 2 attendants. See Freight capacity.

Details for ATR 52C.

Principal dimensions:
Maximum length: 80 ft 3 ins (24.46 m)
Maximum height: 27 ft 6 ins (8.37 m)

Cabin:
Length: 45 ft 10 ins (13.98 m)
Height: 6 ft 1 ins (1.85 m)
Main passenger doors: 5 ft 11 ins x 2 ft 11.4 ins (1.8 x 0.9 m)

Tail unit:
Tailplane span: 24 ft (7.31 m)

Undercarriage:
Wheel base: 31 ft 7.5 ins (9.64 m)

Weights:
Empty, operating: 26,100 lb (11,839 kg)
Maximum zero fuel: 44,092 lb (20,000 kg)
Maximum take-off: 48,500 lb (22,000 kg), or 43,100 lb (19,550 kg) for tactical operations
Maximum landing: 47,070 lb (21,350 kg), or 42,770 lb (19,400 kg) for tactical operations
Payload: 17,110 lb (7,761 kg)

Performance:
FAR 25 balanced take-off field length: 4,530 ft (1,380 m), sea level, ISA, MTOW
Tactical take-off ground run: 1,690 ft (515 m)
FAR landing field length: 3,740 ft (1,140 m) at sea level, ISA, MLW
Tactical landing ground run: 1,150 ft (350 m)

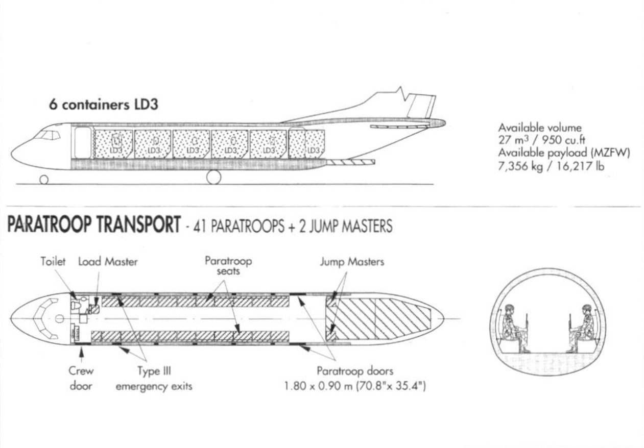

ATR 52C in cargo and paratroop configurations (courtesy ATR)

Freight capacity: In cargo configuration, can carry 6 LD3 containers, 4 pallets of 88 x 108 ins (2.24 x 2.74 m) size, or other loads. Available volume with containers is 953 cu ft (27 m^3), and with pallets 1,271 cu ft (36 m^3).
Freight hold access: Rear ramp cargo door.
Engines: 2 Pratt & Whitney Canada PW127 turboprops, with Hamilton Standard 247 F propellers.
Engine rating: Each 2,750 shp (2,051 kW).
Fuel system: 11,023 lb (5,000 kg).
Mission equipment: Allowance of 882 lb (400 kg).

ATR 72

First flight: 27 October 1988.
Certification: 25 September 1989.
First delivery: 27 October 1989.
Role: Regional airliner.

★ Aims
★ Larger development of the ATR 42, incorporating additional composites (more carbonfibre in the wings).

Details for ATR 72-200, *with ATR 72-210 in italics where different.*

Principal dimensions:
Wing span: 88 ft 9 ins (27.05 m)
Maximum length: 89 ft 1.5 ins (27.17 m)
Maximum height: 25 ft 1 ins (7.65 m)

Cabin:
Length: 63 ft (19.21 m)
Width: 8 ft 5.2 ins (2.57 m), 7 ft 5 ins (2.263 m) at floor
Height: 6 ft 3.2 ins (1.91 m)
Volume: 2,683.9 cu ft (76 m^3)

Wings:
Area: 656.6 sq ft (61 m^2)
Aspect ratio: 12

Undercarriage:
Wheel base: 35 ft 5 ins (10.8 m)
Wheel track: 13 ft 5.5 ins (4.1 m)
Turning radius: 64 ft 10 ins (19.76 m)

Weights:
Empty, operating: 27,337 lb (12,400 kg), *27,447 lb (12,450 kg)*
Maximum zero fuel: 43,430 lb (19,700 kg)
Maximum take-off: 47,400 lb (21,500 kg)
Maximum landing: 47,070 lb (21,350 kg)
Payload: 16,093 lb (7,300 lb), *15,983 lb (7,250 kg)*

Performance:
Maximum cruise speed: 279 kts (321 mph) 516 km/h, *280 kts (322 mph) 518 km/h*
Balanced take-off field length: 4,626 ft (1,410 m), *3,953 ft (1,205 m),* sea level, ISA
Balanced take-off field length (3,000 ft, 915 m altitude): 5,735 ft (1,748 m) at 46,517 lb (21,100 kg) take-off weight, *4,845 ft (1,477 m) at MTOW,* ISA + 10°C.
Landing field length required at destination: 3,963 ft (1,208 m), *3,451 ft (1,052 m),* sea level, ISA
Maximum operational cruise altitude: 25,000 ft (7,600 m)
Range with 66 passengers: 1,200 naut miles (1,382 miles) 2,222 km for ATR 72-200 only

Sales: 151 ordered by September 1994.
Passengers: Typically 66 passengers at 31 ins (79 cm) seat pitch and with either 137.5 cu ft (3.9 m^3) forward cargo area or 2 separate forward areas of 106 cu ft (3m^3) and 99 cu ft (2.8 m^3); 74 passengers at 30 ins (76 cm) seat pitch and with 56.5 cu ft (1.6 m^3) forward cargo area; or 70 passengers at 31 ins (79 cm) seat pitch and with 2 separate forward cargo areas of 74 cu ft (2.1 m^3) and 67 cu ft (1.9 m^3). All have a rear cargo area of 169.5 cu ft (4.8 m^3).
Wing control surfaces: Similar to ATR 42 but with the addition of vortex generators on the wings and tailplane.
Engines: 2 Pratt & Whitney Canada PW124B turboprops for ATR 72-200, and PW127s for ATR 72-210, with Hamilton Standard 14 SF 11 and 247 F 4-blade propellers respectively.
Engine rating: Each 2,160 shp (1,611 kW) and 2,475 shp (1,846 kW) respectively.
Fuel system: 11,023 lb (5,000 kg).

Aircraft variants:
ATR 72-200 has PW124B engines.
ATR 72-210 has PW127 engines and a more advanced flight deck among other improvements. French certified 15 December 1992, US certified 18 December 1992, and German certified 24 February 1993.
ATR 72-500 is a proposed further improved version, with more powerful engines and 6-blade propellers. Similar cabin improvements to the ATR 42-500. 350 kts (403 mph) 648 km/h cruise speed anticipated.

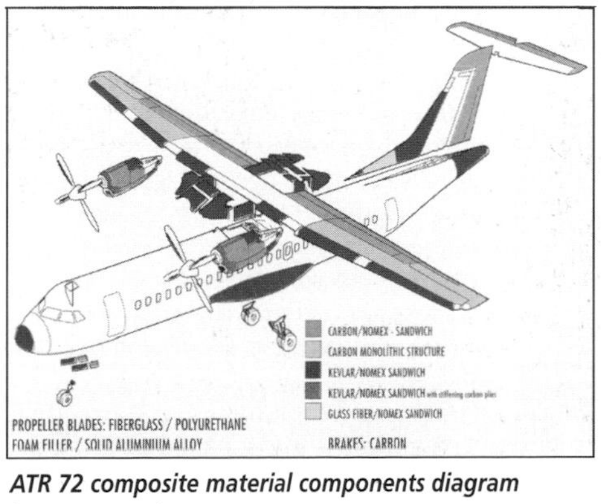

ATR 72 composite material components diagram (courtesy ATR)

ATR 72 in CSA livery

ATR 82

First flight: Advanced definition phase in early 1995. Further development has been slowed
Role: Larger-capacity and higher-performance development of the ATR regional airliners.
Passengers: 84 seats at 31 ins (79 cm) pitch.
Engines: 2 derated Allison AE2100 turboprops or similar.
Fuel system: 11,023 lb (5,000 kg).

Details for ATR 82.

Principal dimensions:
Wing span: 96 ft 7.5 ins (29.452 m)
Maximum length: 105 ft 10 ins (32.267 m)

Cabin:
Width: 8 ft 5.2 ins (2.57 m), or 7 ft 7 ins (2.263 m) at the floor
Height: 6 ft 3 ins (1.91 m)

Undercarriage:
Wheel base: 46 ft 8 ins (14.217 m)
Wheel track: 13 ft 10 ins (4.22 m)

Weights:
Empty, operating: 40,578 lb (18,406 kg)
Maximum take-off: 68,474 lb (31,060 kg)
Payload: 22,720 lb (10,306 kg)

Performance:
Cruise speed: 335 kts (386 mph) 620 km/h
Take-off field length: 4,593 ft (1,400 m), MTOW, sea level, ISA
Landing field length: 4,200 ft (1,280 m) at MLW, sea level
Range with full payload: 1,000 naut miles (1,151 miles) 1,852 km

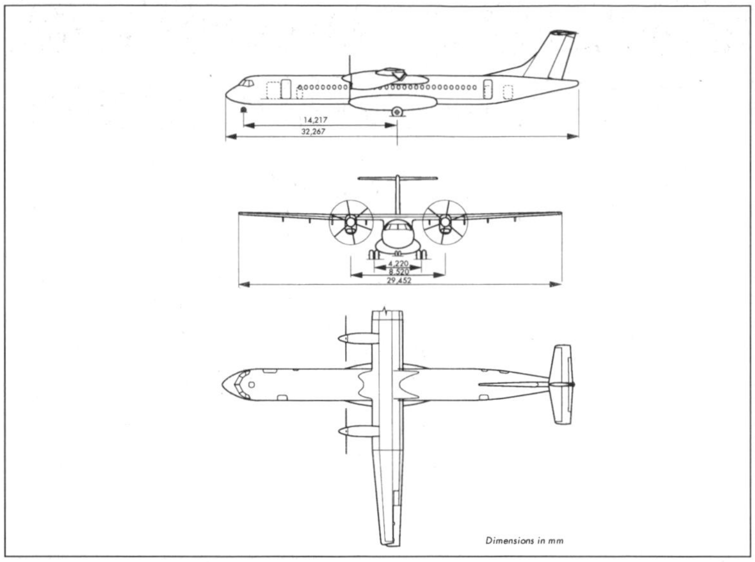

ATR 82 general arrangement (courtesy ATR)

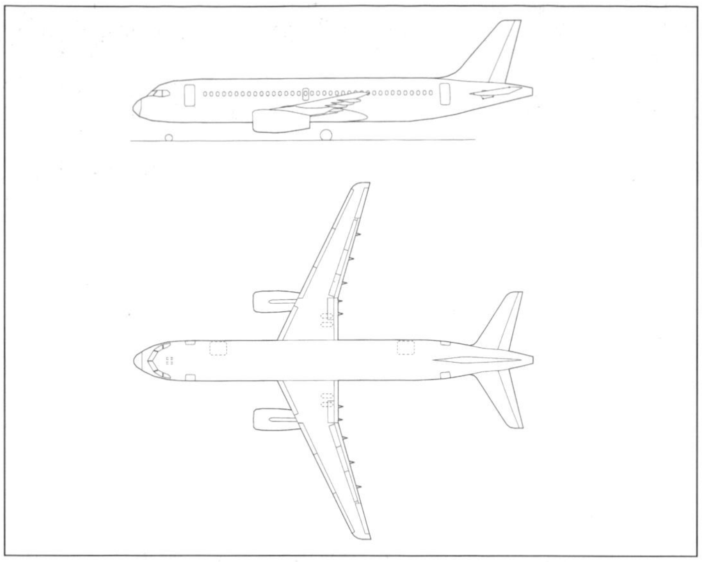

Fokker/Daimler-Benz/AVIC/KCADC Future Aircraft Project-X (courtesy Fokker)

Fokker/Daimler-Benz/AVIC/ Korean Commercial Aircraft Development Consortium (Netherlands/Germany/ China/South Korea)

Corporate address: See Combat section for company details.
Information: Fedde Holwerda (European Project Director).

● Activities

● To jointly develop and produce a new airliner in the 100-120 seat range, partly to complement the existing Fokker range and supplement the lower end of the Airbus range.

Future Aircraft Project-X

★ Aims

⋆ To start with a 120 seat version, with later "stretched" or shortened versions.
⋆ Basic weight of 120,370 lb (54,600 kg).
⋆ An extended range version could fly 2,600 naut miles (2,994 miles) 4,815 km.
⋆ 2 engines in the 20,000 to 24,000 lbf (89 to 106.7 kN) range.

▲ Development

▲ 15 May 1995. Start of a feasibility study into a new 100-120 seat airliner, to enter service after the year 2000, following 6 March 1995 MoU between Daimler-Benz and Samsung. Study conducted in Europe and Asia.

Special Aircraft Transport International Company GIE (SATIC) (France/Germany)

Corporate address: Joint venture of Aerospatiale of France and Daimler-Benz Aerospace Airbus of Germany (which see).
Founded: October 1991.
Information: M-C Granet (Aerospatiale – *telephone* +33 61 93 81 97) and D. Plath (Daimler-Benz – *telephone* +49 40 74 37 30 17)

SATIC Airbus A300-600ST (Super Transporter) "Beluga"

First flight: 13 September 1994 (lasting 4 hours and 21 minutes).
Certification: September 1995, after a test programme lasting about 400 hours.

Fully painted SATIC Airbus A300-600ST "Beluga" (See also cover photograph)

First delivery: 1995.
Role: Freighter for outsized cargoes, based on the Airbus A300-600R.

★ Aims

⋆ To replace Super Guppy outsized freighters used to transport sections of Airbus airliners between manufacturing companies and the Toulouse and Hamburg assembly plants.
⋆ Relocation of the cockpit to a position below and 4 ft 11 ins (1.5 m) forward of the main cargo deck, allowing roll-on loading and roll-off unloading of the aircraft section payloads. This reduces turnaround times to just 45 minutes, compared with 2 to 3 hours for the Super Guppy.

Sales: 4 ordered by Airbus Industrie, to be delivered at yearly intervals from 1995. Built by Sogerma-Socea at Toulouse. To be operated by Airbus Skylink. Expectations are to sell a further 15-20 to other operators, military and civil.
Freight hold volume: Larger fuselage cross-section than any other aircraft, offering a main-deck volume of 49,440 cu ft (1,400 m^3).
Freight hold capacity: Largest cargo in terms of volume will be A330 and A340 rear fuselage sections, while heaviest will be A330 and A340 wings. In addition to commercial Airbus loads, a military derivative could carry 2 CH-53 or 8 BO 105 helicopters. Lower deck capacity for 10 LD3 or 5 LD1/6 containers.
Freight hold access: Largest door ever installed on an aircraft.
Tail surfaces: Taller (3 ft 8 ins, 1.12 m) vertical tail, modified from the A340, with a leading-edge extension. The tailplane is strengthened and given auxiliary fins to improve stability in flight.
Fuselage: Upper fuselage cross-section of 24 ft 3 ins (7.8 m). In addition to the basic Airbus airframe for modification, new airframe components are produced by Latécoère (also lead contractor for integration), Aerostructures of the UK (nose door), CASA, Daimler-Benz, Elbe Flugzeugwerke, Hurel-Dubois and Sogerma-Socea.
Engines: 2 General Electric CF6-80C2A8 turbofans.
Engine rating: Each 59,000 lbf (262.45 kN).

DETAILS FOR A300-600ST.

Principal dimensions:
Wing span: 147 ft 1 ins (44.836 m)
Maximum length: 184 ft 3 ins (56.158 m)
Height with nose door raised: 56 ft 7 ins (17.247 m)
Fuselage diameter: 24 ft 3 ins (7.8 m)

Cabin:
Length: 123 ft 8 ins (37.7 m)
Width: 24 ft 3 ins (7.4 m)
Volume: 49,440 cu ft (1,400 m^3)

Weights:
Maximum take-off: 330,693 lb (150,000 kg)
Payload: 100,310 lb (45,500 kg)

Performance:
Cruise speed: 420 kts (484 mph) 778 km/h
Range: 900 naut miles (1,035 miles) 1,666 km

Helicopters and Autogyros

AMAX (Australia)

Corporate address: 5 Utrecht Court, Donvale, 3111.
Telephone: +61 3 842 3132
Facsimile: +61 3 841 8177

AMAX Eagle and Double Eagle series

Role: Open cockpit, plans or kit-built autogyros.
Airframe materials: Principally aluminium alloy tubing. 2-blade rotor.
Engine: Typically up to 115 hp (85.75 kW) with pusher propeller for the single-seaters and up to 140 hp (104.4 kW) for the Double Eagle TT.

DETAILS FOR EAGLE.

Principal dimensions:
Rotor diameter: 26 ft (7.92 m)
Fuselage length: 10 ft (3.05 m)
Maximum height: 8 ft 4 ins (2.54 m)

Undercarriage:
Type: Fixed nosewheel type

Weights:
Empty, operating: 410 lb (186 kg)
Maximum take-off: 720 lb (326 kg)

Performance:
Maximum speed: 87 kts (100 mph) 161 km/h
Cruise speed: 65 kts (75 mph) 121 km/h
Maximum climb rate: 1,100 ft (335 m) per minute
Take-off distance: 50 ft (15 m)
Operating ceiling: 10,000 ft (3,050 m)
Range: 174 naut miles (200 miles) 322 km

Fuel system: 45 litres.
Aircraft variants:
Eagle and Eagle TT are the single-seat versions.
Double Eagle TT is the tandem two-seater, with more powerful engine.

VTOL Aircraft Pty Ltd (Australia)

Corporate address: PO Box 5195C Newcastle West, 2302 NSW.
Telephone: +61 49 43 5348
Facsimile: +61 49 62 3806
Information: Duan A. Philips (Chairman of Directors).

VTOL Aircraft Phillicopter

First flight: 1971.
Role: Light utility helicopter.
Crew/passengers: 2.
Cockpit: Dual controls. Independent collective throttle. Removable doors. Insulated, heated and ventilated.
Optional equipment: Night lights, cabin heater, cargo hook, sprayboom, spray tanks, cargo racks, and auxiliary fuel tanks.
Rotor system: 2-blade main rotor with semi-rigid underslung teetering hub to reduce rotor vibration and control force feed-back. Main blades are mounted 3° above horizontal to minimize blade flexing. Main rotor blades are foam-filled metal, with straight chord and zero twist. Primary gearbox is coupled to the engine by gear flex coupling. Drive shaft from the reduction box to the tail rotor is coupled to the main rotor by an overrun clutch and automatic centrifugal clutch. Rotor brake may be fitted to the clutch drum. Spiral bevel gears in primary and tail rotor gearboxes. Helical gears in the reduction box drive to the main rotor. Spiral bevel gears for tail rotor take-off. Main rotor/engine rpm ratio is 1:5.66.
Tail rotor characteristics: 2-blade teetering. No rotor brake fitted at present. Tail rotor/engine ratio is 1:1.

DETAILS FOR PHILLICOPTER

Principal dimensions:
Rotor diameter (main): 25 ft 6 ins (7.77 m)
Maximum length, rotors turning: 29 ft (8.84 m)
Fuselage length: 23 ft 2.5 ins (7.07 m)
Maximum height: 8 ft 6 ins (2.59 m)

Cabin:
Width: 3 ft 10 ins (1.17 m)

Main rotor:
Blade chord: 8 ins (20.3 cm)
Blade area: each 8 sq ft (0.74 m^2)
Rotor disc: 510 sq ft (47.38 m^2)

Tail rotor:
Diameter: 4 ft 8 ins (1.42 m)

Undercarriage:
Type: Fixed skid type, with elastomeric anchorage. Ground handling wheels
Skid track: 6 ft (1.83 m)

Weights:
Empty, operating: 1,000 lb (453.6 kg)
Maximum take-off and landing: 1,550 lb (703 kg)

Performance:
Never-exceed speed (VNE): 110 kts (126 mph) 203 km/h
Cruise speed: 75 kts (86 mph) 139 km/h
Maximum climb rate: 1,200 ft (366 m) per minute at 40 kts forward speed, 400 ft (122 m) per minute vertical at sea level
IGE hovering ceiling: 8,000 ft (2,440 m)
Ceiling: 16,000 ft (4,875 m), service, OGE
Range with full payload: 375 naut miles (432 miles) 694 km/h, including optional tanks

VTOL Aircraft Phillicopter

Tail surfaces: Horizontal and vertical stabilizers, 3 sq ft (0.28 m^2) and 2 sq ft (0.186 m^2) respectively.
Engine: Textron Lycoming O-360 piston engine. Alternative Teledyne Continental O-300 or fuel-injected IVO-360-A1A.
Engine rating: 180 hp (134 kW), 175 hp (130.5 kW) and 180 hp (134 kW) respectively.
Fuel system: 91 litres. Optional 91 litre central tank for fuel or for crop spraying chemicals.
Electrical system: 12 volt engine-driven generator/alternator.
Flight avionics/instrumentation: Range of conventional instruments.

Helicópteros do Brasil SA (Helibras) (Brazil)

Corporate address: Caixa Postal 184, 37500-000 Itajubá, MG.
Telephone: +55 35 622 3366
Facsimile: +55 11 283 2978 (information).
Founded: 1978.

● Activities

● Largest shareholder is Eurocopter France. Recent activities include assembly of the Eurocopter Dauphin, Ecureuil, Fennec and Panther for the armed forces of Brazil and Paraguay, police and other government agencies in Brazil and abroad, plus civil operators. (The Ecureuil, known locally as the HB-350 Esquilo, is however reportedly to be replaced in the basic training role with the Brazilian Army because of its operating costs, though it will continue to be used for advanced training.)
● Other activities include overhaul and repair.

Bell Helicopter Textron Canada (Canada)

Corporate address: 12,800 rue de l'Avenir, Mirabel, Quebec J7J 1R4.
Telephone: +1 514 437 2763
Facsimile: +1 514 437 6010
Telex: 05-52827
Founded: 1984.
Employees: Over 1,300.

● Activities

● Bell Helicopter Textron Inc (see USA) moved its assembly line for commercial helicopters to Canada in 1986, where a production facility had been completed the previous year as a division of Textron Canada Ltd. BHTL's 1,000th helicopter (a TwinRanger) was delivered to Niagara Helicopters on 5 May 1994.

Bell 206B-3 JetRanger III and TH 67 Creek

First flight: 8 December 1962 for the original JetRanger prototype. JetRanger III appeared in 1977.
Role: Light civil helicopter, with military variants.

Details for JetRanger III

Principal dimensions:
Rotor diameter (main): 33 ft 4 ins (10.16 m)
Maximum length, rotors turning: 39 ft 1 ins (11.91 m)
Fuselage length: 31 ft 2.5 ins (9.51 m) to tailguard
Maximum height: 9 ft 6 ins (2.9 m) standard skid, 10 ft 5 ins (3.18 m) high skid, to above rotor head

Cabin:
Length: 7 ft 9.5 ins (2.37 m), from forward seats and leg room to (and including) aft baggage shelf
Width: 4 ft 2 ins (1.27 m)
Height: 4 ft 2 ins (1.27 m)
Volume: about 40 cu ft (1.13 m^3) aft cabin volume, 16 cu ft (0.45 m^3) baggage compartment volume

Main rotor:
Blade chord: 1 ft 1 ins (0.33 m)
Blade area: each 18.05 sq ft (1.677 m^2)
Rotor disc: 872.7 sq ft (81.08 m^2)
Rpm: Up to 394

Tail rotor:
Diameter: 5 ft 5 ins (1.65 m)

Undercarriage:
Type: Fixed twin skids (standard and high), with inflatable emergency floats available. Optional ground handling wheels with lift tube
Skid base: 8 ft 3.5 ins (2.53 m) standard
Skid track: 6 ft 5 ins (1.96 m) standard skids

Weights:
Empty: 1,625 lb (737 kg)
FAA normal take-off: 3,200 lb (1,451 kg)
FAA take-off, external load: 3,350 lb (1,519 kg)
External payload: 1,500 lb (680 kg)

Performance (normal gross weight, *with data for 2,600 lb, 1,179 kg take-off weight in italics*):
Maximum allowable speed: 122 kts (140 mph) 226 km/h, *130 kts (150 mph) 241 km/h,* at sea level, IAS
Maximum continuous speed: 115 kts (132 mph) 213 km/h, *121 kts (139 mph) 224 km/h,* sea level
Maximum climb rate: 1,280 ft (390 m) per minute, *2,080 ft (634 m) per minute,* sea level
IGE hovering ceiling: 12,800 ft (3,900 m), *18,800 ft (5,730 m)*
OGE hovering ceiling: 8,800 ft (2,680 m), *14,600 ft (4,450 m)*
Certified altitude: 13,500 ft (4,115 m), *20,000 ft (6,095 m)*
Range at sea level: 365 naut miles (420 miles) 676 km, *385 naut miles (443 miles) 713 km,* sea level at long-range cruise speed, no reserves
Range at 5,000 ft (1,525 m): 395 naut miles (455 miles) 731 km, *435 naut miles (501 miles) 805 km,* sea level at long-range cruise speed, no reserves

Sales: Over 7,600 Model 206B JetRangers and derivatives have been built, including OH-58s and TH-67s for the US Army and TH-57s for the US Navy.
Details: JetRanger III.
Crew/passengers: 5.
Optional equipment: High undercarriage skids or emergency flotation gear, dual controls, external cargo hook (or provisions only), flight instrument group (attitude indicator, directional gyro, rate of climb, turn and bank), bleed air heater/defogger. environmental control system, rescue hoist, litter installation, particle separator, engine intake baffles, searchlight (Nightsun), wire strike protection system, and engine fire protection system. Navigation/communication equipment (see Avionics).
Rotor system: Semi-rigid, 2-blade, see-saw (teetering) type main rotor with precone and underslung feathering axis. All-metal, moisture proofed and epoxy encapsulated blades. Flap restraints. Hydraulic boost

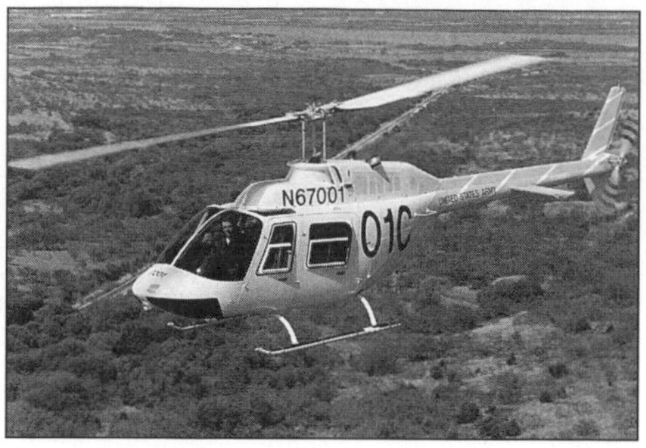

Bell TH-67 Creek US Army pilot trainer

system (pump and reservoir module). Mechanical flight control linkages throughout. Transmission drive system comprises focused pylon mounting; freewheeling unit between engine and main transmission; gearbox, tail rotor with 2.3:1 spiral bevel gear reduction; hydraulic pump for boost controls; main transmission 2-stage 15.22:1 planetary reduction; oil cooler; oil filter with replaceable cartridge; and constant-pressure oil pump. Optional tied-down assemblies for main and tail rotors.
Tail rotor characteristics: Semi-rigid, 2-blade, see-saw type.
Tail surfaces: Vertical fin (6 ft 6 ins, 1.98 m) and fixed horizontal stabilizer.
Airframe materials: Cabin is a semi-monocoque structure using bonded aluminium honeycomb. Monocoque tailboom structure.
Engine: Allison 250-C20J turboshaft.
Engine rating: 420 shp (313 kW) take-off, 370 shp (275 kW) maximum continuous.
Transmission rating: 317 shp (236 kW) take-off, 270 shp (201 kW) maximum continuous.
Fuel system: 344 litres.
Electrical system: 28 volt DC system with 150 amp starter-generator, and 13 amp-hour ni-cd battery (optional 17 amp-hour heavy duty battery and 13 amp-hour auxiliary battery). Volt regulator.
Flight avionics/instrumentation: Conventional flight and engine instrumentation and monitoring systems standard. Options include VHF transceiver/VOR with audio switching panel and more, Omni/LOC, ADF, encoding altimeter, and transponder.
Aircraft variants:
JetRanger III is the current civil version, still in production despite appearance of the new Model 407.
TH-67 Creek is the new US Army single-rotor pilot trainer, with an advanced cockpit display system embedded in the rear of the right-hand seat to provide a second student with a full view of primary flight and navigation instruments. Commercial avionics suite, providing dual pilot IFR capability. Crashworthy seats. 137 ordered, the first 2 delivered on 15 October 1993 and 52 delivered by September 1994.

Bell 206L-4 LongRanger IV

First flight: 11 September 1974 in original form. Current LongRanger IV was certified in October 1992.
Role: Multi-mission light helicopter, for corporate transport, medical support, law enforcement, off-shore support and more, developed as a lengthened JetRanger.
Sales: Well over 1,300.
Crew/passengers: Pilot plus 6 passengers. 4-passenger executive and 2 litter/2 sitting casualty medevac layouts optional.
Optional equipment: Dual controls. Cargo hook with 2,000 lb (907 kg) capacity.
Rotor system: Focused pylon mounted with Noda-Matic cabin suspension system to reduce rotor-induced vibration and cabin noise levels. Freewheeling unit. Kaflex (non-lubricated) input drive shaft.
Tail surfaces: Similar to JetRanger but with sweptback endplates on the horizontal stabilizer.
Engine: Allison 250-C30P turboshaft.
Engine rating: 650 shp (485 kW) take-off, 557 shp (415 kW) maximum continuous.
Transmission rating: 490 shp (365 kW) take-off, 370 shp (276 kW) maximum continuous.
Fuel system: 419 litres.
Flight avionics/instrumentation: Single pilot IFR with Rockwell Collins or SFENA autopilot.

Details for LongRanger.

Principal dimensions:
Rotor diameter (main): 37 ft (11.28 m)
Maximum length, rotors turning: 42 ft 8.5 ins (13.02 m)
Fuselage length: 33 ft (10.06 m)
Maximum height: 10 ft 3.5 ins (3.14 m) to above rotor head

Cabin:
Length: 9 ft (2.74 m)
Width: 4 ft 2 ins (1.27 m)
Height: 4 ft 2 ins (1.27 m)

Main rotor:
Blade chord: 1 ft 1 ins (0.33 m)
Rotor disc: 1,075 sq ft (99.89 m^2)
Rpm: 394

Tail rotor:
Diameter: 5 ft 5 ins (1.65 m)

Undercarriage:
Skid track: 7 ft 8 ins (2.34 m)
Skid base: 9 ft 10.9 ins (3.02 m)

Weights:
Empty: 2,274 lb (1,031 kg)
FAA normal take-off: 4,450 lb (2,018 kg)
FAA take-off with external load: 4,550 lb (2,064 kg)
External payload: 2,000 lb (907 kg)

Performance (normal gross weight, *with data for 3,600 lb, 1,633 kg take-off weight in italics*):
Long-range cruise speed at average gross weight (sea level): 112 kts (129 mph) 207 km/h, *116 kts (134 mph) 215 km/h,* ISA
Maximum continuous power cruise speed at gross take-off weight (5,000 ft, 1,525 m): 107 kts (123 mph) 198 km/h, *122 kts (140 mph) 226 km/h,* ISA + 20° C
IGE hovering ceiling: 10,000 ft (3,050 m), *over 20,000 ft (6,100 m)* at ISA; or 6,600 ft (2,010 m), *16,700 ft (5,090 m)* at ISA + 30° C
OGE hovering ceiling: 6,500 ft (1,980 m), *16,600 ft (5,060 m)* ISA; or 3,100 ft (945 m), *11,500 ft (3,505 m)* at ISA + 30° C
Ceiling: 10,000 ft (3,050 m), *over 20,000 ft (6,100 m),* ISA
Range at average gross weight (sea level): 321 naut miles (370 miles) 594 km, *334 naut miles (385 miles), 619 km,* ISA
Range at average gross weight (5,000 ft, 1,525 m): 357 naut miles (411 miles) 661 km, *382 naut miles (440 miles) 707 km*
Duration: 3.7 hours loiter at sea level at 52 kts, *4.5 hours loiter at 5,000 ft at 52 kts*

Bell 206L-4 LongRanger IV

Bell 206LT TwinRanger

Bell 206LT TwinRanger

Certification: 19 November 1993 (twin-engine Category A one engine inoperative capability and Category B operations).
Role: Twin-engined production version of the LongRanger.

▲ Development

▲ Production version of the Tridair Helicopters Gemini ST conversion of LongRanger (see Tridair), produced under a licence agreement with Tridair and the Tridair/Kawada Industries limited partnership.
Details: Similar to LongRanger except as follow.
Engines: 2 Allison 250-C-20R turboshafts.
Engine rating: Each 450 shp (335.6 kW) 5-minute rating, 380 shp (283.4 kW) maximum continuous. OEI rating 450 shp (335.6 kW).
Transmission rating: 490 shp (365.4 kW) 5-minute rating, 370 shp (276 kW) maximum continuous. OEI rating 490 shp (365.4 kW).
Fuel system: 426.6 litres.
Electrical system: 28 volt DC system with 2 x 150 amp starter-generators, and 28 amp-hour ni-cd battery (optional 17 amp-hour heavy duty battery and 13 amp-hour auxiliary battery). Volt regulator.

DETAILS FOR TWINRANGER ARE SIMILAR TO LONGRANGER, EXCEPT.

Weights:
Empty: 2,748 lb (1,246 kg)

Performance (normal gross weight, *with data for 3,600 lb,1,633 kg take-off weight in italics*):
Maximum continuous cruise speed: 106 kts (122 mph) 196 km/h, *110 kts (127 mph) 204 km/h,* sea level
Economical cruise speed: 108 kts (124 mph) 200 km/h, *112 kts (129 mph) 207 km/h,* average gross weight, sea level
IGE hovering ceiling: 10,000 ft (3,050 m), *over 20,000 ft (6,100 m)* standard day; or 7,700 ft (2,347 m), over 20,000 ft (6,100 m) at standard day + 20° C
OGE hovering ceiling: 6,900 ft (2,100 m), *over 20,000 ft (6,100 m)* standard day; or 4,700 ft (1,433 m), *18,900 ft (5,760 m)* standard day + 20° C
Ceiling: 10,000 ft (3,050 m), *over 20,000 ft (6,100 m),* standard day; or 7,700 ft (2,347 m), *14,800 ft (4,510 m)* ISA + 20° C
Range: 250 naut miles (288 miles) 463 km, *259 naut miles (298 miles) 480 km,* long-range cruise speed, sea level, no reserves

Bell 212

Role: Multi-purpose, including offshore support, executive transport, air taxi, border patrol, search and rescue, and more.

▲ Development

▲ Commercial version of the US forces UH-1N and Canadian CH-135 military helicopters, also operated by other armed forces.
Sales: Well over 700 in worldwide commercial operation, including a growing number certified for IFR; has been IFR certified in the USA, UK, Norway and Canada. Originally from US production lines, it was the first US-manufactured helicopter to be ordered by China (1979), with 10 currently operated by the CAAC in offshore support, geophysical applications and forestry work.
Crew/passengers: Pilot and 14 passengers.
Size of main loading door: 6 ft 2 ins x 4 ft 1 ins (1.88 x 1.24 m) sliding doors to the main cabin.
Rotor system: Semi-rigid, 2-blade, see-saw (teetering) type main rotor with underslung feathering axis. Gyroscopic stabilizer bar.
Tail surfaces: Automatic variable incidence horizontal stabilizer.
Engines: Pratt & Whitney Canada PT6T-3B Twin Pac twinned turboshafts.
Engine rating: Combined rating of 1,800 shp (1,342 kW) at take-off, 1,600 shp (1,193 kW) maximum continuous.
Transmission rating: 1,290 shp (962 kW) take-off, 1,134 shp (845.6 kW) maximum continuous.
Fuel system: 817 litres standard usable capacity, with 2 optional auxiliary tanks of either 75.7 or 341 litres each.
Electrical system: 28 volt DC system with 2 starter-generators derated to 150 amp, and 40 amp-hour ni-cd battery. Single-phase AC supply via solid-state inverters.
Hydraulic system: 2 supplies, each 1,000 psi.
Braking system: Optional rotor brake.
Radar: Optional weather radar.
Flight avionics/instrumentation: Some IFR equipped with ADF, DME, marker beacon/glideslope, transponder, VHF transceivers, and VOR/LOC/RMI receivers. Automatic flight stabilization. Optional flight director.

DETAILS FOR 212.

Principal dimensions:
Rotor diameter (main): 48 ft 2 ins (14.68 m)
Maximum length, rotors turning: 57 ft 3 ins (17.45 m)
Fuselage length: 41 ft 8.5 ins (12.71 m)
Maximum height: 12 ft 9.5 ins (3.9 m) to above rotor head

Cabin:
Length: 7 ft 8 ins (2.34 m)
Width: 8 ft (2.44 m)
Height: 4 ft 1 ins (1.24 m)

Main rotor:
Blade chord: 1 ft 11.5 ins (0.6 m)
Rotor disc: 1,810 sq ft (168.12 m^2)

Tail rotor:
Diameter: 8 ft 6 ins (2.59 m)

Undercarriage:
Type: Fixed skids. Optional emergency inflatable floats or full floats. Ground handling wheels available
Skid track: 8 ft 8 ins (2.64 m)

Weights:
Empty: 5,997 lb (2,720 kg), without IFR avionics
Maximum take-off: 11,200 lb (5,080 kg)
External payload: 5,000 lb (2,268 kg)

Performance:
Maximum cruise speed: 100 kts (115 mph) 185 km/h
Maximum climb rate: 1,320 ft (400 m) per minute
IGE hovering ceiling: 4,750 ft (1,448 m)
Ceiling: 14,200 ft (4,328 m), service
Range with standard fuel: 241 naut miles (278 miles) 447 km

IFR-equipped Bell 212s have an above-fuselage fin for better roll-yaw control during manual flying

Bell 230

First flight: 12 August 1991 (first prototype as a converted Bell 222).
Role: Commercial helicopter for utility, air ambulance, off-shore support, executive transport and other roles. Special multi-purpose military, paramilitary and police version has been demonstrated, carrying search radar and suited to search and rescue, maritime surveillance, over-the-horizon targeting, EEZ control, transport, inter-ship liaison and more.

▲ Development

▲ Certified under Transport Canada and the FAA in 1992 as a greatly improved derivative of the Bell 222.
Crew/passengers: Typically 10 seats in utility layout (including the crew) with foldable seatback, 6 or 8 seats in executive, or 2 litters and 3 seated persons in air ambulance.
Cockpit: Collective-mounted throttles.
Baggage compartment: 500 lb (227 kg) capacity, 37.2 cu ft (1.05 m^3) compartment aft of cabin.
Optional equipment: Emergency flotation system with watertight tailboom, life jackets and stowage of a life-raft; primary flotation actuation system consists of immersion switch assemblies mounted in the belly of the helicopter. Particle separator. 2,800 lb (1,270 kg) cargo hook.
Rotor system: Advanced design, high-inertia rotor blades with quiet, swept tips and over 9 ft (2.7 m) rotor-to-ground clearance. Elastomeric pitch change. Flapping bearings. Noda-Matic cabin suspension system to reduce rotor-induced vibration and cabin noise levels. Rotor system is capable of starts and stops in winds up to 60 kts. Main rotor blades have stainless steel spars, stainless steel leading- and Nomex honeycomb trailing-edges, and glassfibre skins. Glass-fibre straps in each blade for structural redundancy.
Tail rotor characteristics: 2-blade, stainless steel.
Tail surfaces: Horizontal stabilizer, with endplates, has leading-edge slats.
Airframe materials: Primarily aluminium alloy.
Safety features: Energy-absorbing crew seats. Rupture-resistant, drop-tested, fuel cells with self-sealing break-away fittings.
Engines: 2 Allison C30G/2 turboshafts.
Engine rating: Each 700 shp (522 kW) take-off for 5 minutes, and 622 shp (464 kW) maximum continuous. OEI 779 shp (581 kW) for 2.5 minutes. Engine containment/fire protection systems.
Transmission rating: 925 shp (690 kW) take-off, 875 shp (652 kW) maximum continuous, at mast. Single engine 735 shp (548 kW).
Fuel system: 710 litres usable with wheel under-carriage, with 182 litre auxiliary fuel option. 935 litres usable with skid gear, with same auxiliary option.
Electrical system: 28 volt DC supply via 2 starter-generators de-rated to 180 amps. 24 volt, 28 amp-hour ni-cd battery.

Hydraulic system: Standard dual hydraulic systems.
Radar: See Aircraft variants.
Flight avionics/instrumentation: Single-pilot IFR certified without autopilot. Bell 230 is the world's first commercial helicopter to receive full IFR certification using a head-up display (HUD). Standard avionics include AlliedSignal Bendix/King Gold Crown III communications. Optional EFIS and automatic flight control system.
Aircraft variants:
Bell 230 commercial helicopter, as detailed.
Bell 230 Special Mission Demonstrator resulted from a combined effort by Bell and Heli-Dyne Systems Inc. Options for the Special Missions version include Honeywell SPZ-7000 digital automatic flight control system; Honeywell EDZ-705 digital EFIS; Trimble Navigation TNL 7880 airborne VLF/Omega/GPS navigation system; a tactical communications suite with UHF, VHF/AM/FM, HF/SSB transceivers and IFF transponder; AlliedSignal Bendix/King RDR 1500B search and surveillance radar in the nose; Electro Optical System 2602 airborne infra-red imaging system; Flight Visions FV 2000/H HUD; Spectrolab SX-5 Starburst searchlight; 300 lb (136 kg) capacity rescue hoist powered by a 28 volt electric motor; and starboard-side sliding door that folds for clearing sponson. 6-month trial by the Demonstrator with the Chilean Navy (leased) included operating off ships at sea, high altitude operations and cold-weather evaluations in the Antarctic Ocean. This was followed by a demonstration tour of South America.

Bell 230 Special Missions Demonstrator, with nose radar and wheels retracted

DETAILS FOR COMMERCIAL 230.

Principal dimensions:
Rotor diameter (main): 42 ft (12.8 m)
Maximum length, rotors turning: 50 ft 6 ins (15.39 m)
Fuselage length: 42 ft 7 ins (12.98 m) nose to tailguard
Maximum height: 12 ft 2 ins (3.71 m)

Cabin:
Length: 7 ft 1 ins (2.16 m)
Width: 4 ft 10 ins (1.47 m)
Height: 4 ft 9 ins (1.45 m)

Main rotor:
Blade chord: 2 ft 2 ins (0.66 m)
Rotor disc: 1,385 sq ft (128.7 m^2)

Tail rotor:
Diameter: 6 ft 10.5 ins (2.09 m)

Undercarriage:
Type: Retractable wheels with hydraulic mainwheel brakes, or fixed skids

Weights:
Empty: 5,000 lb (2,268 kg) skid undercarriage, 5,097 lb (2,312 kg) with wheels
Normal take-off: 8,400 lb (3,810 kg), the same with external load
External payload: 2,800 lb (1,270 kg)

Performance (gross weight, *with data for 7,000 lb, 3,175 kg take-off weight in italics,* wheel or skid undercarriage as detailed)**:**
Maximum continuous cruise speed: 141 kts (162 mph) 261 km/h with wheels, 137 kts (158 mph) 254 km/h with skids, both at sea level
Economical cruise speed: 138 kts (159 mph) 256 km/h with wheels, 134 kts (154 mph) 248 km/h with skids, both at sea level, average cruise weight and standard fuel
IGE hovering ceiling: 12,400 ft (3,780 m), *17,700 ft (5,395 m),* standard day
OGE hovering ceiling: 7,300 ft (2,225 m), *13,400 ft (4,085 m),* standard day
Ceiling: 15,500 ft (4,725 m), *20,000 ft (6,100 m),* service
Ceiling, OEI 30-minute power: 7,700 ft (2,347 m), *14,100 ft (4,300 m),* standard day
Range at long-range cruise speed: 301 naut miles (346 miles) 557 km with wheels, 385 naut miles (443 miles) 713 km with skids, both at sea level, no reserves, standard fuel
Range at long-range cruise speed (with auxiliary fuel): 379 naut miles (436 miles) 702 km with wheels, at sea level, no reserves

Bell 407 and 407T

First flight: 21 April 1995 (modified LongRanger). June 1995 for prototype 407. September 1995 for first production 407.
Role: Light helicopters, to complement and later replace the LongRanger.

★ Aims
★ Based on the LongRanger but with new fuselage side panels to provide an extra 7 ins (18 cm) of cabin width,

▲ Development
▲ December 1995. Certification of the Bell 407, with first deliveries in February 1996.
▲ 1996. Certification and first deliveries of the 407T.
Sales: 105 firm orders for the Bell 407s by early 1995. First delivery to Niagara Helicopters. IPTN of Indonesia is also to assemble the 407 under license.
Crew/passengers: 7, with main cabin 3-abreast seating.
Cabin: Larger windows than LongRanger.
Rotor system: 4-blade composites main rotor and dynamic system taken from the military Bell OH-58 Kiowa Warrior.
Airframe materials: Additional composite materials used in the cabin (compared with LongRanger) to strengthen its structure and reduce possible corrosion.
Engine: Allison 250-C47M turboshaft for the Bell 407, rated at 790 shp (589 kW) at take-off and 704 shp (525 kW) maximum continuous, and 2 Allison 250-C22Bs of 490 shp (365 kW) take-off and 430 shp (320 kW) maximum continuous for the Bell 407T. Both have FADEC.

Bell 407 development aircraft, a modified LongRanger with a Kiowa Warrior rotor system (Bell Helicopter Textron)

Transmission rating: 670 shp (500 kW) for the 407.
Aircraft variants:
Bell 407 is the single-engined model.
Bell 407T is the twin-engined model.

DETAILS FOR 407, UNLESS STATED.

Principal dimensions:
Rotor diameter (main): 35 ft (10.67 m)

Weights:
Maximum take-off: 5,000 lb (2,268 kg), or nearly 5,510 lb (2,500 kg) for 407T.

Performance (estimated)**:**
Maximum cruise speed: 138 kts (159 mph) 256 km/h
OGE hovering ceiling: 8,000-8,500 ft (2,440-2,590 m) ISA
Range: 370-380 naut miles (426-437 miles) 685-703 km

Bell 412EP

First flight: 1979 (development helicopter, as a modified Bell 212).
Role: Civil and military utility, plus specialized search and rescue, law enforcement and more.
Sales: Including those built under licence by Agusta of Italy and IPTN of Indonesia, a total of over 400 Bell 412s are in operation in 6 continents; delivery of 100 412EPs began in August 1994 to the Canadian Department of National Defence as CH-146 Griffons under the utility tactical transport programme (deliveries at about 3 per month); first squadrons were No 417 at Cold Lake and No 439 at Bagotville for SAR, entering service in Spring 1995. Original deliveries began with the 412 in 1981, followed by the 412SP Special Performance in 1985 and 412HP High Performance in 1990. The 412EP (electric modification) was introduced in 1993.
Crew/passengers: Pilot plus 14 passengers/troops, or 1 or 2 pilots plus 2 litters and 3 attendants or 6 litters and 2 attendants, or cargo.
Cockpit: Collective-mounted throttles.
Freight, internal: 220 cu ft (6.23 m^3) in the cabin, and 28 cu ft (0.79 m^3) in the baggage compartment.
Cabin access: 6 ft 2 ins x 4 ft 1 ins (1.88 x 1.24 m) sliding doors to the main cabin.
Optional equipment: Cargo hook, with 4,500 lb (2,041 kg) capacity, searchlight, rotor brake, high skid undercarriage, emergency floats, snow skis, heated windshield, heavy duty heater, loudspeakers, hydraulic or electric rescue hoist, FLIR, weather/search radar, wire strike protection system, and more.
Rotor system: 4-blade main rotor system, with elastomeric bearings that eliminate both mechanical hinges and viscous dampers. New pendulum dampers on the rotor hub to reduce 4/rev vibrations at higher cruise speed. Unlimited life composite main blades that are individually interchangeable and easily foldable for storage. Main and tail rotor hubs have 5,000 hour retirement lives.
Tail rotor characteristics: 2-blade semi-rigid.
Tail surfaces: Automatic variable incidence horizontal stabilizer.
Flight control system: Collective, cyclic and anti-torque system with self-adjustable elevator, hydraulically servo-assisted system with dual servo actuators for pitch and roll, and single anti-torque servo actuator.
Safety features: Energy absorbing seats, and rupture resistant fuel cells.
Engines: Pratt & Whitney Canada PT6T-3D Twin Pac turboshafts. Helicopter operating range –40° to +52° C.
Engine rating: Combined 1,800 shp (1,342 kW).
Transmission: 5,000 hours time between overhauls.

Fuel system: 2 fuel systems. 1,249 litres, plus 2 optional auxiliary tanks for either 617 or 151 litres each.
Electrical system: 2 independent AC and DC systems. 2 x 200 amp, 28 volt DC starter-generators. 2 x 450 volt-amp, 115/26 volt, 400 Hz single-phase inverters to power AC buses. 34 amp-hour (24 volt) ni-cd battery.
Hydraulic system: 2 redundant flight control hydraulic systems, each capable of operating flight control servo-actuators in case of the failure of the other. Directional control system servo-actuator operated by 1 system.
Flight avionics/instrumentation: Can be IFR equipped. AlliedSignal Bendix/King Gold Crown III communications. 3-axis dual digital stability augmentation/altitude hold system, and 2 computer operated digital automatic flight control subsystems (AFCS) which operate simultaneously in roll/pitch control capabilities (1 with short term yaw control capability); optional 4-axis coupled with EFIS (latter with colour displays, sensor sources and navigation mapping capabilities) for search and rescue, programmed search patterns, mark on target, auto approach to hover and more. Typical avionics can be dual VHF-AM/FM, HF comm, dual VOR/ILS/MB, ADF, DME, IFF or TDR and encoding ALT, area nav or Doppler or inertial system navigation, radar altimeter, weather radar and ELT.
Expendable weapons and equipment: Can be armed with rocket and gun pods, missiles and more (see also Agusta).
Aircraft variants:
412EP is the current production model, as detailed, featuring PT6T-3D instead of PT6T-3B engines, improvements to the main transmission and better utilization of engine power. Also licensed to Agusta in Italy and IPTN in Indonesia (latter as NBell-412). Agusta versions include the EP, EP Maritime Patrol with FLIR and low-light-level TV and more, and EP Griffon.
CH-146 is a version of the 412EP (sometimes referred to as the 412CF) for the Canadian Forces, with fully integrated cockpit designed and manufactured by Canadian Marconi, with dual ARC-210 VHF/UHF, ARC-217 HF, and ARC-164 UHF/AM communications equipment, and ADF, DME, VOR/ILS/marker, Doppler, IFF transponder, and GPS navigation equipment. Other features are a rescue hoist, cargo hook, wire strike protection system, armoured floor and seat provisions, plus FLIR, Nightsun, skis and a heavy duty cabin heater for cold weather operations.

Bell 412EP in CH-146 Griffon configuration for the Canadian Forces

Details for 412EP.

Principal dimensions:
Rotor diameter (main): 45 ft 11 ins (14 m)
Maximum length, rotors turning: 56 ft 2 ins (17.11 m)
Fuselage length: 45 ft 11 ins (14 m)
Maximum height: 12 ft 1 ins (3.68 m) to above rotor head

Main rotor:
Blade chord: 1 ft 4 ins (0.406 m), narrowing to 8.5 ins (0.215 m) at the tip
Rotor disc: 1,662 sq ft (154.4 m^2)
Rpm: 314

Tail rotor:
Diameter: 8 ft 7 ins (2.62 m)

Undercarriage:
Type: Fixed skids, with fixed nosewheel type optional
Skid track: 8 ft 10 ins (2.69 m)

Weights:
Empty: 6,100 lb (2,767 kg), fully equipped CH-146 7,511 lb (3,407 kg), Agusta-Bell AB 412EP 6,425 lb (2,914 kg)
Maximum take-off and landing: 11,900 lb (5,398 kg)
Payload: 4,500 lb (2,041 kg) on the cargo hook

Performance (MTOW):
Never-exceed speed (VNE): 140 kts (161 mph) 259 km/h
Typical cruise speed: 122 kts (140 mph) 226 km/h
Long-range cruise speed: 118 kts (136 mph) 219 km/h at sea level, 130 kts (150 mph) 241 km/h at 5,000 ft (1,525 m)
Maximum climb rate: 1,780 ft (542 m) per minute
IGE hovering ceiling: 10,200 ft (3,109 m) ISA, 6,200 ft (1,890 m) ISA + 20° C
OGE hovering ceiling: 5,200 ft (1,585 m) ISA
Ceiling: 17,700 ft (5,395 m), service
Range: 350 naut miles (403 miles) 648 km at sea level, 402 naut miles (463 miles) 745 km at 5,000 ft (1,525 m)
Duration: 4 hours

Bell 430

First flight: 25 October 1995 (54 minute flight).
Role: Longer and re-engined derivative of the Bell 230 for commercial use.

★ Aims
★ Based on the 230 intermediate twin, but with changes as noted below.

▲ Development
▲ November 1995. Expected certification.
Sales: Deliveries from late 1995, with 24 helicopters to be built in 1996, 36 in 1997 and 55 per year from 1998. IPTN of Indonesia is also to assemble the helicopter under licence.
Crew/passengers: 1 or 2 crew plus 6-8 passengers or litters and attendants.
Rotor system: 4-blade bearingless rotor system based on the 680 rotor design. Redesigned rotating controls and mast to accommodate the 4-blade system and a simplified pylon support system replacing the nodal beam type.
Fuselage: Compared with 230, has a 1 ft 6 ins (0.46 m) plug aft of the cockpit, providing increased cabin space (particularly useful for the emergency medical transport capability).
Engines: 2 Allison 250-C40 turboshafts.
Engine rating: Each 734 shp (547 kW).
Transmission rating: 1,045 shp (779 kW) take-off, 995 shp (742 kW) continuous. Single-engine 2-minute rating 770 shp (574 kW).
Fuel system: 935 litres usable with skid under-carriage, and 710 usable with wheels. Optional 182 litre auxiliary tank.
Radar: Optional weather radar.
Flight avionics/instrumentation: Dual-pilot IFR instrumentation for the development prototype includes Rogerson Kratos integrated instrument display system (IIDS) with 2 colour active matrix liquid crystal displays, Rogerson Kratos EFIS with 2 or 4 colour active matrix 5 ins (12.7 cm) LCD screens (each can be configured for either EADI or EHSI), Bendix/King KAV 485 ALT/VSI to interface with the KCP 520 flight control computer and provide for autopilot altitude and climb rate/descent selection and hold functions, Bendix/King autopilot and KLN 90B GPS. AlliedSignal Bendix/King Gold Crown radios with ADF and transponder. Voice activated ICS panel. AlliedSignal Bendix/King automatic flight control system (AFCS) optional for enhanced VFR or IFR flying. Eyebrow panel has master caution/ warning indicators, engine out and rpm warning and selectors for engine start, engine fire suppression and engine FADEC interface. Pilot/co-pilot panels with electromechanical primary flight instruments are basic fit when optional EFIS is not installed. Selection switches on cyclic and collective control heads to select IIDS pages, change radio frequencies and engage/ disengage the automatic flight control system.

Bell 430 intermediate twin

Details for 430.

Principal dimensions:
Rotor diameter (main): 42 ft (12.8 m)
Maximum length, rotors turning: 50 ft 6 ins (15.39 m)
Fuselage length: 44 ft 1 ins (13.44 m), nose to tailguard
Airframe width: 11 ft 4 ins (3.45 m)
Maximum height: 12 ft 9.5 ins (3.9 m) to above rotor head

Cabin:
Volume: 223.9 cu ft (6.34 m^3), including cockpit

Weights:
Empty, operating: 5,040 lb (2,286 kg) skids, 5,144 lb (2,333 kg) wheels
Maximum take-off: 8,600 lb (3,901 kg)
Useful load: 3,400 lb (1,550 kg)
Payload: 2,800 lb (1,270 kg) on cargo hook

Performance (MTOW, estimated):
Never-exceed speed (VNE): 150 kts (173 mph) 278 km/h IAS
Continuous cruise speed: 140 kts (161 mph) 259 km/h
IGE hovering ceiling: 15,200 ft (4,633 m) ISA, 12,600 ft (3,840 m) ISA + 20° C
OGE hovering ceiling: 9,650 ft (2,941 m) ISA, 6,350 ft (1,935 m) ISA + 20° C
Range: 366 naut miles (421 miles) 678 km with standard fuel, sea level, no reserves

Canadian Home Rotors Inc (Canada)

Corporate address: 4 Roy Street, Ear Falls, Ontario P0V 1T0.
Telephone: +1 807 222 2474
Information: Doug Fulford (Vice President).

Canadian Home Rotors Baby Belle

Role: Two-seat light homebuilt helicopters.
Cockpit: Bubble enclosure.
Sales: Made available as plans and kits for home construction/assembly. Can$41,967.38 (1994) for complete kit, or can be purchased as a series of smaller kits. Building time estimated at 1,200 hours.

Canadian Home Rotors Baby Belle

Rotor system: 2-blade stainless steel main rotor with bonded and riveted skins. Main transmission is supplied assembled ready to bolt on. Includes swashplate, slider cross, cooling fan, over-running clutch and drum. Nickel-plated balance beam assembly. Tailrotor driveshaft kit contains everything to couple the main transmission to the tail rotor gearbox, including pillow block bearings and constant velocity coupling.
Airframe materials: Principally 4130 chromoly tubing, aluminium sheet, and aluminium alloy skids.
Engine: Textron Lycoming O-320 piston engine, with the engine modification kit supplied with everything needed to convert it to vertical operation.
Engine rating: 150-160 hp (112-119.3 kW).
Fuel system: 68 litres.
Electrical system: Engine starter-generator.
Flight avionics/instrumentation: Dual engine and rotor tachometer, manifold pressure, vertical airspeed, compass, hour meter, airspeed indicator, sensitive altimeter, Quad-4 cylinder head temperature, and bank indicator instrumentation.

DETAILS FOR BABY BELLE.

Principal dimensions:	**Weights:**
Rotor diameter (main): 25 ft (7.62 m)	Empty: 900 lb (408 kg)
Maximum length: 29 ft 8 ins (9.04 m)	Maximum take-off: 1,400 lb (635 kg)
Maximum height: 8 ft 9 ins (2.67 m)	Payload: 500 lb (227 kg)
Main rotor:	**Performance:**
Blade chord: 8 ins (0.203 m)	Maximum speed: 87 kts (100 mph) 161 km/h
Tail rotor:	Cruise speed: 74 kts (85 mph) 137 km/h
Diameter: 4 ft (1.22 m)	Normal climb rate: 1,000 ft (305 m) per minute
	IGE hovering ceiling: 7,000 ft (2,133 m)
	Ceiling: 10,000 ft (3,050 m)
	Range: 174 naut miles (200 miles) 322 km

Eurocopter Canada Ltd (Canada)

Corporate address: 1100 Gilmore Road, PO Box 250, Fort Erie, Ontario L2A 5M9.
Telephone: +1 905 871 7772
Facsimile: +1 905 871 3320
Founded: 1984, originally as MBB Helicopter Canada.
Information: Guylaine Gauvin (marketing services).

● Activities

● As a subsidiary of Eurocopter International, Eurocopter Canada has the mandate for Canada and undertakes marketing, repair and overhaul of Eurocopter helicopters, including the AS 350 BA and B2 Ecureuil, AS 355 Ecureuil, AS 365 Dauphin 2, BO 105 LS A-3 and CBS, and BK 117. New programmes include the preparation and development of options for the EC-135. It also has production facilities, where assembly of helicopters is undertaken, including the BO 105 LS for which it is the principal authority. Details of Eurocopter helicopters can be found in the Multi-national section.

IMP Aerospace Ltd (Canada)

Corporate address: Suite 400, 2651 Dutch Village Road, Halifax, Nova Scotia B3L 4T1.
Telephone: +1 902 873 2250
Facsimile: +1 902 873 2249 (repair), 4433 (maintenance)
Founded: 1970.

● Activities

● Undertakes maintenance, repair and modification of aircraft for both Canadian and foreign forces. Among recent work has been the upgrade of 6 or 7 Canadian anti-submarine CH-124A Sea Kings to CH-124B standard, with new digital ASN-123 Tac/Nav, ARR-75 sonobuoy receiver and UYS-503 processor.

Rotary Air Force Marketing Inc (Canada)

Corporate address: PO Box 1236, Kindersley, Saskatchewan S0L 1S0.
Telephone: +1 306 463 6030
Facsimile: +1 306 463 6032

Rotary Air Force 1000, 2000 and GT

Role: Single- and Two-seat kit-built autogyros respectively.
Details: RAF 2000, except under Aircraft variants.
Rotor system: 2-blade foam/aluminium/composites rotor, with pre-rotator to reduce take-off distance.
Airframe materials: Aluminium alloy tubing and composites.
Engine: Subaru EA82 modified auto engine.
Engine rating: 98-130 hp (73-97 kW).
Fuel system: 87 litres.
Aircraft variants:
RAF 1000 is the single-seat version, with a 98 hp (73 kW) Subaru engine and 475 lb (215.5 kg) empty weight.

Rotary Air Force 2000GT autogyro (Geoffrey P. Jones)

RAF 2000 is the basic Two-seater, as detailed.
RAF 1000GT and 2000GT are versions of the basic models with balanced engines, modified exhaust systems and improved levels of trim.

DETAILS FOR RAF 2000.

Principal dimensions:
Rotor diameter (main): 30 ft (9.14 m)
Fuselage length: 13 ft 7 ins (4.14 m)
Maximum height: 8 ft 2 ins (2.49 m)

Main rotor:
Rotor disc: 706 sq ft (65.59 m^2)

Weights:
Empty: 560 lb (254 kg)
Maximum take-off: 1,125-1,300 lb (510-590 kg)

Performance:
Cruise speed: 70-83 kts (80-95 mph) 128-153 km/h
Maximum climb rate: 1,200 ft (366 m) per minute
Take-off distance: 75-350 ft (23-107 m)
Landing distance: 1-10 ft (0.3-3 m)
Ceiling: 10,000 ft (3,050 m)
Range: 278 naut miles (320 miles) 515 km
Duration: 4 hours 25 minutes

China National Helicopter Corporation (China)

● Activities

● A department of AVIC which administers China's helicopter activities, including those of Changhe, Harbin and the Chinese Helicopter Research and Development Institute. It oversees conceptual studies, R&D, testing, production, after sales service, marketing and modifications.

Changhe Aircraft Industries Corporation (China)

Corporate address: PO Box 109, Jingdezhen, Jianhxi 333002.
Telephone: +86 798 442 019
Facsimile: +86 798 441 460

Changhe Z-8

First flight: 11 December 1985, with certification on 8 April 1989.
Role: Civil heavy transport helicopter, suited also to search and rescue, firefighting and survey. Possible military use (though described in the brochure as a commercial helicopter), including for anti-submarine, anti-ship and minelaying with the appropriate equipment installed.

▲ Development

▲ Based on the French Aerospatiale SA 321 Super Frelon, of which the air force retains more than 13 for transport, anti-submarine, and search and rescue roles.
Sales: Believed only to be in civil operation in very small number in 1995, though underwent military trials from 1989.
Crew/passengers: 2 or 3 flight crew plus 39 passengers, or 27 equipped troops, 15 litters and attendant, 11,023 lb (5,000 kg) of cargo, wheeled vehicles or other loads.
Cabin access: Hydraulic rear ramp/door for straight-in loading, plus starboard-side sliding door.
Optional equipment: 605 lb (275 kg) rescue hoist, suppressant tank for firefighting, and other equipment appropriate to its role.
Rotor system: 6-blade main rotor, with drag and flapping hinges and damper. Zhongnan gearbox.
Tail rotor characteristics: 5-blade type.

DETAILS FOR Z-8.

Principal dimensions:
Rotor diameter (main): 62 ft (18.9 m)
Maximum length, rotors turning: 75 ft 6.8 ins (23.035 m)
Maximum height: 21 ft 10 ins (6.66 m) above rotating rotors

Main rotor:
Blade area: each 54.89 sq ft (5.1 m^2)
Rotor disc: 3,019.06 sq ft (280.48 m^2)

Tail rotor:
Diameter: 13 ft 1 ins (4 m)

Weights:
Empty, operating: 16,644 lb (7,550 kg)
Normal take-off: 23,350 lb (10,592 kg)
Maximum take-off: 28,660 lb (13,000 kg)
Payload: 11,023 lb (5,000 kg)

Performance (MTOW, except where shown)**:**
Maximum cruise speed: 134 kts (154 mph) 248 km/h
Long-range cruise speed: 125 kts (144 mph) 232 km/h
Climb rate, one engine out: 1,300 ft (396 m) per minute, sea level
IGE hovering ceiling: 6,230 ft (1,900 m), or 18,000 ft (5,500 m) at 19,840 lb (9,000 kg) weight
OGE hovering ceiling: 14,435 ft (4,400 m) at 19,840 lb (9,000 kg) weight
Ceiling: 10,000 ft (3,050 m), or 19,700 ft (6,000 m) at 19,840 lb (9,000 kg) weight
Range with full fuel: 432 naut miles (497 miles) 800 km
Duration: over 4 hours

Fuselage: Hull type, with high-mounted tailboom and side-mounted stabilizing floats, to permit safe alighting on water in an emergency. Not believed to be intended for fully amphibious operations, due in part to the fixed undercarriage.
Airframe materials: Metal stressed skin.
Engines: 3 Changzhou Lan Xiang WZ6 turboshafts.
Engine rating: Each 1,550 shp (1,156 kW) OEI rating.
Transmission rating: 4,120 shp (3,072 kW).
Fuel system: 3,900 litres standard, with 1,900 litres of auxiliary fuel available in optional cabin tanks for ferry flights.
Radar: Sea surveillance radar would be used for military maritime and search and rescue roles.
Flight avionics/instrumentation: Includes KJ-8 autopilot.
Expendable weapons and equipment: Could include sonobuoys, missiles, torpedoes, depth bombs, mines and other weapons and equipment appropriate to role.

Changhe Aircraft Industries Corporation Z-8 (courtesy Changhe)

Harbin Aircraft Manufacturing Corporation (China)

Corporate address: See Combat section for company details.

Harbin Z-9 (or Zhi-9) Haitun

Role: Light twin-turboshaft helicopter, as a licence-built Eurocopter AS 365N Dauphin 2, for passenger or cargo transport, medevac, off-shore support, maritime surveillance and rescue, forestry protection, survey and more.
Sales: Assembly of 50 Z-9As covered under the technical licence originally signed with Aerospatiale were completed in 1992. Current production version is the Z-9B, first flown on 16 January 1992 and certified on 30 December that year.
Details: Z-9A.
Crew/passengers: 2 crew plus 10-12 passengers, or 4 litters and 2 seats, or 2 litters and 5 seats..
Cockpit: Dual controls.
Cabin access: 6 jettisonable doors.
Loading facilities: 12 tie-down rings flush on the cabin floor, with maximum 3,307 lb (1,500 kg) loading each. Baggage hold beetween the cabin and the tailboom, with starboard door.
Optional equipment: Includes rescue hoist.

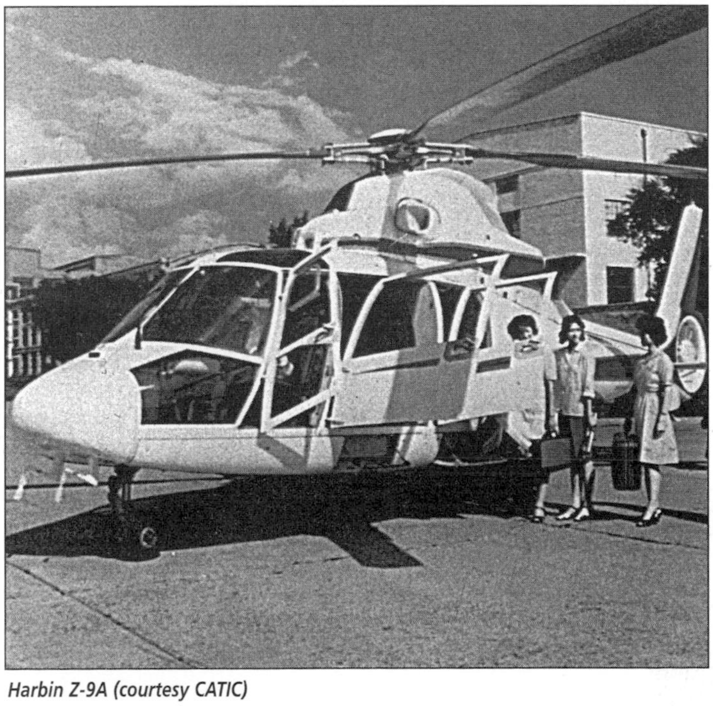

Harbin Z-9A (courtesy CATIC)

Rotor system: 4-blade composites main rotor. Rotor head comprises a glassfibre starflex, glassfibre clamping plate, elastomeric bearing and frequency matcher with no flapping/clamping hinges and no need for lubrication. Each blade (Nomex honeycomb core, glassfibre spar leading-edge, glassfibre/carbonfibre skin and stainless steel leading-edge strip) is attached to the hub by 2 pins.
Airframe materials: Semi-monocoque, with some metal honeycomb sandwich construction, and composites for inspection panels and fairings.
Engines: 2 Turbomeca Arriel 1C or 1C1 turboshafts. Fire detection

and extinguishing systems installed. Oil 26.5 lb (12 kg).
Engine rating: 669 shp (499 kW) take-off, 594 shp (443 kW) maximum continuous, and 696 shp (519 kW) intermediate emergency power.
Fuel system: 1,140 litres standard, with 180 litre optional auxiliary tanks and 475 litre optional ferry tanks.
Braking system: Hydraulic disc, for differential or symmetrical braking to main wheels.
Flight avionics/instrumentation: 3-axis autopilot, coupler flight governor, and appropriate instruments and control boxes for single-pilot IFR use of the radio systems.

Harbin Polar Star

▲ Development

▲ This was a co-operative project between Harbin and the Nanjing University of Aeronautics and Astronautics to design a lightweight helicopter of similar size to the Bell 206, undertaken in about 1992. It did not succeed and was abandoned.

DETAILS FOR Z-9A.

Principal dimensions:
Rotor diameter (main): 11.93 m (39 ft 2 ins)
Maximum length, rotors turning: 44 ft 10.5 ins (13.68 m)
Maximum height: 11 ft 6.5 ins (3.52 m) above rotor head

Cabin:
Area: 45.2 sq ft (4.2 m^2), with loading of 125 lb/sq ft (610 kg/ m^2)

Main rotor:
Aerofoil section: OA2
Blade chord: 1 ft 3 ins to 1 ft 4 ins (0.385 to 0.406 m)
Rotor disc: 1,204.5 sq ft (111.9 m^2)
Twist angle: 10°
Rpm: 349 rpm (at 6,000 rpm engine shaft speed), with 350-360 rpm in flight

Tail rotor:
Aerofoil section: NACA 63A
Diameter: 2 ft 11 ins (0.89 m)
Twist angle: –7°

Undercarriage:
Type: Hydraulically retractable, with castering/ self-centring twin nosewheels

Weights:
Empty: 4,354 lb (1,975 kg) standard helicopter, excluding any optional equipment
Maximum take-off: 8,488 lb (3,850 kg)
Payload: 4,107 lb (1,863 kg)
Maximum slung payload: 3,748 lb (1,700 kg)

Performance:
Maximum speed: 165 kts (190 mph) 306 km/h
Fast cruise speed: 158 kts (182 mph) 293 km/h
Normal cruise speed: 140 kts (162 mph) 260 km/h
Maximum climb rate: 827 ft (252 m) per minute vertical, 1,516 ft (462 m) per minute normal
IGE hovering ceiling: 6,400 ft (1,950 m) at take-off power, ISA
OGE hovering ceiling: 3,345 ft (1,020 m) at take-off power, ISA
Ceiling: 13,123 ft (4,000 m) service (at maximum continuous power and Vr=1 m/sec)
Range: 491 naut miles (565 miles) 910 km with standard fuel, 572 naut miles (658 miles) 1,060 km with auxiliary tank, both without reserves

Aerospatiale Avions (France)

Corporate address: 37 boulevard de Montmorency, 75781 Paris Cedex 16.
Telephone: +33 1 42 24 24 24
Facsimile: +33 1 42 24 26 19
Founded: 1 January 1970.
Employees: 14,000.
Information: André Bloch.

■ Facilities

■ *Meaulte* (employing 1,000), for the manufacture of light alloy parts, assembly by automatic riveting, and integration of sub-assemblies; *Nantes* (employing 2,000), for structural composites, machining of large parts, fuselage assembly, and chemical milling and metal coating; *Saint-Nazaire* (employing 2,000) for assembly of fuselage sections and structures, panel manufacture, sheet metal flexible manufacturing cell, and pipes and tubes; and *Toulouse* (employing 9,000), as the operational centre, R&D, information processing, systems and avionics, product support, manufacture of steel and titanium parts, assembly of pylons, manufacture of electrical equipment, final assembly lines, and commercial aircraft cabin layouts.

● Activities

● From the beginning of 1995, a reorganization of the Aerospatiale group's activities has created 3 new branches plus the Missile division. The new branches are *Aircraft* (incorporating the present aircraft activities plus maintenance, Socata and several subsidiaries), *Space and Defence* and *Helicopter* (Eurocopter activities).
● Has a 37.9% holding in the Airbus Industrie consortium, is a 50% shareholder in ATR, owns 60% of Eurocopter Holding SA, participates in the Eurofar tilt-rotor transport project (no prototype yet built and flight testing will not take place until about the year 2000, thereby not justifying inclusion in this edition), owns Socata (see General Aviation section), and has launched a supersonic transport research programme in association with British Aerospace for a 250-passenger airliner capable of Mach 2.05 and 10,000 km range, plus similar exploratory work with Germany, Italy, Japan, Russia, the UK and USA.

Bruno Guimbal (France)

● Activities

● The single demonstrator G2 Cabri two-seat light helicopter, designed by Eurocopter engineer Bruno Guimbal, is continuing to undergo modification and test flying, having first flown on 11 April 1992. In conversation with the Editor, Mr Guimbal stated that the demonstrator was "delightful to fly" but he wished for no further publicity at this time. In respecting these wishes, WA&SD will report only that the G2 has made steady and cautious progress and was flying again in late 1994 after a 2-month lay-up during which the engine installation was worked on. Some 150 minor and medium changes have been introduced to the helicopter (none concerning the rotor) since 1993. Powered by a 150 hp (112 kW) Textron Lycoming O-320, the G2 has a 3-blade main rotor with Spheriflex hub, "Fenestron" type tail rotor and a composites pod and boom airframe.

Hindustan Aeronautics Limited (HAL) (India)

Corporate address: See Combat section for company details.

HAL built Chetak (Denis Hughes)

● Activities

● The Helicopter division of the Bangalore Complex has been the last production centre for the French Aerospatiale SA 315B Lama and SA 316B Alouette III helicopters, known by the Indian names Cheetah and Chetak respectively. Some 600 of the 2 helicopters have been built in India, with production continuing in 1995, with recent deliveries including 2 Cheetahs and 2 Chetaks handed over to the Namibian Air Force on 2 December 1994.
● A tandem two-seat attack helicopter is also under development, featuring the typical stub-wing armament and chin gun turret.

HAL Advanced Light Helicopter

First flight: 20 August 1992 (30 August officially) for first prototype, 8 April 1993 for second prototype, 28 May 1994 for third and October 1995 for fourth.
Role: Commuter and VIP transport, disaster relief, medevac/medecare, offshore support, search and rescue, and underslung load carrying. Armed military versions for anti-tank, close air support, anti-ship, and anti-submarine. Unarmed military versions for observation, casualty evacuation, assault, logistic support, and training.

★ Aims

★ Intended for domestic and export markets.
★ Capable of deck operations.

HAL advanced light helicopter (courtesy HAL)

★ Integrated dynamic system. Anti-resonance isolation system (ARIS) to isolate rotor-induced vibrations from the fuselage.

▲ Development

▲ Designed and developed by HAL in partnership with Eurocopter Deutschland (formerly MBB).

▲ Full-scale wooden mock-up was followed by a metal mock-up, an interface check rig, and finally a ground test vehicle as a non-flying helicopter to prove the endurance of the drive train and test systems.

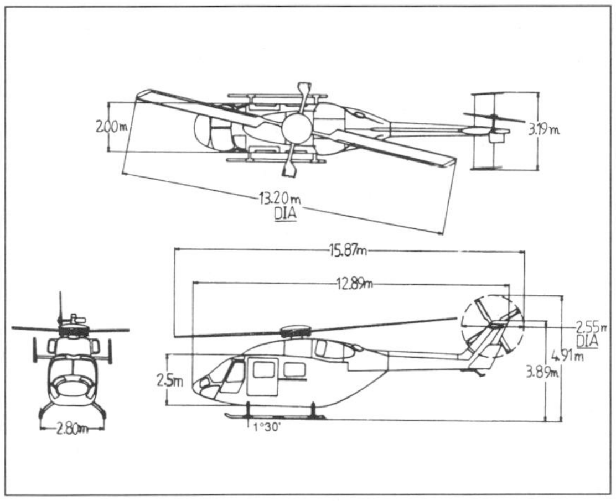

HAL advanced light helicopter general arrangement (courtesy HAL)

Sales: 3 flying prototypes by June 1995, with fourth to follow. 254 accumulated flying hours by late 1994.
Crew/passengers: 2 crew plus 10-14 passengers, or 6 VIPs with foldable table, or 4 litters and 2 ambulatory patients plus all essential medical equipment, spotlights and rescue hoist in medical layout.
Freight, internal/external: Maximum 3,307 lb (1,500 kg). Baggage volume 76.3 cu ft (2.16 m^3).
Cabin access: Sliding doors to main cabin, with hinged doors to cockpit.
Optional equipment: To include cargo hook, emergency medical equipment, oxygen, rescue hoist, pressure refuelling, and nosewheel brakes.
Rotor system: Advanced hingeless system, with 4-blade main rotor (flexible glassfibre blades). FEL type (fibre elastomer) rotor hub with composite upper and lower starplates, titanium centre piece and elastomeric bearings. Blades can be folded manually in 15 minutes by 5 persons. Blades have ballistic tolerance against 12.7 mm bullet strikes. Integrated dynamic system has all upper controls enclosed in the main gearbox housing to offer some protection against small arms fire.
Tail rotor characteristics: 4-blade, stiff in plane, bearingless, incorporating flex beam concept with a high thrust capability. Tailboom can be folded for offshore operation.
Tail surfaces: Horizontal stabilizer with endplates.
Flight control system: Dual controls. Integrated control and stability augmentation system; actuators with hydraulic servos. 4-axis automatic flight control system.
Fuselage: Conventional semi-monocoque structure.
Airframe materials: Composites used in all secondary and some parts of the primary structures, comprising some 29% of structural weight and 60% surface area.
Safety features: 4 nitrogen gas inflatable floats for the skids optional, for emergency alighting on water. Kinetic energy absorption through undercarriage and controlled deformation of the fuselage, plus crew crashworthy seats in military versions, allowing for 9.5 m/second vertical impact and 6 m/second lateral. For operation in threat areas, optional armour protection from 7.62-mm bullets. IR suppressors for engines. Self-sealing fuel tanks against 7.62-mm strikes. Optional chaff/flare dispensers.
Engines: Initial prototypes each have 2 Turbomeca TM333-2B turboshafts, each 1,000 shp (746 kW). In January 1995, HAL contracted LHTEC for CTS800s, each 1,300 shp (969 kW) for testing.
Transmission rating: 1,435 shp (1,070 kW) maximum continuous.
Fuel system: 3 main tanks and 2 supply tanks, with total usable 1,400 litres.
Electrical system: 2 AC subsystems, each with a 5/10 kVA alternator. 2 DC subsystems, each with a 6 kW starter-generator.
Hydraulic system: 3 systems, at 2,988 psi. Systems 1 and 2 for duplicated main and tail rotor flight control actuators. System 3 powers undercarriage, brakes, deck lock harpoon, and optional utility equipment.
Braking system: Hydraulic.
Radar: Weather radar, and Doppler navigation.
Flight avionics/instrumentation: Standard instrumentation and comm/nav package meeting BCAR definition of minimum IFR kit, including V/UHF comm, UHF standby, intercom, ADF, gyromagnetic compass with RMI, radio altimeter, IFF, flight and navigation instruments, ASI, VSI, altimeter, LCD panel for systems, centralized warning panel, and AFCS. Range of optional equipment, including Omega, VHF (FM), HF (SSB), V/UHF homing, FLIR, night vision goggles and RWR.

DETAILS FOR ALH.

Principal dimensions:
Rotor diameter (main): 43 ft 4 ins (13.2 m)
Maximum length, rotors turning: 52 ft 1 ins (15.87 m)
Fuselage length: 42 ft 4 ins (12.89 m)
Width, blades folded: 10 ft 5.5 ins (3.19 m)
Maximum height: 16 ft 1.5 ins (4.91 m) rotors turning with wheel undercarriage, 16 ft 4 ins (4.98 m) with skids.

Cabin:
Width: 6 ft 5.5 ins (1.97 m)
Height: 4 ft 8 ins (1.42 m)
Volume: 258.86 cu ft (7.33 m^3)

Main rotor:
Aerofoil section: DMH3 and DMH4 (outer/inner)
Rotor disc: 1,473 sq ft (136.85 m^2)
Rpm: 314

Tail rotor:
Diameter: 8 ft 4.5 ins (2.55 m)
Rpm: 1,564

Undercarriage:
Type: Retractable nosewheel or fixed skid
Wheel base: 14 ft 4 ins (4.37 m)
Wheel track: 9 ft 2 ins (2.8 m)

Weights:
Empty: 5,400 lb (2,450 kg)
Maximum take-off: 11,023 lb (5,000 kg), with growth potential for 11,464 lb (5,200 kg) in offshore role
Payload: 5,512 lb (2,500 kg)

Performance (MTOW):
Never-exceed speed (VNE): 165 kts (180 mph) 305 km/h
Maximum speed: 151 kts (174 mph) 280 km/h
Cruise speed: 135 kts (155 mph) 250 km/h
Maximum climb rate: 1,770 ft (540 m) per minute
Range with full fuel: 486 naut miles (559 miles) 900 km. with 2 minutes reserve
Duration: 4 hours 40 minutes, with 20 minutes reserve

PT Industri Pesawat Terbang Nusantara (IPTN) (Indonesia)

Corporate address: See Airliners section for company details.

● Activities

● In addition to its airliner programmes, IPTN undertakes licence production of the Bell 412, and Eurocopter BO-105 and Super Puma, and signed an agreement with Bell in 1995 covering regional work and support for the new Bell 407T and 430.

Agusta SpA (Italy)

Corporate address: Via Giovanni Agusta 520, 21017 Cascina Costa di Samarate (VA).
Telephone: +39 331 229111
Facsimile: +39 331 229605, 222595
Founded: 1923, as the original Agusta production and maintenance facility at Cascina Costa. Currently part of the Finmeccanica group.
Employees: About 6,000.
Information: Leonardo Monti (Marketing and Sales Promotion Manager – *telephone* +39 331 229970, *facsimile* +39 331 229920).

■ Facilities

■ Anagni (FR), Benevento, Brindisi, Frosinone and Monteprandone (AP) in the north of Italy, and Cascina Costa di Samarate (VA), Sesto Calende (VA), Somma Lombardo (VA) and Vergiate (VA) in central and southern Italy.

● Activities

● In addition to the helicopters detailed here, Agusta collaborates with Westland of the UK in the EH-101 programme, and participates in the 4-nation NH-90 programme (see Multi-National at the end of this section).

● Since first signing an agreement with Bell of the USA in 1952, Agusta has produced various Bell helicopters under licence. This collaboration continues, currently joined also by helicopters from Boeing, McDonnell Douglas and Sikorsky.

• The Sesto Calende (VA) works undertakes development and production of SIAI-Marchetti aeroplanes.

• Agusta Service has a customer support network based in 3 main centres in Italy, Belgium and the USA, plus 23 Service Centres in other countries. 2 new Maintenance and Support facilities at Manila (Philippines) and Bierset (Belgium). The Components Overhaul Centre in Zaventem, (Belgium), opened in February 1994. Spare parts distribution is based on 3 computer-linked supply centres at Somma Lombardo, Philadelphia and Bierset.

• Agusta Service Engineering, in co-operation with the ILS organization, updates configurations of Agusta helicopters, developing mid-life improvement packages, avionics upgrades and other modifications.

SUBSIDIARIES

SIAI-Marchetti
Corporate address: Via Indipendenza 2, 21018 Sesto Calende (VA).

● Activities

• See Combat section for its fixed-wing programmes.

Agusta Aerospace Corporation
HQ address: Travose, Philadelphia, PA 19047, USA.

Agusta Aerospace Services SA
HQ address: Liege Airport, Belgium.

ASSOCIATED COMPANIES

E.H. Industries Ltd
Address: London, UK.

E.H. Industries Inc
Address: Washington, USA.

N.H. Industries SARL
Address: Aix-en-Provence, France.

Agusta A 109C, CM, K2, KM, MAX and Power

First flight: 4 August 1971, with delivery of the initial production A 109A in 1976.
Role: Civil and military multi-purpose light helicopter, currently available in 6 individual versions with 3 different engine options.
Sales: Over 600 of all versions.
Details: The new A 109 Power, with other versions detailed under Aircraft variants. A 109 Power and A 109C data in the specification box.
Crew/passengers: Pilot and passenger or 2 pilots in the cockpit, with main cabin accommodation for 6 persons. Additional space aft of the rear seats allows for extra baggage, ferry tanks, or easy conversion to an EMS role with 1 or 2 longitudinal litters and 2 medical attendants. Cabin width permits a seat between the litters, and the co-pilot seat is reversible for an additional medical attendant. Optional 4/5-seat VIP, 6-seat executive or 6-seat utility layouts.
Baggage compartment: 33.55 cu ft (0.95 m^3) aft of cabin.
Optional equipment: Dual controls, rotor brake, 2,205 lb (1,000 kg) fixed cargo hook, 441 lb (200 kg) rescue hoist, windshield wiper, snow skis, removable emergency floats, slump protection pads, sliding doors, extended-range fuel tanks, particle separator, engine fire extinguishers, bleed air heating, air conditioning, and sound proofing. See also Avionics.
Rotor system: 4-blade main rotor with drooped leading edges and high inertia, composite material and interchangeable blades. Fully articulated rotor head with titanium hub connected to composite grips through a single elastomeric bearing on each blade.
Tail rotor characteristics: Full authority 2-blade semi-rigid tail rotor.
Flight control system: Collective, cyclic, anti-torque system with collective-synchronized elevator. Hydraulically servo assisted by dual hydraulically actuated swashplate cylinders.
Airframe materials: Aluminium alloy and honeycomb structure.
Engines: 2 Pratt & Whitney Canada PW206C turboshafts with FADEC.
Engine rating: Each 640 shp (477 kW) take-off for 5 minutes, 562 shp (419 kW) maximum continuous, 732 shp (546 kW) OEI for 2.5 minutes and 670 shp (500 kW) OEI 30 minutes.
Transmission rating: 900 shp (671 kW) maximum continuous, 560 shp (418 kW) OEI maximum continuous, and 640 shp (477 kW) OEI for 2.5 minutes.
Fuel system: 605 litres, with provision for an additional 273 litres of auxiliary fuel for extended range.
Electrical system: 2 fully independent AC and DC systems. See Aircraft variants.
Hydraulic system: 2 independent flight control hydraulic systems, each capable of operating swashplate actuators in the event of a failure. 2 utility hydraulic systems with 2 accumulators for undercarriage, rotor brake, wheel brakes and nosewheel centring device.
Radar: Optional colour weather radar.
Flight avionics/instrumentation: Single or dual pilot IFR capability is expandable with a flight director and autotrim, and GPS, integrated with the 3-axis AFCS. Other options include radar altimeter and ELT. Liquid crystal displays available for navigation management or for engines monitoring and for caution and warning presentation. See Aircraft variants.
Aircraft variants:
A 109C is a pilot and 6-7 passenger executive/corporate helicopter, suited also to Medevac. 2 x 450 shp (335.6 kW) take-off rating Allison 250-C20R/1 turboshafts. 550 litres of usable fuel, with 150 litres optional for extended range. Certified for single pilot IFR operation. IFR equipment includes 3-axis autopilot, dual VHF, dual VOR, DME, ADF, TDR and EHSI. Optional flight director and colour weather radar.
Coastal Patrol variant of the A 109C has armoured seats; 550 litres of usable fuel plus optional 150 or 200 litre auxiliary tank and optional self-sealing; pintle-mounted 7.62-mm machine-gun; 4-axis autopilot with automatic approach to hovering to permit easy rescue operations; FLIR; 360° search radar with display information interfaced with LRN 85 VHF Omega, VOR, DME and flight path computer; chaff/flare dispensers; radar warning, and more. Electrical power with 2 x 150 amp (28 volt DC) starter-generators, 3 x 250 volt-amp (115/26 volt AC, 400 Hz) static inverters, and 22 amp-hour battery.
A 109CM is a multi-role military version, capable of carrying 4 or 8 anti-armour missiles and HeliTOW 2. Alternative weapons include rocket and gun pods. APX334 or Helios gyrostabilized sight, FLIR and night vision goggles. Collins CMS-80 cockpit management system. Electrical power with 2 x 160 amp (28 volt DC) starter-generators, 2 x 250 volt-amp or high-load 600 volt-amp (115/26 volt AC, 400 Hz) static inverters, and 27 amp-hour (24 volt) ni-cd battery. Users include the Belgian Army.

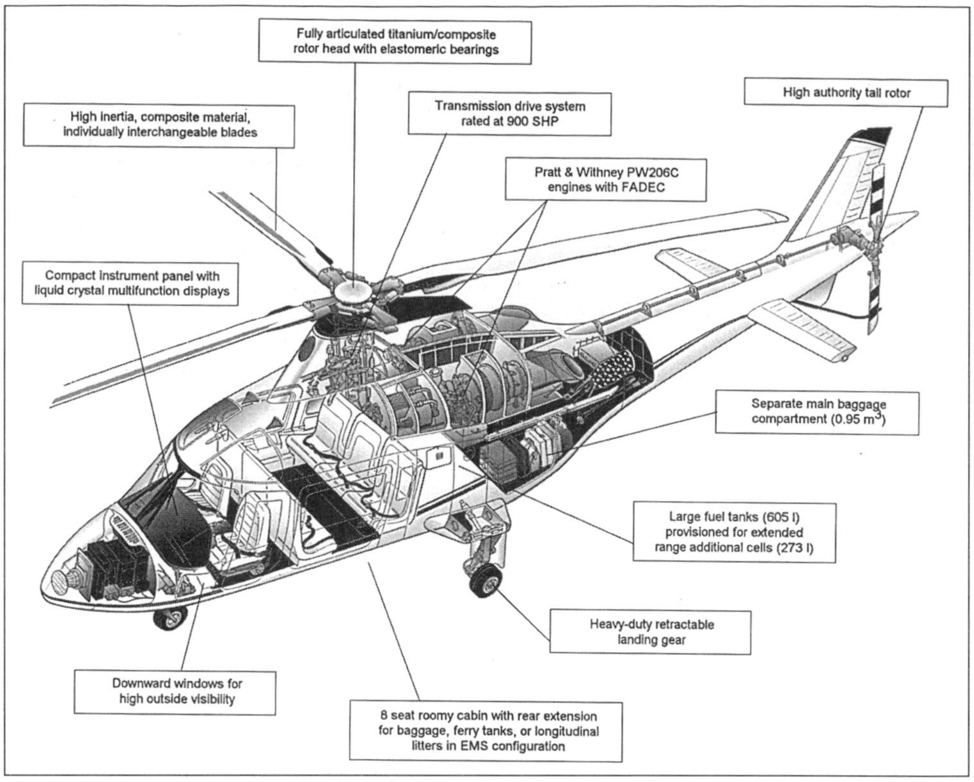

Agusta A 109 Power technical features (courtesy Agusta)

Agusta A 109 Power

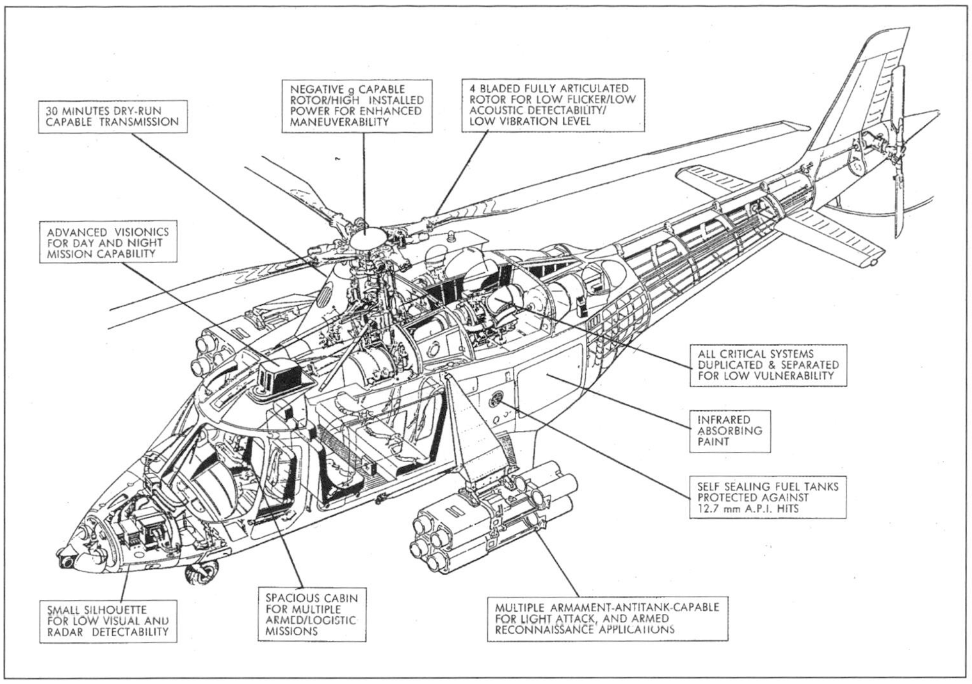

Agusta A 109CM technical features (courtesy Agusta)

A 109 G. di. F is a coast guard version with several of the surveillance and detection systems of the Coastal Patrol, and can have a pintle-mounted MG-3 machine gun.
A 109K2 is a multi-purpose helicopter for hot-and-high operations, using 2 x 632 shp (471 kW) maximum continuous rated Turbomeca Arriel 1K1 engines. AlliedSignal Bendix/King Silver Crown avionics package. Typical roles are medevac and rescue. Can operate up to 20,000 ft (6,100 m) and in 50° C temperature.
A 109K2 Law Enforcement is based on the A 109K2 but has removable equipment suited to its police work, including cargo hook, rescue hoist, wire strike protection, SX16 searchlight, MA3 retractable light, external loudspeakers, emergency floats, EMS options, and more.
A 109KM is a military version based on the A 109K2, and was developed with the European army light multi-role helicopter philosophy in mind. Equipment and armament options are similar to those of the A 109CM, but with performance differences due to the Arriel engines. Electrical power with 2 x 160 amp (28 volt DC) starter-generators, 2 x 250 volt-amp or high-load 600 volt-amp (115/26 volt AC, 400 Hz) static inverters or alternative 6 kVA alternator plus a standby 250 volt-amp inverter, and 22 amp-hour (24 volt) ni-cd battery.
A 109MAX is a dedicated Emergency Medical Service helicopter, allowing full exploitation of its capabilities and accommodation. 1 or 2 pilots, 1 litter plus 3 assistants or 2 litters and 2 assistants, and medical equipment.
A 109 Power is the latest version of the A 109 family. Take-off in Category A without any load reductions from elevated helipads. A-109K2 cabin length, redesigned retractable undercarriage that increases available internal space, improved aerodynamics, new digital control engines, and new cockpit instrumentation with LCDs.

DETAILS FOR A 109 POWER, *WITH A 109C IN ITALICS WHERE DIFFERENT.*

Principal dimensions:
Rotor diameter (main): 36 ft 1 ins (11 m)
Maximum length, rotors turning: 42 ft 9.5 ins (13.035 m)
Maximum length, rotor stopped: 37 ft 7 ins (11.46 m), *37 ft 6.5 ins (11.44 m)*
Maximum height: 11 ft 2 ins (3.4 m), *11 ft 6 ins (3.5 m)*

Cabin:
Length: 6 ft 11 ins (2.1 m), *5 ft 4 ins (1.63 m)*
Width: 5 ft 2 ins (1.58 m), *4 ft 9 ins (1.44 m)*
Height: 4 ft 2.5 ins (1.28 m)
Volume: 180.1 cu ft (5.1 m^3), *156.1 cu ft (4.42 m^3)*

Main rotor:
Aerofoil section: NACA 23011
Blade area: each 19.81 sq ft (1.84 m^2)
Rotor disc: 1,022.89 sq ft (95.03 m^2)

Tail rotor:
Diameter: 6 ft 7 ins (2 m)

Undercarriage:
Type: Heavy duty retractable, with nosewheel. See Optional equipment
Wheel base: *11 ft 7 ins (3.535 m)*

Weights:
Empty, basic: 3,428 lb (1,555 kg)
Maximum take-off: 5,996 lb (2,720 kg)
Maximum take-off, external load: 6,614 lb (3,000 kg)
Useful load: *2,491 lb (1,130 kg)*

Performance:
Never-exceed speed (VNE): 168 kts (193 mph) 311 km/h
Maximum cruise speed: 160 kts (184 mph) 296 km/h, *152 kts (175 mph) 282 km/h at 5,000 ft (1,525 m)*
Maximum climb rate: 2,160 ft (658 m) per minute, *1,693 ft (516 m) per minute*
Climb rate, OEI: *354 ft (108 m) per minute*
IGE hovering ceiling: 15,330 ft (4,672 m), *11,400 ft (3,474 m)*
OGE hovering ceiling: 12,220 ft (3,725 m), *8,000 ft (2,438 m)*
Ceiling: 20,000 ft (6,100 m), *15,000 ft (4,572 m)*, service
Ceiling, OEI: 12,600 ft (3,840 m), *7,000 ft (2,133 m)*, service
Range: 502 naut miles (578 miles) 930 km, at 5,000 ft (1,525 m), best speed, 878 litres of fuel and no reserve, *420 naut miles (483 miles) 778 km, at 5,000 ft (1,525 m) and long-range cruise speed*
Duration: 4 hours 46 minutes, *4 hours 20 minutes*, conditions as for range

Agusta A 119 Koala

Role: Single-engined, widebody passenger and utility helicopter.
Crew/passengers: Pilot and 7 passengers. EMS configuration for 2 litters and 2 medical attendants.
Baggage compartments: Small compartment of "almost half a cubic metre" accessible from inside the cabin. External access to the main 33.55 cu ft (0.95 m^3) baggage area in the tail section, of 7 ft 6.5 ins (2.3 m) length.
Cabin access: Large sliding doors.
Rotor system: High inertia main rotor with "on condition" blades of composite materials. Low vibration, low maintenance, fully-articulated main rotor hub, of titanium, with composite grips and elastomeric bearings.
Airframe materials: Aluminium alloy.
Engine: Unspecified 800 shp (596.6 kW) turboshaft with FADEC.

DETAILS FOR KOALA.

Principal dimensions:
Rotor diameter (main): 36 ft 1 ins (11 m)

Cabin:
Length: 6 ft 11 ins (2.1 m)
Width: 5 ft 3.5 ins (1.61 m)
Height: 4 ft 2.5 ins (1.28 m)
Volume: 121.84 cu ft (3.45m^3)

Weights:
Maximum take-off: 5,732 lb (2,600 kg)
Maximum take-off, external load: 5,997 lb (2,720 kg)
Useful load: 2,720 lb (1,234 kg), or 2,985 lb (1,354 kg) with external load

Performance (MTOW):
Never-exceed speed (VNE): 150 kts (173 mph) 278 km/h
Maximum cruise speed: 133 kts (153 mph) 246 km/h
IGE hovering ceiling: 7,875 ft (2,400 m)
OGE hovering ceiling: 4,035 ft (1,230 m)
Ceiling: 13,910 ft (4,240 m), service
Range: 360 naut miles (414 miles) 667 km
Duration: 3 hours 48 minutes

Agusta's new A 119 Koala, launched in 1994

Agusta A 129 Mangusta and International

First flight: 11 September 1983. 9 January 1995 for the A 129 International.
Role: Day and night attack and reconnaissance, escort, fire support, area suppression, and air-to-air combat.

★ Aims
★ Low detectability (visual, acoustic, IR and radar

Agusta A 129 International

signatures), good detection of the enemy (visual, electronic warning), high agility and manoeuvrability, nap-of-the-earth performance, and passive/active electronic countermeasures.

★ High survivability (see Safety features).

Sales: Deliveries to the Italian Army began in October 1990 against 60 ordered, with 30 delivered by early 1995; 15 Italian Mangustas are being upgraded to have undernose gun turrets and Stinger AAMs. Additional 30 required in both attack and scout configurations, the latter with mast-mounted sights, but doubts have been expressed as to whether more than 60 helicopters will be funded.

Crew: 2, in tandem stepped cockpits, with pilot at rear.

Rotor system: 4-blade main rotor, each blade having a Nomex and carbonfibre main spar, Nomex honeycomb leading/trailing edges, composites skin and stainless steel leading-edge strip. Fully articulated rotor head with titanium hub connected to composite grips through a single elastomeric bearing on each blade.

Tail rotor characteristics: 2-blade, delta hinged.

Airframe materials: Wide use of composites for the fuselage, amounting to some 45% of structural weight.

Safety features: 12.7-mm ballistic tolerance by double/triple vital systems redundancy, system separation, components designed to operate after being hit, armour plating, composites materials, transmission operation without oil, protected flight controls, and automatic reconfiguration. Crew protected against ground fire of up to 23-mm calibre. Can operate in contaminated (NBC) environments without the crew wearing special protective suits. MIL-STD-1290 crashworthiness, with crew survival and minimum aircraft damage after a 36 ft (11 m) per second crash impact, achieved through energy absorbing undercarriage, Martin Baker seats, fuel cells and airframe; crew protection via roll bars, A-shaped reinforced frame and cyclic stick installation; and energy egress (pyrotechnic, both sides).

Engines: *Mangusta*: 2 Rolls-Royce Mk 1004 turboshafts, each 881 shp (657 kW) take-off and 825 shp (615 kW) maximum continuous. *International*: 2 LHTEC (Allison/AlliedSignal) T800-LHT-800 turboshafts, each 1,335 shp (996 kW) take-off, 1,240 shp (925 kW) intermediate, and 1,404 shp (1,045 kW) OEI contingency. Sand and NBC filters. Infra-red suppressor system.

Transmission rating: 1,300 shp (970 kW) for Mangusta and 1,797 shp (1,340 kW) for International.

Fuel system: 1,653 lb (750 kg).

Hydraulic system: 2 independent flight control hydraulic systems of 3,000 psi, each capable of operating swashplate actuators in the event of a failure. 2 utility hydraulic systems with 2 accumulators for rotor brake and wheel brakes.

De-icing system: Blades and engines.

Flight avionics/instrumentation: Computerized, digital integrated management system (IMS), based on the MIL 1553B digital databus architecture, with automatic performance computation, systems monitoring, weapon control, autonomous navigation, and automatic flight control that allows hands-off operation (manual reversion). Information is presented in both cockpits on multi-function displays, but conventional instrumentation is provided for back-up. Integrated INS, GPS and Doppler navigation. Night vision system comprises thermal image cameras, integrated helmet and display, sighting system, flight symbology, and NVG cockpit. Sight and pilot night vision system integration allows the crew to detect, identify and engage targets at extended stand-off ranges during day or night or in adverse weather conditions. HeliTOW sight, or mast-mounted sight. Honeywell FLIR carried in the steerable nose turret is slaved to the crew's integrated helmet and display sighting systems (IHADSS). International has a new second generation FLIR (83 x mag), state-of-the-art CCD TV (126 x mag), laser rangefinder/designator, automatic target tracker, and video recorder.

Self-protection systems: Chaff/flare dispensers, IR and radar jammers, and radar and laser warning receivers.

Fixed guns: Only International has a 3-barrel 20-mm Gatling-type gun under the nose in a Lockheed Martin/GIAT turret as standard, to allow quick off-axis engagement (with 500 rounds of ammunition), but 15 Italian Army Mangustas are receiving similar guns as retrofits.

Number of weapon pylons: 4 under the stub-wings, each 661 lb (300 kg) capacity, with 2° up and 10° down movement to assist weapon launching.

Expendable weapons and equipment: Up to a 2,646 lb (1,200 kg) load. Choice of up to 8 TOW 2A or Hellfire anti-armour missiles (or mix), or alternative Hot for Mangusta; 4 launchers for 76 x 70-mm or 38 x 81-mm rockets (Mangusta can also deploy 68-mm rockets); air-to-air missiles (Javelin, 8 Mistral, AIM-9L Sidewinder or 4 Stinger for Mangusta, but Stinger for International), and with 15 Italian Army Mangustas receiving Stingers along with the gun turret retrofit detailed above; and 20-mm gun pods. On-the-field armament reconfiguration, and armament mixing capability.

Aircraft variants:

Mangusta is the standard Italian Army version.

International uses more powerful engines, has a higher transmission rating, a standard undernose gun, and some avionics upgrading.

DETAILS FOR MANGUSTA, *WITH INTERNATIONAL IN ITALICS.*

Principal dimensions:
Rotor diameter (main): 39 ft 0.5 ins (11.9 m), *the same*
Maximum length, rotors turning: 47 ft 0.5 ins (14.33 m)
Fuselage length: 40 ft 10 ins (12.452 m), *the same*
Maximum height: 11 ft (3.35 m) above rotor head

Main rotor:
Rotor disc: 1,197 sq ft (111.2 m^2)

Tail rotor:
Diameter: 7 ft 7.5 ins (2.32 m), *8 ft 2.5 ins (2.5 m)*

Undercarriage:
Type: Fixed tailwheel type (see Safety features)
Wheel base: 23 ft 1 ins (7.03 m)
Wheel track: 7 ft 4 ins (2.23 m), *the same*

Weights:
Empty, operating: 5,575 lb (2,529 kg)
Maximum take-off: 9,039 lb (4,100 kg), *11,023 lb (5,000 kg)*
Anti-tank mission weight: 8,708 lb (3,950 kg)

Performance (Mangusta for anti-tank mission, sea level, ISA + 20° C, *and International at MTOW*):
Maximum speed: 149 kts (172 mph) 275 km/h
Cruise speed: 135 kts (155 mph) 250 km/h, *150 kts (173 mph) 278 km/h at sea level, ISA*
Maximum climb rate: 2,009 ft (612 m) per minute, *2,225 ft (678 m) per minute, sea level, and 1,062 ft (324 m) per minute, ISA, vertical climb rate*
Climb rate, OEI: *905 ft (276 m) per minute, sea level, ISA*
IGE hovering ceiling: 10,300 ft (3,140 m), *13,800 ft (4,200 m) ISA or 7,800 ft (2,380 m) ISA + 25° C, maximum continuous power*
OGE hovering ceiling: 6,200 ft (1,890 m), *10,800 ft (3,290 m) ISA, 4,400 ft (1,340 m) ISA + 25° C, maximum continuous power*
Ceiling: 15,500 ft (4,725 m)
Range: *303 naut miles (349 miles) 561 km, internal fuel, no reserve, sea level*
Self-deploy range: *over 540 naut miles (621 miles) 1,000 km using external fuel tanks and carrying 4 AAMs.*
Duration: 2 hours 30 minutes

Agusta-Bell AB-206B JetRanger III

Licence-built version of the Bell JetRanger III, with a 450 shp (335.6 kW) Allison 250-C20R/4 turboshaft engine. Sometimes referred to as the AB-206R. Among the most recent customers is the Turkish Army, which began receiving 20 for training in April 1995.

Agusta-Bell AB-212 Naval/Skyshark

Though based on the Bell 212, the *Naval* is an Agusta-missionized version which operates with the Italian Navy and the armed forces of various other NATO countries and in South America. Roles can include shore or corvette/frigate-based anti-submarine search and attack, anti-ship, OTHT, surface surveillance, SAR, transport and liaison. Can undertake independent electronic warfare, anti-submarine and anti-ship missions. An upgraded version is the *Skyshark*, developed with engine and airframe improvements, including the use of PT6T-3D Twin Pac engines. It has digital MIL 1553B databus architecture, 4-axis AFCS, autonomous navigation (INS, GPS, air data systems), 360° search/track radar, FLIR/TV, variable depth sonar, and torpedoes or Sea Skua missiles. Maximum take-off weight is 11,200 lb (5,080 kg), cruise speed is 110 kts (127 mph) 204 km/h, and it has a range of 308 naut miles (355 miles) 571 km.

Agusta-Bell AB-212 Naval

Agusta-Bell AB-412EP, Griffon and Maritime Patrol

Licence-built versions of the Bell 412EP and Griffon, plus an Agusta-developed dedicated maritime patrol version with a 600 lb (272 kg) rescue hoist, FLIR, high-resolution TV camera, 4-axis AFCS, high-intensity night search light, 360° search radar, and new integrated avionics system. The Maritime Patrol version accommodates 2 pilots, plus a radar/FLIR/LLLTV console operator and a rescue hoist operator. Can still transport 14 equipped troops or 3 to 6 litters plus 2 attendants.

Agusta-developed AB-412EP Maritime Patrol version of the Bell 412EP

Agusta-Boeing CH-47C

The Italian licence-built version of the CH-47C Chinook was originally produced under the Elicotteri Meridionali SpA company name, which acquired the production rights a year after forming with Agusta assistance. Powered by 2 x 3,750 shp (2,796 kW) 10-minute take-off rated AlliedSignal T55-L-712E turboshafts, it has a maximum take-off weight of 50,000 lb (22,680 kg), a useful load of 27,015 lb (12,254 kg), and maximum external cargo load of 28,000 lb (12,700 kg). Typical 3 flight crew plus 33 troops, but optional 44-50 or 59 in high-density arrangements. Alternatively, 24 litters and 2 attendants. Agusta has also developed firefighting and Emergency Surgery Flying Centre variants.

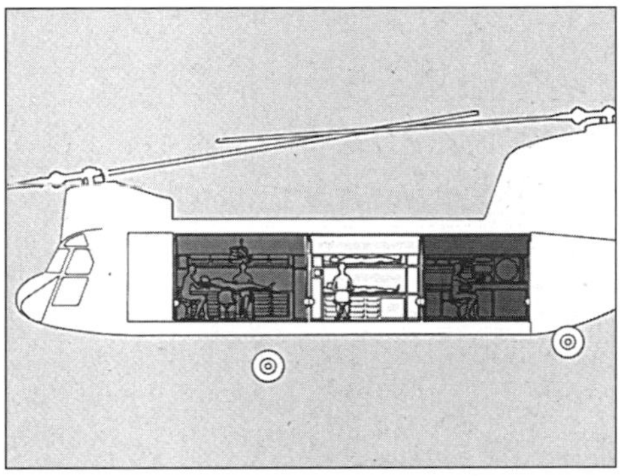

Agusta-Boeing CH-47C in Emergency Surgery Flying Centre configuration, developed jointly by Agusta and the Hospital Division of COGEFAR (courtesy of Agusta)

Agusta-McDonnell Douglas AMD-500E

50 McDonnell Douglas MD 500Es were produced by Agusta for use as basic trainers by the Italian Air Force, which is responsible for training helicopter pilots for all branches of the Italian armed forces. All delivered.

Agusta-McDonnell Douglas AMD-520N

This is a licence-built McDonnell Douglas MD 520N, characterized by having a NOTAR anti-torque system. It incorporates graphite and Kevlar lightweight composite components. Has 13% more power than the AMD-500, allowing it to carry an extra 280 lb (127 kg) of payload. Due to its higher safety and low noise level, it is particularly suited to police operations, passenger carrying and aerial work. Available.

Agusta-Sikorsky SH-3D, S-61N and HH-4F Combat SAR

SH-3Ds built by Agusta are operated by the Italian Navy and other NATO and Latin America and Middle/Far East nations. The HH-3F, typically for search and rescue, remained in production in 1995 in the modernized Combat SAR version, meeting the requirements of the Italian Air Force and having a night rescue capability. Agusta is also modernizing the US Navy's SH-3H fleet to extend operating life into the next century.

Dragon Fly srl (Italy)

Corporate address: Via Raffaello 1/A, 22060 Cucciago (Co).
Telephone: +39 31 725 190
Facsimile: +39 31 787 642
Founded: 1993.
Employees: 35.
Information: Arnaldo P. Ratto.

Dragon Fly

Role: Two-seat light helicopter. Also suited to training and other roles.

★ Aims

★ Wherever possible, developed and tested in accordance with FAR 27 requirements. Type certification under Very Light Rotorcraft specifications was underway in mid-1995.

Sales: Cost 148,000,000 lire (1995) delivered fly-away. Production rate of 3 per month (factory capacity for 8 a month). 2 pre-production helicopters were delivered to a French company in December 1993 for development testing. First full production helicopter was delivered to an Italian operator in April 1994. Now also used in Belgium, Czech Republic, France, Germany, New Zealand and Turkey. Can be shipped in kit form upon request.

Dragon Fly two-seat light helicopters

Crew/passengers: 2, with dual controls.
Freight, internal: Baggage compartment.
Optional equipment: Electric trim (lateral). Chip detectors for the main and tail rotor transmission.
Rotor system: 2-blade, semi-rigid of see-saw (teetering) type. Metal blades. Transmission uses a centrifugal clutch and 2 V belts.
Tail rotor characteristics: 2-blade, metal.
Tail surfaces: T-tail, with horizontal stabilizer above the fin.
Flight control system: Conventional mechanical.
Airframe materials: Welded titanium frame. Tailboom and undercarriage skids of aluminium alloy. Composite cabin and engine bay structures.
Engine: Dragon Fly/Hirth F30A26AK 2-stroke piston engine.
Engine rating: 105 hp (78 kW).
Fuel system: 64 litres.
Electrical system: Starter-generator.
Flight avionics/instrumentation: Full VFR instrumentation and including altimeter, airspeed indicator, bank indicator and compass. Engine and fuel instruments, and malfunction warning lights. Optional fuel pressure indicator, engine fire warning light, radio transceiver, and cabin intercom.

DETAILS FOR DRAGON FLY.

Principal dimensions:
Rotor diameter (main): 21 ft 8 ins (6.6 m)
Fuselage length: 18 ft 3 ins (5.561 m)
Maximum height: 7 ft 9 ins (2.358 m)

Main rotor:
Aerofoil section: NACA 0012
Rotor disc: 368.1 sq ft (34.2 m)
Rpm: 500

Tail rotor:
Diameter: 3 ft 8 ins (1.12 m)

Undercarriage:
Type: Fixed twin skids, with ground handling wheels. Optional floats
Skid base: 7 ft 5 ins (2.26 m)
Skid track: 5 ft 1 ins (1.55 m)

Weights:
Empty: 507 lb (230 kg)
Maximum take-off: 992 lb (450 kg), or 1,102 lb (500 kg) emergency or with floats

Performance:
Never-exceed speed (VNE): 80 kts (92 mph) 150 km/h
Cruise speed: 59 kts (68 mph) 110 km/h
Maximum climb rate: 1,870 ft (570 m) per minute at normal MTOW, 1,280 ft (390 m) at emergency MTOW
IGE hovering ceiling: 10,500 ft (3,200 m), at normal MTOW, 6,725 ft (2,050 m) at emergency MTOW
OGE hovering ceiling: 6,560 ft (2,000 m) at normal MTOW, 4,755 ft (1,450 m) at emergency MTOW
Range: 178 naut miles (205 miles) 330 km at cruise speed, 60 litres of fuel
Duration: 3.5 hours at normal MTOW, or 2.5 hours at emergency MTOW

Elisport srl (Italy)

Corporate address: Strada Traforo del Pino 104, 10132 Torino.
Telephone: +39 11 8999565, 8999618
Facsimile: +39 11 8999618, 8981144

Elisport CH-7 Angel

Role: Single-seat, ultralight helicopter. Can also be used for agricultural work.

▲ Development

▲ Developed from the Augusto Cicarè CH-6.
Sales: Marketed by Aerosport. Kit 47,000,000 lire without engine, 43,000,000 lire also without cabin, and 40,000,000 lire also without cabin and instruments.

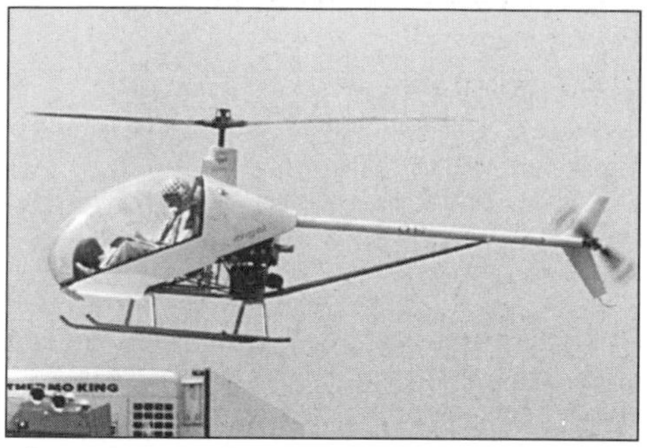

Elisport CH-7 Angel

Rotor system: 2-blade semi-rigid main rotor, with composite blades.
Tail rotor characteristics: 2-blade, aluminium. NACA 63014, symmetrical, aerofoil.
Tail surfaces: Fixed dorsal/ventral fin, with tailskid.
Flight control system: Push-pull, without cables.
Fuselage: Pod and boom type.
Airframe materials: Welded 4130 steel tube frame, and bolted aluminium alloy tailboom and skids. Composites cabin.
Engine: Rotax 582 or similar engine.
Engine rating: 64.4 hp (48 kW).
Transmission: Cardanic gear and transmission box.
Fuel system: 40 litres.
Flight avionics/instrumentation: Instruments for altitude, vertical speed, engine/rotor rpm, water temperature, gearbox oil temperature, and dual EGT.

Details for Angel.

Principal dimensions:
Rotor diameter (main): 20 ft 3 ins (6.17 m)
Length: 23 ft 1.5 ins (7.15 m)
Fuselage width: 2 ft 8 ins (0.82 m)
Maximum height: 7 ft 2.3 ins (2.19 m)

Cabin:
Width: 2 ft 6 ins (0.76 m)

Main rotor:
Aerofoil section: NACA 8-H-12, asymmetric
Rotor disc: 321.6 sq ft (29.88 m)

Tail rotor:
Diameter: 3 ft 4.5 ins (1.03 m)

Undercarriage:
Type: Fixed twin skids, with ground handling wheels
Skid track: 5 ft 4 ins (1.64 m)

Weights:
Empty: 452 lb (205 kg)
Maximum take-off: 794 lb (360 kg)

Performance:
Never-exceed speed (VNE): 80 kts (92 mph) 149 km/h
Cruise speed: 59 kts (68 mph) 110 km/h
Maximum climb rate: 1,970 ft (600 m) per minute
IGE hovering ceiling: 6,890 ft (2,100 m)
OGE hovering ceiling: 4,920 ft (1,500 m)
Ceiling: 11,500 ft (3,500 m)
Range: 148 naut miles (170 miles) 275 km
Duration: 3 hours

Fuji Heavy Industries Ltd (Japan)

Corporate address: See Combat section for company details.

Fuji-Bell 205B and UH-1J

First flight: 1988 for 205B.
Role: Intermediate civil and military general-purpose helicopters.

▲ Development

▲ Having manufactured 56 civil Model 204B/B-2s under a licensing agreement with Bell (sold co-operatively by Fuji and Mitsui Bussan Aerospace Co), plus military UH-1Hs, Fuji is now undertaking production of the Model 205B civil helicopter (upgraded Bell 205) primarily for utility and flying-crane work. Production 205Bs became available in the latter part of 1995. Earlier, in 1993, deliveries began of the UH-1J, an upgraded version of the UH-1H for the JGSDF and powered by a 1,500 shp (1,118.6 kW) T53-K-70 turboshaft built by Kawasaki.

Details: Model 205B.
Crew/passengers: 1 pilot plus 14 passengers.
Engine: AlliedSignal T5317B turboshaft.
Engine rating: 1,800 shp (1,342 kW).
Aircraft variants:
205B is the current civil version, with emphasis on good hot-and-high performance.
UH-1J is a military transport, for up to 13 troops. Slightly larger than the UH-1H, uses AH-1S rotors, has upgraded avionics integrated via the 1553B databus, improved armour protection, IR suppression, wire strike protection system, NVG capability, and more.

Details for 205B.

Principal dimensions:
Rotor diameter (main): 48 ft (14.63 m)
Maximum length, rotors turning: 57 ft 3.25 ins (17.46 m)
Width: 9 ft 4.8 ins (2.86 m), skids
Maximum height: 12 ft 9.8 ins (3.91 m)

Weights:
Empty: 5,324 lb (2,415 kg)
Maximum take-off: 10,500 lb (4,763 kg)

Performance (estimated):
Maximum speed: 130 kts (150 mph) 241 km/h
Cruise speed: 122 kts (140 mph) 226 km/h
Maximum climb rate: 2,530 ft (770 m) per minute
IGE hovering ceiling: 19,500 ft (5,945 m)
OGE hovering ceiling: 15,200 ft (4,635 m)
Ceiling: 20,000 ft (6,100 m), service
Range: 310 naut miles (357 miles) 574 km

Fuji-Bell AH-1S

Licence-built version of the Bell AH-1S (actual AH-1F) HueyCobra, following evaluation of 2 US-built helicopters during 1979-80. Agreement was signed in 1982, and 91 are planned for the JGSDF, of which 78 had been delivered by 1995. 1,800 shp (1,342 kW) AlliedSignal T53-L-703 turboshaft offers a never-exceed speed of 170 kts (196 mph) 315 km/h and a mission radius of 123 naut miles (142 miles) 228 km.

Japan Aircraft Manufacturing Co Ltd (Japan)

Corporate address: 3175 Shova-machi, Kanazawa-ku, Yokohama 236
Telephone: +81 45 773 5111
Facsimile: +81 45 771 1807
Telex: 3822 267 NIPPI J
Founded: 11 October 1934.
Employees: About 1,688.

DIVISIONS

Aircraft

● Activities

● Known also as Nippi, the company has a broad-based aerospace business that currently includes component and sub-assembly construction for many of the licence-built and indigenous aircraft produced in Japan (including the forward fuselage for the CH-47J), while its Atsugi works (28 Soyagi 2-chome, Yamato City, Kanagawa Prefecture, 242) specializes in maintenance, overhaul, and modification. Foreign sub-contracting includes the construction of elevators for the Boeing 757, wing inspar ribs for the 767 and 777, and the underwing fuselage Y barrel for the McDonnell Douglas MD-11.

Space Equipment

Aerial Target Systems

Boat

Industrial Equipment

Kawasaki Heavy Industries Ltd (Japan)

Corporate address: See Combat section for company details.

● Activities

● In addition to the details below, the BK117 developed jointly with Germany (now Eurocopter as partner) can be found in the Multi-national section. The military/civil twin-rotor Kawasaki-Boeing KV107IIA is no longer in production, with the final delivery having taken place on 16 February 1990. Manufacture of CH-47J Chinooks continues, to replace KV107s with the Japan Air and Ground Self-Defence Forces. Deliveries started in 1986 and all 16 JASDF CH-47Js have been delivered, plus a substantial number of the 42 required for the JGSDF. Production also continues of the OH-6D, a licence-built McDonnell Douglas MD 500D for the JGSDF/JMSDF, plus civil examples. In addition, Kawasaki is prime contractor on the OH-X scout/observation helicopter programme for the JGSDF, expected to replace the OH-6D with the JGSDF.

Kawasaki OH-X Kongata Kansoku

First flight: July 1996.
Role: Armed scout and observation, with attack capabilities.

▲ Development

▲ Contracts valued at about 82 billion yen have been awarded to Kawasaki (prime contractor, with 60% stake), Fuji (20%) and Mitsubishi (20%) by Japan's

Kawasaki OH-X Kongata Kansoku armed scout/observation helicopter (Bill Hobson)

Technical Research and Development Agency for the development and construction of 4 flying and 3 static test OH-X prototypes plus 20 engines for the flying prototypes, ground testing and certification.
▲ 1991. OH-X airframe and XTSI-1 engine development was started. Mitsubishi MG-5 was developed as a prototype to the XTSI-1 engine, developing about 600 shp (447 kW).
▲ October 1992. Design began, completed the following year.
▲ September 1994. A mock-up of the OH-X was put on show by Kawasaki, having been built the previous year.
▲ May 1997. Delivery of the first prototype to the Japan Defence Agency for testing.
▲ 1999. Scheduled completion of the development programme.
▲ 2000. Initial deliveries to the JGSDF.
Sales: JGSDF is expected to acquire up to 200.
Crew: 2, in tandem stepped cockpits, with the pilot in the forward cockpit.
Rotor system: 4-blade bearingless rotor system, with composites blades.
Tail rotor characteristics: 8-blade ducted type.
Tail surfaces: Tall tailfin and constant-chord horizontal stabilizers.
Safety features: Rotor and transmission systems are ballistic tolerant. Crashworthy seating. Armour protection. Wire cutter just ahead of the roof sight.
Engines: 2 Mitsubishi XTSI-1 turboshafts. IR suppressors at the engine nozzles.
Engine rating: Each 800 shp (597 kW).
Flight avionics/instrumentation: Fully integrated, with 2 flat-panel multi-function displays in each cockpit. Roof-mounted sighting system houses an IR imager, laser rangefinder and colour TV camera.
Self-protection systems: Radar warning receiver in the nose. IR jammer on the rear fuselage, aft of the rotor pylon fairings.
Fixed guns: No turreted gun on the mock-up.
Number of weapon pylons: 4, under the stub wings for various weapons, including air-to-air missiles.

Undercarriage:
Type: Fixed tailwheel type

Weights:
Maximum take-off: estimated at 7,700 lb (3,500 kg)

Mitsubishi Heavy Industries Ltd (Japan)

Mitsubishi SH-60J anti-submarine helicopter

Mitsubishi MH2000 drawing

Mitsubishi RP1 demonstrator

Corporate address: See Combat section for company details.

● Activities

● In addition to its fixed-wing and engine programmes, and a 20% stake in the new OH-X helicopter programme (see Kawasaki), Mitsubishi is constructing the Sikorsky SH-60J (S-70B-3) anti-submarine helicopter for the JMSDF to replace the HSS-2B (last HSS-2B was delivered in 1990), and the UH-60J search and rescue helicopter for the JMSDF/ JASDF. The first SH-60J flew on 10 May 1991, and well over 50 had been ordered by 1995 against a requirement for 100, with deliveries from August 1991. First flight of a component-assembled UH-60J was on 20 December 1989 (at the Sikorsky plant), followed by a second in February 1990. The JMSDF requires 18 UH-60Js, while the JASDF requires 46, of which about a third had been delivered by early 1995. All H-60J helicopters are powered by T700-IHI-401C turboshafts. A new 8-passenger helicopter is the projected MH2000.

Mitsubishi RP1

The Mitsubishi RP1 was originally produced as a one-off technology demonstrator, based on a highly modified Sikorsky S-76 airframe and powered by 2 x 600 shp (447 kW) Mitsubishi MG-5 turboshafts driving a Mitsubishi 4-blade rotor (see OH-X entry). Progress into a production helicopter under a 3-year programme has been considered, initially for civil operation, requiring full airframe and engine development.

Daewoo Heavy Industries Ltd (South Korea)

Corporate address: See Combat section for company details.

● Activities

● In addition to the programmes detailed in the Combat section, DHI was to begin deliveries in 1995 of its MK-30, a modification of the Russian Mil Mi-171 and 172 meeting FAR Part 29 standards. Principal changes concern the fuselage and cabin layouts, plus upgraded avionics, the former encompassing a longer nose with less glazing and better general streamlining, plus features to increase safety during emergency alighting on water. The MK-30 results from a 1993 agreement with Kazan of Russia, with the prototype flying in about mid-1995. Standard seating for 28 in a modern interior, with a 9-11 seat executive layout also offered.
● Under South Korea's foreign military purchases, DHI has produced components for Bell Canada and Westland Super Lynx Mk 99 helicopters.

Korean Air (South Korea)

Corporate address: Chung-ku, Namdaemun Ro 2KA, 118 Marine Centre, Seoul.
Telephone: +82 2 751 7114
Founded: Aerospace Division was founded in 1976.

● Activities

● The Aerospace division of the commercial airline operator, Korean Air Lines (KAL), undertakes the licensed manufacture of helicopters and fixed-wing aircraft, constructs light aircraft of its own development (see General Aviation), and produces components for a large number of the world's major aircraft manufacturers. These include components for the Airbus A330/340, new generation Boeing 737s and the 777, and McDonnell Douglas MD-11 and MD-95.
● Helicopter activities initially centred on the McDonnell Douglas MD 500, completing over 300 and thereafter continuing to manufacture airframes for the US company. It also jointly developed the 520MK Black Tiger, an armed MD 500 with a larger main rotor, many avionics upgrades to enhance day and night capability, and extra fuel for longer range. Currently, it is also assembling and delivering 80 Sikorsky UH-60Ps for the South Korean Army.

PZL-Świdnik S.A. (Poland)

Full name: Wytwórnia Sprzetu Komunikacy Jnego PZL-Świdnik S.A.
Corporate address: AL. Lotników Polskich 1, 21-045 Świdnik.
Telephone: +48 81 132-49, 120-61
Facsimile: +48 81 135-05, 133-58, 121-73
Telex: 0642301 WSK PL
Founded: 1951.
Employees: About 5,000.
Information: Ryszard Cukierman (Sales Manager).

PZL-Świdnik/Mil Mi-2 (NATO name *Hoplite*) and Kania

Details: For the Mi-2, except under Sales and Aircraft variants.
First flight: 22 September 1961 (Mil-built prototype); 4 November 1965 for the first Mi-2 built in Poland.
Role: Civil and military multi-purpose light helicopter.
Sales: PZL-Świdnik became the sole manufacturer of the Mi-2 after Mil passed all development, production and marketing to Poland in 1964. Production continued in 1995, but only in small quantities. More than 5,450 had been built by early 1995, most having gone to the former Soviet Union. Other customers/users have included Bulgaria, Cuba, Czech Republic, Djibouti, Egypt, Germany (former East), Hungary, Iraq, Latvia, Libya, Myanmar, Nicaragua, North Korea, Poland, Romania, Slovakia and Syria. 232 were in service with the Polish armed forces in 1994, plus about 150 more with Polish civil operators. Kania sales stand at about 10 production helicopters, including most recently 2 to Cyprus in 1991 and the 1995 delivery of 4 to the Polish Ministry of the Interior for border patrol and policing.
Crew/passengers: See Aircraft variants. Cockpit glazing is electrically heated.
Size of main loading door: Largest door is 3 ft 6 ins x 3 ft 8 ins (1.065 x 1.115 m) on the port side. 2 further cabin doors (1 each side).
Rotor system: 3-blade metal (with some honeycomb structure) main rotor with anti-flutter weights, balance plates and hydraulic dampers. Flapping, drag and pitch hinges. Freewheeling unit. Rotor brake. Electric blade de-icing on most versions.
Tail rotor characteristics: 2-blade, with own gearbox. Electric blade de-icing on most versions.
Flight control system: Cyclic and collective systems have hydraulic pitch control boosters operating at 943 psi. Variable incidence horizontal stabilizers.
Airframe materials: Metal.
Engines: 2 PZL-Rzeszów GTD-350 free-turbine turboshafts. Bleed-air intake de-icing. Freon fire extinguishing system.
Engine rating: 394.25 shp (294 kW), or 281.6 shp (210 kW) cruise.
Fuel system: 600 litres. Optional 2 x 238 litre auxiliary tanks carried on the fuselage sides.
Electrical system: Principal AC supply via 2 engine-driven 3 kW starter-generators and a 16 kVA 3-phase alternator. 2 x 24 volt, 28 amp-hour lead-acid batteries for DC supply.
Braking system: Main wheels.

DETAILS FOR MI-2.

Principal dimensions:
Rotor diameter (main): 47 ft 7 ins (14.5 m)
Maximum length, rotors turning: 57 ft 2 ins (17.42 m)
Fuselage length: 37 ft 5 ins (11.4 m)
Maximum height: 12 ft 4 ins (3.75 m) to above rotor head

Cabin:
Length: 7 ft 5.5 ins (2.27 m)
Width: 3 ft 11 ins (1.2 m)
Height: 4 ft 7 ins (1.4 m)

Main rotor:
Blade chord: 1 ft 4 ins (0.4 m)
Blade area: each 25.8 sq ft (2.4 m^2)
Rotor disc: 1,791 sq ft (166.4 m^2)

Tail rotor:
Diameter: 8 ft 10 ins (2.7 m)

Undercarriage:
Type: Fixed, with twin nosewheels. Options include attached skis and possibly emergency flotation aids
Main wheel tyre size: 600 x 180 mm
Nose wheel tyre size: 400 x 125 mm
Wheel base: 8 ft 11 ins (2.71 m)
Wheel track: 10 ft (3.05 m)

Weights:
Empty: 5,070-5,290 lb (2,300-2,400 kg), depending on role
Maximum take-off: 7,825-8,157 lb (3,550-3,700 kg), depending on role
Payload: 1,764 lb (800 kg)

Performance:
Cruise speed: 108 kts (124 mph) 200 km/h
Long-range cruise speed: 103 kts (118 mph) 190 km/h
Maximum climb rate: 886 ft (270 m) per minute, sea level
IGE hovering ceiling: 6,550 ft (2,000 m)
OGE hovering ceiling: 3,275 ft (1,000 m)
Ceiling: 13,125 ft (4,000 m)
Range with full fuel: 430 naut miles (495 miles) 796 km, with 1,076 litres of fuel and no reserve, at 1,650 ft (500 m) altitude
Range with full payload: 92 naut miles (106 miles) 170 km, at 1,650 ft (500 m) altitude
Duration: 2 hours 45 minutes with 600 litres of fuel, at 1,650 ft (500 m) altitude

PZL-Świdnik Mi-2RM (Piotr Butowski)

Flight avionics/instrumentation: Basic conventional equipment including radio altimeter, radio compass, gyro compass and transceivers. Equipment varies among versions, with the Mi-2B having improved AlliedSignal Bendix/King avionics.
Self-protection systems: Military versions can have warning systems and presumably chaff/flares.
Fixed guns: See Aircraft variants.
Expendable weapons and equipment: See Aircraft variants.
Aircraft variants:
Mi-2 Platan is a mine-laying version, mainly converted from Mi-2Ts and Mi-2URNs.
Mi-2B is the export version for Middle East countries, with AlliedSignal Bendix/King avionics. Empty weight 5,070 lb (2,300 kg).
Mi-2Ch Chekla (chemiczny, chemical) has radiation reconnaissance and WDZ-80 smokescreen laying equipment. Mainly converted from Mi-2Ts and Mi-2Ds.
Mi-2D Przetacznik (dowódczy, command) is an airborne command post, with R-111 radio communication, cipher, and telephone equipment added.
Mi-2FM Kajman (fotogrametryczny) is a photogrammetry version. 2 built.
Mi-2P is the standard passenger version, accommodating the pilot plus 8 passengers. With seats removed, the cabin can accommodate 1,543 lb (700 kg) of cargo.
Mi-2R (rolniczy) is the agricultural version, used for normal or ultra low volume spraying or dusting. Chemical hoppers are carried on the fuselage sides, each carrying 500 litres of liquid (using sprayabooms) or 375 kg (827 lb) of dry chemicals vented from below. Typical swath width with spraybooms is up to 150 ft (45 m). Empty weight 5,230 lb (2,372 kg).
Mi-2RL (ratownictwa ladowego) is a land rescue version.
Mi-2RM Anakonda (ratownictwa morskiego) is a sea rescue variant with a 2-person electric winch over the port side door, and air-droppable dinghies. 9 in service with Polish Naval Aviation.
Mi-2Ro (rozpoznawczy) is the military photographic reconnaissance version.
Mi-2RS Padalec (rozpoznania skazen) is for contamination reconnaissance.
Mi-2S (sanitarny) is a medevac version, with 4 litters and an attendant or 2 litters and 2 sitting patients. Empty weight 5,313 lb (2,410 kg).
Mi-2Sz (szkolny) is for training, with dual controls.
Mi-2T is the basic transport version, with payloads including 1,764 lb (800 kg) sling load using an underfuselage cargo hook.
Mi-2URN Zmija (uzbrojony, rakiety niekierowane, armed with unguided missiles) appeared in 1973. Similar to Mi-2US but with 2 Mars 2 rocket launchers (each with 16 x 57-mm rockets) instead of the gun pods. Simple PKV gunsight.

PZL-Świdnik Mi-2R (rolniczy) agricultural helicopter (Piotr Butowski)

Mi-2URP Salamandra (uzbrojony, rakiety przeciwpancerne, armed with anti-tank missiles) appeared in 1976. As for Mi-2URN but with 4 x 9M14M Malyutka (AT-3 *Sagger*) wire-guided anti-tank missiles instead of rocket launchers.
Mi-2URPG Gniewosz (G for Gad) is similar to Mi-2URP but has 4 Gad (9M32 Strela 2, AS-7 *Grail*) portable anti-aircraft missiles added to the lower part of the ATGM pylons.
Mi-2US Adder (uzbrojony, strzelecki, armed with cannon) has NS-23KM cannon installed in the port side of the fuselage plus 4 gun pods (each with 7.62-mm machine-guns) suspended under the side pylons. 2 other PK type 7.62-mm machine-guns are flexibly installed in the cabin. Appeared in 1973 but probably no longer in service.
UMi-2Ro is a reconnaissance training version.
Kania first flew on 3 June 1979 as an upgraded Mi-2, developed with Allison of the USA which supplies its 250-C20 turboshaft engines. Despite the recent order for 4, and interest for an EMS variant, the programme is unlikely to continue for very much longer unless further firm orders are gained.

PZL-Świdnik W-3 Sokól

First flight: 16 November 1979 (piloted by Wieslaw Mercik); see 6 May 1982 under Development.
Role: Civil and military intermediate multi-purpose helicopter.

▲ Development

▲ 1971. Polish-Soviet agreement signed covering an order for a Polish-designed intermediate-sized helicopter. Chief designer Stanislaw Kaminski, now Cezary Kaminski.
▲ 16 November 1979. First prototype (c/n 30.01.02) used for ground fatigue tests. Performed a flight.
▲ 6 May 1982. First true flight of the W-3 (prototype c/n 30.01.03).
▲ May 1984. New higher technical requirements prepared.
▲ 1987. First flight of a production helicopter (c/n 30.02.01).
▲ 26 September 1988. Temporary Polish certificate.
▲ 17 March 1990. First flight of a combat version, the W-3U Salamandra.
▲ 10 April 1990. Full Polish certification.
▲ December 1992. Russian certification.
▲ 31 May 1993. US FAA certification for the PZL W-3A.
Sales: About 88 built by late 1995, including 6 prototypes and at least 37 for export. 20 delivered to Aeroflot between 1988-90 but further Soviet orders cancelled. 12 to Myanmar, 1 to Germany (c/n 37.05.03, registration D-HSNA), 1 to Nigeria and 3 to Citair of South Korea in late 1995/early 1996. In addition, a W-3RM has been ordered by Petrobaltic. First delivery for the Polish armed forces took place in July 1989 (standard W-3 for the 18th Rescue-Communication Flight of Naval Aviation). In early 1995 the Polish armed forces operated 4 W-3RM Anakondas, 10 W-3W Huzars and about 10 standard W-3s. First 5 W-3Ws were delivered to the 47th Training Helicopter Regiment on 12 May 1994, the remainder in July 1994. Since 1991, leased W-3s have undertaken a forest firefighting role in Spain.
Crew/passengers: 2 crew in basic transport layout, with single pilot VFR operation for the W-3A. Typically 12 passengers, or 5 VIPs, or 4 litters and an attendant in medevac role. See Aircraft variants for other layouts.
Freight, external: Up to 4,630 lb (2,100 kg) sling load.
Cabin access: Sliding door on the port side of the cabin, 3 ft 11 ins x 3 ft 1.5 ins (1.2 x 0.95 m). W-3L Traszka has an additional and larger starboard door.
Optional equipment: Dual controls, and flat plate windshield.
Rotor system: 4-blade glassfibre/epoxy fully-articulated main rotor, with Salomon damper to delete oscillatory loads for minimal vibration. Blade de-icing. Optional blade folding (manual).
Tail rotor characteristics: 3-blade glassfibre/epoxy.
Tail surfaces: Non-moving vertical and horizontal.
Engines: 2 PZL-Rzeszów PZL-10W free-turbine turboshafts. Air inlets have de-icing.
Engine rating: Each 887.7 shp (662 kW).
Transmission rating: 1,800 shp (1,342 kW) take-off. Emergency OEI rating 1,150 shp (857 kW).
Fuel system: 1,720 litres standard. Optional 1,100 litre auxiliary tank available to some versions.
Hydraulic system: Dual systems, each 1,305 psi, for main and tail rotor control boosters.
Braking system: Main wheel discs.
Radar: See Aircraft variants.
Flight avionics/instrumentation: IFR equipped. See also Aircraft variants. 2-axis flight control system, with 3-4 axis optional.
Expendable weapons and equipment: See Aircraft variants.
Aircraft variants:
W-3 Sokól (Falcon) is the standard version, as detailed. Single example of a mountain-rescue version with skis added to the undercarriage, a 595 lb (270 kg) electric winch and equipped to carry paratroops, was involved in an accident on 11 August 1994. VIP version accommodates 5 persons.
W-3 Erka is a medical helicopter. Single example (SP-SUE, c/n 32.02.10) was built in 1988.
W-3A was modified to meet US FAR-29 regulations. Changes to the hydraulic and electrical systems. Avionics include AlliedSignal Bendix/King KTR 908 and KHF 950 com radios, KDF 806 radiocompass, KRA 405 radio altimeter, weather radar, KNR 63A VOR/LOC/GS/MB receiver, KA 35A marker beacon receiver, and KXP 756 transponder. Larger main wheels. First prototype (c/n 36.04.20, side number 420; ex SP-PSK, ex SP-SSK) is currently used by the Polish Ministry of Internal Affairs in VIP form.
W-3RM Anakonda (ratowniczy morski, sea rescue) has 3 inflatable flotation bags on each side of the fuselage, plus a fixed float beneath the tailboom, additional door glazing, a containerized dinghy, French electric winch

PZL-Świdnik W-3RM Anakondas (Piotr Butowski)

DETAILS FOR W-3W HUZAR.

Principal dimensions:
Rotor diameter (main): 51 ft 6 ins (15.7 m)
Maximum length, rotors turning: 61 ft 10 ins (18.85 m)
Fuselage length: 46 ft 7.5 ins (14.21 m)
Maximum height: 12 ft 5 ins (3.8 m) to above rotor head

Cabin:
Length: 10 ft 6 ins (3.2 m)
Width: 5 ft 1.5 ins (1.56 m)
Height: 4 ft 7 ins (1.4 m)
Volume: 222.48 cu ft (6.3 m^3)

Main rotor:
Blade chord: 1 ft 5 ins (0.44 m)
Blade area: each 31.2 sq ft (2.9 m^2)
Rotor disc: 2,084 sq ft (193.6 m^2)
Rpm: 268

Tail rotor:
Diameter: 9 ft 11 ins (3.03 m)
Rpm: 1,342

Undercarriage:
Type: Fixed, with twin castoring/self-centring nosewheels. Options include attached skis and emergency flotation aids
Main wheel tyre size: 500 x 250 mm
Nose wheel tyre size: 400 x 150 mm
Wheel base: 11 ft 8 ins (3.55 m)
Wheel track: 10 ft 4 ins (3.15 m)

Weights:
Maximum take-off: 14,100 lb (6,400 kg)
Payload: 4,630 lb (2,100 kg)

Performance:
Never-exceed speed (VNE): 140 kts (161 mph) 260 km/h
Cruise speed: 127-130 kts (146-149 mph) 235-240 km/h, clean
Cruise speed with suspended armament: 116 kts (134 mph) 215 km/h
Maximum climb rate: 1,970 ft (600 m) per minute, clean
OGE hovering ceiling: 6,890 ft (2,100 m)
Ceiling: 16,075 ft (4,900 m) with armament
Range: 373 naut miles (429 miles) 690 km, clean
Range with armament: 270 naut miles (311 miles) 500 km

of 595 lb (270 kg) capacity, starboard racks for 3 marker bombs, and 3 searchlights.

First prototype (c/n 39.04.11, side number 0411) flew in April 1991 and production started in 1992. Polish Navy has 4 and the Ministry of Internal Affairs has 1.

W-3L Traszka (Newt, nickname Long) was to be a stretched version for 14 troops. Cabin length increased by 4 ft 5 ins (1.35 m), sliding doors on both sides of the cabin, 1,000 shp (746 kW) engines, and provision for armament. Abandoned through lack of orders.

W-3MS and W-3MW are combat helicopter projects based on the W-3's engines, rotors and transmission system, but with no cargo cabin. Presented by the Institute of Aviation in Warsaw, they are in very early stages of development. W-3MS is an anti-tank helicopter, and W-3MW is for naval strike. Israeli missiles and sight/tracking system have been suggested.

W-3U Salamandra (U for uzbrojony, armed) had the armament system of the Mil Mi-24V *Hind-E*. Each outrigger carried 2 Polish Mars-8 rocket pods and 2 Russian tube-launched 9M114 Shturm (AT-6 *Spiral*) anti-tank missiles. GSh-23 twin barrel 23-mm cannon was installed in the starboard side of the nose. Single W-3U Salamandra was built in 1990 (c/n 36.03.17, side number 0317). Because of lack of interest from the Polish Air Force, in 1992 it was stripped of armament and exported to Myanmar.

W-3U-1 Aligator is an anti-submarine version, expected after 1997, to replace the Mi-14PL *Haze-A*.

W-3WB Huzar (WB for wsparcia bojowego, combat support) is the most developed armed version of the W-3. Single prototype was tested in South Africa, where the Kentron company provided the weapon system, including the GA-1 20-mm cannon installed in an undernose turret with 300 rounds of ammunition (angle of fire 90° azimuth, +12°/–60° elevation), and ZT-35 anti-tank missiles, plus the fire control system with helmet sight. Standard armament on outriggers comprises 2 Polish-made Mars-2 rocket packs with 16 x 57-mm rockets each, and 2 x 4-tube launchers for ZT-35 Grot (Arrowhead) laser-guided anti-tank missiles. 1 Grot launcher may be replaced by a Gad (Reptile) launcher with 2 x 9M32M Strzaía (SA-7 *Grail*) AAMs or similar. Can alternatively carry Polish ZR-8 submunition dispensers and Platan mine-laying packs. Fire control system is based on a roof-mounted sight with monochrome TV camera and IR imager, while a laser rangefinder is optional. Other options are IR suppressors, light crew armour and upgraded navigation system. Programme halted through lack of orders.

W-3W Huzar (wsparcia, support) is a low-cost variant of W-3WB, purchased by Polish Army Aviation. Polish-built systems only and no anti-tank missiles. Standard armament comprises a fixed GSh-23L twin-barrel 23-mm cannon plus outrigger stores. Each of the 4 pylons can carry a 4-tube Grom (Thunder; a Polish-built weapon derived from the Russian Igla-1 and Igla-M portable SAMs) or 2-tube Gad system, or Mars-2 16-round 57-mm rocket pod or S-8 80-mm launcher, or ZR-8MB1 submunition dispensers. Elbit is offering a Rafael thermal-imaging system and upgrades to enhance night attack capability.

PZL-Świdnik SW-4

First flight: 1995.
Role: Light utility helicopter.
Crew/passengers: Pilot and 3-4 passengers, or alternative layouts according to role.
Rotor system: 3-blade fully articulated main rotor. Elastomeric hub.
Tail rotor characteristics: 2-blade.
Tail surfaces: Horizontal stabilizer with endplates, probably variable incidence. Dorsal and ventral tailfins, the latter with tailguard.
Airframe materials: About 20% of the airframe comprises glassfibre composites.
Engine: Allison 250-C20R/2 free-turbine turboshaft. Optional 650 shp (485 kW) Pratt & Whitney Canada PW206 for later production examples. Engine access by removing upper fuselage fairing.
Engine rating: 450 shp (335.6 kW), 380 shp (283 kW) for normal cruise.
Transmission rating: Same as engine rating.

DETAILS FOR SW-4.

Principal dimensions:
Rotor diameter (main): 29 ft 6 ins (9 m)
Maximum length, rotors turning: 34 ft 7 ins (10.55 m)
Fuselage length: 27 ft (8.238 m)
Maximum height: 9 ft 8 ins (2.939 m)

Cabin:
Length: 7 ft 8 ins (2.34 m)
Width: 4 ft 10 ins (1.48 m)
Height: 4 ft 4 ins (1.32 m)

Main rotor:
Rotor disc: 685 sq ft (63.62 m²)

Tail rotor:
Diameter: 4 ft 11 ins (1.5 m)

Undercarriage:
Type: Skids
Skid track: 6 ft 7 ins (2 m)

Weights:
Empty, operating: 1,656 lb (751 kg)
Maximum take-off: 3,748 lb (1,700 kg) with Allison engines

Performance (Allison engines):
Maximum speed: 132 kts (152 mph) 245 km/h
Cruise speed: 130 kts (149 mph) 240 km/h at 1,640 ft (500 m), 70% power
IGE hovering ceiling: 11,500 ft (3,500 m)
OGE hovering ceiling: 9,500 ft (2,900 m)
Ceiling: 21,300 ft (6,500 m)
Range with full fuel: 324 naut miles (373 miles) 600 km with 450 litres fuel, no reserve

PZL-Świdnik SW-4 without rotors fitted (Ryszard Jaxa-Malachowski)

Fuel system: 450 litres. Auxiliary tank optional.
Flight avionics/instrumentation: AlliedSignal Bendix/King suite for VFR operation, with optional IFR instrumentation.
Aircraft variants:
SW-4 was unveiled in December 1994. Production is expected to begin in 1996, with certification in 1997.
Twin-engined version is under study because of pending restrictions on the use of single-engined helicopters over built-up areas.

IAR-SA Brasov (Romania)

Corporate address: 1 Aeroportului, 2200 Brasov, PO Box 198.
Telephone: +40 68 15 00 15
Facsimile: +40 68 15 13 04, 15 06 23
Telex: 61266
Founded: Established in 1968 as ICA Brasov, with foundations in IAR of 1925. Now a publicly owned stock company.
Employees: 2,930.
Information: Dan Bunesco (Marketing-Military Systems).

● Activities

- Aircraft manufacturing and repair, including production of various gliders/motorgliders and the licence-built Puma. Builds spare parts for the IAR 316B (Alouette), having produced 280 (including 70 for export to France and Angola), and components for the Rombac 1-11 airliner.
- Future plans include the upgraded Puma 2000 and IS-28M2 glider modernization, production of the IAR 46 lightplane and development of the Noga VI business jet (see General Aviation section), and production of 96 Bell AH-1 HueyCobras (see Bell).

IAR 330L Puma and Puma 2000

Role: Medium helicopter for VIP, paramilitary, medevac, firefighting, armed/unarmed military, naval and coast guard uses, as a licence-built version of the former Aerospatiale AS 330 Puma.
Sales: Some 180, of which over 100 have been exported to France, Pakistan, South Africa and Sudan.
Details: IAR 330L Puma.
Crew/passengers: 2 pilots with dual controls for IFR or 1 pilot for VFR flying, with optional third crew seat. Standard seating for 16-20 passengers or troops, with optional layouts including those for 8 and 12 VIPs (additional side windows), or 1-2 pilots plus 6 litters and 7 seated patients/attendants. See Optional equipment.
Cabin access: Sliding door each side, 4 ft 5 ins x 4 ft 5 ins (1.35 x 1.35 m).
Optional equipment: Includes hydraulic hoist, cargo sling, emergency flotation gear, sand filters, parachute installation, litter installation, external fuel tanks, Alcan 1500-1800 LTF or Bamby Bucket 1589 LT (with short term retardant system) firefighting installation, icing detection system, and Locator B or Spectrolab SX-16 searchlight.
Rotor system: 4 composite blade (with stainless steel leading edges) fully-articulated main rotor. Yaw damper. 3 hydraulic servo control units. Freewheeling unit. Folding blades. Rotor brake. Optional electric blade de-icing.
Tail rotor characteristics: 5-blade, metal. Optional electric blade de-icing.
Airframe materials: Metal.
Engines: 2 Turbomeca Turmo IV CA turboshafts, built by Turbomecanica.
Engine rating: 1,495 shp (1,115 kW) take-off, 1,555 shp (1,160 kW) maximum emergency, 1,381 shp (1,030 kW) intermediate emergency, and 1,261 shp (940 kW) maximum continuous.
Fuel system: 1,544 litres standard, with optional

IAR-330L Puma with weapon outriggers (courtesy IAR)

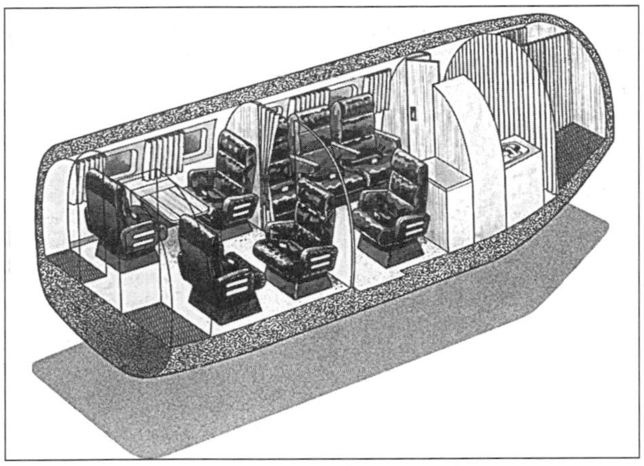

IAR-330L Puma 8-seat VIP cabin layout (courtesy IAR)

2 x 350 litre tanks. Additionally, 1 or 2 auxiliary cabin tanks can be adopted, each 215 litres.

Electrical system: 200 volt, 400 Hz, 3-phase AC supply via 1 or 2 x 20 kVA alternators. 28.5 volt DC supply via 2 transformer rectifiers. Battery for self-start, and also for emergency AC power supply using an inverter.

Hydraulic system: Dual systems, each 2,495 psi.

Braking system: Wheel (disc) and parking brakes. Rotor brake.

Radar: AlliedSignal Bendix/King RDR 1400C, Collins WXT-250B or Honeywell Primus 40/50 weather radar. Optional AlliedSignal Bendix/King RDR 1500 surveillance radar.

Flight avionics/instrumentation: Autopilot, able to be integrated with navigation and microwave landing system. Radio and navigation equipment in 2 standards encompasses Collins VHF, UHF, HF (or ABS), VOR/ILS/marker, ADF, ATC transponder, DME, and SAR-MDF; Elno or Silec head-set; Team ICS; Wuslsberg VHF-FM; TRT or Collins radio altimeter; Racal Doppler; Chelton homing; GPS-IPG or Trimble GPS; VLF Omega; Decca navigator; Cossor IFF; and ELP or Jolliet ELT. Optional night vision goggles and roof sight.

Self-protection systems: Optional laser and radar warning system, and chaff/flare dispensers.

Fixed guns: Turret-mounted 20-mm cannon with helmet control or 2 x 23-mm cannon in pods on the forward fuselage.

Number of weapon pylons: Military versions can have fuselage-side outriggers, each with 2 NATO standard pylons.

Expendable weapons and equipment: Various weapon options including 2 x 4 anti-armour missiles, 4 launchers each with 9 x 70-mm rockets or 16 x 57-mm rockets or 2 x 122-mm rockets, 7.62-mm machine-gun pods each with 550 rounds of ammunition, land or sea mines, air-to-air missiles or 100 kg bombs. Smoke launchers.

Aircraft variants:

IAR 330L Puma has been the production version since 1977.

Puma 2000 is an upgraded variant of the 330L, with higher powered engines, Hellfire anti-armour missiles among other weapon options, modernized flight deck, and greatly enhanced avionics integrated by Elbit and using the MIL-STD-1553B databus. Hands on cyclic and stick (HOCAS) controls. EFIS displays and HUD. Optional El-Op MSIS (multi-sensor stabilized integrated system) including FLIR and TV imaging. Laser rangefinder and target designator.

DETAILS FOR IAR 330L.

Principal dimensions:
Rotor diameter (main): 49 ft 6 ins (15.08 m)
Maximum length, rotors turning: 59 ft 9 ins (18.22 m)
Fuselage length: 48 ft 7.5 ins (14.82 m) nose to end of tail rotor
Width, blades folded: 11 ft 11 ins (3.62 m)
Maximum height: 16 ft 10.5 ins (5.14 m) to top of tail rotor

Cabin:
Length: 19 ft 10 ins (6.05 m)
Width: 5 ft 11 ins (1.8 m)
Height: 5 ft 1 ins (1.55 m)
Volume: 402.6 cu ft (11.4 m^3)

Main rotor:
Blade chord: 2 ft (0.6 m)
Blade area: each 43.06 sq ft (4 m^2)
Rotor disc: 1,902 sq ft (176.7 m^2)
Rpm: 265

Tail rotor:
Diameter: 10 ft (3.04 m)

Undercarriage:
Type: Retractable (semi-exposed), with twin wheels on each unit. Brakes. Optional ski type
Wheel base: 13 ft 3.5 ins (4.05 m)
Wheel track: 9 ft 10 ins (3 m)

Weights:
Empty: 7,970 lb (3,615 kg)
Maximum take-off: 16,314 lb (7,400 kg)
Useful load: 8,287 lb (3,759 kg)
Payload: 7,055 lb (3,200 kg) sling load

Performance (MTOW):
Never-exceed speed (V_{NE}): 142 kts (163 mph) 263 km/h
Maximum cruise speed: 139 kts (160 mph) 258 km/h
Normal cruise speed: 134 kts (154 mph) 248 km/h
Maximum climb rate: 1,200 ft (366 m) per minute
IGE hovering ceiling: 7,545 ft (2,300 m) ISA, 5,250 ft (1,600 m) ISA + 20° C
OGE hovering ceiling: 5,575 ft (1,700 m) ISA, 3,445 ft (1,050 m) ISA + 20° C
Ceiling: 15,750 ft (4,800 m), service
Range: 297 naut miles (342 miles) 550 km, no reserve
Duration: 3.15 hours at 70 kts (81 mph) 130 km/h

Kamerton-N Ltd (Russia)

Corporate address: Tsiolkovskogo Str 2, Shchelkovo-3, 141100, Moscow region.
Telephone: +7 095 526 3243

● Activities

- Development of the Ratnik autogyro was undertaken in association with the Chkalov Air Force Science and Research Institute.

Kamerton-N Ratnik

First flight: Undergoing flight trials in 1995.

Role: Light autogyro, with potential applications including sport and leisure, pipeline and border patrol, surveillance, rescue, air ambulance (1 litter), and armed.

Crew/passengers: 2 persons, side-by-side in a fully-enclosed and highly-glazed cabin.

Cabin access: Large doors, virtually all glazing.

Rotor system: 2-blade main rotor. Pre-rotator possible for jump take-off.

DETAILS FOR RATNIK ARE PROVISIONAL.

Principal dimensions:
Rotor diameter: 29 ft 6 ins (9 m)
Length: 16 ft 3 ins (4.95 m), nose to rudder
Height: 8 ft 2 ins (2.5 m) to top of duct

Undercarriage:
Type: Fixed nosewheel type. Can operate from unpaved airstrips

Weights:
Take-off: 1,100-1,323 lb (500-600 kg)

Performance:
Maximum speed: 81 kts (93 mph) 150 km/h
Minimum speed: 19 kts (22 mph) 35 km/h
Ceiling: 13,120 ft (4,000 m)
Range: 135 naut miles (155 miles) 250 km
Duration: 3 hours

Artist's impression of the Kamerton-N Ratnik (Bill Hobson)

Tail surfaces: Tall rudder is duct mounted immediately behind the propeller.

Engine: 67 hp (50 kW) Samson 760 piston engine, driving a 3-blade pusher propeller in a duct ring. Alternatively, 2 x 64.4 hp (48 kW) Rotax 582 2-cylinder 2-stroke piston engines.

Expendable weapons and equipment: Light weapon (possibly tube-launched) can be carried on an outrigger above each main undercarriage leg.

Kamov Group (Russia)

Full name: Vertoletnyi Nauchno-Tekhnicheskiy Kompleks Imeni N.I. Kamova.
Corporate address: March 8th Street, 140007 Lyubertsy, Moscow Region.
Telephone: +7 095 700 32 04
Facsimile: +7 095 700 30 71
Founded: 1947.

Kamov Ka-25 (NATO name *Hormone)*

First hovering flight: 26 April 1961 (piloted by Dmitri Yefremov). First full circle flight 21 May 1961.
Role: Ship-borne anti-submarine warfare (ASW) helicopter, used also in sea target acquisition, minesweeping, SAR and other roles.
Chief designer: Yuri Lazarenko.

▲ Development

▲ 20 February 1958. Governmental order for a heavy ship-borne ASW helicopter.
▲ 25 April 1965. First production helicopter flew in Ulan-Ude.
▲ November 1965. Factory tests completed.
▲ 19 September 1968. Sea trials of *Moskva* ASW cruiser with 14 Ka-25s on board.
▲ 1972. Ka-25 officially accepted into service with the Soviet Navy.
▲ 1977. Serial production completed.

Sales/users: About 250 manufactured between 1965-77 at the Ulan-Ude plant, of which between 80 and 100 were still in service with CIS naval forces in early 1995. 5 went to India, 9 to Syria, and others to Bulgaria, former Yugoslavia and Vietnam.
Details: Ka-25B *Hormone-A* unless stated.
Flight crew: Pilot on port side, next to the navigator/ASW systems officer.
Passengers/troops: Ka-25B can carry up to 4 people in an emergency situation. Ka-25PS accommodates 1 attendant and 2 litters. Civil Ka-25K accommodates 12 passengers.
Cabin access: Rearward sliding door on port side, 3 ft 6 ins (1.07 m) high and 3 ft 11 ins (1.20 m) wide.
Rotor characteristics: 2 coaxial contra-rotating 3-blade rotors. Steel rotor head. D-1 rotor blades of aluminium alloy. Blades fold manually; provision for automatic electric folding system weighing 243-265 lb (110-120 kg). Electric blade de-icing.
Tail rotor characteristics: No tail rotor.
Tail surfaces: Central fin and toed inward endplates (15°) with rudders.
Flight control system: AP-114 autopilot; hydraulic boosters.
Fuselage: Conventional semi-monocoque.
Safety features: Inflatable pontoons can be mounted on each leg.
Engines: 2 Mars/Glushenkov GTD-3M turboshafts, each 1,000 shp (746 kW); GTD-3F engines on early helicopters, each 900 shp (671 kW). OEI emergency rating is 40% greater.
Engine rating: See above.
Fuel system: Fuel in 3 tanks under the cabin floor. Provision for 2 external auxiliary tanks.
Electrical system: 2 STG-6 (27 volt, 6 kW) DC generators and 1 SGS-40U (400 Hz, 40 kW) AC generator. 2 stand-by batteries.
Radar: Ka-25B has Initsiativa-2K navigation/attack radar in an undernose radome. Ka-25Ts has Uspekh-2A (NATO *Big Bulge*) radar.
Flight avionics/instrumentation: Baykal search/attack system. Flight/navigation avionics provide all-weather, day and night operations. AP-144 4-channel autopilot operates during the entire mission,

Kamov Ka-25Ts Hormone-B features a large undernose radome. Note the flotation gear (Piotr Butowski)

providing automatic hovering. KS-3B course system, ARK-9 radio compass, and RV-3M altimeter. Additional ARK-U2 radio compass on Ka-25PS. 2 UHF R-860 com radios of 54 naut miles (62 miles) 100 km range, and 324 naut miles (372 miles) 600 km range HF R-842. SPU-7 intercom. SRZO-2 IFF.
Combat equipment (standard): For search operations the Ka-25B can carry either Oka-2 dipping sonar housed in the bottom of the fuselage aft of the cabin or an APM-60 Orsha magnetic anomaly detector (MAD) suspended under the tailboom, plus sonobuoys housed inside the weapons bay (36 x RGB-NM type or 8 x RGB-N type). ESM usually carried above the tailboom.

DETAILS FOR KA-25B.

Principal dimensions:
Rotor diameter: 51 ft 8 ins (15.74 m) each
Fuselage length: 31 ft 4 ins (9.55 m) approximately
Fuselage length, Ka-25K: 32 ft 3 ins (9.832 m)
Maximum height: 17 ft 8 ins (5.373 m)

Cabin:
Length: 12 ft 11 ins (3.95 m)
Width: 4 ft 3 ins (1.30 m) floor, 4 ft 10 ins (1.48 m) maximum
Height: 4 ft 1 ins (1.25 m) maximum
Volume: 257.8 cu ft (7.3 m^3)

Tail unit:
Span, maximum: 12 ft 4 ins (3.76 m)

Undercarriage:
Type: 4-leg, fixed (partially retractable for Ka-25Ts); single wheel on each leg
Wheel base: 9 ft 11 ins (3.02 m)
Main wheel track: 11 ft 7 ins (3.52 m)
Front wheel track: 4 ft 7 ins (1.41 m)

Weights:
Normal take-off: 15,653 lb (7,100 kg)
Maximum take-off: 15,873 lb (7,200 kg)
Payload (Ka-25K): 4,409 lb (2,000 kg)

Performance:
Maximum operating speed: 119 kts (137 mph) 220 km/h
Cruise speed: 108 kts (124 mph) 200 km/h
Flight altitude: 33 ft (10 m) to 12,140 ft (3,700 m)
Maximum climb rate: 1,378 ft (420 m) per minute, at sea level, nominal weight and rating
OGE hovering ceiling: 1,640 ft (500 m)
Normal range: 243 naut miles (279.6 miles) 450 km
Duration: 2 hrs 30 mins
Patrol duration 100 km from ship: 1 hour

Fixed weapons: None.
Expendable weapons and equipment: Weapons bay. Standard weapon variations are a single 450-mm AT-1 anti-submarine torpedo; or 4 PLAB-250-120, or 8 PLAB-50-65, or 36 PLAB-MK depth charges; or a single nuclear depth charge. Sonobuoys (see earlier)
Aircraft variants:
Ka-25B (baykal or search/attack system) *Hormone-A.* is the standard ASW version, as described.
Ka-25BShZ (buksir shnurovykh zaryadov) is the mine-sweeping version. 8 built in 1974.
Ka-25PS (poiskovo-spasatelnyi, search-rescue) *Hormone-C* is the utility and search and rescue version. Converted from Ka-25B, with rotatable searchlights at the fuselage sides, hoist, additional search radio compass and a red/white paint scheme.
Ka-25Ts (tseleukazatel, target acquisition) *Hormone-B.* is a special version for target acquisition and over-the-horizon mid-course guidance for ship-to-ship missiles. Bulged undernose radome and partially retracted undercarriage to avoid signals interference.
Ka-25TL, Ka-25TI or Ka-25IV, are each used as a data collecting point, tracking the flight path of intercontinental ballistic missiles.
Ka-25K (kran, crane) is the civil utility/crane conversion of Ka-25B. Prototype only, of 1967.

Kamov Ka-27 and Ka-28 (NATO name *Helix-A and D)*

First hovering flight: 8 August 1973 (piloted by Yevgeni Laryushin). First full circle flight 24 December 1973.
Role: Ship-based ASW, search and rescue, and armed surveillance.
Chief designer: Yuri Lazarenko.

★ Aims

★ Patrol duration of 2 hours at a distance of 200 km from the ship.
★ Ability to carry search equipment and weapons simultaneously (Ka-25 takes one or the other).

Sales/users: Series production undertaken at the Kumertau (Kirgizstan) aviation plant between 1978 and September 1981. About 100 are in the service with the Russian Navy. 13 Ka-28s bought by India, and a dozen or so went to the former Yugoslavia and Vietnam.
Flight crew: Pilot and navigator side-by-side, with an ASW weapon systems officer in the cabin.
Cabin access: Rearward sliding doors at both sides, with bulged windows, or through the cabin.
Passengers/troops: 12 persons in Ka-27PS.
Loading facilities: Ka-27PS has a winch at the port cabin door, of 661 lb (300 kg) capacity.
Main rotor characteristics: 2 coaxial, contra-rotating, 3-blade fully-articulated rotors. Asymmetric blade aerofoils, with ground adjustable tabs. Bottom rotor has vibration dampers. D2-4 composite blades with automatic folding. Titanium/steel rotor head. Rotor brake. Electrical de-icing of the blades.
Tail surfaces: Tailplane with elevators. Inward toed endplates, each with a rudder and fixed leading-edge slat.
Flight control system: Hydraulic, with no manual back-up. Differential collective pitch yaw control.
Fuselage: Watertight, in case of an emergency ditching.
Construction materials: Aluminium alloy, with extensive use of titanium and composite materials.
Engines: 2 Klimov/Izotov TV3-117VK turboshafts side-by-side above the cabin compartment. Air intake de-icing. APU.

Details for Ka-27 *Helix-A*.

Principal dimensions:
Rotor diameter: 52 ft 2 ins (15.9 m) each
Maximum length, rotors folded: 40 ft 2 ins (12.25 m)
Fuselage length: 37 ft 1 ins (11.3 m)
Width, blades folded: 13 ft 1 ins (4 m)
Height: 17 ft 8 ins (5.4 m) to above rotor head

Cabin:
Length: 14 ft 10 ins (4.5 m)
Width: 5 ft 3 ins (1.6 m)
Height: 4 ft 4 ins (1.32 m)

Main rotor:
Blade chord: 1 ft 7 ins (0.48 m)
Rotor disc: 2,136.6 sq ft (198.5 m^2)

Undercarriage:
Type: 4 fixed legs, each with a single wheel; forward pair castering. Large flotation gear on each side of the lower fuselage and ahead of the main undercarriage legs. Optional wheel/skis
Main wheel tyre size: 600 x 180 mm
Nose wheel tyre size: 400 x 150 mm
Wheel base: 9 ft 11 ins (3.02 m)
Main wheel track: 11 ft 6 ins (3.5 m)
Front wheel track: 4 ft 7 ins (1.4 m)

Weights:
Normal take-off: 23,589 lb (10,700 kg)
Maximum take-off: 26,455 lb (12,000 kg)
Payload (Ka-27PS): 6,614 lb (3,000 kg)

Performance:
Maximum operating speed: 146 kts (168 mph) 270 km/h
Cruise speed: 124 kts (143 mph) 230 km/h
Ceiling: 11,480 ft (3,500 m)
Range with maximum fuel: 648 naut miles (745.6 miles) 1,200 km
Normal range: 378 naut miles (435 miles) 700 km
Patrol duration at a distance of 200 km: 2 hours 15 minutes
Maximum duration (Ka-27PS): 4 hours 30 minutes

Kamov Ka-27PS Helix-D SAR helicopter. Note the flotation bag container (below) and additional fuel tank (above) on the cabin side, and two marker bombs just behind the main undercarriage (Piotr Butowski)

Kamov Ka-27PV patrol/combat helicopter (Piotr Butowski)

Engine rating: Each 2,225 shp (1,659 kW) maximum.
Fuel system: 8,113 lb (3,680 kg) of fuel inside 16 tanks under the cabin floor; provision for 2 auxiliary tanks on the cabin sides.
Electrical system: Principal AC supply via 2 generators. DC supply via AC using 2 rectifiers. 2 batteries, able to back-up either supply, with inverters for AC.
Hydraulic system: 3, 2 of which are principally main and stand-by systems for the servos.
Braking system: Hydraulic, as a second function of the main hydraulic system and with back-up from the third.
Radar: Osminog, an unsophisticated radar with no search/attack functions, in the undernose radome.
Flight avionics/instrumentation: NKV-27 navigation system using DISS Doppler nav radar mounted under the tailboom. 3-axis autopilot. Pre-programmed flight path, and autonomous flight back to the ship with no support of ship systems. PKV-27 flight-attitude autopilot provides automatic hovering at altitude of more than 82 ft (25 m).
Fixed weapons: None.
Mission equipment (standard): Osminog search/attack system. Ros dipping sonar housed in the bottom of the fuselage, aft of the cabin. MAD suspended under the tailboom.
Expendable weapons and equipment: Include AT-1 or APR-2 torpedo, PLAB-250-120 depth charges, KAB-250PL guided depth charges or nuclear depth charge. Sonobuoys.
Aircraft variants:
Ka-27 (Ka-252PL) *Helix-A*, named as Ka-27PL by some, is the basic anti-submarine version, as detailed.
Ka-27PS *Helix-D* is the search and rescue version, with ASW equipment removed. 2 radio signal buoys suspended under the tailboom, and an LPG-300 winch at the cabin door. Carries life-rafts, and containers with clothes, food, medicines, etc.
Ka-27K ASW version has the new Kamerton-1M search/attack system. Widened flight deck with flat-plate glazing as for Ka-29. Prototype only.
Ka-27PV (pogranichnyi variant) is intended for armed border surveillance, particularly over coastal areas. Externally similar to Ka-27PS but with the weapon racks of the Ka-29. Under test in 1994-95.
Ka-28 is the export version of Ka-27 *Helix-A*.

Kamov Ka-29 (NATO name *Helix-B*)

First flight: 1976.
Role: Ship-based assault and transport helicopter.

▲ Development

▲ 1974. Official request of Soviet Navy.
▲ 1985. Initial deployment with the Northern and Pacific fleets of the Soviet Navy.
Sales/users: Serial manufacturing undertaken by Kumertau (Kirgizstan) aviation plant. About 30 in service with the Russian Navy and not exported by 1995.
Flight crew: Pilot and weapon system operator side-by-side. Access to the cockpit via rearward sliding doors at both sides or through the cabin. Flight deck is about 15.75 ins (40 cm) wider than for the Ka-27, with 3 flat-plate front glazed panels.
Passengers/troops: Up to 16 troops on folding seats inside the cabin.
Freight, internal: 4,409 lb (2,000 kg).
Freight, external: 8,818 lb (4,000 kg).
Cabin access: Doors at port side, divided horizontally into 2 sections.
Main rotor characteristics: As for Ka-27.
Tail surfaces: As for Ka-27.
Safety features: Armoured flight deck and engine compartment.
Engines: As for Ka-27.
Flight avionics/instrumentation: As for Ka-27.
Radar: None.
Weapon system avionics/instrumentation: Shturm-V anti-tank guided missile system, with electro-optical sight window under the starboard side of the fuselage nose and radio guidance sensor to port. ASP-17VK gun sight. Optionally laser range-finder. ESM.
Self-protection systems: L-166 (NATO *Hot Brick*) infra-red jammer on some aircraft, located aft of the APU compartment.
Fixed weapons: NUV-1UM stand with flexible GShG-7.62 4-barrel Gatling type 7.62-mm machine-gun and 1,800 rounds of ammunition at the doors on the starboard side. Fire angles –31°/0° in elevation, 28° to port and 30° to starboard. Optional 2A42 30-mm single-barrel cannon with 250 rounds on the port weapon rack.
Number of weapon pylons: 4.
Expendable weapons and equipment: Up to 8 x 9M114 Kokon (AT-6 *Spiral*) tube-launched, guided, anti-tank missiles of the Shturm-V system, in 2 x 4-tube clusters. Unguided weapons include 2 or 4 B-8 rocket launchers, each with 20 x 80-mm rockets, UPK-23-250 gun packs, bombs, incendiary tanks, etc. Maximum weapons load is 4,409 lb (2,000 kg).
Aircraft variants:
Ka-29 (Ka-252TB, transportno-boyevoi, combat-transport) *Helix-B* is a ship-borne transport and assault helicopter.
See also Ka-31 Airborne Early Warning and Control (AEW&C) helicopter.

Ka-29 Helix-B showing B-8V-20 rocket launchers (20 x 80 mm rockets each) and the undernose anti-tank missile control system sensors (covered window of the optical sight and antenna of the radio-command guidance system). Note the two flush-folded searchlights above the sight window (Piotr Butowski)

Ka-29 Helix-B transport/combat assault helicopter (Piotr Butowski)

DETAILS FOR KA-29.

Principal dimensions:
Rotor diameter: 52 ft 2 ins (15.9 m) each
Maximum length, rotors folded: 40 ft 2 ins (12.25 m)
Fuselage length: 37 ft 1 ins (11.3 m)
Width, blades folded: 19 ft 1 ins (5.82 m)
Width, blades folded, outriggers removed: 12 ft 5 ins (3.8 m)
Maximum height: 17 ft 10 ins (5.44 m)

Tail unit:
Span: 11 ft 11.5 ins (3.65 m)

Undercarriage:
Main wheel tyre size: 600 x 180 mm
Nose wheel tyre size: 400 x 150 mm
Wheel base: 9 ft 11 ins (3.02 m)
Main wheel track: 11 ft 6 ins (3.5 m)
Front wheel track: 4 ft 7 ins (1.4 m)

Weights:
Normal take-off: 24,250 lb (11,000 kg)
Maximum take-off: 25,353 lb (11,500 kg)
Maximum take-off with external load: 27,778 lb (12,600 kg)
Payload: 4,409 lb (2,000 kg) maximum internal, 8,816 lb (4,000 kg) maximum external

Performance:
Max operating speed: 151 kts (174 mph) 280 km/h
Cruise speed: 127 kts (146 mph) 235 km/h
Ceiling: 14,108 ft (4,300 m), service
OGE hovering ceiling: 12,140 ft (3,700 m)
Maximum climb rate: 3,050 ft (930 m) per minute, sea level
Ferry range: 400 naut miles (460 miles) 740 km
Normal range: 248 naut miles (286 miles) 460 km
Duration: 4 hours 30 minutes
Patrol duration at distance of 200 km: 2 hrs 15 mins

Kamov Ka-31 number 032 fully-equipped prototype undergoing State Acceptance Trials, with radar in lowered position

Kamov Ka-31

First flight: Possibly 1988.
Role: AEW&C helicopter based on the Kamov Ka-29 *Helix B,* originally ship-based, but proposed also for ground forces. Designed for detection of aircraft and surface ships, plotting their position and sending the information to the command post on board ship.

▲ Development

▲ 1992. 031 and 032 (see Sales/users) spotted on the *Admiral Kuznetsov* aircraft carrier. State acceptance trials completed.

Sales/users: 3 prototypes were known in early 1995, all bearing civil Aeroflot registration and side numbers 208, 031 and 032. The 208 was probably used only for testing the mechanism for lowering the underfuselage rectangular radar antenna and for testing the undercarriage retracting system (having reduced equipment and aerials compared with 031 and 032 prototypes; an example being the equipment cooling fan).
Flight crew: 2
Mission equipment: The NNIIRT radar detects and traces small targets, including air targets flying at very low altitude. The 18 ft (5.5 m) wide rectangular radar antenna has an area of 64.5 sq ft (6 m^2). In cruise position the antenna is folded away horizontally with the bottom of fuselage. When operating, the antenna is lowered, put into a vertical position and rotated about the axis every 10 seconds. The undercarriage legs are raised in order to avoid the disturbances found with Ka-25Ts *Hormone-B.* The radar unit operates in decametre range. The unit is capable of tracing up to 20 targets simultaneously; it detects a fighter aircraft at the distance of 54-81 naut miles (62-93 miles) 100-150 km, whereas surface ships can be detected at up to 135 naut miles (155 miles) 250 km.
Fixed weapons: None.
Expendable weapons and equipment: None.
Engines, rotors, transmission: As for Ka-29.
Aircraft variants:
Ka-31 (Ka-252RLD, radio-lokatsyonnogo dozora, radar surveillance). As detailed.

DETAILS FOR KA-31.

Principal dimensions: as for Ka-29

Undercarriage:
Type: 4 legs partially retractable to avoid signals interference

Weights:
Maximum take-off: 27,558 lb (12,500 kg)

Performance:
Cruise speed: 119 kts (137 mph) 220 km/h
Operating altitude: up to 11,485 ft (3,500 m)
Operation radius: up to 54 naut miles (62 miles) 100 km
Operation duration: 2 hours 30 minutes

Kamov Ka-32 (NATO name *Helix-C)*

First flight: 11 January 1980.
Role: Civil transport, flying-crane, offshore support, vertrep, rescue, maritime patrol and firefighting.
Sales: In addition to Russian-operated helicopters, exports include those to Bulgaria, South Korea and Yemen. South Korean Ka-32s (1 Ka-32A1 and 1 Ka-32T) are for forestry and firefighting roles, joining other Kamovs used by the government, and were despatched in an An-124 in mid-1995.

Kamov Ka-32A1 with hugely bulged cockpit door windows, wheel/skis, rescue hoist and other equipment (Piotr Butowski)

DETAILS FOR KA-32.

Principal dimensions: See Ka-27.

Weights:
Empty: 14,330 lb (6,500 kg)
Maximum take-off, external load: 27,778 lb (12,600 kg)
Payload: 11,000 lb (5,000 kg) sling load, 8,819 lb (4,000 lb) in cabin

Performance:
Maximum speed: 135 kts (155 mph) 250 km/h
Cruise speed: 124 kts (143 mph) 230 km/h
OGE hovering ceiling: 11,500 ft (3,500 m)
Ceiling: 19,700 ft (6,000 m), service
Range: 432 naut miles (497 miles) 800 km
Duration: 4.5 hours

Details: Generally similar to Ka-27, except as described below.
Crew/passengers: 2 flight crew plus optional third crew member. Up to 13 passengers in the Ka-32A and 16 in Ka-32T. Alternative layouts include litters for a medevac role.
Engines: 2 Klimov/Izotov TV3-117V or VMA turboshafts side-by-side above the cabin compartment. Air intake de-icing. APU.
Engine rating: Each 2,190 shp (1,633 kW).
Fuel system: 2,180 litres. Optional 2 x 410 litre auxiliary tanks carried with the main underfloor tanks to keep the cabin clear. Further auxiliary tanks have recently been made available as outrigger-mounted external containers that transverse the standard box tanks on the fuselage sides.
Radar: See Aircraft variants.
Flight avionics/instrumentation: Similar to Ka-27.
Aircraft variants:
Ka-32A is an upgrade to obtain Cat A and B certification under Russian NLGB-2 and US FAR-29/33 regulations. Certified in Russia in 1993 and available since 1994. Electronic flight deck optional, with Canadian Marconi EFIS, AFCS, GPS and Doppler. Upgraded systems, modified undercarriage featuring 620 x 180 mm and 480 x 200 mm main/nose wheels, and using 2 Klimov TV3-117VMA turboshafts. Fuel capacity is decreased if pressure refuelling is selected.
Ka-31A1 is a firefighting variant, with equipment including firefighting gear, hugely blistered cockpit door windows for good downward vision, 661 lb (300 kg) capacity electric rescue hoist and optional wheel/skis. See photograph.

Ka-32K (kran) is a utility/flying-crane variant, with a retractable gondola to allow the co-pilot to visually take control of delicate manoeuvring. Possibly no more successful from a sales viewpoint than the earlier Ka-25K. Same bulged windows as Ka-32A1.
Ka-32S carries the NATO name *Helic-C* and is intended for several maritime roles, including SAR, vertrep, ice surveillance and patrol. Based on the Ka-32T but with upgraded avionics for IFR flying, including radar in a chin cylindrical radome.
Ka-32T is the basic utility version (also *Helix-C)*.

Kamov Ka-50 and Ka-52 Werewolf (NATO name *Hokum)*

First hovering flight: 17 June 1982 (piloted by Nikolai Bezdetnov). First full circle flight 27 July 1982 (piloted by Yevgeni Laryushin).
Role: Single-seat anti-tank and attack helicopter (Ka-50) and two-seat training and combat variant (Ka-52).

★ Aims

★ Autonomous operation, at least 2 weeks without refitting at main base.

▲ Development

▲ 1975. Work started.
▲ December 1977. Preliminary design accepted.
▲ May 1980. Full-scale mock-up accepted by common committee of the Air Force and Ministry of Air Industry.
▲ 17 June 1982. First flight of the first prototype, side number 010.
▲ Comparative tests of Ka-50 and Mi-28 .
▲ 3 April 1985. First prototype crashed; pilot Yevgeni Laryushin killed.
▲ Summer 1992. First production helicopter left Arsenyev plant.
▲ August 1992. First public presentation (fly-pass only) during MosAeroshow in Zhukovsky.
▲ 1993. State acceptance trials completed.
▲ Early 1995. Not in operational service but used for squadron development; possible IOC in 1996.
▲ Late 1995. First flight expected of the V-80Sh2 version (see Aircraft variants).

Sales/users: 4 prototypes built (1 lost) by Kamov test facility in Lyubertsy outside Moscow; production started 1992 at Arsenyev plant. Due to financial cuts, production was interrupted after 12 had been built. 4 bought for the Russian army aviation in 1994 and delivered to the Torzhok evaluation and training centre. Further aircraft will be built in single- and two-seat versions, with an expected eventual in-service ratio of 60% single-seaters to 40% two-seaters.
Details: Ka-50.
Flight crew: Single pilot. MKS-3 or WMKS-4 suit.
Cockpit: Hermetic, fully protected by 2-layer steel armour. 2 flat-plate side windows and a single plate windscreen, all armoured. Cockpit protected from 20-mm calibre ammunition fired from a distance.

Kamov Ka-50 Werewolf, the first-ever single-seat combat helicopter, with undercarriage lowered (Piotr Butowski)

Cluster of 6 Vikhr missiles on a Ka-50. Note the wingtip fairing containing UV-26 chaff/flare dispensers (Piotr Butowski)

Flexible 30 mm 2A42 cannon on the starboard side of a Ka-50 (Piotr Butowski)

Ejection seat: Zvezda K-37, operated at speeds from zero to 189 kts (217 mph) 350 km/h, and from zero altitude. Rotor blades are detached by means of explosive charges installed in the blade fastenings.
Main rotor characteristics: 2 coaxial contra-rotating 3-blade rotors, with swept tips. All-composite blades; titanium heads.
Wing/tail surfaces: 2-spar stub-wings, with no high-lift devices. Each wing has 2 armament pylons, and ECM/flare fairings at the wingtips with small vertical plates. All-moving, slightly swept tailfin. The tail unit is not a main structural element, and tests proved that the helicopter can fly after the tailboom has been torn off.
Flight control system: Mechanical, with hydraulic actuators.
Fuselage: Main structural element is a composite glassfibre box beam, 3 ft 3 ins (1 m) in both width and height. Inside this structure are fuel tanks and cannon ammunition. Outside, at both sides, are attached the equipment modules covered by external panels that form the external outline of the airframe.
Construction materials: About 35% by weight comprises composite materials.
Safety features: Armour protection (about 705 lb, 320 kg total weight) for the cockpit, engine bays, etc. Ejection seat (see before). Undercarriage provides for vertical landings of 33 ft (10 m) per second. Crashworthy seat/s. Fuel tanks filled with polyurethane foam.
Engines: 2 widely separated Klimov TV3-117VK turboshafts. AI 9K APU. Dust filters. Infra-red suppression cool air mixers can be fitted to the engine nozzles.
Engine rating: Each 2,200 shp (1,640.5 kW).
Fuel system: Provision for 4 underwing fuel tanks.
Flight refuelling probe: None.
Flight avionics/instrumentation: Integrated PNPrK flight-navigation-attack system, which uses 4 Orbita digital computers. Inertial navigation, short-range radio navigation, DISS Doppler navigation radar, ARK-22 radio compass, and SOS-V1 angle-of-attack dumper. Head-up display (HUD). Data link for receiving information from reconnaissance helicopters, presented on the map display and HUD.
Mission avionics: Shkval fire control unit designed for detecting and automatically tracking small movable targets (such as tanks and helicopters) as well as for aiming and automatic homing of Vikhr guided missiles. The electro-optical Shkval unit includes 3 coupled modes: a TV channel for observation and tracking targets, Prichal laser rangefinder/target designator, and laser beam riding system for Vikhr missile. With additional equipment (for instance, a container with radio-location and FLIR unit), the Shkval may also be used at night. The widow of the Shkval system is located in the helicopter nose. The pilot has a helmet mounted sight slaved to the Shkval unit. Export versions may be offered with French avionics as an option.
Radar: None.
Fixed weapons: Shipunov 2A42 30-mm cannon, originally built for the BMP-2 armoured personnel carrier, mounted on the starboard side of the fuselage. An hydraulic control system moves the barrel in elevation (about +10°/–35°); aiming in azimuth is effected by means of positioning the whole helicopter. This gun aiming system was chosen because the angular speed of the helicopter is much greater than the horizontal speed of the cannon barrel. However, the barrel can also be moved by several degrees in azimuth, but for cannon stabilization only.
Ammunition: 500 rounds (280 rounds in Ka-52, see Aircraft variants).
Number of weapon pylons: 4
Expendable weapons and equipment: Typical weapon load includes 2 x 6-round clusters of 9A4172 Vikhr-M (AT-12) supersonic laser-beam riding anti-tank guided missiles (ATGM) on the inner wing pylons and 2 x B-8 launchers (containing 20 x 80-mm S-8 unguided rockets) on the outer pylons. ATGM clusters are carried in adjustable pods; they can be lowered by 10°, thus reducing the length of the missile path to the target. Vikhr is a supersonic laser-beam riding missile of 8-10 km range. Modified Vikhr-M, with a 12-15 km range, is under development. Alternative weapons include laser-guided Kh-25ML (AS-10 *Karen*) and anti-radar Kh-25MP (AS-12 *Kegler*) ASMs, UPK-23-250 gun packs, rocket launchers, bombs, etc. Against airborne target, R-73 (AA-11 *Archer*) AAMs and Igla V portable SAMs can be carried.
Self-protection systems: Infra-red suppression cool-air mixers on engine nozzles. UV-26 chaff/flare dispensers with 26-mm PPI-26 flares or PPR-26 radar decoys at the wingtips (2 x 32-rounds dispensers in each wingtip fairing). The flares are launched automatically according to the programmed sequence controlled by the L-140 system and Beryoza radar warning receiver.
Aircraft variants:
Ka-50 (V-80Sh1, izdelye 800) *Hokum-A*, as detailed.
Ka-52 *Hokum-B* is a side-by-side two-seat trainer version, under development. Full-scale mock-up was shown in August 1995 in Zhukovsky. First flight expected in 1996.
Ka-52 (V-80Sh2) is a two-seat combat-reconnaissance version of the Ka-52 trainer. Reduced cockpit armour, and 2A42 gun with 280 rounds. Ejection seats for both crew members, with simultaneous use. Armed with Vikhr-M ATGMs. Miilimtre-waxe radar. 2 uprated TV3-17F turboshafts. Speed 162 kts (186 mph) 300 km/h. Hovering ceiling 11,800 ft (3,600 m). Range 248 naut miles (286 miles) 460 km. First flight expected in 1996.

Details for Ka-50 *Hokum-A*.

Principal dimensions:
Rotor diameter: 47 ft 4 ins (14.43 m) each
Maximum length, rotors turning: 52 ft 4.5 ins (15.96 m)
Fuselage length: 49 ft 3 ins (15.0 m)
Wing span: 24 ft 1 ins (7.34 m)
Maximum height: 16 ft 2 ins (4.93 m)

Undercarriage:
Type: Retractable nosewheel type in order to reduce the aerodynamic drag and radar signature. Twin nosewheels and single main wheels. Nosewheels semi-retract.
Main wheel tyre size: 700 x 250 mm
Nose wheel tyre size: 400 x 150 mm
Wheel base: 16 ft 1 ins (4.91 m)
Wheel track: 8 ft 9 ins (2.67 m)

Weights:
Normal take-off: 21,605 lb (9,800 kg)
Maximum take-off: 23,810 lb (10,800 kg)
External load: 6,614 lb (3,000 kg)

Performance:
Maximum speed in a shallow dive: 189 kts (217 mph) 350 km/h
Maximum level flight speed: 167 kts (193 mph) 310 km/h
Backward flight speed: 49 kts (56 mph) 90 km/h
Sideways flight speed: 43 kts (50 mph) 80 km/h
Maximum climb rate at 8,200 ft (2,500 m): 1,970 ft (600 m) per minute
G limit: 3.0
OGE hovering ceiling: 13,125 ft (4,000 m)
Practical range: 243 naut miles (280 miles) 450 km

Kamov V-60R

First flight: Project only in early 1995.
Role: Reconnaissance helicopter to be used to support the Ka-50/52.

▲ Development

▲ Mid-1980s. Programme initiated to match the capabilities of the US LHX (Light Helicopter Experimental).
▲ V-60 project won the Soviet competition against the Mil Mi-36 project.
Flight crew: Probably 2.
Airframe, engines, rotors, dimensions, weights and performance: Probably close to the civil Ka-62 (which see).
Mission sensors: Samshit all-weather, round-the-clock suite for reconnaissance and designation of ground targets. 3 modes: television, thermo-vision and laser. Data link for transmitting data to attack helicopters and ground command posts.
Aircraft variants:
V-60R military reconnaissance/target designation helicopter. See general details.
Fighter helicopter derivative project probably exists.
Ka-62 is the derived civil multi-purpose version, which see.

Kamov Ka-62

First flight: Late 1995.
Role: Civil multi-purpose helicopter, derived from the military V-60 project.

▲ Development

▲ September 1990. Full-scale mock-up presented for the first time. Officially adopted under Russia's "civil aviation for the year 2000" planning.

Details for Ka-62.

Principal dimensions:
Rotor diameter: 44 ft 3.5 ins (13.5 m)
Fuselage length: 43 ft 6 ins (13.25 m)
Maximum height: 13 ft 5.5 ins (4.1 m)

Cabin:
Length: 10 ft 10 ins (3.30 m)
Width: 5 ft 9 ins (1.75 m)
Height: 4 ft 3 ins (1.30 m)

Tail unit
Stabilizer span: 9 ft 10 ins (3.00 m)

Undercarriage:
Type: Retractable, with single mainwheels and twin small tailwheels
Wheel base: 15 ft 6 ins (4.725 m)
Wheel track: 8 ft 2.5 ins (2.50 m)

Weights:
Maximum take-off: 13,228 lb (6,000 kg)

Performance:
Max operating speed: 162 kts (186 mph) 300 km/h
Cruise speed: 143 kts (165 mph) 265 km/h
Maximum climb rate: 2,560 ft (780 m) per minute, sea level
OGE hovering ceiling: 9,515 ft (2,900 m)
Ceiling: 18,045 ft (5,500 m), service
Normal range: 421 naut miles (485 miles) 780 km, at 6,560 ft (2,000 m) altitude
Maximum range, with auxiliary tanks: 567 naut miles (652 miles) 1,050 km

Kamov Ka-62 for fatigue testing (Piotr Butowski)

▲ August 1993. First Ka-62 prototype shown in Zhukovsky while awaiting its first flight, which had not taken place by early 1995.
▲ 1994. General Electric followed Rolls-Royce Turbomeca in providing engines for export versions.
▲ 1996. Certification expected.
Sales/users: Production planned at the Ulan-Ude aircraft plant in Siberia, near Lake Baikal.
Flight crew: 1 or 2.
Passengers: 16 maximum or litters plus attendants.
Freight, internal: Up to 4,409 lb (2,000 kg).
Freight, external: Up to 5,512 lb (2,500 kg).
Cabin access: 4 ft 3 ins x 4 ft 1 ins (1.30 x 1.25 m) doors on both sides of the fuselage, plus smaller doors.
Main rotor characteristics: 4-blade main rotor on the Ka-62 prototype; 5-blade rotor on the Ka-62M.
Tail fan characteristics: Fan-in-fin type.
Construction materials: Wide use of composites, including rotor blades, fuselage panels, tailboom, vertical tail and tail fan.
Safety features: Crashworthy seats and undercarriage.
Engines: 2 Rybinsk/Novikov RD-600 turboshafts in Ka-62 (see Aircraft variants).
Engine rating: 1,300 shp (969 kW) each at 6,000 rpm take-off and 1,000 shp (745.7 kW) cruise.
Fuel system: 1,450 litres. Provision for auxiliary tanks.
Aircraft variants:
Ka-62 (V-62) is the multi-purpose helicopter for the CIS home market, powered by 2 Rybinsk/Novikov RD-600s.
Ka-62G/M are export versions, at least the "G" having 2 General Electric CT7-2D/2D1 turboshafts, each 1,625 shp (1,212 kW), and a 5-blade main rotor. The GE engines will be built at Lynn in Massachusetts.
Ka-62R is an export version with Rolls-Royce Turbomeca RTM322 turboshafts, each 2,100 shp (1,566 kW), and a 5-blade main rotor.

Kamov Ka-115

Role: Civil light helicopter; under development. Intended uses include law enforcement, EMS, SAR and transport. Production from 1997. No other details were known at the time of writing.

Kamov Ka-126 and Ka-128 (NATO name *Hoodlum-B*)

First flight: 19 October 1988 (pre-production Ka-126).
Role: Light transport and agricultural helicopter.
Chief designer: S. V. Mikheev.

★ Aims

★ Turboshaft developments of the twin piston-engined Ka-26, offering reduced weight, higher performance, lower fuel consumption, and reduced noise/vibration levels.
Details: Ka-126, except under Aircraft variants.
Crew/passengers: Pilot, but with provision for a co-pilot or passenger in the non-detachable cockpit. Detachable cabin module for up to 6 persons, or the seats can be folded against the sides for cargo loading via the rear clamshell doors. Medevac module can accommodate 2 litters and 3 sitting casualties/attendants.
Optional equipment: Dual controls, 1,000 litre chemical hopper and spraybars/spreader for agricultural purposes, cargo hook, and more.
Rotor system: 2 non-folding, contra-rotating, 3-blade rotors with hydraulic dampers and standard de-icing. Original plastics blades and hinged rotor head are to be upgraded to newly designed glass/carbonfibre blades and a composites/titanium hingeless rotor head. Rotor brake. Standard filters.
Tail surfaces: Tailplane, and twin inward-toed endplate fins with rudders.
Flight control system: Hydraulic control actuators, with manual reversion.
Fuselage: Pod and twin boom type, with the area aft of the cockpit left free for the optional attachment of one of various cabin modules or equipment loads. Leaving the area open permits lighter-weight crane operations. Detachable cabin modules can include those for passenger transport or medevac roles, or the space can be occupied by agricultural equipment including a chemical hopper with spraybars or dry chemical spreader, a cargo platform, or sling cargo.
Airframe materials: Mostly aluminium alloy, with some use of composites and steel.
Engine: OMSK/Kobchyenko TV-O-100 free-turbine turboshaft. Bleed air intake de-icing.
Engine rating: 700 shp (522 kW).
Fuel system: 800 litres standard. Capacity can rise to 1,120 litres with 2 cabin-side auxiliary tanks.
Electrical system: 27 volt DC supply, with 40 amp-hour stand-by battery. AC supply via a 16 kVA generator, used in part for powering the agricultural gear. Secondary AC supply with 2 static inverters.
Hydraulic system: Single system for rotor control.
Braking system: Pneumatic brakes on rear wheels.
Flight avionics/instrumentation: Basic equipment includes ADF, emergency locator beacon and radar altimeter.

Details for Ka-126.

Principal dimensions:
Rotor diameter: 42 ft 8 ins (13 m) each
Maximum length, rotors turning: 42 ft 8 ins (13 m)
Airframe length: 25 ft 6 ins (7.775 m)
Maximum height: 13 ft 7.5 ins (4.15 m)

Cabin module:
Length: 6 ft 8 ins (2.04 m)
Width: 4 ft 2 ins (1.28 m)
Height: 4 ft 7 ins (1.4 m)

Main rotor:
Blade chord: 10 ins (0.25 m)
Rotor disc: 1,428.4 sq ft (132.7 m^2) each

Undercarriage:
Type: 4-leg fixed type, with single wheels on each unit. Small forward castering/self-centring wheels. Optional wheel/skis and flotation gear at the fuselage nose and rear legs
Main wheel tyre size: 595 x 185 mm
Nose wheel tyre size: 300 x 125 mm
Wheel base: 11 ft 5 ins (3.48 m)
Wheel track: 8 ft 5 ins (2.56 m) main

Weights:
Empty: 4,221 lb (1,915 kg)
Maximum take-off: 7,165 lb (3,250 kg)
Payload: 2,204 lb (1,000 kg) internal or external

Performance:
Never-exceed speed (VNE): 97 kts (112 mph) 180 km/h
Cruise speed: 86 kts (99 mph) 160 km/h
Maximum climb rate: 1,300 ft (396 m) per minute, or 50 ft (15 m) per minute vertical
IGE hovering ceiling: 3,280 ft (1,000 m), ISA
Ceiling: 16,400 ft (5,000 m), service
Range with full standard fuel: 340 naut miles (391 miles) 630 km
Range with full payload: 137 naut miles (157 miles) 253 km

Kamov Ka-126 (Piotr Butowski)

Aircraft variants:
Ka-126 single-turboshaft helicopter, as detailed.
Ka-128 is the much-improved derivative, with a 732 shp (546 kW) Turbomeca Arriel 1D1 turboshaft. Transmission rating 732 shp (546 kW). FAA certification 1996? Reduced empty weight over single-engined Ka-126, at 4,012 lb (1,820 kg). Other weights similar. Very substantial increase in climb rates, hovering/service ceilings and range with maximum payload, including an expected IGE hovering ceiling of 5,250 ft (1,600 m) and OGE hovering ceiling of 2,460 ft (750 m), both ISA, and range with 1,000 kg payload of nearly 200 naut miles (230 miles) 370 km.

Kamov Ka-226

Role: Twin-engined and refined development of the Ka-128, for similar uses.

▲ Development
▲ 1995. Planned FAA certification.
Rotor system: Similar to Ka-128. New system under development.
Tail surfaces: Reconfigured surfaces of less angular form.
Fuselage: More streamlined, with lengthened nose and small ventral windows deleted.

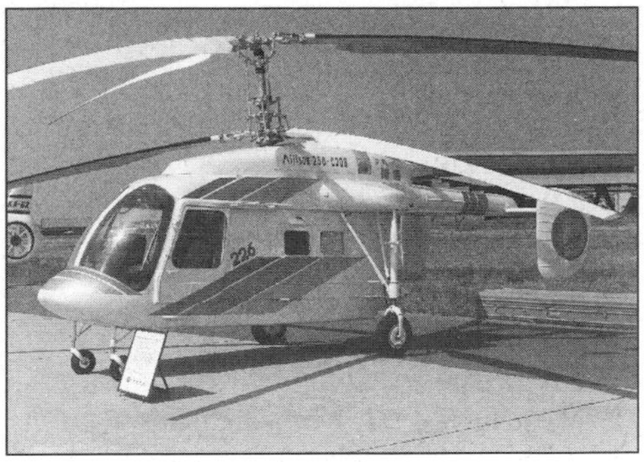

Kamov Ka-226 (Piotr Butowski)

Engines: 2 Allison 250-C20B turboshafts.
Engine rating: Each 420 shp (313.3 kW) at take-off.
Transmission rating: 840 shp (626 kW).
Fuel system: 750 litres, with 2 x 160 litre auxiliary tanks as for Ka-128.
Flight avionics/instrumentation: AlliedSignal Bendix/King or other suite, for VFR or IFR operation.

Details for Ka-226 are similar to Ka-126, except.

Principal dimensions:
Airframe length: 26 ft 7 ins (8.1 m)

Weights:
Empty, operating: 4,303 lb (1,952 kg)
Maximum take-off: 7,495 lb (3,400 kg)
Payload: 2,866 lb (1,300 kg)

Performance:
Cruise speed: 100 kts (115 mph) 185 km/h
Maximum climb rate: 1,771 ft (540 m) per minute
IGE hovering ceiling: over 6,550 ft (2,000 m), ISA
OGE hovering ceiling: 4,200 ft (1,280 m), ISA
Ceiling: over 16,400 ft (5,000 m), service
Range: 325 naut miles (374 miles) 600 km with 750 litres of fuel
Duration: over 4.5 hours with 750 litres of fuel, no reserve

Kazan Helicopter Production Association (Russia)

Corporate address: 420085, Kazan.
Telephone: +7 8432 54 45 52, 54 46 41, 54 46 91
Facsimile: +7 8432 54 52 52
Telex: 224 848 AGAT SU
Founded: 1940s.
Information: Marat Ajupov (Marketing Department Manager).

Kazan/Mil Ansat fuselage mock-up at the Paris Air Show (courtesy Kazan)

● Activities
● Principal past and current manufacturer of Mil helicopters, including exports from 1956. In 1980 received the Golden Mercury award for development of the aircraft industry.
● Uses computer-aided design, some robotic and other advanced manufacturing techniques, and has extensive engineering and test facilities, but until 1994 undertook production only. However, it has now added helicopter design and development to its business activities, and introduced a fuselage mock-up of its first totally new helicopter, the Ansat, at the Paris Air Show in mid-1995, which is a joint project with Mil.

Kazan/Mil Ansat

Role: Twin-turboshaft light multi-purpose helicopter.
Chief designer: Alexei Stepanov.
Crew/passengers: Pilot and 4-6 passengers, with the option of 8 passengers for short journeys, or 2 litters and 2 attendants.
Freight, internal: 2,205 lb (1,000 kg) in the main cabin with the seats removed.
Freight, external: 2,645 lb (1,200 kg) sling load.
Engines: 2 Pratt & Whitney Canada/Klimov PK206A turboshafts, with FADEC.
Engine rating: Each 640 shp (477 kW) take-off.

Details for Ansat.

Principal dimensions:
Rotor diameter (main): 37 ft 9 ins (11.5 m)

Weights:
Maximum take-off: 7,275 lb (3,300 kg)
Payload: 2,205 lb (1,000 kg) internal; 2,646 lb (1,200 kg) sling load

Performance:
Cruise speed: 143 kts (164 mph) 265 km/h
OGE hovering ceiling: 9,845 ft (3,000 m)
Ceiling: 16,400 ft (5,000 m), service
Range with full fuel: 313 naut miles (360 miles) 580 km
Duration: 3.3 hours

Mil Moscow Helicopter Plant (Russia)

Corporate address: 2 Sokolnichesky Val, 107113, Moscow.
Telephone: +7 095 2649083, 2644382
Facsimile: +7 095 2644762
Telex: 412144 Mil SU
Founded: 1947.

● Activities

● Mil-designed helicopters are produced in association with various closely-linked production facilities, including the Kazan Helicopter Production Association that produces the Mi-8, Mi-14, Mi-17 and Mi-171 (which see); Rostvertol PLC (5 Novatorov, 344038, Rostov-on-Don – *telephone* +7 8632 317493/317371, *facsimile* +7 8632 310039/317491) which produces the Mi-26 and 26T, Mi-28 and Mi-35; and the Joint Stock Company Ulan-Ude Aviation Manufacturing Plant (1 Khorinskaya Street, Ulan-Ude 670009 – *telephone* +7 30122 3-74-75, *facsimile* +7 30122 3-01-47) which produces the Mi-8FT, Mi-8AMT and Mi-171 (well as the Kamov Ka-62 and Sukhoi Su-25UBK). Others are Arsenyev and Viatka plants.

● Mil participates in Euromil with Eurocopter, Kazan and Klimov, to develop, produce and market the Mi-38 (which see).

Mil Mi-6 and Mi-22 (NATO name *Hook)*

Details: For Mi-6.
First flight: 5 June 1957 (piloted by Rafail Kaprelyan).
Role: Heavy transport, medevac, firefighting, and airborne command post.

★ Aims

★ Cabin cargo hold compatible with the An-12 *Cub*.

▲ Development

▲ October 1957. World payload-to-height record set, at 26,464 lb (12,004 kg) to 7,979 ft (2,432 m) altitude.
▲ July-October 1959. First stage of State Acceptance Tests.
▲ July 1961. Shown publicly for the first time at Tushino airfield in Moscow.
▲ 21 September 1961. Record speed of 173 kts (199 mph) 320 km/h set, the first helicopter record over 300 km/h.
▲ 1962. Record payload of 44,350 lb (20,117 kg).
▲ 1963. Mi-6A officially commissioned into the Soviet Air Force.

Sales: First helicopters (reportedly about 30) built in 1958 at Factory No 23 in Moscow-Fili. Mass production (about 860) at Rostov-on-Don Factory No 168 (now Rostvertol). In service with the CIS armed forces, and more than 60 exported to Algeria, Egypt, Ethiopia, India, Indonesia, Iraq, Pakistan, Peru, Poland (3 helicopters; no longer used), Syria and Vietnam. Out of production.
Crew/passengers: 5 flight crew (2 pilots, navigator, radio operator and engineer), plus an assault equipment operator in military versions. Standard Mi-6A can carry 61 fully-armed troops. Mi-6TP has 65 folding seats, Mi-6P has 80 seats, and Mi-6S has 41 litters and 2 attendants.
See Aircraft variants, and Freight internal.
Freight, internal: ATL and ATP artillerey vehicles, trucks, jeeps, etc.
Cabin access: Hydraulically-operated rear clamshell doors. Single passenger door and 9 windows on starboard and 2 doors and 7 windows on port side of the fuselage.
Size of main loading door: 8 ft 10 ins x 8 ft 8 ins (2.7 x 2.65 m) rear opening. Largest side door 5 ft 7 ins x 2 ft 7 ins (1.7 x 0.8 m).
Rotor system: 5-blade steel main rotor with flapping and drag hinges. Fixed tabs. Metal swashplate. Electric blade de-icing.
Tail rotor characteristics: 4-blade metal AV-63-Kh6 tail rotor.
Wing/tail surfaces: Adjustable wings (2 position) attached to the fuselage sides to relieve the rotor by producing some 20% of required lift in cruise flight. For powered cruise the port wing is set to +14° 15′. With the engines off (autorotation), the port wing is set to +4° 15′. Since the rotor generated air flow is not symmetrical, the angle of the wings has to be asymmetrical; the starboard wing setting is always greater by 1° 30′. Ground adjustable horizontal stabilizer (+5° 30′, –7° 30′). Tailboom tip acts as the vertical fin. Wings are detacted for flying-crane duties.
Airframe materials: Metal.
Engines: 2 Aviadvigatel/Solovyov D-25V turboshafts.
Engine rating: Each 5,500 shp (4,100 kW) take-off.
Transmission rating: R-7 main gearbox, designed by Pavel Solovyov.
Fuel system: 8,150 litres (13,922 lb, 6,315 kg) standard in 11 bag tanks inside the fuselage, plus 4,500 litres (7,694 lb, 3,490 kg) in 2 metal tanks on the fuselage sides. Provision for 4,500 litres of auxiliary fuel in a metal cabin tank. Maximum fuel weight 29,310 lb (13,295 kg).
Flight avionics/instrumentation: Typical Russian flight/navigation/communications equipment for all-weather operations (no radar), plus astrocompass. AP-34B autopilot (AP-31 earlier). SRO-2 IFF.
Self-protection systems: Some military helicopters have a pack of 2 ASO-2 chaff/flare dispensers on each side of the fuselage, with a total of 128 projectiles.
Fixed guns: NUV-1M turret with flexible 12.7-mm machine-gun in the glazed nose.
Ammunition: 150 rounds.

Mil Mi-6VKP Hook-B airborne command post. Note the tailboom aerials, rear clamshell doors, wings and external tanks (Piotr Butowski)

Number of weapon pylons: None.
Aircraft variants:
Mi-6 covers the initial small production series built at Factory No 23 in Moscow from 1958. TV-2V engines, based on the Kuznetsov TV-2 turboprop core.
Mi-6A basic production version, manufactured at Rostov-on-Don Factory No 168. D-25Vs of the same rating but lighter. Wings added.
Mi-6AYa and Mi-6BUS, see Mi-22.
Mi-6P (passazhirskiy, has airliner-type seats for 80 passengers, and rectangular instead of circular windows.
Mi-6PS (poiskovo-spasatelnyi) of 1977 appearance is a military rescue/evacuation version.
Mi-6PZh (1967) and Mi-6PZh2 (1971) are firefighting versions. 21,000 litres of water in a single 12,000 litre metal cabin tank plus 6 x 1,500 litre bag tanks suspended beneath the fuselage.
Mi-6S (sanitarnyi) is a medevac version for 41 litters and 2 attendants.
Mi-6TP (transportno-passazhirskiy) is a convertible cargo/passenger version, with 65 folding seats.
Mi-6TZ (toplivo-zapravshchik) of 1977 is a tanker version (ground use), used during the Afghan conflict.
Mi-6VKP (vozdushnyi komandnyi punkt, airborne command post) or Mi-6VzPU (vozdushnyi punkt upravlenya, airborne control post) are named by NATO as *Hook B*. 4 small plate-type aerials arranged symmetrically around the tailboom plus a rectangular frame aerial. Usual starboard metal fuel tank is deleted, its place taken by a cooler in front of the undercarriage gear and a small tank behind. Some have additional small aerials.
Mi-22 *Hook-C* is an airborne command post, derived from the Mi-6 (see Mi-6VKP and Mi-6VzPU). Sword type aerial under the front fuselage and no tailboom aerials. Mi-6VKP fuselage cooler deleted, with the starboard metal fuel tank reinstated. According some sources, *Hook-C* is designated Mi-6BUS and Mi-6AYa.

DETAILS FOR Mi-6A.

Principal dimensions:
Rotor diameter (main): 114 ft 10 ins (35 m)
Maximum length, rotors turning: 136 ft 11 ins (41.739 m)
Fuselage length: 108 ft 10 ins (33.165 m)
Maximum height: 32 ft 4 ins (9.86 m)
Wing span: 50 ft 2 ins (15.3 m), with 376.74 sq ft (35 m^2) area

Cabin:
Length: 38 ft 5 ins (11.726 m)
Width: 9 ft 11 ins (3.014 m)
Height: 6 ft 7 ins to 8 ft 8 ins (2.012 to 2.647 m)
Volume: 2,825 cu ft (80 m^3)

Main rotor:
Aerofoil section: NACA 230M and high-speed TsAGI P-57-9 (root/centre and tips)
Rotor disc: 10,356 sq ft (962.1 m^2)

Tail rotor:
Diameter: 20 ft 8 ins (6.3 m)

Undercarriage:
Type: Fixed, with twin nosewheels
Main wheel tyre size: 1,325 x 480 mm
Nose wheel tyre size: 720 x 310 mm
Wheel base: 29 ft 10 ins (9.095 m)
Wheel track: 24 ft 7 ins (7.502 m)

Weights:
Empty: 60,054 lb (27,240 kg)
Normal take-off: 89,287 lb (40,500 kg)
Maximum take-off: 93,696 lb (42,500 kg), raised to 97,003 lb (44,000 kg) for final production helicopters.
Payload: 13,228-26,455 lb (6,000-12,000 kg), nominal/maximum

Performance:
Maximum speed: 162 kts (186 mph) 300 km/h
Cruise speed: 135 kts (155 mph) 250 km/h
OGE hovering ceiling: 3,280 ft (1,000 m)
Ceiling: 14,765 ft (4,500 m), service
Range with 17,632 lb (8,000 kg) payload: 335 naut miles (385 miles) 620 km, without auxiliary fuel, 5% reserve
Range with auxiliary fuel: 783 naut miles (901 miles) 1,450 km

Mil Mi-8 (NATO name *Hip*)

First flight: 24 June 1961.
Role: Medium civil/military transport, armed assault, minelaying, reconnaissance, airborne command/control post, electronic warfare, firefighting, ambulance, agricultural, and more.

▲ Development

▲ May 1960. Ordered as a turbine powered replacement for Mi-4 *Hound*.
▲ 24 June 1961. First flight of the single-engined (Ivchenko AI-24V) prototype.
▲ 2 August 1962. First hovering flight of the twin-engined (Izotov TV2-117s) prototype.
▲ 9 October 1963. First flight of the prototype with a 5-blade main rotor.
▲ 3 November 1964. State acceptance trials completed.
▲ 1965. First production Mi-8 helicopter left the factory in Kazan.

Sales: About 6,500 helicopters have been built by the Kazan and Ulan-Ude factories, and production continues. Some 1,400 have been exported to 57 countries, with recent recipients including Algeria (47 combat equipped) and Mexico (navy 8). Mi-8s took part in the first phase of the Afghanistan conflict but were soon replaced by Mi-8MTs with more powerful engines. In some countries local improvements have been applied; for instance, in Egypt the air intakes of Mi-8Ts are protected by British particle separators, whereas nav/weather radar units have been installed on Finnish Mi-8Ts. Mi-8SMV serves only with CIS armed forces (more than 50), while 2 Mi-8PPAs are in Czech Air Force and 1 in Slovakian service.
Crew/passengers: 2 pilots, plus flight engineer between the cockpit and main cabin. 28 passengers in the Mi-8P (seat pitch 29 ins, 74 cm, with 12 ins, 30 cm aisle), and 24 equipped troops on tip-up seats or 8,818 lb (4,000 kg) of cargo in the Mi-8T. In an air ambulance role, the helicopter can carry 12 litters, 1 attendant and all necessary equipment. See Aircraft variants.
Freight, external: Both passenger and cargo versions can be fitted with external slings for carrying bulky loads or for use as air cranes. Set of available cables make it possible to select the suspension height of a sling load. The crane boom installed enables the helicopter to be used for rescue, using the electric winch.

Mil Mi-8TV Hip-Cs with 4 rocket packs (Piotr Butowski)

Cabin access: Clamshell freight loading doors at the rear of the cabin, are considerably larger on military variants than civil. Mi-8P has a central airstair door of 2 ft 7 ins x 4 ft 3 ins (0.785 x 1.285 m). Port-side sliding door of 2 ft 8 ins x 4 ft 7 ins (0.82 x 1.4 m).
Optional equipment: 331 lb (150 kg) LPG-150M electric hoist, typically on Mi-8T.
Rotor system: Aluminium alloy, 5-blade main rotor, with balance tabs. Flapping and drag hinges. Forward incline off horizontal of 4° 30′. Current helicopters have pendulum vibration damping. Nitrogen pressurized blade spar crack warning system.
Tail rotor characteristics: 3-blade metal, on starboard side (except Mi-8MT/MTV series).
Tail surfaces: Ground adjustable horizontal stabilizer. Tailfin formed from the rear of the tailboom.
Flight control system: Mechanical, with hydraulic boosters.
Airframe materials: D16AT and V95 duralumin, other aluminium alloys, magnez alloy and steel.
Engines: Currently 2 Klimov/Isotov TV2-117AG (formerly TV2-117A) turboshafts, side-by-side above the cabin.
Engine rating: Each 1,500 shp (1,119 kW).

Current production Mi-8AT with nose weather radar. Note the flight data recorder near the Doppler navigation box under the tailboom, and main rotor vibration damper (Piotr Butowski)

Transmission: 3-stage VR-8A main reduction gearbox, ratio 62.5:1. Weight 1,730 lb (785 kg).
Fuel system: Fuel in a 445 litre collector tank above the cabin and 2 fixed external tanks at the fuselage sides. External tanks are of 2 variants; short tanks are 745 litres (starboard) and 680 litres (port); long tanks are 1,140 litres (starboard) and 1,030 litres (port). For ferrying, 1 or 2 additional tanks (915 litres each) can be carried in the cabin, raising volume to 4,445 litres (weighing 7,599 lb; 3,447 kg) and fairly easily installed/removed under field conditions.
Electrical system: 27 volt DC system via 2 x 18 kW starter-generators plus 6 x 28 amp-hour batteries. AC system at 400 Hz via a generator, plus 3-phase back-up.
Hydraulic system: Basic and stand-by systems operating on AMG-10 oil, pressure 653 to 943 psi.
Braking system: Pneumatic brakes.
Radar: Weather radar in the nose for some versions, including current production Mi-8AT and some MTVs.
Flight avionics/instrumentation: AP-34B autopilot for course, altitude, roll and pitch stabilization. ARK-9 and ARK-U2 automatic radio compass, A-037 (earlier RV-3) altimeter, and DIV-1 Doppler navigation. Standard communications equipment includes R-842 (or Yadro-1 in civil versions) and R-860 (earlier R-833, or Baklan-20 for civil versions) radios, and SPU-7 intercom.
Fixed guns: Mi-8TB/TBK have 12.7 mm nose-mounted Afanasyev A-12.7 flexible machine-gun.
Ammunition: 700 rounds.
Number of weapon pylons: Military Mi-8Ts can have outriggers with a total of 4 pylons, while Mi-8TB/TBKs have 6 plus an additional 4 or 6 anti-armour missiles on over-rigger launch rails.
Expendable weapons and equipment: Military Mi-8TV usually carries 4 x UB-16-57UD rocket packs, each with 16 x 57-mm S-5 rockets. Mi-8TB usually carries 6 UB-32 rocket packs (total 192 rockets) and 4 x 9M17P Skorpion (AT-2 *Swatter*) anti-armour missiles, while Mi-8TBK has 6 UB-32s and 6 x 9M14M Malyutka (AT-3 *Sagger*) missiles. Bombs. See Aircraft variants.

Aircraft variants:
V-8 *Hip-A* prototype had a single AI-24V engine and 4-blade main rotor.
V-8A *Hip-B* prototype of 1962 had 2 x TV2-117 engines and a 4-bladed rotor.

DETAILS FOR *HIP-C*.

Principal dimensions:
Rotor diameter (main): 69 ft 10 ins (21.288 m)
Maximum length, rotors turning: 82 ft 9 ins (25.244 m)
Fuselage length: 59 ft 7 ins (18.168 m) or 60 ft 7 ins (18.31 m) with weather radar in nose
Maximum height: 18 ft 7 ins (5.654 m), or 14 ft 4 ins (4.38 m) to above rotor hub

Cabin (Mi-8T, *with Mi-8P in italics*):
Length: 25 ft 8 ins (7.82 m) including rear doors, 17 ft 6 ins (5.34 m) excluding doors, *20 ft 10 ins (6.36 m)*
Width: 7 ft 8 ins (2.34 m) maximum
Width at floor: 6 ft 9 ins (2.06 m), *the same*
Height: 5 ft 11 ins (1.8 m)

Main rotor:
Aerofoil section: NACA 230
Blade chord: 1 ft 8.5 ins (0.52 m)
Rotor disc: 3,832 sq ft (356 m^2)
Rpm: 192

Tail rotor:
Diameter: 12 ft 9.75 ins (3.908 m)

Undercarriage:
Type: Fixed, with twin steerable nosewheels. Tyre pressure can be autonomously increased using the pneumatic system and air in the struts. Optional streamline fairings for mainwheels
Main wheel tyre size: 865 x 280 mm (KT-97-3 type)
Nose wheel tyre size: 595 x 185 mm (K2-116 type)
Wheel base: 14 ft (4.258 m)
Wheel track: 15 ft 9 ins (4.8 m)

Weights:
Empty: 16,248 lb (7,370 kg) for Mi-8P, 15,069-16,006 lb (6,835-7,260 kg) for Mi-8T
Normal take-off: 24,471 lb (11,100 kg)
Maximum take-off: 26,455 lb (12,000 kg)
Payload: 8,818 lb (4,000 kg) internal, 6,614 lb (3,000 kg) external

Performance:
Maximum speed: 135 kts (155 mph) 250 km/h at normal take-off weight, 124 kts (143 mph) 230 km/h at maximum
Cruise speed: 121 kts (140 mph) 225 km/h at normal take-off weight
IGE hovering ceiling: 5,905 ft (1,800 m)
OGE hovering ceiling: 2,790 ft (850 m)
Ceiling: 14,765 ft (4,500 m), service
Range with ferry fuel: 532 naut miles (612 miles) 985 km at 1,640 ft (500 m), 30 minutes reserve
Range with 4,469 lb (2,027 kg) fuel: 281 naut miles (323 miles) 520 km, altitude/reserve as above
Range with passengers: 229 naut miles (264 miles) 425 km, 20 minutes reserve

Mi-8AT *Hip-C* is a current production version (Ulan-Ude factory), with TV2-117AG engines.
Mi-8FT has replaced Mi-8T in Ulan-Ude production. TV2-117F engines.
Mi-8K is a reconnaissance and artillery spotting version. Large window for photographic camera in the rear cabin doors.
Mi-8MT, MTV-1/-2/-3 are Kazan-produced helicopters upgraded to Mi-17 standard, identified by a port-side tail rotor. MTV-1 has high-altitude engines. See Mi-17 entry.
Mi-8P (V-8AP in prototype form) *Hip-C* is a passenger version. Rectangular cabin windows.
Mi-8PA appeared in 1980. Export version of Mi-8P for a Japanese customer, with TV2-117F engines.
Mi-8PD (punkt dowodzenia) is a Polish airborne command post conversion.
Mi-8R is a reconnaissance version.
Mi-8S and Mi-8PS (S for salon) *Hip-C* are VIP versions for 7-11 passengers, based on the Mi-8T or Mi-8P. Some communications equipment added to Mi-8PS.
Mi-8T (V-8AT in prototype form) *Hip-C* is a standard civil and military transport version. Circular cabin windows. Both Mi-8T and Mi-8P have many sub-variants depending on equipment, including crane, medical, firefighting (4,409 lb, 2,000 kg of water in suspended rubber tank), and agricultural. Military helicopters can be used for minelaying. Replaced in production at Ulan-Ude by Mi-8FT.
Mi-8TB (transportno-boyevoi, transport-combat) *Hip-E* appeared in 1975 as a military assault transport with extended armament, including 6 rocket packs and 4 missiles. A-12.7 machine gun.
Mi-8TBK *Hip-F* became the export version of Mi-8TB, with 6 x 9M14M missiles plus other weapons. Received by Germany and Nicaragua.
Mi-8TG has TV2-117TG turboshaft engines adapted for liquid methane fuel, standard aircraft fuel and any mixture of the two. Flew 1987 as the first methane fuelled helicopter in the world.
Mi-8TP is a military executive helicopter, with upgraded communication equipment, produced by Ulan-Ude. Additional R-832 radio equipment (2 sword-type aerials under the front fuselage and tailboom) plus R-111 unit with rod type aerial lowered under the fuselage.
Mi-8TS (tropichesky sukhoi, tropical dry) is an export version for hot and dusty climates, used by Syria from 1973.
Mi-8TV (vooruzhonnyi, armed) *Hip-C* appeared in 1968. As Mi-8T but with provision for weapon pylons carrying 4 x UB-16-57UD rocket packs or bombs.
Mi-8VKP (vozdushnyi komandnyi punkt, airborne command post) or Mi-8VzPU (vozdushnyi punkt upravlenya, airborne control post) *Hip-D* carries distinctive equipment boxes on the racks. 2 frame type aerials installed symmetrically above the rear fuselage, plus a new aerial installed under the tailboom.
Mi-8SMV *Hip-J* is a communications jamming helicopter. R-949 fixed jamming equipment in 2 box-shaped transmitting antennae on each side of the fuselage, in place of windows, with 54 naut miles (62 miles) 100 km range when operating at 3,280 ft (1,000 m). Also has 4 containers, each with 8 releasable single-use jammers that operate for 1 hour at a range of 1,312-3,937 ft (400-1,200 m).
Mi-8PPA *Hip-K* is a radar jamming version. Pack of 6 cruciform dipole antennae on each side of the rear fuselage. Row of 6 heat-exchangers under the fuselage nose, with boxes for batteries ahead of the main undercarriage. 3 radar jamming stations, SPS-63, SPS-66 and SPS-68 (SPS stand for samolotnaya pomekhovaya stantsya, airborne jamming station).
Mi-9 *Hip-G* is an airborne command post. See separate entry.

Mil Mi-9 (NATO name *Hip-G*) and Mi-19

First flight: About 1977.
Role: Tactical airborne command posts.
Sales: More than 100 Mi-9s are used by CIS land forces. Some are with Hungary and 8 were supplied to the former East Germany for service from May 1984. No data for Mi-19.
Mission equipment: Mi-9 has Ivolga (golden oriole, therefore Mi-8IV) command system, including R-826 HF radio equipment (2 plate-type aerials along the bottom of the fuselage), R-802 UHF (mast-type aerial under the front fuselage), R-405 radio-link (hockey-type aerial on the port side of the rear fuselage and another under the tailboom), R-856 and R-832 (aerials on the tailboom), plus R-111 relay equipment (aerial normally folded along the bottom of the fuselage ready for unfolding in flight).
Aircraft variants:
Mi-9 *Hip-G* command post is based on Mi-8 *Hip-C*.
Mi-19 command post is based on the Mi-8MT (Mi-17) *Hip-H*.

Mil Mi-9 Hip-G tactical command post (Cezary Piotrowski, via Piotr Butowski)

Mil Mi-14 (NATO name *Haze*)

First flight: July 1967.
Role: Shore-based anti-submarine amphibious helicopter, with mine-countermeasures and search and rescue variants.
Sales: Production ended in about 1987, after some 230 had been manufactured at Kazan. About 130 remain with CIS naval forces (36 with the Black Sea Fleet remaining in Russia). Other recipients were Bulgaria, Cuba, East Germany, Libya, North Korea, Poland (13), Syria, Vietnam, and former Yugoslavia.
Crew/passengers: 2 pilots, technician, and navigator/weapon systems or rescue equipment operator.
Cabin access: Sliding port door.
Standard equipment: MSK-3M sea suits, LAS-5M-3 dinghy, and electric winch; Mi-14PL and Mi-14BT have an LPG-2 (early series) or LPG-150 external winch with a lifting capacity of 331 lb (150 kg), while Mi-14PS has an LPG-300 winch that is retracted inside the cabin, with a 661 lb (300 kg) lifting capacity.
Rotor system: Mi-17 dynamics.
Fuselage: Watertight boat-type hull with side sponsons.
Engines: 2 Klimov/Isotov TV3-117M turboshafts. AI-9V APU.
Engine rating: Each 1,950 shp (1,454 kW) at take-off, with emergency rating of 2,225 shp (1,659 kW).
Transmission: VR-14 3-stage main gearbox. Weight 1,786 lb (810 kg), ratio 78:1.
Fuel system: 3,795 litres of fuel in a single collector tank in the engine bay aft of the main gearbox and 6 tanks under the cabin floor. Additional 500 litre tank can be installed inside the cabin for ferry flights.
Radar: Initsiativa-2M (I-2M, or I-2ME for export) nav/search/attack radar in an undernose radome. See below.
Flight avionics/instrumentation: SAU-14 automatic control system, with AP34-B autohover in Mi-14PL but not in Mi-14PS. ARK-9 and ARK-U2 radio compasses, RV-3 radio altimeter, and DISS-15 Doppler navigation radar. SRZO-2 IFF. Radio communication equipment comprises R-842M and R-860 in Mi-14PL, Karat-M-24 and R-832M in Mi-14PS. SPU-7 intercom. Mi-14PL *Haze-A* has a Kalmar attack system that interfaces the Initsiativa radar, Oka-2 sonar, Orsha (APM-60) magnetic anomaly detector (MAD) and radio sonobuoys systems. PK-025 data link for group operations.
Expendable weapons and equipment: Mi-14PL *Haze-A* has a weapons bay, with armament choices of a single AT-1 ASW torpedo or APR-2 torpedo, 8 depth bombs, or a nuclear depth bomb. For search operations, 2 cassettes can be carried, each containing 18 RGBN-MN-1 sonobuoys.
Aircraft variants:
Mi-14PL (protivo-lodochnyi) *Haze-A* is the standard ASW version, powered by TV3-117M engines. Tail rotor on the port side. MAD antenna mounted in a lower position on final examples.
Mi-14PLM *Haze-A* has updated equipment, particularly a USK rescue container as standard.
Mi-14BT (buksir-tralshchik) *Haze-B* is the mine countermeasures version, equipped with a towed SKT trawl for cutting the cables of anchored mines, other types of trawls (acoustic, electromagnetic, etc). Can also tow small boats (for instance, landing craft and rescue rafts).
Mi-14PS (poiskovo-spasatelnyi) *Haze-C* is a search and rescue version. ASW equipment is removed from the cabin, providing room for 20 life-rafts, which can be dropped to survivors and towed in a train. Also deploys floating containers with clothes, food, medicines, etc. On-board accommodation for 19 survivors. Compared with the Mi-14PL, it has no magnetometer, the tail rotor is to starboard, 2 large searchlights are installed on the front fuselage and another under the tailboom (some have another in the nose), the port-side cabin door is enlarged, and a 661 lb (300 kg) 3-person rescue hoist is installed. Last production Mi-14PSs have a third fairing under the tailboom, housing a TV camera (the other 2 are for the DISS-15 and searchlight).
Mi-14PX is the Polish Mi-14PL converted in June 1990 for search and rescue (Poland had previously lost half its fleet of 4 Mi-14PSs). Searchlights added, some rescue equipment located inside the cabin, but all the ASW equipment retained, allowing its use only for training purposes. 1 only, side number 1003.
Mi-14 Eliminator III is a German-Russian conversion of the ex-GDR mine-sweeping Mi-14BT *Haze-B* for firefighting, with internal tanks for 4,500 litres of water and 500 litres of

Mil Mi-14PS Haze-C (Piotr Butowski)

DETAILS FOR Mi-14PL *HAZE-A*.

Principal dimensions:
Rotor diameter (main): 69 ft 10 ins (21.294 m)
Maximum length, rotors turning: 83 ft 1 ins (25.315 m)
Fuselage length: 60 ft 3 ins (18.376 m)
Maximum height: 22 ft 9 ins (6.936 m)

Main rotor:
Aerofoil section: NACA 23012

Tail rotor:
Diameter: 12 ft 10 ins (3.908 m)

Undercarriage:
Type: Retractable 4-unit type, with single nosewheels and twin mainwheels, retracted into the fuselage (nosewheels) or side nacelles (mainwheels). Tail rotor is protected from the ground by a tail support with a float of 6.53 cu ft (0.185 m^3) volume. 2 inflatable floats of 141 cu ft (4 m^3) volume on the fuselage sides to keep the helicopter stable when alighting on water. Can float in sea state 2, with side winds up to 33 ft (10 m) per second
Main wheel tyre size: 600 x 180 mm
Nose wheel tyre size: 480 x 200 mm
Wheel base: 13 ft 6 ins (4.128 m)
Wheel track: 9 ft 3 ins (2.82 m) main, 3 ft 10 ins (1.17 m) nose

Weights:
Empty: 19,620 lb (8,902 kg), or 19,400 lb (8,800 kg) for Mi-14BT *Haze-B*, or 19,447 lb (8,821 kg) for Mi-14PS *Haze-C*.
Normal take-off: 28,660 lb (13,000 kg)
Maximum take-off: 30,865 lb (14,000 kg)
Payload: 6,614 lb (3,000 kg) for Mi-14PS *Haze-C*

Performance:
Maximum permissible speed: 135 kts (155 mph) 250 km/h
Maximum speed: 124 kts (143 mph) 230 km/h at sea level, or 130 kts (149 km/h) 240 km/h at 3,280 ft (1,000 m)
Ceiling: 13,125 ft (4,000 m), service
Normal range: 432 naut miles (497 miles) 800 km
Maximum range: 613 naut miles (705 miles) 1,135 km, with 7% reserve
Duration: 5 hours 56 minutes maximum

Mil Mi-14PS Haze-C for SAR, with side floats inflated (Piotr Butowski)

foam suppression agents. With 2 pumps capable of a combined 3,900 litres per minute working rate, the helicopter sucks water when afloat and releases it through the weapon bay doors. First shown publicly during ILA-94 in Berlin, May 1994.

Mil Mi-17 (Mi-8MT), Mi-18, Mi-171 and Mi-172 (NATO name *Hip-H*)

First flight: 1976.
Role: Medium transport, ambulance, rescue and assault helicopter, derived from the Mi-8 but with TV3-117 engines and a port tail rotor.

Mil Mi-17MD with weapon pylons, chaff/flare dispensers, and reconfigured nose housing 8A-813C weather radar (Piotr Butowski)

▲ Development

▲ 1977. Entered service with Soviet armed forces.
Sales: Approx 2,500 built at Kazan and Ulan-Ude, with 810 exported (with recent recipients including 8 Mi-17s for Sri Lanka). Presently, production is going very slowly (for instance, in 1994 no helicopters were ordered by Russian Army Aviation, and only 15 were delivered to the Russian Ministry of Interior).
Crew/passengers: As for Mi-8 *Hip-C*, except optional 6 extra seats installed along the cabin centreline, making 30 seats.
Engines: 2 Klimov/Isotov TV3-117MT turboshafts (or 117VMs for the Mi-8MTV and derivatives). AI-9V APU. Infra-red suppression cool air mixers can be fitted to the engine nozzles.
Engine rating: Each 1,900 shp (1,417 kW) take-off.
Transmission: VR-14 3-stage main gearbox, weighing 1,785 lb (810 kg), with ratio 78:1.
Fuel system: As for Mi-8 *Hip-C*.
Radar: Optional 8A-813 weather radar in the nose. Mi-17MD has 8A-813C radar. See below.
Flight avionics/instrumentation: DISS-32-90 Doppler navigation radar under tailboom, A-723 long-range radio navigation system, ARK-15M and ARK-U2 radio compasses, ZPU-24 course selector, and A-037 altimeter. R-842 (or Yadro-1 for civil versions) and R-863 (or Baklan-20 for civil versions) radios.
Self-protection systems: Some military helicopters have ASO-2V chaff/flare dispensers (4 cassettes under the tailboom or 6 on the rear fuselage sides, each cassette containing 32 PPI-26-1 flares). Provision for L-166V infra-red jammer (NATO *Hot Brick*) on top of the fuselage aft of the engine bay. See Engines.
Fixed guns: A-12.7 flexible 12.7-mm single-barrel machine-gun in the nose on some military versions. AKS-2A photo gun.
Number of weapon pylons: 6 BD3-57KRVM pylons on fuselage truss outriggers.
Expendable weapons and equipment: Armed military versions can typically have 4 x B-8V-20 rocket launchers, each with 20 x 80-mm S-8 rockets. Other weapon options include bombs, KMGU-2 submunitions dispensers, incendiary tanks, and UPK-23 gun packs. Provision for a flexibly-mounted machine-gun at the cabin rear emergency door and troops firing through the cabin windows.
Aircraft variants:
Mi-18 (first with this designation) was the first prototype with TV3-117 engines. Mi-8 airframe combined with engines, transmissions and rotors of Mi-14 *Haze*. Appeared 1976.
Mi-8MT *Hip-H* became the standard version for the Russian armed forces. TV3-117MT turboshafts, as detailed.
Mi-8MA Arktika is equipped for Polar region operations.
Mi-8MB Bissektr is a rescue/medical version, used during the Afghanistan conflict.
Mi-8MTV *Hip-H* is the hot-and-high equivalent of Mi-8MT, but powered by TV3-117VM engines. Produced by Kazan in several subversions, as the civil Mi-8MTV-1; military Mi-8MTV-2 with military communication-equipment and optional armoured flight deck, plus provision for fuselage-side weapon racks and a flexibly-mounted machine-gun at the nose; Mi-17-1V export equivalents of both Mi-8MTV-1 and Mi-8MTV-2; Mi-17-1VA export medical (flying ambulance) version of the Mi-17-1V; Mi-8MTV-3 for both civil and military use, with minor changes in electrical system and equipment compared with Mi-8MTV-1/-2; and Mi-172 export version of Mi-8MTV-3, certified according to the requirements of India and featuring Series 2 engines, upgraded avionics with GPS, DME, ILS, VOR, weather radar and more, full de-icing, and air conditioning.
Mi-8AMT is similar to the Mi-8MTV-1, but manufactured at Ulan-Ude.
Mi-17 *Hip-H* is the export Mi-8MT.
Mi-17M is the export version built by Kazan for both civil and military use. TV3-117VM engines. Up to an 11,023 lb (5,000 kg) external load, DISS Doppler radar antenna in the tailboom, and reconfigured main cabin doors.
Mi-17MD (D for *desantnyi*, air landing) is a derivative of Mi-17M to carry 36-40 troops. Wider port side door (4 ft 1 ins, 1.25 m) and 2 ft 9 ins (0.83 m) door added to the starboard side. Reconfigured nose, housing 8A-813C weather radar. Prototype (c/n 95448) was shown at the June 1995 Paris Air Show.
Mi-17P is the export passenger version, with 24 airliner-type seats and rectangular cabin windows.
Mi-17Z-2 (Z for zastavba) is an electronic intelligence version of Mi-17 prepared in the Czech Republic. 2 large drum antennae on outriggers each side of the fuselage.
Mi-18 (second use) covered 2 prototypes converted by Kazan from Mi-8MTs (c/n 93038 and 93114) in 1980 to Afghan conflict requirements. Fuselage lengthened by 39.3 ins (100 cm), and later given a retractable undercarriage and an additional starboard sliding door. Maximum speed 146 kts (168 mph) 270 km/h, and payload 11,023 lb (5,000 kg).
Mi-171 is the export Mi-8AMT built at Ulan-Ude.
Mi-172 is the export version of Mi-8MTV-3 (see Mi-8MTV).
MK-30, see Daewoo of South Korea.
Mi-17P and other electronic warfare versions, see separate entry.

Mil Mi-8/17 vibration damper, now standard for current prodution helicopters (Piotr Butowski)

Mil Mi-8/17 rear loading ramp (Piotr Butowski)

Details for Mi-8MT *Hip-H*, except where indicated.

Principal dimensions:
Rotor diameter (main): 69 ft 10 ins (21.294 m)
Maximum length, rotors turning: 83 ft 1 ins (25.31 m)
Fuselage length: 59 ft 9 ins (18.219 m) without nose radar.
Maximum height: 18 ft 7 ins (5.65 m)

Cabin:
Length: 17 ft 6 ins (5.34 m) excluding doors
Width: 7 ft 8 ins (2.34 m)
Height: 5 ft 11 ins (1.8 m)

Tail rotor:
Diameter: 12 ft 10 ins (3.908 m)

Weights:
Empty: 15,554-15,873 lb (7,055-7,200 kg)
Normal take-off weight: 24,471 lb (11,100 lb)
Maximum take-off: 28,660 lb (13,000 kg)
Payload: 11,023 lb (5,000 kg) or 9,921 lb (4,500 kg) for early examples internal, 8,818 lb (4,000 kg) external

Performance (without outriggers and IR suppressors):
Maximum speed: 135 kts (155 mph) 250 km/h at 1,650 ft (500 m), normal take-off weight
Cruise speed: 119-130 kts (137-149 mph) 220-240 km/h, or 116-124 kts (134-143 mph) 215-230 km/h for Mi-171 at normal/maximum take-off weights respectively
OGE hovering ceiling: 5,775 ft (1,760 m), 13,060 ft (3,980 m) for Mi-8MTV
Ceiling: 16,405 ft (5,000 m), 19,685 ft (6,000 m) for Mi-8MTV, 18,700 ft (5,700 m) for Mi-8MTV with de-icing operating, and 19,685 ft (6,000 m) for Mi-171 at normal take-off weight
Range with normal fuel: 313 naut miles (360 miles) 580 km
Maximum range: 594 naut miles (684 miles) 1,100 km, or 624 naut miles (718 miles) 1,155 km for Mi-171

Mil Mi-8MT/Mi-17 electronic warfare variants (NATO name *Hip-K*)

Role: Electronic countermeasures and electronic intelligence, based on *Hip-H*.
Sales: CIS, and Hungary (2 Mi-17Ps).
Mission equipment: Jamming equipment with active phase scanning aerials in several configurations, mounted on the fuselage (large vertical panel each side) and tailboom. Digital signal processing.
Aircraft variants:
Mi-17P is the designation stated in official Kazan material (Mi-17PI and PG are of the same source). Equipped with izdelye 1, izdelye 2 and izdelye 3 jamming units. Izdelye 1, operating in F frequency (wavelength 7.5 through 10 cm), generates jamming signals in the sector covered by 30° azimuth and 12° elevation. Izdelye 2 operates in D frequency (15-30 cm) in the same sectors. Izdelye 3 operates in B frequency (60-100 cm), generating jamming signals over 120° azimuth and 30° elevation. Maximum 4 hours continuous operation. Mi-17P also has electronic intelligence equipment, able to detect F and D-band radars in sector 180° x 30°. (Note that the designation Mi-17P is also used for passenger versions of exported Mi-17 helicopters.)
Mi-17PI has 1 unit capable of jamming up to 8 sources simultaneously. It operates in D frequency (15-30 cm) and over a 30° azimuth and 11° elevation sector.
Mi-17PG operates in frequency ranges H and I (3-5 cm) and jams up to 8 sources over a sector 25° azimuth and 12° elevation . The principal characteristic of this unit is its capability of jamming not only the pulse type radars (as former types) but also continuous and quasi continuous radars.
Mi-8MTSh, Mi-8MTPSh, Mi-8MTU, Mi-8MTA, Mi-8MTP, Mi-8MTPB, Mi-8MTR, Mi-8MTI, Mi-8MTPI are designations of EW versions of Mi-8MT used by the Russian armed forces.

Mil Mi-8MTI electronic warfare helicopter, with a large vertical array each side of the mid-fuselage, and smaller rectangular types at the tailboom root (Piotr Butowski)

Mil Mi-24, Mi-25 and Mi-35 (NATO name *Hind*)

First flight: 19 September 1969 (piloted by Herman Alfyorov).
Chief designer: Vyacheslav Kuznetsov; now Alexei Ivanov.
Role: Helicopter gunship with assault capability, observation and spotting, reconnaissance, and NBC sampling.

▲ Development
▲ 1967. Competition opened for a combat-transport helicopter, virtually a flying personnel carrier. Between Kamov Ka-25F and Mil V-24.
▲ November 1970. First flight of a production helicopter.
▲ Autumn 1972. Mi-24A production started, the first built in large quantities.
▲ 1976. Mi-24D with separated pilot and WSO cockpits appeared.
▲ 1978. Mi-24V appeared, with new weapon system and high-altitude engines.
Sales/users: Manufactured between 1970-89 at Arsenyev (for Soviet use), and between 1976-89 at Rostov-on-Don (mainly for export, although small quantities for Soviet use). More than 2,300 were produced in total, of which about 1,250 are currently in service with CIS armed forces, and about 700 were exported. Former WarPact countries (except Romania) received Mi-24Ds from 1978 and later Mi-24Vs, while former East Germany also received Mi-24Ps (East Germany received 51 Mi-24s, which were withdrawn from service after Germany united, 2 going to the USA for testing). Czechoslovakia bought 61 Mi-24s, survivors now split as 36 in the Czech Republic, and 19 in Slovakia. Poland currently has 29 Mi-24s. Mi-24As, Mi-24Ds (designated Mi-25) and Mi-24Vs (designated Mi-35) were sold to Afghanistan, Algeria, Angola, Cambodia, Chad, Cuba, Ethiopia, India, Iran, Iraq, North Korea, Libya, Mozambique, Nicaragua, Peru, Sri Lanka, Syria, Vietnam, and both Yemens. A few Mi-24s taken in Chad by the French army were delivered to the USA, while in December 1988 a Nicaraguan Mi-25 flew to Honduras and was later passed to the USA. A single Mi-24 is in the UK (originally flown from Afghanistan to Pakistan in 1988). According to some reports, Croatia is said to have received a number of used Mi-24s. Russian Ministry of Internal Affairs has contracted Rostvertol to convert a number of Mi-24s into unarmed and unarmoured helicopters for an internal security role. In 1995, the sale of 12 Mi-24s to Bulgaria was agreed.
Details: Generally for Mi-24V *Hind-E*, unless stated.
Crew/passengers: 2 crew, as a weapon system operator (WSO) in the front lower cockpit and pilot to his rear. Room for a mechanic on a jump seat in the passage between the flight deck and cabin. 8 troops on 2 x 4-place benches along the sides of the aft cabin, with horizontally divided (upward/downward opening) doors on both sides, the lower sections forming steps for rapid troop deployment and airborne operations.
Cockpits: Tandem stepped cockpits, each having a bulletproof flat plate windscreen and rounded canopy. Armour fragmentation shield between the cockpits. Armoured seats. Dual controls.
Rotor system: 5-blade main rotor derived from the Mi-8/17 (which see). Hydraulic dampers. Steel rotor head. De-icing.
Tail rotor characteristics: 3-blade, on starboard side of tailfin (port side on Mi-24 and first Mi-24A helicopter). Adjustable blade angle-of-attack, between 7° 55' and –25°. De-icing standard.
Wing/tail surfaces: Trapezoid anhedral wings, with ventral endplates carrying the outer missile pylons.
Flight control system: Mechanical.
Fuselage: All metal, semi-monocoque, with hermetic troop cabin connected to the cockpits.
Airframe materials: Steel, aluminium alloys, magnesium alloys and titanium.
Engines: Typically 2 x 2,225 shp (1,659 kW) Klimov/Isotov TV3-117VM turboshafts, side-by-side above the cabin, with TV2-117s (each 1,700 shp, 1,268 kW) in helicopters built up to 1972, TV3-117s in Mi-24As and Mi-24Ds, and 2,190 shp (1,633 kW) TV3-117VMAs in the last production series. Dust filters standard since 1976. Infra-red suppression cool air mixers can be fitted to the exhaust outlets. 5 mm armour protection. APU.
Transmission: VR-24 3-stage main transmission gearbox, weight 1,830 lb (830 kg), ratio 62.5:1.
Fuel system: 5 bag tanks, Nos 1 and 2 located side-by-side inside the fuselage above the wings, vertical No 3 below them, and Nos 4 and 5 under the cabin floor. Total capacity is 2,130 litres. Provision for 2 or 4 x 500 litre underwing

Slovakian Mil Mi-24V Hind-E (Piotr Butowski)

auxiliary fuel tanks. Early versions, up to Mi-24D, can carry 2 auxiliary tanks (total 1,700 litres) inside cabin (not with external fuel).

Electrical system: 36/115/208 volt, 400 Hz, AC supply via 3 generators. 27 volt DC supply.

Flight avionics/instrumentation: SAU-V24-1 automatic control system, including VUAP-1 autopilot plus autohover. US-450K speedometer, War-30MK climb meter, KI-13K compass, UKT-2 roll/pitch angle indicator, RV-5 altimeter, ARK-15M and ARK-U2 radio compasses, and DISS-15D Doppler nav radar. R-860 (or R-863) and Karat-M24 communication radios, SPU-8 intercom, and RI-65 voice warning device. Shturm-V anti-tank system with electro-optical sight under the starboard side of the fuselage nose, and Raduga-F radio guidance antenna on the left side. Falanga-V system with smaller RG antenna on Mi-24D and earlier versions. ASP-17 gun sight. SRO-2 Khrom IFF transponder (NATO name *Odd Rods*).

Self-protection systems: SPO-15 Beryoza radar warning receiver (SPO-10 Sirena on early versions). L-166V infra-red countermeasures jammer (NATO name *Hot Brick*) aft of engine/APU compartment. ASO-2I chaff/flare dispensers, originally as 4 x 32 round cassettes under the tailboom, later as 3 cassettes on each side of the fuselage aft of the wings. See Engines and Mi-35M under Aircraft variants.

Fixed guns: 4-barrel 12.7 mm Yakushev/Borzov YakB-12.7 (9A624) machine-gun In a USPU-24 undernose turret (60° azimuth, 60° downward and 20° upward movement). USPU-24 and Aist sight make up the SPSV-24 gun armament system. (See Mi-35M under Aircraft variants.)

Ammunition: 1,470 rounds.

Number of weapon pylons: 2 under each wing, plus 1 beneath each wingtip endplate with dual launchers for ATGMs only.

Expendable weapons and equipment: 4 tube-launched 9M114 Kokon (AT-6 *Spiral*) anti-armour missiles of the Shturm-V system are suspended beneath the wingtip pylons, while a further 4 Kokons can be carried on the 2 outer underwing pylons. Strela and Igla portable anti-aircraft missiles or R-60 (AA-8 *Aphid*) AAMs can be carried for use against low-speed airborne targets. Unguided weapons carried on the 4 wing pylons include bombs, KMGU submunition dispensers, UPK-23-250 cannon packs, rocket packs, incendiary tanks, etc. Maximum weapons load is 2,646 lb (1,200 kg). Mi-24D and earlier versions are armed with 4 x 9M17P Skorpion (AT-2 *Swatter*) anti-armour missiles of the Falanga-V anti-tank system. (See Mi-35M under Aircraft variants.)

Aircraft variants:

Mi-24 *Hind-B* was the pre-series model. Conventional wide flight deck with side-by-side seating for the crew behind flat-plate glazing, TV2-117 engines, wings with no anhedral, and no wingtip ATGM pylons.

Mi-24A *Hind-A* was the first large-scale production version. TV3-117 engines, anhedral wings, and wingtip pylons added.

Mi-24U *Hind-C* became the training variant of Mi-24A.

Mi-24B was similar to the Mi-24A, but with a 4-barrel YakB-12.7 machine-gun instead of the A-12.7. Small quantity production.

Mi-24D *Hind-D* introduced a major fuselage redesign that characterized all *Hinds* thereafter. Front fuselage was completely reshaped, with separate tandem cockpits for the pilot and WSO. Became the most widespread version.

Mi-24DU *Hind-D* is the training version of Mi-24D, but with the nose machine-gun deleted.

Mi-24V *Hind-E* is similar to Mi-24D, but introduced the Shturm-V ATGM system and TV3-117V high-altitude engines.

Mi-24VP *Hind-E* is similar to Mi-24V, but with a nose-mounted flexible twin-barrel 23-mm GSh-23 cannon instead of the YakB-12.7 machine-gun.

Mi-24P *Hind-F* is similar to Mi-24V, but with a fixed twin-barrel 30-mm GSh-2-30 cannon on the starboard side of the front fuselage instead of the flexible YakB-12.7 machine-gun.

Mi-24R *Hind-G1* is a nuclear, biological and chemical (NBC) reconnaissance/sampling version. No weapon system. Ground material retrieving mechanisms under the modified wingtip endplates, for scientific analysis.

Mi-24RR is a derivative of Mi-24R, specializing in radiation reconnaissance.

Mi-24RKh is a further derivative of Mi-24R.

Mi-24K *Hind-G2* is an artillery spotting and combat reconnaissance helicopter. No weapon system.

Mil Mi-35M, displayed at the June 1995 Paris Air Show (Piotr Butowski)

Undernose electro-optical sight, large AFA-100 photographic camera inside the cabin, and radio data link.

A-10 is the official name of the first Mi-24 prototype when used to set a series of world records.

Mi-25 is the export designation of the Mi-24D, mainly for Third World countries, but among WarPact countries the original Soviet designations were retained.

Mi-35 is the export designation of the Mi-24V.

Mi-35P is the export designation of the Mi-24P.

Mi-35M is the designation for the proposed upgrade of existing Mi-24/Mi-25/Mi-35s. Also known as *Mi-24VM* for the Russian armed forces. Prototype was exhibited at the June 1995 Paris Air Show, featuring an Mi-28 main and tail rotors, shortened wings, fixed undercarriage, and armed with the Ataka-V anti-tank guided missile system and Igla-V anti-aircraft missiles. Prototype Mi-35M has a fire control system developed by Sextant Avionique and Thomson-TTD Optronic which integrates Chlio FLIR with TWM 1410 displays for night operations and VH-100 HUD. 3 basic upgrade stages proposed, as follows:

Mi-35M1 brings helicopters to the standard of the last production Mi-24VP, introducing a GSh-23L cannon with 450 rounds, Shturm-V anti-tank missile system, L-166V infra-red active jammer, Beryoza RWR, and more. Additionally, the Shturm-V can also use modern 9M120 missiles of the Ataka-V system developed initially for Mi-28 *Havoc*. Moreover, Mi-35M1 will use APU-8/4-U 8-tube missile clusters (developed for Mi-28), allowing shorter wings with 4 instead of 6 pylons, with a consequent weight reduction. Pilot and weapon system operator will also have ONV-2 (ochki nochnogo videnya) night vision goggles. The modernization includes improved TV3-117VMA engines, with increased power during hot-and-high operations. New KAU-115 hydraulic actuators replace old KAU-110 units to improve manoeuvring. Additional oil coolers will be installed in the main gear lubricating system. New BD3-UV armament pylons have built-in mechanical hoisting devices. Optional GPS and other navigation upgrades. Many of the modifications have already been tested and are ready for implementation. Weight reducing measures

Details for Mi-24V *Hind-E.*

Principal dimensions:
Rotor diameter (main): 56 ft 9 ins (17.3 m)
Maximum length, rotors turning: 70 ft 1 ins (21.35 m)
Fuselage length: 57 ft 5 ins (17.51 m)
Maximum height: 17 ft 11 ins (5.47 m), or 14 ft 7 ins (4.44 m) to above rotor head
Wing span: 22 ft 5 ins (6.84 m)

Cabin:
Length: 9 ft 3 ins (2.825 m)
Width: 4 ft 9 ins (1.46 m)
Height: 3 ft 11 ins (1.2 m)

Main rotor:
Aerofoil section: NACA 230
Blade chord: 1 ft 11 ins (0.58 m) constant
Rotor disc: 2,530 sq ft (235.06 m^2)
Rpm: 240

Tail rotor:
Diameter: 12 ft 10 ins (3.908 m)
Weight: 260 lb (118 kg)

Wings:
Incidence: 19°
Anhedral: 12°

Undercarriage:
Type: Retractable, with twin steerable nosewheels (see Mi-35M1 under Aircraft variants)
Main wheel tyre size: 720 x 320 mm
Nose wheel tyre size: 480 x 200 mm
Wheel base: 14 ft 5 ins (4.39 m)
Wheel track: 9 ft 11 ins (3.03 m)

Weights:
Empty: 18,387 lb (8,340 kg)
Normal take-off: 24,692 lb (11,200 kg)
Maximum take-off: 25,353 lb (11,500 kg)
Maximum overload: 26,015 lb (11,800 kg)
Payload: 5,291 lb (2,400 kg), or 1,764-3,307 lb (800-1,500 kg) internal load

Performance:
Maximum speed: 181 kts (208 mph) 335 km/h
Cruise speed: 151 kts (174 mph) 280 km/h
OGE hovering ceiling: 6,560 ft (2,000 m)
Ceiling: 15,090 ft (4,600 m), service
G limits: 1.8
Normal range: 243 naut miles (280 miles) 450 km
Ferry range: 607 naut miles (699 miles) 1,125 km
Duration: 2 hours 35 minutes

Mil Mi-24P Hind-F with a fixed GSh-2-30 cannon. Note the split cabin door (Piotr Butowski)

are under test, and may include new composite rotors similar to those on Mi-28, with elastomeric bearings, offering a 661 lb (300 kg) saving and similar increase in lift. A fixed undercarriage may be selected to reduce weight by 187-198 lb (85-90 kg). Base weight of Mi-35M1 is 18,409 lb (8,350 kg), normal take-off weight 24,471 lb (11,100 kg), maximum speed 162-173 kts (186-199 mph) 300-320 km/h, cruising speed 146-151 kts (168-174 mph) 270-280 km/h, OGE hovering ceiling 6,890 ft (2,100 m) ISA, practical ceiling 15,090 ft (4,600 m), and range with 5% fuel reserve 227 naut miles (261 miles) 420 km.

Mi-35M2 offers 9M39 Igla-V anti-aircraft missiles, GSh-23V cannon with water cooling (eliminating cooling pauses), and new radio equipment for communication with ground troops as well as new anti-tank missile radio guidance link. Base weight will be reduced to 17,747 lb (8,050 kg), and ceilings will be 8,200 ft (2,500 m) hovering and 16,400 ft (5,000 m) practical.

Mi-35M3 has the PNK-24 flight/navigation system and Tor-24 fire control system, both developed from the PrPNK-28 system of the Mi-28. Mak-UFM infra-red warning device (as used by Su-24M and Su-35), as well as the flare launching system combined with this unit (the previous L166 active infra-red jamming system is thought to be ineffective against modern anti-aircraft missiles). Base weight will be 18,078 lb (8,200 kg), maximum speed 162 kts (186 mph) 300 km/h, hovering ceiling 7,875 ft (2,400 m), practical ceiling 15,750 ft (4,800 m), and range 227 naut miles (261 miles) 420 km with 5% reserve.

Mi-24 Ecology is used for surveying water levels and oil spills, with specialized equipment. Modified from a military helicopter by Polyot.

Mi-24 Security covers a number of Mi-24s with weapons and armour removed for an internal security role, probably with the Moscow police. In addition to new communications equipment, other items include a searchlight at the nose, loudspeakers under the wings, and a fixed undercarriage.

Mil Mi-26 and Mi-27 (NATO name *Halo*)

First flight: 14 December 1977.
Role: Very heavy transport, tanker, medevac and firefighting helicopter. Airborne command post for Mi-27.
Chief designer: Alexei Samusenko.

★ Aims

- ★ Range of 800 km with a 15,000 kg payload.
- ★ Empty weight equal to half of the maximum take-off weight.

▲ Development

- ▲ 1985. Initial operational capability.
- ▲ 1995. FAA certification anticipated.

Sales: Produced by Rostvertol since the early 1980s, and production continues. More than 100 built, mainly for Soviet/Russian military aviation. In 1994 the Russian armed forces had about 35 Mi-26s, Belarus 15 (65th Helicopter Regiment in Kobryn), and Ukraine 20 (344th Helicopter Regiment in Kalinov). 10 are also used by the 126th Squadron of the Indian Air Forces (first delivered in June 1986), and over 12 civil Mi-26s are used in Canada. Both Rostvertol and Mil have surplus Mi-26s in store. Mi-26Ts are currently undertaking United Nations humanitarian operations.
Details: Principally Mi-26, except where stated.

Mil Mi-26, the world's largest production helicopter (Piotr Butowski)

Crew/passengers: Pilot, co-pilot, navigator, engineer and assault systems operator, or 4 crew in the civil Mi-26T. Pressurized cockpit. Unpressurized cabin accommodates 68 fully-equipped paratroops (can jump from above 985 ft, 300 m altitude at speeds up to 154 kts, 177 mph, 285 km/h), or 79-80 troops. Medevac layout for 80 litters and 3 attendants.
Freight, internal: Alternative to passengers can be up to 44,092 lb (20,000 kg) of containers, pallets, weapons or vehicles.
Cabin access: Rear loading ramp, plus doors on the fuselage port side.
Loading facilities: Roller tracks and 2 LG-1500 electric winches inside the cabin. 11,023 lb (5,000 kg) capacity hoist, with second optional.
Rotor system: 8-blade main rotor, with metal/composites blades. Titanium rotor head. Electric de-icing.
Tail rotor characteristics: 5-blade, glassfibre. Titanium rotor head. Electric de-icing.
Flight control system: Hydraulic. Fly-by-wire system is under development.
Airframe materials: Includes aluminium-lithium alloys.
Engines: 2 Ivchenko PROGRESS/Zaporozhye D-136 turboshafts side-by-side above the cabin. Dust filters standard, and infra-red suppression cool air mixers optional for military helicopters. TA-8V APU.
Engine rating: Each 11,400 ehp (8,501 ekW) at take-off.
Transmission: VR-26 main gearbox, weight 8,025 lb (3,640 kg), with ratio 62.5:1.
Fuel system: 20,194 lb (9,160 kg) of fuel in the main tanks located under the cabin floor, plus 25,265 lb (11,460 kg) of auxiliary fuel in 4 tanks inside the cabin for ferry flights.
Electrical system: 28 volt DC supply.
Hydraulic system: Dual, each 3,002 psi.
Radar: Weather radar in the nose radome.
Flight avionics/instrumentation: PKV-26-1 flight control system, with autohover. DISS Doppler navigation. Optional GPS. Military variants have coded radio communication equipment. Closed circuit TV provided to monitor external payloads.
Self-protection systems: Provision for armour plating to protect the flight deck, fuel tanks, engines and main gearbox. Chaff/flare dispensers on the fuselage sides. Infra-red jammer.
Fixed guns: Provision for flexible mounting of troops'

DETAILS FOR Mi-26.

Principal dimensions:
Rotor diameter (main): 105 ft (32 m)
Maximum length, rotors turning: 131 ft 4 ins (40.025 m)
Airframe length: 110 ft 8 ins (33.727 m)
Width, blades folded: 26 ft 9 ins (8.15 m)
Maximum height: 26 ft 9 ins (8.145 m)

Cabin:
Length: 39 ft 8 ins (12.1 m) excluding ramp, or 49 ft 3 ins (15 m) including ramp
Width: 10 ft 8 ins (3.25 m)
Height: 9 ft 7 ins to 10 ft 5 ins (2.91 to 3.17 m)
Volume: 4,273 cu ft (121 m^3)

Main rotor:
Aerofoil section: TsAGI
Blade length: 45 ft 11 ins (14 m)
Blade chord: 2 ft 7.5 ins (0.8 m)
Blade weight: 826 lb (375 kg)
Rotor disc: 8,656.9 sq ft (804.25 m^2)
Rpm: 132.7

Tail rotor:
Diameter: 25 ft (7.61 m)
Rpm: 552

Undercarriage:
Type: Fixed, with steerable nosewheels. Twin wheels on each unit. Main legs of hydraulically-adjustable length to make loading easier. Protective support under tailboom
Main wheel tyre size: 1,120 x 450 mm
Wheel base: 29 ft 4 ins (8.95 m)
Wheel track: 23 ft 6 ins (7.17 m)

Weights:
Empty: 62,325 lb (28,270 kg)
Normal take-off: 109,349 lb (49,600 kg)
Maximum take-off: 123,459 lb (56,000 kg)
Payload: 33,069 lb (15,000 kg) nominal, 44,092 lb (20,000 kg) internal, external or mix

Performance:
Maximum speed: 159 kts (183 mph) 295 km/h
Cruise speed: 138 kts (158 mph) 255 km/h, at 1,640 ft (500 m)
IGE hovering ceiling: 3,280 ft (1,000 m), with 11,245 lb (5,100 kg) payload, ISA
OGE hovering ceiling: 5,580 ft (1,700 m), ISA. Also quoted by Rostvertol as 5,900 ft (1,800 m)
Ceiling: 15,090 ft (4,600 m) at nominal take-off weight, 11,810 ft (3,600 m) at MTOW, both service
Range with full fuel: 362 naut miles (416 miles) 670 km, with 30 minutes reserve. Also quoted by Rostvertol as 800 km with 5% reserve
Range with full payload: 254 naut miles (292 miles) 470 km
Ferry range: 972 naut miles (1,118 miles) 1,800 km. Also quoted by Rostvertol at 1,920 km with 4 auxiliary tanks, sea level

Mil Mi-26TM, with a gondola aft of the nosewheels (Piotr Butowski)

machine-guns (7.62-mm) in the blisters of the cargo compartment.

Aircraft variants:
Mi-26 is the basic military transport/assault helicopter, as detailed.
Mi-26A has an upgraded PNK-90 flight/navigation system.
Mi-26M is a projected upgraded version with D-137 turboshafts (derivatives of the Muravchenko/PROGRESS D-27 propfan), all-composite main rotor blades, and an advanced flight/navigation system. Maximum payload raised to 48,500 lb (22,000 kg), OGE hovering ceiling 9,185 ft (2,800 m), and service ceiling 19,350 ft (5,900 m).
Mi-26MS is a projected flying hospital version, with surgical, pre-operating, ambulance and other compartments in the cabin.
Mi-26P is a projected 70 passenger version.
Mi-26T is the civil transport helicopter. Assault equipment, armour, flare dispensers, IR jammer and military communications systems removed.
Mi-26TM is a flying-crane version, with a glazed gondola for the pilot/sling load operator under the front fuselage, aft of the nosewheels, or a larger gondola under the upswept tail.
Mi-26TP (P for pozharnyi, firefighting) has an externally suspended 15,000 litre tank.
Mi-26TS (S for sertifitsyrovannyi, certified) is similar to Mi-26T, but adapted for international certification.
Mi-26TZ (Z for zapravshchik, tanker) delivers over 14,000 litres of fuel and 1,040 litres of lubricants to ground-based tanks, vehicles, etc, in inaccessible areas. First flight was expected in 1993, but not flown by early 1995.
Mi-27 is an airborne command post, intended to replace the Mi-6VKP/Mi-22. Details first released in 1990 by the US Department of Defense, then stated to be under development. 2 prototypes built.

Mil Mi-28 (NATO name Havoc)

First flight: 10 November 1982 (experimental helicopter 012, crewed by Gurgen Karapetyan and V. Tsygankov).
Chief designer: Initially Mark Vainberg and Ye. Yablonsky, now Andrei Yermakov.
Role: Attack. Can operate for 15 days away from base.

▲ Development
▲ 1980. Project begun.
▲ January 1988. First prototype proper built (032).
▲ Early 1992. Full-scale mock-up of Mi-28N accepted.
▲ 6 May 1993. Loop performed by 012, piloted by G. Karapetyan, with a roll a few days later.
▲ 1995. First flight of Mi-28N expected.

Sales: 2 experimental helicopters (012 and 022) and 2 prototypes (032 and 042) built by Moscow Mil design bureau works. First 3 production helicopters were manufactured by Rostvertol at Rostov on Don under Mil/Rostvertol initiative, without an order for the Russian armed forces.
Crew/passengers: 2 crew in tandem, with the weapon system operator/navigator forward and the pilot at the rear. The WSO enters the cockpit via a port side rearward opening jettisonable door, while the pilot uses a similar starboard door. Cockpit is armoured with titanium and ceramic plates, and the bullet resistant flat plate glazing is 50-mm thick at the front and 35-mm thick at the sides; wipers are installed on the front panels. Cockpit can withstand direct hits from 7.62-mm and 12.7-mm machine gun bullets, or fragments from 20-mm cannon shells. Armour fragmentation shield between the cockpits. A small fuselage hatch can be used, if necessary, for loading cargo or 2 or 3 passengers for ferrying, or for removing downed pilots from a battle area. See Safety features.

Mil Mi-28 second prototype. Note the 2A42 cannon with ammunition containers that move with it, optical sight and laser rangefinder/designator turret above, and spherical radome (Piotr Butowski)

Rotor system: 5-blade high-lift main rotor, with elastomeric bearings (2° freedom), dampers (hydraulic) and droop stops (mechanical). Each blade is entirely composites constructed, with a glassfibre spar and honeycomb core, the leading edge protected by titanium. Full-span trailing-edge tab. Titanium rotor head. 5° forward shaft tilt. Blades electrically de-iced. Main rotor blades and wings are detached for transportation by An-22 or Il-76 (requiring 1.5 hours to reassemble), but only the rotor is removed with the An-124 (requiring 30 minutes to reassemble).
Tail rotor characteristics: 4-blade rotor, comprising 2 separate 2-blade rotors (glassfibre) set in scissors configuration, with 45° between the closest intersection. Elastomeric bearings. Electrically de-iced.
Wing/tail surfaces: Anhedral wing (of light alloy except for composites leading/trailing edges) on each side of the mid-fuselage, each with 2 stores pylons and a streamlined container housing electronic sensors and IR flare dispensers. 2-position port-side horizontal stabilizer at the top of the fin. Manually-operated weapon winching system built into the wings.
Flight control system: Mechanical, with hydraulic actuators. Pilot flight controls are arranged for maximum ease, on the pitch-throttle lever, stick and port-side panel.
Airframe materials: Light alloy, except for composites wing and tail unit leading/trailing edges, and a small number of non-structural components including the fuselage access door. Titanium and ceramic plate armour for the cockpit, and titanium protecting other vital areas.
Safety features: Undercarriage has strong energy-absorbing shock absorbers to enable survivable landings at vertical speed equal to 39 ft (12 m) per second. Armoured crew seats, with belts that tighten automatically at high g loading. If a failure occurs at altitude, allowing crew escape by parachute, the cockpit doors are jettisoned, the wings are also jettisoned together with their loads, and a door sill sleeve is air-inflated to protect the crew from protruding structures and help them clear the helicopter.
Engines: 2 Klimov/Isotov TV3-117VMA turboshafts. IR suppression cool air mixers on the exhaust outlets. Air intake dust filters are standard. Engines are set apart and low down in order to reduce the profile and help survivability of the other engine should one be hit. AI-9V APU between the engines at the tailboom root; can be used to power the electric, hydraulic and pneumatic systems for autonomous operations away from base.
Engine rating: Each 2,225 shp (1,659 kW).

DETAILS FOR MI-28, WITH MI-28N *IN ITALICS.*

Principal dimensions:
Rotor diameter (main): 56 ft 5 ins (17.2 m)
Maximum length, rotors turning: 69 ft 5 ins (21.155 m)
Fuselage length: 55 ft 10 ins (17.01 m)
Maximum height: 15 ft 5 ins (4.7 m), or 12 ft 7 ins (3.823 m) to above rotor head
Wing span: 16 ft (4.88 m)

Main rotor:
Blade chord: 2 ft 2.5 ins (0.67 m)
Rotor disc: 2,500 sq ft (232.3 m^2)
Rpm: 242

Tail rotor:
Diameter: 12 ft 7 ins (3.84 m)

Undercarriage:
Type: Fixed, with castring tailwheel. Single wheels, with low pressure tyres
Main wheel tyre size: 720 x 320 mm
Tail wheel tyre size: 480 x 200 mm
Wheel base: 36 ft 1 ins (11 m)
Wheel track: 7 ft 6 ins (2.29 m)

Weights:
Empty: 17,846 lb (8,095 kg)
Normal take-off: 22,928 lb (10,400 kg), *23,589 lb (10,700 kg)*
Maximum take-off: 25,353-25,706 lb (11,500-11,660 kg)
Useful load: 5,180 lb (2,350 kg)

Performance:
Maximum speed: 162 kts (186 mph) 300 km/h, *175 kts (201 mph) 324 km/h**
Cruise speed: 143 kts (165 mph) 265 km/h
Rearward/sideways speed: 54 kts (62 mph) 100 km/h
Maximum climb rate: 2,677 ft (816 m) per minute, sea level
OGE hovering ceiling: 11,810 ft (3,600 m), *12,140 ft (3,700 m)**
Ceiling: 19,030 ft (5,800 m), *18,700 ft (5,700 m)*, service
Hover turn rate: 45° per second
G limits: +3, –0.5
Normal range: 248 naut miles (286 miles) 460 km, *235 naut miles (270 miles) 435 km*
Combat radius: 108 naut miles (124 miles) 200 km, no auxiliary fuel, 10 minutes at target, 5% reserve
Ferry range: 599 naut miles (690 miles) 1,110 km with auxiliary fuel, at 25,706 lb (11,660 kg) weight, 5% reserve
Duration: 2 hours

*Higher performance for Mi-28N is according to official Russian data. Reasons for such gains are unclear

Mil Mi-28 fourth prototype, with 16 missiles and 2 x C-8V-20 rocket pods. Note the rounded fairings shown on the second prototype each side of the turret for LLLTV and FLIR have been deleted (Piotr Butowski)

Fuel system: Standard internal capacity of 2,948 lb (1,337 kg) in self-sealing polyurethane foam filled tanks, with self-tightening latex protectors. Optional 4 underwing auxiliary tanks, raising total capacity to 6,876 lb (3,119 kg).
Electrical system: All Mi-28 systems are duplicated. 208 volt DC supply via 2 generators attached to the main gearbox; by this system (rather than engine-driven), electrical power is not interrupted should both engines fail and the helicopter rely on autorotation. See Engines.
Hydraulic system: Duplicated, at 2,204 psi.
Flight avionics/instrumentation: PrPNK-28 weapon/flight/navigation control system (PrPNK means *pritselno-pilotazhno-navigatsionnyi kompleks*). KOPS (meaning kombinirovannaya obzorno-pritselnaya sistema) precision electro-optical unit to identify, acquire and track targets at long range and establish the optimum positioning for rockets or missile launch via the airborne digital computer, is installed on a gyro-stabilized platform at the nose and has 2 optical channels (wide and narrow) and a very narrow optical TV channel. The axis of observation is adjustable in azimuth within ±110°, and vertically from 13° elevation through to 40° downward. Laser rangefinder is combined with KOPS. Pilot can use a helmet-mounted target designator. Mi-28N will be equipped with a mast-mounted radar system for night and bad weather observation and fire control. The search-aiming unit will have optical, TV and thermal channels (each wide and narrow). Mi-28 can fly nap-of-the-earth (NOE) missions at 50 ft (15 m) altitude. IFR instrumentation, plus CRT for the TV channel and pilot HUD. Autopilot to allow day/night and adverse weather operations, with autohover, autostabilization and hover/heading hold for stabilized missile firing. On-board fault monitoring system.
Self-protection systems: Radar and laser warning receivers, electronic active jammer, and UV-26 flare dispensers.
Fixed guns: Single-barrel 30-mm 2A42 cannon is mounted in the NPPU-28 undernose turret and can be moved within the same azimuth/elevation/downward range as the KOPS, in synchronization. Weight of the turret with ammunition is 1,366 lb (620 kg).
Ammunition: 300 rounds in 2 boxes on the cannon sides and moving with the cannon to delete the need for flexible feed chutes (1994 information quoted 250 rounds). Standard land force ammunition.
Number of weapon pylons: 4 under the wings.
Expendable weapons and equipment: Up to 4,409 lb (2,000 kg). Standard anti-tank armament comprises 16 x 9M114 Kokon (*AT-6 Spiral*) missiles of the Shturm-V system or improved 9M120 ATGMs of the Ataka-V system. Other weapons include C-8 (80-mm) and C-13 (122-mm) rocket packs, bombs of up to 500 kg, incendiary tanks, KMGU submunition dispensers, minelaying containers, UPK-23 and GUV cannon/gun packs, etc.
Aircraft variants:
Mi-28 *Havoc* is the standard version, as described.
Mi-28N is the all-weather day and night version. Millimetre-wave radar. Full-scale mock-up accepted in 1992. First flight expected 1995. Both versions will enter Russian service.

Mil Mi and Mi-34 VAZ (NATO name *Hermit*)

First flight: 17 November 1986.
Chief designer: M. N. Tischenko.
Role: Light training and sport helicopter, suited also to transport, police, ambulance and other work. Aerobatic version available, capable of manoeuvres including the Nesterov loop.

▲ Development

▲ September 1994. A police variant, the Mi-34P, began operations with the Moscow City Police under the auspices of the Russian Ministry of internal affairs.
Sales: In production since late 1993 at Arsenyev. Over 60 ordered, with 30-50 having been expected to be delivered during 1994-95, the first 3 for the Moscow Mayor's office and thereafter mainly for police and ambulance work. Shown at the Sao Paulo Air Show against Brazil's military trainer requirement. Mi-34 VAZ is a Rostvertol variant.
Crew/passengers: Pilot and 3 passengers, with other layouts for training, cargo carrying and EMS hospital (litter plus attendant).
Optional equipment: Dual controls.
Rotor system: 4-blade composites rotor, with only flapping and cyclic pitch hinges, connected to the rotor head via flexing steel straps. De-icing standard.
Tail rotor characteristics: 2-blade, composites. De-icing standard.
Tail surfaces: Both versions have a starboard tail rotor and port dorsal/ventral fixed fin with tailskid, plus a constant-chord horizontal stabilizer.
Flight control system: Mechanical for Mi-34, and hydraulic for Mi-34 VAZ.
Fuselage: Mi-34 has a more rounded appearance than Mi-34 VAZ, the latter featuring reduced lower nose glazing and a more sharply swept windshield.
Airframe materials: Light alloy.
Engines: *Mi-34* has a 325 hp (242 kW) AOOT M14V-26 9-cylinder radial piston engine (45 kg per hour fuel consumption). *Mi-34 VAZ* has 2 x 230 hp (171.5 kW) Wankel-derived VAZ-430 rotary piston engines, capable of starting without pre-heating at –25° C and of using different fuels (68 kg per hour fuel consumption). See Aircraft variants for Mi-34A.
Fuel system: 282.2 lb (128 kg) for Mi-34. 245 litres in Mi-34 VAZ. Optional similar capacity auxiliary fuel. Permits inverted flight.
Flight avionics/instrumentation: Conventional instruments, includes ADF and radio altimeter. At least Mi-34 VAZ has a navigation system suited to day/night and poor weather flying.
Aircraft variants:
Mi-34 with AOOT engine, as detailed.
Mi-34A will have an Allison 250-C20 turboshaft engine.
Mi-34P is a police version of Mi-34.
Mi-34 VAZ is being marketed by Rostvertol, featuring twin VAZ motorcar engine-developed VAZ-430 rotary engines (Wankel type).

DETAILS FOR Mi-34, *WITH Mi-34 VAZ IN ITALICS.*

Principal dimensions:
Rotor diameter (main): 32 ft 10 ins (10 m), *37 ft 5 ins (11.4 m)*
Fuselage length: 28 ft 7 ins (8.71 m), *31 ft 2 ins (9.5 m)*
Maximum height: 9 ft 1 ins (2.76 m), *10 ft (3.05 m) to above rotor head*

Cabin:
Length: *7 ft 10 ins (2.4 m)*
Width: *5 ft 3 ins (1.6 m)*
Height: *4 ft 3 ins (1.3 m)*

Main rotor:
Blade chord: 9 ins (0.22 m)
Rotor disc: 845 sq ft (78.5 m^2)

Tail rotor:
Diameter: 4 ft 10 ins (1.48 m), *4 ft 11 ins (1.5 m)*

Undercarriage:
Type: Fixed skids. Trainer variant has 3-wheel gear
Skid track: 6 ft 9 ins (2.06 m), *7 ft 10 ins (2.4 m)*

Weights:
Normal take-off: 2,822 lb (1,280 kg), or 2,425 lb (1,100 kg) for aerobatics
Maximum take-off: 2,976 lb (1,350 kg), *4,321 lb (1,960 kg)*
Payload: See Performance. Can have sling loads

Performance:
Maximum speed: *108-119 kts (124-137 mph) 200-220 km/h*
Cruise speed: 86-97 kts (99-112 mph) 160-180 km/h, *97 kts (112 mph) 180 km/h*
OGE hovering ceiling: 3,280 ft (1,000 m), *4,920 ft (1,500 m) at MTOW, ISA, or 2,625 ft (800 m) at ISA + +25° C*
Ceiling: 14,765 ft (4,500 m) service
G limits: over +3
Range: 194 naut miles (224 miles) 360 km with a 320 lb (145 kg) payload and 5% reserve, *324 naut miles (373 miles) 600 km with a 750 lb (340 kg) payload and 30 minutes reserve, or 43 naut miles (50 miles) 80 km with a 1,213 lb (550 kg) payload and 30 minutes reserve*
Duration: *5 to 5 hours 30 minutes with maximum standard fuel, 705 lb (320 kg) payload, with 30 minutes reserves*

Mil Mi-34 VAZ mock up, with Euromil Mi-38 mock up to its rear (Piotr Butowski)

Mil Mi-38 - See Multi-national

Mil Mi-40

Role: Assault helicopter.

★ Aims

⋆ "Flying armoured personnel carrier", based on the Mi-28N but with an armoured cabin for 8 troops added.
⋆ High combat survivability due to duplicated systems, critical components masked by non-critical parts, low IR visibility, self-defence system, and 360° gunfire coverage.
⋆ All-weather, day and night operations.

▲ Development

▲ September 1992. Project announced during MosAeroshow in Zhukovsky.
Crew/passengers: 2 flight crew plus up to 8 troops (10 originally). Provision for a rear gunner in a heavily glazed rear-of-cabin position.
Cabin access: Horizontally split cabin door each side, allowing rapid troop deployment and use of the lower doors as airsteps.
Rotor system: Similar to Mi-28.
Engines: Similar to Mi-28.
Fuel system: 2,579 lb (1,170 kg). Provision for auxiliary tanks.
Flight avionics/instrumentation: Weapon system avionics similar to Mi-28. 8-millimetre-wave mast-mounted radar.
Fixed guns: Flexibly-mounted 23-mm GSh-23 cannon in an undernose turret, plus a 12.7-mm machine-gun under the rear cabin.
Expendable weapons and equipment: Up to 8 anti-tank missiles plus 4 rocket pods.

DETAILS FOR MI-40.

Principal dimensions:
Rotor diameter (main): 56 ft 5 ins (17.2 m)
Fuselage length: 52 ft 6 ins (16 m)
Width, blades folded: 13 ft 7 ins (4.15 m)
Maximum height: 15 ft 1 ins (4.6 m) without tail rotor

Tail rotor:
Diameter: 12 ft 7 ins (3.84 m)

Undercarriage:
Type: Retractable, with twin nosewheels
Wheel base: 13 ft 7 ins (4.15 m)
Wheel track: 9 ft 10 ins (3 m)

Weights:
Empty: 18,012 lb (8,170 kg)
Normal take-off: 24,471 lb (11,100 kg)
Maximum take-off: 26,235 lb (11,900 kg)

Performance:
Maximum speed: 170 kts (195 mph) 314 km/h
Cruise speed: 140 kts (162 mph) 260 km/h
OGE hovering ceiling: 10,825 ft (3,300 m)
Ceiling: 18,210 ft (5,550 m), service
Range with standard fuel: 216 naut miles (249 miles) 400 km, with 5% reserve
Range with auxiliary tanks: 518 naut miles (597 miles) 960 km, with 5% reserve

Mil Mi-40 model (Piotr Butowski)

Mil Mi-46

Role: Heavy transport helicopter, plus flying crane version.

★ Aims

⋆ Exact replacement for old Mi-6s and Mi-10s.
⋆ Service time 1,500-1,800 hours per year.

▲ Development

▲ 1992. Project announced.
Sales: Estimated requirement for 200-270 helicopters for CIS use and 60-70 for export.
Rotor system: 7-blade main rotor.
Tail rotor characteristics: 5-blade.
Engines: Mi-46T is to have 2 Aviadvigatel/ Reshetnikov turboshafts, each 8,000 shp (5,965 kW) at take-off. Mi-46K is currently projected with 3 engines, but twin-engined version is also possible.
Aircraft variants:
Mi-46 is the military transport version.
Mi-46T is the civil freight/passenger version.
Mi-46K is a flying crane, without the normal cargo cabin. The fuselage aft of the cockpit is shallow, principally required only to support the engines and tail unit/rotor. Possible (speculation only) access to limited storage or seating space in the shallow fuselage, as provided in the Mi-10. An aft-facing gondola, accessible from the cockpit, allows the helicopter to be controlled while the co-pilot looks directly at the sling load and ground. In 3-engined configuration, hovering will be possible with 1 engine shut down. The main undercarriage legs are long (by necessity to meet the stub wings) and given a wide track, allowing the helicopter to be manoeuvred over a load.

Mil Mi-52

Role: Very light helicopter.

▲ Development

▲ 1993. Displayed in model form.
▲ 1996. Possible start of production by Mil.
Crew/passengers: Pilot forward and 2 passengers on a rear bench seat.
Rotor system: 4-blade composites main rotor.
Tail rotor characteristics: 2-blade, composites.
Tail surfaces: T-tail, with fixed dorsal/ventral fin and horizontal stabilizer. Skid under the fin.
Fuselage: Conventional pod and boom type.
Engine: Possibly Wankel-derived VAZ-430 rotary piston engine.
Engine rating: 230 hp (171.5 kW).

DETAILS FOR MI-52.

Principal dimensions:
Rotor diameter (main): 32 ft 10 ins (10 m)
Fuselage length: 28 ft 7 ins (8.71 m)

Undercarriage:
Type: Fixed nosewheel type, with cantilever legs and wheel fairings.

Weights:
Maximum take-off: 2,535 lb (1,150 kg)
Payload: 550 lb (250 kg)

Performance:
Cruise speed: 92 kts (106 mph) 170 km/h
Range: 216 naut miles (248.5 miles) 400 km

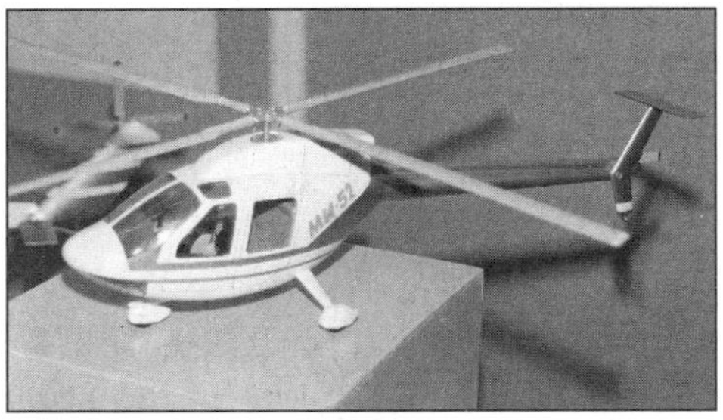

Model of the Mil Mi-52 (Piotr Butowski)

Mil Mi-54

Role: Civil light utility helicopter project, suited to Category A operations.
Sales: Could be available by 1998, marketed principally to offer a more modern alternative to the Mi-2 and replace helicopters of Mi-4 size.
Crew/passengers: 1 or 2 pilots plus 10-11 passengers,

DETAILS FOR MI-46T, *WITH MI-46K IN ITALICS.*

Principal dimensions:
Rotor diameter (main): 90 ft 7 ins (27.6 m)
Fuselage length: 86 ft 3 ins (26.3 m)
Maximum height: 22 ft 6 ins (6.95 m) without tail rotor

Tail rotor:
Diameter: 20 ft 4 ins (6.2 m)

Undercarriage:
Type: Fixed, with twin wheels on each unit
Wheel track: 16 ft 5 ins (5 m)

Weights:
Empty: 35,715 lb (16,200 kg), or *43,431 lb (19,700 kg) in 3-engined Mi-46K configuration*
Maximum take-off: 66,139 lb (30,000 kg), *or 80,468 lb (36,500 kg) in 3-engined Mi-46K configuration*
Payload: 26,455 lb (12,000 kg). *Similar hovering payload for Mi-46K with 1 of 3 engines shut down*

Performance:
Cruise speed: 146 kts (168 mph) 270 km/h
OGE hovering ceiling: 7,545 ft (2,300 m), *and the same for Mi-46K in 3-engined configuration,* MTOW
Range with full fuel: 405 naut miles (466 miles) 750 km
Range with 22,046 lb (10,000 kg) payload: 216 naut miles (249 miles) 400 km, with 30 minutes reserve
Range with 24,251 lb (11,000 kg) payload, Mi-46K: *216 naut miles (249 miles) 400 km, in 3-engined configuration*

Details for Mi-54.

Principal dimensions:
Rotor diameter (main): 44 ft 3.5 ins (13.5 m)
Airframe length: 43 ft 4 ins (13.2 m)
Maximum height: 11 ft 8 ins (3.55 m)

Undercarriage:
Type: Fixed, with twin nosewheels and single mainwheels attached to small fuselage-side sponsons
Wheel base: 12 ft 10 ins (3.9 m)
Wheel track: 9 ft 10 ins (3 m)

Weights:
Maximum take-off: 8,818 lb (4,000 kg)
Payload: 2,646 lb (1,200 kg)

Performance:
Maximum speed: 151 kts (174 mph) 280 km/h
Cruise speed: 140 kts (162 mph) 260 km/h
OGE hovering ceiling: 6,562 ft (2,000 m), MTOW, ISA
Range with full payload: 243 naut miles (279 miles) 450 km
Range with full fuel in main tanks: 432 naut miles (497 miles) 800 km

Model of the Mil Mi-54 (Piotr Butowski)

smaller number of VIPs, or litters and attendants in a medevac layout.
Rotor system: 4-blade composites main rotor with sweptback tips. Likely to have elastomeric bearings and hydraulic drag damper, and rotor brake.
Tail rotor characteristics: 4-blade, composites.
Tail surfaces: Horizontal stabilizer.
Fuselage: Modern streamlined appearance. 3 doors each side.
Engines: 2 Saturn AL-32 turboshafts.
Engine rating: Each 770 shp (574 kW).
Fuel system: Standard, plus auxiliary tanks.

Mil Mi-58

Role: Medium civil helicopter, with many features of an enlarged Mi-54.

★ Aims
★ Probably viewed as a potential successor to the Mi-8, to complement the smaller Mi-54.

▲ Development
▲ 1995. Details first given at the Paris Air Show.
▲ 1998. Tentative early production delivery date.

Crew/passengers: 2 pilots plus up to 20 passengers in 3 or 4 abreast cabin layout. VIP and medevac versions are likely to follow.
Rotor system: 5-blade composites main rotor.
Tail rotor characteristics: 2 x 2-blade rotors set on a single shaft in "scissors" configuration.
Engines: 2 Klimov TV3-117VMA-SB3 turboshafts.
Engine rating: Each 2,190 shp (1,633 kW).

Atlas Aviation (South Africa)

Corporate address: See Combat section for company details.

Atlas CSH-2 Rooivalk (Red Kestrel)

First flight: 11 February 1990.
Role: Anti-armour, deep penetration, close air support, heliborne escort and reconnaissance.

★ Aims
★ Rugged attack helicopter based on elements of Puma dynamics, capable of day/night and adverse/dusty weather operation.
★ Detection avoidance through low radar, visual, infra-red and acoustic signatures. If detected, avoid being struck through high manoeuvrability, enhanced by an automatic flight control system. If struck, sustain flight through tolerance to battle damage by dual redundancy or multiple load paths in critical avionics, flight and structural systems. If crash becomes unavoidable, high survivability for the crew (see Safety features).
★ 30 year upgradable lifespan.

▲ Development
▲ 1984. Design began, bearing little relationship to the earlier XH-1 Alpha experimental attack helicopter built using Alouette III dynamics.

Atlas/Denel Rooivalk (courtesy Denel/Atlas)

Sales: 16 for the South African Air Force, delivered from March 1996 for a single squadron. Proposed, but not selected for the British Army Air Corps, in association with Marshall of Cambridge Aerospace.

Atlas/Denel Rooivalk with ZT-3 anti-armour missiles and 20-mm GA151 cannon

Crew: Pilot (rear cockpit) and weapons system officer/commander.
Cockpit: Hands on collective and stick controls (HOCAS). 23° forward downward view. Interchangeable cockpits. Vibration level (4/Rev 100 KCAS) 0.021g.
Rotor system: 4-blade composites main rotor. Main rotor blade flapping hinge offset 3.8%. Dry-run capability on all transmission gearboxes. Optional deicing system.
Tail rotor characteristics: 5-blade, composites, starboard mounted.
Wing surfaces: Stub wings. Horizontal stabilizer with leading-edge slat to port side of tailfin.
Fuselage: Large access panels, wings and cowlings double as work platforms.
Airframe materials: Mostly metal but with some composites.
Safety features: Crashworthy structure and energy absorbing seats, resulting in crew survival at sink rates of up to 33 ft (10 m) per second. Crash sensors cut off fuel and electrical supplies.
Engines: 2 Topaz turboshafts, derived from the Turbomeca Makila 1A1. Optional RTM 322s.
Engine rating: Each 2,000 shp (1,492 kW) take-off, and 2,300 shp (1,715 kW) for 30 seconds emergency rating. IR suppressors. Sand filters.
Fuel system: 3,238 lb (1,469 kg) internal capacity. Inner wing stations can each carry 750 litre or 625 litre drop tanks. Hot turnaround, with full refuel and rearm within 15 minutes.
Electrical system: All systems operate in silent battery mode.
No APU or GPU necessary for maintainability.
Flight avionics/instrumentation: MIL-STD-1553B digital databuses for integration of multi-function cockpit displays (2 in each cockpit for production helicopters, 3 in the demonstrator) and crew-avionics interface. MIL-STD-1760 Class 2 databus permits adoption of a wide range of weapon systems. Stores management system. Automatic flight control system, with autohover and autoland. Pre-programmable computerized mission planning with digital moving map display, secure voice/image/data communications (with data link), HUD for both crew, and night vision compatibility. Nose-mounted stabilized target detection and tracking system (TDATS) with LLLTV, FLIR, laser rangefinder, and autotracking. Sextant Avionique avionics for SAAF helicopters, including 6.25 ins (16 cm) square liquid crystal displays, helmet-mounted sight/displays (stroke, raster and light intensified images on the visor), laser gyro navigation system, stand-by instruments and more. INS, GPS and Doppler navigation. Video cassette recorder. Built-in test and evaluation (BIT/BITE) for LRUs, and automatic fault detection and systems status monitoring with

maintenance modes (HUMS). Designed to operate at nap-of-the-earth (NOE) altitudes of 15-50 ft (4.5-15 m) for 90% of its life. Optional Bowman radios and mast-mounted payloads.
Self-protection systems: Threat detection, warning and jamming.
Fixed guns: Universal cannon interface with single-barrel F2 high speed 20-mm cannon or double-barrel GAD high speed 20-mm cannon with selectable 2,200 rounds per minute fire rate (helmet look-shoot capability). Effective range 6,560 ft (2,000 m) against ground and air targets. Options include hydraulically-steerable 20-mm Kentron GA-1 Rattler or Armscor MG 151 cannon under the nose. Alternative 30-mm cannon.
Ammunition: 400 or 700 rounds.
Number of weapon pylons: Each stub-wing has a tip and 2 articulated stores pylons.
Expendable weapons and equipment: Standard NATO weapons interface, adaptable to carry any weapons mix. Total of 8 or 16 ZT-4 (or presumably ZT-3) tandem-warhead, laser-guided or electro-optical fire and forget anti-armour missiles with 4.3 naut mile (5 mile) 8 km range, or tandem warhead ZT-35s with a 2.7 naut mile (3.1 mile) 5 km stand-off range, in 4-round packs. Alternatively (or as a mix), 4 Darter air-to-air missiles (2 at each wingtip), 68-mm high-velocity rockets in packs of 22 (typically 44 or 88 carried), or other loads including drop tanks. Optional anti-ship capability.

DETAILS FOR ROOIVALK.

Principal dimensions:
Rotor diameter (main): 51 ft 1.5 ins (15.58 m)
Maximum length, rotors turning: 61 ft 5.5 ins (18.731 m)
Fuselage length: 53 ft 9 ins (16.389 m)
Maximum height: 17 ft (5.187 m), and 14 ft 7 ins (4.447 m) over tail rotor
Wing span: 17 ft 1 ins (5.198 m)

Main rotor:
Rotor disc: 2,052 sq ft (190.6 m^2)

Tail rotor:
Diameter: 10 ft (3.042 m)

Undercarriage:
Type: Fixed, with tailwheel. Two-stage, energy absorbing main legs for survivability in a vertical crash
Wheel base: 38 ft 7.5 ins (11.772 m)
Wheel track: 9 ft 1.5 ins (2.78 m)

Weights:
Empty: 13,029 lb (5,910 kg)
Maximum take-off: 19,290 lb (8,750 kg). Growth potential to 20,738 lb (9,400 kg)
Payload: 3,022 lb (1,371 kg) when carrying full fuel

Performance:
Never-exceed speed (VNE): 167 kts (192 mph) 309 km/h
Fast cruise speed: 150 kts (173 mph) 278 km/h
Sideways speed: 45 kts (52 mph) 83 km/h
Maximum climb rate: 2,200 ft (670 m) per minute
Climb rate, OEI: 1,680 ft (512 m) per minute
IGE hovering ceiling: 18,200 ft (5,547 m)
OGE hovering ceiling: 16,500 ft (5,030 m)
Ceiling: 20,000 ft (6,100 m)
G limits: Believed to be +2.6, –1.5 structural design, and +2.2 aerodynamic/system
Range with full internal fuel: 378 naut miles (435 miles) 700 km
Range with auxiliary fuel: 680 naut miles (783 miles) 1,260 km, or 610 naut miles (702 miles) 1,130 km ferry range with 45 minutes reserve
Duration: 3 hours 36 minutes at sea level, ISA, without drop tanks

Atlas Puma Gunship

Role: Anti-armour, long-range troop deployment, heliborne escort, reconnaissance, area suppression and self defence.

★ Aims
★ Modular, low-cost weapon suite for the Puma, intended to adapt the helicopter for a primary gunship role but still suited to a secondary transport role.
Crew: Pilot and weapon system officer in a gunship role.
Safety features: Armoured crew seats, self-sealing fuel tanks effective against 12.7-mm hits, intumescent paints to protect critical areas and components against direct fire flame temperatures of 1,100°C for over 10 minutes, engine protection by an engine separation shield capable of deflecting 7.62-mm ammunition, and optional ballistic panels for the cockpit floor and sides and other critical areas.
Engines: 2 Turbomeca Turmo IVC turboshafts.
Engine rating: Each 1,496 shp (1,115 kW) take-off, and 1,560 shp (1,163 kW) for 2.5 minute OEI max contingency.

Atlas/Denel Puma Gunship

Fuel system: 2,646 lb (1,200 kg) internal.
Flight avionics/instrumentation: Nose-mounted sighting system for target acquisition and to guide the cannon and missiles during daylight, with optional night capability. Night vision compatible cockpit. HSS and HSOS (see Fixed guns). Reduced pilot workload via centralized control of the navigation, communications, weapons system and EW avionics functions (using the MIL-STD-1553B databus), pilot interface with multi-function displays operated by soft keys, computerized pre-programmed mission planning, digital mission data base with intelligent information, data transfer from mission planning via the data transfer unit, and manual data input via the control and display unit. Standard avionics are the helicopter mission computer (HMC), MFDs, DTU, CDU, attitude and heading reference system (AHRS), GPS, radar altimeter, and digital automatic flight control system.
Self-protection systems: Passive EW suite with option of radar, laser, missile approach, and hostile fire warning. Optional chaff/flare dispensers.
Fixed guns: Computer-controlled, hydraulically actuated turreted TC-20 20-mm cannon, aimed by a helmet sighting system (HSS) or helicopter stabilized optronic sight (HSOS), for self defence. Firing angles ±110° azimuth, –60° downward and 0° upward. Weight of system 365 lb (165.5 kg).
Ammunition: 400 rounds of MG-151 ammunition.
Number of weapon pylons: Tubular weapons beam carried each side of the fuselage, each with 2 pylons.
Expendable weapons and equipment: Choice according to role. For area suppression, HR-68 pods each with 18 x 68-mm rockets (or other rockets) plus the cannon. For anti-armour, 8 x ZT-3 laser-guided missiles in 2 x 4-round packs (option of TOW or similar) on the outer pylons, aimed by the HSOS, plus 2 rocket pods and the cannon.

DETAILS FOR PUMA GUNSHIP.

Principal dimensions: As for standard Puma, except:
Maximum length, rotors turning: 51 ft 5 ins (15.672 m)
Width over pylon weapons: 17 ft 5 ins (5.301 m)

Weights:
Empty: 9,747 lb (4,421 kg)
Maximum take-off: 16,314 lb (7,400 kg)

Performance:
Fast cruise speed: 136 kts (157 mph) 252 km/h anti-tank at sea level, ISA, or 131 kts (151 mph) 243 km/h anti-tank at 6,000 ft (1,830 m), 30° C, both at 13,448 lb (6,100 kg) weight
OGE hovering ceiling: 12,000 ft (3,660 m) and 8,800 ft (2,680 m), conditions as above respectively
Range with full fuel: 348 naut miles (401 miles) 644 km and 352 naut miles (405 miles) 652 km, conditions as above respectively

Westland Group plc (UK)

Corporate address: Yeovil, Somerset BA20 2YB.
Telephone: +44 1935 75222
Facsimile: +44 1935 702131, 702133
Telex: 46277 WHLYEO G
Founded: 4 July 1935 as Westland Aircraft Ltd, having begun aviation activities as Westland Aviation Works on 3 April 1915.
Information: Chris Loney (Group Director of Public Relations).

DIVISIONS

<u>Westland Aerospace Ltd</u>
HQ address: East Cowes, Isle of Wight PO32 6RH
Telephone: +44 1983 294101
Facsimile: +44 1983 291006

● Activities
● Design, manufacture and qualification of advanced composite and metallic flight critical structures and components, including for the Airbus A340, Boeing 737, and McDonnell Douglas C-17 and MD-11. Nacelle manufacture includes those for the C-130J, Dash 8, Dornier 328, Jetstream 41, and Saab 2000.

Westland Engineering Ltd
HQ address: Yeovil, Somerset BA20 2YB.
Telephone: +44 1935 75222
Facsimile: +44 1935 704021

● Activities
● Helicopter dynamics, engine and aeroplane components. Programmes include machined parts for the Boeing 777, having previously supplied bolts and hollow pins for the B747, 757 and 767; Boeing 727 spare part wing panels, and Super Transporter door frames.

Westland Helicopters Ltd
HQ address: Yeovil, Somerset BA20 2YB.
Telephone: +44 1935 75222
Facsimile: +44 1935 702131, 702133
Telex: 46277 WHLYEO G

● Activities
● Manufactures helicopters, including the Sea King based on the US Sikorsky design and Apache from McDonnell Douglas; 67 Apaches were selected for the British Army Air Corps on 13 July 1995, differing mainly from the US helicopter in having Rolls-Royce Turbomeca RTM322 engines. In addition, the WS 70L is a Westland-offered version of the Sikorsky UH-60L Black Hawk, 88 of which had been requested by Saudi Arabia. However, in July 1995, the programme was still in abeyance and there was no immediate prospect of start of manufacture.
● 50% stake in EH Industries EH 101, with Agusta of Italy.

Westland Industries Ltd
HQ address: Winterstroke Road, Weston-super-Mare, Avon BS24 9AB.
Telephone: +44 1934 635555, 642411
Facsimile: +44 1934 612201

● Activities
● Component manufacture. Subsidiaries are Westland Design Services for subcontract design and engineering for aerospace, rail and engineering industries; Westland Heliport for operating London Heliport; Westland Industrial Products for component and subassembly manufacture; and Westland Systems Assessment for operational analysis and systems assessment. Westland Industrial Products has recently fitted GPS, Tacan, VOR, DME and more to 40 RAF Puma helicopters, under a £3.5 million contract from Racal Avionics.

Westland Technologies Ltd
HQ address: PO Box 27, Yeovil, Somerset BA20 2YJ.
Telephone: +44 1935 75181
Facsimile: +44 1935 27600

● Activities
● Principal subsidiary is Normalair-Garrett, producing control systems and associated aerospace components.

Westland Lynx, Battlefield Lynx and Super Lynx

First flight: 21 March 1971 (first of 13 prototypes).
Role: Army general-purpose, utility and armed attack/support; naval anti-submarine, anti-surface-vessel, EEZ and convoy protection, vertrep, over-the-horizon targeting, electronic surveillance and warfare, search and rescue, pollution control and VIP transport.

★ Aims
★ Naval versions can operate in sea state 6 and in 40 kts side or tail winds and up to 50 kts winds from ahead for take-off and landing. In ASW role, can be used for autonomous operations or with other aircraft and ships, for submarine detection, classification, localization and attack in all weathers, by day or night.

Westland Lynx AH Mk 9 with the British Army

▲ Development
▲ 2 April 1968. Lynx became 1 of 3 helicopters covered under an Anglo-French agreement between Westland (70% workshare) and Aerospatiale (30%).
▲ 1986. Lynx set an absolute world helicopter speed record at 216.45 kts (249.1 mph) 400.87 km/h.
Sales: 374 production Lynx of all versions by mid-July 1995, delivered to the Argentine (2 Mk 23 for ASW), Brazilian (9 Mk 21 and 9 Mk 21A Super Lynx for ASV), Danish (8 Mk 80 and 2 Mk 90 for SAR/patrol, actually ordered by the Air Force, with uses including recent flying from new IS86 Thetis class offshore patrol vessels), French (26 HAS Mk 2(FN) and 14 HAS Mk 4(FN) for ASW/ASV), German (19 Mk 88 for ASW), South Korean (12 Mk 99 Super Lynx for ASW/ASV), Netherlands (6 Mk 25 for SAR, 10 Mk 27 and 8 Mk 81 for ASW), Nigerian (3 Mk 89 for ASW/SAR), Portuguese (5 Mk 95 Super Lynx for ASW) and British (60 HAS Mk 2 and 30 HAS Mk 3) navies. Army versions to the British Army Air Corps (113 AH Mk 1, 4 AH Mk 5 and 11 AH Mk 7 for utility/anti-tank, plus 16 AH Mk 9 for utility), Norwegian Air Force (6 Mk 86 for SAR) and Qatar Police (3 Mk 28 for utility). Of these, only Argentina and Qatar no longer operate the helicopter. The export Battlefield Lynx is generally similar to the British AH Mk 9, while export Super Lynx customers are Brazil (9 Mk 21As, with 5 existing Lynx Mk 21/21As being upgraded to the new standard), South Korea (Mk 99) and Portugal (Mk 95), as already detailed. Pakistan now operates 3 ex-Royal Navy HAS Mk 3s from Type 21 frigates, and Portugal has received 2 ex-Royal Navy HAS Mk 3s. Westland is undertaking a programme to extend cold weather operations of Norwegian Lynx operated north of the Arctic Circle for fishery protection and SAR, by lowering operating limits from –26° C to at least –30° C. A Lynx life extension programme is being developed. Reports in September 1995 suggest the Royal Australian Navy is being offered a LHTEC T800-powered Super Lynx.

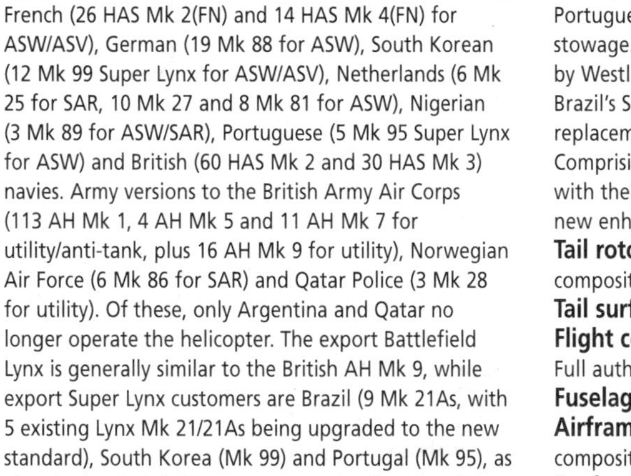

Westland Lynx HAS Mk 3, with 4 Sea Skua missiles

Details: Principally based on newest naval Super Lynx, except where indicated.
Crew/passengers: 2 or 3 crew. Up to 8 passengers in a VIP role, or 8 survivors for SAR, or 3 litters (typically) and an attendant.
Freight, external: 3,000 lb (1,360 kg) cargo hook.
Cabin access: Sliding door, with entrance of 4 ft 6 ins x 3 ft 11 ins (1.37 x 1.19 m).
Optional equipment: Includes dual controls, harpoon deck securing system, and a 600 lb (272 kg) hydraulic rescue hoist above the large sliding door.
Rotor system: Advanced BERP, aerodynamically efficient, 4-blade, semi-rigid main rotor with swept tips. Provides low vibration, high performance, and the high control power and quick response needed for control in turbulence over a rolling flight deck. Negative pitch facility provides 3,000 lb (1,360 kg) downward thrust to hold the helicopter steady on deck until secured, aided by the low centre of gravity of the low profile gearbox and minimal rotor height. Blades evolved from the British Experimental Rotor Programme (BERP), and made of carbon and glassfibre composite components protected from erosion by titanium and nickel shields. These offer a threefold increase in fatigue life over the original steel blades, a 70% reduction in operator maintenance effort, and the potential to increase the maximum thrust by up to 40%. Standard on Super Lynx, the blades have been retrofitted to British, French, German, Netherlands, Norwegian and Portuguese Lynx helicopters. Main rotor folds for stowage. A new main rotor head has been developed by Westland to reduce maintenance, first fitted to Brazil's Super Lynx. Available also as a retrofit replacement, the new head reduces life cycle costs. Comprising several major sub-assemblies (compared with the existing monobloc), the head is fabricated in a new enhanced grade of titanium alloy.
Tail rotor characteristics: 4-blade, metal or composite, on port side of fin.
Tail surfaces: Starboard, fixed.
Flight control system: Hydraulic rotor head controls. Full authority rotor speed control by each engine.
Fuselage: Folding tail pylon.
Airframe materials: Light alloy, with limited use of composites for fairings, doors and panels.
Engines: 2 Rolls-Royce Gem 42 series turboshafts.
Engine rating: Each 1,120 shp (835 kW).
Transmission rating: 1,840 shp (1,372 kW). Optional engine diffusers for IR suppression.
Fuel system: 990 litres in 5 main tanks plus a further 214 litres under the cabin bench seat as standard, with the option of 2 x 436 litre tanks for long-endurance missions. Army Lynx variants only have the 5 main tanks as standard, with all other tanks as optional for extended range or ferrying respectively (bench or ferry, not both).
Electrical system: 28 volt DC supply via 2 engine-driven starter-generators and alternator. 24 volt ni-cd battery for back-up and emergency engine start (23 or 40 amp-hour). 200 volt, 400 Hz, 3-phase AC supply via 2 alternators.
Hydraulic system: 2 principal systems, each 2,050 psi, plus a third if sonar, hoist or MAD is part of the equipment.
Braking system: Sprag pivoting and locking type, to prevent movement on deck.
Radar: Chin-mounted 360° track-while-scan radar, able to detect small targets among strong sea clutter and electronic counter-measures. Typically GEC-Marconi Seaspray Mk 3 (as fitted to South Korean Mk 99s) or AlliedSignal Bendix/King RDR 1500 (as fitted

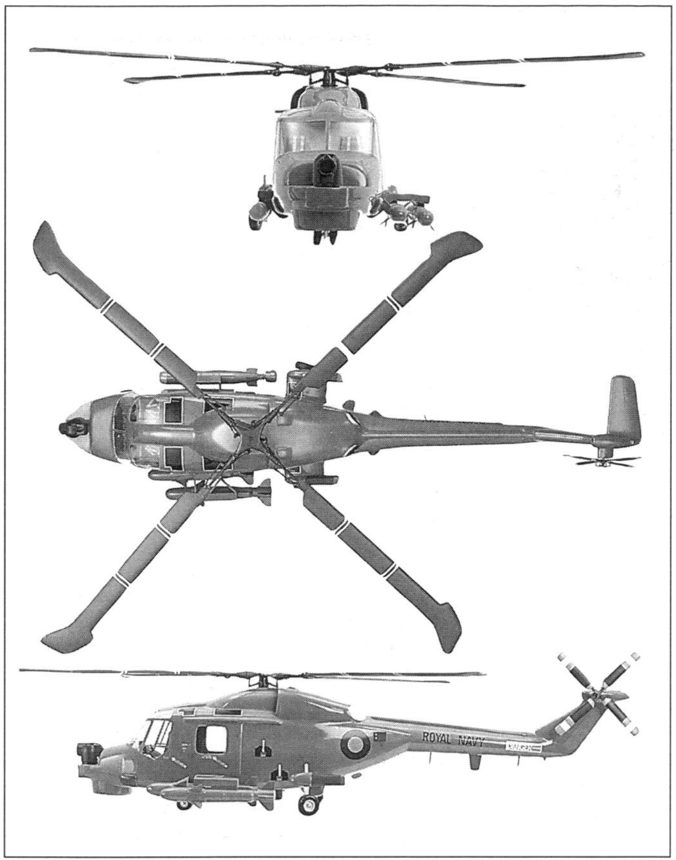

Westland Lynx HMA Mk 8, with BERP blades, Sea Owl passive thermal identification system, and Sea Skuas/torpedo (courtesy Westland)

to Portuguese Mk 95s).
Flight avionics/ instrumentation: GEC-Marconi automatic flight control system, providing transition to and from hover and Doppler hover control. Tactical air navigation system (TANS N or Super TANS) and Doppler. Typical other instrumentation includes DME, VOR/ILS, Tacan, and I-band transponder. IFF. Mission equipment to suit customer, with the recommended suite now upgraded, with options including MAD, passive radar detection system, and dipping sonar (AlliedSignal Bendix/King AQS-18 or Thomson-Sintra HS-312); Super Lynx has the capability of carrying future advanced low-frequency sonar. Target classification is assisted by electronic support measures and the radar. A major cockpit upgrade was launched by Westland in 1994, designed to progressively introduce glass cockpit elements to ease Super Lynx flying and operations. The upgrade has panel mounted displays to enhance tactical and situation awareness. Radar is enhanced using liquid crystal displays. FLIR can also be integrated into the cockpit display, while tactical navigation is enhanced by GPS. New equipment will be NVG compatible. Multi-sensor reconnaissance pod, camera and night viewing devices for an electronic surveillance/warfare role (typically Vinten or Agiflite), with cabin space and electrical capacity for a range of passive and active EW systems.
Self-protection systems: Vinten Vicon 78 chaff dispenser.
Number of weapon pylons: Detachable rack each side of the cabin, with 2 pylons per rack.
Expendable weapons and equipment: 4 Sea Skua or 2 Penguin anti-ship missiles for ASV, 2 homing torpedoes (Sting Ray, Mk 44, Mk 46) and depth charges for ASW. Could carry 4 Stinger AAMs.
Aircraft variants (currently used only):
AH Mk 1 is the original British Army version with Gem 2 engines. Many upgraded to Mk 7s.
AH Mk 7 improved British Army version, with Gem 42 engines, enhanced systems, composite tail rotor blades and more. Now with BERP main blades.
AH Mk 9 is the latest British Army version, similar to Battlefield Lynx. First Army version with wheel undercarriage. Advanced composite rotor blades. Gem 42 engines with exhaust diffusers for IR suppression.
HAS Mk 3 is a Royal Navy version, being upgraded by Westland to HAS Mk 8 standard. Seaspray Mk 1 radar. Gem 41 engines. Includes subvariants for Antarctic and Gulf operations.
HMA Mk 8 (HMA = helicopter maritime attack) is a Royal Navy version by conversion of Mk 3s and sub-variants, with Racal Avionics RAMS 4000 central tactical system with CRTs, GEC-Sensors Sea Owl passive thermal identification system, upgraded Orange Crop ESM, GPS and much more, integrated by the MIL-STD-1553B databus. Primarily for an anti-surface vessel attack role. First of 44 entered service in January 1995. Initial conversions by Westland, thereafter by the Royal Navy's Fleetlands works using Westland kits. Under an £18.8 million contract from the British Ministry of Defence, Westland provided a new radar processor, entering service with the Royal Navy from October 1994.
Battlefield Lynx is the export Army equivalent of Super Lynx. No orders to date, though British AH Mk 9 is similar. Gem 42-1 engines. BERP main rotors. Wheel undercarriage. 8 TOW, Hellfire or HOT anti-tank missiles, or 2 Giat 20-mm cannon pods, or 2 x 7.62-mm machine-guns in each of 2 pods, or 2 pods with 19 x 2.75-in rockets each. Also, can have normal cabin pintle 7.62-mm machine-gun. Enhanced flight and defence aid avionics. Empty weight 7,006 lb (3,178 kg). Same maximum take-off weight as Super Lynx.
Lynx Recce Helicopter is a Westland study for a conversion package to allow a specialized reconnaissance version of the Army Lynx, incorporating a modern mast-mounted sight and mission management system. Prime mission would be identification and designation of targets for attack helicopters.

DETAILS FOR SUPER LYNX.

Principal dimensions:
Rotor diameter (main): 42 ft (12.8 m)
Maximum length, rotors turning: 50 ft (15.24 m)
Maximum length, rotor and tail folded: 35 ft 7 ins (10.85 m)
Width, blades folded: 9 ft 8 ins (2.95 m)
Maximum height: 12 ft 0.5 ins (3.67 m), or 10 ft 8 ins (3.25 m) with rotor and tail folded

Cabin:
Length: 6 ft 9 ins (2.06 m)
Width: 5 ft 10 ins (1.78 m)
Height: 4 ft 8 ins (1.42 m)
Volume: 5.21 cu ft (184 m^3)

Main rotor:
Rotor disc: 128.71 sq ft (1,385.4 m^2)

Tail rotor:
Diameter: 7 ft 9 ins (2.36 m)

Undercarriage:
Type: Fixed, with twin steerable nosewheels. Main units toe outward by 27°, but are manually aligned and locked for deck handling. Optional flotation equipment. Maximum vertical descent rate 7.5 ft (2.3 m) per second
Wheel base: 9 ft 11 ins (3.02 m)
Wheel track: 9 ft 2 ins (2.8 m)

Weights:
Empty: 7,255 lb (3,291 kg)
Empty, equipped: 7,782 lb (3,530 kg) ASW, 8,495 lb (3,853 kg) ASW search and attack with 3 crew and 1 torpedo, 7,984 lb (3,621 kg) ASV, 7,813 lb (3,544 kg) OTHT, 7,789 lb (3,533 kg) SAR
Operating, minus fuel: 9,226 lb (4,185 kg) for ASW with 2 Mk 46 torpedoes, 9,577 lb (4,344 kg) ASW search and attack, 9,640 lb (4,373 kg) for ASV with 4 Sea Skua, 8,311 lb (3,770 kg) OTHT with 2 auxiliary tanks, 8,329 lb (3,778 kg) SAR
Maximum take-off: 11,300 lb (5,126 kg)
Take-off (SAR): 10,063 lb (4,564 kg)

Performance (MTOW):
Cruise speed: 137 kts (158 mph) 254 km/h
Maximum climb rate: 1,776 ft (541 m) per minute at 90 kts
Climb rate, OEI: 396 ft (121 m) per minute at 80 kts
IGE hovering ceiling: 8,859 ft (2,700 m) ISA, or 3,874 ft (1,180 m) at ISA + 15°C
OGE hovering ceiling: 6,726 ft (2,050 m) ISA, 1,116 ft (340 m) at ISA + 15°C
Range: 285 naut miles (328 miles) 528 km *standard tanks*, 437 naut miles (503 miles) 810 km *with 1 auxiliary tank*, 590 naut miles (679 miles) 1,093 km *with 2 auxiliary tanks*, all with 20 minutes reserve
Maximum range (SAR): 340 naut miles (391 miles) 630 km
Radius of action (ASV): Typically up to 160 naut miles (184 miles) 300 km with missiles, at sea level, ISA +15°C, 20 minutes fuel reserve.
Radius of action (ASW): Typically up to 120 naut miles (138 miles) 220 km with 2 torpedoes, at sea level, ISA + 15°C, 20 minutes fuel reserve
Radius of action (SAR): Typically up to 150 naut miles (173 miles) 280 km *with standard fuel*, or 260 naut miles (299 miles) 480 km *with auxiliary tanks*, carrying 3 crew, hoist and 4 survivors, at sea level, ISA + 15°C, 20 minutes fuel reserve
Duration (ASV): Typically 3.25 hours at sea level, ISA +-15°C, 20 minutes fuel reserve.
Time on station (ASW): Typically 2 hours at 20 naut miles (23 miles) 37 km from ship, with dipping sonar and 1 torpedo, at sea level, ISA + 15°C, 20 minutes fuel reserve.
Duration (SAR): Typically 3.7 hours at sea level, ISA +- 15°C, 20 minutes fuel reserve

Westland Sea King and Commando

First flight: 7 May 1969 (HAS Mk 1).
Role: Medium multi-role. 23 different variants are available, including ASW, ASV, SAR, troop/VIP transport, logistic support, airborne early warning, electronic warfare, and Commando assault.

★ Aims
★ Licence developed and manufactured variants of the US Sikorsky S-61.

▲ Development
▲ 19 August 1969. First HAS Mk 1 entered service with 700S Squadron, RNAS Culdrose, Royal Navy.

Westland Sea King Mk 43B for SAR with the Royal Norwegian Air Force

Sales: 328 delivered as Australia (navy, 10 Mk 50s and 2 Mk 50As for utility/SAR), Belgium (air force 5 Mk 48s for SAR), Egypt (air force, 6 Mk 47s for ASW, 5 Mk 70s and 19 Mk 72s for utility, and 4 Mk 73s for ECM), Germany (navy, 22 Mk 41s for SAR/ASW), India (navy, 12 Mk 42s and 3 Mk 42As for ASW, 20 Mk 42Bs for ASW/ASV, and 6 Mk 42Cs for utility), Norway (air force, 10 Mk 43s, 1 Mk 43A, 3 Mk 43Bs and 2 new Mk 43Bs for SAR), Pakistan (navy, 6 Mk 45s for ASV), Qatar (air force, 8 Mk 74s for ASV and 4 Mk 92s for utility/VIP), and UK (air force, 19 HAR Mk 3s and 6 new Mk 3As for SAR; navy, 56 HAS Mk 1s, 21 Mk 2s, 30 HAS Mk 5s and 5 HAS Mk 6s for ASW, plus 40 HC Mk 4s for utility; ETPS 1 HC Mk 4 for utility; and RAE [now DE&RA] 2 HC Mk 4X for utility). In addition, Pakistan has received 1 ex-RN HAS Mk 5. 7 Australian Sea Kings (used during the 1994 Sydney bush fires) are being upgraded under a £27.6 million contract, with a Life of Type Extension (LOTE) programme that includes an avionics update and airframe modifications to extend service life to at least 2008. Five Belgium SAR Sea Kings have been upgraded under a £4.5 million contract with AlliedSignal Bendix/King RDR 1500B search radar, FLIR Systems 2000F FLIR, and Racal RNS-252 navigation computer system integrated with the Canadian Marconi CMA 3012 GPS.

Details: Currently offered advanced version of Sea King, unless stated.

Crew/passengers: 4 crew and 16 (22 possible) survivors in SAR version; 2 crew and 28 troops (can be extended by some 50% for seated/standing troops), or 9 litters and 2 attendants or cargo (see below) in transport/logistic version; 3 crew and up to 15 VIPs with luxurious interior fittings in VIP transport version; 4 crew in AEW version; 3 crew in ASV and 4 crew in ASW versions.

Cockpit: Dual controls.

Freight, internal: 8,682 lb (3,943 kg) in transport version.

Freight, external: 8,000 lb (3,629 kg) cargo sling instead of troops or internal freight in transport role.

Cabin access: Sliding cargo door.

Size of main loading door: 5 ft x 5 ft 8 ins (1.52 x 1.73 m) starboard side, with smaller door to port.

Optional equipment: Includes fixed head undercarriage, no sponsons for overland operatons, troop seats, 1 or 2 x 600 lb (272 kg) hoists, cargo hook, litters, waterproof floor, parachute monorail,

Rotor system: Fixed main rotor head with 5 composite blades. Rotor brake. Optional powered folding main rotor head weighing 165 lb (75 kg).

Tail rotor characteristics: 6-blade.

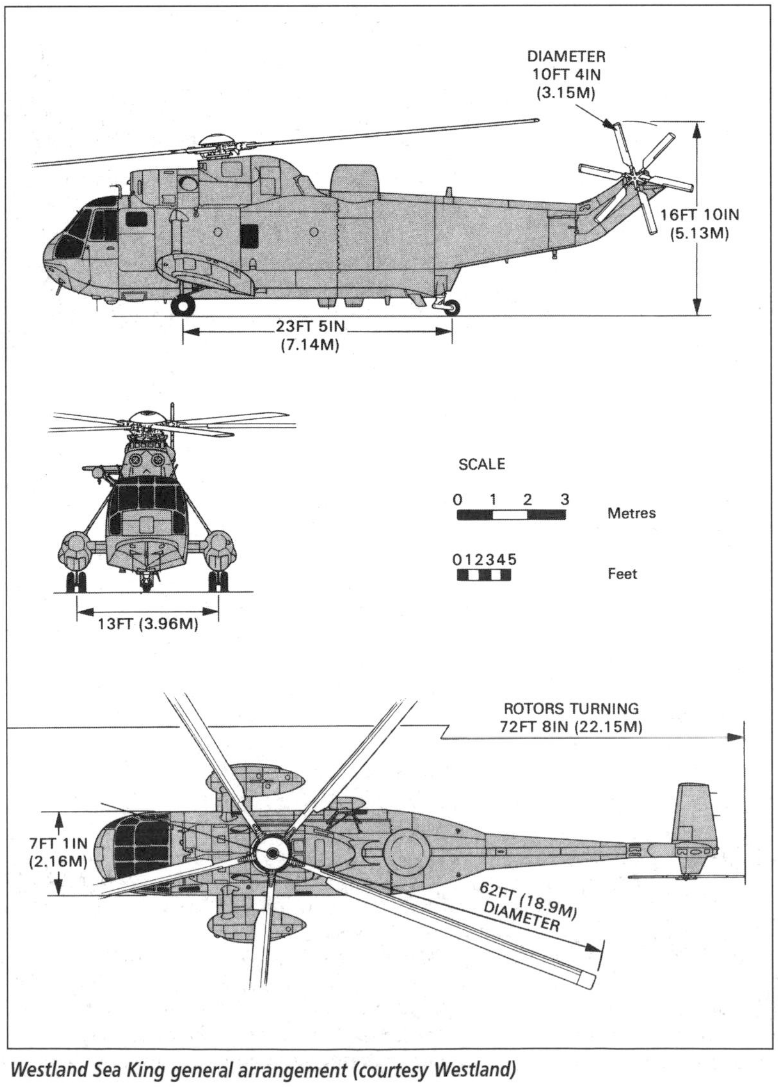

Westland Sea King general arrangement (courtesy Westland)

Fuselage: Semi-monocoque with sponsons (overland version can have sponsons deleted). Folding tail for shipborne use.

Construction materials: Light alloy (stressed skin) airframe. See Rotors.

Engines: 2 Rolls-Royce Gnome H1400-1 turbo-shafts. Electric and hot air anti-icing. Optional sand filters and foreign object deflector.

Engine rating: 1,660 shp (1,238 kW).

Transmission rating: Main gearbox has an emergency lubrication system.

Fuel system: 6,456 lb (2,928 kg), with gravity and pressure refuelling/defuelling and fuel jettison system. Optional auxiliary fuel system (864 litres).

Electrical system: 2 x 20 kVA 200/115 Hz alternators, 2 x 200 amp transformer rectifiers, and a 40 amp-hour battery. Optional third 20 kVA alternator.

Hydraulic system: 2 systems for rotor control at 1,500 psi, plus system for undercarriage retraction, rotor folding and brake and equipment operation, 3,000 psi.

Braking system: Mainwheel brakes.

Radar: AlliedSignal Bendix/King RDR 1300 forward looking or RDR 1500 360° dorsal radar for SAR. Thorn-EMI Searchwater for AEW (fully stabilized and scanning through 360°), including third alternator. MEL Supersearcher for ASW and ASV role.

Flight avionics/instrumentation: Dual pilot IFR. 2 sets of flight instruments, 2 sets of engine instruments, 1 set of general instruments, fire warning, advisory fuel management, caution and identification panels. Automatic flight control system, with fully automatic transition from forward flight to hover and an ability to hover precisely at heights up to 140 ft (43 m) reference to Doppler; auxiliary hover trim facility enables the helicopter to be accurately. positioned. Radio equipment comprises dual Rockwell Collins ARC-182 VHF/UHF and HF9000 HF; Racal Doppler 91 and B6922-1 intercom; and IFF. Navigation equipment comprises Racal RNS-252 tactical navigation computer; AlliedSignal Bendix/King KDF 806 ADF, KNR 634R VOR/ILS, and KDM 706A DME; Smiths/Honeywell APN-198 radar altimeter; Chelton 7 UHF and VHF homing; and ARNAV Series 7000 Loran-C. FLIR 2000 for SAR role. Racal MIR 2 ESM for AEW role. I-band transponder for ASW and ASV role; optional MAD (as used by Royal Navy). AlliedSignal Bendix/King AQS-18(V) or Thomson Sintra HS 312 dipping sonar for ASW role.

Fixed guns: Optional cabin-mounted machine-gun.

Expendable weapons and equipment: Exocet, Sea Eagle, Sea Skua, Harpoon, Otomat or Penguin anti-ship missiles, torpedoes (including Sting Ray), 4 Mk 11 depth charges, Clevite simulator, 2 marine markers, 4 smoke floats, and Ultra Electronics mini sonobuoys.

Aircraft variants:

Sea King AEW Mk 2A is the Royal Navy's airborne early warning version for operations from *Invincible* class carriers (converted from former HAS Mk 2As). Searchwater radar scanner in an external air-pressurized Kevlar fabric container, which is hydraulically rotated to the horizon when the helicopter is in transit or static, and to the vertical, below wheel level, when deployed.

HAR Mk 3A is an RAF SAR version with Thorn-EMI AR15955/2 radar.

HAR Mk 5 is a SAR only version, 4 being converted from HAS Mk 5s.

HAS Mk 5 is a Royal Navy ASW and SAR version with Thorn-EMI Sea Searcher radar, built new and by conversion of older model Sea Kings. Racal Orange Crop ESM. See Mk 6.

HAS Mk 6 is the latest Royal Navy version for ASW, operated from 1989. Some new, others upgraded from HAS Mk 5s using Westland kits. GEC-Marconi 2069 dipping sonar with enhanced digital processing and with sonar and sonobuoy information presented on a CRT, Orange Reaper ESM, internally mounted MAD, and many other improvements.

HC Mk 4 is a Commando type with the Royal Navy, as are the ETPS (Empire Test Pilots' School) Mk 4 and former RAE Mk 4Xs (RAE is now named Defence Evaluation & Research Agency).

Exported Sea Kings are to varying equipment standards, according to roles detailed under Sales. Latest advanced model is detailed.

Commando is a tactical assault derivative of Sea King, to which it differs in equipment. Fixed head undercarriage and no sponsons for its mainly overland role. Commando operators include Egypt, Qatar and India.

DETAILS FOR CURRENTLY OFFERED SEA KING.

Principal dimensions:
Rotor diameter (main): 62 ft (18.9 m)
Maximum length, rotors turning: 72 ft 8 ins (22.15 m)
Fuselage width: 7 ft 1 ins (2.16 m)
Maximum height: 16 ft 10 ins (5.13 m) to top of tail rotor

Cabin:
Length: 24 ft 11 ins (7.59 m)
Width: 6 ft 6 ins (1.98 m)
Height: 6 ft 3.5 ins (1.92 m)
Volume: 990 cu ft (28.03 m^3)

Main rotor:
Aerofoil section: NACA 0012
Blade chord: 1 ft 6.2 ins (0.46 m)
Blade area: each 43 sq ft (3.99 m^2)
Rotor disc: 2,921 sq ft (271.4 m^2)
Rpm: 209

Tail rotor:
Diameter: 10 ft 4 ins (3.15m)

Undercarriage:
Type: Retractable twin mainwheels (into sponsons) and fixed tailwheel. Optional emergency flotation system for overwater operations, and sea anchor.
Wheel base: 23 ft 5 ins (7.14 m)
Wheel track: 13 ft (3.96 m)

Weights:
Empty: 12,009 lb (5,447 kg), except overland version without sponsons is 11,963 lb (5,426 kg)
Maximum take-off: 21,400 lb (9,707 kg)
Payload: 8,692 lb (3,943 kg) maximum

Performance (ISA):
Never-exceed speed (VNE): 122 kts (140 mph) 226 km/h
Cruise speed: 110 kts (127 mph) 204 km/h
Maximum climb rate: 1,850 ft (564 m) per minute
IGE hovering ceiling: 5,600 ft (1,707 m)
OGE hovering ceiling: 3,500 ft (1,067 m)
Operating ceiling: 10,000 ft (3,050 m)
Range with full fuel: 800 naut miles (921 miles) 1,482 km
Duration: 7 hours maximum, no reserve
On station: 1 hour 45 minutes for ASV at 100 naut miles (115 miles) 185 km from base, or 2 hours for ASW at 125 naut miles (144 miles) 231 km from base

Wombat Gyrocopters (UK)

Corporate address: The Chalet, Higher Fraddon, Indian Queens, St Columb, Cornwall.
Telephone: +44 1726 860662
Information: Chris Julian.

Wombat Gyrocopter

Role: Single-seat autogyro, currently under test.
Rotor system: 2-blade, gimballed teetering rotor. Will be offered with optional rotor pre-spin.
Tail surfaces: Small fin and large rudder.
Construction materials: Aluminium alloy blades. Metal tube fuselage structure, with fairing. Glassfibre and foam composite rudder.
Engine: Rotax 582UL piston engine. Optional electric starting. 3-blade pusher propeller.

Wombat Gyrocopter (Geoffrey P. Jones)

Engine rating: 64.4 hp (48 kW).
Fuel system: 77 litres.

DETAILS FOR GYROCOPTER.

Principal dimensions:
Rotor diameter: 22 ft 10 ins (6.96 m)
Fuselage length: 12 ft (3.66 m)
Maximum height: 7 ft 6 ins (2.29 m)

Weights:
Empty: 352 lb (160 kg)
Maximum take-off: 700 lb (318 kg)

Performance:
Maximum speed: 90 kts (103 mph) 167 km/h
Cruise speed: 75 kts (86 mph) 138 km/h
Maximum climb rate: 1,100 ft (335 m) per minute
Ceiling: 10,000 ft (3,050 m), service
Duration: 5 hours

Air Command International Inc (USA)

Corporate address: PO Box 1345, 702 Cooper Drive, Wylie, TX 75098.
Telephone: +1 214 442 6694
Facsimile: +1 214 442 9174

Air Command Commander series

Role: Single and two-seat kit-built autogyros.
Details: Principally for the Commander Tandem 1000, except under Aircraft variants.
Sales: Kit (US$15,994 in 1994) incorporates the engine and propeller. Kit takes approximately 100 working hours to assemble.
Crew/passengers: Pilot and passenger in tandem.
Rotor system: 2-blade rotor.
Tail surfaces: Vertical and horizontal surfaces.
Airframe materials: Metal tubes and composites.
Engine: Arrow 1,000 cc piston engine.
Engine rating: 100 hp (74.6 kW).
Fuel system: 45 litres.
Aircraft variants:
Commander 447 was designed to be a single-seat ultralight autogyro, with a 40 hp (30 kW) Rotax 447 engine. A Sport model was developed with higher performance.
Commander 503 is a single-seat Experimental category autogyro, taking typically just 28 working hours to assemble from a US$8,938 (1994 cost) kit. Rotax 503 engine. A Sport model was developed with higher performance.
Commander 582 is similar to the 503, also with a 23 ft (7.01 m) rotor, but uses a Rotax 582 engine. Kit US$9,760 (1994 cost). Can be built as a two-seater for an additional cost. A Sport model was developed with higher performance.
Commander Tandem 1000 is the two-seater, as detailed.

Air Command International Commander 503 (Geoffrey P. Jones)

DETAILS FOR COMMANDER TANDEM 1000.

Principal dimensions:
Rotor diameter: 27 ft (8.23 m)
Airframe length: 13 ft 5 ins (4.09 m)
Maximum height: 8 ft 11 ins (2.72 m)

Weights:
Empty: 380 lb (172 kg)
Maximum take-off: 1,000 lb (454 kg)

Performance:
Maximum speed: 91 kts (105 mph) 169 km/h
Cruise speed: 65 kts (75 mph) 121 km/h
Maximum climb rate: 1,000 ft (305 m) per minute
Ceiling: 10,000 ft (3,050 m), service
Take-off distance: 300 ft (91 m)

Aircraft Designs Inc (USA)

Corporate address: 5 Harris Court, Building S, Monterey, CA 93940.
Telephone: +1 408 649 6212
Facsimile: +1 408 649 5738

Aircraft Designs Bumble Bee

Role: Single-seat ultralight autogyro.
Sales: Available in plans and kit forms, the latter at $US5,500 (1994 cost?). Typical assembly time is 400 working hours.
Rotor system: 2-blade rotor, using NACA 8-H-12 aerofoil. Aluminium alloy and composites construction (foam, glassfibre and epoxy). Pre-rotator.
Tail surfaces: Horizontal and vertical surfaces.
Airframe materials: Aluminium alloy tube open

Details for Bumble Bee.

Principal dimensions:
Rotor diameter: 23 ft (7.01 m)
Airframe length: 12 ft 6 ins (3.81 m)
Maximum height: 7 ft 6 ins (2.29 m)

Weights:
Empty, operating: 213-230 lb (97-104 kg)
Maximum take-off: 500 lb (227 kg)

Performance:
Maximum speed: 56 kts (65 mph) 105 km/h
Cruise speed: 35 kts (40 mph) 64 km/h
Maximum climb rate: 1,500 ft (457 m) per minute
Ceiling: 12,000 ft (3,660 m)
Range: 56 naut miles (65 miles) 105 km
Duration: 1 hour

structure. Composite tail.
Engine: 40 hp (30 kW) Rotax 447 piston engine, with 2-blade pusher propeller.
Fuel system: 19 or 38 litres.

Aircraft Designs Sportster

Role: Two-seat (side-by-side) Experimental category autogyro.
Sales: Plans only. Typical construction time is 1,500 working hours.
Rotor system: 2-blade rotor, using NACA 8-H-12 aerofoil. Pre-rotator. Rotor brake.
Tail surfaces: Twin fins and rudders.
Airframe materials: Aluminium alloy tubing and sheet, except for composites used for the wheel fairings and part of the tail.
Engine: Typically Textron Lycoming O-320 piston engine, but with other possibilities.

Details for Sportster.

Principal dimensions:
Rotor diameter: 28 ft (8.53 m)
Airframe length: 12 ft (3.66 m)
Maximum height: 8 ft (2.44 m)

Weights:
Empty: 650 lb (295 kg)
Maximum take-off: 1,100 lb (499 kg)

Performance:
Maximum speed: 78 kts (90 mph) 145 km/h
Cruise speed: 65 kts (75 mph) 121 km/h
Maximum climb rate: 1,000 ft (305 m) per minute
Ceiling: 12,000 ft (3,660 m), service
Range: 130 naut miles (150 miles) 241 km

Engine rating: 150 hp (112 kW) for the O-320.
Fuel system: 64 litres.

Alturair (USA)

Corporate address: 1405 North Johnson, El Cajon, CA 92020.
Telephone: +1 619 449 1570
Facsimile: +1 619 442 0481
Information: Frank G. Verbeke (President).

● Activities

● Offers factory completed or components for the BD-5 Experimental category aircraft, Globe Swift components, and air pressure jet helicopters, the Rotorair 2 being detailed below.

Alturair Rotorair 2

Role: Two-seat air-pressure helicopter, without need of a conventional transmission or tailrotor.

★ Aims

★ See diagram: Gas turbine engine *A* drives an air compressor *B* to produce compressed air. This air is ducted via a flexible pipe *C* into a rotor distribution hub *D*. Hollow rotor blades *E* and *F* direct this air to the fixed jet nozzles *G*. These nozzles are orientated tangentially to the rotor disc and expel the compressed air to produce blade rotation. Exhaust from the turbine is directed over the tailfin *H* to provide yaw and directional control.
Rotor system: All-metal hollow blades. Rotor hub is simple, as no transmission is required. A series of

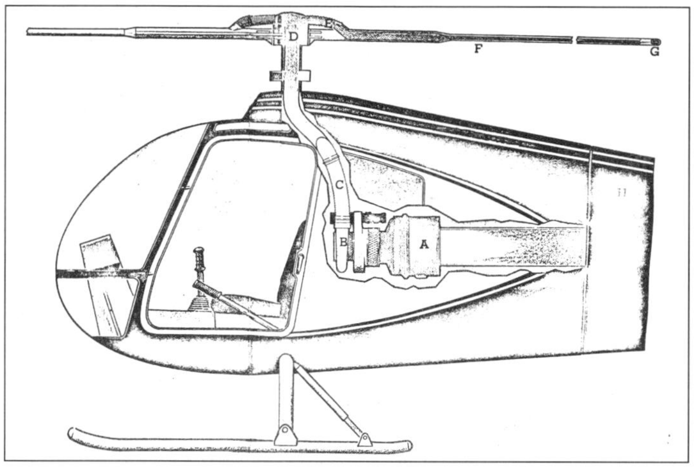

Alturair Rotorair 2 air pressure jet helicopter (courtesy Alturair)

torsion, tension straps unload all centrifugal stresses from the hub and there is no hinging of the blade roots.
Airframe materials: Lightweight glassfibre fuselage shell.
Engine: The gas turbine engine drives a load compressor directly. A load control valve is installed at the compressor intake for simple power control. Operation of the turbine is automatic from a single switch.
Engine rating: 250 shp (186.4 kW).
Fuel system: 227 litres.

Details for Rotorair z.

Principal dimensions:
Rotor diameter: 34 ft (10.36 m)
Airframe length: 10 ft (3.05 m)
Fuselage width: 4 ft (1.22 m)
Maximum height: 7 ft 6 ins (2.29 m)

Undercarriage:
Type: Fixed skids.
Skid track: 6 ft (1.83 m)

Weights:
Empty: 600 lb (272 kg)
Maximum take-off: 1,400 lb (635 kg)

Performance:
Maximum speed: 87 kts (100 mph) 161 km/h
Cruise speed: 74 kts (85 mph) 137 km/h
Maximum climb rate: 900 ft (274 m) per minute
Hovering ceiling: 6,000 ft (1,830 m)
Ceiling: 16,000 ft (4,875 m)
Range: 217 naut miles (250 miles) 402 km

American SportsCopter International Inc (USA)

Corporate address: 875 Middle Ground Blvd, Newport News, VA 23606.
Telephone: +1 804 873 4914
Facsimile: +1 804 873 3711

American SportsCopter UltraSport 254, 331 and 496

Role: Single-seat ultralight (UltraSport 254 and 331) and two-seat (UltraSport 496) Experimental category light helicopters.

★ Aims

★ Intended for FAA certification under the SportPlane category. Prior to certification, the helicopters are offered as kits. Also being marketed from 656 Jian Shing Road, Taichung, Taiwan (*telephone* +886 4 20 72199, *facsimile* +886 4 2072198).

▲ Development

▲ 1994. Several changes were introduced to the UltraSport prior to production, including deletion of the tail rotor ducted fan, extension of the tailboom and raising it by 6 ins (0.15 m), the tail rotor was moved aft and a new horizontal tail unit added to produce progressively higher download as forward speed increases, the Hirth 2703 was chosen as the standard engine, and new upgraded Thomas type couplings fitted at each end of the tail rotor drive shaft, which permit the tailboom to flex at designed locations.
Sales: Kit (meeting FAA 51% amateur built requirements) deliveries were scheduled to start in December 1995, with at least 10 per month thereafter

American SportsCopter UltraSport 496

planned. Kit price US$31,900. Quoted assembly time of under 60 working hours.
Rotor system: 2-blade, high inertia teetering main rotor, with composites blades. Blades fold. Suspended type cyclic stick.
Tail rotor characteristics: 2-blade, composites, no

DETAILS FOR ULTRASPORT 254, *WITH 496 IN ITALICS WHERE DIFFERENT.*

Principal dimensions:
Rotor diameter (main): 21 ft (6.4 m), *23 ft (7.01 m)*
Maximum length, rotor folded: 16 ft 8 ins (5.08 m), *17 ft 8 ins (5.38 m)*
Maximum height: 7 ft 6 ins (2.29 m)

Tail rotor:
Diameter: 2 ft 7 ins (0.79 m)

Undercarriage:
Type: Fixed twin skids
Skid track: 7 ft (2.13 m)

Weights:
Empty: 252 lb (114 kg), *395 lb (179 kg)*
Maximum normal take-off: 525 lb (239 kg), *875 lb (397 kg)*

Performance:
Never-exceed speed (VNE): 55 kts (63 mph) 102 km/h, *90 kts (104 mph) 167 km/h*
Maximum speed: *85 kts (98 mph) 158 km/h*
Cruise speed: 55 kts (63 mph) 102 km/h, *56 kts (65 mph) 105 km/h*
Maximum climb rate: 1,000 ft (305 m) per minute
IGE hovering ceiling: 10,800 ft (3,290 m), *the same*
OGE hovering ceiling: 7,000 ft (2,135 m), *the same*
Ceiling: 12,000 ft (3,660 m), *the same*
Range: 65 naut miles (75 miles) 121 km, *130 naut miles (150 miles) 241 km*
Duration: 1 hour 15 minutes, *2 hours*

longer a ducted fan, but still protected by a flat shroud to guard the tail rotor blades during autorotation or in extreme tail-low manoeuvres.
Airframe materials: Composites fuselage.
Engine: Göbler-Hirthmotoren Hirth 2703 piston engine for UltraSport 254 and 331, and F30 for 496.
Engine rating: 55 hp (41 kW) and 95 hp (71 kW) respectively.
Transmission rating: 65 hp (48.5 kW) main, and 15 hp (11.2 kW) spiral bevel tail. Main is dual stage planetary drive type, with closed loop lubrication and cooling, and with greater than 3:1 power weight ratio.
Fuel system: 19 litres for UltraSport 254, and 38 litres for the others.
Aircraft variants:
UltraSport 254 is the single-seat ultralight version.
UltraSport 331 is a single-seat growth version of 254, meeting FAA Experimental FAR Pt 21.191(g).
UltraSport 496 is the two seater.

Barnett Rotorcraft Co (USA)

Corporate address: 4307 Olivehurst Avenue, Olivehurst, CA 95961.
Telephone: +1 916 742 7416
Facsimile: +1 916 743 6866

Barnett J4B

Role: Single-seat homebuilt autogyro.
Sales: Plans and kits are available, the latter at US$6,500 (1994 cost), taking typically 300 working hours to assemble.
Rotor system: 2-blade, aluminium alloy.
Tail surfaces: Fin, large rudder and tailplane.
Airframe materials: Welded 4130 steel tube, glassfibre nacelle, and fabric covered tail surfaces.
Engine: Teledyne Continental A65 to O-200 piston engine, with a pusher propeller.
Engine rating: 65-100 hp (48.5-74.6 kW).
Fuel system: 51 litres.

DETAILS FOR J4B.

Principal dimensions:
Rotor diameter: 23 ft (7.01 m)
Airframe length: 12 ft 4 ins (3.76 m)
Maximum height: 7 ft 8 ins (2.34 m)

Main rotor:
Rotor disc: 416.6 sq ft (38.7 m²)

Weights:
Empty: 441 lb (200 kg)
Maximum take-off: 850 lb (386 kg)

Performance:
Maximum speed: 104 kts (120 mph) 193 km/h
Cruise speed: 84 kts (97 mph) 156 km/h
Take-off distance: 150 ft (46 m)
Landing distance: up to 20 ft (6 m)
Maximum climb rate: 1,500 ft (457 m) per minute
Ceiling: 12,000 ft (3,660 m), service
Range: 234 naut miles (270 miles) 434 km

Barnett J4B-2

Role: Two-seat homebuilt autogyro.
Sales: Plans and kits are available, the latter at US$7,500 (1994 cost), taking typically 300 working hours to assemble.
Rotor system: Similar to J4B.
Engine: Typically Teledyne Continental O-200 or Textron Lycoming O-360 piston engine.
Engine rating: 100-180 hp (74.6-134 kW).
Fuel system: 64 litres.

DETAILS FOR J4B-2.

Principal dimensions:
Rotor diameter: 25 ft 4 ins (7.72 m)
Airframe length: 13 ft 8 ins (4.17 m)
Maximum height: 8 ft 1 ins (2.46 m)

Main rotor:
Rotor disc: 505.4 sq ft (46.95 m²)

Weights:
Empty: 512 lb (232 kg)
Maximum take-off: 1,085 lb (492 kg)

Performance:
Maximum speed: 97 kts (112 mph) 180 km/h
Cruise speed: 81 kts (93 mph) 150 km/h
Take-off distance: 300 ft (91 m)
Landing distance: up to 20 ft (6 m)
Maximum climb rate: 500 ft (152 m) per minute
Ceiling: 8,000 ft (2,440 m), service
Range: 173 naut miles (199 miles) 320 km

Bell Helicopter Textron Inc (USA)

Corporate address: PO Box 482, Fort Worth, TX 76101.
Telephone: +1 817 280 4686
Facsimile: +1 817 280 2330
Founded: 1935 as Bell Aircraft Corporation, with Bell Helicopter Company becoming an operating branch of Textron Inc in 1960 and a fully-absorbed subsidiary on 3 January 1982.
Employees: About 7,400 worldwide.
Information: Carl Harris (Director of Public Affairs), or Bob Leder (*telephone* +1 817 280 8415). Also *telephone* +1 817 280 3182 for international marketing, and +1 817 280 3263 for military business development.

● Activities

● More than 33,000 helicopters built over nearly 50 years. Bell Helicopter Textron moved its assembly line for commercial helicopters to Canada in 1986, where a production facility had been completed the previous year as a division of Textron Canada Ltd. Details of the JetRanger III, LongRanger IV, TwinRanger, 212, 230, 407, 412EP and 430 can, therefore, be found under Canada, including military versions of these helicopters such as the TH-67 Creek trainer. In addition, IPTN of Indonesia, Agusta of Italy and Fuji of Japan produce licence-built variants of Bell helicopters (which see).
● Bell is teamed with Boeing to develop and produce the V-22 Osprey tilt-rotor for US military service.

Bell UH-1HP Huey II

First flight: 1992.
Role: Upgrade of the UH-1.

★ Aims

★ Joint modernization programme between Bell and AlliedSignal to extend the life of the UH-1H for service into the next century. Bogan Aerotech is responsible for bringing value added enhancements to the programme.
★ Engine and airframe upgrade package offered as parts kits to military and civil operators, with the option of the operator undertaking the work.
★ Huey II has the internal payload increased by 642 lb (291 kg), and has good hot day/high altitude performance.
★ Upgraded engine (see Engine), and upgraded transmission, gearbox, rotor blades, tailboom and drive system to handle the additional 400 shp (298 kW) of power.
Sales: Interest includes possible upgrade of about 130 US Army National Guard UH-1s (though this might not include the new engine), and other operators worldwide including German Police UH-1Ds (13 initially, used for border patrol and EMS).
Standard equipment: Breeze-Eastern hoist for rescue capability.
Optional equipment: Includes armoured crew seats and IR suppressor.
Rotor system: Upgrades include use of Bell 212 blades. See diagram. Reports suggest USMC UH-1Hs might receive AH-1W+4 four-blade rotors.
Engine: AlliedSignal T53-L-703 turboshaft. Heli-Conversions particle separator.
Engine rating: 1,800 shp (1,342 kW) military for 30 minutes, 1,500 shp (1,118 kW) normal.
Transmission rating: 1,290 shp (962 kW) for 5 minutes, 1,134 shp (846 kW) maximum continuous.

Details for Huey II.

Principal dimensions:
Rotor diameter (main): 48 ft (14.63 m)
Maximum length, rotors turning: 56 ft 0.5 ins (17.1 m)
Fuselage length: 44 ft 10 ins (13.67 m), including tail rotor
Maximum height: 15 ft 1 ins (4.6 m)

Weights:
Empty: 5,440 lb (2,468 kg)
Maximum take-off: 10,500 lb (4,762 kg) with internal payload, or 11,200 lb (5,080 kg) with external payload
Useful load: 5,060 lb (2,295 kg)

Performance:
Never-exceed speed (VNE): 112 kts (129 mph) 207 km/h at 9,500 lb (4,309 kg) gross weight, or 106 kts (122 mph) 196 km/h at 10,500 lb (4,762 kg)
Average cruise speed: 109 kts (126 mph) 202 km/h
Maximum climb rate: 1,690 ft (515 m) per minute at 10,500 lb (4,762 kg), or 2,070 ft (631 m) per minute at 9,500 lb (4,309 kg), both at sea level static
Vertical climb rate: 460 ft (140 m) per minute at 10,500 lb (4,762 kg), 1,190 ft (363 m) per minute at 9,500 lb (4,309 kg), both at sea level static
OGE hovering ceiling: 5,600 ft (1,707 m) ISA and 1,200 ft (366 m) at 35° C at 10,500 lb (4,762 kg), or 10,700 ft (3,260 m) ISA and 3,900 ft (1,189 m) at 35°C at 9,500 lb (4,309 kg)
Ceiling: 16,100 ft (4,910 m) at 10,500 lb (4,762 kg), 19,000 ft (5,790 m) at 9,500 lb (4,309 kg)
Operational radius: 102 naut miles (117 miles) 189 km at sea level static, 30 minutes reserve at maximum endurance speed, at 10,500 lb (4,762 kg).
Duration: 2.8 hours

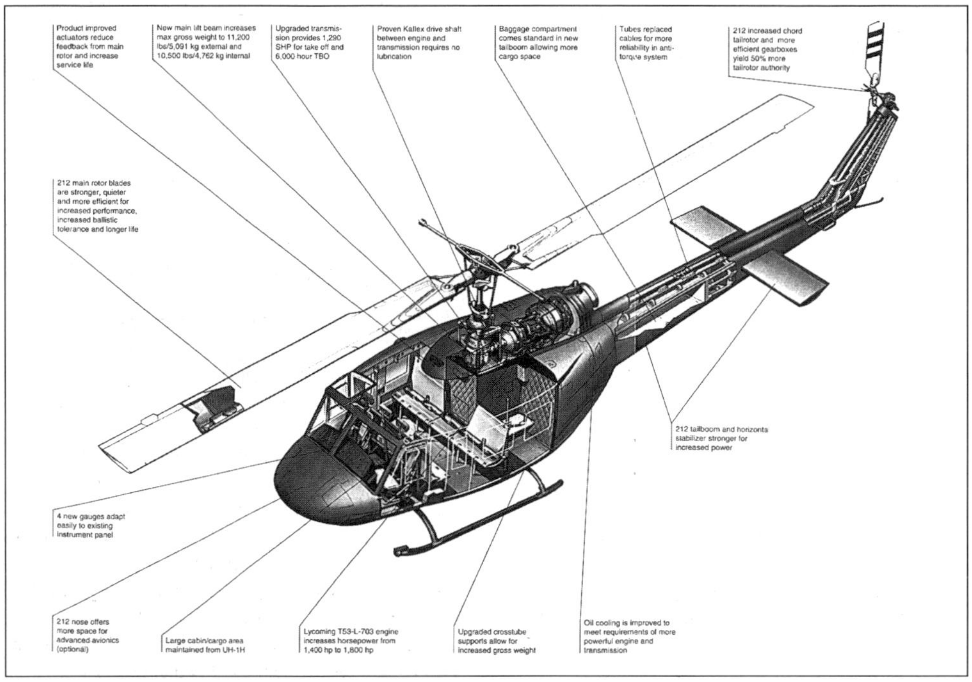

Bell Huey II upgrade features (courtesy Bell Helicopter Textron)

Bell Huey II upgrade of the UH-1

Fuel system: 1,435 lb (651 kg).
Flight avionics/instrumentation: Rockwell Collins suite. Night vision capability is enhanced with Westinghouse FLIR and a Phaostron NVG compatible cockpit. Avionics Specialties Inc turbine monitoring system and Smiths liquid crystal fuel quantity indication system.

Bell AH-1F HueyCobra

Details for AH-1F.

Principal dimensions:
Rotor diameter (main): 44 ft (13.41 m)
Maximum length, rotors turning: 53 ft 1 ins (16.18 m)
Maximum height: 13 ft 5 ins (4.09 m) to above rotor head
Wing span: 10 ft 9 ins (3.28 m)

Main rotor:
Rotor disc: 1,520.2 sq ft (141.23 m^2)

Tail rotor:
Diameter: 8 ft 6 ins (2.59 m)

Undercarriage:
Type: Twin fixed skids
Skid track: 7 ft (2.13 m)

Weights:
Empty: 6,600 lb (2,993 kg)
Maximum take-off and landing: 10,000 lb (4,536 kg)

Performance:
Maximum speed: 122 kts (141 mph) 227 km/h
Maximum climb rate: 1,620 ft (494 m) per minute
Ceiling: 12,200 ft (3,718 m), HIGE and service
G limits: +2.5, –0.5
Range: 273 naut miles (315 miles) 507 km

Note: Manufacture of new AH-1Fs is to restart through licence production in Romania (see Sales), whilst Fuji of Japan produces the helicopter as the AH-1S. However, all US production has ended, with Bell now concentrating on twin-engined models. The description below is, therefore, brief.
First flight: 7 September 1965 as the prototype of the original AH-1G.
Role: Attack, anti-armour, fire support, fire suppression, and heliborne escort.
Sales: Currently used by the US Army (with other models), Israel (with other models), Japan (still under construction as the Fuji-built AH-1S), Jordan, South Korea, Pakistan and Thailand. In addition, in 1995 an agreement was signed with Romania for the licence production of 96 by IAR at Brasov, with Turbomecanica building the dynamics, for delivery from 1999. Various upgrading programmes for existing helicopters have taken place, including 52 US Army Bell AH-1F HueyCobras having their night combat capability improved with the addition of Hughes Cobra-NITE (or C-NITE) targeting systems installed at Camp Humphries in South Korea (C-NITE has also been adopted by Japan, South Korea, Pakistan and the US Army National Guard for their AH-1F/S types, while Israel has a Tamam Precision Instruments Industries-produced thermal imaging system). C-NITE allows TOW missiles to be launched at night, in adverse weather or through smoke, haze and dust. Other upgrades have taken place under the US Army Cobra Fleet Life Extension and other programmes, but all single-engine HueyCobra production by Bell in the USA has ended.

Bell AH-1F HueyCobra in US service

Crew: 2, in tandem stepped cockpits. Flat-plate anti-glint glazing. Jettisonable doors and windows for emergency escape.
Rotor system: 2-blade, composite, with swept tips.
Tail rotor characteristics: 2-blade, to starboard.
Safety features: Include blade and airframe tolerance to 23-mm strikes.
Engine: AlliedSignal T53-L-703 turboshaft.
Engine rating: 1,800 shp (1,342 kW).
Fuel system: 980 litres.
Hydraulic system: 2 systems, each 1,500 psi.
Flight avionics/instrumentation: Includes AN/ASN-128 Doppler, HSI, digital fire control computer, laser rangefinder, automatic target tracker, pilot's Kaiser HUD, IFF, Hughes LAAT stabilized sighting system, Cobra-NITE (or C-NITE) targeting systems, and much more.
Self-protection systems: AN/ALQ-144 IR jammer, radar warning, chaff/flare dispensers, and IR reflective paint.
Fixed guns: General Electric Universal Turret System, with M-197 20-mm 3-barrel Gatling type cannon for close range of up to 1.08 naut miles (1.25 miles) 2 km.
Ammunition: 750 rounds.
Number of weapon pylons: 4, under the stub wings.
Expendable weapons and equipment:
8 TOW anti-armour missiles under outer pylons, and rockets or up to 4 AAMs on the inner pylons.

Bell AH-1W SuperCobra and AH-1W+4

DETAILS FOR AH-1W.

Principal dimensions:
Rotor diameter (main): 48 ft (14.63 m)
Maximum length, rotors turning: 58 ft (17.68 m)
Fuselage length: 45 ft 6 ins (13.87 m)
Maximum height: 14 ft 2 ins (4.31 m)
Wing span: 10 ft 9 ins (3.28 m)

Main rotor:
Aerofoil section: Modified Wortmann FX-083
Blade chord: 2 ft 9 ins (0.84 m)
Blade area: each 66 sq ft (6.13 m^2)
Rotor disc: 1,809.7 sq ft (168.1 m^2)
Rpm: 311

Tail rotor:
Diameter: 9 ft 9 ins (2.97 m)
Rpm: 1,460

Undercarriage:
Type: Fixed twin skids. Provision for ground handling wheels
Skid track: 7 ft 4 ins (2.24 m)

Weights:
Empty: 10,265 lb (4,656 kg)
Maximum take-off: 14,750 lb (6,690 kg)
Useful load: 4,550 lb (2,064 kg)
Payload: 1,661 lb (753 kg) of stores

Performance:
Maximum speed: 170 kts (196 mph) 315 km/h
Cruise speed: 137 kts (158 mph) 254 km/h
Vertical climb rate: 645 ft (196 m) per minute in air-to-air configuration, mid-mission weight, intermediate rated power
Climb rate, OEI: 800 ft (244 m) with AAMs, ISA
OGE hovering ceiling: 3,000 ft (914 m) with 4 TOW and 4 Hellfire missiles, full ammunition and rockets
Ceiling: 14,750 ft (4,500 m), HIGE and service
G limits: +2.5, –0.5
Range: 317 naut miles (365 miles) 587 km

Details: For AH-1W, except under Aircraft variants.
Role: Attack, anti-armour, fire support, fire suppression, and heliborne escort.
Sales: 145 new and earlier AH-1T SeaCobra conversions were operated by the US Marine Corps by late 1994, when an additional 85 were planned at a rate of 12 per year. Other operators are Taiwan (42 firm/options) and Turkey (10). During Operation Desert Storm, US Marine Corps AH-1Ws accounted for 97 tanks, 104 armoured vehicles, 16 bunkers, and 2 anti-aircraft artillery sites, achieving a 92% mission readiness rate under conditions that reached 57-63° C.
Crew: 2, in tandem stepped and armoured cockpits. Dual controls.
Rotor system: 2-blade main rotor, with aluminium alloy blades, and elastomeric and Teflon coated bearings. Rotor brake. A four-blade rotor without hinges and of bearingless type, developed for the AH-1W+4 and offered as an option for Venom, may be fitted to existing USMC AH-1Ws. It has composite blades and 2 composite yokes, and possesses a ballistic tolerance to hits from 23-mm shells.
Tail rotor characteristics: 2-blade, metal.
Wing surfaces: Similar style to HueyCobra, of NACA 0030/0024 aerofoil section.
Flight control system: Hydraulic.
Fuselage: Ultra-slim fuselage cross-section feature of all HueyCobra/SuperCobra types.
Airframe materials: Metal.
Engines: 2 General Electric T700-GE-401 turboshafts.
Engine rating: Each 1,626 shp (1,212 kW) take off.
Transmission rating: 2,032 shp (1,515 kW) take-off, 1,725 shp (1,286 kW) maximum continuous.
Fuel system: 1,161 litres, usable. 295 or 379 litre auxiliary fuel tanks carried under the stub wings. System survives 23-mm shell hits.
Electrical system: 115 volt AC supply comprises principal single-phase and back-up 3-phase, at 400 Hz, plus a single-phase for AAMs. 3 inverters. 28 volt DC supply via 2 generators and 2 x 24 volt batteries.
Hydraulic system: 3 systems, each 3,000 psi.
Flight avionics/instrumentation: Tamam Precision Instruments Industries night targeting system (NTS), first delivered on a US Marine Corps AH-1W in June 1994, integrates the TOW/Hellfire missile systems with FLIR, laser rangefinder/designator, automatic target tracker, TV and video recorder. With NTS, SuperCobra can detect, acquire, track, range, designate and attack targets at night, in adverse weather or limited visibility; NTS can also designate targets for all NATO aircraft that use laser-guided weapons. Kaiser HUD. Helmet-mounted display integrates the NVGs with targeting and navigation cues and also the helmet sight system to control the turret. ADF, Tacan, radar beacon system, radar altimeter, GPS, IFF and much more. For precise target location, the navigation system also includes Teledyne AN/APN-217 Doppler. Airborne Target Handover System can work in conjunction with other helicopters and aeroplanes. Multi-function displays, mission data loader, and onboard systems monitoring and diagnostics; see Integrated Weapon System under Aircraft variants.

Bell AH-1W SuperCobra

Self-protection systems: Dual radar warning, laser warning, missile warning, IR jammers, dual chaff/flare dispensers, and IR reflective paint.
Fixed guns: General Electric Universal Turret System with 110° azimuth, 18° elevation and 50° depressed angle of tracking, with M-197 20-mm 3-barrel Gatling type cannon for close range of up to 1.08 naut miles (1.25 miles) 2 km. Fired by either crew member, able to be slaved to their helmet-mounted sights. Rate of fire 675 rounds per minute.
Ammunition: 750 rounds of M-50 or improved 20 mm HEI ammunition.
Number of weapon pylons: 2 under each stub wing, with 3 planned for new wings (as for Venom). AN/ALE-39 chaff dispenser above each wing.
Expendable weapons and equipment: Dual anti-armour capability, with up to 8 TOW II or Hellfire missiles. Other store options/additions include 2.75-in rockets with submunition warheads or 5-in Zuni rockets, CBU-55B fuel air bombs, GPU-2A 20-mm gun pods, M-188 smoke grenade dispenser, SUU-44 flare dispenser, 295 or 378 litre auxiliary fuel tanks, or Maverick air-to-ground, 2 x AIM-9L Sidewinder air-to-air and 2 x AGM-122A Sidearm anti-radiation missiles.
Aircraft variants:
AH-1W is the standard in-service version, as described.
AH-1W+4 is the designation of SuperCobra after being fitted with a performance-enhancing 4-blade main rotor, offering improved manoeuvrability and agility, reduced vulnerability, greater payload, greater reliability through simplicity of design, 70% reduction in rotor vibration, and easier maintenance. Revised tail stabilizer with endplates, moved aft. Prototype has been tested. Offers increases in empty and take-off weights to 10,400 lb (4,717 kg) and 16,800 lb (7,620 kg) respectively, 3,914 lb (1,775 kg) stores load, maximum and cruise speeds of 210 kts (242 mph) 389 km/h and 148 kts (170 mph) 274 km/h respectively, G limit of +3.2, and vertical climb rate of 1,740 ft (530 m) per minute. See Rotor system.

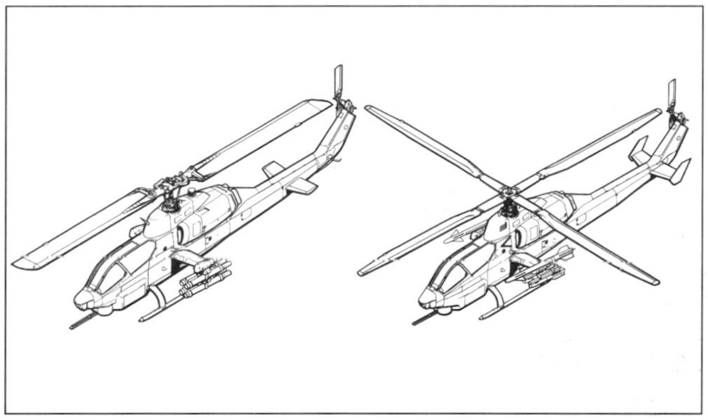

Bell AH-1W (left) and AH-1W+4 (right) (courtesy Bell Helicopter Textron)

Integrated Weapon System "glass cockpit" upgrade for USMC AH-1Ws will include an integrated weapon management system, advanced mission computer, digital moving map display, colour multi-function displays, hands on throttle/collective/cyclic (HOTCC), and more. 7 competing teams (Boeing withdrew in 1994), with the winner expected to be declared in 1995. Redeliveries to begin before the end of the decade.
Venom was the version of SuperCobra offered to the British Army Air Corps, with GEC advanced fully-integrated digital cockpit. Not selected.

Bell OH-58D Kiowa Warrior

Role: Armed reconnaissance and "hunter-killer" attack, but remaining capable of troop or cargo transport and medevac.

★ Aims

★ OH-58D Kiowa programme was initiated as an upgrade of existing US Army OH-58A Kiowas. Modification of OH-58Ds to armed Kiowa Warrior configuration began in 1987, including some 15 designated "Prime Chance" and shipped to the Persian Gulf for operations from US Navy vessels, where they accumulated about 7,500 hours NVG flight time. Later, 115 OH-58Ds took part in Desert Shield/Storm, flying nearly 9,000 hours and achieving a 92% full mission capability. All Kiowas are becoming armed Kiowa Warriors.

▲ Development

▲ 21 September 1981. Bell was awarded a US Army helicopter improvement (AHIP) contract, to upgrade OH-58As to OH-58D standard, with redeliveries from

Details for Oh-58D.

Principal dimensions:
Rotor diameter (main): 35 ft (10.67 m)
Maximum length, rotors turning: 42 ft 2 ins (12.85 m)
Fuselage length: 33 ft (10.06 m)
Width, blades folded: 6 ft 5.5 ins (1.97 m)
Maximum height: 12 ft 11 ins (3.94 m), including MMS

Main rotor:
Blade chord: 9.5 ins (0.24 m)
Blade area: each 14.83 sq ft (1.38 m^2)
Rotor disc: 962 sq ft (89.37 m^2)
Rpm: 395

Tail rotor:
Diameter: 5 ft 5 ins (1.65 m)
Rpm: 2,381

Undercarriage:
Type: Twin fixed skids
Skid track: 7 ft 6 ins (2.29 m)

Weights:
Empty: 3,289 lb (1,492 kg)
Maximum take-off: 5,500 lb (2,495 kg)
Payload: 2,000 lb (907 kg) sling load

Performance:
Maximum speed: 128 kts (147 mph) 236 km/h
Cruise speed: 114 kts (131 mph) 211 km/h
Maximum climb rate: 1,600 ft (488 m) per minute, at sea level, ISA
IGE hovering ceiling: 10,000 ft (3,050 m), ISA
OGE hovering ceiling: 6,900 ft (2,100 m), ISA
Ceiling: 15,000 ft (4,570 m), service
Range: 223 naut miles (257 miles) 414 km

Bell OH-58D Kiowa Warrior

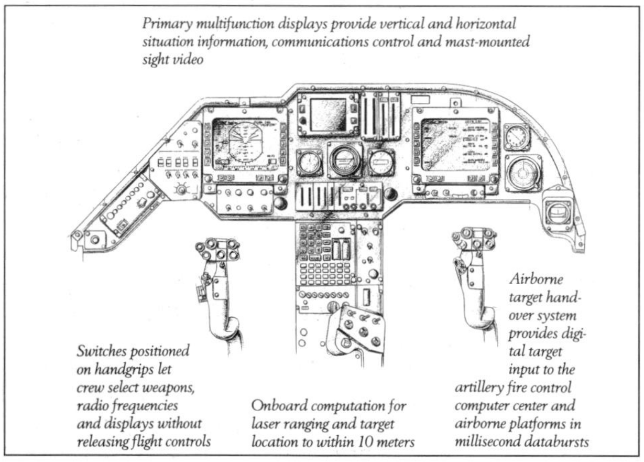
Primary multifunction displays provide vertical and horizontal situation information, communications control and mast-mounted sight video
Switches positioned on handgrips let crew select weapons, radio frequencies and displays without releasing flight controls
Onboard computation for laser ranging and target location to within 10 meters
Airborne target hand-over system provides digital target input to the artillery fire control computer center and airborne platforms in millisecond databursts

Bell OH-58D advanced cockpit (courtesy Bell Helicopter Textron)

1985. Subsequent further requirements raised the OH-58D Kiowa specification to armed Kiowa Warrior standard.

Sales: 308 OH-58Ds had been delivered at the time of writing, of 366 contracted modifications, the latter including 15 under FY1994 and 24 under FY1995 funding.

Crew/passengers: 2. Main cabin can accommodate 6 equipped troops, or 6 litters for medevac (when radius is 50 naut miles).
Freight, external: Sling load on a 2,000 lb (907 kg) capacity cargo hook.
Rotor system: 4-blade main rotor, with elastomeric bearings, composites yokes and all-composites blades, and able to survive hits from 0.50-in shells. Rotor folding (MMS detachment) for fast air deployment by transport aircraft, taking 2 persons 10 minutes or 4 persons 7 minutes (2 helicopters can be deployed in a C-130 Hercules).
Tail rotor characteristics: Two blade, on port side of fin.
Flight control system: Hydraulic.
Engine: Allison 250-C30R or X turboshaft.
Engine rating: 650 shp (484.7 kW).
Transmission rating: 637 shp (475 kW).
Fuel system: 424 litres.
Electrical system: AC supply comprises the main 3-phase 120/208 volt, 400 Hz, alternator. 28 volt DC supply via the AC supply using a transformer rectifier. Stand-by single-phase 115 volt, 400 Hz AC inverter, and 20 volt DC starter-generator.
Hydraulic system: 2 systems, each 1,000 psi.
Flight avionics/instrumentation: McDonnell Douglas/Northrop Mast-Mounted Sight (MMS) as a fully-integrated multi-sensor equipment package. It includes a high-resolution and low-light level TV camera, IR thermal imaging sensor for navigation/target acquisition/designation at night or under obscured conditions, laser rangefinder/designator for precise target location/guidance of Hellfire missiles and Copperhead artillery rounds or hand-off to Cobra for TOW engagement, and boresight assembly for quick in-flight sensor alignment. These functions provide the OH-58D with day/night, adverse weather and extended stand-off range reconnaissance, surveillance, intelligence gathering, and threat and target damage assessment capabilities. The MMS has a quick-release capability. Other OH-58D avionics in the "all glass cockpit" with multi-function displays include (from 1991 redeliveries) video recorder for storing TV and IR imagery from the mission and with cockpit playback capability, data transfer system with data-loading module for pre-mission storing of navigation waypoints and radio frequencies, night vision goggle (NVG) flight reference symbology display, Have-Quick UHF and SINCGARS FM anti-jam radios, and displays to align and fire weapons. AN/ASN-157 Doppler strapdown INS. GPS. Hands on cyclic and collective controls. 3-axis stability and control augmentation system, with AHRS.
Self-protection systems: Latest standard configuration has IR seeker jammer, pulse and CW radar warning receivers, laser warning detector, and inherent IR suppression.
Number of weapon pylons: 2 Universal weapons pylons.
Expendable weapons and equipment: When armed, can carry 4 Hellfiire anti-armour missiles, 4 Stinger AAMs, 2 x 7-round Hydra 70 rocket pods, 2 x 0.5-in machine-guns, or a mix.

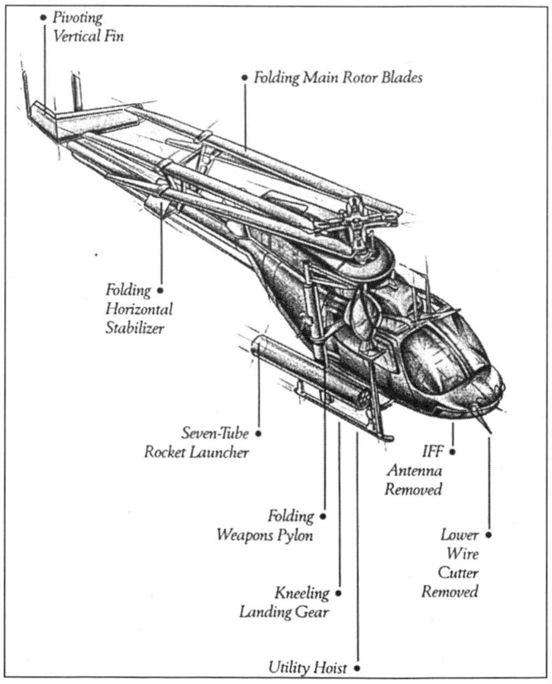

Bell OH-58D prepared for air transportability (courtesy Bell Helicopter Textron)

Bell Helicopter Textron Inc and The Boeing Company – Helicopters Division (USA)

Corporate addresses: See Combat section for company details.

Bell Boeing V-22 Osprey

First flight: 19 March 1989 for AC No 1, 9 August 1989 for AC No 2, 6 May 1990 for AC No 3, 21 December 1989 for AC No 4 (lost on 20 July 1992), and 11 June 1991 for AC No 5.
Role: Vertical-lift tilt-rotor transport and multi-purpose aircraft, combining the flying attributes of a helicopter and aeroplane.

★ Aims

★ Original programme requirements were for 552 MV-22As for the US Marine Corps for combat assault and assault support; 50 HV-22As for the US Navy for combat SAR, special warfare and logistics support; 80 CV-22As for the US Air Force for long-range special operations; and 231 MV-22As for the US Army for medevac, combat support and special operations.

▲ Development

▲ December 1981. Development initiated by the US Department of Defense, with Bell and Boeing receiving a preliminary design contract in April 1983 under the joint services tiltrotor or JVX programme.
▲ 6 May 1990. First cross-country flight by AC No 2, covering 1,210 naut miles (1,393 miles) 2,241 km between Dallas and Wilmington (Del).
▲ 4-7 December 1990. AC Nos 3 and 4 undertook the first sea trials on board USS *Wasp*.
▲ 7 June 1992. Completion of 4 months of climatic trials, subjecting AC No 4 to weather extremes that included temperatures from –54° to +49° C.
▲ December 1996. First flight of the first of 4 EMD production-representative aircraft, construction having begun in 1994. 2 existing ESD aircraft will be modified

Bell Boeing V-22 Osprey AC No 2

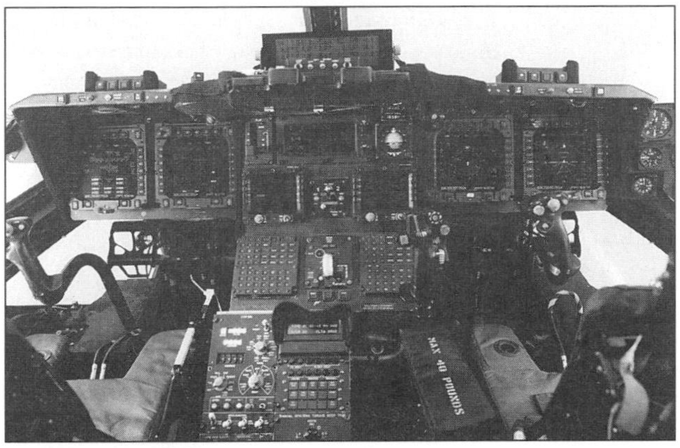

Bell Boeing V-22 Osprey flight deck

to support flight testing of EMDs, while the remaining 2 will be used as mockups and ground demonstrators. ▲ 2001. Anticipated initial operational capability with MV-22A.

Sales: Current DoD procurement stands at 425 USMC MV-22As, 48 USN HV-22As and 50 USAF CV-22As, though the US Army also requires 231 MV-22As. US$497 million was included in the FY1995 DoD defence budget to continue the engineering and manufacturing development programme. Japan might become the first export customer, with a projected requirement for 4 SAR-equipped V-22s for the JMSDF.

Crew/passengers: 2 flight crew. 24 troops or 12 litters plus attendants, depending on role. Crashworthy seats.

Cockpit/cabin: Pressurized to permit operation in NBC contaminated areas.

Freight, external: 10,000 lb (4,536 kg) on single cargo hook, 15,000 lb (6,804 kg) on dual hooks.

Cabin access: Ramp/door under the upswept rear fuselage. Starboard-side fuselage door.

Rotor system: 2 x 3-blade high-twist proprotors mounted with engines and transmissions at the tips of the wings, the proprotors turning in opposite directions (direction of rotation prevents impact of disintegrating parts in an accident from striking the cockpit/cabin). Proprotor tip speed 661.9 ft (201.75 m) per second. Complete propulsion assemblies tilt from horizontal to vertical attitude (through 90° plus a further 7° 30′ aft rotation) for vertical, transitional and horizontal flight. Cyclic control swashplates are controlled asymmetrically for yaw and symmetrically for forward/rearward flight in hovering mode, making sideways flight possible. Elastomeric bearings. Proprotors are interconnected by shafts through the wing, to allow both to function in the event of an engine failure. Blades of graphite/glassfibre construction. Automatic, powered blade folding and blade de-icing.

Wing/tail surfaces: High-mounted and slightly swept-forward wings, with ailerons and single-slotted flaperons that droop during hovering mode. Wings designed to separate from the fuselage under extreme crash loads, so that the inertia of the engines and transmissions are instantly relieved. Twin fin/rudder tail unit, with elevator.

Flight control system: Triple computer and MIL-STD-1553B databus-controlled digital fly-by-wire system (triple redundant), with triple self-monitored primary and automatic processors. Shielded from EMI, EMP and directed energy weapons. Automatic flight envelope protection features.

Airframe materials: About three-fifths composite materials, principally graphite/epoxy, with the remainder metal.

Safety features: All critical systems are triple redundant and separated, some designed to withstand ballistic impact or are armour protected. Extensive built-in fire protection, and nitrogen inerting to prevent explosion (see Fuel system). Forward fuselage constructed to preclude crumpling into the cockpit or digging into the earth in an accident.

Engines: 2 Allison T406-AD-400 turboshafts. APU. Spraymat type inlet ice protection.

Engine rating: Each 6,150 shp (4,586 kW).

Transmission rating: 4,570 shp (3,408 kW) take-off for MV-22A and 4,970 shp (3,706 kW) for HV-22A/CV-22A. 5,920 shp (4,414 kW) emergency OEI.

Fuel system: 4,649 litres in the sponsons and 2,979 litres in the wings. 9,221 litres of auxiliary fuel for self deployment. OBIGGS for tanks.

Flight refuelling probe: Fixed probe in the starboard side of the nose.

Electrical system: AC supply via 2 x 40 kVA generators. DC supply via 50/80 kVA variable-frequency generators and rectifiers. 15 amp-hour lead-acid battery.

Hydraulic system: 2 principal and 1 back-up systems, each 5,000 psi.

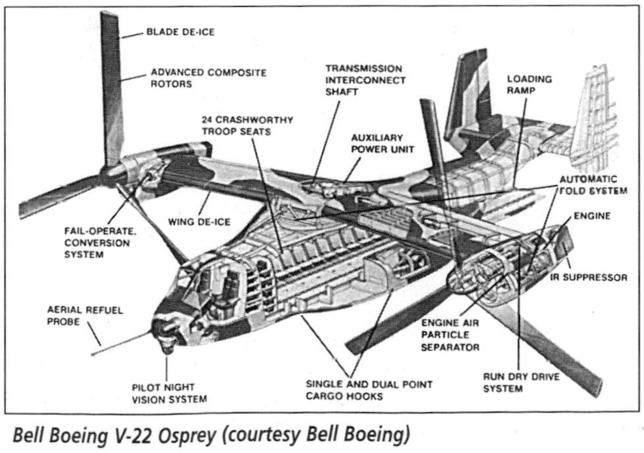

Bell Boeing V-22 Osprey (courtesy Bell Boeing)

Braking system: Multi-disc carbon.

Oxygen system: On-board oxygen generating system.

Radar: Texas Instruments AN/APQ-174 in offset nose radome.

Flight avionics/instrumentation: Advanced digital cockpit, with 6-screen EFIS. 2 mission computers, AHRS, VOR/ILS, Tacan, digital moving map, radar altimeter and more. Pilot night vision and integrated helmet display systems. FLIR for CV-22A and MV-22A.

Self-protection systems: IR and radar warning receivers, missile threat detectors, and chaff/flare dispensers. Up to 75% lower acoustic signature than a helicopter.

DETAILS FOR V-22.

Principal dimensions:
Proprotor diameter: Each 38 ft (11.58 m)
Maximum length, proprotors turning: 83 ft 10 ins (25.55 m)
Fuselage length: 57 ft 4 ins (17.48 m), excluding nose probe
Fuselage length stowed, wings fore and aft: 62 ft 7 ins (19.08 m)
Width, proprotors turning: 84 ft 7 ins (25.78 m)
Width, blades folded: 18 ft 5 ins (5.61 m)
Maximum height: 21 ft 9 ins (6.63 m), nacelles vertical
Height to top of fins: 17 ft 8 ins (5.38 m)
Height when stowed: 17 ft 11 ins (5.46 m)

Cabin:
Length: 24 ft 2 ins (7.37 m)
Width: 5 ft 11 ins (1.8 m)
Height: 6 ft (1.83 m)
Volume: 858 cu ft (24.3 m^3) usable

Main rotor:
Blade chord: 2 ft 11.5 ins (0.9 m) root, 1 ft 10 ins (0.56 m) tip
Blade area: 261.52 sq ft (24.3 m^2)
Rotor disc: 2,268 sq ft (210.7 m^2)

Undercarriage:
Type: Retractable, with steerable nosewheels. Twin wheels on each unit. Maximum 14.7 ft (4.5 m) per second impact
Wheel base: 21 ft 7.5 ins (6.59 m)
Wheel track: 15 ft 2.6 ins (4.63 m) over outer wheels

Weights:
Empty: 33,140 lb (15,032 kg)
Maximum take-off: 47,500 lb (21,545 kg) for vertical take-off, 55,000 lb (24,948 kg) STOL, and 60,500 lb (27,442 kg) self-deployment
Payload: 20,000 lb (9,072 kg) internal (see Freight, external)

Performance:
Maximum speed: 275 kts (317 mph) 510 km/h in horizontal flight at sea level or 313 kts (361 mph) 581 km/h at best height, and 100 kts (115 mph) 185 km/h in helicopter attitude at sea level
Maximum climb rate: 2,320 ft (707 m) per minute
Vertical climb rate: 1,090 ft (332 m) per minute
OGE hovering ceiling: 14,200 ft (4,328 m)
Ceiling: 26,000 ft (7,925 m), service
Ceiling, OEI: 11,300 ft (3,444 m)
Range: 515 naut miles (593 miles) 954 km, amphibious assault
Self-deployment range: 2,100 naut miles (2,418 miles) 3,892 km

Aircraft variants:

CV-22A for long-range special operations (LRSOF) with the US Air Force.

HV-22A for combat SAR, special warfare and logistics support with the US Navy.

MV-22A for combat assault and assault support with the US Marine Corps, and medevac, combat support and special operations with the US Army.

Other possible roles include ASW with the US Navy, flight refuelling tanker and possessing the ability to hover over a supply ship to replenish for further operations, airborne early warning with an over-fuselage saucer radome, and commercial operations into airports and vertiports.

The Boeing Company – Helicopters Division (USA)

Corporate address: See Combat section for company details.

● Activities

• In addition to the Chinook programme (detailed next), Boeing collaborates with Bell Helicopter Textron on the V-22 Osprey, and with Sikorsky on the RAH-66 Comanche.

• Factory activities also include production of composite and composite/aluminium wing sub-assemblies for Boeing 737, 747, 757 and 767 transports, and the design and production of fixed leading-edges for the 777.

• In April 1992 Boeing received a contract for 242 H-46 Sea Knight night-vision goggle kits, followed in December by a contract for 442 engine condition control system kits, all delivered by Spring 1994. Additionally, on 29 July 1992 Boeing received a contract to design, test, verify and validate flight test improved dynamic components for the H-46. In April 1993, it received a contract for 114 dynamic component upgrade production kits, now increased to 298, for completion by 1998. These upgrades followed earlier increased fuel capacity and emergency flotation kits.

Boeing CH-46E Sea Knight (courtesy Boeing)

Boeing H-47 Chinook

First flight: 21 September 1961 (YHC-1B/YCH-47A prototype).
Role: Heavy-lift transport helicopter, primarily for the movement of troops, artillery, ammunition, fuel, water, barrier materials, equipment and supplies on the battlefield, with secondary medevac, aircraft recovery, firefighting, paratroop drop, heavy construction, civil development, SAR and disaster relief.
Sales/users: Boeing-produced military Chinooks operate with the US Army, US Army National Guard, US Army Reserve and 11 other nations. Others built by Agusta in Italy and Kawasaki in Japan operate with 7 nations. A further 13 Chinooks went to commercial operators. Current CH-47Ds and MH-47Es with US forces were produced by upgrade of earlier versions, first flown on 11 May 1979 and first delivered to the 101st Airborne Division at Fort Campbell, Ky, on 28 February 1983, with IOC by the 159th Aviation Assault Battalion on 28 February 1984. All US CH-47D/MH-47Es had been delivered by November 1995, totalling 481.
Details: Principally CH-47D, except as indicated.
Crew/passengers: 2 pilots plus provision for a combat commander. 33 to 55 troops, or 24 litters and 2 attendants.
Freight, internal: Weapon systems, freight or vehicles instead of troops.
Freight, external: Forward and aft cargo hooks, each 17,000 lb (7,711 kg) capacity, and centre hook of 26,000 lb (11,793 kg) capacity.
Cabin access: Rear ramp/door, 6 ft 6 ins high x 7 ft 7 ins wide (1.98 m x 2.31 m). Door can be open in flight or

DETAILS FOR CH-47D, *WITH MH-47E IN ITALICS.*

Principal dimensions:
Rotor diameter: Each 60 ft (18.29 m)
Maximum length, rotors turning: 99 ft (30.18 m)
Fuselage length: 51 ft (15.54 m), *52 ft 1 ins (15.88 m) plus 16 ft 6 ins (5.03 m) for the refuelling probe*
Width, blades folded: 12 ft 5 ins (3.78 m)
Maximum height: 18 ft 11.5 ins (5.78 m) to top of aft hub

Cabin:
Length: 30 ft 6 ins (9.3 m)
Width: 7 ft 6 ins (2.29 m)
Height: 6 ft 6 ins (1.98 m)
Volume: 1,474 cu ft (41.74 m^3)

Main rotor:
Aerofoil section: VR7/8
Blade chord: 2 ft 8 ins (0.81 m)
Blade area: each 80 sq ft (7.43 m^2)
Rotor disc: each 2,827.5 sq ft (262.68 m^2)
Rpm: 225

Undercarriage
Type: Fixed, with 4 units, forward units having twin wheels. Castering rear wheels, the starboard steerable. Fuselage inclined upwards by 1.56° from tail to nose when on the ground.
Wheel base: 22 ft 6 ins (6.86 m)
Wheel track: 11 ft 11 ins (3.63 m) to outside of wheels

Weights:
Empty: 23,401 lb (10,614 kg), *26,918 lb (12,210 kg)*
Maximum take-off: 50,000 lb (22,680 kg), *54,000 lb (24,494 kg)*
Useful load: 26,599 lb (12,065 kg)

Performance (at 50,000 lb):
Maximum speed (V_{CMP}): 145 kts (167 mph) 269 km/h
Cruise speed: 143 kts (165 mph) 265 km/h at sea level, *140 kts (161 mph) 259 km/h*
Maximum climb rate: 1,522 ft (464 m) per minute, *1,841 ft (561 m) per minute, sea level*
IGE hovering ceiling: 8,200 ft (2,499 m) ISA, or 4,350 ft (1,326 m) at ISA + 20° C, *9,800 ft (2,987 m) ISA*
OGE hovering ceiling: 4,950 ft (1,509 m) ISA, or 500 ft (152 m) ISA + 20° C, *5,500 ft (1,676 m) ISA*
Ceiling: 8,450 ft (2,575 m), *10,150 ft (3,094 m)*, service
Range: 230 naut miles (265 miles) 426 km, sea level, ISA
Self-deployment range: *1,260 naut miles (1,451 miles) 2,333 km*
ODA team extraction radius (MH-47E): *505 naut miles (581 miles) 935 km*

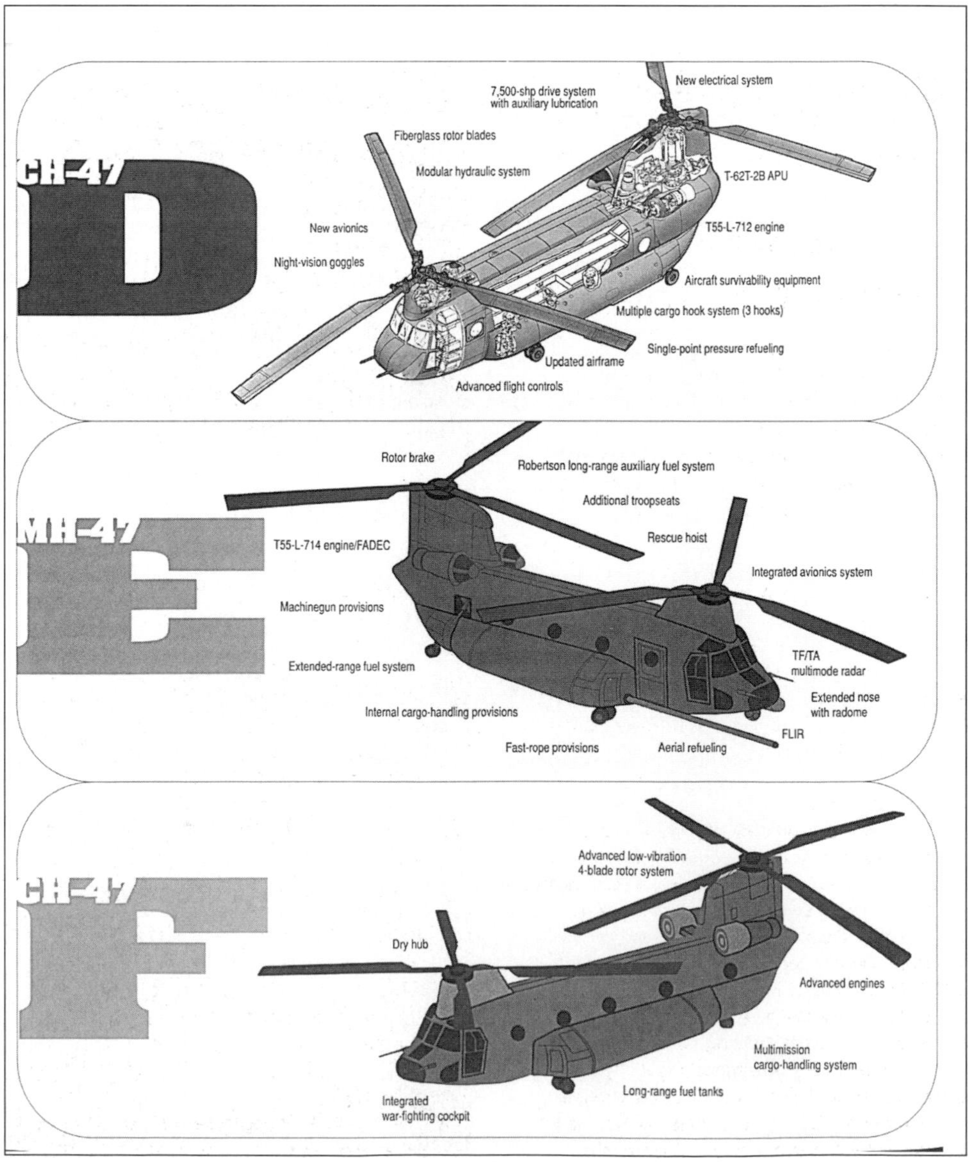

Boeing CH-47D, MH-47E and CH-47F Chinook features (courtesy Boeing)

Boeing CH-47D International Chinook (courtesy Boeing)

removed. Door each side of the fuselage, the larger starboard door of 5 ft 6 ins x 3 ft (1.68 x 0.91 m).
Rotor system: 2 contra-rotating and intermeshing 3-blade rotors in tandem, with flapping and drag hinges. Blades of glassfibre construction. Manual blade folding. Tolerance to hits from 23-mm shells.
Flight control system: Hydraulic.
Fuselage: Watertight underfloor area for buoyancy.
Engines: 2 x AlliedSignal T55-L-712 turboshafts.
Engine rating: Each 3,750 shp (2,796 kW) maximum, 3,000 shp (2,237 kW) continuous. APU.
Transmission rating: Maximum 7,500 shp (5,593 kW).
Fuel system: 3,899 litres in fuselage pods. Optional 3 x 3,028 litre auxiliary tanks in the cabin.
Electrical system: Includes 2 x 40 kVA transmission-mounted alternators.
Hydraulic system: Principal system for controls, at 3,000 psi. Utility supply at 3,350 psi.
Braking system: Hydraulic disc.
Flight avionics/instrumentation: IFR equipped. Includes AFCS with autostabilization and hold, gyromagnetic compass, Tacan, ADF, VOR/glideslope/marker beacon receiver, ADF, IFF, radar altimeter, and more. RAF Chinooks have Racal Super TANS INS with GPS. Chinook International modernizations for the Netherlands were the first with "glass" cockpit displays, as offered on new Internationals.
Self-protection systems: Chaff/flare dispensers, IR jammers, radar and/or missile approach warning receivers are available, as adopted by the UK.
Fixed guns: Can carry cabin-mounted machine-guns. See MH-47E.

Aircraft variants:
CH-47D is the main current version, as detailed.
CH-47D International is the "new-build" export equivalent of the US Army CH-47D, built in Japan as the Kawasaki CH-47J. Also available in MH-47E type. Lengthened fuselage, at 52 ft 1 ins (15.88 m), and available with advanced digital cockpit with multi-function displays and electronic flight instruments. Typical accommodation for 44 troops or 24 litters. 28,000 lb (12,700 kg) payload. T55-L-712-SSB engines of 4,400 shp (3,281 kW) initially, but now standardized on T55-L-714As of 4,867 shp (3,629 kW) maximum and 4,168 shp (3,108 kW) continuous ratings. 30 new CH-47D Internationals delivered to East Asian forces, 3 to the UK and 6 to the Netherlands.
CH-47 International Chinook modernization covers the modernizing of nearly 60 early model Chinooks of Greece (9 Agusta-built CH-47Cs, modernized 1993-95), the Netherlands (7 ex-Canadian CH-47Cs, the first handed over in September 1994), Spain (9 CH-47Cs, modernized 1991-93) and the UK (over 30 Chinook HC Mk 1s to HC Mk 2 standard, modernized 1993-95) to US Army CH-47D configuration. Upgraded CH-47s for the Netherlands are the first to incorporate the new advanced "glass" cockpit.
MH-47E is the US Special Operations Chinook, with the prototype delivered in May 1991. 51 earmarked for conversion within the CH-47D total procurement (including 1 prototype), though initial procurement is believed to have been restricted to 25 (delivered by late 1994) to perform clandestine long-range airlift insertion/extraction missions into hostile territory. Same dimensions as the CH-47D International, T55-L-714 engines of 4,867 shp (3,629 kW) maximum and 4,168 shp (3,108 kW) continuous ratings, extended range fuel system, auxiliary tanks, inflight refuelling capability, internal cargo handling system, and provision for 7.62-mm Miniguns and an 0.50-in machine-gun, and an integrated avionics system with FLIR, multi-mode radar and global communications and navigation. Can complete a 5 hour 30 minute covert mission over a 300 naut mile (345 mile) 555 km radius at low level, day or night, in adverse weather, over any terrain. 7,828 litres of fuel standard, with 3 x 3,028 litres auxiliary tanks optional.
CH-47F is a new advanced version, with new fuel-efficient 5,000 shp (3,728 kW) engines, low vibration 4-blade rotor and dry hub, redesigned aft rotor pylon for faster removal, integrated "war fighting" cockpit, multi-mission cargo handling system, and long-range fuel tanks. Intended, at least initially, as an upgrade of existing helicopters.

The Boeing Company and Sikorsky Aircraft (USA)

Corporate addresses: See Combat section for Boeing company details and Sikorsky later in this section.

Boeing Sikorsky RAH-66 Comanche

First flight: Expected 30 November 1995 (roll out of the first of 2 YRAH-66 prototypes took place on 25 May 1995). First flight of the second prototype expected September 1998.
Role: All-weather multi-role battlefield helicopter, with primary mission of armed reconnaissance. Can be configured for air combat and light attack.

★ Aims
★ To provide the US Army with an armed reconnaissance helicopter of low observability, combined with speed and agility, intended to replace the AH-1, OH-6 and OH-58.
★ 1 Comanche can be transported by C-130, 3 by C-141, 4 by C-17 and 8 by C-5. Can be loaded on or off a C-130 in 22 minutes.

▲ Development
▲ 21 June 1988. Demonstration/validation phase was initiated by a request for proposals for the LHX (Light Helicopter Experimental). Boeing and Sikorsky teamed against competing Bell and McDonnell Douglas.
▲ 5 April 1991. Dem/val contract go-ahead for prototypes went to the Boeing and Sikorsky team.
▲ 2003. Production decision.
Sales: 2 flying (second base-MEP equipped) and 2 static test prototypes. Funding for 6 pre-production Comanches with early operational capability (EOC), for operational evaluation from the year 2001 with a specially formed US Army unit; these will not carry weapons but will have the reconnaissance mission equipment package (MEP). Following evaluation they

Boeing Sikorsky YRAH-66 at roll out

will be given more powerful processors and armament, and redelivered for full operational use. Army requirement for 1,292 Comanches, with low-rate production beginning in about 2004 and IOC in 2007.

Crew: 2 in tandem, the rear WSO raised, in sealed and pressurized cockpits. Sidestick cyclic pitch controllers. Conventional collective controls.
Rotor system: 5-blade bearingless main rotor, having composite blades with swept tips.
Tail rotor characteristics: 8-blade Fantail rotor system of composite construction. Tolerance to 12.7-mm hits. Can operate for 30 minutes on 7 blades.
Tail surfaces: T-tail of composites, with horizontal stabilizer above the fin.
Flight control system: Dual triplex redundant fly-by-wire.
Airframe materials: Composites crashworthy structure, ballistically tolerant up to 23-mm gunfire.
Safety features: Crashworthy crew seats can withstand 38 ft (11.6 m) per second vertical impact.
Engines: 2 x LHTEC T800 turboshafts.
Engine rating: Each 925 shp (690 kW).
Transmission rating: 2,054 shp (1,532 kW) maximum.

DETAILS FOR COMANCHE.

Principal dimensions:
Rotor diameter (main): 39 ft 0.5 ins (11.90 m)
Maximum length, rotors turning: 46 ft 10 ins (14.28 m)
Fuselage length: 43 ft 4 ins (13.22 m)
Maximum height: 11 ft 1.5 ins (3.39 m)

Main rotor:
Rotor disc: 1,197.04 sq ft (11.2 m^2)

Tail rotor:
Diameter: 4 ft 6 ins (1.37 m)
Blade chord: 6.69 ins (17 cm)

Undercarriage:
Type: Retractable tailwheel type. Main units can "kneel" to lower height for transportation by freighter
Wheel track: 7 ft 7 ins (2.31 m)

Weights:
Empty: 7,500 lb (3,402 kg)
Maximum take-off: 17,174 lb (7,790 kg) for self-deployment, or 10,112 lb (4,587 kg) for primary mission.
Useful load: 2,612 lb (1,185 kg)

Performance (at 4,000 ft, 1,220 m, 35° C):
Dash speed: >177 kts (204 mph) 328 km/h
Vertical climb rate: 1,182 ft (360 m) per minute
Masking: 1.6 seconds
180° hover turn to target: 4.7 seconds
Snap turn to target at 80 kts: 3 seconds
G limits: +3.5,–1
Range for self-deployment: 1,260 naut miles (1,451 miles) 2,334 km

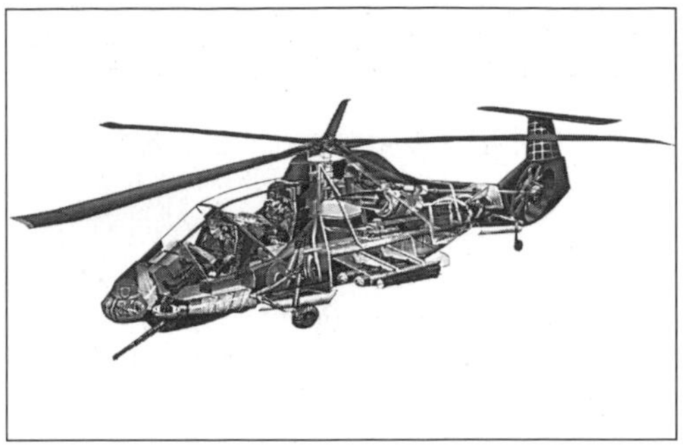

Boeing Sikorsky RAH-66 with anhedral stub wings only (courtesy Boeing Sikorsky)

Fuel system: 984 litres internally, but boosted to 4,542 litres with external fuel tanks for self-deployment.
Electrical system: Triple.
Hydraulic system: Triple.
Radar: Westinghouse Longbow fire-control radar.
Flight avionics/instrumentation: Provides real-time reconnaissance information. Advanced cockpit management system organizes and displays intelligence and allows rapid digital transmission of critical battle-field information to the tactical field commander. Targeting by second-generation focal-plane-array FLIR, low-light-level TV, laser rangefinder/designator, and aided target detection/classification. Night vision/adverse weather pilotage system with the FLIR and image intensifiers. Mission equipment has some commonality with the F-22A, and adopts a highly refined version of the digital map system used on the F-117A; Harris fibre-optic databus, 3D digital map, controls and multi-function liquid crystal displays (6 x 8 ins, 15 x 20 cm – 2 in each cockpit for tactical/map information), and a smaller LCD for weapons and fuel data. MIL-STD-1553B and additional databus, as well as the fibre-optic databus previously mentioned. Hamilton Standard flight control computer, air vehicle interface computer, and 35° x 52° field of view helmet-integrated display and sighting system (also a Kaiser system). On-board diagnostic system and self-healing digital mission electronics. Navigation system has inputs from GPS, Litton AHRS, radar altimeter and more. IFF. Anti-jam communications, including Have Quick.
Self-protection systems: Integrated IR suppression, low acoustic/visual signatures, and reduced cross section. "A breakthrough" heat-suppression system minimizes threats from heat-seeking missiles. Protection against blowing sand, high temperatures, electromagnetic interference, and NBC (nuclear, biological and chemical) agents.
Fixed guns: General Electric stowable turreted 20-mm Gatling-type gun. Rates of fire are 750 or 1,500 rounds per minute.

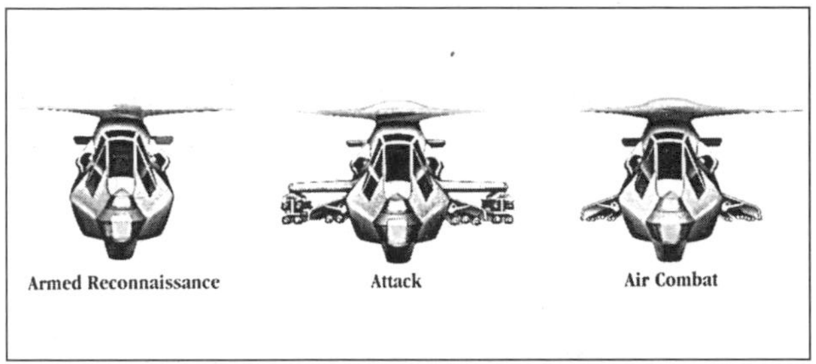

Boeing Sikorsky RAH-66 in internally armed configuration for reconnaissance (left), with full attack armament (centre), and with anhedral stub wings for air combat (courtesy Boeing Sikorsky)

Ammunition: 500 rounds.
Number of weapon pylons: Removable anhedral stub wings for an air combat role, with added larger stub wings to carry anti-armour missiles or other weapons in attack configuration (see diagram).
Expendable weapons and equipment: Internal 4 Hellfire anti-armour and 2 Stinger air-to-air missiles. Internal plus external weapons total 14 Hellfires or 18 Stingers, or 62 x 2.75-ins rockets.

Ken Brock Manufacturing Inc (USA)

Corporate address: 11852 Western Avenue, Stanton, CA 90680.
Telephone: +1 714 898 4366
Facsimile: +1 714 894 0811

Ken Brock KB-2 Freedom Machine

Role: Single-seat autogyro.
Sales: Plans and kits, the latter US$10,000 (1994 cost) and taking typically 50 working hours to assemble.
Rotor system: 2-blade.
Airframe materials: Aluminium alloy, but can have a wooden tail unit.
Engine: McCulloch or Volkswagen piston engine.
Engine rating: Typically 90 hp (67 kW).
Fuel system: 34 litres.

Ken Brock Manufacturing KB-2 Freedom Machine

DETAILS FOR KB-2.

Principal dimensions:
Rotor diameter: 22 ft (6.71 m)
Fuselage length: 11 ft 3 ins (3.43 m)
Maximum height: 6 ft 8 ins (2.03 m)

Main rotor:
Aerofoil section: Clark Y
Rotor disc: 380 sq ft (35.3 m²)

Weights:
Empty: 240 lb (109 kg)
Maximum take-off: 650 lb (295 kg)

Performance:
Maximum speed: 78-82 kts (90-95 mph) 145-153 km/h
Cruise speed: 52-61 kts (60-70 mph) 97-113 km/h
Take-off distance: 220 ft (67 m)
Landing distance: 15 ft (5 m)
Maximum climb rate: 1,200 ft (366 m) per minute
Ceiling: 12,000 ft (3,660 m)
Range: 130 naut miles (150 miles) 241 km
Duration: 2 hours

Ken Brock KB-3

Role: Single-seat ultralight autogyro.
Sales: As for KB-2.
Rotor system: 2-blade rotor.
Engine: Rotax 582 piston engine.
Engine rating: 64.4hp (48 kW).
Fuel system: 19 litres.

DETAILS FOR KB-3.

Principal dimensions:
Rotor diameter: 22 ft (6.71 m)
Fuselage length: 11 ft (3.35 m)
Maximum height: 7 ft 7 ins (2.31 m)

Main rotor:
Rotor disc: 380 sq ft (35.3 m²)

Weights:
Empty: 250 lb (113 kg)
Maximum take-off: 600 lb (272 kg)

Performance:
Maximum speed: 55 kts (63 mph) 101 km/h
Cruise speed: 52 kts (60 mph) 97 km/h
Maximum climb rate: 700 ft (213 m) per minute
Ceiling: 12,000 ft (3,660 m)
Range: 87 naut miles (100 miles) 161 km

B W Rotor Company Inc (USA)

Corporate address: PO Box 391, Towanda, KS 67144.

B W Rotor Sky Cycle

Role: Single-seat ultralight pressure jet helicopter.
Sales: Plans offered.
Rotor system: 2-blade rotor, without the need for a helicopter transmission.
Engines: 2 x G8-20 pressure jets.
Fuel system: 57 litres.

DETAILS FOR SKY CYCLE.

Principal dimensions:
Rotor diameter: 22 ft (6.71 m)
Fuselage length: 5 ft (1.52 m)
Maximum height: 7 ft (2.13 m)

Main rotor:
Rotor disc: 380 sq ft (35.3 m²)

Weights:
Empty: 95 lb (43 kg)
Maximum take-off: 500 lb (227 kg)

Performance:
Maximum speed: 52 kts (60 mph) 96 km/h
Cruise speed: 43 kts (50 mph) 80 km/h
Maximum climb rate: 975 ft (297 m) per minute
Ceiling: 12,000 ft (3,660 m)
Range: over 87 naut miles (100 miles) 161 km

Craft Aerotech (USA)

Corporate address: 1843 South 14th Street West, Missoula, MT 59801.
Telephone: +1 406 543 8133

Craft Aerotech 200

Role: 2+ seat rotorcraft.
Sales: Plans or kit.
Rotor system: 2-blade.
Airframe materials: Metal tube and composites.
Engines: 2 x 52 hp (38.8 kW) Rotax 503 piston engines or a single Subaru.
Fuel system: 113 litres.

DETAILS FOR AEROTECH 200.

Principal dimensions:
Rotor diameter: 27 ft 4 ins (8.33 m)
Fuselage length: 15 ft (4.57 m)
Maximum height: 8 ft 6 ins (2.59 m)

Weights:
Empty: 650 lb (295 kg)
Maximum take-off: 1,000 lb (454 kg)

Performance:
Maximum speed: 87 kts (100 mph) 161 km/h
Cruise speed: 78 kts (90 mph) 145 km/h
Take-off distance: 100 ft (31 m)
Maximum climb rate: 1,000 ft (305 m) per minute
Ceiling: 12,000 ft (3,050 m)
Range: 217 naut miles (250 miles) 402 km

The Enstrom Helicopter Company (USA)

Corporate address: PO Box 490, 2209 22nd Street, Twin County Airport, Menominee, MI 49858.
Telephone: +1 906 863 1200
Facsimile: +1 906 863 6821
Founded: 1959.
Information: Bill May (Marketing Director).

● Activities

- Enstrom has signed an agreement with Wuhan Helicopter Corporation of China to allow licence production of up to 100 helicopters of all models a year.

Enstrom F28F and 280FX

First flight: 1962 for the original F28. F28F certified on 31 December 1980.
Role: Light helicopters, mainly for civil use but suited to external cargo, military, police and agricultural roles.
Sales: Large number in operation, including 12 F28Fs recently delivered to Colombia for a training role under US Army foreign military sales.
Crew/passengers: Pilot and 2 passengers, with optional dual controls.
Freight, internal: 6.3 cu ft (0.178 m^3) baggage compartment, capacity of 108 lb (49 kg).
Optional equipment: Includes spray and dry chemical agricultural equipment (29 ft 8 ins to 36 ft 4 ins, 9.04 to 11.07 m booms), with a 151 litre hopper carried each side of the fuselage, exhaust silencer, cargo hook, and floats.
Rotor system: 3-blade, metal, high inertia, fully articulated main rotor. Low tip speed and low disc loading. Fail safe rotor hub featuring closed cycle hydraulic dampers, and total protection from mast

Enstrom F28F-P Sentinel police helicopter, without searchlight

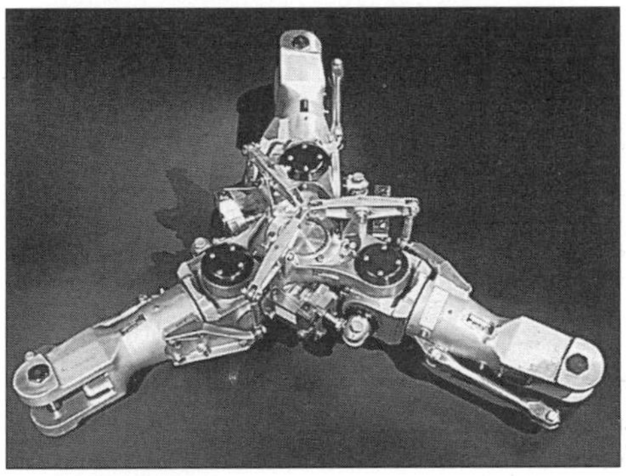

Enstrom F28F/280FX rotor hub (courtesy Enstrom)

bumping. Rotating controls are inside the fuselage. V belt drive from engine to transmission; transmission chip detectors.
Tail rotor characteristics: 2-blade, teetering, to port side of tailboom.
Tail surfaces: Small horizontal surface on each side of the boom, 280FX having endplate fins.
Fuselage: Kick-in access steps.
Airframe materials: Steel tube main structure, aluminium alloy and glassfibre cabin area skins, and aluminium alloy stressed skin tailboom.
Engine: Textron Lycoming HIO-360-F1AD turbocharged piston engine. Starter motor.
Engine rating: 225 hp (168 kW).
Fuel system: 159 litres. Optional 49 litre auxiliary tank in the baggage compartment.
Electrical system: F28F has a 12 volt engine-driven alternator. 280FX has a 24 volt supply, which is optional for F28F.
Flight avionics/instrumentation: Customer choice of avionics. Full range of standard instruments, including airspeed indicator, compass, altimeter, turn/bank indicator, tachometer and much more.
Aircraft variants:
F28F is the standard version.
F28F-P Sentinel is the police variant, offered with police communication equipment, optional searchlight to the starboard side of the fuselage, and optional FLIR. Features 280FX stabilizer endplates.
280FX became available in 1985, based on the F28F but with various cabin and airframe refinements, most obviously a reshaped air intake above the cabin, endplate fins to the tail stabilizer, and faired skids.

DETAILS FOR F28F, WITH 280FX IN ITALICS WHERE DIFFERENT.

Principal dimensions:
Rotor diameter (main): 32 ft (9.75 m)
Maximum length, rotors turning: 29 ft 3 ins (8.91 m)
Maximum height: 9 ft (2.74 m)

Main rotor
Aerofoil section: NACA 0013.5
Blade chord: 9.5 ins (0.24 m)
Rotor disc: 804 sq ft (74.69 m^2)

Tail rotor:
Diameter: 4 ft 8 ins (1.42 m)

Undercarriage:
Type: Fixed, high energy-absorbing twin skids, with retractable ground handling wheels. Optional floats
Skid track: 7 ft 3 ins (2.21 m)

Weights:
Empty: 1,570 lb (712 kg), *1,585 lb (719 kg)*
Maximum take-off: 2,600 lb (1,179 kg)
Useful load: 1,030 lb (467 kg), *1,015 lb (460 kg)*

Performance:
Maximum cruise speed: 97 kts (112 mph) 180 km/h, *102 kts (117 mph) 188 km/h*
Economic cruise speed: 89 kts (102 mph) 164 km/h, *93 kts (107 mph) 172 km/h*
Maximum climb rate: 1,450 ft (442 m) per minute at 2,350 lb (1,066 kg) weight, or 1,150 ft (350 m) per minute at MTOW
IGE hovering ceiling: 13,200 ft (4,023 m) at 2,350 lb (1,066 kg), or 7,700 ft (2,347 m) at MTOW
OGE hovering ceiling: 8,700 ft (2,650 m) at 2,350 lb (1,066 kg)
Ceiling: 12,000 ft (3,660 m) maximum approved
Range with full fuel: 241 naut miles (277 miles) 446 km, *261 naut miles (300 miles) 483 km,* no reserve
Duration: 3 hours 30 minutes

Enstrom 480 Turbine

Role: Turboshaft-powered light helicopter, suited also to utility, law enforcement, patrol, training and more.
Crew/passengers: Pilot and 4 passengers, pilot and 3 passengers in executive layout with more leg room (front starboard seat removed), 2 pilots for training (starboard seat moved outboard and dual controls fitted) plus 1 passenger, or the pilot plus cargo when the starboard front seat is removed and the rear seat folded. Front seats are adjustable, as are the pedals.
Rotor system: Similar to 280FX. Main rotor hub and blades weigh over 300 lb (136 kg).
Safety features: Crashworthy features, including seats, fuel system and skids.

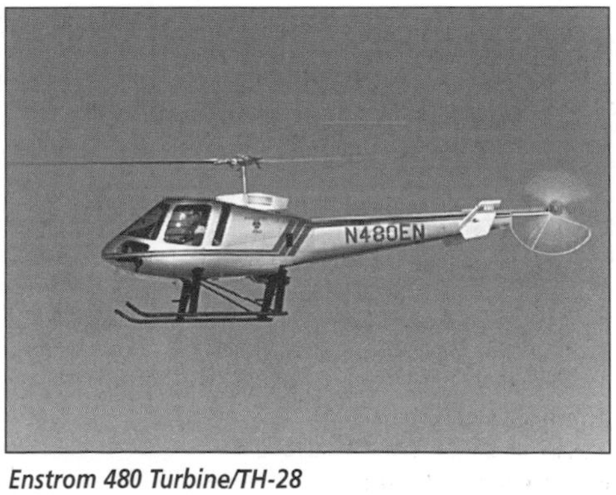

Enstrom 480 Turbine/TH-28

Details for 480 Turbine.

Principal dimensions:
Rotor diameter (main): 32 ft (9.75 m)
Fuselage length: 29 ft 10 ins (9.09 m)
Fuselage width: 5 ft 10 ins (1.78 m)
Maximum height: 8 ft 6 ins (2.59 m) to top of tail rotor

Tail rotor:
Diameter: 5 ft 0.5 ins (1.53 m)

Undercarriage:
Type: As for 280FX
Skid track: 8 ft 1 ins (2.46 m)

Weights:
Empty: 1,675 lb (760 kg), with standard equipment
Maximum take-off: 2,850 lb (1,293 kg)
Useful load: 1,175 lb (5,333 kg)

Performance:
Never-exceed speed (VNE): 121 kts (140 mph) 225 km/h
Cruise speed: 114 kts (131 mph) 211 km/h at 2,500 lb (1,134 kg) weight, or 106 kts (122 mph) 196 km/h at 2,850 lb (1,293 kg), both at 3,000 ft (915 m)
Maximum climb rate: 1,580 ft (482 m) per minute at 2,500 lb weight, 1,450 ft (442 m) at 2,850 lb weight
IGE hovering ceiling: 14,000 ft (4,267 m) at 2,500 lb weight, or 10,000 ft (3,050 m) at 2,850 lb weight
OGE hovering ceiling: 12,000 ft (3,660 m) at 2,500 lb weight, or 6,900 ft (2,103 m) at 2,850 lb weight
Ceiling: 13,000 ft (3,960 m), service
Range: 412 naut miles (475 miles) 764 km at 2,500 lb, or 382 naut miles (440 miles) 708 km at 2,850 lb, no reserve, at sea level
Duration: 5 hours at 2,500 lb, or 4.7 hours at 2,850 lb, no reserve, at sea level

Engine: Allison 250-C20W turboshaft.
Engine rating: 420 shp (335.6 kW), derated to 285 shp (212.5 kW) maximum for 5 minutes and 256 shp (191 kW) continuous. Derating allows full take-off power to above 13,000 ft (3,960 m) or over 49° C. Standard Pall Land Marine particle separator which removes 93% of dust, sand or foreign objects in the air inlet.
Fuel system: 341 litres in 2 interconnected tanks.
Flight avionics/instrumentation: VFR or IFR.

Aircraft variants:
480 Turbine is the standard model, as detailed.
TH-28 is the designation of a three-seat military version with crashworthy features. Intended mainly for training and patrol.

Farrington Aircraft Corporation (USA)

Corporate address: 4460 Shemwell Road, Paducah, KY 42003.
Telephone: +1 502 898 2403
Facsimile: +1 502 898 8691

Farrington Twinstar

Role: Two-seat sporting autogyro.
Sales: Kits for US$9,995 (1994 cost), taking typically 250 hours to assemble.
Rotor system: 2 blades.
Airframe materials: Welded steel tube structure, with composites fairing and tail unit.

Details for Twinstar.

Principal dimensions:
Rotor diameter: 28 ft (8.53 m)
Fuselage length: 12 ft (3.66 m)
Maximum height: 8 ft (2.44 m)

Weights
Empty: 700 lb (318 kg)
Maximum take-off: 1,200 lb (544 kg)

Performance:
Maximum speed: 78 kts (90 mph) 145 km/h
Cruise speed: 56 kts (65 mph) 105 km/h
Minimum flight speed: 20 kts (23 mph) 37 km/h
Take-off distance: 200 ft (61 m)
Landing distance: up to 50 ft (15 m)
Maximum climb rate: 700-1,000 ft (213-305 m) per minute
Ceiling: 10,000 ft (3,050 m)
Range: 78 naut miles (90 miles) 145 km

Engine: Textron Lycoming O-320 piston engine.
Engine rating: 150-160 hp (112-119 kW).
Fuel system: 68 litres

Global Helicopter Technology Inc (USA)

Corporate address: 5070 South Collins, Suite 206, Arlington, TX 76018.
Telephone: +1 817 557 3391
Facsimile: +1 817 557 3392
Information: Dan Pettus (President).

● Activities

● Offers the Huey 800 conversion for the Bell UH-1H, requiring no expensive tooling and only 200 working hours. Based principally on the installation of a LHTEC T800 turboshaft engine, the kit also includes the reduction gearbox, inlet duct and exhaust duct; electronics bay engine FADEC and interface unit; torque limit override, manual mode fuel beep, collective position control input, and throttle position control input for the collective engine controls; ECU channel select switch, EIU channel select switch, ignition select switch, press to test, and output speed beep for the engine control panel; and gas producer speed, dual tach, turbine temperature, engine oil temperature/pressure, torque, and reduction gearbox oil temperature/pressure instrumentation for the instrument panel. The conversion is said to offer over 50% better mission endurance, and pilot workload is reduced through automatic starting, automatic engine and aircraft limit protection, and simplification of emergency procedures. On 22 April 1993, the Huey 800 demonstrator flew non-stop and unrefuelled from Oxnard, California to Georgia, breaking the world helicopter distance record by over 521 naut miles (600 miles) 965 km. On an Army hot/high mission, the Huey 800 is said to carry a 1,000 lb (454 kg) payload 240 naut miles further than the UH-1H, with benefits for other missions. Using 2 auxiliary fuel tanks, it can self-deploy over 1,000 naut miles. Possible options include various avionics, safety and survivability, special equipment and performance items, the latter including high efficiency rotor blades.

Global Huey 800 UH-1H conversion (courtesy Allison)

Groen Brothers Aviation Inc (USA)

Corporate address: 1784 West 500 South, Salt Lake City, Utah 84104.
Telephone: +1 801 973 0195
Facsimile: +1 801 973 4027
Information: Hank Parry.

Groen Brothers Hawk series

First flight: 26 September 1992 (Hawk I prototype).
Role: Single to five-seat autogyros with many uses including transport, utility, survey, aerial photography, flight training, agricultural, military/law enforcement, ground attack, unmanned surveillance and more.

▲ Development

▲ Hawk I prototype was built to evaluate the rotor system (patent pending) designed by Groen Brothers.
Sales: Hawk II costs US$150,000. Hawk V and Nighthawk each cost US$230,000.
Details: Hawk II, except under Aircraft variants.
Crew/passengers: Pilot and passenger side-by-side in the enclosed cabin.
Rotor system: 2-blade teetering rotor. High inertia blades of light alloy. System applies infinitely variable collective pitch control to the semi-rigid rotor. For take-off, the rotor is pre-rotated from the propeller drive shaft to optimum speed; when the pilot pitches the blades the drive is automatically disconnected and

Groen Brothers Hawk I prototype (courtesy Groen Brothers)

the rotor continues to spin under its own momentum, providing vertical lift. With a little forward thrust imparted by the propeller, the autogyro performs a zero-roll lift-off and the rotor then autorotates.
Wing/tail surfaces: Stub wings mounting the tailbooms and main undercarriage units. Twin fins/rudders and an adjoining tailplane and elevator.
Airframe materials: Aluminium alloy, with stressed skin monocoque fuselage and glassfibre non-structural fairings.
Engine: Textron Lycoming IO-360 mounted in the rear of the fuselage pod, driving a 3-blade variable-pitch pusher propeller.
Engine rating: 220 hp (164 kW).
Fuel system: 151 litres.
Electrical system: Starter-generator.
Hydraulic system: For undercarriage retraction.
Flight avionics/instrumentation: IFR equipped.
Aircraft variants:
Hawk I is the single-seater, similar to the Hawk II detailed but with a smaller cabin. Version used for development and testing. 121 litres of fuel. Uses include agricultural and military.
Hawk II is the two-seat commercial-use version, as detailed. 1996 FAA certification anticipated.
Hawk V has accommodation for 2 in front and up to 3 on the rear bench seat in the lengthened cabin. 465 hp (347 kW) engine. IFR equipped. Gross weight 3,300 lb (1,497 kg), useful load 1,400 lb (635 kg), and maximum speed 139 kts (160 mph) 257 km/h.
Night Hawk is a military/law enforcement IFR-equipped version with 2 seats in tandem. Similar engine and performance as Hawk V, but with a 1,500 lb (680 kg) useful load. Can have FLIR, searchlights, police radios, GPS, bullet-proof protection package, and more.
Ramjet UAV Hawk version is proposed to meet the US Navy requirement for an unmanned vertical launch and recovery vehicle for surveillance and communications relay. Based on Hawk II, it would have ramjet-tipped rotor blades. Requirements are for a 100 naut mile range, 150 kts maximum speed with a 200 lb (91 kg) payload, and 5 hours duration.

DETAILS FOR HAWK II.

Principal dimensions:
Rotor diameter: 34 ft (10.36 m)
Maximum length, rotors turning: 34 ft (10.36 m)
Fuselage length: 16 ft 8 ins (5.08 m)
Width, over stub wings: 8 ft 5.5 ins (2.57 m)
Maximum height: 8 ft 8.5 ins (2.65 m)

Undercarriage:
Type: Retractable, with nosewheel. Mainwheels protrude slightly when retracted

Weights:
Maximum take-off: 2,050 lb (930 kg)
Useful load: 800 lb (363 kg)

Performance (provisional):
Maximum speed: 139 kts (160 mph) 257 km/h
Cruise speed: 122 kts (140 mph) 225 km/h
Take-off distance/ground roll over a 50 ft (15 m) obstacle: 0-150 ft (0-46 m)
Landing distance/ground roll over a 50 ft (15 m) obstacle: 0-50 ft (0.15 m)
Maximum climb rate: 1,000 ft (305 m) per minute
Ceiling: 16,000 ft (4,875 m), service
Range: 486 naut miles (560 miles) 901 km at cruise speed

Hinchman Aircraft Company (USA)

Corporate address: PO Box 56, Monrovia, IN 46157.
Telephone: +1 317 996 3157
Facsimile: +1 317 996 3148

Hinchman H-1 Racer

Role: Single-seat autogyro.
Sales: Plans and kits, the latter US$10,500 (1994 cost), taking typically 150 working hours to assemble.
Rotor system: 2-blade.
Airframe materials: Metal tubing.
Engine: Rotax 503 or similar.
Engine rating: 49.5 hp (37 kW).
Fuel system: 19 litres.

DETAILS FOR H-1 RACER.

Principal dimensions:
Rotor diameter: 25 ft (7.62 m)
Fuselage length: 10 ft 9 ins (3.28 m)
Maximum height: 7 ft 11 ins (2.41 m)

Weights:
Empty: 300 lb (136 kg)
Maximum take-off: 550 lb (249 kg)

Performance:
Maximum speed: 74 kts (85 mph) 137 km/h
Cruise speed: 56 kts (65 mph) 105 km/h
Take-off distance: 500 ft (152 m)
Maximum climb rate: 1,200 ft (366 m) per minute
Ceiling: 10,000 ft (3,050 m)
Range: 56 naut miles (65 miles) 105 km

Hiller Aircraft Corporation (USA)

Corporate address: 7980 Enterprise Drive, Newark, CA 94560.
Telephone: +1 510 744 1500
Facsimile: +1 510 744 1600
Founded: Original Hiller Aircraft Division of Hiller Industries was founded in 1942, becoming Hiller Helicopters in 1948. The present company was established in 1994, after Jeffrey Hiller (son of the founder) led an investment consortium to purchase back the assets from Rogerson Hiller Corporation.
Employees: 25.
Information: Craig Smith.

● Activities

- In addition to producing three-seat UH-12E3s and the new five-seat UH-12E5, Hiller has purchased the STCs from Soloy allowing the installation of the Allison 250-C20 turboshaft into UH-12s and Bell Model 47s.

Hiller UH-12E3 and E3T, and UH-12E5 and E5T

First flight: 1958 for original UH-12E. 2 June 1995 for the first new-production UH-12E3 (N101BX); January 1995 for UH-12E5.
Role: Utility helicopters, with uses including transport, agricultural spraying and dusting, forestry work, construction, law enforcement and training.
Sales: Initial production by the new company covers

First new production Hiller UH-12E3

Hiller UH-12E5 type five-seat helicopter

20 UH-12E3/5s for a Thai investment group. Spare part production for over 1,000 older UH-12s still flying began in September 1994, supplementing spares bought from Rogerson Hiller.
Crew/passengers: 3 or 5 seats, according to version (see Aircraft variants). Optional internal or external litter.
Standard equipment: Long list includes a cargo hook hard point.
Optional equipment: Long list includes dual controls, quick-release cargo hook, cyclic control grip, spray system, spreader system, night lighting equipment, loudspeaker. remote searchlight, cargo racks, hydraulic drive kit (turbine only), auto re-ignition kit (turbine only), and particle separator (turbine only).
Rotor system: 2-blade main rotor, with a retention bolt and drag link attaching blade to rotor head. Electrically controlled trim system.
Tail rotor characteristics: 2 blades.
Engine: See Aircraft variants.
Fuel system: 174 litres standard, plus 1 or 2 x 76 litre auxiliary tanks.
Electrical system: Lead-acid battery. Optional ni-cd battery with monitor. Alternator. External power receptacle.

DETAILS FOR UH-12E3T, *WITH UH-12E5 IN ITALICS WHERE DIFFERENT.*

Principal dimensions:
Rotor diameter (main): 35 ft 5 ins (10.79 m)
Maximum length, rotors turning: 40 ft 8.5 ins (12.41 m)
Fuselage length: 28 ft 6 ins (8.69 m), *29 ft 9.5 ins (9.08 m)*
Maximum height: 10 ft 1 ins (3.08 m) to above rotor hub, *9 ft 5 ins (2.87 m) to above blade root*

Tail rotor:
Diameter: 5 ft 6 ins (1.68 m)

Undercarriage:
Type: Fixed twin skids. Standard ground handling wheels. Optional amphibious gear
Skid track: 7 ft 6 ins (2.29 m)

Weights:
Empty: 1,640 lb (744 kg), *1,936 lb (878 kg)*
Maximum take-off: 3,100 lb (1,406 kg)
Payload: 1,460 lb (662 kg), *1,214 lb (551 kg)*

Performance:
Never-exceed speed (VNE): 83 kts (96 mph) 154 km/h
Maximum cruise speed: 78 kts (90 mph) 145 km/h
Maximum climb rate: 1,518 ft (463 m) per minute, *1,290 ft (393 m) per minute*
Vertical climb rate: 967 ft (295 m) per minute, *740 ft (225 m) per minute*
IGE hovering ceiling: 11,300 ft (3,444 m) at 2,800 lb (1,270 kg) weight, or 8,600 ft (2,621 m) at MTOW, *10,400 ft (3,170 m) at 2,800 lb (1,270 kg) weight or 7,300 ft (2,225 m) at MTOW*
OGE hovering ceiling: 8,700 ft (2,652 m) at 2,800 lb (1,270 kg) weight or 5,600 ft (1,707 m) at MTOW, *6,800 ft (2,075 m) at 2,800 lb (1,270 kg) weight, 3,800 ft (1,158 m) at MTOW*
Ceiling: 14,000 ft (4,267 m), *15,000 ft (4,575 m)*, both at 2,800 lb (1,270 kg) weight, service
Range at maximum cruise speed: 149 naut miles (171.9 miles) 276 km with standard fuel or 227 naut miles (319 miles) 513 km with auxiliary fuel, *201 naut miles (232 miles) 373 km with standard fuel or 376 naut miles (433 miles) 697 km with auxiliary fuel*
Duration at maximum cruise speed: 1.91 hours with standard fuel or 3.54 hours with auxiliary fuel, *2.7 hours with standard fuel, 5 hours with auxiliary fuel*

Flight avionics/instrumentation: Optional radio, ADF, transponder, instantaneous vertical speed indicator, and artificial horizon.
Aircraft variants:
UH-12E3 is the basic three-seat utility helicopter, with a 345 hp (257 kW) Textron Lycoming VO-540-C2A piston engine derated to 305 hp (227 kW).
UH-12E3T is the turbine version of the three-seater, with a 420 shp (313 kW) Allison 250-C20B turboshaft derated to 301 shp (224 kW).
UH-12E5 is the new five-seater, the prototype of which flew in January 1995. Same engine as E3. First production UH-12E5 was to be completed in June 1995.
UH-12E5T is the five-seat turbine version, with the same engine as the E3T.

Jaffe Helicopter Inc (USA)

Corporate address: 1770 Sky Place Boulevard, International Airport, San Antonio, TX 78216.
Telephone: +1 210 821 6301
Facsimile: +1 210 822 7766
Telex: 767438 COMTRAN UD

● Activities
● Offers the 222SP as an upgrade of the Bell 222, based around the use of Allison 250-C30G turboshaft engines of 650 shp (485 kW). Also available are upgrades of the avionics and interior.

Kaman Aerospace Corporation (USA)

Corporate address: PO Box 2, Bloomfield, CT 06002.
Telephone: +1 203 243 7547, 8311
Facsimile: +1 203 243 7514
Founded: December 1945 as Kaman Aircraft Corporation.
Employees: 1,200, at its Bloomfield, Moosup and Gilman (CT), Jacksonville (FL) and Tuscon (AZ) facilities.
Information: J. Kenneth Nasshan (Assistant Vice President, Director of Public Relations – *telephone* +1 203 243 7319); Elizabeth K. Healy (Public Relations representative).

● Activities
● Subsidiary of Kaman Corporation. In addition to its own helicopters, Kaman is a major components subcontractor for military aircraft that include the F-14, A-6, F-22, Comanche, C-17, B-1B and V-22, while its commercial subcontracting includes wing structures and other components for Boeing aircraft. It also manufactures fairings and thrust reversers for commercial jets and components for the Space Shuttle.

Kaman SH-2G Super Seasprite

First flight: 28 December 1989 (first SH-2G was a modified SH-2F used for development as the sole YSH-2G). First actual SH-2G was delivered to the US Navy on 21 March 1989.
Role: Anti-submarine helicopter, with secondary SAR and utility roles.

▲ Development
▲ Upgraded version of the SH-2F Seasprite, with more advanced and powerful engines and enhanced mission equipment.
Sales: Only 6 newly-built SH-2Gs, representing the final helicopters on the SH-2F production line. All others by upgrade of SH-2Fs, completed in 1994. Only in service with the US Navy Reserve, though 10 surplus ex-US Navy SH-2Fs have been acquired by Egypt after upgrade to SH-2G standard (have AQS-18A dipping sonar). Turkey (navy) is receiving 14 ex-US Navy SH-2Fs under EMS; unclear whether these will be upgraded.

Kaman SH-2G Super Seasprite

Crew/passengers: 3 crew plus room for 1 passenger. Removal of the sonobuoy launcher allows for 4 passengers or 2 litters.
Optional equipment: Includes 4,000 lb (1,814 kg) cargo hook and 600 lb (272 kg) capacity rescue hoist.
Rotor system: 4-blade main rotor with titanium hub and retention straps. Blades have a light alloy D-section leading-edge spar, honeycomb trailing-edge pocket and glassfibre skin. Each blade incorporates a Kaman servo flap. Manual blade folding.
Tail rotor characteristics: 4-blade.
Tail surfaces: Fixed incidence tailplane.
Airframe materials: Conventional monocoque structure.
Engines: 2 General Electric T700-GE-401 turboshafts.
Engine rating: Each 1,690 shp (1,260 kW) intermediate rating.

DETAILS FOR SH-2G.

Principal dimensions:
Rotor diameter (main): 44 ft (13.41 m)
Maximum length, rotors turning: 52 ft 6 ins (16 m)
Fuselage length: 40 ft 2 ins (12.24 m), or 38 ft 4 ins (11.68 m) folded
Width, blades folded: 12 ft 3 ins (3.73 m)
Maximum height: 15 ft 1 ins (4.6 m), or 13 ft 7 ins (4.14 m) folded

Main rotor:
Rotor disc: 1,521.11 sq ft (141.32 m^2)

Tail rotor:
Diameter: 8 ft 1 ins (2.46 m)

Undercarriage:
Type: Retractable main units, fixed tailwheel
Wheel base: 16 ft 9 ins (5.11 m)
Wheel track: 10 ft (3.05 m)

Weights:
Empty: 8,430 lb (3,824 kg)
Maximum take-off: 13,500 lb (6,123 kg)
Useful load: 5,070 lb (2,300 kg)

Performance:
Maximum speed: 141 kts (162 mph) 261 km/h at 5,000 ft (1,525 m)
Maximum climb rate: 2,070 ft (631 m) per minute at sea level
Climb rate, OEI: 1,305 ft (398 m) per minute at sea level
IGE hovering ceiling: 17,600 ft (5,365 m)
OGE hovering ceiling: 14,600 ft (4,450 m)
Ceiling: 20,400 ft (6,220 m), or 12,080 ft (3,680 m) OEI, service
Range: 540 naut miles (622 miles) 1,000 km, 20 minutes reserve
Duration: 5.3 hours with max. fuel, 20 minutes reserve

Fuel system: 1,779 litres. 1 or 2 x 378 litre external auxiliary fuel tanks.
Electrical system: Includes T-62 APU and dual 30 kVA alternators.
Radar: LN-66 HP.
Flight avionics/instrumentation: Integrated cockpit with 1553B databus. Communications comprises AN/APX-72 IFF/SIF, intercom, AN/ARC-159 radios and KY-58 secure voice; optional AN/ARC-182 radio. Instruments comprise K884059 attitude and K884058 HSI. Navigation comprises AN/ASN-50 AHRS, AN/APN-217(V)3 Doppler, AN/APQ-107 Radalt warning system, AN/APN-171 radar altimeter, MB-1 stand-by compass, AN/ARN-118 Tacan, AN/ASN-150 Tacnav and DF-301E UHF/VHF-DF. Standard mission equipment comprises AN/ALE-39 ECM, AN/ALR-66 ESM, and K884100 interface converter unit. Optional mission equipment comprises AN/AAQ-16 FLIR, AN/ALQ-144 IR countermeasures, AN/ARR-47 missile detectors, AN/ALE-39 chaff/flare dispensers, and AQH-11 mission tape recorder. AN/ASN-150 tactical management system. ASW equipment comprises AN/UYS-503 acoustic data processor, AN/ASQ-81(V)2 MAD, AN/ARN-146 on-top position indicator, K682770 sonobuoy launcher, AN/ARR-84 sonobuoy receiver, AN/ASQ-188 torpedo presetter and AN/AKT-22(V)6 Xmtr/multiplexer. Standard Mission equipment for all US Navy SH-2Gs. Optional equipment on some US Navy SH-2Gs. Export SH-2Gs may have both standard and optional equipment, according to governmental approval.
Fixed guns: Can have a 7.62-mm machine-gun in each cabin door.
Number of weapon pylons: 2.
Expendable weapons and equipment: 1 or 2 Mk 50 (or Mk 46) torpedoes, 8 marine markers, and DIFAR and DICASS sonobuoys.

Kaman K-MAX "Aerial Truck"

First flight: 23 December 1991.
Role: Designed for the repetitive lift and torque loading requirements of external load operations, including logging, firefighting, agricultural, construction, reforestation and oil/mineral exploration.

▲ Development

▲ 30 August 1994. FAA certification after more than

Kaman K-MAX "Aerial Truck"

800 hours of test flying and thousands of hours of structural fatigue tests. Canadian certified.
Sales: Production to mid-1996 assigned to customers, with at least 1 produced each month through 1996. Initially offered under a special lease programme to take the helicopter into the market place, but now offered under direct sale at US$3.5 million (1994 dollars). Initial deliveries to US customers began in late 1994. Operated in the USA by Erikson Air Crane, Louisiana-Pacific Corporation, Scott Paper Company, Wescor Forest Products Company and Weyerhaeuser by July 1995, and others to Midwest Helicopters of Canada and Helog and HeliSuisse of Switzerland, with Heli-Union of France likely to lease a helicopter for oil exploration in Bolivia, among operators. Japan is seen as a likely market. Military deliveries are possible.

Crew: Pilot only, on an energy absorbing seat designed for 20 g downward and 16 g forward impact; energy absorbing cyclic stick for added safety.
Freight, external: 5,000 lb (2,268 kg) can be lifted to 8,000 ft (2,440 m) out of ground effect, and 6,000 lb (2,722 kg) to lower altitudes. Spray rig for agricultural work and a 2,500 litre bambi-bucket for firefighting.
Rotor system: 2 side-by-side intermeshing, contra-rotating rotors (Synchro-lift), with composite blades, with electrical servo-flap control that eliminates the need for hydraulic boost systems or artificial stability augmentation. Bearingless rotors are specifically designed for infinite life and ruggedness. Blades can be folded by removal of drag damper pins. Single transmission for both rotors.
Tail rotor characteristics: Not fitted.
Tail surfaces: Horizontal stabilizer with endplates mounted at mid-fuselage, and vertical fin with inset rudder.
Flight control system: See Rotor system.
Airframe materials: Light alloy. Removable tailcone.
Engine: Textron Lycoming T5317A-1 turboshaft, with particle separator.
Engine rating: 1,800 shp (1,342 kW) design rating, but derated to 1,500 shp (1,118.6 kW).
Transmission rating: 1,500 shp (1,118.6 kW).
Fuel system: 863 litres.
Hydraulic system: None.
Braking system: Mainwheels.

DETAILS FOR K-MAX.

Principal dimensions:
Rotor diameter: Each 48 ft 4 ins (14.73 m)
Maximum length, rotors turning: 52 ft (15.9 m)

Main rotor:
Rpm: Normally 270 maximum

Undercarriage:
Type: Fixed nosewheel type, with a plate at each wheel for landing on soft ground
Wheel base: 13 ft 6 ins (4.11 m)
Wheel track: 11 ft 8 ins (3.56 m)

Weights:
Empty: 4,800 lb (2,177 kg)
Maximum take-off: 11,500 lb (5,216 kg)
Typical mission weight: 10,694 lb (4,850 kg), with pilot, 1.5 hours of fuel and 5,000 lb hook load
Payload: up to 6,000 lb (2,722 kg). See Freight, external

Performance:
Never-exceed speed (VNE): 100 kts (115 mph) 185 km/h without an external load, or 80 kts (92 mph) 148 km/h with an external load
Maximum climb rate: 2,500 ft (762 m) per minute
OGE hovering ceiling: 25,000 ft (7,620 m) estimated, with 6,000 lb (2,722 kg) load, ISA

McDonnell Douglas Corporation – Helicopter Systems (USA)

Corporate address: See Combat section for company details.

McDonnell Douglas MD 500E, MD 530F and Defender

First flight: 28 January 1982 (MD 550E) and 22 October 1982 (MD 530F).
Role: MD 500E and MD 530F are light utility helicopters, used for executive transportation, cargo lifting, law enforcement, patrol and other roles. Defender is a military and paramilitary member of the same family, with more specialized equipment, armament and crashworthy fuselage structure.
Sales: About 4,650 of all civil and military versions (including past and present MD 500 and 530 variants and military/paramilitary Defenders). Military users of currently-available Defender variants include Colombia, the Philippines and the US Army (AH-6 and MH-6 types).
Details: For MD 500E and MD 530F, as appropriate, except under Aircraft variants.
Crew/passengers: Pilot plus up to 4 passengers. 270° potential visibility from the cockpit, due to extensive glazing. Optional 4-seat executive, litter or other layouts including cargo carrying in the aft compartment.
Freight, external: Cargo hook with a 2,000 lb (907 kg) capacity.
Cabin access: 2 doors each side of the fuselage.
Optional equipment: Includes dual controls, searchlight, wire strike kit, cargo hook or underfuselage cargo pod.
Rotor system: Fully articulated 5-blade type, of metal. Fail-safe main rotor and steel strap rotor retention system. Manual folding.
Tail rotor characteristics: Metal, 2-blade standard, with optional 4-blade Quiet Tail Rotor for MD 500E.
Tail surfaces: Ventral and dorsal fins, with T-mounted horizontal stabilizer with endplate fins of 5 ft 5 ins (1.65 m) span.
Flight control system: Mechanical.
Airframe materials: Metal.
Engine: *MD 500E* has an Allison 250-C20B or C-20R turboshaft of 420 shp (313.3 kW) but derated to 375 shp (280 kW) for take-off and 350 shp (261 kW) continuous. *MD 530F* has an Allison 250-C30 turboshaft of 650 shp (485 kW) but derated to 425 shp (317 kW) for take-off up to 50 kts, 375 shp (280 kW) above 50 kts and 350 shp (261 kW) maximum continuous.
Engine rating: See above.
Transmission rating: 350 shp (261 kW) maximum continuous.
Fuel system: 242 litres usable, weighing 403 lb (183 kg). Self-sealing tanks and 79 litre auxiliary tank optional.
Flight avionics/instrumentation: Standard VFR. Optional avionics to customer requirements, and include radar, FLIR, air communications system and scanner/alert system.
Aircraft variants:
MD 500E is the standard lower-powered version, with a choice of 250-C20B or R engines.
MD 530F is the hot day/high altitude version with more engine power, increased diameter rotors for extra thrust and directional control at high altitudes, and 8 ins (0.2 m) extended tailboom.
MG Defender is offered in paramilitary and fully-militarized versions. Paramilitary is for law enforcement, patrol and similar missions and can be lightly armed. The fully militarized versions, again based on the MD 500E and MD 530F, are for day/night and adverse weather operations, capable of nap-of-the-earth anti-armour, armed support, day/night

DETAILS FOR MD 500E, *WITH MD 530F IN ITALICS.*

Principal dimensions:
Rotor diameter (main): 26 ft 5 ins (8.05 m), *27 ft 5 ins (8.36 m)*
Maximum length, rotors turning: 30 ft 10 ins (9.35 m), *32 ft 7 ins (9.93 m)*
Fuselage length: 24 ft 7 ins (7.49 m), *the same*
Fuselage width: 4 ft 7 ins (1.4 m)
Maximum height: 8 ft 9.5 ins (2.69 m), or 9 ft 9.5 ins (3 m) with extended undercarriage, *the same*

Cabin:
Length: 8 ft (2.44 m)
Width: 4 ft 3.5 ins (1.31 m)

Main rotor:
Blade chord: 6.75 ins (0.17 m)
Blade area: each 6.67 sq ft (0.62 m^2), *6.96 sq ft (0.647 m^2)*
Rotor disc: 547.81 sq ft (50.89 m^2), *587.5 sq ft (54.58 m^2)*
Rpm: 492, *477*

Tail rotor:
Diameter: 4 ft 7 ins (1.4 m), *4 ft 10 ins (1.47 m)*
Rpm: 2,933, *2,848*

Undercarriage:
Type: Fixed skids, with extended gear optional, *the same*. Optional floats or emergency buoyancy floats. Can land on a 20° slope
Skid track: 6 ft 3.5 ins (1.92 m), *the same*

Weights:
Empty: 1,481 lb (672 kg) standard, 1,417 lb (643 kg) industrial, *1,591 lb (722 kg) standard*
Maximum take-off: 3,000 lb (1,361 kg), *3,100 lb (1,406 kg)*
Maximum take-off, external load: 3,550 lb (1,610 kg), *3,750 lb (1,700 kg)*
Useful load: 1,519 lb (689 kg) normal category, or 2,069 lb (938 kg) external load operations, *1,509 lb (684 kg) normal category, or 2,159 lb (979 kg) external load operations*

Performance (MD 500E with C20B engine, *MD 530F with C30*)**:**
Never-exceed speed (VNE): 152 kts (175 mph) 281 km/h at sea level, *the same*
Maximum cruise speed: 135 kts (155 mph) 249 km/h at sea level or 133 kts (153 mph) 246 km/h at 5,000 ft (1,525 m), *134 kts (154 mph) 247 km/h at sea level or 135 kts (155 mph) 249 km/h at 5,000 ft (1,525 m)*
Maximum climb rate: 1,770 ft (539 m) per minute at sea level and ISA or 1,776 ft (541 m) per minute ISA + 20° C, *2,069 ft (630 m) per minute sea level and ISA or 2,061 ft (628 m) per minute ISA + 20° C*
IGE hovering ceiling: 8,500 ft (2,590 m) ISA or 6,000 ft (1,830 m) ISA + 20° C, *14,300 ft (4,360 m) ISA or 12,000 ft (3,660 m) ISA + 20° C*
OGE hovering ceiling: 6,000 ft (1,830 m) ISA or 3,100 ft (945 m) ISA + 20° C, *12,000 ft (3,660 m) ISA or 9,750 ft (2,970 m) ISA + 20° C*
Ceiling: 16,000 ft (4,875 m) certified service limit, *the same*
Range: 239 naut miles (275 miles) 442 km at sea level or 264 naut miles (304 miles) 489 km at 5,000 ft (1,525 m), *206 naut miles (237 miles) 381 km at sea level or 232 naut miles (267 miles) 430 km at 5,000 ft (1,525 m)*
Duration: 2.7 hours at sea level, *2 hours at sea level*

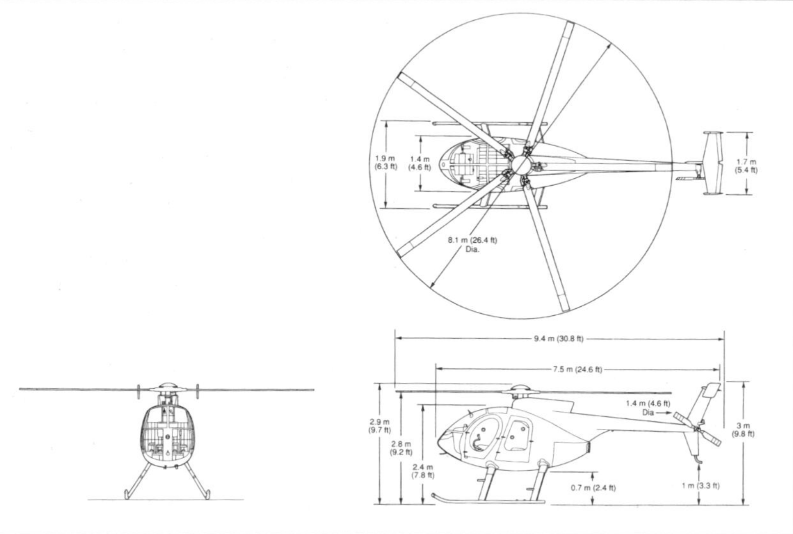

McDonnell Douglas MD 500E (courtesy McDonnell Douglas)

surveillance and other specialized missions in addition to utility work. Fully militarized models each have a fully integrated cockpit using 1553B digital databus interfacing, with multi-function displays, data transfer unit with ground loader, and hands on lever and stick control (incorporating weapon firing). Autopilot, AHRS, Doppler navigator, ADF/VOR, radar altimeter, transponder and optional ground proximity warning system. Other options include a TOW sighting system for use with TOW 2 anti-armour missiles, FLIR, laser ranger, IFF, and radar warning receiver. NATO standard pylons on outriggers. Other weapon choices are launchers for 2.75-in rockets, 7.62-mm machine-gun pods or Stinger AAMs.
TOW Defender specializes in an anti-armour role, with 4 TOW 2 missiles and a sighting system. Any choice of MD 500E/530F engine.
Nightfox is a variant of either fully militarized MG Defender, specializing in night operations and using FLIR and NVG.

McDonnell Douglas MD 500 series Defender operated by the Philippine Air Force, with rocket pods

McDonnell Douglas MD 520N and MD 520N Defender

First flight: 1 May 1990 (prototype, following trials with a modified OH-6A NOTAR from 17 December 1981).
Role: MD 520N is a light utility helicopter, used for executive transportation, cargo lifting, law enforcement, patrol and other roles. Defender is a military and paramilitary member of the same family, with more specialized equipment, armament and crashworthy fuselage structure.
Sales: Over 80 delivered from a total of more than 200 firm orders/options. In addition, some US Army special operations AH-6s and MH-6s have been converted to NOTAR.
Crew/passengers: Pilot and up to 4 passengers for MD 520N, with optional VIP interior.
Freight, external: Optional cargo hook of 2,000 lb (907 kg) capacity.
Optional equipment: As for MD 500E/530F.
Rotor system: Fully articulated 5-blade type, of metal. Fail-safe main rotor and steel strap rotor retention system. Manual folding.
Anti-torque system: NOTAR (no tail rotor) anti-torque system consists of an enclosed variable-pitch fan

DETAILS FOR MD 520N, *WITH DEFENDER IN ITALICS WHERE DIFFERENT.*

Principal dimensions:
Rotor diameter: 27 ft 5 ins (8.36 m)
Maximum length, rotors turning: 32 ft 1 ins (9.78 m)
Fuselage length: 25 ft 6 ins (7.77 m)
Fuselage width: 4 ft 7 ins (1.4 m)
Maximum height: 9 ft 8 ins (2.95 m)
Cabin: Similar to MD 500E/530F but with a lowered mid-cabin divider and some other changes to enhance visibility

Undercarriage:
Type: Fixed skids, with extended gear optional, *the same*. Optional floats or emergency buoyancy floats.
Skid track: 6 ft 3.5 ins (1.92 m)

Weights:
Empty: 1,586 lb (719 kg) standard, 1,486 lb (674 kg) industrial
Maximum take-off: 3,350 lb (1,520 kg) normal category
Maximum take-off, external load: 3,850 lb (1,746 kg)
Useful load: 1,864 lb (845 kg) industrial, normal category, or 2,364 lb (1,072 kg) industrial, external load

Performance (MTOW, normal category)**:**
Never-exceed speed (VNE): 152 kts (175 mph) 281 km/h
Cruise speed: 123 kts (142 mph) 229 km/h at sea level or 124 kts (143 mph) 230 km/h at 5,000 ft (1,525 m), *125 kts (144 mph) 232 km/h at sea level or 120 kts (138 mph) 222 km/h at 5,000 ft (1,525 m)*
Maximum climb rate: 1,546 ft (471 m) per minute at sea level, ISA, or 1,280 ft (390 m) ISA + 20° C
IGE hovering ceiling: 9,300 ft (2,835 m) ISA, 5,100 ft (1,554 m) ISA + 20° C
OGE hovering ceiling: 5,600 ft (1,705 m) ISA, 1,400 ft (427 m) ISA + 20° C
Ceiling: 20,000 ft (6,100 m) certificated
Range: 197 naut miles (227 miles) 365 km at sea level, or 210 naut miles (242 miles) 389 km at 5,000 ft (1,525 m), *202 naut miles (233 miles) 375 km at sea level or 210 naut miles (242 miles) 389 km at 5,000 ft (1,525 m)*
Duration: 2.2 hours

(with 13 thermoplastic blades) driven from the main transmission, a circulation control tailboom, direct-jet thruster and vertical stabilizers mounted at the tips of a horizontal aerofoil tailplane. The port stabilizer is controlled by the anti-torque pedals, the starboard being servo operated. In operation, fan-created low air pressure is forced through 2 circulation control slots in the boom, causing the main rotor downwash to "hug" the contour of the boom, providing the majority of the anti-torque force required in a hover by creating a lateral lift that counteracts main rotor torque. Remaining anti-torque and directional control are provided by the direct-jet thruster, which uses part of the fan-created air pressure, controlled by anti-torque pedal input. The NOTAR system permits greater manoeuvrability, precise directional control even in extreme crosswinds, increases safety both in the air and on the ground, and gives considerable noise reduction. Static mast hub support.
Tail surfaces: See before.
Flight control system: Mechanical, without hydraulic boost.
Airframe materials: Similar to MD 530F but with a new NOTAR lightweight graphite composite tailboom.
Safety features: Defender has crashworthy structure.
Engine: Allison 250-C20R turboshaft.
Engine rating: 450 shp (313 kW), derated to 425 shp (317 kW) for take-off and 375 shp (280 kW) maximum continuous.
Fuel system: 242 litres/
Flight avionics/instrumentation: As for MD 500E/530F.
Aircraft variants:
MD 520N is the civil version.
MD 520N Defender is the military version, similar in role and equipment options to the MD 500 series Defender.

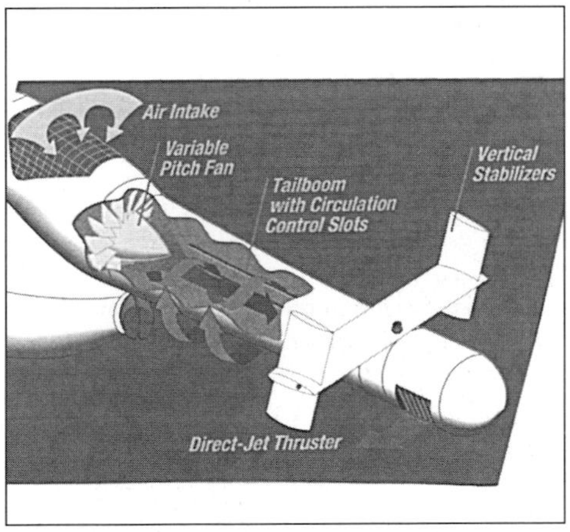

McDonnell Douglas MD 520N NOTAR system (courtesy McDonnell Douglas)

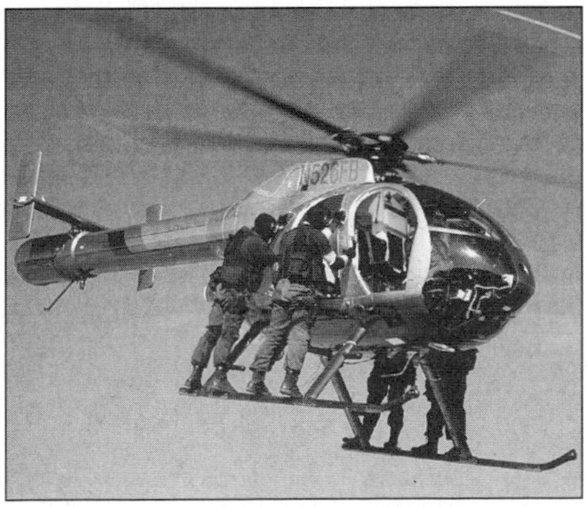

McDonnell Douglas MD 520N carrying officers from the Phoenix police for rapid deployment

McDonnell Douglas MD 600N (formerly MD 630N)

First flight: 22 November 1994. US certification anticipated for the third quarter of 1996, with delivries thereafter.
Role: 7/8-seat stretched version of the MD 520N, intended for utility, offshore work, VIP transport, law enforcement and tour operators. Military version is envisaged.

▲ Development

▲ Prototype based on an MD 520N but with a 2 ft 6 ins (0.76 m) cabin plug and a 2 ft 4 ins (0.71 m) tailboom plug, plus replacement of an underseat fuel tank with a below cabin floor tank, to achieve the required dimensions and cabin volume.
▲ First of a new series of McDonnel Douglas multi-role light helicopters.
Sales: 150-180 expected to be ordered before the turn of the century.
Freight, external: 3,000 lb (1,361 kg) external hook capacity.
Rotor system: 6-blade main rotor.
Anti-torque system: NOTAR (see MD 520N).
Engine: Allison 250-C47 turboshaft.
Engine rating: 790 shp (589 kW), derated to 600 shp (447 kW).
Transmission rating: 600 shp (447 kW).
Fuel system: 454 litres.

McDonnell Douglas MD 600N

DETAILS FOR MD 600N.

Principal dimensions:
Rotor diameter: 27 ft 5 ins (8.36 m)
Maximum length, rotors turning: 36 ft 9 ins (11.2 m)
Fuselage length: 30 ft 6 ins (9.3 m)
Width, blades folded: 6 ft 6 ins (1.98 m)
Maximum height: 9 ft 8 ins (2.95 m)

Undercarriage:
Type: As for MD 520N
Skid track: 6 ft 3.5 ins (1.92 m)

Weights:
Empty: 1,930 lb (875 kg)
Maximum take-off: 4,100 lb (1,860 kg)
Maximum take-off, external load: 4,680 lb (2,123 kg)
Useful load: 2,170 lb (984 kg) internal, 2,750 lb (1,248 kg) external.

Performance:
Never-exceed speed (VNE): 152 kts (175 mph) 282 km/h
Maximum cruise speed: 134 kts (154 mph) 248 km/h
Maximum climb rate: 1,700 ft (518 m) per minute
IGE hovering ceiling: 10,500 ft (3,200 m)
OGE hovering ceiling: 6,800 ft (2,070 m)
Operating ceiling: 20,000 ft (6,100 m)
Range: 335-400 naut miles (386-460 miles) 621-740 km
Duration: 3.7 hours

McDonnell Douglas MD 900 Explorer and Combat Explorer

First flight: 18 December 1992 (first prototype), 17 September 1993 (second), 16 December 1993 (third) and 3 August 1994 (fourth). FAA certification 2 December 1994. IFR and UK certification 1995.
Role: Commercial and military light helicopter.
Sales: Well over 100 firm orders and a large number of options, the former including 17 for 3 Japanese customers. First delivery on 16 December 1994 (first of 5 for Petroleum Helicopters), followed by an air ambulance version for Rocky Mountain Helicopters. 20 Explorers are being delivered during 1995. Production rate of 48 per year from 1997.
Crew/passengers: 8 seats, including crew of 1 or 2.
Freight, internal: 51.4 cu ft (1.46 m^3) baggage compartment, if closed off.
Cabin access: Cabin door each side, 4 ft 2 ins (1.27 m) wide, large enough to allow loading of a standard 4 ft (1.22 m) pallet with a forklift vehicle. Opening 4 ft 4 ins (1.32 m) if door removed.
Rotor system: 5-blade bearingless composite rotor, with titanium leading-edge abrasion strip and carbonfibre flexbeam Iblade retention straps. Detachable swept tips with balance-tracking-weights.
Anti-torque system: NOTAR (see MD 520N).
Flight control system: Hydraulic actuators.
Airframe materials: Typical McDonnell Douglas light alloy A-frame structure, with composites skin, fairings and access doors. Deep keel beams that extend the full length of the helicopter for added safety.
Safety features: Energy-absorbing crew seats (16 g forward and 20 g downward).
Engines: 2 x 650 shp (485 kW) Pratt & Whitney Canada PW206A turboshafts. Alternatively, 2 x 641 shp (478 kW) Turbomeca Arrius 2C turboshafts. Single-engine operation capability.
Transmission rating: Planetary transmission. 900 shp (671 kW) continuous, 1,000 shp (746 kW) for 5 minutes, and 575 shp (429 kW) for 2.5 minutes OEI.
Fuel system: 602 litres usable. Self-sealing fuel lines. Provision for 666 litre tank.
Electrical system: Dual DC starter-generators. Battery.
Flight avionics/instrumentation: Advanced avionics. Dual pilot or single-pilot operation. Integrated Instrument Display System (IIDS) with colour liquid crystal displays for engine, rotor track and balance data, and records engine exceedences and allows maintainers to automatically monitor engine trend analysis, giving advanced warning of potential problems.
Aircraft variants:
MD 900 Explorer is the civil version, as detailed.
Combat Explorer is the military version, for possibly production delivery from 1997. NightHawk electro-optical surveillance and targeting multi-sensor system, with daylight and infra-red sighting, laser ranging and laser designation capabilities, also useful in navigation and search/seizure operations as well as threat location and identification; can use co-ordinates supplied by radar or GPS. FLIR. Armament includes Hellfire anti-armour missiles, 2.75-in rocket launchers and guns

Details for MD 900 Explorer.

Principal dimensions:
Rotor diameter: 33 ft 10 ins (10.31 m)
Maximum length, rotors turning: 38 ft 10 ins (11.84 m)
Fuselage length: 32 ft 4 ins (9.86 m)
Cabin width: 5 ft 4 ins (1.62 m)
Maximum height: 12 ft (3.66 m)

Cabin:
Length: 12 ft 11 ins (3.94 m) to instrument panel, including baggage compartment. 6 ft 3 ins (1.91 m) main cabin alone. 14 ft (4.26 m) flat floor space
Width: 4 ft 9 ins (1.45 m)
Height: 4 ft 1 ins (1.24 m)
Volume: 172.5 cu ft (4.88 m^3) main cabin

Main rotor:
Rotor disc: 899.04 sq ft (83.52 m^2)

Undercarriage
Type: Fixed skids, mounted on dampers to minimize ground resonance
Skid track: 7 ft 4 ins (2.24 m)

Weights:
Empty: 3,265 lb (1,480 kg), standard configuration
Maximum take-off: 6,000 lb (2,721 kg)
Maximum take-off, external load: 6,740 lb (3,057 kg)
Useful load: 2,565 lb (1,163 kg) standard configuration
Payload: 3,000 lb (1,360 kg) externally

Performance (PW206As, preliminary estimates):
Never-exceed speed (VNE): 160 kts (184 mph) 296 km/h at sea level
Cruise speed: 145 kts (167 mph) 268 km/h at sea level
Maximum climb rate: 2,800 ft (853 m) per minute
Vertical climb rate: 1,350 ft (411 m) per minute
Climb rate, OEI 1,000 ft (305 m) per minute
IGE hovering ceiling: 12,800 ft (3,900 m) ISA, 9,550 ft (2,910 m) ISA + 20° C
OGE hovering ceiling: 11,300 ft (3,445 m) ISA, 7,100 ft (2,165 m) ISA + 20° C
Ceiling: 18,000 ft (5,485 m), or 10,500 ft (3,200 m) OEI
Range: 286-315 naut miles (329-363 miles) 530-583 km at 5,000 ft (1,525 m), ISA
Duration: 3 to 3.5 hours, at 5,000 ft (1,525 m), ISA

Performances achieved during certification/testing:
Forward flight: 177 kts (204 mph) 328 km/h
Sideways flight: 40 kts (46 mph) 74 km/h
G loading: +3
Banked turns: 60°
Climb rate: 2,800 ft (853 m) per minute
Descent rate: 2,000 ft (610 m) per minute
Autorotational descent: 4,600 ft (1,402 m) per minute/ 148 kts
Sideslips: ±16° at 100 kts

McDonnell Douglas MD 900 Combat Explorer

Integrated display system, with weather radar, VOR/ADF/GPS navigation, IFF, VHF/UHF/HF communications, and RWR. Operational weight 6,900 lb (3,130 kg), maximum permitted speed 150 kts (172 mph) 278 km/h, maximum duration 3 to 3.35 hours, hovering OGE 10,700 ft (3,261 m) and IGE 12,600 ft (3,840 m), ISA.

McDonnell Douglas AH-64D Longbow Apache

First flight: 15 April 1992 for first AH-64D prototype without radar. Original YAH-64 development prototype first flew on 30 September 1975.
Role: Day/night and adverse weather attack helicopter, designed to survive in a mid-to-high intensity battlefield and be self-deployable. Also suited to air combat, coastal defence, air defence suppression, deep strike, joint air attack, armed reconnaissance, fire support and more.

▲ Development

▲ 4 prototypes appeared in 1992-93, followed in 1994 by 2 prototypes of the anticipated AH-64C version with many AH-64D features but minus the Longbow radar and upgraded engines. That same year the US Army adandoned the AH-64C designation, deciding instead to designate all modernized Apaches as AH-64Ds whether fitted or not with Longbow radar. The AH-64Cs are, therefore, the fifth and sixth AH-64D prototypes.
Sales: All remaining active US Army, US Army National Guard and US Army Reserve AH-64As (of 821 delivered) are being upgraded to the current AH-64D, the programme starting in 1996 and not expected to be completed until the year 2010. In addition, new or ex-US Army AH-64As were ordered by Egypt (24 + 12), Greece, Israel, Kuwait (16 required), Saudi Arabia and the United Arab Emirates (30). 30 AH-64Ds were ordered by the Netherlands on 7 April 1995, for delivery from 1998, with 12 US Army AH-64As being loaned from 1996 until these arrive. On 13 July 1995 the British Government ordered 67 AH-64Ds for the British Army Air Corps, to be built by Westland.
Crew: 2 in tandem, the pilot to the rear in a 1 ft 7 ins (0.48 m) upward-stepped cockpit to improve forward vision. Fragmentation protection barrier between the cockpits. Boron armour protection against 12.7-mm hits.
Rotor system: 4-blade main rotor with swept tips. Metal/composites blades that fold, with tolerance to 23-mm hits. Electric blade de-icing. Steel blade/hub retention straps with elastomeric bearings.
Tail rotor characteristics: 2 teetering 2-blade rotors, with 55° separation in "scissors" configuration, on the port side of the fin.
Tail surfaces: Horizontal stabilizer with automatically adjusting incidence, for optimum position during hover and all other flying modes.
Flight control system: Principal redundant hydraulic system, with fly-by-wire back-up.
Safety features: Can survive 12.7-mm gunfire hits for a minimum of 30 minutes continued flight, and some components can survive 23-mm strikes.
Engines: 2 General Electric T700-GE-701C turboshafts. IR suppression, and particle separators. AlliedSignal 36-155 (BH) APU for engine start-up.
Engine rating: Each 1,890 shp (1,409 kW) take-off and 1,662 shp (1,239.4 kW) maximum continuous. Emergency OEI contingency rating of 1,940 shp (1,447 kW).

McDonnell Douglas AH-64D Longbow Apache

Transmission: Can continue without oil for 60 minutes.
Fuel system: 2,442 lb (1,108 kg) maximum internal. 5,980 lb (2,712 kg) maximum external auxiliary.
Electrical system: Increased AC power on AH-64D by use of 2 x 70 kVA (instead of 35 kVA) engine-driven generators. 2 transformer rectifiers for DC supply. Back-up battery.
Hydraulic system: Twin, at 3,000 psi.
Braking system: Mainwheel hydraulic.
Radar: Mast-mounted Longbow fire control radar (360°). In under 30 seconds the crew unmasks the radar dome for a single radar scan, then remasks. As the scan is completed, onboard processors have *detected* the precise location, speed and direction of movement of up to 256 targets, *classified* the targets as tracked or wheeled, air defence, helicopters or aeroplanes, *prioritized* the most dangerous or priority targets in the target array, and *displayed* the target information and indicated the highest threat targets. All target information, plus its own identification/location/time, are then transmitted to command elements via digital data burst through the improved data modem. The battle area is then divided, and priority fire zones and attack teams assigned.
Flight avionics/instrumentation: Integrated GPS, HF radio, target acquisition and designation sight (TADS) and pilot night vision sensor (PNVS), inertial navigation, radar frequency interferometer, and Longbow fire control radar. TADS provides the co-pilot/gunner with the capabilities for target search, detection, recognition, and laser designation by means of direct-view optics, TV and FLIR sensors that may be used individually or in combination. PNVS provides thermal imaging capabilities that enable nap-of-the-earth (NOE) flight. TADS/PNVS are carried at the nose, and AH-64D introduces reliability improvements. AN/ASN-157 Doppler navigation, with AHRS. Terrain profiling/avoidance. Airborne target handover system (ATHS). SINCGARS radio and GPS were first deployed in AH-64As of the 5-501st Aviation Regiment, in 1993. Cockpit CRTs and crew integrated helmet and display sighting system (IHADSS). AH-64D also features enhanced fire control computer, and antennae relocation to improve NOE communication and improve IFF. Fault detection and location system (FDLS). All systems are integrated through a MIL-STD-1553B multiplex databus system. The AH-64D upgrade also introduces improved data modem, manprint crewstation (provides increased crew effectiveness, ease of maintenance, automated data transfer, and enhanced situation awareness), new weapons processor, and mission planning console. AFCS, with autohover (see Tail surfaces).

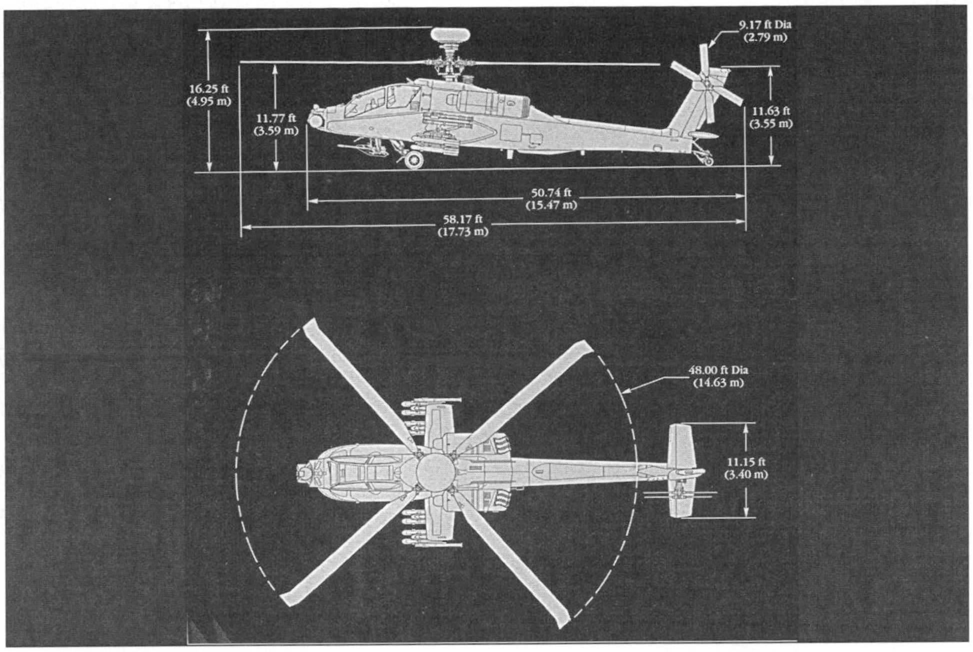

McDonnell Douglas AH-64D Longbow Apache general arrangement (courtesy McDonnell Douglas)

Self-protection systems: Radar and laser warning, radar and infra-red jammers, and chaff dispensers.
Fixed guns: McDonnell Douglas 30-mm M230 Chain Gun automatic cannon, with reliability upgrade on the AH-64D.
Ammunition: 1,200 rounds.

Number of weapon pylons: 4 under the stub wings, with an additional dual AAM launchers on the tips.
Expendable weapons and equipment: 16 Hellfire anti-tank missiles or 76 x 2.75-in rockets typically. 4 AIM-92 Stinger AAMs on wingtip launchers, with alternative 2 Sidewinders or 4 Mistrals. AAMs can also be carried on the main pylons. Maverick is among other possible weapon choices.
Aircraft variants:
AH-64A Apache was the original production version, as delivered to the US Army and all foreign customers prior to the Netherlands and the UK. Will remain the principal version with the US Army while upgrading to AH-64D takes place. T700-GE-701 engines of 1,570 shp (1,170.7 kW) maximum continuous and 1,723 shp (1,285 kW) maximum contingency.
AH-64D Longbow Apache is the current version, either by conversion of AH-64As or newly built (as for the Netherlands and UK). Features Longbow radar and more powerful engines, as detailed. Improved electrical, navigation and vapour cooling systems, plus EMI hardening.
Westland Longbow Apache is the version for the British Army Air Corps (67 ordered), featuring RTM322 engines. Could have new helmet display and sighting system and defence aid suite. Performance should be generally similar, as the Westland-built transmission will be the same type as that in the US Apache.

DETAILS FOR AH-64D.

Principal dimensions:
Rotor diameter (main): 48 ft (14.63 m)
Maximum length, rotors turning: 58 ft 2 ins (17.73 m)
Fuselage length: 50 ft 9 ins (15.47 m) from TADS/PNVS nose to turning tail rotor
Maximum height: 16 ft 3 ins (4.95 m) to top of Longbow radar

Main rotor:
Blade chord: 1 ft 9 ins (0.53 m)
Rotor disc: 1,809.5 sq ft (168.11 m^2)

Tail rotor:
Diameter: 9 ft 2 ins (2.79 m)

Undercarriage:
Type: Fixed, with castering and self-centring tailwheel. Main units can "kneel" to lower height for air transportation. Can sustain landings at 42 ft (12.8 m) per second
Main wheel tyre size: 8.50-10
Tail wheel tyre size: 5.00-4
Wheel base: 34 ft 9 ins (10.59 m)
Wheel track: 6 ft 8 ins (2.03 m)

Weights:
Empty: 11,800 lb (5,352 kg)
Primary mission take-off: 16,491 lb (7,480 kg)
Maximum take-off, for ferrying: 22,283 lb (10,107 kg)

Performance (primary mission weight):
Never-exceed speed (V_{NE}): 197 kts (227 mph) 364 km/h
Maximum speed: 141 kts (162 mph) 261 km/h at sea level and ISA (transmission limit), or 143 kts (165 mph) 265 km/h at 4,000 ft (1,220 m)
Cruise speed: 141 kts (162 mph) 261 km/h at sea level and ISA (transmission limit), or 133 kts (153 mph) 246 km/h at 4,000 ft (1,220 m) and 35° C
Maximum climb rate: 3,090 ft (942 m) per minute at sea level and ISA (transmission limit), or 2,290 ft (698 m) per minute at 4,000 ft (1,220 m) and 35° C
Vertical climb rate: 1,555 ft (474 m) per minute at sea level and ISA (transmission limit), or 1,025 ft (312 m) per minute at 4,000 ft (1,220 m) and 35° C
IGE hovering ceiling: 13,500 ft (4,115 m) ISA, or 9,130 ft (2,783 m) at 35° C
OGE hovering ceiling: 9,810 ft (2,990 m) ISA, 6,120 ft (1,865 m) at 35° C
Range with internal fuel: 220 naut miles (253 miles) 407 km at sea level and ISA, or 234 naut miles (269 miles) 433 km at 4,000 ft (1,220 m) and 35° C, both with 30 minutes reserve
Duration: Design mission 1.83 hours. Maximum 3.2 hours at sea level and ISA or 3.3 hours at 4,000 ft (1,220 m) and 35° C

Perch Inc (USA)

Corporate address: 12451 Oak Plank Road, Jacksonville, FL 32220.
Telephone: +1 904 693 1551

Perch Nolan 51-HJ

Role: Single-seat homebuilt helicopter.
Sales: Kit costing US$17,995 without engine, instruments and avionics. Typically 250 working hours to assemble.
Rotor system: 2 co-axial, contra-rotating, pendulum type, with gimbal control for pitch/yaw.
Tail surfaces: Horizontal stabilizer on a high boom, with endplates and large tabs.
Airframe materials: Main structure is welded steel tubing.
Engines: 2 Rotax 503 piston engines.
Engine rating: Each 49.6 hp (37 kW).
Fuel system: 38 litres.

DETAILS FOR 51-HJ.

Principal dimensions:
Rotor diameter: Each 13 ft 6 ins (4.11 m)
Fuselage length: 14 ft 3 ins (4.34 m)

Undercarriage:
Type: Twin fixed skids

Weights:
Empty: 481 lb (218 kg)
Maximum take-off: 800 lb (363 kg)
Useful load: 320 lb (145 kg)

Performance:
Cruise speed: 52 kts (60 mph) 97 km/h

Piasecki Aircraft Corporation (USA)

Corporate address: Second Street West, Essington, PA 19029-0360.
Telephone: +1 610 521 5700
Facsimile: +1 610 521 5935
Founded: June 1955.
Information: John Piasecki.

● Activities
● Include marketing rights for the PZL Swidnik W-3A in the Americas and Pacific rim. Is developing, under US Army contract, a vectored thrust ducted propeller system for the Apache and SuperCobra, aimed at demonstrating increased performance and agility. A separate programme is defining Piasecki's concept for a new US Marine Corps medium-lift replacement (MLR) type.

Revolution Helicopter Corp Inc (USA)

Corporate address: 1905 West Jesse James Road, Excelsior Springs, MO 64024.
Telephone: +1 816 637 2800
Facsimile: +1 816 637 7936
Founded: January 1991.
Information: Nicole Raulie (Public Relations).

Revolution Mini-500

First flight: 1992.
Role: Single-seat light helicopter, offered in kit form but can be factory assembled. Military version also delivered, and has demonstrated law enforcement capabilities.
Sales: 364 orders/deposits received by April 1995. First delivery of a production helicopter (No 0001 – following factory assembly) 12 July 1994. A single example of a military version was delivered to an unspecified "major military weapons contractor" on 16 August 1994. Further military orders are anticipated. Kit costs US$28,850 (April 1995 cost), shipped with everything needed for VFR flight, including engine and instruments.
Crew: Pilot only, up to 250 lb (113 kg) weight. Can accommodate pilots over 6 ft (1.83 m) tall.
Standard equipment: Includes full flight and engine instrumentation, landing and navigation lights, and ground handling wheels.
Optional equipment: Includes chip detector for the main transmission and tail rotor gearbox.
Rotor system: 2-blade semi-rigid, teetering. Blades of composite construction, with solid aluminium leading-edge, foam core and Kevlar skins. Yoke control system, which eliminates the conventional swashplate. 2.25-ins chromoly steel drive shaft (nickel plated), with control rods inside. Sprag clutch to allow immediate autorotation in the event of engine failure. Spiral-bevel ring and pinion drive line to main rotor, with 4.857:1 speed reducing ratio.
Tail rotor characteristics: 2-blade, free to teeter, rigid interplane. Aluminium alloy blades. Precone angle 2°. Spiral-bevel gears drive line to tail rotor.
Tail surfaces: Dorsal/ventral fin, with T-mounted horizontal stabilizer with endplates.
Flight control system: Conventional mechanical.
Airframe materials: Tubular steel fuselage structure, with foam/glassfibre cabin.

DETAILS FOR MINI-500.

Principal dimensions:
Rotor diameter (main): 19 ft (5.79 m)
Maximum length, rotors turning: 22 ft 6 ins (6.86 m)
Fuselage length: 18 ft (5.49 m)
Fuselage width: 3 ft (0.91 m)
Maximum height: 8 ft 1 ins (2.46 m)

Cabin:
Length: 4 ft 3 ins (1.3 m)
Width: 2 ft 10.5 ins (0.88 m)
Height: 4 ft 5 ins (1.35 m)

Main rotor:
Blade chord: 8 ins (0.2 m)
Rpm: 550

Tail rotor:
Diameter: 3 ft 10 ins (1.17 m)
Rpm: 2,671

Undercarriage:
Type: Fixed twin skids
Skid track: 5 ft 3 ins (1.6 m)

Weights:
Empty: 330 lb (150 kg)
Maximum take-off: 820 lb (372 kg)
Useful load: 400 lb (181 kg)

Performance:
Never-exceed speed (VNE): 130 kts (150 mph) 241 km/h
Demonstrated level speed: On 25 August 1994, the factory demonstrator with doors removed recorded 96 kts (111 mph) 179 km/h
Maximum cruise speed: 82 kts (95 mph) 153 km/h
Cruise speed at 75% power: 65 kts (75 mph) 121 km/h
Maximum climb rate: 1,100 ft (335 m) per minute
IGE hovering ceiling: 5,500 ft (1,675 m)
OGE hovering ceiling: 7,500 ft (2,285 m)
Ceiling: 10,000 ft (3,050 m), service
Range: 196 naut miles (225 miles) 361 km
Duration: 3 hours maximum

Revolution Mini-500 used in police work

Engine: Rotax 582 piston engine.
Engine rating: 67 hp (50 kW).
Transmission: 2 Kevlar belt-drives from engine to transmission.
Fuel system: 57 litres.
Electrical system: For engine starting, clutch engagement, instruments, lighting and comm/nav systems.
Flight avionics/instrumentation: Airspeed indicator, hourmeter, magnetic compass, slip and bank indicator, vertical speed indicator, altimeter, dual rotor and engine tachometer, and engine coolant temperature gauge. Optional AlliedSignal Bendix/King Crown KLX-135 GPS/comm and KT76A transponder.
Expendable weapons and equipment: Mini-500 in military paint scheme has been shown with dummy rocket launchers on undercarriage outriggers.

Robinson Helicopter Company (USA)

Corporate address: 2901 Airport Drive, Torrance, CA 90505.
Telephone: +1 310 539 0508
Facsimile: +1 310 539 5198
Founded: 1971.
Employees: Over 700.
Information: Milly Donahue (Sales Manager).

Robinson R22

First flight: 28 August 1975.
Role: Lightweight helicopter for transport and pleasure, flight training, aerial photography, law enforcement, agriculture and more.

★ Aims

★ Originally designed as a low-cost and inexpensive-to-operate helicopter for mainly personal owner-operator use but with many other potential applications.

▲ Development

▲ 16 March 1979. FAA certification.
Sales: Production deliveries began in October 1979. More than 2,400 sold. 1994 deliveries were 89 R22s.
Crew/passengers: Pilot and passenger. Dual controls standard (T-bar cyclic), with removable passenger controls optional. Throttle synchronizer. Baggage stowed in a compartment under each seat.
Freight, external: Belly hardpoint optional.
Optional equipment: Apollo DTM-3 spray gear, with 24 ft (7.32 m) sprayboom and 151 litre undercarriage-attached chemical hopper.
Rotor system: 2-blade teetering type (elastomeric teeter stop limits blade teetering during start-up and shut down in windy days), with tri-hinge rotor head that eliminates lag hinges, dampers and hydraulic struts. Flexures, teflon-lined bearings and sealed ball bearings eliminate need for grease fittings. Maintenance-free flex couplings are used in place of universal joints and gear couplings in the main and tail drive system. Each blade has a hardened stainless steel spar and leading edge (latter for erosion protection), and an aft portion of light alloy honeycomb and bonded aluminium alloy skin. Rotor brake standard. Optional rpm governor. Sprag clutch.
Tail rotor characteristics: 2-blade, metal.
Tail surfaces: Fin, with a small horizontal stabilizer on the starboard side.
Flight control system: Push-pull tubes and bell cranks.
Airframe materials: Primary structure of welded steel tubing and riveted aluminium alloy. Aluminium alloy monocoque tailboom. Glassfibre and thermoplastics used for secondary structures.
Engine: Textron Lycoming O-320-B2C piston engine. New electronic throttle governor based on the R44 governor (sensing only engine rpm; previous governor sensed rotor rpm and applied both collective and throttle inputs to control rpm), incorporated on all new helicopters from s/n 2520 and offered as a retrofit kit.
Engine rating: 160 hp (119.3 kW).
Transmission: 131 hp (97.7 kW) take-off, 124 hp (92.5 kW) continuous. V-belts drive from engine, with sprag clutch. Main gearbox chip and temperature, and tail gearbox chip warning lights.
Fuel system: 72 litres standard. 40 litre auxiliary tank.
Electrical system: 12 volt DC supply with starter-generator.
Flight avionics/instrumentation: Includes as standard a clock, magnetic compass, digital OAT gauge, hourmeter, carb air temperature gauge, fuel quantity gauge, cylinder head gauge, oil temperature and pressure gauges, ammeter, AlliedSignal Bendix/King KY 197 comm transceiver, intercom, rate-of-climb indicator, airspeed indicator, dual rotor and engine tachometer, altimeter, and manifold pressure gauge.

DETAILS FOR R22 BETA.

Principal dimensions:
Rotor diameter (main): 25 ft 2 ins (7.67 m)
Maximum length, rotors turning: 28 ft 9 ins (8.76 m)
Fuselage length: 20 ft 8 ins (6.3 m)
Cabin width: 3 ft 8 ins (1.12 m)
Maximum height: 8 ft 11 ins (2.72 m)

Cabin:
Length: 4 ft 3.5 ins (1.3 m)
Width: 3 ft 7 ins (1.09 m)
Height: 4 ft (1.22 m)

Main rotor:
Aerofoil section: NACA 63-015
Blade chord: 7.2 ins (0.18 m)
Rotor disc: 497.4 sq ft (46.21 m^2)

Tail rotor:
Diameter: 3 ft 6 ins (1.07 m)

Undercarriage:
Type: Fixed twin skids, with ground handling wheels
Skid track: 6 ft 4 ins (1.93 m)

Weights:
Empty, equipped: 835 lb (379 kg)
Maximum take-off: 1,370 lb (621 kg)
Crew and baggage: 420 lb (191 kg)

Performance:
Never-exceed speed (VNE): 102 kts (118 mph) 190 km/h
Cruise speed: 96 kts (110 mph) 177 km/h
Maximum climb rate: 1,000 ft (305 m) at sea level
IGE hovering ceiling: 6,970 ft (2,125 m)
OGE hovering ceiling: 5,200 ft (1,585 m)
Ceiling: 14,000 ft (4,265 m)
Range: over 173 naut miles (200 miles) 322 km, no reserve
Range with auxiliary fuel: over 260 naut miles (300 miles) 483 km
Duration: 2.2 hours, no reserve, standard fuel

Warning lights for low fuel, main gearbox temperature and chip, tail gearbox chip, low oil pressure, low voltage alternator, rotor rpm (and horn warning) and rotor brake engaged. Options include transponder, remote altitude encoder, Loran-C, nav/comm. ADF, headsets. artificial horizon, directional gyro, vertical compass, and millibar altimeter. See also Aircraft variants (particularly IFR trainer).

Aircraft variants:
R22 was the initial production version, with 150 hp (112 kW) Textron Lycoming O-320-A2C engine.
R22 Alpha superseded R22, introducing a 160 hp (119.3 kW) O-320-B2C engine. 124 hp (92.5 kW) take-off and continuous transmission rating.
R22 Beta is the currently available standard version, as detailed. Same engine but with higher transmission rating for take off.
R22 Mariner is equipped with utility floats, has corrosion proofing throughout, special handling wheels, and gauge/nozzle for checking float pressure. Floats installation adds about 33 lb (15 kg) to empty weight. VNE 95 kts (109 mph) 176 km/h. Optional equipment includes alternative aft battery provision (for operations without floats), belly tie-down ring, main rotor blade supports, wind deflectors, 2-man life-raft, I-Com IC-M56 marine radio, I-Com IC 3230 radio, and single pilot multiple radio control panel.
R22 IFR trainer configuration was conceived for instrument flight training, and includes an artificial horizon, encoding altimeter, turn co-ordinator, HSI, digital clock, ADF, nav/comm, transponder and marker beacon. DME optional.
R22 law enforcement configuration optionally adds a 1.5 million candlepower searchlight with dual lamps, public address speaker and siren, 70 amp alternator (exchange) for use with the searchlight, single pilot multiple radio control panel and dual pilot multiple radio to the basic R22 Beta.

Osaka Aviation Robinson R44 Astro used during the Kobe, Japan, earthquake relief efforts in January 1995

Robinson R22 Beta

Robinson R44 Astro

First flight: 30 March 1990.
Role: Light civil helicopter, with other potential applications including law enforcement, air taxi, sightseeing, aerial photography, reporting, construction support and agricultural spraying. Basically a four-seat development of the R22.

▲ Development
▲ 10 December 1992. FAA certification.
Sales: Production deliveries began in early 1994, with nearly 200 operating in 20 countries by mid-1995. US deliveries started in July 1995.
Crew/passengers: 4 persons, including pilot. Lap belt and shoulder strap restraints are designed for high forward g loads.
Details: Similar to R22; except as described below.
Engine: Textron Lycoming O-540 piston engine.
Engine rating: 260 hp (194 kW), derated to 225 hp (168 kW) for take-off and 205 hp (153 kW) continuous.
Transmission: Automatic clutch engagement to simplify and reduce start-up procedure, and reduce chances of overspeed.
Fuel system: 116 litres standard. Auxiliary tank of 69.3 litres.
Flight avionics/instrumentation: Includes as standard a clock, artificial horizon, magnetic compass, digital OAT gauge, hourmeter, cylinder head gauge, oil temperature and pressure gauges, ammeter, AlliedSignal Bendix/King KY 197 comm transceiver, intercom, rate-of-climb indicator, airspeed indicator, dual rotor and engine tachometer, altimeter, and manifold pressure gauge. Warning lights for low fuel, main gearbox temperature and chip, tail gearbox chip, low oil pressure, low voltage alternator, rotor rpm (and horn warning), voltage, and rotor brake and starter engaged. Optional are Jet Electronics 305-1AL artificial horizon or artificial horizon w/slip skid indicator (exchange – required for Part 135 air taxi operation), turn co-ordinator, Jet Electronics 205-1AL directional gyro (required for Part 135 air taxi operation), PAI-700 vertical compass (exchange), LC-2 digital clock (exchange), millibar altimeter (replaces standard in-Hg), AlliedSignal Bendix/King KT76A transponder and KT70 Mode S transponder (latter required for Part 135 air taxi operation), remote altitude encoder (used with KT76A and required for Part 135 air taxi operation), GPS, AlliedSignal Bendix/King nav/comm (KX155 with KI203 indicator), AlliedSignal Bendix/King ADF, Pointer 3000 or 4000 ELT and more.

DETAILS FOR R44 ASTRO.

Principal dimensions:
Rotor diameter (main): 33 ft (10.06 m)
Maximum length, rotors turning: 38 ft 7 ins (11.76 m)
Fuselage length: 29 ft 9 ins (9.07 m) to end of tail rotor guard
Fuselage width: 4 ft 2.5 ins (1.28 m)
Maximum height: 10 ft 9 ins (3.28 m)

Main rotor:
Rotor disc: 855.3 sq ft (79.46 m^2)

Tail rotor:
Diameter: 4 ft 10 ins (1.47 m)

Undercarriage:
Type: Crashworthy gear
Skid track: 7 ft 2 ins (2.18 m)

Weights:
Empty: 1,400 lb (635 kg)
Maximum take-off: 2,400 lb (1,088 kg)
Payload: 816 lb (370 kg) with standard fuel

Performance:
Cruise speed: 113 kts (130 mph) 209 km/h
Maximum climb rate: over 1,000 ft (305 m) per minute
IGE hovering ceiling: 6,400 ft (1,950 m) at MTOW
OGE hovering ceiling: 5,100 ft (1,555 m) at 2,200 lb (998 kg)
Ceiling: 14,000 ft (4,265 m)
Range: 347 naut miles (400 miles) 644 km approximately, no reserve

RotorWay International (USA)

Corporate address: 4141 West Chandler Boulevard, Chandler, AZ 85226.
Telephone: +1 602 961 1001
Facsimile: +1 602 961 1514
Founded: 1 June 1990 (present company).
Information: John Netherwood (President).

● Activities

● The current Exec 162F has been available since August 1994, replacing the former Exec 90 kit-helicopter.

RotorWay Exec 162F

Role: Two-seat, light, kit-built helicopter.

★ Aims

★ In comparison with the Exec 90, it has a redesigned and more comfortable cabin, adding 2 cu ft (0.0565 m^3) of volume, providing more leg room. Door apertures are widened to improve accessibility (door can be removed). The current version of the engine introduces dual electronic ignition, electronic fuel injection, and FADEC.
Sales: Became available in kit form from August 1994. Kit (US$56,000 in October 1994) comes complete (including RotorWay engine and many prefabricated components), requiring only paint and avionics. Marketed in the USA and over 33 foreign countries. Over 20 kits shipped by October 1994 (following some 310 Exec 90s).
Crew/passengers: 2, side-by-side, with dual controls,
Rotor system: 2-blade. The blades have asymmetric aerofoil section and are of aluminium-alloy construction, attached to an aluminium alloy teetering hub by retention straps. Elastomeric bearings.

DETAILS FOR EXEC 162F.

Principal dimensions:
Rotor diameter (main): 25 ft (7.62 m)
Fuselage length: 22 ft (6.71 m)
Maximum height: 8 ft (2.44 m)

Tail rotor:
Diameter: 4 ft (1.22 m)

Undercarriage:
Type: Twin fixed skids. Ground handling wheels. Optional Full Lotus floats
Skid track: 5 ft 5 ins (1.65 m)

Weights:
Empty: 975 lb (442 kg)
Maximum take-off: 1,500 lb (680 kg)
Crew: 425 lb (193 kg)
Equipped useful load: 525 lb (238 kg)

Performance:
Maximum speed: 100 kts (115 mph) 185 km/h at sea level, ISA
Cruise speed: 82 kts (95 mph) 153 km/h
Maximum climb rate: 1,000 ft (305 m) per minute
IGE hovering ceiling: 7,000 ft (2,135 m)
OGE hovering ceiling: 5,000 ft (1,525 m)
Ceiling: 10,000 ft (3,050 m), service
Range: 156 naut miles (180 miles) 290 km, cruise speed
Duration: 2 hours with maximum fuel, cruise speed

RotorWay Exec 162F with optional floats

Tail rotor characteristics: 2-blade, each with steel spar and aluminium alloy skins.
Tail surfaces: Revised design dorsal/ventral fin. Small horizontal stabilizer with endplates mounted mid-way along the boom.
Flight control system: Dual push-pull cable controlled swashplate for cyclic pitch control.
Airframe materials: Welded 4130 chromoly tubular steel tube structure, with wrap-round non-structural glassfibre cabin enclosure. Aluminium alloy monocoque tailboom.
Engine: RotorWay RI 162F piston engine.
Engine rating: 150 hp (112 kW).
Fuel system: 64.4 litres.
Flight avionics/instrumentation: Kit comes with the instrument panel, digital display monitor, engine instruments, rotor tachometer, and flight instruments. Avionics optional.

Schweizer Aircraft Corporation (USA)

Corporate address: See Reconnaissance section for company details.

● Activities

● In addition to the helicopters below and the aeroplanes in the Reconnaissance section, Schweizer supports over 135 Hughes Model 269 series helicopters (predecessor of the Model 300) operating with 75 different US agencies.

Schweizer Model 300C series

First flight: June 1984. Originally flown in August 1969 as the Hughes 300C, itself developed from the Hughes 300 of 1964.
Details: Principally for Model 300C.
Role: Civil and military light utility helicopter.
Sales: Well over 3,300 Model 300 types built by Hughes and Schweizer, with the latter producing over 500 since 1984 as the licence holder.
Crew/passengers: 3 persons side-by-side, with optional dual controls. 100 lb (45 kg) of baggage. Can be configured for litter carrying.
Freight, external: 900 lb (408 kg) sling load, or alternative 200 lb (91 kg) capacity freight racks.
Optional equipment: Simplex agricultural equipment for liquid or dry chemicals.
Rotor system: 3-blade (metal), fully articulated main rotor, with elastomeric dampers.
Tail rotor characteristics: 2-blade (metal spar, glassfibre skin), teetering.
Tail surfaces: Ventral fin and starboard dihedral stabilizer.

DETAILS FOR MODEL 300C.

Principal dimensions:
Rotor diameter (main): 26 ft 10 ins (8.18 m)
Maximum length, rotors turning: 30 ft 10 ins (9.4 m)
Fuselage length: 22 ft 2.2 ins (6.76 m) from tip of skids to tailskid
Fuselage width: 4 ft 3 ins (1.3 m)
Maximum height: 8 ft 8.5 ins (2.65 m)

Main rotor:
Aerofoil section: NACA 0015
Blade chord: 6.75 ins (0.17 m)
Blade area: each 7.55 sq ft (0.702 m^2)
Rotor disc: 565.5 sq ft (52.54 m^2)

Tail rotor:
Diameter: 4 ft 3 ins (1.3 m)

Undercarriage:
Type: Energy absorbing fixed twin skids. Provision for ground handling wheels and floats
Skid base: 8 ft 3 ins (2.51 m)
Skid track: 6 ft 6.5 ins (1.99 m)

Weights:
Empty: 1,100 lb (499 kg)
Maximum take-off: 2,050 lb (930 kg) normal category
Typical operating weight: 1,700 lb (771 kg)
Maximum take-off, external load: 2,150 lb (975 kg)
Useful load: 950 lb (431 kg) normal category, 1,050 lb (476 kg) external load operations

Performance:
Never-exceed speed (V_{NE}): 91 kts (105 mph) 168 km/h at sea level
Maximum cruise speed: 86 kts (99 mph) 159 km/h at sea level and typical operating weight, or 79 kts (91 mph) 146 km/h at sea level and MTOW
Maximum climb rate: 1,305 ft (398 m) per minute at typical operating weight, 750 ft (229 m) per minute at MTOW
IGE hovering ceiling: 10,800 ft (3,292 m) at typical operating weight, or 5,800 ft (1,768 m) at MTOW
OGE hovering ceiling: 8,600 ft (2,621 m) at typical operating weight, or 2,750 ft (838 m) at MTOW
Ceiling: 10,200 ft (3,108 m)
Range: 224 naut miles (258 miles) 415 km at typical operating weight, or 195 naut miles (224 miles) 361 km at MTOW, both at 4,000 ft (1,220 m), no reserve, standard fuel
Duration: 3.8 hours at typical operating weight, or 3.4 hours at MTOW, no reserve, standard fuel

Flight control system: Mechanical, with electric cyclic trimming system.
Airframe materials: Steel tubing structure, with metal enclosure.
Safety features: Energy absorbing skids, crushable sub-floor, and yielding seat structure.
Engine: Textron Lycoming HIO-360-D1A piston engine.
Engine rating: 190 shp (141.6 kW).
Transmission: Electrically tensioned multi-belt and pulley reduction drive from engine.
Fuel system: 113.6 litres standard capacity, raised to 185.5 litres with auxiliary fuel tank.

Schweizer Model 300C

Electrical system: 24 volt supply via an alternator and battery.
Flight avionics/instrumentation: Can include ADF, transponders and transceiver.
Aircraft variants:
Model 300C is the basic version, as detailed.
Model 300C Sky Knight is a police version, with optional night flying equipment, dual controls, searchlight, IR sensor, loudspeaker and siren, police communications, exhaust muffler, 28 volt electrical system to power the equipment, and much more. Among the latest deliveries was a third to the Cleveland Police Department in June 1995.
Model 300CB is the new training version, the first going to Helicopter Adventures. FAA certified in August 1995. Offers lower operating costs due to extended times on the life-limited components, standard right-hand pilot-in-command, and a 180 hp (134 kW) HO-360-C1A carburettor engine. 132 litres of fuel. 1,750 lb (794 kg) gross weight.
TH-300C is a military dual-control trainer, as used by Thailand.

Schweizer Model 330

First flight: June 1988.
Role: Light utility and training helicopter, with good hot-and-high performance. Other roles similar to Model 300C, including law enforcement and agricultural.
Crew/passengers: 3 seats for training and 4 for utility. Dual or 3 sets of controls are available for training.
Rotor system: 3-blade, fully articulated main rotor, with elastomeric dampers.
Tail rotor characteristics: 2-blade (metal spar, glassfibre skin), teetering.
Tail surfaces: Horizontal stabilizer with endplates on boom, and tall ventral and smaller dorsal fins.
Engine: Allison 250-C20W turboshaft.
Engine rating: 420 shp (313.3 kW), derated to 235 shp (175 kW) take-off for 5 minutes, 220 shp (164 kW) maximum continuous.
Fuel system: 227 litres.

Schweizer Model 330 turbine helicopter

DETAILS FOR MODEL 330.

Principal dimensions:
Rotor diameter (main): 26 ft 10 ins (8.18 m)
Maximum length, rotors turning: 30 ft 10 ins (9.4 m)
Fuselage length: 22 ft 4.5 ins (6.82 m) from nose to ventral fin
Fuselage width: 5 ft 8 ins (1.72 m)
Maximum height: 9 ft 6.5 ins (2.91 m)

Cabin:
Width: 5 ft 7 ins (1.7 m)
Height: 4 ft 5 ins (1.35 m)

Undercarriage:
Type: Fixed twin skids with streamline legs
Skid track: 6 ft 10 ins (2.08 m)

Weights:
Empty: 1,120 lb (508 kg)
Typical operating weight: 1,900 lb (862 kg)
Maximum take-off: 2,230 lb (1,012 kg)
Useful load: 1,110 lb (503 kg)

Performance:
Never-exceed speed (VNE): 108 kts (124 mph) 200 km/h at sea level
Typical cruise speed: 100 kts (115 mph) 185 km/h at typical operating weight, 94 kts (108 mph) 174 km/h at MTOW
IGE hovering ceiling: 14,000 ft (4,267 m) at typical operating weight, 8,200 ft (2,500 m) at MTOW, zero wind
OGE hovering ceiling: 11,300 ft (3,444 m) at typical operating weight, 5,900 ft (1,798 m) at MTOW
Ceiling: 12,000 ft (3,660 m) pressure altitude
Range: 269 naut miles (310 miles) 498 km at typical operating weight, 252 naut miles (290 miles) 467 km at MTOW, both with no reserve
Duration: 3.6 hours at typical operating weight, 3.4 hours at MTOW, both with no reserve

Sikorsky Aircraft (USA)

Corporate address: 6900 Main Street, PO Box 9729, Stratford, CT 06497-9129.
Telephone: +1 203 386 4000
Facsimile: +1 203 386 7300
Founded: Foundations in the Sikorsky Aero Engineering Corporation of 1923. Sikorsky Aviation Corporation founded on 3 October 1928, becoming a division of United Technologies Corporation in 1929 (and remaining a division to this day).
Employees: 11,500.
Information: William Tuttle (Manager, Public Relations – *telephone* +1 203 386 5261).

● Activities

- Specializes in the development and manufacture of intermediate to heavy helicopters (9,900-70,400 lb, 4,500-32,000 kg), used by all 5 branches of the US armed forces and civil/military operators worldwide.
- Licensing agreements established production lines for Sikorsky-based helicopters in the UK (Westland), Italy (Agusta, continuing with the HH-3F, typically in the modernized Combat SAR version), Japan (Mitsubishi) and South Korea (Korean Air for H-60 Black Hawk and Daewoo-Sikorsky Aerospace for the S-76). Out-of US-production Sikorsky helicopters still in major service include the SH-3D/G/H Sea King, of which the Brazilian Navy is expected to acquire 6 ex-US Navy helicopters in 1996, these and its existing SH-3Ds receiving new AN/AQS-18(V) dipping sonar. Sea Kings of other nations also undergo periodic upgrading.
- Developing the RAH-66 Comanche with Boeing (see Boeing Sikorsky).
- Upgrade programmes for Sikorsky helicopters include the CH-53 2000 offered by MATA Helicopters in Israel, as being applied to Israeli Air Force CH-53s. The life extension programme includes considerable avionics upgrades, with features such as a new mission computer, 2 multi-function displays, moving map display, HUD, NVG, and HOCAS. In a US programme, USAF MH-53J Pave low III special operations forces helicopters have received a service life extension programme to upgrade hydraulics, wiring and the structure for an increase in gross weight to 50,000 lb (22,680 kg), completed August 1995. Further upgrades for Pave Low IIIs are introducing the Integrated Defense Avionics System (IDAS) and Multi-mission Advanced Tactical Terminal (MATT) systems, to integrate the helicopter's EW systems with off-board OTH intelligence via the MATT receiver, shown on a digital map display.

Sikorsky S-70A/C, H-60 Black Hawk series and derivatives

First flight: 17 October 1974.
Role: UH-60L is principally for troop assault and redeployment, artillery support, medevac, logistic and utility. Use of ESSS (see Number of weapon pylons) provides substantial attack and suppression capability. Specialized variants of H-60 include those for search/rescue and electronic warfare.

▲ Development

▲ 23 December 1976. UH-60A selected for production against the competing Boeing UH-61A, to meet the US Army Utility Tactical Transport Aircraft System (UTTAS) requirement.

Sales: The 2,000th H-60 series helicopter was rolled out by Sikorsky in May 1994 (including all US Army, US Air Force, US Navy, Coast Guard and export variants described in this and the SH-60 entries) and production continues. Current production for the US Army is against a US$1.54 billion contract for 300 UH-60s produced during FY1992-96. Exports or transfers include those to Argentina (VIP, with VIII Brigada Aérea), Australia, Brunei, Colombia, Egypt, Hong Kong (various roles including utility, police and firefighting with the Government Flying Service), Israel, Japan, Jordan, South Korea, Mexico, Morocco, Philippines, Saudi Arabia, and Turkey.
Details: Principally for the current UH-60L, unless stated.
Crew/passengers: 2 flight crew on armour-protected and crashworthy seats (optional gunner in the cabin) and a fully-equipped 11-person infantry squad (14 possible), able to be airlifted in demanding 4,000 ft (1,220 m) elevations and 35°C temperatures or in desert and arctic climates. Alternatively, 4 or 6 litters or internal/external freight.
Freight, external: 9,000 lb (4,082 kg) sling load.
Size of main loading doors: 5 ft 9 ins x 4 ft 6 ins (1.75 x 1.37 m).
Optional equipment: 600 lb (272 kg) capacity rescue hoist.
Rotor system: 4-blade main rotor, with 3° forward tilt. Each blade has a 20° swept tip and comprises a titanium spar, Nomex honeycomb core and composites trailing edge and skins, with titanium/nickel leading-

DETAILS FOR UH-60L BLACK HAWK.

Principal dimensions:
Rotor diameter (main): 53 ft 8 ins (16.36 m)
Maximum length, rotors turning: 64 ft 10 ins (19.76 m)
Fuselage length: 50 ft 0.75 ins (15.26 m)
Length, rotors and pylon folded: 41 ft 4 ins (12.6 m)
Fuselage width: 7 ft 9 ins (2.36 m)
Maximum height: 16 ft 10 ins (5.13 m)
Air-transportable height: 8 ft 11.75 ins (2.74 m)

Cabin:
Length: 12 ft 7 ins (3.84 m)
Width: 6 ft 2 ins (1.88 m)
Height: 4 ft 6 ins (1.37 m)
Volume: 410 cu ft (11.6 m^3)

Main rotor:
Blade chord: 1 ft 8.75 ins (0.53 m)
Blade area: each 46.7 sq ft (4.34 m^2)
Rotor disc: 2,262 sq ft (210.147 m^2)

Tail rotor:
Diameter: 11 ft (3.35 m)
Cant angle: 20° inward

Undercarriage:
Type: Fixed tailwheel type. Some are ski equipped
Main wheel tyre size: 26 x 10.0-11
Tail wheel tyre size: 15 x 6.0-6
Wheel base: 28 ft 11.75 ins (8.83 m)
Wheel track: 8 ft 10.6 ins (2.7 m)

Weights:
Empty: 11,516 lb (5,224 kg)
Mission gross weight: 17,432 lb (7,907 kg)
Maximum take-off: 22,000 lb (9,979 kg) alternate gross weight
Maximum take-off, external load: 23,500 lb (10,659 kg)
Maximum take-off, ferry flight: 24,500 lb (11,113 kg)
Payload: 9,000 lb (4,082 kg) external sling load

Performance:
Never-exceed speed (V_{NE}): 195 kts (225 mph) 361 km/h
Maximum cruise speed: 152 kts (175 mph) 282 km/h at 4,000 ft (1,220 m) and 35° C, or 159 kts (183 mph) 294 km/h at 2,000 ft (610 m) and 21° C, or 155 kts (178 mph) 287 km/h at sea level
Cruise speed, OEI: 112 kts (129 mph) 207 km/h
Vertical climb rate: 963 ft (293 m) per minute at 95% IRP, or 1,550 ft (472 m) per minute at 95% MRP at 4,000 ft (1,220 m) and 35° C, or 2,750 ft (838 m) per minute at 2,000 ft (610 m) and 21° C, or over 3,000 ft (915 m) per minute at sea level
IGE hovering ceiling: 9,500 ft (2,895 m) at 35° C
OGE hovering ceiling: 7,650 ft (2,332 m) at 35° C, or 9,375 ft (2,858 m) at 21° C, or 11,125 ft (3,390 m) ISA.
Ceiling: 19,150 ft (5,837 m), service, ISA
Self-deployment range: 1,150 naut miles (1,324 miles) 2,130 km
Duration: 2.3 hours

edge anti-erosion strip. 18° blade twist. Bifilar vibration damper over rotor head. Blade de-icing. New 16% wider-chord blades with 20° drooped tips will become available from 1997, to enhance hovering. Monobloc titanium rotor head with elastomeric bearings and hydraulic drag dampers.

Tail rotor characteristics: Cross-beam layout, with 2 separate superimposed 2-blade composite rotors set at 90°. 20° inward cant to widen CG range and offer some lift.

Tail surfaces: Electrically controlled 14 ft 4.6 ins

Sikorsky MH-60K special operations helicopter

(4.39 m) variable-incidence tailplane, set at 34° in hover in concert with the rotor downwash. Fin area permits a controlled emergency landing in the event of tail rotor failure or loss.

Flight control system: Hydraulic.

Airframe materials: Metal, but with composite floors, doors, fairings and other non-structural components.

Safety features: Built-in tolerance to small arms fire and most medium-calibre high-explosive projectiles, as well as specially designed airframe and undercarriage features, for a high degree of battlefield survivability. Wire strike protection. Can survive a 38 ft (11.6 m) per second vertical impact rate, or a simultaneous 20g longitudinal/10g vertical impact.

Engines: 2 General Electric T700-GE-701C turboshafts. APU.

Engine rating: Each 1,870 shp (1,394 kW) maximum, 1,620 shp (1,208 kW) continuous, and 1,940 shp (1,447 kW) contingency.

Transmission rating: 3,400 shp (2,535 kW).

Fuel system: 1,363 litres usable. 2 x 700 litre internal or 2 x 871 litre ESSS-carried auxiliary fuel tanks.

Electrical system: 2 AlliedSignal generators, plus a 17 amp-hour ni-cd battery.

Radar: See Aircraft variants.

Flight avionics/instrumentation: Automatic flight control system, with digital 3-axis autopilot and autostabilization (see MH-60K). Navigation equipment includes AN/ASN-128 Doppler, radar altimeter, ADF, VOR/marker beacon/glideslope, and gyro compass; some have AN/ARN-148 Omega. Wide range of communica-tion equipment.

Self-protection systems: IR jammer, radar warning and chaff/flare.

Fixed guns: 2 pintle-mounted 7.62-mm M134 Miniguns in the cabin, or 0.50- in guns.

Number of weapon pylons: External Stores Support System (ESSS), consisting of removable stub wings that attach to the fuselage sides (above the cabin), have 2 pylons each for auxiliary fuel tanks, weapons or other stores. ESSS attachment is built into the airframe structure.

Expendable weapons and equipment: Using ESSS, can carry over 10,000 lb (4,536 kg) of stores, including auxiliary fuel tanks, ECM pods, up to 16 Hellfire anti-armour missiles (with 16 more carried internally for reload), guns, and mine dispensers.

Aircraft variants:

EH-60C is the designation of 66 UH-60As modified for electronic warfare with the US Army and Army National Guard under the Special Electronics Mission Aircraft programme. Originally EH-60As as redelivered from 1987, and subsequently becoming EH-60Cs, they were fitted with the AN/ALQ-151(V)2 Quick Fix IIB airborne ECM surveillance and detection/jamming suite, installed by Tracor's Flight Systems division at Mojave. 2 dipole antennae on each tailboom side and a large underfuselage whip aerial. Capable of locating AM/FM, continuous wave and single sideband signals. Has transmitters to jam VHF emissions and radar signals. Data link to down link with command or interface with other EH-60s. 2 equipment operators in the main cabin. 32 now being upgraded with Advanced Quick Fit and other changes including T700-GE-701C engines. Hover infra-red suppressor. Self-protection with missile and radar warning, infra-red jammer, and chaff/flare dispensers. Funding being requested for a command and control variant with AN/ASC-15B(V)1 communications equipment.

HH-60G combat rescue helicopter (see MH-60G).

MH-60G Pave Hawk is a special operations version for the USAF. Based on the UH-60 but with aerial refuelling capability and internal auxiliary fuel, mission-unique communication and navigation equipment (including AN/APN-239 radar, Doppler, inertial navigation, Tacan, map display, secure HF and satellite communications), fast rope system, 7.62-mm and 0.50-in calibre armament, and tow plates to facilitate air transportability. Empty weight 12,330 lb (5,593 kg), maximum take-off/landing weight 22,000 lb (9,979 kg), and ferry weight 24,500 lb (11,113 kg). V_{MCP}/V_{BR}/V_{BE} 150/135/79 kts respectively, service ceiling 14,200 ft (4,328 m), and hovering ceiling OGE 4,000 ft (1,220 m) at 35°C and mid-mission point or 4,300 ft (1,310 m) ISA. 103 produced for dual combat search and rescue and special operations, but 82 were later redesignated HH-60Gs for combat rescue.

MH-60K special operations helicopter for the US Army has a useful load of 10,000 lb (4,536 kg), 1,363-2,271 litres of internal fuel and 1,741 litres of external, a 130 kts maximum cruise speed, 120 kts best range speed, and range without refuelling of 755 naut miles. Superseded the MH-60A with the 160th Special Operations Aviation Regiment. 4 crew plus 12 troops with no internal auxiliary fuel or 7 troops with internal auxiliary fuel. Based on the UH-60A, but with UH-60L-type engines/transmission. Fully integrated cockpits and avionics, night/all-weather capability, precise navigation, aerial refuelling, digital automatic flight control computer with coupled automatic approach/depart/hover functions, and electromagnetic environment protection compatible with shipborne operations. AN/APQ-174A radar. FLIR. Full self-protection systems, including missile and laser warning, infra-red and radio jammers, chaff/flare dispensers, 0.50-in calibre guns, and can mount Stinger AAMs.

MH-60L is a 4-crew heavily armed special operations helicopter (very few prepared), used to escort the MH-60K. Operated during Desert Storm. Typically 4 Hellfires, rocket pods, 2 x 30-mm cannon and 2 x 7.62-mm Miniguns, with provision for grenade launchers and Stinger AAMs. AlliedSignal RDR-1400C weather radar, Stormscope, GEC-Marconi HUD, AN/AAQ-16 FLIR and laser designator. GPS, satcom, secure communications and much more. Flight refuelling probe.

UH-60A Black Hawk was the original US Army assault transport version, with 1,560 shp (1,163 kW) T700-GE-700 engines. Maximum gross weight 20,250 lb (9,185 kg) , but with a 24,500 lb (11,113 kg) maximum weight for ferrying. Same roles as noted for UH-60L.

UH-60J is a Japanese (Mitsubishi built) combat search and rescue helicopter for the Air and Maritime Self Defence forces. Variant of the S-70A but with T700-IHI-401C turboshafts.

UH-60L Black Hawk is the current US Army assault transport helicopter, having superseded the UH-60A in production in 1989. As detailed. 24% more power and new gearbox.

UH-60P is the South Korean assembled (Korean Air) equivalent of UH-60L. Variant of the S-70A.

UH-60Q is a required US Army medevac version with a high standard of navigation equipment including weather radar, Tacan, GPS, Doppler and inertial

navigation. Other equipment includes FLIR, searchlight and self-protection systems. Prototype evaluated 1993-94.
VH-60/N Presidential transport; 9 VIP transports with the US Marine Corps.
S-70A is the international variant of the UH-60. Design gross weight 16,825 lb (7,632 kg), and maximum gross weight 22,000 lb (9,979 kg). T700-GE-701A engines.
S-70C is similar to the S-70A/UH-60 but commercially certified and offered for both civil and military use. 24 went to China as S-70C-2s but were withdrawn from use through lack of spares. 14 went to Taiwan as utility helicopters for the Air Force. S-70C(M)-1s have also gone to Taiwan (Navy) as Thunderhawks for ASW, with APS-128 radar, dipping sonar and ESM. General Electric CT7-2 engines.

Sikorsky S-70B, SH-60B Seahawk and derivatives

First flight: 12 December 1979.
Role: All-weather, autonomous anti-submarine (ASW) and anti-surface surveillance and targeting (ASST) for Seahawk, with secondary vertrep, SAR, communications relay and medevac. See Aircraft variants for roles of derivatives.

▲ Development

▲ Derivative of the Army UH-60 Black Hawk, to meet the US Navy LAMPS III requirement for a ship-borne light multi-purpose helicopter. 5 prototypes.
Sales: See Aircraft variants.
Details: SH-60B Seahawk.
Crew: 3, as the pilot and co-pilot/airborne tactical officer in the cockpit, and sensor operator in the main cabin. No seat armour. Dual controls.
Cabin access: Starboard sliding door to main cabin.
Standard equipment: 6,000 lb (2,721 kg) capacity cargo hook, and 600 lb (272 kg) capacity rescue hoist. RAST (recovery assist, secure and traverse) system for assisted landing and stowage on deck.
Rotor system: Similar to Black Hawk. Electric blade folding and rotor brake.
Airframe materials: Similar to Black Hawk but with anti-corrosion features compatible with seaborne operations. Tail folds for stowage.
Engines: 2 General Electric T700-GE-401C turboshafts.
Engine rating: Each 1,870 shp (1,394 kW) maximum, 1,620 shp (1,208 kW) continuous, and 1,940 shp (1,447 kW) contingency.
Transmission rating: 3,400 shp (2,535 kW).
Fuel system: 2,233 litres standard. 2 x 454 litre auxiliary tanks. Capable of hover refuelling.
Radar: Texas Instruments AN/APS-124 search radar with undernose radome.
Flight avionics/instrumentation: Communications include AN/ARC-159(V)2 UHF and AN/ARC-174(V)2 HF radio, Sierra Research AN/ARQ-44 data link for tactical link with the parent ship's ATACO (the ship can operate the helicopter's radar and acoustic processor, relaying data back to the helicopter via the 2-way data link), and IFF transponders. Navigation systems include AN/ARN-118(V) Tacan, AN/APN-217 Doppler radar, AN/ARA-50 UHF/DF, radar altimeter and provision for GPS. Texas Instruments radar (see above) and AN/ASQ-81(V)2 MAD bird carried on a tailboom pylon, launchers on port side of fuselage for 25 passive or active sonobuoys of several types, Rospatch AN/AAR-94 99-channel receiver, AN/UYS-2 acoustic processor (with selectable full-band, quarter-band and eighth-band verniers), AN/ALQ-142 ESM in corner-nose pods (offers passive surface contacts), and magnetic tape memory unit. Some have AN/AAS-44 forward-looking infra-red sensors with laser designators (compatible with Hellfire) or other FLIR. See Aircraft variants for avionics/equipment of other variants.

Sikorsky HH-60J Jayhawk

Expendable weapons and equipment: 2 x Mk 46 or Mk 50 torpedoes, or Penguin AGM-119B (Mk 2 Mod 7) anti-ship missiles interfacing with the MIL-STD-1553B digital databus architecture. Hellfire anti-armour missiles will be integrated from 1996 for small targets (trials conducted with an M299 launcher at Patuxent River test centre).
Aircraft variants:
HH-60H is a combat search and rescue/special warfare support helicopter, entering US Navy service in 1989. Primary mission for special warfare support is a 200 naut mile radius of action with 8 troops, mid-mission hover at 3,000 ft (915 m) at 35° C and 147 kts cruise. Primary mission for combat SAR (strike recovery) is 250 naut miles radius, 4 survivors, and same hover/cruise. Communications are dual UHF/VHF/FM radios, HF radio, IFF and VHF/UHF/HF/IFF crypto computers. Navigation and tactical data systems as for SH-60F. Mission subsystems are 6,000 lb (2,721 kg) cargo hook, NVG compatible lighting, rescue hoist, 2 x M60D 7.62-mm machine-guns, and automatic approach, coupled hover and automatic departure. Survivability systems are IR jammer, 2 chaff/flare dispensers, radar and laser warning receivers, missile plume detector, AN/ARD-6 emergency locator, and hover IR suppressor system (HIRSS). New increase in armament includes Hellfire anti-armour missiles on M299 launchers, 2.75-in rocket launchers, and gun pods. 36 delivered.
HH-60J Jayhawk is a medium range recovery (MMR) multi-mission helicopter for the US Coast Guard, for offshore SAR, law enforcement, drug interdiction, logistics, aids to navigation, marine environment protection and military readiness. Can carry 3 auxiliary fuel tanks. 4 crew and 6 survivors for SAR. Compatible with helicopter decks of *Hamilton* and *Bear* class cutters. Avionics include AlliedSignal Bendix/King RDR-1300C search/weather radar, VHF/UHF ADF, Tacan, Tacnav, radar altimeter, VOR/ILS and GPS provisions. Same communications as HH-60H. Triple redundant hydraulic and electrical systems. 300 naut mile radius of action. First flown 8 August 1989 and delivered from March 1990. 42 delivered.
SH-60B Seahawk was the first production version for the US Navy, first flying in LAMPS III production form on 11 February 1983, with the initial delivery on 24 March that year to HSL-41. Equipment integration by IBM (now Loral Federal Systems Division). Eventual upgrading to SH-60R anticipated. 188 ordered. As detailed.
SH-60F is a CV Helo variant of Seahawk for the US Navy, intended for close-quarter (inner zone) ASW protection for aircraft carrier battle groups. Deployed from 1991. Primary mission is with 4 crew, 1 internal and 1 external auxiliary fuel tank and 2 x Mk 50 torpedoes (can carry 3), at 21,800 lb (9,888 kg) take-off, offering a dash speed of 133 kts and a 4.2 hour endurance at sea level, tropical day. Mission equipment comprises AN/AQS-13F dipping sonar with AN/UYS-2 digital acoustic processing and 1,500 ft (457 m) depth capability, sonobuoy launcher and storage carousel, 99-channel sonobuoy receiver, on-board sonobuoy processing, and mission tape recorder system. Mission subsystems are rescue hoist, automatic approach, coupled hover and automatic departure. Communications are dual UHF/VHF/FM radios, HF radio and tactical data link. Navigation systems comprise Tacan, Tacnav, Doppler radar, radar altimeter and provision for GPS. Tactical data systems are dual redundant AN/ASN-150 mission computers, MIL-STD-1553B digital databus architecture, multi-function keypad access and cockpit video displays.
74 helicopters. To be withdrawn over coming years and converted into SH-60Rs and extra HH-60Hs.

DETAILS FOR SH-60B SEAHAWK, UNLESS STATED.

Principal dimensions:
Rotor diameter (main): 53 ft 8 ins (16.36 m)
Maximum length, rotors turning: 64 ft 10 ins (19.76 m)
Fuselage length: 50 ft 0.75 ins (15.26 m)
Length, folded: 41 ft 0.6 ins (12.5 m)
Width, folded: 10 ft 9 ins (3.28 m)
Maximum height: 17 ft 0.2 ins (5.18 m) over tail rotor
Height, folded: 13 ft 3 ins (4.04 m)
Cabin: See Black Hawk

Tail rotor:
Diameter: 11 ft (3.35 m)

Undercarriage:
Type: Similar to Black Hawk, but with twin tailwheels moved forward towards cabin. Emergency flotation gear
Wheel base: 15 ft 10 ins (4.83 m)
Wheel track: 8 ft 10.6 ins (2.7 m)

Weights:
Empty, operating: 13,648 lb (6,190 kg)
Mission maximum take-off: 21,110 lb (9,575 kg) for ASW, 19,226 lb (8,721 kg) ASST
Maximum take-off: 21,884 lb (9,927 kg)
Payload: 4,100 lb (1,860 kg) internal, 6,000 lb (2,721 kg) external

Performance:
Dash speed: 145 kts (167 mph) 268 km/h
Cruise speed (HH-60J): 146 kts (168 mph) 270 km/h
Vertical climb rate: 700 ft (213 m) per minute at sea level, 32°C
Vertical climb rate OEI: 450 ft (137 m) per minute at sea level, 32°C
Radius of action (HH-60J): 300 naut miles (345 miles) 555 km
Duration: 3.5 to 6 hours
On-station time (HH-60J): 1 hour 30 minutes at 300 naut miles radius in interdiction role, or 45 minutes in MRR role.

Sikorsky SH-60FCV Helo helicopter from USS Theodore Roosevelt

SH-60J is the Mitsubishi-built S-70B-3 with T700-IHI-401C engines, for ship- (*Yukikaze* class destroyers) and shore-based ASW with the JMSDF. RAST equipped. Production continuing, with 80-100 needed.

SH-60R is the forthcoming combined designation of SH-60Bs and Fs after upgrade into a single new variant for LAMPS and CV Helo operations, featuring Hughes and Thomson Sintra developed AN/AQS-22 Airborne Low Frequency Sonar (ALFS) dipping sonar system with high-speed reel, Hughes transmitter/receiver and AN/UYS-2 acoustic processor, interfacing through a MIL-STD-1553B databus with current displays. AN/AYK-14 computer and new ESM are among other changes. 7.62-mm gun. First conversions are expected to be funded from FY1998.

S-70B is the international variant of Seahawk, as the S-70B-1 with AQS-13F dipping sonar for the Spanish Navy (6, designated HS.23), S-70B-2 with role adaptable weapon system (RAWS) for the Royal Australian Navy and fitted with Thorn EMI Super Searcher radar and a full range of other avionics including internal ASQ-504(V) MAD and DHS-901 data link (16, half built by ASTA), S-70B-6 Aegean Hawk for the Hellenic Navy (5 plus 3 options) with APS-143(V)3 radar, AQS-18(V)3 dipping sonar and ESM, and S-70B-7 for the Royal Thai Navy for maritime patrol and SAR (6, initially without dipping sonar, sonobuoys, ESM or Penguin). Fairey Hydraulics Decklock system is under trial for the S-70B.

Aegean Hawk, see S-70B-6 above.

S-70C(M)1 Thunderhawk is the Taiwanese Navy ASW variant with APS-128PC radar, AQS-18(V) dipping sonar

Sikorsky S-76 series

First flight: 13 March 1977.
Role: Civil/military passenger and utility transport, offshore work, medevac, search and rescue, and training.
Sales: Over 400 of all versions. Users of the S-76C include several commercial operators, the Royal Hong Kong Auxiliary Air Force (2), Spanish Air Force (8 for IFR pilot training) and the Japan Maritime Safety Agency (2 in 1994-95 for SAR). Lloyd Helicopter Group operates 5 S-76s with SPZ-7600 for SAR on behalf of the RAAF.
Details: For the S-76C.
Crew/passengers: 1 or 2 crew plus 12-13 passengers (14 persons in total) or 4 or more in executive/business layouts, or 2 litters and 4 seats. 4 crew in SAR configuration.
Freight, internal: Baggage compartment area 38 cu ft (1.08 m^3).
Cabin access: Optional sliding cabin doors (instead of normal hinged) can be opened in flight up to 125 kts.
Optional equipment: Includes dual controls, external cargo hook, SX-16 Nightsun 360° searchlight, 600 lb (272 kg) capacity and 200 ft (61 m) long rescue hoist.
Rotor system: 4-blade fully-articulated main rotor. Each blade has a 30° swept tip and comprises a titanium spar, Nomex honeycomb core and composites trailing edge and skins, with titanium/nickel leading-edge anti-erosion strip. High twist. Bifilar vibration damper system over rotor head. Blade de-icing. Monobloc titanium rotor head with elastomeric bearings and hydraulic drag dampers. Optional manual blade folding and rotor brake.
Tail rotor characteristics: Cross-beam layout, with 2 separate superimposed 2-blade composite rotors set at 90°.
Tail surfaces: 10 ft (3.05 m) span horizontal stabilizer.
Flight control system: Hydraulic.
Airframe materials: Metal, but with many composite non-structural components.
Engines: 2 Turbomeca Arriel 1S1 turboshafts. Optional particle separators.
Engine rating: Each 792 shp (591 kW) for 2.5 minutes emergency OEI at sea level, 723 shp (539 kW) take-off and maximum continuous, and 668 shp (498 kW) normal cruise.
Transmission rating: 1,300 shp (969 kW).
Fuel system: 1,064 litres standard. 208 litre auxiliary tank available.
Electrical system: DC supply via a transmission-driven 7.5 kVA generator and AC via a static inverter for IFR-equipped helicopters when more electrical power is required. 2 x 200 amp starter-generators when VFR equipped. 17 amp-hour ni-cd battery standard, with optional 34 amp-hour.
Hydraulic system: 3,000 psi.
Radar: At customer's request. For SAR is typically a Honeywell Primus 700/701 radar with precision surface mapping, weather detection and beacon mode.
Flight avionics/instrumentation: VFR or IFR (Cat A IFR for FAR Part 29 requirements). Available avionics include Honeywell SPZ-7600 dual digital AFCS with fully coupled autopilot, automatic search/mark on target and approach to hover, and Doppler coupled hover (also controllable by a hoist operator for SAR); EFIS complete flight profile and multi-faceted display system; Racal R-Nav-2; and FLIR for search and rescue. Other choices, at customer's request, include different AFCS, DME, ADF, radar altimeter, and so on.
Expendable weapons and equipment: See H-76 Eagle (below).
Aircraft variants:

H-76 Eagle appeared in 1985 in armed multi-role and naval versions as a military variant of the S-76B. Wide range of specialized mission avionics available, including mast or roof mounted sighting system with laser rangefinder, FLIR, HUD, and self-protection warning, jamming and other systems. Provision for armoured crew seats and self-sealing fuel tanks. Multi-purpose pylon system (MPPS) for the carriage of TOW or Hellfire anti-armour missiles, anti-ship missiles and torpedoes, Stinger AAMs, rockets, guns and mine dispensers and more. No known purchasers.

Sikorsky S-76C operated by the Spanish Air Force as the HE.24 for IFR flying training

Details for S-76C.

Principal dimensions:
Rotor diameter (main): 44 ft (13.41 m)
Maximum length, rotors turning: 52 ft 6 ins (16 m)
Fuselage length: 43 ft 4.4 ins (13.22 m)
Fuselage width: 7 ft (2.13 m)
Maximum height: 14 ft 5.8 ins (4.418 m) over tail rotor, or 11 ft 8.9 ins (3.58 m) over main rotor hub

Cabin:
Length: 8 ft 1 ins (2.46 m)
Width: 6 ft 4 ins (1.93 m)
Height: 4 ft 5 ins (1.35 m)
Floor area: 45 sq ft (4.18 m^2)
Volume: 204 cu ft (5.78 m^3)

Main rotor:
Blade chord: 1 ft 3.5 ins (0.39 m)
Rotor disc: 1,520.53 sq ft (141.262 m^2)

Tail rotor:
Diameter: 8 ft (2.44 m)

Undercarriage:
Type: Retractable, with nosewheel. Optional low pressure tyres and emergency flotation gear
Main wheel tyre size: 14.5 x 5.5-6
Nose wheel tyre size: 13 x 5.0-4
Wheel base: 16 ft 5 ins (5 m)
Wheel track: 8 ft (2.44 m)

Weights:
Empty, standard equipment: 6,282 lb (2,849 kg)
Maximum take-off: 11,700 lb (5,307 kg)
Useful load: 5,418 lb (2,457 kg)

Performance:
Maximum speed: 155 kts (178 mph) 287 km/h at sea level
Cruise speed: 145 kts (167 mph) 269 km/h, normal
Typical search speed for SAR: 90 kts (104 mph) 167 km/h at sea level
Maximum climb rate: 1,460 ft (445 m) per minute at sea level
Ceiling: 11,800 ft (3,600 m), service
Ceiling, OEI: 2,070 ft (631 m), service
Range: 430 naut miles (495 miles) 796 km at 138 kts and 3,000 ft (915 m), standard fuel, ISA, no reserve, or 366 naut miles (421 miles) 678 km) at the same speed and altitude, with 30 minutes reserve

S-76 was the initial production model with 650 shp (484.7 kW) Allison 250-C30 turboshaft engines. Variants included the Mark II with detail changes that included those to improve maintenance and provide slightly higher engine and transmission ratings, and the Utility. Subsequent Arriel turboshaft retrofits to existing S-76s produced the S-76A+. Out of production.

S-76B has Pratt & Whitney Canada PT6B-36A turboshafts, each 981 shp (731.5 kW) at take-off, for better performance and payload in hot-and-high applications. Can use Honeywell SPZ-7000 digital AFCS with EFIS or similar.

S-76C is the latest version and introduced French Arriel 1S1 engines, offering greater payload and enhanced reliability without sacrificing range. Retains the increased structural gross weight capability and uprated drive train of the S-76B.

Sikorsky S-80, CH-53E Super Stallion and MH-53E Sea Dragon

First flight: 1 March 1974 for Super Stallion.
Role: Heavy-lift transport, amphibious assault and vertical on-board delivery (VOD) for Super Stallion, and principally mine countermeasures for Sea Dragon.
Sales: 170 CH-53Es and 50 MH-53Es ordered for the US Marine Corps and Navy, with deliveries of CH-53Es from 16 June 1981. Japan has received 11 S-80Ms.
Details: CH-53E Super Stallion, except where indicated.
Crew/passengers: 3 crew and 55 troops for all models, including Sea Dragon if required. Alternative payloads include freight internally or sling loads including crippled aircraft for deck-clearing or recovery.
Freight, external: 36,000 lb (16,329 kg) cargo hook.
Cabin access: Hydraulic rear ramp/door for straight-in loading/unloading.
Rotor system: 7-blade fully-articulated main rotor. Blades, with 14° twist, have titanium spar, Nomex honeycomb core and composites skins. Steel/titanium rotor head. Rotor brake. Hydraulic blade folding. "Blade inspection method" spar-cracking detection system.
Tail rotor characteristics: 4-blade rotor, mounted on the port side of a 20° outward-canted large fin. Aluminium alloy blades. Rotor position provides lift as well as anti-torque forces, and increases the CG range.
Tail surfaces: Composites fin. Strut-braced, tapering horizontal stabilizer to starboard. Stabilizer is cranked to allow for the angle of the fin. Area of the fin would permit controlled landing in the event of tail rotor loss or failure.
Flight control system: Hydraulic.
Fuselage: Sealed, to allow flotation in an emergency alighting. Hydraulic tail folding for ship stowage.
Airframe materials: Principally metal, but with composites cockpit area and fairings.
Engines: 3 General Electric T64-GE-416 turboshafts. 4,750 shp (3,542 kW) T64-GE-419s are expected to be installed in a CH/MH retrofit programme. APU.
Engine rating: Each 4,380 shp (3,266 kW).
Transmission rating: 13,140 shp (9,798 kW).
Fuel system: 3,850 litres. Provision for 2 x 2,460 litre auxiliary tanks on the sponsons. In-flight refuelling and hover refuelling to extend range and self deploy.

Sikorsky CH-53E Super Stallion with external tanks

Sikorsky MH-53E Sea Dragon preparing for a towing mission

DETAILS FOR CH-53E, *WITH MH-53E IN ITALICS WHERE DIFFERENT.*

Principal dimensions:
Rotor diameter (main): 79 ft (24.08 m)
Maximum length, rotors turning: 99 ft 0.5 ins (30.18 m)
Length, folded: 60 ft 6 ins (18.44 m)
Fuselage length: 73 ft 4 ins (22.35 m)
Fuselage width: 8 ft 10 ins (2.69 m)
Maximum width (excluding rotors): 23 ft 11 ins (7.29 m), *27 ft 7 ins (8.41 m)*
Width, folded: 28 ft 5 ins (8.66 m)
Maximum height: 28 ft 4 ins (8.64 m)
Height, folded: 18 ft 7 ins (5.66 m)

Cabin:
Length: 30 ft (9.14 m)
Width: 7 ft 6 ins (2.29 m)
Height: 6 ft 6 ins (1.98 m)

Main rotor:
Blade chord: 2 ft 6 ins (0.76 m)
Rotor disc: 4,901.7 sq ft (455.383 m^2)

Tail rotor:
Diameter: 20 ft (6.1 m)
Cant angle: 20°

Undercarriage:
Type: Retractable, with castering nosewheels. Twin wheels on each unit
Wheel base: 27 ft 3 ins (8.31 m)
Wheel track: 13 ft (3.96 m)

Weights:
Empty: 33,373 lb (15,138 kg), *36,336 lb (16,482 kg)*
Maximum take-off: 69,750 lb (31,638 kg)
Maximum take-off, external load: 73,500 lb (33,339 kg)
Payload: 32,000 lb (14,515 kg) basic mission
Useful load (MH-53E): *26,000 lb (11,793 kg) influence sweep mission*

Performance:
Maximum speed: 170 kts (196 mph) 315 km/h at sea level
Cruise speed: 150 kts (173 mph) 278 km/h at sea level
Maximum climb rate: 2,500 ft (762 m) per minute with a 25,000 lb (11,340 kg) payload
IGE hovering ceiling: 11,550 ft (3,520 m)
OGE hovering ceiling: 9,500 ft (2,896 m)
Ceiling: 18,500 ft (5,659 m)

Flight refuelling probe: 21 ft 11.5 ins (6.7 m), retracting to 10 ft 6 ins (3.2 m).
Electrical system: 115 volt AC supply via 3 alternators, at 400 Hz. 28 volt DC supply via 2 x 200 amp transformer rectifiers.
Hydraulic system: 3,000 psi; 4,000 psi for engine start-up system.
Flight avionics/instrumentation: AFCS with 4-axis autopilot and dual digital automatic flight control system computers, complete with automatic approach and departure from a coupled hover features. Some retrofitted with AN/APN-217 Doppler, FLIR and GPS. Future upgrades might include colour displays, AHRS, Omega and ground proximity warning system.
Self-protection systems: Expected to receive missile warning and chaff/flare systems.
Fixed guns: See Aircraft variants.
Expendable weapons and equipment: Sidewinder AAMs have been tested for self protection.

Aircraft variants:
CH-53E Super Stallion is the US Marine Corps/US Navy heavy-lift transport version, as detailed.
MH-53E Sea Dragon is a US Navy airborne mine countermeasures (AMCM) helicopter based on the CH-53E, primarily to sweep mined areas to free a shipping lane. Has extra large composites sponsons, each holding 6,056 litres of fuel to permit a 4-hour towing mission, plus reserve. Internal range extension tanks (7 x 1,136 litre) are available. To increase response time and offer self-deployment, a flight refuelling probe is provided. Internal 30,000 lb (13,600 kg) tension tow boom and hydraulic winch for deployment of minesweeping systems. Specialized electrical, hydraulic (additional hydraulic system for AMCM gear) and environmental control systems, and dual digital automatic flight control system computers, complete with automatic tow-tension and skew-angle hold while under tow, and automatic approach and departure from a coupled hover features. Can tow mechanical, acoustic and magnetic hydrofoil sweeping gear through the water. Folding blades and tail pylon. Can also perform vertical on-board delivery (VOD). Can carry a cabin gun. Upgrade has begun to retrofit GPS, 2 horizontal situation colour displays and mission data loader. Delivered from 26 June 1986 and initially operated by HM-14. First sea deployment began on 9 December 1989.
S-80E is the international export version of CH-53E.
S-80M is the international export version of MH-53E.

Sikorsky S-92 Helibus

First flight: 1998.
Role: Civil and military medium transport, offshore, search and rescue, and utility helicopter.

▲ Development

▲ 12 June 1995. Full-scale development launched. 2 civil and 3 military configured prototypes to be built. Risk-sharing partners are Embraer of Brazil (4%, responsible for the sponsons and fuel system), Gamesa of Spain (7%, responsible for the rear fuselage and upper and transmission fairings), Jingdezhen Helicopters of China (2%, responsible for the tail unit), Mitsubishi of Japan (7.5%, responsible for the centre fuselage), and Taiwan Aerospace (6.5%, responsible for the cockpit).
▲ 2000. Anticipated certification under FAR/JAR Part 29.
Crew/passengers: 2 flight crew and 19-22 passengers (3 abreast) in S-92C form, with 7 cabin windows per side. Military/utility version with rear ramp/door loading will have only 2 cabin windows per side.
Freight, internal: Square-section cabin, large enough for 3 LD3 standard containers in the S-92IU.
Freight, external: 10,000 lb (4,536 kg) sling load for the S-92IU and military versions.
Rotor system: 4-blade main rotor, developed from the Black Hawk rotor head. New blades have 30° and 20° tip-droop.

Sikorsky S-92C Helibus mock-up

Details for S-92.

Principal dimensions:
Rotor diameter (main): 53 ft 8 ins (16.36 m)
Maximum length, rotors turning: 66 ft 3 ins (20.19 m)
Fuselage length: 54 ft 2 ins (16.51 m)
Fuselage width: 7 ft 1 ins (2.16 m)
Maximum height: 15 ft 2 ins (4.62 m)

Cabin:
Length: 18 ft 7 ins (5.67 m)
Width: 6 ft 7 ins (2 m)
Height: 6 ft (1.83 m)
Volume: 596 cu ft (16.877 m^3)

Tail rotor:
Diameter: 11 ft (3.35 m)

Undercarriage:
Type: Retractable. Twin wheels on each unit
Wheel base: 22 ft 7 ins (6.88 m)
Wheel track: 11 ft 5 ins (3.48 m)

Weights:
Empty: 14,815 lb (6,720 kg)
Maximum take-off: 24,100 lb (10,931 kg) with internal load, and 26,500 lb (12,020 kg) for the military version with external fuel tanks

Performance (provisional):
Cruise speed: 155 kts (178 mph) 287 km/h
Best range speed: 140 kts (161 miles) 259 km/h
IGE hovering ceiling: 12,700 ft (3,870 m)
OGE hovering ceiling: 8,300 ft (2,530 m)
Ceiling: 15,000 ft (4,572 m), service
Range: 510 naut miles (587 miles) 945 km for the S-92C, and 480 naut miles (553 miles) 890 km for the utility version with auxiliary fuel

Tail rotor characteristics: Developed from the Black Hawk rotor. Inward-canted rotor position provides lift as well as anti-torque forces, and increases the CG range.
Engines: 2 General Electric CT7-6D turboshafts for the S-92C and CT7-8s for the S-92IU. Rolls-Royce Turbomeca RTM322s may be offered as options.
Engine rating: Each 1,750 shp (1,305 kW) for CT7-6D. or 1,900 shp (1,417 kW) for CT7-8, take-off.
Transmission: Mil of Russia is supplying the gearbox.
Fuel system: 2,196 litres, housed in sponson tanks.
Electrical system: Dual.
Hydraulic system: Dual.
Flight avionics/instrumentation: IFR. Hamilton Standard AFCS. "Glass cockpit", incorporating Lockheed Standard EFIS with 6 displays. Integrated avionics. GEC-Marconi HUMS (health usage monitoring system).
Aircraft variants:
S-92C is the civil version, with CT7-6D engines. First version to be developed. Baggage volume 110 cu ft (3.1 m^3)
S-92IU is the international export utility version, with CT7-8 engines.
S-92M is the likely international military designation.

SnoBird Aircraft Inc (USA)

Corporate address: 8850 South-West Hiway 3, Suite 108, Fort Orchard, WA 98366.
Telephone: +1 206 674 2497
Facsimile: +1 206 232 9624

SnoBird Adventurer 636D-4, Charger 582S, Exciter 503S and Stealth Charger 582SE

Details: Exciter 503S, except under Aircraft variants.
Role: Single-seat ultralight autogyro.
Sales: Kits costing US$10,200 (1994 cost), requiring typically 80 working hours to assemble.
Rotor system: 2-blade.
Airframe materials: Metal tubing, with composites tail.
Engine: Rotax 503 piston engine.
Engine rating: 49.6 hp (37 kW).
Fuel system: 27 litres.
Aircraft variants:
Adventurer 636D-4 is a tandem two-seat autogyro with a Honda/CAM 100 engine. Assembly time is typically 150 working hours.
Charger 582S is a single-seat autogyro with a Rotax 582 engine.
Exciter 503S is the ultralight autogyro, as detailed.
Stealth Charger 582SE is a single-seat autogyro with a Rotax 582 engine driving a 6-blade propeller.

Details for Exciter 503S.

Principal dimensions:
Rotor diameter: 23 ft (7.01 m)
Fuselage length: 11 ft 11 ins (3.63 m)
Maximum height: 7 ft 4 ins (2.24 m)

Main rotor:
Rotor disc: 415 sq ft (38.55 m^2)

Weights:
Empty: 253 lb (155 kg)
Maximum take-off: 504 lb (229 kg)

Performance:
Maximum speed: 56 kts (65 mph) 105 km/h
Cruise speed: 52 kts (60 mph) 97 km/h
Take-off distance: 100 ft (30 m)
Landing distance: 20 ft (6 m)
Maximum climb rate: 700 ft (213 m) per minute
Ceiling: 10,000 ft (3,050 m)
Range: 69 naut miles (80 miles) 129 km

Sport Copter Inc (USA)

Corporate address: 34012 North Honeyman Road, Scappoose, OR 97056.
Telephone: +1 503 286 5462
Facsimile: +1 503 285 6222

Sport Copter Lightning, Sport Copter II and Vortex

Details: Vortex, except under Aircraft variants.
Role: Single-seat autogyro.
Sales: Kits costing US$12,000 (1994 cost), requiring typically 50 working hours to assemble.
Rotor system: 2-blade, with steel spar, wooden core and aluminium alloy skins.
Tail surfaces: Large fin and rudder, and small horizontal stabilizer with endplates.
Airframe materials: Steel tubing, with glassfibre cockpit fairing.
Engine: Rotax 582 or other engine.
Engine rating: 64.4 hp (48 kW).
Fuel system: 38 litres.
Aircraft variants:
Lightning is a single-seat ultralight autogyro with a Rotax 503 engine. 19 litres of fuel. Similar general appearance to Vortex.
Sport Copter II is a new two-seat autogyro of very streamlined appearance, with a shock-absorbing undercarriage and a Subaru converted automobile engine. Kit costs US$25,000 (1994 cost).
Vortex is a single-seat autogyro, as detailed.

Sport Copter Vortex is similar to the former Vancraft autogyro, seen here with floats (Geoffrey P. Jones)

Details for Vortex.

Principal dimensions:
Rotor diameter: 25 ft (7.62 m)
Fuselage length: 12 ft (3.66 m)
Maximum height: 8 ft 4 ins (2.54 m)

Main rotor:
Rotor disc: 490.8 sq ft (45.6 m^2)

Weights:
Empty: 350 lb (159 kg)
Maximum take-off: 760 lb (345 kg)

Performance:
Maximum speed: 87 kts (100 mph) 115 km/h
Cruise speed: 69 kts (80 mph) 129 km/h
Take-off distance: up to 200 ft (61 m)
Maximum climb rate: 1,200 ft (366 m) per minute
Ceiling: 13,000 ft (3,960 m)
Range: 147 naut miles (170 miles) 275 km

Star Aviation Inc (USA)

Corporate address: 821 Lone Star Drive, New Braunfels, TX 78130-2932.
Telephone: +1 210 608 9001

Star Aviation LoneStar Sport Helicopter

Details for LoneStar Sport Helicopter.

Principal dimensions:
Rotor diameter (main): 21 ft 5 ins (6.53 m)
Fuselage length: 13 ft 11 ins (4.24 m)
Maximum height: 7 ft 3 ins (2.21 m)

Weights:
Empty: 420 lb (191 kg)
Maximum take-off: 750 lb (340 kg)

Performance:
Maximum speed: 78 kts (90 mph) 145 km/h
Cruise speed: 56 kts (65 mph) 105 km/h
Maximum climb rate: 600 ft (183 m) per minute

Role: Single-seat very light helicopter.
Sales: Kit built.
Rotor system: 2-blade main rotor. Composites blades. Pushrod cyclic/collective control.
Tail rotor characteristics: 2-blade, with cable control.
Airframe materials: Principally an aluminium alloy open structure, with the engine and main rotor supported by a 4 ins (10 cm) square vertical structural member.
Engine: Rotax 582.
Engine rating: 64.4 hp (48 kW).
Transmission: Multiple belt system.
Fuel system: About 33 litres.

Tridair Helicopters Inc (USA)

Corporate address: 3000 Airway Avenue, Costa Mesa, CA 92626.
Telephone: +1 714 540 3000
Facsimile: +1 714 540 1042
Information: Doug D. Daigle (President).

● Activities

● In addition to the Gemini ST LongRanger twin-engine conversions detailed below, Bell Helicopter Textron is manufacturing a newly-built production version as the Bell 206LT TwinRanger, under a licence agreement with Tridair and the Tridair/Kawada Industries limited partnership. See Canada.

Details for Gemini ST.

Weights:
Empty, operating: 2,640 lb (1,197 kg)
Normal maximum take-off: 4,250 lb (1,928 kg)
Maximum take-off: 4,450 lb (2,018 kg)
Useful load: 1,610 lb (730 kg) standard configuration
Maximum external load: 2,000 lb (907 kg)

Performance:
Long-range cruise speed: 112 kts (129 mph) 207 km/h at MTOW, 118 kts (136 mph) 219 km/h at 3,600 lb (1,633 kg), both at 5,000 ft (1,525 m)
Maximum continuous cruise speed: 101 kts (116 mph) 187 km/h at MTOW, 116 kts (134 mph) 215 km/h at 3,600 lb (1,633 kg)
IGE/OGE hovering ceiling: 10,000 ft (3,050 ft) at MTOW, 15,000 ft (4,575 m) at 3,600 lb (1,633 kg), both ISA and ISA + 20°C
Ceiling: 10,000 ft (3,050 m) at MTOW, 20,000 ft (6,100 m) at 3,600 lb (1,633 kg)
Range: 246 naut miles (283 miles) 455 km at MTOW, 280 naut miles (322 miles) 518 km at 3,600 lb (1,633 kg), both sea level, long-range cruise speed, no reserve

Tridair Gemini ST

First flight: 16 January 1991.
Role: Major modification of the Bell LongRanger, meeting FAA Pt 29 standards. With the latest FAA approval, the Gemini ST conversion can now be carried out to the 206L-1, L-3 and L-4 models of LongRanger. Certified to FAA Part 27, 36 and 29 Cat A operation.

▲ Development

▲ November 1993. Received its first FAA certification (STC) as a conventional twin-engined helicopter.
▲ 12 September 1994. Gemini ST received FAA certification to operate 1 or both engines in all phases of flight, validating it as the world's first single/twin aircraft.
Details: Main modifications to the LongRanger are detailed below.
Cockpit: 2 throttles are mounted on each collective. Electric throttle releases allow throttles to be advanced above the start position or retarded below idle or cutoff. N2 governor switches allow adjustments, up or down, of both engines independently or simultaneously. The start switch is located on the pilot cyclic, allowing engine start without removing hands from the primary flight controls. Heating and air conditioning kit.

Tridair Gemini ST twin-engined conversion of the LongRanger

Rotor system: K-flex driveshaft, with 5,000 hours TBO. Rotor brake.
Tail surfaces: Horizontal stabilizer is extended about 3 ins (8 cm) on each side and the port vertical fin is toed inward. The stabilizer has a doubler bonded on the underside to strengthen it for the increased load factor.
Airframe materials: Cowls have been changed and are of fire-resistant carbonfibre wafer material.
Engines: 2 Allison 250-C20R turboshafts. Standard particle separators. Standard engine fire loops for each engine. Engine fire suppression is available as an approved kit. Each engine inlet has an anti-ice system, selectable in the cockpit.
Engine rating: Each 450 shp (335.6 kW) take-off, 380 shp (283 kW) maximum continuous.
Transmission rating: 435 shp (324 kW) take-off (5 minutes), and 370 shp (276 kW) maximum continuous. Soloy combining gearbox, with 2 independent, gear-driven oil pumps to provide oil during operation of either engine. 2 independent oil systems. 2 electric oil-cooling fans. Freewheeling clutches are mounted on the output shaft.
Fuel system: 427 litres. Modified system. Rupture resistant fuel cells.
Electrical system: Battery compartment is enlarged to allow either a 24 amp hour Marathon TSP-9117A ni-cd or Gill G639E lead-acid battery. These heavier batteries eliminate the need for ballast plates. Dual independent electrical systems provide redundant power for the equipment. 2 x 30 VDC 150 amp starter-generators provide power through 2 generator control units to 5 buses, to a 28 volt system.
Flight avionics/instrumentation: Flight instruments remain unchanged. Engine, fuel and electric instruments are of all new technology, provided by Transicoil. Caution and warning annunciator light panel is only slightly larger than the original.

Vertical Aviation Technologies Inc (USA)

Corporate address: PO Box 2527, Sanford, FL 32772-2527.
Telephone: +1 407 322 9488
Facsimile: +1 407 330 2647

● Activities

● Repair, maintenance and modification of Sikorsky helicopters.
● Various programmes include the *Elite* upgrade of the Sikorsky S-55 with an AlliedSignal TPE331-3 turboshaft engine, and other S-55 (and ex-military H-19) modifications to produce the agricultural *Bearcat*, AT-55 *Defender* assault and utility military transport, external-lift *Heavy Lift*, *Heli-Camper* with sleeping accommodation for 4, *Nite-Writer* with a computerized aerial advertising system, *Vistaplane* for passenger or medevac roles, and the *Aggressor*. The latter, offered in piloted and unmanned forms, has been reconfigured to represent a Russian-built Mil Mi-24 *Hind-E*.

Vertical Aviation Technologies Hummingbird

Role: 4-seat, kit-built modernized development of the Sikorsky S-52-3.

▲ Development

▲ Variant is being marketed by the Danubian Aircraft Co in Hungary.

Vertical Aviation Technologies Hummingbird (Geoffrey P. Jones)

Sales: Kit for US$86,000 (1994 cost), with engine. Typical assembly time is 1,000-1,500 working hours.
Rotor system: 4-blade main rotor; 5-blade rotor may follow.
Tail rotor characteristics: 2-blade.
Airframe materials: Metal, of new construction (including a revised nose), but kit has a number of Sikorsky parts.
Engine: Aluminium V-8 piston engine. Other engines are under consideration, including an Allison turboshaft.
Engine rating: 260 hp (194 kW).
Fuel system: 216 litres.

DETAILS FOR HUMMINGBIRD.

Principal dimensions:
Rotor diameter (main): 33 ft (10.06 m)
Maximum length, rotors turning: 39 ft 9 ins (12.12 m)
Fuselage length: 30 ft 5 ins (9.27 m)
Maximum height: 9 ft 5 ins (2.87 m)

Main rotor:
Rotor disc: 855.3 sq ft (79.46 m²)

Undercarriage:
Type: Fixed quadricycle

Weights:
Empty: 1,700 lb (771 kg)
Maximum take-off: 2,700 lb (1,225 kg)

Performance:
Maximum speed: 96 kts (110 mph) 177 km/h
Cruise speed: 82-85 kts (95-98 mph) 153-158 km/h
Maximum climb rate: 1,200 ft (366 m) per minute
Ceiling: 11,000 ft (3,350 m)
Range: 304 naut miles (350 miles) 563 km

Vertech (USA)

Corporate address: PO Box 511, Fallston, MD 21047.
Telephone: +1 410 557 8465
Facsimile: +1 410 692 5902

Vortech G-1B, Kestrel, MEG-2XH, Shadow and Skylark I

Details: For Kestrel, with the other dissimilar models detailed under Aircraft variants.
Role: Single-seat, ultralight, pressure-jet helicopter.
Sales: Plans or kit, the latter at US$9,995 (1994 cost).
Rotor system: 2-blade rotor with pressure jets, making a tail rotor unnecessary.
Tail surfaces: Large fin at the end of the boom.
Airframe materials: Tubular metal open structure.
Engines: 2 x G8-2-20 pressure jets.
Engine rating: Each 47 lbf (0.209 kN).
Fuel system: 19 litres.

DETAILS FOR KESTREL.

Principal dimensions:
Rotor diameter: 24 ft (7.32 m)
Fuselage length: 12 ft (3.66 m)
Maximum height: 7 ft (2.13 m)

Weights:
Empty: 200 lb (91 kg)
Maximum take-off: 475 lb (215 kg)

Performance:
Maximum speed: 82 kts (95 mph) 153 km/h
Cruise speed: 55 kts (63 mph) 101 km/h
Maximum climb rate: 900 ft (274 m) per minute
Ceiling: 12,500 ft (3,810 m)
Range: 43 naut miles (50 miles) 80 km

Aircraft variants:
G-1B is a single-seat ultralight helicopter, powered by a Kawasaki 440B piston engine. Offered in plans and kit forms.
Kestrel is a pressure-jet helicopter, as detailed.
MEG-2XH is a strap-on helicopter, with a 2-blade pressure-jet rotor system. Offered in plans and kit forms.
Shadow is a two-seat autogyro, with an enclosed cabin. Textron Lycoming O-320 engine. Kit only.
Skylark I is a single-seat open helicopter, with a Rotax 582 engine. Kit only.

Multi-national Aircraft

Eurocopter Holding S.A. (France/Germany)

● Activities
● The capital of the Eurocopter Group is shared on 2 levels. Eurocopter Holding S.A. is owned by Aerospatiale of France (60%) and Daimler-Benz Aerospace of Germany (40%). It has a 75% share in Eurocopter S.A.

Eurocopter S.A. (France/Germany)

Corporate address: 72 Boulevard de Courcelles, 75017 Paris, France.
Telephone: +33 1 49 34 44 44
Facsimile: +33 1 49 34 44 47
Founded: 16 January 1992.
Information: Jean Louis Espes (Press and Information Senior Manager – *facsimile* +33 1 49 34 45 10).

● Activities
● A general management organization for the Eurocopter Group, with Eurocopter Holding having a 75% share and Aerospatiale a 25% share.
● Eurocopter S.A. itself owns the 2 national industrial subsidiaries of Eurocopter France and Eurocopter Deutschland, as well as a marketing organization known as Eurocopter International. Another wholly owned subsidiary branch of Eurocopter SA is Eurocopter Participations.
● Group delivered 149 helicopters in 1994 and received 133 orders for new helicopters and 62 orders for second-hand helicopters. See also Euromil and NH Industries.

SUBSIDIARIES

Eurocopter Deutschland
HQ address: Postfach 9801140, Munich 80, Germany.
Telephone: +49 89 60 00-64 88
Facsimile: +49 89 60 00-44 37

● Activities
● Tasked with development and production of helicopters of German origin. Research projects include those to reduce the noise levels, weights, fuel consumption and operating costs of next-generation helicopters, while also increasing cruise speed.

To offer full all-weather capability, it is also developing the Heli-Radar, a rotor-mounted rotating synthetic aperture radar (ROSAR) that will provide a synthetical view for the crew. Main plants at Donauwörth and Ottobrunn.

<u>Eurocopter France</u>
HQ address: PO Box 13, 13725 Marignane, France.
Telephone: + 33 42 85 85 85
Facsimile: +33 42 85 85 00

● Activities
- Main plants at La Courneuve and Marignane.

<u>Eurocopter International</u>
HQ address: 72 Boulevard de Courcelles, 75017 Paris, France.

● Activities
- Promotion and marketing of the product range. Created in 1991 as an Economic Interest Group (GIE).

<u>Eurocopter Participants</u>
HQ address: PO Box 13, 13725 Marignane, France.

● Activities
- Monitors all foreign subsidiaries and participations of the Group in the helicopter field.

RELATED ORGANIZATIONS
<u>American Eurocopter Corp</u>
<u>Eurocopter Canada Ltd</u>
<u>Eurocopter International Japan</u>
<u>Eurocopter Service Japan</u>
<u>Eurocopter Southern Africa</u>
<u>Eurocopter Tiger GmbH</u>

Eurocopter AS 332 Super Puma and AS 532 Cougar

First flight: 13 September 1978.
Role: Civil transport (AS 332 Super Puma) and military multi-role (AS 532 Cougar).
Sales: Approximately 500 civil and military Super Pumas/Cougars have been ordered from some 43 countries, the latest including 2 AS 332 L2s for Vietnam for offshore oilfield support and 4 Cougars for the French Rapid Reaction Force (2 transport, 1 SAR and 1 Horizon). 20 AS 532ULs are also being licence-built for Turkish Army Aviation (TKK), for delivery 1995-98. First operator of the AS 332 L2 Super Puma Mk 2 was Helikopter Service A/S, for oil exploration support over the North Sea.
Details: AS 332 L2 Super Puma Mk 2, unless stated.
Crew/passengers: 2-3 crew and 19-24 passengers. 2 pilots are required for IFR flying, but single-pilot VFR is allowable under DGAC Cat B conditions. Alternative layouts for 12 litters plus 4 seats, and 8-15 VIPs.

Eurocopter AS 332 L2 Super Puma Mk 2s

DETAILS FOR AS 332 L2 SUPER PUMA.

Principal dimensions:
Rotor diameter (main): 53 ft 2 ins (16.2 m)
Maximum length, rotors turning: 63 ft 11.75 ins (19.5 m)
Fuselage length: 55 ft 1 ins (16.79 m) including tail rotor
Width, blades folded: 12 ft 8 ins (3.86 m)
Maximum height: 16 ft 4 ins (4.97 m)

Cabin:
Length: 25 ft 10 ins (7.87 m)
Width: 5 ft 11 ins (1.8 m)
Height: 4 ft 9 ins (1.45 m)

Main rotor:
Rotor disc: 2,217.36 sq ft (206 m^2)

Tail rotor:
Diameter: 10 ft 4 ins (3.15 m)

Undercarriage:
Type: Retractable, with twin self-centring nosewheels. Optional emergency flotation gear for offshore operations, housed in the sponsons.
Wheel base: 17 ft 4 ins (5.28 m)
Wheel track: 9 ft 10 ins (3 m)

Weights:
Empty: 10,274 lb (4,660 kg)
Normal maximum take-off: 20,503 lb (9,300 kg)
Useful load: 10,229 lb (4,640 kg)

Performance:
Never-exceed speed (VNE)**:** 170 kts (195 mph) 315 km/h
Cruise speed: 151 kts (174 mph) 280 km/h at sea level
Maximum climb rate: 1,299 ft (396 m) per minute at sea level
IGE hovering ceiling: 10,761 ft (3,280 m)
OGE hovering ceiling: 6,922 ft (2,110 m)
Ceiling: 17,000 ft (5,180 m), service
Range with standard fuel: 448 naut miles (515 miles) 830 km
Range with auxiliary tanks: 648 naut miles (745 miles) 1,200 km

Eurocopter AS 332 L2 Super Puma Mk 2 EFIS cockpit

FN Herstal 621 gun pod on a Cougar. Note the emergency floats in the sponsons

Freight, external: 9,921 lb (4,500 kg).
Cabin access: Sliding door each side, size 4 ft 3 ins x 4 ft 5 ins (1.3 x 1.35 m).
Optional equipment: Includes rescue winch, cable cutter, bubble observation windows, APU, and automatic transition and hover modes.
Rotor system: 4-blade main rotor with a Spheriflex rotor head, elastomeric bearings and Kevlar retention straps. Composites blades with parabolic tips.
Tail rotor characteristics: 4-blade, to starboard. Similar type of rotor head to main rotor, and composite blades.
Tail surfaces: Port-side horizontal stabilizer, with leading-edge inverted slot.
Flight control system: Hydraulic.
Fuselage: Side sponsons can house auxiliary fuel, emergency floats, life rafts, etc.
Airframe materials: Crashworthy structure incorporating composite materials.
Engines: 2 Turbomeca Makila 1A2 turboshafts.
Engine rating: Each 2,109 shp (1,572 kW) maximum contingency and 1,845 shp (1,375 kW) maximum take-off.
Transmission rating: 3,232 shp (2,410 kW), or 2,234 shp (1,666 kW) OEI.
Fuel system: Crash-proof fuel system. 2,020 litres standard. Auxiliary fuel in sponsons (each 325 litres), cabin tank (600 litres) and central crashworthy tank (320 litres). For ferrying, up to 5 x 475 litre tanks can be carried in the cabin.
Electrical system: AS 532 U2 Cougar has 2 x 30/40 kVA, 115/200 volt, 400 Hz alternators for AC supply, and 2 x 26 volt transformer rectifiers for DC. 43 amp-hour ni-cd battery. 4 hour stand-by battery. Hydraulically powered emergency electrical supply.
Hydraulic system: 2 independent systems with stand-by electric pumps.
Radar: Optional weather radar, including AlliedSignal Bendix/King RDR-1400 or -1500 for SAR.
Flight avionics/instrumentation: SFIM 165 dual-redundant 4-axis digital autopilot. Integrated digital avionics with EFIS. Optional GPS. HUMS.
Expendable weapons and equipment: See Aircraft variants.
Aircraft variants:
<u>AS 332 L1 Super Puma</u> is a Mk 1 civil version, still marketed. Articulated main rotor of 51 ft 2 ins (15.6 m) diameter, and fuselage length 53 ft 5.5 ins (16.29 m) when including the standard 5-blade tail rotor. Makila 1A1 engines, each 1,875 shp (1,400 kW) maximum contingency. Normal accommodation for 2 crew and 10-12 passengers, with 20-24 in high density layout.
<u>AS 532 U2 Cougar</u> is the long-range military utility equivalent of the L1, offered with a wide range of optional nav/comm and radar equipment. Up to 28 troops. 2 have been fitted with battlefield surveillance radar for trials with the French Army under the Horizon programme; a production Horizon has been ordered for the French Rapid Reaction Force.
<u>AS 332 L2 Super Puma Mk 2</u> is the latest civil version, with a composites fuselage plug to increase cabin length. New and larger main rotor and 4-blade tail

rotor, both with Spheriflex heads. Makila 1A2 engines, new transmission, and integrated digital avionics with EFIS.
AS 532U2 Cougar Mk 2 is the military utility equivalent of the L2 Super Puma Mk 2. Up to 29 troops. SAR versions can have radar, FLIR, automatic search pattern/autohover, and more.
AS 532A2 Cougar Mk 2 is the current armed military version, offered with MAD, sonar, sonobuoys, 2 torpedoes or anti-ship missiles for naval use, and FN Herstal 621 gun pods or other guns/cannon, and rocket launchers for army/air force use.

Eurocopter AS 350 Ecureuil, AStar and AS 550 Fennec

First flight: 27 June 1974.
Role: Light multi-role civil helicopter (Ecureuil and Astar) and armed/unarmed military helicopter (Fennec).
Sales: Around 2,000 Ecureuils and Fennecs, with recent customers including the Algerian Air Force which received 9 civil Ecureuils; Fennec sales reached 269 to 23 countries by September 1994, in both single and AS 555 twin-engined versions. The French Army has ordered 6 new Fennecs for anti-armour missions. Ecureuil has also been built by Helibras in Brazil as the Esquilo/Fennec.
Details: AS 350 B2 Ecureuil, except where stated and under Aircraft variants.
Crew/passengers: Pilot plus 5 passengers. Alternatively, pilot, doctor, medical attendant and patient plus complete medical equipment for EMS; some of the medical equipment can be carried in the 3 baggage compartments with a combined capacity of 35.3 cu ft (1 m^3).
Freight, external: 2,557 lb (1,160 kg) sling load. 2,000 lb (907 kg) sling load for AS 350 BA.
Rotor system: 3-blade (manually folding) composites main rotor, with Starflex bearingless rotor head.
Tail rotor characteristics: 2-blade, starboard.
Tail surfaces: Dorsal and ventral fins, and horizontal stabilizer with inverted aerofoil section.
Airframe materials: Light alloy, but with extensive use of composites for the cabin area, cowlings and rotors.
Engine: Turbomeca Arriel 1D1 turboshaft.
Engine rating: 732 shp (546 kW) maximum.
Transmission rating: 590 shp (440 kW).
Fuel system: 540 litres.
Electrical system: 4.5 kW starter-generator. 16 amp-hour ni-cd battery.
Hydraulic system: 580 psi.
Flight avionics/instrumentation: Rockwell Collins, Honeywell or SFIM autopilot. Avionics to customer's requirements for VFR or IFR flying.
Aircraft variants:
AS 350 BA has a Turbomeca Arriel 1B engine of 640 shp (447 kW). Hinged or optional sliding cabin doors. Empty weight 2,526 lb (1,146 kg), maximum weight 4,630 lb (2,100 kg), and maximum weight with sling load 4,960 lb (2,250 kg). Cruise speed is 126 kts.
AS 350 B2 has a more powerful Arriel 1D1 engine and upgraded transmission, as detailed. Referred to as SuperStar in America.
AS 350 B3 is a new variant, featuring an 858 shp (640 kW) Arriel 2 turboshaft and new tail rotor of wider chord.
AS 350D AStar is the name for Ecureuil marketed in America, with an AlliedSignal LTS101-600A-3 turboshaft of 615 shp (458.6 kW).
AS 550 A2 Fennec is the military battlefield version, with Arriel 1D1 engine and self-sealing fuel tanks. Dimensionally similar to Ecureuil, except all versions of Fennec are 10 ft 11.5 ins (3.34 m) high due to taller undercarriage skids. Can be equipped with axial weapons such as a 20 mm gun and rocket pods. Standard sliding doors. Instrument panel adapted to tactical flight, and internal/external provision for flight using night vision goggles. Can still carry 5 troops or a sling load. Armed with a 20-mm cannon and rocket launcher, it can perform a tactical mission out to 27 naut miles (31 miles) 50 km, loiter for 2 hours and 10 minutes, and return with 20 minutes fuel reserve.
AS 550 C2 Fennec is the anti-armour or air-to-air version. Can be equipped with 4 missiles and can still carry 5 troops or a sling load. HeliTOW sighting system and TOW missiles for anti-armour. Can have a night vision system. Armed with 4 missiles, it can perform day/night missions lasting 2 hours 30 minutes with 20 minutes reserve. Arriel 1D1.
AS 550 M2 Fennec is the unarmed naval variant. Arriel 1D1.
AS 550 S2 Fennec is the armed naval variant. Arriel 1D1.
AS 550 U2 Fennec is the reconnaissance/observation version, also suited to utility and training tasks. Arriel 1D1.

Details for AS 350 B2.

Principal dimensions:
Rotor diameter (main): 35 ft 1 ins (10.69 m)
Maximum length, rotors turning: 42 ft 5.5 ins (12.94 m)
Fuselage length: 35 ft 10.5 ins (10.93 m), including tail rotor
Width, blades folded: 8 ft 4 ins (2.53 m)
Maximum height: 10 ft 3.5 ins (3.14 m)

Cabin:
Length: 7 ft 11 ins (2.42 m)
Width: 5 ft 5 ins (1.65 m) maximum
Height: 4 ft 5 ins (1.35 m)

Main rotor:
Blade chord: 1 ft 1.8 ins (0.35 m)
Rotor disc: 966.06 sq ft (89.75 m^2)
Rpm: 394

Tail rotor:
Diameter: 6 ft 1 ins (1.86 m)

Undercarriage:
Type: Fixed twin skids. Emergency flotation gear on the skids.
Skid track: 7 ft 1.5 ins (2.17 m)

Weights:
Empty: 2,542 lb (1,153 kg)
Normal maximum take-off: 4,960 lb (2,250 kg)
Maximum take-off, external load: 5,511 lb (2,500 kg)

Performance:
Never-exceed speed (VNE): 155 kts (178 mph) 287 km/h
Cruise speed: 133 kts (153 mph) 246 km/h at sea level
Maximum climb rate: 1,675 ft (510 m) per minute
IGE hovering ceiling: 9,840 ft (3,000 m)
OGE hovering ceiling: 7,545 ft (2,300 m)
Ceiling: 15,100 ft (4,600 m), service
Range: 360 naut miles (416 miles) 670 km

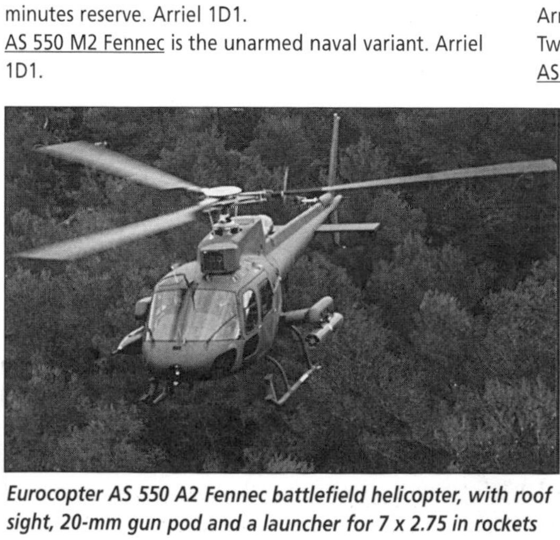

Eurocopter AS 550 A2 Fennec battlefield helicopter, with roof sight, 20-mm gun pod and a launcher for 7 x 2.75 in rockets

Eurocopter AS 355 Ecureuil 2, TwinStar and AS 555 Fennec

First flight: 28 September 1979.
Role: Twin-engined version of the AS 350/550.

★ Aims
★ Particularly suited to missions requiring high performance with OEI, such as rooftop take-off, harbour pilot drop-off, work on power lines and pylons, and offshore connections (sea rescue).
Sales: Many hundreds delivered for civil and military operation; Fennec sales reached 269 to 23 countries by September 1994, in both AS 550 and twin-engined AS 555 versions. Has also been built by Helibras in Brazil as the Esquilo/Fennec. Among recent customers is the Argentine Navy, which received 4 Fennecs from March 1995.
Details: AS 355 N Ecureuil 2.
Crew/passengers: Pilot plus 5 passengers. Alternatively, pilot, doctor, medical attendant and patient plus complete medical equipment for EMS; some of the medical equipment can be carried in the 3 baggage compartments with a combined capacity of 35.3 cu ft (1 m^3). Volume and comfort are identical to other Ecureuil versions.
Freight, external: 2,500 lb (1,134 kg) sling load.
Rotor system: 3-blade (manually folding) composites main rotor, with Starflex bearingless rotor head. Combiner gearbox, with freewheels.
Tail rotor characteristics: Similar to Ecureuil.
Tail surfaces: Similar to Ecureuil.
Airframe materials: Similar to Ecureuil.
Engines: 2 Turbomeca Arrius 1A1 (TM 319) turboshafts with FADEC.
Engine rating: Each 520 shp (388 kW) max contingency, 479 shp (357 kW) take off.
Fuel system: 730 litres usable.
Electrical system: 2 starter-generators.
Flight avionics/instrumentation: Rockwell Collins, Honeywell or SFIM autopilot. Avionics to customer's requirements for VFR or IFR flying.
Aircraft variants:
AS 355 F2 Ecureuil 2 is a twin-engined version of Ecureuil, differing from the AS 355 N in having 2 Allison 250-C20F turboshafts (each 420 shp, 313 kW). Known in America as the TwinStar. Particularly suited to performing offshore liaisons, flying over built-up areas and in inhospitable zones.
AS 355 N Ecureuil 2 is the principal civil version, with Arrius 1A1 engines. As detailed. Also known as TwinStar in America.
AS 555 AN Fennec is a twin-Arrius 1A1-engined version of AS 550 A2 Fennec military battlefield helicopter. Similar armament. Armed with a 20-mm cannon and rocket launcher, it can perform a tactical mission out to 27 naut miles (31 miles) 50 km, loiter fo 1 hours and 30 minutes, and return with 20 minutes fuel reserve.
AS 555 CN Fennec is a twin-Arrius 1A1-engined version of the AS 550 C2 Fennec for anti-armour or air-to-air missions. Similar armament.
AS 555 MN Fennec is a twin-Arrius 1A1-engined version of the AS 550 M2 Fennec unarmed naval helicopter. Suited to small-tonnage vessel operations. Can be used for maritime parol, SAR (with hoist), and OTH targeting.
AS 555 SN Fennec is a twin-Arrius 1A1-engined version of the AS 550 S2 Fennec armed naval helicopter. Capable of operating from low-

tonnage vessels. Can perform (at low cost) maritime surveillance, OTH targeting, submarine attack and sea support missions. Weapons can include a lightweight torpedo. AlliedSignal Bendix/King RDR-1500B radar, Doppler, 3-axis autopilot and more. Recommended cruise speed 110 kts (127 mph) 204 km/h, radius of action 150 naut miles (173 miles) 278 km, and maximum endurance 4 hours.
AS 555 UN Fennec is a twin Arrius 1A1-engined version of AS 550 U2 Fennec for unarmed reconnaissance/observation, utility (including transporting commandos) and IFR training. Basically an unarmed AS 555 AN.

DETAILS FOR AS 355 N ECUREUIL.

Principal dimensions: Similar to Ecureuil
Cabin: Similar to Ecureuil
Main rotor: Similar to Ecureuil
Tail rotor: Similar to Ecureuil
Undercarriage: Similar to Ecureuil

Weights:
Empty: 3,045 lb (1,381 kg)
Normal maximum take-off: 5,600 lb (2,540 kg)
Maximum take-off, external load: 5,732 lb (2,600 kg)

Performance (ISA):
Never-exceed speed (VNE): 150 kts (172 mph) 278 km/h
Cruise speed: 120 kts (139 mph) 223 km/h at sea level
Maximum climb rate: 1,355 ft (414 m) per minute at sea level
IGE hovering ceiling: 8,530 ft (2,600 m)
OGE hovering ceiling: 5,085 ft (1,550 m)
Ceiling: 13,125 ft (4,000 m)
Range: 390 naut miles (448 miles) 722 km with standard fuel

Eurocopter AS 355 N Ecureuil 2 in UK police use, with FLIR and searchlight

Eurocopter AS 365N2 Dauphin 2 and AS 565 Panther

First flight: 29 February 1984 (AS 365 M Panther prototype).

Eurocopter AS 365 N2 Dauphin 2 (M.P. Guillot Marine Nationale)

Eurocopter AS 565 MA Panther operating in the SAR role, with nose radar, searchlight and rescue hoist (M.P. Guillot Marine Nationale)

Role: Multi-purpose civil passenger, offshore liaison, VIP, freight and aerial photography (Dauphin 2) and armed/unarmed military and naval (Panther) helicopters.
Sales: Some 600 of all civil/military models (including development, fly-by-wire and other research, and out-of-production models of the SA/AS 365/565/366). Among the latest customers is the United Arab Emirates, which has purchased 7 armed naval Panthers. The Fench Navy recently ordered 4 new AS 565 MAs and SAs for coastal patrol and ASW. Also built in China by Harbin, currently in Z-9B form.
Details: Principally for AS 365 N2 Dauphin 2, unless stated.
Crew/passengers: Pilot plus 12 passengers, or 4, 5 or 6 passengers in VIP and business layouts. For EMS, 2 or 4 litters plus attendants.
Freight, external: 3,527 lb (1,600 kg) sling load.
Optional equipment: Includes rescue hoist.
Rotor system: 4-blade composites main rotor, with Starflex hub. Manual folding blades, with tabs. Rotor brake.
Tail rotor characteristics: Fenestron fan-in-fin tail rotor composites. 11 blades.
Tail surfaces: Large fin. Horizontal stabilizer, with endplates toed to port by 10°.
Flight control system: Hydraulic.
Airframe materials: Principally alloy or alloy/Nomex composite sandwich construction, but with all-composites fenestron, fin, fairings and nose.
Engines: 2 Turbomeca Arriel 1C2 turboshafts.
Engine rating: Each 763 shp (569 kW) maximum contingency, and 737 shp (550 kW) maximum take-off.
Fuel system: 1,135 litres standard. 180 litre auxiliary tank in hold. 475 litre ferry tank can be positioned in the cabin, replacing the aft seating.
Electrical system: 2 x 4.8 kW starter-generators. 2 inverters for AC supply at 400 Hz. 27 amp-hour ni-cd battery.
Hydraulic system: Dual supplies, each 870 psi.
Braking system: Hydraulic disc.
Radar: Optional.
Flight avionics/instrumentation: 2 pilot IFR. SFIM 155 duplex autopilot, with optional coupler. Wide range of optional avionics, including EFIS screens, VOR/ILS, ADF and transponder.
Aircraft variants:
AS 365 N2 Dauphin 2 is the civil transport version, as detailed. Certified for VFR operations in 1989.
AS 366 G1 variant was delivered to the US Coast Guard between November 1984 and April 1989 as a short-range recovery helicopter (97 full production HH-65As plus 2 of 4 AS 366G development helicopters), for operation from small vessels (cutters and icebreakers) and shore. 4 crew (pilot/commander, co-pilot, flight mechanic and rescuer). US military designated HH-65A Dolphin; they differ from typical AS 365N types in having 2 x 684 shp (510 kW) AlliedSignal LTS101-750B-2 turboshafts and much US equipment. Capable of all-weather operations. FLIR and rescue hoist. Mission weight 6,700 lb (3,039 kg).
AS 565AA Panther is the military battlefield helicopter and air-to-air version. Armament can include 20-mm cannon pods, rocket launchers or up to 8 Mistral AAMs. All Panthers use 748 shp (558 kW) take-off rated Arriel 1M1 turboshafts or the latest 849 shp (633 kW) Arriel 2Cs, and have crashworthy fuel systems and equipment choices that include self-protection systems.
AS 565 CA Panther is the military anti-armour version with roof sight and HOT missiles. Arriel 1M1 turboshafts or the latest 849 shp (633 kW) Arriel 2Cs.
AS 565 MA Panther is the unarmed naval version. Can be used for many roles including maritime patrol and surveillance (with radar), SAR (with hoist), and OTH

DETAILS FOR AS 365 N2 DAUPHIN 2.

Principal dimensions:
Rotor diameter (main): 39 ft 2 ins (11.94 m)
Maximum length, rotors turning: 44 ft 10.5 ins (13.68 m)
Fuselage length: 38 ft 2 ins (11.63 m)
Width, blades folded: 10 ft 6.5 ins (3.21 m)
Maximum height: 13 ft 0.25 ins (3.97 m)

Cabin:
Length: 7 ft 7 ins (2.3 m)
Width: 6 ft 3.5 ins (1.92 m)
Height: 4 ft 7 ins (1.4 m)
Volume: 176.57 cu ft (5 m^3), plus 21.19 cu ft (0.6 m^3) in the hold

Main rotor:
Blade chord: 1 ft 3 ins (0.385 m)
Rotor disc: 1,204.48 sq ft (111.9 m^2)
Rpm: 350

Tail rotor:
Diameter: 3 ft 7.25 ins (1.1 m)

Undercarriage:
Type: Retractable, with twin self-centring nosewheels. Emergency flotation gear for offshore missions
Main wheel tyre size: 15 x 6.00
Wheel base: 11 ft 10 ins (3.61 m)
Wheel track: 6 ft 3 ins (1.9 m)

Weights:
Empty: 4,936 lb (2,239 kg)
Normal maximum take-off: 9,369 lb (4,250 kg)

Performance (ISA):
Never-exceed speed (VNE): 155 kts (178 mph) 2 87 km/h
Cruise speed: 151 kts (173 mph) 279 km/h at sea level
Maximum climb rate: 1,339 ft (408 m) per minute at sea level
IGE hovering ceiling: 6,560 ft (2,000 m)
OGE hovering ceiling: 3,937 ft (1,200 m)
Ceiling: 12,140 ft (3,700 m), service
Range: 464 naut miles (534 miles) 860 km at sea level, with standard fuel

targeting. Arriel 1M1 turboshafts or the latest 849 shp (633 kW) Arriel 2Cs.

AS 565 SA Panther is the armed naval version and can perform maritime surveillance, OTH targeting, submarine detection and attack, anti-ship, SAR and sea support missions. For ASW, the principal detection system is either sonar or MAD, with 2 torpedoes for attack. Agrion 15 radar and 4 x AS 15TT missiles for ASV. Typically AlliedSignal Bendix/King RDR-1500 or Omera ORB 32 surveillance radar for search and rescue. Arriel 1M1 turboshafts or the latest 849 shp (633 kW) Arriel 2Cs.

AS 565 SB Panther is a search and rescue variant, with 849 shp (633 kW) Arriel 2C turboshafts or the latest 849 shp (633 kW) Arriel 2Cs.

AS 565 UA Panther is the military utility version for unarmed reconnaissance/observation, transporting commandos or sling loads, SAR, litter-carrying, and IFR training. Other roles can include conversion for electronic missions. Arriel 1M1 turboshafts or the latest 849 shp (633 kW) Arriel 2Cs.

Panther 800 has 1,335 shp (995.5 kW) LHTEC T800-LHT-800 turboshafts, and first appeared in 1992 as a proposed version for the US Army, offered in co-operation with the former Vought.

Eurocopter BO 105 and EC Super Five

First flight: 16 February 1967.

Role: Civil and military light helicopter, with armed versions. Mainly used for rescue, offshore, law enforcement, emergency medical and executive/utility applications.

Sales: Very large number and continuing, with new-operator deliveries in 1995 including 2 EC Super Fives to EMERCOM in Russia for EMS and SAR. Military operators include the German Army, whose PAH-1s have recently been upgraded with new blades and other improvements (take-off weight increased to 5,511 lb, 2,500 kg); many have digital avionics and HOT 2 anti-armour missiles on light launchers, but plans to retrofit roof sights for night operations were cancelled. 28 Spanish BO 105ATHs are receiving new blades, NVG cockpits, GPS and HOT missiles to enhance their anti-armour capabilities, plus either radar and infra-red warning receivers or chaff/flare dispensers.

Details: BO 105 CBS, unless stated.

Crew/passengers: Pilot plus 4-5 passengers. Rear bench seat is removable for cargo or to allow 1 or 2 litters.

Eurocopter EC Super Five version of the BO 105 CBS

Eurocopter BO 105 P (PAH-1), now upgraded for continued German Army service

Freight, external: 1,984 lb (900 kg).

Cabin access: Rear clamshell doors for internal cargo, with complete access to the cabin, able to accept long loads projecting out under the boom. Side sliding doors.

Optional equipment: Dual controls. Steerable searchlight for SAR, or FLIR, IR searchlight and loudspeaker for law enforcement. Many other options.

Rotor system: 4-blade (manually foldable) hingeless rigid main rotor (System Bölkow), with a single-piece drop-forged titanium rotor head with 4 titanium inner sleeves to which the fibre composites blades are bolted (each blade has a titanium anti-erosion shell on the drooped leading edge). Lead-lag and flapping motions are absorbed by the inherent elasticity of the blades. The inner sleeves are retained within the rotor head by flexible tension-torsion straps attached to 2 quadruple retaining nuts located in the head centre to take up the centrifugal forces. Pendulum absorbers, acting as vibration dampers, are fixed to the blade roots.

Tail rotor characteristics: 2-blade, mounted to port. Same construction as the main blades, but with stainless steel protection shells.

Tail surfaces: Small horizontal stabilizer with endplate fins towards the rear of the tailboom.

Flight control system: Hydraulic.

Airframe materials: Mainly metal, with some secondary structures of composites.

Safety features: Crashworthy structure, with realistic survivability in an impact of 26 ft (8 m) per second sink rate and 49 ft (15 m) per second forward speed.

Engines: 2 Allison 250-C20B turboshafts (same for Super Five).

Engine rating: Each 420 shp (313.3 kW).

Transmission rating: Separate and independent drive shaft for each engine up to the main transmission.

Fuel system: 1,005 lb (456 kg) standard (same for Super Five and LS A-3); 570 litres usable. Fully separated feed to each engine. Auxiliary tanks can be carried in the cargo compartment.

Electrical system: Dual 28 volt DC supply via starter-generators. 25 amp-hour ni-cd battery.

Hydraulic system: Dual hydraulic boost system containing 2 independent modules. 1,500 psi.

Radar: Optional weather radar.

Flight avionics/instrumentation: Stability Augmentation System (pitch and roll axis) is standard. Avionics to customer's choice.

Expendable weapons and equipment: See Sales.

Aircraft variants:

BO 105 CBS basic version, as detailed.

BO 105 LS A-3 is generally similar to the BO 105 CBS but has 500 shp (373 kW) Allison 250-C28C engines for improved hot-and-high performance, with OEI rating of 550 shp (410 kW).

Super Lifter is a new variant of the BO 105 LS A-3, certified in 1995. It has EC Super Five blades and a new tail rotor developed from the BK 117 C-1. Intended primarily for external lift and sling load work, it has a maximum normal weight of 6,283 lb (2,850 kg) and a 2,868 lb (1,300 kg) cargo hook.

EC Super Five is the latest and principal production version, quoted as "the new BO 105 CBS", offering improved main rotor blades, upgraded main transmission for increased OEI performance, and additional equipment including standard dual controls. New rotor blades provide up to 330 lb (150 kg) more thrust, lower vibration level and reduced fuel consumption. Additional equipment package weighs 37.6 lb (17 kg).

DETAILS FOR BO 105 CBS, LS A-3 AND EC SUPER FIVE, UNLESS SPECIFIED.

Principal dimensions:
Rotor diameter (main): 32 ft 3.5 ins (9.84 m)
Maximum length, rotors turning: 38 ft 11 ins (11.86 m)
Fuselage length: 28 ft 11 ins (8.81 m), tail rotor vertical
Width, blades folded: 8 ft 3.5 ins (2.53 m)
Maximum height: 9 ft 10 ins (3 m)

Cabin:
Width: 4 ft 7 ins (1.4 m)
Height: 4 ft 1.25 ins (1.25 m)
Useful volume: about 127.13 cu ft (3.6 m^3)

Main rotor:
Aerofoil section: NACA 23012 for CBS and LS A-3, and DM-H4/H3 for Super Five
Blade chord: 10.63 ins (0.27 m)
Rotor disc: 818.59 sq ft (76.05 m^2)
Rpm: 424

Tail rotor:
Diameter: 6 ft 3 ins (1.9 m)
Rpm: 2,220

Undercarriage:
Type: Fixed skids. Crashworthiness by the ability to absorb energy by elastic and plastic deformation

Weights:
Empty: 2,868 lb (1,301 kg) for CBS, 2,910 lb (1,320 kg) for Super Five, and 3,153 lb (1,430 kg) for LS A-3
Normal maximum take-off: 5,511 lb (2,500 kg) for CBS and Super Five, and 5,732 lb (2,600 kg) for LS A-3
External payload: 1,984 lb (900 kg) for CBS and Super Five, and 2,205 lb (1,000 kg) for LS A-3

Performance:
Never-exceed speed (VNE): 131 kts (150 mph) 242 km/h for CBS, 135 kts (155 mph) 250 km/h for Super Five, 129.5 kts (149 mph) 240 km/h for LS A-3
Cruise speed: 130 kts (149 mph) 240 km/h for CBS, 131 kts (151 mph) 243 km/h for Super Five, and 129 kts (149 mph) 239 km/h for LS A-3, all at sea level
Maximum climb rate: 1,457 ft (444 m) per minute for CBS, 1,614 ft (492 m) per minute for Super Five, and 1,810 ft (552 m) per minute for LS A-3, all at sea level
IGE hovering ceiling: 5,000 ft (1,524 m) for CBS, 8,000 ft (2,438 m) for Super Five, and 11,500 ft (3,500 m) for LS A-3
OGE hovering ceiling: 8,365 ft (2,550 m) for LS A-3
Ceiling: 10,000 ft (3,050 m) for CBS, 17,000 ft (5,182 m) for Super Five, and 20,000 ft (6,100 m) for LS A-3, all service
Range: 299 naut miles (345 miles) 555 km for CBS, 304 naut miles (350 miles) 564 km for Super Five, and 278 naut miles (320 miles) 515 km for LS A-3, all at sea level with standard fuel
Duration: 3.4 hours for CBS, 3.5 hours for Super Five and 3 hours for LS A-3, all at sea level with standard fuel

Eurocopter EC 135

First flight: 15 February 1994 (S-01); second pre-production (S-02) first flew on 16 April 1994; third pre-production (S-03) flew on 28 November 1994.
Role: Light multi-purpose helicopter.

Eurocopter EC 135 S-01

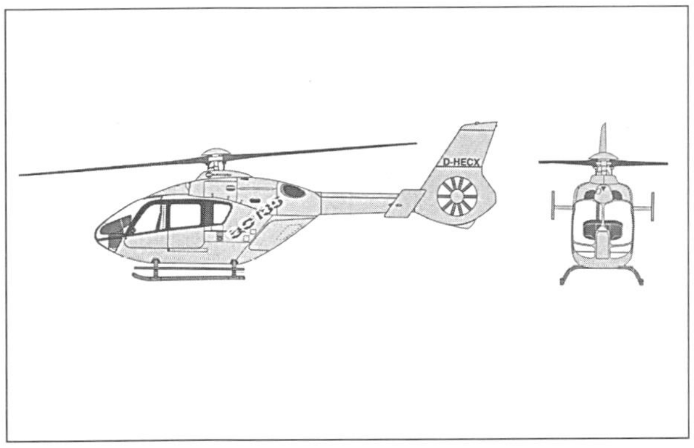

Eurocopter EC 135 general arrangement (courtesy Eurocopter)

Details for EC 135.

Principal dimensions:
Rotor diameter (main): 33 ft 5.5 ins (10.2 m)
Maximum length, rotors turning: 39 ft 9.5 ins (12.13 m)
Fuselage length: 33 ft 4 ins (10.16 m)
Width, without rotors: 8 ft 8 ins (2.65 m)
Maximum height: 12 ft 4 ins (3.75 m)

Tail rotor:
Diameter: 3 ft 3.5 ins (1 m)

Undercarriage
Type: Fixed twin skids.
Skid track: 6 ft 11 ins (2.1 m)

Weights:
Empty: 3,020 lb (1,370 kg) basic version
Normal maximum take-off: 5,511 lb (2,500 kg)
Maximum take-off, external load: 5,952 lb (2,700 kg)

Performance (ISA):
Never-exceed speed: 155 kts (178 mph) 287 km/h
Cruise speed: 140 kts (162 mph) 260 km/h at sea level
Maximum climb rate: 1,594 ft (486 m) per minute at sea level
IGE hovering ceiling: 15,600 ft (4,750 m)
OGE hovering ceiling: 13,450 ft (4,100 m)
Ceiling: 20,000 ft (6,100 m), service
Ceiling, OEI: 12,795 ft (3,900 m), service
Cat A clear heliport, OEI: 11,155 ft (3,400 m)
Cat A restricted/elevated heliport: 8,695 ft (2,650 m)
Range: 386 naut miles (444 miles) 715 km with standard tanks
Duration: 4 hours at sea level, standard tanks

★ Aims

★ Meets current and new transport category operating regulations, with certification to JAR Part 27 (LBA/DGAC) and FAA Part 27, including the requirement for systems segregation and Cat A requirements of Appendix C. Low noise level, 6 dB lower than the new ICAO limit in Annex 16. Can operate in -30° C to +54° C conditions. Main objectives are to make the helicopter more economical by simplifying maintenance procedures and reduce direct operating and life cycle costs, whilst increasing performance.
Sales: Anticipated sales of 900 over many years.
Crew/passengers: Pilot and 4-6 passengers. Crash-resistant seats.
Freight, external: 2,645 lb (1,200 kg).
Loading facilities: Cabin sliding doors and cockpit hinged doors. 2 large and removable rear clamshell doors for rear loading capability and carrying long items.
Rotor system: Advanced hingeless and bearingless main rotor system. No rotor head in the accepted sense, but has 4 aerodynamically optimized composite blades with an integrated glassfibre flexbeam and control cuff, and the rotor shaft with blade attachment flange, which is a single-piece forging. Conventional hub elements are replaced by the elastic properties of the flexbeam. No flap and lag hinges, their functions undertaken by stiffness tuning in the flexbeam. Rotor tilted forward by 5°.
Tail rotor characteristics: Enhanced Fenestron anti-torque system.
Tail surfaces: Horizontal stabilizer, with swept endplate fins, towards the end of the tailboom.
Flight control system: Hydraulic, with electric SAS servos.
Airframe materials: Extensive use of Kevlar/carbonfibre in the structure.
Engine: 2 x 696 shp (519 kW) Turbomeca Arrius 2B or 551 shp (411 kW) Pratt & Whitney Canada PW206B turboshafts, each quoted at maximum rating. Each has FADEC. S-01 has the Arrius engines fitted, S-02 the PW206Bs.
Engine rating: See above.
Transmission: Anti Resonance Isolation System (ARIS).
Fuel system: 1,239 lb (562 kg) standard. Optional 100 litre auxiliary fuel tanks.
Electrical system: Dual, redundant.
Hydraulic system: Dual, redundant.
Radar: Optional weather radar.
Flight avionics/instrumentation: IFR provisions.

Eurocopter EC-145 and EC-165

★ Aims

★ For possible launch in 1997, these are projected replacements for the BK 117 and AS 365 Dauphin in the 4,500 kg class.

Eurocopter SA 342 Gazelle

First flight: 7 April 1967.
Role: Light utility, anti-armour, air-to-air and training helicopter.
Details: SA 342M Gazelle.

★ Aims

★ French Army SA 342M anti-armour helicopters are receiving Viviane sighting systems to enhance their night capability. Very low rate production is being maintained. New rotor blades.
Engine: Turbomeca Astazou XIV M1 turboshaft.
Engine rating: 858 shp (640 kW) maximum contingency, 592 shp (441 kW) maximum take-off.
Fuel system: 545 litres usable.
Flight avionics/instrumentation: Now with Viviane roof sight with direct path, infra-red channel and laser rangefinder, making it possible to launch Hot 2 anti-armour missiles effectively by day or night.
Expendable weapons and equipment: The many armament possibilities for Gazelles in general include Hot 2 anti-armour and 4 Mistral infra-red homing air-to-air missiles (the latter as carried by a number of French Army Gazelle ATAMs, each having a Sextant T200 sight).
Aircraft variants:
SA 342L2 was developed as an export version with NVG cockpit.
SA 342M is the French Army version, being upgraded and built.

Details for SA 342M.

Principal dimensions:
Rotor diameter (main): 34 ft 4.5 ins (10.48 m)
Maximum length, rotors turning: 39 ft 1 ins (11.91 m)
Fuselage length: 31 ft 3 ins (9.53 m)
Width, blades folded: 6 ft 7 ins (2 m)
Maximum height: 10 ft 5.5 ins (3.19 m)

Weights:
Empty: 2,224 lb (1,009 kg)
Normal maximum take-off: 4,629 lb (2,100 kg)

Performance:
Never-exceed speed (VNE): 151 kts (174 mph) 280 km/h
Cruise speed: 132 kts (152 mph) 245 km/h at sea level
Maximum climb rate: 1,515 ft (462 m) per minute at sea level
IGE hovering ceiling: 10,335 ft (3,150 m)
OGE hovering ceiling: 7,775 ft (2,370 m)
Ceiling: 14,600 ft (4,450 m), service
Range: 362 naut miles (416 miles) 670 km at sea level, standard fuel

Eurocopter SA 342M Gazelle with Viviane roof sight

Eurocopter Tiger (Tigre)

First flight: 27 April 1991.
Role: Anti-armour (HAC) and combat support (HAP).

★ Aims

★ Can operate in NBC conditions and continue flying after a nuclear electromagnetic pulse.

▲ Development

▲ Programme has been funded by France and Germany to meet the requirements of their armies.
▲ 30 June 1995. The bi-national Memorandum of Understanding for the industrialization phase of the Tiger programme and its Trigat weapon system was signed.

Eurocopter Tiger HAC with Trigat, Mistrals and a 30-mm gun pod

▲ 1999. Production deliveries will start.

Sales: Original requirement was for 427 for the French and German forces, comprising 140 HACs and 75 HAPs for France, and 212 for Germany as PAH-2s or UHUs.

Crew: 2 in tandem and stepped cockpits, with the pilot forward. Crash-resistant and armoured seats. Dual controls.

Cockpit: Virtually flat glass windscreens to prevent sun glint.

Rotor system: 4-blade main hingeless, failsafe, rotor. Based on a rigid, soft in plane rotor concept. Fibre composites blades, hub with titanium centrepiece and lower/upper fibre composites plates, conical/radial elastomeric bearings, and viscoelastic lead-lag dampers. SARIB vibration suppressor. Blades have ballistic tolerance.

Tail rotor characteristics: 3-blade, to starboard. Composites blades.

Wing/tail surfaces: Small stub wings with anhedral outer panels for weapon/fuel carriage. Horizontal stabilizer towards the rear of the boom, with endplate fins toed to port.

Fuselage: Lower fuselage structure of crash-dedicated design and materials to enhance survivability.

Airframe materials: 80% carbon/carbon or carbon/Kevlar composites. Frames and beams are Kevlar and carbon laminates. Panels are self-stabilized sandwich structures, comprising carbon and Kevlar skins filled with Nomex honeycomb. Fabrics are impregnated with epoxy resins. Low IR reflection paint.

Safety features: 90% protection in crashes in MIL-STD-1290. Crew will survive 34 ft (10.5 m) per second vertical, 26 ft (8 m) per second lateral, and 39 ft (12 m) per second longitudinal impact.

Engines: 2 MTU/Turbomeca/Rolls-Royce MTR 390 turboshafts, with FADEC. IR suppressor in which exhaust gas is diluted with cold air and diverted upwards. Armour plate between engines.

Engine rating: Each 1,555 shp (1,160 kW) super contingency, 1,170 shp (872.5 kW) maximum continuous.

Transmission: Main gearbox can dry run for 30 minutes.

Fuel system: 1,354 litres usable as standard. Self-sealing tanks, self-sealing breaking zones in the fuel lines. Maximum internal and external fuel is 3,472 lb (1,575 kg).

Electrical system: AC supply via 2 x 20 kVA alternators (30 kVA optional). DC supply via 2 x 300 amp, 28 volt transformer rectifiers and 2 x 23 amp-hour ni-cd batteries.

Hydraulic system: 2 autonomous and 1 auxiliary systems.

Flight avionics/instrumentation: Dual redundant MIL-STD-1553B databus architecture. AFCS comprises 2 redundant digital computers controlling the 4 axes (pitch, roll, yaw and collective). CDU (control and display unit) at each crew station for communications, navigation, radio navigation and systems status. The operating radio frequencies are displayed on a liquid crystal radio frequency indicator (RFI). A removable data insertion device (DID) is inserted in the CDU, allowing mission preparation at a ground station. Radio communication equipment is controlled either directly via the databus or via remote terminal units (depending on type). Information from/to radio communications and utility systems such as engines, electrical systems, hydraulics and fuel systems are collated by 2 remote terminal units, permitting monitoring by the crew during the mission. Anomalies of any sub-system are detected, and recorded in the removable mission data transfer systems for postflight evaluation and maintenance purposes; the crew may be informed immediately. Interfacing with the basic helicopter bus, the dual redundant mission computers serve also as bus controllers for the specific redundant MIL-STD-1553B interfacing the sights and weapons. Navigation subsystem comprises 2 identical strap-down navigation units with 3-axis ring laser gyros and silicon accelerometers, 2 magnetometers, 2 air data units, radio altimeter, 4-beam Doppler radar, GPS, and low air speed sensors. Digital map generator. 2 colour multi-function displays (6 x 6 ins, 15 x 15 cm) with function keys and a helmet sight/display for each crew member. HAC has an Osiris mast-mounted sight with IRCCD infra-red channel, CCD TV camera and laser rangefinder (flight tested on a Panther), and nose-mounted FLIR with 40° x 30° field of view. HAP has a roof-mounted sight with infra-red camera and TV, direct optical channel, and laser rangefinder. HAP can have a head-up sight/display, and an automatic air surveillance and warning system (DAV) based on a pulse Doppler radar.

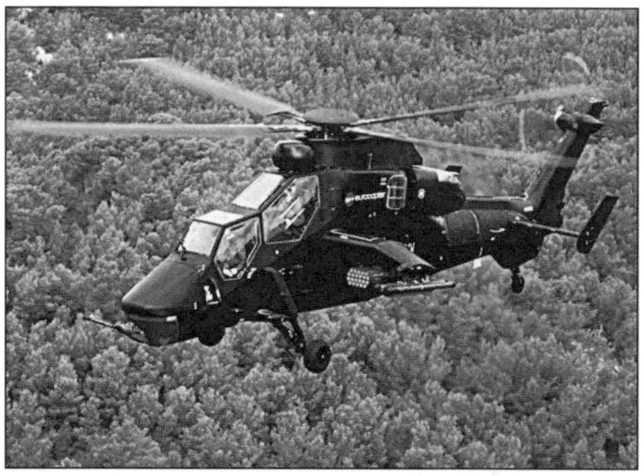

Eurocopter HAP, showing its turreted 30-781 gun

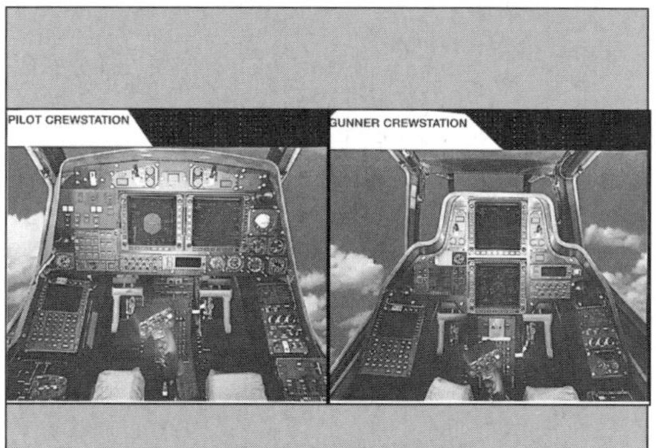

Pilot's and gunner's cockpits on the Eurocopter Tiger

Self-protection systems: Radar and laser warning receivers.

Fixed guns: Turreted 30-781 30-mm gun for HAP. Air-to-air and air-to-ground fire control system, with ±90° azimuth and ±30° elevation.

Ammunition: 450 rounds.

Number of weapon pylons: 4, 2 under each stub wing.

Expendable weapons and equipment: Mission configurations for HAC are 8 Hot plus 4 Mistral or Stinger Missiles, 8 Trigat plus 4 Mistral or Stinger Missiles, 4 Trigat plus 4 Hot and 4 Mistral or Stinger Missiles, or 2 ferry tanks on the inner pylons. Mission configurations for HAP are the turreted gun with 450 rounds of ammunition, gun plus 4 Mistrals, gun plus 44 rockets and 4 Mistrals, gun plus 68 rockets, or 2 ferry tanks.

Aircraft variants:

HAC (Hélicoptère Anti-Char) has been designed as a highly mobile and survivable weapon system, fitted with fire-and-forget anti-armour missiles for use by day or night and in adverse weather. Requirements include to identify and engage ground targets by day and night at up to 2.7 naut miles (3.1 miles) 5 km or more; low detectability, with use of a mast-mounted sight; and self-defence with 4 AAMs.

HAP (Hélicoptère d'Appui et de Protection) is intended to offer day and night protection to anti-armour helicopters against enemy helicopters and light armoured vehicles using the short-range 30-mm wide angle turreted gun, and engage medium/long-range air threats with Mistrals. In combat support, it uses its short-range gun and medium/long-range 68-mm rockets. Fourth Tiger prototype, HAP configured, first flew on 19 December 1994 with an active weapon system.

UHU is a possible anti-armour and/or combat support version for Germany, which could take the place of the expected German PAH-2 version.

DETAILS FOR TIGER.

Principal dimensions:
Rotor diameter (main): 42 ft 8 ins (13 m)
Fuselage length: 45 ft 11 ins (14 m)
Maximum height: 12 ft 6 ins (3.81 m) to above rotor head

Tail rotor:
Diameter: 8 ft 10.ins (2.7 m)

Undercarriage:
Type: High energy absorbing undercarriage
Wheel base: 25 ft 1.25 ins (7.65 m)
Wheel track: 7 ft 10.5 ins (2.4 m)

Weights:
Empty: 7,275 lb (3,300 kg) basic
Design mission: 11,905 lb (5,400 kg)
Alternative gross: 13,228 lb (6,000 kg)

Performance (sea level, ISA at design mission weight):
Design limit speed: 161 kts (185 mph) 298 km/h for HAC, 174 kts (200 mph) 322 km/h for HAP
Cruise speed: 124 kts (143 mph) 230 km/h
Armed flight speed: 145 kts (167 mph) 269 km/h for HAC, 155 kts (178 mph) 287 km/h for HAP
Maximum climb rate: 2,106 ft (642 m) per minute for HAC, 2,264 ft (690 m) per minute for HAP
Vertical climb rate: 1,023 ft (312 m) per minute for HAC, 1,260 ft (384 m) per minute for HAP
Yaw rate: 40° per second
OGE hovering ceiling: 10,500 ft (3,200 m) for HAC, 11,480 ft (3,500 m) for HAP
Maximum range, internal fuel: 432 naut miles (497 miles) 800 km for HAC and HAP
Design mission duration: 2 hours 50 minutes for HAC and HAP
Maximum duration, internal fuel: 3 hours 25 minutes for HAC and HAP

Eurocopter/CATIC/Singapore Technologies Aerospace (France/Germany/China/Singapore)

Corporate addresses: See Combat section for details of CATIC and Singapore Technologies Aerospace.

EC-120

First flight: 9 June 1995.
Role: Light civil helicopter.

▲ Development

▲ 20 October 1992. Development contract was signed, enabling the development phase to begin in January 1993. Joint multi-national team was established at Marignane.
▲ 1997. Anticipated certification and first deliveries.
Crew/passengers: Pilot and 4 passengers.
Rotor system: Spheriflex 3-blade main rotor. Composite blades. Main gearbox with integral rotor-mast is attached directly to the main structure.

Details for EC-120.

Principal dimensions:
Rotor diameter (main): 33 ft 5.5 ins (10.2 m)
Fuselage length: 37 ft 10 ins (11.54 m)
Width, blades folded: 7 ft 10.5 ins (2.4 m)
Maximum height: 10 ft 9 ins (3.27 m)

Cabin:
Length: 5 ft 11 ins (1.8 m)
Width: 4 ft 11 ins (1.5 m)
Height: 4 ft 3.5 ins (1.31 m)

Main rotor:
Blade chord: 10.24 ins (0.26 m)

Tail rotor:
Diameter: 2 ft 5.5 ins (0.75 m)

Undercarriage:
Type: Fixed twin skids

Weight:
Empty: 1,874 lb (850 kg)
Maximum: 3,417 lb (1,550 kg)
Maximum take-off, external load: 3,858 lb (1,750 kg)
Payload: 1,543 lb (700 kg)

Performance:
High cruise speed: 130 kts (149 mph) 240 km/h
IGE hovering ceiling: 13,125 ft (4,000 m)
OGE hovering ceiling: 10,500 ft (3,200 m)
Ceiling: 16,000 ft (4,875 m), service
Range: 378 naut miles (435 miles) 700 km
Duration: 5 hours

EC-120 during its first flight in June 1995

Tail rotor characteristics: 8-blade fenestron type, with composites blades.
Tail surfaces: Small horizontal stabilizer under the tailboom. Fin.
Airframe materials: Extensive use of composites. CATIC/Harbin, which have a 24% share in the programme, are responsible for design and production of the complete fuselage structure, fully equipped, including fuel and hydraulic systems. Singapore Technologies Aerospace, with a 15% share, is responsible for the tailboom, the composites structure for the fenestron tail rotor, and cabin doors. Eurocopter, as 61% share team leader, is in overall charge of design, ground and flight testing, including design and production of the dynamic components, avionics package, electric systems, overall integration, final assembly and certification.
Engine: Turbomeca Arrius 1F turboshaft. Optional Pratt & Whitney PW200 turboshaft.
Engine rating: 500 shp (373 kW).
Fuel system: 400 litres.

Eurocopter/Kawasaki (Germany/Japan)

Corporate addresses: See Combat section for Kawasaki company details.

Eurocopter/Kawasaki BK 117

First flight: 13 June 1979.
Role: Light multi-purpose helicopter used for passenger and freight transport, VIP transport, law enforcement, SAR, EMS, firefighting and more.
Sales: Several hundred sold, and also licence-built by IPTN in Indonesia and assembled from Kawasaki kits in South Korea. Assembly lines in Germany and Japan.
Details: Principally for the BK 117 B-2.
Crew/passengers: Pilot and 7-10 passengers or 2 litters in an EMS role.
Freight, external: 2,645 lb (1,200 kg)
Cabin access: Sliding door on each side of the fuselage and rear clamshell doors.
Optional equipment: Includes dual controls.
Rotor system: 4-blade hingeless rigid main rotor (System Bölkow), with fibre composites blades. Optional manual blade folding. See BO 105 for a detailed description of the System Bölkow rotor system. Separate and independent main transmission drive shaft for each engine. Rotor brake in German-built BK 117s, otherwise optional.
Tail rotor characteristics: 2-blade, mounted to port. Fibre composites blades.
Tail surfaces: Horizontal stabilizer towards rear of tailboom, with large swept endplate fins toed to starboard.
Flight control system: Hydraulic. Fly-by-wire system has been test flown.
Airframe materials: High percentage of composites for the secondary structure, including cabin doors, nose access door, some of the lower fuselage shells, hydraulic/main transmission/engine cowlings, horizontal stabilizer and endplates.
Safety features: Crashworthy structure, able to survive a 26 ft (8 m) per second vertical and 49 ft (15 m) per second forward speed.
Engines: 2 AlliedSignal LTS101-750 B-1 turboshafts.
Engine rating: Each 550 shp (410 kW) maximum, or 593 shp (442 kW) OEI rating for 2.5 minutes.
Transmission rating: 987 shp (736 kW) for take-off and 847 shp (632 kW) maximum continuous. 770 shp (574 kW) emergency OEI rating for 2.5 minutes.
Fuel system: 710 litres, weighing 1,230 lb (558 kg). Auxiliary fuel tank raises capacity by 353 lb (160 kg). Fully separated system for each engine.
Electrical system: Dual 28 volt DC supply via 2 x 150 amp engine-driven starter-generators. 1 or 2 inverters for AC supply. 25 amp-hour ni-cd battery.
Hydraulic system: Dual system with 2 independent modes. 1,500 psi.
Radar: See below.

Details for BK 117 B-2.

Principal dimensions:
Rotor diameter (main): 36 ft 1 ins (11 m)
Maximum length, rotors turning: 42 ft 8 ins (13 m)
Fuselage length: 32 ft 6 ins (9.91 m) tail rotor vertical
Width, blades folded: 8 ft 10 ins (2.7 m)
Maximum height: 11 ft 0.25 ins (3.36 m)

Cabin:
Length: 9 ft 11 ins (3.02 m)
Width: 4 ft 10.75 ins (1.49 m) maximum
Height: 4 ft 2 ins (1.28 m) maximum
Volume: 176.57 cu ft (5 m^3)

Main rotor:
Blade chord: 12.6 ins (0.32 m)
Rotor disc: 1,022.89 sq ft (95.03 m^2)

Tail rotor:
Diameter: 6 ft 5 ins (1.956 m)

Undercarriage:
Type: Fixed twin skids. Crashworthiness through energy absorption by elastic or plastic deformation. Ground handling wheels. Optional emergency flotation gear, skis or skid plates
Skid track: 7 ft 10.5 ins (2.4 m)

Weights:
Empty: 3,818 lb (1,732 kg)
Maximum take-off: 7,385 lb (3,350 kg)

Performance (MTOW, ISA):
Never-exceed speed (VNE): 150 kts (172 mph) 278 km/h
Maximum cruise speed: 133 kts (153 mph) 247 km/h at sea level
Maximum climb rate: 1,770 ft (540 m) per minute at sea level
IGE hovering ceiling: 8,200 ft (2,500 m)
OGE hovering ceiling: 4,200 ft (1,280 m)
Ceiling: 10,000 ft (3,050 m), service
Ceiling, OEI: 4,200 ft (1,280 m)
Range: 291 naut miles (335 miles) 540 km with standard fuel, at sea level
Duration: 2.9 hours with standard fuel, at sea level

Eurocopter/Kawasaki BK 117 C-1

Flight avionics/instrumentation: Space for a variety of different communication, navigation and instrument fits of conventional or electronic types, for both VFR and IFR operations. Different types of radar, a fully-digitalized AFCS with or without coupled flight director and flight management systems can be fitted, as well as VFR/IFR instrumentation.

Aircraft variants:

BK 117 B-2 is the current LTS101-engined version, as detailed.

BK 117 C-1 is a later version with Arriel 1E engines, first flown on 6 April 1990 and delivered from 1993. 708 shp (528 kW) maximum take-off, 692 shp (516 kW) maximum continuous, and 751 shp (560 kW) OEI rating. Better hot-and-high performance, and 10,000 ft (3,050 m) IGE hover ceiling. Enhancement programme has been conducted, affecting mainly the rotor systems and to increase engine and transmission OEI ratings.

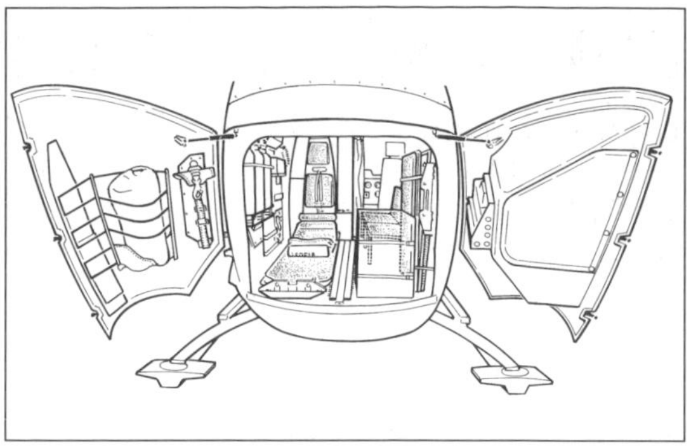

Eurocopter/Kawasaki BK 117 C-1 in EMS layout (courtesy of Eurocopter)

Euromil (France/Germany/Russia)

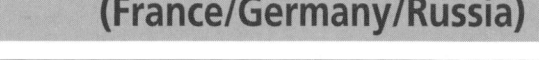

Corporate addresses: See Eurocopter and Mil for company details.

● Activities

● On 18 December 1992, an initial agreement was signed between Mil, Kazan, the Klimov/St Petersburg engine bureau and Eurocopter for joint development, manufacturing and marketing of the Mi-38. Each organization has a 25% shareholding. The venture was formalized in September 1993.

Euromil Mi-38

First flight: 1996?
Chief designer: Aleksei Ivanov; leading designer N. Chalov.
Role: Medium multi-purpose helicopter, to replace the Mi-8/17 family.

Euromil Mi-38 (Piotr Butowski)

★ Aims

★ 2 or 3 times more cost efficient than the Mi-8/17, easier maintenance and greater reliability.
★ All weather, day or night operation.
★ Built according to FAR 29 standards.
★ Integrated digital flight/navigation systems.

▲ Development

▲ 1985. Model shown on Soviet TV.
▲ Summer 1992. Full-scale mock-up shown.
▲ 1999. Western certification anticipated.

Crew/passengers: 2 crew plus up to 30 passengers. Possible pilot only for cargo carrying.
Freight, internal: 11,023 lb (5,000 kg).
Freight, external: 13,228 lb (6,000 kg).
Cabin access: Clamshell rear doors, and front fuselage side door of 5 ft 7 ins x 4 ft 11 ins (1.7 x 1.5 m). Hatch in cabin floor for sling load or air-drop operations.
Loading facilities: Optional cabin floor roller system and cargo hoist. Optional closed circuit TV system for remote viewing of external loads and handling.
Optional equipment: Includes emergency floats, rescue hoist and cargo handling equipment.
Rotor system: 6-blade composites main rotor, with elastomeric bearings and hydraulic drag dampers. Titanium rotor head. Elecric de-icing.
Tail rotor characteristics: 2 x 2-blade composite rotors, in scissors configuration. Electric de-icing.
Tail surfaces: Horizontal stabilizer has inset tabs.
Engines: 2 Klimov/Sarkisov TVA-3000 turboshafts.
Engine rating: Each 2,500 shp (1,864 kW) for take-off, with 3,750 shp (2,796 kW) OEI emergency rating for 30 seconds. VD-100 APU.
Fuel system: Underfloor bag tanks. Optional external auxiliary fuel tanks.
Electrical system: AC supply via 3 generators. DC supply from AC via transformer rectifiers. 2 batteries.
Hydraulic system: 3 systems, with redundancy.
Radar: Weather/navigation radar.
Flight avionics/instrumentation: Advanced flight deck with 2 large CRT displays each for the pilot and co-pilot, a central CRT display and 2 small displays. Integrated digital flight/navigation systems, linked via a central computer. Autopilot, with autostabilization, autohover and auto-landing. Navigation equipment includes Doppler, GPS, ILS and radio compass. Equipment health monitoring and warning system. See Loading facilities.

DETAILS FOR MI-38.

Principal dimensions:
Rotor diameter (main): 69 ft 3 ins (21.1 m)
Maximum length, rotors turning: 82 ft 8 ins (25.2 m)
Fuselage length: 65 ft 5 ins (19.95 m)
Maximum height: 17 ft 1 ins (5.2 m) to above rotor head

Cabin:
Length: 22 ft 4 ins (6.8 m) excluding ramp
Width: 7 ft 8 ins (2.34 m) maximum, 7 ft 3 ins (2.2 m) at floor
Height: 5 ft 11 ins to 6 ft 1 ins (1.8 to 1.85 m)

Main rotor:
Rotor disc: 3,764 sq ft (349.67 m^2)

Tail rotor:
Diameter: 12 ft 7 ins (3.84 m)

Undercarriage
Type: Retractable, with twin nosewheels. Optional emergency inflatable floats
Wheel base: 17 ft (5.17 m)
Wheel track: 14 ft 9 ins (4.5 m)

Weights:
Normal take-off: 31,306 lb (14,200 kg)
Maximum take-off: 34,392 lb (15,600 kg)
Payload: 11,023 lb (5,000 kg) internal, 13,228 lb (6,000 kg) external

Performance:
Maximum speed: 148 kts (171 mph) 275 km/h
Cruise speed: 135 kts (155 mph) 250 km/h
OGE hovering ceiling: 8,200 ft (2,500 m)
Ceiling: 17,060 ft (5,200 m), service
Range with full internal fuel: 432 naut miles (497 miles) 800 km, with a 7,716 lb (3,500 kg) payload, 30 minutes reserve
Range with 5,000 kg payload: 175 naut miles (202 miles) 325 km, 30 minutes reserve
Range with auxiliary fuel: 702 naut miles (808 miles) 1,300 km, with a 3,968 lb (1,800 kg) payload, 30 minutes reserve

European Helicopter Industries Ltd (Italy/UK)

Corporate address: 500 Chiswick High Road, London W4 5RG, England.
Telephone: +44 181 995 8221
Facsimile: +44 181 995 5207, 5990
Founded: 1980.

● Activities

- Jointly and equally owned by Agusta of Italy and Westland of the UK to develop and produce the EH 101.
- EH Industries Inc (1735 Jefferson Davis Highway, Suite 805, Arlington, VA 22202, USA – *telephone* +1 703 412 8000, *facsimile* +1 703 412 8010) is a US subsidiary. McDonnell Douglas is proposing a variant of EH 101 to meet the requirements for a US forces Medium Lift Replacement Helicopter.

EH Industries EH 101

First flight: 9 October 1987.
Role: Medium multi-role helicopter, with Naval, Utility, SAR and Civil variants.
Sales: 22 for the RAF and 44 known as Merlin HAS 1s for the Royal Navy to replace Sea Kings. Italian Navy confirmed an order for 16 in October 1995, with 8 probably to follow. Saudi Arabia is a likely early export customer (naval). Several commercial operators have expressed interest. Production deliveries to start in mid-1996; June 1998 delivery to RNAS Culdrose and from 1999 for the RAF.
Crew/passengers: Flight crew of 2, plus an observer and systems operators for ASW. Naval version can carry

EH Industries EH 101 sixth pre-production helicopter in Italian Naval form, during sea trials with Giuseppe Garibaldi

8 litters and 10 seated casualties over extended ranges in a SAR role. Military transport version will accommodate 30 to 45 troops (latter without seating) or 16 litters plus attendants. The civil Heliliner accommodates 30 passengers (4 abreast) or has a VIP interior.
Freight, internal: 9,500 lb (4,309 kg) for Utility; NATO pallets can be loaded via the side door, or vehicle, trailer, guns, ammunition, etc via the ramp.
Freight, external: 12,000 lb (5,443 kg) capacity cargo hook; 10,000 lb (4,535 kg) load for Utility.
Cabin access: Forward, port passenger door of 5 ft 7 ins x 3 ft (1.7 x 0.91 m). Sliding cargo door on starboard side of 5 ft 1 ins x 6 ft (1.55 x 1.83 m). Utility and SAR versions have an hydraulically-operated rear ramp/door, of 6 ft 11 ins x 5 ft 11 ins (2.1 x 1.8 m).
Loading facilities: Reinforced floor for cargo use. Roller strips and ball matting can be installed in the Utility versions to ease loading.
Standard equipment: Deck lock.
Optional equipment: Hydraulic hoist, electric standby hoist, searchlight, emergency flotation system, and more.
Rotor system: 5-blade main rotor system using both composites and metal components. Rotor head assembly incorporates multiple load paths for both lift and centrifugal loads. Ballistically tolerant composite blades. Active control structural response (ACSR) system to control rotor-induced vibration. Heated blade de-icing. Automatic blade folding. Can offer negative thrust for ship operations.
Tail rotor characteristics: 4-blade tail rotor to port. Ballistically tolerant composite blades. Manual or automatic blade folding is optional.
Fuselage: Modular construction, comprising cockpit, main cabin, sponsons, rear ramp when fitted, rear fuselage, tail unit and upper deck structure. Naval variant has automatic tail folding. Reconfigured rear fuselage and boom for ramp-equipped Utility and SAR versions.
Airframe materials: Extensive use of composites, including the tail unit made of carbon epoxy and Kevlar epoxy skinned sandwich panels over a central skeleton of metal or foam cored composite ribs and longerons, with a Kevlar/Nomex/Kevlar sandwich forward fairing and leading edge.
Safety features: Major systems are duplicated or triplicated.
Engines: 3 General Electric CT7-6 turboshafts standard for Heliliner and civil utility helicopters, each 2,000 shp (1,491 kW) at take-off. 3 Rolls-Royce Turbomeca RTM322s for Merlins and optional for Utility, each 2,100 shp (1,566 kW) take-off and 1,870 shp (1,394 kW) maximum continuous. 3 General Electric/Alfa Romeo Avio/FiatAvio T700/T6As for Italian naval helicopters, each 2,040 shp (1,521 kW) take-off and 1,807 shp (1,348 kW) maximum continuous.
Engine rating: See above.

EH Industries EH 101 in military Utility form, with rear ramp

Transmission rating: 5,200 shp (3,878 kW) maximum take-off and continuous, and 3,840 shp (2,863 kW) OEI maximum continuous.
Fuel system: 3,137 litres standard. 1,514 litre or 3,028 litre auxiliary tank for self-ferry. Crashworthy. Fuel tank inerting and dry bay protection can be fitted.
Flight refuelling probe: Bolt-on (4 hours) air-to-air refuelling package is available.
Electrical system: 2 twin-channel 90 kVA generators, either able to supply all helicopter and mission systems. APU-driven 25 kVA generator can maintain power to essential flight systems.
Hydraulic system: 3 independent supplies for flight control servos, able to operate independently in an emergency. 3,000 psi.
Braking system: Hydraulic.
Radar: 360° search and tracking radar for naval roles and SAR. Merlin has GEC-Marconi Blue Kestrel. AlliedSignal Bendix/King weather radar for civil versions. For EEZ patrol, radar can scan 30,000 sq miles (77,700 sq km) per hour.
Flight avionics/instrumentation: Avionics system is integrated through digital databuses on military variants. Digital AFCS incorporates duplex architecture and provides automatic stabilization and autopilot facilities, allowing both single pilot VFR and IFR operation. EFIS cockpit with colour CRTs. Optional digital map display. Autonomous navigation system, with Doppler and GPS-INS. FLIR (for SAR/ASST roles), VDUs and NVG compatible. For naval roles, can have secure data link, Ferranti-Thomson Sintra FLASH/AQS-950 dipping sonar and advanced sonobuoy processing system, Normalair-AlliedSignal sonobuoy dispenser with 10 sonobuoy capacity, MAD and ESM/ECCM. Normalair-AlliedSignal mission recording system. Health and usage monitoring (HUMS). Automated stores management.
Self-protection systems: Provision on military Utility for IR suppression, radar and laser warning, and chaff/flare.
Fixed guns: Machine-guns can be pintle-mounted at the cabin doors or fixed externally for suppressive fire.
Expendable weapons and equipment: Naval version can carry 4 homing torpedoes, mines, or 2 anti-ship missiles including Harpoon, Sea Eagle,

---

DETAILS FOR EH 101.

Principal dimensions:
Rotor diameter (main): 61 ft (18.59 m)
Maximum length, rotors turning: 74 ft 10 ins (22.8 m)
Fuselage length: 64 ft (19.51 m)
Fuselage length, folded (naval): 51 ft 8 ins (15.75 m)
Fuselage width: 9 ft 2 ins (2.8 m) over cabin, 14 ft 11 ins (4.55 m) over sponsons
Fuselage width, folded (naval): 17 ft 6 ins (5.33 m)
Maximum height: 21 ft 9 ins (6.63 m)
Maximum height, folded (naval): 17 ft 1 ins (5.21 m)

Cabin:
Length: 21 ft 4 ins (6.5 m) civil/utility, or 23 ft 3 ins (7.09 m) naval
Width: 7 ft 5 ins (2.26 m)
Height: 6 ft 2 ins (1.88 m)
Volume: 970 cu ft (27.47 m^3) utility, 1,024 cu ft (29 m^3) naval
Baggage bay (civil): 135 cu ft (3.82 m^3)

Main rotor:
Rotor disc: 2,923 sq ft (271.56 m^2)

Tail rotor:
Diameter: 13 ft 2 ins (4.01 m)

Undercarriage:
Type: Retractable, with steerable nosewheels. Twin wheels on each unit. Allows landings of 12 ft (3.7 m) per second without deformation
Wheel base: 22 ft 11 ins (7 m)

Weights:
Maximum take-off: 31,500 lb (14,288 kg)
Useful load: 12,518 lb (5,678 kg) for naval, 12,300 lb (5,579 kg) for Heliliner, and 11,800 lb (5,352 kg) for civil offshore support

Performance (typical):
Never-exceed speed (VNE): 167 kts (192 mph) 309 km/h, also quoted as a dash speed for the SAR variant
Cruise speed: 150 kts (173 mph) 278 km/h
Best range cruise speed: 142 kts (163 mph) 263 km/h
Ceiling: 15,000 ft (4,575 m), service
Radius of action (military utility): 320 naut miles (368 miles) 593 km with 18 troops, or 190 naut miles (219 miles) 352 km with 30 troops
Radius of action (civil offshore support): 180 naut miles (207 miles) 333 km
Range (civil): 480 naut miles (553 miles) 889 km with 30 passengers, at cruise speed
Range (SAR): 800 naut miles (921 miles) 1,480 km
Ferry range (utility): 864 naut miles (994 miles) 1,600 km with auxiliary fuel tanks
Duration: 5 hours for naval, up to 9 hours for SAR

Exocet and Marte Mk 2. Military utility can have AAMs, rocket pods and a chin turret for a steerable 12.7-mm gun.

Aircraft variants:
Civil variant is offered in EH 101-500 utility with rear ramp and EH 101-300 Heliliner passenger versions. CT7-6 engines. A VIP layout has 4 armchairs in the forward cabin and 2 sofas in the aft. Heliliner will comply to JAROPS 3, Class 1 for offshore take-off.
Naval variant offers fully autonomous, all-weather and day/night capability, and can operate from shore or 3,500 tonne frigates with winds of up to 50 kts in any direction. Possible naval missions include ASW, ASV, ASST, OTH targeting and surveillance, electronic warfare, airborne early warning, mine-countermeasures/deployment and SAR. Known as Merlin to the Royal Navy.
SAR variant can carry 4 crew and 30 survivors, or 4 litters and 4 seated survivors plus 2,205 lb (1,000 kg) of specialised equipment. Can also be configured for 16 litters and a medical team for casevac, or as a transport carrying a 20-strong search team in Arctic clothing. Hydraulic hoist plus electric standby hoist. Rear ramp. Doppler hover and automatic search modes. Winchman hover trim control.
Utility version, like SAR, has a rear ramp. CT7-6 or RTM322 engines. See Self-protection systems. Optional armour. Military utility missions include tactical troop lift, logistic support, combat search and rescue, casualty evacuation, and command and control.

NH Industries (France/Germany/Italy/Netherlands)

Corporate address: Le Quatuor, Bâtiment C, 42 Route de Galice, 13082 Aix-en-Provence Cedex 2, France.
Telephone: +33 42 95 97 02
Facsimile: +33 42 95 97 49
Founded: March 1992.
Information: Alain Gauthier (Commercial Department Manager).

● Activities

● NH Industries is prime contractor for design and development, industrialization, production and logistic support of the NH90 helicopter, and is responsible for marketing and sales. The 4 contributing companies to this international programme are Agusta (26.9%), Eurocopter Deutschland (24%), Eurocopter France (42.4%) and Fokker (6.7%).
● An international programme office, respresenting the 4 participating governments, was founded in February 1992 as NAHEMA (NAto HElicopter Management Agency).

NH Industries NH90

First flight: Expected December 1995.
Role: Tactical transport helicopter (TTH) and multi-role NATO frigate helicopter (NFH).

★ Aims

★ To meet the needs of the navies of France, Germany, Italy and the Netherlands, the armies of France, Germany and Italy, and the air forces of Germany and Italy.

▲ Development

▲ Following studies by a NATO Industrial Advisory Group during 1983-84, and feasibility and pre-definition studies thereafter, the governments of the participating nations signed a memorandum of understanding in December 1990 for full development of a Naval/Tactical helicopter. NHI was founded to manage this joint venture.
▲ Programme includes the production of a ground test vehicle, 3 prototypes in a common basic configuration (PT1-3), a TTH with full mission systems (PT4) and an NFH (PT5) with specific mission systems. All PTs to fly by Spring 1997. Production decision late 1997, allowing deliveries in 2000.
▲ 28 September 1995. The ground test vehicule made its first run at Cascina.

Sales: Planned procurement of 182 NFHs and 544 TTHs by the named services.
Crew/passengers: Can be pilot only for VFR and IFR operations. More typically, NFH has a crew of 3 comprising the pilot, tactical co-ordinator (in co-pilot position) and systems operator (Senso). Fourth crew station optional, allowing for 2 pilots and a separate Tacco position next to the Senso. 2 crew for the TTH. 14-20 troops or up to 12 litters in TTH.
Cockpit: Side-stick controllers.
Freight, internal: Maximum >5,511 lb (2,500 kg) of cargo, or a light tactical vehicle with crew.
Cabin access: Large sliding door each side, plus a rear ramp/door.
Standard equipment: Rescue hoist.
Rotor system: Advanced 4-blade main rotor. Composites blades and titanium main rotor hub with elastomeric bearings. Blade de-icing. Dynamic system has 30 minutes dry running capability. NFH has auto blade folding.
Tail rotor characteristics: 4-blade (composites).
Tail surfaces: Horizontal stabilizer mounted to starboard under the tail rotor pylon and fin.
Flight control system: Quadruplex fly-by-wire.
Airframe materials: All-composites crashworthy fuselage, with low IR signature.
Engines: 2 x 2,100 shp (1,566 kW) Rolls-Royce Turbomeca RTM322-01/9 turboshafts in each of the first prototypes. 2 x 2,400 shp (1,790 kW) General Electric/Alfa Romeo Avio/FiatAvio T700/T6Es will be retrofitted to the first prototype in 1997 for comparative evaluation. APU for engine start and ECS ground operation.
Transmission rating: 3,084 shp (2,400 kW).
Fuel system: Crash-resistant self-sealing tanks.
Electrical system: AC supply via 4 generators. DC supply from AC using transformer rectifiers. 2 batteries.
Radar: See Aircraft variants.
Flight avionics/instrumentation: Avionics integration based on dual MIL-STD-1553B digital databuses, with 8 x 8 ins (20 x 20 cm) multi-function colour displays for flight and mission functions. Automatic monitoring and diagnostic system.

NH Industries NH90 in NFH form

Expendable weapons and equipment: See Aircraft variants.

Aircraft variants:
NFH is the naval variant for ASW, ASUW, OTH targeting, AAW support, vertrep, SAR, troop transport and minelaying. Basic and mission avionics, including advanced mission flight aids, autopilot, MAD, dipping sonar and sonobuoys, Ferranti-Thomson Sintra AQS-950 acoustic processor, tactical radar, tactical FLIR, passive and active threat protection, and equipped for day/night and adverse weather operations in a severe ship movement environment. ASW and ASV weapons. Automatic main rotor blade and tail pylon folding. Deck handling system.
TTH is the tactical transport version, capable also of heliborne operations, SAR and combat SAR, medevac, special operations, electronic warfare, airborne command post, parachuting, VIP transport and training. Has a digital map system, FLIR, helmet-mounted display and sight, NVGs, obstacle warning system, weather radar, IR jammer, chaff/flare dispensers, laser and radar warning receivers, and missile launch detector. Optional VHF/FM data link and fuselage side weapon carriers. Armoured pilots' seats. Cable cutter. NBC, EMI and laser protection. Crashworthiness to MIL-STD-1290 (85% potential survivability). Single pilot IFR/IMC.

DETAILS FOR NH 90.

Principal dimensions:
Rotor diameter (main): 53 ft 6 ins (16.3 m)
Maximum length, rotors turning: 64 ft 2.25 ins (19.563 m)
Fuselage length: 52 ft 1.5 ins (15.885 m)
Width: 14 ft 2.5 ins (4.366 m) without main rotor
Maximum height: 17 ft 10 ins (5.44 m)

Cabin:
Length: 13 ft 2 ins (4 m)
Width: 6 ft 7 ins (2 m)
Height: 5 ft 2 ins (1.58 m)

Main rotor:
Blade chord: 2 ft 1.5 ins (0.65 m)
Rotor disc: 2,246.1 sq ft (208.67 m^2)

Tail rotor:
Diameter: 10 ft 6 ins (3.2 m)

Undercarriage:
Type: Retractable, with twin nosewheels. Crashworthy. NFH has emergency flotation gear
Wheel base: 19 ft 11 ins (6.083 m)

Weights:
Empty, operating: 14,171 lb (6,428 kg)
Mission gross: 20,062 lb (9,100 kg) for NFH, 19,180 lb (8,700 kg) for TTH
Mission payload: >6,614 lb (3,000 kg)
Maximum payload: 10,140 lb (4,600 kg) maximum

Performance:
Dash speed: 162 kts (186 mph) 300 km/h at 3,280 ft (1,000 m) and ISA + 15° C for TTH or sea level and ISA +10°C for NFH
Maximum cruise speed: 140 kts (162 mph) 260 km/h for NFH with weapons at sea level and ISA + 10°C, 157 kts (180 mph) 290 km/h for TTH at 3,280 ft, 1,000 m and ISA + 15°C
IGE hovering ceiling: 11,800 ft (3,600 m) for TTH, ISA
OGE hovering ceiling: 9,840 ft (3,000 m) for TTH, ISA
Maximum operating ceiling: 19,685 ft (6,000 m) at ISA +15° C for TTH or ISA + 10°C for NFH
Maximum range: 540 naut miles (621 miles) 1,000 km for TTH at 3,280 ft (1,000 m) and ISA + 15°C, or 502 naut miles (578 miles) 930 km for NFH at sea level and ISA + 10° C,
Duration: 4 hours with 20 minutes reserve for NFH on ASW mission, or 4 hours 15 minutes with 20 minutes reserve for NFH on ASUW mission, or 2 hours 30 minutes for TTF (all with conditions as for range)

Aero Boero S. A. (Argentina)

Corporate address: *Plant 1:* Brasil y Alem, 2421 Morteros (Córdoba). *Plant 2:* Av.9 de Julio 1101, 2400 San Francisco (Córdoba). Also Rua André Cavalcante, 13A Rio de Janeiro, RJ, Brazil.
Telephone: *Plant 1:* +54 562 22121 or 22690. *Plant 2:* +54 564 22972 or 24118. *Brazil:* +55 21 224 0450
Facsimile: *Plant 1:* +55 562 22121. Brazil: + 55 21 224 2933
Founded: 1959.
Information: Hector A. Boero (President).

Aero Boero AB 115 and AB 115/150

First flight: February 1973.
Role: Training, agricultural (AB 115/150) and recreational.
Crew/passengers: 3.
Baggage capacity: *AB 115*: 7.42 cu ft (0.21 m^3), *AB 115/150*: 7.06 cu ft (0.2 m^3)
Chemical tank/hopper: *AB 115/150:* 280 litres of insecticide in an underfuselage pod.
Wing characteristics: High-wing monoplane with bracing struts. Conventional controls.
Construction materials: All duralumin wing and spar, and reinforced SAE 4130 steel tube fuselage structure with Dacron fabric skin.
Engine: *AB 115:* Textron Lycoming O-235-C2A, *AB 115/150:* O-320-A2B.
Engine rating: *AB 115:* 115 hp (85.75 kW) at 2,800 rpm, *AB 115/150:* 150 hp (112 kW) at 2,700 rpm.
Fuel system: 2 x 57 litre tanks.
Flight avionics/instrumentation: Ready to fit any radio, navigation or IFR instruments.
Aircraft variants:
AB 115 is the basic model, not used for agricultural work.
AB 115/150 is the higher powered model, suitable also for agricultural work.

DETAILS FOR AB 115, WITH AB 115/150 AS INDICATED.

Principal dimensions:
Wing span: 35 ft 9 ins (10.9 m)
Maximum length: 23 ft 3 ins (7.08 m)
Maximum height: 6 ft 11 ins (2.1 m) *at rest,* 9 ft 9 ins (2.98 m) *flying attitude*
Wings:
Aerofoil section: NACA 23012
Area: 186 sq ft (17.28 m^2)
Aspect ratio: 6.87
Undercarriage:
Type: Fixed, with tailwheel
Weights:
Empty: 1,226 lb (556 kg)
Maximum take-off: 1,768 lb (802 kg)
Payload: 542 lb (246 kg)
Performance:
Maximum speed: 119 kts (137 mph) 220 km/h
Cruise speed: 92 kts (106 mph) 170 km/h *for AB 115,* 97 kts (112 mph) 180 km/h *for AB 115/150*
Stall speed: 46 kts (53 mph) 85 km/h *without flaps,* 38 kts (44 mph) 70 km/h *with flaps.* Electrical stall warning
Landing speed: 42 kts (48 mph) 77 km/h
Take-off distance: 328-427 ft (100-130 m) *for AB 115,* 279-328 ft (85-100 m) *for AB 115/150*
Landing distance: 263 ft (80 m) *for AB 115,* 246 ft (75 m) for *AB 115/150*
Maximum climb rate: 670 ft (204 m) per minute *for AB 115,* 787 ft (240 m) per minute *for AB 115/150*

Aero Boero AB 180 PSA two-seater for a military preselection role

Aero Boero AB 180 AG, PSA and RVR

Role: Agricultural (AB 180 AG), glider-towing (RVR), military preselection (PSA) and recreational. AB 180 RVR can climb at 590 ft (180 m) per minute towing a Standard class glider, or 394 ft (120 m) per minute towing a two-seater.
Details: Similar to AB 115, except as quoted:
Crew/passengers: Up to 3 (AG/RVR), with PSA having 2 in tandem.
Baggage capacity: 7.42 cu ft (0.21 m^3). AB 180 PSA has 7.35 cu ft (0.208 m^3) or 55 lb (25 kg).
Chemical tank/hopper: AB 180 AG has 320 litres of insecticide in an underfuselage pod.
Wing control surfaces: AB 180 RVR is fitted with extra large flaps.
Engine: Textron Lycoming O-360-A1A.
Engine rating: 180 hp (134 kW) at 2,700 rpm.
Fuel system: 2 x 88 litre tanks.

DETAILS FOR AB 180.

Principal dimensions: As for AB 115 except:
Wing span: 35 ft 4.5 (10.78 m) *for AS 180 PSA*
Undercarriage:
Wheel track: 5 ft 11 ins (1.8 m)
Weights:
Empty: 1,415 lb (642 kg) *for AB 180 AG,* 1,327 lb (602 kg) *for RVR*
Maximum take-off: 2,209 lb (1,002 kg) *for AB 180* AG, 1,861 lb (844 kg) *for PSA,* 1,962 lb (890 kg) *for RVR*
Payload: 794 lb (360 kg) *for AB 180 AG,* 635 lb (288) *for RVR,* 534 lb (242 kg) *for PSA*
Performance:
Maximum speed: 113 kts (130 mph) 210 km/h *for AB 180 AG,* 132 kts (152 mph) 245 km/h *for PSA and RVR*
Cruise speed: 89 kts (103 mph) 165 km/h *for AB 180 AG,* 114 kts (131 mph) 211 km/h *for PSA,* 107 kts (123 mph) 198 km/h *for RVR*
Stall speed, clean: 46 kts (53 mph) 85 km/h *for AB 180 AG,* 43.5 kts (50 mph) 80 km/h *for PSA,* 44.5 kts (51 mph) 82 km/h *for RVR*
Stall speed, with flaps: 43 kts (49 mph) 79 km/h *for AB 180 AG and RVR,* 42 kts (48 mph) 77 km/h *for PSA.* Electrical stall warning
Landing speed: 48 kts (55 mph) 88 km/h *for AB 180* AG, 45 kts (52 mph) 84 km/h *for RVR*
Take-off distance: 492-820 ft (150-250 m) *for AB 180 AG,* 378 ft (115 m) light *for PSA,* 279-394 ft (85-120 m) *for RVR*
Landing distance: 394 ft (120 m) *for AB 180 AG,* 279 ft (85 m) *for PSA,* 289 ft (88 m) *for RVR*
Maximum climb rate: 453 ft (138 m) per minute *for AB 180 AG,* 1,024 ft (312 m) per minute *for PSA and RVR*
G limits: +4.4, -1.9 *for AB 180 PSA*
Ceiling: 23,000 ft (7,000 m) *for AB 180 RVR*
Range: 541 naut miles (623 miles) 1,002 km *for AB 180 PSA*
Duration: 4 hours to 4 hours 45 minutes

Aero Boero AB 260 AG

First flight: 23 December 1972.
Role: Agricultural aircraft.
Crew/passengers: Pilot only normally, second person can be carried.
Baggage capacity: 7.42 cu ft (0.21 m^3).
Chemical tank/hopper: 550 litres of insecticide.
Dispersal equipment: Wing-installed spraybars, with underwing atomizers.
Wing characteristics: Low monoplane wings with upper bracing struts, wing fences and down-turned wingtips.
Construction materials: Duralumin wings. SAE 4130 steel fuselage structure, with duralumin and composites skins.
Engine: Textron Lycoming O-540-H2B5D.
Engine rating: 260 hp (194 kW) at 2,700 rpm.
Fuel system: 2 x 120 litre tanks.

Aero Boero AB 260 AG agricultural aircraft

DETAILS FOR AB 260AG.

Principal dimensions:
Wing span: 35 ft 9 ins (10.9 m)
Maximum length: 23 ft 11.5 ins (7.3 m)
Maximum height: 6 ft 5.5 ins (1.97 m)
Wings:
Aerofoil section: NACA 23012
Area: 186 sq ft (17.28 m^2)
Aspect ratio: 6.87
Undercarriage:
Type: Fixed, with tailwheel
Weights:
Empty: 1,521 lb (690 kg)
Maximum take-off: 2,976 lb (1,350 kg)
Payload: 1,455 lb (660 kg)
Performance:
Maximum speed: 135 kts (155 mph) 250 km/h
Cruise speed: 119 kts (137 mph) 220 km/h
Stall speed: 49 kts (56 mph) 90 km/h *without flaps*, 43.5 kts (50 mph) 80 km/h *with flaps*. Electrical stall warning
Landing speed: 49 kts (56 mph) 90 km/h
Take-off distance: 591-886 ft (180-270 m)
Landing distance: 492 ft (150 m)
Maximum climb rate: 984 ft (300 m) per minute

Eagle Aircraft Pty Ltd (Australia)

Corporate address: PO Box 586, Fremantle, Western Australia 6160 (also: Cockburn Road, Henderson, Western Australia 6166).
Telephone: +69 9 410 1077
Facsimile: +69 9 410 2430
Founded: 1985.
Information: Denis Macneall (Manager, Sales and Marketing).

● Activities

- The company made its debut in the USA in 1995.

Eagle Aircraft Eagle X-TS

Eagle Aircraft Eagle X-TS two-seater, clearly showing the overwing fences and turbulators

First flight: March 1988.
Certification: 21 September 1993 by the CAA of Australia to meet JAR-VLA.
Role: Recreation, ab-initio training, and fire spotting and surveillance (see Sales).
Sales/users: Production deliveries started November 1993. First 6 sold to the Western Australian Department of Conservation and Land Management (CALM) for use in forestry surveillance and bush firefighting, requiring to operate from short unsealed bush runways. 7 sold to Malaysian flying training schools. 1995 cost US$98,000.
Crew/passengers: 2, side-by-side.
Cockpit: The cockpit area is specially strengthened with Kevlar to become a high-strength capsule with good penetration resistance. Dual controls.
Baggage capacity: 99 lb (45 kg) in containers behind each seat and on the hat rack.
Wing characteristics: Straight, with no anhedral/dihedral, and raised wingtips. Overwing fences and 8 small turbulators. Stall strips on leading edges.
Wing control surfaces: Slotted ailerons and flaps.
Tail control surfaces: Elevators and rudder, with tabs.
Canard: Has a higher angle of incidence than the mainplane. As the aircraft approaches a stall, the canard stalls first, resulting in a loss of lift forward of the centre of gravity. This causes the nose to drop and the aircraft to enter a shallow dive, which allows the airspeed to increase. If the pilot takes no corrective action, the aircraft enters into a phugoid flight on a smooth glide ratio which should enable the aircraft to be landed safely. In addition, because the canard stalls ahead of the mainplane, the ailerons are still effective in the stall and there is no noticeable wing drop. Also, X-TS is said to be exceptionally spin resistant. Full-width single-slotted flaps.
Construction materials: Carbon cloth, Kevlar, Nomex honeycomb and special vinylester resins for resistance to corrosion and fatigue. See also Cockpit.
Engine: Teledyne Continental IO-240-A.
Engine rating: 125 hp (93.2 kW) at 2,800 rpm.
Fuel system: 102 litres. Fuel consumption 23 litres per hour at 75% power.
Electrical system: 12 volt DC incorporating 60 amp alternator.
Braking system: Cleveland discs on main units.
Flight avionics/instrumentation: Full range of flight and engine instruments, and an electric elevator trim. Standard options include navigation systems (GPS, ADF), and gyro instruments (DG, AH and T&B). VHF radio is standard, and an ATC transponder is an option.

Details for Eagle X-TS.

Principal dimensions:
Wing span: 23 ft 6 ins (7.16 m)
Maximum length: 21 ft 5 ins (6.53 m)
Maximum height: 7 ft 5 ins (2.27 m)
Wings:
Aerofoil section: Roncz
Area: 56.5 sq ft (5.25 m^2)
Aspect ratio: 9.77
Canard:
Span: 16 ft (4.88 m)
Undercarriage:
Type: Fixed, with nosewheel
Turning circle: 17 ft 1 ins (5.21 m)
Weights:
Empty: 948 lb (430 kg)
Maximum take-off: 1,433 lb (650 kg)
Payload: 485 lb (220 kg)
Performance:
Never-exceed speed: 165 kts (190 mph) 305 km/h CAS
Maximum speed: 130 kts (150 mph) 241 km/h TAS
Cruise speed: 120 kts (138 mph) 222 km/h TAS, at 75% power
Stall speed: 45 kts (52 mph) 83 km/h *full flaps,* 55 kts (63 mph) 102 km/h *clean.*
Take-off over a 50ft (15 m) obstacle: 1,040 ft (317 m)
Landing over a 50ft (15 m) obstacle: 1,168 ft (356 m)
Maximum climb rate: 1,066 ft (325 m) per minute at sea level
G limits: +3.8, -1.9 limit; +8.55, -4.27 ultimate
Ceiling: 15,000 ft (4,570 m)
Range: 507 naut miles (584 miles) 940 km at 75% power, 594 naut miles (683 miles) 1,100 km at 55% power
Duration: 6 hours at 60% power

Gippsland Aeronautics Pty Ltd (Australia)

Corporate address: PO Box 881, Latrobe Valley Airfield, Morwell 3840, Victoria.
Telephone: +61 51 74 3086
Facsimile: +61 51 74 0956
Founded: 1971.
Information: Peter Furlong (Director).

● Activities

- CAA approved manufacture and maintenance facility.
- Aircraft design, modification and manufacture. Modification programmes have covered a wide variety of aircraft, from wooden homebuilts to pressurized turboprops.

Details for Airvan.

Principal dimensions:
Wing span: 40 ft 6 ins (12.34 m)
Maximum length: 28 ft 9 ins (8.76 m)
Maximum height: 12 ft (3.66 m)
Cabin:
Length: 13 ft 4 ins (4.06 m)
Width: 4 ft 2 ins (1.27 m)
Height: 3 ft 11 ins (1.19 m)
Area: 54 sq ft (5 m^2) floor area, 37 sq ft (3.44 m^2) of floor space available for cargo
Volume: 180 cu ft (5.1 m^3)
Height to sill: 2 ft 10 ins (0.86 m)
Undercarriage:
Type: Fixed, with nosewheel or twin floats
Weights:
Empty: 1,900 lb (862 kg)
Maximum take-off: 4,000 lb (1,814 kg)
Performance:
Cruise speed: 125 kts (144 mph) 232 km/h, at 75% power
Stall speed: 53 kts (61 mph) 98 km/h, *with flaps*
Climb rate: about 750 ft (229 m) per minute
Range: 680 naut miles (782 miles) 1,259 km at 1 litre/min fuel burn and 120 kts cruise

Gippsland GA-8 Airvan

First flight: 3 March 1995.
Role: Utility, for quick change from passengers to freight, and capable of operating from short bush strips.
Certification: Will be certified to FAR Pt 23.
Crew/passengers: Pilot plus 7 passengers.
Main cabin loading: Single door on port side, forward sliding, size 3 ft 7 ins x 3 ft 6 ins (1.09 x 1.07 m).
Wing characteristics: Based on the GA-200 wing but high mounted with one strut each side.
Wing control surfaces: Conventional.
Tail control surfaces: Include rudder with sweepback of 18.8°.
Engine: Textron Lycoming IO-540 or Teledyne Continental IO-550.
Engine rating: 300 hp (224 kW); interim 250 hp (186 kW) in prototype.
Fuel system: 340 litres.

Gippsland GA-8 Airvan

Gippsland AG-Trainer cockpit

Gippsland GA-200 and AG-Trainer

Certification: 1 March 1991, on the basis of Australian CAO 101.16 and 101.22, incorporating FAR 23, making certification in both normal and agricultural categories.
Role: Agricultural, and dual-control agricultural trainer (AG-Trainer).
Sales/users: 20 sold by October 1994, with production was at one per month. Aircraft operating in Australia, China and New Zealand.
Crew: Pilot. Second seat for the loader driver or to allow aerial viewing by the farmer. Side-by-side seating arrangement to minimize centre of gravity shift with the cockpit load and to utilize the wide fuselage width.
Cockpit: Dual controls in AG-Trainer.
Baggage capacity: Storage compartment under the passenger seat.
Chemical hopper: 800 litres. Transparent rear face, to allow the pilot to view the contents. Constructed of glassfibre and Derakane 411 chemically resistant vinylester resin. Gippsland multi-role door/hopper outlet, suitable for operation with both solids and liquids. AG-Trainer has 750 litres capacity (see Aircraft variants).
Safety equipment: Crashworthy structure, to provide a "good fly-on" capability following an obstacle strike. The forward fuselage has been optimized to "progressively crumple" in a sudden forward deceleration, protecting the cockpit. "Pilot behind load" configuration. Upward opening doors, preventing the opening edge from jamming in a closed position by the ground in the event of an overturn.
Wing characteristics: Low mounted, with strut bracing to save approximately 100 lb (45 kg) weight over a cantilever spar design. Wingtip shape evolved to provide the best possible swath width without compromising aircraft performance.
Wing control surfaces: Gap-sealed ailerons. Single-slotted flaps. Take-off flap setting 15°; landing flap (max) setting 38°. Flaps can be used in normal operations and significantly reduce turn radius with fully loaded aircraft. With flaps extended, there is said to be no noticeable change in pitch trim, due to the incorporation of a simple interconnect system which applies bias to the elevator trim spring at such times.
Tail control surfaces: Horn-balanced elevators and rudder.

Gippsland GA-200 agricultural aircraft

Construction materials: All metal wings with full-depth laminated fail-safe spars; the outboard section is joined to the inner section at the strut intersections by load distribution doublers. This allows the relatively easy replacement of the outer wing panels.
All of the aircraft's components are corrosion proofed and leading edges consist of replaceable segments to minimize "down time" due to bird strikes or other minor impacts. The wingtips are also removable. Welded SAE 4130 chromium molybdenum steel tube fuselage assembly, to which metal side panels are attached by half-turn Druz fasteners from the engine bay back to the rear of the cockpit. The rear fuselage upper turtledeck is easily opened for inspection, maintenance and cleaning.
Engine: Textron Lycoming O-540-H2A5 or O-540-A1D5.
Engine rating: 260 hp (194 kW) for H2A5, limited to 250 hp (186.4 kW) at 2,575 rpm for noise considerations. 250 hp for A1D5.
Fuel system: 200 litres (usable) of premium grade auto fuel or Avgas carried in 2 wing tanks plus a 12 litre header tank.
Electrical system: 14 volt, 55 amp auto alternator with internal voltage regulation supplies an auto or R-35 aviation battery. A 28 volt night working light system is available, which is virtually independent of the electrical system, consisting of 2 retractable underwing 600 watt lights powered by a separate 28 volt, 55 amp auto alternator mounted on the engine rear accessory case.
Braking system: Cleveland disc. Hydraulic "lock off" parking brake.
Flight avionics/instrumentation: Arranged in a small panel in front of the pilot.
Aircraft variants:
GA-200 is the standard agricultural aircraft, as detailed.
AG-Trainer is a dedicated dual-control trainer varant, used in the "Spray Safe" agricultural training programme. Used as a conventional agricultural aircraft between training. 50 litres less hopper capacity due to the second set of rudder pedals.

DETAILS FOR GA-200.

Principal dimensions:
Wing span: 39 ft 4 ins (11.984 m)
Maximum length: 24 ft 6.5 ins (7.48 m)
Maximum height: 7 ft 7.7 ins (2.33 m)
Wings:
Area: 197 sq ft (18.3 m^2)
Aspect ratio: 6.816
Dihedral: 7°
Undercarriage:
Type: Fixed, with steerable and castoring tailwheel
Weights:
Empty, operating: 1,698 lb (770 kg), including oil and usable fuel
Maximum take-off: 2,900 lb (1,315 kg) certified
Typical agricultural take-off: 3,750 lb (1,700 kg)

Performance:
Ferry cruise speed: 100 kts (115 mph) 185 km/h at MTOW, clean, 1,000 ft altitude, ISA, at 2,420 engine rpm
Stall speed at MTOW: 54 kts (62 mph) 100 km/h *clean*, 49 kts (57 mph) 91 km/h *with 38° flaps*
Stall speed at typical landing weight: 45 kts (52 mph) 84 km/h *clean*, 41 kts (47 mph) 76 km/h *with 38° flaps*
Landing speed: 50-55 kts (58-63 mph) 93-102 km/h *with full flaps*
Take-off distance: 1,380 ft (420 m) approximately, with full hopper, zero wind and 15° C at sea level
Landing distance: 650 ft (200 m) approximately, with full flaps and light weight
Maximum climb rate: 970 ft (296 m) per minute at MTOW, clean, sea level, ISA
Roll rate: 2 seconds from 45° bank through 45° bank the other way at normal working airspeeds

Jabiru Aircraft Pty Ltd (Australia)

Corporate address: PO Box 5186, Bundaberg West 4670, Queensland.
Telephone: +61 71 55 1778, 71 52 8663/2029
Facsimile: +61 71 55 2669
Information: Phillip Ainsworth (Joint Managing Director).

● Activities

- Produces the Jabiru 1600 and 2000 engines, in addition to the Jabiru LSA (Australian ultralight) and ST light aircraft.

Jabiru Aircraft Jabiru LSA and ST

First flight: 1989.
Certification: 1 October 1991 under CAO 101.55 (by which time deliveries of production aircraft had begun).
Role: General aviation lightplane (ST in Australia and export), and ultralight (LSA, Australia only).
Crew/passengers: 2, side-by-side, with dual controls.
Wing control surfaces: Ailerons and slotted flaps.
Tail control surfaces: Elevators and inset rudder.
Construction materials: Glassfibre, with metal bracing struts.
Engine: 1 Jabiru 1600 with dual ignition, with a 54 ins (1.37 m) wooden propeller.
Engine rating: 60 hp (44.7 kW) at 3,300 rpm.
Fuel system: 50 litres. Fuel consumption at cruise is 11-12 litres per hour.
Flight control system: Mechanical.
Electrical system: 12 volt DC/100 watt and 20 amp-hour battery.
Braking system: Hydraulic disc on main units.
Flight avionics/ instrumentation: VFR.
Aircraft variants:
LSA is the Australian-only ultralight version.
ST is the general aviation model, available to the Australian and export markets.

Jabiru lightplane used by an aero club

Details for Jabiru ST with wheel fairings and one pilot.

Principal dimensions:
Wing span: 26 ft 4 ins (8.034 m)
Maximum length: 16 ft 5 ins (5.004 m)
Maximum height: 6 ft 7 ins (2.013 m)
Wings:
Aerofoil section: NACA 4412
Area: 85 sq ft (7.9 m^2)
Aspect ratio: 8.16
Undercarriage:
Type: Fixed, with nosewheel
Weights:
Empty: 517 lb (235 kg)
Maximum take-off: 946 lb (430 kg)
Performance:
Never-exceed speed (Vne): 116 kts (133 mph) 215 km/h
Maximum speed: 98 kts (113 mph) 181 km/h
Cruise speed: 90 kts (104 mph) 167 km/h at 75% power
Stall speed: 40 kts (46 mph) 74 km/h *with full flaps*, 45 kts (52 mph) 84 km/h *clean*
Take-off distance: 903 ft (275 m)
Landing distance: 525 ft (160 m)
Maximum climb rate: 800 ft (244 m) per minute
G limits: +6.6. -3.3 ultimate
Ceiling: 15,000 ft (4,570 m)
Range: 360 naut miles (414 miles) 667 km
Duration: 4 hours

Seabird Aviation Australia Pty Ltd (Australia)

Corporate address: Hervey Bay Airport, PO Box 618, Pialba 4655, Queensland.
Telephone: +61 71 25 3144
Facsimile: +61 71 25 3123
International representation: AeroSystems Corporation Pty Ltd, 71 Grey Street, PO Box 3283, South Brisbane 4101, Queensland (*telephone*: +61 7 846 2330).
Information: Don Adams (Managing Director).

Seabird Seeker SB7L multi-purpose aircraft

Seabird Seeker SB7L

First flight: 1 October 1989 (as SB5 prototype).
Certification: 24 January 1994 to CAA FAR 23 standards.
Role: Multi-role, including agriculture, border patrol, customs and security surveillance, drug control, survey, fire spotting, game park observation, news gathering, medevac, photographic, pipe and power line patrol, search and rescue, tourism and training.
Sales/users: Available since 1994.
Crew: 2. Three-seat arrangement has been under development.
Cockpit: Dual controls. Removable "gullwing" doors, and removable right-hand seat and controls for installing special mission equipment, 100 litre agricultural spray tank or a litter.
Baggage capacity: 15 cu ft (0.42 m^3). Total load behind seats and in compartment 96 lb (43 kg).
Wing characteristics: Braced high-mounted. 2 underwing hard points for attaching a total of 264 lb (120 kg) of stores.
Wing control surfaces: Slotted ailerons and slotted flaps (20°, 40°).
Tail control surfaces: Single-piece elevator (with tab) and rudder (with tab).
Construction materials: Aluminium alloy wings, boom and tail, with FRP wingtips. Roll cage (of chromoly tubular steel) cabin structure, with FRP non-load bearing skins. FRP dorsal and ventral finlets.
Engine: Textron Lycoming O-360-B2C, with a 5 ft 10 ins (1.78 m) Bishton BB-177 wood/epoxy fixed-pitch 2-blade pusher propeller or electric constant-speed 3-blade propeller.
Engine rating: 160 hp (119.3 kW).
Fuel system: 160-182 litres, of which 148-170 are usable. Analysis undertaken in 1994 to increase fuel to 182 litres. Fuel flow 40 litres per hour at 75% power, or 22 litres per hour at patrol power of 68 hp (50.7 kW).
Flight control system: Mechanical.
Electrical system: 70 amp.
Braking system: Cleveland toe brakes.
Flight avionics/instrumentation: VFR standard. Options include IFR instrumentation and avionics, Garmin GPS/moving map, KX15/K1208 nav/com, KR87 ADF/KI-227 ADF and more. FLIR is an option for surveillance, among other equipment. Emergency locator transponder (ELT) in fin.
Aircraft variants:
SB7L is the current standard version, with noise certification that meets US and European standards. Wide range of features and options, including camera/store drop hatch, vertical and oblique camera mounts, wing hard points, medevac conversion, low-volume sprayer, and searchlight/loudspeaker.

Details for SB7L.

Principal dimensions:
Wing span: 36 ft 4 ins (11.07 m)
Maximum length: 23 ft (7.01 m)
Maximum height: 8 ft 2 ins (2.49 m)
Cabin:
Length: 7 ft 3 ins (2.21 m)
Width: 3 ft 8 ins (1.12 m)
Height: 3 ft 7 ins (1.09 m)
Wings:
Aerofoil section: $63_2$215 modified
Area: 141 sq ft (13.1 m^2)
Aspect ratio: 9.36
Undercarriage:
Type: Fixed, with tailwheel. Floats under development in 1994
Turning circle: 15 ft 1 ins (4.6 m)
Weights:
Empty, operating: 1,332 lb (604 kg) prototype, 1,301 lb (590 kg) production aircraft (approximately)
Maximum take-off: 1,977 lb (897 kg); analysis undertaken in 1994 to increase AUW to 2,039 lb (925 kg)
Disposable load with maximum fuel: 392 lb (178 kg) prototype
Maximum disposable load: 646 lb (293 kg) prototype, 670 lb (304 kg)) production aircraft, increasing to 732 lb (332 kg) at 925 kg AUW (see MTO).
Crew weight range (total): 176-423 lb (80-192 kg)
Performance:
Cruise speed: 112 kts (129 mph) 207 km/h, 75% power
Patrol speed: 65 kts (75 mph) 120 km/h CAS
Stall speed: 58 kts (67 mph) 108 km/h *clean*
Take-off distance (ISA): 867 ft (264 m) at sea level, 1,016 ft (310 m) at 2,000 ft airfield altitude, 1,194 ft (364 m) at 4,000 ft altitude, 1,407 ft (429 m) at 6,000 ft altitude
Landing distance: 650 ft (198 m)
Maximum climb rate (ISA): 944 ft (288 m) per minute at sea level, 813 ft (248 m) per minute at 2,000 ft, 688 ft (210 m) per minute at 4,000 ft, 567 ft (173 m) per minute at 6,000 ft
G limits: +3.8, -1.52
Range: 394 naut miles (453 miles) 730 km at 75% power (with reserve), or 449 naut miles (517 miles) 832 km at patrol power (with reserve)
Duration: 3.55 hours at 75% power, 6.9 hours at patrol power

Skyfox Aviation (Australia)

Corporate address: PO Box 910, Caloundra, Queensland 4551.
Telephone: +61 74 91 5355
Facsimile: +61 74 91 8237
Founded: Hadaro International Pty Ltd began manufacturing light aircraft in Australia under the trading name Skyfox in 1991.
Employees: 25.
Information: James A. K. Cassels (Marketing).

Skyfox Aviation Skyfox series

First flight: 6 September 1989.
Certification: June 1993 for the CA-25 under JAR-VLA.
Role: STOL leisure, ab-initio training, surveillance, and more.
Sales/users: 100th built in November 1994. 2 exported to Switzerland and 2 to Thailand. Cost $59,000 for the CA-25 (1994 cost).
Crew/passengers: 2 persons, with dual controls.
Baggage capacity: Compartment aft of the cabin, with outside access.
Wing control surfaces: All flying ailerons carried behind and slightly below the wings.
Tail control surfaces: Elevators and rudder.
Construction materials: Fuselage of welded 4130 chromoly steel tubing, skinned with Stits Polyfibre fabric. Wings have fabric-covered 6061-T6 aluminium spars (2) and plywood ribs, and moulded downturned glassfibre wingtips. Wings fold in line with the fuselage (4 minutes by 1 person).

Skyfox Aviation CA-25 Skyfox

Engine: Rotax 912 piston engine.
Engine rating: 77.8 hp (58 kW).
Fuel system: 52 litres.
Flight avionics/instrumentation: Full VFR panel of instruments and a 760-channel VHF radio.

Aircraft variants:
CA-21 production ended in 1991. VW Aeropower engine.
CA-22 is a current production ultralight, certified under Australian Civil Aviation Order 101.55. Rotax 912 engine. See Recreational section.
CA-25 is the general aviation version, certified under JAR-VLA.
CA-25N is a new nosewheel undercarriage variant of the CA-25, entering production in early 1995.

DETAILS FOR CA-25.

Principal dimensions:
Wing span: 31 ft 3 ins (9.52 m)
Maximum length: 18 ft 4.5 ins (5.6 m), or 21 ft 6.5 ins (6.57 m) folded
Maximum height: 6 ft 1.5 ins (1.87 m)
Cabin:
Width: 3 ft 4 ins (1.02 m)
Wings:
Area: 124.6 sq ft (11.58 m^2)
Aspect ratio: 7.84
Undercarriage:
Type: Fixed tailwheel, with 18 x 6–8 ins low-pressure mainwheel tyres
Weights:
Empty: 640 lb (290 kg)
Maximum take-off: 1,150 lb (522 kg)
Performance:
Maximum speed: 95 kts (109 mph) 176 km/h at 5,000 ft (1,525 m)
Cruise speed: 85 kts (98 mph) 157 km/h, 75% power
Loiter speed: 50 kts (58 mph) 93 km/h, 50% power
Stall speed: 43 kts (50 mph) 80 km/h
Take-off and landing distance: 400 ft (122 m)
Maximum climb rate: 800 ft (244 m) per minute
Ceiling: 10,000 ft (3,050 m), service
Range: 323 naut miles (372 miles) 598 km, 70% power
Duration: 4 hours at 70% power, 7.4 hours at 50% power

HOAC Austria (Austria)

Full name: HOAC Austria Flugzeugwerk Wr. Neustadt Gesellschaft mhH.
Corporate address: A-2700 Wiener Neustadt, N.A. Ottostrasse 5.
Telephone: +43 2622 26 700
Facsimile: +43 2622 26 780
Founded: 1981.
Employees: 60.
Information: Andreas Klement (Sales Department).

● Activities
- HOAC also produces the HK 36 Super Dimona motorglide (see Gliders section).
- New aircraft are a Stelio Frati-designed four-seater based on the SF.260 type, the airframe being constructed by Mikoyan in Russia, and the DV-40.

DIVISIONS
Diamond Aircraft Industries Canada:
HQ Address: Ontario, Canada.
Employees: 250.

● Activities
- Founded as a subsidiary to produce aircraft for the North American market. Production of the DA 20 version of the DV 20 began 29 June 1994.

HOAC DV 20 and DA 20 Katana

First flight: 16 March 1991 (as LF 2000). 17 December 1992 first flight of the DV 20 Katana prototype proper, following the 2 earlier development aircraft.
Certification: 26 April 1993 in Austria.
Role: Recreational and training lightplane, developed to JAR-VLA using experience gained from production of the Dimona and Super Dimona motorgliders. DV 20 built in Austria by HOAC, DA 20 built in Canada by subsidiary Diamond Aircraft Industries Canada.
Sales/users: 159 DV 20s had been sold by February 1995, with 100 delivered by March 1995. 180 DA 20s sold by the same date. Production rate is 1.5 aircraft per week in Austria. Austrian price with standard equipment ATS 1,068,165 (ex works, excluding taxes and dues).
Crew: 2, side-by-side.
Cockpit: Entry via the single-piece upward/backward hinging canopy.
Baggage capacity: Baggage shelf in the cockpit.
Wing characteristics: Upswept wingtips. Optional folding wings to help storage and transport.

HOAC Austria DV 20 Katana (courtesy HOAC/Heinz Zeggl)

Wing control surfaces: Ailerons and flaps (15°, 40°).
Tail control surfaces: T-tail with elevator (with tab) and large rudder. Small ventral tailfin.
Construction materials: Composites, including a carbonfibre I-beam main spar. Some components have been produced in the Czech Republic and Hungary.
Engine: Rotax 912 A, with a 5 ft 7 ins (1.7 m) Hoffmann constant-speed propeller.
Engine rating: 80 hp (59.6 kW).
Fuel system: 55 litre tank standard, 80 litre optional, of which 79 litres usable.
Flight control system: Mechanical, with electrically-operated flaps.
Electrical system: 12 volt.
Braking system: Hydraulic disc, toe operated.
Flight avionics/instrumentation: VFR. Wide range of optional Becker or AlliedSignal avionics and equipment, including various nav/com and Garmin GPS.
Aircraft variants: DV 20 and DA 20, see Role.

DETAILS FOR DV 20 KATANA.

Principal dimensions:
Wing span: 35 ft 5 ins (10.8 m), 7 ft 1 ins (2.16 m) width with wings folded
Maximum length: 23 ft 3.5 ins (7.1 m)
Maximum height: 6 ft 11 ins (2.1 m)
Cockpit:
Width: 3 ft 7 ins (1.1 m)
Wings:
Aerofoil section: Wortmann FX-63-137 modified, laminar flow
Area: 124.86 sq ft (11.6 m^2)
Aspect ratio: 10.06
Undercarriage:
Type: Fixed, with nosewheel. Wheel fairings are optional
Turning circle: 16 ft 9 ins (5.1 m)
Weights:
Empty: 1,091 lb (495 kg)
Maximum take-off: 1,609 lb (730 kg)
Useful load: 518 lb (235 kg)
Performance:
Never-exceed speed (Vne): 157 kts (181 mph) 291 km/h
Maximum speed: 125 kts (144 mph) 232 km/h
Cruise speed: 122 kts (140 mph) 225 km/h at 75% power
Stall speed: 55 kts (63 mph) 102 km/h *clean*, 44 kts (51 mph) 81 km/h *with flaps*
Take-off distance: 673 ft (205 m)
Landing distance: 800 ft (244 m)
Maximum climb rate: 787 ft (240 m) per minute.
G limits: +4.4, -2.2
Ceiling: over 16,400 ft (5,000 m)
Range: 491 naut miles (565 miles) 910 km at 75% power, with reserve
Noise emission: 55.6 dB maximum at continuous power

HOAC DV 40

Role: Four-seat light aircraft being developed as a long-term project. Known details in early 1995 were single engine, and designed for high levels of efficiency, safety and performance. More details expected at the end of 1995.

Promavia S.A. (Belgium)

Details of this company and its Jet Squalus, ATTA-3000 and ARA-3600 aircraft are to be found in the Combat Section. Promavia also promotes the Jet Squalus as an ab-initio trainer for future airline and business jet pilots, and offers the Jet Air Academy concept. Dimensions, weights and performance for the civil Jet Squalus are similar to those of the military version (which see).

Promavia Jet Squalus for civil pilot training

★ Aims

⋆ Student pilots train with an airline-type instrument panel, and in a turbine engine environment.
⋆ More sophisticated function modes of the avionics system can be gradually introduced, culminating in the full use of EFIS, FMS and weather radar.
⋆ Avionics and panel layout at customer's choice. Typically, an avionics package would be based on the Collins Pro Line II radios and include VHF-com (dual), VHF-nav (VOR/LOC/GS/MKR) (dual), ADF with dual RMI, transponder with encoding altimeter, DME, radio altimeter, FMS with multiple sensors (VOR/DME, VLF/Omega, etc), weather radar with EHSI display, 3-axis autopilot and flight director, EFIS (CRT) display, audio control/intercom, and altitude alerter/preselector.

★ Jet Air Academy Aims

⋆ Flight training on the Jet Squalus.
⋆ Efficient organization and management of training, based on a computerized Training Management System, enabling the completion of training in 12 months.
⋆ For former military pilots, general aviation pilots and flight engineers, a derivative airline conversion course has been developed which includes evaluation of entry knowledge, refresher ground training, civil air law and regulation, civil IFR procedures, training in civilian avionics and navigation systems, etc, crew co-ordination/CRM techniques, airline company procedures, and review of the ab-initio syllabus and preparation for examinations.
⋆ 3 month duration, with 200 hours classroom (including CBT), 50 hours CPT training and 50 hours flight training in the Jet Squalus.

Indústria Aeronáutica Neiva S.A. (Brazil)

Corporate address: Rua Nossa Senhora de Fátima 360, Caixa Postal 10, 18608-900 Botocatu (SP).
Telephone: +55 149 21 2122 and 5077
Facsimile: +55 149 22 1285 and 21 2110
Founded: 12 October 1954 (see Activities).
Information: Adriano Bruder di Creddo (Technical publications).

● Activities

● Sub-contracted by Embraer in 1975 to build the single- and twin-engined light aircraft licensed from Piper of the USA.
● Incorporated by Embraer in March 1980, when all engineering and production tooling for the Embraer/Piper line and for the Ipanema agricultural aircraft were transferred to Botucatu.
● Over 2,380 aircraft of all types (including early gliders, then Regentes, Universals and others) have been built by Neiva since 1956.

DETAILS FOR EMB-202 IPANEMA.

Principal dimensions:
Wing span: 38 ft 4 ins (11.69 m)
Maximum length: 24 ft 3.5 ins (7.43 m)
Maximum height: 7 ft 3.5 ins (2.22 m)
Wings:
Aerofoil section: NACA 23015 modified
Area: 214.6 sq ft (19.94 m^2)
Undercarriage:
Type: Fixed, with tailwheel
Weights:
Empty, equipped: 2,249 lb (1,020 kg)
Maximum take-off: 3,968 lb (1,800 kg) *restricted category,* 3,418 lb (1,550 kg) *normal*
Useful load: 1,720 lb (780 kg) *restricted,* 1,168 lb (530 kg) *normal.*
Performance:
Maximum speed: 121 kts (139 mph) 224 km/h *restricted category,* 124 kts (143 mph) 230 km/h *normal*
Cruise speed: 111 kts (128 mph) 206 km/h *restricted,* 115 kts (132 mph) 213 km/h *normal* , at 75% power and 6,000 ft (1,830 m)
Stall speed: 55 kts (64 mph) 102 km/h *clean, restricted,* 50 kts (58 mph) 93 km/h *clean, normal;* 53 kts (61 mph) 99 km/h 30° *flaps, restricted,* 50 kts (58 mph) 93 km/h 30° *flaps, normal*
Take-off distance: 1,162 ft (354 m) *restricted,* 656 ft (200 m) *normal,* all sea level, ISA
Landing distance: 558 ft (170 m) *restricted,* 502 ft (153 m) *normal,* all sea level, ISA
Maximum climb rate: 928 ft (283 m) per minute *normal*
Ceiling: 11,400 ft (3,470 m) *restricted*
Range: 506 naut miles (583 miles) 939 km

Embraer/Neiva EMB-202 Ipanema

First flight: 30 July 1970 (as EMB-200 prototype).
Certification: 14 December 1971 for the original EMB-200 version.
Role: Single-seat agricultural aircraft.
Sales/users: Production of all models stood at 738 by February 1995 (first 10 delivered in 1972, and high point production was 1975, when 81 were delivered). 401 EMB-201As were built up to 1992, with 60 EMB-202s produced since.
Chemical hopper: 950 litres, 1,653 lb (750 kg).
Dispersal equipment: Micronair atomizers, or spreader/dusting or spray booms. Atomizers and booms near the wing trailing edges, dusting equipment below the fuselage. Various options including ram air pressure generator for the liquid application equipment and lightweight applicators including the Micronair AU5000 with rotary atomizers.
Wing characteristics: Low-mounted cantilever, with substantial dihedral and down-turned wingtips. Leading edges and wingtips are detachable for quick replacement if damaged.
Wing control surfaces: Frise ailerons and slotted flaps.
Tail control surfaces: Elevators (starboard tab) and rudder.
Construction materials: Welded steel tube structure and mainly metal (some glassfibre) skins.
Engine: Textron Lycoming IO-540-K1J5D or Teledyne Continental IO-550, with a 7 ft (2.13 m) constant-speed propeller.

Embraer EMB-202 Ipanema with spray booms, built by Neiva

Engine rating: 300 hp (224 kW)
Fuel system: 292 litres, of which 264 litres are usable. Consumption 69 litres per hour at 75% power, 6,000 ft (1,830 m) altitude.
Flight control system: Mechanical/manual.
Electrical system: 28 volt DC, with a 28 volt/35 amp alternator and 2 x 43 amp-hour batteries.
Braking system: Hydraulically operated disc.
Flight avionics/instrumentation: VFR (ADF and VHF). Can be fitted optionally with Bendix King KX99 transceiver and Garmin 55 AVD GPS.

Embraer/Neiva EMB-720D Minuano

Role: 6/7-seat lightplane, based on the Piper PA-32-301 Saratoga.
Sales/users: Well over 300 sold, including several to air taxi operators. First 12 delivered in 1975.
Engine: Textron Lycoming IO-540-K1G5.
Engine rating: 300 hp (224 kW).

DETAILS FOR EMB-720D MINUANO.

Principal dimensions:
Wing span: 36 ft 2 ins (11.02 m)
Maximum length: 27 ft 8 ins (8.43 m)
Maximum height: 8 ft 2 ins (2.49 m)
Weights:
Empty: 2,095 lb (950 kg)
Maximum take-off: 3,600 lb (1,633 kg)
Performance:
Maximum speed: 147 kts (169 mph) 272 km/h
Cruise speed: 123 kts (142 mph) 228 km/h at 55% best economy power
Stall speed: 58 kts (67 mph) 108 km/h *with flaps.*
Range: up to 890 naut miles (1,024 miles) 1,650 km at 55% best economy power

Embraer/Neiva EMB-810D Cuesta

Role: Six passenger lightplane, based on the Piper PA-34-220T Seneca III.
Sales/users: Over 850 sold. The Brazilian Air Force operates 33 for communications in "C" model form.
Engines: 2 Teledyne Continental L/TSIO-360KBs.
Engine rating: Each 220 hp (164 kW).

Details for EMB-810D Cuesta.

Principal dimensions:
Wing span: 38 ft 11 ins (11.86 m)
Maximum length: 28 ft 7 ins (8.72 m)
Maximum height: 9 ft 11 ins (3.02 m)
Weights:
Empty: 3,197 lb (1,447 kg)
Maximum take-off: 4,751 lb (2,155 kg)
Performance:
Maximum speed: 196 kts (226 mph) 363 km/h
Cruise speed: 180 kts (207 mph) 334 km/h at 55% power
Stall speed: 64 kts (74 mph) 118 km/h
Range: 920 naut miles (1,059 miles) 1,705 km at 55% power

Airtech Canada Aviation Services Ltd (Canada)

Airtech Canada DHC-3 Otter/1000 hp

Corporate address: PO Box 415, Suite 103, Peterborough, Ontario K9J 6Z3.
Telephone: +1 705 743 9483
Facsimile: +1 705 749 0841
Founded: 1977.
Information: Bernard J. LaFrance (General Manager).

● Activities

- Design, engineering, assembly, manufacture and marketing of aircraft and aviation products.
- Principal products/services are the conversion/completion of fixed and rotary wing aircraft for medevac uses, re-engining the DHC-2 Beaver and DHC-3 Otter, repair/maintenance/overhaul of small aircraft, and design/manufacture/testing/installation of specialized aircraft and aviation modifications, parts and assemblies.
- Holds Canadian STA and US STC for the DHC-2 Beaver/600 hp conversion and the DHC-3 Otter/1000 hp conversion. The conversions can be undertaken by Airtech or by a third party using an Airtech kit.
- For the medevac role, has developed or custom engineered and installed a number of portable and semi-dedicated and dedicated air ambulance interiors and patient restraint systems.

Airtech Canada DHC/1000 hp Otter

Certification: Received the STA in 1983.
Role: Re-engined Otter.
Sales/users: 12 completed by early 1995.
Engine: WSK Kalisz ASz-62IR-M18 radial piston engine.
Engine rating: 967 hp (721 kW).

Details for DHC/1000 hp Otter.

Principal dimensions:
Wing span: 58 ft (17.68 m)
Maximum length: 42 ft (12.8 m)
Maximum height: 12 ft 7 ins (3.84 m) *landplane*, 15 ft (4.57 m) *seaplane*
Weights:
Empty: 4,925 lb (2,234 kg) *landplane*, 5,300 lb (2,404 kg) *seaplane*
Maximum take-off: 8,000 lb (3,629 kg)
Performance:
Never-exceed speed (Vne): 157 kts (181 mph) 291 km/h IAS *landplane*, 146 kts (168 mph) 270 km/h IAS *seaplane*
Maximum normal speed (Vno): 125 kts (144 mph) 233 km/h IAS *landplane*, 116 kts (134 mph) 216 km/h IAS *seaplane*
Take-off distance: 440 ft (134 m) *landplane*, 478 ft (146 m) *seaplane*, at sea level
Maximum climb rate: 1,680 ft (512 m) per minute *landplane*, 1,570 ft (478 m) per minute *seaplane*, at sea level
Ceiling: 17,500 ft (5,335 m) *landplane*, 15,700 ft (4,785 m) *seaplane*, service
Range: 677 naut miles (780 miles) 1,255 km at 112 kts and 10,000 ft (3,050 m), 405 bhp (302 kW), *landplane*

Conair Aviation Ltd (Canada)

Corporate address: PO Box 220, Abbotsford, British Columbia V2S 4NY.
Telephone: +1 604 855 1171
Facsimile: +1 604 855 1017
Information: Lorna Thomassen.

● Activities

- Converts aeroplanes and helicopters mainly for firefighting duties, but also for insect and oil control, and other roles involving spraying and aerial discharge. In addition to those for customers, it operates its own fleet of aircraft.
- Conversion can involve structural inspection and modification, systems replacement, upgraded avionics and (in the case of Turbo Firecat) replacement of original radial engines with turboprops.
- Systems have been fitted to aircraft as diverse as the DC-6B and C-130. Principal products are the Firecat, a firefighting modification of the Grumman Tracker former ASW aircraft, with a cabin retardant tank and optional foam injection system; and the Turbo Firecat, introducing P&WC PT6A-67AF turboprops and with a similar compartmentalized tank for 3,456 litres of retardant. The F27 Firefighter is a conversion of the Fokker Friendship, also suited to fire detection, spraying and other activities. For helicopters, Conair produces the Helitanker, a belly retardant tank that is installed beneath the fuselage, refilled via a tank in the main cabin or on the ground, or while hovering.

Zenair Ltd (Canada)

Corporate address: Huronia Airport, Midland, Ontario L4R 4K8.
Telephone: +1 705 526 2871
Facsimile: +1 705 526 8022
Founded: 1974.
Information: Sebastien C. Heintz (President of Zenith Aircraft Company).

● Activities

- In addition to the certified CH 2000, Zenair offers a range of experimental aircraft for home construction (see Recreational section).

DIVISIONS
<u>**Zenith Aircraft Company**</u>
HQ Address: Mexico Memorial Airport, Mexico, MO 65265-0650, USA
Telephone: +1 314 581 9000
Facsimile: +1 314 581 0011

Zenair Zenith CH 2000

Certification: 26 July 1994 (Canadian), 31 July 1994 (FAA); JAR/VLA.
Role: Two-seat training (dual controls), business and pleasure.
Sales/users: US$69,900 (1995). Deliveries began in September 1994.
Wing control surfaces: Ailerons and flaps.
Tail control surfaces: All moving type, with elevator trim control.
Flight control system: Mechanical, but electric flaps.
Construction materials: Metal.
Engine: Textron Lycoming O-235-N2C piston engine, with a 6 ft (1.83 m) Sensenich 2-blade metal propeller.
Engine rating: 116 hp (86.5 kW).
Fuel system: 106 litres. Optional 2 x 53 litre wing tanks in place of fuselage tank.
Electrical system: 12 volt, 60 amp, with heavy duty battery.
Braking system: Cleveland wheels and hydraulic disc toebrakes.
Flight avionics/instrumentation: Terra TX-760D comm transceiver and TRT-250D transponder, AT 3000 encoder, airspeed indicator, altimeter, fluid magnetic compass, static air source, hour meter and more. Stall warning system. Options include gyro package, Terra TGPS-440D GPS, TMA 350D audio/marker panel, TX 200D nav receiver with or without glideslope and tri-nav indicator, and TDF 100D ADF. Optional IFR, Trainer or Cross-Country packages.

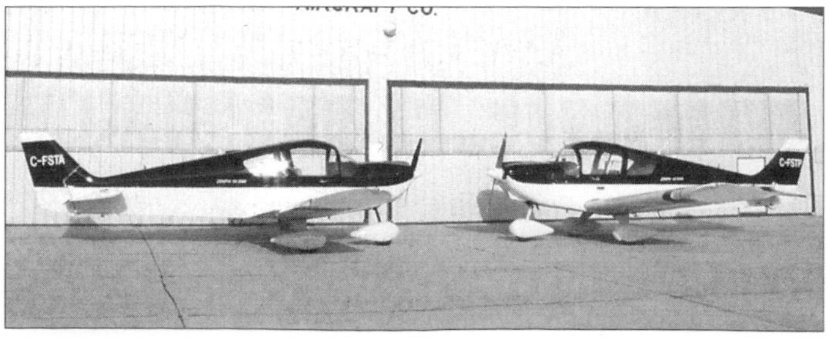

Zenair Zenith CH 2000 trainers

Details for Zenith CH 2000.

Principal dimensions:
Wing span: 28 ft 10 ins (8.79 m)
Maximum length: 23 ft (7.01 m)
Maximum height: 6 ft 10 ins (2.08 m)
Cabin:
Width: 3 ft 10 ins (1.17 m)
Wings:
Area: 137 sq ft (12.73 m^2)
Undercarriage:
Type: Fixed, with steerable nosewheel. Optional wheel fairings
Weights:
Empty: 1,000 lb (454 kg) standard
Maximum take-off: 1,550 lb (703 kg)
Useful load: 550 lb (249 kg)
Performance:
Never-exceed speed (Vne): 147 kts (170 mph) 273 km/h
Cruise speed: 100 kts (115 mph) 185 km/h at 75% power
Stall speed: 44 kts (50 mph) 81 km/h
Take-off distance over a 50 ft (15 m) obstacle: 1,550 ft (473 m)
Landing distance over a 50 ft (15 m) obstacle: 1,300 ft (396 m)
Maximum climb rate: 780 ft (238 m) per minute
G limits: +4.4, -2.2
Range: 434 naut miles (500 miles) 804 km, 75% power, no reserve

Empresa Nacional de Aeronáutica (ENAER) (Chile)

Corporate address: See Combat section for company details.

ENAER T-35 Pillán

First flight: 6 March 1981.
Role: Military and civil basic flying, aerobatic and instrument trainer.

● Aims

● Low engineering and development costs by basing the design on modified structural components and systems from existing Piper aircraft (principally the Cherokee, with Dakota and Saratoga inputs), resulting in few exclusively Pillán assemblies being needed. This makes the availability of replacement components and avionics easy and low cost.
Sales/users: First flight of a production Pillán on 28 December 1984 (3 months after production began), as a T-35A for the Chilean Air Force. Out of production but available to order. 145 built, with all 60 T-35As and 20 Bs still in Air Force use in early 1995. Panama received 10 T-35Ds, Paraguay 15 T-35Ds, and Spain has 37 T-35Cs in use of 40 assembled by CASA, locally known as E.26 Tamiz trainers.
Crew: 2, at a total weight of 380 lb (172 kg).
Cockpit: Tandem, with the instructor's rear seat stepped up by 8.66 ins (220 mm) for visual control over the student.
Wing control surfaces: Ailerons (with port tab) and single-slotted flaps.
Tail control surfaces: Variable incidence tailplane. Single-section elevator and rudder, with tabs.
Engine: Textron Lycoming IO-540-K1K5 piston engine, with 6 ft 4 ins (1.93 m) Hartzell HC-C3YR 3-blade propeller.
Engine rating: 300 hp (223.7 kW).
Fuel system: 291 litres in 2 wing tanks, of which 278 litres are usable; weighing 432 lb (196 kg) of usable fuel, 30 lb (13.6 kg) of unusable fuel.
Flight control system: Mechanical for ailerons, elevator and rudder, the remainder electrical but with electric or mechanical tailplane incidence.
Electrical system: DC supply using a 28 volt 70 amp alternator and 24 volt 15.5 amp-hour acid lead battery. Optional static inverter for AC supply. Socket on starboard fuselage side for electrical power from an external source.
Hydraulic system: 1,800 psi (for undercarriage actuation).
Flight avionics/instrumentation: Standard avionics include Collins audio selector box, VHF, VOR, transponder and ADF. Audio stall warning is activated at 5-8 kts above the aerodynamic stall speed. Many optional AlliedSignal Bendix/King avionics.
Aircraft variants:
T-35A and T-35C are primary trainers for Chile and Spain respectively, the latter assembled by CASA and known as E.26 Tamiz.
T-35B and T-35D are the Chilean and export instrument training versions respectively.
T-35S was a one-off single-seater.

Details for Pillán.

Principal dimensions:
Wing span: 8.84 m (29 ft)
Maximum length: 26 ft 3 ins (8 m)
Maximum height: 8 ft 8 ins (2.64 m)
Wings:
Aerofoil section: NACA 65_2415
Area: 147.36 sq ft (13.69 m^2)
Undercarriage:
Type: Retractable, with steerable nosewheel
Weights:
Empty: 2,050 lb (930 kg)
Maximum take-off and landing: 2,950 lb (1,338 kg)
Maximum aerobatic: 2,900 lb (1,315 kg)
Performance:
Maximum permissible speed: 241 kts (277 mph) 447 km/h
Maximum speed: 180 kts (207 mph) 333 km/h
Cruise speed: 138 kts (159 mph) 255 km/h at 55% power
Stall speed: 62 kts (72 mph) 114 km/h
Landing speed: 65 kts (75 mph) 120 km/h
Take-off distance: 940 ft (287 m)
Take-off distance over a 50 ft (15 m) obstacle: 1,620 ft (494 m)
Landing distance over a 50 ft (15 m)obstacle: 1,670 ft (509 m)
Maximum climb rate: 1,525 ft (465 m) per minute at sea level
Time to 10,000 ft (3,050 m): 8 minutes 48 seconds
Inverted flight time: 40 minutes tested
G limits: +6, -3
Ceiling: 19,160 ft (5,839 m) service, 20,500 ft (6,248 m) absolute
Range at 55% power: 650 naut miles (748 miles) 1,204 km, at 12,000 ft and 45 minutes reserve, or 735 naut miles (845 miles) 1,362 km at 12,000 ft and no reserve
Duration: 5.6 hours at 55% power

ENAER T-35 Pillán (Denis Hughes)

ENAER Ñamcu

First flight: April 1989.
Certification: Meets FAR Pt 23 requirements.
Role: Aerobatic lightplane, club trainer and utility aircraft. Also offered in homebuilt kit form.
Sales/users: Production began in 1995. Also being built in the Netherlands

ENAER Ñamcu (Eaglet) now also offered in kit form (Denis Hughes)

Crew/passengers: 2 persons.
Cockpit: Dual controls. 2 upward-hinging doors form the centre section of the canopy.
Baggage capacity: 22 lb (10 kg) behind seats.
Wing control surfaces: Ailerons and flaps.
Tail control surfaces: Elevators (starboard tab) and rudder.
Construction materials: Glassfibre, carbonfibre and foam composites.
Engine: Textron Lycoming O-235-N2C piston engine, with a 5 ft 10 ins (1.78 m) 2-blade fixed-pitch propeller.
Engine rating: 116 hp (86.5 kW).
Fuel system: 100 litres.
Electrical system: 12 volt 70 amp alternator and 12 volt 35 amp-hour acid lead battery.
Braking system: Cleveland hydraulic disc on main units.
Flight avionics/instrumentation: VFR. Optional upgrade to IFR.

Details for Ñamcu.

Principal dimensions:
Wing span: 27 ft 3 ins (8.31 m)
Maximum length: 23 ft 1.5 ins (7.05 m)
Maximum height: 7 ft 11 ins (2.42 m)
Wings:
Aerofoil section: NACA 63_2415
Area: 107.746 sq ft (10.01 m2)
Undercarriage:
Type: Fixed, with steerable nosewheel
Weights:
Empty: 1,203 lb (546 kg)
Maximum take-off and landing: 1,764 lb (800 kg)
Performance:
Maximum permissible speed: 177 kts (203 mph) 328 km/h
Maximum speed: 127 kts (146 mph) 235 km/h
Cruise speed: 103 kts (118 mph) 191 km/h, at 75% power
Stall speed: 50 kts (58 mph) 93 km/h *with flaps*, 56 kts (65 mph) 104 km/h *clean*
Take-off distance: 1,000 ft (304 m)
Landing distance: 580 ft (177 m)
Maximum climb rate: 970 ft (295 m) per minute
G limits: +4.4, -2.2
Ceiling: 14,010 ft (4,270 m)
Range with full fuel: 500 naut miles (575 miles) 926 km at cruise speed
Duration: 3.6 hours

Harbin Aircraft Manufacturing Corporation (China)

Corporate address: See Combat section for company details.

Harbin Y11B

First flight: 25 December 1990.
Certification: 1993 (CAAC). Designed to FAR Pt 23.
Role: Light general-purpose transport, suited to short-haul passenger and cargo operations, agricultural, forestry and geological survey roles.
Sales/users: Y11B had not entered series production against sales by early 1995. Over 40 of the earlier Y11 model were completed.

Harbin Y11B during spray trials (courtesy Harbin)

Crew/passengers: 1 or 2 pilots plus 7 passengers.
Wing control surfaces: Ailerons (starboard tab) and double-slotted flaps.
Tail control surfaces: Elevators and rudder, with tabs.
Engines: 2 Teledyne Continental TSIO-550-A1B piston engines, with 7 ft 10 ins (2.4 m) Hartzell PHC-C3YF-2KUF/FC 3-blade propellers.
Engine rating: Each 350 hp (261 kW).
Fuel system: 992 lb (450 kg).
Flight avionics/instrumentation: AlliedSignal Bendix/King VFR and IFR nav/comm.

DETAILS FOR Y11B.

Principal dimensions:
Wing span: 56 ft 0.5 ins (17.08 m)
Maximum length: 39 ft 5 ins (12.017 m)
Maximum height: 17 ft 7 ins (5.356 m)
Wings:
Area: 367.69 sq ft (34.16 m^2)
Aspect ratio: 8.54
Undercarriage:
Type: Fixed, with self-centring nosewheel. Twin mainwheels
Weights:
Empty: 5,520 lb (2,504 kg)
Normal take-off: 7,716 lb (3,500 kg), overload 8,598 lb (3,900 kg)
Maximum landing: 7,716 lb (3,500 kg)
Payload: 1,984–2,645 lb (900–1,200 kg)
Performance:
Maximum speed: 143 kts (165 mph) 265 km/h at 9,840 ft (3,000 m), MCP
Maximum cruise speed: 127 kts (146 mph) 235 km/h at 9,840 ft (3,000 m), MCP
Take-off distance: 1,427 ft (435 m), with 656 ft (200 m) roll
Landing distance: 1,739 ft (530 m), with 902 ft (275 m) roll
Maximum climb rate: 1,102 ft (336 m) per minute at sea level, MCP
Climb rate, OEI: 108 ft (33 m) per minute at sea level
Ceiling: 19,685 ft (6,000 m)
Ceiling, OEI: 6,890 ft (2,100 m)
Range with full fuel: 583 naut miles (671 miles) 1,080 km, at 9,840 ft (3,000 m), optimum cruise speed
Range with full payload: 162 naut miles (186 miles) 300 km, at 9,840 ft (3,000 m), optimum cruise speed

Nanchang Aircraft Manufacturing Company (China)

Corporate address: See Combat section for company details.

Nanchang CJ-6A

First flight: 27 August 1958.
Role: Primary piston-engined trainer.
Sales/users: Over 1,500 serving with the Air Force of the People's Liberation Army, and exported (sometimes as the PT-6A) to Albania, Bangladesh, Cambodia, North Korea, Tanzania and Zambia. Thought to remain in low-rate production.
Crew: Instructor and student in tandem. Rear seat is not raised.
Construction materials: Metal.
Engine: South Aero Engine Company HS6A radial piston engine.
Engine rating: 285 hp (212.5 kW).
Fuel system: 100 litres.

Nanchang CJ-6A

DETAILS FOR CJ-6A.

Principal dimensions:
Wing span: 33 ft 6 ins (10.22 m)
Maximum length: 27 ft 9 ins (8.46 m)
Maximum height: 10 ft 8 ins (3.25 m)
Undercarriage:
Type: Retractable, with nosewheel
Weights:
Empty: 2,414 lb (1,095 kg)
Maximum take-off: 3,086 lb (1,400 kg)
Performance:
Maximum speed: 160 kts (184 mph) 297 km/h
Take-off distance: 91 ft (280 m)
Maximum climb rate: 1,245 ft (380 m) per minute
Ceiling: 20,500 ft (6,250 m)
Duration: 3.6 hours

Nanchang N-5A

First flight: 26 December 1989.
Certification: 12 August 1992.
Role: Agricultural spraying and dusting.
Sales/users: In production, with several operational in China.
Crew/passengers: Pilot, with a tandem seat to the rear for ferrying a support operative as required.
Pressurization system: Cockpit has a low level of pressurization to prevent chemicals entering during operations.
Chemical tank/hopper: In the forward fuselage, with a maximum 2,116 lb (960 kg) load of liquid or dry chemicals. Contents can be dumped in 5 seconds in an emergency.
Dispersal equipment: Full-span spraybars to the rear of the wing trailing edges, with low-to-high settings for liquids.
Safety equipment: Wire cutter on the nosewheel leg and ahead of the windshield. Wire deflector from the windshield to the fin. Crashworthy fuselage.
Wing control surfaces: Ailerons (with tabs) and single-slotted flaps.
Tail control surfaces: Elevators and rudder, all with tabs.
Flight control system: Mechanical, except for electrically actuated flaps and elevator tabs.
Construction materials: Metal, except for glassfibre hopper.
Engine: Textron Lycoming IO-720-D1B piston engine. An N-5A development is using a South Aero Engine Company HS6K radial of 400 hp (298.3 kW).
Engine rating: 400 hp (298 kW).
Fuel system: 315 litres.
Electrical system: AC generator and 30 amp-hour battery.
Braking system: Mainwheel hydraulic discs.
Flight avionics/instrumentation: AlliedSignal Bendix/King KY 96A VHF transceiver, with optional KHF 950 HF/SSB. Stall warning system. Other equipment is available upon request.

DETAILS FOR N-5A.

Principal dimensions:
Wing span: 44 ft (13.418 m)
Maximum length: 34 ft 5 ins (10.487 m)
Maximum height: 12 ft 3 ins (3.733 m)
Wings:
Aerofoil section: Modified LS(1)-0417
Area: 279.9 sq ft (26 m^2)
Aspect ratio: 6.92
Undercarriage:
Type: Retractable, with nosewheel
Weights:
Empty: 2,927 lb (1,328 kg)
Maximum take-off: 4,960 lb (2,250 kg) normal, 5,400 lb (2,450 kg) overload
Performance:
Maximum speed: 111 kts (127 mph) 205 km/h
Spray speed: 92 kts (106 mph) 170 km/h typically
Stall speed: 57 kts (65 mph) 105 km/h *clean*, 47 kts (53 mph) 86 km/h *with flaps*
Take-off distance: 994 ft (303 m)
Landing distance: 807 ft (246 m)
Maximum climb rate: 843 ft (257 m) per minute
Ceiling: 12,300 ft (3,750 m), service
Range with full payload: 135 naut miles (155 miles) 250 km, with 45 minutes reserve
Duration: 1.8 hours

Shijiazhuang Aircraft Manufacturing Corporation (China)

Corporate address: PO Box 164, Shijiazhuang, Hebei 050062.
Telephone: +86 311 0744251

Shijiazhuang Y5B

First flight: 2 June 1989 for the Y5B, although other Y5 models of this licence-built Antonov An-2 have been built since 1957.
Role: Agricultural spraying and spreading biplane.
Crew: 1 or 2.
Chemical tank/hopper: 3,307 lb (1,500 kg) load of liquid or dry chemicals.
Spray equipment: Full span spraybars below the trailing-edges of the lower wings.
Safety equipment: Cable cutter above the cockpit.
Wing characteristics: Wire-braced biplane.
Engine: WSK Kalisz ASz-62IR-16 radial piston engine, or a licence-built version as the South Aero Engine Company HS5.
Engine rating: 967 hp (721 kW).
Flight avionics/instrumentation: AlliedSignal Bendix/King comm radios, ADF and more.

DETAILS FOR Y5B.

Principal dimensions:
Wing span: 59 ft 7.5 ins (18.176 m) upper, 46 ft 9 ins (14.236 m) lower
Maximum length: 41 ft 7.5 ins (12.688 m)
Maximum height: 17 ft 7 ins (5.35 m)
Wings:
Area: 468.72 sq ft (43.546 m^2) upper, 301.17 sq ft (27.98 m^2) lower
Aspect ratio: 7.59 upper wing, 7.24 lower wing
Undercarriage:
Type: Fixed, with tailwheel
Weights:
Normal take-off: 11,574 lb (5,250 kg)
Payload: 3,307 lb (1,500 kg)
Performance (at normal take-off weight):
Maximum speed at 5,575 ft (1,700 m): 138 kts (159 mph) 256 km/h clean, 119 kts (137 mph) 220 km/h with spreading gear, 116 kts (134 mph) 215 km/h with spray gear
Maximum speed at sea level: 129 kts (149 mph) 239 km/h clean, 111 kts (128 mph) 205 km/h with spreading gear, 108 kts (125 mph) 200 km/h with spray gear
Stall speed: 52 kts (59 mph) 95 km/h
Take-off distance: 502 ft (153 m) clean, 564 ft (172 m) with spreading gear, 600 ft (183 m) with spray gear
Landing distance: 574 ft (175 m) clean, 525 ft (160 m) with spreader gear, 515 ft (157 m) with spray gear, with brakes
Maximum climb rate: 590 ft (180 m) per minute clean, 394 ft (120 m) per minute with spreading gear, 374 ft (114 m) per minute with spray gear, all at sea level
Ceiling: 14,765 ft (4,500 m) clean, 11,350 ft (3,460 m) with spreading gear, 10,660 ft (3,250 m) with spray gear, all service
Technical range: 456 naut miles (525 miles) 845 km clean, at 3,280 ft (1,000 m), fuel consumption 1,102 lb (500 kg)

Aviones de Colombia S.A. (Colombia)

Corporate address: Entrada 1, Aeropuerto Eldorado, Bogatá.
Telephone: +57 1 413 8300
Facsimile: +57 1 413 8075

● Activities

● Has assembled and marketed particular Cessna aircraft. Developed a side-by-side two-seat agricultural training version of the Cessna AgTruck, as the AgTrainer, and began production in 1992 of its own single-seat agricultural aircraft as the AC-05 Pijao (Teledyne Continental IO-520-D engine and 1,060 litre hopper).

El Gavilán S.A. (Colombia)

Corporate address: Apartado Aéreo 6781, Carrera 3 No 56-19, Santafé de Bogatá, DC.
Telephone: +57 1 676 1101
Facsimile: +57 1 676 0290, 0650
Founded: 1991.
Information: Eric C. Leaver (General Manager).

● Activities

● Aero-Mercantil S.A. is El Gavilán's holding company. Aero-Mercantil itself has other subsidiaries, all engaged in General Aviation activities. One provides maintenance for aircraft and engines, another charters aeroplanes and helicopters to the oil industry, and a third runs a flying school.
● Development of Gavilán 358 was assisted by General Aviation Technical Services of Lock Haven, USA.

El Gavilán Gavilán 358

First flight: 27 April 1990. First prototype was subsequently lost in an accident due to engine failure after the crankshaft broke.
Role: Utility, suitable for operations from short unprepared runways.
Sales/users: Deliveries to begin in July 1996.
Crew/passengers: Pilot and 7 passengers, 4 litters and an attendant, parachutists or freight. 3 doors, one a large double door for cargo.
Wing control surfaces: Ailerons and 3-position flaps (15°, 30° and 40°).
Tail control surfaces: Horn-balanced elevators and rudder. Starboard elevator has a trim tab, and a spring tab is provided for directional trimming.
Flight control system: Cables and pushrods.
Construction materials: Tubular steel truss fuselage structure, with aluminium alloy skins. 2-spar wings of aluminium alloy (strut braced) and aluminium alloy tail unit.
Engine: Textron Lycoming TIO-540-W2A piston engine, with 7 ft (2.13 m) 3-blade propeller.
Engine rating: 350 hp (261 kW).
Fuel system: 454 litres, in the wings.
Flight avionics/instrumentation: Standard gyro instruments including attitude indicator and gyro compass. Night-flying lights. Standard comm equipment is VHF radio, VOR and ADF.

El Gavilán Gavilán 358

DETAILS FOR GAVILÁN 358.

Principal dimensions:
Wing span: 42 ft (12.8 m)
Maximum length: 31 ft 3 ins (9.53 m)
Maximum height: 12 ft 4 ins (3.76 m), or 15 ft 6 ins (4.72 m) with floats
Wings:
Aerofoil section: NACA 4412
Area: 204 sq ft (18.95 m^2)
Aspect ratio: 8.65
Undercarriage:
Type: Fixed, with castering nosewheel. Optional floats
Weights:
Empty: 2,800 lb (1,270 kg) standard VFR equipped
Maximum take-off and landing: 4,500 lb (2,132 kg)
Useful load: 1,700 lb (771 kg)
Payload: 980 lb (444.5 kg) with full fuel
Performance:
Design maximum diving speed: 203 kts (233 mph) 376 km/h CAS
Cruise speed at 10,000 ft (3,050 m): 135 kts (155 mph) 250 km/h at 75% power, 130 kts (150 mph) 241 km/h at 65% power, 126 kts (145 mph) 233 km/h at 55% power, all TAS
Stall speed: 69 kts (80 mph) 128 km/h *clean*, 58 kts (67 mph) 108 km/h *with 40 ° flaps*, CAS
Take-off distance: 900 ft (274 m) with 15° flaps
Landing distance: 643 ft (196 m)
Maximum climb rate: 900 ft (274 m) per minute
Ceiling: 25,000 ft (7,620 m), service
Range: 770 naut miles (886 miles) 1,426 km at 75% power, 870 naut miles (1,001 miles) 1,611 km at 65% power, 945 naut miles (1,088 miles) 1,750 km at 55% power, with 30 minutes reserve

Aero Vodochody Ltd (Czech Republic)

Corporate address: See Combat section for details.

Aero Ae 270 Ibis

First flight: 1995.
Certification: 1996 to FAR Pt 23 Normal requirements.
Role: Short-haul transport and general utility.
Crew/passengers: 2 crew and 8 passengers in the corporate version, pilot plus 2,645 lb (1,200 kg) of cargo, combi or other interiors including 4-passenger executive.
Wing control surfaces: Ailerons, single-slotted Fowler flaps, and roll-control spoilers.
Tail control surfaces: Elevators and rudder (with trim tab). Floatplane has finlets on the tailplane.
Construction materials: Metal.
Engine: See Aircraft variants.
Fuel system: 1,146 litres.
Electrical system: 28 volt DC, via a 250 amp engine-driven starter-generator. 37 amp-hour battery.
Hydraulic system: 2,175 psi.
De-icing system: Wing and tail leading edges, windshield, engine air intake, propeller blades, pitot static system and stall warning sensor.

Aero Ae 270 P Ibis mock-up (courtesy Aero)

DETAILS FOR AE 270 P.

Principal dimensions:
Wing span: 45 ft 3 ins (13.8 m)
Maximum length: 40 ft 2 ins (12.24 m)
Maximum height: 15 ft 9 ins (4.79 m)
Cabin:
Length: 16 ft 4 ins (4.98 m)
Width: 4 ft 9 ins (1.44 m)
Height: 4 ft 5.5 ins (1.36 m)
Volume: 264.9 cu ft (7.5 m^3)
Passenger/cargo door size: 4 ft 1 ins x 4 ft 1 ins (1.25 x 1.25 m)
Wings:
Area: 226 sq ft (21 m^2)
Aspect ratio: 9.07
Weights:
Empty: 3,942 lb (1,788 kg)
Maximum take-off: 7,275 lb (3,300 kg)
Performance:
Cruise speed: 206 kts (237 mph) 381 km/h at sea level, 220 kts (254 mph) 408 km/h at 13,125 ft (4,000 m)
Stall speed: 80 kts (92 mph) 148 km/h *clean*, 61 kts (71 mph) 113 km/h *with flaps*
Take-off distance over a 50 ft (15 m) obstacle: 1,637 ft (499 m)
Landing distance over a 50 ft (15 m) obstacle: 2,799 ft (853 m)
Maximum climb rate: 1,614 ft (492 m) per minute
Ceiling: 31,825 ft (9,700 m), service
Range: 1,188 naut miles (1,367 miles) 2,200 km at 19,685 ft (6,000 m), with 45 minutes reserve

Flight avionics/instrumentation: Standard flight, navigation and engine instrumentation and cockpit arrangement complies with FAR Pt 23. Optional equipment for VFR and IFR. Autopilot will become an option for single-pilot IFR.
Aircraft variants:
Ae 270 P has an 850 shp (634 kW) Pratt & Whitney Canada PT6A-42 turboprop engine, retractable nosewheel undercarriage, and pressurization.
Ae 270 FP is an amphibious floatplane version of Ae 270 P.
Ae 270 W has a 778 shp (580 kW) Walter M601 turboprop, fixed undercarriage and is not pressurized.
Ae 270 FW is an amphibious floatplane version of Ae 270 W.

Letecké opravny Kbely (LOK) (Czech Republic)

Corporate address: Touzimská 583, 197 03 Praha 9, Kbely.
Telephone: +42 2 850 1251-9
Facsimile: +42 2 850 78 06
Telex: 121 407 loc c
Information: Dipl-Ing Václav Renc (Chief Sales and Marketing Manager–*telephone* +42 2 850 7685).

● Activities

● LOK had expected to be privatized, with resulting changes to the plant. However, by August 1995 this had still not been finalized and the Family Air lightplane project had been stopped before realizing its first flight. LOK continues, therefore, as a state-owned aircraft repair works.

Moravan Inc (Czech Republic)

Moravan Zlin Z 50 LS (Tána Vesela/Moravan)

Corporate address: 765 81 Otrokovice.
Telephone: +42 67 922041, 924351
Facsimile: +42 67 922340, 922191
Founded: 1934 as Zlinská Letecká Akciová Spolecnost, its name changing to Moravan in 1949. Products continue to be known as Zlins.
Information: Katerina Trávníckova (Marketing).

Moravan Zlin Z 50 LS

First flight: 18 July 1975 in original Zlin Z 50 L form.
Certification: Certified in Czech Republic, Bulgaria, Germany, Hungary, Sweden and the UK.
Role: Single-seat basic and advanced aerobatics, operated in Normal, Aerobatic and Utility categories.
Wing control surfaces: 2-segment mass balanced ailerons on each wing (no flaps), inner with geared tabs and the port outer with a ground adjustable tab.
Tail control surfaces: Elevators with trim and geared tabs, and rudder with geared tab.
Flight control system: Ailerons and elevators operated by rods, rudder by cables.
Engine: Textron Lycoming AEIO-540-L1B5D piston engine, with a 6 ft 7 ins (2 m) 3-blade Hoffmann HO-V123K-V/200AH wooden propeller.
Engine rating: 300 hp (224 kW) take-off.
Fuel system: 60 litres in the fuselage. Wingtip auxiliary tanks of 50 litres each for non-aerobatic flying. Suited to inverted flight (as is oil system).
Electrical system: Alternator and 12 amp-hour battery. External power socket for engine starting.
Braking system: Mechanical mainwheel brakes actuated by rudder pedals.

DETAILS FOR ZLIN Z 50 LS.

Principal dimensions:
Wing span: 28 ft 2 ins (8.58 m)
Maximum length: 21 ft 8.5 ins (6.62 m)
Maximum height: 6 ft 9.5 ins (2.07 m)
Undercarriage:
Type: Fixed, with tailwheel
Weights:
Empty: 1,323 lb (600 kg) Aerobatic, 1,345 lb (610 kg) Normal
Maximum take-off: 1,675 lb (760 kg) Aerobatic, 1,852 lb (840 kg) Normal
Performance (Aerobatic, MTOW):
Never-exceed speed (Vne): 181 kts (209 mph) 337 km/h CAS
Maximum speed: 166 kts (191 mph) 308 km/h at 1,640 ft (500 m), ISA
Maximum cruise speed: 148 kts (171 mph) 275 km/h at 1,640 ft (500 m), ISA
Stall speed: 56 kts (64 mph) 103 km/h, CAS
Take-off over a 50 ft (15 m) obstacle: 984 ft (300 m), ISA, sea level, dry concrete runway
Landing over a 50 ft (15 m) obstacle: 1,740 ft (530 m), ISA, sea level, idle engine power, dry concrete runway
Maximum climb rate: 2,755 ft (840 m) per minute
G limits: +9, - 6 Aerobatic; +3.8, -1.5 Normal
Ceiling: 26,820 ft (8,175 m), service, ISA
Range: 318 naut miles (366 miles) 590 km, at 1,640 ft (500 m), ISA, Normal category

Moravan Zlin Z 137 T photographed in 1994 on the 60th anniversary of the Zlin/Moravan company (Tána Vesela/Moravan)

Moravan Zlin Z 137 T

First flight: 6 September 1981 in prototype Z 37 form.
Role: Agricultural (spraying, spreading and forest protection), plus firefighting.
Crew/passengers: Pilot. Seat for a maintenance engineer aft of the hopper, or area can be used for carrying cargo.
Chemical tank/hopper: 1,000 litres of liquid or 1,984 lb (900 kg) of dry chemicals. Attachment under the fuselage allows for the transportation of suspended equipment.
Spray equipment: Pneumatically-powered spray gear (swath width 131 ft, 40 m), spreader (swath width 98.5 ft, 30 m), dusting gear and fire-bombing equipment, plus Micronair atomizers. Emergency discharge of hopper in 5 seconds.
Safety equipment: Wire cutter on each mainwheel leg and windscreen.
Wing control surfaces: Fixed leading-edge slats, double-slotted 2-segment trailing-edge flaps (5° retracted, 15° take-off, 40° landing), and statically-balanced slotted ailerons (port trim tab).
Tail control surfaces: Single-piece elevator, with trim tab.
Flight control system: Mechanical, except for pneumatic flap actuation and electric elevator trim.
Construction materials: Welded steel tube fuselage structure, with metal skinning forward and fabric aft. All metal wings, but with fabric on the trailing-edge of the ailerons. Metal tail unit, except for mostly fabric-covered elevator and partially fabric-covered rudder. Guaranteed technical airframe service life of 4,500 hours.
Engine: Motorlet Walter M 601Z turboprop, with an 8 ft 3 ins (2.5 m) Avia Hamilton V 508 Z 3-blade propeller.
Engine rating: 520 shp (387.8 kW) take-off.
Fuel system: 2 x 175 litre tanks in the wings. Underwing attachments for 4 x 125 litre auxiliary fuel tanks for ferry flights or transporting to site.
Electrical system: 28 volt DC, with a starter generator. Auxiliary source is an accumulator.
Braking system: Mainwheel hydraulic drum brakes. Parking brake.
Aircraft variants:
Z 137 T, as detailed.
Z 137 T-2 is a two-seat training model.

DETAILS FOR Z 137 T.

Principal dimensions:
Wing span: 44 ft 9 ins (13.63 m)
Maximum length: 34 ft 4 ins (10.46 m)
Maximum height: 11 ft 6 ins (3.5 m) to propeller
Wings:
Area: 287.29 sq ft (26.69 m^2)
Aspect ratio: 6.96
Undercarriage:
Type: Fixed, with steerable tailwheel (±15°) that can also swivel 360°.
Weights:
Empty: 2,899 lb (1,315 kg)
Maximum take-off: 5,567 lb (2,525 kg)
Performance:
Maximum speed: 118 kts (135 mph) 218 km/h
Cruise speed: 103 kts (118 mph) 190 km/h
Operating speed: 78-89 kts (90-103 mph) 145-165 km/h IAS
Stall speed: 42 kts (48 mph) 77 km/h with flaps, IAS
Take-off over a 50 ft (15 m) obstacle: 1,995 ft (608 m), grass
Landing over a 50 ft (15 m) obstacle: 2,356 ft (718 m)
Maximum climb rate: 827 ft (252 m) per minute
G limits: +3.2, -1.28
Ceiling: 18,045 ft (5,500 m)
Range: 186 naut miles (214 miles) 345 km at 4,982 lb (2,260 kg) and cruise speed
Range with auxiliary fuel: 664 naut miles (765 miles) 1,231 km
Duration: 1 hour 55 minutes at 1,640 ft (500 m)

Moravan Zlin Z 142 and Z 242

First flight: 29 December 1978 for Z 142.
Details: Principally Z 142 C.
Role: Two-seat basic and advanced civil and military training, aerobatics, night and IFR training, glider and banner towing, observation and patrol. Can be operated in Aerobatic, Normal and Utility categories.

Moravan Zlin Z 242 L (Tána Vesela/Moravan)

Sales/users: Current Z 142 C was put into production in 1992, following more than 750 earlier Z 42, Z 142 and Z 43 types.
Baggage capacity: 44 lb (20 kg).
Wing characteristics: Slightly swept-forward wings (4° 20').
Wing control surfaces: Slotted flaps and ailerons, latter with ground adjustable tabs.
Tail control surfaces: Horn-balanced single-piece elevator with trim tabs, and rudder with ground adjustable tab.
Flight control system: Ailerons and elevator are rod controlled, rudder rod/cable.
Construction materials: Metal structure, with metal skins except for composite mid-fuselage panels. Guaranteed technical airframe service life of 3,500 hours.
Engine: LOM Prague M 337 AK piston engine, with an 6 ft 7 ins (2 m) Avia Hamilton Standard V 500 A propeller.
Engine rating: 206.5 hp (154 kW).
Fuel system: 2 x 60 litres in wings. 2 x 50 litre wingtip auxiliary tanks. 5 litre aerobatic tank in the centre fuselage.
Electrical system: 28 volt DC, via engine-driven 600 W dynamo. Auxiliary 25 amp-hour lead-acid battery.
Braking system: Mainwheel hydraulic disc brakes.
Flight avionics/instrumentation: 7 optional approved packages based on AlliedSignal Silver Crown equipment.
Aircraft variants:
Z 142 C has been the current production version since 1992.
Z 142 CAF is the Czech Air Force training version.
Z 242 L is basically a 200 hp (149 kW) Textron Lycoming AEIO-360-A1B6 engined version of the Z 142 C, though other changes include straight wings of 30 ft 8 ins (9.34 m) span, length reduced to 22 ft 9.5 ins (6.94 m), 55 litre wingtip tanks, and a 1.6 kW generator and 19 amp-hour battery for electrical power. Weights are the same but performance is slightly higher.

DETAILS FOR Z 142C.

Principal dimensions:
Wing span: 30 ft 0.5 ins (9.16 m)
Maximum length: 24 ft 0.5 ins (7.33 m)
Maximum height: 9 ft 0.25 ins (2.75 m)
Wings:
Aerofoil section: NACA $63_2416.5$
Area: 141.55 sq ft (13.15 m^2)
Aspect ratio: 6.38
Undercarriage:
Type: Fixed, with steerable nosewheel
Weights:
Empty: 1,609 lb (730 kg)
Maximum take-off: 2,138 lb (970 kg) Aerobatic, 2,403 lb (1,090 kg) Normal
Performance (Normal category):
Maximum speed: 123 kts (142 mph) 228 km/h at 1,640 ft (500 m), ISA
Maximum cruise speed: 109 kts (126 mph) 202 km/h, 75% power, at 1,640 ft (500 m), ISA
Economic cruise speed: 100 kts (115 mph) 186 km/h, 65% power, at 1,640 ft (500 m), ISA
Stall speed: 56 kts (64 mph) 103 km/h, *with flaps*
Take-off distance: 827 ft (252 m)
Landing distance: 722 ft (220 m)
Maximum climb rate: 826 ft (252 m) per minute
G limits: +6, –3.5 Aerobatic; +3.8, –1.5 Normal
Ceiling: 14,175 ft (4,320 m), service
Range: 413-522 naut miles (475-601 miles) 765-967 km, according to cruise speed, at 1,640 ft (500 m)

Moravan Zlin Z 143 L

First flight: 24 April 1992.
Certification: 1994.
Role: Four-seater, based on the Z 242 L. Similar roles to Z 142 C, but also including air taxi, tourist, light business and family flying.
Sales/users: Recently entered series production.
Baggage capacity: 132 lb (60 kg).
Engine: Textron Lycoming O-540-J3A5 piston engine, with a 6 ft 5 ins (1.96 m) MTV-9-B/195-45a 3-blade propeller. An Avia M 337 AK engined version is anticipated.
Engine rating: 235 hp (175 kW).
Fuel system: 2 x 60 litre wing tanks. 2 x 50 litre auxiliary tiptanks.
Electrical system: As for Z 242 L.

Moravan Zlin Z 143 L (Tána Vesela/Moravan)

Details for Z 143 L.

Principal dimensions:
Wing span: 33 ft 3 ins (10.136 m)
Maximum length: 24 ft 10 ins (7.577 m)
Maximum height: 9 ft 6.5 ins (2.91 m)
Wings:
Area: 159 sq ft (14.776 m^2)
Aspect ratio: 6.953
Weights:
Empty: 1,830 lb (830 kg)
Maximum take-off: 2,976 lb (1,350 kg) Normal, 2,380 lb (1,080 kg) Aerobatic
Performance (Utility category):
Maximum speed: 144 kts (166 mph) 267 km/h at sea level
Cruise speed: 127 kts (146 mph) 235 km/h at 75% power, 117 kts (134 mph) 216 km/h at 60% power, at sea level
Stall speed: 54 kts (62 mph) 100 km/h
Take-off distance: 558 ft (170 m)
Landing distance: 1,000 ft (305 m)
Maximum climb rate: 1,457 ft (444 m) per minute
G limits: +4.4, -1.76 Aerobatic; +3.8, -1.5 Normal
Ceiling: 18,700 ft (5,700 m)
Range: 259 naut miles (298 miles) 480 km at 65% power, 295 naut miles (340 miles) 548 km at 58% power, both at 10,000 ft (3,050 m)

MSP Air spol sro (Czech Republic)

MSP Air WK 94 (Peter R. March)

Corporate address: Pavla Hanuse 299, Hradec Králové 500 02.
Telephone: +42 49 383 92, 401 60
Facsimile: +42 49 381 62

MSP Air WK 94

Role: Side-by-side two-seat lightplane.
Wing characteristics: Forward swept, dihedral wings. Conventional flight controls.
Engine: Rotax 532 piston engine in the prototype.
Engine rating: 64.4 hp (48 kW).

Details for WK 94.

Principal dimensions:
Wing span: 42 ft (12.8 m)
Maximum length: 29 ft 6 ins (9 m)
Weights:
Empty: 547 lb (248 kg)
Maximum take-off: 992 lb (450 kg)
Performance:
Maximum speed: 86 kts (99 mph) 160 km/h
Cruise speed: 49-70 kts (56-81 mph) 90-130 km/h
Minimum speed: 34 kts (39 mph) 62 km/h
Maximum climb rate: 787 ft (240 m) per minute
G limits: +4, -2
Duration: 3 hours

Arab Organization for Industrialization (AOI) (Egypt)

Corporate address: See Combat section for details.

AOI Helwan 2

Certification: Tested and approved to civil aviation regulations.
Role: Two-seat multi-purpose, including sporting, light cargo, reconnaissance, aerial photography, survey, patrol, law enforcement, and agricultural.
Engine: 80 hp (59.7 kW) piston engine.
Flight avionics/instrumentation: VHF transceiver, magnetic compass, altimeter, airspeed indicator, artificial horizon, and ambient temperature indicator. Options include G meter, rate of climb/descent indicator, turn/bank indicator, turn/slip indicator, GPS, fuel gauge, tachometer and more.

Details for Helwan 2.

Principal dimensions:
Wing span: 32 ft 10 ins (10 m)
Maximum length: 19 ft 8 ins (6 m)
Maximum height: 7 ft 3 ins (2.2 m)
Weights:
Empty: 727 lb (330 kg)
Maximum take-off: 1,146 lb (520 kg)
Performance:
Maximum speed: 97 kts (112 mph) 180 km/h
Cruise speed: 76 kts (87 mph) 140 km/h
Landing distance: 263 ft (80 m)
Ceiling: 9,840 ft (3,000 m)
Range: 324 naut miles (373 miles) 600 km

AOI Helwan 3 (courtesy AOI)

AOI Helwan 2 (courtesy AOI)

AOI Helwan 3

Certification: Tested and approved to civil aviation regulations.
Role: Multi-purpose, including sporting, light cargo, reconnaissance, aerial photography, survey, patrol, law enforcement and agricultural.
Crew/passengers: 2 seats, side by side. Dual controls.
Engine: Textron Lycoming O-320-A2B piston engine.
Engine rating: 150 hp (112 kW).
Fuel system: 100 litres.
Flight avionics/instrumentation: VHF transceiver, magnetic compass, altimeter, airspeed indicator, engine indicators, fuel gauge, and ambient temperature indicator. Options include G meter, rate of climb/descent indicator, turn/bank indicator, artificial horizon, GPS and more.

Details for Helwan 3.

Principal dimensions:
Wing span: 36 ft 1 ins (11 m)
Maximum length: 21 ft 4 ins (6.5 m)
Wings:
Area: 172.22 sq ft (16 m^2)
Aspect ratio: 7.56
Weights:
Empty: 1,102 lb (500 kg)
Maximum take-off: 1,653 lb (750 kg)
Performance:
Maximum speed: 135 kts (155 mph) 250 km/h
Economic cruise speed: 97 kts (112 mph) 180 km/h
Minimum speed: 41 kts (47 mph) 75 km/h
Glide ratio: 15
G limits: +4.2, –2
Ceiling: 16,400 ft (5,000 m)
Range: 405 naut miles (466 miles) 750 km
Duration: 4 hours

Ethiopian Airlines S.C. (Ethiopia)

Corporate address: PO Box 1755, Addis Ababa.
Telephone: +251 1 612222
Facsimile: +251 1 611474

● **Activities**

● Its aircraft manufacturing division is constructing the Ag-Cat Corporation Ag-Cat Turbine as the Eshet, for domestic use and for sale to other African countries with the exception of Algeria, South Africa and Tunisia.

Valmet Aviation Industries Inc (Finland)

Corporate address: FIN-35600 Halli.
Telephone: +358 42 8291
Facsimile: +358 42 829600
Founded: April 1921.

● Activities

- Operating group of Valmet Corporation, specializing in training aircraft, maintenance, components and assemblies (for Saab). Is also manufacturing parts for, and will assemble, F/A-18C Hornets and engines ordered for the Finnish Air Force.
- Production of the four-seat multi-purpose training and utility L-90 TP RediGO was thought to have ended in December 1994 after 30 production aircraft, of which 10 went to the Finnish Air Force for liaison duties. Others were exported to at least 2 customers (including Mexico's naval aviation school), while a surveillance version with radar had been tested by September 1994 and was then about to be delivered to a customer. However, 2 or more RediGOs were built in 1995, for the Eritrean Republic Air Force.

Valmet L-90 TP RediGO, with a 450 shp (336 kW) Allison 250-B17F turboprop engine (courtesy Valmet)

Arc Atlantique Aviation (France)

Arc Atlantique RF 47 (courtesy Arc Atlantique)

Corporate address: Tours St Symphorien Airport, 37100, Tours.
Telephone: +33 47 51 25 64
Facsimile: +33 47 54 29 49
Information: André Daout.

Arc Atlantique (Fournier) RF 47

First flight: 9 April 1993.
Certification: Undergoing certification under JAR/VLA in 1995.
Role: Two-seat lightplane.
Details: Specifications from June 1995.
Sales/users: About 25 "serious intentions" to order certified aircraft had been received by August 1995. Not available in kit form.
Baggage capacity: Compartment for 44 lb (20 kg).
Wing control surfaces: Ailerons and slotted flaps.
Tail control surfaces: Elevators with trim tab, and rudder.
Construction materials: Principally plywood, but with some composites and fabric.
Engine: Limbach L 2400 EB1 piston engine, with an MT 155 105-1A 2-blade propeller.
Engine rating: 86 hp (64 kW).
Fuel system: 84 litres, of which 80 are usable.
Electrical system: 25 amp alternator and 27 amp-hour battery.
Flight avionics/instrumentation: AlliedSignal Bendix/King KX 125 nav/comm 760 channel transceiver, 200 channel nav receiver (OBS optional), and optional KX 155-KLX 135. Other options are Becker or Narco equipment, GPS and intercom.

DETAILS FOR RF 47.

Principal dimensions:
Wing span: 32 ft 10 ins (10 m)
Maximum length: 21 ft 1.5 ins (6.44 m)
Maximum height: 7 ft 3.5 ins (2.22 m)
Wings:
Area: 117.65 sq ft (10.93 m^2)
Aspect ratio: 9.15
Undercarriage:
Type: Fixed, with nosewheel
Weights:
Empty: 870 lb (395 kg)
Maximum take-off: 1,367 lb (620 kg)
Performance:
Never-exceed speed (Vne): 125 kts (143 mph, 230 km/h
Maximum speed: 108 kts (124 mph) 200 km/h
Cruise speed: 97 kts (112 mph) 180 km/h
Stall speed: 46 kts (53 mph) 85 km/h *clean*, 42 kts (49 mph) 78 km/h with 30° *full flaps*
Take-off over a 50 ft (15 m) obstacle: 1,495 ft (455 m)
Landing over a 50 ft (15 m) obstacle: 1,362 ft (415 m)
Maximum climb rate: 787 ft (240 m) per minute
Ceiling: 16,400 ft (5,000 m)
Duration: 5-6 hours

Aviasud Industries (France)

Corporate address: Zone Industrielle La Palud, 83600 Fréjus Cedex.
Telephone: +33 94 40 19 00
Facsimile: +33 94 52 12 23
Founded: Aviasud has been building aircraft since 1980.
Information: Bernard Collin (President).

● Activities

- In addition to the aircraft detailed below, the Mistral is licence-built in Brazil by Ultraleger for the Brazilian domestic market, and a new side-by-side (staggered) two-seat Cessna-type cabin monoplane is to be launched in 1996, featuring also a nosewheel undercarriage and folding wings. This new aircraft had not been designated by August 1995.

Aviasud AE 206 Mistral

Aviasud AE 206 Mistral and AE 207 Mistral Twin

First flight: 1985.
Role: Ultralight for pilot training, aerial photography, surveillance, agricultural spraying, and banner towing.
Sales/users: Some 250 delivered by August 1995, including about 30 Mistral Twins. No Mistrals had been built in 1995 up to October of that year, when production restarted against orders. Mistral Twin is now only available to order and is not series built. See introduction for Brazilian Mistral construction.
Crew/passengers: 2 seats, side by side.
Control surfaces: All moving bottom wings act as large size ailerons. Slab tailplane with tab and rudder. Manual control.
Construction materials: Mostly composites, but with wooden wing ribs.
Engine: 64.4 hp (48 kW) Rotax 582.
Fuel system: 60 litres.
Aircraft variants:
AE 206 Mistral is the standard version, as described.
AE 206 US was produced as an "Ultra Silent" version, with 3.48:1 reduction gear and a larger propeller.
AE 207 Mistral Twin is a twin-engined version, mainly for aerial work such as surveillance and advertising. Rotax 503 mounted as a pusher on the upper wing, to supplement the existing Rotax 582. Maximum take-off weight 992 lb (450 kg).

DETAILS FOR AE 206.

Principal dimensions:
Wing span: 30 ft 10 ins (9.4 m)
Maximum length: 19 ft 4.5 ins (5.9 m)
Maximum height: 7 ft 4.5 ins (2.25 m)
Wings:
Aerofoil section: NACA 23012
Area: 176.53 sq ft (16.4 m^2)
Aspect ratio: 5.39
Weights:
Empty: 452 lb (205 kg)
Maximum take-off: 860 lb (390 kg)
Performance:
Cruise speed: 70 kts (81 mph) 130 km/h
Minimum speed: 30 kts (34.5 mph) 55 km/h
Take-off distance: 263 ft (80 m)
Maximum climb rate: 787 ft (240 m) per minute
Ceiling: 15,000 ft (4,575 m)
Range: 286 naut miles (329 miles) 530 km

Aviasud AE 209 Albatros

First flight: 1991.
Role: Ultralight monoplane.
Sales/users: Production aircraft No 102 was being assembled in early August 1995.
Crew/passengers: 2 seats, side-by-side, slightly offset to provide more shoulder room.

Aviasud AE 209 Albatros

DETAILS FOR AE 209.

Principal dimensions:
Wing span: 31 ft 10 ins (9.7 m)
Maximum length: 24 ft 2 ins (7.36 m)
Maximum height: 7 ft (2.13 m)
Wings:
Area: 166.84 sq ft (15.5 m^2)
Aspect ratio: 6.07
Undercarriage:
Type: Fixed, with tailwheel. Optional skis. Nosewheel undercarriage version is to be offered
Weights:
Empty: 452 lb (205 kg) with Rotax 503, 507 lb (230 kg) with Rotax 582, and 573 lb (260 kg) with Rotax 912
Maximum take-off: 904 lb (410 kg) with Rotax 503, 992 lb (450 kg) with Rotax 582 and Rotax 912
Performance:
Maximum speed: 76 kts (87 mph) 140 km/h with Rotax 503, 86 kts (99 mph) 160 km/h with Rotax 582, and 94 kts (109 mph) 175 km/h with Rotax 912
Take-off distance: 246 ft (75 m) with a Rotax 582
Landing distance: 213 ft (65 m) with a Rotax 582
Maximum climb rate: 659 ft (201 m) per minute with Rotax 503, 827 ft (252 m) per minute with Rotax 582, and 1,083 ft (330 m) per minute with Rotax 912
Ceiling: 15,000 ft (4,575 m) with a Rotax 582
Range: 281 naut miles (323 miles) 520 km with a Rotax 582

Baggage capacity: 15.89 cu ft (0.45 m^3) behind seats.
Wing characteristics: Can be folded for stowage and transportation by 1 person in under a minute.
Control surfaces: 3-axis, with slab tailplane.
Flight control system: Manual.
Construction materials: Composites (including carbonfibre and Tedlar, and with vacuum or pressure lamination) as well as traditional building methods.
Engine: See Aircraft variants.
Fuel system: 60 litres.
Aircraft variants:
AE 209-50 has a 49.6 hp (37 kW) Rotax 503 engine.
AE 209-64 has a Rotax 64.4 hp (48 kW) 582 engine.
AE 209-80 has a 77.8 hp (58 kW) Rotax 912 engine.
Nosewheel undercarriage version is to be offered.

Dassault Aviation (France)

Corporate address: See Combat section for company details.

● Activities

● As of 15 August 1994, Dassault had delivered 1,116 Falcon jets, including models no longer available. These comprised 226 Falcon 10s and 100s to 174 customers, 476 Falcon 20s to 237 customers, 38 Falcon 200s to 32 customers, 239 Falcon 50s to 180 customers and 137 Falcon 900s to 99 customers, while by then Dassault held 50 options on the Falcon 2000. In addition to passenger transport, Falcons have been used for medevac, maritime surveillance (including F20Gs as HH-25A Guardians with the US Coast Guard, F20s as Gardians with the French Navy and F900s with Japan), photogrammetry, navaid calibration, cargo, electronic monitoring (Canada, Norway and Pakistan), scientific research, military training and more.

Dassault Falcon 50 and 50EX

First flight: 7 November 1976.
Certification: 27 February 1979.
Role: 3-turbofan transcontinental, medium-sized business jet. Successor to the Falcon 20.
Details: Principally for Falcon 50, except under Aircraft variants.
Crew/passengers: Crew of 2 (flight), plus a third cockpit seat, and typically 8 or 9 passengers with a 4-seat front lounge and a 2 seats and sofa rear lounge. Up to 12 passengers with wardrobe and galley removed. Front or rear toilet. Maximum cabin pressure differential 8.85 psi.

Dassault Falcon 50

Baggage capacity: Pressurized compartment of 90 cu ft (2.55 m^3), for up to 2,205 lb (1,000 kg).
Wing control surfaces: Aileron, double-slotted flaps, leading-edge slat, and 3 spoiler/air brakes per wing.
Tail control surfaces: Variable-incidence tailplane, elevators and inset rudder.
Construction materials: Metal, except for carbonfibre ailerons.
Engines: 3 AlliedSignal TFE731-3-1C turbofans.
Engine rating: Each 3,700 lbf (16.46 kN).
Fuel system: 15,520 lb (7,040 kg).
Radar: Honeywell Primus 400 weather radar.
Flight avionics/instrumentation: Rockwell Collins 86C EFIS and 80F autopilot. Choice of long-range navigation and avionic equipment, including satellite communications.
Aircraft variants:
Falcon 50 is the standard version, as detailed.
Falcon 50EX (extended performance) version was launched on 26 April 1995 and will first fly in 1996, with deliveries from 1997. Features 4,250 lbf (18.9 kN) AlliedSignal TFE731-40 turbofans. Time to climb to 41,000 ft (12,500 m) will be 23 minutes. Additional 400 naut miles of range at Mach 0.8. Rockwell Collins Pro Line 4 EFIS (4 screens) and 3 Sextant Avionique liquid crystal engine indicators.

DETAILS FOR FALCON 50.

Principal dimensions:
Wing span: 61 ft 10.5 ins (18.86 m)
Maximum length: 60 ft 9 ins (18.52 m)
Maximum height: 22 ft 10.5 ins (6.975 m)
Fuselage diameter: 6 ft 8 ins (2.03 m)
Cabin:
Length: 23 ft 6 ins (7.16 m)
Width: 6 ft 1.1 ins (1.86 m), or 5 ft 3 ins (1.59 m) at floor
Height: 5 ft 10.87 ins (1.8 m)
Volume: 530 cu ft (15 m^3)
Wings:
Area: 503.75 sq ft (46.8 m^2)
Aspect ratio: 7.6
Undercarriage:
Type: Retractable, with steerable nosewheels. Twin wheels on each unit
Weights:
Empty, equipped: 20,200 lb (9,163 kg)
Maximum take-off: 38,800 lb (17,600 kg)
Maximum landing: 35,715 lb (16,200 kg)
Payload: 4,750 lb (2,155 kg)
Performance:
Maximum permitted operating speed (Vmo): 351-370 kts (403-425 mph) 650-685 km/h IAS
Maximum operating Mach number (Mmo): Mach 0.86
Maximum cruise speed: Mach 0.82 at 35,000 ft (10,650 m), or 470 kts (541 mph) 870 km/h at 31,000 ft (9,450 m)
Landing speed: 123 kts (142 mph) 228 km/h at MLW, or 102 kts (117 mph) 189 km/h with 8 passengers and NBAA IFR reserves, both CAS
Balanced field length: 4,700 ft (1,430 m) at MTOW, or 4,462 ft (1,360 m) with 8 passengers and maximum fuel, both at sea level and ISA
Landing field length: 4,922 ft (1,500 m) at MLW, or 3,560 ft (1,085 m) with 8 passengers and NBAA IFR reserves
Time to climb to 39,000 ft (11,890 m): 30 minutes
Range with 8 passengers: 3,148 naut miles (3,622 miles) 5,830 km with NBAA IFR reserves, or 3,510 naut miles (4,039 miles) 6,500 km with 45 minutes LR reserves

Dassault Falcon 900B and 900EX

First flight: 21 September 1984. Falcon 900EX first flew on 1 June 1995.
Certification: 1986.
Role: 3-turbofan intercontinental, medium-sized, widebody business jet.
Details: Principally for Falcon 900B, except under Aircraft variants.
Crew/passengers: 2 flight crew. Up to 19 passengers. Maximum cabin pressure differential 9.28 psi.
Baggage capacity: 127.13 cu ft (3.6 m^3).
Wing control surfaces: Aileron, double-slotted flaps, leading-edge slat, and 3 spoiler/air brakes per wing. A laminar-flow wing was tested on a Falcon 900 in 1994.
Tail control surfaces: Variable-incidence tailplane, elevators and inset rudder.
Construction materials: Greater use of composites than Falcon 50.
Engines: 3 AlliedSignal TFE731-5BR-1C turbofans.
Engine rating: Each 4,750 lbf (21.13 kN).

Dassault Falcon 900EX, first flown in June 1995

Dassault Falcon 2000

Fuel system: 19,158 lb (8,690 kg).
Radar: Honeywell Primus 870 colour weather radar.
Flight avionics/instrumentation: Bi-directional time multiplexed digital databus, driven by the dual Honeywell SPZ 800 autopilot, connects the laser inertial reference systems that provide heading and attitude reference, air data systems, dual flight management system with incorporated database and 2 sets of EFIS with advanced symbology. FMS may also drive the digital Rockwell Collins Pro Line II radios.
Aircraft variants:
Falcon 900B is the standard version, as detailed.
Falcon 900EX is the extended performance version, for delivery from April 1996 (10 ordered by February 1995). Can carry 8 passengers with the regulation NBAA-IFR reserves over a range of 4,500 naut miles. AlliedSignal TFE731-60 turbofans, each 5,000 lbf (22.24 kN), and the latest Honeywell Primus 2000 avionics. 2 FMSs, with an optional third. HUD optional. Fuel capacity 20,285 lb (9,200 kg). 20% of the total investment from Alenia, AlliedSignal, Hellenic Aircraft Industries, Honeywell, Latécoère and Sabca.

DETAILS FOR FALCON 900B.

Principal dimensions:
Wing span: 63 ft 5 ins (19.33 m)
Maximum length: 66 ft 4 ins (20.21 m)
Maximum height: 24 ft 9.5 ins (7.55 m)
Cabin:
Length: 39 ft (11.9 m)
Width: 7 ft 8.1 ins (2.34 m), or 6 ft 1.2 ins (1.86 m) at floor
Height: 6 ft 1.6 ins (1.87 m)
Volume: 1,267.8 cu ft (35.9 m^3)
Wings:
Area: 527.43 sq ft (49 m^2)
Aspect ratio: 7.63
Weights:
Empty, equipped: 22,608 lb (10,255 lb)
Maximum take-off: 45,503 lb (20,640 kg)
Maximum landing: 42,000 lb (19,050 kg)
Payload: 4,784 lb (2,170 kg)
Performance:
Maximum permitted operating speed (Vmo): 351-370 kts (403-425 mph) 650-685 km/h IAS
Maximum operating Mach number (Mmo): Mach 0.84-87
Maximum cruise speed: Mach 0.85 at 36,000 ft (10,970 m), or 513 kts (590 mph) 950 km/h at 36,000 ft (10,970 m)
Landing speed: 132 kts (152 mph) 244 km/h at MLW, or 106 kts (122 mph) 196 km/h with 8 passengers and NBAA IFR reserves, both CAS
Balanced field length: 4,955 ft (1,510 m) at MTOW, or 4,675 ft (1,425 m) with 8 passengers and maximum fuel, both at sea level and ISA
Landing field length: 5,840 ft (1,780 m) at MLW, or 3,800 ft (1,160 m) with 8 passengers and NBAA IFR reserves
Range with 8 passengers: 3,995 naut miles (4,598 miles) 7,400 km with NBAA IFR reserves

Dassault Falcon 2000

First flight: 4 March 1993.
Certification: 30 November 1994 for JAR 25.
Role: Twin-turbofan, transcontinental, widebody business jet; combines Falcon 50 economy with Falcon 900 comfort.
Sales/users: Customer deliveries began early 1995. First operated by Flicape of South Africa.
Crew/passengers: 2 flight crew (plus a third crew member on a jump seat) and up to 19 passengers. Basic layout is with a forward lounge with 4 seats and 2 tables and a rear lounge with 2 seats, a table and a sofa which is convertible to a couch. Other layouts include a "two and a half" lounge arrangement.
Baggage capacity: 141.26 cu ft (4 m^3), with the option of a further 49.4 cu ft (1.4 m^3) unpressurized volume.
Airframe: Falcon 900 forward fuselage and undercarriage, with wings that only slightly differ from those of the Falcon 50/900.
Engines: 2 CFE Company CFE738-1-1B turbofans.
Engine rating: Each 5,725 lbf (24.47 kN).
Fuel system: 6,865 litres, weighing 12,155 lb (5,513 kg).
Radar: Weather radar.
Flight avionics/instrumentation: Rockwell Collins Pro Line 4, with 7.25 ins (18 cm) EFIS (4 screens) and autopilot, dual comm/nav, AHRS, ADS, ADF, DME and radio altimeter. 3 Sextant Avionique liquid crystal engine indicators. Honeywell FMZ-2000 FMS. Optional HUD for Cat III landing, and TCAS.

DETAILS FOR FALCON 2000.

Principal dimensions:
Wing span: 63 ft 5 ins (19.33 m)
Maximum length: 66 ft 4.5 ins (20.23 m)
Maximum height: 22 ft 11 ins (6.98 m)
Cabin:
Length: 26 ft 2 ins (7.98 m)
Width: 7 ft 8 ins (2.34 m), maximum
Height: 6 ft 2 ins (1.87 m)
Volume: 1,024 cu ft (29 m^3)
Wings:
Area: 527.4 sq ft (49 m^2)
Aspect ratio: 7.625
Weights:
Empty, equipped: 19,700 lb (8,935 kg)
Maximum take-off: 35,000 lb (15,875 kg)
Maximum landing: 33,000 lb (14,968 kg)
Performance:
Maximum operating Mach number: Mach 0.87
Balanced field length: 5,365 ft (1,635 m) with 8 passengers, full fuel, sea level, ISA + 15° C
Landing distance: 2,560 ft (780 m) with 8 passengers, sea level, FAR 91, IFR
Initial climb: 41,000 ft (12,500 m)
Maximum certified altitude: 47,000 ft (14,330 m)
Range: 3,000 naut miles (3,455 miles) 5,560 km with 8 passengers, NBAA-IFR reserves, at Mach 0.8

Dassault Multirole Falcon

Role: Generic term for any version of Falcon when equipped for special roles other than passenger transport, including aerial photography, medevac, calibration, etc. Special systems can also be applied to transport versions for partial or complementary special functions, such as infra-red surveillance, medevac, light cargo transport, etc. Some roles can be operated with a single pilot.

Avions Mudry et Cie (France)

Avions Mudry CAP 10B (courtesy Avions Mudry)

Corporate address: Aérodrome de Bernay, BP 214, 27300 Bernay.
Telephone: +33 32 43 47 34
Facsimile: +33 32 43 47 90
Founded: 1958.
Information: Dominique Roland (Managing Director).

● Activities

- Specializes in single and two-seat aerobatic aircraft, although the CAP 10 B is also widely used for training and the CAP 10 R is for glider towing. The new CAP 232 has replaced the CAP 231 EX and, like EX, has a carbonfibre wing instead of wood. Only the CAP 10B and CAP 232 are currently in production.

	Seats	a) Wing span b) Wing area	Length	Engine	Empty weight	MTOW	Maximum speed kts (mph) km/h	Stall speed kts (mph) km/h	a) Climb rate per minute b) Service ceiling	Roll rate	G limits	Range naut miles (miles) km
CAP 10 B	2	a) 26 ft 5.5 ins (8.06 m) b) 116.79 sq ft (10.85 m^2)	23 ft 6 ins (7.16 m)	180 hp (134 kW) Textron Lycoming AEIO-360-B2F	1,212 lb (550 kg)	1,830 lb (830 kg) utility	146 (168) 270	43.5 (50) 80 with flaps, IAS	a) 1,575 ft (480 m) b) 16,075 ft (4,900 m)		+6, –4.5	540 (621) 1,000
CAP 232	1	a) 24 ft 3 ins (7.40 m) b) !09.8 sq ft (10.2 m^2)	22 ft 2 ins (6.75 m)	300 hp (224 kW) AEIO-540 L1B5D	1,300 lb (590 kg)	1,808 lb (820 kg)	189 (217) 350	57 (65) 105	a) 3,540 ft (1,080 m)	420° per second	±10	648 (745) 1,200

Reims Aviation S.A. (France)

Corporate address: Aérodrome de Reims-Prunay, BP 2745, 51062, Reims Cedex.
Telephone: +33 26 48 46 88
Facsimile: +33 26 49 13 60
Telex: 830 754 F
Founded: Out of Max Holste, originally (but no longer) with Cessna as a 49% shareholder after a February 1960 agreement to produce small Cessna aircraft for European and African markets.
Information: Max Boilami (public relations) and Gérard Bodin (Area Sales Manager).

● Activities

● In addition to building the F 406, Reims was considering re-entering the single-engined aircraft business in line with Cessna's decision, but had not decided up to August 1995, while still also producing parts under sub-contract for Airbus, ATR and Dassault.

Reims F 406

First flight: 22 September 1983.
Certification: 21 December 1984.
Role: Unpressurized utility, commuter, executive, cargo, ambulance, target-towing and training (Caravan II); maritime patrol and surveillance, frontier patrol, pollution control and geo-survey (Vigilant). Based on the Cessna Conquest.
Sales/users: Production deliveries started in 1985 and continued in 1995.
Crew/passengers: 2 crew plus 12 passengers, 6 VIPs, litters or other loads depending on role.
Cargo capacity: Up to a 3,445 lb (1,563 kg) load. Optional large cargo door. Under-fuselage cargo pod is available of 45.9 cu ft (1.3m^3) capacity.

Reims F 406 Vigilant for pollution control with SLAR and line scanner (courtesy Reims)

Wing control surfaces: Ailerons (port trim tab) and Fowler flaps.
Tail control surfaces: Horn-balanced elevators and rudder, with tabs.
Engines: 2 Pratt & Whitney Canada PT6A-112 turboprops, with 7 ft 9 in (2.36 m) propellers.
Engine rating: Each 500 shp (373 kW).
Fuel system: 1,823 litres, of which 1,798 litres are usable.
Electrical system: 28 volt, with 2 engine-driven starter generators and a 39 amp-hour battery.
Hydraulic system: 1,740 psi.
Braking system: Hydraulic disc.
Radar: AlliedSignal Bendix/King RDS 82 weather radar optional. Similar make 1500 radar on French customs aircraft, and GEC-Marconi Seaspray 2000 on Scottish Fishery Protection Agency aircraft (known as Vigilants).
Flight avionics/instrumentation: AlliedSignal Bendix/King Silver Crown, with optional Gold Crown. Other options, include IFR.

DETAILS FOR CARAVAN II.

Principal dimensions:
Wing span: 49 ft 6 ins (15.088 m)
Maximum length: 39 ft (11.893 m)
Maximum height: 13 ft 2 ins (4.008 m)
Cabin:
Length: 18 ft 9 ins (5.712 m) with cockpit
Width: 4 ft 8 ins (1.42 m)
Height: 4 ft 3.5 ins (1.306 m)
Wings:
Aerofoil section: NACA 23018, 23012 (root/tip)
Area: 252.74 sq ft (23.48 m^2)
Aspect ratio: 9.685
Undercarriage:
Type: Retractable, with nosewheel
Weights:
Empty: 5,033 lb (2,283 kg)
Maximum take-off and landing: 9,850 lb (4,468 kg)
Useful load: 4, 892 lb (2,219 kg) maximum
Performance:
Maximum operating speed: 230 kts (265 mph) 426 km/h, design
Stall speed: 98 kts (113 mph) 182 km/h *clean*, 77 kts (89 mph) 143 km/h *landing configuration*, design
Take-off distance: 1,726 ft (526 m)
Maximum climb rate: 1,850 ft (564 m) per minute
Ceiling: 30,000 ft (9,145 m), service
Range with full fuel: 1,152 naut miles (1,326 miles) 2,135 km, with 45 minutes reserve

Avions Robin (France)

Corporate address: 1 route de Troyes, 21121 Darois
Telephone: +33 80 44 20 50
Facsimile: +33 80 35 60 80
Founded: 1969.
Information: Didier Bougarel (Sales Manager).

Robin 200

First flight: 1971 for HR 200/120 B, on which Robin 200 is based.

Robin 200 two-seat lightplane

Role: Two-seat lightplane and trainer.
Sales/users: Production was reinstated in mid-1993, with 18 delivered that year and 17 in 1994.
Cockpit: Entrance via steps and a forward-sliding canopy. Dual controls.
Wing control surfaces: Ailerons and slotted flaps.
Tail control surfaces: Slab tailplane with tabs and rudder.
Flight control system: Manual, except electric flaps.
Construction materials: Metal.
Engine: Textron Lycoming O-235-L2A piston engine.
Engine rating: 118 hp (88 kW).
Fuel system: 120 litres.
Braking system: Disc brakes.
Flight avionics/instrumentation: Can be equipped with a comprehensive set of navaids and blind-flying instruments. VFR night-time illumination is standard.

DETAILS FOR ROBIN 200.

Principal dimensions:
Wing span: 27 ft 4 ins (8.33 m)
Maximum length: 21 ft 9.5 ins (6.64 m)
Maximum height: 6 ft 4.5 ins (1.94 m)
Cabin:
Width: 3 ft 7 ins (1.1 m) at elbow level
Wings:
Area: 134.55 sq ft (12.5 m^2)
Aspect ratio: 5.55
Undercarriage:
Type: Fixed, with steerable nosewheel. Wheel fairings
Weights:
Empty: 1,157 lb (525 kg)
Maximum take-off: 1,719 lb (780 kg)
Performance:
Cruise speed: 120 kts (139 mph) 223 km/h at 75% power, best altitude
Take-off over a 50 ft (15m) obstacle: 1,674 ft (510 m)
Landing over a 50 ft (15m) obstacle: 1,460 ft (445 m)
Maximum climb rate: 768 ft (234 m) per minute
Ceiling: 12,800 ft (3,900 m)
Range: 567 naut miles (652 miles) 1,050 km at 75% power, best altitude, no reserve

Robin DR 400 series

First flight: May 1972.
Certification: 1977.
Role: 2, or 2+2 or four-seat lightplanes.
Sales/users: Well over 1,300 of the series are flying, used by aero clubs, flying schools and private pilots. 49 DR 400s were built in 1994, as for the previous year, with 41 ordered in 1995 (up to July).
Cockpit: Entrance via a forward-sliding canopy. Dual controls. From mid-1993, third window on the rear fuselage was deleted from the /120 and /140 B models.
Baggage capacity: Accessible from the outside on Major and Regent. Capacity 88 lb (40 kg) for Cadet, Dauphins and Major, and 132 lb (60 kg) for Regent and Remos.
Wing control surfaces: Ailerons, flaps and ventral airbrakes.
Tail control surfaces: Slab tailplane with tabs and horn-balanced rudder.
Flight control system: Manual, except for electric flaps.
Construction materials: Wooden airframe, with some composite parts. Wings covered with Dacron fabric.
Engine: See Aircraft variants. New engine cowling from mid-1993.
Fuel system: Optional auxiliary tank is available to the Dauphin 4, Major, Regent and Remo, to increase range by almost 30% without reducing cabin space.

Robin DR 400/140 B Dauphin 4

Flight avionics/instrumentation: Instrument panel designed to integrate a large choice of optional equipment.
Aircraft variants:
DR 400/100 Cadet is the two-seater, powered by a 112 hp (83.5 kW) Textron Lycoming O-235 piston engine and with 110 litres of fuel. Empty weight 1,168 lb (530 kg), gross weight 1,764 lb (800 kg), maximum speed 132 kts (152 mph) 245 km/h, stalling speed 42 kts (49 mph) 78 km/h, climb rate 816 ft (249 m) per minute, and range 510 naut miles (587 miles) 945 km.
DR 400/120 Dauphin 2+2 has 2+2 seating. It is powered by a 118 hp (88 kW) Textron Lycoming O-235 piston engine and has 110 litres of fuel. Empty weight 1,179 lb (535 kg), gross weight 1,984 lb (900 kg), maximum speed 130 kts (150 mph) 241 km/h, stalling speed 44 kts (51 mph) 82 km/h, climb rate 590 ft (180 m) per minute, and range 500 naut miles (576 miles) 928 km.
DR 400/140 B Dauphin 4 is a four-seater, as detailed in the main data box. 155 hp (116 kW) O-320 engine, and 110 litres of fuel standard and 160 with auxiliary tankage.
DR 400/160 Major is a four-seater, powered by a 160 hp (119 kW) Textron Lycoming O-320 piston engine and with 190 litres of fuel standard and 240 litres with auxiliary tankage. Empty weight 1,256 lb (570 kg), gross weight 2,315 lb (1,050 kg), maximum speed 146 kts (168 mph) 271 km/h, stalling speed 50 kts (58 mph) 93 km/h, climb rate 836 ft (255 m) per minute, and range 826 naut miles (950 miles) 1,530 km on standard fuel and 1,026 naut miles (1,180 miles) 1,900 km with auxiliary fuel.
DR 400/180 Regent is a four-seater, powered by a 180 hp (134 kW) Textron Lycoming O-320 piston engine and with 190 litres of fuel standard and 240 litres with auxiliary tankage. Empty weight 1,323 lb (600 kg), gross weight 2,425 lb (1,100 kg), maximum speed 150 kts (173 mph) 278 km/h, stalling speed 51 kts (59 mph) 95 km/h, climb rate 826 ft (252 m) per minute, and range 785 naut miles (904 miles) 1,455 km on standard fuel and 975 naut miles (1,121 miles) 1,805 km with auxiliary fuel.
DR 400/180 R Remo 180 is a four-seater suited also to glider towing, powered by a 180 hp (134 kW) Textron Lycoming O-320 piston engine and with 110 litres of fuel standard and 160 litres with auxiliary tankage. Empty weight 1,235 lb (560 kg), gross weight 2,205 lb (1,000 kg), maximum speed 146 kts (168 mph) 270 km/h, stalling speed 47 kts (54 mph) 87 km/h, climb rate 1,102 ft (336 m) per minute, and range 426 naut miles (491 miles) 790 km on standard fuel and 610 naut miles (702 miles) 1,130 km with auxiliary fuel.
DR 400/200 R Remo 200 is a four-seater suited also to glider towing, powered by a 200 hp (149 kW) Textron Lycoming O-320-A1B6 piston engine and with 110 litres of fuel standard and 160 litres with auxiliary tankage. Empty weight 1,367 lb (620 kg), gross weight 2,425 lb (1,100 kg), cruise speed at 75% power and 5,500 ft (1,675 m) is 135 kts (155 mph) 250 km/h, stalling speed 45 kts (52 mph) 84 km/h at 1,774 lb (800 kg) weight and with flaps, climb rate 1,124 ft (312 m) per minute while towing a 300 kg glider, and range 383 naut miles (441 miles) 710 km on standard fuel and 561 naut miles (646 miles) 1,040 km with auxiliary fuel.

DETAILS FOR DR 400/140 B DAUPHIN 4.

Principal dimensions:
Wing span: 28 ft 7 ins (8.72 m)
Maximum length: 22 ft 10 ins (6.96 m)
Maximum height: 7 ft 4 ins (2.23 m)
Cabin:
Width: 3 ft 7.3 ins (1.1 m) at elbow level
Wings:
Area: 146.39 sq ft (13.6 m^2)
Aspect ratio: 5.59
Weights:
Empty: 1,278 lb (580 kg)
Maximum take-off: 2,204 lb (1,000 kg)
Useful load: 926 lb (420 kg)
Performance:
Maximum speed: 143 kts (165 mph) 265 km/h
Maximum cruise speed: 117 kts (133 mph) 215 km/h
Stall speed: 47 kts (54 mph) 87 km/h
Take-off over a 50 ft (15 m) obstacle: 1,591 ft (485 m)
Landing over a 50 ft (15 m) obstacle: 1,541 ft (470 m)
Maximum climb rate: 865 ft (264 m) per minute
Ceiling: 14,000 ft (4,265 m), service
Range: 464 naut miles (534 miles) 860 km with standard fuel, 740 naut miles (851 miles) 1,370 km with auxiliary fuel

Robin 2160

Certification: 1978. Certified to FAR Pt 23 Aerobatic category.
Role: Two-seat aerobatic lightplane, also suited to basic training and cross-country flying.
Sales/users: Production reinstated in December 1993, with 6 delivered in 1994.
Cockpit: Entrance via a forward-sliding (jettisonable) canopy. Dual controls.

Robin 2160 aerobatic monoplane

Wing control surfaces: Ailerons and slotted flaps.
Tail control surfaces: Slab tailplane with tabs and horn-balanced rudder.
Flight control system: Manual, except for electric flap control.
Construction materials: Aluminium alloy, semi-monocoque structure.
Engine: Textron Lycoming O-320-D2A piston engine, with a Sensenich 74DM6S5-2-64 propeller.
Engine rating: 160 hp (119 kW).
Fuel system: 120 litres, or optional 160 litre tank.
Electrical system: 12 volt, 24 amp-hour battery.
Braking system: Cleveland discs.
Flight avionics/instrumentation: Standard and optional equipment includes airspeed indicator, altimeter, stall warning horn, ball-type slip indicator, magnetic compass, tachometer, accelerometer, AlliedSignal Bendix/King KX155-38 VHF/VOR, KI 208 VOR indicator, KT 76A transponder, GPS and more.

DETAILS FOR 2160.

Principal dimensions:
Wing span: 27 ft 4 ins (8.33 m)
Maximum length: 23 ft 3.5 ins (7.1 m)
Maximum height: 7 ft (2.13 m)
Wings:
Area: 140 sq ft (13 m^2)
Aspect ratio: 5.34
Undercarriage:
Type: Fixed, with steerable and auto-centring nosewheel. Wheel fairings
Weights:
Empty: 1,213 lb (550 kg)
Maximum take-off: 1,764 lb (800 kg) Aerobatic, 1,984 lb (900 kg) Utility.
Performance (Aerobatic category):
Maximum cruise speed: 131 kts (150 mph) 242 km/h at 75% power and 8,500 ft (2,590 m)
Stall speed: 46 kts (53 mph) 85 km/h, with flaps
Take-off over a 50 ft (15 m) obstacle: 1,345 ft (410 m)
Maximum climb rate: 1,023 ft (312 m) per minute
G limits: +6, -3
Ceiling: 15,000 ft (4,575 m), service
Range: 430 naut miles (494 miles) 796 km at 65% power and 11,000 ft (3,350 m), or 363 naut miles (418 miles) 673 km at 75% power and 8,500 ft (2,590 m), both with standard fuel and 45 minutes reserve.

Robin R 3000/160

First flight: 1980.
Role: Four-seat lightplane.
Sales/users: 2 delivered in 1994, following 3 in 1993.
Cockpit: Entrance via retractable step and a forward-sliding canopy. Dual controls. 2 storage boxes under the panel.
Baggage capacity: 15.2 cu ft (0.43 m^3), for 88 lb (40 kg).
Wing characteristics: Winglets to minimize induced drag.

Robin R 3000/160 (courtesy Avions Robin)

Wing control surfaces: Ailerons and slotted flaps.
Tail control surfaces: T-tail with elevator and tabs, and rudder.
Flight control system: Manual, except for electric flaps.
Construction materials: Aluminium alloy.
Engine: Textron Lycoming O-360-A2A piston engine.
Engine rating: 160-180 hp (119-134 kW).
Fuel system: 225 litres.
Electrical system: 12 volt, 60 amp alternator, and 12 volt battery.
Braking system: Hydraulic disc.
Flight avionics/instrumentation: Standard and optional equipment includes airspeed indicator, altimeter, stall warning horn, ball-type slip indicator, magnetic compass, tachometer, and more. Annunciator panel with push to test, pitot heat, flaps down, starter engaged, alternator inoperative, fuel level low, selector off, fuel pressure low and oil pressure low.

DETAILS FOR R 3000/160.

Principal dimensions:
Wing span: 32 ft 2.25 ins (9.81 m)
Maximum length: 24 ft 7.75 ins (7.51 m)
Maximum height: 8 ft 8.75 ins (2.66 m)
Wings:
Area: 155.75 sq ft (14.47 m^2)
Aspect ratio: 6.65
Undercarriage:
Type: Fixed, with steerable and auto-centring nosewheel
Weights:
Empty: 1,433 lb (650 kg)
Maximum take-off: 2,535 lb (1,150 kg)
Useful load: 1,102 lb (500 kg)
Performance:
Maximum speed: 146 kts (168 mph) 270 km/h at sea level
Maximum cruise speed: 138 kts (158 mph) 255 km/h at 75% power and optimum height
Economic cruise speed: 129 kts (148 mph) 238 km/h at 65% power
Stall speed: 49 kts (57 mph) 91 km/h, with flaps
Take-off over a 50 ft (15 m) obstacle: 1,854 ft (565 m)
Landing over a 50 ft (15 m) obstacle: 1,772 ft (540 m)
Maximum climb rate: 875 ft (267 m) per minute, at sea level
G limits: +6, -3
Ceiling: 15,000 ft (4,575 m), service
Range: 869 naut miles (1,000 miles) 1,610 km, at 65% power

Robin X-4 and New four-seater

Aircraft variants:
X-4 is the company technology demonstrator, first flown on 25 February 1991. It has been used to test various aerofoils, including the NASA natural-laminar-flow type in 1994, said to have been highly successful. It has also undertaken drag reduction and enhanced control trials, and has been used to test both composite and combined metal-composite components.
New four-seater has spawned from X-4 trials, and is expected to be a high-performance aircraft with a constant-speed propeller and retractable undercarriage. Construction of the prototype was about 50% complete by July 1995, with the first flight anticipated for 1996.

Socata (France)

Full name: Société de Construction d'Avions de Tourisme et d'Affaires.
Corporate address: See Combat section for company details.

● Activities

● A description of the Omega can be found in the Combat section. In addition, Socata promotes the Skytruck PT for passenger, troop, paratroop/parachutist and cargo transport and medical evacuation roles, details of which can be found under PZL (Poland) in the Airliner section.

Socata TB 30 Epsilon

First flight: 22 December 1979.
Role: Tandem two-seat primary and basic training, screening, formation and aerobatic flying.
Sales/users: Still being promoted in 1995.
Wing control surfaces: Ailerons with tabs (port aileron split) and single-slotted flaps.
Tail control surfaces: Horn-balanced elevators with tabs, and rudder with ground-adjustable tab.
Flight control system: Push-pull rods, manual trims actuated by cables, and electrically actuated flaps.
Construction materials: Metal, except for polyester fabric covering on the elevators and rudder.
Engine: Textron Lycoming AEIO-540-L1B5D piston engine, with a 6 ft 6 ins (1.98 m) Hartzell 2-blade propeller. Christen inverted flight system, for 2 minutes of inverted flight.

Socata Epsilon in Portuguese service

Engine rating: 300 hp (224 kW).
Fuel system: 210 litres.
Electrical system: Busbars distribution. 28 volt, 70 amp alternator. 24 volt, 16 amp-hour ni-cd battery.
Flight avionics/instrumentation: Equipped for blind flying.
Expendable weapons and equipment: Can carry light weapons on 4 underwing pylons when fitted.

DETAILS FOR EPSILON.

Principal dimensions:
Wing span: 26 ft (7.92 m)
Maximum length: 24 ft 11 ins (7.59 m)
Maximum height: 8 ft 7.5 ins (2.63 m)
Wings:
Area: 96.88 sq ft (9 m^2)
Aspect ratio: 6.97
Undercarriage:
Type: Retractable, with castering nosewheel
Weights:
Empty, equipped: 2,046 lb (928 kg) average
Maximum take-off and landing: 2,755 lb (1,250 kg)
Performance:
Never-exceed speed (Vne): 281 kts (323 mph) 520 km/h
Maximum cruise speed: 206 kts (237 mph) 381 km/h at sea level, ISA
Stall speed: 63 kts (72 mph) 116 km/h, landing configuration
Time to 10,000 ft (3,050 m): 7 minutes 40 seconds
G limits: +6.7, -3.35

Socata Rallye 235 F

Role: Basic and instrument training, glider and banner towing, liaison and observation, for use in normal and utility categories.
Crew/passengers: 4 persons. Dual yoke controls.
Baggage capacity: 99 lb (45 kg).
Wing control surfaces: Ailerons with tabs, flaps and leading-edge automatic slats.
Tail control surfaces: Single-piece elevator and rudder, with tabs.
Flight control system: Push-pull rods and cables, but with electrically actuated flaps.
Construction materials: Metal.
Engine: Textron Lycoming O-540-B4B5 piston engine, with a 6 ft 8 ins (2.03 m) Hartzell 2-blade propeller.
Engine rating: 235 hp (175 kW).
Fuel system: 280 litres, of which 270 litres are usable.
Electrical system: 28 volt, 70 amp alternator. 24 volt, 18 to 23 amp-hour ni-cd battery.
Flight avionics/instrumentation: VFR and IFR, according to equipment.

DETAILS FOR RALLYE 235 F.

Principal dimensions:
Wing span: 31 ft 11.5 ins (9.74 m)
Maximum length: 23 ft 10.5 ins (7.28 m)
Maximum height: 9 ft 2 ins (2.8 m)
Wings:
Area: 132.18 sq ft (12.28 m^2)
Aspect ratio: 7.73
Undercarriage:
Type: Fixed, with nosewheel
Weights:
Empty: 1,587 lb (720 kg) average
Maximum take-off and landing: 2,755 lb (1,250 kg)
Useful load: 1,168 lb (530 kg)
Performance:
Maximum cruise speed: 129 kts (149 mph) 239 km/h at 6,000 ft (1,830 m)
Best economy cruise speed: 122 kts (141 mph) 227 km/h at 8,000 ft (2,440 m)
Climb to 10,000 ft (3,050 m): 14 minutes, ISA

Socata Rallye 235 F (courtesy Socata)

Wing control surfaces: Ailerons with tabs, and flaps.
Tail control surfaces: Slab tailplane with anti-balance tab, and rudder with ground-adjustable tab.
Flight control system: Push-pull rods and cables, manual trim actuated by cables and electrically actuated flaps.
Construction materials: Metal.
Engine: Textron Lycoming IO-360-A1B6 piston engine, with a 6 ft 2 ins (1.88 m) Hartzell 2-blade propeller.
Engine rating: 200 hp (149 kW)
Fuel system: 210 litres, of which 204 litres are usable.
Electrical system: 28 volt, 70 amp alternator. 24 volt, 10 amp-hour ni-cd battery. VHF-VOR feeder. VHF antenna.
Flight avionics/instrumentation: VFR or IFR, according to equipment.
Aircraft variants:
Tampico Club TB9 is the low power model, with a 160 hp (119 kW) O-320-D2A engine and 158 litres of fuel. Same dimensions as TB200. Empty weight 1,426 lb (647 kg) and MTOW 2,337 lb (1,060 kg). Maximum cruise speed 107 kts (123 mph) 198 km/h.
Tobago TB10 has a 180 hp (134 kW) O–360-A1AD engine and 210 litres of fuel. Same dimensions as TB200. Empty weight 1,543 lb (700 kg) and MTOW 2,535 lb (1,150 kg). Maximum cruise speed 127 kts (146 mph) 235 km/h.
Tobago XL TB200 is the highest powered version, as detailed.

Details for Trinidad TB20.

Principal dimensions:
Wing span: 32 ft 0.5 ins (9.77 m)
Maximum length: 25 ft 3.5 ins (7.71 m)
Maximum height: 9 ft 4 ins (9.35 m)
Cabin: As for Tobago.
Wings:
Area: 128.09 sq ft (11.9 m^2)
Aspect ratio: 8.02
Undercarriage:
Type: Retractable, with steerable nosewheel
Weights:
Empty: 1,764 lb (800 kg) average
Maximum take-off and landing: 3,086 lb (1,400 kg)
Useful load: 1,323 lb (600 kg)
Performance:
Maximum speed: 167 kts (192 mph) 309 km/h
Maximum cruise speed: 163 kts (188 mph) 301 km/h at 8,500 ft (2,590 m)
Best economy cruise speed: 157 kts (181 mph) 290 km/h at 8,500 ft (2,590 m)
Stall speed: 70 kts (81 mph) 130 km/h *clean*, 59 kts (68 mph) 110 km/h *in landing configuration*
Take-off over a 50 ft (15 m) obstacle: 2,100 ft (640 m)
Landing over a 50 ft (15 m) obstacle: 1,772 ft (540 m)
Maximum climb rate: 1,200 ft (366 m) per minute
Climb to 8,000 ft (2,440 m): 9 minutes, ISA
Ceiling: 20,000 ft (6,100 m)
Range: 885 naut miles (1,019 miles) 1,640 km at 8,000 ft (2,440 m) and 75% power, 966 naut miles (1,112 miles) 1,790 km at 12,000 ft (3,660 m) and 65% power

Socata Tampico Club TB9, Tobago TB10 and Tobago XL TB200

First flight: 9 March 1979 (TB9), 23 February 1977 (TB10) and 27 March 1991 (TB200).

Socata Tobago XL TB200

Certification: 26 April 1979 (TB10).
Role: Basic and instrument flying, proficiency training, and cross-country flying, for operation in the normal category.
Details: Principally for Tobago XL TB200.
Crew/passengers: 4 or 5 persons. Dual yoke controls.
Baggage capacity: 143 lb (65 kg).

Details for Tobago XL TB200.

Principal dimensions:
Wing span: 32 ft 0.5 ins (9.77 m)
Maximum length: 25 ft 3 ins (7.7 m)
Maximum height: 9 ft 11 ins (3.02 m)
Cabin:
Length: 8 ft 3.5 ins (2.53 m)
Width: 4 ft 2.5 ins (1.28 m)
Height: 3 ft 8 ins (1.12 m)
Wings:
Area: 128.09 sq ft (11.9 m^2)
Aspect ratio: 8.02
Undercarriage:
Type: Fixed, with steerable nosewheel. Wheel fairings
Weights:
Empty: 1,576 lb (715 kg) average
Maximum take-off and landing: 2,535 lb (1,150 kg)
Useful load: 959 lb (435 kg)
Performance:
Maximum speed: 140 kts (161 mph) 259 km/h
Maximum cruise speed: 130 kts (149 mph) 240 km/h at 8,500 ft (2,590 m)
Best economy cruise speed: 115 kts (132 mph) 213 km/h at 8,500 ft (2,590 m)
Stall speed: 53 kts (61 mph) 98 km/h, with flaps
Take-off over a 50 ft (15 m) obstacle: 1,558 ft (475 m)
Landing over a 50 ft (15 m) obstacle: 1,476 ft (450 m)
Maximum climb rate: 940 ft (286 m) per minute
Climb to 6,000 ft (1,830 m): 10 minutes, ISA
Ceiling: 13,000 ft (3,960 m)
Range: 648 naut miles (746 miles) 1,200 km at 65% power, with 45 minutes reserve

Socata Trinidad TB20 and TB21

First flight: 14 November 1980 (TB20).
Certification: 18 December 1981.
Role: Advanced instrument training, proficiency training, cross-country flying and business use for TB20, and long-distance and high-speed liaison, cross-country and business for TB21. For use in Normal category.
Crew/passengers: 4 or 5 persons.

Socata Trinidad TB20 (rear) and TB21 (foreground)

Details: Principally for TB20.
Baggage capacity: 143 lb (65 kg).
Control surfaces: Generally as for Tobago.
Construction materials: Metal.
Engine: Textron Lycoming IO-540-C4D5D piston engine, with 6 ft 8 ins (2.03 m) Hartzell 2-blade propeller.
Engine rating: 250 hp (186.4 kW).
Fuel system: 336 litres, of which 326 are usable.
Flight avionics/instrumentation: VFR and IFR, according to equipment.
Aircraft variants:
Trinidad TB20, as detailed.
Trinidad TB21 is similar to TB20 but has a turbocharged TIO-540-AB1AD engine.

Socata TBM 700 and TBM 700 S

First flight: 14 July 1988.
Certification: 31 January 1990. Part 23 Amdt 34 certified for IFR into known icing conditions.
Role: Pressurized business aircraft, and multi-mission aircraft for liaison, training, aerial photography, medevac, target towing, ECM, freight carrying, patrol and law enforcement, and coast watch.
Details: TBM 700, except under Aircraft variants.
Crew/passengers: 6 or 7 including pilot/s.
Cabin: Environmental control system provided by engine bleed-air and bootstrap system. Pressure differential 6.2 psi. 3 emergency oxygen bottles under the seats. Pilot masks with microphone and 4/5 passenger masks.
Baggage capacity: 110 lb (50 kg) in the unpressurized nose compartment, 220 lb (100 kg) in the pressurized aft compartment.
Wing control surfaces: Ailerons (port trim tab), single-slotted Fowler flaps and spoilers.
Tail control surfaces: Balanced elevators and rudder, with trim tabs.
Flight control system: Push-pull rods and cables, except for electric flaps and trim tabs.
Construction materials: Mostly metal, with Nomex honeycomb used in the construction of the tail and control surfaces. Composites wing leading edges and tips, and undercarriage doors.

Socata TBM 700 in French Air Force use

Engine: Pratt & Whitney Canada PT6A-64 turboprop, with a 7 ft 7 ins (2.31 m) Hartzell HC-E4N-3/E9083S(K) 4-blade constant-speed, reverse control, propeller. Foreign object damage (FOD) protection with inertial separator.
Engine rating: 700 shp (522 kW).
Fuel system: 1,100 litres, of which 1,066 are usable.
Electrical system: Bus distribution. 28 volt system with a 5.6 kW starter-generator and auxiliary alternator. 40 amp-hour ni-cd battery.
Braking system: Hydraulic disc.
De-icing system: Pneumatic for wing, tailplane and fin leading edges. Electric for propeller, pitots and windshield. Hot gas for engine air inlets.
Radar: See Aircraft variants and Avionics.
Flight avionics/instrumentation: Variety of avionics suites from Sextant Avionique, AlliedSignal Bendix/King, Magnavox, RCA and Rockwell Collins, according to requirements and role. Options include VHF, UHF, V/UHF, HF, VOR/ILS, Tacan, GPS, Loran, ADF and GNS comm/nav. EFIS. Transponder and IFF. HF and INMARSAT-C. AlliedSignal Bendix/King KFC 275 autopilot and KAS 297C vertical speed/altitude preselector.
Aircraft variants:
TBM 700, as detailed. For aerial photography, it can have a vertically-mounted Leica/Wild or Zeiss camera in the cabin and vertical viewfinder; for freight carrying the floor is reinforced with bonded metal doublers, and tie-down points are available in the 63.57 cu ft (1.8 m³) volume cabin; hard point for an Alkan 6170 B pylon is available under the fuselage for target towing equipment or an ECM unit; a gyrostabilized underfuselage turret can be carried housing an infra-red camera and a video camera for patrol and law enforcement, with an operator's station in the cabin; AlliedSignal RDR 1500 B radar and other equipment (including rescue) for coast watch; etc.
TBM 700S is a stretched version for 2 additional passengers or a 3,417 lb (1,550 kg) useful load. Cabin length increased to 16 ft 11.5 ins (5.169 m), and a 4 ft 1 ins x 3 ft 9 ins (4.05 x 3.77 m) cargo door is installed. PT6A of 850 shp (634 kW).

DETAILS FOR TBM 700 MULTI-MISSIONS.

Principal dimensions:
Wing span: 41 ft 7 ins (12.68 m)
Maximum length: 34 ft 11 ins (10.645 m)
Maximum height: 14 ft 3.5 ins (4.355 m)
Cabin:
Length: 13 ft 3.5 ins (4.05 m)
Width: 3 ft 11.5 ins (1.21 m)
Height: 4 ft (1.22 m)
Wings:
Area: 193.75 sq ft (18 m²)
Aspect ratio: 8.93
Undercarriage:
Type: Retractable, with steerable nosewheel
Weights:
Empty: 4,100 lb (1,860 kg) average
Maximum take-off: 6,579 lb (2,984 kg)
Maximum landing: 6,250 lb (2,835 kg)
Useful load: 2,513 lb (1,140 kg)
Performance:
Maximum cruise speed: 300 kts (345 mph) 555 km/h at 26,000 ft (7,925 m)
Economic cruise speed: 243 kts (280 mph) 450 km/h at 30,000 ft (9,145 m)
Stall speed: 61 kts (71 mph) 113 km/h
Required runway length over a 50 ft (15 m) obstacle: 2,133 ft (650 m)
Maximum climb rate: 1,875 ft (572 m) per minute at sea level
Climb to 20,000 ft (6,100 m): 11 minutes 45 seconds, ISA
Ceiling: 30,000 ft (9,145 m) certified
Range: 1,170 naut miles (1,347 miles) 2,166 km with 6 persons and 132lb (60 kg) of baggage, or 1,650 naut miles (1,900 miles) 3,055 km with 4 persons and full fuel, both at 240 kts and FL300, with 45 minutes reserve

Extra Flugzeugbau GmbH (Germany)

Corporate address: Flugplatz Dinslaken Schwarze Heide, 46569 Hünxe.
Telephone: +49 2858 91370
Facsimile: +49 2858 913730
Employees: 60.
Information: Wolfgang Lukas.

Extra 300 series

First flight: 6 May 1988.
Certification: 16 May 1990.
Role: Pilot only (Extra 300 S) or tandem 2-seat unlimited aerobatic competition monoplane.
Details: Principally for the Extra 300.
Wing control surfaces: Ailerons.
Tail control surfaces: Elevators (starboard trim tab) and horn-balanced rudder.
Flight control system: Push-pull rod and cable.
Construction materials: Composites wings and tail unit. Steel tube fuselage structure, with aluminium and fabric skins.
Engine: Textron Lycoming AEIO-540-L1B5 piston engine, with an MTV-9-B-C/C200-15 3-blade constant-speed propeller.
Engine rating: 300 hp (224 kW).
Fuel system: 158 litres usable.
Electrical system: 12 volt generator. Battery.

Extra 300L

Aircraft variants:
Extra 300 2-seater, as detailed.
Extra 300 S is a single-seat variant of the Extra 300, with a 24 ft 7 ins (7.5 m) wing span and new ailerons, length of 21 ft 10 ins (6.65 m), and maximum cruise speed of 185 kts (213 mph) 343 km/h. Roll rate 380° per second.
Extra 300L is a low-wing monoplane (instead of mid-wing), although wing area remains similar. Deeper ailerons. Fuselage shortened by some 10-12 ins (25-30 cm). Many other small changes, including carbon seats, electric rear-seat adjustment, etc. Roll rate increased to 400° per second.

DETAILS FOR EXTRA 300.

Principal dimensions:
Wing span: 26 ft 3 ins (8 m)
Maximum length: 23 ft 4.5 ins (7.12 m)
Maximum height: 8 ft 7 ins (2.62 m)
Wings:
Aerofoil section: MA-15/MA-12 (root/tip)
Area: 115.17 sq ft (10.7 m²)
Aspect ratio: 5.981
Undercarriage:
Type: Fixed, with steerable tailwheel. Mainwheel fairings
Weights:
Empty: 1,470 lb (666 kg)
Maximum take-off and landing: 2,094 lb (950 kg) Normal category, or 1,918 lb (870 kg) Aerobatic
Performance:
Never-exceed speed (Vne): 220 kts (253 mph) 407 km/h
Maximum speed: 185 kts (213 mph) 343 km/h
Maximum cruise speed: 178 kts (205 mph) 330 km/h
Maximum manoeuvre speed: 158 kts (182 mph) 292 km/h
Stall speed: 55 kts (63.5 mph) 102 km/h
Maximum climb rate: 3,200 ft (975 m) per minute
Roll rate: 340° per second.
G limits: ±8 with 2 crew at 1,918 lb (870 kg) MTOW, or ±10 with pilot only at 1,810 lb (821 kg) MTOW, or +6, -3 Normal category
Range: 415 naut miles (478 miles) 768 km with 45 minutes reserve
Duration: 2 hours 30 minutes

Extra 400

First flight: Expected around October 1995.
Certification: 1996 (designed to FAR 23), including IFR and flying into known icing conditions.
Role: Pressurized six-seat touring high-wing monoplane.
Construction materials: Composites.
Engine: Teledyne Continental TSIOL-550-A engine.
Engine rating: 350 hp (261 kW).
Fuel system: 470 litres.

DETAILS FOR EXTRA 400.

Principal dimensions:
Wing span: 34 ft 5.5 ins (11.5 m)
Maximum length: 30 ft 10 ins (9.39 m)
Maximum height: 10 ft 2 ins (3.09 m)
Cabin:
Width: 4 ft 7 ins (1.39 m)
Height: 4 ft 1 ins (1.24 m)
Weights:
Empty: 2,769 lb (1,256 kg)
Maximum take-off: 4,409 lb (2,000 kg)
Payload: 1,217 lb (552 kg)
Performance:
Maximum speed: 259 kts (298 mph) 480 km/h
Cruise speed: 243 kts (280 mph) 450 km/h at 75% power
Stall speed: 60 kts (69 mph) 111 km/h with full flaps
Range: 918 naut miles (1,057 miles) 1,700 km with 6 persons, or 1,404 naut miles (1,616 miles) 2,600 km with 5 persons

Burkhart Grob Luft-und Raumfahrt GmbH & Co KG (Germany)

Corporate address: See Reconnaissance section for company details.

Grob G 115 series

First flight: November 1985.
Certification: 22 March 1987.
Role: Lightplanes, trainers and aerobatic (not G 115 C) aircraft.
Details: G 115 T, except under Aircraft variants.
Crew/passengers: 2 seats, side by side. Control sticks.
Wing control surfaces: Ailerons and flaps.
Tail control surfaces: Balanced elevators (port trim tab) and rudder.
Flight control system: Manual, except for electric flaps.
Construction materials: Composites.
Engine: Textron Lycoming AEIO-540-D4A5 piston engine, with a 3-blade constant-speed propeller.
Engine rating: 260 hp (194 kW).
Fuel system: 280 litres usable.
Flight avionics/instrumentation: Customer choice. Can be IFR equipped.
Aircraft variants:
G 115 C is the Utility version, not intended for aerobatic training. 160 hp (119 kW) Textron Lycoming O-320-D1A with a Sensenich 2-blade fixed-pitch propeller, or 180 hp (134 kW) O-360-A1F6 engine with a Hartzell/McCauley 2-blade constant-speed propeller. Fixed undercarriage. Control wheels, with sticks optional.
G 115 D is an Aerobatic aircraft, also suited to Utility. Choice of 160 hp (119 kW) Textron Lycoming AEIO-320-D1B engine with a Hoffmann 2-blade propeller, or 180 hp (134 kW) AEIO-360-B1F engine with a Hoffmann 3-blade propeller. Fixed undercarriage. Control sticks. Recent orders include that placed by the Royal Navy under the name Heron, to replace the Chipmunk for pilot screening.

Grob G 115 D2 for Royal Navy flying grading by Shorts (courtesy Shorts)

DETAILS FOR GROB G 115 T.

Principal dimensions:
Wing span: 32 ft 10 ins (10 m)
Maximum length: 26 ft 11 ins (8.2 m)
Maximum height: 8 ft 5 ins (2.57 m)
Wings:
Aerofoil section: Eppler 696
Area: 131.42 sq ft (12.2 m^2)
Aspect ratio: 8.2
Undercarriage:
Type: Retractable, with steerable nosewheel
Weights:
Empty: 1,874 lb (850 kg)
Maximum take-off: 2,866 lb (1,300 kg)
Payload: 772 lb (350 kg)
Performance:
Maximum speed: 178 kts (205 mph) 330 km/h
Cruise speed: 165 kts (190 mph) 306 km/h, at 75% power and 5,000 ft (1,525 m), ISA
Stall speed: 57 kts (66 mph) 106 km/h
Take-off over a 50 ft (15 m) obstacle: 1,840 ft (561 m) at sea level, ISA
Maximum climb rate: 1,400 ft (427 m) per minute
G limits: +6, -4
Range: 707 naut miles (814 miles) 1,310 km at 45% power and 5,000 ft (1,525 m), ISA, 45 minutes reserve

G 115 T is an Aerobatic version with a retractable undercarriage, as detailed. Launch customer is the United Arab Emirates Air Force, which ordered 12 plus 12 options for a ground-attack training role, for delivery from 1997.

Grob GF 200, GF 300 and GF 350

Details: For GF 200, except under Aircraft variants.
First flight: 26 November 1991.
Certification: Complies to FAR Pt 23, with JAR/FAR certification anticipated for the end of 1995.
Role: Pressurized lightplane.
Crew/passengers: Pilot plus 3 or 4 passengers.
Baggage capacity: 110 lb (50 kg).
Wing characteristics: Multi-curvature leading edge and straight trailing edge, with upturned wingtips.
Wing control surfaces: Fowler flaps.
Tail control surfaces: T-tail, with variable incidence tailplane and elevators. Dorsal and ventral fins, with a ventral rudder only in production form.
Construction materials: Composites.
Engine: Teledyne Continental piston engine, with a pusher propeller at the tail driven by a carbonfibre reinforced plastics shaft.
The engine is installed on the aircraft's centre of gravity and its position reduces noise. Prototype had a Textron Lycoming TIO-540.
Engine rating: 310 hp (231 kW).
Fuel system: 350 litres.
Electrical system: 28 volt, 70 amp.
Aircraft variants:
GF 200 is the initial production version, as detailed.
GF 300 is an intended six-seat turboshaft version, with pressurization and a de-icing system. Cruise speed 243 kts (280 mph) 450 km/h.
GF 350 is an intended six/eight-seat version, with twin turboshafts and a cruise speed of 302 kts (348 mph) 560 km/h.

Grob GF 200 prototype (courtesy Grob)

DETAILS FOR GROB GF 200.

Principal dimensions:
Wing span: 36 ft 1 ins (11 m)
Maximum length: 28 ft 6.5 ins (8.7 m)
Maximum height: 11 ft 3 ins (3.42 m)
Wings:
Area: 134.55 sq ft (12.5 m^2)
Aspect ratio: 9.68
Undercarriage:
Type: Retractable, with nosewheel
Weights:
Maximum take-off: 3,748 lb (1,700 kg)
Payload: 1,323 lb (600 kg)
Performance:
Maximum cruise speed: 226 kts (261 mph) 420 km/h at 8,000 ft (2,440 m)
Cruise speed, 75% power: 202 kts (232 mph) 374 km/h at 22,000 ft (6,700 m)
Take-off distance: 1,188 ft (362 m)
Maximum climb rate: 1,221 ft (366 m) per minute
Range at 45% power: 1,272 naut miles (1,464 miles) 2,356 km at 13,000 ft (3,960 m), or 1,244 naut miles (1,431 miles) 2,304 km at 22,000 ft (6,700 m), both with 45 minutes reserve

RFB Rhein-Flugzeugbau GmbH (Germany)

Corporate address: See Combat section for company details.

RFB MFI-10 C Vipan

▲ Development

▲ MFI-Vipan was designed to a specification of the Royal Swedish Aeroclub and Swedish Board of Defence, first appearing in 1961.
Role: Four-seat STOL utility lightplane.
Wing control surfaces: Frise ailerons and split flaps.
Tail control surfaces: Variable-incidence tailplane. Single-piece horn-balanced elevator, and rudder with tab.
Construction materials: Fuselage has a steel tube cabin structure, with all other construction of metal sandwich using 2 thin aluminium sheets bonded to an aluminium honeycomb core.
Engine: Textron Lycoming IO-360-A piston engine, with a 3-blade constant-speed propeller.
Engine rating: 200 hp (149 kW).
Fuel system: 200 litres.

RFB MFI-10C Vipan (courtesy RFB)

Details for RFB Vipan, under Normal category.

Principal dimensions:
Wing span: 34 ft 10 ins (10.61 m)
Maximum length: 26 ft (7.92 m)
Maximum height: 7 ft (2.13 m)
Wings:
Area: 168.99 sq ft (15.7 m^2)
Aspect ratio: 7.17
Undercarriage:
Type: Fixed, with steerable tailwheel
Weights:
Empty: 1,433 lb (650 kg)
Maximum take-off: 2,586 lb (1,173 kg)
Performance:
Maximum permissible diving speed: 163 kts (187 mph) 302 km/h
Maximum speed: 132 kts (152 mph) 244 km/h at sea level
Cruise speed: 124 kts (143 mph) 230 km/h at 75% power and 7,500 ft (2,300 m)
Landing speed: 46 kts (53 mph) 85 km/h
Take-off distance: 509 ft (155 m)
Maximum climb rate: 748 ft (228 m) per minute
Ceiling: 15,750 ft (4,800 m), service
Range: 594 naut miles (683 miles) 1,100 km
Note: *Under Utility category operations, landing speed and take-off distance are reduced, and service ceiling and climb rate are increased

Ruschmeyer Aircraft Production KG (Germany)

Corporate address: Segelfliegerweg 41, D-49324 Melle-Flugplatz.
Telephone: +49 54 22 94 93-0
Facsimile: +49 54 22 94 93-99
Founded: 1987.

Ruschmeyer R90 series

First flight: 8 August 1988.
Certification: June 1992 (LBA), 24 June 1994 (FAA) for R90-230 RG. Certified to FAR/JAR Pt 23 Amdt 24.
Details: Principally for R90-230 RG.
Role: Touring lightplane and basic IFR trainer for private and commercial pilots.
Crew/passengers: 4 persons. Dual controls.
Cockpit: Gull-wing doors.
Baggage capacity: 28.25 cu ft (0.8 m^3) for 110 lb (50 kg). Accessible from outside.
Wing characteristics: Low mounted, with leading-edge stall strips and upturned wingtips for improved lateral stability.
Wing control surfaces: Ailerons with some differential movement, and 3-position Fowler flaps (port tab).
Tail control surfaces: Elevators (port trim/anti-servo tab) and rudder.
Flight control system: Push-pull rods. Electric flaps.
Construction materials: BASF Palatal A430 resin fibre composite material (RFCM), even for primary structures. Ruschmeyer claims for RFCM include durability up to 72 ° C, improved material strength, and structural field repair without special tools. Airframe structure is certified for 18,000 flight hours, while tests have simulated 54,000 hours without structural fatigue.
Engine: Textron Lycoming IO-540-C4D5 piston engine, with 4-blade constant-speed propeller. By flat rating the engine to 2,400 rpm, by employing a special acoustically high damping exhaust system, and by use of the MTV-14-B propeller, noise levels are 8.1 dB below ICAO Annex 16 Chapter 6 and 10.2 dB below ICAO Annex 16 Chapter 10 limits.
Engine rating: 230 hp (171.5 kW).
Fuel system: 250 litres, of which 236 litres are usable.

Ruschmeyer R90-230 RG

Aircraft variants:
R90-180 RG will be certified in 1996. 4 seats, 180 hp (134 kW) O-360 engine and retractable undercarriage. Gross weight 2,535 lb (1,150 kg). Maximum speed 130 kts (150 mph) 240 km/h.
R90-230 FG is a fixed undercarriage version of the R90-230 RG. Empty weight 1,874 lb (850 kg).
R90-230 RG is a retractable gear version of FG.
R90-300 T-RG is under development for production in 1998. Four-seater, with a supercharged 300 hp (224 kW) engine and 400 litres of fuel. Gross weight 3,417 lb (1,550 kg). Maximum speed 240 kts (276 mph) 445 km/h.
R90-420 AT is a four-seat turboprop version, first flown on 2 November 1993. Deliveries from 1997. 470 shp (350 kW) Allison 250-B20 turboprop engine. Gross weight 3,197 lb (1,450 kg). Maximum cruise speed 243 kts (280 mph) 450 km/h. Noise level 14 dB(A) below ICAO limit.

Details for Ruschmeyer R90-230 RG.

Principal dimensions:
Wing span: 31 ft 2 ins (9.5 m)
Maximum length: 26 ft (7.93 m)
Maximum height: 8 ft 11.5 ins (2.73 m)
Cabin:
Length: 9 ft 4.5 ins (2.86 m)
Width: 3 ft 9 ins (1.14 m)
Height: 4 ft 1 ins (1.24 m)
Wings:
Aerofoil section: Wortmann laminar flow
Area: 139.28 sq ft (12.94 m^2)
Aspect ratio: 6.97
Undercarriage:
Type: Retractable, with nosewheel. Trailing link type, with electrohydraulic actuation
Turning radius: 20 ft 6 ins (6.24 m)
Weights:
Empty: 1,980 lb (898 kg)
Maximum take-off and landing: 2,976 lb (1,350 kg)
Useful load: 996 lb (452 kg)
Performance:
Maximum speed: 175 kts (201 mph) 324 km/h
Cruise speed: 168 kts (193 mph) 311 km/h at 6,000 ft (1,830 m) and 85% power, or 144 kts (166 mph) 267 km/h at 9,000 ft (2,740 m) and 55% power, or 110 kts (126 mph) 204 km/h at 3,000 ft (915 m) at 38% power
Stall speed: 67 kts (77 mph) 124 km/h *clean*, 58 kts (67 mph) 107 km/h *in landing configuration*
Take-off over a 50 ft (15 m) obstacle: 1,706 ft (520 m)
Landing over a 50 ft (15 m) obstacle: 1,575 ft (480 m) at 2,557 lb (1,160 kg)
Maximum climb rate: 1,140 ft (347 m) per minute at MTOW
Climb to 10,000 ft (3,050 m): 12 minutes at MTOW
G limits: +3.8, -1.52 certified;. +9 design
Ceiling: 16,000 ft (4,875 m) at MTOW, 20,000 ft (6,100 m) at 2,425 lb (1,100 kg) AUW
Range: 870 naut miles (1,001 miles) 1,611 km, with 45 minutes reserve
Duration: 7.8 hours

Ruschmeyer R95

Certification: Intended for certification under JAR 23 Normal category.
Role: Next-generation, pressurized, 5 passenger, cross-country light aircraft. Will be offered with a variety of engine, interior and exterior options.
Baggage capacity: More area than R90.
Engine: Turbocharged piston or turboprop engine choices.
De-icing system: Capable of flying into known icing conditions.
Flight avionics/ instrumentation: Latest avionics as standard.

Details for R95.

Cabin: Larger than R90
Weights:
Empty: 2,712 lb (1,230 kg)
Maximum take-off: 4,409 lb (2,000 kg)
Useful load: 1,697 lb (770 kg)
Performance:
Maximum cruise speed: 259 kts (298 mph) 480 km/h
Economical cruise speed: 238 kts (274 mph) 440 km/h
Maximum climb rate: 1,300 ft (396 m) per minute
Ceiling: 17,700-24,000 ft (5,400-7,300 m)
Range: 1,403 naut miles (1,615 miles) 2,600 km

Ganz AVIA Kft (Hungary)

Corporate address: 1087 Budapest, Kõbányal út 21 (office); PO Box 62, 1475 Budapest (postal address).
Telephone: +36 1 210 1150
Facsimile: +36 1 133 7783
Founded: Development institute of the Ganz Machinery Works Holding Ltd.
Information: Miklós Deák (Managing Director).

Ganz AVIA GAK-22 Dino

First flight: October 1993.
Certification: Meets JAR/FAR Pt 23 Aerobatic requirements.
Role: Two-seat light multi-purpose and aerobatic biplane, with dual controls. Suited to private, training, agricultural, light transport and military uses.
Sales/users: The prototype was tested between October 1993 and October 1994. As a result of these tests, a new aircraft has been constructed with a 180 hp (134 kW) engine, suited to aerobatics. Considerable interest has been expressed in the Dino, though by

Ganz AVIA GAK-22 Dino

November 1994 contracts had not been concluded. The price for the production aircraft will be GBP 61,000.
Baggage capacity: Luggage rack.
Wing characteristics: Negative stepped biplane, with cantilever surfaces. Intended to avoid spinning.
Wing control surfaces: Combined ailerons-flaps on the lower wings only.
Tail control surfaces: One-piece horn-balanced elevator with tab and a horn-balanced rudder.
Flight control system: Push rods. Combined control system between the ailerons-flaps and elevator, resulting in the ailerons-flaps being lowered when the elevator is raised.
Construction materials: Fuselage has a welded steel tube structure, with aluminium skins for the cabin area, fabric at the rear and a composites engine cowling. Wings have 3 ft 7 ins (1.09 m) negative stagger and are single-spar structures of aluminium alloy, but with fabric covering aft of the leading edge. Tail surfaces are of similar construction to the wings, though the moving surfaces are fabric covered.
Engine: Textron Lycoming O-235-H2C piston engine in the prototype, with a 5 ft 11 ins (1.8 m) Mühlbauer 2-blade propeller. 180 hp (134 kW) engine in production aircraft, with a variable-pitch propeller for Aerobatics.
Engine rating: 115 hp (85.75 kW).
Fuel system: 100 litres, weighing 176 lb (80 kg).
Flight avionics/instrumentation: To customer's requirements.
Aircraft variants:
GAK-22 Dino is the two-seater, as detailed.
Four-seat version was expected to fly in prototype form in the latter part of 1995.

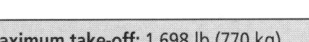

DETAILS FOR GAK-22 DINO 115 HP PROTOTYPE.

Principal dimensions:
Wing span: 25 ft 3 ins (7.7 m)
Maximum length: 20 ft 2 ins (6.1 m)
Maximum height: 8 ft 6.5 ins (2.6 m)
Wings:
Area: 150.69 sq ft (14 m^2)
Undercarriage:
Type: Fixed, with nosewheel. Cantilever spring main legs. Wheel fairings
Weights:
Empty: 948 lb (430 kg)
Maximum take-off: 1,587 lb (720 kg)
Performance:
Maximum speed: 105 kts (121 mph) 195 km/h
Cruise speed: 97 kts (112 mph) 180 km/h
Take-off distance: 771 ft (235 m)
Range: 378 naut miles (435 miles) 700 km

Bharat Heavy Electricals Ltd (India)

Corporate address: Heavy Electrical Equipment Plant, Ranipur (Hardwar) 249 403 U.P.
Telephone: +91 133 426457, 427350-427359
Facsimile: +91 133 426462, 426254
Information: H. W. Bhatnagar (General Manager – Aviation).

BHEL Swati

First flight: 17 November 1990 (with a Rolls-Royce Continental O-240-A engine and tailwheel undercarriage).
Certification: January 1992. Designed to comply with FAR Pt 23 Utility and Normal categories.
Role: Two-seat lightplane, suited also to training and other uses. Designed by the Technical Centre of Directorate General of civil aviation in India.
Details: Production version.
Wing control surfaces: Ailerons and plain flaps.
Tail control surfaces: Elevators and rudder.

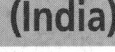

Bharat (BHEL) Swati

DETAILS FOR BHEL SWATI IN UTILITY CATEGORY.

Principal dimensions:
Wing span: 30 ft 3 ins (9.2 m)
Maximum length: 23 ft 8 ins (7.21 m)
Maximum height: 9 ft 1.5 ins (2.78 m)
Wings:
Aerofoil section: NASA GA(W)-1
Area: 128.74 sq ft (11.96 m^2)
Aspect ratio: 7.077
Undercarriage:
Type: Fixed, with steerable nosewheel
Weights:
Empty: 1,168 lb (530 kg)
Maximum take-off: 1,698 lb (770 kg)
Performance:
Never-exceed speed (Vne): 145 kts (167 mph) 268 km/h
Maximum and cruise speed: 105 kts (121 mph) 195 km/h
Stall speed: 41 kts (48 mph) 76 km/h
Take-off distance: 850 ft (259 m)
Landing distance: 660 ft (201 m)
Maximum climb rate: 670 ft (204 m) per minute
G limits: +4.4, –1.76
Ceiling: 10,000 ft (3,050 m), service
Range: 245 naut miles (282 miles) 453 km
Duration: 2 hours 45 minutes

Flight control system: Manual.
Construction materials: Fuselage of chromoly steel tube, with fabric covering aft and metal and composites forward. Metal tail surfaces. Wooden wings.
Engine: Textron Lycoming O-235-N2C piston engine, with a 5 ft 10 ins (1.78 m) Hoffmann HO 14-178115 fixed-pitch, 2-blade, wood/composites propeller.
Engine rating: 116 hp (86.5 kW).
Fuel system: 90 litres.
Braking system: Hydraulic mainwheel brakes.
Flight avionics/instrumentation: VFR instrumentation. Optional radio.

Hindustan Aeronautics Limited (HAL) (India)

Corporate address: See Combat section for company details.

HAL HPT-32 Deepak

First flight: 6 January 1977.

HAL HPT-32 Deepak (Denis Hughes)

Role: Two-seat primary trainer, designed to replace the HT-2. Also capable of other training roles. Utility roles include towing.
Sales/users: Production for the Indian armed forces began in about 1980. An estimated 110 are in Indian Air Force use and 8 in Navy.
Wing control surfaces: Ailerons (with geared and ground tabs) and plain flaps.

Details for HPT-32 Deepak.

Principal dimensions:
Wing span: 31 ft 2 ins (9.5 m)
Maximum length: 25 ft 4 ins (7.72 m)
Maximum height: 9 ft 5 ins (2.88 m)
Wings:
Area: 161.46 sq ft (15 m^2)
Aspect ratio: 6.017
Undercarriage:
Type: Fixed, with nosewheel
Weights:
Empty: 1,962 lb (890 kg)
Maximum take-off and landing: 2,755 lb (1,250 kg)
Performance:
Maximum cruise speed: 115 kts (132 mph) 213 km/h at 10,000 ft (3,050 m)
Stall speed: 60 kts (68 mph) 110 km/h with flaps
Take-off distance: 1,135 ft (345 m)
Landing distance: 722 ft (220 m)
Maximum climb rate: 1,100 ft (335 m) per minute at sea level
G limits: +6, –3
Ceiling: 18,000 ft (5,500 m)
Range: over 400 naut miles (460 miles) 740 km

Tail control surfaces: Single-piece elevator (with geared and trim tabs) and rudder (with trim tab).
Flight control system: Mechanical.
Construction materials: Metal.
Engine: Textron Lycoming AEIO-540-D4B5 piston engine.
Engine rating: 260 hp (194kW).
Fuel system: 220 litres plus a small collector tank.
Electrical system: 28 volt DC supply, with 70 amp alternator. 24 volt ni-cd battery.
Braking system: Hydraulic discs.
Flight avionics/instrumentation: Includes UHF and VHF communications.

National Aeronautical Laboratory (NAL) (India)

Corporate address: PO Bag 1779, Kodihalli, Bangalore 560 017.
Telephone: +91 80 573351

● Activities

● Include the development of the Hansa, now in production by Taneja, and joint development of the M-102 Duet with Myasishchev of Russia (see Multinational section), for production at Smolensk and Nasik (latter by HAL).

Taneja Aerospace and Aviation Ltd (TAAL) (India)

TAAL (NAL) Hansa (courtesy TAAL)

Corporate address: 305 Mota Chambers, 9 Cunningham Road, Bangalore 560 052.
Telephone: +91 80 2250751, 2258619, 2258730
Facsimile: +91 80 2253214
Telex: 0845-8624
Founded: Subsidiary of The Indian Seamless Metal Tubes Ltd company, and the first private sector company in India to venture into aircraft manufacturing, starting its manufacturing activities in April 1993 and flying its first aircraft (a licence-built Partenavia P.68 Observer 2) on 17 March 1994.
Information: Vinod Singel.

■ Facilities

■ Production plant at Hosur in Tamilnadu.

● Activities

● In addition to aircraft manufacturing, maintenance and servicing, TAAL has started a Flying Training Academy to train aircraft maintenance engineers and civil pilots.
● Under licence from Partenavia of Italy, TAAL manufactures in India the P68-C, P68C-TC, P68 Observer and AP68TP-600 Viator. Plans called for 6 aircraft in the year 1994-95, 7 in 1995-96 and 10 per year thereafter. Potential capacity is 24 aircraft a year. 4 ordered by October 1994, with 5 then in negotiation. Exports are anticipated to Bangladesh and Sri Lanka.
● TAAL is manufacturing the Hansa, developed by NAL with TAAL participation.

TAAL (NAL) Hansa

First flight: 17 November 1993.
Certification: FAR Pt 23.
Role: Two-seat lightplane and trainer, with dual controls.
Sales/users: Manufacture started in 1995.
Wing control surfaces: Ailerons and flaps.
Tail control surfaces: Horn-balanced elevators (port tab) and rudder.
Construction materials: Composites.
Engine: Teledyne Continental IO-240 piston engine.
Engine rating: 125 hp (93.2 kW).
Fuel system: 220.5 lb (100 kg).

Details for TAAL Hansa.

Principal dimensions:
Wing span: 34 ft 4 ins (10.47 m)
Maximum length: 23 ft 9.5 ins (7.25 m)
Maximum height: 8 ft 10 ins (2.7 m)
Wings:
Area: 134.23 sq ft (12.47 m^2)
Aspect ratio: 8.79
Undercarriage:
Type: Fixed, with nosewheel
Weights:
Empty: 1,235 lb (560 kg)
Maximum take-off: 1,874 lb (850 kg)
Payload: 463 lb (210 kg)
Performance:
Maximum cruise speed: 115 kts (132 mph) 213 km/h at sea level
Stall speed: 53 kts (61 mph) 98 km/h *clean*, 47 kts (54 mph) 87 km/h *with flaps*
Maximum climb rate: 699 ft (213 m) per minute at sea level
Duration: 4 hours

H.F. Dorna Co (Iran)

Corporate address: No 4 Satary St, Mirmotahary Avenue, Seyed Khandan, Tehran 15419.
Telephone: +98 21 868704
Facsimile: +98 21 862590
Founded: 1989.
Information: Y. Antesary (Managing Director).

H.F. Dorna Two

First flight: 1995.
Certification: Meets JAR-VLA requirements.
Role: Two-seat composites touring lightplane.
Wing characteristics: Low-wing monoplane, with constant chord.
Wing control surfaces: Ailerons and plain flaps.
Tail control surfaces: Elevators (with trim) and rudder.
Flight control system: Pushrod and cables, except for electric trim and possibly flaps.
Engine: Teledyne Continental IO-240 piston engine, with an MT Propeller fixed- or variable-pitch 2-blade propeller.
Engine rating: 125 hp (93 kW).
Fuel system: About 130 litres.
Electrical system: 12 volt DC supply, via a 60 amp alternator and 12 volt, 35 amp-hour battery.
Braking system: Mainwheel brakes.
Flight avionics/instrumentation: Conventional VFR.

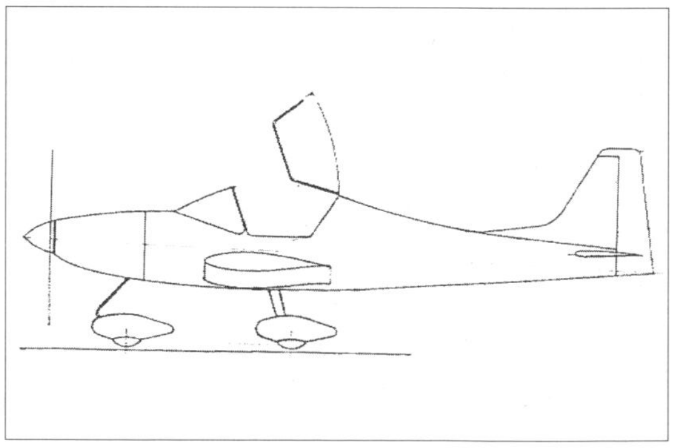

H.F.Dorna Two (courtesy Dorna)

Details for H.F. Dorna Two.

Principal dimensions:
Wing span: 30 ft 6 ins (9.3 m)
Maximum length: 19 ft 9 ins (6.017 m)
Maximum height: 6 ft 5 ins (1.96 m)
Wings:
Area: 117.11 sq ft (10.88 m^2)
Aspect ratio: 7.949
Undercarriage:
Type: Fixed, with nosewheel. Cantilever mixed construction legs, with composites wheel fairings
Weights:
Empty: 877 lb (398 kg)
Maximum take-off and landing: 1,451 lb (658 kg)
Performance:
Never-exceed speed (Vne): 217 kts (249 mph) 402 km/h
Maximum speed: 174 kts (200 mph) 322 km/h at 12,000 ft (3,660 m)
Long-range cruise speed: 122 kts (140 mph) 225 km/h
Stall speed: 46 kts (53 mph) 84 km/h with flaps
Take-off distance: 703 ft (214 m)
Landing distance: 800 ft (244 m)
Maximum climb rate: 1,699 ft (518 m) per minute at sea level
Ceiling: 14,000 ft (4,270 m)
Range with full fuel: 781 naut miles (899 miles) 1,448 km

Israel Aircraft Industries Ltd (IAI) (Israel)

Corporate address: See Combat section for company details.

IAI 1125 Astra SP and SPX

First flight: 19 March 1984 (Astra), 16 August 1994 for the new Astra SPX.
Certification: 29 August 1985 to FAR Pt 26 through Amdt 54 and Pt 36.
Role: Business jets.
Sales/users: Deliveries of the current Astra SP started in 1990. $8,179,000 for the basic Astra SP (June 1994). Deliveries of Astra SPX began in 1995, initially to Hewlett-Packard. Just under $9 million for the Astra SPX.
Details: Principally for Astra SP, except under Aircraft variants.
Crew/passengers: 2 crew (with dual controls) plus 6 to 9 passengers.
Baggage capacity: 55 cu ft (1.5 m^3), for 1,102 lb (500 kg).
Pressurization system: 8.9 psi cabin differential.
Wing control surfaces: Ailerons, spoilers, Fowler flaps and leading-edge slats (latter deploying to 25° automatically with the flaps or under certain height, angle of attack and/or speed conditions). Leading-edge pneumatic de-icing boots.
Tail control surfaces: Variable-incidence tailplane. Elevators and rudder, with tabs. Tailplane de-icing.
Flight control system: Manual/hydraulic, except for electric flaps and slats.
Construction materials: Metal, but with considerable use of composites for parts of the wings and tail, wing/body fairings, most control surfaces, tailcone, and several panels and access doors. GAMESA of Spain is constructing the fuselage and wing sections.
Engines: 2 AlliedSignal TFE731-3A-200G turbofans.
Engine rating: Each 3,700 lbf (16.46 kN).
Fuel system: 4,900 litres usable, with 378 litres available in a removable auxiliary tank that does not reduce cabin volume. 9,365 lb (4,248 kg) by weight usable fuel with auxiliary tank.

IAI 1125 Astra SP

IAI Astra Galaxy

Electrical system: 28 volt DC supply via 2 engine-driven starter-generators. AC supply from DC via 2 single-phase inverters. 2 x 24 volt ni-cd batteries, used partly for engine starting.
Hydraulic system: Dual systems, each 3,000 psi.
Braking system: Multi disc, with anti-skid.
Radar: Colour weather radar.
Flight avionics/instrumentation: Electronic and mechanical, including 5-screen (6 ins, 15 cm) Rockwell Collins EFIS 86C. APS 85 digital autopilot, air data system, dual AHS 85 AHRS and more.
Aircraft variants:
Astra SP, as detailed.
Astra SPX first flew on 16 August 1994. Certified 1995. 2 x 4,250 lbf (18.9 kN) AlliedSignal TFE731-40 turbofans. Revised wings. Maximum Mach number and normal cruise speed are likely to be about Mach 0.87 and Mach 0.82 respectively, although the prototype has attained Mach 0.92. Range about 2,970 naut miles (3,420 miles) 5,500 km with 4 passengers.

DETAILS FOR ASTRA SP.

Principal dimensions:
Wing span: 52 ft 8 ins (16.05 m)
Maximum length: 55 ft 7 ins (16.94 m)
Maximum height: 5.54 m (18 ft 2 ins)
Cabin:
Length: 22 ft 6 ins (6.86 m)
Width: 4 ft 11 ins (1.5 m)
Height: 5 ft 7 ins (1.7 m)
Wings:
Aerofoil section: Sigma 2
Area: 316.6 sq ft (29.41 m^2)
Aspect ratio: 8.759
Undercarriage:
Type: Retractable, with nosewheels. Twin wheels on each unit. Trailing-link main gear
Weights:
Empty: 13,225 lb (6,000 kg) basic operating
Maximum take-off: 23,500 lb (10,660 kg)
Maximum landing: 20,700 lb (9,390 kg)
Useful load: 10,425 lb (4,728 kg)
Payload: 2,775 lb (1,258 kg)
Performance:
Maximum operating Mach number: Mach 0.855
Maximum cruise speed: Mach 0.8 or 455 kts (524 mph) 842 km/h at 19,000 lb (8,618 kg) cruise weight, or 463 kts (533 mph) 857 km/h at 16,000 lb (7,257 kg) cruise weight, both at 35,000 ft (10,670 m)
Stall speed: 132 kts (152 mph) 244 km/h *clean* IAS, or 97 kts (112 mph) 180 km/h *landing configuration* IAS
Balanced field length: 5,250 ft (1,600 m)
Landing distance over a 50 ft (15 m) obstacle: 2,720 ft (829 m)
Maximum climb rate: 3,700 ft (1,128 m) per minute, at sea level
Climb rate, OEI: 1,010 ft (308 m) per minute
Maximum operating altitude: 45,000 ft (13,715 m)
Range: 3,202 naut miles (3,687 miles) 5,930 km, ISA, VFR reserves

IAI Astra Galaxy

First flight: Late 1995.
Certification: 1996, to FAR Pt 25 Amdt 75 initially, and FAR Pt 34 and Pt 36 later.
Role: Convertible widebody business jet and corporate shuttle. Developed with Yakovlev of Russia as a risk-sharing partner.
Sales/users: Deliveries from 1997. Hewlett-Packard has placed a deposit for 2, probably making 1 firm order and 20 deposits by early 1995.
Crew/passengers: Convertible interior allows 2 flight crew plus 8 passengers in an executive layout, changed to 19 passengers in a corporate shuttle layout. Galley and toilet.
Baggage capacity: 150 cu ft (4.25 m^3)
Construction materials: Similar construction to Astra SP. Yakovlev is producing the fuselage and tail unit at Saratov.
Engines: 2 Pratt & Whitney Canada PW306A turbofans. AlliedSignal 36-150(IAI) APU (first delivery August 1995).
Engine rating: Each 5,700 lbf (25.36 kN).
Fuel system: 7,874 litres.
Flight avionics/instrumentation: Rockwell Collins Pro Line 4 digital suite, incorporating EFIS with 4 (7.25 ins, 18 cm) CRTs, dual ADC 850 air data computers and dual AHC 85E AHRS.

DETAILS FOR GALAXY.

Principal dimensions:
Wing span: 57 ft 2 ins (17.42 m)
Maximum length: 63 ft 4 ins (19.3 m)
Maximum height: 21 ft (6.4 m)
Cabin:
Length: 24 ft 3 ins (7.39 m)
Width: 7 ft 2 ins (2.2 m) maximum
Height: 6 ft 3 ins (1.9 m)
Weights:
Empty: 17,770 lb (8,060 kg)
Maximum take-off: 33,450 lb (15,173 kg)
Maximum landing: 27,500 lb (12,473 kg)
Payload: 4,200 lb (1,905 kg)
Performance:
Maximum operating Mach number (Mmo): Mach 0.85
Maximum cruise speed: Mach 0.82
Balanced field length: 6,030 ft (1,838 m)
Landing field length: 3,400 ft (1,036 m)
Maximum operating altitude: 45,000 ft (13,715 m)
Range: 3,699 naut miles (4,258 miles) 6,850 km with 4 passengers and NBAA IFR reserves

Israviation Ltd (Israel)

Corporate address: Industrial Park, Tel-Hai, PO Box 90001, Upper Galilee
Telephone: +972 6 949033
Facsimile: +972 6 950173
Founded: Wholly owned subsidiary of Euraviation Holding S.A. of Luxembourg (see also Euraviation S.A. of Switzerland).
Employees: Expected to rise to 200 engineers and technicians at the Airport of Kiryat-Shmona facility in Northern Israel for production.
Information: Stephane Juffa (President).

Euraviation (Israviation) ST-50

First flight: 7 December 1994.
Certification: 1996 to FAR Pt 23 through Amdt 45 and CAAI regulations.
Role: Pressurized business and private aircraft.

● Development

● ST-50 programme is financed by Euraviation Holding and by the Israeli Government.

● Cirrus Design Corporation of Duluth, Minnesota, USA, provided the initial technology know-how, with the aerodynamic concept based on the Cirrus VK-30. Cirrus is a major sub-contractor to Israviation, producing the proof-of-concept prototype. Core engineering was conducted at Duluth, where both companies' engineering teams combined their efforts, but this has now transferred to Israel.

DETAILS FOR ST-50.

Principal dimensions:
Wing span: 39 ft (11.89 m)
Maximum length: 26 ft (7.92 m)
Maximum height: 11 ft 8 ins (3.56 m)
Cabin:
Length: 10 ft 5 ins (3.18 m)
Width: 5 ft (1.52 m)
Height: 4 ft 4 ins (1.32 m)
Wings:
Area: 165 sq ft (15.33 m^2)
Aspect ratio: 9.22
Undercarriage:
Type: Retractable, with nosewheel. Trailing-link main gear
Weights:
Empty: 3,050 lb (1,383 kg)
Maximum take-off: 5,000 lb (2,268 kg)
Useful load: 1,950 lb (884 kg)
Performance:
Cruise speed: 280 kts (322 mph) 518 km/h at 30,000 ft (9,150 m)
Stall speed: 61 kts (71 mph) 113 km/h, with flaps
Take-off distance: 1,400 ft (427 m)
Landing distance: 1,200 ft (366 m)
Maximum climb rate: 1,800 ft (549 m) per minute at sea level
G limits: +3.8, -1.9 clean
Ceiling: 31,000 ft (9,450 m)
Range: 1,100 naut miles (1,266 miles) 2,037 km, with 45 minutes reserve

Sales/users: Launch cost US$1 million for each of the first 30 aircraft, thereafter likely to be $1.2 million. 40 to be produced in the first year, and 110 in the second. In addition to the original proof-of-concept prototype, 2 further aircraft built to full specification joined the test programme in 1995. Euraviation is undertaking European sales, and Cirrus is undertaking North American sales. Deliveries from 1996.
Crew/passengers: 5 persons. Being certified for single pilot operation in all weather conditions.
Baggage capacity: 300 lb (136 kg), with internal access. Volume 26 cu ft (0.74 m^3).
Pressurization system: 6 psi cabin differential.
Wing control surfaces: Ailerons, Fowler flaps and trim tab.
Tail control surfaces: Tailplane with elevator and pitch trim system. Dorsal and ventral fins, with rudder.
Construction materials: Entirely composites.
Engine: Pratt & Whitney Canada PT6A-135/7 turboprop, driving a 7 ft 4 ins (2.24 m) MTV-9-E-C-F-R 3-blade pusher propeller through a Kamatics driveshaft equipped with flexible couplings.
Engine rating: 810 shp (608 kW), derated to 500 shp (373 kW).
Fuel system: 662 litres, of which 643 litres are usable.
Electrical system: Engine-driven starter-generator (230 amp), 130 amp secondary alternator, and 24 volt, 43 amp-hour lead-acid battery.
De-icing: Complete de-icing/anti-icing system.
Radar: Weather radar.
Flight avionics/instrumentation: ARNAV ICDS 2000 integrated avionics SmartSuite, with 4 flat-panel colour liquid crystal displays (8 x 6 ins, 20 x 15 cm) for primary flight information, multi-function (with WxLink weather graphics) and EICAS displays for engine, navigation, flight planning, weather radar and communications information. Back-up conventional gauges. Fully integrated flight management system, with AHRS, computers and including IFR certified Loran and GPS receiver. ICDS 2000 uses the ARNAV high speed communications bus and ARINC 429 databus. Options include ARNAV System 6 VHF DataLink flight following/air traffic management system, and satcom.

Euraviation (Israviation) ST-50 proof-of-concept aircraft

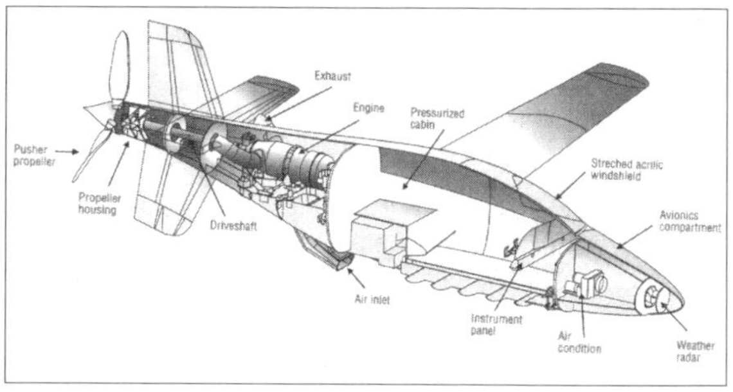

Euraviation (Israviation) ST-50 layout (courtesy Euraviation)

General Avia Costruzioni Aeronautiche srl (Italy)

Corporate address: Via Ubaldo Comandini 38, 00173 Rome
Information: Alessandro Ghisleni (Sales Manager)
Telephone: +39 6 72 31 651
Facsimile: +39 6 72 34 536

General Avia F.22 Pinguino series and F.220 Airone

First flight: 13 June 1989 (F.22/A prototype).
Certification: 1993.
Details: Principally F.22/C, except under Aircraft variants.
Role: Two-seat light aircraft and trainer.
Wing control surfaces: Ailerons and flaps.
Tail control surfaces: Horn-balanced elevators (port trim tab) and rudder.
Flight control system: Manual, except for electric flaps.
Construction materials: Metal.
Engine: Textron Lycoming IO-360-A1A piston engine.
Engine rating: 180 hp (134 kW).
Fuel system: 160 litres. Provision for auxiliary fuel.
Flight avionics/instrumentation: AlliedSignal Bendix/King Silver Crown.
Aircraft variants:
F.22/A Pinguino has a 116 hp (86.5 kW) Textron Lycoming O-235-N2C engine and 105 litres of fuel. Optional retractable undercarriage.
F.22/B Pinguino has a 160 hp (119 kW) Textron Lycoming O-320-D2A engine and 135 litres of fuel. Optional retractable undercarriage.
F.22/C Pinguino is the high-powered version, as detailed.
F.22/R Pinguino-Sprint has a 160 hp (119 kW) O-320-D1A as standard and features a constant-speed propeller and retractable undercarriage.
F.220 Airone is basically a four-seat development of the F.22, with a cabin-type fuselage and doors replacing the sliding canopy. 200 hp (149 kW) IO-360-A1A engine and 245 litres of fuel. Retractable undercarriage. Full development delayed.

General Avia F.22/B Pinguino (Austin J. Brown)

DETAILS FOR F.22/C.

Principal dimensions:
Wing span: 27 ft 11 ins (8.5 m)
Maximum length: 24 ft 3 ins (7.4 m)
Maximum height: 9 ft 4 ins (2.84 m)
Wings:
Area: 116.47 sq ft (10.82 m^2)
Aspect ratio: 6.677
Undercarriage:
Type: Fixed, with steerable nosewheel. Optional retractable undercarriage
Weights:
Empty: 1,411 lb (640 kg)
Maximum take-off: 1,984 lb (900 kg)
Performance:
Maximum speed: 165 kts (190 mph) 305 km/h
Stall speed: 54 kts (62 mph) 100 km/h, with flaps
Take-off distance: 656 ft (200 m)
Landing distance: 788 ft (240 m)
Maximum climb rate: 1,476 ft (450 m) per minute
Ceiling: 19,000 ft (5,800 m), service
Range: 702 naut miles (808 miles) 1,400 km, with standard fuel

Partenavia Costruzioni Aeronautiche SpA (Italy)

Corporate address: See Airliners section for company details.

Partenavia P 68 C, P 68 C-TC and Observer 2

First flight: 25 May 1970 in original P68 Victor form.
Role: Twin piston-engined transport for private and commercial use. Observer 2 for observation, patrol and similar roles.
Details: For P 68 C-TC, except under Aircraft variants.
Sales/users: At least 341 P 68 series aircraft built, with simultaneous production in India by Taneja (which see).

Partenavia P68 Observer 2 with nose sensor

Crew/passengers: 6 or 7 persons, with seats quickly removable for cargo carrying. Options include club seating with folding table and refreshment unit, litters for an air ambulance role, parachutist modifications, photogrammetry camera and tracking hatches, etc.
Baggage capacity: 19.78 cu ft (0.56 m^3) for 400 lb (181 kg), with a large baggage/freight door (also used as an emergency exit).
Wing control surfaces: Ailerons and single-slotted flaps.
Tail control surfaces: Slab tailplane and rudder, both with tabs.
Flight control system: Rod and cable, except for electric flaps.
Construction materials: Principally metal, with glassfibre wing/body fairings.
Engines: 2 Textron Lycoming TIO-360-C1A6D turbocharged piston engines, with Hartzell constant-speed propellers.
Engine rating: Each 210 hp (156.6 kW).
Fuel system: 538 litres, of which 520 litres are usable.
De-icing system: Standard.
Radar: See avionics.
Flight avionics/instrumentation: Instrument panel, with annunciator panel warning light system, accommodates sophisticated avionics packages including autopilot/flight directors, weather radar, HF, etc. VFR/IFR, with options including AlliedSignal Bendix/King Silver Crown or Rockwell Collins suite.
Aircraft variants:
P 68 C has a 200 hp (149 kW) IO-360-A1B6 engine. Empty operating weight 2,711 lb (1,230 kg), maximum speed 174 kts (200 mph) 322 km/h, and service ceiling 19,200 ft (5,850 m).
P 68 C-TC is a turbocharged variant of the P 68 C, as detailed. Offers improved hot-and-high performance. OEI ceiling of 14,500 ft (4,420 m) is about twice that of the P 68 C.
P 68 Observer 2 is an observation and patrol variant of P 68 C, with a unique highly-glazed plexiglas cabin for good forward and downward visibility. Can carry weather radar, FLIR, SLAR and more, the standard transparent nose giving way to a thimble fairing when a nose sensor is carried (see photograph). Upturned wingtips to improve minimum control and stalling speeds, and offer better OEI handling.
P 68-TC Observer is the turbocharged variant.

Details for P 68 C-TC.

Principal dimensions:
Wing span: 39 ft 4.5 ins (12 m)
Maximum length: 31 ft 4 ins (9.55 m)
Maximum height: 11 ft 2 ins (3.4 m)
Wings:
Aerofoil section: NACA 63-3515
Area: 200.21 sq ft (18.6 m^2)
Aspect ratio: 7.74
Undercarriage:
Type: Fixed, with steerable nosewheel. Wheel fairings
Weights:
Empty: 2,866 lb (1,300 kg)
Maximum take-off: 4,387 lb (1,990 kg)
Useful load: 1,521 lb (690 kg)
Performance:
Maximum speed: 195 kts (225 mph) 361 km/h at 17,500 ft (5,335 m)
Cruise speed: 172 kts (198 mph) 318 km/h at 75% power, or 149 kts (172 mph) 276 km/h at 55% power, both at 12,000 ft (3,660 m)
Minimum control speed: 63 kts (73 mph) 117 km/h
Stall speed: 65 kts (75 mph) 120 km/h *clean*, 57 kts (66 mph) 106 km/h *with full flaps*
Take-off distance: 755 ft (230 m)
Landing distance: 705 ft (215 m)
Maximum climb rate: 1,555 ft (474 m) per minute at sea level
Climb rate, OEI: 295 ft (90 m) per minute at sea level
Ceiling: 27,000 ft (8,230 m)
Range: 775 naut miles (892 miles) 1,436 km at 75% power, or 1,020 naut miles (1,174 miles) 1,890 km at 55% power, both at 12,000 ft (3,660 m)

Partenavia AP 68 TP-600 Viator

Partenavia AP 68 TP-600 Viator

First flight: 29 March 1985.
Role: Unpressurized small commuter, charter and utility transport, also suited to air ambulance, surveillance and maritime patrol, photogrammetry, remote sensing (2 belly openings are available for photographic or sensor equipment), paratrooping and multi-engine training.
Sales/users: Also built in India by Taneja (which see).
Crew/passengers: 2 pilots plus 9 passengers.
Wing control surfaces: Ailerons (with trim tabs) and single-slotted flaps. Leading-edge stall strips.
Tail control surfaces: Elevators with vortex generators and rudder, all with trim tabs.
Flight control system: Rod and cable, except for electric flaps.
Construction materials: Metal.
Engines: 2 Allison 250-B17C turboprops, with Hartzell 3-blade constant-speed propellers.
Engine rating: Each flat-rated at 328 shp (245 kW).
Fuel system: 840 litres; 1,488 lb (675 kg) useful fuel by weight.
Electrical system: 28 volt DC supply via 2 starter-generators. 24 volt, 29 amp-hour battery.
De-icing system: For flying surfaces and engines.
Radar: Colour weather radar.
Flight avionics/instrumentation: Standard IFR avionics. 3-axis autopilot. Instrument panel with annunciator panel warning light system, HF, etc.

Details for Viator.

Principal dimensions:
Wing span: 39 ft 4.5 ins (12 m)
Maximum length: 37 ft (11.27 m)
Maximum height: 11 ft 11 ins (3.63 m)
Cabin:
Length: 17 ft 4 ins (5.29 m)
Width: 3 ft 8.5 ins (1.13 m)
Height: 4 ft 1.5 ins (1.265 m)
Volume: 229.55 cu ft (6.5 m^3)
Wings:
Aerofoil section: NACA 63-3515
Area: 200.21 sq ft (18.6 m^2)
Aspect ratio: 7.74
Undercarriage:
Type: Retractable, with nosewheel
Weights:
Empty: 3,571 lb (1,620 kg)
Maximum take-off: 6,614 lb (3,000 kg)
Maximum landing: 6,283 lb (2,850 kg)
Payload: 1,918 lb (870 kg)
Performance:
Maximum speed: 220 kts (254 mph) 409 km/h at 12,000 ft (3,660 m)
Maximum-range cruise speed: 180 kts (207 mph) 334 km/h at 12,000 ft (3,660 m)
Stall speed: 80 kts (92 mph) 148 km/h *clean*, 65 kts (75 mph) 121 km/h *with flaps*
Take-off distance: 1,313 ft (400 m)
Landing distance: 1,050 ft (320 m)
Maximum climb rate: 1,650 ft (503 m) per minute
Ceiling: 26,000 ft (7,925 m), service, or 11,400 ft (3,475 m) OEI
Range: 899 naut miles (1,034 miles) 1,665 km at 12,000 ft (3,660 m), 178 kts, with 1,200 lb (545 kg) payload and 45 minutes fuel reserve

Partenavia PD 93 Idea

Certification: Aerodynamic, structural and system design meets FAR Pt 23 Utility category.
Role: Four-seat training and utility monoplane, also suited to photogrammetry, air ambulance, firefighting and other aerial work.
Baggage capacity: 220 lb (100 kg).
Wing control surfaces: Ailerons and slotted flaps.
Tail control surfaces: Slab tailplane with tabs and balanced rudder.
Construction materials: Quoted as all metal, but including new materials.

Engine: Textron Lycoming IO-360-A1B6 piston engine, with a 3-blade, variable-pitch, constant-speed composites propeller.
Engine rating: 200 hp (149 kW).
Fuel system: 250 litres.

Partenavia PD 93 Idea (courtesy Partenavia)

DETAILS FOR PD 93 IDEA.

Principal dimensions:
Wing span: 36 ft 1 ins (11 m)
Maximum length: 26 ft 3 ins (8 m)
Maximum height: 10 ft 6 ins (3.2 m)
Wings:
Area: 183.52 sq ft (17.05 m^2)
Aspect ratio: 7.1
Undercarriage:
Type: Fixed, with nosewheel. Retractable option may become available.
Weights:
Empty: 1,697 lb (770 kg) equipped
Maximum take-off and landing: 2,755 lb (1,250 kg)
Useful load: 1,058 lb (480 kg)
Payload: 838 lb (380 kg)
Performance:
Maximum diving speed: 200 kts (230 mph) 370 km/h CAS
Maximum speed: 144 kts (166 mph) 267 km/h
Cruise speed: 122-137 kts (140-158 mph) 226-254 km/h, at 55-75% power
Stall speed: 56 kts (65 mph) 104 km/h *clean*, 47 kts (54 mph) 87 km/h with *full flaps*
Maximum climb rate: 950 ft (290 m) per minute
G limits: +4.4, -1.76 manoeuvring limit
Ceiling: 18,000 ft (5,485 m), service
Range: 945 naut miles (1,087 miles) 1,750 km at 55% power and 12,000 ft (3,660 m)

Rinaldo Piaggio (Italy)

Full name: Industrie Aeronautiche E Meccaniche Rinaldo Piaggio SpA.
Corporate address: Via Cibrario 4, 16154 Genova Sestri, Genoa.
Telephone: +39 10 64811
Facsimile: +39 10 6520160
Founded: 1884, with aeronautics from 1915.
Information: Dr Ing Paolo Chiarlone (Sales Technical Support – *Telephone* +39 10 6481 243).

● Activities

- Subcontractor to AMX, Alenia, Dassault and Panavia.
- Produces the Rolls-Royce Gem, Spey and Viper, and AlliedSignal T53 and T55 engines under licence, and has a share in the RTM 322. Also produces shelters.
- Production of the P.166-DL3SEM multi-role aircraft (which first flew in 1976) is now only to order, with 2 aircraft delivered in 1995.

SUBSIDIARY
Piaggio Aviation Inc
HQ Address: Dover, DE, USA.

Piaggio P.180 Avanti

First flight: 23 September 1986.
Certification: 7 March 1990 (RAI/FAA Pt23).
Role: Turboprop business aircraft.
Sales/users: 26 delivered since September 1990, with customers including the Italian Air Force and at least 11 others. 17-20 for delivery 1996-97.
Crew/passengers: 1 or 2 pilots, plus 9 passengers. Alternative layouts include a 5-VIP arrangement.
Pressurization system: 9 psi maximum cabin differential.
Baggage compartment: 44.14 cu ft (1.25 m^3).
Wing control surfaces: Ailerons (starboard trim tab), and co-ordinated flaps on both the wings and canards.
Tail control surfaces: Variable-incidence tailplane, with elevators (with tabs). Rudder with trim tab.
Flight control system: Mechanical, except for electric flaps and trim.
Construction materials: Metal and composites, with carbonfibre or Kevlar and epoxy used in the construction of the tail and tailcone, nose and canards, outer wing flaps, undercarriage doors and engine fairings.
Engines: 2 Pratt & Whitney Canada PT6A-66 turboprops, with 7ft 1ins (2.16 m) Hartzell 5-blade constant-speed pusher propellers.
Engine rating: Each flat-rated to 850 shp (633.8 kW).
Fuel system: 1,600 litres.
Electrical system: 2 starter-generators (400amp, 28 volt). 38 amp-hour ni-cd battery.
Radar: Rockwell Collins WXR-840 weather radar.
Flight avionics/instrumentation: Rockwell Collins suite with 3-screen EFIS-85B, APS-65A autopilot, dual VHF-22A transceivers, dual VIR-32 VOR/LOC/GLS/MKR receivers, marker beacons, ADF-462 ADF, glideslope, dual DME-42, dual TDR-90 transponders, ALT-55B radio altimeter, dual MCS-65 compasses, dual RMI-3337s, and ADS-85 air data system.

Piaggio P.180 Avanti

DETAILS FOR AVANTI.

Principal dimensions:
Wing span: 46 ft 0.5 ins (14.03 m)
Maximum length: 47 ft 3.5 ins (14.41 m)
Maximum height: 13 ft 0.75 ins (3.97 m)
Cabin:
Length: 14 ft 7.2 ins (4.45 m)
Width: 6 ft 0.8 ins (1.85 m)
Height: 5 ft 8.9 ins (1.75 m)
Volume: 375.04 cu ft (10.62 m^3)
Wings:
Area: 172.22 sq ft (16 m^2)
Aspect ratio: 12.303
Undercarriage:
Type: Retractable, with twin steerable nosewheels
Weights:
Empty: 7,500 lb (3,402 kg)
Maximum take-off: 11,550 lb (5,239 kg)
Maximum landing: 10,946 lb (4,965 kg)
Useful load: 4,100 lb (1,860 kg)
Payload: 2,000 lb (907 kg)
Performance:
Maximum operating Mach number (Mmo): 1Mach 0.67
Maximum speed: 395 kts (455 mph) 732 km/h at high altitude
Stall speed: 109 kts (126 mph) 202 km/h *clean*, 93 kts (107 mph) 173 km/h *landing configuration*
Take-off over a 50 ft (15 m) obstacle: 2,850 ft (870 m)
Landing over a 50 ft (15 m) obstacle: 2,860 ft (872 m)
Maximum climb rate: 2,950 ft (900 m) per minute, at sea level
Ceiling: 41,000 ft (12,500 m)
Range: 1,400 naut miles (1,612 miles) 2,592 km, at 39,000 ft (11,900 m) with reserves

SIAI Marchetti (Italy)

Corporate address: See Combat section for company details.

SIAI-Marchetti SF600A Canguro

First flight: 30 December 1978.
Role: Multi-purpose transport.
Crew/passengers: 1 or 2 pilots (dual controls). 9 folding passenger seats in the main cabin, or room for 10 troops or paratroops, or 2 litters and attendants in ambulance configuration.
Wing control surfaces: Ailerons and double-slotted flaps.
Tail control surfaces: Elevators (electric and manual trim) and rudder (manual trim).
Flight control system: Cable, but with electric aileron and elevator trim, and electric flaps.
Engine: 2 Allison 250-B17F1 turboprops, with Hartzell 3-blade propellers.
Engine rating: Each 450 shp (335.6 kW).
Fuel system: 1,024 litres.
De-icing system: Optional.
Radar: Optional weather radar. See Aircraft variants.
Flight avionics/instrumentation: Instrument panel offers space for double instruments, and options include autopilot.

SIAI-Marchetti SF600A Canguro

Aircraft variants:
SF600A roles, in addition to transport, can include photogrammetry with 1 or 2 Wild or Zeiss cameras and high precision navigation systems, and maritime early warning and surveillance with a 360° scanning radar or SLAR and FLAR.

DETAILS FOR SF600A.

Principal dimensions:
Wing span: 49 ft 2 ins (15 m)
Maximum length: 40 ft 1 ins (12.21 m)
Maximum height: 14 ft 1 ins (4.3 m)
Cabin:
Length: 16 ft 8.5 ins (5.09 m)
Width: 3 ft 11 ins (1.2 m)
Height: 4 ft 1 ins (1.25 m)
Volume: 279 cu ft (7.9 m^3)
Cargo door size: Sliding door 4 ft 10.5 ins x 3 ft 8.5 ins (1.48 x 1.12 m), openable in flight
Wings:
Area: 258.33 sq ft (24 m^2)
Aspect ratio: 9.375
Undercarriage:
Type: Fixed, with steerable nosewheel
Weights:
Empty: 4,674 lb (2,210 kg), operating (cargo)
Maximum take-off: 7,947 lb (3,605 kg)
Performance:
Maximum speed: 173 kts (199 mph) 320 km/h at 5,000 ft (1,525 m)
Cruise speed: 165 kts (190 mph) 306 km/h
Stall speed: 67 kts (77 mph) 124 km/h, with flaps
Take-off distance: 1,444 ft (440 m)
Landing distance: 984 ft (300 m)
Maximum climb rate: 1,260 ft (384 m) per minute
G limits: +3.5, -1.4
Ceiling: 20,000 ft (6,100 m), service
Range: 930 naut miles (1,070 miles) 1,722 km

Sivel Aeronautica (Italy)

Corporate address: Via Aldo Moro, 10-25124 Brescia.
Telephone: +39 30 2291232
Facsimile: +39 30 224563

Sivel SD27 Corriedale

Certification: Certified under JAR-VLA.
Role: Two-seat private, aero club and training aircraft.
Sales/users: US$70,000 (in late 1994). 5 pre-series aircraft in 1994, followed by full production in 1995.
Baggage capacity: Shelf area aft of seats.
Wing control surfaces: Ailerons and flaps.
Tail control surfaces: Elevators and rudder.
Construction materials: Welded chromoly steel tubing for the main cabin area structure, with a composites shell, with an aluminium alloy monocoque tailcone and tail unit.
Engine: Rotax 912 piston engine, with a 5 ft 7 ins (1.7 m) Elica 2-blade propeller.
Engine rating: 77.8 hp (58 kW).
Fuel system: 80 litres usable.
Aircraft variants:
SD27 is the standard initial production version, as detailed.
Aerobatic version first flew in 1995 with a 160 hp (119 kW) engine.
4-seat touring version is anticipated for 1996.
Future version will have a 125 hp (93.2 kW) Teledyne Continental IO-240 engine.

Sivel SD27 Corriedale (courtesy Sivel)

Sivel SD28

First flight: 1995.
Role: Private/aerobatic monoplane.
Crew/passengers: 2 persons, side by side. Dual controls. Baggage area aft of seats.
Wing characteristics: Low-mounted, constant chord. Dihedral 7°
Wing control surfaces: Ailerons and flaps.
Tail control surfaces: Elevators (with trim) and rudder.
Flight control system: Mechanical.
Construction materials: Metal.
Engine: Textron Lycoming AEIO-320-D piston engine, with a Mühlbauer propeller.
Engine rating: 160 hp (119.3 kW).
Fuel system: 160 litres.
Flight avionics/instrumentation: VFR. To customer's requirements.

DETAILS FOR SIVEL SD27.

Principal dimensions:
Wing span: 32 ft 10 ins (10 m)
Maximum length: 21 ft 7 ins (6.57 m)
Maximum height: 9 ft 1 ins (2.76 m)
Cabin:
Width: 3 ft 7.3 ins (1.1 m)
Wings:
Area: 134.55 sq ft (12.5 m^2)
Aspect ratio: 8
Undercarriage:
Type: Fixed, with swivelling nosewheel
Weights:
Empty: 816 lb (370 kg)
Maximum take-off: 1,367 lb (620 kg)
Performance:
Never-exceed speed (Vne): 132 kts (152 mph) 245 km/h
Maximum speed: 105 kts (121 mph) 195 km/h
Cruise speed: 95 kts (109 mph) 176 km/h at 75% power and 8,000 ft (2,440 m)
Stall speed: 45 kts (52 mph) 83 km/h *clean*, 41 kts (47.5 mph) 76 km/h *with flaps*
Take-off distance: 492 ft (150 m)
Landing distance: 328 ft (100 m)
Maximum climb rate: 925 ft (282 m) per minute at sea level
Ceiling: 13,125 ft (4,000 m)
Range: 540 naut miles (621 miles) 1,000 km
Duration: 6 hours

DETAILS FOR SD28.

Principal dimensions:
Wing span: 27 ft 7 ins (8.4 m)
Maximum length: 22 ft 4 ins (6.8 m)
Maximum height: 9 ft 1 ins (2.76 m)
Wings:
Area: 107.6 sq ft (10 m^2)
Aspect ratio: 7.01
Undercarriage:
Type: Fixed, with nosewheel
Weights:
Empty: 1,168 lb (530 kg)
Maximum take-off: 1,764 lb (800 kg)
Performance:
Maximum speed: 145 kts (166 mph) 268 km/h
Range with full fuel: 550 naut miles (633.5 miles) 1,019 km, at 135 kts cruise speed

Costruzioni Aeronautiche Tecnam srl (Italy)

Corporate address: 1a Traversa via G. Pascoli, 80026 Casoria (NA).
Telephone: +39 81 7583210, 758854, 7588751
Facsimile: +39 81 7584528
Founded: 1986. Member of the Associazione Italiana Costruttori Aerodine da Diporto e Sportive (AICA).
Information: Giovanni Pascale.

● Activities

- Other work includes manufacture of ATR 42-72 stabilizers, MD-90 fuselage panels, P 68 fuselage, and other smaller parts for aeroplanes and helicopters.

Tecnam P92 Echo

First flight: 1993.
Certification: A version with a 1,146 lb (520 kg) gross weight was certified under JAR-VLA regulations in late 1994.
Role: Two-seat ultralight/JAR-VLA monoplane, with dual controls.
Sales/users: Production at 6 per month.
Wing control surfaces: Frise ailerons and half-span flaps (0-35°).
Tail control surfaces: Slab tailplane with trim/anti-balance tab.
Flight control system: Manual, except for electric flaps and trim.
Construction materials: Metal frames, spars, ribs and skins, except for glassfibre wing leading edges and wing/fin tips, and Dacron fabric on the tailplane aft of the alloy spar to minimize mass-balancing, ailerons and flaps.
Engine: 3 choices: 64.4 hp (48 kW) Rotax 582 piston engine, 77.8 hp (58 kW) Rotax 912, or 80 hp (59.7 kW) Limbach L 2000.

Tecnam P92 Echo

DETAILS FOR P92 ECHO WITH ROTAX 912 ENGINE.

Principal dimensions:
Wing span: 31 ft 6 ins (9.6 m)
Maximum length: 20 ft 8 ins (6.3 m)
Maximum height: 7 ft 6.5 ins (2.3 m)
Wings:
Area: 142.08 sq ft (13.2 m^2)
Aspect ratio: 6.98
Undercarriage:
Type: Fixed, with steerable nosewheel
Weights:
Empty: 620 lb (281 kg)
Maximum take-off: 1,100 lb (499 kg), or 1,146 lb (520 kg) under JAR-VLA
Useful load: 480 lb (218 kg)
Performance:
Maximum speed: 113 kts (130 mph) 209 km/h
Cruise speed: 89 kts (103 mph) 166 km/h at 65% power
Stall speed: 32 kts (37 mph) 60 km/h
Take-off distance: 262 ft (80 m)
Landing distance: 300 ft (92 m)
Maximum climb rate: 1,100 ft (335 m) per minute
Duration: 4.5 hours

Engine rating: See above.
Fuel system: 2 x 30 litre tanks in the composite wing leading edges.
Electrical system: 170 W alternator. 12 volt, 15 amp-hour battery.
Braking system: Hydraulic disc brakes with cockpit brake lever. Parking brake.
Flight avionics/instrumentation: Airspeed indicator, altimeter, magnetic compass, bank indicator, engine speed indicator and temperature gauge. Wide instrument panel allows for extra equipment up to IFR.

Terzi Aerodine (Italy)

Corporate address: Piazzale A. Baiamonti 1, 20154 Milan.
Facsimile: +39 2 3360 7996

● Activities
● Also produces the T30E Katana homebuilt (see Recreational Aircraft section).

Terzi T-9 Stiletto

First flight: 1990.
Certification: Designed to JAR-VLA.
Role: Two-seat lightplane.
Wing control surfaces: Ailerons and 3-position flaps. Wings are detachable.
Tail control surfaces: Slab tailplane and rudder.
Flight control system: Manual.
Construction materials: Principally metal, but with a glassfibre cabin enclosure and cantilever undercarriage legs.
Engine: Rotax 912A piston engine, with a 2-blade wooden propeller.
Engine rating: 77.8 hp (58 kW).
Fuel system: 80 litres.
Electrical system: Alternator and battery.
Braking system: Hydraulic disc brakes.

DETAILS FOR T-9 STILETTO.

Principal dimensions:
Wing span: 33 ft 8 ins (10.26 m)
Maximum length: 22 ft 6 ins (6.85 m)
Maximum height: 7 ft 6.5 ins (2.3 m)
Wings:
Aerofoil section: Wortmann FX67-K-150/17
Area: 132.4 sq ft (12.3 m^2)
Aspect ratio: 8.558
Undercarriage:
Type: Fixed, with castering nosewheel.
Weights:
Empty: 837.5 lb (380 kg)
Maximum take-off: 1,433 lb (650 kg)
Performance:
Maximum speed: 108 kts (124 mph) 200 km/h
Cruise speed: 88 kts (101 mph) 162 km/h at 60% power
Stall speed: 40 kts (46 mph) 74 km/h with flaps
Take-off over a 50 ft (15 m) obstacle: 625 ft (190 m)
Landing over a 50 ft (15 m) obstacle: 575 ft (175 m)
Maximum climb rate: 800 ft (244 m) per minute at sea level

Korean Air (South Korea)

Corporate address: See Helicopter section for company details.

Korean Air Chang-Gong 91

First flight: 22 November 1991.
Certification: 31 August 1993.
Role: Four-seat lightplane.
Crew/passengers: Pilot and 3 passengers, with a fifth rear seat suited to a child.
Baggage capacity: 100 lb (45 kg) aft of the seats.
Wing control surfaces: Frise ailerons (with tabs) and slotted flaps (0-40°).
Tail control surfaces: Slab tailplane with geared tab, and rudder.
Construction materials: Principally metal, but with composites in the tail unit.
Engine: Textron Lycoming IO-360-A1B6 piston engine, with a Hartzell 2-blade constant-speed propeller.
Engine rating: 200 hp (149 kW).
Fuel system: 212 litres.
Electrical system: 14 volt DC supply via an engine-driven alternator.
Braking system: Disc brakes.
Flight avionics/instrumentation: AlliedSignal Bendix/King suite, with KX155 comm/nav, ADF, DME, transponder, marker beacon receiver and more.

DETAILS FOR CHANG-GONG 91.

Principal dimensions:
Wing span: 33 ft 5 ins (10.2 m)
Maximum length: 25 ft 5 ins (7.74 m)
Maximum height: 8 ft 10 ins (2.7 m)
Cabin:
Length: 10 ft (3.05 m)
Width: 3 ft 10 ins (1.17 m)
Wings:
Aerofoil section: NACA 63_2-415
Area: 160 sq ft (14.86 m^2)
Aspect ratio: 7
Undercarriage:
Type: Fixed, with steerable nosewheel
Weights:
Empty: 1,850 lb (839 kg)
Maximum take-off and landing: 2,700 lb (1,225 kg)
Performance:
Maximum speed: 183 kts (210 mph) 339 km/h at sea level
Cruise speed: 102-118 kts (117-136 mph) 189-220 km/h at 5,000 ft (1,525 m)
Stall speed: 63 kts (73 mph) 117 km/h *clean*, 54 kts (62 mph) 100 km/h with *full flaps*
Take-off distance: 2,050 ft (625 m)
Landing distance: 411 ft (125 m)
Maximum climb rate: 738 ft (225 m) per minute at sea level
Ceiling: 16,500 ft (5,025 m)
Range: 810 naut miles (932 miles) 1,500 km

Korean Air Chang-Gong 91

Aeroplastika uab (Lithuania)

Corporate address: J. Bakanausko 29, 3019 Kaunas.
Telephone: +370 770 8446
Facsimile: +370 770 5733
Founded: 1991.
Information: Algimantas Remeika (Director).

Aeroplastika LAK-X

First flight: 2 August 1992.
Role: Composites lightplane.
Sales/users: Also available as a kitplane.
Crew/passengers: 2 persons side-by-side under a hinged bubble canopy.
Wing control surfaces: Ailerons and flaps.
Tail control surfaces: Elevators and rudder.
Construction materials: All composites, principally glassfibre and foam sandwich construction but also with spar caps and undercarriage legs of unidirectional glassfibre/epoxy.
Engine: 5 piston engine options, the LAK-XE having either a 77.8 hp (58 kW) Rotax 912, 100 hp (74.5 kW) Rotax 914 or 93 hp (69.4 kW) Limbach L 2400; the LAK-XA having a 114 hp (85 kW) PZL-Rzeszów PZL-F.4A235B31 or 125 hp (93.2 kW) Teledyne Continental IO-240-A.
Engine rating: See above.
Fuel system: 85 litres for the LAK-XE and 100 litres for the LAK-XA.
Aircraft variants:
LAK-XA has a larger engine, greater fuel capacity and heavier weights, as detailed in the table.
LAK-XE has a Rotax or Limbach engine, and an empty and gross weight of 882 lb (400 kg) and 1,433 lb (650 kg) respectively. G limits +5, -2.5.

Aeroplastika LAK-X

DETAILS FOR LAK-XA.

Principal dimensions:
Wing span: 35 ft 0.5 ins (10.68 m)
Maximum length: 23 ft (7 m)
Maximum height: 7 ft 3 ins (2.2 m)
Wings:
Area: 129.7 sq ft (12.05 m^2)
Aspect ratio: 9.466
Undercarriage:
Type: Fixed, with nosewheel. Streamline wheel fairings
Weights:
Empty: 970 lb (440 kg)
Maximum take-off: 1,587 lb (720 kg)
Performance:
Maximum speed: 130 kts (149 mph) 240 km/h
Cruise speed: 108 kts (124 mph) 200 km/h
Stall speed: 44.5 kts (51 mph) 82 km/h, with flaps
Take-off and landing distance: 492 ft (150 m)
Maximum climb rate: 984 ft (300 m) per minute at sea level
G limits: +4, -2
Range: 459 naut miles (528 miles) 850 km

Dornier Seastar Malaysia Sdn Bhd (Malaysia)

Corporate address: Tingkat 4, Bangunan KPDM, No 1, Jalan Sulaiman, 50000 Kuala Lumpur.
Telephone: +60 3 2731828, 2732673
Facsimile: +60 3 2731826
Founded: 1993.
Information: Abdul Razak Jantan.

● Activities

● This company (formerly known as Flitestar Anokagai), jointly owned by Malaysian organizations and Conrado Dornier, expects to put the German-designed twin-engined Seastar CD2 amphibian into production for various roles including passenger transport (14 persons), cargo carrying, ambulance, SAR, maritime patrol and more. The original prototype first flew in 1984. Production was anticipated to start in 1996, following completion of the manufacturing plant near Penang. However, reports suggest a major backer pulled out of the programme in 1995. A new partner was then being sought both in Malaysia and elsewhere, allowing the possibility that production could be transferred to another country. Full details of the Seastar will be given in the next edition of WA&SD, once full manufacture has begun.

SME Aviation Sdn Bhd (Malaysia)

Correspondence address: Lot No 14643, Locked Bag 222, 47000 Sg. Buloh, Selangor Darul Ehsan.
Telephone: +60 3 6561778
Facsimile: +60 3 6561832
Founded: September 1993, as a subsidiary of SME Technologies Sdn Bhd (SMET). SME Aerospace Sdn Bhd (SMEA) is another subsidiary of SMET, having begun operations in 1992 as an aircraft parts manufacturer.
Information: Amirudin Ab Ghani (General Manager).

SME MD3-160

First flight: 12 August 1983.
Certification: 22 January 1991 (FOCA) and 2 September 1992 by the FAA to FAR Pt 21.29.
Role: Leisure, and basic and aerobatic training.
Sales/users: 5 manufactured by MDB Flugtechnik AG of Switzerland (the designer and developer), of which 2 are operating in Malaysia and 1 in the USA. 40 being built in Malaysia in 1995, with production increasing thereafter. 20 ordered for the Royal Malaysian Air Force and 20 for the Indonesian Air Force.
Crew/passengers: 2 persons, side by side. Forward sliding canopy.
Wing control surfaces: Single-slotted mass-balanced ailerons (with tabs) and flaps.
Tail control surfaces: Mass balanced rudder and slab elevator (with tabs) are the same modules as the flaps and ailerons.
Flight control system: Mechanical, except for electric flaps.
Construction materials: Aluminium alloy, including bonded honeycomb. Modular construction, with interchangeable airframe parts. Airframe is built by SMEA (see Founded).
Engine: Textron Lycoming O-320-D2A piston engine, with a 6 ft 2 ins (1.88 m) Sensenich (or McCauley) propeller. Optional 160 hp (119 kW) AEIO-320-D2B or 116 hp (86.5 kW) O-235-N2A.
Engine rating: 160 hp (119 kW).
Fuel system: 148 litres.
Electrical system: 28 volt DC supply via a belt-driven 60 amp alternator and 24 volt battery.
Flight avionics/instrumentation: Certified for VFR. VOR/LOC, transponder and blind encoder. Optional avionics are available. Full range of standard instruments, including directional gyro, artificial horizon, airspeed indicator, altimeter, vertical speed indicator, and turn and bank indicator.

SME MD3-160

DETAILS FOR MD3-160.

Principal dimensions:
Wing span: 32 ft 9.6 ins (10 m)
Maximum length: 23 ft 3.6 ins (7.1 m)
Maximum height: 9 ft 7.2 ins (2.92 m)
Wings:
Aerofoil section: NACA $64_2$15-414
Area: 161.46 sq ft (15 m^2)
Aspect ratio: 6.67
Undercarriage:
Type: Fixed, with steerable (30° port, 44° starboard) nosewheel. Optional glassfibre fairings
Weights:
Empty: 1,411 lb (640 kg)
Maximum take-off: 2,028 lb (920 kg) Utility, 1,852 lb (840 kg) Aerobatic
Maximum landing: 1,964 lb (891 kg)
Performance (Aerobatic category):
Never-exceed speed (Vne): 175 kts (201 mph) 324 km/h
Maximum cruise speed: 137 kts (158 mph) 254 km/h at sea level
Maximum range cruise speed: 104 kts (120 mph) 193 km/h
Manoeuvring speed (Va): 121 kts (139 km/h) 224 km/h
Stall speed: 56 kts (65 mph) 104 km/h *clean*, 47 kts (54 mph) 87 km/h *with flaps*, both with idle power
Take-off distance: 541 ft (165 m)
Landing distance: 568 ft (173 m)
Maximum climb rate: 985 ft (300 m) per minute at sea level
G limits: +6, -3 Aerobatic, +4.4, -2.2 Utility
Range: 507 naut miles (584 miles) 938 km at 10,000 ft (3,050 m)
Duration: 4 hours 49 minutes at 10,000 ft (3,050 m)

Pacific Aerospace Corporation Ltd (PAC) (New Zealand)

Corporate address: Hamilton Airport, Private Bag HN3027, Hamilton.
Telephone: +64 7 843 6144
Facsimile: +64 7 843 6134
Founded: 1982, following the merger of NZAIL and James Aviation Ltd.
Employees: 90.
Information: John Scott (Marketing Manager).

● Activities

- Much of PAC's business is concerned with manufacture of details and structural components in support of the parent companies, notably ASTA (which owns 75.1% of PAC) and Lockheed-Martin (24.9%).
- Approved to manufacture details and/or assemblies for the Boeing 747 and 777, Airbus A330 and A340, McDonnell Douglas MD-11 and Hornet, and more.

PAC CT4/E Airtrainer

First flight: 23 February 1972; 14 December 1991 for the latest CT4/E.
Certification: CT4 was originally designed to meet FAR Pt 23, for aerobatic aircraft, and also to meet British AvP970 in many respects. 8 May 1992 for the latest CT4/E, under FAR Pt 23 Amdt 36.
Role: Two/three-seat trainer.
Sales/users: Marketing is centred on the CT4/E, originally developed for the USAF EFS requirement. 114 CT4As and Bs were produced for the RTAF, RAAF, RNZAF and Ansett/BAe Flying Training School at Tamworth, Australia.
Baggage capacity: 170 lb (77 kg) utility, 100 lb (45 kg) aerobatic.
Wing control surfaces: Ailerons (16.5° up, 10.5° down) and single-slotted flaps (30° maximum deflection).
Tail control surfaces: Shielded horn-balanced elevator (25° up, 15° down) and rudder, both with trims.
Flight control system: Pushrods and cables.
Construction materials: All metal, except for Kevlar wing root fairings.
Engine: Textron Lycoming AEIO-540-L1B5 piston engine, with a 6 ft 4 ins (1.93 m) Hartzell 3-blade propeller.
Engine rating: 300 hp (224 kW).
Fuel system: 204.5 litres, of which 202 litres are usable. Optional long-range wingtip tanks (2 x 77 litres).
Electrical system: Alternator with a rating of 70 amps at 28 volt DC. 24 volt lead-acid battery.
Flight avionics/instrumentation: Engine and electrical monitoring instruments, flight instruments and radio equipment. Duplicated instruments are altimeter, airspeed indicator, turn and bank indicator, and vertical speed indicator.
Aircraft variants:
CT4/B has a 210 hp (156.6 kW) Teledyne Continental IO-360-H piston engine.
CT4/C turboprop version has an Allison 250-B17G. Development completed but programme discontinued pending a launch customer.
CT4/E is the current piston-engined version, essentially similar to the original CT4/A but with a single-piece carry-through structure and the wing moved 2.5 ins (6.4 cm) further forward. Higher performance than the previous CT4/B.

PAC CT4/E Airtrainer

DETAILS FOR CT4/E.

Principal dimensions:
Wing span: 26 ft (7.92 m)
Maximum length: 23 ft 5.75 ins (7.16 m)
Maximum height: 8 ft 6 ins (2.59 m)
Cabin:
Length: 8 ft 11 ins (2.72 m)
Width: 3 ft 7.5 ins (1.1 m)
Height: 4 ft 6.7 ins (1.38 m)
Wings:
Aerofoil section: NACA 23008 (modified) root, NACA 4412 tip
Area: 129 sq ft (11.98 m^2)
Aspect ratio: 5.24
Undercarriage:
Type: Fixed, with steerable nosewheel
Weights:
Empty: 1,675 lb (760 kg)
Maximum take-off and landing: 2,600 lb (1,179 kg)
Performance:
Maximum speed: 163 kts (188 mph) 302 km/h
Cruise speed: 152 kts (175 mph) 281 km/h at 75% power
Stall speed: 44 kts (51 mph) 82 km/h, with full flaps
Take-off distance: 612 ft (187 m)
Landing distance: 552 ft (169 m)
Maximum climb rate: 1,830 ft (558 m) per minute
G limits: +6, -3
Ceiling: 18,200 ft (5,550 m)
Range: 535 naut miles (616 miles) 991 km

PAC CR-750 Cresco

First flight: 28 February 1979 for prototype Cresco.
Certification: 9 April 1984 for the earlier Cresco 08-600.
Role: Multi-role, for agricultural, firebombing, casevac, utility, passenger, cargo and rainmaking roles. Design and construction follows closely that of the FU24.
Sales/users: 11 Crescos for users in New Zealand and 3 exported to Bangladesh. Current version is the CR-750.

PAC CR-750 Cresco undertaking agricultural work

Crew/passengers: 6 seats civil, 8 military, using an optional passenger kit. 2 litters and 2 attendants, or 2 litters, 3 sitting casualties and an attendant in an air ambulance role.
Chemical tank/hopper: 4,976 lb (2,257 kg) dry chemical payload, or 1,800 litres liquids. Hopper removable in 5 man-hours by experienced personnel, to offer a cargo area.
Dispersal equipment: Pressure via an hydraulically driven pump mounted beneath the hopper opening, with cockpit control. Micronair spray equipment with wind-driven rotary atomizer units for typically up to 160 litres per minute application rate, or Transland boom and nozzle equipment for up to 1,272 litres per minute. Transland Swathmaster for very high application rates. Also aerial spreading of solids via a range of dispersal equipment, including the ultra high application Easton hopper outlet (clamshell type), the high volume Transland solid spreader with gate box and electrically-driven actuator, and the medium volume Transland Swathmaster with gate box and agitator. Controllable fire bombing door with minimum discharge time of 3 seconds.
Safety equipment: Optional wire cutter and deflector cable.
Engine: Pratt & Whitney Canada PT6A-34AG turboprop, with a 3-blade metal constant-speed propeller.
Engine rating: 750 shp (559 kW).
Fuel system: 544 litres, of which 520 litres are usable.

Details for CR-750 Cresco.

Principal dimensions:
Wing span: 42 ft (12.8 m)
Maximum length: 35 ft 9 ins (10.9 m)
Maximum height: 11 ft 11 ins (3.63 m)
Cabin cargo area:
Length: 11 ft 10 ins (3.61 m)
Width: 3 ft 6 ins (1.07 m)
Height: 4 ft 2.5 ins (1.28 m)
Rear access door size: 39 x 38 ins (99 x 94 cm)
Wings:
Area: 294 sq ft (27.31 m^2)
Aspect ratio: 6
Weights:
Empty: 2,820 lb (1,279 kg)
Maximum take-off: 8,256 lb (3,744 kg) agricultural and rainmaking roles, or 6,450 lb (2,926 kg) utility cargo and passengers
Useful load: 5,331 lb (2,418 kg) agricultural and rainmaking roles, or 3,525 lb (1,599 kg) utility cargo and passengers
Performance:
Maximum cruise speed: 157 kts (181 mph) 291 km/h at sea level, ISA
Cruise speed (75% power): 141 kts (162 mph) 261 km/h at sea level
Stall speed: 61.3 kts (70.6 mph) 114 km/h with full flaps at MTOW, 36 kts (42 mph) 67 km/h with full flaps at 3,000 lb (1,360 kg) landing weight
Take-off distance: 800 ft (244 m) unstick with a 1.5 tonne payload, 1,300 ft (396 m) unstick with a 2.2 tonne payload
Landing distance: 805 ft (245 m) ground roll with a 6,450 lb (2,926 kg) load and reverse propeller
Maximum climb rate: 1,658 ft (505 m) per minute with a 3,172 lb (1,438 kg) utility payload
Ceiling: 29,000 ft (8,840 m) clean, or 25,900 ft (7,900 m) with spraygear, both at 6,450 lb (2,926 kg), absolute
Range: 364 naut miles (420 miles) 676 km at 75% power, 7,000 lb (3,175 kg) weight with spraygear
Ferry range: 2,040 naut miles (2,350 miles) 3,782 km
Duration: 3 hours 5 minutes at 60% power
Typical load performance: 24,545 litres of liquid chemicals per hour (1,800 litres per trip), or 30 tonnes of dry chemicals per hour (2.2 tonnes per trip), using an airstrip 3.5 to 8.1 naut miles (4 to 9.3 miles) 6.5 to 15 km from the drop zone, at sea level

Electrical system: 28 volt, 150 amp generator, and 2 x 12 volt lead-acid batteries.
Braking system: Hydraulic. Parking brake.
Flight avionics/instrumentation: Instruments include an altimeter, magnetic compass, airspeed indicator, turn and slip indicator and much more. Optional avionics in basic and advanced Narco and AlliedSignal Bendix/King suites.

PAC FU24-954 Fletcher

First flight: 1954 for original US prototype.
Certification: 1955. Meets FAR Pt 23.
Role: Agricultural, firebombing, rainmaking, utility, aerial survey, photography and more.
Sales/users: 307 built.
Crew/passengers: 6 seats civil, 8 military, using an optional passenger kit. 2 litters and 2 attendants, or 2 litters, 3 sitting casualties and an attendant in an air ambulance role. Dual controls.
Chemical tank/hopper: 1,294 litres of liquid chemicals or up to 2,343 lb (1,063 kg) of dry chemicals.
Dispersal equipment: Micronair ultra-low volume spray equipment with wind-driven rotary atomizer units for typically up to 160 litres per minute application rate, or low volume spray equipment. Also aerial spreading of solids via a range of dispersal equipment, including the ultra high application Easton hopper outlet (clamshell type), the high volume Transland solid spreader with gate box and agitator, and the medium volume Transland Swathmaster with gate box and agitator. Controllable fire bombing door with minimum discharge time of 3 seconds.
Safety equipment: Seat collapse point of 25g. Optional wire cutter and deflector cable.
Wing control surfaces: Plain ailerons (25° up, 10° down) and single-slotted flaps (4 position, 40° maximum deflection).
Tail control surfaces: Slab tailplane (20° up, 5° down) with trim and anti-balance tab. Unbalanced rudder.
Flight control system: Mechanical, except for electric elevator trim.
Construction materials: Metal, stressed skin.
Engine: Textron Lycoming IO-720-A1A or A-1B piston engine, with a 7 ft 2 ins (2.18 m) Hartzell 3-blade constant-speed propeller. AlliedSignal TFE331-450 turboprop is under consideration.
Engine rating: 400 hp (298 kW).
Fuel system: 259 litres, of which 242 litres are usable. Optional integral tanks of 282 litres, of which 263 litres are usable. Optional methanol fueled conversion kit.

Details for FU24-954.

Principal dimensions:
Wing span: 42 ft (12.8 m)
Maximum length: 32 ft 8.75 ins (9.98 m)
Maximum height: 9 ft 4 ins (2.84 m)
Cabin cargo area:
Length: 10 ft (3.05 m)
Width: 4 ft (1.22 m)
Height: 4 ft 3 ins (1.3 m)
Cargo door size: As for Cresco.
Wings:
Aerofoil section: NACA 4415
Area: 294 sq ft (27.31 m^2)
Aspect ratio: 6
Undercarriage:
Type: Fixed, with steerable nosewheel
Weights:
Empty: 2,662 lb (1,207 kg)
Maximum take-off: 5,430 lb (2,463 kg) Agricultural, 4,860 lb (2,204 kg) Normal
Payload: 1,556 lb (705 kg) Normal, 2,126 lb (964 kg) Agricultural, both with full fuel
Performance:
Never-exceed speed (Vne): 143 kts (164 mph) 265 km/h
Maximum speed: 126 kts (145 mph) 233 km/h at sea level
Maximum cruise speed: 113 kts (130 mph) 209 km/h at 75% power
Spray speed: 90-115 kts (104-132 mph) 167-212 km/h
Swath width: 70-80 ft (21-24 m) liquid, 25-50 ft (7.5-15 m) dry
Stall speed: 55 kts (64 mph) 102 km/h *clean*, 49 kts (57 mph) 91 km/h *with flaps*
Take-off distance: 800 ft (244 m)
Landing distance: 680 ft (207 m)
Maximum climb rate: 920 ft (280 m) per minute at sea level
G limits: +3.8, -1.5
Ceiling: 16,000 ft (4,875 m), service
Range: 305 naut miles (351 miles) 565 km at MTOW and sea level, 60% power, clean
Duration: 3.77 hours at MTOW and 5,000 ft (1,525 m), 60% power, clean

Electrical system: 28 volt, 70 amp alternator and 2 x 12 volt batteries.
Flight avionics/instrumentation: Similar to Cresco.

Aeronautical Industrial Engineering and Project Management Company Ltd (Nigeria)

Corporate address: General Aviation Service Centre, PO Box 5662, Old Kaduna Airport, Kaduna.
Telephone: +234 62 236676
Facsimile: +234 62 237325
Founded: 1979.

● Activities

● AIEP manufactures under licence a variant of the Van's RV-6A, known as the Air Beetle (see Recreational section). T18 basic version (as built for the Nigerian Air Force as a trainer) has a 180 hp (134 kW) Textron Lycoming O-360-A1A engine.

Pakistan Aeronautical Complex (PAC) (Pakistan)

Corporate address: See Combat section (Multi-national) for company details. The Mushshak and Shahbaz are products of the Aircraft Manufacturing Factory.

PAC Mushshak and Shahbaz

Certification: Meet FAR Pt 23 in Normal, Utility and Aerobatic categories.
Role: Multi-purpose civil/military lightplanes, capable of several roles including training (basic, instrument, aerobatic, night flying, navigation and formation), crop spraying, army co-operation, observation, border patrol, and forward area support with droppable containers. Licence-built Saab versions of the Saab Safari and Supporter (see Aircraft variants).
Sales/users: Large number built, including some 220 Mushshaks for the Pakistan armed forces. In late 1994, 3 were given to Oman and 6 to Syria.
Details: Principally for Mushshak.
Crew/passengers: 2 crew, side by side, under an upward-hinged canopy. Large baggage compartment in the rear of the cabin can be used instead to accommodate a third person.
Wing control surfaces: Ailerons (starboard servo tab) and flaps.
Tail control surfaces: Slab tailplane with trim/anti-servo tab, and rudder with tab.
Flight control system: Mechanical, except for electric flaps.
Construction materials: Principally metal, but with some use of glassfibre. 8,300 hour structural life.
Engine: Textron Lycoming IO-360-A1B6 piston engine, with a 6 ft 2 ins (1.88 m) Hartzell 2-blade constant-speed propeller.
Engine rating: 200 hp (149 kW).
Fuel system: 182 litres.
Flight avionics/instrumentation: Typically VHF, UHF and ADF.

Pakistan Aeronautical Complex Mushshak

Expendable equipment/stores: Can carry up to 661 lb (300 kg) of external stores (including pylons) at 6 stations (inner stressed for 330lb, 150 kg; the remainder for 220lb, 100 kg), including machine-gun or rocket pods, light missiles or relief containers.
Aircraft variants:
Mushshak is the main military production version, developed from the Saab Safari/Supporter, but can undertake civil roles. Textron Lycoming engine. As detailed.
Shahbaz is an upgraded version of Mushshak, with a 210 hp (156.6 kW) Teledyne Continental TSIO-360MB piston engine and a McCauley 2-blade metal propeller. 6 underwing stations. Length 23 ft 6 ins (7.16 m).

DETAILS FOR MUSHSHAK.

Principal dimensions:
Wing span: 29 ft (8.84 m)
Maximum length: 23 ft (7.01 m)
Maximum height: 8 ft 6.5 ins (2.6 m)
Wings:
Area: 128.1 sq ft (11.9 m^2)
Aspect ratio: 6.57
Undercarriage:
Type: Fixed, with nosewheel
Weights:
Empty: 1,424 lb (646 kg)
Maximum take-off: 2,645 lb (1,200 kg) Normal, 2,480 lb (1,125 kg) Utility, and 1,980 lb (898 kg) Aerobatic
Performance (Normal category):
Never-exceed speed (Vne): 197 kts (226 mph) 364 km/h
Maximum speed: 125 kts (144 mph) 232 km/h
Cruise speed: 110 kts (127 mph) 204 km/h at 75% power, sea level
Stall speed: 66 kts (76 mph) 122 km/h *clean* and engine idling, 60 kts (69 mph) 111 km/h *with 38° flaps* and zero thrust
Take-off distance: 850 ft (259 m) with 10° flaps
Landing distance: 530 ft (162 m) including 1 second delay before braking
Maximum climb rate: 710 ft (216 m) per minute at sea level
Time to 6,000 ft (1,830 m): 11.5 minutes
G limits: +4.8, -2.4, or +6, -3 for Aerobatic category
Ceiling: 10,400 ft (3,170 m), or 18,800 ft (5,730 m) for Aerobatic category
Duration: 5 hours 10 minutes at 65% power, with reserve

Western Pacific Aviation Corporation (Philippines)

Corporate address: RPMCI Hangar, Manila Domestic Airport, PO Box 7633, Airport Airmail Exchange Office, Domestic Road, Pasay City.
Telephone: +63 2 832 3375, 2777
Facsimile: +63 2 833 0605
Information: R. P. Moscardon.

● Activities

● WPAC produces the Skyfox, which is similar in most respects to the SkyStar Kitfox (originally licensed to Philippine Aircraft Company Inc by Denney Aerocraft in 1987). WPAC has the capability to produce quantities to order, and was also expected to begin development of its own aircraft in 1995.

Instytut Lotnictwa (Poland)

Corporate address: See Combat section for company details.

Instytut Lotnictwa I-23

First flight: Expected 1995.
Certification: 1996 to JAR 23.
Role: Four-seat lightplane.
Sales/users: Deliveries from 1997, with expected production rate of 100 per year by the end of the decade.
Wing control surfaces: Ailerons and single-slotted flaps.
Tail control surfaces: Elevators (port tab) and 2-section rudder (with tab).
Flight control system: Mechanical.

DETAILS FOR I-23.

Principal dimensions:
Wing span: 29 ft 4 ins (8.94 m)
Maximum length: 22 ft 2 ins (6.76 m)
Maximum height: 7 ft 10.5 ins (2.4 m)
Wings:
Area: 107.64 sq ft (10 m^2)
Aspect ratio: 7.992
Undercarriage:
Type: Retractable or optional fixed, with nosewheel
Weights:
Empty: 1,217 lb (552 kg)
Maximum take-off: 2,095 lb (950 kg)
Performance:
Maximum speed: 162 kts (186 mph) 300 km/h
Economical cruise speed: 135 kts (155 mph) 250 km/h
Stall speed: 59 kts (68 mph) 109 km/h
Take-off distance: 541 ft (165 m)
Landing distance: 400 ft (122 m)
Maximum climb rate: 1,000 ft (306 m) per minute
Ceiling: 14,425 ft (4,400 m)
Range with full fuel: 810 naut miles (932 miles) 1,500 km

Construction materials: Principally glassfibre, carbonfibre and epoxy.
Engine: Textron Lycoming O-320-D1A piston engine. Other engines in the 115-200 hp (85.75-149 kW) range.
Engine rating: 160 hp (119 kW).
Fuel system: 150 litres.
Electrical system: 12 volt, with alternator and battery.
Flight avionics/instrumentation: AlliedSignal Bendix/King VFR suite. Options include IFR suite, 2-axis autopilot, GPS and DME.

PZL-Mielec S.A. (Poland)

Corporate address: See Combat section for company details.

PZL-Mielec M-18 Dromader series

First flight: 27 August 1976.
Certification: FAR Pt 23, with certification in 11 countries. In addition, many US distributors and companies possess Supplemental Type Certificates allowing installation of enlarged fuel tanks, PW&C PT6A-45AG turboprop engine and a two-seat training cockpit. New M-18B received the revised Polish BB-120 Type Certificate in February 1994.
Role: Agricultural and forestry work. Later can include firefighting, fire patrol, neutralizing contaminated soil, and spraying against diseases and pests.
Sales/users: Many hundreds built and widely exported 45 for delivery in 1995.
Crew/passengers: Pilot in a sealed cockpit to prevent chemical ingress. Separate cabin aft for a passenger, providing also the space required for a second cockpit in the training version.
Chemical tank/hopper: 2,500 litres of liquid chemical or up to 2,976 lb (1,350 kg) of dry chemicals.
Dispersal equipment: 58 ft 1 ins (17.7 m) sprayboom. Alternative atomizer, spreader, or water-bombing equipment. Water bombing dump time (2,500 litres) is 2.5 seconds.
Safety equipment: Cockpit can withstand a 40g impact. Cable cutters.
Wing control surfaces: Slotted ailerons (with trim tabs) and 2-section slotted flaps (15° for landing – see also M-18B).
Tail control surfaces: Elevators and rudder, with trim tabs.
Flight control system: Pushrod and cable, except for hydraulic flaps.
Construction materials: Metal, with some use of corrugated skins.

PZL-Mielec M-18A Dromader

Details for M-18A Dromader.

Principal dimensions:
Wing span: 58 ft 1 ins (17.7 m)
Maximum length: 31 ft 1 ins (9.47 m)
Maximum height: 12 ft 2 ins (3.7 m)
Wings:
Aerofoil section: NACA 4416/4412 (root/tip)
Area: 430.6 sq ft (40 m^2)
Aspect ratio: 7.83
Undercarriage:
Type: Fixed, with castering and lockable tailwheel
Weights:
Empty: about 5,977 lb (2,710 kg)
Maximum take-off: 9,260 lb (4,200 kg) Normal FAR Pt 23, 10,362 lb (4,700 kg) Restricted, and 11,684 lb (5,300 kg) Cam 9 max
Performance (with dry chemical equipment):
Maximum speed: 128 kts (147 mph) 237 km/h
Work speed: 92 kts (106 mph) 170 km/h
Stall speed: 65 kts (74 mph) 119 km/h *clean*, 59 kts (68 mph) 109 km/h *with flaps*
Take-off distance: 624 ft (190 m) at 9,300 lb (4,218 kg) weight, or 1,503 ft (458 m) with 5,600 lb (2,540 kg) hopper load
Landing distance: 985 ft (300 m)
Maximum climb rate: 1,358 ft (414 m) per minute without equipment, at 9,300 lb (4,218 kg) weight
G limits: +3.4, -1.4 to FAR Pt 23
Ceiling: 21,300 ft (6,500 m)
Range with full fuel: 524 naut miles (603 miles) 970 km

Engine: WSK Kalisz ASz-62IR-M18 radial piston engine, with a 10 ft 10 ins (3.3 m) 4-blade propeller.
Engine rating: 967 hp (721 kW).
Fuel system: 720 litres.
Electrical system: 100 amp generator and 25 amp-hour ni-cd battery.
Hydraulic system: Up to 1,987 psi for the agricultural equipment, brakes and flaps.
Braking system: Hydraulic disc. Parking brake.
Aircraft variants:
M-18A is the main production version, as described.
M-18AS is the designation of the M-18A when used for two-seat training purposes, fitted with an attachable instructor's cockpit in the rear cabin area. Glassfibre canopy extension. Reduced-capacity hopper.
M-18B is the new model, designed for firefighting at up to 11,684 lb (5,300 kg) AUW. Primary changes are a modified tailplane and elevator control system, incorporation of elastic interconnection between the ailerons and rudder control systems, and wing flap deflection increased for landing (30°) and take-off. All these modifications result in enhanced lateral stability, improved manoeuvring, steeper landing descent path, landing distance reduced by about 200 m, ability to take-off with a 4,853 lb (2,200 kg) payload, and reduced need to use elevator trim, with K-9 engine and larger AW-2 propeller.
M-18C and D are new models with 1,200hp (895kW) K-9 engines.
Turboprop version, see Certification. See also Melex.

PZL-Mielec M-20 Mewa

First flight: 25 July 1979 with PZL-Rzeszów PZL-F6A350 engines, and 13 October 1988 with Teledyne Continentals.
Certification: 22 September 1983 with PZL engines, and 12 December 1988 with Teledyne Continentals.
Role: Passenger, air taxi, executive, light cargo, ambulance and reconnaissance/patrol. Developed from the Piper Seneca II.

PZL-Mielec M-20 Mewa

Crew/passengers: See Aircraft variants. Additional seat for a seventh person is optional.
Baggage capacity: Compartments in the nose and in the cabin behind the seats. See Aircraft variants.
Wing control surfaces: Frise ailerons and single-slotted flaps.
Tail control surfaces: Slab tailplane with trim tab, and balanced rudder with anti-servo tab.
Construction materials: Metal.
Engines: 2 Teledyne Continental TSIO-360-KB piston engines. Optional APU for special missions.
Engine rating: Each 220 hp (164 kW).
Fuel system: 371 litres standard, of which 352 litres are usable. Optional long-range auxiliary tanks to increase capacity to 484 litres, of which 465 litres are usable. Extra long-range wingtip tanks.
Electrical system: 24 volt, with alternators and battery.
Hydraulic system: 2 systems, at 2,233 psi for the undercarriage and 1,500 psi for brakes.
Braking system: Disc brakes. Parking brake.
De-icing system: Fitted.
Radar: Optional weather radar.
Flight avionics/instrumentation: Current model offered with AlliedSignal Bendix/King suite. ELT.

Options include GPS, area navigation and autopilot, but not all options (these and others including air conditioning) can be carried with 6 passengers on board; the new M-20-04 remedies this by having a higher MTOW.
Aircraft variants:
Current versions are based on the M-20-03:
Passenger/air taxi has seating for the pilot, 5 forward-facing passengers and 88 lb (40 kg) of baggage in 17.66 cu ft (0.5 m^3) of space.
Service/light cargo version carries the pilot, 1 passenger and 750 lb (340 kg) of cargo in 141 cu ft (4 m^3) of space.
Club/executive version has the pilot and 5 opposite-facing seats, table, fold-down armrests and refreshment console.
Ambulance version carries the pilot plus 1 litter or an incubator and 2 attendants, and attachment fittings and supply system for in-flight-usable medical equipment. Special arrangement of the doctor's seat.
Reconnaissance/patrol version has various configurations for maritime/border patrol, police work, SAR, and environmental pollution control. Special optional equipment includes external radio/radar/FLIR/UV detectors, aerial camera, high-power searchlight and loudspeakers.
M-20-04 is a new version that first flew in 1995. Maximum take-off weight is 4,750 lb (2,155 kg). Strengthened main spar and fuselage structure, and 28 volt electrical system. Can carry the full range of options with full passenger load.

Details for the current Mewa.

Principal dimensions:
Wing span: 38 ft 11 ins (11.86 m)
Maximum length: 27 ft 7 ins (8.72 m)
Maximum height: 9 ft 11 ins (3.02 m)
Cabin:
Width: 4 ft 1 ins (1.24 m)
Height: 3 ft 6 ins (1.07 m)
Wings:
Aerofoil section: NACA 652-415
Area: 206.45 sq ft (19.18 m^2)
Aspect ratio: 7.33
Undercarriage:
Type: Retractable, with steerable nosewheel
Weights:
Empty: 2,910 lb (1,320 kg)
Maximum take-off: 4,563 lb (2,070 kg)
Maximum landing: 4,343 lb (1,970 kg)
Payload: 1,080 lb (490 kg)
Performance:
Maximum speed: 194 kts (224 mph) 360 km/h
Cruise speed: 168 kts (193 mph) 311 km/h at 45% power, at 24,800 ft (7,560 m)
Stall speed: 67 kts (77 mph) 124 km/h *clean*, 61 kts (70 mph) 112 km/h *with landing flaps*
Take-off over a 50 ft (15 m) obstacle: 1,457 ft (444 m)
Landing over a 50 ft (15 m) obstacle: 2,150 ft (655 m)
Maximum climb rate: 1,500 ft (456 m) per minute near ground
Ceiling: 25,000 ft (7,620 m)
Range: 669 naut miles (770 miles) 1,240 km with standard fuel, 989 naut miles (1,139 miles) 1,833 km with optional fuel, 45% power, 45 minutes reserve

PZL-Mielec M-26 Iskierka

First flight: 15 July 1986 (with original PZL engine).
Certification: 26 October 1991 (Polish). Meets FAR Pt 23 requirements.
Role: Civil and military basic (VFR and IFR), professional licence, preliminary, navigation and aerobatic trainer.

PZL-Mielec M-26 Iskierka

Sales/users: Production began in late 1994/early 1995. First 10 completed by mid-1995. Melex undertakes US sales.
Crew: 2, in tandem, with the instructor in the raised rear cockpit.
Baggage capacity: Behind rear seat.
Wing control surfaces: Frise ailerons and single-slotted flaps.
Tail control surfaces: Elevators (with starboard trim tab) and rudder.
Construction materials: Metal. Uses M-20 Mewa assemblies, such as elements of the wings, vertical tail, fuselage and undercarriage.
Engine: Textron Lycoming AEIO-540-L1B5D piston engine, with a 6 ft 3 ins (1.9 m) 3-blade propeller.
Engine rating: 300 hp (224 kW).
Fuel system: 597 lb (271 kg).
Electrical system: 100 amp alternator and 25 amp-hour battery.

Details for Iskierka.

Principal dimensions:
Wing span: 28 ft 2.5 ins (8.6 m)
Maximum length: 27 ft 3 ins (8.3 m)
Maximum height: 9 ft 8.5 ins (2.96 m)
Wings:
Area: 150.69 sq ft (14 m^2)
Aspect ratio: 5.28
Undercarriage:
Type: Retractable, with nosewheel
Weights:
Empty: 2,072 lb (940 kg)
Maximum take-off: 3,086 lb (1,400 kg)
Performance:
Never-exceed speed (Vne): 207 kts (239 mph) 385 km/h
Maximum speed: 178 kts (205 mph) 330 km/h
Stall speed: 60 kts (69 mph) 110 km/h, with flaps
Take-off over a 50 ft (15 m) obstacle: 1,870 ft (570 m)
Landing over a 50 ft (15 m) obstacle: 2,247 ft (685 m)
Maximum climb rate: 1,380 ft (420 m) per minute
Range: 874 naut miles (1,006 miles) 1,620 km, with 30 minutes reserve

Hydraulic system: As for Mewa.
Braking system: Mainwheel hydraulic discs. Parking brake.
Flight avionics/instrumentation: AlliedSignal Bendix/King suite now standard. Provision for gunsight, gun camera and armament control system.
Expendable weapons and equipment: 2 pylons for light bombs or weapon pods.

PZL-Mielec An-2 Antek (NATO name *Colt*)

The Antonov An-2 passenger, agricultural and general purpose biplane first flew in 1947. It has been licence-built in Poland since 1960, with more than 12,000 delivered to civil and military users in some 20 countries, although the vast majority have been sold to the former USSR. A description of the Chinese derivative of the An-2 can be found under Shijiazhuang Y5B.

PZL-Warszawa Okëcie (Poland)

Corporate address: See Combat section for company details.

PZL-Warszawa Okëcie PZL-104 Wilga series

First flight: 24 April 1962.
Role: Multi-purpose short take-off lightplane, including passenger, ambulance, agricultural, patrol, survey and aerial towing. (Special missions variant of Wilga 80-S developed by Terra-Scan in the USA, with Wescam IR system.)
Sales/users: Approaching 1,000 built and widely exported.
Crew/passengers: Pilot and 3 passengers or other layouts according to role.
Details: Principally for Wilga 35 and 80.
Wing control surfaces: Slotted ailerons (starboard tab), slotted flaps and leading-edge slats. Ailerons can droop for landing.
Tail control surfaces: Single-piece elevator with tab and rudder.
Flight control system: Manual/mechanical.
Construction materials: Metal.
Engine: WSK Kalisz AI-14RA radial piston engine in Wilga 35, and AI-14RA-KAF with repositioned carburettor in Wilga 80. PZL 2-blade wooden propeller.
Engine rating: 251.3 hp (187.4 kW).
Fuel system: 195 litres. 90 litre auxiliary tank can be fitted in the cabin, in place of the rear seats.
Electrical system: DC supply via a generator and ni-cd battery.
Hydraulic system: 565 psi for brakes.
Braking system: Hydraulic.
Flight avionics/instrumentation: Polish or AlliedSignal Bendix/King nav/comm.
Aircraft variants:
Wilga 35 is the basic version, meeting BCAR certification standards. Wilga 35A is equipped for towing up to 3 gliders, Wilga 35H has Airtech twin floats, and Wilga 35R is for agricultural use.
Wilga 35M is a much more powerful version, with a

PZL-Warszawa Okëcie PZL-104 Wilga 80

360 hp (268 kW) Aerostar M-14P engine and PZL-144 propeller.
Wilga 80 is similar to Wilga 35 except for the carburettor and slightly differing dimensions, and is to FAR 23 certification standard. A, H and R versions as for Wilga 35.
Wilga 80-550 is a version of the Wilga 80 with a 300 hp (224 kW) Teledyne Continental IO-550 horizontally-opposed engine (instead of radial) and other changes, to improve general performance. Developed and marketed by Melex in the USA, it is also produced by PZL using Melex kits.

Details for Wilga 35.

Principal dimensions:
Wing span: 36 ft 9 ins (11.2 m)
Maximum length: 26 ft 7 ins (8.1 m)
Maximum height: 9 ft 8.5 ins (2.96 m)
Wings:
Aerofoil section: NACA 2415
Area: 166.84 sq ft (15.5 m^2)
Aspect ratio: 7.98
Undercarriage:
Type: Fixed, with steerable tailwheel. Tall, pivoted, main legs. Low pressure main types. Optional floats or skis
Weights:
Empty: 1,995 lb (905 kg) ± 1
Maximum take-off and landing: 2,866 lb (1,300 kg)
Performance:
Never-exceed speed (Vne): 150 kts (173 mph) 279 km/h
Maximum speed: 104 kts (120 mph) 192.5 km/h
Cruise speed: 89 kts (103 mph) 165 km/h at 1,860 rpm
Stall speed: 38 kts (44 mph) 70 km/h with 44° flaps
Take-off distance: 437 ft (133 m) on grass
Landing distance: 472 ft (144 m) on grass
Maximum climb rate: 905 ft (276 m) per minute at sea level
Ceiling: 13,000 ft (3,960 m), service
Range with full fuel: 275 naut miles (316 miles) 510 km

PZL-Warszawa Okëcie PZL-105L Flaming

First flight: 19 December 1989 (original M-14P engine).
Certification: Meets FAR Pt 23 standards.
Role: Multi-purpose short take-off lightplane, including passenger, ambulance, agricultural, patrol, survey and aerial towing. Designed to replace Wilga, offering a larger cabin for 6 persons and better performance.
Crew/passengers: Pilot and up to 5 passengers or other layouts according to role. 992 lb (450 kg) of freight with all passenger seats removed.
Wing characteristics: Strut-braced (instead of Wilga's cantilever).
Wing control surfaces: Single-slotted flaperons (port tab) and single-slotted Fowler flaps. Mass balanced.
Tail control surfaces: Cantilever tailplane (instead of Wilga's strut braced). Elevators (port trim tab) and rudder (ground-adjustable tab). Mass balanced.
Flight control system: Pushrods and cables, except for electric flaps and elevator tab.
Construction materials: Metal, other than the glassfibre wingtips, rudder tip and elevator tips.
Engine: Textron Lycoming IO-720-A1B piston engine, with a Hartzell 3-blade propeller.
Engine rating: 400 hp (298 kW).
Fuel system: 270 litres, weight 419 lb (190 kg).
Electrical system: 28 volt DC supply, via an engine-driven 24 volt, 70 amp alternator and 15 amp-hour ni-cd battery.
Braking system: Hydraulic disc.
Flight avionics/instrumentation: Includes audio amplifier, ADF, gyro compass, dual nav/comm, marker receiver, and optional transponder and RMI/HSI. Polish or AlliedSignal.

Details for Flaming.

Principal dimensions:
Wing span: 42 ft 7 ins (12.98 m)
Maximum length: 28 ft 7 ins (8.7 m)
Maximum height: 9 ft 0.5 ins (2.76 m)
Wings:
Aerofoil section: NASA GA(W)-1
Area: 181.91 sq ft (16.9 m^2)
Aspect ratio: 9.969
Undercarriage:
Type: Fixed, with steerable tailwheel. Glassfibre cantilever legs instead of Wilga's pivoting type. Similar float/ski options to Wilga
Weights:
Empty: 2,646 lb (1,200 kg)
Maximum take-off: 4,079 lb (1,850 kg)
Performance:
Maximum speed: 140 kts (161 mph) 260 km/h
Cruise speed: 119-132 kts (137-152 mph) 220-245 km/h
Stall speed: 55 kts (63 mph) 102 km/h
Take-off distance: 620 ft (189 m)
Landing distance: 515 ft (157 m)
Maximum climb rate: 1,102 ft (336 m) per minute at sea level
G limits: +3.8, -1.52
Ceiling: 15,290 ft (4,660 m)
Range: 518 naut miles (597 miles) 960 km

PZL-Warszawa Okëcie PZL-105L Flaming (courtesy PZL-Warszawa Okëcie/Lech Zielaskowski)

PZL-Warszawa Okëcie PZL-106BT-601 Kruk

First flight: 18 September 1985.
Role: Agricultural and firefighting.
Sales/users: All production of the piston-engined Kruk and turboprop-engined Kruk was halted in about 1991-92. Production of the turbine Kruk restarted in 1994, offering a new larger 1,500 litre chemical hopper.
Crew: Pilot, with jump-seat to transport a mechanic to site. For training, a second cockpit can be fitted ahead of the standard cockpit and a small training hopper installed. Cockpit sealed to prevent chemical ingress.
Chemical tank/hopper: Glassfibre, with 1,500 litre liquid capacity or 2,866 lb (1,300 kg) of dry chemicals.
Dispersal equipment: Spraybars for liquids, with fan-driven pump. Alternative atomizer or spreader equipment. Load dump time is about 5 seconds. Swath width 147 ft (45 m) with atomizer, 98 ft (30 m) with nozzles.
Safety equipment: Designed to allow the pilot to survive a 40g impact. Steel roll-over cage, and cable cutters on the undercarriage and windshield. Cable deflector from the windshield cutter to the tail.
Engine: Motorlet Walter M601D turboprop, with an Avia 3-blade propeller.

DETAILS FOR PZL-106BT-601 KRUK.

Principal dimensions:
Wing span: 49 ft 3 ins (15 m)
Maximum length: 33 ft 11 ins (10.34 m)
Maximum height: 14 ft 3 ins (4.34 m)
Wings:
Aerofoil section: NACA 2415
Area: 341.1 sq ft (31.69 m^2)
Aspect ratio: 7.19
Undercarriage:
Type: Fixed, with tailwheel
Weights:
Empty: 3,703 lb (1,680 kg)
Maximum take-off: 7,716 lb (3,500 kg)
Performance (equipped):
Maximum speed: 116 kts (133 mph) 215 km/h
Spray speed: typically 91 kts (105 mph) 170 km/h
Stall speed: 49 kts (56 mph) 90 km/h
Take-off and landing distance: 886 ft (270 m)
Maximum climb rate: 1,181 ft (360 m) per minute at sea level
Range: 486 naut miles (559 miles) 900 km

Engine rating: 724 shp (540 kW).
Fuel system: Ferry fuel can be carried in the hopper.

PZL-Warszawa Okëcie PZL-110 and PZL-111 Koliber

First flight: 18 April 1978 (original low-powered PZL-Rzeszów PZL-F.4A-engined version).
Role: Pleasure, training, aerial towing and more, originally based on the Socata Rallye.
Sales/users: 14 PZL-110 Kolibers were ordered in 1994, with production of the Koliber continuing and range expanding.
Crew/passengers: 4 persons. Dual controls. Entrance via a sliding canopy.
Wing control surfaces: Balanced ailerons (with ground adjustable tabs), Fowler flaps and automatic leading-edge slats.
Tail control surfaces: Balanced elevator (with tab) and rudder (with ground adjustable tab).

PZL-Warszawa Okëcie PZL-106BT-601 Turbo-Kruk (Courtesy PZL-Warszawa Okëcie)

Flight control system: Mechanical, except for electric flaps.
Construction materials: Metal, with corrugated skins adopted by the elevator, flaps and rudder.
Engine: See Aircraft variants.
Fuel system: 105 litres basic for PZL-110, but with the option of 177 litres. 170 litres are basic for the Koliber 235.
Electrical system: 12 volt for all versions except Koliber 150A, which is 24 volt. Supply via an alternator and battery.
Hydraulic system: For brakes only.
Braking system: Hydraulic disc.
Flight avionics/instrumentation: Include ADF, VOR, turn and bank indicator, attitude and direction gyros, and UHF transceiver. Koliber 150A has a higher standard of avionics and can undertake IFR and night flying.
Aircraft variants:
PZL-110 Koliber 150 has a 150 hp (112 kW) Textron Lycoming O-320-E2A piston engine, with a 5 ft 10 ins (1.78 m) Sensenich 74DM6 2-blade constant-speed propeller.
PZL-110 Koliber 150A has a higher-standard of avionics and uprated electrical system, as required for IFR. Sold in North America as the Koliber II by Cadmus Corporation, No 1 Northfield Plaza, Northfield, IL (*telephone* +1 708 446 2644). FAR Pt 23 Amdt 23 certification.
PZL-111 Koliber 160 has a 160 hp (119 kW) Textron Lycoming piston engine.
PZL-111 Koliber 180 has a 180 hp (134 kW) Textron Lycoming piston engine.

PZL-Warszawa Okëcie PZL-110 Koliber 150A

DETAILS FOR THE KOLIBER 150A.

Principal dimensions:
Wing span: 32 ft (9.75 m)
Maximum length: 24 ft 2 ins (7.37 m)
Maximum height: 9 ft 2 ins (2.8 m)
Wings:
Aerofoil section: Modified NACA 63A-416
Area: 136.49 sq ft (12.68 m^2)
Aspect ratio: 7.497
Undercarriage:
Type: Fixed, with castering nosewheel
Weights:
Empty: 1,208 lb (548 kg)
Maximum take-off: 1,874 lb (850 kg)
Performance:
Never-exceed speed (Vne): 145 kts (167 mph) 270 km/h
Maximum cruise speed: 104 kts (119 mph) 192 km/h
Stall speed: 48 kts (56 mph) 89 km/h *clean*, 43 kts (49 mph) 79 km/h *with flaps*, IAS
Take-off over a 50 ft (15 m) obstacle: 1,312 ft (400 m)
Landing over a 50 ft (15 m) obstacle: 984 ft (300 m)
Maximum climb rate: 866 ft (264 m) per minute at sea level
G limits: +4.4, -1.8
Ceiling: 12,150 ft (3,700 m), service
Range with full fuel: 448 naut miles (516 miles) 830 km

PZL-111 Koliber 200 has a 200 hp (149 kW) Textron Lycoming piston engine.
PZL-111 Koliber 235 has a 235 hp (175 kW) Textron Lycoming O-540-B4B5 piston engine.

PZL-Warszawa Okëcie (Agrolot Foundation) PZL-126P Mrówka

Role: Very small and light, low-volume agricultural aircraft, also suited to pest and disease control, forest and pipe/powerline patrol, survey, and more. First flown in 1990. PZL requested that this aircraft should be cancelled from the book.

PZL-Warszawa Okëcie PZL-140 Orzel

Role: 2,700 nautmile (3,107 mile) 5,000 km range, pressurized seven-seat business aircraft, at the design stage. PT6A turboprops. PZL requested that this aircraft should be cancelled from the book.

Aerostar S.A. (Romania)

Full name: Grup Industrial Aeronautic Aerostar S.A.
Corporate address: str. Condorilor nr 9, Bacau 5500.
Telephone: +40 34 130070
Facsimile: +40 34 161113
Founded: 1953, taking its current name in 1991.
Employees: About 7,000.
Information: Dumitru Biceri (Commercial Director).

● Activities

● In addition to Yak-52 production (confirmed as being marketed as the Yak-52 by Aerostar and not the widely quoted Iak-52), the company produces M-14P and M-14V26 aero-engines, the RU-19A-300 engine/APU, low-power diesel engines for agricultural machinery and domestic applications, metal buildings, and undercarriages and systems for other Romanian-built aircraft. It is also teamed with IAI's Bedek division in the upgrade of Romanian MiG-21s.

- Production of avionics.
- The AG-6 agricultural aircraft programme has been terminated.

Aerostar Yak-52

First flight: 1978.
Role: Fully aerobatic military and civil trainer, built under Yakovlev licence.
Sales/users: More than 1,700 in use worldwide.
Crew: 2 in tandem, with dual controls. No rear-instructor elevation.
Delivered with: Towing bars (for hand and car towing), false undercarriage (used for transportation), anchor devices and cables, cockpit lock, cover, spare parts, manuals, tools and wooden transport box. Warranty covers 300 flying hours in 15 months, with no more than 3 months in the producer's wooden box.
Wing control surfaces: Slotted ailerons (with ground-adjustable tabs) and split flaps.
Tail control surfaces: Elevators (port trim tab) and rudder (ground-adjustable tab).
Flight control system: Pushrod and cables, except for pneumatic flaps.
Construction materials: Aluminium alloy and steel, but with fabric covering for the ailerons, elevators and rudder. Airframe life of 5,000 flying hours or 20 years.

Yak-52 (Piotr Butowski)

Details for Aerostar Yak-52.

Principal dimensions:
Wing span: 30 ft 6 ins (9.3 m)
Maximum length: 25 ft 5 ins (7.745 m)
Maximum height: 8 ft 10 ins (2.7 m)
Wings:
Area: 161.46 sq ft (15 m^2)
Aspect ratio: 5.766
Undercarriage:
Type: Retractable, with nosewheel. Mainwheel legs retract forward and nosewheel aft, leaving all 3 wheels exposed to prevent serious damage in a wheels-up landing. Optional skis
Weights:
Empty: 2,204 lb (1,000 kg)
Maximum take-off: 2,844 lb (1,290 kg)
Performance:
Maximum speed: 162 kts (186 mph) 300 km/h at 1,640 ft (500 m)
Stall speed: about 48 kts (56 mph) 90 km/h with flaps
Take-off distance: 560 ft (170 m)
Landing distance: 656 ft (200 m)
Maximum climb rate: 1,476 ft (450 m) per minute at sea level
G limits: +7, -5
Ceiling: 13,125 ft (4,000 m)
Range with full fuel: 297 naut miles (341 miles) 550 km

Engine: Aerostar M-14P radial piston engine, with a 7 ft 10 ins (2.4 m) V-530TA-D35 2-blade variable-pitch propeller. Engine life of 2,250 flying hours, propeller life of 800 flying hours or 12 years.
Engine rating: 360 hp (268 kW).
Fuel system: 122 litres. Collector tank for inverted flight.
Electrical system: 27 volt DC supply, via an engine-driven 3 kW generator. 12 volt battery. 36 volt, 400 Hz AC supply via 2 inverters.
Braking system: Pneumatic brakes.
Flight avionics/instrumentation: Gyro and radio compasses, VHF comm and more.

CPCA (Romania)

Corporate address: As for Avioane in Combat section.
Telephone: +40 51 123059

CPCA DK-10 Dracula

First flight: May 1996.
Certification: To meet FAR Pt 23 standards.
Role: Two-seat lightplane and trainer, with sliding canopy.
Sales/users: Anticipated cost is $78,000.
Baggage capacity: 0.17 cu ft (6 m^3) aft of the seats.
Wing control surfaces: Ailerons (port trim tab) and slotted flaps.
Tail control surfaces: Horn-balanced elevators and rudder, all with trim tabs.
Flight control system: Mechanical, except for hydraulic flaps and electric tabs.
Construction materials: Metal.
Engine: Textron Lycoming O-320-A1A piston engine, with a Hartzell 2-blade constant-speed propeller.
Engine rating: 150 hp (112 kW).
Fuel system: 92 litres.
Electrical system: DC supply via a 28 volt engine-driven starter-generator. 24 volt battery.
Hydraulic system: 3,046 psi.
Braking system: Mainwheel hydraulic.
Flight avionics/instrumentation: AlliedSignal Bendix/King DME, VOR/ILS, marker beacon receiver, VHF comm and transponder.

Details for DK-10 Dracula.

Principal dimensions:
Wing span: 27 ft 6 ins (8.38 m)
Maximum length: 22 ft 11 ins (6.98 m)
Maximum height: 6 ft 11 ins (2.1 m)
Wings:
Aerofoil section: NACA 23-023/23-012 (root/tip)
Area: 107.64 sq ft (10 m^2)
Aspect ratio: 7.022
Undercarriage:
Type: Retractable, with steerable nosewheel
Weights:
Empty: 1,080 lb (490 kg)
Maximum take-off and landing: 1,653 lb (750 kg)
Payload: 406 lb (184 kg)
Performance (provisional):
Maximum speed: 163 kts (187 mph) 302 km/h
Stall speed: 58 kts (66 mph) 107 km/h *clean*, 52 kts (59 mph) 96 km/h *with flaps*
Maximum climb rate: 750 ft (228 m) per minute at sea level
Ceiling: 16,400 ft (5,000 m)
Range with full fuel: 540 naut miles (620 miles) 1,000 km

IAR-SA Brasov (Romania)

Corporate address: See IAR-SA Brasov in the Helicopter section for company details. See also Gliders/Motorgliders.

IAR 46

First flight: 1993.
Role: Two-seat lightplane for private use.

IAR-SA Brasov IAR 46 (courtesy IAR-SA Brasov)

Details for IAR-46.

Principal dimensions:
Wing span: 37 ft 6 ins (11.42 m)
Maximum length: 25 ft 9 ins (7.85 m)
Maximum height: 7 ft 1 ins (2.15 m)
Wings:
Area: 149.29 sq ft (13.87 m^2)
Aspect ratio: 9.403
Undercarriage:
Type: Retracting main wheels, fixed tailwheel
Weights:
Empty: 1,168 lb (530 kg)
Maximum take-off: 1,653 lb (750 kg)
Performance:
Maximum speed: 110 kts (126 mph) 204 km/h
Economical cruise speed: 89 kts (103 mph) 165 km/h
Stall speed: 42 kts (48 mph) 78 km/h
Take-off distance: 775 ft (235 m)
Landing distance: 330 ft (100 m)
Maximum climb rate: 1,980 ft (604 m) per minute
Ceiling: 16,400 ft (5,000 m)
Range: 458 naut miles (528 miles) 850 km

Wing control surfaces: Ailerons and plain flaps.
Tail control surfaces: T-tail with elevators (with tabs) and large rudder.
Flight control system: Mechanical.
Construction materials: Principally metal, but with fabric covering the elevators and rudder, and glassfibre fairings.
Engine: Rotax 912 A piston engine, with a 5 ft 7 ins (1.7 m) 2-blade composites propeller.
Engine rating: 77.8 hp (58 kW).
Fuel system: 78 litres.
Flight avionics/instrumentation: VFR instrumentation. Options at customer's request.

IAR-SA Brasov Noga VI (courtesy IAR-SA Brasov)

IAR Noga VI

First flight: Expected in 1997.
Certification: 1998 to FAR Pt 23/25.
Role: Business jet. Designed in association with the French Aeronautical Design Company.
Sales/users: 2 flying prototypes plus static test airframes.
Crew/passengers: 6 to 8, including pilot(s).
Wing control surfaces: Ailerons, flaps and spoilers.
Tail control surfaces: Elevators and inset rudder.
Construction materials: Aluminium alloy, with some use of composites.
Engines: 2 Williams-Rolls FJ44 turbofans.
Engine rating: Each 1,900 lbf (8.45 kN).
Fuel system: 2,777 lb (1,260 kg).

Details for Noga VI.

Principal dimensions:
Wing span: 37 ft 9 ins (11.5 m)
Maximum length: 41 ft 10 ins (12.75 m)
Maximum height: 14 ft 6 ins (4.42 m)
Wings:
Area: 184.6 sq ft (17.15 m^2)
Aspect ratio: 7.71
Undercarriage:
Type: Retractable, with steerable nosewheel
Weights:
Empty: 5,212 lb (2,364 kg)
Maximum take-off: 9,449 lb (4,286 kg)
Payload: 1,638 lb (743 kg)
Performance:
Maximum operating Mach number (Mmo): Mach 0.82
Maximum speed: 470 kts (541 mph) 870 km/h
Best range cruise speed: 413 kts (476 mph) 765 km/h
Maximum climb rate: 3,800 ft (1,158 m) per minute at sea level
Ceiling: 41,000 ft (12,500 m)
Range: 1,700 naut miles (1,958 miles) 3,148 km at best range speed

Aeropract (Russia)

Corporate address: PO Box 9863, Samara 443008.
Telephone: +7 8462 638291

Aeropract A-21M Solo (Igor Vakhruchev)

Aeropract A-21M Solo

Role: Small and light single-seat private low-wing monoplane, with potential for other uses including aeroclub, agricultural and forest/pipeline patrol.
Control surfaces: Conventional.
Engine: Rotax 503 piston engine, with a 2-blade propeller with spinner.
Engine rating: 45.6 hp (34 kW).
Fuel system: 48 lb (22 kg).

Details for Solo.

Principal dimensions:
Wing span: 21 ft 10 ins (6.65 m)
Maximum length: 15 ft 6 ins (4.73 m)
Maximum height: 5 ft 10.5 ins (1.794 m)
Wings:
Area: 64.58 sq ft (6 m^2)
Aspect ratio: 7.37
Undercarriage:
Type: Fixed, with a steerable nosewheel. Wheel fairing shown on the nosewheel only
Weights:
Maximum take-off: 717 lb (280 kg)
Performance:
Maximum speed: 103 kts (118 mph) 190 km/h
Minimum control speed: 43 kts (50 mph) 80 km/h
Maximum climb rate: 984 ft (300 m) per minute
Range with full fuel: 116 naut miles (133.5 miles) 215 km

Aeroprogress Inc (Russia)

Corporate address: See Combat section for company details.

Aeroprogress T-101 Gratch series, T-106, T-110, T-112 and T-132

Details: For T-101 Gratch, except under Aircraft variants.
First flight: 7 December 1994.
Role: Military and civil STOL passenger and cargo transport, with other uses including agricultural, firefighting, air ambulance, survey and photographic.
Sales/users: Production by MAPO-MiG. Aeroprogress stated orders for 275 T-101s by early 1995, including 200 utility and airborne troop transports for air forces, 25 for the Russian Contingency Ministry and 50 for agricultural work. In addition, Aeroprogress stated that interest had been shown by the Austrian Air Force.
Crew/passengers: 10 persons, including 1 or 2 pilots. Other layouts available.
Wing control surfaces: Ailerons (30° up, 14° down – port trim tab), slotted flaps (40° landing) and 2-section automatic leading-edge slats.
Tail control surfaces: Elevators (port trim tab) and rudder (with tab).
Flight control system: Pushrod and cables, except for electric flaps and slats.
Construction materials: Metal.
Engine: OMSK/Glushenkov TVD-10B turboprop, with AV-24AN 3-blade constant-speed propeller.
Engine rating: 1,011 shp (754 kW).
Fuel system: 1,200 litres.
Electrical system: 120/208 volt AC supply, at 400 Hz, via an alternator. DC supply. 24 volt ni-cd batttery.
Hydraulic system: 2,132 psi, for braking system only.
Braking system: Mainwheel hydraulic brakes and anti-skid devices.
Flight avionics/instrumentation: VFR or IFR. Includes AP-93 autopilot, ADF, marker beacon receiver, radio altimeter and back-up VBM-1PB altimeter, A-723 radio and Grom satellite navigation, ELT, digital air data system, gyro horizon, and compass.
Aircraft variants:
T-101 is the standard transport with a TVD-10B engine, as detailed.
T-101E is a westernized model, with a 1,424 shp (1,062 kW) Pratt & Whitney Canada PT6A-65AR turboprop with Hartzell propeller. AlliedSignal TPE331-14A is a possible alternative. MTOW 12,500 lb (5,670 kg).
T-101L is a skiplane version.
T-101P is a firefighting floatplane.

Details for T-101.

Principal dimensions:
Wing span: 59 ft 8 ins (18.18 m)
Maximum length: 49 ft 4 ins (15.04 m)
Maximum height: 21 ft 11 ins (6.67 m)
Cabin:
Length: 13 ft 9 ins (4.2 m)
Width: 5 ft 3 ins (1.6 m)
Height: 5 ft 11 ins (1.8 m)
Wings:
Aerofoil section: P-11-14
Area: 469.63 sq ft (43.63 m^2)
Aspect ratio: 7.575
Undercarriage:
Type: Fixed, with tailwheel. Optional floats, amphibious floats, or skis
Weights:
Empty: 7,341 lb (3,330 kg)
Maximum take-off and landing: 12,125 lb (5,500 kg)
Payload: 3,527 lb (1,600 kg)
Performance:
Maximum speed: 165 kts (189 mph) 305 km/h at 9,850 ft (3,000 m)
Long-range cruise speed: 127 kts (146 mph) 235 km/h at 9,850 ft (3,000 m)
Take-off over a 50 ft (15 m) obstacle: 2,018 ft (615 m)
Landing over a 50 ft (15 m) obstacle: 1,214 ft (370 m)
Ceiling: 11,810 ft (3,600 m), service
Range with full fuel: 713 naut miles (820 miles) 1,320 km

T-101Skh is a highly modified low-wing agricultural aircraft. Seems unlikely that both this and the T-203 Pchel will be marketed.
T-101S is an armed military assault transport, with weapons/stores carried on 4 underwing pylons and possibly on new stub-wings (latter each have a wingtip and pylon station).
T-101V is a more powerful floatplane version, with 1,380 shp (1,029 kW) OMSK/Glushenkov TVD-20 turboprop. Prototype was expected to be completed by Summer 1995. US amphibious floats, expected to be licence-built in Russia. Wing span increased to 60 ft 8 ins (18.5 m), MTOW 12,599 lb (5,715 kg) and maximum speed 151 kts (174 mph) 280 km/h.
T-106 is a twin-engined development of Gratch, with a 65 ft 3 ins (19.9 m) wing span, 51 ft 5 ins (15.678 m) length, and powered by 2 TVD-10B or PT6A turboprops. MTOW 13,120 lb (5,950 kg).
T-110 is a lengthened version of T-106.
T-112 is a dedicated cargo version of T-106, with a rear ramp/door and small cabin windows.
T-132 is an amphibious flying-boat development of T-106, with a single-step hull, wing floats, power plant mounted above the wings, and nose radar.

Aeroprogress T-101 Gratch

Aeroprogress T-121 Grif

Certification: Will be to AP-23/FAR Pt 23 Normal category.
Role: Projected passenger/cargo transport, suited also to agricultural, SAR, parachute, firefighting, aerial photography and training. Uses elements of PZL aircraft, including the An-2 and the wings of the M-18 Dromader.
Crew/passengers: Crew of 1 or 2 plus 9 passengers typically, or up to 12 maximum.
Construction materials: Metal, with some composite fuselage panels.

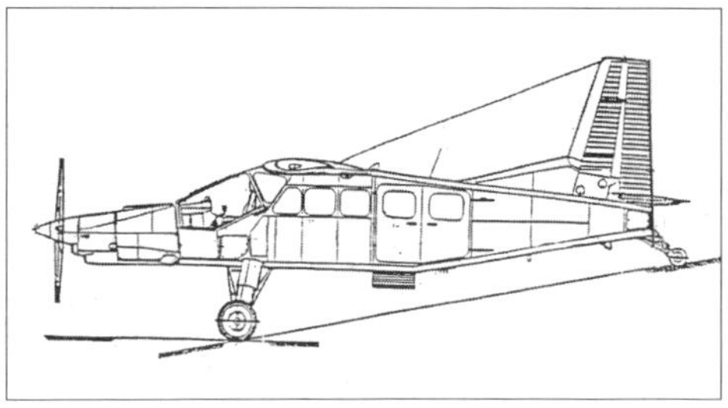

Aeroprogress T-121 Grif (courtesy Aeroprogress)

Engine: OMSK/Glushenkov TVD-10B turboprop, with AV-24AN 3-blade constant-speed propeller.
Engine rating: 1,011 shp (754 kW).
Fuel system: 1,100 litres.

DETAILS FOR T-121 GRIF.

Principal dimensions:
Wing span: 58 ft 1 ins (17.7 m)
Maximum length: 45 ft 11 ins (14 m)
Maximum height: 17 ft 1 ins (5.2 m)
Cabin:
Length: 14 ft 9 ins (4.5 m)
Width: 5 ft 3 ins (1.6 m)
Height: 5 ft 11 ins (1.8 m)
Wings:
Area: 430.56 sq ft (40 m²)
Weights:
Empty: 7,165 lb (3,250 kg) with fuel
Maximum take-off: 10,582 lb (4,800 kg)
Performance:
Maximum cruise speed: 156 kts (180 mph) 290 km/h
Stall speed: 60 kts (69 mph) 110 km/h
Maximum climb rate: 885 ft (270 m) per minute
Ceiling: 13,125 ft (4,000 m)
Range with full fuel: 810 naut miles (932 miles) 1,500 km

Aeroprogress T-130 Fregat

Aeroprogress T-130 Fregat and T-134

Details: For T-130, except under Aircraft variants.
First flight: Anticipated for November 1995.
Role: Amphibious flying-boat for passengers, cargo, SAR, forest patrol and firefighting. Possible armed military use with CIS Frontier forces.
Sales/users: Possible series production in China.
Crew/passengers: 2 crew and up to 15 passengers or other layouts.
Airframe characteristics: Strut-braced, constant-chord wings. 2-step flying-boat hull with side stabilizing sponsons that probably offer some lift. Water rudder to the rear of the second step.
Wing control surfaces: Ailerons and single-slotted flaps.

DETAILS FOR T-130 FREGAT WITH M601E ENGINES.

Principal dimensions:
Wing span: 59 ft 8 ins (18.2 m)
Maximum length: 50 ft 10 ins (15.5 m)
Maximum height: 15 ft 1 ins (4.6 m)
Cabin:
Length: 14 ft 9 ins (4.5 m)
Width: 5 ft 3 ins (1.6 m)
Height: 6 ft 1 ins (1.85 m)
Undercarriage:
Type: Retractable, with steerable nosewheel
Weights:
Maximum take-off and landing: 12,900 lb (5,850 kg)
Payload: 3,307 lb (1,500 kg)
Performance:
Maximum speed: 216 kts (249 mph) 400 km/h
Cruise speed: 189 kts (217 mph) 350 km/h
Take-off distance: 771 ft (235 m) land, 787 ft (240 m) water
Landing distance: 591 ft (180 m) land, 722 ft (220 m) water
Range with full fuel: 983 naut miles (1,130 miles) 1,820 km
Range with full payload: 297 naut miles (342 miles) 550 km

Tail control surfaces: Elevators (starboard trim tab) and rudder (with tab).
Flight control system: Pushrods and cables, except for electric tabs.
Construction materials: Aluminium alloy.
Engines: Either 2 Motorlet Walter M601E or Pratt & Whitney Canada PT6A turboprops, pylon-mounted above the wings in tandem.
Engine rating: Each 751 shp (560 kW) for the M601Es.
Fuel system: 1,000 litres.
Aircraft variants:
T-130 is the principal version, as detailed.
T-134 is similar but intended mainly for coast guard use.
Retractable undercarriage, with tailwheel.

Aeroprogress T-201 Aist and T-203 Pchel

Details: For T-201, except under Aircraft variants.
First flight: 1995.
Role: STOL utility aircraft, developed from the T-101 Gratch. Some differences are detailed below.
Wing control surfaces: High-lift wings with ailerons, 4-section spoilers and double-slotted flaps.
Engine: Pratt & Whitney Canada PT6A-67K turboprop.
Fuel system: 1,400 litres.
Flight avionics/instrumentation: Enhanced avionics, including provision for weather radar.
Aircraft variants:
T-201 Aist is the standard high-wing utility version, as detailed.
T-203 Pchel is an agricultural development, with entirely new low-mounted strut-braced wings with spraybooms. Reintroduces leading-edge automatic slats. Payload 5,070 lb (2,300 kg). Documentation suggests the TVD-20 engine, but as this was dropped for T-201, it is likely that T-203 has the PT6A also.

Aeroprogress T-201 Aist

DETAILS FOR T-201 AIST.

Principal dimensions:
Wing span: 65 ft 3 ins (19.9 m)
Maximum length: 49 ft 6 ins (15.1 m)
Wings:
Area: 471.24 sq ft (43.78 m²)
Aspect ratio: 9.05
Weights:
Empty: 7,495 lb (3,400 kg)
Maximum take-off and landing: 12,565 lb (5,700 kg)
Payload: 4,409 lb (2,000 kg) of cargo
Performance:
Maximum speed: 175 kts (202 mph) 325 km/h
Stall speed: 61 kts (70 mph) 113 km/h *clean* at 3,280 ft (1,000 m)
Take-off distance: 968 ft (295 m)
Landing distance: 525 ft (160 m)
Maximum climb rate: 1,378 ft (420 m) per minute
Ceiling: 13,125 ft (4,000 m)
Range with full fuel: 739 naut miles (851 miles) 1,370 km

Aeroprogress T-204 Condor

First flight: Not yet flown. Programme begun in November 1993.
Role: STOL passenger/cargo transport, with variants for ambulance/medevac, patrol and aerial photography.
Crew/passengers: 2 crew plus 9-12 passengers or 2,866 lb (1,300 kg) of cargo.
Wing control surfaces: Ailerons (port trim tab), 4-section spoilers, 2-section flaps and 2-section leading-edge slats.
Tail control surfaces: Horn-balanced elevators and rudder, all with trim tabs.
Flight control system: Pushrods and cables, except for electric trim.
Construction materials: Metal.
Engines: 2 Pratt & Whitney Canada PT6A-34AC turboprops, with 5-blade automatic variable-pitch propellers.
Engine rating: Each 750 shp (559.3 kW).
Fuel system: 1,200 litres.
Electrical system: 27 volt DC supply from engine-driven generators. 2 x 40 amp-hour batteries. Converters for AC.
Braking system: Hydraulic disc.
Radar: Provision for weather radar.
Flight avionics/instrumentation: Provision for autopilot and satellite navigation.

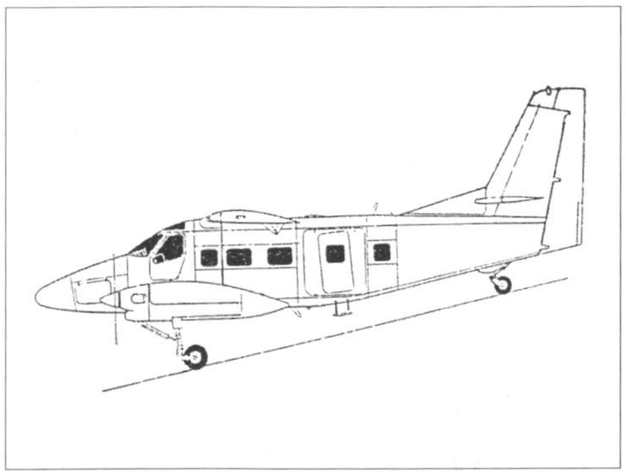

Aeroprogress T-204 Condor (courtesy Aeroprogress)

DETAILS FOR T-204 CONDOR.

Principal dimensions:
Wing span: 59 ft 8.5 ins (18.2 m)
Maximum length: 44 ft 9 ins (13.65 m)
Maximum height: 15 ft 8 ins (4.76 m)
Cabin:
Length: 13 ft 9 ins (4.2 m)
Width: 5 ft 3 ins (1.6 m)
Height: 5 ft 11 ins (1.8 m)
Wings:
Aerofoil section: R-P-14
Area: 469.63 sq ft (43.63 m^2)
Aspect ratio: 7.59
Undercarriage:
Type: Retractable, with tailwheel. Twin wheels on each main unit
Weights:
Empty: 7,937 lb (3,600 kg)
Maximum take-off and landing: 12,654 lb (5,740 kg)
Performance:
Maximum speed: 190 kts (219 mph) 352 km/h at 12,125 lb (5,500 kg)
Ceiling: 19,700 ft (6,000 m)
Range with full fuel: 415 naut miles (478 miles) 770 km, with a 2,072 lb (940 kg) payload, at 9,850 ft (3,000 m)

Proposed Aeroprogress T-282 transport, accommodating 18-24 passengers or cargo, and with a rear ramp/door. 2 OMSK/Glushenkov TVD-10B or TVD-20 turboprops (courtesy Aeroprogress)

Aeroprogress T-205

First flight: Not yet flown.
Role: Utility transport.
Crew/passengers: Crew of 1 or 2 plus 9-15 passengers or 3,528 lb (1,600 kg) of cargo.
Engine: Pratt & Whitney Canada PT6A-67K turboprop. Alternative NPO Saturn AL-34.
Aircraft variants:
T-205 is offered in 3 principal forms, with a standard side entrance door, rear ramp/door, or with the rear section of the fuselage hinging to one side.

DETAILS FOR T-205.

Weights:
Maximum take-off: 12,565 lb (5,700 kg)
Performance:
Maximum speed: 184 kts (211 mph) 340 km/h
Stall speed: 51 kts (59 mph) 95 km/h
Balanced field length: 1,968 ft (600 m)
Ceiling: 13,125 ft (4,000 m)
Range with full fuel: 702 naut miles (808 miles) 1,300 km

Aeroprogress T-401 Sokol

First flight: Anticipated late 1995.
Role: Light general-purpose aircraft, also suited to training, agricultural, law enforcement and patrol/survey work.
Crew/passengers: 6 persons, or the pilot, 1 litter and 2 attendants in an air ambulance role.
Wing control surfaces: Ailerons and flaps.
Tail control surfaces: Elevators (port trim tab) and highly swept rudder (with trim tab). Swept finlets on the tailplane of the floatplane version.
Flight control system: Mechanical.
Construction materials: Metal.
Engine: AOOT M-14PR radial piston engine. Optional Textron Lycoming horizontally-opposed piston engine or Allison 250-B17C turboprop.
Engine rating: 360 hp (268.5 kW).
Fuel system: 350 litres.

Aeroprogress T-401 Sokol

DETAILS FOR T-401 SOKOL.

Principal dimensions:
Wing span: 44 ft 10 ins (13.66 m)
Maximum length: 29 ft 2 ins (8.9 m)
Maximum height: 14 ft 5 ins (4.39 m)
Cabin:
Length: 14 ft 6 ins (4.41 m)
Width: 4 ft 5 ins (1.34 m)
Height: 4 ft 1 ins (1.25 m)
Wings:
Aerofoil section: MS (1) 3M
Area: 215.28 sq ft (20 m^2)
Aspect ratio: 9.329
Undercarriage:
Type: Fixed, with steerable nosewheel. Wheel fairings. Optional floats or skis
Weights:
Empty: 3,152 lb (1,430 kg)
Maximum take-off and landing: 4,475 lb (2,030 kg)
Payload: 992 lb (450 kg)
Performance:
Maximum speed: 157 kts (180 mph) 290 km/h at 9,450 ft (3,000 m)
Stall speed: 68 kts (78 mph) 125 km/h *with flaps*
Take-off distance: 840 ft (255 m)
Landing distance: 764 ft (233 m)
Maximum climb rate: 853 ft (260 m) per minute
Ceiling: 13,125 ft (4,000 m), service
Range with full fuel: 880 naut miles (1,013 miles) 1,630 km

Aeroprogress T-407 Skborets

First flight: 1995.
Role: Light utility aircraft, with the usual range of alternative missions.
Sales/users: Prototype was built at the associated Krunichev works.
Crew/passengers: Pilot and 6 passengers, cargo or litters.
Wing control surfaces: Slotted ailerons and slotted flaps.
Tail control surfaces: Elevators (starboard trim tab) and rudder.
Flight control system: Mechanical.
Construction materials: Metal.

DETAILS FOR T-407 SKBORETS.

Principal dimensions:
Wing span: 39 ft 9 ins (12.12 m)
Maximum length: 32 ft 10 ins (10 m)
Maximum height: 14 ft 5 ins (4.4 m)
Cabin:
Length: 14 ft 1 ins (4.3 m) including cockpit
Width: 4 ft 5 ins (1.34 m)
Height: 4 ft 3 ins (1.3 m)
Wings:
Aerofoil section: P-II
Area: 270.6 sq ft (25.14 m^2)
Aspect ratio: 5.843
Undercarriage:
Type: Fixed, with nosewheel
Weights:
Empty: 2,756 lb (1,250 kg)
Maximum take-off: 4,586 lb (2,080 kg)
Payload: 1,323 lb (600 kg)
Performance:
Maximum cruise speed: 116 kts (134 mph) 215 km/h
Take-off over a 50 ft (15 m) obstacle: 1,805 ft (550 m)
Landing over a 50 ft (15 m) obstacle: 1,312 ft (400 m)
Ceiling: 13,125 ft (4,000 m), service
Range with full fuel: 961 naut miles (1,106 miles) 1,780 km

Engine: AOOT M-14P radial piston engine. Optional Teledyne Continental horizontally-opposed piston engine or Allison 250-B17 turboprop.
Engine rating: 360 hp (268.5 kW).
Fuel system: 380 litres.

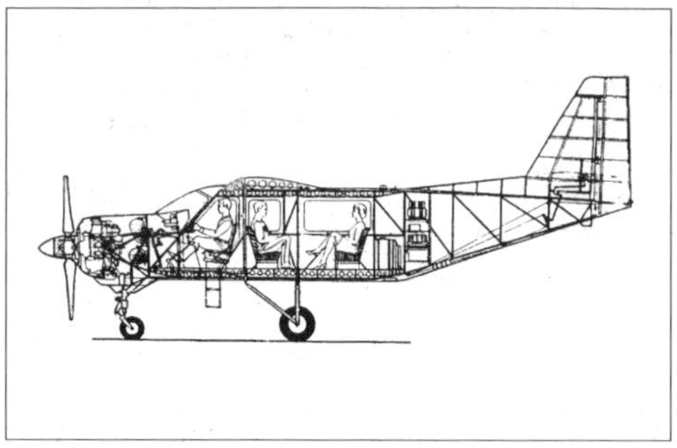

Aeroprogress T-407 Skborets (courtesy Aeroprogress)

Aeroprogress T-433 Flamingo and T-435 Korvet

Details: For Flamingo except under Aircraft variants.
First flight: 1995.
Role: Civil/military five-seat light amphibious flying-boat, also suited to SAR, EEZ patrol and more.
Airframe characteristics: Single-step hull, mid-mounted wings, high-mounted tailplane and pylon-mounted tractor engine in a streamline pod.
Wing control surfaces: Ailerons (with trim tabs) and single-slotted 2-section flaps.
Tail control surfaces: Elevators (with port trim tab) and rudder (with trim tab).
Flight control system: Mechanical.
Construction materials: Metal.
Engine: AOOT M-14P radial piston engine. Optional Allison turboprop.
Engine rating: 360 hp (268.5 kW).
Fuel system: 300 litres.
Braking system: Mainwheel pneumatic brakes.
Aircraft variants:
T-433 Flamingo, as detailed.
T-435 Korvet appears to be a derivative of the T-433 but with a tailwheel undercarriage and wide nose strakes.

DETAILS FOR T-433 FLAMINGO.

Principal dimensions:
Wing span: 46 ft 7 ins (14.2 m)
Maximum length: 34 ft 10 ins (10.62 m)
Maximum height: 12 ft 10 ins (3.9 m)
Wings:
Aerofoil section: P-301
Area: 222.6 sq ft (20.68 m^2)
Aspect ratio: 9.75
Undercarriage:
Type: Retractable, with steerable nosewheel
Weights:
Empty: 3,241 lb (1,470 kg)
Maximum take-off and landing: 4,519 lb (2,050 kg)
Payload: 882 lb (400 kg)
Performance:
Typical cruise speed: 113-130 kts (130-149 mph) 210-240 km/h
Stall speed: 62 kts (72 mph) 115 km/h at sea level, clean
Take-off distance: 673 ft (205 m) land, 984 ft (300 m) water
Landing distance: 738 ft (225 m) land, 886 ft (270 m) water
Ceiling: 13,125 ft (4,000 m)
Range with full fuel: 594 naut miles (684 miles) 1,100 km at sea level, no reserve

Aeroprogress T-433 Flamingo (courtesy Aeroprogress)

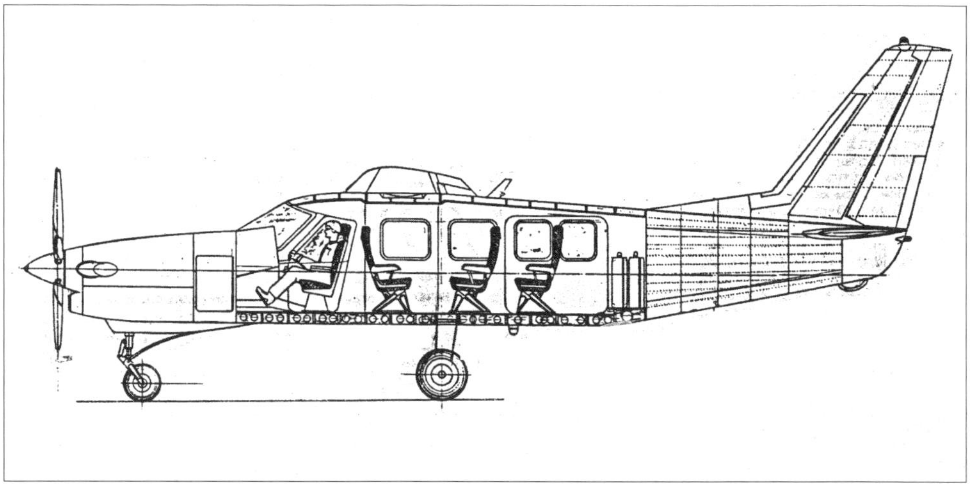

Aeroprogress T-610 Voyage (courtesy Aeroprogress)

Aeroprogress T-610 Voyage

First flight: Anticipated for March 1996.
Role: STOL multi-purpose, including passenger, cargo, parachuting, air ambulance, patrol, photography and more.
Sales/users: Prototype built at Tushino.
Crew/passengers: 11-12 persons in passenger form.
Wing control surfaces: Ailerons (with trim tabs), 2-section flaps and spoilers.
Tail control surfaces: Elevators (port trim tab) and rudder (with trim tab).
Flight control system: Pushrod and cable.
Construction materials: Metal.
Engine: Motorlet Walter M601E turboprop for the prototypes. Production aircraft will have either a 700 shp (522 kW) OMSK/Kobchyenko TV-O-100, similarly rated NPO Saturn AL-34 or 600 shp (447.4 kW) Pratt & Whitney Canada PT6A-114 turboprop.
Engine rating: 751 shp (560 kW).
Fuel system: 1,300 litres.
Aircraft variants:
T-610, as detailed.
T-610B is the floatplane version, with amphibious floats and tailplane finlets.
Projected derivatives of the T-610 include T-611 with an underfuselage cargo pod, T-613 with a tailwheel undercarriage, low-wing and twin-engined T-621, high-wing and twin-engined T-620, and T-680 flying-boat.

DETAILS FOR T-610.

Principal dimensions:
Wing span: 53 ft (16.16 m)
Maximum length: 39 ft 7.5 ins (12.08 m)
Maximum height: 14 ft 5 ins (4.4 m)
Cabin:
Length: 17 ft 4 ins (5.28 m)
Width: 5 ft 3 ins (1.6 m)
Height: 4 ft 7 ins (1.4 m)
Wings:
Aerofoil section: P-301
Area: 301.39 sq ft (28 m^2)
Aspect ratio: 9.327
Undercarriage:
Type: Fixed, with steerable nosewheel. Optional floats or skis
Weights:
Empty: 4,310 lb (1,955 kg)
Maximum take-off: 8,378 lb (3,800 kg)
Payload: 2,425 lb (1,100 kg)
Performance:
Maximum speed: 178-189 kts (205-217 mph) 330-350 km/h
Cruise speed: 146-157 kts (168-180 mph) 270-290 km/h
Stall speed: 76 kts (87 mph) 140 km/h
Take-off distance: 886 ft (270 m)
Landing distance: 1,050 ft (320 m)
Maximum climb rate: 1,100 ft (366 m) per minute at sea level
Range with full fuel: 1,258 naut miles (1,448 miles) 2,330 km

Aeroprogress T-910 Kuryer

First flight: Mock-up only in 1995.
Role: Pressurized business jet.
Crew/passengers: 2 crew plus 6-10 passengers.
Wing control surfaces: Ailerons, flaps and spoilers.
Tail control surfaces: Variable-incidence tailplane. Elevators and inset rudder.
Flight control system: Mechanical, except for electro-hydraulic spoilers and electric tailplane.
Construction materials: Metal.
Engines: 2 Ivchenko PROGRESS AI-25TL turbofans. APU.
Engine rating: Each 3,792 lbf (16.87 kN).
Fuel system: 4,550 litres.
Electrical system: 115 volt supply, at 400 Hz.
Hydraulic system: Dual systems.
Radar: Weather radar.
Flight avionics/instrumentation: IFR.

Details for T-910 Kuryer.

Principal dimensions:
Wing span: 55 ft 9 ins (17 m)
Maximum length: 50 ft (15.24 m)
Maximum height: 16 ft 9 ins (5.1 m)
Wings:
Aerofoil section: P204-14 and P196K (root/tip)
Area: 346.6 sq ft (32.2m^2)
Aspect ratio: 8.98
Weights:
Empty: 12,566 lb (5,700 kg)
Maximum take-off: 21,385 lb (9,700 kg)
Performance:
Maximum speed: 421 kts (485 mph) 780 km/h at 26,250 ft (8,000 m)
Stall speed: 125 kts (143 mph) 230 km/h, with flaps
Take-off distance: 1,640 ft (500 m)
Landing distance: 1,312 ft (400 m)
Range with full fuel: 2,430 naut miles (2,795 miles) 4,500 km at 39,370 ft (12,000 m), with reserve

Aeroric Science and Production Enterprise (Russia)

Corporate address: 2 Sibirskaya Street, 86, Nizhny Novgorod 603089.
Telephone: +7 8312 44 19 65

● Activities

• Has designed and developed the nine-seat Dingo amphibious lightplane of unusual layout, able to operate from virtually any type of surface due to its air cushion landing system. With a 1,100 shp (820.3 kW) Pratt & Whitney Canada PT6A-65B turboprop and pusher propeller as its main power system, it also has a 250 shp (186.4 kW) TBA-200 auxiliary engine for the air cushion. The Sokol Joint Stock Company at Nizhny Novgorod is undertaking production, beginning with a series of 13 pre-series aircraft after first flight of the prototype in 1995.

Avia Ltd (Russia)

Corporate address: 13/4 Cominterna Street, Moscow 127327.
Telephone: +7 095 184 4377
Facsimile: +7 095 184 4377

Avia Akkord

First flight: April 1994.

Avia Akkord in fixed twin-float layout (Piotr Butowski)

Certification: Designed to FAR Pt 23 standards.
Role: Land. float or amphibious lightplane for passengers, cargo and air ambulance work.
Sales/users: Produced by Sokol at Nizhny Novgorod.
Crew/passengers: Pilot and 4 passengers. Baggage compartment aft of the rear seats. Ambulance version carries the pilot, 1 litter, a medical attendant and equipment.
Engines: 2 VAZ-4133A rotary piston engines, with 6 ft 7 ins (2 m) 2-blade propellers. Other engines can be fitted.
Engine rating: Each 150 hp (112 kW).
Fuel system: 661 lb (300 kg).
Flight avionics/instrumentation: Wide choice of avionics, including EFIS and GPS.

Details for Akkord.

Principal dimensions:
Wing span: 37 ft 1 ins (11.3 m)
Maximum length: 26 ft 3 ins (8 m) with wheels only
Maximum height: 10 ft 6 ins (3.2 m) wheels, 11 ft 10 ins (3.6 m) amphibious
Wings:
Area: 161.46 sq ft (15 m^2)
Aspect ratio: 8.51
Undercarriage:
Type: Fixed, with nosewheel. Optional twin floats. Provision for adding electrically-lowering twin floats outside of the mainwheels, allowing amphibious operations
Weights:
Empty: 2,050 lb (930 kg) wheels, 2,358 lb (1,070 kg) amphibious
Maximum take-off: 3,836 lb (1,740 kg)
Performance:
Cruise speed: 146 kts (168 mph) 270 km/h wheels
Economical cruise speed: 97 kts (112 mph) 180 km/h amphibious
Take-off distance: 574 ft (175 m) land, 853 ft (260 m) water
Range with full fuel: 1,242 naut miles (1,429 miles) 2,300 km at economical cruise speed

Aviatika Joint Stock Company (Russia)

Corporate address: 33a Leningradsky Prospect, Moscow 125284
Telephone: +7 095 945 56 54
Facsimile: +7 095 945 29 00
Founded: 1991.
Information: Igor Pyankov (President).

● Activities

• Aviatika was founded to unite a number of enterprises specializing in aviation and related fields. It began when the Moscow Dementyev Aviation Production Association (producing MiG fighters), Gromov Flight Research Institute (major testing facility) and the Moscow Aviation Institute (leading university) united their potential to produce civil light aircraft in accordance with Russia's conversion programme. On 17 February 1993, Aviatika (as the first Russian commercially operated aircraft building company) received a Russian State Certificate as a designer of light civil aircraft.
• 6 projects have been realized, the 890, 890A, 890U, 900, 910 and 920, the latter a single-seat glider.

Aviatika-890, -890A, -890U and -920

Details: Aviatika-890, except under Aircraft variants (unless stated).
First flight: 1990 (Michail Markov established a world time-to-climb to 3,000 m record for this category of aircraft in August 1990).
Certification: Meets JAR-VLA and FAR Pt 23 regulations.
Role: Light multi-purpose sporting, training, ecological monitoring, survey and agricultural biplane. Aviatika-890A is an autogyro variant by application of a conversion kit. Aviatika-920 is a glider.
Sales/users: In production. 150 sold by late 1994 to customers in the CIS and 12 other countries.
Crew/passengers: Pilot only in the Aviatika-890; 2 persons in the Aviatika-890U.
Cockpit: Optional side doors, 1 jettisonable in flight. Seat is adapted for use of a backpack parachute, but a BRS ballistic parachute system can be mounted on the central post.
External equipment: 265 lb (120 kg) payload as external stores carried on 4 attachment points as: under the engine mounts (132 lb, 60 kg), under the belly (220 lb, 100 kg), lower wingtips (each 99 lb, 45 kg).
Wing control surfaces: Full-width, lower-wing ailerons.
Tail control surfaces: Small tailplane and fin, large elevators (with ground-adjustable tab) and rudder (with similar tab).
Construction materials: Aluminium alloy, steel and titanium, with fabric-covered flying surfaces. Glassfibre

Aviatika-890U (left) and 890

cockpit fairing. All essential components of the airframe (fittings, control linkages, etc) are located externally for easy inspection.
Engine: 64.4 hp (48 kW) Rotax 582 or 77.8 hp (58 kW) Rotax 912 piston engine, with a 2-blade pusher propeller.
Fuel system: 50 litres. Optional 55 litre auxiliary tank installed on the under-engine mounts (see External equipment above).
Flight avionics/instrumentation: Flight and engine instruments. VHF transceiver at customer's request.
Aircraft variants:
Aviatika-890 is the single-seat multi-purpose version, as detailed.
Aviatika-890 agricultural is used for the protection of arable, green and forest plantations from pests and disease. Ultra-low-volume and biological Micronair AU-7000 atomizer system uses only 3.3 lb (1.5 kg) of chemical per pass, or more when required. Swath width 46 ft (14 m)
Aviatika-890U is the side-by-side two-seat version.
Aviatika-890A is an autogyro version, either sold as such or by conversion of a standard 890 using a gyro assembly unit. Similar roles to 890. Rotax 912 engine. 23 ft 7.5 ins (7.2 m) 2-blade rotor.
Aviatika-920 is a simple training glider, using 90% Aviatika-890 components. 32 ft 10 ins (10 m) monoplane wing. Simple undercarriage. Lift-drag ratio 15. Minimum rate of descent 3.6 ft (1.1 m) per second.

Details for Aviatika-890 with a Rotax 582.

Principal dimensions:
Wing span: 26 ft 7 ins (8.11 m) upper wing
Maximum length: 17 ft 5.5 ins (5.32 m) including pitot
Maximum height: 7 ft 5 ins (2.25 m)
Wings:
Area: 153.82 sq ft (14.29 m^2)
Undercarriage:
Type: Fixed, with nosewheel. Provision for floats or skis
Weights:
Empty: 474 lb (215 kg)
Maximum take-off: 992 lb (450 kg)
Performance (at MTOW):
Maximum speed: 70 kts (81 mph) 130 km/h
Cruise speed: 49-65 kts (56-75 mph) 90-120 km/h
Stall speed: 35 kts (41 mph) 65 km/h
Take-off distance: 164 ft (50 m)
Landing distance: 361 ft (110 m)
Maximum climb rate: 985 ft (300 m) per minute
G limits: +7.5, -3.75 at 694 lb (315 kg), or +6, -4 ultimate; +5, -2.5 or +4, -2 limit (same conditions)
Ceiling: 14,765 ft (4,500 m), service
Range with full fuel: 146 naut miles (167 miles) 270 km
Range with auxiliary fuel: 297 naut miles (341 miles) 550 km
Duration: 3.5 hours

Aviatika-900 Acrobat

First flight: 22 February 1993.
Role: Single-seat aerobatic competition monoplane. Has set 5 FAI-accredited records.
Sales/users: Avialable.
Wing control surfaces: Ailerons (port ground-adjustable tab), and manoeuvre flaps used for longitudinal control (direct lift control).
Tail control surfaces: Horn-balanced elevators (starboard ground-adjustable tab) and rudder (similar tab).
Construction materials: All metal. Cantilever wings and strut-braced tailplane.

Aviatika-900 Acrobat

Engine: AOOT M-14P radial piston engine.
Engine rating: 360 hp (268.5 kW).

Details for Aviatika-900.

Principal dimensions:
Wing span: 23 ft 5.5 ins (7.15 m)
Maximum length: 18 ft 8.5 ins (5.7 m)
Maximum height: 9 ft 10 ins (3 m)
Wings:
Aerofoil section: Symmetrical
Area: 107.64 sq ft (10 m^2)
Aspect ratio: 5.11
Undercarriage:
Type: Fixed, with steerable tailwheel. Cantilever spring-type main legs
Weights:
Empty: 1,301 lb (590 kg)
Maximum take-off and landing: 1,576 lb (715 kg)
Performance:
Maximum speed: 202 kts (233 mph) 375 km/h
Take-off and landing speed: 59 kts (68 mph) 110 km/h
Stall speed: 58 kts (67 mph) 107 km/h
Take-off distance: 220 ft (66 m)
Landing distance: 394 ft (120 m)
Maximum climb rate: 4,530 ft (1,380 m) per minute at sea level
G limits: ±11

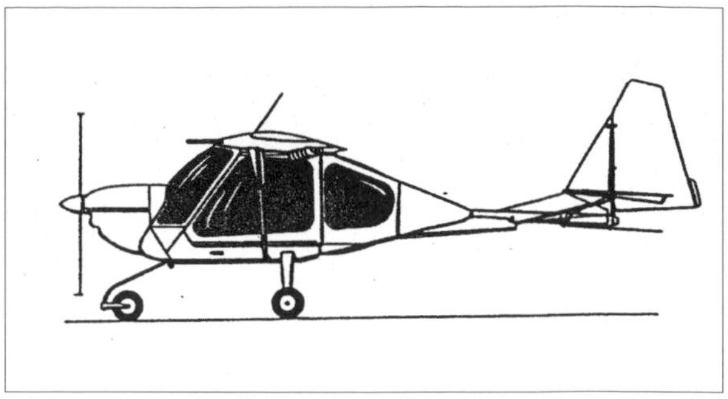

Aviatika-910 (courtesy Aviatika)

Aviatika-910

Certification: Developed to comply with JAR-VLA.
Role: Sporting, training and utility monoplane.
Crew/passengers: 2 persons. Seat can be reclined and 1 of the dual controls removed, providing space for a litter or long item of cargo.
Cockpit: Jettisonable sliding doors, and side hatches for access to the cargo compartment
Baggage/cargo capacity: Large cargo compartment, equipped with a retractable floor to allow use of camera and video equipment as required.
Wing characteristics: Braced, high-mounted. Folding. Higher aspect ratio than Aviatika-890 wing.
Wing control surfaces: Wide-span flaperon.
Tail control surfaces: As for Aviatika-890.
Construction materials: Wings have a spar constructed of large diameter tubing, with ribs and leading/trailing-edges of stamped metal sheet. Identical tail unit to the Aviatika-890. Large diameter tube tailboom. Glassfibre engine cowling. Outer parts of the wings, flaperons and tail covered with cotton fabric.
Engine: Rotax 912 piston engine.
Engine rating: 77.8 hp (58 kW).

Details for Aviatika-910.

Principal dimensions:
Wing span: 35 ft 3 ins (10.73 m)
Maximum length: 19 ft 6 ins (5.95 m)
Maximum height: 7 ft 1 ins (2.15 m)
Wings:
Area: 120.56 sq ft (11.2 m^2)
Undercarriage:
Type: Fixed, easily converted between nosewheel and tailwheel in the field
Weights:
Empty: 750 lb (340 kg)
Maximum take-off: 1,213 lb (550 kg)
Performance:
Maximum speed: 81 kts (93 mph) 150 km/h
Cruise speed: 70 kts (81 mph) 130 km/h
Take-off distance: 378 ft (115 m)
Landing distance: 427 ft (130 m)
Maximum climb rate: 164 ft (50 ft) per minute

Beriev Joint Stock Company (Russia)

Corporate address: See Combat section for all company details.

Beriev Be-103

First flight: 1995.
Role: Light passenger/cargo amphibian, also suited to urgent medical care, tourism, business, fire survey and ecological monitoring.
Crew/passengers: Pilot and 5 passengers. Alternatively, pilot and passenger plus 882 lb (400 kg) of cargo, pilot and 3 seats for casualties/attendant plus a litter in ambulance configuration, or pilot and 3 other crew in patrol layout.
Wing characteristics: Low-mounted, almost delta-planform wings with water-displacing characteristics for amphibious operations. Floats not required.
Wing control surfaces: Ailerons only.
Tail control surfaces: Slab mid-mounted tailplane

Beriev Be-103 light amphibian (Piotr Butowski)

Details for Be 103.

Principal dimensions:
Wing span: 41 ft 9 ins (12.72 m)
Maximum length: 34 ft 11 ins (10.65 m)
Maximum height: 12 ft 2.5 ins (3.72 m)
Cabin:
Length: 9 ft 10 ins (3 m)
Width: 4 ft 5 ins (1.34 m)
Height: 4 ft 2 ins (1.26 m)
Volume: 146.56 cu ft (4.15 m^3)
Wings:
Aerofoil section: NACA 2412M.
Area: 270.17 sq ft (25.1 m^2)
Aspect ratio: 6.46
Undercarriage:
Type: Retractable, with steerable nosewheel. (originally designed with a tail wheel undercarriage.)
Weights:
Empty: 2,667 lb (1,210 kg)
Maximum take-off: 3,968 lb (1,800 kg)
Payload: 882 lb (400 kg)
Performance:
Maximum speed: 157 kts (180 mph) 290 km/h
Cruise speed: 124 kts (143 mph) 230 km/h
Stall speed: 54 kts (62 mph) 100 km/h
Take-off distance: 1,279 ft (390 m) from water, 706 ft (215 m) from shore
Landing distance: 1,149 ft (350 m) to water, 624 ft (190 m) to shore
Maximum climb rate: 1,279 ft (390 m) per minute
Range with full fuel: 1,404 naut miles (1,615 miles) 2,600 km
Range with full payload: 270 naut miles (311 miles) 500 km

with starboard tab, plus rudder with tab.
Flight control system: Manual, with electric tab.
Construction materials: All metal.
Engine: 2 AOOT M-17 turbo-supercharged and fuel-injected pistons, carried on fuselage-mounted pylons, with 3-blade variable-pitch propellers.
Engine rating: Each 175 hp (130.5 kW) at take-off, 160 hp (119.3 kW) cruise.
Fuel system: 450 litres.
Electrical system: 27 volt DC system and 36 volt/400Hz AC system, with generators, rectifiers and a 25 amp-hour battery.
Pneumatic system: 710 psi.
Braking system: On main units.
Flight avionics/instrumentation: Digital flight control/navigation system.

Ilyushin Aviation Complex (Russia)

Corporate address: See Combat section for company details.

Ilyushin Il-103

First flight: 17 May 1994.
Certification: 1995. Designed to meet FAR Pt 23, IAC and AR requirements.
Role: Private, business, training, and coast guard/law enforcement patrol. Aerobatic version is the Il-103SPO.
Sales/users: Expected sales of 1,000 in the CIS and 500 in the west (partnered with Fairchild of the USA). Main production at Lukhovitsy (initial batch of 70).
Crew/passengers: 2 folding front seats and a rear bench for 2 or 3 more passengers. Gullwing doors. Unrestricted access to the baggage hold for fast loading/unloading. Accommodation for 485 lb (220 kg) of cargo with the rear seats taken out.
Wing control surfaces: Ailerons and single-slotted flaps.
Tail control surfaces: Single-piece horn-balanced elevator with trim tab, and horn-balanced rudder.
Flight control system: Pushrod and cables, except for electric tab.
Construction materials: Metal, except for glassfibre wing, tail tips and tab.
Engine: Teledyne Continental IO-360-ES piston engine, with a 6 ft 4 ins (1.93 m) Hartzell 2-blade variable-pitch propeller.
Engine rating: 210 hp (157.6 kW).
Fuel system: 100 litres. Capable of inverted flight.
Electrical system: 27 volt DC supply, via an 1,800 kW generator. 25 amp-hour battery.
Hydraulic system: For the brakes.
Braking system: Hydraulic multi-disc type.
Flight avionics/instrumentation: VFR. Flight/navigation equipment for precise navigation and landing approach under CAT I. Can be equipped with western avionics at the customer's request.

Details for Il-103 (utility).

Principal dimensions:
Wing span: 34 ft 8 ins (10.56 m)
Maximum length: 26 ft 3 ins (8 m)
Maximum height: 10 ft 4 ins (3.14 m)
Cabin:
Length: 8 ft 8 ins (2.65 m)
Width: 4 ft 3 ins (1.3 m)
Height: 4 ft 2 ins (1.27 m)
Wings:
Area: 158.34 sq ft (14.71 m^2)
Aspect ratio: 7.581
Undercarriage:
Type: Fixed, with castering nosewheel and shimmy damper
Weights:
Empty: 1,687 lb (765 kg)
Maximum take-off: 2,888 lb (1,310 kg)
Payload: 871 lb (395 kg)
Performance:
Maximum speed: 135 kts (155 mph) 250 km/h utility
Cruise speed: 121.5 kts (140 mph) 225 km/h
Stall speed: 60 kts (69 mph) 110 km/h *clean*, 51 kts (59 mph) 95 km/h *with flaps*
Take-off over a 50 ft (15 m) obstacle: 1,706 ft (520 m)
Landing over a 50 ft (15 m) obstacle: 1,575 ft (480 m)
Maximum climb rate: 1,083 ft (330 m) per minute, at sea level
G limits: +4.4, -2.2
Range with full fuel: 577 naut miles (665 miles) 1,070 km, with reserve

Ilyushin Il-103 (courtesy Ilyushin)

Interavia Joint Stock Company (Russia)

Corporate address: 18-b Otkritoye Road, Moscow 107370.,
Telephone: +7 095 168 88 19
Facsimile: +7 095 292 65 11

Interavia I-1L

Role: Two-seat lightplane, suited to private use, training, cargo carrying, ecological monitoring and survey, photography, SAR, agricultural and patrol. A variant of the Aviotechnica SL-90 Leshii (see Multi-national section).
Sales/users: In production at the Lukhovitsy Machine Building Plant since 1994.
Baggage/cargo capacity: 35.31 cu ft (1 m^3).
Wing characteristics: Forward-swept wings, with slight dihedral.
Wing control surfaces: Ailerons and plain flaps.
Tail control surfaces: Elevators (starboard tab) and rudder.
Flight control system: Mechanical.
Construction materials: Metal and fabric.
Engine: Textron Lycoming O-320-E2A piston engine.
Engine rating: 140 hp (104.4 kW).
Flight avionics/instrumentation: Customer's choice.

Interavia I-1L (Piotr Butowski)

Details for I-1L.

Principal dimensions:
Wing span: 32 ft 10 ins (10 m)
Maximum length: 22 ft (6.7 m)
Undercarriage:
Type: Fixed, with tailwheel
Weights:
Maximum take-off: 1,808 lb (820 kg)
Payload: 396 lb (180 kg)
Performance:
Maximum speed: 97 kts (111 mph) 180 km/h
Landing speed: 51 kts (59 mph) 95 km/h
Take-off distance: 1,480 ft (450 m) grass
Landing distance: 1,312 ft (400 m) grass
G limits: +6, 3
Ceiling: 13,125 ft (4,000 m), service
Range with full fuel: 324 naut miles (373 miles) 600 km

Interavia I-3

Role: Unlimited aerobatic aircraft, suited also to training.
Crew/passengers: Pilot under a small bubble canopy, but capable of being converted into a 2-seater with full flight and engine instruments and controls in under 1 hour using an interchangeable modular unit.
Wing control surfaces: Drooping ailerons (with tabs).
Tail control surfaces: Horn-balanced elevators and rudder (ground-adjustable tab on rudder).
Flight control system: Probably mechanical.
Construction materials: Metal.
Engine: AOOT M-14P radial piston engine, with a 3-blade wooden propeller.
Engine rating: 360 hp (268.5 kW).

DETAILS FOR I-3.

Principal dimensions:
Wing span: 26 ft 7 ins (8.1 m)
Maximum length: 22 ft (6.7 m)
Wings:
Area: 124.22 sq ft (11.54 m^2)
Aspect ratio: 5.69
Undercarriage:
Type: Fixed, with tailwheel. Cantilever spring main legs
Weights:
Empty: 1,676 lb (760 kg)
Maximum take-off: 2,344 lb (1,063 kg)
Performance:
Maximum speed: 189 kts (217 mph) 350 km/h
Take-off distance: 860 ft (262 m) grass
Landing distance: 1,565 ft (477 m) grass
Maximum climb rate: 2,165 ft (660 m) per minute
G limits: +12, -10 pilot only; +10, -8 as a 2-seater

Khrunichev State Space Research Center (Russia)

Corporate address: 18 Novozavodskaya Street, Moscow 121309.
Telephone: +7 095 145 8343
Facsimile: +7 095 145 5900
Founded: 1994 for the Aviation Department. Closely affiliated with Aeroprogress.
Information: Evgeny P. Gruin (Chief Designer, Aviation Department).

Khrunichev T-201 Sterh and T-205

Role: Proposed developments of the Aeroprogress T-101 Gratch.

Model of the Khrunichev T-205

Aircraft variants:
T-201 has a 1,424 shp (1,062 kW) Pratt & Whitney Canada PT6A-65AR turboprop. MTOW 11,464 lb (5,200 kg). Range with full fuel 891 naut miles (1,025 miles) 1,650 km.
T-205 has a PT6A-67K turboprop with Hartzell propeller, with possibly a 1,300 shp (969.4 kW) RKBM TVD-1500 turboprop as an alternative. MTOW 12,566 lb (5,700 kg), maximum speed 183 kts (211 mph) 340 km/h and range with full fuel 702 naut miles (808 miles) 1,300 km.

Khrunichev T-411 Volverin

First flight: 10 November 1993 as the Aeroprogress T-411.

Khrunichev T-411 Volverine

Role: STOL-capable "wide-body" multi-purpose lightplane. Designed to be simple, reliable, relatively inexpensive and efficient.
Sales/users: This Aeroprogress design was taken over by Khrunichev, and is also produced in the USA by Washington Aeroprogress as the Wolverine. Production started in 1994.
Crew/passengers: Pilot plus 3/4 passengers or 661 lb (300 kg) of cargo. Spacious baggage hold. 2 passengers and baggage with maximum fuel. Starboard front seat and rear bench seat can be folded or removed to allow other roles such as ambulance and patrol.
Wing control surfaces: Ailerons (with tabs), slotted flaps and fixed leading-edge slats.
Tail control surfaces: Elevators with trim tabs and rudder.
Flight control system: Mechanical, but with electric tabs.
Construction materials: Metal structure, with metal and Dacron fabric covering.
Engine: Teledyne Continental TSIO-550-B piston engine, with a Hartzell 3-blade variable-pitch propeller.
Engine rating: 350 hp (261 kW).
Fuel system: 330.5 lb (150 kg) normal, 661 lb (300 kg) maximum.
Electrical system: 24 volt DC supply via an engine-driven generator. 25 amp-hour battery.
Flight avionics/instrumentation: AlliedSignal Bendix/King nav/comm for single-pilot VFR. Instrumentation includes indicated speed indicator, altimeter, magnetic compass, gyro horizon, marker beacon receiver, and more.
Aircraft variants:
Khrunichev T-411 Volverine, as detailed, is a re-engined and slightly larger development of the Aeroprogress T-411. Also produced in the USA as the Wolverine.
Aeroprogress T-411 Aist-2 is the original version of the T-411, with a 360 hp (268.5 kW) AOOT M-14P radial engine.

DETAILS FOR VOLVERINE.

Principal dimensions:
Wing span: 41 ft 9 ins (12.73 m)
Maximum length: 30 ft 10 ins (9.4 m)
Maximum height: 9 ft 2 ins (2.8 m)
Cabin:
Length: 9 ft 8 ins (2.94 m)
Width: 4 ft 2 ins (1.27 m)
Height: 4 ft 3 ins (1.3 m)
Cargo door size: 4 ft x 2 ft 1.5 ins (1.22 x 0.65 m)
Wings:
Aerofoil section: NACA 23011
Area: 261.56 sq ft (24.3 m^2)
Aspect ratio: 6.67
Undercarriage:
Type: Fixed, with steerable and lockable tailwheel. Optional floats
Weights:
Maximum take-off: 3,417 lb (1,550 kg)
Payload: 794 lb (360 kg)
Performance:
Maximum cruise speed: 108 kts (124 mph) 200 km/h
Stall speed: 43 kts (50 mph) 80 km/h
Take-off over a 50 ft (15 m) obstacle: 740 ft (225 m)
Landing over a 50 ft (15 m) obstacle: 1,150 ft (350 m)
Maximum climb rate: 945 ft (288 m) per minute
Ceiling: 9,850 ft (3,000 m)
Range with full fuel: 324 or 594 naut miles (373 or 683 miles) 600 or 1,100 km with normal or maximum fuel respectively

Khrunichev T-415 and T-417 Pegasus

Role: Light cargo or passenger transports.
Crew/passengers: 1 or 2 pilots, with dual controls, plus up to 6 passengers or cargo. Large loading door.
Engine: *T-415:* 360 hp (268.5 kW) AOOT M-14P radial piston engine. *T-416*: 350 hp (261 kW) Teledyne Continental TSIO-550 horizontally-opposed engine.
Fuel system: 661 lb (300 kg).
Flight avionics/instrumentation: AlliedSignal Bendix/King for at least the T-417.
Aircraft variants:
T-415 is a variant of the T-417 with an M-14P engine.
T-417 is the Teledyne Continental engined model, as detailed.

DETAILS FOR T-417.

Principal dimensions: No external dimensions quoted in received brochure
Cabin:
Length: 11 ft 10 ins (3.6 m)
Width: 4 ft 3 ins (1.3 m)
Height: 4 ft 1 ins (1.25 m)
Weights:
Maximum take-off: 4,365 lb (1,980 kg)
Payload: 1,323 lb (600 kg)
Performance:
Maximum speed: 165 kts (189 mph) 305 km/h
Take-off over a 50 ft (15 m) obstacle: 1,116 ft (340 m)
Landing over a 50 ft (15 m) obstacle: 1,610 ft (490 m)
Range with full fuel: 1,074 naut miles (1,236 miles) 1,990 km
Range with full payload: 459 naut miles (528 miles) 850 km

Khrunichev T-415

Khrunichev T-420 Strizh and T-422 Yastreb

Role: Twin-engined passenger and cargo transports. Programmes initiated in August 1994.
Aircraft variants:
T-420 Strizh is a twin-boom design, with straight-in loading via either an upward-hinging rear section of the fuselage pod or via a rear ramp/door. Twin fins and adjoining tailplane. Wings have straight leading-edges and forward-swept outer panel trailing-edges. Conventional, winglet or fuel tank wing tips. 4 piston or turboprop engine options, as 2 x 360 hp (268.5 kW) AOOT M-14P radials (base T-420), 420 shp (313 kW) Allison 250-B17C turboprops (T-420A), 350 hp (261 kW) Teledyne Continental TSIO-550-B piston engines (T-420C), or 210 hp (156.6 kW) Teledyne Continental TSIO-360s (for rear ramp/door freighter). MTOW and payload of the T-420A are 6,834 lb (3,100 kg) and 3,307 lb (1,500 kg) respectively. 6-8 passengers as an alternative to freight.
T-422 Yastreb has a conventional fuselage and tail unit, and 2 TSIO-550-B piston (T-422), Allison 250-B17 turboprop (T-422A), or AOOT M-14P radial engines (T-422M). Generally similar accommodation and weights, though MTOW of the T-422 is slightly lower at 6,614 lb (3,000 kg).

Khrunichev T-430 Sprinter

First flight: 1995?
Role: Business and multi-purpose aircraft. T-430 Sprinter is the production version of the Aeroprogress T-602 Orel.
Crew/passengers: 1 or 2 crew plus up to 9 passengers.
Engines: 2 AOOT M-14P radial piston engines, with 7 ft 10 ins (2.4 m) 3-blade propellers.
Engine rating: Each 360 hp (268.5 kW).
Fuel system: 1,587 lb (720 kg)

DETAILS FOR T-602 OREL PROTOTYPE.

Principal dimensions:
Wing span: 44 ft 10 ins (13.66 m)
Maximum length: 39 ft 9 ins (12.12 m)
Undercarriage:
Type: Retractable, with twin nosewheels
Weights:
Empty: 4,365 lb (1,980 kg)
Maximum take-off: 7,055 lb (3,200 kg)
Payload: 1,763 lb (800 lb) maximum
Performance:
Maximum cruise speed: 173 kts (199 mph) 320 km/h
Economical cruise speed: 130 kts (149 mph) 240 km/h
Take-off distance: 1,250 ft (380 m) paved, 1,542 ft (470 m) unpaved
Landing distance: 1,560 ft (475 m) paved, 1,772 ft (540 m) unpaved
Ceiling: 13,125 ft (4,000 m)
Range with full payload: 853 naut miles (982 miles) 1,580 km
Duration: 7 hours with full payload

NPO Molniya (Russia)

Full name: Molniya Scientific and Industrial Enterprise.
Corporate address: 4 Novoposelkovaja, Moscow 123459.
Telephone: +7 095 493 3335, 493 5093, 497 4760
Facsimile: +7 095 492 9371
Information: Michael Gofin (Marketing Director).

● Activities

- To supplement reduced work on the Buran Space Shuttle programme, Molniya now develops civil aircraft.
- Molniya-1 is being series built, Molniya-100 and -300 have undergone design studies, and Molniya-400 and -1000 Heracles (see Airliners section) are still at the feasibility stage.

Molniya-1

First flight: 18 December 1992.
Certification: 1995?
Role: Light general-purpose transport, including passenger, ambulance and dual-control training.
Sales/users: First batch of 20 has been completed.
Crew/passengers: 6 persons, including the pilot. Other layouts include 4-person business, and a litter and 2 medical attendants in an ambulance role.
Wing characteristics: Low-mounted, to the rear of the cabin. Wings foldable or detachable.
Control surfaces: On each of the canards, wings, twin vertical and adjoining tailplane. Use of 3 sets of horizontal surfaces in tandem helps resist spin at high angles of attack.
Engine: AOOT M-14PM-1 radial piston engine mounted in the rear of the fuselage pod, with a 3-blade pusher propeller. Alternative Teledyne Continental TSIOL-550-B piston engine. Allison 250-B17F turboprop under consideration.

Molniya-1 (Piotr Butowski)

Engine rating: 360 hp (268.5 kW).
Fuel system: 485 lb (220 kg)

Projected Molniya-100 multi-purpose transport, with 2 crew and 15 passengers or 8 business passengers, or 4 litters and 2 attendants in an air ambulance role. All cabin seating can be removed for freight carrying. Wing span 46 ft 11 ins (14.3 m), length 41 ft (12.48 m), MTOW 9,480 lb (4,300 kg), payload 3,307 lb (1,500 kg), and maximum speed 216 kts (248 mph) 400 km/h on the power of 2 x 435 hp (324 kW) Teledyne Continental GTSIO-520-K piston engines (Piotr Butowski)

Molniya-300 high-performance business and commuter aircraft, with 2 crew and 15 commuter passengers or 6 business passengers. Wing span 44 ft 1 ins (13.44 m), length 43 ft 4 ins (13.2 m), MTOW 14,990 lb (6,800 kg), payload 2,976 lb (1,350 kg), maximum speed 502 kts (578 mph) 930 km/h, and range 1,565-2,755 naut miles (1,800-3,170 miles) 2,900-5,100 km on the power of 2 Russian 2,700 lbf (12 kN) turbofans or US Allisons (Piotr Butowski)

DETAILS FOR MOLNIYA-1.

Principal dimensions:
Wing span: 27 ft 11 ins (8.5 m)
Maximum length: 25 ft 9.5 ins (7.86 m)
Maximum height: 7 ft 7 ins (2.3 m)
Width, wings detached or folded: 11 ft 10 ins (3.6 m)
Undercarriage:
Type: Fixed, with nosewheel. Optional skis
Weights:
Maximum take-off: 3,836 lb (1,740 kg)
Payload: 1,113 lb (505 kg)
Performance:
Maximum speed: 216 kts (249 mph) 400 km/h
Cruise speed: 135-173 kts (155-199 mph) 250-320 km/h
Landing speed: 67.5 kts (78 mph) 125 km/h
Take-off distance: 1,148 ft (350 m)
Range with full fuel: 648 naut miles (745 miles) 1,200 km
Range with full payload: 270 naut miles (311 miles) 500 km at 270 km/h cruise

Myasishchev Design Bureau (Russia)

Corporate address: See Combat section for all company details.

Note: Details of the Myasishchev M-102 Duet can be found under Multi-national, and the M-150 in the Airliners section.

Myasishchev M-101T Gzhel and M-103

Details: M-101T, except under Aircraft variants.
First flight: 31 March 1995.
Certification: To conform to local AP-23 and US FAR Pt 23 certification requirements.
Role: Pressurized passenger, passenger/cargo, cargo or ambulance light transport.
Sales/users: Production at Sokol.
Crew/passengers: Pilot and passenger or 2 pilots, plus 6 other persons.
Wing control surfaces: Ailerons (with tabs) and flaps.
Tail control surfaces: Elevators and rudder, with tabs.
Engine: Motorlet Walter M 601F turboprop, with a 7 ft 6 ins (2.3 m) AV-510 5-blade propeller.
Engine rating: 778 shp (580 kW) at take-off, 670.5 shp (500 kW) cruise.
Aircraft variants:
M-101T Gzhel has as standard a Motorlet Walter engine, but a PT6A may be offered later.

Myasishchev M-101T Gzhel (Piotr Butowski)

M-103 is a projected twin-engined derivative of the M-101T.

DETAILS FOR M-101T GZHEL.

Principal dimensions:
Wing span: 42 ft 8 ins (13 m)
Maximum length: 32 ft 6 ins (9.9 m)
Maximum height: 12 ft 2.5 ins (3.72 m)
Undercarriage:
Type: Retractable, with nosewheel. Can operate from prepared or unprepared airstrips
Weights:
Maximum take-off: 6,614 lb (3,000 kg)
Payload: 1,389 lb (630 kg)
Performance:
Cruise speed: 270 kts (311 mph) 500 km/h
Required runway length: 1,640-1,969 ft (500-600 m) unimproved
Operating ceiling: 26,250 ft (8,000 m)
Range with full fuel: 1,620 naut miles (1,864 miles) 3,000 km
Range with full payload: About 540 naut miles (621 miles) 1,000 km

Myasishchev M-500

First flight: Not yet flown at the time of writing.
Role: Agricultural and forestry, with variants suited to cargo carrying, air mail, patrol, ambulance, aerial photography, primary pilot training and business flights.

★ Aims
★ 67.8 hectares per flight hour productivity in an agricultural role. Up to 48% cost reduction per hectare in comparison with the An-2.
★ Recoupment of capital investment in the M-500 is estimated at 2.11 years at 540 flying hours per year, or 1.87 years at 1,000 flying hours per year.
★ 5,000 flying hours airframe life.

Crew/passengers: 1 pilot. Optional second seat.
Chemical tank/hopper capacity: 2,094 lb (950 kg), loaded through the top of the fuselage, aft of the cockpit.
Spray equipment: Carried at the trailing-edge of the wings.
Wing characteristics: Straight, low mounted, with dihedral. Winglets.
Wing control surfaces: Ailerons and flaps.
Tail control surfaces: Continuous elevator and balanced rudder, with tabs.
Fuel system: Consumption in ACO, 190 g/hp per hour.

DETAILS FOR M-500.

Principal dimensions:
Wing span: 50 ft 11 ins (15.52 m)
Maximum length: 34 ft 9 ins (10.6 m)
Maximum height: 11 ft 9 ins (3.57 m)
Undercarriage:
Type: Fixed, with tailwheel
Weights:
Empty: 2,844 lb (1,290 kg)
Normal take-off: 5,512 lb (2,500 kg)
Allowable take-off: 6,393 lb (2,900 kg)
Payload: 2,094 lb (950 kg)
Performance:
Spray speed: 65-113 kts (75-130 mph) 120-210 km/h
Take-off distance: 1,476 ft (450 m) from unpaved airfield, 1,411 ft (430 m) from concrete, 30° temperature
Landing distance: 1,592 ft (485 m) unpaved or paved, 30° temperature
Operating altitude for spraying: 3.2 to 98 ft (1 to 30 m)
Ferry range: 540 naut miles (621 miles) 1,000 km, with reserve
Duration: 2 hours, with reserve

JSC National Institute of Aviation Technologies (Russia)

Corporate address: 24 Petrovka Street, Moscow 103051.
Telephone: +7 095 200 7601
Facsimile: +7 095 292 6511
Information: V. P. Pushkov.

● Activities
● Has completed the initial design phase of an amphibious transport aircraft, intended to operate in remote areas (such as Siberia). Powered by 2 x 1,380 shp (1,029 kW) OMSK/Glushenkov TVD-20 turboprop engines, it has a single-step flying-boat hull and T-tail mounted on twin fins. Loading is via a rear ramp/door, with extra headroom provided at the entrance by upward-hinging roof sections. Wing span is quoted at 65 ft 8 ins (20 m) and range with 5,510 lb (2,500 kg) of cargo is 323 naut miles (373 miles) 600 km.

JSC Pony (Russia)

Corporate address: 17/17-20 Kolokolnicov Street, Moscow 103045.
Telephone: +7 095 925 6276
Facsimile: +7 095 928 6102

Pony and Prize

First flight: December 1994 (Pony).
Certification: 1996? for (Pony). Meets JAR-VLA.
Role: Two-seat (Pony) and four-seat (Prize) amphibians.
Engines: 1 x 77.8 hp (58 kW) Rotax 912A (Pony) and 2 x Teledyne Continental IO-240 or Textron Lycoming O-235 piston engines (Prize).
Aircraft variants:
Pony is the two-seater, currently under test. Retractable tailwheel undercarriage, with permanent floats.
Prize is the twin-engined and four-seat development, not built at the time of writing.

Pony amphibian (Piotr Butowski)

Details for Pony.

Principal dimensions:
Wing span: 36 ft 1 ins (11 m)
Maximum length: 27 ft 7 ins (8.4 m)
Maximum height: 9 ft 4 ins (2.84 m)
Wings:
Area: 177.6 sq ft (16.5 m^2)
Aspect ratio: 7.33
Weights:
Empty: 1,202 lb (545 kg)
Maximum take-off: 1,653 lb (750 kg)
Performance:
Maximum speed: 81 kts (93 mph) 150 km/h
Take-off distance: 395 ft (120 m) land, 985 ft (300 m) water
Landing distance: 265 ft (80 m) land, 395 ft (120 m) water
Maximum climb rate: 470 ft (144 m) per minute
Duration: 3.5 hours

Sukhoi Design Bureau (Russia)

Corporate address: See Combat section for company details.

Sukhoi Su-26M, Su-29 and Su-31

Role: Competition aerobatics and training. All related to the original Su-26M.
Wing control surfaces: Wide-span ailerons (each with a ground-adjustable tab and 2 hanging balance tabs).
Tail control surfaces: Horn-balanced elevators and rudder, each with a ground-adjustable tab on Su-26M.
Flight control system: Pushrods and cables.
Construction materials: Over 50% composites for Su-26M, 60% Su-29 and 70% Su-31.
Engine: See Aircraft variants.
Aircraft variants:
Su-26M first appeared in 1984 and is in production as a single-seat competition aircraft, of which about 70 had been built by 1995 for domestic use and export (as Su-26MX). 390 hp (291 kW) AOOT radial piston engine, with a Mühlbauer 3-blade variable-pitch propeller and 263 litres of fuel (63 litres for competition flying). Pilot seat reclined by 45°. Wing span 25 ft 7 ins (7.8 m) and length 22 ft 6 ins (6.845 m). MTOW 2,205 lb (1,000 kg). Never-exceed speed (Vne) 243 kts (280 mph) 450 km/h, rate of climb 3,545 ft (1,080 m) per minute at sea level, and roll rate above 360° per second. G limits +12, -10 normal.
Su-29 is a two-seat aerobatic trainer, also suited to competition. First flown in 1991. Same AOOT engine as Su-26M but with an MTV-3-8-S/L250-21 propeller and 276 litres of fuel (63 litres for competition flying). Wing span 26 ft 11 ins (8.2 m) and length 23 ft 11 ins (7.285 m). MTOW 2,654 lb (1,204 kg) with 2 crew. Same Vne and G limits as Su-26M, and rate of climb 3,150 ft (960 m) per minute at sea level.
Su-29LL or KS is a "flying" laboratory version for testing the Zvezda KS-38 lightweight ejection seat. Also used for training and maintaining military/civil pilot skills. MTOW 2,601 lb (1,180 kg). Vne 237 kts (273 mph) 440 km/h. G limit 7.5. The KS-38 ejection seat can be used during take-off at a minimum speed of 27-32 kts (31-37 mph) 50-60 km/h, as well as in flight at altitudes of over 33 ft (10 m), or 131 ft (40 m) for inverted flight. Maximum speed for ejection is 216 kts (248 mph) 400 km/h, and maximum altitude 16,400 ft (5000 m).
Su-29M is a production version of the Su-29LL, featuring the KS-38 ejection seat as standard instead of a parachute.
Su-31T is the latest version, first flying in 1992. Pilot seat reclined by 35°. Same AOOT engine but with an MTV-9 propeller. 78 litres of fuel for competition flying, with 200 litres in the wings for ferry flights or a 210 litre underbelly tank. Exported as Su-31X.
Su-31M is similar to the basic Su-31T but with a KS-38 ejection seat.
Su-31U is the only version to feature a retractable undercarriage.

Model of the Sukhoi Su-38 agricultural aircraft, based on the Su-29 and now under construction in prototype form. AOOT M-14P engine. 1,543 lb (700 kg) payload. Model shows the single-seat layout, the two-seat layout having a larger canopy (Piotr Butowski)

Sukhoi Su-31 (Piotr Butowski)

Details for Su-31T.

Principal dimensions:
Wing span: 25 ft 7 ins (7.8 m)
Maximum length: 22 ft 8 ins (6.9 m)
Maximum height: 9 ft 1 ins (2.76 m)
Wings:
Aerofoil section: Symmetrical.
Area: 127 sq ft (11.8 m^2)
Aspect ratio: 5.16
Undercarriage:
Type: Fixed, with steerable tailwheel. Cantilever spring main legs
Weights:
Empty: 1,433 lb (650 kg)
Maximum take-off: 2,134 lb (968 kg)
Performance:
Never-exceed speed (Vne): 243 kts (280 mph) 450 km/h
Maximum speed: 178 kts (205 mph) 330 km/h
Stall speed: 61 kts (71 mph) 113 km/h
Take-off distance: 361 ft (110 m)
Landing distance: 984 ft (300 m)
Maximum climb rate: 4,724 ft (1,440 m) per minute at sea level
Roll rate: 400° per second
G limits: +12, -10 normal

Sukhoi Su-39

First flight: 1996.
Role: Single piston or turboprop engined primary trainer developed from the Su-26, Su-29 and Su-31 series.
Sales/users: Proposed as a replacement for the Yakovlev Yak-52 basic trainer. Orders for 1,500 aircraft reported.

Sukhoi Su-39 (Piotr Butowski)

Crew: 2 in tandem cockpits (instructor at rear).
Crew escape: Lightweight Zvezda/Sukhoi KS-38 ejection seats.
Expendable weapons and equipment: Suspended on 2 underwing pylons.
Engine: AOOT M-14P radial piston engine, with an MTV-9 propeller. Under consideration are the 400 hp (298 kW) RPD-VAZ-4304, 435 hp (324 kW) Teledyne Continental GTSIO-520, and 350 hp (261 kW) Textron Lycoming TIO-540.
Fuel system: 320 litres of internal fuel, with provision for 2 x 100 litre drop tanks.
Braking system: Mainwheel brakes.

Details for Su-39 with AOOT engine (unless stated).

Principal dimensions:
Wing span: 27 ft 11 ins (8.5 m)
Maximum length: 23 ft 11 ins (7.285 m)
Maximum height: 8 ft 6.5 ins (2.6 m)
Wings:
Aerofoil section: NACA 23012
Area: 131.33 sq ft (12.20 m^2)
Aspect ratio: 5.92
Undercarriage:
Type: Retractable, with nosewheel
Weights:
Empty, operating: 1,874 lb (850 kg)
Nominal take-off: 2,866 lb (1,300 kg)
Maximum take-off: 3,307 lb (1,500 kg)
Performance:
Never-exceed speed (Vne): 286 kts (329 mph) 530 km/h
Maximum speed: 200 kts (230 mph) 370 km/h at sea level, or 205 kts (236 mph) 380 km/h with the VAZ engine, or 211 kts (242 mph) 390 km/h with the TC, or 197 kts (227 mph) 365 km/h with the TL
Landing speed: 59 kts (68 mph) 110 km/h
Take-off distance: 755 ft (230 m)
Landing distance: 1,148 ft (350 m)
Maximum climb rate: 2,660 ft (810 m) per minute at sea level, or 2,953 ft (900 m) with the VAZ engine, or 3,248 ft (990 m) with the TC, or 2,560 ft (780 m) with the TL
G limits: +9, -6
Ceiling: 13,125 ft (4,000 m)
Range with internal fuel: 648 naut miles (746 miles) 1,200 km

OTHER SUKHOI PROJECTS

S-21: 6/10 passenger supersonic business jet with 3 Aviadvigatel D-21A1 turbofans.
S-51: 50/68-passenger supersonic transport, with 4 R-51 turbojet engines. Prototype to be flown around 2005.
S-80: See Airliners section.
S-84: Four-seat lightplane with a 350 hp (261 kW) Teledyne Continental TSIOL-550-B piston engine and pusher propeller at the tail.
S-986: Twin AOOT M-14P-engined light transport for a crew of 1 or 2 and 8/9 passengers or cargo. Also suited to other roles, including firefighting and agricultural.

JSC Technoavia (Russia)

Corporate address: 7A Kronshtadsky Bvld, Moscow 125212.
Telephone: +7 095 452 5822
Facsimile: +7 095 452 5694
Founded: 1991.

Technoavia SP-91 Slava and SP-95

Role: Interchangeable single or two-seat aerobatic competition and training aircraft.
Sales/users: Production tooling for the SP-95 at Smolensk was underway in 1995.
Details: SP-95, except under Aircraft variants.
Wing control surfaces: SP-91 has drooping ailerons, each with 2 hanging balance tabs. SP-95 is probably similar.
Tail control surfaces: SP-91 has horn-balanced elevators and rudder (with ground-adjustable tab). SP-95 is probably similar.
Construction materials: Metal, with corrugated skins for part of the wings and the control surfaces.
Engine: AOOT M-14P radial piston engine, with a 3-blade controllable-pitch propeller.
Engine rating: 360 hp (268.5 kW).
Aircraft variants:
SP-91 Slava became the prototype to the production SP-95, its similarity to the Sukhoi Su-26M/29/31 series explained by sharing the same designer. 5 completed for trials, with 3 operating in the USA and 1 in the UK. AOOT M-14P engine.
SP-95 is the production version, as detailed.

Technoavia SP-91 Slava (Piotr Butowski)

DETAILS FOR SP-95.

Principal dimensions:
Wing span: 27 ft 7 ins (8.4 m)
Maximum length: 23 ft (7 m)
Wings:
Area: 125.94 sq ft (11.7 m^2)
Aspect ratio: 6.03
Undercarriage:
Type: Fixed, with tailwheel
Weights:
Empty: 1,763 lb (800 kg)
Maximum take-off: 2,380 lb (1,080 kg)
Performance:
Never-exceed speed (Vne): 243 kts (280 mph) 450 km/h
Maximum speed: 162 kts (186 mph) 300 km/h
Stall speed: 57 kts (65 mph) 105 km/h
Take-off distance: 230 ft (70 m)
Landing distance: 492 ft (150 m)
G limits: +11, -9 with 2 crew, or +12,-10 as a single-seater
Climb rate: 3,350 ft (1,020 m) per minute
Range with full fuel: 702 naut miles (807 miles) 1,300 km

Technoavia SM-92 Finist (Piotr Butowski)

Technoavia SM-94 is a six-seat and AOOT M-14P-powered variant of the Yakovlev Yak-18T (Piotr Butowski)

Technoavia SM-92 Finist

First flight: 28 December 1993.
Certification: Meets FAR/JAR Pt 23 standards.
Role: STOL light transport, agricultural, survey and other work.
Sales/users: 4 flying prototypes. Series production at Smolensk, with deliveries from January 1995. Hundreds ordered.
Crew/passengers: Pilot plus 6 passengers, or 2 litters and a medical attendant in an air ambulance role, or 1,324 lb (600 kg) of cargo or equipment for specialist roles.
Wing control surfaces: Frise ailerons (with ground-adjustable tabs) and 3-position, 2-section Fowler flaps.
Tail control surfaces: Horn-balanced elevators (starboard trim tab) and rudder (with ground-adjustable tab).
Flight control system: Mechanical, except for electric flaps.
Construction materials: Metal, with corrugated skins on tail control surfaces.
Engine: AOOT M-14P radial piston engine, with a Mühlbauer MTV-3 variable-pitch 3-blade propeller.
Engine rating: 360 hp (268.5 kW).
Fuel capacity: 380 litres.
Flight avionics/instrumentation: AlliedSignal Bendix/King ADF, GPS, transponder and VHF comm. Specialist equipment to customer's requirements.

DETAILS FOR SM-92.

Principal dimensions:
Wing span: 47 ft 11 ins (14.6 m)
Maximum length: 30 ft 2 ins (9.2 m)
Undercarriage:
Type: Fixed, with steerable/castering tailwheel. Optional floats or wheel/skis
Weights:
Empty: 3,307 lb (1,500 kg)
Maximum take-off: 5,181 lb (2,350 kg)
Payload: 1,323 lb (600 kg)
Performance:
Cruise speed: 108-124 kts (124-143 mph) 200-230 km/h
Stall speed: 54 kts (63 mph) 100 km/h with maximum flaps
Take-off and landing distance: 656 ft (200 m)
Maximum climb rate: 1,181 ft (360 m) per minute
Range with full fuel: 702 naut miles (808 miles) 1,300 km

Tupolev Joint Stock Company (Russia)

Corporate address: See Combat section for company details. See also Airliners and Reconnaissance sections.

Tupolev Tu-24

First flight: 1995?
Role: Multi-purpose lightplane, with versions for patrol, communications and law enforcement (P), fisheries/wildlife protection and survey (R), air ambulance (S), agricultural (SH), general passenger/parachutist/cargo transport (T), and training (U).
Crew/passengers: Pilot and 5 passengers or other loads.
Chemical tank/hopper: Tu-24SH can carry 1,984 lb (900 kg) of chemicals in a cabin-mounted hopper.
Dispersal system: Tu-24SH has a retractable atomizer system, allowing a clean configuration for ferrying.
Wing control surfaces: Drooping ailerons, flaps and leading-edge automatic slats.
Tail control surfaces: Horn-balanced elevators (port trim tab).
Construction materials: Metal.

Tupolev Tu-24 (Piotr Butowski)

Engine: AOOT M-14PS radial piston engine, with a 3-blade variable-pitch propeller.
Engine rating: 360 hp (268.5 kW).
Fuel system: 154 lb (70 kg).

OTHER TUPOLEV PROJECTS
Tu-34: Six-seat STOL multi-purpose transport, with 2 Allison or Turbomeca turboprop engines with pusher propellers on forward-swept wings. First flight anticipated 1997-98. To be built at the new Kyrgyzstan-Russian factory.
Tu-54: Typical braced low-wing single-seat agricultural aircraft, using a 360 hp (268.5 kW) AOOT M-14P radial piston engine and VISh-9 3-blade propeller. 5 prototypes are being constructed, with the first to fly in about 1996. 1,765 lb (800 kg) chemical hopper. Full details in the next edition of WA&SD, once it has appeared.

DETAILS FOR TU-24.

Principal dimensions:
Wing span: 42 ft 8 ins (13 m)
Maximum length: 30 ft 4 ins (9.25 m)
Wings:
Area: 301.39 sq ft (28 m^2)
Aspect ratio: 6.04
Undercarriage:
Type: Fixed, with tailwheel
Weights:
Maximum take-off: 4,629-4,850 lb (2,100-2,200 kg)
Payload: 1,764 lb (800 kg) of freight or 1,984 lb (900 kg) of agricultural chemicals
Performance:
Maximum speed: 127 kts (146 mph) 235 km/h
Spray speed: 65-75 kts (74-87 mph) 120-140 km/h
Balanced runway length: 1,968 ft (600 m)
Maximum climb rate: 886 ft (270 m) per minute
Ceiling: 9,850 ft (3,000 m)
Range with full fuel: 1,080 naut miles (1,242 miles) 2,000 km

Yakovlev Aircraft Corporation (Russia)

Corporate address: See Combat section for all company details.

Yakovlev Yak-18T

First flight: 1967 (a development of the Yak-18 tandem 2-seat trainer of 1946 first appearance).
Role: Light multi-purpose, including passengers, light cargo, ambulance and training.
Sales/users: Large number built for civil and military use, with continued limited production against orders from the Philippine Air Force and others.
Crew/passengers: 4 persons, or 2 persons plus light cargo, or the pilot, an attendant and 1 litter in ambulance layout (using the baggage door to load the patient).
Cockpit: Dual controls.
Baggage hold: To the rear of the seats, with its own loading door.
Wing control surfaces: Slotted ailerons (with tabs) and split flaps.
Tail control surfaces: Elevators (with tabs) and rudder.
Construction materials: Mostly metal, with fabric covering for the outer wings, ailerons and all of the wire-braced tail.
Engine: AOOT M-14P radial.
Engine rating: 360 hp (268.5 kW).
Fuel system: 208 litres.
Flight control system: Mechanical, with hydraulic flap actuation.
Braking system: Pneumatic on mainwheels.
Flight avionics/instrumentation: VFR.

DETAILS FOR YAK-18T.

Principal dimensions:
Wing span: 36 ft 7.5 ins (11.16 m)
Maximum length: 27 ft 6 ins (8.39 m)
Maximum height: 9 ft 2 ins (2.8 m)
Wings:
Aerofoil section: Clark YH
Aspect ratio: 6.62
Area: 202.36 sq ft (18.8 m^2)
Undercarriage:
Type: Retractable, with non-steerable nosewheel
Weights:
Maximum take-off: 3,638 lb (1,650 kg)
Payload: 961 lb (436 kg)
Performance:
Maximum speed: 159 kts (183 mph) 295 km/h
Cruise speed: 135 kts (155 mph) 250 km/h
Take-off distance: 1,312 ft (400 m)
Landing distance: 1,641 ft (500 m)
Maximum climb rate: 984 ft (300 m) per minute
Ceiling: 18,050 ft (5,500 m)
Range with full fuel: 486 naut miles (559 miles) 900 km

Yakovlev Yak-18T (Piotr Butowski)

Yakovlev Yak-54

First flight: 24 December 1993.
Role: Aerobatic trainer and sports competition, as a 2-seat development of the Yak-55M.
Sales/users: Marketed by Hyundai-Yak Aerospace Company Ltd (see Multi-national). 3 prototypes flown by September 1994. Production at Saratov.
Crew: 2, or pilot only for competition flying.
Cockpit: Tandem, under a single bubble canopy.
Wing characteristics: Mid-wing monoplane with no anhedral/dihedral.
Wing control surfaces: Large horn-balanced ailerons only, with hanging balance tabs.
Tail control surfaces: Horn-balanced elevators and rudder (with tab).
Construction materials: Metal.
Engine: AOOT M-14P radial, with a 3-blade variable-pitch propeller.
Engine rating: 360 hp (268.5 kW).

DETAILS FOR YAK-54.

Principal dimensions:
Wing span: 26 ft 9 ins (8.16 m)
Maximum length: 22 ft 8 ins (6.91 m)
Wings:
Aerofoil section: Symmetrical
Area: 138.75 sq ft (12.89 m^2)
Undercarriage:
Type: Fixed, with tailwheel
Weights:
Empty:
Maximum take-off: 2,183 lb (990 kg), or 1,874 lb (850 kg) as a single-seater for competitions
Performance:
Maximum speed: 243 kts (280 mph) 450 km/h
Stall speed: 60 kts (69 mph) 110 km/h
Maximum climb rate: 2,955 ft (900 m) per minute
Roll rate: 6 rad per second, 345° per second
G limits: +9, -7
Ceiling: 13,125 ft (4,000 m)
Ferry range: 378 naut miles (435 miles) 700 km

Yakovlev Yak-55M (Piotr Butowksi)

Yakovlev Yak-55M

First flight: About 1989.
Role: Aerobatics.
Sales/users: Yak-55M is the only currently built Yak-55 version, in production since 1991.
Crew: Pilot only.
Wing/Tail characteristics: As for Yak-54. Yak-55M wings are somewhat similar to the refined Yak-55 wings, but with even more taper, rounded tips, and with tabs under the ailerons instead of inset. Yak-55M tail is more angular than for Yak-55.
Construction materials: Metal.
Engine: As for Yak-54, but with a 2-blade controllable-pitch propeller.
Fuel system: 120 litres.

DETAILS FOR YAK-55M, *WITH YAK-55 DIMENSION/WEIGHT DIFFERENCES IN ITALICS.*

Principal dimensions:
Wing span: 26 ft 7 ins (8.1 m), *26 ft 11 ins (8.2 m)*
Maximum length: 23 ft (7 m), *24 ft 6.5 ins (7.48 m)*
Maximum height: 9 ft 2 ins (2.8 m), *7 ft 6.5 ins (2.3 m)*
Wings:
Aerofoil section: Symmetrical
Area: 137.78 sq ft (12.8 m^2), *153.92 sq ft (14.3 m^2)*
Aspect ratio: 5.13
Undercarriage:
Type: Fixed, with tailwheel
Weights:
Empty: *1,411 lb (640 kg)*
Maximum take-off: 1,852 lb (840 kg)
Performance:
Never-exceed speed (Vne): 243 kts (280 mph) 450 km/h
Maximum speed: 173 kts (199 mph) 320 km/h
Stall speed: 59.5 kts (68.5 mph) 110 km/h
Maximum climb rate: 3,150 ft (960 m) per minute
Take-off and landing distance: 1,476 ft (450 m)
G limits: +9, -6
Roll rate: 6 rad per second, 345° per second

Yakovlev Yak-58

First flight: 26 December 1993.
Role: Business and executive transport, air-taxi, light cargo carrying, training, liaison, patrol of forests/gas and oil pipelines, EEZ/fishery survey, and ecological work. Cabin allows future modification to ambulance and other roles.
Sales/users: Marketed by Hyundai-Yak Aerospace Company Ltd (see Multi-national).
Crew/passengers: Seats for 6 in the all-passenger cabin layout.
Wing characteristics: Low mounted and constant chord, with down-turned wingtips. Supports the tail booms.
Wing control surfaces: Ailerons and flaps.
Tail control surfaces: Tall twin boom unit, with twin inward-toed fins/rudders and a joining tailplane with elevator.
Fuselage: Central nacelle type, with rear-mounted engine. Large doors.
Engine: Shrouded AOOT M-14PT radial, with a 3-blade variable-pitch pusher propeller.
Engine rating: 360 hp (268.5 kW).
Flight control system: Mechanical, except hydraulic flaps.
Flight avionics/ instrumentation: VFR.

Yakovlev Yak-58 over Tbilisi

Details for Yak-58.

Principal dimensions:
Wing span: 41 ft 8 ins (12.7 m)
Maximum length: 28 ft 1 ins (8.55 m)
Maximum height: 10 ft 4.5 ins (3.16 m)
Wings:
Area: 215.28 sq ft (20 m^2)
Undercarriage:
Type: Retractable, with nosewheel.
Weights:
Empty: 2,800 lb (1,270 kg)
Maximum take-off: 4,630 lb (2,100 kg)
Payload: 992 lb (450 kg)
Performance:
Maximum cruise speed: 162 kts (186 mph) 300 km/h
Long-range cruise speed: 154 kts (177 mph) 285 km/h
Take-off distance: 2,001 ft (610 m)
Landing distance: 1,969 ft (600 m)
Ceiling: 13,125 ft (4,000 m)
Range with full payload: 539 naut miles (621 miles) 1,000 km, with 45 minutes reserve

Yakovlev Yak-112

First flight: 20 October 1992.
Role: Passenger carrying, light cargo and mail carrying, glider towing, powerline/forest patrolling, air ambulance, fish reserve survey and agricultural.
Sales/users: One of 3 aircraft being marketed by Hyundai-Yak Aerospace (see Multi-national). Production underway at Irkutsk and Saratov aviation factories in Russia. Many hundreds ordered.
Crew/passengers: 4.
Wing characteristics: Strut-braced, high wing with down-turned wingtips.
Wing control surfaces: Ailerons.
Tail control surfaces: Horn-balanced elevators and rudder.

Yakovlev Yak-112 (Piotr Butowski)

Construction materials: Much use of composites.
Engine: Teledyne Continental IO-360-ES piston engine, with a Hartzell 2-blade propeller. Optional Textron Lycoming IO-540-D4B5.
Engine rating: 200 hp (149 kW).
Flight avionics/instrumentation: AlliedSignal radio communications, flight control and navigation systems for all-weather, day and night flying.

Details for Yak-112.

Principal dimensions:
Wing span: 33 ft 7.5 ins (10.25 m)
Maximum length: 22 ft 10 ins (6.96 m)
Maximum height: 9 ft 6 ins (2.9 m)
Wings:
Area: 150.69 sq ft (14 m^2)
Aspect ratio: 7.5
Undercarriage:
Type: Fixed, with nosewheel.
Weights:
Empty: 1,709 lb (775 kg)
Maximum take-off: 2,778 lb (1,260 kg)
Payload: 595 lb (270 kg)
Performance:
Maximum cruise speed: 135 kts (155 mph) 250 km/h
Long-range cruise speed: 103 kts (118 mph) 190 km/h
Take-off distance: 1,641 ft (500 m)
Landing distance: 1,641 ft (500 m)
Ceiling: 13,125 ft (4,000 m)
Range with full fuel: 1,080 naut miles (1,243 miles) 2,000 km, with 45 minutes reserve
Range with full payload: 459 naut miles (528 miles) 850 km, with 45 minutes reserve

Aerotek (South Africa)

Full name: Manufacturing and Aeronautical Systems Technology.
Corporate address: PO Box 395, Pretoria 0001.
Telephone: +27 12 841 2780, 4866
Facsimile: +27 12 86 8803, 841 4332
Information: Tommy Dent (Sales Manager).

Aerotek Hummingbird

First flight: 8 May 1993.
Certification: Meets FAR Pt 23 requirements.

Aerotek Hummingbird (courtesy Aerotek)

Role: Light aircraft, designed as a very stable, observation platform, capable of low-speed flight.
Crew/passengers: 2 seats, with possibility for a third seat in the payload area in an emergency. Four-seat version is envisaged.
Wing control surfaces: Plain ailerons (25% chord) and split flaps (25% chord).
Tail control surfaces: Single elevator and rudder. Tailplane, elevator and rudder are removable for transportation.
Flight control system: Pushrod and cables.
Construction materials: Glassfibre and Nomex.
Engine: Textron Lycoming O-360-A3A piston engine, with a 2-blade fixed-pitch pusher propeller.
Engine rating: 180 hp (134 kW).
Fuel system: 160 litres.
Braking system: Mainwheels brake independently.
Flight avionics/ instrumentation: VFR, with various options.

Details for Hummingbird.

Principal dimensions:
Wing span: 37 ft 9 ins (11.5 m)
Maximum length: 21 ft 8 ins (6.6 m)
Maximum height: 7 ft 10.5 ins (2.4 m)
Cabin:
Width: 4 ft 2 ins (1.27 m) maximum
Wings:
Aerofoil section: NASA GAW-1
Area: 185.67 sq ft (17.25 m^2)
Aspect ratio: 7.67
Undercarriage:
Type: Fixed, with steerable nosewheel
Weights:
Empty: 1,433 lb (650 kg)
Maximum take-off: 2,425 lb (1,100 kg)
Useful load: 992 lb (450 kg)
Performance:
Maximum speed: 120 kts (138 mph) 222 km/h
Cruise speed: 100 kts (115 mph) 185 km/h at 70% power
Stall speed: 38 kts (44 mph) 71 km/h with flaps
Take-off and landing distance: < 820 ft (250 m)
Maximum climb rate: > 1,000 ft (305 m) per minute
Ceiling: 15,000 ft (4,575 m)
Duration: 4.5 hours at cruise speed

ASL Hagfors Aero AB (Sweden)

Corporate address: Flygplatsen, S-683 93 Rada.
Telephone: +46 563 602 20

●Activities

● The former Aviation Scotland ARV-1 Super2 lightplane is now available from Highlander Aircraft in the USA as a kitplane, in conjunction with ASL which offers it as the certified Opus 280. See Recreational section for further details.

Malmö Forsknings & Innovations AB (MFI) (Sweden)

Corporate address: Kantyxegatan 21, S-213 76 Malmö.
Telephone: +46 40 21 99 50

● Activities

● Intended production of the two-seat MFI-11 lightplane, first flown in 1992 as a modernized MFI-9B, has been shelved. Production of the two or four-seat BA-14B lightplane has also been delayed.

Euraviation S.A. (Switzerland)

Corporate address: 7 rue Roi-Victor-Amé, 1227 Geneva.
Telephone: +41 22 342 24 88
Facsimile: +41 22 342 31 61
Founded: Subsidiary of Euraviation Holding S.A. of Luxembourg.
Information: Eric del Marmol (General Manager).

● Activities

● European sales and support for the Israviation ST-50 (see Israel).

FFA Flugzeugwerke Altenrhein A.G. (Switzerland)

Corporate address: 9423 Altenrhein.
Telephone: +41 71 43 51 11
Facsimile: +41 71 43 53 30
Founded: 1948.

FFA AS 202 Bravo series

First flight: 7 March 1969 (for AS 202/15 prototype).
Certification: 12 December 1975 for the current AS 202/18A and 1995 for the current AS 202/32TP.
Role: Light private, training and towing aircraft. AS 202/18A is capable of aerobatics.
Crew/passengers: 2 persons side-by-side with dual controls, with the capability of a third person in non-aerobatic form.
Baggage capacity: 220.5 lb (100 kg) of baggage.
Wing control surfaces: Ailerons (with ground adjustable tabs) and single-slotted flaps.
Tail control surfaces: Elevators (starboard trim tab) and balanced rudder (with tab).
Flight control system: Mechanical, except for electric tabs on the AS 202/18A2 and A4.
Construction materials: Metal, but with glassfibre used in the construction of the engine cowls and fairings.
Engine: See Aircraft variants.
Fuel system: 170 litres. AS202/32TP adds 2 x 57 litre wingtip tanks.
Electrical system: Standard 12 volt supply, via an engine-driven alternator, though AS 202/18A3 has a 24 volt supply, and all models have the option of a 28 volt supply.
Braking system: Mainwheel hydraulic disc brakes.
Flight avionics/instrumentation: Customer's choice, with options including autopilot and blind-flying equipment
Aircraft variants:
AS 202/18A current piston-engined version made its maiden flight on 22 August 1974. 180 hp (134 kW) Textron Lycoming AEIO-360-B1F piston engine, with a Hartzell 2-blade constant-speed or Hoffmann 3-blade propeller.
AS 202/32TP Turbine Bravo was certified in 1995 for utility roles, though it is also aerobatic capable. Main differences are the use of a 420 shp (313.3 kW) Allison 250-B17D turboprop engine and the adoption of wingtip tanks, raising empty weight and performance.

FFA AS 202/18A Bravo (Denis Hughes)

Details for AS 202/18A.

Principal dimensions:
Wing span: 32 ft 1 ins (9.78 m)
Maximum length: 24 ft 7 ins (7.5 m)
Maximum height: 9 ft 3 ins (2.81 m)
Wings:
Aerofoil section: Modified NACA $63_2618/\ 63_2415$
Area: 149.19 sq ft (13.86 m^2)
Aspect ratio: 6.901
Undercarriage:
Type: Fixed, with steerable nosewheel
Weights:
Empty: 1,565 lb (710 kg)
Maximum take-off: 2,381 lb (1,080 kg)
Performance:
Never exceed speed (Vne): 172 kts (198 mph) 320 km/h
Maximum speed: 130 kts (150 mph) 241 km/h
Stall speed: 62 kts (72 mph) 115 km/h *clean*, 49 kts (56 mph) 90 km/h *with flaps*
Take-off distance: 706 ft (215 m)
Landing distance: 689 ft (210 m)
Maximum climb rate: 800 ft (244 m) per minute at sea level
G limits: +4.4, -2.2
Range with full fuel: 615.5 naut miles (708 miles) 1,140 km

Pilatus Aircraft Ltd (Switzerland)

Corporate address: See Combat section for company details.

Pilatus PC-6/B2-H4 Turbo Porter

First flight: 4 May 1959 for PC-6 piston-engined prototype.
Certification: Complies with US CAR Part 3 category Normal. Swiss Type Certificate F56-10. Aerial work (agricultural, firefighting, etc) certified under CAR 8. Certified noise level to ICAO Annex 16 is 75.3 dB(A).
Role: Super-STOL utility aircraft, with varied roles including passenger/cargo transport, photogrammetry, air ambulance, liaison, survey, SAR, supply dropping, parachuting, firefighting, cloud seeding, towing and agricultural.
Sales/users: Many hundreds in civil and military use in over 50 countries.
Crew/passengers: Pilot and 7-10 passengers or 10 parachutists or litters.
Agricultural/firefighting equipment: Any Turbo Porter can be temporarily converted for an agricultural role in a few hours. Two ag versions are available: the first has an integral stainless steel tank installed in the cabin with 1,125 litre capacity, Simplex pump with impellers, and 62-nozzle sprayboom or 2-6 micronairs; the second self-contained system uses 2 underwing Micronair spray pods of 189 litres each and Micronair AU 4000 atomizers with variable output of 0-30 litres per minute. For firefighting, each water load dropped can extinguish an area of fire measuring 66 ft (20 m)

Pilatus PC-6/B2-H4 Turbo Porter in Ecuadorian service

wide and 200-390 ft (60-120 m) long, depending on the altitude of flight.

Other equipment: Vertically (through floor hatch) or horizontally (through the sliding door) mounted camera for a photogrammetric role, with conversion from standard transport configuration taking 1 man-hour. For a relief role, supplies weighing up to 661 lb (300 kg) can be air-dropped through the floor hatch.

Wing control surfaces: Ailerons (with geared tabs) and double-slotted flaps.

Tail control surfaces: Variable-incidence tailplane, elevator (with Flettner tabs) and rudder.

Flight control system: Mechanical, except for electric tailplane and flaps.

Construction materials: All components are corrosion protected. Aluminium parts (including skin) are Alodine treated and other metals are cadmium-plated or coated with baked enamel.

Engine: Pratt & Whitney Canada PT6A-27 turboprop, with an 8 ft 5 ins (2.57 m) Hartzell HC-B3TN-3D reversing constant-speed 3-blade propeller.

Engine rating: 680 shp (507 kW), flat rated to 550 shp (410 kW).

Fuel system: 644 litres standard. 2 x 243.5 litre underwing tanks optional.

Electrical system: 30 volt starter-generator. 24 volt, 34 or 40 amp-hour ni-cd battery.

Flight avionics/instrumentation: Customer's choice. VFR or IFR. Basic instrumentation includes altimeter, airspeed indicator, vertical speed indicator, and magnetic compass.

DETAILS FOR TURBO PORTER.

Principal dimensions:
Wing span: 52 ft 1 ins (15.87 m)
Maximum length: 35 ft 9 ins (10.9 m)
Maximum height: 10 ft 6 ins (3.2 m)
Cabin:
Length: 7 ft 7 ins (2.3 m)
Width: 3 ft 10 ins (1.16 m)
Height: 4 ft 2.5 ins (1.28 m)
Wings:
Aerofoil section: NACA 64-514
Area: 324.53 sq ft (30.15 m^2)
Aspect ratio: 8.35
Undercarriage:
Type: Fixed, with steerable and lockable tailwheel. Optional wheel/skis or floats
Weights:
Empty: 2,800 lb (1,270 kg), standard configuration, with usable fuel, without passenger seats or radio.
Maximum take-off: 6,173 lb (2,800 kg), or 5,732 lb (2,600 kg) with wheel/ski undercarriage
Maximum landing: 5,864 lb (2,660 kg)
Payload: 2,083 lb (945 kg) excluding options
Performance:
Never-exceed speed (Vne): 151 kts (174 mph) 279 km/h CAS
Maximum cruise speed: 125 kts (144 mph) 232 km/h at sea level
Manoeuvring speed: As for cruise
Stall speed: 58 kts (67 mph) 108 km/h *clean,* 52 kts (60 mph) 97 km/h *with flaps,* CAS
Take-off distance: 646 ft (197 m) at sea level
Landing distance: 417 ft (127 m) at sea level
Maximum climb rate: 1,010 ft (308 m) per minute at sea level
G limits: +3.58, -1.43
Ceiling: 29,000 ft (8,840 m), service
Range: 500 naut miles (575 miles) 926 km at 10,000 ft (3,050 m), optimum cruise speed, no reserve
Range with 2 underwing tanks: 870 naut miles (1,001 miles) 1,611 km
Duration: 4 hours 20 minutes, or 7 hours 35 minutes with underwing tanks

Pilatus PC-12

Pilatus PC-12

First flight: 31 May 1991.

Certification: 30 March 1994 (FAR Pt 23 Normal category to Amdt 42).

Role: Pressurized utility and business aircraft.

Sales/users: At least 45 orders/options by the start of 1995.

Crew/passengers: 9 or 10 (6 in business configuration), including 1 or 2 pilots respectively. Dual controls available.

Baggage capacity: 39.55 cu ft (1.12 m^3)

Pressurization system: 5.8 maximum cabin differential.

Wing control surfaces: Mass-balanced ailerons (with ground-adjustable trim tabs) with sealed aileron/wing gap, and 3-position Fowler flaps (0° up, 15° take-off, 40° landing).

Tail control surfaces: Variable-incidence tailplane, elevators and rudder (with Flettner tab).

Flight control system: Mechanical, except for electric tailplane, flaps and rudder tab.

Construction materials: Principally metal, but with Kevlar/glassfibre winglets, glassfibre/honeycomb sandwich engine cowling, and Kevlar honeycomb and glassfibre dorsal and ventral fin fairings. 20,000 flying hours or 27,000 landings fatigue life.

Engine: Pratt & Whitney Canada PT6A-67B turboprop, with an 8 ft 9 ins (2.67 m) Hartzell HC-E4A-3D/E10477K constant-speed 4-blade propeller.

Engine rating: 1,605 shp (1,197 kW) thermodynamic power, flat rated at 1,200 shp (894.8 kW).

Fuel system: 1,540 litres, of which 1,522 litres are usable.

Electrical system: 28 volt DC supply via a primary 300 amp starter-generator and back-up 100 amp generator. 24 volt, 40 amp-hour ni-cd battery. 7 DC distribution power buses. 115/26 volt AC supply with 2 power buses, at 400 Hz, via 2 x 150 volt static inverters.

Hydraulic system: 3,000 psi for undercarriage only.

Radar: Optional colour weather radar.

Flight avionics/instrumentation: Can operate under VFR and IFR by day and night, and fly into known icing conditions. Standard equipment (primarily AlliedSignal Bendix/King) is KFC 325 integrated AFCS with EFIS, including KMC 321 mode controller, EFS 40 (4 ins, 10 cm displays for EADI and EHSI), KX 155 comm/nav transceivers (2 each), KN 63 DME, KR 87 digital ADF, KNI 582 RMI, KI 204 COI, KR 21 marker receiver and lights, KT 71 transponder, KEA 130A encoding altimeter, Narco ELT-910 emergency locator transmitter and more. Full range of flight/engine and other instruments. Wide range of optional avionics.

Aircraft variants:
PC-12 is the basic passenger version, as detailed.
PC-12F is the freighter version, with a 3,086 lb (1,400 kg) payload.

DETAILS FOR PC-12.

Principal dimensions:
Wing span: 52 ft 9 ins (16.08 m)
Maximum length: 47 ft 2 ins (14.38 m)
Maximum height: 14 ft (4.26 m)
Cabin:
Length: 16 ft 11 ins (5.16 m)
Width: 5 ft (1.53 m)
Height: 4 ft 9 ins (1.45 m)
Cargo area volume: 326.3 cu ft (9.24 m^3), for up to 3,086 lb (1,400 kg) of cargo
Cargo door size: 4 ft 7 ins x 4 ft 4 ins (1.4 x 1.32 m)
Wings:
Aerofoil section: NASA LS(1)-417 mod
Area: 277.82 sq ft (25.81 m^2)
Aspect ratio: 10.018
Undercarriage:
Type: Retractable , with steerable nosewheel (±12° with pedals, ±60° with differential braking).
Turning radius: 33 ft 10 ins (10.31 m) wingtip, 13 ft 6 ins (4.12 m) nosewheel
Weights:
Empty: 5,260 lb (2,386 kg) with 11 seats
Maximum take-off and landing: 8,818 lb (4,000 kg)
Useful load: 3,602 lb (1,634 kg)
Payload: 2,639 lb (1,197 kg) based on 200 naut mile range and 45 minutes reserve
Performance:
Maximum cruise speed: 269 kts (310 mph) 498 km/h at 20,000 ft (6,100 m)
Stall speed: 84 kts (97 mph) 156 km/h *clean,* 60 kts (69 mph) 111 km/h *landing configuration,* both at 40° bank angle
Take-off distance: 1,020 ft (310 m) at sea level, ISA
Landing distance: 1,395 ft (425 m) at sea level, ISA
Maximum climb rate: 2,080 ft (634 m) per minute at sea level
G limits: +3.4, -1.36 *clean,* or +2, -0 *with flaps lowered*
Ceiling: 35,000 ft (10,670 m) service, 30,000 ft (9,150 m) operating altitude
Range: 2,050 naut miles (2,360 miles) 3,796 km, at 222 kts cruise speed and operating altitude
Duration: 9 hours 30 minutes, at 222 kts and operating altitude

Chichester-Miles Consultants Ltd (CMC) (UK)

Corporate address: West House, Ayot St Lawrence, Welwyn, Hertfordshire AL6 9BT.
Telephone: +44 1438 820341
Facsimile: +44 1438 820030

● Activities

● Has developed the Leopard four-seat business jet, now powered by 2 Williams International FJX turbofans. First flown in 1988. Intended for production but not undertaken to date.

FLS Aerospace Ltd (UK)

Corporate address: Bournemouth International Airport, Christchurch, Dorset BH23 6NW.
Telephone: +44 1202 500200
Facsimile: +44 1202 593271
Information: Anders Toft (Managing Director).

●Activities

● FLS is negotiating the sale of the Optica multi-role and observation aircraft and the Sprint aerobatic primary trainer with several interested parties. Total of 22 Opticas have been built over the years, of which 4 are currently in Spain on fire protection work, 2 hangared in the USA, 1 in the Middle East and 1 privately owned. 3 Sprints have been completed.

Nash Aircraft Ltd (UK)

Corporate address: Trading Estate, Farnham, Surrey GU9 9NU.
Telephone: +44 1252 723688
Information: Richard Nash.

Nash Petrel

First flight: 8 November 1980.
Certification: BCAR Section K.
Role: 2-seat (dual control) light tourer, trainer and glider tug.
Wing control surfaces: Ailerons and slotted flaps.
Tail control surfaces: Elevators and rudder.

DETAILS FOR PETREL.

Principal dimensions:
Wing span: 29 ft 4 ins (8.94 m)
Maximum length: 20 ft 5 ins (6.22 m)
Maximum height: 7 ft 4 ins (2.24 m)
Wings:
Area: 136 sq ft (12.63 m^2)
Undercarriage:
Type: Fixed, with steerable nosewheel
Weights:
Empty: 1,190 lb (540 kg)
Maximum take-off: 1,680 lb (762 kg)
Performance:
Cruise speed: 105 kts (121 mph) 194 km/h
Stall speed: 45 kts (52 mph) 84 km/h *clean,* 40 kts (46 mph) 74 km/h *with full flaps*
Maximum climb rate: 1,100 ft (335 m) per minute

Flight control system: Manual.
Engine: 118-180 hp (88-134 kW) Textron Lycoming engine.
Fuel system: 104.5 litres.
Braking system: Hydraulic disc.

Short Brothers PLC (UK)

Corporate address: PO Box 241, Airport Road, Belfast BT3 9DZ, Northern Ireland.
Telephone: +44 1232 458444
Facsimile: +44 1232 732974, 454406
Founded: 1908, becoming a division of Bombardier Inc in 1989 as the European branch of the aerospace and defence business.
Employees: About 10,000 worldwide.
Information: Alec McRitchie (communications and public affairs).

●Activities

● Worldwide operations, structured into 5 main business units as Aircraft Division, Support Services Division, Nacelle Systems Division, Defence Systems Division and Shorts Missile Systems Ltd. Support Services Division (incorporating the recently acquired Airwork Ltd) provides flying training using Grob G 115 D-2 trainers. Short is also allied with Hurel-Dubois in the International Nacelle Systems EEIG (INS) concern.

● No longer producing Tucano trainers or Shorts 330 transports, its main airframe building business concentrates on the production of the fuselage and empennage of the Learjet 45, and centre fuselage, wing components and engine nacelles of the Canadair Regional Jet. It also produces wings for the Fokker 70 and 100 as a risk-sharing partner and manufactures components for the complete range of Boeing airliners. New programmes include an agreement with British Aerospace to take a 10% share in the UK work on the European FLA transport, and work with Westland on the Longbow Apache for the British Army.

Slingsby Aviation Ltd (UK)

Corporate address: Kirkbymoorside, York YO6 6EZ.
Telephone: +44 1751 432474
Facsimile: +44 1751 431173
Information: Nicola Richards (Sales and Marketing Executive).

● Activities

● Member of the ML Holdings PLC group of companies.
● Offers a comprehensive professional pilot training programme in addition to the sale of Firefly aircraft and sub-contract component manufacture.

Slingsby T67 Firefly series

First flight: 15 May 1981 as the T67A, a licence-built Fournier RF6B.
Certification: All current models are certified to FAR 23 Amdt 27, with T67M260 certified to JAR 23 and FAR 23 Amdt 42. Approved to British BCAR Section K, Issue 6, Chapters 2-2 to 2-5.
Role: Civil and military pilot trainer, aerobatic and private aircraft.
Sales/users: Over 160 delivered to military and commercial academies and other customers in 13 countries, including the T67M260 as the new Enhanced Flight Screener (EFS) aircraft for the USAF.
Crew/passengers: Side-by-side 2 seats, with dual controls.
Baggage capacity: 66 lb (30 kg).
Wing control surfaces: Mass-balanced Frise-type ailerons and fixed-hinge flaps (18° take-off, 40° landing).
Tail control surfaces: Mass-balanced elevator (port trim tab).
Flight control system: Manual, except for optional electric (instead of manual) trim tab.

Slingsby T67M260 (T-3A) Firefly

Construction materials: Glassfibre fuselage of conventional frame and top-hat stringer construction, with stainless steel firewall. All glassfibre wings with double skin (inner corrugated), with flaps having Kevlar skins. Glassfibre tail unit. Tailplane incorporates a built-in VOR antenna, the fin a VHF antenna.
Engine: See Aircraft variants.
Fuel system: 159 litres in wing tanks, or optionally 113 litres in the fuselage for T67C1/C2 and T67M Mk 2.
Flight avionics/instrumentation: Colour coded ASI, altimeter, VSI, electric turn co-ordinator, artificial horizon and directional gyro, accelerometer, engine tachometer, compass and more.

Aircraft variants:
T67C is the low cost aerobatic training variant, offering the same airframe and g limits as the other models. 160 hp (119 kW) Textron Lycoming O-320-D2A piston engine, with a 2-blade fixed-pitch metal propeller. Fuel in the fuselage or wings. No inverted fuel/oil systems. Recommended for a flying syllabus of about 70 hours.
T67M Mk 2 is the lowest powered of the M military models, with a 160 hp (119 kW) AEIO-320-D1B piston engine and constant-speed propeller. Inverted fuel and oil systems. Recommended for a military flying syllabus of about 80 hours.
T67M200 is broadly similar to the T67M260 but with a 200 hp (149 kW) AEIO-360-A1E engine and 3-blade constant-speed composites propeller. Fuel and oil systems for sustained inverted flight. Recommended for a military flying syllabus of about 100 hours.
T67M260 has a 260 hp (194 kW) AEIO-540-D4A5 piston engine and constant-speed propeller. Electric trim standard. Known in USAF service as the T-3A.

DETAILS FOR T67C, *WITH T67M260 IN ITALICS WHERE DIFFERENT.*

Principal dimensions:
Wing span: 34 ft 9 ins (10.59 m)
Maximum length: 24 ft (7.32 m), *24 ft 10 ins (7.55 m)*
Maximum height: 7 ft 9 ins (2.36 m)
Wings:
Aerofoil section: NACA 23015. 23013 (root/tip)
Area: 136 sq ft (12.63 m^2)
Aspect ratio: 8.88
Undercarriage:
Type: Fixed, with steerable nosewheel
Weights:
Empty: 1,510 lb (685 kg), *1,750 lb (794 kg)*
Maximum take-off and landing: 2,150 lb (975 kg), *2,525 lb (1,145 kg)*
Performance:
Never exceed speed (Vne): 180 kts (207 mph) 333 km/h, *195 kts (224 mph) 361 km/h*
Maximum speed: 127 kts (146 mph) 235 km/h, *152 kts (175 mph) 281 km/h at sea level*
Stall speed: 49 kts (57 mph) 91 km/h, *52 kts (60 mph) 96 km/h*, with flaps
Take-off distance: 1,100 ft (335 m), *913 ft (278 m)*, ISA
Landing distance: 1,142 ft (348 m), *1,226 ft (374 m)*, ISA
Maximum climb rate: 900 ft (274 m) per minute, *1,380 ft (420 m) per minute*, at sea level
G limits: +6, -3
Range: 554 naut miles (638 miles) 1,026 km, *407 naut miles (468 miles) 753 km*, 60-65% power at 8,000 ft (2,440 m)
Duration: 7 hours 20 minutes, *5 hours 40 minutes*, best economy speed at 8,000 ft (2,440 m)

Advanced Aerodynamics & Structures Inc (AASI) (USA)

Corporate address: 3060 Airport Way, Long Beach, CA 90806.
Telephone: +1 310 988 2088
Facsimile: +1 310 988 2238
Employees: About 300.
Information: Gene Comfort (Senior Vice President and General Manager).

AASI Jetcruzer 450, 500 and 650

Details: Jetcruzer 450 and 500, except under Aircraft variants.
First flight: 11 January 1989. First production-standard Jetcruzer 450 flew on 2 September 1992.
Certification: 4 June 1994 to FAR Pt 23.
Role: Business and multi-purpose aircraft, including military, cargo carrying, ambulance and radar-equipped SAR.
Sales/users: 66 orders by August 1995, with deliveries from late 1995. Cost US$1.1 million for 6-seat version and 1.5 million for 12 seat version.
Crew/passengers: 6 persons (including pilot/s), five-seat executive layout with toilet, or litter and 2 attendants in a medevac role. Dual controls.
Baggage capacity: 25.25 cu ft (0.715 m^3)
Pressurization system: 5.78 psi maximum cabin differential for Jetcruzer 500.
Wing characteristics: Rear-mounted main wings with compound sweep (34° at roots) and winglets. Spin resistant.
Wing control surfaces: Ailerons. No flaps.
Tail control surfaces: Rudders in winglets.

AASI Jetcruzer 450

Flight control system: Pushrods, torque tubes and bellcranks.
Construction materials: Metal wings and canards, graphite composite fuselage with embedded copper and aluminium screen lightning protection.
Engine: Pratt & Whitney Canada PT6A-42A turboprop, with a 6 ft 8 ins (2.03 m) Hartzell 3-blade constant-speed pusher propeller.
Engine rating: 850 shp (633.8 kW).
Fuel system: 833 litres for Jetcruzer 500.
Electrical system: Engine-mounted 300 amp starter-generator. 2 x 24 volt batteries.
Braking system: Hydraulic.
Radar: Optional colour weather radar.
Flight avionics/ instrumentation: Includes IFR standard package with AlliedSignal Silver Crown equipment including 3 ins (7.6 cm) ADI and HSI, dual VHF comm CNI, dual nav with RNAV VOR/ILS and G/S, GPS, transponder, marker beacon, and ADF. Optional avionics include single or dual EFIS (4 ins, 10 cm), Loran, radar altimeter, storm scope, DME, autopilot, and more. Standard flight instruments include ADI, HSI, airspeed indicator, altimeter, turn and bank indicator, and vertical speed indicator. Range of engine/fuel instruments.
Aircraft variants:
Jetcruzer 450 is the unpressurized model, formerly with a 680 shp (507 kW) PT6A-27 turboprop engine.
Jetcruzer 500 (no longer 500P) is the pressurized model.
Jetcruzer 650 is a stretched twelve-seat long-range development, with a 750 shp (559.3 kW) PT6A-135A engine. Length increased to 34 ft (10.36 m). MTOW 6,500 lb (2,948 kg). Possible production in 1996.

AASI Stratocruzer 1250-ER

First flight: Prototype was structurally complete by August 1995.
Role: 12-seat intercontinental business jet. Cost US$3.5 million.
Engine: 2 Rolls-Royce Williams FJ44 turbofans.
Engine rating: Each 1,900 lbf (8.45 kN).

DETAILS FOR JETCRUZER 450.

Principal dimensions:
Wing span: 42 ft 2 ins (12.85 m)
Maximum length: 28 ft 2 ins (8.59 m)
Maximum height: 10 ft 5 ins (3.18 m)
Canard span: 18 ft 9 ins (5.72 m)
Cabin:
Length: 12 ft 2 ins (3.71 m)
Width: 4 ft 1 ins (1.24 m)
Height: 4 ft 10 ins (1.47 m)
Volume: 203.5 cu ft (5.76 m^3)
Wings:
Aerofoil section: NACA 2412
Area: 193.2 sq ft (17.95 m^2)
Aspect ratio: 9.22
Undercarriage:
Type: Retractable, with steerable nosewheel
Weights:
Empty: 2,980 lb (1,352 kg)
Maximum take-off: 5,000 lb (2,268 kg)
Maximum landing weight: 4,750 lb (2,154 kg)
Payload: 2,020 lb (916 kg)
Performance:
Maximum speed: 320 kts (368 mph) 593 km/h
Maximum cruise speed: 310 kts (357 mph) 574 km/h
Stall speed: 58 kts (67 mph) 108 km/h
Take-off distance: 980 ft (299 m)
Landing distance: 950 ft (290 m)
Maximum climb rate: 2,634 ft (803 m) per minute at MTOW
Ceiling: 30,000 ft (9,140 m)
Range with full fuel: 1,478 naut miles (1,702 miles) 2,737 km at economical cruise speed
Duration: 4.8 hours at 310 kts

DETAILS FOR STRATOCRUZER.

Principal dimensions:
Wing span: 46 ft (14.02 m)
Maximum length: 36 ft (10.97 m)
Maximum height: 13 ft 3 ins (4.08 m)
Weights:
Empty: 5,850 lb (2,653 kg)
Maximum take-off: 12,500 lb (5,670 kg)
Performance:
High cruise speed: 418 kts (482 mph) 775 km/h
Stall speed: 81 kts (93 mph) 150 km/h
Take-off distance: 4,100 ft (1,250 m)
Landing distance: 3,650 ft (1,113 m)
Maximum climb rate: 3,650 ft (1,113 m) per minute
Ceiling: 45,000 ft (13,700 m)
Range with full fuel: 3,213 naut miles (3,700 miles) 5,954 km

Ag-Cat Corporation (USA)

Corporate address: Malden Industrial Park, Building 167, Malden, MO 63863.
Telephone: +1 314 276 5770
Facsimile: +1 314 276 5776
Founded: 1995 from the previous Malden Ag-Craft Inc.
Information: Joe Kosier (Vice President, Sales and Marketing).

● Activities

- New owner and manufacturer of the former Schweizer Ag-Cat series.

Ag-Cat Corporation Ag-Cat series

First flight: 27 May 1957 (Original Grumman Ag-Cat).
Role: Single-seat piston and turboprop agricultural biplanes, capable also of fire bombing.
Sales/users: Some 2,600 Ag-Cats of all versions had been built by Grumman and Schweizer since 1958. Now built by Ag-Cat.
Chemical tank/hopper: See Aircraft variants.
Safety equipment: Cockpit strengthened and padded in case of overturn, and pressurized to prevent chemicals entering during spraying operations.
Wing control surfaces: Ailerons on all wings, the lower port having a ground-adjustable tab.
Tail control surfaces: Horn-balanced elevators and rudder, with ground-adjustable tabs.
Flight control system: Mechanical.
Construction materials: Metal, including welded steel-tube fuselage and tail structures and aluminium wings, except for fabric covering on part of the undersurface of the wings and the wire-braced tail unit. Glassfibre wingtips.
Engine: See Aircraft variants.

Ag-Cat Corporation Ag-Cat with a P&W radial engine

Electrical system: All have a 24 volt supply. APU external power receptacle.
Braking system: Hydraulic disc brakes. Parking brake.
Aircraft variants:
Ag-Cat 450B has a 450 hp (335.6 kW) Pratt & Whitney R-985 radial engine and 242 litres of fuel. 43.4 cu ft (1.23 m^3) and 1,230 litres hopper. 25 ins (63.5 cm) wide gate. Solid system controls. Trailing-edge spray system and bottom loader. Other equipment available. Certified gross weight 5,200 lb (2,359 kg), MTOW (CAM 8) 7,020 lb (3,184 kg), maximum useful load (CAM 8) 3,395 lb (1,540 kg), and working speed 100 kts (115 mph) 185 km/h.
Ag-Cat 600B has a 600 hp (447.4 kW) Pratt & Whitney R-1340 radial engine, with 303 litres of fuel. 53.4 cu ft (1.51 m3) and 1,514 litres hopper. 38 ins (96.5 cm) wide gate. Navigation lights. Trailing-edge spray system and bottom loader. Other equipment available. Weights and speeds as quoted for Ag-Cat 450B except maximum useful load (CAM 8) 3,370 lb (1,529 kg).
Ag-Cat Turbine has either a 680 shp (507 kW) Pratt & Whitney Canada PT6A-15AG or 750 shp (559.3 kW) PT6A-34AG turboprop and 454 litres of fuel. Hopper, gate and spray system as for Ag-Cat 600B.

DETAILS FOR AG-CAT TURBINE.

Principal dimensions:
Wing span: 42 ft 5 ins (12.93 m) upper
Maximum length: 33 ft 1 ins (10.08 m) (3 point attitude)
Maximum height: 12 ft 1 ins (3.68 m)
Wings:
Aerofoil section: NACA 4412
Area: 392.7 sq ft (36.48 m^2)
Undercarriage:
Type: Fixed, with steerable tailwheel
Weights:
Empty: 3,150 lb (1,429 kg) standard
Certified gross weight: 5,200 lb (2,359 kg)
Maximum take-off (CAM 8): 7,020 lb (3,184 kg)
Useful load (CAM 8): 3,870 lb (1,755 kg)
Performance:
Spray speed: 113 kts (130 mph) 209 km/h
Stall speed: 56 kts (64 mph) 103 km/h
Take-off over a 50 ft (15 m) obstacle: 900 ft (274 m) with 680 hp engine at certified gross weight
Landing over a 50 ft (15 m) obstacle: 1,333 ft (406 m)
Range with full fuel: 172 naut miles (198 miles) 319 km

Air Tractor Inc (USA)

Corporate address: PO Box 485, Olney, TX 76374.
Telephone: +1 817 564 5616
Facsimile: +1 817 564 2348
Founded: 1958.

Air Tractor AT-401B, AT-402, AT-502 series, AT-503 and AT-802

Details: AT-401B, except under Aircraft variants.
Role: Single-seat agricultural aircraft, capable of fire bombing.
Sales/users: Over 200 delivered since 1987.
Cockpit: 3-piece windshield optional. Nylon mesh seat cover.
Chemical tank/hopper: Vinylester (Derakane) 1,514 litre hopper, with in-ferry-flight hopper rinse system. Window.

Air Tractor AT-401B (courtesy Air Tractor)

Dispersal equipment: 2 ins (5 cm) stainless steel spray system with streamline booms (41 nozzles). Sprayboom swath width 80 ft (24.4 m). Transland 2.5 ins (6.4 cm) bottom loading valve. Agrinautics 2 ins (5 cm) spray pump with Transland on-off valve. 5-blade ground-adjustable AT-4300 spray fan, partly to increase fluid flow consistency for more volume per acre. 39 ins (96.5 cm) Transland gate box. Optional 8-unit Micronair mini-atomizer, Transland 22358 extra high volume spreader, Transland 54401 NorCal Swathmaster, 40 extra nozzles for high-volume spraying, Crop Hawk Flowmaster, 3 ins (7.62 m) spray system, and fire-bombing dump door and vent.
Safety equipment: Energy-absorbing spring undercarriage, burst-resistant fuel tanks, 5,000 lb (2,268 kg) pilot restraint system, heavy wall overturn structure, optimum battery location, ergonomic seat, and flexible fuel line construction. Optional retractable 600 watt landing light.
Wing characteristics: Low-mounted, with Hoerner wingtips to increase span and swath width, and offer faster climb rate and better control. Stall resistant wings, with steel spar caps.
Wing control surfaces: Ailerons (with boost tabs) that droop by 10° when the Fowler high-lift flaps are fully extended.
Tail control surfaces: Horn-balanced elevators and rudder (all with boost tabs).
Flight control system: Mechanical, except for electric flaps.
Construction materials: Metal, except for glassfibre wing/body fairings and wingtips. Reinforced wing leading edges.
Engine: Pratt & Whitney R-1340 radial piston engine, with 2-blade constant-speed propeller. Can be converted to have a new or used turboprop engine.
Engine rating: 600 hp (447.4 kW).
Fuel system: 477 litres. Optional ferry fuel system.
Electrical system: 35 amp alternator.
Braking system: Cleveland 4-piston brakes.
Flight avionics/instrumentation: Options include Narco ELT, AlliedSignal Bendix/King KY 196 comm radio and KX 115 nav/comm.
Aircraft variants:
AT-401B, as detailed.
AT-402 has a 680 shp (507 kW) Pratt & Whitney PT6A-15AG turboprop engine, with a Hartzell 3-blade constant-speed propeller. Fuel capacity 644 litres standard, with higher options. 250 amp starter-generator, and 2 x 24 volt/21 amp-hour batteries. Similar hopper and dispersal equipment to AT-401B. MTOW 7,860 lb (3,565 kg) and useful load 4,121 lb (1,869 kg). Similar spray speed. Cruise speed 140 kts (162 mph) 261 km/h at 8,000 ft (2,440 m). Some 170 delivered by 1995.
AT-502 introduced an 1,892 litre hopper. Engine, fuel

capacity, starter-generator, etc, are similar to AT-402, although the PT6A-34AG is an alternative engine. Wing span 50 ft (15.24 m). MTOW 9,200 lb (4,173 kg) and useful load 5,077 lb (2,303 kg). Typical spray speed is 104-126 kts (120-145 mph) 193-233 km/h, and cruise speed 144 kts (166 mph) 267 km/h using 475 shp at 8,000 ft (2,440 m). 267 of all AT-502 versions (see below) had been delivered by 1995.

AT-502A is a variant of AT-502, with a 1,100 shp (820 kW) PT6A-47R turboprop and 818 litres of fuel. Wing span increased to 52 ft (15.85 m), providing an 85 ft (26 m) swath width. MTOW 10,480 lb (4,753 kg) and useful load 5,910 lb (2,680 kg). Working speed 104-130 kts (120-150 mph) 193-241 km/h and cruise speed 152 kts (175 mph) 282 km/h using 475 shp at 8,000 ft (2,440 m).

AT-502B has AT-502A's wings combined with a PT6A-15AG engine and 644 litre fuel capacity. MTOW 9,700 lb (4,400 kg) and useful load 5,403 lb (2,450 kg). Virtually identical working and cruise speeds to AT-502.

AT-503 was developed as a tandem two-seater with full cockpit duplication, based on AT-502 with a PT6A-34AG engine. Used for work and ag pilot training.

AT-802 first flew in 1990 and is the largest of the Air Tractor range. It is a two-seater for both agricultural and firefighting roles, the latter having a computerized fire gate and 3,104 litre hopper plus 68 litre foam tank. The agricultural hopper is 3,028 litres. Same MTOW as AT-802A, but useful load of 9,190 lb (4,168 kg) as a fire bomber and 9,540 lb (4,327 kg) for agricultural work. 1,424 shp (1,062 kW) PT6A-67R turboprop, with 961 litres of fuel. Some 25 AT-802/As will have been deliveredby late 1995.

AT-802A is a single-seat version of AT-802, with a 9,330 lb (4,232 kg) useful load as a fire bomber and 9,680 lb (4,391 kg) for agricultural uses. Unchanged hopper capacities. The firefighting version is sometimes referred to as the AT-802AF.

Air Tractor AT-802 (courtesy Air Tractor)

DETAILS FOR AT-401B, *WITH AT-802A*
AGRICULTURAL VERSION IN ITALICS.

Principal dimensions:
Wing span: 51 ft (15.54 m), *58 ft (17.68 m)*
Maximum length: 27 ft (8.23 m), *35 ft 8 ins (10.87 m)*
Maximum height: 8 ft 6 ins (2.59 m), *11 ft (3.35 m)*
Wings:
Area: 306 sq ft (28.43 m^2), *391 sq ft (36.33 m^2)*
Aspect ratio: 8.5, *8.6*
Undercarriage:
Type: Fixed, with castering/lockable tailwheel.
Weights:
Empty: 4,244 lb (1,925 kg), *6,320 lb (2,866 kg)*, both with spray equipment
Maximum take-off: 7,860 lb (3,565 kg), *16,000 lb (7,257 kg)*
Maximum landing: 6,000 lb (2,721 kg), *16,000 lb (7,257 kg)*
Useful load: 3,725 lb (1,690 kg), *9,680 lb (4,391 kg)*
Performance:
Maximum speed: 135 kts (156 mph) 250 km/h at sea level
Cruise speed: 124 kts (143 mph) 230 km/h at 4,000 ft (1,220 m), *166 kts (191 mph) 307 km/h at 8,000 ft (2,440 m) empty of chemical*
Spray speed: typically 104-122 kts (120-140 mph) 193-226 km/h, *113-139 kts (130-160 mph) 209-257 km/h*
Stall speed: 64 kts (73 mph) 119 km/h clean, 53 kts (61 mph) 98 km/h with flaps, 47 kts (54 mph) 87 km/h as usually landed, all at MLW *88 kts (101 mph) 163 km/h clean, 76 kts (87 mph) 140 km/h with flaps, 53 kts (61 mph) 99 km/h as usually landed, all at MTOW*
Take-off distance: 1,318 ft (402 m), *1,900 ft (580 m)*, both at MTOW
Maximum climb rate: 1,100 ft (335 m) per minute at sea level, at 6,000 lb weight, *780 ft (238 m) per minute at MTOW and 1,220 shp*
Range: 547 naut miles (630 miles) 1,014 km at 132 mph and 8,000 ft, no reserves, *529 naut miles (610 miles) 981 km at economical cruise speed*

American Aviation Inc (USA)

Corporate address: 3608 South Davison Boulevard, Spokane, Washington 99204.
Telephone: +1 509 838 5354
Facsimile: +1 509 838 0831
Information: John Ely (Director of Marketing).

● Activities

● Markets FAA certified Aerodynamic Speed Stacks for retrofit to the Piper Cheyenne I, II and IIXL, said to reduce drag and increase true airspeed by 5-8 knots, and last longer because of their high temperature, high strength construction. They also improve boundary layer relief.

● American Aviation's Turbine Division markets a Pitot Cowling System for the same aircraft.

American Champion Aircraft Corporation (USA)

Corporate address: PO Box 37, 32032 Washington Avenue, Highway D, Rochester, WI 53167.
Telephone: +1 414 534 6315
Facsimile: +1 414 534 2395
Information: Jerry Mehlhaff (President).

● Activities

● Offers a range of Dacron-covered two-seat high-wing cabin monoplanes, all based on former Bellanca/Champion aircraft. These are the Explorer (new version of the Citabria) with a 150 hp (112 kW) Textron Lycoming O-320 piston engine, Scout with a 180 hp (134 kW) O-360 engine and Super Decathlon with a 180 hp (134 kW) AEIO-360 engine.

● Company President, Jerry Mehlhaff, has also reportedly agreed to co-produce the *John Doe* as a homebuilt kit in co-operation with its designer, Steve Nusbaum. This is another high-wing braced cabin monoplane (though a single-seater). The kit is expected to cost about US$20,000 without engine and propeller. Information from American Aircraft Engineering Research Company.

Angel Aircraft Corporation (USA)

Corporate address: Municipal Airport, 1410 Arizona PL SW, Orange City, IA 51041-7453.
Telephone: +1 712 737 3344
Facsimile: +1 712 737 3399

● Activities

● This company developed the Model 44 Angel, to be distributed by TradeLink Inc of Roanoke, Texas. Designed by Carl Mortenson, a former missionary pilot and mechanic, it was conceived to fit between single-engined STOL lightplanes and STOL twins of Twin Otter type, for missionary and other work in remote areas (operating from unprepared strips), and also for marketing as an executive aircraft. Certification to FAR Pt 23 for day, night, VFR and IFR in the Normal category was received on 20 October 1992. It is unclear whether production aircraft have yet been completed (13 originally anticipated by the end of 1995).

Angel Aircraft Model 44 Angel

Role: STOL missionary, utility and executive aircraft (see introduction).
Crew/passengers: 8, or 6 with reclining seats.
Engines: 2 Textron Lycoming IO-540-M1C5 piston engines, with 6 ft 4 ins (1.93 m) Hartzell 3-blade constant-speed pusher propellers.
Engine rating: Each 300 hp (224 kW).
Fuel system: 844 litres.
Flight avionics/instrumentation: AlliedSignal Bendix/King Silver Crown and Garmin GPS.

Angel Aircraft Model 44 Angel (courtesy Angel Aircraft)

Details for Angel.

Principal dimensions:
Wing span: 40 ft (12.19 m)
Maximum length: 33 ft 3 ins (10.13 m)
Maximum height: 11 ft 6 ins (3.5 m)
Wings:
Area: 225.2 sq ft (20.92 m^2)
Aspect ratio: 7.08
Undercarriage:
Type: Retractable, with castering nosewheel, suited to use from rough strips
Weights:
Empty: 3,880 lb (1,760 kg)
Maximum take-off: 5,800 lb (2,631 kg)
Useful load: 1,920 lb (871 kg)
Performance:
Maximum speed: 180 kts (207 mph) 333 km/h
Cruise speed: 158 kts (182 mph) 293 km/h at 55% power and 15,000 ft (4,575 m)
Stall speed: 71 kts (82 mph) 132 km/h *clean and power off*, 51 kts (59 mph) 95 mph *in landing configuration and power on*
Take-off distance: 658 ft (201 m) minimum roll
Landing distance: 568 ft (174 m) minimum roll with brakes
Maximum climb rate: 1,330 ft (405 m) per minute
Ceiling: 20,500 ft (6,250 m)
Range with full fuel: 1,415 naut miles (1,629 miles) 2,620 km at 55% cruise and 8,000 ft (2,440 m)
Duration: 9.3 hours (range conditions)

Arctic Aircraft Company (USA)

Corporate address: PO Box 190141, Anchorage International Airport, AK 99519.
Telephone: +1 907 243 1580

● Activities

● Markets the two-seat Arctic Tern and four-seat Privateer, both strut-braced and high-wing cabin monoplanes, the latter in both factory finished and kit forms.

Aviat Inc (USA)

Corporate address: The Airport, Box 1149, Afton, WY 83110.
Telephone: +1 307 886 3151

●Activities

● Markets the A-1 Husky as a metal and fabric, strut-braced and high-wing two-seat cabin monoplane, with a 180 hp (134 kW) Textron Lycoming O-360-C1G piston engine. A new variant with clipped wings and inverted fuel and oil systems is the Acro-Husky.
● Also markets the Eagle II aerobatic biplane as a kit (see Recreational section), and offers a range of single- and two-seat Pitts Special aerobatic biplanes.

Avtek Corporation (USA)

Corporate address: 4680 Calle Carga, Camarillo, CA 93010.
Telephone: +1 805 482 2700
Facsimile: +1 805 987 0068
Founded: 1982.
Information: Quinten E. Ward (President).

Avtek 400A

First flight: 17 September 1984 for proof-of-concept prototype.
Certification: 1996.
Role: Pressurized, all-composites business jetfan.
Sales/users: 80 ordered by 1995. Basic price US$1.75 million IFR equipped.
Crew/passengers: Pilot plus 5 or 8 passengers.
Baggage capacity: 22 cu ft (0.62 m^3) in the nose compartment and 44 cu ft (1.24 m^3) aft cabin.
Pressurization system: 7.6 psi maximum cabin differential.
Wing characteristics: Rear-mounted, high aspect ratio, sweptback wings. Thick strakes between the engine nacelles and the fuselage.
Wing control surfaces: 2-section ailerons, with inner sections also used for pitch-axis trim.
Canard control surfaces: Elevators on the canard. The canard contributes to lift, while providing horizontal stability. High position minimizes airflow interference with the main wings at take-off and landing attitudes.
Tail control surfaces: Rudder only.
Flight control system: Mechanical, with pushrods, except for electric trim.
Construction materials: Kevlar and Nomex as the basic airframe materials (72%), with mainly carbonfibre/graphite for the remainder.
Engines: 2 Pratt & Whitney Canada PT6A-3 turboprops, with 6 ft 4 ins (1.93 m) 4-blade Kevlar pusher propellers.
Engine rating: Each 680 shp (507 kW).
Fuel system: 1,003 litres.
Electrical system: 28 volt DC generators.
Hydraulic system: 2,000 psi.
Radar: Optional colour weather radar.
Flight avionics/instrumentation: Customer's choice, including IFR, EFIS and EICAS.
Aircraft variants:
400A business aircraft, as detailed.
419 Express is a projected 19-passenger airliner development, with 1,173 shp (875 kW) PT6A-45 engines.
Explorer is a special mission version proposed by Valmet of Finland.

Avtek 400A

Details for Avtek 400A.

Principal dimensions:
Wing span: 35 ft (10.67 m)
Maximum length: 39 ft 4 ins (11.99 m)
Maximum height: 11 ft 4 ins (3.45 m)
Cabin:
Length: 15 ft 1 ins (4.6 m), including cockpit
Width: 4 ft 7 ins (1.4 m)
Height: 4 ft 6 ins (1.37 m)
Main door size: 3 ft 10 ins x 2 ft 6 ins (1.17 x 0.76 m)
Wings:
Area: 144.2 sq ft (13.4 m^2)
Canard: 48.7 sq ft (4.52 m^2)
Undercarriage:
Type: Retractable, with steerable nosewheel.
Weights:
Empty: 3,644 lb (1,653 kg) basic IFR, 3,779 lb (1,714 kg) equipped
Maximum take-off and landing: 6,500 lb (2,948 kg)
Performance:
Maximum speed: 363 kts (418 mph) 673 km/h
Stall speed: 72 kts (83 mph) 134 km/h
Take-off over a 50 ft (15 m) obstacle: 1,520 ft (464 m)
Landing over a 50 ft (15 m) obstacle: 1,280 ft (390 m)
Maximum climb rate: 4,630 ft (1,410 m) per minute
Ceiling: 42,500 ft (12,950 m)
Range with full fuel: 1,921 naut miles (2,213 miles) 3,561 km, with NBAA reserves

Ayres Corporation (USA)

Corporate address: PO Box 3090, 1 Rockwell Avenue, Albany, GA 31706.
Telephone: +1 912 833 1440
Facsimile: +1 912 439 9790
Information: Terry Humphrey.

Ayres 600 Thrush

Role: Agricultural aircraft, with optional fire bomber equipment.
Sales/users: Operating in a large number of countries.
Crew/passengers: Pilot, or optional second seat with dual controls. Adjustable mesh seating.
Cockpit: Optional aft-of-cockpit bubble windows.
Chemical tank/hopper: 1,514 litres liquid, 53 cu ft (1.5 m^3) dry chemicals, in a clear-vision glassfibre hopper.
Dispersal equipment: Universal spray system with external 2 ins (5 cm) stainless steel plumbing. 2 ins

(5 cm) Transland pump, streamline sprayborns with 68 nozzles, and 2 ins (5 cm) port-side loader. Optional Micronair AU500 installation, smoker installation, Crop Hawk flow meter, Weath Aero fan assembly, Micronair application monitor, and Transland stainless steel spreader.
Safety equipment: Sealed cockpit. Massive overturn structure. Undercarriage wire cutters. Cockpit wire deflector and deflector cable from canopy to fin.
Wing control surfaces: Ailerons (with servo tabs) and flaps.
Tail control surfaces: Elevators and rudder.
Flight control system: Mechanical, except for electric flaps.
Construction materials: Metal, with 4130 chromoly tubular steel fuselage structure and upper/lower steel spar caps. Quick detach alclad aluminium fuselage skins, and stainless steel bottom fuselage skins. Wing root seals and fairings. Glassfibre cockpit canopy.
Engine: Pratt & Whitney R-1340 radial piston engine, with a Hamilton Standard 12D40 constant-speed propeller with new EAC AG100-2 blades.

Ayres 600 Thrush (courtesy Ayres)

Engine rating: 600 hp (447.4 kW).
Fuel system: 394 litres usable. Optional 863 litre and ferry fuel systems.
Electrical system: 24 volt, 50 amp alternator and 24 volt battery.
Braking system: Cleveland 4-piston disc brakes.

Ayres Turbo Thrush

Ayres Turbo Thrush with quick release panels removed (courtesy Ayres)

Role: Agricultural aircraft, with optional fire bomber equipment. See Aircraft variants.
Details: Similar to 600 Thrush, except as detailed below.
Chemical tank/hopper: 1,514 litres liquid, 53 cu ft (1.5 m^3) dry chemicals, in a clear-vision glassfibre hopper. Optional 1,931 litre, 68.2 cu ft (1.93 m^3) hopper.
Dispersal equipment: Similar to 600 Thrust, but with 2.5 ins (6.4 cm) port-side loader.
Engine: Pratt & Whitney Canada PT6A in the 500 to 1,230 shp (373-917 kW) range. Alternatively, an AlliedSignal TPE331-6 or -10 turboprop in the 750 to 940 shp (559 to 701 kW) range.
Fuel system: 863 litres usable.
Electrical system: 24 volt system, with 200 amp starter-generator and dual 24 volt batteries.
Braking system: Cleveland dual caliper disc brakes.
Aircraft variants:
P&WC engined versions are S2R-T11 (500 shp, 373 kW PT6A-11AG), S2R-T15 (680 shp, 507 kW PT6A-15AG), S2R-T34 (750 shp, 559 kW PT6A-34AG) and S2R-T65 (1,230 shp, 917 kW PT6A-65AG). The latter is used by the US State Department as a special mission NEDS (narcotics eradication delivery systems) aircraft.
AlliedSignal engined versions are the S2R-G6 (750 shp, 559 kW TPE-331-6) and S2R-G10 (940 shp, 701 kW TPE331-10).
Vigilante is an AlliedSignal-engined special surveillance, support and law enforcement version.

DETAILS FOR 600 THRUSH.

Principal dimensions:
Wing span: 47 ft 6 ins (14.48 m)
Maximum length: 29 ft 4.5 ins (8.95 m)
Maximum height: 9 ft 2 ins (2.79 m)
Wings:
Area: 350 sq ft (32.516 m^2)
Aspect ratio: 6.45
Undercarriage:
Type: Fixed, with steerable/lockable tailwheel
Weights:
Empty: 4,250 lb (1,928 kg)
Typical operating: 8,000 lb (3,629 kg)
Performance:
Never-exceed speed (Vne): 138 kts (159 mph) 256 km/h
Cruise speed: 113 kts (130 mph) 209 km/h at 70% power and 4,000 ft (1,220 m)
Spray speed: 100-117 kts (115-135 mph) 185-217 km/h
Stall speed: 45 kts (52 mph) 84 km/h in usual landing configuration
Take-off distance: 1,320 ft (402 m) at 7,900 lb (3,583 kg)
Landing distance: 600 ft (183 m) as usually landed
Maximum climb rate: 1,040 ft (317 m) per minute at sea level, at 6,000 lb (2,722 kg) AUW
Ferry range: 350 naut miles (403 miles) 648 km at 70% power

DETAILS FOR TURBO THRUSH.

Principal dimensions:
Wing span: 44 ft 5 ins (13.54 m) short span, 47 ft 6 ins (14.48 m) long span
Maximum length: 33 ft (10.06 m)
Maximum height: 9 ft 2 ins (2.79 m)
Wings:
Area: 326.6 sq ft (30.34 m^2) short span, 350 sq ft (32.516 m^2) long span
Weights:
Empty: 4,200 lb (1,905 kg)
Typical operating: 9,700 lb (4,400 kg)
Performance (PT6A-34AG):
Never-exceed speed (Vne): 138 kts (159 mph) 256 km/h
Cruise speed: 130 kts (150 mph) 241 km/h at 55% power
Spray speed: 78-130 kts (90-150 mph) 145-241 km/h
Stall speed: 50 kts (57 mph) 92 km/h as usually landed
Take-off distance: 1,200 ft (366 m) at typical operating weight
Landing distance: 500 ft (153 m) as usually landed
Maximum climb rate: 1,740 ft (530 m) per minute at 6,000 lb (2,721 kg) weight
Ferry range: 668 naut miles (770 miles) 1,239 km

Cessna Aircraft Company (USA)

Corporate address: See Combat section for company details, and a description of the 526 CitationJet trainer.

● Activities

● In January 1995 Cessna announced that it had delivered 121 Citations and received orders for 203 more during 1994, plus orders for 139 Caravans. Total Citation deliveries exceed 2,200.

Cessna "restart" lightplanes

Cessna plans to reintroduce into production several of its former lightplanes, namely the 172 Skyhawk, 182 Skylane, 206 Stationair and Turbo 206, with manufacture at a new facility in Independence, Kansas. These new aircraft will have many improvements over the previous models, including new engines and control systems, electronic ignition, fuel injection, reconfigured instrumentation, new AlliedSignal Bendix/King avionics including GPS as standard, new interiors, etc. No new aircraft of these types have yet been built, and published photographs of a 172 "restart prototype" with a Textron Lycoming IO-360 that flew on 19 April 1995 showed only an old repainted model used for development testing (Cessna requested WA&SD not to publish this photograph). Several 172s had been ordered by Summer 1995, as the first reintroduced model, but deliveries will not take place until about December 1996, 10 years after 172 production was suspended. The 182, 206 and Turbo 206 will be added during 1997.

Cessna 208 Caravan series

Cessna Caravan with cargo pod (courtesy Cessna)

First flight: 9 December 1982.
Certification: 1984.
Role: Commuter, business, cargo, bush operations, ambulance, utility, military/government multi-purpose and specialized missions.
Sales/users: Military and civil/commercial use in many countries. Largest customer is Federal Express, which will have received 40 Caravans (as Cargomasters) and 250 Super Cargomasters by May 1996.
Crew/passengers: See Aircraft variants.
Wing control surfaces: Ailerons (with trim), single-slotted flaps and spoilers.
Tail control surfaces: Horn-balanced elevators (with trim tabs) and rudder. Tailplane has vortex generators.
Flight control system: Cables, bell cranks and push-pull rods, but with electric flaps.
Construction materials: Metal.
Engine: See Aircraft variants.
Fuel system: 1,270 litres.
Electrical system: 2 power sources, the primary 200 amp engine-driven starter-generator and a back-up 75 amp alternator. 24 volt lead-acid (45 amp-hour) or optional ni-cd (40 amp-hour) battery.
Hydraulic system: For brakes.

Radar: Optional AlliedSignal Bendix/King RDS-81 colour weather radar in a wing pod.
Flight avionics/instrumentation: ADF, transponder and navigation receiver, with options at customer's request. Flight and engine instruments. Independent pitot static systems on pilot and co-pilot air speed indicators, as well as on VSI and altimeter instruments.
Aircraft variants:
Caravan is the basic version, with a 600 shp (447 kW) Pratt & Whitney Canada PT6A-114 turboprop and 3-blade constant-speed propeller. Length 37 ft 7 ins (11.46 m), useful load 4,110 lb (1,864 kg) and range 1,085 naut miles (1,249 miles) 2,009 km. 12 ft 8 ins (3.86 m) cabin length, with 254 cu ft (7.19 m^3) volume plus optional 82.7 cu ft (2.37 m^3) external cargo pod. Maximum seating for 14, or 10 under FAR Pt 23.
Caravan Floatplane is an amphibious or straight float version of Caravan, with a 3,140 lb (1,424 kg) useful load. No cargo pod, but up to 300 lb (136 kg) of baggage in the floats. Take-off run on water 2,025 ft (617 m). Tailplane finlets.
Grand Caravan is the largest version. 675 shp (503 kW) PT6A-114A turboprop. Propeller as Caravan. Seating for 14 persons, or 9 plus 2 crew under FAR Pt 23 regulations when passenger seat pitch is 36 ins (91 cm). Features a quick-change interior, requiring 30 minutes to convert the passenger interior for all cargo. As detailed.
Super Cargomaster is based on the Grand Caravan but is intended for cargo operations, as required by Federal Express. 2 crew. Standard use of the cargo pod.
U-27A is a military version of Caravan for the US foreign military sales programme. Missions can include troop transport, reconnaissance, medevac, rescue/relief, surveillance and other special roles with appropriate equipment installed in the cabin. Can have a roll-up door.

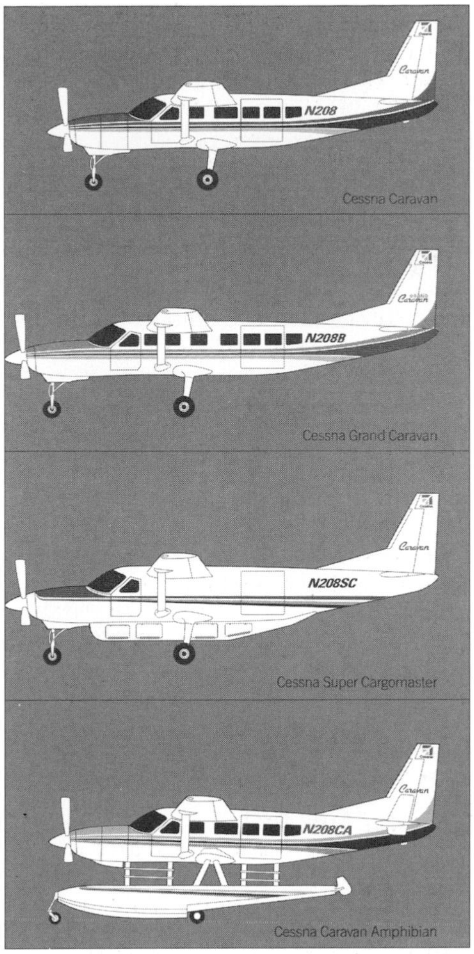

Cessna Caravan, Grand Caravan, Super Cargomaster and Caravan Amphibian (courtesy Cessna)

DETAILS FOR GRAND CARAVAN.

Principal dimensions:
Wing span: 52 ft 1 ins (15.88 m)
Maximum length: 41 ft 7 ins (12.67 m)
Maximum height: 14 ft 10 ins (4.52 m)
Cabin:
Length: 16 ft 8 ins (5.08 m)
Width: 5 ft 2 ins (1.57 m)
Height: 4 ft 3 ins (1.3 m)
Volume: 340 cu ft (9.63 m^3), plus standard use of an external cargo pod of 111.5 cu ft (3.16 m^3), with 1,090 lb (494 kg) capacity
Wings:
Aerofoil section: NACA 23017.424, 23012 (root/tip)
Area: 279.4 sq ft (25.96 m^2)
Aspect ratio: 9.72
Undercarriage:
Type: Fixed, with steerable nosewheel
Weights:
Empty: 4,550 lb (2,064 kg)
Maximum take-off: 8,750 lb (3,969 kg)
Maximum landing: 8,500 lb (3,856 kg)
Useful load: 4,235 lb (1,921 kg)
Performance:
Cruise speed: 175 kts (202 mph) 324 km/h at 10,000 ft (3,050 m)
Stall speed: 61 kts (71 mph) 113 km/h, engine idling
Take-off distance: 1,405 ft (428 m) roll, ISA
Landing distance: 915 ft (279 m) roll, ISA
Maximum climb rate: 925 ft (282 m) per minute at sea level
Ceiling: 28,800 ft (6,950 m)
Range: 963 naut miles (1,109 miles) 1,783 km at 10,000 ft (3,050 m), with 45 minutes reserve

Cessna CitationJet

First flight: 29 April 1991.
Certification: March 1993.
Role: Business jet.

100th Cessna CitationJet roll out

Sales/users: 100th production aircraft was rolled-out unpainted on 8 March 1995. Engine and airframe enhancement programme by Williams and Cessna have been completed on all delivered aircraft, bringing them up to the latest production standard.
Radar: RDR-2000 weather radar with digital colour display.
Flight avionics/instrumentation: Standard avionics include dual nav receivers, dual transponders, and Honeywell SPZ-5000 digital flight director/autopilot with 2 EFIS screens (5 ins, 12.7 cm square). SPZ-5000 incorporates a new microprocessor that integrates 3 computers into a single unit.

Cessna Citation VII

First flight: 1991.
Certification: 1992
Role: Mid-size business jet.
Sales/users: 53 customer deliveries by late April 1995.
Radar: Primus 870 Doppler colour weather radar.
Flight avionics/instrumentation: Honeywell SPZ-8000 flight director/autopilot, comprising a duplex autopilot, EFIS with 4 colour screens (5 x 6 ins, 12.7 x 15 cm) and radar. Optional Wulfsberg GNS-X flight management system for VOR/DME, Loran-C, GPS, VLF/Omega, and IRS/INS. New Magnum Edition of Citation VII has upgraded avionics and systems

Cessna Citation VII (courtesy Cessna)

Cessna Citation X

First flight: 21 December 1993.
Certification: 1996.
Role: Long-range business jet.
Sales/users: Production line opened on 6 June and the first production configured aircraft flew on 27 September 1994. Deliveries from January 1996.
Flight avionics/instrumentation: Dual flight management system, dual AHRS, Honeywell GPS, and Primus 2000 autopilot/flight director system with 5 screen EFIS (7 x 8 ins, 18 x 20 cm) comprising PFDs, MFDs and EICAS.

Cessna Citation X (courtesy Cessna)

Cessna Citation Bravo

First flight: 19 April 1995.
Certification: April 1996.
Role: Business jet.
Sales/users: Deliveries from June 1996.
Radar: RDR-2000 colour weather radar.
Flight avionics/instrumentation: Combination of Honeywell and AlliedSignal. Standard avionics include Honeywell Primus 1000 with dual digital flight directors and dual colour PFDs (8 x 7 ins, 20 x 18 cm). Optional

Cessna Citation Bravo (courtesy Cessna)

(Pax=Passengers)	CitationJet	Citation VII	Citation X	Citation Bravo	Citation Excel	Citation Ultra
Crew + Pax	2 + 6	2 + 10	2 + 9/12	2 + 6/10	2 + 6/8	2 + 8
Engine x 2	Rolls-Royce Williams FJ44	AlliedSignal TFE731-4R-2S	Allison AE 3007C	P&WC PW530A	P&WC PW545A	P&WC JT15D-5D
Engine rating (each)	1,900 lbf (8.45 kN)	4,140 lbf (18.42 kN)	6,400 lbf (28.47 kN)	2,750 lbf (12.23 kN)	3,640 lbf (16.19 kN)	3,045 lbf (13.55 kN)
Usable fuel	3,220 lb (1,460 kg)	7,385 lb (3,350 kg)	13,000 lb (5,896 kg)	4,860 lb (2,204 kg)	6,540 lb (2,966 kg)	5,814 lb (2,637 kg)
Wing span	46 ft 9 ins (14.25 m)	53 ft 6 ins (16.3 m)	63 ft 11 ins (19.48 m)	52 ft 2 ins (15.9 m)	55 ft 8 ins (16.97 m)	52 ft 2 ins (15.9 m)
Length	42 ft 7 ins (12.98 m)	55 ft 6 ins (16.92m)	72 ft 2 ins (22 m)	47 ft 2 ins (14.38 m)	52 ft 1 ins (15.88 m)	48 ft 11 ins (14.91 m)
Height	13 ft 8 ins (4.17 m)	16 ft 10 ins (5.13 m)	18 ft 11 ins (5.77 m)	15 ft (4.57 m)	17 ft 4 ins (5.28 m)	15 ft (4.57 m)
Cabin length pressure vessel	15 ft 9 ins (4.8 m)	23 ft 10 ins (7.26 m)	28 ft 6 ins (8.67 m)	20 ft 11 ins (6.37 m)	23 ft (7.01 m)	17 ft 4 ins (5.28 m)
Cabin width	4 ft 10 ins (1.47 m)	5 ft 8 ins (1.73 m)	5 ft 8 ins (1.73 m)	4 ft 11 ins (1.49 m)	5 ft 7 ins (1.7 m)	4 ft 10.4 ins (1.48 m)
Cabin height	4 ft 9 ins (1.45 m)	5 ft 8 ins (1.73 m)	5 ft 10 ins (1.77 m)	4 ft 8 ins (1.42 m)	5 ft 8 ins (1.73 m)	4 ft 7.3 ins (1.41 m)
Cabin pressurization differential	8.5 psi	9.3 psi	9.3 psi	8.7 psi	9.3 psi	8.9 psi
Weight empty lb (kg)	6,275 (2,846)	11,700 (5,307)	20,200 (9,163)	8,383 (3,802)	10,463 (4,746)	9,250 (4,196)
Maximum take-off weight lb (kg)	10,400 (4,717)	22,450 (10,183)	34,500 (15,649)	14,300 (6,486)	18,700 (8,482)	16,300 (7,394)
Maximum landing weight lb (kg)	9,700 (4,399)	20,000 (9,072)	31,000 (14,061)	13,500 (6,123)	17,400 (7,892)	15,200 (6,895)
Payload lb (kg)	805-1,625 (365-737)	1,165-2,400 (528-1,089)	1,200 (544) with full fuel	857-2,217 (388-1,005)	1,000-2,040 (454-925)	1,036-2,550 (470-1,156)
Mmo	Mach 0.7 at 30,500 ft	Mach 0.851 at 36,525 ft	Mach 0.9 at 37,000 ft	Mach 0.7 at 27,880 ft and above	Mach 0.75 indicated	Mach 0.75 indicated
Maximum cruise speed kts (mph) km/h	383 (441) 709 at 33,000 ft and 8,500 lb	476 (548) 881 at 37,000 ft and 18,000 lb	Mach 0.9 at 37,000 ft	394 (454) 730 at 31,000 ft and 11,850 lb	430 (495) 796 at 35,000 ft	430 (495) 796 at 35,000 ft and 13,000 lb
Stall speed kts (mph) km/h at MLW	82 (95) 152 in landing configuration	97 (112) 180 CAS in landing configuration		84 (97) 156 CAS in landing configuration	86 (99) 159 in landing configuration	82 (95) 152 with 35° flaps
Maximum climb rate ft (m) per minute	3,311 (1,009)	4,442 (1,354)	4,000 (1,220)	2,980 (908)	3,691 (1,125)	4,230 (1,290)
Ceiling ft (m)	41,000 (12,500)	51,000 (15,545)	51,000 (15,545)	43,000 (13,105)	45,000 (13,715)	45,000 (13,715)
Take-off distance, MTOW ft (m)	3,080 (939)	4,690 (1,430)	5,580 (1,700)	3,400 (1,036)	3,414 (1,040)	3,180 (970)
Landing distance, MLW ft (m)	2,750 (838)	2,910 (887)	3,500 (1,067)	3,010 (917)	3,315 (1,010)	2,800 (854)
Range naut miles (miles) km	1,485 (1,710) 2,750	2,220 (2,556) 4,111 with 6 pax and 45 minutes reserve	3,300 (3,800) 6,111 at 34,500 lb	1,900 (2,188) 3,519 with 4 pax + crew and 45 minutes hold	2,055 (2,366) 3,806 with 4 pax + crew and 45 minutes hold	1,960 (2,257) 3,630 with 5 pax + crew

MFD. Pedestal-mounted GNS-X long-range navigation system with GPS and VNAV. AlliedSignal CNI5000 radio package, including dual comms, navs, Mode S transponders and DMEs, ADF and radio altimeter. Loral cockpit voice recorder, angle of attack, and digital clock.

Cessna Citation Excel

First flight: Expected March 1996.
Certification: Expected March 1997.
Role: Business jet.
Sales/users: Deliveries from December 1997. Over 50 ordered by February 1995. Delivery positions sold to 1999.
Radar: Colour weather radar.
Flight avionics/instrumentation: Same PFD/MFDs as Citation X. Standard avionics built around the Honeywell Primus 1000 system, with Global GNS-X flight management system with colour CDU display, GPS and VNAV.

Cessna Citation Excel (courtesy Cessna)

Cessna Citation Ultra

Certification: June 1994.
Role: Business jet, also selected for crew training by Korean Air Lines.
Sales/users: 41 by July 1995, following 259 of the previous Citation V (from which Ultra became the new model).
Flight avionics/instrumentation: Primus 1000 digital flight control system, with 2 PFDs (8 x 7 ins, 20 x 18 cm) and central MFD. Standard avionics include a coupled vertical navigation system, dual altitude reporting systems, dual DME and dual transponders, Global GNS-X/ES flight management system with GPS and with an expanded keyboard and colour CDU display. Cockpit voice recorder.

Cessna Citation Ultra (courtesy Cessna)

Cirrus Design Corporation (USA)

Corporate address: 4515 Taylor Circle, Duluth, MN 55811.
Telephone: +1 218 727 2737
Facsimile: +1 218 727 2148
Information: Alan Klapmeier (President).

● Activities

● The Cirrus VK30 turboprop kitplane (first flown in 1988 and 45 kits delivered by 1995) provided the aerodynamic concept behind the Israviation ST-50, which see under Israel. Cirrus is a major sub-contractor to Israviation, undertaking core engineering and producing the ST-50 proof-of-concept prototype. The unpressurized VK30 itself is similar in design concept to the pressurized ST-50, accommodating 4 or 5 persons but powered by a lower rated Allison 250-B17C turboprop, 300-350 hp (224-261 kW) Teledyne Continental, or LPE TIIV-650 or TGIIV-650 piston engine.

Cirrus SR20

First flight: 21 March 1995.
Certification: Anticipated for 1996, under FAR Pt 23.
Role: Four-seat composites light aircraft.
Sales/users: US$2,500 deposits taken to reserve delivery positions. US$130,000 cost (1995).
Wing control surfaces: Ailerons (starboard tab) and flaps.

Cirrus SR20 (Geoffrey P. Jones)

Tail control surfaces: Horn-balanced elevators and rudder.
Construction materials: Composites. Improved crashworthiness, with energy absorbing structures, special engine mount and firewall structure. Designed with a ballistic recovery system.
Engine: Teledyne Continental IO-360-ES piston engine, with a 6 ft 4 ins (1.93 m) 3-blade propeller
Engine rating: 200 hp (149 kW).
Fuel system: 227 litres usable.
Flight avionics/instrumentation: IFR equipped. Optional flat-panel technology.

DETAILS FOR SR20.

Principal dimensions:
Wing span: 35 ft (10.67 m)
Maximum length: 25 ft (7.62 m)
Maximum height: 9 ft 2 ins (2.79 m)
Cabin:
Length: 10 ft 10 ins (3.3 m)
Width: 4 ft (1.22 m)
Height: 4 ft 2 ins (1.27 m)
Undercarriage:
Type: Fixed, with nosewheel. Wheel fairings
Weights:
Empty: 1,740 lb (789 kg)
Maximum take-off: 2,900 lb (1,315 kg)
Useful load: 1,160 lb (526 kg)
Performance:
Cruise speed: 160 kts (184 mph) 296 km/h
Stall speed: 55 kts (64 mph) 102 km/h
Take-off over a 50 ft (15 m) obstacle: 1,650 ft (503 m)
Landing over a 50 ft (15 m) obstacle: 1,400 ft (427 m)
Maximum climb rate: 1,000 ft (305 m) per minute
Range with full fuel: 800 naut miles (921 miles) 1,481 km

Classic Aircraft Corporation (USA)

Corporate address: Capital City Airport, MI 48906.
Telephone: +1 517 321 7500
Facsimile: +1 517 321 5845
Information: D. C. Kettles.

●Activities

● This company offers the Waco Classic YMF Super biplane, as a modernized development of the 1930s Waco Model F open-cockpit commercial three-seater. Power is provided by a reworked 275 hp (205 kW) Jacobs R-755-D2 radial piston engine.

Colemill Enterprises Inc (USA)

Corporate address: PO Box 60627, Cornelia Fort Airpark, Nashville, TN 37206.
Telephone: +1 615 226 4256
Facsimile: +1 615 226 4702
Information: Bill Colbert or Ralph Peeler.

● Activities

● Said to be the largest aircraft modification company in the USA, Colemill undertakes conversions of Beech, Cessna and Piper light aircraft aimed at improving performance. After conversion they are renamed as:
Foxstar is the conversion of Beech C, D, E and 58 Barons, with 300 hp (224 kW) Teledyne Continental IO-550-C altitude compensating engines. 4-blade Q-tip propellers, governors and synchrophaser. New propeller spinners. Winglets. Shadin digital fuel system. Includes vacuum pumps, starters, alternators, mounts, and fuel and oil hoses. US$94,750 with factory new engines, US$73,900 with remanufactured engines.
President 600 is the conversion of A55 and B55 Barons, with 300 hp (224 kW) Teledyne Continental IO-520-E engines with belt-driven generators or alternators, new Hartzell 3-blade propellers and Woodward or McCauley governors. Pumps, starters, mounts and hoses as for Foxstar. US$73,500 with factory new engines, US$57,500 with remanufactured engines.
President II is similar to President 600, but with IO-550-E engines and Shadin fuel computer. US$84,500 with factory new engines, US$67,500 with remanufactured engines.
Starfire is the conversion of Beech A36, S35, V35, E33A and F33A Bonanzas. 300 hp (224 kW) IO-550-B engines, Q-tip propeller, new spinner, and fuel computer, pump, starter, etc as for Foxstar. US$44,900 with factory new engine, US$34,900 with remanufactured engine.
Bearcat is the conversion of the Cessna 310R with IO-550-A engines, Shadin digital fuel computer, pumps, starters, etc. Uses existing propellers and governors. US$72,500 with factory new engines, US$52,900 with remanufactured engines.
Executive 600 is the conversion of the Cessna 310 (F-Q) with IO-520-E engines with belt-driven alternator and new 3-blade McCauley propellers and governors, plus pumps, starters, etc. US$73,500 with factory new engines, US$57,500 with remanufactured engines.
Executive II is the conversion of the Cessna 310 (F-Q) and is similar to Executive 600 but with IO-550-E engines, new McCauley 3-blade threadless hub propellers, Shadin fuel computer, etc. US$84,500 with factory new engines, US$67,500 with remanufactured engines.
Panther Navajo is the conversion of Piper PA-31 and C/R Navajos with 350 hp (261 kW) Textron Lycoming TIO-540 turbocharged engines, new Hartzell 4-blade Q-tip propellers, governors and synchrophaser. Propeller spinners. Unfeathering accumulators. Shadin digital fuel computer. Pumps, mounts and hoses. US$141,500 with factory new engines, US$116,000 with overhauled engines. US$5,500 for Zip Tip winglets with landing lights.
Panther II is the conversion of Piper Chieftains with TIO-540s and other items as for Panther Navajo. US$141,500 with factory new engines, US$116,000 with overhauled engines. US$5,500 for Zip Tip winglets with landing lights.
Panther III is also for Chieftains but covers only the propellers, governors, synchrophaser, spinners, fuel computer and Zip Tips. US$37,500.

Commander Aircraft Company (USA)

Corporate address: Wiley Post Airport, Hangar 8, 7200 NW 63rd Street, Bethany, OK 73008.
Telephone: +1 405 495 8080
Facsimile: +1 405 495 8383
Founded: 1988.
Information: Herbert B. Franck.

Commander 114B

Certification: 4 May 1992.
Role: Four-seat high-performance lightplane and trainer, the latest new development of the original Rockwell Commander 112/114 series.
Sales/users: 93 delivered by early 1995, with 50 more expected that year.
Baggage capacity: 200 lb (91 kg).
Wing control surfaces: Ailerons and single-slotted flaps.
Tail control surfaces: Elevators and rudder, both with trim.
Flight control system: Electric flaps.
Engine: Textron Lycoming IO-540-T4B5 piston engine, with a McCauley Black Mac 3-blade constant-speed propeller.
Engine rating: 260 hp (194 kW).
Fuel system: 265 litres.
Electrical system: 28 volt, with 85 amp alternator and battery.
Flight avionics/instrumentation: Can be IFR equipped. Standard avionics include AlliedSignal Bendix/King KMA 24-03 audio panel, KX-155 digital nav/comm with GS or LOC indicator, and KT-76A

DETAILS FOR COMMANDER 114B.

Principal dimensions:
Wing span: 32 ft 9.1 ins (9.99 m)
Maximum length: 24 ft 11 ins (7.59 m)
Maximum height: 8 ft 5 ins (2.57 m)
Cabin:
Length: 6 ft 3 ins (1.91 m)
Width: 3 ft 11 ins (1.19 m)
Height: 4 ft 1 ins (1.24 m)
Wings:
Aerofoil section: Laminar flow
Area: 152 sq ft (14.12 m^2)
Aspect ratio: 7.06
Undercarriage:
Type: Retractable, with steerable and lockable nosewheel
Turning circle: 28 ft 5.5 ins (8.67 m)
Weights:
Empty: 2,044 lb (927 kg)
Maximum take-off: 3,250 lb (1,474 kg)
Useful load: 1,216 lb (551 kg)
Performance:
Maximum speed: 164 kts (189 mph) 304 km/h
Cruise speed: 155 kts (178 mph) 287 km/h at 65% power
Stall speed: 61 kts (71 mph) 113 km/h *clean*, 56 kts (65 mph) 104 km/h *landing configuration*
Take-off distance: 1,040 ft (317 m)
Landing distance: 720 ft (220 m)
Maximum climb rate: 1,070 ft (326 m) per minute at sea level
Ceiling: 16,800 ft (5,120 m)
Cruise range: 725 naut miles (834 miles) 1,342 km at 55% power

transponder. Other standard equipment includes Terra AT-3000 altitude encoder and ELT. Large range of optional avionics, including 2-axis AFCS. Full standard flight/engine instruments.

Aircraft variants:

114AT Advanced Trainer, for primary training.

114B, as detailed.

114TC is a turbocharged version.

Commander Aircraft Commander 114B

Excalibur Aviation Company (USA)

Corporate address: 8337 Mission Road, San Antonio, TX 78214.
Telephone: +1 210 927 6201
Facsimile: +1 210 927 6287
Information: Michael M. Davis.

● Activities

● Excaliber offers conversions aimed at increasing the cruise speed of the Beech Queen Air by up to 23 kts (27 mph) 43 km/h or increase range by 50%.

Aircraft variants:

Queenaire 800 is the conversion of Queen Air Models 65, A65 and 80 to have 400 hp (298 kW) Textron Lycoming IO-720-A1B engines and new Hartzell 3-blade constant-speed propellers, low drag cowlings and full-closure undercarriage doors. Cruise speed of 201 kts (231 mph) 372 km/h at 75% power and 8,300 ft (2,530 m), and 1,535 ft (468 m) per minute climb.

Queenaire 8800 is the conversion of Queen Air Models A80, B80 and 88 to the same standard. Same cruise speed, and climb of 1,490 ft (454 m) per minute.

Gevers Aircraft Inc (USA)

Corporate address: PO Box 430, Brownsburg, IN 46112.
Telephone: +1 317 852 2735, 217 367 5550
Founded: 1988.
Information: David E. Gevers (President) or Robert L. Glasa (Marketing, Investment Manager).

● Activities

● Developing an innovative six-seat and twin-engined general aviation aircraft known as Genesis, designed with telescopic wings and reconfigurable undercarriage for selection between wheels, skis and an amphibious hull. Both the wings and undercarriage can be converted in flight to suite the mission, conditions and environment. By early 1995 Gevers was ground testing a complete propeller drive system and was optimizing the aerodynamic configuration using finite element fluid flow analysis. A full description will be given in a later edition of WA&SD, once construction of a prototype has begun.

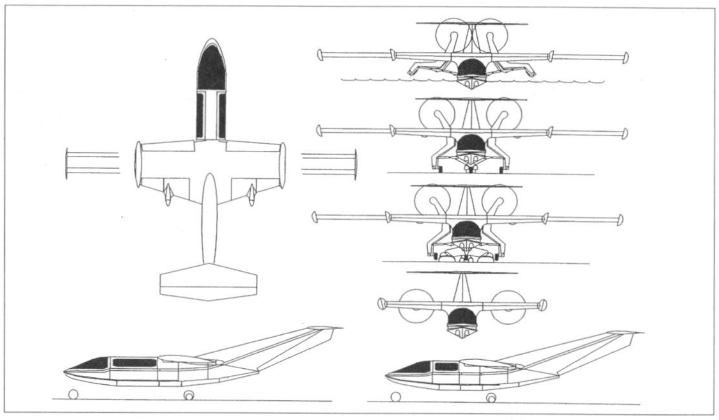

Gevers Genesis with telescopic wings and reconfigurable undercarriage (courtesy Gevers)

Global Aircraft Corporation (USA)

Corporate address: PO Box 800, Starkville, MS 39759.
Telephone: +1 601 324 2800
Information: Michael Smith (President).

● Activities

● Global is flight testing its three-seat composites low-wing GT-3 Trainer, powered by a 160 hp (119 kW) engine. It anticipates FAA certification in 1996. Intended for primary and instrument training, it has a 141 kts (162 mph) 261 km/h cruise speed and a range of 810 naut miles (932 miles) 1,500 km on 170 litres of fuel.

Gulfstream Aerospace Corporation (USA)

Corporate address: PO Box 2206, Savannah, GA 31402-2206.
Telephone: +1 912 965 3000
Facsimile: +1 912 965 3775
Information: Julie Stone (Marketing Communications - *telephone* +1 912 965 3865, *facsimile* +1 912 965 3084).

■ Facilities

■ Production facilities at Savannah (Georgia), Oklahoma City (Oklahoma) and Mexicali (Mexico), with service and completion centres in Savannah and Long Beach (California).

● Activities

● In addition to Gulfstream aircraft, the company constructs wings for the Jetstream 41.

Gulfstream Aerospace Gulfstream IV series

First flight: 19 September 1985.
Certification: 22 April 1987.
Role: Pressurized, long-range and high-capacity business jet, with special mission military variants.
Sales/users: 270 delivered by June 1995 of all versions.
Details: For Gulfstream IV-SP, except under Aircraft variants.
Crew/passengers: 2 flight crew plus attendant and typically 13 business passengers, with maximum of 19.
Baggage capacity: 169 cu ft (4.79 m^3), for 2,000 lb (907 kg).
Pressurization system: 9.45 psi maximum cabin differential.
Wing control surfaces: Aileron (port trim tab), single-slotted Fowler flap and 3 spoilers (for aileron assist, lift dumping and speedbrake) per wing. Stall strip and 4 vortillons per wing.
Tail control surfaces: Elevators (with trim tabs) and rudder.
Flight control system: Hydraulic, with manual back-up.
Construction materials: Principally metal, but with composites control surfaces (except flaps) and some other components.
Engines: 2 Rolls-Royce Tay Mk 611-8 turbofans. AlliedSignal GTCP 36-100 APU.
Engine rating: Each 13,850 lbf (61.61 kN).
Fuel system: 29,500 lb (13,381 kg).
Electrical system: 115/200 volt AC supply, at 400 Hz, via 2 alternators. 28 volt DC supply via converters. 2 x 24 volt, 40 amp-hour ni-cd batteries.
Hydraulic system: Dual, each 3,000 psi.
Radar: Colour weather radar.
Flight avionics/instrumentation: Honeywell SPZ8000 digital avionics package including AFCS, FMZ800 Phase II flight management system with six 8 ins (20 cm) square colour CRTs, dual ADCs, dual flight guidance system including autothrottles, dual air data computers, and dual PZ800 performance

Gulfstream Aerospace C-20G used as a priority operational support aircraft by the US Navy. Features an hydraulic 63 x 82 ins (1.6 x 2.08 m) cargo door

computers. Dual laser INS. AHRS. Dual VOR/LOC/GS/marker beacon receivers, dual DME, dual ADF and more. Options include GPS, VLF Omega and TCAS.

Aircraft variants:

Gulfstream IV was the initial version, replaced by IV-SP from September 1992.

Gulfstream IV-B is a projected longer-range model being studied in association with Textron Aerostructures, as announced at the September 1994 Farnborough Air Show. 4,600 naut mile (5,297 mile) 8,519 km range. Programme on a year-long hold in mid-1995.

Gulfstream IV-MPA is a Multi-Purpose Aircraft and the newest available model of the range, offering a quick-change interior for high or low density seating, cargo or combinations. Based on the IV-SP/C-20G. Maximum 26 passengers, or executive layouts, or 4,800 lb (2,177 kg) of cargo. Optional large cargo door.

Gulfstream IV-SP entered service in 1992. As detailed.

SRA-4 is a little used generic term for aircraft modified for special missions (mainly military). Current aircraft are based on IV-SP. These can include electronic warfare (among the latest being 2 fully-camouflaged aircraft delivered to Sweden from August 1995 for sigint), airways flight inspection, SAR, training, special weather applications, anti-submarine and maritime patrol, medevac, transport and more. The US Army operates a C-20F, the US Navy and USMC C-20Gs (see IV-MPA for similar loads) and the USAF C-20Hs for transport purposes. Other users include Turkey.

Gulfstream Aerospace Gulfstream V

First flight: Rolled out 22 September 1995.
Certification: Expected October 1996.
Role: Pressurized, long-range (global) business jet, as a larger and more powerful development of the Gulfstream IV.
Sales/users: Inital aircraft to cost US$29.5 million. Deliveries from late 1996. Some 60 already ordered.
Crew/passengers: 2 flight crew, attendant plus typically 13-15 business passengers, with 19 maximum.
Baggage capacity: 226 cu ft (6.4 m^3), for 2,500 lb (1,134 kg).
Engines: 2 BMW Rolls-Royce BR710-48 turbofans. AlliedSignal RE220 APU.
Engine rating: Each 14,750 lbf (65.61 kN).
Fuel system: 41,000 lb (18,597 kg).
Flight avionics/instrumentation: Generally similar to IV-SP, but with a Honeywell/GEC-Marconi 2020 HUD; AlliedSignal CAS-67A TCAS II, Mk VI GPWS and maintenance-data acquisition system; and Rockwell Collins communications, navigation and transponder suite, incorporating the RT-4220 integrated radio-tuning unit with liquid-crystal display. Will have "office in the sky" capability using IBM satellite communications.

Gulfstream Aerospace Gulfstream V

DETAILS FOR GULFSTREAM IV-SP.

Principal dimensions:
Wing span: 77 ft 10 ins (23.72 m)
Maximum length: 88 ft 4 ins (26.92 m)
Maximum height: 24 ft 5 ins (7.44 m)
Cabin:
Length: 45 ft 1 ins (13.74 m)
Width: 7 ft 4 ins (2.24 m)
Height: 6 ft 2 ins (1.88 m)
Volume: 1,525 cu ft (43.18 m^3)
Wings:
Area: 950 sq ft (88.26 m^2)
Aspect ratio: 6.38
Undercarriage:
Type: Retractable, with steerable nosewheels. Twin wheels on each unit.
Weights:
Empty: 35,500 lb (16,100 kg)
Maximum take-off: 74,600 lb (33,838 kg)
Maximum landing: 66,000 lb (29,937 kg)
Payload: 6,500 lb (2,948 kg)
Performance:
Maximum operating Mach number (Mmo): Mach 0.88
Cruise speed: Mach 0.8 normal
Take-off distance: 5,450 ft (1,662 m) sea level, ISA
Landing distance: 3,190 ft (972 m) sea level, ISA, MLW
Maximum climb rate: 4,122 ft (1,256 m) per minute at sea level
Normal cruise altitude: 45,000 ft (13,715 m)
Range: 4,220 naut miles (4,859 miles) 7,815 km with 3 crew and 8 passengers, NBAA IFR reserve
Duration: 9 hours 27 minutes, conditions as for range

DETAILS FOR GULFSTREAM V.

Principal dimensions:
Wing span: 93 ft 6 ins (28.5 m)
Maximum length: 96 ft 5 ins (29.39 m)
Maximum height: 25 ft 4 ins (7.72 m)
Cabin:
Length: 50 ft 1 ins (15.27 m)
Width: 7 ft 4 ins (2.24 m)
Height: 6 ft 2 ins (1.88 m)
Volume: 1,669 cu ft (47.26 m^3)
Wings:
Larger and more efficient than IV-SP's but of basically similar configuration
Area: 1,137 sq ft (105.63 m^2)
Aspect ratio: 7.69
Weights:
Basic operating weight: 46,800 lb (21,228 kg) with 3 crew
Maximum take-off: 89,000 lb (40,370 kg)
Maximum landing: 72,000 lb (32,658 kg)
Payload: 6,500 lb (2,948 kg)
Performance:
Maximum operating Mach number (Mmo): Mach 0.9
Normal cruise speed: Mach 0.8
Take-off distance: 5,870 ft (1,790 m) sea level, ISA
Landing distance: 2,950 ft (900 m) sea level, ISA, MLW
Maximum climb rate: 4,188 ft (1,276 m) per minute at sea level
Cruise altitude: 41,000 ft (12,500 m) initial, 51,000 ft (15,550 m) final
Range: 6,500 naut miles (7,485 miles) 12,038 km with 8 passengers and 4 crew at Mach 0.8, NBAA IFR reserve
Duration: 14 hours 38 minutes, conditions as for Range

Integrated Systems Aero Engineering Inc (ISAE) (USA)

Corporate address: 1850 North 600 West, Logan, UT 84321.
Telephone: +1 801 753 2224
Facsimile: +1 801 753 2975
Information: Dave Repko (Sales & Marketing Manager).

ISAE Omega II

Certification: Intended FAR Pt 23 Aerobatic category.
Role: Tandem two-seat aerobatic lightplane, developed from the Streak 90 Palomino.
Sales/users: Originally offered as a kit, but now undergoing certification.
Baggage capacity: 120 lb (54 kg).
Wing control surfaces: Frise type ailerons and plain flaps (15°, 30° or 40°).
Tail control surfaces: Elevators (with tab) and rudder.
Flight control system: Push-pull rods, torque tubes and cables. Electric tab.
Construction materials: All metal.
Engine: 200 hp (149 kW) Textron Lycoming AEIO-360-A1E6 for kit-built aircraft, with a 300 hp (224 kW) AEIO-540-L for certificated aircraft.
Fuel system: 170 litres usable in 2 wing tanks, and with a collector tank and flop-tube pickup for inverted capability.
Electrical system: 24 volt.
Braking system: Disc brakes.

ISAE Omega II (courtesy ISAE)

Details for Omega II with 200 hp (149 kW) engine.

Principal dimensions:
Wing span: 28 ft 4 ins (8.64 m)
Maximum length: 24 ft 6 ins (7.47 m)
Maximum height: 9 ft 6 ins (2.9 m)
Wings:
Aerofoil section: Laminar flow
Area: 106.8 sq ft (9.92 m^2)
Aspect ratio: 7.51
Undercarriage:
Type: Retractable, with steerable nosewheel. Hydraulic actuation, with emergency "fall" into locked position
Weights:
Empty: 1,350 lb (612 kg)
Maximum take-off: 2,100 lb (952.5 kg)
Useful load: 750 lb (340 kg)
Performance:
Maximum speed: 187 kts (215 mph) 346 km/h
Cruise speed: 176 kts (202 mph) 326 km/h at 75% power and 6,000 ft (1,830 m)
Stall speed: 59 kts (68 mph) 110 km/h
Take-off distance: 1,100 ft (336 m)
Landing distance: 1,200 ft (366 m), dry pavement, with brakes
Maximum climb rate: 2,000 ft (610 m) per minute at sea level
Roll rate: 110° per second
Range: 660 naut miles (760 miles) 1,223 km

Kestrel Aircraft Company (USA)

Corporate address: PO Box 720960, Max Westheimer Airport, Norman, OK 73070.
Telephone: +1 405 573 0090

● Activities

● Offers the Kestrel as a four or six-seat cantilever high-wing cabin monoplane, with either fixed or retractable nosewheel undercarriage (or floats). Roll out of the prototype took place on 21 April 1995. Basic KL-1A has a 160 hp (119.3 kW) Textron Lycoming IO-360-ES piston engine, providing a 124 kts (143 mph) 229 km/h cruise speed at 75% power, but other versions have engines up to a 325 hp (242.4 kW) TSIO-550-B.

Lake Aircraft Inc (USA)

Corporate address: Laconia Airport, 50 Airport Road, Gilford, NH 03246.
Telephone: +1 603 524 5868
Facsimile: +1 603 524 5728
Founded: 1959.

International marketing: 606 North Dyer Blvd, Kissimmee Airport, Kissimmee, FL 34741.
Telephone: +1 407 847 9000
Facsimile: +1 407 847 4516
Information: Haig Hogopian (Vice President, International Marketing & Sales).

■ Facilities

■ Also at Renton Airport, 500 W Perimeter Road, Renton, WA 98055.

● Activities

● Over 1,300 amphibians delivered of all past and current versions.

Lake Renegade (courtesy Lake)

Lake Renegade, Turbo Renegade, Seawolf, Seafury, Turbo Seafury and Lean Machine

Certification: 1983 for the current Renegade.
Role: Civil and military, single-engined, passenger and utility amphibians.
Details: For Turbo Renegade, except under Aircraft variants.
Crew/passengers: 4 persons, including pilot/s. Dual controls.
Baggage capacity: 200 lb (91 kg).
Airframe characteristics: Single-step hull, with a retractable rudder.
Wing control surfaces: Ailerons (with ground-adjustable trim tabs) and single-slotted flaps.
Tail control surfaces: Elevators, and rudder (with tabs). Port elevator is split into 2 sections, the smaller outer section used also for trimming.
Flight control system: Manual, except for hydraulic flaps and port elevator trim section.
Construction materials: Metal.
Engine: Textron Lycoming TIO-540-AA2AD, with a 6 ft 4 ins (1.93 m) Hartzell Q-tip pusher propeller.
Engine rating: 270 hp (201 kW).
Fuel system: 288 litres, with 341 litres optional.
Electrical system: 12 volt supply, via an engine-driven alternator and 30 amp-hour battery.
Hydraulic system: 1,250 psi for undercarriage, flaps and elevator trim.
Braking system: Disc brakes.
Flight avionics/instrumentation: Avionics to customer's requirements. Can include full IFR equipment, dual nav/comm, RNAV, ADF, autopilot, etc. Full range of engine instruments.
Aircraft variants:
Renegade seats 6 and is powered by a 250 hp (186.4 kW) Textron Lycoming IO-540-C4B5 piston engine.
Turbo Renegade is a four-seater with a turbocharged engine, as detailed. Expected to be licence-built in China by the Chengdu Asia Water Aircraft Company, following delivery of 11 US-built aircraft to China.
Seafury and Turbo Seafury are versions of Renegade and Turbo Renegade for salt water operations, also having sea survival equipment.
Seawolf is a military version, equipped with underwing NATO standard pylons and stores, designed to meet the special mission needs of government agencies and military organizations. Can be radar equipped.
Lean Machine is a reduced cost version of Renegade, mainly for commercial use. US$118,000 with basic instrumentation. No wing fuel tanks, allowing a 99 lb (45 kg) increase in payload. 15 orders are needed to launch production.

Details for Turbo Renegade.

Principal dimensions:
Wing span: 38 ft 4 ins (11.68 m)
Maximum length: 29 ft 8 ins (9.04 m)
Maximum height: 10 ft (3.05 m)
Cabin:
Length: 10 ft 4 ins (3.15 m)
Width: 3 ft 5 ins (1.04 m)
Height: 3 ft 7 ins (1.09 m)
Wings:
Aerofoil section: NACA 4415
Area: 164 sq ft (15.24 m^2)
Aspect ratio: 8.96
Undercarriage:
Type: Retractable, with swivelling nosewheel
Weights:
Empty: 2,075 lb (941 kg)
Maximum take-off: 3,140 lb (1,424 kg)
Useful load: 1,065 lb (483 kg)
Performance:
Cruise speed: 155 kts (178 mph) 287 km/h at 75% power
Stall speed: 55 kts (64 mph) 102 km/h *clean*, 49 kts (57 mph) 91 km/h *landing configuration*
Take-off distance: 880 ft (268 m) *land*, 1,250 ft (381 m) *water*
Landing distance: 475 ft (145 m) *land*, 600 ft (183 m) *water*
Maximum climb rate: 900 ft (274 m) per minute at sea level, MTOW
Ceiling: 23,800 ft (7,255 m) service, or 20,000 ft (6,100 m) certified
Range: 1,120 naut miles (1,290 miles) 2,074 km

Learjet Inc (USA)

Corporate address: One Learjet Way, PO Box 7707, Wichita, KS 67277.
Telephone: +1 316 946 2000, 2450
Facsimile: +1 316 946 2220, 3235
Founded: 1962, becoming a subsidiary of Bombardier in 1990 as part of the Aerospace Group – North America.
Employees: Over 3,700.

Learjet 31A

First flight: 11 May 1987 (prototype).
Certification: 12 August 1988 to FAR Pt 25 transport category, including day, night, VFR, IFR, FAA FAR Pt 91 Category II and flight into known icing.
Role: Pressurized light corporate jet.
Sales/users: 69 completed by mid-1995, following earlier Learjet 31s. The 100th aircraft of the 31/31A series was rolled out in November 1994.
Details: For Learjet 31A, except under Aircraft variants.
Wing characteristics: Cambered leading edge. Winglets.
Wing control surfaces: Ailerons (with geared balance tabs plus port electric trim tab), single-slotted flaps and spoilers.
Tail control surfaces: Variable-incidence tailplane. Elevators, and rudder (with trim tab).
Flight control system: Mechanical, except for electrically controlled and hydraulically actuated flaps and spoilers, and electric trim tabs.
Construction materials: Metal.
Electrical system: DC supply via 2 x 30 volt, 400 amp, engine-driven starter-generators. 2 x 24 volt, 40 amp-hour lead-acid batteries for engine starting and emergency bus operation. 3,000 VA AC supply, with 115/26 volt auto-transformers, providing 26 volts.
Hydraulic system: 1,500 psi.
Radar: AlliedSignal Bendix/King RDS 82 VP.
Flight avionics/instrumentation: AlliedSignal Bendix/King suite including KFC 3100 AFCS, 5 tube EFIS 50, dual Series III VHF transceivers, dual Series III VOR/ILS nav receivers, ADF, Series III DME, dual Mode S transponder, dual central air data computers with digitally interfaced displays, dual AHRS, and radar altimeter. Universal UNS-1M FMS.
Aircraft variants:
Learjet 31A, as detailed.
Learjet 31A/ER is the extended-range model, with a 20 ft 7 ins (6.27 m) cabin length, 16,500 lb (7,484 kg) MTOW, 4,653 lb (2,111 kg) of usable fuel, and performance differences.

Learjet 35A

Certification: 1974.
Role: Pressurized, multi-mission corporate jet.
Details: Generally similar to Learjet 31A except as detailed below and in table.
Radar: Honeywell Primus 450 colour weather radar.
Flight avionics/instrumentation: Rockwell Collins suite, including ADF, dual DME, dual transponders, dual nav receivers, and dual comm receivers. AlliedSignal Bendix/King HF.
Aircraft variants:
Learjet 35A, as detailed.
Multi-mission versions for mainly military uses include those for priority operational support (includes the USAF's C-21A), target-towing, medevac, calibration and other utility roles (UC-35A), reconnaissance (RC-35A) and maritime patrol and rescue (PC-35A).

Learjet 45 over Californian sand dunes

Learjet 45

First flight: Rolled out 14 September 1995.
Certification: December 1996 to FAR Pt 25 transport category, including day, night, VFR, IFR, and flight into known icing.
Role: Mid-size pressurized corporation jet and crew trainer.
Sales/users: Over 100 ordered by mid-1995, for delivery from the end of 1996.
Control surfaces: Similar to Learjet 31A except both ailerons have electric trim tabs.
Undercarriage: Unlike previous Learjets, Learjet 45 has air-oil trailing-link shock-struts and steer-by-wire nosewheel steering (±55%).
Hydraulic system: 3,000 psi, for undercarriage and uplocks, main gear doors, brakes, flaps, thrust reversers and spoilers.
Radar: Honeywell Primus 650 weather radar, with optional Primus 870.
Flight avionics/instrumentation: Honeywell Primus 1000 avionics suite, and dual Primus II nav/comm/identification radio pulse package. Primus 1000 includes 4 EFIS screen displays, each 8 x 7 ins (20 x 18 cm), as 2 PFDs, an MFD and EICAS. Heart of Primus 1000 is the integrated avionics computer, combining the EFIS and EICAS processor, flight director and digital autopilot in a single LRU. Primus II includes a liquid-crystal flat display which also provides back-up navigation and engine displays.

Learjet 60

First flight: 15 June 1992 for first production aircraft.

Pax=Passengers	Learjet 31A	Learjet 35A	Learjet 45	Learjet 60
Crew + Pax	2 + 10	2 + 7/9	2 + 10	2 + 6/9
Engine x 2	AlliedSignal TFE731-2-3B turbofans	AlliedSignal TFE731-2-2B turbofans	AlliedSignal TFE731-20 turbofans	Pratt & Whitney Canada PW305A turbofans
Engine rating (each)	3,500 lbf (15.57 kN)	3,500 lbf (15.57 kN)	3,500 lbf (15.57 kN)	4,600 lbf (20.46 kN)
Usable fuel lb (kg)	4,124 (1,871)		6,000 (2,722)	4,471 litres
Wing span	43 ft 8 ins (13.31 m)	39 ft 6 ins (12.04 m)	47 ft 10 ins (14.58 m)	43 ft 9 ins (13.34 m)
Length	48 ft 8 ins (14.83 m)	48 ft 8 ins (14.83 m)	57 ft 11.75 ins (17.65 m)	58 ft 8 ins (17.88 m)
Height	12 ft 3 ins (3.73 m)	12 ft 4 ins (3.76 m)	14 ft 0.75 ins (4.29 m)	14 ft 8 ins (4.47 m)
Wing area sq ft (m^2)	264.51 (24.57)	253.3 (23.53)		264.5 (24.57)
Cabin Length pressure vessel	21 ft 9 ins (6.63 m)	21 ft 9 ins (6.63 m)	24 ft 9.5 ins (7.56 m)	23 ft 1 ins (7.04 m)
Cabin width	4 ft 11 ins (1.5 m)	4 ft 11 ins (1.5 m)	5 ft 1 ins (1.55 m)	5 ft 11 ins (1.8 m)
Cabin height	4 ft 4 ins (1.32 m)	4 ft 4 ins (1.32 m)	4 ft 11 ins (1.5 m)	6 ft 8 ins (1.73m)
Cabin pressurization differential	9.4 psi	9.4 psi	9.4 psi	
Weight empty lb (kg)	10,653 (4,832)	10,119 (4,590)	11,700 (5,307)	13,750 (6,237)
Maximum take-off weight lb (kg)	15,500 (7,031)	18,300 (8,300)	19,500 (8,845)	23,100 (10.478)
Maximum landing weight lb (kg)	15,300 (6,940)	15,300 (6,940)	19,200 (8,709)	19,500 (8,845)
Payload with maximum fuel lb (kg)	1,865 (846)	1,783 (809)	1,650 lb (748 kg)	1,290 (585)
Mmo	Mach 0.81	Mach 0.81		
Maximum cruise speed kts (mph) km/h	481 (554) 891 ±3% at 13,500 lb	460 (530) 852	464 (534) 859 ±5%	479 (552) 887 at 18,000 lb
Stall speed kts (mph) km/h	93 (107) 172, landing configuration			
Maximum climb rate ft (m) per minute, MTOW, sea level, ISA	5,480 (1,670)	4,340 (1,323)		4,500 (1,372)
Maximum operating altitude ft (m)	51,000 (15,545)	41,000 (12,500)	51,000 (15,545)	51,000 (15,545)
Take-off distance, ft (m), MTOW, sea level, ISA	2,930 (893)		4,200 (1,280) ±5%	5,350 (1,631)
Landing distance, MLW, sea level, ISA ft (m)	2,767 (843)		2,990 (911) ±5%, to FAR 91	
Range naut miles (miles) km	1,561 (1,797) 2,891 ±4% VFR, with 2 crew + 4 pax, 45 minutes reserve	2,196 (2,528) 4,067 with 2 crew + 4 pax, 45 minutes reserve	2,200 (2,533) 4,074 ±5%, with 2 crew + 4 pax, 45 minutes reserve	2,750 (3,166) 5,093 VFR, with 2 crew + 4 pax, 45 minutes reserve
FAR Pt 36 noise levels Take-off, Sideline, Approach EPNdb	79.5/80.9, 87.2/87.4, 92.6			70.8, 87.7

Certification: 15 January 1993. FAR Pt 25 transport category, including day, night, IFR, and flight into known icing.
Role: Transcontinental corporate jet.
Sales/users: 51 delivered by mid-1995, including 20 since September 1994 (when they operated in 8 countries).
Baggage capacity: 58.7 cu ft (1.66 m^3) for 640 lb (290 kg).
Radar: Digital weather radar.
Flight avionics/instrumentation: Rockwell Collins Pro Line 4 digital suite, including integrated 4 CRT screen EFIS, AMS-850 avionics management system to centralize cockpit control (by providing EFIS, radar and TCAS control and radio management as well as flight management capability), dual channel digital fail-passive autopilot, dual flight directors, dual AHRS, dual digital central air data computers and cockpit voice recorder. Universal UNS1-B optional.

Learjet 60

Maule Air Inc (USA)

Corporate address: 2099 GA Highway, 133 South Moultrie, GA 31768.
Telephone: + 1 912 985 2045
Facsimile: +1 912 890 2402
Employees: Some 100.
Information: Gary Black.

Maule M-7, MT-7, MXT-7 and M-8 series

Maule MXT-7-420 Starcraft (Courtesy Maule)

Role: STOL-capable four or five-seat leisure and business aircraft, also suited to cargo carrying, glider and banner towing, instruction, law enforcement and more.
Sales/users: Over 1,800 Maule aircraft have been produced since 1962.
Details: All current aircraft are strut-braced, high-wing cabin monoplanes of identical length, height, cabin dimensions, gross weight, baggage and cargo capacity, and fuel capacity.
Crew/passengers: See Aircraft variants. Dual controls. Standard double cargo door.
Baggage capacity: 250 lb (113 kg).
Wing control surfaces: Ailerons and flaps. Flap settings -7°, 0°, 24°, 40° and 48°, although M-7-235 floatplane and M-8s do not have the 48° setting.
Tail control surfaces: Elevators (port trim tab) and rudder (servo tab, linked to ailerons).
Construction materials: All aluminium wing. Fuselage and tail group of alloy steel tubing with trusses welding, Ceconite fabric covered.
Engine: See Aircraft variants.
Fuel system: 265 litres.
Electrical system: 60 amp engine-driven alternator and 12 volt battery. 100 amp starter-generator and 24 volt battery on Starcrafts.
Braking system: Hydraulic. Parking brakes.
Flight avionics/instrumentation: Standard avionics include EBC102A ELT, AlliedSignal Bendix/King KT-76A transponder and KX-125-01 nav/comm, and Narco AR-850 altitude encoder. Standard instruments include altimeter, airspeed indicator, rate of climb indicator, tachometer and more. Wide range of optional equipment includes DME, marker beacon, ADF, GPS and autopilot.
Aircraft variants:
MX-7-180B Star Rocket is a four-seat (plus optional jump seat) taildragger, with a 180 hp (134 kW) Textron Lycoming O-360-C1F engine or optionally a 160 hp (119 kW) engine. Optional skis and floats. 32 ft 11 ins (10.03 m) wing span. US$105,850.
M-7-235B Super Rocket is a five-seat taildragger, with a 235 hp (175 kW) Textron Lycoming O-540-J1A5D engine. Optional skis and floats. 33 ft 8 ins (10.26 m) wing span. US$118,062. Alternative O-540-B4B5 low compression engine adds US$2,500. Version with an IO-540-W1A5D engine is US$125,062.
MXT-7-180 Starcraft is a four-seater (plus optional jump seat) with a nosewheel undercarriage. 180 hp (134 kW) Textron Lycoming O-360-C1F engine or optionally a 160 hp (119 kW). Optional skis and floats. 32 ft 11 ins (10.03 m) wing span. US$115,353.
MT-7-235 Super Rocket is a five-seater with nosewheel undercarriage, with a 235 hp (175 kW) Textron Lycoming IO-540-W1A5D engine. 32 ft 11 ins (10.03 m) wing span. US$135,707.
M-8-235 Star Rocket Spring Gear is a four-seat plus optional jump seat) taildragger with an O-540-J1A5D engine. 32 ft 11 ins (10.03 m) wing span. US$123,369. Alternative O-540-B4B5 low compression engine adds US$2,500. Version with an IO-540 is US$130,369.
MX-7-420 Starcraft is a taildragger with 4/5 seats and a 420 shp (313 kW) Allison 250-B17C turboprop engine. 32 ft 11 ins (10.03 m) wing span. US$450,000.
MXT-7-420 Starcraft is a nosewheel version of MX-7-420. US$490,000.
M-7-420 Starcraft is an amphibious version with Edo floats. US$550,000.

DETAILS FOR M-8-235 STAR ROCKET.

Principal dimensions:
Wing span: 32 ft 11 ins (10.03 m)
Maximum length: 23 ft 6 ins (7.16 m)
Maximum height: 6 ft 4 ins (1.93 m)
Cabin:
Width: 3 ft 6 ins (1.07 m)
Wings:
Area: 165.6 sq ft (15.38 m^2)
Aspect ratio: 6.54
Weights:
Empty: 1,535 lb (696 kg)
Maximum take-off: 2,500 lb (1,134 kg)
Useful load: 900 lb (408 kg)
Maximum cargo: 770 lb (349 kg)
Performance:
Cruise speed: 139 kts (160 mph) 257 km/h at 75% power
Stall speed: 35 kts (40 mph) 65 km/h
Take-off over a 50 ft (15 m) bstacle: 600 ft (183 m)
Landing over a 50 ft (15 m) obstacle: 500 ft (153 m)
Maximum climb rate: 2,000 ft (610 m) per minute at sea level, with pilot only and 50% fuel
Ceiling: 20,000 ft (6,100 m)
Range: 747 naut miles (860 miles) 1,384 km with O-540 engine

Mid-Continent Aircraft Corporation (USA)

Mid-Continent King Cat

Corporate address: Drawer L, Hayti, MO 63851.
Telephone: +1 314 359 0500
Facsimile: +1 314 359 0538
Founded: 1949.
Information: Richard Reade (President).

● Activities

● Mid-Continent markets the King Cat, a Schweizer/Ag-Cat Corporation Ag-Cat C converted to use a 1,200 hp (895 kW) Wright R radial engine with a new 3-blade propeller. With the 1,893 litre/67 cu ft (1.897 m^3) hopper, it has a working speed of 87-113 kts (100-130 mph) 161-209 km/h. Options include a 38 ins (97 cm) gatebox and wide spreader. In addition, a 2,271 litre hopper is available, and the company now also offers AlliedSignal modifications.
● Authorized distributor of the Ag-Cat/Schweizer Ag-Cat, Ayres Thrush and Cessna agricultural aircraft. The business is divisionalized into large international aircraft parts sales and FAA approved repair station Class 1, 2 and 3 DFQR172D; insurance brokerage for agricultural aircraft; and refurbishment of the Stearman trainer into MCMD Custom Specials with 220, 300 and 450 hp (164, 224 and 336 kW) engines. It also operates 4 agricultural aircraft.

Moller International (USA)

Corporate address: 1222 Research Park Drive, Davis, CA 95616.
Telephone: +1 916 756 5086
Facsimile: +1 916 767 5179
Founded: 1983.
Information: Jack Allison.

● Activities

● In 1989 Moller demonstrated a unique experimental and piloted "power lift" aircraft called Volantor M200X, with VTOL flying capability. The circular craft is powered by 8 Moller single-rotor rotary engines (each developing 65 hp, 48.5 kW weighing only 45 lb, 20.4 kg) and has a company-developed electronic stabilization and fly-by-wire control system. This has made over 150 flights. Resulting from the trials, Moller has built the newly configured prototype of the M400 Skycar, a four-seat composite VTOL aircraft intended for volume production at a unit price of about US$995,000. This is being considered for FAA certification under the new Powered lift-normal category. First flight may take place by the end of 1995. A two-seat variant was shown at the 1995 Paris Air Show in model form as the M200 Skycar.

● The company has also developed and patented a ducted-fan hover-capable unmanned airborne robotic vehicle (Aerobot), originally designed for aircraft damage assessment. Both electric and fuel-powered models have been flown, and Aerobots have been delivered to 3 customers, with uses including civil construction inspection.

● Moller's MR 530 twin-rotor liquid-cooled 1,060 cc rotary engine is now producing 160 hp (119.3 kW). Low rate production is expected to start in 1995.

Moller M400 Skycar, awaiting engines. Paul Moller suggested to WA&SD the possibility of the first flight at the end of 1995

Moller M200 and M400 Skycar

Details: For M400, except under Aircraft variants.
First flight: Late 1995?
Role: 4-seat VTOL lightplane.
Wing characteristics: Rear-mounted short-span wing, with aerodynamic lift also generated by the body shape.
Construction materials: Composites. Twin emergency ballistic parachutes.
Engines and control: 8 Moller MR 530 twin-rotor rotary engines, carried in pairs in each of the 4 power pods. Each engine drives a 7-blade variable-speed fan, with VTOL achieved by 2 sets of computer-reconfigured variable lift vanes at the rear of each pod to redirect thrust. The vanes, each assembly with 4 independent servo-motors, also perform the functions of ailerons and elevators by symmetrical and differential application. Computer fly-by-wire stabilization.
Engine rating: Each 160 hp (119.3 kW).
Fuel system: 227 litres.
Flight avionics/instrumentation: 3 redundant and independent computer systems for flight management and control. EFIS.
Aircraft variants:
M200 Skycar is a proposed two-seater with 2 main power pods forward and 3 smaller pods on the rear wing.
M400 Skycar, as detailed. See also the introduction.

Details for M400 Skycar.

Principal dimensions:
Wing span: 9 ft (2.74 m)
Maximum length: 18 ft (5.49 m)
Maximum height: 6 ft (1.83 m)
Weights:
Maximum take-off: 2,500 lb (1,134 kg)
Payload: 740 lb (336 kg) with full fuel
Performance (projected):
Maximum speed: 353 kts (407 mph) 655 km/h
Cruise speed: 308 kts (355 mph) 571 km/h
Take-off and landing area: 35 ft (10.67 m) diameter
Maximum climb rate: 7,150 ft (2,180 m) per minute
Operational ceiling: 30,000 ft (9,150 m)
Range: 781 naut miles (900 miles) 1,448 km
Noise level: 65 dBA at 500 ft (152 m)

Mooney Aircraft Corporation (USA)

Corporate address: PO Box 72, Louis Schreiner Field, Kerrville, TX 78028.
Telephone: +1 210 896 6000;
Direct sales +1 800 456 3033
Facsimile: +1 210 896 7333;
Direct sales +1 210 896 8180
Founded: 5 July 1946.
Information: Jeffrey Dunbar (Vice-President, Sales).

● Activities

● Mooney marked production of its 10,000th aircraft in 1994.

Mooney M20 series

First flight: 1976 for the original Mooney 201.
Details: For the MSE, except under Aircraft variants and table.
Role: 4-seat lightplane.
Baggage capacity: 120 lb (54.4 kg). Also, rear seats can be removed for carrying light cargo.
Wing control surfaces: Ailerons and single-slotted flaps.
Tail control surfaces: Variable incidence tailplane (fin moves with tailplane). Elevators and

Mooney M20R Ovation (courtesy Mooney)

forward-swept rudder.
Flight control system: Manual, except electric flaps. Optional electric trimming.
Construction materials: Metal.
Engine: Textron Lycoming IO-360-A3B6D piston engine, with a 6 ft 2 ins (1.88m) McCauley 2-blade constant-speed propeller.
Engine rating: 200 hp (149 kW).
Fuel system: 242 litres usable.
Electrical system: 70 amp alternator and 24 volt battery (10 amp-hour).
Braking system: Hydraulic disc. Parking brake.
Flight avionics/instrumentation: Blind-flying instrumentation. Selection of AlliedSignal Bendix/King avionics packages, with or without DME, RNAV, EFIS and GPS. Other options include flight control system/autopilot, ADF, RMI, Mode C transponder, radar altimeter, and Goodrich stormscope.
Aircraft variants:
ATS is an advanced trainer, similar to MSE.
MSE (M-20J), as detailed above. Maximum take-off weight 2,900 lb (1,315 kg) and maximum speed 175 kts (202 mph) 324 km/h at sea level. Duration 7 hours.
TLS is a lengthened and IFR-equipped four-seater, with a turbocharged Textron Lycoming TIO-540-AF1A engine. First appeared in 1989. Redesigned interior in 1994. Cruise speed 220 kts (253 mph) 407 km/h at 25,000 ft (7,620 m).Duration 7 hours.
Ovation (M20R) was unveiled on 27 April 1994, first flew in May, certified July, and the initial 21 (of 31 ordered) were delivered that year. Combines the TLS airframe and interior with a 280 hp (209 kW) Teledyne Continental IO-550-G5B engine. Fuel capacity 337 litres, of which 314 litres are usable. Baggage 125 lb (56.7 kg). 2 x 24 volt lead-acid batteries. Composites sandwich cabin side panels to reduce vibration and noise.

Details for M20R Ovation.

Principal dimensions:
Wing span: 36 ft 1 ins (11 m)
Maximum length: 26 ft 9 ins (8.15 m)
Maximum height: 8 ft 4 ins (2.54 m)
Wings:
Area: 175 sq ft (16.26 m^2)
Aspect ratio: 7.4
Undercarriage:
Type: Retractable (electric), with steerable nosewheel
Weights:
Empty: 2,269 lb (1,029 kg)
Maximum take-off: 3,368 lb (1,527 kg)
Maximum landing weight: 3,200 lb (1,451 kg)
Useful load: 1,143 lb (519 kg)
Performance:
Maximum cruise speed: 190 kts (219 mph) 352 km/h at 9,000 ft (2,745 m)
Stall speed: 66 kts (76 mph) 122 km/h *clean*, 59 kts (68 mph) 110 km/h *in landing configuration*
Maximum climb rate: 1,200 ft (366 m) per minute at sea level
Ceiling: 20,000 ft (6,100 m), service
Range: 1,129 naut miles (1,300 miles) 2,090 km
Duration: 6.7 hours, with reserve

Piper Aircraft Corporation (USA)

Corporate address: 2926 Piper Drive, Vero Beach, FL 32960.
Telephone: +1 407 567 4361
Facsimile: +1 407 778 2144
Founded: 1936. Became a subsidiary of Newco Pac Inc in 1995.
Employees: About 540.
Information: Kimberley von Hagen (Marketing Manager).

● Activities

● Piper expected to deliver 173 aircraft to customers in 1995, 42 more than in 1994.

Piper PA32R-301 Saratoga II HP

	PA18-150 Super Cub	PA28-161 Warrior III	PA28-181 Archer III	PA28R-201 Arrow	PA28-236 Dakota	PA32R-301 Saratoga II HP	PA34-220T Seneca IV	PA44-180 Seminole	PA46-350P Malibu Mirage
Role	Lightplane and trainer	Lightplane and trainer	Lightplane	Lightplane and trainer	Lightplane	Lightplane and business aircraft	Twin-engined lightplane and trainer	Twin-engined lightplane and trainer	Pressurized business aircraft
Passengers	2 in tandem	4	4	4	4	6	6	4	6
Engines	Textron Lycoming O-320-A2B	Textron Lycoming O-320-D3G	Textron Lycoming O-360-A4M	Textron Lycoming O-360-C1C6	Textron Lycoming O-540-J3A5D	Textron Lycoming IO-540-K1G5	2 x Teledyne Continental TSIO/ LTSIO-360-KBs	2 x Textron Lycoming IO-360-A1H6s	Textron Lycoming TIO-540-AE2A
Engine rating	150 hp (112 kW)	160 hp (119.3 kW)	180 hp (134 kW)	200 hp (149 kW)	235 hp (175 kW)	300 hp (224 kW)	Each 220 hp (164 kW)	Each 180 hp (134 kW)	350 hp (261 kW)
Propeller	6 ft 2 ins (1.88 m) Sensenich 2-blade, fixed-pitch	6 ft 2 ins (1.88 m) Sensenich 2-blade, fixed-pitch	6 ft 4 ins (1.93 m) Sensenich 2-blade, fixed-pitch	McCauley 2-blade, constant-speed	6 ft 8 ins (2.03 m) Hartzell 2-blade, constant-speed	Hartzell, constant-speed	6 ft 4 ins (1.93 m) McCauley 3-blade, constant-speed	6 ft 2 ins (1.88 m) Hartzell 2-blade, constant-speed	6 ft 8 ins (2.03 m) Hartzell 2-blade, constant-speed
Usable fuel	135.5 litres	182 litres	182 litres	272.5 litres	273 litres	386 litres	466 litres	409 litres	454 litres
Wing span	35 ft 2 ins (10.72 m)	35 ft (10.67 m)	35 ft 5 ins (10.8 m)	35 ft 5 ins (10.8 m)	35 ft 5 ins (10.8 m)	36 ft 2 ins (11.02 m)	38 ft 11 ins (11.86 m)	38 ft 7 ins (11.76 m)	43 ft (13.11 m)
Length	22 ft 7 ins (6.88 m)	23 ft 9.5 ins (7.25 m)	24 ft (7.32 m)	24 ft 8 ins (7.52 m)	24 ft 8 ins (7.52 m)	27 ft (8.23 m)	28 ft 7 ins (8.71 m)	27 ft 7 ins (8.41 m)	28 ft 7 ins (8.71 m)
Height	5 ft 9 ins (1.75 m)	7 ft 4 ins (2.23 m)	7 ft 4 ins (2.23 m)	7 ft 11 ins (2.41 m)	7 ft 2 ins (2.18 m)	8 ft 6 ins (2.59 m)	9 ft 11 ins (3.02 m)	8 ft 6 ins (2.59 m)	11 ft 6 ins (3.51 m)
Wing area sq ft (m^2)	178.5 (16.58)	170 (15.79)	170 (15.79)	170 (15.79)	170 (15.79)	178.3 (16.56)	208.7 (19.39)	183.8 (17.08)	175 (16.26)
Cabin length		8 ft 2 ins (2.49 m)	8 ft 2 ins (2.49 m)	8 ft 2 ins (2.49 m)	8 ft 2 ins (2.49 m)	10 ft 4 ins (3.15 m)	10 ft 4.25 ins (3.156 m)	8 ft 1 ins (2.46 m)	12 ft 4 ins (3.759 m)
Cabin width		3 ft 5.25 ins (1.05 m)	3 ft 5.75 ins (1.06 m)	3 ft 5.75 ins (1.06 m)	3 ft 5.75 ins (1.06 m)	4 ft 1 ins (1.24 m)	4 ft 0.75 ins (1.238)	3 ft 5.5 ins (1.054 m)	4 ft 1 ins (1.24 m)
Cabin height		3 ft 8.25 ins (1.12 m)	3 ft 9 ins (1.14 m)	3 ft 8.75 ins (1.137 m)	3 ft 8.75 ins (1.137 m)	3 ft 6 ins (1.07 m)	3 ft 6 ins (1.07 m)	4 ft 1 ins (1.24 m)	3 ft 11 ins (1.19 m)
Baggage lb (kg)	50 (22.7)	200 (91)	200 (91)	200 (91)	200 (91)	200 (91)	200 (91)	200 (91)	200 (91)
Cabin pressurization differential	N/A	N/A	N/A	N/A	N/A	N/A	N/A	N/A	5.5 psi
Weight empty lb (kg)	1,062 (482)	1,491 (676)	1,639 (743)	1,798 (816)	1,610 (730)	2,364 (1,072)	2,852 (1,294)	2,593 (1,176)	3,048 (1,382)
Maximum take-off weight lb (kg)	1,750 (793)	2,447 (1,110)	2,550 (1,156)	2,750 (1,247)	3,000 (1,361)	3,600 (1,633)	4,750 (2,154)	3,800 (1,723)	4,300 (1,950)
Average useful load lb (kg)	688 (312)	956 (434)	919 (417)	952 (432)	1,401 (635)		1,921 (871)	1,207 (547)	1,270 (576)
Maximum speed kts (mph) km/h	113 (130) 29	127 (146) 235	129 (149) 239	152 (175) 282	148 (170) 274	166 (191) 307	196 (226) 363	202 (232) 373	232 (267) 430
Cruise speed kts (mph) km/h	100 (115) 185 at 75% power and 5,000 ft	126 (145) 233 at 75% power	125 (144) 232 at 65% power and 12,000 ft	143 (165) 265 at 75% power	144 (166) 267 at 75% power	159 (183) 294 at economical cruise power	193 (222) 357 at optimum altitude, 75% power	162 (187) 300 at 75% power	225 (259) 417 high speed cruise
Stall speed kts (mph) km/h	38 (43) 70 *with flaps*	50 (58) 93 IAS *clean*, 44 (51) 82 IAS *with full 40° flaps*	50 (58) 93 IAS *clean*, 45 (52) 83 IAS *with full 40° flaps*	60 (69) 111 IAS *clean*, 55 (64) 102 IAS *with full 40° flaps*	65 (75) 120 IAS *clean*, 56 (65) 104 IAS *with full 40° flaps*	65 (75) 120 IAS *clean*, 60 (69) 111 IAS *with full 40° flaps*	67 (77) 124 IAS *clean*, 64 (74) 119 IAS *with full 40° flaps*	57 (66) 106 IAS *clean*, 55 (64) 102 IAS *with full 40° flaps*	71 (82) 132 CAS *clean*, 60 (69) 111 IAS *with full 40° flaps*
Maximum climb rate ft (m) per minute	960 (293)	644 (196)	667 (203)	831 (253)	1,110 (338)	1,116 (340)	1,400 (427)	1,340 (408)	1,218 (371)
Service ceiling ft (m)	19,000 (5,790)	11,000 (3,353)	13,236 (4,034)	16,200 (4,938)	17,500 (5,334)	15,588 (4,751)	25,000 (7,620) approved	15,000 ft (4,572)	25,000 (7,620) approved
Take-off distance, MTOW ft (m)	200 (61) *with flaps*	1,650 (503) over a 50 ft (15 m) obstacle	1,210 (369) over a 50 ft (15 m) obstacle	1,600 (488) over a 50 ft (15 m) obstacle	1,216 (371) over a 50 ft (15 m) obstacle	1,768 (539) over a 50 ft (15 m) obstacle	1,210 (369) over a 50 ft (15 m) obstacle	1,520 (464) over a 50 ft (15 m) obstacle	2,375 (724) over a 50 ft (15 m) obstacle
Landing distance, MLW ft (m)	350 (107) *with flaps*	1,160 (354) over a 50 ft (15 m) obstacle	1,390 (424) over a 50 ft (15 m) obstacle	1,525 (465) over a 50 ft (15 m) obstacle	1,725 (526) over a 50 ft (15 m) obstacle	1,520 (463) over a 50 ft (15 m) obstacle	1,978 (603) over a 50 ft (15 m) obstacle	1,238 (378) over a 50 ft (15 m) obstacle	1,964 (599) over a 50 ft (15 m) obstacle
Range naut miles (miles) km	399 (460) 740 at 75% power	520 (598) 963 at 55% power, 7,000 ft and 45 minutes reserve	580 (667) 1,074 at 55% power, 12,500 ft and 45 minutes reserve	795 (915) 1,472 at 55% power, 10,000 ft and 45 minutes reserve	750 (863) 1,389 at 55% power, 45 minutes reserve	860 (990) 1,593 at 152 kts long-range cruise speed	990 (1,140) 1,833 at 168 kts and optimum altitude	751 (864) 1,390	1,450 (1,669) 2,685 at 168 kts long-range cruise speed

Piper PA18-150 Super Cub, with production just ended

Piper PA34-220T Seneca IV

Piper PA46-350P Malibu Mirage

Raisbeck Engineering Inc (USA)

Corporate address: 4411 South Ryan Way, Seattle, WA 98178.
Telephone: 800 537 7277 (within US, Canada and Mexico), or +1 206 723 2000 (international)
Facsimile: +1 206 723 2884
Founded: 1974.
Information: Robert P. Steinbach (Vice President Sales/Service).

● Activities

● Raisbeck offers a range of enhancements for Beech King Airs and Super King Airs, and by 1995 had installed over 5,000 individual systems. These systems are known as Quiet Turbofan Propellers (for B300, 300C and 350), Ram Air Recovery Systems (300, 300LW), Enhanced Performance Leading Edges (200, B200 series), Composite Exhaust Stack Fairings (100, A100 and B100), Dual Aft Body Strakes (F90 and F90-1), Fully-Enclosed MLG Doors (E90), Wing Lockers (C90, C90-1, C90A and C90B) and Gross Weight Increase (90, A90 and B90). In addition, on 31 March 1995 Raisbeck made the first delivery of its new Learjet Aft Fuselage Locker, an entirely external fairing to the existing fuselage that begins as a rearward extension of the horizontal fuselage keel beam and rolls into a 17 ins (43 cm) deep ventral fin, replacing the aircraft's current fin. Within the 18 ft (5.49 m) fairing is an 8 ft (2.44 m) drawer which deploys sideways to carry 300 lb (136 kg) of cargo.

Raisbeck-produced Learjet Aft Fuselage Locker on a Learjet 36A

Raytheon Aircraft Company (USA)

Corporate address: See Airliners section for company details.

● Activities

● Details of the Beech 1900D Airliner can be found in the Airliners section. Despite the merger of Beech and Hawker aircraft within Raytheon Aircraft, the individual products retain their original names.
● The Beech Mk II (a derivative of the Pilatus PC-9) was announced to be winner of the US JPATS competition on 22 June 1995, and details can be found in the Combat section under Pilatus.
● 361 aircraft were delivered in 1994, comprising, 317 civil/commercial and 44 military including 133 turbine business aircraft.
● Production of the Beech Starship 2000A eight/nine-seat business jetprop ended in 1995 after 53 aircraft. Production of the Hawker business jets is continuing with emphasis on the Hawker 800, although development of a new light business aircraft started in 1995, as the 390 Premier I.

Beech Starship 2000A, taken out of production in 1995

Beech Bonanza F33A, A36 and B36TC

First flight: Prototype Bonanza Model 35 first flew on 22 December 1945. Model 33 Debonair first flew in September 1959, from which the F33 later evolved. Model 36 appeared in 1968, followed by the A36 in 1983. B36TC appeared in 1982.
Role: Utility, commercial training and business.
Baggage capacity: 37 cu ft (1.05 m^3) cabin compartment for 400 lb (181 kg), and 10 cu ft (0.28 m^3) for 70 lb (32 kg).
Wing control surfaces: Ailerons (with trim tabs) and 3-position single-slotted flaps. Vortex generators.
Tail control surfaces: Elevators (with trim tabs) and rudder (with ground-adjustable tab).
Flight control system: Mechanical, except for electric flaps.
Construction materials: Metal.
Electrical system: 28 volt, with 60 amp alternator and 15.5 amp-hour battery.
Flight avionics/instrumentation: Standard avionics include AlliedSignal Bendix/King KX-155-39 760-channel comm transceiver with audio amplifier, 200-channel nav receiver with KI-208 VOR/LOC converter indicator, microphone, cabin speaker, headset, and nav/comm antennae. Many options. Range of engine and flight instruments.
Aircraft variants:
<u>F33A</u> is a four-seater with a 285 hp (212.5 kW) IO-550-BB engine and 6 ft 8 ins (2.03 m) propeller. Generally similar dimensions to A36. MTOW 3,400 lb (1,542 kg). Manual aileron trim control.
<u>A36</u>, as detailed above and in tables.
<u>A36AT</u> is the commercial training version for airline use, with a Hartzell propeller, engine flat rated to 290 hp (216 kW) and other changes.
<u>B36TC</u> is a turbocharged version of A36, with a 300 hp (224 kW) TSIO-520-UB engine and 6 ft 6 ins (1.98 m) propeller. Maximum speed 213 kts (245 mph) 394 km/h and MTOW 3,850 lb (1,746 kg).

Beech Bonanza B36TC

Beech Baron 58

Certification: 1969.
Role: High-performance private and business aircraft.

Beech Baron 58

Baggage capacity: 18 cu ft (0.51 m^3) in nose for 300 lb (136 kg), 12 cu ft (0.34 m^3) centre cabin for 200 lb (91 kg), 37 cu ft (1.05 m^3) rear compartment for 400 lb (181 kg), and 10 cu ft (0.28 m^3) extended rear compartment for 120 lb (54 kg).
Wing control surfaces: Ailerons (port trim tab) and single-slotted flaps.
Tail control surfaces: Elevators and rudder, all with trim tabs.
Flight control surfaces: Manual, except for electric flaps.
Construction materials: Metal.
Electrical system: 28 volt, with 2 x 60 amp alternators and 2 x 12 volt, 25 amp-hour batteries.
Flight avionics/instrumentation: Standard avionics include AlliedSignal Bendix/King KX-155-39 760-channel comm transceiver with audio amplifier, 200-channel nav

receiver with KI-208 VOR/LOC converter indicator, KR-87 ADF with KI-227-00 indicator and combined loop/sense antenna, microphone, headset, cabin speaker, and nav/comm antennae. Many options. Range of engine and flight instruments.

Beech King Air C90B and C90SE

First flight: King Air C90 dates from 1970, with C90B from 1991.
Role: Pressurized business aircraft.
Baggage capacity: 53.5 cu ft (1.51 m^3) aft for 350 lb (158 kg), and 26.8 cu ft (0.76 m^3) with aft toilet.
Electrical system: 3-bus system with automatic load shedding, solid state generator controllers and a 34 amp-hour ni-cd battery. 2 Flite-Tronics 250VA inverters.
Wing control surfaces: Ailerons (port trim tab) and 3-position single-slotted flaps. Aileron cable tension regulator.
Tail control surfaces: Elevators and rudder, all with trim tabs.
Flight control system: Manual, except for electric flaps.
Construction materials: Metal.
Flight avionics/instrumentation: AlliedSignal Bendix/King avionics, including dual KY-196As with dual antennae, single or dual VOR/ILS nav (VHF), ADF, dual Mode S transponders, DME, encoding altimeter, audio/marker beacon and cockpit voice recorder. Many options, including AlliedSignal package with CNI-5000 system.
Aircraft variants:
C90B accommodates a pilot plus 6 or 7 passengers. McCauley 4-blade propellers and Rockwell Collins Pro Line II avionics, with optional AlliedSignal Silver/Gold Crown. Standard WXR-270 colour weather radar and APS-65 flight director/autopilot.
C90SE is the new lower-cost and reduced specification version; see above details and table. First delivery September 1994.

Beech King Air C90SE

Beech Super King Air B200 series

First flight: 1972 for the original Super King Air 200.
Certification: 1981 for B200.
Role: Pressurized business, cargo, and military special mission aircraft.
Sales/users: 1,500th commercial Super King Air B200 series aircraft was delivered in 1995.
Baggage capacity: 53.5 cu ft (1.51 m^3) aft for 550 lb (249 kg).
Wing control surfaces: Ailerons (port trim tab) and single-slotted flaps. Yaw damper system. Aileron cable tension regulator.
Tail control surfaces: Elevators and rudder, all with trim tabs.
Flight control system: Manual, except for electric flaps.
Construction materials: Metal.
Electrical system: 2 x 28 volt (250 amp) starter-generators and a 24 volt (34 amp-hour) ni-cd battery. AC supply via inverters.
Radar: Rockwell Collins WXR-270 colour weather radar standard, with AlliedSignal Bendix/King RDS 84VP optional.
Flight avionics/instrumentation: Standard Rockwell Collins Pro Line II suite with 4 ins (10 cm) EFIS 84 flight control system. Includes APS-65H autopilot. Optional Pro Line II with EFIS-85B(14) or AlliedSignal Gold Crown. Other options.
Aircraft variants:
B200 is the standard version, as detailed.
B200C is generally similar but features a large cargo door.
B200CT is a merger of C and T features.
B200SE was certified in mid-1995 as a lower cost version, having 3-blade propellers and WXR-270 radar as an option.
B200T offers removable wingtip tanks for an additional 401 litres of fuel. A *maritime patrol* version with specialized equipment serves with the armed forces or government agencies of Algeria, France, Germany, Japan, Malaysia, Peru, Puerto Rico, and Uruguay.
C-12 is the US armed forces designation for their support transport models. More specialized versions include the US Army's RC-12 Guardrail series of specially-equipped comint aircraft with numerous aerials and antennae.

Beech Super King Air B200

Beech Super King Air 350

First flight: 1988.
Role: Pressurized business, cargo, and military special mission aircraft.
Baggage capacity: 54 cu ft (1.53 m^3) aft for 550 lb (249 kg).
Wing control surfaces: Ailerons (port trim tab) and single-slotted flaps. Yaw damper system. Aileron cable tension regulator.
Tail control surfaces: Elevators and rudder, all with trim tabs.
Flight control system: Manual, except for electric flaps. Dual pushrod trim tab actuators.
Construction materials: Metal.
Electrical system: 2 x 28 volt (300 amp) starter-generators and a 24 volt (34 amp-hour) ni-cd battery. AC supply via inverters.
Radar: WXR-270 colour weather radar.
Flight avionics/instrumentation: Standard Rockwell Collins Pro Line II suite and including APS-65J autopilot with FIS-85 5 ins (12.7 cm) flight director system. Optional Pro Line II with EFIS-85B(14). Other options.
Aircraft variants:
350, as detailed above and in table.
350C features a large cargo door with integral airstair door, and dry chemical toilet facing forward.
RC-350 Guardian is a multi-sensor version offering elint/comint, surveillance radar, synthetic aperture radar, FLIR, long-range electro-optical or remote spectroscopy sensors.

Beech T-1A Jayhawks at Reese AFB

Beech Beechjet 400A

First flight: 1986, derived from the Mitsubishi Diamond II. 400A version first flew 22 September 1989.
Role: Pressurized business jet and trainer.
Baggage capacity: Total of 58.4 cu ft (1.65 m^3) in forward, aft and external aft positions, for 950 lb (431 kg).
Wing control surfaces: Ailerons, single- and double-slotted Fowler flaps, and spoilers (for aileron assist, lift-dumping and speed brakes). Dual flap asymmetrical detection system.
Tail control surfaces: Variable-incidence tailplane. Elevators and rudder (with tab).
Flight control system: Mechanical primary surfaces, hydraulic/mechanical spoilers, and electric roll trim, pitch trim and yaw trim. Hydraulic flaps.
Construction materials: Aluminium alloy and steel used for skin and structure.
Electrical system: 28 volt DC supply via 2 x 400 amp starter-generators. 24 volt, 36 amp-hour ni-cd battery. 2 AC inverters (50 VA, 115 and 26 volt).
Radar: Rockwell Collins WXR-840.
Flight avionics/instrumentation: Rockwell Collins Pro Line 4 flight control system with FIS-870 display and FCS-850 flight control system and including APS-850A autopilot. FMS-850 flight management system with data base unit, and VLF/Omega/RNAV. Dual VHF comm, single or dual VOR/ILS, ADF, dual marker beacons, dual glideslope, dual DMEs, dual transponders, radio altimeter, etc.
Aircraft variants:
400A, as detailed.
400T is a military training version for the JASDF, with long-range navigation systems and other changes.
T-1A Jayhawk is the USAF version for training aerial tanker crews. 180 ordered, with 114 delivered by August 1995, at which time US Navy pilots had started training with USAF aircrew.

Hawker 800

First flight: 26 May 1983.
Certification: 4 May 1984.
Role: Mid-size business jet.
Baggage capacity: 40-71 cu ft (1.13-2.01 m^3), with optional pannier for 28 cu ft (0.79 m^3) of external capacity.
Wing control surfaces: Ailerons (with tabs) and 4-position double-slotted flaps. Upper/lower speedbrakes.
Tail control surfaces: Elevators and rudder, all with tabs.
Flight control system: Manual, except for hydraulic flaps.
Construction materials: Metal.
Electrical system: DC supply via 2 x 30 volt starter-generators. 2 x 24 volt, 23 amp-hour ni-cd batteries, plus a 4 amp-hour battery for instrument back-up. 3 AC inverters and 2 alternators.
Radar: Honeywell Primus 870 weather radar. Optional Rockwell Collins TWR-850 turbulence weather radar.
Flight avionics/instrumentation: Honeywell suite is standard, including dual RNZ-850 integrated navigation

unit, AA-300 radio altimeter, dual AHZ-600 AHRS, dual ADZ-810 air data computer, dual EDZ-817 flight director with MDZ-817 multifunction display, digital DFZ-800 AFCS, FMS with dual FMZ-800 and dual Omega/VLF sensors, GPS, etc. Options include TCAS, GPWS and 5 ins (12.7 cm) LCD with articulating arms. Optional Rockwell Collins suite.

Aircraft variants:

800, as detailed above and in the table.
800XP extended performance model appeared in 1995, featuring 4,660 lbf (20.72 kN) TFE731-5BR engines for an additional 14 kts, faster climb, 500 lb (227 kg) extra payload and improved environmental system.
C-29A is a USAF model for flight inspection work.
U-125 is the JASDF designation for its flight inspection and SAR (U-125A) versions.

Hawker 800 in U-125A SAR form, handed over to the JASDF on 28 February 1995. Equipment includes 360° search radar, FLIR, thermal imager, marker flare dispensing system, dinghy, large observation windows and rescue equipment dropping capability

Hawker 1000

First flight: 16 June 1990.
Role: Pressurized business aircraft.
Baggage capacity: 76 cu ft (2.15 m^3).
Electrical system: DC supply via 2 x 30 volt starter-generators. 2 x 26 volt, 43 amp-hour ni-cd batteries, plus a 5 amp-hour battery for instrument back-up. 2 alternators.
Flight avionics/instrumentation: As Hawker 800, but with dual Laseref III AHRS, FMS with dual FMZ-900 and dual Laseref III inertial sensors, and other changes.

Pax=Passengers	Bonanza A36	Baron 58	King Air C90SE	King Air B200	King Air 350	Beechjet 400A	Hawker 800	Hawker 1000
Crew + Pax	1 + 3-5.	1 + 3-5.	1 + 5-6. Max occupancy limit is 13	1 + 7-8. Max occupancy limit is 15	1 + 9. Max occupancy limit is 17	2 + 7-9.	2 + 8-9.	2 + 8-12.
Engine/s	Teledyne Continental IO-550-B	2 x Teledyne Continental IO-550-C	2 x Pratt & Whitney Canada PT6A-21 turboprops	2 x Pratt & Whitney Canada PT6A-42 turboprops	2 x Pratt & Whitney Canada PT6A-60A turboprops	2 x Pratt & Whitney Canada JT15D-5 turbofans	2 x AlliedSignal TFE731-5R-1H turbofans	2 x Pratt & Whitney Canada PW305B turbofans
Engine rating	300 hp (224 kW)	Each 300 hp (224 kW)	Each 550 shp (410 kW)	Each 850 shp (633.8 kW)	Each 1,050 shp (783 kW)	Each 2,900 lbf (12.9 kN)	Each 4,300 lbf (19.13 kN)	Each 5,266 lbf (23.42 kN)
Propeller/s	6 ft 8 ins (2.03 m) McCauley 3-blade constant-speed	6 ft 3 ins (1.91 m) 3-blade, constant-speed	7 ft 9 ins (2.36 m) Hartzell 3-blade, constant-speed	7 ft 10 ins (2.39 m) Hartzell 4-blade, auto feathering with synchrophaser	8 ft 9 ins (2.69 m) 4-blade, auto feathering with synchrophaser	N/A	N/A	N/A
Usable fuel	280 litres	628 litres standard, 734 litres optional	2,573 lb (1,167 kg)	2,059 litres	2,040 litres	2,774 litres	5,648 litres	6,440 litres
Wing span	33 ft 6 ins (10.21 m)	37 ft 10 ins (11.53 m)	50 ft 3 ins (15.32 m)	54 ft 6 ins (16.61 m)	57 ft 11 ins (17.65 m)	43 ft 6 ins (13.26 m)	51 ft 4 ins (15.65 m)	51 ft 5 ins (15.67 m)
Length	27 ft 6 ins (8.38 m)	29 ft 10 ins (9.09 m)	35 ft 6 ins (10.82 m)	43 ft 9 ins (13.34 m)	46 ft 8 ins (14.22 m)	48 ft 5 ins (14.76 m)	51 ft 2 ins (15.6 m)	53 ft 11 ins (16.43 m)
Height	8 ft 7 ins (2.62 m)	9 ft 9 ins (2.97 m)	14 ft 3 ins (4.34 m)	15 ft (4.57 m)	14 ft 4 ins (4.37 m)	13 ft 11 ins (4.24 m)	17 ft 7 ins (5.36 m)	17 ft 1 ins (5.21 m)
Wing area sq ft (m^2)	181 (16.82)	199.2 (18.51)	293.94 (27.31)	303 (28.15)	310 (28.8)	241.4 (22.43)	374 (34.75)	374 (34.75)
Cabin length	12 ft 7 ins (3.84 m)	12 ft 7 ins (3.84 m) including rear baggage compartment	12 ft 11 ins (3.94 m) excluding cockpit	16 ft 8 ins (5.08) excluding cockpit	19 ft 6 ins (5.94 m) excluding cockpit	15 ft 6 ins (4.72 m) excluding cockpit	21 ft 4 ins (6.5 m)	24 ft 5 ins (7.44 m)
Cabin width	3 ft 6 ins (1.07 m)	3 ft 6 ins (1.07 m)	4 ft 6 ins (1.37 m)	4 ft 4 ins (1.3 m)	4 ft 4 ins (1.3 m)	4 ft 11 ins (1.5 m)	6 ft (1.83m) maximum	6 ft (1.83m) maximum
Cabin height	4 ft 2 ins (1.27 m)	4 ft 2 ins (1.27 m)	4 ft 9 ins (1.45 m)	4 ft 9 ins (1.45 m)	4 ft 9 ins (1.45 m)	4 ft 9 ins (1.45 m)	5 ft 9 ins (1.75 m)	5 ft 9 ins (1.75 m)
Cabin pressurization differential	N/A	N/A	5 psi	6.5 psi	6.5 psi	9 psi	8.6 psi	8.6 psi
Weight empty lb (kg)	2,295 (1,041)	3,570 (1,619)	6,225 (2,823)	8,358 (3,791) basic operating	9,062 (4,110)	10,050 (4,558)	16,000 (7,257) typical operating	18,000 (8,164) typical operating
Maximum take-off weight lb (kg)	3,650 (1,655)	5,500 (2,494)	10,100 (4,581)	12,500 (5,670)	15,000 (6,804)	16,100 (7,303)	27,400 (12,428)	31,000 (14,061)
Maximum landing weight lb (kg)	3,650 (1,655)	5,400 (2,449)	9,600 (4,354)	12,500 (5,670)	15,000 (6,804)	15,700 (7,121)	23,350 (10,591)	25,000 (11,340)
Useful load lb (kg)	1,368 (620)	1,954 (886)	3,935 (1,785)	4,432 (2,010)	6,038 (2,739)	5,850 (2,653) at ramp weight	11,520 (5,225)	13,100 (5,942)
Maximum speed kts (mph) km/h	184 (212) 340	208 (239) 385	249 (286) 461	294 (338) 544	315 (363) 583	468 (539) 866. Mach 0.78 Mmo	457 (526) 846	465 (535) 861
Maximum cruise speed kts (mph) km/h	176 (202) 326 at 6,000 ft and 3,400 lb	203 (234) 376 at 5,000 ft and 5,200 lb	247 (284) 457 at 16,000 ft	289 (333) 535	308 (354) 570 at 18,000 ft	443 (510) 820 at 23,000 ft	437 (503) 809 at 37,000 ft	452 (521) 837
Stall speed kts (mph) km/h	68 (78) 126 IAS *clean,* 59 (68) 110 IAS *with 30° flaps*	84 (97) 156 IAS *clean,* 75 (86) 139 IAS *with flaps*	88 (101) 163 *clean,* 78 (90) 145 *with flaps*	99 (114) 183 IAS *clean,* 75 (86) 139 IAS *with flaps*	96 (111) 178 *clean,* 81 (94) 150 *with flaps*	110 (127) 204 *clean,* 92 (106) 171 *with full flaps*	92 (106) 171 *landing configuration*	89 (103) 165 *landing configuration*
Maximum climb rate ft (m) per minute	1,208 (368) at MTOW	1,735 (529) at MTOW	2,003 (611) at MTOW	2,450 (747) at MTOW	2,731 (832) at MTOW	3,770 (1,150) at MTOW	3,500 (1,067)	3,577 (1,090
Ceiling ft (m)	18,500 (5,640)	20,688 (6,305) at MTOW	28,900 (8,810)	35,000 (10,668)	above 35,000 ft (10,668)	45,000 (13,715)	41,000 (12,500) certified	43,000 (13,106)
Take-off distance, ft (m)	971 (296) with 12° flaps, at MTOW	1,400 (427) at MTOW	1,885 (575) at MTOW	1,856 (566)	3,300 (1,006) required field length	4,290 (1,308) field length at MTOW	5,600 (1,707) at MTOW, sea level	5,950 (1,814) at MTOW, sea level
Landing distance, ft (m)	920 (281) at MLW	1,425 (435) at MLW	1,401 (427) at MLW	1,760 (537)	1,338 (408)	3,514 (1,072) at MLW	2,800 (853) at MLW	2,850 (869) at MLW
Range naut miles (miles) km	785 (904) 1,454 at 12,000 ft	1,348 (1,552) 2,496	1,400 (1,612) 2,592 at 29,000 ft	2,023 (2,329) 3,746	1,894 (2,180) 3,507 at 35,000 ft	1,693 (1,949) 3,135 at 45,000 ft	2,474 (2,850) 4,580	3,011 (3,468) 5,576 with 8 pax and NBAA IFR fuel reserve

Raytheon 390 Premier I

Role: Six-seat light business jet. Programme launched in 1995, with the first flight scheduled for 1997 and deliveries from 1998.
Flight control system: Fly-by-light, with fibre-optic signalling.
Construction materials: Composites fuselage.
Engines: 2 Williams Rolls-Royce FJ44-2 turbofans, allowing 461 kts (530 mph) 854 km/h cruise speed and 1,500 naut mile (1,725 mile) 2,775 km range.
Engine rating: Each 2,300 lbf (10.23 kN)
Flight avionics/instrumentation: Rockwell Collins Pro Line 21 suite, with flat-panel displays.

Shadin Company Ltd (USA)

Corporate address: 14280 23rd Avenue N, Minneapolis, MN 55447-4910.
Telephone: +1 612 544 6422

● Activities

● This new company is marketing a development of the Bücker Bü.181 Bestmann/Helwan Gomhouria as the S-10 Aeropony.

Sherpa Aircraft Manufacturing Inc (USA)

Corporate address: 17350 SW Shaw Street, Aloha, OR 97007.
Telephone: +1 503 649 5673
Information: Glen Gordon.

Sherpa Aircraft Sherpa (courtesy Sherpa)

● Activities

● This company has developed the Sherpa, which is currently undergoing FAA certification.

Sherpa Aircraft Sherpa

Role: Five-seat utility aircraft.
Construction materials: Tubular steel, fabric covered.
Engine: Textron Lycoming IO-720 piston engine.
Engine rating: 400 hp (298 kW).
Fuel system: 458 litres.
Flight avionics/instrumentation: Options will include 2-axis autopilot.

DETAILS FOR SHERPA.

Principal dimensions:
Wing span: 42 ft 7 ins (12.98 m)
Wings:
Area: 258 sq ft (23.97 m^2), or 300 sq ft (27.87 m^2) with flaps extended
Undercarriage:
Type: Fixed, with tailwheel. Optional large Tundra tyres, floats or skis
Weights:
Empty: 2,585 lb (1,172 kg)
Maximum take-off: 4,750 lb (2,154 kg)
Useful load: 2,165 lb (982 kg)
Performance:
Cruise speed: 139 kts (160) 296 km/h
Slow speed: about 39 kts (45 mph) 73 km/h
Take-off distance: 135 ft (41 m) at 3,000 lb AUW
Landing distance: 145 ft (44 m) at 3,000 lb AUW

Sierra Industries Inc (USA)

Corporate address: Garner Municipal Airport, PO Box 5184, Uvalde, TX 78802-5184.
Telephone: +1 210 278 4381
Facsimile: +1 210 278 7649

● Activities

● Offers a series of Cessna Citation enhancement products, as follows:
Eagle 400SP Modification is for Citation 500/501SPs and includes the Eagle modification, Longwing (if Model 500), installation of JT15D-4 engines, reinstallation of existing thrust reversers, new Silver de-ice boots, 12,500 lb (5,670 kg) MTOW, spar modification if due and exterior paint.
Eagle 400SP Modification (to existing Eagles) for Models 500/501SP, includes installation of JT15D-4 engines, reinstallation of existing thrust reversers, new Silver de-ice boots, 12,500 lb (5,670 kg) MTOW, spar modification if due and exterior paint.
Silver Edition Eagle Modification for Models 500/501SPs includes full Eagle modification, Longwing modification (if Model 500), single-pilot authorization, new wing leading-edge de-ice boots, 12,500 lb (5,670 kg) MTOW authority, exterior paint, wingtip recognition lights, spar modification if due, new heated leading-edge panels, and flap seals.
Longwing modification for Model 500 includes 38 ins (97 cm) wingspan increase, single-pilot authorization, new wing leading-edge de-ice boots, 12,500 lb (5,670 kg) MTOW authority, paint on affected areas and fuel to 3,807 lb (1,727 kg).
Single pilot authorization for the Model 500 for aircraft already equipped with the Eagle or Longwing modifications.
Wingtip mounted recognition lights for Models 500/501SP.
Spar modification to eliminate reoccuring inspections.
JT15D-1A or 1B engine updates to Models 500/501SP.
Radome modification to Models 500/501SP.
Landing gear warning horn cutout switch for Models 500/501.
Avionics master switch for Model 500.
Citation inlet and exhaust covers for Models 500/501SP.

Staudacher Aircraft Inc (USA)

Corporate address: 2648 East Beaver Road, Kawkawlin, MI 48631.

● Activities

● Custom builds aerobatic aircraft. Recent 300GS uses a 320 hp (238 kW) Textron Lycoming IO-540-KIE5D engine, has an empty weight of 1,280 lb (580 kg) and has a maximum speed of 178 kts (205 mph) 330 km/h.

Swearingen Aircraft Inc (USA)

Corporate address: 1234 99th Street, San Antonio, TX 78214.
Telephone: +1 210 921 0055
Facsimile: +1 210 921 0198
Founded: 1953.

● Activities

● Swearingen and the Sino Aerospace Investment Corporation of Taiwan have formed Sino-Swearingen Aircraft (SSAC) to certificate and manufacture the SJ30, with final assembly at Martinsburg, West Virginia.

Swearingen SJ30

First flight: 13 February 1991.
Certification: To be certified for day, night, VFR, IFR and flight into known icing conditions.
Role: Seven/eight-seat light business jet.
Details: For SJ30-1
Pressurization system: 12 psi cabin differential.
Wing control surfaces: Ailerons (trim tabs), Fowler slotted flaps and leading-edge slats. Airbrakes.
Tail control surfaces: Variable-incidence tailplane. Elevators and rudder (trim tab).
Flight control system: Manual, except for electric tailplane, flaps and trim tabs. Hydraulic slats and electro-hydraulic airbrakes.
Construction materials: Metal. Composites and bonding are not part of any load path.
Engines: 2 Williams Rolls-Royce FJ44 turbofans.
Engine rating: Each 1,900 lbf (8.45 kN).
Fuel system: 1,893 litres.
Electrical system: 2 engine-driven generators and a 38 amp-hour battery. Inverters for AC supply. Second battery for emergency power.

Sino-Swearingen SJ30-1

Radar: RDS-81 colour weather radar.
Flight avionics/instrumentation: AlliedSignal Bendix/King Gold Crown III suite, including 2 tube EFS 40 and KFC-400 digital autopilot/flight director.

Details for SJ30-1.

Principal dimensions:
Wing span: 36 ft 4 ins (11.07 m)
Maximum length: 42 ft 7 ins (12.98 m)
Maximum height: 13 ft 11 ins (4.24 m)
Cabin:
Length: 11 ft 10 ins (3.61 m)
Width: 4 ft 8 ins (1.42 m)
Height: 4 ft 3.5 ins (1.3 m)
Wings:
Area: 165 sq ft (15.33 m^2)
Weights:
Empty: 6,210 lb (2,817 kg)
Maximum take-off: 10,400 lb (4,717 kg)
Maximum landing: 9,880 lb (4,481 lb
Performance:
Maximum operating Mach number (Mmo): Mach 0.82
Maximum cruise speed: Mach 0.77 or 445 kts (512 mph) 824 km/h
Stall speed: 81 kts (93 mph) 150 km/h at MLW
Take-off balanced field length: 3,330 ft (1,015 m)
FAA landing distance: 2,500 ft (762 m)
Maximum climb rate: 3,920 ft (1,195 m) per minute
Operating altitude: 43,000 ft (13,106 m)
Range: 2,076 naut miles (2,389 miles) 3,845 km at Mach 0.72, NBAA VFR

Options include 4 tube EFIS, GPS, step-up WX radar, etc
Aircraft variants:
SJ30-1, as detailed.
SJ30-2 is a new version with 2,300 lbf (10.23 kN) FJ44-2C engines, offering Mach 0.83 high cruise speed

Thurston Aeromarine Corporation (USA)

Corporate address: 24 Ledge Road, Cumberland Foreside, ME 04110.
Telephone: +1 207 829 6108
Information: David Thurston.

● Activities

● Deliveries started in 1995 of the metal/composites Teal III two-seat amphibian, powered by the 180 hp (134 kW) Textron Lycoming O-360-A1F6D piston engine. The 4-seat Seafire with a 250 hp (186 kW) engine is expected to enter production in 1996, and in the following year the eight-seat Seamaster could become available, powered by 2 Allison 250-B17F turboprop engines.

Tradewind Turbines Corporation (USA)

Corporate address: PO Box 31930, Amarillo, TX 79120-1930.
Telephone: +1 806 376 5203
Facsimile: +1 806 376 9725
Information: David M. Welch.

● Activities

● This company produces the Prop-Jet Bonanza, by modifying the Beech A36 Bonanza to have a 450 shp (335.6 kW) Allison 250-B17F/2 turboprop engine. Since October 1989, Tradewind Turbines has converted over 20 aircraft, including those prior to March 1992 that were given 420 shp (313 kW) engines. The current version has a maximum and cruise speed at 15,000 ft (4,575 m) of 220 kts (253 mph) 407 km/h.

Tradewind Turbines Prop-Jet Bonanza

Vazar Aerospace (USA)

Corporate address: 3025 Eldridge Avenue, Bellingham, WA 98225.
Telephone: +1 206 671 7817
Facsimile: +1 206 671 7820
Information: S. Vaughan.

● Activities

● This company produces the Dash 3 Turbine Otter, by replacing the original P&W R1340 radial engine of the de Havilland Canada Otter with a 750 shp (559 kW) Pratt & Whitney Canada PT6A-135 turboprop driving a Hartzell 3-blade propeller. Other changes affect the fuel system, heater, battery source (2 x 24 volt lead-acid batteries), electrical system, and engine instruments, with some modification also to the airframe. Cruise speed is thereby raised from 105 kts (121 mph) 195 km/h to 144 kts (166 mph) 267 km/h at 10,000 ft (3,050 m).

Vazar Aerospace Dash 3 Turbine Otter (courtesy Vazar)

Washington-Aeroprogress Inc (USA)

Corporate address: 8535 Perimeter Road South, Boeing Field, Seattle, Washington 98108.
Telephone: +1 206 762 0190
Facsimile: +1 206 768 0661
Founded: 1994.
Information: Vadim Karpan (International Sales Manager).

● Activities

● Adapts, promotes and markets Russian-developed aircraft to Western markets (developed by Aeroprogress, Roks-Aero, Khrunichev Space Centre Aviation Division and others – see Aeroprogress). Currently offers the T-411 Wolverine, which it manufactures in kit form but plans to certificate. Wolverine is based on the Aeroprogress T-411 but is modified for the North American market by using US-made materials, avionics, wheels, brakes, etc. Also purchases Western materials used by the Russian companies detailed above.
● Working on certification in the USA of the Aeroprogress T-101 (as the Westernized T-201). The Corshun and Grif are also to be assembled, either at Seattle or Vancouver in Canada. Actively seeking international partners.

Wipaire Inc (USA)

Corporate address: 8520 River Road, Inver Grove Heights, MN 55076.
Telephone: +1 612 451 1205
Facsimile: +1 612 451 1786

● Activities

● In addition to installing its range of Wipline floats suited to aircraft from the Cessna 185 to the de Havilland Canada Twin Otter, the company also undertakes airframe modifications, conversions from piston to turboprop power, engine/propeller updates, interior conversions, cabin extensions, STOL kits and more.

Aviotechnica Ltd (Bulgaria/Russia)

Corporate address: PO Box 423, Trakia, Plovdiv 4000, Bulgaria.
Telephone: +359 32 83 10 40
Founded: 1991, as a 49% Bulgarian and 51% Russian venture. Russian shareholders are Interavia and Lukhovitsy Machine Building Plant.

● Activities

● Produces the SL-90 Leshii, a two/three-seat lightplane powered by a 110 hp (82 kW) M-3 piston engine (or other engine, including Textron Lycoming) and first flown in 1990. A smaller span and more powerful development is the Interavia I-1L (which see).

Baoshan Iron & Steel Complex and Venga Aerospace Systems Inc (China/Canada)

Corporate address: *Baoshan:* Baosteel Administrative Building, Shanghai 201900, China. *Venga:* PO Box 665, 61 Cameron, Hudson, Quebec J0P 1H0, Canada
Telephone: *Baoshan:* +86 21 664859. *Venga:* +1 514 458 5659

● Activities

● On 23 February 1994, Baoshan and Venga signed a Memorandum of Understanding to support a joint venture programme intended to develop, build and market the Timberwolf composites turboprop sporting aircraft, and a composites jet trainer based on the existing Venga TG-10 Bushfire programme, with a factory in Shanghai. Can-Aero International Ltd (*telephone* +1 905 573 3031) had been assigned to undertake marketing.

Hyundai-Yak Aerospace Co Ltd (South Korea/Russia)

Corporate address: #140-2, Gye-Dong, Chongro-Ku, Seoul, South Korea.
Telephone: +82 2 746 7371
Facsimile: +82 2 746 7398

● Activities

● To develop, market and sell a range of small and medium size aircraft. Initial products are the Yak-54, Yak-58 and Yak-112 (see Yakovlev in the Russian section).

Myasishchev/National Aeronautical Laboratory (Russia/India)

Myasishchev M-102 Duet mock-up (Piotr Butowski)

Corporate addresses: See Combat section for all company details.

Myasishchev M-102 Duet/National Aeronautical Laboratory Saras

First flight: 1996 (Myasishchev prototype).
Role: Multi-purpose, as a regional transport, for business or cargo, or configured for patrol, ambulance, aerial photography, environmental monitoring and other specialized missions.

★Aims

★For hot-and-high operations (quoted as airfields at 6,560 ft, 2,000 m and up to 45° C), with concrete or unpaved runways.

▲ Development

▲ Development programme is funded by the Russian Government/Myasishchev (initially a reported $13.3 million), the Indian Government/NAL (initially a reported $15.6 million, including a substantial share from the Department of Science and Technology), and with perhaps a further $31 million required from private investors.

▲1993. Agreement signed between Myasishchev and NAL for joint development of a regional transport, following earlier individual programmes of similar type.

Sales/users: 3 prototypes, 2 built in Russia and 1 in India. Production lines at Smolensk in Russia and Nasik in India (from 1997-98).
Crew/passengers: 1 or 2 pilots. Maximum of 14 passengers in the main cabin, at 31 ins (79 cm) seat pitch. Business version could carry 9 passengers, with additional amenities including tables, galley, etc. 6 litters and 2 seated attendants in ambulance layout.
Baggage capacity: 38.85 cu ft (1.1 m^3).
Pressurization system: 8 psi cabin differential.
Wing control surfaces: Ailerons and flaps.
Tail control surfaces: Elevators (starboard tab) and rudder (with tab).
Flight control system: Mechanical/manual but with electric flaps and tabs.
Construction materials: Aluminium alloy, except for composites ailerons, flaps, wingtips, wing-root fairings, tail unit, nosecone and engine cowls. Fuselage and undercarriage built in Russia, wings and tail unit in India. 20,000 flying hours or 20 years life.
Engines: Optional OMSK TVD-20M or Pratt & Whitney Canada PT6A-65P engines, with 7 ft 1 ins (2.16 m) Hartzell 6-blade handed constant-speed pusher propellers.
Engine rating: Each in the 1,380 shp (1,029 kW) range.
Fuel system: 1,500 litres in wing tanks. System by Secondo Mona of Italy.
Electrical system: 28 volt DC supply, with 2 x 9kW starter-generators and emergency 40 amp-hour ni-cd. 115 volt/400Hz AC supply, with 2 inverters.
Hydraulic system: 3,000 psi.
De-icing system: Electrical.
Radar: Weather type.
Flight avionics/instrumentation: IFR, using an integrated digital system. Includes EFIS displays, flight control computer, and GPS navigation. Conventional back-up instruments. The expected supplier of avionics will be either AlliedSignal Bendix/King or Rockwell Collins.
Aircraft variants:
Duet is the Russian name, Saras the Indian.

Principal dimensions:
Wing span: 48 ft 3 ins (14.7 m)
Maximum length: 46 ft 11 ins (14.3 m)
Maximum height: 16 ft 9 ins (5.10 m)
Cabin:
Length: 21 ft 4 ins (6.5 m)
Width: 5 ft 10 ins (1.77 m)
Height: 5 ft 7 ins (1.7 m)
Volume: 565 cu ft (16 m^3)
Undercarriage:
Type: Retractable, with twin steerable nosewheels
Weights:
Maximum take-off: 12,566 lb (5,700 kg)
Maximum landing: 12,566 lb (5,700 kg)
Payload: 2,866 lb (1,300 kg)
Performance:
Cruise speed: 297 kts (342 mph) 550 km/h
Stall speed: 92 kts (106 mph) 170 km/h
Take-off distance: 1,247 ft (380 m), ISA
Landing distance: 1,673 ft (510 m), ISA
Take-off distance over a 50 ft (ISM) obstacle: 1,969 ft (600 m), ISA
Landing distance over a 50 ft (ISM) obstacle: 1,969 ft (600 m), ISA
Maximum climb rate: 2,660 ft (810 m) per minute.
Operating ceiling: 29,525 ft (9,000 m)
Range: typically 1,080 naut miles (1,243 miles) 2,000 km, with reserve

Recreational Aircraft

This section details aircraft available for amateur construction and ultralights/microlights. A number of the aircraft are also available in ready-assembled form from the manufacturer and can be used for training, patrol, agricultural and other professional roles. Aircraft originally produced as "homebuilts" but now certificated can be found in the General Aviation section. Helicopters and autogyros available for amateur construction are detailed in the main Helicopters section. Addresses and Telephone/Facsimile numbers are given for the first entry of each company.

Australia

AAW Aerolite 1+1

Address: Australian Aviation Works, 5 Utrecht Court, Donvale, W. Australia 3111.
Telephone: +61 3 8423132
Facsimile: +61 3 8418177
Type: Single-seat, high-wing cabin monoplane, with fixed nosewheel undercarriage.
Construction: Wood, metal tube and fabric.
Wing span: 30 ft (9.14 m)
Length: 17 ft 6 ins (5.33 m)
Empty weight: 350 lb (159 kg)
Gross weight: 680 lb (308 kg)
Recommended engine: 49.6 hp (37 kW) Rotax 503, 64.4 hp (48 kW) Rotax 532, 65 hp (48.5 kW) Rotax 582 or 73.8 hp (55 kW) Rotax 618.
Maximum speed: 87 kts (100 mph) 161 km/h
Cruise speed: 65 kts (75 mph) 121 km/h
Range: 208 naut miles (240 miles) 386 km
Take-off distance: 300 ft (92 m)
Climb rate: 900 ft (274 m) per minute
Availability: Plans and kits.
Comments: Microlight or homebuilt, with option of a second seat.

AAW Aeromax 1700 Sport

Type: Single-seat, open cockpit, strut-braced parasol monoplane, with fixed tail-dragger undercarriage.
Construction: Wood, metal tube and fabric.
Wing span: 30 ft (9.14 m)
Length: 17 ft 6 ins (5.33 m)
Empty weight: 350 lb (159 kg)
Gross weight: 680 lb (308 kg)
Recommended engine: 50-100hp (37.3-74.6 kW)
Maximum speed: 87 kts (100 mph) 161 km/h
Cruise speed: 65 kts (75 mph) 121 km/h
Stall speed: 34 kts (39 mph) 63 km/h
Range: 208 naut miles (240 miles) 386 km/h
Take-off distance: 300 ft (92 m)
Climb rate: 900 ft (274 m) per minute
Availability: Plans.
Comments: Modified Australian version of the PFA Luton LA.4 Minor (see UK).

AAW Karatoo C Model

Type: Side-by-side 2-seat high-wing cabin monoplane, with fixed tail-dragger undercarriage.
Construction: Wood, metal tube and fabric.
Wing span: 33 ft (10.06 m)
Length: 20 ft 6 ins (6.25 m)
Empty weight: 700 lb (318 kg)
Gross weight: 1,300 lb (590 kg)
Recommended engine: 105 hp (78.3 kW)
Maximum speed: 96 kts (110 mph) 177 km/h
Cruise speed: 83 kts (95 mph) 153 km/h
Range: 434 naut miles (500 miles) 804 km
Take-off distance: 300 ft (92 m)
Climb rate: 1,000 ft (305 m) per minute
Availability: Plans.
Comments: Australian version of Jesse Anglin's Karatoo. Partial kits for wings and ailerons available.

AAW Spacewalker I

Type: Single-seat, open cockpit low-wing monoplane, with fixed tail-dragger undercarriage.
Construction: Wood, tube and fabric.
Wing span: 26 ft (7.92 m)
Length: 17 ft 3 ins (5.26 m)
Empty weight: 540 lb (245 kg)
Gross weight: 850 lb (386 kg)
Recommended engine: 65 hp (48.5 kW) Teledyne Continental.
Maximum speed: 109 kts (125 mph) 201 km/h
Cruise speed: 97 kts (112 mph) 180 km/h
Stall speed: 33 kts (38 mph) 61 km/h
Range: 260 naut miles (300 miles) 482 km
Take-off distance: 300 ft (92 m)
Climb rate: 850 ft (259 m) per minute
Availability: Plans.
Comments: Jesse Anglin's design from the USA. Also available is the tandem-seat Spacewalker II. See also Warner Revolution I and II under USA.

AAW Spacewalker I (Geoffrey P Jones)

Australian Light Wing PR

Address: Howard Hughes Engineering Pty Ltd, PO Box 89, Ballina, NSW 2478.
Telephone: +61 66 86 8658
Facsimile: +61 66 86 8343
Type: Tandem 2-seat, braced high-wing cabin monoplane, with a fixed tail-dragger or float undercarriage.
Construction: Steel tube, alloy and fabric.
Wing span: 31 ft 10 ins (9.7 m)
Length: 19 ft 1 ins (5.82 m)
Empty weight: 476 lb (216 kg), 584 lb (265 kg) with floats.
Gross weight: 881 lb (400 kg), 992 lb (450 kg) with floats.
Recommended engine: 65 hp (48.5 kW) Rotax 532.
Maximum speed: 80 kts (92 mph) 148 km/h
Cruise speed: 65 kts (75 mph) 120 km/h
Stall speed: 29 kts (34 mph) 54 km/h
Range: 149 naut miles (172 miles) 276 km
Take-off distance over a 50 ft obstacle: 1,000 ft (305 m)
Climb rate: 900 ft (274 m) per minute
Availability: Kits and factory complete.
Comments: Prototype Light Wing first flew in June 1986.

Australian Light Wing PR on floats (Geoffrey P Jones)

Australian Light Wing GR-912

Type: Side-by-side 2-seat, high-wing cabin monoplane, with fixed tail-dragger undercarriage.
Construction: Steel tube, alloy and fabric.
Wing span: 31 ft 2 ins (9.5 m)
Length: 18 ft 4 ins (5.6 m)
Empty weight: 551 lb (250 kg)
Gross weight: 992 lb (450 kg)
Recommended engine: 77.8 hp (58 kW) Rotax 912
Maximum speed: 105 kts (121 mph) 194 km/h
Cruise speed: 70 kts (81 mph) 130 km/h
Stall speed: 38 kts (44 mph) 71 km/h
Range: 300 naut miles (345 miles) 555 km
Take-off distance: 328 ft (100 m)
Climb rate: 750 ft (230 m) per minute
Availability: Kits and factory complete.
Comments: Optional flaps. A further and similar version, the GA-55, is also produced.

Corby/CSN Starlet CJ-1

Address: John C. Corby, 34 Coronet Court, North Rocks, Sydney, NSW 2151 (also USA: CSN, 510 NW 46th Terrace, Plantation, FL 33317).
Telephone: USA: +1 305 581 8835
Type: Single-seat low-wing monoplane, with fixed tail-dragger undercarriage.
Construction: Wood.
Wing span: 18 ft 6 ins (5.64 m)
Length: 14 ft 9 ins (4.5 m)
Empty weight: 450 lb (204 kg)
Gross weight: 710 lb (322 kg)
Recommended engine: 60 hp (44.7 kW) Volkswagen.
Maximum speed: 139 kts (160 mph) 257 km/h
Cruise speed: 113 kts (130 mph) 209 km/h
Stall speed: 43 kts (49 mph) 79 km/h
Range: 231 naut miles (266 miles) 428 km
Take-off distance: 350 ft (107 m)
Climb rate: 1,050 ft (320 m) per minute
Availability: Plans.
Comments: Designed by Australian John Corby. Plans also available in the USA.

Corby Starlet built by Ray Downs in California (Geoffrey P Jones)

Kimberley Sky-Rider

Address: Gareth J. Kimberley, 211 Fowler Road, Illawong, NSW 2234.
Telephone: +61 2 543 2348
Type: Single-seat, high-wing, open microlight, with a fixed tail-dragger undercarriage.
Construction: Steel and alloy tube, and fabric.
Wing span: 32 ft 4 ins (9.86 m)
Length: 19 ft 6 ins (5.94 m)
Empty weight: 195 lb (88.5 kg)
Gross weight: 400 lb (181 kg)
Recommended engine: 20 hp (15 kW) Fuji-Robin or Rotax of equivalent size.
Maximum speed: 43 kts (50 mph) 80 km/h

Cruise speed: 39 kts (45 mph) 72 km/h
Stall speed: 19 kts (21 mph) 34 km/h
Range: 70 naut miles (80 miles) 129 km
Take-off distance: 246 ft (75 m)
Climb rate: 300 ft (92 m) per minute
Availability: Plans.
Comments: Designed in 1977. 194 sets of plans sold in 20 countries worldwide by early 1995.

Kimberley Sky-Rider homebuilt microlight.

Moyes Dragonfly

Address: Moyes Microlites Pty Ltd, 2-4 Taylor St, Waverley, NSW 2024 (also 1805 Dean Still Rd, Davenport, FL 33837, USA).
Telephone: +61 2 387 5114 (USA: +1 813 424 0070)
Facsimile: +61 2 387 4472 (USA: +1 813 424 0070)
Type: Tandem 2-seat, high-wing microlight, with fixed tail-dragger undercarriage.
Construction: Alloy tube and fabric.
Wing span: 34 ft 8 ins (10.57 m)
Length: 20 ft (6.1 m)
Empty weight: 330 lb (150 kg)
Gross weight: 800 lb (363 kg)
Recommended engine: 65 hp (48.5 kW) Rotax 582
Maximum speed: 65 kts (75 mph) 121 km/h
Cruise speed: 52 kts (60 mph) 97 km/h
Range: 87 naut miles (100 miles) 161 km
Climb rate: 1,400 ft (427 m) per minute
Availability: Kits.
Comments: Built to tow unpowered microlights and hang-gliders. Also available in the USA.

Skyfox Aviation CA-22 Skyfox

Address: Skyfox Aviation, PO Box 910, Caloundra, Queensland 4551.
Telephone: +61 74 91 5355
Facsimile: +61 74 91 8237
Type: 2-seat, high-wing cabin microlight, with fixed tail-dragger undercarriage.
Construction: Steel, alloy and fabric.
Wing span: 31 ft 3 ins (9.53 m)
Length: 18 ft 5 ins (5.61 m)
Empty weight: 640 lb (290 kg)
Gross weight: 992 lb (450 kg)
Recommended engine: 77.8 hp (58 kW) Rotax 912
Maximum speed: 95 kts (109 mph) 176 km/h
Cruise speed: 85 kts (98 mph) 157 km/h
Stall speed: 40 kts (46 mph) 74 km/h
Range: 288 naut miles (331 miles) 533 km
Take-off distance: 400 ft (122 m)
Climb rate: 940 ft (287 m) per minute
Availability: Factory complete aircraft.
Comments: Microlight version of the CA-25, which is certificated under JAR/VLA.

Skyfox Aviation CA-22 Skyfox microlight

Slepcev Storch

Address: Nestor Slepcev, VRBAS, Beechwood, NSW 2446.
Facsimile: +61 65 85 6458
Type: Tandem 2-seat, high-wing cabin monoplane, with fixed tail-dragger undercarriage.
Construction: Metal, steel tube and fabric.
Wing span: 33 ft 8 ins (10.26 m)
Length: 31 ft 4 ins (10.39 m)
Empty weight: 618 lb (280 kg)
Gross weight: 996 lb (452 kg)
Recommended engine: 75 hp (56 kW) Rotax 618
Maximum speed: 68 kts (78 mph) 126 km/h
Cruise speed: 56 kts (65 mph) 105 km/h
Stall speed: 16 kts (18 mph) 29 km/h
Range: 87 naut miles (100 miles) 161 km
Climb rate: 1,200 ft (366 m) per minute
Availability: Kits.
Comments: 75% replica of the WWII Fieseler Storch.

Thruster Aircraft T.300

Address: Thruster Aircraft (Australia) Pty Ltd, PO Box 172, Ingleburn, NSW 2565
Type: Side-by-side 2-seat, open high-wing microlight, with fixed tail-dragger undercarriage.
Construction: Alloy, tube and fabric.
Wing span: 31 ft 6 ins (9.6 m)
Length: 18 ft (5.49 m)
Empty weight: 396 lb (180 kg)
Gross weight: 516 lb (234 kg)
Maximum speed: 70 kts (81 mph) 130 km/h
Cruise speed: 59 kts (68 mph) 109 km/h
Range: 196 naut miles (226 miles) 363 km
Availability: Kits or factory complete aircraft.
Comments: T.500 version with enclosed rear fuselage also available, both a development of the Thruster Gemini.

Thruster T.300/TST Mk.1 built in UK (Geoffrey P Jones)

Canada

Aces High Cuby 1

Address: Aces High Light Aircraft Ltd, RR #1, London, Ontario N6A 4B5.
Telephone: +1 519 652 3020
Facsimile: +1 519 652 3020
Type: Single-seat high-wing cabin microlight, with fixed tail-dragger undercarriage.
Construction: Steel tube and fabric.
Wing span: 33 ft 6 ins (10.21 m)
Length: 18 ft 3 ins (5.56 m)
Empty weight: 250 lb (113 kg)
Gross weight: 850 lb (386 kg)
Recommended engine: 26 hp (19 kW) Rotax 277 (50 hp, 37.3 kW Rotax 503 for larger 2-seat Cuby II).
Maximum speed: 83 kts (95 mph) 153 km/h
Cruise speed: 48 kts (55 mph) 89 km/h
Stall speed: 25 kts (28 mph) 45 km/h
Range: 174 naut miles (200 miles) 322 km
Take-off distance: 150 ft (46 m)
Climb rate: 700 ft (213 m) per minute
Availability: Kits.
Comments: Several engine options for the single-seat Cuby 1. Side-by-side 2-seat Cuby II is similar, and both models have float and ski undercarriage options.

Aces High Cuby II two-seater (Geoffrey P Jones)

ASAP Chinook Plus 2

Address: 905 Kal Lake Road, Vernon, British Columbia V1T 6V4.
Telephone: +1 604 549 1102
Facsimile: +1 604 549 7111
Type: Tandem 2-seat high-wing microlight, with fixed tail-dragger undercarriage.
Construction: Steel tube and fabric.
Wing span: 32 ft (9.75 m)
Length: 17 ft 8 ins (5.38 m)
Empty weight: 380 lb (172 kg)
Gross weight: 900 lb (408 kg)
Recommended engine: 65 hp (48.5 kW) Rotax 582
Maximum speed: 83 kts (95 mph) 153 km/h
Cruise speed: 72 kts (83 mph) 134 km/h
Range: 259 naut miles (298 miles) 479 km
Take-off distance: 250 ft (77 m)
Climb rate: 1,200 ft (366 m) per minute
Availability: Kits.
Comments: Smaller Rotax 503 engine optional. Over 650 estimated to have been completed and flown.

ASAP Beaver RX-550

Type: Tandem 2-seat, open high-wing microlight, with fixed nosewheel undercarriage.
Construction: Steel tube and fabric.
Wing span: 35 ft (10.67 m)
Length: 21 ft (6.4 m)
Empty weight: 450 lb (204 kg)
Gross weight: 1,110 lb (503 lb)
Recommended engine: 65 hp (48.5 kW) Rotax 582
Maximum speed: 70 kts (80 mph) 129 km/h
Cruise speed: 56 kts (65 mph) 105 km/h
Stall speed: 26 kts (29 mph) 47 km/h
Range: 104 naut miles (120 miles) 193 km
Take-off distance: 400 ft (122 m)
Climb rate: 800 ft (244 m) per minute
Availability: Kits.
Comments: Variant of the Spectrum Beaver RX-550, a 2-seat training version of the Beaver RX-28. some 2,000 completed and flown.

ASAP Beaver RX-550 two-seat microlight (Geoffrey P Jones)

Avionnerie Cyclone

Address: Avionnerie Lac St-Jean Inc, 373 de la Friche, Dolbeau, Quebec G8L 2T3.
Telephone: +1 418 276 7903
Facsimile: +1 418 276 9079
Type: 4-seat, high-wing cabin monoplane based on a Cessna 185, with options for nosewheel, tail-dragger or float undercarriage.

Construction: Metal.
Wing span: 38 ft (11.58 m)
Length: 26 ft (7.92 m)
Empty weight: 1,700 lb (771 kg)
Gross weight: 3,000 lb (1,361 kg)
Recommended engine: 230 hp (171.5 kW) Teledyne Continental
Maximum speed: 148 kts (170 mph) 274 km/h
Cruise speed: 137 kts (158 mph) 254 km/h
Stall speed: 51 kts (58 mph) 94 km/h
Range: 756 naut miles (870 miles) 1,400 km
Take-off distance: 750 ft (229 m)
Climb rate: 1,300 ft (396 m) per minute
Availability: Partial kits.
Comments: Cessna-type fuselage with redesigned wings. Engine options from 145-350 hp (108-261 kW).

Circa Reproductions Nieuport 11

Address: Circa Reproductions, Graham Lee, General Delivery, Lamont, Alberta T0B 2R0.
Telephone: +1 403 895 2975
Type: Single-seat biplane replica, with fixed tail-dragger undercarriage.
Construction: Metal, steel tube and fabric.
Wing span: 21 ft 6 ins (6.55 m)
Length: 16 ft 4 ins (4.98 m)
Empty weight: 350 lb (159 kg)
Gross weight: 675 lb (306 kg)
Recommended engine: 46 hp (34.3 kW) Rotax
Maximum speed: 82 kts (94 mph) 151 km/h
Cruise speed: 70 kts (80 mph) 129 km/h
Stall speed: 23 kts (26 mph) 42 km/h
Range: 173 naut miles (200 miles) 322 km
Take-off distance: 125 ft (38 m)
Climb rate: 850 ft (259 m) per minute
Availability: Plans and kits.
Comments: 87% scale replica. Lighter microlight version for 40 hp (30 kW) Rotax available (Nieuport 11UL). Also 87% scale Nieuport 12.

Nieuport replica with a Rotax 503 engine, built by Randal Berardi (Geoffrey P Jones)

Back Forty Developments Tundra

Address: Back Forty Developments Ltd, RR 4, Campbellford, Ontario K0L 1L0.
Telephone: +1 705 653 2219
Type: Tandem 2-seat, open high-wing microlight, with fixed tail-dragger undercarriage.
Construction: Metal, steel tube and fabric.
Wing span: 32 ft (9.75 m)
Length: 19 ft (5.79 m)
Empty weight: 385 lb (175 kg)
Gross weight: 850 lb (386 kg)
Recommended engine: 64 hp (47.7 kW) Rotax 532
Maximum speed: 83 kts (95 mph) 153 km/h
Cruise speed: 61 kts (70 mph) 113 km/h
Range: 121 naut miles (140 miles) 225 km
Take-off distance: 200 ft (61 m)
Climb rate: 800 ft (244 m) per minute
Availability: Kits.

Custom Flight North Star

Address: Custom Flight Components Ltd, RR1, Perkinsfield, Ontario L0L 2J0
Telephone: +1 705 526 9626
Facsimile: +1 705 526 2529
Type: Tandem 2-seat, high-wing cabin monoplane based on the Piper Super Cub, with fixed tail-dragger or float undercarriage.
Construction: Metal, steel tube and fabric.
Wing span: 36 ft 4 ins (11.07 m)
Length: 22 ft 6 ins (6.86 m)
Empty weight: 1,170 lb (531 kg)
Gross weight: 2,200 lb (998 kg)
Recommended engine: 150 hp (112 kW) Textron Lycoming
Maximum speed: 122 kts (140 mph) 225 km/h
Cruise speed: 100 kts (115 mph) 185 km/h
Range: 521 naut miles (600 miles) 965 km
Take-off distance: 280 ft (86 m)
Climb rate: 1,100 ft (335 m) per minute
Availability: Kits.
Comments: Piper PA-18 Super Cub lookalike, built with modern materials.

Custom Flight North Star on floats (Geoffrey P Jones)

Elmwood Aviation Christavia Mk.1

Address: R.B. Mason, RR #4, Elmwood Drive, Belleville, Ontario K8N 4Z4.
Telephone: +1 613 967 1853
Type: Tandem 2-seat, strut-braced high wing cabin monoplane, with fixed tail-dragger undercarriage.
Construction: Alloy tube and wood.
Wing span: 32 ft 6 ins (9.9 m)
Length: 20 ft 8 ins (6.3 m)
Empty weight: 745 lb (338 kg)
Gross weight: 1,300 lb (590 kg)
Recommended engine: 65 hp (48.5 kW) Teledyne Continental A65
Maximum speed: 104 kts (120 mph) 193 km/h
Cruise speed: 87 kts (100 mph) 161 km/h
Stall speed: 31 kts (35 mph) 57 km/h
Range: 304 naut miles (350 miles) 563 km
Take-off distance: 350 ft (107 m)
Climb rate: 850 ft (259 m) per minute
Availability: Plans and kits.
Comments: First flown 3 October 1981. Over 130 known to be flying. Several built for work in the mission field.

Elmwood Aviation Christavia Mk.4

Type: 4-seat strut-braced highwing cabin monoplane, with fixed tail-dragger undercarriage.
Construction: Alloy tube and wood.
Wing span: 35 ft 6 ins (10.82 m)
Length: 23 ft (7 m)
Empty weight: 1,100 lb (500 kg)
Gross weight: 2,150 lb (975 kg)
Recommended engine: 150 hp (112 kW) Textron Lycoming O-320
Maximum speed: 111 kts (128 mph) 206 km/h
Cruise speed: 102 kts (118 mph) 190 km/h
Stall speed: 34 kts (39 mph) 63 km/h
Range: 347 naut miles (400 miles) 643 km
Take-off distance: 450 ft (137 m)
Climb rate: 800 ft (244 m) per minute
Availability: Plans and kits.
Comments: 4-seat development of Christavia Mk.1. First flown 3 January 1986. For missionary work.

Elmwood Christavia Mk.4 prototype

Falconar/Mignet HM.293

Address: Falconar Air Engineering, 11343 104 Street, Edmonton, Albert T5G 2K7.
Telephone: +1 403 479 3515
Facsimile: +1 403 447 4634
Type: Single-seat, tandem-wing version of the Pou-du-Ciel, with fixed tail-dragger undercarriage.
Construction: Wood.
Wing span: 20 ft (6.1 m)
Length: 13 ft (3.96 m)
Empty weight: 350 lb (159 kg)
Gross weight: 600 lb (272 kg)
Recommended engine: 60 hp (44.7 kW) Volkswagen
Maximum speed: 96 kts (110 mph) 177 km/h
Cruise speed: 78 kts (90 mph) 145 km/h
Stall speed: Does not stall
Range: 260 naut miles (300 miles) 483 km
Take-off distance: 150 ft (46 m)
Climb rate: 1,400 ft (427 m) per minute
Availability: Plans and some components.
Comments: Larger version of the HM.290 single-seater. Plans for both redrawn from originals by Henri Mignet in the 1940s. Folding wings.

Falconar/Mignet HM.360

Type: Single-seat, tandem-wing homebuilt version of the Pou-du-Ciel, with fixed tail-dragger undercarriage.
Construction: Wood.
Wing span: 21 ft (6.4 m)
Length: 13 ft (3.96 m)
Empty weight: 390 lb (177 kg)
Gross weight: 700 lb (318 kg)
Recommended engine: 100 hp (74.6 kW) Teledyne Continental
Maximum speed: 109 kts (125 mph) 200 km/h
Cruise speed: 83 kts (95 mph) 153 km/h
Stall speed: Does not stall
Range: 286 naut miles (330 miles) 530 km
Take-off distance: 130 ft (40 m)
Climb rate: 1,500 ft (457 m) per minute
Availability: Plans and some components.
Comments: Largest single-seat version of the Pou-du-Ciel. 2-seat development is the HM.380.

Falconar/Mignet HM.360 with a McCulloch engine and enclosed cockpit, built by Jack McWhorter in Florida (Geoffrey P Jones)

Falconar Cubmajor

Type: Tandem 2-seat, high-wing cabin monoplane, with fixed tail-dragger undercarriage.

Construction: Wood.
Wing span: 35 ft (10.67 m)
Length: 23 ft 10 ins (7.26 m)
Empty weight: 900 lb (408 kg)
Gross weight: 1,400 lb (635 kg)
Take-off distance: 250 ft (77 m)
Recommended engine: Teledyne Continental C-85
Maximum speed: 100 kts (116 mph) 187 km/h
Cruise speed: 91 kts (105 mph) 169 km/h
Stall speed: 44 kts (50 mph) 81 km/h
Range: 239 naut miles (275 miles) 442 km
Climb rate: 860 ft (262 m) per minute
Availability: Plans and kit components.
Comments: Version of the Luton L.5 Major that dates from 1939. Several built in Britain from Phoenix-supplied plans.

Falconar Jodel F.9

Type: Single-seat, open cockpit, low-wing monoplane, with fixed tail-dragger undercarriage.
Construction: Wood.
Wing span: 23 ft (7.01 m)
Length: 17 ft 11 ins (5.46 m)
Empty weight: 402 lb (182 kg)
Gross weight: 660 lb (300 kg)
Recommended engine: 60 hp (44.7 kW) Volkswagen
Maximum speed: 122 kts (140 mph) 225 km/h
Cruise speed: 87 kts (100 mph) 161 km/h
Stall speed: 26 kts (30 mph) 49 km/h
Range: 365 naut miles (420 miles) 676 km
Take-off distance: 328 ft (100 m)
Climb rate: 600 ft (183 m) per minute
Availability: Plans and kit components.
Comments: Canadian version of the classic Jodel D.9 (see France). A more streamlined and larger-engined version is the Falconar F.10.

Falconar Jodel F.9 built by George Pearce at Trochu, Alberta

Falconar F.12A Cruiser

Type: Side-by-side 2-seat (optional third child seat), low-wing cabin monoplane, with fixed tail-dragger undercarriage.
Construction: Wood.
Wing span: 28 ft (8.53 m)
Length: 22 ft 6 ins (6.86 m)
Empty weight: 898 lb (407 kg)
Gross weight: 1,800 lb (816 kg)
Recommended engine: 150 hp (112 kW) Textron Lycoming O-320
Maximum speed: 161 kts (185 mph) 298 km/h
Cruise speed: 139 kts (160 mph) 257 km/h
Stall speed: 37 kts (42 mph) 68 km/h
Range: 486 naut miles (560 miles) 900 km
Take-off distance: 300 ft (92 m)
Climb rate: 1,100 ft (335 m) per minute
Availability: Plans and some components.
Comments: Design based on the Jodel D.11 (see France) and developed in Canada as the Falconar F.11.

Falconar ARV-1K Golden Hawk

Type: Tandem 2-seat, pusher-engined canard type, with fixed nosewheel undercarriage.
Construction: Composites and metal.
Wing span: 34 ft (10.36 m)
Length: 14 ft (4.27 m)
Empty weight: 500 lb (227 kg)
Gross weight: 990 lb (449 kg)
Recommended engine: 55 hp (41 kW) Hirth 2703
Maximum speed: 113 kts (130 mph) 209 km/h
Cruise speed: 87 kts (100 mph) 101 km/h
Range: 217 naut miles (250 miles) 402 km
Take-off distance: 250 ft (77 m)
Climb rate: 800 ft (244 m) per minute
Availability: Kits.
Comments: Complete kit including engine, propeller and instruments.

ADAM (Falconar) RA.14 Loisirs/Maranda

Address: Designed by Roger Adam in France but marketed by Falconar Air Engineering.
Type: 2/3-seat, high-wing cabin monoplane, with fixed tail-dragger undercarriage.
Construction: Wood.
Wing span: 31 ft 9 ins (9.68 m)
Length: 22 ft (6.71 m)
Empty weight: 1,100 lb (500 kg)
Gross weight: 1,850 lb (840 kg)
Recommended engine: 150 hp (112 kW) Textron Lycoming O-320
Maximum speed: 113 kts (130 mph) 200 km/h
Cruise speed: 100 kts (115 mph) 185 km/h
Stall speed: 39 kts (45 mph) 73 km/h
Range: 347 naut miles (400 miles) 643 km
Climb rate: 1,300 ft (395 m) per minute
Availability: Kits and plans.

Adam RA-14 Loisirs (Leisure) (Geoffrey P Jones)

Murphy Aircraft Maverick

Address: Murphy Aircraft Mfg. Ltd, Unit 1, 8155 Aitken Road, Chilliwack, British Columbia V2R 4H5.
Telephone: +1 604 792 5855
Facsimile: +1 604 792 7006
Type: Side-by-side 2-seat, high-wing cabin microlight/homebuilt, with fixed tail-dragger undercarriage.
Construction: Metal.
Wing span: 29 ft 6 ins (8.99 m) (standard wing)
Length: 20 ft 8 ins (6.3 m)
Empty weight: 395 lb (179 kg)
Gross weight: 950 lb (431 kg)

Murphy Maverick in un-painted form at Sun 'n Fun 1993 (Geoffrey P Jones)

Recommended engine: 53 hp (39.5 kW) Rotax 503 (as for details) or 65 hp (48.5 kW) Rotax 582
Maximum speed: 104 kts (120 mph) 193 km/h
Cruise speed: 70 kts (80 mph) 129 km/h
Stall speed: 28 kts (32 mph) 52 km/h
Range: 191 naut miles (220 miles) 354 km
Take-off distance: 150 ft (46 m)
Climb rate: over 600 ft (183 m) per minute
Availability: Kits.
Comments: Introduced in 1993. Microlight category in some countries.

Murphy Aircraft Rebel

Type: 3-seat, high-wing STOL cabin monoplane, with fixed tail-dragger, float or ski undercarriage.
Construction: Semi-monocoque alloy.
Wing span: 30 ft (9.14 m)
Length: 21 ft 6 ins (6.55 m)
Empty weight: 650-900 lb (295-408 kg)
Gross weight: 1,057-1,650 lb (479-748 kg)
Recommended engine: 80 hp (59.7 kW) Rotax 912 or other engines up to a 160 hp (119.3 kW) Textron Lycoming (as for details)
Maximum speed: 131 kts (151 mph) 243 km/h
Cruise speed: 104 kts (120 mph) 193 km/h
Stall speed: 35 kts (40 mph) 65 km/h
Range: 691 naut miles (795 miles) 1,280 km
Take-off distance: 300 ft (92 m)
Climb rate: 1,200 ft (366 m) per minute
Availability: Kits.
Comments: First flown in 1990. Rugged STOL bush aeroplane with engine options.New Murphy Aircraft SR 2500 Super Rebel has a 150-210 hp (112-157 kW) engine.

Murphy Rebel (Geoffrey P Jones)

Murphy Aircraft Renegade II

Type: Tandem 2-seat, open cockpit microlight biplane, with fixed tail-dragger undercarriage.
Construction: Sheet alloy, tubing, composites and wood.
Wing span: 21 ft 4 ins (6.5 m)
Length: 18 ft 6 ins (5.64 m)
Empty weight: 375-425 lb (170-193 kg)
Gross weight: 850 lb (385 kg)
Recommended engine: 53 hp (39.5 kW) Rotax 503
Maximum speed: 104 kts (120 mph) 193 km/h
Cruise speed: 61 kts (70 mph) 113 km/h
Stall speed: 32 kts (36 mph) 58 km/h
Range: 213 naut miles (245 miles) 394 km
Take-off distance: 150 ft (46 m) (solo)
Climb rate: 700 ft (213 m) per minute
Availability: Kits and plans.
Comments: First flown in May 1985. Lighter version of the Renegade Spirit, complying with Canadian microlight regulations.

Murphy Aircraft Renegade Spirit

Type: Tandem 2-seat, open cockpit biplane, with fixed tail-dragger undercarriage.
Construction: Sheet alloy, tubing, composites and wood.
Wing span: 21 ft 4 ins (6.5 m)
Length: 18 ft 6 ins (5.64 m)
Empty weight: 460 lb (209 kg)
Gross weight: 950 lb (431 kg)
Recommended engine: 80 hp (59.7 kW) Rotax 912 (as for details given) or 64 hp (47.7 kW) Rotax 582

Maximum speed: 104 kts (120 mph) 193 km/h
Cruise speed: 74 kts (85 mph) 137 km/h
Stall speed: 32 kts (36 mph) 58 km/h
Range: 206 naut miles (237 miles) 381 km
Climb rate: 900 ft (274 m) per minute
Availability: Kits and plans.
Comments: First flown 6 May 1987. Darryl Murphy's most successful homebuilt to date, with an estimated 500 completed.

Murphy Renegade Spirit with radial-type cowling (Geoffrey P Jones)

Norman Aviation Nordic II

Address: Norman Aviation, CP 61032, Levis, Quebec G6V 8X3.
Telephone: +1 418 833 4337
Facsimile: +1 418 833 7057
Type: Side-by-side 2-seat high-wing cabin monoplane, with fixed tail-dragger undercarriage.
Construction: Alloy tube and fabric.
Wing span: 33 ft 8 ins (10.26 m)
Length: 19 ft (5.79 m)
Empty weight: 600 lb (272 kg)
Gross weight: 1,058 lb (480 kg)
Recommended engine: 71 hp (53 kW) Subaru EA 81
Maximum speed: 113 kts (130 mph) 209 km/h
Cruise speed: 70 kts (80 mph) 129 km/h
Stall speed: 31 kts (35 mph) 57 km/h
Range: 347 naut miles (400 miles) 643 km
Take-off distance: 150 ft (46 m)
Climb rate: 600 ft (183 m) per minute
Availability: Kits and plans.
Comments: Very similar to the Nordic VI, the ready-to-fly version. Over 400 Nordic aircraft now flying, including some in Bolivia and Australia.

Norman Aviation Nordic II

Norman Aviation Nordic VII

Type: Single-seat, high-wing cabin monoplane, with fixed tail-dragger undercarriage.
Construction: Alloy tube and fabric.
Wing span: 30 ft (9.14 m)
Length: 16 ft 6 ins (5.03 m)
Empty weight: 270 lb (122 kg)
Gross weight: 800 lb (363 kg)
Recommended engine: 65 hp (48.5 kW) Rotax 582
Maximum speed: 91 kts (105 mph) 169 km/h
Cruise speed: 78 kts (90 mph) 145 km/h
Range: 260 naut miles (300 miles) 482 km
Climb rate: 1,600 ft (487 m) per minute
Availability: Kits.
Comments: Norman Aviation's first single-seater.

Norman Aviation Karatoo J-6

Type: Side-by-side 2-seat, high-wing cabin monoplane, with fixed tail-dragger undercarriage or floats.
Construction: Wood and alloy tube.
Wing span: 33 ft 8 ins (10.26 m)
Length: 19 ft (5.79 m)
Empty weight: 620 lb (281 kg)
Gross weight: 1,058 lb (480 kg)
Recommended engine: 71 or 90 hp (53 or 67 kW) Subaru
Maximum speed: 113 kts (130 mph) 210 km/h
Cruise speed: 78 kts (90 mph) 145 km/h
Stall speed: 33 kts (38 mph) 61 km/h
Range: 347 naut miles (400 miles) 643 km
Take-off distance: 200 ft (61 m)
Climb rate: 500 ft (152 m) per minute
Availability: Kits.
Comments: Modified version of Jesse Anglin's Karatoo.

Norman Aviation Karatoo J-6.

Paxman's Aerocraft Viper

Address: Paxman's Northern Lite, PO Box 1155, Glenwood, Alberta T0K 2R0.
Telephone: +1 403 626 3490
Facsimile: +1 403 626 3490
Type: Side-by-side 2-seat low-wing cabin monoplane, with fixed tail-dragger undercarriage.
Construction: Wood and fabric.
Wing span: 27 ft (8.23 m)
Length: 20 ft 6 ins (6.25 m)
Empty weight: 585 lb (265 kg)
Gross weight: 1,050 lb (476 kg)
Recommended engine: 100 hp (74.6 kW) Suzuki-Turbo
Maximum speed: 109 kts (125 mph) 200 km/h
Cruise speed: 96 kts (110 mph) 177 km/h
Stall speed: 42 kts (48 mph) 78 km/h
Range: 508 naut miles (585 miles) 941 km
Take-off distance: 300 ft (92 m)
Climb rate: 1,500 ft (457 m) per minute
Availability: Plans and kits.
Comments: Prototype first flew in 1994.

Pegazaire-100 STOL

Address: Pegase Aero Enr., 437 rte 309 Nord, Mont-St-Michel, Quebec J0W 1P0.
Telephone: +1 819 586 2350
Facsimile: +1 819 586 2350
Type: Side-by-side 2-seat, STOL high-wing cabin monoplane, with fixed tail-dragger undercarriage.
Construction: Steel tube, aluminium and fabric.
Wing span: 29 ft 6 ins (9 m)
Length: 22 ft 6 ins (6.86 m)
Empty weight: 795 lb (360 kg)
Gross weight: 1,350 lb (612 kg)
Recommended engine: 100 hp (74.6 kW) CAM-100 (also Rotax 912 or Teledyne Continental A65)
Maximum speed: 106 kts (122 mph) 196 km/h
Cruise speed: 91 kts (105 mph) 169 km/h
Stall speed: 16 kts (18 mph) 29 km/h
Range: 382 naut miles (440 miles) 708 km
Climb rate: 1,350 ft (411 m) per minute
Availability: Kits and plans.
Comments: Wide cabin and leading-edge slats. Different engine/airframe combinations meet both Canadian ultralight and homebuilt requirements.

Pegazair-100 STOL with CAM-100 engine (Geoffrey P Jones)

Replica Plans SE.5A

Address: Replica Plans, PO Box 346, Yarrow, British Colombia V0X 2A0.
Telephone: +1 604 823 6428
Facsimile: +1 604 532 9822
Type: 85% replica World War 1 biplane, with fixed tail-dragger undercarriage.
Construction: Wood.
Wing span: 23 ft 4 ins (7.11 m)
Length: 18 ft 2 ins (5.54 m)
Empty weight: 750 lb (340 kg)
Gross weight: 1,150 lb (522 kg)
Recommended engine: Teledyne Continental C85
Maximum speed: 96 kts (110 mph) 177 km/h
Cruise speed: 74 kts (85 mph) 137 km/h
Stall speed: 31 kts (35 mph) 57 km/h
Range: 217 naut miles (250 miles) 402 km
Take-off distance: 400 ft (122 m)
Climb rate: 600 ft (183 m) per minute
Availability: Plans.
Comments: First flown in the 1970s. Also suitable for engines of 65-115 hp (48.5-85.75 kW).

Replica Plans SE.5A built by Ken Garrett in the UK (Geoffrey P Jones)

Streamline Welding 10-200 Ultimate Competitor

Address: Streamline Welding, 296 Homewood Avenue, Hamilton, Ontario L8P 2M9.
Telephone: +1 905 526 9990
Facsimile: +1 519 823 1834
Type: Single-seat competition/aerobatic biplane, with fixed tail-dragger undercarriage.
Construction: Steel tube, alloy, wood and fabric.
Wing span: 16 ft (4.88 m)
Length: 17 ft 4 ins (5.28 m)
Empty weight: 925 lb (420 kg)
Gross weight: 1,350 lb (612 kg)
Recommended engine: Textron Lycoming IO-360
Maximum speed: 191 kts (220 mph) 354 km/h
Cruise speed: 148 kts (170 mph) 273 km/h
Stall speed: 52 kts (60 mph) 97 km/h
Range: 434 naut miles (500 miles) 804 km
Take-off distance: 450 ft (137 m)
Climb rate: 2,000 ft (610 m) per minute
Availability: Kits.
Comments: Basic Ultimate 10 Dash 100 first flew on 6 October 1985 with a 100 hp (74.6 kW) Teledyne Continental. Other version is the 10-300 Ultimate Winner for engines of up to 350 hp (261 kW).

10-200 Streamline Welding 10-200 Ultimate Competitor (Geoffrey P Jones)

Streamline Welding 20-300 Ultimate Companion

Type: Tandem 2-seat competition/aerobatic biplane, with fixed tail-dragger undercarriage.
Construction: Steel tube, alloy, wood and fabric.
Wing span: 19 ft 6 ins (5.94 m)
Length: 21 ft (6.4 m)
Empty weight: 1,200 lb (544 kg)
Gross weight: 2,000 lb (907 kg)
Recommended engine: 300 or 350 hp (224 or 261 kW) Textron Lycoming
Maximum speed: 217 kts (250 mph) 402 km/h
Cruise speed: 165 kts (190 mph) 306 km/h
Stall speed: 46 kts (53 mph) 86 km/h
Range: 434 naut miles (500 miles) 804 km
Take-off distance: 600 ft (183 m)
Climb rate: 3,000 ft (914 m) per minute
Availability: Kits.
Comments: Available as 20-300E (exhibition) and 20-300T (Trainer).

Ultravia Pelican Club S

Address: Ultravia Aero International, 300-D Airport Road, Mascouche, Quebec J7K 3C1.
Telephone: +1 514 953 1491
Facsimile: +1 514 966 6299
Type: Side-by-side 2-seat, high-wing cabin monoplane, with fixed tail-dragger or nosewheel undercarriage.
Construction: Composites and sheet alloy.
Wing span: 34 ft 5 ins (10.49 m)
Length: 19 ft 6 ins (5.94 m)
Empty weight: 500 lb (227 kg)
Gross weight: 1,000 lb (453 kg)
Recommended engine: 64.4 hp (48 kW) Rotax 582 for the S and 77.8 hp (58 kW) Rotax 912 for the GS model
Maximum speed: 100 kts (115 mph) 185 km/h
Cruise speed: 87 kts (100 mph) 161 km/h
Stall speed: 31 kts (35 mph) 57 km/h
Range: 434 naut miles (500 miles) 804 km
Take-off distance: 300 ft (92 m)
Climb rate: 800 ft (244 m) per minute
Availability: Kits.
Comments: First flown in May 1982. Lightest of 4 versions now available, the S as a microlight and GS as a homebuilt.

Ultravia Pelican Club PL

Type: Side-by-side 2-seat, high-wing cabin monoplane, with fixed nosewheel undercarriage. Tail-dragger and float options also available.
Construction: Composites and sheet alloy.
Details: Principally for PL-912.
Wing span: 29 ft 6 ins (8.99 m)
Length: 19 ft 6 ins (5.94 m)
Empty weight: 700 lb (318 kg)
Gross weight: 1,250 lb (567 kg)
Recommended engine: 77.8 hp (58 kW) Rotax 912 for PL-912 model, and 100 hp (74.6 kW) Rotax 914 for new PL-914
Maximum speed: 117 kts (135 mph) 217 km/h
Cruise speed: 104 kts (120 mph) 193 km/h
Stall speed: 38 kts (43 mph) 70 km/h
Range: 260 naut miles (300 miles) 482 km
Take-off distance: 450 ft (137 m)
Climb rate: 950 ft (290 m) per minute
Availability: Kits.
Comments: Nosewheel undercarriage version suitable for pilot training. New PL-914 model with a 100 hp (74.6 kW) Rotax 914 is faster but heavier, and options include a floatplane version.

Ultravia Pelican Club PL-912 with fixed nosewheel undercarriage (Geoffrey P Jones)

Western Aircraft PGK-1 Hirondelle

Address: Western Aircraft Supplies, 623 Markerville Rd North East, Calgary, Alberta T2E 5X1.
Telephone: +1 403 275 3513
Facsimile: +1 403 276 3087
Type: Side-by-side 2-seat, low-wing cabin monoplane, with fixed tail-dragger undercarriage.
Construction: Wood, glassfibre and fabric.
Wing span: 26 ft (7.92 m)
Length: 20 ft 7 ins (6.27 m)
Empty weight: 944 lb (428 kg)
Gross weight: 1,475 lb (700 kg)
Recommended engine: 115 hp (85.75 kW) Textron Lycoming
Maximum speed: 123 kts (142 mph) 229 km/h
Cruise speed: 117 kts (135 mph) 217 km/h
Stall speed: 52 kts (60 mph) 97 km/h
Range: 521 naut miles (600 miles) 965 km
Take-off distance: 750 ft (230 m)
Climb rate: 1,000 ft (305 m) per minute
Availability: Plans and some components.
Comments: First flown on 27 June 1976. Examples mainly in North America but first European example was flown in France in 1994.

Zenair Zenith CH-200

Address: Zenair Ltd, Huronia Airport, Midland, Ontario L4R 4K8 (or USA: Zenith Aircraft Co., Mexico Memorial Airport, Mexico, MO 65265-0650).
Telephone: +1 705 526 2871 (USA: +1 314 581 9000)
Facsimile: +1 705 526 8022 (USA: +1 314 581 0011)
Type: Side-by-side 2-seat, low-wing cabin monoplane, with fixed nosewheel or tail-dragger undercarriage.
Construction: Metal, with some glassfibre.
Wing span: 23 ft (7 m)
Length: 20 ft 6 ins (6.25 m)
Empty weight: 970 lb (440 kg)
Gross weight: 1,500 lb (680 kg)
Recommended engine: 100-150 hp (74.6-112 kW) Textron Lycoming
Maximum speed: 145 kts (167 mph) 269 km/h
Cruise speed: 132 kts (152 mph) 245 km/h
Stall speed: 47 kts (54 mph) 87 km/h
Range: 347 naut miles (400 miles) 643 km
Take-off distance: 600 ft (183 m)
Climb rate: 1,700 ft (518 m) per minute
Availability: Plans.
Comments: Prototype designed by Chris Heintz and first flown on 22 March 1970. Hundreds flying world-wide. Other variants include the CH-250 long-range version, the single-seat CH-100, and the Acro CH-150 and CH-180 aerobatic versions.

Zenair Zenith CH-200 (Geoffrey P Jones)

Zenair Zenith CH-300 (Tri-Z)

Type: 3/4-seat low-wing cabin monoplane, with fixed nosewheel undercarriage.
Construction: Metal and some glassfibre.
Wing span: 26 ft 7 ins (8.1 m)
Length: 22 ft 6 ins (6.86 m)
Empty weight: 1,140 lb (517 kg)
Gross weight: 1,850 lb (859 kg)
Recommended engine: 125-180 hp (93.2-134 kW) Textron Lycoming
Maximum speed: 130 kts (150 mph) 241 km/h
Cruise speed: 109 kts (125 mph) 201 km/h
Stall speed: 45 kts (51 mph) 82 km/h
Range: 521 naut miles (600 miles) 965 km
Take-off distance: 650 ft (198 m)
Climb rate: 800 ft (244 m) per minute
Availability: Plans and custom ordered kits. Commercially built version is the Zenair CH-2000.

Zenith Aircraft CH-601 Zodiac and Super Zodiac

Address: See Zenair
Type: Side-by-side 2-seat, low-wing cabin monoplane, with fixed nosewheel or tail-dragger undercarriage.
Construction: Metal.
Wing span: 23 ft (7 m) for HDS version
Length: 19 ft (5.79 m)
Empty weight: 570 lb (259 kg) for HDS
Gross weight: 1,200 lb (544 kg) for HDS
Recommended engine: 80 hp (59.7 kW) Rotax 912
Maximum speed: 135 kts (155 mph) 249 km/h
Cruise speed: 113 kts (130 mph) 209 km/h
Stall speed: 51 kts (58 mph) 94 km/h
Range: 347 naut miles (400 miles) 643 km
Take-off distance: 550 ft (168 m)
Climb rate: 1,030 ft (314 m) per minute
Availability: Plans or kits.
Comments: Original CH-601 was first flown in June 1984, and the latest CH-601 HDS flew August 1991.

CH-601 HDS Super Zodiac with nosewheel undercarriage and CH-601 HDS tail-dragger behind.

Zenith Aircraft Zenair CH-701 STOL

Type: Side-by-side 2-seat, high-wing utility cabin monoplane, with fixed nosewheel, tail-dragger, float or ski undercarriage.
Construction: Metal.
Wing span: 27 ft (8.23 m)
Length: 20 ft (6.1 m)
Empty weight: 460 lb (209 kg)
Gross weight: over 960 lb (435 kg)
Recommended engine: 65 or 80 hp (48.5 or 59.7 kW) Rotax (details for 80 hp).
Maximum speed: 83 kts (95 mph) 153 km/h
Cruise speed: 74 kts (85 mph) 137 km/h
Stall speed: 25 kts (28 mph) 45 km/h
Range: 234 naut miles (270 miles) 434 km
Take-off distance: 75-115 ft (23-35 m)
Climb rate: 1,400 ft (427 m) per minute
Availability: Kits and plans.
Comments: Prototype first flew in 1986. Over 400 flying in 36 countries. Type certificated in Israel and Mexico.

Zenair CH-701 STOL homebuilt utility in bare metal finish (Geoffrey P Jones)

Chile

ENAER Ñamcu

Address: Empresa Naçional de Aeronáutica, Avda J.M.Carrera, 11087 Paradero 36½, Santiago.
Telephone: +56 2 5282823, 5282735 and 5282599.
Facsimile: +56 2 5282699
Type: Side-by-side 2-seat, low-wing cabin monoplane, with fixed nosewheel undercarriage.
Availability: Kits.
Comments: Ñamcu (Eaglet) was originally designed for commercial production as an inexpensive club trainer (see General Aviation section). Now also available in kit form.

China

Beijing University Mifeng-11

Address: Beijing University of Aeronautics and Astronautics, PO Box 85, 37 Xue Yuan Road, Haidian District, Beijing 100083.
Type: 2/3-seat, high-wing utility microlight, with fixed nosewheel undercarriage.
Construction: Steel tube, metal and composites.
Wing span: 28 ft 6 ins (8.69 m)
Length: 19 ft 10 ins (6.05 m)
Empty weight: 397 lb (180 kg)
Recommended engine: 62 hp (46.2 kW) Rotax 532
Maximum speed: 90 kts (103 mph) 166 km/h
Range: 474 naut miles (546 miles) 878 km with auxiliary tank.
Availability: Not known.
Comments: First flown in May 1991. The Mifeng-11 (Bee-11) is the latest of a succession of Mifeng microlights by Beijing University that commenced in the early 1980s.

HAMC HFY-5

Address: PO Box 201, 15 Youxie Street, Pingfang, Harbin 150066.
Telephone: +86 451 8602122
Facsimile: +86 451 8602061
Type: 2-seat "propulsive wing" microlight, with fixed nosewheel undercarriage.
Construction: Composites.
Wing span: 32 ft 10 ins (10 m)
Gross weight: 750 lb (340 kg)
Recommended engine: 109 lbf (0.49 kN)
Maximum speed: 70 kts (81 mph) 130 km/h
Take-off distance: 131 ft (40 m)
Availability: Kits or assembled.
Comments: Prototype first flew on 8 October 1994. Claimed to be versatile, collapsible and low cost, suited to aerial observation, express delivery and aerial advertising.

Colombia

Agrocopteros MXP-740

Address: Agrocopteros Ltda, Apartado Aereo 1789, Calle 20 N8A-18, Cali.
Telephone: +57 3 825110 and 833519
Facsimile: +57 3 842002
Type: Side-by-side 2-seat, high-wing cabin monoplane, with fixed nosewheel undercarriage.
Construction: Metal.
Wing span: 29 ft 6 ins (9 m)
Length: 21 ft 3 ins (6.5 m)
Empty weight: 616 lb (280 kg)
Gross weight: 1,200 lb (544 kg)
Recommended engine: 80 hp (59.7 kW) Rotax 912
Maximum speed: 83 kts (95 mph) 153 km/h
Cruise speed: 74 kts (85 mph) 137 km/h
Stall speed: 31 kts (35 mph) 57 km/h
Range: 369 naut miles (425 miles) 684 km
Take-off distance: 100 ft (31 m)
Climb rate: 1,000 ft (305 m) per minute
Availability: Kits and complete aircraft.
Comments: Version of the Zenair CH-701 STOL. Also available is the MXP-640 (a version of the Zenair CH-601 Zodiac). Also produced in Slovakia as the Ekoflug MXP-740 (Address: Ekoflug sro, P O Box G-19, 043 49 Kosice 1).

Czech Republic

Inteco VM-23 Variant

Address: Inteco, Velkomoravska 1469, Stare Mesto, CS-686 03 Uherske Hrasdiste.
Type: 4-seat, high-wing cabin monoplane, with fixed tail-dragger undercarriage.
Construction: Steel tube, metal and fabric.
Wing span: 35 ft 5 ins (10.8 m)
Length: 24 ft 5 ins (7.45 m)
Empty weight: 992 lb (450 kg)
Gross weight: 1,984 lb (900 kg)
Recommended engine: 140 hp (104.4 kW) LOM M.332
Maximum speed: 108 kts (124 mph) 200 km/h
Cruise speed: 86 kts (99 mph) 160 km/h
Range: 400 naut miles (460 miles) 740 km
Take-off distance: 590 ft (180 m)
Climb rate: 728 ft (222 m) per minute
Availability: Prototype only to date – possible commercial production.
Comments: By glider designer and manufacturer Jiri Valny. Inteco hopes to obtain FAR 23 certification.

Interwork TL-32 Typhoon

Address: Inter Work, Civil Aviation Services Division of Colsys Ltd, Bustehradska 109, 272 03 Kladno.
Telephone: +42 312 2757
Type: Side-by-side 2-seat, high-wing monoplane microlight/homebuilt, with fixed nosewheel undercarriage.
Construction: Steel tube and composites.
Wing span: 35 ft 1 ins (10.7 m)
Length: 19 ft 4 ins (5.9 m)
Empty weight: 430 lb (195 kg)
Gross weight: 882 lb (400 kg)
Recommended engine: 40 hp (30 kW) Rotax 447
Maximum speed: 59 kts (68 mph) 110 km/h
Cruise speed: 49 kts (56 mph) 90 km/h
Stall speed: 25 kts (28 mph) 45 km/h
Range: 189 naut miles (217 miles) 350 km
Take-off distance: 164 ft (50 m)
Climb rate: 400 ft (122 m) per minute (gross)
Availability: Kits or assembled.
Comments: Good visibility and 3-axis control.

Interwork TL-32 Typhoon

Interwork TL-132 Condor

Type: Side-by-side 2-seat, high-wing monoplane microlight/homebuilt, with fixed tail-dragger undercarriage.
Construction: Steel tube and fabric.
Wing span: 34 ft 9 ins (10.6 m)
Length: 16 ft 11 ins (5.16 m)
Recommended engine: 45.6 hp (34 kW) Rotax 503 for microlight version (option of Rotax 912 or Hirth F30).
Maximum speed: 97 kts (112 mph) 180 km/h
Cruise speed: 73 kts (84 mph) 135 km/h
Stall speed: 30 kts (34 mph) 55 km/h
Climb rate: 395 ft (120 m) per minute
Availability: Kits or assembled.
Comments: Stylish aircraft that can be built as a microlight or experimental homebuilt.

Jora

Address: JORA spol. sro, Vraclav 565 42.
Telephone & Facsimile: +42 468 8224
Type: Side-by-side 2-seat, semi-enclosed high-wing microlight/homebuilt, with fixed nosewheel undercarriage.
Construction: Composites and wood.
Wing span: 35 ft 5 ins (10.8 m)
Length: 24 ft 7 ins (7.5 m)
Empty weight: 441 lb (200 kg)
Gross weight: 926 lb (420 kg)
Recommended engine: 50 hp (37 kW) Rotax 503
Maximum speed: 89 kts (103 mph) 165 km/h
Cruise speed: 43-84 kts (50-96 mph) 80-155 km/h
Stall speed: 25 kts (28 mph) 45 km/h
Range: 216 naut miles (248 miles) 400 km
Take-off distance: 164 ft (50 m)
Climb rate: 590 ft (180 m) per minute
Availability: Kits.
Comments: Said to have good low-speed handling.

Jora microlight

Letov LK-2 Sluka

Address: Letov a.s., Aeronautical Products Division, Beranovych 65, 199 02 Prague 9.
Telephone: +42 2 858 75 78
Facsimile: +42 2 859 05 53
Type: Single-seat, high-wing monoplane microlight, with fixed nosewheel undercarriage.
Construction: Aluminium and steel tube, composites and fabric.
Wing span: 30 ft 2 ins (9.2 m)
Length: 16 ft 10 ins (5.12 m)
Empty weight: 331 lb (150 kg)
Gross weight: 551 lb (250 kg)
Recommended engine: 41.6 hp (31 kW) Rotax 447
Maximum speed: 54 kts (62 mph) 100 km/h
Cruise speed: 38 kts (43 mph) 70 km/h
Stall speed: 24 kts (27 mph) 43 km/h
Range: 129 naut miles (149 miles) 240 km
Take-off distance: 164 ft (50 m)
Climb rate: 690 ft (210 m) per minute
Availability: Kits and assembled.
Comments: Prototype first flew in February 1991.

Letov LK-3 Nova

Type: Side-by-side 2-seat, semi-enclosed high-wing microlight/homebuilt, with fixed nosewheel undercarriage.
Construction: Alloy and steel tube, composites and fabric.
Wing span: 34 ft 5 ins (10.5 m)
Length: 19 ft 3 ins (5.9 m)
Empty weight: 441 lb (200 kg)
Gross weight: 860 lb (390 kg)
Recommended engine: 64.4 hp (48 kW) Rotax 582
Maximum speed: 59 kts (68 mph) 110 km/h
Cruise speed: 43 kts (50 mph) 80 km/h
Stall speed: 26 kts (30 mph) 48 km/h
Range: 94 naut miles (108 miles) 175 km
Take-off distance: 197 ft (60 m)
Climb rate: 787 ft (240 m) per minute
Availability: Kits and assembled.
Comments: Prototype first flew in 1993.

Letov LK-3 Nova registered in the UK (Geoffrey P Jones)

Motorlet Praha M-7

Address: J. Vycital, Motorlet Praha, clen Aeroklubu Havlickuv Brod, Soucasne.
Type: Side-by-side 2- seat, high-wing microlight/homebuilt, with fixed nosewheel undercarriage.
Construction: Metal and composites.
Recommended engine: Walter M-202
Comments: First flown in September 1994. No other information available.

OK Fly Lesus

Address: OK Fly sro., PO Box 60, 261 05 Pribram 5
Telephone & Facsimile: +42 42 306 27 229
Type: Side-by-side 2-seat, high-wing monoplane, with fixed nosewheel undercarriage.
Construction: Composites.
Wing span: 32 ft 2 ins (9.8 m)
Length: 20 ft 4 ins (6.2 m)
Empty weight: 617 lb (280 kg)
Gross weight: 992 lb (450 kg)
Recommended engine: 50 hp (37 kW) Rotax 503 (optionally other Rotax and Hirth engines).
Maximum speed: 108 kts (124 mph) 200 km/h
Cruise speed: 86 kts (99 mph) 160 km/h
Stall speed: 34 kts (39 mph) 63 km/h
Range: 324 naut miles (373 miles) 600 km
Take-off distance: 590 ft (180 m)
Climb rate: 590 ft (180 m) per minute
Availability: Commercial production planned.
Comments: OK Fly has specialized in hang-glider skin and wind-surf sail production for 15 years. First flight of the prototype Lesus was expected in 1995.

France

Air Creation SX GT582 ES

Address: Air Creation, Aerodrome de Lanas, 07200 Aubenas.
Type: Tandem 2-seat microlight with flex-rogallo wing and trike.
Construction: Alloy tube and fabric.
Wing span: 32 ft 10 ins (10 m)
Length: 9 ft 10 ins (3 m)
Empty weight: 344 lb (156 kg)
Recommended engine: 53 hp (39.5 kW) Rotax 582 EC
Maximum speed: 65 kts (75 mph) 120 km/h
Range: 162 naut miles (186 miles) 300 km
Availability: Commercially built or as kits.
Comments: One of a range of single and tandem-seat Air Creation microlights, some with optional fuselage pods. Over 1,000 of all types sold.

Air Creation flexwing microlights at Granville, France (Geoffrey P Jones)

Alpha 2000

Address: ICM, Immeuble le Centaure, Route de Carnon, avenue de la Mer, 34970 Lattes.
Telephone: +33 67 20 00 05
Facsimile: +33 67 20 00 46
Type: Single-seat homebuilt with canard, with fixed nosewheel undercarriage.
Construction: Composites.
Wing span: 15 ft 10.5 ins (4.84 m)
Length: 13 ft 7 ins (4.15 m)
Empty weight: 187 lb (85 kg)
Gross weight: 397 lb (180 kg)
Recommended engines: 2 x 25 hp (18.6 kW) Limbach 277
Maximum speed: 162 kts (186 mph) 300 km/h
Availability: Plans may be available.
Comments: Completed in 1993 by a team led by Philippe Monestier and Georges Bosc, after over 5,000 man hours of work.

Alpha 2000 single-seat canard monoplane (Geoffrey P Jones)

Ameur Aviation Balbuzard II

Address: Ameur Aviation Technologie, Lieu dit de Cavone, 20129 Bastelicaccia.
Telephone: +33 95 20 03 54 or 95 20 03 16
Facsimile: +33 95 20 05 80
Type: Side-by-side 2-seat cabin monoplane, with pusher engine, V-tail and retractable nosewheel undercarriage.
Construction: Composites.
Wing span: 23 ft (7.01 m)
Length: 17 ft 7 ins (5.35 m)
Empty weight: 507 lb (230 kg)
Gross weight: 1,069 lb (485 kg)
Recommended engine: 100 hp (74.5 kW) Rotax 914
Maximum speed: 228 kts (263 mph) 423 km/h
Cruise speed: 173 kts (199 mph) 320 km/h
Stall speed: 54 kts (62 mph) 99 km/h
Range: 228 naut miles (262 miles) 423 km
Climb rate: 1,378 ft (420 m) per minute
Availability: Kits.
Comments: Prototype was expected to fly in 1995. Rotax 912 powered version was the Balbuzard I.

Ameur Aviation Balbuzard I displayed part-completed at Moulins in July 1994 (Geoffrey P Jones)

BILOUIS 01

Address: Louis Pena, Les Hts de Saubagnacq, 6 imp Grand Piton, 40100 Dax
Type: Tandem 2-seat low-wing monoplane, with retractable tail-dragger undercarriage.
Construction: Steel tube, wood and fabric.
Wing span: 27 ft 7 ins (8.4 m)
Length: 21 ft 2 ins (6.45 m)
Empty weight: 1,279 lb (580 kg)
Gross weight: 1,896 lb (860 kg)
Recommended engine: 200 hp (149 kW) Textron Lycoming
Cruise speed: 135 kts (155 mph) 250 km/h
Climb rate: 2,360 ft (720 m) per minute
Availability: Plans.
Comments: Two-seat development of the Capena, stressed to +8, -6g and first flown at Dax in June 1991.

CAPENA 01

Address: Louis Pena, Les Hts de Saubagnacq, 6 imp Grand Piton, 40100 Dax.
Type: Single-seat, aerobatic monoplane, with fixed tail-dragger undercarriage.
Construction: Wood.
Wing span: 26 ft 6 ins (8.08 m)
Length: 17 ft 8 ins (5.39 m)
Empty weight: 970 lb (440 kg)
Gross weight: 1,213 lb (550 kg)
Recommended engine: 200 hp (149 kW) Textron Lycoming
Cruise speed: 175 kts (202 mph) 325 km/h
Climb rate: 3,150 ft (960 m) per minute
Availability: Plans.
Comments: Designed by French aerobatic pilot Louis Pena. First flown in 1985.

Capena 01 prototype (Geoffrey P Jones)

CATA LMK.1 Oryx

Address: Construction Aeronautique de Technologie Avancee, Aerodrome de Muret-Lherm, 31600 Muret.
Telephone: +33 62 23 03 90
Type: Side-by-side 2-seat, low-wing monoplane, with retractable nosewheel undercarriage.
Construction: Composites.
Wing span: 25 ft 10 ins (7.87 m)
Length: 20 ft 11 ins (6.37 m)
Empty weight: 1,058 lb (480 kg)
Gross weight: 1,764 lb (800 kg)
Recommended engine: 160 hp (119 kW) Textron Lycoming O-320-B1E
Maximum speed: 200 kts (230 mph) 370 km/h
Cruise speed: 160 kts (184 mph) 296 km/h
Stall speed: 60 kts (69 mph) 110 km/h
Range: 918 naut miles (1,056 miles) 1,700 km
Take-off distance: 1,476 ft (450 m)
Climb rate: 1,358 ft (414 m) per minute
Availability: Complete kits less engine, instruments and radio (FF 185,000).
Comments: Prototype first flew on 18 September 1994.

CATA LMK.1 Oryx built by Yvon Laignel and Gilbert Matheley

Buse'Air 150

Address: Chantier Djicat, ZA Leucate Village, 11370 Leucate.
Telephone: +33 68 40 01 41
Facsimile: +33 68 40 09 96
Type: Side-by-side 2-seat high-wing cabin monoplane, with fixed nosewheel undercarriage.
Construction: Composites.
Wing span: 34 ft (10.36 m)
Length: 21 ft (6.4 m)
Empty weight: 485 lb (220 kg)
Gross weight: 992 lb (450 kg)
Recommended engine: 64.4 hp (48 kW) Rotax 582 (also Hirth F.30 or Limbach 2000)
Maximum speed: 92 kts (106 mph) 170 km/h
Cruise speed: 76 kts (87 mph) 140 km/h
Stall speed: 33 kts (38 mph) 60 km/h
Range: 260 naut miles (300 miles) 483 km
Climb rate: 846 ft (258 m) per minute
Availability: Kits.
Comments: Five partial kits. Microlight version available, as is a version with larger engine in the JAR/VLA category. Folding wings.

Buse'Air 150; behind is a partly complete fuselage (Geoffrey P Jones)

C.L.7 Speed

Address: Centre National RSA, Aerodrome Montauban, 82000 Montauban.
Type: High performance, side-by-side 2-seat, low-wing monoplane, with retractable tail-dragger undercarriage.
Construction: Wood.
Wing span: 23 ft 11 ins (7.3 m)
Length: 19 ft 8 ins (6.0 m)
Empty weight: 882-937 lb (400-425 kg)
Gross weight: 1,543-1,587 lb (700-720 kg)
Recommended engine: 160 or 180 hp (119.3-134 kW) Textron Lycoming
Maximum speed: 194-205 kts (224-236 mph) 360-380 km/h
Cruise speed: 162-173 kts (186-199 mph) 300-320 km/h
Stall speed: 54 kts (62 mph) 100 km/h
Range: 648 naut miles (745 miles) 1,200 km
Availability: Plans once the prototype has flown.
Comments: A French homebuilt for touring.

C.L.8 RSA Club

Address: Centre National RSA.
Type: Side-by-side 2-seat, low-wing monoplane, with fixed nosewheel undercarriage.
Construction: Wood.
Wing span: 26 ft 11 ins (8.2 m)
Length: 19 ft 8 ins (6 m)
Empty weight: 661 lb (300 kg)
Gross weight: 1,213 lb (550 kg)
Recommended engine: 115 hp (85.75 kW) Textron Lycoming O-235
Maximum speed: 148 kts (171 mph) 275 km/h
Cruise speed: 124 kts (143 mph) 230 km/h
Stall speed: 46 kts (53 mph) 85 km/h
Range: 486 naut miles (559 miles) 900 km
Availability: Plans.
Comments: Designed by Louis Cariou against a joint FNA/RSA requirement for a new French flying club trainer complying with FAR 23. First flown late 1994.

C.L.8 RSA Club prototype (Geoffrey P Jones)

CQR.1 Roitelet/Wren

Address: Centre National RSA.
Type: Single-seat, parasol-wing microlight/homebuilt, with fixed tail-dragger undercarriage.
Construction: Wood.
Recommended engine: 25 hp (19 kW) Rotax 277 or 41.6 hp (31 kW) Rotax 447
Availability: Plans.
Comments: Designed by Charles Roussoulieres at Montauban and first flown in June 1991.

Cobra 200A

Address: Avionics, 3 place Armand Goujon, 78200 Mantes-la-Jolie (or c/o Jean Poirot, 68 rue de Longchamp, 75116 Paris).
Telephone: +33 34 77 09 91
Facsimile: +33 34 78 59 20
Type: Tandem 2-seat, competition/aerobatic monoplane, with fixed tail-dragger undercarriage.
Construction: Steel tube fuselage and wood/fabric wings.
Wing span: 26 ft 6 ins (8.08 m)
Length: 19 ft 11 ins (6.08 m)
Empty weight: 1,213 lb (550 kg)
Gross weight: 1,830 lb (830 kg)
Recommended engine: 200 hp (149 kW) Textron Lycoming AEIO-360
Maximum speed: 227 kts (261 mph) 420 km/h
Cruise speed: 151 kts (174 mph) 280 km/h
Stall speed: 49 kts (56 mph) 90 km/h
Range: 378 naut miles (435 miles) 700 km
Take-off distance: 410 ft (125 m)
Climb rate: 2,950 ft (900 m) per minute
Availability: Plans and some components.
Comments: Increasingly popular in France, with at least 6 examples flying. Stressed to +10, -9g.

Cobra 200A built by Jean Poirot which first flew in May 1991 (Geoffrey P Jones)

Colomban MC 15 CriCri

Address: Michel Colomban, 37bis rue Lakanal, 92500 Rueil-Malmaison.
Telephone: +33 1 47 51 88 76
Type: Single-seat, twin-engined, aerobatic monoplane, with fixed nosewheel undercarriage.
Construction: Light alloy.
Wing span: 16 ft 1 ins (4.9 m)
Length: 12 ft 10 ins (3.91 m)
Recommended engines: 2 x 15 hp (11.2 kW) JPX PUL 212
Maximum speed: 159 kts (183 mph) 295 km/h
Cruise speed: 108 kts (124 mph) 200 km/h
Stall speed: 39 kts (45 mph) 72 km/h
Range: 216 naut miles (248 miles) 400 km
Take off distance: 328 ft (100m)
Climb rate: 1,280 ft (390 m) per minute
Availability: Plans.
Comments: Nearly 600 sets of plans sold, with about 100 aircraft flying.

Colomban MC 15 CriCri built by the Auffredou brothers at Troyes (Geoffrey P Jones)

Colomban MC-100 Banbi

Type: Side-by-side 2-seat, low-wing monoplane, with fixed nosewheel undercarriage.
Construction: Metal.
Wing span: 21 ft 9 ins (6.63 m)
Length: 17 ft 9 ins (5.4 m)
Empty weight: 518 lb (235 kg)
Gross weight: 992 lb (450 kg)
Recommended engine: 80 hp (59.7 kW) Rotax 912
Maximum speed: 162 kts (186 mph) 300 km/h
Cruise speed: 135 kts (155 mph) 250 km/h
Stall speed: 43 kts (50 mph) 80 km/h
Range: 567 naut miles (652 miles) 1,050 km
Climb rate: 1,378 ft (420 m) per minute
Availability: Plans plus some components (see Dyn'Aero MCR-01).
Comments: Designed by Michel Colomban. Prototype first flown on 15 July 1994. Detachable wings for easy storage.

Colomban MC-100 Banbi (Geoffrey P Jones)

Croses EC-3 Pouplume

Address: Emilien Croses, 63 route de Davaye, 71000 Charnay-les-Macon.
Telephone: +33 85 38 07 31
Type: Single-seat, tandem-wing biplane, with fixed tail-dragger undercarriage.
Construction: Wood and fabric.
Wing span: 25 ft 7 ins (7.8 m)
Length: 9 ft 10 ins (3 m)
Empty weight: 243-309 lb (110-140 kg)
Gross weight: 485-573 lb (220-260 kg)
Recommended engine: Converted 2-stroke motor-cycle engine of 10.5-18 hp (8-13.4 kW), but more recently a converted Volkswagen engine (Pouplume Sport) or small Rotax types.
Maximum speed: 38 kts (44 mph) 70 km/h
Cruise speed: 27 kts (31 mph) 50 km/h
Stall speed: Will not stall.
Availability: Plans.
Comments: Probably the first practical modern microlight, first flown in June 1961. Fixed rear wing and pivoting forward wing, without ailerons or elevators.

Croses EC-6 Criquet (Locust)

Type: Side-by-side 2-seat, tandem-wing homebuilt (also microlight version as the EC-6L), with fixed tail-dragger undercarriage.
Construction: Wood, fabric and glassfibre.
Wing span: 25 ft 7 ins (7.8 m)
Length: 15 ft 3 ins (4.65 m)
Empty weight: 639 lb (290 kg)
Gross weight: 1,213 lb (550 kg)
Recommended engine: 90 hp (67 kW) Teledyne Continental or Rotax 503 for microlight version.
Maximum speed: 115 kts (132 mph) 213 km/h
Cruise speed: 86 kts (99 mph) 160 km/h
Stall speed: Will not stall.
Climb rate: 1,000 ft (305 m) per minute
Availability: Plans.
Comments: Prototype first flew on 6 July 1965. Very popular Pou-du-Ciel type, with at least 30 completed and flown in France. Developed into the EC-8 Tourisme and EC-9 Paras Cargo.

Croses EC-6 Criquet at Marennes in France (Geoffrey P Jones)

Croses Airplume

Address: Yves Croses, 35 avenue de Saxe, 69006 Lyon.
Type: Tandem 2-seat, open cockpit Pou-du-Ciel microlight, with fixed tail-dragger undercarriage.
Construction: Composites, wood and fabric.
Wing span: 25 ft 11 ins (7.9 m)
Length: 17 ft 1 ins (5.2 m)
Empty weight: 383 lb (174 kg)
Recommended engine: 35 hp (26 kW) Cuyuna, Limbach or Rectimo.
Maximum speed: 70 kts (81 mph) 130 km/h
Range: 239 naut miles (275 miles) 442 km
Availability: Kits and plans.
Comments: Developed by Emilien Croses' son. Utilized for aerial crop dusting.

Croses Airplume microlight built from a kit. (Geoffrey P Jones)

Denise RD.20/150 Raid Driver

Address: Robert Denize, 17 rue de l'Abbe Borreau, 78400 Chatou.
Type: 2-seat, low-wing cabin monoplane, with tail-dragger undercarriage.
Construction: Wood and fabric.
Wing span: 27 ft 11 ins (8.5 m)
Length: 22 ft 8 ins (6.9 m)
Empty weight: 1,102 lb (500 kg)
Gross weight: 1,631 lb (740 kg)
Recommended engine: 150 hp (112 kW) Textron Lycoming IO-320
Maximum speed: 151 kts (174 mph) 280 km/h
Cruise speed: 108 kts (124 mph) 200 km/h
Range: 324 naut miles (373 miles) 600 km
Availability: Plans.
Comments: Developed from the RD.105 built between 1957 and 1963. RD.20/150 prototype was built between 1986 and 1989.

RD.20/150 prototype at the 1994 RSA Rally at Moulins (Geoffrey P Jones)

Druine D.5 Turbi

Address: Avions Roger Druine, 10 avenue Aristide Briand, 94100 St Maur.
Type: Tandem 2-seat, low-wing monoplane, with fixed nosewheel undercarriage.
Construction: Wood and fabric.
Wing span: 28 ft 6 ins (8.7 m)
Length: 22 ft 6 ins (6.86 m)
Empty weight: 617 lb (280 kg)
Gross weight: 1,091 lb (495 kg)
Recommended engine: 65 hp (48.5 kW) Teledyne Continental or Walter Mikron
Maximum speed: 84 kts (96 mph) 155 km/h
Cruise speed: 65 kts (75 mph) 120 km/h
Range: 345 naut miles (397 miles) 640 km
Availability: Plans.
Comments: 2-seat development of the Turbulent, first flown on 20 December 1951.

Druine D.31 Turbulent

Type: Single-seat, low-wing monoplane, with fixed tail-dragger undercarriage.
Construction: Wood.
Wing span: 21 ft 7 in (6.58 m)
Length: 17 ft 6 in (5.33 m)
Empty weight: 395 lb (179 kg)
Gross weight: 619 lb (281 kg)
Take-off distance: 310 ft (95 m)
Recommended engine: Volkswagen conversions.
Maximum speed: 109 kts (126 mph) 202 km/h
Cruise speed: 76 kts (88 mph) 141 km/h
Stall speed: 39 kts (44 mph) 71 km/h
Range: 216 naut miles (248 miles) 400 km
Climb rate: 450 ft (137 m) per minute
Availability: Plans.
Comments: Classic homebuilt also commercially produced in Britain by Rollason.

Druine D.31 Turbulent single-seat homebuilt (Geoffrey P Jones)

Druine D.60 Condor

Type: Side-by-side 2-seat, low-wing cabin monoplane, with fixed tail-dragger undercarriage.
Construction: Wood and fabric.
Wing span: 30 ft 2 ins (9.2 m)
Length: 21 ft 6 ins (6.55 m)
Empty weight: 664 lb (301 kg)
Gross weight: 1,102 lb (500 kg)
Recommended engine: 90 or 100 hp (67 or 74.6 kW) Teledyne Continental
Maximum speed: 97 kts (112 mph) 180 km/h
Cruise speed: 86 kts (99 mph) 160 km/h
Range: 351 naut miles (404 miles) 650 km
Availability: Plans.
Comments: First flown November 1954. Most Condors were commercially built by Rollason in Britain.

Duruble RD-03 Edelweiss 150

Address: Roland Duruble, 40 rue de Paradis, Les Essarts, 76530 Grand-Couronne.
Telephone: +33 35 32 20 63
Type: 2/4-seat low-wing cabin monoplane, with retractable nosewheel undercarriage.
Construction: Duralumin.

Wing span: 28 ft 11 ins (8.82 m)
Length: 22 ft 7 ins (6.88 m)
Empty weight: 1,124 lb (510 kg)
Gross weight: 2,227 lb (1,010 kg)
Recommended engine: 150 hp (112 kW) Textron Lycoming.
Maximum speed: 148 kts (171 mph) 275 km/h
Cruise speed: 128 kts (148 mph) 238 km/h
Stall speed: 57 kts (66 mph) 105 km/h
Range: 593 naut miles (685 miles) 1,100 km
Take-off distance over a 50 ft obstacle: 1,675 ft (510 m)
Climb rate: 1,160 ft (354 m) per minute
Availability: Plans.
Comments: Developed from the 2-seat RD-02 and designed to FAR 23 standard. Prototype first flew in 1982.

Duruble RD-03 Edelweiss built by Serge Gastan assisted by M Duruble (Geoffrey P Jones)

Dyn'Aero CR.100

Address: Dyn'Aero SA, 19 rue de l'Aviation, 21121 Darois.
Telephone: +33 80 35 60 62
Facsimile: +33 80 35 60 63
Type: Side-by-side 2-seat, aerobatic low-wing monoplane, with fixed tail-dragger undercarriage.
Construction: Wood and fabric.
Wing span: 27 ft 11 ins (8.5 m)
Length: 23 ft 4 ins (7.1 m)
Empty weight: 1,213 lb (550 kg)
Gross weight: 1,874 lb (850 kg), 1,675 lb (760 kg) for aerobatics
Recommended engine: 180 hp (134 kW) Textron Lycoming AEIO-360
Maximum speed: 205 kts (236 mph) 380 km/h
Cruise speed: 165 kts (190 mph) 306 km/h
Take-off distance: 492 ft (150 m)
Climb rate: 1,575 ft (480 m) per minute
Availability: Kits.
Comments: Designed by Chris Robin and first flown on 27 August 1992 at Dijon (Darois).

Dyn'Aero CR.100 prototype (Geoffrey P Jones)

Dyn'Aero MCR-01 Banbi

Type: Side-by-side 2-seat, low-wing monoplane, with fixed nosewheel undercarriage.
Construction: Composites.
Wing span: 21 ft 9 ins (6.63 m)
Length: 17 ft 9 ins (5.4 m)
Empty weight: 518 lb (235 kg)
Gross weight: 992 lb (450 kg)
Recommended engine: 80 hp (59.7 kW) Rotax 912
Maximum speed: 162 kts (186 mph) 300 km/h
Cruise speed: 135 kts (155 mph) 250 km/h
Stall speed: 43 kts (50 mph) 80 km/h
Range: 567 naut miles (652 miles) 1,050 km
Take-off distance: 574 ft (175 m)
Climb rate: 1,378 ft (420 m) per minute
Availability: Kits.
Comments: Kit version of the Colomban MC-100.

Grinvalds G.801 Orion

Address: Club Orion, c/o Michel Suire, 9 rue des Hirondelles, 91210 Draveil.
Type: 4-seat cabin monoplane with pusher engine and retractable nosewheel undercarriage.
Construction: Composites.
Wing span: 29 ft 6 ins (9 m)
Length: 21 ft 10 ins (6.65 m)
Empty weight: 1,340 lb (608 kg)
Gross weight: 2,310 lb (1,048 kg)
Recommended engine: 200 hp (149 kW) Textron Lycoming IO-360
Maximum speed: 178 kts (205 mph) 330 km/h
Cruise speed: 162 kts (186 mph) 300 km/h
Stall speed: 60 kts (69 mph) 111 km/h
Range: 1,618 naut miles (1,864 miles) 3,000 km, with auxilliary tanks fitted.
Take-off distance over a 50 ft obstacle: 1,800 ft (548 m)
Climb rate: 885 ft (270 m) per minute
Availability: Plans.
Comments: G-801 plans and access to moulds are still available via Club Orion.

Grinvalds G-801 Orion built by Jean-Dominique Leullier (Geoffrey P Jones)

Grunberg/Mignet HM.293

Address: Rodolphe Grunberg, 47310 Roquefort.
Telephone: +33 53 91 67 90
Type: Single-seat, tandem-wing, Pou-du-Ciel-type microlight, with fixed tail-dragger undercarriage.
Construction: Wood and fabric.
Wing span: 20 ft (6.1 m)
Length: 13 ft (3.97 m)
Empty weight: 265 lb (120 kg)
Gross weight: 485 lb (220 kg)
Recommended engine: 32 hp (24 kW) Rotax
Availability: Plans and kits.
Comments: Updated microlight version of the classic Mignet design. See also Mignet/Falconar HM.293.

Humbert Moto-du-Ciel

Address: Ets Humbert, rue du Menil, 88160 Ramonchamps.
Telephone: +33 29 25 05 75
Facsimile: +33 29 25 98 97
Type: Tandem-seat, high-wing microlight, with fixed nosewheel undercarriage. Optional cabin.
Construction: Steel tube, wood and composites.
Wing span: 37 ft 1 ins (11.3 m)
Length: 21 ft 4 ins (6.5 m)
Empty weight: 381 lb (173 kg)
Gross weight: 866 lb (393 kg)
Recommended engine: 1,600cc Volkswagen
Maximum speed: 59 kts (68 mph) 110 km/h
Cruise speed: 52 kts (60 mph) 96 km/h
Stall speed: 27 kts (31 mph) 50 km/h
Range: 378 naut miles (435 miles) 700 km
Climb rate: 590 ft (180 m) per minute
Availability: Plans and kits.
Comments: First flown in March 1985. Also now available with Rotax engines and optional cockpit pod.

Humbert Moto-du-Ciel fitted with enclosed cockpit (Geoffrey P Jones)

Humbert Le Tetras

Type: Side-by-side 2-seat, high-wing cabin microlight/homebuilt, with fixed tail-dragger undercarriage.
Construction: Steel tube, metal and composites.
Wing span: 37 ft 1 ins (11.3 m)
Length: 21 ft 4 ins (6.5 m)
Empty weight: 529 lb (240 kg)
Gross weight: 992 lb (450 kg)
Recommended engine: 72 hp (53.7 kW) HW2000 for microlight, or 80 hp (59.7 kW) Rotax 912
Maximum speed: 86 kts (99 mph) 160 km/h
Cruise speed: 65 kts (75 mph) 120 km/h
Stall speed: 35 kts (41 mph) 65 km/h
Take-off distance: 246 ft (75 m)
Climb rate: 395 ft (120 m) per second
Availability: Kits.

Tetras homebuilt in the microlight category (Geoffrey P Jones)

Jacques Coupe JC-01

Address: Avions Jacques Coupe, La Trute, Azay-le-Cher, 37270 Montlouis-sur-Loire.
Telephone: +33 47 50 41 84
Type: Side-by-side 2-seat, low-wing cabin monoplane, with fixed tail-dragger undercarriage.
Construction: Wood and fabric.
Wing span: 27 ft 5 ins (8.35 m)
Length: 21 ft (6.4 m)
Empty weight: 728 lb (330 kg)
Gross weight: 1,279 lb (580 kg)
Recommended engine: 65 hp (48.5 kW) Teledyne Continental A65-8F
Maximum speed: 108 kts (124 mph) 200 km/h
Cruise speed: 76 kts (87 mph) 140 km/h
Stall speed: 25 kts (28 mph) 45 km/h
Take-off distance: 295 ft (90 m)
Availability: Plans.
Comments: Prototype first flew on 16 March 1976 (see JC-200 for nosewheel version).

Jacques Coupe JC-01 prototype (Geoffrey P Jones)

Jacques Coupe JC-200

Type: Side-by-side 2-seat, low-wing cabin monoplane, with fixed nosewheel undercarriage.
Construction: Wood and fabric.
Wing span: 27 ft 5 ins (8.35 m)
Length: 21 ft (6.4 m)
Empty weight: 1,102 lb (500 kg)
Gross weight: 1,653 lb (750 kg)
Recommended engine: 100 hp (74.5 kW) Teledyne Continental
Maximum speed: 108 kts (124 mph) 200 km/h
Cruise speed: 86 kts (99 mph) 160 km/h
Stall speed: 24 kts (28 mph) 45 km/h
Take-off distance: 328 ft (100 m)
Availability: Plans and possibly kits.
Comments: Prototype JC-2 first flew in May 1981. Several JC-200s completed since.

JCC Aviation J.300

Address: JCC Aviation, Zone Industrial, Bd. de l'Avenir, 37530 Nazelles.
Type: Side-by-side 2-seat, high-wing cabin microlight/homebuilt, with fixed tail-dragger undercarriage.
Construction: Alloy tube, wood and fabric.
Wing span: 33 ft 6 ins (10.2 m)
Length: 17 ft 3 ins (5.27 m)
Empty weight: 331 lb (150 kg)
Gross weight: 992 lb (450 kg)
Recommended engine: 60 hp (44.7 kW) Arrow GT500 or 77.8 hp (58 kW) Rotax 912
Maximum speed: 86 kts (99 mph) 160 km/h
Cruise speed: 73 kts (84 mph) 135 km/h
Stall speed: 30 kts (34 mph) 55 km/h
Climb rate: 490 ft (150 m) per minute
Availability: Kits.
Comments: Excellent short-field performance.

JCC AviationJ.300 on approach to land (Geoffrey P Jones)

Jodel D.9 Bebe

Address: SAB, Aerodrome Beaune Challanges, 21200 Beaune (also from Falconar Air Engineering in Canada).
Telephone: +33 80 22 01 51
Facsimile: +33 80 24 19 43
Type: Single-seat, low-wing monoplane, with fixed tail-dragger (some have nosewheel) undercarriage.
Construction: Wood and fabric.
Wing span: 23 ft (7.0 m)
Length: 17 ft 11 ins (5.45 m)
Empty weight: 419 lb (190 kg)
Gross weight: 705 lb (320 kg)
Recommended engine: 40 hp (30 kW) Volkswagen
Maximum speed: 87 kts (100 mph) 160 km/h
Cruise speed: 74 kts (85 mph) 137 km/h
Stall speed: 35 kts (41 mph) 65 km/h
Range: 216 naut miles (248 miles) 400 km
Take-off distance: 360 ft (110 m)
Climb rate: 750 ft (230 m) per minute
Availability: Plans and kits.
Comments: Original Jodel design of Joly and Delemontez first flew in January 1948. Canadian version is the Falconar F-9.

Jodel D.9 with enclosed cockpit built by Jean Valette (Geoffrey P Jones)

Jodel D.11

Type: Side-by-side 2-seat, low-wing cabin monoplane, with fixed tail-dragger undercarriage.
Construction: Wood and fabric.
Wing span: 27 ft (8.23 m)
Length: 17 ft 11 ins (5.45 m)
Empty weight: 750 lb (340 kg)
Gross weight: 1,239 lb (562 kg)
Recommended engine: 65-90 hp (48.5-67 kW) Teledyne Continental
Maximum speed: 93 kts (107 mph) 173 km/h
Cruise speed: 87 kts (100 mph) 161 km/h
Stall speed: 43 kts (50 mph) 80 km/h
Range: 260 naut miles (299 miles) 482 km
Take-off distance: 500 ft (152 m)
Climb rate: 500 ft (152 m) per minute
Availability: Kits and plans.
Comments: Developed for commercial production by several companies. Canadian versions are the Falconar F-11 (2 seats) and F-12 (3 seats).

Jodel D.11 built in the UK (Geoffrey P Jones)

Jodel D.18

Type: Side-by-side 2-seat, low-wing cabin monoplane, with fixed tail-dragger undercarriage.
Construction: Wood and fabric.
Wing span: 24 ft 7 ins (7.5 m)
Length: 18 ft 8 ins (5.7 m)
Empty weight: 551 lb (250 kg)
Gross weight: 1,014 lb (460 kg)
Recommended engine: 1,600cc Volkswagen or Limbach
Maximum speed: 135 kts (155 mph) 250 km/h
Cruise speed: 92 kts (106 mph) 170 km/h
Stall speed: 39 kts (45 mph) 72 km/h
Range: 459 naut miles (528 miles) 850 km
Take-off distance over a 50 ft obstacle: 590 ft (180 m)
Climb rate: 590 ft (180 m) per minute
Availability: Plans and some components.
Comments: Developed from the Delemontez-Cauchy DC-01 and first flown on 21 May 1984. Extremely popular homebuilt in France. Nosewheel undercarriage version is the D.19 and larger D.20 is under development.

Jodel D.150 Mascaret

Type: Side-by-side 2-seat, sport tourer low-wing monoplane, with fixed tail-dragger undercarriage.
Construction: Wood and fabric.
Wing span: 20 ft 8 ins (6.3 m)
Length: 20 ft 8 ins (6.3 m)
Empty weight: 750 lb (340 kg)
Gross weight: 1,587 lb (720 kg)
Recommended engine: 100-115 hp (74.6-85.75 kW)
Cruise speed: 117 kts (135 mph) 217 km/h
Range: 521 naut miles (600 miles) 965 km
Climb rate: 630 ft (190 m) per minute
Availability: Plans and some components.
Comments: 61 aircraft originally built commercially by SAN at Bernay, France.

Jonathan Souricette (Mousetrap)

Address: Association Jonathan/Planapar, Aerodrome de la Ferte Alais, 91590 Cerny.
Telephone: +33 1 64 57 68 14 or +33 1 47 20 46 46
Type: Single-seat, open cockpit microlight, with fixed tail-dragger undercarriage.
Construction: Wood and styrofoam.
Wing span: 29 ft 6 ins (9 m)
Length: 18 ft 8 ins (5.7 m)
Empty weight: 220 lb (100 kg)
Gross weight: 441 kg (200 kg)
Recommended engine: 22 hp (16.4 kW) JPX PUL 425
Maximum speed: 65 kts (75 mph) 120 km/h
Cruise speed: 54 kts (62 mph) 100 km/h
Stall speed: 23 kts (26 mph) 42 km/h
Range: 270 naut miles (310 miles) 500 km
Take-off distance: 328 ft (100 m)
Climb rate: 225-490 ft (70-150 m) per minute
Availability: Plans and kits.
Comments: Easy to build microlight designed by Michel Barry.

Jonathan Souricette being man-handled (Geoffrey P Jones)

JP Marie JPM.01 Medoc

Address: Didier Marie, 35 rue de Caumont, Residence l'Aigiliere, 76520 Quevreville-la-Poterie.
Type: Side-by-side 2-seat low-wing monoplane, with fixed nosewheel undercarriage.
Construction: Wood.
Wing span: 24 ft 7 ins (7.5 m)
Length: 20 ft 4 ins (6.2 m)
Empty weight: 462 lb (210 kg)
Gross weight: 1,014 lb (460 kg)
Recommended engine: 68 hp (50.7 kW) Limbach 1700
Maximum speed: 103 kts (118 mph) 190 km/h
Cruise speed: 92 kts (106 mph) 170 km/h
Stall speed: 43 kts (50 mph) 80 km/h
Range: 367 naut miles (422 miles) 680 km
Climb rate: 787 ft (240 m) per minute
Availability: Plans.
Comments: First flown in 1991. Several engine options.

Junqua RJ.03 Ibis

Address: Junqua-Diffusion Internationale, c/o SCAM, 69 rue Garibaldi, 94100 Saint-Maur.
Telephone: +33 1 42 83 45 79
Facsimile: +33 1 42 83 00 65
Type: Tandem 2-seat monoplane, with canard. Fixed nosewheel undercarriage.
Construction: Wood and foam.
Wing span: 20 ft 5 ins (6.22 m)
Length: 16 ft 1 ins (4.9 m)
Empty weight: 573 lb (260 kg)
Gross weight: 1,036 lb (470 kg)
Recommended engine: 2,000cc Volkswagen or Limbach
Maximum speed: 140 kts (161 mph) 259 km/h
Cruise speed: 110 kts (127 mph) 204 km/h
Stall speed: 52 kts (60 mph) 96 km/h
Range: 432 naut miles (497 miles) 800 km
Take-off distance: 1,706 ft (520 m)
Climb rate: 617 ft (188 m) per minute
Availability: Plans (FF 2,950)
Comments: Developed from the RJ.02 Volucelle. Prototype Ibis first flew on 25 May 1991.

Junqua RJ.03 Ibis prototype (Geoffrey P Jones)

Jurca MJ.2 Tempete

Address: 3 Allées des Bordes, 94430 Chevennevieres (also from the USA: Ken Heit, 1733 Kansas, Flint, MI 48506)
Telephone: +33 1 45 94 01 38 (USA: +1 313 232 5395)
Type: Single-seat, aerobatic low-wing monoplane, with fixed tail-dragger undercarriage.
Construction: Wood and fabric.
Wing span: 19 ft 8 in (6 m)
Length: 19 ft (5.8 m)
Empty weight: 639 lb (290 kg)
Gross weight: 948 lb (430 kg)
Recommended engine: 65 hp (48.5 kW) Teledyne Continental. Variety of other engine options up to 180 hp (134 kW).
Maximum speed: 104 kts (120 mph) 193 km/h
Cruise speed: 89 kts (102 mph) 165 km/h
Stall speed: 48 kts (55 mph) 90 km/h
Range: 269 naut miles (310 miles) 500 km
Take-off distance: 820 ft (250 m)
Climb rate: 558 ft (170 m) per minute
Availability: Plans.
Comments: Prototype first flew on 27 June 1956.

Jurca MJ.2D Tempete with 90 hp (67 kW) Teledyne Continental engine (Geoffrey P Jones)

Jurca MJ.5 Sirocco

Type: Tandem 2-seat, low-wing aerobatic monoplane, with fixed or retractable tail-dragger undercarriage.
Construction: Wood and fabric.
Wing span: 23 ft (7 m)
Length: 20 ft 2 ins (6.15 m)
Empty weight: 948 lb (430 kg)
Gross weight: 1,499 lb (680 kg)
Take-off distance: 820 ft (250 m)
Recommended engine: 115 hp (85.75 kW) Textron Lycoming. Variety of other engine options up to 180 hp (134 kW).
Maximum speed: 127 kts (146 mph) 235 km/h
Cruise speed: 116 kts (134 mph) 215 km/h
Stall speed: 43 kts (50 mph) 80 km/h
Range: 477 naut miles (550 miles) 1,018 km
Climb rate: 820 ft (250 m) per minute
Availability: Plans.
Comments: Developed from the MJ.2 and first flown on 3 August 1962.

Jurca MJ.53 Autan

Type: Side-by-side 2-seat, aerobatic low-wing monoplane. with retractable tail-dragger undercarriage.
Construction: Wood.
Wing span: 24 ft 11 ins (7.6 m)
Length: 21 ft 4 ins (6.5 m)
Empty weight: 1,323 lb (600 kg)
Gross weight: 1,860 lb (844 kg)
Recommended engine: 180 hp (134 kW) Textron Lycoming
Cruise speed: 130 kts (149 mph) 240 km/h
Stall speed: 49-54 kts (56-62 mph) 90-100 km/h
Range: 521 naut miles (600 miles) 965 km
Climb rate: 985 ft (300 m) per minute
Availability: Plans.
Comments: Developed from the Sirocco. First flew 20 December 1991.

Jurca MJ.53 Autan built by F Melani at Salon, France (Geoffrey P Jones)

Jurca MJ.10 Spitfire

Type: 75% scale Spitfire replica.
Construction: Wood.
Wing span: 27 ft 8 ins (8.43 m)
Length: 23 ft 5 ins (7.14 m)
Empty weight: 1,450 lb (658 kg)
Gross weight: 2,860 lb (1,297 kg)
Recommended engine: 105 hp (78.5 kW) Teledyne Continental
Maximum speed: 124 kts (143 mph) 230 km/h
Cruise speed: 113 kts (130 mph) 210 km/h
Stall speed: 60 kts (69 mph) 110 km/h
Range: 432 naut miles (497 miles) 800 km
Availability: Plans.
Comments: One of Jurca's many World War II fighter replicas. Also available in 75% scale are the MJ.8 (Fw-190), MJ.9 (Bf-109) and MJ.12 (P-40).

MJ.77 Gnatsum (Mustang)

Type: 75% scale P.51 Mustang replica.
Construction: Wood.
Wing span: 27 ft 10 ins (8.48 m)
Length: 21 ft 6 ins (6.55 m)
Empty weight: 2,200 lb (998 kg)
Gross weight: 2,860 lb (1,297 kg)
Recommended engine: 200-360 hp (149-268.5 kW) Geschwender
Cruise speed: 151 kts (175 mph) 280 km/h
Climb rate: 1,500 ft (457 m) per minute
Availability: Plans.
Comments: See also MJ.10 Spitfire.

Jurca MJ.100 Spitfire

Type: Full-scale homebuilt Spitfire replica.
Construction: Wood or metal tube.
Wing span: 36 ft (10.97 m)
Length: 29 ft 11 in (9.12 m)
Empty weight: 3,900 lb (1,769 kg)
Gross weight: 5,060 lb (2,295 kg)
Recommended engine: 690 hp (514.5 kW) Hispano Suiza V.12 or V-12 Allison
Maximum speed: 308 kts (355 mph) 571 km/h
Cruise speed: 261 kts (300 mph) 483 km/h
Range: 434 naut miles (500 miles) 804 km
Climb rate: 3,500 ft (1,065 m) per minute
Availability: Plans.
Comments: One of Marcel Jurca's full-scale World War II fighter replicas that include the MJ.80 (Fw-190) and MJ.90 (Bf-109).

Jurca MJ.100 Spitfire replica built at Reims and first flown in October 1994

Kieger AK.1

Address: André Kieger, 85 route de Bischwiller, 67500 Hagenau.
Type: Side-by-side 2-seat, low-wing monoplane, with tail-dragger undercarriage.
Construction: Wood
Wing span: 27 ft 5 ins (8.35 m)
Length: 20 ft 5 ins (6.22 m)
Empty weight: 772 lb (350 kg)
Gross weight: 1,235 lb (560 kg)
Recommended engine: 80 hp (59.7 kW) Limbach L2000
Cruise speed: 95 kts (109 mph) 176 km/h
Range: 475 naut miles (546 miles) 880 km
Availability: Plans.
Comments: First flown on 17 March 1989.

Kieger AK.01 prototype built by André Kieger (Geoffrey P Jones)

Kitair Helios-5-TR

Address: Kitair, ZA St. Pouange, 10120 St Andre
Telephone: +33 25 41 90 34
Facsimile: +33 25 41 71 11
Type: Side-by-side 2-seat, high-wing monoplane, with fixed nosewheel undercarriage.

Construction: Wood and composites.
Wing span: 36 ft 1 ins (11 m)
Length: 19 ft 8 ins (6 m)
Empty weight: 340 lb (154 kg)
Gross weight: 992 lb (450 kg)
Recommended engine: 50 hp (37.3 kW) Rotax 503 or 64.4 hp (48 kW) Rotax 582
Maximum speed: 81 kts (93 mph) 150 km/h
Cruise speed: 65 kts (75 mph) 120 km/h
Stall speed: 27 kts (31 mph) 50 km/h
Availability: Kits.
Comments: Detachable wings to facilitate road transportation.

Helios-5-TR marketed in kits by Kitair (Geoffrey P Jones)

KOENIG AK.09 Faucon

Address: Koenig Engineering, 49 route du Mont St. Odile, 67220 Breitenbach.
Telephone: +33 88 58 95 78
Facsimile: +33 88 58 95 77
Type: Side-by-side 2-seat, low-wing microlight/homebuilt, with fixed nosewheel undercarriage.
Construction: Composites.
Wing span: 27 ft 3 ins (8.3 m)
Length: 19 ft 8 ins (6 m)
Empty weight: 286 lb (125 kg)
Gross weight: 992 lb (450 kg)
Recommended engine: 50 hp (37.3 kW) Rotax 503 or 64.4 hp (48 kW) Rotax 582 for microlight version, or 77.8 hp (58 kW) Rotax 912 for JAR/VLA version (data for microlight).
Maximum speed: 97 kts (112 mph) 180 km/h
Cruise speed: 86 kts (99 mph) 160 km/h
Stall speed: 30 kts (34 mph) 55 km/h
Range: 432 naut miles (497 miles) 800 km
Take-off distance: 213 ft (65 m)
Climb rate: 885 ft (270 m) per minute
Availability: Kits.
Comments: First flown in 1993. Available as microlight or in JAR/VLA category. Also available from a German supplier.

Koenig AK.09 Faucon prototype (Geoffrey P Jones)

La Mouette Paramotor SR.210

Address: La Mouette, ZA- 1, rue de la Petite-Fin, 21121 Fontain-les-Dijon.
Telephone: +33 80 56 66 47
Facsimile: +33 80 55 42 01
Type: Single-seat ram-air parachute with shrouded engine and propeller attached to the pilot.
Construction: Alloy tube and fabric.
Empty weight: 44 lb (20 kg)
Gross weight: 220 lb (100 kg)
Recommended engine: Solo 210
Climb rate: 275 ft (84 m) per minute
Availability: Commercially built by La Mouette.
Comments: First flown on 8 October 1993 and over 70 built. Also the Paramotor ZR.250 with Zenoah 250 engine.

La Mouette Paramotor SR.210

La Mouette/ULM Cosmos Phase II

Type: Tandem 2-seat rogallo wing microlight, with trike and pusher engine.
Construction: Alloy tube and fabric.
Wing span: 34 ft 9 ins (10.6 m)
Empty weight: 309 lb (140 kg)
Gross weight: 772 lb (350 kg)
Recommended engine: 50 hp (37.3 kW) Rotax
Maximum speed: 70 kts (81 mph) 130 km/h
Cruise speed: 41 kts (47 mph) 75 km/h
Stall speed: 25 kts (28 mph) 45 km/h
Range: 113 kts (130 mph) 210 km
Climb rate: 985 ft (300 m) per minute
Availability: Commercially manufactured.
Comments: First flown in March 1991. Over 200 sold.

ULM Cosmos Phase II (Geoffrey P Jones)

Lascaud Bifly

Address: Ets D. Lascaud, 41 rue de Crussol, 07500 Granges-les-Valence.
Telephone: +33 75 44 47 02
Type: Single-seat, tandem-wing microlight.
Construction: Wood and fabric.
Wing span: 20 ft 4 ins (6.19 m)
Length: 10 ft 8 ins (3.25 m)
Empty weight: 143 lb (65 kg)
Gross weight: 353 lb (160 kg)
Recommended engine: 22 hp (16.4 kW) JPX PUL 425
Maximum speed: 65 kts (75 mph) 120 km/h
Cruise speed: 38 kts (43 mph) 70 km/h
Stall speed: 16.5 kts (19 mph) 30 km/h
Range: 89 naut miles (102 miles) 165 km
Take-off distance: 131 ft (40 m)
Climb rate: 590 ft (180 m) per minute
Availability: Kits.
Comments: Microlight version of the classic Henri Mignet Pou-du-Ciel formula.

Lefebvre MP.205 Busard

Address: Robert Lefebvre, 393 rue Pierre Cardinal, La Paillade, 34100 Montpellier.
Type: Single-seat, low-wing racing monoplane, with fixed tail-dragger undercarriage.
Construction: Wood.
Wing span: 19 ft 8 ins (6 m)
Length: 17 ft 7 ins (5.35 m)
Empty weight: 527 lb (239 kg)
Gross weight: 760 lb (345 kg)
Recommended engine: 90 hp (67 kW) Teledyne Continental
Maximum speed: 156 kts (180 mph) 290 km/h
Stall speed: 40 kts (45 mph) 74 km/h
Range: 242 naut miles (279 miles) 450 km
Availability: Plans.
Comments: Original Max Plan MP.204 first flew on 5 June 1952. First MP.205 built by M. Lefebvre flew in 1975. Other versions with different engines.

Lefebvre MP.207 Busard with 100 hp (74.6 kW) Teledyne Continental engine built by I Rieti (Geoffrey P Jones)

Lucas L.5

Address: Emile Lucas, 7 Allée des Acacias, 60330 Lagny-le-Sec.
Type: Side-by-side 2-seat (also 3 or 4 seat) cabin low-wing monoplane, with either fixed nosewheel or retractable tail-dragger undercarriage.
Construction: Metal.
Wing span: 30 ft 2 ins (9.2 m)
Length: 20 ft 8 ins (6.3 m)
Empty weight: 1,036 lb (470 kg)
Gross weight: 1,587 lb (720 kg)
Recommended engine: 115 hp (85.75 kW) Textron Lycoming O-235
Maximum speed: 146 kts (168 mph) 270 km/h with retractable gear
Cruise speed: 138 kts (158 mph) 255 km/h
Range: 499 naut miles (575 miles) 925 km
Take-off distance: 920 ft (280 m)
Climb rate: 985 ft (300 m) per minute
Availability: Plans and some components.
Comments: Prototype first flew on 13 August 1976. Many versions built with different capacity engines.

Lucas L.5 built by M. Devicq with 4 seats and 180hp (134 kW) Textron Lycoming (Geoffrey P Jones)

Lucas L.6

Type: Tandem 2-seat, low-wing cabin monoplane, with either retractable tail-dragger or nosewheel undercarriage. Suitable for use as a motor-glider with wingtip extensions.

Construction: Metal.
Wing span: 31 ft 2 ins (9.5 m)
Length: 23 ft (7 m)
Empty weight: 992 lb (450 kg)
Gross weight: 1,499 lb (680 kg)
Recommended engine: 80 hp (59.7 kW) Limbach
Maximum speed: 108 kts (124 mph) 200 km/h
Cruise speed: 86 kts (99 mph) 160 km/h
Range: 540 naut miles (621 miles) 1,000 km
Take-off distance: 985 ft (300 m)
Availability: Plans and some components.
Comments: First flown 4 September 1991. Suitable for other engines.

Mecavia Onyx Biplace

Address: Mecavia, 26 rue Galpin Thiou, 37000 Tours.
Telephone: +33 47 61 18 30
Type: Tandem 2-seat, canard monoplane with winglets, pusher engine and fixed nosewheel undercarriage.
Construction: Composites.
Recommended engine: 50 hp (37.3 kW) Rotax 503, 65 hp (48.5 kW) Rotax 582 or 80 hp (59.7 kW) Hirth F.30
Availability: Kits.
Comments: Developed from the single-seat Piel CP.150 Onyx.

Mecavia Onyx canard just prior to its first flight in 1994 (Geoffrey P Jones)

Mignet HM.1000 Balerit

Address: Société d'Exploitation des Aéronefs Henri Mignet, Logis des Pierrières, St Romain-de-Benêt, 17600 Saujon.
Type: Tandem-wing, 2-seat, Pou-du-Ciel type microlight.
Wing span: 23 ft 11 ins (7.3 m)
Length: 16 ft 5 ins (5 m)
Empty weight: 386 lb (175 kg)
Gross weight: 628 lb (285 kg)
Recommended engine: 46 hp (34 kW) Rotax 503
Maximum speed: 78 kts (90 mph) 145 km/h
Cruise speed: 70 kts (81 mph) 130 km/h
Stall speed: Does not stall
Range: 216 naut miles (248 miles) 400 km
Take-off distance: 300 ft (91 m)
Climb rate: 1,230 ft (376 m) per minute
Availability: Complete aircraft and kits.
Comments: Sold in large numbers in France for sporting use and air work including aerial surveillance by the Armée de l'Air.

Mignet HM.1000 Balerit, 24 of which have been sold to the French Armée de l'Air (Geoffrey P Jones)

Nickel & Foucard NF-2 Asterix

Address: Rudy Nickel, 106 avenue Chateau-Fleury, 26100 Romans.
Type: Tandem 2-seat monoplane with pivoting wing, pusher propeller and fixed nosewheel undercarriage.
Construction: Wood, fabric and some styrofoam.
Wing span: 24 ft 7 ins (7.5 m)
Length: 16 ft 11 ins (5.15 m)
Empty weight: 441 lb (200 kg)
Gross weight: 824 lb (374 kg)
Recommended engine: 45 hp (33.6 kW) Citroen Visa converted motorcar engine or other type.
Maximum speed: 78 kts (90 mph) 145 km/h
Cruise speed: 70 kts (81 mph) 130 km/h
Stall speed: 33 kts (38 mph) 60 km/h
Range: 189 naut miles (217 miles) 350 km
Take-off distance: 492 ft (150 m)
Climb rate: 492 ft (150 m) per minute
Availability: Plans.
Comments: Prototype built by Rudy Nickel and Joseph Foucard first flew in 1987. Several completed in France.

Nickel & Foucard NF-2 Asterix fitted with a Rotax 582 engine (Geoffrey P Jones)

Nicollier HN.433 Menestrel

Address: Avions H. Nicollier, 13 rue de Verdun, 25000 Besancon.
Telephone: +33 81 53 57 01
Type: Single-seat, low-wing monoplane, with a tail-dragger undercarriage.
Construction: Wood and fabric.
Wing span: 23 ft (7 m)
Length: 17 ft 5 ins (5.3 m)
Empty weight: 443 lb (201 kg)
Gross weight: 727 lb (330 kg)
Recommended engine: 39 hp (29 kW) Rectimo-VW (also other 30-50 hp, 22.4-37.3 kW engines)
Maximum speed: 103 kts (118 mph) 190 km/h
Cruise speed: 92 kts (106 mph) 170 km/h
Stall speed: 26 kts (30 mph) 48 km/h
Range: 278 naut miles (320 miles) 515 km
Take-off distance: 395 ft (120m)
Climb rate: 590 ft (180 m) per minute
Availability: Plans and some components.
Comments: Prototype first flew on 25 November 1962. Redesigned version, HN.434, also available.

Nicollier HN.500 Bengali

Type: Side-by-side seating, low-wing cabin monoplane homebuilt, with fixed nosewheel undercarriage.
Construction: Wood.
Wing span: 27 ft 6 ins (8.39 m)
Length: 20 ft 4 ins (6.2 m)
Recommended engine: 100 hp (74.6 kW) Teledyne Continental O-200
Cruise speed: 105 kts (121 mph) 195 km/h
Availability: Plans.
Comments: First flown on 9 June 1988.

Nicollier HN.700 Menestrel II

Type: 2-seat, low-wing monoplane, with tail-dragger undercarriage.
Construction: Wood and fabric.
Wing span: 25 ft 7 ins (7.8 m)
Length: 17 ft 5 ins (5.3 m)
Empty weight: 622 lb (282 kg)
Gross weight: 1,102 lb (500 kg)
Recommended engine: 80 hp (59.7 kW) Limbach
Maximum speed: 101 kts (116 mph) 187 km/h
Cruise speed: 95 kts (109 mph) 176 km/h
Stall speed: 43 kts (50 mph) 80 km/h
Range: 540 naut miles (621 miles) 1,000 km
Take-off distance: 600 ft (183 m)
Climb rate: 1,280 ft (390 m) per minute (2 crew)
Availability: Plans and some components.
Comments: 2-seat development of HN.433 and 434.

Nicollier HN.700 Menestrel II built at Reims (Geoffrey P Jones)

Nogaro Midour

Address: Aero Club de Bas Armagnac, Aerodrom BP.17, 32110 Nogaro.
Telephone: +33 62 09 00 69
Facsimile: +33 62 09 01 32
Type: Tandem 2-seat, low-wing monoplane trainer and glider tug. Fixed nosewheel undercarriage.
Construction: Wood and composites.
Wing span: 28 ft 7 ins (8.72 m)
Length: 22 ft 4 ins (6.8 m)
Empty weight: 1,213 lb (550 kg)
Gross weight: 1,742 lb (790 kg)
Recommended engine: 180 hp (134 kW) Textron Lycoming O-360
Maximum speed: 162 kts (186 mph) 300 km/h
Cruise speed: 103 kts (118 mph) 190 km/h
Take-off distance: 460 ft (140 m)
Climb rate: 730 ft (220 m) per minute
Availability: Plans.
Comments: Designed at Nogaro by members of the Aero Club de Bas Armagnac, utilizing some Robin components. Specially silenced engine with 4-blade Hoffmann propeller.

Nogaro Midour prototype built between 1991 and 1994 (Geoffrey P Jones)

Ollivier Collivier

Address: Charles Ollivier, 85450 Chaille-les-Marais.
Type: 4-seat low-wing cabin monoplane, with retractable tail-dragger undercarriage.
Construction: Wood and fabric.
Wing span: 28 ft 7 ins (8.72 m)
Length: 22 ft 10 ins (6.96 m)
Empty weight: 1,433 lb (650 kg)
Gross weight: 2,425 lb (1,100 kg)
Recommended engine: 180 hp (134 kW) Textron Lycoming O-320
Maximum speed: 170 kts (196 mph) 315 km/h
Cruise speed: 150 kts (173 mph) 278 km/h

Length: 15 ft 9 ins (4.8 m)
Recommended engine: 120 hp (89.5 kW) Limbach
Cruise speed: 175 kts (202 mph) 325 km/h
Stall speed: 58 kts (66 mph) 106 km/h clean, 48 kts (56 mph) 89 km/h with flaps
Range: 540 naut miles (621 miles) 1,000 km
Availability: Prototype was still under construction in early 1995. Kits are expected.
Comments: One-eighth scale model was displayed for the first time at the RSA Moulins in 1994. Prototype under construction by Claude Bire.

Quaissard GQ-01 Monogast

Address: Gaston Quaissard, 4 rue Boileau, 01000 Bourg-en-Bresse.
Type: Single-seat, high-wing cabin monoplane, with fixed tail-dragger undercarriage.
Construction: Wood and fabric.
Wing span: 24 ft 1 ins (7.33 m)
Length: 18 ft 4 ins (5.58 m)
Recommended engine: 47 hp (35 kW) Volkswagen 1,600cc
Maximum speed: 81 kts (93 mph) 150 km/h
Cruise speed: 70 kts (81 mph) 130 km/h
Stall speed: 35 kts (41 mph) 65 km/h
Availability: Plans.
Comments: Prototype first flew on 15 November 1983.

Quaissard GQ-01 Monogast built by Daniel Labruisie (Geoffrey P Jones)

SMAN Petrel

Address: 2 rue du Parc en Escop, 56400 Auray.
Telephone: +33 97 24 83 10
Facsimile: +33 97 24 86 12
Type: Side-by-side 2-seat amphibian.
Construction: Composites, stainless steel, alloy and fabric.
Wing span: 27 ft 11 ins (8.5 m)
Length: 19 ft 11 ins (6.07 m)
Empty weight: 386 lb (175 kg)
Gross weight: 992 lb (450 kg)
Recommended engine: 64 hp (47.7 kW) Rotax 532 (or 582)
Maximum speed: 81 kts (93 mph) 150 km/h
Cruise speed: 60 kts (70 mph) 112 km/h
Stall speed: 31 kts (36 mph) 57 km/h
Range: 208 naut miles (240 miles) 386 km
Take-off distance: 165 ft (50 m) land, 328 ft (100 m) water.
Climb rate: 787 ft (240 m) per minute.
Availability: Kits and factory assembled.
Comments: Developed from the Tisserand Hydroplum II.

Stern/Mallick SM-01 Vega

Address: Rene Stern, 10 rue du Château, 57730 Folscherville.
Telephone: +33 87 92 25 49
Type: Side-by-side 2-seat, low-wing monoplane, with fixed tail-dragger undercarriage.
Construction: Wood and fabric.
Wing span: 24 ft 11 ins (7.6 m)
Length: 19 ft 4 ins (5.9 m)
Empty weight: 1,014 lb (460 kg)
Gross weight: 1,499 lb (680 kg)
Recommended engine: 115 hp (85.75 kW) Textron Lycoming O-235
Maximum speed: 140 kts (162 mph) 260 km/h
Cruise speed: 113 kts (130 mph) 210 km/h
Stall speed: 45 kts (51 mph) 82 km/h
Range: 521 naut miles (600 miles) 965 km
Availability: Plans.
Comments: Developed from the Stern ST-87 with the assistance of Richard Mallick.

Stern/Mallick SM-01 Vega prototype which first flew in 1992 (Geoffrey P Jones)

Stern ST-87 Europlane

Type: Side-by-side 2-seat, low-wing monoplane, with fixed nosewheel undercarriage.
Construction: Wood and fabric.
Wing span: 24 ft 11 ins (7.6 m)
Length: 19 ft 4 ins (5.9 m)
Empty weight: 842 lb (382 kg)
Gross weight: 1,323 lb (600 kg)
Recommended engine: 80 hp (59.7 kW) Limbach
Maximum speed: 135 kts (155 mph) 250 km/h
Cruise speed: 103 kts (118 mph) 190 km/h
Stall speed: 43 kts (50 mph) 80 km/h
Range: 499 naut miles (575 miles) 975 km
Availability: Plans.
Comments: Developed from the single-seat ST-80 Balade. First flown on 7 June 1991.

Germany

C-Con Delta Dart II

Address: C-Con GmbH, Weiler Weg 4, D-8873 Ichenhausen.
Type: Tandem 2-seat, pusher-engined homebuilt, with rear delta wings and endplate fins/rudders, forward canard and retractable nosewheel undercarriage.
Construction: Composites.
Wing span: 20 ft 6 ins (6.25 m)
Length: 18 ft 2 ins (5.54 m)
Empty weight: 408 lb (185 kg)
Gross weight: 882 lb (400 kg)
Recommended engine: 65 hp (48.5 kW) Arrow
Maximum speed: 119 kts (137 mph) 220 km/h
Range: 755 naut miles (870 miles) 1,400 km
Availability: Prototype to date.
Comments: Futuristic aircraft that first flew in 1992.

Cosy Europe Cozy Classic

Address: Uli Wolter, Cosy Europe, Ahornstrasse 10, D-86510 Ried.
Telephone: +49 8233 60594
Facsimile: +49 8233 20150
Type: 2/3-seat canard type, with a pusher engine and retractable nose gear and fixed main wheels.
Construction: Mostly composites.
Wing span: 26 ft 4 ins (8.03 m)
Length: 17 ft 9 ins (5.4 m)
Empty weight: 960 lb (435 kg)
Gross weight: 1,750 lb (794 kg)
Recommended engine: 150-160 hp (112-119.3 kW) Textron Lycoming O-320/IO-320
Maximum speed: 195 kts (225 mph) 362 km/h
Cruise speed: 162 kts (187 mph) 301 km/h
Stall speed: 58 kts (67 mph) 108 km/h
Range: 868 naut miles (1,000 miles) 1,609 km
Take-off distance: 1,476 ft (450 m)
Climb rate: 1,500 ft (457 m) per minute
Availability: Plans and kits.
Comments: Cosy Europe purchased the design rights to the Cozy from Nat Puffer in 1987. Original US Cozy first flew on 19 July 1982. French kits are available from Stratifies Composites Aeronautiques of Bourges.

Stratifies Composites kit-built Cosy Europe Cosy Classic (Geoffrey P Jones)

Dallach Sunrise II

Address: Dallach Flugzeuge GmbH, Stauferstrasse 10, D-7076 Wissgoldingen.
Telephone: +49 7114 41127
Type: Tandem 2-seat microlight, with fixed tail-dragger undercarriage, available as low-wing monoplane or biplane.
Construction: Steel tube, wood and fabric.
Wing span: 42 ft 11 ins (13.08 m)
Length: 17 ft 5 ins (5.31 m)
Empty weight: 331 lb (150 kg)
Gross weight: 728 lb (330 kg)
Recommended engine: 40 hp (30 kW) KKHD
Maximum speed: 81 kts (93 mph) 150 km/h
Cruise speed: 65 kts (75 mph) 121 km/h
Stall speed: 22 kts (25 mph) 41 km/h
Climb rate: 570 ft (175 m) per minute
Availability: Kits and assembled.
Comments: Biplane version has a shorter wing span.

Dallach Sunrise II biplane (Geoffrey P Jones)

Funk FK.6

Address: B & F Technik Vertriebs GmbH, Hofheimer Strasse 67, 6238 Hofheim/Ts.7.
Telephone: +49 619 24090
Type: Single-seat, high-wing monoplane, with a pusher engine, V-tail and fixed tail-dragger undercarriage.
Construction: Metal, composites and fabric.
Wing span: 36 ft 1 ins (11 m)
Length: 17 ft 9 ins (5.41 m)
Empty weight: 331 lb (150 kg)
Gross weight: 551 lb (250 kg)
Recommended engine: 22 hp (16.4 kW) Hirth 263-A
Maximum speed: 81 kts (93 mph) 150 km/h
Cruise speed: 65 kts (75 mph) 121 km/h
Range: 404 naut miles (466 miles) 750 km

Take-off distance: 230 ft (70 m)
Climb rate: 700 ft (213 m) per minute
Availability: Plans.
Comments: Built as a private project at MBB's Speyer factory and first flown in early 1985.

Funk FK.6 single-seat microlight (Geoffrey P Jones)

Funk FK.9

Type: 2-seat, high-wing monoplane, with a tail-dragger undercarriage.
Construction: Steel tube and fabric, some wood and foam.
Wing span: 32 ft 2 ins (9.8 m)
Length: 19 ft 2 ins (5.85 m)
Empty weight: 441 lb (200 kg) (Rotax 503), 507 lb (230 kg) (Rotax 912)
Gross weight: 992 lb (450 kg)
Engine: 46 hp (34.3 kW) Rotax 503 DCDI or 80 hp (59.7 kW) Rotax 912 UL
Maximum speed: 89 kts (103 mph) 165 km/h
Cruise speed: 86 kts (99 mph) 160 km/h
Range: 341 naut miles (393 miles) 633 km
Take-off distance: 328 ft (100 m)
Climb rate: 1,365 ft (415 m) per minute
Availability: Kits without engine, instruments, seats.
Comments: Folding wings. In production since 1991. Won 1994 World Microlight Championships in Poland.

Funk FK.9 (Geoffrey P Jones)

Leichtflugzeug Sky Walker

Address: Leichtflugzeug GmbH & Co KG, Osemundstrasse 22, D-5982 Neuenrade.
Type: Tandem 2-seat, high-wing microlight/homebuilt, with pusher engine and fixed nosewheel undercarriage or floats.
Construction: Steel tube and fabric.
Wing span: 33 ft 3 ins (10.13 m)
Length: 18 ft 8 ins (5.69 m)
Empty weight: 392 lb (178 kg)
Gross weight: 833 lb (378 kg)
Recommended engine: 50 hp (37.3 kW) Rotax 503 (option for Rotax 582 or Sauer UL2100)
Maximum speed: 65 kts (75 mph) 121 km/h
Stall speed: 31 kts (35 mph) 57 km/h
Range: 247 naut miles (285 miles) 458 km
Climb rate: 590 ft (180 m) per minute
Availability: Kits and assembled.
Comments: Used by the Helmond Police in the Netherlands.

LO-Fluggeratebau LO-120

Address: LO-Fluggeratebau GmbH, Aspachstrasse 14, D-7981 Berg/Effishofen.
Type: Tandem 2-seat high-wing homebuilt/microlight, with pusher engine, twin tail boom and inverted V tail unit. Fixed nosewheel undercarriage.
Construction: Steel tube, composites and fabric.
Wing span: 39 ft 4 ins (12 m)
Length: 22 ft 11 ins (7 m)
Empty weight: 331 lb (150 kg)
Gross weight: 616 lb (280 kg)
Recommended engine: 38 hp (28.3 kW) Rotax 337
Maximum speed: 54 kts (62 mph) 100 km/h
Cruise speed: 52 kts (60 mph) 96 km/h
Range: 215 naut miles (248 miles) 400 km
Availability: Kits.
Comments: Version is the LO-120S Bausalz I, which has a longer wing span (49 ft 2 ins, 15 m), increased length (24 ft 7 ins, 7.5 m) and 52 hp (38.8 kW) Rotax engine, giving higher gross weight and better performance.

Platzer Kiebitz

Type: Tandem 2 seat microlight/homebuilt biplane, with tail-dragger undercarriage.
Construction: Steel tube fuselage and wood/composite wings.
Empty weight: 463 lb (210 kg)
Gross weight: 882 lb (400 kg)
Recommended engine: 74 hp (55.2 kW) Sauer VW UL2100
Cruise speed: 59 kts (68 mph) 110 km/h
Stall speed: 35 kts (41 mph) 65 km/h
Availability: Plans and kits.
Comments: Designed by Michael Platzer and loosely based on the FW Stieglitz.

Platzer Kiebitz built by Frank Liborius (Geoffrey P Jones)

Tandem Aircraft Sunny

Address: Tandem Aircraft KG, Am Flugplatz, D-88348 Saulgau.
Telephone: +49 7581 8479
Facsimile: +49 7581 8169
Type: 2-seat, positive-stagger biplane micro-light interlinked box-wing configuration, with pusher engine and fixed under-carriage (single seat version also available).
Construction: Alloy tube, stainless steel and fabric.
Wing span: 22 ft (7 m)
Length: 12 ft 5 in (3.8 m)
Empty weight: 414 lb (188 kg)
Gross weight: 881 lb (400 kg)
Take-off distance: 300 ft (92 m)
Recommended engine: 64 hp (47.7 kW) Also suitable to Rotax engines of 60-80 hp (44.7-59.7 kW)
Maximum speed: 81 kts (93 mph) 150 km/h
Cruise speed: 70 kts (81 mph) 130 km/h
Stall speed: claimed not to stall but minimum speed of 30 kts (34 mph) 55 km/h
Range: 173 naut miles (200 miles) 321 km
Climb rate: 1020 ft (310 m) per minute
Availability: Commercially built but kits of the single-seat version available Aug 1995.
Comments: First flown in 1990. Over 100 sold in Germany and France.

Tandem Aircraft Sunny tandem-seat variant (Geoffrey P Jones)

Italy

Eurofly FireFox

Address: Eurofly, Via Ca' Onorai 50, 35015 Galliera Veneta (PD).
Telephone: +39 49 5965464
Type: Tandem 2-seat, high-wing microlight, with pusher engine and fixed nosewheel undercarriage.
Construction: Alloy tube and fabric.
Wing span: 28 ft 3 ins (9.6 m)
Length: 20 ft 4 ins (6.2 m)
Empty weight: 331 lb (150 kg)
Gross weight: 794 lb (360 kg)
Recommended engine: 48 hp (35.8 kW) Rotax 503
Maximum speed: 70 kts (81 mph) 130 km/h
Cruise speed: 57 kts (65 mph) 105 km/h
Stall speed: 22 kts (25 mph) 40 km/h
Range: 113 naut miles (130 miles) 210 km
Climb rate: 787 ft (240 m) per minute
Availability: Factory produced.
Comments: Simplified version of the FireFox is the BasicFox.

Eurofly FireFox being operated in Slovenia (Geoffrey P Jones)

Ferrari ULM Olimpios

Address: Ferrari ULM, Via Garibaldi, 104/A, 35040 Castelbaldo (PD).
Telephone: +39 425 57316
Facsimile: +39 425 546422
Type: Side-by-side 2-seat, high-wing microlight monoplane, with fixed nosewheel undercarriage.
Construction: Metal or composites.
Wing span: 32 ft 10 ins (10 m)
Length: 20 ft 8 ins (6.3 m)
Empty weight: 595 lb (270 kg)
Gross weight: 992 lb (450 kg)
Recommended engine: 64 hp (47.7 kW) Rotax 582
Maximum speed: 162 kts (186 mph) 300 km/h
Cruise speed: 108 kts (124 mph) 200 km/h
Stall speed: 33 kts (38 mph) 60 km/h
Range: 324 naut miles (372 miles) 600 km
Climb rate: 787 ft (240 m) per minute
Availability: Kits and complete aircraft.

Ferrari ULM Tucano

Type: Single-seat, high-wing microlight, with fuselage pod, tail-boom, pusher engine and fixed nosewheel undercarriage.
Construction: Metal and fabric.

Wing span: 33 ft 4 ins (10.17 m)
Length: 19 ft (5.8 m)
Empty weight: 441 lb (200 kg)
Gross weight: 838 lb (380 kg)
Recommended engine: 64 hp (47.7 kW) Rotax 582
Maximum speed: 92 kts (106 mph) 170 km/h
Cruise speed: 76 kts (87 mph) 140 km/h
Stall speed: 33 kts (38 mph) 60 km/h
Range: 151 naut miles (174 miles) 280 km
Climb rate: 885 ft (270 m) per minute
Availability: Kits and complete aircraft.
Comments: Over 150 sold.

Lucchini Speedy

Address: Lucchini & c, Via le Valeggio 2, 46100 Mantova.
Telephone: +39 376 328569 or 220661
Type: Single-seat, high-wing microlight, with pusher engine and fixed nosewheel undercarriage.
Construction: Metal.
Wing span: 25 ft 11 ins (7.9 m)
Length: 19 ft 8 ins (6 m)
Empty weight: 397 lb (180 kg)
Gross weight: 661 lb (300 kg)
Recommended engine: 52 hp (38.8 kW) Rotax 462 or 64 hp (47.7 kW) Rotax 582
Maximum speed: 113 kts (130 mph) 210 km/h
Cruise speed: 86 kts (99 mph) 160 km/h
Stall speed: 28 kts (33 mph) 52 km/h
Climb rate: 885 ft (270 m) per minute
Availability: Kits and complete aircraft.
Comments: 2-seat version under development.

Maefin TopFun

Address: Maefin, Luigi Muciarelli, Pozzuolo Umbro (PG).
Telephone: +39 75 957134 or +39 376 800235 (North Italy)
Type: Side-by-side 2-seat, high-wing microlight/homebuilt, with fixed nosewheel undercarriage.
Construction: Metal, composites and fabric.
Wing span: 30 ft 4 ins (9.24 m)
Length: 18 ft 11 ins (5.77 m)
Empty weight: 540 lb (245 kg)
Gross weight: 992 lb (450 kg)
Recommended engine: 64.4 hp (48 kW) Rotax 582 or 77.8 hp (58 kW) Rotax 912
Maximum speed: 86 kts (99 mph) 160 km/h
Cruise speed: 76 kts (87 mph) 140 km/h
Stall speed: 22 kts (25 mph) 40 km/h
Range: 162 naut miles (186 miles) 300 km
Climb rate: 1,180 ft (360 m) per minute
Availability: Kits.
Comments: Quick-build kit.

Maefin TopFun microlight (Geoffrey P Jones)

Nike Aerdelta PUL 10

Address: Nike Aerdelta SRL, Via Sabbionara 5, I-40064 Ozzano Emilia, Bologna.
Telephone: +39 51 796910
Facsimile: +39 51 796988
Type: Side-by-side 2-seat, flying-wing homebuilt, with pusher engine and retractable nosewheel undercarriage.
Construction: Steel tube and composites.
Wing span: 32 ft 10 ins (10 m)
Length: 13 ft (3.95 m)
Empty weight: 540 lb (245 kg)
Gross weight: 992 lb (450 kg)
Recommended engine: 64 hp (47.7 kW) Rotax 582
Maximum speed: over 108 kts (124 mph) 200 km/h
Cruise speed: 84 kts (96 mph) 155 km/h
Stall speed: 33 kts (38 mph) 60 km/h
Range: 350 naut miles (403 miles) 648 km
Take-off distance: 493 ft (150 m)
Availability: Kits.
Comments: Derived from the Canadian Ultraflight Lazair microlight and the PUL 9. PUL 10 first flew in July 1990. Also suitable for military use and unmanned operations. Manufactured by Nurflügel in Germany.

Nike Aeronautica PUL 10 (Geoffrey P Jones)

Rodaro Storch

Address: Aergroup Blue Sky, Via Provinciale, 27030 Mezzana Bigli (PV).
Telephone: +39 384 88097
Facsimile: +39 384 88466
Type: Single or side-by-side two-seat high-wing microlight, with fixed nosewheel undercarriage.
Construction: Metal and composites.
Wing span: 33 ft 2 ins (10.1 m)
Length: 20 ft (6.1 m)
Recommended engine: 52 hp (38.8 kW) Rotax 503
Maximum speed: 78 kts (90 mph) 145 km/h
Cruise speed: 62 kts (71 mph) 115 km/h
Stall speed: 30 kts (34 mph) 55 km/h
Availability: Kits.

Rodaro Storch microlight

Terzi T30E Katana

Address: Terzi Aerodine,Piazzale A. Baiamonti 1, 20154 Milan
Telephone: +39 2 3360 7996
Type: Single-seat, competition/aerobatic monoplane, with fixed tail-dragger undercarriage.
Construction: Alloy wings and tail, with steel tube fuselage covered with composite shells.
Wing span: 25 ft 6 ins (7.77 m)
Length: 22 ft (6.7 m)
Empty weight: 1,450 lb (658 kg)
Gross weight: 1,940 lb (880 kg)
Recommended engine: 400 hp (298 kW) Textron Lycoming IO-720 (T30C has 300 hp, 224 kW IO-540).
Maximum speed: 273 kts (314 mph) 505 km/h
Cruise speed: 194 kts (224 mph) 360 km/h
Stall speed: 53 kts (61 mph) 98 km/h
Range: 217 naut miles (250 miles) 402 km
Climb rate: 4,525 ft (1,380 m) per minute
Availability: Plans and kits.
Comments: Designed by Pietro Terzi. First flown on 16 January 1991. Available certificated to FAR 21.

Terzi T30C Katana competition/aerobatic homebuilt (Geoffrey P Jones)

Lithuania

Kensgaila VK-8 Ausra

Address: V. Kensgaila Aircraft Enterprize, Roziu 87, Panevezys 5306.
Telephone: +7 1254 60774
Type: Side-by-side 2-seat, agricultural monoplane, with fixed tail-dragger undercarriage.
Construction: Metal and composites.
Wing span: 48 ft 8 ins (14.83 m)
Length: 32 ft 10 ins (10 m)
Empty weight: 2,513 lb (1,140 kg)
Gross weight: 4,850 lb (2,200 kg)
Recommended engine: 360 hp (268 kW) AOOT M-14P radial
Maximum speed: 119 kts (137 mph) 220 km/h
Cruise speed: 97 kts (112 mph) 180 km/h
Stall speed: 39 kts (44 mph) 71 km/h
Range: 258 naut miles (298 miles) 480 km
Climb rate: 985 ft (300 m) per minute
Comments: First flown in 1989. First seen at the 5th National Homebuilt Convention at Riga in 1989.

Poland

Alpha/Janowski Marco J-5

Address: Jaroslav Janowski, Zaklad Filialny, Zgerz, UL Dadowa 13/17, Wlasciciel, Marold AG-Triesen, Gus 0850589, Poland, or Alpha Aeronautics, Balicka 176-190, PL-30-149 Krakow.
Telephone: +48 12 37 44 17 or 37 40 00
Type: Single-seat monoplane, with pusher engine, tail-boom and V-tail. Option of retractable single main wheel with wingtip outriggers or fixed tail-dragger undercarriage.
Construction: Composites.
Wing span: 26 ft 9 ins (8.16 m)
Length: 15 ft 3 ins (4.66 m)
Empty weight: 363 lb (165 kg)
Gross weight: 640 lb (290 kg)
Recommended engine: 25 hp (18.6 kW) KFM 107ER
Maximum speed: 113 kts (130 mph) 210 km/h
Cruise speed: 91 kts (105 mph) 169 km/h
Stall speed: 42 kts (48 mph) 78 km/h
Range: 295 naut miles (340 miles) 547 km
Take-off distance: 655 ft (200 m)
Climb rate: 605 ft (185 m) per minute
Availability: Kits.
Comments: First flown in Poland on 30 October 1983.

Marco J-5 built in Germany (Geoffrey P Jones)

Orlinski RO-7 Orlik

Address: Roman Orlinski, ul Lesna 4, PL-82-200 Malbork.
Type: Single-seat, low-wing monoplane, with fixed tail-dragger undercarriage.
Construction: Steel tube and wood.
Wing span: 24 ft 11 ins (7.6 m)
Length: 18 ft (5.5 m)
Empty weight: 485 lb (220 kg)
Gross weight: 705 lb (320 kg)
Recommended engine: 65 hp (48.5 kW) Walter Mikron III
Maximum speed: 81 kts (93 mph) 150 km/h
Cruise speed: 49 kts (56 mph) 90 km/h
Stall speed: 39 kts (45 mph) 73 km/h
Range: 215 naut miles (248 miles) 400 km
Take-off distance: 328 ft (100 m)
Climb rate: 984 ft (300 m) per minute
Availability: Plans and some components.

Antoniewski AT-1

Address: M. Antoniewski, Sorboq, Warsaw 00-682, Poland Hoza 50.
Type: Single-seat, low-wing monoplane, with tail-dragger undercarriage.
Construction: Wood, steel tube, composites and fabric.
Wing span: 25 ft (7.62 m)
Length: 17 ft (5.2 m)
Empty weight: 300 lb (136 kg)
Gross weight: 600 lb (272 kg)
Recommended engine: Limbach
Cruise speed: 65 kts (75 mph) 120 km/h estimated
Range: 304 naut miles (350 miles) 563 km
Availability: No details.
Comments: Prototype was flown from Warsaw to the July 1991 RSA rally at Moulins, France.

Antoniewski AT-1 (Geoffrey P Jones)

Spain

Aero-Jean AJ.1/RF-5 Serrania

Address: Aero-Jean SA, PO Box 40, 23280 Beas de Seguria (or France: Avions Rene Fournier, 37270 Athée-Nitray).
Telephone: (France: +33 47 50 68 30)
Facsimile: (France: +33 47 50 24 22)
Type: Tandem 2-seat, low-wing monoplane motor-glider, with retractable single main-wheel undercarriage and outriggers.
Construction: Wood.
Wing span: 45 ft (13.72 m), 28 ft (8.53 m) with wingtips folded.
Length: 29 ft (8.84 m)
Empty weight: 925 lb (420 kg)
Gross weight: 1,431 lb (650 kg)
Recommended engine: Limbach L2000 E01
Maximum speed: 135 kts (155 mph) 250 km/h
Cruise speed: 113 kts (130 mph) 210 km/h
Stall speed: 42 kts (49 mph) 78 km/h
Range: 485 naut miles (558 miles) 900 km
Take-off distance: 656 ft (200 m)
Climb rate: 625 ft (190 m) per minute
Availability: Kits.
Comments: Kit version of the French Fournier RF-5 produced in Spain under licence.

Bücker Prado Jungmann

Address: Bücker Prado SL, PO Box 1239, Albacete (also USA: Krybus Aviation, PO Box 14, Santa Paula, CA 93060)
Telephone: +34 67 508325 (USA: +1 805 525 8764)
Facsimile: +34 67 210581 (USA: +1 805 525 1147)
Type: Tandem 2-seat, aerobatic biplane, with fixed tail-dragger undercarriage.
Construction: Steel tube, wood and fabric.
Wing span: 24 ft 3 ins (7.4 m)
Length: 22 ft 1 ins (6.73 m)
Empty weight: 993 lb (450 kg)
Gross weight: 1,587 lb (720 kg)
Recommended engine: 125-150 hp (93.2-112 kW) Tigre G-IV or Textron Lycoming O-360
Maximum speed: 104 kts (120 mph) 193 km/h
Cruise speed: 96 kts (111 mph) 179 km/h
Stall speed: 39 kts (45 mph) 73 km/h
Range: 193 naut miles (222 miles) 357 km
Climb rate: 1,705 ft (520 m) per minute
Availability: Kits.
Comments: Kits fabricated using original jigs for Bücker/CASA Bu.131.

Bücker Prado Jungmann during final fitting out at Albacete (Geoffrey P Jones)

Bücker Prado Jungmeister

Type: Single-seat, aerobatic biplane, with fixed tail-dragger undercarriage.
Construction: Steel tube, wood and fabric.
Wing span: 21 ft 8 ins (6.6 m)
Length: 19 ft 9 ins (6 m)
Empty weight: 925 lb (420 kg)
Gross weight: 1,342 lb (609 kg)
Recommended engine: Scarab or Textron Lycoming O-360
Maximum speed: 117 kts (135 mph) 217 km/h
Cruise speed: 107 kts (123 mph) 198 km/h
Stall speed: 44 kts (50 mph) 80 km/h
Range: 260 naut miles (300 miles) 482 km
Climb rate: 2,100 (640 m) per minute
Availability: Kits.
Comments: Classic pre-war aerobatic aircraft now available again in kit form.

Sweden

Andreasson BA-4B

Address: Bjorn Andreasson, Collins Vag 22B, S-23600 Hollviksnas.
Type: Single-seat, open or enclosed cockpit, aerobatic biplane with fixed tail-dragger undercarriage.
Construction: Metal, with optional wood wings.
Wing span: 17 ft 7 ins (5.34 m)
Length: 15 ft (4.6 m)
Empty weight: 600 lb (272 kg)
Gross weight: 827 lb (375 kg)
Recommended engine: 100 hp (74.6 kW) Rolls-Royce Continental O-200-A or other type.
Maximum speed: 122 kts (140 mph) 225 km/h
Cruise speed: 104 kts (120 mph) 193 km/h
Stall speed: 33 kts (38 mph) 61 km/h
Range: 152 naut miles (175 miles) 281 km
Climb rate: 2,000 ft (610 m) per minute
Availability: Plans.
Comments: Several built in the UK, including by Crosby Aircraft.

Andreasson BA-4B with Textron Lycoming IO-320 engine (Geoffrey P Jones)

Switzerland

Brändli BX-2 Cherry

Address: BX-Aviation, c/o Max Brändli, Hoeweg 2, CH-2553 Safnern.
Telephone: +41 32 55 18 23
Facsimile: +41 32 55 18 23
Type: Side-by-side 2-seat monoplane, with retractable nosewheel undercarriage.
Construction: Wood and foam composites.
Wing span: 22 ft 11 ins (7 m)
Length: 17 ft 5 ins (5.3 m)
Empty weight: 700 lb (318 kg)
Gross weight: 1,213 lb (550 kg)
Recommended engine: 90 hp (67 kW) Teledyne Continental A65 or Rotax 912
Maximum speed: 141 kts (162 mph) 260 km/h
Cruise speed: 109 kts (125 mph) 200 km/h
Stall speed: 45 kts (52 mph) 84 km/h
Range: 500 naut miles (575 miles) 805 km
Take-off distance: 985 ft (300 m)
Climb rate: 590 ft (180 m) per minute
Availability: Plans and some components.
Comments: Prototype first flew on 24 April 1982. Quickly detachable wings and tail for trailering.

Brändli BX-2 Cherry built by Hans Brandstatter in Austria with a Rotax 912 engine (Geoffrey P Jones)

Brügger MB-2 Colibri 2

Address: Max Brügger, CH-1724 Zenauva.
Telephone: +41 37 33 29 20
Type: Single-seat, low-wing monoplane, with fixed tail-dragger undercarriage.
Construction: Wood and fabric.
Wing span: 19 ft 8 ins (6 m)
Length: 15 ft 9 ins (4.8 m)
Empty weight: 474 lb (215 kg)
Gross weight: 727 lb (330 kg)
Recommended engine: 40 hp (30 kW) 1,600cc Volkswagen
Maximum speed: 96 kts (111 mph) 180 km/h
Cruise speed: 86 kts (99 mph) 160 km/h
Stall speed: 33 kts (38 mph) 60 km/h
Range: 269 naut miles (310 miles) 500 km
Take-off distance: 656 ft (200 m)
Climb rate: 590 ft (180 m) per minute
Availability: Plans.

Comments: Prototype first flew on 1 May 1970. An all-metal Colibri 3 was built but not continued. Over 280 Colibri 2s are under construction or flying in Europe.

Brügger MB-2 Colibri 2 based at Limoges, France (Geoffrey P Jones)

UK

AMF Super Chevvron 2-45CS

Address: AMF Microflight Ltd, Membury Airfield, Lambourne, Berkshire RG16 7TJ.
Telephone: +44 1488 72224
Facsimile: +44 1488 72224
Type: Side-by-side 2-seat, low-wing microlight-trainer, with fixed nosewheel undercarriage. Floats available outside of UK.
Construction: Composites.
Wing span: 39 ft 8 ins (12.1 m)
Length: 23 ft (7.01 m)
Empty weight: 408 lb (185 kg)
Gross weight: 860 lb (390 kg)
Recommended engine: 45 hp (33.6 kW) Limbach-AMF L-550E
Maximum cruise speed: 70 kts (81 mph) 130 km/h
Range: 200 naut miles (230 miles) 370 km
Take-off distance: 300 ft (92 m)
Climb rate: 700 ft (213 m) per minute
Availability: Factory built.
Comments: Prototype Chevvron first flew in 1983. 39 Chevvron 2-32Cs built but production now centred on the new Super Chevvron.

AMF Chevvron 2-32C; Super Chevvron looks similar (Geoffrey P Jones)

CFM Streak Shadow

Address: CFM Metal-Fax Ltd, Unit 2D, Eastlands Industrial Estate, Leiston, Suffolk IP16 4LL.
Telephone: +44 1728 832353 or 833076
Facsimile: +44 1728 832944
Type: Tandem 2-seat, high-wing monoplane, with pusher engine and fixed nosewheel undercarriage.
Construction: Composites, wood and metal.
Wing span: 28 ft (8.53 m)
Length: 21 ft (6.4 m)
Empty weight: 388 lb (176 kg)
Gross weight: 900 lb (408 kg)
Recommended engine: 64.4 hp (48 kW) Rotax 582
Maximum speed: 105 kts (121 mph) 195 km/h
Cruise speed: 87 kts (100 mph) 161 km/h
Stall speed: 25 kts (28 mph) 45 km/h
Range: 347 naut miles (400 miles) 643 km
Climb rate: 1,800 ft (550 m) per minute
Availability: Kits.
Comments: See Laron Aviation Technologies for US built versions of the CFM Shadow range. Prototype first flew in 1983. 250 sold in 36 countries.

Designer David Cook with a CFM Streak Shadow.

Europa Aviation Europa

Address: Europa Aviation Ltd, Unit 2A, Dove Way, Kirby Mills Industrial Estate, Kirbymoorside, N. Yorks YO6 6NR.
Telephone: +44 1751 431773
Facsimile: +44 1751 431706
Type: Side-by-side 2-seat monoplane, with retractable single main wheel and wingtip outriggers. See caption.
Construction: Composites.
Wing span: 26 ft (7.92 m)
Length: 19 ft 2 ins (5.84 m)
Empty weight: 680 lb (308 kg)
Gross weight: 1,300 lb (590 kg)
Recommended engine: 80 hp (59.7 kW) Rotax 912
Maximum speed: 144 kts (166 mph) 267 km/h
Cruise speed: 126 kts (145 mph) 233 km/h
Stall speed: 39 kts (45 mph) 73 km/h
Range: 434 naut miles (500 miles) 805 km
Take-off distance: 600 ft (183 m)
Climb rate: 800 ft (244 m) per minute
Availability: Kits.
Comments: First flown in September 1992. Nearly 230 kits sold by July 1995.

New tri-gear version of the Europa (Geoffrey P Jones)

Isaacs Fury II

Address: John O. Isaacs, 23 Linden Grove, Chandlers Ford, Eastleigh, Hants SO5 1LE.
Telephone: +44 1703 260885
Type: Single-seat, 70% scale representation of a Hawker Fury biplane, with fixed tail-dragger undercarriage.
Construction: Wood and fabric.
Wing span: 21 ft (6.4 m)
Length: 19 ft 3 ins (5.87 m)
Empty weight: 710 lb (322 kg)
Gross weight: 1,000 lb (454 kg)
Recommended engine: 125 hp (93.2 kW) Textron Lycoming O-290
Maximum speed: 100 kts (115 mph) 185 km/h
Cruise speed: 87 kts (100 mph) 161 km/h
Stall speed: 33 kts (38 mph) 61 km/h
Range: 173 naut miles (200 miles) 321 km
Take-off distance: 400 ft (122 m)
Climb rate: 1,600 ft (488 m) per minute
Availability: Plans.
Comments: Designed by John Isaacs. First flown 30 August 1963. About 30 completed and flown worldwide.

Isaacs Fury II built by Graham Jones, in Persian AF colours (Geoffrey P Jones)

Isaacs Spitfire

Type: 60% scale representation of a Spitfire, with fixed tail-dragger undercarriage.
Construction: Wood and fabric.
Wing span: 22 ft 1 ins (6.75 m)
Length: 19 ft 3 ins (5.87 m)
Empty weight: 805 lb (365 kg)
Gross weight: 1,100 lb (499 kg)
Recommended engine: 100 hp (74.6 kW) Teledyne Continental
Maximum speed: 130 kts (150 mph) 241 km/h
Cruise speed: 116 kts (134 mph) 216 km/h
Stall speed: 45 kts (52 mph) 84 km/h
Range: 174 naut miles (200 miles) 321 km
Take-off distance: 600 ft (183 m)
Climb rate: 1,100 ft (335 m) per minute
Availability: Plans.
Comments: First flown on 5 May 1975.

Mainair Blade 503 and 582

Address: Mainair Sports Ltd, Unit 2, Alma Industrial Estate, Regent Street, Rochdale, Lancashire OL12 0HQ.
Telephone: +44 1706 55134
Facsimile: +44 1706 31561
Type: Tandem 2-seat, flex-wing microlight, with pusher engine and fixed nosewheel undercarriage.
Construction: Alloy tube and fabric.
Wing span: 34 ft 6 ins (10.52 m)
Length: 9 ft 2 ins (2.8 m)
Empty weight: 463 lb (210 kg)
Gross weight: 860 lb (390 kg)
Recommended engine: 50 hp (37.3 kW) Rotax 503 or 64.4 hp (48 kW) Rotax 582-2V
Maximum speed: 91 kts (105 mph) 169 km/h
Cruise speed: 43-61 kts (50-70 mph) 80-113 km/h
Stall speed: 25 kts (28 mph) 45 km/h
Availability: Completed aircraft.
Comments: In-flight trimmer and aerodynamic fins on the wheel spats give the Blade good handling in turbulent air.

Mainair Blade two-seater (Paul Tomlin)

Mainair Mercury

Type: Single or tandem 2-seat flex-wing monoplane, with pusher engine and fixed nosewheel undercarriage.

Construction: Alloy tube and fabric.
Wing span: 34 ft 9 ins (10.6 m)
Length: 11 ft 4 ins (3.46 m)
Empty weight: 328 lb (149 kg)
Gross weight: 728 lb (330 kg)
Recommended engine: 51 hp (38 kW) Rotax 462, 50 hp (37.3 kW) Rotax 503 or 64.4 hp (48 kW) Rotax 582
Maximum speed: 77 kts (89 mph) 143 km/h
Cruise speed: 43-52 kts (50-60 mph) 80-97 km/h
Stall speed: 25 kts (28 mph) 45 km/h
Range: 434 naut miles (500 miles) 804 km with long-range tank.
Climb rate: 490 ft (150 m) per minute (dual)
Availability: Kit or ready built.
Comments: Aerodynamic fuselage pod can be fitted to the trike unit.

Nipper Kits Nipper Mk.III

Address: Nipper Kits & Components Ltd, Foxley, Blackness Lane, Keston, Kent BR2 6HL.
Telephone: +44 1689 858351
Type: Single-seat, mid-wing, aerobatic homebuilt, with fixed nosewheel undercarriage.
Construction: Steel tube, wood and fabric.
Wing span: 19 ft 8 ins (6 m)
Length: 15 ft (4.57 m)
Empty weight: 465 lb (211 kg)
Gross weight: 750 lb (340 kg), 685 lb (311 kg) for aerobatics.
Recommended engine: 60 hp (44.7 kW) 1,834cc Volkswagen
Maximum speed: 100 kts (115 mph) 185 km/h
Cruise speed: 78 kts (90 mph) 145 km/h
Stall speed: 34 kts (39 mph) 63 km/h
Range: 139 naut miles (160 miles) 257 km, or 304 naut miles (350 miles) 563 km with tip tanks.
Take-off distance: 280 ft (86 m)
Climb rate: 650 ft (198 m) per minute
Availability: Plans and some components.
Comments: Developed from the Avions Fairey Tipsy Nipper. Other engine fits now available.

Nipper with tip-tanks (Geoffrey P Jones)

Pegasus AX-3

Address: Pegasus Aviation, Elm Tree Park, Marlborough, Wiltshire SN8 1PS.
Telephone: +44 1672 861578
Facsimile: +44 1672 861550
Type: Side by side 2-seat monoplane, with nosewheel undercarriage.
Construction: Glassfibre.
Wing span: 32 ft 2 ins (9.8 m)
Length: 15 ft 1 ins (5 m)
Empty weight: 430 lb (195 kg)
Gross weight: 860 lb (390 kg)
Recommended engine: 52 hp (38.8 kW) Rotax 503
Maximum speed: 65 kts (75 mph) 121 km/h
Cruise speed: 52 kts (60 mph) 97 km/h
Stall speed: 27 kts (31 mph) 50 km/h
Take-off distance: 100 ft (31 m)
Climb rate: 433 ft (132 m) per minute
Availability: Factory built.
Comments: Unlike other aircraft from Pegasus, this is a 3-axis control type.

Pegasus AX-3

Pegasus Chaser-S

Type: Single-seat, flex-wing microlight, with nosewheel trike.
Construction: Alloy tube, fabric and composites.
Wing span: 26 ft 7 ins (8.1 m)
Length: 16 ft 1 ins (4.9 m) wing bag.
Empty weight: 220 lb (100 kg)
Gross weight: 485 lb (220 kg)
Recommended engine: 35 hp (26 kW) Rotax 337, or 40 hp (30 kW) Rotax 447 or 508
Maximum speed: 80-82 kts (92-95 mph) 148-153 km/h
Cruise speed: 48-61 kts (55-70 mph) 89-113 km/h, depending on engine.
Stall speed: 30 kts (34 mph) 55 km/h
Take-off distance over a 50 ft obstacle: 285-312 ft (87-95 m)
Availability: Factory built.

Pegasus Quantum 15 Super Sport 582 LN

Type: 2-seat flex-wing microlight/light aircraft, with nosewheel trike.
Construction: Alloy tube, Mylar and Kevlar fabric, and composites.
Wing span: 34 ft (10.35 m)
Gross weight: 858 lb (390 kg)
Recommended engine: 54 hp (40 kW) Rotax 582
Maximum speed: 73 kts (84 mph) 135 km/h
Cruise speed: 55 kts (63 mph) 101 km/h
Stall speed: 23 kts (26 mph) 42 km/h
Take-off distance: 280 ft (85 m)
Climb rate: 666 ft (203 m) per minute
Availability: Factory built, or kit for export only.
Comments: Also available in Sport and Clubman versions with differing wings and engines.

Pegasus Quasar

Type: 2-seat, flex-wing microlight/light aircraft, with nosewheel trike.
Construction: Alloy tube, Trilam or Mylar and Kevlar fabric, and composites.
Wing span: 34 ft (10.35 m)
Length: 9 ft 3 ins (2.82 m) for trike.
Empty weight: 385 lb (175 kg)
Gross weight: 858 lb (390 kg)
Recommended engine: 54 hp (40 kW) Rotax 582
Maximum speed: 69 kts (80 mph) 129 km/h
Cruise speed: 52 kts (60 mph) 97 km/h
Stall speed: 23 kts (26 mph) 42 km/h
Take-off distance over a 50 ft obstacle: 575 ft (175 m)
Climb rate: 666 ft (203 m) per minute
Availability: Factory built.

Pegasus Quasar

PFA Currie Wot

Address: Popular Flying Association, Terminal Building, Shoreham Airport, Shoreham-by-Sea, Sussex BN43 5FF.
Telephone: +44 1273 461616
Facsimile: +44 1273 463390
Type: Single-seat biplane, with fixed tail-dragger undercarriage.
Construction: Wood and fabric.
Wing span: 22 ft 1 ins (6.73 m)
Length: 18 ft 4 ins (5.59 m)
Empty weight: 550 lb (249 kg)
Gross weight: 900 lb (408 kg)
Recommended engine: 65 hp (48.5 kW) Walter Mikron or 90 hp (67 kW) Teledyne Continental C90
Maximum speed: 83 kts (95 mph) 153 km/h
Cruise speed: 70 kts (80 mph) 129 km/h
Stall speed: 35 kts (40 mph) 65 km/h
Range: 208 naut miles (240 miles) 386 km
Take-off distance: 500 ft (152 m)
Climb rate: 600 ft (183 m) per minute
Availability: Plans.
Comments: Designed by J. R. Currie in 1937. Plans sold via the PFA.

PFA Currie Wot with Teledyne Continental A-65 engine (Geoffrey P Jones)

PFA/Luton LA.4 Minor

Type: Single-seat, parasol-wing monoplane, with fixed tail-dragger undercarriage.
Construction: Wood and fabric.
Wing span: 25 ft (7.62 m)
Length: 20 ft 9 ins (6.32 m)
Empty weight: 390 lb (177 kg)
Gross weight: 750 lb (340 kg)
Recommended engine: Volkswagen, Teledyne Continental or Textron Lycoming, between 50 and 100 hp (37.3 and 74.6 kW).
Maximum speed: 65 kts (75 mph) 121 km/h
Cruise speed: 60 kts (69 mph) 111 km/h
Stall speed: 25 kts (28 mph) 45 km/h
Range: 173 naut miles (200 miles) 321 km
Take-off distance: 300 ft (92 m)
Climb rate: 350 ft (107 m) per minute
Availability: Plans.
Comments: Classic homebuilt design from 1936. See also Falconar Cubmajor (Canada).

PFA/Luton LA.4 Minor with Textron Lycoming O-145 engine (Geoffrey P Jones)

Sherwood Ranger ST

Address: TCD Ltd, Larkfield, Retford Road, Mattersey, Doncaster, S. Yorkshire DN10 5HG (USA: Sherwood America Aviation, 904 Silver Spur Road, Ste 333, Rolling Hills Estates, CA 90274).
Telephone: +44 1777 817975 (USA: +1 310 325 3422)
Facsimile: +44 1302 752643 (USA: +1 310 378 7685)
Type: Single/tandem-seat biplane, with fixed tail-dragger undercarriage.
Construction: Wood, tube and fabric.
Wing span: 23 ft (7.01 m)
Length: 20 ft (6.1 m)
Empty weight: 500 lb (227 kg)
Gross weight: 1,000 lb (454 kg)
Recommended engine: 64.4 hp (48 kW) Rotax 582 (Rotax 503 for lighter "LW" series).
Maximum speed: 83 kts (95 mph) 153 km/h
Cruise speed: 78 kts (90 mph) 145 km/h
Stall speed: 33-37 kts (38-42 mph) 61-68 km/h
Range: 182 naut miles (210 miles) 338 km
Take-off distance: 700 ft (214 m)
Climb rate: 1,200 ft (366 m) per minute
Availability: Kits.
Comments: First flown in October 1992. Folding wings, and also available as the LW microlight.

Sherwood Ranger two-seat biplane prototype (Geoffrey P Jones)

Smith Acro Advanced

Address: Barry Smith, 2 Wrentree Close, Redcar, Cleveland TS10 4SB
Telephone: +44 642 475631 or 470322
Type: Single-seat aerobatic monoplane, with fixed tail-dragger undercarriage.
Construction: Steel tube, wood and composites.
Wing span: 19 ft 10 ins (6.05 m)
Length: 15 ft 11 ins (4.85 m)
Empty weight: 490 lb (222 kg)
Gross weight: 750 lb (340 kg)
Recommended engine: 68 hp (50.7 kW) 2.1 litre Acro Aerobatic Volkswagen conversion
Cruise speed: 113-122 kts (130-140 mph) 209-225 km/h
Stall speed: 42 kts (48 mph) 78 km/h
Range: 391 naut miles (450 miles) 724 km
Take-off distance: 656 ft (200 m)
Climb rate: 1,500 ft (457 m) per minute
Availability: prototype only.
Comments: Intended for affordable competition aerobatics up to advanced level. Designed by Barry Smith.

Smith Aero Advanced (Geoffrey P Jones)

Speedtwin Developments Speedtwin Mk.I

Address: Speedtwin Developments Ltd, Upper Cae Garw Farm, Trellech, Monmouth, Gwent NP5 4PJ.
Telephone: +44 1600 860165
Facsimile: +44 1600 860813
Type: Tandem 2-seat, aerobatic monoplane, with twin engines and fixed tail-dragger undercarriage.
Construction: Metal.
Wing span: 26 ft (7.92 m)
Length: 22 ft 10 ins (6.96 m)
Empty weight: 1,410 lb (640 kg)
Gross weight: 2,250 lb (1,020 kg) or 2,000 lb (907 kg) for aerobatics.
Recommended engines: 2 x 100 hp (74.6 kW) Teledyne Continental O-200
Maximum speed: 155 kts (178 mph) 286 km/h
Cruise speed: 139 kts (160 mph) 257 km/h
Stall speed: 59 kts (68 mph) 110 km/h
Range: 1,129 naut miles (1,300 miles) 2,092 km
Take-off distance: 540 ft (165 m)
Climb rate: 1,200 ft (366 m) per minute
Availability: Kits.
Comments: First flown in 1992. Speedtwin Mk.II has 2 x 160 hp (119.3 kW) Textron Lycomings.

Speedtwin Mk.I prototype (Geoffrey P Jones)

Taylor JT.1 Monoplane

Address: 79 Springwater Road, Leigh-on-Sea, Essex SS9 5BW.
Telephone: +44 1702 521484
Type: Single-seat, open or enclosed cockpit, low-wing monoplane, with fixed tail-dragger undercarriage.
Construction: Wood and fabric.
Wing span: 21 ft (6.4 m)
Length: 15 ft (4.57 m)
Empty weight: 430 lb (195 kg)
Gross weight: 660 lb (299 kg)
Recommended engine: 40 hp (30 kW) 1,500cc Volkswagen
Maximum speed: 100 kts (115 mph) 185 km/h
Cruise speed: 87 kts (100 mph) 161 km/h
Stall speed: 35 kts (40 mph) 65 km/h
Range: 252 naut miles (290 miles) 466 km
Take-off distance: 600 ft (183 m) from grass, 350 ft (107 m) paved.
Climb rate: 1,000 ft (305 m) per minute
Availability: Plans.
Comments: First flight 4 July 1959. Engines in the 40-60 hp (30-44.7 kW) range are suitable. Over 113 completed and flown worldwide.

Taylor JT.2 Titch

Type: Single-seat racing monoplane, with fixed tail-dragger undercarriage.
Construction: Wood, aluminium and fabric.
Wing span: 18 ft 9 ins (5.72 m)
Length: 16 ft 2 ins (4.93 m)
Empty weight: 505 lb (229 kg)
Gross weight: 760 lb (345 kg)
Recommended engine: 85 hp (63.4 kW) Teledyne Continental C85 (also suitable for 105 hp, 78.3 kW Textron Lycoming)
Maximum speed: 174 kts (200 mph) 322 km/h
Cruise speed: 139 kts (160 mph) 257 km/h
Stall speed: 52 kts (59 mph) 95 km/h
Range: 330 naut miles (380 miles) 611 km
Take-off distance: 600 ft (183 m) from grass, 350 ft (107 m) paved.
Climb rate: 1,100-2,000 ft (335-610 m) per minute
Availability: Plans.
Comments: Prototype first flew on 4 January 1967. Used for Formula One air racing and by Vic Davies for European city-to-city records. Over 33 completed worldwide.

Taylor Titch "Special" with tip tanks, flown on record breaking flights by Vic Davies (Geoffrey P Jones)

Whittaker MW.5 Sorcerer

Address: Mike Whittaker, Dawlish Cottage, Pincots Lane, Wickwar, Wotton-under-Edge, Gloucestershire GL12 8NY.
Telephone: +44 1454 294598
Type: Single-seat, high-wing monoplane, with tail-dragger undercarriage.
Construction: Steel tube, wood and fabric.
Wing span: 28 ft (8.53 m)
Length: 15 ft 9 ins (4.8 m)
Empty weight: 308 lb (140 kg)
Gross weight: 528 lb (239 kg)
Recommended engine: 50 hp (37.3 kW) Fuji-Robin
Maximum speed: 85 kts (98 mph) 158 km/h
Cruise speed: 61 kts (70 mph) 113 km/h
Range: 149 naut miles (172 miles) 276 km
Availability: Plans.
Comments: Microlight or homebuilt category. Rotax 503 and 532 engines optional. Over 18 completed and flown.

Whittaker MW.6 Merlin

Type: Tandem 2-seat, high-wing monoplane, with fixed nosewheel undercarriage.
Construction: Alloy tube and fabric.
Wing span: 32 ft (9.75 m)
Length: 17 ft 6 ins (5.33 m)
Empty weight: 400 lb (181 kg)
Gross weight: 800 lb (363 kg)
Recommended engine: 50 hp (37.3 kW) Robin, 50 hp (37.3 kW) Rotax 503 or 64.4 hp (48 kW) Rotax 532
Maximum speed: 100 kts (115 mph) 185 km/h
Cruise speed: 70 kts (80 mph) 129 km/h
Range: 104 naut miles (120 miles) 193 km
Availability: Plans.
Comments: Development of MW.5. Over 25 completed and flown.

Whittaker MW.7

Type: Single-seat, aerobatic monoplane, with fixed tail-dragger undercarriage.
Construction: Alloy tube and fabric.
Wing span: 22 ft (6.71 m)
Length: 15 ft (4.57 m)
Empty weight: 320 lb (145 kg)
Gross weight: 540 lb (245 kg)
Recommended engine: 64 hp (47.7 kW) Rotax 532
Maximum speed: 100 kts (115 mph) 185 km/h
Cruise speed: 78 kts (90 mph) 145 km/h
Range: 220 naut miles (253 miles) 407 km
Availability: Plans.
Comments: First flown in August 1988. One of the few available aerobatic microlights.

Whittaker MW.7 built by Kim Wilcox (Geoffrey P Jones)

Whittaker MW.8

Type: Single-seat monoplane, with pusher engine and fixed nosewheel undercarriage.
Construction: Alloy tube, wood and fabric.
Wing span: 29 ft 6 ins (8.99 m)
Length: 18 ft 4 ins (5.59 m)
Empty weight: 400 lb (181 kg)
Gross weight: 680 lb (308 kg)
Recommended engine: 42.9 hp (32 kW) Rotax 508
Availability: Plans.
Comments: Suitable for precision flying competitions, with good cockpit visibility, good fuel economy, and flaps for spot landings. First flown in 1993.

Whittaker MW.8 prototype (Geoffrey P Jones)

USA

Ace Aircraft Baby Ace D

Address: Ace Aircraft Co, 05-134th Street, Chesapeake, WV 25315.
Telephone: +1 304 949 3098
Type: Single-seat, parasol-wing monoplane, with fixed tail-dragger undercarriage.
Construction: Steel tube, wood and fabric.
Wing span: 26 ft 5 ins (8.05 m)
Length: 17 ft 9 ins (5.41 m)
Empty weight: 575 lb (261 kg)
Gross weight: 950 lb (431 kg)
Recommended engine: Teledyne Continental A65 or other engine of 65 or 85 hp (48.5 or 63.4 kW)
Maximum speed: 96 kts (110 mph) 177 km/h
Cruise speed: 87 kts (100 mph) 161 km/h
Stall speed: 30 kts (34 mph) 55 km/h
Range: 304 naut miles (350 miles) 563 km
Take-off distance: 250 ft (77 m)
Climb rate: 1,200 ft (366 m) per minute
Availability: Plans and kits.
Comments: Originally designed by "Ace" Corben in the 1930s, and updated to Model D form (first flying in 1956). Over 350 completed.

Ace Baby Ace Model D (Geoffrey P Jones)

Ace Aircraft Junior Ace E

Type: Side-by-side 2-seat open cockpit version of the Baby Ace Model D, with parasol wing and fixed tail-dragger undercarriage.
Construction: Steel tube, wood and fabric.
Wing span: 26 ft (7.92 m)
Length: 18 ft (5.49 m)
Empty weight: 809 lb (367 kg)
Gross weight: 1,335 lb (606 kg)
Recommended engine: 85 hp (63.4 kW) Teledyne Continental C85
Maximum speed: 113 kts (130 mph) 209 km/h
Cruise speed: 91 kts (105 mph) 169 km/h
Stall speed: 39 kts (44 mph) 71 km/h
Range: 304 naut miles (350 miles) 563 km
Take-off distance: 400 ft (122 m)
Climb rate: 500 ft (153 m) per minute
Availability: Plans and kits.

Acro Sport Acro-Sport I

Address: Acro Sport Inc, PO Box 462, Hales Corner, WI 53130
Telephone: +1 414 529 2609
Type: Single-seat competition/aerobatic biplane, with fixed tail-dragger undercarriage.
Construction: Steel tube, wood and fabric.
Wing span: 19 ft 7 ins (5.97 m)
Length: 17 ft 6 ins (5.33 m)
Empty weight: 733 lb (332 kg)
Gross weight: 1,350 lb (612 kg)
Recommended engine: 180 hp (134 kW) Textron Lycoming IO-360
Maximum speed: 132 kts (152 mph) 245 km/h
Cruise speed: 113 kts (130 mph) 209 km/h
Stall speed: 44 kts (50 mph) 81 km/h
Range: 304 naut miles (350 miles) 563 km
Take-off distance: 150 ft (46 m)
Climb rate: 1,800-3,500 ft (549-1,067 m) per minute
Availability: Plans and components.
Comments: Designed for construction by school students. First flown on 11 January 1972. The Super Acro Sport, suitable for unlimited International level aerobatics, is generally similar but with a different wing section.

Acro Sport Acro-Sport I built in the UK with an IO-360 engine (Geoffrey P Jones)

Acro Sport Acro-Sport II

Type: Tandem 2-seat aerobatic biplane, with fixed tail-dragger undercarriage.
Construction: Steel tube, wood and fabric.
Wing span: 21 ft 8 ins (6.6 m)
Length: 18 ft 10 ins (5.74 m)
Empty weight: 875 lb (397 kg)
Gross weight: 1,520 lb (689 kg)
Recommended engine: 180 hp (134 kW) Textron Lycoming IO-360-A4B or similar.
Maximum speed: 124 kts (143 mph) 230 km/h
Cruise speed: 107 kts (123 mph) 198 km/h
Stall speed: 46 kts (53 mph) 86 km/h
Range: 260 naut miles (300 miles) 483 km
Take-off distance: 300 ft (92 m)
Climb rate: 1,500 ft (457 m) per minute
Availability: Plans and components.
Comments: 2-seat development of the Acro Sport I. First flown on 9 July 1978. An estimated 74 completed and flown.

Acro Sport Pober Junior Ace

Type: Side-by-side 2-seat, parasol-wing monoplane, with fixed tail-dragger undercarriage.
Construction: Steel tube, wood and fabric.
Wing span: 34 ft (10.36 m)
Length: 20 ft (6.1 m)
Empty weight: 750 lb (340 kg)
Gross weight: 1,320 lb (599 kg)
Recommended engine: Teledyne Continental C65, A/C85 or other type.
Maximum speed: 113 kts (130 mph) 209 km/h
Cruise speed: 70 kts (80 mph) 129 km/h
Stall speed: 39 kts (45 mph) 73 km/h
Range: 217 naut miles (250 miles) 402 km
Take-off distance: 350 ft (107 m)
Climb rate: 500 ft (152 m) per minute
Availability: Plans and components.
Comments: Updated version of the 1930s design by "Ace" Corben (see Ace Aircraft Co.).

Acro Sport Pober Pixie

Type: Single-seat, open cockpit parasol-wing monoplane, with fixed tail-dragger undercarriage.
Construction: Steel tube, wood and fabric.
Wing span: 29 ft 10 ins (9.09 m)
Length: 17 ft 3 ins (5.26 m)
Empty weight: 543 lb (246 kg)
Gross weight: 900 lb (408 kg)
Recommended engine: 60 hp (44.7 kW) Limbach SL1700, other Volkswagens or Teledyne Continental C65.
Maximum speed: 90 kts (103 mph) 166 km/h
Cruise speed: 72 kts (83 mph) 134 km/h
Stall speed: 26 kts (30 mph) 49 km/h
Range: 252 naut miles (290 miles) 466 km
Take-off distance: 300 ft (92 m)
Climb rate: 500 ft (152 m) per minute
Availability: Plans and components.
Comments: Designed by ex-EAA President Paul Poberezny. First flown in July 1974.

Acro Sport Pober Pixie built in Belgium by M. Haegeman (Geoffrey P Jones)

Acro Sport Pober Super Ace

Type: Single-seat, parasol-wing monoplane, with fixed tail-dragger undercarriage.
Construction: Steel tube, wood and fabric.
Wing span: 27 ft 4 ins (8.32 m)
Length: 18 ft 5 ins (5.61 m)
Empty weight: 685 lb (311 kg)
Gross weight: 1,030 lb (467 kg)
Take-off distance: 350 ft (107 m)
Recommended engine: 85 hp (63.4 kW) Teledyne Continental A/C85
Maximum speed: 139 kts (160 mph) 257 km/h
Cruise speed: 96 kts (110 mph) 177 km/h
Stall speed: 33 kts (38 mph) 61 km/h
Range: 217 naut miles (250 miles) 402 km
Climb rate: 500 ft (152 m) per minute
Availability: Plans and components.

Acro Sport Nesmith Cougar I

Type: Side-by-side 2-seat, high wing monoplane, with fixed tail-dragger undercarriage.
Construction: Sheet metal, steel tube, wood and fabric.
Wing span: 20 ft 6 ins (6.25 m)
Length: 18 ft 11 ins (5.77 m)
Empty weight: 624 lb (283 kg)
Gross weight: 1,250 lb (567 kg)
Recommended engine: Teledyne Continental A/C85
Maximum speed: 152 kts (175 mph) 282 km/h
Cruise speed: 104 kts (120 mph) 193 km/h
Stall speed: 46 kts (53 mph) 86 km/h
Range: 521 naut miles (600 miles) 965 km
Take-off distance: 800 ft (244 m)
Climb rate: 1,300 ft (396 m) per minute
Availability: Plans and components.
Comments: Over 100 completed, mainly in N. America.

Acro Sport Nesmith Cougar I built by Ken Dannenburg (Geoffrey P Jones)

Adventure Air 2 + 2 Amphibian

Address: Adventure Air, Carroll County Airport, PO Box 368, Berryville, AR 72616-0368.
Telephone: +1 501 423 5350
Facsimile: +1 501 423 5366
Type: 2 + 2 seat, amphibious monoplane, with pusher engine mounted above the wing and retractable nosewheel undercarriage.
Construction: Composites.
Wing span: 35 ft (10.67 m)
Length: 24 ft (7.32 m)
Empty weight: 1,800 lb (816 kg)
Gross weight: 3,000 lb (1,361 kg)
Recommended engine: 200 hp (149 kW) Textron Lycoming
Maximum speed: 137 kts (158 mph) 254 km/h
Cruise speed: 113 kts (130 mph) 209 km/h
Stall speed: 47 kts (54 mph) 87 km/h
Range: 1,390 naut miles (1,600 miles) 2,575 km with optional 189 litre wing tanks.
Take-off distance: 700 ft (214 m) land, 1,000 ft (305 m) water.
Climb rate: 800 ft (244 m) per minute
Availability: Kits.
Comments: First flown in 1993. Other available models include the Super Adventurer and Adventurer 4-Place. Engine options include 210 hp (156.6 kW) Teledyne Continental, 220 hp (164 kW) Ford V.8 and 230 hp (171.5 kW) Chevrolet 4.3L.

Adventure Air 2 + 2 Amphibian (Geoffrey P Jones)

Adventure Air Adventure Twin

Type: Side-by-side 2-seat, amphibious monoplane, with twin wing-mounted engines and retractable nosewheel undercarriage.
Construction: Composites.
Wing span: 35 ft (10.67 m)
Length: 24 ft (7.32 m)
Empty weight: 1,850 lb (839 kg)
Gross weight: 3,100 lb (1,406 kg)
Take-off distance: 650 ft (198 m) land, 1,000 ft (305 m) water.
Recommended engines: 2 x 100 hp (74.6 kW) CAM100
Maximum speed: 130 kts (150 mph) 241 km/h
Cruise speed: 117 kts (135 mph) 217 km/h
Stall speed: 47 kts (54 mph) 87 km/h
Range: 1,173 naut miles (1,350 miles) 2,172 km
Climb rate: 850 ft (259 m) per minute
Availability: Kits.
Comments: Prototype expected to fly in 1995. Other suitable engines include 150 and 160 hp (112 and 119.3 kW) Textron Lycomings.

AeroCad AeroCanard

Address: AeroCad Inc, 1445 Crater Lane, Yadkinville, NC 27055.
Telephone: +1 910 961 2238
Facsimile: +1 910 961 2238
Type: 4-seat monoplane with canards, winglets, pusher engine, and nosewheel undercarriage (retractable nosewheel, fixed main units).
Construction: Composites.
Wing span: 28 ft 2 ins (8.59 m)
Length: 16 ft 9 ins (5.11 m)
Empty weight: 1,080 lb (490 kg)
Gross weight: 2,050 lb (930 kg)
Recommended engine: 200 hp (149 kW) Textron Lycoming IO-360
Maximum speed: 196 kts (225 mph) 362 km/h
Cruise speed: 178 kts (205 mph) 330 km/h
Stall speed: approx 61 kts (70 mph) 113 km/h
Range: 869 naut miles (1,000 miles) 1,609 km
Take-off distance: 1,000 ft (305 m)
Climb rate: 1,500 ft (457 m) per minute
Availability: Kits.
Comments: Prototype scheduled to fly early 1995.

Aerocar Mini-Imp

Address: Aerocar Associates, Box 1171, Longview, WA 98632.
Telephone: +1 206 425 9874
Type: Single-seat monoplane, with engine in mid-fuselage and tail mounted pusher propeller, inverted V-tail and retractable nosewheel undercarriage.
Construction: Metal and composites.
Wing span: 25 ft (7.62 m)
Length: 16 ft (4.88 m)
Empty weight: 500 lb (227 kg)
Gross weight: 850 lb (386 kg)
Recommended engine: 100 hp (74.6 kW) Teledyne Continental O-200
Maximum speed: 174 kts (200 mph) 322 km/h
Cruise speed: 152 kts (175 mph) 282 km/h
Stall speed: 48 kts (55 mph) 89 km/h
Range: 434 naut miles (500 miles) 805 km
Take-off distance: 600 ft (183 m)
Climb rate: 1,500 ft (457 m) per minute
Availability: Plans.
Comments: Designed by Moulton "Molt" Taylor. A similar version, constructed of Taylor Paper Glass and called the Micro-Imp, is also available.

Aerocar Coot-A

Type: Side-by-side 2-seat, amphibious monoplane, with retractable nosewheel undercarriage.
Construction: Metal, composites and wood.
Wing span: 34 ft (10.36 m)
Length: 22 ft (6.71 m)
Empty weight: 1,450 lb (658 kg)
Gross weight: 1,950 lb (885 kg)
Take-off distance: 200 ft (61 m) land, 600 ft (183 m) water.
Recommended engine: 180 hp or 220 hp (134 or 164 kW) Franklin
Maximum speed: 122 kts (140 mph) 225 km/h
Cruise speed: 104 kts (120 mph) 193 km/h
Range: 434 naut miles (500 miles) 804 km
Climb rate: 1,000-1,250 ft (305-381 m) per minute
Availability: Plans.
Comments: Prototype first flew in February 1971.

Aerocar Coot-A built by Lionel Parrera at Petaluma, California (Geoffrey P Jones)

Aero Designs Pulsar

Address: Aero Designs Inc, 11910 Radium Street, San Antonio, TX 78216
Telephone: +1 210 308 9332
Facsimile: +1 210 308 9329
Type: Side-by-side 2-seat monoplane, with fixed nosewheel or tail-dragger undercarriage.
Construction: Composites.
Wing span: 25 ft (7.62 m)
Length: 19 ft 6 ins (5.94 m)
Empty weight: 460 lb (209 kg)
Gross weight: 900 lb (408 kg)
Recommended engine: 64.4 hp (48 kW) Rotax 582
Maximum speed: 122 kts (140 mph) 225 km/h
Cruise speed: 113 kts (130 mph) 209 km/h
Stall speed: 39 kts (45 mph) 209 km/h
Range: 434 naut miles (500 miles) 804 km
Take-off distance: 800 ft (244 m)
Climb rate: 1,000 ft (305 m) per minute
Availability: Kits.
Comments: 2-seat version of the Star-Lite, designed by Mark Brown, which is no longer available. Prototype Pulsar first flew on 3 April 1988.

Aero Designs Pulsar built by Martin Faro (Geoffrey P Jones)

Aero Designs Pulsar XP

Type: Side-by-side 2-seat monoplane, with fixed nosewheel or tail-dragger undercarriage.
Construction: Composites.
Wing span: 25 ft (7.62 m)
Length: 19 ft 6 ins (5.94 m)
Empty weight: 510 lb (231 kg)
Gross weight: 960 lb (435 kg)
Recommended engine: 80 hp (59.7 kW) Rotax 912
Maximum speed: 139 kts (160 mph) 257 km/h
Cruise speed: 122 kts (140 mph) 225 km/h
Stall speed: 40 kts (46 mph) 74 km/h
Range: 521 naut miles (600 miles) 965 km
Take-off distance: 800 ft (244 m)
Climb rate: 1,200 ft (366 m) per minute
Availability: Kits.
Comments: More powerful version of the Pulsar. Quick-build kits available.

Aerolites AeroMaster AG

Address: Aerolites Inc, 12104 David Road, Welsh, LA 70591.
Telephone: +1 318 734 3865
Facsimile: +1 318 734 3865
Type: Single-seat, low-wing monoplane for agricultural spraying, with fixed tail-dragger undercarriage.
Construction: Composites, steel tube and fabric.
Wing span: 28 ft 8 ins (8.74 m)
Length: 18 ft 6 ins (5.64 m)
Empty weight: 425 lb (193 kg)
Gross weight: 1,000 lb (454 kg)
Recommended engine: 64.4 hp (48 kW) Rotax 582
Maximum speed: 83 kts (95 mph) 153 km/h
Cruise speed: 65 kts (75 mph) 121 km/h
Range: 130 naut miles (150 miles) 241 km
Availability: Kits.
Comments: Kit includes Spray Miser CDA ag system. 56 kts (65 mph) 105 km/h spray speed; 113.5 litre tank covers up to 120 acres.

Aerolites Aeromaster AG (Geoffrey P Jones)

Aerolites Ag Bearcat

Type: Single-seat high-wing monoplane for agricultural spraying, with fixed tail-dragger undercarriage.
Construction: Composites, steel tube and fabric.
Wing span: 30 ft 4 ins (9.25 m)
Length: 18 ft 6 ins (5.64 m)
Empty weight: 380 lb (172 kg)
Gross weight: 900 lb (408 kg)
Recommended engine: 65 hp (48.5 kW) Rotax 582
Maximum speed: 78 kts (90 mph) 145 km/h
Cruise speed: 61 kts (70 mph) 113 km/h
Stall speed: 31 kts (35 mph) 57 km/h
Range: 121 naut miles (140 miles) 225 km
Take-off distance: 500 ft (152 m)
Climb rate: 1,000 ft (305 m) per minute
Availability: Kits.
Comments: Available for use with Spray Miser CDA ag system.

Aerolites Bearcat

Type: Single-seat, parasol wing monoplane, with fixed tail-dragger undercarriage.
Construction: Composites, steel tube and fabric.
Wing span: 30 ft 4 ins (9.25 m)
Length: 18 ft 6 ins (5.64 m)
Empty weight: 300 lb (136 kg)
Gross weight: 750 lb (340 kg)
Recommended engine: 42 hp (31.3 kW) Rotax 447
Maximum speed: 65 kts (75 mph) 121 km/h
Cruise speed: 55 kts (63 mph) 101 km/h
Stall speed: 28 kts (32 mph) 52 km/h
Range: 104 naut miles (120 miles) 193 km
Take-off distance: 100 ft (31 m)
Climb rate: 700 ft (213 m) per minute
Availability: Kits.
Comments: Microlight representation of the 1930s Corben Baby Ace.

Aero-Systems Cadet STF

Address: Aero-Systems, 9031 Suncrest Street, Wichita, KS 67212.
Telephone: +1 316 722 2494
Type: Side-by-side 2-seat replica of the 1941 Culver Cadet monoplane, with retractable tail-dragger undercarriage.
Construction: Steel tube, wood and fabric.
Wing span: 27 ft (8.23 m)
Length: 18 ft (5.49 m)
Empty weight: 785 lb (356 kg)
Gross weight: 1,350 lb (612 kg)
Recommended engine: 90 hp (67 kW) Teledyne Continental
Maximum speed: 152 kts (175 mph) 282 km/h
Cruise speed: 113 kts (130 mph) 209 km/h
Stall speed: 47 kts (54 mph) 87 km/h
Range: 452 naut miles (520 miles) 836 km
Take-off distance: 800 ft (244 m)
Climb rate: 800 ft (244 m) per minute
Availability: Plans.

Aero Wood Avocet 1-A

Address: Aero Wood Specialities Inc, 4950 County Road 1510, Pomona, MO 65789.
Telephone: +1 417 257 2422
Facsimile: +1 417 257 2239
Type: 4-seat amphibious monoplane, with pusher engine and retractable nosewheel undercarriage.
Construction: Metal and composites.
Wing span: 39 ft (11.89 m)
Length: 26 ft 3 ins (8 m)
Empty weight: 1,960 lb (889 kg)
Gross weight: 3,520 lb (1,597 kg)
Recommended engine: 300 hp (224 kW) Textron Lycoming IO-540
Maximum speed: 143 kts (165 mph) 265 km/h
Cruise speed: 135 kts (155 mph) 249 km/h
Range: 782 naut miles (900 miles) 1,448 km
Take-off distance: 700 ft (214 m)
Climb rate: 1,200 ft (366 m) per minute
Availability: Kits.
Comments: Designed in 1993 to have exceptional visibility and large payload capacity.

Aerovant Acroduster 1

Address: Aerovant Aircraft Corp, 2342 Jonquil Place, Rockford, IL 61107.
Telephone: +1 815 877 4508
Type: Single-seat aerobatic biplane, with fixed tail-dragger undercarriage.
Construction: Steel tube, wood and fabric.
Wing span: 19 ft (5.79 m)
Length: 15 ft 9 ins (4.8 m)
Empty weight: 740 lb (336 kg)
Gross weight: 1,190 lb (540 kg)
Recommended engine: 200 hp (149 kW) Textron Lycoming
Maximum speed: 156 kts (180 mph) 290 km/h
Cruise speed: 143 kts (165 mph) 266 km/h
Stall speed: 61 kts (70 mph) 113 km/h
Range: 260 naut miles (300 miles) 482 km
Climb rate: 3,000 ft (914 m) per minute
Availability: Plans.
Comments: Formerly the Stolp SA-700 Acroduster. Rights purchased by Walt Peters of Aerovant in April 1990.

AFI Prescott Pusher II

Address: Tom Prescott, Aviation Franchising International (AFI), San Antonio, TX.
Type: 2-seat cabin monoplane, with pusher engine, T-tail and retractable nosewheel undercarriage.
Construction: Steel tube and metal.
Wing span: 29 ft 4 ins (8.94 m)
Length: 20 ft 3 ins (6.17 m)
Empty weight: 1,400 lb (635 kg)
Gross weight: 2,400 lb (1,089 kg)
Recommended engine: 180 hp (134 kW) Textron Lycoming
Maximum speed: 207 kts (238 mph) 383 km/h
Cruise speed: 156 kts (180 mph) 290 km/h
Stall speed: 64 kts (73 mph) 118 km/h
Range: 869 naut miles (1,000 miles) 1,609 km
Take-off distance over a 50 ft obstacle: 1,725 ft (526 m)
Climb rate: 950 ft (290 m) per minute
Comments: Revised version of the Pusher. May be produced commercially and certificated.

AFI Prescott Pusher prototype in 1986 (Geoffrey P Jones)

Air Magic Spitfire

Address: Air Magic Ultralights, Hangar 594, Ellingston Airfield, Houston, TX 77034.
Telephone: +1 713 482 8124
Facsimile: +1 713 484 0005
Type: Single-seat microlight, with fixed nosewheel undercarriage.
Construction: Steel tube, fabric and glassfibre.
Wing span: 30 ft (9.14 m)
Length: 17 ft 10 ins (5.44 m)
Empty weight: 252 lb (114 kg)
Gross weight: 550 lb (249 kg)
Recommended engine: 40 hp (30 kW) Rotax 447
Maximum speed: 56 kts (65 mph) 105 km/h
Cruise speed: 48 kts (55 mph) 89 km/h
Range: 104 naut miles (120 miles) 193 km
Take-off distance: 100 ft (31 m)
Climb rate: 700 ft (213 m) per minute
Availability: Factory built microlight and kit.
Comments: Air Magic also sells the faster Spitfire Super Sport, 2-seat Spitfire II and Spitfire II Elite with a Rotax 582.

Aircraft Designs Stallion

Address: Aircraft Designs Inc, 5 Harris Court Building S, Monterey, CA 93940.
Telephone: +1 408 649 6212
Facsimile: +1 408 649 5738
Type: 4-seat high-wing monoplane, with retractable nosewheel undercarriage (possibly optional floats and skis).
Construction: Welded steel frame and composites (including honeycomb core).
Wing span: 35 ft 6 ins (10.82 m)
Length: 25 ft (7.62 m)
Empty weight: 1,900 lb (862 kg)
Gross weight: 3,300 lb (1,497 kg)
Recommended engine: 280 hp (209 kW) Teledyne

Continental IO-550-G
Maximum speed: 209 kts (241 mph) 388 km/h
Cruise speed: 195 kts (224 mph) 360 km/h
Stall speed: 60 kts (69 mph) 111 km/h
Range: 1,303 naut miles (1,500 miles) 2,414 km
Take-off distance: 800 ft (244 m)
Climb rate: 1,500 ft (457 m) per minute
Availability: Kits.
Comments: Designed by Martin Hollmann. Prototype construction began in August 1990, with the first flight in 1994. Can be used for cargo carrying.

Aircraft Designs Stallion 4-seat homebuilt.

Aircraft Spruce & Speciality One Design

Address: Aircraft Spruce & Speciality Inc, PO Box 424, Fullerton, CA 92632.
Telephone: +1 714 870 7551
Facsimile: +1 714 871 7289
Type: Single-seat aerobatic monoplane, with fixed tail-dragger undercarriage.
Construction: Steel tube, metal, composites and fabric.
Wing span: 19 ft 4 ins (5.89 m)
Length: 17 ft (5.18 m)
Empty weight: 740 lb (336 kg)
Gross weight: 1,140 lb (517 kg)
Recommended engine: 160 hp (119.3 kW) Textron Lycoming
Maximum speed: 160 kts (184 mph) 296 km/h
Cruise speed: 139 kts (160 mph) 257 km/h
Stall speed: 44 kts (50 mph) 81 km/h
Range: 304 naut miles (350 miles) 563 km
Take-off distance: 250 ft (77 m)
Climb rate: 2,000 ft (610 m) per minute
Availability: Plans and kits.
Comments: First flown in 1994. Designed for single-class competition aerobatics.

Aircraft Technologies Acro 1

Address: Aircraft Technologies Inc, 4265 Lilburn Industrial Way, Lilburn, GA 30247.
Telephone: +1 404 806 9098
Type: Single-seat aerobatic monoplane, with fixed tail-dragger undercarriage.
Construction: Composites.
Wing span: 19 ft 4 ins (5.89 m)
Length: 17 ft (5.18 m)
Empty weight: 750 lb (340 kg)
Gross weight: 1,222 lb (554 kg)
Recommended engine: 200 hp (149 kW) Textron Lycoming IO-360
Maximum speed: 243 kts (280 mph) 451 km/h
Cruise speed: 222 kts (255 mph) 410 km/h
Stall speed: 48 kts (55 mph) 89 km/h
Climb rate: 2,700 ft (823 m) per minute
Availability: Plans and kits.
Comments: Developed for the International Aerobatic Club "One Design" competition. 2-seat version, the Atlantis, shown part complete at Sun 'n Fun '95.

AkroTech Giles G-200

Address: AkroTech Aviation Inc, 1260-5 NW Perimeter Road, Troutdale, OR 97060.
Telephone: +1 503 666 2284
Facsimile: +1 503 666 2375
Type: Single-seat aerobatic monoplane, with fixed tail-dragger undercarriage.
Construction: Composites.
Wing span: 20 ft (6.1 m)
Length: 18 ft (5.49 m)
Empty weight: 750 lb (340 kg)
Gross weight: 1,150 lb (522 kg)
Recommended engine: 200 hp (149 kW) Textron Lycoming
Maximum speed: 220 kts (253 mph) 407 km/h
Cruise speed: 184 kts(212 mph) 341 km/h
Stall speed: 48 kts (55 mph) 89 km/h
Take-off distance: 300 ft (92 m)
Climb rate: 3,500 ft (1,080 m) per minute
Availability: Kits.
Comments: Two-seat version flew September 1995 as the G-202.

AkroTech Giles G-200 (Geoffrey P Jones)

Alturair BD-5

Address: Alturair, 1780 Joe Crosson Drive, Hangar B, El Cajon, CA 92020.
Telephone: +1 619 449 1570
Facsimile: +1 619 442 0481
Type: Single-seat, low-wing monoplane, with pusher engine and retractable nosewheel undercarriage.
Construction: Metal.
Wing span: 17 ft (5.18 m)
Length: 13 ft 7 ins (4.14 m)
Take-off distance: 600 ft (183 m)
Recommended engine: 90 hp (67 kW) Honda, 70 hp (52.2 kW) Zenoah or others up to 150 hp (112 kW).
Maximum speed: 195-202 kts (225-232 mph) 362-373 km/h
Cruise speed: 174-199 kts (200-229 mph) 322-369 km/h
Stall speed: 62 kts (71 mph) 114 km/h
Range: 499 naut miles (575 miles) 925 km
Climb rate: 1,900 ft (579 m) per minute
Availability: Re-worked original Bede kits.
Comments: Support company for Jim Bede's homebuilt project of the 1970s.

Aviat Eagle II

Address: Aviat Inc, The Airport, Box 1149, Afton, WY 83110.
Telephone: +1 307 886 3151
Facsimile: +1 307 886 9674
Type: Tandem 2-seat aerobatic biplane, with fixed tail-dragger undercarriage.
Construction: Steel tube, wood and fabric.
Wing span: 19 ft 11 ins (6.07 m)
Length: 18 ft 6 ins (5.64 m)
Empty weight: 1,025 lb (465 kg)
Gross weight: 1,600 lb (726 kg)
Recommended engine: 200 hp (149 kW) Textron Lycoming AEIO-360-AID
Maximum speed: 160 kts (184 mph) 296 km/h
Cruise speed: 137 kts (158 mph) 254 km/h
Stall speed: 51 kts (58 mph) 94 km/h
Range: 330 naut miles (380 miles) 611 km
Take-off distance: 800 ft (244 m)
Climb rate: 2,120 ft (646 m) per minute
Availability: Kits.
Comments: Hundreds previously sold by Christen Industries as the Christen Eagle II. First flew in February 1977.

Aviat Eagle II built by Arnold Timmerman in Germany (Geoffrey P Jones)

Avid Bandit

Address: Avid Aircraft Inc, PO Box 728, Caldwell, ID 83606.
Telephone: +1 208 454 2600
Facsimile: +1 208 454 8608
Type: Side-by-side 2-seat, cabin monoplane, with fixed nosewheel or tail-dragger undercarriage.
Construction: Steel tube and fabric.
Wing span: 29 ft 11 ins (9.12 m)
Length: 17 ft 11 ins (5.46 m)
Empty weight: 425 lb (193 kg)
Gross weight: 950 lb (431 kg)
Take-off distance: 300 ft (92 m)
Recommended engine: 50 hp (37.3 kW) Rotax 503 or 64.4 hp (48 kW) Rotax 582
Maximum speed: 117 kts (135 mph) 217 km/h
Cruise speed: 65 kts (75 mph) 121 km/h
Stall speed: 33 kts (36 mph) 58 km/h
Range: 295 naut miles (340 miles) 547 km
Take-off distance: 300 ft (92 m) grass
Climb rate: 550 ft (168 m) per minute
Availability: Kits.
Comments: Microlight version of the Avid Mark IV.

Avid Catalina

Type: 3-seat amphibian, with retractable tail-dragger undercarriage.
Construction: Steel tube and fabric.
Wing span: 36 ft (10.97 m)
Length: 19 ft 5 ins (5.92 m)
Empty weight: 600 lb (272 kg)
Gross weight: 1,200 lb (544 kg)
Recommended engine: 65 hp (48.5 kW) Rotax 582 or 100 hp (74.6 kW) AMW
Maximum speed: 78 kts (90 mph) 145 km/h
Cruise speed: 65 kts (75 mph) 121 km/h
Stall speed: 32 kts (36 mph) 58 km/h
Range: 316 naut miles (364 miles) 585 km
Take-off distance: 300 ft (92 m) land, 756 ft (230 m) water
Climb rate: 750 ft (229 m) per minute
Availability: Kits.
Comments: Developed from the Avid Amphibian, which first flew on 12 July 1985.

Avid Catalina

Avid Magnum

Type: Side-by-side 2-seat, or 2+1, cabin monoplane, with fixed tail-dragger undercarriage.
Construction: Steel tube and fabric.
Wing span: 32 ft (9.75 m)
Length: 21 ft (6.4 m)
Empty weight: 1,025 lb (465 kg)
Gross weight: 1,750 lb (794 kg)
Recommended engine: 160 hp (119.3 kW) Textron Lycoming O-320
Maximum speed: 130 kts (150 mph) 241 km/h
Cruise speed: 113 kts (130 mph) 209 km/h
Stall speed: 32 kts (36 mph) 58 km/h
Range: 434 naut miles (500 miles) 804 km
Take-off distance: 250 ft (77 m)
Climb rate: 1,000 ft (305 m) per minute
Availability: Kits.
Comments: Suitable for floats and skis.

Avid Magnum

Avid Mark IV Speedwing

Type: Side-by-side 2-seat, cabin monoplane with aerobatic or STOL capabilities, with fixed nosewheel or tail-dragger undercarriage.
Construction: Steel tube and fabric.
Wing span: 23 ft 11 ins (7.3 m)
Length: 17 ft 11 ins (5.46 m)
Empty weight: 510 lb (231 kg)
Gross weight: 1,050 lb (476 kg)
Recommended engine: 64.4 hp (48 kW) Rotax 582. Rotax 912 or Subaru are options.
Maximum speed: 130 kts (150 mph) 241 km/h
Cruise speed: 96 kts (110 mph) 177 km/h
Stall speed: 40 kts (46 mph) 74 km/h
Range: 492 naut miles (566 miles) 911 km
Take-off distance: 300 ft (92 m)
Climb rate: 850 ft (259 m) per minute
Availability: Kits.
Comments: Aerobatic and STOL versions.

Barney Oldfield Baby Lakes

Address: Barney Oldfield Aircraft Co (BOAC), PO Box 228, Needham, MA 0219.
Telephone: +1 617 444 5480
Type: Single-seat biplane, with fixed tail-dragger undercarriage.
Construction: Metal, wood and fabric.
Wing span: 16 ft 8 ins (5.08 m)
Length: 13 ft 9 ins (4.19 m)
Empty weight: 475 lb (215 kg)
Gross weight: 850 lb (386 kg)
Recommended engine: 85 hp (63.4 kW) Teledyne Continental
Maximum speed: 117 kts (135 mph) 217 km/h
Cruise speed: 103 kts (118 mph) 190 km/h
Stall speed: 44 kts (50 mph) 81 km/h
Range: 217 naut miles (250 miles) 402 km
Take-off distance: 300 ft (92 m)
Climb rate: 2,000 ft (610 m) per minute
Availability: Plans and kits.
Comments: Sport biplane representation of the Great Lakes Biplane of the 1930s. Also available are the 108 hp (80.5 kW) Textron Lycoming-powered Super Baby Lakes and the slightly larger and similarly powered Buddy Baby Lakes.

Barney Oldfield Great Lakes Sport Trainer

Type: Tandem 2-seat sport biplane, with fixed tail-dragger undercarriage.
Construction: Steel tube, wood and fabric.
Wing span: 26 ft 8 ins (8.13 m)
Length: 20 ft 4 ins (6.2 m)
Empty weight: 1,025 lb (465 kg)
Gross weight: 1,618 lb (734 kg)
Recommended engine: 125 hp (93.2 kW) Textron Lycoming O-320
Maximum speed: 120 kts (138 mph) 222 km/h
Cruise speed: 109 kts (125 mph) 201 km/h
Stall speed: 37 kts (42 mph) 68 km/h
Range: 295 naut miles (340 miles) 547 km
Take-off distance: 300 ft (92 m)
Climb rate: 1,200 ft (366 m) per minute
Availability: Plans and kits.
Comments: Manufactured commercially by several companies since the first flight in the 1930s.

Barney Oldfield Great Lakes Sport Trainer (Geoffrey P Jones)

Bede Aircraft BD-4

Address: Bede Aircraft Corporation, Spirit of St Louis Airport, Chesterfield, MO 63005.
Telephone: +1 314 537 2312
Facsimile: +1 314 536 2822
Type: 4-seat, high-wing cabin monoplane with either nosewheel or tail-dragger undercarriage.
Construction: Metal.
Wing span: 25 ft (7.62 m)
Length: 21 ft 6 ins (6.55 m)
Empty weight: 1,140 lb (517 kg)
Gross weight: 2,500 lb (1,134 kg)
Recommended engine: 180 hp (134 kW) Textron Lycoming IO-360
Maximum speed: 179 kts (206 mph) 332 km/h
Cruise speed: 126 kts (145 mph) 233 km/h
Stall speed: approximately 55 kts (63 mph) 102 km/h
Range: 679 naut miles (782 miles) 1,258 km
Take-off distance: 450 ft (138 m)
Climb rate: 1,800 ft (549 m) per minute
Availability: Plans and kits.
Comments: First flown in the early 1970s. Similar but smaller single-seat BD-6 also revived.

Bede BD-4 tail-dragger (Geoffrey P. Jones)

Bede Aircraft BD-12A

Type: Tandem 2-seat, low-wing monoplane, with pusher engine and retractable nosewheel undercarriage.
Construction: Metal and composites.
Wing span: 22 ft (6.71 m)
Length: 19 ft 6 ins (5.94 m)
Empty weight: 590 lb (268 kg)
Gross weight: 1,220 lb (553 kg)
Recommended engine: 80-100 hp (59.7-74.6 kW) range
Maximum speed: 160 kts (184 mph) 296 km/h
Cruise speed: 149 kts (172 mph) 277 km/h
Range: 816 naut miles (940 miles) 1,512 km
Take-off distance: 850 ft (259 m)
Climb rate: 1,110 ft (338 m) per minute
Availability: Kits.
Comments: 1994 development of the BD-5. A larger four-seat development, the BD-14A with 150 hp (112 kW) engine, is also under development.

Bede Jet Corp BD-10 (Peregrine PJ-2)

Address: Bede Jet Corporation, Spirit of St Louis Airport, Chesterfield, MO 63005.
Telephone: +1 314 537 2333
Facsimile: +1 314 536 2822
Type: Tandem 2-seat twin-jet monoplane, with twin tailfins and retractable nosewheel undercarriage.
Construction: Metal and composites.
Wing span: 21 ft 6 ins (6.55 m)
Length: 28 ft 11 ins (8.81 m)
Empty weight: 1,580 lb (717 kg)
Gross weight: 4,140 lb (1,878 kg)
Recommended engines: 2 x 2,850 lbf (12.68 kN) General Electric CJ.610 turbojets
Maximum speed: 805 kts (926 mph) 1,490 km/h
Cruise speed: 539 kts (620 mph) 998 km/h
Stall speed: 92 kts (106 mph) 171 km/h
Range: 1,599 naut miles (1,840 miles) 2,961 km
Take-off distance: 600 ft (183 m)
Climb rate: 10,000 ft (3,050 m) per minute
Availability: Kits.
Comments: Design bought in 1995by Peregrine Flight International and further sale of civil BD-10 kits ended. Certified variant expected as PJ-2, though a prototype was involved in an accident on 4 August 1995.

Bede Jet Corp BD-10 prototype at Oshkosh in 1992 (Geoffrey P Jones)

Bede BD-5

Address: BD Micro-Technologies Inc, 1260 Wade Road, Siletz, OR 97380.
Telephone: +1 503 444 1343
Type: Single-seat low-wing monoplane, with pusher engine and retractable nosewheel undercarriage.
Construction: Metal.
Wing span: 17 or 21 ft (5.18 or 6.4 m)
Length: 12 ft (3.66 m)
Empty weight: 510 lb (231 kg)
Gross weight: 890 lb (404 kg)
Recommended engine: Engines of greatly varying power can be installed, including a turboprop. Details for a 95 hp (70.8 kW) engine.
Maximum speed: 209 kts (240 mph) 386 km/h
Cruise speed: 174 kts (200 mph) 322 km/h
Stall speed: 68 kts (78 mph) 126 km/h
Range: 825 naut miles (950 miles) 1,529 km
Take-off distance: 1,250 ft (381 m)
Climb rate: 1,900 ft (579 m) per minute
Availability: Partial kits and plans.
Comments: Set up by Ed "Skeeter" Karnes to cater for existing BD-5 builders and provide new kit components.

Bede BD-5 built by Bob Sauser (Geoffrey P Jones)

Bounsall Super Prospector

Address: Bounsall Aircraft, PO Box 506, Mesquite, NV 89024.
Type: Single-seat, parasol-wing STOL monoplane, with fixed tail-dragger undercarriage.
Construction: Steel tube, wood and fabric.
Wing span: 29 ft 8 ins (9.04 m)
Length: 19 ft 4 ins (5.89 m)
Empty weight: 470 lb (213 kg)
Gross weight: 860 lb (390 kg)
Recommended engine: 60 hp (44.7 kW) HAPI
Maximum speed: 87 kts (100 mph) 161 km/h
Cruise speed: 78 kts (90 mph) 145 km/h
Stall speed: 31 kts (35 mph) 57 km/h
Range: 260 naut miles (300 miles) 482 km
Take-off distance: 300 ft (92 m)
Climb rate: 800 ft (244 m) per minute
Availability: Plans and kits.
Comments: Cheap to purchase STOL bush-plane.

Bowdler Aviation Supercat

Address: Bowdler Aviation Inc, 1370 Howell Road, Beavercreek, OH 45434-6828.
Telephone: +1 513 426 9868
Type: Single-seat, low-wing microlight/homebuilt, with fixed tail-dragger undercarriage.
Construction: Wood, composites and fabric.
Wing span: 27 ft 4 ins (8.33 m)
Length: 15 ft 10 ins (4.83 m)
Empty weight: 325 lb (147 kg)
Gross weight: 650 lb (295 kg)
Recommended engine: 40 hp (30 kW) Rotax 447
Maximum speed: 74 kts (85 mph) 137 km/h
Cruise speed: 61 kts (70 mph) 113 km/h
Stall speed: 28 kts (32 mph) 52 km/h
Range: 121 naut miles (140 miles) 225 km
Take-off distance: 150 ft (46 m)
Climb rate: 900 ft (274 m) per minute
Availability: Plans and kits.
Comments: First flown in May 1984 and originally marketed by First Strike of Piggott, Arkansas, before Bowdler took over.

Bowdler Aviation Supercat (Geoffrey P Jones)

Bowers Fly Baby 1-A

Address: Peter M. Bowers, 10458 18th Avenue South, Seattle, WA 98168.
Telephone: +1 206 242 2582
Type: Single-seat low-wing monoplane, with fixed tail-dragger undercarriage.
Construction: Wood and fabric.
Wing span: 28 ft (8.53 m)
Length: 18 ft 11 ins (5.77 m)
Empty weight: 605 lb (274 kg)
Gross weight: 925 lb (420 kg)
Recommended engine: 85 hp (63.4 kW) Teledyne Continental C85
Maximum speed: 104 kts (120 mph) 193 km/h
Cruise speed: 87 kts (100 mph) 161 km/h
Range: 208 naut miles (240 miles) 386 km
Take-off distance: 250-230 ft (76-107 m)
Climb rate: 1,050 ft (320 m) per minute
Availability: Plans.
Comments: Prototype first flew on 27 July 1960, subsequently winning an EAA design contest. Biplane version, the Fly Baby 1-B, also available.

Bowers Fly Baby 1-A built in the UK with a Teledyne Continental C90 engine (Geoffrey P Jones)

Bradley Aerobat

Address: Bradley Aerospace, 960 Muri Avenue, Chico, CA 95926.
Telephone: +1 916 899 7918
Type: Single-seat, aerobatic monoplane, with fixed nosewheel or tail-dragger undercarriage.
Construction: Metal.
Wing span: 18 ft (5.49 m)
Length: 13 ft 6 ins (4.11 m)
Empty weight: 300 lb (136 kg)
Gross weight: 540 lb (245 kg)
Recommended engine: 64.4 hp (48 kW) Rotax 582 to 100 hp (74.5 kW) Rotax 914
Maximum speed: 171 kts (197 mph) 317 km/h
Cruise speed: 122 kts (140 mph) 225 km/h
Range: 173 naut miles (200 miles) 322 km
Take-off distance: 150 ft (46 m)
Climb rate: 1,300 ft (396 m) per minute
Availability: Kits.
Comments: STOL option.

Bronson Ultralight

Address: Bill Bronson, 2540 Hillcrest Drive, High Ridge, MO 63049.
Telephone: +1 314 677 4047
Type: Single-seat, high-wing monoplane, with fixed tail-dragger undercarriage.
Construction: Steel tube and fabric.
Recommended engine: Bronson "half" Volkswagen engine.
Availability: Plans.
Comments: Instructions on engine and microlight aircraft construction.

Bronson Ultralight cockpit area and "half" Volkswagen engine

Brutsche Freedom 180 STOL

Address: Brutsche Aircraft Corporation, 475 E. 900 S, Ste 108, m/s 67, Salt Lake City, UT 84111.
Telephone: +1 801 355 8060
Facsimile: +1 801 328 2060
Type: 4-seat, high-wing cabin monoplane, with fixed tail-dragger undercarriage.
Construction: Metal.
Wing span: 31 ft (9.45 m)
Length: 24 ft 1 ins (7.34 m)
Empty weight: 1,175 lb (533 kg)
Gross weight: 2,150 lb (975 kg)
Recommended engine: 180 hp (134 kW) Textron Lycoming O-360
Maximum speed: 170 kts (196 mph) 315 km/h
Cruise speed: 167 kts (192 mph) 309 km/h at 8,000 ft (2,440 m)
Stall speed: 40 kts (46 mph) 74 km/h
Range: 801 naut miles (922 miles) 1,483 km
Climb rate: 1,425 ft (434 m) per minute
Availability: Kits (available late 1995).
Comments: STOL utility aircraft with full-span Fowler flaps. To conform to FAA Part 23 Utility Category.

Buckeye Eagle 447

Address: Buckeye Powered Parachute Inc, 16111 Linden Road, Argos, IN 46501.
Telephone: +1 219 892 5566
Facsimile: +1 219 892 5566
Type: Single-seat trike and ram-air parachute.
Construction: Steel tube, composites and fabric.
Wing span: 35 ft 6 ins (10.82 m)
Length: 8 ft 9 ins (2.67 m)
Empty weight: 220 lb (100 kg)
Gross weight: 500 lb (227 kg)
Recommended engine: 40 hp (30 kW) Rotax 447. Alternative Rotax 503.
Maximum and cruise speed: 23 kts (26 mph) 42 km/h
Range: 43 naut miles (50 miles) 80 km
Take-off distance: 150 ft (46 m)
Climb rate: 500 ft (152 m) per minute
Availability: Kits.
Comments: Two-seat Buckeye Dream Machine 503 and 582 also available.

Buckeye Eagle 447 (Geoffrey P Jones)

Buethe Barracuda

Address: Buethe Enterprises Inc, PO Box 486, Cathedral City, CA 92234.
Telephone: +1 619 324 9455
Type: Side-by-side 2-seat, low-wing monoplane, with retractable nosewheel undercarriage.
Construction: Wood and glassfibre.
Wing span: 24 ft 10 ins (7.57 m)
Length: 21 ft 6 ins (6.55 m)
Empty weight: 1,540 lb (699 kg)
Gross weight: 2,300 lb (1,043 kg)
Recommended engine: 250 hp (186.4 kW) Textron Lycoming IO-540
Maximum speed: 181 kts (208 mph) 335 km/h
Cruise speed: 143 kts (165 mph) 266 km/h
Stall speed: 56 kts (64 mph) 103 km/h
Range: 695 naut miles (800 miles) 1,287 km
Take-off distance: 800 ft (244 m)
Climb rate: 2,500 ft (762 m) per minute
Availability: Plans and kits.

Comments: Designed by Dr William Buethe and first flown on 29 June 1975.

Buethe Barracuda (Geoffrey P Jones)

Butterfly Banty

Address: Butterfly Aero, 1333 Garrard Creek Road, Oakville, WA 98568.
Telephone: +1 206 273 9202
Facsimile: +1 206 273 5082
Type: Single-seat, parasol-wing monoplane microlight, with fixed tail-dragger undercarriage.
Construction: Wood, aluminium and fabric.
Wing span: 32 ft (9.75 m)
Length: 18 ft 10 ins (5.74 m)
Empty weight: 237 lb (108 kg)
Gross weight: 500 lb (227 kg)
Recommended engine: 25 hp (19 kW) Rotax 277
Maximum speed: 52 kts (60 mph) 97 km/h
Cruise speed: 43 kts (50 mph) 80 km/h
Stall speed: 20 kts (23 mph) 37 km/h
Range: 78 naut miles (90 miles) 145 km
Take-off distance: 220 ft (67 m)
Climb rate: 400 ft (122 m) per minute
Availability: Plans.
Comments: Easy to build microlight.

CADI 2001

Address: Composite Aircraft Design Inc, 5085 South Arville Street, Las Vegas, NV 89118.
Telephone: +1 702 876 4352
Type: 4-seat, low-wing monoplane, with tail-mounted propeller, T-tail, winglets and a retractable nosewheel undercarriage.
Construction: Composites.
Wing span: 27 ft (8.23 m)
Length: 24 ft (7.32 m)
Empty weight: 1,800 lb (816 kg)
Gross weight: 3,000 lb (1,361 kg)
Recommended engine: 300 hp (224 kW) Textron Lycoming IO-540 or other engines.
Maximum speed: 261 kts (300 mph) 483 km/h
Cruise speed: 217 kts (250 mph) 402 km/h
Range: 868 naut miles (1,000 miles) 1,609 km
Take-off distance: 2,000 ft (610 m)
Availability: Kits.
Comments: First example yet to be completed and flown.

Carlson Sparrow Ultralight

Address: Carlson Aircraft Inc, 50643 S.R. 14, East Palestine, OH 44413-0088
Telephone: +1 216 426 3934
Facsimile: +1 216 426 1144
Type: Single-seat, high-wing microlight, with fixed nosewheel undercarriage.
Construction: Steel tube and fabric.
Wing span: 30 ft 2 ins (9.19 m)
Length: 16 ft 9 ins (5.11 m)
Empty weight: 254 lb (115 kg)
Gross weight: 504 lb (229 kg)
Recommended engine: 25 hp (19 kW) Rotax 277
Maximum speed: 55 kts (63 mph) 101 km/h
Cruise speed: 50 kts (58 mph) 93 km/h
Stall speed: 30 kts (34 mph) 55 km/h
Range: 173 naut miles (200 miles) 322 km
Take-off distance: 140 ft (43 m)
Climb rate: 750 ft (229 m) per minute
Availability: Kits.
Comments: Design by Ernest W. Carlson. His Sparrow Sport Special is similar but a full homebuilt with larger engine (50 hp, 37 kW Rotax 503), with higher weights and performance, and tail-dragger undercarriage.

Carlson Sparrow Sport Special, the only Sparrow with a tailwheel (Geoffrey P Jones)

Carlson Sparrow II

Type: Side-by-side 2-seat, high-wing monoplane, with fixed nosewheel undercarriage.
Construction: Steel tube and fabric.
Wing span: 31 ft 6 ins (9.6 m)
Length: 18 ft (5.49 m)
Empty weight: 510 lb (231 kg)
Gross weight: 1,050 lb (476 kg)
Recommended engine: 64.4 hp (48 kW) Rotax 582
Maximum speed: 113 kts (130 mph) 209 km/h
Cruise speed: 96 kts (110 mph) 177 km/h
Stall speed: 30 kts (34 mph) 55 km/h
Range: 260 naut miles (300 miles) 483 km
Take-off distance: 125 ft (39 m)
Climb rate: 1,000 ft (305 m) per minute
Availability: Kits.
Comments: Enlarged 2 seat version of the Sparrow Ultralight. Also similar is the Sparrow-ette with Rotax 582, shorter span and lower gross weight.

Carlson Sparrow II XTC

Type: Side-by-side 2-seat, high-wing monoplane, with fixed nosewheel undercarriage.
Construction: Steel tube and fabric.
Wing span: 31 ft 2 ins (9.5 m)
Length: 18 ft (5.49 m)
Empty weight: 600 lb (272 kg)
Gross weight: 1,250 lb (567 kg)
Recommended engine: 82 hp (61 kW) Mosler 82X or 85 hp (63.4 kW) Teledyne Continental
Maximum speed: 113 kts (130 mph) 209 km/h
Cruise speed: 96 kts (110 mph) 177 km/h
Stall speed: 32 kts (37 mph) 60 km/h
Range: 347 naut miles (400 miles) 643 km
Take-off distance: 150 ft (46 m)
Climb rate: 1,100 ft (335 m) per minute
Availability: Kits.
Comments: Ailerons and flaps replaced by flaperons.

Carlson Skycycle

Type: Single-seat low-wing monoplane, with fixed tail-dragger undercarriage.
Construction: Metal and fabric.
Wing span: 20 ft (6.1 m)
Length: 15 ft 10 ins (4.83 m)
Empty weight: 295 lb (134 kg)
Gross weight: 450 lb (204 kg)
Recommended engine: 55 hp (41 kW) Textron Lycoming O-145A
Maximum speed: 95 kts (109 mph) 175 km/h
Cruise speed: 87 kts (100 mph) 161 km/h
Stall speed: 32 kts (37 mph) 60 km/h
Range: 173 naut miles (200 miles) 322 km
Comments: Adaptation of the 1945 Skycycle design.

Cassagneres Ryan STA

Address: Ev Cassagneres, 430 Budding Ridge, Cheshire, CT 06410.
Telephone: +1 203 272 2127
Type: Tandem 2-seat, low-wing monoplane, with fixed tail-dragger undercarriage.
Construction: Metal and fabric.
Wing span: 30 ft (9.14 m)
Length: 21 ft 6 ins (6.55 m)
Empty weight: 1,023 lb (464 kg)
Gross weight: 1,575 lb (714 kg)
Recommended engine: 125 hp (93.2 kW) Menasco C-4
Maximum speed: 122 kts (140 mph) 225 km/h
Cruise speed: 104 kts (120 mph) 193 km/h
Range: 304 naut miles (350 miles) 563 km
Take-off distance: 525 ft (160 m)
Climb rate: 850 ft (259 m) per minute
Availability: Plans.
Comments: Plans enable a builder to re-create an example of this classic design of the 1930s. Engine option includes the CASA Tigre.

CEI Free Spirit Mk.II

Address: CEI, 345 Woodside Way, Auburn CA 95603
Telephone: +1 916 878 6867.
Type: Side-by-side 2-seat, or 2+1, low-wing monoplane, with retractable nosewheel undercarriage.
Construction: Composites.
Wing span: 29 ft 6 ins (8.99 m)
Length: 20 ft 8 ins (6.3 m)
Empty weight: 950 lb (431 kg)
Gross weight: 1,850 lb (839 kg)
Recommended engine: 210 hp (156.6 kW) Teledyne Continental IO-360
Maximum speed: 230 kts (265 mph) 426 km/h
Cruise speed: 191 kts (220 mph) 354 km/h
Stall speed: 55 kts (63 mph) 102 km/h
Range: 1,216 naut miles (1,400 miles) 2,253 km
Take-off distance: 600 ft (183 m)
Climb rate: 2,000 ft (610 m) per minute
Availability: Kits.
Comments: Designed by Richard Cabrinha. Prototype Cabrinha Free Spirit Mk I first flew in July 1986 with a 150 hp (112 kW) Textron Lycoming. Mk II first flew in 1991. Ordered by Pakistan for pilot training.

CGS Hawk Classic

Address: CGS Aviation Inc, PO Box 470635, Broadview Hts, OH 44147.
Telephone: +1 216 632 1424
Facsimile: +1 216 632 1207
Type: Single-seat high-wing microlight/homebuilt, with pusher engine and fixed tail-dragger undercarriage.
Construction: Steel tube and fabric.
Wing span: 28 ft 10 ins (8.79 m)
Length: 20 ft 8 ins (6.3 m)
Empty weight: 253 lb (115 kg)
Gross weight: 600 lb (272 kg)
Take-off distance: 100 ft (31 m)
Recommended engine: 41.6 hp (31 kW) Rotax 447
Maximum speed: 78 kts (90 mph) 145 km/h
Maximum cruise speed: 65 kts (75 mph) 121 km/h
Stall speed: 26 kts (30 mph) 49 km/h
Range: 130 naut miles (150 miles) 241 km
Climb rate: 800 ft (244 m) per minute
Availability: Kits.
Comments: Larger engine and nosewheel undercarriage optional.

CGS Hawk II Classic

Type: Tandem 2-seat, high-wing microlight/homebuilt, with pusher engine and nosewheel undercarriage.
Construction: Steel tube and fabric.
Wing span: 29 ft (8.84 m)
Length: 20 ft 8 ins (6.3 m)
Empty weight: 335 lb (152 kg)
Gross weight: 800 lb (363 kg)

Recommended engine: 50 hp (37.3 kW) Rotax 503 or 64.4 hp (48 kW) Rotax 582
Maximum speed: 78 kts (90 mph) 145 km/h
Maximum cruise speed: 65 kts (75 mph) 121 km/h
Stall speed: 31 kts (35 mph) 57 km/h
Range: 152 naut miles (175 miles) 281 km
Take-off distance: 200 ft (61 m)
Climb rate: 700 ft (213 m) per minute
Availability: Kits.
Comments: Suitable for flight training. Tail-dragger undercarriage optional.

CGS Hawk II Classic

CGS Ag-Hawk

Type: Single-seat, high-wing microlight/homebuilt for agricultural spraying, with pusher engine and fixed nosewheel undercarriage.
Construction: Steel tube and fabric.
Wing span: 28 ft 10 ins (8.79 m)
Length: 20 ft 8 ins (6.3 m)
Empty weight: 285 lb (129 kg)
Gross weight: 700 lb (318 kg)
Recommended engine: 40 hp (30 kW) Rotax 447, 45.6 hp (34 kW) Rotax 503 or 64.4 hp (48 kW) Rotax 582
Maximum speed: 78 kts (90 mph) 145 km/h
Cruise speed: 61 kts (70 mph) 113 km/h
Stall speed: 26 kts (30 mph) 49 km/h
Range: 130 naut miles (150 miles) 241 km
Climb rate: 900 ft (274 m) per minute
Availability: Kits.

CGS Ag-Hawk with spray-gear fitted.

CGS Hawk II Arrow

Type: Tandem 2-seat, high-wing microlight/homebuilt, with pusher engine and fixed nosewheel undercarriage.
Construction: Steel tube and fabric.
Wing span: 29 ft (8.84 m)
Length: 22 ft 2 ins (6.76 m)
Empty weight: 350 lb (159 kg)
Gross weight: 830 lb (376 kg)
Recommended engine: 49.6 hp (37 kW) Rotax 503
Maximum speed: 78 kts (90 mph) 145 km/h
Cruise speed: 61 kts (70 mph) 113 km/h
Stall speed: 31 kts (35 mph) 57 km/h
Range: 130 naut miles (150 miles) 241 km
Take-off distance: 200 ft (61 m)
Climb rate: 700 ft (213 m) per minute
Avajlability: Kits.
Comments: Also available as the single-seat CGS Hawk Arrow with a Rotax 447 engine.

Collins Dipper Amphibian

Address: Collins Aero, 238 Fairville Road, RD1, Chadds Ford, PA 19317.
Telephone: +1 215 388 2393
Type: Side-by-side 2-seat, high-wing amphibian, with pylon mounted pusher engine and retractable nosewheel undercarriage.
Construction: Metal and glassfibre.
Wing span: 33 ft 4 ins (10.16 m)
Length: 25 ft 4 ins (7.72 m)
Empty weight: 1,060 lb (481 kg)
Gross weight: 1,760 lb (798 kg)
Take-off distance: 600 ft (183 m)
Recommended engine: 150 or 180 hp (112 or 134 kW) Textron Lycoming O-360
Maximum speed: 120 kts (138 mph) 222 km/h
Cruise speed: 100 kts (115 mph) 185 km/h
Stall speed: 39 kts (45 mph) 73 km/h
Range: 499 naut miles (575 miles) 925 km
Climb rate: 1,400 ft (427 m) per minute
Availability: Plans.
Comments: Designed by Willard Collins. Prototype first flew on 24 August 1982. Cessna 150 wings and part fuselage utilized.

Cosmos Echo 12

Address: Cosmos, 8710 Carefree Highway, Peoria, AZ 85382.
Telephone: +1 602 931 4991
Type: Single-seat, open trike microlight, with pusher engine and pivoting rogallo wing.
Construction: Steel tube and fabric.
Wing span: 32 ft (9.75 m)
Length: 8 ft (2.44 m)
Empty weight: 246 lb (112 kg)
Gross weight: 600 lb (272 kg)
Recommended engine: 40 hp (30 kW) Rotax 447
Maximum speed: 76 kts (87 mph) 140 km/h
Cruise speed: 39 kts (45 mph) 73 km/h
Range: 130 naut miles (150 miles) 241 km
Take-off distance: 100 ft (31 m)
Availability: Kits and factory complete aircraft.
Comments: Also available are the similar tandem two-seat Magnum 21 Bidlum and Chronos 16 BiPhase II, both Rotax 503 powered.

Co-Z Mark IV

Address: Co-Z Development Corporation, 2046 N. 63rd Place, Mesa, AZ 85205.
Telephone: +1 602 981 6401
Type: 4-seat canard monoplane design, with pusher engine and nosewheel undercarriage (retractable nosewheel).
Construction: Composites.
Wing span: 28 ft 1 ins (8.56 m)
Length: 16 ft 11 ins (5.16 m)
Empty weight: 1,050 lb (476 kg)
Gross weight: 2,050 lb (930 kg)
Recommended engine: 180 hp (134 kW) Textron Lycoming O-360A
Maximum speed: 200 kts (230 mph) 370 km/h
Cruise speed: 178 kts (205 mph) 330 km/h
Range: 869 naut miles (1,000 miles) 1,609 km
Take-off distance: 1,200 ft (366 m)
Climb rate: 1,500 ft (457 m) per minute
Availability: Plans and kit components.
Comments: Nathan Puffer's design developed from his Cosy Classic, which in turn was a side-by-side 2-seat development of the Rutan Long-EZ. (See Cosy Classic under Germany.)

Craft 200 FW

Address: Craft Aerotech, 1843 S. 14th Street West, Missoula, MT 59801.
Telephone: +1 406 543 8133
Type: Side-by-side 2-seat, high-wing monoplane, with twin pusher engines and fixed nosewheel undercarriage.
Construction: Composites, metal and fabric.
Wing span: 30 ft 6 ins (9.3 m)
Length: 18 ft (5.49 m)
Empty weight: 700 lb (318 kg)
Gross weight: 1,200 lb (544 kg)
Recommended engines: 2 x 49.6 hp (37 kW) Rotax 503 or similar.
Maximum speed: 122 kts (140 mph) 225 km/h
Cruise speed: 104 kts (120 mph) 193 km/h
Stall speed: 44 kts (50 mph) 81 km/h
Range: 608 naut miles (700 miles) 1,126 km
Take-off distance: 650 ft (198 m)
Climb rate: 1,000 ft (305 m) per minute
Availability: Kits.

Cvjetkovic CA-65 Skyfly

Address: Anton Cvjetkovic, 5324 W. 121 Street, Hawthorne, CA 90250.
Telephone: +1 310 643 6931
Type: Side-by-side 2-seat, low-wing monoplane, with retractable tail-dragger undercarriage.
Construction: Wood and fabric.
Wing span: 25 ft (7.62 m)
Length: 19 ft (5.79 m)
Empty weight: 900 lb (408 kg)
Gross weight: 1,500 lb (680 kg)
Recommended engine: 125 hp (93.2 kW) Textron Lycoming O-290
Maximum speed: 156 kts (180 mph) 290 km/h
Cruise speed: 135 kts (155 mph) 249 km/h
Stall speed: 48 kts (55 mph) 89 km/h
Range: 434 naut miles (500 miles) 804 km
Take-off distance: 450 ft (137 m)
Climb rate: 1,000 ft (305 m) per minute
Availability: Plans.
Comments: The CA-65 first flew July 1965. An all-metal version is optional. A single-seater from Anton Cvjetkovic is the CA-61 Mini-Ace.

Cvjetkovic CA-65 Skyfly prototype

D'Apuzzo D-201 Sportwing

Address: Nick d'Apuzzo Airplane Designs, 1029 Blue Rock Ln, Blue Bell, PA 19422.
Telephone: +1 215 646 4792
Type: Tandem 2-seat sport biplane, with fixed tail-dragger undercarriage.
Construction: Steel tube and fabric.
Wing span: 27 ft (8.23 m)
Length: 21 ft 7 ins (6.59 m)
Empty weight: 1,303 lb (591 kg)
Gross weight: 1,900 lb (862 kg)
Recommended engine: 160 hp (119.3 kW) Textron Lycoming IO-360
Maximum speed: 115 kts (132 mph) 212 km/h
Cruise speed: 106 kts (122 mph) 196 km/h
Stall speed: 41 kts (47 mph) 76 km/h
Range: 312 naut miles (360 miles) 579 km
Take-off distance: 420 ft (128 m)
Climb rate: 1,050 ft (320 m) per minute
Availability: Plans and partial kits.
Comments: Developed by Nicholas E. D'Apuzzo from his earlier PJ-260 Senior Aero Sport.

DFE Ascender III-A

Address: DFE Ultralights, RD 1, Box 185, Vanderbilt, PA 15486.
Telephone: +1 412 529 0450
Facsimile: +1 412 529 0596
Type: Single-seat open microlight, with trike and canard.
Construction: Steel tube and fabric.
Wing span: 33 ft (10.06 m)
Length: 12 ft 4 ins (3.76 m)
Empty weight: 165 lb (75 kg)
Gross weight: 425 lb (193 kg)
Recommended engine: 22 hp (16.4 kW) Zenoah G25
Maximum speed: 48 kts (55 mph) 89 km/h
Cruise speed: 35 kts (40 mph) 64 km/h
Stall speed: 18 kts (20 mph) 32 km/h
Range: 130 naut miles (150 miles) 241 km
Take-off distance: 125 ft (38 m)
Climb rate: 400 ft (122 m) per minute
Availability: Kits.
Comments: Also available with the 35 hp (26 kW) Cuyuna 430 in the Ascender III-B and III-C versions.

Dickey E-Racer

Address: Shirl Dickey Enterprises, PO Box 1184, Yarnell, AZ 85362.
Telephone: +1 602 427 6384
Type: 2-seat canard monoplane, with pusher engine and retractable nosewheel undercarriage.
Construction: Composites.
Wing span: 26 ft 2 ins (7.98 m)
Length: 17 ft (5.18 m)
Empty weight: 1,000 lb (454 kg)
Gross weight: 1,800 lb (816 kg)
Recommended engine: 240 hp (179 kW) Buick V-8 converted motorcar engine.
Maximum speed: 209 kts (240 mph) 386 km/h
Cruise speed: 191 kts (220 mph) 354 km/h
Range: 869 naut miles (1,000 miles) 1,609 km
Take-off distance: 1,200 ft (366 m)
Climb rate: 2,500 ft (762 m) per minute
Availability: Plans.
Comments: 4 examples completed and flown by 1994.

Dong In Wizard

Address: Dong In Industries, Granby Sports Park, PO Box 771, Granby, CO 80446.
Telephone: +1 303 887 2434
Type: Side-by-side 2-seat, high-wing microlight/homebuilt, with pusher engine, twin tails and fixed nosewheel undercarriage.
Construction: Steel tube, composites, wood and fabric.
Wing span: 30 ft 8 ins (9.35 m)
Length: 19 ft 8 ins (5.99 m)
Empty weight: 462 lb (210 kg)
Gross weight: 924 lb (419 kg)
Recommended engine: 64.4 hp (48 kW) Rotax 582
Maximum speed: 104 kts (120 mph) 193 km/h
Cruise speed: 78 kts (90 mph) 145 km/h
Range: 234 naut miles (270 miles) 434 km
Take-off distance: 164 ft (50 m)
Climb rate: 1,350 ft (411 m) per minute
Availability: Kits. See also Laron Star Streak.

Dyke Delta JD-2

Address: Dyke Aircraft, 2840 Old Yellow Springs Road, Fairborn, OH 45324.
Telephone: +1 513 878 9832
Type: 4-seat, delta wing monoplane, with retractable nosewheel undercarriage.
Construction: Steel tube, glassfibre and Poly-Fiber fabric.
Wing span: 22 ft 2 ins (6.76 m)
Length: 19 ft (5.79 m)
Empty weight: 1,060 lb (481 kg)
Gross weight: 1,950 lb (885 kg)
Recommended engine: 180 hp (134 kW) Textron Lycoming O-360 or others.
Maximum speed: 174 kts (200 mph) 322 km/h
Cruise speed: 156 kts (180 mph) 290 km/h
Range: 550 naut miles (633 miles) 1,018 km
Take-off distance: 700 ft (214 m)
Climb rate: 2,000 ft (610 m) per minute
Availability: Plans and partial kits.
Comments: Designed by John W. Dyke and developed from his JD-1 flying wing. First flown in July 1966. An estimated 40 examples completed and flown.

Dyke Delta JD-2 (Geoffrey P Jones)

Early Bird Jenny

Address: Early Bird Aircraft Co, 125 Stearman Court, Erie, CO 80516.
Telephone: +1 303 665 5169
Type: Tandem 2-seat, 67% Curtiss JN replica microlight/homebuilt biplane, with fixed tail-dragger undercarriage.
Construction: Steel tube or aluminium alloy and fabric.
Wing span: 27 ft 6 ins (8.38 m)
Length: 18 ft 4 ins (5.59 m)
Empty weight: 419 lb (190 kg)
Gross weight: 800 lb (363 kg)
Recommended engine: 45.6 hp (34 kW) Rotax 503
Maximum speed: 61 kts (70 mph) 113 km/h
Cruise speed: 52 kts (60 mph) 97 km/h
Range: 156 naut miles (180 miles) 289 km
Take-off distance: 250 ft (77 m)
Climb rate: 450 ft (137 m) per minute
Availability: Plans and kits.
Comments: Kits available from Falconar (see under Canada).

Early Bird Spad XIII

Type: Single-seat 75% replica SPAD XIII biplane, with fixed tail-dragger undercarriage.
Construction: Steel tube, composites and fabric.
Wing span: 20 ft 5 ins (6.22 m)
Length: 15 ft 6 ins (4.72 m)
Empty weight: 520 lb (236 kg)
Gross weight: 750 lb (340 kg)
Recommended engine: 60 hp (44.7 kW) converted Geo Metro motorcar engine.
Maximum speed: 78 kts (90 mph) 145 km/h
Cruise speed: 70 kts (80 mph) 129 km/h
Stall speed: 39 kts (45 mph) 73 km/h
Range: 234 naut miles (270 miles) 434 km
Take-off distance: 300 ft (92 m)
Climb rate: 600 ft (183 m) per minute
Availability: Plans.

Earthstar Thunder Gull J

Address: Earthstar Aircraft Inc, Star Route 313, Santa Margarita, CA 93453.
Telephone: +1 805 438 5235
Type: Single-seat high-wing monoplane, with pusher engine and fixed nosewheel undercarriage.
Construction: Metal and fabric.
Wing span: 20 ft (6.1 m)
Length: 16 ft 6 ins (5.03 m)
Empty weight: 245 lb (111 kg)
Gross weight: 550 lb (249 kg)
Recommended engine: 25 hp (19 kW) Rotax 277 (optional Rotax 447 or 503)
Maximum speed: 55 kts (63 mph) 101 km/h
Cruise speed: 48 kts (55 mph) 89 km/h
Stall speed: 23 kts (26 mph) 42 km/h
Range: 156 naut miles (180 miles) 289 km
Take-off distance: 125 ft (39 m)
Climb rate: 700 ft (213 m) per minute
Availability: Kits.
Comments: Designed and engineered by Mark Beierle. Wings fold for trailering.

Earthstar Thunder Gull J flown from California to Oshkosh in 1992. (Geoffrey P Jones)

Earthstar Thunder Gull JT2

Type: Tandem 2-seat, high-wing monoplane, with pusher engine and fixed nosewheel undercarriage.
Construction: Metal and fabric.
Wing span: 24 ft (7.32 m)
Length: 17 ft (5.18 m)
Empty weight: 392 lb (178 kg)
Gross weight: 850 lb (386 kg)
Recommended engine: 49.6 hp (37 kW) Rotax 503 (optional Rotax 447)
Maximum speed: 104 kts (120 mph) 193 km/h
Cruise speed: 74 kts (85 mph) 137 km/h
Stall speed: 32 kts (37 mph) 60 km/h
Range: 278 naut miles (320 miles) 515 km
Take-off distance: 200 ft (61 m)
Climb rate: 800 ft (244 m) per minute
Availability: Kits and factory completed.
Comments: Suitable for pilot training and stressed to +6/-4g.

Eklund Thorpe T-18

Address: Eklund Engineering, PO Box 1510, Lockeford, CA 95237.
Telephone: +1 209 727 0318
Facsimile: +1 209 727 0873
Type: Single-seat low-wing monoplane, with fixed tail-dragger undercarriage.
Construction: Sheet metal.
Wing span: 20 ft 10 ins (6.35 m)
Length: 18 ft 11 ins (5.77 m)
Empty weight: 923 lb (419 kg)
Gross weight: 1,500 lb (680 kg)
Recommended engine: 150 hp (112 kW) Textron Lycoming
Maximum speed: 159 kts (183 mph) 294 km/h
Cruise speed: 156 kts (180 mph) 290 km/h
Stall speed: 52 kts (60 mph) 97 km/h
Range: 460 naut miles (530 miles) 853 km
Take-off distance: 1,000 ft (305 m)
Climb rate: 1,200 ft (366 m) per minute
Availability: Plans.
Comments: The late John Thorpe's classic all-metal homebuilt design that first flew on 12 May 1964. Some parts available – see Sport Aircraft T-18.

Eklund Thorpe T-18 built by Mr. G. Humbyrd at Billings, Montana (Geoffrey P Jones)

Evans VP-1

Address: Evans Aircraft, Box 744, La Jolla, CA 92038.
Type: Single-seat, open cockpit low-wing monoplane homebuilt, with fixed tail-dragger undercarriage.
Construction: Wood, fabric and glassfibre.
Wing span: 24 ft (7.32 m)
Length: 18 ft (5.49 m)
Empty weight: 475 lb (215.5 kg)
Gross weight: 675 lb (340 kg)
Recommended engine: 40-60 hp (30-44.7 kW) Volkswagen
Maximum speed: 83 kts (95 mph) 153 km/h
Cruise speed: 65 kts (75 mph) 121 km/h
Stall speed: 35 kts (40 mph) 65 km/h
Range: 173 naut miles (200 miles) 322 km
Take-off distance: 500 ft (153 m)
Climb rate: 600 ft (183 m) per minute
Availability: Plans.
Comments: Designed by Bud Evans for easy building and flying. Originally called the Volksplane. Plans for the 2-seat VP-2 are also available.

Evans VP-1 built by John Penney, the first to be completed in the UK (Geoffrey P Jones)

Experimental Aviation Berkut

Address: Experimental Aviation, 3025 Airport Avenue, Santa Monica, CA 90405
Telephone: +1 310 391 1943
Facsimile: +1 310 391 8645
Type: Tandem 2-seat, canard monoplane, with pusher engine and retractable nosewheel undercarriage.
Construction: Composites.
Wing span: 26 ft 8 ins (8.13 m)
Length: 18 ft 6 ins (5.64 m)
Empty weight: 1,035 lb (469 kg)
Gross weight: 2,000 lb (907 kg)
Recommended engine: 205 hp (153 kW) Textron Lycoming IO-360-B1A
Maximum speed: 215 kts (248 mph) 399 km/h
Cruise speed: 191 kts (220 mph) 354 km/h
Stall speed: 61 kts (70 mph) 113 km/h
Range: 1,067 naut miles (1,228 miles) 1,976 km
Take-off distance: 1,000 ft (305 m)
Climb rate: 2,000 ft (610 m) per minute
Availability: Kits.
Comments: Designed by Dave Ronneberg and first flown on 11 July 1991. 50 kits under construction in early 1995.

Experimental Aviation Berkut prototype (Geoffrey P Jones)

Express Design Express FT

Address: Express Design Inc, PO Box 609, Redmond, OR 97756.
Telephone: +1 503 548 2723
Facsimile: 503 548 2949
Type: 4-seat, low-wing cabin monoplane, with fixed nosewheel undercarriage.
Construction: Composites.
Wing span: 31 ft 6 ins (9.6 m)
Length: 26 ft (7.92 m)
Empty weight: 1,700 lb (771 kg)
Gross weight: 2,850 lb (1,293 kg)
Recommended engine: 200 hp (149 kW) Textron Lycoming IO-360, or other engines including the LPE TIIV-600.
Maximum speed: 174 kts (200 mph) 322 km/h
Cruise speed: 169 kts (195 mph) 314 km/h
Stall speed: 55 kts (63 mph) 102 kts
Range: 1,303 naut miles (1,500 miles) 2,414 km
Take-off distance: 700 ft (214 m)
Climb rate: 1,200 ft (366 m) per minute
Availability: Kits.
Comments: Formerly the Wheeler Express. New Express Series 90 has a 20% larger horizontal tail and 300 hp (224 kW) Textron Lycoming.

Express Design Loadmaster

Type: 6-seat, low-wing monoplane, with under-fuselage cargo pod and fixed nosewheel undercarriage.
Construction: Composites.
Wing span: 31 ft (9.45 m)
Length: 26 ft (7.92 m)
Empty weight: 1,825 lb (828 kg)
Gross weight: 3,200 lb (1,451 kg)
Recommended engine: 260 hp (194 kW) Textron Lycoming IO-540
Maximum speed: 196 kts (225 mph) 362 km/h
Cruise speed: 187 kts (215 mph) 346 km/h
Stall speed: 68 kts (78 mph) 126 km/h
Range: 1,216 naut miles (1,400 miles) 2,253 km
Take-off distance: 700 ft (214 m)
Climb rate: 1,250 ft (381 m) per minute
Availability: Kits.
Comments: Only 6-seat homebuilt currently available. Prototype first flew in 1993.

Express Design Loadmaster with under-fuselage cargo pod (Geoffrey P Jones)

Ferguson F-2

Address: Ferguson Aircraft Inc, 2431 Ferguson Pl, Dallas, GA 30132.
Telephone: +1 404 443 2747
Type: 2-seat, high-wing monoplane, with pusher engine and fixed tail-dragger undercarriage.
Construction: Steel tube and fabric.
Wing span: 30 ft (9.14 m)
Length: 21 ft 3 ins (6.48 m)
Empty weight: 430 lb (195 kg)
Gross weight: 900 lb (408 kg)
Recommended engine: 65 hp (48.5 kW) AMW
Maximum speed: 78 kts (90 mph) 145 km/h
Cruise speed: 61 kts (70 mph) 113 km/h
Range: 174 naut miles (200 miles) 322 km
Take-off distance: 200 ft (610 m)
Climb rate: 1,300 ft (396 m) per minute
Availability: Kits.

Fighter Escort Wings P-51

Address: Fighter Escort Wings, Ardmore Airpark, #206 Gene Autry, OK 73436.
Telephone: +1 405 389 5452
Facsimile: +1 405 389 5451
Type: Single-seat or 1+1 low-wing fighter representation, with retractable tail-dragger undercarriage.
Construction: Composites.
Wing span: 25 ft 5 ins (7.75 m)
Length: 21 ft 3 ins (6.48 m)
Empty weight: 1,200 lb (544 kg)
Gross weight: 2,000 lb (907 kg)
Recommended engine: 160-300 hp (119.3-224 kW) liquid cooled V-6 or V-8
Maximum speed: 217 kts (250 mph) 402 km/h
Cruise speed: 182 kts (210 mph) 338 km/h
Stall speed: 48 kts (55 mph) 89 km/h
Range: 651 naut miles (750 miles) 1,207 km
Take-off distance: 900 ft (275 m)
Climb rate: 1,000 ft (305 m) per minute
Availability: Kits.
Comments: Two-thirds scale P-51 Mustang replica designed by Ron Renzelman. First flown in 1992.

Fighter Escort Wings P-51 representation (Geoffrey P Jones)

Fisher Avenger

Address: Fisher Aero Corp, 7118 State Route 335, Portsmouth, OH 45662.
Telephone: +1 614 820 2219
Facsimile: +1 614 820 2219
Type: Single-seat low-wing monoplane, with fixed tail-dragger undercarriage.
Construction: Wood and fabric.
Wing span: 27 ft (8.23 m)
Length: 16 ft 3 ins (4.95 m)
Empty weight: 250-280 lb (113.5-127 kg)
Gross weight: 600 lb (272 kg)
Recommended engine: 25hp (19 kW) Rotax 277 or 41.6 hp (31 kW) Rotax 477.
Maximum speed: 78 kts (90 mph) 145 km/h
Cruise speed: 70 kts (80 mph) 129 km/h
Range: 130 naut miles (150 miles) 241 km
Climb rate: 900 ft (274 m) per minute
Availability: Plans and kits.
Comments: Unveiled in 1994.Performance data with Rotax 447.

Fisher Celebrity

Type: Tandem seat, open cockpit biplane homebuilt, with fixed tail-dragger undercarriage.
Construction: Wood, steel tube and fabric.
Wing span: 22 ft (6.71 m)
Length: 17 ft (5.18 m)
Empty weight: 600 lb (272 kg)
Gross weight: 1,000-1,250 lb (454-567 kg)
Recommended engine: 100 hp (74.6 kW) Teledyne Continental O-200, or other Teledyne Continental, Textron Lycoming or Volkswagen engines above 65 hp (48.5 kW).
Maximum speed: 100 kts (115 mph) 185 km/h
Cruise speed: 87 kts (100 mph) 161 km/h
Stall speed: 35 kts (40 mph) 65 km/h
Range: 173 naut miles (200 miles) 322 km
Take-off distance: 300 ft (92 m)

Climb rate: 1,200 ft (366 m) per minute
Availability: Kits.
Comments: Quick-build and partial kits available. Prefabricated components also include J-3 Cub type cowling.

Fisher Culex

Type: Tandem 2-seat, mid-wing monoplane, with fixed tail-dragger undercarriage.
Construction: Wood.
Wing span: 30 ft (9.14 m)
Length: 20 ft 4 ins (6.2 m)
Empty weight: 950-1,000 lb (431-454 kg)
Gross weight: 1,750 lb (794 kg)
Recommended engines: 2 x 80 hp (59.7 kW) Limbach 2000
Maximum speed: 130 kts (150 mph) 241 km/h
Cruise speed: 113 kts (130 mph) 209 km/h
Stall speed: 52 kts (60 mph) 97 km/h
Range: 677 naut miles (780 miles) 1,255 km
Take-off distance: 250-350 ft (77-107 m)
Climb rate: 1,500 ft (457 m) per minute
Availability: Plans and kits.

Fisher Horizon 2

Type: Tandem 2-seat, high-wing monoplane, with fixed nosewheel undercarriage.
Construction: Wood, steel tube and fabric.
Wing span: 26 ft (7.92 m)
Length: 19 ft 8 ins (5.99 m)
Empty weight: 570 lb (259 kg)
Gross weight: 1,050 lb (476 kg)
Recommended engine: 80 hp (59.7 kW) Limbach, or other engines of 65-115 hp (48.5-85.85 kW)
Maximum speed: 96 kts (110 mph) 177 km/h
Cruise speed: 83 kts (95 mph) 153 km/h
Stall speed: 31 kts (35 mph) 57 km/h
Range: 217 naut miles (250 miles) 402 km
Take-off distance: 250 ft (77 m)
Climb rate: 900 ft (274 m) per minute
Availability: Plans and kits.
Comments: Development of the Horizon 1. Has slotted flaps and ailerons for greater control with less drag, a lower stall and faster cruise speeds.

Fisher Horizon 2 with port wing folded (Geoffrey P Jones)

Fisher Mariah

Type: Tandem 2-seat, low-wing monoplane, with fixed nosewheel undercarriage.
Construction: Wood and fabric.
Wing span: 25 ft (7.62 m)
Length: 20 ft (6.1 m)
Empty weight: 800 lb (363 kg)
Gross weight: 1,300 lb (590 kg)
Recommended engine: 85 hp (63.4 kW) Teledyne Continental or other engines.
Maximum speed: 130 kts (150 mph) 241 km/h
Cruise speed: 113 kts (130 mph) 209 km/h
Range: 339 naut miles (390 miles) 627 km
Take-off distance: 400 ft (122 m)
Climb rate: 1,200 ft (366 m) per minute
Availability: Plans and kits.

Fisher Youngster

Type: Single-seat biplane, with fixed tail-dragger undercarriage.
Construction: Steel tube and fabric.
Wing span: 18 ft (5.49 m)
Length: 15 ft 6 ins (4.72 m)
Empty weight: 400 lb (181 kg)
Gross weight: 650 lb (295 kg)
Recommended engine: 45.6 hp (34 kW) Rotax 503
Maximum speed: 87 kts (100 mph) 161 km/h
Cruise speed: 74 kts (85 mph) 137 km/h
Take-off distance: 200 ft (61 m)
Climb rate: 750 ft (229 m) per minute
Availability: Plans and kits.
Comments: 50-65 hp (37.3-48.5 kW) VW model is the Youngster V.

Fisher Flying Products FP-303

Address: Fisher Flying Products, PO Box 468, Edgeley, ND 58433.
Telephone: +1 701 493 2286
Facsimile: +1 701 493 2539
Type: Single-seat low-wing microlight, with fixed tail-dragger undercarriage.
Construction: Wood, tube and fabric.
Wing span: 27 ft 8 ins (8.43 m)
Length: 16 ft 6 ins (5.03 m)
Empty weight: 230-240 lb (104.5-109 kg)
Gross weight: 450 lb (204 kg)
Recommended engine: 25 hp (19 kW) Rotax 277
Maximum speed: 52 kts (60 mph) 97 km/h
Cruise speed: 39-52 kts (45-60 mph) 72-97 km/h
Stall speed: 22 kts (25 mph) 41 km/h
Range: 72 naut miles (83 miles) 134 km
Take-off distance: 125 ft (38 m)
Climb rate: 750 ft (229 m) per minute
Availability: Kits.

Fisher Flying Products FP-505 Skeeter

Type: Single-seat parasol-wing microlight, with fixed tail-dragger undercarriage.
Construction: Wood, tube and fabric.
Wing span: 28 ft (8.53 m)
Length: 16 ft 6 ins (5.03 m)
Empty weight: 250 lb (113.4 kg)
Gross weight: 500 lb (227 kg)
Recommended engine: 25 hp (19 kW) Rotax 277
Maximum speed: 54 kts (62 mph) 100 km/h
Cruise speed: 48 kts (55 mph) 89 km/h
Stall speed: 23 kts (26 mph) 42 km/h
Range: 156 naut miles (180 miles) 289 km
Take-off distance: 150 ft (46 m)
Climb rate: 750 ft (229 m) per minute
Availability: Kits.
Comments: Rotax 447 or 503 engine also suitable.

Fisher Flying Products FP-606 Sky Baby

Type: Single-seat parasol-wing microlight, with fixed nosewheel undercarriage.
Construction: Wood and fabric.
Wing span: 28 ft 10 ins (8.79 m)
Length: 17 ft 4 ins (5.28 m)
Empty weight: 250 lb (113.4 kg)
Gross weight: 500 lb (227 kg)
Recommended engine: 25 hp (19 kW) Rotax 277 or larger.
Maximum speed: 74 kts (85 mph) 137 km/h
Cruise speed: 65 kts (75 mph) 121 km/h
Stall speed: 23 kts (26 mph) 42 km/h
Range: 95 naut miles (110 miles) 177 km
Take-off distance: 150 ft (46 m)
Climb rate: 700 ft (213 m) per minute
Availability: Kits.
Comments: Introduced in 1987. An average builder should be able to complete an FP-606 in 500 hours. Optional quick-build kit for 300 hour build-time.

Fisher Flying Products Classic

Type: Tandem 2-seat biplane, with fixed tail-dragger undercarriage.
Construction: Wood and fabric.
Wing span: 22 ft (6.71 m)
Length: 16 ft 9 ins (5.11 m)
Empty weight: 400 lb (181 kg)
Gross weight: 850 lb (386 kg)
Recommended engine: 64.4 hp (48 kW) Rotax 582
Maximum speed: 87 kts (100 mph) 161 km/h
Cruise speed: 74 kts (85 mph) 136 km/h
Stall speed: 34 kts (39 mph) 63 km/h
Range: 195 naut miles (225 miles) 362 km
Take-off distance: 200 ft (61 m)
Climb rate: 900 ft (274 m) per minute
Availability: Kits.
Comments: Development of the single-seat FP-404 EXP. Classic first flew on 25 March 1987.

Fisher Flying Products Classic tandem-seat biplane (Geoffrey P Jones)

Fisher Flying Products Dakota Hawk

Type: Side-by-side 2-seat, cabin monoplane, with fixed tail-dragger undercarriage.
Construction: Wood.
Wing span: 28 ft 6 ins (8.69 m)
Length: 19 ft (5.79 m)
Empty weight: 600 lb (272 kg)
Gross weight: 1,150 lb (522 kg)
Recommended engine: 77.8 hp (58 kW) Rotax 912 (option for Teledyne Continental 65 or 85 or Subaru conversion).
Maximum speed: 87 kts (100 mph) 161 km/h
Cruise speed: 78 kts (90 mph) 145 km/h
Stall speed: 31 kts (35 mph) 57 km/h
Range: 217 naut miles (250 miles) 402 km
Take-off distance: 350 ft (107 m)
Climb rate: 850 ft (259 m) per minute
Availability: Kits.
Comments: Introduced in 1992. Folding wings.

Fisher Flying Products Dakota Hawk (Geoffrey P Jones)

Fisher Flying Products R-80 Tiger Moth

Type: Tandem seat, open cockpit replica biplane homebuilt, with fixed tail-dragger undercarriage.

Construction: Wood, composites and fabric.
Wing span: 23 ft (7.01 m)
Length: 19 ft (5.79 m)
Empty weight: 560 lb (254 kg)
Gross weight: 1,150 lb (522 kg)
Recommended engine: 100 hp (74.6 kW) Mid-West AE100R
Maximum speed: 96 kts (110 mph) 177 km/h
Cruise speed: 78 kts (90 mph) 145 km/h
Range: 217 naut miles (250 miles) 402 km
Take-off distance: 300 ft (92 m)
Climb rate: 800 ft (244 m) per minute
Availability: Kits.
Comments: Unveiled in 1994 as a scale representation of the DH.82 Tiger Moth. Rotax or Subaru engine options.

Fisher Flying Products Super Koala

Type: Side-by-side 2-seat, high-wing monoplane, with fixed tail-dragger undercarriage.
Construction: Wood and fabric (see Comments).
Wing span: 31 ft (9.45 m)
Length: 18 ft 1 ins (5.51 m)
Empty weight: 400 lb (181 kg)
Gross weight: 830 lb (376 kg)
Recommended engine: 64.4 hp (48 kW) Rotax 582 (option for Rotax 503)
Maximum speed: 74 kts (85 mph) 137 km/h
Cruise speed: 70 kts (80 mph) 129 km/h
Stall speed: 28 kts (32 mph) 52 km/h
Range: 195 naut miles (225 miles) 362 km
Take-off distance: 150 ft (46 m)
Climb rate: 1,100 ft (335 m) per minute
Availability: Kits.
Comments: Geodetic wooden structure, with option for steel tube fuselage structure. Development of the single-seat FP-202 Koala microlight.

Flightstar II

Address: Flightstar Inc, Ellington Airport, PO Box 760, Ellington, CT 06029.
Telephone: +1 203 875 8185
Facsimile: +1 203 870 5499
Type: Side-by-side 2-seat monoplane, with fixed nosewheel or floats undercarriage.
Construction: Steel tube, fabric and composites.
Wing span: 32 ft 6 ins (9.91 m)
Length: 19 ft (5.79 m)
Empty weight: 420 lb (191 kg)
Gross weight: 970 lb (440 kg)
Recommended engine: 49.6 hp (37 kW) Rotax 503 (option for Rotax 582)
Maximum speed: 87 kts (100 mph) 161 km/h
Cruise speed: 56 kts (65 mph) 105 km/h
Stall speed: 32 kts (36 mph) 58 km/h
Range: 156 naut miles (180 miles) 289 km
Take-off distance: 200 ft (61 m)
Climb rate: 700 ft (213 m) per minute
Availability: Kits.
Comments: Tom Peghiny's design supercedes the Aviastar II (see Flightstar Spyder). Rotax 582 installation recommended for float flying.

Flightstar International Flightstar II

Flightstar Spyder

Type: Single-seat high-wing monoplane, with fixed tail-dragger undercarriage.
Construction: Composites, tube and fabric.
Wing span: 30 ft (9.14 m)
Length: 16 ft 6 ins (5.03 m)
Empty weight: 280 lb (127 kg)
Gross weight: 650 lb (295 kg)
Recommended engine: 41.6 hp (31 kW) Rotax 447
Maximum speed: 87 kts (100 mph) 161 km/h
Cruise speed: 52 kts (60 mph) 97 km/h
Stall speed: 23 kts (26 mph) 42 km/h
Range: 173 naut miles (200 miles) 322 km
Take-off distance: 180 ft (55 m)
Climb rate: 1,000 ft (305 m) per minute
Availability: Kits.
Comments: Flightstar ultralight was introduced in 1982. In the mid-1980s it was manufactured under licence by Pampas Bull in Argentina as the Aviastar. More powerful version is the Flightstar Formula.

Flightworks Capella

Address: Flightworks Corporation, 4211-C Todd Lane, Austin TX 78744.
Telephone: +1 512 441 8844
Facsimile: +1 512 441 1997
Type: Single-seat, high-wing monoplane, with fixed tail-dragger or nosewheel undercarriage.
Construction: Aluminium alloy, tube and fabric.
Wing span: 27 ft 6 ins (8.38 m)
Length: 17 ft 4 ins (5.28 m)
Empty weight: 340-360 lb (154-163 kg)
Gross weight: 625 lb (283 kg)
Recommended engine: 49.6 hp (37 kW) Rotax 503
Maximum speed: 80 kts (92 mph) 148 km/h
Cruise speed: 71 kts (82 mph) 132 km/h
Stall speed: 33 kts (38 mph) 61 km/h clean, 29 kts (33 mph) 53 km/h with flaps.
Range: 137 naut miles (158 miles) 254 km
Take-off distance: 130-150 ft (40-46 m)
Climb rate: 830 ft (253 m) per minute
Availability: Kits.

Flightworks Capella XS

Type: Side-by-side 2-seat, high-wing monoplane, with fixed tail-dragger or nosewheel undercarriage.
Construction: Aluminium alloy, tube and fabric.
Wing span: 28 ft 6 ins (8.69 m)
Length: 18 ft 5 ins (5.61 m)
Empty weight: 490 lb (222 kg)
Gross weight: 1,100 lb (499 kg)
Recommended engine: 64.4 hp (48 kW) Rotax 582
Maximum speed: 93 kts (107 mph) 172 km/h
Cruise speed: 83 kts (95 mph) 153 km/h
Stall speed: 32 kts (37 mph) 60 km/h
Range: 413 naut miles (476 miles) 766 km
Take-off distance: 230 ft (71 m)
Climb rate: 930 ft (283 m) per minute
Availability: Kits.
Comments: Similar Rotax 912 version is the Capella XLS.

Flightworks Capella XS flown by aerobatic pilot Duane Cole. (Geoffrey P Jones)

Clutton Fred

Address: Eric Clutton, 913 Cedar Lane, Tullahoma, TN 37388.
Type: Single-seat, parasol-wing monoplane, with fixed tail-dragger undercarriage.
Construction: Wood, aluminium and fabric.
Wing span: 22 ft 6 ins (6.86 m)
Length: 16 ft (4.88 m)
Empty weight: 550 lb (249 kg)
Gross weight: 800 lb (363 kg)
Recommended engine: 65 hp (48.5 kW) Teledyne Continental or Volkswagen
Maximum speed: 74 kts (85 mph) 137 km/h
Cruise speed: 61 kts (70 mph) 113 km/h
Range: 173 naut miles (200 miles) 322 km
Take-off distance: 900 ft (275 m)
Climb rate: 500 ft (152 m) per minute
Availability: Plans.
Comments: Designed in the UK by Eric Clutton. Fred stands for "Flying Run-about Experimental Design". First flown on 3 November 1963. Series I, II & III versions.

Fred monoplane with Volkswagen engine (Geoffrey P Jones)

Freewing Freebird Mk.V

Address: Freewing Aerial Robotics Corporation, Technical Advance Program, Building 340-1300, University of Maryland, College Park, MD 20742.
Telephone: +1 301 314 7794
Facsimile: +1 301 314 9592
Type: Side-by-side 2-seat, high-wing monoplane, with fixed tail-dragger undercarriage.
Construction: Steel tube, composites and fabric.
Wing span: 33 ft 4 ins (10.16 m)
Empty weight: 670 lb (304 kg)
Gross weight: 1,050 lb (476 kg)
Recommended engine: 100 hp (74.6 kW) Mid-West AW100R rotary
Maximum speed: 69 kts (80 mph) 129 km/h
Cruise speed: 61 kts (70 mph) 113 km/h
Stall speed: 26 kts (30 mph) 49 km/h
Range: 112 naut miles (130 miles) 209 km
Take-off distance: 200 ft (61 m)
Availability: Plans.
Comments: Developed from other experimental light aircraft with pivoting main wing, helping to give a smooth ride in turbulence. Earlier open-frame Freebird Mk IV has a 100 hp (74.6 kW) pusher engine and 65 kts (75 mph) 121 km/h maximum speed.

Freewing Freebird Mk.V at Sun 'n Fun 1993. (Geoffrey P Jones)

Golden Circle T-Bird I

Address: Golden Circle Air Inc, 11691 NW 46th, Grimes, IA 50111.
Telephone: +1 515 986 4181
Type: Single-seat, high-wing monoplane, with pusher engine and fixed tail-dragger undercarriage.
Construction: Steel tube and fabric.
Wing span: 31 ft 9 ins (9.68 m)
Length: 18 ft (5.49 m)
Empty weight: 272 lb (123 kg)
Gross weight: 572 lb (259 kg)
Recommended engine: 49.6 hp (37 kW) Rotax 503
Maximum speed: 78 kts (90 mph) 145 km/h
Cruise speed: 56 kts (65 mph) 105 km/h
Stall speed: 26 kts (30 mph) 49 km/h
Range: 87 naut miles (100 miles) 161 km
Climb rate: 900 ft (274 m) per minute
Availability: Kits.
Comments: Successor to the Teratorn Tierra microlights. Also available are the 2-seat T-Bird Side-by-Side, the T-Bird Tandem and 3-seat T-Bird III, all with Rotax 582 engines.

Golden Circle T-Bird predecessor, the Tierra (Geoffrey P Jones)

Great Plains Sonerai I

Address: Great Plains Aircraft, PO Box 545, Boys Town, NE 68010.
Telephone: +1 402 493 6507
Facsimile: +1 402 493 6507
Type: Single-seat mid-wing monoplane, with fixed tail-dragger undercarriage.
Construction: Aluminium alloy, steel tube and fabric (glassfibre engine cowls).
Wing span: 16 ft 8 ins (5.08 m)
Length: 16 ft 8 ins (5.08 m)
Empty weight: 440 lb (200 kg)
Gross weight: 750-1,000 lb (340-454 kg)
Recommended engine: 60 hp (44.7 kW) Volkswagen or larger.
Maximum speed: 148 kts (170 mph) 274 km/h
Cruise speed: 126 kts (145 mph) 233 km/h
Stall speed: 35 kts (40 mph) 65 km/h
Range: 217-260 naut miles (250-300 miles) 402-483 km
Take-off distance: 600 ft (183 m)
Climb rate: 1,000 ft (305 m) per minute
Availability: Plans and kits.
Comments: Designed by John Monnett and first flown in July 1971.

Great Plains Sonerai II

Type: Tandem 2-seat, mid-wing monoplane, with fixed tail-dragger or nosewheel undercarriage.
Construction: Aluminium alloy, steel tube and fabric (glassfibre engine cowls).
Wing span: 18 ft 8 ins (5.69 m)
Length: 18 ft 10 ins (5.74 m)
Empty weight: 500 lb (227 kg)
Gross weight: 1,150 lb (522 kg)
Recommended engine: 60-82 hp (44.7-61 kW) Volkswagen
Maximum speed: 152 kts (175 mph) 282 km/h
Cruise speed: 130 kts (150 mph) 241 km/h
Range: 304 naut miles (350 miles) 563 km
Take-off distance: 900 ft (274 m)
Climb rate: 500 ft (152 m) per minute
Availability: Plans and kits.
Comments: 2-seat development of the Sonerai I. Also available are 4 other 2-seat versions, as the low-wing L, lengthened LS (20 ft 4 ins, 6.2 m), LT with a standard 2,180 cc VW, and lengthened LTS with the 2,180 cc engine.

Great Plains (formerly Monnett) Sonerai II built in Belgium (Geoffery P Jones)

Green Sky Micro Mong

Address: Green Sky Adventures Inc, 2377 Cream Ridge Road, Orwell, OH 44076.
Telephone: +1 216 293 6624
Facsimile: +1 216 293 6321
Type: Single-seat biplane, with fixed tail-dragger undercarriage.
Construction: Metal and fabric.
Wing span: 19 ft 6 ins (5.94 m)
Length: 14 ft (4.26 m)
Empty weight: 320 lb (145 kg)
Gross weight: 650 lb (295 kg)
Take-off distance: 200 ft (61 m)
Recommended engine: 49.6 hp (37 kW) Rotax 503
Maximum speed: 96 kts (110 mph) 177 km/h
Cruise speed: 74 kts (85 mph) 137 km/h
Stall speed: 39 kts (45 mph) 73 km/h
Range: 173 naut miles (200 miles) 322 km
Climb rate: 1,000 ft (305 m) per minute
Availability: Plans and kits. Ultralight version also available.

Green Sky Zippy Sport

Type: Single-seat high-wing monoplane, with fixed tail-dragger undercarriage.
Construction: Metal, wood and fabric.
Wing span: 26 ft 4 ins (8.03 m)
Length: 17 ft 10 ins (5.44 m)
Empty weight: 421 lb (191 kg)
Gross weight: 680 lb (308 kg)
Recommended engine: 49.6 hp (37 kW) Rotax 503
Maximum speed: 104 kts (120 mph) 193 km/h
Cruise speed: 87 kts (100 mph) 161 km/h
Stall speed: 35 kts (40 mph) 65 km/h
Range: 260 naut miles (300 miles) 483 km
Take-off distance: 350 ft (107 m)
Climb rate: 700 ft (213 m) per minute
Availability: Plans.
Comments: Introduced by Gerald Olenik in 1992 to appeal to homebuilders who like mixed construction.

Green Sky Zippy Sport (Geoffrey P Jones)

Grega GN-1 Aircamper

Address: John W. Grega, 255 Grand Blvd, Bedford, OH 44146-2146.
Telephone: +1 216 232 5790
Type: Tandem-seat, parasol-wing monoplane, with fixed tail-dragger undercarriage.
Construction: Steel tube and wood.
Wing span: 29 ft (8.84 m)
Length: 18 ft 1 ins (5.51 m)
Empty weight: 650 lb (295 kg)
Gross weight: 1,100 lb (499 kg)
Take-off distance: 300-400 ft (92-122 m)
Recommended engine: 65 hp (48.5 kW) Teledyne Continental
Maximum speed: 100 kts (115 mph) 185 km/h
Cruise speed: 78 kts (90 mph) 145 km/h
Stall speed: 22-31 kts (25-35 mph) 41-56 km/h
Range: 304 naut miles (350 miles) 563 km
Climb rate: 500 ft (152 m) per minute
Availability: Plans plus some components.
Comments: Revised version of the Pietenpol Aircamper of 1920s origin. First flown in 1963, with an estimated 500 examples completed.

Grega GN-1 Aircamper two-seater (Geoffrey P Jones)

Halsted Saffire

Address: Barry Halsted, 17542 Briarwood Street, Fountain Valley, CA 92708.
Telephone: +1 714 962 9921
Type: Tandem 2-seat, low-wing monoplane, with retractable nosewheel undercarriage.
Construction: Metal.
Wing span: 28 ft (8.53 m)
Length: 25 ft (7.62 m)
Empty weight: 1,625 lb (737 kg)
Gross weight: 2,350 lb (1,066 kg)
Recommended engine: Teledyne Continental IO-360-C
Maximum speed: 183 kts (211 mph) 339 km/h
Cruise speed: 178 kts (205 mph) 330 km/h
Stall speed: 60 kts (69 mph) 111 km/h
Range: 700 naut miles (806 miles) 1,296 km
Take-off distance over a 50 ft obstacle: 1,600 ft (488 m)
Climb rate: 1,200 ft (366 m) per minute
Availability: Plans.
Comments: Prototype first flew on 24 November 1990. Won "Plans-Built Champion" award at EAA Oshkosh 1991.

Halsted Saffire two-seat homebuilt

Highlander Aircraft Highlander

Address: Highlander Aircraft Corporation, 2255 Orkla Drive, Golden Valley, MN 55427.
Telephone: +1 612 593 0341
Facsimile: +1 612 546 5640
Type: Side-by-side 2-seat monoplane, with fixed nosewheel undercarriage.
Construction: Aluminium alloy.
Wing span: 28 ft 6 ins (8.69 m)
Length: 18 ft (5.49 m)
Empty weight: 715 lb (324 kg)
Gross weight: 1,165 lb (528 kg)
Recommended engine: 77.8 hp (58 kW) Rotax 912
Maximum speed: 97 kts (112 mph) 180 km/h
Cruise speed: 90 kts (104 mph) 167 km/h
Stall speed: 54 kts (62 mph) 100 km/h clean, 48 kts (55 mph) 88 km/h with flaps
Range: 370 naut miles (426 miles) 685 km
Take-off distance: 600 ft (183 m)
Climb rate: 800 ft (244 m) per minute
Availability: Kits.
Comments: UK design by Richard Noble as the ARV Super2, later the Aviation Scotland ARV-1 Super2. Now built in conjunction with Sweden, where it is certificated as the Opus 280.

British-registered Super2, the type now offered as the Highlander kit plane (Geoffrey P Jones)

Hipp's Superbirds J-3 Kitten

Address: Hipp's Superbirds Inc, PO Box 266, Saluda, NC 28773.
Telephone: +1 704 749 9134
Facsimile: +1 704 749 3986
Type: Single-seat, high-wing microlight, with fixed tail-dragger undercarriage.
Construction: Steel tube, wood and fabric.
Wing span: 30 ft (9.14 m)
Length: 16 ft 4 ins (4.98 m)
Empty weight: 252 lb (114 kg)
Gross weight: 500 lb (227 kg)
Recommended engine: 25 hp (19 kW) Rotax 277
Maximum speed: 55 kts (63 mph) 101 km/h
Cruise speed: 51 kts (59 mph) 95 km/h
Stall speed: 26 kts (30 mph) 49 km/h
Range: 104 naut miles (120 miles) 193 km
Climb rate: 800 ft (244 m) per minute
Availability: Plans and kits.
Comments: Introduced in 1984. Also available is the J-5 Super Kitten with 39.6 hp (29.5 kW) Rotax 447 and perhaps the Super Kitten homebuilt.

Hipps Superbird J-3 Kitten built in France (Geoffrey P Jones)

Hipp's Superbirds J-4 Sportster

Type: Single-seat, parasol-wing microlight, with fixed tail-dragger undercarriage.
Construction: Wood, steel tube and fabric.
Wing span: 28 ft (8.53 m)
Length: 16 ft 4 ins (4.98 m)
Empty weight: 240 lb (109 kg)
Gross weight: 500 lb (227 kg)
Recommended engine: 25 hp (19 kW) Rotax 277
Maximum speed: 55 kts (63 mph) 101 km/h
Cruise speed: 51 kts (59 mph) 95 km/h
Range: 104 naut miles (120 miles) 193 km
Climb rate: 800 ft (244 m) per minute
Availability: Plans and kits.
Comments: Smaller and more basic development of the J-3 Kitten. Also available with wheel spats, faired turtle-deck, etc. Also offered is the heavier Super Sportster homebuilt, with a Rotax 447 engine.

Hipp's Superbirds Reliant

Type: Single-seat, high-wing microlight, with fixed tail-dragger undercarriage.
Construction: Wood, steel tube and fabric.
Wing span: 30 ft (9.14 m)
Length: 16 ft 4 ins (4.98 m)
Empty weight: 254 lb (115 kg)
Gross weight: 500 lb (227 kg)
Recommended engine: 25 hp (19 kW) Rotax 277
Maximum speed: 55 kts (63 mph) 101 km/h
Cruise speed: 52 kts (60 mph) 97 km/h
Range: 104 kts (120 miles) 193 km/h
Climb rate: 800 ft (244 m) per minute
Availability: Kits.
Comments: More refined version of the J-3 Kitten, introduced in 1987. Also available is the Reliant SX homebuilt with a Rotax 447 engine, offering 87 kts (100 mph) 161 km/h maximum speed.

Hirt Trio

Address: Hirt Aircraft, PO Box 2134, Hemet, CA 92546-2134.
Telephone: +1 909 925 3404
Type: Side-by-side 2-seat, forward-swept-wing monoplane with canard, and fixed nosewheel undercarriage.
Construction: Composites.
Wing span: 30 ft (9.14 m)
Length: 21 ft 6 ins (6.55 m)
Empty weight: 1,050 lb (476 kg)
Gross weight: 1,650 lb (748 kg)
Recommended engine: 160 hp (119.3 kW) Textron Lycoming
Maximum speed: 156 kts (180 mph) 290 km/h
Cruise speed: 150 kts (173 mph) 278 km/h
Stall speed: 48 kts (55 mph) 89 km/h
Range: 695 naut miles (800 miles) 1,287 km
Take-off distance: 950 ft (290 m)
Climb rate: 1,000 ft (305 m) per minute
Availability: Plans and kits once test flying completed.
Comments: Prototype first flew in 1994. Twin control yokes.

Historical Aircraft P-51D

Address: Historical Aircraft Corporation, 536 Star Lane South, St. Paul, MN 55075.
Telephone: +1 612 451 3283
Type: Single-seat 62.5% fighter representation, with retractable tail-dragger undercarriage.
Construction: Steel tube and composites.
Wing span: 24 ft (7.32 m)
Length: 20 ft 8 ins (6.3 m)
Empty weight: 1,354 lb (614 kg)
Gross weight: 1,960 lb (889 kg)
Recommended engine: 230 hp (171.5 kW) Ford V-8 conversion
Maximum speed: 222 kts (255 mph) 410 km/h
Cruise speed: 187 kts (215 mph) 346 km/h
Range: 608 naut miles (700 miles) 1,126 km
Take-off distance: 1,800 ft (550 m)
Climb rate: 2,300 ft (700 m) per minute
Availability: Kits.
Comments: Other scale representations available from Historical Aircraft include the AU-1 Corsair, P-40 Tomahawk and PZL P.11c. An 85% scale Ryan STA is also available.

Howland H-2 Honey Bee

Address: Howland Aero Designs, 333 E. Highbanks Road, No.22, Debary, FL 32713.
Telephone: +1 407 668 2216
Facsimile: +1 407 668 2217
Type: Single-seat biplane, with fixed tail-dragger undercarriage.
Construction: Steel tube, wood and fabric.
Wing span: 19 ft (5.79 m)
Length: 15 ft 9 ins (4.8 m)
Empty weight: 315 lb (143 kg)
Gross weight: 550 lb (249 kg)
Recommended engine: 40 or 60 hp (30 or 44.7 kW) Hirth
Maximum speed: 55 kts (63 mph) 101 km/h
Cruise speed: 50 kts (58 mph) 93 km/h
Stall speed: 21 kts (24 mph) 39 km/h
Range: 156 naut miles (180 miles) 289 km
Take-off distance: 100 ft (31 m)
Climb rate: 800 ft (244 m) per minute
Availability: Kits and plans.
Comments: Neat aerobatic microlight sport biplane, stressed to +8, -6g.

New Howland HP-40 Warhawk; details received too late for inclusion (Geoffrey P Jones)

Howland H-3 Pegasus

Type: Single-seat, low-wing microlight, with fixed tail-dragger undercarriage.
Construction: Steel tube, wood and fabric.
Wing span: 25 ft (7.62 m)
Length: 15 ft (4.57 m)
Empty weight: 252-276 lb (114-125 kg)
Gross weight: 555 lb (252 kg)
Recommended engine: 31 hp (23 kW) Hirth 263, Rotax 227 or 447
Maximum speed: 52-71 kts (60-82 mph) 97-132 km/h
Cruise speed: 48 kts (55 mph) 89 km/h
Stall speed: 24 kts (27 mph) 44 km/h
Range: 156 naut miles (180 miles) 289 km
Take-off distance: 200 ft (61 m)
Climb rate: 600 ft (183 m) per minute
Availability: Kits and plans.
Comments: Kit construction takes 250 hours +.

Hummel Bird

Address: Morry Hummel,509 E. Butler, Bryan, OH 43506-0880.
Telephone: +1 419 636 3390.
Type: Single-seat, low-wing monoplane, with fixed tail-dragger or nosewheel undercarriage.
Construction: Metal.
Wing span: 21 ft (6.4 m)
Length: 13 ft 4 ins (4.06 m)

Empty weight: 268 lb (122 kg)
Gross weight: 540 lb (245 kg)
Recommended engine: 30 hp (22.4 kW) half Volkswagen
Maximum speed: 104 kts (120 mph) 193 km/h
Stall speed: 39 kts (45 mph) 73 km/h
Range: 172 naut miles (200 miles) 322 km
Take-off distance: 300 ft (92 m)
Climb rate: 1,000 ft (305 m) per minute
Availability: Plans.
Comments: Diminutive single-seater modified from the Watson Windwagon. First flown in June 1981.

Hummel Bird with nosewheel undercarriage, built in Canada (Geoffrey P Jones)

Hurricane Co Hurricane

Address: Hurricane Co Inc, 23055 Airport Road N.E., Aurora, OR 97002.
Telephone: +1 503 678 5740
Facsimile: +1 503 678 2771
Type: Single-seat, high-wing microlight, with fixed nosewheel undercarriage.
Construction: Metal and fabric.
Wing span: 28 ft 7 ins (8.71 m)
Length: 16 ft 10 ins (5.13 m)
Empty weight: 252 lb (114 kg)
Gross weight: 515 lb (234 kg)
Recommended engine: 41.6 hp (31 kW) Rotax 447
Maximum speed: 55 kts (63 mph) 101 km/h
Cruise speed: 52 kts (60 mph) 97 km/h
Range: 87 naut miles (100 miles) 161 km
Take-off distance: 120 ft (37 m)
Climb rate: 800 ft (244 m) per minute
Availability: Kits.
Comments: Also available are ClipWing-HP (Rotax 503 DIDC) and Two Place (Rotax 582 DIDC)

Innovation Genesis

Address: Innovation Engineering Inc, 8970 Harrison Street, Davenport, IA 52804.
Telephone: +1 319 386 6966
Facsimile: +1 319 386 4569
Type: Side-by-side 2-seat, high-wing microlight, with pusher engine and fixed nosewheel undercarriage.
Construction: Composites, steel tube and fabric.
Wing span: 26 ft 8 ins (8.13 m)
Length: 18 ft 6 ins (5.64 m)
Empty weight: 480 lb (218 kg)
Gross weight: 1,200 lb (544 kg)
Recommended engine: 64.4 hp (48 kW) Rotax 582 (as for details), or Rotax 503, 618 or 912
Maximum speed: 104 kts (120 mph) 193 km/h
Cruise speed: 78 kts (90 mph) 145 km/h
Range: 543 naut miles (625 miles) 1,005 km
Take-off distance: 200-350 ft (61-107 m)
Climb rate: 900 ft (274 m) per minute (solo)
Availability: Kits.

Javelin Wichawk

Address: Javelin Aircraft Co Inc, Municipal Airport, Augusta, KS 67010.
Telephone: +1 316 733 1011
Type: 2/3-seat biplane, with fixed tail-dragger undercarriage.
Construction: Metal, wood and fabric.
Wing span: 24 ft (7.01 m)
Length: 19 ft 3 ins (5.87 m)
Empty weight: 1,280-1,400 lb (581-635 kg)
Gross weight: 2,200 lb (998 kg)
Recommended engine: 180 hp (134 kW) Textron Lycoming O-360
Maximum speed: 122 kts (140 mph) 225 km/h
Cruise speed: 110 kts (127 mph) 204 km/h
Stall speed: 50 kts (57 mph) 92 km/h
Range: 434 naut miles (500 miles) 804 km
Take-off distance: 150 ft (46 m)
Climb rate: 1,700 ft (518 m) per minute
Availability: Plans.
Comments: Prototype first flew on 24 May 1971. Hundreds under construction or flying.

Javelin V6 STOL

Type: 4-seat, high-wing cabin monoplane, with fixed tail-dragger undercarriage.
Construction: Metal tubing, metal sheet and fabric.
Wing span: 32 ft (9.75 m)
Length: 22 ft 4 ins (6.81 m)
Empty weight: 1,250 lb (567 kg)
Gross weight: 2,200 lb (998 kg)
Recommended engine: 230 hp (171.5 kW) Ford converted auto engine.
Maximum speed: 122 kts (140 mph) 225 km/h
Cruise speed: 113 kts (130 mph) 209 km/h
Stall speed: 45 kts (52 mph) 84 km/h
Range: 564 naut miles (650 miles) 1,046 km
Take-off distance: 150 ft (46 m)
Climb rate: 1,700 ft (518 m) per minute
Availability: Plans.

Kelly Hatz CB-1

Address: Dudley R. Kelly, Rt. 4, Box 194, Versailles, KY 40383.
Telephone: +1 606 873 5253
Type: Tandem 2-seat biplane, with fixed tail-dragger undercarriage.
Construction: Wood, steel tube and fabric.
Wing span: 25 ft 4 ins (7.72 m)
Length: 19 ft (5.79 m)
Empty weight: 850-875 lb (386-397 kg)
Gross weight: 1,600 lb (726 kg)
Recommended engine: 100 hp (74.6 kW) Teledyne Continental O-200, 115 hp (85.75 kW) Textron Lycoming O-235 or others.
Maximum speed: 91 kts (105 mph) 169 km/h
Cruise speed: 74 kts (85 mph) 137 km/h
Stall speed: 35 kts (40 mph) 65 km/h
Range: 174 naut miles (200 miles) 322 km
Take-off distance: 400 ft (122 m)
Climb rate: 750 ft (229 m) per minute
Availability: Plans.
Comments: Designed by John D. Hatz and first flown on 19 April 1968.

Kelly Hatz CB-1 biplane (Geoffrey P Jones)

Kelly-D

Type: Tandem 2-seat biplane, with fixed tail-dragger undercarriage.
Construction: Wood, steel tube and fabric.
Wing span: 26 ft 4 ins (8.03 m)
Length: 19 ft 3 ins (5.87 m)
Empty weight: 950 lb (431 kg)
Gross weight: 1,600 lb (726 kg)
Recommended engine: 115 hp (85.75 kW) Textron Lycoming O-235
Maximum speed: 91 kts (105 mph) 169 km/h
Cruise speed: 78 kts (90 mph) 145 km/h
Stall speed: 39 kts (45 mph) 73 km/h
Range: 243 naut miles (280 miles) 450 km
Take-off distance: 400 ft (122 m)
Climb rate: 800 ft (244 m) per minute
Availability: Plans.

Kemmeries Tukan

Address: Kemmeries Aviation, Ultralight Flight Center, Pleasant Valley Airport, 8710 West Carefree hwy, Peoria, AZ 85382.
Telephone: +1 602 566 8026
Facsimile: +1 602 561 2287
Type: Single-seat trike (with option for 1+1 seating) microlight, with pusher engine and pivoting Rogallo wing.
Construction: Steel tube and fabric.
Wing span: 35 ft (10.67 m)
Length: 8 ft (2.44 m)
Empty weight: 254 lb (115 kg)
Gross weight: 769 lb (349 kg)
Recommended engine: 41.6 hp (31 kW) Rotax 447
Maximum speed: 61 kts (70 mph) 113 km/h
Cruise speed: 24-53 kts (28-61 mph) 45-98 km/h
Stall speed: 20 kts (23 mph) 37 km/h
Range: 61 naut miles (70 miles) 112 km
Climb rate: 750 ft (229 m) per minute
Availability: Plans and kits.
Comments: In production since 1987. Also agents for the French Air Creation and Cosmos/La Mouette microlights.

Kemmeries Tukan single-seat trike.

Keuthan Buccaneer II

Address: Keuthan Aircraft, 910 Airport Road, Merritt Island, FL 32952.
Telephone: +1 407 452 2000
Facsimile: +1 407 452-7111
Type: Side-by-side 2-seat, high-wing amphibian, with retractable tail-dragger undercarriage.
Construction: Composites, steel tube and fabric.
Wing span: 29 ft 8 ins (9.04 m)
Length: 22 ft 4 ins (6.81 m)
Empty weight: 575 lb (261 kg)
Gross weight: 1,150 lb (522 kg)
Take-off distance: 275 ft (84 m) land, 300 ft (92 m) water
Recommended engine: 64.4 hp (48 kW) Rotax 582 (Rotax 618 and 912 optional)
Maximum speed: 78 kts (90 mph) 145 km/h
Cruise speed: 63 kts (73 mph) 117 km/h
Stall speed: 37 kts (42 mph) 68 km/h
Range: 217 naut miles (250 miles) 402 km
Climb rate: 650 ft (198 m) per minute
Availability: Kits.
Comments: Also available is the single-seat Buccaneer SX with either Rotax 503 or 582 engine.

Keuthan Buccaneer II 2-seat amphibian with wheels retracted

Keuthan Sabre I

Type: Single-seat, high-wing, pusher-engined monoplane, with fixed undercarriage of nosewheel, tail-dragger or float types.
Construction: Steel tube and fabric.
Wing span: 29 ft 8 ins (9.04 m)
Length: 20 ft 1 ins (6.12 m)
Empty weight: 345 lb (156 kg)
Gross weight: 755 lb (342 kg)
Recommended engine: Rotax 503 (Rotax 447 and 582 options)
Maximum speed: 78 kts (90 mph) 145 km/h
Cruise speed: 56 kts (65 mph) 105 km/h
Stall speed: 26 kts (29 mph) 47 km/h
Range: 217 naut miles (250 miles) 402 km
Take-off distance: 125 ft (39 m) land
Climb rate: 1,100 ft (335 m) per minute
Availability: Kits.
Comments: Also available is the similar side-by-side 2-seat Sabre II, suitable for Rotax 582, 618 or 912 engines.

Keuthan Sabre I

Keuthan Zephyr II

Type: Tandem two-seat, high-wing monoplane, with fixed tail-dragger undercarriage.
Construction: Steel tube and fabric.
Wing span: 29 ft 8 ins (9.04 m)
Length: 22 ft 6 ins (6.86 m)
Empty weight: 475 lb (215 kg)
Gross weight: 1,100 lb (499 kg)
Recommended engine: 64.4 hp (48 kW) Rotax 582 (options are the Rotax 618 and 912)
Maximum speed: 78 kts (90 mph) 145 km/h
Cruise speed: 63 kts (73 mph) 117 km/h
Stall speed: 29 kts (33 mph) 53 km/h
Range: 217 naut miles (250 miles) 402 km
Take-off distance: 125 ft (39 m)
Climb rate: 1,100 ft (335 m) per minute
Availability: Kits.
Comments: Wings are easily detachable for transport and storage.

Kolb Firestar I

Address: Kolb Company Inc, R.D. 3, Box 38, Phoenixville, PA 19460.
Telephone & Facsimile: +1 215 948 4136
Type: Single-seat high-wing microlight, with pusher engine and fixed tail-dragger undercarriage.
Construction: Steel tube and fabric.
Wing span: 27 ft 6 ins (8.38 m)
Length: 21 ft 3 ins (6.48 m)
Empty weight: 275 lb (125 kg)
Gross weight: 550 lb (250 kg)
Recommended engine: 39.6 hp (29.5 kW) Rotax 447
Maximum speed: 55 kts (63 mph) 101 km/h
Cruise speed: 48 kts (55 mph) 89 km/h
Stall speed: 26 kts (29 mph) 47 km/h
Take-off distance: 125 ft (39 m)
Climb rate: 1,000 ft (305 m) per minute
Availability: Kits.
Comments: Also available are the tandem 2-seat Firestar II and the STOL Mark III 2-seater with larger wings and Rotax 582 engine.

Kolb Firestar I built by Steve Anderson at Everett, WA

Lancair 320 Mk.II

Address: Lancair International Inc, 2244 Airport Way, Redmond, OR 97756
Telephone: +1 503 923 2233
Facsimile: +1 503 923 2255
Type: Side-by-side 2-seat, low-wing monoplane, with retractable nosewheel undercarriage.
Construction: Composites.
Wing span: 23 ft 6 ins (7.16 m)
Length: 21 ft (6.4 m)
Empty weight: 1,090 lb (494 kg)
Gross weight: 1,685 lb (764 kg)
Recommended engine: 180 hp (134 kW) Textron Lycoming IO-360
Maximum speed: 222 kts (255 mph) 410 km/h
Cruise speed: 200 kts (230 mph) 370 km/h
Stall speed: 55 kts (63 mph) 102 km/h
Range: 990 naut miles (1,140 miles) 1,834 km
Take-off distance: 690 ft (210 m)
Climb rate: 1,950 ft (594 m) per minute
Availability: Kits.
Comments: Designed by Lance Niebaur. Prototype Lancair 200 first flew in June 1984. Kits sold in 34 countries. 160 hp (119.3 kW) Textron Lycoming O-320 option also available.

Lancair IV

Type: Four-seat low-wing monoplane, with retractable nosewheel undercarriage and pressurized cabin option.
Construction: Composites.
Wing span: 30 ft 3 ins (9.22 m)
Length: 25 ft (7.62 m)
Empty weight: 1,900 lb (862 kg)
Gross weight: 3,200 lb (1,451 kg)
Recommended engine: 350 hp (261 kW) Teledyne Continental TSIO 550-B (twin turbo-charged, twin intercooled).
Maximum speed: 296 kts (341 mph) 548 km/h
Cruise speed: 230 kts (265 mph) 426 km/h
Stall speed: 65 kts (75 mph) 121 km/h
Range: 921 naut miles (1,060 miles) 1,706 km
Take-off distance: 1,200 ft (366 m)
Climb rate: 2,600 ft (792 m) per minute
Availability: Kits.
Comments: First flown in 1990, and currently holds 4 national Aeronautic Association World Records.

Lancair ES

Type: 4-seat low-wing monoplane, with fixed nosewheel undercarriage.
Construction: Composites.
Wing span: 35 ft 6 ins (10.82 m)
Length: 25 ft (7.62 m)
Empty weight: 1,700 lb (771 kg)
Gross weight: 2,900 lb (1,315 kg)
Recommended engine: 200 hp (149 kW) Teledyne Continental IO-360-ES
Maximum speed: 191 kts (220 mph) 354 km/h
Cruise speed: 167 kts (192 mph) 309 km/h
Stall speed: 47 kts (54 mph) 87 km/h
Range: 1,042 naut miles (1,200 miles) 1,931 km
Take-off distance: 800 ft (244 m)
Climb rate: 1,250 ft (381 m) per minute
Availability: Kits.
Comments: A joint venture company has been formed between Lancair and a Malaysian organization to gain FAR Pt 23 certification for the new Lancair ESP, and sell production-assembled examples with 200 hp (149 kW) engines. Development of the ESP will produce a higher-powered version with retractable undercarriage.

Lancair ES with fixed undercarriage introduced in 1993 (Geoffrey P Jones)

Laron Shadow & Streak Shadow

Address: Laron Aviation Technologies Inc, PO Box 5026, Borger, TX 79008-5026.
Telephone: +1 806 273 8513
Facsimile: +1 806 273 8375
Type: Tandem 2-seat, high-wing monoplane, with pusher engine and fixed nosewheel undercarriage.
Construction: Composites, wood and metal.
Details: Shadow (A), Streak Shadow (B).
Wing span: (A) 32 ft 11 ins (10.03 m), (B) 28 ft (8.53 m)
Length: (A) and (B) 21 ft (6.4 m)
Empty weight: (A) 349 lb (158 kg), (B) 388 lb (176 kg)
Gross weight: (A) 824 lb (374 kg), (B) 900 lb (408 kg)
Recommended engine: (A) 45.6 hp (34 kW) Rotax 503, (B) 64.4 hp (48 kW) Rotax 583
Maximum speed: (A) 89 kts (102 mph) 164 km/h, (B) 105 kts (121 mph) 195 km/h
Cruise speed: (A) 78 kts (90 mph) 145 km/h, (B) 87 kts (100 mph) 161 km/h
Stall speed: (A) 22 kts (25 mph) 41 km/h, (B) 27 kts (31 mph) 50 km/h
Range: (A) 169 naut miles (195 miles) 313 km, (B) 279 naut miles (322 miles) 518 km
Take-off distance: (A) and (B) 100 ft (31 m)
Climb rate: (A) 700 ft (213 m), (B) 1,100 ft (335 m) per minute
Availability: Kits.
Comments: Manufactured in the USA under licence from CFM of Leiston, UK.

Laron Streak Shadow (Geoffrey P Jones)

Laron Star Streak

Type: Tandem 2-seat, high-wing monoplane, with pusher engine and fixed nosewheel undercarriage.
Construction: Composites, wood and metal.
Wing span: 30 ft (9.14 m)
Length: 21 ft (6.4 m)
Empty weight: 400 lb (181 kg)
Gross weight: 900 lb (408 kg)
Recommended engine: 85 hp (63.4 kW) Hirth F-30
Maximum speed: 123 kts (141 mph) 227 km/h
Cruise speed: 106 kts (122 mph) 196 km/h
Stall speed: 31 kts (35 mph) 57 km/h
Range: 269 naut miles (310 miles) 499 km
Take-off distance: 100 ft (31 m)
Climb rate: 2,100 ft (640 m) per minute
Availability: Kits.
Comments: Also available is the similar Wizard built under licence from Dong-In Industrial Co of Seoul, Korea. See Dong-In Wizard.

Light Miniature LM-1

Address: Light Miniature Aircraft, 19695 NW 80th Drive, Okeechobee, FL 34972.
Telephone: +1 813 467 0933
Type: Single-seat high-wing monoplane, with fixed tail-dragger undercarriage.
Construction: Wood, metal and fabric.
Wing span: 27 ft (8.23 m)
Length: 17 ft 8 ins (5.38 m)
Empty weight: 335 lb (152 kg)
Gross weight: 600 lb (272 kg)
Take-off distance: 200 ft (61 m)
Recommended engine: 39.6 hp (29.5 kW) Rotax 447, or others including the 45 hp (33.6 kW) Zenoah.
Maximum speed: 56 kts (65 mph) 105 km/h
Stall speed: 21 kts (24 mph) 39 km/h
Range: 139 naut miles (160 miles) 257 km
Climb rate: 600 ft (183 m) per minute
Availability: Plans and kits.
Comments: LM-1A and LM-1X are scale representations of the Piper J-3, with differing spans (LM-1A detailed). The LM-2X is a 75% Taylorcraft representation and the LM-2X-2P is a 2-seater.

Light Miniature LM-2X 75% scale Taylorcraft replica (Geoffrey P Jones)

Light Miniature LM-3X

Type: Single-seat high-wing monoplane, with fixed tail-dragger undercarriage.
Construction: Steel tube and fabric.
Wing span: 30 ft (9.14 m)
Length: 17 ft 6 ins (5.33 m)
Empty weight: 325 lb (147 kg)
Gross weight: 600 lb (272 kg)
Recommended engine: 39.6 hp (29.5 kW) Rotax 447
Maximum speed: 65 kts (75 mph) 121 km/h
Cruise speed: 56 kts (65 mph) 105 km/h
Stall speed: 24 kts (27 mph) 44 km/h
Range: 95 naut miles (110 miles) 177 km
Take-off distance: 100 ft (31 m)
Climb rate: 600 ft (183 m) per minute
Availability: Plans and kits.
Comments: 75% scale Aeronca representation. Also available is the LM-5X Super Cub representation with either 100 hp (74.6 kW) or 65 hp (48.5 kW) Rotax 582.

Lightning Bug

Address: Lightning Bug Aircraft Corporation, PO Drawer 40, Sheldon, SC 29941.
Telephone: +1 803 549 1800
Facsimile: +1 803 846 8584
Type: Single-seat low-wing monoplane, with fixed tail-dragger undercarriage.
Construction: Composites.
Wing span: 17 ft 10 ins (5.44 m)
Length: 17 ft 5 ins (5.31 m)
Empty weight: 475 lb (215 kg)
Gross weight: 800 lb (363 kg)
Recommended engine: 90 hp (67 kW) AMW 750
Maximum speed: 217 kts (250 mph) 402 km/h
Cruise speed: 196 kts (225 mph) 362 km/h
Stall speed: 74 kts (85 mph) 137 km/h
Range: 764 naut miles (880 miles) 1,416 km
Take-off distance: 800 ft (244 m)
Climb rate: 1,200 ft (366 m) per minute
Availability: Kits.
Comments: First example built by Nick Jones. Capable of aerobatics. Nosewheel undercarriage version also available.

Lightning Bug built by J. L. Murphy at Cape Canaveral, Florida (Geoffrey P Jones)

Lockwood Air Cam

Address: Lockwood Aviation Inc, 280 Hendricks Way, Sebring, FL 33870
Telephone: +1 813 655 5100
Facsimile: +1 813 655 6225
Type: Tandem 2-seat, high-wing monoplane, with twin pusher engines and fixed tail-dragger undercarriage.
Construction: Metal and fabric.
Wing span: 32 ft 4 ins (9.86 m)
Length: 21 ft (6.4 m)
Empty weight: 740 lb (336 kg)
Gross weight: 1,300 lb (590 kg)
Recommended engines: 2 x 64.4 hp (48 kW) Rotax 582s, or 75hp (56 kW) Rotax 618s
Maximum speed: 78 kts (90 mph) 145 km/h with Rotax 582s
Cruise speed: 39-65 kts (45-75 mph) 72-121 km/h
Range: 130 naut miles (150 miles) 241 km
Take-off distance: 250 ft (77 m)
Climb rate: 1,000 ft (305 m) per minute with Rotax 582s
Availability: Kits.

Lockwood Air Cam (Geoffrey P Jones)

Loehle P-40

Address: Loehle Aircraft Corporation, Shipmans Creek Road, Wartrace, TN 37183.
Telephone: +1 615 857 3419
Facsimile: +1 615 857 3908
Type: Single-seat low-wing monoplane, with retractable tail-dragger undercarriage.
Construction: Wood and fabric.
Wing span: 28 ft 8 ins (8.74 m)
Length: 22 ft 10 ins (6.96 m)
Empty weight: 550 lb (249 kg)
Gross weight: 885 lb (401 kg)
Recommended engine: 64.4 hp (48 kW) Rotax 582
Maximum speed: 87 kts (100 mph) 161 km/h
Cruise speed: 74 kts (85 mph) 137 km/h
Stall speed: 28 kts (32 mph) 52 km/h
Range: 273 naut miles (315 miles) 507 km
Take-off distance: 150 ft (46 m)
Climb rate: 1,200 ft (366 m) per minute
Availability: Kits.
Comments: Option for fixed undercarriage. Curtiss P-40 representation, based on the Loehle 5151 fuselage.

Loehle 5151 RG Mustang

Type: Single-seat low-wing monoplane, with retractable tail-dragger undercarriage.
Construction: Wood and fabric.
Wing span: 27 ft 5 ins (8.36 m)
Length: 22 ft 10 ins (6.96 m)
Empty weight: 588 lb (267 kg)
Gross weight: 885 lb (401 kg)
Recommended engine: 64.4 hp (48 kW) Rotax 582
Maximum speed: 87 kts (100 mph) 161 km/h
Cruise speed: 74 kts (85 mph) 137 km/h
Stall speed: 26 kts (30 mph) 49 km/h
Range: 273 naut miles (315 miles) 507 km
Take-off distance: 150 ft (46 m)
Climb rate: 1,200 ft (366 m) per minute
Availability: Kits.
Comments: Developed from the fixed undercarriage Loehle 5151 Mustang, an approximate 75% scale Mustang representation which first flew on 30 January 1986.

Loehle 5151 RG Mustang with undercarriage extended (Geoffrey P Jones)

Loehle Sport Parasol

Type: Single-seat parasol-wing microlight, with fixed tail-dragger undercarriage.
Construction: Wood and fabric.
Wing span: 25 ft 6 ins (7.77 m)
Length: 18 ft 5 ins (5.61 m)
Empty weight: 252 lb (114 kg)
Gross weight: 548 lb (249 kg)
Recommended engine: 49.6 hp (37 kW) Rotax 503
Maximum speed: 74 kts (85 mph) 137 km/h
Cruise speed: 56 kts (65 mph) 105 km/h
Stall speed: 26 kts (30 mph) 49 km/h
Range: 174 naut miles (200 miles) 322 km
Take-off distance: 100 ft (31 m)
Climb rate: 750 ft (229 m) per minute
Availability: Kits.
Comments: Introduced into the Loehle range in 1992 as a cheap to purchase, simple to build and easy to fly microlight.

Loehle Sport Parasol (Geoffrey P Jones)

Marquart MA-5 Charger

Address: Ed Marquart, Box 3032, Riverside, CA 92519-3032.
Telephone: +1 909 683 9582
Type: Tandem 2-seat, aerobatic biplane, with fixed tail-dragger undercarriage.
Construction: Steel tube and fabric.
Wing span: 24 ft (7.32 m)
Length: 19 ft 6 ins (5.94 m)
Empty weight: 1,000 lb (454 kg)
Gross weight: 1,550 lb (703 kg)
Recommended engine: 125 hp (93.2 kW) Textron Lycoming or others up to 180 hp (134 kW) O-360 (as detailed).
Maximum speed: 126 kts (145 mph) 233 km/h
Cruise speed: 117 kts (135 mph) 217 km/h
Stall speed: 37 kts (42 mph) 68 km/h
Range: 390 naut miles (450 miles) 724 km
Take-off distance: 400-600 ft (122-183 m)
Climb rate: 1,800 ft (549 m) per minute
Availability: Plans.
Comments: Classic sport biplane design by Edward Marquart.

Marquart MA-5 Charger (Geoffrey P Jones)

Merlin Aircraft Merlin GT-582

Address: Merlin Aircraft Inc, 509 Airport Road, Muskegon, MI 49441.
Telephone: +1 616 798 1622
Facsimile: +1 616 798 2370
Type: Side-by-side 2-seat, high-wing monoplane, with fixed tail-dragger undercarriage.
Construction: Steel tube and fabric.
Wing span: 30 ft (9.14 m)
Length: 20 ft (6.1 m)
Empty weight: 480 lb (218 kg)
Gross weight: 1,300 lb (590 kg)
Recommended engine: 64.4 hp (48 kW) Rotax 582
Maximum speed: 96 kts (110 mph) 177 km/h
Cruise speed: 74 kts (85 mph) 137 km/h
Stall speed: 32 kts (36 mph) 58 km/h
Range: 289 naut miles (333 miles) 536 km
Take-off distance: 85 ft (26 m)
Climb rate: 1,200 ft (366 m) per minute
Availability: Kits.
Comments: Originally the Canadian Macair Merlin. Available in STOL configuration with 25 kts (28 mph) 45 km/h stall speed. Also available are CAM 100 and other Rotax powered versions with varying designations.

Merlin Aircraft Merlin GT 618 (Geoffrey P Jones)

Mirage Celerity

Address: Mirage Aircraft Inc, 3936 Austin Street, Klamath Falls, OR 97603.
Telephone: +1 503 884 4011
Type: Side-by-side 2-seat, low-wing cabin monoplane, with retractable tail-dragger undercarriage.
Construction: Composites and wood.
Wing span: 23 ft 10 ins (7.26 m)
Length: 21 ft 6 ins (6.55 m)
Empty weight: 1,169 lb (530 kg)
Gross weight: 1,825 lb (828 kg)
Take-off distance: 800 ft (244 m)
Recommended engine: 160 hp (119.3 kW) Textron Lycoming O-320-B1A
Maximum speed: 191 kts (220 mph) 354 km/h
Cruise speed: 178 kts (205 mph) 330 km/h
Stall speed: 46 kts (53 mph) 86 km/h
Range: 869 naut miles (1,000 miles) 1,609 km
Climb rate: 1,800 ft (549 m) per minute
Availability: Plans and some components.
Comments: Designed by Larry Burton and first flown on 18 May 1985.

Mirage Celerity built by Larry Burton (Geoffrey P Jones)

Montana Coyote Mountain Eagle

Address: Montana Coyote Inc, 3302 Airport Road, Helena, MT 59601.
Telephone: +1 406 449 3556
Type: Side-by-side 2-seat, high-wing cabin monoplane, with fixed tail-dragger undercarriage.
Construction: Wood, steel tube, composites and fabric.
Wing span: 37 ft (11.28 m)
Length: 25 ft (7.62 m)
Empty weight: 1,100 lb (499 kg)
Gross weight: 2,000 lb (907 kg)
Recommended engine: 150 hp (112 kW) Textron Lycoming O-320
Maximum speed: 109 kts (125 mph) 201 km/h
Cruise speed: 91 kts (105 mph) 169 km/h
Stall speed: 31 kts (35 mph) 57 km/h
Range: 391 naut miles (450 miles) 724 km
Take-off distance: 350 ft (107 m)
Climb rate: 1,250 ft (381 m) per minute
Availability: Kits.
Comments: First flown in Spring 1991 with 125 hp (93.2 kW) Honda Prelude engine. New variant in 1994 named the Mountain Eagle.

Montana Coyote prototype (Geoffrey P Jones)

Morrisey 2000

Address: Morrisey Aircraft Co, PO Box 27889, Las Vegas, NV 89126.
Telephone: +1 702 251 5551
Type: Tandem 2-seat, low-wing monoplane, with fixed nosewheel undercarriage.
Construction: Metal.
Wing span: 30 ft (9.14 m)
Length: 20 ft (6.1 m)
Empty weight: 975 lb (442 kg)
Gross weight: 1,600 lb (726 kg)
Recommended engine: 115 hp (85.75 kW) Textron Lycoming O-235
Maximum speed: 115 kts (132 mph) 212 km/h
Cruise speed: 109 kts (125 mph) 201 km/h
Stall speed: 37 kts (42 mph) 68 km/h
Range: 304 naut miles (350 miles) 563 km
Take-off distance: 500 ft (153 m)
Climb rate: 1,000 ft (305 m) per minute
Availability: Kits and as a certificated assembled aircraft.
Comments: Original Morrisey 1000C Nifty first flew in 1948. Many subsequent modifications and commercial builders, including Varga which built the Kachina.

Morrisey 2000 (Geoffrey P Jones)

Mountaineer Dual 175

Address: Mountain Trikes, PO Box 557, Finkle Road, Millerton, NY 12546.
Telephone: +1 518 789 6550
Facsimile: +1 518 789 6775
Type: Tandem 2-seat, trike microlight, with pusher engine and shift Rogallo wing.
Construction: Alloy tube and fabric.
Wing span: 33 ft 4 ins (10.16 m)
Length: 11 ft (3.35 m)
Empty weight: 250 lb (113 kg)
Gross weight: 750 lb (340 kg)
Recommended engine: 49.6 hp (37 kW) Rotax 503 UL-DCDI
Maximum speed: 58 kts (67 mph) 108 km/h
Cruise speed: 43 kts (50 mph) 80 km/h
Take-off distance: 250 ft (77 m)
Climb rate: 900 ft (274 m) per minute
Availability: Kits.
Comments: Also available in a single-seat Rotax 277-powered version, as the Mountaineer Mite Lite.

Mustang Aeronautics Midget Mustang

Address: Mustang Aeronautics, PO Box 1685, Troy, MI 48099.
Telephone: +1 810 589 9277
Facsimile: +1 510 588 6788
Type: Single-seat low-wing monoplane, with fixed tail-dragger undercarriage.
Construction: Metal.
Wing span: 18 ft 6 ins (5.64 m)
Length: 16 ft 5 ins (5 m)
Empty weight: 680 lb (308 kg)
Gross weight: 1,000 lb (454 kg)
Recommended engine: 150 hp (112 kW) Textron Lycoming O-320 (option for 100 hp, 74.5 kW O-200)
Maximum speed: 200 kts (230 mph) 370 km/h
Cruise speed: 187 kts (215 mph) 346 km/h
Stall speed: 54 kts (62 mph) 100 km/h
Range: 347 naut miles (400 miles) 643 km
Take-off distance: 450 ft (138 m)
Climb rate: 2,200 ft (670 m) per minute
Availability: Plans and kits.
Comments: Originally designed by David Long in the 1940s and updated for sale as a homebuilt in the 1950s by Robert Bushby.

Midget Mustang built by Jim Spear at Reno, NV (Geoffrey P Jones)

Mustang Aeronautics Mustang II

Type: Side-by-side 2-seat, low-wing monoplane, with fixed tail-dragger undercarriage.
Construction: Metal.
Wing span: 24 ft 4 ins (7.42 m)
Length: 19 ft 6 ins (5.94 m)
Empty weight: 1,100 lb (499 kg)
Gross weight: 1,600 lb (726 kg)
Recommended engine: 180 hp (134 kW) Textron Lycoming IO-360 (option for 160 hp, 119.3 kW O-320)
Maximum speed: 191 kts (220 mph) 354 km/h
Cruise speed: 182 kts (210 mph) 338 km/h
Stall speed: 52 kts (60 mph) 97 km/h
Range: 456 naut miles (525 miles) 845 km
Take-off distance: 450 ft (138 m)
Climb rate: 1,800 ft (549 m) per minute
Availability: Plans and kits.
Comments: Two-seat development of the Midget Mustang, first flown on 9 July 1966. Also examples with retractable nosewheel undercarriage.

Mustang II two-seater (Geoffrey P Jones)

National Aeronautics Cassutt IIIM

Address: National Aeronautics Co, 5611 Kendall Court, #4, Arvada, CO 80002.
Telephone & Facsimile: +1 303 940-8442
Type: Single-seat mid-wing monoplane racer, with fixed tail-dragger undercarriage.
Construction: Wood, steel tube and fabric.
Wing span: 15 ft (4.57 m)
Length: 16 ft (4.88 m)
Empty weight: 500 lb (227 kg)
Gross weight: 850 lb (386 kg)
Recommended engine: Teledyne Continental C85 or O-200
Maximum speed: 200 kts (230 mph) 370 km/h
Cruise speed: 165 kts (190 mph) 306 km/h
Stall speed: 59 kts (67 mph) 108 km/h
Range: 391 naut miles (450 miles) 724 km
Take-off distance: 450 ft (138 m)
Climb rate: 1,500 ft (457 m) per minute
Availability: Plans and kits.
Comments: Prototype designed and built by Capt Tom Cassutt in 1954 for air racing. Examples built in UK by Airmark Ltd. Aerobatic, and regularly raced at Reno.

National Aeronautics Cassutt IIIM built in the UK (Geoffrey P Jones)

O'Neill Magnum V8

Address: O'Neill Airplane Co, 791 Livingston, Carlyle, IL 62231.
Telephone: +1 618 594 2681
Type: 6-seat, high-wing cabin monoplane, with unusual 4-wheel fixed undercarriage.
Construction: Metal.
Wing span: 36 ft (10.97 m)
Length: 25 ft 10 ins (7.87 m)
Empty weight: 1,900 lb (862 kg)
Gross weight: 3,800 lb (1,724 kg)
Recommended engine: 380 hp (283.4 kW) Ford V8 conversion
Maximum speed: 161 kts (185 mph) 298 km/h
Cruise speed: 122 kts (140 mph) 225 km/h
Range: 347 naut miles (400 miles) 643 km
Take-off distance: 1,000 ft (305 m)
Climb rate: 1,500 ft (457 m) per minute
Availability: Plans and some components.
Comments: Large cargo-carrying homebuilt with swing-tail for loading out-sized items. Only the prototype completed by 1995.

Osprey Aircraft Osprey II

Address: Osprey Aircraft, 3741 El Ricon Way, Sacramento, CA 95825.
Telephone: +1 916 483 3004
Type: Side-by-side 2-seat, mid-wing amphibian, with pylon mounted pusher engine and retractable nosewheel undercarriage.
Construction: Composites and wood.
Wing span: 26 ft (7.92 m)
Length: 20 ft 6 ins (6.25 m)
Empty weight: 970 lb (440 kg)
Gross weight: 1,560 lb (707 kg)
Take-off distance: 400 ft (122 m) land, 520 ft (159 m) water.
Recommended engine: 150 hp (112 kW) Textron Lycoming O-320
Maximum speed: 113 kts (130 mph) 209 km/h
Cruise speed: 95 kts (109 mph) 175 km/h
Stall speed: 52 kts (60 mph) 97 km/h
Range: 313 naut miles (360 miles) 579 km
Climb rate: 1,000 ft (305 m) per minute
Availability: Plans and kits.
Comments: Designed by George Pereira and developed from the Osprey I. Prototype Osprey II first flew from water in April 1973.

Osprey II built in the UK by Arthur and John Zwetsloot (Geoffrey P Jones)

Osprey Aircraft GP-4

Type: Side-by-side 2-seat, low-wing cabin monoplane, with retractable nosewheel undercarriage.
Construction: Wood.
Wing span: 24 ft 8 ins (7.52 m)
Length: 21 ft 6 ins (6.55 m)
Empty weight: 1,248 lb (566 kg)
Gross weight: 1,985 lb (900 kg)
Recommended engine: 200 hp (149 kW) Textron Lycoming IO-360
Maximum speed: 217 kts (250 mph) 402 km/h
Cruise speed: 209 kts (240 mph) 386 km/h
Stall speed: 57 kts (65 mph) 105 km/h
Range: 955 naut miles (1,100 miles) 1,770 km
Take-off distance: 300 ft (92 m)
Climb rate: 2,200 ft (670 m) per minute
Availability: Plans and kits.
Comments: Another George Pereira homebuilt design, first flying in 1984.

Pacific Aerosystem Sky Arrow 1450L

Address: Pacific Aerosystem Inc, 5760 Chesapeake Ct, San Diego, CA 92123.
Telephone: +1 619 571 1441
Facsimile: +1 619 571 0803
Type: Tandem 2-seat, high-wing monoplane, with pusher engine and either fixed nosewheel undercarriage or floats.
Construction: Composites.

Pacific Aerosystem Sky Arrow 1450L (Geoffrey P Jones)

Wing span: 31 ft 6 ins (9.6 m)
Length: 24 ft 11 ins (7.59 m)
Empty weight: 770 lb (349 kg)
Gross weight: 1,450 lb (658 kg)
Recommended engine: 77.8 hp (58 kW) Rotax 912
Maximum speed: 80 kts (92 mph) 148 km/h
Cruise speed: 68 kts (78 mph) 126 km/h
Range: 304 naut miles (350 miles) 563 km
Take-off distance: 500 ft (153 m)
Climb rate: 800 ft (244 m) per minute
Availability: Kits.
Comments: Also the 1450A with 920 lb (417 kg) empty weight.

ParaPlane PSE-2

Address: ParaPlane Corp, 68 Stacey Haines Road, Medford, NJ 08055.
Telephone: +1 609 261 1234
Facsimile: +1 609 261 9116
Type: Single-seat powered parachute, with fixed nosewheel trike.
Construction: Metal and fabric.
Wing span: 30 ft 6 ins (9.3 m)
Length: 6 ft 6 ins (1.98 m)
Empty weight: 235 lb (107 kg)
Gross weight: 554 lb (251 kg)
Recommended engine: 45.6 hp (34 kW) Rotax 503
Maximum speed: 24 kts (28 mph) 45 km/h
Cruise speed: 24 kts (28 mph) 45 km/h
Range: 21.7 naut miles (25 miles) 40 km
Take-off distance: 100 ft (31 m)
Climb rate: 650 ft (198 m) per minute
Availability: Kits.
Comments: Another ParaPlane variant is the PM-2, powered by twin 15 hp (11.2 kW) Solo engines.

Parascender 1-447

Address: Parascender Technologies Inc, 828 North Hoagland Blvd, Kissimmee, FL 34741-4518.
Telephone: +1 407 935 0775
Facsimile: +1 407 935 0778
Type: Single-seat powered parachute, with fixed nosewheel undercarriage trike.
Construction: Steel tube and fabric.
Wing span: 36 ft 6 ins (11.13 m)
Length: 8 ft 9 ins (2.67 m)
Empty weight: 205 lb (93 kg)
Gross weight: 455 lb (206 kg)
Take-off distance: 100 ft (31 m)
Recommended engine: 39.6 hp (29.5 kW) Rotax 447
Maximum speed: 23 kts (26 mph) 42 km/h
Climb rate: 450 ft (137 m) per minute
Availability: Kits.
Comments: Other single-seat and 2-seat variants are Rotax 503 powered, plus the Para-Ag agricultural model for spray applications.

Parker Teenie Two

Address: Calvin Parker, Box 2092, Harker Heights, TX 76543.
Telephone: +1 817 698 3283
Facsimile: +1 817 698 1207
Type: Single-seat low-wing monoplane, with fixed nosewheel undercarriage.
Construction: Metal.
Wing span: 18 ft (5.49 m)
Length: 12 ft 10 ins (3.91 m)
Empty weight: 310 lb (140 kg)
Gross weight: 590 lb (267 kg)
Recommended engine: 65 hp (48.5 kW) Volkswagen or other VWs
Maximum speed: 122 kts (140 mph) 225 km/h
Cruise speed: 104 kts (120 mph) 193 km/h
Range: 347 naut miles (400 miles) 643 km
Take-off distance: 600 ft (183 m)
Climb rate: 1,000 ft (305 m) per minute
Availability: Plans and kits of raw materials.

Parker Teenie Two in France (Geoffrey P Jones)

Pazmany PL-2

Address: Pazmany Aircraft Corporation, PO Box 80051, San Diego, CA 92138.
Telephone: +1 619 224 7330
Type: Side-by-side 2-seat, low-wing cabin monoplane, with fixed nosewheel undercarriage.
Construction: Aluminium alloy.
Wing span: 28 ft (8.53 m)
Length: 19 ft 3.5 ins (5.9 m)
Empty weight: 900 lb (408 kg)
Gross weight: 1,445 lb (655 kg)
Recommended engine: 108 hp (80.5 kW) Textron Lycoming O-235
Maximum speed: 125 kts (144 mph) 232 km/h
Cruise speed: 111 kts (128 mph) 206 km/h
Stall speed: 47 kts (54 mph) 87 km/h
Range: 331 naut miles (381 miles) 613 km
Take-off distance: 700 ft (214 m)
Climb rate: 1,200 ft (366 m) per minute
Availability: Plans.
Comments: Designed by Ladislao Pazmany, developed from the single-seat PL-1 and first flown on 4 April 1969. As well as over 100 homebuilt examples flying, PL-2s have been built by the Air Forces of Vietnam, Thailand and Korea.

Pazmany PL-2 built by the Republic of Korea Air Force.

Pazmany PL-4A

Type: Single-seat low-wing monoplane, with T-tail and fixed tail-dragger undercarriage.
Construction: Metal.
Wing span: 26 ft 8 ins (8.13 m)
Length: 16 ft 2 ins (4.93 m)
Empty weight: 578 lb (262 kg)
Gross weight: 850 lb (386 kg)
Recommended engine: 54 hp (40.25 kW) Volkswagen
Maximum speed: 96 kts (110 mph) 177 km/h
Cruise speed: 87 kts (100 mph) 161 km/h
Stall speed: 42 kts (48 mph) 78 km/h
Range: 243 naut miles (280 miles) 450 km
Take-off distance: 560 ft (171 m)
Climb rate: 650 ft (198 m) per minute
Availability: Plans.
Comments: Prototype first flew on 12 July 1972. Examples built by air cadets in Argentina and Canada.

Pazmany PL-9 Stork

Type: Tandem 2-seat, high-wing monoplane, with fixed tail-dragger undercarriage.
Construction: Metal and fabric.
Wing span: 36 ft (10.97 m)
Length: 24 ft 3.5 ins (7.4 m)
Empty weight: 1,132 lb (513 kg)
Gross weight: 1,673 lb (759 kg)
Take-off distance: 250 ft (77 m)
Recommended engine: 150 hp (112 kW)
Maximum speed: 101 kts (116 mph) 187 km/h
Cruise speed: 83 kts (95 mph) 153 km/h
Range: 288 naut miles (332 miles) 534 km
Climb rate: 1,400 ft (427 m) per minute
Availability: Plans.
Comments: Representation of a German WW2 Fieseler Storch.

Performance Mountain Goat

Address: Performance Engineering, 4970 Owens Drive, #612, Pleasanton, CA 94588.
Telephone: +1 415 373-9396
Type: 2-seat, high-wing cabin monoplane, with fixed tail-dragger undercarriage.
Construction: Steel tube, composites and fabric.
Wing span: 36 ft (10.97 m)
Length: 22 ft 6 ins (6.86 m)
Empty weight: 1,070 lb (485 kg)
Gross weight: 2,170 lb (984 kg)
Recommended engine: 160 hp (119.3 kW) Textron Lycoming O-320
Maximum speed: 132 kts (152 mph) 245 km/h
Cruise speed: 115 kts (132 mph) 212 km/h
Stall speed: 31 kts (35 mph) 57 km/h
Range: 869 naut miles (1,000 miles) 1,609 km
Take-off distance: 120 ft (37 m)
Climb rate: 1,700 ft (518 m) per minute
Availability: Kits.
Comments: Bush plane with good high- and low-speed performance.

Peris JN-1

Address: Nancy Peris, 149 South Eastland Drive, Lancaster, PA 17602.
Telephone: +1 71 393 5928
Type: Single-seat high-wing microlight, with fixed tail-dragger undercarriage.
Construction: Composites, steel tube and wood.
Wing span: 30 ft (9.14 m)
Length: 17 ft 4 ins (5.28 m)
Empty weight: 320 lb (145 kg)
Gross weight: 600 lb (272 kg)
Recommended engine: 38 hp (28.3 kW) Kawasaki 440
Maximum speed: 56 kts (65 mph) 105 km/h
Cruise speed: 52 kts (60 mph) 97 km/h
Range: 96 naut miles (110 miles) 177 km
Take-off distance: 250 ft (77 m)
Climb rate: 600 ft (183 m) per minute
Availability: Plans.
Comments: Conventional single-seat microlight design.

Phantom XI

Address: Phantom Sport Airplane Corporation, PO Box 1684, Carthage, NC 28327
Telephone: +1 910 947 4744
Facsimile: +1 910 944 7449
Type: Single-seat high-wing microlight, with fixed nosewheel undercarriage.
Construction: Steel tube and fabric.
Wing span: 28 ft 6 ins (8.69 m)
Length: 16 ft 9 ins (5.11 m)
Empty weight: 250 lb (113 kg)
Gross weight: 510 lb (231 kg)
Recommended engine: 39.6 hp (29.5 kW) Rotax 447
Maximum speed: 53 kts (61 mph) 98 km/h
Cruise speed: 48 kts (55 mph) 89 km/h

Take-off distance: 100 ft (31 m)
Climb rate: 800 ft (244 m) per minute
Availability: Kits.
Comments: Phantom X2 is a 2-seat version with a Rotax 503 engine, 30 ft (9.14 m) span and 950 lb (431 kg) gross weight.

Pietenpol Sky Scout

Address: Don Pietenpol, 1604 Meadow Circle SE, Rochester, MN 55904-5251.
Telephone: +1 507 289 2436
Type: Single-seat, parasol-wing monoplane, with fixed tail-dragger undercarriage.
Construction: Wood and fabric.
Wing span: 27 ft 3 ins (8.31 m)
Length: 16 ft 2 ins (4.93 m)
Empty weight: 320 lb (145 kg)
Gross weight: 520 lb (236 kg)
Recommended engine: 20 hp (14.9 kW)
Maximum speed: 54 kts (62 mph) 100 km/h
Cruise speed: 48 kts (55 mph) 89 km/h
Range: 87 naut miles (100 miles) 161 km
Take-off distance: 150 ft (46 m)
Climb rate: 200 ft (61 m) per minute
Availability: Plans.
Comments: Designed shortly after the famous Pietenpol Aircamper in the 1930s. Plans for the separate 2-seat Aircamper also available (see also Grega Aircamper).

Preceptor N-3 Pup

Address: Preceptor Aircraft Corporation, 1230 Shepard Street, Hendersonville, NC 28792.
Telephone: +1 704 697 8284
Facsimile: +1 704 696 3739
Type: Single-seat high-wing microlight, with fixed tail-dragger undercarriage.
Construction: Steel tube and fabric.
Wing span: 30 ft 6 ins (9.3 m)
Length: 16 ft 6 ins (5.03 m)
Empty weight: 254 lb (115 kg)
Gross weight: 535 lb (243 kg)
Take-off distance: 150 ft (46 m)
Recommended engine: 40 hp (30 kW) 2-cylinder 1083 Defiant built by TEC.
Maximum speed: 55 kts (63 mph) 101 km/h
Cruise speed: 52 kts (60 mph) 97 km/h
Stall speed: 24 kts (27 mph) 44 km/h
Range: 130 naut miles (150 miles) 241 km
Climb rate: 600 ft (183 m) per minute
Availability: Plans and kits.
Comments: Representation of a Piper Cub. Oshkosh Grand Champion in its class in 1993. Preceptor Sport is a lighter 25 hp (18.6 kW) version.

Preceptor N-3/L-4 Super Pup

Type: Single-seat high-wing monoplane, with fixed tail-dragger undercarriage.
Construction: Steel tube and fabric.
Wing span: 26 ft (7.92 m)
Length: 16 ft 6 ins (5.03 m)
Empty weight: 330 lb (150 kg)
Gross weight: 630 lb (286 kg)
Recommended engine: 50 hp (37.3 kW)
Maximum speed: 88 kts (101 mph) 163 km/h
Cruise speed: 74 kts (85 mph) 137 km/h
Stall speed: 31 kts (35 mph) 57 km/h
Range: 260 naut miles (300 miles) 482 km
Take-off distance: 300 ft (92 m)
Climb rate: 800 ft (244 m) per minute
Availability: Plans and kits.
Comments: More powerful version of the N-3 Pup. Also as a representation of a Piper liaison aircraft.

Preceptor Stinger with TEC engine, first flown in April 1995. Details received too late for full inclusion.

Preceptor Ultra Pup

Type: Tandem 2-seat, high-wing monoplane, with fixed tail-dragger undercarriage.
Construction: Steel tube and fabric.
Wing span: 30 ft 6 ins (9.3 m)
Length: 17 ft 3 ins (5.26 m)
Empty weight: 450 lb (204 kg)
Gross weight: 1,050 lb (476 kg)
Recommended engine: 60 hp (44.7 kW) Preceptor Gold built by TEC.
Maximum speed: 96 kts (110 mph) 177 km/h
Cruise speed: 78 kts (90 mph) 145 km/h
Stall speed: 31 kts (35 mph) 57 km/h
Range: 304 naut miles (350 miles) 563 km
Take-off distance: 300 ft (92 m)
Climb rate: 1,500 ft (457 m) per minute
Availability: Plans and kits.
Comments: Folding wings. Can also be configured as a microlight trainer.

Progressive SeaRey

Address: Progressive Aerodyne Inc, 520 Clifton Street, Orlando, FL 32808.
Telephone: +1 407 292 3700
Facsimile: +1 407 292 5555
Type: Side-by-side 2-seat, high-wing amphibian, with pusher engine and retractable tail-dragger undercarriage.
Construction: Steel tube, composites and fabric.
Wing span: 29 ft 10 ins (9.09 m)
Length: 22 ft 5 ins (6.83 m)
Empty weight: 590 lb (268 kg)
Gross weight: 1,150 lb (522 kg)
Take-off distance: 175 ft (54 m)
Recommended engine: 64.4 hp (48 kW) Rotax 582
Maximum speed: 91 kts (105 mph) 169 km/h
Cruise speed: 70 kts (80 mph) 129 km/h
Stall speed: 32 kts (37 mph) 60 km/h
Climb rate: 700 ft (213 m) per minute
Availability: Kits.
Comments: Also suitable for Rotax 912 or AMW engines.

Progressive SeaRey with wheels retracted (Geoffrey P Jones)

Prostar PT.2C

Address: Prostar Aircraft Inc, PO Box 760, Beeville, TX 78104.
Telephone: +1 512 358 7670
Facsimile: +1 512 358 8128
Type: Side-by-side 2-seat, high-wing cabin monoplane, with fixed tail-dragger undercarriage.
Construction: Metal, composites and fabric.
Wing span: 32 ft 6 ins (9.91 m)
Length: 22 ft (6.71 m)
Empty weight: 800 lb (363 kg)
Gross weight: 1,550 lb (703 kg)
Take-off distance: 300 ft (92 m)
Recommended engine: 150 hp (112 kW) Textron Lycoming O-320
Maximum speed: 113 kts (130 mph) 209 km/h
Cruise speed: 100 kts (115 mph) 185 km/h
Range: 260 naut miles (300 miles) 482 km
Climb rate: 1,200 ft (366 m) per minute
Availability: Kits.

Prowler Jaguar

Address: Prowler Aviation Inc, 3707 Meadow View Drive, Redding, CA 96002.
Telephone: +1 916 365 4524
Type: Tandem 2-seat, low-wing monoplane, with retractable tail-dragger undercarriage.
Construction: Metal.
Wing span: 25 ft 5 ins (7.75 m)
Length: 21 ft (6.4 m)
Empty weight: 1,560 lb (708 kg)
Gross weight: 2,500 lb (1,134 kg)
Recommended engine: 350 hp (261 kW) Rodeck V8 conversion
Maximum speed: 261 kts (300 mph) 483 km/h
Cruise speed: 217 kts (250 mph) 402 km/h
Stall speed: 52 kts (60 mph) 97 km/h
Range: 1,042 naut miles (1,200 miles) 1,931 km
Take-off distance: 1,100 ft (336 m)
Climb rate: 2,500 ft (762 m) per minute
Availability: Kits.
Comments: Developed from George Morse's Prowler, which first flew in 1985.

Prowler Jaguar prototype

Quad City Challenger II Special

Address: Quad City Aircraft Corporation, 3610 Coaltown Road, Moline, IL 61265.
Telephone: +1 309 764 3515
Type: Tandem 2-seat, high-wing monoplane, with pusher engine and fixed nosewheel undercarriage.
Construction: Metal and fabric.
Wing span: 26 ft (7.92 m)
Length: 20 ft (6.1 m)
Empty weight: 350 lb (159 kg)
Gross weight: 850 lb (386 kg)
Recommended engine: 49.6 hp (37 kW) Rotax 503
Maximum speed: 87 kts (100 mph) 161 km/h
Cruise speed: 74 kts (85 mph) 137 km/h
Stall speed: 32 kts (37 mph) 60 km/h
Range: 191 naut miles (220 miles) 354 km
Take-off distance: 250-300 ft (77-92 m)

Climb rate: 1,000 ft (305 m) per minute
Availability: Kits.
Comments: Other Challenger models are the single-seat Challenger UL (Rotax 277), Challenger Special (Rotax 447) and the 2-seat Challenger II (Rotax 447).

Quad City Challenger II Special (Geoffrey P Jones)

Questair Venture

Address: Questair Inc, 3800 McAree Road, Waukegan, IL 60087.
Telephone: +1 708 244 0005
Facsimile: +1 708 244 0007
Type: Side-by-side 2-seat, low-wing monoplane, with retractable nosewheel undercarriage.
Construction: Metal.
Wing span: 27 ft 6 ins (8.38 m)
Length: 16 ft 3 ins (4.95 m)
Empty weight: 1,240 lb (562 kg)
Gross weight: 2,000 lb (907 kg)
Recommended engine: 280 hp (209 kW) Teledyne Continental IO-550-G or similar.
Maximum speed: 265 kts (305 mph) 491 km/h
Cruise speed: 240 kts (276 mph) 444 km/h
Stall speed: 62 kts (71 mph) 115 km/h
Range: 999 naut miles (1,150 miles) 1,850 km
Take-off distance: 1,000 ft (305 m)
Climb rate: 2,500 ft (762 m) per minute
Availability: Kits.
Comments: Prototype Venture first flew on 1 July 1987. Also available is the Questair Spirit with fixed nosewheel undercarriage, 210 hp (156.6 kW) Teledyne Continental IO-360 engine, and 198 kts (228 mph) 367 km/h cruise speed. Robert McLallen, head of Questair, was killed in an accident on 21 January 1995 (along with Henry Bouley), while flying a Venture powered by a 300 hp (224 kW) Bouley engine.

Questair Venture with retractable undercarriage (Geoffrey P Jones)

Quicksilver MX Sprint

Address: Quicksilver Enterprises Inc, PO Box 1572, Temecula, CA 92593.
Telephone: +1 909 676 6886
Facsimile: +1 909 676 4883
Type: Single-seat open trike microlight, with pusher engine.
Construction: Steel tube and fabric.
Wing span: 28 ft (8.53 m)
Length: 18 ft 1 ins (5.51 m)
Empty weight: 250 lb (113 kg)
Gross weight: 525 lb (238 kg)
Recommended engine: 39.6 hp (29.5 kW) Rotax 447
Maximum speed: 47 kts (54 mph) 87 km/h
Cruise speed: 43 kts (50 mph) 80 km/h
Range: 73 naut miles (84 miles) 135 km
Climb rate: 900 ft (274 m) per minute
Availability: Kits.
Comments: Successor to Eipper. Similar single-seater is the Quicksilver MX Sport with spats and fuselage pod. 2-seat versions are the MX.II Sprint and MXL.II Sprint, both with Rotax 503 engines.

Quicksilver MX Sprint single seater (Geoffrey P Jones)

Quicksilver GT 400

Type: Single-seat high-wing microlight, with fixed nosewheel undercarriage.
Construction: Steel tube and fabric.
Wing span: 30 ft (9.14 m)
Length: 19 ft 9 ins (6.02 m)
Empty weight: 276 lb (125 kg)
Recommended engine: 39.6 hp (29.5 kW) Rotax 447
Maximum speed: 53 kts (61 mph) 98 km/h
Cruise speed: 50 kts (58 mph) 93 km/h
Range: 67 naut miles (78 miles) 125 km
Take-off distance: 80 ft (25 m)
Climb rate: 1,000 ft (305 m) per minute
Availability: Kits.
Comments: 2-seat version is the Quicksilver GT 500, the first homebuilt design to be certificated in the USA under new FAA regulations.

Quicksilver GT 400 (Geoffrey P Jones)

Quick Flight Quiet Bird

Address: Flight Shack, PO Box 61252, Lakeport, NH 03247.
Telephone: +1 603 279 3480
Type: Single-seat microlight, with fixed nosewheel undrcarriage.
Wing span: 34 ft (10.36 m)
Empty weight: 240 lb (109 kg)
Gross weight: 495 lb (225 kg)
Maximum speed: 52 kts (60 mph) 97 km/h
Range: 174 naut miles (200 miles) 322 km
Availability: Kit.

Quikkit Glass Goose

Address: Quikkit Corporation, 9002 Summer Glen No. B, Dallas, TX 75243.
Telephone: +1 214 349 0462
Facsimile: +1 214 349 0462
Type: Side-by-side 2-seat, biplane amphibian, with pusher engine and retractable nosewheel undercarriage.
Construction: Composites.
Wing span: 27 ft (8.23 m)
Length: 19 ft 6 ins (5.94 m)
Empty weight: 900 lb (408 kg)
Gross weight: 1,800 lb (816 kg)
Recommended engine: 160 hp (119.3 kW) Textron Lycoming O-320
Maximum speed: 139 kts (160 mph) 257 km/h
Cruise speed: 126 kts (145 mph) 233 km/h
Stall speed: 44 kts (50 mph) 81 km/h
Range: 955 naut miles (1,100 miles) 1,770 km
Take-off distance: 700 ft (214 m)
Climb rate: 1,500 ft (457 m) per minute
Availability: Kits.
Comments: Improved derivative of the Aero Composites Sea Hawker, which first flew in 1982. Quikkit introduced the Glass Goose in 1992.

Quikkit Glass Goose amphibian (Geoffrey P Jones)

Raceair Skylite

Address: Raceair, 2331 Dodgeville Road, Rome, OH 44085
Telephone: +1 216 563 3387
Type: Single-seat parasol-wing microlight, with fixed tail-dragger undercarriage.
Construction: Steel tube and fabric.
Wing span: 29 ft 2 ins (8.89 m)
Length: 17 ft 6 ins (5.33 m)
Empty weight: 240 lb (109 kg)
Gross weight: 520 lb (236 kg)
Recommended engine: 25 hp (19 kW) Rotax 277
Maximum speed: 52 kts (60 mph) 97 km/h
Cruise speed: 41 kts (47 mph) 76 km/h
Stall speed: 22 kts (25 mph) 41 km/h
Range: 78 naut miles (90 miles) 144 km
Take-off distance: 400 ft (122 m)
Climb rate: 400 ft (122 m) per minute
Availability: Plans.
Comments: Easy to build microlight.

Raceair Skylite (Geoffrey P Jones)

RagWing Trainer

Address: RagWing/Roger Mann, 312 Gilstrap Drive, Liberty, SC 29657.
Telephone: +1 803 843 1324
Facsimile: +1 803 843 9916
Type: Tandem 2-seat, parasol-wing monoplane, with fixed tail-dragger undercarriage.
Construction: Wood and fabric.
Wing span: 28 ft 6 ins (8.69 m)
Length: 17 ft (5.18 m)
Empty weight: 450 lb (204 kg)
Gross weight: 900 lb (408 kg)
Recommended engine: 70 hp (52.2 kW) Sprint
Maximum speed: 91 kts (105 mph) 169 km/h
Cruise speed: 70 kts (80 mph) 129 km/h

Stall speed: 35 kts (40 mph) 65 km/h
Range: 226 naut miles (260 miles) 418 km
Take-off distance: 200 ft (61 m)
Climb rate: 650 ft (198 m) per minute
Availability: Plans and kits.
Comments: Designed as a representation of the Pietenpol Aircamper and to complement the single-seat 35 hp (26 kW) Kawasaki-powered RagWing.

RagWing Special

Type: Single-seat biplane, with fixed tail-dragger undercarriage.
Construction: Wood and fabric.
Wing span: 18 ft (5.49 m)
Length: 14 ft 9 ins (4.5 m)
Empty weight: 254 lb (115 kg)
Gross weight: 550 lb (249 kg)
Recommended engine: 35 hp (26 kW) Kawasaki 440
Maximum speed: 55 kts (63 mph) 101 km/h
Cruise speed: 48 kts (55 mph) 89 km/h
Range: 108 naut miles (125 miles) 201 km
Climb rate: 850 ft (259 m) per minute
Availability: Plans and kits.
Comments: Available as a microlight or experimental homebuilt.

Rand-Robinson KR-1

Address: Rand-Robinson Engineering Inc, 15641 Product Lane, Ste A5, Huntington Beach, CA 92649.
Telephone: +1 714 898 3811
Facsimile: +1 714 890 1658
Type: Single-seat low-wing monoplane, with either fixed or retractable tail-dragger undercarriage.
Construction: Composites and wood.
Wing span: 17 ft (5.18 m)
Length: 12 ft 9 ins (3.89 m)
Empty weight: 375 lb (170 kg)
Gross weight: 750 lb (340 kg)
Recommended engine: 90 hp (67 kW) Volkswagen
Maximum speed: 191 kts (220 mph) 354 km/h
Cruise speed: 130 kts (150 mph) 241 km/h
Stall speed: 39 kts (45 mph) 73 km/h
Range: 1,216 naut miles (1,400 miles) 2,253 km
Take-off distance: 400 ft (122 m)
Climb rate: 1,500 ft (457 m) per minute
Availability: Plans and kits.
Comments: Designed by Ken Rand and Stuart Robinson and first flown in February 1972. One of the first homebuilts to make extensive use of composite construction.

Rand-Robinson KR-1 built by Richard Shirley (Geoffrey P Jones)

Rand-Robinson KR-2

Type: Side-by-side 2-seat, low-wing monoplane, with either fixed or retractable tail-dragger undercarriage. Tri-gear available.
Construction: Composites and wood.
Wing span: 20 ft 8 ins (6.3 m)
Length: 14 ft 6 ins (4.42 m)
Empty weight: 480 lb (217 kg)
Gross weight: 900 lb (408 kg)
Recommended engine: 2,100cc Volkswagen
Maximum speed: 174 kts (200 mph) 322 km/h
Cruise speed: 156 kts (180 mph) 290 km/h
Stall speed: 39 kts (45 mph) 73 km/h
Range: 1,390 naut miles (1,600 miles) 2,575 km
Take-off distance: 350 ft (107 m)
Climb rate: 1,000 ft (305 m) per minute
Availability: Plans and kits.
Comments: Developed from the KR-1 and first flown in July 1974. New version is the KR-2S with 16 in (0.41m) longer fuselage, higher canopy, 23 ft (7 m) wing span and suitable for 76 hp (56.7 kW) Volkswagen engine.

RANS S-4 and S-5 Coyote

Address: Rans Co, 4600 Highway 183 Alternate, Hays, KS 67601.
Telephone: +1 913 625 6346
Facsimile: +1 913 625 2795
Type: Single-seat high-wing monoplane, with fixed undercarriage and option for tail-dragger or nosewheel.
Construction: Steel tube and fabric.
Wing span: 29 ft 6 ins (8.99 m)
Length: 17 ft (5.18 m)
Empty weight: 290 lb (131.5 kg)
Gross weight: 587 lb (266 kg)
Recommended engine: 41.6 hp (31 kW) Rotax 447
Maximum speed: 83 kts (95 mph) 153 km/h
Cruise speed: 48 kts (55 mph) 89 km/h
Stall speed: 24 kts (27 mph) 44 km/h
Range: 74 naut miles (85 miles) 136 km
Take-off distance: 60 ft (18.5 m)
Climb rate: 800 ft (244 m) per minute
Availability: Kits.
Comments: Rans S-4 is the taildragger and S-5 the nosewheel version. Rotax 503 engine is optional. Designed by Randy Schlitter, now company President.

Rans S-4 Coyote

Rans S-6 Coyote II

Type: Side-by-side 2-seat, high-wing monoplane, with fixed nosewheel or tail-dragger undercarriage.
Construction: Steel tube and fabric.
Wing span: 34 ft 6 ins (10.52 m)
Length: 20 ft (6.1 m)
Empty weight: 440 lb (200 kg)
Gross weight: 930 lb (422 kg)
Recommended engine: 64.4 hp (48 kW) Rotax 582 (options for Rotax 503 and 912)
Maximum speed: 104 kts (120 mph) 193 km/h
Cruise speed: 78 kts (90 mph) 145 km/h
Stall speed: 33 kts (38 mph) 61 km/h
Range: 191 naut miles (220 miles) 354 km
Take-off distance: 145 ft (45 m)
Climb rate: 1,000 ft (305 m) per minute
Availability: Kits.
Comments: Available in microlight or homebuilt/experimental category. A Super Six Coyote II model with a larger wing span has been produced for aerial mapping over the Amazon, equipped with a 35 mm camera.

Rans S-6-ESA Coyote II built in the UK with a Rotax 582 engine (Geoffrey P Jones)

Rans S-7 Courier

Type: Tandem 2-seat, high-wing monoplane, with fixed tail-dragger undercarriage.
Construction: Steel tube and fabric.
Wing span: 29 ft 3 ins (8.92 m)
Length: 21 ft (6.4 m)
Empty weight: 520 lb (236 kg)
Gross weight: 1,025 lb (465 kg)
Recommended engine: 64.4 hp (48 kW) Rotax 582
Maximum speed: 104 kts (120 mph) 193 km/h
Cruise speed: 70 kts (80 mph) 129 km/h
Stall speed: 31 kts (35 mph) 57 km/h
Range: 208 naut miles (240 miles) 386 km
Take-off distance: 175 ft (54 m)
Climb rate: 750 ft (229 m) per minute
Availability: Kits.
Comments: Prototype first flew in October 1985.

Rans S-7 Courier

Rans S-9 Chaos

Type: Single-seat, mid-wing monoplane, with fixed tail-dragger undercarriage.
Construction: Steel tube and fabric.
Wing span: 22 ft (6.71 m)
Length: 15 ft 8 ins (4.78 m)
Empty weight: 320 lb (145 kg)
Gross weight: 670 lb (304 kg)
Recommended engine: 49.6 hp (37 kW) Rotax 503SC
Maximum speed: 113 kts (130 mph) 209 km/h
Cruise speed: 74 kts (85 mph) 137 km/h
Stall speed: 26 kts (29 mph) 47 km/h
Range: 147 naut miles (170 miles) 273 km
Take-off distance: 200 ft (61 m)
Climb rate: 800 ft (244 m) per minute
Availability: Kits.
Comments: Also available is the 2-seat Rans S-10 Sakota with a Rotax 582, 960 lb (435 kg) gross weight and 24 ft (7.32 m) wing span.

Rans S-9 Chaos

Rans S-12 Airaile

Type: Side-by-side 2-seat, high-wing monoplane, with pusher engine and fixed nosewheel undercarriage.
Construction: Steel tube and fabric.
Wing span: 31 ft (9.45 m)
Length: 20 ft 4 ins (6.2 m)
Empty weight: 410 lb (186 kg)
Gross weight: 920 lb (417 kg)
Recommended engine: 49.6 hp (37 kW) Rotax 503SC
Maximum speed: 87 kts (100 mph) 161 km/h
Cruise speed: 56 kts (65 mph) 105 km/h
Stall speed: 26 kts (30 mph) 49 km/h
Range: 226 naut miles (260 miles) 418 km
Take-off distance: 275 ft (84 m)
Climb rate: 500 ft (152 m) per minute
Availability: Kits.
Comments: Introduced in 1991. The single-seat Rans S-14 Airaile has smaller dimensions and a Rotax 447 engine.

Rans S-12 Airaile side-by-side two-seat homebuilt (Geoffrey P Jones)

Rans S-16 Shekari

Type: Side-by-side 2-seat, mid-wing aerobatic monoplane, with fixed tail-dragger undercarriage.
Construction: Composites, steel tube and fabric.
Wing span: 25 ft (7.62 m)
Length: 19 ft 11 ins (6.07 m)
Empty weight: 590 lb (268 kg)
Gross weight: 1,200 lb (544 kg)
Recommended engine: 77.8 hp (58 kW) Rotax 912
Maximum speed: 148 kts (170 mph) 274 km/h
Cruise speed: 113 kts (130 mph) 209 km/h
Range: 334 naut miles (385 miles) 619 km
Take-off distance: 325 ft (99 m)
Climb rate: 1,000 ft (305 m) per minute
Availability: Kits.
Comments: First flown in 1994. Similar in external appearance to the Rans S-10 Sakota but stressed for aerobatics. Spatted undercarriage and 25 ft (7.62 m) wing span.

Redfern Fokker DR.1

Address: Walter Redfern, S-211 Spenser, Post Falls, ID 83854.
Telephone: +1 208 773 8280
Type: Single-seat triplane replica, with fixed tail-dragger undercarriage.
Construction: Wood, steel tube and fabric.
Wing span: 23 ft 8 ins (7.21 m)
Length: 19 ft (5.79 m)
Empty weight: 1,112 lb (504 kg)
Gross weight: 1,455 lb (660 kg)
Recommended engine: 145 hp (108 kW) Warner radial
Maximum speed: 104 kts (120 mph) 193 km/h
Cruise speed: 87 kts (100 mph) 161 km/h
Range: 260 naut miles (300 miles) 482 km
Climb rate: 2,000 ft (610 m) per minute
Availability: Plans.
Comments: Over 5,000 sets of plans sold. One of 4 Walter Redfern replicas of World War I aircraft. Others are the Nieuport 17, Nieuport 24 and DH-2.

Redfern Fokker DR.1 Triplane replica built by Ned and James Butler (Geoffrey P Jones)

Repeat Aircraft DH.88 Comet

Address: Bill Turner, Repeat Aircraft, PO Box 3427, Riverside, CA 92519.
Type: Tandem 2-seat, low-wing monoplane replica, with retractable tail-dragger undercarriage.
Construction: Wood.
Wing span: 44 ft (13.41 m)
Recommended engines: 2 x Gipsy Queens
Cruise speed: 139 kts (160 mph) 257 km/h
Stall speed: 63 kts (72 mph) 116 km/h
Take-off distance: 1,500 ft (458 m)
Climb rate: 2,500 ft (762 m) per minute
Availability: One-off replica of the 1934 Comet *Grosvenor House*.
Comments: Built by Repeat Aircraft for Tom Wathen and first flown on 28 November 1993. Other replicas built have been the Brown B-2 (1934), GeeBee Model Z (1931) and Miles and Attwood Special (1933).

Repeat Aircraft DH.88 Comet replica (Geoffrey P Jones)

Rotor-Wings Flaglor Scooter

Address: Rotor-Wings & Flying Machines, 10405 Button Quail, Austin, TX 78758-5032.
Telephone: +1 512 837 4041
Type: Single-seat high-wing monoplane, with fixed tail-dragger undercarriage.
Construction: Wood.
Wing span: 28 ft (8.53 m)
Length: 15 ft 6 ins (4.72 m)
Empty weight: 346 lb (157 kg)
Gross weight: 650 lb (295 kg)
Recommended engine: 40 hp (30 kW) Volkswagen
Maximum speed: 78 kts (90 mph) 145 km/h
Cruise speed: 65 kts (75 mph) 121 km/h
Stall speed: 31 kts (35 mph) 57 km/h
Range: 152 naut miles (175 miles) 281 km
Climb rate: 600 ft (183 m) per minute
Availability: Plans.
Comments: Prototype first flew in June 1967.

Sabre Aircraft Sabre

Address: Sabre Aircraft Inc, 1001 W. Monona Drive, Phoenix, AZ 85027.
Telephone: +1 602 582 6308
Facsimile: +1 602 925 6688
Type: Single, or 2-seat open framed trike, with pusher engine and high shift Rogallo wing.
Construction: Steel tube and fabric.
Wing span: 34 ft (10.36 m)
Length: 10 ft (3.05 m)
Empty weight: 205 lb (93 kg)
Gross weight: 600 lb (272 kg)
Recommended engine: 32 hp (23.9 kW) Kawasaki
Maximum speed: 43 kts (50 mph) 80 km/h
Cruise speed: 40 kts (46 mph) 74 km/h
Range: 87 naut miles (100 miles) 161 km
Take-off distance: 100 ft (31 m)
Climb rate: 1,000 ft (305 m) per minute
Availability: Kits.
Comments: Optional Rotax 447 or 503 engine.

St.Croix Pietenpol Aerial

Address: St Croix Aircraft, 5957 Seville Street, Lake Oswego, OR 97034.
Telephone: +1 503 636 4153
Type: Tandem 2-seat biplane, with fixed tail-dragger undercarriage.
Construction: Wood, steel tube and fabric.
Wing span: 29 ft 6 ins (8.99 m)
Length: 19 ft 6 ins (5.94 m)
Empty weight: 900 lb (408 kg)
Gross weight: 1,400 lb (635 kg)
Recommended engine: 145 hp (108 kW) Teledyne Continental O-300
Maximum speed: 91 kts (105 mph) 169 km/h
Cruise speed: 74 kts (85 mph) 137 km/h
Range: 130 naut miles (150 miles) 241 km
Take-off distance: 250 ft (77 m)
Climb rate: 1,000 ft (305 m) per minute
Availability: Plans.
Comments: Biplane development of the Pietenpol Aircamper. Latter aircraft also available in plans form from St.Croix. Other St.Croix aircraft are the single-seat Excelsior Ultralight and a Sopwith Triplane replica.

Ron Sands Fokker DR-1

Address: Ron Sands, 89 Forrest Road, Mertztown, PA 19539.
Telephone: +1 610 682-6788
Facsimile: +1 610 682-6788
Type: Single-seat replica triplane, with fixed tail-dragger undercarriage.
Construction: Metal, wood and fabric.
Wing span: 23 ft 8 ins (7.21 m)
Length: 19 ft (5.79 m)
Empty weight: 1,150 lb (522 kg)
Gross weight: 1,600 lb (726 kg)
Recommended engine: 110 hp (82 kW) Le Rhone
Maximum speed: 104 kts (120 mph) 193 km/h
Cruise speed: 96 kts (110 mph) 177 km/h
Range: 217 naut miles (250 miles) 402 km
Take-off distance: 300 ft (92 m)
Climb rate: 1,800 ft (549 m) per minute
Availability: Plans.
Comments: Full-scale replica of the WWI Fokker DR.1 Triplane. Suitable for Warner and Textron Lycoming engines. Other Ron Sands replicas are the Fokker D-VIII and 1929 Primary Glider.

Seawind 3000

Address: Seawind/S.N.A. Inc, PO Box 607, Kimberton, PA 19442-0607.
Telephone: +1 610 983 3377
Facsimile: +1 610 983 3335
Type: 4-seat amphibian, with retractable nosewheel undercarriage.
Construction: Composites.
Wing span: 35 ft (10.67 m)
Length: 27 ft (8.23 m)
Empty weight: 2,300 lb (1,043 kg)
Gross weight: 3,200 lb (1,451 kg)
Recommended engine: 300 hp (224 kW) Textron Lycoming IO-540
Maximum speed: 174 kts (200 mph) 322 km/h
Cruise speed: 166 kts (191 mph) 307 km/h

Stall speed: 61 kts (70 mph) 113 km/h
Range: 1,268 naut miles (1,460 miles) 2,349 km
Take-off distance: 650 ft (198 m) land, 1,060 ft (323 m) water.
Climb rate: 1,250 ft (381 m) per minute
Availability: Kits.
Comments: Development of the Canadian Seawind 2000. Production prototype first flew on 23 August 1982.

Seawind 2000 from which the Seawind 3000 was developed (Geoffrey P Jones)

Sequoia F.8L Falco

Address: Sequoia Aircraft Corporation, 2000 Tomlynn Street, PO Box 6861, Richmond, VA 23230.
Telephone: +1 804 353 1713
Facsimile: +1 804 359 2618
Type: Side-by-side 2-seat, low-wing monoplane, with retractable nosewheel undercarriage.
Construction: Wood.
Wing span: 26 ft 3 ins (8 m)
Length: 21 ft 4 ins (6.5 m)
Empty weight: 1,212 lb (550 kg)
Gross weight: 1,880 lb (853 kg)
Recommended engine: 160 hp (119.3 kW) Textron Lycoming IO-320-B1A
Maximum speed: 184 kts (212 mph) 341 km/h
Cruise speed: 165 kts (190 mph) 306 km/h
Stall speed: 54 kts (62 mph) 100 km/h
Range: 869 naut miles (1,000 miles) 1,609 km
Take-off distance: 1,150 ft (351 m)
Climb rate: 1,140 ft (347 m) per minute
Availability: Plans and kits.
Comments: Homebuilt version of Stelio Frati's Italian production aircraft. Also available is the all-metal 300 hp (224 kW) 300 Sequoia.

Sequoia F.8L Falco (Geoffrey P Jones)

Six-Cuter Skye-Ryder Aerochute

Address: Six-Chuter Inc, PO Box 8331, Yakima, WA 98908.
Telephone: +1 509 966 8211
Facsimile: +1 509 966 4284
Type: Single- or 2-seat, open framed trike, with fixed undercarriage, pusher engine and ram-air parachute.
Construction: Composites, steel tube and fabric.
Wing span: 36 ft 6 ins (11.13 m)
Length: 12 ft 4 ins (3.76 m)
Empty weight: 231 lb (105 kg)
Gross weight: 420 lb (191 kg)
Recommended engine: 39.6 hp (29.5 kW) Rotax 447 or 49.6 hp (37 kW) Rotax 503
Maximum and cruise speed: 23 kts (26 mph) 42 km/h
Stall speed: Stall resistant.
Range: 45 naut miles (52 miles) 83 km
Take-off distance: 100 ft (31 m)
Climb rate: 700 ft (213 m) per minute
Availability: Kits.
Comments: Designed by Larry Neiborsky in 1991. 2-seater is the Aerochute 2.

Skystar Kitfox Classic IV

Address: Skystar Aircraft Corporation, 100 N. Kings Road, Nampa, ID 83687.
Telephone: +1 208 466 1711
Facsimile: +1 208 466 7194
Type: Side-by-side 2-seat, high wing cabin monoplane, with fixed tail-dragger undercarriage.
Construction: Steel tube and fabric.
Wing span: 32 ft (9.75 m)
Length: 18 ft 5 ins (5.61 m)
Empty weight: 495 lb (225 kg)
Gross weight: 1,050 lb (476 kg)
Recommended engine: 49.6 hp (37 kW) Rotax 503 (optional Rotax 582 or 912)
Maximum speed: 83 kts (95 mph) 153 km/h
Cruise speed: 74 kts (85 mph) 137 km/h
Stall speed: 32 kts (36 mph) 58 km/h
Range: 139 naut miles (160 miles) 257 km
Take-off distance: 200 ft (61 m)
Climb rate: 425 ft (130 m) per minute
Availability: Kits.
Comments: Latest version of the Denney Kitfox series. Prototype Kitfox first flew on 7 May 1984. Kitfox IV introduced in mid-1991 and previously sold as the Kitfox XL.

Skystar Kitfox Classic IV on floats (C. Denney).

Skystar Kitfox Series 5

Type: Side-by-side 2-seat, high-wing cabin monoplane, with fixed tail-dragger undercarriage.
Construction: Steel tube and fabric.
Wing span: 32 ft (9.75 m)
Length: 19 ft 2 ins (5.84 m)
Empty weight: 705 lb (320 kg)
Gross weight: 1,200 lb (544 kg)
Recommended engine: 64.4 hp (48 kW) Rotax 582 (optional Rotax 618, 912 and 914)
Maximum speed: 96 kts (110 mph) 177 km/h
Cruise speed: 87 kts (100 mph) 161 km/h
Stall speed: 35 kts (40 mph) 65 km/h
Range: 400 naut miles (460 miles) 740 km
Take-off distance: 250 ft (77 m)
Climb rate: 570 ft (174 m) per minute
Availability: Kits.
Comments: Long-wing (details above) and short wing versions available and including the Kitfox Speedster and Kitfox Safari.

Skystar Kitfox Series 5 (C. Denney)

Skystar Kitfox Vixen

Type: Side-by-side 2-seat, high-wing cabin monoplane, with fixed nosewheel undercarriage.
Construction: Steel tube and fabric.
Wing span: 29 ft (8.84 m) short-wing, 32 ft (9.75 m) long wing.
Length: 20 ft 3 ins (6.17 m)
Empty weight: 725 lb (329 kg)
Gross weight: 1,200 lb (544 kg)
Recommended engine: 77.8 hp (58 kW) Rotax 912
Maximum speed: 104 kts (120 mph) 193 km/h
Cruise speed: 97 kts (112 mph) 180 km/h
Stall speed: 39 kts (44 mph) 71 km/h
Range: 534 naut miles (615 miles) 989 km
Take-off distance: 340 ft (104 m)
Climb rate: 700 ft (213 m) per minute
Availability: Kits.
Comments: Details for the short-wing version at gross weight. Developed for Skystar by Harry Riblett and the first nosewheel undercarriage Kitfox.

Skystar Kitfox Vixen (C. Denney)

Sky Technology Sky Car

Address: Kenneth G. Wernicke, Sky Technology Vehicle Design & Development Company, Fort Worth, Texas.
Type: 4-seat low-wing monoplane, with stub wings and endplates, twin fins, and fixed nosewheel undercarriage. Designed to operate as an automobile or aircraft.
Construction: Composites.
Wing span: 8 ft 6 ins (2.59 m)
Length: 21 ft (6.4 m)
Gross weight: 1,400 lb (635 kg)
Recommended engine: 180 hp (134 kW) Mazda rotary in proof-of-concept version and 475 hp (354 kW) in production type.
Maximum speed: 189 kts (217 mph) 349 km/h
Cruise speed: 152 kts (175 mph) 282 km/h
Range: 521 naut miles (600 miles) 965 km
Take-off distance: 980 ft (299 m)
Availability: Proof-of-concept prototype under construction.
Comments: Project under development – current project status uncertain.

Sky Technology Sky Car mock-up.

Sorrell SNS-7 Hiperbipe

Address: Sorrell Aircraft Co Ltd, 16525 Tilley Road South, Tenino, WA 98589.
Telephone: +1 206 264 2866
Facsimile: +1 206 264 2154
Type: Side-by-side 2-seat, reverse stagger aerobatic cabin biplane, with aerofoil shaped fuselage and fixed tail-dragger undercarriage.
Construction: Metal and fabric.
Wing span: 22 ft 10 ins (6.96 m)
Length: 20 ft 10 ins (6.35 m)
Empty weight: 1,236 lb (561 kg)
Gross weight: 1,911 lb (867 kg)
Recommended engine: 180 hp (134 kW) Teledyne Continental IO-360-B1E
Maximum speed: 149 kts (172 mph) 227 km/h
Cruise speed: 139 kts (160 mph) 257 km/h
Stall speed: 43 kts (49 mph) 79 km/h clean
Range: 436 naut miles (502 miles) 807 km
Take-off distance: 400 ft (122 m)
Climb rate: 1,500 ft (457 m) per minute
Availability: Kits.

Sorrell SNS-7 Hiperbipe (Geoffrey P Jones)

Sorrell SNS-8 Hiperlight

Type: Single-seat, reverse stagger biplane microlight, with fixed tail-dragger undercarriage.
Construction: Metal and fabric.
Wing span: 22 ft (6.71 m)
Length: 15 ft 8 ins (4.78 m)
Empty weight: 247 lb (112 kg)
Gross weight: 500 lb (227 kg)
Recommended engine: 25 hp (19 kW) Rotax 277
Maximum speed: 54 kts (62 mph) 100 km/h
Cruise speed: 52 kts (60 mph) 97 km/h
Range: 173 naut miles (200 miles) 321 km
Take-off distance: 175 ft (54 m)
Climb rate: 650 ft (198 m) per minute
Availability: Kits.
Comments: Other single-seat Sorrell aircrafts are the SNS-8 EXP (Rotax 447) and the SNS-2 Guppy (Rotax 377). 2-seat version is the SNS-9 EXP II (Rotax 503).

Spencer Amphibian Air Car

Address: Spencer Aircraft Inc, PO Box 327, Kansas, IL 61933.
Telephone: +1 217 948 5505
Facsimile: +1 708 883 0123
Type: 4-seat, high-wing amphibian, with pusher engine, fixed wingtip floats and retractable nosewheel undercarriage.
Construction: Wood, steel tube, composites and fabric.
Wing span: 37 ft 4 ins (11.38 m)
Length: 26 ft 5 ins (8.05 m)
Empty weight: 2,190 lb (993 kg)
Gross weight: 3,200 lb (1,451 kg)
Recommended engine: 300 hp (224 kW) Teledyne Continental IO-520 or 285 hp (212.5 kW) Teledyne Continental Tiara.
Maximum speed: 135 kts (155 mph) 249 km/h
Cruise speed: 122 kts (140 mph) 225 km/h
Stall speed: 38 kts (43 mph) 70 km/h
Range: 695 naut miles (800 miles) 1,285 km
Take-off distance: 700 ft (214 m)
Climb rate: 1,050 ft (320 m) per minute
Availability: Plans and kits.
Comments: Original Air Car patent received in January 1950. Spencer Amphibian Air Car Inc was sold to Robert F. Kerans on 15 July 1988. By January 1992 an estimated 37 were flying.

Spencer Amphibian Air Car (Geoffrey P Jones)

Sport Aircraft (Sunderland) S-18

Address: Sport Aircraft Inc, 44211 Yucca, Unit A, Lancaster, CA 93535.
Telephone: +1 805 949 2312
Type: Side-by-side 2-seat, low-wing monoplane, with fixed tail-dragger undercarriage.
Construction: Metal.
Wing span: 20 ft 10 ins (6.35 m)
Length: 19 ft 4 ins (5.89 m)
Empty weight: 923 lb (419 kg)
Gross weight: 1,600 lb (726 kg)
Recommended engine: 150 hp (112 kW) Textron Lycoming
Maximum speed: 159 kts (183 mph) 295 km/h
Cruise speed: 143-156 kts (165-180 mph) 266-290 km/h
Stall speed: 55 kts (63 mph) 101 km/h
Range: 460 naut miles (530 miles) 853 km
Take-off distance: 900 ft (275 m)
Climb rate: 1,200 ft (366 m) per minute
Availability: Plans and kits.
Comments: Sport Aircraft took over the sale of plans and kits of the classic Thorpe T-18 Tiger from Sunderland Aircraft, who had developed a modified version as the S-18. See Eklund Engineering Thorpe T-18 (USA).

Sport Racer

Address: Sport Racer Inc, 14 Hawthorne Road, Valley Center, KS 67147.
Telephone: +1 316 755 0659
Type: Tandem 2-seat, mid-wing monoplane, with fixed tail-dragger undercarriage.
Construction: Metal, composites and wood.
Wing span: 22 ft (6.71 m)
Length: 21 ft (6.4 m)
Empty weight: 1,175 lb (533 kg)
Gross weight: 1,825 lb (828 kg)
Recommended engine: 230 hp (171.5 kW) Javelin Ford auto conversion.
Maximum speed: 200 kts (230 mph) 370 km/h
Cruise speed: 152 kts (175 mph) 282 km/h
Range: 456 naut miles (525 miles) 845 km
Take-off distance: 1,600 ft (488 m)
Climb rate: 900 ft (274 m) per minute
Availability: Plans.
Comments: Homebuilt suitable for racing and aerobatics. 4 examples completed and flown by early 1995.

Stallings Air Master

Address: Jerry Stallings, 7822 Gulfton, Houston, TX 77036.
Telephone & Facsimile: +1 713 780 1123
Type: Side-by-side 2-seat, low-wing monoplane, with retractable nosewheel undercarriage.
Construction: Composites.
Wing span: 26 ft 6 ins (8.08 m)
Length: 21 ft (6.4 m)
Gross weight: 1,885 lb (855 kg)
Recommended engine: 150 hp (112 kW) Textron Lycoming O-320
Maximum speed: 207 kts (238 mph) 383 km/h
Cruise speed: 174 kts (200 mph) 322 km/h
Range: 869 naut miles (1,000 miles) 1,609 km
Climb rate: 2,000 ft (610 m) per minute
Availability: Plans.
Comments: A blend of Glasair and Lancair for the homebuilder with limited funds was the reported design philosophy behind the Air Master. First flown in 1994.

Starfire Firebolt

Address: Starfire Aviation Inc, 907 South Hohokam Drive, Tempe, AZ 85281.
Telephone: +1 602 731 9419
Type: Tandem 2-seat, aerobatic biplane, with fixed tail-dragger undercarriage.
Construction: Steel tube, wood and fabric.
Wing span: 24 ft (7.32 m)
Length: 21 ft (6.4 m)
Empty weight: 1,354 lb (614 kg)
Gross weight: 2,000 lb (907 kg)
Recommended engine: 340 hp (254 kW) Textron Lycoming IO-540
Maximum speed: 186 kts (214 mph) 344 km/h
Cruise speed: 176 kts (202 mph) 325 km/h
Range: 521 naut miles (600 miles) 965 km
Take-off distance: 400 ft (122 m)
Climb rate: 4,000 ft (1,220 m) per minute
Availability: Plans.
Comments: Highly modified Skybolt. Enclosed cockpit option.

Steen Skybolt

Address: Steen Aero Lab, 1210 Airport Road, Marion, NC 28752.
Telephone: +1 704 652 7382
Facsimile: +1 704 652 7382
Type: Tandem 2-seat, sport biplane, with fixed tail-dragger undercarriage.
Construction: Wood, steel tube and fabric.
Wing span: 24 ft (7.32 m)
Length: 19 ft (5.79 m)
Empty weight: 1,250 lb (567 kg)
Gross weight: 2,000 lb (907 kg)
Recommended engine: 260 hp (194 kW) Textron Lycoming IO-540-D4A5
Maximum speed: 156 kts (180 mph) 290 km/h
Cruise speed: 139 kts (160 mph) 257 km/h
Stall speed: 52 kts (60 mph) 97 km/h
Range: 391 naut miles (450 miles) 724 km
Take-off distance: 300 ft (92 m)
Climb rate: 3,500 ft (1,067 m) per minute
Availability: Plans.

Comments: Designed by Lamar Steen and first flown in October 1970. Design rights purchased by Hale Wallace in 1990.

Steen Pitts S1-C Special

Type: Single-seat, open or enclosed cockpit, sport biplane, with fixed tail-dragger undercarriage.
Wing span: 17 ft 4 ins (5.28 m)
Length: 15 ft 6 ins (4.72 m)
Empty weight: 830 lb (376 kg)
Gross weight: 1,150 lb (522 kg)
Take-off distance: 300 ft (92 m)
Recommended engine: 200 hp (149 kW) Textron Lycoming AEIO-360
Maximum speed: 161 kts (185 mph) 298 km/h
Cruise speed: 152 kts (175 mph) 282 km/h
Stall speed: 56 kts (64 mph) 103 km/h
Range: 268 naut miles (309 miles) 497 km
Climb rate: 2,800 ft (853 m) per minute
Availability: Plans.
Comments: Rights to Curtiss Pitts' famous 1944 design were taken over by Steen Aero Lab in December 1994. Previously manufactured by Aviat. Rights to the 2-seat S-2 version are still held by Aviat.

Steen Pitts S-1 Special – line up of Pitts in 1994 on the 50th anniversary of the type's first flight (Geoffrey P Jones)

Stewart S-51D Mustang

Address: Stewart 51 Inc, 3120 Airport West Drive, Vero Beach, FL 32960.
Telephone: +1 407 778 0051
Facsimile: +1 407 778 0051
Type: Tandem 2-seat, low-wing monoplane representing the P-51, with retractable tail-dragger undercarriage.
Construction: Metal.
Wing span: 26 ft (7.92 m)
Length: 22 ft (6.71 m)
Empty weight: 2,200 lb (998 kg)
Gross weight: 2,960 lb (1,343 kg)
Recommended engine: 400 hp (298 kW) V-8
Maximum speed: 230 kts (265 mph) 426 km/h
Cruise speed: 204 kts (235 mph) 378 km/h
Stall speed: 57 kts (65 mph) 105 km/h
Range: 573 naut miles (660 miles) 1,062 km
Take-off distance: 1,370 ft (418 m)
Climb rate: 2,400 ft (732 m) per minute
Availability: Kits.
Comments: Designed by Jim Stewart as a 70% scale Mustang fighter replica. First flown in May 1985.

Stoddard-Hamilton Glasair Super IIRG

Address: Stoddard-Hamilton Aircraft Inc, 18701 58th Avenue NE, Arlington, WA 98223.
Telephone: +1 206 435 8533
Facsimile: +1 206 435 9525
Type: Side-by-side 2-seat, low-wing cabin monoplane, with retractable nosewheel undercarriage.
Construction: Composites.
Wing span: 23 ft 4 ins (7.11 m)
Length: 20 ft 9 ins (6.32 m)
Empty weight: 1,325 lb (601 kg)
Gross weight: 2,200 lb (998 kg)
Recommended engine: 180 hp (134 kW) Textron Lycoming
Maximum speed: 217 kts (250 mph) 402 km/h
Cruise speed: 204 kts (235 mph) 378 km/h
Stall speed: 44 kts (50 mph) 81 km/h
Range: 1,390 naut miles (1,600 miles) 2,575 km
Take-off distance: 380 ft (116 m)
Climb rate: 2,700 ft (823 m) per minute
Availability: Kits.
Comments: Stretched version of the Glasair II, introduced in 1993. RG = retractable gear.

Stoddard-Hamilton Glasair Super IIRG (Geoffrey P Jones)

Stoddard-Hamilton Glasair Super IIFT and TD

Type: Side-by-side 2-seat, low-wing cabin monoplane, with fixed nosewheel (FT) or fixed tail-dragger (TD) undercarriage.
Construction: Composites.
Details: Principally for TD.
Wing span: 23 ft 4 ins (7.11 m)
Length: 20 ft 9 ins (6.32 m)
Empty weight: 1,200 lb (544 kg)
Gross weight: 2,100 lb (953 kg)
Recommended engine: 180 hp (134 kW) Textron Lycoming
Maximum speed: 202 kts (232 mph) 373 km/h
Cruise speed: 195 kts (224 mph) 360 km/h
Stall speed: 44 kts (50 mph) 81 km/h
Range: 1,303 naut miles (1,500 miles) 2,414 km
Take-off distance: 350 ft (107 m)
Climb rate: 2,700 ft (823 m) per minute
Availability: Kits.
Comments: Prototype first flew in 1979. Claimed as the first pre-moulded composite kitplane. Prototype now preserved in the EAA Museum.

Stoddard-Hamilton Glasair III

Type: Side-by-side 2-seat, low-wing cabin monoplane, with retractable nosewheel undercarriage.
Construction: Composites.
Wing span: 23 ft 3 ins (7.09 m)
Length: 21 ft 4 ins (6.5 m)
Empty weight: 1,625 lb (737 kg)
Gross weight: 2,500 lb (1,134 kg)
Recommended engine: 300 hp (224 kW) Textron Lycoming (turbocharged Textron Lycoming TIO-540 option available).
Maximum speed: 252 km/h (290 mph) 467 km/h
Cruise speed: 239 kts (275 mph) 443 km/h
Stall speed: 65 kts (74 mph) 119 km/h
Range: 1,113 naut miles (1,281 miles) 2,061 km
Take-off distance: 700 ft (214 m)
Climb rate: 2,400 ft (732 m) per minute
Availability: Kits.
Comments: Introduced in 1987, offering higher performance. Wingtip extensions available. Fully aerobatic.

Stoddard-Hamilton GlaStar

Type: Side-by-side 2-seat, high-wing cabin monoplane, with fixed nosewheel or tail wheel undercarriage.
Construction: Metal and composites.
Wing span: 35 ft (10.67 m)
Length: 22 ft (6.71 m) fuselage
Empty weight: 1,100 lb (499 kg)
Gross weight: 1,900 lb (862 kg)
Recommended engine: 125 hp (93.2 kW) Teledyne Continental IO-240-A
Maximum speed: 135 kts (156 mph) 251 km/h
Cruise speed: 130 kts (150 mph) 241 km/h
Stall speed: 42 kts (48 mph) 78 km/h clean
Range: 712 naut miles (820 miles) 1,319 km
Availability: Kits.
Comments: First flown on 29 November 1994. Possible for certification and commercial production for flight training. Folding wings.

Stoddard-Hamilton GlaStar

Stoddard-Hamilton Turbine 250/III

Type: Side-by-side 2-seat, low-wing cabin monoplane, with retractable nosewheel undercarriage.
Construction: Composites.
Wing span: 23 ft 4 ins (7.11 m)
Length: 22 ft (6.71 m)
Empty weight: 1,650 lb (748 kg)
Gross weight: 2,500 lb (1,134 kg)
Recommended engine: 450 hp (335.6 kW) Allison 250 turboprop
Maximum speed: 287 kts (330 mph) 531 km/h
Cruise speed: 243 kts (280 mph) 450 km/h
Stall speed: 61 kts (70 mph) 113 km/h
Range: 1,042 naut miles (1,200 miles) 1,931 km
Take-off distance: 600 ft (183 m)
Climb rate: 4,200 ft (1,280 m) per minute
Availability: Kits.
Comments: Known initially as the SH/Arocet AT-9 Stalker. Possible use for military training applications. Development in association with Becktold Aircraft.

Stoddard-Hamilton Turbine 250/III

Stolp SA-300 Starduster Too

Address: Stolp Starduster Corporation, 4301 Twining Street, Riverside, CA 95209.
Telephone: +1 800 833 9102
Facsimile: +1 909 784 0072
Type: Tandem 2-seat biplane, with fixed tail-dragger undercarriage.
Construction: Wood, steel tube and fabric
Wing span: 24 ft (7.32 m)
Length: 21 ft 9 ins (6.63 m)
Empty weight: 1,139 lb (517 kg)

Gross weight: 2,000 lb (907 kg)
Recommended engine: 180 hp (134 kW) Textron Lycoming O-360, or others.
Maximum speed: 174 kts (200 mph) 322 km/h
Cruise speed: 100 kts (115 mph) 185 km/h
Stall speed: 51 kts (58 mph) 94 km/h
Range: 521 naut miles (600 miles) 965 km
Take-off distance: 700 ft (214 m)
Climb rate: 1,800 ft (549 m) per minute
Availability: Plans and kits.
Comments: Louis Stolp design, first flown in November 1957. 2-seat version derived from the original SA-100 single-seat Starduster (now the SA-101, plans for which are still available).

Stolp SA-300 Starduster Too built in the USA but now flown in UK (Geoffrey P Jones)

Stolp SA-500 Starlet

Type: Single-seat high-wing monoplane, with fixed tail-dragger undercarriage.
Construction: Wood, steel tube and fabric.
Wing span: 25 ft (7.62 m)
Length: 17 ft (5.18 m)
Empty weight: 700 lb (318 kg)
Gross weight: 1,058 lb (480 kg)
Recommended engine: 85-125 hp (63.4-93.2 kW), typically 108 hp (80.5 kW) Textron Lycoming.
Maximum speed: 113 kts (130 mph) 209 km/h
Cruise speed: 78 kts (90 mph) 145 km/h
Stall speed: 42 kts (48 mph) 78 km/h
Range: 521 naut miles (600 miles) 965 km
Take-off distance: 400 ft (122 m)
Climb rate: 1,000 ft (305 m) per minute
Availability: Plans and kits.
Comments: Prototype first flew on 1 June 1969.

Stolp SA-500 Starlet built in UK in the early 1970s (Geoffrey P Jones)

Stolp SA-750 Acroduster Too

Type: Tandem 2-seat, enclosed or open cockpit, aerobatic biplane, with fixed tail-dragger undercarriage.
Construction: Wood, steel tube and fabric.
Wing span: 21 ft 5 ins (6.53 m)
Length: 18 ft 6 ins (5.64 m)
Empty weight: 1,050 lb (476 kg)
Gross weight: 1,950 lb (885 kg)
Recommended engine: 200 hp (149 kW) Textron Lycoming IO-360
Maximum speed: 161 kts (185 mph) 298 km/h
Cruise speed: 135 kts (155 mph) 249 km/h
Stall speed: 48 kts (55 mph) 89 km/h
Take-off distance: 700 ft (214 m)
Climb rate: 2,300 ft (701 m) per minute
Availability: Plans and kits.
Comments: Developed from the Stolp SA-700 Acroduster single-seater first flown in 1973.

Stolp SA-900 V-Star

Type: Single-seat, open cockpit aerobatic biplane, with fixed tail-dragger undercarriage.
Construction: Wood, steel tube, glassfibre and fabric.
Wing span: 23 ft (7.01 m)
Length: 17 ft 2 ins (5.23 m)
Empty weight: 700 lb (318 kg)
Gross weight: 1,000 lb (454 kg)
Recommended engine: 60-125 hp (44.7-93.2 kW) Teledyne Continentals
Maximum speed: 78 kts (90 mph) 145 km/h
Cruise speed: 65 kts (75 mph) 121 km/h
Stall speed: 31 kts (35 mph) 57 km/h
Range: 239 naut miles (275 miles) 442 km
Take-off distance: 400 ft (122 m)
Climb rate: 600 ft (183 m) per minute
Availability: Plans and kits.
Comments: Low cost, low power aerobatic design, as a biplane version of the SA-500 Starlet.

Superdrone Henderson Little Bear

Address: Superdrone Aviation Inc, Sky Manor Road, RD 2, PO Box 52, Pittstown, NJ 08867.
Telephone: +1 908 996 7916
Facsimile: +1 908 996 7964
Type: Tandem 2-seat, high-wing monoplane, with fixed tail-dragger undercarriage.
Construction: Steel tube and fabric.
Wing span: 35 ft 3 ins (10.74 m)
Length: 22 ft 4 ins (6.81 m)
Empty weight: 649 lb (294 kg)
Gross weight: 1,220 lb (553 kg)
Recommended engine: 65 hp (48.5 kW) Teledyne Continental
Maximum speed: 74 kts (85 mph) 137 km/h
Cruise speed: 61 kts (70 mph) 113 km/h
Stall speed: 28 kts (32 mph) 52 km/h
Range: 295 naut miles (340 miles) 547 km
Take-off distance: 400 ft (122 m)
Climb rate: 800 ft (244 m) per minute
Availability: Kits.
Comments: Piper Cub representation.

Super Stinker

Address: Super Stinker Inc, 1611 S. Eisenhower, Suite B, Wichita, KS 67209.
Telephone: +1 316 945 7343
Facsimile: +1 316 945 7341
Type: Single-seat aerobatic aircraft.
Comments: Latest Pitts' design. First 10 homebuilt kits will be sold at $44,500 (not including engine, propeller and covering). No other information available at the time of writing.

Swick T

Address: Swick Aircraft, Rt.1, Box 203, McKinney, TX 75070.
Telephone: +1 214 347 2596
Type: Side by side 2-seat, high-wing cabin monoplane, with fixed tail-dragger undercarriage.
Construction: Wood and steel tube.
Wing span: 27 ft 6 ins (8.38 m)
Length: 22 ft 3 ins (6.78 m)
Empty weight: 900 lb (408 kg)
Gross weight: 1,280 lb (581 kg)
Recommended engine: 180 hp (134 kW)
Maximum speed: 122 kts (140 mph) 225 km/h
Cruise speed: 113 kts (130 mph) 209 km/h
Range: 339 naut miles (390 miles) 627 km
Take-off distance: 400 ft (122 m)
Climb rate: 1,800 ft (549 m) per minute
Availability: Plans.

TEAM Air-Bike

Address: TEAM Inc, 10790 Ivy Bluff Road K, Bradyville, TN 37026.
Telephone: +1 615 765 5397
Facsimile: +1 615 765 7234
Type: Single-seat, high-wing microlight, with fixed tail-dragger. undercarriage.
Construction: Wood, steel tube and fabric.
Wing span: 26 ft (7.92 m)
Length: 16 ft (4.88 m)
Empty weight: 225 lb (102 kg)
Gross weight: 440 lb (200 kg)
Recommended engine: 22 hp (16.4 kW) Zenoah
Never exceed speed: 70 kts (80 mph) 129 km/h
Cruise speed: 42 kts (48 mph) 77 km/h
Range: 87 naut miles (100 miles) 161 km
Take-off distance: 160 ft (49 m)
Climb rate: 430 ft (131 m) per minute
Availability: Kits.
Comments: Basic open framed, sit-astride microlight. Also Rotax 277 or 447 engines.

TEAM Air-Bike (Geoffrey P Jones)

TEAM Hi-MAX

Type: Single-seat, high-wing microlight/homebuilt, with fixed tail-dragger undercarriage.
Construction: Wood and fabric.
Wing span: 25 ft (7.62 m)
Length: 16 ft (4.88 m)
Empty weight: 319 lb (145 kg)
Gross weight: 560 lb (254 kg)
Recommended engine: Various types, including the 25 hp (19 kW) Rotax 227, 41.6 hp (31 kW) Rotax 447 and 42 hp (31.3 kW) Zenoah G50. Details for the Zenoah.
Maximum speed: 87 kts (100 mph) 161 km/h
Cruise speed: 61 kts (70 mph) 113 km/h
Stall speed: 26 kts (30 mph) 49 km/h
Range: 104 naut miles (120 miles) 193 km
Take-off distance: 100 ft (31 m)
Climb rate: 1,200 ft (366 m) per minute
Availability: Plans and kits.
Comments: Common components with the miniMAX series. Introduced in 1987. Various designations denote engine selection.

TEAM Hi-MAX single-seater (Geoffrey P Jones)

TEAM miniMAX

Type: Single-seat, mid-wing microlight/homebuilt, with either open or enclosed cockpit and fixed tail-dragger undercarriage.
Construction: Wood and fabric.
Wing span: 25 ft (7.62 m)
Length: 16 ft (4.88 m)
Empty weight: 250-400 lb (113-181.4 kg) according to version.
Gross weight: 500-700 lb (227-317.5 kg) according to version.
Recommended engine: Typical options for 7 different models of the miniMax basic design are:
1030R Max 103UL - 25 hp (19 kW) Rotax 277 (open cockpit).
1100R miniMax - 41.6 hp (31 kW) Rotax 447 (open cockpit).
1200Z - 42 hp (31.6 kW) Zenoah G50 (open cockpit).
1300Z - 42 hp (31.6 kW) Zenoah G50 (enclosed cockpit).
1500R - 41.6 hp (31 kW) Rotax 447 (open cockpit).
1550V V-Max - 50 hp (37.3 kW) Volkswagen 1,600cc modified auto engine (open cockpit).
1600R - 41.6 hp (31 kW) Rotax 447 (enclosed cockpit).
Maximum speed: 87 kts (100 mph) 161 km/h
Cruise speed: 65 kts (75 mph) 121 km/h
Stall speed: 23 kts (26 mph) 42 km/h
Range: 104-173 naut miles (120-200 miles) 193-322 km
Take-off distance: 150 ft (46 m)
Climb rate: 650-1,200 ft (198-366 m) per minute
Availability: Plans and kits.
Comments: Tennessee Engineering and Manufacturing (TEAM) flew Wayne Ison's miniMax prototype in February 1985.

TEAM miniMax with Zenoah G50 engine, open cockpit and spatted undercarriage (Geoffrey P Jones)

Titan Tornado Sport

Address: Titan Aircraft, 2730 Walter Main Road, Geneva, OH 44041.
Telephone: +1 216 466 0602
Facsimile: +1 216 466 7550
Type: Single-seat high-wing monoplane, with pusher engine and fixed nosewheel undercarriage.
Construction: Metal, composites and fabric.
Wing span: 20 ft (6.1 m)
Length: 18 ft 6 ins (5.64 m)
Empty weight: 325 lb (147 kg)
Gross weight: 700 lb (318 kg)
Recommended engine: 41.6 hp (31 kW) Rotax 447 (option for 25 hp, 19 kW Rotax 277 for microlight version)
Maximum speed: 91 kts (105 mph) 169 km/h
Cruise speed: 70 kts (80 mph) 129 km/h
Range: 217 naut miles (250 miles) 402 km
Take-off distance: 200 ft (61 m)
Climb rate: 1,200 ft (366 m) per minute
Availability: Kits.
Comments: Microlight version, the Tornado UL 103, also available.

Titan Tornado Sport single-seater at Sun 'n Fun in 1993 (Geoffrey P Jones)

Titan Tornado II Trainer

Type: Tandem 2-seat, high-wing monoplane, with fixed nosewheel undercarriage.
Construction: Metal, composites and fabric.
Wing span: 23 ft 6 ins (7.16 m)
Length: 19 ft (5.79 m)
Empty weight: 440 lb (200 kg)
Gross weight: 900 lb (408 kg)
Take-off distance: 250 ft (77 m)
Recommended engine: 49.6 hp (37 kW) Rotax 503
Maximum speed: 104 kts (120 mph) 193 km/h
Cruise speed: 74 kts (85 mph) 137 km/h
Range: 217 naut miles (250 miles) 402 km
Climb rate: 1,400 ft (427 m) per minute
Availability: Kits.
Comments: Titan Tornado II with 64.4 hp (48 kW) Rotax 582 has higher gross weight and cruise speed. At least 30 examples of both types were flying in 1995.

Tri-R KIS

Address: Tri-R Technologies Inc, 1114 E. 5th Street, Oxnard, CA 93030.
Telephone: +1 805 385 3680
Facsimile: +1 805 483 8366
Type: Side-by-side 2-seat, low-wing cabin monoplane, with fixed nosewheel undercarriage.
Construction: Composites.
Wing span: 23 ft (7.01 m)
Length: 22 ft (6.71 m)
Empty weight: 680 lb (308 kg)
Gross weight: 1,200 lb (544 kg)
Recommended engine: 80 hp (59.7 kW) Limbach L2000 (option for 100 hp, 74.6 kW CAM-100)
Maximum speed: 130 kts (150 mph) 241 km/h
Cruise speed: 117 kts (135 mph) 217 km/h
Stall speed: 48 kts (55 mph) 89 km/h
Range: 521 naut miles (600 miles) 965 km
Take-off distance: 1,000 ft (305 m)
Climb rate: 1,000 ft (305 m) per minute
Availability: Kits.
Comments: Designed by Rich Trickel and first flown in 1991. Keep It Simple = KIS. Also suitable for Teledyne Continental IO-240 engine.

Tri-R KIS built in the UK with CAM-100 engine (Geoffrey P Jones)

Tri-R KIS TD

Type: Side-by-side 2-seat, low-wing monoplane, with fixed tail-dragger undercarriage.
Construction: Composites.
Wing span: 23 ft (7.01 m)
Length: 22 ft (6.71 m)
Empty weight: 812 lb (368 kg)
Gross weight: 1,450 lb (658 kg)
Recommended engine: 108 hp (80.5 kW) Teledyne Continental O-235
Maximum speed: 156 kts (180 mph) 290 km/h
Cruise speed: 143 kts (165 mph) 266 km/h
Stall speed: 57 kts (65 mph) 105 km/h
Range: 651 naut miles (750 miles) 1,207 km
Take-off distance: 600 ft (183 m)
Climb rate: 1,300 ft (396 m) per minute
Availability: Kits.
Comments: 2 other 2-seat versions of KIS are the Super and TR-1, with Teledyne Continental IO-240 engines and available with nosewheel or tail-dragger undercarriages. Higher empty weights and speeds.

Tri-R KIS TR-4 Cruiser

Type: 4-seat low-wing monoplane, with fixed nosewheel undercarriage.
Construction: Composites.
Wing span: 29 ft (8.84 m)
Length: 25 ft (7.62 m)
Empty weight: 1,200 lb (544 kg)
Gross weight: 2,400 lb (1,089 kg)
Take-off distance: 1,200 ft (366 m)
Recommended engine: 180 hp (134 kW) Textron Lycoming O-360. Other engines of 160-200 hp (119-149 kW) available.
Maximum speed: 165 kts (190 mph) 306 km/h
Cruise speed: 152 kts (175 mph) 282 km/h
Stall speed: 48 kts (55 mph) 89 km/h
Range: 738 naut miles (850 miles) 1,368 km
Climb rate: 1,100 ft (335 m) per minute
Availability: Kits.
Comments: First flown in 1994. Kit parts manufactured by High Tech Composites. Build time 1,500 hours.

Turner T-40A

Address: Turner Aircraft Inc, Rte 4, Box 115AB3, Grandview, TX 76050.
Telephone: +1 817 783 5350
Type: Side-by-side 2-seat, low-wing monoplane, with fixed tail-dragger or nosewheel undercarriage.
Construction: Wood.
Wing span: 27 ft 8 ins (8.43 m)
Length: 20 ft (6.1 m)
Empty weight: 1,050 lb (476 kg)
Gross weight: 1,600 lb (726 kg)
Recommended engine: 125 hp (93.2 kW) Textron Lycoming
Maximum speed: 148 kts (170 mph) 274 km/h
Cruise speed: 128 kts (147 mph) 237 km/h
Stall speed: 51 kts (58 mph) 94 km/h
Range: 412 naut miles (475 miles) 764 km
Take-off distance: 1,250 ft (381 m)
Climb rate: 850 ft (259 m) per minute
Availability: Plans.
Comments: Single-seat Turner T-40 first flew in April 1961. 2-seat T-40A first flew in July 1966, and was further developed into the Super T-40 with a blister canopy for more modern appearance.

Turner T-40A built by Dean Meadows at La Mesa, CA (Geoffrey P Jones)

Two Wings Mariner UL

Address: Two Wings Aviation, 6821 167th Avenue, Forest Lake, MN 55025.
Telephone: +1 612 464 2099
Type: Single 1- (optional 2-) seat, amphibious biplane, with pusher engine and retractable tail-dragger undercarriage.
Construction: Metal and fabric.
Wing span: 28 ft 6 ins (8.69 m)
Length: 18 ft 9 ins (5.72 m)
Empty weight: 304 lb (138 kg)
Gross weight: 950 lb (431 kg)
Recommended engine: 39.6 hp (29.5 kW) Rotax 447
Maximum speed: 54 kts (62 mph) 100 km/h
Cruise speed: 48 kts (55 mph) 89 km/h
Stall speed: 26 kts (30 mph) 49 km/h
Range: 65 naut miles (75 miles) 120 km
Take-off distance: 150 ft (46 m)
Climb rate: 800 ft (244 m) per minute
Availability: Kits.
Comments: Also available is the Mariner EXP with a 60 hp (44.7 kW) Subaru engine.

Two Wings Mariner UL with 65 hp (48.5 kW) Rotax 582 (Geoffrey P Jones)

Two Wings Mariner Mono EXP

Type: Single- (optional 2-) seat, shoulder-wing amphibian, with pylon-mounted pusher engine behind the cockpit and retractable tail-dragger undercarriage.
Construction: Metal and fabric.
Wing span: 30 ft (9.14 m)
Length: 18 ft 9 ins (5.72 m)
Empty weight: 380 lb (172 kg)
Gross weight: 900 lb (408 kg)
Recommended engine: 60 hp (44.7 kW) Subaru
Maximum speed: 87 kts (100 mph) 161 km/h
Cruise speed: 74 kts (85 mph) 137 km/h
Range: 347 naut miles (400 miles) 643 km
Take-off distance: 200 ft (61 m)
Climb rate: 1,000 ft (305 m) per minute
Availability: Kits.
Comments: Also available as a microlight with a 39.6 hp (29.5 kW) Rotax 447 engine. Designed by Larry Seivert in 1984.

US Aviation Cloud Dancer

Address: US Aviation, 265 Echo Lane, South St Paul, MN 55075.
Telephone: +1 612 450 0930
Facsimile: +1 612 450 0930
Type: Single-seat, pusher-engined monoplane, with V-tail and fixed tail-dragger undercarriage.
Construction: Metal and fabric.
Wing span: 40 ft (12.19 m)
Length: 20 ft (6.1 m)
Empty weight: 253 lb (115 kg)
Gross weight: 520 lb (236 kg)
Take-off distance: 120 ft (37 m)
Recommended engine: 25 hp (19 kW) Rotax 277
Maximum speed: 55 kts (63 mph) 101 km/h
Cruise speed: 48 kts (55 mph) 89 km/h
Stall speed: 22-24 kts (25-27 mph) 41-44 km/h
Range: 217 naut miles (250 miles) 402 km
Climb rate: 600 ft (183 m) per minute
Availability: Kits.
Comments: Designed by Erwin Rodger of Ultra Sail (US) Aviation, and first flown in 1983. Also available is the similar Cumulus.

US Aviation Cloud Dancer microlight (Geoffrey P Jones)

US Light Aircraft Hornet

Address: US Light Aircraft Corporation, 27080 Rancho Ballena Lane, Ramona, CA 92065.
Telephone & Facsimile: +1 619 789 8607
Type: Tandem 2-seat, high-wing monoplane, with pusher engine and fixed nosewheel undercarriage.
Construction: Metal and fabric.
Wing span: 27 ft 6 ins (8.38 m)
Length: 20 ft (6.1 m)
Empty weight: 490 lb (222 kg)
Gross weight: 1,000 lb (454 kg)
Recommended engine: 55 hp (41 kW) Hirth
Maximum speed: 104 kts (120 mph) 193 km/h
Cruise speed: 70 kts (80 mph) 129 km/h
Range: 347 naut miles (400 miles) 643 km
Take-off distance: 200 ft (61 m)
Climb rate: 700 ft (213 m) per minute
Availability: Kits.
Comments: Introduced by Jim Millett in 1983.

Van's RV-3

Address: Van's Aircraft Inc, PO Box 160, North Plains, OR 97133.
Telephone: +1 503 647 5117
Facsimile: +1 503 647 2206
Type: Single-seat, low-wing monoplane, with fixed tail-dragger undercarriage.
Construction: Metal.
Wing span: 19 ft 11 ins (6.07 m)
Length: 19 ft (5.79 m)
Empty weight: 750 lb (340 kg)
Gross weight: 1,100 lb (499 kg)
Recommended engine: 150 hp (112 kW) Textron Lycoming O-320
Maximum speed: 182 kts (210 mph) 338 km/h
Cruise speed: 152 kts (175 mph) 282 km/h
Stall speed: 45 kts (52 mph) 84 km/h
Range: 445 naut miles (512 miles) 824 km
Take-off distance: 250 ft (77 m)
Climb rate: 2,000 ft (610 m) per minute
Availability: Plans and kits.
Comments: Designed by Richard VanGrunsven and first flown in 1972.

Van's RV-4

Type: Tandem 2-seat, low-wing monoplane, with fixed tail-dragger undercarriage.
Construction: Metal.
Wing span: 23 ft (7.01 m)
Length: 20 ft 4.5 ins (6.21 m)
Empty weight: 905 lb (411 kg)
Gross weight: 1,500 lb (680 kg)
Recommended engine: 160 hp (119.3 kW) Textron Lycoming O-320
Maximum speed: 178 kts (205 mph) 330 km/h
Cruise speed: 143 kts (165 mph) 266 km/h
Stall speed: 47 kts (54 mph) 87 km/h
Range: 565 naut miles (650 miles) 1,046 km
Take-off distance: 450 ft (138 m)
Climb rate: 1,650 ft (503 m) per minute
Availability: Plans and kits.
Comments: Two-seat development of the Van's RV-3 and first flown on 21 August 1979. One of the world's most popular homebuilts, with over 470 flying and 1,500 under construction.

Van's RV-4 based in UK (Geoffrey P Jones)

Van's RV-6A

Type: Side-by-side 2-seat, low-wing monoplane, with fixed nosewheel undercarriage.
Construction: Metal.
Wing span: 23 ft (7.01 m)
Length: 19 ft 11 ins (6.07 m)
Empty weight: 985 lb (447 kg)
Gross weight: 1,600 lb (726 kg)
Recommended engine: 160 hp (119.3 kW) Textron Lycoming O-320
Maximum speed: 174 kts (200 mph) 322 km/h
Cruise speed: 144 kts (166 mph) 267 km/h
Stall speed: 48 kts (55 mph) 89 km/h
Range: 660 naut miles (760 miles) 1,223 km
Take-off distance: 525 ft (160 m)
Climb rate: 1,650 ft (503 m) per minute
Availability: Plans and kits.
Comments: Prototype RV-6 2-seater derived from the RV-4 first flew in June 1986. Nosewheel undercarriage RV-6A first flew in July 1988. Candidate for certification. Built commercially in Nigeria as the Air Beetle.

Van's RV-6A with 180 hp (134 kW) Textron Lycoming engine (Geoffrey P Jones)

Velocity Aircraft Velocity

Address: Velocity Aircraft, 200 W. Airport Drive, Sebastian, FL 32958.
Telephone: +1 407 589 1860
Facsimile: +1 407 589 1893
Type: 4-seat monoplane with canard, winglets, pusher engine and nosewheel undercarriage (fixed main gear and retractable nosewheel).
Construction: Composites.
Wing span: 28 ft 7 ins (8.71 m)
Length: 16 ft 6 ins (5.03 m)
Empty weight: 1,250 lb (567 kg)
Gross weight: 2,250 lb (1,021 kg)
Recommended engine: 200 hp (149 kW) Textron Lycoming IO-360
Maximum speed: 200 kts (230 mph) 370 km/h
Cruise speed: 174 kts (200 mph) 322 km/h
Stall speed: 64 kts (73 mph) 118 km/h
Range: 1,042 naut miles (1,200 miles) 1,931 km
Take-off distance: 850 ft (259 m)
Climb rate: 1,100 ft (335 m) per minute
Availability: Kits.

Comments: Dan Maher design debuted at Sun 'n Fun in 1985. A variant is the Velocity RG.

Velocity prototype with fixed main and retractable nose gear (Geoffrey P Jones)

Velocity 173

Type: Four-seat monoplane with canard, winglets, pusher engine and fixed nosewheel undercarriage.
Construction: Composites.
Wing span: 31 ft (9.45 m)
Length: 19 ft 3 ins (5.87 m)
Empty weight: 1,300 lb (590 kg)
Gross weight: 2,400 lb (1,089 kg)
Recommended engine: 200 hp (149 kW) Textron Lycoming IO-360
Maximum speed: 171 kts (197 mph) 317 km/h
Cruise speed: 162 kts (187 mph) 301 km/h
Stall speed: 59 kts (67 mph) 108 km/h
Range: 1,129 naut miles (1,300 miles) 2,092 km
Take-off distance: 750 ft (229 m)
Climb rate: 1,000 ft (305 m) per minute
Availability: Kits.
Comments: New fully fixed undercarriage version of the Velocity, but also available in fully retractable form as the Velocity 173RG.

Viking Dragonfly

Address: Viking Aircraft Ltd, PO Box 646, Elkhorn, WI 53121.
Telephone: +1 414 728 7861
Facsimile: +1 414 728 7862
Type: Side-by-side 2-seat monoplane, with fixed tail-dragger undercarriage (main wheels located in wingtip fairings).
Construction: Composites.
Wing span: 22 ft (6.71 m)
Length: 19 ft (5.79 m)
Empty weight: 610 lb (277 kg)
Gross weight: 1,150 lb (522 kg)
Recommended engine: 60 hp (44.7 kW) Volkswagen 1,835cc
Maximum speed: 143 kts (165 mph) 265 km/h
Cruise speed: 104 kts (120 mph) 193 km/h
Stall speed: 42 kts (48 mph) 78 km/h
Range: 434 naut miles (500 miles) 804 km
Take-off distance over 50 ft obstacle: 1,200 ft (366 m)
Climb rate: 850 ft (259 m) per minute
Availability: Plans and kits.
Comments: Dragonfly prototype first flew on 16 June 1980. 3 versions, the Mk I (see illustration), Mk II with main undercarriage legs under the inboard section of the wings for operation on narrow taxiways and unprepared strips, and the Mk III with fixed nosewheel gear.

Viking Dragonfly Mk I

Viking Aircraft Cygnet

Type: Side-by-side two-seat, shoulder-wing monoplane, with fixed tail-dragger undercarriage.
Construction: Metal, wood and fabric.
Wing span: 30 ft (9.14 m)
Length: 19 ft (5.79 m)
Empty weight: 585 lb (265 kg)
Gross weight: 1,100 lb (499 kg)
Recommended engine: 60 hp (44.7 kW) Volkswagen
Maximum speed: 94 kts (108 mph) 174 km/h
Cruise speed: 87 kts (100 mph) 161 km/h
Stall speed: 42 kts (48 mph) 78 km/h
Range: 339 naut miles (390 miles) 627 km
Take-off distance: 700 ft (214 m)
Climb rate: 580 ft (177 m) per minute
Availability: Plans.
Comments: Originally the Sisler SF-2 Whistler and first flown in 1973. Name changed to Cygnet with design modifications soon after. In 1983 HAPI Engines acquired the rights, when also dealer for the Viking Dragonfly.

Volmer VJ-22 Sportsman

Address: Volmer Aircraft, Box 5222, Glendale, CA 91201.
Telephone: +1 818 247 8718
Type: Side-by-side 2-seat, shoulder-wing amphibian, with pylon mounted pusher engine above the wings and retractable tail-dragger undercarriage.
Construction: Wood and fabric.
Wing span: 36 ft 6 ins (11.13 m)
Length: 24 ft (7.32 m)
Empty weight: 1,000 lb (454 kg)
Gross weight: 1,500 lb (680 kg)
Take-off distance: 350 ft (107 m) land, 1,000 ft (305 m) water.
Recommended engine: 90 hp (67 kW) Teledyne Continental C90
Maximum speed: 96 kts (110 mph) 177 km/h
Cruise speed: 74 kts (85 mph) 137 km/h
Stall speed: 39 kts (45 mph) 73 km/h
Range: 260 naut miles (300 miles) 482 km
Climb rate: 600 ft (183 m) per minute
Availability: Plans.
Comments: Volmer Jensen's 22nd design (previous types were mostly gliders) and first flown on 22 December 1958. Uses wings from Aeronca Champion or Chief.

Volmer VJ-24W SunFun

Type: Single-seat, open framed high-wing microlight, with fixed tail-dragger undercarriage.
Construction: Steel tube and fabric.
Wing span: 36 ft 6 ins (11.13 m)
Length: 18 ft 6 ins (5.64 m)
Empty weight: 165 lb (75 kg)
Gross weight: 345 lb (156 kg)
Recommended engine: 15 hp (11.2 kW) Yamaha
Maximum speed: 35 kts (40 mph) 64 km/h
Cruise speed: 24 kts (28 mph) 45 km/h
Stall speed: 13 kts (15 mph) 24 km/h
Range: 26 naut miles (30 miles) 48 km
Take-off distance: 100 ft (31 m)
Climb rate: 350 ft (107 m) per minute

Volmer VJ-24W SunFun

Availability: Plans.
Comments: VJ-24's predecessor, the VJ-23 Swingwing, was the first modern microlight. David Cook flying a VJ-23 was the first person to fly a powered hang-glider across the English Channel, on 9 May 1978.

Wag-Aero Sport Trainer

Address: Wag-Aero Inc, 1216 North Road, Box 181, Lyons, WI 53148.
Telephone: +1 414 763 9586
Facsimile: +1 414 763 7595
Type: Tandem 2-seat, high-wing monoplane, with fixed tail-dragger undercarriage.
Construction: Steel tube and fabric.
Wing span: 36 ft (10.97 m)
Length: 22 ft 4 ins (6.81 m)
Empty weight: 720 lb (327 kg)
Gross weight: 1,400 lb (635 kg)
Recommended engine: 85 hp (63.4 kW) Teledyne Continental
Maximum speed: 89 kts (102 mph) 164 km/h
Cruise speed: 82 kts (94 mph) 151 km/h
Stall speed: 34 kts (39 mph) 63 km/h
Range: 191 naut miles (220 miles) 354 km
Take-off distance: 208 ft (64 m)
Climb rate: 490 ft (150 m) per minute
Availability: Plans and kits.
Comments: Modern representation of the Piper Cub, also suitable for Franklin or Textron Lycoming engines. Special shortened and strengthened wing for the Acro Trainer aerobatic version.

Wag-Aero Sport Acro Trainer built in the UK (Geoffrey P Jones)

Wag-Aero Sportsman 2 + 2

Type: 4-seat (2 + 2) high-wing cabin monoplane, with fixed tail-dragger undercarriage.
Construction: Steel tube and fabric.
Wing span: 35 ft 9 ins (10.9 m)
Length: 23 ft 4 ins (7.11 m)
Empty weight: 1,080 lb (490 kg)
Gross weight: 2,200 lb (998 kg)
Recommended engine: 150 hp (112 kW) Textron Lycoming
Maximum speed: 112 kts (129 mph) 208 km/h
Cruise speed: 108 kts (124 mph) 200 km/h
Stall speed: 33 kts (38 mph) 61 km/h
Range: 582 naut miles (670 miles) 1,078 km
Take-off distance: 361 ft (110 m)
Climb rate: 800 ft (244 m) per minute
Availability: Plans and kits.
Comments: Modern representation of the Piper PA-14 Family Cruiser. Optional hinged turtle-deck for loading long loads such as a litter.

Wag-Aero Wag-A-Bond

Type: Side-by-side 2-seat, high-wing cabin monoplane, with fixed tail-dragger undercarriage.
Construction: Steel tube and fabric.
Wing span: 29 ft 4 ins (8.94 m)
Length: 18 ft 9 ins (5.72 m)
Empty weight: 725 lb (329 kg)
Gross weight: 1,450 lb (658 kg)
Recommended engine: 115 hp (85.75 kW) Textron Lycoming O-235
Maximum speed: 118 kts (136 mph) 219 km/h

Cruise speed: 108 kts (124 mph) 200 km/h
Stall speed: 39 kts (45 mph) 73 km/h
Range: 738 naut miles (850 miles) 1,368 km
Take-off distance: 415 ft (127 m)
Climb rate: 850 ft (259 m) per minute
Availability: Plans and kits.
Comments: Modern representation of the Piper Vagabond. The Classic model is suitable for 65-100 hp (48.4-74.6 kW) engines and the Traveler for 108-115 hp (80.5-85.75 kW) engines.

Wainfan Facetmobile

Address: Barnaby Wainfan, 4358 Tulane Avenue, Long Beach, CA 90808.
Telephone: +1 310 425 3338
Type: Single-seat scale-representation of an F-117 stealth fighter, with fixed nosewheel undercarriage.
Construction: Alloy tube and fabric.
Wing span: 15 ft (4.57 m)
Length: 19 ft 6 ins (5.94 m)
Empty weight: 370 lb (168 kg)
Gross weight: 620 lb (281 kg)
Recommended engine: 49.6 hp (37 kW) Rotax 503
Cruise speed: 52 kts (60 mph) 97 km/h
Stall speed: 18-22 kts (20-25 mph) 32-411 km/h
Range: 173 naut miles (200 miles) 32 km
Availability: Prototype to date.
Comments: Designed by Barnaby and Lynne Wainfan with Rick Dean. First flown on 22 April 1994. 2-seat version under development.

Warner Revolution 1

Address: Warner Aerocraft Inc, 7801 North Armenia Avenue, Tampa, FL 33604-3824.
Telephone: +1 813 932 6111
Facsimile: +1 813 932 6112
Type: Single-seat, low-wing monoplane, with fixed tail-dragger undercarriage.
Construction: Wood, steel tube and fabric.
Wing span: 26 ft (7.92 m)
Length: 17 ft (5.18 m)
Empty weight: 500 lb (227 kg)
Gross weight: 750 lb (340 kg)
Recommended engine: 65 hp (48.5 kW) Teledyne Continental
Maximum speed: 100 kts (115 mph) 185 km/h
Cruise speed: 91 kts (105 mph) 169 km/h
Stall speed: 37 kts (42 mph) 68 km/h
Range: 260 naut miles (300 miles) 482 km
Take-off distance: 300 ft (92 m)
Climb rate: 800 ft (244 m) per minute
Availability: Plans and kits.
Comments: Version of the former Country Air Space-Walker. Tandem 2-seat version, the Revolution II, uses a 100 hp (74.6 kW) Textron Lycoming O-235.

Warner Revolution I (Geoffrey P Jones)

Watson Windwagon

Address: Mayona Watson, Route 1, Box 50, Newcastle, TX 76372.
Telephone: +1 817 846 3295
Type: Single-seat, open or enclosed cockpit, low-wing monoplane, with fixed nosewheel undercarriage.
Construction: Metal.
Wing span: 18 ft (5.49 m)
Length: 13 ft (3.96 m)
Empty weight: 273 lb (124 kg)
Gross weight: 485 lb (220 kg)
Recommended engine: 30 hp (22.4 kW) half Volkswagen
Maximum speed: 117 kts (135 mph) 217 km/h
Cruise speed: 87 kts (100 mph) 161 km/h
Stall speed: 35 kts (40 mph) 65 km/h
Range: 173 naut miles (200 miles) 322 km
Take-off distance: 250 ft (77 m)
Climb rate: 400 ft (122 m) per minute
Availability: Plans.
Comments: Prototype first flew on 19 April 1977 (see similar Hummel Bird).

Watson Windwagon built in Canada (Geoffrey P Jones)

Weedhopper DeLuxe Ultralight

Address: Weedhopper Inc, PO Box 1377, Clinton, MO 39056.
Telephone: +1 601 924 0806
Type: Single-seat, open-framed, high-wing microlight, with fixed nosewheel undercarriage.
Construction: Steel tube and fabric.
Wing span: 28 ft (8.53 m)
Length: 18 ft 3 ins (5.56 m)
Empty weight: 252 lb (144 kg)
Gross weight: 500 lb (227 kg)
Recommended engine: 39.6 hp (29.5 kW) Rotax 447
Maximum speed: 54 kts (62 mph) 100 km/h
Cruise speed: 43 kts (50 mph) 80 km/h
Stall speed: 25 kts (28 mph) 45 km/h
Range: 65 naut miles (75 miles) 120 km
Climb rate: 900 ft (274 m) per minute
Availability: Kits.
Comments: Developed in 1978.

White Lightning WLAC-1

Address: White Lightning Aircraft Corporation, PO Box 497, Walterboro, SC 29488-0497.
Telephone & Facsimile: +1 803 549 1800
Type: 4-seat low-wing monoplane, with retractable nosewheel undercarriage.
Construction: Composites.
Wing span: 27 ft 8 ins (8.43 m)
Length: 23 ft 4 ins (7.11 m)
Empty weight: 1,350 lb (612 kg)
Gross weight: 2,400 lb (1,089 kg)
Recommended engine: 210 hp (156.6 kW) Teledyne Continental IO-360
Maximum speed: 243 kts (280 mph) 451 km/h

White Lightning WLAC-1 prototype (Geoffrey P Jones)

Cruise speed: 215 kts (247 mph) 398 km/h
Stall speed: 79 kts (90 mph) 145 km/h clean
Range: 1,738 naut miles (2,000 miles) 3,218 km
Take-off distance: 1,200 ft (366 m)
Climb rate: 1,500 ft (457 m) per minute
Availability: Kits.
Comments: Designed by Howell "Nick" Jones and originally named the Jones White Lightning. Prototype first flew on 8 March 1986. 10 examples completed and flown by 1995.

Wings Unlimited Kingfisher

Address: Wings Unlimited, 6230 Rock Island Road, Charlotte, NC 28278.
Telephone: +1 704 588 9249
Type: Side-by-side 2-seat, high-wing amphibian, with pylon-mounted engine and retractable tail-dragger undercarriage.
Construction: Wood, steel tube, glassfibre and fabric.
Wing span: 36 ft 1 ins (11 m)
Length: 23 ft 7 ins (7.19 m)
Empty weight: 1,050 lb (476 kg)
Gross weight: 1,600 lb (726 kg)
Recommended engine: 100 hp (74.5 kW) Teledyne Continental O-200A, or other including the 115 hp (85.75 kW) Textron Lycoming O-235
Maximum speed: 83 kts (95 mph) 153 km/h
Cruise speed: 74 kts (85 mph) 137 km/h
Stall speed: 33 kts (38 mph) 61 km/h
Range: 243 naut miles (280 miles) 450 km
Take-off distance: 1,000 ft (305 m) land, 2,000 ft (610 m) water.
Climb rate: 700 ft (214 m) per minute
Availability: Plans.
Comments: Originally the Anderson Kingfisher and first flown on 24 April 1969. Later marketed by Richard Warner Aviation before Wings Unlimited. Super Kingfisher version has a 150 hp (112 kW) Textron Lycoming and much improved performance.

Wings Unlimited (Anderson) Kingfisher amphibian (Geoffrey P Jones)

Wolf W-11 Boredom Fighter

Address: Donald Wolf, 17 Chestnut Street, Huntington, NY 11743.
Telephone: +1 516 427 9678
Type: Single-seat biplane, with fixed tail-dragger undercarriage.
Construction: Wood and fabric.
Wing span: 20 ft (6.1 m)
Length: 15 ft 8.5 ins (4.79 m)
Empty weight: 473 lb (215 kg)
Gross weight: 770 lb (349 kg)
Recommended engine: 65 hp (48.5 kW) Teledyne Continental A65 or others.
Maximum speed: 102 kts (118 mph) 190 km/h
Cruise speed: 95 kts (109 mph) 175 km/h
Stall speed: 37 kts (42 mph) 68 km/h
Range: 382 naut miles (440 miles) 708 km
Take-off distance: 250 ft (77 m)
Climb rate: 1,200 ft (366 m) per minute
Availability: Plans.
Comments: Styled like a WWI fighter, Donald Wolf's prototype first flew on 30 August 1979.

Gliders and Motorgliders

Designation	a) Crew b) Materials	a) Aerofoil b) Wing aspect ratio	a) Span ft-ins (m) b) Wing area sq ft (m^2)	Length ft-ins (m)	Weights lb (kg): a) empty b) maximum c) ballast (max)	Wing loading lb/sq ft (kg/m^2): a) minimum b) maximum	a) Minimum rate of sink ft (m)/sec b) at speed of kts (mph) km/h	a) Best glide ratio b) at speed of kts (mph) km/h	Speeds kts (mph) km/h: a) stalling b) maximum c) cruise	a) Engine b) Fuel capacity litres	Comments
Type: G: Glider MGS: Motorglider, self-launch MGN: Motorglider, no self-launch											
Australia											
Manufacturer: Moyes Microlights Pty Ltd. 2-4 Taylor Street, Waverley 2024, NSW - (tel: +61 2 387 5114)											
Tempest (G)	a) 1 b) Tubes and fabric	b) 12	a) 42-6 (12.95) b) 150 (13.92)	21 (6.4)	a) 220 (100) b) 440 (200)	b) 2.93 (14.32)	a) 2.83 (0.86)		b) 70 (80) 129		Kits available.
Austria											
Manufacturer: HOAC Austria Flugzeugwerk Wiener Neustadt GmbH. NA Ottostrasse 5, A-2700 Wiener Neustadt - (tel: +43 2622 26700)											
HK 36 R Super Dimona (MGS)	a) 2 b) Composites	a) FX 63-137 b) 17.5	a) 53-2 (16.2) b) 164.7 (15.3)	23-4 (7.1)	a) 1,202 (545) b) 1,698 (770)	b) 10.3 (50.3)	a) 3.71 (1.13)	a) 28	b) 141 (162) 261 c) 108 (124) 200	a) Front-mounted 80 hp (59.7 kW) Rotax 912 A b) 79	Production continues. Also usable for aero-towing.
Brazil											
Manufacturer: Aeromot Industria Mecanico-Metallurgica Ltda. 1200 Avenue das Industrias, BR-90200-290 Porto Alegre - RS - (tel: +55 51 3371344)											
AMT-100 Ximango (MGS)	a) 2 b) Glassfibre	a) NACA 64.3.618 b) 16.32	a) 57-4 (17.47) b) 201.3 (18.7)	25-10.5 (7.89)	a) 1,323 (600) b) 1,764 (800)	a) 7.39 (36.09) b) 8.76 (42.78)	a) 3.08 (0.94) b) 54 (62) 100	a) 30 b) 59 (69) 110	a) 41 (47) 76 b) 132 (152) 245 never-exceed c) 103 (118) 190	a) Front-mounted 80 hp (59.7 kW) Limbach L 2000 EO1 b) 90	Production continues. Based on French RF-10 design.
AMT-200 Super Ximango (MGS)	a) 2 b) Glassfibre	a) NACA 64.3.618 b) 16.32	a) 57-4 (17.47) b) 201.3 (18.7)	26-5 (8.05)	a) 1,334 (605) b) 1,874 (850)	a) 7.39 (36.09) b) 9.31 (45.45)	a) 3.08 (0.94) b) 57 (65) 105	a) 31 b) 59 (69) 110	a) 41 (47) 76 b) 132 (152) 245 never-exceed c) 111 (127) 205	a) Front-mounted 80 hp (59.7 kW) Rotax 912 A2 b) 90	Production continues.
Manufacturer: IPE-Industria Projetos e Estruturas Aeronáutics Ltda. CP7931, 80021, Curitiba, Paraná											
IPE-02b Nhapecan II (G)	a) 2 b) Composites	b) 16	a) 54-5 (16.6) b) 185.1 (17.2)	28 (8.54)	a) 750 (340) b) 1,235 (560)		a) 2.46 (0.75) b) 38 (43.5) 70	a) 32 b) 48 (55) 88	a) 37 (42.5) 68 b) 108 (124) 200		Many built, including 80th as prototype IPE-02c Nhapecan III.
China											
Manufacturer: Shenyang Sailplane Factory. 17 Shen-Liao East Road, Shenyang, Liaoning 110021											
HU-1 Seagull (MG)	a) 2 b) Aluminium alloy with limited wood, glassfibre and fabric	a) Eppler E 603 b) 16.35	a) 55-10 (17) b) 190.3 (17.68)	25 (7.62)	a) 1,323 (600) b) 2,315 (1,050)	b) 12.16 (59.39)	a) 4.92 (1.5) b) 43 (50) 80	a) 20	a) 46 (53) 85 b) 121 (140) 225 never-exceed	a) Overwing-mounted 116 hp (86.5 kW) Lycoming O-235-N2A	Used mainly for aerial photography and survey, carrying appropriate equipment.

HOAC Austria HK 36 R Super Dimona (P. F. Selinger)
(page 511)

Aeromot AMT-200 Super Ximango
(page 511)

Designation	a) Crew b) Materials	a) Aerofoil b) Wing aspect ratio	a) Span ft-ins (m) b) Wing area sq ft (m^2)	Length ft-ins (m)	Weights lb (kg): a) empty b) maximum c) ballast (max)	Wing loading lb/sq ft (kg/m^2): a) minimum b) maximum	a) Minimum rate of sink ft (m)/sec b) at speed of kts (mph) km/h	a) Best glide ratio b) at speed of kts (mph) km/h	Speeds kts (mph) km/h: a) stalling b) maximum c) cruise	a) Engine b) Fuel capacity litres	Comments
Type: G: Glider **MGS:** Motorglider, self-launch **MGN:** Motorglider, no self-launch											
China											
Manufacturer: Shenyang Sailplane Factory (Continued)											
HU-2 Petrel 650B (MGS)	a) 2 or 3 b) Wood and fabric	a) Göttingen 535 b) 11.34	a) 48-11 (14.92) b) 211.3 (19.63)	23 (7.02)	a) 1,069 (485) b) 1,653 (750)	b) 7.82 (38.2)			a) 33 (37.5) 60 b) 73 (84) 135 c) 54 (62) 100	a) Front-mounted 80 hp (59.7 kW) Limbach L 2000 EO1	Many built since 1990. Resembles a conventional high-wing lightplane.
X-9 Jian Fan (G)	a) 2 b) Aluminium alloy and wood	a) Göttingen 535 b) 11	a) 47-4 (14.42) b) 203.4 (18.9)	24-1 (7.34)	a) 507 (230) b) 838 (380)	b) 4.12 (20.1)	a) 3.15 (0.96) b) 32.5 (37) 60	a) 17 b) 36 (42) 67	a) 24.5 (28) 45 b) 81 (93) 150		Many built for training.
X-10 Qian Jin (G)	a) 1 b) Glassfibre and wood	a) NACA 43012A b) 18.63	a) 52-6 (16) b) 147.9 (13.74)	25 (7.63)	a) 556 (252) b) 754 (342)	b) 5.1 (24.9)	a) 2.46 (0.75) b) 37 (42) 68	a) 26 b) 38 (43.5) 70	a) 32.5 (37.5) 60 b) 135 (155) 250		Club type. Modified version of the SZD-8/14 Jaskolka.
Czech Republic											
Manufacturer: Aerotechnik. Podnik UV Svazarmu, 68604 Kunovice - (tel: +42 632 5122)											
L 13 SEH Vivat (SDM has twin-wheel undercarriage) (MGS)	a) 2 b) Metal	a) NACA 63_2 A615 and 63_2 A612 b) 14	a) 55-1.5 (16.8) b) 217.4 (20.2)	27-3 (8.3)	a) 1,102 (500) b) 1,587 (720)	b) 7.29 (35.6)	a) 3.61 (1.1) b) 51 (59) 95	a) 25 b) 54 (62) 100	a) 32.5 (37.5) 60 b) 111 (127) 205 c) 92 (106) 170	a) Front-mounted 65 hp (48.5 kW) Mikron III AE b) 50	Production continues with single-wheel semi-retractable or twin-wheel fixed undercarriage.
L 13 SL Vivat (SDL with twin-wheel undercarriage) (MGS)	a) 2 b) Metal	a) NACA 63_2 A615 and 63_2 A612 b) 14	a) 55-1.5 (16.8) b) 217.4 (20.2)	27-3 (8.3)	a) 1,102 (500) b) 1,587 (720)	b) 7.29 (35.6)	a) 3.61 (1.1) b) 51 (59) 95	a) 25 b) 54 (62) 100	a) 32.5 (37.5) 60 b) 111 (127) 205 c) 93 (107) 172	a) Front-mounted 67 hp (50 kW) Limbach L 2000 EO1 b) 50	Production continues with single-wheel semi-retractable or twin-wheel fixed undercarriage.
Manufacturer: Inteco. Velkomoravská 1469, 68604 Uherské Hradisté - (tel: +42 632 61186)											
L 213 A (G)	a) 1 b) Metal	b) 12.44	a) 41-3 (12.57) b) 136.7 (12.7)	24 (7.31)	a) 507 (230) b) 772 (350)	b) 5.76 (28.14)	a) 3.94 (1.2) b) 48 (55) 88	b) achieved at 60 (69) 111	a) 38 (44) 70 b) 189 (217) 350 possibly never-exceed		Fully aerobatic +8/-6g.
Manufacturer: Let Aeronautical Works. 68604 Kunovice - (tel: +42 632 411111)											
L 13 Blanik (G)	a) 2 b) Metal	a) NACA 63_2 A615 and 63_2 A612 b) 13.7	a) 53-2 (16.2) b) 206.1 (19.15)	27-7 (8.4)	a) 644 (292) b) 1,102 (500)	a) 4.08 (19.9) b) 5.35 (26.1)	a) 2.79 (0.85) b) 37 (42.5) 68	a) 28 b) 46 (53) 86	a) 32.5 (37.5) 60 b) 129 (149) 240		2,600 built between 1956 and 1981.

Aerotechnik L 13 SL Vivat (J. Ewald) (page 512)

Inteco L 213 A (P. F. Selinger) (page 512)

Designation	a) Crew b) Materials	a) Aerofoil b) Wing aspect ratio	a) Span ft-ins (m) b) Wing area sq ft (m²)	Length ft-ins (m)	Weights lb (kg): a) empty b) maximum c) ballast (max)	Wing loading lb/sq ft (kg/m²): a) minimum b) maximum	a) Minimum rate of sink ft (m)/sec b) at speed of kts (mph) km/h	a) Best glide ratio b) at speed of kts (mph) km/h	Speeds kts (mph) km/h: a) stalling b) maximum c) cruise	a) Engine b) Fuel capacity litres	Comments
Type: G: Glider **MGS:** Motorglider, self-launch **MGN:** Motorglider, no self-launch											
Czech Republic											
Manufacturer: Let Aeronautical Works (Continued)											
L 23 Super Blanik (G)	a) 2 b) Mostly metal	a) NACA 63_2 A615 and 63_2 A612 b) 13.7 (16.5 with wingtips)	a) 53-2 (16.2) or 59-8.5 (18.2) with anhedral wingtips b) 206.1 (19.15) or 215.6 (20.03) with wingtips	27-11 (8.5)	a) 683 (310) or 690 (313) with wingtips b) 1,124 (510)	b) 5.45 (26.63) or 5.22 (25.5) with wingtips	a) 2.69 (0.82) b) 43 (50) 80	a) 28 (32 with wingtips)	a) 32 (37) 59 b) 135 (155) 250 or 124 (143) 230 with wingtips		In production since 1988. Semi-aerobatic as single-seater, +6/-3g.
L 33 Solo (G)	a) 1 b) Metal	b) 18.12	a) 46-4 (14.12) b) 118.4 (11)	21-9 (6.62)	a) 463 (210) b) 750 (340)	a) 4.94 (24.1) b) 6.33 (30.9)	a) 2.17 (0.66) b) 37 (42.5) 68	a) 32.6 b) 49 (56) 90	a) 35 (40) 64 b) 134 (154) 248		In production.
Manufacturer: Orlican Aircraft. 56537 Chocen											
VSO-10 Gradient (G)	a) 1 b) Glassfibre, wood and metal	a) FX 61-163 b) 18.75	a) 49-2.5 (15) b) 129.2 (12)	23 (7)	a) 551 (250) b) 838 (380) c) 123.5 (56)	b) 6.49 (31.7)	a) 2.10 (0.64) b) 39 (45) 73	a) 36 b) 49 (56) 90	a) 37 (42.5) 68 b) 135 (155) 250		225 built between 1976 and 1989.
France											
Manufacturer: SA Centrair. BP 44, F-36300 Le Blanc											
Marianne (G)	a) 2 b) Composites	a) OAP 1 and OAP 2 b) 20	a) 60-10 (18.54) b) 184.9 (17.18)	29-6 (9)	a) 895 (406) b) 1,347 (611)	a) 5.12 (25) b) 7.28 (35.56)	a) 2.07 (0.63) b) 46 (53) 85	a) 42 b) 57 (65) 105	a) 40 (46) 73 b) 140 (162) 260		Built since 1985.
101 Club (G)	a) 1 b) Composites	a) OAP 1 and OAP 2 b) 21.43	a) 49-2.5 (15) b) 113 (10.5)	22-4.5 (6.82)	a) 540 (245) b) 1,003 (455)	b) 8.87 (43.3)	a) 2.13 (0.65) b) 39 (45) 72	a) 38 b) 50 (57) 92	b) 135 (155) 250		Non-retractable monowheel, no water ballast in wings and no instruments.
Pégase A (G)	a) 1 b) Composites	a) OAP 1 and OAP 2 b) 21.43	a) 49-2.5 (15) b) 113 (10.5)	22-4.5 (6.82)	a) 553 (251) b) 1,003 (455)	b) 8.87 (43.3)	a) 2.2 (0.67) b) 43 (50) 80	a) 40 b) 53 (61) 98	b) 135 (155) 250		Hundreds built. Generally similar to 101 Club but with instruments and retractable monowheel.
Pégase B (G)	a) 1 b) Composites	a) OAP 1 and OAP 2 b) 21.43	a) 49-2.5 (15) b) 113 (10.5)	22-4.5 (6.82)	a) 564 (256) b) 1,113 (505) c) 160 litres of water	b) 9.85 (48.1)	a) 2.13 (0.65) b) 45 (52) 83	a) 40 b) 55 (63) 102	b) 135 (155) 250		Version of Pégase A with water ballast in wings.
Pégase D (G)	a) 1 b) Composites	a) OAP 3 and OAP 2 b) 21.43	a) 49-2.5 (15) b) 113 (10.5)	22-4.5 (6.82)	a) 551 (250) b) 1,113 (505) c) 160 litres of water	a) 6.25 (30.5) b) 9.85 (48.1)	a) 1.97 (0.6) b) 47 (54) 87	a) 41 b) 58 (66) 107	a) 39 (45) 72 b) 135 (155) 250		Certified in 1986. Based on Pégase B type.

Let L 23 Super Blanik (A. Wilsch) (page 513)

Let L 33 Solo (J. Ewald) (page 513)

Designation	a) Crew b) Materials	a) Aerofoil b) Wing aspect ratio	a) Span ft-ins (m) b) Wing area sq ft (m²)	Length ft-ins (m)	Weights lb (kg): a) empty b) maximum c) ballast (max)	Wing loading lb/sq ft (kg/m²): a) minimum b) maximum	a) Minimum rate of sink ft (m)/sec b) at speed of kts (mph) km/h	a) Best glide ratio b) at speed of kts (mph) km/h	Speeds kts (mph) km/h: a) stalling b) maximum c) cruise	a) Engine b) Fuel capacity litres	Comments
Type: G: Glider **MGS:** Motorglider, self-launch **MGN:** Motorglider, no self-launch											
France											
Manufacturer: Avions René Fournier. F-37270 Athée sur Cher - (tel: +33 47 50 68 30)											
RF-5 (MGS)	a) 2 b) Wood and fabric	a) NACA 23015 and NACA 23012 b) 12.5	a) 45-1 (13.74) b) 162.75 (15.12)	25-7 (7.8)	a) 926 (420) b) 1,433 (650)	b) 8.77 (42.8)			a) 42.5 (49) 78 c) 113 (130) 210	Front-mounted 80 hp (59.7 kW) Limbach L 2000 EO1	Has been built under licence in Spain and Germany.
Manufacturer: Issoire-Aviation SA.											
PIK-20E2F (MGS)	a) 1 b) Composites	a) FX-67-K-170 and FX-67-K-150 b) 22.5	a) 49-2.5 (15) b) 107.6 (10)	21-5 (6.53)	a) 683 (310) b) 1,036 (470) c) 176.4 (80)	b) 9.63 (47)	a) 2.3 (0.7) b) 48 (55) 88	a) 41 b) 63 (73) 117	a) 41 (47) 75 b) 154 (177) 285 without power	a) Mid-fuselage, retractable 43 hp (32 kW) Rotax 505 b) 30	Version of the earlier production Finnish PIK-20E.
PIK-30 (MGS)	a) 1 b) Composites	a) FX-67-K-170 and FX-67-K-150 b) 27.2	a) 55-9 (17) with removable wingtips b) 114.4 (10.63)	Believed to be 21-5 (6.53)	a) 683 (310) b) 1,014 (460)	b) 8.86 (43.27)	a) 1.77 (0.54) b) 41 (47) 75	a) 45 b) 59 (68) 110	a) 38 (44) 70 b) 103 (118) 190	a) Mid-fuselage, retractable 43 hp (32 kW) Rotax 505 b) 29	Qualifies for 17 m Open Class and, with wingtips removed, 15 m Class.
Manufacturer: Sarl La Mouette. 1 rue de la Petite Fin, 21121 Fontaine-lès-Dijon											
Atlas 21M (MG)	b) Aluminium alloy	b) 5.2	a) 34-9 (10.6) b) 231.4 (21.5)		a) 92.6 (42) b) 772 (350)		a) 5.91 (1.8)	a) 6	a) 21 (24) 38 c) 35 (40) 65		Based on the company's hang glider experience. First flight in 1987.
Chronos (MG)	b) Aluminium alloy	b) 8.6	a) 36-1 (11) b) 150.7 (14)		b) 661 (300)		a) 6.56 (2)	a) 8	c) 70 (81) 130		First flight in 1988.
Germany											
Manufacturer: EIS. Dahlemer - Binz, D-53949 Dahlem											
RF-9 (MGS)	a) 2 b) Wood	b) 16.627	a) 56.9 (17.3) b) 193.75 (18)	26-5 (8.06)	a) 1,146 (520)) b) 1,642 (745)	b) 8.48 (41.39)	a) 2-62 (0.8)	a) 29	a) 38 (44) 70 c) 103 (118) 190	a) Front-mounted 80 hp (59.7 kW) Rotax 912A3	French Fournier RF-9, formerly marketed by ABS.
Manufacturer: Flugwissenschaftliche Vereinigung Aachen (1920) e. V. Templergraben 55, D-52062 Aachen - (tel: +49 241 806824)											
FVA-27 (G)	a) 1 b) Glassfibre, carbonfibre and aramid	a) Canard: FX 67 K-170, Wing: HQ 21M2/25 b) Canard: 13.9, Wing: 29.2	a) 49-3 (15) b) 82.9 (7.7) (Wing plus Canard 102.25/9.5 m²)	13-1.5 (4)	a) 573 (260) approx b) 1,058 (480) c) 220 (100)	a) 7.11 (34.7) b) 10.34 (50.5)			b) 151 (174) 280		Canard glider with pilot rescue system. Under construction. First flight expected in 1999.

Orlican VSO-10 Gradient (J. Ewald)
(page 513)

Centrair Marianne (J. Ewald)
(page 513)

Designation	a) Crew b) Materials	a) Aerofoil b) Wing aspect ratio	a) Span ft-ins (m) b) Wing area sq ft (m^2)	Length ft-ins (m)	Weights lb (kg): a) empty b) maximum c) ballast (max)	Wing loading lb/sq ft (kg/m^2): a) minimum b) maximum	a) Minimum rate of sink ft (m)/sec b) at speed of kts (mph) km/h	a) Best glide ratio b) at speed of kts (mph) km/h	Speeds kts (mph) km/h: a) stalling b) maximum c) cruise	a) Engine b) Fuel capacity litres	Comments
Type: G: Glider **MGS:** Motorglider, self-launch **MGN:** Motorglider, no self-launch											
Germany											
Manufacturer: Frank + Waldenberger. An der Kühlweid 3, D-76661 Philippsburg											
H 101 Salto (G)	a) 1 b) Glassfibre	a) FX 66-17-All-182 b) 21.8	a) 43-8 or 50-10 (13.3 or 15.5) b) 92.35 or 98 (8.58 or 9.1)	18-8.5 (5.7)	a) 401-412 (182-187) b) 617-683 (280-310)	a) 6.7-6.96 (32.7-34)	a) 2.3 (0.7) b) 39 (45) 72	a) 35-36 b) 51 (58) 94	a) 33.5-38 (39-44) 62-70 b) 135-151 (155-174) 250-280		Originally based on Hütter H-30 Gfk.
Manufacturer: Glaser-Dirks Flugzeugbau GmbH. Im Schollengarten 19-20, D-76646 Bruchsal - (tel: +49 7257 8910)											
DG-300 Elan (Acro) (G) See Comments for DG 303	a) 1 b) Glassfibre	a) HQ-21 mod b) 21.91	a) 49-3 (15) b) 110.5 (10.27)	22-4 (6.8)	a) 540 (245) b) 1,157 (525) c) 419 (190)	a) 6.19 (30.2) b) 10.47 (51.1)	a) 1.94 (0.59) b) 42 (48.5) 78	a) 42 b) 66 (76) 122	a) 35 (40.5) 65 b) 146 (168) 270		452 built from 1983; production continues as DG 303 with winglets and Acro versions. Fully aerobatic (+7/-5g) at 370 kg. Club versions with fixed under carriage and no ballast.
DG-400 (MGS)	a) 1 b) Glassfibre	a) FX 67-K-170/17 b) 27.24 with 17 m wing; 22.5 with 15 m wing	a) 55-9 (17) or 49-3 (15) b) 113.8 or 107.6 (10.57 or 10)	22-11.5 (7)	a) 675-683 (306-310) b) 1,014-1,058 (460-480) c) 198 (90)	a) 7.46 (36.4) for 17 m wing b) 8.91 (43.5) for 17 m wing, 9.83 (48) for 15 m wing	a) 1.77 (0.54) for 17 m wing, 1.97 (0.6) for 15 m wing b) 43 (50) 80	a) 45 for 17 m wing, 42 for 15 m wing b) 59 (68) 110	a) 34 (39.5) 63 for 17 m wing, 35 (41) 65 for 15 m wing b) 146 (168) 270 unpowered	a) Mid-fuselage, retractable Rotax 505 b) 20 standard	290 built from 1981-1992.
DG-500 Elan Trainer. Replaced by new DG-505 Orion version in 1995. (G)	a) 2 b) Glassfibre and carbonfibre	a) FX 73-K-170/17 b) 19.5 (23.3 for Orion). See Comments	a) 59-1 (18) or 65-8 (20) for Orion b) 178.7 (16.6) or 189.4 (17.6) for Orion. See Comments	28-5 (8.66)	a) 860 (390) b)1,356 (615) or 1,653 (750) for Orion	a) 5.8 (28.3) b) 7.58 (37)	a) 1.8 (0.55) approx for Orion b) 43 (50) 80 approx for Orion	a) 44 approx for Orion	a) 35 (40.5) 65 b) 146 (168) 270		Aerobatic (+7/-5g). Constructed at Elan in Slovenia. DG-500 replaced by DG 505 Orion in 1995 with 17.2, 18 and 20 m span wings (20 m data given).
DG-500 M (MGS)	a) 2 b) Glassfibre and carbonfibre	a) FX 73-K-170/17 b) 26.5	a) 72-2 (22) b) 196.9 (18.29)	28-5 (8.66)	a) 1,190 (540) b) 1,819 (825) c) 220 (100)	a) 6.86 (33.5) b) 9.24 (45.1)	a) 1.67 (0.51) b) 43 (50) 80	a) 47 b) 59 (68) 110	a) 37 (42.5) 68 b) 146 (168) 270 c) 81 (93) 150	a) Mid-fuselage, retractable 60 hp (44.7 kW) Rotax 535 b) 78	53 built since 1987. Production continues.

Frank + Waldenberger H 101 Salto (J. Ewald) (page 515)

Glaser-Dirks DG-300 Elan Acro (J. Ewald) (page 515)

Designation	a) Crew b) Materials	a) Aerofoil b) Wing aspect ratio	a) Span ft-ins (m) b) Wing area sq ft (m²)	Length ft-ins (m)	Weights lb (kg): a) empty b) maximum c) ballast (max)	Wing loading lb/sq ft (kg/m²): a) minimum b) maximum	a) Minimum rate of sink ft (m)/sec b) at speed of kts (mph) km/h	a) Best glide ratio b) at speed of kts (mph) km/h	Speeds kts (mph) km/h: a) stalling b) maximum c) cruise	a) Engine b) Fuel capacity litres	Comments
Type: **G:** Glider **MGS:** Motorglider, self-launch **MGN:** Motorglider, no self-launch											
Germany											
Manufacturer: Glaser-Dirks Flugzeugbau GmbH (Continued)											
DG-500/20 Elan Winglets (G)	a) 2 b) Glassfibre and carbonfibre	a) FX 73-K-170/17 b) 22.7	a) 65-7.5 (20) b) 189.2 (17.58)	28-5 (8.66)	a) 970 (440) b) 1,653 (750) c) 353 (160)	a) 6.14 (30) b) 8.75 (42.7)	a) 1.74 (0.53) b) 43 (50) 80	a) 44 b) 59 (68) 110	a) 31 (36) 57 b) 145 (168) 270		4 built since 1994. Production continues. Constructed by Elan of Slovenia.
DG-500/22 Elan (G)	a) 2 b) Glassfibre and carbonfibre	a) FX 73-K-170/17 b) 26.5	a) 72-2 (22) b) 196.9 (18.29)	28-5 (8.66)	a) 981 (445) b) 1,653 (750) c) 353 (160)	a) 5.94 (29) b) 8.4 (41)	a) 1.67 (0.51) b) 43 (50) 80	a) 47 approx b) 59 (68) 110	a) 31.5 (36) 58 b) 146 (168) 270		17 built since 1989. Production continues. Built by Elan of Slovenia.
DG-600 (G)	a) 1 b) Carbonfibre and aramid	a) HQ 35 mod b) 20.55 (24.94 with 17 m wings)	a) 49-3 (15) or 55-9 (17 m) with detachable wingtips b) 117.9 (10.95) or 124.75 (11.59) with wingtips	22-5 (6.83)	a) 567 (257) or 573 (260) with wingtips b) 1,157 (525) c) 419 (190)	a) 6.0 (29.3) b) 9.81 (47.9) or 9.28 (45.3) with wingtips	a) 1.84 (0.56) or 1.64 (0.5) with wingtips	a) 45 or 49 with wingtips	a) 35 (40) 64 or 33.5 (38.5) 62 with wingtips b) 146 (168) 270		60 of all versions built between 1987-1993.
DG-600 M (MGS)	a) 1 b) Carbonfibre and aramid	a) HQ 35 mod b) 20.55 (24.94 with 17 m wings	a) 49-3 (15) or 55-9 (17 m) with detachable wingtips b) 117.9 (10.95) or 124.75 (11.59) with wingtips	22-5 (6.83)	a) 672 (305) or 683 (310) with wingtips b) 1,157 (525) c) 265 (120)	a) 7.21 (35.2) or 6.88 (33.6) with wingtips b) 9.81 (47.9) or 9.28 (45.3) with wingtips	a) 1.97 (0.6) or 1.74 (0.53) with wingtips b) 48 (55) 88 or 45 (52) 84 with wingtips	a) 45 or 49 with wingtips b) 65 (75) 120 or 62 (71) 115 with wingtips	a) 38.5 (44.5) 71 or 37.5 (43) 69 with wingtips b) 146 (168) 270 c) 65 (75) 120	a) Mid-fuselage, retractable 24 hp (18 kW) Rotax 275 b) 22	52 of all M versions built from 1989-1993. Self launch only up to 970 lb (440 kg).
DG-600/18 (G)	a) 1 b) Carbonfibre and aramid	a) HQ 35 mod/HQ 37 b) 27.24	a) 59-1 (18) b) 127.1 (11.81)	22-5 (6.83)	a) 578 (262) b) 1,058 (480) c) 419 (190)	a) 5.94 (29) b) 9.81 (47.9)	a) 1.61 (0.49)	a) 50 b) 59 (68) 110	a) 33.5 (39) 62 b) 146 (168) 270		Built from 1992-93 (see DG-600).
DG-600/18M Evolution (MGS)	a) 1 b) Carbonfibre and aramid	a) HQ 35 mod/HQ 37 b) 27.24	a) 59-1 (18) b) 127.1 (11.81)	22-5 (6.83)	a) 699 (317) b) 1,058 (480) c) 265 (120)	a) 6.88 (33.6) b) 8.32 (40.6)	a) 1.67 (0.51) b) 45 (52) 83	a) 50 b) 59 (68) 110	a) 37 (42.5) 68 b) 146 (168) 270 c) 65 (75) 120	a) Mid-fuselage, retractable 24 hp (18 kW) Rotax 275 b) 22	Built from 1991-93 (see DG-600 M). Self-launch only up to 970 lb (440 kg).
DG-800 A (MGS)	a) 1 b) Carbonfibre and aramid	a) DU 89-138/14 and DU-92-137-14 b) 27.43 or 21.07 in 15 m span form	a) 59-1 (18) or 49-3 (15) b) 127.1 (11.81) or 115 (10.68) in 15 m span form	23-0.5 (7.02)	a) 723 (328) or 710 (322) in 15 m span form b) 1,157 (525) c) 265 (120)	a) 7.07 (34.5) or 7.7 (37.6) in 15 m span form b) 9.11 (44.5) or 10.08 (49.2) in 15 m span form	a) 1.64 (0.5) or 1.94 (0.59) in 15 m span form b) 41 (47) 76 or 43 (50) 80 in 15 m span form	a) 50 or 45 approx in 15 m span form b) 59 (68) 110 or 63 (72) 116 in 15 m span form	a) 37 (42.5) 68 or 39 (45) 72 in 15 m span form b) 146 (168) 270	a) Mid-fuselage, retractable 43 hp (32 kW) Rotax 505 b) 52	30 built since 1991. Production continues.

Glaser-Dirks DG-400 (P. F. Selinger) (page 515)

Glaser-Dirks DG-500 M (J. Ewald) (page 515)

Designation	a) Crew b) Materials	a) Aerofoil b) Wing aspect ratio	a) Span ft-ins (m) b) Wing area sq ft (m²)	Length ft-ins (m)	Weights lb (kg): a) empty b) maximum c) ballast (max)	Wing loading lb/sq ft (kg/m²): a) minimum b) maximum	a) Minimum rate of sink ft (m)/sec b) at speed of kts (mph) km/h	a) Best glide ratio b) at speed of kts (mph) km/h	Speeds kts (mph) km/h: a) stalling b) maximum c) cruise	a) Engine b) Fuel capacity litres	Comments
Type: G: Glider **MGS:** Motorglider, self-launch **MGN:** Motorglider, no self-launch											
Germany											
Manufacturer: Glaser-Dirks Flugzeugbau GmbH (Continued)											
DG-800 B (MGS)	a) 1 b) Carbonfibre and aramid	a) DU 89-138/14 and DU-92-137-14 b) 27.43 or 21.07 in 15 m span form	a) 59-1 (18) or 49-3 (15) b) 127.1 (11.81) or 115 (10.68) in 15 m span form	23-0.5 (7.02)	a) 723 (328) or 710 (322) in 15 m span form b) 1,157 (525) c) 265 (120)	a) 7.07 (34.5) or 7.7 (37.6) in 15 m span form b) 9.11 (44.5) or 10.08 (49.2) in 15 m span form	a) 1.64 (0.5) or 1.94 (0.59) in 15 m span form b) 41 (47) 76 or 43 (50) 80 in 15 m span form	a) 50 or 45 approx in 15 m span form b) 59 (68) 110 or 63 (72) 116 in 15 m span form	a) 37 (42.5) 68 or 39 (45) 72 in 15 m span form b) 146 (168) 270	a) Mid-fuselage, 50 hp (37.3 kW) MWAE 50 with retractable propeller b) 52	1 built in 1994. Production continues.
DG-800 S (G)	a) 1 b) Carbonfibre and aramid	a) DU 89-138/14 and DU-92-137-14 b) 27.43 or 21.07 in 15 m span form	a) 59-1 (18) or 49-3 (15) b) 127.1 (11.81) or 115 (10.68) in 15 m span form	22-5 (6.83)	a) 578 (262) or 564 (256) in 15 m span form b) 1,157 (525) c) 419 (190)	a) 5.94 (29) or 6.45 (31.5) in 15 m span form b) 9.11 (44.5) or 10.08 (49.2) in 15 m span form	a) 1.54 (0.47) or 1.8 (0.55) in 15 m span form b) 38 (44) 71 or 40 (46.5) 75 in 15 m span form	a) 50 or 45 in 15 m span form b) 59 (68) 110 or 63 (72) 116 in 15 m span form, all approx	a) 34 (39.5) 63 or 36 (41) 66 in 15 m span form b) 146 (168) 270		12 built since 1993. Production continues.
Manufacturer: Burkhart Grob Luft und Raumfahrt GmbH & Co KG. Am Flugplatz, D-86874 Tussenhausen-Mattsies - (tel: +49 8268 998 0)											
G 103 C Twin III acro (G)	a) 2 b) Glassfibre	a) HQ 32 - E583 mod b) 18.5	a) 59-1 (18) b) 188.6 (17.52)	26-10 (8.18)	a) 838 (380) b) 1,323 (600)	a) 5.26 (25.7) b) 7.03 (34.3)	a) 2.1 (0.64) b) 39.5 (45) 73	a) 38 b) 59 (68) 109	a) 34 (39.5) 63 b) 151 (174) 280		First produced in 1976 as G 103 A with Eppler 60.3 aerfoil.

Glaser-Dirks DG-800 A (18m) (J. Ewald) (page 516)

Grob G 103 C Twin III acro (J. Ewald) (page 517)

LTB Gerhard Nitsche Avo 68 (J. Ewald) (page 518)

Grob G 109 B (J. Ewald) (page 518)

Designation	a) Crew b) Materials	a) Aerofoil b) Wing aspect ratio	a) Span ft-ins (m) b) Wing area sq ft (m^2)	Length ft-ins (m)	Weights lb (kg): a) empty b) maximum c) ballast (max)	Wing loading lb/sq ft (kg/m^2): a) minimum b) maximum	a) Minimum rate of sink ft (m)/sec b) at speed of kts (mph) km/h	a) Best glide ratio b) at speed of kts (mph) km/h	Speeds kts (mph) km/h: a) stalling b) maximum c) cruise	a) Engine b) Fuel capacity litres	Comments
Type: G: Glider MGS: Motorglider, self-launch MGN: Motorglider, no self-launch											
Germany											
Manufacturer: Burkhart Grob Luft und Raumfahrt GmbH & Co KG (continued)											
G 103 C Twin III (details for SL version) (MGS)	a) 2 b) Glassfibre	a) HQ 32 - E583 mod b) 18.5	a) 59-1 (18) b) 188.6 (17.52)	26-10 (8.18)	a) 1,014 (460) b) 1,565 (710)	b) 8.3 (40.5)	a) 2.1 (0.64) b) 42 (51) 82	a) 38 b) 57 (66) 106	a) 37 (42.5) 68 b) 151 (174) 280	a) Mid-fuselage, retractable 43 hp (32 kW) Rotax 505	Twin III and the aerobatic Acro versions are gliders for clubs and training purposes. The SL is powered.
G 109 B (MGS)	a) 2 b) Glassfibre	b) 15.9	a) 57-1 (17.4) b) 204.5 (19)	26-7 (8.1)	a) 1,367 (620) b) 1,874 (850)	b) 9.16 (44.7)	a) 3.61 (1.1) b) 58 (71) 108	a) 28 b) 62 (71) 115	a) 40 (45.5) 73 b) 130 (149) 240 c) 103 (118) 190	a) Front-mounted 90 hp (67 kW) Grob G2500	Vigilant T.1 military version for the RAF with a 75 hp (56 kW) Limbach engine was for bought for Air Cadet use.
Manufacturer: Jürgen Lutz.											
Libelle (G)	a) 1 b) Glassfibre, carbonfibre and wood	b) 7.6	a) 34-5.5 (10.5) b) 156.1 (14.5)	23-5.5 (7.15)	a) 148 (67) b) 346 (157)	a) 1.8 (8.8) b) 2.21 (10.8)	a) 2.62 (0.8)	a) 15	a) 19 (22) 35 b) 49 (56) 90		Homebuilt microlight glider.
Manufacturer: LTB Gerhard Nitsche. D-83246 Unterwössen											
Avo 68 (MGS)	a) 2 b) Wood and steel tube	a)NACA/Gö b) 13.6	a) 54-9 (16.68) b) 222.8 (20.7)	24-7 (7.5)	a) 1,080 (490) b) 1,510 (685)	a) 5.63 (27.5) b) 6.76 (33)	a) 3.41 (1.04) b) 40 (47) 75	a) 22 b) 49 (56) 90	a) 32.5 (37.5) 60 b) 89 (103) 165 c) 79 (91) 147	a) Front mounted Limbach L 1700 E1 b) 40, with 80 planned	Austrian Alpha design reintroduced. New prototype with a Rotax 912 A, suited to aero-towing, flew 1994.

Grob G 103 SL Twin III engine detail (page 518)

Lutz Libelle (P. F. Selinger) (page 518)

Neumann ULF-1 (P. F. Selinger) (page 519)

Designation	a) Crew b) Materials	a) Aerofoil b) Wing aspect ratio	a) Span ft-ins (m) b) Wing area sq ft (m^2)	Length ft-ins (m)	Weights lb (kg): a) empty b) maximum c) ballast (max)	Wing loading lb/sq ft (kg/m^2): a) minimum b) maximum	a) Minimum rate of sink ft (m)/sec b) at speed of kts (mph) km/h	a) Best glide ratio b) at speed of kts (mph) km/h	Speeds kts (mph) km/h: a) stalling b) maximum c) cruise	a) Engine b) Fuel capacity litres	Comments
Type: G: Glider **MGS:** Motorglider, self-launch **MGN:** Motorglider, no self-launch											
Germany											
Manufacturer: Heinz Neumann and Dieter Reich. Fichtenstrasse 7, D-85084 Reichertshofen - (tel: +49 8453 467)											
ULF-1 (G)	a) 1 b) Wood, fabric and glassfibre	a) FX 63-137/18-15% b) 8	a) 34-1.5 (10.4) b) 144.2 (13.4)	18-2.5 (5.55)	a) 99 (45) b) 298 (135)	b) 2.05 (10)	a) 2.62 (0.8)	a) 15	a) 17.5 (20) 32 b) 38 (43) 70		Microlight glider. Drawings available. About 10 built.
Manufacturer: Rolladen Schneider Flugzeugbau GmbH. Postfach 1130, D-63323 Egelsbach											
LS4B (G)	a) 1 b) Glassfibre	a) Lemke b) 21.4	a) 49-3 (15) b) 113 (10.5)	22-5 (6.83)	a) 529 (240) b) 1,157 (525) c) 375 (170)	a) 6.04 (29.5) b) 10.24 (50)	a) 1.97 (0.6) b) 40.5 (47) 75	a) 41 b) 54 (62) 100	a) 37 (42.5) 68 b) 151 (174) 280		About 900 of all versions of the LS4 built since 1980.
LS6 (G)	a) 1 b) Glassfibre, carbonfibre and aramid	a) Lemke b) 21.4	a) 49-3 (15) b) 113 (10.5) See Comments	21-10 (6.66)	a) 551 (250) b) 1,157 (525) c) 353 (160)	b) 10.24 (50)	a) under 1.97 (0.6)	43	a) 35 (40.5) 65 b) 146 (168) 270		Several versions developed, including LS6A with 5.5 litre water ballast in tailfin, LS6B with carbon-fibre wings in place of glass-fibre and the LS6-17.5 with 57 ft 5 ins (17.5 m) wings. New LS 6C with 59 ft (18 m) wings.
LS7 WL (G)	a) 1 b) Glassfibre, carbonfibre and aramid	a) Lemke b) 23.1	a) 49-3 (15) b) 104.7 (9.73)	21-10 (6.66)	a) 529 (240) b) 1,071 (486) c) 375 (170)	a) 6.55 (32) b) 10.24 (50)		43	a) 37 (42.5) 68 b) 146 (168) 270		Production began in 1988. WL=winglets.

Rolladen Schneider LS4 (P. F. Selinger) (page 519)

Rolladen Schneider LS6 (J. Ewald) (page 519)

Rolladen Schneider LS7 (J. Ewald) (page 519)

Scheibe SF25 C Rotax-Falke (J. Ewald) (page 520)

Designation	a) Crew b) Materials	a) Aerofoil b) Wing aspect ratio	a) Span ft-ins (m) b) Wing area sq ft (m²)	Length ft-ins (m)	Weights lb (kg): a) empty b) maximum c) ballast (max)	Wing loading lb/sq ft (kg/m²): a) minimum b) maximum	a) Minimum rate of sink ft (m)/sec b) at speed of kts (mph) km/h	a) Best glide ratio b) at speed of kts (mph) km/h	Speeds kts (mph) km/h: a) stalling b) maximum c) cruise	a) Engine b) Fuel capacity litres	Comments
Type: G: Glider **MGS:** Motorglider, self-launch **MGN:** Motorglider, no self-launch											
Germany											
Manufacturer: Rolladen Schneider Flugzeugbau GmbH (continued)											
LS8 (G)	a) 1 b) Glassfibre, carbonfibre and aramid	a) Lemke (see comments) b) 21.4	a) 49-3 (15) b) 113 (10.5)	22-0.5 (6.72)	a) 529 (240) b) 1,157 (525) c) 397 (180)	a) 6.76 (33) b) 10.24 (50)		43	a) 36 (41) 66 b) 146 (168) 270		LS6 wing section, but wings without flaps.
LS9 (MGS)	a) 1 b) Glassfibre, carbonfibre and aramid	a) Lemke (LS-6) b) 28.4	a) 59-1 (18) b) 122.7 (11.4)	22-5 (6.83)				a) about 50		a) Mid fuselage Rotax	Based on LS-4 fuselage and LS-6C wings. First flight 1995.
Manufacturer: Scheibe-Flugzeugbau GmbH. August-Pfaltz-Strasse 23, D-85221 Dachau - (tel: +49 8131 72083/72084)											
SF 25C Falke 2000 (MGS)	a) 2 b) Wood and steel tube	a) Mü b) 13.8	a) 50-2.5 (15.3) b) 195.9 (18.2)	24-11 (7.6)	a) 959 (435) b) 1,433 (650)	b) 7.31 (35.7)	a) 3.28 (1)	a) 23	a) 35 (40.5) 65 b) 103 (118) 190 c) 92 (106) 170	a) Front-mounted 80 hp (59.7 kW) Limbach L 2000 EA b) 55 Note. IorAvia of Thionville-Yutz, France, modifies SF 25-S and SF 28 for aero-towing, with Limbach 2400EB1 engines.	About 1,000 SF 25 Falkes built since 1966 in 1, 2 and 3 wheel versions, including SF 25-S with a feathering Hoffmann propeller, Falke 76. Falke 88, Falke 90 with a Limbach SL 1700 EA engine and SF 25E Super-Falke with 18 m wings.
SF 25C Rotax-Falke (MGS)	a) 2 b) Wood and steel tube	a) Mü b) 13.8	a) 50-2.5 (15.3) b) 195.9 (18.2)	24-11 (7.6)	a) 959 (435) b) 1,433 (650)	b) 7.31 (35.7)	a) 3.28 (1)	a) 23	a) 35 (40.5) 65 b) 103 (118) 190 c) 97 (112) 180	a) Front-mounted 80 hp (59.7 kW) Rotax 912A b) 55	1, 2 and 3 wheel versions available.
SF 28A Tandem-Falke (MGS)	a) 2 b) Wood and steel tube	b) 14.4	a) 53-6 (16.3) b) 195.9 (18.5)	26-7 (8.1)	a) 904 (410) b) 1,345 (610)	b) 6.76 (33)	a) 2.95 (0.9) b) 38 (44) 70	a) 27 b) 51 (59) 95	a) 32.5 (37.5) 60 unpowered b) 103 (118) 190	a) Front-mounted 65 hp (48.5 kW) Limbach SL 1700 EAI b) 40	Tandem instead of side-by-side seating.
SF 34B (G)	a) 2 b) Glassfibre	a) FX 61-184 and FX 60-126 b) 17	a) 51-10 (15.8) b) 159.3 (14.8)	24-7 (7.5)	a) 728 (330) b) 1,190 (540)	a) 5.33 (26) b) 7.48 (36.5)	a) 2.3 (0.7) b) 40.5 (47) 75	a) 35 b) 51 (59) 95	a) 35 (40.5) 65 b) 135 (155) 250		Now produced in France.
SF 36R (MGS)	a) 2 b) Glassfibre	a) FX 61-184 and FX 60-126 b) 17.1	a) 53-6 (16.3) b) 167.9 (15.6)	23-7.5 (7.2)	a) 1,135 (515) b) 1,576 (715)	b) 9.38 (45.8)	a) 2.95 (0.9) b) 43 (50) 80	a) 28 b) 51 (59) 95	a) 40.5 (47) 75 b) 113 (130) 210 c) 97 (112) 180	a) Front-mounted 80 hp (59.7 kW) Rotax 912A b) 70	First prototypes in 1981 with Limbach engines.

Scheibe SF34 B (P. F. Selinger) (page 520)

Scheibe SF36 (J. Ewald) (page 520)

Designation	a) Crew b) Materials	a) Aerofoil b) Wing aspect ratio	a) Span ft-ins (m) b) Wing area sq ft (m²)	Length ft-ins (m)	Weights lb (kg): a) empty b) maximum c) ballast (max)	Wing loading lb/sq ft (kg/m²): a) minimum b) maximum	a) Minimum rate of sink ft (m)/sec b) at speed of kts (mph) km/h	a) Best glide ratio b) at speed of kts (mph) km/h	Speeds kts (mph) km/h: a) stalling b) maximum c) cruise	a) Engine b) Fuel capacity litres	Comments
Type: G: Glider **MGS:** Motorglider, self-launch **MGN:** Motorglider, no self-launch											
Germany											
Manufacturer: Schempp-Hirth Flugzeugbau GmbH. Krebenstrasse 25, D-73230 Kirchheim/Teck - (tel: +49 7021 2441)											
Discus a (G)	a) 1 b) Glassfibre and carbonfibre	a) Horstmann, Quast, Althaus, Holighaus b) 21.3	a) 49-3 (15) b) 113.9 (10.58)	20-10 (6.35)	a) 496 (225) b) 1,157 (525) c) 370 (168)	b) 10.16 (49.6)	a) 1.94 (0.59) b) 42 (48) 78	a) 54 b) 54 (62) 100	a) 36 (41) 66 b) 135 (155) 250		558 Discus gliders of all types built since 1984, and production continues. Discus a has a narrow fuselage.
Discus b and CS (G)	a) 1 b) Glassfibre and carbonfibre	a) Horstmann, Quast, Althaus, Holighaus b) 21.3	a) 49-3 (15) b) 113.9 (10.58)	21-7 (6.58)	a) 507 (230) b) 1,157 (525) c) 370 (168)	a) 6.04 (29.5) b) 10.16 (49.6)	a) 1.94 (0.59) b) 44 (51) 82	a) 43 b) 52 (60) 97	a) 37.5 (43) 69 b) 135 (155) 250		CS built at Orlican in Czech Republic.
Discus bM (MGS)	a) 1 b) Glassfibre and carbonfibre	a) Horstmann, Quast, Althaus, Holighaus b) 21.3	a) 49-3 (15) b) 113.9 (10.58)	21-7 (6.58)	a) 694 (315) b) 1,157 (525) c) 370 (168)	a) 7.56 (36.9) b) 10.16 (49.6)	a) 2.2 (0.67)	a) 42.5	a) 41 (47.5) 76 b) 135 (155) 250 c) 81 (93) 150	a) Mid-fuselage 48 hp (35.8 kW) Rotax 463 with a retractable propeller b) 29	About 6 built since 1991. Production continues.
Discus bT (MGN)	a) 1 b) Glassfibre and carbonfibre	a) Horstmann, Quast, Althaus, Holighaus b) 21.3	a) 49-3 (15) b) 113.9 (10.58)	21-7 (6.58)	a) 606 (275) b) 992 (450) c) 370 (168)	a) 6.96 (34) b) 8.7 (42.5)		a) 43	a) 34 (39.5) 63 b) 135 (155) 250	a) Mid-fuselage, retractable 20.8 hp (15.5 kW) Solo	138 built since 1988. Production continues.
Duo-Discus (G)	a) 2 b) Glassfibre, carbonfibre and aramid	a) Wortmann, Althaus, Holighaus b) 24.4	a) 65-7.5 (20) b) 176.5 (16.4)	28-3.5 (8.62)	a) 882 (400) b) 1,543 (700)	a) 6.0 (29.3) b) 8.75 (42.7)	a) 1.97 (0.6) b) 38 (43) 70		a) 37 (42.5) 68 b) 135 (155) 250		About 25 built since 1993. Production continues.
Janus (G)	a) 2 b) Glassfibre	a) FX 67-K-170/150 b) 20	a) 59-8.5 (18.2) b) 178.7 (16.6)	28-1.5 (8.57)	a) 838 (380) b) 1,367 (620) c) 529 (240)	a) 5.57 (27.2) b) 7.64 (37.3)	a) 2.3 (0.7) b) 49 (56) 90	a) 39.5 b) 59 (68) 110)	a) 38 (43.5) 70 b) 119 (137) 220		About 250 of all Janus glider versions built since 1974. Flying T-tail.
Janus B (G)	a) 2 b) Glassfibre	a) FX 67-K-170/150 b) 20	a) 59-8.5 (18.2) b) 178.7 (16.6)	28-3.5 (8.62)	a) 816 (370) b) 1,367 (620) c) 529 (240)	a) 5.49 (26.8) b) 7.64 (37.3)	a) 2.3 (0.7) b) 49 (56) 90	a) 39.5 b) 59 (68) 110	a) 38 (43.5) 70 b) 119 (137) 220		Conventional T-tail.
Janus C (G)	a) 2 b) Glassfibre and carbonfibre	a) FX 67-K-170/150 b) 20	a) 65-7.5 (20) b) 186.2 (17.3)	28-3.5 (8.62)	a) 805 (365) b) 1,543 (700) c) 529 (240)	a) 5.2 (25.4) b) 8.3 (40.5)	a) 1.97 (0.6) b) 49 (56) 90	a) 43 b) 59 (68) 110	a) 35 (40.5) 65 b) 135 (155) 250		Built since 1979 and production continues.
Janus Ce (G)	a) 2 b) Glassfibre and carbonfibre	a) FX 67-K-170/150 b) 20	a) 65-7.5 (20) b) 186.2 (17.3)	28-3.5 (8.62)		a) 5.2 (25.4) b) 8.3 (40.5)	a) 1.97 (0.6) b) 49 (56) 90	a) 43 b) 59 (68) 110	a) 35 (40.5) 65 b) 135 (155) 250		Ce has larger rudder and airbrakes, and retractable main wheel.

Schempp-Hirth Discus bT (J. Ewald) (page 521)

Schempp-Hirth Duo-Discus (J. Ewald) (page 521)

Designation	a) Crew b) Materials	a) Aerofoil b) Wing aspect ratio	a) Span ft-ins (m) b) Wing area sq ft (m²)	Length ft-ins (m)	Weights lb (kg): a) empty b) maximum c) ballast (max)	Wing loading lb/sq ft (kg/m²): a) minimum b) maximum	a) Minimum rate of sink ft (m)/sec b) at speed of kts (mph) km/h	a) Best glide ratio b) at speed of kts (mph) km/h	Speeds kts (mph) km/h: a) stalling b) maximum c) cruise	a) Engine b) Fuel capacity litres	Comments
Type: G: Glider MGS: Motorglider, self-launch MGN: Motorglider, no self-launch											
Germany											
Manufacturer: Schempp-Hirth Flugzeugbau GmbH (Continued)											
Janus CM (MGS)	a) 2 b) Glassfibre and carbonfibre	a) FX 67-K-170/150 b) 20	a) 65-7.5 (20) b) 186.2 (17.3)	28-3.5 (8.62)	a) 1,058 (480) b) 1,543 (700)	b) 8.3 (40.5)	a) 2.23 (0.68) b) 52 (60) 97	a) 43.5 b) 61 (70) 113	a) 39.5 (46) 73 b) 135 (155) 250	a) Mid-fuselage, retractable 59 hp (44 kW) Rotax 535A b) 44	Built since 1982.
Janus CT (MGN)	a) 2 b) Glassfibre and carbonfibre	a) FX 67-K-170/150 b) 20	a) 65-7.5 (20) b) 186.2 (17.3)	28-3.5 (8.62)	a) 981 (445) b) 1,543 (700) c) 529 (240)	a) 6.12 (29.9) b) 8.3 (40.5)	a) 2.23 (0.68) b) 52 (60) 97	a) 43.5 b) 61 (70) 113	a) 36 (41) 66 b) 135 (155) 250	a) Mid-fuselage, retractable 26 hp (19.4 kW) Solo 2350, driving a 5-blade folding propeller b) 18	17 built since 1983.
Nimbus 3D (G)	a) 2 b) Glassfibre and carbonfibre	a) Wortmann, Althaus, Holighaus b) 36	a) 80-8.5 (24.6) b) 181.4 (16.85)	28-3.5 (8.62)	a) 1,069 (485) b) 1,653 (750) c) 370 (168)	a) 6.76 (33) b) 9.11 (44.5)		a) 57	a) 37 (42.5) 68 b) 148 (171) 275		13 built from 1986-1993.
Nimbus 3DT (MGN)	a) 2 b) Glassfibre and carbonfibre	a) Wortmann, Althaus, Holighaus b) 36	a) 80-8.5 (24.6) b) 181.4 (16.85)	28-3.5 (8.62)	a) 1,168 (530) b) 1,764 (800) c) 370 (168)	a) 7.41 (36.2) b) 9.73 (47.5)		a) 57	a) 37 (42.5) 68 b) 148 (171) 275	a) Mid-fuselage, retractable 26 hp (19.4 kW) Solo 2350, driving a 5-blade folding propeller b) 18	25 built from 1986-1993.
Nimbus 4 (G)	a) 1 b) Glassfibre, carbonfibre and aramid	a) Wortmann, Althaus, Holighaus b) 39.1	a) 86-7.5 (26.4) b) 191.6 (17.8)	25-8 (7.82)	a) 1,058 (480) b) 1,653 (750) c) 714 (324)	a) 6.33 (30.9) b) 8.62 (42.1)	a) 1.57 (0.48) b) 46 (53) 86	a) 60 b) 59 (68) 110	a) 35 (40) 64 b) 154 (177) 285		6 built since 1990. Production continues.
Nimbus 4D (G) See Comments for Nimbus 4DT	a) 2 b) Glassfibre, carbonfibre and aramid	a) Wortmann, Althaus, Delft, Holighaus b) 39.1	a) 86-11 (26.5) b) 193.3 (17.96)	28-7 (8.72)	a) 1,157 (525) b) 1,653 (750) c) 362 (164)	a) 6.84 (33.4) b) 8.56 (41.8)		a) 60 approx			In production since 1994, alongside Nimbus 4DT (MGN) version with a mid-fuselage, retractable Solo engine.
Nimbus 4DM (MGS)	a) 2 b) Glassfibre, carbonfibre and aramid	a) Wortmann, Althaus, Delft, Holighaus b) 39.1	a) 86-11 (26.5) b) 193.3 (17.96)	28-7 (8.72)	a) 1,312 (595) b) 1,764 (800) c) 362 (164)	a) 7.64 (37.3) b) 9.11 (44.5)		a) 60 approx		a) Mid-fuselage 59 hp (44 kW) Rotax 535A driving a retractable propeller b) 44	In production since 1994.

Schempp-Hirth Janus C (J. Ewald) (page 521)

Schempp-Hirth Janus CM (P. F. Selinger) (page 522)

Designation	a) Crew b) Materials	a) Aerofoil b) Wing aspect ratio	a) Span ft-ins (m) b) Wing area sq ft (m²)	Length ft-ins (m)	Weights lb (kg): a) empty b) maximum c) ballast (max)	Wing loading lb/sq ft (kg/m²): a) minimum b) maximum	a) Minimum rate of sink ft (m)/sec b) at speed of kts (mph) km/h	a) Best glide ratio b) at speed of kts (mph) km/h	Speeds kts (mph) km/h: a) stalling b) maximum c) cruise	a) Engine b) Fuel capacity litres	Comments
Type: G: Glider **MGS:** Motorglider, self-launch **MGN:** Motorglider, no self-launch											
Germany											
Manufacturer: Schempp-Hirth Flugzeugbau GmbH (Continued)											
Nimbus 4M (MGS)	a) 1 b) Glassfibre, carbonfibre and aramid	a) Wortmann, Althaus, Holighaus b) 39.1	a) 86-7.5 (26.4) b) 191.6 (17.8)	25-8 (7.82)	a) 1,261 (572) b) 1,764 (800) c) 714 (324)	a) 7.43 (36.3) b) 9.2 (44.9)		a) 60 approx	a) 38 (44) 70 b) 154 (177) 285	a) Mid-fuselage, retractable 43 hp (32 kW) Rotax 505A	10 built since 1986. Production continues.
Nimbus 4T (MGN)	a) 1 b) Glassfibre, carbonfibre and aramid	a) Wortmann, Althaus, Holighaus b) 39.1	a) 86-7.5 (26.4) b) 191.6 (17.8)	25-8 (7.82)	a) 1,157 (525) b) 1,764 (800) c) 714 (324)	a) 6.9 (33.7) b) 9.2 (44.9)	a) 1.64 (0.5) b) 49 (56) 90	a) 60 approx b) 59 (68) 110	a) 36.5 (42) 67 b) 154 (177) 285	a) Mid-fuselage, retractable 27 hp (20 kW) Solo	10 built since 1990. Production continues.
Standard Cirrus (G)	a) 1 b) Glassfibre	a) FX S 02-196/FX 66-17AII-182 b) 22.5	a) 49-3 (15) b) 107.6 (10)	20-10 (6.35)	a) 463 (210) b) 728 (330) c) 132.3 (60)	a) 5.57 (27.2) b) 6.76 (33)	a) 2.13 (0.65) b) 40.5 (47) 75	a) 37 b) 51 (59) 95	a) 33.5 (39) 62 b) 119 (137) 220		About 700 Cirrus gliders of all versions built from 1969-1978, also by Grob, Lanaverre of France and developed by Jastreb in the former Yugoslavia under licence and sold since 1979.
Ventus a and b (G)	a) 1 b) Glassfibre and carbonfibre	a) Wortmann, Althaus, Holighaus b) 23.7	a) 49-3 (15) b) 102.4 (9.51)	Ventus a 20-10 (6.35) Ventus b 21-7 (6.58)	a) 485 (220) b) 948 (430) c) 370 (168)	a) 6.35 (31) b) 9.26 (45.2)	a) 2.17 (0.66) b) 49 (56) 90	a) 43.5 b) 63 (73) 117	a) 35 (40.5) 65 b) 135 (155) 250		323 Ventus gliders of all versions built from early 1980s to 1994. Ventus a has a narrow fuselage.
Ventus b/16.6 (G)	a) 1 b) Glassfibre and carbonfibre	a) Wortmann, Althaus, Holighaus b) 27.7	a) 54-5.5 (16.6) b) 107.2 (9.96)	21-7 (6.58)	a) 503 (228) b) 948 (430) c) 370 (168)	a) 6.25 (30.5) b) 8.85 (43.2)	a) 2.1 (0.64) b) 47 (53) 86	a) 46.5 b) 56 (64) 103	a) 32.5 (37.5) 60 b) 135 (155) 250		Removable wingtips, with Hänle airbrakes.
Ventus bT (MGN)	a) 1 b) Glassfibre and carbonfibre	a) Wortmann, Althaus, Holighaus b) 27.7	a) 54-5.5 (16.6) b) 107.2 (9.96)	21-7 (6.58)	a) 580 (263) b) 948 (430) c) 370 (168)	a) 6.94 (33.9) b) 8.85 (43.2)		a) 46.5	a) 33 (38) 61 b)135 (155) 250	a) Mid-fuselage, retractable Solo engine	179 built from 1983-1994 (all Ventus Turbo).
Ventus c (G)	a) 1 b) Glassfibre, carbonfibre and aramid	a) Wortmann, Althaus, Holighaus b) 30.2	a) 49-3 (15) standard. Can be fitted with wing extensions allowing for spans of 16.6 and 17.6 m b) 102.4 (9.51), or 107.2 (9.96) or 109.25 (10.15)	21-7 (6.58)	a) 538 (244) b) 1,102 (500) c) 370 (168)	b) 10.10 (49.3) with 17.6 m wings		a) 48	a) 31.5 (36) 58 b) 135 (155) 250		Built from 1986-1994. Removable wingtips made available. S-H airbrakes. 5 litre water ballast tank in the tailfin.

Schempp-Hirth Nimbus 3DT (P. F. Selinger) (page 522)

Schempp-Hirth Nimbus 4DT (J. Ewald) (page 522)

Designation	a) Crew b) Materials	a) Aerofoil b) Wing aspect ratio	a) Span ft-ins (m) b) Wing area sq ft (m²)	Length ft-ins (m)	Weights lb (kg): a) empty b) maximum c) ballast (max)	Wing loading lb/sq ft (kg/m²): a) minimum b) maximum	a) Minimum rate of sink ft (m)/sec b) at speed of kts (mph) km/h	a) Best glide ratio b) at speed of kts (mph) km/h	Speeds kts (mph) km/h: a) stalling b) maximum c) cruise	a) Engine b) Fuel capacity litres	Comments
Type: G: Glider MGS: Motorglider, self-launch MGN: Motorglider, no self-launch											
Germany											
Manufacturer: Schempp-Hirth Flugzeugbau GmbH (Continued)											
Ventus cM (MGS)	a) 1 b) Glassfibre, carbonfibre and aramid	a) Wortmann, Althaus, Holighaus b) 30.2	a) 57-9 (17.6) b) 109.25 (10.15)	21-7 (6.58)	a) 683 (310) b) 948 (430) c) 370 (168)	a) 7.76 (37.9) b) 8.68 (42.4)		a) 48	a) 35 (40) 64 b) 146 (168) 270	a) Mid-fuselage, retractable 27 hp (20 kW) Solo engine	109 built between 1988-1994.
Ventus cT (MGN)	a) 1 b) Glassfibre, carbonfibre and aramid	a) Wortmann, Althaus, Holighaus b) 30.2	a) 57-9 (17.6) b) 109.25 (10.15)	21-7 (6.58)	a) 637 (289) b) 948 (430) c) 370 (168)	a) 7.37 (36) b) 8.68 (42.4)		a) 48	a) 34 (39.5) 63 b) 146 (168) 270	a) Mid-fuselage, retractable 20.8 hp (15.5 kW) Solo engine	Built between 1987-1994.
Ventus 2a and 2b (G)	a) 1 b) Glassfibre, carbonfibre and aramid	a) Wortmann, Althaus, Delft, Holighaus b) 23.3	a) 49-3 (15) b) 104.4 (9.7)	20-10 (6.35) for Ventus 2a, 21-7 (6.58) for Ventus 2b	a) 496 (225) for Ventus 2a, 507 (230) for Ventus 2b b) 1,157 (525)	a) 6.43 (31.4) b) 11.08 (54.1)					In production since 1994. Ventus 2a has a narrow fuselage.
Ventus 2c (G) Ventus 2c motorgliders See Comments	a) 1 b) Glassfibre, carbonfibre and aramid	a) Wortmann, Althaus, Delft, Holighaus b) 29.4	a) 59-1 (18) or 49-3 (15); details for 18 m b) 118.4 (11)	22-6 (6.87)	a) 560 (254) b) 1,102 (500) c) 397 (180)	a) 5.2 (25.4) b) 9.31 (45.45)					First flight 1995.Ventus 2cT (MGN) and 2cM (MGS) have retractable engines. 2cMi abandoned. 2cT first flew 29 March 1995.

Schempp-Hirth Standard Cirrus (P. F. Selinger)
(page 523)

Schempp-Hirth Ventus 2c, first flown 29 March 1995
(page 524)

Schempp-Hirth Ventus cM (J. Ewald)
(page 524)

Schleicher ASH 25 (J. Ewald)
(page 525)

Designation	a) Crew b) Materials	a) Aerofoil b) Wing aspect ratio	a) Span ft-ins (m) b) Wing area sq ft (m2)	Length ft-ins (m)	Weights lb (kg): a) empty b) maximum c) ballast (max)	Wing loading lb/sq ft (kg/m2): a) minimum b) maximum	a) Minimum rate of sink ft (m)/sec b) at speed of kts (mph) km/h	a) Best glide ratio b) at speed of kts (mph) km/h	Speeds kts (mph) km/h: a) stalling b) maximum c) cruise	a) Engine b) Fuel capacity litres	Comments
Type: G: Glider **MGS:** Motorglider, self-launch **MGN:** Motorglider, no self-launch											
Germany											
Manufacturer: Alexander Schleicher Segelflugzeugbau GmbH & Co. Huhnrain 1, D-36163 Poppenhausen - (tel: +49 6658 890)											
ASH 25 (G)	a) 2 b) Glassfibre, carbonfibre and aramid	a) HQ 17-14.38, DU 84-132V3 b) 38.32, or 39.82 with wingtips	a) 82 (25) or 84 (25.6) with wingtips b) 175.6 (16.31) or 177.2 (16.46) with wingtips	29-6 (9)	a) 1,058 (480) or 1,067 (484) with wingtips b) 1,653 (750) c) 397 (180)	a) 6.9 (33.7) b) 9.42 (46) or 9.34 (45.6) with wingtips	a) 1.38 (0.42) b) 40.5 (47) 75	a) 58 or 60 with wingtips b) 51 (59) 95	a) 35 (40.5) 65 b) 151 (174) 280		108 built since 1986. Production continues.
ASH 25 E (MGN)	a) 2 b) Glassfibre, carbonfibre and aramid	a) HQ 17-14.38, DU 84-132V3 b) 38.32, or 39.82 with wingtips	a) 82 (25) or 84 (25.6) with wingtips b) 175.6 (16.31) or 177.2 (16.46) with wingtips	29-6 (9)	a) 1,168 (530) or 1,177 (534) with wingtips b) 1,653 (750) c) 309 (140)	a) 7.37 (36) b) 9.42 (46) or 9.34 (45.6) with wingtips	a) 1.44 (0.44) b) 42 (49) 78	a) 58 or 60 with wingtips b) 51 (59) 95	a) 37 (42.5) 68 b) 151 (174) 280	a) Mid-fuselage, retractable 24 hp (17.9 kW) Rotax 277	64 built from 1987-1994.
ASH 25 M (MGS)	a) 2 b) Glassfibre, carbonfibre and aramid	a) HQ 17-14.38, DU 84-132V3 b) 38.32, or 39.82 with wingtips	a) 82 (25) or 84 (25.6) with wingtips b) 175.6 (16.31) or 177.2 (16.46) with wingtips	29-6 (9)	a) 1,168 (530) or 1,177 (534) with wingtips b) 1,653 (750) c) 309 (140)	a) 7.37 (36) b) 9.42 (46) or 9.34 (45.6) with wingtips	a) 1.44 (0.44) b) 42 (49) 78	a) 58 or 60 with wingtips b) 51 (59) 95	a) 37 (42.5) 68 b) 151 (174) 280	a) Mid-fuselage 60 hp (44.7 kW) Mid-West rotary engine driving a retractable propeller	First built in 1994. Production continues.
ASH 26 (G)	a) 1 b) Glassfibre, carbonfibre and aramid	a) DU 89-134/14 b) 27.74	a) 59-1 (18) b) 125.7 (11.68)	23-1.5 (7.05)	a) 617 (280) b) 1,157 (525) c) 386 (175)	a) 6.14 (30) b) 9.22 (45)	a) 1.57 (0.48) b) 46 (53) 85	a) 50 approx b) 48 (55) 88	a) 33.5 (39) 62 b) 146 (168) 270		11 built since 1993. Production continues.
ASH 26 E (MGS)	a) 1 b) Glassfibre, carbonfibre and aramid	a) DU 89-134/14 b) 27.74	a) 59-1 (18) b) 125.7 (11.68)	23-1.5 (7.05)	a) 772 (350) b) 1,157 (525) c) 220 (100)	a) 7.54 (36.8) b) 9.22 (45)	a) 1.57 (0.48) b) 46 (53) 85	a) 50 approx b) 52 (60) 96	a) 37 (42.5) 68 b) 146 (168) 270	a) Mid-fuselage 50 hp (37.3 kW) Mid-West AE 50R rotary engine driving a retractable propeller	20 built since 1993. Production continues. Engine removable.
ASK 13 (G)	a) 2 b) Wood, steel tube and fabric	a) Gö 535/549 mix, Gö 541 b) 14.63	a) 52-6 (16) b) 188.4 (17.5)	26-10 (8.18)	a) 653 (296) b) 1,058 (480)	a) 4.44 (21.7) b) 5.61 (27.4)	a) 2.3 (0.7) b) 32.5 (38) 60	a) 27 b) 46 (53) 85	a) 31-33 (36-38) 57-61 b) 108 (124) 200		600 built from 1966 to 1980, plus 90 also produced by JUBI, Oerlinghausen after 1980.
ASK 21 (G)	a) 2 b) Glassfibre	a) FX S02-196, FX 60-126 b) 16.1	a) 55-9 (17) b) 193.2 (17.95)	27-5 (8.35)	a) 794 (360) b) 1,323 (600)	a) 4.92 (24) b) 6.84 (33.4)	a) 2.23 (0.68) b) 41 (47) 76	a) 34 b) 49 (56) 90	a) 35-40 (41-46) 65-74 b) 151 (174) 280		610 built since 1979. Production continues. Aerobatic (+6.5/-4g). Called the Vanguard in RAF Air Cadet use.

Schleicher ASH 25 BL (a binder powered motor glider version of ASH 25) (P. F. Selinger) (page 525)

Schleicher ASH 26 E (J. Ewald) (page 525)

Designation	a) Crew b) Materials	a) Aerofoil b) Wing aspect ratio	a) Span ft-ins (m) b) Wing area sq ft (m^2)	Length ft-ins (m)	Weights lb (kg): a) empty b) maximum c) ballast (max)	Wing loading lb/sq ft (kg/m^2): a) minimum b) maximum	a) Minimum rate of sink ft (m)/sec b) at speed of kts (mph) km/h	a) Best glide ratio b) at speed of kts (mph) km/h	Speeds kts (mph) km/h: a) stalling b) maximum c) cruise	a) Engine b) Fuel capacity litres	Comments
Type: G: Glider **MGS:** Motorglider, self-launch **MGN:** Motorglider, no self-launch											
Germany											
Manufacturer: Alexander Schleicher Segelflugzeugbau GmbH & Co (Continued)											
ASK 23 B (G)	a) 1 b) Glassfibre	a) FX 61-168, FX 60-126 b) 17.44	a) 49-3 (15) b) 138.9 (12.9)	23-1.5 (7.05)	a) 529 (240) b) 838 (380)	a) 4.92 (24) b) 6.03 (29.46)	a) 2.17 (0.66) b) 40 (46) 74	a) 34 b) 49 (56) 90	a) 35 (40) 64 b) 116 (134) 215		137 built since 1983 (ASK 23 and 23B). Production continues. Aerobatic (+5.3/-2.65g).
ASW 20 (G)	a) 1 b) Glassfibre	a) FX 62-K-131 mod, FX 60-126 b) 21.43	a) 49-3 (15) b) 113 (10.5)	22-4.5 (6.82)	a) 573 (260) b) 1,001 (454) c) 265 (120)	a) 6.55 (32) b) 8.81 (43)	a) 1.94 (0.59) b) 46 (52) 84	a) 42 b) 54 (62) 100	a) 37 (42.5) 68 b) 143 (165) 265		865 built from 1977 to 1990. Also built by Centrair in France in different versions.
ASW 20 L (G)	a) 1 b) Glassfibre	a) FX 62-K-131 mod, FX 60-126 b) 24.9	a) 54-5 (16.59) b) 118.9 (11.05)	22-4.5 (6.82)	a) 589 (267) b) 838 (380) c) None	a) 6.25 (30.5) b) 7.05 (34.4)	a) 1.8 (0.55) b) 43 (50) 80	a) 45.5 b) 49 (56) 90	a) 35 (40) 64 b) 135 (155) 250		As above.
ASW 22 B (G)	a) 1 b) Glassfibre, carbonfibre and aramid	a) HQ 17-14.38, DU 84-132V3 b) 38.32	a) 82 (25) b) 175.6 (16.31)	26-7 (8.1)	a) 1,003 (455) b) 1,653 (750) c) 485 (220)	a) 6.6 (32.2) b) 9.42 (46)	a) 1.31 (0.4) without ballast b) 40.5 (47) 75	a) 60 without ballast b) 62 (71) 115	a) 36 (41) 66 b) 151 (174) 280		42 built since 1981, including BLs detailed next. Production continues.
ASW 22 BL (G)	a) 1 b) Glassfibre, carbonfibre and aramid	a) HQ 17-14.38, DU 84-132V3 b) 41.81	a) 86-7.5 (26.4) b) 179.4 (16.67)	26-7 (8.1)	a) 990 (449) b) 1,653 (750)	a) 6.49 (31.7) b) 9.22 (45)	a) 1.31 (0.4) b) 40.5 (47) 75	a) about 60 b) 62 (71) 115	a) 36 (41) 66 b) 151 (174) 280		As above but with wingtips.
ASW 22 BE (MGS)	a) 1 b) Glassfibre, carbonfibre and aramid	a) HQ 17-14.38, DU 84-132V3 b) 38.32	a) 82 (25) b) 175.6 (16.31)	26-7 (8.1)	a) 1,202 (545) b) 1,786 (810)	a) 7.72 (37.7) b) 10.18 (49.7)	a) 1.41 (0.43) b) 43 (50) 80	a) 60 b) 62 (71) 115	a) 37 (42.5) 68 b) 151 (174) 280 c) 70 (81) 130	a) Mid-fuselage, retractable 49 hp (36.5 kW) Rotax 505A	25 built from 1986 to 1994, including BLE detailed next.
ASW 22 BLE (MGS)	a) 1 b) Glassfibre, carbonfibre and aramid	a) HQ 17-14.38, DU 84-132V3 b) 41.81	a) 86-7.5 (26.4) b) 179.4 (16.67)	26-7 (8.1)	a) 1,210 (549) b) 1,786 (810)	a) 7.6 (37.1) b) 9.95 (48.6)	a) 1.41 (0.43) b) 43 (50) 80	a) about 60 b) 62 (71) 115	a) 37 (42.5) 68 b) 151 (174) 280 c) 70 (81) 130	a) Mid-fuselage, retractable 49 hp (36.5 kW) Rotax 505A	Version of ASW 22 BE with wingtips.
ASW 24 (G)	a) 1 b) Glassfibre, carbonfibre and aramid	a) DU 84-158 b) 22.5	a) 49-3 (15) b) 107.6 (10)	21-6 (6.55)	a) 507 (230) b) 1,102 (500) c) 342 (155)	a) 6.14 (30) b) 10.24 (50)	a) 1.9 (0.58) b) 46.5 (53) 86	a) 43.5 b) 70 (81) 130	a) 38 (44) 70 b) 151 (174) 280		223 built since 1987. Production continues. ASW 24 B version has winglets. Aerobatic (+5.3/-2.65g).

Schleicher ASK 23 B (J. Ewald)
(page 526)

Schleicher ASW 20 (P. F. Selinger)
(page 526)

Designation	a) Crew b) Materials	a) Aerofoil b) Wing aspect ratio	a) Span ft-ins (m) b) Wing area sq ft (m²)	Length ft-ins (m)	Weights lb (kg): a) empty b) maximum c) ballast (max)	Wing loading lb/sq ft (kg/m²): a) minimum b) maximum	a) Minimum rate of sink ft (m)/sec b) at speed of kts (mph) km/h	a) Best glide ratio b) at speed of kts (mph) km/h	Speeds kts (mph) km/h: a) stalling b) maximum c) cruise	a) Engine b) Fuel capacity litres	Comments
Type: G: Glider **MGS:** Motorglider, self-launch **MGN:** Motorglider, no self-launch											
Germany											
Manufacturer: Alexander Schleicher Segelflugzeugbau GmbH & Co (Continued)											
ASW 24 E (MGS)	a) 1 b) Glassfibre, carbonfibre and aramid	a) DU 84-158 b) 22.5	a) 49-3 (15) b) 107.6 (10)	21-6 (6.55)	a) 606 (275) b) 1,102 (500) 1,014 (460) max for self-launch c) 342 (155)	a) 7.05 (34.4) b) 10.24 (50)	a) 1.9 (0.58) b) 46.5 (53) 86	a) 43.5 b) 70 (81) 130	a) 40.5 (47) 75 b) 151 (174) 280	a) Mid-fuselage, retractable 24 hp (17.9 kW) Rotax 275	54 built from 1988-1993. Aerobatic (+5.3/-2.65g).
ASW 24 TOP (MGS)	a) 1 b) Glassfibre, carbonfibre and aramid	a) DU 84-158 b) 22.5	a) 49-3 (15) b) 107.6 (10)	21-6 (6.55)	a) 606 (275) b) 1,102 (500) c) 342 (155)	a) 7.05 (34.4) b) 10.24 (50)			a) 40.5 (47) 75 b) 151 (174) 280	a) Mid-fuselage Fischer pod with König engine driving a folding propeller	8 modified by Fischer & Entwicklungen of Germany. Production continues.
ASW 27 (G)	b) Glassfibre, carbonfibre, aramid and polyethylene	a) DU 89-134/14, DU 92-131/14 mod b) 25	a) 49-3 (15) b) 96.9 (9)	21-6 (6.55)	a) 496 (225) b) 1,102 (500) c) 397 (180)	a) 6.72 (32.8) b) 11.38 (55.56)	a) 1.71 (0.52)	a) 48 b) 54 (62) 100	a) 38 (44) 70 b) 151 (174) 280		First flight 3 April 1995.
Manufacturer: Stemme GmbH & Co KG. Flugplatz Strausberg, D-15344 Strausberg - (tel: +49 3341 311170)											
S10 (MGS)	a) 2 b) Composites	a) HQ 41/14.35 b) 28.2	a) 75-5.5 (23) b) 201.3 (18.7)	27-7.5 (8.42)	a) 1,411 (640) b) 1,874 (850)	a) 7.84 (38.3) b) 9.28 (45.3)	a) 1.8 (0.55) b) 46 (53) 85	a) 50 b) 57 (65) 105	a) 38 (44) 70 b) 146 (168) 270 c) 89 (103) 165 or 121 (140) 225 with variable-pitch propeller	a) Mid-fuselage 93 hp (69.4 kW) Limbach L 2400 ED1D driving a front folding propeller b) 90 or 120 optional	62 built since 1986. Production continues.
S10 VC (MGS)	a) 2 b) Composites	a) HQ 41/14.35 b) 28.2	a) 75-5.5 (23) b) 201.3 (18.7)	27-7.5 (8.42)	a) 1,477 (670) b) 2,161 (980)	a) 8.32 (40.6) b) 10.73 (52.4)	a) 1.97 (0.6) b) 48 (55) 88	a) 50 b) 59 (68) 109	a) 40.5 (47) 75 b) 146 (168) 270 c) 89 (103) 165 or 121 (140) 225 with variable-pitch propeller	a) Mid-fuselage 93 hp (69.4 kW) Limbach L 2400 ED1D driving a front folding propeller b) 120	3 built since 1990. Production continues. Version of S10 as a multi-purpose sensor platform, with underwing pods provided by Gepard Sensor Technologies of Switzerland housing TV, FLIR and other possible payloads (also known as S10 gsm).

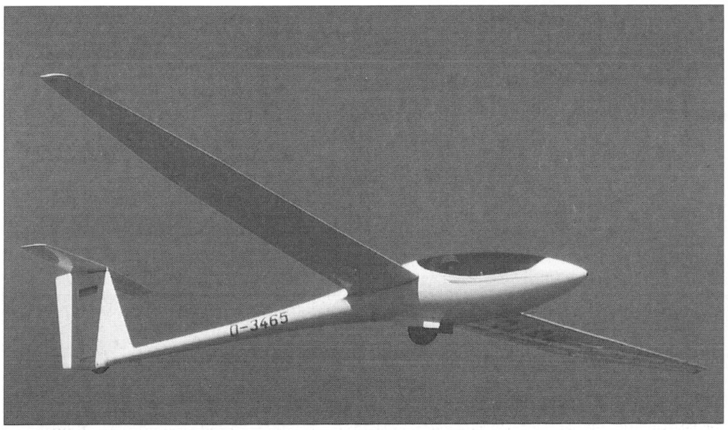

Schleicher ASW 24 (J. Ewald) (page 526)

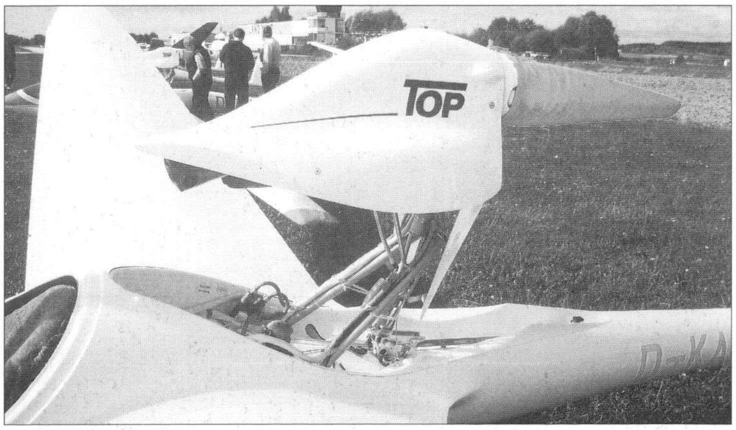

Schleicher ASW 24 TOP (P. F. Selinger) (page 527)

Designation	a) Crew b) Materials	a) Aerofoil b) Wing aspect ratio	a) Span ft-ins (m) b) Wing area sq ft (m^2)	Length ft-ins (m)	Weights lb (kg): a) empty b) maximum c) ballast (max)	Wing loading lb/sq ft (kg/m^2): a) minimum b) maximum	a) Minimum rate of sink ft (m)/sec b) at speed of kts (mph) km/h	a) Best glide ratio b) at speed of kts (mph) km/h	Speeds kts (mph) km/h: a) stalling b) maximum c) cruise	a) Engine b) Fuel capacity litres	Comments
Type: G: Glider **MGS:** Motorglider, self-launch **MGN:** Motorglider, no self-launch											
Germany											
Manufacturer: Technoflug GmbH. Dr-Kurt-Steim-Strasse 6, D-78713 Schramberg-Sulgen - (tel: +49 7422 8423)											
Piccolo b (MGS)	a) 1 b) Glassfibre	a) FX 63-137 b) 16.6	a) 43-7.5 (13.3) b) 114.1 (10.6)	20-7 (6.28)	a) 397 (180) b) 655 (297)	b) 5.73 (28)	a) 2.95 (0.9)	a) 23 b) 42 (48) 78	a) 29.5 (34) 54 b) 92 (106) 170 c) 65-73 (75-84) 120-135	a) 23 hp (17.15 kW) Solo 2350 BS behind wing with folding 3-blade pusher propeller b) 22.5	About 100 built since 1986 as the production version of the Neukom AN 20K. Fulfils JAR motorglider and microlight specifications. Strut-braced wings.
Manufacturer: TWI Flugzeuggesellschaft mbH. (No longer operating)											
Taifun 17 E II (MGS)	a) 2 b) Glassfibre	a) FX 67-K-170/17 b) 16.4	a) 55-9 (17) b) 189.4 (17.6)	25-6 (7.78)	a) 1,345 (610) b) 1,874 (850)	b) 9.89 (48.3)	a) 3.12 (0.95) b) 46 (53) 85	a) 30 b) 62 (71) 115	a) 39 (45) 72 b) 135 (155) 250	a) Front-mounted 90 hp (67 kW) Limbach L 2400 EB1B b) 90	Ex-Valentin type. Produced by FFT. Side-by-side seating.
Kiwi (G or MGS)	a) 1 b) Composites	a) FX 61-163/FX 60-126 b) 20.4	a) 49-3 (15) b) 118.7 (11.03)	22-4 (6.8)	a) 452 (205) as glider b) 838 (380) as MGS	b) 7.07 (34.5) as MGS	a) 1.9 (0.58) as glider	a) 37 as glider	a) 33.5 (39) 62 b) 132 (152) 245	a) Mid-fuselage, retractable 24 hp (17.9 kW) König SC 430 on a Fischer & Entwicklungen TOP system	Ex-Valentin type. Glider or motorglider with TOP system. Produced by FFT.

Schleicher ASW 27 (P. F. Selinger)
(page 527)

Stemme S10 VC
(page 527)

Technoflug Piccolo b (P. F. Selinger)
(page 528)

Lithuanian Factory of Aviation LAK 12 (J. Ewald)
(page 529)

Designation	a) Crew b) Materials	a) Aerofoil b) Wing aspect ratio	a) Span ft-ins (m) b) Wing area sq ft (m^2)	Length ft-ins (m)	Weights lb (kg): a) empty b) maximum c) ballast (max)	Wing loading lb/sq ft (kg/m^2): a) minimum b) maximum	a) Minimum rate of sink ft (m)/sec b) at speed of kts (mph) km/h	a) Best glide ratio b) at speed of kts (mph) km/h	Speeds kts (mph) km/h: a) stalling b) maximum c) cruise	a) Engine b) Fuel capacity litres	Comments
Type: G: Glider **MGS:** Motorglider, self-launch **MGN:** Motorglider, no self-launch											
Hungary											
Manufacturer: Autó-Aeró Közlekedéstechnikai Vállalat, Szombathely, Zanati ut.4											
Góbé R-26SU (G)	a) 2 b) Metal and fabric	a) Göttingen 549 mod b) 10.9	a) 45-11 (14) b) 193.75 (18)	29-6 (9)	a) 529 (240) b) 970 (440)	b) 5 (24.4)	a) 3.18 (0.97) b) 40.5 (47) 75	a) 23.2 b) 43.5 (50) 80	a) 33.5 (39) 62 b) 103 (118) 190		Large number built.
India											
Manufacturer: Technical Centre, Civil Aviation Department. Nr Safdarjung Airport, New Delhi 110003 - (tel: +91 133 611504)											
ATS-1 Ardhra (G)	a) 2 b) Wood and fabric	a) FX 61-184 b) 12.46	a) 54-1.5 (16.5) b) 235 (21.83)	28-3 (8.61)	a) 723 (328) b) 1,120 (508)	b) 4.77 (23.28)	a) 2.53 (0.77) b) 39 (45) 72	a) 28 b) 49 (56) 90	a) 33 (38) 61 b) 113 (130) 210		Most built by HAL. Production completed.
Lithuania											
Manufacturer: Lithuanian Factory of Aviation (LAK). Pociūnai, 4340 Prienai - (tel: +7 370 49 51575)											
LAK 12 (G)	a) 1 b) Glassfibre	a) FX 67-K-170/150 b) 28.5	a) 67 (20.42) b) 157.5 (14.63)	23-9 (7.23)	a) 794 (360) b) 1,433 (650) c) 419 (190)	a) 6.14 (30) b) 9.1 (44.43)	a) 1.57 (0.48) b) 40.5 (47) 75	a) 48 b) 62 (71) 115	a) 35 (41) 65 b) 135 (155) 250		Built since 1979. Production continues.
LAK 17 Nida (G)	a) 1 b) Glassfibre and carbonfibre	a) VAG/KTU 92-130 (150)/15 b) 24.83	a) 49-3 (15) b) 97.52 (9.06)	21-1 (6.42)	a) 461 (209) b) 899 (408) c) 163 litres	a) 6.14 (30) b) 9.22 (45)	a) 1.74 (0.53) b) 43.5 (50) 80	a) 45 b) 62 (71) 115	a) 38 (44) 70 b) 135 (155) 250		Built since 1992. Production continues.
Netherlands											
Manufacturer: HB Aviation International. Maraboeweg 8, NL-8218 AH Lelystad Airport - (tel: +31 3200 88030)											
HB 23/2400 Hobbyliner/ Scanliner (MGS)	a) 2 b) Wood, steel and composites	a) FX 61-184, FX 60-126 b) 14	a) 53-10 (16.41) b) 205.3 (19.07)	24-1.5 (7.35)	a) 1,168 or 1,213 (530 or 550) b) 1,676 (760)	b) 8.16 (39.85)	a) 4.59 (1.4) b) 60 (69) 111	a) 18 b) 63 (72) 116	a) 40.5 (47) 75 b) 108 (124) 200 c) 93 (107) 172	a) Mid-fuselage 110 hp (82 kW) VW-HB-2400 b) 100 Note. Aero-towing versions are available.	About 60 built. Production continues. Aerobatic +5/-3g at 1,653 lb (750 kg) take-off weight. Scanliner is an observation aircraft with a full glass cockpit. Built in Austria.
Norway											
Manufacturer: Lunds Tekniske. PO Box 463, 8601 Mo - (tel: +47 75 152100)											
Silhouette (MGS)	a) 1 b) Composites	b) 13.46 or 18.69 with wing extensions	a) 41 (12.5) with wing extensions b) 90 (8.36) with wing extensions	19-3 (5.87)	a) 578 (262) without wing extensions b) 825 (374)	b) 9.16 (44.74) with wing extensions			a) 45.5 (52.5) 84 b) 121 (140) 225 c) 104 (120) 193	a) Front-mounted 40 hp (29.8 kW) Rotax 447 or 50 hp (37.3 kW) Rotax 503	Homebuilt light aircraft with standard wings, or a homebuilt motorglider with wing extensions.

Lithuanian Factory of Aviation LAK 17 Nida (P. F. Selinger) *(page 529)*

HB Aviation HB 23/2400 Hobbyliner *(page 529)*

Designation	a) Crew b) Materials	a) Aerofoil b) Wing aspect ratio	a) Span ft-ins (m) b) Wing area sq ft (m2)	Length ft-ins (m)	Weights lb (kg): a) empty b) maximum c) ballast (max)	Wing loading lb/sq ft (kg/m2): a) minimum b) maximum	a) Minimum rate of sink ft (m)/sec b) at speed of kts (mph) km/h	a) Best glide ratio b) at speed of kts (mph) km/h	Speeds kts (mph) km/h: a) stalling b) maximum c) cruise	a) Engine b) Fuel capacity litres	Comments
Type: G: Glider **MGS:** Motorglider, self-launch **MGN:** Motorglider, no self-launch											
Poland											
Manufacturer: DWL KK Ltd. Warsaw (marketed in the USA by Solaire North America Ltd. 41 Cottonwood Lane, Hilton Head Island, SC 29926)											
PW-2D Gapa D (G)	a) 1 b) Glassfibre and fabric	b) 9.5	a) 36-1 (11) b) 136.7 (12.7)	18-1 (5.5)	a) 243 (110) b) 485 (220)	b) 3.55 (17.32)	a) 3.6 (1.1) b) 28 (33) 52	a) 16 b) 38 (43) 70	b) 81 (93) 150		Certified to JAR 22 Utility category. G limits +5.3/ -2.65.
Manufacturer: MDM-Company, ul. Bachu 30m908, PL-02-743 Warsaw - (tel: +48 30 201 10)											
MDM-1 Fox (G)	a) 2 b) Composites	a) NACA 64.412 b) 15.88	a) 45-11 (14) b) 132.7 (12.33)	22-8 (6.91)	a) 739 (335) b) 1,168 (530)	b) 8.81 (43)					Fully aero-batic: +7.5/ -5.5g with two crew, or +10/-7.5g with pilot only.
Manufacturer: Politechnika Warszawska - Warsaw University of Technology, Institute of Aeronautics and Applied Mechanics.ul. Nowowiejska 22/24, PL-00-665 Warsaw - (tel: +48 2 6285748)											
PW-4 Pelikan (MGS)	a) 2 b) Glassfibre and fabric	b) 13.95	a) 53-2 (16.2) b) 202.4 (18.8)	26-3 (8)	a) 1,102 (500) b) 1,587 (720)	b) 7.84 (38.3)	a) 3.94 (1.2) b) 46.5 (53) 86	a) 20 b) 51 (59) 95	a) 38 (44) 70	a) Mid-fuselage 80 hp (59.7 kW) Limbach L 2000 EC1 driving a pusher propeller b) 40	Prototype first flew in December 1990.
Manufacturer: PDPS PZL-Bielsko. ul. Cieszynska 325, PL-43-300 Bielsko-Biala - (tel: +48 30 25021)											
SZD-48-3 Jantar Standard 3 (G)	a) 1 b) Glassfibre	a) NN-8 b) 21.1	a) 49-3 (15) b) 114.7 (10.66)	22-6 (6.85)	a) 573 (260) b) 1,190 (540) c) 331 (150)	a) 6.27 (30.6) b) 10.37 (50.65)	a) 1.97 (0.6) b) 40.5 (47) 75	a) 40 b) 51 (59) 95	a) 38 (44) 70 b) 154 (177) 285		345 built since 1983. Production continues. Semi aerobatic (+5.3/-2.65g).

HB Aviation HB 23/2400 Scanliner (page 529)

MDM-Company MDM-1 Fox (J. Ewald) (page 530)

Politechnika Warszawska PW-4 Pelikan (Wojciech Fraczek) (page 530)

PDPS PZL-Bielsko SZD-48-3 Jantar Standard 3 (P. F. Selinger) (page 530)

Designation	a) Crew b) Materials	a) Aerofoil b) Wing aspect ratio	a) Span ft-ins (m) b) Wing area sq ft (m^2)	Length ft-ins (m)	Weights lb (kg): a) empty b) maximum c) ballast (max)	Wing loading lb/sq ft (kg/m^2): a) minimum b) maximum	a) Minimum rate of sink ft (m)/sec b) at speed of kts (mph) km/h	a) Best glide ratio b) at speed of kts (mph) km/h	Speeds kts (mph) km/h: a) stalling b) maximum c) cruise	a) Engine b) Fuel capacity litres	Comments
Type: G: Glider MGS: Motorglider, self-launch MGN: Motorglider, no self-launch											
Poland											
Manufacturer: PDPS PZL-Bielsko (Continued)											
SZD-50-3 Puchacz (G)	a) 2 b) Glassfibre	a) FX 61-168/60-1261 b) 15.3	a) 54-8 (16.67) b) 195.5 (18.16)	27-6 (8.38)	a) 74 (360) b) 1,257 (570)	a) 5.02 (24.5) b) 6.43 (31.4)	a) 2.3 (0.7) b) 40.5 (47) 75	a) 30 b) 46 (53) 85	a) 32.5 (37.5) 60 b) 116 (134) 215		286 built since 1979. Production continues. Semi aerobatic (+5.3/-2.65g).
SZD-51-1 Junior (G)	a) 1 b) Glassfibre	a) FX S02-196/SO2/1-158 b) 18	a) 49-3 (15) b) 134.7 (12.51)	21-11.5 (6.69)	a) 496 (225) b) 838 (380)	a) 4.18 (20.4) b) 6.23 (30.4)	a) 1.77 (0.54)	a) 35 b) 38 (43.5) 70	a) 32.5 (37.5) 60 b) 119 (137) 220		193 built since 1979. Production continues. Semi aerobatic (+5.3/-2.65g).
SZD-54 Perkoz (G)	a) 2 b) Glassfibre	a) NN-8 b) 18.7	a) 57-5 (17.5) b) 176.1 (16.36)	26-3 (8)	a) 805 (365) b) 1,290 (585)	b) 7.32 (35.76)	a) 2.2 (0.67)	a) 35	a) 32.5 (37.5) 60 b) 146 (168) 270		Prototype first flew in 1991.
SZD-55-1 (G)	a) 1 b) Glassfibre	a) NN-27 b) 23.44	a) 49-3 (15) b) 103.33 (9.6)	22-6 (6.85)	a) 474 (215) b) 1,102 (500) c) 430 (195)	a) 5.84 (28.5) b) 10.67 (52.1)	a) 1.77 (0.54) b) 43 (49) 79.5	a) 44 b) 64 (74) 119	a) 36 (41) 66 b) 138 (158) 255		63 built since 1988. Production continues. Semi aerobatic (+5.3/-2.65g).

PDPS PZL-Bielsko SZD-50-3 Puchacz (P. F. Selinger) *(page 531)*

PDPS PZL-Bielsko SZD-51-1 Junior (J. Ewald) *(page 531)*

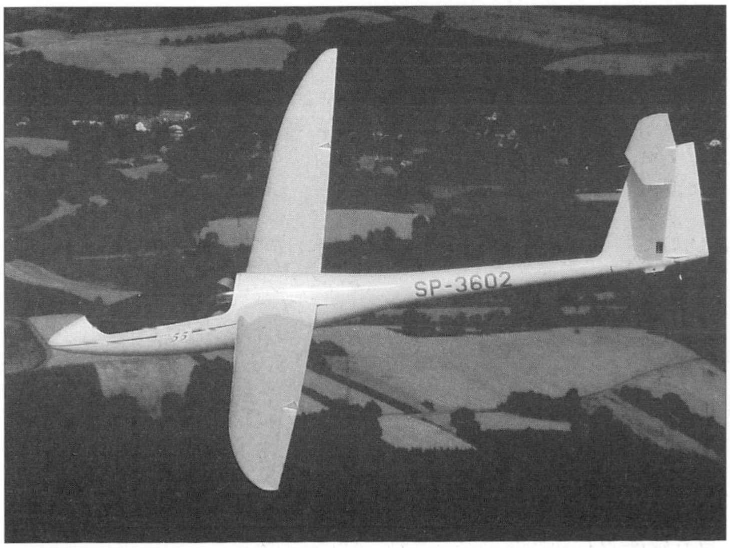

PDPS PZL-Bielsko SZD-55-1 (J. Ewald) *(page 531)*

PDPS PZL-Bielsko SZD-56 Diana *(page 532)*

Designation	a) Crew b) Materials	a) Aerofoil b) Wing aspect ratio	a) Span ft-ins (m) b) Wing area sq ft (m²)	Length ft-ins (m)	Weights lb (kg): a) empty b) maximum c) ballast (max)	Wing loading lb/sq ft (kg/m²): a) minimum b) maximum	a) Minimum rate of sink ft (m)/sec b) at speed of kts (mph) km/h	a) Best glide ratio b) at speed of kts (mph) km/h	Speeds kts (mph) km/h: a) stalling b) maximum c) cruise	a) Engine b) Fuel capacity litres	Comments
Type: G: Glider MGS: Motorglider, self-launch MGN: Motorglider, no self-launch											
Poland											
Manufacturer: PDPS PZL-Bielsko (Continued)											
SZD-56 Diana (G)	a) 1 b) Carbonfibre and aramid	a) NN-27-13 b) 27.57	a) 49-3 (15) b) 87.83 (8.16)	22-7 (6.88)	a) 386 (175) b) 904 (410) c) 353 (160)	a) 5.84 (28.5) b) 10.24 (50)	a) 1.61 (0.49) b) 39 (45) 72	a) 48.5 b) 60 (70) 112	a) 34 (39.5) 63 b) 140 (162) 260		2 built since 1990. Production continues.
SZD-59 Acro (G)	a) 1 b) Glassfibre	a) NN-8 b) 17.8, or 21.1 with wing extensions	a) 43-4 (13.2), or 49-3 (15) with wing extensions b) 105.5 (9.8) or 114.7 (10.66) with wing extensions	22-6 (6.85)	a) 584 (265), or 595 (270) with wing extensions b) 838 (380) or 1,190 (540) with wing extensions c) 331 (150) with wing extensions	a) 7 (34.2) or 6.35 (31) with wing extensions b) 7.95 (38.8) or 10.38 (50.7) with wing extensions	a) 2.3 (0.7) or 2.53 (0.77) with wing extensions b) 46 (53) 85 or 52 (60) 97 with wing extensions	a) 36 or 40 with wing extensions b) 57 (66) 106 or 67 (77) 124 with wing extensions	a) 40 (46) 74 or 44.5 (51) 82 with wing extensions b) 151 (174) 280 or 154 (177) 285 with wing extensions		2 built since 1991. Production continues. Fully aerobatic (+7/-5g).
Manufacturer: PZL-Swidnik S.A., Polish Aviation Works. Al. Lotnikóv Polskich 1, PL-21-045 Swidnik - (tel: +48 81 13249)											
PW-5 Smyk (G)	a) 1 b) Glassfibre	a) NN 18-17 b) 17.8	a) 44-1 (13.44) b) 109.4 (10.16)	20-4 (6.2)	a) 366 (166) b) 617 (280)	b) 5.63 (27.5)	a) 2.1 (0.64) b) 39.5 (45) 73	a) 32.5 b) 43 (50) 80	a) 33.5 (39) 62 b) 119 (137) 220		In production since 1992. Prototype built by Politechnika Warszawska.
Manufacturer: WSK PZL-Krosno. ul. Zwirki i Wiguri 6, PL-38-400 Krosno - (tel: +48 131 22911)											
KR-03A Puchatek (G)	a) 2 b) Aluminium alloy and fabric	a) FX S02/1-158 b) 13.7	a) 53-10 (16.4) b) 209.25 (19.44)	28-4 (8.63)	a) 739-772 (335-350) b) 1,190 (540)	a) 4.38 (21.39) b) 5.69 (27.77)	a) 2.56 (0.78) b) 41 (47) 75	a) 27 b) 46 (53) 85	a) 32 (37) 59 b) 108 (124) 200		About 51 built since 1986. Production continues. Semi aerobatic (+5.3/-2.65g).

PDPS PZL-Bielsko SZD-59 Acro (page 532)

WSK PZL-Krosno KR-03A Puchatek (page 532)

PZL-Swidnik PW-5 Smyk (Krysztof Janusz) (page 532)

Swift-S1 (J. Ewald) (page 533)

Designation	**a) Crew** **b) Materials**	**a) Aerofoil** **b) Wing aspect ratio**	**a) Span** ft-ins (m) **b) Wing area** sq ft (m^2)	**Length** ft-ins (m)	**Weights** lb (kg): **a) empty** **b) maximum** **c) ballast** (max)	**Wing loading** lb/sq ft (kg/m^2): **a) minimum** **b) maximum**	**a) Minimum rate of sink** ft (m)/sec **b) at speed of** kts (mph) km/h	**a) Best glide ratio** **b) at speed of** kts (mph) km/h	**Speeds** kts (mph) km/h: **a) stalling** **b) maximum** **c) cruise**	**a) Engine** **b) Fuel capacity** litres	**Comments**
Type: G: Glider **MGS:** Motorglider, self-launch **MGN:** Motorglider, no self-launch											
Poland											
Manufacturer: Swift - (sales and information from: Güntert + Kohlmetz GmbH. Bruchsaler Strasse 52, D-76646 Bruchsal, Germany) - (tel: +49 7257 1071)											
Swift-S1 (G)	a) 1 b) Glassfibre	a)NACA 64_1412 b) 13.8	a) 41-7 (12.68) b) 126.3 (11.73)	22-8 (6.91)	a) 639 (290) b) 904 (410)	a) 6.02 (29.4) b) 7.15 (34.9)	a) 3.12 (0.95) b) 46.5 (53) 86	a) 28 b) 68 (78) 126	a) 39 (45) 72 b) 155 (178) 287		25 built. Production continues. Fully aerobatic (+10/-7.5g)
Romania											
Manufacturer: IAR SA. 1 Aeroportului Street, PO Box 198, 2200 Brasov - (tel: +40 68 150015)											
IAR-35 (G)	a) 1 b) Aluminium alloy	a) NACA 642-015 b) 13.3	a) 39-4 (12) b) 116.25 (10.8)	21-4 (6.5)	a) 573 (260) b) 838 (380)	b) 7.21 (35.2)	a) 3.94 (1.2) b) 51 (59) 95	a) 27 b) 54 (62) 100	a) 46 (53) 85 b) 205 (236) 380		Built since 1989. Production continues. Fully aerobatic (+7.4/-7g).
IS-28B2 (G)	a) 2 b) Aluminium alloy	a) FX 61-163 and FX 60-126 b) 15.84	a) 55-9 (17) b) 196.33 (18.24)	27-9 (8.45)	a) 882 (400) b) 1,300 (590)	b) 6-63 (32-3)	a) 2.56 (0.78) b) 46 (53) 85	a) 34 b) 54 (62) 100	a) 38 (44) 70 b) 124 (143) 230		In production. +6.5/-4g single seat aerobatic.
IS-28 M2A and IS-28 M2RS (MGS)	a) 2 b) Aluminium alloy and glassfibre	a) FX 61-163/-126 b) 15.84	a) 55-9.5 (17) b) 196.33 (18.24)	22-11.5 (7)	a) 1,235 (560) b) 1,676 (760) for M2A	b) 8.54 (41.7) for M2A	a) 3.94 (1.2) b) 43 (50) 80 for M2A	a) 27 b) 54 (62) 100 for M2A	a) 36 (41) 66 b) 100 (115) 185 c) 92 (106) 170 for M2A	a) Front-mounted 80 hp (59.7 kW) Limbach L 2000 EO1. New Rotax powered version is IS-28 M2RS b) 40-60	Production continues. Semi aerobatic (+5.3/-2.65g).

IAR IAR-35 (P. F. Selinger)
(page 533)

IAR IS-28 M2 80 HP variant of IS-28M2A (J. Ewald)
(page 533)

Aviatika 920
(page 534)

Celair Ltd Celstar CG-1 (J. Ewald)
(page 534)

Designation	a) Crew b) Materials	a) Aerofoil b) Wing aspect ratio	a) Span ft-ins (m) b) Wing area sq ft (m²)	Length ft-ins (m)	Weights lb (kg): a) empty b) maximum c) ballast (max)	Wing loading lb/sq ft (kg/m²): a) minimum b) maximum	a) Minimum rate of sink ft (m)/sec b) at speed of kts (mph) km/h	a) Best glide ratio b) at speed of kts (mph) km/h	Speeds kts (mph) km/h: a) stalling b) maximum c) cruise	a) Engine b) Fuel capacity litres	Comments
Type: G: Glider **MGS:** Motorglider, self-launch **MGN:** Motorglider, no self-launch											
Romania											
Manufacturer: IAR SA. (Continued)											
IS-29D2 (G)	a) 1 b) Aluminium alloy	a) FX 61-163 and FX 60-126 b) 21.84	a) 49-3 (15) b) 110.9 (10.3)	24 (7.3)	a) 529 (240) b) 794 (360)	b) 7.15 (34.9)	a) 1.9 (0.58) b) 42 (48) 78	a) 37 b) 50 (58) 93	a) 41 (47) 75 b) 121 (140) 225		In production.
Russia											
Manufacturer: Aviatika JSC. 33a Leningradsky prospect, Moscow 125284 - (tel: +7 095 5654)											
Aviatika 920 (G)	a) 1 b) Metal, fabric and glassfibre	a) 1-14 b) 9.96	a) 32-10 (10) b) 108.07 (10.04)	17-5 (5.3)	a) 227 (103) b) 441 (200)	b) 4.08 (19.9)	a) 3.61 (1.1)	a) 15	a) 24.5 (28) 45		Developed from the Aviatika 890 aeroplane.
South Africa											
Manufacturer: Celair Ltd. PO Box 77, Ermelo 2350, Transvaal											
Celstar CG-1 (G)	a) 1 b) Composites	a) FX 71-L-150/25 b) 11.7	a) 36-3 (11.05) b) 110.8 (10.3)	21-4 (6.5)	a) 584 (265) b) 826 (375)	b) 7.46 (36.4)	a) 2.95 (0.9)	a) 23	a) 43.5 (50) 80 b) 175 (201) 324		Aerobatic and competition glider (±10g).
United Kingdom											
Manufacturer: Kenilworth International Ltd. 7 The Willows, Bangor BT19 7XZ - (tel: +44 1247 453783)											
Mechta Me-7 (G)	a) 1 b) Glassfibre	a) FX 61-157 b) 20.6	a) 41-8 (12.7) b) 82.88 (7.7)	17-5.5 (5.3)	a) 265 (120) b) 551 (250)	a) 4.79 (23.4) b) 6.64 (32.4)	a) 2.56 (0.78) b) 43.5 (50) 80	a) 32 b) 51 (59) 95	a) 33.5 (39) 62 b) 119 (137) 220		Production version of Russian Russia 2. 5° forward wingsweep.
United States of America											
Manufacturer: Advanced Soaring Concepts Inc. 4730 Calle Quetzal, Camarillo, CA 93012 - (tel: +1 805 389 3434)											
Falcon (G)	a) 1 b) Glassfibre, carbonfibre and aramid		a) 49-3 (15)					a) 44			Kit glider.
American Spirit (G)	a) 1 b) Glassfibre, carbonfibre and aramid		a) 49-3 (15) b) 106.2 (9.87)	21-6 (6.55)	a) 505 (229) b) 1,157 (525)	b) 10.89 (53.19)		a) 42	b) 117 (135) 217 c) 61 (70) 113.		Available as a kit. New prototype 18 m version is the XL.
Manufacturer: Aero Dovron Inc. 8718 150th Court North, Palm Beach Gardens, FL 33418 - (tel: +1 407 575 1259)											
Mini Straton D-7 (MGS)	a) 1 b) Glassfibre, wood and fabric	b) 11.9	a) 35-5 (10.8) b) 105.5 (9.8)	19-8 (5.99)	a) 242 (110) b) 462 (210)	b) 4.45 (21.75)		a) 14	a) 24 (27) 44 b) 54 (62) 100 c) 43 (50) 80	a) 24 hp (17.9 kW) Trabant or Rotax 277 engine behind wings driving a pusher propeller.	Available as a kit. Built in Czech Republic.

Kenilworth Mechta Me-7 (J. Ewald) (page 534)

Advanced Soaring Concepts American Spirit XL, possibly the first glider flown with a boron fiber main spar (P. F. Selinger) (page 534)

Designation	a) Crew b) Materials	a) Aerofoil b) Wing aspect ratio	a) Span ft-ins (m) b) Wing area sq ft (m^2)	Length ft-ins (m)	Weights lb (kg): a) empty b) maximum c) ballast (max)	Wing loading lb/sq ft (kg/m^2): a) minimum b) maximum	a) Minimum rate of sink ft (m)/sec b) at speed of kts (mph) km/h	a) Best glide ratio b) at speed of kts (mph) km/h	Speeds kts (mph) km/h: a) stalling b) maximum c) cruise	a) Engine b) Fuel capacity litres	Comments
Type: G: Glider **MGS:** Motorglider, self-launch **MGN:** Motorglider, no self-launch											
United States of America											
Manufacturer: ARACO. 1121 Lewis Avenue, Sarasota, FL 34237 - (tel: +1 813 365 3860)											
Windex 1200 (MGS)	a) 1 b) Composites	a) R-R17 b) 19.75	a) 39-8 (12.1) b) 79.6 (7.4)	16-1 (4.9)	a) 330 (150) b) 683 (310)	b) 8.58 (41.9)	a) 2.13 (0.65) b) 40.5 (47) 75	a) 38 b) 54 (62) 100	a) 35 (41) 65 b) 146 (168) 270 c) 113 (130) 209	a) Tail-mounted 24 hp (17.9 kW) König	Kit MGS. Fully aerobatic at +9/-7g, at below 250 kg.
Manufacturer: Bright Star Gliders Inc. 48 Barham Avenue, Santa Rosa, CA 95407 - (tel: +1 707 576 7627)											
Swift (foot-launched motorized hang glider)	b) Composites	b) 11.5	a) 39 (11.89) b) 135 (12.54)	10 (3.05)				a) 24	b) 55 (63) 101 c) 46 (53) 85	a) Optional 24 hp (17.9 kW) König SC 430	Kit glider and/or motorglider.
Manufacturer: Group Genesis Inc. 1530 Pole Lane Road, Marion, OH 43302 - (tel: +1 614 387 9464)											
Genesis I (G)	a) 1 b) Composites	a) Roncz G-74S b) 20.1	a) 49-3 (15) b) 120.5 (11.19)	13-9 (4.2)	a) 500 (227) b) 1,157 (525)	a) 5.02 (24.5) b) 9.6 (46.8)	a) 1.9 (0.58) b) 45 (52) 83	a) 43 b) 65 (75) 120	b) 157 (180) 290		Kit glider. First example built in 1994.
Manufacturer: Marske Aircraft Corporation. 975 Loire Valley Drive, Marion, OH 43302											
Monarch F (G)	a) 1 b) Wood and composites	a) NACA 43012A b) 9.7	a) 42-7 (12.98) b) 186 (17.27)	12-6 (3.81)	a) 220 (100) b) 450 (204)	b) 2.42 (11.81)	a) 2.5 (0.76) b) 26 (30) 48	a) 20 b) 35 (40) 64	a) 21 (24) 39 b) 61 (70) 113 c) 39 (45) 72		Plans and kits are available. Pilot in 100-230 lb (45-104 kg) range.
Pioneer II-D (G)	a) 1 b) Wood, fabric and composites	a) NACA 33012/33010 mod b) 12.6	a) 42.7 (12.98) b) 144 (13.38)	12-6 (3.81)	a) 350 (159) b) 600 (272)	b) 4.17 (20.34)	a) 2.1 (0.64)	a) 35	a) 31 (35) 57 approx b) 113 (130) 209 c) 83 (95) 153		Latest version, available in plans and kit forms.
Manufacturer: Jim Maupin Ltd. 24201 Rowel Court, Tehachapi, CA 93561											
Carbon Dragon (G)	a) 1 b) Wood and Composites	a) Culver b) 12.9	a) 44 (13.41) b) 150 (13.94)	20 (6.1) approx	a) 144 (65.3) b) 300-335 (136-152)		a) 1.67 (0.51)	25	b) 61 (70) 112		Built from available plans. Foot launched.
Windrose (MGS)	a) 1 b) Wood and composites	b) 17.9	a) 41-6 (12.65) b) 96 (8.92)	21-7 (6.58)	a) 512 (232) b) 700 (317.5)	a) 7.29 (35.59)	a) 2.3 (0.7) b) 40 (46) 74	a) 29 b) 45.5 (52) 84	b) 114 (132) 212 c) 87 (100) 161	a) Rear of cockpit pod-mounted 35 hp (26 kW) Cuyuna UL-II-02 b) 19	Plans and kits of this self-launching motorglider are available.
Windrose II (MGS)	a) 1 b) Wood and composites		a) 49-2 (14.98) b) 102 (9.47)	21-7 (6.58)	a) 512 (232) b) 740 (336)	b) 7.25 (35.42)	a) 2.3 (0.7)		c) 114 (132) 212	a) Rear of cockpit pod-mounted 46 hp (34.3 kW) Rotax 503 b) 19	Plans for this larger-span version of Windrose are available.

Group Genesis Genesis I (page 535)

Jim Maupin Woodstock (page 536)

Designation	a) Crew b) Materials	a) Aerofoil b) Wing aspect ratio	a) Span ft-ins (m) b) Wing area sq ft (m^2)	Length ft-ins (m)	Weights lb (kg): a) empty b) maximum c) ballast (max)	Wing loading lb/sq ft (kg/m^2): a) minimum b) maximum	a) Minimum rate of sink ft (m)/sec b) at speed of kts (mph) km/h	a) Best glide ratio b) at speed of kts (mph) km/h	Speeds kts (mph) km/h: a) stalling b) maximum c) cruise	a) Engine b) Fuel capacity litres	Comments
Type: G: Glider **MGS:** Motorglider, self-launch **MGN:** Motorglider, no self-launch											
United States of America											
Manufacturer: Jim Maupin Ltd. (Continued)											
Woodstock (G)	a) 1 b) Wood and fabric	a) IRV Culver b) 14.5	a) 39 (11.89) b) 104.7 (9.73)	19 (5.79)	a) 235 (106.6) b) 450 (204)	b) 4.3 (20.98)	a) 2.62 (0.8)	a) 24	a) 13 (15) 24 b) 87 (100) 161 c) 68 (78) 126		Plans and kits available.
Manufacturer: Rensselaer Polytechnic Institute. Troy, New York											
RP3 (G)	a) 2 b) Composites	a) FX 67-170 b) 17	a) 54 (16.46) b) 180 (16.7)	17 (5.18)	a) 650 (295)		a) 3.05 (0.93) b) 39 (45) 72	a) 33 b) 44.5 (51) 82	a) 37 (42) 68		Crew side-by-side or pilot in the centre.
Manufacturer: Ron Sands. 89 Forrest Road, Mertztown, PA 19539 - (tel: +1 610 682 6788)											
Primary Glider 1929 (G)	a) 1 b) Tube, wood and fabric		a) 32 (9.75) b) 160 (14.86)	17-8 (5.38)	a) 175 (79.4) b) 375 (170)	b) 2.34 (11.44)			b) 39 (45) 72 c) 33 (38) 61		Plans available. Suitable for descending flights.
Manufacturer: Schweizer Aircraft Corporation. PO Box 147, Elmira, New York 14902 - (tel: +1 607 739 3821)											
SGS 1-36 Sprite (G)	a) 1 b) Aluminium alloy	a) FX 61-163, FX 60-126 b) 15	a) 46-2 (14.07) b) 140.72 (13.07)	20-7 (6.27)	a) 475 (216) b) 710 (322)	b) 5.045 (24.63)	a) 2.25 (0.69) b) 36.5 (42) 67.5	a) 31 b) 46 (53) 85	a) 30.5 (35) 56 b) 105 (121) 195		Out of production but supported by the company.
SGS 2-33A (G)	a) 2 b) Metal	b) 11.8	a) 51 (15.54) b) 219.5 (20.39)	25-9 (7.85)	a) 600 (272) b) 1,040 (471.7)	b) 4.74 (23.14)	a) 3.1 (0.94) b) 36.5 (42) 67.5	a) 22.25 b) 45 (52) 83.5	a) 30.5 (35) 56 b) 85 (98) 157		Training glider. Out of production but supported by the company.
SGM 2-37 (MGS)	a) 2 b) Aluminium alloy	a) FX 61-163, FX 60-126 b) 18.1	a) 59-6 (18.14) b) 195.71 (18.182)	27-6 (8.38)	a) 1,260 (571.5) b) 1,850 (839)	b) 9.45 (46.15)	a) 3.8 (1.16) b) 52 (60) 96.5	a) 22 b) 54 (62) 100	a) 44 (50) 81 b) 116 (133) 214 gliding	a) Front-mounted 112 hp (83.5 kW) Textron Lycoming O-235-L2C, or 150-180 hp (112-134 kW) O-320/O-360	Delivered to the USAF's Academy at Colorado Springs as TG-7A (12 delivered).

Buoyant Aircraft (Airships)

The term Buoyant Aircraft is a more up-to-date and meaningful expression for Airships, as many can operate 'heavy'. However, to retain plain and familiar language, the term Airship has been used in the entries that follow.

Advanced Hybrid Aircraft (Australia)

Corporate address: 96 Rankins Road, Kensington, Victoria 3031.
Telephone: +61 3 372 1998
Facsimile: +61 3 391 9569
Information: Bruce N. Blake P.Eng, MRAeS, C.Eng, BE(Aero), LAME (Manager).

AHA Albatross RPMB

First flight: 1987.
Role: Non-rigid fully functioning, remotely piloted mini blimp (RPMB), 80% scale proof-of-concept vehicle assisting in the Hornet programme. Has operated at more than 25% heaviness.

★ Aims

★ To prove that the combination of aerostatic and aerodynamic lift generation is viable.
★ To show the airship will operate stably and under full control from very low to maximum speeds.
★ To prove the airship can taxi on the field, with little need for ground crew.

▲ Development

▲ The prospects of increased productivity for hybrid buoyant airships is stated by AHA to be good, with the expectation of increased speed and greater disposable load for a given helium volume over EQ (equilibrium) airships.

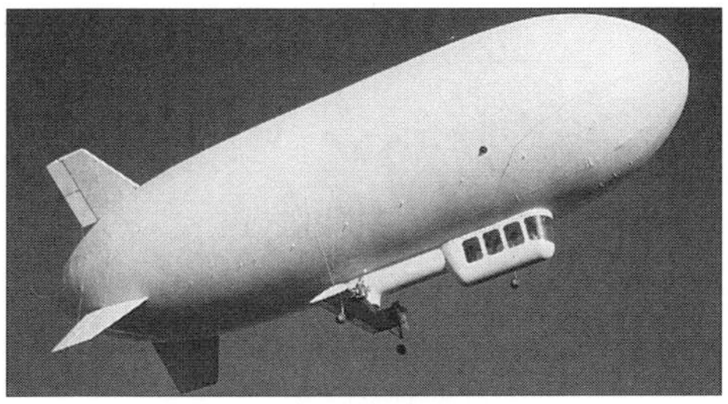

Advanced Hybrid Aircraft Albatross RPMB

AHA Hornet LV

First flight: Not yet flown.
Role: Non-rigid, hybrid, leisure/sports airship (LV – leisure variant).

★ Aims

★ To operate at 50% heaviness, with only half of the total lift provided by the helium filled envelope.
★ At take-off, with the wings vectored at +30°, aerodynamic lift boosted by the vectored thrust will allow a very short ground run and a steep climb.

▲ Development

▲ A market study estimates the sale of 60 LV units in kit form per year, primarily in the USA and EU. The company's business plan is to raise A$1m for commercialization of this airship.
Crew: Pilot in small enclosed gondola.
Length: 50 ft (15.24 m)
Width over winglets: 22 ft 6 ins (6.86 m)
Height: 16 ft (4.88 m)
Envelope: Volume 4,300 cu ft (121.76). Advertising area 730 sq ft (67.8 m^2).
Surface area: 1,570 sq ft (145.86 m^2)
Ballonet/s maximum volume: 430 cu ft (12.18 m^3)
Gross aerostatic lift: 270 lb (122.5 kg) at 5% ballonets inflation.
Take-off weight: 540 lb (245 kg) maximum
Empty weight: 336 lb (152.4 kg)
Empty weight (heaviness) at mast: 66 lb (29.94 kg)
Maximum normal heaviness: 270 lb (122.5 kg)
Disposable load: 204 lb (92.53 kg)
Engines: 2 Konig SC 430 pistons. Fuel in the strut-tank assembly.
Propellers: 2, 4 ft 6 ins (1.37 m) diameter each.
Stabilizers/winglets: 4 stabilizers at tail. 2 winglet assemblies carrying engines, able to vector engine thrust by +30° for steep climb.
Maximum airspeed: 51 kts (59 mph) 94 km/h
Minimum airspeed: 30 kts (34 mph) 56 km/h
Maximum climb rate: 2,000 ft (610 m) per minute

AHA Hornet LV two-seater

First flight: Not yet flown.
Role: Non-rigid, hybrid, leisure/sports and advertising airship. FAA Experimental Category.

★ Aims

★ 2-seat and larger version of the LV.
★ See LV entry.
Length: 68 ft (20.73 m)
Diameter: 17 ft (5.18 m)
Width over winglets: 30 ft 6 ins (9.30 m)
Winglet chord: 4 ft 6 ins (1.37 m^3
Envelope: Volume 10,750 cu ft (304.4 m^3)
Ballonet/s maximum volume: 15% of envelope.
Take-off weight: 1,350 lb (612.3 kg)
Heaviness: Maximum of 50% of take-off weight.
Buoyancy: 675 lb (306 kg)
Disposable load: 510 lb (231.3 kg)
Engines: 2x 100 hp (74.6 kW) Mid-West AE100R pistons. +30° vectoring through tilt of winglets.
Maximum airspeed: 72 kts (83 mph) 133 km/h
Minimum airspeed: 29 kts (33.5 mph) 54 km/h
Operating altitude: 5,000 ft (1,525 m)

AHA Hornet AW

First flight: Not yet flown.
Role: Non-rigid, hybrid airship. Applications for the AW (aerial work) commercial version of Hornet may include aerial survey, mapping, surveillance, and electronic news gathering, where at present small to medium sized fixed and rotary winged aircraft are used. It can also fulfil advertising and promotion roles.

★ Aims

★ To offer a wide speed range, and lower acquisition and operating costs than helicopters.
★ Quieter and with longer endurance than helicopters.
★ Twin-engine reliability, permitting low altitude operations over built-up areas.
★ Increased thrust vectoring compared to LV (see Engines).
★ To gain BCAR Q or FAA P-8110-2 certification.

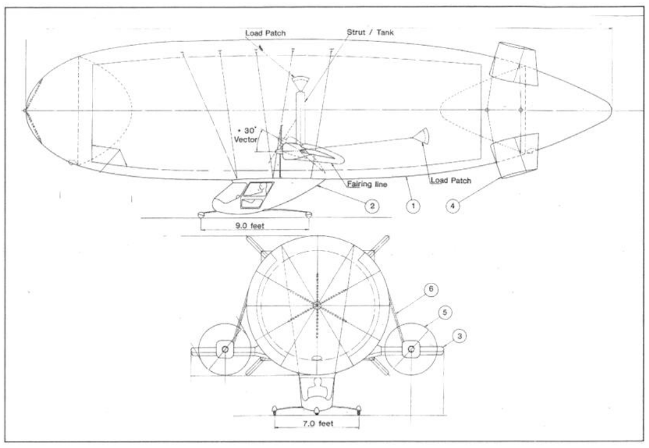

Advanced Hybrid Aircraft Hornet LV, showing: 1 Envelope assembly, 2 Gondola, 3 Winglet, 4 Stabilizer, 5 Propeller 6 Strut-tank assembly

Length: 100 ft (30.48 m)
Diameter: 20 ft (6.10 m)
Width over winglets: 30 ft 2 ins (9.19 m)
Winglet chord: 4 ft 1 ins (1.24 m)
Envelope: Volume 22,000 cu ft (623 m^3)
Ballonet/s maximum volume: 20% of envelope.
Take-off weight: 2,822 lb (1,280 kg)
Heaviness: Maximum 56% of take-off weight.
Buoyancy: 1,235 lb (560 kg)
Disposable load: 941 lb (427 kg)
Engines: 4x 100 hp (74.6 kW) Mid-West AE100R pistons. +45° vectoring through tilt of wings.
Maximum airspeed: 81 kts (93 mph) 150 km/h
Minimum airspeed: 33 kts (38 mph) 61 km/h
Operating altitude: 7,000 ft (2,135 m)

AHA 1200 Light Utility

First flight: Not yet flown.
Role: Non-rigid, hybrid airship, specially designed for use in the general aviation field and for light cargo carrying, where low maintenance and low operational costs are paramount. A medium lift, robust and short take-off airship could access unprepared airfields in Third World countries, and in disaster areas. Also advertising and surveillance.

★ Aims

★ Provision for the carriage of unusual cargoes, by the structural design of the spine of the tricycle assembly.
★ Carriage of internal and external loads.
★ To gain BCAR Q or FAA P-8110-2 certification.
Length: 98 ft 6 ins (30.02 m)
Diameter: 24 ft 6 ins (7.47 m)
Width over winglets: 19 ft 5 ins (5.92 m)
Winglet chord: 4 ft 8 ins (1.42 m)
Envelope: Volume 42,400 cu ft (1,200 m^3)
Ballonet/s maximum volume: 25% of envelope.
Take-off weight: 3,166 lb (1,436 kg)
Heaviness: Maximum 25% of take-off weight.
Buoyancy: 2,381 lb (1,080 kg) at 10% ballonet inflation.
Disposable load: 950 lb (431 kg)
Engines: 2x 100 hp (74.6 kW) Mid-West AE100R pistons.
Maximum airspeed: 41 kts (47 mph) 76 km/h
Minimum airspeed: 19 kts (22 mph) 35 km/h
Operating altitude: 9,000 ft (2,745 m)

21st Century Airships Inc (Canada)

Corporate address: Box 177, 180 Main street, Newmarket, Ontario L3Y 4X1.
Telephone: +1 905 898 6274
Facsimile: +1 905 898 7245
Information: Hokan Colting (Chairman/CEO)

21st Century Airships SPAS 13

First flight: 13 May 1994.
Role: Semi-rigid helium airship demonstrator (C-FRLM).

★ Aims

⋆ To demonstrate the advantages of a spherical airship, with the crew/passengers seated inside the envelope in a spacious cabin.
⋆ To show the envelope to be extremely helium-tight, and thereby cost efficient.
⋆ Steering and altitude control through varied and deflected thrust, the technology having been developed and patented by the company.

▲ Development

▲ The latest spherical airship built by the company, following on from SPAS 1 and subsequent airships with external gondolas.
Crew/Passengers: Pilot and 1 passenger occupying an internal cabin with 96 sq ft (8.92 m^2) of panoramic window area. 2 ground crew required.
Diameter: 43 ft (13.11 m)
Height: 45 ft (13.72 m) including undercarriage.
Envelope: Outside load-bearing envelope made of Spectra fabric, said to be ten times stronger than steel of the same weight. Second inner envelope of Mylar film and reinforced with Kevlar, and containing helium gas.
Take-off weight: 2,403 lb (1,090 kg)
Empty weight: 1,596 lb (724 kg)
Engines: 2x 50 hp (37.3 kW) Rotax 503s.
Propellers: 2x 6 ft (1.83 m) diameter 3-blade.
Control vanes: 4 surfaces behind each engine deflect air for ascending/descending.
Maximum airspeed: 26 kts (30 mph) 48 km/h
Cruise speed: 16.5 kts (19 mph) 30 km/h

21st Century Airships SPAS 13 demonstrator

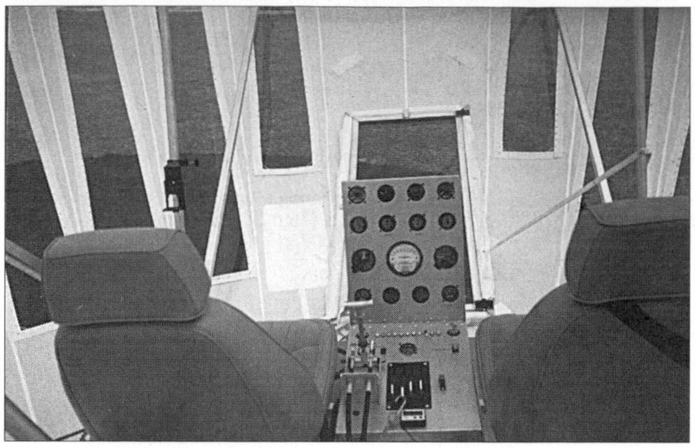

SPAS 13 cockpit. A pressure gauge, showing pressure of water inside the combined cabin and ballonet, is included on the instrument panel. The lever is for dumping emergency ballast, while another activates a helium release system. The vane control lever is not shown

Engine, propeller and vane layout on SPAS 13

21st Century Airships 5-seater

First flight: Not yet flown.
Role: Advertising and aerial filming.

★ Aims

⋆ Internal built-in cabin, and envelope/control technologies demonstrated on SPAS 13.

▲ Development

▲ Under development as a larger spherical airship.
Crew/Passengers: Pilot and 4 passengers in internal cabin. 2 ground crew required.
Diameter: 53 ft (16.15 m)
Height: 55 ft (16.76 m) including undercarriage.
Envelope: Probably similar to SPAS 13.
Engines: 2x 90 hp (67.1 kW) engines.
Propellers: Possibly in shrouds.
Control vanes: Steering and altitude control through varied and deflected thrust (see SPAS 13).
Maximum airspeed: 30 kts (35 mph) 56 km/h
Cruise speed: 22 kts (25 mph) 40 km/h

21st Century Airships 10-seater

First flight: Not yet flown.
Role: Sightseeing passenger rides.

★ Aims

⋆ Internal built-in cabin with partially glass bottom. Offers passengers a high level of comfort, with 360° views through wrap-round windows.

▲ Development

▲ Based on SPAS 13 and 5-seater technology.
Crew/Passengers: Pilot and 10 passengers. 2 ground crew.
Diameter: 64 ft (19.51 m)
Height: 66 ft (20.1 m) including undercarriage.
Envelope: Probably similar to SPAS 13.
Engines: 2x 140 hp (104.4 kW) engines.
Propellers: In shrouds.
Control vanes: Steering and altitude control through varied and deflected thrust (see SPAS 13).
Maximum airspeed: 30 kts (35 mph) 56 km/h
Cruise speed: 22 kts (25 mph) 40 km/h

Drawing of the cockpit/cabin for the 21st Century Airships 10-seater glass bottom airship

Pan Atlantic Aerospace Corp (Canada)

Corporate address: 881 Lady Helen Place, Suite 302, Ottawa (Nepean), Ontario K1Z 5L3.
Telephone: +1 613 722 1454
Facsimile: +1 613 722 1691
Information: Fredrick Ferguson (CEO – Nord-Am Research Corporation), Nick Baumberg (Office Manager/Communications – Pan Atlantic Aerospace Corp).

● Activities

● Pan Atlantic Aerospace Corp is a research company focusing on a number of airship projects. None has yet reached the construction stage, with exception of the one-third scale LESA and the LEAP drones, and the company is engaged in setting up financing. The CAS is likely to be the first project to carry forward, though HASP is a current programme at the conceptual stage.
● Prototype and manufacturing phase of CAS is not expected to remain in Canada and planning is underway to relocate the project.

Pan Atlantic Aerospace Cargo Airship System (CAS)

First flight: First pre-production vehicle flights unlikely to be before 1997.
Role: Patented large cargo-carrying airship, aimed at high value, low density cargo markets.

★ Aims

★ Segmented pressure airship to provide a net payload of up to 500 tons (508 tonnes) and built in sizes of up to 1,700 ft (518 m) length. Uses LEAP technology (which see).
★ To operate at costs approximately one-third that of low-cost fixed-wing cargo aircraft.
★ To operate in all weather conditions and to meet and exceed 35fps gust loads.
★ Utilize articulation, modern high strength and lightweight materials, and allow effective load transfer throughout the module envelopes.
★ To maximize volume and payload without building a craft much beyond 200 ft (61 m) height, a long high fineness radio design is chosen. Although such a design has higher aerodynamic bending moments from flight and gust loads, CAS will take these loads and remain structurally sound through modularization.

▲ Development

▲ Approximately $10m spent in first phase of development, including two 50 ft (15.24 m) scaled flying drones, wind tunnel analyses, final design definition, simulation, market and business feasibility, etc.
▲ 18 month phase begun, to include detailed engineering, conclude market-user commitments, and complete manufacturing contracts.
Length: 1,500 ft (457.2 m)
Diameter: 200 ft (61 m)
Envelope: 6 modules, front powered control module section and rear tail section 350 ft x 200 ft (106.7 x 61 m) max diameter each, and 4 payload modules 200 ft x 200 ft. Total volume 39,793,500 cu ft (1,126,825 m^3). Fabric assumed to be Dacron and Tedlar laminate for weight calculations**. Use of Kevlar or Spectra would reduce projected weights.
Fineness ratio: 7.5:1
Drag coefficient: 0.026
Ballonets maximum volume: 20% of total volume.
Gross buoyancy: 1,965,800 lb (891,671 kg) with all ballonets fully inflated.
Empty weight: 420,000 lb (190,500 kg)**
Payload: 1,284,000 lb (582,400 kg) net available payload (containers + cargo).
Engines: 4x 6,000 shp (4,474 kW) Allison GMA 2100 turboprops.
Fuel: 238,000 lb (107,955 kg) for 4,000 mile range at cruise speed, with 10% fuel reserves.
Maximum airspeed: 82.5 kts (95 mph) 153 km/h
Cruise speed: 66 kts (76 mph) 122 km/h
Duration: 52.6 hours
Range: 3,476 naut miles (4,000 miles) 6,437 km

Pan Atlantic Aerospace High Altitude Satellite Platform (HASP)

First flight: Not yet flown. Conceptual project only.
Role: High-altitude robotic platform for surveillance, communications and other equipment payloads.

★ Aims

★ 2 HASP airships per system, with one or other operating in 6-week cycles.
★ LEAP type technology for envelope.
★ 70,000 ft (21,335 m) operating altitude.
Engines: 4

Pan Atlantic Aerospace Long Endurance Airship Platform (LEAP)

First flight: 9 December 1990. Completed flight trials.
Role: Long Endurance Articulating Powered (LEAP), remotely piloted, drone airship. Suitable as a platform for TV and motion picture cameras, radar and IR systems, over-the-horizon transmitters, high-intensity lights, pollution probes, geodetic survey equipment, etc.

★ Aims

★ On-board stability augmentation to ease piloting fatigue during lengthy operations.
★ Low cost, energy efficient and environmentally safe surveillance through remotely controlled guidance.

▲ Development

▲ Result of 3 years R&D of pre-production prototypes.
Crew: No on-board crew. 1 ground-based operator. Multiple and redundant radio control transmission and frequencies provide back-up assurance for added flight safety.
Length: 67 ft (20.42 m)
Diameter: 11 ft (3.4 m)
Envelope: Modular design, consisting 3 separate sections, for simplified inflation, ground handling, and increased structural integrity. Total volume 5,339 cu ft (151.18 m^3). Carbonfibre stiffeners at nose.
Surface area: 2,655.5 sq ft (246.7 m^2)
Ballonet: Automatic ballonet operation. Volume 7.5% of total volume.
Total lift: 335.3 lb (152.1 kg)
Gross weight: 263.3 lb (119.5 kg)
Payload: 72 lb (32.6 kg), maintained at various altitudes for up to 6 hours.
Engines: 3 remotely-controlled 1.5 hp (1.12 kW) engines mounted on the front section, individually controlled for precise low speed manoeuvrability and hover control.
Fuel: Main fuel cells above side engines.
Canards: Engines and horizontal/ventral canards attached to an aluminium or carbonfibre support yoke. Fixed ventral canard, and vectored horizontal canards.
Tail surfaces: Cruciform fins and active rudders.
Maximum airspeed: 26 kts (30 mph) 48 km/h

Pan Atlantic Aerospace Long Endurance Manned Solar Airship (LEMS)

First flight: Not yet flown. Programme on hold.
Role: Solar-electric powered version of the multi-segmented long fineness ratio airship (see Aims for projected roles, and Motive power).

★ Aims

★ Initial model designed to operate at low or high altitudes, over short or long ranges, and to remain stationary or fly forwards, offering multi-role capabilities.
★ Adapt to wind loads by bending in flight.
★ Minimize hangar size, and storage costs, by modular construction.
★ Eventual aim is to undertake extreme long endurance missions with LEMS types.
★ To promote the solar airship to a single sponsor-user. Follow-on production will be marketed for long term surveillance, environmental research and monitoring, advertising and peace-time military roles.

▲ Development

▲ Design definition prepared by Mr Ferguson, following LESA project (which see).
Crew: Single pilot operation.
Length: 141 ft (43 m) initial model.
Height: 22 ft (6.6 m) approximately, initial model.
Envelope: 3 inter-connected modules. Solar cells mounted on the top surface.
Motive power: Derived from on-board solar cells, converting sunlight energy into electricity to power electric motors for propulsion. On-board batteries are charged during daylight; the stored electrical energy in the batteries used for propulsion during weak or low light conditions. Solar cells are mounted on the top surface of the airship.

Pan Atlantic Aerospace Long Endurance Solar Airship (LESA)

First flight: 8 October 1991.
Role: One-third scale, electric-powered, radio-controlled drone airship, to assist in the LEMS programme (which see).

▲ Development

▲ 1991, Nord-Am initiated design and fabrication.
Length: 48 ft (14.63 m)
Envelope: 6-segment, long fineness ratio.

Pan Atlantic Aerospace Magnus 60

First flight: Programme on hold while awaiting financing.
Role: Rotating spherical VTOL, low speed, highly manoeuvrable, heavy-lift airship. To be used for low-level aerial animated advertising and capable of precise station keeping.

★ Aims

★ Exploit the Magnus effect, in which lift is generated by a spherical object that rotates while moving in a horizontal direction. This enables the development of an airship that is said to have superior qualities compared to conventional airships.

Conceptual drawing of Pan Atlantic Aerospace CAS airships at a terminal

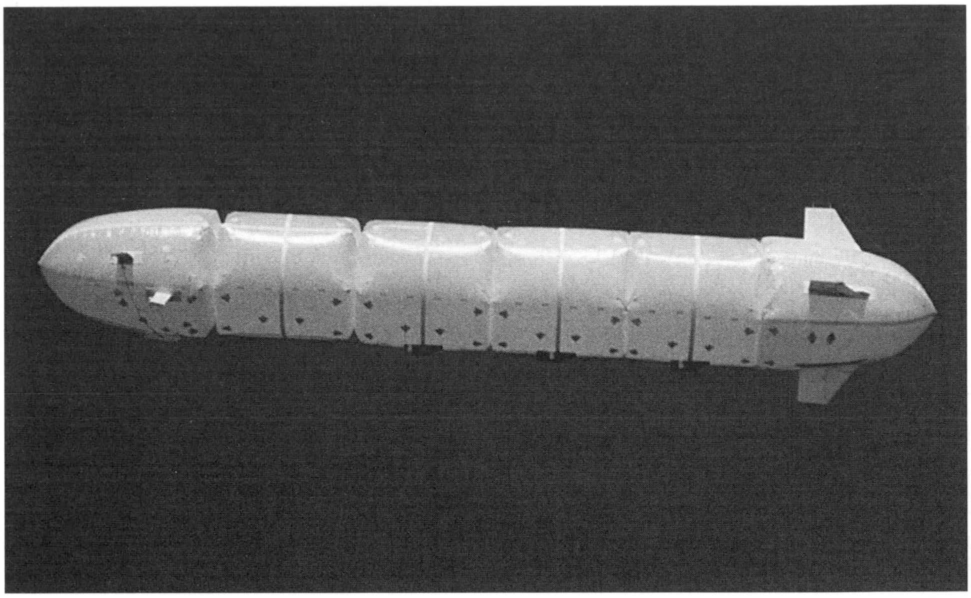

Pan Atlantic Aerospace LESA

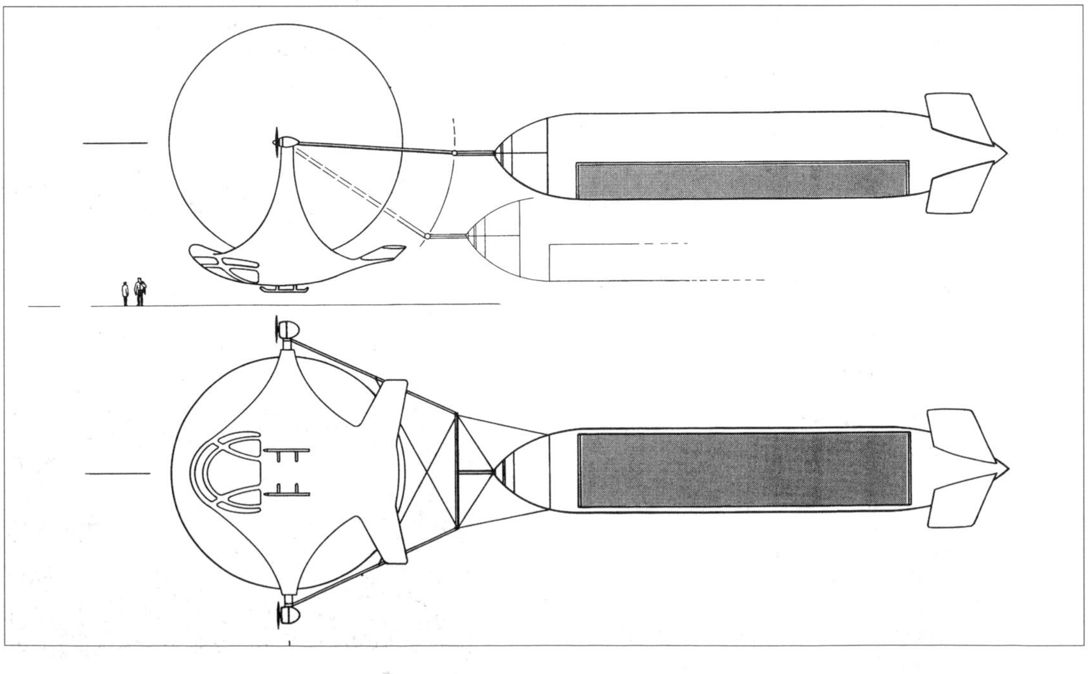

Pan Atlantic Aerospace Magnus 60, seen from the side and below

★ To compete with standard advertising airships for aerial advertising work.
★ Does not require mooring masts or large ground crews.
★ Anticipated to be approximately 50% less expensive than similar size standard airships.
★ Operate precision hover.
★ Can be dismantled for transport to advertising locations.
★ Statically stable in pitch and roll, easy to pilot, good control power in yaw, and precise low speed manoeuvring.

▲ Development

▲ Initially invented and developed during 1979-88 by Mr Ferguson (CEO of Nord-Am Research Corp), and scale tested during 1981-86.
▲ Originally designed to provide helicopter-like performance and intended to act as an aerial crane to move heavy and oversized loads.
▲ Pan Atlantic Aerospace subsequently prepared design definition for an advertising version, with an electronic advertising panel on a towed aerostat, joined to Magnus 60 by light aluminium or plastic tubing.
▲ Full scale pre-production unit direct cost $5m. Production unit cost $2m, estimated.

Crew: 2, plus video equipment, etc in enclosed cabin gondola.
Diameter: 60 ft (18.3 m) maximum.
Envelope: Volume 113,097 cu ft (3,203 m^3). As forward speed increases, sphere rotation is started and lift is generated by the Magnus effect. The effect lift is sufficient to counteract the 600 lb (272 kg) negative buoyancy that the engines had been lifting and all engine thrust is thereafter dedicated to propel the airship forward. Climb and descent is controlled by sphere rotation speed, ballonet volume and engine pitch settings. A safety valve in the envelope allows quick release of helium gas.
Surface area: 11,310 sq ft (1,050.7 m^2)
Ballonet maximum volume: 11,310 cu ft (320.26 m^3)
Lift volume: 101,787 cu ft (2,882.28 m^3)
Gross lift: 6,484 lb (2,941 kg)
Net lift: 1,084 lb (491.7 kg)
Empty weight: Envelope 1,414 lb (641.4 kg). Ballonet 44 lb (20 kg)
Payload: over 1,000 lb (453.6 kg)
Engines: 2 pivoting engines (90°), positioned vertically for take-off, each controlled separately by the pilot using a stick and twist grip. As airship climbs, the pilot moves the controls forward to pivot both engines forward (see Envelope for rotation). Differential engine power settings achieve directional control.
Cruise speed: 30.5 kts (35 mph) 56 km/h approximately.
Duration: 4.5 hours

Beijing University of Aeronautics and Astronautics (China)

Address: PO Box 85, 37 Xue Yuan Road, Haidian District, Beijing 100083.
Telephone: +86 1 2017251
Facsimile: +86 1 2010994

● Activities

● The BUAA has a small research group that has produced a series of Mifeng (Bee) aircraft, mostly microlights and the Mifeng-6 hot-air airship. The latter first flew on 20 December 1985 and at least 4 have been constructed, used for aerial photography, power line lifting, research and recreation/sport. However, despite this, it is believed that there is no formal airship manufacturing in China. The Mifeng-6 accommodates 4 persons, is 110 ft (33.7 m) long, has an envelope volume of 105,300 cu ft (2,983 m^3), and the Rotax 447 engine is used not only for power but also to inflate the envelope. Burners provide the heat needed for buoyancy variation.

BUAA Mifeng-6 hot-air airship

Huahang Airship Development Group (China)

Address: PO Box 307, Jingmen, Hubei 434535.
Telephone: +86 7267 32525
Facsimile: +86 7267 32551

● Activities

● In August 1990 this Group flew an impressive non-rigid helium airship with a 70,600 cu ft (2,000 m^3) envelope volume and 2 vectoring Rotax 503 engines with shrouded propellers, known as the FK-4, recognized as having been the first passenger-carrying airship of its kind built in China. Suited to advertising, surveillance, aerial broadcasting, photography, sightseeing and other roles, it might have been expected to lead to further examples being constructed but no indication of this has been received. Meanwhile, in 1992 a small robotic airship was flown as the FK-6, with a volume of 3,100 cu ft (88 m^3).

Shanghai Aircraft Research Institute (China)

Address: PO Box 232-003, Long Hua Airport Building, Shanghai 200232.
Telephone: +86 21 4390811
Facsimile: +86 21 4390584

● Activities

● This research organization has built 2 robotic helium airships as the Shen Zhou-1 and -2, flown since 1992. They are each powered by 3x 2.5 hp (1.9 kW) engines driving shrouded propellers, all attached to the gondola and able to vector for vertical or horizontal control in addition to providing propulsion (Shen Zhou-2 has 2 vectoring and 1 fixed engine). The cruciform tail fins carry movable control surfaces. Envelope volumes of the Shen Zhou-1 and -2 are 1,024 cu ft (29 m^3) and 1,060 cu ft (30 m^3) respectively. Uses, apart from research that might lead to the development of a large airship, could include surveillance.

Kubicek Ltd (Czech Republic)

Corporate address: Francouzská 81, 602 00 Brno.
Telephone: + 42 5 45 21 19 17
Facsimile: +42 5 45 21 30 74
Information: Dipl ing Ales Kubicek (Owner), Michael Suchy (Sales Manager).

● Activities

● Producer of lighter-than-air craft since 1983, the last 5 years as a private company.
● Offers 11 standard types of hot-air balloons and a hot-airship, plus constructs special shape envelopes and other cool-air inflatables such as tents. Kubicek is looking to build an improved hot-air airship for another customer.

Kubicek AV-1

First flight: 16 October 1993 (*OK-3040*)
Role: Hot-air airship.

▲ Development

▲ First modern Czech airship, produced for TICO Prague.
▲ September 1994. AV-1 had accumulated 50 flying hours.

Crew: Pilot and passenger.
Length: 114 ft 10 ins (35 m)
Height of envelope: 39 ft 4 ins (12 m)
Envelope: Volume 98,880 cu ft (2,800 m^3).
Weight of envelope: 430 lb (195 kg)
Weight of gondola: 529 lb (240 kg)
Engine: 1x 50 hp (37.3 kW) Rotax 503 piston engine.
Propeller: 1 Justra-Stratos 4-blade pusher.
Burners: 2 Kubicek-kovo H3s.
Maximum airspeed: 13.5 kts (15.5 mph) 25 km/h
Duration: 1.5 hours

Kubicek AV-1 produced for TICO

Aerazur (France)

Corporate address: 58 boulevard Gallieni, 92137 Issy-les-Moulineaux Cedex.
Telephone: +33 1 41 23 24 25
Facsimile: +33 1 46 48 74 79
Information: Jean-Pierre Fetu (Director, international marketing).

● Activities:

- Designs and constructs envelopes for other airship manufacturers, including Westinghouse (which see).

GEFA-FLUG GmbH (Germany)

Corporate address: Weststrasse 14, D-52074 Aachen.
Telephone: +49 241 87 40 26 or 27
Facsimile: +49 241 87 52 06
Information: Karl Ludwig Busemeyer (Managing Director).

● Activities

- Concentrating on hot-air airship development, partly government funded.
- Intention to gain type certification for a 105,944 cu ft (3,000 m^3) hot-air airship to be used for environmental research projects and advertising.
- Operates 2 hot-air airships and 6 hot-air balloons in Europe.

GEFA-FLUG AS 80 GD

First flight: 1990.
Role: 2-seat hot-air airship for environmental projects and advertising.

▲ Development

▲ Based on the Thunder & Colt AS 80 Mk II.
Crew: 2 in a semi-enclosed gondola.
Length: 118 ft 1.3 ins (36 m)
Diameter: 37 ft 8.8 ins (11.5 m)
Height: 44 ft 9.4 ins (13.65 m)
Envelope: Volume 79,460 cu ft (2,250 m^3). Advertising area 3,014 sq ft (280 m^2).
Surface area: 10,656 sq ft (990 m^2)
Take-off weight: 1,477 lb (670 kg)
Empty weight: 419 lb (190 kg) including tail unit.
Engine: 52 hp (38.8 kW) Rotax 462

GEFA-FLUG AS 80 GD 2-seat hot-air airship

Cruise speed: 24 kts (28 mph) 45 km/h
Duration: 60 minutes

WDL Luftschiffgesellschaft mbH (Germany)

Corporate address: Flughafen, 45470 Mülheim/Ruhr.
Telephone: +49 208 37 80 80
Facsimile: +49 208 3 78 08 33 or 41
Information: Arnold D. Beier (marketing, sales, operations).

● Activities

- WDL corporate group comprises 7 aviation companies offering:

WDL 1B 8-seat airship in Asahi markings

- Development of airships and a shipyard for complete construction (WDL is an officially authorized manufacturer of airships).
- Airship operation for advertising, promotion and observation tasks.
- Advertising from the air with slogans and banners towed by aircraft.
- Scheduled flight services for passengers and freight.
- Authorized (by LBA) technical department for aircraft up to 20t. All work including major repairs and basic overhauls.
- Electronics and instrument service.
- Group of inspection engineers.

WDL 1

First flight: mid-1970s.
Role: Helium airship for advertising.
Crew/Passengers: 8 persons, including pilot.
Length: 190 ft 3 ins (58 m)
Width: 53 ft 9 ins (16.4 m)
Height: 62 ft (18.9 m)
Envelope: Total volume 227,038 cu ft (6,429 m^3).
Engines: 2x 210 hp (156.6 kW) Teledyne Continental piston engines.
Cruise speed: 30-50 kts (35-57 mph) 55-90 km/h
Operating altitude: 1,000-6,000 ft (300-1,800 m)

WDL 1B

First flight: 30 August 1988.
Role: Helium airship for advertising, promotion and observation.
Crew/Passengers: 8 persons, including pilot. Total air/ground crew comprises 20.
Length: 196 ft 10 ins (60 m)
Width: 53 ft 9 ins (16.4 m)
Height: 63 ft 4 ins (19.3 m)
Envelope: Total volume 254,266 cu ft (7,200 m^3). Gondola and envelope are painted with customer/corporate colours/logo. Also prepared for advertising lightshows at night, with a 108 x 26 ft (33 x 8 m) screen each side holding a total of approximately 10,000 different coloured bulbs controlled by a computer unit in the airship.
Empty weight: 11,244 lb (5,100 kg)
Payload: 2,600 lb (1,180 kg)
Engines: 2x 210 hp (156.6 kW) Teledyne Continental piston engines.
Cruise speed: 30-58 kts (35-65 mph) 55-105 km/h
Operating altitude: 1,000-6,000 ft (300-1,800 m)
Duration: 22 hours

Zeppelin Luftschifftechnik GmbH (Germany)

Corporate address: Zeppelin Werftgelände, Leutholdstrasse, D-88045 Friedrichshafen
Telephone: +49 7541 202 0
Facsimile: +49 7541 202 516
Information: Wolfgang Hagenlocher (project manager).

● Activities

- Founded in 1993 for the development and production of New Technology (NT) airships.
- Parent company, Luftschiffbau Zeppelin GmbH, originally founded in 1908 and still exists under the auspices of the Zeppelin Foundation. Shareholders in ZLT include ZF Friedrichshafen AG and Zeppelin Metallwerke GmbH, and share capital is $3.5m.

Zeppelin NT series LZ N07

First flight: Scheduled for early 1997.
Role: Rigid helium airship for passenger/freight carrying; monitoring/control/surveillance operations for environmental protection, fishery surveillance and more; atmospheric and marine chemistry, atmospheric physics, gravimetric measurements and other research tasks; TV; traffic control; advertising and other missions.

★ Aims

★ Based on the rigid airframe principle. Majority of the static and dynamic loads are carried by the rigid structure. Thereby, the airship remains fully manoeuvrable even if internal pressure drops.
★ Safety by redundant configuration of structure, envelope and systems.
★ Non-flammable helium lifting gas.
★ Improved performance, especially maximum speed.
★ All year availability due to all-weather capability.
★ Environmentally friendly, with low noise level and low pollutants emission due to economic fuel consumption.
★ High manoeuvrability, resulting in reduced ground

crew requirements.
★ Cabin and cockpit free from noise and vibration.
★ Engine arrangement substantially reduces effects of lateral gusts during slow approach, ensuring a controlled and accurate landing.

▲ Development

▲ LZ N07 is the demonstration model for the NT series.
▲ Assembly of the prototype began May 1995.
▲ Production 225 ft (68.6 m) long NT is expected to cost $6m.
▲ First commercial NT expected to take off in 1998, with further production from 1999 following FAA approval. Realistic operating cost of approximately $1,800 per hour.

Crew/Passengers: 2 crew plus 12 passengers. Cabin avionics include weather radar and a stormscope. Galley and wardrobe.
Length: 225 ft (68.4 m)
Diameter: 46 ft 5 ins (14.16 m) maximum
Envelope and structure: Total volume 254,266 cu ft (7,200 m^3). Multi-layer laminate envelope using Dacron, Mylar and Tedlar. 3 gas cells, each consisting a cylindrical section of the outer envelope and an integrated lifting-gas cell together with a corresponding section of the air chamber, which passes through the lower region of the airship. Rigid primary structure extends over the entire length, and all major assemblies (such as engines, tail units and gondola) are attached to it. The low-weight longerons and frames are principally

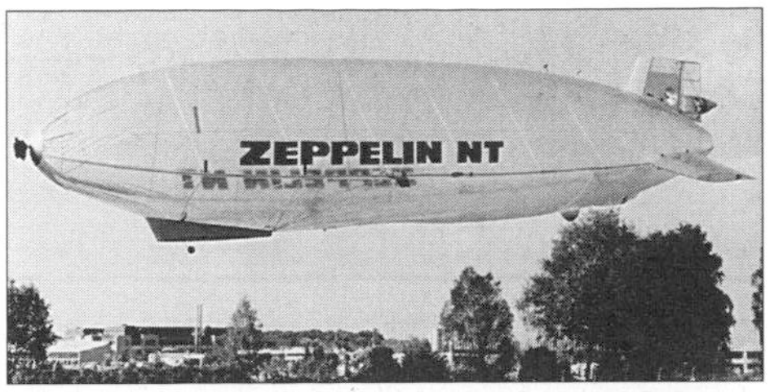

Zeppelin NT, 10 metre-long robotic proof-of-concept model tested in 1991

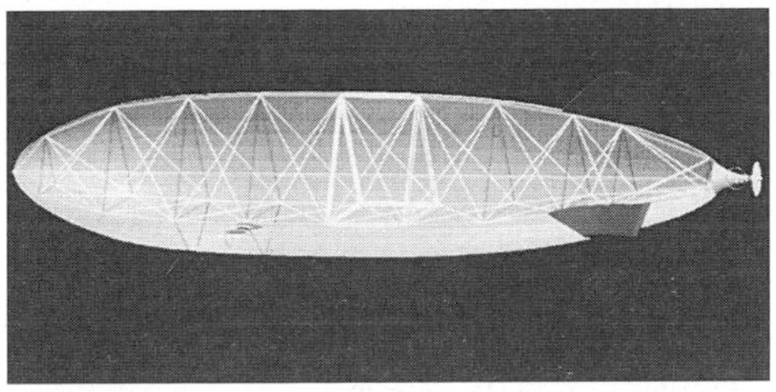

Structure for the production Zeppelin NT airship

of aluminium alloy and carbonfibre respectively.
Maximum gross weight: 15,322 lb (6,950 kg) for 1,000 m cruising altitude.
Payload: 4,078 lb (1,850 kg) for 1,000 m cruising altitude.
Engines: 2 side-mounted 200 hp (149 kW), Textron Lycoming engines mounted as vectored thrust units, and a similar stern-mounted unit capable of delivering lateral thrust together with vectored/horizontal thrust for exact pitch and yaw control. Fly-by-wire control.
Stabilizers: Controlled using fly-by-wire systems.
Maximum airspeed: 76 kts (87 mph) 140 km/h
Cruise speed: 62 kts (71 mph) 115 km/h
Maximum altitude: 8,200 ft (2,500 m)
Duration: 18 hours at 70 km/h, or 36 hours at 70 km/h with reduced payload.

Zeppelin NT series LZ N30

First flight: Not yet flown.
Role: Passenger carrying.

▲ Development

▲ Under development.

Crew/Passengers: 2 crew plus 84 passengers.
Length: 361 ft (110 m)
Diameter: 74 ft (22.5 m) maximum
Envelope: Total volume 1,060,400 cu ft (30,000 m^3)
Maximum gross weight: 66,140 lb (30,000 kg)
Payload: 33,069 lb (15,000 kg)
Engines: 3, type not yet defined.
Maximum airspeed: 76 kts (87 mph) 140 km/h
Cruise speed: 67 kts (78 mph) 125 km/h
Maximum altitude: 9,800 ft (3,000 m)
Duration: 23 hours at 70 km/h, or 82 hours at 70 km/h with reduced payload.

Szolcsák Airships Hungary (Hungary)

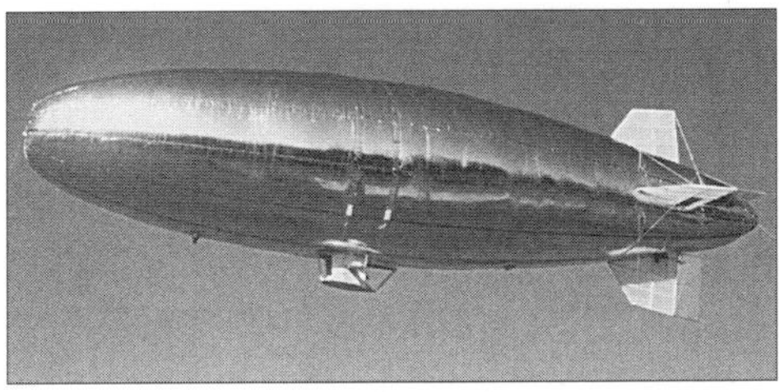

Szolcsák SG-05 remotely-controlled electric airship

Corporate address: H-3231 Gyöngyössolymos, Virág, u.35.
Telephone: +36 37 370 480
Facsimile: +36 37 374 021
Information: Gyula Szolcsák.

● Activities

● Has produced a small remotely-controlled airship with electric power as the SG-05. Under development is a hybrid airship as the SV-01.

Szolcsák Airships Hungary SG-05

First flight: 1994.
Role: Experimental, non-rigid, remotely-controlled airship.
Crew: None
Length: 15 ft 6 ins (4.73 m)
Diameter: 4 ft 2 ins (1.27 m)
Envelope: Volume 128.19 cu ft (3.63 m^3)
Engines: 2x SPEED 500 electric motors.

Szolcsák Airships Hungary SV-01

First flight: Not flown in early 1995.
Role: Experimental, flat-bodied, remotely-controlled, hybrid airship.

▲ Development

▲ Under development in 1995.

Crew: None
Length: 39 ft 5 ins (12 m)
Width: 13 ft 9 ins (4.2 m)
Height: 9 ft 6 ins (2.9 m)
Envelope: Volume 423.78 cu ft (3.6 m^3)
Engines: 4 Mabuchi 540 electric motors.

Aerostatika – Scientific & Industrial Enterprise (Russia)

Corporate address: 31-1-315 Krylatiskaya Street, 121614 Moscow.
Telephone: +7 095 415 26 30
Facsimile: +7 095 415 26 30
Information: Alexander Kirilin (President).

● Activities

● 4 airships under development.

Aerostatika 01

First flight: August 1994.
Role: Multi-functional small-volume gas airship for manned, remotely controlled and tethered \aerostat uses.

▲ Development

▲ 20 take-offs and landings performed during August and September 1994.

Crew: Pilot only with a 154 lb (70 kg) payload (see Payload).
Length: 75 ft (22.88 m)
Envelope: Volume 13,066 cu ft (370 m^3)
Fineness ratio: 4:1
Payload: 154 lb (70 kg) with a pilot, 220 lb (100 kg) in remotely-controlled form, or 330 lb (150 kg) as a tethered and unmanned aerostat.
Engines: 2x 28 hp (20.9 kW) RM2-640 piston engines.
Maximum airspeed: 40 kts (47 mph) 75 km/h
Operating altitude: 3,280 ft (1,000 m)

Dolgoprudny Automation Systems Design Bureau (Russia)

Corporate address: 1 Letnaya Street, 141700 Dolgoprudny, Moscow Region.
Telephone: +7 095 408 89 09
Facsimile: +7 095 408 75 11
Information: P. P. Dementyev (Chief Designer).

Dolgoprudny Automation (DKBA) DP-800 Ecology

First flight: 1995 or 1996.
Role: Experimental, semi-rigid, helium airship, designed as a part of a technical programme for the Aviation Department in accordance with a Government decision. Many possible roles, including search and rescue, surveillance, mapping, promotional, tourism, environmental protection, broadcasting, traffic control, fishery protection, fire-watch and fire-fighting.

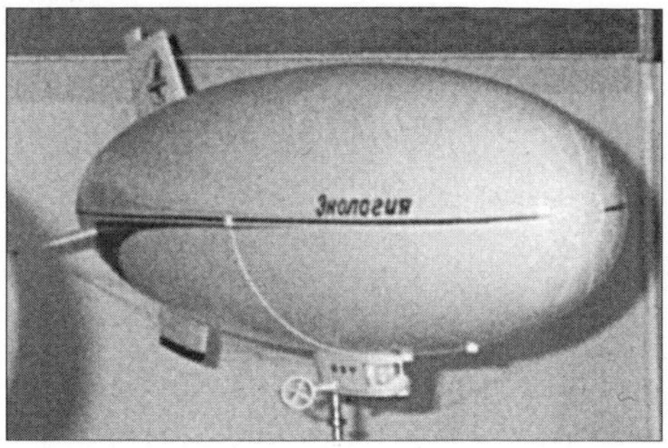

Model of the Dolgoprudny Automation DP-800 Ecology, seen at Farnborough 1994

★ Aims

★ Zero take-off and landing runs, though short runs are optional. The airship is towed to the take-off field using a special collapsible mooring mast on a tractor chassis.
★ Aerostatic balancing.
★ Flight without relying on lifting gas.
★ Management of propeller thrust vectoring and control surfaces.
★ Use of modern materials and on-board equipment.
★ Conforms to British Standards of Airworthiness for airships; its manoeuvrability is said to be similar to that of non-aerobatic aeroplanes.
★ Day and night flights in accordance with Level 1 category ICAO.

▲ Development

▲ This programme covers a wide range of tasks, including the validation/testing of new technical decisions, technologies and materials; manuals for the designers; norms of airworthiness and other documents, which are necessary for the creation and legal certification of airships in Russia; the development of methods and programmes for testing, demands for the testing of airship ports, and technical tasks for designing and constructing support buildings; creation of a training centre for simulating the flight dynamics and for aircrew training; the construction of 2 experimental airships with load-carrying capacity of up to 3 tonnes.
▲ Project has been approved, and all scientific and research work is complete. A mock-up of the cockpit has been built, all technical documents printed, the test stand is ready, and the development of technological processes for attachments was virtually finished by early 1995.

Crew/Passengers: All-metal semi-monocoque gondola, divided into 6 separate compartments: cockpit for 2 pilots, under-cockpit accessory compartment, the cabin for 12 passengers, under-cabin 3-section ballast tank, engine bay and tail compartments. Ground crew of 3-5, excluding truck drivers.
Length: 205 ft (62.5 m) – some sources say 62 m.
Diameter: 51 ft 8 ins (15.75 m)
Height: 72 ft 2 ins (22 m) overall
Envelope: Russian rubberized diagonally-plied fabric (2-ply) of Kapron type with aluminium coating, offering gas permeability of up to 3 l/m^2 per day. Volume 283,895 cu ft (8,039 m^3). Calculated lifetime is 16,000 hours under gas over 5 years (including 2 years in storage), with further usage in accordance with technical conditions. The single leg undercarriage beneath the gondola is from an Mi-24 helicopter.
Ballonet/s volume: 26% of envelope.
Fineness ratio: Believed to be 3.95:1
Take-off weight: 18,520 lb (8,400 kg)
Empty weight: 11,354 lb (5,150 kg)
Maximum load: 6,619 lb (3,000 kg) including fuel and ballast.
Engines: 2x 325 hp (242.4 kW) M-14V-26 radial piston engines from a Ka-26 helicopter, giving 275 hp (205 kW) for cruise. Engine power is transmitted through side pylons to the 2 propellers.
Propellers: 2 shrouded AV-83 4-blade, reversible/variable-pitch propellers, of 4 ft 11 ins (1.5 m) diameter. Propellers can be vectored ±120°.
Fuel: 2,205 lb (1,000 kg), of minimum 91 octane (B-91/115, Oil-100 and OM-270).
Stabilizers: Cruciform tail, with metal framework covered with fabric. Operation of the elevators and rudders is mechanical, accomplished from the control-wheel column in the gondola cockpit, with no pedal operation. Remote control can be installed if required by customers.
Maximum airspeed: 62.5 kts (71 mph) 115 km/h
Ceiling: 8,850 ft (2,700 m)
Duration: 44.7 hours
Range: 723.5 naut miles (832.5 miles) 1,340 km

Dolgoprudny Automation (DKBA) DP-6000 Vityaz

Role: Very large passenger and/or cargo airship. Can be adapted for various military roles, including AEW housing phased-array radars, airborne communications and relay, intelligence, search and rescue, and more.

★ Aims

★ Projected very large airship with a 20-tonne carrying capacity, using experience gained from building the DP-800.

▲ Development

▲ Development started in 1993.

Crew/Passengers: 2-deck gondola of 106 ft 7 ins (32.5 m) length, accommodating 144 passengers in the commercial or military transport models, or 84 passengers and cargo in the mixed-load layout, or all cargo. Gondola appears to have a detachable lower/central portion, able to accept a passenger or cargo pod or have a heavy-cargo platform attached for outsized loads including long vehicles in a flying-crane configuration. The gondola also houses a modern cockpit, crew utility and rest areas, toilets, passenger galley and bar, power unit, and a ballast bay.
Length: 411 ft 7 ins (125.46 m)
Envelope: 4 gas compartments.
Engines: 2x 800 hp (597 kW) or 1,000 hp (746 kW) diesel engines driving 2 shrouded and vectoring propellers on the rear cabin sides, plus 1 or 2x 2,500 shp (1,864 kW) TV7-117 turboshaft engines driving a shrouded cruise propeller/s from the rear of the gondola.
Propellers: See Engines.
Stabilizers: Cruciform tail fins with electrically-powered elevators and rudders.
Cruise speed: 54 kts (62 mph) 100 km/h with a 20-tonne payload.
Ceiling: 9,850 ft (3,000 m) with a 12-tonne payload.
Range: 1,890 naut miles (2,175 miles) 3,500 km at 3,280 ft (1,000 m) altitude.

Myasishchev Design Bureau (Russia)

Corporate address: See Combat section.

● Activities

● Airship work includes a proposed 6 crew and 28 passenger semi-rigid hybrid with 2 TVD-100 turbo-props, as the KRUI-3. Volume 706,300 cu ft (20,000 m^3), length 279 ft (85 m) and take-off weight 30,887 lb (14,000 kg).

The Thermoplane Design Bureau, Moscow Aviation Institute (Russia)

Corporate address: 4 Volokolamskoe Shosse, 125871 Moscow.
Telephone: +7 095 158 79 16 or 158 41 27
Facsimile: + 7 095 158 29 77
Telex: 411746 Sokol SU
Information: Dr Leon P. Poniaev (Deputy General Director).

Thermoplane ALA-40

First flight: 1993.
Role: One-fifth scale test and proof-of-concept model of the ALA-600. Also proposed for aerial inspection of above-ground oil, gas and heating pipelines, road traffic control, pollution control, TV and radio broadcasting, medical and police services, rescue, and tourism. Advertising space offered on the lower envelope skin.

★ Aims

★ To prove the design concept, leading eventually to the production of very large Thermoplanes capable of carrying many passengers or bulky/heavy freight (including harvested produce, vehicles, building sections and generators) in difficult weather conditions (as found in Siberia, the far North and far East regions of Russia), in areas of sparse population and few, if any, roads or railways. These regions often have high-velocity winds with substantial changes in direction, and long periods of very low temperatures with freezing fog, snow and ice. However, they are remote areas rich in mineral resources including oil, gas, gold, diamonds, forests and more.
★ An unballasted airship with the ability to operate on an ecologically friendly basis, without the need for the usual complex of ground bases, hangars and mooring posts.
★ To show the wheel or disc configuration offers smaller, lighter and stronger airships, compared to conventional types, with improved distribution of stress loads. Designers claim a 200 m diameter Thermoplane could carry a 500 tonnes load, which they say would require a conventional airship length of approximately 700 m.
★ Dual gas system (see Envelope). The recyclable nature of the engine gas is to provide ecologically clean operations.
★ Very smooth aerodynamic surface minimizes turbulence and drag and allows a new system of adaptive blowing flow control to improve aerodynamic qualities, dampening stress loads and distortion.

▲ Development

▲ 1980. Russian LTA Thermoplane Design Bureau formed. LTA-Dirigible Programme was initially headed by Professor S. Eger but currently led by Professor Yuri Ryzhov. Programme funded from the outset by a

consortium that includes the oil and gas company Ritek, the Energy Resource Fund, the gold and diamond company Nika, Aviastar, and the Moscow Aviation Institute.
▲ 1989. Design work completed.
▲ End 1991. Construction of the first of 3 ALA-40s (*4001*) neared completion at the Aviastar Industrial Complex plant.
▲ Mid 1992. Full ground test programme began; the static and dynamic tests at the Flight Test Control Aero Centre.
▲ 1994. Second ALA-40 (*4002*) completed at Ulyanovsk, for ground and flight tests in 1995.
Crew: Occupy a gondola fabricated from a converted Mi-2 helicopter.
Envelope diameter: 131 ft 3 ins (40 m)
Envelope height: 52 ft 6 ins (16 m)
Envelope: Total volume 376,450 cu ft (10,660 m^3), of which 204,800 cu ft (5,800 m^3) is helium/hydrogen. Centre section holds the helium (or hydrogen) in spherical cells to give lift equal to the empty weight of the vehicle. Remaining volume filled with high-temperature gas from the propulsive engines, providing the additional lift needed to carry the payload. See ALA-600.
Payload: 4,410-7,715 lb (2,000-3,500 kg)
Engines: 2 engines mounted with the gondola for propulsion, plus another on the forward envelope to assist stability.
Propellers: 2 propulsive propellers plus a series of 4 small horizontally-mounted propellers around the envelope for extra lift and control.
Stabilizer: Large tailplane-type surface at rear, plus 2 twin vertical rudders and a series of other fins and elevators on the undersurface.
Maximum airspeed: 59 kts (68 mph) 110 km/h
Ceiling: 6,550 ft (2,000 m)

Thermoplane ALA-600

First flight: Possibly end 1995.
Role: Passenger or heavy-lift freight carrying. Unusual proposals from potential customers have included a one-off de luxe hospital version with surgery facilities for use in remote areas, and a cruise Sky Ship luxury airborne hotel with accommodation for 150-200 guests.

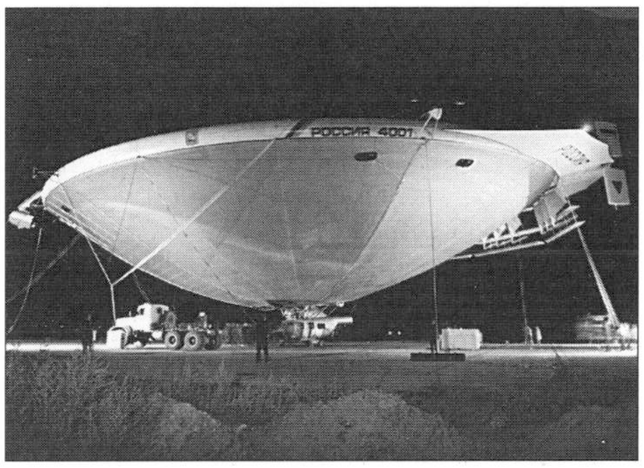

Thermoplane ALA-40 (4001)

★ Aims

★ To carry a 600 tonnes load over 5,000 km.
★ See ALA-40 for flight expectations.

▲ Development

▲ To be in service by the end of the 1990s or 2000.
▲ May be developed as an international co-operative programme. Approaches for EU investment and co-operation have already been made.
▲ Russian government has guaranteed to fund design and development, following a visit to see the first ALA-40 by President Boris Yeltsin in 1992.
▲ Analysis indicates that 25-35 ALA-600s operating from European and Tyumen bases could provide potential profits of US$15-18m during 1997-2005.
Crew/Passengers: Active crew of 4 in an under-envelope cabin, with rest rooms and facilities for replacement crews on long flights. Freight (see Payload) or up to 150–200 passengers (see also Role).
Length: 689 ft (210 m)
Envelope diameter: 650 ft (198 m)
Envelope height: 269 ft (82 m)
Envelope: Centre section holds helium (or hydrogen) in spherical cells to give lift equal to the empty weight of the vehicle. Remaining volume filled with high-temperature gas from the propulsive turboprop engines, providing the additional lift needed to carry the payload. Multi-layer thermoplastic and carbonfibre ribbon power tor, and film and fibre skin based on Terlon.
Take-off weight: 2,645,500 lb (1,200,000 kg)
Payload: 1,322,700 lb (600,000 kg) carried on a huge 115 ft (35 m) diameter under-envelope platform with ramps.
Engines: Possibly 12 turboprop engines, 6 on the canard and 6 on the rear tail complex. Investigations are underway into new energy efficient and ecologically friendly engines with the flame-safe inhibitor of hydrogen fuel.
Propellers: Contra-rotating.
Fuel: see Engines.
Stabilizers: Canard with multiple control surfaces and multiple fins supporting the forward engines. Rear very-large-area horizontal tail surface, with inset ventral and dorsal fins supporting rudders and the rear-mounted pusher engines.
Maximum airspeed: 108 kts (124 mph) 200 km/h
Ceiling: 23,000 ft (7,000 m)
Range: 2,700 naut miles (3,100 miles) 5,000 km with full load.

Airspeed Airships (UK)

Corporate address: 4 Amberleaze Drive, Pembury, Tunbridge Wells, Kent TN2 4HF.
Telephone: +44 1892 833839
Facsimile: +44 1892 510229
Information: Nigel Wells.

● Activities

● Produces remotely-piloted airships. 4 built by early 1995, of which 1 has been sold.

Airspeed AS 400

Role: Non-rigid, unmanned, remotely-piloted airship for air-to-gound TV link and real-time monitoring, aerial photography, survey work, surveillance, advertising and more.

Airspeed Airships AS 400

Crew: None
Length: 26 ft (7.92 m)
Diameter: 5 ft 3 ins (1.6 m) maximum
Envelope: Volume 494 cu ft (14 m^3).
Payload: 13.2 lb (6 kg), including video and 35 mm camera equipment.
Engine: 2x 2 hp (1.49 kW) Irvine engines.
Maximum airspeed: 19 kts (22 mph) 35 km/h
Operating ceiling: 600 ft (183 m)
Range: 0.65 naut miles (0.75 miles) 1.2 km

Cameron Balloons Ltd (UK)

Corporate address: St John's Street, Bedminster, Bristol BS3 4NH.
Telephone: +44 117 9637216
Facsimile: +44 117 9661168
Information: Philip Dunnington (Sales Director).

● Activities

● Cameron Balloons took over Thunder & Colt in late 1994 and made it a division, though it retains its name for marketing purposes.

Cameron DG-14

First flight: 1989.
Role: Non-rigid, for advertising, photographic, surveillance and recreational use.

★ Aims

★ To offer significantly better cost/performance ratio than other helium airships.
★ Though normally moored to a portable mast when not in flight, its low height allows it to enter a standard aircraft hangar without deflation for maintenance or protection, preserving helium.

▲ Development

▲ 20 February 1991. Received BCAR 31 certification.
Crew: Pilot (see Payload) plus 2 ground crew.
Length: 62 ft 2 ins (18.95 m)
Diameter: 22 ft 7 ins (6.88 m) maximum

Height: 26 ft 4 ins (8.03 m) including gondola.
Envelope: Double laminated nylon. Volume 12,000 cu ft (340 m^3).
Ballonets: Main and tail.
Payload/ballast: Lifting capacity at 15°C at sea level is the pilot of 180 lb (81.6 kg) weight plus 90 lb (41 kg) of disposable ballast.
Engine: 570 cc König piston engine, with electric start. Vertical vectoring of the fan for control, which reduces the take-off roll to a few feet and cushions landing.
Propeller: 6-blade ducted fan.
Fuel: 23 litres.

Cameron DG-14 helium airship

Maximum airspeed: 26 kts (30 mph) 48 km/h
Operating ceiling: 2,800 ft (850 m)
Duration: 2 hours

Cameron DP60, DP70, DP80 and DP90

First flight: 1986.
Role: Hot-air airships for recreation and advertising.

▲ Development

▲ DP series gained 1st, 2nd and 3rd places in 1990 World Hot-Air Championships.
Crew/Passengers: Pilot or pilot and passenger. Aluminium gondola with a full-height polycarbonate windscreen. Intercom system is standard.
Length: *DP60* 100 ft (30.48 m), *DP70* 106 ft (32.31 m), *DP80* 111 ft (33.83 m), *DP90* 115 ft (35.05 m)
Width: *DP60* 37 ft (11.28 m), *DP70* 39 ft (11.89 m), *DP80* 40 ft (12.19 m), *DP90* 42 ft (12.80 m)
Height: *DP60* 45 ft (13.72 m), *DP70* 48 ft (14.63 m), *DP80* 50 ft (15.24 m), *DP90* 51 ft (15.54 m)
Envelope: Lower and centre sections of high tenacity ripstop nylon, upper third of Hyperlast. Volumes: *DP60* 60,000 cu ft (1,700 m^3), *DP70* 70,000 cu ft (1,982 m^3), *DP80* 80,000 cu ft (2,265 m^3), *DP90* 90,000 cu ft (2,548 m^3). Each side of the envelope can have an advertising display of approximately: *DP60* 936 sq ft (86.96 m^2), *DP70* 1,033 sq ft (95.97 m^2), *DP80* 990 sq ft (91.97 m^2), *DP90* 1,066 sq ft (99.03 m^2).
Engine: 570 cc König is standard on the DP60 and DP70 and optional on the DP80 and DP90. One Rotax 582UL with hush kit is standard on the DP80 and DP90.
Propeller: 3-blade pusher in a shroud.
Propane tanks: Choice covers 2 Worthingtons containing 77 litres, 2 Cameron 599s containing 85 litres, or 2 Cameron 426s containing 108 litres.
Maximum airspeed: 15 kts (17 mph) 27 km/h

Cameron DP80 hot-air airship

Lindstrand Balloons Ltd (UK)

Corporate address: Maesbury Road, Oswestry, Shropshire SY10 8ZZ.
Telephone: +44 1691 671717
Facsimile: +44 1691 671122
Information: Tina Lewis. Per Lindstrand (Managing Director).

Lindstrand AS 300

First Flight: 5 February 1993.
Role: Pressurized, non-rigid hot-air airship.

★ Aims

★ Can be operated in winds up to 10 kts by an experienced crew.
★ Designed to carry a 1,653 lb (750 kg) raft slung beneath it from 6 points on the envelope.
★ Largest hot-air airship so far built.
★ New envelope shape (see Develpment) to give better aerodynamics (less drag and leaves fins protruding further into the airflow, and on a longer torque arm, resulting in improved turn performance).
★ New fin geometry resulting in a much stiffer fin without increased weight or the use of non-fabric stiffeners.
★ New air distributing system for the tail plane to ensure constant fin buoyancy during flight and less air loss.
★ A new catenary load curtain developed using finite element analysis programme, which could simulate flight motions. This enables the elimination of pitch instability.
★ Precise control by thrust reverser (see Engine).

▲ Development

▲ AS 300 created for Operation Canopée, which undertakes botanic research of rainforests.
▲ Follows on from the AS 261 which flew 260 hours and performed excellent work in South America and Africa.
▲ 1992. Lindstrand Balloons received the order to build the new AS 300 envelope and update the gondola.
▲ 1993. Delivery. Used for its intended purpose in Summer 1993 in Borneo but political difficulties prevented plans for its use elsewhere. Thereafter based in France, and made an appearance (non-competitive) at the 1994 World Airship Championships.
Crew/Passengers: 7 persons, including pilot. Stainless steel spaceframe gondola, capable of being split into 5 sections for airlift by Twin Otter.
Length: 167 ft 2 ins (50.96 m)
Diameter: 59 ft 9 ins (18.20 m) maximum
Width: 67 ft 3 ins (20.50 m) maximum
Height: 68 ft 10 ins (20.98 m)
Envelope: Volume 300,960 cu ft (8,522.2 m^3). The main hull of the envelope is pressurized using a 5 hp (3.7 kW) Honda engine driving a multi-blade fan. Pressure is regulated by 2 fabric pressure relief valves forward of the gondola. Hull shape is maintained using a Kevlar catenary system to distribute the loads from the gondola into the top of the envelope. Fins have a separate pressurization system fed by a multi-blade fan belt driven off the propulsion system. Fin shape is maintained by multiple internal formers. Stability of the fins by using a large footprint at the base of the fins, attaching all the internal formers to the main hull and by a tip tube giving longitudinal stiffness at the fin tip. Rigging lines facility to secure the fin tips to the main hull. Entire envelope is manufactured from HTN 90. An emergency 5 hp (3.7 kW) electric fan can supply either the main hull or fins.

Lindstrand AS 300 hot-iar airship

Fineness ratio: 2.8:1
Total lift: 5,952 lb (2,700 kg) maximum
Weights: Envelope 904 lb (410 kg). Gondola 1,173 lb (532 kg) dry. Propane capacity 849 lb (385 kg). Avgas 99.2 lb (45 kg).
Engine: 100 hp (74.6 kW) Teledyne Continental O-200 piston engine. (See also Envelope.) Thrust reverser installed behind the pusher propeller consisting of 2 air vanes that swing into the propwash by lever control. This results in a 60% effective reverse thrust which can also make the airship go backwards.
Propeller: 4-blade Hoffmann.
Fuel: See Weights
Maximum airspeed: Over 20 kts (23 mph) 37 km/h

Lindstrand HS 110

First flight: 1 May 1995.
Role: Hot-air airship solely for advertising purposes.

★ Aims

★ Optimized for low maintenance and ease of handling in the air and transportation on the ground.
★ Set-up time from a trailer is under 30 minutes.
★ Refuelling without envelope deflation.

▲ Development

▲ 3 orders by January 1995.
Crew/Passengers: 2 persons side-by-side, in a glassfibre/Kevlar/carbonfibre gondola; 1 person only when extra propane is carried or when single pilot flight is desired. 2 ground crew.
Length: 111 ft 7 ins (34 m)
Diameter: 43 ft 4 ins (13.2 m)
Width: 48 ft 6 ins (14.78 m) over fins.
Height: 51 ft 10 ins (15.8 m) overall.
Envelope: Manufactured from high-tenacity polyamide fabric coated with a high temperature polyurethane solution; jointing technique is a double-fell twin needle seam reinforced with load tape. Volume 110,358 cu ft (3,125 m^3). Twin burners of modified JetStream type and can be fired individually or as a pair to give more longitudinal control (see Fuel).

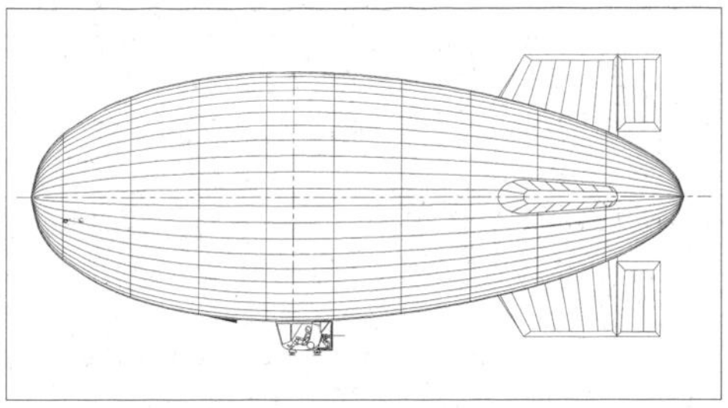

Lindstrand HS 110 2-seat hot-air airship

Twin catenary load curtain. Advertising can be directly on the hull or on 2 side banners of 72 ft (22 m) length (area 3,230 sq ft, 300 m^2) and 1 under the chin of 13 ft x 13 ft (4 m x 4 m) and with an area of 150 sq ft (14 m^2). Banners can be changed in under 1 hour using Velcro and have a weight penalty of 45 lb (20 kg).
Surface area: 15,000 sq ft (1,393.5 m^2)
Fineness ratio: 2.575:1
Empty weight: 375 lb (170 kg)
Engine: 65 hp (48.5 kW) Arrow GT500.
Propeller: 3-blade composites type.
Fuel: 35 litres for the engine. 176 lb (80 kg) of gas for envelope inflation; further 88 lb (40 kg) can be carried instead of the passenger.
Stabilizer: 4 fins, inflated via a fan at the gondola, have much higher air pressure than the hull and thereby stay rigid even under full turns.
Maximum airspeed: 20 kts (23 mph) 37 km/h
Advertising cruise speed: 10-12 kts (11.5-14 mph) 19-22 km/h
Duration: up to 2 hours on standard fuel; almost 3.5 hours with extra propane.

Thunder & Colt (UK)

Corporate address: St John's Street, Bedminster, Bristol BS3 4NH.
Telephone: +44 1179 532 772
Facsimile: +44 1179 663 638
Information: Alan Noble.

● Activities

● Thunder & Colt's parent organization, Airborne Group, went into receivership on 7 November 1994. Cameron Balloons has taken over the company as a division of its operations, though the GA 42 has gone to ABC. Work has been concentrated at Bristol, although the AS 80 Mk II and AS 105 Mk II will continue to be marketed as Thunder & Colt types.

Thunder & Colt AS 80 Mk II

First flight: 1988.
Role: Recreational, pressurized hot-air airship.
Crew/Passengers: Pilot or pilot and passenger. Stainless steel and aluminium gondola, with polycarbonate windscreen.
Length: 101 ft 8 ins (31 m)
Diameter: 40 ft 8 ins (12.40 m) maximum

Thunder & Colt (Cameron) AS 80 Mk II

Envelope: Volume 75,000 cu ft (2,123.76 m^3). Twin catenary system to distribute loads from the gondola and engine to the envelope. Envelope constructed of HTN 90K. Envelope pressurized via an electric fan and air scoop aft of the propeller.
Fineness ratio: 2.5:1
Gross lift: 1,323 lb (600 kg)
Weights: Envelope 419 lb (190 kg). Gondola 463 lb (210 kg) dry. Propane 242 lb (110 kg) maximum.
Engine: 52 hp (38.8 kW) Rotax 462 piston engine.
Propeller: 2-blade pusher type.
Maximum airspeed: 20 kts (23 mph) 37 km/h
Duration: 2.5 hours

Thunder & Colt AS 105 Mk II

Role: Recreational, pressurized hot-air airship.
Crew/Passengers: Pilot or pilot and passenger. Stainless steel and aluminium gondola, with polycarbonate windscreen.
Length: 111 ft 7 ins (34 m)
Diameter: 45 ft 6 ins (13.87 m) maximum
Envelope: Volume 105,000 cu ft (2,973 m^3). Twin catenary system to distribute loads from the gondola and engine to the envelope. Envelope constructed of HTN 90K. Envelope pressurized via an electric fan and air scoop aft of the propeller.
Fineness ratio: 2.5:1
Weights: Envelope 469 lb (212.7 kg). Gondola 463 lb (210 kg) dry. Propane 242 lb (110 kg) maximum.
Engine: 52 hp (38.8 kW) Rotax 462 piston engine.
Propeller: 2-blade pusher type.
Maximum airspeed: 20 kts (23 mph) 37 km/h
Duration: 2.5 hours

American Blimp Corporation (USA)

Corporate address: Suite 5, 1900 N-E 25th Avenue, Hillsboro, OR 97124.
Telephone: +1 503 693 1611
Facsimile: +1 503 681 0906
Information: Charles Ehrler (Executive Vice-President).

● Activities

● ABC expects to sell 3 airships per year.

ABC GA 42

First flight: 2 September 1987.
Role: Non-rigid helium airship for surveillance, advertising and promotions, broadcasting, training and other tasks.

★ Aims

★ Fly-by-wire control system.

▲ Development

▲ Designed by Thunder & Colt and built in association with Airborne Industries. Taken over by ABC.
▲ Certified to BCAR CAP 471 Section Q.
Crew/Passengers: 2 crew. Enclosed aluminium gondola.
Length: 90 ft 3 ins (27.5 m)
Diameter: 30 ft 2 ins (9.2 m)
Envelope: Volume 42,000 cu ft (1,189 m^3). Envelope of polyamide, with polyurethane coating. Aluminium battens. Twin catenary curtains to distribute loads from the gondola and engine to the envelope. Advertising area 1,187 sq ft (110.25 m^2) approximately.
Ballonets: 2 (1 in each end), inflated with air via an engine-driven fan. Volume 11,000 cu ft (311.48 m^3).
Gross lift: 2,425 lb (1,100 kg)
Maximum heaviness: 220 lb (100 kg) static
Engine: 74.6 kW (100 hp) Teledyne Continental O-200-B piston engine.
Propeller: 4-blade Hoffmann.
Fuel: 130 litres
Stabilizers: Glassfibre cruciform tail fins, with movable control surfaces on the horizontal and ventral fins.
Cruise speed: 27-40 kts (31-46 mph) 50-74 km/h
Maximum climb rate: 1,300 ft (396 m) per minute
Ceiling: 9,500 ft (2,900 m)
Duration: 7.5 hours

ABC A-60+ Lightship

First flight: 9 April 1988 (prototype designated A-50).
Role: Non-rigid helium airship, principally for aerial advertising. Has gyrostabilized camera mounting and real-time datalink for broadcasting work.

▲ Development

▲ 18 May 1990. FAA certification.
▲ November 1989. First flight of a production A-60, delivered to Virgin Lightships in May 1990 but recalled and redelivered about November that year.
▲ 1991. FAA certification for the A-60+, with an 8,000 cu ft (226.5 m^3) increase in envelope volume for improved hot and high performance.
▲ 1993. A-60 fleet modified to A-60+ standard to offer additional disposable load.
▲ In early 1995 Virgin operated 4 Lightships, together with a very large number of hot-air balloons for advertising purposes. 5 other A-60+s operated by Lightship America, Hutchinson Communications, Beijing Oriental Air Service, and in Brazil. 10th A-60+ completed in 1995, with 2 more then under construction.
Crew/Passengers: Pilot and 4 passengers in an enclosed gondola.
Length: 128 ft (39 m)
Diameter: 32 ft 10 ins (10 m)
Envelope: Dacron and Mylar envelope, with urethane film internal helium bladder. Volume 68,000 cu ft (1,925 m^3). Internal illumination of banner signs; an A-60+ has flown with a computer-controlled lightbulb lightsign. 2 side advertising banners 90 ft x 22 ft (27.43 m x 6.7 m) each, plus a belly banner 20 ft x 20 ft (6.1 m x 6.1 m).
Ballonet: 1, 20% of envelope volume.
Fineness ratio: 3.8:1
Gross buoyancy: 4,144 lb (1,880 kg)
Dynamic lift: 250 lb (113.4 kg)
Gross useful lift: 1,364 lb (618.7 kg) standard, at 2,500 ft (760 m)
Empty weight: 2,780 lb (1,261 kg)
Engines: 2x 80 hp (59.6 kW) Limbach L 2000 piston engines mounted on outriggers from the gondola; no vectoring.
Propellers: 5 ft (1.52 m) diameter Muhlbauer 3-blade pusher propellers.
Fuel: 280 litres.
Stabilizers: Cruciform tail fins with movable control surfaces.

American Blimp Corporation A-60+ Lightship (Virgin Lightships)

Maximum airspeed: 46 kts (53 mph) 85 km/h
Cruise speed: 35 kts (40 mph) 64 km/h
Maximum climb rate: 1,660 ft (506 m) per minute
Maximum rate of descent: 1,400 ft (427 m) per minute
Ceiling: 10,000 ft (3,050 m)
Take-off distance: 366 ft (112 m) or more
Duration: 15 hours at cruise

ABC A-130 Lightship

First flight: August 1996.
Role: Non-rigid helium airship.

★ Aims
★ A-130 designation indicates the envelope volume, at 130,000 cu ft. Larger A-150 and A-170 variants are planned for surveillance.

▲ Development
▲ In advanced design in early 1995.
Crew/Passengers: Pilot and 8 passengers in a lengthened version of the A-60+ gondola, with identical pilot station.
Envelope: New type of third-generation single-layer heat-sealed material, requiring no separate internal helium bladder. Volume 130,000 cu ft (3,681 m^3. Envelope lifetime 10 years.
Ballast: Water ballast system for pitch/trim and buoyancy control.
Engines: 2 x 200 hp (149 kW) Textron Lycoming IO-360 piston engines

Barnes Airships (USA)

Corporate address: Route 2, Box 86, Statesville, NC 28677.
Telephone: +1 704 876 2378
Facsimile: +1 704 876 1251
Information: Bill Meadows.

● Activities
● The Whispership was dismantled in early 1995, for work on its power plant.

Barnes Whispership

First flight: 1991.
Role: Non-rigid, experimental airship.

★ Aims
★ Probably low noise and low power requirement.
Crew/Passengers: Pilot and passenger in a gondola with a float.
Length: 56 ft (17.1 m)
Diameter: 19 ft (5.8 m)
Height: 23 ft (7 m) overall
Envelope: 12,000 cu ft (340 m^3)
Fineness ratio: 2.94:1
Gross lift: 603 lb (273.5 kg)
Empty weight: 304 lb (138 kg)
Engine: 5 hp (3.7 kW) piston engine.
Fuel: Standard capacity can be increased to extend duration.
Maximum airspeed: 28 kts (32 mph) 51.5 km/h
Cruise speed: 22 kts (25 mph) 40 km/h
Ceiling: 3,000 ft (914 m)
Duration: 10 hours normal at cruise speed.

Goodyear Airship Operations (USA)

Address: 841 Wingfoot Lake Road, Mogadore, OH 44278.
Telephone: +1 216 796 7920
Facsimile: +1 216 796 8399
Information: Michael Wittman.

● Activities
● Goodyear airships are primarily for marketing and sales promotions for its parent Tire & Rubber Company.
● Operates 3 airships: *Spirit of Akron* based near the corporate headquarters in Ohio; *Stars & Stripes* based at Pompano Beach, Florida; and *Eagle* based in Carson, California.
● The last airship designed and engineered by Goodyear (but completed by Loral – which see) was GZ-22 *Spirit of Akron*, launched in 1989. However, Goodyear has not been in the airship manufacturing business since the latter 1980s, having sold its rights to Loral in 1987. It continues to carry out repair and rebuild work, under licence from Loral which owns the rights. The other 2 airships are rebuilt GZ-20s.

Loral Defense Systems – Akron (USA)

Corporate address: 1210 Massillon Road, Akron, OH 44310.
Telephone: +1 216 796 8825
Facsimile: +1 216 796 7230
Information: Ron Browning (Programmes Director).

● Activities
● Loral holds the Type Certificates to former Goodyear airships, and is under contract to Goodyear to supply engineering and technical support to the Goodyear airship operations, itself also licensing work to Goodyear (see Goodyear).

Loral GZ-22

First flight: 1989.
Role: Helium airship for advertising, promotional and broadcasting work.

▲ Development
▲ See Goodyear entry.
Crew/Passengers: Pilot and 6 passengers in a steel framed and composites skinned (honeycomb-shaped non-metallic aramid paper/resin and impregnated aramid fibre woven cloth) gondola, with a retractable undercarriage.
Length: 205 ft 6 ins (62.64 m)
Width: 47 ft (14.33 m)
Height: 60 ft 2 ins (18.34 m)
Envelope: Neoprene-impregnated polyester 2-ply fabric. Volume 247,800 cu ft (7,017 m^3). 8,064 Night Sign lights.
Gross weight: 15,000 lb (6,804 kg) maximum
Engines: 2x 420 shp (313.2 kW) Allison 250-B17C turboprops.
Propellers: 2x 5 ft 10 ins (1.78 m) Hartzell 3-blade propellers, vectorable +75° and –30° .
Stabilizers: X configuration. Aluminium alloy structure covered with heat shrinkable polyester fabric and coated with polyurethane paint.

Loral GZ-22 Spirit of Akron, operated by Goodyear

Maximum airspeed: 56 kts (65 mph) 105 km/h
Cruise speed: 26-35 kts (30-40 mph) 48-64 km/h
Ceiling: 10,000 ft (3,050 m)
Operating altitude: 1,000-3,000 ft (305-915 m)

Raven Industries Inc (USA)

Corporate address: Box 1007, Sioux Falls, SD57117-1007.
Telephone: +1 605 336 2750

● Activities

● Raven constructs balloons and offers fabric. It built the *Earthwinds Hilton* twin-balloon (upper helium and lower air-filled for ballasting) for a non-stop world circumnavigation and research flight. The project has been supported by NASA and other official organizations from the USA and Russia. The 3-person pressurized gondola that is attached below the upper balloon was constructed by Scaled Composites Inc of Mojave, California. The crew includes Larry Newman, who successfully achieved with others the first-ever balloon transatlantic and transpacific flights in August 1978 and November 1981 respectively. The *Earthwinds Hilton* made a 7 hour test flight on 12 January 1994 and the world flight attempt was expected in 1995. No further details will be recorded here, as this is not an airship.

TCOM LP (USA)

Corporate address: 7115 Thomas Edison Drive, Columbia, Maryland 21046.

● Activities

● Builds non-rigid, helium-filled aerostats used mainly as tethered radar platforms for airborne tracking and surveillance. A principal operator is the US Customs Service, while South Korea is the main overseas customer. Details have emerged of the TCOM AEW aerostat used by the Israeli Air Force. It is 230 ft (70 m) high and 131 ft (40 m) in diameter, and carries a Westinghouse radar for long-range surveillance. Deployment in southern Israel began in 1991.

James Thompson (USA)

Address: 1700 Citizens Plaza, Louisville, KY 40202.
Telephone: +1 502 566 0504
Facsimile: +1 502 589 0148

James Thompson *N99TW*

First Flight: Expected 1995.
Role: Non-rigid helium airship, built as a one-off homebuilt.

▲ Development

▲ Inflated at Tillamook, Oregon, on 30 June 1994, when some last minute adjustments and completion of control rigging were all that remained before first flight. By October 1994 the Winter weather was setting in, making flight testing unlikely.
Crew/Passengers: 2 persons in a steel tube and composites, cable-suspended, gondola.
Length: 82 ft (25 m)
Diameter: 26 ft (7.92 m)
Envelope: Volume 28,000 cu ft (792.87 m^3), including ballonets.
Fineness ratio: 3.15:1
Ballonets: 2, each 2,000 cu ft (56.63 m^3) air capacity, providing pitch trim. Maximum combined capacity 3,456 cu ft (97.86 m^3).
Take-off weight: 1,534 lb (695.8 kg) estimated
Ballast: 180 lb (81.65 kg) of lead shot or sand.
Engine: 1,200 cc Honda liquid-cooled piston engine, with belt reduction drive.
Propeller: Fixed-pitch wooden propeller in a shroud.
Stabilizers: 3 aluminium alloy tube/fabric fins, in inverted Y configuration, each with a movable control surface.

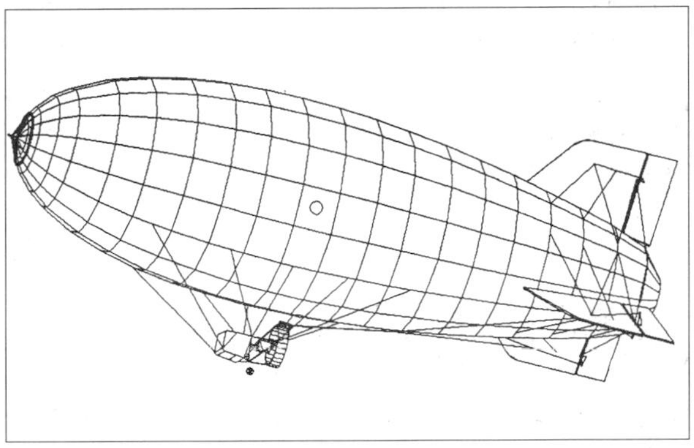

James Thompson N99TW homebuilt airship

Maximum airspeed: 35 kts (40 mph) 65 km/h expected
Ceiling: 4,000 ft (1,220 m) expected

Ulita Industries Inc (USA)

Corporate address: PO Box 412, Sheboygan, WI 53082-0412.

● Activities

● Manufacturer of balloons and fabrics.
● Among several airship projects begun, the Cloud Cruiser is the nearest to fulfillment. However, expected progress looked likely to be delayed in early 1995 due to non-aviation matters.

Ulita UM10-23 Cloud Cruiser

First flight: Not flown at time of writing.
Role: Non-rigid helium airship for sale as a kit for recreational use; assembled and certified airships may be available later.

★ Aims

★ Inexpensive kit for homebuilders.
Crew/Passengers: Pilot and passengers with dual controls.
Length: 83 ft 7 ins (25.48 m)
Envelope diameter: 22 ft 9 ins (6.93 m)
Height: 29 ft 5 ins (8.97 m) overall
Envelope: Volume 23,250 cu ft (658.37 m^3)
Ballonets: 2, totalling 5,115 cu ft (144.84 m^3)
Fineness ratio: 3.6:1
Gross aerostatic lift: 1,423 lb (645.5 kg)
Empty weight: 941 lb (426.8 kg)
Payload: 410 lb (186 kg) including crew.
Engines: 2x 24 hp (17.9 kW) König SC 430 piston engines.
Propellers: 2x 3 ft 6 in (1.07 m) diameter 3-blade propellers in vectoring shrouds.
Fuel: 61-98 litres.
Stabilizers: 2 large ventral tailfins and an adjoining tailplane, with rudders and elevators.
Maximum airspeed: 39 kts (45 mph) 72 km/h
Ceiling: 8,000 ft (2,438 m)

UPship – The Dirigible Airship (USA)

Corporate address: Rt 2, Box 53-4, Elba, AL 36323.
Telephone: +1 205 897 6132
Information: Jesse Blenn (Director).

UPship 100

First flight: Not expected until 1999.
Role: Semi-rigid, helium homebuilt airship, intended to become a commercial venture.

★ Aims

★ Advanced design, with undisclosed innovations.
★ Good low-speed handling and good control throughout the speed range.
★ No ground-crew mooring capability.

▲ Development

▲ Design began in 1989 and has been completed. Development is underway. Mock-ups of the gondola and fins have been fabricated.
▲ Construction of the UPship 100-001 prototype is expected to start in about 1997 and take 2 years.
▲ Venture capital is being sought.
Length: 100 ft (30.5 m)
Diameter: 20 ft (6.1 m)
Height: 24 ft 8 ins (7.52 m)
Envelope: Polyester envelope, with 3 inner helium cells of Mylar film. Aluminium alloy girder keel. Volume over 21,900 cu ft (620 m^3)
Ballonet: 20% of envelope volume. For trimming in pitch.
Gross lift: 1,200 lb (544.3 kg)

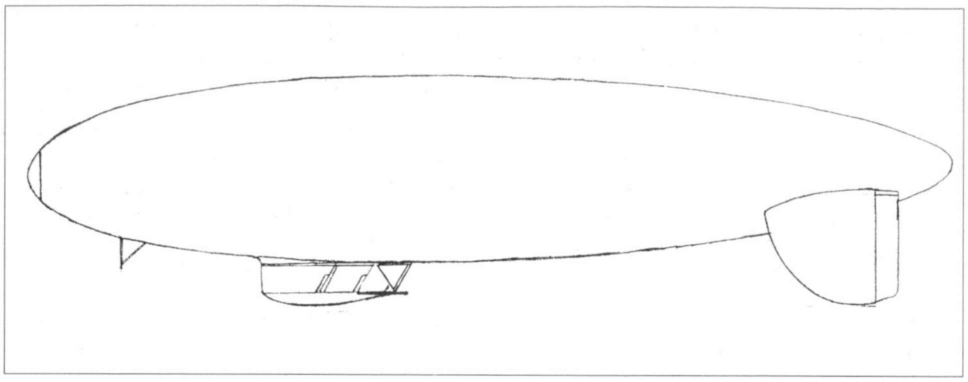

Empty weight: 800 lb (363 kg)
Engines: 3x 5 hp (3.73 kW) Honda GX140 piston engines.
Fuel: 66.25 litres.
Stabilizers: Inverted V twin fins with active control surfaces. Carbonfibre/balsawood construction, with polyester skins.
Maximum airspeed: 28.5 kts (33 mph) 53 km/h
Cruise speed: 25 kts (29 mph) 46 km/h at 70% power.
Ceiling: Up to 6,000 ft (1,825 m)
Duration: Up to 20 hours at cruise speed

UPship 100-001 semi-rigid helium homebuilt airship

US Lighter Than Air Corporation (USA)

Address (US): 750 Commercial Street, Eugene, OR 97402.
Telephone: +1 503 683 4983
Facsimile: +1 503 484 4299
Information: Ray Olma (President/CEO).

■ Facilities

■ US-LTA is a Canadian owned company, registered as a US corporation. The corporate office is at 1160 Skana Drive, Delta, BC V4M 2L4, Canada.
■ Engineering and manufacturing is at 750 Commercial Street, Eugene, OR 97402.
■ The airship is hangared and operated from Tillamook, OR.

US-LTA 138-S

First flight: 28 October 1987.
Role: Non-rigid helium airship for advertising, research and pollution monitoring.

▲ Development

▲ 1990. Prototype certified by the FAA.
▲ Summer 1992. Prototype used for oceanographic research under short-term contract from the Naval Research Laboratory (NRL), with missions including suspending a 700 lb (317 kg) sled carrying research equipment while off the Pacific coast. Success led to further contracts in 1993-95.
▲ 4 July 1993. First production example was lost in an accident at Manhattan.
▲ 1995. Tailfins, gondola and other components are completed for a further example and long-lead items for others.

Crew/Passengers: 6 persons in a steel tube and composites gondola.
Length: 160 ft (48.8 m)
Diameter: 42 ft (12.8 m)
Height: 57 ft (17.4 m) overall
Envelope: Dacron/polyurethane outer skin bonded with an internal non-woven material. Volume 138,000 cu ft (3,907.7 m^3).
Ballonets: 2 inside the helium cell.
Take-off weight: 8,386 lb (3,803 kg)
Empty weight: 5,865 lb (2,660 kg)
Payload: 2,520 lb (1,143 kg)
Engine: 300 hp (224 kW) Textron Lycoming IO-540-K1A5 piston engine.
Propeller: Hartzell 3-blade, pusher, reversible-pitch propeller in a shroud.
Fuel: 386 litres.
Stabilizers: 3 tailfins of aluminium/fabric, each with a movable control surface.
Maximum airspeed: 56.5 kts (65 mph) 105 km/h
Cruise speed: 30 kts (35 mph) 56 km/h, economical
Maximum climb rate:
Ceiling: 9,000 ft (2,750 m)
Duration: 14.5 hours at economical cruise speed.

US Lighter Than Air 138-S prototype at Tillamook (A.W.L. Nayler)

Westinghouse Airships Inc (USA)

Corporate address: PO Box 17193, Mail Stop 1780, Baltimore, MD 21203.
Telephone: +1 410 765 3000
Facsimile: +1 410 765 2950
Information: E. Judson Brandreth

■ Facilities

■ Successor to Airship Industries of the UK, maintaining an engineering/design centre in Luton, England, as well as a main operating base and flight operations and support centre in Weeksville, North Carolina, USA.
■ WAI operates within the Airborne Early Warning Systems Division of the Electronic Systems Group.

Westinghouse Airships Skyship 500HL

First flight: 30 July 1987.
Role: Non-rigid helium airship, used by Airship International (operating from Orlando, Florida) primarily for aerial advertising, with secondary sight-seeing, alongside a Skyship 600 and a WDL 1B.

★ Aims

★ Greater lift capability than Skyship 500.

▲ Development

▲ 2 airships, based on the former Airship Industries Skyship 500 but modified to incorporate the larger Skyship 600 envelope to increase load under hot and high conditions, and also with gondola changes.

Crew/Passengers: 1 or 2 pilots in an enclosed composites gondola.
Length: 193 ft 7 ins (59 m)
Diameter: 49 ft 10 ins (15.2 m)
Height: 66 ft 7 ins (20.3 m) overall
Envelope: Aerazur-manufactured envelope of 1-ply polyester fabric, with a polyurethane/titanium dioxide outer coating against UL deterioration, and with a polyvinylidene chloride inner film attached with polyurethane. Volume 235,000 cu ft (6,654 m^3). Composites nose dome with mooring attachments.
Ballonets: 2, accounting for 26% of envelope volume.
Ballast: Water ballast in tanks and non-disposable ballast beneath seats in containers.
Disposable load: 3,120 lb (1,415 kg) maximum structural. An extra 1,191 lb (540 kg) can be carried (envelope mounted only). Typical disposable load comprises crew and basics 1,000 lb (453.5 kg), mission avionics 1,570 lb (712 kg), and fuel 550 lb (249.5 kg) at cruise altitude.
Engines: 2x 204 hp (152.1 kW) Porsche 930/10 piston engines.
Propellers: 5-blade propulsors in shrouds, able to vector vertically for near V/STOL and hovering flight.
Fuel: 842 lb (382 kg) maximum usable capacity.
Electrical load: 10 kW.
Stabilizers: Cruciform tail with elevators and rudders, of composites construction.
Maximum airspeed: 55 kts (63 mph) 102 km/h
Cruise speed: 35 kts (40 mph) 65 km/h, economical
Cruise altitude: 3,000-5,000 ft (915-1,525 m)
Ceiling: 8,000 ft (2,440 m)
Duration: 8 hours without reballasting or refuelling, allowing 20% reserves.

Westinghouse Airships Skyship 600

First flight: 6 March 1984.
Role: Non-rigid helium airship for surveillance, border patrol, interdiction, crowd control, police, training, and limited military tasks including command/control/communications.

▲ Development

▲ 1 September 1984. CAA Certificate of Airworthiness gained.
▲ 8 January 1987. C of A for passenger carrying gained.
▲ 1987-88. Skycruise sight-seeing flights undertaken in Europe, Australia and USA.
▲ 1989. FAA type certificate gained in the USA, the first ever for a commercial airship.
▲ 15 September 1993. First flight of the first Skyship 600 in UK military service (ZH762) after receiving a new envelope. Reports suggested possible trial surveillance use over Northern Ireland.

▲ August 1994. ZH762 (see above) handed to UK MoD's Flight Test Evaluation Centre at Boscombe Down, where British Army has been conducting further evaluation before taking it permanently. Trials due to end in 1995.
Crew/Passengers: 2 pilots plus up to 13 passengers in an enclosed composites gondola or mission equipment.
Length: 193 ft 7 ins (59 m)
Diameter: 49 ft 10 ins (15.2 m)
Height: : 66 ft 7 ins (20.3 m) overall
Envelope: Aerazur-manufactured envelope of 1-ply polyester fabric, with a polyurethane/titanium dioxide outer coating against UL deterioration, and with a polyvinylidene chloride inner film attached with polyurethane. Volume 235,000 cu ft (6,654 m^3). Composites nose dome with mooring attachments.
Ballonets: 2, acounting for 26% of envelope volume.
Ballast: Water ballast in tanks and non-disposable ballast beneath seats in containers.
Disposable load: 3,625 lb (1,644 kg) maximum structural. Typical disposable load is 3,195 lb (1,449 kg), comprising 1,150 lb (521.5 kg) crew and basics, 1,200 lb (544 kg) mission avionics and 845 lb (383.5 kg) fuel at cruise altitude.
Engines: 2x 255 hp (190.2 kW) Porsche 930/67 piston engines.
Propellers: 5-blade propulsors in shrouds, able to vector –90° and +120° vertically for near V/STOL and hovering flight.
Fuel: 1,067 lb (484 kg) maximum usable capacity.
Electrical load: 10 kW.
Stabilizers: 4 tail surfaces with elevators and rudders, of composites construction.
Maximum airspeed: 55 kts (63 mph) 102 km/h
Cruise speed: 35 kts (40 mph) 65 km/h, economical
Cruise altitude: 5,000 ft (1,525 m)
Duration: 10 hours without reballasting or refuelling, allowing 20% reserves.

Westinghouse Skyship 600-01 over Cardington (A.W.L. Nayler)

Westinghouse Airships Sentinel S1000

First flight: 26 June 1991.
Role: Non-rigid helium airship for airborne early warning, anti-air warfare (AAW), anti-surface warfare (ASUW) with highly sophisticated surface radars including inverse synthetic array systems, mine countermeasures, naval blockade, maritime patrol, fisheries protection, surveillance, policing, drug interdiction, command/control/communications, disaster communications, fire-watch patrol, and more. Commercial applications can include advertising and transportation. Prototype was to be used in the S5000 development programme.

★ Aims

★ The world's largest flying airship in early 1995.
★ Large increase in payload over earlier WAI airships.
★ GEC-Marconi fly-by-light (fibre optic) system (see Development), to reduce potential electromagnetic influence to a minimum, thereby eliminating envelope wires and uncommanded control inputs caused by electromagnetic interference.
★ Various valves that maintain the pressure in the envelope are pneumatically controlled, further reducing wires and cables.
★ One-half linear scale model of the Sentinel S5000.
★ Design emphasizes safety and mission performance.
★ Over 1,500 lb (680 kg) of fuel can be used without reballasting, contributing to its long-on-station duration.
★ Equipped for AEW, the 7 m antenna can detect 3 m^2 targets at ranges beyond 130 naut miles and provide extended-range radar coverage out to 350 naut miles against conventional targets.
★ Equipped with a maritime surveillance radar, at 1,500 m altitude small craft may be detected to ranges up to the horizon at 70 naut miles.
★ A full suite of communications equipment makes the airship a command and control centre to co-ordinate the application of other airborne and surface units in the interdiction of suspected smugglers and poachers.
★ Very low noise signature, offering a stealthy night aircraft to photograph illegal activity and off-load enforcement officers or recover personnel.
★ Can be equipped with missiles to defend itself and the friendly naval battle group.

▲ Development

▲ 11 April 1992. First flown with the completed fly-by-light flight control system. Upon certification by the FAA (see below), it became the first and thereby only aircraft of any type approved to fly with this type of system. Has 3-axis autopilot, and autostabilization is to be incorporated into the S5000.
▲ October 1992. UHF communications relay trial took place under US Defense Advanced Research Projects Agency (DoD) funding, in co-operation with US Navy warships.
▲ 22 October 1993. FAR Part 21 certification gained for single-pilot operations.
▲ Trials airship in the S5000 development programme.
▲ 2 August 1995. S1000 was destroyed in a hangar fire.
Crew/Passengers: 2 pilots, operating the flight controls with modern side-stick controllers, and the autopilot provides full instrument flight capability. 2 or 3 mission specialists. Kevlar gondola, with the cabin portion aft of the cockpit approximately 22.6 x 8.4 x 6.3 (6.9 x 2.6 x 1.9 m), providing space for mission equipment, as well as bunks and galleys for extended duration missions. Requires 60% of the Skyship 600's ground crew needs.
Length: 222 ft (67.67 m)
Diameter: 54 ft 9 ins (16.69 m)
Height: 66 ft 3 ins (20.2 m) overall
Envelope: Tedlar outer ply, impervious to UV radiation. Heat bonded seaming. Volume 354,000 cu ft (10,024 m^3).
Ballonets maximum volume: Approximately 24% of envelope volume.
Disposable load: 8,715 lb (3,953 kg) maximum structural. Typical disposable load is 6,505 lb (2,951 kg), comprising 1,150 lb (521.5 kg) crew and basics, 3,812 lb (1,729.5 kg) mission avionics and 1,543 lb (700 kg) fuel.
Engines: 2x 255 hp (190.2 kW) Porsche 930/67 piston engines.
Propellers: 5-blade propulsors in shrouds, able to vector –90° and +120° vertically for near V/STOL and hovering flight.
Fuel: 2,498 lb (1,133 kg) maximum usable capacity
Electrical load: 20 kW.
Stabilizers: X configured tail fins. Any one control surface provides sufficient control for mooring in the event of battle damage.
Maximum airspeed: 58 kts (67 mph) 107 km/h
Cruise speed: 35 kts (40 mph) 65 km/h, economical
Cruise altitude: 8,000 ft (2,440 m) maximum. Typical cruise altitude is 4,000 ft (1,220 m).
Duration: 18 hours without reballasting or refuelling, allowing 20% reserves. Easily capable of a 24 hrs mission with auxiliary fuel.

Westinghouse Sentinel S1000, the first of the Sentinel range to fly

Westinghouse Airships Sentinel S1240

First flight: Not yet flown.
Role: Similar to S1000 but with greater load capability.
Length: 238 ft (72.54 m)
Diameter: 59 ft (18 m)
Height: 70 ft 10 ins (21.6 m)
Envelope: Volume 438,000 cu ft (12,400 m^3)
Ballonets: 30% of envelope volume.
Disposable load: 12,282 lb (5,571 kg) maximum structural. Typical disposable load 7,501 lb (3,402 kg), comprising 1,150 lb (521.5 kg) crew and basics, 4,808 lb (2,180.5 kg) mission avionics and 1,543 lb (700 kg) fuel.
Engines: 2x 315 hp (235 kW) Porsche 930 type piston engines, or possibly 300 hp (223.7 kW) Zoche diesel engines.
Propellers: Possibly 5-blade propulsors in shrouds, able to vector –90° and +120° vertically for near V/STOL and hovering flight.
Fuel: 2,498 lb (1,133 kg) maximum usable capacity.
Electrical load: 20 kW.
Maximum airspeed: 55 kts (63 mph) 102 km/h
Cruise speed: 35 kts (40 mph) 65 km/h, economical
Cruise altitude: 10,000 ft (3,050 m) maximum. Typical cruise altitude 8,000 ft (2,440 m).
Duration: 18 hours without reballasting or refuelling, allowing 20% reserves. Possible 32 hours with auxiliary fuel.

Westinghouse Airships Sentinel S5000

First flight: Anticipated 1997.
Role: Non-rigid helium airship for AEW with the US Navy; current military designation YEZ-2A.

★ Aims

★ To develop an autonomous and long-endurance AEW system able to communicate and co-operate with US Naval assets worldwide.
★ Use of GEC-Marconi fly-by-light control system, and autopilot and autostabilization (see S1000 for benefits).
★ Stable, vibration-free environment for use of highly sensitive equipment.
★ Pressurized forward sections of the gondola to increase structural strength, enhance crew comfort, and provide extra protection against chemical and biological attack.
★ Capable of detection, classification, identification and tracking of surface and low altitude/high speed airborne targets in a sea clutter environment, particularly cruise missiles. Other potential roles could include communications relay, over-the-horizon targeting, and anti-narcotics operations.

▲ Development

▲ 1985. Naval Air Systems Command began the Naval Airship Program to study the viability of a modern airborne early warning airship, having operated similar types up to the early 1960s. Initial feasibility contracts were awarded to Boeing, Goodyear and Westinghouse.
▲ August 1986. Request for proposals issued by the Navy. Boeing eventually pulled out its rigid design from the programme.
▲ 5 June 1987. Naval Air Systems Command issued a contract to the Westinghouse/Airship Industries consortium worth nearly $169 million for an operational development model of its proposed Sentinel 5000.
▲ October 1988. Programme taken over by DARPA (see S1000) of the Department of Defense, subsequently becoming a "very large airship now under design for the Air Defense Initiative program", with the S1000 performing as a scale vehicle.
▲ 1990. Westinghouse Airships took over Airship Industries' half share in the Sentinel programme, after the British company went into liquidation in September 1990.
▲ 1994. Design review completed. First flight date slipped from 1994 to about 1997.
▲ UN Navy expected to require a minimum of 5 further S5000s, produced from about 1998.

Crew: Up to 15 crew in a triple-deck 85 ft (26 m) long gondola with pressurized forward sections (see illustration), with an ultra-modern cockpit containing multifunction and multimenu colour display technology.

Westinghouse Sentinel S5000 gondola, showing: 1 Crew entry and replenishment bay , with an advanced winch mechanism overhead to lift refuelling hoses and supply nets (or people in SAR role), 2 Maintenance area with access to engines, 3 Airlock leading from the unpressurized maintenance bay to the 5-crew galley, 4 Combat Information Centre (CIC) with up to six decision and display workstations, 5 Cockpit entered by short ladder from the CIC, 6 Crew semi-private quarters for up to fifteen persons as well as a restroom and shower facilities, 7 Recreational area equipped with stereo system, VCR, sofa and aerobic equipment

Length: 425 ft (129.54 m)
Diameter: 105 ft (32 m)
Height: 152 ft (46.33 m)
Envelope: Multi-layer Tedlar/urethane/clear Mylar film/urethane/Dacron Polyester cloth/urethane fabric envelope, with Hytrel bonding, designed to last over a decade. Volume 2,500,000 cu ft (70,790 m^3).
Disposable load: 60,350 lb (27,374 kg) maximum structural. Typical disposable load 49,000 lb (22,226 kg) at cruise altitude, comprising 6,000 lb or 3,500 lb (2,721 kg or 1,587 kg) crew and basics, 12,500 lb or 25,000 lb (5,670 kg or 11,340 kg) of mission avionics, and 30,500 lb or 20,500 lb (13,835 kg or 9,299 kg) of fuel.
Engines: 2 cruise 2,400 hp (1,790 kW) CRM diesel engines in the gondola (weighing 4,000 lb/1,814 kg), driving a vectoring, shrouded propulsor each side. 1 1,870 shp (1,394.5 kW) General Electric CT7-9 turboprop "turbo-sprint" engine in the rear of the gondola, driving a pusher propeller to provide maximum speed for short intervals, increased manoeuvrability and enhanced stability for low speed, low altitude flight operations.
Propellers: See Engines.
Fuel: 39,000 lb (17,690 kg) maximum usable capacity.
Electrical load: 200 or 600 kW.
Stabilizers: X configuration, with 2 movable surfaces per fin, controlled by fibre optics.
Maximum airspeed: 82-90 kts (94-104 mph) 152-167 km/h
Cruise speed: 40 kts (46 mph) 74 km/h, economical
Cruise altitude: 13,000 ft (3,960 m) maximum. Typical cruise altitude 5,000 ft (1,525 m).
Duration: 82 or 26 hours maximum without reballasting or refuelling, allowing 20% reserves (respective typical fuel loads as stated under Disposable load). Possible 30 days mission with replenishment arrangements.

Westinghouse Airships Sentinel/ US Navy Projection

▲ Development

▲ A US Navy design study has projected a 25,000 lb (11,340 kg) airship (compared to 12,500 lb/5,670 kg for S5000) with a 3 million cu ft envelope capacity.

Worldwide Aeros Corporation (USA)

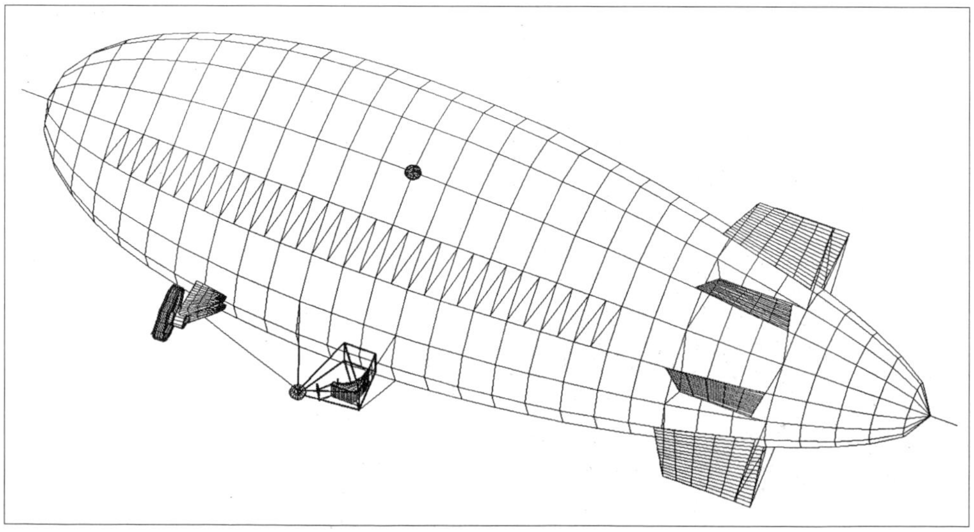

Worldwide Aeros Corporation Aeros-20 ultralight airship

Corporate address: 485 Aviator Drive, Atwater, CA 95301.
Telephone: +1 209 357 7000 or 3708
Facsimile: +1 209 357 0591
Information: Irina Svirid.

■ Facilities

■ Formed in Europe in 1987, but transferred to Atwater in the USA in 1993.
■ Atwater operation incorporates manufacturing facilities at the closing Castle Air Force Base, R&D, general management and the marketing division.

● Activities

● Designer and manufacturer of lighter-than-air craft.
● Producer of tethered aerostats used for advertising, ecological monitoring and surveillance.
● Developed tethered modular airborne air pollution control stations and systems for radiation monitoring, known as Guard. Used for transboundary air pollution monitoring at the border of Poland and the Ukraine

and for radiation monitoring after the Chernobyl nuclear accident.
• Has branches in 6 countries and over 300 employees.

Aeros-20

Role: Non-rigid, helium, ultralight airship for advertising, pilot training, aerial photography, recreational/sporting, sightseeing, ecological monitoring, border patrol and surveillance.

★ Aims

★ Claimed to be the only production airship in the world whose operation does not require pilot's certification.
★ 8-fin stabilizer layout claimed to increase stability 1.5 times compared to 4-fin layout.
★ Altitude change and safe landing during free flight by helium valve control cable and water ballast control pedal.
★ Full compliance with FAR Part 103 -Ultralight Vehicles and the provisions provided in the Airship Design Criteria, No FAA-D-8110-2.
★ Simplicity of operation, flight and docking safety.
★ Outside storage using a small, lightweight mast.
★ Automatic landing system allows the pilot to land without any ground crew. The airship lands on a prepared anchor site. It is pulled down to the ground by a cable extended from the gondola. An electric winch is installed on the anchor site.

Crew: Pilot. Gondola is an open tubular structure; gondola covering is optional. Under normal conditions, 2 people can handle the airship on the ground (see Aims).
Length: 56 ft 4 ins (17.18 m)
Diameter: 17 ft 8 ins (5.38 m) maximum
Height: 23 ft (7.01 m) overall
Envelope: 2 fabric options: Vectran base, and Lavsan fabric and film base. Volume variable, up to 9,180 cu ft (260 m^3); minimum volume 8,300 cu ft (235 m^3). Shape and static superpressure maintained by 2 longitudinal elastic belts. Advertising banners on the envelope, each 12 ft 6 ins x 40 ft (3.8 x 12.2 m), with a total area of 982 sq ft (91.2 m2). Nose mooring attachment.
Surface area: 2,659 sq ft (247 m^2)
Ballonet/s: None.
Fineness ratio: 3.2:1
Empty weight: 350 lb (159 kg)

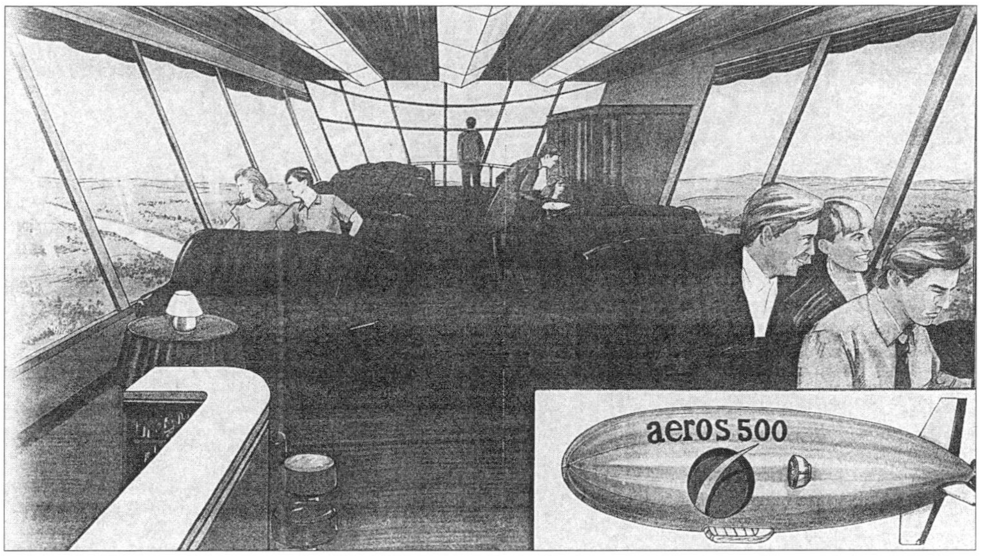

Impression of a Worldwide Aeros Corporation-500 rigid helium/hydrogen airship

Engine: 28 hp (20.9 kW) Rotax 277 suspended from the nose section of the envelope. Installed on a rotating mount, allowing a thrust angle change of 120° left and right and 60° up and down. Optional electric starter.
Propeller: 3-blade, fixed-pitch composites, in a shroud.
Diameter: 4 ft 11 ins (1.5 m).
Fuel: 18 litres.
Stabilizers: 8, with no rudders or elevators. Fabric and tube construction, attached to the envelope and positioned with flying wires.
Maximum airspeed: 39 kts (45 mph) 72 km/h
Cruise speed: 32.4 kts (37.3 mph) 60 km/h at 70% power
Ceiling: 3,650 ft (1,110 m)

Aeros-40

Role: Non-rigid, helium, kit-built airship for mainly recreational use.
Crew/Passengers: 2. Aluminium tubing gondola, with composites cover.
Length: 68 ft 4 ins (20.82 m)
Diameter: 21 ft 4 ins (6.49 m) maximum
Height: 30 ft (9.14 m) overall
Envelope: Vectran based fabric. Volume 16,250 cu ft (460.15 m^3). Advertising panels 16 ft 6 ins x 50 ft (5 x 15.24 m), with a total area of 825 sq ft (76.63 m^2).
Surface area: 3,900 sq ft (362.3 m^2)
Ballonet/s maximum volume: 1,765 cu ft (50 m^3). 75 denier polyester fabric construction. Inflated with air from the propeller.
Fineness ratio: 3.2:1
Engine: 52 hp (38.8 kW) Rotax 503 piston engine. Thrust control as for Aeros-20 (which see).
Propeller: 3-blade, fixed-pitch composites, in a shroud.
Diameter: 4 ft 11 ins (1.5 m).
Fuel: 39 litres.
Maximum airspeed: 47 kts (54 mph) 87 km/h
Cruise speed: 39 kts (45 mph) 72 km/h
Ceiling: 4,000 ft (1,220 m)

Worldwide Aeros Corporation Aeros-50-02 at Castle Air Force Base, with an open gondola (Vadim Sokolov/Aeros)

Aeros-50

Role: Semi-rigid, helium airship for advertising, monitoring and research. Can also be used in tethered form as part of the Guard system (see Activities).

★ Aims

★ Full compliance with FAA requirements (Airship Design Criteria No FAA-P-8110-2).
★ Exceptional manoeuvrability and control, and low operational expense, coupled with high reliability at low cost.
★ Minimum ground crew or, using ground mooring equipment, no ground handling crew.

Crew/Passengers: Pilot in an aluminium and composites enclosed gondola. Prototype (*50-02* illustrated) has an open gondola.
Length: 77 ft 5 ins (23.60 m)
Envelop diameter: 26 ft 3 ins (8.00 m)
Width: 35 ft 8 ins (10.87 m) overall
Height: 39 ft 5 ins (12.01 m) overall
Envelope: Vectran based fabric of 5.9 oz/sq yd weight. Volume 26,246 cu ft (743.2 m^3). 2 catenary belts distribute gondola and propeller thrust loads. Rigid nosecone, with 3 ft 7 ins (1.09 m) ring-shaped mooring unit attached.
Ballonets maximum volume: 3,000 cu ft (84.95 m^3) each, forward and rear. Inflated with air via a duct behind the pusher propeller. 75 denier polyester fabric.
Envelope weight: 537 lb (243.6 kg) including nosecone, valves and ballonets 50% inflated (excluding gondola and tail surfaces).
Engine: 80 hp (59.7 kW) Rotax 912A.

Propeller: 3-blade pusher with adjustable pitch in an aluminium shroud. Propeller diameter 6 ft (1.83 m). 2.273:1 drive reduction ratio.
Fuel: 60.5 litres
Stabilizers: 4 fins, each 86 sq ft (7.99 m^2), with rudders.
Maximum airspeed: 78 kts (90 mph) 145 km/h
Cruise speed: 61 kts (70 mph) 113 km/h
Ceiling: 5,000 ft (1,525 m)
Duration: 8 hours
Range: 521 naut miles (600 miles) 966 km

Aeros-500

First flight: Not yet flown.
Role: Rigid, all-metal, helium/hydrogen airship, intended as a comfortable tourist carrier or flying ecological laboratory.

★ Aims

- ★ Automatic take-off and mooring without using ground control commands. Mooring speed: horizontal 2.4-4 m per second, vertical 0.5-1 m per second.
- ★ Low cabin noise due to the distance of the engines from the gondola.
- ★ Metal envelope allowing use in adverse climatic conditions.
- ★ Helium/hydrogen combination.
- ★ Control at cruise speed by tail fins, at lower speed using nose duct engine and side vectoring propeller units. Static control of trim by blowing air into the ballonets.
- ★ 15,000 flight hour life (15 years).

Crew/Passengers: 2 pilots, 4 stewardesses and 20 passengers. All-composites gondola, accommodating the control section and a passenger cabin with 2 rows of chairs, a bar and viewing screen.
Length: 177 ft 2 ins (54 m)
Envelope diameter: 59 ft (18 m)
Width: 72 ft 2 ins (22 m) over tail
Height: 77 ft 5 ins (23.6 m) overall
Envelope: Made from 0.15 mm duralumin sheets, strengthened by 8 frames and 4 spars. Interior is divided into sections of polymeric film reinforced with glassfibre yarns. The film is attached to the panelling so that longitudinal canals are formed between the film and the envelope providing warm air circulation and thereby maintaining a desirable outer surface temperature and preventing ice formation. Volume 300,175 cu ft (8,500 m^3).
Ballonets: Air filled, fore and aft, each 81,224 cu ft (2,300 m^3).
Fineness ratio: 3.0:1.
Engines: 1,200 hp (895 kW) main engine driving a reversible-pitch shrouded pusher propeller. 2x 500 hp (373 kW) side engines driving shrouded propellers that are able to rotate through 360° for thrust vectoring. To ensure good manoeuvrability at inverse speeds there is an impulse duct engine.
Stabilizers: X-shape tail surfaces, shown in Aeros tests to be more efficient at small angles of attack than cruciform.
Maximum airspeed: 108 kts (125 mph) 201 km/h
Cruise speed: 64 kts (74 mph) 119 km/h
Ceiling: 14,750 ft (4,500 m)
Range: 810 naut miles (932 miles) 1,500 km at cruise speed.
Duration: 18 hours

Worldwide Aeros Corporation/Aeroplast (USA/Ukraine)

Corporate address: Aeros: 485 Aviator Drive, Atwater, CA 95301.
Telephone: Aeros: +1 209 357 7000 or 3708
Facsimile: Aeros: +1 209 357 0591
Information: Aeros: Irina Svirid.

● Activities

- ● Joint programme to develop the D1 and D4 cargo airships, based upon former-Soviet designs initiated in the 1970s.

Aeros-Aeroplast D1 and D4

Role: Rigid, helium, multi-purpose cargo carrier, flying crane, ship escort, tourism and other work.

★ Aims

- ★ Control by both aerodynamic and engine power.
- ★ No weather, wind speed or visibility restrictions to flying.
- ★ Vertical or short-run landing.
- ★ Mooring to the rotating platform of the tower, followed by automatic mast-mooring.
- ★ De-icing using thermal air and electric impulse.
- ★ Open air storage.
- ★ 60,000 flight hours or 20 years life.

▲ Development

- ▲ Programmes initiated in the former USSR in the 1970s.
- ▲ Construction of the prototype D1 began October 1995.

Crew/Passengers/Load: 3-level gondola, the bottom level housing the undercarriage equipment. Compartment above is for the pilots, navigator, flight engineer and cargo platform operator, with stairs leading to the crew living compartment and an auxiliary compartment. Cargo carried in a container either fixed in the cargo compartment or mounted on the cargo suspension platform, or without a container on the platform, or carried as a slung load. Cargo compartment 52 ft 6 ins x 20 ft 4 ins x 10 ft 10 ins (16 x 6.2 x 3.3 m) for D1, 164 ft x 52 ft 6 ins x 11 ft 6 ins (50 x 16 3.5 m) for D4. Cargo compartment volume 11,560 cu ft (327.34 m^3) for D1. Cargo carrying facilitated by an undercarriage with a wheel track and wheel base of (respectively) 20 ft 4 ins and 65 ft 9 ins (8.2 and 20.05 m) for the D1, and 78 ft 9 ins and 170 ft 7ins (24 and 52 m) for the D4.
Length of envelope: 275 ft 7 ins (84 m) for D1, 551 ft 2 ins (168 m) for D4.
Length overall: 311 ft 8 ins (95 m) for D1.
Diameter: 82 ft (25 m) for D1, 164 ft (50 m) for D4.
Height overall: 108 ft 3 ins (33 m) for D1.
Envelope: Semi-monocoque, with active rigid hull made of 3-ply carbonplastic panels. Volume 971,155 cu ft (27,500 m^3) for D1, and 7,769,230 cu ft (220,000 m^3) for D4.
Surface area: 57,800 sq ft (5,370 m^2) for D1.
Ballonets: Constructed of Vectran cloth/adhesive/ethylene-vynalalcohol-Copolmere 15/protective agent sandwich.
Payload (fuel and cargo): 27,558 lb (12,500 kg) for D1, 275,580 lb (125,000 kg) for D4.
Engines: 1x 3,600 shp (2,685 kW) General Electric T64 turboprop engine at the tail of the hull and 2x 300 hp (224 kW) Zoche ZO 02A side engines in vectoring shrouds (+120°, –90°) for D1, and 1x 6,000 hp (4,474 kW) aft engine and 2x 1,000 hp (746 kW) side engines for D4.
Stabilizers/wings: Large T-tail, incorporating elevators and a rudder. Canards towards the nose of the hull.
Vertical tailfin area: 1,722 sq ft (160 m^2) for D1.
Horizontal tailfin area: 1,076 sq ft (100 m^2) for D1.
Maximum airspeed: 151 kts (174 mph) 280 km/h
Cruise speed: 124 kts (143 mph) 230 km/h
Mooring speed: 10-16.5 ft (3-5 m) per second horizontal, 1.6-3.3 ft (0.5-1 m) per second vertical.
Ceiling: 11,800 ft (3,600 m) for D1, 19,670 ft (6,000 m) for D4.
Range: Approximately 540 naut miles (621 miles) 1,000 km with a 10,000 kg payload, or 2,160 naut miles (2,485 miles) 4,000 km with a 2,000 kg payload for the D1.

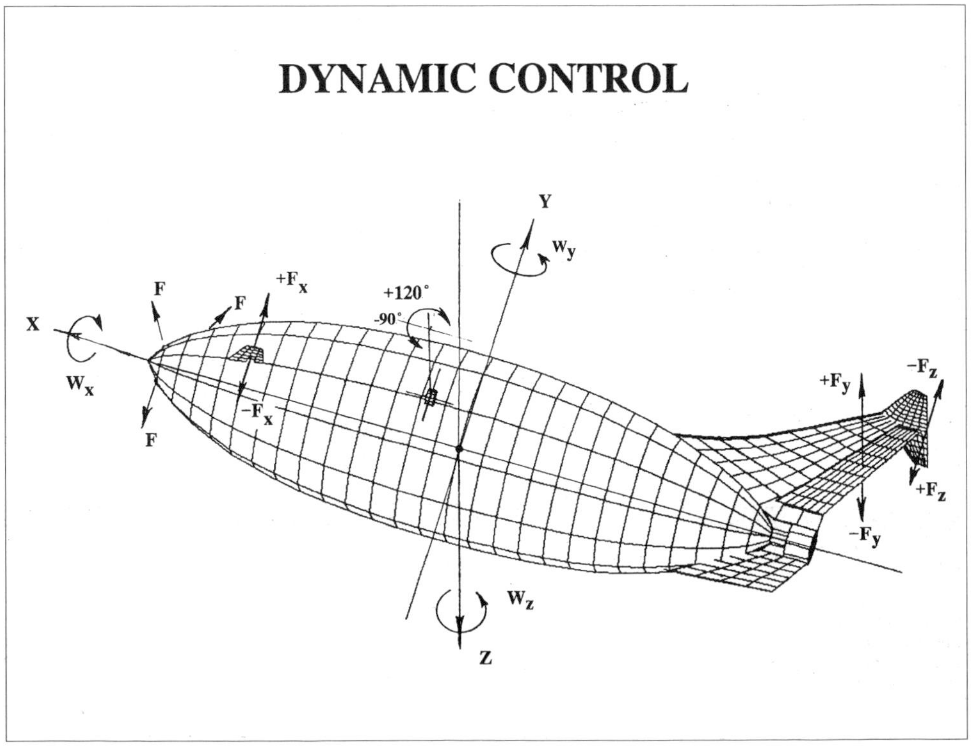

Worldwide Aeros/Aeroplast D1 dynamic control drawing

The Chief Editor would like to acknowledge The Airship Association Ltd (6 Kings Road, Cheriton, Folkestone, Kent CT20 3LG, England), both in the UK and USA.

Engines (Civil and Military)

Designation (type of engine)	**Power output** (normally take-off rating for piston, turboprop and turboshaft, unless stated)	**Specific Fuel Consumption** (S F C)	**a) Max RPM b) Pressure or Compression ratio**	**a) EGT** (unless stated to be MGT, TET, TGT or TIT) **b) Primary fuel type or Octane rating**	**Dry weight** lb (kg)	**a) Length** ins (mm) **b) Width** ins (mm) **c) Height** ins (mm)	**Current aircraft users, and comments**
Australia							
Jabiru Aircraft Pty Ltd, PO Box 5186. Bundaberg West 4670, Queensland							
Jabiru 1600 (4-cyl, air-cooled, direct-drive piston)	60 hp (44.7 kW)	0.46 lb/hp/hr (280 g/kW/hr)	a) 3,300 b) 9.5:1	a) 600-680° C b) Avgas 100 LL or Mogas	124 (56)	a) 20.94 (532) b) 22.6 (574) c) 18.58 (472)	Aircraft up to 1,100 lb (499 kg) gross.
Jabiru 2000 (4-cyl, air-cooled, direct-drive piston)	75 hp (55.93 kW)	0.46 lb/hp/hr (280 g/kW/hr)	a) 3,300 b) 9.5:1	a) 600-680° C b) Avgas 100 LL or Mogas	128 (58)	a) 21.57 (548) b) 22.87 (581) c) 18.58 (472)	Aircraft up to 1,250 lb (567 kg) gross.
Austria							
Bombardier-Rotax GmbH. A-4623 Gunskirchen							
447 UL-SCDI 1V (2-cyl, 2-stroke, fan-cooled piston)	39.6 hp (29.5 kW) at 6,500 rpm	0.82 lb/hp/hr (500 g/kW/hr) at 6,800 rpm	a) 6,800 b) 9.6:1 th; 6.3:1 ef	a) 460-580° C b) MON 83, RON 91	71.9 (32.6)*	a) 21.38 (543) b) 20.59 (523) c) 16.38 (416)	For experimental and ultralight uncertified aircraft. Not certified. *With carburettor and exhaust. Bore 2.66 ins (67.5 mm); stroke 2.4 ins (61 mm).
447 UL-SCDI 2V (2-cyl, 2-stroke, fan-cooled piston)	41.6 hp (31.0 kW) at 6,500 rpm	0.81 lb/hp/hr (493 g/kW/hr) at 6,800 rpm	a) 6,800 b) 9.6:1 th; 6.3:1 ef	a) 460-580° C b) MON 83, RON 91	72.75 (33)*	a) 21.38 (543) b) 20.59 (523) c) 16.38 (416)	For experimental and ultralight uncertified aircraft. Not certified. *With carburettor and exhaust. Bore 2.66 ins (67.5 mm); stroke 2.4 ins (61 mm).
503 UL-DCDI 1V (2-cyl, 2-stroke, fan-cooled piston)	45.6 hp (34.0 kW) at 6,500 rpm	0.83 lb/hp/hr (505 g/kW/hr) at 6,800 rpm	a) 6,800 b) 10.8:1 th	a) 460-580° C b) MON 83, RON 91	84.4 (38.3)*	a) 21.89-22.2 (556-564) b) 20.2 (513) c) 16.77 (426)	For experimental and ultralight uncertified aircraft. Not certified. *With carburettors and exhaust. Bore 2.84 ins (72 mm); stroke 2.4 ins. (61 mm).
503 UL-DCDI 2V (2-cyl, 2-stroke, fan-cooled piston)	49.6 hp (37.0 kW) at 6,500 rpm	0.81 lb/hp/hr (493 g/kW/hr) at 6,800 rpm	a) 6,800 b) 10.8:1 th	a) 460-580° C b) MON 83, RON 91	84.4 (38.3)*	a) 21.89-22.2 (556-564) b) 20.2 (513) c) 16.77 (426)	For experimental and ultralight uncertified aircraft. Not certified. *With carburettors and exhaust. Bore 2.84 ins (72 mm); stroke 2.4 ins (61 mm).
582 UL-DCDI (2-stroke, liquid-cooled piston, with rotary valve inlet)	64.4 hp (48 kW) at 6,500 rpm, 53.6 hp (40 kW) at 6,000 rpm	0.66 lb/hp/hr (401 g/kW/hr) at 6,800 rpm	a) 6,800 b) 11.5:1 th	a) 500-620° C b) MON 83, RON 91	75.6 (34.3)*	a) 22.91-23.27 (582-591) b) 17.2 (437) c) 17.32 (440)	For experimental and ultralight uncertified aircraft. Not certified. *With carburettors and exhaust. Bore 2.99 ins (76 mm); stroke 2.52 ins (64 mm).
618 UL-DCDI (2-cyl, 2-stroke liquid-cooled piston, with rotary valve inlet)	73.8 hp (55 kW) at 6,750 rpm, 54 hp (40 kW) at 5,300 rpm	0.65 lb/hp/hr (395 g/kW/hr) at 7,000 rpm	a) 7,000 b) 11.5:1 th; 5.95:1 ef	a) 500-620 ° C b) MON 85, RON 95	85.75 (38.9)*	a) 23.9-28.27 (607-718) b) 22.6 (574)	For experimental and ultralight uncertified aircraft. Not certified. *With carburettors and exhaust. Bore 2.99 ins (76 mm); stroke 2.68 ins (68 mm).
912 UL-DCDI (4-cyl, 4-stroke, liquid/air-cooled piston)	77.8 hp (58 kW) at 5,500 rpm, 80 hp (59.6 kW) at 5,800 rpm for 5 minutes	0.44 lb/hp/hr (268 g/kW/hr) at 5,800 rpm	a) 5,800 for 5 minutes b) 9.0:1	a) 850° C maximum b) RON 90 unleaded or AKI 87 minimum, Avgas 100 LL	121.9 (55.3) with gearbox	a) 22.79 (579) b) 22.68 (576) c) 14.82 (376.5)	For experimental and ultralight uncertified aircraft. Not certified. Bore 3.13 ins (79.5 mm); stroke 2.4 ins (61 mm).
912 A2/3/4 and 912 F2/3/4 (4-cyl, 4-stroke, liquid/air-cooled piston)	77.8 hp (58 kW), 80 hp (59.6 kW) for 5 minutes for 912 A	0.44 lb/hp/hr (268 g/kW/hr) at 5,800 rpm	a) 5,500 b) 9.0:1	a) 850° C maximum b) RON 90 unleaded or AKI 87 minimum, Avgas 100 LL	126.3 (57.3)	a) 22.79 (579) b) 22.68 (576) c) 14.82 (376.5)	912 A2/3/4 certified to JAR-22. 912 F2/3/4 for FAR-33 certification. Bore 3.13 ins (79.5 mm); stroke 2.4 ins (61 mm).
914 UL-DCDI (4-cyl, 4-stroke, liquid/air-cooled piston)	100 hp (74.6 kW) at 5,500 rpm, 115 hp (85.7 kW) at 5,800 rpm for 5 minutes	0.42 lb/hp/hr (255 g/kW/hr)	a) 5,800 for 5 minutes b) 9.0:1	a) 850° C maximum b) MON 85, RON 95, Avgas 100 LL	150.4 (68.2)*	a) 26.85 (682) b) 24.84 (631) c) 14.27 (362.5)	For experimental and ultralight uncertified aircraft. Non-certified. Production began 1995. *With gearbox, intake silencer, exhaust, and truss assembly. Bore 3.13 ins (79.5 mm); stroke 2.4 ins (61 mm).
Belgium							
Techspace Aero SA. B-4041 Herstal (Milmort)							
Produces components for CFM56, TM333, Tyne, GE and P&W engines, and assemblies.							On 21 December 1994 Techspace Aero received FAR-145 for maintenance, repair and testing of commercial engines.

Designation (type of engine)	Power output (normally take-off rating for piston, turboprop and turboshaft, unless stated)	Specific Fuel Consumption (S F C)	a) Max RPM b) Pressure or Compression ratio	a) EGT (unless stated to be MGT, TET, TGT or TIT) b) Primary fuel type or Octane rating	Dry weight lb (kg)	a) Length ins (mm) b) Width ins (m) c) Height ins (mm)	Current aircraft users, and comments
Brazil							
Celma-Cia Electromecanica. Rua Alice Hervê 356, Bingen, Caixa Postal 90341, CEP 25669-900, Petrópolis, RJ							
RB168 Spey Mk 807 (twin-shaft turbofan)	11,030 lbf (49.06 kN)	0.659 lb/lbf/hr (18.67 g/kNs)	b) 16.8:1	a) 585° C maximum EGT, 1,107° C maximum MGT b) JP-1, JP-4 and JP-5	2,417 (1,096)	a) 96.7 (2,456) b) 32.5 (826)	Builds the Spey under licence from Rolls-Royce for the Embraer AM-X with Fiat co-operation. Celma overhauls various General Electric, Pratt & Whitney and CFM engines.
Indústria Mecânica E Aeronáutica Ltda (IMAER). 18600 Botucatú, SP							
IMAER 1000 (2-cyl, air-cooled, piston)	40 hp (29.8 kW)				86 (39)	a) 14.6 (370) b) 30.1 (764) c) 16.14 (410)	Light and very light aircraft. Offered with either electronic or magneto ignition.
IMAER 2000 (4-cyl, air-cooled piston)	80 hp (59.66 kW)				up to 178.5 (81)	a) 23.2 (590) b) 30.1 (764) c) 17.6 (447)	Light and very light aircraft. Offered with either or both electronic and magneto ignition. Certificated.
Canada							
Canadian Airmotive Inc. 7400 Wilson Avenue, Delta, BC, V4G 1E5							
CAM 100 (4-cyl, 4-stroke piston, with reduction gear)*	100 hp (74.6 kW)	0.41 lb/hp/hr (249 g/kW/hr)	b) 9.2:1	b) Minimum 90 Octane (unleaded)	203 (92.1)	a) 32 (813) b) 20.47 (520) c) 25.2 (641)	*Modified from a 1,488 cc Honda Civic motorcar engine. Available in converted form.
Hawker-Siddeley Canada – Orenda Division. 3160 Derry Road East, Mississauga, Ontario L4T 1A9							
Orenda 600 (V-8, liquid-cooled, piston)	600 hp (447.4 kW) take-off, 500 hp (373 kW) continuous		a) 4,400 crankshaft				Formerly Thunder Engines Thunder. To have FADEC and to be certified.
Pratt & Whitney Canada Inc. 1000 Marie-Victorin, Longueuil, Quebec J4G 1A1							
JT15D-1 (twin-shaft turbofan) See Comments for D-1A/B	2,200 lbf (9.79 kN) take-off	0.54 lb/lbf/hr (15.3 g/kNs)	b) 10:1	a) 960° C MGT b) JP-1, JP4, JP-5	514 (233.1)	a) 56.6 (1,438) b) 27 (693)	Citation/Citation I. D-1 certified in 1971. D-1B introduced 1983. D-1A /D-1B have dry weight of 519 lb (235.4 kg) and length of 59.3 ins (1,506 mm). Out of production.
JT15D-4 (twin-shaft turbofan) See Comments for D-4B/C/D	2,500 lbf (11.12 kN) take-off	0.562 lb/lbf/hr (15.92 g/kNs)	b) 10:1		557 (252.7)	a) 60.4 (1,534) b) 27.3 (693)	D-4 engines on Corvette, Citation II and Mitsubishi Diamond. Similar but heavier (568 lb, 257.6 kg) and longer (63.3 ins, 1,608 mm) D-4B on Citation SII; D-4C for prolonged inverted flight and with electronic fuel control (575 lb, 260.8 kg dry weight and 60.4 ins, 1,534 mm length) on Agusta S.211; and D-4D hot and high version (560 lb, 254 kg) on Diamond 1A. In production in D-4/4C models.
JT15D-5/-5A (twin-shaft turbofan) See Comments for D-5B	2,900 lbf (12.9 kN) to 26.7° C	0.551 lb/lbf/hr (15.61 g/kNs)			632 (286.7)	a) 60.4 (1,534) b) 27 (686)	D-5 on Beech Beechjet 400A, Cessna T-47A and Scaled Composites Ares. D-5A on Citation V. Similar but heavier (643 lb, 292 kg) and slightly longer (27.3 ins, 693 mm) D-5B on Beech T-1A Jayhawk. In production.
JT15D-5C (twin-shaft turbofan)	3,190 lbf (14.19 kN) take-off	0.573 lb/lbf/hr (16.23 g/kNs)			665 (301.6)	a) 60.4 (1,534) b) 27.3 (693)	Agusta S.211A and Rockwell Ranger 2000. In production.
JT15D-5D (twin-shaft turbofan)	3,045 lbf (13.55 kN) to 26.7° C	0.56 lb/lbf/hr (15.86 g/kNs) take-off			627 (284.4)	a) 63 (1,600) b) 27 (686)	Citation V Ultra. In production.
JT15D-5F (twin-shaft turbofan)	2,900 lbf (12.90 kN) to 26.7° C	0.551 lb/lbf/hr (15.61 g/kNs) take-off			635 (288)	a) 60.4 (1,534) b) 27 (686)	Beech TBA. In production.
PT6A-11 (free-turbine turboprop with 3 axial and 1 centrifugal stages)	500 shp (373 kW) at 2,200 rpm	0.647 lb/shp/hr (394 g/kW/hr)	a) 2,200		328 (148.8)	a) 62 (1,575) approx b) 19 (483) approx c) 21 (533) approx	Piper Cheyenne 1/1A and T-1040. Single stage compressor turbine; single stage power turbine (as those below until indicated).
PT6A-11AG (free-turbine turboprop with 3 axial and 1 centrifugal stages)	500 shp (373 kW) at 2,200 rpm	0.647 lb/shp/hr (394 g/kW/hr)	a) 2,200	b) Includes diesel	330 (149.7)	a) 62 (1,575) b) 19 (483) c) 21 (533)	Ayres Turbo-Thrush, Ag-Cat Turbine, Weatherly 620TB.
PT6A-15AG (free-turbine turboprop with 3 axial and 1 centrifugal stages)	680 shp (507 kW) take-off, 620 shp (462.3 kW) cruise at 2,200 rpm	0.602 lb/shp/hr (366 g/kW/hr)	a) 2,200	b) Includes diesel	328 (148.8)	a) 62 (1,575) b) 21.5 (546) c) 21 (533)	Air Tractor AT-400, Ayres Turbo-Thrush, Ag-Cat Turbine.

Designation (type of engine)	Power output (normally take-off rating for piston, turboprop and turboshaft, unless stated)	Specific Fuel Consumption (S F C)	a) Max RPM b) Pressure or Compression ratio	a) EGT (unless stated to be MGT, TET, TGT or TIT) b) Primary fuel type or Octane rating	Dry weight lb (kg)	a) Length ins (mm) b) Width ins (mm) c) Height ins (mm)	Current aircraft users, and comments
Canada							
Pratt & Whitney Canada Inc (continued)							
PT6A-21 (free-turbine turboprop with 3 axial and 1 centrifugal stages)	550 shp (410 kW) at 2,200 rpm	0.630 lb/shp/hr (383 g/kW/hr)	a) 2,200		328 (148.8)	a) 62 (1,575) b) 21.5 (546) c) 21 (533)	Beech King Air C90.
PT6A-25 (free-turbine turboprop with 3 axial and 1 centrifugal stages)	560 shp (417.6 kW) take-off, 550 shp (410 kW) cruise at 2,200 rpm	0.630 lb/shp/hr (383 g/kW/hr)	a) 2,200		341 (154.7)	a) 62 (1,575) approx b) 21.5 (546) approx c) 24.8 (630) approx	Beech T-34C and PZL-130TE Orlik.
PT6A-25A (free-turbine turboprop with 3 axial and 1 centrifugal stages)	560 shp (417.6 kW) take-off, 550 shp (410 kW) cruise at 2,200 rpm	0.630 lb/shp/hr (383 g/kW/hr)	a) 2,200		343 (155.6)	a) 62 (1,575) b) 21.5 (546) c) 24.8 (630)	Beech T-34C-1, Pilatus PC-7, PZL-130T Orlik and Daewoo KTX-1. Identical to PT6A-25 except some castings of different alloy, hence weight difference.
PT6A-25C (free-turbine turboprop with 3 axial and 1 centrifugal stages)	750 shp (559.3 kW) take-off, 700 shp (522 kW) cruise at 2,200 rpm	0.595 lb/shp/hr (362 g/kW/hr)	a) 2,200		346 (156.9)	a) 62 (1,575) b) 21.5 (546) c) 24.8 (630)	EMB-312 Tucano, PZL-130TD Orlik, pre-production Atlas Ace and Pilatus PC-7 Mk II.
PT6A-27 (free-turbine turboprop with 3 axial and 1 centrifugal stages)	680 shp (507 kW) take-off, 620 shp (462.3 kW) cruise at 2,200 rpm	0.602 lb/shp/hr (366 g/kW/hr)	a) 2,200 b) 6.7:1		328 (148.8)	a) 62 (1,575) b) 21.5 (546) c) 21 (533.4)	Beech 99A and B99, DHC-6 Twin Otter Series 300, EMB-110, Frakes Mallard, Harbin Y-12 II, Let L-410A, Turbo Porter PC-6/B2-H2, Viking Air Turbo Beaver and Jetcruzer 450.
PT6A-34AG (free-turbine turboprop with 3 axial and 1 centrifugal stages)	750 shp (559.3 kW) take-off, 700 shp (522 kW) cruise at 2,200 rpm	0.595 lb/shp/hr (362 g/kW/hr)	a) 2,200		331 (150.1)	a) 62 (1,575) b) 21.5 (546) c) 21 (533.4)	Air Tractor AT-402/AT-502, Ayres Turbo-Thrush T-34, Frakes Turbo Cat A/C, Fieldmaster, Pacific Aero Cresco 750, Ag-Cat. Similarly rated PT6A-34A for Atlas Ace. Similarly rated PT6A-34B was for Beech T-44A, with all magnesium alloy castings replaced by aluminium alloy castings.
PT6A-41 (free-turbine turboprop with 3 axial and 1 centrifugal stages)	850 shp (633.8 kW) at 2,000 rpm	0.591 lb/shp/hr (359.5 g/kW/hr)	a) 2,000		403 (182.8)	a) 67 (1,702) b) 19.4 (493) c) 22.1 (561.3)	Beech Super King Air 200, Piper Cheyenne III. Single stage compressor turbine; two stage power turbine (as for those below until indicated). Similar PT6A-41AG used on Frakes Turbo Cat, with dry weight of 412 lb (186.9 kg).
PT6A-42 (free-turbine turboprop with 3 axial and 1 centrifugal stages)	850 shp (633.8 kW) at 2,000 rpm	0.601 lb/shp/hr (365.6 g/kW/hr)	a) 2,000		403 (182.8)	a) 67 (1,702) b) 19.4 (493) c) 22.1 (561.3)	Beech Super King Air B200, Aero Ae 270 Ibis and AASI Jetcruzer 500.
PT6A-45R (free-turbine turboprop with 3 axial and 1 centrifugal stages)	1,197 shp (892.6 kW) at 1,700 rpm, 956 shp (713 kW) cruise at 1,425 rpm	0.553 lb/shp/hr (336 g/kW/hr)	a) 1,700		448 (203.2)	a) 71.9 (1,826) b) 19.4 (493) c) 22.1 (561.3)	Air Tractor AT-503, Shorts 330/C-23A Sherpa, USAC Turbo Express (DC-3 conversion). Hot end upgrade. Water/methanol removed. Earlier and lighter 1,173 shp (874.7 kW) at 1,700 rpm PT6A-45A/B used by Frakes Mohawk 298 and Shorts 330; PT6A-45B has increased water/methanol injection for take-off.
PT6A-60A (free-turbine turboprop with 3 axial and 1 centrifugal stages)	1,050 shp (783 kW) take-off, 1,000 shp (745.7 kW) cruise at 1,700 rpm	0.548 lb/shp/hr (333.3 g/kW/hr)	a) 1,700	b) Jet A, Jet A-1, Jet B, Wide-cut or JP-4	475 (215.5)	a) 72 (1,829) b) 19 (483) c) 22 (559)	Beech King Air 300 and King Air 350, and Daewoo KTX-1.
PT6A-61 (free-turbine turboprop with 3 axial and 1 centrifugal stages)	850 shp (633.8 kW) at 2,000 rpm	0.591 lb/shp/hr (359.5 g/kW/hr)	a) 2,000	b) Jet A, Jet A-1, Jet B, Wide-cut or JP-4	429 (194.6)	a) 67.5 (1,715) b) 19 (483) c) 22 (559)	Piper Cheyenne IIIA.
PT6A-62 (free-turbine turboprop with 3 axial and 1 centrifugal stages)	950 shp (708.4 kW) take-off, 900 shp (671 kW) cruise at 2,000 rpm	0.567 lb/shp/hr (345 g/kW/hr)	a) 2,000	b) Jet A, Jet A-1, Jet B, Wide-cut or JP-4	456 (206.8)	a) 70.5 (1,791) b) 19 (483) c) 20.5 (521)	Pilatus PC-9, PZL-130TC Orlik and HTT-35.

Designation (type of engine)	Power output (normally take-off rating for piston, turboprop and turboshaft, unless stated)	Specific Fuel Consumption (S F C)	a) Max RPM b) Pressure or Compression ratio	a) EGT (unless stated to be MGT, TET, TGT or TIT) b) Primary fuel type or Octane rating	Dry weight lb (kg)	a) Length ins (mm) b) Width ins (m) c) Height ins (mm)	Current aircraft users, and comments
Canada							
Pratt & Whitney Canada Inc (continued)							
PT6A-64 (free-turbine turboprop with 4 axial and 1 centrifugal stages)	700 shp (522 kW) at 2,000 rpm	0.703 lb/shp/hr (428 g/kW/hr)	a) 2,000		456 (206.8)	a) 70 (1,778) b) 19 (483) c) 22 (559)	TBM 700.
PT6A-65AG (free-turbine turboprop with 4 axial and 1 centrifugal stages)	1,300 shp (969.4 kW) at 1,700 rpm, 956 shp (712.9 kW) cruise at 1,425 rpm	0.516 lb/shp/hr (314 g/kW/hr)	a) 1,700		486 (220.4)	a) 75 (1,905) b) 19 (483) c) 22 (559)	Ayres Turbo Thrush T65 and Croplease Firemaster.
PT6A-65B (free-turbine turboprop with 4 axial and 1 centrifugal stages)	1,100 shp (820.3 kW) take-off, 1,000 shp (745.7 kW) cruise at 1,700 rpm	0.536 lb/shp/hr (326 g/kW/hr)	a) 1,700 b) 10:1	b) Jet A, Jet A-1, Jet B, Wide-cut or JP-4	481 (218.2)	a) 75 (1,905) b) 19 (483) c) 22.5 (571.5)	Beech 1900 Airliner and C-12J, PZL M-28 Skytruck PT, and Beriev Be-32. 1,376 shp (1,026 kW) PT6A-65R used by Shorts 360.
PT6A-65AR (free-turbine turboprop with 4 axial and 1 centrifugal stages)	1,424 shp (1,062 kW) at 1,700 rpm, 956 shp (712.9 kW) at 1,425 rpm	0.509 lb/shp/hr (310 g/kW/hr)	a) 1,700	b) Jet A, Jet A-1, Jet B, Wide-cut or JP-4	486 (220.4)	a) 75 (1,905) b) 19 (483) c) 22 (559)	AMI Cargo Master (DC-3 conversion), Shorts 360, C-23B, and Aeroprogress T-101 Gratch.
PT6A-66 (free-turbine turboprop with 4 axial and 1 centrifugal stages)	1,485 shp (1,107 kW) flat-rated to 850 shp (633.8 kW) at 2,000 rpm	0.642 lb/shp/hr (390.5 g/kW/hr)	a) 2,000		456 (206.8) standard rotation, 470 (213.2) reverse rotation	a) 70 (1,778) b) 19.4 (493) c) 22.5 (571.5)	Avanti.
PT6A-67 (free-turbine turboprop with 4 axial and 1 centrifugal stages)	1,200 shp (894.8 kW) take-off, 1,000 shp (745.7 kW) cruise at 1,700 rpm	0.547 lb/shp/hr (333 g/kW/hr)	a) 1,700		506 (229.5)	a) 74 (1,880) b) 19 (483) c) 22 (559)	Beech RC-12K.
PT6A-67A (free-turbine turboprop with 4 axial and 1 centrifugal stages)	1,200 shp (894.8 kW) take-off, 1,000 shp (745.7 kW) cruise at 1,700 rpm	0.547 lb/shp/hr (333 g/kW/hr)	a) 1,700		506 (229.5)	a) 76 (1,930) b) 19 (483) c) 22 (559)	Beech Starship 1.
PT6A-67AG (free-turbine turboprop with 4 axial and 1 centrifugal stages) See Comments	1,350 shp (1,006.7 kW) take-off, 1,220 shp (909.75 kW) cruise at 1,700 rpm	0.528 lb/shp/hr (321 g/kW/hr)	a) 1,700		520 (235.9)	a) 76 (1,930) b) 19 (483) c) 22 (559)	New version of PT6A-67A series. Single stage compressor turbine; single stage power turbine. Previous 1,424 shp (1,062 kW) PT6A-67AF for Conair Turbo Firecat.
PT6A-67B (free-turbine turboprop with 4 axial and 1 centrifugal stages)	1,200 shp (894.8 kW) take-off, 1,000 shp (745.7 kW) cruise at 1,700 rpm	0.552 lb/shp/hr (335.8 g/kW/hr)	a) 1,700		515 (233.6)	a) 76 (1,930) b) 19 (483) c) 22 (559)	Pilatus PC-12. Single stage compressor turbine; two stage power turbine (as below until indicated).
PT6A-67D (free-turbine turboprop with 4 axial and 1 centrifugal stages)	1,279 shp (953.75 kW) take-off, 1,106 shp (824.7 kW) cruise at 1,700 rpm	0.530 lb/shp/hr (322.4 g/kW/hr)	a) 1,700		515 (233.6)	a) 74 (1,880) b) 19 (483) c) 22 (559)	Beech 1900D Airliner.
PT6A-67R (free-turbine turboprop with 4 axial and 1 centrifugal stages)	1,424 shp (1,062 kW) at 1,700 rpm, 1,020 shp (760.6 kW) cruise at 1,425 rpm	0.520 lb/shp/hr (316.3 g/kW/hr)	a) 1,700		515 (233.6)	a) 76 (1,930) b) 19 (483) c) 22 (559)	Basler Turbo 67 (DC-3 conversion), Shorts 360-300.

Designation (type of engine)	Power output (normally take-off rating for piston, turboprop and turboshaft, unless stated)	Specific Fuel Consumption (S F C)	a) Max RPM b) Pressure or Compression ratio	a) EGT (unless stated to be MGT, TET, TGT or TIT) b) Primary fuel type or Octane rating	Dry weight lb (kg)	a) Length ins (mm) b) Width ins (mm) c) Height ins (mm)	Current aircraft users, and comments
Canada							
Pratt & Whitney Canada Inc. (continued)							
PT6A-68A (free-turbine turboprop with 4 axial and 1 centrifugal stages)	1,300 shp (969.4 kW) take-off, 1,250 shp (932.1 kW) cruise at 2,000 rpm	0.540 16/shp/hr (328.5 g/kW/hr) for PTEA-68 (see Comments)	a) 2,000		572 (259.5)	a) 72.2 (1,834) b) 19 (483) c) 22.5 (571.5)	Northrop Grumman/Embraer EMB-312H Super Tucano. 1,250 shp (932.1 kW) at 2,000 rpm PT6A-68 is of similar weight and size, and is used by the Beech/Pilatus PC-9 II JPATS.
PT6A-112 (free-turbine turboprop with 3 axial and 1 centrifugal stages) See Comments	500 shp (372.9 kW)	0.637 lb/shp/hr (387.5 g/kW/hr)	a) 1,900		326 (147.9)	a) 62 (1,575) b) 21.5 (546) c) 21 (533).	Cessna Conquest I, Reims F 406 Caravan II. Single stage compressor turbine; single stage power turbine. Engine related to the PT6A-11 series
PT6A-114 (free-turbine turboprop with 3 axial and 1 centrifugal stages)	600 shp (447.4 kW) at 1,900 rpm	0.640 lb/shp/hr (389 g/kW/hr)	a) 1,900		345 (156.5)	a) 62 (1,575) b) 21.5 (546) c) 21 (533)	Cessna 208/208B Caravan I. Single stage compressor turbine; single stage power turbine. Engine related to the PT6A-11 series.
PT6A-114A (free-turbine turboprop with 3 axial and 1 centrifugal stages)	675 shp (503.3 kW) at 1,900 rpm	0.616 lb/shp/hr (375 g/kW/hr)	a) 1,900		350 (158.8)	a) 62 (1,575) b) 21.5 (546) c) 21 (533)	Single stage compressor turbine; single stage power turbine. Engine related to the PT6A-11 series.
PT6A-135 (free-turbine turboprop with 3 axial and 1 centrifugal stages)	750 shp (559.3 kW) take-off, 700 shp (522 kW) cruise at 1,900 rpm	0.585 lb/shp/hr (356 g/kW/hr)	a) 1,900		338 (153.3)	a) 62 (1,575) b) 21.5 (546) c) 21 (533)	Embraer EMB-121 Xingu A1, Israviation ST-50, Piper Cheyenne IIXL, Schafer Comanchero, Vardax Resources Turbo Otter. Single stage compressor turbine; single stage power turbine. Engine related to PT6A-34 series.
PT6A-135A (free-turbine turboprop with 3 axial and 1 centrifugal stages)	750 shp (559.3 kW) take-off, 700 shp (522 kW) cruise at 1,900 rpm	0.585 lb/shp/hr (356 g/kW/hr)	a) 1,900		338 (153.3)	a) 62 (1,575) b) 21.5 (546) c) 21 (533)	Beech King Air F90-1, Dornier Seastar, Vazer Dash 3 Turbine Otter. Comments as above.
PT6B-35H (free-turbine turboshaft)	675 shp (503.3 kW) take-off	0.657 lb/shp/hr (400 g/kW/hr)	a) 6,188 shaft		307.8 (139.6)	a) 59.2 (1,504) b) 19.5 (495)	Available.
PT6B-36 (free-turbine turboshaft)	1,033 shp (770.3 kW) 30 minutes (OEI), 981 shp (731.5 kW) take-off	0.581 lb/shp/hr (353 g/kW/hr) take-off	a) 6,409 shaft		372 (168.7)	a) 59.2 (1,504) b) 19.5 (495)	Sikorsky S-76B.
PT6B-36A/B (free-turbine turboshaft)	981 shp (731.5 kW) take-off at 6,409 rpm, 887 shp (661.4 kW) max continuous	0.581 lb/shp/hr (353 g/kW/hr) take-off	a) 6,409 shaft	b) JP-4	384 (174) for 36A, 386 (175) for 36B	a) 59.2 (1,504) b) 19.5 (495)	Sikorsky S-76B. PT6B-36B in production. PT6C was developed to offer direct drive; not listed as available.
PT6T-3 Twin Pac (twinned free-turbine turbo-shafts driving a single output shaft through identical geartrains in a common reduction gearbox)	1,800 shp (1,342 kW) take-off at 6,600 rpm, 1,600 shp (1,193 kW) max continuous but power restricted in user helicopters by transmission (see Comments)	0.595 lb/shp/hr (362 g/kW/hr)	a) 6,600 shaft	b) JP-4	648 (294)	a) 65.8 (1,671) b) 43.5 (1,105) c) 32.6 (828)	Bell CUH-1N and UH-1N. Plus Bell/Agusta-Bell 212, restricted to 1,290 shp (962 kW) take-off; and S-58T restricted to 1,505 shp (1,122 kW) take-off.
PT6T-3B Twin Pac (as above)	1,800 shp (1,342 kW) take-off at 6,600 rpm, 1,600 shp (1,193 kW) max continuous	0.600 lb/shp/hr (365 g/kW/hr)	a) 6,600 shaft	b) JP-4	660 (299.4)	a) 65.8 (1,671) b) 43.5 (1,105) c) 32.6 (828)	Bell/Agusta-Bell 212, Bell 412/412SP.

Designation (type of engine)	Power output (normally take-off rating for piston, turboprop and turboshaft, unless stated)	Specific Fuel Consumption (S F C)	a) Max RPM b) Pressure or Compression ratio	a) EGT (unless stated to be MGT, TET, TGT or TIT) b) Primary fuel type or Octane rating	Dry weight lb (kg)	a) Length ins (mm) b) Width ins (m) c) Height ins (mm)	Current aircraft users, and comments
Canada							
Pratt & Whitney Canada Inc (continued)							
PT6T-3BE (as above)	1,800 shp (1,342 kW) take-off, 1,600 shp (1,193 kW) max continuous	0.600 lb/shp/hr (365 g/kW/hr)	a) 6,600 shaft	b) JP-4	665 (301.6)	a) 65.8 (1,671) b) 43.5 (1,105) c) 32.6 (828)	Bell/Agusta-Bell 412/412HP.
PT6T-3D (as above)	1,800 shp (1,342 kW) take-off at 6,600 rpm, 1,600 shp (1,193 kW) max continuous	0.595 lb/shp/hr (362 g/kW/hr)	a) 6,600 shaft	b) JP-4	690 (313)	a) 65.8 (1,671) b) 43.5 (1,105) c) 32.6 (828)	Bell 412EP.
PT6T-6 (as above)	1,875 shp (1,398 kW) take-off at 6,600 rpm, 1,675 shp (1,249 kW) max continuous	0.591 lb/shp/hr (359 g/kW/hr)	a) 6,600 shaft	b) JP-4	660 (299.4)	a) 65.8 (1,671) b) 43.5 (1,105) c) 32.6 (828)	Agusta-Bell 212/212ASW, S-58T.
PT6T-6B (as above)	1,875 shp (1,398 kW) take-off at 6,600 rpm, 1,675 shp (1,249 kW) max continuous	0.591 lb/shp/hr (359 g/kW/hr)	a) 6,600 shaft	b) JP-4	665 (301.6)	a) 65.8 (1,671) b) 43.5 (1,105) c) 32.6 (828)	Agusta-Bell 412.
PW118 (free-turbine turboprop)	1,800 shp (1,342.3 kW) take-off, 1,512 shp (1,127.5 kW) at 1,300 rpm	0.523 lb/shp/hr (318 g/kW/hr) take-off	a) 1,300 b) 11.8:1	b) Conforming to CPW204	861 (390.5)	a) 81 (2,057) approx b) 25 (635) approx c) 31 (787) approx	EMB-120RT, EMB-120ER Advanced.
PW118A (free-turbine turboprop)	1,800 shp (1,342.3 kW) take-off, 1,512 shp (1,127.5 kW) at 1,300 rpm	0.528 lb/shp/hr (321 g/kW/hr) take-off	a) 1,300 b) 11.8:1	b) Conforming to CPW204	866 (393)	a) 81 (2,057) approx b) 25 (635) approx c) 31 (787) approx	EMB-120ER Advanced.
PW119B and C (free-turbine turboprop) Data for PW119C (see Comments)	2,180 shp (1,626 kW) take-off, 1,734 shp (1,293 kW) cruise at 1,300 rpm	0.513 lb/shp/hr (312 g/kW/hr) at maximum take-off	a) 1,300 b) 11.8:1	b) Conforming to CPW204	916 (415.5)	a) 81 (2,057) approx b) 25 (635) approx c) 33 (838) approx	Dornier 328. PW119C offers 5% extra thermodynamic power for the Dornier 328-120.
PW120 (free-turbine turboprop)	2,000 shp (1,491.4 kW) take-off, 1,619 shp (1,207 kW) cruise at 1,200 rpm	0.509 lb/shp/hr (310 g/kW/hr) at take-off	a) 1,200 b) 11.8:1	b) Conforming to CPW204	921 (417.75)	a) 84 (2,134) approx b) 25 (635) approx c) 31 (787) approx	ATR 42.
PW120A (free-turbine turboprop)	2,000 shp (1,491.4 kW) take-off, 1,651 shp (1,231 kW) cruise at 1,200 rpm	0.509 lb/shp/hr (310 g/kW/hr) at take-off	a) 1,200 b) 11.8:1	b) Conforming to CPW204	933 (423.2)	a) 84 (2,134) approx b) 25 (635) approx c) 31 (787) approx	DHC-8 Dash 8-100.
PW121 (free-turbine turboprop)	2,150 shp (1,603.25 kW) take-off, 1,700 shp (1,267.7 kW) cruise at 1,200 rpm	0.500 lb/shp/hr (304 g/kW/hr) at take-off	a) 1,200 b) 11.8:1	b) Conforming to CPW204	936 (424.6)	a) 84 (2,134) approx b) 25 (635) approx c) 31 (787) approx	ATR 42-200, DHC-8 Dash 8-100.
PW121A (free-turbine turboprop)	2,200 shp (1,640.5 kW) take-off, 1,700 shp (1,267.7 kW) cruise at 1,200 rpm	0.496 lb/shp/hr (302 g/kW/hr) at take-off	a) 1,200 b) 11.8:1	b) Conforming to CPW204	957 (434)	a) 84 (2,134) approx b) 25 (635) approx c) 31 (787) approx	ATR 42-320.

Designation (type of engine)	Power output (normally take-off rating for piston, turboprop and turboshaft, unless stated)	Specific Fuel Consumption (S F C)	a) Max RPM b) Pressure or Compression ratio	a) EGT (unless stated to be MGT, TET, TGT or TIT) b) Primary fuel type or Octane rating	Dry weight lb (kg)	a) Length ins (mm) b) Width ins (mm) c) Height ins (mm)	Current aircraft users, and comments
Canada							
Pratt & Whitney Canada Inc (continued)							
PW123 (free-turbine turboprop)	2,380 shp (1,775 kW) take-off, 2,030 shp (1,514 kW) cruise at 1,200 rpm	0.494 lb/shp/hr (300.5 g/kW/hr) at take-off	a) 1,200 b) 14.4:1	b) Conforming to CPW204	992 (450)	a) 84 (2,134) approx b) 26 (660.4) approx c) 33 (838) approx	DHC-8 Dash 8-311.
PW123AF (free-turbine turboprop)	2,380 shp (1,775 kW) take-off, 2,030 shp (1,514 kW) cruise at 1,200 rpm	0.494 lb/shp/hr (300.5 g/kW/hr) at take-off	a) 1,200 b) 14.4:1	b) Conforming to CPW204	992 (450)	a) 84 (2,134) approx b) 26 (660.4) approx c) 33 (838) approx	CL-215T, CL-415.
PW123B (free-turbine turboprop)	2,500 shp (1,864.25 kW) take-off, 2,030 shp (1,514 kW) cruise at 1,200 rpm		a) 1,200	b) Conforming to CPW204	992 (450)	a) 84 (2,134) approx b) 26 (660.4) approx c) 33 (838) approx	DHC-8 Dash 8-314.
PW123C (free-turbine turboprop)	2,150 shp (1,603.25 kW) take-off, 1,950 shp (1,454 kW) cruise at 1,200 rpm	0.508 lb/shp/hr (309 g/kW/hr)	a) 1,200	b) Conforming to CPW204	992 (450)	a) 84 (2,134) approx b) 26 (660.4) approx c) 33 (838) approx	DHC-8 Dash 8-201
PW123D (free-turbine turboprop)	2,150 shp (1,603.25 kW) take-off, 1,950 shp (1,454 kW) cruise at 1,200 rpm	0.508 lb/shp/hr (309 g/kW/hr)	a) 1,200	b) Conforming to CPW204	992 (450)	a) 84 (2,134) approx b) 26 (660.4) approx c) 33 (838) approx	DHC-8 Dash 8-202.
PW123E (free-turbine turboprop)	2,380 shp (1,775 kW)						DHC-8 Dash 8-300E.
PW124B (free-turbine turboprop)	2,400 shp (1,790 kW) take-off, 2,088 shp (1,557 kW) cruise at 1,200 rpm	0.492 lb/shp/hr (299 g/kW/hr) at take-off	a) 1,200 b) 14.4:1	b) Conforming to CPW204	1,060 (480.8)	a) 84 (2,134) approx b) 26 (660.4) approx c) 33 (838) approx	ATR 72-200.
PW125B (free-turbine turboprop)	2,500 shp (1,864.25 kW) take-off, 2,030 shp (1,514 kW) cruise at 1,200 rpm	0.486 lb/shp/hr (296 g/kW/hr) at take-off	a) 1,200 b) 14.4:1	b) Conforming to CPW204	1,060 (480.8)	a) 84 (2,134) approx b) 26 (660.4) approx c) 33 (838) approx	Fokker 50-100.
PW126 (free-turbine turboprop)	2,653 shp (1,978.3 kW) take-off, 2,083 shp (1,553.3 kW) cruise at 1,200 rpm	0.485 lb/shp/hr (295 g/kW/hr) at max contingency	a) 1,200 b) 14.4:1	b) Conforming to CPW204	1,060 (480.8)	a) 84 (2,134) approx b) 26 (660.4) approx c) 33 (838) approx	Jetstream ATP.
PW126A (free-turbine turboprop)	2,662 shp (1,985 kW) take-off, 2,081 shp (1,552 kW) cruise at 1,200 rpm	0.484 lb/shp/hr (294.4 g/kW/hr) at take-off	a) 1,200 b) 14.7:1	b) Conforming to CPW204	1,060 (480.8)	a) 84 (2,134) approx b) 26 (660.4) approx c) 33 (838) approx	Jetstream ATP.
PW127 (free-turbine turboprop)	2,750 shp (2,050.7 kW) take-off, 2,132 shp (1,590 kW) cruise at 1,200 rpm	0.481 lb/shp/hr (292.6 g/kW/hr) at take-off	a) 1,200	b) Conforming to CPW204	1,060 (480.8)	a) 84 (2,134) approx b) 26 (660.4) approx c) 33 (838) approx	ATR 72-210.
PW127B (free-turbine turboprop)	2,750 shp (2,050.7 kW) take-off, 2,132 shp (1,590 kW) cruise at 1,200 rpm	0.481 lb/shp/hr (292.6 g/kW/hr) at take-off	a) 1,200	b) Conforming to CPW204	1,060 (480.8)	a) 84 (2,134) approx b) 26 (660.4) approx c) 33 (838) approx	Fokker 50-300, Fokker 60 Utility.

Designation (type of engine)	Power output (normally take-off rating for piston, turboprop and turboshaft, unless stated)	Specific Fuel Consumption (S F C)	a) Max RPM b) Pressure or Compression ratio	a) EGT (unless stated to be MGT, TET, TGT or TIT) b) Primary fuel type or Octane rating	Dry weight lb (kg)	a) Length ins (mm) b) Width ins (m) c) Height ins (mm)	Current aircraft users, and comments
Canada							
Pratt & Whitney Canada Inc (continued)							
PW127C (free-turbine turboprop)	2,750 shp (2,050.7 kW) take-off, 2,132 shp (1,590 kW) cruise at 1,200 rpm	0.481 lb/shp/hr (292.6 g/kW/hr) at take-off	a) 1,200	b) Conforming to CPW204	1,060 (480.8)	a) 84 (2,134) approx b) 26 (660.4) approx c) 33 (838) approx	Xi'an Y7-200A and Ilyushin Il-114.
PW127D (free-turbine turboprop)	2,750 shp (2,050.7 kW) take-off, 2,132 shp (1,590 kW) cruise at 1,200 rpm	0.481 lb/shp/hr (292.6 g/kW/hr) at take-off	a) 1,200	b) Conforming to CPW204	1,060 (480.8)	a) 84 (2,134) approx b) 26 (660.4) approx c) 33 (838) approx	Jetstream 61.
PW127E (free-turbine turboprop)	2,400 shp (1,789.7 kW) take-off, 2,132 shp (1,590 kW) cruise at 1,200 rpm	0.497 lb/shp/hr (302 g/kW/hr)	a) 1,200	b) Conforming to CPW204	1,060 (480.8)	a) 84 (2,134) approx b) 26 (660.4) approx c) 33 (838) approx	ATR 42-500.
PW150 (turboprop)	6,000-7,000 shp (4,474-5,220 kW)						De Havilland Dash 8-400. Three-stage LP, axial-flow compressor driving second-stage HP turbine, centrifugal HP compressor driving first-stage HP turbine, and high power/low speed gearbox.
PW206A (free-turbine turboshaft)	650 shp (484.7 kW) for 2.5 minutes OEI at 6,000 rpm, 500 shp (373 kW) take-off and max continuous at 6,000 rpm	0.543 lb/shp/hr (330 g/kW/hr)	a) 6,000 shaft b) 8:1	b) JP-4	237 (107.5)	a) 35.9 (912) b) 19.7 (500) c) 22.3 (566)	MD Explorer.
PW206B (free-turbine turboshaft)	551 shp (411 kW) for 2.5 minutes OEI at 5,898 rpm, 414 shp (308.7 kW) take-off and max continuous	0.548 lb/shp/hr (333 g/kW/hr)	a) 5,898 shaft b) 8:1	b) JP-4	246.7 (111.9)	a) 41 (1,041) b) 19.7 (500) c) 24.7 (627)	EC 135.
PW206C (free-turbine turboshaft)	640 shp (477.3 kW) for take-off for 5 minutes, 562 shp (419 kW) max continuous and 732 shp (546 kW) OEI for 2.5 minutes	0.543 lb/shp/hr (330 g/kW/hr)	a) 6,000 shaft	b) JP-4		a) 35.9 (912) b) 19.7 (500) c) 22.3 (566)	Agusta A 109 Power.
PW300 turboprop See Comments						.	Programme on hold. May become active
PW305A (twin-shaft turbofan)	4,679 lbf (20.81 kN) to 33.9° C	0.388 lb/lbf/hr (10.99 g/kNs) take-off	b) 12.9:1	b) JP-1, JP-4, JP-5. Conforms to CPW204	992.9 (450.4)	a) 65 (1,651) b) 34.3 (871) c) 43.8 (1,113)	Learjet 60. Certified December 1992. Development and production collaboration between P&WC and MTU of Germany.
PW305B (twin-shaft turbofan)	5,266 lbf (23.42 kN) to 23.5° C	0.391 lb/lbf/hr (11.075 g/kNs) maximum take-off	b) 12.9:1	b) JP-1, JP-4, JP-5. Conforms to CPW204	993 (450.4)	a) 81.5 (2,070) b) 36.5 (927) c) 45.2 (1,148)	Raytheon Hawker 1000. Certified January 1993.
PW306A (twin-shaft turbofan)	5,700 lbf (25.36 kN) to 31° C	0.394 lb/lbf/hr (11.16 g/kNs) take-off	b) 12.7:1	b) JP-1, JP-4, JP-5. Conforms to CPW204	1,043 (473.1)	a) 81.5 (2,070) b) 36.5 (927) c) 45.2 (1,148)	IAI Astra Galaxy. Larger fan and other changes to PW305 models. Certification anticipated 1996.
PW530A (advanced high by-pass ratio twin-shaft turbofan)	2,750 lbf (12.23 kN)	0.468 lb/lbf/hr (13.26 g/kNs)			605 (274.4)	a) 60 (1,524) b) 27.6 (701) c) 34.4 (874)	Cessna Citation Bravo. Specifically designed for quiet operation, fuel efficiency and high productivity benefits to the corporate jet operator. Design began 1992. First engine run October 1993. First flight on B720 testbed May 1994. Certification anticipated December 1995.
PW545A (advanced high by-pass ratio twin-shaft turbofan)	3,640 lbf (16.19 kN)	0,436 lb/lbf/hr (12.35 g/kNs)			765 (347)	a) 68 (1,727) b) 38.4 (975)	Cessna Excel. Design started April 1994. First engine run December 1994. Certification anticipated December 1996.
T74 and T400							Military versions of the PT6A-20/27 (for Beech U-21s) and PT6T (for UH-1N/CUH-1N/VH-1N) respectively.

Designation (type of engine)	**Power output** (normally take-off rating for piston, turboprop and turboshaft, unless stated)	**Specific Fuel Consumption** (S F C)	**a) Max RPM b) Pressure or Compression ratio**	**a) EGT** (unless stated to be MGT, TET, TGT or TIT) **b) Primary fuel type or Octane rating**	**Dry weight** lb (kg)	**a) Length** ins (mm) **b) Width** ins (mm) **c) Height** ins (mm)	**Current aircraft users, and comments**
China (People's Republic of)							
Beijing University of Aeronautics and Astronautics. 37 Xue Yuan Road, Beijing 100083							
WP11 (single-shaft turbojet)	1,875 lbf (8.34 kN)					b) 23.3 (593) approx	Aircraft and UAVs. Based on the French Turbomeca Marboré but with a higher rating.
Changzhou Lan Xiang Machinery Works. Changzhou, Jiangsu 213123							
WZ6 (free-turbine turboshaft)	1,550 shp (1,156 kW) OEI rating	0.63 lb/shp/hr (383 g/kW/hr) estimated			660 (300) approx	a) 78 (1,980) approx b) 28.2 (717) approx	Z-8. 20% power reserve at sea level.
China National South Aeroengine Company (CNSAC). Zhuzhou, Hunan 412002							
HS5 (9-cyl, 4-stroke, air-cooled, radial piston)	967 hp (721 kW) take-off at 2,200 rpm, 792.5 hp (591 kW) cruise	0.671 lb/hp/hr (408 g/kW/hr) minimum at take-off, 0.626-0.671 lb/hp/hr (381-408 g/kW/hr) cruise	a) 1,511 propeller b) 6.4:1		1,276.5 (579)	a) 52.28 (1,328) b) 54.33 (1,380)	Shijiazhuang Y-5. Chinese-built ASz-62IR-16.
HS6 (9-cyl, 4-stroke, air-cooled, radial piston	285-400 hp (212.5-298.3)		a) 1,849 propeller rpm estimated b) 5.9:1 estimated		441 (200)	a) 37.64 (956) b) 38.78 (985)	CJ-6A, Haiyan, Y-11 and was to be used on an N-5A development in the most powerful HS6K form.
WJ6 (turboprop)	4,250 eshp (3,167 kW)				2,646 (1,200)		Shannxi Y8. WJ6A rated at 4,550 eshp (3,393 ekW).
WJ9 (turboprop)	680 shp (507.1 kW)						No known applications by early 1995, although reportedly intended for a Y-12 variant and other working aircraft.
Dongan Engine Manufacturing Company. Harbin							
WJ5A-1 (single-shaft turboprop)	2,900 ehp (2,162.5 ekW) ±3% take-off at 15,600 rpm ±150	not more than 1,715 lb (778 kg) per hour max rating	a) 15,600 ±150 or 14,050 ± 225 idling		1,323 (600) net, 1,587 (720) including accessories		Y7-100 and Y7H-500.
WJ5A-1G (single-shaft turboprop)		9% fuel reduction					Y7-200B. Sometimes referred to as WJ5E.
WJ5A-1(M) (single-shaft turboprop)	2,790 shp (2,080.5 kW)						Y7H.
Liming Engine Manufacturing Corporation. 6 Dongta Street, Dadong District, Shenyang, Liaoning 110043							
WP6/6A/6B (turbojet)	5,400 lbf (24.03 kN) and 5,512 lbf (24.52 kN) typical dry ratings for WP6A and B respectively, 8,267 lbf (36.776 kN) and 8,930 lbf (39.72 kN) with afterburning for WP6A and B respectively	1.6 lb/lbf/hr (45.24 g/kNs) with afterburning and 0.97 lb/lbf/hr (27.48 g/kNs) typical dry rating for WP6A	b) 7.44:1		1,599 (725)	a) 215.87 (5,483) b) 26.3 (668) c) 37.4 (950)	J-6/JJ-6 and Q-5, plus CK1C (ChangKong 1C) supersonic target UAV. Based on Russian Tumansky RD-9.
WP7C (twin-shaft turbojet)	9,590 lbf (42.66 kN) dry, 13,625 lbf (60.6 kN) with afterburning			b) RP-1, RP-2		a) 181.1 (4,600) c) 42.72 (1,085)	J-7/J-7 II.
WP7F (twin-shaft turbojet)	9,920 lbf (44.13 kN) dry, 14,330 lbf (63.75 kN) with afterburning			b) RP-1, RP-2		a) 181.1 (4,600) c) 42.72 (1,085)	J-7E.
WS6 (twin-shaft turbofan)	15,983 lbf (71.1 kN) dry, 27,448 lbf (122.1 kN) with afterburning	0.62 lb/lbf/hr (17.56 g/kNs) dry, 2.26 lb/lbf/hr (64 g/kNs) with afterburning	b) 14.44:1	a) 1,177° C (TIT)	4,629 (2,100)	a) 183.23 (4,654) b) 53.94 (1,370) nozzle diameter	No known current applications.

Designation (type of engine)	Power output (normally take-off rating for piston, turboprop and turboshaft, unless stated)	Specific Fuel Consumption (S F C)	a) Max RPM b) Pressure or Compression ratio	a) EGT (unless stated to be MGT, TET, TGT or TIT) b) Primary fuel type or Octane rating	Dry weight lb (kg)	a) Length ins (mm) b) Width ins (m) c) Height ins (mm)	Current aircraft users, and comments
China							
Liyang Machinery Corporation. PO Box 5, Pingba, Guizhou 561102							
WP7B (twin-shaft turbojet)	9,689 lbf (43.1 kN) dry, 13,443 lbf (59.8 kN) with afterburning	1.01 lb/lbf/hr (28.61 g/kNs) dry, 2.00 lb/lbf/hr (56.67 g/kNs) with afterburning	b) 8.85:1	a) 1,800° C b) RP-1, RP-2	2,447 (1,110)	a) 181.1 (4,600) c) 42.72 (1,085)	Chengdu J-7/F-7A. Power to weight ratio 5.5.
WP7B M batch (twin-shaft turbojet)	9,689 lbf (43.1 kN) dry, 13,443 lbf (59.8 kN) with afterburning	1.01 lb/lbf/hr (28.61 g/kNs) dry, 2.00 lb/lbf/hr (56.67 g/kNs) with afterburning	b) 8.85:1	a) 1,800° C b) RP-1, RP-2	2,447 (1,110)	a) 181.1 (4,600) c) 42.72 (1,085)	Chengdu J-7/F-7B. Power to weight ratio 5.5.
WP7B (BM) (twin-shaft turbojet)	9,689 lbf (43.1 kN) dry, 13,443 lbf (59.8 kN) with afterburning	1.01 lb/lbf/hr (28.61 g/kNs) dry, 2.00 lb/lbf/hr (56.67 g/kNs) with afterburning	b) 8.85:1	a) 1,800° C b) RP-1, RP-2	2,409.6 (1,093)	a) 181.1 (4,600) c) 42.72 (1,085)	Chengdu J-7/F-7L and F-7M. Power to weight ratio 5.6.
WP13 (twin-spool turbojet)	9,037 lbf (40.2 kN) dry, 14,815 lbf (65.9 kN) with afterburning	0.961 lb/lbf/hr (27.22 g/kNs) dry, 2.245 lb/lbf/hr (63.61 g/kNs) with afterburning	b) 8.9:1	a) 1,900° C b) RP-1, RP-2	2,496 (1,132)	a) 181.1 (4,600) c) 42.72 (1,085)	Chengdu J-7/F-7III. Power to weight ratio 5.9.
WP13A II (twin-spool turbojet)	9,600 lbf (42.7 kN) dry, 14,815 lbf (65.9 kN) with afterburning	0.99 lb/lbf/hr (28.06 g/kNs) dry, 2.196 lb/lbf/hr (62.22 g/kNs) with afterburning	b) 8.9:1	a) 1,900° C b) RP-1, RP-2	2,648.6 (1,201.4)	a) 202.76 (5,150) b) 35.71 (907) c) 42.72 (1,085)	Chengdu J-8 II/F-8 II. Power to weight ratio 5.6. 15,432 lbf (68.65 kN) with afterburning WP 13B possibly in F-8 II.
WP13F (twin-spool turbojet – new version)	9,690 lbf (43.1 kN) dry, 14,815 lbf (65.9 kN) with afterburning	0.99 lb/lbf/hr (28.06 g/kNs) dry, 2.05 lb/lbf/hr (58.06 g/kNs) with afterburning	b) 9.0:1	a) 1,870° C b) RP-1, RP-2	2,413 (1,094.5)	a) 181.1 (4,600) c) 42.72 (1,085)	Chengdu J-7/F-7M, F-7 III. Power to weight ratio 6.
Xi'an Aero-Engine Corporation. PO Box 13, Xi'an, Shaanxi 710021							
WP8 (turbojet)	20,945 lbf (93.167 kN)				6,907 (3,133)		Xi'an H-6.
WS9 (twin-shaft turbofan)	12,550 lbf (55.83 kN) dry, 20,515 lbf (91.26 kN) with afterburning	0.675 lb/lbf/hr (19.12 g/kNs) dry, 2.03 lb/lbf/hr (57.5 g/kNs) with afterburning	a) 12,640 b) 20:1	a) 1,167° C MGT, 634-726 ° C EGT b) Kerosene	4,061 (1,842)	a) 205 (5,205) b) 32.45 (824.23) c) 43.0 (1,093.32)	Jianjiji-Hongzhaji JH-7. Based on the Rolls-Royce Spey 202.
Czech Republic							
Aerotechnik. Podnik UV Svazarmu, 68604, Kunovice							
Mikron IIIS (4-cyl, inverted piston)	65 hp (48.5 kW) take-off		a) 2,600		up to 154.3 (70)		L-13SEH/SDM Vivat in Mikron IIIS AE form with electric starter/alternator.
LOM Prague. 270 Cernokostelecká Street, 100 38 Prague 10-Malesice							
M 132 A (4-cyl, inverted, inline piston). Basic version without super-charger (see Comments)	120.7 hp (90 kW) at 2,700 rpm, 94 hp (70 kW) cruise at 2,500 rpm. (Power ±2.5%)	0.46 lb/hp/hr (280 g/kW/hr)	a) 2,700 b) 6.3:1	b) min 78	231.5 (105) ±2%	a) 41.42 (1,052) b) 16.73 (425) c) 27.1 (688)	For light sports aerobatic aircraft (single or multi-engined). Flick rolls forbidden. A and AL refer to basic engines, capable of basic aerobatics with 5 secs of inverted flight. AR for basic aerobatics/5 secs inverted flight. AK with oil system adapted for full aerobatic inverted flight. AK1/2/3 similar to AK except 1.7 kW alternator instead of dynamo.
M 137 A (6-cyl, inverted, inline piston). Basic version without super-charger (see Comments)	177.7 hp (132.5 kW) at 2,750 rpm, 138 hp (103 kW) at 2,580 rpm. (Power ±2.5%)	0.492 lb/hp/hr (299 g/kW/hr)	a) 2,750 b) 6.3:1	b) min 78	312 (141.5) ±2.5%	a) 52.91 (1,344) b) 17.44 (443) c) 24.8 (630)	For light sports aerobatic aircraft. Flick rolls allowed. A, AL and AZ types, for full aerobatics and inverted flight. AZ has specially adapted crankshaft and other changes.
M 332 AK (4-cyl, inverted, inline piston). Aerobatic modification (see Comments)	138.1 hp (103 kW) at 2,700 rpm. 98.6 hp (73.5 kW) at 2,400 rpm. (Power ±2.5%)	0.457 lb/hp/hr (278 g/kW/hr)	a) 2,700 b) 6.3:1	b) min 78	227 (103) ±2%	a) 43.39 (1,102) b) 16.73 (425) c) 25.79 (655)	For light sports aircraft. Inverted flight allowed. Flick rolls forbidden. A, AR and AK types. AR supplied without 600W dynamo/adapted drive for a 3 kW alternator.
M 337 AK (6-cyl, inverted, inline piston). Aerobatic modification (see Comments)	206.5 hp (154 kW) at 2,750 rpm, 138.8 hp (103.5 kW) at 2,400 rpm. (Power ±2.5%)	0.48 lb/hp/hr (292 g/kW/hr)	a) 2,700 b) 6.3:1	b) min 78	337.3 (153)	a) 55.51 (1,410) b) 17.48 (444) c) 24.72 (628)	For light sports aircraft. Inverted flight allowed. Flick rolls forbidden. A, AK, AK1/2/3 types (see M 132 A for meaning).

Designation (type of engine)	**Power output** (normally take-off rating for piston, turboprop and turboshaft, unless stated)	**Specific Fuel Consumption** (S F C)	**a) Max RPM b) Pressure or Compression ratio**	**a) EGT** (unless stated to be MGT, TET, TGT or TIT) **b) Primary fuel type or Octane rating**	**Dry weight** lb (kg)	**a) Length** ins (mm) **b) Width** ins (mm) **c) Height** ins (mm)	**Current aircraft users, and comments**
Czech Republic							
Motorlet a.s. 158 01 Praha 5, Jinonice							
Walter M202 (2-cyl, 2-stroke, air-cooled piston, with reduction gear)	64.4 hp (48 kW) for 5 minutes, 55 hp (41 kW) maximum continuous	0.715 lb/hp/hr (435 g/kW/hr) cruise	a) 2,355 propeller b) 8.4:1 effective	b) min 96 Octane	79.37 (36) ±1.5%	a) 16.69 (424) b) 22.28 (566) c) 16.77 (426)	Light and ultralight aircraft. In production since 1994.
Walter M601D (free-turbine turboprop)	724 shp (540 kW), 657 shp (490 kW) cruise	0.648 lb/shp/hr (394 g/kW/hr)	a) 2,080 propeller b) 6.55:1	a) 568° C b) Aviation kerosene	425.5 (193) ±2%	a) 65.94 (1,675) b) 23.23 (590) with exhaust nozzle c) 25.59 (650)	L-410UVP, PZL-106BT-601 Turbo-Kruk in M601D-1 form. In production since 1983.
Walter M601E (free-turbine turboprop)	751 shp (560 kW), 657 shp (490 kW) cruise	0.649 lb/shp/hr (395 g/kW/hr)	a) 2,080 propeller b) 6.65:1	a) 572° C b) Aviation kerosene	441 (200) ±2%	a) 65.94 (1,675) b) 23.23 (590) with exhaust nozzle c) 25.59 (650)	L-410UVP-E and possibly T-130 Fregat and T-610 Voyage. In production since 1985.
Walter M601F (free-turbine turboprop)	778 shp (580 kW), 670.5 shp (500 kW) cruise	0.633 lb/shp/hr (385 g/kW/hr)	a) 2,080 propeller b) 6.65:1	a) 567° C b) Aviation kerosene	445.3 (202) ±2%	a) 65.94 (1,675) b) 23.23 (590) with exhaust nozzle c) 25.59 (650)	L-420, Aero Ae 270 Ibis, Myasishchev M-101T Gzhel in M601F-22 form. Certified in 1993.
Walter M601T (free-turbine turboprop for aerobatic aircraft)	751 shp (560 kW), 657 shp (490 kW) cruise	0.649 lb/shp/hr (395 g/kW/hr)	a) 2,080 propeller b) 6.65:1	a) 572° C b) Aviation kerosene	445.3 (202) ±2%	a) 65.94 (1,675) b) 23.23 (590) with exhaust nozzle c) 25.59 (650)	PZL-130TB Orlik. In production since 1993.
Walter M601Z (free-turbine turboprop)	512.3 shp (382 kW), 328.5 shp (245 kW) cruise	0.949 lb/shp/hr (577 g/kW/hr)	a) 1,900 propeller b) 6.08:1	a) 524° C b) Aviation kerosene	434.3 (197) ±2%	a) 65.94 (1,675) b) 23.23 (590) with exhaust nozzle c) 25.59 (650)	Z 37T Agro Turbo. In production since 1984.
Walter M602 (triple-shaft free-turbine turboprop)	1,823.8 shp (1,360 kW), 1,609 shp (1,200 kW) cruise	0.575 lb/shp/hr (350 g/kW/hr)	a) 1,320 propeller b) 12.4:1	a) 511° C b) Aviation kerosene	1,257 (570) ±1.5%	a) 101 (2,565) b) 29.65 (753) c) 33.54 (852)	L-610. Under development flight testing in early 1995.
Walter M701c-500 (turbojet)	1,963 lbf (8.731 kN), 1,577 lbf (7.014 kN) cruise	1.14 lb/lbf/hr (32.29 g/kNs)	a) 15,400 gas generator b) 4.34:1	a) 680° C b) Aviation kerosene	738.5 (335) ±2.5%	a) 83.19 (2,113) b) 35.0 (889) c) 38.58 (980)	L-29. Manufactured 1960-1995.
PDS Kovovyroba sro. Veleslavinská 26, 160 00 Praha 6							
See Comments							Manufactures engines for paragliders.
Ústav pro vyzkum motorovych vozidel. Lihovarská 12, 190 00 Praha 9							
M-115 and M-125 aircraft engines							Manufacturer of these engines.
Egypt							
ABECO (Arab British Engine Company). PO Box 71, Helwan							
Offers overhaul and repair to Astazou XIVH, TV2-117A, Gnome H-1400, VO-540-C2A							
A.O.I Engine Factory (Arab Organisation for Industrialisation). PO Box 12, Helwan El Hammamat							
Larzac 04 (turbofan, assembly, testing, overhaul and repair in co-operation with SNECMA)							
PT6A-25E (free-turbine, triple-stage, axial and centrifugal turboprop)	750 shp (559.3 kW) max continuous at 2,200 rpm (31° C), 700 shp (522 kW) max cruise (29° C)	0.595 lb/shp/hr (362 g/kW/hr)	b) 6.7:1				Tucano. Assembly, testing, overhaul and repair under licence from P&WC.
France							
Sarl JPX. ZI Nord, BP13, 72320 Vibraye							
4T 60A (4-cyl, air-cooled piston)	65 hp (48.5 kW)		a) 3,200 b) 8.2:1	b) 100 LL or auto fuel	161 (73)	a) 25.59 (650) b) 31.69 (805)	ATL and Jodel types. A lighter version is the 4T 60AES. Converted Volkswagen auto engine.

Designation (type of engine)	**Power output** (normally take-off rating for piston, turboprop and turboshaft, unless stated)	**Specific Fuel Consumption** (S F C)	**a) Max RPM b) Pressure or Compression ratio**	**a) EGT** (unless stated to be MGT, TET, TGT or TIT) **b) Primary fuel type or Octane rating**	**Dry weight** lb (kg)	**a) Length** ins (mm) **b) Width** ins (m) **c) Height** ins (mm)	**Current aircraft users, and comments**
France							
Sarl JPX (continued)							
4TX 75 (4-cyl, air-cooled piston)	75 hp (56 kW)		a) 2,800 b) 8.7:1	b) 100 LL or auto fuel	165.3 (75)		Light aircraft.
PUL 212 (1-cyl, 2-stroke piston)	18 hp (13.42 kW)		a) 6,000		17.4 (7.9)		Experimental category homebuilt aircraft.
PUL 425 (2-cyl, 2-stroke piston)	22 hp (16.4 kW)		a) 4,600		46.3 (21) with reduction gear		Experimental category homebuilt aircraft.
Microturbo S.A. Chemin du pont de Rupé, BP 2089-31019 Toulouse Cedex							
TRS 18 (single-shaft turbojet)	326 lbf (1.45 kN)	1.3 lb/lbf/hr (37 g/kNs)	a) 48,750 b) 4.5:1	a) 860° C b) JP-8	89.3 (40.5)	a) 22.2 (564) b) 12.05 (306) c) 13.37 (339.5)	Details refer mainly to TRS 18-1. TRS 18 models used on Bede BD-5J, several prototype and experimental aircraft such as Microjet, and currently on UAVs and missiles. More powerful Microturbo engines are available, such as TRI 60-5 and TRI 60-20. Microturbo also produces auxiliary power systems for aircraft and other uses.
Rectimo Aviation SA. Aeroport de Chambery - Aix les Bains, F-73420 Viviers du Lac							
4 AR-1200 (4-cyl, 4-stroke, air-cooled piston)	37.5 hp (28 kW) at 3,600 rpm, 27 hp (20 kW) cruise at 3,200 rpm	0.59 lb/hp/hr (360 g/kW/hr)	a) 3,600 b) 7:1	b) 80 Octane	134.5 (61)	a) 14.17 (360) b) 29.53 (750) c) 21.65 (550)	Light aircraft and motorgliders. Often quoted 4 AR-1600 follow-up engine was never commercialized.
SNECMA–Société Nationale d'Étude et de Construction de Moteurs d'Aviation. 2 boulevard du Général Martial Valin, 75724 Paris Cedex 15							
Atar 08K50 (single-shaft turbojet)	11,023 lbf (49 kN)	0.97 lb/lbf/hr (27.48 g/kNs)		b) TR0, TR4	2,546 (1,155)	a) 15.51 (3,950) b) 43.86 (1,114) master cross section	Super Etendard.
Atar 09C (single-shaft turbojet)	9,702 lbf (43.16 kN) dry, 13,672 lbf (60.82 kN) with afterburning	1.00 lb/lbf/hr (28.33 g/kNs) dry, 2.01 lb/lbf/hr (57.03 g/kNs) with afterburning	b) 4.5:1	a) 890° C TIT b) TR0/AG or AIR 3405, TR4/AG or AIR 3407	3,197 (1,450)	a) 234 (5,944) forward flange to exhause nozzle b) 44.09 (1,120) master cross section	Mirage III and V.
Atar 09K50 (single-shaft turbojet)	11,060 lbf (49.2 kN) dry, 15,846 lbf (70.49 kN) with afterburning	0.97 lb/lbf/hr (27.47 g/kNs) dry, 1.967 lb/lbf/hr (55.72 g/kNs) with afterburning	b) 6.15:1	a) 930° C TIT, 930° C TET b) TR0/AG or AIR 3405, TR4/AG or AIR 3407	3,505 (1,590)	a) 234.02 (5,944) forward to aft flanges b) 40.47 (1,028) master cross section	Mirage III and V upgrades, Mirage F1, Mirage 50 and Cheetah.
M53-5 (single-shaft turbofan)	12,235 lbf (54.43 kN) dry, 19,840 lbf (88.26 kN) with afterburning	0.87 lb/lbf/hr (24.64 g/kNs) dry	b) 9.8:1	b) TR0	3,241 (1,470)	b) 41.53 (1,055)	Early production Mirage 2000.
M53-P2 (single-shaft turbofan)	14,400 lbf (64.05 kN) dry, 21,400 lbf (95.19 kN) with afterburning	0.91 lb/lbf/hr (25.78 g/kNs) dry, 2.08 lb/lbf/hr (58.92 g/kNs) with afterburning	b) 9.8:1	a) 862° C EGT, 1,327° C TET b) TR0	3,340 (1,515)	a) 191.3 (4,859) b) 31.89 (810) c) 41.5 (1,054)	Mirage 2000 built after 1985.
M88-2 and M88-3 (twin-shaft turbofan) Details for M88-2 (see Comments)	11,250 lbf (50.04 kN) dry, 16,850 lbf (74.95 kN) with afterburning	0.8 lb/lbf/hr (22.66 g/kNs) dry, 1.8 lb/lbf/hr (51 g/kNs) with afterburning	b) 24.5:1	a) 1,577° C TIT b) TR0	1,977 (896.75)	a) 139.29 (3,538) b) 32.7 (831), 27.4 (696) inlet diameter	Rafale. Power/weight ratio 8.5:1. 3-stage LP compressor with inlet guide vanes, 6-stage HP compressor with variable vanes, annular combustion chamber, cooled single-stage HP and LP turbines, radial afterburner and convergent nozzle. M88-3 for production Rafales of 19,560 lbf (87 kN) with afterburning.
M138 (turboshaft)	8,582-10,058 shp (6,400-7,500 kW)						Possibly FLA. Based on the M88 core. Optimized for Mach 0.72 at 9,500 m altitude and Mach 0.68 cruise. Still in the study phase. Development could start in 1977, for flight testing early next century.

Designation (type of engine)	**Power output** (normally take-off rating for piston, turboprop and turboshaft, unless stated)	**Specific Fuel Consumption** (S F C)	**a) Max RPM** **b) Pressure or Compression ratio**	**a) EGT** (unless stated to be MGT, TET, TGT or TIT) **b) Primary fuel type or Octane rating**	**Dry weight** lb (kg)	**a) Length** ins (mm) **b) Width** ins (mm) **c) Height** ins (mm)	**Current aircraft users, and comments**
France							
Turbomeca. Bordes 64511 Cedex							
Arriel 1 (free-turbine turboshaft) See Comments	640-725.5 shp (477-541 kW) See Comments	0.573 lb/shp/hr (349 g/kW/hr) for Arriel 1A and 1B	a) 6,000 shaft for Arriel 1A and 1B b) 9:1 for Arriel 1A and 1B		264.5 (120) including accessories for Arriel 1A and 1B	a) 42.91 (1,090) for Arriel 1A and 1B b) 16.93 (430) for Arriel 1A and 1B c) 22.4 (569) for Arriel 1A and 1B	AS 350 and AS 365C (Arriel 1A/B), AS 365N (640 shp, 477 kW Arriel 1C), AS 365/X 380, A 109K and S-76A+ (700 shp, 522 kW Arriel 1C1, 1K, 1M and 1S), AS 365N2 (737 shp, 550 kW Arriel 1C2), AS 350 (684 shp, 510 kW Arriel 1D), AS 350B2, AS 550 Fennec and Kamov Ka-128 (732 shp, 546 kW Arriel 1D1), BK 117 C-1 (737.6 shp, 550 kW Arriel 1E), A 109K2 (737.6 shp, 550 kW Arriel 1K1), AS 565 Panther (748 shp, 558 kW Arriel 1M1), and S-76C (723 shp, 539 kW Arriel 1S1). Some 3,400 Arriel engines had been produced by August 1994, totalling over 5.5 million flight hours.
Arriel 2 (free-turbine turboshaft) See Comments	858 shp (640 kW)						Sikorsky S-76C+ and possibly Dauphin N, Ecureuil and Panther. First flown on an S-76C on 30 June 1994 at the subsidiary CGTM. Equipped with FADEC.
Arrius 1/1A1 (free-turbine turboshaft)	479 shp (357 kW) take off, 520 shp (388 kW) max emergency				191.8 (87)	a) 30.79 (782) b) 14.17 (360) c) 21.26 (540)	AS 355N. Has FADEC.
Arrius 1D (turboprop variant of the Arrius turboshaft)	488 shp (364 kW), flat rated for Omega to 360 shp (268 kW)			244.7 (111)	a) 32.52 (826) b) 18.74 (476) c) 23.23 (590)		TB 31 Omega. Previously known as the Arrius 1A2. Has FADEC.
Arrius 1F (free-turbine turboshaft)	500 shp (373 kW)					a) 30.79 (782) b) 14.17 (360) c) 21.26 (540)	EC 120. Single engine application, with hydromechanical control. Development began in 1993.
Arrius 1M (free-turbine turboshaft)	479 shp (357 kW) take-off				191.8 (87)	a) 30.79 (782) b) 14.17 (360) c) 21.26 (540)	AS 555 Fennec. Military version of Arrius 1, in service with the French Air Force and French Army's ALAT.
Arrius 2B (free-turbine turboshaft)	696 shp (519 kW)						EC 135. First flight on 15 February 1994.
Arrius 2C (free-turbine turboshaft)	641 shp (478 kW) take-off						Alternative engine for the MD 900 Explorer. First flown in an Ecureuil test-bed in February 1993. To fly in an Explorer in 1996.
Arrius 2D (free-turbine turboshaft)	600 shp (447 kW)			b) Jet JP-1, JP-4 and Jet B			Latest engine for Omega.
Astazou III (single-shaft, single-stage axial and single-stage centrifugal turboshaft)	523-591 shp (390-441 kW) max continuous	0.643-0.65 lb/shp/hr (391-395 g/kW/hr) maximum			324-331 (147-150)	a) 56.42 (1,433) b) 18.11 (460) c) 18.11 (460)	SA 341 Gazelle. SA 341F2 variant uses a 643.7 shp (480 kW) Astazou IIIPA, the maximum rating for a Astazou III type.
Astazou XIVH (single-shaft, two-stage axial and single-stage centrifugal turboshaft)	591.4 shp (441 kW) in SA 341 flat-rated to 55 °C, 872 shp (650 kW) in SA 342 maximum power and flat-rated to trans-mission				352.7 (160)	a) 57.87 (1,470) b) 18.11 (460) c) 18.11 (460)	SA 341 and SA 342J/K/L Gazelle. Flat-rated to transmission limitations on SA 342.
Astazou XIVM1 and M2 (single-shaft, two-stage axial and single-stage centrifugal turboshaft)	858.25 shp (640 kW) maximum power, 592 shp (441 kW) take-off					a) 57.87 (1,470) b) 18.11 (460) c) 18.11 (460)	SA 342L2 Gazelle.
Astazou XVI (single-shaft turboprop)	965 shp (720 kW) in XVIG form	0.525 lb/shp/hr (319 g/kW/hr) in XVIG form	a) 43,000		503 (228) equipped in XVIG form	a) 80.59 (2,047) incl propeller b) 21.5 (546) intake	Pucará (XVIG), early Jetstream and others. XVIG capable of inverted flight.
Artouste III (single-shaft turboshaft)	590 shp (440 kW), flat-rated to 55° C in IIID form	0.747 lb/shp/hr (454 g/kW/hr)	b) 5.2:1		392.4 (178)	a) 71.46 (1,815) b) 19.96 (507) c) 24.68 (627)	SA 315 Lama and SA 316B and C Alouette III (401 lb, 182 kg and 563.2 shp, 420 kW Artouste IIIB for HAL Cheetah and Chetak), and SA 316C Alouette III (IIID).

Designation (type of engine)	Power output (normally take-off rating for piston, turboprop and turboshaft, unless stated)	Specific Fuel Consumption (S F C)	a) Max RPM b) Pressure or Compression ratio	a) EGT (unless stated to be MGT, TET, TGT or TIT) b) Primary fuel type or Octane rating	Dry weight lb (kg)	a) Length ins (mm) b) Width ins (m) c) Height ins (mm)	Current aircraft users, and comments
France							
Turbomeca (continued)							
Makila (free-turbine turboshaft)	1,777-1,877 shp (1,325-1,400 kW) Makila 1A1 max contingency, 2,109 shp (1,572 kW) Makila 1A2 max contingency, 1,845 shp (1,375 kW) max take-off, 938.7 shp (700 kW) cruise	0.563 lb/shp/hr (342 g/kW/hr) Makila 1A1 cruise			463 (210)	a) 54.92 (1,395) b) 20.24 (514)	Rooivalk (as Topaz upgrade of Makila 1A1), AS 332 Super Puma and AS 532 Cougar in Makila 1A and 1A1 (higher max contingency rating) versions. New Makila 1A2, in Super Puma II and Cougar II, has 1,845 shp (1,376 kW) take-off and 1,657.5 shp (1,236 kW) max continuous ratings. Makila 1A2 is the first commercial turboshaft to be certified with a super contingency rating (30 seconds).
TM 333 (free-turbine turboshaft)	1,001.7 shp (747 kW) take-off for TM 333 2B	0.529 lb/shp/hr (322 g/kW/hr) take-off for TM 333 2B	a) 6,000 shaft		344 (156) for TM 333 2B	a) 41.14 (1,045) b) 17.87 (454) c) 28.03 (712)	TM 333 1A is the base variant, with the TM 333 1M for the AS 565 Panther military helicopter. TM 333 2B has been selected for the Indian HAL Advanced Light Helicopter, with an initial 14 engines delivered for 5 prototypes by late 1994 (first flown on an ALH on 22 July 1992).
Groupement Turbomeca-SNECMA. 2 boulevard du Général Martial Valin, 75724 Paris Cedex 15							
Larzac 04-6 (twin-shaft turbofan)	2,965 lbf (13.19 kN)	0.716 lb/lbf/hr (20.28 g/kNs)	a) 22,570 b) 10.53:1	a) 1,130° C TET b) TR0, TR4, TR5	650.4 (295) basic	a) 46.73 (1,187) fwd to aft flanges b) 17.78 (451.6) c) 30.39 (772)	Alpha Jet.
Larzac 04-20 (twin-shaft turbofan)	3,174 lbf (14.12 kN)	0.745 lb/lbf/hr (21.11 g/kNs)	a) 23,330 b) 11.13:1	a) 1,160° C TET b) TR0, TR4, TR5	650.4 (295) basic	a) 46.73 (1,187) fwd to aft flanges b) 17.78 (451.6) c) 30.39 (772)	Alpha Jet (C20), MiG-AT or UTS/MiG-80 export version (R20, with different nozzle and fuel control and interface). R20 mockup first fitted to left side of MiG in 1994. First production engines fitted in France for initial MiG ground runs in January 1995, then shipped to Russia for first flight and subsequent exhibit at Le Bourget.
Germany							
Göbler-Hirthmotoren GmbH & Co KG. PO Box 62, 71724 Benningen/Neckar							
Hirth F 23A (2-cyl, 2-stroke, horizontally opposed, fan-cooled piston)	39.6 hp (29.5 kW) at 5,500 rpm		a) 6,500 b) 9.3:1	a) 732° C b) 95 ROZ, 85 MOZ unleaded	52.9 (24)	a) 12.78 (324.5) b) 22.91 (582) c) 13.82 (351)	Ultralights, Experimental category aircraft.
Hirth F 30 (4-cyl, 2-stroke, horizontally opposed piston, with available fan-cooling)	93.9 hp (70 kW) at 5,700 rpm		a) 6,500 b) 9.3:1	a) 732° C b) 95 ROZ, 85 MOZ unleaded	83.8 (38)	a) 16.24 (412.5) b) 22.91 (582) c) 14.72 (374).	Ultralights, ultralight helicopters and Experimental category aircraft.
Hirth F 263 R53 (2-cyl, 2-stroke, inline piston)	27.6 hp (20.6 kW) at 6,000 rpm		a) 6,500 b) 9.5:1	a) 732° C b) 95 ROZ, 85 MOZ unleaded	59.5 (27)	a) 15.16 (385) b) 17.8 (452) c) 13.9 (353)	Ultralights.
Hirth 2702 R 55 (2-cyl, 2-stroke, fan-cooled, inline piston)	39.4 hp (29.4 kW) at 5,700 rpm		a) 6,500 b) 9.3:1	a) 732° C b) 95 ROZ, 85 MOZ unleaded	72.75 (33)	a) 14.84 (377) b) 21.81 (554) c) 14.8 (376)	Ultralights, Experimental category aircraft.
Hirth 2703 R 35 (2-cyl, 2-stroke, fan-cooled, inline piston)	54.2 hp (40.4 kW) at 6,200 rpm		a) 6,500 b) 9.3:1	a) 732° C b) 95 ROZ, 85 MOZ unleaded	72.75 (33)	a) 14.84 (377) b) 21.81 (554) c) 14.8 (376)	Ultralights, ultralight helicopters and Experimental category aircraft.
Hirth 2704 R05 (2-cyl, 2-stroke, fan-cooled, inline piston)	39.6 hp (29.5 kW) at 4,700 rpm		a) 6,500 b) 9.2:1	a) 732° C b) 95 ROZ, 85 MOZ unleaded	66.1 (30)	a) 16.22 (412) b) 22.68 (576) c) 15.1 (383)	Ultralights, Experimental category aircraft.
Hirth 2706 R05 (2-cyl, 2-stroke, fan-cooled, inline piston)	61.7 hp (46 kW) at 6,300 rpm		a) 6,500 b) 9.3:1	a) 732° C b) 95 ROZ, 85 MOZ unleaded	66.6 (30.2)	a) 16.22 (412) b) 21.93 (557) c) 15.1 (383)	Ultralights, Experimental category aircraft.
Hirth 2706 R06 (2-cyl, inline piston)						a) 21.91 (556.5) b) 14.84 (377) c) 15.35 (390)	Estimated. Under development in 1995.

Designation (type of engine)	Power output (normally take-off rating for piston, turboprop and turboshaft, unless stated)	Specific Fuel Consumption (S F C)	a) Max RPM b) Pressure or Compression ratio	a) EGT (unless stated to be MGT, TET, TGT or TIT) b) Primary fuel type or Octane rating	Dry weight lb (kg)	a) Length ins (mm) b) Width ins (mm) c) Height ins (mm)	Current aircraft users, and comments
Germany							
Dieter König GmbH & Co Motorenbau KG. Friedrich-Olbricht-Damm 72, D-13627 Berlin-Charlottenburg							
SC 430 (3-cyl, 2-stroke radial piston with direct or reduction drive)	24 hp (17.9 kW)	10.8 litres/hr	a) 4,300 b) 7.4:1	a) 150° C b) 100 LL or Super gasoline with Pb	33 (15)	a) 11.42 (290) b) 18.1 (480)	Ultralights.
SD 570 (4-cyl, 2-stroke radial piston)	28 hp (20.9 kW)	12 litres/hr	a) 4,300 b) 7.4:1	a) 150° C b) 100 LL or Super gasoline with Pb	44 (20)	a) 13.78 (350) b) 18.11 (460)	Ultralights.
Limbach Flugmotoren GmbH. Kotthausenerstrasse 5, 53639 Königswinter 21, Sassenberg							
L 275E (2-cyl, 2-stroke, air-cooled piston)	24 hp (18 kW)		a) 7,300	b) 90 Octane	16.53 (7.5)	a) 8.9 (226) b) 5.4 (390) c) 7.4 (187)	Ultralights.
L 550E (4-cyl, 2-stroke piston)	50 hp (37.3 kW)		a) 7,500	b) 90 Octane	34 (15.4)		Lightplanes and ultralights.
SL 1700 series (4-cyl, 4-stroke, air-cooled piston)	typically 64 hp (51 kW) take-off		b) 8:1	b) 90 Octane	161 (73)	a) 24.33 (618) b) 30.1 (764) c) 14.49 (368)	Lightplanes and motorgliders. Certified and non-certified models.
L 1800 series (4-cyl, 4-stroke, air-cooled piston)	typically 66 hp (49 kW) take-off		b) 7.5:1	b) Mogas and 100 LL	154.5 (70) approx	a) 24.33 (618) b) 30.1 (764)	Lightplanes and motorgliders.
L 2000 series (4-cyl, 4-stroke, air-cooled piston)	80 hp (59.7 kW) take-off		b) 8.5-8.9:1	b) Mogas and 100 LL	154.3-158 (70-72)	a) 24.33 (618) b) 30.1 (764)	Lightplanes and many motorgliders, including the Fournier RF-5 in L 2000EO1 form.
L 2400 series (4-cyl, 4-stroke, piston)	typically 93-130 hp (69.4-97 kW)		b) 8.5:1	b) RON 96 minimum. Latest L 2400EFI uses unleaded auto fuel	typically 181 (82) for EB models, or 187.5 (88) for L 2400-EFI		Lightplanes and motorgliders, the many types including the Stemme S10 and Arc RF47. Certified JAR-22. Series of at least 9 models, the latest being the100 hp (74.6 kW) L 2400EFI with electronic fuel injection and solid state ignition, certified under JAR-VLA. Anticipated future derivatives of the EFI could include a turbocharged, geared 160 hp (119.4 kW) model
MTU. PO Box 50 0640, 80976 München							
See comments							Partner in several multi-national programmes, including Eurojet, International Aero Engines, MTR and Turbo-Union. Also participates in GE and P&W programmes.
Sauer Motorenbau GmbH. 55270 Ober-Olm, Nieder-Olmer-Str 16							
SE 1800 E1S (4-cyl, horizontally opposed, air-cooled, direct drive piston)	54 hp (40.3 kW) at 3,000 rpm, 44 hp (32.8 kW) cruise at 2,600 rpm	0.506 lb/hp/hr (308 g/kW/hr)	a) 3,200 b) 8.8:1	a) 600° C b) 93 Octane	139.6 (63.3)	a) 21.65 (550) b) 30.1 (765) c) 11.18 (284)	Fournier RF4, Scheibe SF 25, Stark-Turbulent Jodel Bebe, Tipsy Nipper.
SF 2500 H1S (4-cyl, horizontally opposed, air-cooled, shaft drive piston)	103 hp (76.7 kW) at 3,200 rpm, 80 hp (59.7 kW) cruise	0.506 lb/hp/hr (308 g/kW/hr)	a) 3,400 b) 9.5:1	a) 650° C b) 97 Octane	176.4 (80)	a) 23.62 (600) b) 30.71 (780) c) 10.24 (260)	Stemme S10.
SS 2100 H1S (4-cyl, horizontally opposed, air-cooled, direct drive piston)	80 hp (59.7 kW) at 3,000 rpm, 65 hp (48.5 kW) cruise at 2,700 rpm	0.496 lb/hp/hr (302 g/kW/hr)	a) 3,200 b) 9.5:1	a) 650° C b) 95 Octane	167.6 (76)	a) 23.62 (600) b) 31.1 (790) c) 11.61 (295)	Fournier RF, Scheibe SF 25, Jodel D18.
ST 2500 H1S (4-cyl, horizontally opposed, air-cooled, direct drive piston)	92 hp (68.6 kW) at 3,000 rpm, 75 hp (56 kW) cruise at 2,700 rpm	0.496 lb/hp/hr (302 g/kW/hr)	a) 3,200 b) 9.5:1	a) 650° C b) 95 Octane	174.2 (79)	a) 23.62 (600) b) 30.71 (780) c) 11.61 (295)	Bölkow Junior, Fournier RF, Jodel D18, Valentin TL17.
Michael Zoche Antriebstechnik. Keferstrasse 13, 80802 München							
ZO 01A (4-cyl piston in radial form)	147.5 hp (110 kW)	0.37 lb/hp/hr (225 g/kW/hr) max power, 0.362 lb/hp/hr (220 g/kW/hr) 70% cruise	a) 2,500 b) 17:1	a) 550° C inlet temperature b) Diesel 2, JP-4, JP-5, JP-8 or Jet A	185.2 (84)	a) 32.44 (824) b) 25.35 (644) c) 21.85 (555)	Compact aero diesel engine incorporating the latest cylinder technology as well as refinements such as tungsten counterweights and full aerobatic pressure lubrication.
ZO 02A (8-cyl piston in radial form)	295 hp (220 kW)	0.37 lb/hp/hr (225 g/kW/hr) max power, 0.362 lb/hp/hr (220 g/kW/hr) 70% cruise	a) 2,500 b) 17:1	a) 550° C inlet temperature b) Diesel 2, JP-4, JP-5, JP-8 or Jet A	271 (123)	a) 36.77 (934) b) 25.35 (644) c) 25.35 (644)	Compact aero diesel engine incorporating the latest cylinder technology as well as refinements such as tungsten counterweights and full aerobatic pressure lubrication.

Designation (type of engine)	Power output (normally take-off rating for piston, turboprop and turboshaft, unless stated)	Specific Fuel Consumption (S F C)	a) Max RPM b) Pressure or Compression ratio	a) EGT (unless stated to be MGT, TET, TGT or TIT) b) Primary fuel type or Octane rating	Dry weight lb (kg)	a) Length ins (mm) b) Width ins (m) c) Height ins (mm)	Current aircraft users, and comments
Germany							
Michael Zoche Antriebstechnik (continued)							
ZO 03A (2-cyl piston)	68 hp (51 kW)	0.386 lb/hp/hr (235 g/kW/hr) max power, 0.378 lb/hp/hr (230 g/kW/hr) 75% cruise	a) 2,500 b) 17:1	a) 550° C inlet temperature b) Diesel 2, JP-4, JP-5, JP-8 or Jet A	121.25 (55)	a) 29.53 (750) b) 21.85 (555) c) 15.94 (405)	Compact aero diesel engine incorporating the latest cylinder technology as well as refinements such as tungsten counterweights and full aerobatic pressure lubrication.
India							
Gas Turbine Research Establishment. Suranjan Das Road, CV Raman Nagar, Bangalore 560 093							
Kaveri (turbofan)	11,530 lbf (51.3 kN) dry, 18,078 lbf (80.4 kN) with afterburning approximately		b) 22:1	a) 1,427° C TET			For production examples of the HAL LCA.
Italy							
Arrow Engineering Srl. Via Badiaschi 25, 29100 Piacenza							
AE 270 AC (1-cyl, 2-stroke, air-cooled piston)	35 hp (26.07 kW) at 6,800 rpm	6-8 litres per hour	a) 6,800		79.4 (36)	a) 18.11 (460) b) 14.88 (378) c) 14.96 (380)	Experimental category homebuilts and ultralights. 267 cc. Bore 2.94 ins (74.6 mm), stroke 2.4 ins (61 mm). Planetary reduction gear ratio 0.321.
AE 430 (2-cyl piston)	28 hp (21 kW) at 6,500 rpm				24.25 (11)		For UAVs.
AE 530 AC (2-cyl, 2-stroke, air-cooled piston)	68 hp (50.7 kW) at 6,800 rpm	8-12 litres per hour	a) 6,800		110.23 (50)	a) 18.94 (481) b) 19.29 (490) c) 18.23 (463)	Experimental category homebuilts and ultralights. 533 cc. Planetary reduction gear ratio 0.361.
AE 1070 AC (4 cyl, piston)	120 hp (89.5 kW) at 6,800 rpm	8-14 litres per hour	a) 6,800		143.3 (119)	a) 20.51 (521) b) 19.3 (490) c) 18.03 (458)	Experimental category homebuilts. 1,066 cc. Helical reduction gear ratio 0.327.
GP250 (1-cyl, 2-stroke, air-cooled piston)	34 hp (25 kW) max power	up to 6 litres per hour	a) 6,800		57.32 (26)	a) 18.11 (460) b) 14.57 (370) c) 14.96 (380)	Experimental category homebuilts and ultralights.
GP500 (2-cyl, 2-stroke, air-cooled piston)	65 hp (48.5 kW)	up to 10 litres per hour	a) 6,800		79.4 (36)	a) 19.69 (500) b) 19.69 (500) c) 17.76 (451)	Experimental category homebuilts and ultralights.
GP654 (2-cyl, 4-stroke, air-cooled V piston)	55 hp (41 kW)	up to 6 litres per hour	a) 6,500		132.3 (60)	a) 27.64 (702) b) 16.97 (431) c) 18.11 (460)	Experimental category homebuilts and ultralights.
GP1000 (4-cyl, air-cooled piston)	120 hp (89.5 kW)	up to 14 litres per hour	a) 6,800		143.3 (65)	a) 20.51 (521) b) 19.3 (490) c) 18.03 (458)	Experimental category homebuilts and ultralights.
GP1500 (6-cyl, air-cooled piston)	180 hp (134 kW)	up to 14 litres per hour	a) 6,800		193 (87.5)	a) 32.3 (821) b) 19.3 (490) c) 18.03 (458)	Experimental category homebuilts and ultralights.
CRM. Via Manzoni 12, 20121 Milan							
CRM 18D/SS (18-cyl, 4-stroke, liquid-cooled, turbocharged diesel)	2,400 hp (1,790 kW)				4,000 (1,814)	a) 132.7 (3,370) b) 53.15 (1,350) c) 51.34 (1,304)	Sentinel 5000 buoyant aircraft.
FiatAvio. Via Nizza 312, 10127 Turin							
See Comments							Partner in several multi-national programmes, including Eurojet, International Aero Engines and Turbo-Union. Also participates in GE and P&W programmes.
IAME. Engine production ended in 1993							
KFM 107 MAXI (2-cyl, 2-stroke piston)	30 hp (22.4 kW)	8.3 litres per hour at 6,080 rpm	a) 6,300		42-50 (19-11.5)	a) 17.12 (435) b) 17.3 (440) c) 10 (253)	Experimental category homebuilt aircraft and ultralights. Out of production.
KFM 112 (4-cyl, 4-stroke piston)	60 hp (44.7 kW)	11-16 litres per hour	a) 3,200		119 (54)	a) 23 (583) b) 23.7 (603) c) 15 (380)	Experimental category homebuilt aircraft and ultralights. Out of production.
Industrie Aeronautiche E Meccaniche Rinaldo Piaggio SpA. Via Cibrario 4, 16154 Genoa							
See Comments							Produces Rolls-Royce Gem, Spey and Viper, and AlliedSignal T53 and T55 engines under licence, and has a share in the RTM 322.

Designation (type of engine)	**Power output** (normally take-off rating for piston, turboprop and turboshaft, unless stated)	**Specific Fuel Consumption** (S F C)	**a) Max RPM b) Pressure or Compression ratio**	**a) EGT** (unless stated to be MGT, TET, TGT or TIT) **b) Primary fuel type or Octane rating**	**Dry weight** lb (kg)	**a) Length** ins (mm) **b) Width** ins (mm) **c) Height** ins (mm)	**Current aircraft users, and comments**
Italy							
VM Motori SpA, Via Ferrarese 29, 44042 Cento (Fe)							
TPJ 1304HF, 1306HF and 1308HF (4, 6 and 8-cyl, 4-stroke, liquid-cooled, turbo-charged pistons)	207, 315 and 423.75 hp (154, 235 and 316 kW)		a) 2,640 b) 18:1	b) JP-4, JP-5, JP-8, Jet A or others	408, 535.7 and 657 (185, 243 and 298)		No other details supplied.
Japan							
Ishikawajima-Harima Heavy Industries Co Ltd. Shin Ohtemachi Building, 2-1, Ohtemachi 2-Chome, Chiyoda-ku, Tokyo 100							
Produces under licence the P&W F100 for the F-15J, Allison T56 for the P-3C, GE T700 for the H-60J, and is a partner in the GE90, IAE V2500, PW4000 and RJ500.							IHI produced 610 GE J79s for F-104/F-4s to 1980, 391 GE T64s for the P-2J and PS/US-1 to 1982, GE T58s for HSS-2/S-61/V-107 helicopters, and 426 TF40 turbofans for F-1/T-2s to 1987. The FJR710 5-tonne class high bypass ratio turbofan development project was completed in 1982, and 4 were fitted to the experimental NAL STOL aircraft.
F3-IHI-30 (twin-shaft turbofan)	3,682 lbf (16.38 kN) take-off	0.7 lb/lbf/hr (19.83 g/kNs)	b) 11:1		749.5 (340)	a) 79.61 (2,022) overall b) 22.05 (560)	T-4. Developed as an R&D project of the Japan Defence Agency. Series production began in 1987.
J3-IHI-7D (turbojet)	3,417 lbf (15.2 kN)				838 (380)	a) 81.89 (2,080) overall b) 24.8 (630) c) 37.87 (962).	P-2J and T1B. 247 delivered to 1980.
Kawasaki Heavy Industries Ltd. World Trade Center Building, 4-1, 2-Chome Hamamatsucho, Minato-ku, Tokyo 105							
In addition to producing parts for the F100, PW4000, RB211-524 and V2500, Kawasaki builds versions of the AlliedSignal T53 and T-55, and participates in the RJ500.							Also produces Spey/Olympus/Tyne gas generators.
KT5311A (free-turbine turboshaft)	1,100 shp (820.3 kW)					a) 47.6 (1,209) b) 23 (584.2) c) 24.33 (618)	UH-1B and Fuji-Bell 204B. Production began in 1967 and has ended.
T53-K-13B and KT5313B (free-turbine turboshaft)	1,400 shp (1,044 kW)				551 (250)	a) 47.6 (1,209) b) 23 (584.2) c) 26.1 (663)	UH-1H (T53) and Fuji-Bell 204B-2 (KT53). Production began in 1973.
T53-K-703 (free-turbine turboshaft)	1,485 shp (1,107 kW)				544.5 (247)	a) 47.6 (1,209) b) 23 (584.2) c) 26.1 (663)	AH-1S and UH-1J.
T55-K-712 (free-turbine turboshaft)	4,626 shp (3,450 kW) OEI rating, 3,149 shp (2,348 kW) continuous				750 (340)	a) 47.09 (1,196) b) 24.25 (615.9)	CH-47J. Production began in 1984.
Ramjet, as part of Combined Cycle Engine (See Comments)							Experimental ramjet to be tested in 1995, following tests of a 2.4 ins (60 mm) diameter scale model ramjet combustor at Pratt & Whitney by the Japanese Hypersonic Transport Propulsion Research System Corp. The R&D programme will eventually develop a combined ramjet and turbojet to form a Combined Cycle Engine suited to a Mach 5 hypersonic transport.
Mitsubishi Heavy Industries Ltd. 5-1 Marunouchi 2-Chome, Chiyoda-ku, Tokyo 100							
Takes part in the PW4000, RJ500 and V2500 multi-national programmes							Produced CT63-M-5A/250-218A turboshaft engines under licence from Allison from 1967-77 (still produces parts for 250 series engines) and P&W JT8D-M-9 turbofans for the C-1 from 1971-81 (still produces parts for the JT8D). Developing XTSI-1 for OH-X.
Poland							
Instytut Lotnictwa. Aleja Krakowska 110/114, 02-256 Warszawa							
D-18A (twin-shaft turbofan)	3,970 lbf (17.65 kN)	0.74 lb/lbf/hr (20.96 g/kNs)	b) 8.09:1	b) Jet A-1	838 (380)	a) 76.38 (1,940) b) 29.53 (750) c) 35.43 (900)	

Designation (type of engine)	Power output (normally take-off rating for piston, turboprop and turboshaft, unless stated)	Specific Fuel Consumption (S F C)	a) Max RPM b) Pressure or Compression ratio	a) EGT (unless stated to be MGT, TET, TGT or TIT) b) Primary fuel type or Octane rating	Dry weight lb (kg)	a) Length ins (mm) b) Width ins (m) c) Height ins (mm)	Current aircraft users, and comments
Poland							
Instytut Lotnictwa (continued)							
K-15 Kaszub (axial-flow turbojet)	3,307 lbf (14.72 kN)	1.007 lb/lbf/hr (28.52 g/kNs)	b) 5.3:1	a) 730° C b) Jet A-1, TS-1, PSM-2	772 (350)	a) 61.42 (1,560) b) 28.54 (725) c) 35.12 (892)	I-22 Iryda. Also produced by PZL-Rzeszów.
K-16 (turbojet)	3,527 lbf (15.69 kN)						Under development for Iryda types.
K-18 (turbojet)	3,968 lbf (17.65 kN)						Under development for Iryda M-93.
PZL Kalisz - see WSK Kalisz							
PZL-Rzeszów Wytwórnia Sprzetu Komunikacy Jnego (Transport Equipment Enterprise). ul. Hetmanska 120, 35-078 Rzeszow, PO Box 340							
GTD-350 standard model (free-turbine turboshaft)	394.25 shp (294 kW) at 43,200 gas generator rpm, 281.6 shp (210 kW) cruise at 39,375 gas generator rpm	0.815 lb/shp/hr (496 g/kW/hr) at take-off	a) See Power output b) 6.05:1 at take-off	b) TS-1, TS-2, Jet A-1	307 (139.3)	a) 54.53 (1,385) b) 24.65 (626) c) 29.92 (760)	Mi-2 built by PZL-Swidnik.
GTD-350W upgraded model (free-turbine turboshaft)	419.7 shp (313 kW) at above rpm, 281.6 shp (210 kW) at above rpm	0.815 lb/shp/hr (496 g/kW/hr) at take-off	a) See Power output b) 6.05:1 at take-off	b) TS-1, TS-2, Jet A-1	307 (139.3)	a) 54.53 (1,385) b) 24.65 (626) c) 29.92 (760)	As above. GTD-350P version of the engine was only a prototype and not put into series production.
PZL-3S (7-cyl, air-cooled radial piston, with single-speed supercharger and direct drive)	591.4 hp (441 kW) at 2,200 rpm, 406.3 hp (303 kW) cruise at 2,000 rpm	0.536-0.727 lb/hp/hr (326-442 g/kW/hr)	a) 2,200 b) 6.4:1	b) min 91 Octane	906 (411)	a) 43.7 (1,110) b) 49.88 (1,267)	PZL-106 Kruk, Ag-Cat, Ayres Thrush Commander S-2R, de Havilland Canada DHC-2 Beaver.
PZL-3SR (7-cyl, air-cooled radial piston, with single-speed supercharger and propeller drive reduction gear – ratio 0.7)	591.4 hp (441 kW) at 2,200 rpm, 406.3 hp (303 kW) cruise at 2,000 rpm	0.536-0.727 lb/hp/hr (326-442 g/kW/hr)	a) 1,540 propeller b) 6.4:1	b) min 91 Octane	983.3 (446)	a) 50 (1,270) b) 49.88 (1,267)	PZL-106BR Kruk.
PZL-5 (turbojet)	2,425 lbf (10.79 kN)						I-22 Iryda. Formerly SO-3W22.
PZL-10W (free-turbine turboshaft)	887.7 shp (662 kW) at 29,156 gas generator rpm, 690.6 shp (515 kW) cruise at 27,865 gas generator rpm	0.60 lb/shp/hr (365 g/kW/hr)	a) See Power output b) 7.3:1	b) T-1, T-2, TS-1, RT, PSM-2, Jet A-1	311 (141)	a) 73.82 (1,875) b) 29.13 (740) left-hand version, 30.12 (765) right hand version c) 23.43 (595)	PZL-Swidnik Sokól.
PZL-F.2A120C1 (2-cyl, horizontally opposed piston)	59 hp (44 kW) at 3,200 rpm	0.513 lb/hp/hr (312 g/kW/hr)	b) 8.5:1	b) 100 LL	129 (58.5)	a) 24.8 (630) b) 31.3 (795) c) 20.47 (520)	SZD-41 Ogar. PZL-F engines based on design documentation of US Franklin Engine Co Inc.
PZL-F.4A235B31 (4-cyl, horizontally opposed piston)	114 hp (85 kW) at 2,800 rpm	0.513 lb/hp/hr (312 g/kW/hr)	b) 8.5:1	b) 100 LL	227 (103)	a) 29.53 (750) b) 31.3 (795) c) 25.2 (640)	Aeroplastika LAK-X.
PZL-F.6A350C1L and -C1R (6-cyl, horizontally opposed piston)	202.5 hp (151 kW) at 2,800 rpm	0.436 lb/hp/hr (265 g/kW/hr)	b) 10.5:1	b) 100 LL	330.7 (150)	a) 37.8 (960) b) 31.3 (795) c) 24.8 (630)	M-20 Mewa. C1R is right-hand rotation version.
SO-3W (single-shaft turbojet)	2,425 lbf (10.8 kN)	1.1 lb/lbf/hr (31.16 g/kNs)	b) 5.0:1	b) PSM-2, TS-1, Jet A-1	771.6 (350) max	a) 83.15 (2,112) b) 29.92 (760) c) 30.67 (779)	TS-11 Iskra.
TWD-10B (free-turbine turboprop)	945 shp (705 kW) at 29,600 gas generator rpm, 770 shp (574 kW) cruise at 28,400 gas generator rpm	0.613 lb/shp/hr (373 g/kW/hr)	b) 7.4:1	b) T-1, T-2, TS-1, RT, PSM-2, Jet A-1	507 (230)	a) 81.10 (2,060) b) 21.85 (555) c) 35.43 (900)	PZL-Mielec M-28.

Designation (type of engine)	**Power output** (normally take-off rating for piston, turboprop and turboshaft, unless stated)	**Specific Fuel Consumption** (S F C)	**a) Max RPM b) Pressure or Compression ratio**	**a) EGT** (unless stated to be MGT, TET, TGT or TIT) **b) Primary fuel type or Octane rating**	**Dry weight** lb (kg)	**a) Length** ins (mm) **b) Width** ins (mm) **c) Height** ins (mm)	**Current aircraft users, and comments**
Poland							
WSK Kalisz – Wytwórnia Sprzetu Komunikacyjnego "PZL-Kalisz". ul. Czestochowska 140, 62-800 Kalisz							
AI-14RA (9-cyl, 4-stroke, air-cooled, radial piston with pneumatic starting)	251.3 hp (187.4 kW) take-off at 2,350 rpm, 212.7 hp (158.6 kW) cruise at 2,050 rpm	0.57-0.625 lb/hp/hr (347-380 g/kW/hr) take-off, 0.536-0.582 lb/hp/hr (326-354 g/kW/hr) cruise	a) 1,849 propeller rpm b) 5.9:1	b) min 91 Octane with tetraethyl lead (max 2.5 g/ 1 kg of fuel); B-91/115 and 100 L	441 (200)	a) 37.64 (956) b) 38.78 (985)	Wilga 35 and Gawron; suitable for ambulance/ tourist/and other aircraft.
AI-14RA-KAF (9-cyl, 4-stroke, air-cooled, radial piston with pneumatic starting)	251.3 hp (187.4 kW) take-off at 2,350 rpm, 212.7 hp (158.6 kW) cruise at 2,050 rpm	0.57-0.625 lb/hp/hr (347-380 g/kW/hr) take-off, 0.536-0.582 lb/hp/hr (326-354 g/kW/hr) cruise	a) 1,849 propeller rpm b) 5.9:1	b) min 91 Octane with tetraethyl lead (max 2.5 g/1 kg of fuel); B-91/115 and 100 L	441 (200)	a) 37.64 (956) b) 38.78 (985)	Wilga 80; suitable for ambulance/tourist/and other aircraft. Identical to AI-14RA but with repositioned carburettor.
AI-14RC (9-cyl, 4-stroke, air-cooled, radial piston with electric starting)	251.3 hp (187.4 kW) take-off at 2,350 rpm, 212.7 hp (158.6 kW) cruise at 2,050 rpm	0.57-0.625 lb/hp/hr (347-380 g/kW/hr) take-off, 0.536-0.582 lb/hp/hr (326-354 g/kW/hr) cruise	a) 1,849 propeller rpm b) 5.9:1	b) min 91 Octane with tetraethyl lead (max 2.5 g/ 1 kg of fuel); B-91/115 and 100 L	441 (200) + 2%	a) 37.64 (956) b) 38.78 (985)	For ambulance/tourist/and other aircraft. Similar to RA but has electric starting.
AI-14RD (9-cyl, 4-stroke, air-cooled, radial piston with electric starting)	273.2 hp (203.7 kW) take-off at 2,400 rpm, 234.7 hp (175 kW) cruise at 2,100 rpm	0.582-0.625 lb/hp/hr (354-380 g/kW/hr) take-off, 0.559-0.603 lb/hp/hr (340-367 g/kW/hr) cruise	a) 1,888 propeller b) 5.9:1	b) min 91 Octane with tetraethyl lead (max 2.5 g/ 1 kg of fuel); B-91/115 and 100 L	441 (200)	a) 37.64 (956) b) 38.78 (985)	Wilga; suitable for ambulance, tourist, agricultural and other aircraft.
AI-14RDP (9-cyl, 4-stroke, air-cooled, radial piston with pneumatic starting)	273.2 hp (203.7 kW) take-off at 2,400 rpm, 234.7 hp (175 kW) cruise at 2,100 rpm	0.582-0.625 lb/hp/hr (354-380 g/kW/hr) take-off, 0.559-0.603 lb/hp/hr (340-367 g/kW/hr) cruise	a) 1,888 propeller b) 5.9:1	b) min 91 Octane with tetraethyl lead (max 2.5 g/ 1 kg of fuel); B-91/115 and 100 L	441 (200)	a) 37.64 (956) b) 38.78 (985)	Wilga; suitable for ambulance, tourist, agricultural and other aircraft.
ASz-62IR-16 (9-cyl, 4-stroke, air-cooled, radial piston)	967 hp (721 kW) take-off at 2,200 rpm, 792.5 hp (591 kW) cruise	0.671 lb/hp/hr (408 g/kW/hr) minimum at take-off, 0.626-0.671 lb/hp/hr (381-408 g/kW/hr) cruise	a) 1,511 propeller b) 6.4:1	b) min 91 Octane with tetraethyl lead (max 3.3 g/ 1 kg of fuel); B-91/115 and 100 LL	1,276.5 (579)	a) 52.28 (1,328) b) 54.33 (1,380)	An-2 and Y-5B. Based on Russian ASh-62.
ASz-62IR-M18 (9-cyl, 4-stroke, air-cooled, radial piston)	967 hp (721 kW) take-off at 2,200 rpm, 792.5 hp (591 kW) cruise	0.671 lb/hp/hr (408 g/kW/hr) minimum at take-off, 0.626-0.671 lb/hp/hr (381-408 g/kW/hr) cruise	a) 1,511 propeller b) 6.4:1	b) min 91 Octane with tetraethyl lead (max 3.3 g/ 1 kg of fuel); B-91/115 and 100 LL	1,250 (567)	a) 44.49 (1,130) b) 54.33 (1,380)	M-18 Dromader. Version for retrofitting to the DHC-3 Otter has a vacuum pump. WSK Kalisz has not applied any special designation to this version beyond "ASz-62IR-M18 for DHC-3 Otter".
K8-AA (9-cyl, 4-stroke, radial piston with direct drive and pneumatic starting)	273.2 hp (203.7 kW) take-off at 2,400 rpm, 234.7 hp (175 kW) cruise at 2,100 rpm	0.582-0.625 lb/hp/hr (354-380 g/kW/hr) take-off, 0.559-0.603 lb/hp/hr (340-367 g/kW/hr) cruise	a) 2,400 propeller b) 5.9:1	b) min 91 Octane with tetraethyl lead (max 2.5 g/1 kg of fuel); B-91/115 and 100 L	441 (200)	a) 39.15 (994.5) b) 38.78 (985)	Adjusted for aerobatics. Version of the AI-14R.
K9-AA (9-cyl, 4-stroke, air-cooled, radial piston with electric starting)	1,153 hp (860 kW) take-off at 2,300 rpm, 936.3 hp (698.2 kW) cruise at 2,150 rpm	0.694 lb/hp/hr (422 g/kW/hr) minimum at take-off, 0.649-0.694 lb/hp/hr (395-422 g/kW/hr) cruise	a) 1,580 propeller b) 6.4:1	b) min 91 Octane with tetraethyl lead (max 3.3 g/1 kg of fuel); B-91/115 and 100 LL	1,257 (570)	a) 44.49 (1,130) b) 54.33 (1,380)	M-24 Super Dromader; suitable for tourist and ambulance aircraft. Version of the ASz-62R developed by WSK Kalisz.
K9-BA (9-cyl, 4-stroke, air-cooled, radial piston with electric starting)	1,153 hp (860 kW) take-off at 2,300 rpm, 936.3 hp (698.2 kW) cruise at 2,150 rpm	0.694 lb/hp/hr (422 g/kW/hr) minimum at take-off, 0.649-0.694 lb/hp/hr (395-422 g/kW/hr) cruise	a) 1,580 propeller b) 6.4:1	b) min 91 Octane with tetraethyl lead (max 3.3 g/1 kg of fuel); B-91/115 and 100 LL	1,257 (570)	a) 44.49 (1,130) b) 54.33 (1,380)	DC-3 conversions and suitable for tourist and ambulance aircraft. Hydraulic and vacuum pumps. Can use feathering propeller.

Designation (type of engine)	**Power output** (normally take-off rating for piston, turboprop and turboshaft, unless stated)	**Specific Fuel Consumption** (S F C)	**a) Max RPM b) Pressure or Compression ratio**	**a) EGT** (unless stated to be MGT, TET, TGT or TIT) **b) Primary fuel type or Octane rating**	**Dry weight** lb (kg)	**a) Length** ins (mm) **b) Width** ins (m) **c) Height** ins (mm)	**Current aircraft users, and comments**
Poland							
WSK Kalisz – Wytwórnia Sprzetu Komunikacyjnego "PZL-Kalisz" (continued)							
K9-BB (9-cyl, 4-stroke, air-cooled, radial piston with electric starting)	1,153 hp (860 kW) take-off at 2,300 rpm, 936.3 hp (698.2 kW) cruise at 2,150 rpm	0.694 lb/hp/hr (422 g/kW/hr) minimum at take-off, 0.649-0.694 lb/hp/hr (395-422 g/kW/hr) cruise	a) 1,477 propeller b) 6.4:1	b) min 91 Octane with tetraethyl lead (max 3.3 g/1 kg of fuel); B-91/115 and 100 LL	1,257 (570)	a) 44.49 (1,130) b) 54.33 (1,380)	M-24 Super Dromader and suitable for tourist and ambulance aircraft.
K9-BC (9-cyl, 4-stroke, air-cooled, radial piston with electric starting)	1,153 hp (860 kW) take-off at 2,300 rpm, 936.3 hp (698.2 kW) cruise at 2,150 rpm	0.694 lb/hp/hr (422 g/kW/hr) minimum at take-off, 0.649-0.694 lb/hp/hr (395-422 g/kW/hr) cruise	a) 1,580 propeller b) 6.4:1	b) min 91 Octane with tetraethyl lead (max 3.3 g/1 kg of fuel); B-91/115 and 100 LL	1,257 (570)	a) 44.49 (1,130) b) 54.33 (1,380)	An-2 and Kruk.
Romania							
Aerostar S.A. Grup Industrial Aeronautic Bacau. Str. Condorilor nr. 9, cod 5500, Bacau							
M-14P (9-cyl, air-cooled radial piston)	360 hp (268 kW) at 2,900 rpm, 180 hp (134 kW) at 1,850 rpm cruise	0.386 lb/hp/hr (235 g/kW/hr) maximum, 0.258 lb/hp/hr (157 g/kW/hr) minimum	a) 2,900 b) 6.3:1	b) B-91/115 (91 Octane)	471.8 (214)	a) 36.38 (924) b) 38.78 (985) c) 38.78 (985)	AG 6, SM-92 Finist, Su-26, Su-29, Su-31, Yak-18T, Yak-50, Yak-52, Yak-53, Yak-54, Yak-55 and Wilga 35M.
M-14V26 (9-cyl, air-cooled radial piston)	325 hp (242kW) at 2,800 rpm, 190 hp (142 kW) at 2,350 rpm cruise	0.38 lb/hp/hr (231 g/kW/hr)	a) 2,850 b) 6.3:1 (±0.1%)	b) B-91/115 (91 Octane)	560 (254)	a) 43.39 (1,102) b) 38.78 (985) c) 38.78 (985)	Ka-26, Mi-34.
Russia							
AOOT OKBM. Voroshilov Street 22, 394086 Voronezh							
M-14PF (9-cyl, 4-stroke, air-cooled, radial piston driving a tractor propeller)	390 hp (291 kW) take-off at 2,900 rpm, 310 hp (231.2 kW) cruise at 2,400 rpm	0.474 lb/hp/hr (288 g/kW/hr)	a) 1,975 propeller minimum b) 6.3:1 (±0.1%)	b) B-91/115 of 91 Octane	472 (214)	a) 36.38 (924) ±3 mm b) 38.78 (985) ±3 mm	Su-26M, Su-29, Su-31, Su-38, Yak-54, Yak-55 and others. General Designer of AOOT is Anatoly Bakanov.
M-14PM-1 (9-cyl, 4-stroke, air-cooled, radial piston with an updated gearbox and a pusher propeller)	360 hp (268.5 kW) take-off at 2,900 rpm, 290 hp (216.25 kW) cruise at 2,400 rpm	0.463 lb/hp/hr (282 g/kW/hr)	a) 2,600 propeller minimum b) 6.3:1 (±0.1%)	b) B-91/115 of 91 Octane	472 (214)	a) 39.92 (1,014) b) 38.78 (985)	Molniya-1; Aeroprogress T-401 for M-14PR model.
M-14PT (9-cyl, 4-stroke, air-cooled, radial piston driving a pusher propeller)	360 hp (268.5 kW) take-off at 2,900 rpm, 290 hp (216.25 kW) cruise at 2,400 rpm	0.463 lb/hp/hr (282 g/kW/hr)	a) 1,900 propeller minimum b) 6.3:1 (±0.1%)	b) B-91/115 of 91 Octane	472 (214)	a) 38.19 (970) b) 38.78 (985)	Yak-58; Tu-34 uses M-14PS. Generator up to 8 hp/6 kW, and up to an additional 6.7 hp/5 kW power take-off drive to conditioning system compressor.
M-14VI (9-cyl, 4-stroke, air-cooled, radial piston with planetary gear-box, centrifugal blower and forced cylinder cooling fan)	370 hp (276 kW) take-off at 2,950 rpm, 190 hp (141.7 kW) cruise at 2,620 rpm	0.496-0.54 lb/hp/hr (302-328 g/kW/hr)	a) 865 output shaft rpm b) 6.3:1 (±0.1%)	b) A76 of 76 Octane	577.6 (262)	a) 43.39 (1,102) b) 38.78 (985)	Airships, and an amphibious motorboat on an air cushion "Bars". M-14V-26 for Mi-34 of 325 hp (242.4 kW).
M-17 (4-cyl, 4-stroke, air-cooled, horizontally-opposed piston with turbo-supercharger and low-pressure fuel injection)	175 hp (130.5 kW) take-off at 2,950 rpm, 160 hp (119.3 kW) cruise at 2,880 rpm; power can be boosted to 200 hp (149 kW)	0.386 lb/hp/hr (235 g/kW/hr)	a) 2,950 propeller minimum	b) B-91/115 of 91 Octane	242.5 (110)	a) 39.37 (1,000) b) 32.68 (830) c) 21.65 (550)	Be-103, Il-103 and Yak-112.

Designation (type of engine)	Power output (normally take-off rating for piston, turboprop and turboshaft, unless stated)	Specific Fuel Consumption (S F C)	a) Max RPM b) Pressure or Compression ratio	a) EGT (unless stated to be MGT, TET, TGT or TIT) b) Primary fuel type or Octane rating	Dry weight lb (kg)	a) Length ins (mm) b) Width ins (mm) c) Height ins (mm)	Current aircraft users, and comments
Russia							
AOOT OKBM (continued)							
M-17F (4-cyl, 4-stroke, air-cooled, horizontally-opposed piston with turbo-supercharger and low-pressure fuel injection and an electric starter)	200 hp (149 kW) take-off at 2,450 rpm, 150 hp (112 kW) nominal rating at 2,270 rpm	0.408 lb/hp/hr (248 g/kW/hr)	a) 2,450 propeller minimum	b) B-91/115 of 91 Octane	286.6 (130)	a) 41.34 (1,050) b) 32.68 (830) c) 21.65 (550)	Be-103, Il-103, RT-6, Tu-34 and Yak-112.
M-18-02 (2-cyl, 2-stroke, air-cooled piston with hand or electric starter)	55 hp (41 kW) take-off at 2,500 rpm, 37 hp (27.6 kW) nominal rating at 2,100 rpm	0.772 lb/hp/hr (469 g/kW/hr)	a) 2,200 output shaft rpm b) 7.2:1	b) AN 93 of 93 Octane, with MC 20 oil	61.73 (28)	a) 13.78 (350) b) 19.69 (500) c) 19.69 (500)	Ultralight aircraft and powered gliders.
M-25-01 (9-cyl, 4-stroke, air-cooled, radial piston, with fuel injection, turbo-supercharger and automatic control system (see Comments)	430 hp (320.7 kW) take-off at 2,900 rpm, 300 hp (223.7 kW) nominal rating at 2,460 rpm	0.408 lb/hp/hr (248 g/kW/hr)	a) 1,900 propeller minimum b) 6.3:1 (±0.1%)	b) A 76 of 76 Octane	485 (220)	a) 45.28 (1,150) b) 38.78 (985)	Molniya, Su-26, T-401 Sokol, M-500, Yak-18T, Yak-54, Yak-55M and Yak-58. Turbo-supercharger to maintain engine power up to the design flight altitude. Electric or compressed air starting. May be equipped with 4 hp or 8 hp (3 kW or 6 kW) generator.
M-25 (9-cyl, 4-stroke, air-cooled, radial piston, with fuel injection and automatic control system (see Comments)	430 hp (320.7 kW) take-off at 2,900 rpm, 360 hp (268.5 kW) nominal rating at 2,460 rpm	0.408 lb/hp/hr (248 g/kW/hr)	a) 1,900 propeller minimum b) 6.3:1 (±0.1%)	b) A 76 of 76 Octane	485 (220)	a) 45.28 (1,150) b) 38.78 (985)	Finist, Molniya, Su-26, T-401 Sokol, M-500, Yak-18T, Yak-54, Yak-55M and Yak-58.Electric or compressed air starting. May be equipped with 4 hp or 8 hp (3 kW or 6 kW) generator.
Joint Stock Company "Aviadvigatel", JSC Perm Motors. 93 Komsomolsky Prospect, GSP 624, Perm 614600 (Also JSC Rybinskie Motors detailed below under Aviadvigatel, from D-30KP)							
D-25V (free-turbine turboshaft)	5,500 shp (4,100 kW) take-off (-2%) at 9,950 rpm (+150/-100), up to ISA +15° C	0.65 lb/shp/hr (396 g/kW/hr)	a) 10,580 b) 5.6:1 (±0.2)	a) 555° C b) TC-1, T-1 and T-2 PP	2,738 (1,242) + 2%	a) 107.76 (2,737) without transmission, 217.99 (5,537 with transmission b) 42.76 (1,086) c) 45.59 (5,537)	Mi-6, Mi-6A, Mi-10, Mi-10K.
D-30 (twin-shaft turbofan)	14,991 lbf (66.69 kN) take-off (-2%) at 11,600 rpm (+50/-100), up to ISA +15° C	0.62 lb/lbf/hr (17.56 g/kNs) maximum	a) 11,650 b) 18.4:1 (±0.2)	a) 620° C b) T-1, TC-1	3,417 (1,550) + 2%	a) 156.81 (3,983) ±10 mm b) 41.34 (1,050)	Mid-range Tu-134, and M-55 Mystic. Quoted by Aviadvigatel as a by-pass turbojet.
D-30 II (twin-shaft turbofan with thrust reverser)	14,991 lbf (66.69 kN) take-off (-2%) at 11,550 rpm (+50/-100), up to ISA +15° C	0.62 lb/lbf/hr (17.56 g/kNs) maximum	a) 11,600 b) 18.4:1 (±0.2)	a) 620° C b) T-1, TC-1	3,891 (1,765) + 2%	a) 186.36 (4,733.5) ±10 mm b) 41.34 (1,050)	Mid-range Tu-134A and Tu-134B. Quoted by Aviadvigatel as a by-pass turbojet.
D-30 III (twin-shaft turbofan with thrust reverser)	14,991 lbf (66.69 kN) take-off (-2%) at 11,500 rpm (+50/-100), up to ISA +15° C	0.625 lb/lbf/hr (17.7 g/kNs) maximum	a) 11,550 b) 19.8:1 (±0.2)	a) 600° C b) T-1, PT	3,990 (1,810) + 2%	a) 166.75 (4,235.5) ±10 mm b) 41.34 (1,050)	Mid-range Tu-134A3 and Tu-134B3. Quoted by Aviadvigatel as a by-pass turbojet.
D-30F6 (twin-shaft turbofan with afterburner) (See Comments for D-30F8)	20,944 lbf (93.17 kN) dry, 34,172 lbf (152 kN) with afterburning	0.72 lb/lbf/hr (20.39 g/kNs)	a) 11,200 b) 21.3:1	a) 840° C b) T-6	5,353 (2,428) +2%	a) 279 (7,087) b) 60.63 (1,540)	MiG-31. Quoted by Aviadvigatel as a by-pass turbojet. D-30F8 of 38,580 lbf (171.62 kN) with afterburning on MiG-31M.
Joint Stock Company "Aviadvigatel", JSC Rybinskie Motors							
D-30KP (twin-shaft turbofan)	26,455 lbf (117.68 kN) take-off, up to ISA +15° C, 6,062 lbf (26.97 kN) cruise, at 11,000 m altitude and Mach 0.8	0.7 lb/lbf/hr (19.83 g/kNs) cruise	a) 10,620 b) 18.44:1	a) 1,154° C take-off b) TC-1, T-1, PT	5.088 (2,308)	a) 214.49 (5,448) b) 57.28 (1,455)	Il-76. Quoted by Aviadvigatel as a by-pass turbojet.

Designation (type of engine)	Power output (normally take-off rating for piston, turboprop and turboshaft, unless stated)	Specific Fuel Consumption (S F C)	a) Max RPM b) Pressure or Compression ratio	a) EGT (unless stated to be MGT, TET, TGT or TIT) b) Primary fuel type or Octane rating	Dry weight lb (kg)	a) Length ins (mm) b) Width ins (mm) c) Height ins (mm)	Current aircraft users, and comments
Russia							
Joint Stock Company "Aviadvigatel", JSC Rybinskie Motors (continued)							
D-30KP II (twin-shaft turbofan)	26,455 lbf (117.68 kN) take-off, to ISA+ 23° C, 6,062 lbf (26.97 kN) cruise, at 11,000 m altitude and Mach 0.8	0.7 lb/lbf/hr (19.83 g/kNs) cruise	a) 10,710 b) 19.2:1	a) 1,123° C cruise b) TC-1, T-1, PT	5,110 (2,318)	a) 214.49 (5,448) b) 57.28 (1,455)	Quoted by Aviadvigatel as a by-pass turbojet.
D-30KPV (twin-shaft turbofan)	26,455 lbf (117.68 kN) take-off, to ISA+ 23° C, 6,062 lbf (26.97 kN) cruise, at 11,000 m and Mach 0.8	0.7 lb/lbf/hr (19.83 g/kNs) cruise	a) 10,710 b) 20.1:1	a) 1,123° C cruise b) TC-1, T-1, PT	5,090 (2,309)	a) 214.49 (5,448) b) 57.28 (1,455)	Beriev A-40/Be-40. Quoted by Aviadvigatel as a by-pass turbojet.
D-30KU (twin-shaft turbofan)	24,250 lbf (107.88 kN) take-off, to ISA + 21° C, 6,062 lbf (26.97 kN) cruise, at 11,000 m altitude and Mach 0.8	0.7 lb/lbf/hr (19.83 g/kNs) cruise	a) 10,470 b) 17.2:1	a) 1,113° C at take-off b) TC-1, T-1, PT	5,088 (2,308)	a) 224.33 (5,698) b) 57.28 (1,455)	Long-range Il-62M. Quoted by Aviadvigatel as a by-pass turbojet.
D-30KU II (twin-shaft turbofan)	24,250 lbf (107.88 kN) take-off, to ISA + 30° C, 6,062 lbf (26.97 kN) cruise, at 11,000 m altitude and Mach 0.8	0.7 lb/lbf/hr (19.83 g/kNs) cruise	a) 10,550 b) 17.82:1	a) 1,084° C b) TC-1, T-1, PT	5,110 (2,318)	a) 224.33 (5,698) b) 57.28 (1,455)	Long-range Il-62M. Quoted by Aviadvigatel as a by-pass turbojet.
D-30KU-154 II (twin-shaft turbofan)	23,149 lbf (103 kN) take-off, 6,062 lbf (26.97 kN) cruise, to ISA + 30° C	0.7 lb/lbf/hr (19.83 g/kNs) cruise	a) 10,420 b) 17.22:1	a) 1,065° C b) TC-1, T-1, PT	5,082 (2,305)	a) 224.33 (5,698) b) 57.28 (1,455)	Tu-154M. Quoted by Aviadvigatel as a by-pass turbojet.
D-100 (twin-shaft turbofan)	41,888 lbf (186.33 kN) take-off	0.544 lb/lbf/hr (15.41 g/kNs) cruise at 11,000 m altitude and Mach 0.8	b) 36.7:1 climb	a) 547° C b) Kerosene	7,385-7,716 (3,350-3,500)	a) 163.78 (4,160) b) 92.52 (2,350) fan	Advanced aircraft, including Il-106.
D-110B (twin-shaft propfan with a contra-rotating fan gearbox drive)	44,092 lbf (196.14 kN) take-off	0.52 lb/lbf/hr (14.73 g/kNs) cruise at 11,000 m altitude and Mach 0.8	b) 31.4:1 climb	a) 548° C b) Kerosene	7,760 (3,520)	a) 161.42 (4,100) b) 105.12 (2,670) fan	Advanced aircraft.
D-112 (reverse-flow propfan with contra-rotating fan direct drive)	46,297 lbf (205.95 kN) take-off	0.51 lb/lbf/hr (14.45 g/kNs) cruise at 11,000 m altitude and Mach 0.8)	b) 36.1:1 climb	a) 548° C b) Kerosene	7,937 (3,600)	b) 113 (2,870) fan	Advanced aircraft.
D-200 (twin-rotor piston with liquid cooling)	220 hp (164 kW) at 2,700 rpm	0.507 lb/hp/hr (308 g/kW/hr)	a) 2,835 b) 9.4:1	b) 91 Octane minimum	352.7 (160)	a) 39 (990) b) 24.53 (623) c) 27.17 (690)	Yak-112 I.
Joint Stock Company "Aviadvigatel", JSC Perm							
PS-90A or D-90A (twin-shaft turbofan with fan reverser)	35,274-35,583 lbf (156.9-158.3 kN) take-off, to 30° C, 7,716 lbf (34.32 kN) cruise, at 11,000 m altitude and Mach 0.8	0.595 lb/lbf/hr (16.85 g/kNs) cruise	a) 12,400 b) 35.5:1	a) 1,367° C b) TS-1, RT	6,504 (2,950)	a) 195.43 (4,964) b) 74.8 (1,900)	Il-86 re-engined, Il-96-300, Tu-154M2, and Tu-204. PS-90AT for Tu-330 and PS-90A76 for Il-76MF.
Joint Stock Company "Aviadvigatel", JSC Rybinskie Motors							
PS-90A12 (twin-shaft turbofan with fan reverser)	26,455 lbf (117.68 kN) take-off, to +30° C, 5,070 lbf (22.56 kN) cruise, at 11,000 m and Mach 0.8	0.582 lb/lbf/hr (16.485 g/kNs) cruise	a) 11,800 b) 25:1	a) 1,285° C b) TS-1, RT	5,070 (2,300)	a) 187.24 (4,756) b) 65.75 (1,670)	Yak-242.

Designation (type of engine)	Power output (normally take-off rating for piston, turboprop and turboshaft, unless stated)	Specific Fuel Consumption (S F C)	a) Max RPM b) Pressure or Compression ratio	a) EGT (unless stated to be MGT, TET, TGT or TIT) b) Primary fuel type or Octane rating	Dry weight lb (kg)	a) Length ins (mm) b) Width ins (mm) c) Height ins (mm)	Current aircraft users, and comments
Russia							
Joint Stock Company "Aviadvigatel", Pratt & Whitney and MTU							
PS-90P (See Multi-national)							
Enterprise named after "V. Chernyshov". 7 Vishnevaya Str., 123362 Moscow.							
See Comments							One of the leading aircraft engine manufacturing plants in Russia, producing the Klimov RD-33 and TV7
Klimov Corporation. 13 Kantemirovskaya Street, 184100 St Petersburg							
TV2-117A/AG (free-turbine turboshaft) (See Comments)	1,500-1,700 shp (1,120 – 1,270 kW), 1,000 shp (746 kW) cruise for A	0.683 lb/shp/hr (415 g/kW/hr) cruise	a) 12,000 shaft b) 6.6:1		745.2 (338)	a) 111.6 (2,835) b) 21.54 (547) c) 29.33 (745)	Mi-8. TV2-117TG of similar output used by Mi-8TG and Mi-38, able to use liquefied petroleum gas or kerosene. TG can also use diesel, butane/propane gas or other fuels. Mi-8FT has TV2-117Fs.
TV3-117 (free-turbine turboshaft)	1,900 shp (1,417 kW) for TV3-117MT	0.57 lb/shp/hr (347 g/kW/hr) for TV3-117V/VK/VMA			628.3 (285) TV3-117MT	a) 82.09 (2,085) TV3-117MT b) 25.2 (640) TV3-117MT c) 28.54 (725) TV3-117MT	Ka-27 and Ka-28 (TV3-117BK of 2,170 shp, 1,618 kW). Mi-8, Mi-14, Mi-17 and Mi-24 (TV3-117MT). Ka-32 (TV3-117V of 2,190 shp, 1,633 kW). Ka-27, Ka-29, Ka-31 and Ka-50 (TV3-117VK of 2,225 shp, 1,659 kW). Mi-17M, Mi-17V, Mi-24, Mi-25, Mi-28, Mi-35, Mi-40, Mi-171 and Mi-172 (TV3-117VM of 2,225 shp, 1,659 kW). Ka-32A, Mi 58 and late Mi-24s (TV3-117VMA of 2,190 shp, 1,633 kW).
TV7-117 (free-turbine turboprop)	2,500 shp (1,864 kW) take-off to 35° C, 1,799.6 shp (1,342 kW) cruise for TV7-117-3 version	0.397 lb/shp/hr (241.5 g/kW/hr) for TV7-117-3 version	b) 16:1	a) 1,242° C TET for TV7-117-3 version	1,146.4 (520) for TV7-117-3 version	a) 84.37 (2,143) for TV7-117-3 version b) 34.8 (886) for TV7-117-3 version c) 37 (940) for TV7-117-3 version	An-140, Myasishchev M-150 and Il-114 for TV7-117-3 version (formerly TV7-117S). Engine features low fuel consumption and electronic automatic control system. A version said to be intended to replace Chinese WJ5s is the L-3000. TV7-117M2 version is rated at 2,800 shp (2,088 kW).
TVA-3000 (turboshaft)	2,500 shp (1,864 kW), 3,750 shp (2,796 kW) OEI						Mi-38. Formerly known as the TV7-117V.
RD-33 (twin-shaft turbojet)	11,100 lbf (49.42 kN) dry, 18,300 lbf (81.4 kN) with afterburning	0.77 lb/lbf/hr (21.81 g/kNs) dry, 2.1 lb/lbf/hr (59.48 g/kNs) with afterburning	b) 20:1	a) 1,397° C TET	2,326 (1,055)	a) 166.54 (4,230) b) 39.37 (1,000)	MiG-29, Chengdu Super 7, and South African Mirage F1-Cs as SMR95s. Possibly for MiG-21 upgrade.
RD-33K (twin-shaft turbojet)	19,400 lbf (86.3 kN) with afterburning						MiG-29K, MiG-29M and MiG-33. 22,050 lbf (98.07 kN) with afterburning version under test in 1994-5.
RD-33 "Third Generation" (see Comments). Engine is believed to be known as the RD-33-191.							Modernized, with several design features introduced to allow 1,200 hours (instead of 800 hours) between overhauls, improved reliability and lower maintenance costs. The fan rotor, centre HP compressor drum and three-stage labyrinth seals of the combustion camber have been strengthened, and some bearings have also been strengthened.
RD-35M (turbofan)	4,945 lbf (22 kN)						Yak-130. Developed from DV-2S.
OMSK Aircraft Engine Design Bureau "Mars". 644021 Omsk 21							
Glushenkov GTD-3F and 3M (free-turbine turboshaft)	900 shp (671 kW) for 3F and 1,000 shp (746 kW) for 3M		b) 7.3:1 estimated		311 (141) approx	a) 73.82 (1,857) b) 21.13 (740) c) 23.43 (545)	Ka-25 (early models 3F, later 3M). See also PZL-Rzeszów PZL-10W.
Glushenkov TVD-10B/BA (free-turbine turboprop)	1,011 shp (754 kW) as TVD-10B, 1,059 shp (790 kW) as TVD-10BA		b) 7.4:1 estimated		507 (230) approx for TVD-10B	a) 81.1 (2,060) b) 21.85 (555) c) 35.34 (900)	T-101 Gratch, T-501 and possibly T-106. See also PZL-Rzeszów TWD-10B.
Glushenkov TVD-20 (turboprop)	1,380 shp (1,029 kW) take-off	0.506 lb/shp/hr (308 g/kW/hr)			628.3 (285)	a) 69.68 (1,770) b) 33.46 (850) c) 33.27 (845)	T-101V and T-201 Aist, and T-203 Pchel and T-282.
Kobchyenko TV-O-100 (free-turbine turboshaft) (See Comments for TVD-100 turboprop)	700 shp (522 kW)	0.646 lb/shp/hr (393 g/kW/hr)	a) 6,000 shaft b) 9.2:1	a) 1,027° C TET	352.7 (160)	a) 50.2 (1,275) b) 30.71 (780) c) 28.94 (735)	Ka-126 and T-282. One of three choices for production T-610 Voyage and possibly S-86, both in TVD-100 turboprop form.

Designation (type of engine)	Power output (normally take-off rating for piston, turboprop and turboshaft, unless stated)	Specific Fuel Consumption (S F C)	a) Max RPM b) Pressure or Compression ratio	a) EGT (unless stated to be MGT, TET, TGT or TIT) b) Primary fuel type or Octane rating	Dry weight lb (kg)	a) Length ins (mm) b) Width ins (mm) c) Height ins (mm)	Current aircraft users, and comments
Russia							
RKBM - Rybinsk Engine Building Design Office.152903 Rybinsk, Jaroslavskaya oblast							
DN-200 (3-cyl, 2-stroke diesel)	200 hp (149 kW) take-off at 4,700 rpm, 100 hp (74.6 kW) cruise at 3,700 rpm	0.375 lb/hp/hr (228 g/kW/hr)	a) 2,700	b) Kerosene, TS-1, diesel, DL, DZ	291 (132)	a) 31.5 (800) b) 26.38 (670) c) 16.34 (415)	Yak-112.
Kolesov RD-36-51V (high-altitude turbojet)	15,432 lbf (68.65 kN)	0.88 lb/lbf/hr (24.93 g/kNs)	b) 15.4:1	a) 1,167° C b) T-1, TS-1 and T-8		a) 194.88 (4,950) b) 58.5 (1,486)	M-17.
Novikov RD-38K (turbojet)	6,581 lbf (29.27 kN)	1.5 lb/lbf/hr (42.5 g/kNs)	a) 12,200 b) 5:1	a) 997° C b) T-1 and TS-1	491.6 (223)	a) 63.11 (1,603) b) 23.23 (590) diam of inlet	An-71, and A-40 booster.
Novikov RD-41 (single-shaft turbojet)	9,039 lbf (40.21 kN)	1.4 lb/lbf/hr (39.66 g/kNs)	a) 17,500 b) 6.28:1	a) 1,197° C b) Kerosene, T-1 and TS-1	617.3 (280)	a) 62.76 (1,594) b) 25 (635) diam of inlet	Yak-141.
RD-600 (free-turbine turboshaft)	1,300 shp (969.4 kW) take-off at 6,000 rpm, 1,000 shp (745.7 kW) cruise	0.461 lb/shp/hr (280 g/kW/hr)	a) 41,500 b) 14.4:1	a) 1,257° C b) Kerosene, T-1 and TS-1	529 (240)	a) 49.21 (1,250) b) 24.41 (620) c) 29.92 (760)	Ka-62 and Yamal. RKBM Model number TVD RD-600V.
TVD-1500B (free-turbine turboprop)	1,300 shp (969.4 kW) take-off at 1,700 rpm, 1,000 shp (745.7 kW) cruise at 1,500 rpm	0.454 lb/shp/hr (276 g/kW/hr)	a) 41,500 b) 14.4:1	a) 1,257° C b) Kerosene, T-1 and TS-1	529 (240)	a) 77.36 (1,965) b) 24.41 (620) c) 29.92 (760)	An-38, possibly Khrunichev T-205, and Sukhoi S-80.
Dobrynin VD-19 (single-shaft turbojet)	24,250 lbf (107.88 kN) dry, 28,660 lbf (127.49 kN) with afterburning	0.82 lb/lbf/hr (23.23 g/kNs) dry, 2.05 lb/lbf/hr (58.07 g/kNs) with afterburning	a) 6,850 b) 11:1	a) 897° C b) Kerosene, T-1 and TS-1	6,063 (2,750)	a) 310.75 (7,893) b) 55.12 (1,400)	Tu-I28.
Joint-Stock Company Samara Scientific-Technical Complex "NK Engines". 443026 Samara							
NK-8 (twin-shaft turbofan)	20,945 lbf (93.17 kN)	0.62 lb/lbf/hr (17.56 g/kNs)	a) 7,050 HP spool and 5,170 LP spool b) 10.25:1	a) 927° C TIT b) Kerosene (Hu, 10250 kcal/kg)	5,115 (2,320)	a) 222.78 (5,658) b) 53.35 (1,355) fan, 56.77 (1,442) engine	Il-62.
NK-8-2 (twin-shaft turbofan)	20,945 lbf (93.17 kN)	0.59 lb/lbf/hr (16.71 g/kNs)	a) 6,820 HP spool and 5,165 LP spool b) 9.6:1	a) 927° C TIT b) Kerosene (Hu, 10250 kcal/kg)	4,740 (2,150)	a) 222.78 (5,658.5) b) 53.35 (1,355) fan, 56.77 (1,442) engine	Tu-154.
NK-8-2U (twin-shaft turbofan)	23,145 lbf (102.97 kN)	0.58 lb/lbf/hr (16.43 g/kNs)	a) 7,060 HP spool and 5,390 LP spool b) 10.7:1	a) 982° C TIT, 308° C EGT b) Kerosene (Hu, 10250 kcal/kg)	4,784 (2,170)	a) 208.19 (5,288) incl thrust reverser b) 53.35 (1,355) fan, 56.77 (1,442) engine	Tu-154.
NK-8-4 (twin-shaft turbofan)	23,145 lbf (102.97 kN)	0.59 lb/lbf/hr (16.71 g/kNs)	a) 6,940 HP spool and 5,380 LP spool b) 10.3:1	a) 982° C TIT, 335.5° C EGT b) Kerosene (Hu, 10250 kcal/kg)	4,938 (2,240)	a) 200.83 (5,101) b) 53.35 (1,355) fan, 56.77 (1,442) engine	Il-62 and Tu-154.
NK-8-4K (twin-shaft turbofan)	23,145 lbf (102.97 kN)	0.61 lb/lbf/hr (17.28 g/kNs)	b) 10.3:1	a) 971° C TIT b) Kerosene (Hu, 10250 kcal/kg)	4,850 (2,200)	b) 53.35 (1,355) fan, 56.77 (1,442) engine	Orlyonok (Eaglet) ground effect Ekranoplan.
NK-22 (twin-shaft turbofan)	28,660 lbf (127.49 kN) dry, 44,090 lbf (196.14 kN) with afterburning	0.69-1.8 lb/lbf/hr (19.54-50.99 g/kNs)	a) 7,670 HP spool and 5,400 LP spool b) 14.75:1	a) 1,117° C TIT b) Kerosene	7,804 (3,540)	a) 293.54 (7,456) b) 53.35 (1,355) fan, 65.75 (1,670) engine	Tu-22M.
NK-25 (turbofan)	31,526 lbf (140.2 kN) dry, 55,155 lbf (245.18 kN) with afterburning						Tu-22M3.
NK-32 (triple-shaft turbofan)	30,865 lbf (137.3 kN) dry, 55,115 lbf (245.18 kN) with afterburning		b) 28.4:1	a) 1,357° C TET	7,495 (3,400) approx	a) 236.22 (6,000) approx	Tu-160 and Yak-43. Quoted as a bypass turbojet.

Designation (type of engine)	Power output (normally take-off rating for piston, turboprop and turboshaft, unless stated)	Specific Fuel Consumption (S F C)	a) Max RPM b) Pressure or Compression ratio	a) EGT (unless stated to be MGT, TET, TGT or TIT) b) Primary fuel type or Octane rating	Dry weight lb (kg)	a) Length ins (mm) b) Width ins (mm) c) Height ins (mm)	Current aircraft users, and comments
Russia							
Joint-Stock Company Samara Scientific-Technical Complex "NK Engines" (continued)							
NK-44 (triple-shaft turbofan)	97,000 lbf (431.51 kN)	0.302 lb/lbf/hr (8.554 g/kNs)	a) 9,012 HP spool and 6,323 LP spool b) 36.5:1	a) 1,340° C TIT and 449° C EGT b) Kerosene (Hu, 10250 kcal/kg)	18,519 (8,400)	a) 153.54 (3,900) b) 129.92 (3,300)	
NK-62M (unducted propfan)	55,100 lbf (245.2 kN)						Myasishchev MGS-6 and MGS-8
NK-63 (ducted propfan)	66,140 lbf (294.2 kN)						Myasishchev MGS-6 and MGS-8
NK-86 (twin-shaft turbofan)	29,320 lbf (130.43 kN)	0.53 lb/lbf/hr (15.01 g/kNs)	a) 7,270 HP spool and 5,510 LP spool b) 13.4:1	a) 987° C TIT b) Kerosene (Hu, 10250 kcal/kg)	4,828 (2,190)	a) 250.28 (6,357) b) 57.28 (1,455) fan, 62.99 (1,600) engine	Il-86.
NK-89 (turbofan)	23,150 lbf (102.97 kN) at take-off						Tu-156, to use LNG fuel.
NK-92 (triple-shaft turbofan)	39,685 lbf (176.53 kN)						Il-106.
NK-93 (triple-shaft geared propfan)	39,678 lbf (176.5 kN) take-off	0.49 lb/lbf/hr (13.89 g/kNs) at 11,000 m and Mach 0.75	b) 37:1		8,046 (3,650)	a) 216.54 (5,500) approx b) 124.02 (3,150) c) 124.02 (3,150)	Certification expected in 1997. Another version of the same engine is designated NK-92 as a turbofan.
Samara Machine-Building Design Bureau							
NK-12 (single-shaft turboprop)	11,844 ehp (8,832 ekW) take-off at 8,200 rpm 10,728 ehp (8,000 ekW) cruise	0.496 lb/ehp/hr (302 g/ekW/hr) take-off, 0.397 lb/ehp/hr (241.5 g/ekW/hr) cruise	a) 8,200 b) 9.2-12.5:1	a) 852° C MGT, 462° C EGT b) T-1, TS-1, T-2, RT	6,614 (3,000)	a) 308.35 (7,832) b) 54.13 (1,375) c) 59.06 (1,500)	Tu-95.
NK-12M (single-shaft turboprop)	14,805 ehp (11,040 ekW) take-off at 8,300 rpm, 9,870 ehp (7,360 ekW) cruise	0.448 lb/ehp/hr (272.5 g/ekW/hr) take-off, 0.355 lb/ehp/hr (216 g/ekW/hr) cruise	a) 8,300 b) 9.5-13:1	a) 927° C MGT, 515° C EGT b) T-1, TS-1, T-2, RT	6,680 (3,030)	a) 308.35 (7,832) b) 54.13 (1,375) c) 59.06 (1,500)	Tu-95.
NK-12MA (single-shaft turboprop)	14,805 ehp (11,040 ekW) take-off at 8,300 rpm, 12,337 ehp (9,200 ekW) cruise	0.448 lb/ehp/hr (272.5 g/ekW/hr) take-off, 0.355 lb/ehp/hr (216 g/ekW/hr) cruise	a) 8,300 b) 9.5-12.5:1	a) 927° C MGT, 515° C EGT b) T-1, TS-1, T-2, RT	6,757 (3,065)	a) 303.82 (7,717) b) 54.13 (1,375) c) 59.06 (1,500)	An-22.
NK-12MK (single-shaft turboprop)	13,818 ehp (10,304 ekW) take-off at 8,400 rpm, 12,337 ehp (9,200 ekW) cruise	0.456 lb/ehp/hr (277 g/ekW/hr) take-off, 0.485 lb/ehp/hr (295 g/ekW/hr) cruise	a) 8,400 b) 9.7-11:1	a) 905° C MGT, 552° C EGT b) T-1, TS-1, T-2, RT	6,757 (3,065)	a) 303.82 (7,717) b) 54.13 (1,375) c) 59.06 (1,500)	Orlyonok (Eaglet) ground effect Ekranoplan.
NK-12MV (single-shaft turboprop)	14,805 ehp (11,040 ekW) take-off at 8,300 rpm, 9,870 ehp (7,360 ekW) cruise	0.448 lb/ehp/hr (272.5 g/ekW/hr) take-off, 0.355 lb/ehp/hr (216 g/ekW/hr) cruise	a) 8,300 b) 9.5-13:1	a) 927° C MGT, 515° C EGT b) T-1, TS-1, T-2, RT	6,680 (3,030)	a) 308.35 (7,832) b) 54.13 (1,375) c) 59.06 (1,500)	Tu-95/Tu-142, Tu-114 and Tu-126.
P-032MR (2-cyl, 2-stroke, air-cooled piston with reduction gearbox and silencer)	31.5 hp (23.5 kW) take-off at 7,000 crankshaft rpm, 22.93 hp (17.1 kW) cruise at 6,300 crankshaft rpm	0.806 lb/hp/hr (490 g/kW/hr)	a) 7,300 crankshaft b) 7.24:1	b) 82 Octane	57.3 (26)	a) 19.88 (505) without silencer b) 17.99 (457) without silencer c) 14.69 (373) without silencer	Lightplanes and microlights.
P-065 (2-cyl, 2-stroke, air-cooled piston with reduction gearbox and silencer)	63hp (47 kW) take-off at 7,000 crankshaft rpm, 45.9 hp (34.2 kW) cruise at 6,300 crankshaft rpm	0.806 lb/hp/hr (490 g/kW/hr)	a) 7,300 crankshaft b) 7.24:1	b) 82 Octane	125.7 (57)	a) 27.17 (690) without silencer b) 27.36 (695) without silencer c) 19.09 (485) without silencer	Light aircraft.

Designation (type of engine)	Power output (normally take-off rating for piston, turboprop and turboshaft, unless stated)	Specific Fuel Consumption (S F C)	a) Max RPM b) Pressure or Compression ratio	a) EGT (unless stated to be MGT, TET, TGT or TIT) b) Primary fuel type or Octane rating	Dry weight lb (kg)	a) Length ins (mm) b) Width ins (mm) c) Height ins (mm)	Current aircraft users, and comments
Russia							
NPO Saturn. 13 Kasatkin Street, 129301 Moscow							
Lyulka AL-21F-3/3A (izdelye 89) (single-shaft turbojet)	17,196 lbf (76.49 kN) dry, 24,692 lbf (109.84 kN) with afterburning	0.76 lb/lbf/hr (21.53 g/kNs) dry, 1.86 lb/lbf/hr (52.68 g/kNs)	b) 14.8:1	a) 1,112° C TET	4,420 (2,005)	a) 203.15 (5,160) b) 34.84 (885)	MiG-23B, Su-17, Su-20, Su-22UM3K and Su-24.
Lyulka AL-31F (izdelye 99V) (twin-shaft turbofan)	16,755 lbf (74.53 kN) dry, 27,558 lbf (122.59 kN) with afterburning	0.67 lb/lbf/hr (18.98 g/kNs) dry	b) 23:1	a) 1,427° C TET	3,373 (1,530)	a) 194.88 (4,950) b) 48.03 (1,220)	Su-27, Su-30, Su-33, Su-34 (initially) and Su-35 (initially).
Lyulka AL-32 (turboshaft)	770 shp (574 kW)						
AL-34 (pusher turboprop)	variously rated at 542-700 shp (404-522 kW)						Possibly for the Sukhoi S-86, Aeroprogress T-205 and T-610 Voyage, and other Russian light transports.
AL-35F (twin-shaft turbofan)	30,865 lbf (137.3 kN)						Su-33 expected, Su-34 and Su-35. Also known as AL-31FM.
AL-41F (advanced turbofan)	40,785 lbf (181.4 kN) approx	low consumption			low weight		Mikoyan I-42. To have vectoring nozzles.
Soyuz. Luzhnetskaya nab 2/4, 119048 Moscow							
GTE-400 (turboshaft)	400 shp (298 kW)						May be fitted to a new Kamov helicopter.
Tumansky R-11F-300, R-11F2-300 and R-11F2S-300/F2SK-300 (twin-shaft turbojet)	12,676 lbf (56.39 kN), 13,614 lbf (60.56 kN) and 13,669 lbf (60.8 kN) with afterburning respectively					a) 181.1 (4,600) c) 42.72 (1,085)	MiG-21.
Gavrilov R-13-300 (twin-spool turbojet)	9,370 lbf (41.68 kN) dry, 14,308 lbf (63.65 kN) with afterburning						MiG-21MF and SM.
Tumansky R-15BD-300	24,692 lbf (109.84 kN) with afterburning						MiG-25.
Gavrilov R-25-300 (twin-spool turbojet)	9,039 lbf (40.21 kN) dry, 15,100 lbf (67.18 kN) with afterburning						MiG-21bis (izdelye 75 and 75P versions).
Khachaturov R-27F2M-300 (twin-shaft turbojet) See Comments	14,330 lbf (63.75 kN) dry, 22,046 lbf (98.07 kN) with afterburning				3,307 (1,500)	a) 190.94 (4,850) b) 41.73 (1,060)	MiG-23MS, S and UB. R-27V-300 was the non-afterburning and vectoring-thrust derivative produced for the Yak-36M/38, of smaller dimensions but increased unaugmented thrust.
Khachaturov R-29-300 (turbojet)	18,298 lbf (81.4 kN) dry, 28,660 lbf (127.5 kN) with afterburning		a) 8,800 HP turbine b) 13.1:1		4,145 (1,880)	a) 195.3 (4,960) b) 35.91 (912)	MiG-23M, MF and BN.
Khachaturov R-29B-300 and BS-300 (turbojet)	17,637 lbf (78.46 kN) dry, 25,353 lbf (112.78 kN) with afterburning		a) 8,800 HP turbine b) 12.4:1		3,880 (1,760)		MiG-27, export MiG-23BN and Su-22 (see below). Developed for optimum low-altitude performance, with two nozzle settings only. R-29BS-300 powers the Su-22UM3.
Khachaturov R-35-300 (turbojet)	18,850 lbf (83.85 kN) dry, 28,660 lbf (127.49 kN) with afterburning		b) 13.1:1				MiG-23ML, MLA, MLD, P and PD. Derived from the R-29-300.
Kobchyenko R-79V-300 (twin-shaft turbofan with thrust vectoring)	24,250 lbf (107.88 kN) dry, 34,172 lbf (152.01 kN) with afterburning	0.66 lb/lbf/hr (18.69 g/kNs) without afterburning		a) 1,600+° C TET	6,060 (2,750) approx	a) 205.865 (5,229) b) 67.559 (1,716)	Yak-141. Uprated version being developed with FADEC despite uncertainty of Yak-141, designated R-79M and rated at approximately 39,680 lbf (176.5 kN).

Designation (type of engine)	Power output (normally take-off rating for piston, turboprop and turboshaft, unless stated)	Specific Fuel Consumption (S F C)	a) Max RPM b) Pressure or Compression ratio	a) EGT (unless stated to be MGT, TET, TGT or TIT) b) Primary fuel type or Octane rating	Dry weight lb (kg)	a) Length ins (mm) b) Width ins (mm) c) Height ins (mm)	Current aircraft users, and comments
Russia							
Soyuz (continued)							
Gavrilov R-95Sh (non-afterburning variant of R-13-300)	9,039 lbf (40.21 kN)						Su-25. Replaced on Su-25BM by R-195s offering lower IR signature and increased thrust.
R-123-300 (twin-shaft turbofan)	3,152 lbf (14.02 kN) class						No known applications by early 1995.
R-126-300 (turbofan)							Tu-324.
Gavrilov R-195 (twin-shaft turbojet)	9,921 lbf (44.13 kN)				2,182.5 (990)	a) 129.92 (3,300) b) 35.98 (914)	Su-25BM (upgraded) and last series Su-25UB, and Su-39.
Gavrilov R-195FS (twin-shaft turbojet with afterburning)	9,259 lbf (41.19 kN) dry, 13,669 lbf (60.8 kN) with afterburning					a) 129.92 (3,300) b) 35.98 (914)	Sukhoi S-54. Afterburning variant of the R-195.
TV116-300 (single-shaft turboprop or turboshaft)	1,080 shp (805 kW)				330.7 (150)	a) 31.5 (800) b) 16.5 (420)	No known applications in early 1995.
TVD-450 (turboprop)	450 shp (335.6 kW)						One candidate for the Sukhoi S-86. Could be built by Mars?
Slovakia							
Povazské Strojárne a.s. 017 34 Povazská Bystrica							
DV-2 (twin-shaft mixed flow turbofan)	4,851 lbf (21.58 kN)	0.61 lb/lbf/hr (17.28 g/kNs)	b) 13.3:1	a) 1,110° C MGT b) Jet A-1	1,045 (474)	a) 67.76 (1,721) without jetpipe b) 39.13 (994) c) 40.83 (1,037)	L-39 MS, L-59 E and M-99 Orkan. Company co-operated with Ukrainian Ivchenko PROGRESS ZMKB in DV-2 development from 1980-89. Since then, has been producing and developing engines fully independently.
DV-2A (twin-shaft mixed flow turbofan)	5,510 lbf (24.51 kN)	0.593 lb/lbf/hr (16.81 g/kNs)	b) 15.49:1	a) 1,115° C MGT b) Jet A-1	992 (450)	a) 67.76 (1,721) without jetpipe b) 39.13 (994) c) 40.83 (1,037)	New project. L-159 and PZL-Mielec M-99 Orkan.
DV-2S (military RD-35) (twin-shaft mixed flow turbofan)	4,851 lbf (21.58 kN)	0.586 lb/lbf/hr (16.61 g/kNs)	b) 14.28:1	a) 1,064° C MGT	992 (450)	a) 88.11 (2,238) b) 32.28 (820) c) 41.34 (1,050)	New project. Yak-130 UTS.
Sweden							
Turbomin AB. Författarvägen 19, S-161 40 Bromma							
TN 300 (single-shaft turbojet)	65 lbf (0.29 kN) dry, 78 lbf (0.347 kN) with afterburning	1.4 lb/lbf/hr (39.7 g/kNs) dry, 2.8 lb/lbf/hr (79.3 g/kNs) with afterburning	b) 3.5:1	a) 800° C b) Jet A/A-1, JP-5, JP-8, diesel Class 1	13.2 (6)	a) 19.7 (500), 27.6 (700) with afterburner b) 6.5 (165) c) 6.5 (165)	Gliders, UAVs and target drones. Other Turbomin engines include the 17 lbf (0.075kN) TN 75 turbojet for ultra small UAVs and target drones.
Volvo Aero Corporation. Trollhättan							
RM6C (Avon Mk 60) (Single spool turbojet)	12,450 lbf (55.4 kN) dry, 17,085 lbf (76 kN) with afterburning	0.93 lb/lbf/hr (26.3 g/kNs) dry, 1.85 lb/lbf/hr (52.4 g/kNs) with afterburning	b) 8.25:1	a) 770° C b) JP-8	3,946 (1,790)	a) 320.5 (8,140)	J35J Draken.
RM8A (twin-shaft turbofan)	14,750 lbf (65.61 kN) dry, 26,000 lbf (115.7 kN) with afterburning	0.62 lb/lbf/hr (17.7 g/kNs) dry, 2.47 lb/lbf/hr (70 g/kNs) with afterburning	b) 16.5:1	b) JP-4, JP-5	4,630 (2,100)	a) 242.2 (6,153) b) 40.6 (1,030) inlet c) 49.61 (1,260)	AJS37 Viggen.
RM8B (twin-shaft turbofan)	16,200 lbf (72.06 kN) dry, 28,110 lbf (125.04 kN) with afterburning	0.64 lb/lbf/hr (18.13 g/kNs) dry, 2.52 lb/lbf/hr (71.4 g/kNs) with afterburning	b) 16.5:1	b) JP-4, JP-5	4,895 (2,220)	a) 245.0 (6,223) b) 40.6 (1,030) inlet c) 49.61 (1,260)	JA37 Viggen.
RM12 (axial flow turbofan)	12,141 lbf (54 kN) dry, 18,105 lbf (80.54 kN) with afterburning	0.842 lb/lbf/hr (23.85 g/kNs)	b) 27.2:1	a) 867° C b) MIL-T-5624 grade JP-5	2,325 (1,055)	a) 159.1 (4,040) b) 33.46 (850) c) 43.31 (1,100)	JAS39 Gripen.

Designation (type of engine)	Power output (normally take-off rating for piston, turboprop and turboshaft, unless stated)	Specific Fuel Consumption (S F C)	a) Max RPM b) Pressure or Compression ratio	a) EGT (unless stated to be MGT, TET, TGT or TIT) b) Primary fuel type or Octane rating	Dry weight lb (kg)	a) Length ins (mm) b) Width ins (mm) c) Height ins (mm)	Current aircraft users, and comments
Turkey							
Tusas Engine Industries Inc (TEI). P.K. 610 Eskisehir							
F110-GE-100 (twin-shaft turbofan)	16,760 lbf (74.55 kN) dry, 28,000 lbf (124.55 kN) with afterburning		b) 30.4:1	a) 935° C b) MIL-T-5624 grade JP-4, JP-5, JP-8	3,911 (1,774)	a) 182.3 (4,630) max envelope b) 46.5 (1,181) max envelope	F-15, F-16. Joint venture company between GE Aircraft Engines of USA and Turkish shareholders.
F110-GE-129 (twin-shaft turbofan)	17,155 lbf (76.31 kN) dry, 29,000 lbf (129.0 kN) with afterburning		b) 30.7:1	a) 980° C b) As for F110-GE-100	As for F110-GE-100	a) As for F110-GE-100 b) As for F110-GE-100	F-15E, F-16C/D.
Ukraine							
Ivchenko PROGRESS ZMKB. 330068 Zaporozhye							
AI-20D series 4 (single-shaft turboprop)	5,180 ehp (3,863 ekW) take-off at 12,300 rpm, 2,990 ehp (2,230 ekW) cruise at 8,000 m altitude and 630 km/h	0.443 lb/ehp/hr (270 g/ekW/hr)	a) 12,300 b) 7.36:1	a) 952° C MGT b) Kerosene RT, TC-1, T-1	2,381 (1,080)	a) 121.89 (3,096) b) 33.15 (842) c) 46.46 (1,180)	An-8, Be-12.
AI-20D series 5 (single-shaft turboprop)	5,180 ehp (3,863 ekW) take-off at 12,300 rpm, 2,850 ehp (2,125 ekW) cruise at 8,000 m altitude and 540 km/h	0.432 lb/ehp/hr (263 g/ekW/hr)	a) 12,300 b) 7.62:1	a) 937° C MGT b) Kerosene RT, TC-1, T-1	2,293 (1,040)	a) 121.89 (3,096) b) 33.15 (842) c) 46.46 (1,180)	An-32
AI-20M (single-shaft turboprop)	4,250 ehp (3,169 ekW) take-off at 12,300 rpm, 2,700 ehp (2,013 ekW) cruise at 8,400 m altitude and 630 km/h	0.434 lb/ehp/hr (264 g/ekW/hr)	a) 12,300 b) 7.62:1	a) 900° C MGT b) Kerosene RT, TC-1, T-1	2,293 (1,040)	a) 121.89 (3,096) b) 33.15 (842) c) 46.46 (1,180)	An-12 and Il-18D.
AI-24 (single-shaft turboprop)	2,550 ehp (1,902 ekW) take-off at 15,100 rpm, 1,650 ehp (1,230 ekW) cruise at 6,000 m altitude and 504 km/h	0.509 lb/ehp/hr (310 g/ekW/hr)	a) 15,100 b) 6.4:1	a) 877° C MGT b) Kerosene RT, TC-1, T-1	1,323 (600)	a) 92.36 (2,346) b) 26.65 (677) c) 42.32 (1,075)	An-24.
AI-24T (single-shaft turboprop)	2,820 ehp (2,103 ekW) take-off at 15,800 rpm, 1,650 ehp (1,230 ekW) cruise at 6,000 m altitude and 504 km/h	0.518 lb/ehp/hr (315 g/ekW/hr)	a) 15,800 b) 7.05:1	a) 877° C MGT b) Kerosene RT, TC-1, T-1	1,323 (600)	a) 92.36 (2,346) b) 26.65 (677) c) 42.32 (1,075)	An-24, An-26 and An-30.
AI-24VT (single-shaft turboprop)	2,820 ehp (2,103 ekW) take-off at 15,800 rpm, 1,650 ehp (1,230 ekW) cruise at 6,000 m altitude and 360 km/h, ISA + 15° C	0.527 lb/ehp/hr (321 g/ekW/hr)	a) 15,800 b) 7.05:1	a) 877° C MGT b) Kerosene RT, TC-1, T-1	1,323 (600)	a) 92.36 (2,346) b) 26.65 (677) c) 42.32 (1,075)	An-24, An-26 and An-30.
AI-25 series 2E (twin-shaft turbofan)	3,307 lbf (14.71 kN) take-off, 443 lbf (1.97 kN) cruise at 6,000 m and 550 km/h, ISA	0.795 lb/lbf/hr (22.52 g/kNs)	b) 8.1:1	a) 939° C MGT b) Kerosene RT, TC-1, T-1	767 (348)	a) 78.46 (1,993) b) 32.28 (820) c) 35.28 (896)	Yak-40.
AI-25TL (twin-shaft turbofan)	3,792 lbf (16.87 kN) take-off, 1,135 lbf (5.05 kN) cruise at 8,000 m altitude and 550 km/h, ISA	0.815 lb/lbf/hr (23.08 g/kNs)	b) 9.6:1	a) 977° C MGT b) Kerosene RT, TC-1, T-1	882 (400)	a) 132.2 (3,358) b) 38.78 (985) c) 37.72 (958)	L-39.

Designation (type of engine)	**Power output** (normally take-off rating for piston, turboprop and turboshaft, unless stated)	**Specific Fuel Consumption** (S F C)	**a) Max RPM b) Pressure or Compression ratio**	**a) EGT** (unless stated to be MGT, TET, TGT or TIT) **b) Primary fuel type or Octane rating**	**Dry weight** lb (kg)	**a) Length** ins (mm) **b) Width** ins (mm) **c) Height** ins (mm)	**Current aircraft users, and comments**
Ukraine							
Ivchenko PROGRESS ZMKB (continued)							
D-18T series 3 (triple-shaft turbofan)	51,654 lbf (229.78 kN) ideal take-off, to 30° C, 10,714 lbf (47.66 kN) ideal cruise at 11,000 m altitude and Mach 0.8, ISA	0.57 lb/lbf/hr (16.145 g/kNs)	b) 25:1	a) 1,337° C MGT b) Kerosene RT, TC-1, T-1	9,039 (4,100)	a) 212.6 (5,400) b) 109.92 (2,792) c) 115.63 (2,937)	An-124 and An-225. Volga-Dnepr cargo airline funded from 1994 an engine life extension programme, increasing service hours from 1,000 to 4,000.
D-18T1 (triple-shaft turbofan)	57,320 lbf (254.98 kN) max contingency (OEI), 48,149 lbf (214.18 kN) take-off, to 30° C, 11,596 lbf (51.58 kN) cruise at 11,000 m altitude and Mach 0.8, ISA + 10° C	0.615 lb/lbf/hr (17.42 g/kNs)	b) 29.6:1 max contingency, 25:1 normal	a) 1,477° C max contingency, 1,337° C MGT b) Kerosene RT, TC-1, T-1	9,039 (4,100)	a) 212.6 (5,400) b) 109.92 (2,792) c) 116.22 (2,952)	An-218.
D-18TM (triple-shaft turbofan)	55,775 lbf (248 kN) at take-off to 30° C, 11,575 lbf (51.5 kN) cruise at 11,000 m altitude and Mach 0.8, ISA	0.585 lb/lbf/hr (16.57 g/kNs)	b) 28.8:1	a) 1,322° C b) Kerosene RT, TC-1, T-1	10,472 (4,750)	a) 224.41 (5,700) b) 117.4 (2,982) c) 117.56 (2,986)	An-218.
D-18TR (triple-shaft turbofan)	60,627 lbf (269.7 kN) at take-off to 30° C, 12,015 lbf (53.45 kN) cruise at 11,000 m altitude and Mach 0.8, ISA	0.585 lb/lbf/hr (16.57 g/kNs)	b) 30.3:1	a) 1,337° C b) Kerosene RT, TC-1, T-1	10,472 (4,750)	a) 224.41 (5,700) b) 117.4 (2,982) c) 117.56 (2,986)	An-218.
D-27 (propfan)	14,000 ehp (10,440 ekW) take-off at 8,394 rpm, to 30° C, 6,750 ehp (5,033 ekW) cruise at 7,135 rpm at 11,000 m altitude and Mach 0.7, ISA	0.287 lb/ehp/hr (175 g/ekW/hr)	a) 8,394 b) 22.15:1	a) 1,397° C MGT b) Kerosene RT, TC-1, T-1	3,638 (1,650)	a) 165.531 (4,204.5) b) 49.57 (1,259) c) 53.82 (1,367)	An-70T, An-180 and Yak 46 – 20.
D-36 series 1 (triple-shaft turbofan)	14,330 lbf (63.745 kN) ideal take-off, ISA, 3,527 lbf (15.69 kN) ideal cruise at 8,000 m altitude and Mach 0.75, ISA	0.65 lb/lbf/hr (18.41 g/kNs)	b) 20:1	a) 1,237° C MGT b) Kerosene RT, TC-1, T-1	2,438 (1,106)	a) 136.594 (3,470) b) 60.67 (1,541) c) 67.382 (1,711.5)	Yak-42 and An-72.
D-127 (free-turbine turboshaft)	14,500 ehp (10,813 ekW) take-off at 8,314 rpm, 7,250 ehp (5,406 ekW) cruise at 7,135 rpm	0.401 lb/ehp/hr (244 g/ekW/hr)	a) 8,314 b) 24.3:1	a) 1,366° C MGT b) Kerosene RT, TC-1, T-1	2,866 (1,300)	a) 143.94 (3,656) b) 24.65 (626) intake	Project engine in 1995.
D-136 (free-turbine turboshaft)	11,400 ehp (8,500 ekW) take-off at 8,300 rpm, 6,100 ehp (4,549 ekW) cruise	0.531 lb/ehp/hr (323 g/ekW/hr)	a) 8,700 b) 18.4:1	a) 1,229° C MGT b) Kerosene RT, TC-1, T-1	2,315 (1,050)	a) 146.26 (3,715) b) 55.24 (1,403) c) 44.61 (1,133)	Mil Mi-26 and Mi-26T.
D-236 (geared propfan)	10,850 shp (8,090 kW)						Tested on a Yak-42E-LL.
D-436T1 (triple-shaft turbofan)	16,865 lbf (75 kN) ideal take-off, to 30° C, 3,307 lbf (14.71 kN) cruise at 11,000 m altitude and Mach 0.75, ISA	0.608 lb/lbf/hr (17.22 g/kNs)	b) 23.2:1	a) 1,249° C MGT b) Kerosene RT, TC-1, T-1	3,197 (1,450)	a) 164.13 (4,169) b) 71.73 (1,822) c) 77.13 (1,959)	Be-200 and Tu-334-100.

Designation (type of engine)	Power output (normally take-off rating for piston, turboprop and turboshaft, unless stated)	Specific Fuel Consumption (S F C)	a) Max RPM b) Pressure or Compression ratio	a) EGT (unless stated to be MGT, TET, TGT or TIT) b) Primary fuel type or Octane rating	Dry weight lb (kg)	a) Length ins (mm) b) Width ins (mm) c) Height ins (mm)	Current aircraft users, and comments
Ukraine							
Ivchenko PROGRESS ZMKB (continued)							
D-436T2 (triple-shaft turbofan)	18,078 lbf (80.42 kN) ideal take-off, to 30° C, 3,527 lbf (15.69 kN) cruise at 11,000 m and Mach 0.75, ISA	0.61 lb/lbf/hr (17.28 g/kNs)	b) 24.2	a) 1,277° C MGT b) Kerosene RT, TC-1, T-1	3,197 (1,450)	a) 164.13 (4,169) b) 71.73 (1,822) c) 77.13 (1,959)	Tu-334-200
D-727 (triple-shaft turbofan)	24,990 lbf (111.17 kN) max contingency (OEI), to 30° C, 25,353 lbf (112.78 kN) take-off, to 30° C, 5,070 lbf (22.56 kN) cruise at 11,000 m altitude and Mach 0.8, ISA	0.534 lb/lbf/hr (15.13 g/kNs)	b) 34:1 max contingency, 30:1 normal	a) 1,444° C max contingency, 1,372° C MGT b) Kerosene RT, TC-1, T-1	5,732 (2,600)	a) 196.85 (5,000) b) 85.94 (2,183) intake	Project engine.
DV-2 (twin-shaft turbofan)	4,850 lbf (21.58 kN) take-off at 15° C, 1,852 lbf (8.24 kN) cruise at 6,000 m altitude and Mach 0.5, ISA	0.78 lb/lbf/hr (22.1 g/kNs)	b) 13.5:1	a) 1,183° C MGT b) Kerosene RT, TC-1, T-1	992 (450)	a) 141.73 (3,600) b) 39.13 (994) c) 40.83 (1,037)	L-59, K-8 Karakorum for Chinese service, and Yak-130.
DV-2F (twin-shaft turbofan)	4,850 lbf (21.58 kN) dry, at <24° C, 8,113 lbf (36.1 kN) with afterburning at <24° C	0.63 lb/lbf/hr (17.84 g/kNs)	b) 13.5:1	a) 1,147° C MGT b) Kerosene RT, TC-1, T-1	1,389 (630)	a) 123.23 (3,130) b) 39.13 (994) intake c) 40.83 (1,037)	Project engine. Afterburning provides supersonic possibilities.
DV-12 (free-turbine turboshaft)	7,500 ehp (5,592.75 ekW) take-off at 11,440 rpm, to 28° C, 3,750 ehp (2,796 ekW) cruise at ISA	0.498 lb/ehp/hr (303 g/ekW/hr)	a) 11,440 b) 15.3:1	a) 1,147° C MGT b) Kerosene RT, TC-1, T-1	1,488 (675)	a) 98.43 (2,500) b) 18.9 (480) intake	Project engine.
DV-22 (twin-shaft turbofan)	8,532 lbf (37.95 kN) take-off, 1,720 lbf (7.65 kN) cruise at 11,000 m altitude and Mach 0.8	0.66 lb/lbf/hr (18.69 g/kNs)	b) 18:1	a) 1,147° C MGT b) Kerosene RT, TC-1, T-1	1,543 (700)	a) 94.49 (2,400) b) 40.16 (1,020) intake	Project engine, possibly for Il-108.
United Kingdom							
Mid-West Engines. Hangar SE38, Gloucestershire Airport, Staverton, Gloucestershire GL51 6SR							
AE50R (single-rotor rotary)	50 hp (37.3 kW)	9 litres per hour average	a) 7,500	a) 950° C maximum b) 94+ Octane	72.75 (33)	a) 23 (585) b) 10 (254) across mounting plate c) 11.4 (290) including gearbox	Certified JAR-22.
AE50T (2-cyl, 2-stroke piston)	50 hp (37.3 kW)	12 litres per hour average	a) 6,000		84 lb (38)	a) 22 (560) including gearbox b) 9.5 (242) across mounting plate c) 14.8 (377)	Aimed at the German motor-glider market. To be certified JAR-22 in 1995.
AE75T (3-cyl, 2-stroke piston)	75 hp (56 kW)	20 litres per hour average	a) 6,750 b) 10.9:1	b) Premix 100 LL	110 (50)	a) 26.67 (677) b) 10 (254) across mounting plate c) 14.8 (377)	Super2. Certified JAR-E.
AE100R (twin-rotor rotary)	100 hp (74.6 kW)	18 litres per hour average	a) 7,500	a) 950° C b) 94+ Octane	117 (53)	a) 28.74 (730) b) 11.22 (285) across mounting plate c) 13.78 (350)	To be certified under JAR-E in 1995.

Designation (type of engine)	Power output (normally take-off rating for piston, turboprop and turboshaft, unless stated)	Specific Fuel Consumption (S F C)	a) Max RPM b) Pressure or Compression ratio	a) EGT (unless stated to be MGT, TET, TGT or TIT) b) Primary fuel type or Octane rating	Dry weight lb (kg)	a) Length ins (mm) b) Width ins (mm) c) Height ins (mm)	Current aircraft users, and comments
United Kingdom							
Rolls-Royce plc. 65 Buckingham Gate, London SW1E 6AT							
RB211-524G (triple-shaft turbofan)	58,000 lbf (258.0 kN) flat rated at 30° C	0.57 lb/lb/hr (16.145 g/kNs) cruise	b) 33.0:1		9,670 (4,386)	a) 125 (3,175) b) 86.3 (2,192) fan	B747-400.
RB211-524H (triple-shaft turbofan)	60,600 lbf (269.57 kN) flat rated at 30° C	0.57 lb/lbf/hr (16.145 g/kNs)	b) 33.0:1		9,670 (4,386)	a) 125 (3,175) b) 86.3 (2,192) fan	B747-400, B767-300.
RB211-535C (triple-shaft turbofan)	37,400 lbf (166.37 kN) flat rated at 29° C	0.646 lb/lbf/hr (18.3 g/kNs) cruise	b) 21.1:1		7,294 (3,308)	a) 118.5 (3,010) b) 73.2 (1,859) inlet	B757-200.
RB211-535E4/E4-B (triple-shaft turbofan)	40,100-43,100 lbf (178.38-191.72 kN) flat rated at 29° C	0.598 lb/lbf/hr (16.94 g/kNs) cruise	b) 25.8:1		7,264 (3,295)	a) 117.9 (2,994) b) 74.5 (1,892) inlet	B757-200 and Tupolev Tu-224. B757-200 also offered with RB211-535E4-B of 43,100 lbf (191.72 kN).
Gem 2 (free-turbine turboshaft)	900 shp (671.1 kW) max contingency, 750 shp (559.3 kW) max continuous	0.65 lb/shp/hr (396 g/kW/hr)	b) 12.0:1		330 (149.7)	a) 43.2 (1,097) b) 22.6 (574) c) 23.5 (597)	Naval and multi-role Lynx. Out of production. Includes Mk 1001.
RR 1004 (free-turbine turboshaft)	944 shp (704 kW) max contingency, 881 shp (657 kW) take-off, 825 shp (615.2 kW) max continuous	0.525 lb/shp/hr (319 g/kW/hr)	a) 27,000 output speed b) 10.8:1		360 (163.3)	a) 42 (1,067) b) 22.6 (574) c) 23.5 (597)	Agusta A129 Mangusta. Produced under licence by Rinaldo Piaggio in Italy.
Gem 41–2 (free-turbine turboshaft)	1,120 shp (835 kW) max contingency, 1,000 shp (745.7 kW) take-off, 890 shp (663.7 kW) max continuous	0.51 lb/shp/hr (310 g/kW/hr)	b) 12.02:1		404 (183.25)	a) 43.2 (1,097) b) 22.6 (574) c) 23.5 (597)	Naval Lynx. Out of production.
Gem 42 (free-turbine turboshaft)	1,120 shp (835 kW) max contingency, 1,000 shp (745.7 kW) take-off, 890 shp (663.7 kW) max continuous	0.51 lb/shp/hr (310 g/kW/hr)	a) 6,164 output speed b) 12.02:1		404 (183.25)	a) 42 (1,067) b) 22.6 (574) c) 23.5 (597)	Current production standard for all Lynx applications, including Super Lynx and Battlefield Lynx. UK MoD and French programme to update in-service Gem 2s and 41s to this standard.
Gnome H.1400-1T (free-turbine turboshaft)	1,535 shp (1,145 kW) max contingency at ISA + 30° C, 1,050 shp (783 kW) max continuous	0.627 lb/shp/hr (381 g/kW/hr)	a) 19,500 output speed b) 8.6:1		332 (150.6)	a) 54.8 (1,392) b) 22.7 (577) c) 21.6 (549)	Advanced versions of Westland Sea King and Commando. Optimized for hot-weather operations. Current production model. New deliveries to RAF starting 1994 ensure Gnome service until at least 2,020.
Pegasus 11 (twin-shaft, vectored thrust turbofan)	21,500 lbf (95.64 kN) nominal with normal hover bleed	Details not available	b) 14.6:1		3,113 (1,412), 3,179 (1,442) naval versions, minus nozzles	a) 98.83 (2,510) minus nozzles b) 48.05 (1,220) over fan casing	RAF two-seat Harriers and naval Sea Harriers. Weight 3,734 lb (1,694 kg) installed. See Pegasus 11-61 for length with nozzles.
Pegasus 11-21 (twin-shaft, vectored thrust turbofan)	21,450, 21,550 or 21,750 lbf (95.42, 95.86 or 96.75 kN), with a nominal 22,000 lbf (97.86 kN) output	Details not available	b) 15.3:1		3,240 (1,470), minus nozzles, 3,960 lb (1,796 kg) installed	a) 98.83 (2,510) minus nozzles b) 48.05 (1,220) over fan casing	Harrier II/AV-8B. RAF uses Mk 105 of 21,550 lbf. Naval Mk 106 and Spanish Mk 152-42 of similar power. Early USMC AV-8Bs and some Italian aircraft use 21,450 lbf F402-RR-406A version.
Pegasus 11-61 (twin-shaft, vectored thrust turbofan)	23,800 lbf (105.89 kN) at sea level, ISA conditions	Details not available	b) 16.3:1		4,180 (1,896) 4,260 (1,932) installed	a) 137.2 (3,485) with nozzles b) 48.05 (1,220) intake	USMC AV-8Bs delivered from late 1990 and Italian AV-8Bs. Ordered for Spanish aircraft. US military designation F402-RR-408A. For Harrier II Plus.
RB163 Spey Mk 511-8/F113-RR-100 (twin-shaft turbofan)	11,400 lbf (50.71 kN) flat rated at 23.5° C	0.8 lb/lbf/hr (22.66g/kNs)	b) 18.4:1		2,483 (1,126)	a) 109.6 (2,784) b) 32.5 (826) fan	Gulfstream II/III/SMA-3. US military designation F113-RR-100. Civil Spey.

Designation (type of engine)	Power output (normally take-off rating for piston, turboprop and turboshaft, unless stated)	Specific Fuel Consumption (S F C)	a) Max RPM b) Pressure or Compression ratio	a) EGT (unless stated to be MGT, TET, TGT or TIT) b) Primary fuel type or Octane rating	Dry weight lb (kg)	a) Length ins (mm) b) Width ins (mm) c) Height ins (mm)	Current aircraft users, and comments
United Kingdom							
Rolls-Royce plc (continued)							
RB163 Spey Mk 512-14DW (twin-shaft turbofan)	12,550 lbf (55.83 kN) wet, flat-rated at 25° C	0.82 lb/lbf/hr (23.23 g/kNs)	b) 21.2:1		2,609 (1,183)	a) 109.6 (2,784) b) 37.1 (942)	BAC One-Eleven Series 475 and 500, Romaero Rombac 1-11.
RB168 Spey Mk 202 (twin-shaft turbofan)	12,250 lbf (54.49 kN) dry, 20,515 lbf (91.26 kN) with afterburning				4,093 (1,856)	a) 204.9 (5,204) b) 32.5 (826)	Xi'an Jianjiji Hongzhaji JH-7. Military Spey.
RB168 Spey Mk 250/251 (twin-shaft turbofan)	11,995 lbf (53.36 kN)				2,740 (1,243)	a) 117 (2,972) b) 32.5 (826)	Nimrod MR (Mk 250) for maritime operations, Nimrod R (Mk 251) for high altitude operations.
RB168 Spey Mk 807 (twin-shaft turbofan)	11,030 lbf (49.06 kN)	0.659 lb/lbf/hr (18.67 g/kNs) take-off maximum	b) 16.8:1	a) 585° C maximum EGT, 1,107° C maximum MGT b) JP-1, JP-4 and JP-5	2,417 (1,096)	a) 96.7 (2,456) b) 32.5 (826)	AMX, built under licence by FiatAvio in Italy and Celma-Cia in Brazil.
Tay 611 (twin-shaft turbofan)	13,850 lbf (61.61 kN) flat-rated at 30° C	0.69 lb/lbf/hr (19.54 g/kNs)	b) 15.8:1		2,951 (1,339)	a) 94.7 (2,405) b) 44 (1,118) fan	Gulfstream IV/IV-SB. Tay designed around core and external gearbox of RB183 Mk 555.
Tay 620 (twin-shaft turbofan)	13,850 lbf (61.61 kN) take-off, 2,550 lbf (11.34 kN) cruise at 35,000 ft and Mach 0.8	0.69 lb/lbf/hr (19.54 g/kNs)	b) 15.8:1		3,185 (1,445)	a) 94.7 (2,405) b) 44 (1,118) fan	Fokker 70 and Fokker 100, latter service entry from late 1994.
Tay 650 (twin-shaft turbofan)	15,100 lbf (67.17 kN) take-off, 2,950 lbf (13.12 kN) cruise at 35,000 ft and Mach 0.8	0.69 lb/lbf/hr (19.54 g/kNs)	b) 16.2:1		3,340 (1,515)	a) 94.8 (2,408) b) 44.8 (1,138) fan	Fokker 100 in Tay 620-15 form. Tay 650-14 to re-engine BAC One-Eleven and for Romaero Airstar 2500.
Tay 651 (twin-shaft turbofan) See comments for Tay 670	15,400 lbf (68.50 kN), flat rated at 28 C°	As above, at higher altitude and speed	b) 16.6:1		3,380 (1,533)	a) 94.8 (2,408) b) 44.8 (1,138) fan	Re-engined 727-100. Service entry December 1992. Tay 670 for re-engined DC-9.
Trent 764 (triple-shaft turbofan)	64,000 lbf (284.69 kN)	0.565 lb/lbf/hr (16.0 g/kNs)	b) 39.0:1		10,550 (4,785)	a) 154 (3,912) b) 97.4 (2,474) fan	MD-12. Service entry 1995. Trent has growth potential of over 100,000 lbf (444.83 kN). Owes much of design to RB211, but with increased diameter and improved wide-chord fan, increased-flow compressors and FADEC.
Trent 768 (triple-shaft turbofan)	67,500 lbf (300.26 kN), flat rated at 30 C°	0.565 lb/lbf/hr (16.0 g/kNs)	b) 35.16:1		14,350 (6,509) basic engine weight	a) 154 (3,912) b) 97.4 (2,474) fan	Airbus A330.
Trent 772 (triple-shaft turbofan)	71,000 lbf (315.83 kN), flat rated at 30 C°	0.565 lb/lbf/hr (16.0 g/kNs)	b) 36.84:1		14,350 (6,509) basic engine weight	a) 154 (3,912) b) 97.4 (2,474) fan	Airbus A330. Gained 90 minutes ETOPS clearance by the JAR in February 1995, ahead of airline operations.
Trent 775 (triple-shaft turbofan)	75,150 lbf (334.29 kN), flat rated at 30 C°	0.565 lb/lbf/hr (16.0 g/kNs)	b) 39.03		14,350 (6,509) basic engine weight	a) 154 (3,912) b) 97.4 (2,474) fan	Airbus A330.
Trent 875 (triple-shaft turbofan)	77,900 lbf (346.52 kN), flat rated at 30 C°	0.557 lb/lbf/hr (15.78 g/kNs)	b) 36.0:1		18,086 (8,204)	a) 172 (4,369) b) 110 (2,794)	777. First delivery to Boeing February 1995. Derated thrust model to suit customers' requirements.
Trent 877 (triple-shaft turbofan)	80,080 lbf (356.22 kN), flat rated at 33 C°	0.557 lb/lbf/hr (15.78 g/kNs)	b) 37:1		18,086 (8,204)	a) 172 (4,369) b) 110 (2,794)	777.
Trent 884 (triple-shaft turbofan)	86,400 lbf (384.33 kN), flat rated at 30 C°	0.557 lb/lbf/hr (15.78 g/kNs)	b) 40:1		18,086 (8,204)	a) 172 (4,369) b) 110 (2,794)	777 and Tu-304.
Trent 890 (triple-shaft turbofan)	91,300 lbf (404.13 kN), flat rated at 30 C°	0.557 lb/lbf/hr (15.78 g/kNs)	b) 42.7:1		18,086 (8,204)	a) 172 (4,369) b) 110 (2,794)	777. Certification of Trent 800 at 90,000 lbf (400.35kN) gained January 1995. First flown on a B747 on 29 March 1995.
Tyne RTy 20 Mk 21 (twin-shaft turboprop)	6,100 ehp (4,549 ekW)	0.485 lb/shp/hr (295 g/kW/hr)	b) 13.5:1		2,391 (1,084)	a) 108.72 (2,762) b) 55 (1,397)	Atlantic/Atlantique. Produced internationally in Europe. In production.

Designation (type of engine)	Power output (normally take-off rating for piston, turboprop and turboshaft, unless stated)	Specific Fuel Consumption (S F C)	a) Max RPM b) Pressure or Compression ratio	a) EGT (unless stated to be MGT, TET, TGT or TIT) b) Primary fuel type or Octane rating	Dry weight lb (kg)	a) Length ins (mm) b) Width ins (mm) c) Height ins (mm)	Current aircraft users, and comments
United Kingdom							
Rolls-Royce plc (continued)							
Tyne RTy 20 Mk 22 (twin-shaft turboprop)	6,100 ehp (4,549 ekW)	0.485 lb/shp/hr (295 g/kW/hr)	b) 13.5:1			a) 108.72 (2,762) b) 55 (1,397)	Transall C-160
Tyne RTy 20 Mk 801 (twin-shaft turboprop)	4,860 shp (3,624 kW)						G222T. Derated.
Viper 20 Mk 545 (single-shaft turbojet)	3,360 lbf (14.95 kN)	1.00 lb/lbf/hr (28.33 g/kNs)	b) 5.6:1		790 (358.3)	a) 71.1 (1,806) b) 24.55 (624)	I-22/M-93/M-95?/M-97? Iryda.
Viper 600 Mk 632 (single-shaft turbojet)	3,970 lbf (17.66 kN)	0.97 lb/lbf/hr (27.48 g/kNs)	b) 5.95:1		830 (376.4)	a) 71.1 (1,806) b) 29 (737) c) 35.5 (902)	Orao and IAR 93A (632-41), IAR 99 Soim (632-41M), MB-326K and MB-339 (632-43), and G-4 Super Galeb (632-46).
Viper 600 Mk 633 (single-shaft turbojet)	5,030 lbf (22.37 kN), with afterburning					a) 71.1 (1,806) b) 29 (737) c) 35.5 (902)	Mk 632 with afterburning. Orao (633-41) and IAR 93B (633-47).
Viper 600 Mk 680-43 (single-shaft turbojet)	4,360 lbf (19.39 kN)	0.98 lb/lbf/hr (27.76 g/kNs)	b) 6.75:1		836 (379.2)	a) 71.1 (1,806) b) 29 (737) c) 35.5 (902)	MB 339C.
Viper 600 Mk 680-582 (single-shaft turbojet)	4,000 lbf (17.79 kN)		b) 6.75:1		836 (379.2)	a) 71.1 (1,806) b) 29 (737) c) 35.5 (902)	T Bird II. TBO 4,500 hrs. Improved maintainability.
United States of America							
AlliedSignal Engines. 111 South 34th Street, PO Box 52181, Phoenix, AZ 85072-2181							
500 Series Common Core (compact, lightweight family of engines in turboprop, turboshaft and turbofan forms)	7,500 eshp (5,593 ekW) as turboprop and turboshaft, with growth variants to 11,000 eshp (8,203 ekW) being studied. Up to 18,000 lbf (80 kN) as turbofan.						Turboprop for a new generation of high-speed regional aircraft. Turboshaft for large cargo and transport helicopters. Turbofan for regional jetliners. Derived from ALF502/LF507.
ALF502L (twin-shaft turbofan)	7,500 lbf (33.362 kN) take-off	0.414-0.428 lb/lbf/hr (11.73-12.12 g/kNs)	b) 13.6:1		1,311 (594.7)	a) 58.56 (1,487) b) 41.7 (1,059)	Canadair 600 Challenger.
ALF502R-3 (twin-shaft turbofan)	6,700 lbf (29.8 kN) take-off	0.411 lb/lbf/hr (11.64 g/kNs)	b) 11.6:1		1,336 (606)	a) 56.8 (1,443) b) 41.7 (1,059)	BAe 146.
ALF502R-3A/4/5 (twin-shaft turbofan)	6,970 lbf (31 kN) take-off	0.408 lb/lbf/hr (11.56 g/kNs)	b) 11.6 to 12:1		1,336 (606)	a) 56.8 (1,443) b) 41.7 (1,059)	BAe 146.
ALF502R-6 (twin-shaft turbofan)	7,500 lbf (33.36 kN) take-off	0.415 lb/lbf/hr (11.75 g/kNs)			1,336 (606)	a) 58.6 (1,487) b) 41.7 (1,059)	BAe 146.
F124 and F125 see TFE1042-70							
LF507-1F (turbofan)	7,000 lbf (31.14 kN) to 23.3° C	0.406 lb/lbf/hr (11.5 g/kNs)	b) 13:1		1,385 (628.2)	a) 58.6 (1,487) b) 41.7 (1,059)	Avro RJ. Dispatch reliability 99.93%. F for FADEC controlled. For Cat III capable regional jets.
LF507-1H (turbofan)	7,000 lbf (31.14 kN) to 23.3° C	0.406 lb/lbf/hr (11.5 g/kNs)			1,375 (623.7)	a) 58.6 (1,487) b) 41.7 (1,059)	Yak-40TC. H for Hydromechanical controlled growth derivative, certified in October 1991.
LTP101-700A-1A (free-turbine turboprop)	700 eshp (522 ekW)	0.55 lb/eshp/hr (335 g/ekW/hr) take-off	a) up to 1,950 output		335 (152)	a) 36 (914.4) b) 21 (533.4)	Piaggio P.166-DL3, PAC Cresco, and various re-engined aircraft. Lower rated but otherwise similar 620 eshp (462.3 ekW) LTP101-600A-1A also for P.166-DL3.

Designation (type of engine)	Power output (normally take-off rating for piston, turboprop and turboshaft, unless stated)	Specific Fuel Consumption (S F C)	a) Max RPM b) Pressure or Compression ratio	a) EGT (unless stated to be MGT, TET, TGT or TIT) b) Primary fuel type or Octane rating	Dry weight lb (kg)	a) Length ins (mm) b) Width ins (mm) c) Height ins (mm)	Current aircraft users, and comments
United States of America							
AlliedSignal Engines (continued)							
LTS101-600A-2 (turboshaft version of the LTP 101)	615 shp (458.6 kW) take-off	0.571 lb/shp/hr (347 g/kW/hr)	a) 6,000		253 (114.75)	a) 30.9 (785) b) 23.6 (599.4)	AS 350D Astar. Plus I and Plus II variants of the LTS101 range incorporate component upgrades.
LTS101-600A-3 (turboshaft version of the LTP 101)	615 shp (458.6 kW) take-off	0.582 lb/shp/hr (354 g/kW/hr)	a) 6,000		265 (120.2)	a) 30.9 (785) b) 23.6 (599.4)	AS 350D AStar.
LTS101-750B-1 (turboshaft version of the LTP 101)	550 shp (410 kW) take-off	0.577 lb/shp/hr (351 g/kW/hr)	a) 6,000		297 (134.7)	a) 32.36 (822) b) 24.7 (627.4)	BK 117B.
LTS101-750B-2 (turboshaft version of the LTP 101)	684 shp (510 kW) take-off	0.57 lb/shp/hr (347 g/kW/hr)	a) 6,000		271 (123)	a) 32.36 (822) b) 24.7 (627.4)	HH-65A Dolphin.
T53-L-13B/T5313B (free-turbine turboshaft)	1,400 shp (1,044 kW) take-off	0.58 lb/shp/hr (353 g/kW/hr)			540 (245)	a) 47.6 (1,209) b) 23 (584)	UH-1/CH-118 and AH-1 in military T53 form. Bell 205A.
T5317A/A-1 (free-turbine turboshaft)	1,500 shp (1,118.6 kW) take-off	0.59 lb/shp/hr (359 g/kW/hr)			564 (256)	a) 47.6 (1,209) b) 23 (584)	Kaman K-max. Commercial version of T53-L-703.
T53-L-701 (turboprop)	1,400 shp (1,044 kW)	0.6 lb/shp/hr (365 g/kW/hr)			688 (312)	a) 58.4 (1,483) b) 23 (584)	OV-1 Mohawk.
T53-L-703/T5317B (free-turbine turboshaft)	1,800 shp (1,342.3 kW) take-off	0.6 lb/shp/hr (365 g/kW/hr)			545 (247.2)	a) 47.6 (1,209) b) 23 (584)	AH-1, UH-1, and Fuji-Bell 205B. See also Kawasaki.
T5508D/LTC4B-8D (free-turbine turboshaft)	2,930 shp (2,185 kW), transmission limit 2,250 shp (1,678 kW)	0.592 lb/shp/hr (360 g/kW/hr)		b) JP-4, JP-5, JP-8 and CITE	605 (274.4)	a) 44 (1,118) b) 24 (609.6)	Bell 214.
T55-L-11-712E (free-turbine turboshaft)	3,750 shp (2,796 kW) See comments	0.53 lb/shp/hr (322 g/kW/hr)	b) 8.2:1	b) JP-4, JP-5 and CITE	710 (322)	a) 46.5 (1,181) b) 24.25 (616)	CH-47C Chinook. 3,400 shp (2,535 kW) military for 30 minutes, 3,000 shp (2,237 kW) max continuous.
T55-L-712 and 712-SSB (free-turbine turboshaft)	3,750 shp (2,796 kW) normal maximum for 712, 4,400 shp (3,281 kW) for SSB	0.53 lb/shp/hr (322 g/kW/hr)		b) JP-4, JP-5, JP-8 and CITE	750 (340.2)	a) 46.5 (1,181) b) 24.25 (616)	CH-47D/J Chinook.
AL5512 (free-turbine turboshaft)	4,075 shp (3,039 kW) take-off	0.53 lb/shp/hr (322 g/kW/hr)			780 (354)	a) 44 (1,118) b) 24.25 (616)	Commercial Chinook. Civil derivative of T55-L-712.
T55-L-714 (free-turbine turboshaft)	5,000 shp (3,729 kW) max contingency	0.503 lb/shp/hr (306 g/kW/hr)	b) 9.3:1	b) JP-4, JP-5, JP-8 and CITE	800 (363)	a) 46.5 (1,181) b) 24.25 (616)	MH-47E
T55-L-714A (free-turbine turboshaft)	6,000 shp (4,474 kW)			b) JP-4, JP-5, JP-8 and CITE		a) 46.5 (1,181) b) 24.25 (616)	CH-47D Chinook. Selected by Boeing for all new CH-47D sales internationally. Features elimination of magnesium for better operation in salt-water environments, improved torque measurement system, improved FADEC and longer life rotating components.
T55-L-71X and T55ACE (see comments)							Two new free-turbine turboshafts, details of which had not been received at the time of writing.
TFE731-2/2A/2B/2J/2L/2N (twin-shaft turbofan)	3,500 lbf (15.57 kN) take-off to 22.2° C, 755 lbf (3.36 kN) cruise at 40,000 ft and Mach 0.8	0.815 lb/lbf/hr (23.1 g/kNs) cruise	b) 14:1		743 (337)	a) 59.83 (1,519) b) 34.2 (869) c) 39.36 (1,000)	AT-3 Tzu-Chung, C-101EB, K-8 Karakorum, Learjet 31A/35A/36A/C-21, Pampa and Pampa 2000-International.

Designation (type of engine)	Power output (normally take-off rating for piston, turboprop and turboshaft, unless stated)	Specific Fuel Consumption (S F C)	a) Max RPM b) Pressure or Compression ratio	a) EGT (unless stated to be MGT, TET, TGT or TIT) b) Primary fuel type or Octane rating	Dry weight lb (kg)	a) Length ins (mm) b) Width ins (mm) c) Height ins (mm)	Current aircraft users, and comments
United States of America							
AlliedSignal Engines (continued)							
TFE731-3/3A/3B/3J (twin-shaft turbofan)	up to 3,700 lbf (16.46 kN) to 24.4° C take-off, up to 844 lbf (3.75 kN) cruise (as before)	0.816-0.835 lb/lbf/hr (23.1-23.65 g/kNs) cruise	b) 14.6:1		754-775 (342-351.5)	a) 59.7 (1,516) b) 34.2 (869) c) 39.36 (1,000)	BAe 125-700, C-101BB, Citation III/VI, Falcon 50, JetStar II, Learjet 55/56, Sabreliner 65A and Westwind/1125 Astra SP.
TFE731-4 (twin-shaft turbofan)	4,000 lbf (17.8 kN) take-off, 929 lbf (4.13 kN) cruise (as before)	0.796 lb/lbf/hr (22.54 g/kNs) cruise			822 (373)	a) 58.15 (1,477) b) 34.2 (869) c) 39.36 (1,000)	Citation VII and G-5 Super Galeb. TFE731-4-1T in L-139, rated at 4,080 lbf (18.15 kN), and with dry weight of 822 lb (373 kg) and 0.518 lb/lbf/hr (14.67 g/kNs) TFC.
TFE731-5/5A/5B/5J (twin-shaft turbofan)	4,300-4,750 lbf (19.13-21.13 kN) take-off, up to 1,052 lbf (4.68 kN) cruise (as above)	0.756-0.802 lb/lbf/hr (21.414-22.72 g/kNs) cruise			852-899 (386-408)	a) 65.54 (1,665) for TFE731-5 b) 33.79 (858) c) 40.52 (1,029)	C-101CC/DD, Citation V Ultra, re-engined Falcon 20, Falcon 900/900B, and Raytheon Hawker 800. 4,660 lbf (20.72 kN) TFE731-5BR in Hawker 800XP.
TFE731-20 (twin-shaft turbofan)	3,500 lbf (15.57 kN) take-off to 33.9° C, 876 lbf (3.9 kN) cruise (as above)	0.728 lb/lbf/hr (20.62 g/kNs)	b) 14.3:1		836 (379.2)	a) 59.65 (1,515) b) 34.2 (869) c) 39.36 (1,000)	Learjet 45.
TFE731-40 (twin-shaft turbofan)	4,250 lbf (18.9 kN) take-off to 24.4°C, 1,010 lbf (4.49 kN) cruise (as above)	0.457 lb/lbf/hr (12.94 g/kNs)	b) 22:1 cycle pressure ratio		885 (401)	a) 51.03 (1,296) without spinner c) 28.2 (716) fan housing, 22.37 (568) from centre of spinner to bottom of accessory case.	Falcon 50EX and Astra SPX. Certified in 1995. 24% increase in cruise altitude thrust and 7% reduction in cruise TSFC relative to TFE731-3. N1 control full authority digital control with hydromechanical back-up with integral synchronization and APR. ARINC 429 glass cockpit interface.
TFE731-60 (twin-shaft turbofan)	5,000 lbf (22.24 kN) take-off to 32.2°C, 1,120 lbf (4.98 kN) cruise (as above)	0.405 lb/lbf/hr (11.47 g/kNs)	b) 22:1 cycle pressure ratio		988 (448)	a) 72.01 (1,829) c) 32.68 (830) fan housing, 24.18 (614) from centre of spinner to bottom of accessory case.	Falcon 900EX. Certified in 1995. Completed high-altitude performance tests in 1994. Utilizes a larger wide-chord damperless fan. 17% increase in cruise altitude thrust and 12% reduction in TSFC relative to TFE 731-5. N1 control as for TFE731-40.
TFE1042-70 (twin-shaft turbofan)	6,025 lbf (26.8 kN) dry, 9,460 lbf (42.08 kN) with afterburning	0.8 lb/lbf/hr (22.7 g/kNs)			1,360 (616.9)	a) 140.2 (3,561) b) 30.8 (782) nozzle	Han Hsiang Ching-Kuo.
F124-GA-100 (twin-shaft turbofan)	6,300 lbf (28.02 kN) dry	0.81 lb/lbf/hr (22.94 g/kNs) typical	b) 19.4:1	a) 1,366° C TIT	1,100 lb (499 kg) approx	a) 66.8 (1,697) b) 30 (762) c) 36 (914)	L-159, to fly in April 1996.
F124X (twin-shaft turbofan)	8,120 lbf (36.12 kN)						
F124XX (twin-shaft turbofan)	11,500 lbf (51.16 kN)						
F125-GA-100 (twin-shaft turbofan)	9,250 lbf (41.15 kN)	2.06 lb/lbf/hr (58.35 g/kNs) with afterburning	b) 18.45:1	a) 1,372° C TIT	1,360 (617)	a) 140.2 (3,561) b) 30.8 (782) c) 33.4 (848)	Han Hsiang Ching-Kuo.
F125X (twin-shaft turbofan)	12,250 lbf (54.49 kN) with afterburning						No further information available at the time of writing.
F125XX (twin-shaft turbofan)	16,000 lbf (71.17 kN) with afterburning						No further information available at the time of writing.
TPE331-5/5A/6 series (single-shaft turboprop)	840 shp (626.4 kW) take-off, with 776 shp (578.66 kW) gearbox limit	0.56 lb/shp/hr (340.6 g/kW/hr)	b) 10.37:1	a) 1,005° C TIT	360 (163.3)	b) 21 (533) c) 26 (660)	Includes Ayres Turbo-Thrush, C-212 and Do 228.
TPE331-8 (single-shaft turboprop)	715 shp (533.2 kW) flat rated to 36° C	0.572 lb/shp/hr (348 g/kW/hr)		a) 1,005° C TIT	370 (168)	b) 21 (533) c) 26 (660)	Cessna Conquest and Conquest II.

Designation (type of engine)	Power output (normally take-off rating for piston, turboprop and turboshaft, unless stated)	Specific Fuel Consumption (S F C)	a) Max RPM b) Pressure or Compression ratio	a) EGT (unless stated to be MGT, TET, TGT or TIT) b) Primary fuel type or Octane rating	Dry weight lb (kg)	a) Length ins (mm) b) Width ins (mm) c) Height ins (mm)	Current aircraft users, and comments
United States of America							
AlliedSignal Engines (continued)							
TPE331-10/10R/10U (single-shaft turboprop)	1,000 shp (745.7 kW) take-off, with 900 shp (671 kW) gearbox limit	0.558 lb/shp/hr (339 g/kW/hr)		a) 1,005° C TIT	375 (170)	b) 21 (533) c) 26 (660)	Ayres Turbo-Thrush, C-212, Jetstream 31, Merlin III and other types.
TPE331-11U (single-shaft turboprop)	1,000 shp (745.7 kW) take-off, with 1,100 shp (820.3 kW) gearbox limit	0.558 lb/shp/hr (339 g/kW/hr)		a) 1,005° C TIT	405 (183.7)	b) 21 (533) c) 26 (660)	Merlin 23, Metro 23 and Expediter.
TPE331-12U (single-shaft turboprop)	1,100 shp (820.3 kW) take-off	0.547 lb/shp/hr (332.7 g/kW/hr)		a) 1,005° C TIT	407 (184.6)	b) 21 (533) c) 26 (660)	Metro 23, C-26, Jetstream Super 31, and RAF Tucano. TPE331-12D variant on HTT-35.
TPE331-14A/B and /15 (single-shaft turboprop)	1,645 shp (1,227 kW)	0.502 lb/shp/hr (305 g/kW/hr)		a) 1,005° C TIT	620 (281.2)	b) 21 (533) c) 26 (660)	PA-42-1000 Cheyenne 400 and upgraded S-2 Tracker.
TPE331-14GR/HR (single-shaft turboprop)	1,650 shp (1,230 kW)	0.502 lb/shp/hr (305 g/kW/hr)		a) 1,005° C TIT	620 (281.2)	b) 21 (533) c) 26 (660)	An-38 and Jetstream 41.
TPE331-14F (single-shaft turboprop)	Derated 750 shp (559.3 kW)						Grob G-520 Strato 1.
TPE331-25/61 and 71 (single-shaft turboprop)	575 shp (428.8 kW) take-off, 445 shp (332 kW) cruise	0.66 lb/shp/hr (401.5 g/kW/hr)	b) 8:1	a) 987° C TIT	335 (152)	b) 21 (533) c) 26 (660)	MU-2B and other early models, and various re-engined aircraft.
Allison Engine Company. PO Box 420, Speed Code U10C, Indianapolis, IN 46206-0420							
Rolls-Royce plc of the UK agreed to purchase the Allison Engine Company in November 1994. Allison continues to operate under its own name as a member of Rolls-Royce's Aerospace Group. Allison has also established the Allison Advanced Development Co to undertake US classified or restricted access programmes.							
250-B17C (free-turbine turboprop)	420 shp (313.2 kW) take-off, 369 shp (275 kW) normal cruise, sea level static	0.657 lb/shp/hr (400 g/kW/hr)	b) 7.2:1	a) 810° C MGT b) Jet	195 (88.5)	a) 45 (1,143) b) 19.4 (493) c) 22.6 (574)	Nomad, Turbine Islander, Turbostar, Viator and more.
250-B17D (free-turbine turboprop)	420 shp (313.3 kW) take-off, 369 shp (275 kW) normal cruise, sea level static	0.657 lb/shp/hr (400 g/kW/hr)	b) 7.2:1	a) 810° C MGT b) Jet	198 (89.8)	a) 45 (1,143) b) 19.4 (493) c) 22.6 (574)	Fuji T-5, SF.260TP, AS 202/32TP Turbine Brave, Turbo Pillán and more. In production. Allison Series II engine.
250-B17F (free-turbine turboprop)	450 shp (335.6 kW) take-off, 380 shp (283.4 kW) normal cruise, sea level static	0.613 lb/shp/hr (373 g/kW/hr)	b) 7.91:1	a) 810° C MGT b) Jet	205 (93)	a) 45 (1,143) b) 19.4 (493) c) 22.6 (574)	Beech A36, Cessna P210, Nomad, SF 600A Canguro, RediGO, SF.260TP, Ruschmeyer 90-420 AT, Turbine Islander and Defender 4000 and MSSA. In production. Allison Series II engine.
250-C20B/F/J/W (free-turbine turboshaft)	420 shp (313.3 kW) take-off, 370 shp (276 kW) normal cruise, sea level static	0.650 lb/shp/hr (395 g/kW/hr)	b) 7.1:1	b) Jet	161 (73)	a) 38.8 (985) b) 19.4 (493) c) 23.2 (589)	A 109A, Bell 47G re-engined, BO 105CBS, Fantrainer 400, Hiller UH-12E3T and UH-12E5T, JetRanger, Ka-226, Kania, LongRanger, MD 500/Defender, EC Super Five. In production. Allison Series II engines. Military designation T63-A-720 for Allison engine in OH-58C. 250-C20W for Enstrom 480.
250-C20R (free-turbine turboshaft)	450 shp (335.6 kW) take-off, 380 shp (283 kW) normal cruise, sea level static	0.608 lb/shp/hr (370 g/kW/hr)	b) 7.9:1	b) Jet	173 (78.5)	a) 38.8 (985) b) 19.4 (493) c) 23.2 (589)	A 109C/EOA, AB-206B, MD 500E/Defender, MD 520N, PZL-Swidnik SW-4, Tridair Gemini ST conversions, TwinRanger. In production. Allison Series II engines.
250-C20R/9 (free-turbine turboshaft)	550 shp (410 kW) 30 seconds OEI, 465 shp (346.75 kW) take-off, 400 shp (298 kW) max continuous, sea level static		b) 8.4:1	b) Jet	195 (88.5)	a) 38.8 (985) b) 19.4 (493) c) 23.2 (589)	Has FADEC. In production. Allison Series II engine.

Designation (type of engine)	Power output (normally take-off rating for piston, turboprop and turboshaft, unless stated)	Specific Fuel Consumption (S F C)	a) Max RPM b) Pressure or Compression ratio	a) EGT (unless stated to be MGT, TET, TGT or TIT) b) Primary fuel type or Octane rating	Dry weight lb (kg)	a) Length ins (mm) b) Width ins (mm) c) Height ins (mm)	Current aircraft users, and comments
United States of America							
Allison Engine Company (continued)							
250-C22B (free-turbine turboshaft)	490 shp (365 kW) take-off, 430 shp (320 kW) continous						Bell 407T.
250-C28B/C (free-turbine turboshaft)	500 shp (373 kW) take-off, 494 shp (368.4 kW) normal cruise, sea level static	0.606 lb/shp/hr (369 g/kW/hr)	b) 8.4:1	b) Jet	233 (105.7)	a) 47.3 (1,201) b) 21.9 (557) c) 25.1 (638)	BO 105LS, LongRanger. In production. Allison Series III engines.
250-C30G (free-turbine turboshaft)	650 shp (484.7 kW) take-off	0.592 lb/shp/hr (360 g/kW/hr)	b) 8.6:1	b) Jet	240 (109)	a) 41 (1,041) b) 21.9 (557) c) 25.1 (638)	Bell 230, MD 530, S-76.
250-C30M/P/S (free-turbine turboshaft)	650 shp (484.7 kW) take-off, 600 shp (447.4 kW) normal cruise, sea level static (see Comments)	0.592 lb/shp/hr (360 g/kW/hr)	b) 8.6:1	b) Jet	250 (113.4) C30M, 245 (111) C30P 251 (114) C30S,	a) 41 (1,041) b) 21.9 (557) c) 25.1 (638)	MD 530F, MD Defender, LongRanger III/IV. In production. C-30R or X used on Bell 406/OH-58 (military designation T703-AD-700). C30S has lower cruise ratings (for example, 418 shp/312 kW at 75% power, compared to 450 shp/335.5 kW for C30M/P). Allison Series IV engines.
250-C40/47 (as above)	734 shp (547 kW) for 250-C40, 790 shp (589 kW) at take-off and max continuous for 250-C47		b) 9.2:1	b) Jet	280 (127)		Bell 407 and 430, and MD600. In production. Growth derivatives of C20R/9, with FADEC. Allison Series IV engines.
AE100 (free-turbine turboprop)	5,000 shp (3,729 kW)						Reported derivative engine of the AE2100.
AE 2100A (free-turbine turboprop)	4,152 shp (3,096 kW) at 1,100 propeller rpm	0.416 lb/shp/hr (253 g/kW/hr) take-off	a) 15,375 (1,100 propeller) b) 16.6:1	a) 852° C MGT b) Jet A/A-1	1,578 (715.8)	a) 115.68 (2,938) b) 30.9 (785) c) 52.52 (1,334)	Saab 2000. ATR–82?
AE 2100C (free-turbine turboprop)	3,271 shp (2,365 kW) at 1,100 propeller rpm	0.430 lb/shp/hr (262 g/kW/hr)	a) 15,375 (1,100 propeller) b) 16.6:1	a) 831° C MGT b) ASTM D 1655 JET A/A-1	1,578 (715.8)	a) 115.68 (2,938) b) 32.69 (830) c) 47.41 (1,204)	N-250-100.
AE 2100D3 (free-turbine turboprop)	4,591 shp (3,424 kW)	0.426 lb/shp/hr (259 g/kW/hr)	a) 14,268 (1,021 propeller) b) 16.6:1	a) 852° C MGT b) Jet A/A-1	1,655 (750.7)	a) 115.65 (2,938) b) 25.4 (645) c) 46.4 (1,179)	C-130J. AE 2100 is candidate for P-3 Orion II and other ASW fleet modernization.
AE 3007A (twin-shaft turbofan)	7,630 lbf (33.94 kN)	0.386 lb/lbf/hr (10.92 g/kNs) uninstalled	b) 18.3:1	a) 888° C MGT b) Jet A	1,608 (729)	a) 115.08 (2,923) b) 46.14 (1,172) c) 55.7 (1,415)	Embraer EMB-145.
AE 3007C (twin-shaft turbofan)	6,400 lbf (28.47 kN)	0.378 lb/lbf/hr (10.735 g/kNs)	b) 18:1 take-off	a) 888° C MGT b) Jet A	1,588 (720.3)	a) 115.08 (2,923) b) 46.14 (1,172) c) 55.7 (1,415)	Citation X.
AE 3008 (twin-shaft turbofan)	8,000 lbf (35.59 kN)					b) 38.5 (978) fan	Active growth programme for 50-seat regional jet.
AE 3009 (twin-shaft turbofan)	8,500-9,000 lbf (37.81-40 kN)					b) 38.5 (978) fan	Active growth programme for 50-seat regional jet.
AE 3010 (twin-shaft turbofan)	9,500-11,000 lbf (42.26-48.93 kN)					b) 38.5 (978) fan	Active growth programme for 70-100 seat regional jet.
AE 3012 (twin-shaft turbofan)	12,000-14,000 lbf (53.38-62.28 kN)					b) 38.5 (978) fan	Active growth programme for 70-100 seat regional jet.
AE 301X (twin-shaft turbofan)	10,000 lbf (44.48 kN)					b) 38.5 (978) fan	Demonstrator.
501-D22 (civil) and T56-A-7/-10WA (military) (axial flow, single-shaft turboprop)	4,050 eshp (3,020 ekW) at 13,820 rpm, 2,390 eshp (1,782 ekW) at 84%	0.522 lb/eshp/hr (318 g/ekW/hr) take-off	a) 13,820 (1,020 propeller) b) 9.5:1	a) 971° C TIT b) Jet A/A-1, JP-4, JP-5, JP-8	1,835 (832)	a) 146.1 (3,711) b) 27.2 (691) c) 39 (991), 42 (1,067) for T56-A-10WA	C-130B/E/F (T56-A-7), L-100 Commercial Hercules (501-D22), P-3A Orion (T56-A-10WA). Series II engines.

Designation (type of engine)	Power output (normally take-off rating for piston, turboprop and turboshaft, unless stated)	Specific Fuel Consumption (S F C)	a) Max RPM b) Pressure or Compression ratio	a) EGT (unless stated to be MGT, TET, TGT or TIT) b) Primary fuel type or Octane rating	Dry weight lb (kg)	a) Length ins (mm) b) Width ins (mm) c) Height ins (mm)	Current aircraft users, and comments
United States of America							
Allison Engine Company (continued)							
501-D22A/C/G (civil) and T56-A-14/-15/-16/-423/-425 (military) (axial flow, single-shaft turboprop)	4,910 eshp (3,661 ekW) at 13,820 rpm, 3,275 eshp (2,442 ekW) at 75%	0.501 lb/eshp/hr (305 g/ekW/hr) take-off	a) 13,820 (1,020 propeller, except 1,106 for E-2C and C-2A) b) 9.5:1	a) 1,077° C TIT b) MIL-T-5624 grades JP-4, JP-5, JP-8	1,820 (825.5)	a) 146.9 (3,731) b) 27.2 (691) c) 39 (991), 42 (1,067) for T56-A-14 and 501-D22C/G	Convair 580A (501-D22G), CV5800 (501-D22G), C-2 Greyhound (T56-A-425), E-2C Hawkeye (T56-A-425), C-130H/H-30 (T56-A-15), C-130F/T and EC-130Q (T56-A-16/-423), L-100-20/-30 (501-D22A), Tracor Super Guppy-201. In addition, T56-A-422s on E-2C/C-2As were designated T56-A-425s, and T56-A-426s on E-2A/Bs and C-2As are retired or modified to other configurations. T56-A-14LFE/ALFE for CP-140 Aurora are commercially improved versions of military T56-A-14. T56-A-15LFE is latest production and commercially improved version of military T56-A-15 for C-130H/H-30. Series III engine.
T56-A-427 (military), Allison Model 501-M71D but no civil equivalent (axial flow, single-shaft turboprop)	5,250 eshp (3,915 ekW) at 14,239 rpm, 4,062 eshp (3,029 ekW) at 75%	0.473 lb/eshp/hr (288 g/ekW/hr) take-off	a) 14,239 (1,106 propeller) b) 14.1:1	a) 813° C max compensated turbine temperature b) JP-4, JP-5, JP-8	1,940 (880)	a) 146.8 (3,729) b) 27.2 (691) c) 39 (991)	E-2C+. Series IV engine.
T406-AD-400 (axial flow turboshaft)	6,150 shp (4,586 kW) at 15,000 rpm, 3,600 shp (2,684 kW) at 12,750 rpm	0.405 lb/shp/hr (246 g/kW/hr)	a) 15,000 b) 16.6:1	a) 1,204° C MGT b) JP-5	970.5 (440.2)	a) 77.94 (1,980) b) 24.5 (622) c) 33.35 (847)	Bell-Boeing V-22 Osprey. Allison Model 501-M80C. 21 delivered for ground and flight tests for V-22 programme. 12 more in final production configuration, for delivery in 1996, to be incorporated in the V-22 EMD flight test programme.
Allison-AlliedSignal Partnership (LHTEC)							
CTS800 (free-turbine turboshaft)	1,300 shp (970 kW)						Flight testing on the HAL Advanced Light Helicopter (ALH). Production engines could be delivered from 1998. Commercial version of the T800.
T800-LHT-800 (free-turbine turboshaft)	1,335 shp (995.5 kW) at 23,000 rpm, 1,038 shp (774 kW) cruise at similar rpm	0.45 lb/shp/hr (274 g/kW/hr)	a) 23,000 b) 14.0:1	a) 603° C EGT, 868° C MGT b) JP-4. JP-5	310 (140.6)	a) 31.5 (800) b) 21.7 (551) c) 26.1 (663)	UH-1H, RAH-66, A 129 International, and Panther 800.
T800-LHT-801 (free-turbine turboshaft)	1,550 shp (1,156 kW) at 23,000 rpm, 1,218 shp (908 kW) cruise at similar rpm	0.46 lb/shp/hr (280 g/kW/hr)	a) 23,000 b) 14.0:1	a) 618° C b) JP-4, JP-5	330 (149.7)	a) 32 (813) b) 22.3 (566) c) 26.8 (681)	UH-1H, RAH-66.
Alturdyne. 8050 Armour Street, San Diego, CA 92111							
A650 series (rotary piston)	250 hp (186.4 kW) at 6,000 rpm	0.551 lb/hp/hr (335 g/kW/hr)	a) 2,700 propeller b) 10.0:1	b) Gasoline 100 Octane	188 (85.3)	a) 26.5 (673) b) 15 (381) c) 26 (660)	
AT62 (military T62) (turboshaft)	200 shp (149 kW) at 6,000 rpm		a) 6,000 b) 5.0:1	a) 649° C b) Aviation kerosene	100 (45.4)	a) 24 (610) b) 12 (305)	Suitable for helicopters, in addition to ground and industrial applications.
CFE Company. 111 South 34th Street, PO Box 62332, Phoenix, AZ 85082-2332							
CFE738-1-1B (high bypass, twin spool turbofan)	5,725 lbf (25.47 kN) to 30° C take-off, 1,464 lbf (6.514 kN) cruise	0.38 lb/lbf/hr (10.76 g/kNs) at 5,725 lbf SLS. 0.642 lb/lbf/hr (18.13 g/kNs) at 1,464 lbf	b) 35:1	b) Aviation kerosene	1,325 (601)	a) 99.24 (2,520) b) 43 (1,092) c) 47.3 (1,201)	Dassault Falcon 2000.
Dyna-Cam Aero Engine Corporation. PO Box 1159, Torrance, CA 90505-0159							
DC/375 (12-cyl piston)	200 hp (149 kW) at 2,000 rpm	0.43 lb/hp/hr (262 g/kW/hr) take-off, 0.40 lb/hp/hr (243 g/kW/hr)	a) 2,000 b) 8.0:1	a) 732° C b) 80 Octane Avgas or auto fuel	265 (120.2)	a) 40 (1,016) b) 15 (381)	Small 4-seat lightplanes, kit aircraft and helicopters.
General Electric Aircraft Engines. One Neumann Way, Evendale, OH 45215-6301							
GE90 (twin-shaft turbofan)	84,700 lbf (376.77 kN) for baseline engine intended for the 777 "B" market, rising in stages to over 115,000 lbf (511.55 kN) growth derivative.		b) 39.3:1			a) 193 (4,902) flange to flange b) 123 (3,124) fan	Boeing 777 "B" market for 84.7 K thrust engine. Derated variant will offer 75 K thrust. Leading to uprated 92 K for 777 "B" and 777 stretch, and featuring LP system design improvements and improved HPT materials. Growth engines are planned as 95-97 K for 777 stretch and "C" market, and featuring improved turbomachinery; 105 K engine with higher p/p fan with destaged core for 777 stretch growth and "C" market; and 115+ K engine, with larger fan with destaged core for 777 stretch growth.

Designation (type of engine)	Power output (normally take-off rating for piston, turboprop and turboshaft, unless stated)	Specific Fuel Consumption (S F C)	a) Max RPM b) Pressure or Compression ratio	a) EGT (unless stated to be MGT, TET, TGT or TIT) b) Primary fuel type or Octane rating	Dry weight lb (kg)	a) Length ins (mm) b) Width ins (mm) c) Height ins (mm)	Current aircraft users, and comments
United States of America							
General Electric Aircraft Engines (continued)							
CF6-80A and A1 (twin-shaft turbofan)	48,000 lbf (213.52 kN), 10,320 lbf (45.91 kN) cruise (as above)	0.344 lb/lbf/hr (9.74 g/kNs)	b) 28:1	a) 1,330° C	8,496 (3,854)	a) 157.4 (3,998) c) 105.3 (2,674.5)	A310 and 767.
CF6-80A2 and A3 (twin-shaft turbofan)	50,000 lbf (222.42 kN)		b) 29:1	a) 1,330° C	8,420-8,496 (3,819-3,854)	a) 157.4 (3,998) c) 105.3 (2,674.5)	A310 and 767.
CF6-80C2A series (twin-shaft turbofan)	52,460-61,500 lbf (233.36-273.57 kN)	0.329 lb/lbf/hr (9.32 g/kNs) approx	b) 30.4:1		9,135 (4,144) approx	a) 160.9 (4,087)	A300 and A310. CF6-80C2 series has a dispatch reliability rate of 99.92% based on a rolling average for 12 months to July 1994. CF6-80C2 series powered 588 aircraft by September 1994.
CF6-80C2B series (twin-shaft turbofan)	51,570-59,750 lbf (229.4-265.79 kN),	0.329 lb/lbf/hr (9.32 g/kNs) approx	b) 30.4:1		9,135 (4,144) approx	a) 160.9 (4,087)	An-218, 747 and 767. F103-GE-102, equivalent to the CF6-80C2B1.
CF6-80C2D1F (twin-shaft turbofan)	60,960 lbf (271.17 kN) at 30° C	0.34 lb/lbf/hr (9.63 g/kNs)	b) 30.4:1			a) 160.9 (4,087)	767 AWACS and MD-11.
CF6-80E1A2 (twin-shaft turbofan)	67,500 lbf (300.26 kN)	0.327 lb/lbf/hr (9.262 g/kNs)	b) 32.6:1		10,627 (4,820)	a) 173.5 (4,407)	A330. Entered service January 1994. Dispatch reliability rate of 99.75% based on a rolling average for 12 months to July 1994.
CF6-80E1A3 (twin-shaft turbofan)	72,000 lbf (320.28 kN)	0.34 lb/lbf/hr (9.63 g/kNs)	b) 34.6:1		10,627 (4,820)	a) 173.5 (4,407)	A330. A 70,000 lbf (311.38 kN) version has been defined for A330 growth requirements. CF6-80E1 received 120 minute ETOPS approval in April 1994.
CF34-1A (twin-shaft turbofan)	8,650 lbf (38.48 kN)					a) 103 (2,616) b) 49 (1,245)	Challenger 601-1A.
CF34-3A (twin-shaft turbofan)	8,729 lbf (38.83 kN) normal take-off		b) 14:1			a) 103 (2,616) c) 49 (1,245)	Challenger 601-3A. Airflow 34 lb (15.4 kg) per second. 14-stage compressor.
CF34-3A1 (twin-shaft turbofan)	8,729 lbf (38.83 kN) normal take-off, 9,220 lbf (41.01 kN) with Automatic Power Reserve	0.357 lb/lbf/hr (10.11 g/kNs)				a) 103 (2,616) b) 49 (1,245)	Canadair Regional Jet. Challenger 601-3R and Canadair Special Edition. Dispatch reliability rate of 99.99%.
CF34-3B (twin-shaft turbofan)	8,729 lbf (38.83 kN) normal take-off to 30° C, APR as above	0.346 lb/lbf/hr (9.8 g/kNs)				a) 103 (2,616) b) 49 (1,245)	Next-generation Challenger 604. Certification June 1995. Incorporating 3B1 improvements.
CF34-3B1 (twin-shaft turbofan)	8,729 lbf (38.83 kN) normal take-off, 9,220 lbf (41.01 kN) with Automatic Power Reserve, flat rated to 30° C.	2-3% improvement over CF34-3A1 version				a) 103 (2,616) b) 49 (1,245)	Canadair Regional Jet. June 1995 certification. New stage 1 compressor rotor design. Increased hot-day ratings and top climb thrust over CF34-3A1 version.
CF34-8C (twin-shaft turbofan)	12,000-14,000 lbf (53.38-62.28 kN)	Up to 8% improvement over CF34-3A version	b) 19:1			b) 45.59 (1,158)	Proposed for the Canadair CRJ-X. Growth version of the CF34. Provides base for a new engine range in the 13,000-18,000 lbf (57.83-80 kN) class. Airflow 50 lb (22.7 kg) per second. 11-stage compressor. Core ran late 1995.
CJ610 (turbojet)	2,850-3,100 lbf (12.68-13.79 kN) take-off	0.97-0.99 lb/lbf/hr (27.48-28.04 g/kNs)			399-421 (181-191)	a) 45.4-51.1 (1,153-1,298) b) 17.7 (450) flange	Learjet 24/25 series, Bede/Peregrine BD-10 types, and 1123 Westwind.
CT7-2A/C (turboshaft)	1,625 shp (1,212 kW) take-off	0.473 lb/shp/hr (288 g/kW/hr)			442 (200.5)	a) 47 (1,194) b) 26 (660.4) max envelope	Bell 214ST (2A) and S-70C (2C).
CT7-2D/2D1 (turboshaft)	1,625 shp (1,212 kW) take-off	0.473 lb/shp/hr (288 g/kW/hr)			442-466 (200.5-211.4)	a) 47 (1,194) b) 26 (660.4) max envelope	Kamov Ka-62G and S-70C.
CT7-5A (turboprop)	1,735 shp (1,294 kW) take-off, 1,312 shp (978.4 kW) cruise				783 (355)	a) 96 (2,438) b) 29 (736.7)	Saab 340.

Designation (type of engine)	Power output (normally take-off rating for piston, turboprop and turboshaft, unless stated)	Specific Fuel Consumption (S F C)	a) Max RPM b) Pressure or Compression ratio	a) EGT (unless stated to be MGT, TET, TGT or TIT) b) Primary fuel type or Octane rating	Dry weight lb (kg)	a) Length ins (mm) b) Width ins (mm) c) Height ins (mm)	Current aircraft users, and comments
United States of America							
General Electric Aircraft Engines (continued)							
CT7-6/6A/6D (turboshaft)	2,000 shp (1,491.4 kW) take-off	0.47 lb/shp/hr (286 g/kW/hr) max continuous to 15° C			466 (211.4)	a) 47 (1,194) b) 26 (660.4) max envelope	Commercial EH 101 and S-92 (S-92 IV will have CT7-8).
CT7-7A (turboprop)	1,700 shp (1,267.7 kW) take-off, 1,312 shp (978.4 kW) cruise				783 (355)	a) 96 (2,438) b) 29 (736.7)	CN-235.
CT7-9 series (turboprop)	1,750 shp (1,305 kW) take-off, 1,411-1,499 shp (1,052-1,118 kW) cruise				805 (365.1)	a) 96 (2,438) b) 29 (736.7)	CN-235, L-610G and Saab 340. CT7-9B for Sukhoi S-80 of 1,870 shp (1,394.5 kW) maximum. CT7-9D has an Automatic Power Reserve of 1,940 shp (1,446.7 kW), greater than for the 9B/9C.
F101-GE-102 (turbofan with afterburning)	30,780 lbf (136.92 kN)				4,400 (1,996)	a) 181 (4,597) b) 55 (1,397)	B-1B. 2.76 unscheduled engine-caused shop visits per 1,000 flight hours over a 12-month rolling average.
F103-GE-100/101 (twin-shaft turbofan)	52,500 lbf (233.54 kN) to 26° C	0.376 lb/lbf/hr (10.65 g/kNs)	b) 30.1:1	a) 1,330° C	8,490 (3,851)	a) 173 (4,394) c) 105.3 (2,674.5)	767 AWACS, E-4B and KC-10. Military version of the CF6-50E. Powered 59 KC-10As and 4 E-4Bs by June 1994. 0.163 unscheduled engine-caused shop visits per 1,000 flight hours over a 12-month rolling average.
F103-GE-102 (twin-shaft turbofan)	56,700 lbf (252.22 kN)		b) 30.1:1	a) 1,330° C		a) 173 (4,394) c) 105.3 (2,674.5)	VC-25A. No engine-caused shut-downs or unscheduled shop visits by June 1994. Equivalent to the CF6-80C2B1.
F110-GE-100 (twin-shaft turbofan)	28,000 lbf (124.55 kN) with afterburning					a) 181.9 (4,620) b) 46.5 (1,181)	F-16C/D and F-16N. Powered 1,428 aircraft by June 1994, not including those with Israel.
F110-GE-129 (twin-shaft turbofan)	17,000 lbf (75.62 kN) dry, 29,000 lbf (128.93 kN) with afterburning		b) 31:1 approx			a) 181.9 (4,620) b) 46.5 (1,181)	F-16C/D and FS-X. All USAF F-16C/Ds procured in fiscal year 1994 have this engine. Powered 151 aircraft by June 1994, with 1.99 unscheduled engine-caused shop visits per 1,000 flight hours over a 12-month rolling average.
F110-GE-400 (twin-shaft turbofan)	16,000 lbf (71.17 kN) dry, 27,000 lbf (120.1 kN) with afterburning					a) 181.9 (4,620) b) 46.5 (1,181)	F-14B/D. Powered 104 aircraft by June 1994, with 1.11 unscheduled engine-caused shop visits per 1,000 flight hours over a 12-month rolling average.
F118-GE-100 (twin-shaft turbofan)	19,000 lbf (84.518 kN)						B-2A. 93 engines delivered by June 1994.
F118-GE-101 (twin-shaft turbofan)	19,000 lbf (84.518 kN)						U-2S.
F404-GE-400 (twin-shaft turbofan)	16,000 lbf (71.17 kN) with afterburning					a) 158.8 (4,034) b) 34.8 (884)	F/A-18, X-29, X-31A EFM, Super Skyhawk (in non-afterburning 100D form) and Gripen in RM12 form. F404-GE-100D has 11,000 lbf (48.93 kN) rating and no afterburning.
F404-GE-402 (twin-shaft turbofan)	17,700 lbf (78.73 kN) with afterburning		b) 26:1		2,282 (1,035)	a) 158.8 (4,034) b) 34.8 (884)	F/A-18. 0.8 unscheduled engine-caused shop visits per 1,000 flight hours for the whole of the F404 series of engines over a 12-month rolling average. F404s of all models powered 1,119 aircraft by June 1994.
F404-GE-F1D2 (twin-shaft turbofan)	10,800 lbf (48.04 kN). No afterburning					b) 34.8 (884)	F-117A.
F404-GE-F2J3 (twin-shaft turbofan)	18,100 lbf (80.51 kN) with afterburning					a) 158.8 (4,034) b) 34.8 (884)	HAL LCA.
F414-GE-400 (twin-shaft turbofan)	22,000 lbf (97.86 kN) with afterburning						F/A-18E/F. Delivery of first flight-test engines to US Navy in mid-1995, with the first flight late that year. Six development engines had accumulated over 2,200 ground test hours by June 1994. F414 fan provides 16% increased airflow over F404, and the core is based on the F412 turbine design.

Designation (type of engine)	Power output (normally take-off rating for piston, turboprop and turboshaft, unless stated)	Specific Fuel Consumption (S F C)	a) Max RPM b) Pressure or Compression ratio	a) EGT (unless stated to be MGT, TET, TGT or TIT) b) Primary fuel type or Octane rating	Dry weight lb (kg)	a) Length ins (mm) b) Width ins (mm) c) Height ins (mm)	Current aircraft users, and comments
United States of America							
General Electric Aircraft Engines (continued)							
J79-GE-19 (single-shaft turbojet)	11,870 lbf (52.8 kN) dry, 17,900 lbf (79.62 kN) with afterburning	1.98 lb/lbf/hr (55.8 g/kNs) take-off		b) JP-4 and JP-5	3,847 (1,745)	a) 208.69 (5,300) b) 39.06 (992) compressor	Aeritalia F-104S.
J85-GE-5 (single-shaft turbojet)	2,680 lbf (11.92 kN) dry, 3,850 lbf (17.13 kN) with afterburning	1.03 lb/lbf/hr (29.17 g/kNs) dry, 2.2 lb/lbf/hr (62.32 g/kNs) with afterburning			584 (264.9)	a) 104.6 (2,657) incl after-burner b) 21 (533)	T-38 Talon.
J85-GE-21 series (single-shaft turbojet)	3,500 lbf (15.57 kN) dry, 5,000 lbf (22.24 kN) with afterburning	1 lb/lbf/hr (28.325 g/kNs) dry, 2.13 lb/lbf/hr (60.33 g/kNs) with afterburning	b) 8.3:1	a) 977° C TIT	684 (310.25)	a) 112.5 (2,858) incl afterburner b) 21 (533)	F-5E/F and RF-5E.
T64-GE-7A (axial-flow turboshaft with direct drive)	3,936 shp (2,935 kW)	0.466 lb/shp/hr (283 g/kW/hr) maximum	12.5:1		720 (326.6)	a) 79 (2,007) b) 20 (508) max envelope c) 32.5 (825.5)	H-53. Being improved to T64-GE-100 standard.
T64-GE-10 (free-turbine turboprop)	2,970 shp (2,215 kW)	0.5 lb/shp/hr (304 g/kW/hr)	12.5:1		1,167 (529.3)	a) 113 (2,870) c) 46 (1,168)	P-2J and PS/US-1 as the T64-IHI-10 built by Ishikawajima.
T64-GE-100 (axial-flow turboshaft)	4,330 shp (3,229 kW) max at 28° C, military rated at 4,090 shp (3,050 kW)	0.487 lb/shp/hr (296 g/kW/hr) maximum	14:1		720 (326.6)	a) 79 (2,007) b) 20 (508) c) 32.5 (825.5)	CH-53C and MH-53J.
T64-GE-413 (axial-flow turboshaft)	3,925 shp (2,927 kW)	0.466 lb/shp/hr (283 g/kW/hr) maximum	14:1		720 (326.6)	a) 79 (2,007) b) 20 (508) c) 32.5 (825.5)	CH-53D.
T64-GE-415/416/A (axial-flow turboshaft)	4,380 shp (3,266 kW) max at 15° C, military rated at 4,110 shp (3,065 kW)	0.466 lb/shp/hr (283 g/kW/hr) maximum	14:1		720 (326.6)	a) 79 (2,007) b) 20 (508) max envelope c) 32.5 (825.5)	H-53E and RH-53D.
T64-GE-419 (axial-flow turboshaft)	4,750 shp (3,542 kW) max at 15° C, military rated at 4,560 shp (3,400 kW)	0.474 lb/shp/hr (288 g/kW/hr)	14:1		755 (342.5) self-contained lube cooler	a) 79 (2,007) b) 20 (508) max envelope c) 32.5 (825.5)	H-53E retrofit.
T64/P4D (free-turbine turboprop)	3,400 shp (2,535 kW) max take-off, flat rated to 45° C, 2,745 shp (2,047 kW) max continuous	0.484 lb/shp/hr (294 g/kW/hr) take-off	a) 1,260 propeller		1,188 (539)	a) 110.14 (2,798) b) 20.1 (510.5) c) 46 (1,168.5)	G222/C-27A. Power to weight ratio 2.86. Similar to the CT64, which see, and the T64 series of turboshafts.
T700-GE-401 (free-turbine turboshaft)	1,723 shp (1,285 kW) max contingency, 1,437 shp (1,071.5 kW) max continuous	0.471 lb/shp/hr (287 g/kW/hr) max continuous	a) 21,000 output b) 15:1		434 (197)	a) 46 (1,168) b) 25 (635) c) 23 (584)	AH-1W, SH-2G and early SH-60B.
T700-GE-401C (free-turbine turboshaft)	1,940 shp (1,447 kW) max contingency, 1,620 shp (1,208 kW) max continuous	0.459 lb/shp/hr (279 g/kW/hr) max continuous	a) 21,000 output b) 15:1		458 (207.75)	a) 46 (1,168) b) 25 (635) c) 23 (584)	SH-60B, HH-60H and HH-60J Jayhawk.
T700-GE-700 (free-turbine turboshaft)	1,560 shp (1,163 kW), 1,324 shp (987.3 kW) max continuous	0.47 lb/shp/hr (286 g/kW/hr) max continuous	a) 21,000 output b) 15:1		437 (198.2)	a) 46 (1,168) b) 25 (635) c) 23 (584)	UH-60A.
T700-GE-701 (free-turbine turboshaft) For 701A, see Comments	1,723 shp (1,285 kW) max contingency, 1,570 shp (1,170.7 kW) max continuous	0.466 lb/shp/hr (283.5 g/kW/hr) max continuous	a) 21,000 output b) 15:1			a) 46 (1,168) b) 25 (635) c) 23 (584)	AH-64. T700-GE-701A is an alternative for export S-70A.

Designation (type of engine)	Power output (normally take-off rating for piston, turboprop and turboshaft, unless stated)	Specific Fuel Consumption (S F C)	a) Max RPM b) Pressure or Compression ratio	a) EGT (unless stated to be MGT, TET, TGT or TIT) b) Primary fuel type or Octane rating	Dry weight lb (kg)	a) Length ins (mm) b) Width ins (mm) c) Height ins (mm)	Current aircraft users, and comments
United States of America							
General Electric Aircraft Engines (continued)							
T700-GE-701C (free-turbine turboshaft)	1,940 shp (1,447 kW) max contingency, 1,620 shp (1,208 kW) max continuous	0.459 lb/shp/hr (279 g/kW/hr) max continuous	a) 21,000 output b) 15:1		456 (207)	a) 46 (1,168) b) 25 (635) c) 23 (584)	H-60/WS-70L and AH-64D.
T700/T6A (free-turbine turboshaft)	2,040 shp (1,521 kW) max take-off, 1,807 shp (1,348 kW) max continuous						Italian Navy EH 101. Developed by GE, Alfa Romeo Avio and FiatAvio of Italy.
T700/T6E (free-turbine turboshaft)	2,400 shp (1,790 kW)						NH90. Being developed by GE, Alfa Romeo Avio and FiatAvio of Italy, with participation of EGT (UK) and Hamilton Standard (USA). Flight tests from early 1997. Has larger compressor, increasing engine airflow by about 10%. FADEC. Future derivatives could power potential growth versions of the Apache, Black Hawk and S-92.
TF34-GE-100 (twin-shaft turbofan)	9,065 lbf (40.32 kN)	0.37 lb/lbf/hr (10.48 g/kNs)	b) 21:1	a) 1,225° C EGT b) JP-4 and JP-5	1,440 (653.2)	a) 100 (2,540) b) 49 (1,245)	A-10A.
TF34-GE-400 (twin-shaft turbofan)	9,275 lbf (41.26 kN)	0.363 lb/lbf/hr (10.28 g/kNs)	b) 21:1	a) 1,225° C EGT b) JP-4 and JP-5	1,478 (670.4)	a) 100 (2,540) b) 52 (1,321)	S-3B, EA-3A, US-3A and potentially Boeing EX.
TF39-GE-1C (turbofan)	43,000 lbf (191.28 kN)		b) 26:1	a) 871° C LP TIT	7,900 (3,583)	a) 271 (6,883) b) 100 (2,540)	C-5A and C-5B. Powered 104 aircraft by June 1994. 0.166 unscheduled engine-caused shop visits per 1,000 flight hours over a 12-month rolling average.
In-Tech International Inc. 7500 West Park Drive, Spokane, WA 99204-5726							
TDIL 210 (3-cyl, 2-stroke, liquid-cooled, diesel, inline piston)	650 hp (484.7 kW) at 4,800 rpm, 450 hp (335.6 kW) cruise at 3,800 rpm	0.36 lb/hp/hr (219 g/kW/hr)	a) 2,060 propeller b) 15.3:1	a) 816° C b) Jet A, JP-4, diesel	580 (263.1)	a) 50.5 (1,283) b) 18 (457) c) 25.5 (648)	Formerly known as Merlyn.
LHTEC (Light Helicopter Turbine Engine Company) – see Allison-AlliedSignal partnership							
Light Power Engine Corporation. PO Drawer 3350, Morgantown, WV 26503							
ZM 200 Series III-200 (inverted, fuel injected, inline piston, with direct drive)	150 hp (112 kW) at 2,700 rpm				229 (103.9)	a) 39 (991) b) 10 (254) c) 23 (584)	Turbocharged version is the 175 hp (130.5 kW) at 2,700 rpm ZM 200 Series TIII-200.
ZM 400 Series IVG-400 (fuel injected, V piston, with gear reduction drive)	420 hp (313.2 kW) at 4,300 rpm				430 (195)	a) 42 (1,067) b) 21 (533) c) 22 (559)	Inverted, direct drive versions of same dimensions but 370 lb (167.8 kg) dry weight, are the 230 hp (171.5 kW) ZM 400 Series IIV-400A and ZM 400 Series IIV-400 B.
ZM 500 Series IIV-500 (inverted V8, liquid-cooled piston, with direct drive)	320 hp (238.6 kW) at 2,750 rpm. 240 hp (179 kW) cruise at 2,400 rpm	0.39 lb/hp/hr (237 g/kW/hr)	a) 2,750 b) 10.2:1	b) 100 LL	480 (217.7)	a) 43.8 (1,113) b) 24 (610) c) 27 (686)	Turbocharged version is the TIIV-500, weighing 490 lb (222.3 kg) dry and offering 320 hp (238.6 kW) at 2,700 rpm.
ZM 500 Series IVG-500A (fuel injected, V piston, with gear reduction drive)	450 hp (335.6 kW) at 4,300 rpm				550 (249.5)	a) 43.8 (1,113) b) 23 (584) c) 24 (610)	Similar IVG-500B offers 500 hp (373 kW) at 4,500 rpm.
ZM 500 Series TIVG-500 (turbocharged, fuel injected, V piston, with gear reduction drive)	500 hp (373 kW) at 4,300 rpm				550 (249.5)	a) 53 (1,346) b) 23 (584) c) 24 (610)	
ZM 500 Series IIV-560 (inverted, fuel injected, V piston, with direct drive)	350 hp (261 kW) at 2,700 rpm				480 (217.7)	a) 43.8 (1,113) b) 24 (610) c) 24 (610)	

Designation (type of engine)	Power output (normally take-off rating for piston, turboprop and turboshaft, unless stated)	Specific Fuel Consumption (S F C)	a) Max RPM b) Pressure or Compression ratio	a) EGT (unless stated to be MGT, TET, TGT or TIT) b) Primary fuel type or Octane rating	Dry weight lb (kg)	a) Length ins (mm) b) Width ins (mm) c) Height ins (mm)	Current aircraft users, and comments
United States of America							
Light Power Engine Corporation (continued)							
ZM 500 Series IVG-560 (fuel injected, V piston, with gear reduction drive)	560 hp (417.6 kW) at 4,500 rpm				560 (254)	a) 43.8 (1,113) b) 23 (584) c) 24 (610)	
ZM 600 Series IVG-600 (fuel injected, V piston, with gear reduction drive)	600 hp (447.4 kW) at 4,500 rpm				562 (255)	a) 43.8 (1,113) b) 23 (584) c) 24 (610)	The turbocharged variant is the TIVG-600, of similar power output, 580 lb (263 kg) weight, and 53 ins (1,346 mm) length.
ZM 600 Series TIIV-600 (turbocharged, inverted, fuel injected, liquid-cooled, V8 piston, with direct drive)	380 hp (283.4 kW) at 2,750 rpm. 285 hp (212.5 kW) cruise at 2,400 rpm		a) 2,750 b) 10.2:1	b) 100 LL	496 (225)	a) 43.8 (1,113) b) 24 (610) c) 27 (686)	Express. The non-turbocharged version is the IIV-600 of 380 hp (283.4 kW) at 2,700 rpm, with dry weight of 486 lb (220.4 kg), and width and height of 25 ins (635 mm) and 24 ins (610 mm) respectively.
ZM 600 Series TIIV-650 (turbocharged, inverted, fuel injected, liquid-cooled, V8 piston, with direct drive)	500 hp (373 kW) at 2,750 rpm, 375 hp (279.6 kW) cruise at 2,400 rpm	0.39 lb/hp/hr (237 g/kW/hr)	a) 2,750 rated hp, 3,200 max b) 10.2:1	b) 100 LL	536 (243)	a) 43.8 (1,113) b) 24 (610) c) 27 (686)	Lancair IV, Cirrus, Glasair III. Non-turbocharged version is the IIV-650 of 450 hp (335.6 kW) at 2,700 rpm, with dry weight of 506 lb (229.5 kg), and width 25 ins (635 mm).
ZM 600 Series TGIIV-650 (turbocharged, inverted, fuel injected, liquid-cooled, V piston)	650 hp (484.7 kW) at 4,300 rpm (propeller 2,750 rpm), 480 hp (358 kW) cruise at 3,100 rpm	0.39 lb/hp/hr (237 g/kW/hr)	a) 2,750 b) 10.2:1	b) 100 LL	613 (278) with all connections and accessories, ready to run	a) 43.8 (1,113) b) 24 (610) c) 27 (686)	Cirrus.
Moller International. 1222 Research Park Drive, Davis, CA 95616							
MR 530 PA and PL (single rotor, piston)	75 hp (55.9 kW)	0.6 lb/hp/hr (365 g/kW/hr)	a) 7,500 b) 8.9:1		78 (35.4) for 530 PA and 52 (23.6) for 530 PL	a) 11 (279) b) 11 (279) for 530 PA and 10 (254) for 530 PL c) 10 (254) for 530 PA and 9 (229) for 530 PL	530 cc. PA is air cooled, PL is liquid cooled.
MR 1060 PL (twin rotor, liquid-cooled, piston)	160 hp (119 kW)	0.6 lb/hp/hr (365 g/kW/hr)	a) 7,500 b) 8.9:1		74 (33.6)	a) 15 (381) b) 10 (254) c) 9 (229)	Moller Skycar. Produces more than 1.5 hp per pound weight. Ducted fan VTOL application. Round shape and small size allow it to be placed in the centre of the duct behind the fan hub where it directly drives the fan without a gearbox. Low rate initial production late 1995.
Mosler Motors Inc. 140 Ashwood Road, Hendersonville, NC 28739							
Range of piston engines (4-stroke and air-cooled)	40-82 hp (29.8-61 kW)						Users include Kitfox with a 65 hp (48.5 kW) Mosler 65X.
NSI Propulsion Systems LLC. 19132 59th Drive NE, Arlington, WA 98223							
NSI/Suber EA81-98-TBI (1,800 cc, 4-cyl, 4-stroke, water/ethylene glycol-cooled piston, based on Subaru EA81 auto engine)	98 hp (73 kW) at 5,200 rpm continuous	0.49 lb/hp/hr (298 g/kW/hr) at 5,043 rpm continuous		b) all auto and aviation grades	212 (96.2)*	a) 23 (584) mount to prop flange b) 27 (686) c) 15.5 (394) minus exhaust	Approved for Kitfox Models III/IV, Speedster, Vixen, Murphy Rebel, Glastar, Cessna 120/140/150/152, and Zodiac 601/90. Components available for DIY conversion of Subaru engines. Not certified. *Includes exhaust muffler and tailpipes, mounts, wiring harness and more. 58 EA81s sold by November 1994 plus many individual kits. Complete engine package US$7,950; firewall forward propulsion system US$10,660 in 1995.
NSI/Suber EA81-118-TBI (as above)	118 hp (88 kW) at 5,800 rpm	0.51 lb/hp/hr (310 g/kW/hr) continuous at 5,800 rpm		b) auto unleaded premium or aviation 90 or 100 LL	214 (97.1)*	a) 23 (584) mount to prop flange b) 27 (686) c) 15.5 (394) minus exhaust	Aircraft and other details as above*. Not certified. Complete engine package US$8,950; firewall forward propulsion system US$12,160 in 1995.
NSI/Suber Turbo EA81-120-EFI (as above, based on Turbo Subaru EA81)	120 hp (89.5 kW) at 4,800 rpm continuous	0.44 lb/hp/hr (268 g/kW/hr) cruise at 3,800 rpm, estimated		b) all auto and aviation grades	222 (100.7)*	a) 23 (584) b) 27 (686) c) 20 (508)	Aircraft as above. Not certified. *Includes stainless steel exhaust pipe, mounts, wiring harness and more. Complete engine package US$9,850; firewall forward propulsion system US$12,850 in 1995.

Designation (type of engine)	Power output (normally take-off rating for piston, turboprop and turboshaft, unless stated)	Specific Fuel Consumption (S F C)	a) Max RPM b) Pressure or Compression ratio	a) EGT (unless stated to be MGT, TET, TGT or TIT) b) Primary fuel type or Octane rating	Dry weight lb (kg)	a) Length ins (mm) b) Width ins (mm) c) Height ins (mm)	Current aircraft users, and comments
United States of America							
NSI Propulsion Systems LLC (continued)							
NSI/Suber EJ22-160-EFI (2,200 cc, 4-cyl, 4-stroke, water/ ethylene glycol-cooled piston, based on Subaru EJ22)	160 hp (119.3 kW) at 5,500 rpm	0.4 lb/hp/hr (243 g/kW/hr) cruise at 4,200 rpm estimated		b) all auto and aviation grades	272 (123.4)*	a) 25 (635) b) 29 (737) c) 16.5 (419) minus muffler	Aircraft as above. Not certified. *Includes exhaust muffler and tailpipes, mounts, wiring harness and more. Complete engine package US$10,950; firewall forward propulsion system US$14,500 in 1995. Production engines shipped from February 1995.
NSI/Suber Turbo EJ22-200-EFI (as above, with turbocharger)	200 hp (149 kW) at 5,200 rpm and 6,000 ft above sea level	0.4 lb/hp/hr (243 g/kW/hr) cruise at 3,800 rpm estimated		b) all auto and aviation grades	284 (128.8)*	a) 25 (635) b) 29 (737) c) 17.75 (451)	Aircraft as above. Not certified. *Includes stainless steel exhaust pipe, mounts, wiring harness and more. Complete engine package US$13,950; firewall forward propulsion system US$16,950 in 1995. Production engines shipped from April 1995.
Pop's Props. 331 Avenue F - Hilltop, Bloomington, IL 61704							
Volkswagen conversion (2-cyl opposed)		5.7 litres per hour	a) 3,450 b) 7.1:1	b) 92 Octane	86 (39)	a) 16 (406) b) 30 (762) c) 14 (356)	For light and ultralight aircraft. Plans built only (plans US$19.95).
Pratt & Whitney. 400 Main Street, East Hartford, CT 06108							
F100-PW-100 (twin-shaft turbofan)	14,670 lbf (65.26 kN) dry, 23,770 lbf (105.74 kN) with afterburning		b) 25:1	a) 1,399° C MGT	3,033 (1,376)	a) 191.2 (4,855) without spinner b) 46.5 (1,181)	F-15. Original P&W designation JTF22.
F100-PW-200 (twin-shaft turbofan)	14,590 lbf (64.9 kN) dry, 23,770 lbf (105.74 kN) with afterburning	2.17 lb/lbf/hr (61.47 g/kNs) max power	b) 25:1	a) 1,399° C MGT b) JP-4, JP-5, JP-8, Jet A	3,234 (1,467)	a) 191 (4,851) without spinner b) 46.5 (1,181) c) 46.5 (1,181)	F-15 and F-16.
F100-PW-220 (twin-shaft turbofan)	14,590 lbf (64.9 kN) dry, 23,770 lbf (105.74 kN) with afterburning		b) 25:1	a) 1,399° C MGT b) P-4, JP-5, JP-8, Jet A	3,200 (1,452)	a) 191 (4,851) without spinner b) 46.5 (1,181) c) 46.5 (1,181)	F-15 and F-16.
F100-PW-220E (twin-shaft turbofan)	14,590 lbf (64.9 kN) dry, 23,770 lbf (105.74 kN) with afterburning		b) 25:1	b) P-4, JP-5, JP-8, Jet A	3,151 (1,429)	a) 191 (4,851) without spinner b) 46.5 (1,181) c) 46.5 (1,181)	First of two improvement programmes underway by retrofit for existing USAF F100-PW-100 and 200 engines to bring them to F100-PW-220 standard.
F100-PW-220P (twin-shaft turbofan)	16,700 lbf (74.287 kN) dry, 27,000 lbf (120.1 kN) with afterburning			b) P-4, JP-5, JP-8, Jet A	3,365 (1,526.33)	a) 191 (4,851) without spinner b) 46.5 (1,181) c) 46.5 (1,181)	Further planned upgrade version to introduce F100-PW-229 features.
F100-PW-229 (twin-shaft turbofan)	17,800 lbf (79.18 kN) dry, 29,100 lbf (129.445 kN) with afterburning	2.05 lb/lbf/hr (58.07 g/kNs)	b) 32:1	b) P-4, JP-5, JP-8, Jet A	3,740 (1,696)	a) 191 (4,851) without spinner b) 46.5 (1,181) c) 46.5 (1,181)	F-15 and F-16.
F117-PW-100 (twin-spool turbofan)	41,700 lbf (185.5 kN) take-off flat rated to 30.6° C, 35,330 lbf (157.16 kN) max continuous, 8,250 lbf (36.7 kN) cruise at ISA+10° C	0.5998 lb/lbf/hr (16.99 g/kNs)	b) 30.8:1	a) 1,425° C combustor exit temperature	7,100 (3,221)	a) 141.4 (3,592) flange to flange, 146.8 (3,729) spinner tip to flange b) 84.5 (2,146) c) 84.5 (2,146)	C-5 and C-17. Military variant of the PW2040.
New F117 (provisionally PW2643 commercial designation)	43,000 lbf (191.28 kN)						
F119-PW-100 (twin-spool, counter-rotating, low-bypass ratio, axial-flow turbofan)	Dry rating classified, 35,000 lbf (155.69 kN) class with afterburning	classified	classified	a) classified b) JP-8	classified	a) classified b) classified c) classified	F-22, and also Lockheed Martin X-32 in 30,000 lbf (133.45 kN) F119-PW-220+ form. Fitted with 2D convergent/divergent exhaust nozzles (±20°) with independent throat and exit area actuation and pitch-axis thrust vectoring. Offers high supersonic speed without afterburning.

Designation (type of engine)	Power output (normally take-off rating for piston, turboprop and turboshaft, unless stated)	Specific Fuel Consumption (S F C)	a) Max RPM b) Pressure or Compression ratio	a) EGT (unless stated to be MGT, TET, TGT or TIT) b) Primary fuel type or Octane rating	Dry weight lb (kg)	a) Length ins (mm) b) Width ins (mm) c) Height ins (mm)	Current aircraft users, and comments
United States of America							
Pratt & Whitney (continued)							
J52-P-408/408A (twin-spool turbojet)	11,200 lbf (49.82 kN)				2,318 (1,051)	a) 118.9 (3,020) b) 32.06 (814)	EA-6B Prowler and A-4 Skyhawk respectively.
J52-P-409 (twin-spool turbojet)	12,000 lbf (53.38 kN)						EA-6B Prowler re-engined under the ADVCAP improvement programme. This engine is still offered.
JT3D-3/3B (turbofan variant of J57)	18,000 lbf (80.07 kN)	0.535 lb/lbf/hr (15.15 g/kNs)	b) 13:1		4,340 (1,969)	a) 137 (3,479) b) 53.14 (1,350)	DC-8-50, Super 61/62, and E-8C.
JT8D-209 (twin-spool turbofan)	18,500 lbf (82.29 kN) to 25° C take-off, 4,945 lbf (22 kN) cruise at 35,000 ft and Mach 0.8	0.724 lb/lbf/hr (20.51 g/kNs) cruise	b) 17.4:1		4,533 lb (2,056)	a) 154.2 (3,917) b) 49.2 (1,250)	DC-9 Super 81 and MD-81. Derived from the previous JT8D-9 but with advanced low-pressure compressor features. OEI rating 19,250 lbf (85.63 kN).
JT8D-217/217A/217C (twin-spool turbofan)	20,000 lbf (88.97 kN) normal take-off, rated up to 25° C for -217 and 29° C for -217A, 18,000 lbf (80 kN) max continuous	0.51 lb/lbf/hr (14.45 g/kNs) take-off	b) 18.6:1		4,470 (2,028)	a) 154.2 (3,917) b) 49.2 (1,250)	DC-9 Super 82, MD-82 and MD-88. JT8D-217A take-off power up to 29° C or 5,000 ft. OEI rating of 20,850 lbf (92.75 kN) to 28.9° C. Cruise rating of 5,240 lbf (23.31 kN) at 35,000 ft and Mach 0.8.
JT8D-217C (twin-spool turbofan)	20,000 lbf (88.97 kN) take-off, 5,240 lbf (23.31 kN) cruise at 35,000 ft and Mach 0.8	0.736 lb/lbf/hr (20.85 g/kNs)	b) 18.6:1		4,612 (2,092)	a) 154.2 (3,917) b) 49.2 (1,250) fan tip	MD-82 and MD-87.
JT8D-218B (twin-spool turbofan)						a) 154.2 (3,917) b) 49.2 (1,250) fan tip	Development initiated in March 1994, offering improved environmental performance and durability.
JT8D-219 (twin-spool turbofan)	21,000 lbf (93.41 kN)	0.737 lb/lbf/hr (20.88 g/kNs)	b) 19.2:1		4,612 (2,092)	a) 154.2 (3,917) b) 49.2 (1,250) fan tip	MD-80ADV, MD-83 and MD-88. OEI rating 21,700 lbf (96.53 kN). 2% reduction in fuel burn than JT8D-217A.
JT9D-7R4 series (twin-shaft turbofan)	48,000-56,000 lbf (213.52-249.1 kN) take-off without water injection, 11,250-12,250 lbf (50.04-54.49 kN) cruise at above conditions	0.615-0.639 lb/lbf/hr (17.42-18.1 g/kNs)	b) 23.4-26.7	a) up to 1,300° C TIT	8,905-9,135 (4,039-4,144)	a) 132.7 (3,370) b) 97 (2,464)	A300-600 (highest power version original launch engine), A310 (launch engine) and alternative choice for 767.
JT9D-70A series (twin-shaft turbofan)	53,000 lbf (235.76 kN) take-off to 30° C without water injection, 11,950 lbf (53.16 kN) cruise at above conditions	0.631 lb/lbf/hr (17.87 g/kNs)	b) 24.5:1	a) up to 1,370° C	9,155 (4,152)	a) 132.2 (3,357) b) 97 (2,464)	747.
PW2037 (twin-shaft turbofan)	38,250 lbf (170.1 kN) take-off, flat-rated to 30.6° C, 35,330 lbf (157.16 kN) max continuous, 8,250 lbf (36.7 kN) cruise at ISA +10° C	0.342 lb/lbf/hr (9.69 g/kNs) take off (sea level static TSFC)	b) 27:1	a) 1,405° C combustor exit temperature	7,300 (3,311)	a) 141.4 (3,592) flange to flange, 146.8 (3,729) spinner tip to flange b) 78.5 (1,994) fan tip, 84.8 (2,154) fan inlet case flange	757-200. Introduced FADEC technology to commercial aviation. New performance improvement configuration is the first to use second-generation single crystal turbine blades. Approved for 180 minutes ETOPS.
PW2040 (twin-shaft turbofan)	41,700 lbf (185.5 kN) take-off flat rated to 30.6° C, 35,330 lbf (157.16 kN) max continuous, 8,250 lbf (36.7 kN) cruise at ISA +10° C	0.352 lb/lbf/hr (9.97 g/kNs) (sea level static TSFC)	b) 28:1	a) 1,425° C combustor exit temperature	7,300 (3,311)	a) 141.4 (3,592) flange to flange, 146.8 (3,729) spinner tip to flange b) 78.5 (1,994) fan tip, 84.8 (2,154) fan inlet case flange	757.

Designation (type of engine)	Power output (normally take-off rating for piston, turboprop and turboshaft, unless stated)	Specific Fuel Consumption (S F C)	a) Max RPM b) Pressure or Compression ratio	a) EGT (unless stated to be MGT, TET, TGT or TIT) b) Primary fuel type or Octane rating	Dry weight lb (kg)	a) Length ins (mm) b) Width ins (mm) c) Height ins (mm)	Current aircraft users, and comments
United States of America							
Pratt & Whitney (continued)							
PW2337 (twin-shaft turbofan)	38,250 lbf (170.1 kN) take-off	0.565 lb/lbf/hr (15.95 g/kNs)	b) 27.6-31.8	a) 1,405° C combustor exit temperature	7,300 (3,311)	a) 141.4 (3,592) flange to flange, 146.8 (3,729) spinner tip to flange b) 78.5 (1,994) fan tip, 84.8 (2,154) fan inlet case flange	Il-96M.
PW2643 (twin-shaft turbofan)	43,000 lbf (191.28 kN)						New military F117 engine.
PW4050 (twin-spool turbofan)	50,000 lbf (222.42 kN) take-off, 48,120 lbf (214.05 kN) max continuous	0.348 lb/lbf/hr (9.86 g/kNs) take-off (sea level static TSFC)	b) 26.3:1		9,213 (4,179)	a) 153.6 (3,901) b) 96.98 (2,463)	767-200/200ER. PW4000 series is 180 minutes ETOPS approved with FADEC for 767, A300 and A310. Basic dispatch reliability for PW4000 series is 99.88%.
PW4052 (twin-spool turbofan)	52,200 lbf (232.2 kN) to 33.3° C, 49,820 lbf (221.61 kN) max continuous	0.351 lb/lbf/hr (9.94 g/kNs) take-off (sea level static TSFC)	b) 27.5		9,213 (4,179)	a) 153.6 (3,901) b) 96.98 (2,463)	767-200/200ER.
PW4056 (twin-spool turbofan)	56,750 lbf (252.4 kN) take-off to 33.3° C in the Boeing 747, 56,000 lbf (249.1 kN) take-off in the Boeing 767	0.359 lb/lbf/hr (10.17 g/kNs) take-off (sea level static TSFC)	b) 29.7:1		9,213 (4,179)	a) 153.6 (3,901) b) 96.98 (2,463)	747-400, 767-200/200ER/300/300ER.
PW4060 (twin-spool turbofan)	60,000 lbf (266.9 kN) take-off to 33.3° C, 50,250 lbf (223.53 kN) max continuous	0.365 lb/lbf/hr (10.34 g/kNs) take-off (sea level static TSFC)	b) 31.2:1		9,213 (4,179)	a) 153.6 (3,901) b) 96.98 (2,463)	747 and 767-200ER/300ER.
PW4062 (twin-spool turbofan)	62,000 lbf (275.8 kN) to 30° C		b) 27.5-32.3:1 for PW4000 series		9,400 (4,264) for PW4000 series	a) 132.7 (3,371) for PW4000 series b) 94 (2,388) fan tip	747 and 767.
PW4074 (twin-spool turbofan)	74,000 lbf (329.17 kN) to 30° C		b) 34.2:1			a) 191.7 (4,869) b) 112 (2,845)	777.
PW4077 (twin-spool turbofan)	77,000 lbf (342.52 kN)		b) 34.2:1			a) 191.7 (4,869) b) 112 (2,845)	777.
PW4084 (twin-spool turbofan)	84,000 lbf (373.66 kN) to 30°C (see comments)		b) 34.2:1		14,700 (6,667)	a) 191.7 (4,869) b) 112 (2,845)	777. Certified April 1994. Programme for 90,000 lbf (400.35 kN) variant announced. Growth potential for 100,000 lbf (444.83 kN); first run at 90,000 lbf (400.35 kN) on a 777 on 29 September 1994. ETOPS capable at entry into service from June 1995.
PW4090 (twin-spool turbofan)	90,000 lbf (400.35 kN)		b) 34.2:1			a) 191.7 (4,869) b) 112 (2,845)	B model and A stretch 777. Programme begun in 1994 to certify this engine by mid-1996.
PW4152 (twin-spool turbofan)	52,000 lbf (231.3 kN) take-off, 49,200 lbf (218.86 kN) max continuous	0.348 lb/lbf/hr (9.86 g/kNs) take-off (sea level static TSFC)	b) 27.1:1		9,332 (4,233)		A310-200/300.
PW4156A (twin-spool turbofan)	56,000 lbf (249.1 kN) take-off to 30° C, 50,000 lbf (222.45 kN) max continuous	0.359 lb/lbf/hr (10.17 g/kNs) take-off (sea level static TSFC)	b) 29.7:1		9,332 (4,233)		A300-600 and A310-300.
PW4158 (twin-spool turbofan)	58,000 lbf (258 kN) take-off to 30° C, 50,000 lbf (222.45 kN) max continuous	0.365 lb/lbf/hr (10.34 g/kNs) take-off (sea level static TSFC)	b) 31:1		9,332 (4,233)		A300-600/600R.

Designation (type of engine)	Power output (normally take-off rating for piston, turboprop and turboshaft, unless stated)	Specific Fuel Consumption (S F C)	a) Max RPM b) Pressure or Compression ratio	a) EGT (unless stated to be MGT, TET, TGT or TIT) b) Primary fuel type or Octane rating	Dry weight lb (kg)	a) Length ins (mm) b) Width ins (mm) c) Height ins (mm)	Current aircraft users, and comments
United States of America							
Pratt & Whitney (continued)							
PW4164 (twin-spool turbofan)	64,000 lbf (284.7 kN)						A330.
PW4168 (twin-spool turbofan)	68,000 lbf (302.48 kN) to 30° C		b) 32:1		11,700 (5,307)	a) 163.1 (4,143) b) 100 (2,540) fan tip	A330. Growth potential to 74,000 lbf (329.17 kN).
PW4460 (twin-spool turbofan)	60,000 lbf (266.9 kN) take-off to 30° C, 50,300 lbf (223.75 kN) max continuous	0.37 lb/lbf/hr (10.48 g/kNs)	b) 32.3:1		9,332 (4,233)		MD-11.
PW4462 (twin-spool turbofan)	62,000 lbf (275.8 kN) to 30° C		b) 27.5-32.3:1 for PW4000 series				MD-11.
TF33-P-3 (military designation of the JT3D-2 turbofan)	17,000 lbf (75.62 kN)	0.52 lb/lbf/hr (14.73 g/kNs)			3,900 (1,769)	a) 137 (3,479) b) 53.14 (1,350)	B-52H.
TF33-PW-100/100A (military designation of the JT3D-8B turbofan)	21,000 lbf (93.41 kN)	0.56 lb/lbf/hr (15.86 g/kNs)	b) 15.6:1		4,790 (2,173)	a) 142 (3,607) b) 54.06 (1,373)	E-3B/C Sentry.
Ross Manufacturing. Tucson, AZ							
Mazda 13B (RX-7 rotary auto engine conversion)	180 hp (134kW)				265 (120.3) with accessories		Weight quoted includes the propeller speed reduction unit.
RotorWay International. 4141 W. Chandler Boulevard, Chandler, AZ 85226							
RI 162F (4-cyl horizontally opposed piston)	150 hp (111.9 kW) at 4,250 rpm		b) 9.4:1	b) 92 Octane premium unleaded auto fuel	180 (81.6)	a) 30 (762) b) 21 (533) c) 21 (533)	Exec 162F. Incorporates FADEC.
Sport Plane Products Inc. 420 Harbor Drive, Naples, FL 33940							
Nelson H63C (4-cyl, 2-stroke, air-cooled piston)	43 hp (32 kW) take-off and cruise (2 hp, 1.49 kW used by cooling fan)	17 litres per hour	a) 4,000 b) 8:1		83 (37.6)*	a) 20 (508) b) 23.8 (604.5) c) 14.8 (376)	Light helicopter. *With Kevlar and carbon shrouds, saving 3 lb (1.36 kg) weight. Sport Plane Products Inc is the exclusive distributer of Nelson Engines.
Nelson H63CP (4-cyl, 2-stroke, air-cooled piston)	48 hp (36 kW) take-off, 45 hp (33.6 kW) cruise	23.5 litres per hour maximum power, 16 litres per hour cruise	a) 4,400 take-off, 4,000 cruise b) 8:1		68 (31)		Light aeroplane version of the previous engine.
Nelson H63CP twin installation (see Comments)	96 hp (71.6 kW) take-off, 90 hp (67 kW) cruise		a) 2,400 take-off for propeller shaft	b) 80-90 Octane lead-free auto fuel	200 (91)* including adjustable-pitch propeller		Twin engine installation driving a single propeller, to fit or be adapted to standard engine cowlings for up to 125 hp (93.2 kW) installations. Initial installation in a Glastar. First displayed at the July-August 1995 Oshkosh Fly-In. *Including adjustable-pitch propeller.
Teledyne Continental Motors. PO Box 90, Mobile, Alabama 36601							
O-200 (4-cyl, horizontally-opposed, air-cooled piston with direct drive)	100 hp (74.6 kW) at 2,750 rpm max continuous		b) 7.0:1	b) 80/87	188 (85.3)	a) 28.5 (724) b) 31.56 (802) c) 23.18 (589)	Cessna 150, Champion Lancer, Taylorcraft F19. Bore 4.06 ins (103.1 mm); stroke 3.87 ins (98.3 mm).
IO-240-A (4-cyl, horizontally-opposed, air-cooled piston with direct drive)	125 hp (93.2 kW) take-off at 2,800 rpm (+5%, -0%), 94 hp (70.1 kW) recommended cruise at 2,550 rpm		b) 8.5:1	b) 100/100 LL	246 (111.6) with standard equipment	a) 30.3 (770) b) 31.4 (798) c) 23.5 (597)	Bore 4.44 ins (112.8 mm); stroke 3.87 ins (98.3 mm); displacement 240 cu ins. Dual magnetos ignition.
O-300-A/C/D (6-cyl, horizontally-opposed piston with direct drive)	145 hp (108 kW) at 2,700 rpm max continuous		b) 7.0:1	b) 80/87	270 (122.5) for A/C and 272 (123.4) for D.	a) 39.75 (1,010) for A/C b) 31.5 (800) c) 23.25 (591) for A/C	Bore 4.06 ins (103.1 mm); stroke 3.87 ins (98.3 mm). Length for O-300-D is 36 ins (914 mm) and height is 27 ins (686 mm).

Designation (type of engine)	Power output (normally take-off rating for piston, turboprop and turboshaft, unless stated)	Specific Fuel Consumption (S F C)	a) Max RPM b) Pressure or Compression ratio	a) EGT (unless stated to be MGT, TET, TGT or TIT) b) Primary fuel type or Octane rating	Dry weight lb (kg)	a) Length ins (mm) b) Width ins (mm) c) Height ins (mm)	Current aircraft users, and comments
United States of America							
Teledyne Continental Motors (continued)							
IO-360-A/AB/C/CB/D/DB (6-cyl, horizontally-opposed, air-cooled piston with direct drive)	210 hp (156.6 kW) at 2,800 rpm max continuous		b) 8.5:1	b) 100/100 LL	294 (133.4)	a) 34.6 (879) b) 31.4 (798) c) 24.33 (618)	Cessna 337 and Cessna 172 XP for IO-360 series. Bore 4.44 ins (112.8 mm); stroke 3.87 ins (98.3 mm).
IO-360-ES (6-cyl, horizontally-opposed, air-cooled piston with direct drive)	210 hp (156.6 kW) take-off at 2,800 rpm (+5%, -0%), 157 hp (117 kW) recommended cruise at 2,500 rpm		b) 8.5:1	b) 100/100 LL	330 (149.7) with standard equipment	a) 36.32 (922.5) b) 33.05 (839.5) c) 26.22 (666)	Bore 4.44 ins (112.8 mm); stroke 3.87 ins (98.3 mm); displacement 360 cu ins. TCM dual magnetos ignition.
IO-360-G/GB/H/HB/J/JB/K/KB (6-cyl, horizontally-opposed, air-cooled piston with direct drive)	210 hp (156.6 kW) take-off at 2,800 rpm, 195 hp (145.4 kW) at 2,600 rpm max continuous		b) 8.5:1	b) 100/100 LL	294 (133.4)	a) 34.6 (879) b) 31.4 (798) c) 24.33 (618)	Bore 4.44 ins (112.8 mm); stroke 3.87 ins (98.3 mm).
TSIO-360-A/AB (6-cyl, horizontally-opposed, air-cooled, turbo-charged piston with direct drive)	210 hp (156.6 kW) at 2,800 rpm max continuous		b) 7.5:1	b) 100/100 LL	300 (136)	a) 35.84 (910) b) 33.03 (839) c) 23.75 (603)	Cessna T337, Mooney 231/252, Piper Seneca and Turbo Arrow for TSIO-360 series. Bore 4.44 ins (112.8 mm); stroke 3.87 ins (98.3 mm).
TSIO-360-C/CB (as above)	225 hp (167.8 kW) at 2,800 rpm max continuous		b) 7.5:1	b) 100/100 LL	300 (136)	a) 35.84 (910) b) 33.03 (839) c) 23.75 (603)	Bore 4.44 ins (112.8 mm); stroke 3.87 ins (98.3 mm).
TSIO-360-D/DB (6-cyl, horizontally-opposed, air-cooled, turbo-charged piston with direct drive)	225 hp (167.8 kW) at 2,800 rpm max continuous		b) 7.5:1	b) 100/100 LL	278 (126)	a) 34.6 (879) b) 31.4 (798) c) 24.33 (618)	Bore 4.44 ins (112.8 mm); stroke 3.87 ins (98.3 mm).
L/TSIO-360-E/EB (as above)	200 hp (149 kW) at 2,575 rpm max continuous		b) 7.5:1	b) 100/100 LL	352 (159.7)	a) 56.58 (1,437) b) 31.4 (798) c) 26.44 (672)	Bore 4.44 ins (112.8 mm); stroke 3.87 ins (98.3 mm).
TSIO-360-F/FB (as above)	200 hp (149 kW) at 2,575 rpm max continuous		b) 7.5:1	b) 100/100 LL	359 (162.8)	a) 56.58 (1,437) b) 31.3 (795) c) 26.44 (672)	Bore 4.44 ins (112.8 mm); stroke 3.87 ins (98.3 mm).
TSIO-360-GB/LB (as above)	210 hp (156.6 kW) at 2,700 rpm max continuous		b) 7.5:1	b) 100/100 LL	354 (160.6)	a) 33.57 (853) b) 33.88 (861) c) 31.9 (810)	Bore 4.44 ins (112.8 mm); stroke 3.87 ins (98.3 mm).
TSIO-360-MB (as above)	210 hp (156.6 kW) at 2,700 rpm max continuous		b) 7.5:1	b) 100/100 LL	412 (186.9)	a) 42.78 (1,087) b) 35.78 (909) c) 32.93 (836)	Bore 4.44 ins (112.8 mm); stroke 3.87 ins (98.3 mm).
TSIO-360-H/HB (as above)	210 hp (156.6 kW) at 2,800 rpm max continuous		b) 7.5:1	b) 100/100 LL	313 (142)	a) 35.34 (898) b) 31.38 (797) c) 22.43 (570)	Bore 4.44 ins (112.8 mm); stroke 3.87 ins (98.3 mm).
L/TSIO-360-KB (as above)	220 hp (164 kW) at 2,800 rpm max continuous		b) 7.5:1	b) 100/100 LL	359 (162.8)	a) 56.58 (1,437) b) 31.3 (795) c) 26.44 (672)	Bore 4.44 ins (112.8 mm); stroke 3.87 ins (98.3 mm).
O-470-G (6-cyl, horizontally-opposed piston with direct drive)	240 hp (179 kW) at 2,600 rpm max continuous		b) 8.0:1	b) 91/96	431 (195.5)	a) 37.56 (954) b) 33.58 (853) c) 26.69 (678)	Bore 5 ins (127 mm); stroke 4 ins (102 mm).
O-470-J (as above)	225 hp (167.8 kW) at 2,550 rpm max continuous		b) 7.0:1	b) 80/87	380 (172.4)	a) 36.03 (915) b) 33.32 (846) c) 27.75 (705)	Bore 5 ins (127 mm); stroke 4 ins (102 mm).
O-470-K/L (as above)	230 hp (171.5 kW) at 2,600 rpm max continuous		b) 7.0:1	b) 80/87	404 (183.25)	a) 36.03 (915) b) 33.56 (852) c) 27.75 (705)	Bore 5 ins (127 mm); stroke 4 ins (102 mm).

Designation (type of engine)	Power output (normally take-off rating for piston, turboprop and turboshaft, unless stated)	Specific Fuel Consumption (S F C)	a) Max RPM b) Pressure or Compression ratio	a) EGT (unless stated to be MGT, TET, TGT or TIT) b) Primary fuel type or Octane rating	Dry weight lb (kg)	a) Length ins (mm) b) Width ins (mm) c) Height ins (mm)	Current aircraft users, and comments
United States of America							
Teledyne Continental Motors (continued)							
O-470-M (as above)	240 hp (179 kW) at 2,600 rpm max continuous		b) 8.0:1	b) 91/96	409 (185.5)	a) 43.31 (1,100) b) 33.56 (852) c) 19.62 (498)	Bore 5 ins (127 mm); stroke 4 ins (102 mm).
O-470-R (as above)	230 hp (171.5 kW) at 2,600 rpm max continuous		b) 7.0:1	b) 80/87	401 (181.9)	a) 36.03 (915) b) 33.56 (852) c) 28.42 (722)	Bore 5 ins (127 mm); stroke 4 ins (102 mm).
O-470-S (as above)	230 hp (171.5 kW) at 2,600 rpm max continuous		b) 7.0:1	b) 100/100 LL	412 (186.9)	a) 36.03 (915) b) 33.56 (852) c) 28.42 (722)	Bore 5 ins (127 mm); stroke 4 ins (102 mm).
O-470-U (as above)	230 hp (171.5 kW) at 2,400 rpm max continuous		b) 8.6:1	b) 100/100 LL	412 (186.9)	a) 36.03 (915) b) 33.56 (852) c) 28.42 (722)	Bore 5 ins (127 mm); stroke 4 ins (102 mm).
IO-470-C (as above)	250 hp (186.4 kW) at 2,600 rpm max continuous		b) 8.0:1	b) 91/61	431 (195.5)	a) 37.93 (963) b) 33.58 (853) c) 26.81 (681)	Bore 5 ins (127 mm); stroke 4 ins (102 mm).
IO-470-D/E (as above)	260 hp (194 kW) at 2,625 rpm max continuous		b) 8.6:1	b) 100/100 LL	426 (193.2)	a) 43.31 (1,100) b) 33.56 (852) c) 19.75 (502)	Bore 5 ins (127 mm); stroke 4 ins (102 mm).
IO-470-F (as above)	260 hp (194 kW) at 2,625 rpm max continuous		b) 8.6:1	b) 100/100 LL	426 (193.2)	a) 37.22 (945) b) 33.56 (852) c) 23.79 (604)	Bore 5 ins (127 mm); stroke 4 ins (102 mm).
IO-470-H (as above)	260 hp (194 kW) at 2,625 rpm max continuous		b) 8.6:1	b) 100/100 LL	431 (195.5)	a) 38.14 (969) b) 33.58 (853) c) 26.81 (681)	Bore 5 ins (127 mm); stroke 4 ins (102 mm).
IO-470-J/K (as above)	225 hp (167.8 kW) at 2,600 max continuous		b) 7.0:1	b) 80/87	401 (181.9)	a) 38.14 (969) b) 33.39 (848) c) 26.81 (681)	Bore 5 ins (127 mm); stroke 4 ins (102 mm).
IO-470-L (as above)	260 hp (194 kW) at 2,625 rpm max continuous		b) 8.6:1	b) 100/100 LL	430 (195)	a) 43.17 (1,097) b) 33.56 (852) c) 19.75 (502)	Bore 5 ins (127 mm); stroke 4 ins (102 mm).
IO-470-M (as above)	260 hp (194 kW) at 2,625 rpm max continuous		b) 8.6:1	b) 100/100 LL	430 (195)	a) 47.16 (1,198) b) 33.56 (852) c) 19.75 (502)	Bore 5 ins (127 mm); stroke 4 ins (102 mm).
IO-470-N (as above)	260 hp (194 kW) at 2,625 rpm max continuous		b) 8.6:1	b) 100/100 LL	433 (196.4)	a) 38.14 (969) b) 33.58 (853) c) 26.81 (681)	Bore 5 ins (127 mm); stroke 4 ins (102 mm).
IO-470-S (as above)	260 hp (194 kW) at 2,625 rpm max continuous		b) 8.6:1	b) 100/100 LL	426 (193.2)	a) 41.41 (1,052) b) 33.56 (852) c) 19.75 (502)	Bore 5 ins (127 mm); stroke 4 ins (102 mm).
IO-470-U (as above)	260 hp (194 kW) at 2,625 rpm max continuous		b) 8.6:1	b) 100/100 LL	423 (191.9)	a) 44.14 (1,121) b) 33.86 (860) c) 19.75 (502)	Bore 5 ins (127 mm); stroke 4 ins (102 mm).

Designation (type of engine)	Power output (normally take-off rating for piston, turboprop and turboshaft, unless stated)	Specific Fuel Consumption (S F C)	a) Max RPM b) Pressure or Compression ratio	a) EGT (unless stated to be MGT, TET, TGT or TIT) b) Primary fuel type or Octane rating	Dry weight lb (kg)	a) Length ins (mm) b) Width ins (mm) c) Height ins (mm)	Current aircraft users, and comments
United States of America							
Teledyne Continental Motors (continued)							
IO-470-V/VO (as above)	260 hp (194 kW) at 2,625 rpm max continuous		b) 8.6:1	b) 100/100 LL	423 (191.9)	a) 43.69 (1,110) b) 33.56 (852) c) 19.75 (502)	Bore 5 ins (127 mm); stroke 4 ins (102 mm).
IO-520-A/J (as above)	285 hp (212.5 kW) at 2,700 rpm max continuous		b) 8.5:1	b) 100/100 LL	431 (195.5)	a) 41.41 (1,052) b) 33.56 (852) c) 19.75 (502)	Aero Commander 500, Cessna 185/188/206/207/210/310, Beech Baron 55/58, Beech Bonanza 33/35/36, Bellanca Viking 300, and Navion for IO-520 series. Bore 5.25 ins (133 mm); stroke 4 ins (102 mm).
IO-520-B/BA/BB (as above)	285 hp (212.5 kW) at 2,700 rpm max continuous		b) 8.5:1	b) 100/100 LL	422 (191.4)	a) 39.71 (1,009) b) 33.58 (853) c) 26.71 (678)	Bore 5.25 ins (133 mm); stroke 4 ins (102 mm).
IO-520-C/CB (as above)	285 hp (212.5 kW) at 2,700 rpm max continuous		b) 8.5:1	b) 100/100 LL	415 (188.2)	a) 42.88 (1,089) b) 33.56 (852) c) 19.75 (502)	Bore 5.25 ins (133 mm); stroke 4 ins (102 mm).
IO-520-D (as above)	300 hp (223.7 kW) take-off at 2,850 rpm, 285 hp (212.5 kW) at 2,700 rpm max continuous		b) 8.5:1	b) 100/100 LL	430 (195)	a) 37.36 (949) b) 35.46 (901) c) 23.79 (604)	Bore 5.25 ins (133 mm); stroke 4 ins (102 mm).
IO-520-E (as above)	300 hp (223.7 kW) take-off at 2,850 rpm, 285 hp (212.5 kW) at 2,700 rpm max continuous		b) 8.5:1	b) 100/100 LL	427 (193.7)	a) 47.66 (1,211) b) 33.56 (852) c) 19.75 (502)	Bore 5.25 ins (133 mm); stroke 4 ins (102 mm).
IO-520-F (as above)	300 hp (223.7 kW) take-off at 2,850 rpm, 285 hp (212.5 kW) at 2,700 rpm max continuous		3b) 8.5:1	b) 100/100 LL	430 (195)	a) 41.41 (1,052) b) 35.91 (912) c) 19.75 (502)	Bore 5.25 ins (133 mm); stroke 4 ins (102 mm).
IO-520-K (as above)	300 hp (223.7 kW) take-off at 2,850 rpm, 285 hp (212.5 kW) at 2,700 rpm max continuous		b) 8.5:1	b) 100/100 LL	428 (194)	a) 40.91 (1,039) b) 33.56 (852) c) 19.75 (502)	Bore 5.25 ins (133 mm); stroke 4 ins (102 mm).
IO-520-L (as above)	300 hp (223.7 kW) take-off at 2,850 rpm, 285 hp (212.5 kW) at 2,700 rpm max continuous		b) 8.5:1	b) 100/100 LL	431 (195.5)	a) 40.91 (1,039) b) 33.56 (852) c) 23.25 (591)	Bore 5.25 ins (133 mm); stroke 4 ins (102 mm).
IO-520-M/MB (as above)	285 hp (212.5 kW) at 2,700 rpm max continuous		b) 8.5:1	b) 100/100 LL	413 (187.3)	a) 46.8 (1,189) b) 33.56 (852) c) 20.41 (518)	Bore 5.25 ins (133 mm); stroke 4 ins (102 mm).
TSIO-520-B/BB (6-cyl, horizontally-opposed, turbo-charged piston with direct drive)	285 hp (212.5 kW) at 2,700 rpm max continuous		b) 7.5:1	b) 100/100 LL	423 (191.9)	a) 39.75 (1,010) b) 33.56 (852) c) 20.32 (516)	Beech Bonanza V35TC, Baron 58TC and 58P, Cessna T206/P210/303/T310/340/401/402/414 for TSIO-520 series. Bore 5.25 ins (133 mm); stroke 4 ins (102 mm).
TSIO-520-C/H (as above)	285 hp (212.5 kW) at 2,700 rpm max continuous		b) 7.5:1	b) 100/100 LL	433 (196.4)	a) 40.91 (1,039) b) 33.56 (852) c) 20.04 (509)	Bore 5.25 ins (133 mm); stroke 4 ins (102 mm).
TSIO-520-D/DB (as above)	285 hp (212.5 kW) at 2,700 rpm max continuous		b) 7.5:1	b) 100/100 LL	423 (191.9)	a) 43.25 (1,099) b) 33.58 (853) c) 22.34 (567)	Bore 5.25 ins (133 mm); stroke 4 ins (102 mm).
TSIO-520-E/EB (as above)	300 hp (223.7 kW) at 2,700 rpm, max continuous		b) 7.5:1	b) 100/100 LL	421 (191)	a) 39.75 (1,010) b) 33.56 (852) c) 20.32 (516)	Bore 5.24 ins (133 mm); stroke 4 ins (102 mm).

Designation (type of engine)	Power output (normally take-off rating for piston, turboprop and turboshaft, unless stated)	Specific Fuel Consumption (S F C)	a) Max RPM b) Pressure or Compression ratio	a) EGT (unless stated to be MGT, TET, TGT or TIT) b) Primary fuel type or Octane rating	Dry weight lb (kg)	a) Length ins (mm) b) Width ins (mm) c) Height ins (mm)	Current aircraft users, and comments
United States of America							
Teledyne Continental Motors (continued)							
TSIO-520-G (as above)	300 hp (223.7 kW) take-off at 2,700 rpm, 285 hp (212.5 kW) at 2,600 rpm max continuous		b) 7.5:1	b) 100/100 LL	433 (196.4)	a) 40.91 (1,039) b) 33.56 (852) c) 20.04 (509)	Bore 5.24 ins (133 mm); stroke 4 ins (102 mm).
TSIO-520-J/JB/N/NB (as above)	310 hp (231 kW) at 2,700 rpm max continuous		b) 7.5:1	b) 100/100 LL	412 (186.9)	a) 54.36 (1,381) b) 33.56 (852) c) 22.5 (572)	Bore 5.24 ins (133 mm); stroke 4 ins (102 mm).
TSIO-520-K/KB (as above)	285 hp (212.5 kW) at 2,700 rpm max continuous		b) 7.5:1	b) 100/100 LL	412 (186.9)	a) 54.36 (1,381) b) 33.56 (852) c) 20.32 (516)	Bore 5.24 ins (133 mm); stroke 4 ins (102 mm).
TSIO-520-L/LB (as above)	310 hp (231 kW) at 2,700 rpm max continuous		b) 7.5:1	b) 100/100 LL	540 (244.9)	a) 50.62 (1,286) b) 33.56 (852) c) 20.02 (509)	Bore 5.25 ins (133 mm); stroke 4 ins (102 mm).
TSIO-520-M/P (as above)	310 hp (231 kW) take-off at 2,700 rpm, 285 hp (212.5 kW) at 2,600 rpm max continuous		b) 7.5:1	b) 100/100 LL	436 (197.8)	a) 40.91 (1,039) b) 33.56 (852) c) 20.04 (509)	Bore 5.25 ins (133 mm); stroke 4 ins (102 mm).
TSIO-520-R (as above)	310 hp (231 kW) take-off at 2,700 rpm, 285 hp (212.5 kW) at 2,600 rpm max continuous		b) 7.5:1	b) 100/100 LL	436 (197.8)	a) 40.91 (1,039) b) 33.56 (852) c) 23.54 (598)	Bore 5.25 ins (133 mm); stroke 4 ins (102 mm).
TSIO-520-T (as above)	310 hp (231 kW) at 2,700 rpm max continuous		b) 7.5:1	b) 100/100 LL	426 (193.2)	a) 38.2 (970) b) 33.56 (852) c) 32.26 (819)	Bore 5.25 ins (133 mm); stroke 4 ins (102 mm).
TSIO-520-UB (as above)	300 hp (223.7 kW) at 2,700 rpm max continuous		b) 7.5:1	b) 100/100 LL	536 (243)	a) 44.73 (1,136) b) 33.56 (852) c) 28.86 (733)	Bore 5.25 ins (133 mm); stroke 4 ins (102 mm).
TSIO-520-VB (as above)	325 hp (242.4 kW) at 2,700 rpm max continuous		b) 7.5:1	b) 100/100 LL	456 (206.8)	a) 39.25 (997) b) 33.56 (852) c) 20.41 (518)	Bore 5.25 ins (133 mm); stroke 4 ins (102 mm).
TSIO-520-WB (as above)	325 hp (242.4 kW) at 2,700 rpm max continuous		b) 7.5:1	b) 100/100 LL	539 (244.5)	a) 50.62 (1,286) b) 33.56 (852) c) 20.02 (509)	Bore 5.25 ins (133 mm); stroke 4 ins (102 mm).
L/TSIO-520-AE (as above)	250 hp (186.4 kW) at 2,400 rpm max continuous		b) 8.5:1	b) 100/100 LL	365 (165.6)	a) 38.07 (967) b) 33.29 (846) c) 21.38 (543)	Bore 5.25 ins (133 mm); stroke 4 ins (102 mm).
TSIO-520-AF (as above)	310 hp (231.2 kW) take-off at 2,600 rpm, 285 hp (212.5 kW) at 2,600 rpm max continuous		b) 7.5:1	b) 100/100 LL	418 (189.6)	a) 40.31 (1,024) b) 33.56 (852) c) 23.45 (596)	Bore 5.25 ins (133 mm); stroke 4 ins (102 mm).
TSIO-520-BE (as above)	310 hp (231.2 kW) at 2,600 rpm max continuous		b) 7.5:1	b) 100/100 LL	442 (200.5)	a) 42.64 (1,083) b) 42.5 (1,080) c) 33.5 (851)	Bore 5.25 ins (133 mm); stroke 4 ins (102 mm).
TSIO-520-CE (as above)	325 hp (242.4 kW) at 2,700 rpm max continuous		b) 7.5:1	b) 100/100 LL	527 (239)	a) 41 (1,041) b) 34 (864) c) 25 (635)	Bore 5.25 ins (133 mm); stroke 4 ins (102 mm).
GTSIO-520-C (6-cyl, horizontally-opposed, turbocharged piston with geared drive)	340 hp (253.5 kW) at 3,200 rpm max continuous		b) 7.5:1	b) 100/100 LL	481 (218.2)	a) 42.56 (1,081) b) 34.04 (865) c) 23.1 (587)	Aero Commander 685, Cessna 404/421A/421B/421C for GTSIO-520 series. Bore 5.25 ins (133 mm); stroke 4 ins (102 mm).
GTSIO-520-D/H (as above)	375 hp (279.6 kW) at 3,400 rpm max continuous		b) 7.5:1	b) 100/100 LL	508 (230.4)	a) 42.56 (1,081) b) 34.04 (865) c) 26.78 (680)	Bore 5.25 ins (133 mm); stroke 4 ins (102 mm).

Designation (type of engine)	Power output (normally take-off rating for piston, turboprop and turboshaft, unless stated)	Specific Fuel Consumption (S F C)	a) Max RPM b) Pressure or Compression ratio	a) EGT (unless stated to be MGT, TET, TGT or TIT) b) Primary fuel type or Octane rating	Dry weight lb (kg)	a) Length ins (mm) b) Width ins (mm) c) Height ins (mm)	Current aircraft users, and comments
United States of America							
Teledyne Continental Motors (continued)							
GTSIO-520-K (as above)	435 hp (324.4 kW) at 3,400 rpm max continuous		b) 7.5:1	b) 100/100 LL	600 (272.2)	a) 56.25 (1,429) b) 34.04 (865) c) 26.18 (665)	Bore 5.25 ins (133 mm); stroke 4 ins (102 mm).
GTSIO-520-L/N (as above)	375 hp (279.6 kW) at 3,350 rpm max continuous		b) 7.5:1	b) 100/100 LL	557 (252.7)	a) 43.87 (1,114) b) 34.04 (865) c) 26.41 (671)	Bore 5.25 ins (133 mm); stroke 4 ins (102 mm).
GTSIO-520-M (as above)	375 hp (279.6 kW) at 3,350 rpm max continuous		b) 7.5:1	b) 100/100 LL	545 (247.2)	a) 43.87 (1,114) b) 34.04 (865) c) 26.8 (681)	Bore 5.25 ins (133 mm); stroke 4 ins (102 mm).
IO-550-A (6-cyl, horizontally-opposed, air-cooled piston with direct drive)	300 hp (223.7 kW) at 2,700 rpm max continuous		b) 7.5:1	b) 100/100 LL	414 (187.8)	a) 46.8 (1,189) b) 33.56 (852) c) 20.41 (518)	Beech Baron 58 and Bonanza A36 for IO-550 series. Bore 5.25 ins (133 mm); stroke 4.25 ins (108 mm).
IO-550-B (as above)	300 hp (223.7 kW) at 2,700 rpm max continuous		b) 8.5:1	b) 100/100 LL	422 (191.4)	a) 37.97 (964) b) 33.56 (852) c) 27.32 (694)	Bore 5.25 ins (133 mm); stroke 4.25 ins (108 mm).
IO-550-C (as above)	300 hp (223.7 kW) at 2,700 rpm max continuous		b) 8.5:1	b) 100/100 LL	433 (196.4)	a) 43.31 (1,100) b) 33.56 (852) c) 19.78 (502)	Bore 5.25 ins (133 mm); stroke 4.25 ins (108 mm).
IO-550-D (as above)	300 hp (223.7 kW) at 2,700 rpm max continuous		b) 7.5:1	b) 100/100 LL	422 (191.4)	a) 36.74 (933) b) 33.56 (852) c) 23.79 (604)	Bore 5.25 ins (133 mm); stroke 4.25 ins (108 mm).
IO-550-E (as above)	300 hp (223.7 kW) at 2,700 rpm max continuous		b) 7.5:1	b) 100/100 LL	426 (193.2)	a) 43.91 (1,115) b) 33.56 (852) c) 19.75 (502)	Bore 5.25 ins (133 mm); stroke 4.25 ins (108 mm).
IO-550-F (as above)	300 hp (223.7 kW) at 2,700 rpm max continuous		b) 7.5:1	b) 100/100 LL	423 (191.9)	a) 40.91 (1,039) b) 33.56 (852) c) 19.75 (502)	Bore 5.25 ins (133 mm); stroke 4.25 ins (108 mm).
IO-550-G (as above)	280 hp (208.8 kW) take-off at 2,500 rpm, 210 hp (156.6 kW) cruise at 75% power (2,300 rpm)		b) 7.5:1	b) 100/100 LL	465 (210.9)*	a) 46.8 (1,189) b) 33.56 (852) c) 20.41 (518.4)	Bore 5.25 ins (133 mm); stroke 4.25 ins (108 mm). Dual magnetos ignition. *With standard equipment (may vary with specification).
IO-550-L (as above)	300 hp (223.7 kW) at 2,700 rpm max continuous		b) 7.5:1	b) 100/100 LL	423 (191.9)	a) 40.91 (1,039) b) 33.56 (852) c) 23.25 (591)	Bore 5.25 ins (133 mm); stroke 4.25 ins (108 mm).
TSIO-550-A (6-cyl, horizontally-opposed, air-cooled, turbo-charged piston with direct drive)	360 hp (268.5 kW) at 2,600 rpm max continuous		b) 7.5:1	b) 100/100 LL	425 (192.8)	a) 42.64 (1,083) b) 42.5 (1,080) c) 33.5 (851)	Bore 5.25 ins (133 mm); stroke 4.25 ins (108 mm).
TSIOL-550-A (as above)	350 hp (261 kW) at 2,700 rpm max continuous		b) 7.5:1	b) 100/100 LL	402 (182.3)	a) 42.65 (1,083) b) 42.5 (1,080) c) 33.5 (851)	Users include new Extra 400, and Grob Strato 2 at 402 hp (300 kW). Bore 5.25 ins (133 mm); stroke 4.25 ins (108 mm).
TSIO-550-B (as above)	350 hp (261 kW) at 2,700 rpm		b) 7.5:1	b) 100/100 LL	566 (256.7)	a) 42.75 (1,086) b) 42.2 (1,072) c) 33.6 (853)	Bore 5.25 ins (133 mm); stroke 4.25 ins (108 mm).
Voyager 550 (6-cyl, horizontally-opposed, liquid-cooled piston with direct drive)	350 hp (261 kW) at 2,700 rpm		b) 7.5:1	b) 100/100 LL	504 (228.6)		Bore 5.25 ins (133 mm); stroke 4.25 ins (108 mm). Fuel-injected.
Voyager T-550 (6-cyl, horizontally-opposed, liquid-cooled piston with direct drive)	300 hp (223.7 kW) at 2,500 rpm		b) 7.5:1	b) 100 LL	450 (204.1)		Beech Bonanza modification. Bore 5.25 ins (133 mm); stroke 4.25 ins (108 mm). Turbocharged and fuel-injected.

Designation (type of engine)	Power output (normally take-off rating for piston, turboprop and turboshaft, unless stated)	Specific Fuel Consumption (S F C)	a) Max RPM b) Pressure or Compression ratio	a) EGT (unless stated to be MGT, TET, TGT or TIT) b) Primary fuel type or Octane rating	Dry weight lb (kg)	a) Length ins (mm) b) Width ins (mm) c) Height ins (mm)	Current aircraft users, and comments
Unites States of America							
Teledyne Continental Motors (continued)							
Voyager GT-550 (as above, but geared drive)	400 hp (298.3 kW)		b) 7.5:1	b) 100 LL	550 (249.5)		Piper Chieftain modification. Bore 5.25 ins (133 mm); stroke 4.25 ins (108 mm).
Teledyne CAE, 1330 Laskey Road, Toledo, OH 43612-0971							
J69-T-25A (single-shaft turbojet)	1,025 lbf (4.56 kN)	1.14 lb/lbf/hr (32.3 g/kNs)	a) 21,730		364 (165.1)	a) 35.39 (900) b) 22.3 (566)	Cessna T-37B. Based on French Turbomeca Marboré.
Textron Lycoming Reciprocating Engines. 652 Oliver Street, Williamsport, PA 17701							
O-235 series (4-cyl, 4-stroke, piston with direct drive) See Comments	105-118 hp (78.3-88 kW)*		b) 6.75-8.5:1	b) 80, 87 or 100 Octane*	215-218 (97.52-98.9)*	a) 29-29.56 (738-751)* b) 32 (813) c) 22.4 (569)	Light aircraft, including the Robin 200 and DR 400 Dauphin among many examples. *Depending on model.
O-320 series (4-cyl, 4-stroke, piston with direct drive, some models with fuel injection) See Comments	150-160 hp (112-119.3 kW) at 2,700 rpm*		b) 7-9:1	b) 80, 87, 91, 96 or 100 Octane*	243-271 (110.2-123)*	a) 29-33.6 (738-853)* b) 32.24-32.68 (819-830), mostly the former c) 19.22-23 (488-584)	Light aircraft. Some models have fuel injection, and some are suited to aerobatics and helicopter applications. For example, the Robinson R22 helicopter uses the 160 hp (119.3 kW) O-320-B2C, derated to 131 hp (97.7 kW). *Depending on model.
O-360 series (4-cyl, 4-stroke, piston with direct drive, some models with fuel injection and/or turbocharging) See Comments	180-210 hp (134.2-156.6 kW) typically throughout series, depending on model, except for TIO-360-C, which is rated much higher		b) 7.3-8.7:1 typically, but with HIO-360-D1A at 10:1	b) Mostly 100 Octane, but some models 91 and 96 Octane	265-348 (120.2-157.9)*	a) 29.8-35.82 (757-910)* b) 33.37-36.25 (847-920.75)* c) 19.22-24.84 (488-631)*	Light aircraft, many examples including the Slingsby Firefly trainers. Some models have fuel injection, others are turbocharged; TIO-360-C has both. Some are suited to aerobatics, and there are helicopter models, including the HIO-360-D1A and the HIO-360-F1AD, as fitted to the Enstrom F28. *Depending on model.
O-540 series (6-cyl, 4-stroke, piston with direct drive, some models with fuel injection and/or turbocharging) See Comments	235-360 hp (175.2-268.5 kW)*		b) 7.2-8.7:1	b) 80, 87, 91, 96 and 100	366-549 (166-249)*	a) 37.22-53.21 (945.4-1,351.5)* b) Mostly 33.37-34.7 (847.5-881), but with models up to 46.5 (1,181.5) c) 19.6-30.33 (498-770)	Light and twin aircraft, two of many examples being the Malibu Mirage and Islander. Some models have fuel injection, some are turbocharged and fuel injected. Others are suited to aerobatics, and there are helicopter models including that used by the Robinson R44. *Depending on model.
IO-541 series (6-cyl, 4-stroke piston with fuel injection and turbocharging)	380 or 425 hp (283.4 or 317 kW) for TIO-541-E and TIGO-541-E respectively		b) 7.3:1	b) 100 Octane	596 or 704 (270.3-319.3) respectively	a) 50.7 or 57.6 (1,288-1,462) respectively b) 34.86 or 35.66 (885-906) respectively c) 22.65-25.2 (575.3-639)	Light aircraft and twins. TIGO-541-E is a geared engine.
IO-720 (8-cyl, 4-stroke, fuel injected piston with direct drive)	400 hp (298.3 kW)		b) 8.7:1	b) 100 Octane	568 (257.6)	a) 46.4 (1,179) b) 34.25 (870) c) 22.53 (572)	
Thermo-Jet Standard Inc. PO Box 55976, Houston, TX 77055							
J-8-200 (twin air inlets, valveless pulse jet)	up to 30 lbf (0.133 kN)	5.2 lb/lbf/hr (147 g/kNs)	a) 65 Hertz Comb freq	b) Propane	11 (5)	a) 56 (1,422) b) 8 (20.3) c) 8 (20.3)	UAV and target drone. Can be used for recreational aircraft.
J-10-200 (as above)	up to 50 lbf (0.222 kN)	5.2 lb/lbf/hr (147 g/kNs)	a) 65 Hertz Comb freq	Propane	19.5 (8.845)	a) 70 (1,778) b) 10 (254) c) 10 (254)	UAV and target drone. Can be used for recreational aircraft.
J-13-200 (as above)	up to 90 lbf (0.40 kN)	5.2 lb/lbf/hr (147 g/kNs)	a) 56 Hertz Comb freq	b) Propane	33 (14.97)	a) 91 (2,311) b) 13 (330) c) 13 (330)	UAV and target drone. Can be used for recreational aircraft.
Multi-national							
Joint Stock Company "Aviadvigatel", Pratt & Whitney and MTU.							
PS-90P (twin-shaft turbofan with fan reverser)	38,830 lbf (172.6 kN) take-off, to +30° C, 7,716 lbf (34.32 kN) cruise at 11,000 m altitude and Mach 0.8	0.574 lb/lbf/hr (16.26 g/kNs) cruise	a) 12,400 b) 38.8:1	a) 1,354° C b) IS-1, RT	6,504 (2,950)	a) 195.43 (4,964) b) 75.59 (1,920)	Suited to the Il-76, Il-96M, Tu-204 and Tu-330.

Designation (type of engine)	Power output (normally take-off rating for piston, turboprop and turboshaft, unless stated)	Specific Fuel Consumption (S F C)	a) Max RPM b) Pressure or Compression ratio	a) EGT (unless stated to be MGT, TET, TGT or TIT) b) Primary fuel type or Octane rating	Dry weight lb (kg)	a) Length ins (mm) b) Width ins (mm) c) Height ins (mm)	Current aircraft users, and comments
Multi-national							
BMW Rolls-Royce GmbH. Hohemarkstrasse 60-70, 61440 Oberursel, Germany							
BR710-48 (twin-shaft turbofan)	14,680 lbf (65.3 kN) for Bombardier, flat rated at 35° C, 14,900 lbf (66.28 kN) for Gulfstream, take-off, ISA +20° C	0.64 lb/lbf/hr (18.13 g/kNs)	b) 25.7:1		4,640 (2,105)	a) 200.8 (5,100) b) 48 (1,220) fan	Gulfstream GV in BR710-48-A1-10 form from December 1996. Bombardier Global Express in BR710-48-A2-20 form from late 1997. BR710 first ran 1 September 1994, following BR700 core engine on 14 August 1993. First German jet engine ordered for series production for civil aircraft.
BR715-55 (turbofan)	19,883 lbf (88.45 kN)	0.62 lb/lbf/hr (17.56 g/kNs)	b) 32.1:1			b) 55 (1,397) fan	BR715-55 chosen for MD-95, to enter service 1998. Certification 1997. Alternative engine for Tu-334. Volvo has taken a 4.5% stake. Further variant is BR715-58.
CFM International SA. 2 Blvd du Général Martial Valin, 75724 Paris Cedex 15, France							
CFM56-2 series (twin-shaft turbofan)	22,000 lbf (97.86 kN) take-off for CFM56-2B/C1/C3/C5/C6, 24,000 lbf (106.76 kN) take-off for CFM56-2/2A, latter which has 5,188 lbf (23.98 kN) cruise	0.651-0.661 lb/lbf/hr (18.44-18.72 g/kNs)	b) 31.2:1 for CFM56-2C1/C3/C5/C6		4,822 (2,187) for CFM56-2A, 4,635 (2,102) for CFM56-2C1/C3/C5/C6	a) 95.67 (2,430) b) 68.3 (1,735) fan	DC-8 Super 71, 72 and 73 (110 aircraft). Entered commercial service April 1982. Dispatch reliability 99.94%. Engine-caused shop visit rate 0.115 (yearly rolling average). Military versions on KC-135R, C-135FR, KE-3A, export E-3, RC-135 and E-6A (405 aircraft). Entered service June 1984. US military designation F108. Engine-caused shop visit rate 0.022 (yearly rolling average). CFM56-2-C1/C5 take-off rating flat rated to 30° C, C3/C6 to 41.1° C.
CFM56-3B series (twin-shaft turbofan)	18,500-20,000 lbf (82.29-88.97 kN) take-off, flat rated to 30° C, 4,400-5,050 lbf (19.57-22.42 kN) cruise	0.655 lb/lbf/hr (18.55 g/kNs) cruise	b) 25.5:1 for re-rated B1, 27.5:1 for B1, 28.8:1 for B2		4,276-4,301 (1,940-1,951)	a) 92.91 (2,360) b) 60 (1,524) fan	737-300, 737-400 and 737-500 (1,483 aircraft by September 1994). Low 18,500 lbf re-rating for 737-500. Entered service December 1994. Dispatch reliability 99.96%, with 36 million flight hours by above date. Engine-caused shop visit rate 0.075 (yearly rolling average), including CFM56-3C1.
CFM56-3C1 (twin-shaft turbofan)	23,500 lbf (104.54 kN) take-off, flat rated to 30° C, 5,370 lbf (23.89 kN) high cruise	0.655 lb/lbf/hr (18.55 g/kNs) cruise	b) 30.6:1		4,301 (1,951)	a) 92.91 (2,360) b) 60 (1,524) fan	737-400. Could become the standard version for the 737, derated when needed to suit 737-500.
CFM56-5A series (twin-shaft turbofan)	22,000-26,500 lbf (97.86-117.88 kN) take-off, flat rated to 30° C, 5,000 lbf (22.24 kN) cruise	0.596 lb/lbf/hr (16.88 g/kNs) cruise	b) 31.4:1		4,975-4,995 (2,257-2,266)	a) 95.35 (2,422) b) 68.3 (1,735) fan	A319 and A320 (305 aircraft by September 1994). Entered service April 1988. Dispatch reliability 99.94%. Engine-caused shop visit rate 0.068 (yearly rolling average).
CFM56-5B series (twin-shaft turbofan)	22,000-31,000 lbf (97.86-137.9 kN) take-off, 5,840 lbf (25.98 kN) cruise. (30,000 lbf 5B1 and 31,000 lbf 5B2 rated to 30° C, 27,000 lbf 5B4 rated to 45° C)	0.596 lb/lbf/hr (16.88 g/kNs) cruise	b) 35.4:1		5,250 (2,381)	a) 102.4 (2,601) b) 68.3 (1,735) fan	A319, A320 and A321. Entered service April 1994. Dispatch reliability in first few months 99.85%. CFM56-5B equipped with DAC (double annular combustor) underwent testing in late 1994. First CFM56-5B DAC entered service in 1995. DAC provides a 40%+ reduction in oxides of nitrogen emissions. CFM56-5BX improvements will be incorporated from Spring-Summer 1996.
CFM56-5BX (twin-shaft turbofan)		3% improvement over CFM56-5B					Ground testing began in mid-1995. Certification expected March 1996 and service entry later that year. Will serve as core for future CFM56 programmes, including the CFM56-7. New high pressure compressor, and redesigned high and low pressure turbines.
CFM56-5C series (twin-shaft turbofan)	31,200-34,000 lbf (138.79-151.24 kN) take-off, flat rated to 30° C, 6,910 lbf (30.74 kN) cruise	0.567 lb/lbf/hr (16.06 g/kNs)	b) 37.4:1	a) 975° C EGT for CFM56-5C2/G, -5C3/G and 5C4	8,645 (3,921) propulsion weight system	a) 103 (2,616) b) 72.28 (1,836) fan	A340. Entered service March 1993. Dispatch reliability 99.7%. Engine-caused shop visit rate 0.009 (yearly rolling average). Highest rated CFM56-5C4 version was certified in October 1994.
CFM56-7B18 to B26 series (twin-shaft turbofan)	18,500-26,400 lbf (82.29-117.44 kN) take-off, flat rated to 30° C	New wide-chord fan and advanced booster will increase airflow and, with core improvements, reduce SFC by about 5%	32.3-32.6:1		5,205 (2,361)	a) 98.7 (2,506) b) 61 (1,549) fan	Proposed for 737-500, 700 and 800. Ground testing began May 1995. First flight in a 747 testbed in early 1996, with certification October 1996. Reduced maintenance costs by up to 15% compared to CFM56-3C1. Uses CFM56-5BX core.

Designation (type of engine)	Power output (normally take-off rating for piston, turboprop and turboshaft, unless stated)	Specific Fuel Consumption (S F C)	a) Max RPM b) Pressure or Compression ratio	a) EGT (unless stated to be MGT, TET, TGT or TIT) b) Primary fuel type or Octane rating	Dry weight lb (kg)	a) Length ins (mm) b) Width ins (mm) c) Height ins (mm)	Current aircraft users, and comments
Multi-national							
CFM International SA (continued)							
CFM56 "Lite" (turbofan)	16,000-20,000 lbf (71.17-88.97 kN) range	0.6-0.63 lb/lbf/hr (17-17.84 g/kNs) at 35,000 ft and Mach 0.8, ISA					Proposed within the NSE (New Small Engine) study for service entry around the turn of the century. Stage 3 -18 EPNdB noise; ICAO -50% for Nox emissions; long duct mixed flow nacelle; FADEC controls. Based on M88 core and possible future applications include RJ70/85/100, Euroflug, Regioliner, Fokker 70 and 130, and other 70-130 seat airliners.
CFM56-XX (turbofan)	40,000-50,000 lbf (177.9-222.4 kN) range						For service entry on new aircraft introduced beyond the year 2000. Launch expected in late 1995, for growth A340 and other types. Core rating 43,000 lbf (191.28 kN). SNECMA to lead development.
Eurojet Turbo GmbH. Inselkammerstrasse 5, D-82008 Unterhaching, Germany							
EJ200 (two-spool turbofan)	13,500 lbf (60 kN) dry, 20,250 lbf (90 kN) with afterburning, rising to 23,000 lbf (102.31 kN)	0.74-0.81 lb/lbf/hr (20.96-22.94 g/kNs) dry, 1.66-1.73 lb/lbf/hr (47-49 g/kNs) with afterburning	b) 26:1	a) about 1,527°C	2,180-2,280 (989-1,034)	a) 157 (3,988) b) 29 (737) inlet	Eurofighter 2000. Company is a consortium of Rolls-Royce (UK), MTU (Germany), FiatAvio (Italy), and ITP (Spain). First EJ200 flown 1994. Completion of Initial Certification Testing 1998. Production deliveries 1999.
International Aero Engines AG. Corporate Center II, 628 Hebron Avenue, Glastonbury, CT 06033-2595, USA							
V2500-A1 (twin-shaft turbofan)	25,000 lbf (111.21 kN)	0.581 lb/lbf/hr (16.46 g/kNs)	b) 29.4:1		5,074 (2,302)	a) 126 (3,200) b) 63 (1,600) fan	A320-200. IAE is a collaborative venture of Rolls-Royce, MTU, FiatAvio, Pratt & Whitney and JAEC.
V2522-A5 (twin-shaft turbofan)	22,000 lbf (97.86 kN)	0.575 lb/lbf/hr (16.29 g/kNs) cruise	b) 25.4:1		5,139 (2,331)	a) 126 (3,200) b) 63.5 (1,613) fan	A319.
2522-D5 (twin-shaft turbofan)	22,000 lbf (97.86 kN), flat rated to 30° C	0.574 lb/lbf/hr (16.26 g/kNs)	b) 24.9:1		5,252 (2,382)	a) 126 (3,200) b) 63.5 (1,613) fan	MD-90-10
V2524-A5 (twin-shaft turbofan)	23,500 lbf (104.54 kN), flat rated to 55° C	0.547 lb/lbf/hr (16.26 g/kNs)	b) 27.1:1		5,139 (2,331)	a) 126 (3,200) b) 63.5 (1,613) fan	Proposed for A319.
V2525-D5 (twin-shaft turbofan)	25,000 lbf (111.21 kN), flat rated to 30° C	0.574 lb/lbf/hr (16.287 g/kNs) cruise	b) 27.7:1		5,252 (2,382)	a) 126 (3,200) b) 63.5 (1,613) fan	MD-90-10 and 30
V2527-A5 (twin-shaft turbofan)	26,500 lbf (117.88 kN), flat rated to 46° C	0.574 lb/lbf/hr (16.287 g/kNs)	b) 27.7:1		5,139 (2,331)	a) 126 (3,200) b) 63.5 (1,613) fan	A320-200.
V2528-D5 (twin-shaft turbofan)	28,000 lbf (124.55 kN), flat rated at 30° C	0.574 lb/lbf/hr (16.287 g/kNs)	b) 30.4:1		5,252 (2,382)	a) 126 (3,200) b) 63.5 (1,613) fan	MD-90-10,-30, -40 and -50
V2530-A5 (twin-shaft turbofan)	30,000 lbf (133.45 kN), flat rated 30° C	0.574 lb/lbf/hr (16.287 g/kNs)	b) 31.4:1		5,139 (2,331)	a) 126 (3,200) b) 63.5 (1,613) fan	A321-100.
V2530-W5 (twin-shaft turbofan)	31,500 lbf (140.12 kN)						Growth study for re-engining 727.
V2533 (twin-shaft turbofan)	33,000 lbf (146.79 kN)				5,139 (2,331)	a) 126 (3,200) b) 63.5 (1,613) fan	A321-200 growth derivative (formerly V253X-A5).
ITEC (International Turbine Engine Corporation) -Joint venture by AlliedSignal (which see) and Han Hsiang of Taiwan							
MTR – MTU Turbomeca Rolls-Royce GmbH. Inselkammerstrasse 5, D-82008 Unterhaching, Germany							
MTR 390 (free-turbine turboshaft)	1,285 shp (958 kW) at 6,000 or 8,000 rpm, 1,170 shp (872.5 kW) max continuous	0.46 lb/shp/hr (280 g/kW/hr)	a) 27,000 direct drive output, 8,000 with reduction gearbox b) 14:1		372.6 (169)	a) 42.44 (1,078) b) 29.1 (739) envelope diameter c) 26.85 (682)	Eurocopter Tiger and Panther. First run December 1989. Engine qualification testing completed August 1993. To gain civil certification. Suitable for Bell 442, EC500/600 and HAL ALH.
Pratt/Klimov – see Pratt & Whitney Canada and Klimov St Petersburg, Russia							
Producing the PT6A in Russia as the PK6A. Other types following.							

Designation (type of engine)	Power output (normally take-off rating for piston, turboprop and turboshaft, unless stated)	Specific Fuel Consumption (S F C)	a) Max RPM b) Pressure or Compression ratio	a) EGT (unless stated to be MGT, TET, TGT or TIT) b) Primary fuel type or Octane rating	Dry weight lb (kg)	a) Length ins (mm) b) Width ins (mm) c) Height ins (mm)	Current aircraft users, and comments
Multi-national							
Rolls-Royce Turbomeca Ltd. 4-5 Grosvenor Place, London SW1X 7HH, England							
Adour 102 (twin-shaft turbofan)	5,240 lbf (23.31 kN) dry, 7,305 lbf (32.5 kN) with afterburning	0.74 lb/lbf/hr (20.96 g/kNs)			1,552 (704)	a) 117 (2,970) b) 30 (762) c) 41 (1,041)	Jaguar (French, UK).
Adour 104 (twin-shaft turbofan)	5,270 lbf (23.44 kN) dry, 7,900 lbf (35.14 kN) with afterburning*				1,572 (713)	a) 117 (2,970) b) 30 (762) c) 41 (1,041)	Jaguar (UK). *Turbine gas temperature modification can increase power to 5,350 lbf (23.8 kN), 8,100 lbf (36.03 kN) with afterburning.
Adour 151 (twin-shaft turbofan without afterburning)	5,240 lbf (23.31 kN)		b) 11.0:1		1,220 (533.4)	a) 77 (1,956) b) 30 (762) c) 41 (1,041)	BAe Hawk T.Mk 1/1A.
Adour 801A (twin-shaft turbofan with afterburning)	7,305 lbf (32.5 kN) with afterburning				1,552 (704)	a) 117 (2,970) b) 30 (762) c) 41 (1,041)	Built in Japan by IHI as TF40 to power Mitsubishi F-1/T-2.
Adour 804 (twin-shaft turbofan with afterburning)	8,040 lbf (35.76 kN) with afterburning				1,572 (713)	a) 117 (2,970) b) 30 (762) c) 41 (1,041)	Jaguar International (Ecuador, India and Oman).
Adour 811 (twin-shaft turbofan with afterburning)	8,400 lbf (37.37 kN) with afterburning		b) 11.3:1		1,633 (741)	a) 117 (2,970) b) 30 (762) c) 41 (1,041)	Jaguar International (assembled by HAL in India).
Adour 815 (twin-shaft turbofan with afterburning)	8,400 lbf (37.37 kN) with afterburning				1,627 (738)	a) 117 (2,970) b) 30 (762) c) 41 (1,041)	Jaguar International (Nigeria and Oman).
Adour 851 (twin-shaft turbofan without afterburning)	5,240 lbf (23.31 kN)				1,252 (568)	a) 77 (1,956) b) 30 (762) c) 41 (1,041)	Hawk Mk 50 (Finland, Indonesia and Kenya).
Adour 861/861A (twin-shaft turbofan without afterburning)	5,710 lbf (25.4 kN)	0.74 lb/lbf/hr (20.96 g/kNs)	b)11.3:1		1,272 (577), or 1,240 (562) basic engine weight	a) 77 (1,956) b) 30 (762) c) 41 (1,041)	Hawk Mk 60 (Abu Dhabi, Dubai, South Korea, Kuwait, Saudi Arabia, Switzerland and Zimbabwe). Mk 861A has addition of fuel dip for weapons firing. Fan diameter 22.3 ins (566 mm).
Adour 871 (twin-shaft turbofan without afterburning)	5,990 lbf (26.65 kN)	078 lb/lbf/hr (22.09 g/kNs)	b) 11.3:1		1,299 (589)	a) 77 (1,956) b) 30 (762) c) 41 (1,041)	Hawk Mk 100 and Mk 200. Also PZL-Mielec M-99 Orkan. Matched to give more thrust at high speeds/low level and on hot day conditions.
F405-RR-401 (twin-shaft turbofan without afterburning)	5,990 lbf (26.65 kN)					a) 77 (1,956) b) 30 (762) c) 41 (1,041)	T-45A Goshowk production aircraft, with aircraft carrier capability. Modified Mk 871. US military designation. Goshawk prototype used F405-RR-400 (Adour 861-49) of 5,450 lbf (24.24 kN)
RTM322 (twin-shaft turboshaft)	2,100 shp (1,566 kW) take-off, 1,892 shp (1,411 kW) max continuous	0.48 lb/shp/hr (292 g/kW/hr)	b) 14.7:1		529 (240) civil	a) 46.1 (1,171) b) 23.8 (604)	EH 101, Kamov Ka-62R, NH 90, UH-60/SH-60, and Westland Apache. Also collaborating in programme are Rinaldo Piaggio of Italy and MTU of Germany. Lucas FADEC fitted in 1994. Civil version has max continuous SFC of 0.453 lb/shp/hr (276 g/kW/hr) and military 0.449 lb/shp/hr (273 g/kW/hr). Military dry weight is 539 lb (244 kg). Envelope diameter 25.9 ins (658 mm).
Turbo-Union Ltd. PO Box 3, Filton, Bristol BS12 7QE, England							
RB199 Mk 101 (three-shaft turbofan)	8,700 lbf (38.70 kN) dry, 14,840 lbf (66.01 kN) with afterburning		a) 18,000 HP shaft b) 23.1:1 approx	a) 1,327° C TET	1,980 (898)	a) 127 (3,226) b) 34.25 (870)	Initial Tornado IDS deliveries to European air forces.
RB199 Mk 103 (three-shaft turbofan)	9,100 lbf (40.5 kN) dry, 16,000 lbf (71.2 kN) with afterburning	0.649 lb/lbf/hr (18.38 g/kNs)	b) 23.5:1	a) 1,327° C TET	2,103 (954) without thrust reverser	a) 126 (3,200) to nozzle exit b) 37 (940)	Tornado IDS.
RB199 Mk 104 (three-shaft turbofan)	9,100 lbf (40.5 kN) dry, 16,410 lbf (73 kN) with afterburning	0.649 lb/lbf/hr (18.38 g/kNs)	b) 23.5:1	a) 1,327° C TET	2,151 (976) without thrust reverser	a) 142 (3,607) incl longer jetpipe b) 37 (940)	Tornado ADV. Derivative Mk 104D used on BAe EAP and Mk 104E used on Eurofighter 2000 prototypes as RB199-122s.

Designation (type of engine)	Power output (normally take-off rating for piston, turboprop and turboshaft, unless stated)	Specific Fuel Consumption (S F C)	a) Max RPM b) Pressure or Compression ratio	a) EGT (unless stated to be MGT, TET, TGT or TIT) b) Primary fuel type or Octane rating	Dry weight lb (kg)	a) Length ins (mm) b) Width ins (mm) c) Height ins (mm)	Current aircraft users, and comments
Multi-national							
Turbo-Union Ltd. (continued)							
RB199 Mk 105 (three-shaft turbofan)	9,550 lbf (42.5 kN) dry, 16,700 lbf (74.3 kN) with afterburning	0.65 lb/lbf/hr (18.41 g/kNs)	b) 24.5:1		2,183 (990) with thrust reverser	a) 130 (3,302) b) 29.6 (752) intake	Tornado ECR. Available for the Tornado IDS.
RB199 Mk 122 (three-shaft turbofan)	Could provide up to 18,000 lbf (80.1 kN) as the enhanced engine						Eurofighter 2000. Under development also for Tornado.
Williams-Rolls Inc. 2280 West Maple Road, PO Box 200, Walled Lake, MI 48390, USA							
FJ44 (twin-shaft turbofan)	1,900 lbf (8.45 kN), 506 lbf (2.251 kN) max cruise	0.758 lb/lbf/hr (21.47 g/kNs) max cruise			447 (202.75)	a) 40.3 (1,024) b) 23.7 (602)	CitationJet, SJ30, Saab SK-60 (re-engined, re-entering service 1996), Jet Squalus and Tiro Trainer.Growth capability being studied. Company is a partnership between Williams International of USA and Rolls-Royce of UK.
F129 (military version of FJ44, as above)	1,500 lbf (6.672 kN)	0.48 lb/lbf/hr (13.6 g/kNs)					Derated FJ44, used first in Cessna 526 JPATS trainer.

Bombardier-Rotax 582 UL 2-stroke piston engine (page 555)

Pratt & Whitney Canada JT15D turbofan (page 556)

Pratt & Whitney Canada PW305 series advanced turbofan (page 562)

Pratt & Whitney Canada PT6T-3D Twin Pac turboshaft (page 560)

LOM Prague M337 inverted piston engine
(page 564)

SNEMCA M88-2 turbofan
(page 566)

Turbomeca Arriel 1D turboshaft
(page 567)

Turbomeca Makila 1A1 turboshaft
(page 568)

Göbler-Hirthmotoren Hirth F 30 piston engine with fan cooling
(page 568)

Instytut Lotnictwa D-18A turbofan
(page 571)

PZL-Rzeszów GTD-350 turboshaft
(page 572)

PZL-Rzeszów PZL-F.6A350C1L piston engine
(page 572)

WSK Kalisz ASz-62IR radial piston engine
(page 573)

JSC Aviadvigatel D-30F6 afterburning turbofan (by-pass turbojet)
(page 575)

JSC Aviadvigatel PS-90A turbofan
(page 576)

JSC Aviadvigatel D-200 piston engine
(page 576)

Klimov RD-33 turbojet (Piotr Butowski)
(page 577)

Samara Machine Building Design Bureau MK-12MV turboprop
(page 579)

Ivchenko PROGRESS ZMKB AI-20D series 5 turboprop
(page 582)

Povazské Strojárne DV-2 turbofan
(page 581)

Ivchenko PROGRESS ZMKB D-27 propfan
(page 583)

Ivchenko PROGRESS ZMKB D-136 turboshaft
(page 583)

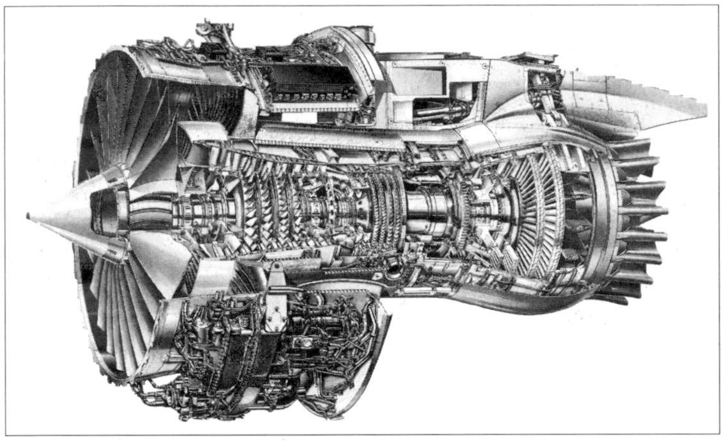

Rolls-Royce RB211-524H turbofan cutaway drawing
(page 585)

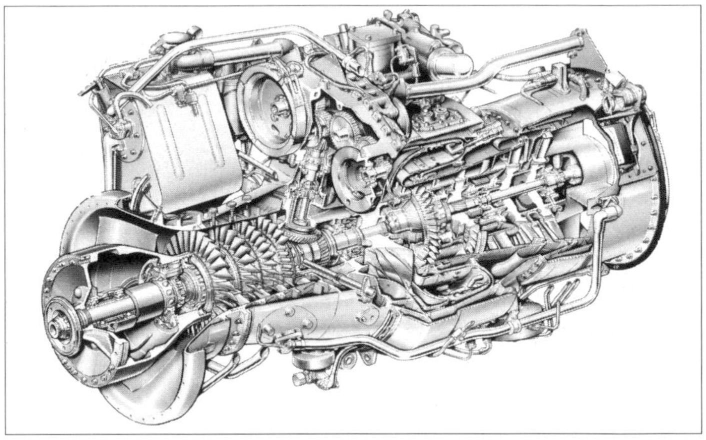

Rolls-Royce RR 1004 turboshaft
(page 585)

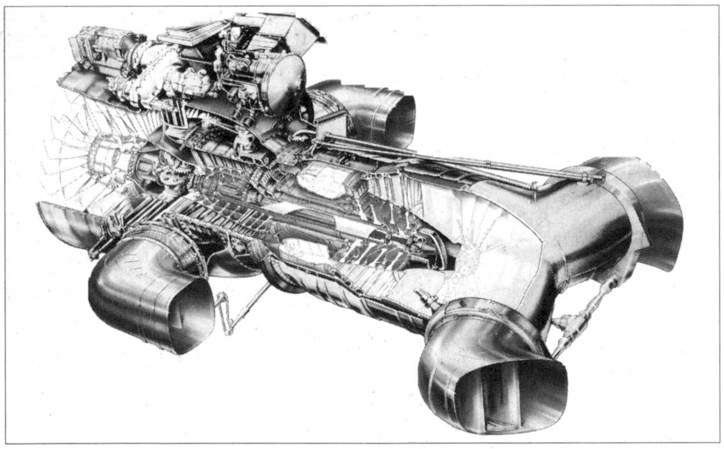

Rolls-Royce Pegasus vectored thrust turbofan cutaway drawing
(page 585)

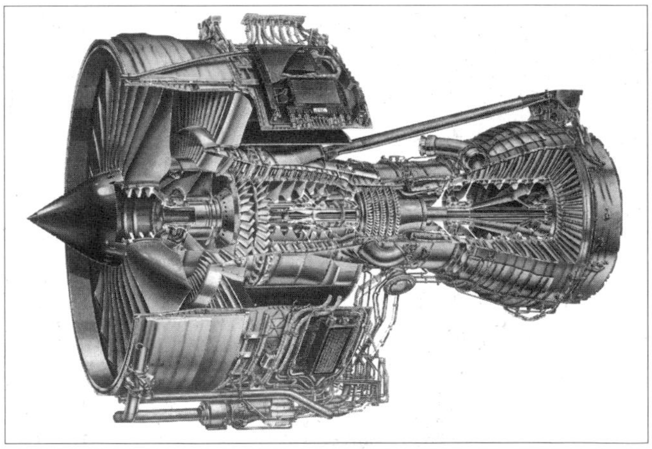

Rolls-Royce Trent 800 cutaway drawing
(page 586)

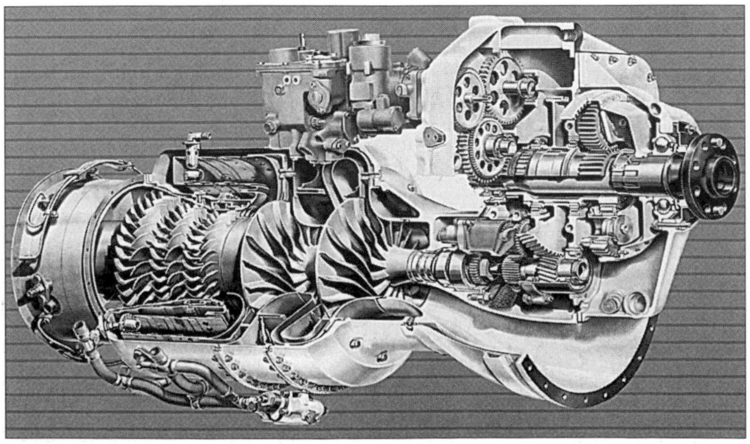

AlliedSignal TPE331-5/5A turboprop cutaway drawing
(page 589)

Allison 250-B17F turboprop
(page 590)

Allison-AlliedSignal Partnership T800-LHT-801 turboshaft
(page 592)

CFE Company CFE738 turbofan
(page 592)

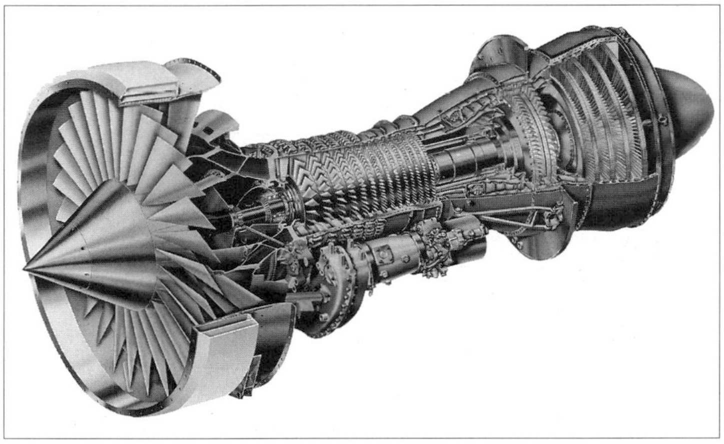

General Electric CF34 turbofan drawing
(page 593)

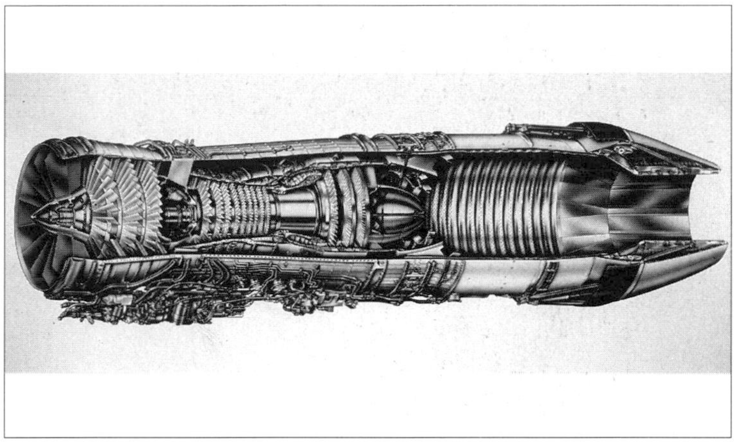

General Electric F110-GE-129 turbofan drawing
(page 594)

NSI Propulsion Systems Suber EA81 package with spur gear drive
(page 597)

Pop's Props Volkswagen conversion
(page 598)

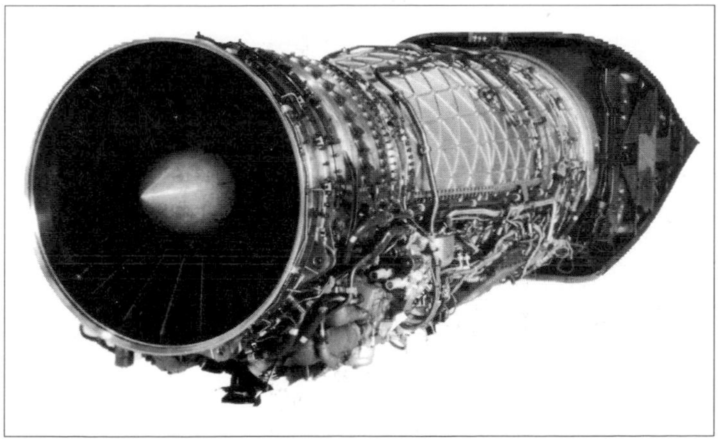

Pratt & Whitney F119-PW-100 twin spool turbofan
(page 598)

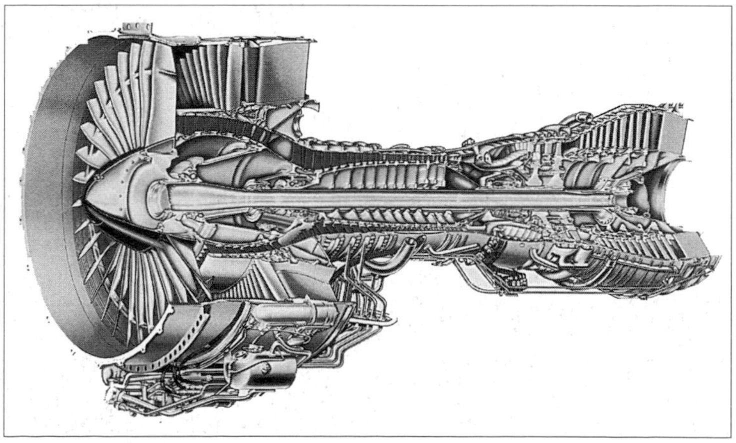

Pratt & Whitney PW2000 turbofan drawing
(page 599)

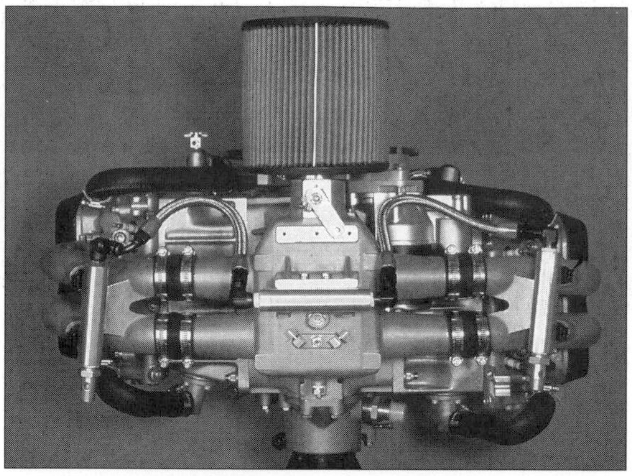

RotorWay International RI 162F piston engine (page 601)

Teledyne Continental IO-550-G piston engine (page 606)

JSC Aviadvigatel, Pratt & Whitney and MTU PS-90P turbofan (page 607)

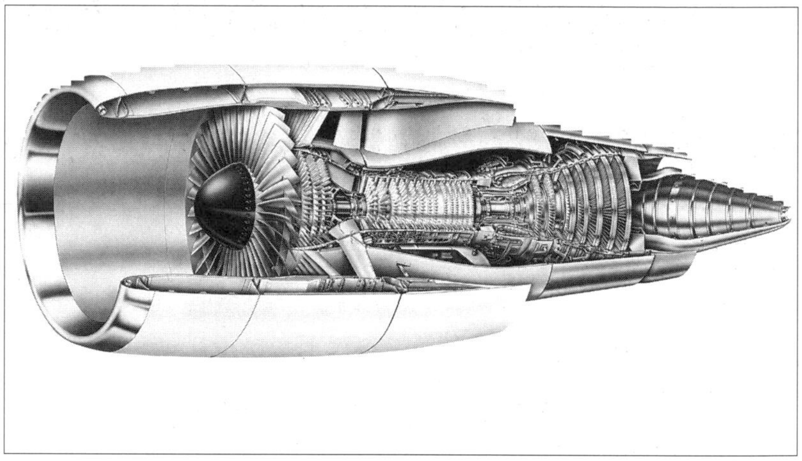

General Electric CF6-80C2 turbofan drawing (page 593)

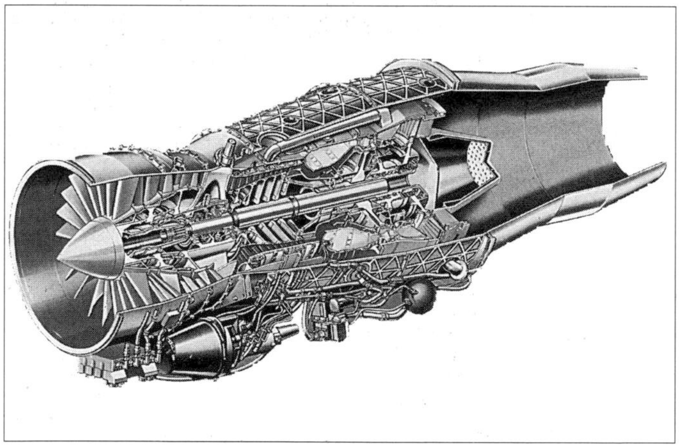

Eurojet EJ200 turbofan cutaway drawing (page 609)

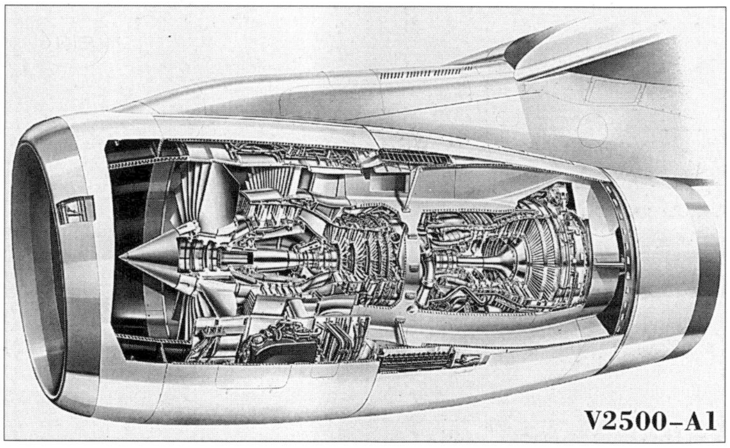

International Aero Engines V2500-A1 turbofan in an airliner nacelle cutaway drawing (page 609)

MTR 390 turboshaft (*Phototheque Turbomeca*) (page 609)

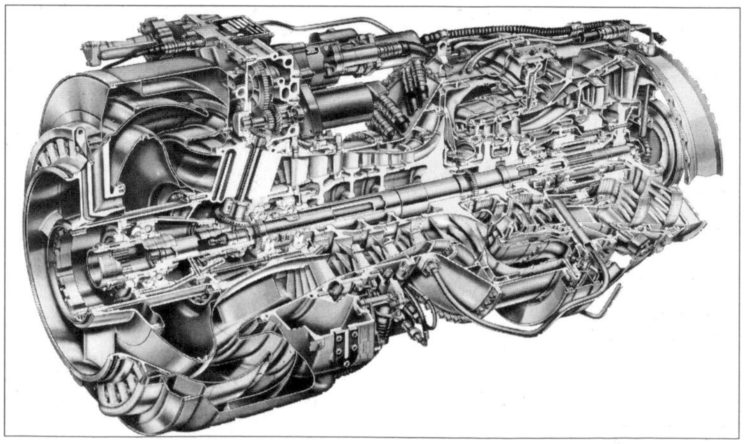

Rolls-Royce Turbomeca RTM322 turboshaft cutaway drawing (page 610)

Missiles

Missiles are listed by nation, then alphabetically by designation

Air-to-surface

Manufacturer	Designation	a) Length ins (m) b) Span ins (cm)	a) Diameter ins (cm) b) Weight lb (kg)	Range naut miles (km)	Speed	Control	Propulsion	Guidance	a) Warhead lb (kg) b) Fuzing	Platform(s)
Argentina										
Instituto de Investigaciones Cientificas y Tecnicas de las Fuerzas Armadas (CITEFA) Zufriategui 4380, 1603 Villa Martelli Buenos Aires	Martin Pescador (MP-1000 – see platforms)	a) 115.8 (2.94) b) 28.7 (73.0)	a) 8.6 (21.9) b) 308.6 (140.0)	1.35 – 4.85 (2.5 – 9.0)	Mach 1+ at impact	Moving canard fins	Solid-propellant rocket	Radio command	a) 88 (40) HE (HE = high explosive)	A-4, A 109 and Pucará. MP-1000 is wire-guided, with 3.2 naut miles (6km) range
Brazil										
Avibras Industria Aerospacial Antiga Estrada de Paraibuna km 118, PO Box 229, 12201-970 Sao Jose dos Campos	MAS-1 Carcara	a) 47.2 (1.20) b) 16.5 (42.0)	a) 4.9 (12.5) b) 99.2 (45.0)				Solid-propellant rocket	Television	a) HE	
France										
Matra 37 avenue Louis-Breguet, F-78146 Velizy-Villacoublay Cedex	Anti-Radar Futur (ARF)		b) 395? (180?)	c.54 (c.100)	Supersonic		Integrated rocket/ramjet	Passive radar homing	a) HE	
Matra 37 avenue Louis-Breguet, F-78146 Velizy-Villacoublay Cedex	Apache	a) 200.8 (5.10) b) 112.2 (285)	b) 2,651 (1,200)	75.6 (140)	Subsonic		Turbojet	Inertial with updates + millimetre wave active radar homing	a) 10 kriss submunitions	Mirage F1, Mirage 2000, Rafale, Tornado
Aerospatiale Division Engins Tactiques 2 rue Beranger, F-92322, Chatillon-sous-Bagneux	Armat	a) 152.4 (3.87) b) 47.2 (120.0)	a) 15.8 (40.0) b) 1,213 (550)	21.5 – 65 (40 – 120)		Moving tail fins	Solid-propellant rocket	Passive radar homing	a) 331 (150) HE	Mirage III, Mirage F1, Mirage 2000, Jaguar, Atlantique
Aerospatiale Division Engins Tactiques 2 rue Beranger, F-92322, Chatillon-sous-Bagneux	AS.30 Laser	a) 143.7 (3.65) b) 39.4 (100.0)	a) 13.5 (34.2) b) 1,146 (520)	5.4 (10)	Mach 1.4		Two-stage solid-propellant rocket	Semi-active laser homing	a) 529 (240) HE or SAP b) Contact & delayed action fuzes	Mirage F1, Mirage 2000, Super Etendard, Jaguar, F-16, Rafale
Aerospatiale Division Engins Tactiques 2 rue Beranger, F-92322, Chatillon-sous-Bagneux	ASLP	a) c.200 (c.5.1)		432 – 648 (800 – 1,200)	Mach 3.0	Cruciform moving tail fins	Liquid propellant ramjet with integral solid-propellant rocket booster		a) Variable-yield nuclear	Studied as ASMP replacement
Aerospatiale Division Engins Tactiques 2 rue Beranger, F-92322, Chatillon-sous-Bagneux	ASMP	a) 211.8 (5.38) b) 37.8 (96.0)	a) 15.0 (38.0) b) 1,896 (860)	135 (250)	Mach 3.0	Cruciform moving tail fins	Liquid propellant ramjet with integral solid-propellant rocket booster	Inertial + terrain mapping	a) 300kT nuclear	Mirage 2000D & N, Mirage IVP, Super Etendard, Rafale
Aerospatiale Division Engins Tactiques 2 rue Beranger, F-92322, Chatillon-sous-Bagneux	ASSM				Subsonic		Solid propellant rocket	Inertial + GPS, or inertial + semi-active laser, IIR, or radar homing	a) 551 (250) or 2,205 (1,000) unitary warhead or submunitions	
Matra 37 avenue Louis-Breguet, F-78146 Velizy-Villacoublay Cedex	ASSM	a) 118 (3) b) 22.8 (58)	b) 661 (300)	8.1+ (15+)			Undecided (unpowered or solid-propellant rocket)	Inertial + GPS	a) HE bomb?	
Aerospatiale Division Engins Tactiques 2 rue Beranger, F-92322, Chatillon-sous-Bagneux	Asura	a) 197.0 (5.00)	b) 1,951 (885)	216 (400)	Mach 3.0	Cruciform moving tail fins	Liquid propellant ramjet with integral solid-propellant rocket booster	Inertial + IIR terminal homing	a) 529 (230) HE penetrator	
Matra 37 avenue Louis-Breguet, F-78146 Velizy-Villacoublay Cedex	250kg BLG	a) 142.1 (3.61) b) 56.3 (143.0)	a) 12.8 (32.4) b) 551 (250)			Moving canards	None	Semi-active laser homing	a) HE	Mirage F1, Mirage 2000, Jaguar
Matra 37 avenue Louis-Breguet, F-78146 Velizy-Villacoublay Cedex	400kg BLG	a) 139.4 (3.54) b) 56.3 (143.0)	a) 15.9 (40.3) b) 1,036 (470)			Moving canards	None	Semi-active laser homing	a) HE	Mirage F1, Mirage 2000, Jaguar

Manufacturer	Designation	a) Length ins (m) b) Span ins (cm)	a) Diameter ins (cm) b) Weight lb (kg)	Range naut miles (km)	Speed	Control	Propulsion	Guidance	a) Warhead lb (kg) b) Fuzing	Platform(s)
France										
Matra 37 avenue Louis-Breguet, F-78146 Velizy-Villacoublay Cedex	400kg PE BLG	a) 143.3 (3.64) b) 56.3 (143.0)	a) 15.4 (39.1) b) 992 (450)			Moving canards	None	Semi-active laser homing	a) HE penetrating	Mirage F1, Mirage 2000, Jaguar
Matra 37 avenue Louis-Breguet, F-78146 Velizy-Villacoublay Cedex	Arcole	a) 172.1 (4.37) b) 67.7 (172.0)	a) 18.0 (45.7) b) 2,138 (970)	c. 5.4 (c. 10)		Moving canards	None	Semi-active laser homing	a) HE penetrating	Mirage F1, Mirage 2000, Jaguar
Société des Ateliers Mecaniques de Pont-sur-Sambre (SAMP) 37 Grand Rue, F-59138 Pont-sur-Sambre	MP 22 Excalibur	a) 98.4 (2.50) b) 20.3 (51.6)	a) 10.8 (27.3)			Moving canard fins	Solid-propellant rocket	Inertial	a) BL EU2 551 (250) general-purpose bomb	
Matra 37 avenue Louis-Breguet, F-78146 Velizy-Villacoublay Cedex	SCALP	a) 201? (5 .1?) b) 112.2 (285)	a) 24.8 x 20 (63 x 51)	216 – 324 (400 – 600)	Subsonic		Turbojet?	Inertial with updates + IIR terminal homing	Unitary HE	
Germany										
Daimler-Benz Aerospace PO Box 801109 D-81663 Munich	DWS 24	a) 138 (3.5) b) 39.3 (100)	a) 24.8 x. 12.6 (63 x 32) b) 1,323 (600)	5.4 (10)	Subsonic		None	Inertial	a) 49 submunitions (KB-44 armour-piercing, MIFF anti-tank, MUSA fragmentation or MUSPA anti-runway	
Daimler-Benz Aerospace PO Box 801109 D-81663 Munich	DWS 39	a) 138 (3.5) b) 39.3 (100)	a) 24.8 x. 12.6 (63 x 32) b) 1,323 (600)	5.4 (10)	Subsonic		None	Inertial	a) As DWS24 + Bofers MJ-1 fragmentation or MJ-2 anti-tank	Gripen, AJS 37 Viggen
Daimler-Benz Aerospace PO Box 801109 D-81663 Munich	AFDS (Autonomous Free-flight Dispenser System)	a) 147 (3.74) b) c. 39.3 (100)	b) 1,323 (600)	10.8 (20)	Subsonic		None	Inertial + Integrated GPS	a) Submunitions	Tested on F-16
India										
Aeronautical Development Establishment Bangalore	Designation unknown			c.324 (c.600)	Supersonic		Integrated rocket/ramjet	GPS with radar or IR terminal homing?	a) c.990 (c. 450)	
Israel										
Rafael Armament Development Authority PO Box 2082, 31021 Haifa	AGM-142A Have Nap/ Popeye	a) 189.8 (4.82)	a) 20.0 (50.8) b) 2,998 (1,360)	50 (92)	Subsonic?	Moving tail fins	Solid-propellant rocket	Mid-course inertial, + inter-changeable TV or imaging IR seeker	a) 750 (340) HE	F-4, F-15, F-16, F-111, Kfir, B-52
Rafael Armament Development Authority PO Box 2082, 31021 Haifa	Popeye 2 and Popeye 3 Turbo		a) 20? (50.8?)	40.5 (75) for Popeye 2 162 (300) for Popeye 3 Turbo	Subsonic?	Moving tails	Solid-propel-lant rocket for Popeye 2, turbojet or turbofan for Popeye 3 Turbo	Mid-course inertial, + inter-changeable TV or IIR seeker	a) 750 (340) HE for Popeye 2, HE for Popeye 3 Turbo	Popeye 2 on F-4, F-15, F-16, F-111, Kfir & B-52. Popeye 3 Turbo on test
Israel Aircraft Industries PO Box 105, Yahud Industrial Zone 56000	Griffin			5.4 (10)		Moving canard fins	None	Semi-active laser homing	a) Mk82, Mk83, or Mk84 bomb	Kfir
Israel Aircraft Industries PO Box 105, Yahud Industrial Zone 56000	Guillotine			16 (30)		Moving canard fins	None	Semi-active laser homing	a) Mk82 or Mk83 bomb	Kfir
Israel Aircraft Industries PO Box 105, Yahud Industrial Zone 56000	Nimrod	a) 111.8 (2.84) b) 19.7 (50)	a) 8.27 (21.0) b) 220 (100)		Subsonic?	Moving tail fins?	Solid-propellant rocket ?	Semi-active laser homing	a) (15) HE	
Elbit Computers PO Box 5390, 31053 Haifa	Opher	a) 132.3 (3.36) b) 27.5 (70.0)	a) 10.8 (27.3) b) 717 (325)	3.8+ (7+)		Moving canard fins	None	Passive IR homing	a) Mk82 bomb	Kfir
Rafael Armament Development Authority PO Box 2082, 31021 Haifa	Pyramid	a) 109.1 (2.77) b) 46.5 (118.0)	a) 11.4 (29.0) b) 800 (363)		Mach 0.8 average	Aerodynamic	None	TV homing	a) 230kg HE	
TAAS (formerly Israel Military Industries) Advanced Systems Division, PO Box 1044, Ramat Hasharon 47100	Star-1	a) 106.6 (2.71) b) 45.3 (115)	a) 13 (33) b) 401 (182)		Mach 0.8	Moving tail fins	Turbojet	Passive radar homing via broad-band seeker	a) HE	
TAAS (as above)	Cruise missile	b) 45.3? (115?)	a) 13? (33?)	Over 220 (407)	High subsonic	Moving tail fins	Turbojet?	Inertial with GPS + terminal seeker?	a) HE	

Manufacturer	Designation	a) Length ins (m) b) Span ins (cm)	a) Diameter ins (cm) b) Weight lb (kg)	Range naut miles (km)	Speed	Control	Propulsion	Guidance	a) Warhead lb (kg) b) Fuzing	Platform(s)
Italy										
Consorzio Armamenti Spendibili Multi-Uso (CASMU) Via della Quattro Fontane 21A, I-00 184, Roma	Skyshark (rocket-powered, unless stated)	a) 197.0 (5.00) b) 59.0 (150)	b) c.2,200 (c.1,000)	13.5 – 32 (25 – 60)	Subsonic		Solid-propellant rocket	Inertial & GPS + passive IR seeker & datalink	a) 1,100 (500) of submunitions	Tornado, Eurofighter 2000
Consorzio Armamenti Spendibili Multi-Uso (CASMU) Via della Quattro Fontane 21A, I-00 184, Roma	Skyshark (turbojet-powered)	a) 197.0 (5.00) b) 59.0 (150)	b) c.3,300 (c.1,500)	135+ (250+)	Subsonic		Turbojet	Unpowered version has 3.2 – 6.4 (6 – 12)	a) 1,985 (900) of submunitions	Tornado, Eurofighter 2000
Japan										
Mitsubishi Electric/ Japan Technical Research & Development Institute	GCS-1 (Guidance Control Set 1)				Subsonic		None	Passive IIR homing	a) 500 (227) or 1,000 (454) bomb	FS-X
Russia										
GNPP Moscow	KAB-500L	a) 120.0 (3.05) b) 26.4 (67.0)	a) 13.8 (35.0) b) 1,177 (534)			Moving surfaces on tail fins	None	Semi-active laser homing	a) Contains c.430 (195) HE	MiG-27, Su-22, Su-24, Su-25
GNPP Moscow	KAB-500Kr	a) 120.0 (3.05) b) 33.5 (85.0)	a) 13.8 (35.0) b) 1,235 (560)			Moving surfaces on tail fins	None	TV homing	a) Contains c.430 (195) HE	MiG-27, Su-24, Su-25
GNPP Moscow	KAB-1500L-F	a) 181.0 (4.60) b) 51.2 (130.0)	a) 22.8 (58.0) b) 3,440 (1,560)			Moving surfaces on tail fins	None	Semi-active laser homing	a) Contains 2,600 (1180) HE	MiG-27, Su-22, Su-24, Su-25
GNPP Moscow	KAB-1500L-Pr	a) 181.0 (4.60) b) 51.2 (130.0)	a) 22.8 (58.0) b) 3,307 (1,500)			Moving surfaces on tail fins	None	Semi-active laser homing	a) Contains 2,425 (1100) HE	MiG-27, Su-22, Su-24, Su-25
GNPP Moscow	KAB-1500Kr					Moving surfaces on tail fins	None	TV homing	a) HE	
Raduga Dubna	Kh-15 (AS-16 Kickback)	a) c.188.1 (c.4.77) b) 36.2 (92.0)	a) 17.9 (45.5) b) c.2,650 (c.1,200)	81 (150)	Mach 5	Moving tail fins	Solid-propellant rocket	Inertial?	a) Kiloton-range nuclear?	Tu-22M, Tu-160
Raduga Dubna	Kh-15P izdieliye 115 (AS-16 Kickback)	a) c.188.2 (c.4.78) b) 36.2 (92.0)	a) 17.9 (45.5) b) c.2,650 (c.1,200)		Mach 5	Moving tail fins	Solid-propellant rocket	Inertial + passive radar seeker	a) HE	Tu-22M, Tu-160
Raduga Dubna	Kh-22 (AS-4 Kitchen)	a) 458.7 (11.65) b) 118.1 (300.0)	a) 36.2 (92.0) b) 12,742 (5,780)	c.215 (c.400)		Moving tail fins?	Liquid-propellant rocket	Inertial	a) Nuclear	Tu-22M, Tu-95K
Zvezda Kaliningrad	Kh-23/Kh-66 izdieliye 66 (AS-7 Kerry)	a) 141.0 (3.59) b) 30.9 (78.5)	a) 10.8 (27.5) b) 633 (287)	5.4 (10)	1,965 – 2,460 ft/sec (600 – 750 m/sec)	Moving tail fins	Solid-propellant rocket	Radio command	a) 245 (111) HE b) impact fuze	MiG-23, MiG-27, Su-17/20/22, Su-24, Su-25
Zvezda Kaliningrad	Kh-24 (AS-7 Kerry)	a) 141.0 (3.59) b) 30.9 (78.5)	a) 10.8 (27.5) b) c.630 (c.290)	5.4 (10)	1,965 – 2,460 ft/sec (600 – 750 m/sec)	Moving tail fins	Solid-propellant rocket	Passive radar homing	a) 246 (111) HE b) Impact fuze	MiG-23, MiG-27, Su-17/20/22
Zvezda Kaliningrad	Kh-25 izdieliye 69 (AS-10 Karen)	a) 159.1 (4.04)	a) 10.8 (27.5)	5.9 (11)	2,790ft/sec (850m/sec)	Moving canards	Solid-propellant rocket	Semi-active laser homing	a) 198 (90) blast fragmentation	MiG-27, Su-17/20/22, Su-24, Su-25
Zvezda Kaliningrad	Kh-25ML izdieliye 713 (AS-10 Karen)	a) 146.06 (3.71) b) 28.74 (73.0)	a) 10.8 (27.5) b) 660 (300)	5.4 (10)	2,790ft/sec (850m/sec)	Moving canards	Solid-propellant rocket	Semi-active laser homing	a) 198 (90) blast fragmentation	MiG-27, Su-17, Su-24, Su-25, Su-35, Ka-50
Zvezda Kaliningrad	Kh-25MP izdieliye 711 (AS-12 Kegler)	a) 165.0 (4.19)	a) 10.8 (27.5) b) 706 (320)	21.6 (40)	2,790ft/sec (850m/sec)	Moving canards	Solid-propellant rocket	Passive radar seeker	a) 198 (90) blast fragmentation	MiG-23, MiG-27, Su-17, Ka-50
Zvezda Kaliningrad	Kh-25MR izdieliye 715 (AS-10 Karen)	a) 145.28 (3.69)	a) 10.8 (27.5) b) 660 (300)	5.4 (10)	2,790ft/sec (850m/sec)	Moving canards	Solid-propellant rocket	Radio command	a) 198 (90) blast fragmentation	MiG-23BN, MiG-27, Su-17/20/22, Su-24
Zvezda Kaliningrad	Kh-27 PS izdieliye 711 (AS-12 Kegler)			32 (60)		Moving canards	Solid-propellant rocket	Passive radar homing	a) 198 (90) blast fragmentation	MiG-27, Su-17/20/22, Su-24, Su-25, Tu-22M
Raduga Dubna	Kh-28 izdieliye 93 (AS-9 Kyle)	a) 248.40 (6.31) b) 55.1 (140.0)	a) c.18 (c.45) b) 1,576 (715)	46 (85)	Mach 0.8		Liquid-propellant rocket	Passive radar homing	a) 245 (111) HE	Su-17, Su-24
Vympel?	Kh-29D (AS-14 Kedge)	a) 153.5 (3.90) b) 43.3 (110.0)	a) 15.8 (40.0) b) c.1,500 (c.660)					Passive (imaging?) IR homing	a) 705 (320) HE	
Vympel?	Kh-29L izdieliye 63 (AS-14 Kedge)	a) 153.5 (3.90) b) 43.3 (110.0)	a) 15.8 (40.0) b) 1,455 (660)	1 – 5.4 (1.8 –10)			Solid-propellant rocket	Semi-active laser homing	a) 705 (320) HE	MiG-27, Su-17, Su-24, Su-25, Su-33, Su-35

Manufacturer	Designation	a) Length ins (m) b) Span ins (cm)	a) Diameter ins (cm) b) Weight lb (kg)	Range naut miles (km)	Speed	Control	Propulsion	Guidance	a) Warhead lb (kg) b) Fuzing	Platform(s)
Russia										
Vympel?	Kh-29T (AS-14 Kedge)	a) 153.5 (3.90) b) 43.3 (110.0)	a) 15.8 (40.0) b) 1,521 (690)	1.6 – 15 (3 – 28)			Solid-propellant rocket	TV homing	a) 705 (320) HE	MiG-27, MiG-29, Su-17, Su-24, Su-25, Mirage F1
Zvezda Kaliningrad	Kh-31H izdieliye 77 (As-17 Krypton)	a) 185 (4.7) b) 45.3 (115)	a) 14.2 (36.0) b) 1,323 (600)	8 – 60 (15 – 110)	Mach 3.5		Integrated rocket-ramjet	Passive radar homing	a) HE?	MiG-29, SU-25
Zvezda Kaliningrad	Kh-31P	a) 185.0 (4.70) b) 45.3(115)	a) 14.2 (36.0) b) 1,323 (600)	81 (150)	Mach 3.5		Integrated rocket-ramjet	Passive-radar homing	a) 198 (90) HE b) Impact & proximity fuzes?	MiG-21E, MiG-27M, MiG-29M, Su-25, Su-27, Su-30MK, Su-35
Zvezda Kaliningrad	Kh-31U (AS-17 Krypton)	a) 185? (4.7?) b) 45.3? (115?)	a) 14.2 (36.0) b) c.1,401 (c.650?)	8 – 60 (15 – 110)	Mach 3.5		Integrated rocket-ramjet		a) HE	MiG-29, Su-25, Su-30MK, Su-33, Su-35
Raduga Dubna	Kh-55 (AS-15a Kent)	a) 237.8 (6.04) b) 122.0 (310)	a) 20.2 (51.4) b) 2,756 (1,250)	1,350 (2,500)	Subsonic	Moving tail fins	Turbofan	Inertial + terrain matching	a) 200kT nuclear	Tu-95, Tu-160
Raduga Dubna	Kh-55SM (AS-15b Kent)	b) 122.0 (310)	a) 20.2 (51.4) b) 3,307 (1,500)	1,620 (3,000)	Subsonic	Moving tail fins	Turbofan	Inertial + terrain matching	a) 200kT nuclear	Tu-95, Tu-160
Raguda Dubna	Kh-58 izdieliye 112 (AS-11 Kilter)	a) 189? (4.8?) b) 46.1 (117.0)	a) 15.0 (38.0) b) c.1,430 (c.650)	at least 19 (at least 35)	High subsonic	Moving tail fins	Solid-propellant rocket	Autopilot + passive radar homing	a) 328 (149) HE?	MiG-25BM, Su-17, Su-24
Raguda Dubna	Kh-58U (AS-11 Kilter)	a) 189.0 (4.80) b) 46.1 (117.0)	a) 15.0 (38.0) b) c.1,430 (c.650)	54 (100)	High subsonic	Moving tail fins	Solid-propellant rocket	Autopilot + passive radar homing	a) 328 (149) HE?	MiG-25BM, Su-24
Raduga Dubna	Kh-58E (AS-11 Kilter)	a) 189.0 (4.80) b) 46.1 (117.0)	a) 15.0 (38.0) b) 1,433 (650)	19 – 65 (36 – 120) depending on launch altitude and speed	High subsonic	Moving tail fins	Solid-propellant rocket	Autopilot + passive radar homing	a) 328 (149) HE?	Su-22 (two under fuselage); Su-24 (two under wings), Su-25
Raduga Dubna	Kh-58E (AS-11 Kilter) – long-range version	a) 189.0 (4.80) b) 46.1 (117.0)	a) 15.0 (38.0) b) 1,433 (650)	32 – 65 (60 – 120) depending on launch altitude and speed	High subsonic	Moving tail fins	Solid-propellant rocket	Autopilot + passive radar homing	a) 328 (149) HE?	
Raduga Dubna	Kh-59 Ovod (AS-13 Kingpost)	a) 212.6 (5.4) b) 49.2 (12.5)	a) 15.0 (38.0) b) 1,764 (800)	27 (50)		Moving canards	Solid-propellant booster and sustainer	TV + datalink	a) c.331 (150) HE	MiG-27, SU-17, Su-22, SU-24
Raduga Dubna	Kh-59M Ovod-M (AS-18 Kazoo)	a) 224.0 (5.69) b) 51.2 (130.0)	a) 15.0 (38.0) b) 2,028 (920)	62 (115)	350 – 540kts (860 – 1,000 km/h)	Moving canards	Turbofan mounted below fuselage + solid-propellant rocket booster	TV + datalink	a) 705.5 (320) with 617 (280) of submunitions	Su-30MK
Raduga Dubna	Kh-65	a) 237.8 (6.04) b) 122.0 (310.0)	a) 20.2 (51.4) b) 2,755 (1,250)	270 – 324 (500 – 600)	Subsonic	Moving tail fins	Turbofan mounted below rear fuselage		a) 904 (410) HE	
Zvezda Kaliningrad	Kh-66 (AS-7 Kerry)	a) 141? (3.59?) b) 30.9 (78.5)	a) 10.8 (27.5) b) 632? (287?)	5.4 (10)	1,965 – 2,460 ft/sec (600 – 750 m/sec)	Moving tail fins	Solid propellant rocket	Radio command?	a) 245 (111) HE? b) Impact fuze	MiG-21
Raduga Dubna	Kh-101			1,500 (2,778)	Subsonic				a) Conventional?	Tu-95 Bear-H Tu-22M3. Likely replacement for cancelled Kh-90 cruise missile
Raduga Dubna	KSR-5, KSR-5N, KSR-5P (AS-6 Kingfish)	a) 417.0 (10.60) b) 102.4 (260)	a) 36.2 (92) b) 8,700 (3,950)	c.215 (c.400)	Mach 3	Moving tail fins?	Liquid-propellant rocket	Cruise inertial, Attack: active radar seeker (or passive radiation seeker for KSR-5P)	a) 2,205 (1,000) HE for KSR-5, 350kT nuclear for KSR-5N	Tu-16 including anti-ship
Not known	S-25L	a) 130.0 (3.30)	a) 10.2 (26.0) b) c.880 (c.400)	1.6 (3)		Moving canards	Solid-propellant rocket	Semi-active laser homing	a) HE	

Manufacturer	Designation	a) Length ins (m) b) Span ins (cm)	a) Diameter ins (cm) b) Weight lb (kg)	Range naut miles (km)	Speed	Control	Propulsion	Guidance	a) Warhead lb (kg) b) Fuzing	Platform(s)
Russia										
Chelomey Moscow	BL-10 (AS-X-19 Koala)	a) c.390 (c.10)		1,620 (3,000)	Mach 2.5-3				a) Two independently-targetable - 54naut miles (100km) separation – warheads	
South Africa										
Grinaker Avitronics	Guided Boosted Bomb	a) 138 (3.5)	a) 10.75 (27.3) b) 716.5 (325)	9.7 (18) at low level	Subsonic	Moving canard fins	None	Passive radar homing or semi-active laser homing	a) Mk82 bomb	
Sweden										
Saab Missiles S-58 1 88 Linkoping	Autonomous Stand-Off Missile (ASOM)	a) c.168 (c.4.3) b) 55.1? (140?)	a) 19.7? (50?) b) c.1,600 (c.725)		High subsonic	Moving tail fins	Turbojet?	Terrain comparison + imaging IR homing	a) HE	
Saab Missiles S-58 1 88 Linkoping	RB 04E	a) 175.2 (4.45) b) 77.5 (197.0)	a) 19.7 (50.0) b) 1,358 (616)	17.3 (32)			Solid-propellant rocket	Active radar homing	a) 661 (300) fragmentation	Viggen
Saab Missiles S-58 1 88 Linkoping	RB 05A	a) 141.7 (3.60) b) 31.5 (80.0)	a) 11.8 (30.0) b) 672 (305)	4.85 (9)	Supersonic		Liquid-propellant rocket	Command via microwave radio		Viggen
United Kingdom										
GEC-Marconi Dynamics Stanmore, Middlesex, England	Lancelot					Moving wings	Externally-mounted solid-propellant rocket	Semi-active laser homing + optional inertial GPS	a) HE penetrator	Tornado, Eurofighter 2000
GEC-Marconi Dynamics Stanmore, Middlesex, England	Hakim A/ PGM-A			c.27 (c.50)		Moving wings	Externally-mounted solid-propellant rocket	Semi-active laser homing	a) 500 (227) HE blast fragmentation	Mirage 2000
GEC-Marconi Dynamics Stanmore, Middlesex, England	HakimB/ PGM-B			c.27 (c.50)		Moving wings	Two externally-mounted solid-propellant rockets	Semi-active laser homing	a) 1,000 (454) HE blast fragmentation	Mirage 2000
British Aerospace (Defence) Dynamics Division PO Box 19, Six Hills Way, Stevenage, Hertfordshire SG1 2DA	Alarm	a) 166.9 (4.24) b) 28.4 (72.0)	a) 8.7 (22.0) b) 590.8 (268)	24.3 (45)		Cruciform moving tail fins	Solid-propellant rocket	Passive radar homing	a) HE	Tornado, Sea Harrier
United States of America										
Texas Instruments PO Box 405, Lewisville, TX 75067	AGM-45A Shrike	a) 120.0 (3.05) b) 36.0 (91.4)	a) 8.0 (20.3) b) 390 (177)	15.6 – 21.6 (29 – 40)	Mach 2	Moving wings	Solid-propellant rocket	Passive radar homing	a) 145 (66) fragmentation	F-4G, F-16, EF-111, & others
Hughes Missile Systems Old Nogales Highway, PO Box 11337, Tucson, AZ 85734	AGM-65A/B Maverick	a) 98.0 (2.49) b) 28.4 (72.0)	a) 11.8 (30.0) b) 463 (210)	1.6 (3)	Subsonic	Moving tail fins	Dual-thrust solid-propellant rocket	TV homing	a) 125 (57) HEAT b) Impact	F-4, F-5, F-15, F-16, F/A-18, F-111, A-4, A-6, A-7, Harrier II, A-10, Viggen, Hunter, Orao, Super Galeb
Hughes Missile Systems Old Nogales Highway, PO Box 11337, Tucson, AZ 85734	AGM-65D Maverick	a) 98.0 (2.49) b) 28.4 (72.0)	a) 11.8 (30.0) b) 485 (220)	10.8 (20)	Subsonic	Moving tail fins	Dual-thrust solid-propellant rocket	Imaging IR seeker	a) 125 (57) HEAT b) Impact	F-4, F-5, F-15, F-16, F-111, A-7, Harrier II, A-10, Tornado, P-3C-III, MB-339?
Hughes Missile Systems Old Nogales Highway, PO Box 11337, Tucson, AZ 85734	AGM-65E Maverick	a) 98.0 (2.49) b) 28.4 (72.0)	a) 11.8 (30.0) b) 646 (293)	10.8 (20)	Subsonic	Moving tail fins	Dual-thrust solid-propellant rocket	Semi-active laser homing	a) 300 (136) blast-penetrator b) Impact	F-4, F/A-18, A-7, Harrier II, F-117?
Hughes Missile Systems Old Nogales Highway, PO Box 11337, Tucson, AZ 85734	AGM-65F Maverick	a) 98.0 (2.49) b) 28.4 (72.0)	a) 11.8 (30.0) b) 677 (307)	13.5 (25)	Subsonic	Moving tail fins	Dual-thrust solid-propellant rocket	Imaging IR	a) 300 (136) blast-penetrator b) Impact	F/A-18, A-6, A-7, Harrier II
Hughes Missile Systems Old Nogales Highway, PO Box 11337, Tucson, AZ 85734	AGM-65G Maverick	a) 98.0 (2.49) b) 28.4 (72.0)	a) 11.8 (30.0) b) 677 (307)	13.5 (25)	Subsonic	Moving tail fins	Dual-thrust solid-propellant rocket	Imaging IR	a) 300 (136) blast penetrator b) Impact	F-15, F-16, F-111, F-117?
Hughes Missile Systems Old Nogales Highway, PO Box 11337, Tucson, AZ 85734	AGM-65H Maverick	a) 102.4 (2.60) b) 28.4 (72.0)	a) 11.8 (30.0) b) 672 (305)	13.5 (25)	Subsonic	Moving tail fins	Dual-thrust solid-propellant rocket	Millimetre-wave active radar homing	a) 300 (136) blast-penetrator b) Impact	

Manufacturer	Designation	a) Length ins (m) b) Span ins (cm)	a) Diameter ins (cm) b) Weight lb (kg)	Range naut miles (km)	Speed	Control	Propulsion	Guidance	a) Warhead lb (kg) b) Fuzing	Platform(s)
United States of America										
Boeing Defense & Space Group, PO Box 3999, Seattle, WA 98124-2499	AGM-69A SRAM	a) 168.0 (4.27) b) 35.4 (90)	a) 17.5 (44.5) b) 2,230 (1,012)	30 – 91 (55 – 168)	Mach 3		Two-burn solid-propellant rocket	Inertial	a) 200kT W-69 nuclear	B-52, B-1, (missiles retired from alert status in 1990)
McDonnell Douglas Missile Systems St. Louis, Missouri 63166-0516	AGM-84E SLAM	a) 175.0 (4.45) b) 35.8 (91.0)	a) 13.5 (34.3) b) 1,366 (620)	54 (100)	Mach 0.85	Cruciform moving tail fins	Turbojet	Cruise: inertial + radar altimeter + GPS; Attack: active radar homing + datalink	a) 485 (220) HE penetration blast b) Contact (with time delay) + proximity fuzes	F/A-18, F-111, B-52, S-3B
McDonnell Douglas Missile Systems St. Louis, Missouri 63166-0516	AGM-84 SLAM ER	a) 172.0 (4.37)	a) 13.5 (34.3) b) 1,565 (710)		Mach 0.85	Cruciform moving tail fins	Turbojet	Cruise: inertial + radar altimeter + GPS; Attack: active radar homing + datalink	a) Improved HE penetrator b) Contact (with time delay) + proximity fuzes	F/A-18, F-111, B-52
Boeing Defense & Space Group, PO Box 3999, Seattle, WA 98124-2499	AGM-86B & C ALCM	a) 248.8 (6.32) b) 144.1 (366.0)	a) 24.0 (61.0) b) 3,197 (1,450), 3,300?(1,497?) for AGM-86C	1, 080 (2,000) for AGM-86C	Mach 0.6	Elevons	Turbofan	Inertial + tercom	a) 271 (123) W-80 200kT thermonuclear, or 1,000 (454) HE for AGM-86C	B-52, B-1B
Texas Instruments PO Box 405, Lewisville, TX 75067	AGM-88 HARM	a) 164.2 (4.17) b) 44.5 (113.0)	a) 10 (25.4) b) 794 (360)	10 (18.5)	Mach 2+	Cruciform moving tail fins	Solid-propellant rocket	Passive radar homing	a) Modified Shrike fragmentation b) Motorola proximity fuze	F-4G, F-15, F-16, F/A-18, F-111, F-117A. A-6, EA-6B, Tornado
Motorola Scottsdale, Arizona	AGM-122 Sidearm	a) 118.1 (3.00) b) 24.8 (63.0)	a) 5.0 (12.7) b) 201 (91)	4.3 (8)		Cruciform moving canard fins	Solid-propellant rocket	Passive radar homing	a) 22.5 (10.2) HE blast	F-4G, F/A-18, A-4, Harrier II, AH-64, AH-1T
Electronics & Space Corporation St. Louis, Missouri	AGM-123 Skipper II	a) 169.3 (4.30) b) 63.0 (160)	a) 14.0 (35.6) b) 1,283 (582)			Cruciform moving canard fins	Solid-propellant rocket	Semi-active laser homing	a) Mk83 bomb	F/A-18, A-6
Hughes Missile Systems Old Nogales Highway, PO Box 11337, Tucson, AZ 85734	AGM-129 Advanced Cruise Missile	a) 250.0 (6.35) b) 122.0 (310.0)	a) 25.1 – 27.7 (64 – 70.4) b) 2,755 (1,250)	1,620 (3,000)	Subsonic	Moving fins?	Turbofan	Inertial + laser radar	a) 200kT nuclear	B-52H, B-1B, B-2
Rockwell International 1800 Satellite Blvd, Duluth, GA 30136	AGM-130A & B	a) 154.5 (3.92) b) 59.0 (150.0)	a) 18.0 (45.7) b) 2,917 (1,323)	13 – 35 (24 – 65)	Subsonic	Moving fins	Solid-propellant rocket	IR or TV seeker + datalink	a) Mk84 or BLU-109/B bomb (for A), or submunition dispenser (for B)	F-4, F-15E, F-111
Texas Instruments PO Box 405, Lewisville, TX 75067	AGM-154A Joint Stand-Off Weapon (JSOW) -USAF version	a) 156.0 (3.96)	a) 20.9 x 23.6 (53 x 60) b) 1,058 (480)	15 – 40 (28 – 74)			None	Inertial + GPS	a) 6 Textron BLU-108B Sensor Fuzed Weapon Submunitions	F-15E, F-16, F-111, F-117?, B-52
Texas Instruments PO Box 405, Lewisville, TX 75067	GBU-10C, D, E & F Paveway II	a) 170.1 (4.32) b) 66 (168)	a) 18.1 (46.0) b) c.1,985 (c.900)			Moving canard fins	None	Semi-active laser homing	a) Mk84 bomb	Includes F-15E, F-117
Texas Instruments PO Box 405, Lewisville, TX 75067	GBU-10G, H & J Paveway II	a) 167.7 (4.26) b) 66 (168)	a) 14.6 (37.0) b) c.1,985 (c.900)			Moving canard fins	None	Semi-active laser homing	a) BLU-109/B	Includes F-15E, F-117
Texas Instruments PO Box 405, Lewisville, TX 75067	GBU-12B, C & D Paveway II	a) 131.1 (3.33) b) 52.75 (134)	a) 10.75 (27.3) b) 603 (225)			Moving canard fins	None	Semi-active laser homing	a) Mk82 bomb	Includes F-15E, F-117
Texas Instruments PO Box 405, Lewisville, TX 75067	GBU-16A & B	a) 144.9 (3.68) b) 66 (168)	a) 13.8 (35.0) b) c.1,000 (c.454)			Moving canard fins	None	Semi-active laser homing	a) Mk83 bomb	
Rockwell International 1800 Satellite Blvd, Duluth, GA 30136	GBU-15/Mk84	a) 154.0 (3.91) b) 59.0 (149.0)	a) 18.0 (46.0) b) 2,513 (1,141)	0.8 – 44 (1.5 – 82)	Subsonic	Moving canard fins	None	IR or TV seeker + datalink	a) Mk84 or BLU-109/B bomb	F-4, F-15E, F-16, F-111, B-52
Texas Instruments PO Box 405, Lewisville, TX 75067	GBU-24A/B Paveway III	a) 177.0 (c.4.5)				Moving canard fins	None	Semi-active laser homing	a) HE	
Lockheed Martin Missiles & Space PO Box 3504, Sunnyvale, CA 94088-3504	GBU-27B	a) 166.9 (4.24) b) 66.15 (168.0)				Moving fins	None	Semi-active laser homing	a) Penetrator with 529 (240) HE core	F-111, F-117A

Manufacturer	Designation	a) Length ins (m) b) Span ins (cm)	a) Diameter ins (cm) b) Weight lb (kg)	Range naut miles (km)	Speed	Control	Propulsion	Guidance	a) Warhead lb (kg) b) Fuzing	Platform(s)
United States of America										
Lockheed Martin Missiles & Space PO Box 3504, Sunnyvale, CA 94088-3504	GBU-28B	a) 230 (5.84) b) 66.15 (168.0)	a) 14.6 (37.0) b) 5,707 (2,130)			Moving fins	None		a) 675 (306) HE penetrator	F-111
Lockheed Martin & McDonnell Douglas	GBU-30 (formerly JDAM)			10.5 (19.5)		Moving tail fins	None	Inertial + GPS	a) Mk 83, Mk 84, or BLU-109 penetrator bomb	B-1B, B-2, B-52, F-14 F-15, F-16, F/A-18, F-22, P-3
McDonnell Douglas Missile Systems PO Box 516, St Louis, MS 63166-0516	Grand SLAM	a) 209.0 (5.31) b) 95.6 (242.8)	a) 13.5 (34.3) b) c.2,400 (c.1100)	162+ (300+)	Mach 0.85?	Cruciform moving tail fins	Turbojet	Cruise: inertial + radar altimeter + GPS; Attack: IIR terminal homing	a) c.1,000 (450) HE penetrator	Proposed for Tornado, Harrier, Eurofighter 2000
Unknown	Have Slick	a) c.180 (4.60)	b) c.3,100 (c.1,400)	19 (35)			None?	Imaging IR or millimetre-wave homing?	a) c. 2,000 (c.900) of stores – warhead or submunitions	
Loral Vought Systems 1210 Massillon Road, Akron, OH 44315	Hypervelocity missile	a) 113.8 (2.89)	a) 3.8 (9.7) b) 71 (32)	1.6 (3)	0.93miles/sec (1.5km/sec)	Pyrotechnic thrusters	Solid-propellant rocket	Laser or radar command	a) None – kinetic kill by tungsten carbide tip	None
Texas Instruments PO Box 405, Lewisville, TX 75067	JSOW (Joint Stand-off Weapon)	a) 157.0 (3.98) for USN/USMC version, 158 (4.01) for unitary warhead	a) 20.9 x 23.6 (53 x 60) b) 1,058 (480) for USN/USMC version	15 – 40 (28 –74)			None	Inertial + GPS (+IIR terminal homing for unitary version)	a) 145 BLU-97/B combined effect bomblets (shaped charge, blast & incendiary) or BLU-111 HE warhead for unitary version	F/A-18, Harrier II, A-6E
Northrop Grumman & Boeing	Inertial Aided Munition (AIM)					Moving tailfins	None	Inertial	a) Mk 82 bomb	Tested on F-4, A-6
Rockwell International 3800 Satellite Blvd, Duluth GA 30136	Mk 82 GT (GPS-guided Tailkit)				Subsonic		None	GPS	a) Mk 82	B-1B, B-2
Lockheed Martin & Alliant/Texas Instruments	Wind Corrected Munitions Dispenser					Moving tailfins	None		a)Tactical munitions dispenser	B-1B, B-2, B-52, F-15E, F-16
Multi-national										
Aerospatiale/Daimler-Benz?	Aramis			10.8 (20)	Supersonic		Ramjet	Combined passive radar/ passive IR homing?	a) HE	
Texas Instruments/Shorts	Griffin 38			15 – 40 (28 – 74)			Solid propellant rocket	Inertial + Passive IIR homing?	a) 6 Textron BLU-108B Sensor Fuze Weapon submunitions	Proposed for Tornado, Harrier II, Eurofighter 2000
Daimler-Benz/Saab	KEPD 350									Proposed for Tornado, Harrier II, Eurofighter 2000
GEC-Marconi/Kentron	Pegasus			More than 135? (250?)						Proposed for Tornado, Harrier II, Eurofighter 2000
British Aerospace Defence, Dynamics Division/Matra	Storm Shadow	a) 200? (5.1?) b) 112.2 (285.0)	a) 24.8 x 20.0 (63 x 51) b) c.2,650 (c.1,200)	More than 135? (250?)	Subsonic		Turbojet	RLG inertial with updates + IIR homing	a) Unitary kinetic energy HE penetrator warhead	Proposed for Tornado, Harrier II, Eurofighter 2000
Hunting Engineering/ Daimler-Benz	SWAARM 2	a) 130 (3.3) b) 59 (150)	a) 24.8 x 12.6 (63 x 32) b) 992 (450)		Subsonic		None	Inertial + millimetre wave terminal homing	a) 16 Alliant Techsystems SADARM dual-mode (mm wave/IR) submunitions	Proposed for Tornado, Harrier II, Eurofighter 2000

Air-to-air

Manufacturer	Designation	a) Length ins (m) b) Span ins (cm)	a) Diameter ins (cm) b) Weight lb (kg)	Range naut miles (km)	Speed	Control	Propulsion	Guidance	a) Warhead lb (kg) b) Fuzing	Platform(s)
Brazil										
Orbita Sistemas Aeroespaciais Ave Tucunare 125, PO Box 152, 06460-020 Barueri SP	MAA-1 Mol (formerly known as Piranha)	a) 111.0 (2.82) b) 25.6 (65.0)	a) 6.0 (15.2) b) 198.4 (90.0)	5.4 (10)	Mach 2+	Moving canard fins	Single-stage solid-propellant rocket	Passive IR homing	a) 26.5 (12.0) HE fragmentation b) Laser proximity fuze	AMX, Mirage III, F-5
China										
China National Aero-Technology Import and Export Corporation (CATIC) 5 Liangguochang, Dongcheng Qu, Beijing 100010	PL-2B	a) 117.7 (2.99) b) 20.8 (52.8)	a) 5.0 (12.7) b) 167.6 (76.0)	1.6 (3)		Moving canard fins	Solid-propellant rocket	IR homing	a) 24.9 (11.3) blast fragmentation b) IR proximity fuze	J-5, J-6, J-7, JJ-7, J-8II, A-5
China National Aero-Technology Import and Export Corporation (CATIC) 5 Liangguochang, Dongcheng Qu, Beijing 100010	PL-3	a) 117.7 (2.99) b) 20.8 (52.8)	a) 5.0 (12.7) b) 180.8 (82.0)	1.6 (3)		Moving canard fins	Solid-propellant rocket	IR homing	a) 29.7 (13.5) HE blast fragmentation b) IR proximity fuze	J-5, J-6, J-7
China National Aero-Technology Import and Export Corporation (CATIC) 5 Liangguochang, Dongcheng Qu, Beijing 100010	PL-5 and PL-5B	a) 113.8 (2.89) b) 25.9 (65.7)	a) 5.0 (12.7) b) 187.4 (85.0)	8.6 (16)		Moving canard fins	Solid-propellant rocket	Passive IR homing	a) 19.8 (9.0) continuous-rod or HE blast fragmentation b) IR or radio proximity fuze. Improved on PL-5B	J-5, J-7, J-7, A-5
China National Aero-Technology Import and Export Corporation (CATIC) 5 Liangguochang, Dongcheng Qu, Beijing 100010	PL-7 and PL-7B	a) 108.3 (2.75) b) 26.0 (66.0)	a) 6.2 (15.8) b) 198.4 (90.0)			Moving canard fins	Solid-propellant rocket	Passive IR homing	a) 28.6 (13.0) HE fragmentation b) IR proximity fuze	J-7, J-8II, A-5, K-8
Unknown	PL-8	a) 118.1 (3.00) b) 33.9 (86.0)	a) 6.3 (16.0) b) 264.6 (120.0)	2.7 (5)		Moving canard fins	Solid-propellant rocket	Passive IR homing	a) 24.2 (11.0) HE fragmentation b) Laser proximity fuze	
China National Aero-Technology Import and Export Corporation (CATIC) 5 Liangguochang, Dongcheng Qu, Beijing 100010	PL-9	a) 117.7 (2.99) b) 31.9 (81.0)	a) 6.3 (16.0) b) 264.6 (120.0)	2.7 (5)		Moving canard fins	Solid-propellant rocket	Passive IR homing	a) 22.0 (10.0) HE b) Laser proximity fuze	J-7, J-8?
China National Aero-Technology Import and Export Corporation (CATIC) 5 Liangguochang, Dongcheng Qu, Beijing 100010	PL-10	a) 157.1 (3.99) b) 46.1 (117.0)	a) 11.3 (28.6) b) 661.4 (300.0)	8.1 (15)	Mach 3	Moving wings	Single-stage solid-propellant rocket	Semi-active radar homing	a) HE fragmentation b) RF proximity fuze	J-7, J-8?
France										
Aerospatiale Division Engins Tactiques F-92322 Chatillon-sous-Bagneux	ASMP-R	a) 211.8 (5.38) b) 37.8 (96.0)	a) 15.0 (38.0) b) 1,896 (860)	135 (250)	Mach 3.0	Moving tail fins	Liquid-propellant ramjet with integral solid propellant rocket booster	Passive radar homing	a) c.441 (c.200) HE	Projected anti-AEW weapon Mirage 2000?, Rafale?
Matra 37 avenue Louis-Breguet, F-78146 Velizy-Villacoublay Cedex	Air-Air Futur	a) 142 (3.6) b) 22.28 (56.6)	a) 6.7 (17)				Self modulated ramjet		a) HE	Projected long-range, air-to-air missile Mirage 2000?, Rafale?
Matra 37 avenue Louis-Breguet, F-78146 Velizy-Villacoublay Cedex	MICA	a) 122.1 (3.10) b) 22.1 (56.0)	a) 6.3 (16.0) b) 242.5 (110)	32+ (60+)		Moving tail fins + thrust vectoring	Solid-propellant rocket	Inertial with datalink up-dating + semi-active radar or passive IR seeker	a) HE blast fragmentation b) Active radar proximity fuze	Mirage 2000, Rafale
Matra 37 avenue Louis-Breguet, F-78146 Velizy-Villacoublay Cedex	Mistral	a) 71.3 (1.81) b) 7.5 (19.0)	a) 3.6 (9.3) b) 40.6 (18.4)	0.16 – 3.2 (0. 3 – 6)	Mach 2.6	Moving canard fins	Solid-propellant rocket	Passive IR/UV homing	a) 6.5 (2.95) fragmentation b) Contact & active laser proximity fuzes	AS 565 Panther, Gazelle, Tigre, AH-64

Manufacturer	Designation	a) Length ins (m) b) Span ins (cm)	a) Diameter ins (cm) b) Weight lb (kg)	Range naut miles (km)	Speed	Control	Propulsion	Guidance	a) Warhead lb (kg) b) Fuzing	Platform(s)
France										
Matra 37 avenue Louis-Breguet, F-78146 Velizy-Villacoublay Cedex	R.550 Magic 1	a) 107.1 (2.72) b) 26.0 (66.0)	a) 6.2 (15.7) b) 196 (89)	0.15 – 5+ (0.3 – 10+)	Mach 2+	Moving canard fins	Solid-propellant rocket	Passive IR homing	a) 27.5 (12.5) HE fragmentation b) Contact & IR proximity fuzes	Mirage III, Mirage 5, Mirage F1, Mirage 2000, Jaguar, Super Etendard, Alpha Jet, Sea Harrier, MiG-21, MiG-23, Harrier II, A-5, MB-339,Hawk, F-16, J-7, Atlantique
Matra 37 avenue Louis-Breguet, F-78146 Velizy-Villacoublay Cedex	R.550 Magic 2	a) 108.3 (2.75) b) 26.0 (66.0)	a) 6.2 (15.7) b) 198 (90)	0.15 – 5+ (0.3 – 10+)	Mach 2+	Moving canard fins	Solid-propellant rocket	Passive IR homing	a) 27.5 (12.5) HE fragmentation b) Contact & RF proximity fuzes	See Magic 1
Matra 37 avenue Louis-Breguet, F-78146 Velizy-Villacoublay Cedex	Super 530D	a) 149.6 (3.80) b) 24.4 (62.0)	a) 10.4 (26.3) b) 595 (270)	21+ (40+)	Mach 4.5+	Moving tail fins	Solid-propellant rocket	Semi-active radar homing	a) 66 (30) HE fragmentation b) Active radar proximity fuze	Mirage III, Mirage F1, Mirage 2000, Rafale
Matra 37 avenue Louis-Breguet, F-78146 Velizy-Villacoublay Cedex	Super 530F	a) 139.4 (3.54) b) 34.7 (88.0)	a) 10.4 (26.3) b) 540 (245)	19 (35)	Mach 4.5	Moving tail fins	Dual-thrust solid-propellant rocket	Semi-active radar homing	a) 66 (30) HE fragmentation b) Radar proximity fuze	Mirage III, Mirage F1, Mirage 2000, Rafale
Germany										
Daimler-Benz Aerospace PO Box 801109, D-81663 Munich	A3M						Rocket/ramjet	Active radar homing	a) HE	
Bodenseewerke-Geratetechnik PO Box 101155, D-88641 Uberlingen	IRIS-T	a) c.114 (c.2.9)	a) 5.0 (12.7) b) c.190 (c.86)			Thrust vectoring	Solid Propellant rocket	Passive IIR homing	a) HE	Planned for Tornado, Eurofighter 2000
India										
Defence R&D Lab	Astra							Inertial + active radar		LCA
Israel										
Rafael Armament Development Authority PO Box 2082, 31021 Haifa	Python 3	a) 118.1 (3.00) b) 33.9 (86.0)	a) 6.3 (16.0) b) 265 (120)	0.25 – 8 (0.5 – 15)	Mach 3.5	Moving canard fins	Solid-propellant rocket	Passive IR homing	a) 24.25 (11.0) HE fragmentation b) Laser proximity fuze	Kfir, F-4, F-5, F-15, F-16, Mirage III, Mirage F1, Mirage 2000, Pantara, MiG-21-2000, J-7
Rafael Armament Development Authority PO Box 2082, 31021 Haifa	Python 4	a) c.118? (c.3.0?) b) c.20? (c.50?)	a) c.6.3? (16.0?) b) 234 (108)	8.1 (15)			Smokeless solid-propellant rocket	All aspect two-colour passive IR homing		Kfir, F-16
Rafael Armament Development Authority PO Box 2082, 31021 Haifa	Shafrir 2	a) 102.4 (2.60) b) 25.2 (64.0)	a) 6.3 (16.0) b) 205 (93)	2.7 (5)		Moving canard fins	Double-base solid rocket	All-aspect two-colour passive IR homing	a) 24.25 (11.0) HE fragmentation b) Contact & proximity fuzes	F-4, F-15, F-16, Mirage III, Kfir, A-4
Italy										
Alenia Defense Systems Via Tiburtina Km 12,400, PO Box 7083, I-00 131 Roma	Aspide Mk1	a) 145.7 (3.70) b) 39.4 (100.0)	a) 8.0 (20.3) b) 485 (220)	18.9 (35)	Mach 4	Moving wings	Single-stage solid-propellant rocket	Semi-active radar homing	a) 77 (35) fragmentation b) Active-radar proximity fuze	F-104S
Alenia Defense Systems Via Tiburtina Km 12,400, PO Box 7083, I-00 131 Roma	Aspide Mk2	a) 143.7 (3.65) b) 24 (64)	a) 8.4 (21.2) b) 507 (230)	21.6 (40)	Mach 4	Moving wings	Single-stage solid-propellant rocket	Active radar homing	a) 77 (35) fragmentation b) Active-radar proximity fuze	Eurofighter 2000
Japan										
Mitsubishi Electric Mitsubishi Denki Bldg, 2-chome, 2-3 Marunouchi, Chiyoda-ku, Tokyo 100	AAM-3 (Type 90)	a) 118 (3.0) b) 25.2 (64)	b) 201 (91)	2.7 (5)			Solid-propellant rocket	Passive IR homing	a) HE b) Contact & proximity fuzes?	F-4, F-15, FS-X
Mitsubishi Electric Mitsubishi Denki Bldg, 2-chome, 2-3 Marunouchi, Chiyoda-ku, Tokyo 100	XAAM-4	a) c.158 (c.4.0)	b) c.507 (c.230)					Active radar homing		Planned for F-15J

Manufacturer	Designation	a) Length ins (m) b) Span ins (cm)	a) Diameter ins (cm) b) Weight lb (kg)	Range naut miles (km)	Speed	Control	Propulsion	Guidance	a) Warhead lb (kg) b) Fuzing	Platform(s)
Pakistan										
Pakistan Ordnance Factories Wah Cantt, Pakistan	designation unknown			short				Passive IR homing		
Russia										
Fakel/Toropov Moscow	K-5 or K-55 izdieliye I (AA-1 Alkali)	a) 98.4 (2.5) b) 25.75 (65.4)	a) 7.9 (20) b) (83)	0.65 – 5.4 (1.2 – 10)			Solid-propellant rocket	Semi-active radar or passive IR homing	a) 26.4 (12.0) HE	MiG-17PFU, MiG-19PM, MiG-21
Toropov Tushino	R-3S izdieliye 310a (AA-2 Atoll)	a) 111.7 (2.84) b) 20.8 (52.8)	a) 5.0 (12.7) b) 166 (75.3)	0.65 – 4.1 (1.2 – 7.6)	Mach 2.5?	Moving canard fins	Solid-propellant rocket	Passive IR homing	a) 24.9 (11.3) HE blast fragmentation b) Impact & optical proximity fuzes	MiG-21, MiG-23, MiG-27, Su-17, Su-20, Su-22
Toropov Tushino	R-3R izdieliye 320 (AA-2C Atoll)	a) 134.7 (3.42) b) 20.8 (52.8)	a) 5.0 (12.7) b) 184.1 (83.5)	0.5 – 3.8 (1 – 7)	Mach 2.5?	Moving canard fins	Solid-propellant rocket	J-band semi-active radar homing	a) 24.9 (11.3) HE blast fragmentation b) Impact & optical proximity fuzes	MiG-21, MiG-23, MiG-27, Su-17, Su-20, Su-22
Toropov Tushino	R-13M izdieliye 380 (AA-2D Atoll)	a) 113.2 (2.88) b) 23.2 (59.0)	a) 5.0 (12.7) b) 198.0 (89.8)	0.3 – 8.0 (0.6 – 15)	Mach 2.5?	Moving canard fins	Solid-propellant rocket	Passive IR homing	a) 24.9 (11.3) HE blast fragmentation b) Impact & RF proximity fuzes	MiG-21, MiG-23, MiG-27, Su-17, Su-20, Su-22, Su-25
Vympel Moscow	R-23R izdieliye 340 (AA-7 Apex)	a) 175.6 (4.46) b) 39.4 (100.0)	a) 7.9 (20.0) b) 491.6 (223.0)	1 – 19 (1.8 – 35)	3,280 ft/sec (1,000m/sec)	Moving tail fins	Solid-propellant rocket	Semi-active radar homing	a) 77.2 (35.0) HE fragmentation b) Proximity fuze	MiG-23, MiG-25, MiG-29
Vympel Moscow	R-23T izdieliye 360 (AA-7 Apex)	a) 163.8 (4.16) b) 39.4 (100.0)	a) 7.9 (20.0) b) 478? (217?)	1 – c.14.6? (1.8 – c.27?)	3,280 ft/sec (1,000m/sec)	Moving tail fins	Solid-propellant rocket	Passive IR homing	a) 77.2 (35.0) HE fragmentation b) Proximity fuze	MiG-23, MiG-25, MiG-29
Vympel Moscow	R-24R izdieliye 140 (AA-7 Apex)	a) 189.0 (4.80) b) 38.3 (97.2)	a) 7.9 (20.0) b) 551.1 (250.0)	27 (50)	3,280 ft/sec (1,000m/sec)	Moving tail fins	Solid-propellant rocket	Semi-active radar homing	a) 77.2 (35.0) HE fragmentation b) Proximity fuze	MiG-23, MiG-25, MiG-29
Vympel Moscow	R-24T izdieliye 160 (AA-7 Apex)	b) 38.3 (97.2)	a) 7.9 (20.0) b) c.500? (c.230?)		3,280 ft/sec (1,000m/sec)	Moving tail fins	Solid-propellant rocket	Passive IR homing	a) 77.2 (35.0) HE fragmentation b) Proximity fuze	MiG-23, MiG-25, MiG-29
Vympel Moscow	R-27R izdieliye 470 (AA-10 Alamo A)	a) 160.6 (4.08) b) 30.4 (77.2)	a) 9.1 (23.0) b) 557.8 (253.0)	0.25 – 32 (0.5 – 60)		Moving canard fins	Solid-propellant rocket	Inertial + command updates, then semi-active radar homing	a) 86 (39) HE b) Active radar proximity fuze	MiG-29, Su-27, Su-33, Su-35
Vympel Moscow	R-27R1	a) 160.6? (4.08?) b) 30.4? (77.2?)	a) 9.1 (23.0) b) 557.8?			Moving canard fins	Solid-propellant rocket	Inertial + command updates, then semi-Active radar homing	a) 86 (39) HE b) Active radar proximity fuze	MiG-29, Su-27, Su-33, Su-35
Vympel Moscow	R-27T izdieliye 470 (AA-10 Alamo B)	a) 149.5 (3.80) b) 30.4 (77.2)	a) 9.1 (23.0) b) 540.1 (245.0)	9.7 (18)		Moving canard fins	Solid-propellant rocket	Inertial + command updates, then passive IR homing	a) 86 (39) HE b) Active radar proximity fuze?	MiG-29, Su-27, Su-33, Su-35
Vympel Moscow	R-27EA	a) 188.2? (4.78?) b) 31.5? (80?)	a) 10.2 (26.0) b) c.772? (c.350?)			Moving canard fins	Solid-propellant rocket	Inertial + command updates, then active radar homing	a) 86 (39) HE b) Active radar proximity fuze	MiG-29, Su-27, Su-33, Su-35
Vympel Moscow	R-27EM	a) 188.2 (4.78) b) 31.5 (80)	a) 10.2 (26.0) b) 772 (350)	0.25 – 92 (0.5 – 170)		Moving canard fins	Solid-propellant rocket	Inertial + command updates, then passive IR homing	a) 86 (39) HE b) Active radar proximity fuze	MiG-29, Su-27, Su-33, Su-35
Vympel Moscow	R-27ER (AA-10 Alamo C)	a) 188.2 (4.78) b) 31.5 (80.0)	a) 10.2 (26.0) b) 772 (350)	0.25 – 70 (0.5 – 130)		Moving canard fins	Solid-propellant rocket	Inertial + command updates, then semi-active radar homing	a) 86 (39) HE b) Active radar proximity fuze	MiG-29, Su-27, Su-33, Su-35

Manufacturer	Designation	a) Length ins (m) b) Span ins (cm)	a) Diameter ins (cm) b) Weight lb (kg)	Range naut miles (km)	Speed	Control	Propulsion	Guidance	a) Warhead lb (kg) b) Fuzing	Platform(s)
Russia										
Vympel Moscow	R-27ET (AA-10 Alamo D)	b) 31.5? (80?)	a) 10.2 (26.0) b) 772 (350)	0.25 – 70 (0.5 – 130)		Moving canard fins	Solid-propellant rocket	Inertial + command updates, then passive IR homing	a) 86 (39) HE b) Active radar proximity fuze	MiG-29, Su-27, Su-33, Su-35
Vympel Moscow	R-27P	b) 31.5? (80?)					Solid-propellant rocket	Passive radar homing		
Vympel Moscow	R-33 izdieliye 410 (AA-9 Amos)	a) 163.4 (4.15) b) 46.5 (118.0)	a) 15.0 (38.0) b) 1,080 (490)	65 (120)			Solid-propellant rocket	Autopilot + semi-active radar homing	a) 103.6 (47) HE b) Impact & proximity fuzes?	MiG-31, Su-33, option on Su-27
Vympel Moscow	R-33S (AA-9 Amos)	a) c.164 (c.4.2) b) 46.5 (118.0)	a) 15.0 (38.0) b) c.1,300 (c.600)				Solid-propellant rocket	Autopilot + semi-active radar homing	b) Impact & proximity fuzes?	MiG-31, option on Su-27
Vympel Moscow	R-37	a) 161.4 (4.10) b) 27.6 (70.0)	a) 15.0 (38.0) b) 992 (450) anticipated	162 (300)		Moving rear fins		Inertial + active radar homing	a) 132 (60) fragmentation b) Impact & proximity fuzes?	MiG-31M
Bisnovat (now part of Vympel)	R-40R izdieliye 84 (AA-6 Acrid)	a) 245.3 (6.23) b) 57.1 (145.0)	a) 12.2 (31.0)	38 (70)	Mach 4.5	Ailerons + moving canard fins?	Solid-propellant rocket	Semi-active radar homing	a) 83.7 (38.0) HE b) Impact & proximity fuzes?	MiG-25, Su-21
Bisnovat (now part of Vympel)	R-40T izdieliye 84 (AA-6 Acrid)	a) 233.5 (5.93) b) 57.1 (145.0)	a) 12.2 (31.0)	16.2? (30?)	Mach 4.5	Ailerons + moving canard fins?	Solid-propellant rocket	Passive radar homing	a) 83.7 (38.0) HE b) Impact & proximity fuzes?	MiG-25, MiG-31, Su-22
Vympel?	R-40RD (AA-6 Acrid)	a) 245.3 (6.23) b) 57.1 (145.0)	a) 12.2 (31.0) b) 1,016 (461)	1.08 - 43 (2 – 80)	Mach 4.5	Ailerons + moving canard fins?	Solid-propellant rocket	Semi-active radar homing	a) 83.7 (38.0) HE b) Impact & proximity fuzes?	MiG-25, MiG-31, Su-35
Vympel Moscow	R-40TD (AA-6 Acrid)	a) 233.5 (5.93) b) 57.1 (145.0)	a) 12.2 (31.0) b) 992 (450)	16.2? (30?)	Mach 4.5	Ailerons + moving canard fins?	Solid-propellant rocket	Passive radar homing	a) 83.7 (38.0) HE b) Impact & proximity fuzes?	MiG-25, MiG-31, Su-35
Molniya (now part of Vympel)	R-60 izdieliye 62 (AA-8 Aphid)	a) 82.5 (2.09) b) 15.4 (39.0)	a) 4.7 (12.0) b) 95.9 (43.5)	0.16 – 4.0 (0.3 – 7.5)	Mach 2.5?	Moving canard fins	Solid-propellant rocket	Passive IR homing	a) 7.7 (3.5) HE b) Active radar proximity fuze	MiG-21, MiG-23, MiG-25, MiG-27, MiG-31, Mi-24, Su-17, Su-22, Su-24, Su-25, Su-27, Super Galeb, Iryda
Molniya (now part of Vympel)	R-60M & MK (AA-8 Aphid)	a) 84.2 (2.14) b) 15.4 (39.0)	a) 4.7 (12.0) b) 99.2 (45.0)	6.5 (12)	Mach 2.5?	Moving canard fins	Solid-propellant rocket	Passive IR homing	a) 7.7 (3.5) HE b) Laser proximity fuze?	MiG-21, MiG-23, MiG-25, MiG-27, MiG-29, MiG-31, Su-17, Su-22, Su-24, Su-25, Su-35
Novator Ekaterinburg	R-72 AAM-L	a) 236 (6.0); 291 (7.4) with booster	b) 1,654 (750)	216 (400)			Solid-propellant rocket & solid-propellant tandem booster	Inertial + command up-dates, then active-radar terminal homing	a) Adaptive HE fragmenting b) Active-radar proximity fuze	Probably the Su-27 and -35
Molniya (now part of Vympel)	R-73 izdieliye 72 (AA-11 Archer)	a) 114.2 (2.90) b) 20.1 (51.0)	a) 6.7 (17.0) b) 232 (105)	8.1 (15)		Moving canard fins + thrust vectoring	Dual-thrust solid-propellant rocket?	Passive IR homing	a) 16.3 (7.4) b) Active radar proximity fuze	MiG-29, Su-17, Su-27, Su-33, Su-34, Su-35, Ka-50
Molniya/Vympel	R-73E (AA-11 Archer)	a) 114.2 (2.90) b) 20.1 (51.0)	a) 6.7 (17.0) b) 243 (110)	0.15 – 16 (0.3 – 30)		Moving canard fins + thrust-vectoring	Dual-thrust solid-propellant rocket?	Passive IR homing	a) 16.3 (7.4) b) Active radar proximity fuze	MiG-29, Su-27, Su-33, Su-34, Su-35, Ka-50
Vympel Moscow	R-77 RVV-AE izdieliye 170 (AA-12)	a) 141.7 (3.60) b) 13.8 (35.0)	a) 7.9 (20.0) b) 386 (175)	49 (90)	Mach 3	Moving rear lattice control surfaces	Solid-propellant rocket (probably dual-thrust)	Inertial with datalink updates, then active or passive radar homing	a) 39.7 (18.0) HE b) Active radar proximity fuze	MiG-29, MiG-31, Su-25, Su-34, Su-35

Manufacturer	Designation	a) Length ins (m) b) Span ins (cm)	a) Diameter ins (cm) b) Weight lb (kg)	Range naut miles (km)	Speed	Control	Propulsion	Guidance	a) Warhead lb (kg) b) Fuzing	Platform(s)
Russia										
Vympel Moscow	R-77M RVV-AE-PD			86 (160)			Combined rocket/ramjet			
Bisnovat (now part of Vympel)	R-98MR (AA-3 Anab)	a) 168.1 (4.27) b) 51.2 (130.0)	a) 10.8 (27.5) b) 606 (275)	6.5 (12)	Mach 2+		Solid-propellant rocket	Semi-active radar homing	b) Impact & proximity fuzes?	See above
Toropov/Kolumna Machine Construction Design Bureau Tushino	9K32M Strela 2M (SA-7b)	a) 56.7 (1.44)	a) 2.8 (7.2) b) 21.8 (9.8)	0.43 – 2.3 (0.8 – 4.2)	Mach 1.7 (580 m/sec) maximum, Mach 1.49 (500m/sec) average	Two moving canard fins	Improved solid-propellant booster & sustainer	Passive IR homing	a) 2.53 (1.15) fragmentation b) Contact and grazing	Mi-2, Mi-24, Gazelle
Kolumna Machine Construction Design Bureau Tushino	9K310 Igla 1 (SA-16 Gimlet)	a) c.66 (c.1.68)	a) 2.8 (7.2)			Two moving canard fins	Solid-propellant booster & sustainer	Passive IR homing	a) 2.86 (1.3) fragmentation? b) Contact and grazing	Mi-2, Mi-24, Ka-50
Vympel	Unknown			c.16? (c.30?)		Vectored thrust		Passive IR homing	a) HE	New dogfight missile for Russian fighters
South Africa										
Denel, Kentron Division Jochemus Street, Erasmuskloof, PO Box 8322, Hennopsmeer 0046	Darter & A-Darter	a) 108.3 (2.75) b) 26.0 (66.0)	a) 6.2 (15.7) b) 196 (89)	0.15 – 5.4 (0.3 – 10)	Aircraft velocity + 1960ft/sec (600m/sec)	Moving canard fins	Solid-propellant rocket	Passive IR homing	a) 35.3 (16.0) prefragmented HE b) Contact & laser proximity fuzes	Mirage III, Mirage F1, Puma
Denel, Kentron Division Jochemus Street, Erasmuskloof, PO Box 8322, Hennopsmeer 0046	U/Darter	a) 108.3 (2.75) b) 26.0 (66.0)	a) 6.2 (15.7) b) 211.6 (96.0)	0.22 – 5.4 (0.4 – 10.0);	Aircraft velocity + 2,130ft/sec (650m/sec)	Moving canard fins	Solid-propellant rocket	Passive two-colour IR homing	a) 37.5 (17) prefragmented HE b) Contact & laser proximity	Cheetah?
Denel, Kentron Division Jochemus Street, Erasmuskloof, PO Box 8322, Hennopsmeer 0046	LRAAM (Long-Range Anti-Aircraft Missile)	a) c.120 (c.3.0) b) c.16 (c.40)	a) 7.1 (18.0) b) c.287 (c.130)	54+ (100+)	Mach 2.3 - 3.0		Solid-propellant integral rocket/ramjet	Autopilot with datalink + passive IIR homing	a) 44 (20) HE	
Denel, Kentron Division Jochemus Street, Erasmuskloof, PO Box 8322, Hennopsmeer 0046	V3/Kukri	a) 115.8 (2.94) b) 20.9 (53.0)	a) 5.0 (12.7) b) 161.8 (73.4)	0.16 – 1 (0.3 – 2) (low-altitude); 0.16 – 2.2 (0.3 – 4) (high-altitude)	Aircraft velocity + 1640ft/sec (500m/sec)	Moving canard fins	Double-base solid-propellant rocket	Passive IR homing	a) Fragmenta-tion, with Torpex 2A explosive b) Contact & proximity fuzes?	Mirage III, Mirage F1 & conversions
Taiwan										
Chung Shang Institute of Science and Technology Taipei	Tien Chien (Sky Sword I)	a) 113.0 (2.87) b) 25.2 (64.0)	a) 5.0 (12.7) b) 198 (90)	2.7 (5.0)		Moving canard fins	Solid-propellant rocket	Passive IR homing	a) HE blast fragmentation b) Laser proximity fuze	Ching-Kuo, F-5, F-16, Mirage 2000
Chung Shang Institute of Science and Technology Taipei	Tien Chien (Sky Sword II)	a) 141.7 (3.60) b) 29.5 (75.0)	a) 8.0 (20.3) b) 419 (190)	21.6 (40)		Moving wings?	Solid-propellant rocket	Semi-active radar?	a) HE fragmentation b) Radar proximity fuze	Ching-Kuo, F-16?, Mirage 2000?
United Kingdom										
British Aerospace (Defence) Dynamics Division PO Box 19, Six Hills Way, Stevenage, Hertfordshire SG1 2DA	Active Sky Flash	a) 144.1 (3.66) b) 40.2 (102.0)	a) 8.0 (20.3) b) 459 (208)	21.6 (40)	Mach 4	Moving wings	Solid-propellant rocket	Active radar homing	a) 66 (30) fragmentation b) Pulse-Doppler proximity fuze	Proposed for Tornado ADV
Shorts Belfast, N. Ireland	Javelin	a) 54.7 (1.39) b) 10.8 (27.5)	a) 3.0 (7.6) b) 28.0 (12.7)	0.16 – 3.0 (0.3 – 5.5)	Mach 1+	Cruciform moving canard fins	Solid-propellant rocket	SACLOS	a) 6.0 (2.74) fragmentation b) Impact & proximity fuzes	A129
British Aerospace (Defence) Dynamics Division PO Box 19, Six Hills Way, Stevenage, Hertfordshire SG 1 2DA	Sky Flash	a) 144.1 (3.66) b) 40.2(102.0)	a) 8.0 (20.3) b) 423.9 (192.3)	21.6 (40)	Mach 4	Moving wings	Solid-propellant rocket	CW semi-active radar homing	a) 66 (30) continuous-rod b) Radar proximity fuze	Tornado ADV, JA37 Viggen, Mirage 2000-5, tested on F-16
Shorts Belfast, N. Ireland	Starstreak	a) 55.1 (1.4) b) 9.85 (25)	a) 5.0 (12.7) b) 35.3 (16)	0.16 – 3.8 (0.3 – 7)	c. Mach 4 at sustainer burnout	Moving fins	Solid-propellant rocket booster, then unpowered	Laser beam-riding	a) Three dense alloy darts containing HE b) Delayed-action fuze	Proposed for AH-64

Manufacturer	Designation	a) Length ins (m) b) Span ins (cm)	a) Diameter ins (cm) b) Weight lb (kg)	Range naut miles (km)	Speed	Control	Propulsion	Guidance	a) Warhead lb (kg) b) Fuzing	Platform(s)
United States of America										
Raytheon Company Missile Systems Division Hartwell Road, Bedford, MA 01730	AIM-7E (AAM-N-6B) Sparrow	a) 144.0 (3.66) b) 40.0 (101.6)	a) 8.0 (20.3) b) 452 (205)	23.8 (44)	Mach 3.7 at burnout	Moving wings	Solid-propellant rocket	Semi-active radar homing		F-4, F-14, F-15, F-16, F/A-18
Raytheon/General Dynamics	AIM-7F Sparrow	a) 144.0 (3.66) b) 40.0 (101.6)	a) 8.0 (20.3) b) 500 (227)	21.6 (40)		Moving wings	Solid-propellant rocket	Semi-active radar homing	a) 86 (39) continuous-rod b) Impact & RF proximity fuzes	F-4, F-14, F-15, F-16, F/A-18
Raytheon/Hughes	AIM-7M Sparrow	a) 144.0 (3.66) b) 40.0 (101.6)	a) 8.0 (20.3) b) 508 (230)	0.3 – 24.3 (0.6 – 45)	Mach 2.5	Moving wings	Solid-propellant rocket	Semi-active radar homing	a) 86 (39) focussed blast fragmentation b) Impact & active-radar proximity fuzes	F-4, F-14, F-15, F-16, F/A-18, early FS-X?
Raytheon Company Missile Systems Division Hartwell Road, Bedford, MA 01730	AIM-7P Sparrow	a) 144.0 (3.66) b) 40.0 (101.6)	a) 8.0 (20.3) b) 508 (230)	24.3 (45)		Moving wings	Solid-propellant rocket	Command via mid-course data uplink receiver, then semi-active radar homing	a) 86 (39) continuous-rod b) Impact & active-radar proximity fuzes	F-4, F-14, F-15, F-16, F/A-18
Raytheon Company Missile Systems Division Hartwell Road, Bedford, MA 01730	AIM-7R Sparrow	a) 144.0 (3.66) b) 40.0 (101.6)	a) 8.0 (20.3) b) 508 (230)			Moving wings	Solid-propellant rocket	Combined semi-active radar & passive IR seeker		F-4, F-14, F-15, F-16, F/A-18
Ford Aerospace/ Raytheon	AIM-9B Sidewinder	a) 111.4 (2.83) b) 20.9 (53.0)	a) 5.0 (12.7) b) 168 (76)	1.08 (2)		Moving canard fins	Solid-propellant rocket	Passive IR homing	a) 10.0 (4.5) blast-fragmentation b) IR proximity fuze	Widely used by NATO & others
Ford Aerospace/ Raytheon	AIM-9J Sidewinder	a) 120.9 (3.07) b) 22.0 (55.9)	a) 5.0 (12.7) b) 172.0 (78.0)	7.8 (14.5)	Mach 2.5	Moving canard fins	Solid-propellant rocket	Passive IR homing	b) Impact & proximity fuzes?	F-4
Ford Aerospace/ Raytheon	AIM-9L Sidewinder	a) 113.0 (2.87) b) 25.2 (64.0)	a) 5.0 (12.7) b) 190.9 (86.6)	4.32 (8)	Mach 2.5	Moving canard fins	Solid-propellant rocket	Passive IR homing	a) 21.0 (9.5) annular blast-fragmentation b) DSU-21 laser proximity fuze	F-4EJ, C-101, F-14, F-15, F-16, F/A-18, Tornado, Tornado ADV, Sea Harrier, Harrier II, Gripen, AMX, AM-1, P-3, A129, AH-64, Nimrod
Loral/Raytheon	AIM-9M Sidewinder	a) 113.0 (2.87) b) 25.2 (64.0)	a) 5.0 (12.7) b) 190.9 (86.6)	4.32 (8)	Mach 2.5	Moving canard fins	Reduced-smoke solid-propellant rocket	Passive IR homing	a) 21.0 (9.5) blast-fragmentation b) Laser proximity fuze	F-14, F-15, F-16, F/A-18, F-117A, F-22?, A-10A, Sea Harrier
Loral/Raytheon	AIM-9P-1 Sidewinder	a) 120.9 (3.07) b) 25.2 (64.0)	a) 5.0 (12.7) b) 180.8 (82.0)	4.32 (8)	Mach 2.5	Moving canard fins	Solid-propellant rocket	Passive IR homing	a) 26.5 (12.0) blast-fragmentation b) Laser proximity fuze	Used by export customers on various air-craft. Also L-39?, MB-339?, T-bird II?
Loral/Raytheon	AIM-9P-2 Sidewinder	a) 120.9 (3.07) b) 25.2 (64.0)	a) 5.0 (12.7) b) 180.8 (82.0)	4.32 (8)	Mach 2.5	Moving canard fins	Reduced smoke solid-propellant rocket	Passive IR homing	a) 26.5 (12.0) blast-fragmentation b) Laser proximity fuze	See above
Loral/Raytheon	AIM-9P-3 Sidewinder	a) 120.9 (3.07) b) 25.2 (64.0)	a) 5.0 (12.7) b) 180.8 (82.0)	4.32 (8)	Mach 2.5	Moving canard fins	Reduced-smoke solid-propellant rocket	Passive IR homing	a) 26.5 (12.0) blast-fragmentation b) Laser proximity fuze	See above
Loral/Raytheon	AIM-9P-4 Sidewinder	a) 120.9 (3.07) b) 25.2 (64.0)	a) 5.0 (12.7) b) 180.8 (82.0)	4.32 (8)	Mach 2.5	Moving canard fins	Solid-propellant rocket	Passive IR homing	a) 26.5 (12.0) blast-fragmentation b) Laser proximity fuze	See above
Loral/Raytheon	AIM-9R Sidewinder	a) 113.0 (2.87) b) 25.2 (64.0)	a) 5.0 (12.7) b) 191.8 (87.0)	4.32 (8)	Mach 2.5	Moving canard fins	Solid-propellant rocket	Optical-band homing	a) 21.0 (9.5) blast-fragmentation b) Laser proximity fuze	

Manufacturer	Designation	a) Length ins (m) b) Span ins (cm)	a) Diameter ins (cm) b) Weight lb (kg)	Range naut miles (km)	Speed	Control	Propulsion	Guidance	a) Warhead lb (kg) b) Fuzing	Platform(s)
United States of America										
Loral/Raytheon	AIM-9S Sidewinder	a) 113.0 (2.87) b) 25.2 (64.0)	a) 5.0 (12.7) b) 190 (86.0)	4.32 (8)	Mach 2.5	Moving canard fins	Solid-propellant rocket	Passive IR homing	a) 22.5 (10.2) blast-fragmentation b) Laser proximity + impact fuzes	F-15, F-16
Hughes & Raytheon	AIM-9X Sidewinder	a) c.120? (c.3?)	a) 5.0 (12.7) b) c.200? (c.90?)				Solid-propellant rocket	Passive IR homing	a) HE	Planned for USAF fighters, including F-22
Raytheon Company Missile Systems Division Hartwell Road, Bedford, MA 01730	Tail Control Sidewinder	a) 122.0 (3.10) b) 11.0 (28.0)	a) 5.0 (12.7) b) 185.2 (84.0)			Rear fins	Solid-propellant rocket	Passive IR homing		
Hughes Missile Systems Old Nogales Highway, PO Box 11337, Tucson, AZ 85734	AIM-54C Phoenix	a) 169.3 (4.30) b) 36.0 (91.5)	a) 15.0 (38.0) b) 1,020.7 (463.0)	108+ (200 +)	Mach 4+	Moving tail fins	Solid-propellant rocket	Inertial + semi-active & active radar homing	a) 132 (60) HE continuous rod b) Impact & radar proximity fuzes	F-14
Hughes Missile Systems Old Nogales Highway, PO Box 11337, Tucson, AZ 85734	AIM-120A, B&C AMRAAM	a) 144.0 (3.65) b) 21.0 (53.3) -span reduced on C	a) 7.0 (17.8) b) 345.0 (156.5)	30 (55)	Mach 4 at altitude?	Moving tail fins driven by electric actuators	Solid-propellant boost/sustain rocket	Inertial with datalink updating + I-band active-radar homing	a) 48.5 (22.0) HE directed fragmentation b) Active radar proximity fuze	F-4F, F-14, F-15, F-16, F/A-18, F-22, Sea Harrier, Harrier II Plus, Gripen, Eurofighter 2000
Hughes Missile Systems Old Nogales Highway, PO Box 11337, Tucson, AZ 85734	FIM-92A Stinger	a) 59.8 (1.52) b) 3.6 (9.10)	a) 2.8 (7.0) b) 22.3 (10.1)	0.1 – 2.1+ (0.2 – 4+)	Mach 2.2 (maximum)	Cruciform Moving canard fins	Dual-thrust solid-propellant booster & sustainer	Passive IR homing	a) 2.2 (1.0) HE fragmentation b) Contact fuze	Tigre, A109K, A129, Kiowa Warrior, Comanche, AH-64, H-76 Eagle
Loral Aeronutronic Ford Road, Newport Beach, CA 92658	Have Dash	a) c.120 (c.3.0)	b) 397 (180.0)	27? (50?)	Mach 3+?	Rear fins	Solid-propellant rocket prototypes	Active radar & IR homing		
Loral Aeronutronic Ford Road, Newport Beach, CA 92658	Kestrel	a) 63.8 (1.62)	a) 5.0 (12.7) b) 74.0 (33.6)						a) 10 (4.5) blast-fragmentation	Proposed for US Army helicopters
Raytheon	Unknown	a) 72.4 (1.84)	a) 5.0 (12.7) b) 96.1 (43.6)			Moving rear fins?			a) HE	Proposed for US Army helicopters
Multi-national										
British Aerospace (Defence) Dynamics Division PO Box 19, Six Hills Way, Stevenage, Hertfordshire SG 1 2DA	AIM-132 ASRAAM	a) 114.2 (2.90) b) 17.7 (45.0)	a) 6.5 (16.6) b) 192 (87)	<0.15 – c.8 (<0.3 – c.15)		Moving tail fins	Solid-propellant rocket	Inertial + imaging IR homing	a) c.22 (c.10) HE blast fragmentation b) Laser proximity fuze	Harrier, Sea Harrier Eurofighter 2000
BAe/Saab/Thomson-CSF	S225X & S225XR		a) (c.20)	54+ (100+)	Very high	Moving tail fins	Solid-propellant rocket (S225X) or ramjet (S225XR)	Inertial (probably with command link update) + active-radar homing	b) Active-radar or IR-based proximity fuze	Intended as a possible armament for export versions of Eurofighter 2000 and the JAS 39 Gripen

Air-launched anti-ship

Manufacturer	Designation	a) Length ins (m) b) Span ins (cm)	a) Diameter ins (cm) b) Weight lb (kg)	Range naut miles (km)	Speed	Control	Propulsion	Guidance	a) Warhead lb (kg) b) Fuzing	Platform(s)
Brazil										
Avibras Industria Aerospacial Antiga Estrada de Paraibuna km 118, PO Box 229, 12201-970 Sao Jose dos Campos	SM70 Barracuda	a) 204.0 (5.20) b) 47.2 (120.0)	a) 12.6 (32.0)	38? (70?)			Solid-propellant rocket	Inertial mid-course + active-radar terminal homing		Project suspended
China										
China Precision Machinery Import Export Corporation (CPMIEC) 17 Wenchang Hutong, Xidan, PO Box 845, Beijing	C101 (CSS-X-5 Saples)	a) 228.35 (5.80) b) 47.2 (120.0)	a) 29.9 (76.0) b) 4,210 (1,910)	45 (83)	Supersonic	Moving fins	Twin liquid-propellant ramjets & two solid-propellant rocket boosters	Inertial midcourse + active-radar terminal homing	a) 660 (300) semi-armour-piercing (SAP)	H-5, H-6, SH-5

Manufacturer	Designation	a) Length ins (m) b) Span ins (cm)	a) Diameter ins (cm) b) Weight lb (kg)	Range naut miles (km)	Speed	Control	Propulsion	Guidance	a) Warhead lb (kg) b) Fuzing	Platform(s)
China										
China Precision Machinery Import Export Corporation (CPMIEC) 17 Wenchang Hutong, Xidan, PO Box 845, Beijing	Hai Ying 4/C-201 (CSSC-7 Sadback)	a) 289.8 (7.36) b) 108.3 (275.0)	a) 30 (76) b) c.7,275 (c.3,300)	c.73 (135)	Mach 0.8	Aerodynamic	Solid-propellant rocket booster & turbojet sustainer	Autopilot + active radar homing	a) 1,100 (500) HE	H-6?
China Precision Machinery Import Export Corporation (CPMIEC) 17 Wenchang Hutong, Xidan, PO Box 845, Beijing	Ying Ji 1/C-801 (CSSC-N-4 Sardine)	a) 228.4 (5.80) b) 46.5 (118.0)	a) 14.2 (36.0) b) 1,444 (655)	4.4 – 21.6 (8 – 40)	Mach 0.9	Cruciform moving tail fins	Solid-propellant rocket booster & sustainer	Autopilot/ radar altimeter + active radar terminal homing	a) 363 (165) HE	H-6, H-7
China Precision Machinery Import Export Corporation (CPMIEC) 17 Wenchang Hutong, Xidan, PO Box 845, Beijing	Ying Ji 2K/C-802K	a) 252 (6.39) b) 65 (165)	a) 14.2 (36.0) b) c.1,500 (c.680)	6 – 65 (15 – 120)	Mach 0.8 – 0.9	Cruciform moving tail fins	Turbojet & solid-propellant rocket propellant booster	Autopilot/ radar altimeter + active radar terminal homing	a) 363? (165?) HE	H-6, Q/A-5, JH-7, helicopters
China Precision Machinery Import Export Corporation (CPMIEC) 17 Wenchang Hutong, Xidan, PO Box 845, Beijing	YJ-6/C-601 (CAS-1 Kraken)	a) 290.6 (7.38) b) 94.5 (240.0)	a) 30 (76) b) 5,380 (2,440)	86 (160)	Mach 0.9	Aerodynamic	Liquid propellant rocket	Autopilot + active radar seeker	a) 1,131 (513) HE	Q/A-5, JH-7
France										
Aerospatiale Division Engins Tactiques 2 rue Beranger, F-92322 Chatillon-sous-Bagneux	AM.39 Exocet	a) 185.0 (4.70) b) 43.3 (110.0)	a) 13.8 (35.0) b) 1,477 (670)	27 – 38 (50 – 70)	Mach 0.93	Cruciform moving tail fins	Solid-propellant booster & sustainer	Inertial/radar altimeter + active radar seeker	a) 363.7 (165) shaped charge/ fragmentation b) Delay + proximity fuze	AMX, Mirage 5, Mirage F1, Mirage 2000, Jaguar, Atlantique, CN-235, Sea King, Super Frelon, Cougar
Aerospatiale Division Engins Tactiques 2 rue Beranger F-92322, Chatillon-sous-Bagneux	AS.15TT	a) 85.0 (2.16) b) 20.9 (53.0)	a) 7.3 (18.5) b) 212 (96)	8+ (15+)	920ft/sec (280m/sec)	Cruciform moving tail fins	Solid-propellant rocket	Command in azimuth + height control via radio altimeter	a) 65 (29.7) HE (derived from warhead in AS.12)	AS 565 Panther, C-212
Germany										
MBB (now part of Daimler/Benz Aerospace)	AS34 Kormoran	a) 173.2 (4.40) b) 39.4 (100.0)	a) 13.5 (34.4) b) 1,323 (600)	16 (30)	Mach 0.9	Cruciform moving tail fins	Solid-propellant booster & sustainer	Cruise: inertial + radar altimeter; Attack: active radar seeker	a) P-charge 441 (200) HE	Tornado, F-104
Daimler/Benz Aerospace PO Box 801109, D-81663 Munich	Kormoran 2	a) 173.2 (4.40) b) 39.4 (100.0)	a) 13.5 (34.4) b) 1,389 (630)	18.9 (35)	Mach 0.9	Cruciform moving tail fins	Solid-propellant booster & sustainer	Cruise: inertial + radar altimeter; Attack: active radar seeker	a) 485 (220) semi-armour-piercing	Tornado
Israel										
Israel Aircraft Industries PO Box 105, Yahud Industrial Zone 56000	Gabriel Mk III	a) 151.6 (3.85) b) 43.3 (110.0)	a) 13.4 (34.0) b) 1,323 (600)	32+ (60+)	Mach 0.73	Cruciform moving tail fins	Solid-propellant rocket	Cruise: inertial + radar altimeter; Attack: active radar homing	a) 330 (150) HE	F-4, A-4, Kfir, Sea Scan
Italy										
OTO Melara (formerly Sistel) Via Valdilocchi 15, PO Box 337, I-19 100 La Spezia	Marte Mk 2	a) 190.6 (4.84) b) 38.6 (98.0)	a) 7.9 (20) fuselage, 12.4 (31.6) warhead b) 761 (345)	11+ (20+)	820ft/sec (250m/sec)	Cruciform centrebody wings?	Solid-propellant rocket booster & sustainer	Cruise: gyro control; Attack active radar homing	a) 154 (70) SAP b) Contact & proximity fuzes	ASH-3D, MB-339
OTO Melara (formerly Sistel) Via Valdilocchi 15, PO Box 337, I-19 100 La Spezia	Marte Mk 2a	a) 153.5 (3.9) b) 38.6 (98.0)	a) 7.9 (20) body, 12.4 (31.6) warhead b) 573 (260)	11+ (20+)	820ft/sec (250m/sec)	Cruciform centerbody wings?	Sold-propellant rocket	Cruise: gyro control; Attack: active radar homing	a) 154 (70) SAP b) Contact & proximity	MB-339AM
OTO Melara (formerly Sistel) Via Valdilocchi 15, PO Box 337, I-19 100 La Spezia	Marte Mk 2b	a) 153.5 (3.9) b) 38.6 (98.0)	a) 7.9 (20) body, 12.4 (31.6) warhead b) 573 (260)	32 (60)	820ft/sec (250m/sec)	Cruciform centrebody wings?	Sold-propellant rocket	Passive radar homing	a) HE fragmentation	
Japan										
Mitsubishi Electric Mitsubishi Denki Bldg, 2-chome, 2-3 Marunouchi, Chiyoda-ku, Tokyo 100	ASM-1	a) 155.5 (3.95) b) 47.2 (120.0)	a) 13.8 (35.0) b) 1,345 (610)	24+ (45+)	Mach 0.9	Moving tail fins	Solid-propellant rocket	Cruise: inertial + radar altimeter; Attack: active radar homing	a) 331 (150) SAP	F-1, F-4, P-3C

Manufacturer	Designation	a) Length ins (m) b) Span ins (cm)	a) Diameter ins (cm) b) Weight lb (kg)	Range naut miles (km)	Speed	Control	Propulsion	Guidance	a) Warhead lb (kg) b) Fuzing	Platform(s)
Japan										
Mitsubishi Electric Mitsubishi Denki Bldg, 2-chome, 2-3 Marunouchi, Chiyoda-ku, Tokyo 100	ASM-2			80+ (150+)	Subsonic?		Turbojet	Inertial midcourse + imaging IR terminal homing	a) HE	F-1, F-15J, F-16, planned for FS-X
Norway										
Norsk Forsvarsteknologi PO Box 1003, N-3601 Kongsberg	AGM-119 Penguin Mk3	a) 126.0 (3.20) b) 39.4 (100.0)	a) 11.0 (28.0) b) 794 (360)	29.7 (55+)	Mach 0.8	Moving canard fins	Solid-propellant rocket	Inertial + IR homing	a) 264.5 (120) semi-armour-piercing HE b) Delayed-impact fuze	F-16
Norsk Forsvarsteknologi PO Box 1003, N-3601 Kongsberg	Penguin Mk2 Mod 7	a) 118.5 (3.01) b) 55.1 (140.0)	a) 11.0 (28.0) b) 849 (385)	18.3 (34+)	Mach 0.9	Moving canard fins	Dual-thrust solid-propellant rocket	Inertial + IR homing	a) 264.5 (120) semi-armour-piercing HE b) Delayed-impact fuze	Surface ships & SH-60B
Russia										
Raguda Dubna	Kh-15S	a) 188.2 (4.78) b) 36.2 (92.0)	a) 17.9 (45.5) b) 2,646 (1,200)	Max 21.5 – 81 (40 – 150) (depending on launch height and target radar cross-section)	Mach 5 during the attack phase	Moving tail fins	Solid-propellant rocket	Inertial + active-radar terminal homing	a) 330 (150) semi-armour-piercing	Tu-22M, Tu-160
Raduga Dubna	Kh-22M (AS-4 Kitchen)	a) 458.7 (11.65) b) 118.1 (300.0)	a) 36.2 (92.0) b) 12,742 (5,780)	c.215 (c.400)		Moving tail fins?	Liquid-propellant rocket	Inertial + active radar seeker or passive radar seeker	a) HE	Tu-22M, Tu-95K
Zvezda Kaliningrad	Kh-31A izdieliye 77 (AS-17 Krypton)	a) 185.0 (4.70) b) 45.3 (115)	a) 14.2 (36.0) b) 1,323 (600)	27 (50)	Mach 3.5		Integrated rocket-ramjet	Inertial + active-radar homing	a) 198 (90) semi armour piercing	MiG-29, Su-24, Su-25, Su-27, Su-30
Zvezda Kaliningrad	Kh-35 (SS-N-25)	a) 147.6 (3.75) b) 51.2 (130)	a) 16.5 (42.0) b) 1,323 (600)	2.7 – 70 (5 – 130)	985ft/sec (300m/sec)	Moving tail fins	Turbojet? + tandem solid-propellant rocket booster	Inertial mid-course + active radar terminal homing	a) 320 (145) semi-armour-piercing/ incendiary	Tu-142M Bear F, Ka-28, WIGE (eight on fuselage)
Raduga Dubna	Kh-41 3M80 "Moskit"	a) 369.5 (9.39) b) 82.7 (210)	a) 30.0 (76.0) b) c8,700? (c.3,950?)	135 (250)	1,510kts ? (2,800 km/h?)		Integral rocket-ramjet	Inertial mid-course + active or passive radar seeker	a) 704 (320) HE?	Su-33
Raguda Dubna	Kh-58A (AS-11 Kilter)	a) 189? (4.8?) b) 46.1 (117.0)	a) 15.0 (38.0) b) c.1,430 (c.650)	97 (180)	High subsonic	Moving tail fins	Solid-propellant rocket	Autopilot + active radar homing	a) 328 (149) HE?	MiG-25BM, Su-24
Raduga Dubna	Kh-59M – anti-ship version	a) 224.0 (5.69) b) 51.2 (130.0)	a) 15.0 (38.0) b) c.2,030 (c.920)	108 (200)	350 – 540kts (860 – 1,000km/h)	Moving canards	Turbofan mounted below fuse-lage + solid-propellant rocket booster	Autopilot + active radar homing	a) HE	
Raguda Dubna	Kh-65SE	a) 237.8 (6.04) b) 122.0 (310.0)	a) 20.2 (51.4) b) 2,756 (1,250)	135 – 151 (250 – 280) (depending on launch altitude)	Mach 0.48 – 0.77	Moving tail fins	Turbofan mounted below rear fuselage	Inertial + radar seeker	a) 904 (410) semi-armour-piercing	Tu-95 Bear H
Sweden										
Saab Missiles S-58 1 88 Linkoping	RBS15F	a) 171.3 (4.35) b) 55.1 (140.0)	a) 19.7 (50.0) b) 1,318 (598)	80+ (150+)	High subsonic	Moving tail fins	Turbojet	Active radar homing	a) HE	Viggen, Gripen
Taiwan										
Chung Shan Institute of Science & Technology Taipei	Hsiung Feng 2 (air-launched)	b) 35.4 (90.0)	a) 13.4 (34.0)	43 (80)	High subsonic	Cruciform moving tail fins	Turbofan	Inertial + active radar homing	a) 496 (220) semi-armour-piercing HE b) Contact	Ching Kuo, AT-3A
United Kingdom										
British Aerospace (Defence) Dynamics Division PO Box 19, Six Hills Way, Stevenage, Hertfordshire SG 1 2DA	Sea Eagle	a) 163.0 (4.14) b) 47.2 (120.0)	a) 15.8 (40.0) b) 1,301 (590)		High subsonic	Cruciform moving tail fins	Turbojet	Cruise: preset; Attack: active radar homing	a) HE b) Delayed-impact fuze	Sea Harrier, Tornado, Jaguar, Sea King
British Aerospace (Defence) Dynamics Division PO Box 19, Six Hills Way, Stevenage, Hertfordshire SG 1 2DA	Sea Skua	a) 112.2 (2.85) b) 24.4 (62.0)	a) 8.7 (22.2) b) 324 (147)	10 (18)	High subsonic	Cruciform moving canard fins	Solid-propellant rocket	Semi-active radar homing	a) 44 (20) semi-armour-piercing	Lynx, AB.212, SH-3D, H-76, C-212,

Manufacturer	Designation	a) Length ins (m) b) Span ins (cm)	a) Diameter ins (cm) b) Weight lb (kg)	Range naut miles (km)	Speed	Control	Propulsion	Guidance	a) Warhead lb (kg) b) Fuzing	Platform(s)
United States of America										
McDonnell Douglas Missile Systems PO Box 516, St Louis, MS 63166-0516	AGM-84A Harpoon	a) 151.2 (3.84) b) 35.8 (91.0)	a) 13.5 (34.3) b) 1,168 (530)	65 (120)	Mach 0.85	Cruciform moving tail fins	Turbojet	Cruise: inertial + radar altimeter; Attack: active radar homing	a) Naval Weapons Centre 488 (221) penetration blast b) Contact (with time delay) + proximity fuzes	F/A-18, B-52, P-3, S-3, Nimrod, CN-235, Fokker Enforcer Mk2, tested on F-16
McDonnell Douglas Missile Systems PO Box 516, St Louis, MS 63166-0516	AGM-84A Harpoon Block 1D	a) 174.8 (4.44) b) 32.6 (83.0)	a) 13.5 (34.3) b) 1,388 (629.5)	130 (240)	Mach 0.85	Cruciform moving tail fins	Turbojet	Cruise: inertial + radar altimeter; Attack: active radar homing	a) Naval Weapons Centre 488 (221) penetration blast b) Contact (with time delay) + proximity fuzes	See above
Multi-national										
Aerospatiale/Daimler-Benz	Anti-Navire Nouvelle Generation (ANNG)			81 – 108 (150 – 200)	Mach 2.0+	Moving tail fins	Sold-propellant ramjet	Inertial + active radar homing	a) EH	Aircraft, frigates and submarines

Air-launched anti-tank

Manufacturer	Designation	a) Length ins (m) b) Span ins (cm)	a) Diameter ins (cm) b) Weight lb (kg)	Range naut miles (km)	Speed	Control	Propulsion	Guidance	a) Warhead lb (kg) b) Fuzing	Platform(s)
Argentina										
Instituto de Investigaciones Cientificas y Tecnicas de las Fuerzas Armadas (CITEFA) Zufriategui 4380, 1603 Villa Martelli Buenos Aires	Mathogo	a) 39.4 (1.00) b) 17.7 (45.0)	a) 4.0 (10.2) b) 24.9 (11.3)	0.2 – 1.1 (0.35 – 2.1)	295ft/sec (90m/sec)	Wing-mounted spoilers	Solid-propellant booster & sustainer	CLOS via wire	a) 6.2 (2.8) HE	A109
Brazil										
Avibras Industria Aerospacial Antiga Estrada de Paraibuna km 118, PO Box 229, 12201-970 Sao Jose dos Campos	MAC-MP		b) 72.8 (33.0)	5.4 (10)			Solid-propellant rocket	Command via trailing optical fibre	a) HEAT	Helicopters
China										
China North Industries Corporation (NORINCO) 7A Yuetan Nanjie, PO Box 2137, Beijing	Hongjian 8A (Red Arrow 8)	a) 33.86 (0.86) b) 12.6 (32.0)	a) 4.7 (12) b) 0.25 – 1.65 (0.5 – 3.1)	24.7 (11.2)	656 – 787ft/sec (200–240 m/sec)	Deflector in sustainer efflux?	Solid-propellant booster & sustainer	SACLOS	a) 6.6 (3.0) HEAT	Harbin Z-9
China North Industries Corporation (NORINCO) 7A Yuetan Nanjie, PO Box 2137, Beijing	Hongian 8B (Red Arrow 8B)	a) 39.4 (1.0) b) 12.6 (32.0)	a) 4.7 (12) b) 27.5 (12.5)	2.1 (4.0)		Deflector in sustainer efflux	Solid-propellant booster and sustainer	SACLOS via wire	a) Tandem-charge HEAT b) Nose probe	Harbin Z-9?
France										
Aerospatiale Division Engins Tactiques 2 rue Beranger, F-92322, Chatillon-sous-Bagneux, France	AS.11	a) 47.6 (1.21) b) 19.7 (50)	a) 6.5 (16.4) b) 66.1 (30.0)	1.6 (3)		Deflector in sustainer efflux	Solid-propellant rocket	CLOS via wire	a) 9.9 (4.4) HEAT	Alouette, Gazelle,
Aerospatiale Division Engins Tactiques 2 rue Beranger, F-92322, Chatillon-sous-Bagneux, France	AS.12	a) 73.6 (1.87) b) 25.6 (65)	a) 7.1 (18.0) b) 369.3 (167.5)	2.7 (5)		Deflector in sustainer efflux	Solid-propellant rocket	CLOS via wire	a) 66 (20) HEAT	Atlantique, Nimrod, Gazelle, Lynx, AB.212,
India										
Unknown	NAG							Radio command link + imaging IR or millimetric-wave seeker	a) HEAT	Includes helicopters
Russia										
Nepobidimy Kolomna	9K14 Malyutka (AT 3 Sagger)	a) 34.3 (0.87) b) 18.1 (46.0)	a) 4.7 (12.0) b) 24.3 (11.0)	0.25 – 1.6 (0.5 – 3.0)	394ft/sec (120m/sec)	Jetavator nozzles	Solid-propellant rocket	CLOS via wire. SACLOS via wire in Sagger-C	a) 5.9 (2.7) HEAT b) impact	Mi-2URP, Mi-8, Mi-17, Mi-24, Gazelle

Manufacturer	Designation	a) Length ins (m) b) Span ins (cm)	a) Diameter ins (cm) b) Weight lb (kg)	Range naut miles (km)	Speed	Control	Propulsion	Guidance	a) Warhead lb (kg) b) Fuzing	Platform(s)
Russia										
Nudelman Moscow	9M17 Skorpion (AT-2 Swatter A & B)	a) 45.7 (1.16) b) 26.0 (66.0)	a) 5.2 (13.2) b) 69.4 (31.5)	2.16 (4.0)	558ft/sec (170m/sec)	Elevons + moving canard fins	Single-stage solid-propellant rocket?	CLOS via radio command link	a) HEAT b) impact	Mi-8, Mi-17, Mi-24
Nepobidimy Kolomna	9M114 Kokon (AT-6 Spiral)	a) 72.0 (1.83) b) 11.8 (30.0)	a) 5.1 (13.0) b) 77.1 (35.0)	2.7 (5)	1,312ft/sec (400m/sec)	Moving canard fins	Solid-propellant rocket	Radio command	a) 22 (10) HEAT b) Impact	Mi-24, Mi-28, Ka-29, W-3
Nepobidimy Kolomna	9M120 Vikhr (AT-9)	a) 47 (1.2) b) 12.8 (32.5)	a) 4.9 (12.5) b) 37.5 (17)	2.16 (4.0)			Solid-propellant rocket	Laser beam rider	a) c.6.6 (c.3.0) HEAT	Su-25, Mi-28, Mi-35
Nepobidimy Kolomna	9A-4172 Vikhr M (AT-16)	a) 114 (2.9)	a) c.4.9 (c.12.5) b) c.132 (c.60)	4.3 (8.0)	Supersonic		Solid-propellant rocket	Laser beam rider	a) c.18 (c.8.0) Shaped charge	Ka-50
Nepobidimy Kolomna	Vikhr M (modified)			6.5 – 8.1 (12 – 15)	Supersonic		Solid-propellant rocket	Laser beam rider?	a) Shaped charge	Ka-50?
South Africa										
Denel, Kentron Division Jochemus Street, Erasmuskloof, PO Box 8322, Hennopsmeer 0046	ZT3 Swift	a) 53.2 (1.35) b) 15.8 (40.0)	a) 5.0 (12.7) b) 41.9 (19.0)	2.16 (4)		Cruciform rudders	Solid-propellant rocket	CLOS via laser command link	a) HEAT - tandem-charge warhead planned	Puma/Oryx, Rooivalk
Denel, Kentron Division Jochemus Street, Erasmuskloof, PO Box 8322, Hennopsmeer 0046	ZT4	a) 70.9 (1.8)	a) 7.0 (17.8) b) 114.6 (52)	0.27 – 4.3 (0.5 – 8.0)	1,740ft/sec (530m/sec)		Solid-propellant rocket boost/sustain motor	Digital autopilot + semi-active laser homing or millimetre-wave fire-and-forget homing	a) Tandem-shaped charge	Proposed for Rooivalk
Denel, Kentron Division Jochemus Street, Erasmuskloof, PO Box 8322, Hennopsmeer 0046	ZT35	a) 53.2 (1.35) b) 15.8 (40)	a) 5.0 (12.7) b) c.42 (c.19)	2.7 (5)		Rudders	Solid-propellant rocket	CLOS via laser command link?	a) Tandem shaped charge	W-3WB Huzar
Sweden										
Bofors (now part of Saab Missiles)	Bantam	a) 33.4 (0.85) b) 15.75 (40)	a) 4.3 (11.0) b) 16.75 (7.6)	1.08 (2.0)	Subsonic	Trailing-edge spoilers	Solid-propellant rocket	CLOS via wire	a) 4.9 (1.9) HEAT	PAC Mushshak
United States of America										
Rockwell International/ Lockheed Martin	AGM-114A Hellfire	a) 64.0 (1.63) b) 13.0 (33.0)	a) 7.0 (17.8) b) 95 (43)	3.2 (6)	Subsonic	Aerodynamic surfaces on cruciform wings	Solid-propellant rocket	Semi-active laser homing	a) Firestone c.20 (c.9) HEAT	AH-1, AH-64, OH-58D, UH-60, HH-60H
Rockwell International/ Lockheed Martin	AGM-114B Hellfire	a) 64.0 (1.63) b) 13.0 (33.0)	a) 7.0 (17.8) b) 95 (106)	c.5.4 (c.10)	Supersonic	Aerodynamic surfaces on cruciform wings	Solid-propellant rocket	Semi-active laser homing	a) Firestone c.20 (c.9) HEAT	AH-1, AH-64, OH-58D, UH-60, HH-60H
Rockwell International/ Lockheed Martin	AGM-114K Hellfire II	a) 64.0 (1.63) b) 13.0 (33.0)	a) 7.0 (17.8) b) 99 (45)	4.8 (9)	Supersonic	Aerodynamic surfaces on cruciform wings	Solid-propellant rocket	Semi-active laser homing	a) Tandem shaped charge	AH-1, AH-64, OH-58D, UH-60, HH-60H
Westinghouse/ Lockheed Martin	AGM-114 Hellfire Modular Missile System (LBHMMS)	b) 13.0 (33.0)	a) 7.0 (17.8)	4.4? (8?)	Supersonic	Aerodynamic surfaces on cruciform wings	Solid-propellant rocket	Inertial + radar homing	a) Shaped charge	AH-64D
Hughes Missile Systems Old Nogales Highway, PO Box 11337, Tucson, AZ 85734	BGM-71A TOW	a) 46.5 (1.18) b) 13.4 (34.0)	a) 5.9 (14.9) b) 41.7 (18.9)	0.03 – 2.0 (0.065 – 3.75)	1,224ft/sec (312m/sec)	Cruciform rudders	Solid-propellant booster & sustainer	SACLOS	a) 7.7 (3.5) HEAT	AH-1, MD500/530, A109, A129, Lynx, BO 105, Dauphin, Ecureuil
Hughes Missile Systems Old Nogales Highway, PO Box 11337, Tucson, AZ 85734	BGM-71C Improved TOW	a) 55.1 (1.40) b) 13.4 (34.0)	a) 5.9 (14.9) b) 41.9 (19.0)	2 (3.75)	1,224ft/sec (312m/sec)	Cruciform rudders	Solid-propellant booster & sustainer	SACLOS	a) HEAT of increased diameter	AH-1, MD500, A109, A129, Lynx, BO 105, Dauphin, Ecureuil, H-76 Eagle? Griffon?
Hughes Missile Systems Old Nogales Highway, PO Box 11337, Tucson, AZ 85734	BGM-71D TOW 2	a) 55.1 (1.40) b) 13.4 (34.0)	a) 5.9 (14.9) b) 27.6 (12.5)	2 (3.75)	1,224ft/sec (312m/sec)	Cruciform rudders	Solid-propellant rocket booster & sustainer	SACLOS	a) 13.2 (6.0) HEAT	A129, Super Lynx

Manufacturer	Designation	a) Length ins (m) b) Span ins (cm)	a) Diameter ins (cm) b) Weight lb (kg)	Range naut miles (km)	Speed	Control	Propulsion	Guidance	a) Warhead lb (kg) b) Fuzing	Platform(s)
United States of America										
Hughes Missile Systems Old Nogales Highway, PO Box 11337, Tucson, AZ 85734	BGM-71D TOW 2A	b) 13.4 (34.0)	a) 5.9 (14.9)	2 (3.75)	1,224ft/sec (312m/sec)	Cruciform rudders	Solid-propellant rocket booster & sustainer	SACLOS	a) HEAT	A109HA, A129
Multi-national										
Euromissile Dynamics Group (EMDG) 12 rue de la Redoute, F-92260 Fontenay-aux-Roses	ATGW-3LR (Trigat)	a) 59.0 (1.5) b) 17.7 (45.0)	a) 5.0 (12.7) b) 46.3 (21.0)	4.3 (8.0)		Cruciform fins	Solid-propellant rocket	Imaging IR homing	a) Tandem shaped charge	Tigre, A129
Euromissile Dynamics Group (EMDG) 12 rue de la Redoute, F-92260 Fontenay-aux-Roses	HOT 1	a) 50.0 (1.27) b) 12.2 (31.0)	a) 5.4 (13.6) b) 50.7 (23.0)	0.04 – 2.1 (0.075 – 4.0)	787ft/sec (240m/sec)	Deflector in sustainer efflux	Solid-propellant booster & sustainer	SACLOS	a) 13.2 (6.0) HEAT	
Euromissile Dynamics Group (EMDG) 12 rue de la Redoute, F-92260 Fontenay-aux-Roses	HOT 2	a) 51.2 (1.3) b) 12.2 (31.0)	a) 5.9 (15) b) 51.8 (23.5)	2.1 (4.0)		Deflector in sustainer efflux	Solid-propellant booster & sustainer	SACLOS	a) Heavier warhead of increased diameter, containing 9.0lb (4.1kg) of explosive	PAH-1, Tigre, A129, Lynx, Super Lynx
Thomson Thorn Missile Electronics 23-27 rue Pierre Valette F-92245 Malakoff	TAAWS (Thomson Thorn Anti Armour Weapon System)	a) 96.4 (2.45) b) 22.3 (56.6)	a) 16.5 (41.9)		Subsonic	None	None	Dispenser is unguided; submunitions use millimetre wave homing	a) 3 terminally guided submunitions	Proposed for Harrier II, Sea Harrier, Tornado, Eurofighter 2000

Air-to-air Missiles

The drawings are reproduced with the kind permission of Air International/Key Publishing

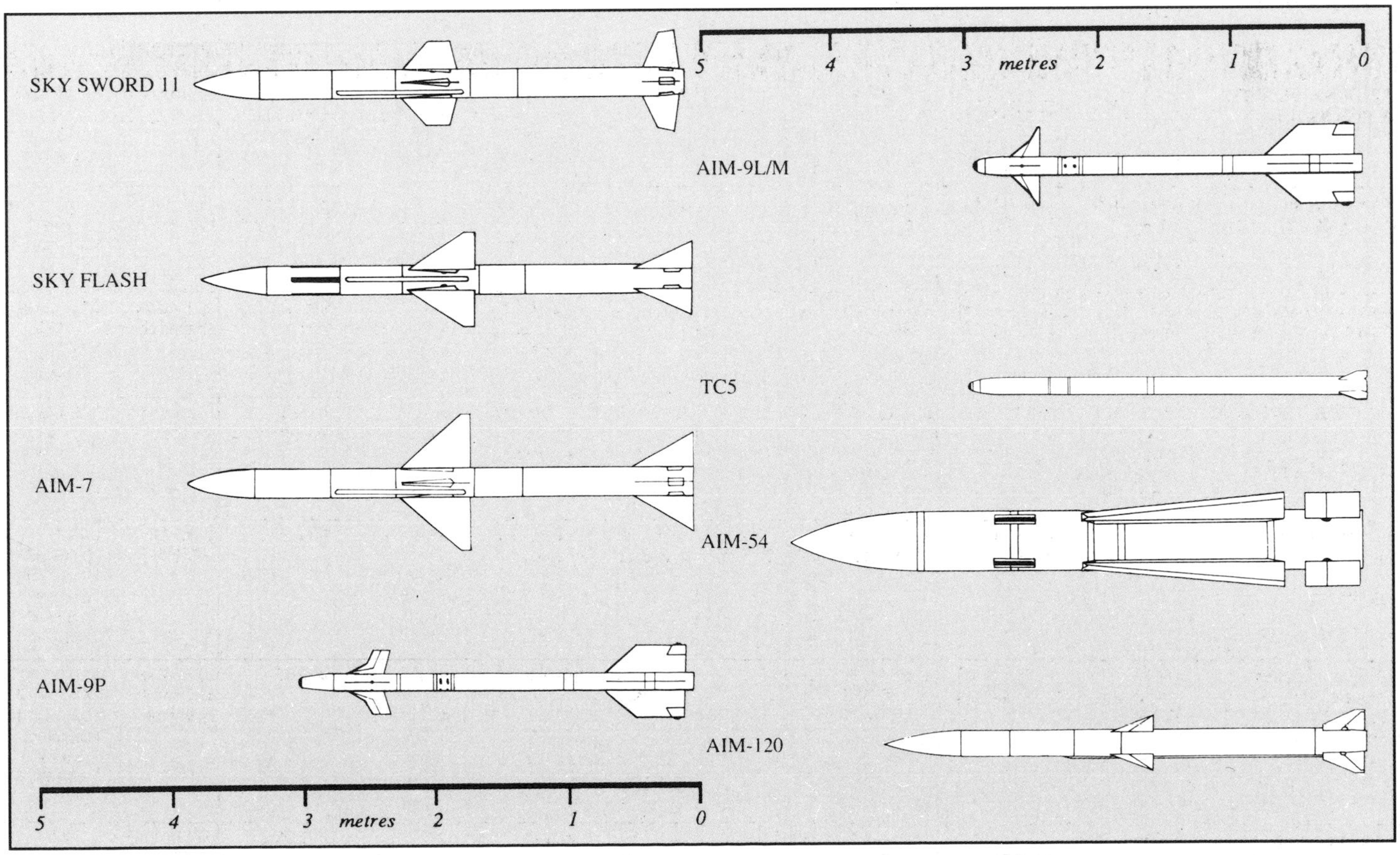

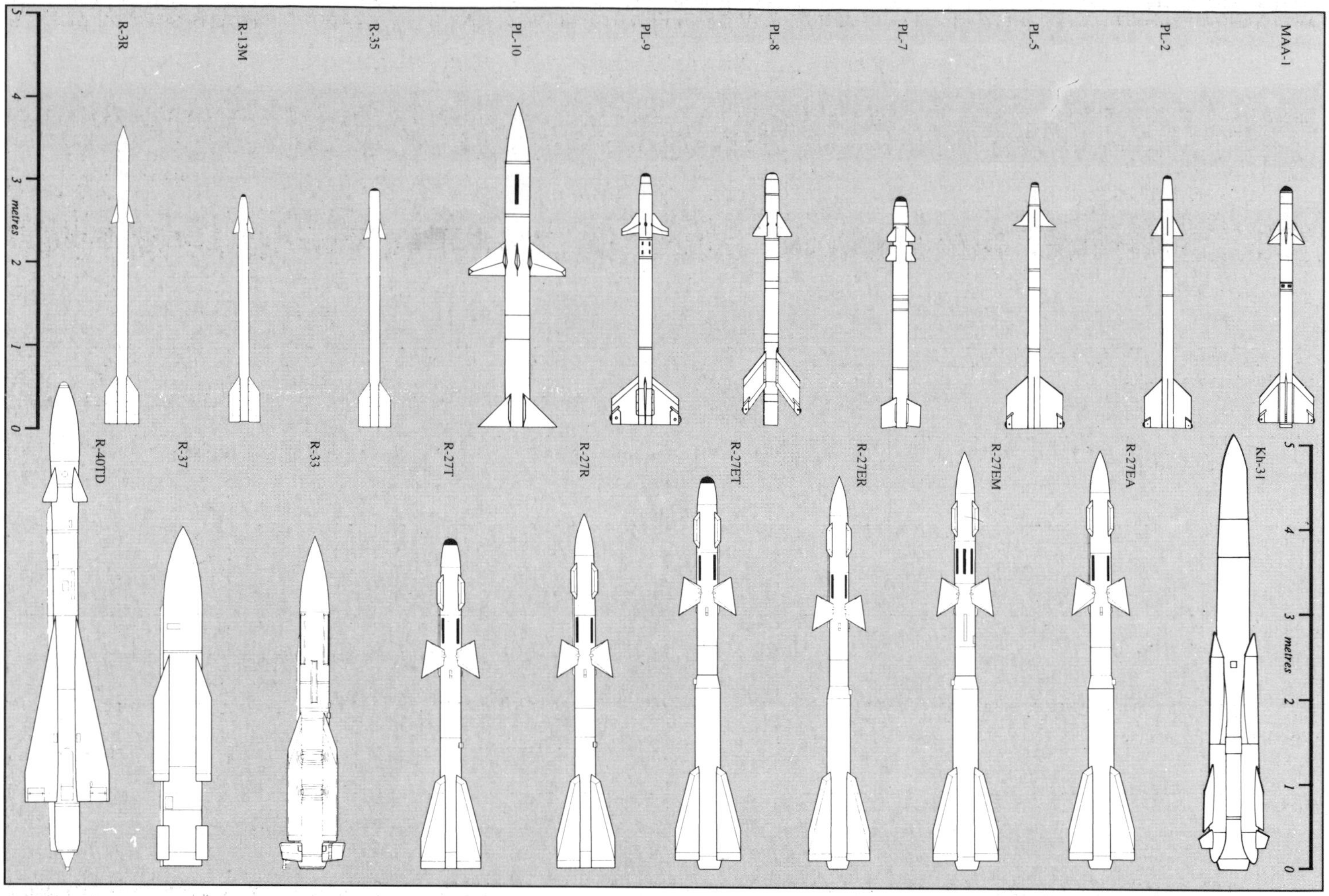

R-3R
R-13M
R-35
PL-10
PL-9
PL-8
PL-7
PL-5
PL-2
MAA-1
R-40TD
R-37
R-33
R-27T
R-27R
R-27ET
R-27ER
R-27EM
R-27EA
Kh-31
metres

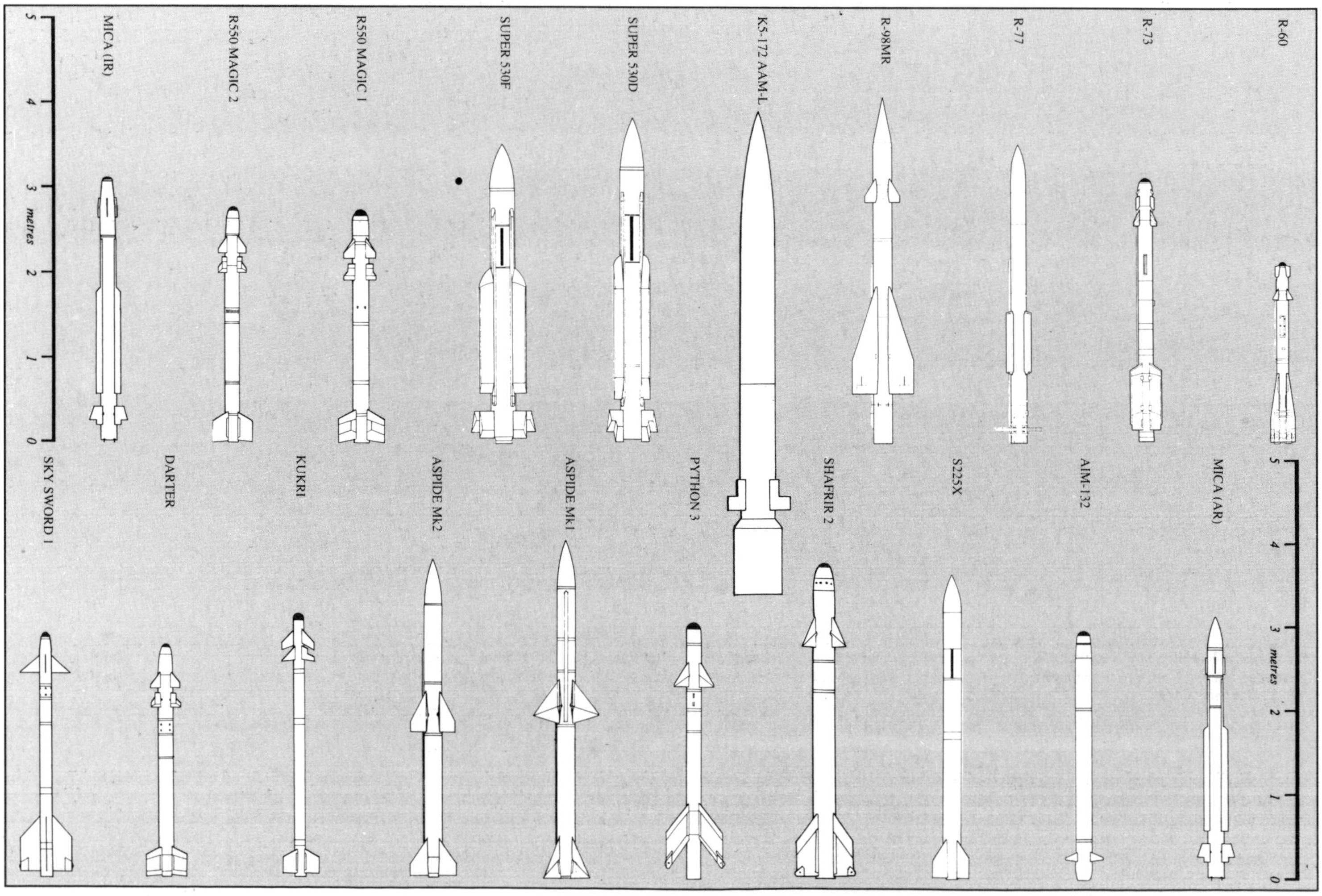

MICA (IR)
R550 MAGIC 2
R550 MAGIC 1
SUPER 530F
SUPER 530D
KS-172 AAM-L
R-98MR
R-77
R-73
R-60
SKY SWORD 1
DARTER
KUKRI
ASPIDE Mk2
ASPIDE Mk1
PYTHON 3
SHAFRIR 2
S225X
AIM-132
MICA (AR)
metres

Airborne Radars

Radars are listed by nation, then alphabetically by designation

Fighter, attack and bomber

Manufacturer	Radar	Role	Type	Operating frequency	Antenna type	a) PRF (Hz) b) Pulse width (microsec)	Operating modes (air-to-air)	Operating modes (air-to-surface)	a) Tracking capacity b) Engagement capacity	a) Maximum range naut miles (km) b) Weight lb (kg)
China										
China Leihua Electronic Technology Research Institute	JL-7	Air-to-air, air-to-ground (secondary)	Pulse (monopulse)	J-band	Paraboloid		Search, track, boresight	Air-to-ground ranging, attack	a) Single target b) Single target	a) Search 16 (30) track 8 (15) b) 254 (115)
China Leihua Electronic Technology Research Institute	JL-10	Multirole	Pulse-Doppler		Planar	a) Low, medium, & high	Look-up, look-down, dogfight	Moving-target attack	a) Single target b) Single target	a) Look-up 32 (60) look-down 29 (54)
China Leihua Electronic Technology Research Institute	SR-4	Air-to-air	Pulse	I/J-band			Search, track, CW illumination	None?	a) Single target b) Single target	b) 88 (40)
Unknown	T.266	Air-to-air?	Pulse?						a) Single target b) Single target	
China Leihua Electronic Technology Research Institute	Type 317	Multirole	Pulse				Include ranging	Ground mapping, terrain avoidance, ranging	a) Single target b) Single target	
China Leihua Electronic Technology Research Institute	Type 317a	Multirole	Pulse (monopulse)						a) Single target b) Single target	b) Lighter than Type 317
Unknown	Unknown	Missile guidance	Pulse?					Search guidance for anti-ship missiles	a) Single target	
France										
Thomson-CSF RCM division 1 blvd Jean Martin, F-78852 Elancourt Cedex	Agave	Multirole	Pulse (monopulse)?	I/J-band	Inverse Cassegrain	a) Variable b) Variable	Search, automatic tracking, ranging	Search, automatic tracking, target designation, mapping, air-to-ground ranging		a) Air 10 – 13.5 (18 – 25) sea 21.5 – 30 (40 – 55) b) 143 (65)
Dassault Electronique 55 quai Marcel Dassault, PO Box 301, F-922214 Saint-Cloud	Aida II	Ranging	Pulse	I/J-band						b) 66 (30)
Dassault Electronique 55 quai Marcel Dassault, PO Box 301, F-922214 Saint-Cloud	Anemone	Multirole	Pulse (monopulse)	I/J-band	Planar		Linear scan search, continuous tracking	Search, track, track-while-scan, air-to-ground ranging, ground mappiing		b) 132 (60)
Dassault Electronique 55 quai Marcel Dassault, PO Box 301, F-922214 Saint-Cloud	Antilope 5/50	Attack		J-band	Planar			Terrain-following and ground-mapping (interlaced if reqd), air-to-air and air-to-surface		
Thomson-CSF RCM division 1 blvd Jean Martin, F-78852 Elancourt Cedex	Cyrano II	Multirole	Pulse (monopulse)	I/J-band	Inverse Cassegrain		Search, track, ranging	Ground mapping, terrain warning, ranging, navigation		
Thomson-CSF RCM division 1 blvd Jean Martin, F-78852 Elancourt Cedex	Cyrano IV & Cyrano IV-1	Multirole	Pulse (monopulse)	I-band (8-10GHz)	Inverse Cassegrain	a) Variable b) Choice of three	Search, track, dogfight, home-on-jam (IV–1 adds MTI look-down mode)			a) 52 (96) b) c.480 (c.217)
Thomson-CSF RCM division 1 blvd Jean Martin, F-78852 Elancourt Cedex	Cyrano IV-2 & Cyrano IV-3	Multirole	Pulse (monopulse)	I-band (8-10GHz)	Inverse Cassegrain	a) Variable? b) Choice of three?		Adds ground mapping, terrain avoidance & ranging		a) 52 (96) b) c.480 (c.217)

Manufacturer	Designation	Role	Type	Operating frequency	Antenna type	a) PRF (Hz) b) Pulse width (microsec)	Operating modes (air-to-air)	Operating modes (air-to-surface)	a) Tracking capacity b) Engagement capacity	a) Maximum range naut miles (km) b) Weight lb (kg)
France										
Thomson-CSF RCM division 1 blvd Jean Martin, F-78852 Elancourt Cedex	Cyrano IV-M & Cyrano IV-M3	Multirole	Pulse (monopulse)	I-band (8-10GHz)	Inverse Cassegrain	a) Variable? b) Choice of three?	Search, track, interception, dogfight, home-on-jam,	Optional contour mapping, terrain avoidance, blind let-down, air-to-ground ranging		a) 52 (96) b) 480 (217)
GIE Radar 1 blvd Jean Martin, F-78852 Elancourt Cedex	RBE2	Multirole	Pulse-Doppler		Phased array	a) Low, medium, & high	Look-up, look-down, track-while-scan, single-target tracking, dogfight	Terrain following, terrain avoidance, fixed & moving target search and track, high-resolution mapping, ranging	a) Several tens b) Several	
Thomson-CSF RCM division 1 blvd Jean Martin, F-78852 Elancourt Cedex	RDC (Radar Doppler Compact)	Multirole	Pulse-Doppler	I-band (8-10 GHz)	Planar	a) Medium & low	All-aspect search & tracking, range-while-search, TWS, single target track, and various combat modes	Ground mapping, DBS, moving target detection, range finding; air-to-sea modes include BVR search and detection, target designation		b) c.220 (c.100)
Thomson-CSF RCM division 1 blvd Jean Martin, F-78852 Elancourt Cedex	RDI	Air-to-air	Pulse-Doppler	I/J-band		a) High				a) 54 (100)
Thomson-CSF RCM division 1 blvd Jean Martin, F-78852 Elancourt Cedex	RDM	Multirole	Pulse-Doppler	I/J-band	Inverse Cassegrain	a) High	Look-up, look-down, track-while-scan	Terrain-avoidance, contour mapping, ranging, sea search		a) 50 (92) against fighter targets
Thomson-CSF RCM division 1 blvd Jean Martin, F-78852 Elancourt Cedex	RDY	Multirole	Pulse-Doppler	I/J-band	Planar	a) Low, medium, & high		Includes air-to-ground & air-to-sea modes	a) 8	
India										
Hindustan Aeronautics PO Box 5150,15/1 Cubbon Rd. Banglalore 560001	Designation unknown	Multirole (for LCA)								
Israel										
Elta Electronic Industries PO Box 330, 77102 Ashdod	EL/M-2001B	Ranging	Pulse	I/J-band			Air-to-air ranging	Air-to-ground ranging	a) n/a b) n/a	b) Under 22 (under 10)
Elta Electronic Industries PO Box 330, 77102 Ashdod	EL/M-2011	Multirole	Pulse-Doppler?		Planar		Search, super-search, vertical scan, boresight	Ranging		a) 8 (15) b) 148 (67)
Elta Electronic Industries PO Box 330, 77102 Ashdod	EL/M-2021B	Multirole	Pulse-Doppler	I/J-band	Planar		Search, track-while-scan, single-target track	Ground mapping, terrain following & avoidance, ranging, DBS	a) Several b) Single	b) 265 (120)
Elta Electronic Industries PO Box 330, 77102 Ashdod	EL/M-2032 & -2032D	Multirole	Pulse-Doppler		Planar		Look-up, look-down, track-while-scan, single-track, slewable ACM, HUD, boresight, and vertical scan	Ranging, MTI, terrain avoidance, sea search, high-resolution SAR mapping and mapping with real-beam, DBS, expand, & freeze	a) Several b) Single	a) Look-up 35 - 55 (65 - 102), look-down 30 - 45 (55 - 83) b) 172 - 220 (78 - 100)
Elta Electronic Industries PO Box 330, 77102 Ashdod	EL/M-2035	Multirole	Pulse-Doppler		Planar		Look-up, look-down, track-while-scan, automatic lock-on, boresight		a) Several b) Single	a) 25 (46) b) 304 (138)

Manufacturer	Radar	Role	Type	Operating frequency	Antenna type	a) PRF (Hz) b) Pulse width (microsec)	Operating modes (air-to-air)	Operating modes (air-to-surface)	a) Tracking capacity b) Engagement capacity	a) Maximum range naut miles (km) b) Weight lb (kg)
Italy										
FIAR Via Montefeltro 8, I-20 156, Milan	Grifo ASV P2801	Multirole	Pulse-Doppler	I/J band	Planar		Search, range-while-search, track-while-scan, single-target track, combat	Track-while-scan, single-target track, sea search, ground mapping, freeze, terrain avoidance, air-to-ground ranging,	a) Several	a) Air 19 (36) large warship 65 (120) b) 150 (68)
FIAR Via Montefeltro 8, I-20 156, Milan	Grifo F, Grifo L & Grifo M3	Multirole	Pulse-Doppler	I/J band	Planar	a) Low, medium, & high	Range-while-search, velocity search, track-while-scan, single-target scan, situational awareness, combat	Real beam & DBS ground mapping, air-to-ground ranging, sea mapping, surface MTI, surface moving target track	a) Several for GrifoF & M3; 8 for Grifo L	b) 165 (75) for Grifo F, c.154? (c.70?) for Grifo M3
FIAR Via Montefeltro 8, I-20 156, Milan	Grifo X	Multirole	Pulse-Doppler	I/J band	Planar	a) Low, medium, & high	Range-while-search, velocity search, track-while-scan, single-target scan, vertical-scan, HUD acquisition, boresight	Ground mapping, terrain avoidance, air-to-ground ranging, DBS	a) Several	b) 154 (70)
FIAR Via Montefeltro 8, I-20 156, Milan	Grifo 7	Air-to-air	Pulse-Doppler	I/J band	Planar	a) Low & medium	Look-up, look-down, supersearch, boresight	Air-to-ground ranging	Single-target?	b) 121 (55)
FIAR Via Montefeltro 8, I-20 156, Milan	Pointer 2500	Ranging		I-band			Ranging	Ranging		
SMA/Tecnasa	SCP-01 Scipio	Multirole	Pulse-Doppler				Air-to-air, air-to-ground, and air-to-sea			b) 161 (73)
FIAR Via Montefeltro 8, I-20 156, Milan	R21G/M1 Setter	Multimode			Paraboloid		Includes look-down			
Japan										
Mitsubishi Electric Mitsubish Denki Bldg 2-chome 2-3 Marúnouchi, Chiyoda-ku Tokyo 100	J/AWG-11 & J/AWG-12	Multimode					Search and ranging for J/AWG-11	Ranging? for J/AWG-11		
Russia										
Unknown	Kinzhal	Attack (pod-mounted on Su-25)								
Phazotron 1 Electrichesky Per, Moscow RF 123 557	Kopyo	Multirole	Pulse-Doppler	I/J-band	Planar		Track-while-scan, plus three automatic lock-on combat modes (vertical 2-bar scan, HUD, & boresight)	Ground & sea search, plus real-beam and synthetic-aperture mapping	a) 8 b) 2	a) Head-on 30 (57) tail-on 18.9 (35) b) 364 (165)
Phazotron 1 Electrichesky Per, Moscow RF 123 557	Kopyo 25	Multirole	Pulse-Doppler	I/J-band	Planar		Air-interception, velocity search, range-while-search, single target track, track-while-scan, HUD/vertical/ slewable search, boresight			
Phazotron 1 Electrichesky Per, Moscow RF 123 557	M-002	Multirole	Pulse-Doppler		Planar?					

Manufacturer	Designation	Role	Type	Operating frequency	Antenna type	a) PRF (Hz) b) Pulse width (microsec)	Operating modes (air-to-air)	Operating modes (air-to-surface)	a) Tracking capacity b) Engagement capacity	a) Maximum range naut miles (km) b) Weight lb (kg)
Russia										
Phazotron 1 Electrichesky Per, Moscow RF 123 557	Moskit	Multirole	Pulse-Doppler		Planar		Look-up & look-down search/track, single-target track, air-combat	Real-beam & DBS ground mapping, fixed sea target indication, moving sea target tracking, sea target designation		a) 8 (15) against a fighter; 38 (70) against a ship b) 88 (40)
Unknown	NO-01 RLPK-27 radar attack system	Air-to-air	Pulse-Doppler						b) At least 2	
Unknown	NO-06 RP-23P	Air-to-air	Pulse-Doppler	J-band					b) Single target	
Kunyavskiy	NO-03 Sapfir-23ML (High Lark 2)	Air-to-air	Pulse-Doppler?	J-band			Version on Mig-23MLD has additional close-combat modes		b) Single target?	a) Search 46 (85) track 30 (55) b) lighter than High Lark
Kirpichev	NO-05 S-500 RP-25 Sapfir-25	Air-to-air	Pulse-Doppler?				Look-up, look-down		b) Single target	a) Search 62 (115) track 43 (80)
Phazotron 1 Electrichesky Per, Moscow RF 123 557	NO-07 S-800 SBI-16 Zaslon (Flash Dance)	Air-to-air	Pulse-Doppler	9.0 – 9.5GHz	Planar		Look-up, look-down		a) 10 b) 4	a) Look-down search 108 (200) track 65 (120) b) More than 2,200 (1,000)
Unknown	NO-08 RP-23MLA	Air-to-air	Pulse-Doppler	J-band					b) Single target	
Phazotron 1 Electrichesky Per, Moscow RF 123 557	NO-10 S-29 Zhuk	Multirole	Pulse-Doppler	I/J-band	Planar		Look-up and look-down	Automatic terrain following and terrain avoidance, real & synthetic aperture ground mapping with 50 – 65 ft(15 – 20 m) resolution	a) 10 b) 4	a) 54+ (100+) maximum, 48 (90) against fighters b) 551 (250)
Phazotron 1 Electrichesky Per, Moscow RF 123 557	NO-11 Zhuk 27	Multirole	Pulse-Doppler	I/J-band	Planar		Range-while-search, track-while-scan, vertical & HUD search, wide-angle, boresight	Real-beam ground mapping, DBS, synthetic-aperture, enlargement, freeze, MTI, moving- target tracking, ranging	a) 10 b) 4	a) Head-on 54 (100) tail-on 30 (55) b) 573 (260)
Phazotron 1 Electrichesky Per, Moscow RF 123 557	Zhuk PH	Multirole	Pulse-Doppler	I/J-band	Phased array		Target detection & velocity measurement, vertical & HUD search, wide-angle, boresight, raid-assessment	Real-beam ground mapping, DBS, synthetic-aperture, enlargement, freeze, MTI, moving-target tracking, terrain avoidance	a) 24 b) 6 – 8	a) 89 (165) in velocity mode, 75 (140) in range mode, 32 (60) against receding targets b) 606 (275)
Phazotron 1 Electrichesky Per, Moscow RF 123 557	Zhuk PH Improved	Multirole	Pulse-Doppler	I/J-band	Phased array		As Zhuk PH	As Zhuk PH	a) 24 b) 6 – 8	a) 132 (245) in velocity mode, 99 (183) in range mode
Phazotron 1 Electrichesky Per, Moscow RF 123 557	NO-19 RP-29 Sapfir 29 (Slot Back)	Air-to-air	Pulse-Doppler		Cassegrain		Look-up & look-down		a) 10 b) Single target	a) Search 54 (100) track 38 (70)
Phazotron 1 Electrichesky Per, Moscow RF 123 557	NO-19E A	Air-to-air	Pulse-Doppler		Cassegrain?					As NO-19 above
Phazotron 1 Electrichesky Per, Moscow RF 123 557	NO-19ME & NO-19M Topaz	Air-to-air	Pulse-Doppler		Cassegrain?				a) 10 b) 2	a) 54 (100) maximum, 38 (70) against surface targets
Unknown	Orion-A	Attack	Pulse?				None			a) 81 (150)

Manufacturer	Radar	Role	Type	Operating frequency	Antenna type	a) PRF (Hz) b) Pulse width (microsec)	Operating modes (air-to-air)	Operating modes (air-to-surface)	a) Tracking capacity b) Engagement capacity	a) Maximum range naut miles (km) b) Weight lb (kg)
Russia										
Leninets St Petersburg	PN-A (Down Beat)	Nav/attack (on Tu-95K-22 & Tu-22M)		I-band						a) 324 (175)
Leninets St Petersburg	PSRS-2 Initsia-tiva-2B,-2K,-2M & -2ME	Nav/attack	Pulse				None	Search & attack		
Nyenartouich	RP-21, RP-21MA, R2L (Spin Scan)	Air-to-air	Pulse	I-band		a) 900–950 (search); 1,750 - 1,850 (track)			a) Single target b) Single target	a) Search 10.8 (20) track 5.4 (10)
Unknown	RP-21M (Spin Scan)	Air-to-air	Pulse	I-band		a) As above	Guidance for RS-2US missile		a) Single target b) Single target	a) As above
Volkov	RP-22, 22M, 22SM Saphir-21 (Jay Bird)	Air-to-air	Pulse	12.80 - 13.2GHz		a) 1,592 – 1,792; 2,042 – 2,048, 2,716 – – 2,725 (for RP-22), –2,726 (for 22M) & – 2,277 (for 22SM) b) 0.3 – 1.0			a) Single target b) Single target	a) Search 16 (30), track 8 (15) for RP-22; search 10.8 (20), track 5.4 (10) for RP-22M; search 10.8–13.5 (20–25), track 7.6– 9.2 (14–17) for RP-22SM
Volkov	RP-25 Smerch A (Fox Fire)	Air-to-air	Pulse	I-band					b) Single target	a) Search 54 (100) track 27 (50) b) More than 1,100 (500)
Kunyavskiy	NO-? S-23 Sapfir-23D-Sh (High Lark)	Air-to-air	Pulse- Doppler?	J-band					b) Single target	b) Search 38 (70) track 30 (55)
A. Golenischev design team	SRD-5 (Scan Fix)	Ranging	Pulse	I-band			Range only		a) Single target b) Single target	
Unknown	SRD-5M (High Fix)	Ranging	Pulse	I-band			Range only		a) Single target b) Single target	a) 4.3 (8.0)
Phazotron 1 Electrichesky Per, Moscow RF 123 557	Super Kopyo	Multirole	Pulse-Doppler	I/J-band	Planar		Look-up, look-down, range-while-search, raid assessment, vertical & HUD search, wide-angle, boresight	Terrain avoid-ance, real-beam ground mapping, DBS, synthetic-aperture, enlargement, freeze, MTI, moving-target tracking, ranging	a) 8 air, 4 surface b) 2	b) 220 (100)
Phazotron 1 Electrichesky Per, Moscow RF 123 557	Super Kopyo PH	Multirole	Pulse-Doppler	I/J-band	Active phased array		Look-up, look-down, with range-while-search, single-target track, air-combat	Rear-beam ground mapping, DBS, 100:1 angular resolution synthetic-aperture		
Unknown	Uspekh-2A (Big Bulge)	Nav/attack (Tu-95RT & Ka-25T)		I-band						a) More than 350 (190)
Phazotron? 1 Electrichesky Per, Moscow RF 123 557	Zaslon-M	Air-to-air	Pulse-Doppler	9–9.5 GHz?	Planar		Look-up, look-down		a) 10 b) 6	a) Better than SBI-16 Zaslon
Leninets St Petersburg	Unknown (for Su-32FN/34)	Multirole	Pulse-Doppler		Phased array					
Note: Little known types include Relyef pulse (?) nav/attack & terrain avoidance for Su-24; a multirole (?), millimetric frequency, air-to-surface observation and fire control (nose-mounted) radar on Mi-28 N; mast-mounted, multirole (?), K-band radar on Mi-40; and Clam Pipe nav/attack radar for the Tu-95MS.										
Sweden										
Ericsson Radar Electronics Bergfotsgatan 2, S-431 84 Molndal	PS-05/A	Multirole	Pulse-Doppler	I/J band	Planar	a) Low, medium, & high	Search, track-while-scan, short-range wide-angle scan	Ground and sea search, ground map-ping, missile fire-control		b) 344 (156)

Manufacturer	Designation	Role	Type	Operating frequency	Antenna type	a) PRF (Hz) b) Pulse width (microsec)	Operating modes (air-to-air)	Operating modes (air-to-surface)	a) Tracking capacity b) Engagement capacity	a) Maximum range naut miles (km) b) Weight lb (kg)
Sweden										
Ericsson Radar Electronics Bergfotsgatan 2, S-431 84 Molndal	PS-46/A	Air-to-air	Pulse-Doppler	I/J band	Cassegrain	a) Low rate for look-up; medium rate for look-down	Look-down, search, track-while-scan, single-target track, automatic & semi-automatic HUD	Air-to-ground ranging, optional ground mapping		a) Look-down 27 (50) b) 661 (300)
Taiwan										
Unknown	Golden Dragon 53	Multirole	Pulse-Doppler	I/J band ?			Look-up, look-down	40:1 Doppler beam sharpening		a) Search 81 (150)
United Kingdom										
GEC Marconi Avionics Crewe Toll, Ferry Road, Edinburgh	AI.24 Foxhunter	Air-to-air	FMICW pulse-Doppler	I-band	Cassegrain		Search, track, target illumination		a) More than 100 (185)	
GEC Marconi Avionics Crewe Toll, Ferry Road, Edinburgh	Blue Fox	Air-to-air	Pulse	I-band	Planar		Search, track	Search, track		
GEC Marconi Avionics Crewe Toll, Ferry Road, Edinburgh	Blue Hawk	Multirole	Pulse-Doppler	9.6 – 9.9GHz	Planar	a) Low, medium, and high (800Hz – 90kHz)	Look-up, look-down, velocity search, HUD field of view, and single target track	Ground mapping with DBS, surface target tracking, freeze-frame, and two sea-search modes		a) Look-up 44 (81) look-down 27 (50) ground mapping 80 (148) b) 236 (107)
GEC Marconi Avionics Crewe Toll, Ferry Road, Edinburgh	Blue Vixen	Multirole	Pulse-Doppler	I-band	Planar	a) Low, medium, and high	Look-up, look-down, TWS, single-target track, air-combat, air-to-air ranging	Sea search, air-to-ground ranging		b) 312 (141.5)
GEC Marconi Avionics Crewe Toll, Ferry Road, Edinburgh	Skyranger	Air-to-air	Pulse	I-band	Paraboloid		Gun & missile			a) 8 (15) b) 88 (40)
United States of America										
Hughes Aircraft Bldg R10 MS 10001, PO Box 92426, Los Angeles, CA 90009	AN/APG-63 & AN/APG-63(V)1 generally similar	Air-to-air	Pulse-Doppler	I-band	Planar	a) Medium & high	Look-down, supersearch, vertical scan, boresight			a) 100+ (185+) b) 494 (224)
Hughes Aircraft Bldg R10 MS 10001, PO Box 92426, Los Angeles, CA 90009	AN/APG-65	Multirole	Pulse-Doppler	I/J-band	Planar	a) Low, medium, & high	Long-range velocity search, range-while-search, single target track, TWS, raid-assessment, HUD acquisition, vertical scan,boresight	Real-beam & DBS mapping, medium-range SAR, fixed & moving target tracking, sea surface search, terrain avoidance, INS update	a) 10 b) 8	a) 39 (72) b) 341 (154.7)
Westinghouse Electric Corp PO Box 17319, MS A255, Baltimore, MD 21203-7319	AN/APG-66	Multirole	Pulse-Doppler	I/J-band	Planar	a) Low rate for look-up; medium rate for look-down	Look-up, look-down, search, track, air-combat search, automatic tracking	Real-beam & DBS ground mapping, scan-freeze, sea search, air-to-ground ranging		a) Look-up 25 – 40 (46 – 74) look-down 20 – 30 (37 – 56) b) 297 (134.7)
Westinghouse Electric Corp PO Box 17319, MS A255, Baltimore, MD 21203-7319	AN/APG-66(V)	Multirole	Pulse-Doppler	I/J-band	Planar	a) Low rate for look-up; medium rate for look-down	Single-target track, multi-target track, look-up search, situational awareness	Rear-beam & DBS ground mapping, MTI, fixed target track, sea search & track	a) Optional 10	a) 25% better than AN/APG-66
Westinghouse Electric Corp PO Box 17319, MS A255, Baltimore, MD 21203-7319	AN/APG-66(V)-2A	Multirole	Pulse-Doppler	I/J-band	Planar	a) Low rate for look-up; medium rate for look-down	As AN/APG-66, buts adds helo detection, raid-awareness, four-target situational awareness, auto/manual primary target acquisition.	As AN/APG-66, but adds ground MTI, fixed target tracking over sea or desert, & medium DBS, combined ground mapping & situational awareness	a) Up to 15	a) 20 - 25% increase in detection range over AN/APG-66 b) 260 (118)

Manufacturer	Radar	Role	Type	Operating frequency	Antenna type	a) PRF (Hz) b) Pulse width (microsec)	Operating modes (air-to-air)	Operating modes (air-to-surface)	a) Tracking capacity b) Engagement capacity	a) Maximum range naut miles (km) b) Weight lb (kg)
United States of America										
Westinghouse Electric Corp PO Box 17319, MS A255, Baltimore, MD 21203-7319	AN/APG-66(V)3	Multirole	Pulse-Doppler	I/J-band	Planar	a) Low rate for look-up; medium rate for look-down	Similar to AN/APG-66(V)/2A?; has CW illuminator for use with AIM-7	Similar to AN/APG-66(V)/2A?		
Westinghouse Electric Corp PO Box 17319, MS A255, Baltimore, MD 21203-7319	AN/APG-66J	Multirole	Pulse-Doppler	I/J-band	Planar	a) Low rate for look-up; medium rate for look-down	Look-up, look-down, search, track, air-combat search, automatic tracking	Real-beam & DBS ground mapping, scan-freeze, & sea search, air-to-ground ranging		a) Look-up 25-40 (46-74); look-down 20-30 (37-56)
Westinghouse Electric Corp PO Box 17319, MS A255, Baltimore, MD 21203-7319	AN/APG-66Z	Multirole	Pulse-Doppler	I/J-band	Planar	a) Low rate for look-up; medium rate for look-down				
Westinghouse Electric Corp PO Box 17319, MS A255, Baltimore, MD 21203-7319	AN/APG-66H	Multirole	Pulse-Doppler	I/J-band	Planar	a) Low rate for look-up; medium rate for look-down	Look-up, look-down, search, track-while-scan, situation awareness single-target track, air-combat search, automatic tracking	Real-beam & DBS ground mapping, scan-freeze, sea search, air-to-ground ranging	a) 8	
Westinghouse Electric Corp PO Box 17319, MS A255, Baltimore, MD 21203-7319	AN/APG-66T	Multirole	Pulse-Doppler	I/J-band	Planar	a) Low rate for look-up; medium rate for look-down	Look-up, look-down, search, track-while-scan, single-target track, air-combat search, 4 dog-fight modes, 2-target situational awareness	Real-beam & DBS ground mapping, ground MTI, scan-freeze, sea search, sea track, air-to-ground ranging		
Westinghouse Electric Corp PO Box 17319, MS A255, Baltimore, MD 21203-7319	AN/APG-66NT & AN/APG-66SR	Multirole	Pulse-Doppler							
Martin Marietta Electronics & Missiles 5600 W. Sand Lake Road, Orlando, FL 32819-8907	AN/APG-67 & AN/APG-67E	Multirole	Pulse-Doppler	I/J-band	Planar	a) Low, medium & high b) Variable	Look-up and look-down, automatic search & track	Real-beam & DBS ground mapping, air-to-ground ranging		a) Look-up 39 (72) look-down 21 (39) for –67; slightly less for –67E b) 271 (123)
Martin Marietta Electronics & Missiles 5600 W. Sand Lake Road, Orlando, FL 32819-8907	AN/APG-67F	Multirole	Pulse-Doppler	I/J-band	Planar	a) Low, medium & high b) Variable	Look-up and look-down, automatic search & track, range-while-search	Real-beam & DBS ground mapping, air-to-ground ranging		a) 80 (148)
Westinghouse Electric Corp PO Box 17319, MS A255, Baltimore, MD 21203-7319	AN/APG-68	Multirole	Pulse-Doppler	I/J-band	Planar	a) Low, medium & high	Look-up, look-down, velocity search, range-while-search, track-while-scan, raid-assessement, air-combat search	Real-beam & DBS ground mapping, fixed and moving-target tracking, sea-search, air-to-ground ranging	a) 10	b) 337 (153)
Westinghouse Electric Corp PO Box 17319, MS A255, Baltimore, MD 21203-7319	AN/APG-68(V)5	Multirole	Pulse-Doppler	I/J-band	Planar	a) Low, medium & high	As AN/APG-68, but adds situational-awareness mode	Real-beam, DBS & SAR ground mapping, fixed and moving-target tracking, and ship-detection, automatic terrain-following	a) 10?	b) c.379 (c.172)
Hughes Aircraft Bldg R10 MS 10001, PO Box 92426, Los Angeles, CA 90009	AN/APG-70	Multirole	Pulse-Doppler	I-band	Planar	a) Medium & high	Range-while-scan, velocity search, single target track, TWS, raid assessment, auto aquisition	Real-beam & high-resolution mapping, precision velocity update, air-to-ground ranging		

Manufacturer	Designation	Role	Type	Operating frequency	Antenna type	a) PRF (Hz) b) Pulse width (microsec)	Operating modes (air-to-air)	Operating modes (air-to-surface)	a) Tracking capacity b) Engagement capacity	a) Maximum range naut miles (km) b) Weight lb (kg)
United States of America										
Hughes Aircraft Bldg R10 MS 10001, PO Box 92426, Los Angeles, CA 90009	AN/APG-71	Air-to-air	Pulse-Doppler		Planar		As AWG-9 but adds BVR target identification and raid-assessment modes	Real-beam & DBS mapping, medium-range SAR, fixed & moving target tracking, sea surface search, terrain avoidance, INS update	a) 10 b) 8	
Hughes Aircraft Bldg R10 MS 10001, PO Box 92426, Los Angeles, CA 90009	AN/APG-73	Multirole	Pulse-Doppler	I/J-band	Planar		Velocity search, range-while-search, single target track, TWS, raid assessment, situational awareness, gun acquisition, vertical scan and target acquisition	Higher resolution in air-to-ground mode; adds terrain-following and clearance		
Westinghouse Norden Systems, PO Box 5300, Norwalk, CT 06856-5300	AN/APG-76	Multirole	Pulse-Doppler	Ku-band	Planar		Look-up and look-down, track-while-scan, velocity & adaptive search, air combat	Real-beam & SAR ground mapping, DBS, & MTI, sea search, sea moving target track, air-to-ground ranging, freeze		a) 80 (148) in ground mapping mode b) 625 (283)
Westinghouse Electric Corp PO Box 17319, MS A255, Baltimore, MD 21203-7319	AN/APG-77	Air-to-air	Pulse-Doppler		VLO electrically-scanned active array		Not known	Not known		
Magnavox 1313 Production Road, Fort Wayne, FN 46808	AN/APQ-104	Air-to-air	Pulse	I/J-band?						
	AN/APQ-110	Terrain-following						Terrain-following		
GE Aerospace (now part of Lockheed Martin)	AN/APQ-113	Attack	Pulse	16.0 – 16.4GHz	Paraboloid	a) 337, 674, 2022 b) 0.4, 1.2, 2.4	Range search, target-acquisition, track	Navigation, weapon-delivery, ranging		
GE Aerospace (now part of Lockheed Martin)	AN/APQ-114	Attack	Pulse		Paraboloid					
Westinghouse Electric Corp PO Box 17319, MS A255, Baltimore, MD 21203-7319	AN/APQ-120	Multirole	Pulse	I/J-band	Paraboloid	a) 500 or 1,000 b) 0.4 or 2.0				b) 619 (281)
Texas Instruments 8505 Forest Lane, PO Box 660246, MS 3134, Dallas, TX 75266	AN/APQ-126(V)	Attack	Pulse	J-band	Paraboloid			Terrain avoidance & following, ground mapping, ranging		
Raytheon 141 Spring Drive, Lexington, MA 02173	AN/APQ-140	Forward-looking		J-band	Planar					
GE Aerospace (now part of Lockheed Martin)	AN/APQ-144	Attack	Pulse		Paraboloid	b) 0.2		Navigation, weapon-delivery, ranging		
Westinghouse Norden Systems PO Box 5300, Norwalk, CT 06856-5300	AN/APQ-148	Attack	Pulse	J-band	Paraboloid + fixed			Terrain following, terrain-avoidance, ground mapping, search, tracking, beacon tracking		b) 507 (230)
Motorola Military & Aerospace Electronics 8201 East McDowell Road, Scottsdale AZ 85257	AN/APQ-150	Attack								
Emerson (now part of Electronics & Space Corporation)	AN/APQ-153	Air-to-air	Pulse	9.3GHz	Paraboloid		As below			b) 110 (50)

Manufacturer	Radar	Role	Type	Operating frequency	Antenna type	a) PRF (Hz) b) Pulse width (microsec)	Operating modes (air-to-air)	Operating modes (air-to-surface)	a) Tracking capacity b) Engagement capacity	a) Maximum range naut miles (km) b) Weight lb (kg)
United States of America										
Westinghouse Norden Systems, PO Box 5300, Norwalk, CT 06856-5300	AN/APQ-156	Attack	Pulse	J-band	Paraboloid + fixed			Terrain following, terrain-avoidance, ground mapping, search, tracking, beacon tracking		b) c.507 (c.230)
Texas Instruments 8505 Forest Lane, PO Box 660246, MS 3134, Dallas, TX 75266	AN/APQ-158	Attack	Pulse	J-band	Paraboloid			Terrain avoidance, terrain following, ground mapping, ranging		
Emerson (now part of Electronics & Space Corporation)	AN/APQ-157	Air-to-air	Pulse		Paraboloid		Search, boresight missile, guns			
Electronics & Space Corporation 8100 W. Florissant Ave, St. Louis, MO 63136	AN/APQ-159(V)-1/ –2/ –3/ –4	Air-to-air	Pulse	I/J-band	Planar	a) Medium for receding targets; high for approaching	Search, boresight missile, guns			b) 139 (63) for AN/APQ-159(V)1
Electronics & Space Corporation 8100 W. Florissant Ave, St. Louis, MO 63136	AN/APQ-159(V)-5	Air-to-air	Pulse	I/J-band	Planar	a) Medium for receding targets; high for approaching	Search, boresight missile, guns			a) Search 18 (34) track 12 (22)
Electronics & Space Corporation 8100 W. Florissant Ave, St. Louis, MO 63136	AN/APQ-159(V)-7	Multirole	Pulse	I/J-band	Planar	a) Medium for receding targets; high for approaching	Search, boresight missile, guns	Adds air-ground		
	AN/APQ-160	Attack								
GE Aerospace (now part of Lockheed Martin)	AN/APQ-161	Attack		J-band	Paraboloid					
Westinghouse Electric Corp PO Box 17319, MS A255, Baltimore, MD 21203-7319	AN/APQ-164	Attack		I/J-band	Phased array			Terrain following, terrain avoidance, navigation, weapon-delivery, high-resolution ground mapping, weather		
GE Aerospace (now part of Lockheed Martin)	AN/APQ-165	Attack		J-band	Paraboloid					
Lockheed Martin Electronics & Missiles 5600 W. Sand Lake Road, Orlando, FL 32819-8907	AN/APQ-169(V1/V2)	Attack				b) Down to 0.25				
Texas Instruments 8505 Forest Lane, PO Box 660246, MS 3134, Dallas, TX 75266	AN/APQ-171	Attack	Pulse		Twin units			Terrain following, terrain-avoidance, ground mapping		
Texas Instruments 8505 Forest Lane, PO Box 660246, MS 3134, Dallas, TX 75266	AN/APQ-172	Forward-looking	Pulse (monopulse)	J-band	Paraboloid			Ground mapping, terrain following		
Hughes Aircraft	AN/APQ-180	Attack	Pulse-Doppler							
Hughes Aircraft Bldg R10 MS 10001, PO Box 92426, Los Angeles, CA 90009	AN/APQ-181	Attack	Synthetic-aperture	12.5 - 18GHz				21 modes, including: terrain following, terrain-avoidance, ground mapping, target detection & tracking, weapon delivery		b) 2,101 (953)

Manufacturer	Designation	Role	Type	Operating frequency	Antenna type	a) PRF (Hz) b) Pulse width (microsec)	Operating modes (air-to-air)	Operating modes (air-to-surface)	a) Tracking capacity b) Engagement capacity	a) Maximum range naut miles (km) b) Weight lb (kg)
United States of America										
Westinghouse Norden Systems, PO Box 5300, Norwalk, CT 06856-5300	AN/APS-130	Attack	Pulse	J-band	Paraboloid + fixed			Terrain following, terrain-avoidance, ground mapping, search, tracking, beacon tracking		
Hughes Aircraft Bldg R10 MS 10001, PO Box 92426, Los Angeles, CA 90009	AN/AWG-9	Air-to-air	Pulse-Doppler	I/J-band	Planar	a) High	Velocity search, range-while-search, track-while-scan		a) 24 b) 6	
Lockheed Martin Electronics & Missiles 5600 W. Sand Lake Road, Orlando, FL 32819-8907	Longbow	Attack		Millimetre-wave	Interferometer			Target detection, classification and missile fire-control		
Texas Instruments 8505 Forest Lane, PO Box 660246, MS 3134, Dallas, TX 75266	Tornado attack radar	Multirole	Pulse	Ku-band			Search, track, air-to-air ranging	Terrain mapping, terrain following		
Lockheed Martin Electronics & Missiles 5600 W. Sand Lake Road, Orlando, FL 32819-8907	Designation not yet assigned	Multirole		I/J band			Look-up, look-down, search, track, boresight, supersearch. vertical	Mapping, DBS, MTI, freeze, sea-search, air-to-ground ranging		a) Look-up 30 (55), look-down 19 (35) – against fighter-sized targets b) 229 (104)
Multi-national										
GEC-Thomson, Daimler-Benz Aerospace Airborne Radars	Airborne Multi-Role Solid-state Active-array Radar (AMSAR)	Technology demonstrator	Pulse-Doppler							
Consortium headed by GEC Marconi Avionics Crewe Toll, Ferry Road, Edinburgh	ECR 90 Euroradar	Multirole	Pulse-Doppler		Planar	a) Low, medium, and high	Look-up, look down	No information available		
Thomson-CSF/Phazotron	Phathom	Multirole	Pulse-Doppler		Active phased array	a) Medium and high	Long-range search, look-up & look-down, boresight, vertical search, HUD acquisition, sector scan, raid assessment	Ground attack, ground mapping, MTI, terrain avoidance, sea search & attack	a) 8 b) 4	b) c.265 (c.120)

Sea, land and air surveillance

Manufacturer	Radar	Role	Type	Operating frequency	Antenna type	a) Scan rate (rpm) b) Peak output (kW)	a) PRF (Hz) b) Pulse width (microsec)	Operating modes	a) Maximum range naut miles (km) b) Weight lb (kg)	Platform(s)
Canada										
Litton Systems Canada 25 City View, Etobicoke, Ontario	AN/APS-503	Sea surveillance	Pulse	9.2 – 9.4GHz	Paraboloid	a) 30 b) 50	a) 400 b) 0.5	Surface search	b) 99 (45)	Sea King
Litton Systems Canada 25 City View, Etobicoke, Ontario	AN/ APS-504(V)3	Sea surveillance	Pulse	9.2 – 9.4GHz	Paraboloid	b) 100	b) 0.5 or 2.4	Surface search		Y-8
Litton Systems Canada 25 City View, Etobicoke, Ontario	AN/ APS-504(V)5	Sea surveillance	Pulse	8.9 – 9.4GHz	Paraboloid	b) 8		Surface search		Do 228MP, CN-235
Litton Systems Canada 25 City View, Etobicoke, Ontario	LASR-2	Sea surveillance	Pulse	9.2 – 9.4GHz	Paraboloid	a) Choice of three b) 100	a) Choice of four b) Choice of two	Surface search	b) 170 (77)	
CAL Corporation 1050 Morrison Drive, Ottawa	Saffire	Ground surveillance	Sideways-looking	9.25GHz	Microstrip	b) 200	a) 550 – 1100 b) 230 nanosec	Surface mapping	b) Various	

Manufacturer	Radar	Role	Type	Operating frequency	Antenna type	a) Scan rate (rpm) b) Peak output (kW)	a) PRF (Hz) b) Pulse width (microsec)	Operating modes	a) Maximum range naut miles (km) b) Weight lb (kg)	Platform(s)
Canada										
CAL Corporation 1051 Morrison Drive, Ottawa	SLAR 100	Ground surveillance	Sideways-looking	9.25GHz		b) 200	a) 800 b) 0.23	Surface mapping	b) 588 (267)	DHC-7, L-188
CAL Corporation 1052 Morrison Drive, Ottawa	SLAR 300	Ground surveillance	Sideways-looking	I/J-band	Microstrip	b) 250		Surface mapping	a) 45 (83)	
China										
China Leihua Electronic Technology Research Institute	Type 698	Sea surveillance	Sideways-looking	I/J-band	Paraboloid			Surface search	a) 32 (60) b) 507 (230)	
France										
Thomson-CSF RCM division 1 blvd Jean Martin, F-78852 Elancourt Cedex	Agrion	Sea surveillance/ missile targeting	Pulse		Paraboloid			Surface search, missile guidance for AS 15TT		Dauphin, AS 565 Panther
Thomson-CSF RCM division 1 blvd Jean Martin, F-78852 Elancourt Cedex	DRAA 2	Sea surveillance/ ASW	Pulse	I/J-band?				Surface search, tracking, coastal mapping, beacon		Alize, Atlantic
LCTAR 6 rue Nieuport, PO Box 86, F-78143 Velizy-Villacoublay Cedex	Horizon	Land surveillance	Pulse-Doppler	I/J-band				High-resolution ground mapping, MTI		AS 532UL Cougar
Thomson-CSF RCM division 1 blvd Jean Martin, F-78852 Elancourt Cedex	Iguane	Sea surveillance	Pulse		Paraboloid			Surface search		Atlantic, Atlantique 2
OMERA-Segid (Now part of Thomson-CSF)	ORB-31D	Sea surveillance/ missile targeting	Pulse		Paraboloid			Surface search, target tracking	a) 43 (80) b) 165 (75)	Super Frelon
OMERA-Segid (Now part of Thomson-CSF)	ORB-32	Sea surveillance/ ASW	Pulse		Paraboloid	b) 80		Surface search, navigation, missile fire-control	a) 49 (90) b) Various	SA 321 Super Frelon, AS 565 Panther
Thomson-CSF RCM division 1 blvd Jean Martin, F-78852 Elancourt Cedex	Raphael TH	Reconnaissance	Sideways-looking					Surface mapping		
Thomson-CSF RCM division 1 blvd Jean Martin, F-78852 Elancourt Cedex	SLAR 2000	Reconnaissance	Sideways-looking					Surface mapping		Mirage F1, Mirage 2000
Thomson-CSF RCM division 1 blvd Jean Martin, F-78852 Elancourt Cedex	Varan	Sea surveillance	Pulse	I-band	Paraboloid	b) Low	b) Several	Surface search	a) 130 (240)	Gardian, Falcon, Dauphin, Cougar
Germany										
Daimler-Benz Aerospace Radar & Radio Division Sedanstrasse 10, D-89070 Ulm (Donau)	Swallow	Land surveillance		45GHz			b) 2 or 70	Surface search, target detection		Helicopters
Israel										
Elta Electronic Industries PO Box 330, 77102 Ashdod	EL/M-2022 & EL/M-2022A	Sea surveillance						Surface search, target detection, ASW?		An-72P, proposed for P-3
Elta Electronic Industries PO Box 330, 77102 Ashdod	EL/M-2075 Phalcon	Air surveillance		L-band	Six airframe-mounted phased arrays		a) Medium & low	Medium PRF search and track, low PRF helicopter detection, long-range search		Boeing 707
Italy										
SMA Villa San Martino a Soffiano, I-50 124 Florence	AM/APS-717	Land & sea surveillance		I/J-band	Planar array			Search, ground mapping		HH-3F
FIAR Via Montefeltro 8, I-20 156, Milan	Creso P2132	Land surveillance	Pulse-Doppler		Planar array			Land surveillance, MTI target detection & tracking		Helicopters
SMA Villa San Martino a Soffiano, I-50 124 Florence	MM/APS-705	Sea surveillance	Pulse	I-band	Paraboloid	a) 20 or 40 b) 25	a) 650, 1,600 b) 0.05, 1.5	Surface search, target tracking, weapon-aiming	b) 176 (80)	AB.212, SH-3D

Manufacturer	Radar	Role	Type	Operating frequency	Antenna type	a) Scan rate (rpm) b) Peak output (kW)	a) PRF (Hz) b) Pulse width (microsec)	Operating modes	a) Maximum range naut miles (km) b) Weight lb (kg)	Platform(s)
Italy										
SMA Villa San Martino a Soffiano, I-50 124 Florence	MM/APS-706	Sea surveillance/ missile targeting	Pulse	I-band	Back-to-back paraboloids			Surface search, navigation, missile fire-control		SH-3D
SMA Villa San Martino a Soffiano, I-50 124 Florence	MM/APS-707	Sea surveillance	Pulse	I-band	Paraboloid			Surface search, surface mapping, target-designation		
Eliradar	MM/APS-784	Sea surveillance	I/J-band					Sea search, ASW, weather		EH 101
Japan										
NEC 5-7-1 Shiba, Minato-ku, Tokyo	NEC-SAR	Land & sea surveillance	Sideways-looking	9.53 GHz				Surface mapping		
Poland										
Unknown	ARS-100	Sea surveillance & navigation			Modified X-band	a) 7.5 – 15			a) 60 (111)	M-28RM, replacing SRN-441XA. Later versions to have ARS-400
Russia										
Vega	Igla	Sea surveillance?	Sideways-looking		Phased array					Il-20
Unknown	Korshun	Sea surveillance/ ASW	Pulse	J-band				Surface search & ASW		Tu-142M Bear F mod 2/3
Unknown	Kvant	Air & land surveillance	Pulse-Doppler?							Yak-44
Vega	Nit	Sea surveillance?	Sideways-looking	J-band (2 cm)	Phased array					Il-20 & 24N
Unknown	NNIIRT	Air & sea surveillance	Pulse-Doppler?	Decametric				Air surveillance (tracks up to 10 targets, surface search)	a) 54-81 (100-150) against a fighter; 135 (250) against ships	Ka-31
Unknown	Sabla & Shompol	Land surveillance	Sideways-looking							MiG-25RBS for Sabla, MiG-25RBSh for Shompol
Unknown	Shtyk	Reconnaissance	Sideways-looking							Su-24MR Fencer-E
Unknown		Land surveillance	Sideways-looking	A-band (125 cm) & H-band (4 cm)						M-55B
Unknown	Type 12-M	Sea surveillance/ ASW								Mi-14PL
Vega	Shmel & Shmel2	Air surveillance	Pulse-Doppler?	S-band		a) 6			a) 108 – 324 (200 – 600) depending on target size & altitude	Shmel on A-50, Il-76 Adnan-9?; Shmel2 on A-50M
Unknown	designation unknown (Flap Jack)	Air surveillance	Pulse?							Tu-126
Unknown	Berkut (Wet Eye)	Sea surveillance/ ASW	J-band							Il-38
Sweden										
Ericsson Microwave Systems/Swedish National Defense Research Establishment (FOA)	Carabas (Coherent All RAdio Band Sensing) & II	Land surveillance	Sideways-looking	20-90 MHz	Towed array for Carabas; rigid booms for Carabas II					Sabreliner trials aircraft
Philips Elektronikindustrier	Hera	Sea surveillance/ missile targeting	Pulse			b) 100		Surface search, navigation, missile fire-control for RBS15		Helicopters

Manufacturer	Radar	Role	Type	Operating frequency	Antenna type	a) Scan rate (rpm) b) Peak output (kW)	a) PRF (Hz) b) Pulse width (microsec)	Operating modes	a) Maximum range naut miles (km) b) Weight lb (kg)	Platform(s)
Sweden										
Ericsson Radar Electronics Bergfotsgatan 2, S-431 84 Molndal	FSR-890 Erieye	Air surveillance		S-band	Phased array		a) Low & medium		b) 2,910 (1,320)	Saab 340 AEW, Fairchild AEW, EMB-120EW, Fokker Kingbird Mk2
United Kingdom										
GEC Marconi Avionics Foxhunter Drive, Linford Wood, Milton Keynes, Buckinghamshire	Argus	Air surveillance	Pulse-Doppler	E/F-band	Twin paraboloids			Air and maritime surveillance		Believed used in Y-8 AEW; developed from radar in Nimrod AEW
MEL (now part of Thorn EMI)	ARI 5954/5955	Sea surveillance/ ASW	Pulse	I-band						Sea King
Racal Avionics 88 Bushey Road, London SW20 0JH	ASR 360	Sea surveillance	Pulse	I/J-band	Slotted waveguide	a) 23 b) 25	b) 0.05, 0.25, 1.0	Surface search		Jetstream 31, Skyvan
GEC Marconi Avionics Crewe Toll, Ferry Road, Edinburgh	Blue Kestrel 5000	Sea surveillance/ ASW	Pulse	I-band	Planar array		a) Selectable		b) 225 (102)	EH 101
GEC Marconi Avionics Crewe Toll, Ferry Road, Edinburgh	Blue Kestrel 6000	Sea surveillance/ ASW	Pulse-Doppler	I-band	Planar array			Includes stand-off target classification & air target detection	b) 276 (125)	
Thorn EMI Electronics 120 Blyth Road, Hayes, Middlesex	Marec II	Sea surveillance	Pulse	9.345GHz	Paraboloid	b) 80	a) 200, 400 b) 0.4, 2.5	Surface search		Do 228
Thorn EMI Electronics 120 Blyth Road, Hayes, Middlesex	Searchwater (ARI 5980)	Sea surveillance	Pulse					Surface search, navigation, target-classification, missile fire-control		Nimrod, Sea King
Thorn EMI Electronics 120 Blyth Road, Hayes, Middlesex	Searchwater 2	Sea surveillance	Pulse					Surface search, navigation, target-classification		Maritime patrol aircraft
Racal Electronics Western Road, Bracknell, Berkshire RG12 1RG	Searchwater 2000 MR & (Searchwater 2000 AEW in brackets) See Platform(s) for GEC Marconi proposal	Sea surveillance (air surveillance)	Pulse-Doppler (both)	I-band (both)						Proposed for P-3 & and reworked Nimrod options for RAF Nimrod replacement (proposed for AEW Mk 7 upgrade of Royal Navy Sea King AEW)
GEC Marconi Avionics Crewe Toll, Ferry Road, Edinburgh		Air surveillance	Pulse-Doppler	I-band			a) Medium			Proposed for AEW Mk 7 upgrade of Royal Navy Sea King AEW
MEL (now part of Thorn EMI)	Sea Searcher (ARI 5991)	Sea surveillance/ ASW								Sea King
GEC Marconi Avionics Crewe Toll, Ferry Road, Edinburgh	Seaspray Mk1/Mk3	Sea surveillance/ missile targeting	Pulse	I-band	Paraboloid	b) 90	a) Choice of three b) Choice of two	Search, navigation, missile guidance for Sea Skua	b) 165 (75)	Lynx, Sea King, AB212, Super Lynx
GEC Marconi Avionics Crewe Toll, Ferry Road, Edinburgh	Seaspray 2000	Sea surveillance	Pulse	I-band	Paraboloid	b) 90	a) Choice of four b) Choice of two	Search, navigation, ground mapping	b) 176 (80)	Reims Vigilant
GEC Marconi Avionics Crewe Toll, Ferry Road, Edinburgh	Seaspray 3000	Sea surveillance/ missile targeting	Pulse	I-band	Paraboloid	b) 90	a) Choice of four b) Choice of two	Search, navigation, missile guidance for Sea Skua	b) 198 (90)	Lynx, Sea King, AB212
GEC Marconi Avionics Crewe Toll, Ferry Road, Edinburgh	Seaspray 4000	Sea surveillance	Pulse	I-band	Paraboloid		a) Selectable b) Selectable	Search, navigation	b) 176 (80)	Fixed & rotary wing maritime-patrol aircraft

Manufacturer	Radar	Role	Type	Operating frequency	Antenna type	a) Scan rate (rpm) b) Peak output (kW)	a) PRF (Hz) b) Pulse width (microsec)	Operating modes	a) Maximum range naut miles (km) b) Weight lb (kg)	Platform(s)
United Kingdom										
Thorn EMI Electronics 120 Blyth Road, Hayes, Middlesex	Skymaster	Air & sea surveillance	Pulse-Doppler	I-band	Paraboloid			Look-up, look-down, surface search		PB-N Defender
Thorn EMI Electronics 120 Blyth Road, Hayes, Middlesex	Super Marec	Sea surveillance	Pulse	9.345GHz?	Paraboloid			Surface search		Do 228MP
MEL (now part of Thorn EMI)	Super Searcher	Sea surveillance	Pulse	I-band	Planar array		b) Choice of three	Surface search, ASW		S-70B, Sea King, EMB-111, Dominie, Do 228MP
United States of America										
Motorola 8201 E. McDowell Road, Scottsdale, Arizona 85257	AN/APS-94F	Reconnaissance	Sideways-looking		Back-to-back slotted waveguides			Ground mapping, MTI	a) 54 (100)	OV-1D, P-3, UH-1
General Electric (now part of Lockheed Martin Electronics & Missiles)	AN/APS-111	Air surveillance	Pulse	UHF (c.400MHz?)	Yagi array					E-2B
Texas Instruments 8505 Forest Lane, PO Box 660246, MS 3134, Dallas, TX 75266	AN/APS-115	Sea surveillance/ ASW		I-band	Two paraboloids					P-3C, US-1A
Texas Instruments 8505 Forest Lane, PO Box 660246, MS 3134, Dallas, TX 75266	AN/APS-116	Sea surveillance/ ASW		I-band	Paraboloid					S-3A, CP-140 Aurora
Texas Instruments 8505 Forest Lane, PO Box 660246, MS 3134, Dallas, TX 75266	AN/APS-124	Sea surveillance/. ASW								SH-60
Texas Instruments 8505 Forest Lane, PO Box 660246, MS 3134, Dallas, TX 75266	AN/APS-127	Sea surveillance			Planar					HU-25A
Eaton Corp.	AN/APS-128	Sea surveillance		9.375GHz	Planar	a) 15 or 60 b) 100	a) 400, 1200, 1600 b) 0.5, 2.4, optional 0.1	Search, weather		E-9A, Do 228MP, C-212MP, EMB-111
Motorola Military & Aerospace Electronics 8201 East McDowell Road, Scottsdale, AZ 85257	AN/APS-131	Sea surveillance	Sideways-looking		Back-to-back slotted waveguides			Sea surface mapping		HU-25A
Texas Instruments 8505 Forest Lane, PO Box 660246, MS 3134, Dallas, TX 75266	AN/APS-134(V)	Sea surveillance/. ASW	Pulse	9.5 – 10.0GHz	Paraboloid	a) 6, 40, 150 b) 500	a) Low, 500, 2000	Surveillance, search, navigation, periscope-detection, track-while-scan	a) 150 (278)	P-3B, C & P, Maritime Enforcer, Maritime Mk2, Sentinel Mk2
Motorola Military & Aerospace Electronics 8201 East McDowell Road, Scottsdale, AZ 85257	AN/APS-135	Sea surveillance	Sideways-looking		Slotted waveguide			Sea surface mapping		HC-130, Fokker Sentinel Mk2
Texas Instruments 8505 Forest Lane, PO Box 660246, MS 3134, Dallas, TX 75266	AN/APS-137(V) & (V)2	Sea surveillance/ ASW		c.9.75GHz	Paraboloid or planar			Includes long-range radar imaging		S-3B, P-3C, US Coast Guard C-130; AN/APS-137(H) in helicopters
General Electric (now part of Lockheed Martin Electronics & Missiles)	AN/APS-138	Air surveillance	Pulse-Doppler	UHF (c.400MHz?)	Yagi array	a) 6		Air surveillance, limited ground surveillance		E-2C, P-3AEW
Lockheed Martin Electronics & Missiles 5600 W. Sand Lake Road, Orlando, FL 32819-8907	AN/APS-139	Air surveillance	Pulse-Doppler	UHF (c.400MHz?)	Yagi array	a) 6?		Air surveillance with improved ECCM, improved ground surveillance		
Telephonics Corp. 770 Park Ave, Huntingdon, NY 11743	AN/APS-143	Sea surveillance		9.3 – 9.5GHz		b) 10	a) 390, 750, 1510, 2500 b) 5.0 & 17.0	Surveillance	b) c.243 (c.110)	DHC-8, Beech 200T
Telephonics Corp. 770 Park Ave, Huntingdon, NY 11743	AN/ APS-143(V)3	Sea surveillance		9.2 – 9.5GHz	Paraboloid or planar	b) 8	a) 400, 800, 1510, 2500 b) 5.0 & 17.0	Surveillance		S-70

Manufacturer	Radar	Role	Type	Operating frequency	Antenna type	a) Scan rate (rpm) b) Peak output (kW)	a) PRF (Hz) b) Pulse width (microsec)	Operating modes	a) Maximum range naut miles (km) b) Weight lb (kg)	Platform(s)
United States of America										
Martin Marietta Electronics & Missiles 5600 W. Sand Lake Road, Orlando, FL 32819-8907	AN/APS-145	Air surveillance	Pulse-Doppler	UHF (c.400MHz?)	Yagi array	a) 5	a) Choice of three?	Air and ground surveillance. Can track over 2,000 targets and control 40 interceptions simultaneously		E-2C, C-130 AEW
Westinghouse Electric Corp PO Box 17319, MS A255, Baltimore, MD 21203-7319	AN/APY-1	Air & sea surveillance	Pulse-Doppler	c.3GHz	Slotted planar array		a) High or low	Elevation scan, non-elevation scan, beyond the horizon, passive, maritime		E-3. See E-3 entry for more details
Westinghouse Electric Corp PO Box 17319, MS A255, Baltimore, MD 21203-7319	AN/APY-2	Air & sea surveillance	Pulse-Doppler	c.3GHz/S-band	Slotted planar array		a) High or low	Elevation scan, non-elevation scan, beyond the horizon, passive, maritlme		E-3, E-767 See E-3 entry for more details
Westinghouse Norden Systems, PO Box 5300, Norwalk, CT 06856-5300	AN/APY-3 JSTARS	Land surveillance	Sideways-looking		Phased array					E-8C SeeE-8C entry for details
Loral Defense Systems 1300 S. Litchfield Rd, Goodyear, AZ	AN/UPD-4 and AN/UPD-9	Reconnais-sance	Sideways-looking	I/J-band	Slotted waveguide			Ground mapping, MTI	a) 30 (55) b) 622 (282)	RF-4
Loral Defense Systems 1300 S. Litchfield Rd, Goodyear, AZ	AN/UPD-8	Reconnais-sance	Sideways-looking	I/J-band	Slotted waveguide			Ground mapping, MTI	a) 50 (93)	RF-4
Hughes Aircraft Bldg R10 MS 10001, PO Box 92426, Los Angeles, CA 90009	ASARS-1 (see platforms)	Reconnais-sance	Sideways-looking	I/J-band				Ground mapping, MTI		U-2S. ASARS-1 used in SR-71A (by Goodyear)
Hughes Aircraft Bldg R10 MS 10001, PO Box 92426, Los Angeles, CA 90009	HISAR	Reconnais-sance	Sideways-looking	I/J-band?				Air-to-air search, wide-area search, strip map, spot, sea surveillance, MTI		Military Beech
Westinghouse Electric Corp PO Box 17319, MS A255, Baltimore, MD 21203-7319	MESA (Multirole Electronically Scanning Aircraft system)	Air, sea & ground surveillance		L-band				Air, sea and surface surveillance		Tested on BAC One-Eleven; offered for C-130, P-3, Boeing 737
Motorola Military & Aerospace Electronics 8201 East McDowell Road, Scottsdale, AZ 85257	SLAMMR	Sea surveillance	Sideways-looking		Slotted waveguide			Sea surface mapping, optional MTI	a) 80 (148)	C-130, Boeing 737
Multi-national										
AlliedSignal/FIAR	RDR-1500B	Land & sea surveillance		9.375GHz	Planar array	b) 10	a) 200 or 800 b) 0.1 or 2.35	Surface search, sea search, terrain mapping, weather-avoidance	a) 160 (300)	A109, AB412, P.166, Do 228MP, AS 555SN Fennec
Thomson-CSF/Daimler-Benz Aerospace	Ocean Master	Sea surveillance			Paraboloid			Surface search, target detection, ASW	b) 159 (72)	fixed & rotary-wing

Navigation and weather

Manufacturer	Radar	Role	Operating frequency	Antenna type	Power output (kW)	a) PRF (Hz) b) Pulse width (microsec)	Operating modes	Display	a) Maximum range naut miles (km) b) Weight lb (kg)	Platform(s)
France										
Thomson-CSF RCM Division 1 blvd Jean Martin, F-78852 Elancourt Cedex	ORB 37	Weather	9.345GHz	Planar	10	b) 2.5 & 0.4	Weather, ground mapping	Monochrome		C-160
Thomson-CSF RCM Division 1 blvd Jean Martin, F-78852 Elancourt Cedex	Arcana	Navigation					Advanced pulse-Doppler air-to-ground modes			Mirage IV-P

Manufacturer	Radar	Role	Operating frequency	Antenna type	Power output (kW)	a) PRF (Hz) b) Pulse width (microsec)	Operating modes	Display	a) Maximum range naut miles (km) b) Weight lb (kg)	Platforms
France										
Thomson-CSF RCM Division 1 blvd Jean Martin, F-78852 Elancourt Cedex	Romeo	Navigation	Millimetre-wave				Navigation, ground mapping?			Helicopters
Germany										
Daimler-Benz Aerospace Radar & Radio Systems Division Sedanstrasse 10, D-89070 Ulm (Donau)	Swallow	Obstacle detection	60GHz			a) Agile b) 2 or 70	Obstacle detection		b) c.110 (50)	Helicopters
Russia										
Unknown	Buran D	Weather	9.345GHz		20	a) 250 - 1500 b) 0.5 - 6	Weather, ground-mapping, beacon-interrogation	Colour	a) 300 (550)	
Phazotron 1 Electrichesky Per, Moscow RF 123 557	Gukol 1, Gukol 2, Gukol 3 & Gukol 4	Navigation & weather	I/J-band, except Gukol 4 which adds U-band		0.5 for Gukol 1, the others all 1.5		Real-beam ground mapping, DBS, synthetic aperture, enlarge, freeze, weather & turbulence detection, hazard warning, beacon interrogation	Colour	a) 189 (350) for Gukol 1, 242 (450) for Gukol 2 & 324 (600) for Gukol 3 & 4 b) 33 (15) for Gukol 1, 55 (25) for Gukol 2, 62 (28) for Gukol 3 & 132 (60) for Gukol 4	Light aircraft, transports & tankers
Unknown	Osminog	Navigation?					No search or attack modes			Ka-27 & Ka-28, Ka-32?
Unknown	PBR-4 Rubin 1	Mapping								Tu-16
Unknown	RBP-4 (Short Horn)	Navigation	14 – 15GHz			a) Choice of four b) Choice of four				Ka-25PL
United States of America										
Honeywell Military Avonics PO Box 312, 2600 Ridgway Parkway, Minneapolis, MN 55440	AN/APN-58E(V)	Multifunction	I/J-band				Weather, navigation, search, beacon homing		b) Typically 185 (84)	C-130, C-135, KC-135, RC-135
AlliedSignal Air Transport Avionics 2100 NW 62nd St, PO Box 9327, FL 33309	AN/APN-215(V) & AN/APN-234	Multifunction					Weather, ground mapping, surface search; AN/APN-234 adds sea search	Colour	a) 240 (445)	Heavy twins, turboprops, helicopters, Schweizer RU-38A
Westinghouse Electric Corp PO Box 17319, MS A255, Baltimore, MD 21203-7319	AN/APN-241	Multifunction	9.3–9.41 GHz	Planar	0.116 peak		Weather, wind-shear, ground mapping, skin paint, beacon, station-keeping, flight plan, traffic collision avoidance	Colour	a) 320? (592?) b) 130.5 (59.2)	C-130H
Texas Instruments 8505 Forest Lane, PO Box 660246, MS 3134, Dallas, TX 75266	AN/APQ-122(V) & (V)5	Multifunction	I-band & K-band; I-band for (V)5				Ground mapping, weather, beacon interrogation		a) 200 (370)	C-130, E-4B
Texas Instruments 8505 Forest Lane, PO Box 660246, MS 3134, Dallas, TX 75266	AN/APQ-122(V)8	Multifunction	I-band & K-band				Ground mapping, terrain following, weather, beacon interrogation		a) 200 (370)	MC-130 Combat Talon I
Texas Instruments 8505 Forest Lane, PO Box 660246, MS 3134, Dallas, TX 75266	AN/APQ-168 & AN/APQ-174	Multifunction					Ground mapping, terrain following, terrain avoidance, ranging. APQ-174 adds weather & beacon		b) 249 (113)	HH-60 for APQ-168. CH-47, MH-47, HH-60, MH-60, V-22 for APQ-174
Electronics & Space Corp. 8100 W. Florissant Ave, St. Louis, MO 63136	AN/APQ-170	Multifunction					As for AN/APQ-174	Four CRTs		MC-130H Combat Talon II

Manufacturer	Radar	Role	Operating frequency	Antenna type	Power output (kW)	a) PRF (Hz) b) Pulse width (microsec)	Operating modes	Display	a) Maximum range naut miles (km) b) Weight lb (kg)	Platform(s)
United States of America										
Electronics & Space Corp. 8100 W. Florissant Ave, St. Louis, MO 63136	AN/APQ-175 & AN/APQ-175X	Multifunction	I/J-band & (K-band for AN/APQ-175)				Ground mapping, weather, beacon			C-130 all-weather inc. delivery system (AWADS) aircraft
AlliedSignal Air Transport Avionics 2100 NW 62nd St, PO Box 9327, FL 33309	AN/APS-133	Multifunction	9.375GHz	Paraboloid	65	a) 200, 800 b) 0.4 - 5	Weather, ground mapping, navigation + air-to-air search & track	Colour	a) 300 (555) b) 100 (45.5)	C-5, C-141, KC-10, C-17, E-3, E-4, E-6
AlliedSignal General Aviation Avionics 400 N Rogers Rd, Olathe, Kansas	KWX-56 (KWX-58 – see platforms)	Multifunction		Planar	7.5	b) 3.5	Weather, ground mapping, navigation	Colour	a) 160 (296)	KWX-58 has similar role, frequency & output
Westinghouse Electric Corp. PO Box 17319, MS A255, Baltimore, MD 21203-7319	LPCR 130-1	Multifunction?			Low power			Colour		C-130
Honeywell Business & Commuter Aviation Systems 8501 Balboa Blvd, PO Box 9028, Van Nuys, CA	Primus 40, 50 & 90	Search for Primus 40 & 50, weather for Primus 90						Colour		IAR Puma for Primus 40 & 50. Y-7 for Primus 90
Honeywell Business & Commuter Aviation Systems 8501 Balboa Blvd, PO Box 9028, Van Nuys, CA	Primus 100 & 200 ColoRadar	Multifunction	9.345GHz	Paraboloid for Primus 100. Planar for Primus 200		b) 4.0 & 10 for Primus 100. 4.0 & 11 for Primus 200	Weather, navigation	Colour	a) 120 (222)	Singles, light twins
Honeywell Business & Commuter Aviation Systems 8501 Balboa Blvd, PO Box 9028, Van Nuys, CA	Primus 300SL ColoRadar	Multifunction	9.375GHz	Planar			Weather, navigation	Colour	a) 300 (556) b) 32.3 – 39.7 (14.7 – 18.0)	Turboprop twins, and small jets, including Citation S/II & Citation VI
Honeywell Business & Commuter Aviation Systems 8501 Balboa Blvd, PO Box 9028, Van Nuys, CA	Primus 450/650	Weather	Planar				Weather			Turboprop twins and small jets
Honeywell Business & Commuter Aviation Systems 8501 Balboa Blvd, PO Box 9028, Van Nuys, CA	Primus 500 ColoRadar	Multifunction	9.375GHz	Planar	10		Weather, navigation, beacon navigation	Colour	a) 200 (370) b) c.27 (12.2)	Fixed-wing aircraft, helicopters
Honeywell Business & Commuter Aviation Systems 8501 Balboa Blvd, PO Box 9028, Van Nuys, CA	Primus 700/701	Multifunction		Planar	10	a) Choice of four b) Choice of six	Weather, navigation, (+ beacon navigation on 701)	Colour	a) 300? (555?)	Most transport types
Honeywell Business & Commuter Aviation Systems 8501 Balboa Blvd, PO Box 9028, Van Nuys, CA	Primus 708A & Primus 800	Multifunction		Planar		b) Two for Primus 708A	Weather, ground mapping, navigation	Colour	a) 300 (555)	Large corporate jet/ turboprops inc ATR-42 for Primus 800
Honeywell Business & Commuter Aviation Systems 8508 Balboa Blvd, PO Box 9028, Van Nuys, CA	Primus 870	Multifunction		Planar			Weather (including turbulence-detection), ground mapping, navigation	Colour	a) 300 (555)	Most transport types, including Raytheon Hawker 1000
AlliedSignal Air Transport Avionics 2100 NW 62nd St, PO Box 9327, FL 33309	RDR-1FB	Multifunction	9.375GHz	Paraboloid	65	a) 200 b) 0.5 & 5.0	Weather, air-to-air mapping, ground mapping, navigation, beacon tracking	Colour	a) 300 (555) b) 107.8 (48.9)	Jet transports
AlliedSignal Air Transport Avionics 2100 NW 62nd St, PO Box 9327, FL 33309	RDR-4A & -4B	Multifunction	I-band	Planar			Weather, navigation (+ wind-sheard detection/ avoidance on -4B)	Colour	a) 320 (593)	737, 747, 757, 767, A300, A310, Yak-142
AlliedSignal Air Transport Avionics 2100 NW 62nd St, PO Box 9327, FL 33309	RDR-150 Colorvision/ Weathervision	Multifunction	9.375GHz	Paraboloid or planar	8	b) 3.5	Weather, ground mapping, navigation	Colour or monochrome	a) 160 (296) b) 18.5 – 23.2 (8.4 – 10.5)	Light/medium twins, helicopters
AlliedSignal Air Transport Avionics 2100 NW 62nd St, PO Box 9327, FL 33309	RDR-160 & RDR-230HP	Multifunction for RDR-160 weather for RDR-230HP	I-band	Paraboloid for RDR-160 & planar for RDR-230HP	6 for RDR 160 & 5 for RDR-230HP		Weather, ground mapping	Colour or monochrome	a) 240 (444) for RDR-230HP b) 15.5 (7.0) for RDR-160	Light/medium twins

Manufacturer	Radar	Role	Operating frequency	Antenna type	Power output (kW)	a) PRF (Hz) b) Pulse width (microsec)	Operating modes	Display	a) Maximum range naut miles (km) b) Weight lb (kg)	Platform(s)
United States of America										
AlliedSignal Air Transport Avionics 2100 NW 62nd St, PO Box 9327, FL 33309	RDR-1100 & RDR-1200	Weather	9.375GHz for RDR-1100	Planar	8 for RDR-1100, 10 for RDR-1200		Weather, ground mapping, navigation for RDR-1100	Colour or monochrome		Light/medium twins. RDR-1200 users incl corporate aircraft
AlliedSignal Air Transport Avionics 2100 NW 62nd St, PO Box 9327, FL 33309	RDR-1400 (see platforms for RDR-1300)	Multifunction	I-band	Planar	10		Weather, ground mapping, navigation, beacon navigation & tracking, search	Colour or monochrome	a) 160 (296) b) 34.1 (15.5)	Helicopters, including AS 532 Cougar, IAR Puma, and HH/MH-60. Do 228,Y-12. RDR-1300 in Sea King MK43
AlliedSignal Air Transport Avionics 2100 NW 62nd St, PO Box 9327, FL 33309	RDR-1500, RDR-1500B & RDR-2000	Search for RDR-1500/B; weather for RDR-2000						Colour for RDR-2000		Cougar, Sea King Mk48, Super Lynx, AS 555SN Fennec, Do 228MP
AlliedSignal General Aviation Avionics 400 N. Rogers Road, Olathe, KS 66062-1212	RDS-81	Weather	9.375GHz	Planar	1	a) 128 – 1026 b) 0.6 – 11.5	Weather	Colour	b) 19 (8.6)	Including An-28, Caravan, CitationJet
AlliedSignal General Aviation Avionics 400 N. Rogers Road, Olathe, KS 66062-1212	RDS-82 & RDS-83	Weather	I/J-band	Planar	1 for RDS-82		Weather	Colour	b) 19.8 (9.0) for RDS-83	W-3A for RDS-82. Heavy piston, light jets for RDS-83
AlliedSignal General Aviation Avionics 400 N. Rogers Road, Olathe, KS 66062-1212	RDS-84VP	Weather	9.345GHz	Planar	1.3	a) 128 – 1086 b) 0.8 – 15.3	Weather	Colour	b) 26.5 (12)	Super King Air
AlliedSignal General Aviation Avionics 400 N. Rogers Road, Olathe, KS 66062-1212	RDS-86	Multifunction	I/J-band	Planar			Weather, navigation	Colour	a) 1,000 (1,850) b) 22 (10)	Heavy corporate aircraft, including Jetstream ATP
Collins Commercial Avionics 400 Collins Rd NE, MS 126-100, Cedar Rapids, IA 52498	RNS-300	Multifunction	9.375GHz		5	b) 1.0 & 5.6	Weather, ground mapping, navigation	Colour	a) 354 (654) b) 28.6 (13.0)	Large twins, jet/turboprop corporate aircraft
Collins Commercial Avionics 400 Collins Rd NE,MS 126-100, Cedar Rapids, IA 52498	RNS-325	Multifunction	9.345GHz		5		Weather, navigation	Colour	a) 300 (555)	Jets & turboprops
Collins Commercial Avionics 400 Collins Rd NE,MS 126-100, Cedar Rapids, IA 52498	TWR-850	Weather	9.345GHz	Planar			Weather	Colour	a) 300 (555) b) 19.8 (9)	Business aircraft, N-250
Honeywell Business & Commuter Aviation Systems 8500 Balboa Blvd, PO Box 9028, Van Nuys, CA	WeatherScout II	Weather	9.345GHz	Paraboloid		b) 4.0 & 10	Weather	Monochrome	a) 120 (222)	Singles, light twins
Collins Commercial Avionics 400 Collins Rd NE, MS 126-100, Cedar Rapids, IA 52498	WXR-200A	Weather	9.375GHz	Paraboloid or planar	5	b) 1.0 & 5.5	Weather	Monochrome	a) 180 (333) b) 22.7 (10.3)	Singles, light twins
Collins Commercial Avionics 400 Collins Rd NE,MS 126-100, Cedar Rapids, IA 52498	WXR-250A (WXR-270 – see platforms)	Multifunction	9.345GHz	Planar	5	b) 1 or 5.5	Weather, navigation	Monochrome	a) 240 (445)	Large twins, corporate jets. WXR-270 users incl Brasilia
Collins Commercial Avionics 400 Collins Rd NE,MS 126-100, Cedar Rapids, IA 52498	WXR-300	Multifunction	9.375GHz		5	b) 1.0 & 5.5	Weather, ground mapping, navigation	Colour	a) 353 (654) b) 28.6 (13.0)	Large twins, jet/turboprop corporate air-craft, includ-ing Raytheon Hawker 800
Collins Commercial Avionics 400 Collins Rd NE,MS 126-100, Cedar Rapids, IA 52498	WXR-700C	Multifunction	5.440MHz	Planar	0.23	a) 180 – 1,440 b) 2.0 – 20	Weather, ground mapping, navigation	Colour	a) 240 (444) b) 74.3 (33.7)	Heavy jet transports
Collins Commercial Avionics 400 Collins Rd NE,MS 126-100, Cedar Rapids, IA 52498	WXR-700X & WXR-700XW	Multifunction	9.330GHz	Planar	0.1	a) 180 – 1,440 b) 1.0 – 20	Weather, navigation. WXR-700XW adds wind-shear	Colour	a) 320 (593) b) 74.3 (33.7)	Heavy jet transports
Collins Commercial Avionics 400 Collins Rd NE,MS 126-100, Cedar Rapids, IA 52498	WXR-840			12 ins (30 cm)				Colour		Avanti, Saab 2000, Seastar

Airport Runway Bearing Strengths

This section provides details of the orientation, length and load-bearing strength of the longest runway at the world's major airports. The criterion adopted in selecting the airports to be included is that they should have a longest runway of at least 6000 ft (1829 m), except where exclusion on this basis would result in a country, self-governing area or capital city not being represented. Note that in this section commas are not used in runway length figures.

Runway weight bearing capacity is shown by one of the following methods:

Pavement Classification Number (PCN) expresses the bearing strength of a runway pavement for unrestricted operations, using the following codes. Type of Pavement: R-Rigid, F-Flexible. Pavement sub-grade category: A-High, B-Medium, C-Low, D-Ultra low. Maximum tyre pressure authorised: W-High, no limit, A-Medium, max 217 psi, Y-Low, max 145 psi, Z-Very low, max 73 psi. Pavement evaluation method: T-Technical evaluation, U-From actual past use by aircraft.

Load Classification Group (LCG) is related to **Load Classification Number (LCN),** LCG I being the greatest strength.

LCG	LCN
I	101-120
II	76-100
III	51-75
IV	31-50
V	16-30
VI	11-15
VII	10 and under

Thousands of Kilogrammes (all-up weight per undercarriage assembly), where S = Single wheel, T = Twin wheel, B = Bogie, DB = Double Bogie. Thus 43S/150B/350DB indicates 43000 kg for single wheel assembly, 150000 kg for single bogie, 350000 kg for double bogie.

All-up weight (AUW) in Kilogrammes

Isolated Single-Wheel (ISWL), maximum permissible weight in Kilogrammes.

Aircraft type, e.g. B747, indicating that the runway is suitable for aircraft having all-up weights no greater than the maximum all-up weight of that type.

THE DETAILS PRINTED BELOW ARE FOR GENERAL REFERENCE AND ARE NOT TO BE USED FOR FLIGHT PLANNING PURPOSES.

Based on material supplied by, and reproduced in part with the kind permission of, British Airways AERAD.

Airport name	Orientation and length of longest runway		Runway LCN/PCN
Afghanistan			
Kabul	11/29	11483 ft (3500 m)	ISWL 55000
Kandahar	05/23	10500 ft (3200 m)	ISWL 20400
Alaska-see also USA			
Anchorage International, AK	06R/24L	10897 ft (3321 m)	PCN 52/F/A/X/T
Fairbanks International, AK	01L/19R	10300 ft (3139 m)	PCN 50/F/A/X/T
Albania			
Tirana (Rinas)	18/36	9022 ft (2750 m)	—
Algeria			
Algiers (Houari Boumedienne)	05/23	11500 ft (3505 m)	43S/45T/74B
Oran (Es Senia)	07/25	9843 ft (3000 m)	ISWL 25000
Tamanrasset	03/21	11811 ft (3600 m)	ISWL 40000
Zarazaitine (In Amenas)	05/23	9843 ft (3000 m)	ISWL 35000
Angola			
Luanda	06/24	12139 ft (3700 m)	LCN 105

Airport name	Orientation and length of longest runway		Runway LCN/PCN
Argentina			
Buenos Aires (Ezeiza)	11/29	10827 ft (3300 m)	172S/220T/386DB
Comodoro Rivadavia	07/25	9022 ft (2750 m)	56S/157B/365DB
Cordoba	18/36	10500 ft (3200 m)	43S/150B/350DB
Mendoza (El Plumerillo)	18/36	9885 ft (3013 m)	60S/160B/330DR
Rio Gallegos	07/25	11647 ft (3550 m)	58S/87T/330DB
Armenia			
Yerevan (Zvartnots)	09/27	12631 ft (3850 m)	PCN 35/R/B/X/T
Australia			
Adelaide	05/23	8294 ft (2528 m)	PCN 72/F/D/U
Alice Springs	12/30	8000 ft (2438 m)	PCN 60/F/B/U
Brisbane	01/19	11483 ft (3500 m)	PCN 97/F/D/T
Cairns	15/33	10489 ft (3197 m)	PCN 90/F/D/U
Canberra	17/35	8800 ft (2682 m)	PCN 45/F/B/U
Darwin International	11/29	10906 ft (3324 m)	PCN 66/F/C/U
Melbourne International	16/34	12000 ft (3658 m)	PCN 79/F/C/U
Perth International	03/21	11300 ft (3444 m)	PCN 55/F/A/T
Sydney (Kingsford Smith)	16R/34L	13000 ft (3962 m)	PCN 67/F/A/U

Airport name	Orientation and length of longest runway		Runway LCN/PCN
Austria			
Graz	17/35	9055 ft (2760 m)	PCN 36/R/B/W/T
Innsbruck	08/26	6562 ft (2000 m)	PCN 45/R/B/W/T
Klagenfurt	10/28	8924 ft (2720 m)	PCN 37.5/R/B/W/T
Linz	09/27	9219 ft (2810 m)	PCN 55/F/C/W/T
Salzburg	16/34	8366 ft (2550 m)	PCN 55/R/B/W/T
Vienna (Schwechat)	16/34	11811 ft (3600 m)	PCN 70/F/C/W
Azerbaijan			
Baku (Bina)	16/34	8858 ft (2700 m)	PCN 25/R/B/X/T
Azores			
Santa Maria	18/36	10000 ft (3048 m)	LCN 200
Bahamas			
Freeport	06/24	11000 ft (3353 m)	PCN 73
Nassau International	14/32	11000 ft (3353 m)	PCN 73
Bahrain			
Bahrain International	12/30	13002 ft (3963 m)	LCN 100
Bangladesh			
Chittagong	05/23	10000 ft (3048 m)	PCN 40/F/C/Y/T
Dhaka (Zia International)	14/32	10500 ft (3200 m)	PCN 75/R/B/W/T
Belarus			
Minsk 2	13/31	11942 ft (3640 m)	PCN 60/R/B/X/T
Belgium			
Antwerp (Deurne)	11/29	4954 ft (1510 m)	PCN 30/F/A/W/U
Brussels (National)	07L/25R	11936 ft (3638 m)	PCN 64/F/A/W/U
Charleroi (Brussels South)	07/25	8366 ft (2550 m)	PCN 56/F/A/W/U
Ostend	08/26	10500 ft (3200 m)	PCN 56/F/A/W/U
Belize			
Belize (Phillip S.W. Goldson International)	07/25	7100 ft (2164 m)	LCN 60
Benin			
Cotonou (Cadjehoun)	06/24	7874 ft (2400 m)	PCN 59/F/B/X/T
Bermuda			
Bermuda	12/30	9660 ft (2944 m)	52S/120T/161B
Bolivia			
Cochabamba (Jorge Wilsterman)	13/31	12467 ft (3800 m)	PCN 48/F/B/X/T
La Paz (J.F. Kennedy International)	09R/27L	13123 ft (4000 m)	PCN 46/R/A/X/U
Santa Cruz (El Trompillo)	15/33	9144 ft (2787 m)	PCN 48/F/C/X/U
Santa Cruz (Viru Viru)	15/33	11482 ft (3500 m)	PCN 57/R/B/X/T
Bosnia-Hercegovina			
Sarajevo	12/30	8530 ft (2600 m)	LCN 80
Botswana			
Gaborone (Seretse Khama International)	08/26	9843 ft (3000 m)	PCN 75/R/B/W/T
Brazil			
Belo Horizonte (Tancredo Neves)	16/34	9843 ft (3000 m)	PCN 60/F/A/W/T
Brasilia	11/29	10496 ft (3199 m)	PCN 76/F/B/X/T
Natal (Augusto Severo)	16L/34R	7447 ft (2270 m)	PCN 41/F/A/X/T
Recife (Guararapes)	18/36	9846 ft (3001 m)	PCN 63/F/B/X/T
Rio de Janeiro (Galeao International)	10/28	13123 ft (4000 m)	PCN 78/R/A/W/T
Sao Jose dos Campos	15/33	8780 ft (2676 m)	PCN 71/F/A/X/T
Sao Paulo (Guarulhos)	09L/27R	12140 ft (3700 m)	PCN 85/F/B/W/T
Bulgaria			
Burgas	04/22	10500 ft (3200 m)	PCN 60/R/B/X/T
Plovdiv	13/31	8202 ft (2500 m)	PCN 38/R/A/X/T
Sofia	09/27	9186 ft (2800 m)	PCN 49/R/B/X/T
Varna	09/27	8202 ft (2500 m)	PCN 60/R/B/X/T
Burkina Faso			
Bobo-Dioulasso	06/24	10827 ft (3300 m)	PCN 57/F/B/X/T
Ouagadougou	04/22	9843 ft (3000 m)	PCN 59/F/B/X/T

Airport name	Orientation and length of longest runway		Runway LCN/PCN
Burundi			
Bujumbura	17/35	11811 ft (3600 m)	PCN 75/F/A/X/U
Caicos Islands			
Grand Turk	11/29	6335 ft (1931 m)	—
Providenciales International	10/28	7600 ft (2316 m)	—
Cambodia			
Phnom-Penh (Pochentong)	05/23	9843 ft (3000 m)	AUW 183000
Cameroun			
Douala	12/30	9350 ft (2850 m)	PCN 59/F/C/X/U
Garoua	09/27	11155 ft (3400 m)	PCN 71/F/C/X/T
Yaounde (Nsimalen)	01/19	11155 ft (3400 m)	PCN 71/F/C/W/U
Canada			
Abbotsford	07/25	8000 ft (2438 m)	PCN 54/F/A/Y/T
Calgary International	16/34	12675 ft (3863 m)	PCN 111/F/D/W/T
Edmonton International	02/20	11000 ft (3353 m)	PCN 93/R/C/W/T
Gander	04/22	10500 ft (3200 m)	PCN 54/F/A/W/T
Goose Bay	08/26	11050 ft (3368 m)	PCN 67/F/A/W/T
Halifax International	06/24	8800 ft (2682 m)	PCN 61/F/B/W/T
Hamilton	12L/30R	8000 ft (2438 m)	PCN 87/F/D/X/T
London	15/33	8800 ft (2682 m)	PCN 70/F/C/X/T
Moncton	11/29	8000 ft (2438 m)	PCN 70/F/C/W/T
Montreal (Dorval)	06L/24R	11000 ft (3353 m)	PCN 70/F/C/W/T
Montreal (Mirabel)	06/24	12000 ft (3658 m)	PCN 68/R/A/W/T
Ottawa	14/32	10000 ft (3048 m)	PCN 67/F/A/W/T
Quebec	06/24	9000 ft (2743 m)	PCN 71/R/C/W/T
Stephenville	10/28	10000 ft (3048 m)	PCN 67/F/A/X/T
Toronto	15/33	11050 ft (3368 m)	PCN 79/R/B/W/T
Vancouver	08/26	11000 ft (3353 m)	PCN 93/R/C/W/T
Winnipeg	18/36	11000 ft (3353 m)	PCN 79/R/B/W/T
Canary Islands			
Gran Canaria (Las Palmas)	03L/21R	10170 ft (3100 m)	LCN 110
Lanzarote	04/22	7874 ft (2400 m)	LCN 71
La Palma	01/19	7218 ft (2200 m)	PCN 34/F/A/W/T
Tenerife Norte (Los Rodeos)	12/30	11155 ft (3400 m)	ISWL 26000
Tenerife Sur (Reina Sofia)	08/26	10500 ft (3200 m)	86B
Cape Verde Republic			
Sal (Amilcar Cabral)	02/20	10729 ft (3270 m)	PCN 58/F/A/W/T
Cayman Islands			
Cayman Brac (Gerrard-Smith)	08/26	6000 ft (1829 m)	PCN 50/F/B/X/U
Grand Cayman (Owen Roberts)	08/26	7000 ft (2134 m)	PCN 50/F/B/W/U
Central African Republic			
Bangui (M'Poko)	17/35	8530 ft (2600 m)	PCN 59/F/B/X/T
Chile			
Punta Arenas (President Ibanez)	07/25	9154 ft (2790 m)	PCN 40/F/A/W/T
Santiago (A.M. Benitez)	17/35	10500 ft (3200 m)	PCN 63/F/B/W/T
China (People's Republic)			
Beijing/Peking	18L/36R	12467 ft (3800 m)	PCN 73/R/B/X/T
Chengdu (Shuangliu)	02/20	9186 ft (2800 m)	PCN 50/R/B/W/T
Guangzhou/Canton	03/21	11089 ft (3380 m)	PCN 58/R/B/X/T
Kunming (Wujiaba)	03/21	11155 ft (3400 m)	PCN 63/R/B/X/T
Lanzhou (Zhongchuan)	18/36	11155 ft (3400 m)	PCN 29/R/A/X/T
Shanghai (Hongqiao)	18/36	10500 ft (3200 m)	PCN 58/R/C/X/T
Shenzhen (Huangtian)	15/33	11155 ft (3400 m)	PCN 72/R/B/W/T
Tianjin (Zhangguizhuang)	16/34	10500 ft (3200 m)	PCN 50/R/B/X/T
Urumqi (Diwopu)	07/25	10500 ft (3200 m)	PCN 52/R/B/W/T
Colombia			
Barranquilla (Cortissoz)	04/22	9843 ft (3000 m)	273DB
Bogota (Eldorado)	12/30	12467 ft (3800 m)	363DB
Cali (Alfonso Bonilla Aragon)	01/19	9843 ft (3000 m)	293DB
Cartagena (R. Nunez)	18/36	8530 ft (2600 m)	77.3B/233DB
Rionegro (J.M. Cordova)	18/36	11483 ft (3500 m)	PCN 82/F/C/X/T

Airport name	Orientation and length of longest runway		Runway LCN/PCN
Comores and Mayotte Islands			
Moroni (Hahaia)	02/20	9514 ft (2900 m)	B747
Congo			
Brazzaville (Maya Maya)	06/24	10827 ft (3300 m)	PCN 69/F/C/X/U
Costa Rica			
Alajuela (Juan Santa Maria)	07/25	9880 ft (3011 m)	B747
Liberia International	07/25	9022 ft (2750 m)	B747
Côte D'Ivoire (Ivory Coast)			
Abidjan (Felix Houphouet Boigny)	03/21	8858 ft (2700 m)	PCN 53/F/A/X/T
Yamoussoukro	05/23	9843 ft (3000 m)	DC-8
Croatia			
Dubrovnik	12/30	10827 ft (3300 m)	LCN 80
Rijeka (Krk)	14/32	8202 ft (2500 m)	LCN 65
Zadar	14/32	8202 ft (2500 m)	LCN 85
Zagreb	05/23	10663 ft (3250 m)	LCN 90
Cuba			
Ciego de Avila	07/25	11483 ft (3500 m)	PCN 57/F/B/X/T
Havana (Jose Marti International)	05/23	13123 ft (4000 m)	PCN 57/F/B/X/T
Santiago de Cuba (Antonio Maceo)	09/27	13123 ft (4000 m)	PCN 50/F/A/X/T
Varadero	06/24	11483 ft (3500 m)	PCN 52/F/A/X/T
Cyprus			
Larnaca	04/22	8858 ft (2700 m)	PCN 80/F/D/W/U
Paphos International	11/29	8858 ft (2700 m)	PCN 80/F/C/W/T
Czech Republic			
Brno (Turany)	10/28	8694 ft (2650 m)	PCN 48/R/A/X/T
Prague (Ruzyne)	06/24	12188 ft (3715 m)	PCN 62/R/B/X/T
Vodochody	10/28	8202 ft (2500 m)	PCN 19/R/B/X/T
Denmark			
Aalborg	08L/26R	8694 ft (2650 m)	PCN 42/R/D/X/U
Billund	09/27	10171 ft (3100 m)	PCN 110/F/A/X/T
Bornholm (Ronne)	11/29	6562 ft (2000 m)	PCN 27/F/B/X/T
Copenhagen (Kastrup)	04L/22R	11811 ft (3600 m)	PCN 70/F/C/X/U
Esbjerg	08/26	8530 ft (2600 m)	PCN 60/F/A/W/T
Tirstrup	10R/28L	8885 ft (2708 m)	PCN 34/R/D/X/U
Vandel	09L/27R	8038 ft (2450 m)	LCN 50
Djibouti			
Djibouti (Ambouli)	09/27	10302 ft (3140 m)	24S/35T/85B
Ecuador			
Guayaquil (Simon Bolivar)	03/21	8005 ft (2440 m)	PCN 63/F/C/X/T
Quito (Mariscal Sucre)	17/35	10236 ft (3120 m)	PCN 42/F/B/X/T
Egypt			
Alexandria	04/22	7218 ft (2200 m)	PCN 48/F/D/X/U
Cairo International	05L/23R	10827 ft (3300 m)	PCN 70/F/B/W/U
Hurghada	16/34	13123 ft (4000 m)	PCN 35/F/C/W/U
Luxor	02/20	9843 ft (3000 m)	PCN 58/F/C/W/U
Sharm-El-Sheikh International	04L/22R	10105 ft (3080 m)	PCN 65/F/B/W/U
El Salvador			
San Salvador (El Salvador International)	07/25	10500 ft (3200 m)	B747
Eritrea			
Asmara	07/25	9843 ft (3000 m)	PCN 40/F/B/X/T
Estonia			
Tallin (Yulemiste)	09/27	9055 ft (2760 m)	PCN 40/F/B/X/T
Ethiopia			
Addis Ababa (Bole International)	07/25	12139 ft (3700 m)	PCN 65/F/D/X/T
Equatorial Guinea			
Malabo (Santo Isabel)	05/23	9649 ft (2941 m)	DC-10

Airport name	Orientation and length of longest runway		Runway LCN/PCN
Falkland Islands			
Mount Pleasant	10/28	8497 ft (2590 m)	PCN 90/F/C/W/T
Faroe Islands			
Vagar	13/31	4101 ft (1250 m)	PCN 28/F/A/X/U
Fiji			
Nadi International	02/20	10500 ft (3200 m)	PCN 59/F/C/X/U
Finland			
Helsinki (Vantaa)	04/22	11286 ft (3440 m)	PCN 58/F/C/W/T
Ivalo	04/22	8202 ft (2500 m)	PCN 58/F/B/X/T
Mariehamn	03/21	6234 ft (1900 m)	PCN 31/F/D/X/T
Oulu	12/30	8202 ft (2500 m)	PCN 36/F/B/X/T
Pori	12/30	6562 ft (2000 m)	PCN 40/F/B/X/T
Rovaniemi	03/21	9843 ft (3000 m)	PCN 45/F/C/W/T
Tampere (Pirkkala)	06/24	8858 ft (2700 m)	PCN 46/F/C/X/T
Turku	08/26	8202 ft (2500 m)	PCN 47/F/B/X/T
France			
Ajaccio (Dell'Oro)	02/20	7933 ft (2418 m)	22S/35T/70B
Basle (Mulhouse)	16/34	12795 ft (3900 m)	25S/33T/85B
Bastia (Poretta)	16/34	8268 ft (2520 m)	45S/50T/65B
Beauvais (Tille)	13/31	7972 ft (2430 m)	23S/29T/50B
Biarritz/Bayonne (Anglet)	09/27	7382 ft (2250 m)	PCN 54/R/D/W/T
Bordeaux (Merignac)	05/23	10170 ft (3100 m)	25S/33T/70B
Brest (Guipavas)	08R/26L	10170 ft (3100 m)	PCN 45/F/C/W/T
Chateauroux (Deols)	04/22	8366 ft (2550 m)	35S/40T/74B
Cherbourg (Maupertus)	11/29	8005 ft (2440 m)	25S/31T/56B
Clermont Ferrand (Aulnat)	08/26	9892 ft (3015 m)	28S/33T/53B
Deauville (St. Gatien)	12/30	8366 ft (2550 m)	20S/28T/50B
Dijon (Longvic)	18/36	7874 ft (2400 m)	17S/22T/37B
Dinard (Pleurtuit-St. Malo)	17/35	7218 ft (2200 m)	20S/27T/45B
Grenoble (St. Geoirs)	09/27	10007 ft (3050 m)	35S/40T/65B
Le Havre (Octeville)	05/23	7546 ft (2300 m)	13S/18T/33B
Le Touquet (Paris-Plage)	14/32	7382 ft (2250 m)	12S/17T/31B
Lille (Lesquin)	08/26	9268 ft (2825 m)	30S/36T/60B
Limoges (Bellegarde)	04/22	8202 ft (2500 m)	PCN 61/F/C/W/T
Lyon (Satolas)	18R/36L	13123 ft (4000 m)	30S/43T/78B
Marseille (Provence)	14L/32R	11483 ft (3500 m)	35S/40T/80B
Metz (Nancy Lorraine)	04/22	8202 ft (2500 m)	PCN 48/F/C/W/T
Montpellier (Frejorgues)	13L/31R	8530 ft (2600 m)	35S/38T/65B
Nantes Atlantique	03/21	9514 ft (2900 m)	27S/33T/53B
Paris (Charles de Gaulle)	10/28	11860 ft (3615 m)	28S/45T/100B
Paris (Le Bourget)	07/25	9843 ft (3000 m)	35S/40T/70B
Paris (Orly)	07/25	11975 ft (3650 m)	40S/45T/90B
Pau Pyrenees	13/31	8202 ft (2500 m)	PCN 45/F/C/W/U
Perpignan (Rivesaltes)	15/33	8202 ft (2500 m)	20S/27T/44B
Reims (Champagne)	07/25	8143 ft (2482 m)	41S/48T/87B
Strasbourg (Entzheim)	05/23	7874 ft (2400 m)	24S/33TJ/72TB
Toulouse (Blagnac)	15R/33L	11483 ft (3500 m)	43S/48T/90B
Tours (St. Symphorien)	02/20	7874 ft (2400 m)	31S/37T/68B
French Antilles			
Fort de France (Le Lamentin)	09/27	10827 ft (3300 m)	45S/45T/75B
Point a Pitre (Le Raizet)	11/29	11499 ft (3505 m)	40S/45T/75B
French Guiana			
Cayenne (Rochambeau)	08/26	10500 ft (3200 m)	PCN 52/F/D/W/U
Gabon			
Franceville (Mvengue)	15/33	10105 ft (3080 m)	PCN 59/F/B/X/T
Libreville	16/34	9843 ft (3000 m)	PCN 59/F/C/X/T
Gambia			
Banjul	14/32	11810 ft (3600 m)	LCN 80/H/J
Georgia			
Tbilisi (Novoalekseevka)	13/31	8202 ft (2500 m)	PCN 44/R/B/X/T
Germany			
Berlin (Schoenefeld)	07R/25L	9843 ft (3000 m)	PCN 140
Berlin (Tegel)	08L/26R	9918 ft (3023 m)	35S/50T/90B
Berlin (Tempelhof)	09L/27R	6942 ft (2116 m)	32S/77T/141B
Bremen	09/27	6673 ft (2034 m)	PCN 62/F/B/X/T
Cologne-Bonn	14L/32R	12467 ft (3800 m)	PCN 75/R/B/W/T
Dresden	04/22	8202 ft (2500 m)	PCN 60/R/A/W/T
Dusseldorf	05L/23R	9843 ft (3000 m)	PCN 73/F/C/W/T
Frankfurt (Main)	07L/25R	13123 ft (4000 m)	PCN 74/R/A/W/T
Friedrichshafen	06/24	7730 ft (2356 m)	AUW 20000

Airport name	Orientation and length of longest runway		Runway LCN/PCN
Germany			
Hamburg	15/33	12028 ft (3666 m)	PCN 65/F/A/W/T
Hannover	09L/27R	12467 ft (3780 m)	PCN 68/R/B/W/T
Munich	08/26	13123 ft (4000 m)	PCN 90/R/A/W/T
Munster-Osnabruck	07/25	7119 ft (2170 m)	PCN 68/F/B/X/T
Nurnberg	10/28	8858 ft (2700 m)	PCN 65/R/B/W/T
Stuttgart	08/26	8366 ft (2550 m)	LCN 90
Ghana			
Accra (Kotoka International)	03/21	11810 ft (3600 m)	PCN 70/F/B/W/T
Gibraltar			
Gibraltar	09/27	6000 ft (1829 m)	LCG III
Greece			
Alexandroupolis (Dimokritos)	07/25	8530 ft (2600 m)	LCN 80
Athens (Central)	15L/33R	11483 ft (3500 m)	LCN 100
Heraklion (Nikos Kazantzakis)	09/27	8793 ft (2680 m)	LCN 60
Ioannina	14/32	7874 ft (2400 m)	LCN 45
Kavala (Megas Alexandros)	05R/23L	9843 ft (3000 m)	LCN 80
Kerkyra (Ioannis Kapodistrias)	17/35	7792 ft (2375 m)	LCN 45
Limnos	04/22	9843 ft (3000 m)	LCN 80
Rhodes (Diagoras)	07/25	10696 ft (3260 m)	LCN 100
Salonika (Makedonia)	10/28	8005 ft (2440 m)	LCN 80
Zakinthos	16/34	7283 ft (2220 m)	PCN 36/F/D/X/U
Greenland			
Narsarsuaq	07/25	6004 ft (1830 m)	PCN 43/R/B/X/U
Sondestrom (Kangerlussuaq)	10/28	9236 ft (2815 m)	12S/71T/80ST/ 150TT/382DDT
Grenada			
Point Salines	10/28	9000 ft (2743 m)	LCN 86
Guatemala			
Guatemala International (La Aurora)	01/19	9800 ft (2987 m)	ISWL 27272
Guinea-Bissau			
Bissau (Osvaldo Vieira)	03/21	10500 ft (3200 m)	LCN 75
Guinea			
Conakry (Gbessia)	06/24	10827 ft (3300 m)	B747
Guyana			
Georgetown (Timehri	06/24	7500 ft (2286 m)	PCN 40/R/A/W/T
Haiti			
Port au Prince (Mais Gate)	09/27	9974 ft (3040 m)	B707
Hawaii-see also USA			
Honolulu International	08L/26R	12360 ft (3767 m)	45S/91T/181B
Honduras			
San Pedro Sula (La Mesa)	03/21	9202 ft (2805 m)	PCN 8/F/C/X/T
Hong Kong			
Hong Kong (Kai Tak)	13/31	11130 ft (3392 m)	PCN 65/F/A/W/T
Hungary			
Budapest (Ferihegy)	13L/31R	12162 ft (3707 m)	PCN 75/R/B/X/T
Iceland			
Akureyi	02/20	6496 ft (1980 m)	LCN 40
Keflavik	11/29	10013 ft (3052 m)	LCN 90
Reykjavik	02/20	5987 ft (1825 m)	LCN 20
India			
Bombay (Jawaliarial Nehru International)	09/27	11447 ft (3489 m)	PCN 65/F/C/W/T
Calcutta (N.S. Chandra Bose International)	01R/19L	11900 ft (3627m)	PCN 63/F/C/W/T
Delhi International	10/28	12500 ft (3810 m)	PCN 55/F/B/W/T
Madras International	07/25	12001 ft (3658 m)	PCN 56/F/C/W/T
Nagpur	14/32	10500 ft (3200 m)	PCN 41/R/B/W/T

Airport name	Orientation and length of longest runway		Runway LCN/PCN
Indian Ocean			
Cocos Island	15/33	8000 ft (2438 m)	PCN 30/F/A/1400/U
Indonesia			
Bali International	09/27	9843 ft (3000 m)	PCN 83/F/C/X/T
Biak (Kaisiepo)	11/29	11713 ft (3570 m)	PCN 81/F/B/X/U
Jakarta (Soekarno-Hatta International)	07R/25L	12008 ft (3660 m)	PCN 120/R/D/W/T
Surabaya (Juanda)	10/28	9843 ft (3000 m)	PCN 73/F/C/X/U
Iran			
Esfahan	08L/26R	14435 ft (4400 m)	LCN 100
Shiraz International	11R/29L	14009 ft (4270 m)	LCN 100
Tabriz	12/30	12000 ft (3658 m)	LCN 70
Tehran (Mehrabad)	11L/29R	13123 ft (4000 m)	PCN 50/F/A/X/T
Zahedan International	17R/35L	14000 ft (4267 m)	LCN 70
Iraq			
Baghdad (Saddam International)	15L/33R	13123 ft (4000 m)	LCN 100
Basrah International	14/32	13123 ft (4000 m)	PCN 72/R/C/W/T
Ireland			
Connaught (Knock)	09/27	7546 ft (2300 m)	PCN 52/F/A/W/T
Cork	17/35	7000 ft (2134 m)	PCN 55/R/C/W/U
Dublin	10/28	8652 ft (2637 m)	PCN 70/R/B/W/T
Kerry	08/26	6562 ft (2000 m)	PCN 44/F/C/W/T
Shannon	06/24	10500 ft (3200 m)	PCN 75/R/C/W/U
Israel			
Elat (J. Hozman)	03/21	6234 ft (1900 m)	PCN 36/F/B/X/T
Jerusalem (Atarot)	12/30	6447 ft (1965 m)	PCN 15 & 28/F/C/X/T
Tel Aviv (Ben Gurion International)	08/26	11998 ft (3657 m)	PCN 84/F/B/Y/U
Italy			
Alghero (Fertilia)	03/21	9843 ft (3000 m)	PCN 80/F/B/W/T
Ancona (Falconara)	04/22	9810 ft (2990 m)	LCN 80
Bergamo (Orio al Serio)	11/29	9186 ft (2800 m)	LCN 90
Bologna	12/30	8038 ft (2450 m)	LCN 100
Brindisi (Casale)	14/32	8622 ft (2628 m)	LCN 90
Cagliari (Elmas)	14/32	9186 ft (2800 m)	PCN 79/F/B/W/T
Catania (Fontanarossa)	08/26	8366 ft (2550 m)	PCN 70/F/B/W/T
Genoa (Sestri)	11/29	9925 ft (3025 m)	ISWL 35000
Milan (Linate)	18L/36R	8005 ft (2440 m)	ISWL 30000
Milan (Malpensa)	17L/35R	12844 ft (3915 m)	PCN 70
Naples	06/24	8661 ft (2640 m)	ISWL 28000
Olbia (Costa Smeralda)	06/24	8022 ft (2445 m)	PCN 60/F/C/W/T
Palermo (Punta Raisi)	07/25	11220 ft (3420 m)	PCN 52/F/B/W/U
Pescara	04/22	7808 ft (2380 m)	PCN 90/F/A/W/T
Pisa	04R/22L	9800 ft (2987 m)	LCN 90
Rimini	13/31	8337 ft (2541 m)	LCN 65
Rome (Ciampino)	15/33	7218 ft (2200 m)	ISWL 35000
Rome (Fiumicino)	16R/34L	12795 ft (3900 m)	LCN 100
Trieste (Ronchi de Legionari)	09/27	9843 ft (3000 m)	PCN 90/F/A/W/T
Turin (Caselle)	18/36	10827 ft (3300 m)	PCN 115/F/B/X/T
Venice (Tessera)	04/22	10827 ft (3300 m)	LCN 100
Verona (Villafranca)	05/23	8717 ft (2657 m)	LCN 90
Jamaica			
Kingston	12/30	8786 ft (2678 m)	70T/136B
Montego Bay (Sangster International)	07/25	8705 ft (2653 m)	PCN 63/F/A/W/T
Japan			
Nagasaki	14/32	9840 ft (2999 m)	PCN 58/F/A/X/T
Nagoya	16/34	8990 ft (2740 m)	PCN 97/F/D/X/T
Osaka (Kansai International)	06/24	11667 ft (3556 m)	PCN 100/F/C/X/T
Tokyo (Haneda)	15/33	10335 ft (3150 m)	PCN 83/F/C/X/T
Tokyo International (Narita)	16/34	13123 ft (4000 m)	PCN 140/F/C/X/T
Jordan			
Amman (Queen Alia International)	08R/26L	12008 ft (3660 m)	—
Amman (Marka)	06/24	10781 ft (3286 m)	LCN 75
Aqaba	02/20	9843 ft (3000 m)	LCN 67
Kazakhstan			
Alma-Ata	05/23	14436 ft (4400 m)	PCN 39/R/B/X/T

Airport name	Orientation and length of longest runway		Runway LCN/PCN
Kenya			
Kisumu	07/25	6693 ft (2040 m)	PCN 35/F/B/X/U
Mombasa (Moi)	03/21	10991 ft (3350 m)	PCNs 28-44-76/F/A/X/T
Nairobi (Jomo Kenyatta)	06/24	13507 ft (4117 m)	PCN 80/F/A/W/U
Korea (Democratic People's Republic)			
Pyongyang (Sunan)	01/19	13123 ft (4000 m)	PCN 53/R/A/W/U
Korea (Republic)			
Cheju International	06/24	9843 ft (3000 m)	PCN 83/F/C/W/T
Pusan (Kimhae International)	18/36	8000 ft (2438 m)	PCN 58/R/D/X/T
Seoul (Kimpo International)	14L/32R	11811 ft (3600 m)	PCN 100/F/C/W/T
Kuwait			
Kuwait International	15L/33R	11483 ft (3500 m)	PCN 63/F/A/W/T
Kyrgystan			
Bishkek (Manas)	08/26	13780 ft (4200 m)	PCN 56/R/A/X/T
Lao People's Democratic Republic			
Vientiane (Wattay)	13/31	9843 ft (3000 m)	PCN 43/R/B/W/T
Latvia			
Riga International	18/36	8366 ft (2550 m)	PCN 49/R/C/W/T
Lebanon			
Beirut	18/36	10663 ft (3250 m)	LCN 120
Leeward Islands			
Antigua	07/25	9000 ft (2743 m)	LCN 80
St. Kitts (Golden Rock)	07/25	8002 ft (2439 m)	LCN 70
Lesotho			
Maseru (Moshoeshoe 1)	04/22	10500 ft (3200 m)	PCN 52/F/B/W/T
Liberia			
Monrovia (Roberts International)	04/22	11000 ft (3353 m)	160B
Libya			
Benghazi (Benina)	15L/33R	11811 ft (3600 m)	LCN 90
Sebha International	13/31	11811 ft (3600 m)	LCN 85
Tripoli International	09/27	11811 ft (3600 m)	LCN 100
Lithuania			
Vilnius	02/20	8202 ft (2500 m)	PCN 33/F/D/X/T
Luxembourg			
Luxembourg	06/24	13123 ft (4000 m)	PCN 65/F/A/W/U
Madagascar			
Antananarivo (Ivato)	11/29	10170 ft (3100 m)	PCN 59/F/B/X/T
Madeira			
Funchal	06/24	5906 ft (1800 m)	PCN 60/F/B/X/T
Porto Santo	01/19	9843 ft (3000 m)	PCN 60/F/C/W/T
Malawi			
Blantyre (Chileka)	10/28	7628 ft (2325 m)	PCN 50/F/A/W/T
Lilongwe (Kamuzu International)	14/32	11614 ft (3540 m)	PCN 80/F/B/W/T
Malaysia and Brunei			
Brunei International (Bandar Seri Begawan)	03/21	12000 ft (3658 m)	LCN 126
Johor Bahru	16/34	11004 ft (3354 m)	PCN 59/F/B/X/U
Kota Kinabalu	02/20	9800 ft (2987 m)	PCN 59/F/B/X/U
Kuala Lumpur International	15/33	12400 ft (3779 m)	PCN 59/F/B/X/T
Penang International	04/22	10000 ft (3048 m)	LCN 70
Maldives			
Male International	18/36	11024 ft (3360 m)	PCN 66/F/A/W/U
Mali			
Bamako (Senou)	06/24	8858 ft (2700 m)	PCN 59/F/B/X/T
Malta			
Luqa	14/32	11627 ft (3544 m)	PCN 100

Airport name	Orientation and length of longest runway		Runway LCN/PCN
Mauritania			
Nouakchott	05/23	9843 ft (3000 m)	PCN 53/F/A/X/T
Mauritius			
Mauritius (Sir Seewoosagar Ramgoolam International)	14/32	8500 ft (2591 m)	PCN 80/F/D/X/T
Mexico			
Acapulco International	10/28	10824 ft (3299 m)	PCN 48/R/B/X/T
Guadalajara (Don Miguel Hidalgo)	10/28	13120 ft (3999 m)	PCN 56/R/B/X/T
Mexico City (B. Juarez Int'l)	05R/23L	12795 ft (3900 m)	PCN 97/F/B/X/U
Monterrey International	11/29	9843 ft (3000 m)	PCN 59/R/B/X/T
Puerto Vallarta	04/22	10171 ft (3100 m)	PCN 48/F/B/X/T
Tijuana	09/27	9711 ft (2960 m)	PCN 59/R/B/X/U
Moldova			
Kishinau	08/26	11778 ft (3590 m)	PCN 26/R/B/Y/T
Mongolia			
Ulaanbaatar (Buyant-Ukhaa)	14/32	10170 ft (3100 m)	PCN 47/R/A/X/U
Morocco			
Agadir (Al Massirah)	10/28	10500 ft (3200 m)	PCN 46/F/A/W/T
Casablanca (Mohamed V)	17/35	12205 ft (3720 m)	32S/58T/100B
Marrakech (Menara)	10/28	10171 ft (3100 m)	PCN 42/F/B/W/U
Quarzazate	12/30	9843 ft (3000 m)	PCN 46/F/A/W/T
Rabat (Sale)	04/22	11483 ft (3500 m)	PCN 41/F/B/W/U
Tangier (Boukhalf)	10/28	11483 ft (3500 m)	PCN 42/F/B/W/U
Mozambique			
Beira	12/30	7874 ft (2400 m)	PCN 44/F/A/X/U
Myanmar			
Yangdon (Mingaladon)	03/21	8100 ft (2469 m)	PCN 50/R/B/W/T
Namibia			
Windhoek International	08/26	14869 ft (4532 m)	LCN 84
Nepal			
Kathmandu (Tribhuvan)	02/20	10007 ft (3050 m)	PCN 54/F/A/W/T
Netherlands			
Amsterdam (Schiphol)	09/27	11330 ft (3453 m)	PCN 82/R/C/1.7/T
Maastricht	04/22	8202 ft (2500 m)	PCN 71/F/C/X/T
Rotterdam	06/24	7218 ft (2200 m)	PCN 42/R/D/X/U
Netherlands Antilles			
Aruba (Reina Beatrix)	11/29	9000 ft (2743 m)	PCN 48/R/A/X/T
Curaçao (Willemstad)	11/29	11188 ft (3410 m)	LCN 100
New Zealand			
Auckland International	05/23	11926 ft (3635 m)	PCN 65/R/B/W/T
Christchurch International	02/20	10784 ft (3287 m)	PCN 60/F/B/X/U
Wellington International	16/34	6350 ft (1935 m)	PCN 49/F/A/X/U
Nicaragua			
Managua (La Mercedes)	09/27	8000 ft (2438 m)	B707
Niger			
Niamey	09/27	9843 ft (3000 m)	PCN 59/F/B/X/T
Nigeria			
Ilorin	05/23	10171 ft (3100 m)	LCN 90
Kaduna	05/23	9843 ft (3000 m)	LCN 100
Kano (Mallam Aminu Int'l)	06/24	10827 ft (3300 m)	LCN 90
Lagos (Murtala Muhammed)	01L/19R	12795 ft (3900 m)	LCN 110
Port Harcourt	03/21	9843 ft (3000 m)	LCN 100
Norway			
Bergen (Flesland)	18/36	8038 ft (2450 m)	PCN 70/F/A/X/T
Hardstad Narvik (Evenes)	18/36	8720 ft (2658 m)	PCN 65/F/A/W/T
Oslo (Fornebu)	06/24	7776 ft (2370 m)	PCN 70/F/B/X/T
Stavanger (Sola)	18/36	8383 ft (2555 m)	PCN 65/F/B/X/T
Torp	18/36	8005 ft (2440 m)	PCN 45/F/B/X/U
Tromso	01/19	7080 ft (2158 m)	PCN 45/F/C/X/T
Oman			
Muscat (Seeb)	08/26	11762 ft (3585 m)	PCN 60/F/A/X/J
Salalah	07/25	10958 ft (3340 m)	PCN 60/F/A/X/U

Airport name	Orientation and length of longest runway		Runway LCN/PCN
Pakistan			
Islamabad (Chaklala)	12/30	9000 ft (2743 m)	LCN 85
Karachi	07L/25R	10500 ft (3200 m)	LCN 83
Lahore	18/36	9000 ft (2743 m)	A300
Nawabshah	02/20	9000 ft (2743 m)	PCN 32/R/C/X/T
Panama and Canal Zone			
Panama (Tocumen)	03R/21L	10007 ft (3050 m)	PCN 140/R/C/X/U
Papua New Guinea			
Port Moresby (Jacksons)	14L/32R	9022 ft (2750 m)	PCN 70/F/C/X/U
Paraguay			
Ascuncion (Silvia Pettirossi)	02/20	11000 ft (3353 m)	PCN 55/F/G/W/T
Peru			
Anta (C.A. Grazziani)	16/34	10007 ft (3050 m)	PCN 19/F/B/Y/U
Cuzco	09/27	11155 ft (3400 m)	PCN 35/F/C/X/U
Juliaca	11/29	13780 ft (4200 m)	PCN 30/F/C/X/T
Lima (Callao) International	15/33	11506 ft (3507 m)	PCN 42/R/A/W/T
Puerto Maldonado	18/36	11483 ft (3500 m)	PCN 69/R/C/X/T
Philippines			
Manila International	06/24	11000 ft (3353 m)	PCN 91/F/D/W/U
Poland			
Gdansk	11/29	9186 ft (2800 m)	PCN 36/R/A/X/U
Krakow	08/26	7874 ft (2400 m)	PCN 31/F/B/X/T
Poznan	11/29	8202 ft (2500 m)	PCN 49/F/A/X/T
Warsaw (Okecie)	15/33	12106 ft (3690 m)	PCN 70/F/C/X/T
Portugal			
Faro	11/29	8169 ft (2490 m)	PCN 80/F/A/W/T
Lisbon	03/21	12483 ft (3805 m)	PCN 80/F/B/W/T
Oporto (Francisco Sa Carneiro)	17/35	11417 ft (3480 m)	PCN 90/F/C/W/T
Puerto Rico			
San Juan (Luis Munoz Marin International)	08/26	10000 ft (3048 m)	PCN 61/F/B/X/T
Qatar			
Doha	16/34	15000 ft (4572 m)	LCN 100
Romania			
Bucharest (Otopeni)	08/26	11483 ft (3500 m)	ISWL 45000
Constanta (Kogalniceanu)	18/36	11483 ft (3500 m)	ISWL 45000
Timisoara (Giarmata)	11/29	11483 ft (3500 m)	ISWL 45000
Russia			
Irkutsk	12/30	9072 ft (2765 m)	PCN 72/R/C/X/T
Khabarovsk	05R/23L	13123 ft (4000 m)	PCN 55/R/B/X/T
Moscow (Sheremetyevo)	07R/25L	12139 ft (3700 m)	PCN 70/R/B/X/T
Moscow (Vnukovo)	02/20	10039 ft (3060 m)	PCN 100/R/C/X/T
Novosibirsk (Tolmachevo)	07/25	11808 ft (3599 m)	PCN 82/R/C/X/T
St. Petersburg (Pulkovo)	10R/28L	12408 ft (3782 m)	PCN 74/R/C/X/T
Vladivostok (Knevichi)	07L/25R	11483 ft (3500 m)	PCN 52/R/B/X/U
Yakutsk	05R/23L	11155 ft (3400 m)	PCN 63/R/C/X/T
Rwanda			
Kigali	10/28	11483 ft (3500 m)	LCN 50
Sao Tome			
Sao Tome	11/29	7284 ft (2220 m)	ISWL 50000
Saudi Arabia			
Al Jouf	10/28	10827 ft (3300 m)	PCN 34/R/B/W/T
Arar (Badanah)	10/28	10007 ft (3050 m)	PCN 35/R/B/W/T
Dhahran	16R/34L	12008 ft (3660 m)	B747
Gassim	15/33	9843 ft (3000 m)	PCN 56/F/A/W/T
Jeddah (King Abdulaziz)	16R/34L	12467 ft (3800 m)	PCN 52/R/B/W/T
Madinah	17/35	12631 ft (3850 m)	PCN 64/F/A/X/T
Riyadh (King Khalid International)	15L/33R	13780 ft (4200 m)	PCN 70/F/B/W/T
Taif	07/25	12254 ft (3735 m)	PCN 53/F/A/W/T
Senegal			
Dakar (Yoff)	18/36	11450 ft (3490 m)	PCN 82/F/C/X/U

Airport name	Orientation and length of longest runway		Runway LCN/PCN
Seychelles			
Seychelles International	13/31	9800 ft (2987 m)	LCN 100
Sierra Leone			
Freetown (Lungi)	12/30	10500 ft (3200 m)	LCN 80
Singapore			
Singapore (Changi)	02L/20R	13123 ft (4000 m)	PCN 72/F/B/W/U
Singapore (Paya Lebar)	02/20	12400 ft (3779 m)	PCN 72/F/B/W/U
Slovak Republic			
Bratislava (Ivanka)	13/31	9678 ft (2950 m)	PCN 50/R/B/X/T
Kosice	01/19	10171 ft (3100 m)	PCN 55/F/A/X/T
Poprad (Tatry)	09/27	8530 ft (2600 m)	PCN 33/R/A/X/T
Slovenia			
Ljubljana	13/31	10827 ft (3300 m)	PCN 110/F/B/X/T
Maribor	15/33	8202 ft (2500 m)	LCN 72
Somalia			
Mogadishu	05/23	10335 ft (3150 m)	PCN 44/F/A/Y/T
South Africa			
Bloemfontein (J.B.M. Hertzog)	02/20	8396 ft (2559 m)	LCN 74
Cape Town (D.F. Malan)	01/19	10500 ft (3200 m)	LCN 74
Durban (Louis Botha)	05/23	8015 ft (2443 m)	LCN 74
Johannesburg (Jan Smuts)	03L/21R	14495 ft (4418 m)	LCN 74
Kimberley (B.J. Vorster)	02/20	9843 ft (3000 m)	LCN 62
Lanseria	06L/24R	10000 ft (3048 m)	LCN 38
Mmabatho	04/22	14764 ft (4500 m)	LCN 100
Upington (Pierre van Ryneveld)	17/35	16076 ft (4900 m)	LCN 74
Spain			
Alicante	10/28	9843 ft (3000 m)	PCN 87/F/B/W/T
Almeria	08/26	10500 ft (3200 m)	LCN 80
Barcelona	06/24	10197 ft (3108 m)	PCN 86/F/A/W/T
Bilbao	12/30	8530 ft (2600 m)	PCN 60/F/B/Y/O
Gerona	02/20	7874 ft (2400 m)	LCN 80
Granada	10/28	9514 ft (2900 m)	PCN 44/F/C/X/U
Ibiza	06/24	9186 ft (2800 m)	LCN 105
Madrid (Barajas)	15/33	13450 ft (4100 m)	PCN 91/F/B/W/T
Malaga	14/32	10500 ft (3200 m)	PCN 60/F/B/X/U
Minorca	01/19	7710 ft (2350 m)	PCN 45/F/A/X/T
Palma	06L/24R	10728 ft (3270 m)	LCN 120
Santiago	17/35	10500 ft (3200 m)	ISWL 35000
Seville	09/27	11024 ft (3360 m)	PCN 75/F/B/W/J
Valencia	12/30	8858 ft (2700 m)	PCN 54/F/C/W/T
Vitoria	04/22	11483 ft (3500 m)	LCN 89
Sri Lanka			
Colombo (Katunayake)	04/22	10991 ft (3350 m)	PCN 85/F/B/X/T
Sudan			
Khartoum	18/36	9843 ft (3000 m)	LCG III
Port Sudan	17/35	8202 ft (2500 m)	ISWL 2500
Surinam			
Paramaribo (Johan A. Pengel)	11/29	11417 ft (3480 m)	PCN 52/F/A/W/T
Swaziland			
Matsapha (Manzini)	07/25	8530 ft (2600 m)	PCN 71/F/C/X/T
Sweden			
Gothenburg (Landvetter)	03/21	10827 ft (3300 m)	PCN 90/F/B/X/T
Malmö (Sturup)	17/35	9186 ft (2800 m)	PCN 80/F/B/X/T
Stockholm (Arlanda)	01/19	10827 ft (3300 m)	PCN 97/R/B/X/T
Switzerland			
Berne (Belp)	14/32	4298 ft (1310 m)	PCN 40/F/B/X/T
Geneva (Cointrin)	05/23	12795 ft (3900 m)	PCN 60/R/B/W/T
Zurich (Kloten)	16/34	12140 ft (3700 m)	PCN 60/R/B/W/T
Syria			
Damascus International	05R/23L	11811 ft (3600 m)	PCN 80/R/C/W/T
Tahiti			
Tahiti	04/22	11204 ft (3415 m)	PCN 53/F/A/W/U

Airport name	Orientation and length of longest runway		Runway LCN/PCN
Taiwan			
Kaohsiung International	09L/27R	10335 ft (3150 m)	PCN 69/R/C/X/T
Taipei International (Chiang Kai Shek)	05L/23R	12008 ft (3660 m)	100S/170T/ 266B/378DB
Tajikistan			
Dushanbe	09/27	10170 ft (3100 m)	PCN 26/R/B/X/T
Tanzania			
Dar-es-Salaam	05/23	9843 ft (3000 m)	PCN 56/F/A/W/T
Kilimanjaro	09/27	11811 ft (3600 m)	LCN 100
Zanzibar (Kisauni)	18/36	8077 ft (2462 m)	PCN 42/F/A/W/T
Tchad			
N'Djamena	05/23	9186 ft (2800 m)	DC-10/30
Thailand			
Bangkok	03L/21R	12139 ft (3700 m)	PCN 126/F/D/W/T
Chiang Mai	18/36	10171 ft (3100 m)	PCN 75/F/D/X/T
Phuket	09/27	9843 ft (3000 m)	PCN 61/F/C/X/T
Songkhla (Hat Yai International)	08/26	10007 ft (3050 m)	PCN 60/F/C/X/T
Togo			
Lome (Tokoin)	05/23	9843 ft (3000 m)	PCN 59/F/B/X/T
Trinidad and Tobago			
Port of Spain (Piarco)	10/28	10500 ft (3200 m)	B747
Tunisia			
Djerba (Zarzis)	09/27	10171 ft (3100 m)	PCN 52/F/B/Y/U
Monastir (Habib Bourguiba International)	08/26	9679 ft (2950 m)	PCN 50/F/B/Y/U
Tozeur (Nefta)	09/27	10581 ft (3225 m)	PCN 48/F/B/Y/U
Tunis (Carthage)	01/19	10500 ft (3200 m)	PCN 56/R/B/W/U
Turkey			
Adana	05/23	9022 ft (2750 m)	PCN 100/F/A/X/T
Ankara (Esenboga)	03R/21L	12310 ft (3752 m)	PCN 58/F/A/X/T
Dalaman (Mugia)	01/19	9843 ft (3000 m)	PCN 100/R/A/W/T
Diyarbakir	16/34	11644 ft (3549 m)	LCN 75
Istanbul (Ataturk)	18/36	9843 ft (3000 m)	PCN 100/R/A/X/T
Izmir (Adnan Menderes)	10/34	10630 ft (3240 m)	PCN 120/F/C/W/T
Turkmenistan			
Ashkhabad	12/30	9843 ft (3000 m)	PCN 20/R/B/X/T
Uganda			
Entebbe	17/35	12001 ft (3658 m)	LCN 100
Ukraine			
Kiev (Borispol)	18R/36L	11483 ft (3500 m)	PCN 62/R/C/X/T
Odessa	16/34	9186 ft (2800 m)	PCN 15/R/B/X/T
United Arab Emirates			
Abu Dhabi International	13/31	13451 ft (4100 m)	LCN 95
Abu Dhabi (Bateen)	13/31	10500 ft (3200 m)	LCN 80
Dubai	12L/30R	13123 ft (4000 m)	PCN 70/F/B/W/T
Fujairah International	11/29	12303 ft (3750 m)	LCN 100
Ras Al Khaimah	16/34	12336 ft (3760 m)	LCN 80
Sharjah International	12/30	12336 ft (3760 m)	LCN 100
United Kingdom			
Aberdeen (Dyce)	16/34	6001 ft (1829 m)	PCN 40/R/B/X/T
Belfast (Aldergrove)	07/25	9110 ft (2777 m)	PCN 71/R/B/W/U
Birmingham International	15/33	7398 ft (2255 m)	PCN 62/F/B/W/T
Bournemouth International	08/26	6030 ft (1838 m)	PCN 46/F/A/X/U
Bristol (Lulsgate)	09/27	6598 ft (2011 m)	PCN 57/F/C/X/U
Bristol (Filton)	09/27	8038 ft (2450 m)	PCN 78/R/D/X/T
Cambridge	05/23	6447 ft (1965 m)	PCN 48/R/B/X/T
Cardiff	12/30	7000 ft (2134 m)	PCN 52/F/A/W/T
East Midlands	09/27	7480 ft (2280 m)	PCN 63/R/C/W/T
Edinburgh	07/25	8400 ft (2560 m)	PCN 74/R/C/W/T
Exeter	08/26	6834 ft (2083 m)	PCN 53/F/B/X/U
Farnborough	07/25	7874 ft (2400 m)	LCG III
Glasgow	05/23	8720 ft (2658 m)	PCN 65/R/B/W/T
Guernsey	09/27	4800 ft (1463 m)	PCN 27/F/C/X/U
Humberside	03/21	7218 ft (2200 m)	PCN 55/F/R/B/X/T
Isle of Man (Ronaldsway)	08/26	5751 ft (1753 m)	PCN 32/F/C/X/T
Jersey	09/27	5597 ft (1706 m)	PCN 34/F/C/X/T
Leeds-Bradford	14/32	7382 ft (2250 m)	PCN 61/R/A/W/T

Airport name	Orientation and length of longest runway		Runway LCN/PCN
United Kingdom			
Liverpool	09/27	7500 ft (2286 m)	PCN 42/R/B/W/J
London (Gatwick)	08R/26L	10364 ft (3159 m)	PCN 78/R/B/W/T
London (Heathrow)	09L/27R	12802 ft (3902 m)	PCN 83/R/A/W/T
London (Stansted)	05/23	10000 ft (3048 m)	PCN 86/R/C/W/T
Luton	08/26	7087 ft (2160 m)	PCN 75/R/D/X/T
Manchester International	06/24	10000 ft (3048 m)	PCN 94/F/C/W/T
Newcastle	07/25	7651 ft (2332 m)	PCN 73/F/C/W/T
Prestwick	13/31	9800 ft (2987 m)	PCN 85/R/C/W/T
Stornoway	18/36	7211 ft (2198 m)	PCN 47/F/A/W/T
Tee-side	05/23	7516 ft (2291 m)	PCN 79/F/D/X/T
United States of America (see separate Alaska and Hawaii)			
Albuquerque, NM	08/26	13375 ft (4077 m)	45S/95D/141DT
Atlanta (Wm. B. Hartsfield), GA	09L/27R	11889 ft (3624 m)	PCN 62/R/B/W/T
Atlantic City, NJ	13/31	10000 ft (3048 m)	39S/55D/159DT
Baltimore (Washington International), MD	15/33	11438 ft (3486 m)	PCN 71/R/B/W/T
Bangor International, ME	15/33	11438 ft (3486 m)	PCN 71/R/B/W/T
Birmingham International, AL	05/23	8000 ft (2438 m)	80S/93D/159DT
Boston (Logan International), MA	15R/33L	10081 ft (3073 m)	PCN 61/F/B/W/U
Buffalo, NY	05/23	8100 ft (2469 m)	34S/89D/204DT
Casper (Natrona City International), WY	03/21	10600 ft (3231 m)	59S/77D/123DT
Charleston, SC	15/33	9000 ft (2743 m)	174D/159DT/ 352DDT
Charlotte (Douglas), NC	18R/36L	10000 ft (3048 m)	PCN 61/R/B/W/T
Chicago (O'Hare) IL	14R/32L	13000 ft (3962 m)	PCN 72/R/C/X/T
Cleveland, OH	05R/23L	9000 ft (2743 m)	PCN 51/R/C/X/T
Colorado Springs, CO	17L/35R	13500 ft (4115 m)	79D/154DT/340DDT
Columbus (Port Columbus International), OH	10R/28L	10700 ft (3261 m)	46S/68D/136DT
Dallas–Fort Worth, TX	17R/35L	13400 ft (4084 m)	PCN 60/R/B/X/U
Denver International, CO	16/34	12000 ft (3658 m)	PCN 76/R/C/W/T
Detroit Metropolitan (Wayne), MI	03L/21R	12000 ft (3658 m)	PCN 70/R/C/X/T
Duluth International, MN	09/27	10152 ft (3094 m)	34S/59D/104DT
Houston International, TX	14L/32R	12000 ft (3658 m)	PCN 71/R/B/X/U
Huntsville, AL	18R/36L	10000 ft (3048 m)	34S/91D/385DDT
Indianapolis International, IN	50L/23R	10005 ft (3049 m)	PCN 56/R/C/X/T
Kansas City International, MO	01L/19R	10801 ft (3292 m)	PCN 62/F/B/W/T
Las Vegas, NV	07L/25R	14505 ft (4421 m)	PCN 71/F/B/X/T
Long Beach, CA	12/30	10000 ft (3048 m)	14S/91D/136DT
Los Angeles International, CA	07L/25R	12090 ft (3685 m)	PCN 70/R/B/W/T
Louisville (Standiford Field) KY	01/19	10000 ft (3048 m)	34S/77D/164DT
Miami International, FL	09R/27L	13000 ft (3962 m)	PCN 63/F/A/X/T
Milwaukee, WI	01L/19R	9690 ft (2953 m)	PCN 70/R/C/W/T
Minneapolis, MN	11R/29R	10000 ft (3048 m)	PCN 61/R/B/X/T
Montgomery, AL	10/28	9001 ft (2743 m)	48S/53D/82DT
Moses Lake (Grant County), WA	14L/32R	13501 ft (4115 m)	45S/91D/181DT
Nashville, TN	13/31	11030 ft (3362 m)	59S/69D/104DT
Newark International, NJ	04R/22L	9300 ft (2835 m)	PCN 62/F/A/W/T
Newburgh (Stewart), NY	09/27	11818 ft (3602 m)	79D/158DT/353DDT
New Orleans, LA	10/28	10080 ft (3072 m)	PCN 94/F/D/X/U
New York (John F. Kennedy), NY	13R/31L	14572 ft (4441 m)	PCN 94/F/A/W/T
New York (La Guardia), NY	04/22	7000 ft (2134 m)	36S/77D/163DT
Niagara Falls International, NY	10L/28R	9125 ft (2781 m)	PCN 46/F/C/X/T
Oakland, CA	11/29	10000 ft (3048 m)	PCN 61/R/A/W/T
Ontario International, CA	08L/26R	12200 ft (3719 m)	PCN 35/R/A/W/U
Orlando, FL	18L/36R	12004 ft (3659 m)	75S/95D/182DT
Philadelphia, PA	09R/27L	10500 ft (3200 m)	91S/95D/159DT
Phoenix (Sky Harbor), AZ	08L/26R	11001 ft (3353 m)	PCN 47/F/B/X/U
Pittsburgh, PA	10R/28L	11500 ft (3505 m)	45S/102D/159DT
Portland International, OR	10R/28L	11011 ft (3356 m)	PCN 63/F/A/X/T
Pueblo Memorial, NM	08L/26R	10500 ft (3200 m)	PCN 26/F/C/X/T
Reno (Cannon International), NV	16R/34L	10000 ft (3048 m)	34S/84D/159DT
St Louis International, KY	12R/30L	11019 ft (3359 m)	PCN 61/R/B/W/T
Salt Lake City, UT	16/34	12000 ft (3658 m)	27S/91D/159DT

Airport name	Orientation and length of longest runway		Runway LCN/PCN
United States of America (see separate Alaska and Hawaii)			
San Antonio International, NM	12R/30L	8500 ft (2591 m)	PCN 57/R/C/X/U
San Diego, CA	09/27	9400 ft (2865 m)	PCN 61/R/A/W/T
San Francisco, CA	10L/28R	11870 ft (3618 m)	PCN 62/F/B/X/T
Seattle Boeing Field (King County International), WA	13R/31L	10000 ft (3048 m)	PCN 34/R/A/X/T
Seattle (Tacoma), WA	16L/34R	11900 ft (3627 m)	PCN 62/F/B/X/T
Tampa International, FL	18R/36L	11002 ft (3353 m)	PCN 58/R/A/W/T
Washington (Dulles), D.C.	01R/19L	11500 ft (3505 m)	PCN 81/R/C/W/U
Uruguay			
Montevideo (Carrasco)	06/24	8858 ft (2700 m)	PCN 60/F/C/W/U
Uzbekistan			
Samarkand	09/27	10171 ft (3100 m)	PCN 29/R/B/X/T
Tashkent (Yuzhnyy)	08L/26R	13123 ft (4000 m)	PCN 61/R/B/X/T
Venezuela			
Caracas (Simon Bolivar)	09/27	11483 ft (3500 m)	B747
Maracaibo (La Chinita)	02R/20L	8169 ft (2490 m)	PCN 53/F/B/W/U
Margarita (Del Caribe)	09/27	10433 ft (3180 m)	AUW 360 tonnes
Vietnam			
Da Nang	17L/35R	10000 ft (3048 m)	PCN 30/F/B/X/U
Hanoi (Noibai)	11/29	10500 ft (3200 m)	PCN 54/R/B/W/U
Ho Chi Minh City (Tansonnhat)	07L/25R	10000 ft (3048 m)	PCN 50/R/B/X/U

Airport name	Orientation and length of longest runway		Runway LCN/PCN
Virgin Islands			
St. Croix (Alexander Hamilton)	09/27	7612 ft (2320 m)	PCN 52/F/B/X/T
St. Thomas	10/28	7000 ft (2134 m)	PCN 36/F/B/X/T
Windward Islands			
St. Lucia (Hewanorra International)	10/28	9000 ft (2743 m)	LCN 100+
Yemen Arab Republic			
Aden International	08/26	10168 ft (3099 m)	PCN 74/F/B/W/U
Sanaa International	18/36	10669 ft (3252 m)	LCN 60
Yugoslavia (Serbia)			
Belgrade	12/30	11155 ft (3400 m)	PCN 65/F/C/X/T
Skopje	16/34	8038 ft (2450 m)	LCN 70
Zaïre			
Kinshasa (Ndjili)	06/24	11811 ft (3600 m)	20S/40T/100B
Kisangani (Bangoka)	13/31	11483 ft (3500 m)	20S/40T/100B
Zambia			
Lusaka International	10/28	13000 ft (3962 m)	LCN 135
Zimbabwe			
Bulawayo	13/31	8491 ft (2588 m)	PCN 40/F/A/X/U
Harare International	05/23	15502 ft (4725 m)	PCN 50/F/A/W/T
Hwange National Park	08/26	14764 ft (4500 m)	PCN 25/F/B/Y/U
Victoria Falls	12/30	7500 ft (2286 m)	PCN 28/F/B/X/U

INDEX

Index of Advertisers

Index

Page numbers in bold refer to company details with addresses. Specific aircraft are listed alphabetically by name or designation whilst the Engine, Missile and Radar sections are indexed by country and company only. Page numbers in italics refer to illustrations.

AIRFORCE

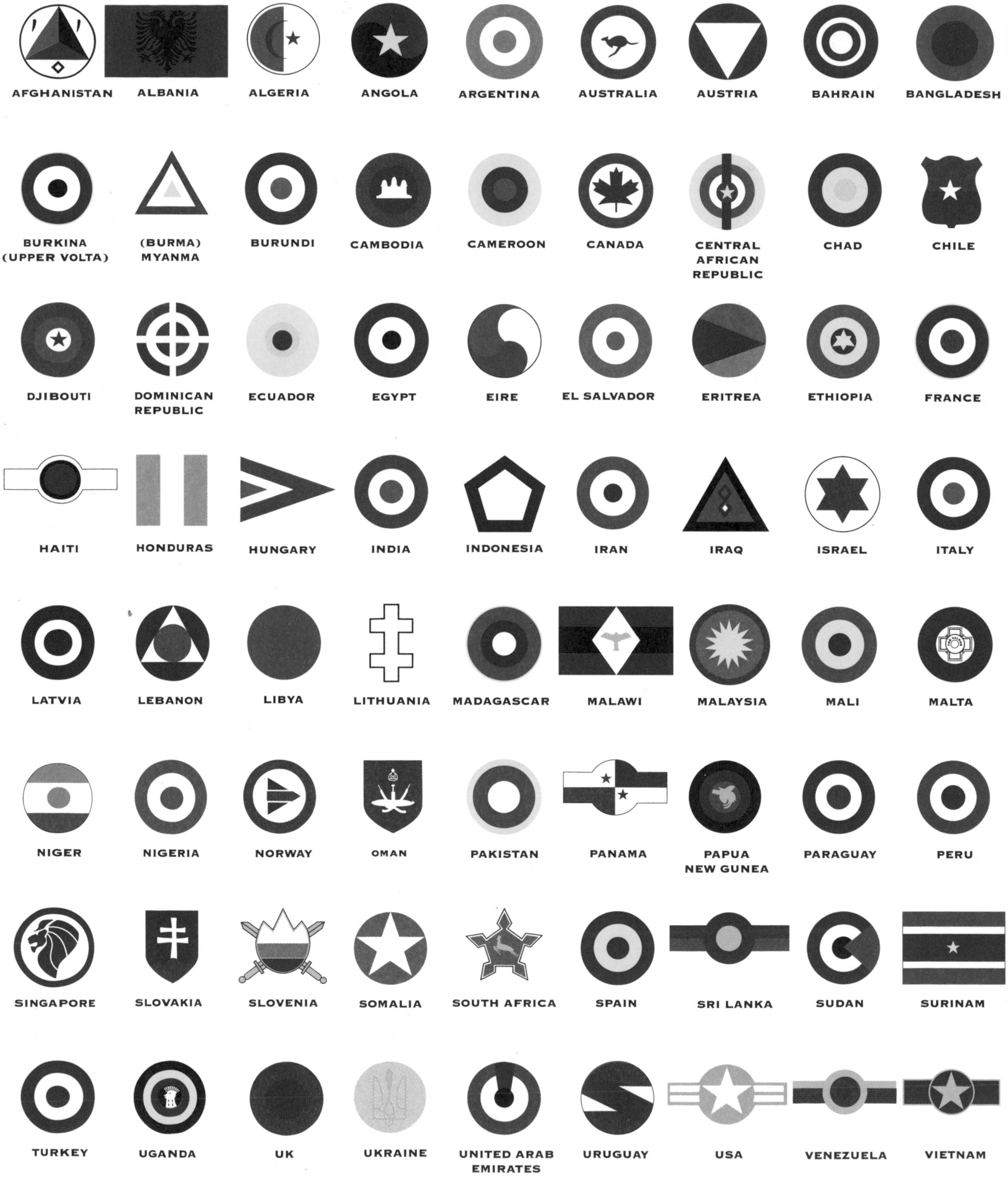
AFGHANISTAN
ALBANIA
ALGERIA
ANGOLA
ARGENTINA
AUSTRALIA
AUSTRIA
BAHRAIN
BANGLADESH
BURKINA (UPPER VOLTA)
(BURMA) MYANMA
BURUNDI
CAMBODIA
CAMEROON
CANADA
CENTRAL AFRICAN REPUBLIC
CHAD
CHILE
DJIBOUTI
DOMINICAN REPUBLIC
ECUADOR
EGYPT
EIRE
EL SALVADOR
ERITREA
ETHIOPIA
FRANCE
HAITI
HONDURAS
HUNGARY
INDIA
INDONESIA
IRAN
IRAQ
ISRAEL
ITALY
LATVIA
LEBANON
LIBYA
LITHUANIA
MADAGASCAR
MALAWI
MALAYSIA
MALI
MALTA
NIGER
NIGERIA
NORWAY
OMAN
PAKISTAN
PANAMA
PAPUA NEW GUNEA
PARAGUAY
PERU
SINGAPORE
SLOVAKIA
SLOVENIA
SOMALIA
SOUTH AFRICA
SPAIN
SRI LANKA
SUDAN
SURINAM
TURKEY
UGANDA
UK
UKRAINE
UNITED ARAB EMIRATES
URUGUAY
USA
VENEZUELA
VIETNAM